Random House
German–English
English–German
Dictionary

Random House
German–English
English–German
Dictionary

Anne Dahl, M.A.
Frankfurt University,
Germanic and Romance
Languages and Literatures

RANDOM
HOUSE

Library of Congress Cataloging-in-Publication Data

Random House German-English English-German dictionary / [edited by] Anne Dahl. — 1st ed.
      p.   cm.
  ISBN 0–679–44808–X
  1. German language—Dictionaries—English.   2. English language—Dictionaries—German.   I. Dahl, Anne.
  PF3640.R35   1997
  433'.21—dc20   96–34407
                                                 CIP

Printed in the United States of America

Random House Web address: http://www.randomhouse.com/

First Edition

9 8 7 6 5 4 3 2 1

New York   Toronto   London   Sydney   Auckland

Foreword

This volume is an addition to the Random House series of bilingual dictionaries. It is a totally new version designed for the American public. For the German spelling we took into account the new regulations adopted by the cultural ministers of the various states of the Federal Republic of Germany in December 1995. For the English spelling we adopted the American version.

The user of this dictionary may find useful lists and tables concerning pronunciation, verbs, abbreviations, etc. in the front, middle, and back of the book.

Contents/Inhalt

Inhalt/Contents

Notes on German Pronunciation

As very few German sounds are exactly like the corresponding English sounds the English equivalents given below represent in most cases only approximately the sounds of the German vowels and consonants.

A. Vowels

Simple vowels are either long or short in German.

They are always long when doubled or followed by *h*, and mostly long when followed by a single consonant.

They are, as a rule, short when followed by a group of consonants.

All long vowels are simple sounds in German, e.g. long *e* in *Fee* is like the first part of the English *a* in *mane*, but does not shift to *i*; long *o* is like the English *o* in *no*, without shifting to *u*.

Short *i* is like *i* in *it*, e.g. *mit*.
Long *i* ,, ,, *i* in *machine*, e.g. *dir*.
Short *e* ,, ,, *e* in *let*, e.g. *fett*.
Long *e* ,, ,, *a* in *late*, e.g. *Fee*.
Long *a* ,, ,, *a* in *alms*, e.g. *Tal*.
Short *o* ,, ,, *o* in *not*, e.g. *flott*.
Long *o* ,, ,, *o* in *no*, e.g. *rot*.
Short *u* ,, ,, *u* in *put*, e.g. *und*.
Long *u* ,, ,, *u* in *rude*, e.g. *Mut*.
Short *ä* ,, ,, *e* in *fell*, e.g. *fällt*.
Long *ä* ,, ,, *a* in *mare*, e.g. *fährt*.

The letters *ie* always represent the long English *ee* sound as in *field*, e.g. *sie*.

ö is pronounced like German *e* with rounded and protruded lips.

ü is pronounced like German *i* with rounded and protruded lips.

Final *e* is always pronounced in German words, e.g. *fette* like English *fetter* (without the *r*-sound).

B. Diphthongs

äu and *eu* resemble the *oi*-sound in *boy*, e.g., *Mäuse*, *Heu*.

ei⎫ are like ⎰*ei* in height⎱ e.g. *Ei*.
ai⎭ ⎱*ai* in aisle ⎰ *Mai*.

au is like *ow* in *how*, e.g. *lau*.

C. Consonants

b, *d* = English *b*, *d* at the beginning of a word or syllable, e.g. *Boden*.

b, *d* = English *p*, *t* in all other cases, e.g. *Lob*, *Abt*, *und*.

ch = (1) Scottish *ch* in 'loch' after *a*, *o*, *u*, e.g. *ach*, *doch*, *Tuch*.

= (2) first sound of 'hew' after the remaining vowels, and consonants, e.g. *ich, echt, Mächte, reich, euch, Gretchen.*
= (3) *k* before 's', e.g. *Fuchs, wachsen, Ochs,* and in some words of Greek origin, e.g. *Christ, Chor, Charakter.*
ck = *k,* e.g. *Lack, wecken.*
g = (1) English *g* at the beginning of a word or syllable, e.g. *gar, legen.*
= (2) *ch* (1) or (2) in all other cases, e.g. *zag, selig, lugte, Berg.* This *g* may also be pronounced like English *g* or *k,* except after *i* and *n.*
ng = English *ng* in *long,* e.g. *lang, singen.*
j = English *y* in *yes,* e.g. *ja, jeder.*
r = There are two regionally different pronunciations: the frontal *r* like the Scottish *r* in *girl,* e.g. *roh, Herr;* and the uvular *r,* nonexistent in English.
s = (1) English *z,* at the beginning of a word or between vowels; e.g. *so, Rose.*
= (2) English voiceless *s* in *hiss,* in all other cases, e.g. *es, ist.*
ss = English voiceless *s* in *hiss,* e.g. *lassen, Fuss, grösser.*
sp, st = English *shp, sht,* at the beginning of a word, e.g. *spät, Stuhl;* in all other cases like English *sp, st.*
th = English *t,* e.g. *Theater.*
v = English *f,* e.g. *vor, Vetter;* in words of Latin origin like English *v,* e.g. *Viktoria.*
w = English *v,* e.g. *wer, wir, Löwe.*
x = English *ks* (never like *gs*), e.g. *Max.*
y = mostly like *ü,* e.g. *Symphonie,* sometimes like *i.*
z, tz = English *ts,* e.g. *zu, Reiz, Sitz, Katze.*
-tion = *-tsyon,* e.g. *Nation.*

Stress

The principal stress in German words rests on the root syllable which is usually the first syllable, e.g. *sa´gen, el´terlich.*

Exceptions are *Forel´le, Holun´der, Wa´cholder, leben´dig,* nouns ending in *-ei,* like *Bettelei´,* and verbs ending in *-ieren,* e.g. *spazier´en.*

The prefixes *be-, ge-, er-, ver-, ent-, zer-,* are unstressed.

The prefix *ant-* has always, and the prefix *un-* has usually the principal stress, e.g. *ant´worten, un´ruhig.*

Exceptions are *unmög´lich, unend´lich.*

Words borrowed from foreign languages retain their original stress, e.g. *Natur´, Dok´tor, Doktor´en, Universität´.*

Compound adverbs have their principal stress on the second part, e.g. *hervor´, dahin´, zusam´men.*

Bemerkungen zur Aussprache des Englischen

Lautzeichen und Lautwerte decken sich im Englischen noch viel weniger als im Deutschen. Derselbe Laut kann durch ganz verschiedene Buchstaben wiedergegeben werden, und derselbe Buchstabe kann ganz verschiedene Laute bezeichnen. Die Schreibweise ist also durchaus kein Führer für die Aussprache. Dennoch dürften einige allgemeine Hinweise nützlich sein.

A. Vokale

Langes *a* ist wie im deutschen *kam*, z.B. *car, alms*.

Kurzes *a* liegt zwischen dem deutschen *a* und *ä*, doch ist der Raum zwischen Zunge und Gaumen grösser als beim deutschen *a*, z.B. *rat, can*.

Ausserdem gibt es ein kurzes dunkles *a*, wobei die zurückgezogene Zunge sich gegen den weichen Gaumen hebt, z.B. *but, some*.

Langes *e* ist ein Diphthong, der mit *e* beginnt und nach *i* hin ausklingt, z.B. *may* = *mee-i*.

Langes halboffenes *o* ist ein Diphthong, der mit *o* beginnt und nach *u* hin ausklingt, z.B. *no* = *noo-u*.

Langes offenes *o* liegt zwischen *a* und *o* (der Laut des *o* in *Gott* verlängert), z.B. *all, or*.

Kurzes offenes *o* klingt nach *a* hin, z.B. *not, god*.

Langes offenes *ö* in Wörtern wie *fir, girl, learn*. Die Zunge bleibt flach in mitterler Lage und der Unterkiefer wird gesenkt.

Auslautendes *e* ist immer stumm im Englischen.

B. Konsonanten

b, d, und *g* werden auch am Ende einer Silbe stimmhaft, d.h. wie am Anfang gesprochen, z.B. *bib, dead, gag*.

j ist ein stimmhaftes *sch* wie in *Genie*, mit einem *d* davor, z.B. *Jew*; derselbe Laut wird oft durch *g* bezeichnet, z.B. *gin*.

r vor Vokalen wird mit der Zungenspitze hervorgebracht, aber nicht gerollt, z.B. *rid, proud*.

s im Anlaut ist immer stimmlos wie im deutschen *ist*, z.B. *so*. Zwischen Vokalen wird es stimmhaft, z.B. *rose*, wie im deutschen *Rose*.

sp und *st* sind niemals wie deutsches *schp* und *scht* zu sprechen.

th ist ein Reibelaut (wie *s*), bei dem sich die Zunge an die oberen Schneidezähne legt. Es ist entweder stimmlos, z.B. *thick*, oder stimmhaft, z.B. *them*.

w ist ein mit den Lippen gebildetes deutsches *w* mit der Zungenstellung für *u*.

z ist immer der stimmhafte s-Laut (wie im deutschen *sie*), z.B. *zest, lazy*.

Abbreviations Used in the Dictionary

Verzeichnis der im Wörterbuch gebrauchten Abkürzungen

a. = adjective, Adjektiv.
adv. = adverb, Adverb, Umstandswort.
Am. = Americanism, Amerikanismus.
ar. = arithmetic, Arithmetik.
arch. = architecture, Baukunst.
art. = article, Artikel, Geschlechtswort.
astro. = astronomy, Astronomie.
avi. = aviation, Aviation.
bes. = besonders, especially.
bio. = biology, Biologie.
bot. = botany, Botanik.
c. = conjunction, Konjunktion, Bindewort.
chem. = chemistry, Chemie.
com. = commercial, Handel.
comp. = computer, Computer.
cp. = compare, vergleiche.
cul. = culinary, Kochkunst.
def. = defective, defektiv.
elek. = electricity, Elektrizität.
etw. = something, etwas.
f. = feminine, weiblich.
fam. = familiär, colloquial.
fig. = figuratively, figurativ.
geol. = geology, Geologie.
geom. = geometry, Geometrie.
gram. = grammar, Grammatik.
her. = heraldry, Heraldik.
hist. = history, Geschichte.
hunt. = hunting, Jagdwesen.
i. = interjection, Empfindungswort.
ir. = irregular, unregelmäßig.
jn. = jemanden, someone.
jm. = jemandem, someone.
jur. = jurisprudence, Rechtswissenschaft.
ling. = linguistics, Linguistik.
lit. = literally, wörtlich.
liter. = literature, Literatur.
m. = masculine, männlich.
math. = mathematics, Mathematik.

mech. = mechanics, Maschinenwesen.
med. = medicine, Medizin.
met. = meteorology, Meteorologie.
mil. = military, Militär.
min. = mining, Bergbau.
mot. = motoring, Autofahren.
mus. = music, Musik.
n. = neuter, sächlich.
nav. = navigation, Schiffahrt.
obs. = obsolete, veraltet.
od. = or, oder.
opt. = optics, Optik.
o.s. = oneself, sich selbst.
p. = participle, Partizipium.
pej. = pejorative, abwertend.
phot. = photography, Photographie.
phys. = physics, Physik.
pl. = plural, Mehrzahl.
pn. = pronoun, Fürwort.
pol. = politics, Politik.
pr. = preposition, Verhältniswort.
print. = printing, Druckereibetrieb.
r. = regular, regelmäßig.
rail. = railway, Eisenbahn.
rel. = religion, Religion.
s. = substantive, Hauptwort.
s.b., sb. = somebody, jemand.
sl. = slang, Slang.
sp. = sports, Sport.
st. = strong, stark.
s.th., sth. = something, etwas.
subj. = subjunctive, Konjunktiv.
theat. = theater, Theater.
tech. = technical, Technik.
tel. = telegraphy, Telegraphie.
tel. = telephone, Fernsprechwesen.
typ. = typography, Buchdruck.
u. = and, und.
v.i. = intransitive verb, intransitives Zeitwort.
v.imp. = impersonal verb, unpersönliches Zeitwort.
v.refl. = reflexive verb, rückbezügliches Zeitwort.
v.t. = transitive verb, transitives Zeitwort.
vulg. = vulgar, vulgär.
Zus. = Zusammensetzung(en), compound word(s).
zool. = zoology, Zoologie.

Notes on Signs

0 Indicates that a German noun has no plural form.

(-,) Indicates that a German noun remains unaltered in the genitive or plural.

(s) Indicates that the German verb is conjugated with *sein*.

(h, s) Indicates that the German verb is conjugated with either *haben* or *sein*. (Where neither of these is mentioned, the verb is conjugated with *haben*.)

~ Indicates the main word at the beginning of each separate entry.

Bemerkungen zu den Zeichen

0 Zeigt an, daß ein deutsches Substantiv keine Pluralform hat.

(-,) Zeigt an, daß ein deutsches Substantiv im Genitiv oder Plural unverändert bleibt.

(s) Zeigt an, daß das deutsche Zeitwort mit 'sein' konjugiert wird.

(h, s) Zeigt an, daß beide Hilfszeitwörter (*haben* und *sein*) zulässig sind. (Wo ein Angabe fehlt, versteht sich die Verbindung mit *haben* von selbst.)

~ Zeigt das Stichwort am Anfang des betreffenden Artikels an.

German–English
Dictionary

A

A, a *n.* the letter A *or* a.
Aal *m.* (-[e]s, -e) eel.
aalen *v.* (sich) ~ *v.refl.* to loaf about; laze.
aalglatt *a. pej.* slippery.
Aas *n.* (-es, Äser) carcass, carrion.
Aasfresser *m.* (-s, -) scavenger.
Aasgeier *m.* (-s, -) vulture.
ab *adv,* off; down; (away) from; ~ *und zu,* from time to time; to and fro; occasionally; *auf und ~,* up and down; *Hut ~* ! hats off!; *pr.* from.
abändern *v.t.* to alter; (*Gesetz*) to amend.
Abänderung *f.* (-, -en) alteration; (*Gesetz*) amendment.
abarbeiten (sich) *v.refl.* to overwork oneself; to work off; to wear out.
Abart *f.* (-, -en) variety.
abartig *a.* abnormal; perverse.
Abartigkeit *f.* (-, -en) abnormality.
Abbau *m.* (-[e]s, 0) working (of a mine); retrenchment; dismantling; cutback; *Preis* ~, reduction of prices.
abbaubar *a.* degradable.
abbauen *v.t.* to work (a mine); to dismantle; to reduce; *Stellen* ~, to abolish; *Beamte* ~, to dismiss.
abbehalten *v.t.st. den Hut* ~, to remain uncovered.
abbeißen *v.t.st.* to bite off.
abbekommen *v.t.st.* to get a share in; *etwas* ~, to get hit, get hurt.
abberufen *v.t.st.* to call back, to recall.
Abberufung *f.* (-, -en) recall.
abbestellen *v.t.* to cancel.
abbezahlen *v.t.* to pay off, to pay up.
abbiegen *v.t. & i.st.* to bend off; to turn off, to branch off.
Abbiegespur *f.* (-, -en) turnoff lane.
Abbild *n.* (-[e]s, -er) copy, image.
abbilden *v.t.* to copy, to portray; *nach dem Leben* ~, to draw from the life.
Abbildung *f.* (-, -en) picture, illustration.
Abbitte *f.* (-, -en) apology; ~ *leisten,* ~ *tun,* to apologize.
abblasen *v.t.st.* to blow off; to sound (a retreat); to call off.
abblättern *v.i.* to shed petals; to flake off.
abblenden *v.t.* (*mot.*) to dim.
Abblendlicht *n.* (-s, -er) low beam.
abblitzen *v.i. jn* ~ *lassen* to send someone packing.
abblühen *v.i.* (*h, s*) to cease flowering; to wither.
abbrechen *v.t.st.* to break off, to pluck off; to cut off; to demolish, to pull down (*Häuser etc.*); *kurz* ~, to cut short; ~ *v.i.st.* to break off, to leave off; to drop a subject.
abbremsen *v.t.* to brake, to slow down.
abbrennen *v.t.ir.* to burn off (away, down); (*Feuerwerk*) to let off; ~ *v.i.ir.* (*s*) to be burnt down; to lose one's property by fire.
abbringen *v.t.ir.* to dissuade; to divert.
abbröckeln *v.t. & l.* (*s*). to crumble away.

Abbruch *m.* (-[e]s, -brüche) demolition; breaking off; pulling down; damage; injury, detriment.
abbuchen *v.t.* (*Bank*) to debit.
Abbuchung *f.* (-, -en) debit entry.
Abbuchungsauftrag *m.* (-s, -träge) debit order.
abbürsten *v.t.* to brush off, to brush.
abbüßen *v.t.* to atone for, to expiate; to serve (*Strafe*).
ABC-Waffen *pl.* ABC-weapons (atomic, biological, chemical).
abdampfen *v.i. fam.* to set off.
abdämmen *v.t.* to dam up; to embank.
abdanken *v.i.* to resign, to abdicate.
Abdankung *f.* (-, -en) abdication.
abdecken *v.t.* to uncover; to unroof; to flay; (*den Tisch*) to clear.
Abdecker *m.* (-s, -) knacker.
abdichten *v.t.* to seal; to plug.
abdienen *v.t.* to pay off by service, to work off; to serve one's time.
abdrängen *v.t.* to force (one) away.
abdrehen *v.t.* (*Gas*) to turn off; (*Elek., Licht, Radio*) to switch off.
abdriften *v.i.* to be blown, to drift off.
abdrosseln *v.t.* to throttle.
Abdruck *m.* (-[e]s, -drücke), impression; copy; (*phot.*) print; cast (*Abguss*), stamp, mark.
abdrucken *v.t.* to take a copy, to print off.
abdrücken *v.t.* to pull the trigger, to fire.
abdüsen *v.i. fam.* to zoom off.
abebben *v.i.* to recede.
Abend *m.* (-s, -e) evening, night; (*Himmelsgegend*) West *m.; gestern* ~, last night; *heute* ~, tonight.
Abendanzug *m.* (-[e]s, -züge), **Abendkleid** *n.* (-[e]s, -er) evening dress.
Abend: ~**blatt** *n.* evening paper; ~**brot** *n.* supper; ~**dämmerung** *f.* twilight, dusk; ~**essen,** supper; ~**land** *n.* West, Occident.
abendländisch *a.* western.
abendlich *a.* evening. . .
Abendmahl *n. das heilige* ~, the Lord's Supper; *das* ~ *empfangen,* to take the sacrament.
Abendrot *n.* sunset glow.
abends *adv.* in the evening.
Abendstern *m.* evening star, Hesperus.
Abenteuer *n.* (-s, -) adventure.
abenteuerlich *a.* adventurous; strange.
Abenteurer *m.* (-s, -)adventurer.
aber *c.* but; ~ *doch,* but yet; ~ *adv.* however.
Aberglaube *m.* (-ns, 0) superstition.
abergläubisch *a.* superstitious.
aberkennen *v.t.ir.* to deprive of *or* disallow, by legal verdict.
Aberkennung *f.* (-, -en) deprivation.
abermalig *a.* reiterated, repeated.
abermals *adv.* again, once more.
abernten *v.t.* to reap (a field).
Aberwitz *m.* (-es, 0); craziness.

3

aberwitzig *a.* crazy.

abfahren *v.t.st.* to cart away; ~ *v.i.ir.* (*s*) to depart, to start, to leave; *auf jemanden* ~ (*fam.*) to be crazy about someone; *jemanden* ~ *lassen* (*fam.*) to send someone packing.

Abfahrt *f.* (-, -en) departure, start; (*Schiff*) sailing.

Abfall *m.* (-[e]s, -fälle) falling off; decrease; garbage, waste, offal, refuse; apostasy; defection.

abfallen *v.i.st.* to fall off; to slope; to desert, to apostatize; *es fällt dabei etwas für mich ab*, I profit by it.

abfällig *a.* derogatory.

Abfallentsorgung *f.* (-, 0) waste management.

Abfallprodukt *n.* (-s, -e) by-product.

Abfallverwertung *f.* (-, 0) recycling.

abfangen *v.t.st.* to catch; to intercept.

abfärben *v.i.* to lose color, to come off (of colors); to stain.

abfassen *v.t.* to compose, to draw up, to draft.

Abfassung *f.* (-, -en) composing, wording.

Abfangjäger *m.* (-e, -) (*mil.*) interceptor (plane).

abfaulen *v.i.* to rot off.

abfedern *v.t.* to absorb, to cushion.

abfegen *v.t.* to wipe, to sweep (off).

abfeilen *v.t.* to file off.

abfertigen *v.t.* to dispatch, to send off; *kurz* ~, to snub, to put down.

Abfertigung *f.* (-, -en), dispatch; clearance.

abfeuern *v.t.* to fire off, to discharge.

abfinden *v.t.st.* to satisfy, to pay off; (sich) ~ (*mit*), *v.refl.* to put up with.

Abfindung *f.* (-, -en) indemnity.

Abfindungssumme *f.* compensation.

abflachen *v.i.* to flatten.

abflauen *v.i.* (*Wind*) to drop; to die down; to subside.

abfliegen *v.i.st.* (*avi.*) to take off.

abfließen *v.i.st.* (*s*) to flow off.

Abflug *m.* (-[e]s, -flüge) take-off; departure.

Abfluß *m.* (-flusses, -flüsse) flowing off; discharge; gutter, drain, waste-pipe.

Abflußrohr *n.* (-s, -e) drainpipe.

abfordern *v.t.* to call away; to demand.

abfragen *v.t.* to test (*quiz*), to inquire of, to get (a thing) out of (one); to retrieve (*comp.*); *eine Lektion* ~, to hear a lesson.

abfressen *v.t.st.* to eat bare, to strip bare.

abfrieren *v.i.st. Mir frieren die Ohren ab.* My ears are freezing. *v.refl.* (*fam.*) *sich einen* ~ to be freezing to death.

Abfuhr *f.* (-, -en) removal; rebuff.

abführen *v.t.* to carry away; (*med.*) to purge; (*Schuld*) to discharge.

abführend *a.* (*med.*) aperient.

Abführmittel *n.* purgative, laxative.

abfüllen *v.t.* to decant, to bottle.

abfüttern *v.t.* to feed; to line (*coat*).

Abgabe *f.* (-, -en) delivery, surrender; tax, duty.

Abgang *m.* (-[e]s, -gänge) departure; (*com.*) deficiency, tare; diminution; (*von Waren*) sale; (*theat.*) exit.

Abgangsprüfung *f.* final examination.

Abgangszeugnis *n.* certificate of completion.

Abgas *n.* (-es, -e) waste gas, exhaust gas.

abgearbeitet *a.* worn out.

abgeben *v.t.st.* to deliver up, to give up, to turn in; *sich* ~ *mit*, to concern oneself about a thing, to

keep company with a person.

abgebrannt *a.* (*fam.*) broke.

abgebrüht *a.* (*fam.*) hardened.

abgedroschen *a.* trite, hackneyed.

abgefeimt *a.* cunning, crafty.

abgegriffen *p. & a.* well-thumbed.

abgehackt *a.* clipped, chopped.

abgehangen *a.* hung.

abgehärmt *a.* haggard.

abgehärtet *a.* tough, hardened.

abgehen *v.i.st.* (*s*) to go off, to depart; (*Schiff*) to sail; to come off; *es geht mir ab*, I lack.

abgehetzt *a.* exhausted.

abgekämpft *a.* worn out, exhausted.

abgekartet *a.* (*fam.*) prearranged.

abgeklärt *a.* (*fig.*) detached.

abgelagert *a.* seasoned, matured.

abgelegen *a.* remote, outlying.

abgelten *v.t.st.* to satisfy, to settle.

abgemacht *a.* settled; ~! done! agreed!

abgemagert *a.* emaciated.

abgemessen *a.* disinclined.

abgeneigt *a.* measured; formal.

Abgeneigtheit *f.* (-, 0) disinclination, aversion.

abgenutzt *a.* worn out, used up; threadbare.

Abgeordnete(r) *m.* (-n, -n) deputy, representative; Member of Parliament.

Abgeordnetenhaus *n.*, **Abgeordnetenkammer** *f.* House of Commons; House of Representatives.

abgepackt *p. & a.* prepacked.

abgerechnet *p.* not counting, exclusive (of), deducting.

abgerissen *p. & a.* ragged; (*fig.*) abrupt.

abgesagt *a.* cancelled.

Abgesandte(r) *m.* (-n, -n) messenger.

Abgesang *m.* farewell, swansong.

abgeschieden *a.* secluded; retired; deceased.

abgeschmackt *a.* tasteless; absurd.

abgesehen *p.* ~ *von*, apart from; ~ *auf*, aimed at.

abgespannt *a.* (*fig.*) exhausted, run down.

abgestanden *p. & a.* stale, flat.

abgestorben *a.* dead, numb.

abgestumpft *a.* blunted; (*fig.*) dull, insensitive.

Abgestumpftheit *f.* (-, 0) dullness.

abgetakelt *a.* (*fig.*) run down.

abgetan *a.* done with, settled; dispatched.

abgetragen *a.* (*Kleider*) threadbare, worn out.

abgewinnen *v.t.st.* to win from; *Geschmack* ~, to get a taste for.

abgewogen *a.* balanced.

abgewöhnen *v.t.* to wean from; *sich etwas* ~, *v.refl.* to give up.

abgezehrt *a.* emaciated.

abgießen *v.t.ir.* to pour off, to decant.

Abglanz *m.* (-es, 0) reflection, image.

Abgott *m.* (-[e]s, -götter) idol.

Abgötterei *f.* (-, 0) idolatry.

abgöttisch *a.* itolatrous.

abgraben *v.t.st.* to drain off.

abgrämen (sich) *v.refl.* to pine away.

abgrasen *v.t.* to graze.

abgrenzen *v.t.* to delimit, to differentiate.

Abgrund *m.* (-[e]s, -gründe) abyss; precipice.

abgründig *a.* inscrutable, dark.

abgucken *v.t.* to learn through observation, to copy.

Abguß *m.* (-gusses, -güsse) cast, copy.
abhacken *v.t.* to chop off.
abhaken *v.t.* to unhook, to check off.
abhalftern *v.t.* to undo the halter; (*fig.*) to criticize.
abhalten *v.t.st.* to detain; to prevent; to keep off; (*Versammlung*) to hold.
abhandeln *v.t.* (*vom Preise*) to beat down; to discuss, to treat of.
abhanden *adv.* not at hand; ~ *kommen*, to be missing, to get lost.
Abhandlung *f.* (-, -en) treatise, paper.
Abhang *m.* (-[e]s, Abhänge) declivity, slope.
abhängen *v.t. & i.* to take down; to depend; to shake off.
abhängig *a.* dependent; addicted; ~ *von* subject to.
Abhängigkeit *f.* (-en, 0) dependence.
abhärmen (sich) *v.refl.* to pine away, to grieve.
abhärten *v.t.* to harden; to toughen.
abhaspeln *v.t.* to reel off.
abhauen *v.t.* to chop off, to cut off, to beat it.
abhäuten *v.t.* to skin.
abheben *v.t.st.* (*Karten*) to cut; (*Geld*) to withdraw; to take off; (sich) ~, to stand out (against).
abheften *v.t.* to file.
abheilen *v.i.* to heal.
abhelfen *v.t.st.* to remedy, to redress.
abhetzen *v.t.* to rush.
Abhilfe *f.* (-, 0) redress, remedy, relief.
abhobeln *v.t.* to plane off.
abhold *a.* averse, ill-disposed (towards).
abholen *v.t.* to fetch, to go for, to call for; *einen vom Bahnhof* ~, to meet a person at the station; ~ *lassen*, to send for.
Abholung *f.* (-, -en) collection.
abholzen *v.t.* to clear a wood.
abhorchen *v.t.* to sound (chest, lungs).
abhören *v.t.* to listen in, to monitor, to tap, to bug.
abirren *v.t.* (*s*) to deviate, to stray.
Abirrung *f.* (-, -en) deviation, aberration.
Abitur *n.* (-s, 0) school-leaving examination.
Abiturient *m.* (-en, -en) candidate for the leaving examination of a secondary school.
abjagen *v.t.* to retrieve; to override, overdrive (a horse); to snatch.
abkanten *v.t.* to bevel.
abkanzeln *v.t.* (*fig.*) to rebuke.
abkapseln *v.refl.* to cut o.s. off.
abkarten *v.t.* to prearrange; *abgekartete Sache*, put-up job, plot, collusion.
abkaufen *v.t.* to buy from.
Abkehr *f.* (-, 0) falling away, desertion.
abkehren (sich), *v.refl.*, to fall away, to desert.
abklappern *v.t.* (*fam.*) to scour (shops), to do (museums).
Abklatsch *m.* (-es, -e) poor imitation.
abklemmen *v.t.* to disconnect, to clamp.
abklingen *v.i.st.* to abate, to ease, to subside.
abklopfen *v.t.* to tap.
abknabbern *v.t.* to nibble off.
abknallen *v.t.* (*fam.*) to shoot down.
abkneifen *v.t.ir.* to pinch (off), to nip (off).
abknicken *v.t.* to snap off; to bend.
abknöpfen *v.t.* to unbutton; (*fam.*) *to get sth. out of sb.*.
abkochen *v.* to boil.
abkommandieren *v.t.* to detail, to send.

abkommen *v.i.st.* (*s*) to deviate; to fall into disuse; *ich kann nicht* ~, I am busy.
Abkommen *n.* (-s, -) agreement.
abkömmlich *a.* available.
Abkömmling *m.* (-s, -e) descendant.
abkoppeln *v.t.* to uncouple.
abkratzen *v.t.* to scrape off, to scratch off, (*fig. fam.*) to kick the bucket.
abkriegen *v.t.* to get (a share of); *etwas* ~, to come in for a scolding.
abkühlen *v.t.* to cool; (sich) ~ *v.refl.* to cool down, to get cool.
Abkühlung *f.* (-, -en) cooling; (*chem.*) refrigeration.
Abkunft *f.* (-, 0) descent, origin; *von guter* ~, of good family.
abkuppeln *v.t.* to uncouple.
abkürzen *v.t.* to shorten, to abridge, to abbreviate; (*math.*) to reduce.
Abkürzung *f.* (-, -en) abbreviation.
Abkürzungsweg *m.* short cut.
abküssen *v.t.* to kiss and hug.
abladen *v.t.st.* to unload, to dump.
Ablage *f.* (-, -n) file; storage.
ablagern *v.t.* to deposit.
Ablagerung *f.* (-, -en) sediment; (*geol.*) deposit.
Ablass *m.* (-lasses, -lässe) (*rel.*) indulgence; *vollkommener* ~, plenary indulgence.
ablassen *v.t.st.* (*vom Preise etwas*) to abate, to take off; (*einen Teich*) to drain; ~ *v.t.st.* to cease, to leave off.
Ablativ *m.* (-[e]s, -e) ablative.
Ablauf *m.* (-[e]s, 0) course, lapse, expiration.
ablaufen *v.t.st.* (*s*) to flow down; to end, to expire; to become due; ~ *v.t.ir.* to wear off by walking; (*den Rang*) ~, to outdo; ~ *lassen*, to snub; *schlecht* ~, to end ill.
ablauschen *v.t.* to overhear.
Ableben *n.* (-s, 0) decease, death.
ablecken *v.t.* to lick off.
ablegen *v.t.* to file, to lay aside; take off, to put down; (*einen Eid*) to take (an oath); (*ein Kleid*) to take off, to cease wearing; (*Rechenschaft*) to account for; *Zeugnis* ~, to bear witness.
Ableger *m.* (-s, -) layer, shoot, cutting.
ablehnen *v.t.* to decline, to refuse, to turn down; (*Richter, Geschworene*) to challenge.
Ablehnung *f.* (-, -en) refusal; (*Richter, Geschworene*) challenge.
ableisten *v.t.* to serve, to perform duly.
ableiten *v.t.* to divert; to derive.
Ableitung *f.* (-, -en) derivation; diversion.
ablenken *v.t.* to avert, to divert, to turn off; (*phys.*) to deflect.
ablernen *v.t.* to learn from.
ablesen *v.t.st.* to read.
Ablesung *f.* (-, -en) reading.
ableugnen *v.t.* to deny, to disown.
Ableugnung *f.* (-, -en) denial, abnegation.
ablichten *v.t.* to copy.
abliefern *v.t.* to deliver.
Ablieferung *f.* (-, -en) delivery.
abliegen *v.i.st.* (*s*) to lie away from.
ablocken *v.t.* to get by coaxing.
ablöschen *v.t.* to wipe.
ablösen *v.t.* to loosen; to take off; to detach; (*die*

Wache) to relieve; (sich) ~ *v.refl* to peel off; to alternate.

Ablösung *f.* (-, -en) loosening; redemption; relief.

abluchsen *v.t.* (*fam.*) to get something out of somebody.

abmachen *v.t.* to undo, to loosen; to arrange, to stipulate.

Abmachung *f.* (-, -en) arrangement, stipulation.

abmagern *v.i.* (*s*) to fall away, to grow lean, thin.

Abmagerungskur *f.* (-, -en) weight-losing diet.

abmähen *v.t.* to mow.

abmalen *v.t.* to paint, to portay; to depict.

Abmarsch *m.* (-[e]s, -märsche) (*mil.*) marching off.

abmarschieren *v.i.* (*s*) to march off.

abmartern *v.t.* to torture; to vex; to worry.

abmatten *v.t.* to fatigue, to tire out.

abmelden (sich) *v.t. & refl.* to report out, to report a person's departure; to cancel.

abmessen *v.t.st.* to measure, to survey.

Abmessung *f.* (-, -en) measurement; proportion, dimension.

abmontieren *v.t.* (*mech.*) to dismantle.

abmühen (sich) *v.refl.* to exert oneself; to struggle.

abmurksen *f.* (*fam.*) to do s.o. in.

abnabeln *v.t.* to cut the umbilical cord.

abnagen *v.t.* to gnaw, to nibble.

Abnäher *m.* (-s, 0) tuck.

Abnahme *f.* (-, -n) decrease; (*einer Maschine*) acceptance.

abnehmen *v.t.st.* to take off *or* away; ~ *v.i.ir.* to decrease, to diminish; to lose weight.

Abnehmer *m.* (-s, -) buyer.

Abneigung *f.* (-, -en) disinclination, aversion, dislike.

abnorm *a.* abnormal.

Abnormität *f.* (-, -en) abnormality, monstrosity.

abnötigen *v.t.* to force (from), to extort (from).

abnutzen *v.t.* to wear out; (sich) ~, *v.refl.* to wear off.

Abnutzung *f.* (-, -en) wear and tear.

Abonnement *n.* (-s, -s) subscription; season ticket; *Jahres* ~, annual subscription; *Monats* ~, monthly subscription; *sein* ~ *aufgeben*, to discontinue one's subscription.

Abonnent *m.* (-en, -en) subscription.

abonnieren *v.t.* to subscribe to.

abordnen, *v.t.* to delegate; (*mil.*) to detail.

Abordnung *f.* (-, -en) delegacy, delegation, deputation.

Abort *m.* (-[e]s, -e) water-closet (W.C.), lavatory; toilet; miscarriage.

abpachten *v.t.* to rent, to farm (from).

abpacken *v.t.* to pack, to wrap.

abpassen *v.t.* to watch for; to choose a fitting time, to time.

abpausen *v.t.* to trace.

abpfeifen *v.t.st.* (*sp.*) to blow the whistle to stop the game.

Abpfiff *m.* (-[e]s, -e) (*sp.*) final whistle.

abpflücken *v.t.* to pluck off; to pick.

abplacken, abplagen (sich) *v.refl.* to tire oneself out, to drudge.

abplatten *v.t.* to flatten.

abplatzen *v.i.* to flake off.

abpralen *v.i.* (s) to rebound; to bounce off; to ricochet.

abpumpen *v.t.* to pump out; to extract (*milk*).

abputzen *v.t.* to clean, to polish.

abquälen *v.t.* to torment, to worry.

abrackern *v.refl.* to slave, to toil.

abraten *v.t.st.* to dissuade (from), to warn (against).

abräumen *v.t.* to clear, to take away, to remove.

abrauschen *v.i.* (*fam.*) to rush off.

abreagieren *v.t.* to work off; *v.refl.* to work off one's feelings.

abrechnen *v.t.* to deduct; ~ *v.i.* to settle (accounts).

Abrechnung *f.* (-, -en) settlement; *auf* ~ on account.

Abrechnungstag *m.* (*Börse*) settling day.

Abrede *f.* (-, -n) agreement; *in* ~ *stellen*, to deny, to dispute.

abreiben *v.t.st.* to rub off, to rub down; to grind (colors).

Abreise *f.* (-, -n) departure.

abreisen *v.i.* (*s*) to depart, to set out, to start.

abreißen *v.t.st.* to tear off; (*Häuser*) to pull down; ~ *v.i.st.* to break off, to snap off.

abrichten *v.t.* (*Pferd*) to break (in); (*Hund*) to train.

abriegeln *v.t.* to bolt.

abringen *v.t.st.* to twist off; (*fig.*) to wrest (a thing) from.

abrinnen *v.i.st.* (*s*) to flow down.

Abriss *m.* (-risses, -risse) sketch, abstract; demolition.

abrollen *v.i.* (*s*) to roll off; ~ *v.t.* to unroll.

abrücken *v.t. & i.* to move away, to move off.

Abruf *m.* (-[e]s, -e) recall; *auf* ~ (*com.*) on call.

abrufen *v.t.st.* to call away *or* off.

abrunden *v.t.* (*Zahlen*) to correct, to round off.

abrupfen *v.t.* to pluck off.

abrupt *a. & adv.* abrupt, abruptly.

abrüsten *v.t.* to disarm.

Abrüstung *f.* (-, -en) disarmament.

abrutschen *v.i.* to glide down, to slip.

Absage *f.* (-, -n) refusal.

absagen *v.t. & i.* to cancel (one's engagement).

absägen *v.t.* to saw off.

absahnen *v.t.* (*fam.*) to skim.

absatteln *v.t.* to unsaddle.

Absatz *m.* (-es, -sätze) (*Treppen~*) landing; (*Waren~*) sale, market; (*Stiefel~*) heel; (*im Druck*) paragraph; *schnellen* ~ *finden*, to have a ready sale.

Absatz: ~**bewegung** (*mil.*) disengagement; ~**genossenschaft**, marketing association; ~**markt**, outlet, market.

absaugen *v.t.* to suck off, to vacuum.

abschaben *v.t.* to scrape off.

abschaffen *v.t.* to abolish, to remove.

Abschaffung *f.* (-, -en) abolition.

abschälen *v.t.* to peel, to pare.

abschalten *v.t.* to turn off.

abschatten *v.t.* to shade.

abschätzen *v.t.* to value; to assess, to estimate.

Abschätzung *f.* (-, -en) estimate, valuation.

Abschaum *m.* (-[e]s, -schäume) scum; dross; (*fig.*) dregs, *pl.*

abschäumen *v.t.* to scum, to skim.

abscheiden *v.t.st.* to secrete; ~*v.i.* (*s*) to die.

Abscheu *m.* (-[e]s, 0) abhorrence, horror.

abscheuern *v.t.* to scrub off.

abscheulich *a.* abominable, detestable.
abschicken *v.t.* to send off, to dispatch.
abschieben *v.t.st.* to shove off; (*fam.*) to move off; to deport.
Abschiebung *f.* (-, -en) (*jur.*) deportation.
Abschied *m.* (-[e]s, -e) discharge; departure, leave; ~ *nehmen*, to bid farewell, to take leave; *einem den* ~ *geben*, to dismiss someone; *seinen* ~ *nehmen*, to resign.
Abschiedsgesuch *n.* resignation.
abschießen *v.t.st.* to shoot off; to fire, to discharge; (*avi.*) to shoot down.
abschinden *v.t.st.* to flay, to skin; (sich) ~ *v.refl.* to tire oneself to death.
abschirmen *v.t.* to shield; to screen off.
abschirren *v.t.* to unharness.
abschlachten *v.t.* to slaughter, to butcher.
abschlaffen *v.i.* (*fam.*) to wilt; to sag.
Abschlag *m.* (-[e]s, -schläge); (*im Preise*) decline; *auf* ~, on account, in part-payment; ~**szahlung**, payment on account.
abschlagen *v.t.st.* to refuse, to deny; (*den Feind*) to repel; (*sein Wasser*) to make water.
abschlägig *a.* negative, refusing; ~*e Antwort f.* refusal, denial.
abschleifen *v.t.st.* to grind off, to polish, to sand.
Abschleppdienst *m.* (-[e]s, -e) towing service.
abschleppen *v.t.* to tow away; to drag off; (sich) ~ *v.refl.* to exert oneself in carrying.
abschließen *v.t.st.* to close, to lock; (*einen Handel*) to conclude (*or* strike) a bargain.
abschließend *a.* definitive, final.
Abschluß *m.* (-schlusses, -schlüsse) close, settlement, conclusion.
Abschlußprüfung *f.* (-, -en) final exam.
Abschlußzeugnis *n.* (-ses, -se) diploma.
abschmecken *v.t.* to taste; to season.
abschmieren *v.t.* to grease, (*fam.*) to copy from.
abschminken *v.t.* to remove make-up; (*fam.*) *das kannst du dir* ~ forget it.
abschnallen *v.t.* to unbuckle.
abschneiden *v.t.st.* to cut off, to clip; to pare; *gut* ~ *v.i.* to come off well.
abschnellen *v.t.* to let fly with a jerk; ~ *v.i.* (*s*) to fly off with a jerk.
Abschnitt *m.* (-[e]s, -e) cut; section; division; chapter, part, (*geom.*) segment.
abschnittweise *adv.* in paragraphs, piece by piece.
abschnüren *v.t.* to cut off.
abschöpfen *v.t.* to skim.
abschrägen *v.t.* (*mech.*) to bevel.
abschrauben *v.t.* to unscrew.
abschrecken *v.t.* to frighten, to deter.
Abschreckung *f.* (-, -en) deterrence.
Abschreckungsmittel *n.* (-s, -) deterrent, determent.
abschreiben *v.t.* to transcribe, to copy; to write off; ~ *v.t.* to cancel an engagement in writing.
Abschreibung *f.* (-en) amortization.
abschreiten *v.t.st.* to measure by steps; (*mil.*) to review.
Abschrift *f.* (-, -en) copy, transcript; *die Richtigkeit der* ~ *wird bezeugt*, certified true copy.
abschriftlich *adv.* in a copy.
abschrubben *v.t.* to scrub off.
abschürfen *v.t.* to graze; to chafe.

abschuppen *v.t.* to scale.
Abschuß *m.* (-sses, -schüsse) shooting; discharge, launching; ~ *rampe f.* (-, -n) launching pad.
abschüssig *a.* steep, precipitous.
abschütteln *v.t.* to shake off.
abschwächen *v.t.* to weaken.
abschwatzen *v.t.* to talk (one) out of (a thing).
abschweifen *v.i.* (*s*) to stray; to digress.
Abschweifung *f.* (-, -en) digression.
abschwellen *v.t.* (*med.*) to go down; (noise) to die down.
abschwenken *v.i.* (*s*) to wheel, to turn aside.
abschwindeln *v.t.* to swindle (a person) out of.
abschwören *v.t.st.* to abjure, to forswear.
Abschwung *m.* (-s, -schwünge) downward trend; (*sp.*) dismount.
absegeln *v.i.* (*s*) to set sail, to put to sea.
absehbar *a.* within sight, foreseeable.
absehen *v.t.st.* to predict, to foresee; to learn by observation; ~ *auf*, to aim at; ~ *von*, to leave out of account, to disregard.
abseifen *v.t.* to soap somebody down.
abseilen *v.t.* to lower with a rope.
abseits *adv.* aside, apart.
Abseits *n.* (-, -) (*sp.*) offside.
absenden *v.t.ir.* to send away, to dispatch.
Absender *m.* (-s, -) sender, consignor.
Absendung *f.* (-, -en) sending, dispatch.
abservieren *v.i.* to clear away; (*fam.*) to throw out.
absetzen *v.t.* to depose; to dismiss; to remove; (*Waren*) to sell; (sich) ~, *v.refl.* (*m.l.*) to disengage.
absetzbar *a.* deductible.
Absetzung *f.* (-, -en) removal, deposition.
absichern *v.t.* to make safe; (*comp.*) to save.
Absicht *f.* (-, -en) view, intention, purpose; *mit der* ~, with a view (to).
absichtlich *a.* intentional, deliberate, ~ *adv.* on purpose.
absichtslos *adv.* unintentionally.
absingen *v.t.st.* to sing, to chant.
absinken *v.i.st.* to sink; (*fig.*) to decline.
absitzen *v.i.st.* (*s*) to dismount, ~ *v.t.* to sit out (a given time).
absolut *a.* absolute, positive; ~ *adv.* absolutely, perfectly.
Absolutismus *m.* (-, 0) absolutism.
Absolution *f.* (-, -en) (*rel.*) absolution.
absolvieren *v.t.* (*Schule*) to graduate from.
absonderlich *a.* particular; singular, odd.
absondern *v.t.* to separate; to set apart; (*med.*) to secrete; (sich) ~ *v.refl.* to seclude oneself, to withdraw; to dissolve partnership.
Absonderung *f.* (-, -en) separation; seclusion, retirement; (*med.*) secretion.
absorbieren *v.t.* to absorb.
abspalten *v.t.* to split off.
abspannen *v.t.* (horse) to unharness.
Abspannung *f.* (-, 0) fatigue.
absparen *v.t. sich* ~, to pinch oneself.
abspeisen *v.t.* to feed; (*fig.*) to put off, to palm off.
abspenstig *a.* ~ *machen*, to alienate (from); ~ *werden*, to fall off from.
absperren *v.t.* to shut off, to cut off; to block; *polizeilich* ~, to cordon off.
Absperrung *f.* (-, -en) isolation; blockage, closure, barrier.

abspielen *v.refl.* to play; to take place, to come off; to pass.

absplittern *v.t.* to splinter; ~ *v.i.* to come off in splinters.

Absprache *f.* (-, -n) agreement, arrangement.

absprechen *v.t.* to deny; ~ *v.i.* to criticize rashly; ~ *v.refl.* to come to an agreement.

abspringen *v.i.st.* (*s*) to leap off, to jump off; to rebound; (*fig.*) to shift, to digress.

Absprung *m.* (-[e]s, -sprünge) (downward) leap, jump; (*sp.*) take-off.

abspulen *v.t.* to wind off, to unwind.

abspülen *v.t.* to wash up.

abstammen *v.i.* (*s*) to descend; to be derived.

Abstammung *f.* (-, -en) descent; derivation.

Abstammungslehre *f.* (-, -n) theory of evolution.

Abstand *m.* (-[e]s, -stände) distance; interval; compensation; ~ *nehmen,* to desist from.

abstatten *v.t.* to render; (*Besuch*) to pay a visit.

abstauben *v.t.* to dust.

abstechen *v.t.st.* to stab; to kill; ~ *v.i.* (*h, s*) to contrast (with).

Abstecher *m.* (-s, -) excursion, trip.

abstecken *v.t.* to mark out, to plot (the course); to define.

abstehen *v.i.st.* to stick out; to give up; (*schal werden*) to get stale.

Absteige *f.* (-, -n) flophouse.

absteigen *v.i.st.* (*s*) to get off; (Hotel) to put up at, to stop at.

Absteiger *m.* (-s, -) (*s*) relegated team.

abstellen *v.t.* to stop (machine); to turn off (gas); to put; to park.

abstempeln *v.t.* to stamp; (*fig.*) to label.

absterben *v.i.st.* (*s*) to die away, out; (*med.*) to mortify; to fade; to go numb.

Absterben *n.* (-s, 0) death, demise, decrease.

Abstieg *m.* (-[e]s, -e) descent; decline; (*sp.*) relegation.

abstillen *v.t.* to wean.

abstimmen *v.i.* to vote, to coordinate; ~ *lassen über etwas,* to put a thing to the vote; ~ *v.t.* to tune.

Abstimmung *f.* (-, -en) voting, ballot.

abstinent *a.* abstinent; non-drinker.

Abstinenz *f.* total abstinence.

Abstinenzler *m.* (-s, -) total abstainer, non-drinker.

abstoppen *v.t.* to stop; (*sp.*) to measure the time.

abstossen *v.t.st.* to thrust off; (*fig.*) to repel; to reject.

abstossend *a.* revolting, repulsive.

Abstossung *f.* (-, -en) repulsion.

atstottern *v.t.* (*fam.*) to pay in installments.

abstrahieren *v.t.* to abstract.

abstrakt *a.* abstract; abstractly.

abstreifen *v.t.* to strip off, to slip off.

abstreiten *v.t.st.* to dispute, to deny.

Abstrich *m.* (-[e]s, -e) deduction; (*med.*) smear; (*mus.*) down-bow.

abstufen *v.t.* to grade, to graduate.

Abstufung *f.* (-, en) gradation.

abstumpfen *v.t.* to blunt; to deaden; (sich) ~ *v.refl.* to grow blunt *or* dulled.

Absturz *m.* (-es, -stürze) precipice; (*avi.*) crash.

abstürzen *v.i.* to fall; (*avi.*) to crash.

abstützen *v.t.* to support.

absuchen *v.t.* to search, to comb, to screen.

Absud *m.* (-[e]s, -e) decoction.

absurd *a.* absurd; ~ *adv.* absurdly.

Abt *m.* (-[e]s, Äbte) abbot.

abtakeln *v.t.* to lay up, dismantle.

abtasten *v.t.* to feel; to palpate.

abtauen *v.t. & i.* to melt away, to thaw, to defrost.

Abtei *f.* (-, -en) abbey.

Abteil *n.* or *m.* (-es, -e) compartment.

abteilen *v.t.* to divide off; to partition off.

Abteilung *f.* (-, -en) division; partition; compartment; department; (*Soldaten*) detachment.

abtippen *v.t.* (*fam.*) to type out.

Äbtissin *f.* (-, -nen) abbess.

abtönen *v.t.* to shade (*Farbe, Ton*).

abtöten *v.t.* to mortify; to destroy; to deaden.

abtragen *v.t.st.* (*Kleider*) to wear out; (*Gebäude*) to demolish, to pull down; (*Hügel*) to level; (*Schuld*) to pay; *den Tisch* ~, to clear away.

abträglich *a.* detrimental, derogatory.

abtrainieren *v.t.* to work off.

Abtransport *m.* (-s, -e) transport, removal.

abtransportieren *v.t.* to take away; to dispatch; to remove.

abtreiben *v.t.st.* to drive off; (*med.*) to procure abortion; ~ *v.i.* to drift off.

Abtreibung *f.* (-, -en) abortion.

abtrennen *v.t.* to separate; to detach; to sever.

abtreten *v.t.st.* to cede, to make over; ~ *v.i.* (*s*) to retire.

Abtretung *f.* (-, -en) abdication, cession.

Abtritt *m.* (-[e]s, -s) exit; (*Abort*) water-closet, urinal.

abtrocknen *v.t.* to dry.

abtröpfeln *v.i.* (*s*) to drip off.

abtropfen *v.i.* to drip off.

abtrotzen *v.t.* to bully (someone) out of.

abtrünnig *a.* renegade, rebellious, apostate.

Abtrünnig(er) *m.* (-n, -n) deserter, renegade.

abtun *v.t.st.* to take off; to dismiss; to settle, to finish; to kill.

abtupfen *v.t.* to dab.

aburteilen *v.i.* to criticize harshly.

abverlangen *v.t.* to ask someone to give (a thing) up, to demand (from).

abwägen *v.t.st.* to weigh, to weigh out.

abwählen *v.t.* to vote out.

abwälzen *v.t.* to shift; (*Schuld*) to exculpate oneself.

abwandeln *v.t.* to adapt, to modify; (*gram.*) to decline, to conjugate.

Abwandlung *f.* (-, -en) modification; (*gram.*) declension, conjugation.

abwarten *v.t.* to await, to wait for .

abwärts *adv.* downward(s).

abwärtsgehen *v.i.st.* to get worse.

Abwärtstrend *m.* (-s, -s) downward trend.

Abwasch *m.* (-s, 0) washing dishes.

abwaschbar *a.* washable.

abwaschen *v.t.st.* to wash off.

Abwasser *n.* (-s, -wässer) waste-water, sewage.

abwechseln *v.t.* to alternate; to vary; ~ *v.i.* to come *or* go by turns.

abwechselnd *a. & adv.* alternate; by turns, in rotation.

Abwechslung *f.* (-, -en) change; variation; *zur* ~,

8

for a change.

abwechslungsreich *a.* varied; eventful.

Abweg *m.* (-e[s], -e) wrong way; *auf ~e geraten*, to go astray.

abwegig *a.* erroneous.

Abwehr *f.* (-, 0) defense; (*mil.*) counter-intelligence; hostility.

abwehren *v.t.* to ward off; to avert.

Abwehr: **~haltung** *f.* (-, -en) (*psych.*) defensiveness; **~kräfte** *pl.* (-) (*med.*) resistance; ~ **mechanismus** *m.* (-, -men) defense mechanism; **~reaktion** *f.* (-, -en) defensive reaction; ~ **spieler** *m.* (-s, -) (*sp.*) defender, defense; ~ **stoffe** *pl.* (-) (*med.*) antibodies.

abweichen *v.i.st.* (s) to deviate, to differ.

abweichend *a.* anomalous, different, divergent; *~e Meinung*, (*law*) dissenting opinion.

Abweichler *m.* (-s, -) deviationist.

Abweichung *f.* (-, -en) deviation; deflection; divergence; *zugelassene ~* (*mech.*) tolerance.

abweisen *v.t.st.* to turn away; to refuse; to reject; to dismiss; to repel.

Abweisung *f.* (-, -en) refusal, rejection; (law) nonsuit.

abwelken *v.i.* (s) to wither, to fade away.

abwenden *v.t.ir.* to turn away (off); to prevent; to avert; (sich) ~ *v.refl.ir.* to turn away (from), to abandon.

abwerfen *v.t.st.* to drop, to throw off, to cast off; (*Gewinn*) to yield a profit; (*Bomben*) to release.

abwerten *v.t.* to devalue.

abwertend *a.* derogatory.

Abwertung *f.* (-, -en) devaluation.

abwesend *a.* absent; ~ *ohne Urlaub* (*mil.*) absent without leave.

Abwesender *m.* (*bes. von der Arbeit*) absentee.

Abwesenheit *f.* (-, -en) absence.

abwetzen *v.t.* to wear off; to rub off.

abwickeln *v.t.* to unwind; to do (business).

Abwicklung *f.* (-, -en) handling.

abwiegeln *v.t.* to calm down (crowd); *v.i.* (pej.) to appease.

abwiegen *v.t.st.* to weigh out.

abwimmeln *v.t.* to get rid of.

abwinken *v.i.* to stop with a hint.

abwirtschaften *v.i.* to come to grief.

abwischen *v.t.* to wipe (off).

abwracken *v.t.* to break up, to scrap.

Abwurf *m.* (-[e]s, -würfe) (*avi.*) (*Bomben*) release.

abwürgen *v.t.* to strangle; to stall.

abzahlen *v.t.* to pay off.

abzählen *v.t.* to tell; to count out.

Abzahlung *f.* (-, -en) installment.

abzapfen *v.t.* to tap; *Blut ~*, to draw blood.

abzäumen, *v.t.* to unbridle.

Abzeichen *n.* (-s, -n) badge; ~ *pl.* insignia.

abzeichnen *v.t.* to mark (out); to draw; to copy a drawing.

Abziehbild *n.* (-[e]s, -er) sticker.

abziehen *v.t.st.* to pull off; to distill; to deduct; to subtract; (*phot.*) to print; (*die Aufmerksamkeit*) to divert; to sharpen; to skin; ~ *v.i.st.* (s) to march off.

abzielen *v.i.* to aim at.

abzirkeln *v.t.* to measure with compasses.

Abzug *m.* (-[e]s, -züge) departure; discount, deduction; (*phot.*) print; (*typ.*) proof.

abzüglich *pr.* (*com.*) less, deducting.

abzugsfähig *a.* deductible.

Abzugsgraben *m.* drain, conduit.

abzwacken *v.t.* to pinch off.

abzweigen *v.i.* (s) to branch off; (sich) ~ *v.refl.* to branch off, to turn off.

Abzweigung *f.* (-, -en) turnoff.

abzwicken *v.t.* to nip off.

abzwingen *v.t.st.* to extort (from).

ach! *i.* alas! ah!

Achat *m.* (-[e]s, -e) agate.

Achse *f.* (-, -n) axle, axletree; axis.

Achsel *f.* (-, -n) shoulder; *die ~n zucken*, to shrug one's shoulders.

Achselhöhle *f.* arm-pit.

Achselklappe *f.* shoulder-strap.

Achselzucken *n.* (-s, 0) shrug (of the shoulders).

acht *a.* eight; ~ *Tage*, a week.

Acht *f.* (-, 0) ban, outlawry; attention, care; *sich in acht nehmen*, to be careful; *achtgeben*, to pay attention.

achtbar *a.* respectable.

achteckig *a.* octagonal.

Achtel *n.* (-s, -) eighth part, eighth.

Achtelnote *f.* eighth note.

achten *v.t.& i.* to mind; to attend to; to consider; to esteem.

ächten *v.t.* to outlaw, to proscribe.

achtenswert *a.* estimable.

achtern *adv.* aft.

Achterdeck *n.* (*nav.*) quarterdeck.

achtfach *a.* eightfold.

achtgeben *v.i.st.* to take care; to pay attention.

achtlos *a.* careless, negligent.

achtsam *a.* attentive, mindful.

Achtstundentag *m.* eight-hour day.

achttägig *a.* for eight days; weekly.

Achtung *f.* (-, 0) attention; esteem, regard.

Ächtung *f.* (-, -en) ostracism, proscription, banning.

achtungswert *a.* estimable, respectable.

achtzehn *a.* eighteen.

achtzig *a.* eighty.

Achtziger *m.* (-s, -) octogenarian.

ächzen *v.i.* to groan.

Acker *m.* (-s, -Äcker) field, soil.

Acker: **~bau** *m.* farming, agriculture; **~land** *n.* arable land.

ackern *v.t.* to plow, to till; (*fam.*) to work hard.

adäquat *a.* appropriate, adequate, suitable.

addieren *v.t.* to sum up, to add up.

Addition *f.* (-, -en) addition; **~szeichen** *n.* sign of addition.

ade! *i.* adieu! good-bye! farewell!.

Adel *m.* (-s, 0) nobility, peerage; (*fig.*) nobleness.

adelig *a.* titled.

adeln *v.t.* (*fig.*) to ennoble, to give sb. a title.

Ader *f.* (-, -n) vein; artery; grain, streak; *zur ~ lassen*, to bleed.

Aderlaß *m.* (-lasses, -lässe) bleeding, blood-letting, phlebotomy.

adieu *adv.* adieu; ~ *sagen*, to bid farewell.

Adjektiv *n.* (-s, -e) adjective.

Adjutant *m.* (-en, -en) adjutant, aide-de-camp.

Adler *m.* (-s, -) eagle.

Adlernase *f.* aquiline *or* hooked nose.

adlig *a.* noble; **die Adligen** *m.pl.* the nobles, the nobility.

Admiral *m.* (-[e]s, -e) admiral.

Admiralität *f.* (-, -en) Board of Admiralty.

adoptieren *v.t.* to adopt.

Adoptivkind *n.* (-[e]s, -er) adopted child.

Adressat *m.* (-en, -en) addressee.

Adreßbuch *n.* (-[e]s, -bücher) directory.

Adresse *f.* (-, -n) address, direction; *per ~,* care of (c/o).

adressieren *v.t.* to address, to direct.

adrett *a.* smart.

Adria *f.* Adriatic.

Adverb *n.* (-s, -ien) adverb.

Advokat *m.* (-en, -en) lawyer, counsel.

Aerodynamik *f.* (-, 0) aerodynamics.

Affäre *f.* (-, -n) affair.

Affe *m.* (-n, -n) ape, monkey.

Affekt *m.* (-s, -e) passion; affection; **im ~** in the heat of the moment.

Affekthandlung *f.* (-, -en) emotive act.

affektieren *v.t.* to affect.

affektiert *a.* (*pej.*) affected.

Affenliebe *f.* blind fondness.

Affenschande *f.* (-, 0) great shame.

Äffin *f.* (-, -nen) she-ape.

affizieren *v.t.* to affect, to influence.

Afghane *m.* (-n, -n) **Afghanin** *f.* (-, -nen); **afghanisch** *a.* Afghan; **Afghanistan** n.(-s).

Afrika *n.* (-s,) Africa; **Afrikaner** (*m.*) (-s, -) **Afrikanerin** *f.* (-, -nen); **afrikanish** *a.* African.

After *m.* (-s, -) anus, backside.

Ägäis *f.* Aegean.

Agent *m.* (-en, -en), **Agentin** *f.* (-, -nen) representative, agent.

Agentur *f.* (-, -en) agency.

Aggregat *n.* (-s, -e) (*tech.*) unit; set.

Aggression *f.* (-, -en) aggression.

Aggressionstrieb *m.* (-s, -e) aggressive drive.

aggresiv *a.* aggressive.

Aggressivität *f.* (-, -en) aggressiveness.

Aggressor *m.* (-s, -en) aggressor.

Ägide *f.* (-, 0) ægis; auspices *pl.*

agieren *v.i.* to act.

Agio *n.* (-s, 0) agio, premium.

Agitation *f.* (-, -en) agitation.

agitieren *v.i.* to agitate.

Agonie *f.* (-, -n) agony.

Agraffe *f.* (-, -n) clasp, brooch.

Agrarland *n.* (-es, -länder) agrarian country.

Agrarpolitik *f.* (-, 0) agricultural policy.

Agronom *m.* (-en, -en) agronomist.

Ägypten *n.* (-s) Egypt; **Ägypter** *m.* (-s, -); **Ägypterin** *f.* (-, -en); **ägyptisch** *a.* Egyptian.

ah! *i.* ah! ha!

Ahle *f.* (-, -n) awl.

Ahn *m.* (-s, -en) ancestor, forefather.

ahnden *v.t.* to punish; to avenge.

Ahne *f.* (-, -n) ancestress.

ähneln *v.i.* to resemble.

ahnen *v.i.* to have a presentiment *or* premonition.

Ahnherr *m.* ancestor.

ähnlich *a.* resembling, similar, alike.

Ähnlichkeit *f.* (-, -en) resemblance, likeness.

Ahnung *f.* (-, -en) premonition, foreboding, presentiment, suspicion, inkling; *keine ~,* not the slightest idea.

abnungslos *a.* unsuspecting.

ahnungsvoll *a.* ominous, awe-inspiring.

Ahorn *m.* (-s, -e) maple.

Ähre *f.* (-, -n) (*bot.*) ear; head; *~n lesen,* to glean.

Aids *n.* (-, 0) AIDS.

Akademie *f.* (-, -en) (*Kunst~*) Academy.

Akademiker *m.* (-s, -) Akademikerin *f.* (-, -nen) university graduate, academician.

akademisch *a.* academic.

Akazie *f.* (-, -n) acacia.

Akklamation *f.* (-, -en) acclamation.

akklimatisieren *v.t.* to acclimatize.

Akkord *m.* (-[e]s, -e) (*mus.*) chord, accord; contract, agreement.

Akkordarbeit *f.* piece work; *im Akkord arbeiten,* to do piecework; **Akkordlohn** *m.* piece(work) rates.

akkreditieren *v.t.* to accredit.

Akkreditierung *f.* (-, -en) accreditation.

Akkumulator *m.* (-s, -en) accumulator, storage battery; battery.

akkurat *a.* precise; meticulous; neat.

Akkusativ *m.* (-s, -e) accusative.

Akne *f.* (-, -n) acne.

Akquisiteur *m.* (-s, -e) agent, canvasser.

Akribie *f.* (-, 0) meticulousness.

Akrobat *m.* (-s, -en) **Akrobatin** *f.* (-, -nen) acrobat.

Akrobatik *f.* (-, 0) acrobatics.

akrobatisch *a.* acrobatic.

Akt *m.* (-[e]s, -e) act; deed; the nude.

Akte *f.* (-, -n) file.

Akten *pl.* acts, deeds, instruments, official documents, dossier.

Akten: ~deckel *m.* file; folder; **~klammer** *f.* paper clip; **~tasche** *f.* brief-case; **~stück** *n.* document; **~zeichen** *n., -nummer f.* file-number, reference-number.

Aktie *f.* (-, -n) share, stock.

Aktien: ~gesellschaft *f.* joint-stock company; **~kapital** share capital.

Aktion *f.* (-, -en) drive, project.

Aktionar *m.* (-[e]s, -e) shareholder.

aktiv *a.* active; *~er Teilhaber* (*com.*) working partner.

Aktiv *n.* (-s, -e) (*gram.*) active voice.

Aktiva *n. pl.* assets.

aktualisieren *v.t.* to update.

Aktualität *f.* (-, -en) relevance (to the present).

aktuell *a.* current.

Akupunktur *f.* (-, -en) acupuncture.

Akustik *f.* (-, 0) acoustics, *pl.*.

akustisch *a.* acoustic.

akut *a.* acute; urgent.

Akzent *m.* (-s, -e) stress, accent.

akzentuieren *v.t.* to stress, to accentuate.

Akzept *n.* (-[e]s, -e) (*com.*) acceptance.

akzeptabel *a.* acceptable.

akzeptieren *v.t.* to accept, to honor.

Alabaster *m.* (-s, 0) alabaster.

Alarm *m.* (-s, 0) alarm.

alarmieren *v.t.* to sound the alarm.

Alaun *m.* (-[e]s, -e) alum.

Albaner *m.* (-s, -,); **Albanerin** *f.* (-, -en); **albanisch** *a.* Albanian; **Albanien** *n.* (-s, 0) Albania.

albern *a.* silly, foolish.

Alchimie f. (-, 0) alchemy.

Alexandriner m. (-s, -) (*poet.*) Alexandrine.

Alge f. (-, -n) seaweed.

Algebra f. (-, 0) algebra.

Algerien n. (-s, 0) Algeria; **Algerier** (m.) (-s, -); **Algerierin** f. (-, -nen); **algerisch** a. Algerian.

Alibi n. (*law*) alibi; *sein ~ nachweisen*, to prove one's alibi.

Alimente n.pl. alimony; (*Scheidungs-*) ~, separation allowance.

alkalisch a. alkaline.

Alkohol m. (-s, -e) alcohol.

alkoholfrei a. non-alcoholic.

Alkoholika pl. alcoholic beverages.

Alkoholiker m. (-s, -) **Alkoholikerin** f. (-, -nen) alcoholic.

alkoholisch a. alcoholic.

alkoholisieren v.t. alcoholize.

Alkoholismus m. (-, 0) alcoholism.

Alkoven m. (-s, -) alcove; recess.

all(er), alle, alles a. all; whole; every.

All n. (-s, 0) the universe.

allbekannt a. notorious.

alle adv. ~ *sein*, to be gone, to be spent.

Allee f. (-, -[e]n) avenue.

Allegorie f. (-, -[e]n) allegory.

allein a. single; along; ~ c. only, but.

Alleinerziehende m. f. (-n, -n) single parent.

Alleingang m. (-s, -gänge) solo; single-handed action.

Alleinherrschaft f. (-, -en) autocracy.

Alleinvertreter m. sole agent.

alleinig a. sole, exclusive.

Alleinsein n. (-s, 0) loneliness.

alleinstehend a. detached, isolated; single, unmarried.

Alleinunterhalter m. (-s, -) solo entertainer.

allemal adv. always, every time; *ein für ~*, once for all.

allenfalls adv. at most, if need be; perhaps.

allenthalben adv. everywhere.

alleräußerst a. farthest, worst.

allerdings adv. indeed, to be sure, however, I admit.

allererst, zu allererst adv. first of all.

Allergie f. (-, -n) allergy.

allergisch a. allergic.

allerhand a. of all kinds.

Allerheiligen(fest) f. (-festes, -feste) All-Hallows, All Saints' Day.

allerlei a. of all kinds.

allerletzt a. last of all.

allerliebst a. charming, exquisite.

allermeist a. & adv. most, most of all; chiefly, mostly.

Allerseelentag m. All Souls' Day.

allerseits adv. on every side, everywhere.

allerwärts adv. everywhere.

Allerweltskerl m. (-s, -e) devil of a fellow.

allerwenigst a. least.

allesamt adv. one and all.

Allesfresser m. (-s, -) omnivore.

Alleskleber m. (-s, -) all-purpose glue.

Alleskönner m. (-s, -) person of many talents.

allezeit adv. always; (at) any time.

Allgegenwart f. (-, 0) omnipresence.

allgegenwärtig a. omnipresent, ubiquitous.

allgegemein a. universal, general, common; *im ~en*, in general; ~ adv. generally.

Allgemeinbegriff m. (-s, -e) general notion.

Allgemeinbesitz m. (-es, 0) common property.

Allgemeinbildung f. (-, 0) all round education.

allgemeingültig a. generally valid.

Allgemeinheit f. (-, -en) universality, generality; general public.

Allgemeinmedizin f. (-, 0) general medicine.

Allgemeinplatz m. (-es, plätze) platitude, cliché.

Allgemeinwohl n. (-s, 0) public welfare.

Allgewalt f. (-, 0) omnipotence.

Allheilmittel n. panacea.

Allianz f. (-, -en) alliance.

alliiert a. allied.

Alliierte m. (-n, -n) ally. .

alljährlich a. yearly, annual; ~ adv. yearly, annually.

Allmacht f. (-, 0) omnipotence.

allmächtig a. omnipotent, almighty.

allmählich a. gradual.

Allotria pl. tomfoolery.

Allparteienregierung f. (-, -en) all-party government.

Allradantrieb m. (-s, -e) all-wheel drive.

allseitig a. in all respects; universal, versatile; ~ adv. on all hands.

Alltag m. (-s, 0) weekday; daily routine.

alltäglich a. daily; (*fig.*) trite, everyday, commonplace.

Alltagstrott m. (-s, 0) daily grind.

allwissend a. omniscient, all-knowing.

allzu adv. too, much too.

Allzweck- all-purpose.

Alm f. (-, -en) Alpine pasture.

Almanach m. (-[e]s, -e) almanac.

Almosen n. (-s, -) alms, charity.

Alp m. (-[e]s, -e), **Alpdrücken** n. nightmare, incubus.

Alpen pl. (-) Alps.

Alphabet n. (-[e]s, -e) alphabet.

alphabetisch a. & adv. alphabetic(al); ~**anordnen** v.t. to aphabetize.

Alphabetisierung f. (-) teaching of literacy skills.

Alptraum m. (-s, -träume) nightmare.

Alraun m. (-[e]s, -e), **Alraune** f. mandrake.

als c. than; as; like; when; but; *sowohl ~ auch*, as well as; ~ *ob*, as if.

alsbald adv. forthwith, directly.

alsdann adv. then.

also adv. thus, so; ~ c. consequently.

alt a. old, ancient; aged; stale.

Alt m. (-[e]s, -e) contralto; ~ n. (-s, 0) dark beer.

Altan m. (-[e]s, -e) balcony.

Altar m. (-[e]s, -, Altäre) altar.

Altarbild n. altar-piece.

altbacken a. stale; outdated.

Altbau m. (-s, -ten) old building.

Alte[r] m. (-n, -n) *die ~n*, the ancients.

Alten: ~**heim** n. (-s, -e) old people's home; ~**pfleger** m. (-s, -) geriatric nurse; ~**tagesstätte** f. (-, -n) old people's day center.

Alter n. (-s, 0) age; old age; *vor alters*, of old, in olden days.

älter a. elderly.

altern *v.i.* (*h, s*) to grow old, to age.

alternativ *a.* alternative.

Alternativbewegung *f.* (-, -en) alternative movement.

Alternative *f.* (-, -n) alternative.

Alters: ~**erscheinung** *f.* sign of old age; ~**grenze** *f.* age limit; ~**heim** *n.* home for the aged; ~**klasse** (*mil.*) age class, age group; ~**rente** *f.* old-age pension; ~**schwäche** *f.* decrepitude; ~**versicherung** *f.* old-age insurance.

Altertum *n.* (-s, -tümer) antiquity.

altertümlich *a.* old-fashioned; antique.

altertumsforschung *f.* (-, 0) archaeology.

Altistin *f.* (-, -nen) alto-singer.

altklug *a.* precocious.

ältlich *a.* elderly, oldish.

altmodisch *a.* old-fashioned.

Altphilologie *f.* (-, 0) classical studies.

altruistisch *a.* altruistic.

Altstadt *f.* (-, -staedte) old town.

Altvordern *pl.* ancestors, progenitors, forbears.

Altweibersommer *m.* Indian summer.

Aluminium *n.* (-s, 0) aluminum.

am = **an dem**.

amalgamieren *v.t.* to amalgamate.

Amazone *f.* (-, -n) Amazon.

Amboß *m.* (-bosses, -bosse) anvil.

ambulanter Kranker *m.* outpatient.

Ambulanz *f.* (-, -en) ambulance; outpatients department.

Ameise *f.* (-, -n) ant.

Ameisen: ~**haufen** *m.* ant-hill; ~**säure** *f.* formic acid.

Amerika *n.* (-s, -s) America; **Amerikaner** *m.* (-s, -); **Amerikanerin** *f.* (-, -nen); **amerikanisch** *a.* American.

Amme *f.* (-, -n) wet-nurse.

Ammenmärchen *n.* (*pej.*) nursery tale.

Ammer *f.* & *m.* (-, -n) yellow-hammer, bunting.

Ammoniak *n.* (-s, 0) ammonia.

Amnestie *f.* (-, -[e]n) amnesty.

Amor *m.* (-, 0) Cupid.

amortisieren *v.t.* to pay off, to redeem (a debt).

Ampel *f.* (-, -n) traffic light.

Ampere: ~**meter** *m.* (*el.*) ammeter; ~**stunde** *f.* ampere-hour.

Amphibie *f.* (-, -n) amphibium.

Amphitheater *n.* (-s, -) amphitheater.

Ampulle *f.* (-, -n) ampule.

amputieren *v.t.* to amputate.

Amsel *f.* (-, -n) blackbird.

Amt *n.* (-[e]s, Ämter) position; charge, employment; office.

Amtfrau *f.* (-, -en) female senior civil servant; vgl. Amtmann.

amtieren *v.i.* to officiate.

amtlich *a.* official.

Amtmann *m.* (-s, -männer) senior civil servant, bailiff, rural magistrate.

Amts: ~**anmassung** *f.* unauthorized assumption of authority; ~**eid** *m.* oath of office; ~**enthebung** *f.* discharge from office; ~**führung** *f.* administration; ~**geheimnis** *n.* official secret; ~**gericht** *n.* local court; ~**gewalt** *f.* official authority; ~**handlung** *f.* official act; ~**inhaber** *m.* officeholder; ~**pflicht** *f.* official duty; ~**richter** *m.* district judge; ~**stunden**

f.pl. office hours; ~**zeit** *f.* term of office.

amtswegen *adv. von* ~, officially, ex officio.

Amulett *n.* (-s, -e) amulet, charm.

amüsant *a.* amusing.

amüsieren *v.t.* to amuse; *sich* ~, to enjoy oneself.

an *pr.* on, by, near, of, against, about, to, at.

Anabolikum *n.* (-s, -lika) anabolic steroid.

Analgesikum *n.* (-s, -sika) analgesic.

analog *a.* analogous.

Analogie *f.* (-, -n) analogy.

Analphabet *m.* (-en, -en) illiterate.

Analphabetentum *n.* illiteracy.

Analyse *f.* (-, -n) analysis.

analysieren *v.t.* to analyse.

analytisch *a.* analytical.

Anämie *f.* (-, -n) anemia.

Ananas *f.* (-, -u. -nasse) pineapple.

Anarchie *f.* (-, -n) anarchy.

anarchistisch *a.* anarchistic.

Anästhesie *f.* (-, -n) anaesthesia.

Anatolien *n.* (-s, 0) Anatolia.

Anatom *m.* (-en, -en) anatomist.

Anatomie *f.* (-, -[e]n) anatomy; dissecting-room, anatomical institute.

anatomisch *a.* anatomical.

anbahnen *v.t.* to pave the way for.

Anbau *m.* (-[e]s, -e) cultivation, culture; extension, wing.

anbauen *v.t.* to cultivate; to add.

Anbeginn *m.* (-s, 0) beginning, outset.

anbehalten *v.t.st.* to keep on.

anbei *adv.* herewith, enclosed, attached.

anbeissen *v.t.* & *i.st.* to bite.

anbelangen *v.t. was mich anbelangt*, for my part.

anbellen *v.t.* to bark at.

anberaumen *v.t.* to appoint, to fix (a day).

anbeten *v.t.* to adore, to worship.

Anbetracht *m. in* ~, considering, seeing.

anbetteln *v.t.* to ask alms of, to importune.

Anbetung *f.* (-, -en) adoration, worship.

anbiedern *v.refl.* sich ~ to ingratiate o.s..

anbieten *v.t.st.* to offer.

anbinden *v.t.st.* to tie; to bind, to fasten; ~ *v.i.* (*mit einem*) to pick a quarrel (with one); *kurz angebunden sein*, to be short with one.

anblasen *v.t.st.* to blow (the fire).

anbleiben *v.i.st.* to stay on.

Anblick *m.* (-[e]s, -e) view, aspect, sight; *beim ersten* ~, at first sight.

anblicken *v.t.* to look at.

anblinzeln *v.t.* to blink at.

anbohren *v.t.* to bore, to pierce, to drill.

anbrechen *v.t.st.* to break, to begin to cut off; ~ *v.i.* (*s*) to break, to begin, to appear.

anbrennen *v.i.ir.* to burn; *angebrannt schmecken*, to taste of burning.

anbringen *v.t.ir.* to apply, to fix; to sell; to lodge (a complaint).

Anbruch *m.* (-[e]s, -brüche) beginning, ~ *der Nacht*, night-fall.

anbrüllen *v.t.* to roar at; to bellow.

anbrummen *v.t.* to growl at.

Ancienität *f.* seniority.

Andacht *f.* (-, -en) devotion, prayers, *pl.*

andächtig *a.* devout, attentive.

Andalusien *n.* (-s, 0) Andalusia.

andauern *v.i.* to last.
andauernd *a.* constant, continual, continuous.
Anden *pl.* Andes.
Andenken *n.* (-s, -) souvenir; memory.
ander *a.* other, second; next.
andererseits *adv.* on the other hand.
andermal *adv.* another time.
ändern *v.t.*, sich ändern *v.refl.* to alter, to change; *ich kann es nicht ~*, I cannot help it.
andernfalls *adv.* otherwise, else.
andernorts *adv.* elsewhere.
anders *adv.* otherwise, else.
anderseits *adv.* on the other side *or* hand.
anderswo *adv.* elsewhere.
anderthalb *a.* one and a half.
Änderung *f.* (-, -en) change, alteration.
anderweitig *a. & adv.* other; in another way.
andeuten *v.t.* to signify, to hint; to intimate.
Andeutung *f.* (-, -en) intimation, suggestion, hint.
andichten *v.t.* to impute falsely.
Andrang *m.* (-[e]s, 0) crowd, throng, rush.
andrängen *v.i.st.* (s) to press forward.
andrehen *v.t.* to turn on; to screw; (*pej.*) to sell.
androhen *v.t.* to threaten, to menace.
Androhung *f.* (-, -en) threat.
andrücken *v.t.* to press towards *or* against.
anecken *v.i. bei jm.* ~ to give offence to sb.
aneignen (sich) *v.refl.* to appropriate.
aneinander *adv.* together; one another.
Anekdote *f.* (-, -n) anecdote.
anekeln *v.t.* to disgust.
Anerbieten *n.* (-s, -) offer, tender.
anerkennen *v.t.ir.* to acknowledge, to recognize; *Schuld nicht ~*, to repudiate a debt.
anerkennenswert *a.* commendable.
Anerkennung *f.* (-, -en) acknowledgement, recognition; appreciation.
anfachen *v.t.* to blow into a flame; (*fig.*) to kindle.
anfahren *v.t.* to convey, to carry; (*fig. einen*) to snub.
Anfahrt *f.* (-, -en) approach (to a building).
Anfall *m.* (-[e]s, -fälle) fit, seizure, attack.
anfallen *v.t.st.* to attack; to accrue; *~de Zinsen pl.* accrued interest.
anfällig *a.* (*fig.*) susceptible; prone.
Anfang *m.* (-[e]s, -fänge) commencement, beginning, opening.
anfangen *v.t.st.* to begin, to commence; to start; ~ *v.i.* to begin; to open.
Anfänger *m.* (-s, -) beginner.
angänglich *a. & adv.* initial, incipient; at first, at the outset, originally.
anfangs *adv.* in the beginning.
Anfangs ~**buchstabe** *m.* initial (letter); ~**gründe** *m.pl.* elements, rudiments.
anfassen *v.t.* to take hold of, to seize.
anfauchen *v.t.* to spit at; (*fig.*) to snap at.
anfaulen *v.i.* (s) to begin to rot, to go bad; **angefault** *a.* half-decayed.
anfechtbar *a.* contestable, disputable, open to criticism.
anfechten *v.i.st* to contest; to challenge; to tempt; to trouble.
Anfechtung *f.* (-, -en) temptation.
anfeinden *v.t.* to attack, to persecute.
anfertigen *v.t.* to manufacture, to make.

anfeuchten *v.t.* to moisten, to dampen.
anfeuern *v.t.* to inflame, to spur on.
anflehen *v.t.* to implore, to beseech.
anfliegen *v.t.st.* to fly to, to land at; *v.i.st.* to approach.
Anflug *m.* (-[e]s, -flüge) approach; blush, flush; tinge, smattering.
anfordern *v.t.* (*mil.*) to request, to order, to ask for.
Anforderung *f.* (-, -en) demand; (*mil.*) requisition.
Anfrage *f.* (-, -n) inquiry, application.
anfragen *v.t.* to inquire, to call for.
anfressen *v.t.st.* to gnaw; to corrode; to eat into.
anfreunden *v.refl.* to become friends.
anfügen *v.t.* to join to; to enclose, to annex, to subjoin.
anfühlen *v.t.* to touch, to feel.
anführen *v.t.* to lead, to conduct, to command; to impose upon, to dupe; to cite, to quote.
Anführer *m.* (-s, -) leader, commander.
Anführung *f.* (-, 0) leadership; command; quotation.
Anführungszeichen *n.* quotation mark.
anfüllen *v.t.* to fill; to replenish.
Angabe *f.* (-, -n) declaration, statement; instruction; (*com.*) entry; (*tennis*) service.
angeben *v.t.st.* to specify; to suggest; to declare, to assert; to denounce; *den Ton ~*, (*fig.*) to set the fashion, *v.i.st.* to brag, to boast.
Angeber *m.* (-s, -) boaster.
Angeberei *f.* (-, -en) bragging, showing off.
angeberisch *a.* boastful, pretentious.
angeblich *a.* pretended, purported, alleged; *adv.* supposedly, allegedly.
angeboren *a.* innate, inborn, congenital.
Angebot *n.* (-[e]s, -e) offer; bid; supply; (*com.*) tender; *~ und Nachfrage*, supply and demand.
angebracht *a.*, proper, appropriate.
angebunden *p.p.* tied to; *kurz ~* abrupt.
angedeihen (lassen) *v.i.st.* to bestow upon.
angegossen *a. wie ~ sitzen/passen* to fit like a glove.
angegraut *a.* graying.
angegriffen *a.* (*Gesundheit*) delicate, weakened, strained.
angeheiratet *a.* by marriage.
angeheitert *a.* tipsy.
angehen *v.t.st.* to apply to; to have to do with, to concern; (*einen um etwas*) to solicit; ~ *v.i.st.* to begin; to be tolerable; to be practicable; *es geht nicht an*, it won't do.
angehend *a.* incipient, prospective.
angehören *v.t.* to belong to.
Angehörige *m.pl.* relatives, relations; *abhängige~pl.* dependents.
Angeklagte[r] *m.* (-n, -n) defendant, accused.
Angel *f.* (-, -n) fishing-rod; (*archaic*) hinge.
angelegen, *sich ~ sein lassen*, to make a point of.
Angelegenheit *f.* (-, -en) affair, matter; *kümmere dich um deine eigenen ~en*, mind your own business.
angeln *v.t.* to fish, to angle; (*fig.*) to fish for.
Angel: ~**punkt** *m.* pivot; ~**rute** *f.* fishing-rod; ~**sachse**; ~**sächsisch** Anglo-Saxon, ~**schnur** *f.* fishing-line.
angemessen *a.* appropriate, suitable, fit, adequate.
angenehm *a.* agreeable, pleasant, acceptable.
angenommen *c.* ~ *dass*, supposing that, assuming that

angepaßt *a.* well adjusted.
angeregt *adv.* lively, animated.
angeschlagen *a.* groggy, weakened.
angeschlossen *p.p.* connected.
angeschmutzt *a.* soiled.
angesehen *a.* distinguished, respected.
angesessen *a.* settled, resident.
Angesicht *n.* (-[e]s, -er) face, countenance; *von ~,* by sight.
angesichts *pr.* in the face of, considering.
angespannt *a.* tense, tight, close.
angestammt *a.* hereditary, ancestral.
Angestellte[r] *m.* (-n, -n) employee.
angestrengt *a.* concentrated.
angetan *a.* ~ *sein von* to be taken with.
angetrunken *a.* tipsy.
angewandt *a.* applied.
angewiesen (auf) *a.* dependent (on).
angewöhnen *v.t.* to accustom; *v.refl.* to get into the habit of.
Angewohnheit *f.* (-, -en) habit, custom.
angleichen *v.t.st.* to assimilate.
angliedern *v.t.* to attach.
Anglikaner *m.* (-s, -); **anglikanisch** *a.* Anglican.
Anglist *m.* (-en, -en) **Anglistin** *f.* (-, -nen) English scholar, Anglicist.
Anglistik *f.* (-, 0) Anglistics, English studies.
Anglizismus *m.* (-, -men) Anglicism.
anglotzen *v.t.* (*fam.*) to stare at.
Angola *n.* (-s, 0) Angola; **Angolaner** *m.* (-s, -); **Angolanerin** *f.* (-, -nen); **angolanisch** *a.* Angolan.
angreifbar *a.* vulnerable, contestable.
angreifen *v.t.st.* to attack; to undertake (*fig.*) to fatigue, to tell upon, to affect.
Angreifer *m.* (-s, -) aggressor.
angrenzen *v.i.* to border (up)on.
angrenzend *a.* adjacent, contiguous.
Angriff *m.* (-[e]s, -e) attack, assault; aggression; *in ~ nehmen,* to start (on).
Angriffskrieg *m.* war of aggression.
angrinsen *v.t.* to grin at.
Angst *f.* (-, Ängste) anxiety, anguish, fright, fear.
ängstigen *v.t.* to frighten, to scare; (sich) ~ *v.refl.* to be frightened; to feel alarmed.
ängstlich *a. & adv.* anxious, uneasy; anxiously; scrupulously.
angucken *v.t.* to look at, to peep at.
angurten *v.t.* to strap in, to buckle up; *v.refl.* to fasten seat belt.
angstvoll *a.* anxious.
anhaben *v.t.st.* to have on, to wear; *er kann ihm nichts ~,* he cannot find anything against him.
anhaften *v.t.* to stick to, to cling to.
Anhalt *m.* (-[e]s, -e) support, hold; clue.
anhalten *v.t.st.* to stop, to arrest; ~ *v.i.st.* to last; ~ *um,* to propose (to), to ask in marriage; to pull up, to draw up.
anhaltend *a.* constant, continuous.
Anhalter *m.* (-s, -) **Anhalterin** *f.* (-, -nen) hitchhiker.
Anhaltspunkt *m.* evidence, clue.
anhand *pr.* with the help of.
Anhang *m.* (-[e]s, -hänge) appendix; supplement; adherents.
anhängen *v.t.* to hang on; to join, to annex, to

affix, to add.
Anhänger *m.* (-s, -) supporter, adherent, follower.
Anhängewagen (Anhänger) *m.* trailer.
anhängig *a.* (*Prozeß*) pendent, pending; *~machen,* to bring (an action against).
anhänglich *a.* attached (to).
Anhängsel *n.* (-s, -) appendage.
anhauchen *v.t.* to breathe on, to blow on.
anhäufen *v.t. & r.* (sich) to heap up; to accumulate.
Anhäufung *f.* (-, -en) accumulation.
anheben *v.t. & i.st.* to begin; to lift, to raise.
Anhebung *f.* (-, -en) increase.
anheften *v.t.* to tack on; to stitch to.
anheimelnd *a.* homely, cozy.
anheimfallen *v.i.st.* (s) to fall to.
anheimstellen *v.t.* to leave to; to submit (to).
anheischig *a. sich ~ machen,* to pledge oneself, to undertake.
anheizen *v.t.* to fire, to fuel, to heat up.
anheuern *v.t.* to sign on.
Anhöhe *f.* (-, -n) rising ground, hill.
anhören *v.t.* to listen to, to attend; *sich ~,* to sound.
Anhörung *f.* (-, -en) hearing.
Anilin *n.* (-s, 0) aniline.
animalisch *a.* animal, bestial.
Animateur *m.* (-s, -e) animator.
animieren *v.t.* to encourage.
Animosität *f.* (-, -en) animosity.
Anis, *m.* (-es, -e) anise, aniseed.
ankämpfen (gegen) *v.i.* to struggle against.
Ankauf *m.* (-[e]s, -käufe) purchase.
ankaufen *v.t.* to purchase, to buy; (sich) ~ *v.refl.* to buy land, to settle at a place.
Anker *m.* (-s, -) anchor; (*el.*) armature; *vor ~gehen,* to cast anchor; *~lichten,* to weigh anchor.
ankern *v.t.* to anchor.
Anker: ~platz *m.* anchorage; **~winde** *f.* windlass, capstan.
anketten *v.t.* to chain (to).
Anklage *f.* (-, -n) accusation, charge; *f. öffentliche ~ (law),* arraignment; *unter ~ stehen (law),* to be on trial, to stand trial (for).
Anklagebank *f.* (-, -bänke) dock.
Anklagebehörde *f.* prosecution.
anklagen *v.t.* to accuse, to impeach.
Anklagepunkt *m.* count (of the indictment).
Anklageschrift *f.* indictment.
Anklagevertreter *m.* counsel for the prosecution.
anklammern (sich) *v.refl.* to cling (to).
Anklang *m.* (-[e]s, -klänge) (*fig.*) approval, kind reception; *Anklänge (an etwas)* reminiscence (of), *pl.*
ankleben *v.t. & i.* to paste on; to stick up; to stick to, to adhere.
ankleiden *v.t.* to dress, to attire; *v.refl.* to get dressed.
Ankleidezimmer *n.* dressing-room.
anklingen *v.i.st.* (*fig.*) to remind one (of).
anklopfen *v.i.* to knock (at the door).
anknabbern *v.t.* to nibble.
anknipsen *v.t.* to switch on.
anknüpfen *v.t.* (*ein Gespräch*) to enter (into a conversation); *Bekanntschaft ~,* to make one's acquaintance.

Anknüpfungspunkt *m.* point of contact, starting-point.

ankommen *v.i.st.* (*s*) to arrive; *auf etwas ~*, to depend upon; *es darauf ~ lassen*, to take a chance; *es nicht darauf ~ lassen*, to take no chances; *es kommt nicht darauf an*, it does not matter.

Ankömmling *m.* (-s, -e) newcomer.

ankoppeln *v.t.* to couple, to hitch, to dock.

ankreiden *v.t. jm. etwas ~* to blame sb.; to make someone pay.

ankreuze *v.t.* to mark with a cross.

ankündigen *v.t.* to announce.

Ankündigung *f.* (-, -en) announcement.

Ankunft *f.* (-, 0) arrival.

Ankunftszeit *f.* (-, -en) time of arrival.

ankuppeln *v.t.* to hitch, to dock.

ankurbeln *v.t.* to put into gear, to crank up; (*fig.*) to start; to boost.

anlächeln *v.t.* to smile at.

anlachen *v.t.* to smile at, to laugh with.

Anlage *f.* (-, -n) (*von Kapital*) investment; (*von Strassen, Gärten*) layout; (*Park*) park, grounds, *pl.*; (*fig.*) talent, disposition; (*Fabrik*) plant; (*in Brief*) enclosure.

anlangen *v.i.* (*s*) to arrive; *~ v.t.* to concern.

Anlaß *m.* (-lasses, -lässe) occasion.

anlassen *v.t.st.* to keep on; to start, to turn on; (sich) *~ v.refl.* to promise.

Anlasser *m.* (-s, -) starter.

anläßlich *pr. mit. Gen.* on the occasion of.

anlasten *v.tr.* to accuse, to blame.

Anlauf *m.* (-[e]s, -läufe) run, start, rush.

anlaufen *v.i.st.* (s) to run against; (*sich trüben*) to tarnish.

Anlaut *m.* (-s, -e) initial sound.

Anlegehafen *m.* port of call.

anlegen *v.t.* (*Kleider, etc.*) to put on; (*Gewehr*) to take aim; to found, to establish; (*Kapital*) to invest; (*Garten*) to lay out; (*Hand*) to set to work; *~ v.i.* (*nav.*) to land.

Anleger *m.* (-s, -) investor.

Anlegestelle *f.* landing place.

anlehnen *v.t.* to lean on *or* upon; (*Tür*) to leave ajar.

Anleihe *f.* (-, -n) loan; *eine ~ machen*, to raise a loan.

anleimen *v.t.* to glue on.

anleinen *v.t.* to put on a leash.

anleiten *v.t.* to guide, in instruct (in).

Anleitung *f.* (-, -en) instruction.

anlernen *v.t.* to train.

Anliegen *n.* (-s, -) concern, request.

anliegend *a.* adjacent, tightfitting.

Anlieger *m.* (-s, -) resident, *~ frei!* residents only!.

anlocken *v.t.* to lure; to attract.

anlöten *v.t.* to solder.

anlügen *v.t.st.* to lie to.

anmachen *v.t.* to fasten to; (*Feuer*) to light; (*Salat*) to dress; (*fam.*) to turn s.o. on; to snap at.

anmalen *v.t.* to paint.

Anmarsch *m.* (-[e]s, -märsche) approach (of an army).

anmassen (sich) *v.refl.* to assume, to arrogate, to usurp; to pretend to.

anmassend *a.* arrogant.

Anmassung *f.* (-, -en) assumption, usurpation, arrogance.

anmelden *v.t.* to enroll, to announce; (sich) *~ v.refl.* (*polizeilich*) to register; to notify.

Anmeldung *f.* (-, -en) enrollment, registration.

anmerken *v.t.* (-, -en) to remark, to note.

Anmerkung *f.* (-, -en) note, footnote, remark.

Anmut *f.* (-, 0) sweetness, charm, grace.

anmuten *v.t.* to give the impression.

anmutig *a.* graceful, charming.

annageln *v.t.* to nail to.

annähen *v.t.* to sew on.

annähern (sich) *v.refl.* to approach

annähernd *a.* approximate; *adv.* almost, nearly.

Annäherung *f.* (-, -en) approach.

Annäherungsversuch *m.* (-s, -e) advance.

Annahme *f.* (-, -n) acceptance; (*an Kindes Statt*) adoption; (*Meinung*) assumption.

Annahmestelle *f.* receiving office.

Annalen *pl.* annals

annehmbar *a.* acceptable, admissible, plausible

annehmen *v.t.st.* to accept; to assume; (*als ausgemacht*) to take for granted; (sich) *~ v.refl.* to take care of, befriend.

Annehmlichkeit *f.* (-, -en) comfort, amenity.

annektieren *v.t.* to annex.

Annexion *f.* (-, -en) annexation.

anno, Anno in the year.

Annonce *f.* (-, -n) advertisement.

annoncieren *v.t.* to advertise.

annullieren *v.t.* to annul; (*law*) to set aside.

Anode *f.* (-, -n) anode.

anöden *v.t.* (*fam*) to bore to death.

anomal *a.* anomalous, abnormal.

Anomalie *f.* (-, -n) anomaly, abnormality.

anonym *a.* anonymous.

Anonymität *f.* (-, en) anonymity.

Anorak *m.* (-s, -s) anorak.

anordnen *v.t.* to order, to dispose, to arrange.

Anordnung *f.* (-, -en) order; arrangement, disposition, alignment.

anorganisch *a.* inorganic.

anormal *a.* abnormal.

anpacken *v.t.* to grasp, to seize.

anpassen *v.t.* to fit to; to try on; to adapt, to accommodate.

Anpassung *f.* (-, 0) adaptation.

anpassungsfähig *a.* adaptable.

Anpassungsfähigkeit *f.* adaptability.

anpeilen *v.t.* to take a bearing; to aim at.

anpfeifen *v.t.st.* to whistle for the start; (*fam.*) to blow s.o. up.

Anpfiff *m.* (-s, -e) whistle for the start; **einen ~ kriegen** to get ticked off.

anpflanzen *v.t.* to plant.

anpöbeln *v.t.* to molest, to mob.

anpochen *v.i.* to knock (at the door).

Anprall *m.* (-[e]s, 0) impact; (*mil.*) shock.

anprallen *v.i.* (s) to crash.

anprangern *v.t.* to denounce (publicly).

anpreisen *v.t.* to commend, to extol.

Anprobe *f.* (-, -en) fitting.

anproben, anprobieren *v.t.* to try on, to fit on.

anpumpen *v.t.* to borrow money from.

Anrainer *m.* (-s, -) neighbor.

anrasen *v.i.* to come racing along/up.

anraten *v.t.st.* to advise.

15

anrechnen *v.t.* to count; to charge; to rate; to impute; ~ *gegen*, to set off against.

Anrecht *n.* (-[e]s, -e) right, claim, title.

Anrede *f.* (-, -n) address; (*Brief*) salutation.

anreden *v.t.* to address, to accost.

anregen *v.t.* to suggest; to stimulate; to mention.

anregend *a.* stimulating.

Anregung *f.* (-, -en) incitement, stimulation; suggestion.

anreichern *v.t.* to enrich.

anreihen (sich) *v.refl.* to join.

Anreise *f.* (-, -n) journey there/here; arrival.

anreisen *v.i.* to travel there/here.

anreizen *v.t.* to incite, to instigate.

Anreiz *m.* (-s, -e) incitement; stimulus.

anrempeln *v.t.* to jostle against.

anrennen *v.i.st.* (s) to run against.

Anrichte *f.* (-, -n) dresser, sideboard.

anrichten *v.t.* to prepare; to arrange; to serve up, to dish up; (*fig.*) to cause, to occasion.

anrüchig *a.* disreputable.

anrücken *v.i.* to approach, to move up.

Anruf *m.* (-s, -e) call.

Anrufbeantworter *m.* (-s, -) answering machine.

anrufen *v.t.st.* to call (to); (*tel.*) to ring up; to call up.

Anrufer *m.* (-s, -); **Anruferin** *f.* (-, -nen) caller.

Anrufung *f.* (-, -en) invocation.

anrühren *v.t.* to touch, to handle.

ans = an das.

ansagen *v.t.* to announce; (*Kartenspiel*) to bid.

Ansager *m.* (-s, -) announcer.

ansammeln (sich) *v.refl.* to gather, to collect.

Ansammlung *f.* (-, -en) collection; pile; crowd.

ansässig *a.* resident, settled, domiciled; ~ *e Briten*, British residents.

Ansatz *m.* (-es, -sätze) start; approach; deposit; (*math.*) statement.

ansatzweise *adv.* to some extent.

ansaufen *v.refl.st.* sich **einen** ~ to get plastered.

ansaugen *v.t.* to suck in.

anschaffen *v.t.* to provide, to procure, to buy.

Anschaffung *f.* (-, -en) procurement; purchase.

anschauen *v.t.* to look at, to view; to contemplate; (sich) ~ *v.refl.* to look over.

anschalten *v.t.* to switch on.

anschaulich *a.* clear; evident; graphic, lucid.

Anschauung *f.* (-, -en) view; experience.

Anschein *m.* (-s, 0) appearance, semblance.

anscheinend *a.* apparent, seeming.

anschicken (sich) *v.refl.* to get ready; to prepare; to set about.

anschieben *v.t.st.* to push.

anschießen *v.t.st.* to shoot and wound.

anschirren *v.t.* to harness.

Anschiß *m.* (-, -e) bawling-out.

Anschlag *m.* (-[e]s, -schläge) (*Mauer~*) poster; *Schätzung*) estimate; (*Komplott*) plot; (*auf das Leben*) attempt.

anschlagen *v.t.st.* to affix; (*Zettel*) to post; (*Saite*) to strike; ~ *v.i.* to prove effectual.

anschleichen *v.refl.st.* to creep up.

anschleppen *v.t.* to drag along.

anschließen *v.t.st.* annex; to fasten with a lock; (sich) ~ *v.refl.st.* to join (a company).

anschließend *adv.* afterwards.

Anschluß *m.* (-schlusses, -schlüsse) (*rail.*, *el.*) connection; ~ *dose*, *f.* connection-box.

Anschlußzug *m.* (-s, -züge) connecting train.

anschmiegen (sich) *v.refl.* to nestle, to snuggle up.

anschmiegsam *a.* affectionate.

anschmieren *v.t.* to smear, to daub; (*vulg.*) to cheat.

anschnallen *v.t.* to buckle up.

anschnauzen *v.t.* (*fam.*) to shout at.

anschneiden *v.t.st.* to cut; to raise (*Frage*).

Anschnitt *m.* (-[e]s, -e) first cut.

anschreiben *v.t.st.* to write (down); to score up; *gut angeschrieben*, favorably known.

Anschrift *f.* (-, -en) address.

Anschuldigung *f.* (-, -en) accusation, charge.

anschwärzen *v.t.* to blacken; (*fig.*) to slander.

anschwellen *v.i.st.* (s) to swell.

anschwemmen *v.t.* to wash ashore.

Anschwemmung *f.* (-, -en) deposit (of flood).

anschwindeln *v.t.* (*fam.*) to lie.

ansehen *v.t.st.* to look at (upon); to consider; to regard.

Ansehen *n.* (-s, 0) appearance; (*Achtung*) esteem, credit, reputation, authority; *von* ~, by sight.

ansehnlich *a.* considerable, siz(e)able; good-looking.

ansetzen *v.t.* to put to; (*Preis*) to fix; (*schätzen*) to rate, to estimate; (*Blätter*) to put forth.

Ansicht *f.* (-, -en) sight, view; inspection; (*Meinung*) opinion; *zur* ~, on approval.

Ansichts(post)karte *f.* picture (post)card.

ansiedeln (sich) *v.t. & refl.* to settle.

Ansied(e)lung *f.* (-, -en) settlement.

Ansiedler *m.* (-s, -) settler, colonist.

Ansinnen *n.* (-s, -) demand, request.

anspannen *v.t.* to stretch; (*Pferde*) to put to; to hitch up; (*fig.*) to exert, to strain.

Anspannung *f.* (-, -en) exertion, strain.

anspielen *v.i.* to hint at, to allude to.

Anspielung *f.* (-, -en) allusion, hint; (*pej.*) insinuation.

Ansporn *m.* (-s, 0) incentive.

anspornen *v.t.* to spur; (*fig.*) to incite.

Ansprache *f.* (-, -en) address, speech.

ansprechen *v.t.st.* to address, to accost; to please, to appeal to.

ansprechend *a.* appealing; attractive.

Ansprechpartner *m.* (-s, -) contact (person).

anspringen *v.i.st.* to start (up); *v.t.st.* to jump at.

Anspruch *m.* (-[e]s, -sprüche) claim, pretension, title.

anspruchslos *a.* unassuming, unpretentious.

anspruchsvoll *a.* demanding, exacting, fastidious.

anspucken *v.t.* to spit at.

anspülen *v.t.* to wash ashore, to deposit.

anstacheln *v.t.* to spur on, to prick, to goad.

Anstalt *f.* (-, -en) institution, establishment; ~*en treffen*, *machen*, to make arrangements; to arrange (for).

Anstand *m.* (-[e]s, -stände) decorum, decency, polite manners; (*Beanstandung*) objection.

anständig *a.* proper; (*pers.*) respectable, decent.

Anständigkeit *f.* (-, -en) propriety, decency.

Anstandsdame *f.* chaperon.

anstandslos *adv.* without hesitation.

anstarren *v.t.* to stare at.

anstatt *pr.* instead of; **–daß** *c.* instead of.

anstauen *v.t.* to dam up; *v.refl.* to accumulate, to build up.

anstaunen *v.t.* to gaze at.

anstechen *v.t.st.* to prick; to puncture; (*ein Faß*) to tap.

anstecken *v.t.* to stick on; to pin; (*mit Krankheit*) to infect; (*Licht*) to light; (*Feuer*) to make fire.

ansteckend *a.* contagious, catching; infectious; communicable.

Ansteckung *f.* (-, -en) contagion, infection.

anstehen *v.t.st.* to stand in line; to queue up; to suit.

ansteigen *v.i.st.* (*s*) to ascend, to rise.

anstelle *pr.* instead.

anstellen *v.t.* to appoint; to arrange; (*Versuch*) to make; (sich) ~ *v.refl.* to behave; to feign, to make believe.

anstellig *a.* handy, skilful.

Anstellung *f.* (-, -en) appointment; (*Stelle*) job, place, situation.

Anstieg *m.* (-[e]s, -e) rise, increase.

anstiften *v.t.* to contrive, to cause; to instigate, to set on.

Anstifter *m.* (-s, -) **Anstifterin** *f.* (-, -nen) instigator.

Anstiftung *f.* (-, -en) incitement.

anstimmen *v.t.* to sing, to strike up.

Anstoß *m.* (-es, -stosse) impulse, stimulus; (*fig.*) offense; (*Fußball*) kickoff; *Stein des ~es m.* stumbling block.

anstoßen *v.t.st.* to push *or* strike against; ~ *v.i.st.* to stumble; to give offense; (*mit den Gläsern*) clink glasses; (*mit der Zunge*) to lisp.

anstößig *a.* offensive, scandalous, shocking.

anstrahlen *v.t.* to illuminate, to floodlight.

anstreben *v.t. & i.* to aspire to.

anstreichen *v.t.st.* to paint, to stain.

Anstreicher *m.* (-s,-) house-painter.

anstrengen *v.t.* to make an effort; to strain; to exert; (*Klage*) to bring an action; (sich) ~ *v.refl.* to exert oneself.

anstrengend *a.* strenuous, demanding, fatiguing.

Anstrengung *f.* (-, -en) exertion, effort.

Anstrich *m.* (-[e]s,' -e) color, painting, paint, coat; (*fig.*) appearance, tinge, air.

Ansturm *m.* (-s, -stürme) rush, attack.

anstürmen *v.i.* (*s*) to attack, to storm at, to rush upon.

ansuchen *v.t.* to apply for, to petition for.

Ansuchen *n.* (-s, -) request, application.

Antagonismus *m.* (-, -men) antagonism.

antanzen *v.i.* (*fam.*) to show up.

antarktisch *a.* Antarctic.

antasten *v.t.* to touch, to handle; to break into (savings).

Anteil *m.* (-[e]s, -e) share, portion; contribution; lot; (*fig.*) interest; ~ *nehmen,* to sympathize with.

anteilig *a. & adv.* proportional(ly).

Anteilnahme *f.* (-, 0) participation; interest; sympathy.

antelephonieren *v.t.* to ring up.

Antenne *f.* (-, -n) (radio) aerial, antenna.

Antezedentien *f.pl.* antecedents.

Anthrazit *m.* (-s, 0) anthracite.

Anthropologe *m.* (-n, -n); **Anthropologin** *f.*

(-, -nen) anthropologist.

Anthroposoph *m.* (-en, -en); **Anthroposophin** *f.* (-, -nen) anthroposophist.

Antialkoholiker *m.* (-s, -) teetotaller.

antiautoritär *a.* antiauthoritarian.

Antibiotikum *n.* (-s, -tika) antibiotic.

Antiblockiersystem, ABS *n.* antilock braking system.

antik *a.* antique.

Antike *f.* (-, 0) classical antiquity.

Antillen *pl.* (-) Antilles.

Antilope *f.* (-, -n) antelope.

Antipathie *f.* (-, -n) antipathy.

antippen *v.t.* to touch lightly, to tap.

Antiqua *f.* (-, 0) (printing) Roman type.

Antiquar *m.* (-[e]s, -e) antiquary; second-hand bookseller.

Antiquariat *n.* (-s, -e) antiquarian second-hand bookshop.

antiquarisch *a. & adv.* second-hand.

Antiquität *f.* (-, -en) antique, curiosity.

Antiquitätenhändler *m.* antique-dealer.

Antiquitätenladen *m.* (-s, -läden) antique shop.

Antisemit *m.* (-en, -en) anti-Semite.

antisemitisch *a.* anti-Semitic.

antiseptisch *a.* antiseptic.

antizipieren *v.t.* to anticipate.

Antlitz *n.* (-es, -e) face, countenance.

Antrag *m.* (-[e]s, -träge) application, proposition, proposal; motion; bill.

Antragsformular *n.* application-form.

Antragsteller *m.* mover, proposer.

antreffen *v.t.st.* to find, to come across.

antreiben *v.t.st.* to drive; to power; to impel; to step up.

antreten *v.t.st.* (*Reise*) to set out upon; *Dienst* ~, to assume duty; ~, *v.i.st.* (*s*) to fall in.

Antrieb *m.* (-[e]s, -e) drive, impulse, motive, propulsion.

Antriebskraft *f.* (-, kräfte) driving power.

Antritt *m.* (-e[s], 0) entrance (upon), beginning.

Antrittsrede *f.* inaugural address.

antun *v.t.st.* to put on; (*fig.*) to inflict; *es einem* ~, to bewitch one.

Antwort *f.* (-, -en) answer, reply.

antworten *v.t.* to answer, to reply.

Antwortschein *m.* (*Post*) reply coupon.

anvertrauen *v.t.* to entrust to, to confide in.

anvisieren *v.t.* to aim at.

anwachsen *v.i.st.* (*s*) to grow to; to grow up; to increase; to swell.

anwählen *v.t.* to dial a number.

Anwalt *m.* (-[e]s, -e, *u.* -wälte); **Anwältin** *f.* (-, -nen) agent; (*Rechts~*) advocate, solicitor, advocate, lawyer, attorney, counsel.

anwandeln *v.t.* to befall, to seize.

Anwandlung *f.* (-, -en) fit, attack; touch.

Anwärter *m.* (-s, -) candidate, expectant.

Anwartschaft *f.* (-, -en) candidacy, expectancy; reversion.

anweisen *v.t.st.* to instruct, to direct; to advise; *auf sich selbst angewiesen sein,* to be thrown on one's own resources.

Anweisung *f.* (-, -en) assignment; instruction, directive; (*Geld~*) order, check, draft.

anwendbar *a.* applicable; practical.

anwenden *v.t.r. & st.* to apply to; to bestow upon; to make use of, to employ.
Anwendung *f.* (-, -en) application, practice, use.
anwerben *v.t.st.* to enlist, to enroll, to hire, to recruit; *sich ~ lassen,* to sign on.
Anwerbung *f.* (-, -en) recruitment.
Anwesen *n.* (-s, -) estate, property.
anwesend *a.* present.
Anwesenheit *f.* (-, 0) presence.
Anwesenheitsliste *f.* (-, -n) attendance list.
anwetzen *v.i.* (*fam.*) to run towards.
anwidern *v.t.* to excite loathing, to disgust.
Anwurf *m.* (-[e]s, -würfe) accusation.
anwurzeln *v.i.* to take roots.
Anzahl *f.* (-, 0) number; quantity.
anzahlen *v.t.* to pay a deposit.
Anzahlung *f.* (-, -en) deposit, down-payment.
anzapfen *v.t.* to tap.
Anzeichen *n.* (-s, -) sign, symptom.
Anzeige *f.* (-, -n) (*Inserat*) advertisement; report (police).
Anzeigeblatt *n.* advertiser, flyer.
anzeigen *v.t.* to report; to indicate; to notify; (*einen*) to denounce; (*Meßapparat*) to read.
anzetteln *v.t.* to plot, to contrive.
anziehen *v.t.st.* to pull; (*spannen*) to tighten, to stretch; (*Kleider*) to put on; (*fig.*) to attract; (sich) *~ v.refl.* to dress.
anziehend *a.* attractive, interesting.
Anziehung *f.* (-, 0) attraction.
Anziehungskraft *f.* (*fig.*) appeal.
Anzug *m.* (-[e]s, -züge) (*Herren~*) suit; (*Damen~*) costume, dress.
anzüglich *a.* insinuating; suggestive, personal.
Anzüglichkeit *f.* (-, -en) insinuating nature; insinuating remark.
anzünden *v.t.* to light; to kindle; to set fire to.
Anzünder *m.* (-s, -) lighter.
anzweifeln *v.t.* to doubt.
anzwinkern *v.t.* to wink at.
apart *a.* out of the common.
Apartment *n.* (-s, -s) studio apartment.
Apathie *f.* (-, 0) apathy.
apathisch *a.* apathetic.
Apfel *m.* (-s, Äpfel) apple.
Apfelmus *n.* applesauce.
Apfelsine *f.* (-, -n) orange.
Apfelwein *m.* cider.
Aphorismus *m.* (-, -men) aphorism.
aphoristisch *a.* aphoristical.
Apologet *m.* (-en, -en) apologist.
Apostel *m.* (-s, -) apostle.
Apostelgeschichte *f.* The Acts of the Apostles *pl..*
Apostroph *m.* (-s, -e) apostrophe.
Apotheke *f.* (-, -n) drugstore; chemist's shop.
Apotheker *m.* (-s, -); **Apothekerin** *f.* (-, -nen) pharmacist.
Apparat *m.* (-[e]s, -e) apparatus, telephone, extension, appliance.
Appell *m.* (-s, -e) roll call; (*fig.*) appeal.
Appellation *f.* (-, -en) appeal.
Appellationsgericht *n.* court of appeal.
appellieren *v.i.* to appeal (to).
Appetit *m.* (-[e]s, -e) appetite.
appetitanregend *a.* appetizing; stimulating the appetite.

appetitlich *a.* appetizing.
appetitlos *a.* without any prejudice.
Appetitlosigkeig *f.* (-, 0) lack of appetite.
applaudieren *v.t.* to applaud.
Applaus *m.* (-es, 0) applause.
apportieren *v.i.* (*von Hunden*) to retrieve.
Appretur *f.* (-, -en) finish, dressing.
approbiert *a.* (*Arzt*) certified.
Aprikose *f.* (-, -n) apricot.
April *m.* (-[e]s, -e) April; *in den ~ schicken,* to make an April fool of.
apropos *adv.* by the way.
Aquädukt *m.od.n.* (-s, -e) aqueduct.
Aquarrell *n.* (-[e]s, -e) water-color.
Aquarellist *m.* (-en, -en) water-colorist.
Äquator *m.* (-s, 0) equator.
Äquatortaufe *f.* (-, -n) crossing-the-line ceremony.
Äquivalent *n.* (-[e]s, -e) equivalent.
äquivalent *a.* equivalent.
Äquivalenz *f.* (-, -en) equivalence.
Ära *f.* (-, 0) era.
Araber *m.* (-s, -); **Araberin** *f.* (-, -nen) Arab; **Arabien** *p.* (-s, 0) Arabia; **arabisch** *a.* Arabian, Arab, Arabic.
arabische Ziffern *f.pl.* arabic numerals.
Arbeit *f.* (-, -en) labor, work, toil; task; (*Bearbeitung*) workmanship; (*Leistung*) performance.
arbeiten *v.i.* to labor, to work; (*Maschine*) to operate; *~ mit,* to work; *~ v.t.* to make, to manufacture.
Arbeiter *m.* (-s, -) workman, laborer, hand, working-man.
Arbeiter: **~bewegung** *f.* labor movement; **~familie** *f.* working-class family; **~gewerkschaft** *f.* labor union.
Arbeiterin *f.* (-, -nen) working-woman.
Arbeitgeber *m.*; **Arbeitgeberin** *f.* (-, -nen) employer.
Arbeitnehmer *m.* employee.
arbeitsam *a.* laborious, industrious.
Arbeits: **~amt** *n.* employment-exchange, labor-exchange; **~anzug** *m.* overalls; **~belastung** *f.* work-load; **~beschaffung** *f.* creation of employment; **~dienst** *m.* labor service; **~dienstpflicht** *f.* compulsory labor service; **~einkommen** *n.* earned income; **~einstellung** *f.* strike; **~erlaubnis** *f.* work permit; **~fähig** *a.* able-bodied, fit to work; *in arbeitsfähigem Zustand,* in operating condition; *arbeitsfähige Mehrheit,* working majority; **~gang** *m.* (*mech.*) operation; **~gebiet** *n.* field; **~gemeinschaft** *f.* working association; **~gericht** *n.* industrial court; **~leistung** *f.* rate of output; (*einer Maschine*) service; **~los** *a.* out of work, unemployed; **~losenunterstützung** *f.* unemployment benefit, dole; **~losenversicherung** *f.* unemployment insurance; **~losigkeit** *f.* unemployment; **~minister** *m.* Minister of Labor; **~scheu** *a.* lazy, shirking; **~streit** *m.* industrial dispute; **~stück** *n.* job; **~stunden** *m.pl.* working hours, hours of work; **~stunde** *f.* **pro Kopf** manhour; **~unfähig** *a.* incapable of work; **~unfähigkeit** *f.* disablement; **~verhältnis** *n.* employment; **~zeit** *f.* working hours; **~zeitverkürzung** *f.* reduction of working hours; **~zimmer** *n.* study.
Archäologe *m.* (-n, -n); **Archäologin** *f.* (-, -nen)

archaeologist.
Archäologie *f.* (-, 0) archaeology.
archäologisch *a.* archaeologic(al).
Arche *f.* (-, -n) ark.
Archipel *m.* (-s, -e) archipelago.
Architekt *m.* (-en, -en); **Architektin** *f.* (-, -nen) architect.
Architektur *f.* (-, -en) architecture.
Archiv *n.* (-[e]s, -e) archives, record office.
Archivar *m.* (-[e]s, -e) keeper of the records, Master of the Rolls.
archivieren *v.t.* to archive.
Areal *n.* (-[e]s, -e) area, surface.
Arg *n.* (0) malice.
arg *a.* arrant; bad; mischievous.
Ärger *m.* (-s, 0) annoyance, vexation, anger, worry, irritation.
ärgerlich *a.* annoying, provoking, vexatious; angry.
ärgen *v.t.* to annoy; to make angry; to vex; *sich ~ über...*, to be annoyed at...
Ärgernis *n.* (-nisses, -nisse) offense, scandal; vexation.
Arglist *f.* (-, 0) deceit, cunning.
arglos *a.* inoffensive, harmless.
Argument *n.* (-s, -e) argument.
Argumentation *f.* (-, -en) argumentation.
argumentieren *v.i.* argue.
Argwohn *m.* (-[e]s, 0) suspicion.
argwöhnen *v.t.* to suspect.
argwönisch *a.* suspicious, distrustful.
Arie *f.* (-, -n) aria.
Arier *m.* (-s, -), **arisch** *a.* Aryan.
Aristokrat *m.* (-en, -en); **Aristokratin** *f.* (-, -nen) aristocrat.
Aristokratie *f.* (-, -[e]n) aristocracy.
aristokratisch *a.* aristocratic.
Arithmetik *f.* (-, 0) arithmetic.
Arithmetiker *m.* (-s, -); **Arithmetikerin** *f.* (-, -nen) arithmetician.
arithmetisch *a.* arithmetical.
Arkade *f.* (-, -n) arcade.
Arktis *f.* (-, 0) Arctic.
arktisch *a.* arctic.
arm *a.* poor.
Arm *m.* (-[e]s, -e) arm; (*Fluß*) branch.
Armatur *f.* (-, -en) armature; fittings; instrument (car).
Armaturenbrett *n.* (-s, -en) instrument panel; dashboard.
Arm: ~band *n.* bracelet; **~banduhr** *f.* wristwatch; **~binde** *f.* band; sling; **~brust** *f.* crossbow.
Arme *m.* & *f.* (-n, -n) poor woman/man.
Armee *f.* (-, -n) army.
Ärmel *m.* (-s, -) sleeve.
Armen: ~haus *n.* poorhouse; **~pflege** *f.* poor relief; **recht** *n.* poor law.
Armenien *n.* (-s, 0) Armenia; **Armenier** *m.* (-s, -); **Armenierin** *f.* (-, -nen); **armenisch** *a.* Armenian.
Arm: ~lehne *f.* arm (of an arm-chair); **~leuchter** *m.* chandelier.
ärmlich *a.* poor, miserable.
Armreif *m.* (-s, -en) bangle.
armselig *a.* needy, miserable; paltry; pathetic.
Armsessel *m.* (-s, -); **Armstuhl** *m.* (-s, -stühle) arm chair.

Armut *f.* (-, 0) poverty, indigence.
Aroma *n.* (-s, -s *or*-ta) flavor, aroma, perfume.
aromatisch *a.* aromatic.
Arrak *m.* (-s, 0) arrack.
Arrangement *m.* (-s, -s) arrangement.
arrangerien *v.t.* to arrange.
Arrest *m.* (-[e]s, -e) detention, arrest, seizure.
Arrestant *m.* (-en, -en) prisoner.
arretieren *v.t.* to detain, to arrest, to take into custody.
arrivieren *v.i.* to arrive, to achieve.
Arrivierte *m.* & *f.* (-n, -n) (*pej.*) parvenu.
arrogant *a.* arrogant.
Arroganz *f.* (-, 0) arrogance.
Arsch *m.* (-es, Ärsche) ass, arse, backside, buttocks.
Arschbacke *f.* buttock.
Arsch: ~kriecher *m.* (*vulg.*) ass-licker; **~kriecherei** *f.* (*vulg.*) ass-licking; **~loch** *n.* asshole.
Arsenal *n.* (-[e]s, -e) arsenal.
Arsenik *m.* (-s, 0) arsenic.
Art *f.* (-, -en) (*Geschlecht*) species, race, stock; (*Sorte*) sort, kind; (*Weise*) way, manner; (*Lebensart*) manners *pl.*; *auf diese ~*, in this way.
Arterie *f.* (-, -en) artery.
Arterienverkalkung *f.* (-, -en) arteriosclerosis.
artfremd *a.* (*bio.*) alien, foreign.
artig *a.* well-behaved, civil, polite.
artesisch *a.* Artesian.
Artigkeit *f.* (-, -en) politeness, courtesy.
Artikel *m.* (-s, -) article; (*com.*) item.
artikulieren *v.t.* articulate.
Artillerie *f.* (-, -[e]n) artillery, ordnance.
Artillerist *m.* (-en, -en) artillery man, gunner.
Artischocke *f.* (-, -n) artichoke.
Artist *m.* (-en, -en); **Artistin** *f.* (-, -nen) artist (circus).
Arznei *f.* (-, -en) medicine, physic.
Arzneikunde *f.* pharmaceutics *pl.*.
Arzt *m.* (-es, Ärzte); **Ärztin** *f.* (-, -nen) physician, doctor.
Arzthelferin *f.* doctor's receptionist.
ärztlich *a.* medical; **~es Attest** *n.* medical certificate; **~e Betreuung** *f.* medical care.
Arztpraxis *f.* (-, -xen) doctor's office.
As *n.* (Asses, Asse) ace.
As *n.* (-, -) (*mus.*) A flat.
Asbest *m.* (-[e]s, -e) asbestos.
Asche *f.* (-, -n) ashes *pl.*.
Aschenbecher *m.* ash-tray.
Aschenbrödel *n.* Cinderella.
Aschermittwoch *m.* Ash-Wednesday.
Asiat *m.* (-en, -en); **Asiatin** *f.* (-, -nen); **asiatisch** *a.* Asian.
Asien *n.* (-s, -) Asia.
Askese *f.* (-, 0) asceticism.
Asket *m.* (-en, -en) ascetic.
asozial *a.* antisocial; asocial.
Asoziale *m.* & *f.* (-n, -n) social misfit.
Aspekt *m.* (-s, -e) aspect.
Asphalt *m.* (-[e]s, -e) asphalt.
asphaltieren *v.t.* to asphalt.
Aspirant *m.* (-en, -en) candidate.
Assessor *m.* (-s, -en) assessor; assistant judge.
assimilieren *v.t.* to assimilate.
Assistent *m.* (-en, -en); **Assistentin** *f.* (-, -nen) assistant.

Assistenzarzt *m.* (-es, -ärzte) **Assistenzärztin** *f.* (-, -nen) junior doctor.

assoziieren (sich) *v.refl.* to enter into partnership (with); *v.t.* to associate.

Ast *m.* (-es, Äste) bough, branch; (*im Holze*) knot.

Aster *f.* (-, -n) aster.

Ästhetik *f.* (-, 0) aesthetics *pl.*

ästhetisch *a.* aesthetic.

Asthma *n.* (-s, 0) asthma.

Asthmatiker *m.* (-s, -) **Asthmatikerin** *f.* (-, -nen) asthmatic.

Astloch *n.* knothole.

Astrologe *m.* (-n, -n) astrologer.

Astrologie *f.* (-, 0 astrology.

Astronom *m.* (-en, -en) astronomer.

Astronomie *f.* (-, 0) astronomy.

astronomisch *a.* astronomical.

Astrophysik *f.* (-, 0) astrophysics.

Asyl *n.* (-[e]s, -e) asylum.

Asylant *m.* (-en, -en) **Asylantin** *f.* (-, -nen) person seeking asylum.

asymmetrisch *a.* asymmetrical.

asynchron *a.* asychronous.

Atelier *n.* (-s, -s) (artist's) studio.

Atem *m.* (-s, 0) breath, breathing; *ausser ~*, out of breath; *den ~ anhalten*, to hold one's breath.

atemlos *a.* breathless.

Atem: ~not *f.* shortness of breath; **~pause** *f.* breathing space; **~zug** *m.* breath.

Äther *m.* (-s, 0) ether.

Atheismus *m.* (0) atheism.

Atheist *m.* (-en, -en) atheist.

ätherisch *a.* ethereal, aerial.

Äthiopien *n.* (-s, 0) Ethopia; **Äthiopier** *m.* (-s, -); **Äthiopierin** *f.* (-, -nen); **äthiopisch** *a.* Ethiopian.

Athlet *m.* (-en, -en) athlete.

Athletik *f.* (-, 0) athletics.

Atlantik *m.* (-s, 0) Atlantic.

Atlas *m.* (-u. -lasses, -lanten) atlas.

Atlas *m.* (-u. -lasses, -lasse) (*Stoff*) satin.

atmen *v.t. & i.* to breathe, to respire.

Atmosphäre *f.* (-, -n) atmosphere.

atmosphärisch *a.* atmospheric.

Atmung *f.* (-, 0) respiration.

Atom *n.* (-[e]s, -e) atom; particle.

Atom . . . atomic.

atomar *a.* atomic.

Atombombe *f.* atomic bomb.

atomisieren *v.t.* to atomize.

Atom: ~kern *m.* atomic nucleus; **~kraft** *f.* nuclear power; **~kraftwerk** *n.* nuclear power plant; **~krieg** *m.* nuclear war; **~macht** *f.* nuclear power; **~müll** *m.* nuclear waste; **~rakete** *f.* nuclear missile; **~sprengkopf** *m.* nuclear warhead; **~waffe** *f.* nuclear weapon; **~waffensperrvertrag** *m.* Nuclear Nonproliferation Treaty; **~zeitalter** *n.* nuclear age.

Attaché *m.* (-s, -s) attaché.

Attacke *f.* (-, -n) attack.

Attentat *n.* (-[e]s, -e) assault, outrage; attempt against one's life.

Attentäter *m.* (-s, -) criminal, assailant.

Attest *n.* (-[e]s, -e) certificate.

attestieren *v.t.* to certify.

attraktiv *a.* attractive.

Attrappe *f.* (-, -n) dummy; fancy box; sham things.

Attribut *n.* (-[e]s, -e) attribute.

atypisch *a.* atypical.

ätzen *v.t.* (*ärztlich*) to cauterize; (*Kunst*) to etch.

ätzend *a.* corrosive; (*fig.*) caustic.

Ätzmittel *n.* corrosive; (*med.*) cautery.

au! *i.* oh!

Aubergine *f.* eggplant.

auch *c.* also, too, even, likewise; *~ nicht*, neither, nor; *sowohl . . . als ~*, as well . . . as . . . , both . . . and.

Audienz *f.* (-, -en) audience.

Auditorium *n.* (-s, -rien) lecture hall, auditorium.

Auerhahn *m.* capercaillie; **Auerochs** *m.* bison, aurochs.

auf *pro.* on, upon, in, at, to, up, into, after; *~ adv.* up, upwards; *~! i.* arise; *~ dass*, in order that; *~ und ab*, up and down; *~ einmal*, at once.

aufarbeiten *v.t.* to catch up; to refurbish; to work up.

aufatmen *v.i.* to breathe again.

aufbahren *v.t.* to lay out.

Aufbahrung *f.* (-, 0) lying in state.

Aufbau *m.* (-[e]s, -e) erection, structure, construction; organization.

aufbauen *v.t.* to erect, to build up.

aufbäumen (sich) *v.refl.* to rear up.

aufbauschen *v.t. & i.* to billow; to puff, to swell up, to exaggerate.

aufbegehren *v.i.* to rise *or* revolt against.

aufbehalten *v.t.st.* to keep on.

aufbekommen *v.t.st.* to get s.th. open.

aufbessern *v.t.* (*Gehalt*) to raise.

aufbewahren *v.t.* to preserve, to keep, to take charge of.

Aufbewahrung *f.* (-, 0) preservation.

aufbieten *v.t.st.* to raise, to summon; (*fig.*) to exert oneself; (*Verlobte*) to publish banns of marriage.

aufbinden *v.t.st.* to untie, to loosen.

aufblähen *v.t.* to puff up; to inflate; to expand.

aufblasbar *a.* inflatable.

aufblasen *v.t.st.* to blow up, to inflate.

aufbleiben *v.i.st.* (*s*) to stay up; to remain open.

aufblenden *v.t. & i* to switch to high beam.

aufblicken *v.i.* to look up.

aufblinken *v.i.* to flash; to glint.

aufblitzen *v.i.* to flash; to sparkle.

aufblühen *v.i.* to bloom; to blossom.

aufbrauchen *v.t.* to consume, to use up.

aufbrausen *v.i.* (*s*) to flare up; to roar; to effervesce; (*fig.*) to fly out.

aufbrausend *a.* hottempered.

aufbrechen *v.t.st.* to break open; *~ v.i.st.* (*s*) to burst open; to set out.

aufbringen *v.t.ir.* (*Truppen, Geld*) to raise; (*erzürnen*) to provoke; (*Kosten*) to defray.

Aufbruch *m.* (-[e]s, 0) departure.

aufbrühen *v.t.* to brew [up].

aufbügeln *v.t.* to iron, to do up.

aufbürden *v.t.* to burden with.

aufdecken *v.t.* to uncover; to disclose.

aufdrängen *v.t.* to thrust upon; sich *~*, *v.refl.* to obtrude oneself (upon).

aufdrehen *v.t.* to turn on.

aufdringen *v.t.st.* to force upon.

aufdringlich *a.* obtrusive; pushy; importunate; insistent.

aufdröseln *v.t.* to unravel.

aufdrücken *v.t.* to impress.

aufeinander *adv.* one after another, one upon another.

Aufenthalt *m.* (-[e]s, -e) stay; abode; (*Verzögerung*) delay; (*rail.*) stop.

Aufenthaltsort *m.* place of residence.

auferlegen *v.t.* to impose (upon).

auferstehen *v.i.st.* (*s*) to rise from the dead.

Auferstehung *f.* (-, 0) resurrection.

auferwecken *v.t.* to raise from the dead, to resuscitate.

aufessen *v.i.st.* (*s*) to eat (up), to finish.

auffahren *v.i.st.* (*s*) to ascend; to start (up).

Auffahrt *f.* (-, -en) (*vor Palästen*) drive, approach.

auffallen *v.i.st.* (*s*) (*einem*) to strike (*fig.*); to stand out.

auffallend, auffällig *a.* striking.

auffangen *v.t.st.* to catch.

Auffanglinie *f.* (*mil.*) holdingline.

auffassen *v.t.* to understand, to take in, to conceive; to interpret (*Rolle*).

Auffassung *f.* (-, -en) comprehension, perception; opinion.

auffindbar *a.* traceable.

auffinden *v.t.st.* to find.

auffischen *v.t.st.* (*fam.*) to fish out.

aufflackern *v.i.* to flicker up; to flare up.

aufflammen *v.i.* (*s*) to flame, to blaze.

auffliegen *v.i.* to fly up.

auffordern *v.t.* to ask, to invite, to request.

Aufforderung *f.* (-, -en) summons; invitation.

aufforsten *v.t.* to reforest.

auffressen *v.t.st.* to eat up, to devour.

auffrischen *v.t.* to refresh; to brush up; to touch up.

Auffrischung *f.* brushing up; (*mil.*) rehabilitation.

aufführen *v.t.* to perform; to represent; (*Einzelnes*) to list, to specify; (sich) ~, *v.refl.* to behave.

Aufführung *f.* (-, -en) performance, representation; behavior.

auffüllen *v.t.* to fill up.

Aufgabe *f.* (-, -n) delivery; (*Brief~*) posting; (*Schul~*) lesson; task; problem; giving up, resignation.

Aufgang *m.* (-[e]s, -gänge) stairs; steps; ascent.

aufgeben *v.t.st.* to give up, to deliver; (*Brief*) to mail; (*Gepäck*) to check; (*Frage, Rätsel*) to propose; (*Plan, Stelle*) to abandon, to resign, to give up.

aufgeblasen *a.* puffed up.

Aufgebot *n.* (-[e]s, -e) (*mil.*) contingent; levy; banns of marriage *pl.*

aufgebracht *a.* angry, provoked (at).

aufgedreht *a.* (*fam.*) in high spirits.

aufgedunsen *a.* bloated, swollen, sodden.

aufgehen *v.i.st.* (*Sonne*) to rise; (*Blüten*) to open; (*Knoten*) to get loose, to come undone; (*Fenster, etc.*) to come open; (*Genähtes*) to give way; (*math.*) to leave no remainder.

aufgeklärt *a.* enlightened; explained.

aufgekratz *a.* (*fam.*) in high spirits.

aufgelegt *a.* disposed (for), minded.

aufgelöst *a.* distraught.

aufgeräumt *a.* merry, in good humor.

aufgeregt *a.* excited, flurried.

Aufgeregtheit *f.* (-, 0) excitement; agitation.

aufgeschlossen *a.* openminded, approachable.

Aufgeschlossenheit *f.* openmindedness.

aufgeschmissen *a.* (*fam.*) ~ **sein** to be stuck.

aufgeweckt *a.* bright, clever.

aufgießen *v.t.st.* to make (tea, coffee); to brew.

aufgliedern *v.t.* to subdivide, to break down into parts.

aufgreifen *v.t.st.* to take up; to pick up.

aufgrund *pr.* on the basis of.

Aufguß *m.* (-gusses, -güsse) infusion.

aufhaben *v.t.st.* to have on; to have to do (school).

aufhaken *v.t.* to unhook, to unclasp.

aufhalsen *v.t.* to saddle (with).

aufhalten *v.t.st.* to hold up; to delay, to detain; (sich) ~ *v.refl.st.* to reside, to stay; (*über etwas*) to find fault with.

aufhängen *v.t.* to hang up; to hang upon; (sich) ~ *v. refl.* to hang oneself.

Aufhänger *m.* loop (clothes); tab; peg (article).

aufhäufen *v.t.* to heap up, to pile; (sich) ~ *v.refl.* to accumulate.

Aufhäufung *f.* (-, -en) accumulation.

aufheben *v.t.st.* to pick up; (*bewahren*) to keep, to preserve; (*sparen*) to save; (*Gesetz*) to abrogate; (*Belagerung*) to raise.

Aufheben *n.* (-s, 0) viel ~s machen, to make a great fuss (about).

Aufhebung *f.* (-, -en) (*eines Gesetzes*) abolition; repeal, rescission.

aufheitern *v.t.* to clear up; to cheer up; (sich) ~ *v.refl.* to clear up; (*fig.*) to grow cheerful.

Aufheiterung *f.* (-, -en) clearing up.

aufheizen *v.t.* to heat up, to inflame.

aufhelfen *v.t.st.* to help up.

aufhellen *v.t.* to brighten; (sich) ~ *v.refl.* to clear up.

aufhetzen *v.t.* to stir up; to incite.

aufholen *v.i.* to catch up (with); to make up.

aufhorchen *v.i.* to listen.

aufhören *v.i.* to cease, to leave off, to stop; *da hört alles auf*, that's the limit.

aufjauchzen *v.i.* to shout with joy.

aufkaufen *v.t.* to buy up.

Aufkäufer *m.* (-s, -) forestaller.

aufkeimen *v.i.* to sprout; to burgeon.

aufklappen *v.t.* to open; to fold back.

aufklären *v.t.* to clear up; (*fig.*) to explain; (*einen*) to enlighten; (*mil.*) to reconnoiter.

Aufklärung *f.* (-, -en) clearing up; enlightenment; explanation; reconnoitering.

aufkleben *v.t.* to paste upon, to stick on.

Aufkleber *m.* (-s, -) sticker.

aufknacken *v.t.* to crack open.

aufknöpfen *v.t.* to unbutton.

aufknoten *v.t.* to undo; to untie.

aufknüpfen *v.t.* to untie; (*einen*) to hang.

aufkochen *v.t.* to bring to the boil.

aufkommen *v.i.st.* (*s*) to come into use. (*für etwas*) to be responsible (for); to prevail against.

aufkrempeln *v.t.* to roll up (sleeves).

aufkriegen *v.t.* to get s.th. open.

aufkündigen *v.t.* to renounce; (*Kapital*) to recall; to cancel.

aufladen *v.t.st.* to load; (*fig.*) to impose, to saddle (with).

Auflage *f.* (-, -n) impost, duty, tax; (*eines Buches*) edition; (*einer Zeitung*) circulation.

Auflagenhöhe *f.* number of copies printed.

auflassen *v.t.st.* to leave open.

auflauern *v.t.* to lie in wait for, to waylay.

Auflauf *m.* (-[e]s, -läufe) crowd; tumult, riot; (*Speise*) soufflé.

auflaufen *v.i.st.* (*s*) (*nav.*) to run aground; (*anwachsen*) to accumulate; *aufgelaufene Summe*, aggregate amount.

aufleben *v.i.* (*s*) to revive.

auflegen *v.i.* to put on; to publish.

auflehnen (sich) *v.refl.* (*gegen*) to rebel against, to oppose.

Auflehnung *f.* (-, -en) insurrection, mutiny.

auflesen *v.t.st.* to pick up, to glean.

aufleuchten *v.i.* to light up.

aufliegen *v.i.st.* to lie; to rest; (sich) ~ *v.refl.st.* to become bed-sore.

auflisten *v.i.* to list.

auflockern *v.t.* to loosen.

Auflockerung *f.* (-, -en) loosening.

auflodern *v.i.* (*s*) to blaze up.

auflösbar *a.* soluble.

auflösen *v.t.* to loosen, to untie; to dissolve, to melt; (*Rätsel*) to solve; (*Brüche*) to reduce; (*mil. Einheiten*) to disband; (sich) ~ *v.refl.* to dissolve, to break up.

Auflösung *f.* (-, -en) solution; (*mil.*) disbandment, deactivation.

aufmachen *v.t.* to open; to unpack; (sich) ~ *v.refl.* to set out (for).

Aufmachung *f.* (-, -en) style; presentation; layout.

Aufmarsch *m.* (-es, -märsche) (*mil.*) review; deployment.

aufmarschieren *v.i.* (*s*) to march up, to deploy.

aufmerken *v.i.* to attend to.

aufmerksam *a.* attentive; ~ *machen auf*, to draw a person's attention to.

Aufmerksamkeit *f.* (-, -en) attention, attentiveness.

aufmöbeln *v.t.* to do up; to pep up; to cheer up.

aufmotzen *v.t.* to soup up.

aufmucken *v.i.* (*fam.*) to balk at s.th.

aufmuntern *v.t.* to encourage, to cheer.

Aufmunterung *f.* (-, -en) encouragement.

aufmüpfig *a. & adv.* (*fam.*) rebellious.

aufnähen *v.t.* to sew on.

Aufnahme *f.* (-, -n) reception, admission; survey; photographing; shooting (film); recording; photo, snapshot.

Aufnahme: ~**gebühr** *f.* entrance fee; ~**prüfung** *f.* entrance examination.

aufnehmen *v.t.st.* to take up; to pick up; to receive; to admit; (*abbilden*) to photograph; (*messen*) to survey; (*Geld*) to borrow; (*Gäste*) to take; *es mit einem* ~, to try conclusions with someone.

aufnötigen *v.t.* to force upon.

aufoktroyieren *v.t.* to impose.

aufopfern *v.t.* to sacrifice.

aufopfernd *a. & adv.* self-sacrificing.

Aufopferung *f.* (-, -en) sacrifice.

aufpäppeln *v.t.* (*fam.*) to feed up.

aufpassen *v.i.* to attend, to look out, to take notice of.

Aufpasser *m.* (-s, -) spy, guard.

aufpeitschen *v.t.* to whip up; to inflame (passion).

aufpflanzen *v.t.* (*Seitengewehr*) to fix; to plant oneself.

aufpfropfen *v.t.* to graft on.

aufpflügen *v.t.* to plow up.

aufpicken *v.t.* to peck up; (*fam.*) to pick up.

aufplatzen *v.i.* to burst open; to open up;

aufplustern *v.t.* to ruffle up; to puff up; *v.refl.* to ruffle its feathers; (*fig.*) to show off.

aufpolieren *v.t.* to polish up.

Aufprall *m.* (-s, -e) impact.

aufprallen *v.i.* to hit; to collide.

Aufpreis *m.* (-es, -e) extra charge.

aufpumpen *v.t.* to pump up, to inflate.

aufputschen *v.t.* (*pej.*) to stimulate; to arouse.

Aufputschmittel *n.* (-s, -) stimulant.

aufquellen *v.i.* to swell up.

Aufputz *m.* (-es, -e) finery, dress.

aufraffen (sich) *v.refl.* to pull oneself together; to bring oneself to do s.th.; to recover; (*fig.*) to pluck up courage.

aufrappeln *v.refl.* (*fam.*) to struggle to one's feet.

aufrauhen *v.t.* to roughen up.

aufrämen *v.t.* to tidy, to remove, to set in order; to clear (a shop); *mit etwas* ~, to make a clean sweep of.

aufrecht *a. & adv.* upright, erect; ~ *erhalten*, to maintain.

Aufrechthaltung *f.* (-, 0) maintenance.

aufrechtstehend *a.* on end, on edge.

aufregen *v.t.* to stir up, to rouse; to incite, to excite; (*nervös*) to flutter.

Aufregung *f.* (-, -en) excitement, stir.

aufreiben *v.t.st.* to rub open, to gall; (*fig.*) to worry; (*vertilgen*) to destroy.

aufreihen *v.t.* to string.

aufreißen *v.t.st.* to tear open; (*Tür*) to fling open; ~ *v.i.st.* to burst, to split.

aufreizen *v.t.* to rouse, to excite.

aufreizend *v.t.* provocative.

Aufreizung *f.* (-, -en) provocation; incitement.

aufrichten *v.t.* to set up; to erect; to straighten up; (*fig.*) to comfort; (sich) ~ *v.refl* to sit up.

aufrichtig *a.* sincere, frank.

Aufrichtigkeit *f.* (-, 0) sincerity.

aufriegeln *v.t.* to unbolt.

Aufriß *m.* (-risses, -risse) sketch.

aufrollen *v.t.* to roll up; to unroll.

aufrücken *v.i.* to move up.

Aufruf *m.* (-[e]s, -e) call, summons.

aufrufen *v.t.st.* to call up, to summon.

Aufruhr *m.* (-[e]s, -e) uproar, insurrection, rebellion.

aufrühren *v.t.* to stir up.

Aufrührer *m.* (-s, -) rebel, mutineer.

aufrührerisch *a.* rebellious.

aufrunden *v.t.* to round off.

aufrüsten *v.i. & v.* to arm.

Aufrüstung *f.* (-, 0) armament.

aufrütteln *v.t.* to shake up, to rouse.

aufs = auf das.

aufsagen *v.t.* to recite.

aufsammeln *v.t.* to pick up, to gather.

aufsässig *a.* recalcitrant, refractory, adverse.

Aufsatz *m.* (-es, -sätze) essay, article; top; (*Tafel*~)

centerpiece; essay, paper.

aufsaugen *v.t.st.* to vacuum; to suck up; to absorb.

aufschauen *v.i.* to look up.

aufscheuchen *v.t.* to frighten, to scare.

aufscheuern *v.t.* to chafe.

aufschichten *v.t.* to pile up, to stack.

aufschieben *v.t.st.* to postpone, to delay, to defer, to put off; to adjourn.

aufschießen *v.i.* to shoot up; to leap up.

Aufschlag *m.* ((-[e]s, -schläge) (*Rock~*) cuff, facings; (*Preis~*) rise, advance; plussage; (*mil.* Geschoss) impact; (*Tennis*) service.

aufschlagen *v.t.st.* (*die Augen*) to cast up; (*Gerüst*) to put up; (*Buch*) to open; (*Wort*) to look up; (*Zelt*) to pitch; *~* (*s*) (*im Preise*) to rise (in price); (*tennis*) to serve.

aufschließen *v.t.st.* to unlock.

aufschlitzen *v.t.* to slit, to slash open; to rip up.

Aufschluß *m.* (-schlusses, -schlüsse) (*fig.*) explanation.

aufschlüsseln *v.t.* to break down (statistics).

aufschlußreich *a.* informative; revealing.

aufschnallen *v.t.* to buckle upon; to unbuckle.

aufschnappen *v.t.* (*fam.*) to pick up.

aufschneiden *v.t.st.* to cut open; (*Buch*) to cut; *~ v.i.st.* to swagger, to brag.

Aufschneider *m.* (-s, -) swaggerer, braggart.

Aufschnitt *m.* (-[e]s, -e) kalter *~*, slices of cold meat.

aufschnüren *v.t.* to unlace.

aufschrauben *v.t.* to unscrew; to screw on.

aufschrecken *v.t.* to startle; *~ v.i.* (*s*) to start, to jump.

Aufschrei *m.* (-[e]s, -e) scream, shriek, outcry.

aufschreiben *v.t.st.* to write down, to take down, to put down.

aufschreien *v.i.st.* to cry out, to scream.

Aufschrift *f.* (-, -en) inscription; direction, address.

Aufschub *m.* (-[e]s, -0) delay, adjournment.

aufschürfen *v.t.* to graze; to bark (knee).

aufschürzen *v.t.* to tuck up.

aufschütteln *v.t.* to shake up, to rouse.

aufschütten *v.t.* to heap up; to pour upon.

aufschwatzen/aufschwätzen *v.t.* to talk s.o. into s.th.

aufschwingen (sich) *v.refl.st.* to soar, to rise.

Aufschwung *m.* (-[e]s, -schwünge) upswing; recovery; boom; rise, progress.

Aufsehen *n.* (-s, 0) looking up; (*fig.*) stir, sensation.

aufsehenerregend *a.* sensational.

Aufseher *m.* (-s, -) guard; inspector.

auf sein *v.i.ir* (*s*) to be up (out of bed); to be open.

aufsetzen *v.t.* (*Hut, Miene*) to put on; (*schriftlich*) to draw up; (sich) *~ v.refl.* to sit up.

Aufsicht *f.* (-, 0) inspection, supervision, superintendence, charge.

aufsichtführend *a.* in charge; on duty.

Aufsichts . . supervisory; *~behörde* *f.* inspectorate; *~rat* *m.* board of directors.

aufsitzen *v.i.st.* (*s*) to sit up; to mount (a horse).

aufspalten *v.t. & i.st.* to split, to cleave.

Aufspaltung *f.* (-, -en) splitting.

aufspannen *v.t.* (*Schirm*) to put up; (*Segel*) to spread; *Saiten ~,* to string.

aufsparen *v.t.* to save, to lay up.

aufsperren *v.t.* to open wide, to throw wide; (*Schlösser*) to pick; (*das Maul*) to gape.

aufspielen (sich) *v.refl.* to swagger; to set up for, *v.i.* to play (music).

aufspießen *v.t.* to spit, to pierce; to impale; to skewer.

aufsprengen *v.t.* to burst open.

aufspringen *v.i.st.* (*s*) to leap up; to crack; (*Hände*) to chap.

aufsprühen *v.t.* to spray on.

aufspulen *v.t.* to wind up.

aufspüren *v.t.* to trace out, to track down.

aufstacheln *v.t.* to goad, to incite.

aufstampfen *v.i.* to stamp (on the ground).

Aufstand *m.* (-[e]s, -stände) rebellion; insurrection, uproar, sedition.

aufständisch *a.* rebellious, seditious.

aufstapeln *v.t.* to pile up.

aufstechen *v.t.st.* to prick; to pick open; (*Geschwür*) to lance.

aufstecken *v.t.* to pin up, to put up (hair); to give up; (*fam.*) to retire.

aufstehen *v.i.st.* (*s*) to get up, to rise; (*aufrecht*) to stand up.

aufsteigen *v.i.st.* (*s*) to rise.

aufsteigend *a.* ascending.

Aufsteiger *m.* social climber; parvenu; (*sport*) promotion side.

aufstellen *v.t.* to set up, to put up, to erect; (*mil.* Einheit) to activate; (*Behauptung*) to make (an assertion) (*Grundsatz*) to lay down; (*Kandidaten*) to nominate.

Aufstellung *f.* (-, -en) (*mil.*) disposition; (*eines Kandidaten*) nomination.

Aufstieg *m.* (-[e]s, -e) ascent, rise; promotion.

aufstöbern *v.t.* (*fig.*) to put up; to track down; to ferret out.

aufstocken *v.t.* to raise; to increase.

aufstöhnen *v.i.* to groan.

aufstören *v.t.* to stir, to disturb, to rouse.

aufstossen *v.t.st.* to push open; *~ v.i.st.* (*s*) to occur to, to meet with; (*Speisen*) to belch, to burp (*fam.*)

aufstrebend *a.* rising; ambitious.

aufstreichen *v.t.st.* to lay on, to spread.

Aufstrich *m.* (*Brot~*) spread.

aufstülpen *v.t.* to turn up, to cock.

aufstützen *v.t.* to prop up; *~ v.i.* to lean (upon).

aufsuchen *v.t.* to go and see, to look up.

auftakeln *v.t.* to rig out.

Auftakt *m.* (-es, -e) upbeat, anacrusis; (*fig.*) prelude, preliminaries *pl.*

auftanken *v.t. & i* to fill up; to refuel.

auftauchen *v.t.* to emerge, to appear.

auftauen *v.t. & i* to thaw.

aufteilen *v.t.* to divide, to parcel out.

Aufteilung *f.* (*–*, en) dividing; sharing.

auftischen *v.t.* to serve up.

Auftrag *m.* (-[e]s, -träge) commission, task, order, mandate; (*mil.*) assignment, mission; *Aufträge annehmen* (*com.*) to accept orders.

auftragen *v.t.st.* to carry up; (*Speise*) to serve up; (*einem etwas*) to charge someone with; (*Farbe*) to lay on; (*Kleider*) to wear out.

Auftraggeber *m.* client, customer (who gives an order).

auftreiben *v.t.st.* (*Geld*) to raise; (*finden*) (*fam.*) to get hold of.

auftrennen *v.t.* to rip up; to undo.

auftreten *v.i.st.* (*s*) to appear, to come forth; to behave.

Auftreten *n.* manner, appearance.

Auftrieb *m.* (-[e]s, -e) buoyancy, lift; impetus (energy).

Auftritt *m.* (-[e]s, -e) (*Theater*) scene, appearance; entrance.

auftrocknen *v.t. & i* to dry up.

auftrumpfen *v.i.* (*fig.*) to fight back.

auftun *v.st.refl.* to open; (*fig.*) to open up; *v.t.st.* to find; (*servieren*) to help.

auftürmen *v.t.* to pile up; (sich) ~ *v.refl.* to tower.

aufwachen *v.i.* (*s*) to wake up.

aufwachsen *v.i.st.* (*s*) to grow up.

Aufwallung *f.* (-, -en) bubbling; ebullition; (*fig.*) emotion, transport.

Aufwand *m.* (-[e]s, -0) expense, display.

aufwärmen *v.t.* to warm up.

aufwarten *v.i.* to wait on; to serve; to visit; ~ *mit*, to offer.

aufwärts *adv.* upward, upwards.

Aufwärtsentwicklung *f.* (-, -en) upward trend.

Aufwartung *f.* (-, -en) (*Bedienung*) attendance; *seine ~ machen*, to pay a visit to somebody.

aufwaschen *v.t.st.* to wash up.

aufwecken *v.t.* to wake up.

aufweichen *v.t.* to moisten, to soak.

aufweisen *v.t.st.* to show, to produce, to exhibit.

aufwenden *v.t.* to spend (upon).

aufwendig *a.* costly, expensive; *adv.* lavishly.

aufwerfen *v.t.st.* (*Frage*) to raise; *sich ~ zu*, to set up for.

aufwerten *v.t.* to revalue, to revalorize.

Aufwertung *f.* (-, -en) revaluation, revalorization.

aufwickeln *v.t.* to wind up.

aufwiegeln *v.t.* to incite (to mutiny), to stir up.

aufwiegen *v.t.st.* to outweigh; to counterbalance.

Aufwind *m.* upwind; *im ~ sein* to be on the upswing.

aufwirbeln *v.t.* to swirl up, to raise.

aufwischen *v.t.* to wipe up.

aufwühlen *v.t.* to agitate; to churn up; to stir.

aufzählen *v.t.* to enumerate.

Aufzählung *f.* (-, -en) enumeration, listing; list.

aufzäumen *v.t.* to bridle.

aufzehren *v.t.* to consume.

aufzeichnen *v.t.* to record; to draw.

Aufzeichnung *f.* (-, -en) note, record.

aufzeigen *v.t.* to point out; to demonstrate, to highlight.

aufziehen *v.t.st.* to draw up, to pull up; (*Uhr*) to wind up; (*Vorhang*) to draw; (*Kinder*) to rear, to bring up; (*Pflanzen*) to cultivate, to grow, to rear; (*foppen*) to rally, to chaff; *v.i.* (*s*) to march up.

Aufzug *m.* (-[e]s, -züge) hoist; (*Fahrstuhl*) elevator; (*Theater*) act; (*Gewind*) attire.

aufzwingen *v.t.st.* to force upon.

Ausgapfel *m.* eyeball; (*fig.*) apple of one's eye, darling.

Auge *n.* (-s, -n) eye; *unter vier ~n*, between ourselves, in private; *aus dem ~ verlieren*, to lose sight of; (*mil.*) *~n geradeaus*, eyes front; *~n rechts*, eyes right.

äugen *v.i.* to peer.

Augen ..., augenärztlich *a.* ophthalmic.

Augen: *~arzt* *m.* ophthalmologist; *~blick* *m.* moment, twinkling.

augenblicklich *a.* instantaneous, momentary; *~ adv.* instantly.

Augen: *~braue* *f.* eyebrow; *~brauenstift* *m.* eyebrow pencil.

augenfällig = augenscheinlich.

Augen: *~glas* *n.* eyeglass; (*des Fernrohrs*) eyepiece; *~höhle* *f.* socket, orbit; *~licht* *n.* eyesight; *~lid* *n.* eyelid; *~maß* *n.* correct eye, estimate; *~merk* *n.* attention; *~nerv* *m.* optic nerve; *~schein* *m.* appearance; view, inspection.

augenscheinlich *a.* evident, apparent.

Augen: *~spiegel* *m.* ophthalmoscope; *~wimper* *f.* eyelash; *~zeuge* *m.* eyewitness; *~zwinkern* *n.* wink.

-äugig *a.* -eyed.

August *m.* (-[e]s, -e) (*Monat*) August.

Auktion *f.* (-, -en) public sale, auction.

Auktionator *m.* (-s, -en) auctioneer.

Aula *f.* (-, -s) (large) hall.

aus *pr.* out of, from, through, about, on, upon, in by; ~ *adv* out, over, up, finished, consumed.

Aus *n. der Ball ging ins ~* the ball was out.

ausarbeiten *v.t.* to elaborate, to perfect, to compose.

ausarten *v.i.* (*s*) to degenerate.

ausatmen *v.t.* to breathe out, to exhale.

ausbaden *v.t.* (*fig.*) to suffer for, to take the rap for (*sl.*).

ausbaggern *v.t.* to excavate; to dredge.

ausbalancieren *v.t.* to balance (out).

Ausbau *m.* (-es, 0) extension, completion.

ausbauen *v.t.* to extend; to finish; (*fig.*) to improve.

ausbedingen *v.t.st.* to stipulate, to reserve.

ausbessern *v.t.* to fix; to mend; to repair.

Ausbesserung *f.* (-, -en) repair, reparation.

ausbeulen *v.t.* to make baggy; to bulge.

Ausbeute *f.* (-, 0) yield; gain, profit.

ausbeuten *v.t.* to exploit.

Ausbeutung *f.* (-, 0) exploitation.

ausbezahlen *v.t.* to pay (out, off).

ausbilden *v.t.* to form; to school, to train, to cultivate; (sich) ~ *v.refl.* to improve one's mind.

Ausbilder *m.* instructor.

Ausbildung *f.* (-, 0) training; *in der ~ sein*, to be in training, under training.

Ausbildungs: *~förderung* *f.* provision of (education) grants; *~platz* *m.* trainee post; apprenticeship; *~stelle* *f.* training center.

ausbitten *v.t.st.* to request, to beg for; *sich ~*, to insist on.

ausblasen *v.t.st.* to blow out.

ansbleiben *v.i.st.* (*s*) to stay away, to fail to appear.

Ausbleiben *n.* (-s, 0) absence.

ausblenden *v.t.* to fade out.

Ausblick *m.* (-[e]s, -e) view, prospect, preview.

ausbomben *v.t.* to bomb out.

ausbooten *v.t.* (*fam.*) to get rid of.

ausborgen *v.t.* (*fam.*) to borrow.

ausbrechen *v.t.st.* to break out; *~v.i.st.* (*s*) to break out.

ausbreiten *v.t.* to spread, to extent; to propagate; (sich) ~ *v.refl.* to gain ground.

Ausbreitung *f.* (-, -en) spreading, propagation.

ausbrennen *v.i.* to burn out.

Ausbruch *m.* (-[e]s, -brüche) outbreak; (*Vulkan*) eruption; outburst.

ausbrüten *v.t.* to hatch; (*fig.*) to breed; to plot.

Ausbuchtung *f.* (-, -en) bulge.

ausbuddeln *v.t.* to dig up.

ausbügeln *v.t.* to iron out; (*fig.*) to make good.

ausbuhen *v.t.* to boo.

Ausbund *m.* (-[e]s, -bünde) best, paragon.

Ausbürgerung *f.* (-, -en) expatriation.

ausbürsten *v.t.* to brush.

Ausdauer *f.* (-, 0) perserverance, endurance.

ausdauernd *a.* perservering, tenacious.

ausdehnbar *a.* expansible, extensible.

ausdehnen *v.t.* to extend, to stretch; (*fig.*) to prolong.

Ausdehnung *f.* (-, -en) extension, expansion, extent; dimension.

ausdenken *v.t.ir.* to contrive, to devise; to imagine.

ausdeuten *v.t.* to interpret, to explain.

Ausdeutung *f.* (-, -en) interpretation.

ausdienen *v.i. ausgedient haben*, to be used up.

ausdiskutieren *v.t.* to discuss s.th. thoroughly.

ausdörren *v.t.* to parch; to dry up.

ausdrehen *v.t.* (*das Gas*) to turn off; (*elektr. Licht*) to switch off.

Ausdruck *m.* (-[e]s, -drücke) expression; term.

ausdrücken *v.t.* to express; (sich) ~ *v.refl.* to express oneself.

ausdrücklich *a.* express, explicit.

ausdruckslos *a.* blank, vacant.

ausdrucksvoll *a.* expressive, significant.

Ausdrucksweise *f.* mode of expression.

ausdunsten, ausdünsten *v.i. & t* to evaporate; (*schwitzen*) to perspire.

Ausdünstung *f.* (-, -en) evaporation; exhalation; (*Schweiss*) perspiration.

auseinander *adv.* apart, asunder; separately.

auseinandernehmen *v.t.* to take to pieces.

Auseinandersetzung *f.* (-, -en) examination; argument; dispute; discussion.

auserkoren *a.* chosen, elect.

auserlesen *v.t.st.* to choose, to select; ~ *a.* select, choice; exquisite.

ausersehen *v.t.st.* to single out.

ausfahren *v.t.st.* (*Flotte*) to put out, to put to sea.

Ausfahrt *f.* (-, -en) exit; departure; drive; (*Tor*) gateway.

Ausfall *m.* (-[e]s, -fälle) falling out; deficiency; (*Ergebnis*) result; (*mil.*) sally; (*im Fechten*) thrust, pass; failure; breakdown.

ausfallen *v.i.st.* (*s*) (*gut oder schlecht*) to turn out; (*Haar*) to come off; not to take place; (*mil.*) to make a sally; (*im Fechten*) to lunge.

ausfallend *a.* aggressive, abusive (verbally).

Ausfallstraße *f.* main road out of the town.

ausfechten *v.t.st.* to fight out.

ausfegen *v.t.* to sweep (out).

ausfeilen *v.t.* to file down; to polish.

ausfertigen *v.t.* to issue; to dispatch; (*Rechnung*) to make out; (*Urkunde*) to execute.

Ausfertigung *f.* (-, -en) dispatch; execution.

ausfindig machen *v.t.* to find out.

ausfliegen *v.i.* to fly out.

ausflippen *v.i.* (*fam.*) to freak out.

Ausflucht *f.* (-, -flüchte) evasion, subterfuge, poor excuse.

Ausflug *m.* (-[e]s, -flüge) outing, trip, excursion.

Ausflügler *m.* (-s, -) excursionist.

Ausflugs: ~**dampfer** *m.* pleasure steamer; ~**lokal** *n.* restaurant for excursionists; ~**ziel** *n.* destination of excursion.

Ausfluß *m.* (-flusses, -flüsse) flowing out; (*Loch etc.*) outlet; (*Mündung*) mouth; (*med.*) discharge; (*phys.*) emanation.

ausformen *v.t.* to shape.

ausformulieren *v.t.* to formulate; to flesh out.

ausforschen *v.t.* to search out.

ausfragen *v.t.* to examine.

ausfransen *v.t.* to fray out.

ausfressen *v.t.* to be up to s.th.

Ausfuhr *f.* (-, -en) exportation, export.

ausführbar *a.* practicable, feasible.

ausführen *v.t.* (*Waren*) to export; (*vollenden*) to perform, to execute; to set forth.

Ausfuhrhandel *m.* export trade.

ausführlich *a.* detailed, ample, full; ~ *adv.* in detail, fully.

Ausfuhr: ~**stelle** *f.* export control office; ~**zoll** *m.* export duty.

Ausführung *f.* (-, -en) (*fig.*) execution; statement.

Ausführungsbestimmung *f.* (executive) regulation.

ausfüllen *v.t.* to fill out; (*Formular*) to complete, to fill up.

Ausgabe *f.* (-, -n) (*eines Buchs*) edition; (*Kosten*) expense; (*Papiergeld*) issue.

Ausgang *m.* (-[e]s, -gänge) going out; (*Ergebnis*) issue, event; (*Ende*) end, conclusion; (*Tür*) way out, exit.

Ausgangs: ~**lage** *f.* initial situation; ~**punkt** *m.* starting point; ~**sperre** *f.* curfew; ~**stellung** *f.* starting position.

ausgeben *v.t.st.* to distribute; (*Buch*) to publish, to edit; (*Geld*) to spend; (*Papiergeld*) to issue; *sich* ~ *für*, to pass oneself off for . . .

ausgebrannt *a.* gutted.

ausgebreitet *a.* extensive.

ausgebucht *a.* booked up.

ausgebufft *a.* (*fam.*) canny; crafty.

Ausgeburt *f.* (-, -en) product, creature.

ausgedehnt *a.* extensive.

ausgedient *a.* superannuated; (*sl.*) worn out; beat up.

ausgefallen *a.* unusual.

ausgeglichen *a.* balanced, harmonious.

ausgehen *v.i.st.* (*s*) to go out; ~ *von*, to originate with; (*Haare, Farbe*) to come out or off, to fade; (*zu Ende gehen*) to run out; *es ist uns ausgegangen*, we are run out of it or short of it.

ausgehungert *a.* starving.

Ausgehverbot *n.* curfew; ~ *aufheben*, to lift the curfew.

ausgelassen *a.* frisky, exuberant; boisterous.

Ausgelassenheit *f.* exuberance; boisterousness.

ausgemacht *a.* downright, agreed; ~*e Sache*, foregone conclusion.

ausgenommen *pr. & adv.* except, save.

ausgeprägt *a.* clear-cut, distinctive.

ausgerechnet *adv.* ~**heute** today of all days.

ausgeschlafen *a.* wide-awake.

ausgeschlossen *a.* out of the question.
ausgeschnitten *a.* low-cut.
ausgesprochen *a.* marked, decided.
ausgestalten *v.t.* to arrange; to formulate.
ausgestorben *a.* extinct; deserted.
ausgestreckt *a.* outstretched.
ausgesucht *a.* choice, exquisite; (*com.*) picked.
ausgewachsen *a.* full-grown.
ausgewogen *a.* balanced.
ausgezeichnet *a.* excellent, first-rate.
ausgiebig *a.* abundant.
ausgießen *v.t.st.* to pour out.
Ausgleich *m.* (-[e]s, -e) settlement; (*el.*) compensation.
ausgleichen *v.t.st.* to equalize, to compensate; to offset; to balance; (*Streit*) to make up.
ausgleiten *v.t.st.* (*s*) to slip.
ausgraben *v.t.st.* to excavate; to dig out; (*Leichnam*) to exhume.
Ausgrabung *f.* (-, -en) excavation; exhumation.
Ausguck *m.* look-out post.
Ausguß *m.* (-gusses, -güsse) sink; gutter; (*Tülle*) spout.
aushaken *v.t.* to unhook; *v.i.* (*fam.*) to have a block (learning); to lose patience.
aushalten *v.t.st.* to hold out; to last; (*pers.*) to hold out, to persevere; ~ *v.t.st.* to endure, to bear, to stand.
aushandeln *v.t.* to negotiate.
aushändigen *v.t.* to hand over.
Aushang *m.* (-s, -hänge) notice.
aushängen *v.t.* to hang out; to unhinge.
Aushängeschild *n.* sign-board.
ausharren *v.i.* to persevere, to hold out.
aushauchen *v.i. & t.* to breathe out, to expire; to exhale.
ausheben *v.t.st.* to lift out; (*Tür*) to unhinge; (*mil.*) to levy (troops).
Aushebung *f.* (-, -en) draft of soldiers, levy.
aushecken *v.t.* to hatch; (*fig.*) to devise.
ausheilen *v.t.* to heal thoroghly.
aushelfen *v.i.st.* to help out; to aid.
Aushilfe *f.* (-, -n) help, assistance, aid; (*Notbehelf*) makeshift, expedient.
aushöhlen *v.t.* to hollow out, to excavate.
ausholen *v.i.* to strike out; (*fig.*) to go far back.
aushorchen *v.t.* to sound, to pump.
aushören *v.t.* to hear the end.
Aushülfe = **Aushilfe**
aushungern *v.t.* to starve, to famish.
auskämmen *v.t.* to comb (out).
auskämpfen *v.t.* to fight out.
auskehren *v.t.* to sweep (out), to brush.
auskennen (sich) *v.refl.* to be at home in; to be knowledgeable.
auskernen *v.t.* (*Früchte*) to stone.
auskippen *v.t.* to empty.
ausklammern *v.t.* (*math.*) to place outside the brackets; to exclude.
auskleiden *v.t.* to undress; (sich) ~ *v.refl.* to undress.
ausklingen *v.i.st.* to die away (of sound).
ausklopfen *v.t.* to beat.
ausklügeln *v.t.* to puzzle out.
auskneifen *v.t.st.* (*s*) (*fam.*) to make oneself scarce.
ausknipsen *v.t.* to turn off.

ausknobeln *v.t.* to figure s.th. out.
auskochen *v.t.* to boil sufficiently; to sterilize; to extract by boiling.
auskommen *v.i.st.* to manage, to get by; (*mit etwas*) to make both ends meet; (*mit einem*) to get on well.
Auskommen *n.* (-s, 0) livelihood.
auskömmlich *a.* sufficient.
auskosten *v.t.* to enjoy s.th. to the full.
auskratzen *v.t.* to scratch out.
auskundschaften *v.t.* to explore, to spy out.
Auskunft *f.* (-, -künfte) information.
Auskunftei *f.* (-, -en) inquiry office.
Auskunfts: **~bureau** *n.* private inquiry office; **~mittel** *n.* expedient.
auskuppeln *v.i.* to declutch.
auskurieren *v.t.* to heal completely.
auslachen *v.t.* to laugh at, to make fun of.
Ausladebahnhof *m.* railhead.
ausladen *v.t.st.* to unload, to discharge; (*Truppen*) to detrain; to cancel an invitation.
Auslage *f.* (-, -n) disbursement; (*Kosten*) expenses; outlay; (*Schaufenster*) window.
Auslagerung *f.* (-, -en) dispersal of industry.
Ausland *n.* (-[e]s, -0) foreign country; *im ~, ins ~,* abroad.
Ausländer *m.* (-s, -) **Ausländerin** *f.* (-, -nen) foreigner; alien; *feindliche ~,* enemy alien.
ausländisch *a.* foreign.
Auslands: **~gespräch** *n.* (*tel.*) international call.
auslassen *v.t.st.* to omit; to melt; (*Wut*) to give vent; (sich) ~ *v.refl.st.* to speak one's mind.
Auslassung *f.* (-, -en) omission.
Auslassungszeichen *n.* (-s, -) apostrophe.
auslasten *v.t.* to use s.th. to full capacity.
Auslauf *m.* possibility/space to run around; exercise.
auslaufen *v.i.st.* (*s*) to run out; to leak; (*nav.*) to put to sea.
Ausläufer *m.* (-s, -) foothill; (*met.*) ridge, trough.
auslangen *v.t.* to leach (soil); to drain, exhaust.
ausleben *v.t.* to fully live (passion); *v.refl.* to live it up.
auslecken *v.t.* to lick out.
ausleeren *v.t.* to empty, to clear.
auslegen *v.t.* to lay out; (*erklären*) to interpret; (*Geld*) to disburse, to advance.
Auslegung *f.* (-, -en) interpretation.
ausleiern *v.i.* to go baggy; to lose its stretch.
ausleihen *v.t.st.* to lend out.
Auslese *f.* (-, -n) selecton.
auslesen *v.t.st.* (-, -n) to select; (*Buch*) to read through.
ausliefern *v.t.* to deliver, to give up.
Auslieferung *f.* (-, -en) delivery; (*von Verbrechern*) extradition.
ausliegen *v.i.st.* (*Zeitungen*) to display.
auslöschen *v.t.* to extinguish, to quench; to efface; ~ *v.i.* to go out.
auslosen *v.t.* to draw lots for; to draw.
auslösen *v.t.* to trigger; to provoke; to redeem, to ransom.
Auslöser *m.* (-s, -) (*phot.*) release; trigger.
Auslosung *f.* (-, -en) draw.
Auslösung *f.* (-, -en) ransom; redemption; (*phot.*) release.

ausloten *v.t.* to sound the depth of; (*fig.*) to sound out.

auslüften *v.t.* to air, to ventilate.

auslutschen *v.t.* to suck out.

ausmachen *v.t.* (*Feuer*) to put out; (*betragen*) to come to, to constitute; *es macht nichts aus*, it does not matter.

ausmalen *v.t.* to paint; to illuminate.

ausmarschieren *v.i.* (*s*) to march out.

Ausmaß *n.* (-es, -e) extent; measurement.

ausmauern *v.t.* to line with brickwork *or* masonry.

ausmergeln *v.t.* to emaciate.

ausmerzen *v.t.* to eradicate, to eliminate.

ausmessen *v.t.st.* to measure.

ausmisten *v.t. & i.* to muck out; (*fig.*) to clean out.

ausmustern *v.t.* to reject; to discharge.

Ausnahme *f.* (-, -n) exception; *keine ~ zulassen*, to admit of no exception; *~gesetz, n.* emergency law.

ausnahmsweise *adv.* by way of exception.

ausnehmen *v.t.st.* to take out; (*Geflügel*) to draw; (*fig.*) to except, to exclude; (sich) *~ v.refl.st.* to show, to look.

ausnehmend *adv.* exceedingly.

ausputzen/ausnützen *v.t.* to take advantage; to utilize fully; to use up.

auspacken *v.t.* to unpack, to open.

auspeitschen *v.t.* to whip.

auspfeifen *v.t.* to hiss.

ausplaudern *v.t.* to blab out, to let out.

ausplündern *v.t.* to plunder, to pillage, to sack.

auspolstern *v.t.* to stuff.

ausposaunen *v.t.* to trumpet forth, to cry up.

ausprägen *v.refl.* to develop; to become more pronounced.

auspressen *v.t.* to press out, to squeeze.

ausprobieren *v.t.* to test.

ausprügeln *v.t.* to cudgel thoroughly.

Auspuff *m.* (-s, -püffe) exhaust.

Auspuff: *~klappe f.* exhaust valve; *~rohr n.* exhaust pipe.

auspumpen *v.t.* to pump (out).

auspusten *v.t.* to blow out.

ausputzen *v.t.* to clean; to prune; (*schmücken*) to trim out, to deck out.

ausquartieren *v.t.* to dislodge.

ausquetschen *v.t.* to squeeze (out).

ausradieren *v.t.* to erase.

ausrangieren *v.i.* to discard.

ausrasten (sich) *v.refl.* to have a rest; (*sl. fig.*) to have a fit.

ausrauben *v.t.* to rob.

ausräuchern *v.t.* to fumigate, to perfume.

ausraufen *v.t.* to pluck out.

ausräumen *v.t.* to remove, to clear away.

ausrechnen *v.t.* to calculate, to compute.

Ausrechnung *f.* (-, -en) calculation, computation.

Ausrede *f.* (-, -n) excuse, subterfuge, evasion.

ausreden *v.t. & i* to finish speaking; (*einem etwas*) to dissuade someone from; (sich) *~ v.refl.* to shuffle, to beat about the bush.

ausreiben *v.t.st.* to rub out.

ausreichen *v.i.* to suffice.

ausreichend *a.* sufficient.

ausreifen *v.i.* to ripen fully.

Ausreise *f.* (-, -n) departure to a foreign country; *~erlaubnis f.* exit permit.

ausreisen *v.i.* to leave the country.

ausreißen *v.t.st.* to tear out, to pull out; *~ v.i.st.* (*fig.*) to run away, to decamp; to desert.

Ausreißer *m.* (-s, -) runaway, deserter.

ausreiten *v.i.st.* (*s*) to ride out, to go for a ride.

ausrenken *v.t.* to dislocate.

ausrichten *v.t.* to achieve; (*mil.*) to dress; *eine Botschaft ~*, to give a message; *etwas ~ lassen*, to leave a message.

Ausritt *m.* (-s, -e) ride.

ausrollen *v.t.* to roll out.

ausrotten *v.t.* to root out *or* up; (*fig.*) to exterminate, to extirpate.

Ausrottung *f.* (-, -en) extirpation, extermination.

ausrücken *v.i.* to march out; to decamp.

Ausruf *m.* (-[e]s, -e) cry, exclamation; proclamation.

ausrufen *v.i.st.* to cry out, to call out; *~ v.t.st.* to proclaim.

Ausrufezeichen/Ausrufungszeichen *n.* exclamation mark.

ausruhen *v.i.* to rest, to repose.

ausrupfen *v.t.* to pluck out.

ausrüsten *v.t.* to equip; to furnish; to fit out.

Ausrüstung *f.* (-, -en) outfit; equipment.

ausrutschen *v.i.* (*s*) to slip; to skid.

Aussaat *f.* (-, -en) sowing; seed-corn.

aussäen *v.t.* to sow; to disseminate.

Aussage *f.* (-, -n) declaration, statement; deposition; (*gram.*) predicate.

aussagen *v.t.* to say, to declare; (*als Zeuge*) to depose, to give evidence.

Aussagesatz *m.* (-es, -sätze) affirmative clause.

Aussatz *m.* (-es, 0) leprosy; scab.

aussätzig *a.* leprous.

Aussätzige[r] *m.* (-n, -n) leper.

aussaugen *v.t.st. or weak* to suck out; (*fig.*) to exhaust, to impoverish.

Aussauger *m.* (-s, -) bloodsucker, extortioner.

ausschaben *v.t.* (*med.*) to curette.

Ausschabung *f.* (*med.*) currettage.

ausschachten *v.i.* to sink.

ausschalten *v.t.* to switch off; to eliminate.

Ausschank *m.* (-[e]s, -0) bar; counter; retail license.

ausschauen *v.i.* to look out; to look.

ausscheiden *v.t.st.* to separate; to secrete; *~ v.i.st.* (*s*) to withdraw.

Ausscheidung *f.* (-, -en) excretion; elimination; excreta; (*sp.*) qualifier.

Ausscheidungsorgan *n.* (-s, -) excretory organ.

Ausscheidungsspiel *n.* (-s, -e) qualifying game.

ausschenken *v.t.* to pour out; to retail.

ausscheren *v.i.* to pull out; to deviate.

ausschiffen *v.t. & i* to disembark, to land.

ausschimpfen *v.t.* to scold; to carry on.

ausschlachten *v.t.* to exploit.

ausschlafen *v.i.st.* to have a good sleep.

Ausschlag *m.* (-[e]s, -schläge) (*der Waage*) turn of the scales; (*Krankheit*) rash; (*Entscheidung*) decision.

ausschlagen *v.t.st.* (*mit etwas*) to line; (*Geschenk*) to decline, to refuse; *~ v.i.* (*s*) (*von Pferden*) to kick; (*Knospen*) to bud, to shoot; (*gut, schlecht*) to turn out, to prove.

ausschlaggebend *a.* decisive, deciding.

ausschließen v.t. to exclude; to expel.

ausschließlich a. exclusive.

ausschlüpfen v.i. to hatch; to emerge.

ausschlürfen v.t. to sip noisily; to suck.

Ausschluß m. (-schlusses, -schlüsse) exclusion, exemption.

ausschmücken v.t. to adorn, to decorate; to embellish.

ausschneiden v.t.st. to cut out.

Ausschnitt m. (-[e]s, -e) cutting out; cut; low neck; (math.) sector.

ausschöpfen v.t. to scoop out; (fig.) to exhaust.

ausschrauben v.t. to unscrew.

ausschreiben v.t.st. to write out, to spell out; (Landtag, etc.) to convene, to summon; (Steuern) to impose; (Stelle) to advertise.

Ausschreibung f. (-, -en) announcement; calling; invitation to apply.

Ausschreitung f. (-, -en) excess.

Ausschuß m. (-schusses, -schüsse) damaged goods pl.; (Komitee) committee, board, panel; dem ~ angehören, to be on the committee.

ausschütteln v.t. to shake out.

ausschütten v.t. to pour out; (fig.) to unburden (one's heart); to pay (dividend).

ausschwärmen v.i. (s) to swarm out; (mil.) to extend.

ausschwatzen v.t. to blab; to talk of.

ausschweifend a. dissolute, licentious.

Ausschweifung f. (-, -en) debauchery.

ausschweigen v.refl.st. to remain silent.

ausschwenken v.t. to rinse.

ausschwitzen v.t. to exude.

aussehen v.i.st. to look; (nach) to look out (for).

Aussehen n (-s, 0) appearance, look.

aus sein v.i.ir. (s) to be out; to be over.

außen adv. on the outside, without; nach ~, outward.

Außenbordmotor m. outboard motor.

aussenden v.t.ir. to send out.

Außenhandel m. foreign trade.

Außenpolitik f. (-, 0) foreign politics, foreign policy.

Außenseite f. outside, exterior.

Außenseiter m. outsider.

Außenstände m.pl. outstanding debts.

Außenwelt f. outer world.

außer pr. without, out of; except; besides; but; ~ c. unless, except that, but that.

außeramtlich a. unofficial.

außerdem adv. besides, moreover.

Außerdienststunden f.pl. off-duty hours.

äußere a. outer, exterior, external.

Äußere n. (-n, 0) external appearance; Minister des Äußern, Minister of Foreign Affairs.

außerehelich a. extra-marital, illegitimate.

außergerichtlich adv. out of court.

außergewöhnlich a. extraordinary.

außerhalb adv. outside, outwardly.

äußerlich a. external, outward; ~ adv. (med.) for external use only!

Äußerlichkeit f. (-, -en) formality.

äußern v.t. to utter, to express; (sich) ~ v.refl. to express oneself.

außerordentlich a. extraordinary; ~er Professor, assistant (associate) professor.

außerplanmäßig a. unscheduled; unbudgeted.

äußerst a. outermost; extreme, utmost; ~ adv. extremely.

außerstande a. unable.

Äußerung f. (-, -en) remark; comment, utterance; pronouncement.

aussetzen v.t. (Kind) to expose; (Belohnung) to promise; (Summe) to settle; (Tätigkeit) to suspend; (rügen) to find fault (with); ~ v.i. to intermit; (mit etwas) to discontinue.

Aussetzung f. (-, -en) suspension; (Summe) settlement.

Aussicht f. (-, -en) view, prospect.

aussichtslos a. without prospects.

Aussichtsturm m. watchtower.

aussieben v.t. to sift out; to screen.

aussiedeln v.t. to resettle; to evacuate.

Aussiedler m.; **Aussiedlerin** f. emigrant.

aussinnen v.t.st. to contrive.

aussöhnen v.t. to reconcile; (sich) ~ v.refl. to become reconciled (to).

Aussöhnung f. (-, -en) reconciliation.

aussondern v.t. to single out.

aussortieren v.t. to assort, to sort (out).

ausspähen v.t. to spy out; v.i. to look out (for).

ausspannen v.t. to relax; to have a break; to stretch, to extend; (Pferd) to unharness; ~ v.i. to take a rest.

aussparen v.t. to leave out; to leave blank.

ausspeien v.t.st. to spit (out).

aussperren v.t. to shut out; to lock out.

Aussperrung f. (-, -en) lockout.

ausspielen (gegen) v.t. to play off against.

ausspionieren v.t. to spy out.

Aussprache f. (-, -n) pronunciation, accent; talk.

aussprechen v.t.st. to pronounce; (äussern) to declare, to utter; (sich) ~ v.refl. to speak one's mind.

aussprengen v.t. (fig.) to divulge, to report.

Ausspruch m. (-[e]s, -sprüche) remark; utterance; sentence, verdict.

ausspucken v.t. to spit out.

ausspülen v.t. to rinse.

ausstaffieren v.t. to equip, to fit out; to dress up, to rig out.

Ausstand m. (-[e]s, -stände) outstanding debts, arrears pl.; (von Arbeitern) strike.

ausständig a. outstanding (money); (Arbeiter) on strike.

ausstatten v.t. to endow; to provide with; (Töchter) to portion off.

Ausstattung f. (-, -en) outfit; dowry (von Büchern) get-up.

ausstäuben v.t. to beat (carpets), to dust.

ausstechen v.t.st. to cut out; (Augen) to put out; (fig.) to supplant.

ausstehen v.t.st. to endure, to undergo; (fig.) to tolerate.

aussteigen v.i.st. (s) to get out, to get off, to alight; (vom Schiffe) to disembark.

Aussteiger m.; **Aussteigerin** f. dropout.

ausstellen v.t. (auf einer Ausstellung) to exhibit; (Wechsel) to draw; (tadeln) to find fault (with).

Aussteller m. (-s, -) (Wechsel~) drawer; (Industrie~) exhibitor.

Ausstellung f. (-, -en) (Industrie~) exhibition;

(*Tadel*) objection.

Ausstellungsraum *m.* (-[e]s, -räume) showroom.

aussterben *v.i.st.* (*s*) to die out; to become extinct.

Aussteuer *f.* (-, -n) dowry, portion, trousseau.

aussteuern *v.t.* to portion, to endow; (*tech.*) to modulate; to control the level.

Ausstieg *m.* (-s, -e) exit; (*fig.*) opting out.

ausstopfen *v.t.* to stuff.

ausstossen *v.t.st.* to expel; to drive out; (*Schrei*) to utter.

ausstrahlen *v.t. & i* (*s*) to radiate.

Ausstrahlung *f.* radiation; charisma; transmission (TV).

ausstrecken *v.t.* to stretch (out).

ausstreichen *v.t.st.* to cross out; to delete; to strike out.

ausstreuen *v.t.* to scatter, to spread.

ausströmen *v.i.* to stream forth; to escape; to emanate.

Ausströmen (*von Gas*) *n.* (-s, 0) escape of gas.

aussuchen *v.t.* to select; to pick out.

Austausch *m.* (-[e]s, -e) exchange, barter.

austauschbar *a.* interchangeable; replaceable.

austauschen *v.t.* to exchange, to barter; to trade.

austeilen *v.t.* to distribute, to issue; (*Gnaden*) administer.

Auster *f.* (-, -n) oyster.

austilgen *v.t.* to extirpate; to obliterate.

Austilgung *f.* (-, -en) extirpation.

austoben *v.refl.* to have a good romp.

austragen *v.t.st.* to carry out; (*Briefe*) to deliver; (*Streit*) to fight out.

Australien *n.* (-s, 0) Australia; **Australier** *m.*; **Australierin** *f.*; **australisch** *a.* Australian.

austreiben *v.t.st.* to exorcize; to drive out; to expel.

Austreibung *f.* exorcism; expulsion.

austreten *v.t.st.* to stamp out; ~ *v.i.st.* (*s*) (*Fluss*) to overflow; (*verlassen*) to retire.

austricksen *v.t.* (*fam.*) to trick.

austrinken *v.t.st.* to drink up.

Austritt *m.* (-[e]s, -e) stepping out; retirement, leaving.

austrocknen *v.t. & i.* (*s*) to dry up; to drain.

austüfteln *v.t.* to work out.

ausüben *v.t.* to exercise, to practise.

Ausübung *f.* (-, 0) exercise, practice.

ausufern *v.i.* to get out of hand.

Ausverkauf *m.* (-[e]s, -käufe) (clearance) sale, selling off.

ausverkauft *a.* sold out.

auswachsen *v.t.* to grow out of.

Auswahl *f.* (-, -en) choice, selection; *eine ~ treffen*, to make a choice.

auswählen *v.t.* to choose, to select.

auswalzen *v.t.* to roll out.

Auswanderer *m.* (-s, -) emigrant.

auswandern *v.i.* (*s*) to emigrate.

Auswanderung *f.* (-, -en) emigration.

auswärtig *a.* foreign; *~e Beziehungen pl.* international relations *pl.*

Auswärtiges Amt *n.* Foreign Office.

auswärts *adv.* outward, outwards; abroad.

auswaschen *v.t.st.* to wash (out).

auswechselbar *a.* interchangeable.

auswechseln *v.t.* to exchange.

Ausweg *m.* -[e]s, -e) way out; outlet; (*fig.*)

expedient.

ausweglos *a. & adv.* hopeless(ly).

Ausweglosigkeit *f.* hopelessness.

ausweichen *v.i.st.* (*s*) to make way for; to avoid, to evade; to turn aside (*von Wagen*).

ausweichend *a.* evasive.

ausweiden *v.t.* to eviscerate, to draw.

ausweinen *v.refl.* to have a good cry.

Ausweis *m.* (-es, -e) ID, identification; *~papier*, identity paper, certificate of identity.

ausweisen *v.i.st.* to expel, to banish; (*erweisen*) to prove; *sich ~*, to prove one's identity.

Ausweisung *f.* (-, -en) expulsion, banishment.

ausweiten *v.t.* to widen, to stretch.

auswendig *a.* outer, exterior; *~ adv.* by heart.

auswerfen *v.t.st.* to cast; (*Gehalt*) to appoint.

auswerten *v.t.* to analyze and evaluate; to make full use of.

Auswertung *f.* (-, -en) analysis and evaluation; utilization.

auswickeln *v.t.* to unwrap.

auswiegen *v.t.st.* to weigh.

auswirken *refl.* to affect.

Auswirkung *f.* effect; consequence.

auswischen *v.t.* to wipe out.

auswringen *v.t.st.* to wring out.

Auswuchs *m.* (-wuchses, -wüchse) growth; excrescence; abuse.

auswuchten *v.t.* to balance (tire).

Auswurf *m.* (-[e]s, -würfe) sputum; excretion; expectoration; (*fig.*) refuse, dregs *pl.*

auszahlen *v.t.* to pay (down).

auszählen *v.t.* to count (up/out).

Auszahlung *f.* (-, -en) payment.

Auszählung *f.* (-, -en) counting.

auszehren *v.t.* to exhaust.

Auszehrung *f.* (-, -en) consumption.

auszeichnen *v.t.* to mark out), to distinguish; to honor.

Auszeichnung *f.* (-, -en) distinction.

ausziehbar *a.* extendible; telescopic.

ausziehen *v.t.st.* to draw *or* pull out; (*chem.*) to extract; (*dehnen*) to stretch, to extend; (*Kleider*) to take off; *~ v.i.st.* to move out; to remove; (*mil.*) to march out; *sich ~*, to undress.

Ausziehtisch *m.* extending table.

Auszubildende *m./f.* (-n, -n) trainee; apprentice.

Auszug *m.* (-[e]s, -züge) (*Wohnungs~*) removal; (*aus einem Buche*) abstract; (*fig.*) extract, summary, digest.

auszugsweise *adv.* in excerpts/extracts.

auszupfen *v.t.* to pluck out; to pull out.

autark *a.* self-sufficient.

Autarkie *f.* (-, 0) self-sufficiency.

authentisch *a.* (*& adv.*) authentic(ally).

Auto *n.* (-s) car, automobile.

Autoatlas *m.* road atlas.

Autobahn *f.* (-, -en) highway, freeway.

Autobiographie *f.* autobiography.

autobiographisch *a.* autobiographical.

Autodidakt *m.* (-en, -en) self-taught person.

Autofahrer *m.*; **autofahrerin** *f.* driver.

autogen *a.* autogenous; *~ Training n.* autogenic training, autogenics.

Autogramm *n.* (-[e]s, -e) autograph.

Autohaltestelle *f.* cab rank, taxi stand.

Autokino *n.* drive-in cinema.
Autoknacker *m.* car burglar.
Autokolonne *f.* convoy.
autokratisch *a.* autocratic.
Automat *m.* (-en, -en) machine; automaton.
Automatik *f.* (-, -en) automatism; automatic system/transmission.
automatisch *a.* (& *adv.*) automatic(ally).
automatisieren *v.t.* automate.
Automatisierung *f.* (-, -en) automation.
Automatismus *m.* (-, -men) automatism.
Automechaniker *m.* mechanic.
Automobil *n.* (-s, -e) motor car; automobile.
Auto: ~**mobilist** *m.* motorist; ~**strasse** *f.* highway.
autonom *a.* autonomous.
Autonummer *f.* registration number.
Autopapiere *pl.* car documents.
Autopsie *f.* (-, -[e]n) coroner's inquest.
Autor *m.* (-s, -en); **Autorin** *f.* (-, -nen) author, writer.
Autorennen *n.* (-s, -) car race.
autorisieren *v.t.* to authorize.
autoritär *a.* authoritarian.
Autorität *f.* (-, -en) authority.
Autorschaft *f.* (-, 0) authorship.
Autoverleih *m.*/**Autovermietung** *f.* car rental.
Autowerkstatt *f.* garage.
Autozubehör *n.* car accessories.
Auwald *m.* riverside forest.
avancieren *v.i.* to rise, to get promoted.
avisieren *v.t.* to advise, to inform.
Avitaminose *f.* (-, -n) (*med.*) avitaminosis.
Axt *f.* (-, Äxte) axe, hatchet.
Azalie *f.* (-, -n) azalea.
Azetylen *n.* (-s, 0) acetylene.
Azteke *m.*; **Aztekin** *f.* Aztec.
Azubi *m.*/*f.* trainee; apprentice.
azurblau, azurn *a.* azure.

B

B, b *n.* the letter B or b; (*mus.*) B flat.
babbeln *v.t.*/*i.* to babble.
Baby *n.* (-s, -s) baby.
Babyausstattung *f.* layette.
babylonisch *a.* Babylonian; ~**es Sprachgewirr** *n.* a babel of languages.
Babysprache *f.* baby talk.
Bach *m.* (-[e]s, -Bäche) brook, rivulet.
Bache *f.* (-, -n) (*hunt.*) wild sow.
Backblech *n.* (-s, -e) baking-sheet.
Bachstelz *f.* (-, -n) wag-tail.
Backbord *n.* larboard, port.
Backe *f.* (-, -n) cheek; jaw; (*mech.*) jaw; buttock.
backen *v.t.* to bake; (*Fische*) to fry; (*Ziegel*) to burn.
Backen ~**bart** *m.* whiskers *pl.*; beard; ~**knochen** *m.* cheekbone; ~**zahn** *m.* molar.
Bäcker *m.* (-s, -) baker.
Bäcker ~**bursche** *m.* (-s, -) baker's boy; ~**gesell** *m.* baker's man.
Bäckerei *f.* (-, -en) bakery.
Back: ~**fisch** *m.* fried fish; girl in her teens, flapper; ~**obst** *n.* dried fruit; ~**ofen** *m.* baking oven; ~**pfanne** *f.* drying pan; ~**pulver** *n.* baking powder; ~**stein** *m.* brick.
Bad *n.* (-es, -Bäder) bath; (*Ort*) watering-place, spa; (*Handlung*) bathe.
Bade: ~**anstalt** *f.* baths *pl.*; public pool; ~**anzug** *m.* bathing suit; ~**kur** *f.* course of mineral waters; ~**mantel** *m.* dressing-gown, bathrobe.
baden *v.t.* & *i.* to bathe.
Bade: ~**ofen** *m.* bathroom boiler (water heater); ~**ort** *m.* spa.
Bade: ~**wanne** *f.* bath, bathtub; ~**tuch** *n.* bath towel; ~**zimmer** *n.* bathroom.
baff *a.* ~**sein** to be flabbergasted.
Bagage (-, 0) *f.* (*fig.*) (*pej.*) bunch, rabble, slut.
Bagatelle *f.* (-, -n) trifle.
bagatellisieren *v.t.* to play down.
Bagger *m.* (-s, -) excavator; ~ **maschine** *f.* dredger, dredging-machine.
baggern *v.t.* to excavate, to dredge.
Bahn *f.* (-, -en) road, path; course; (*Eisen*~) railway, railroad; (*fig.*) career; *mit der* ~, by train.

bahnbrechend *a.* pioneering, epoch-making.
Bahnbrecher *m.* (-s, -) pioneer.
Bahndamm *m.* (-s, -dämme) railroad embankment.
bahnen *v.t.* (Weg) to open a way; (*fig.*) to pave the way for.
Bahn ~**hof** *m.* railway-station; ~**hofsvorsteher** *m.* stationmaster; ~**linie** *f.* line (of railway); ~**steig** *m.* platform; ~**steigkarte** *f.* platform ticket; (*schienengleicher*) **Bahnübergang** *m.* level crossing.
Bahre *f.* (-, -n) stretcher, bier.
Bai *f.* (-, -en) bay.
Baisse *frz.f.* fall in prices, slump; *auf* ~ *spekulieren*, to bear.
Bajonett *n.* (-[e]s, -e) bayonet.
Bakterie *f.* (-, -n) bacterium.
bacteriell *a.* bacterial.
bakteriologisch *a.* bacteriological.
balancieren *v.t.* & *i.* to balance.
bald *adv.* soon, shortly; nearly, almost; ~ . . . , ~ . . . , now . . . , now . . .
Baldachin *m.* (-[e]s, -e) canopy.
in Bälde soon.
baldig *a.* quick, speedy, early.
Baldrian *m.* (-s, 0) valerian.
Balearen *pl.* the Balearic Islands.
Balg *m.* (-[e]s, -Bälge) skin; (*fig.*) brat.
balgen (sich) *v.refl.* to fight; to romp, to scuffle.
Balgerei *f.* (-, -en) fight; scuffle.
Balkan *m.* (-s, 0) the Balkans; the Balkan Mountains.
Balken *m.* (-s, -) beam; rafter.
Balkon *m.* (-s, -e *u.* -s) balcony.
Ball *m.* (-[e]s, -Bälle) ball; globe.
Ballade *f.* (-, -n) ballad.
Ballast *m.* (-es, -e) ballast.
ballen *v.t.* *die Faust* ~, to clench; (sich) ~ *v.refl.* to cluster; to gather.
Ballen *m.* (-s, -) bale, pack; (*Fuss*) ball, bunion.
Ballett *n.* (-[e]s, -e) ballet.
Ballon *m.* (-s, -s) balloon.
Ballsaal *m.* ballroom; ~**spiel** *n.* ball-game.
Ballungs: ~**gebiet** *n.*; ~**raum** *m.*; ~**zentrum** *n.*

conurbation; area of industrial concentration.
Balsam *m.* (-[e]s, -e) balm, balsam.
balsamich *a.* balmy.
Balz *f.* (-, -n) (*Auerhahn*) courting; mating season.
balzen *v.i.* to court, to mate.
Bambus *m.*, **Bambusrohr** *n.* bamboo.
Bammel *m.* (*fam.*) fear.
banal *a.* trite, banal.
Banalität *f.* banality.
Banane *f.* (-, -n) banana.
Banause *m.* (-n, -n) Philistine, lowbrow.
Band *n.* (-[e]s, **-Bänder** *u.* [*fig.*] **Bande**) band;
(*Seiden~*) ribbon; (*Zwirn~*) tape; (*anat.*) ligament;
(*fig.*) tie, bond.
Band *m.* (-es, Bände) (*Buch*) volume; (*Einband*)
binding.
Bandage *f.* (-, -n) bandage, truss.
bandagieren *v.t.* to bandage.
Bande *f.* (-, -n) band, gang; cushions (billiard).
Bande *n.pl.* fetters, chains; ties *pl.*
bändigen *v.t.* to tame; (*Pferd*) to break (in); (*fig.*)
to subdue.
Bandit *m.* (-en, -en) bandit.
Bandscheibe *f.* (intervertebral) disc.
Bandwurm *m.* tape-worm.
bange *a.* afraid, alarmed, uneasy.
bangen *v.imp.* to be afraid of; (*nach*) to long for.
Bangigkeit *f.* (-, -en) anxiety.
Bank *f.* (-, Bänke) bench; (*Schul~*) form; *auf die*
lange ~ schieben, to put off; *durch die ~*, without
exception.
Bank *f.* (-, Banken) (*Geld~*) bank.
bankrott *a.* bankrupt.
Bankrott *m.* (-[e]s, -e) bankruptcy; *betrügerische ~*,
fraudulent bankruptcy.
Bankrottierer *m.* (-s, -) bankrupt.
Bankett *n.* (-s, -e) banquet.
Bank: *~konto* *n.* banking account; *~note* *f.* bank-
note, bank bill.
Bankier *m.* (-s, -s) banker.
Bann *m.* (-[e]s, 0) ban, excommunication.
bannen *v.t.* to banish; (*Geister*) to exorcise.
Banner *n.* (-s, -) banner.
bar *a.* bare; cash, ready money; *gegen ~*, for cash;
~bezahlen, to pay cash.
Bar *f.* (-, -s) bar; nightclub.
Bär *m.* (-en, -en) bear; *der Grosse ~*, The Great Bear.
Baracke *f.* (-, -n) shed, hut.
Barbar *m.* (-en, -en) barbarian.
Barbarei *f.* (-, -en) barbarity; vandalism.
barbarisch *a.* barbarous.
bärbeissig *a.* grumpy.
Barbier *m.* (-[e]s, -e) barber, hairdresser.
barbieren *v.t.* to shave; to cheat.
Barchent *m.* (-[e]s, -e) cotton flannel.
Barde *m.* (-n, -n) bard.
Bärenhaut *f.* bearskin; *auf der ~ liegen*, to be idle.
Barett *n.* (-s, -e) cap.
barfuss, barfüssig *a.* & *adv.* barefoot.
Bargeld *n.* ready money, cash.
barhäuptig *a.* bareheaded.
Bariton *m.* (-s, -e) baritone.
Barkasse *f.* (-, -n) launch.
Barke *f.* (-, -n) barge.
barmherzig *a.* merciful, compassionate; *~e Schwes-*
ter, sister of mercy.

Barmherzigkeit *f.* (-, 0) mercy, compassion.
Barmixer *m.* barman; barkeeper.
Barock *m.* & *a.* baroque.
Barometer *n.* & *m.* (-s, -) barometer; *das ~ steigt*,
the glass is going up.
Baron *m.* (-[e]s, -e) baron.
Baronin *f.* (-, -nen) baroness.
Barren *m.* (-s, -n) (*Metall*) pig, ingot; (*Turnen*) par-
allel bars.
Barriere *f.* (-, -n) barrier.
Barrikade *f.* (-, -n) barricade.
Barsch *m.* (-es, -e *u.* Bärsche) perch.
barsch *a.* harsh, rude, abrupt.
Barschaft *f.* (-, -en) cash, ready money.
Bart *m.* (-[e]s, Bärte) beard.
bärtig *a.* bearded.
bartlos *a.* beardless.
Barzahlung *f.* cash payment.
Basalt *m.* (-[e]s, -e) basalt.
Basar *m.* (-s, -e) bazaar.
Base *f.* (-, -n) (female) cousin; (*chem.*) base.
basieren *v.i.* to be based on.
Basilika *f.* (-, -ken) basilica.
Basilikum *n.* basil.
Basis *f.* (-, 0) basis.
Baskenmütze *f.* (-, -n) beret.
Baß *m.* (Basses, Basse) bass; bass viol.
Baßgeige *f.* bass viol.
Bassist *m.* (-en) bass singer, basso.
Baßschlüssel *m.* (*mus.*) bass clef.
Bast *m.* (-es, -e) bast, inner bark of trees.
Bastard *m.* (-[e]s, -e) bastard.
Bastelei *f.* (-, -en) handicraft work.
basteln *v.i.* to do handicraft.
Bataillon *n.* (-s, -e) battalion.
Batist *m.* (-[e]s, -e) cambric.
Batterie *f.* (-, -[e]n) battery.
Bau *m.* (-es, -e) building, structure; edifice; (*Körper*)
build, frame; cultivation; (*von Tieren*) den, earth;
im ~, under construction.
Bau: *~amt* *n.* Board of Works; *~arbeiten* *pl.* con-
struction work; *~bataillon* *n.* (*mil.*) construction
battalion.
Bauch *m.* (-[e]s, -Bäuche) belly; (*Schiffs~*) bottom;
stomach.
Bauch: *~fell* *n.* peritoneum; *~fellentzündung* *f.*
peritonitis.
bauchig *a.* bellied, bulgy.
Bauchklatscher *m.* belly flop.
Bauchlandung *f.* (*air.*) belly landing.
Bauchnabel *m.* belly button.
Bauch *~redner* *m.* ventriloquist; *~weh* *n.* colic,
stomach ache.
bauen *v.t.* to build; to till; (*Getreide*) to grow;
(*Pflanzen*) to cultivate; *auf jemand ~*, to rely on one.
Bauer *m.* (-n *or* -s, -n) peasant, farmer; (*im Schach*)
pawn; (*Karte*) knave.
Bauer *m.* & *n.* (-s, -) cage (birds).
Bäuerin *f.* (-, -nen) peasant *or* farmer (woman).
bäu(e)risch *a.* rustic; (*fig.*) boorish.
bäuerlich *a.* farming; rural.
Bauern: *~hof* *m.* farmhouse; *~fänger* *m.* con man.
Bauernkrieg *m.* Peasant War.
Bauersfrau *f.* (-, -en) farmer (woman).
Baufach *n.* (-[e]s, 0) architecture.
baufällig *a.* out of repair, tumble-down.

Baufälligkeit *f.* (-, 0) disrepair.
Bau: ~**führer** *m.* overseer (at building works); ~**gerüst** *n.* scaffolding; ~**holz** *n.* timber; ~**kasten** *m.* box of bricks; ~**kunst** *f.* architecture.
baulich *a.* architectural.
Baum *m.* (-[e]s, -Bäume) tree; (*nav.*) boom.
Baumast *m.* knot.
Baumeister *m.* architect; master builder.
baumeln *v.i.* to dangle, to bob.
bäumen (sich) *v.refl.* to prance, to rear.
Baum: ~**grenze** *f.* timber line; ~**krone** *f.* treetop; ~**rinde** *f.* bark; ~**schere** *f.* pruning-shears *pl.*; ~**schule** *f.* nursery; ~**stamm** *m.* trunk.
Baumwolle *f.* cotton.
baumwollen *a.* (made of) cotton.
Baumwollgarn *n.* cotton-yarn.
Baumwollspinnerei *f.* cotton-mill.
Bau: ~**platz** *m.* building-lot; ~**polizei** *f.* building department; ~**rat** *m.* government surveyor (of works).
Bausch *m.* (-es, Bäusche) bolster, pad; compress; *in* ~ *und Bogen*, in the lump.
bauschen *v.i.* to bag; to bulge, to swell out.
bauschig *a.* baggy, puffed out; swollen.
Bau: ~**sparkasse** *f.* building society; ~**stein** *m.* building-stone; ~**stelle** *f.* building site; ~**stelle!** men working!; ~**stil** *m.* architectural style; ~**stoff** *m.* building material; ~**teil** *n.* component; ~**unternehmen** *n.* building firm; ~**unternehmer** *m.* building contractor; ~**vorhaben** *n.* building project; ~**weise** *f.* method of building; ~**werk** *n.* building, structure (bridge).
Bauxit *m.* (-[e]s, -e) bauxite.
Bauzaun *m.* (-s, -zäune) site fence.
Bayer *m.*; **Bayerin** *f.*; **bay(e)risch** *a.* Bavarian; **Bayern** *n.* Bavaria.
Bazillus *m.* (-, Bazillen) bacillus.
B-Dur *n.* (*mus.*) B flat major.
beabsichtigen *v.t.* to intend.
beachten *v.t.* to observe; to follow (rule); to pay attention to.
beachtenswert *a.* noteworthy.
beachtlich *a.* considerable; notable.
Beachtung *f.* observance, following; consideration.
Beamte[r] *m.* (-en, -en); **Beamtin** *f.* (-, -nen) official; civil servant; *höherer* ~, senior official.
beängstigen *v.t.* to alarm.
beängstigend *a.* worrying, alarming; unsettling.
beanspruchen *v.t.* to claim, to demand.
Beanspruchung *f.* (-, -en) *starke* ~, hard wear.
beanstanden *v.t.* to object to; to complain about.
beantragen *v.t.* to apply; to propose.
beantworten *v.t.* to answer, to reply to.
Beantwortung *f.* (-, -en) reply, answer.
bearbeiten *v.t.* to work; to process; (*Angelegenheit*) to attend to, to deal with; (*fig. einen*) to influence.
Bearbeitung *f.* (-, -en) working; revision; treatment.
Bearbeitungsgebühr *f.* (-, -en) handling charge.
Beatmung *f.* (-, 0) (**künstliche**) ~ artificial respiration.
beaufsichtigen *v.t.* to superintend, to control.
Beaufsichtigung *f.* (-, -en) supervision.
beauftragen *v.t.* to charge.
Beauftragte *f./m.* representative; commissioner.
beäugen *v.t.* to eye; to inspect.

bebauen *v.t.* to build on; to cultivate.
Bebauung *f.* development; buildings, cultivation.
beben *v.i.* to quake, to shake, to shiver.
bebildern *v.t.* to illustrate.
Becher *m.* (-s, -) cup, goblet; (*ohne Fuss*) tumbler; (*Würfel*) box.
bechern *v.i.* (*fam.*) to booze.
Becken *n.* (-s, -) basin; (*mus.*) cymbal; (*anat.*) pelvis.
Bedacht *m.* (-[e]s, 0) consideration; *mit* ~, deliberately.
bedacht *a.* ~ **sein auf** to be intent on.
bedächtig *a.* considerate, advised, prudent, circumspect.
Bedächtigkeit *f.* (-, 0) caution, circumspection.
bedachtsam *a.* circumspect.
Bedachung *f.* (-, -en) roofing.
bedanken (sich) *v.refl.* to thank; to decline.
Bedarf *m.* (-[e]s, 0) need, want.
Bedarfsartikel *m.pl.* requisites *pl.*
bedauerlich *a.* deplorable.
bedauerlicherweise *adv.* regrettably, unfortunately.
bedauern *v.t.* to pity; to regret.
bedauernswert *a.* deplorable, pitiable.
bedecken *v.t.* to cover; (sich) ~*v.refl.* to put on one's hat.
Bedeckung *f.* (-, -en) covering; (*mil.*) escort, convoy.
bedenken *v.t.ir.* to consider, to mind, to reflect upon; (*im Testament*) to remember; (sich) ~ *v.refl.ir.* to deliberate; *sich anders* ~, to change one's mind.
Bedenken *n.* (-s, -) doubt; hesitation, scruple.
bedenkenlos *a.* unhesitating; unscrupulous.
bedenkenswert *a.* worthy of consideration.
bedenklich *a.* doubtful, risky; scrupulous.
Bedenkzeit *f.* time for reflection.
bedeuten *v.t.* to signify, to mean; to indicate; *es hat nichts zu* ~, it is of no consequence.
bedeutend *a.* important, considerable.
bedeutsam *a.* significant.
Bedeutung *f.* (-, -en) meaning, significance, sense; consequence, importance.
bedeutungslos *a.* insignificant.
bedienen *v.t.* to serve; to attend; (*Maschinen*) to operate; (sich) ~ *v.refl.* to make use of; (*bei Tische*) to help oneself.
Bedienstete(r) *m./f.* (-n, -n) employee.
Bediente[r] *m.* (-en, -en) servant.
Bedienung *f.* (-, -en) service, attendance; ~**inbegriffen** service included.
Bedienungs: ~**anleitung** *f.* operating instructions; ~**komfort** *m.* ease of operation.
bedingen *v.t.* to stipulate, to involve; to require.
bedingt (**durch**) *a.* conditional (on).
Bedingung *f.* (-, -en) condition; stipulation; terms *pl.*
bedingungslos *a.* unconditional.
Bedingungssatz *m.* conditional clause.
bedrängen *v.t.* to press hard; to oppress, to afflict.
Bedrängnis *f.* (-, -nisse) oppression; affliction; distress.
bedrohen *v.t.* to threaten, to menace.
bedrohlich *a.* threatening.
Bedrohung *f.* (-, -en) threat, menace.
bedrucken *v.t.* to print.

bedrücken *v.t.* to depress, to oppress.
bedrückend *a.* depressing; oppressive.
bedruckt *a.* printed.
bedrückt *a.* depressed.
Bedrückung *f.* (-, -en) depression.
Beduine *m.* (-n, -n); **Beduinen** *f.* (-, -nen) Bedouin.
bedürfen *v.t. & i.ir* to require; to need, to want.
Bedürfnis *n.* (-nisses, nisse) want, need; **Bedürfnisse** *pl.* necessaries *pl.*
Bedürfnisanstalt *f.* public convenience.
bedürfnislos *a.* modest, simple.
Bedürfnislosigkeit *f.* lack of needs.
bedürftig *a.* needy, indigent.
Bedürftigkeit *f.* neediness.
beehren *v.t.* to honor.
beeiden *v.t.* to swear to.
beeilen (sich) *v.refl.* to hurry up, to make haste.
beeindrucken *v.t.* to impress.
beeindruckend *a.* impressive.
beeinflussen *v.t.* to influence.
beeinträchtigen *v.t.* to impair.
beenden, beendigen *v.t.* to finish, to terminate.
Beendigung *f.* (-, -en) conclusion.
beengen *v.t.* to restrict, to narrow, to cramp.
beerben *v.t.* to be someone's heir.
beerdigen *v.t.* to inter, to bury.
Beerdigung *f.* (-, -en) funeral, burial.
Beere *f.* (-, -en) berry.
Beet *n.* (-[e]s, -e) bed, border.
befähigen *v.t.* to enable, to qualify.
befähigt *a.* capable, qualified.
Befähigung *f.* (-, -en) qualification; capacity; caliber.
befahrbar *a.* passable, navigable.
befahren *v.t.st.* to pass over.
befallen *v.t.st.* to befall; to attack.
befangen *a.* biased; self-conscious.
Befangenheit *f.* (-, -en) prejudice; self-consciousness.
befassen (sich) *v.refl.* to occupy oneself with, to engage in.
befehden *v.t.* to make war upon.
Befehl *m.* (-[e]s, -e) command, order; *auf ~ von*, by order of.
befehlen *v.t.st.* to command, to order; to commit.
befehligen *v.t.* to command.
Befehls: *~ausgabe* *f.* (*mil.*) briefing; *~haber* *m.* (-s, -) commanding officer; *~ton* peremptory tone; *~weg* *m.* chain of command.
befestigen *v.t.* to fasten; to fortify.
Befestigung *f.* (-, -en) consolidation; fortification.
befinden *v.t.st.* to find; to deem; (sich) *~ v.refl.* to be; *wie ~ Sie sich?* how are you?; *für tauglich befunden werden*, to be passed as fit.
Befinden *n.* (-s, 0) health; opinion.
befindlich *a.* being; contained.
beflaggen *v.t.* to deck with flags.
beflecken *v.t.* to stain, to spot; (*fig.*) to pollute.
befleissigen (sich) *v.refl.* to bestow pains upon; to apply oneself to.
beflissen *a.* keen, eager, studious, intent (upon).
beflügeln *v.t.* to inspire s.b.
befolgen *v.t.* to follow, to obey; (*Gesetz*) to abide by, to comply with.
Befolgung *f.* (-, 0) observance of; adherence to.

befördern *v.t.* to further, to promote, to advance; to upgrade; (*verschicken*) to forward, to dispatch; to convey.
Beförderung *f.* (-, -en) furtherance, promotion, advancement; forwarding.
Beförderungsmittel *n.* means of transport.
befrachten *v.t.* to load, to charge.
befragen *v.t.* to question, to examine.
Befragung *f.* questioning, examination.
befreien *v.t.* to free, to deliver, to liberate, to release; *vom Erscheinen befreit*, excused from appearing.
Befreier *m.* (-s, -) liberator.
befreit *a.* relieved.
Befreiung *f.* (-, -en) deliverance; exemption.
befremden *v.t.* to appear strange (to), to surprise.
Befremden *n.* (-s, 0) surprise and displeasure.
befremdlich *a.* strange, odd, surprising.
befreunden (sich) *v.refl.* to make friends.
befrieden *v.t.* to bring peace to.
befriedigen *v.t.* to content, to satisfy.
befriedigend *a.* satisfactory.
befriedigt *a.* satisfied.
Befriedigung *f.* (-, -en) satisfaction.
befristen *v.t.* to set a time limit.
befristet *a.* limited in time.
befruchten *v.t.* to impregnate; to fertilize; to pollinate.
Befruchtung *f.* (-, -en) impregnation, fecundation; pollination.
Befugnis *f.* (-, -nisse) authority.
befugt *a.* authorised, competent.
befühlen *v.t.* to feel, to touch.
befummeln *v.t.* (*fam.*) to paw; to grope.
Befund *m.* (-[e]s, Befunde) finding; result.
befürchten *v.t.* to fear, to apprehend.
Befürchtung *f.* (-, -en) fear, apprehension.
befürworten *v.t.* to recommend; to support.
Befürworter *m.*; **Befürworterin** *f.* supporter.
Befürwortung *f.* support.
begabt *a.* gifted, talented.
Begabung *f.* (-, -en) endowment, gift, talent.
begaffen *v.t.* (*fam. pej.*) to gawp, to stare.
begatten (sich) *v.refl.* to pair, to copulate.
Begattung *f.* (-, -en) copulation, mating.
begeben *v.t.st.* (*Wechsel*) to negotiate; (sich) *~ v.refl.st.* to proceed to; (*geschehen*) to come to pass, to happen.
Begebenheit *f.* (-, -en) event, occurrence.
begegnen *v.i.* (s) to meet (with); to happen (to), to befall.
Begegnung *f.* (-, -en) meeting.
begehen *v.t.st.* (*feiern*) to celebrate; (*verüben*) to commit.
Begehren *n.* (-s, 0) desire, wish.
begehren *v.t.* to desire; to request.
begehrenswert *a.* desirable.
begehrlich *a.* desirous, covetous, greedy.
begehrt *a.* much sought-after.
Begehung *f.* (-, -en) perpetration; (*Feier*) celebration.
begeistern *v.t.* to inspire.
begeistert *a.* enthusiastic.
Begeisterung *f.* (-, -en) enthusiasm.
Begier, Begierde *f.* (-, Begierden) desire, appetite.
begierig *a.* desirous; eager.

begießen *v.t.st.* to water; to baste.
Beginn *m.* (-[e]s, 0) beginning, origin.
beginnen *v.t. & i.st.* to begin; to undertake.
beglaubigen *v.t.* to certify, to attest, to confirm, to authenticate; to accredit.
Beglaubigung *f.* (-, -en) certification, attestation.
Beglaubigungsschreiben *n.* letter of accreditation, credentials *pl.*
begleichen *v.t.* to settle; to pay.
Begleit . . . (*mil.*) escort.
Begleit: ~brief *m.* cover(ing) letter; **~erscheinung** *f.* concomitant.
begleiten *v.t.* to accompany, to attend.
Begleiter *m.* (-s, -) companion, attendant.
Begleitung *f.* (-, -en) company, attendants; (*mil.*) escort; retinue; (*mus.*) accompaniment.
beglücken *v.t.* to bless, to make happy.
beglückt *a.* happy, delighted.
beglückwünschen *v.t.* to congratulate.
begnadet *a.* highly gifted.
begnadigen *v.t.* to pardon.
Begnadigung *f.* (-, -en) pardon; amnesty.
begnügen (sich) *v.refl.* to content oneself, to be satisfied (with), to acquiesce (in).
begraben *v.t.st.* to bury.
Begräbnis *n.* (-nisses, -nisse) burial, funeral; tomb, grave.
begreifen *v.t.st.* to include, to contain, to comprise; (*fig.*) to understand, to conceive, to comprehend.
begreiflich *a.* conceivable, intelligible.
begreiflicherweise *adv.* understandably.
begrenzen *v.t.* to bound, to border; to limit.
begrenzt *a.* limited, restricted.
Begrenztheit *f.* (-, 0) limitation.
Begrenzung *f.* (-, -en) boundary, restriction, delimitation.
Begriff *m.* (-[e]s, -e) idea, notion, concept, conception; *im~*, about to, on the point of.
begrifflich *a.* conceptual.
Begriffsbestimmung *f.* definition.
begriffsstutzig *a.* dense, slow-witted.
begründen *v.t.* to found, to establish; to confirm, to prove.
Begründer *m.* founder.
begründet *a.* well-founded, reasonable.
Begründung *f.* reason; founding; establishment.
begrüßen *v.t.* to greet, to salute.
Begrüßung *f.* greeting; welcoming.
begucken *v.t.* to look at.
begünstigen *v.t.* to favor, to patronize.
Begünstiger *m.* (-s, -) (*law*) accessory after the fact.
Begünstigung *f.* (-, -en) encouragement, patronage; advantage, privilege.
begutachten *v.t.* to give an opinion on.
begütert *a.* wealthy, well-to-do.
begütigen *v.t.* to placate; to mollify; to pacify.
behaart *a.* hairy; hirsute.
behäbig *a.* sedate; portly; stout.
behaftet *a.* affected (with), infected (with), to be marked with.
behagen *v.imp.* to please, to suit.
Behagen *n.* (-s, 0) pleasure, comfort.
behaglich *a.* comfortable, pleasing, snug.
behalten *v.t.st.* to keep; to retain.
Behälter *m.* (-s, -) container, receptacle.

behandeln *v.t.* to handle; to deal with; to treat; (*Arzt*) to attend; (*chem.*) to process.
Behandlung *f.* (-, -en) management, treatment.
behangen *a.* decorated (tree).
behängen *v.t.* to hang with.
beharren (bei) *v.i.* to persist in, to stick to.
beharrlich *a.* constant, steady, persevering.
Beharrlichkeit *f.* doggedness; persistence.
behauen *v.t.* to hew.
behaupten *v.t.* to assert, to maintain; (sich) ~ *v.refl.* to keep one's ground.
Behauptung *f.* (-, -en) assertion, statement.
Behausung *f.* (-, -en) lodging, habitation.
beheben *v.t.* to clear away.
beheimatet *a.* to come from a place/country.
beheizbar *a.* heatable.
beheizen *v.t.* to heat.
Behelf *m.* (-[e]s, -e) expedient, shift.
behelfen (sich) *v.refl.st.* to make shift (with); (*ohne etwas*) to do without.
behelfsmäßig *a.* makeshift; temporary.
behelligen *v.t.* to trouble, to importune.
behend(e) *a.* quick, agile, nimble.
Behendigkeit *f.* (-, 0) agility, nimbleness.
beherbergen *v.t.* to accommodate, to put up, to lodge, to shelter.
Beherbergung *f.* accommodation.
beherrschen *v.t.* to reign over, to rule over; to govern; (*Sprache*) to master; (sich) ~ *v.refl.* to control oneself.
Beherrscher *m.* (-s, -) ruler.
beherrscht *a. & .adv.* self-controlled.
Beherrschtheit *f.* self-control.
Beherrschung *f.* (-, 0) control; domination, rule, sway; mastery.
beherzigen *v.t.* to take to heart, to mind.
beherzt *a.* courageous, bold.
behexen *v.t.* to bewitch.
behilflich *a.* helpful, serviceable.
behindern *v.t.* to hinder, to hamper, to impede; to obstruct.
behindert *a.* handicapped.
Behinderte *m. & f.* (-n, -n) handicapped person.
Behörde *f.* (-, -n) authority.
Behördeneigentum *n.* governemt property.
behördlich *a.* official.
Behuf *m.* (-[e]s, 0) *zu diesem ~*, for this purpose.
behufs *pr.* for the purpose of.
behüten *v.t.* to guard, to preserve; to protect; *Gott behüte!* God forbid!
behutsam *a.* careful, cautious, wary.
Behutsamkeit *f.* care, caution.
bei *pr.* at, by, about, near; beside, with, to, in, upon, on.
beibehalten *v.t.* to keep, to retain.
Beiboot *n.* (-s, -e) ship's boat.
beibringen *v.t.ir.* to bring forward; (*Verluste*) to inflict upon; *einem etwas ~*, to teach something to one.
Beichte *f.* (-, -n) confession; ~ *hören*, to confess (one).
beichten *v.t.* to confess.
Beicht: ~kind *n.* penitent; **~stuhl** *m.* confessional; **~vater** *m.* father-confessor.
beide *a.* both, either.
beiderlei *a.* both, of both sorts.

beiderseits *adv.* on both sides.

beidseitig *a.* mutual.

Beifahrer *m.*; **Beifahrerin** *f.* (front-seat) passenger.

Beifall *m.* (-[e]s, 0) approbation, applause; ~ *klatschen*, to applaud.

beifällig *a.* approving, favorable.

beifolgend *a.* annexed, enclosed.

beifügen *v.t.* to add, to enclose.

beigeben *v.t.st. klein* ~, to give in.

Beigeschmack *m.* (-[e]s, 0) (unpleasant) taste.

Beihilfe *f.* (-, 0) assistance; subsidy; ~ *leisten* (*law*) to aid and abet.

beikommen *v.i.st.* (*s*) (*fig.*) to match, to come up to, to approach.

Beil *n.* (-[e]s, -) hatchet.

Beilage *f.* (-, -n) addition; (*eines Briefes*) enclosure; (*Gemüse*) vegetables *pl.*; (*einer Zeitung*) supplement.

beiläufig *a.* casual, incidental; ~ *adv.* by the way, casually, incidentally.

beilegen *v.t.* to add, to enclose; (*Streit etc.*) to settle, to make up; (*zuschreiben*) to attribute.

Beilegung *f.* (-, -en) settlement.

beileibe nicht not for the world.

Beileid *n.* (-[e]s, 0) **Beileidsbezeigung** *f.* condolence.

beiliegen *v.i.st.* to be enclosed.

beiliegend *a.* enclosed, attached.

beim = bei dem.

beimessen *v.t.st.* to impute, to attribute.

beimischen *v.t.* to mix with.

Beimischung *f.* (-, -en) admixture.

Bein *n.* (-[e]s, -e) leg; (*Knochen*) bone; *zweibeinig, dreibeinig*, etc., two-legged, three-legged.

beinahe *adv.* almost, nearly.

Beiname *m.* (-ns, -n) epithet, surname.

Beinbruch *m.* fracture (of a leg).

Beinfreiheit *f.* legroom.

beinern *a.* made of bone, bony.

Beinkleider *n.pl.* trousers *pl.*

Beinschiene *f.* shin pad; splint.

Beipackzettel *m.* instruction leaflet.

beipflichten *v.t.* to agree (with).

Beirat *m.* (-[e]s, -räte) adviser; advisory board.

beirren *v.t.* to confuse; to divert from.

beisammen *adv.* together.

Beischlaf *m.* (-[e]s, 0) sexual intercourse.

Beisein *n.* (-s, 0) presence.

beiseite, beiseits *adv.* aside, apart.

beisetzen *v.t.* (*Leiche*) to bury.

Beisitzer *m.* (-s, -) assessor; assistant judge or magistrate.

Beispiel *n.* (-[e]s, -e) *n.* example; *zum* ~, for instance.

beispielhaft *a.* exemplary.

beispiellos *a.* unparalleled.

beispielshalber *adv.*; **beispielsweise** *adv.* for example; for instance.

beispringen *v.i.st.* (*s*) to assist, to succor.

beißen *v.t. & i.st.* to bite.

beißend *a.* pungent, hot; mordant.

Beißzange *f.* nippers *pl.*

Beistand *m.* (-[e]s, -stände) assistance.

beistehen *v.i.st.* to stand by; to assist, to support.

Beistelltisch *m.* side-table.

Beisteuer *f.* (-, -n) contribution.

beisteuern *v.t.* to contribute (to).

beistimmen *v.i.* to agree with.

Beistrich *m.* comma.

Beitrag *m.* (-[e]s, -träge) contribution, subscription; share.

beitragen *v.t.st.* to contribute (to).

beitragsfrei *a.* noncontributory.

beitragspflichtig *a.* liable to contributions.

beitreiben *v.t.st.* to collect (money); to recover.

beitreten *v.i.st.* (*s*) to accede, to assent; (*einer Gesellschaft*) to join.

Beitritt *m.* (-[e]s, 0) accession; joining.

Beiwagen *m.* (-s, -) side-car.

Beiwerk *n.* (-[e]s, -e) accessories *pl.*

beiwohnen *v.i.* to be present at, to attend; to cohabit.

Beize *f.* (-, -n) (*Mittel*) caustic; wood-stain.

beizeiten *adv.* in time.

beizen *v.t.* (*chem.*) to corrode; (*Fleisch*) to pickle; (*Holz*) to stain; (*med.*) to cauterize.

bejahen *v.t.* to answer in the affirmative.

bejahend *a.* affirmative.

bejahrt *a.* aged, elderly.

Bejahung *f.* (-, -en) affirmation; acceptance.

bejammern *v.t.* to lament, to bemoan, to bewail.

bejammernswert *a.* lamentable, deplorable.

bejubeln *v.t.* to cheer; to acclaim.

bekämpfen *v.t.* to fight against, to combat.

bekannt *a.* well-known; acquainted (with).

Bekannte[r] *m. & f.* (-en, -en) acquaintance.

Bekanntgabe *f.* (-, -en) announcement.

bekanntgeben *v.t.* to announce.

Bekanntheitsgrad *m.* name recognition.

bekanntlich *adv.* as is well-known.

bekanntmachen *v.t.* to announce.

Bekanntmachung *f.* (-, -en) notice.

Bekanntschaft *f.* (-, -en) acquaintance.

bekanntwerden *v.i.st.* to become known.

bekehren *v.t.* to convert.

Bekehrte[r] *m. & f.* (-en, -en) convert.

Bekehrung *f.* (-, -en) conversion.

bekennen *v.t.st.* to admit, to confess, (sich) ~ *v.refl.st* to profess; to acknowledge.

Bekenntnis *n.* (-nisses, -nisse) confession, avowal.

Bekenntnisfreiheit *f.* religious freedom.

Bekenntnisschule *f.* denominational school.

bekifft *a.* stoned.

beklagen *v.t.* to lament, to deplore, to pity; (sich) ~ *v.refl.* to complain (of).

beklagenswert *a.* lamentable, pitiable.

Beklagte[r] *m. & f.* (-en, -en) defendant.

beklatschen *v.t.* to applaud.

bekleben *v.t.* to paste upon.

bekleckern *v.t.* to stain; ~ *v.refl.* to spill over oneself.

bekleiden *v.t.* to clothe, to attire; (*fig.*) to invest (with); (*Amt, Stelle*) to hold, to fill.

Bekleidung *f.* (-, -en) clothing, clothes *pl.*; (*fig.*) investiture.

beklemmend *a. & adv.* oppressive(ly).

Beklemmung *f.* (-, -en)(*der Brust*) oppression (of the chest); (*fig.*) anguish.

beklommen *a.* oppressed, anxious.

beknackt *a.* (*fam.*) lousy; stupid.

beknien *v.t.* to beg.

bekommen *v.t.st.* to obtain, to get, to receive; (~ *v.i.st.* (s) (*einem wohl*) to agree with; *nicht gut* ~, to disagree with.

bekömmlich *a.* beneficial; digestible.

beköstigen *v.t.* to board, to feed.

bekräftigen *v.t.* to confirm, to corroborate.

bekränzen *v.t.* to wreathe, to crown.

bekreuzen, bekreuzigen *v.t.* (sich) ~ *v.refl.* to make the sign of the cross, to cross oneself.

bekritzeln *v.t.* to scribble on.

bekümmern *v.t.* to afflict; (sich) ~ *v.refl.* to concern oneself with.

Bekümmernis *f.* (-, -nisse) affliction.

bekunden *v.t.* to express, to manifest.

belächeln *v.t.* to smile at.

beladen *v.t.st.* to load; (*fig.*) to burden, to charge.

beladen *a.* loaded, laden.

Belag *m.* (-[e]s, -läge) coating; film; surface; (*Zunge*) fur.

belagern *v.t.* to besiege, to beleaguer.

Belagerung *f.* (-, -en) siege.

Belang *m.* (-[e]s, -e) interest.

belangen *v.t.* to concern, to relate to; (*vor Gericht*) to sue.

belanglos *a.* unimportant, trifling.

Belanglosigkeit *f.* (-, -en) unimportance; triviality.

Belangung *f.* (-, -en) prosecution.

belassen *v.t.st.* to let be; to leave.

belastbar *a.* tough, resilient, strong.

Belastbarkeit *f.* ability to withstand stress; load-bearing capacity.

belasten *v.t.* to load, to charge; (*com.*) to debit; *erblich belastet*, tainted by hereditary disease.

belastend *a.* incriminating.

belästigen *v.t.* to trouble, to bother; to molest.

Belästigung *f.* (-, -en) molestation.

Belastung *f.* (-, -en) charge, load; debit; strain; (*el.*) load.

Belastungsprobe *f.* (-, -n) endurance test; stress test.

Belastungszeuge *m.* witness for the prosecution.

belauern *v.t.* to watch s.b. carefully.

belaufen (sich) *v.refl.st.* to amount to, to run to.

belauschen *v.t.* to watch, to overhear.

beleben *v.t.* to animate; to enliven.

belebt *a.* lively, animated; crowded.

Belebung *f.* (-, -en) animation, revival.

belecken *v.t.* to lick.

Beleg *m.* (-[e]s, -e) receipt, voucher, proof.

belegbar *a.* verifiable.

belegen *v.t.* to lay on *or* over; (*Platz*) to reserve, to secure; (*mit Beweisen*) to prove.

Belegschaft *f.* (-, -en) staff.

belegt *a.* (*Zunge*) furred, coated; ~*e Brötchen n.* sandwich.

belehnen *v.t.* to invest.

belehren *v.t.* to inform, to instruct.

belehrend *a.* instructive, didactic.

Belehrung *f.* (-, -en) instruction, lecture.

beleibt *a.* corpulent, stout.

beleidigen *v.t.* to offend, to insult.

beleidigt *a.* insulted, offended.

Beleidigte[r] *m.* (*law*) offended party.

Beleidigung *f.* (-, -en) offense, insult, slander; *tätliche ~* (*law*), assault; *schwere tätliche ~*, assault and battery.

beleihen *v.t.* to grant a loan on the security of.

belesen *a.* well-read.

beleuchten *v.t.* to illumine, to illuminate, to light; (*fig.*) to illustrate.

Beleuchtung *f.* (-, -en) lighting, illumination.

Beleuchtungskörper *m.* light fixture.

beleumdet *a.*; **beleumundet** *a. übel/gut ~ sein* to have a good/bad reputation.

Belgien *n.* (-s, 0) Belgium; **Belgier** *m.*; **Belgierin** *f.*; **belgisch** *a.* Belgian.

belichten *v.t.* (*phot.*) to expose.

Belichtung *f.* (-, -en) (*phot.*) exposure; ~**smesser** *m.* exposure meter.

belieben *v.t.* to like; ~ *v.i.* to please.

Belieben *n.* (-s, 0) pleasure, liking.

beliebig *a.* (with *ein*) any.

beliebt *a.* popular.

Beliebtheit *f.* (-, 0) popularity.

beliefern *v.t.* to supply.

Belieferung *f.* (-, -en) supply.

bellen *v.i.* to bark.

Belletristik *f.* (-, 0) fiction; **belletristisch** *a.* belletristic.

belobigen *v.t.* to praise.

Belobigung *f.* (-, -en) praise.

belohnen *v.t.* to reward, to recompense.

Belohnung *f.* (-, -en) reward, recompense.

belüften *v.t.* to ventilate.

Belüftung *f.* ventilation.

belügen *v.t.* to lie to.

belustigen *v.t.* to amuse, to divert.

belustigt *a.* amused.

Belustigung *f.* (-, -en) amusement, diversion.

bemächtigen (sich) *v.refl.* to take possession of, to seize.

bemäkeln *v.t.* (*fam.*) to criticize.

bemalen *v.t.* to paint (over).

bemängeln *v.t.* to find fault with.

bemannen *v.t.* to man, to equip.

Bemannung *f.* (-, -en) crew.

bemänteln *v.t.* to cover up; (*fig.*) to palliate.

bemerken *v.t.* to remark, to observe; to perceive, to note.

bemerkenswert *a.* remarkable.

Bemerkung *f.* (-, -en) remark, observation, comment.

bemessen *v.t.* to measure according to.

bemitleiden *v.t.* to pity.

bemitleidenswert *a.* pitiable.

bemittelt *a.* well-off, independent.

bemogeln *v.t.* (*fam.*) to cheat.

bemühen *v.t.* to make an effort; *v.refl.* to take pains, to endeavor; to apply (for).

Bemühung *f.* (-, -en) trouble, pains *pl.*; effort.

bemüssigt *adv.* sich ~ fühlen to feel obliged.

bemuttern *v.t.* to mother.

benachbart *a.* neighboring.

benachrichtigen *v.t.* to inform, to advise, to let a person know.

Benachrichtigung *f.* (-, -en) information, advice.

benachteiligen *v.t.* to discriminate against; to put at a disadvantage.

Benachteiligung *f.* (-, -en) prejudice, detriment.

benagen *v.t.* to gnaw at.

benebeln *v.t.* to fog, to befuddle, to cloud.

benehmen (sich) *v.refl.st.* to behave.
Benehmen *n.* (-s, 0) behavior, conduct.
beneiden *v.t.* to envy, to grudge.
beneidenswert *a.* enviable.
benennen *v.t.ir.* to name, to denominate.
Benennung *f.* (-, -en) name, appellation.
benetzen *v.t.* to moisten, to wet.
Bengel *m.* (-s, -) young rascal.
benommen *a.* benumbed, dazed.
benötigen *v.t.* to be in want of, to want.
Benotung *f.* (-, -en) grading; grade.
benutzen *v.t.* to make use of, to take advantage of.
Benutzer *m.* user.
Benutzung *f.* use.
Benzin *n.* (-s, -e) benzine; petrol; gasoline ~**stelle** *f.* petrol station, gasoline station.
Benzol *n.* (-s, -e) benzol(e), benzene.
beobachten *v.t.* to observe, to watch; to keep, to perform.
Beobachter *m.* (-s, -) observer.
Beobachtung *f.* (-, -en) observation; observance.
beordern *v.t.* to order, to command.
bepacken *v.t.* to load, to charge.
bepflanzen *v.t.* to plant.
bequatschen *v.t.* (*fam.*) to talk s.o. into.
bequem *a.* convenient; apt, fit, commodious, comfortable; easy going.
bequemen (sich) *v.refl.* to comply with, to submit.
Bequemlichkeit *f.* (-, -en) convenience, comfort, ease; indolence.
berappen *v.t.* (*fam.*) to pay.
beraten *v.t.st.* to advise; (sich) ~ *v.refl.st.* to consult with, to deliberate.
beratend *a.* advisory.
Berater *m.*; **Beraterin** *f.* consultant; adviser.
beratschlagen (sich) *v.i. & refl.* to discuss; to deliberate, to take counsel.
Beratung *f.* (-, -en) advice, council, conference; consultation.
Beratungstelle *f.* counseling center; advice bureau.
berauben *v.t.* to rob.
Beraubung *f.* robbery.
berauschen *v.t.* to intoxicate; (sich) ~ *v.refl.* to get drunk; ~**de Getränke** *n.pl.* intoxicating liquors.
berauschend *a.* intoxicating.
berechenbar *a.* calculable, predictable.
berechnen *v.t.* to compute, to calculate; (*anschreiben*) to charge; *der Kaffee wird besonders berechnet,* coffee will be extra.
berechnend *a.* (*fam.*) calculating.
Berechnung *f.* (-, -en) computation, calculation.
berechtigen *v.t.* to entitle, to authorize.
berechtigt *a.* justified, legitimate; authorized.
Berechtigung *f.* (-, -en) right; authorization; qualification.
bereden *v.t.* to talk over; discuss.
beredsam *a. & adv.* eloquent(ly).
Beredsamkeit *f.* (-, 0) eloquence.
beredt *a.* eloquent.
Bereich *m. & n.* (-[e]s, -e) reach, area, range; sphere, orbit.
bereichern *v.t.* to enrich; (*fig.*) to enlarge.
Bereicherung *f.* enrichment.
bereifen *v.t.* (*Faß*) to hoop; (*mot.*) to put tires on (a car).

bereinigen *v.t.* to settle.
bereisen *v.t.* to travel around.
bereit *a.* ready, prepared, prompt.
bereiten *v.t.* to prepare, to dress.
bereithalten *v.t.* to have ready; to keep ready.
bereits *adv.* already.
Bereitschaft *f.* (-, -en) readiness, preparedness; flying squad (*Polizei*).
bereitstehen *v.i.st.* to be ready.
bereitstellen *v.t.* to provide; to make available.
Bereitung *f.* (-, -en) preparation.
bereitwillig *a.* ready, willing; ~ *adv.* willingly.
Bereitwilligkeit *f.* (-, 0) willingness.
bereuen *v.t.* to repent; to regret.
Berg *m.* (-[e]s, -e) mountain, hill; *hinter dem ~e halten,* to hold in reserve; *zu Berge stehen,* to stand on end (*Haar*).
bergab *adv.* downhill.
bergan, bergauf *adv.* uphill.
Berg: ~**akademie** *f.* mining academy; ~**amt** *n.* mining bureau; ~**bau** *m.* mining.
bergen *v.t.st.* to save; to salvage; to conceal, to contain.
bergig *a.* mountainous, hilly.
Berg: ~**kette** *f.* mountain-chain *or* range; ~**mann** *m.* miner; ~**leute** *pl.* miners; ~**predigt** *f.* (Christ's) sermon on the Mount; ~**steiger** *m.* mountaineer, alpinist.
Bergung *f.* (-, -en) rescue, saving; salvage.
Berg: ~**wacht** *f.* mountain rescue service; ~**wanderung** *f.* hike in the mountains; ~**werk** *n.* mine.
Bericht *m.* (-[e]s, -e) report, account.
berichten *v.t.* to inform, to send word, to report.
Berichterstatter *m.* reporter.
berichtigen *v.t.* to set right, to correct; (*Rechnung*) to settle.
Berichtigung *f.* (-, -en) correction.
beriechen *v.t.* to smell, to sniff.
berieseln *v.t.* to irrigate; sich ~ lassen constantly have music (etc.) on in the background.
Berieselung *f.* irrigation; (*fig.*) constant exposure to music (etc.).
beritten *a.* mounted.
berlinern *v.i.* to speak Berlin dialect.
Bermudainseln *pl.* Bermudas.
Bernhardiner *m.* (-s, -) St. Bernard (dog).
Bernstein *m.* (-[e]s, 0) amber.
bersten *v.i.st.* (*s*) to break, to burst, to crack.
berüchtigt *a.* notorious, ill-reputed.
berücken *v.t.* to fascinate.
berücksichtigen *v.t.* to regard, to respect, to allow for, to consider.
Berücksichtigung *f.* (-, -en) regard, consideration.
Beruf *m.* (-[e]s, -e *u.* Berufsarten) vocation; calling, trade, profession.
berufen *v.t.st.* to call; to appoint to an office; (*zusammenrufen*) to convene, to convoke; (sich) ~ *v.refl.* to refer to, to invoke.
berufen *a.* competent.
beruflich *a.* professional, vocational.
Berufs ... occupational, professional.
Berufs: ~**beratung** *f.* vocational guidance; ~**diplomat** *m.* career diplomat; ~**spieler** *m.* professional.
Berufung *f.* (-, -en) appointment; vocation; appeal; ~**einlegen,** to lodge an appeal; *einer ~*

stattgeben, to allow an appeal; *eine ~ zurückweisen*, to dismiss an appeal; *~sgericht n.* court of appeal, appelate court.

beruhen *v.i.* to be based on; to rest upon; to depend upon *or* on.

beruhigen *v.t.* to quiet, to calm; (sich) ~ *v.refl.* to compose oneself.

Beruhigung *f.* (-, -en) reassurance.

Beruhigungs: *~mittel n.*, **pille** *f.* sedative, tranquilizer.

berühmt *a.* famous, celebrated.

Berühmtheit *f.* (-, -en) fame, celebrity; renown.

berühren *v.t.* to touch, to handle.

Berührung *f.* (-, -en) contact, touch.

besagen *v.t.* to mean, to signify.

besagt *a.* aforementioned.

besänftigen *v.t.* to soften, to soothe; to mitigate; to placate.

besät *a.* covered with.

Besatz *m.* (-es, -sätze) trimming.

Besatzung *f.* (-, -en) garrison, crew; occupation; *~szone f.* zone of occupation.

Besatzungs . . . occupation—.

besaufen (sich) *v.refl.st.* to get drunk.

Besäufnis *n.* (-ses, -se) (*fam.*) blast.

beschädigen *v.t.* to hurt, to damage.

Beschädigung *f.* (-, -en) damage, hurt.

beschaffen *v.t.* to obtain, to get.

beschaffen *a.* constituted, conditioned; ~ *v.t.* to procure.

Beschaffenheit *f.* (-, -en) properties, condition, quality, constitution.

Beschaffung *f.* (-, 0) obtaining, finding.

beschäftigen *v.t.* to employ, to occupy.

beschäftigt *a.* occupied, busy.

beschäftigen *v.t.* to employ, to occupy.

Beschäftigte *m./f.* (-n, -n) employee.

Beschäftigung *f.* (-, -en) occupation, employment.

beschälen *v.t.* to horse (a mare).

beschämen *v.t.* to shame.

beschämend *a.* shameful, humiliating.

beschämt *a.* ashamed.

Beschämung *f.* (-, 0) shame.

beschatten *v.t.* to shade, to shadow.

beschauen *v.t.* to look at, to view, to inspect.

beschaulich *a.* contemplative.

Beschauung *f.*, **Beschaulichkeit** *f.* (-, -en) contemplation.

Bescheid *m.* (-[e]s, -e) decision; information; answer; ~ *wissen*, to know.

bescheiden *v.t.st.* (*zu sich*) to send for; (sich) ~ *v.refl.st.* to acquiesce (in).

bescheiden *a.* modest, unassuming.

Bescheidenheit *f.* (-, 0) modesty, discretion.

bescheinen *v.t.* to shine.

bescheinigen *v.t.* to attest, to certify.

Bescheinigung *f.* (-, -en) certificate.

bescheißen *v.t.* (*vulg.*) to rip s.b. off.

beschenken *v.t.* to present with.

bescheren *v.t.* to give (presents).

Bescherung *f.* (-, -en) distribution of presents; *eine schöne ~*, a nice mess.

bescheuert *a.* (*fam.*) nuts.

beschickert *a.* (*fam.*) tipsy.

beschießen *v.t.st.* to fire at.

Beschießung *f.* (-, -en) bombardment.

beschimpfen *v.t.* to insult, to swear at.

Beschimpfung *f.* (-, -en) insult, abuse (verbal).

beschirmen *v.t.* to protect, to defend.

Beschiß *m.* (-es, 0) (*vulg.*) rip-off.

beschissen *a.* (*vulg.*) lousy, shitty.

beschlafen *v.t.st.* (*eine Sache*) to sleep upon.

Beschlag *m.* (-[e]s, -schläge) (*metal*) mounting; (*gerichtlicher*) sequestration, seizure, confiscation; (*eines Pferdes*) shoeing; *in ~ nehmen, mit ~ belegen*, to seize, to sequestrate.

beschlagen *v.t.st.* to mount; (*Pferde*) to shoe; (*mit Nägeln*) to nail, to stud.

beschlagen *a.* (*fig.*) versed, skilled.

Beschlagnahme *f.* (-, -en) seizure, sequestration; (*nav.*) embargo; ~ *aufheben*, to derequisition.

beschlagnahmen *v.t.* to impound, to seize.

beschleichen *v.t.* to creep up on; to creep over.

beschleunigen *v.t.* to hasten, to accelerate, to speed up.

Beschleunigung *f.* acceleration; speeding up.

beschließen *v.t.st.* to resolve (upon), to determine.

Beschluß *m.* (-schlusses, -schlüsse) resolution; decree.

beschlußfähig *a.* quorate, *das Haus war ~*, there was a quorum of the House.

Beschlußfähigkeit *f.* presence of a quorum.

beschmeißen *v.t.st.* (*fam.*) to pelt s.b. with.

beschmieren *v.t.* to smear; to spread (sandwich); to grease.

beschmutzen *v.t.* to dirty, to soil.

beschneiden *v.t.st.* to cut, to clip; (*med.*) to circumcise; to prune, (*fig.*) to curtail.

Beschneidung *f.* (-, -en) circumcision; trimming, pruning.

beschönigen *v.t.* to palliate, to gloss over.

beschönigend *a.* palliative.

beschränken *v.t.* to restrict; to circumscribe; to limit; to reduce to.

beschränkt *a.* narrow; dull; half-witted.

Beschränktheit *f.* (-, 0) narrowness; (*fig.*) narrow-mindedness.

Beschränkung *f.* (-, -en) limitation, restriction.

beschreiben *v.t.st.* to describe.

Beschreibung *f.* (-, -en) description.

beschreiten *v.t.st.* to walk along, to step over.

beschriften *v.t.* to label; to inscribe.

beschuldigen *v.t.* to charge with, to accuse of.

Beschuldigte *m./f.* accused.

Beschuldigung *f.* (-, -en) charge, accusation; impeachment.

beschummeln *v.t.* (*fam.*) to cheat.

Beschuß *m.* shelling; shooting.

beschützen *v.t.* to protect, to defend.

Beschützer *m.* (-s, -) protector, patron.

beschwatzen *v.t.* to talk s.b. round; to talk s.b. into s.th.

Beschwerde *f.* (-, -n) trouble; (*Mühe*) hardship; (*Klage*) grievance, complaint; (*Leiden*) complaint; ~ *führen*, to complain (of).

Beschwerdeführer *m.* complainant.

beschweren *v.t.* to burden, to charge; (sich) ~ *v.refl.* to complain (of).

beschwerlich *a.* laborious, troublesome; ~ *fallen*, to molest, to importune.

Beschwerlichkeit *f.* (-, -en) trouble, inconvenience.

beschwichtigen *v.t.* to soothe, to allay.
Beschwichtigung *f.* pacification, mollification.
beschwindeln *v.t.* to cheat, to swindle.
beschwingt *a.* elated, lively.
beschwipst *a.* tipsy.
beschworen *a.* sworn (to).
beschwören *v.t.st.* to confirm by oath; (*bitten*) to entreat; to conjure; (*bannen*) to exorcise.
Beschwörer *m.* (-s, -) conjuror, exorcist.
Beschwörung *f.* (-, -en) confirmation by oath; (*Geister~*) exorcism.
beseelen *v.t.* to animate, to inspirit.
besehen *v.t.st.* to look at, to view.
beseitigen *v.t.* to eliminate, to remove.
beseligen *v.t.* to bless, to enrapture.
Besen *m.* (-s, -) broom.
Besenstiel *m.* broomstick.
besessen *a.* possessed.
besetzen *v.t.* to occupy; (*Stelle*) to fill; (*Platz*) to engage; (*mit Spitzen etc.*) to trim, to border.
besetzt *a.* die Leitung ist besetzt, (*tel.*) the line is busy or occupied.
Besetztzeichen *n.* busy signal.
Besetzung *f.* (-, -en) (*von Stellen*) appointment; occupation.
besichtigen *v.t.* to see, to view, to inspect.
Besichtigung *f.* (-, -en) inspection.
besiedeln *v.t.* to settle in, to colonize.
Besiedlung *f.* settlement.
besiegeln *v.t.* to seal.
besiegen *v.t.* to defeat, vanquish, to conquer.
besingen *v.t.st.* to celebrate, to sing.
besinnen (sich) *v.refl.st.* to recollect, to call to mind; to consider, to reflect.
besinnlich *a.* contemplative.
Besinnung *f.* (-, 0) reflection, consciousness.
besinnungslos *a.* insensible, unconscious.
Besitz *m.* (-es, 0) possession, property; in ~ haben, to be in possession of.
Besitzanspruch *m.* (-s, -sprüche) claim to ownership.
besitzanzeigend *a.* (*ling.*) possessive.
besitzen *v.t.st.* to possess, to own.
Besitzer *m.* (-s, -) proprietor, owner.
Besitzergreifung, Besitznahme *f.* occupation.
besitzlos *a.* destitute.
Besitzstand *m.* standard of living.
Besitzstörungsklage *f.* action of trespass.
Besitzung *f.* (-, -en) possession, estate.
Besitzurkunde *f.* title deed.
besoffen *a.* tipsy, drunk.
besohlen *v.t.* to sole.
besolden *v.t.* to pay.
besoldet *a.* salaried.
Besoldung *f.* (-, -en) salary; pay, stipend.
besonder *a.* (*abgesondert*) separate; peculiar, particular, special.
besonders *adv.* particularly, specially.
besonnen *a.* cautious, discreet.
Besonnenheit *f.* (-, 0) circumspection; calmness.
besorgen *v.t.* to provide; (*befürchten*) to fear.
Besorgnis *f.* (-, -nisse) concern, care; apprehension.
besorgniserregend *a.* alarming.
besorgt *a.* worried, apprehensive, anxious.
Besorgung *f.* (-, -en) commission.

bespannen *v.t.* to cover; to put (horses) to; to string.
bespielbar *a.* playable.
bespielen *v.t.* to record.
bespitzeln *v.t.* to spy on.
Bespitzelung *f.* spying.
bespötteln *v.t.* to rally, to riducule.
besprechen *v.t.st.* to discuss, to talk over; (*bösen Geist*) to conjure; (sich) ~ *v.refl.st.* to confer with.
Besprechung *f.* (-, -en) discussion, conference; review.
besprengen *v.t.* to besprinkle, to water.
bespritzen *v.t.* to splash.
besprühen *v.t.* to spray.
bespucken *v.t.* to spit at.
besser *a. & adv.* better; um so ~, so much the better.
bessergehen *v.i.* to feel better.
bessern *v.t.* to better; to improve, to mend, to repair.
Besserung *f.* (-, -en) improvement; recovery.
best *a.* best; der erste ~e, the first comer; zum ~en, for the benefit; aufs ~e, in the best manner; einen zum ~en haben, to make fun of one.
Bestallung *f.* (-, -en) appointment.
Bestand *m.* (-[e]s, -stände) continuance; amount, number, stock.
beständig *a.* constant, continual; steady.
Bestandsaufnahme *f.* stocktaking.
Bestandteil *m.* constituent (part), component.
bestärken *v.t.* to confirm.
bestätigen *v.t.* to confirm; to rat.fy, to sanction; (*Empfang*) to acknowledge; (sich) ~ *v.refl.* to be confirmed.
Bestätigung *f.* (-, -en) confirmation; acknowledgement.
bestatten *v.t.* to bury, to inter.
Bestattung *f.* (-, -en) burial.
Bestattungsunternehmen *n.* funeral parlor.
bestäuben *v.t.* to pollinate.
Bestäubung *f.* (-, -en) pollination.
bestaunen *v.t.* to marvel at; to gaze at.
bestechen *v.t.st.* to corrupt, to bribe.
bestechend *a.* captivating, tempting.
bestechlich *a.* corrupt.
Bestechung *f.* (-, -en) corruption, bribery.
Bestechungsgeld *n.* (-es, -en) bribe.
Besteck *n.* (-[e]s, -e) (*Tisch~*) fork, knife, and spoon; instruments; (*nav.*) das ~ machen, to prick the chart.
bestehen *v.i.st.* (*aus etwas*) to consist of; (*auf etwas*) to insist on; (*dauern*) to continue, to last; ~ *v.t.st.* to undergo, to endure, to stand; die Prüfung ~, to pass; nicht ~, to fail.
Bestehen *n.* (-s, 0) existence.
bestehend *a.* existing, current.
bestehlen *v.t.st.* to rob, to steal from.
besteigen *v.t.st.* to step upon; to ascend; to mount (a horse).
Besteigung *f.* (-, -en) ascent.
bestellen *v.t.* to order; (*Briefe*) to deliver; (*Plätze*) to book; (*das Feld*) to till; (*einen*) to send for; (*Zeitung*) to take in a paper; (*ernennen*) to appoint.
Bestellschein *m.* order form.
Bestellung *f.* (-, -en) order, command; (*des Feldes*) tillage; auf ~, to order; eine ~ aufnehmen, to take an order.

bestenfalls *adv.* in the best possible case.

bestens *adv.* in the best manner.

besteuern *v.a.* to tax.

Besteuerung *f.* (-, -en) taxation.

bestialisch *a.* bestial; brutal.

Bestialität *f.* bestiality; brutality.

besticken *v.t.* to embroider.

Bestie *f.* (-, -n) beast, brute.

bestimmen *v.t.* to determine; to appoint; to define; to destine (for).

bestimmend *a.* decisive, determining.

bestimmt *a.* fixed; (*entschlossen*) decided; (*gewiß*) certain, positive.

Bestimmung *f.* (-, -en) destination; destiny; regulation, provision; definition.

Bestleistung *f.* (-, -en) best performance.

bestmöglich *a.* best possible.

bestrafen *v.t.* to punish; to chastise; to penalize.

Bestrafung *f.* (-, -en) punishment; penalty.

bestrahlen *v.t.* to irradiate; (*med.*) to treat with X-rays.

Bestrahlung *f.* (-, -en) exposure to rays; (*med.*) X-ray treatment; radiotherapy.

bestreben (sich) *v.refl.* to endeavor.

Bestreben *n.* (-s, 0), **Bestrebung** *f.* (-, -en) endeavor, exertion.

bestreichen *v.t.ir.* to spread over.

bestreiken *v.t.* to go out on strike against.

bestreitbar *a.* disputable.

bestreiten *v.t.st.* to contest, to dispute; *die Kosten ~,* to defray the expenses.

bestreuen *v.t.* to strew, to sprinkle.

bestricken *v.t.* to charm.

bestürmen *v.t.* to storm, to assail; (*fig.*) to importune.

bestürzen *v.t.* to dismay, to perplex, to confound.

bestürzend *a.* dismaying.

bestürzt *a.* dismayed.

Bestürzung *f.* (-, 0) dismay.

Besuch *m.* (-[e]s, -e) visit; (pers.) company, visitors *pl.*

besuchen *v.t.* to call upon, to pay a visit; (*Lokale etc.*) to frequent, to attend.

Besucher *m.* (-s, -) visitor.

besucht *a.* attended (performance), frequented (restaurant).

besudeln *v.t.* to soil, to dirty.

betagt *a.* aged, elderly.

betasten *v.t.* to touch, to handle, to finger.

betätigen *v.t.* to practice; to manifest; *sich ~,* to take an active part in.

betäuben *v.t.* to stun; (*med.*) to anaesthetize.

Betäubung *f.* (-, -en) (*fig.*) stupor, bewilderment, daze, (*med.*) anaesthetization, anaesthesia.

Betäubungsmittel *n.* anaesthetic.

beteiligen *v.t.* to give one his share; *beteiligt sein,* to have a share in; *die Beteiligten,* those concerned; (sich) *~ v.refl.* to participate in; to have an interest in.

beteiligt *a.* involved; *am Gewinn ~ sein* to have a share in the profit.

Beteiligung *f.* participation; involvement; share.

beten *v.i.* to pray; to say one's prayers.

beteuern *v.t.* to assert; to protest.

Beteuerung *f.* assertion; protestation.

betiteln *v.t.* to give a title, to style.

Beton (*frz.*) *m.* (-s, -s) concrete.

betonen *v.t.* to stress; to accent, (*fig.*) to emphasize.

Betonung *f.* (-, -en) stress; accentuation.

betören *v.t.* to infatuate; to bewitch.

Betracht *m.* (-[e]s, 0) consideration, regard; *in ~ ziehen,* to take into consideration *or* account.

betrachten *v.t.* to look at; to consider.

beträchtlich *a.* considerable, important.

Betrachtung *f.* (-, -en) contemplation; examination.

Betrachtungsweise *f.* (-, -n) way of looking at things.

Betrag *m.* (-[e]s, -träge) amount.

betragen *v.t.st.* to amount to; (sich) *~ v.refl.st.* to behave.

Betragen *n.* (-s, 0) behavior, conduct.

betrauen *v.t.* to entrust.

betrauern *v.t.* to mourn for.

Betreff *m.* (-[e]s, 0) subject, re; with regard to.

betreffen *v.t.st.* to concern; *was das betrifft,* as far as that is concerned.

betreffend *a.* concerning.

Betreffende *m./f.* person concerned; ~n *pl.* people concerned.

betreffs *p.* with respect to, concerning.

betreiben *v.t.st.* to urge; (*Geschäft*) to manage, to carry on, to run; (*Beruf*) to pursue.

betreten *v.t.st.* to step on, to enter.

betreten *a.* disconcerted, embarrassed.

betreuen *v.t.* to look after, to take care of.

Betreuung *f.* (-, 0) care.

Betrieb *m.* (-[e]s, -e) management; establishment; works; (*öffentlicher*) service; *in ~ sein,* to operate; *außer ~ setzen,* to put out of action.

betrieblich *a.* internal; company related.

betriebsam *a.* busy, industrious, active.

Betriebs: ~**kapital** *n.* working capital; ~**kosten** *pl.* working expenses; ~**leiter** *m.* manager; ~**rat** *m.* shop steward, works council; ~**vorrat** *m.* stock-in-trade.

betrinken (sich) *v.refl.st.* to get drunk.

betroffen *a.* dismayed, struck, perplexed.

Betroffene *m./f.* person affected; ~n *pl.* people affected.

Betroffenheit *f.* dismay, consternation.

betrüben *v.t.* to afflict; (sich) *~v.refl.* to grieve (at).

Betrug *m.* (-[e]s, 0) fraud, deceit.

betrügen *v.t.st.* to cheat, to deceive; to defraud; to doublecross.

Betrüger *m.* (-s, -) swindler, fraud, deceiver.

Betrügerei *f.* (-, -en) deception; cheating; swindling.

betrügerisch *a.* fraudulent; deceitful.

betrunken *a.* drunk, tipsy, intoxicated.

Betrunkene *m./f.* drunk.

Betrunkenheit *f.* (-, 0) drunkenness.

Bett *n.* (-[e]s, -en) bed.

Bettbelag *m.* bedspread.

Bettdecke *f.* blanket; duvet, quilt.

Bettelei *f.* (-, -en) begging; solicitation.

bettelhaft *a.* beggarly.

Bettelmönch *m.* mendicant friar.

betteln *v.t.* to ask alms, to beg.

bettlägerig *a.* bed-ridden.

Bettler *m.* (-s, -) beggar.

Bett: ~stelle *f.* bedstead; ~**tuch** *n.* sheet; ~**überzug** *m.* bedcover; ~**wäsche** *f.* bed linen; ~**zeug** *n.* bedclothes *pl.*

betucht *a.* well-off.

betulich *a.* fussy; unhurried.

betupfen *v.t.* to dab.

beugen *v.t.* to bend, to bow; (*fig.*) to humble; (*gram.*) to inflect.

Beugung *f.* (-, -en) inflexion.

Beule *f.* (-, -en) bump, bruise.

Beulenpest *f.* bubonic plague.

beunruhigen *v.t.* to disquiet, to harass, to worry.

Beunruhigung *f.* (-, -en) worry, concern.

beurkunden *v.t.* to document, to authenticate, to prove.

beurlauben *v.t.* to grant *or* to give leave of absence; (sich) ~ *v.refl.* to take leave.

Beurlaubung *f.* leave of absence.

beurteilen *v.t.* to judge; to criticize.

Beurteilung *f.* (-, -en) judgment; appraisal, assessment; (*mil.*) efficiency rating.

Beute *f.* (-, 0) booty, spoil, prey.

Beutel *m.* (-s, -) bag, pouch; purse.

beuteln *v.t.* to shake up.

Beutelratte *f.* opossum.

Beuteltier *n.* marsupial.

bevölkern *v.t.* to people, to populate.

Bevölkerung *f.* (-, -en) population.

Bevölkerungsdichte *f.* population density.

bevollmächtigen *v.t.* to authorize.

Bevollmächtigte[r] *m.* (-en, -en) authorized representative, (*Gesandte*) plenipotentiary.

Bevollmächtigung *f.* (-, -en) authorization; (*law*) power of attorney.

bevor *c.* before.

bevormunden *v.t.* to impose one's will on s.b.

bevorstehen *v.i.st.* to impend, to be imminent.

bevorstehend *a.* imminent, coming.

bevorzugen *v.t.* to prefer, to favor, to privilege.

Bevorzugung *f.* (-, -en) preferential treatment.

bewachen *v.t.* to watch over, to guard.

bewachsen *a.* overgrown, cover.

Bewachung *f.* (-, -en) escort, guard.

bewaffnen *v.t.* to arm.

bewaffnet *a.* armed.

Bewaffnung *f.* (-, -en) arming, armament.

bewahren *v.t.* to preserve; to guard, to keep; *Gott bewahre!* God forbid!

bewähren (sich) *v.refl.* to prove oneself; to stand the test.

bewahrheiten *v.t.* (sich) to prove true.

bewährt *a.* proven, tried.

Bewährung *f.* (-, 0) (*law*) probation, verification.

Bewährungsfrist *f.* period of probation; *eine ~ von zwei Jahren erhalten*, to be bound over for two years.

bewaldet *a.* woody.

bewältigen *v.t.* to overcome, to master.

bewandert *a.* knowledgeable, versed, skilled.

Bewandtnis *f.* (-, -nisse) condition, explanation.

bewässern *v.t.* to irrigate.

Bewässerung *f.* (-, -en) irrigation.

bewegen *v.t. & st.* to move; to stir, to induce; *sich ~ v.refl.* to move.

Beweggrund *m.* (-[e]s, -gründe) motive.

beweglich *a.* mobile; movable; versatile; agile; ~*es Vermögen*, movables, movable property, personal estate.

Beweglichkeit *f.* (-, 0) mobility; agility.

bewegt *a.* eventful, turbulent.

Bewegung *f.* (-, -en) motion; movement; commotion; exercise; emotion.

bewegungslos *a.* motionless.

beweinen *v.t.* to weep for, to deplore.

Beweis *m.* (-weises, -weise) proof; evidence; argument; *zum ~ von*, in proof of; ~ *antreten*, to produce evidence; ~ *liefern*, to furnish proof; *als ~ zulassen*, to admit in evidence.

beweisen *v.t.st.* to prove; to demonstrate.

Beweis: ~**grund** *m.* argument; ~**last** *f.* burden of proof.

beweisbar *a.* provable.

bewenden *v.ir.* *es dabei ~ lassen*, to let the matter rest there.

bewerben (sich) *v.refl.st.* to apply for.

Bewerber *m.* (-s, -); *Bewerberin* *f.* (-, -en) applicant.

Bewerbung *f.* (-, -en) application.

Bewerbungsschreiben *n.* letter of application.

bewerkstelligen *v.t.* to manage.

bewerten *v.t.* to assess, to estimate, to value.

Bewertung *f.* assessment, evaluation; grading.

Bewertungsmasstab *m.* criterion of assessment.

bewilligen *v.t.* to consent to, to grant, to concede; **bewilligte Mittel** *pl.* approved funds.

Bewilligung *f.* (-, -en) concession; grant; consent; (*von Geldern*) appropriation of funds.

bewirken *v.t.* to effect, to cause, to bring about.

bewirten *v.t.* to entertain, to treat.

bewirtschaften *v.t.* to manage, to run (business), to cultivate.

Bewirtung *f.* food and service.

bewohnbar *a.* habitable.

bewohnen *v.t.* to inhabit.

Bewohner *m.* (-s, -) inhabitant; (*eines Hauses*) resident, inmate.

bewohnt *a.* occupied; inhabited.

bewölken (sich) *v.refl.* to become overcast.

bewölkt *a.* cloudy, overcast.

Bewölkung *f.* (-, 0) clouds; **zunehmende** ~ increasing cloudiness.

Bewunderer *m.* (-s, -); **Bewunderin** *f.* (-, -nen) admirer.

bewundern *v.t.* to admire.

bewundernswert, bewundernswürdig *a.* admirable.

Bewunderung *f.* (-, 0) admiration.

bewußt *a.* conscious (of); in question.

bewußtlos *a.* unconscious.

Bewußtlosigkeig *f.* (-, 0) unconsciousness.

bewußtmachen *v.t.* to make s.b. realize s.th.

Bewußtsein *n.* (-s, 0) consciousness.

Bewußtseinsspaltung *f.* split consciousness, schizophrenia.

bezahlbar *a.* affordable.

bezahlen *v.t.* to pay, to discharge; (*Wechsel*) to honor.

Bezahlung *f.* (-, 0) payment, pay; *gegen ~*, for payment.

bezähmen *v.t.* to tame; (*fig.*) to restrain, to subdue.

bezaubern *v.t.* to enchant, to bewitch, to charm.

bezaubernd *a.* enchanting.

bezeichnen *v.t.* to mark, to denote; to signify; ~*d*, *a.* characteristic, significant.

Bezeichnung *f.* (-, -en) note, mark, designation.

bezeigen *v.t.* to show, to manifest.

bezeugen *v.t.* to testify.

bezichtigen *v.t.* to charge with, to accuse of.

Bezichtigung *f.* accusation.

beziehen *v.t.st.* to cover; (*Instrument*) to string; (*Geld*) to draw; (*Waren*) to obtain; (*Zeitung*) to take; (*Wohnung*) to move into; (*Hochschule*) to enter; (sich) ~, to refer to; to relate to; (*Himmel*) to become cloudy.

Bezieher *m.* (-s, -) subscriber.

Beziehung *f.* (-, -en) relation, connection; respect; *mit guten* ~*en*, well connected.

beziehungsweise *adv.* respectively.

beziffern (sich) *v.refl.* to amount (to).

Bezirk *m.* (-[e]s, -e) district, area.

Bezug *m.* (-[e]s, -züge) case; (*Waren*) supply; reference; *in* ~ *auf*, with respect to.

bezüglich *a.* respecting, referring to.

Bezugnahme *f.* (-, -n) reference.

Bezugs: ~**bedingungen** *f.pl.* terms of delivery; ~**quelle** *f.* source of supply.

bezuschussen *v.t.* to subsidize.

bezwecken *v.t.* to aim at.

bezweifeln *v.t.* to doubt (of).

bezwingen *v.t.st.* to subdue, to vanquish.

bibbern *v.i.* to shiver, to shake, to tremble.

Bibel *f.* (-, -n) Bible, Scripture.

Bibelspruch *m.* Scripture text.

Biber *m.* (-s, -) beaver.

Bibliograph *m.* (-en, -en) bibliographer.

Bibliographie *f.* (-, -n) bibliography.

Bibliothek *f.* (-, -en) library.

Bibliothekar *m.* (-s, -e); **Bibliothekarin** *f.* (-, -nen) librarian.

biblisch *a.* biblical, scriptural.

bieder *a.* unsophisticated; honest, straightforward.

Biedermann *m.* (-es, -männer) (*pej.*) petty bourgeois.

biegen *v.t. & i.st.* to bend, to bow; to curve; to turn; *sich* ~, to bend, to warp.

biegsam *a.* flexible; supple, pliant.

Biegsamkeit *f.* flexibility.

Biegung *f.* (-, -en) bend, curve.

Biene *f.* (-, -n) bee.

Bienen: ~**königin** *f.* queen bee; ~**korb** *m.* beehive; ~**schwarm** *m.* swarm of bees; ~**stock** *m.* beehive; ~**wachs** *n.* beeswax; ~**zucht** *f.* bee-keeping, apiculture.

Bier *n.* (-[e]s, -e) beer; (*englisches*) ale.

Biest *n.* (-e(s), -er) creature; beast.

bieten *v.t.st.* to bid; to offer.

Bigamie *f.* (-, -n) bigamy.

Bigamist *m.* (-en, -en) bigamist.

bigott *a.* bigoted, over-devout.

Bilanz *f.* balance-sheet.

Bild *n.* (-[e]s, -er) image; picture.

Bildband *m.* (-es, -bände) illustrated book.

Bildbeilage *f.* (-, -n) illustrated supplement.

bilden *v.t.* to form; to shape, to model; to cultivate, to improve; to constitute; (*fig.*) to improve one's mind.

bildend *a.* instructive; (*Kunst*) plastic.

Bilder: ~**buch** *n.* picture book; ~**galerie** *f.* picture gallery; ~**rahmen** *m.* picture frame; ~**stürmer** *m.* iconoclast.

Bildhauer *m.* (-s, -); **Bildhauerin** *f.* (-, -nen) sculptor.

Bildhauerkunst *f.* sculpture.

bildlich *a.* figurative; ~*e Darstellung*, pictorial representation.

Bildnis *n.* (-nisses, -nisse) portrait.

Bildplatte *f.* video disc; **Bildplattenspieler** *m.* video disc player.

Bildregie *f.* camera work.

bildsam *a.* plastic.

Bildsäule *f.* statue.

Bildschirm *m.* (-s, -e) screen.

Bildschnitzer *m.* woodcarver.

bildschön *a.* very beautiful, dazzling.

Bildstörung *f.* interference (TV).

Bildung *f.* (-, -en) formation; constitution; culture; training, education.

Bildungs: ~**chancen** *pl.* educational opportunities; ~**politik** *f.* educational policy; ~**urlaub** *m.* educational leave.

Bildunterschrift *f.* (-, -en) caption.

billard *n.* (-s, -s) billiards *pl.*; billiard table.

Billardstock *m.* cue.

Billett *n.* (-[e]s, -e *or* -s) (*Fahrkarte*) ticket; *ein* ~ *lösen*, to buy a ticket.

billig *a.* equitable, just, fair, reasonable; (*im Preise*) cheap.

billigen *v.t.* to approve (of).

Billigkeit *f.* (-, 0) fairness; cheapness.

Billigung *f.* (-, 0) sanction, approval.

Bimsstein *m.* pumice-stone.

Binde *f.* (-, -n) band; (neck) tie; bandage, sling; sanitary napkin.

Binde: ~**glied** *n.* connecting link; ~**haut** *f.* conjuctiva; ~**hautentzündung** *f.* conjunctivitis; ~**mittel** *n.* binder.

binden *v.t.st.* to bind; to tie, to fasten; (*mil.*) to tie down, to contain; (*fig.*) to engage; (sich) ~, *v.refl.* to commit oneself.

bindend *a.* binding, definite.

Binder *m.* tie.

Bindestrich *m.* (*gram.*) hyphen.

Bindewort *n.* conjunction.

Bindfaden *m.* string, packthread, twine.

Bindung *f.* (-, -en) binding; (*mus.*) ligature; (*fig.*) obligation; restriction.

binnen *pr.* within.

Binnen: ~**hafen** *m.* inland harbor, inland port; basin (of a port); ~**handel** *m.* home trade; ~**land** *n.* inland, interior; ~**meer** *n.* inland sea.

Binse *f.* (-, -n) rush.

Binsenweisheit *f.* (-, -en) truism.

Biochemie *f.* biochemistry.

Biograph *m.* (-en, -en) biographer.

Biographie *f.* (-, -en) biography.

Biologe *m.* (-en, -en); **Biologin** *f.* (-, -nen) biologist.

Biologie *f.* (-, -n) biology.

biologisch *a.* biological; natural; **aus** ~**em Anbau** organically produced.

Biomasse *f.* (-, 0) biomass.

Biotop *n.* (-s, -e) biotope.

Biowissenschaften *pl.* life sciences.

Birke *f.* (-, -n) birch, birch tree.

Birnbaum *m.* pear tree.
Birne *f.* (-, -n) pear; (*el.*) (light-)bulb; ~**nkontakt** *m.* lampholder.
bis *pr.* to, up to, as far as, till, until; ~ *c.* till, until; ~ *dahin*, ~ *jetzt*, so far.
Bisam *m.* (-[e]s, -e) musk; **Bisamratte** *f.* muskrat.
Bischof *m.* (-[e]s, -schöfe) bishop.
bischöflich *a.* episcopal.
Bischofs: ~**mütze** *f.* mitre; ~**sitz** *m.* episcopal see; ~**stab** *m.* crosier.
Bisexualität *f.* bisexuality.
bisexuell *a.* bisexual.
bisher *adv.* hitherto, till now.
bisherig *a.* previous, hitherto, existing.
Biskaya *f.* der Golf von ~ the Bay of Biscay.
Biskuit *m. or n.* (-s, -s, *u.* -e) biscuit; sponge cake.
bislang *adv.* until now.
Biß *m.* (Bisses, Bisse) bite, sting.
bißchen *a.* (-s, 0) *ein* ~, a little.
Bissen *m.* (-s, -) morsel, mouthful.
bissig *a.* biting; (*Hund*) snappish; sarcastic.
Bistum *n.* (-[e]s, -tümer) bishopric.
bisweilen *adv.* sometimes, now and then.
Bittbrief *m.* (-s, -e) letter of request.
Bitte *f.* (-, -n) request, entreaty, prayer.
bitten *v.t.st.* to beg, to request; to pray; to invite; **bitte**, please.
bitter *a.* bitter, stinging.
bitterböse *a.* very wicked; extremely angry.
Bitterkeit *f.* (-, -en) bitterness.
bitterlich *a.* slightly bitter; *adv.* bitterly.
Bittermandel *f.* bitter almond.
Bittersalz *n.* Epsom salt.
Bitt: ~**gesuch** *n.* petition; ~**schrift** *f.* petition, supplication; ~**steller** *m.* petitioner, supplicant.
Biwak *n.* (-s, -e) bivouac.
bizarr *a.* strange, odd.
Bizeps *m.* (-, -e) biceps.
blähen *v.t.* to billow; to inflate, to cause flatulency.
blähend *a.* flatulent.
Blähung *f.* (-, -en) flatulence.
blamabel *a.* shameful, disgraceful.
Blamage *f.* (*frz.*) (-, -n) exposure to ridicule, disgrace.
blamieren *v.t.* to disgrace; to expose to ridicule; (sich)~, to make a fool of oneself.
blanchieren *v.t.* to blanch.
blank *a.* blank; smooth, polished, bright.
blanko *a.* blank (*Scheck*).
Blankvers *m.* blank verse.
Blase *f.* (-, -n) bladder; bubble; blister; flaw (in glass).
Blasebalg *m.* bellows *pl.*
blasen *v.t. & i.st.* to blow; to sound.
Blasenkatarrh *m.* (*med.*) cystitis.
Bläser *m.*; **Bläserin** *f.* wind player.
blasiert *a.* blasé, cloyed.
Blasinstrument *n.* wind instrument.
Blaskappelle *f.*, **Blasorchester** *n.* brass band.
Blasphemie *f.* blasphemy.
blasphemisch *a.* blasphemous.
Blasrohr *n.* blowpipe.
blaß *a.* pale, wan, pallid.
Blässe *f.* (-, 0) paleness, pallor.
Bläßhuhn *n.* coot.

Blatt *n.* (-[e]s, -Blätter) leaf; sheet; blade; newspaper; *vom* ~, at sight; *das* ~ *wendet sich*, the tide turns.
Blatter *f.* (-, -n) blister, pustule; ~**n** *pl.* smallpox.
blättern *v.i.* to leaf through a book.
Blatternarbe *f.* pockmark.
Blätterteig *m.* puff pastry.
Blatt: ~**gold** *n.* gold leaf; ~**laus** *f.* greenfly; ~**pflanze** *f.* foliage plant; ~**säge** *f.* wide-bladed saw; ~**salat** *m.* green salad.
blau *a.* **Blau** *n.* (-s, 0) blue; *ins Blaue*, at random.
Blaubeere *f.* (-, -en) blueberry.
bläulich *a.* bluish.
Blaupause *f.* (*mech.*) blueprint.
Blau: ~**säre** *f.* Prussic acid; ~**strumpf** *m.* bluestocking.
Blaustift *m.* blue pencil.
Blech *n.* (-[e]s, -e) sheet metal; tin plate, tin; (*fam.*) stuff, nonsense.
blechen *v.t./v.i.* (*fam.*) to pay for.
Blechmusik *f.* brass band.
blecken *v.t.* die Zähnen ~ to bare one's teeth.
Blei *n.* (-s, -e) lead; (*fam.*) pencil.
bleiben *v.i.st.* to remain, to stay; to rest; to continue, to keep; ~ *lassen*, to let alone.
bleibend *p. & a.* lasting, permanent.
bleich *a.* pale, wan; faint.
Bleiche *f.* (-, -n) bleaching-(ground).
bleichen *v.t.* to bleach, to whiten; ~ *v.i.* to get bleached.
Bleich: ~**gesicht** *n.* paleface; ~**mittel** *n.* bleaching agent.
Bleichsucht *f.* anemia, chlorosis.
bleichsüchtig *a.* anemic, chlorotic.
bleiern *a.* leaden; (*fig.*) heavy, dull.
bleifrei *a.* unleaded.
Blei: ~**stift** *m.* pencil; ~**stiftspitzer** *m.* pencil sharpener.
Blende *f.* (-, -n) blind, folding-screen; shutter; (*Pferde~*) blinker; (*nav.*) deadlights *pl.*; (*opt.*) diaphragm, aperture.
blenden *v.t.* to blind, to blindfold; to make blind; (*fig.*) to dazzle.
Blenden: ~**einstellung** *f.* (photo) aperture setting; ~**skala** *f.* aperture ring.
Blendung *f.* dazzling; blinding.
Blendwerk *n.* delusion, illusion.
Blesse *f.* blaze.
Blick *m.* (-[e]s, -e) glance, look; view; *auf den ersten* ~, at first sight.
blicken *v.i.* to glance, to look.
Blick: ~**fang** *m.* eye-catcher; ~**feld** *n.* field of vision; ~**kontakt** *m.* eye contact; ~**punkt** *m.* visual focus; point of view; ~**winkel** *m.* angle of view; point of view.
blind *a.* blind; dull; ~*er Alarm*, false alarm; *machen* (*Granate*) to render harmless.
Blinddarm *m.* appendix; ~**entzündung** *f.* appendicitis.
Blinde *m./f.* blind person.
Blindekuh *f.* blindman's buff.
Blindgänger *m.* dud.
Blindheit *f.* (-, 0) blindness.
blindings *adv.* blindly, blindfold.
Blindschleiche *f.* (-, -n) blindworm.
blinken *v.i.* to glitter, to gleam, to twinkle.

Blinker *m.* indicator (car); spoon bait (fishing).
Blinkfeuer *m.* intermittent light.
blinzeln, blinzen *v.i.* to blink, to wink; to twinkle.
Blitz *m.* (-es, -e) lightning; *wie ein ~ aus heiterem Himmel,* out of the blue.
Blitzableiter *m.* lightning conductor; lightning rod.
blitzen *v.i.* to flash, to sparkle.
Blitz: ~**gerät** *n.* flash (photo); ~**krieg** *m.* blitzkrieg; ~**licht** *n.* flashlight.
blitzschnell *a.* swift as lightning.
Block *m.* (-[e]s, -Blöcke) block; log.
Blockade *f.* (-, -n) blockade; *die ~ brechen,* to run the blockade; ~**brecher** *m.* blockade-runner.
Blockhaus *n.* log-cabin.
blockieren *v.t.* to block up, to blockade.
Block: ~**schokolade** *f.* baking chocolate; ~**schrift** *f.* block letters; ~**stunde** *f.* double period (school).
blöde *a.* stupid, imbecile.
Blödsinn *m.* nonsense, trash.
blöken *v.i.* to bleat (sheep); to low (cattle).
blond *a.* fair, blonde.
blondieren *v.t.* to dye blonde.
Blondine *f.* (-, -n) blonde.
bloß *a.* naked, bare; uncovered; mere; ~ *adv.* merely, only; ~ *stellen,* to expose.
Blösse *f.* (-, -n) nakedness, bareness; weak side.
bloß: ~**legen** *v.t.* to uncover; to expose; to reveal; ~**liegen** *v.i.* to be exposed; ~**stellen** *v.t.* to show up.
Bluff *m.* (-s, -s) bluff.
bluffen *v.i.* to bluff.
blühen *v.i.* to bloom, to flower, to blossom; (*fig.*) to flourish.
Blume *f.* (-, -n) flower; (*Wein~*) bouquet; *durch die ~,* figuratively, allusively.
Blumen: ~**ausstellung** *f.* flower show; ~**beet** *n.* flower bed; ~**blatt** *n.* petal; ~**händler** *m.* florist; ~**kohl** *m.* cauliflower; ~**spende** *f.* floral tribute; ~**stock** *m.* flowering pot plant; ~**strauß** *m.* bunch of flowers, bouquet; ~**topf** *m.* flowerpot; ~**zucht** *f.* floriculture; ~**zwiebel** *f.* bulb.
blumig *a.* flowery; (*fig.*) florid.
Bluse *f.* (-, -n) blouse.
Blut *n.* (-[e]s, 0) blood.
Blut: ~**ader** *f.* vein; blood-vessel; ~**alkohol** *m.* blood alcohol level; ~**armut** *f.* anemia; ~**bahn** *f.* blood stream; ~**bild** *n.* blood count; ~**buche** *f.* copper beech, bronze beech; ~**druck** *m.* blood pressure.
blutdürstig *a.* bloodthirsty.
Blüte *f.* (-, -n) blossom, bloom; (*fig.*) prime, heyday.
Blutegel *m.* leech.
bluten *v.i.* to bleed.
Bluter *m.* (-s, -) hemophiliac.
Blüten: ~**kelch** *m.* calyx; ~**knospe** *f.* bud; ~**staub** *m.* pollen.
Blütezeit *f.* prime, golden age.
Blut: ~**erguß** *m.* hematoma, bruise; ~**erkrankheit** *f.* hemophilia; ~**farbstoff** *m.* hemoglobin; ~**gefäß** *n.* blood vessel; ~**gerinnsel** *n.* blood clot.
blutgierig *a.* sanguinary, bloodthirsty.
Blutgruppe *f.* blood group.
blutig *a.* bloody; sanguinary.
Bluthochdruck *m.* (-s, 0) high blood pressure.

blutjung *a.* very young.
Blut: ~**konserve** *f.* unit of stored blood; ~**körperchen** *n.* blood corpuscle; ~**krebs** *m.* leukemia; ~**kreislauf** *m.* blood circulation; ~**lache** *f.* pool of blood.
blutleer, blutlos *a.* bloodless, anemic.
Blutprobe *f.* blood test; blood sample.
Blutrache *f.* vendetta.
blutrünstig *a.* bloody.
Blut: ~**sauger** *m.* vampire; (*fig.*) extortioner, skinflint; ~**schande** *f.* incest.
blutschänderisch *a.* incestuous.
Blutschuld *f.* bloodguilt; capital crime.
Blut: ~**spender** *m.* blood donor.
blutstillend *a.* hemostatic, styptic.
Blut: ~**sturz** *m.,* **Blutung** *f.* hemorrhage; ~**übertragung** *f.* blood transfusion; ~**unterlaufen** *a.* bloodshot; ~**vergiftung** *f.* blood poisoning; ~**vergießen** *n.* bloodshed; ~**verwandt** *a.* consanguineous; ~**verwandter** *m.* blood relationship; ~**verwandtschaft** *f.* consanguinity, blood-relationship.
Blutwurst *f.* black pudding; blood sausage.
b-Moll *n.* B flat minor.
Bö *f.* (-, en) gust.
Bob *m.* (-, -s) bob (sleigh).
Bob: ~**bahn** *f.* bobrun; ~**fahrer** *m.*; ~**fahrerin** *f.* bobber.
Bock *m.* (-[e]s, Böcke) ram; (*anderer Tiere*) buck; trestle; high stool; *einen ~ schiessen,* to make a blunder.
bockbeinig *a.* stubborn.
Bockgestell *n.* trestle.
bockig *a.* stubborn; pigheaded.
Bockleder *n.* buckskin.
Buckshorn *n. einen ins ~ jagen,* to intimidate one.
Boden *m.* (-s, u. Böden) ground; soil; bottom; garret, loft; (*eines Fasses etc.*) head; floor.
Boden: ~**fenster** *n.* dormer window; ~**kammer** *f.* garret, attic.
bodenlos *a.* bottomless.
Boden: ~**rente** *f.* base rent; ~**ständig,** native; ~**satz** *m.* sediment, dregs *pl.*; ~**schätze** *m.pl.* mineral resources.
Bogen *m.* (-s, -) arch, vault; blow; (*math.*) arc; (*Geigen~*) bow; sheet (*Papier*); *in Bausch und ~,* wholesale.
Bogen: ~**gang** *m.* arcade; ~**lampe** *f.* arc lamp; ~**schütze** *m.* archer.
Bohème *f.* Bohemia.
Bohèmien *m.* Bohemian.
Bohle *f.* (-, -n) board, plank.
bohlen *v.t.* to board, to plank.
Böhme *m.*; **Böhmin** *f.*; **böhmisch** *a.* Bohemian; *das sind mir ~e Dörfer,* that is Greek to me.
Böhmen *n.* Bohemia.
Bohne *f.* (-, -n) bean; *dicke ~n,* broad beans; *grüne ~n,* French beans, runner beans.
bohnern *v.t.* to wax.
Bohnenstange *f.* beanpole.
bohren *v.t.* to bore, to drill; *in den Grund ~,* to sink (a ship).
bohrend *a.* gnawing; piercing; probing.
Bohrer *m.* (-s, -) drill.
Bohr: ~**insel** *f.* oil rig; ~**lehre,** ~**schablone** *f.* jig; ~**maschine** *f.* boring machine, drilling machine;

~turm *m.* derrick.
Bohrung *f.* drilling; hole.
böig *a.* gusty.
Boiler *m.* water heater; boiler.
Boje *f.* (-, -n) buoy.
Bolivianer *m.*; **Bolivianerin** *f.*; **bolivianisch** *a.* Bolivian; **Bolivien** *n.* Bolivia.
Böller *m.* (-s, -) small mortar.
Böllerschuß *m.* gun salute.
Bollwerk *n.* bastion, bulwark.
Bolzen *m.* (-s, -) bolt; arrow.
bolzen *v.i.* (*fam.*) to play soccer.
Bolzplatz *m.* (children's) soccer field.
Bombardement *n.* (-s, -s) bombardment.
bombardieren *v.t.* to bombard, to shell, to pound.
Bombardierung *f.* (-, -en) bombing.
Bombast *m.* (-es, 0) bombast.
bombastisch *a.* bombastic, inflated.
Bombe *f.* (-, -n) bomb, shell.
Bomben: ~angriff *m.* bomb attack, bombing raid; **~anschlag** *m.*, **~attentat** *n.* bomb attack; **~drohung** *f.* bomb threat; **~erfolg** *m.* (*fam.*) smash hit; **~flugzeug** *n.* bomber; **~punktwurf** *m.* pinpoint bombing; **~schacht** *m.* bomb rack; **~sicher** *a.* bombproof; **~zielgerät** *n.* bombsight.
Bomber *m.* bomber.
Bon *m.* (-s, -s) voucher; coupon; sales slip.
Bonbon (*frz.*) *n.* (-s, -s) sweet.
bonbonfarben *a.* candy-colored.
Bonmot *n.* (-s, -s) bon mot.
Bonus *m.* (-, -se) discount; bonus point.
Bonze *m.* (-n, -n) (*pej.*) big wig; big wheel.
Boom *m.* (-s, -s) boom.
Boot *n.* (-[e]s, -e) boat.
Boots: ~fahrt *f.* boat trip; **~mann** *m.* boatswain; **~steg** *m.* landing-stage; **~verleih** *m.* boat rentalhire.
Bord *n.* (-s, -e) shelf.
Bord *m.* (-[e]s, -e) board; *an ~*, aboard; *über ~*, overboard.
Bordbuch *n.* logbook.
Bordell *n.* (-[e]s, -e) brothel.
Bordfunk *m.* radio.
Bordfunker *m.* (*avi.*) radio operator.
Bord: ~personal *n.* cabin crew; **~stein** *m.* curb; **~steinkante** *f.* edge of the curb.
Bordüre *f.* (-, -n) edging.
borgen *v.t.* to borrow; to lend.
Borke *f.* (-, -n) bark.
Borkenkäfer *m.* bark beetle.
borniert *a.* narrowminded.
Borniertheit *f.* narrow mindedness.
Borretsch *m.* (-(e)s, 0) borage.
Borsalbe *f.* boric acid ointment.
Börse *f.* (-, -n) purse; stock exchange.
Börsen: ~bericht *m.* market report; **~kurs** *m.* quotation; **~makler** *m.* stockbroker.
Borste *f.* (-, -n) bristle.
borstig *f.* (-, -n) bristly.
Borte *f.* (-, -n) lace trim.
Borwasser *n.* boric acid lotion.
bösartig *a.* malignant; malicious, vicious.
Bösartigkeit *f.* maliciousness, viciousness.
Böschung *f.* (-, -en) embankment, scarp, slope.
böse *a.* bad; evil, ill, wicked; angry.
Bösewicht *m.* (-[e]s, -e[r]) villain.

boshaft *a.* spiteful, malicious.
Bosheit *f.* (-, -n) malice, spite.
Boskop *m.* russet (apple).
Boss *m.* (*fam.*) boss.
böswillig *a.* malevolent, wicked.
Böswilligkeit *f.* malice, maliciousness.
Botanik *f.* (-, 0) botany.
Botaniker *m.* (-s, -) botanist.
botanisch *a.* botanic(al).
botanisieren *v.i.* to botanize.
Bote *m.* (-n, -n) messenger; **~ngang** *m.* errand.
Botschaft *f.* (-, -en) message; news; embassy.
Botschafter *m.* (-s, -) ambassador.
Böttcher *m.* (-s, -) cooper.
Bottich *m.* (-[e]s, -e) vat, coop, tub.
Bouillon *f.* (meat) bouillon broth; **~würfel** *m.* bouillon cube.
Bowle *f.* (-, -n) punch; (*Getränk*) spiced wine, claret cup, iced cup.
Bowling *n.* bowling; **Bowlingbahn** *f.* bowling alley.
boxen *v.i.* to box.
Boxer *m.* (-s, -) boxer, pugilist, prizefighter.
Boykott *m.* boycott.
boykottieren *v.t.* to boycott.
brabbeln *v.i.* (*fam.*) to mumble, to mutter; to bubble.
brach *a.* fallow, unplowed.
Brachfeld *n.* fallow (ground).
brachial *a.* violent; **~e Gewalt** *f.* brute force.
Brachialgewalt *f.* brute force.
Brachland *n.* fallow; uncultivated land.
brachliegen *v.i.* to lie fallow.
brackig *a.* brackish.
Brahmane *m.* Brahman; **Brahmanin** *f.* Brahmanee.
bramarbasieren *v.i.* to swagger, to bully.
Bramsegel *n.* topsail.
Branche *f.* (-, -n) branch, line (of business).
Branchenverzeichnis *n.* classified directory, yellow pages.
Brand *m.* (-[e]s, Brände) combustion; fire, conflagration; (*med.*) gangrene; fuel; firebrand; (*bot.*) blight, mildew; *in ~ stecken*, to set on fire.
Brand: ~brief *m.* urgent letter; **~bombe** *f.* incendiary bomb.
branden *v.i.* to surge, to break.
brandig *a.* blighted, blasted; (*med.*) gangrenous; smelling as if burnt.
Brandlegung *f.* (-, -en) incendiarism.
Brandmal *n.* (-[e]s, -e) stigma.
brandmarken *v.t.* to brand.
Brand: ~mauer *f.* fireproof wall; **~schaden** *m.* damage by fire.
brandschatzen *v.t.* to plunder.
Brand: ~stifter *m.* incendiary; **~stiftung** *f.* arson, incendiarism.
Brandung *f.* (-, -en) breakers *pl.*; surf, surge.
Brandungswelle *f.* (-, -n) breaker.
Brandwunde *f.* burn, scald.
Branntwein *m.* (-[e]s, -e) spirits *pl.*
Branntweinbrenner *m.* distiller.
Brasil *f.* Brasil cigar.
Brasilianer *m.*; **Brasilianerin** *f.*; **brasilianisch** *a.* Brazilian; **Brasilien** *n.* Brazil.
braten *v.t.st.* to roast; to broil, to grill; (*in der*

Pfanne) to fry.

Braten *m.* (-s, -) roast meat.

Bratenfett *n.* dripping.

Bratensoße *f.* gravy.

Brat: ~**kartoffel** *f.* fried potato; ~**ofen** *m.* roasting-oven; ~**pfanne** *f.* frying pan; ~**rost** *m.* gridiron, grill.

Bratsche *f.* (-, -n) viola, bass-viol.

Brat: ~**spieß** *m.* spit; ~**wurst** *f.* sausage.

Brauch *m.* (-[e]s, Bräuche) usage, custom.

brauchbar *a.* useful, serviceable.

brauchen *v.t.* to use, to employ; to need, to want.

brauen *v.t.* to brew.

Brauer *m.* (-s, -) brewer.

Brauerei *f.* (-, -en) brewery.

braun *a.* brown, tawny; (*Pferd*) bay; **Braune** *m.* bay horse.

Bräune *f.* (-, 0) tan; brownness.

bräunen *v.t.* to get a tan; to brown.

Braunkohle *f.* lignite.

bränlich *a.* brownish.

Braunsche Röhre *f.* cathode-ray tube.

Braus *m.* in *Saus und ~ leben*, to revel and riot.

Brausebad *n.* shower bath.

brausen *v.i.* to roar; to buzz; to race, to effervesce.

Brausepulver *n.* effervescent powder.

Braut *f.* (-, Bräute) fiancée; (*am Hochzeitstage*) bride.

Braut: ~**aussteuer** *f.* trousseau; ~**führer** *m.* man who gives away the bride.

Bräutigam *m.* (-s, -e) fiancé; (*am Hochzeitstage*) bridegroom.

Braut: ~**jungfer** *f.* bridesmaid; ~**kleid** *n.* wedding dress; ~**kranz** *m.* bridal wreath.

Braut: ~**nacht** *f.* wedding night; ~**paar** *n.* couple.

brav *a.* honest, good, brave, courageous.

bravo! *i.* bravo! well done!

Bravour *f.* stylishness; **mit** ~ brilliantly.

Bravourleistung *f.* brilliant performance.

bravourös *a. & adv.* brilliant(ly).

Bravourstück *n.* piece of bravura.

Brecheisen *n.* crowbar.

brechen *v.st.* to break; (*Knochen*) to fracture; (*Lichtstrahlen*) to be refracted; to vomit.

Brech: ~**mittel** *n.* emetic; ~**reiz** *m.* retching; nausea.

Brechung *f.* (-, -en) (*opt.*) refraction.

Brei *m.* (-[e]s, -e) porridge; pulp, mush.

breiig *a.* mushy.

breit *a.* broad; wide, large; *weit und* ~, far and wide; ~ *schlagen*, to persuade.

Breite *f.* (-, -n) breadth; width; (*geographische*) latitude.

Breitengrad *m.* degree of latitude.

breitspurig *a.* bumptious.

Brems: ~**backe** *f.* brake shoe; ~**belag** *m.* brake lining.

Bremse *f.* (-, -n) gadfly; brake.

bremsen *v.t.* to apply the brake.

Brems: ~**flüssigkeit** *f.* brake fluid; ~**hebel** *m.* brake arm; ~**klotz** *m.* brake pad; ~**licht** *n.* brake light; ~**scheibe** *f.* brake disc; ~**spur** *f.* skid mark; ~**trommel** *f.* brake drum.

Bremsung *f.* braking.

Bremsweg *f.* braking distance.

brennbar *a.* combustible, inflammable.

brennen *v.t.ir.* to burn, to scorch; (*med.*) to cauterize; (*Kaffee*) to roast; (*Kohlen*) to char; (*Branntwein*) to distill; (*Ziegel*) to bake; ~ *v.i.st.* to burn, to be on fire; (*Wunde*) to smart; (*Nessel*) to sting.

Brennerei *f.* (-, -en) distillery.

Brenn: ~**holz** *n.* firewood; ~**material** *n.* fuel; ~**essel** *f.* stinging nettle; ~**punkt** *m.* focus; ~**stoff** *m.* fuel; ~**spiegel** *m.* burning mirror.

brenzlig *a.* dangerous, risky.

Bresche *f.* (-, -n) breach; gap.

Bretagne *f.* Brittany.

Brett *n.* (-[e]s, -er) board; plank; *mit Brettern verschlagen*, to board up.

Bretter: ~**boden** *m.* wooden floor; ~**bude** *f.* hut, shack; ~**verschlag** *m.* shed; ~**wand** *f.* wooden wall; ~**zaun** *m.* wooden fence.

Brettspiel *n.* (-s, -e) board game.

Brevier *n.* (-s, -e) breviary.

Brezel *f.* (-, -n) pretzel.

Brief *m.* (-[e]s, -e) letter, epistle; *unter* ~ *und Siegel*, under hand and seal.

Brief: ~**beschwerer** *m.* paperweight; ~**bote** *m.* postman; ~**drucksache** *f.* printed paper; ~**freund** *m.*; ~**freundin** *f.* pen pal; ~**kasten** *m.* letter box; mailbox; ~**kastenfirma** *f.* mailbox company; ~**kopf** *m.* letterhead.

brieflich *a. & adv.* by letter.

Brief: ~**marke** *f.* (postage) stamp; ~**markensammler** *m.* stamp collector; ~**papier** *n.* notepaper; ~**porto** *n.* postage.

Briefschaften *f.pl.* letters, papers, documents *pl.*

Brief: ~**steller** *m.* model letter writer; ~**tasche** *f.* wallet; ~**taube** *f.* carrier pigeon; ~**telegramm** *n.* nightletter telegram; ~**träger** *m.* postman; ~**umschlag** *m.* envelope; ~**waage** *f.* postage scale; ~**wechsel** *m.* correspondence.

Bries *n.* (-es, -e) (*cul.*) sweetbreads.

Brigade *f.* (-, -n) brigade.

Brigg *f.* (-, -s) brig.

Brikett *n.* (-s, -s) briquette.

Brillant *m.* (-en, -en) brilliant, diamond.

brillant *a. & adv.* brilliant(ly).

Brillanz *f.* (-, 0) brilliance.

Brille *f.* (-, -n) (pair of) spectacles *pl.*; glasses *pl.*; goggles *pl.*; (*Klosett~*) toilet seat.

Brillen: ~**etui** *n.*; ~**futteral** *n.* spectacle case; ~**gestell** *n.* spectacle frame; ~**schlange** *f.* cobra.

brillieren *v.i.* to shine.

Brimborium *n.* (-s, 0) (*fam. pej.*) hoo-ha.

bringen *v.t.ir.* to bring; to carry; to take; to convey; to conduct; to give, to present; *in Gang* ~, to set going; *zustand(e)* ~, to bring about; *es weit* ~, to get on in the world; *um etwas* ~, to deprive; *ums Leben* ~, to kill, to murder; *ein Opfer* ~, to make a sacrifice.

brisant *a.* (*fig.*) explosive.

Brisanz *f.* (-, 0) (*fig.*) explosiveness.

Brise *f.* (-, -n) breeze.

Britannien *n.* (-s, 0) Britain; Britannia; **Brite** *m.* (-n, -n); **Britin** *f.* (-, -nen); Briton; **britisch** *a.* British.

bröck[e]lig *a.* crumbling.

bröckeln *v.t. & i.* to crumble.

Brocken *m.* (-s, -) fragment; morsel; crumb.

brodeln *v.i.* to bubble.

Brokat *m.* (-[e]s, -e) brocade.

Brom *m.* (-s, 0) bromine.
Brombeere *f.* blackberry.
Brombeerstrauch *m.* bramble.
Bronchialkatarrh *m.* bronchitis.
Bronchie *f.* (-, -n) bronchial tube; broncus.
Bronze *f.* (-, -n) bronze, brass.
Bronzezeit *f.* bronze age.
Brosame *f.* (-, -n) crumb.
Brosche *f.* (-, -n) brooch.
broschiert *a.* paperback.
Broschüre *f.* (-, -n) pamphlet, booklet.
Brösel *m.* (-s, -) crumb.
bröselig *a.* crumbly.
bröseln *v.i.* to crumble.
Brot *n.* (-[e]s, -e) bread; loaf.
Brotaufstrich *m.* sandwich spread.
Brötchen *n.* (-s,-) roll.
Brot: ~**erwerb** *m.* way to earn a living; ~**kasten** *m.* bread bin, breadbox; ~**krume** *f.*; ~**krümel** *m.* breadcrumb; ~**laib** *m.* loaf.
brotlos *a.* unprofitable.
Brot: ~**maschine** *f.* bread slicer; **rinde** *f.* breadcrust; ~**zeit** *f.* lunch break; snack.
Bruch *m.* (-[e]s, Brüche) breach, rupture; (*Bein~*) fracture; (*med.*) rupture, hernia; (*ar.*) fraction; *gemeiner ~,* vulgar *or* common fraction; *in die Brüche gehen,* to break up.
Bruchband *n.* truss.
Bruchbude *f.* (*fam. pej.*) hovel, dump.
brüchig *a.* full of cracks, brittle.
Bruch: ~**landung** *f.* (*avi.*) crash-landing; ~**strich** *m.* fraction line; ~**stück** *n.* fragment; ~**teil** *m.* fraction.
Brücke *f.* (-, -n) bridge.
Brücken: ~**geländer** *n.* railing; ~**kopf** *m.* bridgehead; ~**pfeiler** *m.* pier.
Bruder *m.* (-s, Brüder) brother; (*Mönch*) friar.
Bruderkreig *m.* fratricidal war.
brüderlich *a. & adv.* fraternal.
Brudermord *m.* fratricide.
Brüderschaft *f.* (-, -en) brotherhood.
Brühe *f.* (-, -n) broth, gravy, sauce.
brühen *v.t.* brew; to make (tea).
brühheiß, brühwarm *a.* boiling hot.
brüllen *v.i.* to roar; to bellow, to low.
Brummbär *m.* (*fam.*) grouch.
brummeln *v.i.* (*fam.*) to mumble, to mutter.
brummen *v.i.* to growl, to grumble; to hum; to mumble.
Brummer *m.* (*fam.*); **Brummi** *m.* (*fam.*) truck.
brummig *a.* grumpy.
Brünette *f.* (-, -n) brunette.
Brunft *f.* (-, 0) rut, rutting time.
Brunnen *m.* (-s, -) spring, well; fountain; mineral waters *pl.*
Brunnenkresse *f.* watercress.
Brunst *f.* (-, 0) rut, sexual desire, heat.
brünstig *a.* ardent, fervent; in heat.
Brunszreit *f.* rutting season, heat.
brüsk *a.* brusque; **brüskieren** *v.t.* to snub.
Brust *f.* (-Brüste) breast; bosom, chest.
Brustbild *n.* half-length portrait.
brüsten (sich) *v/refl.* to boast, to brag about.
Brust: ~**fellentzündung,** pleurisy; ~**kasten,** ~**korb** *m.* chest, thorax.
Brustschwimmen *n.* breaststroke.

Brüstung *f.* (-, -en) parapet, balustrade.
Brust: ~**warze** *f.* nipple; ~**wehr** *f.* parapet; ~**wickel** *m.* chest compress.
Brut *f.* (-, -en) brood, hatch; (*Fische*) fry; (*Vögel*) covey; (*fig.*) set, pack.
brutal *a.* brutish, brutal.
Brutalität *f.* brutality.
Brutapparat *m.* incubator.
brüten *a.* to brood, to hatch, to sit (on eggs).
Brüter *m.* breeder (nuclear power).
Bruthenne *f.* (-, -en) sitting hen.
Brutkasten *m.* incubator.
Brutstätte *f.* breeding place; hot bed.
brutto *adv.* gross.
Bruttogewicht *n.* (-[e]s, -e) gross weight.
bst! *i.* hush! hist!
Bube *m.* (-n, -n) boy, lad; knave, rogue; (*in der Karte*) knave, jack.
Bubenstreich *m.* childish prank.
Bubikopf *m.* bobbed hair.
Buch *n.* (-[e]s, Bücher) book; (~ *Papier*) quire; *die Bücher führen,* to keep the books.
Buch: ~**besprechung** *f.* book-review; ~**binder** *m.* bookbinder; ~**deckel** *m.* cover; ~**druck** *m.* printing; ~**drucker** *m.* printer.
Buche *f.* (-, -n) beech, beech tree.
Buchecker *f.* (-, -n) beechnut.
buchen *v.t.* to book, to enter.
Bücher: ~**brett** *n.* bookshelf; ~**ei** *f.* library; ~**schrank** *m.* book-case; ~**stütze** *f.* bookend.
Buchfink *m.* chaffinch.
Büch: ~**führung** *f.* bookkeeping; ~**halter** *m.* book keeper; ~**handel** *m.* book trade; ~**händler** *m.* bookseller; ~**handlung** *f.*; ~**laden** *m.* bookstore; ~**messe** *f.* book fair; ~**prüfer** *m.* auditor; ~**rücken** *m.* spine.
Buchsbaum *m.* (-[e]s, -bäume) box tree.
Buchschuld *f.* (-, -en) book debt.
Buchse *f.* (-, -en) (*elek.*) socket; (*tech.*) bush, liner.
Büchse *f.* (-, -n) box, case; tin; (*Flinte*) rifle, shotgun.
Büchsen: ~**fleisch** *n.* tinned meat; ~**öffner** *m.* can opener, tin opener.
Buchstabe *m.* (-n[s], -n) letter, character; type.
buchstabengetreu *a. & adv.* literal; to the letter.
buchstabieren *v.t.* to spell.
buchstäblich *a.* literal, verbatim; ~ *adv.* literally.
Buchstütze *f.* bookend.
Bucht *f.* (-, -en) creek, bay, inlet, cove.
Buchtitel *m.* title.
Buchung *f.* (-, -en) entry; booking.
Buchweizen *m.* (-s, 0) buckwheat.
Buchzeichen *n.* bookmark.
Buckel *m.* (-s, -) hunchback, hump.
buckeln *v.i.* (*fam. pej.*) to bow and scrape, to kowtow.
bücken (sich) *v.refl.* to bend, to stoop, to bow.
bucklig *a.* hunchbacked.
Bucklige *m./f.* hunchback.
Bückling *m.* (-s, -e) (smoked) herring.
buddeln *v.i.* (*fam.*) to dig.
Buddhismus *m.* Buddhism.
Buddhist *m.*; **Buddhistin** *f.*; **buddhistisch** *a.* Buddhist.
Bude *f.* (-, -n) booth, stall.
Budget *n.* (-s, -s) budget.

Büffet *n.* (-s, -s) sideboard; bar.
Büffel *m.* (-s, -) buffalo.
büffeln *v.i.* to cram, to grind.
Bug *m.* (-[e]s, -e) bow (ship).
Bügel *m.* (-s, -) hanger; earpiece (glasses), hoop, bow.
Bügelbrett *n.* ironing board.
Bügeleisen *n.* iron.
Bügelfalte *f.* crease.
bügeln *v.t.* to iron, to smoothe.
Buggy *m.* stroller.
bugsieren *v.t.* (*fam.*) to shift, to steer.
Bugspriet *n.* (-[e]s, -e) bowsprit.
buhen *v.i.* (*fam.*) to boo.
Buhle *m.* (-n, -n) & *f.* (-, -n) lover.
buhlen *v.i.* to court.
Buhmann *m.* bogey man.
Bühne *f.* (-, -n) stage; scaffold; platform; *zur ~ gehen,* to go on the stage.
Bühnen: ~**anweisung** *f.* stage direction; ~**arbeiter** *m.* stage hand; ~**autor** *m.*; ~**autorin** *f.* playwright; ~**bearbeitung** *f.* stage adaptation; ~**beleuchtung** *f.* stage lighting; ~**bild** *n.* (stage) set; ~**bilder** *m.*; **bildnerin** *f.* set designer; ~**leiter** *m.* stage manager; ~**regisseur** *m.*; **regisseurin** *f.* stage director; ~**stück** *n.* stage play.
Buhruf *m.* boo.
Bukett *n.* (-s, -s) bouquet, bunch of flowers.
Bulette *f.* (-, -n) meatball.
Bulgare *m.*; **Bulgarin** *f.*; **bulgarisch** *a.* Bulgarian; **Bulgarien** *n.* (-s, 0) Bulgaria.
Bullauge *n.* circular porthole.
Bulle *m.* (-en, -en) bull *f.* (-, -n).
bullig *a.* beefy, stocky, chunky, hefty.
Bummel *m.* (-s, -) stroll.
Bummelei *f.* (-, -en) dawdling.
bummeln *v.i.* to stroll; to loaf.
Bummelstreik *m.* go-slow; work to rule.
bums *int.* bang.
bumsen *v.i.* (*fam.*) to crash; to bang; to bash; to screw (vulg.).
Bund *m.* (-[e]s, Bünde) band, tie; league, alliance, confederacy; covenant.
Bund *n.* (-[e]s, -e) bundle, bunch, truss.
Bündel *n.* (-s, -) bundle, bunch, truss, wisp (of straw).
Bundes . . . federal.
Bundes: ~**bürger** *m.*; ~**bürgerin** *f.* citizen of the FRG; ~**ebene** *f.* federal *or* national level; ~**genosse** *m.* confederate, ally; ~**grenzschutz** *m.* Federal Border Police; ~**haus** *n.* Federal Parliament Building; ~**kabinett** *n.* Federal Cabinet; ~**kanzler** *m.* Federal Chancellor; ~**kanzleramt** *n.* Federal Chancellery; ~**lade** *f.* ark of the covenant; ~**land** *n.* (federal) state; province (Austria); ~**liga** *f.* federal division; ~**präsident** *m.* (Federal) President; ~**rat** *m.* Upper House (of the Parliament); ~**regierung** *f.* Federal Government; ~**republic** *f.* Federal Republic; ~**staat** *m.* Federal state; ~**tag** *m.* Lower House (of the Parliament); ~**tagsabgeordnete** *m./f.* member of the Bundestag; ~**tagswahl** *f.* general election; ~**wehr** *f.* (Federal) Armed Forces.
bundesweit *a. & adv.* nationwide.
bündig *a.* concise, terse; convincing.
Bündnis *n.* (-nisses, -nisse) alliance.
bündnisfrei *a.* nonaligned.

Bündnispartner *m.* ally.
Bundweite *f.* waist (size).
Bunker *m.* (-s, -) air-raid shelter; bunker.
bunt *a.* colorful, colored, variegated; motley, parti-colored, spotted; *das ist zu ~,* it goes too far.
Buntdruck *m.* (-[e]s, -e) color printing.
Buntsandstein *m.* red sandstone.
Buntspecht *m.* spotted woodpecker.
Buntwäsche *f.* coloreds.
Bürde *f.* (-, -n) burden, load.
Bureau *n.* (-s, -s *u.* -x) office.
Bureaukratie *f.* bureaucracy.
Burg *f.* (-, -en) castle, stronghold.
Bürge *m.* (-n, -n) bail, guarantee, surety.
bürgen *v.i.* to bail, to answer for, to warrant.
Bürger *m.* (-s, -) citizen, townsman.
Bürgerinitiative *f.* citizens' action group.
Bürgerkreig *m.* civil war.
bürgerlich *a.* civil, civic; ~**es Gesetzbuch** *n.* code of Civil Law.
Bürgerliche *m./f.* (-n, -n) commoner.
Bürger: ~**meister** *m.* mayor; ~**recht** *n.* civic rights *pl.*; freedom (of a city); ~**schreck** *m.* bogey of the middle classes; ~**stand** *m.* middle class(es); ~**steig** *m.* sidewalk.
Bürgertum *n.* (-[e]s, 0) middle class.
Burg: ~**friede** *m.* truce; ~**graben** *m.* moat.
Bürgschaft *f.* (-, -en) bail, surety, security; guarantee, guaranty; *gegen ~ freilassen,* to release on bail; ~ *leisten,* to go bail; ~ *zulassen,* to admit to bail.
Burgund *n.* (-s, 0) Burgundy.
burlesk *a.* burlesque.
Büro *n.* (-s, -s) office.
Büro: ~**arbeit** *f.* paper work; ~**artikel** *m.pl.* office appliances *pl.*; ~**bedarf** *m.* office supplies; ~**gebäude** *n.* office building; ~**klammer** *f.* paper clip.
Bürokrat *m.* bureaucrat; **Bürokratie** *f.* bureaucracy; **bürokratisch** *a.* bureaucratic.
Büro: ~**personal** *n.* office staff; ~**stunden** *pl.*, ~**zeit** *f.* office hours.
Bursch(e) *m.* (-en, -en) fellow, lad.
Burschenschaft *f.* (students) fraternity.
burschikos *a.* pert.
Bürste *f.* (-, -n) brush.
bürsten *v.t.* to brush.
Bürstenbinder *m.* brushmaker.
Bus *m.* (-ses, -se) bus.
Busbahnhof *m.* bus station.
Busch *m.* (-[e]s, Büsche) bush; thicket.
Büschel *m.* (-s, -) tuft; bunch; cluster.
buschig *a.* bushy.
Busch: ~**mann** *m.* Bushman; ~**messer** *n.* machete; ~**windröschen** *n.* wood anemone.
Busen *m.* (-s, -) bosom; breast; heart.
busenfrei *a.* topless.
Busenfreund *m.*; **Busenfreundin** *f.* bosom friend.
Bus: ~**fahrer** *m.* bus driver; ~**haltestelle** *f.* bus stop; ~**linie** *f.* bus route.
Bussard *m.* (-s, -e) buzzard.
Buße *f.* (-, -n) penance, penitence; (*Geld~*) fine, penalty.
büßen *v.t.* to atone for; ~ *v.t.* to suffer, to expiate.
Büßer *m.* (-s, -) penitent.
bußfertig *a.* penitent, repentant.
Bußtag *m.* day of penance.

Buß: ~**geld** *n.* fine; ~**geldbescheid** *m.* notice of fine due.
Büste *f.* (-, -n) bust.
Büstenhalter *m.* (-s, -) bra, brassiere.
Bus: ~**verbindung** *f.* bus service; bus connection; ~**verkehr** *m.* bus service.
Butt *m.* flounder.
Bütte *f.* (-, -n) tub, coop.
Büttenpapier *n.* handmade paper.

Butter *f.* (-, 0) butter.
Butter: ~**blume** *f.* buttercup; ~**faß** *n.* churn.
Butterbrotpapier *n.* greaseproof paper.
Buttermilch *f.* buttermilk.
buttern *v.t.* to butter; to churn.
Buttersemmel *f.* roll and butter.
butterweich *a.* very soft; (*fig.*) vague.
Butzenscheibe *f.* bull's eye window-pane.
Button *m.* (-s, -s) badge.
Byte *n.* (*comp.*) byte.

C

C, c *n.* the letter C or c.
C Celsius C.
Café *n.* (-s, -s) coffee house, café.
Cafeteria *f.* cafeteria.
campen *v.i.* to camp.
Camper *m.*; **camperin** *f.* camper.
Camping *n.* camping.
Camping: ~**bus** *m.* camper; ~**platz** *m.* campground.
Campus *m.* campus.
Caravan *m.* station wagon; trailer.
catchen *v.i.* to do all-in wrestling.
Catcher *m.* all-in wrestler.
CB-Funk *m.* CB radio.
CD *f.* CD.
CD-Spieler *m.* CD player.
C-Dur *n.* C major.
Cellist *m.* (-en, -en) violoncellist.
Cello *n.* (-[s], -s) violoncello.
Ces *n.* (-, 0) (*mus.*) C flat.
C-Flöte *f.* soprano recorder.
Chamäleon *n.* (-s, -s) chameleon.
Champagner *m.* (-s, -) champagne.
Champignon *m.* (-s, -s) champignon, mushroom.
Champion *m.* champion.
Chance *f.* (-, -n) chance.
Chancengleichheit *f.* equal opportunities.
changieren *v.i.* to shimmer.
Chaos *n.* (-, 0) chaos.
chaotisch *a.* chaotic.
Charakter *m.* (-s, Charaktere) character.
Charaktereigenschaft *f.* characteristic; trait.
charakterfest *a.* firm.
charakterisieren *v.t.* to characterize.
Charakteristik *f.* (-, -en) characteristic.
charakteristisch *a.* characteristic.
charakterlos *a.* unprincipled.
Characterzug *m.* (~es, züge) characteristic.
Charisma *n.* charisma; **charismatisch** *a.* charismatic.
charmant *a.* charming.
Charme *m.* charm.
Charta *f.* charter.
Charterflug *f.* charter flight.
chartermaschine *f.* charter plane.
chartern *v.t.* to charter, to hire.
Chassis *n.* chassis.
Chauffeur (*frz.*) *m.* (-s, -e) chauffeur.
Chaussee *f.* (-, -n) highroad.
Chauvi *m.* (*fam. pej.*) male chauvinist.
Chauvinismus *m.* (-, 0) chauvinism.
Chauvinist *m.* (-n, -n) chauvinist.

chauvinistisch *a.* chauvinistic.
checken *v.t.* to check, to examine; (*fam.*) check out.
Chef *m.* (-s, -s) head, principal, boss.
Chefarzt *m.* head physician.
Chefin *f.* (-, -nen) head, leader, boss.
Chef: ~**redakteur** *m.*; ~**redakteurin** *f.* chief editor; ~**sekretärin** *f.* director's secretary.
Chemie *f.* (-, 0) chemistry.
Chemiefaser *f.* synthetic fiber.
Chemikalien *n.pl.* chemicals *pl.*
Chemiker *m.* (-s, -) (analytical) chemist.
chemisch *a. & adv.* chemical; ~**e Reinigung** *f.* dry cleaning; ~**e Wirkung** *f.* chemical action.
Cherub *m.* (-s, ~im) cherub.
Chesterkäse *m.* cheddar cheese.
Chicoree *m.* endive.
Chiffre *f.* (-, -n) cipher.
Chiffretelegramm, code telegram, cipher.
chiffrieren *v.t.* to cipher, to code.
Chile *n.* (-s, 0) Chile.
Chilene *m.*; **Chilenin** *f.*; chilenisch *a.* Chilean.
China *n.* (-s, 0) China.
Chinese *m.*; **Chinesin** *f.*; **chinesisch** *a.* Chinese.
Chinin *n.* (-s, 0) quinine.
Chiropraktiker *m.*; **Chiropraktikerin** *f.* chiropractor.
Chirurg *m.* (-en, -en); **Chirurgin** *f.* (-, -nen) surgeon.
Chirurgie *f.* (-, 0) surgery.
chirurgisch *a.* surgical.
Chitinpanzer *m.* chitinous exoskeleton.
Chlor *n.* (-[e]s, 0) chlorine.
Chlor: ~**kalium** *n.* potassium chloride; ~**kalk** *m.* chloride of lime; ~**kalzium** *n.* calcium chloride.
chloren *v.t.* to chlorinate.
chloroformieren *v.t.* to chloroform.
Cholera *f.* (-, 0) cholera.
cholerisch *a.* choleric.
Chor *m.* (-s, Chöre) chorus; choir.
Choral *m.* (-[e]s, Choräle) chorale.
Choreograph *m.*; **Choreographin** *f.* choreographer.
Choreographie *f.* (-, -n) choreography.
Chor: ~**hemd** *n.* surplice, alb. ~**knabe** *m.* choirboy; ~**leiter** *m.* chorus master; ~**musik** *f.* choral music; ~**sänger** *m.* chorister, ~**stuhl** *m.* (cathedral) stall.
Christ *m.*; **Christin** *f.* Christian.
Christbaum *m.* Christmas tree.
Christdemokrat *m.* (*pol.*) Christian Democrat.
Christengemeinde *f.* Christian community.
Christenheit *f.* (-, 0) Christendom.

Christentum *n.* (-s, 0) Christianity.
Christkind *n.* infant Jesus.
christlich *a.* Christian.
Christliche Wissenschaft *f.* (-,) Christian Science.
Christ: ~**messe** *f.* Christmas Mass; midnight service on Christmas eve; ~**nacht** *f.* Christmas night.
Christus *m.* Christ.
Chrom *n.* (-s, 0) chromium, chrome.
chromatisch *a.* chromatic.
Chromosom *n.* (-s, -en) chromosome.
Chronik *f.* (-, -en) chronicle.
chronisch *a.* chronic.
Chronist *m.* (-en, -en) chronicler.
Chronologie *f.* (-, -[e]n) chronology.
chronologisch *a.* chronological.
Chrysantheme *f.* chrysanthemum.
circa (*zirca*) *adv.* about, nearly.
Cis *n.* (-, 0) (*mus.*) C sharp.
city *f.* (-s, -) city center.
clever *a.* clever, smart; shrewd.
Clou *m.* main point.
Comeback *n.* comeback.

Comicheft *n.* comic.
Computer *m.* (-s, -) computer; *auf* ~ *umstellen* to computerize.
Conférencier *m.* emcee.
Container *m.* container.
Copyright *n.* (-s, -s) copyright.
Cord *m.* corduroy.
Couch *f.* (-, -es) couch.
Couchgarnitur *f.* three-piece suite.
Couchtisch *m.* coffee table.
Coup *m.* coup.
Coupé *n.* (-s, -s) compartment.
Couplet (*frz.*) *n.* (-s, -s) comic song.
Coupon *m.* (-s, -s) coupon, voucher.
Courage *f.* courage, pluck.
couragiert *a.* courageous.
Cousin *m.* (-s, -s) (male) cousin.
Cousine *f.* (-, -n) (female) cousin.
Crême (*frz.*) (-, 0) *f.* & *m.* cream.
cremig *a.* creamy.
Crew *f.* team, crew.
C-Schlüssel *m.* (*mus.*) C clef.
Cutter *m.*; **Cutterin** *f.* editor (film, TV).

D

D, d the letter D or d; (*mus.*) (key of) D.
da *adv.* there; then; ~ *c.* when; because, as, since; *wer* ~? who goes there?
dabehalten *v.t.st.* to keep (here).
dabei *adv.* thereby, near it; on this occasion; ~ *bleibt es,* that is agreed; *was ist* ~? what harm is there in that?
dabei: ~**bleiben** *v.i.st.* to stick to; to stay there; ~**haben** *v.t.st.* to have with one; ~**sein** *v.i.st.* to be there; to take part; ~**sitzen** *v.i.st.* to sit there; ~**stehen** *v.i.st.* to stand by.
dableiben *v.i.st.* (*s*) to stay, to remain.
da capo *i.* encore.
Dach *n.* (-[e]s, Dächer) roof.
Dach: ~**balken** *m.* rafters *pl.*; ~**boden** *m.* loft, garret; ~**decker** *m.* roofer, slater, tiler; ~**garten** *m.* roof garden; ~**gepäckträger** *m.* roof-rack; ~**geschoss** *n.* attic; ~**kammer** *f.* garret, attic; ~**pappe** *f.* roofing, roofing felt; ~**rinne** *f.* gutter.
Dachs *m.* (Dachses, Dachse) badger.
Dachshund *m.* dachshund.
Dach: ~**stuhl** *m.* framework of a roof; ~**ziegel** *m.* tile.
Dackel *m.* dachshund.
dadurch *adv.* thereby.
dafür *adv.* for that, for it; instead; *ich kann nichts dafür,* I cannot help it.
Dafürhalten *n., nach meinem* ~, in my opinion.
dafürkönnen *v.t.st.* *etwas/nichts* ~ to be/not be responsible.
dagegen *adv.* against that, in return, on the other hand.
dagegen: ~**halten** *v.t.st.* to counter, to object; ~**stellen** *v.refl.* to oppose it.
dahaben *v.t.st.* to have here/in the house.
daheim *adv.* at home.
daher *adv.* thence; therefore; along.
dahin *adv.* thither, to that place; *dahin,* gone; lost.
da: ~**hinab** *adv.* down there; ~**hinauf** *adv.* up

there; ~**hinaus** *adv.* out there.
dahinbringen *v.t.ir.* to manage to, to persuade, to prevail upon.
dahin: ~**dämmern** *v.i.* to be semiconscious; ~**eilen** *v.i.* to hurry along; to pass quickly.
dahinein *adv.* in there.
dahin: ~**gehen** *v.i.st.* to pass, to go by; ~**jagen** *v.i.* to race along; ~**kommen** *v.i.st.* (*s*) to come so far; **stellen** *v.t.* *dahingestellt sein lassen,* to leave undecided.
dahinten *adv.* over there.
dahinter *adv.* behind that, after it; *es steckt nichts* ~, there is nothing in it.
dahinter: ~**klemmen** *v.refl.* to buckle down to it; ~**stecken** *v.i.* to be behind it; ~**stehen** *v.i.st.* to support.
dahinziehen *v.i.st.* to drift by; to pass along.
Dahlie *f.* dahlia.
da: ~**lassen** *v.t.st.* to leave there; ~**liegen** *v.i.st.* to lie there.
damalig *a.* then, of that time.
damals *adv.* then, at that time.
Damast *m.* (-es, -e) damask.
Dame *f.* (-, -n) lady, gentlewoman; (*im Kartenspiel*) Queen; (*beim Tanzen*) partner; checkers, drafts.
Damen: ~**abteil** *n.* ladies' compartment; ~**binde** *f.* sanitary napkin.
damenhaft *a.* lady-like.
Damen: ~**mannschaft** *f.* women's team; ~**sattel** *m.* sidesaddle; ~**schneider** *m.* ladies' tailor.
damit *adv.* & *c.* with that; in order that; ~ *nicht,* lest.
dämlich *a.* (*fam.*) foolish.
Damm *m.* (-[e]s, Dämme) levee, dam, dike; mole; causeway; (*rail.*) embankment; (*fig.*) barrier.
Dammbruch *m.* bursting of a dike; rupture of the perineum.
dämmen *v.t.* to dam.
Dämmerlicht *n.* twilight; dim light.

dämmern *v.i.* to grow dusky, to dawn.
Dämmerung *f.* (-, -en) twilight, dusk, dawn.
dämmrig *a.* dim, day is breaking; night is falling.
Dämon *m.* (-s, Dämonen) demon.
dämonisch *a.* demoniac(al).
Dampf *m.* (-[e]s, Dämpfe) vapour; steam; fume.
Dampfdruckmesser *m.* steam pressure gauge.
dampfen *v.i.* to steam.
dämpfen *v.t.* to damp; (*fig.*) to quell; (*Speisen*) to stew.
Dampfer *m.* (-s, -) steamer.
Dämpfer *m.* (-s, -) damper.
Dämpf: ~**kessel** *m.* boiler; ~**kochtopf** *m.* pressure cooker; ~**maschine** *f.* steam engine; ~**schiff** *f.* steam vessel, steamer; ~**schiffahrt** *f.* steam-navigation.
Dampfwalze *f.* steam roller.
Damwild *n.* (-es, 0) fallow deer.
danach *adv.* after that; accordingly; ~ *aussehn*, to look like it.
Däne *m.;* **Dänin** *f.* Dane.
daneben *adv.* near it; besides.
Dänemark *n.* (-s, 0) Denmark.
danieder *adv.* on the ground; down; ~*liegen* *v.i.* to lie prostrate, to be depressed.
dänisch *a.* Danish.
Dank *m.* (-es, 0) thanks *pl.;* acknowledgment; gratitude; vote of thanks.
dankbar *a.* thankful, grateful; profitable.
Dankbarkeit *f.* (-, 0) gratitude.
danke! thank you; ~ *nein*, no, thanks.
danken *v.i.* to thank; ~ *v.t.* (*einem etwas*) to be indebted to one for a thing.
dankenswert *a.* deserving of thanks.
Dankeschön *n.* thank-you.
Dankfest *n.* Thanksgiving Day.
Danksagung *f.* (-, -en) thanksgiving.
Dankschreiben *n.* letter of acknowledgment.
dann *adv.* then; ~ *und wann*, now and then.
daran *adv.* thereon, thereat; by, of, about it; *es ist nichts* ~, it is not true; *er ist* ~, it is his turn.
darankommen *v.i.st. ich komme daran*, it is my turn.
darauf *adv.* thereupon, thereon; on that; after that.
daraus *adv.* out of that, therefrom; thence; *es wird nichts* ~, it won't come to anything.
darben *v.i.* to suffer want; to starve.
darbieten *v.t.st.* to perform, to offer, to present.
Darbietung *f.* presentation, performance.
darbringen *v.t.ir.* to tender, to render, to offer up.
darein *adv.* into it, therein.
darf *s.***dürfen.**
darin(nen) *adv.* therein; in it, in this.
darlegen *v.t.* (*fig.*) to explain, to prove.
Darlehen *n.* (-s, -) loan.
Darlehnskasse *f.* loan bank.
Darm *m.* (-[e]s, Därme) gut; bowels, intestines *pl.*
Darm ... enteric.
Darm: ~**saite** *f.* catgut; ~**spiegelung** *f.* enteroscopy; ~**trägheit** *f.* constipation; ~**verschluß** *m.* ileus.
darnach *s.* **danach.**
darreichen *v.t.* to reach, to hand, to present.
darstellen *v.t.* exhibit; to represent; to personate, to act; (*chem.*) to produce.
Darsteller *m.* (-s, -); **Darstellerin** *f.* (-, -nen)

performer.
Darstellung *f.* (-, -en) presentation, representation, exhibition.
dartun *v.t.st.* to demonstrate.
darüber *adv.* over it, about it; concerning that; above, upwards.
darüber: ~**liegen** *v.i.st.* to be higher; ~**stehen** *v.i.st.* to be above such things.
darum *adv.* around that; therefore, for that reason; ~ *kommen*, to lose.
darunter *adv.* under that, beneath it; below that; among them, between them.
darunter: ~**fallen** *v.i.st.* to be included; to be in the same category; ~**liegen** *v.i.st.* to be lower; ~**setzen** *v.t.* to put (signature) to it.
das *art. pn.* the; that; which.
dasein *v.i.ir.* (*s*) to be present; to exist.
Dasein *n.* (-, 0) existence; presence.
Daseinsberechtigung *f.* right to exist.
daselbst *adv.* there, in that place.
dasitzen *v.i.st.* to sit there.
daß *c.* that; ~ *nicht*, lest.
Datei *f.* (-, -en) data file.
Daten *pl.* data, facts.
Daten: ~**bank** *f.* data bank; ~**erfassung** *f.* data collection; ~**missbrauch** *m.* data abuse; ~**netz** *n.* data network; ~**schutz** *m.* data protection; ~**speicherung** *f.* data storage; ~**technik** *f.* data systems engineering; ~**übermittlung** *f.* data transfer; ~**verarbeitung** *f.* data processing.
datieren *v.t.* to date.
Dativ *m.* (-[e]s, -e) dative (case).
Dattel *f.* (-, -n) date.
Datum *n.* (-[s], Daten) date; *ohne* ~, undated.
Dauer *f.* (-, 0) duration; continuance; *auf die* ~, in the long run.
dauerhaft *a.* durable, lasting.
Dauerkarte *f.* season ticket.
dauern *v.i.* to last, to continue; to abide; *er dauert mich*, I pity him; *es dauert mich*, I regret it.
dauernd *a. & adv.* constant(ly), permanent(ly).
Dauerwelle *f.* perm; permanent wave.
Daumen *m.* (-s, -) thumb.
Daumenschraube *f.* thumbscrew.
Daune *f.* (-, -n) down.
Daunendecke *f.* (-, -n) duvet.
davon *adv.* thereof, therefrom, of that; off, away; ~**kommen**, to get away; ~**tragen**, to obtain, to win.
davor *adv.* before that; for that.
dazu *adv.* thereto, to that, to it; in addition to that; for that purpose; ~ *kommen* *v.i.st.* to arrive, to turn up.
dazuverdienen *v.t.* to earn on the side.
dazwischen *adv.* between them, among them.
dazwischen: ~**fahren** *v.i.st.* to step in; ~**kommen** *v.i.st.* to intervene; ~**liegen** *v.i.st.* to lie in between; ~**reden** *v.i.* to interrupt; ~**treten** *v.i.st.* to intervene.
dealen *v.t.* to sell drugs.
Debatte *f.* (-, -n) debate.
debattieren *v.i.* to debate.
Debüt *n.* (-s, -s) debut; first appearance.
debütieren *v.i.* to make one's debut.
dechiffrieren *v.t.* to decipher; to decode.
Deck *n.* (-[e]s, -e) deck.

Deck: ~**adresse** *f.* cover address; ~**bett** *n.* (-s, -en) duvet; ~**blatt** *n.* cover page; (*Zigarren*) wrapper.

Decke *f.* (-, -n) cover; blanket, coverlet, quilt; (*eines Zimmers*) ceiling; *unter einer* ~ *stecken,* to conspire together.

Deckel *m.* (-s, -) cover; lid; top.

decken *v.t.* to cover, to roof; (*com.*) to reimburse, to refund; *den Tisch* ~, to lay the table.

Deckengemälde *n.* ceiling painting.

Deck: ~**mantel** *m.* (*pej.*) cover; ~**name** *m.* pseudonym; ~**offizier** *m.* warrant officer.

Deckung *f.* (-, -en) (*com.*) reimbursement; (*mil.*) cover; **Golddeckung** *f.* gold backing; *Zahlungsmittel mit Dollardeckung,* dollar-backed instruments.

deckungsgleich *a.* (*geom.*) congruent.

Deckweiß *n.* opaque white.

Deckwort *n.* codeword.

deduktiv *a.* deductive.

de facto *adv.* de facto, in reality.

Defätismus *m.* defeatism.

Defätist *m.* (-en, -en) defeatist.

Defekt *m.* (-[e]s, -e) defect, deficiency; ~ *a.* defective, incomplete.

defensiv *a.* defensive.

Defensive *f.* (-, 0) defensive; *in die* ~*gehen,* to go over to the defensive.

defilieren *v.i.* (*s*) to march past.

definieren *v.t.* to define.

definierbar *a.* definable.

definitiv *a.* final.

Defizit *n.* (-s, -s) deficit, deficiency.

Deformation *f.* deformation; deformity.

deformieren *v.t.* to distort, to deform.

deftig *a.* solid; crude, coarse (speech).

Degen *m.* (-s, -) sword.

degenerieren *v.i.* to degenerate.

degradieren *v.t.* to downgrade; to demote; *zum Gemeinen* ~, to reduce to the ranks.

dehnbar *a.* elastic; (*Begriff*) vague.

dehnen *v.t.* to stretch, to extend.

Dehnung *f.* stretching; lengthening (pronunciation).

Deich *m.* (-[e]s, -e) dike, dam.

Deichsel *f.* (-, -n) pole, shaft.

dein *pn.* thy; your.

deinerseits *adv.* on/for your part.

deinesgleichen, the like of you.

deinetwegen, deinethalben *adv.* on your account, for your sake.

deinetwillen *adv.* um ~ for your sake.

de jure *adv.* de jure, legally.

Dekade *f.* (-, -n) decade.

dekadent *a.* decadent.

Dekadenz *f.* decadence.

Dekan *m.* (-s, -e) dean.

Dekanat *n.* (-s, -e) dean's office.

Deklamation *f.* (-, -en) declamation.

deklamieren *v.t.* to recite, to declaim.

deklarieren *v.t.* to declare.

Deklination *f.* (-, -en) declension.

deklinieren *v.t.* to decline.

Dekolleté *n.* neckline.

dekolletiert *s.* low (-necked).

Dekor *n.* (-s, -e) decoration.

Dekorateur *m.*; **Dekorateurin** *f.* window dresser; interior decorator.

Dekoration *f.* (-, -en) decoration.

dekorieren *v.t.* to decorate; *neu* ~, to redecorate.

Dekret *n.* (-[e]s, -e) decree.

dekretieren *v.t.* to decree.

Delegation *f.* (-, -en) delegation.

delegieren *v.t.* to delegate.

Delegierte *m./f.* (-n, -n) delegate.

delikat *a.* delicious, delicate.

Delikatesse *f.* (-, -n) delicacy, treat.

Delikt *n.* (-[e]s, -e) crime, offence.

Deliquent *m.* (-en, -en) offender.

delirieren *v.i.* to be delirious.

Delirium *n.* (-s, -rien) delirium.

Delle *f.* dent.

Delphin *m.* (-[e]s, -e) dolphin.

Delta *n.* (-s, -s) delta.

dem *art. dative* the.

Demagog[e] *m.* (-en, -en) demagogue.

demagogisch *a.* demagogic(al).

Demarkationslinie *f.* demarcation line.

demaskieren *v.t.* to unmask.

dementieren *v.t.* to deny.

Dementi *n.* (-s, -s) denial.

dementsprechend *adv.* accordingly.

demgegenüber *adv.* held against this.

demgemäss *adv.* accordingly.

demnach *c.* therefore, consequently.

demnächst *adv.* soon after; in the near future.

Demo *f.* demo.

demobilisieren *v.t. u. v.i.* to demobilize.

Demographie *f.* demography.

demographisch *a.* demographic.

Demokrat *m.* (-en, -en) democrat.

Demokratie *f.* (-, 0) democracy.

demokratisch *a.* democratic.

demokratisieren *v.t.* to democratize.

Demokratisierung *f.* democratization.

demolieren *v.t.* to demolish.

Demonstrant *m.*; **Demonstrantin** *f.* demonstrator.

Demonstration *f.* (-, -en) demonstration.

demonstrieren *v.t.* demonstrate.

Demontage *n.* (-, -n) dismantling.

demontieren *v.t.* to dismantle.

demoralisieren *v.t.* to demoralize.

Demoskop *m.*; **Demoskopin** *f.* opinion pollster.

Demoskopie *f.* opinion research.

demoskopisch *a.* ~ **Umfrage** *f.* opinion poll.

Demut *f.* (-, 0) humility, meekness.

demütig *a.* humble; submissive.

demütigen *v.t.* to humble, to humiliate.

Demütigung *f.* (-, -en) humiliation.

demzufolge *adv.* consequently.

den *art. accusative* the.

denkbar *a.* conceivable, imaginable.

denken *v.i.st.* to think (of).

Denken *n.* (-s, 0) thinking; thought.

Denker *m.* thinker.

denkfaul *a.* mentally lazy.

Denkfehler *m.* flaw in one's reasoning.

Denkmal *n.* (-[e]s, -mäler) monument.

Denk: ~**münze** *f.* medal; ~**schrift** *f.* memorial; memoir.

Denkweise *f.* way of thinking.

denkwürdig *a.* memorable.

Denkwürdigkeiten *f.pl.* memoirs.

Denkzettel *m.* refresher, reminder.
denn *c. & adv.* for; then; than.
dennoch *c.* yet, nevertheless.
Denunziant *m.* (-en, -en) informer.
denunzieren *v.t.* to denounce, to inform against.
Deo *n.* **Deodorant** *n.* (-s, -s) deodorant.
Depesche *f.* (-, -n) dispatch, telegram, wire.
deplaciert, deplaziert *a.* out of place.
Deponie *f.* (-, -n) dump.
deponieren *v.t.* to deposit, to depose.
deportieren *v.t.* to deport.
Deportierter *m.* deportee.
Depositen *n.pl.* deposits; **~kasse** *f.* (*Bank*) branch office.
Depot *n.* depot, warehouse.
Depp *m.* fool, idiot.
Depression *f.* (-, -en) depression.
depressiv *a.* depressive.
deprimieren *v.t.* to depress.
deprimierend *a.* depressing.
deprimiert *a.* depressed.
Deputierte[r] *m.* (-en, -en) deputy.
der, die, das, *art.* the; **der, die, das,** *pn.* that, who, which.
derartig *a.* such, of the kind.
derb *a.* compact; coarse.
Derbheit *f.* crudity, coarseness.
derenthalben, derentwegen, derentwillen *adv.* on their (her, whose) account.
dergestalt *adv.* in such a manner, thus.
dergleichen *adv.* such, such like.
Derivat *n.* (-[e]s, -e) (*chem.*) derivative.
derjenige, diejenige, dasjenige *pn.* that, this, he.
derlei *a.* of that kind.
dermassen *adv.* in such a degree *or* manner, so much.
derselbe, dieselbe, dasselbe *pn.* the same; he, she, it; that.
derweil(en) *adv.* while.
Derwisch *m.* (-[e]s, -e) dervish.
derzeit *adv.* at the moment.
derzeitig *a.* for the time being.
Des *n.* (*mus.*) D flat.
Desaster *n.* disaster.
desavouieren *v.t.* to disavow.
Deserteur *m.* (-[e]s, -e) deserter.
desertieren *v.i.* (*s*) to desert.
deshalb *c.* therefore.
Design *n.* (-s, -s) design.
Designer *m.;* **Designerin** *f.* designer.
desillusionieren *v.t.* to disillusion.
Desinfektion *f.* disinfection.
desinfizieren *v.t.* to disinfect.
Desinformation *f.* disinformation.
Desinteresse *n.* lack of interest.
desinteressiert *a.* uninterested.
desodorierend *a.* deodorant.
desolat *a.* wretched.
Despot *m.* (-en, -en) despot, tyrant.
Despotie *f.* (-, -n) despotism.
despotisch *a.* despotic.
Despotismus *m.* (-, 0) despotism.
dessentwegen, dessentwillen *adv.* on that account.
dessenungeachtet *adv.* notwithstanding.
Dessert *n.* (-s, -s) dessert.

destillieren *v.t.* to distill.
desto *adv.* the; ~ *besser,* so much the better.
Destruktion *f.* (-, -en) destruction.
destruktir *a. & adv.* destructive(ly).
deswegen *adv. & c.* therefore.
Detail *n.* (-s, -s) detail, particulars *pl.;* **~handel** *m.* retail trade.
detaillieren *v.t.* to detail, to itemize; to retail.
Detektiv *m.* (-s, -e); **Detektivin** *f.* (-, -nen) detective.
Detektor *m.* (-s, -en) detector.
Detonation *f.* detonation, blast.
detonieren *v.i.* to detonate.
Deut *m.* (-[e]s, -e) doit; farthing.
deuteln *v.t. & i.* to subtilize, to twist the meaning.
deuten *v.i.* to point (at *or* to); ~ *v.t.* to interpret, to explain.
deutlich *a.* clear, distinct; evident, plain.
Deutlichkeit *f.* clarity; distinctness.
deutsch *a.* German.
Deutsch(e) *n.* German (language).
Deutsche *m./f.* (-n, -n) German.
Deutschland *n.* Germany.
Deutschtum *n.* (-s, 0) Germanness.
Deutung *f.* (-, -en) interpretation.
Devise *f.* (-, -n) motto; foreign exchange; **~nzwangswirtschaft,** *f.* foreign exchange control.
devot *a.* obsequious.
Dezember *m.* (-s, -) December.
dezent *a.* quiet, subdued, discreet; *adv.* unostentatiously (dress).
dezentralisieren *v.t.* to decentralize.
Dezentralisierung *f.* decentralization.
Dezernat *n.* (-[e]s, -e) government department.
Dezernent *m.* (-en, -en) head of a government department.
dezimal *a.* decimal.
dezimieren *v.t.* to decimate.
Dia *n.* (-s, -s) slide.
Diabetiker *m.;* **Diabetikerin** *f.* diabetic.
diabolisch *a.* diabolic.
Diadem *n.* (-s, -e) diadem, tiara.
Diagnose *f.* (-, -n) diagnosis.
diagnostizieren *v.t.* to diagnose.
Diagonale *f.* (-, -n) diagonal.
Diagramm *n.* graph, diagram.
Diakon *m.* (-s, -e) deacon.
Diakonissin *f.* (-, -nen) deaconess.
Dialekt *m.* (-[e]s, -e) dialect.
Dialog *m.* (-[e]s, -e) dialogue.
Dialyze *f.* dialysis.
Diamant *m.* (-en, -en) diamond.
Diamantschleifer *m.* diamond cutter.
diametral *a.* diametrical.
Diarrhöe *f.* (-, -n) diarrhea.
Diät *f.* (-, 0) special diet.
Diäten *f.pl.* daily allowance.
Diätetik *f.* dietetics.
Diätetiker *m.* (-s, -); **Diätetikerin** *f.* (-, -nen) dietician.
dicht *a.* dense, solid, compact, close; tight.
Dichte *f.* density.
dichten *v.t.* to make watertight, to caulk.
dichten *v.t. & i.* to write poetry.
Dichter *m.* (-s, -) poet.

Dichterin *f.* (-, -nen) poet.
dichterisch *a.* poetic(al).
dicht: ~**gedrängt** *a.* tightly packed; ~**halten** *v.i.st.* (*fam.*) to keep one's mouth shut.
Dichtkunst *f.* poetry.
Dichtung *f.* (-, -en) poetry; (*mech.*) sealing, gasket.
Dichtungsring *m.* washer.
dick *a.* thick; stout; large, bulky; (*Milch*) curdled.
Dickdarm *m.* large intestine, great gut.
Dicke *f.* (-, 0) thickness, bigness, bulk.
dickflüssig *a.* sticky.
Dickhäuter *m.* pachyderm.
dickhäutig *a.* thick-skinned, callous, dull.
Dickicht *n.* (-[e]s, -e) thicket.
Dickkopf *m.* mule; pig-headed person.
dickköpfig *a.* stubborn, obstinate.
Didaktik *f.* didactics; teaching method.
die *art.pn.* the; that; which.
Dieb *m.* (-[e]s, -e); **Diebin** *f.* (-, -nen) thief.
diebisch *a.* thievish; (*Freude*) devilish.
Diebs (Diebes): ~**bande** *f.* gang of thieves.
Diebstahl *m.* (-[e]s, -stähle) theft, robbery.
Diele *f.* (-, -n) board, plank, deal; hall.
dienen *v.i.* to serve; to be serviceable.
Diener *m.* (-s, -), **Dienerin** *f.* (-, -nen) servant.
dienern *v.i.* (*pej.*) to bow.
Dienerschaft *f.* (-, -en) servants, domestics *pl.*
dienlich *a.* serviceable, useful.
Dienst *m.* (-[e]s, -e) service; employment, office; *im* ~, on duty; *ausser* ~, off duty, retired; ~ *leisten*, to render service.
Dienstag *m.* (-[e]s, -e) Tuesday.
dienstags *adv.* on Tuesdays.
Dienstalter *n.* seniority.
dienstälter *a.* senior.
Dienstantritt *m.* assumption of duty.
dienstbar *a.* subject; subservient; tributary.
Dienst: ~**bezüge** *pl.* salary; ~**bote** *m.* domestic servant; ~**eid** *m.* oath of office.
dienstreifrig *a.* zealous, officious, eager to serve.
dienstfrei *a.* exempt from service; off duty.
Dienst: ~**geheimnis** *n.* professional secret; ~**grad** *m.* (*nav.*) rank; ~**leistung** *f.* service; ~**leistungsbetrieb** *m.* business in the service sector; ~**liste** *f.* (*mil.*) roster.
dienstlich *a.* (*amtlich*) official.
Dienst: ~**mädchen** *n.* servant girl, maidservant; ~**pflicht** *f.* compulsory military service.
dienstpflichtig *a.* liable to service.
Dienstreise *f.* business trip.
Dienstsache *f.* official matter.
Dienst: ~**stelle** *f.* agency; ~**stunden** *f.pl.* duty hours; ~**tauglich** *a.* fit for service; ~**tuend** *a.* on duty; ~**turnus** *m.* work rotation.
dienstunfähig *a.* unfit for work, disabled, invalid.
Dienst: ~**wohnung** *f.* official residence; ~**zeit** *f.* working hours.
dies *s.* dieser.
Dieselmotor *m.* Diesel engine.
dieser, diese, dieses *pn.* this; the latter.
diesbezüglich *a.* referring to this.
diesjährig *a.* of this year, this year's.
diesmal *adv.* this time, for this once.
dies: ~**malig** *a.* present; ~**seitig** *a.* on this side.
diesseits *adv.* (on) this side.
Diesseits *n.* (-, 0) this world.

Dietrich *m.* (-[e]s, -e) picklock, burglar; skeleton key.
diffamieren *v.t.* to slander; to defame.
Diffamierung *f.* defamation.
Differentialrechnung *f.* differential calculus.
Differenz *f.* (-, -en) difference.
differenzieren *v.t.* (*math.*) to differentiate; *v.i.* to differentiate, to make a distinction.
differieren *v.i.* to differ.
diffus *a.* diffuse; vague.
digitalisieren *v.t.* to digitalize.
Diktat *n.* (-s, -e) dictation.
Diktator *m.* dictator.
diktatorisch *a.* dictatorial.
Diktatur *f.* (-, -en) dictatorship.
diktieren *v.t.* to dictate.
Dilettant *m.* (-en, -en) **Dilettantin** *f.* (-, -nen) (*pej.*) amateur.
Dill (-[e]s, -e) (*bot.*) dill.
Dimension *f.* dimension.
Ding *n.* (-[e]s, -e[r]) thing, matter; creature; *guter* ~*e sein*, to be in high spirits.
dingen *v.t.st.* to hire.
dingfest *a.*, ~ *machen*, to arrest.
dinglich *m.* (*law*) real.
Dinkel *m.* (-s, 0) spelt.
Dinosaurier *m.* (-s, -) dinosaur.
Dioxyd *n.* (-s, -e) dioxide.
Diözese *f.* (-, -n) diocese.
Diphtheritis *f.* (-, 0) diphtheria.
Diphthong *m.* (-s, -e) diphthong.
Diplom *n.* (-[e]s, -e) diploma, patent.
Diplomat *m.* (-n, -en) diplomat.
Diplomatie *f.* (-, 0) diplomacy.
diplomatisch *a.* diplomatic.
direkt *a.* direct.
Direktheit *f.* directness.
Direktion *f.* (-, -en) direction, management; board of directors.
Direktive *f.* (-, -n) instruction.
Direktor *m.* (-s, -en); **Direktorin** *f.* (-, -nen) director, manager; headmaster.
Direkt: ~**sendung** *f.*, ~**übertragung** *f.* live broadcast; ~**wahl** *f.* direct election.
Dirigent *m.* (-en, -en) (*mus.*) conductor.
Dirigenten: ~**pult** *n.* conductor's rostrum; ~**stab** *m.* baton.
dirigieren *v.t.* to direct; (*mus.*) to conduct.
Dirne *f.* (-, -n) maid, lass, prostitute.
Dis *n.* (-, 0) (*mus.*) D sharp.
Disharmonie *f.* (-e -[e]n) disharmony.
Diskette *f.* (-, -n) d(*comp.*) floppy disc.
Diskettenlaufwerk *n.* (-s, -e) disc drive.
Diskant *m.* (-[e]s, -e) treble, soprano.
Diskont, Diskonto *m.* (-s, -s *u.* -i) discount.
Diskontsatz *m.* discount rate.
diskontieren *v.t.* to discount.
Diskothek *f.*, **Disko** *f.* disco.
diskreditieren *v.t.* to bring into disrepute.
Diskrepanz *f.* discrepancy.
diskret *a. & adv.* discreet; discreetly.
Diskretion *f.* (-, 0) discretion.
diskriminieren *v.t.* to discriminate against, to disparage.
diskriminierend *a.* disparaging.
Diskriminierung *f.* discrimination.

Diskussion *f.* (-, -en) discussion.
diskutieren *v.t.* to debate, to discuss.
Dispens *m.* (-es, -e) dispensation, license.
dispensieren *v.t.* to dispense (of), to excuse, to exempt (from).
Disponent *m.* (-en, -en) manager.
disponieren *v.i.* to make plans, to plan ahead.
Disposition *f.* (-, -en) arrangement, disposition.
Disput *m.* (-[e]s, -e) dispute.
disputieren *v.i.* to dispute; to argue.
disqualifizieren *v.t.* to disqualify.
Dissertation *f.* (-, -en) thesis, dissertation.
Dissident *m.* (-en, -en); **Dissidentin** *f.* (-, -nen) dissident.
Dissonanz *f.* (-, -en) dissonance, discord.
Distanz *f.* (-, -en) distance.
distanzieren (sich) *v.refl.* to dissociate oneself from.
Distel *f.* (-, -n) thistle.
distinguiert *a.* distinguished, distinguished-looking.
Distrikt *m.* (-[e]s, -e) district.
Disziplin *f.* (-, -en) discipline.
Disziplinar ... disciplinary: **~gewalt** *f.* disciplinary power; **~verfahren** *n.* disciplinary action *or* proceedings.
disziplinieren *v.t.* to discipline; *v.refl.* to discipline oneself.
dito *adv.* (*com.*) ditto.
Dividende *f.* (-, -n) dividend.
dividieren *v.t.* to divide.
Division *f.* (-, -en) (*auch mil.*) division.
Diwan *m.* (-s, -s) divan, sofa.
doch *c.* yet; however; but, nevertheless; *ja* ~! yes, to be sure!; *nicht* ~! certainly not! don't!; yes (after negat. clause).
Docht *m.* (-[e]s, -e) wick.
Dock *n.* (-s. -s *u.* -e) dock, dockyard.
Dogge *f.* (-, -n) Great Dane; mastiff.
dogmatisch *a. & adv.* dogmatic, dogmatically.
Dohle *f.* (-, -n) jackdaw.
Doktor *m.* (-s, -en) doctor; physician.
Doktor: **~arbeit** *f.* dissertation; **~würde** *f.* doctorate.
Doktrinär *m.* (-s, -e) doctrinaire, theorist.
Dokument *n.* (-[e]s, -e) document.
Dokumentarfilm *m.* documentary.
dokumentieren *v.t.* to prove by documentary evidence.
Dolch *m.* (-[e]s, -e) dagger, poniard, dirk.
Dolde *f.* (*bot.*) umbel.
doll *a.* (*fam.*) great; amazing.
Dollar *m.* (-(s), -s) dollar.
dolmetschen *v.t.* to interpret.
Dolmetscher *m.* (-s, -); **Dolmetscherin** *f.* (-, -nen) interpreter.
Dom *m.* (-[e]s, -e) cathedral.
Domäne *f.* (-, -n) domain, crown land.
domestizieren *v.t.* to domesticate.
Domherr *m.* canon, prebendary.
dominant *a.* dominant.
Dominante *f.* (*mus.*) dominant (chord).
Dominanz *f.* dominance.
dominieren *v.i.* to domineer (over).
Dominikaner *m.*; **Dominikanerin** *f.*; **dominikanisch** *a.* Dominican.

Dominikanische Republik *f.* Dominican Republic.
Domino: **~spiel** *n.* dominoes *pl.*; **~stein** *m.* domino.
Domizil *n.* domicile, residence.
Domkapitel *n.* cathedral chapter.
Dompteur *m.*; **Dompteuse** *f.* tamer.
Donau *f.* Danube.
Donner *m.* (-s, -) thunder; *von* ~ *gerührt*, thunderstruck.
donnern *v.i.* to thunder.
Donnerschlag, *m.* thunderclap.
Donnerstag *m.* (-[e]s, -e) Thursday.
donnerstags *adv.* Thursdays.
Donnerwetter *n.*, ~! *i.* wow!; damn it!
doof *a.* stupid, dumb.
Doofheit *f.* stupidity.
dopen *v.t.* to dope.
Doping *n.* doping.
Doppel *n.* (-s, -) duplicate copy; doubles.
Doppel: **~decker** *m.* biplane.
doppeldeutig *a.* ambiguous.
Doppel: **~fenster** *n.* double window; **~flinte** *f.* double-barrelled gun; **~gänger** *m.* double.
doppelläufig *a.* double-barrelled.
Doppel: **~moral** *f.* double standard; **~name** *m.* hyphenated name; **~punkt** *m.* colon.
doppelseitige Lungenentzündung *f.* double pneumonia.
doppelsinnig *a.* ambiguous.
Doppelspiel *n.* (tennis) doubles; (*fig.*) double game.
doppelt *a.* double, twofold; ~*e Buchführung*, bookkeeping by double entry.
doppelzüngig *a.* two-faced.
Doppelzüngigkeit *f.* (-, -en) duplicity.
Dorf *n.* (-[e]s, Dörfer) village.
Dorfbewohner *m.* (-s, -); **Dorfbewohnerin** *f.* (-, -nen) villager.
dörflich *a.* village; rural.
Dorn *m.* (-[e]s, -en *u.* -e) thorn, prickle.
dornig *a.* (*fig.*) thorny.
dörren *v.t.* to dry.
Dörrobst *n.* (-[e]s, 0) dried fruit.
Dorsch *m.* (-[e]s, -e) cod; torsk, codling.
dort *adv.* there, yonder.
dort: **~bleiben** *v.i.st.* to stay there; **~her** *adv.* from there; **~hin** *adv.* there; **~hinab** *adv.* down there; **~hinauf** *adv.* up there; **~hinaus** *adv.* out there.
dortig *a.* of that place; residing there.
Dose *f.* (-, -n) can; box; snuffbox.
Dosenöffner *m.* can opener.
dosieren *v.t.* to dose.
Dosis *f.* (-, Dosen) dose; *zu starke* ~, overdose.
dotieren *v.t.* to endow.
Dotter *m. or n.* (-s, -) yolk.
Dotterblume *f.* marsh marigold.
Double *n.* stand-in; double.
Dozent *m.* (-en, -en); **Dozentin** *f.* (-, -nen) lecturer, university teacher.
Drache *m.* (-n, -n) dragon; (paper) kite.
Drachenfliegen *n.* hang gliding.
Dragoner *m.* (-[e]s, -) dragoon.
Draht *m.* (-[e]s, Drähte) wire; cable.
Drahtbürste *f.* wirebrush.
drahten *v.t.* to wire.

Draht: ~**geflecht** *n.* wire netting; ~**los** *a.* wireless; ~**seil** *n.* wire rope; ~**seilbahn** *f.* cable railway; ~**verhau** *n.* wire entanglements; ~**zange** *f.* pliers *pl.*; ~**zieher** *m.* wirepuller.
drakonisch *a.* Draconian.
drall *a.* strapping; full; rounded.
Drama *n.* (-[e]s, Dramen) drama; (*fig.*) disaster.
Dramatiker *m.* (-s, -) dramatist, playwright.
dramatisch *a.* dramatic.
Dramaturg *m.*; **Dramaturgin** *f.* dramaturge.
Dramaturgie *f.* dramaturgy.
dran = **daran.**
Dränage *f.* (-, -n) drainage.
dranbleiben *v.i.* to hold (tel.); to stick at (work).
Drang *m.* (-[e]s, 0) urge; pressure; impulse.
drängen *v.t.* to throng, to press; to urge.
Drangsal *n.* (-[e]s, -e *u.* f. -, -e) hardship; distress, misery.
drangsalieren *v.t.* to worry, to torment.
dränieren *v.t.* to drain.
drastisch *a.* drastic; strong.
drauf = **darauf.**
Draufgänger *m.* daredevil.
draufgängerisch *a.* daring, audacious.
drauf: ~**gehen** *v.i.st.* (*fam.*) to be killed; to be lost (money); ~**kriegen** *v.t. einen draufkriegen* ~ to get it in the neck; ~**legen** *v.t.* to pay extra; ~**los** *adv.* straight ahead; right away; ~**machen** *v.t. einen draufmachen* ~ to have a ball; ~**stehen** *v.i.st.* to be on it.
draußen *adv.* outside, out of doors.
Drechselbank *f.* turner's lathe.
drechseln *v.t.* to turn (on a lathe).
Drechsler *m.* (-s, -) turner.
Drechslerarbeit, Drechslerei *f.* turnery.
Dreck *m.* (-[e]s, 0) dirt, filth.
dreckig *a.* dirty, muddy, filthy.
Dreck: ~**sack** *m.* (*vulg.*) bastard; ~**schwein** *n.* (*fam.*) filthy swine.
Dreckskerl *m.* swine.
Dreh: ~**bank** *f.* (turner's) lathe; ~**buch** *n*, (Film) script, scenario; ~**brücke** *f.* swing bridge.
drehen *v.t.* to turn; (*Film*) to shoot; (sich) ~ *v.refl.* to turn, to rotate, to revolve; *sich drehen um,* to pivot round.
Dreher *m.* (-s, -) (*mech.*) lathe operator.
Dreh: ~**kreuz** *n.* turnstile; ~**orgel** *f.* barrel organ; ~**punkt** *m.* pivot; ~**schalter** *m.* (*el.*) rotary switch; ~**scheibe** *f.* potter's wheel; (*rail.*) turntable; ~**strom** *m.* three-phase current; ~**tür** *f.* revolving door; ~**stuhl** *m.* swivel chair.
Drehung *f.* (-, -en) turn; revolution.
drei *a.* three.
Dreiachteltakt *m.* (-[e]s, -e) (*mus.*) three-eighth time.
dreibeinig *a.* three-legged.
dreidimensional *a.* three-dimensional.
Dreieck *n.* (-[e]s, -e) triangle.
dreieckig *a.* triangular, three-cornered.
Dreiecksverhältnis *n.* love triangle.
dreierlei *a.* of three kinds.
dreifach *a.* threefold, treble; ~*e Ausfertigung,* triplicate.
Dreifaltigkeit *f.* (-, 0) Trinity.
Dreifuß *m.* (-es, -füsse) tripod; trivet.
dreijährig *a.* three years old; triennial.

Dreiklang *m.* (-[e]s, 0) (*mus.*) triad.
Dreikönigsfest *n.* Twelfth Night; Epiphany.
Dreimächte... tripartite.
dreimal *adv.* three times, thrice.
drein = **darein.**
Dreirad *n.* (-[e]s, -räder) tricycle.
Dreisatz *m.* (*math.*) rule of three.
dreisilbig *a.* trisyllabic.
dreispurig *a.* three-laned.
dreißig *a.* thirty.
Dreißiger *m.* (-s, -) man of thirty years.
dreißiger *a. die ~ Jahre* the thirties.
dreißigjährig *a.* thirty-year.
dreist *a.* bold, brazen.
Dreistigkeit *f.* (-, -en) boldness, brazenness.
Dreivierteltakt *m.* (-[e]s, 0) triple time *or* measure.
Dreizack *m.* (-[e]s, -e) trident.
dreizehn *a.* thirteen.
dreschen *v.t.st.* to thresh, to thrash, to wallop, to bang.
Dresch: ~**flegel** *m.* flail; ~**maschine** *f.* threshing machine; ~**tenne** *f.* threshing floor.
dressieren *v.t.* to break in (horses); to train dogs, etc.
Dressman *m.* male model.
Dressur *f.* (-, -en) breaking in; training.
Drillbohrer *m.* drill.
drillen *v.t.* to drill.
Drillich *m.* (-[e]s, -e) ticking.
Drillichanzug *m.* fatigue dress.
Drilling *m.* (-[e]s, -e) triplet; lantern wheel; three-barrelled gun.
drin = **darin.**
dringen *v.t. & i.st.* to urge; to penetrate.
dringend *a.* urgent.
dringlich *a.* urgent, pressing.
Dringlichkeit *f.* urgency.
drinnen *adv.* inside, within.
dritte *a.* third; ~ *Person* (*law*) third party; ~**Welt** *f.* Third World.
Drittel *n.* (-s, -) third part, third.
drittens *adv.* thirdly.
drittletzt *a.* last but two, antepenultimate.
droben *adv.* above, on high, overhead.
Drogen *pl.* drugs *pl.*.
drogenabhängig *a.* addicted to drugs.
Drogenabhängige *m./f.* (-, -n) drug addict.
Drogenabhängigkeit *f.* drug addiction.
Drogerie *f.* (-, -n) drugstore, pharmacy.
Drogist *m.* (-en, -en) druggist.
Drohbrief *m.* threatening letter.
drohen *v.i.* to threaten, to menace.
drohend *a.* threatening.
Drohne *f.* (-, -n) drone.
dröhnen *v.i.* to boom, to roar.
Drohung *f.* (-, -en) threat, menace.
drollig *a.* droll, odd, funny.
Dromedar *n.* dromedary.
Droschke *f.* (-, -n) hackney carriage.
Drossel *f.* (-, -n) thrush.
drosseln *v.t.* to throttle; to reduce.
drüben, da drüben *adv.* over there.
drüber = **darüber.**
Druck *m.* (-[e]s, -e *u.* Drücke) pressure, compression; oppression; print, impression; ~ *auf einen*

ausüben, to put pressure on someone.
Druck: ~**abfall** *m.* drop in pressure; ~**bogen** *m.* proof (sheet); ~**buchstabe** *m.* printed letter.
Drückeberger *m.* (-s, -) shirker.
druckempfindlich *a.* pressure-sensitive.
drucken *v.t.* to print.
drücken *v.t.* to press, to squeeze; (*Schuhe*) to pinch; (*Preise*) to bring down; (sich) ~ *v.refl.* to shirk work.
drückend *a.* burdensome; heavy; oppressive.
Drucker *m.* (-s, -) printer.
Drücker *m.* (-s, -) trigger; latch.
Druckerei (-, -en) *f.* printing plant.
Drucker: ~**presse** *f.* printing press; ~**schwärze** *f.* printer's ink.
Druckfehler *m.* misprint.
druckfertig *a.* ready for the press.
druckfest *a.* pressure-resistant.
Druck: ~**knopf** *m.* patent fastener; ~**sache** *f.* printed matter; ~**schrift**, print.
drum = **darum**.
drunten *adv.* there below.
drunter und drüber, upside down.
Drüse *f.* (-, -n) gland.
Dschungel *m.* (-s, -) jungle.
du *pn.* thou; you.
Dübel *m.* dowel, peg; **dübeln** *v.t.* to dowel.
Dublee *n.* gold plate.
ducken *v.t.* to duck; to humble; (*sich*) ~, to submit, to stoop.
Duckmäuser (-s, -) *m.* sneak, cringer.
dudeln *v.i.* (*fam.*) to tootle.
Dudelsack *m.* (-[e]s, -säcke) bagpipes.
Dudelsackpfeifer *m.* bagpiper.
Duell *n.* (-[e]s, -e) duel.
duellieren (sich) *v.refl.* to fight a duel.
Duett *n.* (-[e]s, -e) duet.
Duft *m.* (-[e]s, Düfte) scent, fragrance.
duften *v.i.* to smell sweet.
duftend *a.* fragrant.
Duft: ~**stoff** *m.* aromatic substance; ~**wasser** *n.* perfume, scent; ~**wolke** *f.* cloud of perfume.
dulden *v.t.* to endure; to tolerate.
duldsam *a. & adv.* tolerant(ly); patient.
Duldsamkeit *f.* tolerance; patience.
Duldung *f.* tolerance.
dumm *a.* dull, stupid.
dummerweise *adv.* unfortunately; annoyingly.
Dummheit *f.* (-, -en) stupidity; blunder.
Dummkopf *m.* (-[e]s, -köpfe) idiot; blockhead.
dümmlich *a.* simpleminded.
dumpf *a.* hollow, dull; close, musty.
Düne *f.* (-, -n) sandhill, dune.
düngen *v.t.* to manure.
Dünger *m.* (-s, -) dung, manure; fertilizer.
Dunkel *n.* darkness.
Dünkel *m.* (-s, 0) conceit, arrogance.
dunkel *a.* dark, dusky, gloomy; obscure; mysterious.
dünkelhaft *a.* arrogant, conceited.
Dunkelheit *f.* (-, -en) darkness; obscurity.
Dunkelkammer *m.* (*phot.*) darkroom.
dunkeln *v.i.* *es dunkelt*, it is growing dark.
Dunkelziffer *f.* estimated number of unknown cases.
dünken *v.t.imp.* to seem, to appear; to think.

dünn *a.* thin, fine, slender; (*Getränk*) weak; (*Luft*) rare.
Dünndruckpapier *n.* (-s, -e) India paper, Bible paper.
Dünne *f.* (-, 0) thinness; sparseness.
Dunst *m.* (-es, Dünste) haze; mist; vapor; steam; fume (of wine).
Dunstabzug *m.* extractor, range hood.
dünsten *v.t.* to stew, to steam, to braise.
Dunstglocke *f.* blanket of smog.
dunstig *a.* vaporous; hazy.
Duo *n.* (*mus.*) duet; duo.
Duodez *n.* (-es, 0) duodecimo.
düpieren *v.t.* to dupe.
Duplikat *n.* (-[e]s, -e) duplicate.
Dur *n.* (*mus.*) major.
durch *pr.* through, by; ~ *a.* well-done; ~ **und** ~, thoroughly; ~ *und* ~ *nass*, wet through.
durcharbeiten *v.t.* to work through.
durchaus *adv.* by all means, absolutely; ~ *nicht*, by no means.
durchbeißen (sich) ~ *v.refl.st.* (fig.) to fight one's way through; *v.t.st.* to bite through.
durchblättern *v.t.* to skim (a book).
Durchblick *m.* den ~ *haben* to know what's going on.
durchblicken: to look through; ~ *lassen*, to give to understand.
durchbohren *v.t.* to pierce, to perforate.
durchboxen *v.refl.* to fight one's way through.
durchbrechen *v.t. & i.st.* (s) to break through.
durchbrennen *v.i.ir.* (s) (*el.*) to blow, to fuse; (*fig.*) to run away, to abscond.
durchbringen *v.t.ir.* to squander; to get past/through/accepted.
durchbrochen *a.* open (pierced) work.
Durchbruch *m.* (-[e]s, -brüche) breach; (*mil.*) breakthrough.
durchchecken *v.t.ir.* to check thoroughly.
durchdenken *v.t.ir.* to think over.
durchdrängen (sich) *v.refl.* to elbow one's way (through the crowd).
durchdrehen *v.i.* to mince; (*fig.*) to flip; to panic.
durchdringen *v.t.st.* to come through; to penetrate; ~*v.i.st.* (s)(fig.) to prevail.
durchdringend *a.* piercing, penetrating, sharp.
durchdrücken *v.t.* to press s.th. through; to straighten (leg); to manage to get (benefits).
durcheinander *adv.* in a mess; confused.
Durcheinander *n.* (-s, 0) muddle; confusion, mess.
durchfahren *v.i.st.* to pass through.
Durchfahrt *f.* (-, -en) passage, thoroughfare, gateway; transit.
Durchfall *m.* (-[e]s, -fälle) diarrhea.
durchfallen *v.i.st.* (s) to fall through; to fail; to flunk (an examination).
durchfinden *v.t.st.* (sich) to find one's way.
durchfließen *v.i.st.* (s) *u.* *v.t.st.* to flow through.
durchfluten *v.t.* to flood (through).
durchforschen *v.t.* to explore.
Durchforschung *f.* (-, -en) exploration.
durchforsten *v.t.* to sift through.
durchfragen (sich) *v.refl.* to ask one's way through.
durchfressen *v.t.st.* to eat through; to corrode.

durchfrieren *v.i. durchgefroren sein* to be frozen stiff.

Durchfuhr *f.* (-, 0) transit.

durchführbar *a.* practicable; feasible.

Durchführbarkeit *f.* practicability; feasibility.

durchführen *v.t.* to accomplish, to implement, to carry out.

durchfurchen *v.t.* to furrow, to wrinkle; to plow (the sea).

durchfüttern *v.t.* to feed; (*fig.*) to support.

Durchgang *m.* (-[e]s, -gänge) passage, transit; **~slager** *n.* transit camp; **~sverkehr** *m.* transit traffic; **~szoll** *m.* transit duty.

durchgängig *a.* general, common; ~ *adv.* in all cases, generally.

durchgehen *v.t.st.* to peruse, to go through; ~ *v.i.st.* (*s*) to abscond; to bolt.

durchgehend *a.* (*Zug, Fahrkarte*) through.

durchgehends *a.* generally, universally.

durchgeistigen *v.t.* to spiritualize.

durchgreifen *v.i.st.* to crack down (on); to take energetic action.

durchgreifend *a.* determined, energetic.

durchhalten *v.t.* to hold out; ~ *v.i.* to stick it out.

durchhängen *v.i.st.* to sag.

durchhauen *v.t.ir.* to cut through; to flog.

durchhecheln *v.t.* to criticize.

durchhelfen *v.i.st.* to support; (sich) ~ *v.refl.* to make shift.

durchkämpfen *v.t.* to fight out.

durchkommen *v.i.st.* (*s*) to get through; (*Prüfung*) to pass; to succeed; to recover.

durchkönnen *v.i.ir.* to be able to pass.

durchkreuzen *v.t.* to cross; to thwart.

durchlassen *v.t.st.* to let pass, to let through.

durchlässig *a.* permeable.

Durchlässigkeit *f.* permeability.

Durchlaucht *f.* (-, -en) Serene Highness.

Durchlauf *m.* run; flow.

durchlaufen *v.i.st.* (*s*) to run through; ~ *v.t.st.* to wear out (shoes); to run over (a book).

durchlanfend *a.* continuous; in sequence.

Durchlauferhitzer *m.* instantaneous water heater.

durchleben *v.t.* to live through.

durchlesen *v.t.st.* to read through, to peruse.

durchleuchten *v.t.* to screen, to X-ray; to investigate.

durchlöchern *v.t.* to perforate; to riddle.

durchmachen *v.t.* to go through.

Durchmarsch *m.* (-es, -märsche) (troops) transit.

durchmessen *v.t.st.* to cross, to traverse.

Durchmesser *m.* (-s, -) diameter.

durchmogeln *v.refl.* to cheat one's way through.

durchmüssen *v.i.ir.* to have to pass through.

durchmustern *v.t.* to scan, to review.

durchnässen *v.t.* to soak, to wet through.

durchnehmen *v.t.st.* to deal with, to go over.

durchpausen *v.t.* to trace.

durchpeitschen *v.t.* to thrash; (*fig.*) to rush through.

durchprügeln *v.t.* to thrash.

durchqueren *v.t.* to cross.

durchrechnen *v.t.* to calculate, to examine.

durchreiben *v.t.st.* to rub a hole in.

Durchreise *f.* (-, -n) passage, passing through.

durchreisen *v.i.* (*s*) to travel through.

durchreißen *v.t.st.* to tear in half.

durchringen *v.refl.* to make up one's mind.

durchrosten *v.i.* to rust through.

durchs durch das.

Durchsage *f.* announcement.

durchsäuern *v.t.* to leaven thoroughly.

durchschaubar *a.* transparent.

durchschauen *v.i.* to look through; ~ *v.t.* (*fig.*) to see through.

durchscheinen *v.i.st.* (*s*) to shine through; to be transparent.

durchscheinend *a.* translucent.

durchscheuern *v.t.* to wear through.

durchschimmern *v.i.* to shimmer/gleam through.

Durchschlag *m.* (-[e]s, -schläge) (carbon) copy.

durchschlagen *v.i.st.* to penetrate; (*fig.*) to tell, to have effect; (sich) ~ *v.refl.st.* to rough it.

durchschlagend *a.* resounding (success); decisive.

durchschlüpfen *v.i.* (*s*) to slip through.

durchschneiden (sich) *v.refl.st.* to cut.

Durchschnitt *m.* (-[e]s, -e) cut; average.

durchschnittlich *a. & adv.* average; on an average.

durchschreiten *v.t.st.* to stride through.

durchschwitzen *v.t.* to soak with sweat.

durchsehen *v.t.st.* to revise, to look over.

durchseihen *v.t.* to filter, to strain.

durchsein *v.i.ir.* (*s*) to be done with.

durchsetzen *v.t.* (*fig.*) to carry through; to mix with.

durchsetzt (mit) *a.* honeycombed with.

Durchsetzungskraft *f.*, **Durchsetzungsvermögen** *n.* self assertion.

Durchsicht *f.* (-, -en) revision, perusal.

durchsichtig *a.* transparent.

durchsickern *v.i.* (*s*) to trickle through, to ooze through; (*fig.*) to leak through.

durchsieben *v.t.* to sift, to bolt.

durchspielen *v.t.* to go through (a piece of music).

durchsprechen *v.t.st.* to talk (a thing) over.

durchstehen *v.t.st.* to stand; to come through; to get over (illness).

durchstellen *v.i.* to put through (call).

Durchstich *m.* (-[e]s, -e) (*rail.*) cutting, excavation.

durchstöbern *v.t.* to rummage, to ransack.

durchstossen *v.t.st.* to break by thrusting; to pierce, to run through the body.

durchstreichen *v.t.st.* to cross out; to delete.

durchstreifen *v.t.* to roam through.

durchströmen *v.t.* to flow through.

durchsuchen *v.t.* to search, to ransack.

Durchsuchung *f.* (-, -en) search.

Durchsuchungsbefehl *m.* search warrant.

durchtränken *v.t.* to soak with.

durchtrennen *v.t.* to cut, to sever.

durchtrieben *a.* sly; arrant, cunning.

durchwachsen *a.* (*vom Fleisch*) streaked, streaky; (*fig.*) mixed.

Durchwahl *f.* direct dialing.

durchwählen *v.i.* to dial direct.

durchwärmen *v.t.* to warm thoroughly.

durchweg *adv.* throughout.

durchweichen *v.t.* to soak thoroughly, to drench; ~ *v.i.* (*s*) to become soft.

durchwinden *v.t.st.* to entwine; (sich) ~ *v.refl.st.* to struggle through.

durchwischen *v.i.* (*s*) to slip away.

durchwühlen *v.i.* to root up (*fig.*) to ransack.

durchzählen *v.t.* to count up.

durchzucken *v.t.* to flash across; to cross s.b. mind.

Durchzug *m.* (-[e]s, -züge) passage, march through; draft.

dürfen *v.i.ir.* to be allowed; *darf ich?* may I?; *du darfst nicht*, you must not.

dürftig *a.* needy, indigent; scanty, insufficient.

dürr *a.* dry, arid; withered; barren; lean; ~*e Worte*, plain language.

Dürre *f.* (-, -n) drought.

Durst *m.* (-es, 0) thirst.

dursten, dürsten *v.i.* to thirst, to be thirsty; to long for.

durstig *a.* thirsty.

durstlöschend *a.*, **durststillend** *a.* thirst-quenching.

Durststrecke *f.* (*fig.*) lean period.

Dusche *f.* (-, -n) shower.

duschen *vt.* & *i. refl.* to take a shower.

Düse *f.* (-, -n) nozzle; jet.

Dusel *m.* luck, ~ **haben** to be lucky.

düsen *v.i.* (*fam.*) to zoom.

Düsen: ~**antrieb** *m.* jet propulsion; ~**flugzeg** *n.* jet plane; ~**jäger** *m.* jet fighter; ~**triebwerk** *n.* jet engine.

Dussel *m.* dope.

dusselig *a.* stupid.

düster *a.* gloomy.

Düsterkeit *f.* darkness; gloom.

Dutzend *n.* (-s, -e) dozen.

dutzendweise *adv.* by the dozen.

duzen *v.t.* to call s.b. 'du'; *sich* ~, to call each other 'du'.

Dynamik *f.* (-, 0) dynamics *pl.*

dynamisch *a.* dynamic; *adv.* dynamically.

Dynamit *m.* (-s, 0) dynamite.

Dynamomaschine *f.* dynamo.

Dynastie *f.* (-, -en) dynasty.

dynastisch *a.* dynastic(al).

D-Zug *m.* (-[e]s, -züge) fast train.

E

E, e the letter E or e.

Ebbe *f.* (-, -n) ebb, low tide.

ebben *v.i.* to ebb.

eben *a.* even, level; flat; (*math.*) plane; ~ *adv.* just; precisely; ~ *erst*, just now; *ebenso*, just so, quite as.

Ebenbild *n.* (-[e]s, -er) image; likeness.

ebenbürtig *a.* equal.

Ebene *f.* (-, -n) plain; (*math.*) plane, level.

ebenerdig *a.* & *adv.* (at) ground level.

ebenfalls *adv.* likewise, too, also.

Ebenholz *n.* (-es, 0) ebony.

Ebenmaß *n.* (-es, -e) symmetry, regularity.

ebenmäßig *a.* regular, well-proportioned.

ebenso *adv.* just as.

Eber *m.* (-s, -) boar.

Eberesche *f.* mountain ash, roan tree.

ebnen *v.t.* to level, to smoothe.

Echo *n.* (-s, -s) echo.

Echolot *n.* echo sounder.

Echse *f.* saurian; **Eid**~ lizard.

echt *a.* genuine; true; authentic; (*Farben*) fast; (*Perle, Diamant*) real.

Echtheit *f.* genuineness, authenticity.

Ecke *f.* (-, -n) corner; nook; *an allen* ~*n und Enden*, everywhere; *um die* ~ *gehen*, (*fig.*) to go west.

Ecker *f.* (-, -n) acorn.

Eckhaus *n.* corner-house.

eckig *a.* angular; (*fig.*) awkward.

Eck: ~**platz** *m.* corner seat; ~**stein** *m.* corner-stone; ~**stoß** *m.* corner kick; ~**zahn** *m.* canine tooth.

Economyklasse *f.* economy class.

edel *a.* noble; well-born; generous; precious; *die edlen Teile*, the vital parts.

Edelmann *m.* nobleman.

Edelmetall *n.* rare metal, precious metal.

Edelmut *m.* (-[e]s, 0) generosity.

edelmütig *a.* generous.

Edel: ~**stahl** *m.* stainless steel; ~**stein** *m.* precious stone; ~**tanne** *f.* silver-fir, pitch-pine.

Eden, der Garten ~ the Garden of Eden.

Edikt *n.* (-[e]s, -e) edict.

Efeu *m.* (-s, 0) ivy.

Effekt *m.* effect.

Effekten *m.pl.* (*com.*) securities.

effektiv *a.* effective; real.

Effektivität *f.* effectiveness.

Effektivlohn *m.* real wage.

effektvoll *a.* effective; dramatic.

effizient *a.* & *adv.* efficient(ly).

egal *a.* equal; all the same.

Egel *m.* leech.

Egge *f.* (-, -n) harrow.

eggen *v.t.* to harrow.

Ego *n.* ego.

Egoismus *m.* (-, 0) selfishness, egoism.

Egoist *m.* (-en, -en); **Egoistin** *f.* (-, -nen) selfish person, egoist.

egoistisch *a.* selfish, egoistic(al).

Egozentriker *m.*; **Egozentrikerin** *f.* egocentric.

egozentrisch *a.* egocentric.

ehe *c.* before.

Ehe *f.* (-, -n) marriage, wedlock; *aus erster* ~, from the first marriage; *wilde* ~, concubinage.

Eheberatung *f.* marriage counseling.

ehebrechen *v.i.st.* to commit adultery.

Ehebrecher *m.* (-s, -) adulterer.

Ehebrecherin *f.* (-, -nen) adulteress.

ehebrecherisch *a.* adulterous.

Ehebruch *m.* adultery; (*law*) misconduct.

ehedem *adv.* formerly.

Ehe: ~**frau** *f.* wife; ~**gatte** *m.* husband; spouse; ~**gattin** *f.* wife, spouse.

ehe: ~**hälfte** *f.* (*fam.*) better half, spouse; ~**hindernis** *n.* (*marriage*) impediment; ~**leute** *pl.* married people, spouses.

ehelich *a.* matrimonial; legitimate.

ehelichen *v.t.* to marry.

ehelos *a.* unmarried, single.

Ehelosigkeit *f.* (-, 0) celibacy, unmarried state.

ehemalig *a.* former; late.

ehemals *adv.* formerly.

Ehe: ~**mann** *m.* husband; ~**paar** *n.* married couple.

eher *adv.* sooner; rather.

Eherecht *n.* matrimonial law.

ehern *a.* brazen.

Ehescheidung *f.* divorce.

Ehe: ~**stand** *m.* married state, wedlock; ~**vermittlungsinstitut** *n.* marriage bureau; ~**vertrag** *m.* marriage settlement; ~**trennung** *f.* separation; ~**weib** *n.* spouse, wife.

Ehrabschneider *m.* slanderer.

ehrbar *a.* respectable; honorable.

Ehre *f.* (-, -n) honor, reputation.

ehren *v.t.* to honor, to respect

Ehren: ~**amt** *n.* post of honor; ~**amtlich** *a.* unpaid; ~**bürger** *m.* (honorary) citizen; ~**bürgerrecht** *n.* freedom of the city; ~**gericht** *n.* court of honor.

ehrenhaft *a.* honorable.

ehrenhalber *adv.* for honor's sake.

Ehren: ~**handel** *m.* affair of honor; ~**kränkung** *f.* affront, libel, defamation; ~**mann** *m.* man of honor; ~**mitglied** *n.* honorary member.

ehrenrührig *a.* defamatory, calumnious.

ehrenvoll *a.* honorable, creditable.

Ehrenwache *f.* guard of honor.

ehrenwert *a.* respectable.

Ehrenwort *n.* word of honor.

ehrerbietig *a.* respectful, reverential.

Ehrerbietung *f.* (-, 0) reverence.

Ehrfurcht *f.* (-, 0) reverence, awe.

Ehr: ~**gefühl** *n.* sense of honor; ~**geiz** *m.* ambition.

ehrgeizig *a.* ambitious.

ehrlich *a.* honest, fair, faithful.

Ehrlichkeit *f.* (-, 0) honesty, faithfulness.

ehrlos *a.* disgraceful, dishonorable, infamous.

Ehrlosigkeit *f.* (-, 0) infamy.

ehrwürdig *a.* venerable, reverend.

Ei *n.* (-[e]s, -er) egg; *gekochtes* ~, boiled egg (*hartgekocht*, hardboiled, *weichgekocht*, softboiled); *frischgelegtes* ~, newlaid egg.

ei! *i.* ah! why!; indeed!

Eibe *f.* (-, -n) yew(tree).

Eichamt *n.* (-s, -ämter) Bureau of Standards.

Eiche *f.* (-, -n) oak.

Eichel *f.* (-, -n) acorn; glans; (*Karten*) club.

eichelförmig *a.* acorn-shaped.

eichen *v.t.* to adjust, to calibrate, to gauge.

eichen *a.* oaken, oak.

Eichenlaub *n.* oak leaves *pl.*

Eich: ~**hörnchen**, ~**kätzchen** *n.* (-s, -) squirrel; ~**maß** *n.* standard.

Eid *m.* (-es, -e) oath; *einen* ~ *leisten*, to take an oath; *unter* ~, on oath; *an Eides statt, eidesstattlich,* in lieu of an oath.

eidbrüchig *a.* perjured, forsworn.

Eidechse *f.* (-, -n) lizard.

Eiderdaunen *f.pl.* eiderdown.

Eidesformel *f.* formula of an oath.

eidesstattliche Erklärung *f.* statutory declaration.

Eidgenosse *m.*; **Eidgenossin** *f.* Swiss.

Eidgenossenschaft *f.* **die Schweizerische** ~ the Swiss Confederation.

eidgenössisch *a.* Swiss.

eidlich *a.* by oath, upon oath, sworn; ~**e Versicherung** *f.* affidavit; *eine* ~*e Versicherung abgeben*, to make an affidavit.

Eidotter *m. or n.* yolk.

Eier: ~**becher** *m.* egg cup; ~**kuchen** *m.* omelette.

eierlegend *a.* oviparous.

Eier: ~**schale** *f.* eggshell; ~**stock** *m.* ovary.

Eifer *m.* (-s, 0) zeal, ardor; passion.

Eiferer *m.* zealot.

eifern *v.i.* to be zealous.

Eifersucht *f.* (-, 0) jealousy.

Eifersüchtelei *f.* (-, -en) petty jealousy.

eifersüchtig *a.* jealous.

eiförmig *a.* egg-shaped.

eifrig *a.* zealous; ardent, eager.

Eigelb *n.* yolk.

eigen *a.* own; singular, strange, odd.

Eigenart *f.* peculiarity; originality.

eigenartig *a.* original, peculiar.

Eigenbrötler *m.* (-s, -) loner, crank.

Eigendünkel *m.* (-s, 0) self-conceit.

eigenhändig *a.* with one's own hand.

Eigenheim *n.* house of one's own.

Eigenheit *f.* (-, -en) peculiarity, singularity; idiosyncrasy.

eigenmächtig *a.* arbitrary, autocratic.

Eigenname *m.* (-ns, -n) proper name.

Eigennutz *m.* (-es, 0) self-interest.

eigennützig *a.* self-seeking, selfish.

eigens *adv.* particularly, (e)specially.

Eigenschaft *f.* (-, -en) quality, property; attribute; (*chem.*) property; *in seiner Eigenschaft als . . . ,* in his capacity of.

Eigenschaftswort *n.* adjective.

Eigensinn *m.* (-[e]s, 0) obstinacy.

eigensinnig *a. & adv.* obstinate(ly), stubborn(ly).

eigenständig *a. & adv.* independent(ly).

eigensüchtig *a. & adv.* selfish(ly).

eigentlich *a.* actual, proper; real; peculiar; true; ~ *adv.* actually, properly; exactly.

Eigentum *n.* (-[e]s, -tümer) property.

Eigentümer *m.* (-s, -) owner, proprietor.

eigentümlich *a.* peculiar; proper.

Eigentümlichkeit *f.* (-, -en) peculiarity.

Eigentumsrecht *n.* right of possession; copyright.

eigenwillig *a.* self-willed.

eignen (sich) *v.refl.* to suit, to be fit, to be adapted for.

Eignung *f.* suitability, aptitude.

Eignungsprüfung *f.*, **Eignungstest** *m.* aptitude test.

Eilbestellung *f.* express delivery.

Eilbote *m.* courier, express messenger.

Eilbrief *m.* express letter.

Eile *f.* (-, 0) haste, speed, hurry.

Eileiter *m.* Fallopian tube; oviduct.

eilen *v.i.* to hasten, to make haste; *die Sache eilt* (*nicht*), the matter requires (no) dispatch; there is no hurry.

eilend, eilends *a. & adv.* speedy; hastily.

eilfertig *a.* hasty, precipitate, speedy.

Eilgut *n.* express goods; *als* ~ or *mit Eilboten schicken,* to send express.

eilig *a.* hasty, speedy; *ich hab es sehr* ~, I am pressed for time.

Eil: ~**marsch** *m.* forced march; ~**zug** *m.* fast train.

Eimer *m.* (-s, -) bucket.

ein *adv.* in; *ich weiss nicht wo* ~ *und aus,* I am at my

wits' end.
ein, eine, ein *art.* a, an; *unser ~er,* people like you and me; *~er nach dem andern,* one by one; *~s,* one; *in ~em zu,* continuously.
Einakter *m.* one-act piece.
einander *a.* one another, each other; *nach ~,* in succession, one after another.
einarbeiten (sich) *v.refl.* to familiarize oneself (with), to get used to a job.
einarmig *a.* one-armed.
einäschern *v.t.* to cremate.
einatmen *v.t.* to inhale, to breathe.
einäugig *a.* one-eyed.
Einbahnstraße *f.* one-way street.
Einbahnverkehr *m.* one-way traffic.
einbalsamieren *v.t.* to embalm.
Einband *m.* (-[e]s, -bände) cover, binding; *in Leinwand ~,* clothbound; *in Leder ~,* leatherbound.
einbändig *a.* in one volume.
einbauen *v.t.* to build in; to fit; to install.
einbegreifen *v.t.st.* to include.
einbehalten *v.t.st.* to keep back.
einbeinig *a.* one-legged.
einberufen *v.t.st.* to summon (a meeting); (*mil.*) to call up.
Einberufung *f.* summoning; draft.
einbetten *v.t.* to embed.
Einbettzimmer *n.* single room.
einbeulen *v.t.* to dent.
einbeziehen *v.t.* to include.
Einbeziehung *f.* (-, -en) inclusion.
einbiegen *v.t.* to bend inward; *~v.i.* to turn into.
einbilden (sich) *v.refl.* to imagine, to fancy; *sich etwas* (*viel*) *~,* to think a good deal of oneself.
Einbildung *f.* (-, -en) imagination, fancy; conceit.
Einbildungs: ~kraft *f.;* **~vermögen** *n.* imagination, imaginative powers.
einbinden *v.t.st.* to bind (a book).
einblenden *v.t.* to insert; *v.refl.* to go over to.
Einblick *m.* (-s, -e) insight.
einbrechen *v.i.st.* (*s*) to break into; to set in.
Einbrecher *m.* (-s, -) burglar.
einbrennen *v.t.ir.* to burn in; to brand.
einbringen *v.t.ir.* to bring in; to yield; *wieder ~,* to recoup.
Einbruch *m.* (-[e]s, -brüche) burglary; (*mil.*) penetration; *~ der Nacht,* nightfall.
einbruchsicher *a.* burglarproof.
Einbuchtung *f.* (-, -en) bay, recess; dent.
einbürgern *v.t.* to naturalize.
Einbürgerung *f.* naturalization.
Einbuße *f.* (-, -n) loss.
einbüßen *v.t.* to suffer loss; to lose.
einchecken *v.t. & i.* to check in.
eincremen *v.t.* to put cream on.
eindämmen *v.t.* to dam up, to embank, to contain.
eindecken (sich) (*mit*) *v.refl.* to stock up; *v.t.* to swamp.
Eindecker *m.* (-s, -) monoplane.
eindellen *v.t.* to dent.
eindeutig *a.* unambiguous, univocal.
eindeutschen *v.t.* to Germanize.
eindimensional *a.* one-dimensional.
eindösen *v.i.* to doze off.
eindringen *v.i.st.* (*s*) to penetrate.
eindringlich *a.* impressive.

Eindringlichkeit *f.* urgency; impressiveness; forcefulness.
Eindringling *m.* (-s, -e) intruder.
Eindruck *m.* (-[e]s, -drücke) impression.
eindrücken *v.t.* to smash in; to press/push in.
eindrucksvoll *a.* impressive.
einebnen *v.t.* to level.
Einebnung *f.* leveling.
Einehe *f.* monogamy.
eineiig *a.* identical (twins).
einenhalb one and a half.
einengen *v.t.* to restrict; to confine; to cramp.
Einer *m.* (-s) unit; single number, digit.
einerlei *a.* of the same kind, the same; *es ist mir ~,* it's all one to me.
Einerlei *n.* monotony, sameness.
einerseits *adv.* on the one hand.
einfach *a.* single, simple; plain; *~e Buchführung* *f.* bookkeeping by single entry.
Einfachheit *f.* (-, 0) simplicity.
einfädeln *v.t.* to thread; (*fig.*) to contrive, to scheme.
einfahren *v.i.* (*s*) to enter; to descend (into a mine).
Einfahrt *f.* (-, -en) entrance.
Einfall *m.* (-[e]s, -fälle) invasion; idea, whim, fancy.
einfallen *v.i.st.* (*s*) to fall in; to interrupt; to invade; to occur (to one's mind); *es will mir nicht ~,* I can't think of it; (*das*) *fällt mir gar nicht ein!* catch me doing that!
einfallslos *a.* unimaginative.
einfallsreich *a.* imaginative.
Einfalt *f.* (-, 0) simple-mindedness.
einfältig *a.* simple; silly; naïve.
Einfamilienhaus *n.* one-family house.
einfangen *v.t.st.* to catch, to seize.
einfärben *v.t.* to dye.
einfarbig *a.* of one color; plain.
einfassen *v.t.* to set; to mount.
Einfassung *f.* (-, -en) setting; foil.
einfetten *v.t.* to oil, to grease; to lubricate.
einfinden (sich) *v.refl.st.* to turn up.
einflechten *v.t.st.* to mention casually.
einfliegen *v.t.st.* to fly in.
einfließen *v.i.st.* (*eine Bemerkung, ein Wort*) *~ lassen,* to slip in (a word, a remark).
einflößen *v.t.* to imbue, to inspire with.
Einfluß *m.* (-flusses, -flüsse) influence.
einflußreich *a.* influential.
einflüstern *v.t.* to whisper to, to suggest.
einfordern *v.t.* to call in.
einförmig *a.* uniform; monotonous.
Einförmigkeit *f.* (-, -en) uniformity, monotony.
einfrieden, einfriedigen *v.t.* to enclose.
einfrieren *v.t.st.* (*s*) to freeze.
einfügen *v.t.* to insert.
einfühlen *v.refl.; in jmdn. ~* to empathize with.
einfühlsam *a.* understanding, sensitive.
Einfuhr *f.* (-, -en) importation, import.
einführen *v.t.* to import; to introduce.
Einführung *f.* (-, -en) introduction.
Einführungsbesprechung *f.* general orientation.
Einfuhrzoll *m.* import duty.
einfüllen *v.t.* to fill into.
Eingabe *f.* (-, -n) petition; memorial.

Eingang *m.* (-[e]s, -gänge) entrance, entry; way in; preamble.

eingängig *a.* catchy (song).

eingangs *adv.* at the beginning.

eingeben *v.t.st.* (*comp.*) to feed in.

ein: ~**gebildet** *a.* imaginary; conceited; ~**geboren** *a.* native.

Eingebung *f.* (-, -en) inspiration.

eingedenk *a.* mindful of.

eingefallen *a.* gaunt (face); sunken, hollow.

eingefleischt *a.* inveterate; confirmed.

eingehen *v.i.st.* (s) (*Brief*) to come to hand; (*Ehe*) to contract; *eine Wette* ~, to make a bet; to consent to; to decay; to shrink.

eingehend *a.* thorough, exhaustive; (*Post etc.*) incoming.

eingekeilt *a.* wedged in; hemmed in.

eingeklemmt *a.* trapped.

Eingemachte[s] *n.* (-n, 0) preserves *pl.*; (*in Essig*) pickles *pl.*

eingemeinden *v.t.* to incorporate.

eingenommen *a.* ~ *sein von* to be taken; *von sich* ~ *sein* to be full of oneself.

eingerostet *a.* rusty.

eingeschnappt *a.* (*fam.*) huffy.

eingeschneit *a.* snowed in.

eingeschränkt *a.* restrained, limited.

eingeschrieben *a.* registered, enrolled.

eingeschworen *a.* confirmed.

eingestandenermaßen *adv.* avowedly.

Eingeständnis *n.* (-nisses, -nisse) confession, avowal.

eingestehen *v.t.st.* to admit, to confess, to avow.

eingestellt *a.* **fortschrittlich** ~ progressively minded.

Eingeweide *n.* (-s, -) entrails, intestines, bowels *pl.*

eingewöhnen (sich) *v.refl.* to get used to, to accustom oneself to.

eingießen *v.t.st.* to pour in; (*ein Glas*) to pour out.

eingipsen *v.t.* to fix in with plaster, to put in plaster.

eingleisig *a.* single-track.

eingliedern *v.t.* to incorporate, to include; to rehabilitate.

Eingliederung *f.* integration.

eingraben *v.t.st.* to bury; to sink; (sich) ~ *v.refl.* (*mil.*) to entrench.

eingravieren *v.t.* to engrave.

eingreifen *v.i.st.* to intervene; (*von Zahnrädern*) to interlock; to interfere.

Eingriff *m.* (-[e]s, -e) intervention; interference; (*med.*) operation; (*mech.*) mesh.

Einhalt *m.* (-[e]s, 0) ~**gebieten** to stop s.th.

einhalten *v.t.st.* to observe; to stop.

Einhaltung *f.* observance.

einhämmern *v.i.* to hammer on s.th.; *v.t.* to drum into somebody.

einhandeln *v.t.* to purchase, to buy.

einhändig *a.* one-handed, single-handed.

einhändigen *v.t.* to hand (over).

einhängen *v.t.* to hang (up); to take s.b.'s arm.

einhauchen *v.t.* to inspire (with).

einheften *v.t.* to file.

einhegen *v.t.* to enclose.

einheimisch *a.* indigenous; native.

einheimsen *v.t.* (*fam.*) to rake in.

erheiraten *v.i.* to marry into.

Einheit *f.* (-, -en) unity; (*ar.*) unit.

einheitlich *a.* unified, uniform, standardized.

Einheits: ~**format** *n.* standard size; ~**front** *f.* united front; ~**gewerkschaft** *f.* general trade union; ~**preis** *m.* uniform price; ~**staat** *m.* unitary state; ~**tarif** *m.* flat rate.

einheizen *v.t.* to light a fire; (*fig.*) to give s.o. hell.

einhellig *a.* unanimous.

einher *adv.* forth, along, on.

einholen *v.t.* to catch up with; to collect, to get.

Einhorn *n.* (-[e]s, -hörner) unicorn.

einhüllen *v.t.* to wrap up; to cover.

enig *a.* united; ~ *sein* to agree with s.b.

einigen *v.t.* to unite; (sich) ~ *v.refl.* to come to an agreement with.

einige[r], einiges *pn.* some, any; **einige** *pl.* some, a few; *einige hundert*, a hundred odd.

einigermassen *adv.* to a certain extent.

Einigkeit *f.* (-, 0) union, unanimity, concord.

Einigung *f.* (-, -en) agreement, union; unification.

einimpfen *v.t.* to inoculate.

einjagen *v.t.* *einem einen Schrecken* ~, to frighten someone.

einjährig *a.* one year old.

einkalkulieren *v.t.* to take into account.

einkassieren *v.t.* to cash.

Einkauf *m.* (-[e]s, -Käufe) purchase; *Einkäufe machen*, to go shopping.

einkaufen *v.t.* to buy, to purchase; to shop.

Einkaufspreis *m.* purchase price, wholesale price.

Einkaufswagen *m.* shopping cart.

einkehren *v.i.* (s) to stop off.

einkerben *v.t.* to notch.

einkerkern *v.t.* to imprison.

einklagen *v.t.* to sue for.

einklammern *v.t.* to put in brackets.

Einklang *m.* (-[e]s, 0) unison, harmony; *im ~ stehen*, to be in unison, to agree.

einkleiden *v.t.* to clothe s.b.; (*Gedanken*) to put into words.

einklemmen *v.t.* to squeeze in, to jam, to wedge in.

einknicken *v.t.* to bend, to snap.

einkochen *v.t.* (*Frucht*) to preserve, to bottle.

Einkommen *n.* (-s, -) income, revenue.

Einkommensteuer *f.* income tax; ~**erklärung** *f.* income tax return.

einkreisen *v.t.* to encircle; to circumscribe (*mil.*) to envelop.

Einkreisung *f.* (-, -en) encirclement.

Einkünfte *f.pl.* income, revenue, rent.

einladen *v.t.st.* to invite, to bid; (*Güter*) to load.

einladend *a.* inviting, appetizing.

Einladung *f.* (-, -en) invitation.

Einlage *f.* (-, -n) (*Brief*) enclosure; (*Bank*) deposit; (*Schuh*) arch support; (*Zahn*) filling; (*Schneiderei*) wadding.

einlagern *v.t.* to store, to warehouse.

Einlaß *m.* (-lasses, 0) admission; inlet.

einlassen *v.t.st.* to let in; to admit; (sich) ~ *v.refl.* to engage in.

Einlaßkarte *f.* ticket of admission.

Einlauf *m.* (-s, -läufe) enema.

einlaufen *v.i.st.* (s) to shrink; (*Schiff*) to make *or* enter a port; (*Briefe, Gelder*) to come to hand;

nicht einlaufend *a.* unshrinkable; *v.refl.* to warm up.

einleben (sich) *v.refl.* to accustom oneself.

Einlegearbeit *f.* inlaid work, intarsia.

einlegen *v.t.* to lay in, to put in; to inlay; to deposit; (*Früchte etc.*) to preserve, to pickle; (*Berufung*) to lodge; *ein Wort für einen* ~, to intercede for someone.

einleiten *v.t.* to introduce; (*Maßnahmen*) to initiate.

einleitend *a.* introductory.

Einleitung *f.* (-, -en) introduction.

einlenken *v.i.* to relent.

einleuchten *v.i.* to be evident.

einleuchtend *a.* plausible.

einliefern *v.t.* to mail; to take s.o. to the hospital.

einliegend *a.* enclosed, herewith.

einlochen *v.t.* (*fam.*) to put s.b. away, imprison.

einlösen *v.t.* to redeem (a pledge); (*Wechsel*) to honor, to take up. (*Scheck*) to cash.

Einlösung *f.* (-, -en) redemption.

einlullen *v.t.* to lull to sleep.

einmachen *v.t.* to pickle, to preserve.

Einmachglas *n.* preserving jar.

einmal *adv.* once; *auf* ~, all at once, suddenly; *nicht* ~, not even.

Einmaleins *n.* (-, -) multiplication table.

Einmalhandtuch *n.* disposable towel.

einmalig *a.* unique.

Einmannbetrieb *m.* one-man business.

Einmarsch *m.* (-[e]s, -märsche) entry.

einmarschieren *v.i.* (*s*) to march in.

einmauern *v.t.* to wall in.

einmengen (sich) *v.refl.* to meddle (with), to interfere (in).

einmieten (sich) *v.refl.* to take lodgings.

einmischen (sich) *v.refl.* to interfere (in), to meddle (with).

Einmischung *f.* (-, -en) intervention, interference.

einmonatig *a.* one-month (duration).

einmonatlich *a.* monthly.

einmotorig *a.* single-engined.

einmumme(l)n *v.t.* to wrap up.

einmünden *v.i.* to flow into, to debouch.

Einmündung *f.* junction (streets).

einmütig *a.* unanimous.

Einmütigkeit *f.* (-, 0) concord, unanimity.

einnähen *v.t.* to sew in.

Einnahme *f.* (-, -n) receipt, income, revenue; capture, taking; *Einnahmen und Ausgaben*, revenue and expenditure.

Einnahmequelle *f.* source of income/revenue.

einnehmen *v.t.st.* to take; (*fig.*) to charm, to captivate; (*den Kopf*) to disturb.

einnehmend *a.* engaging, charming.

Einnehmer *m.* (-s, -) receiver, collector.

einnicken *v.i.* (*s*) to nod off.

einnisten (sich) *v.refl.* to nest; to install o.s.

Einöde *f.* (-, -n) desert, solitude.

einölen *v.t.* to oil, to grease.

einordnen *v.t.* to arrange; to classify; to file.

einpacken *v.t.* to pack up.

einparken *v.t.* to park.

einpauken *v.t.* (*Studenten*) to coach, to bone up.

einpferchen *v.t.* to be crammed together.

einpflanzen *v.t.* to plant; (*med.*) to implant.

einplanen *v.t.* to plan; to include; to allow for.

einpökeln *v.t.* to salt, to pickle.

einprägen *v.t.* to impress; to stamp.

einprägsam *a.* easily remembered; catchy.

einprogrammieren *v.t.* (*comp.*) to program in.

einquartieren *v.t.* to quarter, to billet.

Einquartierung *f.* (-, -en) soldiers' quarters *pl.*

einquetschen *v.t.* to squeeze.

einrahmen *v.t.* to frame.

einrasten *v.i.* to engage, to click into place.

einräumen *v.t.* to clear away; to concede.

einrechnen *v.t.* to include (in an account).

Einrede *f.* (-, -n) objection, exception; (*law*) plea.

einreden *v.t.* to talk into; ~ *v.i.* to remonstrate.

einregnen *v.i.* *eingeregnet sein*, to be caught in the rain; *es regnet sich ein*, the rain is settling in.

einreiben *v.t.* to rub into.

einreichen *v.t.* to hand in, to submit; *ein Gesuch* ~, to file *or* present a petition.

einreihen *v.t.* to range, to enroll.

einreihig *a.* (*Rock*) single-breasted.

Einreise *f.* (-, -n) entry; ~**erlaubnis** *f.* entry permit.

einreisen *v.i.* to enter (country).

einreissen *v.t.st.* to pull down, to tear, to rend; ~ *v.i.st.* to become a habit.

einreiten *v.i.st.* to ride in; to break in.

einrenken *v.t.* to set (a bone); to arrange.

einrennen *v.t.st.* to force open by running against.

einrichten *v.t.* to arrange or settle; (*Wohnung*) to furnish.

Einrichtung *f.* (-, -en) arrangement, institution; furniture.

Einrichtungsgegenstände *m.pl.* furnishings.

einritzen *v.t.* to carve.

einrosten *v.i.* (*s*) to get rusty.

einrücken *v.i.* (*s*) to march in(to); to enter; ~ *v.i.* to indent; to insert.

einrühren *v.t.* to stir in.

eins *a.* one.

Eins *f.* (-, Einsen) one, grade A.

einsacken *v.i.* to bag; to pocket; to sink in.

einsalzen *v.t.st.* to salt, to cure.

einsam *a.* lonely, solitary.

Einsamkeit *f.* (-, 0) solitude, loneliness.

einsammeln *v.t.* to pick up, to gather in, to collect.

Einsatz *m.* (-[e]s, -sätze) stake, pool; (*mil.*) commitment, employment.

Einsatz: ~**befehl** *m.* combat order; ~**kommando** *n.* task force; ~**leiter** *m.* head of operations; ~**plan** *m.* plan of action; ~**zentrale** *f.* operations center.

einsaugen *v.t.st.* to suck in; to absorb.

einsäumen *v.t.* to hem; to border.

einschalten *v.t.* to insert; (*el.*) to switch on; (*anderen Gang*) to put in another gear.

Einschaltquote *f.* ratings.

einschärfen *v.t.* (*fig.*) to impress.

einschätzen *v.t.* to assess; to estimate.

Einschätzung *f.* assessment, estimation.

einschäumen *v.t.* to lather.

einschenken *v.t.* to pour out, to fill; *einem reinen Wein* ~, to tell one the plain truth.

einscheren *v.i.* to move into a lane (traffic).

einschicken *v.t.* to send in.

einschieben *v.t.st.* to put in, to insert.

einschießen (sich) *v.refl.st.* (*mil.*) to get the range.

einschiffen *v.t. & v.refl.* to embark.

Einschiffung f. (-, -en) embarkation.
einschlafen v.i.st. (s) to go to sleep, to fall asleep.
einschläfern v.t. to lull to sleep.
einschläfernd a. soporific.
Einschlag m. (-[e]s, -schläge) woof, weft; tuck; touch.
einschlagen v.t.st. to beat in; to break; to wrap up; *einen Weg ~*, to take a road; *~ v.i.st. (Blitz)* to strike.
einschlägig a. relevant.
einschleichen (sich) v.refl.st. to creep in.
einschleifen v.t. to cut in.
einschleppen v.t. (Krankheit) to introduce.
einschleusen v.t. to infiltrate.
einschließen v.t.st. to lock up; to enclose; (fig.) to include.
einschließlich a. inclusive.
Einschluß m. (-schlusses, -schlüsse) inclusion; *mit ~ von*, inclusive of, including.
einschmeicheln (sich) v.refl. to ingratiate oneself.
einschmelzen v.t.st. to melt down.
einschmieren v.t. to cream; to grease, to oil.
einschmuggeln v.t. to smuggle.
einschnappen v.i. to click or shut, as in lock or door; (fig.) to go into a huff.
einschneiden v.i.st., to cut; *~d* a. incisive, thorough.
einschneien v.t. to get snowed in.
Einschnitt m. (-[e]s, -e) incision; notch.
einschränken v.t. to confine; to restrain; (sich) *~ v.refl.* to retrench.
Einschränkung f. (-, -en) limitation, restriction; retrenchment.
einschrauben v.t. to screw in.
Einschreibe: ~brief m. registered letter; **~gebühr** f. registration fee.
einschreiben v.t.st. to register; (sich) *~v.refl.st.* to enroll.
Einschreibung f. registration; enrollment.
einschreiten v.i.st. (s) to intervene.
einschrumpfen v.i. (s) to shrink up.
Einschub m. (-[e]s, -schübe) insertion.
einschüchtern v.t. to intimidate.
einschulen v.t. to start school.
Einschuss m. (-es, -schüsse) bullet wound.
einschütten v.t. to pour in.
einschweißen v.t. to weld in; to shrink-wrap.
einschwenken v.i. (mil.) to turn in.
einsegnen v.t. to consecrate; to confirm.
Einsegnung f. (-, -en) consecration, blessing; confirmation.
einsehen v.t.st. to look into, to look over; to understand, to see.
Einsehen n. (-s, 0) *ein ~ haben*, to be reasonable.
einseifen v.t. to soap; (den Bart) to lather; (fig.) to take in.
einseitig a. unilateral; partial, one-sided; biased.
einsenden v.t.ir. to send in.
einsetzen v.t. (mil.) to commit, to employ; (Pflanze) to set up; to insert; (Geld) to stake; (Kraft) to use; (einen) to appoint, to install; *einen zum Erben ~*, to make one one's heir; *~ v.i.* to begin, to set in; (sich) *~ v.refl. (für)* to work hard (for).
Einsicht f. (-, -en) insight; intelligence.
einsichtig a. sensible, well-advised.
einsickern v.i. to seep in.
Einsiedler m. (-s, -) hermit, anchorite.

einsilbig a. monosyllabic; (fig.) taciturn.
einsinken v.i.st. (s) to sink in, to fall in.
einsitzig a. single-seated.
einspannen v.t. (Pferde) to harness to.
einspännig a. drawn by one horse.
einsparen v.t. to save, to economize.
einspeichern v.t. (comp.) to feed in, to input.
einsperren v.t. to lock up; to imprison.
einsprachig a. monolingual.
einspringen v.i. (s) *helfend ~*, to lend a hand; *als Stellvertreter ~*, to step in for someone.
einspritzen v.t. to inject.
Einspritzmotor m. fuel-injection engine.
Einspritzung f. (-, -en) injection.
Einspruch m. protest, objection; appeal.
einsprühen v.t. to spray.
einspurig a. single-lane.
einst adv. once.
einstampfen v.t. to pulp.
Einstand m. to celebrate the start of a new job; debut (sports); deuce (tennis).
einstecken v.t. to pocket; to mail; to put in.
einstehen v.i.st. to answer for, to guarantee.
einsteigen v.i.st. (s) to get in; to get into, to enter (a carriage); *~! i.* take your seats!
einstellbar a. (mech.) adjustable.
einstellen v.t. (mech.) to adjust; (mil.) to enlist; (Radio) to tune; (Zahlungen) to stop; *die Arbeit ~*, to strike; (sich) *~ v.refl.* to appear, to turn up.
einstellig a. one position.
Einstellplatz m. parking space.
Einstellung f. (-, -en) (der Feindseligkeiten) cessation; *~ der Arbeit*, strike; enlistment; (Zahlungen) suspension; attitude, mentality.
Einstellungsgespräch n. job interview.
Einstich m. puncture, prick.
Einstieg m. entrance, entry; (fig.) start, beginning.
einstig a. future; ancient, former.
einstimmig a. unanimous; unison.
Einstimmigkeit f. (-, 0) unanimity.
einstmals adv. once, formerly.
einstöckig a. one-story.
einstossen v.t.st. (Tür) to smash.
einstreichen v.t.st. to pocket.
einstreuen v.t. to intersperse.
einströmen v.i. to pour into.
einstudieren v.t. (Theater) to produce; to rehearse.
einstufen v.t. to classify; to categorize.
Einstufung f. categorization; classification.
einstündig a. one hour (duration).
einstürmen v.i. (auf) to assail.
Einsturz m. (-es, -stürze) collapse.
einstürzen v.i. (s) to collapse; to fall in.
einstweilen adv. for the time being; meanwhile.
einstweilig a. provisional, temporary; *~e Verfügung* f. interim order.
eintägig a. one day (duration).
Eintänzer m. (-s, -) gigolo.
eintauchen v.t. to immerse, to dip, to steep; *~ v.i.* to dive.
eintauschen v.a. to receive in exchange.
einteilen v.t. to divide; to distribute.
Einteilung f. (-, -en) division; distribution; classification.
eintippen v.t. to type in; to key in.
eintönig a. monotonous.

Eintönigkeit *f.* monotony.

Eintopf *m.*, **Eintopfgericht** *n.* stew.

Eintracht *f.* (-, 0) concord; harmony.

einträchtig *a.* harmonious.

Eintrag *m.* (-[e]s, -träge) entry (in a book).

eintragen *v.t.st.* to enter, to yield.

einträglich *a.* profitable, lucrative.

Eintragung *f.* (-, -en) entry, registration.

eintreffen *v.i.st.* (*s*) to arrive; to happen.

Eintreffen *n.* arrival.

eintreiben *v.t.st.* (*Geld*) to call in, to collect.

eintreten *v.i.st.* (*s*) to enter, to join; (*für einen*) to intercede; (*Hindernisse*) to arise, to crop up.

eintrichtern *v.t.* to drum s.th. in.

Eintritt *m.* (-[e]s, 0) entry, entrance; setting in; *freier* ~, free admission.

Eintritts: ~**geld** *n.* admission fee; ~**karte** *f.* ticket.

eintrockenen *v.i.* (*s*) to dry up, to shrivel.

eintrudeln *v.i.* (*fam.*) to drift in.

eintunken *v.t.* to dip, to steep.

einüben *v.t.* to practice, to drill, to train.

einverleiben *v.t.* to annex; to absorb.

Einverleibung *f.* (-, -en) annexation.

Einvernehmen *n.* (-s, 0) understanding; agreement; *im besten* ~ *mit einem*, on the best of terms with one.

einverstanden *a.* agreed; *mit etwas* ~ *sein*, to agree to.

Einverständnis *n.* (-nisses, -nisse) agreement, understanding.

Einwand *m.* (-[e]s, -wände) objection.

Einwanderer *m.* (-s, -) immigrant.

einwandern *v.i.* (*s*) to immigrate.

Einwanderung *f.* (-, -en) immigration.

einwandfrei *a.* flawless; perfect; unobjectionable; ~ *adv.* beyond doubt.

einwärts *adv.* inward, inwards.

einwechseln *v.t.* to change; to substitute (sports).

einwecken *v.t.* to preserve.

Einweckglas *n.* preserving jar.

Einwegflasche *f.* nonreturnable bottle.

Einwegspritze *f.* disposable syringe.

einweichen *v.t.* to soak.

einweihen *v.t.* to inaugurate, to consecrate; to initiate.

Einweihung *f.* (-, -en) opening.

einweisen *v.t.st.* to send s.o. into; to hospitalize; to brief s.o. in; to direct (car).

Einweisung *f.* admission to a hospital; introduction (work).

einwenden *v.t.ir.* to object; to reply.

einwerfen *v.t.st.* (*Scheiben*) to smash, to break; (*fig.*) to object; to insert (coin); to throw in (remark).

einwickeln *v.t.* to wrap up, to envelop; to take s.o. in.

einwilligen *v.t.* to consent, to agree.

Einwilligung *f.* (-, -en) consent, assent.

einwinken *v.t.* to guide in (plane); to direct (car).

enwirken *v.t.* to influence.

einwöchig *a.* one-week (duration); week-old.

Einwohner *m.* (-s, -); **Einwohnerin** *f.* (-, -nen) inhabitant.

Einwohnermeldeamt *n.* residents' registration office.

Einwohnerschaft *f.* population.

Einwurf *m.* (-[e]s, -würfe) objection; insertion (mail); (*des Briefkastens*) slit, slot.

einwurzeln *v.i.* (*s*) to take root.

Einzahl *f.* (-, 0) singular (number).

einzahlen *v.t.* to pay in.

Einzahlung *f.* (-, -en) payment.

einzäunen *v.t.* to fence in.

Einzäunung *f.* (-, -en) enclosure, fence.

einzeichnen *v.t.* to mark.

einzeilig *a.* one-line; single spaced.

Einzel *n.* (-s, -) singles (sports).

Einzel: ~**aktion** *f.* independent action; ~**anfertigung** *f.* custom-made article; ~**ausfstellung** *f.* itemized list; ~**ausgabe** *f.* separate edition; ~**bett** *n.* single bed; ~**erscheinung** *f.* isolated occurrence; ~**exemplar** *n.* unique specimen; ~**fall** *m.* particular care; ~**gänger** *m.*; **gängerin** *f.* loner.

Einzelhaft *f.* (-, 0) solitary confinement.

Einzelhandel *m.* retail trade.

Einzelheit *f.* (-, -en) detail; particulars *pl.*

Einzelkind *n.* only child.

einzeln *a.* odd; single; individual; isolated.

Einzel: ~**stück** *n.* individual piece; ~**verkauf** *m.* (-[e]s, -verkäufe) selling by retail; ~**wesen** *n.* (-s, -) individual; ~**zelle** *f.* single cell; ~**zimmer** *n.* single-room.

Einziehdecke *f.* duvet.

einziehen *v.t.st.* to draw in; (*zur Strafe*) to confiscate; (*Münzen etc.*) to call in, to withdraw; (*Erkundigungen*) to make (inquiries); ~ *v.i.st.* (*s*) to march in; (*Haus*) to move into.

Einziehung *f.* (-, -en) confiscation; collection.

einzig *a.* only; single; sole; ~ *in seiner Art*, unique.

einzigartig *a. & adv.* unique(ly).

Einzigartigkeit *f.* uniqueness.

Einzimmerwohnung *f.* one-room apartment.

Einzug *m.* (-[e]s, -züge) entry, entrance; moving in.

Einzugsbereich *m.*; **Einzugsgebiet** *n.* catchment area; drainage basin.

Einzugsermächtigung *f.* standing order for a direct debit.

einzwängen *v.t.* to squeeze in.

Eis *n.* (Eises, 0) ice; *Frucht* ~, ice cream.

Eis: ~**bahn** *f.* skating rink; ~**bär** *m.* polar bear; ~**bein** *n.* pig's knuckles; ~**berg** *m.* iceberg; ~**beutel** *m.* ice bag; ~**blume** *f.* frost flower; ~**brecher** *m.* icebreaker.

Eischnee *m.* beaten egg white.

Eisdiele *f.* (-, -n) ice-cream parlor.

Eisen *n.* (-s, -) iron.

Eisen: ~**bahn** *f.* railway, railroad; ~**bahnabteil** *n.* railroad compartment; ~**bahndamm** *m.* embankment; ~**bahnendpunkt** *m.* railhead; ~**bahnnetz** *n.* railroad network; ~**bahnschaffner** *m.* railroad conductor; ~**bahnwagen** *m.* railroad car; ~**bergwerk** *n.* iron mine.

Eisenbeton *m.* ferroconcrete, reinforced concrete.

Eisenerz *n.* iron ore.

Eisengießerei *f.* iron-foundry.

Eisenkonstruktion *f.* steel frame.

Eisen: ~**mangel** *m.* iron deficiency; ~**säge** *f.* hacksaw; ~**stange** *f.* iron bar; ~**träger** *m.* iron girder; ~**waren** *pl.* hardware; ~**warengeschäft** *n.* hardware store; ~**zeit** *f.* Iron Age.

eisern *a.* iron, of iron; ~**er Vorhang** *m.* Iron

Curtain.

Eisfach *n.* freezing compartment.

Eisgang *m.* breaking up and floating of the ice.

eisig *a.* icy, glacial; chilly.

eiskalt *a.* icy cold.

Eis: ~**kübel** *m.* ice bucket; ~**kuntslauf** *m.* figure skating; ~**lauf** *m.* skating; ~**pickel** *m.* ice pick.

Eisprung *m.* ovulation.

Eis: ~**regen** *m.* sleet; ~**revue** *f.* ice show; ~**scholle** *f.* ice floe; ~**schrank** *m.* refrigerator; ~**stadion** *n.* ice rink; ~**tanz** *m.* ice dancing; ~**würfel** *m.* ice cube; ~**zapfen** *m.* icicle; ~**zeit** *f.* ice age, glacial period.

eitel *a. & adv.* vain.

Eitelkeit *f.* (-, -en) vanity.

Eiter *m.* (-s, 0) pus.

eitrig *a.* suppurating.

eitern *v.i.* to suppurate.

Eiweiß *n.* (-es, 0) white of an egg, albumen; protein; ~**haltig** *a.* albuminous.

Eiweiß: ~**bedarf** *m.* protein requirement; ~**mangel** *m.* protein deficiency.

eiweißreich *a.* rich in protein.

Eizelle *f.* egg cell; ovum.

Ejakulation *f.* ejaculation.

Ekel *m.* (-s, 0) disgust; revulsion; *n.* nasty person.

ekelerregend *a.* repulsive.

ekelhaft *a.* loathsome, disgusting.

ekeln (sich) *v.refl.* to feel disgusted.

Eklat *m.* sensation; scandal.

eklatant *a.* striking; scandalous.

eklig *a.* disgusting; nauseating.

Eklipse *f.* eclipse.

Ekstase *f.* (-, -n) ecstasy.

Ekzem *n.* (-[e]s, -e) eczema.

Elan *m.* verve; energy.

elastisch *a.* elastic.

Elastizität *f.* elasticity; suppleness.

Elch *m.* (-[e]s, -e) elk; moose.

Elefant *m.* (-en, -en) elephant.

elegant *a.* elegant, stylish; civilized.

Eleganz *f.* (-, 0) elegance.

Elegie *f.* (-, -n) elegy.

elegisch *a.* elegiac; mournful.

elektrifizieren *v.t.* to electrify.

Elektriker *m.* (-s, -) electrician.

elektrisch *a.* electric(al).

elektrisieren *v.t.* to electrify.

Elektrizität *f.* (-, 0) electricity.

Elektrizitätsversorgung *f.* power supply.

Elektrizitätswerk *n.* power station.

Elektroantrieb *m.* electric drive.

Elektroauto *n.* electric car.

Elektroenzephalogramm *n.* EEG; electro-encephalogram.

Elektrode *f.* (-, -n) electrode.

Elektro: ~**gerät** *n.* electrical appliance; ~**installateur** *m.* electrician; ~**kardiogramm** *n.* EKG electrocardiogram; ~**konzern** *m.* electrical company; ~**lyse** *f.* electrolysis; ~**lyt** *m.* electrolyte;

Elektron *n.* (-s, -en) electron.

Elektronen: ~**blitz** *m.* electronic flash; ~**hirn** *n.* electronic brain.

Elektronik *f.* electronics.

Elektro: ~**technik** *f.* electrical engineering; ~**techniker** *m.* electrical engineer.

Element *n.* (-[e]s, -e) element; rudiment; (*el.*) cell.

elementar *a.* elementary; primary.

Elementar: ~**kenntnisse** *pl.* elementary knowledge; ~**teilchen** *pl.* (phys.) elementary particle; ~**unterricht** *m.* elementary instruction.

Elend *n.* (-[e]s, 0) misery; affliction.

elend *a.* miserable, wretched.

Elendsquartier *n.*; **Elendsviertel** *n.* slum.

Eleve *m.*; **Elevin** *f.* student (theater, ballet).

elf *a.* eleven.

Elfe *f.* (-, -n) elf, fairy.

Elfenbein *n.* (-[e]s, 0) ivory; ~**turm** *m.* ivory tower.

elftens *adv.* in the eleventh place.

Elfmeter *m.* penalty (soccer).

eliminieren *v.t.* to eliminate.

elisabethanisch *a.* Elizabethan.

elitär *a.* elitist.

Elite *f.* elite.

Elitedenken *n.* elitism.

Elitetruppen *f.pl.* (*mil.*) crack troops.

Ellbogen *m.* (-s, -) elbow.

Elle *f.* (-, -n) ulna (anatomical); cubit (about 17 to 21 inches.).

ellenlang *a.* (*fam.*) interminable.

Ellipse *f.* (-, -n) ellipse; ellipsis.

elliptisch *a.* elliptical.

Elsaß *n.* (-, 0) Alsace.

Elsässer *m.*; **Elässerin** *f.*; **elsässisch** *a.* Alsatian.

Elster *f.* (-, -n) magpie.

elterlich *a.* parental.

Eltern *pl.* parents *pl.*

Eltern: ~**abend** *m.* parent-teacher meeting; ~**beirat** *m.* parents association; ~**teil** *m.* parent.

Email *n.* (-s, 0) enamel.

emaillieren *v.t.* to enamel.

Emanzipation *f.* emancipation.

Emanzipationsbewegung *f.* liberation movement.

emanzipieren *v.t.* to emancipate.

emanzipiert *a.* emancipated.

Embargo *n.* embargo.

Embolie *f.* embolism.

Embryo *m.* (-s, -nen) embryo.

embryonal *a.* embryonic.

Emigrant *m.*; **Emigrantin** *f.* emigrant; emigré.

emigrieren *v.i.* to emigrate.

Emission *f.* (-, -en) (*Finanz*) issue.

e-Moll *n.* E minor.

Emotion *f.* (-, -en) emotion.

emotional *a.* emotional.

Emotionalität *f.* emotionalism.

Empfang *m.* (-[e]s, -pfänge) reception, receipt.

empfangen *v.t.st.* to receive; ~*v.i.st.* to conceive.

Empfänger *m.* (-s, -); **Empfängerin** *f.* (-, -nen) receiver, recipient; addressee; consignee.

empfänglich *a.* receptive; susceptible.

Empfängnis *f.* (-, 0) conception.

Empfängnisverhütung *f.* contraception; **empfängnisverhütendes Mittel** *n.* contraceptive.

Empfangs: ~**dame** *f.* receptionist; ~**schein** *m.* receipt; ~**zimmer** *n.* reception room, drawing room.

empfehlen *v.t.st.* to recommend; (sich) ~ *v.refl.st.* to take leave; ~ *Sie mich Ihrem Herrn Vater,* please

remember me to your father.
empfehlenswert *a.* recommendable.
Empfehlung *f.* (-, -en) recommendation.
Empfehlungsbrief *m.* ~**schreiben** *n.* letter of recommendation.
empfinden *v.t.st.* to feel, to perceive, to be sensible (of).
empfindlich *a.* sensible; sensitive, touchy; delicate; painful, grievous.
empfindsam *a.* sentimental; sensitive.
Empfindsamkeit *f.* sensitivity; sentimentality.
Empfindung *f.* (-, -en) perception, sensation, feeling.
empfindungslos *a.* insensible, unfeeling.
emphatisch *a.* emphatic(al).
empirisch *a.* empirical.
empor *adv.* upwards, on high, up, aloft.
emporarbeiten (sich) *v.refl.* to work one's way up.
Empore *f.* gallery.
empören *v.t.* to revolt, to shock; (sich) ~ *v.refl.* to rebel.
empörend *a.* outrageous; shocking.
Empörer *m.* (-s, -) insurgent, rebel.
emporkommen *v.i.st.* to rise in the world.
Emporkömmling *m.* (-[e]s, -e) upstart.
emporragen *v.i.* to tower; to rise up.
emporsteigen *v.i.st.* to rise aloft; to climb up.
empört *a.* outraged.
Empörung *f.* (-, -en) rebellion, revolt; indignation.
emsig *a.* assiduous, industrious, busy.
Emsigkeit *f.* industriousness, sedulousness.
E-Musik *f.* serious music.
Endabrechnung *f.* final account.
Ende *n.* (-s, -n) end; close, conclusion; *zu ~ gehen,* to draw to an end.
Endeffekt *m.* **im** ~ in the end.
endemisch *a.* endemic.
enden *v.i. & refl.* (sich) to end, to finish, to terminate, to conclude.
Endergebnis *n.* (-nisses, -nisse) final result.
Endgeschwindigkeit *f.* (-, -en) terminal velocity.
endgültig *a.* definitive, final.
endigen *v.t.* to end, to finish.
Endivie *f.* (-, -n) chicory, endive.
Endkampf *m.* final battle.
Endlagerung *f.* ultimate disposal (of nuclear waste).
endlich *a.* finite; final, ultimate; ~ *adv.* at last, finally.
endlos *a.* endless, infinite.
endogen *a.* endogenous.
Endoskop *n.* endoscope.
End: ~**phase** *f.* final stages; ~**punkt** *m.* final point; terminus; ~**runde** *f.* final; ~**spurt** *m.* final spurt; ~**stadium** *n.* final stage; terminal stage; ~**station** *f.* terminus.
Endung *f.* (-, -en) ending, termination.
Endverbraucher *m.* end user.
Endzweck *m.* final purpose.
Energie *f.* (-, -n) energy.
Energie: ~**bedarf** *m.* energy requirement; ~**gewinnung** *f.* energy production; ~**haushalt** *m.* energy balance; ~**quelle** *f.* energy source; ~**verbrauch** *m.* energy consumption; ~**verschwendung** *f.* waste of energy; ~**versorgung** *f.* energy supply; ~**wirtschaft** *f.* energy industry.

energisch *a.* energetic, vigorous.
eng *a.* narrow, tight, strait; strict.
engagieren *v.t.* to engage; *v.refl.* to commit o.s.; to become involved.
engagiert *a.* committed; involved.
enganliegend *a.* tight(-fitting).
Enge *f.* (-, -n) narrowness, tightness; *in die ~ treiben,* to drive into a corner.
Engel *m.* (-s, -) angel.
Engelsgeduld *f.* patience of a saint.
engherzig *a.* small-minded.
England *n.* (-s, -) England, Britain.
Engländer *m.* (*mech.*) monkey wrench; ~ *m.* (-s, -) Englishman; **Engländerin** *f.* (-, -nen) Englishwoman; **englisch** *a.* English, British.
Englisch *n.* (-, 0) English, the English language.
englisch-deutsch *a.* Anglo-German; English-German (dictionary).
Engpaß *m.* (-es, -pässe) pass; (*fig.*) bottleneck.
en gros (*frz.*) *adv.* wholesale.
Engrospreis *m.* wholesale price.
engstirnig *a.* narrow-minded.
Engstirnigkeit *f.* narrow-mindedness.
Enkel *m.* (-s, -) grandson, grandchild.
Enkelin *f.* (-, -nen) granddaughter.
Enklave *f.* (-, -n) enclave.
enorm *a.* enormous, immense, huge.
en passant *adv.* in passing.
Ensemble *n.* ensemble; company; outfit.
entarten *v.i.* (*s*) to degenerate.
entartet *p. & a.* degenerate.
Entartung *f.* (-, -en) degeneration, degeneracy.
entäußern (sich) *v.refl.* to renounce, to give up.
entbehren *v.t.* to lack, to be without; to want, to miss; to do without.
entbehrlich *a.* unnecessary, dispensable.
Entbehrung *f.* (-, -en) privation.
entbinden *v.t.st.* to deliver (a woman); to disengage; (*fig.*) to release.
Entbindung *f.* (-, -en) childbirth delivery, confinement; disengagement.
Entbindungsklinik *f.* maternity clinic.
entblättern *v.t.* to take the leaves off; *v.refl.* to shed the leaves; (*fig.*) to strip.
entblössen *v.t.* to uncover.
entbrennen *v.i.st.* to break out, to flare up.
entdecken *v.t.* to discover, to detect.
Entdeckung *f.* (-, -en) discovery.
Ente *f.* (-, -n) duck; (*Zeitungs-*) canard.
entehren *v.t.* to dishonor; to violate.
entehrend *a.* disgraceful, degrading.
enteignen *v.t.* to expropriate.
Enteignung *f.* (-, -en) expropriation.
enteisen *v.t.* to de-ice.
Entenbraten *m.* roast duck.
Entenküken *n.* duckling.
Ententeich *m.* duck pond.
enterben *v.t.* to disinherit.
Enterhaken *m.* grapnel.
Enterich *m.* (-s, -e) drake.
entern *v.t.* to board, to grapple.
entfachen *v.t.* to kindle.
entfahren *v.i.st.* (*s*) to escape (sigh).
entfallen *v.i.st.* (*s*) ~ *auf,* to fall to one's share; *es ist mir ~,* I cannot remember.
entfalten *v.t.* to unfold; to develop; (sich) ~ *v.refl.*

to open, to expand.
entfärben (sich) *v.refl.* to lose color; *v.t.* to get the color out.
entfernen *v.t.* to remove; (sich) ~ *v.refl.* to withdraw.
entfernt *a.* remote, distant; far from.
Entfernung *f.* (-, -en) removal; distance.
entfesseln *v.t.* to unchain, to let loose; to unleash.
entfetten *v.t.* to skim.
entflammen *v.t.* to inflame, to kindle.
entflechten *v.t.st.* to disentangle; to break up.
entfliehen *v.i.st.* (s) to run away; to escape.
entfremden *v.t.* to estrange, to alienate.
Entfremdung *f.* (-, -en) estrangement, alienation.
entfrosten *v.t.* to defrost.
entführen *v.t.* to hijack; to abduct; to elope with; (*Kinder*) to kidnap; *sich ~ lassen*, to elope (with s.b.).
Entführer *m.* kidnapper, hijacker.
Entführung *f.* kidnapping; hijacking; abduction.
entgegen *pr.* against, contrary to, in opposition to.
entgegenarbeiten *v.t.* to counteract.
entgegengehen *v.i.st.* (s) to get to meet.
entgegengesetzt *a.* opposite, contrary.
entgegenhalten *v.t.st.* to object.
entgegenkommen *v.i.st.* (s) to come to meet; (*fig.*) to meet (half way).
entgegenkommend *a.* accommodating.
Entgegennahme *f.* (-, 0) receipt.
entgegennehmen *v.t.st.* to accept, to receive.
entgegensehen *v.i.st.* to look forward to.
entgegensetzen *v.t.* to oppose, to contrast.
entgegenstehen *v.i.st.* to be opposed.
entgegenstellen *v.t.* to oppose.
entgegentreten *v.i.st.* (s) (*fig.*) to oppose.
entgegenwirken *v.i.* to counteract.
entgegnen *v.i.* to reply, to retort.
Entgegnung *f.* (-, -en) reply; retort.
entgehen *v.i.st.* (s) to escape, to get off.
entgeistert *a.* dum(b)founded; aghast.
Entgelt *n.* (-[e]s, 0) remuneration.
entgelten *v.t.st.* to pay for.
entgleisen *v.i.* (s) to run off the rails; (*fig.*) to make a slip.
Entgleisung *f.* (-, -en) derailment; slip.
entgleiten *v.i.st.* (s) to slip from.
entgräten *v.t.* to bone.
enthaaren *v.t.* to depilate, to remove hair.
enthalten *v.t.st.* to contain; (sich) ~ *v.refl.st.* to abstain (from), to forbear.
enthaltsam *a.* abstemious, abstinent, continent.
Enthaltsamkeit *f.* (-, 0) abstinence.
Enthaltung *f.* abstention.
enthärten *v.t.* to soften.
enthaupten *v.t.* to behead, to decapitate.
enthäuten *v.t.* to skin.
entheben *v.t.st.* to remove (from office).
enthemmend *a.* disinhibitory.
enthemmt *a.* uninhibited.
enthüllen *v.t.* to unveil; to reveal.
Enthüllung *f.* (-, -en) unveiling (of a statue); (*fig.*) exposure, revelation.
enthülsen *v.t.* to shell.
Enthusiasmus *m.* enthusiasm.
enthusiastisch *a.* enthusiastic.
entjungfern *v.t.* to deflower.

entkalken *v.t.* to decalcify.
entkernen *v.t.* to core, to stone.
entkleiden *v.t.* to undress.
entkommen *v.i.st.* (s) to escape.
entkorken *v.t.* to uncork, to open.
entkräften *v.t.* invalidate; to refute; to weaken.
Entkräftung *f.* debility; exhaustion; refutation.
entkrampfen *v.t.* to ease; to relax.
entladen *v.t.st.* to unload; (sich) *v.refl.* to go off, to burst.
entlang *adv.* along.
entlarven *v.t.* to unmask; to expose.
entlassen *v.t.st.* to dismiss, to discharge.
Entlassung *f.* (-, -en) dismissal; *seine ~ nehmen*, to resign (one's office); *seine ~ beantragen*, to tender one's resignation.
entlasten *v.t.* to unburden, to exonerate, to credit.
Entlastung *f.* (-, -en) exoneration; defense.
Entlastungszeuge *m.* witness for the defense.
entlauben *v.t.* to strip (branch); to defoliate.
entlaufen *v.i.st.* (s) to run away.
entledigen (sich) *v.refl.* to get rid (of); to acquit oneself (of one's duty).
entleeren *v.t.* to empty.
entlegen *a.* remote.
entlehnen *v.t.* to borrow.
entleihen *v.t.st.* to borrow (of, from).
Entleiher *m.* (-s, -) borrower.
entlocken *v.t.* to elicit, to draw from.
entlohnen *v.t.* to pay off.
entlüften *v.t.* to ventilate; (*tech.*) to bleed (brakes).
entmachten *v.t.* to deprive of power.
Entmachtung *f.* deprivation of power.
entmannen *v.t.* to castrate.
entmenscht *a.* inhuman, brutish.
entmilitarisieren *v.t.* to demilitarize.
Entmilitarisierung *f.* demilitarization.
entmündigen *v.t.* (*jur.*) to disenfranchise; to incapacitate.
Entmündigung *f.* incapacitation.
entmutigen *v.t.* to discourage.
Entmutigung *f.* discouragement.
Entnahme *f.* taking (samples); withdrawal (money); removal (organs).
entnehmen *v.t.st.* to take from; to gather (from); (*com.*) to draw upon.
entnerven *v.t.* to enervate.
entnervend *a.* nerve-racking.
entpuppen (sich) *v.refl.* (*als*) to turn out to be.
enträtseln *v.t.* to decipher; to unriddle, to make out.
entrechten *v.t.* to deprive s.o. of his/her rights.
entreißen *v.t.st.* to snatch away (from).
entrichten *v.t.* to pay.
entriegeln *v.t.* to unbolt.
entrinnen *v.i.st.* (s) to escape; *knapp ~*, to have a narrow escape.
entrollen *v.t.* to unroll, to unfurl.
entrosten *v.t.* to derust.
entrückt *a.* carried away; enraptured.
entrümpeln *v.t.* to clear out.
entrüsten *v.t.* to provoke, to exasperate; (sich) ~ *v.refl.* to get indignant, to get angry.
Entrüstung *f.* (-, 0) indignation.
entsaften *v.t.* to extract the juice from.
Entsafter *m.* juicer.

entsagen v.i. to renounce, to waive.
Entsagung f. (-, -en) renunciation.
entschädigen v.t. to indemnify, to compensate; to make up for (fig.).
Entschädigung f. (-, -en) compensation; indemnity; ~ leisten, to make compensation for.
entschärfen v.t. to deactivate; to defuse; to tone down.
Entschärfung f. defusing; deactivation.
entscheiden v.t.st. to decide; (sich) ~ v.refl.st. to come to a decision.
entscheidend a. decisive.
Entscheidung f. (-, -en) decision; ruling; zur ~ bringen, to bring to a head.
entschieden, decided; resolute; definite.
Entschiedenheit f. (-, 0) determination; decisiveness.
entschlacken v.t. to purge; to purify.
entschlafen v.i.st. to pass away.
entschließen (sich) v.refl.st. to resolve, to make up one's mind.
Entschließung f. (-, -en) resolution.
entschlossen a. resolute, determined.
Entschlossenheit f. determination; resolution.
entschlummern v.i. to fall asleep.
entschlüpfen v.i. (s) to escape; to slip out.
Entschluß m. (-schlusses, -schlüsse) resolution.
entschlüsseln v.t. to decipher; to decode.
Entschlüsselung f. deciphering; decoding.
entschuldbar a. excusable; pardonable.
entschuldigen v.t. to excuse; (sich) ~ v.refl. to apologize.
Entschuldigung f. (-, -en) excuse, apology; um ~ bitten, to beg pardon.
entschwinden v.i.st. to vanish.
entsenden v.t.ir. to send off, to despatch.
entsetzen v.t. to depose; to relieve, to raise the siege of; (sich) ~ v.refl. to be shocked.
Entsetzen n. (-s, 0) terror, horror.
entsetzlich a. horrible, terrible, dreadful.
entsetzlen v.t. to decontaminate.
entsichern v.t. to release the safety catch.
entsiegeln v.t. to open, to unseal.
entsinnen (sich) v.refl.st. to remember; to recall to mind.
entsorgen v.t. to dispose of (waste).
Entsorgung f. waste disposal.
entspannen (sich) v.i. or refl. to relax.
Entspannung f. (-, 0) relaxation; détente.
entsprechen v.i.st. to correspond to; to answer, to suit (a purpose).
entsprechend a. corresponding; suitable.
Entsprechung f. correspondence.
entspringen v.i.st. (s) to escape; to arise, to rise.
entstammen v.i. (s) to descend from.
entstehen v.i.st. (s) to begin, to originate, to arise; to result, to spring (from).
Entstehung f. (-, -en) origin, rise.
entsteinen v.t. to stone.
entstellen v.t. to disfigure, to deface; to misrepresent.
Entstellung f. (-, -en) distortion.
enttäuschen v.t. to disappoint.
Enttäuschung f. (-, -en) disappointment.
entthronen v.t. to dethrone.
entvölkern v.t. to depopulate.

entwachsen v.i.st. (s) to outgrow.
entwaffnen v.t. to disarm.
Entwarnung f. (-, -en) (Luftschutz) 'all-clear' signal.
entwässern v.t. to drain.
Entwässerung f. drainage.
entweder c. ~... oder... either... or...
entweichen v.i.st. (s) to escape.
entweihen v.t. to profane, to desecrate.
entwenden v.t. to purloin, to embezzle.
entwerfen v.t.st. to sketch, to design.
entwerten v.t. to cancel; to devalue.
Entwertung f. (-, -en) cancellation, devaluation.
entwickeln v.t. to develop.
Entwicklung f. (-, -en) development; evolution; (phot.) developing.
Entwicklungs: ~abteilung f. planning department; **~dienst** m. development aid service; **~geschichte** f. history of the development; evolution; **~hilfe** f. development aid; **~land** n. developing country; **~störung** f. developmental disturbance.
entwirren v.t. to unravel, to disentangle.
entwischen v.i. (s) to escape.
entwöhnen v.t. to disaccustom; to wean (a child).
entwölken (sich) v.refl. to clear up.
entwürdigen v.t. to disgrace, to degrade.
Entwurf m. (-[e]s, -würfe) sketch, draft, blueprint; erster ~, rough draft.
entwurzeln v.t. to uproot.
entziehen v.t.st. to take away; to deprive of; (sich) ~ v.refl. to withdraw.
Entziehung f. withdrawal.
Entziehungskur f. withdrawal treatment.
entzifferbar a. decipherable.
entziffern v.t. to decipher.
entzücken v.t. to delight; to enrapture, to charm.
Entzücken n. delight.
entzückt a. delighted.
Entzückung f. (-, -en) transport.
Entzug m. withdrawal.
Entzugserscheinung f. withdrawal symptom.
entzündbar a. inflammable.
entzünden v.t. to kindle, to set on fire; (fig.) to inflame; (sich) ~ v.refl. to catch fire.
entzündlich a. inflammable; (med.) inflammatory.
Entzündung f.(-, -en) inflammation.
entzwei adv. in two, in pieces; broken.
entzweien v.t. to disunite, to set at variance; (sich) ~ v.refl. to fall out.
entzweigehen v.i.st. to break (down).
Enzian m. (-[e]s, -e) (bot.) gentian.
Enzyklopädie f. (-, -[e]n) encyclopedia.
enzyklopädisch a. encyclopedic.
Enzym n. enzyme.
Epaulett n. (-s, -s) epaulet.
Epheu = **Efeu** m. ivy.
Epidemie f. (-, -[e]n) epidemic.
epidemisch a. epidemic.
Epigramm n. (-s, -e) epigram.
Epik f. epic poetry.
Epilepsie f. (-, 0) epilepsy.
epileptisch a. epileptic.
Epilog m. (-[e]s, -e) epilogue.
episch a. epic.
Episkopat n. episcopate.
Episode f. (-, -n) episode.

episodenhaft *a.* episodic.
Epistel *f.* (-, -n) epistle.
Epizentrum *n.* epicenter.
epochal *a.* epochal; epoch-making.
Epoche *f.* (-, -n) epoch.
epoche-machend *a.* epoch-making.
Epos *n.* (-, Epen) epic poem; epos.
Equipage *f.* (-, -n) carriage.
er *pn.* he; ~ *selbst*, he himself.
erachten *v.t.* to consider, to think, to be of opinion.
Erachten *n.* (-s, 0) opinion; *meines ~s*, in my opinion, for all I know.
erahnen *v.t.* to suspect; to imagine.
erarbeiten *v.t.* to obtain by labor.
Erbanlage *f.* hereditary disposition.
erbarmen (sich) *v.refl.* to pity.
Erbarmen *n.* (-s, 0) mercy; commiseration, pity.
erbarmenswert, erbarmenswürdig *a.* pitiable.
erbärmlich *a.* wretched; miserable, pitiful.
erbarmungslos *a.* merciless; pitiless, remorseless.
erbauen *v.t.* to build, to erect; (*fig.*) to edify; (sich) ~ *v.refl.* to be edified.
Erbauer *m.* (-s, -) builder, founder.
erbaulich *a.* edifying.
erbberechtigt *a.* entitled to inherit.
Erbe *m.* (-n, -n) heir; *gesetzlicher~,* heir-at-law; *mutmaßlicher* ~, heir presumptive; ~ *n.* (-s, 0) inheritance; heritage.
erbeben *v.i.* to tremble, to shake.
Erbeigenschaft *f.* hereditary characteristic.
erben *v.t.* to inherit, to succeed to.
erbetteln *v.t.* to get by begging.
erbeuten *v.t.* to capture.
Erbfall *m.* case of succession, heritage.
Erbfolge *f.* hereditary succession.
Erbforschung *f.* genetics.
Erbgut *n.* hereditary make-up.
erbieten (sich) *v.refl.st.* to volunteer.
Erbin *f.* (-, -nen) heiress.
erbitten *v.t.st.* to request, to solicit.
erbittern *v.t.* to exasperate, to provoke.
erbittert *a. & adv.* bitter.
Erbitterung *f.* (-, -en) exasperation; bitterness.
Erbkrankheit *f.* hereditary disease.
erblassen *v.i.* (*s*) to turn pale, to pale.
Erblasser *m.* (-s, -) testator.
erbleichen *v.i.st.* (*s*) to pale.
erblich *a.* hereditary.
erblicken *v.t.* to see, to discover.
erblinden *v.i.* (*s*) to go blind.
erblühen *v.i.* (*s*) to bloom; to blossom.
Erbmasse *f.* genotype; genetic make-up; (*jur.*) estate.
erbost *a.* angry; furious.
Erbpacht *f.* hereditary lease.
erbrechen *v.t.st.* to break open; (sich) ~ *v.refl.* to vomit.
Erbrechen *n.* (-s, 0) vomiting.
Erbrecht *n.* law of inheritance.
erbringen *v.t.ir.* to produce.
Erbschaden *m.* hereditary defect.
Erbschaft *f.* (-, -en) inheritance.
Erbschaftssteuer *f.* estate/death duties.
Erbschleicher *m.* legacy hunter.
Erbse *f.* (-, -n) pea.
Erb: ~**stück** *n.* heirloom; ~**sünde** *f.* original sin.

Erbteil *n.* portion (of an inheritance).
Erd: ~**apfel** *m.* potato; ~**anziehung** *f.* earth's gravity; ~**ball** *m.* globe; ~**beben** *n.* earthquake; ~**beere** *f.* strawberry; ~**boden** *m.* ground, soil; earth.
Erde *f.* (-, -n) earth; world; ground, soil; (*fam.*) floor; (*fig.*) dust, clay; (*el.*) earth, ground.
erden *v.t.* to earth, to ground.
Erdenbürger *m.* earth dweller.
erdenken *v.t.ir.* to imagine.
erdenklich *a.* imaginable, conceivable.
Erdgas *n.* natural gas.
Erdgeschoß *n.* ground floor.
erdichten *v.t.* to invent, to feign.
Erd: ~**kabel** *n.* underground cable; ~**kreis** *m.* ~**kugel** *f.* globe; ~**kunde** *f.* geography; ~**nuß** *f.* peanut; groundnut; ~**öl** *n.* petroleum.
erdolchen *v.t.* to stab.
Erdölraffinerie *f.* oil refinery.
Erdreich *n.* earth; soil.
erdreisten (sich) *v.refl.* to make bold.
erdrosseln *v.t.* to strangle, to throttle.
erdrücken *v.t.* to crush; to overwhelm.
erdrückend *a.* overwhelming.
Erd: ~**rutsch** *m.* landslide; land slip; ~**teil** *m.* continent.
Erdtruppen *f.pl.* ground forces.
erdulden *v.t.* to suffer, to endure.
Erd: ~**umdrehung** *f.* rotation of the earth; ~**umfang** *m.* circumference of the earth; ~**umlaufbahn** *f.* orbit.
Erdung *f.* grounding.
Erdzeitalter *n.* geological era.
ereifern (sich) *v.refl.* to get excited.
ereignen (sich) *v.refl.* to happen, to occur.
Ereignis *n.* (-nisses, -nisse) occurrence, event.
ereignislos *a.* uneventful.
ereignisreich *a.* eventful.
ereilen *v.t.* to catch up with s.o.
Erektion *f.* erection.
Eremit *m.* (-en, -en) hermit.
ererben *v.t.* to inherit.
erfahren *v.t.st.* to experience, to suffer; to learn, to hear; ~ *a.* experienced, expert; conversant (with).
Erfahrung *f.* (-, -en) experience; knowledge; practice; *in ~ bringen*, to learn, to be informed, to find out.
erfassen *v.t.* to comprehend, to grasp; to catch.
Erfassung *f.* registration.
erfinden *v.t.st.* to invent; to make up.
Erfinder *m.* (-s, -) inventor.
erfinderisch *a.* inventive.
Erfindung *f.* (-, -en) invention.
Erfindungsgabe *f.* inventiveness.
erfindungsreich *a.* imaginative.
erflehen *v.t.* to implore.
Erfolg *m.* (-[e]s, -e) result, effect, success.
erfolgen *v.i.* (*s*) to take place; to happen.
erfolg: ~**los** *a.* unsuccessful, vain; ~**reich** *a.* successful.
erfolgversprechend *a.* promising.
erforderlich *a.* necessary, required.
erfordern *v.t.* to demand, to require.
Erfordernis *n.* (-nisses, -nisse) requirement, demand.
erforschen *v.t.* to explore, to investigate.
Erforschung *f.* (-, -en) exploration.

erfragen *v.t.* to ascertain by inquiry.
erfreuen *v.t. & refl.* (sich) to rejoice; to cheer, to please.
erfreulich *a.* pleasant; encouraging.
erfreulicherweise *adv.* fortunately.
erfrieren *v.i.st.* (*s*) to freeze (to death).
Erfrierung *f.* frostbite.
erfrischen *v.t.* to refresh.
erfrischend *a.* refreshing.
Erfrischung *f.* (-, -en) refreshment.
erfüllen *v.t.* to fulfil; to accomplish; *seine Pflicht ~*, to do one's duty; *ein Versprechen ~*, to keep a promise.
Erfüllung *f.* (-, 0) fulfilment, accomplishment; *in ~ gehen*, to come true.
Erfüllungsort *m.* settling place.
ergänzen *v.t.* to complete, to supply.
ergänzend *a.* supplementary.
Ergänzung *f.* (-, -en) supplement; supplementation.
ergattern *v.t.* to get hold of.
ergeben *v.t.st.* to yield, to produce; (sich) ~ *v.refl.* to surrender; to result; to devote oneself.
ergeben *a.* devoted, addicted; obedient.
ergebenst *adv.* very truly yours.
Ergebnis *n.* (-nisses, -nisse) result.
ergebnislos *a.* without result.
Ergebung *f.* (-, 0) surrender; submission, resignation.
ergehen *v.i.st. es wird ihm schlimm ~*, he will suffer for it; ~ *lassen*, to issue, to promulgate; *über sich ~ lassen*, to submit to.
ergiebig *a.* productive; fertile, rich.
ergießen (sich) *v.refl.st.* to fall (into); to pour.
ergötzen *v.t.* to amuse, to delight; (sich) ~ *v.refl.* to enjoy oneself.
ergötzlich *a.* delightful, amusing.
ergrauen *v.i.* to turn grey.
ergreifen *v.t.st.* to seize, to take up; (*Flucht*) to take to flight; (*Partei*) to side with; to affect.
ergreifend *a.* moving.
Ergreifung *f.* capture; seizure.
ergriffen *a.* moved; struck, affected.
ergründen *v.t.* to get to the bottom of.
Erguß *m.* (-gusses, -güsse) (*fig.*) effusion; (*Blut ~*) bruise; (*samen~*) ejaculation.
erhaben *a.* raised, elevated; sublime.
Erhalt *m.* receipt.
erhalten *v.t.st.* to maintain; to sustain; to preserve; to receive, to get; to obtain; (sich) ~ *v.refl.* to live *or* subsist on.
erhältlich *a.* obtainable.
Erhaltung *f.* (-, 0) preservation, conservation; maintenance.
erhängen (sich) *v.refl.* to hang oneself.
erhärten *v.t.* to substantiate; to strengthen.
erhaschen *v.t.* to catch, to seize.
erheben *v.t.st.* to lift up; to elevate, to raise; to extoll, to praise; (sich) ~ *v.refl.st.* to rise; *ein Geschrei ~*, to set up a cry; *die Frage ~*, to start the question; *Geld ~*, to raise money; *ins Quadrat ~*, to square.
erheblich *a.* considerable.
Erheblichkeit *f.* (-, 0) relevance.
Erhebung *f.* (-, -en) elevation; promotion; (*Steuer*) levy; (*Nachforschung*) inquiry; (*Aufstand*) insurrection.

erheitern *v.t.* to cheer, to exhilarate.
Erheiterung *f.* (-, -en) amusement, diversion.
erhellen *v.t.* to light up, to clear up; ~ *v.i.* to become evident.
erheucheln *v.t.* to feign.
erhitzen *v.t.* to heat; (sich) ~ *v.refl.* to grow hot; (*fig.*) to get angry.
erhoffen *v.t.* to hope for.
erhöhen *v.t.* to heighten; to enhance; to raise, to increase.
Erhöhung *f.* (-, -en) rise, increase.
erholen (sich) *v.refl.* to recover.
erholsam *a.* restful.
Erholung *f.* (-, -en) recovery; recreation.
Erholungs . . . recreational.
Erholungsstätte *f.* rest center.
erhören *v.t.* to hear; to grant.
erigieren *v.i.* to become erect.
Erika *f.* (*bot.*) heather.
erinnerlich *a. soviel mir ~ ist*, so far as I can recollect.
erinnern *v.t.* to remind; (sich) ~ *v.refl.* to remember; to recollect.
Erinnerung *f.* (-, -en) remembrance; reminiscence.
Erinnerungslücke *f.* gap in one's memory.
Erinnerungswert *m.* sentimental value.
erjagen *v.t.* to get (by hunting).
erkalten *v.i.* (*s*) to cool down.
erkälten (sich) *v.refl.* to catch (a) cold.
Erkältung *f.* (-, -en) cold.
erkämpfen *v.t.* to gain by fighting.
erkennbar *a.* recognizable; visible; discernible.
erkennen *v.t.st.* to perceive; to discern; to realize, to see; to know; to recognize; to decide.
erkenntlich *a.* grateful.
Erkenntnis *f.* (-nisses, -nisse) knowledge; cognition; perception.
Erkennungs: ~dienst *m.* police records department; **~melodie** *f.* theme music; signature tune; **~zeichen** *n.* sign.
Erker *m.* (-s, -) oriel; **~fenster** *n.* bay window.
erklärbar *a.* explicable.
erklären *v.t.* to explain, to interpret; to declare; to account for; (sich) ~ *v.refl.* to declare oneself.
erklärend *a.* explanatory.
erklärlich *a.* explicable; *leicht ~*, easily accounted for, easily explained.
erklärt *a.* professed; sworn.
erklärtermassen *adv.* professedly.
Erklärung *f.* (-, -en) explanation; declaration.
erklecklich *a.* considerable.
erklettern *v.t.* to climb to the top.
erklimmen *v.t.* to climb.
erklingen *v.i.st.* (*s*) to resound, to ring.
erkranken *v.i.* (*s*) to fall ill, to become sick.
Erkrankung *f.* (-, -en) illness, sickness, disease.
erkühnen (sich) *v.refl.* to dare.
erkunden *v.t.* to explore; to find out; (*mil.*) to reconnoiter.
erkundigen (sich) *v.refl.* to make inquiries.
Erkundigung *f.* (-, -en) inquiry.
erlahmen *v.i.* (*s*) to get tired *or* weak.
erlangen *v.t.* to attain; to obtain.
Erlaß *m.* (-lasses, -lasse) remission, pardon; decree.

erlassen *v.t.st.* to issue; (*Gesetz*) to enact; (*nachlassen*) to remit.

erlauben *v.t.* to permit, to allow.

Erlaubnis *f.* (-, 0) permission, leave; *mit ~ von*, by permission of.

erläutern *v.t.* to illustrate, to elucidate; to explain; to annotate.

Erläuterung *f.* (-, -en) explanation; illustration.

Erle *f.* (-, -n) alder.

erleben *v.t.* to live to see; to experience.

Erlebnis *n.* (-nisses, -nisse) experience.

erledigen *v.t.* to deal with; carry out; to settle; (sich) ~ *v.refl.* to be settled.

erledigt *a.* finished; settled.

Erledigung *f.* (-, -en) settlement; execution (of work); errand.

erlegen *v.t.* to kill.

erleichtern *v.t.* to facilitate; to lighten, to ease; to alleviate.

Erleichterung *f.* (-, -en) relief; facilitation; (*von Bestimmungen*) relaxation.

erleiden *v.t.st.* to suffer, to bear.

erlernen *v.t.* to learn.

erlesen *a.* select, choice.

erleuchten *v.t.* to illuminate; to enlighten.

Erleuchtung *f.* (-, -en) illumination.

erliegen *v.i.st.* (*s*) to succumb.

erlogen *a.* false, untrue, forged.

Erlös *m.* (-ses, -se) proceeds *pl.*

erlöschen *v.t.* to extinguish; ~ *v.i.st.* (*s*) to go out; to become void.

erlösen *v.t.* to redeem, to deliver.

Erlöser *m.* (-s, -) Redeemer, Saviour.

Erlösung *f.* (-, -en) redemption.

ermächtigen *v.t.* to empower, to authorize.

Ermächtigung *f.* (-, -en) authorization; ~**sgesetz** *n.* enabling act.

ermahnen *v.t.* to admonish.

Ermahnung *f.* (-, -en) admonition, exhortation.

ermangeln *v.i.* to be wanting; to fail.

Ermangelung *f.* (-, 0) *in ~ von*, in default of.

ermäßigen *v.t.* to abate; to reduce; *zu ermässigten Preisen*, at reduced rates.

Ermäßigung *f.* (-, -en) reduction; abatement.

ermatten *v.i.* (*s*) to grow tired, to slacken.

ermessen *v.t.st.* to measure; to judge.

Ermessen *n.* (-s, 0) judgment; *nach meinem ~*, in my opinion.

Ermessens: ~**frage** *f.* matter of opinion; ~**spielraum** *m.* latitude.

ermitteln *v.t.* to find out, to ascertain.

Ermittlung *f.* (-, -en) inquiry.

Ermittlungs: ~**beamte** *m.*; ~**beamtin** *f.* investigating officer.

ermöglichen *v.t.* to enable; to render possible.

ermorden *v.t.* to murder; (*pol.*) to assassinate.

Ermordung *f.* (-, -en) murder; (*pol.*) assassination.

ermüden *v.t.* to tire, to fatigue; ~*v.i.* (*s*) to get tired.

ermüdend *a.* tiring.

Ermüdung *f.* (-, -en) exhaustion.

ermuntern *v.t.* to encourage; to animate.

ermutigen *v.t.* to encourage.

ermutigend *a.* encouraging.

Ermutigung *f.* (-, -en) encouragement.

ernähren *v.t.* to nourish; to support.

Ernährer *m.*; **Ernährerin** *f.* provider; supporter.

Ernährung *f.* (-, -en) nutrition.

Ernährungs: ~**weise** *f.* diet; ~**wissenschaft** *f.* dietetics.

ernennen *v.t.st.* to nominate, to appoint.

Ernennung *f.* (-, -en) appointment.

erneuen, erneuern *v.t.* to renew, to renovate; to replace.

Erneuerung *f.* (-, -en) renovation; replacement; renewal; revival.

erneut *a.* renewed; once again.

erniedrigen *v.t.* to lower; to humble; (sich) ~ *v.refl.* to degrade oneself.

erniedrigend *a.* humiliating.

Erniedrigung *f.* humiliation.

Ernst *m.* (-es, 0) seriousness.

ernst *a.* earnest, serious, grave, stern; *etwas ~ nehmen*, to take a thing seriously.

Ernstfall *m.* emergency; (*mil.*) case of war; **im ~** in case of emergency.

ernstgemeint *a.* serious; sincere.

ernsthaft *a.* serious, grave.

Ernsthaftigkeit *f.* seriousness.

ernstlich *a.* earnest, serious.

Ernte *f.* (-, -n) harvest; (*Ertrag*) crop.

Ernte: ~**ausfall** *m.* crop failure; ~**dankfest** *n.* harvest festival; ~**ertrag** *m.* yield; ~**maschine** *f.* harvester.

ernten *v.t.* to reap, to harvest.

ernüchtern *v.t.* to sober, to disillusion.

Ernüchterung *f.* disillusionment.

Eroberer *m.* (-s, -); **Eroberin** *f.* (-, -nen) conqueror.

erobern *v.t.* to conquer.

Eroberung *f.* (-, -en) conquest.

eröffnen *v.t.* to open, to begin; to inaugurate; (*fig.*) to disclose, to make known.

Eröffnung *f.* (-, -en) opening, beginning; communication.

Eröffnungs: ~**ausprache** *f.* opening speech; ~**feier** *f.* opening ceremony.

erogen *a.* erogenous.

erörtern *v.t.* to discuss.

Erörterung *f.* (-, -en) discussion.

Erosion *f.* (-, -en) erosion.

Erotik *f.* eroticism.

erotisch *a.* erotic.

Erpel *m.* drake.

erpicht *a.* keen upon; bent (upon).

erpressen *v.t.* to blackmail; to extort.

erpresserisch *a.* blackmailing.

Erpressung *f.* (-, -en) extortion; blackmail.

erproben *v.t.* to try, test.

Erprobung *f.* testing.

erquicken *v.t.* to refresh.

erraten *v.t.* to guess, to divine.

errechnen *v.t.* to compute.

erregbar *a.* excitable; irritable.

erregen *v.t.* to stir up, to arouse; to excite; to provoke; to produce.

erregend *a.* exciting; arousing.

Erreger *m.* (*med.*) pathogen.

erregt *a.* excited; aroused.

Eregung *f.* (-, -en) excitement; arousal.

erreichbar *a.* attainable; within reach.

erreichen *v.t.* to attain, to reach.

erretten *v.t.* to save, to rescue (from).

Erretter *m.* saviour.

Errettung *f.* (-, -en) deliverance.

errichten *v.t.* to build; to erect; to establish.

Errichtung *f.* (-, -en) erection; establishment.

erringen *v.t.st.* to gain; to win.

erröten *v.i.* (s) to blush.

Errungenschaft *f.* (-, -en) achievement; acquisition.

Ersatz *m.* (-es, 0) substitute; compensation, reparation; amends *pl.*

Ersatz: ~anspruch *m.* right of compensation; **~batterie** *f.* spare battery; **handlung** *f.* (psych.) displacement activity; **~rad** *n.* (*mot.*) spare wheel; **~reifen** *m.* spare tire; **~stoff** *m.* substitute; **~teil** *m.* spare (part).

ersaufen *v.i.st.* (*fam.*) to drown.

ersäufen *v.t.* to drown.

erschaffen *v.t.st.* to create.

Erschaffung *f.* (-, 0) creation.

erschellen *v.i.* to sound.

erschauern *v.i.* to tremble.

erscheinen *v.i.st.* (s) to appear; (*Buch*) to come out.

Erscheinung *f.* (-, -en) appearance; apparition; phenomenon; symptom.

Erscheinungsjahr *n.* year of publication.

erschießen *v.t.st.* to shoot (dead).

Erschießung *f.* shooting; (*mil.*) execution.

Erschießungskommando *n.* firing squad.

erschlaffen *v.i.* (s) to slacken.

erschlagen *v.t.st.* to slay.

erschlichen *a.* surreptitious.

erschließen *v.t.st.* to make accessible.

erschöpfen *v.t.* to exhaust.

erschöpfend *a.* exhaustive.

erschöpft *a.* exhausted.

Erschöpfung *f.* (-, 0) exhaustion.

erschrecken *v.t.* to frighten, to startle; *~v.i.st.* (s) to be frightened.

erschrocken *a.* frightened, terrified.

erschüttern *v.t.* to shake, to shock.

erschütternd *a.* deeply distressing; shocking.

Erschütterung *f.* (-, -en) shock; (*fig.*) emotion.

erschweren *v.t.* to aggravate.

erschwerend *a.* complicating; aggravating.

erschwindeln *v.t.* to swindle.

erschwingen *v.t.st.* to afford.

erschwinglich *a.* reasonable; affordable.

ersehen *v.t.st.* to see, to find; to choose.

ersehnen *v.t.* to long for.

ersetzbar *a.* replaceable.

ersetzen *v.t.* to replace, to repair, to compensate; to refund.

Ersetzung *f.* reimbursement; compensation (damage).

ersichtlich *a.* evident, apparent.

ersinnen *v.t.st.* to devise.

esparen *v.t.* to spare, to save.

Ersparnis *f.* (-nisses, -nisse) savings *pl.*

ersprießlich *a.* useful, beneficial.

erst *adv.* first, at first; not until, only.

erstarken *v.i.* (s) to grow strong.

erstarren *v.i.* (s) to grow stiff *or* numb.

erstatten *v.t.* to reimburse; *Bericht ~,* to report (on).

Erstattung *f.* (-, -en) reimbursement.

Erstaufführung *f.* (-, -en) premiere; opening

night.

erstaunen *v.i.* (s) to amaze; to be astonished.

Erstaunen *n.* (-s, 0) amazement; astonishment.

erstaunlich *a.* astonishing, amazing.

erstaunlicherweise *adv.* amazingly.

erstaunt *a.* astonished; amazed.

erstechen *v.t.st.* to stab.

erstehen *v.i.st.* (s) to arise; ~ *v.t.st.* to buy.

Erste-Hilfe-Ausrüstung *f.* first-aid kit.

ersteigen *v.t.st.* to ascend, to climb.

ersteigern *v.t.* to buy at an auction.

Ersteigung *f.* ascent.

erstens *adv.* firstly, in the first place.

erstgeboren *a.* firstborn.

Erstgeburt *f.* (-, -en) primogeniture.

ersticken *v.t.* to suffocate, to choke; ~ *v.i.* (s) to be suffocated.

Erstickung *f.* suffocation; asphyxiation.

erstklassig *a.* first-rate.

erstlich *adv.* firstly, at first.

Erstling *m.* first work.

erstmalig *a.* first; *adv.* for the first time.

erstrahlen *v.i.* to shine.

erstreben *v.t.* to strive after.

erstrebenswert *a.* desirable.

erstrecken (sich) *v.refl.* to extend; to stretch.

Erstschlag *m.* first strike.

erstürmen *v.t.* to take by storm.

ersuchen *v.t.* to request, to beg.

ertappen *v.t.* to surprise, to catch; *auf der Tat ~,* to take in the act.

erteilen *v.t.* to impart, to confer; (*Verweis*) to administer.

Erteilung *f.* granting.

ertönen *v.i.* (s) to (re)sound.

Ertrag *m.* (-[e]s, -träge) produce, yield; proceeds *pl.*; returns *pl.*

Ertragfähigkeit *f.* productiveness.

ertragen *v.t.st.* (*fig.*) to bear, to endure.

erträglich *a.* tolerable, endurable.

entränken *v.t.* to drown.

erträumen *v.refl.* to dream of.

ertrinken *v.i.st.* (s) to get drowned.

Ertrinkende *m./f.* drowning person.

Ertrunkene *m./f.* drowned person.

ertüchtigen *v.t.* to train.

erübrigen *v.t.* to save, to spare; to remain; *sich ~,* to be unnecessary.

eruieren *v.t.* to find out.

Erwachen *n.* awakening.

erwachen *v.i.* (s) to awake.

erwachsen *v.i.st.* (s) to accrue; ~ *a.* grown-up.

Erwachsene[r] *m.* (-n, -n) adult, grown-up person.

Erwachsenenbildung *f.* adult education.

erwägen *v.t.st.* (*fig.*) to weigh, to consider.

Erwägung *f.* (-, -en) consideration; *in ~ ziehen,* to take into consideration; *in ~ dass,* considering, seeing that . . .

erwählen *v.t.* to choose, to elect.

erwähnen *v.t.* to mention.

erwähnenswert *a.* worth mentioning.

Erwähnung *f.* (-, -en) mention.

erwärmen *v.t.* to warm, to heat.

erwarten *v.t.* to expect; to wait for, to await.

Erwartung *f.* (-, -en) expectation.

erwartungs: ~**gemäß** *a.* as expected; ~**voll** *a.* expectant.

erwecken *v.t.* to awaken.

Erweckung *f.* (-, -en) awakening.

erwehren (sich) *v.refl.* to fend off.

erweichen *v.t.* to soften, to mollify.

erweisen *v.t.st.* to prove, to render; (*eine Gunst*) to bestow upon; *sich ~ als,* to turn out to be.

erweitern *v.t.* to widen, to enlarge; to expand; to extend, to amplify.

Erweiterung *f.* (-, -en) enlargement; amplification, expansion; extension.

Erwerb *m.* (-[e]s, 0) acquisition; gain, earnings *pl.*; living.

erwerben *v.t.st.* to acquire, to gain.

erwerbsfähig *a.* able-bodied, capable of earning one's living.

Erwerbsleben *n.* working life.

erwerbslos *a.* unemployed.

Erwerbslosenunterstützung *f.* (-, 0) unemployment benefit, dole.

Erwerbslosigkeit *f.* (-, 0) unemployment.

erwerbsunfähig *a.* unable to work.

Erwerbung *f.* (-, -en) acquisition.

erwidern *v.t.* to return; to reply.

Erwiderung *f.* (-, -en) return; reply.

erwiesen *a.* proved.

erwiesenermassen *adv.* as has been proved.

erwirken *v.t.* to procure.

erwirtschaften *v.t.* to make.

erwischen *v.t.* to catch.

erwünscht *a.* desired, welcome.

erwürgen *v.t.* to strangle, to throttle.

Erz *n.* (-es, -e) ore.

erzählen *v.t.* to tell, to narrate, to relate.

erzählend *a.* narrative.

erzählerisch *a.* narrative.

Erzählung *f.* (-, -en) narrative, tale, story.

Erzbergbau *m.* ore mining.

Erzbergwerk *n.* ore mine.

Erzbischof *m.* archbishop.

erzbischöflich *n.* archiepiscopal.

Erzbistum *n.* archbishopric.

Erzengel *m.* archangel.

erzeugen *v.t.* to beget, to engender, to produce; (*Dampf*) to generate.

Erzeuger *m.* producer; father.

Erzengerland *n.* country of origin.

Erzengerpreis *m.* manufacturer's price.

Erzeugnis *n.* (-nisses, -nisse) (*der Natur*) produce; (*des Geistes*) product.

Erzeugung *f.* (-, -en) generation; production.

Erzfeind *m.* arch enemy.

Erz: ~**gießer** *m.* brass founder; ~**herzog** *m.* archduke; ~**herzogin** *f.* archduchess.

erziehen *v.t.st.* to bring up, to educate.

Erzieher *m.* teacher, tutor.

Erzieherin *f.* (-, -nen) governess.

Erziehung *f.* (-, 0) upbringing; education.

Erziehungs: ~**anstalt** *f.* approved school; ~**berater** *m.* educational adviser; ~**beratung** *f.* child guidance; ~**berechtigte** *m./f.* parent; guardian; ~**wissenschaft** *f.* educational science.

erzielen *v.t.* to obtain; to produce.

erzittern *v.i.* to shake; to tremble.

erzkonservativ *a.* ultraconservative.

erzürnen *v.t.* to anger; *v.i.* (*s*) (sich) ~*v.refl.* to grow angry.

erzwingen *v.t.st.* to force, to enforce.

es *pn.* it; so.

Es *n.* (-, 0) E flat.

E-saite *f.* E-string.

Esche *f.* (-, -n) ash (tree).

Esel *m.* (-s, -) ass; donkey; (*fam.*) idiot.

Eselsbrücke *f.* mnemonic (aid).

Eselsohr *n.* (*fig.*) (*im Buche*) dog's ear.

Eskalation *f.* escalation.

eskalieren *v.i.* to escalate.

Eskapade *f.* escapade.

Eskorte *f.* escort.

eskortieren *v.t.* to escort.

esoterisch *a.* esoteric.

Espe *f.* (-, -n) aspen, quaking aspen.

Esplenlaub *n.* aspen leaves *pl.*

Esprit *m.* wit.

Eßapfel *m.* eating apple.

Essay *m.* essay.

eßbar *a.* edible.

Eßbesteck *n.* knife, fork and spoon.

Esse *f.* (-, -n) smithy; chimney.

essen *v.t. & i.st.* to eat; to dine; to feed.

Essen *n.* (-s, -) food; dinner, meal; *ohne ~ sein,* to go without food.

Essenszeit *f.* mealtime.

essentiell *a.* essential.

Essenz *f.* (-, -en) essence.

Eßgewohnheiten *pl.* eating habits.

Essig *m.* (-[e]s, -e) vinegar.

Essig: ~**gurke** *f.* gherkin; ~**sauer** *a.* acetic; acetate of; ~**saure Tonerde** *f.* aluminium acetate; ~**säure** *f.* acetic acid.

Eß: ~**kastanie** *f.* chestnut; ~**löffel** *m.* tablespoon; *ein ~löffel voll,* one tablespoonful of; ~**lokal** *n.* restaurant; ~**stäbchen** *n.* chopstick; ~**tisch** *m.* diningtable, dinner table; ~**waren** *pl.* edibles, victuals *pl.*; ~**zimmer** *n.* dining room.

Eß-Service *n.* dinnerware.

Este *m.* (-n, -n); **Estin** *f.* (-, -nen) Estonian; **Estland** *n.* (-s, 0) Estonia.

estnisch *a.* Estonian.

Estragon *m.* tarragon.

Estrich *n.* (-[e]s, -e) floor.

etablieren *v.t.* to establish; (sich) ~ *v.refl.* to settle; to set up in business.

Etablissement *n.* (-s, -s) establishment.

Etage *f.* (-, -n) storey, floor, flat.

Etagenwohnung *f.* flat.

Etagenbett *n.* bunk bed.

Etappe *f.* (-, -n) stage; (*mil.*) rear.

Etat (*frz.*) *m.* (-s, -s) budget, estimate.

Etatkürzung *f.* cut in the budget.

Ethik *f.* (-, 0) ethics *pl.*

ethisch *a.* ethical.

ethnisch *a.* ethnic.

Ethnologe *m.*; **Ethnologin** *f.* ethnologist.

Ethnologie *f.* ethnology.

ethnologisch *a.* ethnological.

Etikett *n.* (-s, -s) label.

Etikette *f.* (-, -n) etiquette.

etliche *a.pl.* quite a number of, several.

Etrusker *m.*; **Etruskerin** *f.*; **etruskisch** *a.* Etruscan.

Etui *n.* (-s, -s) case, box.
etwa *adv.* perhaps, nearly, about; say.
etwaig *a.* eventual.
etwas *pn.* something; some, any; ~ *adv.* somewhat.
Etymologie *f.* (-, -en) etymology.
etymologisch *a.* etymological.
euch *pn.* you.
euer *pn.* your; yours; **euresgleichen**, your equals.
Eugenik *f.* (-, -en) eugenics *pl.*
Eule *f.* (-, -n) owl, owlet.
Euphemismus *m.* (-, -men) euphemism.
Euphorie *f.* euphoria.
euphorisch *a.* euphoric; *adv.* euphorically.
Eurasien *n.* Eurasia.
eurethalben, euretwegen, um euretwillen, *adv.* for your sake.
eurige (*der, die, das*) *pn.* yours.
Europa *n.* (-s, 0) Europe.
Europäer *m.*; **Europäerin** *f.*; **europäisch** *a.* European.
Europäische Gemeinschaft *f.* European Community.
Europaparlament *n.* European Parliament.
Europarat *m.* Council of Europe.
Euroscheck *m.* Eurocheque.
Euter *n.* (-s, -) udder, dug.
Euthanasie *f.* euthanasia.
evakuieren *v.t.* to evacuate.
Evakuierte *m./f.* evacuee.
Evakuierung *f.* evacuation.
evangelisch *a.* evangelical; Protestant.
Evangelist *m.* (-en, -en) evangelist.
Evengelium *n.* (-s, Evangelien) gospel.
eventuell *a. & adv.* possible, possibly, in a certain contingency.
evident *a.* obvious.
Evolution *f.* evolution.
evolutionär *a.* evolutionary.
ewig *a.* eternal, everlasting, perpetual; *auf* ~, in perpetuity.
Ewigkeit *f.* (-, -en) eternity.
exakt *a.* exact, accurate; *~e Wissenschaften*, exact sciences.
exaltiert *a.* overexcited, exaggerated, effusive.
Examen *n.* (-s, Examina) examination; *ein ~ bestehen*, to pass an examination.
Examinator *m.* (-s, -en) examiner.
examinieren *v.t.* to examine.
exekutieren *v.t.* to execute.
Exempel *n.* (-s, -) example.
Exemplar *n.* (-[e]s, -e) (*eines Buches*) copy; sample, specimen.
exemplarisch *a.* exemplary.
exerzieren *v.t. & i.* to exercise, to drill.
Exerzierplatz *m.* drill ground.
Exhibitionismus *m.* exhibitionism.
exhibitionistisch *a.* exhibitionist.
exhumieren *v.t.* to exhume.
Exil *n.* exile.
Exilant *m.*; **Exilantin** *f.* exile.

Existentialismus *m.* existentialism.
existentiell *a.* existential.
Existenz *f.* (-, -en) existence, livelihood.
Existenzminimum *n.* subsistence level.
existieren *v.i.* to exist, to subsist.
exklusiv *a. & adv.* exclusive(ly).
Exklusivität *f.* exclusiveness, exclusivity.
Exkurs *m.* digression; excursus.
exmatrikulieren *v.t. u. refl.* to remove s.o.'s name from the university register.
Exorzismus *m.* exorcism.
exotisch *a.* exotic.
expandieren *v.i.* to expand.
expansiv *a.* expansionist; expansionary.
expedieren *v.t.* to dispatch, to forward.
Expedition *f.* (-, -en) expedition.
Experiment *n.* (-[e]s, -e) experiment.
experimentieren *v.t.* to experiment.
Experte *m.*; **Expertin** *f.* expert.
Expertise *f.* expert's report.
explizit *a.* explicit.
explodieren *v.i.* (*s*) to explode.
Explosion *f.* (-, -en) explosion.
Explosionsmotor *m.* internal combustion engine.
explosiv *a.* explosive.
Explosivität *f.* explosiveness.
Exponat *n.* exhibit.
exponiert *a.* exposed.
Export *m.* (-[e]s, -e) export, exportation.
Exporthandel *m.* export trade.
exportieren *v.t.* to export.
Exposé *n.* exposé; outline.
expreß *a. & adv.* express(ly).
Expressionismus *m.* expressionism.
expressionistisch *a.* expressionist; *adv.* expressionistically.
exquisit *a. & adv.* exquisite(ly).
extensiv *a. & adv.* extensive(ly).
extern *a.* external.
Exterritorialität *f.* extraterritoriality.
extra *adv.* extra, besides, over and above; (*fam.*) especially, separately.
Extraausgabe *f.* special edition; additional expense.
Extrablatt *n.* special edition.
Extrakt *m.* (-s, -e) extract.
Extraration *f.* extra ration.
extraterrestrisch *a.* extraterrestrial.
extravagant *a.* flamboyant.
Extravaganz *f.* flamboyance.
Extrem *n.* (-[e]s, -e) extreme.
Extremfall *m.* extreme case.
Extremismus *m.* extremism.
extremistisch *a.* extremist.
Extremitäten *f.pl.* extremities *pl.*
extrovertiert *a.* extrovert(ed).
Exzellenz *f.* (-, -en) Excellency.
Exzentriker *m.*; **Exzentrikerin** *f.* eccentric.
exzentrisch *a.* eccentric.
Exzeß *m.* (-es, -e) excess.

F

F, f the letter F or f.
Fabel *f.* (-, -n) fable, fiction; plot.
fabelhaft *a.* fabulous, amazing.
Fabrik *f.* (-, -en) factory, mill, works *pl.*
Fabrikanlage *f.* factory plant.
Fabrikant *m.* (-en, -en) factory owner; manufacturer.
Fabrikat *n.* (-[e]s, -e) product; make.
Fabrikation *f.* (-, -sarten) production.
Fabrik: ~**gebäude** *n.* factory building; ~**gelände** *n.* factory site.
fabrikmäßig *a. & adv.* by machinery.
Fabrikware *f.* manufactured goods *pl.*
fabrizieren *v.t.* to manufacture, to make.
Facette *f.* (-, -en) facet.
facettieren *v.t.* to cut in facets.
Fach *n.* (-[e]s, Fächer) compartment, partition; drawer, box, shelf; panel; (*im Schreibtisch*) pigeonhole; (*fig.*) province, department; branch, line; (*Lehrfach*) subject.
Fach: ~**arbeiter** *m.* skilled worker; ~**ausdruck** *m.* technical term; ~**berater** *m.* technical adviser *or* consultant; ~**bildung** *f.* professional education.
fächeln *v.t.* to fan.
Fächer *m.* (-s, -) fan.
Fach: ~**frau** *f.* expert; ~**gelehrte** *m./f.* specialist.
fachkundig *a.* knowledgeable.
Fach: ~**lehrer** *m.*; ~**lehrerin** *f.* subject teacher; ~**leute** *pl.* experts.
fachlich *a.* specialist.
Fach: ~**literatur** *f.* specialized/technical literature; ~**mann** *m.* expert.
fachmännisch *a.* expert, specialist, professsional.
fachmäßig *a. & adv.* professional(ly).
Fach: ~**richtung** *f.* field; ~**schule** *f.* professional *or* special school; ~**simpelei** *f.* shoptalk; ~**studium** *n.* professional study; ~**werk** *n.* half-timbered work; ~**wissenschaft** *f.* special branch of science.
Fackel *f.* (-, -n) torch.
Fackelzug *m.* torchlight procession.
fade *a.* flat, tasteless; insipid, dull.
Faden *m.* (-s, Fäden) thread; fathom.
Fadenkreuz *n.* cross-hairs.
Fadennudeln *f.pl.* vermicelli.
fadenscheinig *a.* threadbare; flimsy.
Fagott *n.* (-[e]s, -e) bassoon.
fähig *a.* capable, able; fit, qualified.
Fähigkeit *f.* (-, -en) capacity; ability, faculty, talent.
fahl *a.* pale, ashen; drab; livid.
fahnden *v.i. nach einem* ~, to search for.
Fahne *f.* (-, -n) standard, colors *pl.*, flag, banner.
Fahnenabzug *m.* (*typ.*) galley(-proof).
Fahnen: ~**eid** *m.* oath of allegiance; ~**flucht** *f.* desertion; ~**stange** *f.* flagpole; ~**träger** *m.* standard-bearer.
Fähnrich *m.* (-[e]s, -e) ensign; ~ *zur See*, midshipman.
Fahrausweis *m.* ticket; (*mil.*) travel order, travel permit.
Fahrbahn *f.* road, lane.
fahrbar *a.* practicable (*Straße*); mobile (*Kantine, etc.*).

Fähre *f.* (-, -n) ferry(boat).
fahren *v.t.st.* to drive; to cart, to wheel; to convey; ~ *v.i.st.* (*s*) to ride (in a carriage); to sail; to travel; to go; *aus der Haut* ~, to jump out of one's skin.
fahrend *a.* itinerant.
Fahrer *m.* (-s, -); **Fahrerin** *f.* (-, -nen) driver.
Fahr: ~**erlaubnis** *f.* driver's license; ~**gast** *m.* passenger; ~**geld** *n.* fare; ~**gemeinschaft** *f.* car pool; ~**gestell** *n.* (*avi.*) chassis.
fahrig *a.* fidgety.
Fahrkarte *f.* (-, -n) (*rail.*) ticket.
Fahrkarten: ~**ausgabe** *f.* ticket office; ~**automat** *m.* ticket machine; ~**kontrolle** *f.* ticket inspection; ~**schalter** *m.* ticket office.
fahrlässig *a.* negligent, careless.
Fahrlässigkeit *f.* (-, -en) negligence.
Fährmann *m.* ferryman.
Fahrordnung *f.* (-, -en) rule of the road.
Fahrplan *m.* timetable, schedule.
fahrplanmäßig *a.* regular; *adv.* on time; scheduled, on schedule.
Fahr: ~**preis** *m.* fare; ~**rad** *n.* cycle, bicycle, (*fam.*) bike; ~**schein** *m.* ticket; ~**schule** *f.* driving school; ~**stuhl** *m.* (*im Hotel*) lift; bath chair; ~**weg** *m.* wagon road; driveway.
Fahrt *f.* (-, -en) ride (in a vehicle), drive; journey; (sea) voyage; row; course; *in voller* ~, at full speed.
fahrtauglich *a.* fit to drive.
Fahrtbefehl *m.* (*mil.*) travel order.
Fährte *f.* (-, -n) track, scent; *auf falscher* ~, on the wrong track.
Fahrtenmesser *n.* sheath knife.
Fahrtrichtung *f.* direction.
fahrtüchtig *a.* fit to drive.
Fahrtunterbrechung *f.* stopover.
Fahrtwind *m.* (-es, -e) airflow.
Fahrunterricht *m.* (*mot.*) driving instruction.
Fahr: ~**wasser** *n.* track; channel; ~**zeug** *n.* vehicle.
Faible *n.* (-s, -s) liking; weakness.
fair *a.* fair.
faktisch *a. & adv.* actual(ly).
Faktor *m.* (-s, Faktoren) factor.
Faktur, Faktura *f.* (-, -ren) invoice.
Fakultät *f.* (-, -en) faculty.
fakultativ *a.* optional.
falb *a.* fallow, sorrel, dun.
Falke *m.* (-n, -n) falcon, hawk.
Falkner *m.* falconer.
Fall *m.* (-[e]s, Fälle) *m.* fall, accident; case; *im* ~*e dass*, in case; *den* ~ *setzen*, to suppose; *auf jeden* ~, at all events; *auf keinen* ~, on no account; *zu Fall bringen*, to ruin, to seduce.
Fallbeil *n.* guillotine.
Falle *f.* (-, -n) trap, snare; (*fig.*) pitfall.
fallen *v.i.st.* (*s*) to fall, to drop; (*Preise*) to decline (*com.*) to fail, to break; (*Schuß*) to break; *in die Augen* ~, to catch *or* strike the eye; *ins Gewicht* ~, to be of great weight; *in Ohnmacht*~, to swoon, to faint; *es fällt mir schwer*, I find it hard.
fällen *v.t.* to fell; to cut down; *ein Urteil* ~, to pass a sentence.
fallenlassen *v.t.st.* to abandon; to drop; to let fall.
Fallgeschwindigkeit *f.* rate of fall.

Fallgrube *f.* trap.

Fallhammer *m.* drophammer.

fällig *a.* due, payable; ~ *werden*, to become due; *sofort ~e Schulden*, liquid debts.

Fälligkeit *f.* (-, -en) maturity (*com.*).

Fallobst *n.* windfalls.

falls *adv.* in case (that).

Fallschirm *m.* (-s, -e) parachute.

Fallschirm: ~**absprung** *m.* parachute jump; ~**abwurf** *m.* airdrop; ~**jäger** *m.* (mil.) paratrooper; ~**springen** *n.* parachute jumping; (*sp.*) sky diving; ~**springer** *m.* parachutist; ~**leuchtbombe** *f.* parachute flare; ~**truppen** *pl.* paratroops.

Fall: ~**strick** (*m.*) trap, snare; ~**studie** *f.* case study; ~**tür** *f.* trapdoor.

falsch *a.* false, wrong; forged, counterfeit; (*fig.*) faithless, deceitful; ~ *singen*, to sing out of tune; ~ *spielen*, to cheat at play.

Falsch: ~**aussage** *f.* false testimony; ~**eid** *m.* false oath.

fälschen *v.t.* to falsify; to adulterate; (*Wechsel, Scheck*) to forge; (*Geld*) to counterfeit; *gefälschte Stelle*, surreptitious passage.

Fälscher *m.* forger; counterfeiter.

Falschgeld *n.* counterfeit money.

Falschheit *f.* (-, -en) falsehood, falseness; deceitfulness.

fälschlich *a.* false; ~ *adv.* falsely.

fälschlicherweise *adv.* by mistake; mistakenly.

Falschmeldung *f.* false report; hoax.

Falschmünzer *m.* (-s, -) forger; counterfeiter.

Falschspieler *m.* (-s, -) cardsharper.

Fälschung *f.* (-, -en) fake; forgery.

Falsett *n.* (*mus.*) falsetto.

Faltblatt *n.* leaflet; insert (newspaper).

Faltboot *n.* collapsible boat.

Falte *f.* (-, -n) fold, pleat, crease.

fälteln *v.t.* to pleat.

falten *v.t.* to fold, to pleat; *die Stirn ~*, to knit one's brow; (*Hände*) to join.

Falten: ~**bildung** *f.* folding; wrinkling; ~**gebirge** *n.* fold mountains.

faltenlos *a.* unwrinkled, uncreased.

Faltenrock *m.* pleated skirt.

Faltenwurf *n.* drapery.

Falter *m.* (-s, -) (*Nacht~*) moth; (*Tag~*) butterfly.

faltig *a.* creased; wrinkled; lined.

Falz *f.* fold.

Falzbein *n.* (paper) folder.

falzen *v.t.* to fold; to flute; to groove.

familiär *a.* familiar, intimate.

Familie *f.* (-, -n) family.

Familien: ~**angehörige** *m./f.* member of the family; ~**angelegenheit** *f.* family affair/matter; ~**betrieb** (*m.*) family business; ~**feier** *f.* family party; ~**krach** (*m.*) family row; ~**leben** *n.* family life; ~**name** *m.* family name; ~**unterstützung** *f.* (*mil.*) separation allowance; ~**zulage** *f.* family allowance.

famos *a.* (*fam.*) first-rate, prime.

Fanatiker *m.* (-s, -) fanatic.

fanatisch *a.* fanatic(al).

Fanatismus *m.* (-, 0) fanaticism.

Fanfare *f.* (-, -n) fanfare; flourish of trumpets.

Fang *m.* (-[e]s, Fänge) catch, capture; fang, tusk; claw, talon; thrust, stab.

fangen *v.t.st.* to catch; to seize, to take; (sich) ~ *v.refl.st.* to rally; to recover.

Fangen *n.* ~**spielen** to play tag.

Fangfrage *f.* trick question.

Fangopackung *f.* mud pack.

Farbband *n.* (-[e]s, -bänder) typewriter ribbon.

Farbe *f.* (-, -n) color; dye, paint; hue, complexion.

färben *v.t.* to color, to tinge; to dye.

farbenblind *a.* color-blind.

Farbendruck *m.* color printing.

Färber *m.* (-s, -) dyer, stainer.

farbig *a.* colored.

Farbige *m./f.* colored man/woman.

Farbkasten *m.* (-s, -kästen) color box.

farblich *a.* colored; *adv.* in color.

farblos *a.* colorless.

Farb: ~**schicht** *f.* layer of paint; ~**skala** *f.* color chart; ~**stift** *m.* (-s, -e) crayon; ~**stoff** *m.* dye; coloring.

Färbung *f.* (-, -en) coloration, coloring; tinge, shade.

Farce *f.* (-, -n) farce.

Farn *m.*, **Farnkraut** *n.* fern.

Fasan *m.* (-[e]s, -e[n]) pheasant.

Fasching *m.* (-s, -e) carnival.

Faschismus *m.* (-, 0) fascism.

Faschist *m.* (-en, -en) fascist.

faschistisch *a.* fascist.

faseln *v.i.* (*pej.*) to drivel, to twaddle.

Faser *f.* (-, -n), **Faserstoff** *m.* fiber; **Faserbrett** *n.* fiberboard.

faserig *a.* fibrous; stringy.

fasern (sich) *v.refl.* to fray.

Fassade *f.* (-, -n) façade.

Faß *n.* (Fasses, Fässer) barrel, cask; (*offenes*) tub, vat; *Bier vom ~*, beer on tap.

Fassade *f.* façade; front.

faßbar *a.* tangible, comprehensible.

fassen *v.t.* to lay hold of, to seize; to contain; to conceive, to comprehend; (sich) ~ *v.refl.* to compose oneself; *sich kurz ~*, to be brief; *Edelsteine ~*, to set, to mount; *in Worte ~*, to put into words; *einen Entschluss ~*, to come to a decision.

faßlich *a.* intelligible, easy to understand.

Fasson *f.* (-, -en) shape.

Fassung *f.* (-, -en) setting (of stones); version; wording, draft; composure.

fassungslos *a.* beside oneself; stunned.

Fassungsvermögen *n.* capacity.

fast *adv.* almost, nearly.

fasten *v.i.* to fast.

Fastenzeit *f.* Lent; time of fasting.

Fastnacht *f.* Shrove Tuesday; Shrovetide; carnival.

Fasttag *m.* day of fasting.

Faszination *f.* fascination.

faszinieren *v.t.* to fascinate.

fatal *a.* unlucky, disagreeable; odious.

Fatalismus *m.* fatalism.

Fatalist *m.*; **Fatalistin** *f.* fatalist.

fatalistisch *a.* fatalistic.

Fata Morgana *f.* Fata Morgana; illusion.

Fatzke *m.* (*pej.*) jerk.

fauchen *v.i.* to hiss; to snarl.

faul *a.* putrefied, rotten; lazy, idle, slothful.

faulen *v.i.* (s) to rot, to putrefy.

faulenzen *v.i.* to idle, to loaf; to laze around.

Faulenzer *m.* (-s, -) idler, lazybones.
Faulenzerei *f.* idleness, laziness.
Faulheit *f.* idleness, laziness.
faulig *a.* stagnating; putrefying; rotting; foul, putrid (smell).
Fäulnis *f.* (-, 0) rottenness, putrefaction.
Faul: ~**pelz** *m.* lazybones; ~**tier** *n.* sloth.
Fauna *f.* (-, -nen) fauna.
Faust *f.* (-, Fäuste) fist.
Fäustchen *n.* (-s, -) *sich ins* ~ *lachen*, to laugh in one's sleeve.
Fäustling *f.* mitten.
Fausthandschuh *m.* mitten.
Faustregel *f.* rule of thumb.
Faustschlag *m.* punch.
Fauxpas *m.* faux pas.
favorisieren *v.t.* to favor.
Favorit *m.*; ~**Favoritin** *f.* favorite.
Fax *n.* (-, -(e)) fax.
faxen *v.t.* to fax.
Faxen *pl.* nonsense; ~**machen** to make faces, to clown about.
Fazit *n.* (-s, -s *or* -e) result, sum total.
F-Dur *n.* F-major.
Feature *n.* feature.
Februar *m.* (-s, -e) February.
fechten *v.i.st.* to fight; (*kunstgerecht*) to fence; (*fig.*) to beg one's way.
Fechter *m.* (-s, -) swordsman, fencer.
Feder *f.* (-, -n) feather; pen; spring.
Feder: ~**ball** *m.* badminton; shuttlecock; ~**bett** *n.* feather bed; ~**busch** *m.* plume; crest; ~**halter** *m.* fountain pen.
federleicht *a.* light as a feather.
Federlesen *n.* *nicht viel* ~*s machen*, to make short work of one.
Federmesser *n.* (-s, -) penknife.
federn *v.i.* to rebound; to be elastic.
Federstrich *m.* stroke of the pen.
Federung *f.* springs; suspension (car).
Federzeichnung *f.* pen and ink drawing.
Fee *f.* (-, -n) fairy.
feenhaft *a.* fairy-like.
Fegefeuer *n.* (-s, 0) purgatory.
fegen *v.t.* to sweep.
Fehde *f.* (-, -n) quarrel, feud; challenge.
Fehdehandschuh *m.* gauntlet.
Fehl *m.* (-s, 0) blemish.
fehl *adv.* amiss, wrong.
fehlbar *a.* fallible.
Fehl: ~**besetzung** *f.* miscast; ~**betrag** *m.* deficit; ~**diagnose** *f.* incorrect diagnosis; ~**einschätzung** *f.* misjudgment.
fehlen *v.i.* to be missing; ~ *v.t.* to miss; *was fehlt dir?*, what is the matter with you?
fehlend *a.* missing; absent.
Fehl: ~**entscheidung** *f.* wrong decision; ~**entwicklung** *f.* undesirable development.
Fehler *m.* (-s, -) fault, defect; error, mistake, blunder.
fehlerfrei *a.* faultless.
fehlerhaft *a.* faulty, incorrect.
fehlerlos *a.* flawless.
Fehler: ~**quelle** *f.* source of error; ~**quote** *f.* error rate; ~**zahl** *f.* number of errors.
Fehlgeburt *f.* miscarriage.

fehlgehen *v.i.st.* (*s*) to go wrong.
fehlgreifen *v.i.st.* to make a mistake.
Fehlgriff *m.* mistake; blunder.
Fehlkonstruktion *f.* *eine* ~ *sein* to be badly designed.
Fehlleistung *f.* *Freudsche* ~ (Freudian) slip.
Fehlschlag *m.* miss; failure.
fehlschlagen *v.i.st.* to miscarry, to fail.
Fehlschluß *m.* fallacy.
Fehlstart *m.* false start.
Fehltritt *m.* false step; (*fig.*) error, mistake.
Fehlurteil *n.* (-s, -e) miscarriage of justice.
Fehlzündung *f.* misfire.
Feier *f.* (-, 0) party, celebration; festival; rest.
Feierabend *m.* cessation from work, time of rest in the evening.
feierlich *a.* festive, solemn; ceremonious.
Feierlichkeit *f.* (-, -en) celebration, festivity, ceremony.
feiern *v.i.* to rest from labor; ~ *v.t.* to solemnize; to celebrate.
Feierschicht *f.* cancelled shift.
Feiertag *m.* holiday; *gesetzlicher* ~, public holiday.
feig(e) *a.* cowardly.
Feige *f.* (-, -n) fig.
Feigheit *f.* (-, -en) cowardice.
Feigling *m.* (-[e]s, -e) coward.
feil *a.* for sale, venal; mercenary.
feilbieten *v.t.st.* to offer for sale.
Feile *f.* (-, -n) file.
feilen *v.t.* to file; to refine, to polish.
feilschen *v.t.* to bargain, to haggle.
fein *a.* fine; delicate, elegant, refined; polite, genteel; subtle; *extra* ~, super-fine.
Feinarbeit *f.* detailed work; precision work.
Feind *m.* (-[e]s, -e); **Feindin** *f.* (-, -nen) enemy; adversary, foe.
feind *a.* hostile, inimical.
feindlich *a.* inimical, hostile, adverse.
Feindschaft *f.* (-, -en) enmity, hostility.
feindselig *a.* hostile, malevolent.
Feindseligkeit *f.* (-, -en) hostility.
feinfühlig *a.* sensitive.
Feingefühl *n.* sensitivity.
Feingehalt *m.* (-[e]s, -e) standard (of coins, gold, etc.).
Feinheit *f.* fineness, delicacy, subtlety.
feinkörnig *a.* fine-grained.
Feinkost *f.* (-, 0) delicatessen.
feinmachen *v.refl.* (*fam.*) to dress up.
feinmaschig *a.* finely meshed.
Feinschmecker *m.* (-s, -) gourmet.
feinsinnig *a.* delicate, sensitive.
feist *a.* fat, obese, stout.
feixen *v.i.* (*fam.*) to smirk.
Feld *n.* (-[e]s, -er) field; plain; panel; (*Schach*) square.
Feld: ~**arbeit** *f.* work in the fields; field work; ~**bahn** *f.* field railway; ~**bett** *n.* camp-bed; ~**geistlicher** *m.* army chaplain, padre; ~**geschrei** *n.* war-cry; ~**herr** *m.* general; ~**küche** *f.* field-kitchen; ~**lazarett** *n.* field-hospital; ~**marschall** *m.* field-marshal; ~**messer** *m.* surveyor; *Chef der* ~**polizei** *m.* provost-marshal, ~**post** *f.* army post, field post; ~**postamt** *n.* Army Post Office (APO);

~**spat** *m.* feldspar; ~**stuhl** *m.* camp-stool; ~**Wald-und-Wiesen-** (*fam.*) run-of-the mill; common-or-garden; ~**webel** *m.* sergeant-major; ~**zug** *m.* campaign.

Felge *f.* (-, -n) rim.

Fell *n.* (-[e]s, -e) fur; hide; skin; coat; *ein dickes ~ haben*, to be thick-skinned.

Fels *m.* (Felsen, Felsen), **Felsen** *m.* (-s, -) rock, crag.

felsenfest *a.* firm as a rock.

Felsblock *m.* rock, boulder.

Felsen *m.* (-s, -) rock, cliff.

Felsen: ~**klippe** *f.* rocky cliff; ~**riff** *n.* rocky reef.

felsig *a.* rocky.

Fels: ~**spalte** *f.* crevice; ~**vorsprung** *m.*; ~**wand** *f.* rock face.

Feme *f.* vehmgericht; kangaroo court.

Fememord *m.* lynching.

feminin *a.* feminine, effeminate.

Femininum *n.* (-s, -na) feminine noun.

Feminismus *m.* feminism.

Feminist *m.*; **Feministin** *f.* feminist.

feministisch *a.* feminist.

Fenchel *m.* fennel.

Fenster *n.* (-s, -) window.

Fenster: ~**bank** *f.* ~**brett** *n.* window-sill; ~**kitt** *m.* putty; ~**laden** *m.* shutter; ~**putzer** *m.* window-cleaner; ~**rahmen** *m.* window-frame; ~**scheibe** *f.* window-pane.

Ferien *pl.* vacation, holidays *pl.*; *in den ~*, on holiday.

Ferienkolonie *f.* holiday/vacation camp.

Ferkel *n.* (-s, -) piglet.

Ferkelei *f.* filthy behavior; dirty remark.

ferkeln *v.t.* to farrow.

Ferment *n.* enzyme; ferment.

fern *a. & adv.* far, remote, distant.

Fernaufklärung *f.* (*mil.*) long-range reconnaissance.

Fernbedienung *f.* remote control.

fernbleiben *v.i.st.* to stay away.

Ferne *f.* (-, -n) distance.

ferner *a.* farther, further; ~ *adv.* further, moreover.

fernerhin *adv.* henceforward, henceforth.

Fernfahrer *m.* trucker.

Ferngespräch *n.* long-distance call.

ferngesteuert *a.* remote-controlled.

Fernglas *n.* binoculars.

fernhalten *v.t.st.* to keep off.

fernhin *adv.* to a distance, far away.

Fern: ~**heizung** *f.* long-distance heating; ~**kampfartillerie** *f.* long-range artillery; ~**rohr** *n.* telescope; ~**schreiben** *n.* ~**schreiber** *m.* teletype; ~**sehen** *n.* television; ~**sehapparat** *m.* television set; ~**sicht** *f.* prospect, panorama.

Fernsprechamt *n.* telephone exchange.

Fernsprecher *m.* (-s, -) telephone.

Fernsteuerung *f.* remote control.

Fernsteuerwaffe *f.* guided missile.

Ferse *f.* (-, -n) heel.

fertig *a.* ready; ready-made; finished; *ich bin ~*, I have (am) done; *mit etw. ~ werden*, to finish sth., to get over sth.

Fertig: ~**bau** *m.* prefabricated building; ~**bauweise** *f.* prefabricated construction.

fertigen *v.t.* to manufacture, to make.

Fertig: ~**gericht** *n.* ready-to-serve meal; ~**haus** *n.* prefabricated house.

Fertigkeit *f.* (-, -en) skill, dexterity; fluency.

Fertigstellung *f.* completion.

Fertigteil *n.* prefabricated part.

Fertigungsstraße *f.* production line.

Fertigwaren *f.pl.* finished (*or* manufactured) goods.

Fes *m.* fez.

fesch *a.* smart; dashing; stylish.

Fessel *f.* (-, -n) fetter, shackel; (*des Pferdes*) fetlock, pastern; ~**ballon** *m.* captive balloon.

fesseln *v.t.* to tie up, to chain up; to fetter; (*fig.*) to captivate; (*Blick*) to arrest.

fest *a.* fast; firm; solid; settled, fixed; fortified; ~*er Schlaf*, sound sleep; ~ *Körper*, solid; *sich ~halten*, to hold on; *sich ~legen*, to commit oneself; ~*legen*, to fix, lay down; ~*machen*, to fasten; ~*nehmen*, to arrest; ~*setzen*, ~*stellen*, to establish; *... fest* *a.* resisting; **stoßfest** *a.* shock resisting.

Fest *n.* (-es, -e) feast, festival.

Festbeleuchtung *f.* illumination.

Feste *f.* (-, -n) fastness, stronghold.

Festessen *n.* banquet.

festhalten *v.t.st.* to hold on to.

festigen *v.t.* to strengthen; to consolidate.

Festigkeit *f.* (-, 0) firmness; solidity; constancy; (*Metall*) strength.

Festigung *f.* strengthening; consolidation.

Festival *n.* festival.

fest: ~**klammern** *v.refl.* to cling on to; ~**klemmen** *v.i.* to be stuck; *v.t.* to wedge.

Festkörper *m.* (*phys.*) solid.

Festland *n.* continent.

Festlandsockel *m.* continental shelf.

festlegen *v.t.st.* to fix, to arrange; *v.refl.st.* to commit oneself.

festlich *a.* festive, festival; solemn.

Festlichkeit *f.* (-, -en) festivity, solemnity.

festliegen *v.i.st.* to be stuck; to be tied up (money).

festmachen *v.t.* to fix; to arrange (appointment); to moor.

Festnahme *f.* arrest.

Festplatte *f.* (*comp.*) hard disk.

Festplatz *m.* fairground.

Festpreis *m.* fixed price.

Festrede *f.* (ceremonial) address.

Festschrift *f.* commemorative publication.

festsetzen *v.t.* to fix, to settle, to appoint.

Festspiel *n.* festival.

feststellen *v.t.* to ascertain; to establish.

Festtag *m.* feast, holiday.

Festung *f.* (-, -en) fortress.

Festungs: ~**anlage** *f.* fortification; ~**mauer** *f.* wall of a fortress.

Festzelt *n.* marquee.

Festzug *m.* procession, pageant.

Fete *f.* (-, -en) (*fam.*) party.

Fetisch *m.* (-es, -e) fetish.

Fetischismus *m.* fetishism.

fett *a.* fat; greasy; (*von Speisen*) rich; bold (print).

Fett *n.* (-[e]s, -e) fat; grease.

Fett: ~**druck** *m.* bold face; ~**gedruckt** *a.* bold; ~**gewebe** *n.* fatty tissue; ~**flecken** *m.* grease-spot.

fettig *a.* greasy, fatty.

fettleibig *a.* obese.

Fettleibigkeit *f.* obesity.
Fettsack *m.* (*fam.*) fatso.
Fettsäure *f.* fatty acid.
Fettschicht *f.* layer of fat.
Fettwanst *m.* (*fam.*) paunch.
Fetus *m.* (-, -se) fetus.
Fetzen *m.* (-s, -) shred, tatter, rag.
feucht *a.* moist, wet; damp.
Feuchtigkeit *f.* (-, -en) moisture, humidity.
Feuchtigkeitsmesser *m.* hygrometer.
feuchtigkeitssicher *a.* damp-proof.
feudal *a.* feudal; aristocratic; plush (hotel).
Feuer *n.* (-s, -) fire; (*fig.*) ardor; (*für Zigarren*) light.
Feuer: **~bekämpfung** *f.* fire-fighting; **~bestattung** *f.* cremation; **~eifer** *m.* enthusiasm; zest.
feuerfest *a.* fire-proof.
Feuergefahr *f.* danger of fire.
feuergefährlich *a.* inflammable, combustible.
Feuer: **~gitter** *n.* (*am Kamin*) fireguard; **~kraft** *f.* (*mil.*) fire-power; **~leiter** *f.* fire escape; ladder; **~löscher** *m.* fire extinguisher; **~melder** *m.* fire-alarm.
feuern *v.i.* to fire.
feuerrot *a.* fiery red, red-hot.
Feuersbrunst *f.* (-, brünste) fire, conflagration.
Feuer: **~schein** *m.* glow of fire; **~schlucker** *m.* fire-eater.
feuersicher *a.* fireproof.
Feuer: **~spritze** *f.* fire-hose; **~stein** *m.* flint; **~stelle** *f.* fireplace, hearth; **~teufel** *m.* fire bug; **~tod** *m.* (death at) the stake.
Feuerung *f.* (-, -en) fuel; firing.
Feuer: **~versicherung** *f.* fire insurance; **~wache** *f.* fire-station; **~wehr** *f.* fire-brigade; **~wehrmann** *m.*; **~wehrfrau** *f.* fire fighter; **~werk** *n.* fireworks *pl.*; **~zange** *f.* tongs *pl.*; **~zeug** *n.* lighter.
Feuilleton *n.* arts and leisure section (newspaper).
feurig *a.* fiery; ardent.
Fiasko *n.* (-[s], -s) failure; ~ *machen*, to fail.
Fibel *f.* (-, -n) primer, spelling-book.
Fiber *f.* (-, -n) fiber, filament.
Fichte *f.* (-, -n) spruce; pine(-tree).
ficken *v.i.* (*vulg.*) to fuck.
fidel *a.* (*fam.*) merry, jolly.
Fidschiinseln *pl.* the Fiji Islands.
Fieber *n.* (-s, -) fever; ~ *haben*, to have a temperature.
fieberhaft *a.* feverish.
fieberkrank *a.* feverish.
fiebern *v.i.* to be in a fever.
fiebrig *a.* feverish.
Fiedel *f.* (-, -n) fiddle.
Fiedelbogen *m.* fiddle-stick, bow.
fiedeln *v.t. & n.* to fiddle; to scrape.
fiepen *v.i.* to whimper; to cheep.
fies *a.* nasty, mean.
Figur *f.* (-, -en) figure; diagram; (*Schach*) chessman.
figurativ *a. & adv.* figurative(ly).
figürlich *a.* figured; figurative.
Fiktion *f.* fiction.
fiktiv *a.* fictitious.
Filet *n.* (-s, -s) netting; fillet of beef.
Filiale *f.* branch (establishment).
Filigranarbeit *f.* filigree.
Film *m.* (-s, -s) film; movie, motion-picture.
Filmatelier *n.* studio.

Filmemacher *m.*; **Filmemacherin** *f.* film-maker.
filmen *v.t.* to film, to shoot.
filmisch *a.* cinematic.
Filmverleih *m.* film distribution.
Filter *m. or n.* (-s, -) filter.
filtern, filtrieren *v.t.* to filter, to strain.
Filz *m.* (-es, -e) felt; (*fig.*) niggard.
filzen *v.i.* to felt; (*fig.*) to search, to frisk.
Filzhut *m.* felt-hat.
filzig *a.* felt-like; (*fig.*) stingy, niggardly.
Filzlaus *f.* crab louse.
Filzokratie *f.* (*fam. pej.*) corruption, graft.
Fimmel *m.* craze.
Finale *n.* final; (*mus.*) finale.
Finalsatz *m.* final clause.
Finanzamt *n.* internal revenue office.
Finanzausschuß *m.* finance committee.
Finanzen *f.pl.* finances *pl.*; revenue.
finanziell *a.* financial.
finanzieren *v.t.* to finance.
Finanzierung *f.* financing.
Finanz: **~jahr** *n.* fiscal year; **~mann** *m.* financier; **~minister** *m.* minister of finance; (*in England*) Chancellor of the Exchequer.
Findelhaus *n.* foundling-hospital.
Findelkind *n.* foundling.
finden *v.t.st.* to find; to discover; to meet with; to think, to deem; (sich) ~ *v.refl.st.* to be found; *Vergnügen* ~ *an*, to take pleasure in; *Geschmack* ~ *an*, to like, to relish; *es wird sich* ~, we shall see; *sich* ~ *in*, to put up with.
Finderlohn *m.* reward to the finder.
findig *a.* shrewd, ingenious.
Findling *m.* (-[e]s, -e) foundling.
Finesse *f.* finesse, trick.
Finger *m.* (-s, -) finger; *einem auf die* ~ *sehen*, to watch one closely; *durch die* ~ *sehen*, to wink at.
Finger: **~abdruck** *m.* finger print; **~fertigkeit** *f.* dexterity; **~hakeln** *n.* finger wrestling; **~handschuh** *m.* glove; **~hut** *m.* thimble; (*bot.*) fox-glove; **~knöchel** *m.* knuckle; **~kuppe** *f.* fingertip.
fingern *v.t.* to finger.
Finger: **~nagel** *m.* fingernail; **~satz** *m.* (*mus.*) fingering; **~spitze** *f.* fingertip; **~spitzengefühl** *n.* feeling; **~zeig** *m.* hint.
fingieren *v.t.* to fake.
Fink[e] *m.* (-en, -en) finch.
Finne *m.*; **Finnin** *f.* Finn; **finnisch** *a.* Finnish.
Finnland *n.* (-s, 0) Finland.
finster *a.* dark, obscure; gloomy, dim.
Finsternis *f.* (-, -nisse) darkness, obscurity; eclipse.
Finte *f.* (-, -n) feint; pretense; fib.
Firlefanz *m.* (*fam. pej.*) frippery; nonsense.
firm *a.* (*fam.*) knowledgeable.
Firma *f.* (-, Firmen) firm.
Firmament *n.* (-[e]s, -e) firmament, sky.
Firmen: **~inhaber** *m.* owner of a company; **~name** *m.* trade name; **~sitz** *m.* headquarters; **~wagen** *m.* company car; **~zeichen** *m.* logo.
Firmung *f.* (-, -en) confirmation.
Firnis *m.* (-nisses, -nisse) varnish.
firnissen *v.t.* to varnish.
First *m.* (-es, -e) & *f.* (-, -en) top; ridge of a roof.
Fis *n.* (-, 0) (*mus.*) F sharp.
Fisch *m.* (-es, -e) fish.
Fisch: **~angel** *f.* fishing-hook; **~bein** *n.* whalebone.

80

fischen *v.t.* to fish, to angle; *im Trüben ~,* to fish in troubled waters.

Fischer *m.* (-s, -) fisherman, angler.

Fischerboot *n.* fishing-boat.

Fischerei *f.* fishing.

Fisch: **~fang** *m.* fishing; **~grätenmuster** *n.* herringbone pattern; **~gründe** *pl.* fishing grounds; **~händler** *m.* fishmonger; **~konserve** *f.* canned fish; **~kutter** *m.* fishing trawler; **~laich** *m.* spawn; **~mehl** *n.* fishmeal; **~zucht** *f.* fish farming.

fiskalisch *a.* fiscal.

Fiskus *m.* (-, 0) treasury; government.

Fistel *f.* (-, -n) fistula; (*als Stimme*) falsetto.

Fitness center *n.* health club, gym.

Fittich *m.* (-[e]s, -e) wing, pinion.

Fitzelchen *n.* (*fam.*) scrap.

fix *a.* fixed, firm; (*fig.*) quick, sharp; *~ und fertig,* quite ready.

fixen *v.i.* to fix.

Fixer *m.*; **Fixerin** *f.* fixer.

fixieren *v.t.* to fix, to settle; (*phot.*) to fix; (*einen*) to stare at; *Fixierbad, Fixierlösung* (*phot.*) fixing solution.

Fixstern *m.* (-[e]s, -e) fixed star.

Fjord *m.* fiord.

FKK-Strand *m.* nudist beach.

flach *a.* flat; plain, level; shallow.

Fläche *f.* (-, -n) plain, surface; plane.

Flächen: **~inhalt** *m.* area: **~maß** *n.* square measure; **~raum** *m.* area.

Flachland *n.* lowland.

flach: **~legen** *v.refl.* to lie down; **~liegen** to be flat on one's back.

Flachrelief *n.* low relief.

Flachs *m.* (-es, -e) flax.

flackern *v.i.* to flare, to flicker.

Fladen *m.* flat cake; cowpat; **Fladenbrot** *n.* flat loaf of bread.

Flagge *f.* (-, -n) flag, colors *pl.*

flaggen *v.i.* to hoist the flag(s).

Flair *n.* aura, flair.

Flak *f.* anti-aircraft gun, AA gun.

Flakon *n.od.m.* little bottle.

flambieren *v.t.* to flame.

Flame *m.*; **Flämin** *f.* Fleming.

flämisch *a.* Flemish.

Flamme *f.* (-, -n) flame, blaze; (*Liebchen*) love, sweetheart.

flammen *v.i.* to flame, to blaze.

flammend *a.* flaming.

Flammenwerfer *m.* flame-thrower.

Flandern *n.* Flanders.

Flanell *m.* (-[e]s, -e) flannel.

flanieren *v.i.* to stroll.

Flanke *f.* (-, -n) flank.

Flankenspiel *n.* (*mech.*) backlash.

flankieren *v.t.* to flank.

flapsig *a.* loutish.

Flasche *f.* (-, -n) bottle flask; *auf ~n ziehen,* to bottle.

Flaschen: **~bier** *n.* bottled beer; **~gestell** *n.* bottlerack; **~öffner** *m.* bottle opener.

Flaschenzug *m.* pulley, tackle.

flatterhaft *a.* unsteady, fickle.

Flatterhaftigkeit *f.* fickleness.

flattern *v.i.* to flit, to flutter; (*Fahne*) to wave, to

stream.

flau *a.* flat, insipid; faint; (*com.*) dull.

Flaum *m.* (-[e]s, 0) down.

flaumig *a.* downy.

flauschig *a.* fluffy.

Flause *f.* silly idea.

Flaute *f.* lull; slack period.

Flechte *f.* (-, -n) twist, plait, braid; (*med.*) eczema; (*Pflanze*) lichen.

flechten *v.t.st.* to twist, to plait; (*Kranz*) to wreathe; to weave.

Flechtwerk *n.* wickerwork.

Fleck *m.* (-[e]s, -e) spot; place; patch; blot, stain; tripe.

Flecken *m.* (-s, -) spot, stain; blemish; (*Ort*) market-town, hamlet.

flecken *v.t.* to stain.

Fleckfieber *n.* typhus.

fleckig *a.* spotted, speckled, stained.

fleddern *v.t.* to blunder, to rob.

Fledermaus *f.* bat.

Flegel *m.* (-s, -) lout.

Flegelei *f.* (-, -en) loutish behavior.

flegelhaft *a.* loutish.

Flegeljahre *pl.* awkward age.

flehen *v.i.* to implore, to beseech.

flehend *a.* suppliant.

flehentlich *a. & adv.* imploring(ly), urgent(ly).

Fleisch *n.* (-es, 0) flesh; (butcher's) meat; (*des Obstes*) pulp.

Fleisch: **~beschauer** *m.* inspector of butcher's meat; **~brühe** *f.* broth, beef-tea; gravy.

Fleischer *m.* (-s, -) butcher.

Fleischerei *f.*; **Fleischerladen** *m.* butcher's shop.

Fleischeslust *f.* carnal appetite.

Fleisch: **~extrakt** *m.* extract of meat; **~farbe** *f.* carnation (color).

fleischfressend *a.* carnivorous.

fleischig *a.* plump; fleshy.

Fleisch: **~käse** *m.* meat loaf; **~kloß** *m.* meat ball; **~konserve** *f.* can of meat.

fleischlich *a.* carnal.

fleischlos *a.* meatless.

Fleischpastete *f.* pâté.

Fleischwolf *m.* mincer.

Fleiß *m.* (-es, 0) diligence, application, industry.

fleißig *a.* diligent; industrious.

flektieren *v.t.* to inflect.

fletschen *v.t.* to snarl.

flexibel *a. & adv.* flexible, flexibly.

Flexibilität *f.* flexibility.

Flexion *f.* inflexion.

flicken *v.t.* to mend, to patch, to botch.

Flickendecke *f.* patchwork quilt.

Flickschuster *m.* cobbler.

Flickwerk *n.* patch-up job.

Flickzeug *n.* repair kit.

Flieder *m.* (-s, -) (*spanischer*) lilac.

Fliege *f.* (-, -n) fly.

fliegen *v.i.st.* (*s*) to fly; to rush, to dash; *~lassen,* to fly (a kite), to wave (a flag).

Flieger *m.* (-s, -); **Fliegerin** *f.* (-, -nen) flyer, aviator; pilot.

Fliegerabwehr . . . anti-aircraft-.

Fliegeralarm *m.* air-raid warning.

fliehen *v.i.st.* (*s*) to flee; *~ v.t.st.* to avoid, to shun.

fliehend *a.* sloping (forehead); receding (chin).

Fliehkraft *f.* centrifugal force.

Fliese *f.* (-, -n) tile.

Fließband *n.* assembly line.

fließen *v.i.st.* (s) to flow; (*vom Papier*) to blot.

fließend *a. & adv.* fluent(ly); *-es warmes Wasser*, hot running water.

Fließpapier *n.* blotting-paper.

flimmern *v.i.* to twinkle, to flicker.

flink *a.* brisk, quick, nimble.

Flinte *f.* (-, -n) gun, musket; *die ~ ins Korn werfen*, to give in, to throw in the sponge.

Flipper *m.*; **Flipperautomat** *m.* pinball machine.

flippern *v.i.* to play pinball.

Flittchen *n.* (*fam. pej.*) floozie.

Flitter *m.* frippery.

Flitterwochen *f.pl.* honeymoon.

Flocke *f.* (-, -n) flock; flake (of snow).

flockig *a.* fluffy.

Floh *m.* (-[e]s, Flöhe) flea.

Flor *m.* (-[e]s, -e) (*Trauer-*) crepe, gauze.

Florett *n.* (-[e]s, -s *u.* -e) (fencing) foil.

florieren *v.i.* to flourish, to thrive.

Floskel *f.* (-, -n) flourish (of rhetoric), tirade, phrase; cliché.

floskelhaft *a.* cliché-ridden.

Floß *n.* (-es, Flösse) raft.

Flosse, Floßfeder *f.* (-, -n) fin; flipper; (*fam.*) paw.

flößen *v.t.* to float.

Flöte *f.* (-, -n) flute.

Flötist *m.*; **Flötistin** *f.* flautist, flute-player.

flott *a.* afloat, floating; slick; lively, fast; *wieder ~ machen*, to refloat; *~ leben*, to lead a fast life.

Flotte *f.* (-, -n) fleet, navy.

Flotten: *~***stützpunkt** *m.* naval base; *~***verband** *m.* naval unit.

Flotille *f.* (-, -n) squadron, flotilla.

Flöz *n.* (-es, -e) layer, stratum; seam.

Fluch *m.* (-[e]s, Flüche) curse, malediction; (*aus Gewohnheit*) oath.

fluchen *v.t.* to curse; to swear.

Flucht *f.* (-, 0) flight, escape; (*wilde*) rout; (*Reine*) range, row.

fluchtartig *a. & adv.* hurried(ly), hasty, hastily.

flüchten *v.i.* (s) & *refl.* (sich) ~, to flee, to take to flight; ~ *v.t.* to secure, to carry to a place of safety.

flüchtig *a.* fugitive; (*oberflächlich*) careless, slight, fleeting.

Flüchtigkeit *f.* cursoriness.

Flüchtigkeitsfehler *m.* slip; careless mistake.

Flüchtling *m.* (-[e]s, -e) refugee.

Flüchtlingslager *n.* refugee camp.

Flucht: *~***linie** *f.* vanishing line; *~***versuch** *m.* escape attempt.

Flug *m.* (-[e]s, Flüge) flight.

Flug: *~***bahn** *f.* trajectory; *~***begleiter** *m.*; *~***begleiterin** *f.* flight attendant; *~***blatt** *n.* leaflet.

Flügel *m.* (-s, -) wing; grand piano; leaf (of a door); blade (of a propeller).

Flügeltür *f.* double door.

Fluggast *m.* air-passenger.

flügge *a.* fully fledged.

Flug: *~***geschwindigkeit** *f.* flying speed; *~***gesellschaft** *f.* airline; *~***hafen** *m.* airport; *~***lotse** *m.* air traffic controller; *~***platz** *n.* airfield, airport, *~***preis** *m.* air fare.

flugs *adv.* quickly, instantly.

Flug: *~***sand** *m.* quicksand; *~***schneise** *f.* approach corridor; *~***schreiber** *m.* flight recorder, black box; *~***schrift** *f.* pamphlet; *~***zeug** *n.* aircraft, airplane; *~***zeughalle** *f.* hangar; *~***zeugträger** *m.* (*nav.*) aircraft carrier.

Flugzeug: *~***absturz** *m.* plane crash; *~***besatzung** *f.* crew; *~***entführer** *m.* hijacker; *~***entführung** *f.* hijacking.

Flugziel *n.* destination.

Fluidum *n.* aura.

fluktuieren *v.i.* to fluctuate.

Flunder *m.* (-s, -n) & *f.* (-, -n) flounder.

Flunkerer *m.* (-s, -) liar.

flunkern *v.i.* to brag, to tell fibs.

Flunsch *m.* pout.

Fluoreszenz *f.* fluorescence.

Flur *f.* (-, -en) field, tilled plain; ~ *m.* (-[e]s, -e) (*Haus~*) entrance-hall; corridor.

Fluß *m.* (Flusses, Flüsse) flow; river, stream; flux.

Fluß: *~***abschnitt** *m.* reach; *~***bett** *n.* channel, river-bed; *~***gebiet** *n.* river basin; *~***becken** *n.* river basin; *~***krebs** *m.* cray fish; *~***landschaft** *f.* fluvial topography; *~***mündung** *f.* river mouth; *~***pferd** *n.* hippopotamus; *~***übergang** *m.* river crossing; *~***ufer** *n.* riverbank.

flüssig *a.* fluid, liquid.

Flüssigkeit *f.* (-, -en) fluidity; fluid, liquid.

flüstern *v.t.* to whisper.

Flüster: *~***propaganda** *f.* underground propaganda; *~***ton** *m.* whisper; *~***tüte** *f.* megaphone; *~***witz** *m.* underground joke.

Flut *f.* (-, -en) flood; high tide; (*fig.*) torrent, spate.

fluten *v.i.* to flow.

Flut: *~***licht** *n.* floodlight; *~***welle** *f.* tidal wave.

Fock: *~***mast** *m.* (-es, -e) foremast; *~***segel** *n.* foresail.

Föderalismus *m.* federalism.

föderalistisch *a.* federalist.

Föderation *f.* federation.

föderativ *a.* federal.

fohlen *v.i.* foal.

Fohlen *n.* (-s, -) foal, colt.

Föhn *m.* (-[e]s, -e) scorching south-wind.

Föhre *f.* (-, -n) pine tree.

Folge *f.* (-, -n) succession, series; consequence; (*Zeit*) future, sequel; ~ *leisten*, to comply with; *infolge*, in consequence of, pursuant to; *zufolge*, according to.

Folgeerscheinung *f.* consequence.

folgen *v.i.* (s) to follow, to succeed; to result, to ensue; to obey; *im Folgenden*, hereinafter.

folgendermaßen *adv.* in the following manner.

folgenreich *a.* big with consequences.

folgenschwer *a.* portentous, big with consequences.

folgerecht, folgerichtig *a.* consistent; logical.

Folgerichtigkeit *f.* logicality.

folgern *v.t.* to conclude, to infer.

Folgerung *f.* (-, -en) deduction, conclusion, inference.

Folgeschaden *m.* consequential damage.

folgewidrig *a.* inconsistent.

Folgezeit *f.* time to come, after-ages *pl.*

folglich *adv.* consequently, therefore.

folgsam *a.* obedient; obsequious.

Foliant *m.* (-en, -en) folio (volume).

Folie *f.* (-, -n) foil.

Folio *n.* (-[s], -s *u.* Folien) folio.

folkloristisch *a.* folklore.

Follikel *m.* follicle.

Follikelsprung *m.* ovulation.

Folter *f.* (-, -n) rack, torture.

foltern *v.t.* to put to the rack, to torture; (*fig.*) to torment.

Folterung *f.* torture.

Fön *m.* hair drier.

Fond *m.* rear compartment, back.

Fonds *m.* (-, -) fund, capital, stock.

fönen *v.t.* to blow-dry.

Fontäne *f.* fountain.

foppen *v.t.* to put s.b. on; to hoax.

Förder: ~**anlage** *f.* conveyor; ~**band** *n.* conveyor belt.

Förderer *m.*; **Förderin** *f.* patron.

förderlich *a.* useful, beneficial.

fordern *v.t.* to demand, to claim, to call for; to require; (*zum Duell*) to challenge.

fördern *v.t.* to further, to forward; to promote; (*Bergwerk*) to haul; *zu Tage* ~, to bring to light, to unearth.

förderndes Mitglied *n.* sponsoring member.

Förderschacht *f.* engine-shaft.

Forderung *f.* (-, -en) demand, claim; challenge.

Förderung *f.* (-, -en) furtherance; promotion; hauling, output.

Forelle *f.* (-, -n) trout.

forensisch *a.* forensic.

Form *f.* (-, -en) shape, form, figure; fashion; model, pattern; mold.

Formalität *f.* (-, -en) formality, form.

formal *a.* formal.

Format *n.* (-[e]s, -e) (*Buch*) size; form, shape.

formbar *a.* malleable; soft; pliable.

Formel *f.* (-, -n) formula, form.

formell *a.* & *adv.* formal(ly), in due form.

formen *v.t.* to form, to shape, to mold.

Formenlehre *f.* morphology.

Form: ~**fehler** *m.* irregularity; faux pas; ~**frage** *f.* formality; ~**gebung** *f.* design.

formieren *v.t.* to form.

Formierung *f.* formulation.

förmlich *a.* formal, in due form; ceremonious, stiff; explicit; regular, downright; ~ *adv.* actually; formally.

Förmlichkeit *f.* (-, -en) formality.

formlos *a.* shapeless; informal; rude.

Formular *n.* (-[e]s, -e) (printed) form, schedule.

formulieren *v.t.* to formulate; *neu* ~, to restate.

Formulierung *f.* formulation.

formvollendet *a.* perfectly shaped.

forsch *a.* (*fam.*) vigorous, self-assertive.

forschen *v.i.* to do research, to search, to inquire.

Forscher *m.* (-s, -) researcher, investigator, scholar.

Forschung *f.* (-, -en) research, investigation; ~**srei-sender** *m.* explorer.

Forst *m.* (-es, -e) forest.

Förster *m.* (-s, -) forester, ranger.

Forst: ~**akademie** *f.* school of forestry; ~**amt** *n.* Forestry Commission.

fort *adv.* on; off, gone, away; *in einem* ~, without interruption; *und so* ~, and so on.

fortan *adv.* henceforth.

fortarbeiten *v.i.* to keep on working.

fortbegeben (sich) *v.refl.st.* to leave.

Fortbestand *m.* continuation; continued existence.

fortbestehen *v.i.st.* to continue to exist.

fortbewegen (sich) *v.t.* & *refl.* to move on.

fortbilden (sich) *v.refl.* to continue studying.

Fortbildung *f.* further education/training.

Fortbildungsschule *f.* continuation-school.

fortbleiben *v.i.st.* (*s*) to stay away.

fortbringen *v.t.ir.* to carry away; to help forward.

Fortdauer *f.* (-, 0) continuance.

fortdauern *v.i.* to continue, to last.

fortdürfen *v.i.ir.* to be permitted to go.

fortentwickeln *v.t.* to develop s.th. further.

fortfahren *v.i.st.* (*h*) to continue, to go on.

fortführen *v.t.* to carry on.

Fortgang *m.* (-[e]s, 0) progress, success.

fortgehen *v.i.st.* (*s*) to go away.

Fortgeschrittener *m.* advanced student.

fortgesetzt *a.* & *adv.* continual(ly), constant(ly).

fortjagen *v.t.* to expel; to chase away.

fortkommen *v.i.st.* (*s*) to prosper; *gut, schlecht* ~, to do well, ill.

Fortkommen *n.* (-s, 0) progress, success.

fortlassen *v.t.st.* to allow to go.

fortlaufen *v.i.st.* (*s*) to run away.

fortlaufend *a.* continuous, continual.

fortleben *v.i.* to live on.

fortmachen *v.i.* (sich) ~ *v.refl.* to make off.

fortmarschieren *v.i.* (*s*) to march off *or* on.

fortmüssen *v.i.ir.* to be obliged to go.

fortpflanzen (sich) *v.t.* & *refl.* to reproduce; to propagate; to transmit; (*Krankheit*) to spread.

Fortpflanzung *f.* (-, 0) propagation, reproduction.

Fortpflanzungs . . . reproductive *a.*

fortreisen *v.i.* (*s*) to depart.

fortrennen *v.i.ir.* (*s*) to run off.

fortrücken *v.t.* (*h*) & *i.* (*s*) to move on, to remove; to advance, to make progress.

fortschaffen *v.t.* to carry off, to remove.

fortschicken *v.t.* to send away.

fortschleppen (sich) *v.refl.* to drag oneself on.

fortschreiten *v.i.t.st.* (*s*) to proceed, to make progress; to improve.

fortschreitend *a.* progressive.

Fortschritt *m.* (-[e]s, -e) progress.

fortschrittlich *a.* progressive.

fortsetzen *v.t.* to continue, to pursue.

Fortsetzer *m.* (-s, -) continuer.

Fortsetzung *f.* (-, -en) continuation, sequel.

Fortsetzungsroman *m.* serialized novel.

forttragen *v.t.* to carry away.

fortwährend *a.* & continual(ly).

fortwirken *v.i.* to continue to operate.

fortwollen *v.i.ir.* to want to go.

fortziehen *v.t.st.* to draw away; ~ *v.i.st.* (*s*) to move off; to leave (a house).

fossil *a.* fossilized, fossil.

Fossil *n.* (-[e]s, -ien) fossil.

Foto *n.* photo, picture.

Foto: ~**apparat** *m.* camera; ~**atelier** *n.* photographic studio.

fotogen *a.* photogenic.

Fotograf *m.* (-en, -en); **Fotografin** *f.* (-, -nen)

photographer.

fotographieren *v.t.u.i.* to photograph, to take pictures.

fotographisch *a.* photographic.

Fotokopie *f.* photocopy.

Fotokopierer *m.*, **Fotokopiergerät** *n.* photocopier.

Fotothek *f.* photographic library.

Fötus *m.* fetus.

Foul *n.* foul.

Foyer *n.* lounge, foyer.

Fracht *f.* (-, -en) freight; load; cargo; (*~geld*) freight; *~ bezahlt*, freight paid.

Fracht: ~brief *m.* waybill; **~dampfer** *m.* cargo steamer.

Frachter *m.* freighter, cargo ship.

frachtfrei *a.* freight prepaid; carriage-paid.

Frack *m.* (-[e]s, Fräcke) tailcoat; **~hemd** *n.* dress shirt.

Frage *f.* (-, -n) question; issue; *eine ~ stellen*, to ask a question; *in ~ stellen*, to question; *ohne ~*, unquestionably.

fragen *v.t.* to ask, to demand; *es fragt sich*, it is doubtful, the question is whether . . .

Fragebogen *m.* questionnaire.

Frage: ~wort *n.* interrogative; **~zeichen** *n.* question-mark.

fragil *a.* fragile.

fraglich *a.* questionable; doubtful.

fragwürdig *a.* questionable; dubious.

Fraktion *f.* (-, -en) parliamentary party; faction.

fraktionslos *a.* independent.

Fraktionszwang *m.* obligation to vote according to the party policy.

Frakturschrift *f.* Gothic black letter type.

frank *a.* free, frank, ingenuous.

Franken *n.* Franconia.

frankieren *v.t.* to stamp.

frankiert, franko *a.* prepaid.

Franse *f.* (-, -n) fringe.

fransig *a.* fringed, frayed.

Franziskaner *m.* (-s, -) Franciscan.

Franzose *m.* Frenchman; **Französin** French woman.

französisch *a.* French.

Französisch *n.* French.

frappant *a.* striking.

frappieren *v.t.* to astonish.

frappierend *a.* astonishing, remarkable.

Fräse *f.* milling machine; molding machine; rotary cultivator.

Fraß *m.* food (animals); muck.

fraternisieren *v.i.* to fraternize.

Fratz *m.* (-es, *u.* -en, -en) brat, naughty child; (little) rascal.

Fratze *f.* (-, -n) grimace; caricature.

Frau *f.* (-, -en) woman; wife; lady; (*auf Briefen*) Mrs. (=Mistress).

Frauen: ~arzt *m.* gynecologist; **~bewegung** *f.* women's movement; **~feind** *m.* misogynist; **~haus** *n.* battered wives' refuge; **~held** *m.* womanizer; **~kloster** *n.* nunnery; **~zimmer** *n.* woman, female.

Fräulein *n.* (-s, -) Miss (title); young lady, single lady.

fraulich *a.* feminine; womanly.

Fraulichkeit *f.* femininity; womanliness.

frech *a.* insolent, saucy, shameless.

Frechheit *f.* (-, -en) impudence.

Freesie *f.* freesia.

Fregatte *f.* (-, -n) frigate.

Fregattenkapitän *m.* commander.

frei *a.* free; disengaged; exempt; vacant; *im Freien*, out doors, in the open air; *es steht dir ~*, you are at liberty (to); *es einem ~ stellen*, to leave one at liberty (to); *~ Eisenbahn*, free on rail; *~ Schiff*, free on board; *~e Berufe pl.* the independent professions; *~e Fahrt* (*mot.*) clear road ahead; *~e Wirtschaft*, private enterprise; *aus ~er Hand*, off-hand; *aus ~em Willen*, of one's own free will.

Freibad *n.* outdoor swimming-pool.

freibekommen *v.i.st.* to get time off.

freiberuflich *a.* self-employed; freelance.

Frei: ~betrag *m.* allowance; **~brief** *m.* charter; **~denker** *m.* freethinker.

freien *v.t. & i.* to court, to woo; to marry.

Freier *m.* (-s, -) wooer, suitor.

Freiexemplar *n.* free copy, presentation copy.

Freifrau *f.* baroness.

Freigabe *f.* release.

freigeben *v.t.* to set free, to release.

freigebig *a.* liberal, generous.

Frei: ~geist *m.* freethinker; **~hafen** *m.* freeport; **~handel** *m.* free-trade.

Freihandzeichnen *n.* freehand drawing.

Freiheit *f.* (-, -en) freedom, liberty; *in ~*, at large.

freiheitlich *a.* liberal.

Freiheits: ~beraubung *f.* wrongful detention; **~bewegung** *f.* liberation movement; **~entzug** *m.* imprisonment; **~kämpfer** *m.* freedom fighter; **~rechte** *pl.* civil rights; **~strafe** *f.* imprisonment.

freiheraus *adv.* openly, frankly.

Freiherr *m.* baron.

freiherrlich *a.* baronial.

Freiin *f.* (-, -nen) baron's daughter.

freikaufen *v.t.* to ransom.

freikommen *v.i.st.* to be released.

Freikörperkultur *f.* nudism.

freilassen *v.t.st.* to set free, to release.

Freilauf *m.* freewheel.

freilebend *a.* living in the wild.

freilegen *v.t.* to uncover.

freilich *adv.* indeed, certainly, to be sure, it is true, I admit.

Freilicht: ~bühne *f.*, **~theater** *n.* open-air theater.

freimachen *v.t.* to stamp; *v.refl.* to free *o.s.*; to arrange to be free; to take off one's clothes.

Frei: ~maurer *m.* freemason; **~maurerei** *f.* freemasonry; **~mut** *m.* frankness, candor.

freimütig *a.* candid, frank.

Freiraum *m.* (*psych.*) space to be oneself.

freischaffend *a.* freelance.

Freischärler *m.* (-s, -) guerilla.

freisinnig *a.* liberal.

freisprechen *v.t.st.* to acquit.

Frei: ~sprechung *f.* acquittal; **~staat** *m.* republic; Free State; **stätte** *f.* refuge, asylum; **~stelle** *f.* scholarship (in a school); **~tag** *m.* Friday; **~treppe** *f.* outside stairs.

Freiübungen *f.pl.* callisthenics, light gymnastics *pl.*

Freiwild *n.* fair game.

freiwillig *a.* voluntary, spontaneous.

Freiwillige *m./f.* (-n, -n) volunteer.
Freizeichen *n.* dialtone.
Freizeit *f.* free/leisure time.
Freizeit: ~**beschäftigung** *f.* leisure time activity; ~**kleidung** *f.* casual wear.
freizügig *a.* generous, liberal, permissive.
Freizügigkeit *f.* (-, 0) generosity, liberalness, right of settlement.
fremd *a.* strange, foreign, outlandish.
fremdartig *a.* strange, odd.
Fremde *m./f.* stranger, foreigner; alien.
Fremde *f.* foreign parts; away from home.
Fremden: ~**amt** *n.* visitors' bureau; ~**buch** *n.* visitors' book; hotel register; ~**führer** *m.* guide; ~**legion** *f.* Foreign Legion; ~**verkehr** *m.* tourist traffic.
fremdenfeindlich *a.* xenophobic.
Fremdenfeindlichkeit *f.*, **Fremdenhaß** *m.* xenophobia.
Fremdenverkehr *m.* tourism.
fremdgehen *v.i.st.* (*fam.*) to be unfaithful.
Fremdheit *f.* strangeness.
Fremdherrschaft *f.* (-, -en) foreign domination.
Fremdkörper *m.* foreign body.
Fremdling *m.* (-[e]s, -e) stranger.
Fremdsprache *f.* foreign language.
Fremdsprachen: ~**korrespondent** *m.* ~**korrespondentin** *f.* foreign language correspondent;/ ~**sekretär** *m.* ~**sekretärin** *f.* bilingual/multilingual secretary.
Fremdwort *n.* (-[e]s, -wörter) foreign word.
frenetisch *a.* frenetic.
frequentieren *v.t.* to frequent, to use.
Frequenz *f.* (*elek.*) frequency.
Fresko *n.* (-s, Fresken) fresco(-painting).
fressen *v.t.st.* to eat (animals); to devour.
Fressen *n.* (-s, -) food, meal.
Fresserei *f.* guzzling, stuffing.
Frettchen *n.* (-s, -) ferret.
Freude *f.* (-, -n) joy; enjoyment, pleasure, delight.
Freuden: ~**fest** *n.* celebration; ~**feuer** *n.* bonfire; ~**taumel** *m.* transport of delight.
freudestrahlend *a.* beaming with joy.
freudetrunken *a.* overjoyed, enraptured.
freudig *a.* joyful, joyous, cheerful.
freudlos *a.* joyless, cheerless.
freuen *v.t.* to please; to give pleasure; *das freut mich,* I am glad of that; (sich) ~ *v.refl.* (*über*) to be glad of; (*auf*) to look forward to.
Freund *m.* (-[e]s, -e) friend.
Freundeskreis *m.* circle of friends.
Freundin *f.* (-, -nen) (female) friend.
freundlich *a.* kind, friendly; (*Ort*) cheerful.
freundlicherweise *adv.* kindly.
Freundlichkeit *f.* (-, -en) kindness.
Freundschaft *f.* (-, -en) friendship.
freundschaftlich *a.* amicable, friendly.
Freundschafts: ~**besuch** *m.* goodwill visit; ~**vertrag** *m.* treaty of friendship.
Frevel *m.* (-s, -) crime; outrage.
frevelhaft *a.* mischievous, criminal.
freveln *v.i.* to commit an outrage.
Frevler *m.* (-s, -) transgressor; offender.
Friede[n] *m.* (-dens, 0) peace; *im* ~*n,* at peace.
Friedens: ~**bewegung** *f.* peace movement; ~**bruch** *m.* violation of the peace; ~**nobelpreis** *m.*

Nobel Peace Prize; ~**richter** *m.* Justice of the Peace, J.P.; ~**schluß** *m.* (conclusion of) peace; ~**stifter** *m.* peacemaker; ~**truppe** *f.* peace-keeping force; ~**verhandlungen** *pl.* peace talks; ~**vertrag** *m.* peace treaty.
friedfertig *a.* peaceful, peaceable.
Friedhof *m.* church-yard, cemetery, graveyard.
friedlich *a.* peaceable, peaceful.
friedliebend *a.* peaceable.
frieren *v.i.st.* to freeze; to feel cold.
Fries *m.* (-es, -e) (*arch.*) frieze; (*Zeug*) baize.
frigide *a.* frigid.
Frikadelle *f.* meat-ball.
Frikassee *n.* fricassee.
Friktion *f.* friction.
frisch *a.* fresh; new; (*fig.*) brisk; bright; vigorous; hale.
Frische *f.* (-, 0) freshness; vigor.
Frischzellentherapie *f.* living-cell therapy.
Friseur *m.* (-[e]s, -e); **Friseuse** *f.* (-, -n) hairdresser.
frisieren *v.t.* to dress the hair.
Frist *f.* (-, -en) time-limit; deadline.
fristen *v.t.* (*das Leben*) to get by somehow.
frist: ~**gemäß,** ~**gerecht** *a.* in time.
fristlos *a.* & *adv.* without notice.
Frisur *f.* (-, -en) hair-style, hair-do.
Friteuse *f.* deep fryer.
frivol *a.* & *adv.* frivolous(ly).
froh *a.* joyous, glad, joyful.
frohgelaunt *a.* cheerful.
frohgemut *a.* happy; *adv.* in good spirits.
fröhlich *a.* joyous; merry, cheerful.
fröhlichkeit *f.* cheerfulness.
frohlocken *v.i.* to rejoice; to exult.
Froh: ~**natur** *f.* cheerful person; ~**sinn** *m.* cheerfulness, gaiety.
fromm *a.* pious, religious.
Frömmelei *f.* (-, -en) sanctimoniousness.
Frömmigkeit *f.* (-, 0) piety.
Frondienst *m.*, **Fron(e)** *f.* (-, -en) enforced labor; (*hist.*) corvée.
frönen *v.i.* to indulge in.
Fronleichnamsfest *n.* Corpus Christi-day.
Front *f.* (-, -en) front, façade; face.
frontal *a.* frontal; head-on.
Frontal: ~**angriff** *m.* frontal attack; ~**zusammenstoß** *m.* head-on collision.
Frontantrieb *m.* front-wheel drive (car).
Frosch *m.* (-es, Frösche) frog.
Frosch: ~**könig** *m.* Frog Prince; ~**perspektive** *f.* worm's eye view; ~**schenkel** *m.* frog's leg.
Frost *m.* (-es, Fröste) frost; chill; cold.
Frostbeule *f.* chillblain; frostbite.
frösteln *v.i.* to shiver, to feel chilly.
frostig *a.* frosty; chilly; frigid.
frottieren *v.t.* (*med.*) to rub.
Frotzelei *f.* teasing remark.
frotzeln *v.t.* to tease.
Frucht *f.* (-, Früchte) fruit; (*fig.*) result, effect.
fruchtbar *a.* fruitful, productive, fertile.
Fruchtbarkeit *f.* (-, 0) fruitfulness, fertility; fecundity.
Fruchtblase *f.* amniotic sac.
Früchtchen *n.* (*fam.*) good-for-nothing.
Fruchteis *n.* sundae.

fruchten *v.i.* (*fig.*) to be effectual.
fruchtlos *a.* fruitless; ineffectual.
Frucht: ~**saft** *m.* fruit-juice; ~**salat** *m.* fruit-salad; ~**wasser** *n.* amniotic fluid; ~**wechsel** *m.* rotation of crops; ~**zucker** *m.* fructose.
früh *a. & adv.* early; in the morning.
Früh: ~**aufsteher** *m.* early bird; ~**dienst** *m.* early duty.
Frühe *f.* (-, 0) early morning; *in aller* ~, early in the morning.
Früherkennung *f.* early diagnosis/recognition.
frühestens *adv.* at the earliest.
Früh: ~**geburt** *f.* premature birth; ~**jahr** *n.* spring.
Frühling *m.* (-s, -e) spring.
frühreif *a.* precocious.
Früh: ~**schicht** *f.* early shift; ~**schoppen** *m.* morning drink; ~**stadium** *n.* early stage; ~**start** *m.* early start.
Frühstück *n.* breakfast; ~ *anrichten*, to lay breakfast.
frühstücken *v.i.* to breakfast.
frühzeitig *a.* early, premature; untimely.
Frust *m.* (*fam.*), **Frustration** *f.* frustration.
frustrieren *v.t.* to frustrate.
Fuchs *m.* (Fuchses, Füchse) fox, sorrel horse; (*Student*) freshman.
fuchsen *v.t.* to annoy; *v.refl.* to be annoyed.
Füchsin *f.* vixen.
Fuchsjagd *f.* fox-hunt.
Fuchsschwanz *m.* foxtail; (*mech.*) pad saw.
fuchsteufelswild *a.* hopping mad.
Fuchtel *f.* (-, -n) ferule, rod, *unter der* ~ *stehen* to be under the thumb.
fuchteln *v.i.* to fidget.
Fuder *n.* (-s, -) cart-load.
Fug *m.* (-[e]s, 0) *mit* ~ *und Recht*, with good cause.
Fuge *f.* (-, -n) juncture, joint; groove; (*mus.*) fugue; *aus den* ~*n sein*, to be out of joint.
fügen *v.t.* to join, to unite; (sich) ~ *v.refl.* to be suitable, to be convenient; to submit (to), to conform (to); to chance, to happen.
fügsam *a.* accommodating, docile.
Fügung *f.* (-, -en) contingency; divine Providence.
fühlbar *a.* sensible, perceptible.
fühlen *v.t.* to feel; to be sensible *or* aware of.
Fühler *m.* (-s, -) antenna, feeler, tentacle.
Fühlung *f.* (-, -en) contact; (*mil.*) touch; ~ *haben mit einem*, to be in touch with a person.
Fuhre *f.* (-, -n) conveyance; cartload.
führen *v.t.* to convey, to conduct; to lead, to guide; to manage; (*Bücher*) to keep; (*Waren*) to keep, to deal in; (*betreiben*) to carry on; *die Aufsicht* ~ *über*, to superintend; *den Beweis* ~, to show proof; *das Wort* ~, to be spokesman; *wohin soll das* ~? what we are coming to?
Führer *m.* (-s, -) leader; conductor; guide; pilot; guide-book.
Führer: ~**prinzip** *n.* leadership principle.
Führerschaft *f.* (-, 0) leadership.
Führerschein *m.* (*mot.*) driver's license.
Fuhrmann *m.* wagoner, carrier.
Führung *f.* (-, -en) guidance, conduct; direction, management; (*mil.*) generalship.
Führungs: ~**anspruch** *m.* claim to leadership; ~**aufgabe** *f.* management/leadership function; ~**kraft** *f.* executive; ~**spitze** *f.* top echelons;

~**zeugnis** *n.* certificate of good conduct.
Fuhrwerk *n.* carriage, vehicle.
Fülle *f.* (-, 0) plenty; abundance; *in Hülle und* ~, enough and to spare.
füllen *v.t.* to fill (up); to stuff; (*Zahn*) to stop.
Füllen *n.* (-s, -) foal, colt, filly.
Füller, Füllfeder *f.* fountain pen.
Füllgewicht *n.* net weight.
füllig *a.* corpulent; portly; ample.
Füllung *f.* (-, -en) stuffing, filling; panel.
Füllwort *n.* filler; expletive.
Fummelei *f.* twiddling; petting (erotic).
fummeln *v.i.* (*fam.*) to fumble around; to pet (erotic).
Fund *m.* (-[e]s, -e) find.
Fundament *n.* (-[e]s, -e) foundation.
Fund: ~**büro** *n.* lost and found office; ~**grube** *f.* (*fig.*) treasure house.
fünf *a.* **Fünf** *f.* (-, -en) five.
Fünfeck *n.* (-[e]s, -e) pentagon.
fünfeckig *a.* pentagonal.
fünferlei *a.* of five kinds.
fünffach, fünffältig *a.* fivefold, quintuple.
fünfhundert, five hundred.
Fünfhundertjahrfeier *f.* quincentenary.
Fünfkampf *m.* pentathlon.
Fünfkämpfer *m*; **Fünfkämpfern** *f.* pentathlete.
Fünflinge *pl.* quintuplets *pl.*
fünfte Kolonne *f.* fifth column.
fünftens *adv.* fifthly; in the fifth place.
fünfzehn *a.* fifteen.
fünfzig *a.* fifty.
Fünfziger *m.* (-s, -) quinquagenarian, man of fifty.
fungieren *v.i.* to act as.
Funk *m.* (-s, 0), radio.
Funkamateur *m.* radio ham.
Funkaufklärung *f.* (-, -en) radio intelligence.
Funke[n] *m.* (-ken[s], -ken) spark, sparkle.
funkeln *v.i.* to sparkle, twinkle, blaze.
funkelnagelneu *a.* brand-new.
funken *v.i. & t.* to radio, to send out.
Funker *m.* (-s, -) radio operator.
Funk: ~**gerät** *n.* radio set; ~**meßgerät** *n.* radar; ~**peilung** *f.* radio direction finding; ~**spruch** *m.* walkie-talkie message; ~**telegramm** *n.* radio-telegram; radio.
Funktion *f.* function; functioning, working.
funktional *a.* functional.
Funktionär *m.* **Funktionärin** *f.* official.
funktionieren *v.i.* to function, to work.
Funk: ~**turm** *m.* radio tower; ~**verbindung** *f.* radio contact; ~**verkehr** *m.* radio communication.
für *pr.* for; instead of; (*im Interesse von*) in behalf of; *an und* ~ *sich*, in itself; *Tag* ~ *Tag*, day by day; ~ *sich leben*, to live by oneself; *er* ~ *seine Person*, he, for one; ~ *und wider*, pro and con.
Fürbitte *f.* (-, -n) intercession.
Furche *f.* (-, -n) furrow.
furchen *v.t.* to furrow; (*fig.*) to wrinkle.
Furcht *f.* (-, 0) fear, fright, dread.
furchtbar *a.* terrible, dreadful; awful.
furchteinflößend *a.* frightening, fearsome.
fürchten *v.t.* to fear, to apprehend, to dread; (sich) ~ *v.refl.* to be afraid.
fürchterlich *a.* terrible, frightful.
furchterregend *a.* frightening.

furchtlos *a.* fearless, intrepid.
Furchtlosigkeit *f.* fearlessness.
furchtsam *a.* timid, nervous, shy.
Furchtsamkeit *f.* timidity; fearfulness.
füreinander *adv.* for each other, for one another.
Furie *f.* (-, -n) fury.
Furnier *n.* (-s, -e) veneer.
furnieren *v.t.* to veneer.
Furore *f.* ~**machen** cause a sensation.
Fürsorge *f.* care; welfare.
fürsorgend, fürsorglich *a.* caring, thoughtful, considerate.
Fürsorglichkeit *f.* considerateness, thoughtfulness.
Fürsprache *f.* (-, -n) support; intercession, good offices *pl.*
Fürsprecher *m.* (-s, -) intercessor, mediator.
Fürst *m.* (-en, -en) prince, sovereign.
Fürstenhaus *n.* dynasty.
Fürstentum *n.* principality.
Fürstin *f.* (-, -nen) princess.
fürstlich *a.* princely; sumptuous.
Furt *f.* (-, -en) ford.
Furunkel *m.* furuncle.
Fürwort *n.* (-[e]s, -wörter) (*gram.*) pronoun.
Furz *m.* (*vulg.*) fart.
furzen *v.i.* (*vulg.*) to fart.
Fusel *m.* rotgut.

fusion *f.* (-, -en) fusion; merger.
fusionieren *v.t.* to amalgamate; to merge.
Fuß *m.* (-es, Füsse) foot; base; footing, style; (*Münz~*) standard; *zu ~e*, on foot, afoot; *auf gutem, gespanntem ~e mit einem stehen*, to be on good, strained terms with one.
Fuß: ~**abstreifer** *m.*, ~**arbtreter** *m.* shoescraper; ~**angel** *f.* mantrap; trap; ~**ball** *m.* soccer, football; ~**balltoto** *m.* football pool; ~**boden** *m.* floor.
fussen *v.i.* to rely upon a thing.
Fussel *n.* lint.
fusselig *a.* linty; *sich den Mund ~ reden* to talk one's head off.
Fuß: ~**gänger** *m.* pedestrian; ~**gängerzone** *f.* pedestrian precinct; ~**gelenk** *n.* ankle; ~**leiste** *f.* baseboard; ~**matte** *f.* doormat; ~**note** *f.* footnote; ~**pflege** *f.* chiropody; ~**pilz** *m.* athlete's foot; ~**sohle** *f.* sole; ~**stapfle** *f.* foot-step, trace, track; ~**tritt** *m.* kick; ~**weg** *m.* foot-path.
futsch *a.* (*fam.*) broken.
Futter *n.* (-s, -) lining; food, fodder.
Futteral *n.* (-[e]s, -e) case.
Futterkrippe *f.* manger.
Futtermittel *n.pl.* feed, fodder.
futtern, füttern *v.t.* to line; to feed.
Fütterung *f.* (-, -en) feeding; lining.
Futur (*um*) *n.* (-s, -a) future tense.
futuristisch *a.* futuristic.

G

G, g *n.* the letter G *or* g; (*mus.*) sol.
Gabe *f.* (-, -n) gift, present; donation; alms; talent; (*med.*) dose.
Gabel *f.* (-, -n) fork; (*bot.*) tendril; (*eines Wagens*) thill, shafts *pl.*.
gabeln (sich) *v.refl.* to fork, to bifurcate.
Gabelstapler *m.* forklift.
Gabelung *f.* fork (streets).
Gabentisch *m.* table with presents.
gackern *v.i.* to cluck; to cackle.
gaffen *v.i.* to gape, to stare, to gaze at.
Gag *m.* gag; gimmick.
Gage *f.* (-, -n) salary, pay.
gähnen *v.i.* to yawn.
Gala *f.* (-, 0) gala.
Gala: ~**abend** *m.* gala; ~**diner** *n.* formal dinner; ~**empfang** *m.* gala; formal reception.
Galakleid *n.* full dress, court-dress.
galaktisch *a.* galactic; ~*er Nebel m.* nebula.
galant *a.* polite, courteous; gallant.
Galanterie *f.* (-, -[e]n) gallantry, courtesy.
Galanteriewaren *f.pl.* trinkets, fancy-articles *pl.*
Galaxie *f.* galaxy.
Galeere *f.* (-, -n) galley.
Galerie *f.* (-, -[e]n) gallery.
Gallerist *m.*; **Galleristin** *f.* gallery-owner.
Galgen *m.* (-s, -) gallows, gibbet.
Galgen: ~**frist** *f.* (*fam.*) respite, short delay; ~**strick** *m.*, ~**vogel** *m.* rogue.
Galionsfigur *f.* figurehead.
Gallapfel *m.* (-s, -äpfel) gall-nut.
Galle *f.* (-, 0) gall; bile.
Gallen: ~**blase** *f.* gall-bladder; ~**stein** *m.* gall-stone.
gallertartig *a.* gelatinous.

Gallert(e) *f.* (-, -n) jelly; gelatine.
gallig *a.* bilious.
Galopp *m.* (-[e]s, -e) gallop.
Galoppbahn *f.* race-track.
galoppieren *v.i.* to gallop.
galvanisch *a.* galvanic.
galvanisieren *v.t.* to galvanize.
Galvanismus *m.* (-, 0) galvanism.
Galvanostegie *f.* electroplating.
Gamaschen *f.* (-, -n) gaiters; spats.
Gambe *f.* viola da gamba.
Gammastrahlen *pl.* (*phys.*) gamma rays.
gammelig *a.* rotten; scruffy.
gammeln *v.i.* to bum around.
Gammler *m.*; **Gammlerin** *f.* bum.
Gang *m.* (-[e]s, -Gänge) walk, turn; gait; (*Maschine*) movement; alley, passage, corridor; (*Speisen*) course; (*Verlauf*) progress, course; (*Pferd*) pace; *im ~ sein*, to be in progress; *in vollem ~*, in full swing; *in ~ bringen*, to set going, to start.
gang und gäbe *a.* usual, common.
Gangart *f.* way of walking; gait.
gangbar *a.* passable.
Gängelband *n.* (-[e]s, -bänder) leading-strings *pl.*
gängeln *v.t.* to lead by the nose.
gängig *a.* usual, common; popular.
Gangräne *f.* (-, 0) gangrene.
Gangschaltung *f.* gearshift.
Gangster *m.* gangster; ~**bande** *f.* gang.
Gangway *f.* (*avi.*) steps; gangway.
Gangwerk *n.* (-[e]s, -e) mechanism, movement.
Ganove *m.* (*fam.*) crook.
Gans *f.* (-, Gänse) goose.
Gänse: ~**blume** *f.* daisy; ~**braten** *m.* roast goose;

~füßchen *n.pl.* quotation marks, inverted commas *pl.; es überläuft mich eine ~ haut,* my flesh creeps; **~klein** *n.* (goose) giblets *pl.;* **~marsch** *m.* single file.

Gänserich, Ganser[t] *m.* (-s, -e) gander.

Gänseschmalz *n.* goose dripping.

ganz *a.* whole, entire, all; complete; *~ adv.* quite, entirely, wholly; *eine ~e Note,* a semibreve, whole note; *~e Zahl,* integer; *im ~en,* on the whole.

Ganze *n.* (-n, 0) whole; totality.

Gänze *f. in ~* in its totality.

gänzlich *a.* whole, total; *~ adv.* totally, wholly.

ganz: ~metall *a.* all-metal; **~tägig** *a.* all-day; **~tags** *adv.* all-day; full-time; **~wolle** *a.* all-wool; **~zeitlich** *a.* full-time.

gar *a.* (*gekocht*) done, sufficiently cooked; *~ adv.* quite, very, fully; even; *~ nicht,* not at all, by no means.

Garage *f.* (-, -n) garage.

Garantie *f.* (-, -[e]n) guarantee, warranty; security.

garantieren *v.t.* to warrant, guarantee.

Garaus *m.* (-, 0) knockout blow; *den ~ machen,* to ruin, to do for someone.

Garbe *f.* (-, -n) sheaf.

Garde *f.* (-, -n) guard.

Garderobe *f.* (-, -n) wardrobe; checkroom, cloakroom; clothes *pl.*

Gardine *f.* (-, -n) curtain.

Gardinen: ~leiste *f.,* **~stange** *f.* curtain rail.

garen *v.t.u.i.* to cook.

gären *v.i.st.* to ferment; (*fig.*) to seethe.

Garn *n.* (-[e]s, -e) yarn, thread; *ins ~ gehen,* to fall into the net; *ins ~ locken,* to decoy.

Garnele *f.* (-, -n) shrimp.

garnieren *v.t.* to garnish, to trim.

Garnierung *f.* garnish; garnishing.

Garnison *f.* (-, -en) garrison.

Garnitur *f.* (-, -en) set; (*Besatz*) trimming.

Garn: ~knäuel *n.* ball of thread; **~rolle** *f.* reel; bobbin.

garstig *a.* nasty; naughty.

Garten *m.* (-s, Gärten) garden.

Garten: ~arbeit *f.* gardening; **~bau** *m.* horticulture; **~fest** *n.* garden party; **~haus** *n.* summerhouse; **~lokal** *n.* beer garden; **~messer** *n.* pruning-knife.

Gärtner *m.* (-s, -); **Gärtnerin** *f.* gardener.

Gärtnerei *f.* (-, -en) nursery.

Gärung *f.* (-, 0) fermentation.

Gas *n.* (-es, -e) gas.

gasartig *a.* gaseous.

Gas: ~anzünder *m.* gas-lighter; **~beleuchtung** *f.* gas-lighting; **~brenner** *m.* burner; **~hahn** *m.* gas tap; **~fußhebel** *m.* (*mot.*) accelerator.

gasförmig *a.* gaseous.

Gas: ~blühlicht *n.* incandescent light; **~maske** *f.* gas mask; **~messer** *m.* gas-meter.

Gasometer *m.* (-s, -) gasometer.

Gaspedal *n.* (*mot.*) accelerator.

Gasrohr *n.u.* **Gasröhre** *f.* gas-pipe.

Gasse *f.* (-, -n) street; lane.

Gassen: ~bube *m.* street-boy; **~hauer** *m.* popular song; **~junge** *m.* street urchin.

Gast *m.* (-[e]s, Gäste) guest; visitor; stranger; customer; *Gäste haben,* to have company; *zu ~ bitten,*

to invite (to dinner *or* supper).

gastfrei, gastfreundlich *a.* hospitable.

Gastfreundschaft *f.* hospitality.

Gast: *~geber m.* host; **~geberin** *f.* hostess; **~haus** *n.* restaurant, inn; **~hof** *m.* hotel; **~hörer** *m.* auditor.

gastlich *a.* hospitable.

Gastlichkeit *f.* hospitality.

Gastmahl *n.* banquet, dinner-party.

Gastprofessor *m.* **Gastprofessorin** *f.* visiting professor.

Gastrecht *n.* right to hospitality.

Gastritis *f.* gastritis.

Gastrolle *f.* starring-part.

Gastro: ~nom *m.;* **~nomin** *f.* restaurant owner; **~nomie** *f.* restaurant trade, gastronomy; **~nomisch** *a.* gastronomic.

Gast: ~spiel *n.* guest performance; **~spielreise** *f.* tour; **~stätte** *f.* restaurant; **~vorlesung** *f.* guest lecture; **~wirt** *m.* host, landlord; **~wirtschaft** *f.* inn.

Gatte *m.* (-n, -n) husband, spouse, consort.

Gatter *n.* (-s, -) grate, lattice; railing.

Gattin *f.* (-, -nen) wife, spouse.

Gattung *f.* (-, -en) kind, sort; (*liter.*) genre; (*Naturgeschichte*) species, family genus.

Gattungsname *m.* appellative, generic name.

Gau *m.* (-[e]s, -e) district; county.

Gaudi *f.* (*fam.*) bit of fun.

Gaukelei *f.* (-, -en) juggling; (*fig.*) trick, imposture.

gaukeln *v.i.* to juggle; to sway to and fro, to dangle.

Gaukelspiel *n.* (-[e]s, -e) delusion.

Gaukler *m.* (-s, -) conjurer, juggler.

Gaul *m.* (-[e]s, Gäule) horse, nag.

Gaumen *m.* (-s, -) palate.

Gaumen: ~freude *f.,* **~kitzel** *m.;* **~schmaus** *m.* delicacy.

Gauner *m.* (-s, -) cheat, crook, swindler.

Gaze *f.* (-, -n) gauze.

Gazelle *f.* (-, -n) gazelle.

geachtet *a.* respected.

Geächtete[r] *m.* (-n, -n) outlaw.

Geächze *n.* (-s, 0) groaning.

geädert *a.* veined, veiny.

geartet *a.* disposed; *gut ~,* good-natured.

Geäst *n.* branches.

Gebäck *n.* (-[e]s, -e) pastry.

Gebälk *n.* (-[e]s, -e) beams; rafters; timber-work, frame.

geballt *a.* concentrated; clenched.

Gebärde *f.* (-, -n) gesture.

gebärden (sich) *v.refl.* to behave.

Gebärdensprache *f.* sign language.

Gebaren *n.* behavior, conduct.

gebaren (sich) *v.refl.* to behave.

gebären *v.t.st.* to bear (a child), to give birth to.

Gebärmutter *f.* womb, uterus.

Gebäude *n.* (-s, -) building, edifice.

Gebein *n.* (-[e]s, -e) bones *pl.;* skeleton.

Gebell *n.* (-[e]s, 0) barking.

geben *v.t.st.* to give; to produce; to act, to perform; (*Karten*) to deal; *es gibt,* there is, there are; (sich) ~ *v.refl.st.* to abate; *Achtung ~,* to pay attention; *Nachricht ~,* to send word; *sich Mühe ~,* to take pains; *nichts auf einen ~,* to make no account of a person;

sich zufrieden ~, to rest content (with).

Geber *m.*; **Geberin** *f.* donor; giver.

Gebet *n.* (-[e]s, -e) prayer.

Gebetbuch *n.* prayer-book.

Gebiet *n.* (-[e]s, -e) district, territory; department; (*fig.*) province, sphere.

gebieten *v.t.st.* to command, to order; ~ *v.i.st.* (*über*) to rule; to control; to possess, to dispose of.

Gebieter *m.* master; **Gebieterin** *f.* mistress.

gebieterisch *a.* imperious, peremptory.

Gebietsanspruch *m.* territorial claim.

Gebilde *n.* (-s, -) structure, organization; form; image.

gebildet *a.* cultured; educated.

Gebirge *n.* (-s, -) (range of) mountains.

gebirgig *a.* mountainous.

Gebirgs: ~**ausläufer** *m.* foothill; ~**bach** *m.* mountain stream; ~**kamm** *m.* mountain-ridge; ~**kette** *f.* mountain chain; ~**massiv** *n.* massif; ~**paß** *m.* mountain pass; ~**zug** *m.* mountain range.

Gebiß *n.* (-bisses, -bisse) set of teeth; (*künstliches*) denture.

Gebläse *n.* (*tech.*) fan; blower.

Geblödel *n.* (*fam.*) silly chatter; silly things.

geblümt *a.* flowered.

Geblüt *n.* blood, descent.

geboren *p. & a.* born; *ein ~er Leipziger*, a native of Leipzig; *sie ist eine ~e N.*, her maiden name is N., née N.

geborgen *a.* saved, secure.

Geborgenheit *f.* security.

Gebot *n.* (-[e]s, -e) command(ment), order; (*com.*) offer, bid; *zu ~ stehen*, to be at (someone's) disposal.

Gebotsschild *n.* mandatory sign (traffic).

Gebräu *n.* (-s, -e) mixture, concoction.

Gebrauch *m.* (-[e]s, -bräuche) use, usage; custom; rite; *ausser ~sein*, to be obsolete; *außer ~ kommen*, to fall into disuse.

gebrauchen *v.t.* to use, to employ.

gebräuchlich *a.* usual, customary; ~*er*, more widely used.

Gebrauchsanweisung *f.* directions for use.

gebrauchsfertig *a.* ready-made.

Gebrauchsgegenstand *m.* item of practical use.

gebraucht *a.* second-hand; used.

Gebrauchtwagen *m.* used/second-hand car.

Gebrechen *n.* (-s, -) disability, handicap, infirmity.

gebrechlich *a.* fragile; infirm, weak.

gebrochen *p. & a.* broken, fractured; *mit ~em Herzen*, broken-hearted.

Gebrüder *m.pl.* brothers *pl.*

Gebrüll *n.* (-[e]s, 0) roar; lowing.

gebückt *a.* stooping; bending forward.

Gebühr *f.* (-, -en) duty, due; fee; tax; *eine ~ erheben*, to charge a fee for; *nach ~*, deservedly; *über ~*, unduly.

gebühren *v.i. & refl.* (sich) to be due; to be proper, to be meet.

gebührend *a. & adv.* appropriate(ly).

Gebühren: ~**einheit** *f.* (*tel.*) unit; ~**erhöhung** *f.* increase in charges/fees; ~**ermäßigung** *f.* reduction of charges/fees.

gebührenfrei *a.* free of charges, post-free.

gebührlich *a.* due, suitable, proper.

Geburt *f.* (-, -en) delivery, childbirth; birth; extraction.

Geburten: ~**kontrolle** *f.* birth-control; ~**ziffer** *f.* birthrate.

gebürtig *a.* born, a native of.

Geburts: ~**datum** *n.* date of birth; ~**helfer** *m.*; ~**helferin** *f.* midwife, obstetrician; ~**hilfe** *f.* midwifery, obstetrics *pl.*; ~**land** *n*, native country; ~**ort** *m.* native place, birthplace; ~**schein** *m.* certificate of birth; ~**tag** *m.* birthday; ~**urkunde** *f.* birth certificate.

Gebüsch *n.* (-[e]s, -e) bushes, shrubbery, underwood.

Geck *m.* (-en, -en) dandy, fop.

geckenhaft *a.* foppish, dandyish.

Gedächtnis *n.* (-nisses, 0) memory.

Gedächtnis: ~**lücke** *f.* gap in one's memory; ~**schwund** *m.* loss of memory; amnesia; ~**stütze** *f.* memory aid, mnemonic.

gedämpft *a.* subdued; muted; muffled; low.

Gedanke *m.* (-ns, -n) thought, idea.

Gedanken: ~**blitz** *m.* (*fam.*) brainwave; ~**freiheit** *f.* freedom of thought; ~**gang** *m.* train of thought; ~**lesen** *n.* mind reading.

gedankenlos *a.* thoughtless.

Gedankenlosigkeit *f.* thoughtlessness.

Gedankenstrich *m.* dash.

Gedankenübertragung *f.* telepathy.

gedankenverloren *a.* lost in thought.

gedankenvoll *a.* thoughtful, pensive.

gedanklich *a.* intellectual.

Gedärm *n.* (-[e]s, -e) intestines, bowels *pl.*

Gedeck *n.* (-[e]s, -e) table-cloth; plate; cover (at table), knife and fork.

gedeihen *v.i.st.* (s) to thrive; to prosper.

Gedeihen *n.* (-s, 0) prosperity.

gedeihlich *a.* prosperous; wholesome.

gedenken *v.i. & t.ir.* to think of; to remember; to intend.

Gedenk: ~**feier** *f.* commemoration; ~**minute** *f.* minute's silence; ~**stätte** *f.* memorial; ~**tag** *m.* commemoration day.

Gedicht *n.* (-[e]s, -e) poem.

gediegen *a.* solid; pure; sterling.

Gedränge *n.* (-s, 0) crowd, throng.

gedrängt *a.* crowded; condensed.

gedrückt *a.* depressed.

gedrungen *a.* compact; square-built.

Gedudel *n.* (*pej.*) tooting; noise.

Geduld *f.* (-, 0) patience.

gedulden (sich) *v.refl.* to have patience.

geduldig *a.* patient.

Gedulds: ~**faden** *m. mir reißt der ~* my patience is wearing thin; ~**probe** *f.* trial of one's patience; ~**spiel** *n.* puzzle.

gedungen *a.* hired.

gedunsen *a.* bloated, sodden.

geehrt *a.* honored.

geeignet *a.* fit, adapted, suitable.

Gefahr *f.* (-, -en) danger, peril, risk; ~ *laufen*, to run the risk; *auf eigene ~*, at owner's risk; *auf Ihre ~*, at your peril.

gefährden *v.t.* to endanger, to jeopardize, to imperil.

gefährdet *a.* at risk.

Gefährdung *f.* endangering; jeopardizing.

Gefahren: ~**bereich** *m.* danger area; ~**herd** *m.*,

~quelle f. source of danger; **~zulage** f. danger money.

gefährlich a. dangerous.

Gefährlichkeit f. dangerousness; riskiness.

gefahrlos a. free from danger; safe.

Gefährt n. vehicle.

Gefährte m. (-n, -n); **Gefährtin** f. (-, -nen) companion, comrade, associate, mate.

gefahrvoll a. perilous.

Gefälle n. (-s, -) fall, slope, grade; *starkes ~*, (*mot.*) steep hill down.

gefallen v.i.st. to please, to like; *sich ~ lassen*, to submit to.

Gefallen m. (-s, 0) pleasure; liking; *einen ~ erweisen*, to do a favor.

Gefallene m. soldier killed in action.

gefällig a. pleasing; agreeable, obliging.

Gefälligkeit f. (-, -en) favor.

gefälligst adv. please (ironic; hidden order).

gefallsüchtig a. coquettish.

gefangen a. imprisoned; captured, captive; *~nehmen*, to take prisoner; *~setzen*, to imprison; *sich ~ geben*, to surrender, to give oneself up.

Gefangene[r] m./f. (-n, -n) prisoner, captive.

Gefangennahme f. (-, 0) imprisonment; *ungesetzliche ~*, false imprisonment.

Gefangenschaft f. (-, 0) captivity.

Gefängnis n. (-nisses, -nisse) prison, jail; *ein Jahr ~*, one year's imprisonment; **~strafe** f. sentence of imprisonment; **~wärter** m. warder; **~wärterin** f. wardress.

Gefasel n. (-s, 0) drivel.

Gefäß n. (-es, -e) vessel.

gefaßt a. composed, collected, calm; *~ auf*, prepared, ready for; *sich ~ machen*, to prepare oneself.

Gefecht n. (-[e]s, -e) fight, combat, engagement.

gefedert a. (*mech.*) sprung.

gefeit (gegen) a. immune (from).

Gefieder n. (-s, -) plumage.

gefiedert a. feathered.

Gefilde n. (-s, -) plain, fields pl.

Geflecht n. (-[e]s, -e) texture; wickerwork.

gefleckt a. speckled, spotted.

geflissentlich a. intentional, wilful.

geflochten a. plaited.

Geflügel n. (-s, 0) poultry, fowls pl.

Geflügelhändler m. poulterer.

geflügelt a. winged; *~es Wort* n. familiar quotation.

Geflüster n. (-s, 0) whisper(ing).

Gefolge n. (-s, -) entourage, retinue, suite, attendants pl.

Gefolgschaft f. (-, -en) followers pl.

Gefolgsmann m. vassal; supporter, follower.

gefragt a. in demand, in request.

gefräßig a. voracious, gluttonous, greedy.

Gefräßigkeit f. greediness, gluttony, voracity.

Gefreite[r] m. (-n, -n) private first class; lance-corporal.

gefrieren v.i.st. (s) to freeze.

Gefrierfleisch n. frozen meat.

Gefrierpunkt m. (-[e]s, 0) freezing-point, zero.

Gefrier: schrank m. freezer; **~truhe** f. (chest) freezer.

Gefüge n. (-s, 0) structure; texture; tissue.

gefügig a. pliant; (*fig.*) docile.

Gefühl n. (-[e]s, -e) feeling, sensation.

gefühllos a. numb, unfeeling, insensitive.

gefühlsarm a. (emotionally) cold.

Gefühlsausbruch m. outburst of emotion.

gefühlsbetont a. emotional.

Gefühlsduselei f. (*pej.*) sentimentality.

gefühlsmäßig a. emotional (reaction).

Gefühlsregung f. emotion.

gefühlvoll a. sensitive, feeling, tender.

gefüllt a. filled; stuffed.

gefurcht a. lined; wrinkled.

gefürchtet a. dreaded, feared.

gegeben a. given.

gegebenenfalls adv. should the occasion arise.

Gegebenheit f. condition; fact.

gegen pr. towards; against; versus; to; in exchange for; contrary to; about, nearly; *~ bar*, for cash.

Gegen: ~angriff m. counter-attack; **~antrag** m. counter-motion, counter-proposal; **~besuch** m. return-visit; **~bewegung** f. counter movement.

Gegend f. (-, -en) region; country.

Gegendarstellung f. correction; reply (news).

gegeneinander adv. against each other; against one another.

Gegen: ~entwurf m. alternative draft; **~fahrbahn** f. opposite lane; **~forderung** f. counter-claim; **~gewicht** n. counter-weight; **~gift** n. antidote; **~kandidat** m. rival candidate; **~leistung** f. return, equivalent; **~licht** n. back-lighting; **~maßregel** f. preventive measure; **~mittel** n. antidote, remedy; **~papst** m. antipope; **~partei** f. opposite party; **~probe** f. counter-test; **~satz** m. contrast, opposition, antithesis; **~sätzlich** a. contrary, opposite; **~schlag** m. counter-stroke; **~seite** f. opposite side; opponent.

gegenseitig a. mutual, reciprocal.

Gegen: ~seitigkeit f. reciprocity; **~stand** m. object; subject.

gegenständlich a. representational (art).

gegenstandslos a. invalid; unsubstantiated, unfounded.

Gegen: ~stimme f. vote against, objection; **~stoß** m. counter-thrust; **~stück** n. counterpart; **~teil** n. contrary, reverse; *im ~*, on the contrary.

gegenteilig a. opposite.

gegenüber adv. & pr. opposite (to).

Gegenüber n. (-s, 0) person opposite.

Gegenüberstellung f. confrontation.

Gegenverkehr m. oncoming traffic.

Gegenvorschlag m. counter proposal.

Gegenwart f. (-, 0) presence; (*Zeit*) the present.

gegenwärtig a. current, present; *~ adv.* at present.

Gegenwartsliteratur f. contemporary literature.

gegenwartsnahe a. topical.

Gegenwartsprobleme pl. current problems.

Gegen: ~wehr f. defense, resistance; **~wert** m. equivalent; **~wind** m. headwind; **~wirkung** f. reaction; countereffect.

gegenzeichnen v.t. to countersign.

Gegenzug m. countermove.

gegliedert a. jointed; organized, structured.

Gegner m. (-s, -) opponent, adversary; *sich zum ~ machen*, to antagonize.

gegnerisch a. antagonistic, adverse.

Gegnerschaft f. (-, -en) antagonism; opposition pl.

Gegröle n. raucous singing; bawling.

Gehackte n. ground meat.

Gehalt *m.* (-[e]s, 0) contents *pl.*; value, merit; (*chem.*) proportion of; ~ *n.* (-[e]s, *u.* -hälter) salary, wages *pl.*

Gehaltsliste *f.* payroll.

Gehaltsskala *f.* (-, skalen) salary-scale.

Gehaltsvorschuß *m.* advance (on one's salary).

Gehaltszulage *f.* (-, -n) increase of salary.

gehaltvoll *a.* nourishing, substantial.

Gehänge *n.* (-s, -) festoon, garland.

geharnischt *a.* clad-in-armor; (*fig.*) angry, aggressive.

gehäßig *a.* malicious, spiteful.

Gehäßigkeit *f.* (-, -en) animosity, spitefulness.

gehäuft *a.* heaped.

Gehäuse *n.* (-s, -) case; capsule (*Obst*) core; shell.

gehbehindert *a.* walking disabled.

Gehege *n.* preserve; enclosure.

geheim *a.* secret; clandestine; *ganz ~, ~e Kommandosache,* top secret.

Geheimbund *m.* (-[e]s, -bünde) secret alliance, society.

Geheimdienst *m.* secret service.

Geheimhaltung *f.* observance of secrecy.

Geheimmittel *n.* (-s, -) nostrum, patent medicine.

Geheimnis *n.* (-nisses, -nisse) secret, mystery, arcanum.

Geheimniskrämer *m.* secret-monger.

geheimnisvoll *a.* mysterious.

Geheimpolizei *f.* secret police.

Geheimschrift *f.* (-, -en) cipher; code.

Geheimsprache *f.* (-, -n) secret language.

Geheimtuerei *f.* (-, -en) secretiveness.

Geheiß *n.* (-es, 0) order, command.

gehemmt *a.* inhibited.

gehen *v.i.st.* (*s*) to go, to walk; to sell (*v.i.*); (*Maschinen*) to work; *zum Fischen ~,* to go fishing; *wie geht es Ihnen?,* how are you?; *es geht nicht,* it won't do!; *vor sich ~,* to take place; *sich ~ lassen,* to indulge one's humor.

Geher *m.*; **Geherin** *f.* walker.

geheuer *a.* safe; *nicht ~,* haunted; unsafe.

Geheul *n.* (-[e]s, 0) howl(ing).

Gehilfe *m.* (-n, -n) assistant.

Gehirn *n.* (-[e]s, -e) brain, brains *pl.*

Gehirn: ~**erschütterung** *f.* concussion of the brain; ~**erweichung** *f.* softening of the brain; ~**hautentzündung** *f.* meningitis; ~**schlag** *m.* stroke, apoplexy.

Gehöft *n.* (-[e]s, -e) homestead.

Gehölz *n.* (-es, -e) wood, copse.

Gehör *n.* (-[e]s, 0) hearing; *sich ~ verschaffen,* to make oneself heard; *~ finden,* to be heard; *ein gutes ~,* a good ear.

gehorchen *v.i.* to obey.

gehören *v.i.* to belong; to appertain; (sich) ~ *v.refl.* to be proper.

Gehörgang *m.* auditory duct.

Gehörhilfe *f.* hearing aid.

gehörig *a.* belonging, appertaining; proper, due; ~ *adv.* duly, soundly.

gehörlos *a.* deaf.

Gehörnerv *m.* auditory nerve.

gehörnt *a.* horned; antlered; (*fig.*) cuckolded.

Gehörorgan *n.* organ of hearing.

Gehörrohr *n.* (-s, -e) ear-trumpet.

gehorsam *a.* obedient.

Gehorsam *m.* (-[e]s, 0) obedience.

Gehorsamsverweigerung *f.* (*mil.*) insubordination.

Gehörsinn *m.* sense of hearing.

Gehverwundeter *m.* walking wounded.

Gehsteig *m.* sidewalk.

Geier *m.* (-s, -) vulture.

Geifer *m.* (-s, 0) slaver, slobber; (*fig.*) venom.

geifern *v.i.* to slaver; to foam.

Geige *f.* (-, -n) violin, fiddle.

geigen *v.i.* to play the violin, to fiddle.

Geigen: ~**bogen** *m.* fiddle-stick; bow; ~**kasten** *m.* violin case.

Geiger *m.* (-s, -) violinist, fiddler.

Geigerzähler *m.* (*phys.*) Geiger counter.

geil *a.* (*fam.*) terrific; randy, horny.

Geisel *m.* (-s, -) hostage.

Geiß *f.* (-, -en) goat; roe.

Geiß: ~**blatt** *n.* honeysuckle; ~**bock** *m.* he-goat.

Geissel *f.* (-, -n) whip, lash, scourge.

geißeln *v.t.* to castigate, to scourge, to whip.

Geißelung *f.* castigation; scourging.

Geist *m.* (-es, -er) spirit; wit; mind, intellect; specter, ghost.

Geisterbahn *f.* ghost train.

Geisterfahrer *m.* ghost driver.

Geistergeschichte *f.* ghost story.

geisterhaft *a.* spectral, ghostly.

geistesabwesend *a.* absent-minded.

Geistes: ~**abwesenheit** *f.* absent-mindedness; ~**blitz** *m.* brainwave; ~**gegenwart** *f.* presence of mind; ~**geschichte** *f.* history of ideas; ~**haltung** *f.* attitude.

geisteskrank *a.* mentally ill, insane, of unsound mind.

Geisteskranker *m.* mental patient, mental case.

geistesschwach *a.* feeble-minded, imbecile.

Geistesstörung *f.* mental disorder.

Geisteswissenschaften *pl.* humanities.

Geisteszustand *m.* mental condition.

geistig *a.* (*Getränke*) alcoholic; intellectual, mental; spiritual.

geistlich *a.* sacred; spiritual; ecclesiastical, clerical.

Geistliche[r] *m.* (-n, -n) clergyman, minister.

Geistlichkeit *f.* (-, 0) clergy; priesthood.

geist: ~**los** *a.* spiritless, flat, dull; ~**reich** *a.* witty, gifted, racy, spirited; ~**voll** *a.* ingenious, witty, bright.

Geiz *m.* (-es, 0) meanness, stinginess, avarice.

geizen *v.i.* to be stingy.

Geizhals *m.* miser, niggard.

geizig *a.* avaricious, stingy.

Gejammer *n.* (-s, 0) lamentation.

Gekicher *n.* giggling.

Geklapper *n.* (-s, 0) clatter, rattling.

Geklimper *n.* tinkling.

Geklingel *n.* (-s, 0) tinkling, jingling.

geknickt *a.* (*fam.*) downcast.

Geknister *n.* rustling; crackling.

gekonnt *a.* accomplished.

Gekreisch *n.* (-s, 0) shrieking, screaming.

Gekritzel *n.* scribble.

gekünstelt *a.* artificial, affected.

Gel *n.* gel.

Gelaber *n.* (*fam. pej.*) babbling.

Gelächter *n.* (-s, 0) laughter.

geladen *a.* loaded; charged; furious.
Gelage *n.* (e[e]s, -e) feast; banquet.
Gelähmte *m./f.* paralytic.
Gelände *n.* (-s, -) terrain; **~abschnitt** *m.* (*mil.*) sector.
Gelände: **~fahrt** *f.* cross-country driving; **~fahrzeug** *n.* calmness; composure.
Geländer *n.* (-s, -) railing, balustrade, banisters *pl.*
gelangen *v.i.* (*s*) to arrive at; to attain (to).
gelassen *a.* composed, resigned, quiet, calm.
Gelassenheit *f.* calmness; composure.
Gelatine *f.* gelatine.
geläufig *a.* fluent; common; familiar.
gelaunt *a.* disposed, humored.
Geläute *n.* (-s, -) ringing, peal (of bells).
gelb *a.* yellow; (*Ei*) ~ *n.* yolk; **~es Fieber,** yellow fever.
gelblich *a.* yellowish.
Gelbsucht *f.* jaundice.
Geld *n.* (-[e]s, -er) money; *bares* ~, cash.
Geld: **~angelegenheit** *f.* financial matter; **~anlage** *f.* investment; **~automat** *m.* cash dispenser; **~betrag** *m.* sum, amount; **~beutel** *m.* purse; **~geber** *m.* financial backer; sponsor; **~gier** *f.* greed; **~institut** *n.* financial institution, **~schrank** *m.* safe; **~strafe** *f.* fine; **~stück** *n.* coin, piece of money; **~wechsel** *m.* change.
geldlich *a.* financial.
Geld: **~mittel** *pl.* financial resources; funds; **~prämie** *f.* cash bonus; **~quelle** *f.* source of income; **~schein** *f.* bill.
Gelee *n.* jelly.
gelegen *a.* situated; convenient.
Gelegenheit *f.* (-, -en) occasion, opportunity; ~ *ergreifen,* to take an opportunity.
Gelegenheits: **~arbeiter** *m.* casual worker; **~arbeiten** *pl.* odd jobs; **~kauf** *m.* bargain.
gelegentlich *a.* occasional.
gelehrig *a.* docile, tractable.
Gelehrsamkeit *a.* (-, 0) learning, erudition.
gelehrt *a.* scholarly; learned, erdudite; *die ~en Berufe pl.* the professions.
Gelehrte *m./f.* (-n, -n) scholar.
Geleise *n.* (-s, -) track; (*rail.*) rails *pl.*
Geleit *n.* (-[e]s, -e) escort, safe conduct.
geleiten *v.t.* to conduct, to escort; to convoy.
Geleitzug *m.* (*nav.*) convoy.
Gelenk *n.* (-[e]s, -e) joint, articulation; link.
Gelenkentzündung *f.* arthritis.
gelenkig *a.* agile, flexible, supple.
Gelenkrheumatismus *m.* articular rheumatism.
gelernter Arbeiter *m.* skilled worker.
Geliebte *m.* & *f.* (-n, -n) lover; sweetheart; mistress.
gelieren *v.t.* to jell.
gelind[e] *a.* mild, soft.
gelingen *v.i.st.* (*s*) to succeed, to prosper; *es gelang ihm,* he succeeded (in).
Gelingen *n.* (-s, 0) success.
gellen *v.t.* to yell, to shrill.
gellend *a.* piercing, shrill.
geloben *v.t.* to vow, to promise solemnly.
Gelöbnis *n.* (-nisses, -nisse) vow.
gelöst *a.* relaxed.
gelt *i.* (*fam.*) is it not so? right?
gelten *v.i.st.* to be worth, to be valid; to have

influence; ~ *für,* to pass for; ~ *lassen,* to let pass, to admit; *das gilt nicht!,* it is not fair!.
geltend *p.* & *a.* in force; ~ *machen,* to assert.
Geltung *f.* (-, 0) value; recognition; *zur ~ bringen,* to enforce, to assert; *zur ~ kommen,* to get into favor.
Geltungs: **~bedürfnis** *n.* **~drang** *m.,* **~sucht** *f.* craving for recognition.
Gelübde *n.* (-s, -) vow, solemn promise.
gelungen *a.* (*fam.*) amusing.
gelüsten *v.i.* to long for.
gemach *i.* peace!
Gemach *n.* (-[e]s, -mächer) apartment, chamber.
gemächlich *a.* easy, comfortable.
Gemahl *m.* (-[e]s, -e) consort, husband.
Gemahlin *f.* (-, -nen) consort, wife.
Gemälde *n.* (-s, -) picture, painting.
Gemäldegalerie *f.* picture-gallery.
gemäß *a.* & *p.* according to.
gemäßigt *a.* (*Klima*) temperature; moderate.
Gemäuer *n.* (-s, -) walls *pl.*
Gemecker *n.* bleating, griping, grousing.
gemein *a.* common; low, vulgar, coarse; mean; *der ~e Mann,* the common people; *der ~e Soldat,* the simple soldier.
Gemeinde *f.* (-, -n) community; (*Stadt*) municipality; parish; congregation.
Gemeinde... communal.
Gemeinde: **~rat** *m.* town-council; **~steuer** *f.* rate.
gemeingefährlich *a.* dangerous to the public.
Gemeingut *n.* common property.
Gemeinheit *f.* (-, -en) vulgarity; baseness; dirty trick.
gemeinhin *adv.* commonly.
gemeinnützig *a.* of public utility; *~e Organisation,* non-profitmaking organization.
Gemeinplatz *m.* common-place, truism.
gemeinsam *a.* common; mutual, joint.
Gemeinsamkeit *f.* common feature; point in common.
Gemeinschaft *f.* (-, -en) community.
Gemeinschaftsarbeit *f.* joint work.
Gemeinschaftsgefühl *n.* community spirit.
gemeinschaftlich *a.* common, joint.
Gemeinsinn *m.* public spirit.
gemeint *a.* intended.
gemeinverständlich *a.* generally intelligible, popular.
Gemein: **~wesen** *n.* commonwealth; **~wohl** *n.* public wealth.
Gemenge *n.* (-s, -) mixture, medley; (*fig.*) crowd.
gemessen *a.* measured; formal.
Gemetzel *n.* (-e, -0) slaughter, butchery.
Gemisch *n.* (es, -e) mixture.
gemischtes Doppel *n.* (*Tennis*) mixed double.
Gemme *f.* (-, -n) gem.
Gemotze *n.* (*fam.*) grouching.
Gemse *f.* (-, -n) chamois.
Gemunkel *n.* (-s, 0) secret talk, gossip.
Gemurmel *n.* (-s, 0) murmur(ing).
Gemüse *n.* (-s, -) greens, vegetables *pl.*
Gemüsegarten *m.* vegetable garden.
Gemüsehändler *m.* greengrocer.
Gemüt *n.* (-[e]s, -er) mind, soul, heart, feeling, disposition, nature.
gemütlich *a.* good-natured; cozy, snug.

Gemütlichkeit *f.* (-,0) good-nature; coziness; comfort.

Gemüts: ~**bewegung** *f.* emotion; ~**krankheit** *f.* mental disorder; ~**mensch** *m.* good-natured person; ~**regung** *f.* emotion, ~**ruhe** *f.* peace of mind.

gemütvoll *a.* warm-hearted; sentimental.

Gen *n.* (*bio.*) gene.

genagelt *a.* (*Schuhe*) hobnailed.

genau *a.* close; strict, precise; exact, accurate; *es* ~ *nehmen*, to be particular.

genaugenommen *adv.* strictly speaking.

Genauigkeit *f.* (-, 0) accuracy, precision, exactness.

Gendarm *m.* (-en, -en) gendarme.

Gendarmerie *f.* rural police.

Genealogie *f.* (-, -n) genealogy.

genehm *a.* convenient, acceptable.

genehmigen *v.t.* to approve of.

Genehmigung *f.* (-, -en) approval; assent, sanction; ratification.

geneigt *a.* inclined; prone; favorable.

General *m.* (-[e]s, -e) general; ~ *der Flieger*, air marshal.

General: ~**agent** *m.* agent-general; ~**baß** *m.* (*mus.*) basso continuo; ~**direktor** *m.* general manager; ~**konsul** *m.* consul-general; ~**probe** *f.* final dress rehearsal; ~**stab** *m.* general staff; ~**stabskarte** *f.* ordnance survey map; ~**versammlung** *f.* general meeting ~**vollmacht** *f.* general power of attorney.

Generation *f.* (-, -en) generation.

Generations: ~**konflikt** *m.* new generation; (*bio.*) alteration of generations.

Generator *m.* generator.

generell *a. & adv.* general(ly).

genesen *v.i.st.* (*s*) to recover, to be restored to health.

Genesung *f.* (-, -en) convalescence, recovery; ~**sheim** *n.* convalescent home.

Genetik *f.* genetics.

genetisch *a. & adv.* genetical(ly).

Genf *n.* (-s, 0) Geneva; *der* ~*er See m.* Lake Geneva.

genial *a.* inspired; gifted, brilliant.

Genialität *f.* genius, brilliancy.

Genick *n.* (-[e]s, -e) nape, back of the neck.

Genie *n.* (-s, -s) genius; man of genius.

genieren *v.t.* to molest, to bother; (sich) ~ *v.refl.* to feel embarrassed.

genießbar *a.* edible; palatable.

genießen *v.t.st.* to enjoy; to eat *or* drink.

Genießer *m.* bon vivant.

genießerisch *a. & adv.* appreciative(ly).

Genitalien *pl.* genitals.

Genitiv *m.* (-s, -e) genitive case.

Genius *m.* (-, -Genien) genius.

Genosse *m.* (-nossen, -nossen) **Genossin** *f.* (-, -nen) companion, comrade, partner, mate.

Genossenschaft *f.* (-, -en) cooperative.

genossenschaftlich *a.* cooperative; collective.

Genre *n.* (-s, -s) genre.

Gen: ~**technik** *f.* ~**technologie** *f.* genetic engineering.

genug *a. & adv.* enough, sufficient.

Genüge *f.* (-, 0) *zur* ~, sufficiently; ~ *tun*, to satisfy.

genügen *v.i.* to suffice; to satisfy; *sich* ~ *lassen*, to be satisfied (with).

genügend *a.* sufficient, enough.

genügsam *a.* modest; easily satisfied; frugal.

Genugtuung *f.* (-, -en) satisfaction.

Genus *n.* (-, Genera) gender.

Genuß *m.* (-nusses, -nüsse) consumption; enjoyment; pleasure, delight; use, profit; eating, drinking.

genüßlich *a. & adv.* appreciative(ly).

genußsüchtig, *a.* pleasure-seeking.

Geograph *m.* (-en, -en) geographer.

Geographie *f.* (-, 0) geography.

geographisch *a.* geographical.

Geologe *m.* (-en, -en) geologist.

Geologie *f.* geology.

geologisch *a.* geological.

Geometer *m.* (-s, -) geometrician; surveyor.

Geometrie *f.* (-, -n) geometry.

geometrisch *a.* geometrical.

Gepäck *n.* (-[e]s, -e) luggage, baggage.

Gepäck: ~**abfertigung** *f.* baggage check-in; baggage office; ~**aufbewahrungsstelle** *f.* check-room; ~**aufgabeschein** *m.* registration-slip; ~**netz** *n.* baggage rack; ~**träger** *m.* carrier; porter; ~**wagen** *m.* baggage car.

Gepard *m.* cheetah.

gepflegt *a.* neat, cultured, stylish.

Gepflogenheit *f.* (-, -en) custom, habit.

Geplänkel *n.* (-s, 0) skirmishing, banter.

Geplapper *n.* (-s, 0) babbling, chatter.

Geplätscher *n.* (-s, 0) splashing, plashing; babbling, chit-chat.

Geplauder *n.* (-s, 0) small-talk.

Gepolter *n.* clatter; grumbling.

Gepräge *n.* (-s, -) impression, stamp, coinage.

Gepränge *n.* (-s, 0) pomp, ceremony, pageantry.

gepunktet *a.* spotted; dotted.

gequält *a.* forced, pained.

Gequassel *n.* **Gequatsche** *n.* jabbering.

gerade *a.* straight; direct, right; upright, honest; (*Zahl*) even; ~*aus*, straight on; ~ *heraus*, frankly.

gerade *adv.* just, exactly.

Gerade *f.* straight line; straight arm punch.

geradezu *adv.* bluntly; actually, no less than.

gerad: ~**linig** *a.* straight, rectilineal, rectilinear; ~**sinnig** *a.* upright, straightforward.

Gerangel *n.* scrapping, wrangling.

Geraschel *n.* rustling.

Gerassel *n.* (-s, 0) rattling, din.

Gerät *n.* (-[e]s, -e) tool, implement, appliance, utensil.

geraten *v.i.st.* (*s*) to come, to get (into); to succeed, to turn out well; to prosper; *in Brand* ~, to catch fire; *ins Stocken* ~, to come to a standstill.

geraten *a.* advisable.

Geräteschuppen *m.* toolshed.

Geräteturnen *n.* apparatus gymnastics.

Geratewohl *n.* *aufs* ~, haphazard.

Gerätschaften *f.pl.* tools, implements *pl.*

geraum *a.* long; ~*e Zeit*, (for) a long time.

geräumig *a.* spacious, roomy, ample.

Geräusch *n.* (-[e]s, -e) noise, sound, bustle.

geräusch: ~**los** *a.* noiseless; ~**voll** *a.* noisy.

gerben *v.t.* to tan; to refine.

Gerber *m.* (-s, -) tanner.

Gerberei *f.* tannery.

Gerbsäure *f.* (-, 0) **Gerbstoff** *m.* (-[e]s, -e) tannic acid, tannin.

gerecht *a.* just; righteous, impartial.
gerechtfertigt *a.* justified.
Gerechtigkeit *f.* (-, 0) justice.
Gerechtigkeitsgefühl *n.* sense of justice.
gerechtigkeitsliebend *a.* having a love for justice; fair-minded.
Gerede *n.* (-s, 0) talk, rumor.
geregelt *a.* regular, steady.
gereizt *a.* & *p.* irritated, angry.
Gereiztheit *f.* (-, 0) irritation, anger.
gereuen *v.imp.* es gereut mich, I repent (of it), I regret (it).
Gericht *n.* (-[e]s, -e) court of justice, tribunal; judgment; dish, food; *das jüngste ~*, Doomsday, the Last Judgment; *vor ~ stellen*, to bring to trial, to try.
Gericht: ~**barkeit** *f.* jurisdiction; *streitige ~barkeit*, contentious jurisdiction; ~**beschluß** *m.* court order, ~**entscheidung** *f.* ruling; ~**ferien** *pl.* recess, vacation; ~**gebäude** *n.* courthouse; ~**hof** *m.* court of justice; ~**kosten** *pl.* costs.
gerichtlich *a.* judicial, legal; forensic; *~vorgehen gegen*, to take proceedings against.
Gerichtmedizin *f.* forensic medicine; ~**saal** *m.* courtroom; ~**schreiber** *m.* clerk of the court; ~**stand** *m.* venue; ~**vollzieher** *m.* marshal, bailiff; ~**wesen** *n.* judiciary, judicature.
geriffelt *a.* corrugated, fluted, ribbed.
gering *a.* small, little, mean; scanty, slight, un-important; inferior, poor; *nicht im ~sten*, not in the least.
geringelt *a.* curly, with horizontal stripes.
geringfügig *a.* unimportant, slight; trifling.
Geringfügigkeit *f.* triviality; insignificance.
geringschätzen *v.t.* to think little of.
geringschätzig *a.* disdainful, contemptuous.
Geringschätzung *f.* (-, 0) disdain, contempt, scorn.
gerinnen *v.i.st.* (*s*) to coagulate, to curdle.
Gerinnsch *n.* clot.
Gerippe *n.* (-s, -) skeleton; framework.
gerippt *a.* ribbed, fluted, laid.
gerissen *a.* cunning, crafty.
Germane *m.* **Germanin** *f.* Teuton.
germanisch *a.* Teutonic; Germanic.
germanisieren *v.t.* to germanize.
Germanist *m.*; **Germanistin** *f.* Germanist, German scholar.
Germanistik *f.* German studies.
gern *adv.* with pleasure, willingly, readily, easily; ~**haben**, to be fond of; ~**sehen**, to like; *nicht ~ gesehen*, unwelcome.
Geröll *n.* (-[e]s, -e) rubble, boulders *pl.*
Gerste *f.* (-, -n) barley.
Gerstengraupen *pl.* pearl barley.
Gerstenkorn *n.* barleycorn; (*med.*) sty.
Gerte *f.* (-, -n) switch, rod.
Geruch *m.* (-[e]s, -rüche) smell; scent, odor.
geruchlos, *a.* odorless, unscented.
Geruchs: ~**organ** *n.* olfactory organ; ~**sinn** *m.* sense of smell; ~**tilgendes Mittel** *n.* deodorant.
Gerücht *n.* (-[e]s, -e) rumor, report, news *pl.*; *es geht das ~*, it is rumored.
geruhen *v.i.* to be pleased, to deign.
gerührt *a.* touched; moved.
geruhsam *a.* peaceful; leisurely.
Gerümpel *n.* (-s, 0) junk; trash.

Gerundium *n.* (-s, -dien) gerund.
Gerüst *n.* (-[e]s, -e) scaffold, stage, scaffolding, frame(work).
Ges *n.* (-, 0) (*mus.*) G flat.
gesalzen *a.* salted; (*fig.*) steep.
gesammelt *a.* concentrated; *~e Werke pl.* collected works.
gesamt *a.* whole, total, aggregate.
Gesamt: ~**auflage** *f.* total edition; total circulation; ~**ausgabe** *f.* complete edition; ~**betrag** *m.* sum total; ~**eindruck** *m.* overall impression, ~**ergebnis** *n.* overall result; ~**gewicht** *n.* total weight.
Gesamtheit *f.* (-, 0) totality.
Gesandte *m./f.* (-n, -n) minister, envoy.
Gesandtschaft *f.* (-, -en) legation.
Gesandtschaftsrat *m.* counsellor of legation.
Gesang *m.* (-[e]s, -sänge) singing; song, air; canto (of a long poem).
Gesangbuch *n.* hymn-book.
Gesang: ~**lehrer** *m.*; ~**lehrerin** *f.* singing teacher, voice teacher; ~**unterricht** *m.* singing lesson, voice lesson; ~**verein** *m.* choral society.
gesättigt *a.* (*chem.*) saturated; full.
Gesäß *n.* (-es, -e) bottom, buttocks.
Geschädigte *m.* (*law*) the injured party.
Geschäft *n.* (-[e]s, -e) business; employment, occupation; shop, establishment; transaction.
Geschäftemacher *m.* (*pej.*) profit seeker.
geschäftig *a.* busy, bustling, active.
geschäftlich *a.* business-, commercial; *~e Verbindung haben mit*, to do (transact) business with.
Geschäfts: ~**abschluß** *m.* transaction; ~**aufsicht** *f.* legal control; ~**bedingungen** *pl.* terms of trade; ~**bericht** *m.* company report; ~**brief** *m.* business-letter; ~**bücher** *n.pl.* the books (of a firm); ~**fähigkeit** *f.* (*law*) legal capacity; ~**führer** *m.* manager; ~**mann** *m.* business man; ~**nummer** *f.*, ~**zeichen** *n.* reference (number); ~**ordnung** *f.* rules of procedure; standing order; ~**papiere** *pl.* (*Post*) commercial papers; ~**reise** *f.* business trip; ~**stunden** *f.pl.* office hours; ~**träger** *m.* chargé d'affaires; ~**verkehr** *m.* business dealings *pl.*; ~**zeit** *f.* office-hours *pl.*; ~**zweig** *m.* branch of business.
gescheckt *a.* spotted; skewbald.
geschehen *v.i.st.* (*s*) to come to pass, to occur, to happen; *~ lassen*, to permit; *es geschieht ihm recht*, it serves him right.
Geschehen *n.* events; action.
gescheit *a.* clever, intelligent.
Geschenk *n.* (-[e]s, -e) gift, present.
Geschichte *f.* (-, -n) history; story; (*fam.*) affair.
geschichtlich *a.* historic(al).
Geschichtschreiber *m.* historian.
Geschichtsschreibung *f.* historiography.
Geschichtswissenschaftler *m.*; **Geschichtswissenschaftlerin** *f.* historian.
Geschick *n.* (-[e]s, -e) dexterity, skill; destiny, fate.
Geschicklichkeit *f.* (-, -en) dexterity, adroitness, skill.
geschickt *a.* fit, apt, clever; skilled.
geschieden *a.* divorced.
Geschiedene *m./f.* divorcee.
Geschirr *n.* (-[e]s, -e) vessel; (*Silber*) plate; (*irdenes*) crockery, earthenware; tools *pl.*; (*Pferde~*) harness.
Geschirr: ~**schrank** *m.* cupboard; ~**spüler** *m.* dishwasher; ~**tuch** *n.* dish towel.

Geschlecht *n.* (-[e]s, -er) sex; kind; race; lineage; generation; (*gram.*) gender.

geschlechtlich *a.* sexual.

Geschlechts: ~**krankheit** *f.* venereal disease; ~**reife** *f.* sexual maturity; ~**teile** *m.pl.* genitals *pl.*; ~**trieb** *m.* sexual drive; ~**verkehr** *m.* intercourse; ~**wort** *n.*(gram.) article.

geschliffen *a.* polished; (*Glas*) cut.

geschlossen *a.* close, compact; concentrated; solid, in a body.

Geschlossenheit *f.* unity; uniformity.

Geschmack *m.* (-[e]s, -schmäcke) taste; flavor; liking.

geschmacklos *a.* tasteless; in bad taste.

Geschmacklosigkeit *f.* (-, -en) bad taste.

Geschmacksfrage *f.*, **Geschmacksache** *f.* matter of taste.

Geschmacksverirrung *f.* lapse of taste.

geschmackvoll *a.* tasteful, elegant.

Geschmeide *n.* (-s, -) jewels *pl.*

geschmeidig *a.* flexible, pliant, supple.

Geschmeiß *n.* (-es, 0) (*sl. pej.*) low rabble; vermin.

Geschnatter *n.* cackling; chatter.

geschniegelt *a.* spruce, trim.

Geschöpf *n.* (-[e]s, -e) creature; creation.

Geschoß *n.* (-schosses, -schosse) projectile, missile; storey, floor.

geschraubt *a.* stilted; pretentious.

Geschrei *n.* (-es, -e) screaming; yelling; shouting.

Geschütz *n.* (-es, -e) cannon, gun.

Geschütz: ~**feuer** *n.* gunfire; ~**stand** *m.* emplacement.

geschützt *a.* protected; *m.* turret.

Geschwader *n.* (-s, -) squadron; (*avi.*) wing; *Geschützturm* ~**kommandeur** *m.* wing commander.

Geschwafel *n.* (*pej.*) waffle.

Geschwätz *n.* (-es, 0) gossip; prattle.

geschwätzig *a.* talkative, garrulous.

geschweift *a.* curved; ~*e klammern pl.* parentheses.

geschweige denn, not to mention, let alone.

geschwind *a.* quick, fast, swift.

Geschwindigkeit *f.* (-, -en) quickness, speed; velocity.

Geschwindigkeits: ~**begrenzung** *f.* speed limit; ~**kontrolle** *f.* speed check; ~**messer** *m.* speedometer.

Geschwirr *n.* (-[e]s, 0) whirr, buzz.

Geschwister *pl.* brothers and sisters *pl.*; siblings.

geschwisterlich *a.* brotherly; sisterly.

geschwollen *a.* swollen; pompous, bombastic.

geschworen *a.* sworn.

Geschworene *m./f.* (-n, -n) jury member, juror.

Geschworenengericht *n.* jury.

Geschwulst *f.* (-, -schwülste) tumor; swelling.

geschwungen *a.* curved.

Geschwür *n.* (-[e]s, -e) ulcer, abscess.

Gesell, Geselle *n.* (-[e]n, -[e]n) journeyman; companion, comrade.

gesellen (sich) *v.refl.* to join (with).

gesellig *a.* social, sociable, convivial; ~*e Zusammenkunft f.* social gathering.

Geselligkeit *f.* (-, 0) sociability.

Gesellschaft *f.* (-, -en) society; company; party: *eine ~ gründen*, to form a company.

Gesellschafter *m.* (-s, -) **Gesellschafterin** *f.* (-, -nen) companion; associate; (*com.*) partner;

shareholder.

gesellschaftlich *a.* social.

Gesellschafts: ~**anzug** *m.* evening dress; ~**form** *f.* social system; ~**kritik** *f.* social criticism; ~**ordnung** *f.* social order; ~**politik** *f.* social policy; ~**reise** *f.* conducted tour; ~**spiel** *n.* society game, parlor game; ~**tanz** *m.* ballroom dancing; ~**vertrag** *m.* deed of partnership.

Gesetz *n.* (-es, -e) law, statute; rule.

Gesetzblatt *n.* law gazette.

Gesetz: ~**buch** *n.* code; ~**entwurf** *m.* bill.

Gesetzeskraft *f.* force of law, legal force.

gesetzgebend *a.* legislative; ~*e Körperschaft f.* legislative body.

Gesetz: ~**geber** *m.* legislator; ~**gebung** *f.* legislation; legislature.

gesetzlich *a.* lawful, legal, statutory; ~**geschützt** *a.* legally registered, proprietary.

gesetzlos *a.* lawless, illegal.

Gesetzlosigkeit *f.* (-, -en) anarchy.

gesetzmäßig *a.* lawful, legitimate; legal.

gesetzt *a.* steady; sedate; ~*daß*, suppose, supposing that.

gesetzwidrig *a.* illegal, unlawful, contrary to law.

gesichert *a.* safe, secured.

Gesicht *n.* (-[e]s, -er, *u.* -e) face; countenance; mien; apparition, vision.

Gesichts: ~**ausdruck** *m.* expression, look; ~**farbe** *f.* complexion; ~**kreis** *m.* horizon; (*fig.*) intellectual horizon; ~**punkt** *m.* point of view; ~**zug** *m.* feature.

Gesims *n.* (-simses, -simse) shelf; cornice; mantlepiece.

Gesinde *n.* (-s, 0) servants, domestics *pl.*

Gesindel *n.* (-s, 0) mob, rabble.

gesinnt *a.* minded, disposed.

Gesinnung *f.* (-, -en) intention; disposition, opinion; mind; conviction.

Gesinnungs: ~**genosse** *m.*; ~**genossin** *f.* likeminded person; ~**losigkeit** *f.* lack of principle; ~**wandel** *m.* change of heart.

gesittet *a.* well-behaved; well-mannered.

Gesittung *f.* (-, 0) civilization.

Gesöff *m.* (*pej.*) muck.

gesondert *a.* separate.

gesonnen *a.* disposed, resolved.

Gespann *n.* (-[e]s, -e) team; yoke (of oxen).

gespannt *a. & p.* strained; intent, wrought up; anxious to know; *auf ~em Fuß*, on bad terms.

Gespenst *n.* (-es, -er) specter, ghost.

Gespenster: ~**geschichte** *f.* ghost story; ~**stunde** *f.* witching hour.

gespenstisch *a.* ghostly; eerie.

gesperrt *a.* closed; (*Druck*) spaced; ~ *für Zutritt*, out of bounds, off limits.

Gespött *n.* (-[e]s, 0) mockery, ridicule.

Gespräch *n.* (-[e]s, -e) conversation, talk.

gesprächig *a.* talkative, communicative.

Gesprächs: ~**bereitschaft** *f.* readiness for discussion; ~**fetzen** *m.* fragment of conversation; ~**stoff** *m.* topics of conversation.

gespreizt *a.* pompous; stilted.

gesprenkelt *a.* speckled.

Gespritzte *m.* wine with soda water.

Gespür *n.* feeling; nose.

Gestade *n.* (-s, -) shore, beach, bank.

Gestalt *f.* (-, -en) form, figure, shape; frame; size, stature; fashion, manner.
gestalten *v.t.* to form, to shape; (sich) ~ *v.ref.* to turn out.
gestaltlos *a.* shapeless; formless.
Gestaltung *f.* (-, -en) shaping; fashioning; formation; configuration; condition.
Gestaltungsprinzip *n.* formal principle.
Gestammel *n.* stammering, stuttering.
geständig *a.* confessing; ~*sein*, to confess.
Geständnis *n.* (-nisses, -nisse) confession.
Gestank *m.* (-[e]s, -stänke) stink, stench.
gestatten *v.t.* to permit, to allow.
Geste *f.* (-, -n) gesture.
Gesteck *n.* flower arrangement.
gestehen *v.t.st.* to confess, to avow, to admit.
Gestehungskosten *pl.* prime cost, cost price.
Gestein *n.* (-[e]s, -e) rock.
Gesteinskunde *f.* petrology.
Gestell *n.* (-[e]s, -e) frame; rack, stand; trestle.
gestelzt *a.* stilted; affected.
gestern *adv.* yesterday.
gestiefelt *a.* booted.
Gestik *f.* gestures.
gestikulieren *v.i.* to gesticulate.
Gestirn *n.* (-[e]s, -e) star; constellation.
gestirnt *a.* starred, starry.
gestört *a.* disturbed.
Gestotter *n.* (-s, 0) stammering, stuttering.
Gesträuch *n.* (-[e]s, -e) thicket, shrubs *pl.*
gestreift *a.* striped.
gestreng *a.* strict, severe, rigorous.
gestrichen *a.* painted; deleted; level (measure).
gestrig *a.* yesterday's.
Gestrüpp *n.* (-[e]s, -e) undergrowth.
Gestühl *n.* seats.
Gestüt *n.* (-[e]s, -e) stud-farm.
Gesuch *n.* (-[e]s, -e) application, request; ~ *einreichen*, to make an application; *ein ~ bewilligen*, to grant (approve) an application.
gesucht *a.* in demand; affected; sought-after.
Gesumm *n.* buzzing, humming.
gesund *a.* sound, healthy; well, in good health; (*Ansicht*) sane; (*Speisen, etc.*) wholesome; (*Klima*) salubrious.
gesunden *v.i.* (*s*) to recover (health), to get well.
Gesundheit *f.* (-, 0) health; sanity; ~! Bless you!
gesundheitlich *a.* physical; sanitary.
Gesundheits: ~**pflege** *f.* hygiene.
gesundheitsschädlich *a.* unhealthy.
Gesundheitswesen *n.* public health service.
gesund: ~**schrumpfen** *v.refl.* to pare down (business); ~**stoßen** *v.refl.* to make a pile (business).
Gesundung *f.* recovery.
getäfelt *a.* wainscoted, tiled.
Getier *n.* animals.
getigert *a.* patterned like a tiger.
Getöse *n.* (-s, 0) noise, din.
getragen *a.* used (clothes); solemn, measured.
Getrampel *n.* (-s, 0) trampling.
Getränk *n.* (-[e]s, -e) beverage, drink.
Getränkeautomat *m.* drinks dispenser.
Getränkekarte *f.* list of beverages; wine list.
Getratsche *n.* (*fam.*) gossip, gossiping.
getrauen (sich) *v.refl.* to dare, to venture; *ich getraue mich nicht hinein*, I dare not go in.

Getreide *n.* (-s, -) corn, grain.
Getreidespeicher *m.* grain silo.
getrennt *a.* & *adv.* separate(ly).
getreu *a.* faithful, true, trusty; loyal.
getreulich *a.* & *adv.* faithful(ly).
Getriebe *n.* (-s, -) gears; (*Uhr, Klavier*) works; bustle; ~**kasten** *m.* gear box.
getrost *a.* confident.
Getto *n.* (-s, -s) ghetto.
Getue *n.* (-s, 0) fuss.
Getümmel *n.* (-s, 0) bustle.
getupft *a.* speckled.
Getuschel *n.* whispering, gossiping.
geübt *a.* experienced; practised; expert.
Gewächs *n.* (-es, -e) plant, vegetable; (*Wein*) vintage; (*med.*) growth.
gewachsen *a.* equal to, a match for.
Gewächshaus *n.* greenhouse.
gewagt *a.* risky; daring; risqué.
gewählt *a.* refined, select, choice.
gewahr *a.* aware (of).
Gewähr *f.* (-, 0) guarantee; *ohne* ~, subject to correction.
gewahren *v.t.* to perceive.
gewähren *v.t.* to give, to allow, to grant; *einen ~ lassen*, to let a person alone.
gewährleisten *v.t.* to guarantee.
Gewahrsam *m.* (-s, 0) safe-keeping, safe-custody; *in* ~, under restraint.
Gewährsmann *m.* informant; authority.
Gewalt *f.* (-, -en) power, authority; force, violence; *höhere* ~, act of God.
Gewalt: ~**akt** *m.* act of violence; ~**anwendung** *f.* use of violence.
Gewaltenteilung *f.* separation of powers.
Gewaltherrschaft *f.* tyranny; despotism.
gewaltig *a.* mighty, enormous; tremendous; powerful.
gewaltlos *a.* non-violent.
Gewaltmarsch *m.* forced march.
gewaltsam *a.* forcible, violent; *eines ~en Todes sterben*, to die a violent death.
gewalttätig *a.* violent, outrageous.
Gewalttätigkeit *f.* (-, -en) violence; rowdyism.
Gewaltverbrechen *n.* crime of violence.
Gewaltverbrecher *m.* violent criminal.
Gewaltverzichtsabkommen *n.* nonaggression treaty.
Gewand *n.* (-[e]s, -e *u.* -wänder) robe, garment; drapery.
gewandt *a.* dexterous, smart, agile.
gewärtigen *v.t.* to expect.
Gewäsch *n.* (-es, 0) twaddle.
Gewässer *n.* (-s, -) waters *pl.*
Gewebe *n.* (-s, -) texture, tissue, fabric.
Gewehr *n.* (-[e]s, -e) gun, rifle.
Gewehrkolben *m.* butt.
Gewehrlauf *m.* rifle barrel.
Geweih *n.* (-[e]s, -e) antlers *pl.*
geweiht *a.* consecrated.
Gewerbe *n.* (-s, -) trade; calling; industry.
Gewerbe: ~**freiheit** *f.* freedom of trade; ~**ordnung** *f.* trade regulations *pl.*; ~**schein** *m.* trading license; ~**schule** *f.* technical school; ~**steuer** *f.* trade-tax; ~**treibende** *m./f.* person carrying on a trade.

gewerblich *a.* industrial, commercial.
gewerbetreibend *a.* manufacturing.
gewerbsmäßig *a.* professional.
Gewerkschaft *f.* (-, -en) labor-union.
Gewerkschafter *m.*; **Gewerkschafterin** *f.* labor unionist.
gewerkschaftlich *a.* (labor) union.
Gewerkschaftsbund *m.* federation of labor unions.
Gewerkschaftsmitglied *n.* member of a labor union.
Gewicht *n.* (-[e]s, -e) weight.
Gewichtheben *n.* weight-lifting.
gewichtig *a.* weighty, important.
Gewichts: ~**klasse** *f.* (sp.) weight (class); ~**verlust** *m.* loss of weight; ~**zunahme** *f.* increase of weight.
gewillt *a.* wiling, disposed.
Gewimmel *n.* (-s, 0) swarm, crowd.
Gewimmer *n.* whimpering.
Gewinde *n.* (-s, -) thread.
Gewindebohrer *m.* (*mech.*) tap.
Gewinnn *m.* (-[e]s, -e) gain, profit, advantage; *mit* ~, at a profit; ~ *und Verlustkonto*, profit and loss account; ~**beteiligung** *f.* profit sharing.
Gewinnanteil *m.* dividend.
gewinnbringend *a.* profitable.
gewinnen *v.i.* & *t.st.* to win; to gain, to get, to earn; *über sich* ~, to get oneself to do.
gewinnend *a.* winning, engaging.
Gewinner *m.*; **Gewinnerin** *f.* winner.
Gewinn: ~**los** *n.* winning ticket; ~**spanne** *f.* profit margin; ~**streben** *n.* pursuit of profit; ~**sucht** *f.* greed for profit.
gewinnsüchtig *a.* profiteering.
Gewinnung *f.* mining, extraction, recovery.
Gewinsel *n.* (-s, 0) whimpering, whining.
Gewirr *n.* (-[e]s, 0) confusion; criss-cross; tangle.
Gewisper *n.* (-s, -) whispering.
gewiß *a.* certain; sure; constant, fixed; ~ *adv.* certainly, no doubt.
Gewissen *n.* (-s, -) conscience.
gewissenhaft *a.* conscientious.
Gewissenhaftigkeit *f.* conscientiousness.
gewissenlos *a.* unscrupulous.
Gewissenlosigkeit *f.* unscrupulousness.
Gewissens: ~**biß,** *m.* remorse; ~**freiheit,** *f.* freedom of conscience; ~**konflikt** *m.* moral conflict.
gewissermassen *adv.* so to speak.
Gewißheit *f.* (-, -en) certainty, surety.
Gewitter *n.* (-s, -) (thunder)storm.
gewitz *a.* smart, clever.
gewogen *a.* favorable, kindly disposed.
gewöhnen *v.t.* to accustom.
gewohnt *a.* usual, accustomed, habitual; in the habit of. . .
Gewohnheit *f.* (-, -en) custom; habit.
gewohnheitsmäßig *a.* habitual.
Gewohnheits: ~**recht** *n.* common law; ~**tier** *n.* creature of habit; ~**verbrecher** *m.* habitual criminal.
gewöhnlich *a.* usual; common, vulgar; ~ *adv.* usually, as a rule.
gewohnt *a.* usual; *es* ~ *sein* to be used to.
Gewöhnung *f.* habituation; addiction.
Gewölbe *n.* (-s, -) vault, arch.

gewölbt *a.* vaulted, arched.
Gewühl *n.* (-[e]s, 0) throng, crowd.
gewunden *a.* & *p.* tortuous.
gewürfelt *a.* checked.
Gewürz *n.* (-es, -e) spice; seasoning.
Gewürznelke *f.* clove.
Geysir *m.* (-s, -e) geyser.
Gezänk *n.* (-[e]s, -e) **Gezanke** *n.* (-s, 0) quarrel, squabble.
gezeichnet *a.* (*gez.*) signed.
Gezappel *n.* wriggling.
Gezeiten *pl.* tides.
Gezeitenkraftwerk *n.* tidal powerstation.
Gezeter *n.* (-s, 0) scalding, nagging.
gezielt *a.* specific, deliberate, well-directed.
geziemen (sich) *v.i.* & *refl.* to become, to befit; to be fitting.
geziemend *a.* proper, befitting.
geziert *a.* affecting, finicking, finicky.
Gezirpe *n.* chirping.
Gezwitscher *n.* (-s, 0) chirping, twitter.
gezwungen *a.* constrained, forced.
gezwungenermassen *adv.* of necessity.
Gicht *f.* (-, 0) gout.
Giebel *m.* (-s, -) gable, gable-end.
Gier *f.* (-, 0) raging desire, greed(iness).
gierig *a.* eager, greedy.
Gießbach *m.* torrent.
gießen *v.t.st.* to pour; (*Blumen*) to water; (*Metall*.) to cast, to found; *Öl ins Feuer* ~, to add fuel to the flames.
Gießerei *f.* (-, -en) foundry.
Gießkanne *f.* watering-can.
Gift *n.* (-[e]s, -e) poison; venom (snake); (*fig.*) spite.
giftfrei *a.* non-toxic; non-poisonous.
giftgrün *a.* garnish green.
giftig *a.* poisonous; venomous; toxic; (*fig.*) angry.
Gift: ~**müll** *m.* toxic waste; ~**mülldeponie** *f.* toxic waste dump; ~**pflanze** *f.* poisonous plant.
Gigant *m.* (-en, -en) giant.
gigantisch *a.* gigantic.
Gilde *f.* (-, -n) guild; corporation.
Ginster *m.* (-s, -) broom, furze; gorse.
Gipfel *m.* (-s, -) summit, peak; top; (*fig.*) height, acme.
gipfeln *v.i.* to culminate.
Gips *m.* (-es, -e) gypsum, plaster of Paris.
Gipsabdruck *m.* **Gipsabguß** *m.* plaster-cast.
Gipsverband *m.* plaster-cast.
Giraffe *f.* (-, -n) giraffe.
girieren *v.t.* to endorse (a bill of exchange); to circulate.
Girlande *f.* garland.
Giro *n.* (-[s], -s) endorsement.
Giro: ~**konto** *n.* bank account; ~**verkehr** *m.* clearing house business.
girren *v.i.* to coo.
Gis *n.* (-, 0) G sharp.
Gischt *m.* (-[e]s, -e) foam (wave), spray.
Gitarre *f.* (-, -n) guitar.
Gitter *n.* (-s, -) trellis, grating, grille, lattice.
Glacéhandschuh *m.* kid-glove.
Gladiole *f.* gladiolus.
Glanz *m.* (-es, 0) luster, gloss; polish, sheen; brightness, splendor.

glänzen *v.i.* to glitter; to shine.
glänzend *a.* shining, bright, brilliant.
Glanz: ~**leder** *n.* patent-leather; ~**leistung** *f.* brilliant performance; ~**papier** *n.* glossy paper; ~**stück** *n.* pièce de résistance; ~**zeit** *f.* heyday.
Glas *n.* (-es, Gläser) glass; *buntes* ~, stained glass.
Glasbläser *m.* glass-blower.
Glaser *m.* (-s, -) glazier.
glässern *a.* glassy; of glass.
Glas: ~**glocke** *f.* glass-shade; bell-glass; ~**hütte** *f.* glass-works *pl.*
glasieren *v.t.* to glaze; to varnish.
Glaskörper *m.* (*biol.*) vitrious body.
Glassplitter *m.* splinter of glass.
Glasur *f.* (-, -en) glazing.
Glasware *f.* glass-ware.
glatt *a.* smooth, sleek; ~**rasiert** *a.* clean-shaven.
Glätte *f.* smoothness; slipperiness.
Glatteis *n.* (-es, 0) glare ice; icy ground, icy roads.
glätten *v.t.* to smooth; (*mech.*) to face.
glattgehen *v.i.st.* to go smoothly.
Glatze *f.* (-, -u) bald-head.
Glaube *m.* (~ns, 0) faith, belief, credit; religion; *auf Treu und* ~, in good faith, on trust; *in gutem Glauben,* (*law*) bona fide, in good faith.
glauben *v.t.* to believe, to trust; to think, to suppose.
Glaubens: ~**artikel** *m.* article of faith; ~**bekenntnis** *n.* confession of faith, creed; ~**freiheit** *f.* religious freedom; ~**genosse** *m.* coreligionist; ~**satz** *m.* dogma ~**streit** *m.* religious dispute.
glaubhaft *a.* credible, believable.
Glaubhaftigkeit *f.* credibility.
gläubig *a.* believing; faithful; devout.
Gläubige *m./f.* (-n, -n) (true) believer.
Gläubiger *m.* (-s, -) creditor.
glaublich *a.* credible; probable.
glaubwürdig *a.* credible; authentic.
Glaukom *n.* glaucoma.
glazial *a.* glacial.
gleich *a.* same, equal, like; ~ *adv.* equally, just, alike; at once, directly; *meinesgleichen,* my equals *pl.* people like me.
gleichartig *a.* homogeneous.
gleichbedeutend *a.* synonymous, equivalent.
Gleichberechtigung *f.* (-, 0) equal rights.
gleichbleibend *a.* constant, steady.
gleichen *v.i.st.* to be alike, to resemble; to equal.
gleichermassen *adv.* equally.
gleicherweise *adv.* likewise.
gleichfalls *adv.* likewise, also, equally.
gleichförmig *a.* uniform; conform.
gleichgeschlechtlich *a.* homosexual.
gleichgesinnt *a.* like-minded, congenial.
Gleichgewicht *n.* (-[e]s, 0) balance, equilibrium; *das* ~ *halten,* to keep one's balance.
gleichgültig *a.* indifferent; irrelevant; ~ *wie,* no matter how.
Gleichgültigkeit *f.* (-, 0) indifference.
Gleichheit *f.* (-, 0) equality; likeness.
Gleichheitszeichen *n.* (*ar.*) equal sign.
gleichlaufend *a.* parallel.
gleich: ~**lautend** *a.* identical; ~**machen** *v.t.; dem Boden* ~**machen,** to level; ~**macherisch** *a.* (*pej.*) egalitarian.

Gleichmaß *n.* (es, 0) symmetry, proportion.
gleichmäßig *a.* uniform, regular.
Gleichmut *m.* (-[e]s, 0) equanimity.
gleichmütig *a.* calm, even-tempered.
gleichnamig *a.* bearing the same name.
Gleichnis *n.* (-nisses, -nisse) parable.
gleichordnen *v.t.* to co-ordinate.
gleichrangig *a.* equally important; of equal rank.
Gleichrichter *m.* (-s, -) (*elek.*) rectifier.
gleichsam *adv.* as it were, as if.
Gleichschaltung *f.* (*political*) co-ordination.
gleichschenk(e)lig *a.* (*geom.*) isosceles.
Gleichschritt *m.* marching in step.
gleichseitig *a.* equilateral.
Gleichstellung *f.* (-, -en) equalization.
Gleichstrom *m.* (*elek.*) direct current (D.C.).
Gleichung *f.* (-, -en) equation.
gleichviel *adv.* no matter, all the same.
gleichwertig *a.* equivalent.
gleichwie *c.* as, even as.
gleichwink(e)lig *a.* equiangular.
gleichwohl *c.* yet, however.
gleichzeitig *a.* contemporary; simultaneous.
gleichziehen *v.i.st.* to catch up, to draw level.
Gleis *n.* track; rails; line.
gleißen *v.i.* to blaze.
gleiten *v.i.st.* (*s*) to glide; to slide.
gleitend *a.* sliding; ~*e Arbeitszeit f.* flexible working hours, flexitime.
Gleit: ~**flug** *m.* glide; ~**flugzeug** *m.* glider; ~**klansel** *f.* (*jur.*) escalator clause; ~**mittel** *n.* lubricant; ~**schutz** *m.* antiskid device; ~**sichtgläser** *pl.* multifocal lenses.
Gleitzeit *f.* flextime; flexible working hours; ~**karte** *f.* time card.
Gletscher *m.* (-s, -) glacier.
Gletscher: ~**brand** *m.* glacial sunburn; ~**spalte** *f.* crevasse.
Glied *n.* (-[e]s, -er) limb; member; link; rank, file (of soldiers); *männliches* ~, penis.
Gliederfüßer *m.* (*bio.*) arthropod.
gliedern *v.t.* to articulate; to organize; to structure.
Gliederpuppe *f.* jointed doll; lay-figure.
Gliederschmerz *m.* rheumatic pains.
Gliederung *f.* (-, -en) (*auch mil.*) organization; structure.
Gliedmaßen *pl.* limbs *pl.*
Gliedsatz *m.* subordinate clause.
glimmen *v.i.* to glimmer, to glow.
Glimmer *m.* (-s, 0) glimmer; mica.
glimpflich *a.* gentle, mild, lenient.
glitschen *v.i.* (*s*) to slide, to glide.
glitschig *a.* slippery.
glitzern *v.i.st.* to twinkle; to glitter, to sparkle.
global *a.* global, world-wide; general, overall.
Globus *m.* (-, -ben) globe.
Glocke *f.* (-, -n) bell.
Glocken: ~**blume** *f.* bell flower; ~**schlag** *m.* stroke; ~**spiel** *n.* chimes *pl.*; ~**turm** *m.* bell tower, belfry.
glockig *a.* bell-shaped.
Glöckner *m.* bellringer.
Glorie *f.* (-, 0) glory; ~**nschein** *m.* halo.
glorifizieren *v.t.* to glorify.
Glorifizierung *f.* glorification.
Gloriole *f.* glory; halo, aura.
glorreich *a.* glorious.

Glossar *n.* (-s, -e *u.* -ien) glossary.
Glosse *f.* (-, -n) gloss, commentary.
Glotzaugen *pl.* goggle eyes.
Glotze *f.* tube.
glotzen *v.i.* to stare; to goggle.
Glück *n.* (-[e]s, 0) luck, good luck; happiness, prosperity; fortune; ~ *haben*, to be in luck; *kein* ~ *haben*, to be unlucky; *viel* ~*!* good luck!; *es war ein* ~, it was fortunate; ~ *wünschen*, to wish good luck.
glückbringend *a.* lucky.
Glucke *f.* sitting hen; (*fig.*) mother hen.
glucken *v.i.* to cluck; to brood.
glücken *v.i.* (*s*) to succeed, to prosper.
gluckern *v.i.* to glug; to gurgle.
glücklich *a.* happy, fortunate; lucky.
glücklicherweise *adv.* fortunately; luckily.
glücklos *a.* luckless; unhappy (existence).
Glücksdringer *m.* mascot, lucky charm.
Glückseligkeit *f.* (-, -en) bliss, happiness.
glucksen *v.i.* to chuckle.
glucksen *v.i.* to squelch (wet shoes).
Glücks: ~**fall** *m.* stroke of luck; ~**göttin** *f.* goddess of fortune; Fortune; ~**spiel** *n.* game of chance; ~**strähne** *f.* lucky streak.
glückstrahlend *a.* radiant.
Glückwunsch *m.* congratulation.
Glühbirne *f.* light bulb.
glühen *v.i.* to glow.
glühend *a.* glowing; red-hot; ardent; burning.
Glühwürmchen *n.* glow-worm; fire-fly.
Glut *f.* (-, -en) fire, heat; embers; (*fig.*) fervor, ardor.
Gnade *f.* (-, -n) grace, favor; pardon, mercy.
Gnadengesuch *n.* clemency plea, petition for clemency *or* mercy.
gnadenlos *a.* merciless.
Gnaden: ~**schuß** *m*; ~**stoß** *m.* coup de grâce; ~**tod** *m.* mercy killing.
gnädig *a.* gracious; ~*e Frau*, madam.
Gnom *m.* gnome.
Gobelin *m.* (-s, -s) tapestry.
Gockel *m.* (*fam.*) rooster; cock.
Golanhöhen *pl.* Golan Heights.
Gold *n.* (-[e]s, 0) gold.
Goldbarren *m.* goldbar, ingot.
golden *a.* gold; (*fig.*) golden.
goldhaltig *a.* auriferous.
goldig *a.* (*fam.*) sweet, cute.
Gold: ~**regen** *m.* (*bot.*) laburnum; ~**schmied** *m.* goldsmith; ~**schnitt** *m.* gilt edges; ~**standard** *m.*, ~**währung** *f.* gold standard.
Golf *m.* (-[e]s, -e) gulf; (*Spiel*) golf.
Golf: ~**platz** *m.* golf course, golf links; ~**spieler** *m.* golfer; ~**schläger** *m.* golf club.
Golfstrom *m.* Gulf Stream.
Gondel *f.* (-, -n) gondola.
gönnen *v.t.* not to envy, not to grudge; to allow, to grant.
Gönner *m.* (-s, -) patron.
gönnerhaft *a.* patronizing.
Gonorrhöe *f.* gonorrhoea.
Göre *f.* child, kid; brat.
Gorilla *m.* (-s, -s) gorilla.
Gosse *f.* (-, -n) gutter.
Gotik *f.* (-, 0) Gothic style.
gotisch *a.* Gothic.

Gott *m.* (-s, Götter) God; *um* ~*es willen*, for God's sake; ~*sei Dank!* thank God, thank goodness!; *leider Gottes!* alas!
göttergleich *a.* god-like.
Götterspeise *n.* food of the gods; jelly.
Gottesdienst *m.* public worship, divine service.
gottesfürchtig *a.* pious, God-fearing.
Gotteslästerung *f.* blasphemy.
Gottesurteil *n.* trial by ordeal.
gott: ~**gefällig** *a.* pleasing to God; ~**gewolt** *a.* ordained by God.
Gottheit *f.* (-, -en) deity; divinity.
Göttin *f.* (-, -nen) goddess.
göttlich *a.* divine; godlike.
Göttlichkeit *f.* (-, 0) divinity; divine origin.
gottlos *a.* godless, impious, wicked.
Gottvater *m.* God the Father.
gott: ~**verdammt** *a.* ~**verflucht** *a.* goddamned; ~**verlassen** *a.* godforsaken.
Gottvertrauen *n.* trust in God.
gottvoll *a.* divine; (*fam.*) capital, grand.
Götze *m.* (-n, -n) idol.
Götzendienst *m.* idolatry.
Gouvernante *f.* (-, -n) governess.
Gouverneur *m.* (-s, -e) governor.
Grab *n.* (-[e]s, Gräber) grave, tomb, sepulcher.
Graben *m.* (-s, Gräben) ditch, trench; moat.
graben *v.t.st.* to dig; to engrave, to cut.
Grab: ~**mal** *n.* tomb, sepulchre; ~**rede** *f.* funeral sermon; ~**schrift** *f.* epitaph; ~**stätte** *f.*, ~**stelle** *f.* grave, tomb; ~**stein** *m.* tombstone, gravestone.
Grabung *f.* excavation.
Graburne *f.* funeral urn.
Gracht *f.* canal.
Grad *m.* (-[e]s, -e) degree; grade; rate; *in hohem* ~, highly; *im höchsten* ~, exceedingly, to the last degree.
Gradeinteilung *f.* (-, -en) graduation, scale.
graduieren *v.i.* to graduate.
Graf *f.* (-en, -en) count; (*englischer*) earl.
Gräfin *f.* (-, -nen) countess.
Grafschaft *f.* (-, -en) earldom; county.
Gram *m.* (-[e]s, 0) grief, sorrow.
grämen (sich) *v.refl.* to grieve, to be grieved, to fret, to pine.
grämlich *a.* sullen, morose.
Gramm *n.* (-[e]s, -e) gram.
Grammatik *f.* (-, -en) grammar.
Grammatiker *m.* (-s, -) grammarian.
grammatisch *a.* & *adv.* grammatical(ly).
Grammophon *n.* (-s, -e) gramophone, phonograph; ~**platte** *f.* record.
Granat *m.* garnet.
Granatapfel *m.* pomegranate.
Granate *f.* (-, -n) grenade, shell.
Granattrichter *m.* (shell) crater.
Granatwerfer *m.* mortar.
grandios *a.* terrific.
Granit *m.* (-[e]s, -e) granite.
grantig *a.* grumpy, bad-tempered.
Granulat *n.* granules.
Grapefruit *f.* (-, -s) grapefruit.
Graphik *f.* (-, -en) graphic art; engraving.
Graphiker *m*; **Graphikerin** *f.* graphic designer.
graphisch *a.* graphic; ~*e Darstellung* *f.* graphic representation, graph; ~*es Zeichen* *n.* symbol.

Graphit *m.* (-[e]s, -e) graphite.
Graphologe *m.* (-en, -en) graphologist.
Gras *n.* (-es, Gräser) grass, herbage; *ins ~ beißen,* to bite the dust.
Grasbüschel *n.* tuft of grass.
Grashüpfer *m.* grasshopper.
grasen *v.i.* to graze.
Grashalm *m.* blade of grass.
grassieren *v.i.* to spread, to rage.
gräßlich *a.* ghastly, dreadful, horrible.
Grat *a.* (-[e]s, -e) edge, ridge; (*mech.*) burr.
Gräte *f.* (-, -n) fish-bone.
grätenlos *a.* boneless.
Grätenmuster *n.* herringbone pattern.
Gratifikation *f.* bonus.
grätig *a.* full of (fish-)bones.
gratis *adv.* free of charge.
Grätsche *f.* straddle.
Gratulation *f.* (-, -en) congratulation.
gratulieren *v.i.* to congratulate (on).
Gratwanderung *f.* ridge walk; (*fig.*) balancing act.
grau *a.* gray, grey; grizzled; *~er Star,* cataract.
grauen *v.imp.* to shudder (at); to dawn.
Grauen *n.* (-s, 0) dread, horror; dawn.
grauenhaft, grauenvoll *a.* horrifying, terrible.
gräulich *a.* grayish.
graumeliert *a.* graying.
Graupe *f.* (-, -n) groats *pl.*; pearl barley.
Graupel *f.* (-s, -n) sleet.
graupeln *v.i.imp.* to sleet.
Graus *m.* (-[e]s, 0) horror, dread.
grausam *a.* cruel.
Grausamkeit *f.* (-, -en) cruelty.
Grauschimmel *m.* gray horse; gray mold.
Grausen *n.* horror.
grausen *v.i.imp.* to shudder (at).
grausig *a.* dreadful, gruesome, awful.
Grau: *~tier* *n.* ass; donkey; mule; *~zone* *f.* (*fig.*) grey area.
Graveur *m.* (-[e]s, -e) engraver.
gravieren *v.t.* to engrave.
gravierend *a.* serious, important.
Gravitation *f.* gravitation.
Gravitations: *~feld* *n.* gravitational field; *~gesetz* *n.* law of gravitation.
gravitätisch *a.* grave, solemn.
Grazie *f.* (-, -n) grace, gracefulness; *pl.* Graces.
graziös *a.* graceful, pretty.
Gregorianisch *a.* *~er Gesang* *m.* Gregorian chant.
Greif *m.* (-[e]s, -e) griffin.
greifbar *a.* tangible, palpable; on hand.
greifen *v.t.st.* to seize, to lay hold on; to grasp, to catch.
Greifer *m.* (*tech.*) grab, gripper.
Greif: *~vogel* *m.* bird of prey; *~zange* *f.* tongs.
greis *a.* very old.
Greis *m.* (-es, -e) **Greisin** *f.* (-, -nen) old person.
Greisenalter *n.* old age.
greisenhaft *a.* senile.
Greisenhaftigkeit *f.* senility.
grell *a.* (*Licht, Farbe*) glaring, dazzling.
Gremium *n.* committee.
Genadier *m.* (-s, -e) grenadier.
Grenz: *~abfertigung* *f.* passport control and customs clearance; *~berichtigung* *f.* (-, -en) frontier readjustment.

Grenze *f.* (-, -n) border, frontier, boundary; limit.
grenzen *v.i.* to border on, to adjoin.
grenzenlos *a.* boundless; immense.
Grenzfall *m.* borderline case.
Grenzformalitäten *pl.* passport and customs formalities.
Grenzkontrolle *f.* border check.
Grenzlinie *f.* border.
Greuel *m.* (-s, -) horror, abomination, outrage.
Greueltat *f.* atrocity.
greulich *a.* horrible, heinous.
Grieche *m.*; **Griechin** *f.*; **griechisch** *a.* Greek.
Griechenland *n.* (-s, 0) Greece.
Griesgram *m.* (-[e]s, -e) grumbler.
griesgrämig *a.* morose, sullen, grumbling.
Grieß *m.* (-sses, -sse) semolina *pl.*
Griff *m.* (-[e]s, -e) grip, grasp, hold.
griffbereit *a.* ready to hand.
Griffbrett *n.* (*Geige*) fret-board, neck.
Griffel *m.* (-s, -) (*bot.*) style; slate-pencil.
griffig *a.* handy.
Grill *m.* barbecue.
Grille *f.* (-, -n) cricket (insect); (*fig.*) whim, caprice, fad.
grillen *v.t.* to grill.
Grimasse *f.* (-, -n) grimace, wry face.
Grimm *m.* (-[e]s, 0) fury, rage, wrath.
grimm *a.* grim, furious.
grimmig *a.* grim, furious.
Grind *m.* (-[e]s, -e) scab, scurf.
grinsen *v.i.* to grin, to smirk.
Grippe *f.* (-, 0) (*med.*) influenza (*fam.*) flu.
Grips *m.* (*fam.*) brains.
grob *a.* coarse, gross, thick; clumsy; rude, insolent; rough; *~e Berechnung* *f.* rough calculation.
grobgemahlen *a.* coarsely ground.
Grobheit *f.* rudeness; coarseness.
Grobian *m.* (-s, -e) lout, boor.
gröhlen, grölen *v.i.* to scream, to squall.
Groll *m.* (-[e]s, 0) rancor, grudge, resentment.
grollen *v.i.* to bear a grudge *or* ill-will; (*Donner*) to rumble.
Gros *n.* (-, 0) bulk.
groß *a.* large; (*dick*) big; (*Wuchs*) tall; (*fig.*) great; high, eminent; *~er Buchstabe* *m.* capital (letter); *~tun,* to brag, to give oneself airs.
großartig *a.* grand, sublime.
Großbetrieb *m.* large undertaking.
Größe *f.* (-, -n) size; (*fig.*) greatness, magnitude; quantity.
Groß: *~einkauf* *m.* bulk purchase; *~eltern* *pl.* grandparents *pl.*; *~enkel* *m.* great-grandson.
großenteils *adv.* in large measure.
Größenwahn *m.* megalomania.
Groß: *~grundbesitzer* *m.* large estate owner; *~handel* *m.* wholesale business; *~händler* *m.* wholesale merchant.
großhierzig *a.* magnanimous.
Großherzog *m.* grand-duke.
Großindustrie *f.* big industry *pl.*
Grossist *m.*; **Grossistin** *f.* wholesaler.
großjährig *a.* of age.
Groß: *~kampfschiff* *n.* capital ship; *~macht* *f.* great power; *~maul* *n.* (*fam.*) big mouth.
Großmut *f.* magnanimity, generosity.
großmütig *a.* magnanimous, generous.

Groß: ~**mutter** *f.* grandmother; ~**neffe** *m.* grandnephew; ~**nichte** *f.* grandniece; ~**sprecher** *m.* swaggerer, braggart; ~**sprecherei** *f.* big talk.

groß; ~**sprecherisch** *a.* swaggering, vain-glorious.

Groß: ~ **stadt** *f.* large city.

Groß: ~ **städter** *m.* inhabitant of a large city.

groß: ~**städtisch** *a.* big city (attrib.).

größtenteils *adv.* for the most part.

Groß: ~**tat** *f.* achievement, exploit; ~**vater** *m.* grandfather;

großzügig *a.* on a large scale, generous.

grotesk *a.* grotesque.

Grotte *f.* (-, -n) grotto.

Grübchen *n.* dimple.

Grube *f.* (-, -n) pit; mine; (*fig.*) grave.

Grübelei *f.* (-, -en) pondering; musing.

grübeln *v.i.* to brood, to ponder.

Gruben: ~**klotz** *m.* prop; ~**licht** *n.* miner's lamp.

Grübler *m.* meditative person.

Gruft *f.* (-, Grüfte) tomb, vault.

grummeln *v.i.* to rumble; to mumble.

grün *a.* green; fresh; (*fig.*) unripe; ~*er Tisch,* bureaucracy.

Grün *n.* (-s, 0) green color; verdure.

Grund *m.* (-[e]s, Gründe) ground; bottom; foundation; reason, motive; argument; *auf ~ von,* on the strength of; *von ~ aus,* thoroughly; *im ~e,* after all, at bottom; *auf ~ laufen,* to run aground; *zu ~e richten,* to ruin; *zu ~e gehen,* to perish.

Grund: ~**bedingung** *f.* main condition; ~**begriff** *m.* fundamental notion; ~**besitz** *m.* landed property, real estate; ~**besitzer** *m.* landowner; ~**bestandteil** *m.* main element, essential ingredient; ~**buch** *n.* land register, real estate register; ~**buchamt** *n.* land registry; ~**dienstbarkeit** *f.* (*law.*) encumbrance.

Grund: ~**eigentum** *n.* landed property; ~**eigentümer** *m.* landowner.

gründen *v.t.* to establish, to found, to promote, to float; (sich) ~ *v.refl.* to rest (upon).

Gründer *m.* (-s, -) founder.

grundfalsch *a.* radically wrong *or* false.

Grund: ~**farbe** *f.* ground color, priming; ~**fläche** *f.* base, basis; ~**gedanke** *m.* fundamental idea; ~**gehalt** *m.* basic salary.

Grundgesetz *n.* fundamental law.

grundieren *v.t.* to prime.

Grund: ~**irrtum,** fundamental error; ~**kapital** *n.* initial capital, stock; ~**lage** *f.* foundation, groundwork, substructure, base; ~**legung** *f.* foundation.

gründlich *a.* profound, thorough; solid.

Grund: ~**linie** *f.* basis; base line; ~**lohn** *m.* basic wage.

grundlos *a.* bottomless; groundless.

Gründonnerstag *m.* Maundy-Thursday.

Grund: ~**rechte** *n.pl.* fundamental rights. ~**regel** *f.* basic rule; ~**rente** *f.* ground-rent; ~**riß** *m.* ground-plan; (*Buch*) outline; ~**satz** *m.* principle, maxim.

grundsätzlich *a.* fundamental; ~ *adv.* on principle.

Grund: ~**schule** *f.* primary school, ~**stein** *m.* foundation-stone; ~**steuer** *f.* property tax; ~**stock** *m.* basis, foundation, nucleus; ~**stück** *n.* real estate; ~**ton** *m.* key-note.

Gründung *f.* (-, -en) foundation, establishment.

Grundursache *f.* original cause.

grundverschieden *a.* radically different.

Grund: ~**wasser** *n.* ground water; ~**zahl** *f.* cardinal number; ~**zins** *m.* ground-rent; ~**zug** *m.* main feature.

Grüne *n.* green, countryside.

Grüne *m./f.* member of the Green Party.

Grünen *pl.* the Greens.

grünen *v.i.* to grow green.

grünlich *a.* greenish.

Grünschnabel *m.* greenhorn, sucker.

Grünspan *m.* verdigris.

grunzen *v.i.* to grunt.

Grünzeug *n.* (-es, 0) greens *pl.*

Gruppe *f.* (-, -n) group; (*avi.*) group.

Gruppen: ~**arbeit** *f.* group work; ~**dynamik** *f.* group dynamics; ~**kommandeur** *m.* (*avi.*) group commander ~**therapie** *f.* group therapy.

gruppieren *v.t.* to group.

Gruppierung *f.* (-, -en) grouping (*pol.*) faction.

gruselig *a.* uncanny, creepy.

Gruselgeschichte *f.* horror story.

gruseln *v.t.imp mich gruselt,* my flesh creeps, I shudder.

Gruß *m.* (-es, Grüsse) salutation, greeting; salute; compliment.

grüßen *v.t.* to greet; to salute; ~ *lassen,* to send one's regards.

grußlos *a.* without a word of greeting.

Grütze *f.* (-, 0) groats *pl.*; (*fig.*) brains.

Guatemala *n.* (-s, 0) Guatemala.

Guatelmateke *m.*; **Guatelmatekin** *f.* Guatemalan.

gucken *v.i.* to peep, to look.

Guckloch *n.* spy-hole; peep-hole.

Guerilla *f.* (-, -s) guerilla war; guerilla unit; ~**kämpfer** *m.* guerilla.

Gulasch *n./m.* goulash.

Gulden *m.* (-s, -) florin; (*holländischer*) guilder.

Gully *m.* drain.

gültig *a.* valid, available; good, current; ~ *machen,* to validate.

Gültigkeit *f.* (-, 0) validity, legality.

Gummi *n.* (-s, 0) eraser, rubber.

Gummiband *n.* elastic.

gummieren *v.t.* to gum.

Gummi: ~**knüppei** *m.* truncheon; ~**paragraph** *m.* elastic clause; ~**schuhe** *m.pl.* goloshes *pl.* ~**stiefel** *m.* rubber boot; ~**zelle** *f.* padded cell.

Gunst *f.* (-, 0) favor, kindness; *zu ~en,* in favor of.

günstig *a.* favorable.

Günstling *m.* (-[e]s, -e) favorite.

Gurgel *f.* (-, -n) throat, gullet.

Gurgeln *v.i.* to gargle.

Gurke *f.* (-, -n) cucumber; (*fig.*) lemon; *saure ~,* pickled cucumber, gherkin.

gurren *v.i.* to coo.

Gurt *m.* (-[e]s, -e) strap; seat belt.

Gürtel *m.* (-s, -) belt; (*geog.*) zone.

Gürtel: ~**linie** *f.* waist line; ~**reifen** *m.* radial tire; ~**rose** *f.* (*med.*) shingles *pl.* ~**schnalle** *f.* belt buckle; ~**tier** *n.* armadillo.

gürten *v.t.* to gird, to girdle.

Guß *m.* (Gusses, Güsse); casting, founding; gush, shower; downpour; (*cul.*) icing.

Guß: ~**eisen** *n.* cast-iron; ~**stahl** *m.* cast-steel.

gut *a.* good; well; ~*heißen,* to approve of; *es ~ haben,* to have a good time; ~*schreiben,* to credit, to place to one's credit; *einem etwas zu ~e halten,* to make allowance for a thing; *sich etwas zu ~e tun,* to pride oneself upon; *kurz und ~,* in short; *mit einem ~ stehen,* to be on good terms with a person.

Gut *n.* (-[e]s, Güter) good; property estate; (*com.*) commodity, article, goods *pl.*

Gutachten *n.* (-s, -) expert opinion, expert evidence.

gutartig *a.* good-natured; (*med.*) benign.

Gutdünken *n.* judgment, discretion.

Güte *f.* (-, 0) goodness; (*com.*) (good) quality.

Güter: ~**bahnhof** *m.* goods-station, goods-yard, freight yard; ~**gemeinschaft** *f.* joint property; ~**recht** *n.* property law; ~**trennung** *f.* separation of property; ~**verkehr** *m.* goods traffic; ~**wagen** *m* (*rail.*) truck, freight-car; ~**zug** *m.* goods train, freight train.

gut: ~**gelaunt** *a.* good-humored; ~**gesinnt** well disposed; ~**gläubig,** bona fide, in good faith; credulous.

Gutgläubigkeit *f.* credulity; gullibility.

Guthaben *n.* (-s, -) (credit) balance.

gutheißen *v.t.st.* to approve of.

gutherzig *a.* kind-hearted.

gütig *a.* kind, benignant.

gütlich *a.* amicable.

gutmachen *v.t.* to make good; to correct.

gutmütig *a.* good-natured.

Gutmütigkeit *f.* (-, 0) good-nature.

Gutsbesitzer *m.* (-s, -) land-owner.

Gutschein *m.* (-s, -e) voucher, coupon.

gutschreiben *v.t.* to enter to one's credit.

Gutschrift *f.* credit.

Gutshof *m.* farmyard.

Gutsverwalter *m.* bailiff.

gutsituiert *a.* well-to-do, well-off.

guttun *v.i.st.* to do good.

gutwillig *a.* obliging; willing; friendly.

Gymnasial: ~**bildung** *f.* secondary school education; ~**direktor** *m.* principal of a secondary school; ~**lehrer** *m.* secondary school teacher.

Gymnasiast *m.* (-en, -en) **Gymnasiastin** *f.* highschool student.

Gymnasium *n.* (-s, -ien) secondary school.

Gymnastik *f.* (-, 0) gymnastics *pl.*

gymnastisch *a.* gymnastic.

Gynäkologe *m.*; **Gynäkologin** *f.* gynecologist.

Gynäkologie *f.* gynecology.

gynäkologisch *a.* gynecological.

H

H, h the letter H or h; (*mus.*) B.

Haar *n.* (-[e]s, -e) hair; *die ~e standen ihm zu Berge,* his hair stood on end; *einander in die ~e geraten,* to come to blows; *sich die ~e machen,* to do one's hair.

Haar: ~**ausfall** *m.* loss of hair; ~**bürste** *f.* hairbrush; ~**büschel** *n.* tuft of hair.

haaren *v.i.sich ~,* to lose one's hair.

Haaresbreite *f. um ~* by a hair's breadth.

haarig *a.* hairy; *kurz~,* short-haired; *lang~,* long-haired.

Haarklammer *f.* hair clip.

haarklein *adv.* minutely.

Haarklemme *f.* hair clip.

Haarnadel *f.* hair-pin, bodkin.

haarscharf *a.* very subtle, very keen.

Haarschleife *f.* bow; hair-ribbon.

Haarschopf *m.* shock of hair.

Haarspalterei *f.* (*fig.*) hair-splitting.

haarsträubend *a.* revolting, shocking.

Haar: ~**wasser** *n.* hair-lotion; ~**wuchsmittel** *n.* hair tonic

Habe *f.* (-, 0) property, effects *pl.*; *Hab' und Gut,* goods and chattels *pl.*

haben *v.t.ir.* to have; *da haben wir's!* there we are!

Haben *n.* (-s, -) (*com.*) credit.

Haben: ~**seite** *f.* credit side; ~**zinsen** *pl.* interest on deposits.

Habgier *f.* (-, 0) covetousness, greediness.

habgierig *a.* covetous, greedy.

habhaft *a. ~ werden,* to get hold of.

Habicht *m.* (-[e]s, -e) hawk.

Habilitation *f.* postdoctoral exam.

habilitieren (sich) *v.refl.* to be admitted as lecturer at a German university.

Habsburger *m.* Habsburg.

Habseligkeiten *pl.* meager belongings *pl.*

Habsucht *f.* (-, 0) avarice, covetousness.

habsüchtig *a.* avaricious, covetous.

Hack: ~**beil** *n.* chopper, hatchet; ~**block** *m.* chopping-block; ~**brett** *n.* chopping-board; (*mus.*) dulcimer.

Hacke *f.* (-, -n) hoe, pick(axe), heel.

hacken *v.t.* to chop, to hack, to cleave; to mince; to hoe.

Hackfleisch *n.* ground minced meat.

Hackfrüchte *f.pl.* root crops.

Hackordnung *f.* (*fig.*) pecking order.

Hacksel *m. or n.* (-s, 0) chaff.

Hacksteak *n.* beefburger.

Hader *m.* (-s, -n) quarrel, brawl.

hadern *v.i.* to quarrel, to wrangle.

Hafen *m.* (-s, Häfen) harbor, port, haven.

Hafen: ~**anlagen** *pl.* docks; ~**arbeiter** *m.* docker; ~**gebühren** *f.pl.* harbor dues, port dues; ~**stadt** *f.* sea-port; ~**viertel** *n.* dockland.

Hafer *m.* (-s, 0) oats *pl.*

Hafer: ~**brei** *m.* porridge; ~**mehl** *n.* oatmeal; ~**schleim** *m.* gruel.

Haft *f.* (-, 0) custody, arrest.

Haftanstalt *f.* prison.

haftbar *a.* liable, responsible.

Haftbefehl *m.* warrant (of arrest).

haften *v.i.* to stick, to adhere; ~*für,* to be liable for.

Haftenbleiben *v.i.st.* to stick.

Häftling *m.* (-s, -e) detainee.

Haftpflicht *f.* liability.

haftpflichtig *a.* liable.

Haftung *f.* adhesion, grip; liability; (*un*)*beschränkte ~* (un)limited liability.

Hagebutte *f.* (-, -n) rose-hip.

Hagedorn *m.* hawthorn.

Hagel *m.* (-s, 0) hail.

Hagelkorn *n.* hail-stone.

hageln *v.i.imp.* to hail.

Hagel: ~**schaden** *m.* damage caused by hail; ~**schaden-Versicherung** *f.* hail-insurance; ~**wetter** *n.* hail-storm.

hager *a.* lean, gaunt, meager.

Häher *m.* (-s, -) jay.

Hahn *m.* (-[e]s, Hähne) cock, rooster; faucet; hammer (gun).

Hähnchen *n.* chicken.

Hahnen: ~**fuß** *m.* buttercup; ~**kamm** *m.* cock's-comb ~**kampf** *m.* cockfight; ~**schrei** *m.* cockcrow; ~**trittmuster** *n.* dog-tooth.

Hahnrei *m.* (-[e]s, -e) cuckold.

Hai(fisch) *m.* (-[e]s, -e) shark.

Hain *m.* (-[e]s, -e) grove, wood.

Häkchen *n.* (-s, -) small hook.

Häkelarbeit *f.* crochet-work.

Häkelgarn *n.* crochet yarn.

Häkelmuster *n.* crochet-pattern.

häkeln *v.t.* to crochet.

Häkelnadel *f.* crochet-needle.

Haken *m.* (-s, -) hook, clasp; *das hat einen ~,* there's a snag somewhere.

Hakenkreuz *n.* swastika.

halb *a. & adv.* half; ~*e Note f.* (*mus.*) half note; ~*er Ton m.* semitone; *auf ~em Wege,* halfway.

Halbamtlich *a.* semi-official.

Halbbruder *a.* (-s, -brüder) half-brother.

Halbdunkel *n.* dusk, twilight.

Halbedelstein *m.* half- (*or* semi-) precious stone.

halbe-halbe half-half.

halbfertig *a.* half-finished.

Halbfinale *n.* semifinal.

halbgar *a.* underdone, rare.

Halbgott *m.* demi-god.

Halbheit *f.* (-, -en) half-measure.

halbherzig *a. & adv.* half-hearted(ly).

halbieren *v.t.* to halve; to bisect.

Halbinsel *f.* peninsula.

halb: ~**jährig** *a.* lasting six months; six months old; ~**jährlich** *a.* half-yearly; ~ *adv.* every six months.

Halb: ~**kreis** *m.* semicircle; ~**kugel** *f.* hemisphere.

halblaut *a. & adv.* in a low voice, in an undertone.

Halb: ~**leinen** *n.* half-linen; ~**leiter** *m.* semiconductor; ~**mast** *m.* half-mast; ~**messer** *m.* radius; ~**mond** *m.* half-moon, crescent.

halboffen *a.* ajar.

Halb: ~**schlaf** *m.* light sleep; ~ **schuh** *m.* (low) shoe; ~**seiden** *a.* half-silk; (*fig.*) dubious; ~**steif** *a.* semi-stiff; ~**stiefel** *m.* (*Damen*) ankle boot.

halb: ~**stündig** *a.* half-hour; ~**stündlich** *a.* half-hourly; ~**tags** *a.* part-time.

Halbtags: ~**arbeit** *f.* part-time job; ~**kraft** *f.* part-timer.

halbwegs *adv.* to some extent; reasonably.

Halb: ~**welt** *f.* demimonde; ~**wüchsige** *m./f.* adolescent; teenager; ~**zeit** *f.* half-time.

Halde *f.* (-, -n) declivity, slope; dump.

Hälfte *f.* (-, -n) half; middle.

Halfter *f.* (-, -n) *m. & n.* (-s, -) halter; holster.

halftern *v.t.* to halter, to put a halter on.

Hall *m.* reverberation; echo.

Halle *f.* (-, -n) hall; lobby; foyer.

hallen *v.i.* to sound, to resound, to reverberate, to echo.

Hallenbad *n.* indoor pool.

Hallig *f.* (-, -en) small island off the North Sea coast.

hallo! *i.* hullo!; **Hallo** *n.* fuss.

Halluzination *f.* hallucination.

Halm *m.* (-[e]s, -e) stalk, straw.

Hals *m.* (Halses, Hälse) neck; throat; *vom Halse,* off one's hands; *bis zum Halse,* neck-deep; ~ *über Kopf,* in a rush/hurry; *einen auf dem ~e haben,* to be encumbered with one; *sich vom ~e schaffen,* to get rid of; *um den ~ fallen,* to embrace.

Hals: ~**abschneider** *m.* cut throat; ~**band** *n.* necklace; collar.

halsbrecherisch *a.* break-neck.

Halsentzündung *f.* sore throat.

Hals-Nasen-Ohren-Arzt *m.;* -**Ärztin** *f.* ear, nose and throat specialist.

Halsschlagader *f.* carotid.

halsstarrig *a.* stubborn, obstinate.

Hals: ~**tuch** *n.* scarf, neckerchief; ~-*und Beinbruch!* Break a leg! ~**weh** *n.* sore throat; ~**weite** *f.* collar size; ~**wirbel** *m.* cervical vertebra.

Halt *m.* (-[e]s, -e) hold, footing; halt, stop; support, stay; ~ *machen,* to halt, to stop.

halt! *i.* hold! stop!

haltbar *a.* non perishable; durable.

halten *v.t. & i.st.* to hold; to keep; to contain; to deem, to estimate; (*mil.*) to hold on to; (sich) ~ *v.refl.* to keep (good); to hold one's own; *länger ~* (*von Sachen*), to have longer wear; *viel auf einen ~,* to think highly of one; *den Mund~,* to hold one's tongue; *eine Predigt ~,* to preach a sermon; *eine Rede ~,* to make a speech; *im Zaume ~,* to keep a tight hand on; *Wort ~,* to keep one's word; *sich ~ an,* to have recourse to.

Halter *m.* keeper; owner; holder.

Halterung *f.* holding device.

Halte: ~**schild** *n.* stop sign; ~**signal** *n.* stop signal; ~**stelle** *f.* station, stop; ~**verbot** *n.* no stopping; ~**verbotsschild** *n.* no stopping sign.

haltlos *a.* unsteady, fickle.

Haltung *f.* (-, -en) attitude; bearing; position: (*Körper~*) posture.

Halunke *m.* (-n, -n) scoundrel, rascal.

hämisch *a.* malicious, sneering.

Hammel *m.* (-s, -) wether; mutton; (*fig.*) idiot.

Hammel: ~**braten** *m.* roast mutton; ~**fleisch** *n.* mutton; ~**keule** *f.* leg of mutton; ~**sprung** *m.* (*parl.*) division.

Hammer *m.* (-s, Hämmer) hammer.

hämmerbar *a.* malleable.

hämmern *v.t.* to hammer.

Hammerwerfer *m.* hammer-thrower.

Hämorrhoiden *f.pl.* piles *pl.,* hemorrhoids *pl.*

Hampelmann *m.* jumping jack; (*pej.*) puppet.

hampeln *v.i.* to jump about.

Hamster *m.* (-s, -) hamster, marmot.

Hamsterer *m.* (-s, -) food-hoarder.

Hamster: ~**fahrt** *f.* foraging trip; ~**kauf** *m.* panic buying.

hamstern *v.t.* to hoard.

Hand *f.* (-, Hände) hand; *mit der ~,* by hand; *zu Händen,* attention; *sich die Hände reiben,* to rub one's hands (together); *die ~ drücken,* to shake hands; *aus der ~ in den Mund leben,* to live from hand to mouth; *die Hände in den Schoss legen,* to remain idle; *unter der ~,* underhand, secretly; *die Hände im Spiel haben,* to have a finger in the pie;

bei der ~, zur Hand, at hand.

Hand: **~akten** *pl.* personal files; **~arbeit** *f.* handicraft, craft work; **~bibliothek** *f.* reference library.

handbreit *a.* of a hand's breadth.

Handbremse *f.* handbrake.

Handbuch *n.* manual, handbook.

Hände: **~druck** *m.* handshake; **~klatschen** *n.* applause.

Handel *m.* (-s, 0) trade, traffic, commerce; bargain; affair; *einen ~ abschließen,* to strike a bargain; *~treiben,* to trade; *pl. Händel,* quarrel(s).

handeln *v.i.* to act; to deal; to trade, to do business; to bargain, to chaffer; *es handelt sich um...,* the point in question is...

Handels: **~abkommen** *n.* trade agreement; **~adressbuch** *n.* commercial directory; **~bilanz** *f.* balance of trade; *~einig werden,* to come to terms; **~flotte** *f.* merchant fleet; **~gericht** *n.* commercial court; **~gesellschaft** *f.* trading company; *offene ~gesellschaft,* (general) partnership; **~gesetzbuch** *n.* commercial code; **~hochschule** *f.* business school; **~kammer** *f.* chamber of commerce; **~recht** *n.* commercial law; **~schiff** *n.* merchant ship; **~schiffahrt** *f.* merchant marine; **~schule** *f.* commercial school; **~teil** *(einer Zeitung) m.* business section; **~vertrag** *m.* commercial treaty.

handeltreibend *a.* trading.

händeringend *adv.* despairingly.

Händeschütteln *n.* handshake.

Handfertigkeit *f.* manual skill.

handfest *a.* strong, stout, strapping.

Hand: **~feuerwaffen** *pl.* small arms; **~fläche** *f.* palm of the hand; **~gelenk** *n.* wrist; *etwas aus dem ~ machen,* to do a thing with one's little finger.

handgemein *a.* at close quarters.

Hand: **~gemenge** *n.* hand-to-hand fighting; **~gepäck** *n.* hand-luggage.

hand: **~geschneidert** *a.* hand-tailored; **~greiflich** *a. er wurde ~* he used his fists; obvious; palpable.

Hand: **~granate** *f.* hand grenade; **~griff** *m.* grasp; handle; *(fig.)* knack; **~habe** *f.* handle.

handhaben *v.t.* to handle; to manage.

Handikap *n.* (-s, -s) handicap.

Handkoffer *m.* suitcase.

Handlanger *m.* laborer.

Händler *m.* (-s, -) dealer, tradesman.

handlich *a.* handy; manageable.

Handlung *f.* (-, -en) act, action, deed; trade, *(lit.)* plot.

Handlungs: **~fähigkeit** *f.* ability to act; **~freiheit** *f.* freedom of action; **~reisende(r)** *m.* traveling salesman; **~spielraum** *m.* scope of action; **~unfähigkeit** *f.* inability to act; **~weise** *f.* way of acting, mode of dealing.

Handrücken *m.* the back of one's hand.

Handschelle *f.* handcuff.

Handschlag *m.* handshake.

Handschrift *f.* handwriting; manuscript.

handschriftlich *a.* in manuscript, written.

Hand: **~schuh** *m.* glove; **~streich** *m.* coup de main; **~tasche** *f.* attaché case, handbag; **~teller** *m.* palm of one's hand; **~tuch** *n.* towel; **~umdrehen** *n., im ~,* in no time, *(fig.)* **~voll** *f.* handful; **~werk** *n.* craft, trade, small business; *einem das ~legen,* to render a person innocuous.

Handwerker *m.* (-s, -) craftsman, artisan,

mechanic.

Handwerks: **~betrieb** *m.* trade.

Handwerkszeug *n.* implements, tools *pl.*

Handwörterbuch *n.* concise dictionary.

Handzettel *m.* leaflet.

hanebüchen *a.* outrageous.

Hanf *m.* (-[e]s, 0) hemp.

hänfen *a.* hempen.

Hänfling *m.* (-[e]s, -e) linnet.

Hanfzwirn *m.* hemp-yarn.

Hang *m.* (-[e]s, 0) slope, declivity; propensity, bias, bent.

Hänge: **~back** *f.* flabby cheek; **~bauch** *m.* paunch; **~brücke** *f.* suspension bridge; **~brust** *f.*, **~busen** *m.* sagging breasts; **~lampe** *f.* ceiling lamp; **~matte** *f.* hammock.

hängen *v.i.* to hang; to suspend.

hängend *a.* hanging.

Hansdampf *m.* *~ in allen Gassen* jack of all trades.

Hanse *f.* Hanseatic league.

hänseln *v.t.* to tease.

Hansestadt *f.* Hanseatic town.

Hanswurst *m.* clown, harlequin; buffoon.

Hanteln *f.pl.* dumb bells *pl.*

hantieren *v.t.* to handle, to manage.

hapern *v.i.impers.* to stick, to be amiss.

Happen *m.* (-s, -) morsel.

happig *a.* *(fam.) ~e Preise pl.* fancy prices.

Härchen *n.* tiny hair.

Harem *m.* harem.

Häretiker *m.* heretic.

Harfe *f.* (-, -n) harp.

Harfenist *m.* (-en, -en) harper.

Harke *f.* (-, -n) rake.

harken *v.t.* to rake.

Harlekin *m.* (-s, -s) harlequin.

Harm *m.* (-[e]s, 0) grief, sorrow; injury.

härmen (sich) *v.refl.* to grieve, to pine for.

harmlos *a.* harmless.

Harmlosigkeit *f.* harmlessness; mildness.

Harmonie *f.* (-, -n) harmony; concord.

harmonieren *v.i.* to agree, to harmonize.

Harmonika *f.* (-, -s) accordion.

harmonisch *a.* harmonious.

Harn *m.* (-[e]s, 0) urine.

Harnblase *f.* bladder.

harnen *v.i.* to make water, to urinate.

Harnisch *m.* (-[e]s, -e) armor.

Harnröhre *f.* urethra.

Harnsäure *f.* uric acid.

harntreibend *a.* diuretic.

Harnuntersuchung *f.* urinalysis.

Harnwege *pl.* urinary tract.

Harpune *f.* (-, -n) harpoon.

harren *v.i.* to wait.

harsch *a.* harsh; rough, stiff.

Harsch *m.* crusted snow.

hart *a.* hard; stiff; severe, austere; cruel.

Härte *f.* (-, -n) hardness; severity; cruelty.

Härtefall *m.* case of hardship.

Härtegrad *m.* degree of hardness.

härten *v.t.* to harden; *(Stahl)* to temper, to chill.

Hartfaserplatte *f.* fiberboard.

Hartgummi *m.* hard rubber.

hart: **~herzig** *a.* hard-hearted; **~näckig** *a.* stubborn; headstrong, obstinate.

Hartplatz *m.* hard court.
Hartwurst *f.* dry sausage.
Harz *n.* (-es, -e) resin, rosin.
harzig *a.* resinous.
Hasch *n.* hash.
Hasardspiel *n.* game of chance, gambling.
Haschee *n.* (*cul.*) hash.
haschen *v.t.* to snatch, to seize, to snap up; ~ *v.i.* (*nach*) to aspire to; to smoke hash.
Haschisch *n.* hashish.
Hase *m.* (-n , -n) hare.
Haselnuß *f.* hazel-nut.
Hasenfuß *m.* coward.
Hasenscharte *f.* hare-lip.
Haspel *m.* (-s, -) reel, windlass.
haspeln *v.t. & i.* to reel, to wind on a reel.
Haß *m.* (Hasses, 0) hate, hatred.
hassen *v.t.* to hate.
haßerfüllt *a.* filled with hatred.
hassenswert *a.* hateful.
häßlich *a.* ugly; nasty; hateful.
Häßlichkeit *f.* ugliness; nastiness.
Haßliebe *f.* love-hate relationship.
Hast *f.* (-, 0) haste, hurry, precipitation.
hasten *v.i.* to hasten, to hurry.
hastig *a.* hasty, hurried.
hätscheln *v.t.* to coddle, to caress; to pamper.
Haube *f.* (-, -n) cap; hood.
Haubitze *f.* (-, -n) howitzer.
Hauch *m.* (-[e]s, -e) breath, whiff.
hauchdühn *a.* wafer-thin; flimsy.
hauchen *v.i.* to breathe; to aspirate.
hauchfein *a.* extremely fine.
hauchzart *a.* extremely delicate (fabric).
Hauchlaut *m.* spirant.
Haudegen *m.* warhorse.
Haue *f.* (-, -n) hoe; spanking; ~ *pl.* blows.
hauen *v.t.st.* to hew, to cut; to strike; *einen übers Ohr* ~, to make one pay through the nose.
Hauer *m.* (-s, -) (mine) face worker; fang, tusk.
Haufen *m.* (-ns, -n) heap; pile; crowd, rabble; *über den ~n werfen*, to overthrow.
häufen (sich) *v.refl.* to accumulate.
haufenweise *adv.* in heaps.
Haufenwolke *f.* cumulus cloud.
häufig *a.* frequent; copious, abundant.
Häufigkeit *f.* (-, 0) frequency.
Häufung *f.* (-, 0) accumulation.
Haupt *n.* (-[e]s, Häupter) head; (*fig.*) chief, chieftain.
Haupt . . . chief, main, principal.
Haupt: ~**aktionär** *m.* principal shareholder; ~**buch** *n.* ledger; ~**fach** *n.* main subject; ~**geschäftsstelle** *f.* headquarters, main office; ~**geschäftszeit** *f.* rush hours; ~**inhalt** *m.* summary, substance.
Häuptling *m.* (-[e]s, -e) chieftain.
Haupt: ~**linie** *f.* main line, trunk line; ~**mann** *m.* captain; ~**mast** *m.* mainmast; ~**nenner** *m.* (*ar.*) common denominator; ~**probe** *f.* dress-rehearsal; ~**quartier** *n.* head-quarters *pl.*; ~**rolle** *f.* principal *or* leading part; ~**sache** *f.* main point.
hauptsächlich *a.* chief, principal; ~ *adv.* chiefly, pincipally.
Haupt: ~**saison** *f.* high season, ~**satz** *m.* (*gram.*) principal clause; ~**schlagader** *f.* aorta; ~**schlüssel**

m. master key; ~**schule** *f.* intermediate school; ~**sendezeit** *f.* TV prime time; ~**sorge** *f.* main concern; ~**speicher** *m.* (*comp.*) main memory; ~**stadt** *f.* capital; metropolis; ~**straße** *f.* main street; (*jur.*); ~**täter** *m.* principal; ~**tribüne** *f.* main stand, ~**verhandlung** *f.* (*jur.*) main hearing; ~**verkehrzeit** *f.* rush hour; ~**wohnsitz** *m.* main residence; ~**wort** *n.* noun, substantive.
Haus *n.* (-es, Häuser) house; *zu Hause*, at home; *ich bin für niemanden zu ~e*, I am not in for anybody; *nach ~e*, home; *von ~ aus*, originally.
Haus: ~**angestellte[r]** *m./f.* domestic servant; ~**arbeiten** *pl.* home work; ~**arzt** *m.* family doctor.
hausbacken *a.* unadventurous, boring.
Haus: ~**bau** *m.* house-building; ~**besetzer** *m.* squatter; ~**besetzung** *f.* squatting; squat, ~**besitzer** *m.* landlord; ~**besitzerin** *f.* landlady; ~**brand** *m.* domestic fuel.
Häuschen *n.* (-s, -) *aus dem ~sein*, to be wild.
hausen *v.i.* to dwell; to keep house.
Häusermakler *m.* real estate agent.
Haus: ~**flur** *f.* vestibule, hall; ~**frau** *f.* housewife; ~**friedensbruch** *m.* illegal entry into s.b.'s home.
Hausgebrauch *m.* domestic use; **Hausgemacht** *a.* home-made.
Haus: ~**gemeinschaft** *f.* house community; household; ~**halt** *m.* household; *den ~halt führen*, to keep house; ~**halten** *v.i.* to economize; ~**hälterin** *f.* house-keeper.
haushälterisch *a.* economical, thrifty.
Haushalts . . . housekeeping . . .
Haushalts: ~**ausschuß** *m.* budget committee; ~**jahr** *n.* fiscal year, financial year; ~**kunde** *f.* domestic subjects *pl.*; ~**plan** *m.* budget; ~**voranschlag** *m.* budget estimates; ~**vorstand** *m.* head of the household.
haushoch *a.* as high as a house.
hausieren *v.i.* to go peddling, to hawk.
Hausierer *m.* (-s, -) pedlar, hawker.
Haus: ~**kleid** *n.* house dress; ~**lehrer** *m.* private tutor.
häuslich *a.* domestic; economical, frugal.
Häuslichkeit *f.* (-, 0) home, family life; domesticity.
Haus: ~**macherart** *f.* homemade style; ~**macht** *f.* power base; ~**mädchen** *n.* housemaid; ~**marke** *f.* house wine; ~**meister** *m.* custodian; caretaker; ~**rat** *m.* household goods; ~**ratsversicherung** *f.* house contents insurance; ~**schlüssel** *m.* frontdoor key; ~**schuh** *m.* slipper.
Hausse *f.* bull market; boom.
Haus: ~**suchung** *f.* house search; ~**suchungsbefehl** *m.* search warrant; ~**tier** *n.* domestic animal; ~**tür** *f.* frontdoor; ~**vater** *m.* father of the family; ~**verwalter** *m.* house-manager; ~**wesen** *n.* household.
Haut *f.* (-, Häute) skin, hide; (*auf Flüßigkeit*) film; (*anat.*) membrane; (*fam.*) *gute, ehrliche ~*, good fellow; *aus der ~fahren*, to lose all patience; *sich seiner ~ wehren*, to defend one's own life.
Haut: ~**abschürfung** *f.* graze; ~**arzt** *m.*; ~**ärztin** *f.* dermatologist; ~**ausschlag** *m.* rash.
Häutchen *n.* (-s, -) cuticle, pellicle; film.
häuten *v.refl.* to skin; to shed *or* change one's skin.
hauteng *a.* skin-tight.
Hautevolee *f.* (-, 0) upper crust.

Hautfarbe *f.* complexion.
hautfarben *a.* flesh-colored; skin-colored.
Hautkrankheit *f.* skin disease.
hautnah *a.* immediate, vivid.
Haut: ~**pflege** *f.* skin care; ~**pilz** *m.* fungal infection; ~**schere** *f.* cuticle scissors; ~**transplantation** *f.* skin graft(ing).
Häutung *f.* shedding; sloughing.
Hautwasser *n.* lotion.
Havarie *f.* (-, -en) damage.
H-Bombe *f.* H-bomb.
Hebamme *f.* midwife.
Hebebock *m.* (*mech.*) jack.
Hebebühne *f.* car lift.
Hebel *m.* (-s, -) lever.
Hebel: ~**gesetz** *n.* principle of the lever: ~**kraft** *f.* ~**wirkung** *f.* leverage.
heben *v.t.st.* to raise, to lift; to elevate; (sich) ~ *v.refl.* to **lift**.
hebräisch *a.* Hebrew.
Hebung *f.* (-, -en) lifting, raising; (*fig.*) improvement.
hecheln *v.t.* to pant.
Hecht *m.* (-[e]s, -e) pike.
hechten *v.i.* to do a pike-dive; to do a long fly; to dive full-length.
Heck *n.* (-[e]s, -e) (*nav.*) stern; rear; back; (*avi.*) tail.
Heckantrieb *m.* rear-wheel drive.
Hecke *f.* (-, -n) hedge; thicket.
Heckenrose *f.* dog-rose.
Heckenschütze *m.* (*mil.*) sniper.
heda! *i.* hullo!.
Heer *n.* (-[e]s, -e) army; host; great number; *stehende(s)* ~, standing army.
Heer(es)dienst *m.* military service.
Heerführer *m.* general.
Heerschau *f.* military review, parade.
Hefe *f.* (-, -n) yeast; (*fig.*) dregs *pl.*
Heft *n.* (-[e]s, -e) haft, handle, hilt; (*Schule*) notebook.
heften *v.t.* to fasten; to pin; to stitch; to tack.
Hefter *m.* file.
heftig *a.* violent, vehement.
Heft: ~**klammer** *f.* paper-clip; staple; ~**maschine** *f.* stapling machine; ~**pflaster** *n.* adhesive plaster; ~**verband** *m.* adhesive bandage.
hegen *v.t.* to foster, to cherish; (*Zweifel*) to entertain.
Hegemonie *f.* (-, -n) hegemony.
Hehl *n.* (-[e]s, 0) concealment; *kein ~ daraus machen,* to make no secret of.
Hehler *m.* (-s, -) receiver (of stolen goods).
hehr *a.* sublime, august.
Heide *f.* (-, -n) heath; (*Kraut*) heather.
Heide *m.* (-n, -n); **Heidin** *f.* (-, -nen) pagan, heathen, gentile.
Heidekraut *n.* heather, heath.
Heidelbeere *f.* blueberry; bilberry; whortleberry.
Heidelerche *f.* woodlark.
Heiden: ~**angst** *f.* (*fam.*) *eine ~ haben,* to be scared to death; ~**geld** *n.* no end of money.
Heidentum *n.* (-[e]s, 0) paganism.
heidnisch *a.* heathenish, pagan.
heikel, heiklig *a.* fastidious, delicate, ticklish, thorny.

heil *a.* unhurt; *mit ~er Haut davonkommen,* to come off scot-free.
Heil *n.* (-[e]s, 0) salvation; ~*! i.* hail!; *sein ~ versuchen,* to try one's luck.
Heiland *m.* (-[e]s, -e) Savior, Redeemer.
Heil: ~**anstalt** *f.* medical establishment, sanatorium; ~**bad** *n.* watering place, spa.
heilbar *a.* curable.
heilbringend *a.* salutary.
Heilbutt *m.* halibut.
heilen *v.t.* to cure, to heal; ~ *v.i.* to heal.
heilfroh *a.* (*fam.*) very glad.
heilig *a.* holy; (*geweiht*) sacred; *Heiliger Abend,* Christmas Eve; ~**halten,** to keep holy, to observe religiously.
Heilige *m./f.* (-n, -n) saint.
heiligen *v.t.* to sanctify, to hallow.
Heiligenschein *m.* gloriole, aureole; halo.
Heiligkeit *f.* (-, 0) holiness; sanctity; sacredness.
heiligsprechen *v.t.* to canonize.
Heiligtum *n.* (-[e]s, -tümer) sanctuary.
Heiligung *f.* (-, 0) sanctification.
Heilkraft *f.* healing power.
heilkräftig *a.* healing, curative.
Heilkunde *f.* medicine.
heillos *a.* dreadful.
Heil: ~**mittel** *n.* remedy, medicine; ~**quelle** *f.* mineral spring.
heilsam *a.* wholesome, salutary.
Heilsarmee *f.* Salvation Army.
Heilserum *n.* (-s, 0) anti-toxic serum.
Heilung *f.* (-, -en) cure.
Heilverfahren *n.* (-s, -) medical treatment.
heim *adv.* home.
Heim *n.* (-[e]s, -e) home, homestead.
Heimarbeit *f.* homework, outwork.
Heimarbeiter *m.*; **Heimarbeiterin** *f.* homeworker.
Heimat *f.* (-, -en) homeland, home, native place *or* country.
Heimat: ~**adresse** *f.* home address; **dichter** *m.*, ~**dichterin** *f.* regional writer; ~**erde** *f.* native soil; ~**film** *m.* (sentimental) regional film; ~**hafen** *m.* homeport, port of registry; ~**kunde** *f.* local history, geography and natural history; ~**land** *n.* homeland, home country.
heimatlich *a.* native; home-like.
heimatlos *a.* homeless.
Heimat: ~**museum** *n.* museum of local history; ~**ort** *m.* home town/village; ~**stadt** *f.* home town; ~**vertriebene** *m./f.* expellee.
heimbegleiten *v.t.* to take s.b. home; **heimbringen** *v.t.st.* to take s.b. home; to bring s.th. home.
Heimchen *n.* (-s, -) cricket.
Heimcomputer *m.* home computer.
heimelig *a.* cozy.
Heimfahrt *f.* return, homeward journey.
heimführen *v.t.* to lead home; to marry.
Heimgang *m.* decease.
heimgehen *v.i.st.* (s) to go home.
heimisch *a.* domestic, homelike, homely; native, indigenous.
Heimkehr *f.* return; homecoming.
heimkehren *v.i.* (s) to return home.
Heimkind *n.* institution child.

Heimkunft *f.* return home.
heimlich *a.* secret, clandestine, furtive; private.
Heimlichkeit *f.* (-, -en) secrecy.
Heimlichtuer *m.* **Heimlichtuerin** *f.* (*pej.*) secretive person.
Heimmannschaft *f.* home team.
Heimreise *f.* return.
heimsuchen *v.t.* to visit; to afflict; to punish.
Heimsuchung *f.* (-, -en) affliction.
Heimtücke *f.* (-, 0) malice; treachery.
heimtückisch *a.* malicious; insidious; treacherous.
heimwärts *adv.* homeward(s).
Heim: ~**weg** *m.* way home, return; ~**weh** *n.* homesickness, nostalgia; *Heimweh haben*, to be homesick.
Heimwerker *m.*; **Heimwerkerin** *f.* handyman; do-it-yourselfer.
heimzahlen *v.t. einem etwas* ~, to get even with s.b.
Heinzelmännchen *n.* little people, goblin.
Heirat *f.* (-, -en) marriage; match.
heiraten *v.t.* to marry; ~ *v.i.* to get married.
Heiratsantrag *m.* offer *or* proposal of marriage.
heiratsfähig *a.* marriageable.
Heirats: ~**schwindler** *m.* marriage imposter; ~**urkunde** *f.* marriage certificate; ~**vermittlung** *f.* marriage bureau.
heisa! *i.* hurrah!
heischen *v.t.* to demand, to require.
heiser *a.* hoarse, husky.
Heiserkeit *f.* (-, 0) hoarseness, raucity.
heiß *a.* hot; (*Zone*) torrid; fervent, ardent.
heißblütig *a.* hot-blooded, passionate.
heißen *v.t.st.* to call; to bid, to command; ~ *v.i.st.* to be called; to signify, to mean; *etwas gut* ~, to approve of a thing; *wie heißt das auf französisch?* what do you call this in French?; *das heißt*, that is to say.
heißersehnt *a.* ardently longed-for.
heißgeliebt *a.* dearly loved.
Heißhunger *m.* ravenous hunger; (sudden) craving.
heißhung(e)rig *a.* ravenous, voracious.
heißlaufen *v.i.st.* to run hot; to overheat.
Heiß: ~**luftballon** *m.* hot-air balloon; ~**mangel** *f.* rotary ironer; ~**sporn** *m.* hotspur, firebrand.
heißumkämpft *a.* fiercely embattled.
heißumstritten *a.* highly controversial.
Heißwasserbereiter *m.* water heater.
heiter *a.* cheerful, serene, clear, bright; fair; cheerful.
Heiterkeit *f.* (-, 0) cheerfulness; serenity; hilarity.
Heizanlage *f.* heating system.
heizbar *a.* heatable; with heat.
Heizdecke *f.* electric blanket.
heizen *v.t.* to heat, to make a fire (in), to stoke.
Heizer *m.* (-s, -) (*rail.*) fireman, stoker.
Heiz: ~**gerät** *n.* heater; ~**kessel** *m.* boiler; ~**kissen** *n.* heating pad; ~**körper** *m.* radiator; ~**material** *n.* fuel; ~**öl** *n.* fuel oil; *elektrische* ~*vorrichtung f.* electric heater.
Heizung *f.* (-, -en) heating, firing.
Hektar *m.n.* (-e, -e) hectare.
Hektik *f.* hectic rush, hectic pace.
Hekto... = hecto...
Hektograph *m.* mimeograph.
Held *m.* (-en, -en) hero.

Helden: ~**dichtung** *f.* epic/heroic poetry; ~**epos** *n.* heroic epic.
helden: ~**haft**, ~**mütig** *a.* heroic.
Helden: ~**tod** *m.* heroic death, hero's death; ~**sage** *f.* heroic legend, heroic saga; ~**tum** *n.* heroism.
Heldin *f.* (-, -nen) heroine.
helfen *v.i.st.* to help; to aid, to assist; to avail, to do good, to remedy.
Helfer *m.* (-s, -); **Helferin** *f.* (-, -nen) helper, assistant.
Helfershelfer *m.* (*pej.*) accomplice.
hell *a.* light, clear, bright; *am* ~*en Tage*, in broad day light; ~*er Wahnsinn*, sheer madness.
hellblau *a.* light blue.
Helldunkel *a.* clair-obscure.
Helle *f.* = **Helligkeit**.
Hellebarde *f.* (-, -n) halberd.
Heller *m.* (-s, -) farthing, doit; *bei* ~ *und Pfennig*, to the last cent.
Helligkeit *f.* (-, 0) clearness, brightness.
hellodernd *a.* blazing.
Hellseher *m.*; **Hellseherin** *f.* clairvoyant.
hellsichtig *a.* clear-sighted.
hellwach *a.* wide awake; bright, intelligent.
Helm *m.* (-[e]s, -e) helmet.
Helmbusch *m.* crest, plume.
Hemd *n.* (-[e]s, -en) shirt; (*Frauen*~) chemise.
Hemd: ~**ärmel** *m.* shirt-sleeve.
Hemisphäre *f.* hemisphere.
hemmen *v.t.* to slow, to hinder, to check.
Hemm: ~**nis** *n.* check, obstruction, obstacle; ~**schuh** *m.* obstacle, hindrance.
Hemmung *f.* (-, -en) inhibitions.
Hengst *m.* (-[e]s, -e) horse, stallion.
Hengstfohlen *n.* colt, (male) foal.
Henkel *m.* (-s, -) handle; ear.
henken *v.t.* to hang.
Henker *m.* (-s, -) hangman; executioner.
Henne *f.* (-, -n) hen.
her *adv.* hither, here; *her damit!* out with it!; *hin und* ~, to and fro; *nicht weit* ~ (*sein*), not much to boast of.
herab *adv.* down; downwards.
herablassen (sich) *v.refl.* to condescend.
herablassend *a.* condescending.
Herablassung *f.* (-, 0) condescension.
herabmindern *v.t.* to reduce; to belittle, to disparage.
herabregnen *v.i.* to rain down.
herabsehen *v.i.st.* to look down.
herabsenken *v.refl.* to fall (night); to settle.
herabsetzen *v.t.* to disparage; to reduce.
Herabsetzung *f.* (-, 0) disparagement; reduction, lowering.
herabsteigen *v.i.st.* (*s*) to descend; (*vom Pferde*) to dismount.
herabwürdigen *v.t.* to abase; to disparage; (sich) ~ *v.rel.* to demean oneself.
Heraldik *f.* (-, 0) heraldry.
heran *adv.* on, up, near.
heranbilden *v.t.* to train, to educate.
heranführen *v.t.* (*mil.*) to bring up, to move up.
herangehen *v.i.st.* to go up; to tackle (problem).
herankommen *v.i.st.* to come up to.
heranmachen (sich) (an) *v.refl.* to sidle up to.
herannahen *v.i.* (*s*) to approach.

heranreifen *v.i.* (s) to come to maturity.
heranrücken *v.i.* (s) to advance.
heranwachsen *v.i.st.* (s) to grow up.
herauf *adv.* up, upwards.
heraufbeschwören *v.t.* to conjure up, to precipitate.
heraufsetzen *v.t.* (*Preis*) to put up.
heraufziehen *v.t.st.* to pull up; ~ *v.i.st.* (s) to be approaching.
heraus *adv.* out; ~ ! come out *i; er hat's* ~, he has got the knack of it.
herausbekommen *v.t.st.* to get back (change); to find out.
herausbringen *v.t.ir.* to bring out; to find *or* make out.
herausfinden *v.t.* to find out.
herausfordern *v.t.* to challenge; to provoke.
Herausforderung *f.* (-, -en) challenge; provocation.
Herausgabe *f.* (-, 0) handing over, delivery; publication.
herausgeben *v.t.st.* to give up, to deliver up; to give change; to publish; to edit.
Herausgeber *m.* (-s, -) (*Leiter*) editor; publisher.
herauskommen *v.i.st.* (s) to come out; to tran-spire; *auf eins* ~, to come to the same thing; *dabei kommt nichts heraus*, it's no use, it doesn't pay.
herausnehmen (sich) *v.refl.st.* (*etwas*) to take out, to remove.
herausplatzen *v.i.* (s) (*mit*) to burst out, to blurt out.
herausputzen *v.t.* to dress up, to rig out.
herausreden (sich) *v.refl.* to talk one's way out.
herausrücken *v.i.* (s) (*mit dem Gelde*) to fork out, to come down; (*mit der Sprache*) to speak frankly.
herausschlagen *v.t.st.* to make money.
herausstellen (sich) *v.refl. imp.* to turn out, to become apparent; to emphasize.
herausstreichen *v.t.st.* to delete; to point out.
heraustreten *v.i.st.* (s) to step out; to protrude.
herb *a.* sharp; astringent; dry; (*fig.*) harsh, austere.
herbei *adv.* hither, near; on.
herbeiführen *v.t.* to bring about, to entail.
herbeischaffen *v.t.* to produce, to procure.
herbeimühen *v.t.* to give one the trouble of com-ing here; (sich) ~ *v.refl.* to take the trouble of coming.
Herberge *f.* (-, -n) hostel; inn.
Herbergs: ~**mutter** *f.*; ~**vater** *m.* warden of a youth hostel.
herbestellen *v.t.* to appoint, to send for.
herbitten *v.t.st.* to invite.
herbringen *v.t.ir.* to bring (hither).
Herbst *m.* (-es, -e) autumn, fall.
herbstlich *a.* autumnal.
Herbstzeitlose *f.* (-, -n) (*bot.*) meadow-saffron.
Herd *m.* (-[e]s, -e); stove; fireplace; kitchen-range; (*einer Epidemie*) center.
Herde *f.* (-, -n) (*Schafe*) flock; herd.
Herdentier *n.* gregarious animal.
Herdentrieb *m.* herd instinct.
Herdplatte *f.* hotplate.
herein *adv.* in; ~ ! *i.* come in!.
hereinbitten *v.t.st.* to invite s.b. in.
hereinbrechen *v.i.st.* to befall; to set in.
hereindürfen *v.i.ir.* to be allowed in.

Hereinfall *m.* (*fam.*) hoax; failure.
hereinfallen *v.i.* to be taken in, to be sold.
hereinlassen *v.t.* to let in.
hereinplatzen *v.i.* to burst in.
hereinschneien *v.i.* to snow in; to turn up out of the blue.
hereinsehen *v.i.st.* to look in; to drop in.
hereinstürmen *v.i.* to dash in; to storm in.
herfallen (über) *v.i.st.* to fall upon.
Hergang *m.* (-[e]s, -gänge) proceedings *pl.*, course of events, circumstances *pl.*
hergeben *v.t.st.* to surrender, to give up; (sich) ~ *v.refl.* to lend oneself.
hergebracht *a.* traditional, established.
hergehen *v.i.st.* to happen; (*lustig, etc.*) to be going on..
hergehören *v.t.* to belong to the matter.
hergelaufen *a.* *ein* ~*er Mensch*, undesirable newcomer.
herholen *v.t.* to fetch.
Hering *m.* (-[e]s, -e) herring.
herkommen *v.i.st.* (s) to come on; to come from; to originate in.
herkömmlich *a.* customary, usual, traditional.
Herkunft *f.* (-, 0) descent, origin.
herlegen *v.t.* to put down (here).
herleiern *v.t.* to reel off.
herleiten *v.t.* to conduct; to derive.
hermachen (sich) *v.refl.* (*über*) to fall upon; to set about.
Hermelin *n.* (-[e]s, -e) ermine.
hermetisch *a. & adv.* hermetic(ally).
hernach *adv.* afterwards.
hernehmen *v.t.st.* to take from.
heroben *adv.* up here.
Heroin *n.* (-s, 0) heroin.
heroisch *a. & adv.* heroic(ally).
Herold *m.* (-[e]s, -e) herald.
herplappern *v.t.* to rattle off.
Herr *m.* (-n, -en) master; lord; gentleman; Sir; *Herr Braun*, Mr. (Mister) B.; ~ *werden*, to master, to overcome.
Herreise *f.* (-, 0) journey hither.
herreisen *v.i.* (s) to travel hither.
Herren: ~**abend** *m.* stag evening; ~**ausstatter** *m.* men's outfitter; ~**haus** *n.* manor-house, hall.
herrenlos *a.* stray.
Herrenreiter *m.* gentleman rider.
Herrgott *m.* (*fam.*) the Lord, God.
Herrgottsfrühe *f. in aller* ~ at the crack of the dawn.
herrichten *v.t.* to get ready, to arrange.
Herrin *f.* (-, -nen) mistress, lady.
herrisch *a.* imperious, peremptory.
herrlich *a.* magnificent, splendid.
Herrlichkeit *f.* (-, -en) magnificence, splendor, glory; excellence.
Herrschaft *f.* (-, -en) dominion, mastery; master and mistress; *meine* ~*en*, ladies and gentlemen.
herrschaftlich *a.* high class.
Herrschaftsform *f.* system of government.
herrschen *v.i.* to rule, to govern; to prevail.
herrschend *a.* ruling; reigning; prevailing.
Herrscher *m.* (-s, -) ruler, sovereign.
Herrscherfamilie *f.* dynasty.
Herrschsucht *f.* thirst for power, domineering

nature.

herrschsüchtig *a.* domineering.
herrücken *v.i.* to move near.
herrühren *v.i.* to originate in.
hersagen *v.t.* to recite, to repeat.
herschaffen *v.t.* to procure, to produce.
herschreiben (sich) *v.refl.st.* to date from.
herstellen *v.t.* to manufacture, to produce, to turn out; to restore (to health).
Hersteller *m.* producer; manufacturer.
Herstellung *f.* production; manufacture.
herüben *adv.* over here.
herüber *adv.* over, across, on this side.
herüberkommen *v.i.st.* to come over.
herum *adv.* round; about; *hier* ~, hereabout(s); *die Reihe* ~, each one in his turn.
herumalbern *v.i.* to fool around.
herumärgern *v.refl.* to be plagued.
herumführen *v.t.* to show over a place; *an der Nase* ~, to lead by the nose.
herumkommen *v.i.st.* (s) *weit* ~, to see the world.
herumlaufen *v.i.* to run about.
herumliegen *v.i.* to lie about.
herumlungern, herumstehen, *v.i.* to loaf around.
herumnörgeln *v.i.* to moan; to grumble.
herumpfuschen (an) *v.i.* to tamper with.
herumreichen *v.t.* to hand round.
herumschlagen *v.t.st.* to wrap about; *sich* ~ *mit,* to scuffle with.
herumtrieben (sich) *v.refl.st.* to hang around.
herumtrödeln *v.i.* to dawdle around.
herumziehend *a.* ambulatory.
herunter *adv.* down, off; (*fam.*) low, weak.
herunterbringen *v.t.ir.* to bring down; to reduce; to take it out of a person.
herunterkommen *v.i.st.* (s) to come down; to decay, to go to the bad.
herunterlassen *v.t.* to lower.
heruntermachen *v.t.* to run down.
herunterreißen *v.t.st.* to tear down.
herunterschlucken *v.t.* to swallow.
heruntersteigen *v.i.st.* (s) to descend.
hervor *adv.* forth, out.
hervorbringen *v.t.ir.* to bring forth, to produce; to effect.
hervorgehen *v.i.st.* (s) to proceed; to result; to come off.
hervorheben *v.t.st.* to emphasize; to set off.
hervorragen *v.i.* to stand out; to project.
hervorragend *a.* outstanding.
hervorrufen *v.t.st.* to call forth, to cause.
hervorstechen *v.i.st.* to be prominent.
hervorstechend *a.* striking.
hervorstehen *v.i.st.* to protrude.
hervortreten *v.i.st.* (s) (*fig.*) to excel, to stand pre-eminent.
hervortun (sich) *v.refl.st.* to distinguish oneself.
Herweg *m.* (-[e]s, -e) way here.
Herz, *n.* (-ens, -en) heart; breast; (*kern*) core (*fig.*) courage; *ans* ~*legen,* to urge, to enjoin; *es liegt mir am* ~*en,* I have it at heart; *ich kann es nicht übers* ~*bringen,* I cannot find it in my heart; *von* ~*en,* with all my heart; (*sich*) *etwas zu* ~*en nehmen,* to take a thing to heart.
Herz... cardiac.

Herzanfall *m.* heart attack.
Herzbeschwerden *pl.* heart trouble.
Herzbeutel *m.* pericardium.
Herzbube *m.* jack of hearts.
herzbrechend *a.* heart-rending.
Herzchen *n.* darling, sweetheart.
Herzdame *f.* queen of hearts.
Herzeleid *n.* heart-ache, grief, anguish.
herzen *v.t.* to hug, to caress.
Herzensangelegenheit *f.* affair of the heart.
Herzensbedürfnis *n.* sth. that is very important to s.b.
Herzensbrecher *m.* lady-killer.
herzensgut *a.* kind-hearted, good-hearted.
Herzenslust *f. nach* ~ to one's heart's content.
Herzenswunsch *m.* fondest wish.
herzerfrischend *a.* refreshing.
Herzerweiterung *f.* dilatation of the heart.
Herzfehler *m.* heart defect.
herzhaft *a.* courageous, bold; hearty.
herzig *a.* lovely, sweet, dear.
Herz: ~**infarkt** *m.* heart attack; cardiac infarction, ~**kammer** *f.* ventricle (of the heart); ~**klappe** *f.* valve; ~**klopfen** *n.* heartbeat; palpitation; ~**könig** *m.* king of hearts; ~**kranzgefäß** *n.* coronary vessel.
herzlich *a.* hearty.
Herzlichkeit *f.* warmth, kindness.
herzlos *a.* heartless, callous.
Herzog *m.* (-[e]s, Herzöge) duke.
Herzogin *f.* (-, -nen) duchess.
herzoglich *a.* ducal.
Herzogtum *n.* (-[e]s, -tümer) dukedom, duchy.
Herz: ~**schlag** *m.* heart-throb; heart-failure; ~**schrittmacher** *m.* pace maker; ~**stillstand** *m.* cardiac arrest; ~**versagen** *n.* heart-failure.
herzzerreißend *a.* heart-rending.
heterogen *a.* heterogeneous.
heterosexuell *a.* **Heterosexuelle** *m./f.* heterosexual.
Hetze *f.* (-, -n) hunt, chase; (*fig.*) hurry, rush; agitation; persecution, baiting.
hetzen *v.t.* to hunt; to set on; to agitate; to incite; to bait.
Hetzer *m.* (-s, -) agitator.
hetzerisch *a.* inflammatory.
Hetzjagd *f.* hunt (with hounds); chase.
Heu *n.* (-[e]s, 0) hay.
Heuboden *m.* hay loft.
Heuchelei *f.* (-, -en) hypocrisy.
heucheln *v.t.* to feign, to put on, simulate; ~ *v.i.* to dissemble.
Heuchler *m.* (-s, -) **Heuchlerin** *f.* (-, -nen) hypocrite.
heuchlerisch *a.* hypocritical.
heuer *adv.* this year.
Heuer *f.* pay, wages (sailors).
Heu: ~**ernte** *f.* hay-time, hay-making; ~**gabel** *f.* pitchfork; ~**haufen** *m.* haystack.
Heulboje *f.* whistling buoy.
heulen *v.i.* to howl; to cry, to whine.
Heulsuse *f.* (*fam. pej.*) cry-baby.
heurig *a.* this year's.
Heuschnupfen *m.* (-s, 0) hay fever.
Heuschrecke *f.* (-, -en) grasshopper.
heute *adv.* today.

heutig *a.* this day's, present day.
heutzutage *adv.* nowadays.
Hexe (*hekse*) *f.* (-, -n) witch.
hexen (*heksen*) *v.i.* to practice witchcraft.
Hexen: ~**jagd** *f.* witch-hunt; ~**kessel** *m.* (*fig.*) inferno; ~**meister** *m.* sorcerer; ~**schuß** *m.* lumbago; ~**verfolgung** *f.* witch-hunt.
Hexerei *f.* (-, -en) sorcery, witchcraft.
Hickhack *m.* (*fam.*) squabbling; bickering.
hie *adv.* ~**und da** here and there.
Hieb *m.* (-[e]s, -e) blow, lash, cut, stroke; (*fig.*) hit.
hiebfest *a.* hieb- und stichfest watertight; cast-iron.
hiemit = **hiermit.**
hienieden *adv.* here below.
hier *adv.* here; present; ~*zu Lande*, in this country.
Hierarchie *f.* (-, -[e]n) hierarchy.
hierarchisch *a.* hierarchical.
hierauf *adv.* hereupon; after this.
hieraus *adv.* from this; hence.
hierbei *adv.* at, by, with this.
hierbleiben *v.i.* to stay here.
hierdurch *adv.* by this, hereby.
hierfür *adv.* for this.
hiergegen *adv.* against this.
hierher *adv.* hither, this way; *bis* ~, so far, hitherto.
hierherum *adv.* about here, hereabouts.
hierhin *adv.* this way.
hierin *adv.* in this.
hiermit *adv.* with this, herewith.
hiernach *adv.* after this, according to this.
Hieroglyphe (-*glife*) *f.* (-, -n) hieroglyph.
hierorts *adv.* in this place.
Hiersein *n.* (-s, 0) presence, stay here.
hierüber *adv.* over here; about this.
hierum *adv.* about this.
hierunter *adv.* under this, among these.
hiervon *adv.* of, from this; about this.
hierwider *adv.* against this.
hierzu *adv.* to this; ~ *kommt noch*, add to this.
hierzulande *adv.* (here) in this country.
hiesig *a.* of this place.
hieven *v.t.* to heave.
Hi-Fi-Aulage *f.* hi-fi set.
Hilfe *f.* (-, -n) help, aid, assistance, relief; *erste* ~, first aid; *einem zu* ~ *kommen*, to come to the rescue of; ~ *leisten*, to aid, to assist.
Hilfeleistung *f.* assistance.
Hilferuf *m.* cry for help.
Hilfestellung *f.* support.
hilflos *a.* helpless.
Hilflosigkeit *f.* helplessness.
hilfreich *a.* helpful; benevolent.
Hilfsaktion *f.* relief action.
Hilfsarbeiter *m.* laborer, unskilled worker.
hilfsbedürftig *a.* in need; needy.
Hilfsbedürftigkeit *f.* need; neediness.
hilfsbereit *a.* helpful; ready to help.
Hilfs: ~**fonds** *m.* relief fund; ~**mittel** *n.* resource, expedient; ~**quelle** *f.* resource; ~**truppen** *pl.* auxiliary troops *pl.*; ~**unterstützung** *f.* grant-in-aid; ~**verb**, ~**zeitwort** *n.* auxiliary (verb).
Himalaja *m.* Himalaya.
Himbeere *f.* (-, -n) raspberry.
Himmel *m.* (-s, -) heaven; heavens *pl.*; (*sichtbarer*) sky; (*eines Bettes*) canopy.
Himmelbett *n.* four-poster.

himmelblau *a.* azure, sky-blue.
Himmelfahrt *f.* Ascension; (*Maria*) Assumption.
Himmelfahrtskommando *n.* suicide mission.
Himmelfahrtstag *m.* Ascension-day.
himmelhoch *a.* sky-high.
Himmelreich *n.* kingdom of heaven.
himmelschreiend *a.* crying to heaven.
Himmels: ~**gewölbe** *n.* firmament; ~**körper** *m.* celestial body; ~**richtung** *f.* direction; ~**schrift** *f.* sky-writing.
himmelwärts *adv.* heavenward(s).
himmelweit *a.* & *adv.* vast.
himmlisch *a.* celestial, heavenly.
hin *adv.* thither, there, along; gone, lost; ~ *und her*, to and fro, backwards and forwards; ~ *und wieder*, now and then; ~*und zurück*, there, and back.
hinab *adv.* down.
hinarbeiten *v.i.* to aim at.
hinauf *adv.* up, up to; upstairs.
hinaufarbeiten (sich) *v.refl.* to work one's way up.
hinaufsteigen *v.i.st.* (*s*) to ascend, to step up.
hinaus *adv.* out; *darüber* ~, beyond that.
hinausgehen *v.i.st.* (*s*) to go out; to surpass, to exceed.
hinaus: ~**kommen**, ~**laufen** *v.i.st.* (*s*) *auf dasselbe* ~, to come to the same thing.
hinausschieben *v.t.st.* (*fig.*) to defer, to put off, to postpone.
hinauswerfen *v.t.st.* to throw out.
hinauswollen *v.i.ir.* to want to get out; to be driving at.
hinbegeben (sich) *v.refl.st.* to go to.
Hinblick *m.* (-[e]s, 0) consideration; *im* ~ *auf*, with a view to, in consideration of.
hinbringen *v.t.ir.* to carry to; (*Zeit*) to pass away.
hinderlich *a.* hindering, in the way.
hindern *v.t.* to hinder, to prevent, to impede.
Hindernis *n.* (-nisses, -nisse) hindrance, impediment, obstacle, fence.
Hindernis: ~**lauf** *m.*; ~**rennen** *n.* steeplechase.
Hinderung *f.* (-, -en) hindrance.
hindeuten *v.i.* to point to *or* at.
Hindu *m.* Hindu.
Hinduismus *m.* Hinduism.
hinduistisch *a.* Hindu.
hindurch *adv.* through, throughout; across.
hinein *adv.* in; *in den Tag* ~, at random, at a venture.
hineinarbeiten (sich) *v.refl.* to familiarize oneself with.
hineinbegeben (sich) *v.refl.st.* to enter, to go in.
hineindenken (sich) *v.refl.ir.* to transfer oneself mentally into.
hineinfahren *v.i.st.* to run into.
hineinfinden (sich) *v.refl.* to make the best of a thing.
hineingeh(e)n *v.i.st.* to enter; *es wird nicht mehr* ~, it will hold no more.
hineinstecken, hineintun *v.t.* to put into.
hineinsteigern *v.refl.* to get worked up.
hineinwagen (sich) *v.refl.* to venture in.
hineinziehen *v.t.st.* to pull s.b./s.th. into.
Hinfahrt *f.* (-, -en) journey to, drive, passage to; outward journey.
hinfallen *v.i.st.* (*s*) to fall down.
hinfällig *a.* frail, weak.

hinfliehen *v.i.st.* (*s*) to fly to; to fly away.
hinführen *v.t.* to conduct to, to lead to.
Hingabe *f.* (-, 0) devotion, dedication; surrender.
Hingang *m.* (-[e]s, 0) decease.
hingeben *v.t.st.* to give up; (sich) ~, *v.refl.* to devote oneself (to); to indulge (in).
hingebend *a.* devoted, fond.
Hingebung *f.* (-, 0) resignation; devotion.
hingebungsvoll *a.* devoted.
hingegen *adv.* on the other hand.
hingehen *v.i.st.* (*s*) to go; to pass; ~ *lassen*, to wink at, to let pass.
hingerissen *a.* carried away; spellbound.
hinhalten *v.t.st.* to hold out; to put off, to delude with hopes.
hinken *v.i.* to limp, to halt.
hinkommen *v.i.st.* (*s*) to come to, to get to.
hinlänglich *a.* sufficient, adequate.
hinnehmen *v.t.st.* to put up with.
hinraffen *v.t.* (*fig.*) to carry off, to cut off (in the prime of life).
hinreichen *v.t.* to hand, to offer; ~ *v.i.* to suffice.
hinreichend *a.* sufficient.
Hinreise *f.* (-, -n) journey to, voyage out.
hinreisen *v.i.* (*s*) to travel to.
hinreißen *v.t.st.* to enthrall.
hinreißend *a.* charming, ravishing.
hinrichten *v.t.* to execute.
Hinrichtung *f.* (-, -en) execution.
hinschaffen *v.t.* to convey to.
hinscheiden *v.i.st.* to depart (life).
hinschlagen *v.i.st.* to fall down.
hinschlachten *v.t.* to massacre.
hinschlendern *v.i.* (*s*) to saunter.
hinschwinden *v.i.st.* (*s*) to dwindle.
hinsehen *v.i.* to look.
hinsein *v.i.st.* (*s*) to be lost, to be gone.
hinsetzen *v.t.* to sit down: (sich) ~ *v.refl.* to sit down.
Hinsicht *f.* (-, -en) respect; *in ~ auf. . .*, with regard to.
hinsichtlich *a.* with regard to.
hinsiechen *v.i.* (*h*, *s*) to pine away.
Hinspiel *n.* (sp.) first leg.
hinsterben *v.i.st.* (*s*) to die away.
hinstrecken *v.t.* (*fig.*) to knock down; sich ~, to lie down.
hintan: ~**setzen;** ~**stellen** *v.t.* to put s.th. last; to neglect.
hinten *adv.* behind; in the back; (*nav.*) aft; ~*nach*, afterwards.
hinten: ~**drauf** *adv.* (*fam.*) on the back; ~**über** *adv.* backwards.
hinter *pr.* behind, after; ~*einander*, one after another; ~*s Licht führen*, to dupe; *etwas ~ sich haben*, to have got over a thing.
Hinter: ~**achse** *f.* rear/back axle; ~**ausicht** *f.* rear/back view; ~**ausgang** *m.* rear/back exit; ~**bänkler** *m.* backbencher; ~**bein** *n.* hind-leg.
Hinterbliebene *f./m.* (-n, -n) survivor; ~**n** the bereaved; surviving dependent.
hinterbringen *v.t.st.* to inform.
Hinterdeck *n.* afterdeck.
hinterdrein *adv.* afterwards; after; too late.
Hintere[r] *m.* (-n, -n) backside.
hintere[r] *a.* hind, hinder, back.

hintereinander *adv.* one behind the other; one after another.
hinterfragen *v.i.* to question; to scrutinize.
Hinterfuß *m.* hind-foot.
Hintergedanke *m.* ulterior motive.
hintergehen *v.t.st.* to deceive.
Hintergrund *m.* background.
hintergründig *a.* enigmatic; cryptic; profound.
Hinterhalt *m.*(-[e]s, -e) ambush.
hinterhältig *a.* underhand(ed); crafty.
Hinterhand *f.* hindquarters (animals).
Hinterhaus *n.* backbuilding, outhouse.
hinterher *adv.* afterwards; ~**sein** *v.i.st.*(*s.*) *jm.*~ to pursue s.b. diligently; ~**mit** to be behind with sth.
Hinter: ~**kopf** *m.* back of the head; occiput; ~**land** *n.* hinterland.
hinterlassen *v.t.st.* to leave (behind); to leave word; to bequeath.
Hinterlassene *m./f.* (-n, -n) survivor.
Hinterlassenschaft *f.* (-, -en) inheritance; estate.
hinterlegen *v.t.* to deposit.
Hinterlist *f.* fraud, deceit, cunning.
hinterlistig *a.* cunning, deceitful.
Hintermann *m.* person behind; ~**männer** *pl.* brains behind the operation.
Hintermannschaft *f.* (*sp.*) defense.
Hintern *m.* (-, -) behind, backside; bottom.
Hinterpfote *f.* (-, -n) hind paw.
Hinter: ~**rad** *n.* rear wheel; ~**antrieb** *m.* rear-wheel drive.
hinterrücks *adv.* from behind, insidiously.
hintersinnig *a.* with a deeper meaning, subtle.
Hintersitz *m.* back-seat.
hinterste[r] *a.* hindmost.
Hinter: ~**teil** *n.* behind; backside; (*nav.*) stern; ~**treppe** *f.* back-stairs *pl.*
hintertreiben *v.t.st.* to frustrate.
Hinter: ~**tür** *f.* back-door; loop-hole; ~**wälder** *m.* (-s, -) backwoodsman.
hinterziehen *v.t.st.* to evade (taxes).
hintun *v.t.* to put.
hinüber *adv.* over, across.
hin und her to and fro; back and forth.
Hin- und Rück: ~**fahrt** *f.*, ~**flug** *m.* round trip; ~**reise** *f.*, ~**weg** *m.* journey/way there and back.
hinunter *adv.* down; downstairs.
hinunter: ~**schlucken** *v.t.* to swallow; ~**würgen** *v.t.* to gulp down.
hinwagen (sich) *v.refl.* to venture/to go somewhere.
Hinweg *m.* (-[e]s, -e) way there.
hinweg *adv.* away off; ~! begone!; *über etwas* ~*gehen*, to pass lightly over a thing; ~*raffen*, to cut off, to sweep away; ~*sehen über etwas*, to overlook a thing; *sich über etwas* ~*setzen*, not to mind a thing, to make light of it.
Hinweis *m.* (-weises, -weise) hint; tip; reference.
hinweisen (auf) *v.i.st.* to point out; to refer to.
hinweisend *a.* (*gram.*) demonstrative.
Hinweis: ~**schild** *n.* sign; road sign; ~**tafel** *f.* information board.
hinwerfen *v.t.st.* to throw down; to fling to; to dash off, to utter carelessly.
hinwieder *adv.* again; on the other hand.
hinwirken (auf) *v.i.* to work in the direction of.
Hinz *m.* ~**und Kunz** (*fam. pej.*) every Tom, Dick

and Harry.

hinziehen *v.t.st.* to draw to, to protract; *sich* ~, to drag on.

hinzielen *v.i.* to aim at; (*fig.*) to have in view.

hinzu *adv.* to it; in addition; near.

hinzudenken *v.t.ir.* to supply mentally.

hinzufügen *v.t.* to add; to subjoin.

hinzukommen *v.i.st.* (*s*) to come to; to be added.

hinzurechnen *v.t.* to add to.

hinzusetzen *v.t.* to add, to subjoin.

hinzuziehen *v.t.st.* to include, to add; (*einen Arzt*) to consult.

Hiob *m.* Job.

Hiobspost *f.* (-, -en) bad news.

Hirn *n.* (-[e]s, -e) brain, brains *pl.*

Hirngespinst *n.* (-[e]s, -e) fantasy, chimera.

Hirnhautentzündung *f.* meningitis.

hirnlos *a.* brainless, hare-brained.

hirnrissig *a.* (*fam.*) crack-brained, mad.

Hirnschale *f.* skull, cranium.

hirnverbrannt *a.* mad.

Hirsch *m.* (-[e]s, -e) stag, hart.

Hirsch; ~brunft *f.*; **~brunst** *f.* rut; **~fänger** *m.* hanger, cutlass; **~geweih** *n.* antlers *pl.*, hartshorn; **kalb** *n.* fawn; **~käfer** *m.* stag-beetle; **~kuh** *f.* hind, doe; **~leder** *n.* buckskin.

Hirse *f.* (-, 0) millet.

Hirsebrei *m.* millet gruel.

Hirte *m.* (-en, -en) shepherd.

Hirtenbrief *m.* pastoral letter.

Hirtin *f.* shepherdess.

His (*mus.*) B sharp.

hissen *v.t.* to hoist (up).

Historiker *m.* (-s, -); **Historikerin** *f.* (-, -en) historian.

historisch *a.* historical.

Hitze *f.* (-, 0) heat; hot weather; (*fig.*) ardor, passion; **fliegende~** hot flushes.

hitzebeständig *a.* heat-resistant.

Hitzebläschen *a.* heat spot.

hitzeempfindlich *a.* sensitive to heat.

hitzefrei *a.* **~haben** to have time off from school because of hot weather.

Hitzewelle *f.* heat wave.

hitzig *a.* hot; ardent, fervid; passionate.

Hitzkopf *m.* spit-fire, hotspur.

hitzköpfig *a.* hot-headed.

Hitzschlag *m.* sunstroke.

Hobby *n.* (-s, -s) hobby.

Hobel *m.* (-s, -) plane; slicer (vegetable).

Hobelbank *f.* carpenter's bench.

Hobelmaschine *f.* (-, -n) planer.

hobeln *v.t.* to plane.

Hobelspäne *f.pl.* shavings *pl.*

hoch *a.* highly; lofty, sublime; eminent; *drei Mann* ~, three men strong; *hohe See*, high seas; *hohe Strafe*, heavy penalty; *wenn es* ~ *kommt*, at most; *hoch lebe!* long live!; *ein Hoch n.* (*Wetterkunde*) a high.

hochachten *v.t.* to esteem, to respect, to value.

Hochachtung *f.* (-, 0) esteem, respect.

hochachtungsvoll *adv.* yours faithfully.

Hoch: ~amt *n.* high mass; **~bahn** *f.* overhead railway; **~bau** *m.* overground building; **~burg** *f.* stronghold.

hochdeutsch *a.* High-German.

Hochdruck *m.* high pressure; **~gebiet** *n.* high-pressure area.

Hochebene *f.* plateau, table-land.

hoch: ~fahrend *a.* haughty; **~fein** *a.* superfine; **~fliegend** *a.* (*fig.*) ambitious, lofty.

Hoch: ~format *n.* upright size; **~frequenz** *f.* high frequency; **~gefühl** *n.* (feeling of) elation.

Hochgenuß *m.* treat, delight.

Hochglauz *m.* high gloss; high polish.

hochgradig *a.* to a high degree.

hochhackig *a.* high-heeled.

Hochhaus *n.* high-rise building.

hoch: ~herzig *a.* high-minded, magnanimous; **~kirchlich** *a.* High Church.

Hochkonjunktur *f.* boom (economy).

Hochland *n.* (-[e]s, -e *u* -länder) highland.

Hochleistung *f.* outstanding performance; **~sport** *m.* top-level sport.

höchlich *adv.* highly.

Hochmittelalter *n.* High Middle Ages.

Hochmut *a.* arrogance, haughtiness.

hochmütig *a.* haughty, proud.

hochnäsig *a.* stuck-up; conceited.

Hochofen *m.* blast-furnace.

hochragen *v.i.* to rise up, to tower up.

Hochrechnung *f.* (*Statistik*) projection.

hochrot *a.* light-red, crimson.

Hochsaison *f.* (-, -s) peak season.

hochschätzen *v.t.* to esteem highly.

Hoch: ~schätzung *f.* high esteem; **~schule** *f.* university, college (of university rank).

hochschwanger *a.* far advanced in pregnancy.

Hoch: ~seefischerei *f.* deep-sea fishing; **~seeschlepper** *m.* sea-going tug.

Hochseilakt *m.* tight-rope act.

Hochsitz *m.* raised hide.

Hochsommer *m.* midsummer.

Hoch: ~spannung *f.* high tension *or* voltage; **~spannungsleitung** *f.* high tension cable, power line; **~sprung** *m.* high jump.

hochspielen *v.t.* to blow up (incident).

Hochsprache *f.* (-, -n) standard language.

höchst *a.* & *adv.* highest; extremely; ~*e Zeit*, high time.

Hochstapler *m.* (-s,) **Hochstaplerin** *f.* (-, -nen) swindler, confidence trickster, fraud.

Höchst: ~belastung *f.* maximum load.

hochstehend *a.* high standing.

höchstenfalls *adv.* at most; at the very most.

höchstens *adv.* at most, at best.

Höchst: ~fall *m.* *im~* at the very most; **~form** *f.* top form, top condition; **~geschwindigkeit** *f.* speed limit, top speed; **~genze** *f.* ceiling.

hochstilisieren *v.t.* to build up.

Hochstimmung *f.* festive mood; high spirits.

Höchst: ~leistung *f.* record; **~preis** *m.* maximum price; **~strafe** maximum penalty.

höchstwahrscheinlich *adv.* very probably.

hoch: ~trabend *a.* pretentious; high-sounding, bombastic; **~verdient** *a.* of great merit; **~verehrt** *a.* highly respected.

Hoch: ~verrat *n.* high treason; **~wasser** *n.* flood.

hochwertig *a.* high grade, high-quality.

Hochwürden Reverend Father.

hochwürdig *a.* reverend.

Hochzeit *f.* wedding, marriage.

hochzeitlich *a.* nuptial.

Hochzeitsreise *f.* honeymoon.

hocken *v.i.* to squat.

Hocker *m.* (-s, -) stool.

Höcker *m.* (-s, -) bump.

höckerig *a.* uneven; hunch-backed.

Hode *f.* (-, -n) testicle.

Hodensack *m.* scrotum.

Hof *m.* (-[e]s, Höfe) yard; court; farm; (*um den Mond*) halo; (*opt.*) cornea; *den ~ machen,* to court.

Hofdame *f.* lady-in-waiting.

Hoffart *f.* (-, 0) price, haughtiness.

hoffen *v.i.* to hope; to expect.

hoffentlich *adv.* I hope, hopefully.

Hoffnung *f.* (-, -en) hope; expectation; *sich ~ machen,* to indulge in the hope of; *guter ~sein (von Frauen)* to be expecting a baby.

hoffnungs: **~los** *a.* hopeless, past hope; **~voll** *a.* hopeful; promising.

Hoffnungsschimmer *m.* glimmer of hope.

hofhalten *v.i.* to hold court.

Hofhund *m.* watchdog.

hofieren *v.i.* to court, to flatter.

höfisch *a.* courtly, courtier-like.

höflich *a.* courteous, polite.

Höflichkeit *f.* (-, -en) courteousness, courtesy, politeness.

Höflichkeits: **~besuch** *m.* courtesy visit; **~floskel** *f.* polite phrase.

Höfling *m.* (-s, -e) courtier.

Hof: **~mann** *m.* courtier; **~marschall** *m.* majordomo; **~narr** *m.* jester; **~schranze** *m.* (*pej.*) fawning courtier; **~staat** *m.* royal *or* princely household.

Höhe *f.* (-, -n) height hill; (*Luft, Geogr.*) altitude; (*der Preise*) level; *auf der ~,* up to date; *nicht ganz auf der ~,* not quite up to the mark; *auf der ~ von,* (*nav.*) off.

Hoheit *f.* (-, -en) grandeur; (*Titel*) Highness.

Hoheit: **~abzeichen** *n.* national emblem; **~gewässer** *n.* territorial waters; **~grenze** *f.* limit of territorial waters.

Hoheitsrecht *n.* right of the state.

Hohelied *n.* Song of Solomon.

Höhen: **~angst** *f.* fear of heights; **~krankheit** *f.* altitude sickness; **~kurort** *m.* high-altitude health resort; **~lage** *f.* high altitude; **~luft** *f.* mountain air; **~messer** *m.* (*avi.*) altimeter; **~sonne** *f.* ultraviolet rays *or* lamp; **~steuer** *n.* (*avi.*) elevator; **~zug** *m.* mountain range.

Höhepunkt *m.* climax, acme, peak.

hohl *a.* hollow; concave.

Höhle *f.* (-, -n) cave, cavern.

Höhlen: **~forscher** *m.*; **~forscherin** *f.* speleologist; **~forschung** *f.* speleology; **~malerei** *f.* cave-painting; **~mensch** *m.* cave-dweller.

Hohl: **~kopf** *m.* idiot; dimwit; **~maß** *n.* capacity measure; **~raum** *m.* cavity; **~saum** *m.* hemstitch; **~spiegel** *m.* concave mirror.

Höhlung *f.* (-, -en) hollow, cavity.

Hohlweg *m.* ravine.

Hohn *m.* (-[e]s, 0) scorn; derision.

höhnen *v.t.* to sneer (at).

Hohngelächter *n.* derisive laughter.

höhnisch *a.* scornful, sneering.

hohnlachen *v.i.* to laugh scornfully.

hohnsprechen *v.i.* to scorn; to make a mockery.

hökern *v.i.* to huckster.

Hokuspokus *m.* (-, 0) hocus-pocus.

hold *a.* fair, lovely, propitious.

holdselig *a.* charming, lovely.

holen *v.t.* to fetch; *sich etwas ~,* to catch; *Atem ~,* to breathe; **~lassen,** to send for.

holla! *i.* hullo! hulloa!

Holland *n.* (-s, 0) Holland.

Holländer *m.* (-s, -) Dutchman; Dutch; Dutch cheese.

Holländerin *f.* (-, -nen) Dutchwoman.

holländisch *a.* Dutch.

Hölle *f.* (-, 0) hell.

Höllenangst *f.* mortal fright.

Höllen: **~lärm** *m.* diabolical noise; **~maschine** *f.* infernal machine; **~pein** *f.,* **~qual** *f.* agony; **~qualen** *pl.* **~leiden** to suffer the torments of hell; **~tempo** *n.* breakneck speed.

höllisch *a.* hellish, infernal.

Hollywoodschaukel *f.* swinging garden bench.

Holm *m.* (*sp.*) bar; beam.

holpern *v.i.* to jolt, to be uneven.

holp(e)rig *a.* bumby, rough, rugged; rude.

holterdiepolter *adv.* helter-skelter.

Holunder *m.* (-s, -) elder.

Holz *n.* (-[e]s, Hölzer) wood, lumber, timber; bush, forest.

Holz: **~arbeit** *f.* woodwork; **~arbeiter** *m.* woodworker.

Holz: **~bläser** *m.,* **~bläserin** *f.* woodwind player; **~blasinstrument** *n.* woodwind instrument.

Holzbock *m.* sawing-block, jack.

hölzern *a.* wooden; (*fig.*) clumsy, awkward.

Holzfäler *m.* lumberjack; wood cutter.

Holzfaser *f.* wood fiber; **~stoff** *m.* wood cellulose; wood pulp.

Holzgas *n.* producer gas.

Holz: **~hacker** *m.* wood-chopper; **~hammer** *m.* mallet; **~hammermethode** *f.* (*fam.*) sledge-hammer method, **~handel** *m.* timber-trade; **~händler** *m.* timber-merchant.

holzig *a.* woody, wooded.

Holz: **~klotz** *m.* log; **~kohle** *f.* charcoal; **~pflock** *m.* peg; **~scheit** *m.* stick of wood; **~schnitt** *m.* woodcut; **~schnitzer** *m.* wood-carver; **~schnitzerei** *f.* woodcarving; **~schuh** *m.* clog; **~stoß** *m.* pile of wood; **~span** *m.* wood shaving; **~weg** *m.,* *auf dem ~wege sein,* to be on the wrong track; **~wolle** *f.* wood-wool; **~zellstoff** *m.* wood-pulp.

Holzung *f.* (-, -en) forest, wood.

Homo *m.* gay, homo, queer.

homogen *a.* homogeneous.

Homöopathie *f.* (-, 0) homeopathy.

Homosexualität *f.* homosexuality.

homosexuell *a.* homosexual.

Homosexuelle *m./f.* homosexual.

Honig *m.* (-s, 0) honey.

Honigmelone *f.* honeydew melon.

Honigwabe *f.* honeycomb.

Honorar *n.* (-s, -e) fee; royalty (author); *ein ~ berechnen,* to charge a fee.

Honoratioren *pl.* notabilities; local dignitaries.

honorieren *v.t.* to pay a fee.

honoris causa: *Professor h.c.* honorary professor.

Hopfen *m.* (-s, 0) hop; *an ihm ist ~ und Malz verloren*, he is past hope of amendment.
Hopfenstange *f.* hop-pole; (*fam. von Menschen*) beanpole.
hopp! *i.* hop! jump!
hoppeln *v.i.* to hop.
hopsen *v.i.* (*s*) to jump.
hopsgehen *v.i.st.* (*fam.*) to get broken; to kick the bucket.
hörbar *a.* audible.
horch! *i.* .
horchen *v.i.* to listen, to eavesdrop.
Horcher *m.* eavesdropper.
Horde *f.* (-, -n) horde; mob, gang.
hören *v.t.* to hear; to listen; *schwer ~*, to be hard of hearing; *hören Sie mal*, I say; *das läßt sich ~*, that sounds fair enough; *bei einem Professor ~*, to attend a professor's lectures.
Hörensagen *n.* hearsay; *vom ~*, by hearsay.
Hörer *m.* (-s, -) (*Radio*) listener; (*univ.*) student; (*tel.*) receiver.
Hörerschaft *f.* (-, -en) audience.
hörig *a.* enslaved; bond.
Hörigkeit *f.* (-, 0) bondage.
Horizont *m.* (-[e]s, -e) horizon.
Hormon *n.* (-, -e) hormone; *~drüsen f.pl.* ductless glands.
hormonal *a.* hormonal.
Horn *n.* (-[e]s, Hörner) horn; French horn, bugle.
Hornbläser *m.* **Hornbläserin** *f.* horn player.
Hornbrille *f.* hornrimmed glasses.
Hörnchen *n.* (*Gebäck*) crescent, croissant.
hörnern *a.* of horn.
Hornhaut *f.* cornea (*Auge*); callus.
Hornisse *f.* (-, -n) hornet.
Hornist *m.* (-en, -en) cornet-player.
Horoskop *n.* (-es, -e) horoscope; *das ~ stellen*, to cast a horoscope.
horrend *a.* horrendous.
Hörrohr *n.* ear-trumpet.
Horror *m.* horror.
Hörsaal *m.* lecture-room.
Hörspiel *n.* radio play.
Horst *m.* (-es, -e) eyrie, nest (of a bird of prey).
Hörsturz *m.* (*med.*) aural attack.
Hort *m.* (-[e]s, -e) hoard; (*fig.*) stronghold, retreat; protector; (*Kinder~*) ~, day nursery.
Hortensie *f.* (-, -n) hydrangea.
Hörweite *f.* hearing range; earshot.
Hose *f.* (-, -n) trousers *pl.*, pants; *Knie~* breeches *pl.*, knickerbockers, plus-fours *pl.*
Hosen: *~aufschläge pl.* turn-ups; *~bandorden m.* Order of the Garter; *~boden m.* seat of the trousers; *~schlitz m.* fly; *~träger pl.* suspenders.
Hospital *n.* (-[e]s, Hospitäler) hospital.
Hostie *f.* (-, -n) host, holy wafer.
Hotel *n.* (-s, -s) hotel; *~apartement n.* suite.
Hotel garni *n.* bed-and-breakfast hotel.
Hotelhalle *f.* lobby.
Hub *m.* (-es, Hübe) lift; (*Kolben*) stroke.
Hubbel *m.* bump.
hubbelig *a.* bumpy.
hüben *adv.* on this side; *~ und drüben*, on each (either) side.
Hubraum *m.* cubic capacity.
hübsch *a.* pretty, fair; proper; *das ist nicht ~ von ihm*,

that's hardly fair of him.
Hubschrauber *m.* (-s, -) helicopter; *~landeplatz m.* heliport; helicopter pad.
huckepack *adv.* pick-a-pack; piggy back.
hudeln *v.t.* to bungle, to work sloppily.
Huf *m.* (-[e]s, -e) hoof.
Hufbeschlag *m.* (horse)-shoeing.
Hufe *f.* (-, -n) hide of land.
Hufeisen *n.* horse-shoe.
Hufschmied *m.* blacksmith, farrier; *~e f.* shoeing-forge.
Hüftbein *n.* hip bone.
Hüfte *f.* (-, -n) hip.
Hüftgelenk *n.* hip joint.
Huftier *n.* hoofed animal; ungulate.
Hügel *m.* (-s, -) hill, hillock.
Hügelgrab *n.* barrow; tumulus.
hüg[e]lig *a.* hilly.
Hügelkette *f.* chain/range of hills.
Hugenotte *m.*; **Hugenottin** *f.* Huguenot.
Huhn *n.* (-[e]s, Hühner) chicken; fowl; hen.
Hühnchen *n.* (-s, -) chicken.
Hühner: *~auge n.* corn (on the foot); *~braten m.* roast chicken; *~futter n.* chickensfeed; *~korb m.* hencoop; *~stall m.* chicken-house; *~stange, ~steige, f.* hen-roost.
Huld *f.* (-, 0) grace, favor.
huldigen *v.i.* to pay, render, *or* do homage; to hold (an opinion); to indulge in.
Huldigung *f.* (-, -en) homage, tribute.
huldvoll *a.* benevolent.
Hülfe = **Hilfe**.
Hülle *f.* (-, -n) cover, veil, wrapper; *~und Fülle*, abundance, enough and to spare.
hüllen *v.t.* to cover, to wrap.
Hülse *f.* (-, -n) hull; husk; (*Patronen*) case.
Hülsenfrucht *f.* legume; pulse.
human *a.* humane.
humanisieren *v.t.* to humanize.
Humanisierung *f.* humanization.
Humanismus *m.* (-, 0) humanism; Humanism.
humanitär *a.* humanitarian.
Humanität *f.* (-, 0) humanity.
Humanmedizin *f.* human medecine.
Humbug *m.* (-s, 0) humbug, nonsense.
Hummel *f.* (-, -n) bumble-bee.
Hummer *m.* (-s, -n) lobster.
Hummerkrabbe *f.* king prawn.
Humor *m.* (-s, -e) humor.
Humoreske *f.* (-, -n) humorous sketch.
humorig *a.* humorous.
Humorist *m.*; **Humoristin** *f.* humorist; comedian.
humoristisch *a.* humorous.
humpeln *v.i.* (h, s) to hobble, to limp.
Humpen *m.* (-s, -) tankard.
Hund *m.* (-[e]s, -e) dog, hound; *auf den ~ kommen*, to go to the dogs.
hundelend *a.* wretched, lousy.
Hunde: *~halsband n.* dog-collar; *~hütte f.* kennel; *~kälte f.* bitter, sharp cold; *~kuchen m.* dog-biscuit; *~leben n.* dog's life; *~rasse f.* breed of dog.
hundert *a.* hundred.
Hunderter *m.* hundred-mark-note.
hunderterlei *a.* of a hundred sorts.
hundertfach *a.* hundredfold.
Hundertjahrfeier *f.* centenary; centennial.

Hundertjährige *m./f.* centenarian.
hundertmal *adv.* hundred times.
hundertste *a.* hundredth.
Hündin *f.* (-, -nen) bitch.
hündisch *a.* doglike; servile; mean.
Hundstage *m.pl.* dog-days *pl.*
Hüne *m.* (-n, -n) giant.
Hünengrab *n.* megalithic tomb; barrow.
Hunger *m.* (-s, 0) hunger; ~ *haben,* to be hungry; ~ *leiden,* to starve; ~*s sterben,* to die of hunger, to starve to death.
Hungerleider *m.* (-s, -) starveling.
Hungerlohn *m.* starvation wages, pittance.
hungern *v.i.imp.* to hunger, to be hungry.
Hungersnot *f.* famine.
Hunger: ~streik *m.* hunger strike; **~tod** *m.* starvation.
hungrig *a.* hungry.
Hunne *m.* Hun.
Hupe *f.* (-, -n) horn.
hupen *v.i.* to hoot.
hüpfen *v.i.* (*s*) to hop, to skip.
Hupzeichen *n.* horn-signal.
Hürde *f.* (-, -n) hurdle; pen, fold.
Hure *f.* (-, -n) prostitute, whore.
huren *v.i.* to whore, to fornicate.
Hurerei *f.* (-, 0) whoring, whoredom.
hurra *i.* hurrah!
hurtig *a.* quick, swift, nimble, agile.
Husar *m.* (-en, -en) hussar.
husch *i.* quick!
huschen *v.i.* (*s*) to scurry, to whisk.
hüsteln *v.i.* to cough slightly.
Husten *m.* (-s, 0) cough.
husten *v.i.* to cough.
Hutablage *f.* hat rack.
Hut *m.* (-[e]s, Hüte) hat, bonnet; (*Zucker*) loaf; ~ *f.* keeping, charge, guard; *auf der ~sein,* to be on one's guard.
hüten *v.t.* to guard, to watch, to tend, to keep; (sich)~ *v.refl.* to be on one's guard, to beware (of); *das Bett, das Zimmer ~,* to be confined to one's bed, room.
Hüter *m.* (-s, -) keeper, guardian.
Hut: ~krempe *f.* brim (of a hat); **~macher** *m.* hatter; **~schachtel** *f.* hat-box.
Hütte *f.* (-, -n) hut, cabin; shack; (*Werkhaus*) foundry, smelting works, forge.
Hütten: ~industrie *f.* iron and steel industry; **~käse** *m.* cottage cheese; **~schuh** *m.* slipper-sock; **~werk** *n.* metallurgical plant.
Hüttenwesen *n.* metallurgy.
Hyäne *f.* (-, -n) hyena.
Hyazinthe *f.* (-, -n) hyacinth.
Hydraulik *f.* hydraulics.
hydraulisch *a.* hydraulic.
hydrieren *v.t.* to hydrogenate.
Hydrokultur *f.* hydroponics.
Hygiene *f.* (-, 0) hygiene.
hygienisch *a.* hygienic.
Hymne *f.* (-, -n) hymn.
Hyperbel (-, -n) hyperbole; (*geom.*) hyperbola.
hyperbolisch *a.* hyperbolical.
hyperkorrekt *a.* (*fam.*) hypercorrect.
Hypnose *f.* (-, -n) hypnosis.
hypnotisieren *v.t.* to hypnotize.
Hypochonder *m.* (-s, -) hypochondriac.
Hypochondrie *f.* (-, 0) hypochondria.
hypochondrisch *a.* hypochondriac.
Hypothek *f.* (-, -en) mortgage; *eine ~für verfallen erklären,* to foreclose a mortgage; **~enschuld** *f.* debt on mortgage.
hypothekarisch *a.* hypothecary.
Hypothese *f.* (-, -n) hypothesis.
hypothetisch *a.* hypothetical.
Hysterie *f.* (-, 0) hysteria.
hysterisch *a.* hysterical.

I

I, i *n.* the letter I or i.
iambisch *a.* iambic.
iberisch *a.* Iberian; *Iberische Halbinsel* Iberian Peninsula.
ich *pn.* I, I myself.
Ich *n.* self, ego.
ichbezogen *a.* egocentric.
Ichbezogenheit *f.* egocentricity.
Ich-Form *f.* first person.
Ideal *n.* (-[e]s, -e) ideal; ~ *a.* ideal.
idealisieren *v.t.* to idealize.
Idealismus *m.* idealism.
idealistisch *a.* idealistic.
Idee *f.* (-, -n) idea, notion; *um eine ~ zu lang,* just a thought too long.
ideell *a.* non-material, spiritual.
ideenreich *a.* full of ideas; inventive.
Identifikation *f.* identification.
identifizierbar *a.* identifiable.
identifizieren *v.t.* to identify.
identisch *a.* identical.
Identität *f.* (-, -en) identity; **~skrise** *f.* identity crisis; **~sverlust** *m.* loss of identity.
Ideologe *m.*; **Ideologin** *f.* ideologue.
Ideologie *f.* (-, -n) ideology.
ideologisch *a.* ideological.
Idiom *n.* idiom.
idiomatisch *a.* idiomatic.
Idiot *m.* idiot.
idiotensicher *a.* foolproof.
Idiotie *f.* idiocy.
Idiotin *f.* idiot.
idiotisch *a.* idiotic; stupid.
Idol *n.* idol.
Idyll *n.* (-s, -en) idyll.
Idylle *f.* idyll.
idyllisch *a.* idyllic.
Igel *m.* (-s, -) hedgehog.
Iglu *m./f.* igloo.
Ignorant *m.* (-en, -en) (*fam.*) ignoramus.
Ignoranz *f.* ignorance.
ignorieren *v.t.* to take no notice of; (*einen*) to cut.
ihm *pn.* (to) him; (to) it.
ihn *pn.* him, it.
ihnen *pn.* (to) them.
ihr *pn.* (to) her, their.

ihrerseits *adv.* on their (her) part.

ihresgleichen *pn.* people like her/them; **Ihresgleichen** people like you.

ihrethalben, ihretwegen, um ihretwillen *adv.* for her, their sake; *Ihrethalben, etc* for your sake.

ihrige *pn.* hers, theirs; *Ihrige,* yours.

Ikone *f.* icon.

illegal *a.* illegal.

Illegalität *f.* illegality.

Illumination *f.* illumination.

illuminieren *v.t.* to illuminate; to color.

illusionär *a.* illusory.

illustrieren *v.t.* to illustrate.

Illustrierte *f.* magazine.

Iltis *m.* (-tisses, -tisse) polecat.

im = in dem.

imaginär *a.* imaginary.

Imbiß *m.* (-bisses, -bisse) snack; light meal.

Imbißraum *m.* teashop, snackbar.

imitieren *v.t.* to imitate.

Imker *m.* (-s, -) beekeeper.

Imkerei *f.* beekeeping; apiary.

immanent *a.* inherent.

Immatrikulation *f.* (university) registration.

immatrikulieren *v.t.* to register; to matriculate.

immens *a. & adv.* immense(ly).

immer *adv.* always, ever; *noch ~,* still; *~ besser,* better and better; *~ wieder,* again and again, over and over again; *~zu,* continually.

immerdar *adv.* for ever.

immerfort *adv.* for ever and ever, continually.

Immergrün *n.* (-s, 0) evergreen.

immerhin *adv.* at least; anyhow; at any rate; still, yet.

immer mehr *adv.* more and more.

immerwährend *a.* perpetual.

Immigrant *m.;* **Immigrantin** *f.* immigrant.

immigrieren *v.i.* to immigrate.

Immobilien *pl.* immovables *pl.* real estate.

Immobilienmakler *m.* realtor.

immun *a.* immune.

immunisieren *v.t.* to immunize.

Immunisierung *f.* immunization.

Immunität *f.* (-, -en) immunity.

Immunkörper *m.* (-s, -) antibody.

Imperativ *m.* (-s, -e) imperative.

Imperfekt *n.* imperfect tense.

Imperialismus *m.* imperialism.

imperialistisch *a.* imperialistic.

Imperium *n.* (-s, -rien) empire.

impertinent *a.* impertinent, impudent.

Impetus *m.* impetus; verve; zest.

impfen *v.t.* to vaccinate, to inoculate.

Impfschein *m.* certificate of vaccination.

Impfstoff *m.* vaccine.

Impfung *f.* (-, -en) vaccination.

Implantat *n.* (-s, -e) (*med.*) implant.

implantieren *v.t.* to implant.

Implikation *f.* (-, -en) implication.

implizieren *v.t.* to implicate; (*stillschweigend*) to imply.

implizit *a.* implicit.

Imponderabilien *pl.* imponderables *pl.*

imponieren *v.i.* to impress forcibly, to overawe; *~d a.* impressive.

Imponiergehabe *n.* display behavior; (*fig.*) attempt to impress.

Import *m.* (-s, -en) import; imports.

Importeur *m.* importer.

importieren *v.t.* to import.

imposant *a.* imposing; impressive.

Impotenz *f.* (-, 0) impotence.

imprägnieren *v.t.* to impregnate; to waterproof.

imprägniert *a.* waterproofed.

Imprägnierung *f.* impregnation, waterproofing.

Impression *f.* impression.

Impressionismus *m.* impressionism.

Impressum *n.* imprint; masthead (newspaper).

Improvisation *f.* improvisation.

improvisieren *v.i.* to improvise.

Impuls *m.* (-es, -e) stimulus; impulse.

impulsiv *a.* impulsive.

Impulsivität *f.* impulsiveness.

imstande *adv.* able.

in *pr.* in, into; at; within.

inadäquat *a.* inadequate.

inakzeptabel *a.* unacceptable.

Inangriffnahme *f.* taking in hand.

Inanspruchnahme *f.* (-, -n) strain; demands.

Inbegriff *m.* essence, substance.

inbegriffen *a.* included, inclusive of.

Inbetrieb: *~nahme f.; ~setzung f.* (-, -en) opening.

Inbrunst *f.* (-, 0) fervor; ardor.

inbrünstig *a.* ardent, fervent.

indem *c.* while, when; as, because.

Inder *m.;* **Inderin** *f.* Indian.

indes, indessen *c.* however.

Indianer *m.;* **Indianerin** *f.* (American) Indian; Native American.

indianisch *a.* Indian.

Indien *a.* (-s, -) India.

Indienststellung *f.* (-, -en) (*Kriegsschiff*) commissioning.

indigniert *a.* indignant.

Indigo *m.* (-s, 0) indigo.

Indikativ *m.* (-s, -e) indicative (mood).

indikativisch *a.* indicative.

Indikator *m.* (-s, -en) indicator.

Indio *m.* (-s, -s) Indian (central/south America).

indirekt *a.* indirect.

indisch *a.* Indian.

indiskret *a.* indiscreet, ill-advised.

Indiskretion *f.* (-, -en) indiscretion.

indisponiert *a.* indisposed.

Individualismus *m.* individualism.

individualistisch *a.* individualistic.

Individualität *f.* (-, -en) individuality.

individuell *a.* individual.

Individuum *n.* (-s, -duen) individual.

Indiz *n.* (-es, -zien) indication, sign.

Indizienbeweis *m.* circumstantial evidence.

indoeuropäisch *a.* Indo-European.

indoktrinieren *v.t.* to indoctrinate.

Indonesien *n.* (-s, 0) Indonesia.

Indonesier *m.;* **Indonesierin** *f.;* **indonesisch** *a.* Indonesian.

Indossant *m.* (-en, -en) endorser.

Indossat *m.* (-en, -en) endorsee.

indossieren *v.t.* to endorse.

Induktion *f.* (-, -en) induction.

industrialisieren *v.t.* to industrialize.

Industrie f. (-, -[e]n) industry.
industriell a. industrial.
Industrielle m./f. industrialist.
Industrie- und Handelskammer f. Chamber of Industry and Commerce.
induzieren v.t. to induce.
ineinander adv. with one another; with each other.
ineinandergreifen v.i. (mech.) to mesh.
Ineinanderspiel n. (-[e]s, 0) interplay.
infam a. infamous, scandalous.
Infamie f. (-, 0) infamy, enormity.
Infanterie f. (-, 0) infantry.
Infanterist m. (-en, -en) foot-soldier.
infantil a. infantile.
Infarkt m. infarct.
Infekt m. **Infektion** f. infection.
Infektions: ~**gefahr** f. risk of infection; ~**herd** m. seat of the infection; ~**krankheit** f. (-, -en) contagious disease.
infektiös a. infectious.
infernalisch a. infernal.
infiltrieren v.t. to infiltrate.
Infinitiv m. (-s, -e) infinitive.
infizieren v.t. to infect.
in flagranti adv. in flagrante.
Inflation f. inflation.
inflationär a. inflationary.
Info n. (-s, -s) (fam.) (Informationsblatt) hand-out.
Info f. (-, -s) (fam.) (Information) piece of info.
infolge pr. owing to, in consequence of; ~**dessen** adv. consequently.
Informant m.; **Informantin** f. informant.
Informatik f. (-, 0) computer science.
Informatiker m., **Informatikerin** f. computer scientist.
Information f. (-, -en) information.
Informations: ~**austausch** m. exchange of information; ~**fluß** m. flow of information; ~**schalter** m., ~**stand** m. information desk.
informativ a. informative.
informell a. informal.
informieren v.t. to inform.
infrarot a. infra-red.
Infrastruktur f. infrastructure.
Infusion f. (-, -en) infusion.
Infusorien pl. infusoria.
Ingenieur m. (-s, -e) engineer; ~**büro** n. engineering office.
Ingrimm m. (-[e]s, 0) anger, spite, wrath.
ingrimmig a. angry, wrathful.
Ingwer m. (-s, 0) ginger.
Inhaber m. (-s, -) possessor, holder; occupant; (eines Wechsels) payee, bearer.
Inhaberaktie f. bearer share.
inhaftieren v.t. to imprison.
Inhaftierung f. (-, -en) detention.
Inhalation f. inhalation.
inhalieren v.t. to inhale.
Inhalt m. (-[e]s, -e) contents, tenor, substance; volume; des ~s, to the effect.
inhaltlich a. & adv. material; in substance.
Inhaltsangabe f. summary, synopsis.
inhalt[s]leer, inhalt[s]los a. empty, meaningless.
Inhaltsverzeichnis n. table of contents, index.
inhuman a. inhuman; inhumane.

Initiale f. (-, -n) initial.
Initialzündung f. detonation.
Initiative f. (-, 0) initiative; die ~ ergreifen, to take the initiative.
Initiator m., **Initiatorin** f. initiator.
initiieren v.t. to initiate.
Injektion f. (-, -en) injection; ~**snadel** f. hypodermic needle; ~**sspritze** f. hypodermic syringe.
injiziieren v.t. to inject.
Injurie f. (-, -n) insult.
Inkarnation f. incarnation.
Inkasso n. (-, -s) cashing, collection.
inklusive pr. inclusive of; including.
inkompetent a. incompetent.
Inkonsequenz f. (-s, -en) inconsistency.
Inkrafttreten n. (-s, 0) coming into force.
Inkubation f. incubation; ~**szeit** f. incubation period.
Inkunabel f. (-, -n) incunabula.
Inland n. (-[e]s, 0) inland, interior; im In~ und Ausland, at home and abroad.
Inländer m. (-s, -); **Inländerin** f. (-, -nen) native citizen.
inländisch a. domestic; native, inland; indigenous.
Inlaut m. (-s, -e) medial sound.
Inlett n. (-s, -e) tick, ticking.
inliegend a. enclosed.
inmitten pr. in the midst/middle of.
inne: ~**haben** v.t.ir. to possess; ~**halten** v.i.st. to stop, to pause.
innen adv. within, inside, indoors; nach ~, inwards, inwardly; von ~, (from) within, on the inside; von ~ und aussen kennen, to know the ins and outs of.
Innen: ~**dekoration** f. interior decoration; ~**leben** n. inner life; ~**politik** f. domestic politics; ~**raum** m. interior.
Innenseite f. inside, inner side.
inner a. interior, internal, inner.
Innere n. (-[e]s, 0) inside, interior; Home Office (England), Ministry of the Interior.
Innereien pl. entrails; (cul.) offal.
innerhalb pr. within; inside.
innerlich a. inward; internal, intrinsic.
innerparteilich a. within the party.
innerstaatlich a. internal, domestic.
innerst a. inmost, innermost.
Innerzonen... intrazonal.
innewerden v.refl.st. to become aware of.
innewohnen v.i. to be inherent.
innig a. hearty, heartfelt; intimate.
Innigkeit f. (-, 0) cordiality, fervor.
Innung f. (-, -en) corporation, guild.
inoffiziell a. unofficial.
in petto adv. etw. ~ haben to have s.th. up one's sleeve.
in puncto pr. as regards.
ins = in das.
Insasse m. (-n, -n) inmate (Haus); (Schiff, Abteil) passenger.
insbesondere adv. especially.
Inschrift f. (-, -en) inscription.
Insekt n. (-[e]s, -en) insect.
Insektenlehre f. entomology.
Insektenpulver n. **Insektizid** n. insecticide, insect powder.
Insektenstich m. insect-sting (bee); insect bite

(mosquito).

Insel *f.* (-, -n) island, isle.

Inserat *n.* (-[e]s, -e) advertisement.

inserieren *v.t. & i.* to advertise.

insgeheim *adv.* privately, secretly.

insgemein *adv.* generally, commonly.

insgesamt *adv.* altogether, collectively.

Insignien *pl.* insignia *pl.*, badge of office.

insofern *adv.* in so far as; in this respect.

insolvent *a.* insolvent.

Insolvenz *f.* (-, -en) insolvency.

insoweit *adv.* (in) so far.

Inspektion *f.* inspection; service; *das Auto zur ~ bringen*, to take the car in for service.

inspirieren *v.t.* to inspire.

inspizieren *v.t.* to inspect, to examine.

Installateur *m.* (-s, -e) plumber; electrician *or* gas fitter.

installieren *v.t.* to install.

instandhalten *v.t.st.* to maintain; to service.

Instandhaltung *f.* (-, -en) maintenance.

inständig *a.* instant, urgent.

instandsetzen *v.t.* to enable; to repair.

Instanz *f.* (-, -en) instance; *höhere ~*, superior court; *höchste ~*, highest court of appeal; *in der letzten ~*, in the last resort; *im ~enweg*, through (official) channels.

Instinkt *m.* (-[e]s, -e) instinct.

instinktiv *a. & adv.* instinctive(ly).

instinktmäßig *a. & adv.* instinctive(ly).

Institut *n.* (-[e]s, -e) institute.

Institution *f.* (-, -en) institution.

institutionalisieren *v.t.* to institutionalize.

institutionell *a.* institutional.

instruieren *v.t.* to instruct; to inform.

instruktiv *a.* instructive; informative.

Instrument *n.* (-[e]s, -e) instrument.

Instrumentarium *n.* (-s, -rien) equipment; instrument; apparatus.

instrumentieren *v.t.* (*mus.*) to orchestrate.

Insuffizienz *f.* (-, -en) insufficiency.

inszenieren *v.t.* to stage, to produce (a play); to direct.

Inszenierung *f* (-, -en) staging; direction; production; (*pej.*) engineering.

intakt *a.* intact; in working condition.

Intarsie *f.* (-, -n) intarsia.

integer *a. eine integre Persönlichkeit* a person of integrity.

Integralrechnung *f.* integral calculus.

Integration *f.* (-, -en) integration.

integrieren *v.t.* to integrate.

Integrierung *f.* (-, -en) integration.

Integrität *f.* integrity.

Intellekt *m.* (-s, 0) intellect.

intellektuell *a.* intellectual.

Intellektuelle *m./f.* intellectual.

intelligent *a.* intelligent.

Intelligenz *f.* (-, 0) intelligence.

Intelligenzquotient *m.* (-s, -en) intelligence quotient, IQ.

Intendant *m.* (-en, -en) (*theat.*) manager and artistic director.

intendieren *v.t.* to intend.

Intensität *f.* intensity.

intensiv *a.* intensive; intense.

intensivieren *v.t.* to intensify.

Intensivierung *f.* intensification.

Intensivstation *f.* intensive care unit.

Intention *f.* intention.

interdisziplinär *a.* interdisciplinary.

Intercity *m.* inter-city, IC; *~Express m.* inter-city-express (train) ICE.

interessant *a.* interesting.

Interesse *n.* (-s, -n) interest.

Interessenssphäre *f.* sphere of influence.

Interessent *m.* (-en, -en) prospective customer.

interessieren *v.t.* to interest, to concern; (sich) *~ v.refl.* to take an interest (in).

interessiert *a.* interested; grasping.

Interimsregierung *f.* interim government.

interimistisch *a.* temporary.

Interkontinentalflug *m.* (-s, -flüge) intercontinental flight.

Interkontinentalrakete *f.* intercontinental balistic missile.

Intermezzo *n.* (-[e]s, -s) interlude.

intern *a.* internal.

Internat *n.* (-[e]s, -e) boarding school.

international *a.* international.

internationalisieren *v.t.* to internationalize.

internieren *v.t.* to intern.

Internierte *m./f.* (-ten, -ten) internee.

Internierung *f.* (-, -en) internment.

Internist *m.*; **Internistin** *f.* internist.

interparlamentarisch *a.* interparliamentary.

Interpret *m.*, **Interpretin** *f.* performer, singer; intepreter.

Interpretation *f.* interpretation.

interpretieren *v.i.* to interpret.

Interpunktion *f.* (-, -en) punctuation; *~szeichen n.* punctuation mark.

Interrailkarte *f.* Interrailcard (train).

**Interrogativ . . . a.* interrogative (pronoun etc.).

Intervall *n.* interval.

intervenieren *v.i.* to intervene.

Intervention *f.* intervention.

Interview *n.* interview.

interviewen *v.t.* to interview.

Interviewer *m.*; **Interviewerin** *f.* interviewer.

Interviewte *m./f.* interviewee.

Inthronisation *f.* enthronement.

intim, *a.* intimate.

Intimbereich *m.* genital area; private parts.

Intimität *f.* intimacy.

Intimsphäre *f.* private life.

Intimverkehr *m.* intimate relations.

intolerant *a.* intolerant.

Intoleranz *f.* (-, 0) intolerant.

intonieren *v.t.* to start to sing/to play (music).

intransitiv *a.* intransitive.

intravenös *a.* intravenous.

Intrigant *m.*; **Intrigantin** *f.* schemer, intriguer.

Intrige *f.* intrigue.

intrigieren *v.i.* to plot, to intrigue.

introvertiert *a.* introverted.

Intuition *f.* intuition.

intuitiv *a. & adv.* intuitive(ly).

Invalide *m.* (-n, -n) invalid, disabled person.

Invalidenversicherung *f.* disability insurance.

invariabel *a.* invariable.

Invasion *f.* invasion.

Inventar *n.* (-s, -e) inventory; *das ~ aufnehmen*, to take stock, to inventory.
inventarisieren *v.t.* to inventory.
Inventur *f.* (-, -en) stock-taking.
Inversion *f.* inversion.
investieren *v.t.* to invest.
Investierung *f.* (-, -en) **Investition** *f.* (-, -en) investment.
Investitions: *~güter pl.* capital goods; *~lenkung f.* investment control.
Investmentfonds *m.* investment fund.
inwendig *a.* interior, inner; *~ adv.* inside, within.
inwiefern, inwieweit *adv.* (in) how far.
Inzest *m.* incest.
Inzucht *f.* (-, 0) in-breeding; intermarriage.
inzwischen *adv.* meanwhile.
ionisiert *a.* (*elek.*) ionized.
Ionosphäre *f.* ionosphere.
I-Punkt *m.* dot over the i.
Irak *m.* (-s, 0) Iraq.
Iraker *m.*; **Irakerin** *f.*; **irakisch** *a.* Iraqi.
Iran *m.* Iran.
Iraner *m.*; **Iranerin** *f.*; **iranisch** *a.* Iranian.
irden *a.* earthen.
irdisch *a.* earthly; temporal; worldly.
Ire *m.* (-n, -n) Irishman.
irgend *adv.* at all, possibly; any(where); *wenn ~ möglich*, if at all possible; *~ etwas*, anything, something; *~jemand*, anybody, somebody.
irgendein *pn.* any(one), anybody (*attr.*) some.
irgendwann *adv.* some time.
irgendwas *pn.* something.
irgendwer *pn.* somebody.
irgendwie *adv.* anyhow.
irgendwo *adv.* anywhere, somewhere.
irgendwoher *adv.* from some place (or other).
irgendwohin *adv.* (to) anywhere, somewhere.
Irin *f.* (-, -nen) Irishwoman.
irisch *a.* Irish.
irisieren *v.i.* to iridesce; *~d a.* iridescent.
Irland *n.* (-s, 0) Ireland.
Ironie *f.* (-, 0) irony.
ironisch *a. & adv.* ironical(ly).
ironisieren *v.t.* to ironize.
irrational *a. & adv.* irrational(ly).
Irrationalität *f.* irrationality.
irre *a. & adv.* mad, astray, wrong; insane; *~werden (an)*, to lose confidence (in); *~gehen*, to lose one's way; *~führen*, to lead astray; *sich nicht ~machen lassen*, not to be easily put out *or* perplexed.
Irre *m./f.* (-n, -n) madman, lunatic.
Irre *f. in die ~ gehen* to go astray; to make a mistake;

in die ~ führen to mislead; to deceive.
irreal *a.* unreal.
irreführen *v.t.* to mislead; *~d a.* misleading.
irrelevant *a.* irrelevant.
irremachen *v.t.* to disconcert.
irren *v.i.* to err; to go astray; (sich) *~ v.refl.* to be mistaken.
Irren: *~anstalt f.n.* lunatic asylum, mental institution; *~haus n.* (*fig.*) madhouse.
irreparabel *a.* irreparable.
Irr: *~fahrt f.* odyssey, wandering, vagary; *~garten m.* maze.
Irrglaube *m.* misconception.
irrgläubig *a.* heretical.
irrig *a.* erroneous, wrong, false.
Irritation *f.* irritation.
irritieren *v.t./i.* to irritate; to annoy; to put off.
Irr: *~lehre f.* heresy; false doctrine; *~lehrer m.* heretic; *~licht n.* will-o'-the-wisp, jack o' lantern.
Irrsinn *m.* madness, insanity.
irrsinnig *a.* insane, deranged.
Irrtum *m.* (-[e]s, -tümer) error, mistake; fallacy.
irrtümlich *a. & adv.* incorrect, wrong; mistaken(ly), erroneous(ly).
Irrung *f.* (-, -en) error; misunderstanding, mistake.
Irrwahn *m.* delusion.
Ischias *f.* (-, 0) sciatica.
Ischiasnerv *m.* sciatic nerv.
Islam *m.* (-(s), 0) Islam.
islamisch *a.* Islamic.
Island *n.* (-s, 0) Iceland.
Isländer *m.*; **Isländerin** *f.* Icelander.
isländisch *a.* Icelandic.
Isobare *f.* (-, -n) isobar.
Isolation *f.* isolation; insulation; *~shaft f.* solitary confinement.
Isolator *m.* (-s, -en) insulator.
Isolierband *n.* (*elek.*) insulating tape.
isolieren *v.t.* to isolate; to insulate (electric wire).
Isolierstation *f.* (*med.*) isolation ward.
Isolierung *f.* isolation; insulation; sound proofing.
Isotherme *f.* (-, -n) (*met.*) isotherm.
Isotop *n.* (-s, -e) isotope.
Israel *n.* (-s, 0) Israel.
Israeli *m./f.*; **israelisch** *a.* Israeli.
Israelit *m.*; **Israelitin** *f.*; **israelitisch** *a.* Israelite.
Istbestand *m.* (-[e]s, -bestände) actual stock.
Iststärke *f.* (-, -n) actual strength.
Italien *n.* (-s, 0) Italy.
Italiener *m.* (-s, -); **Italienerin** *f.* (-, -nen); **italienisch** *a.* Italian.
I-tüpfelchen *n.* dot over the i; finishing touch.

J

J, jn. the letter J *or* j.
ja *adv.* yes; aye; even; *er ist ~ mein Bruder*, he is my brother, you know.
Jacht *f.* (-, -en) yacht.
Jacke *f.* (-, -en) jacket; cardigan.
Jackett *n.* (-s, -e) jacket.
Jagd *f.* (-, -en) chase; hunting; shooting; shoot; *auf die ~ gehen*, to go hunting, shooting.
Jagd: *~beute f.* bag; kill; *~falke m.* falcon; *~fieber n.* hunting-fever; *~flinte f.* shotgun; *~flugzeug n.*

fighter; **frevel** *m.* poaching; *~gesellschaft f.* hunting party; *~gesetz n.* game law; *~haus n.* hunting lodge; *~hund m.* gun-dog; hound; *~hütte f.* shooting box; *~saison f.* open season; *~schein m.* hunting *or* shooting license; *~zeit f.* hunting season.
jagen *v.t.* to chase, to hunt; *ins Bockshorn ~*, to bully, to intimidate; *~ v.i.* (*s*) to rush.
Jäger *m.* (-s, -) hunter, sportsman.
Jägerin *f.* huntress.

Jägerlatein *n.* tall stories *pl.*

jäh *a.* steep, precipitous; sudden.

jählings *adv.* suddenly, abruptly.

Jahr *n.* (-[e]s, -e) year; *übers* ~, a year hence; *von* ~ *zu* ~, one year after another; ~ *ein*, ~ *aus*, year in, year out.

Jahrbuch *n.* year-book.

jahrelang *a. & adv.* for years.

jähren (sich) *v.refl.* to be a year ago.

Jahres: ~**ausgleich** *m.* end-of-year adjustment; ~**bericht** *a.* annual report; ~**frist** *f.* a year's time; ~**tag** *m.* anniversary; ~**urlaub** *m.* (*mil.*) annual leave; ~**wende** *f.*, ~**wechsel** *m.* New Year; ~**zahl** *f.* (date of the) year; ~**zeit** *f.* season.

Jahrgang *m.* year; annual set; ~*1902*, persons born in 1902 (*esp. mil.*); (*Wein*) vintage.

Jahrhundert *n.* (-s, -e) century.

Jahrhundertfeier *f.* centenary.

Jahrhundertwende *f.* turn of the century.

jährlich *a.* yearly, annual; ~ *adv.* annually.

Jahrmarkt *m.* fair; fun-fair.

Jahrtausend *n.* (-s, -e) millennium.

Jahrzehnt *n.* (-[e]s, -e) decade.

Jähzorn *m.* violent anger, fit, outburst.

jähzornig *a.* violent-tempered.

Jakob *m.* Jacob, James.

Jakobiner *m.* (-s, -) Jacobin.

Jalousie *f.* (-, -n) Venetian blind.

Jamaika *n.* Jamaica.

Jamaikaner *m.*; **Jamaikanerin** *f.*; **jamaikanisch** *a.* Jamaican.

jambisch *a.* iambic.

Jambus *m.* (-, -ben) iambus; iamb.

Jammer *m.* (-s, 0) lamentation; misery.

Jammer: ~**bild** *n.* miserable sight; ~**gestalt** *f.* pitiful creature; ~**lappen** *m.* (*fig.*) coward.

jämmerlich *a.* pathetic, pitiful, miserable, wretched.

jammern *v.i.* to lament, to moan; ~ *v.t.pers. & imp.* to feel pity, to pity.

jammerschade *a.* a thousand pities.

Jammertal *n.* vale of tears.

jammervoll *a.* deplorable, piteous.

Januar *m.* (-s, -e) January.

Japan *n.* (-s, 0) Japan.

Japaner *m.* (-s, -); **Japanerin** *f.* (-, -nen); **japanisch** *a.* Japanese.

japsen *v.i.* to pant.

Jargon *m.* jargon; slang.

Jasager *m.* yes-man.

Jasmin *m.* (-s, -e) jasmine, jessamine.

Jaspis *m.* (-pisses, -pisse) jasper.

Jastimme *f.* yes-vote.

jäten *v.t.* to weed.

Jauche *f.* (-, -n) liquid manure.

jauchzen *v.i.* to cheer, to shout, to exult.

jaulen *v.i.* to howl, to yowl.

Jause *f.* snack.

jawohl *adv.* yes (indeed).

Jawort *n.* consent.

Jazz *m.* (-es, -e) jazz; ~**band** *f.* jazzband.

je *adv.* ever; *von* ~*her*, from the remotest times; ~ *nachdem*, according to; ~*nach*, in proportion to; ~*zwei*, two at a time; every two; ~ *zwei Mark*, two shillings each; ~ *mehr desto besser*, the more the better.

Jeans *pl./f.* jeans.

jedenfalls *adv.* at all events, at any rate.

jeder, jede, jedes *pn.* every, every one, each.

jedermann *pn.* (-[e]s) every one, everybody.

jederzeit *adv.* always, at any time.

jedesmal *adv.* every *or* each time; ~ *wenn*, whenever.

jedoch *c.* yet, however, nevertheless.

jedweder *pn.* each, every one.

jeglicher, jegliche, jegliches *pn.* every, each.

jeher *adv.* *seit*~, *von*~ always; from time immemorial.

jemals *adv.* ever, at any time.

jemand *pn.* (-es) somebody, anyone.

Jemen *n./m.* Yemen.

jener, jene, jenes *pn.* that, that one, the former; yon, yonder.

jenseit(s) *pr.* beyond, over, on the other side (of).

jenseitig *a.* being on the other side, opposite.

Jenseits *n.* (-, 0) the other world; hereafter.

Jesuit *m.* (-en, -en) Jesuit.

Jesuitisch *a.* Jesuitical.

Jet *m.* (-[s], -s) jet.

jetten *v.i.* to jet.

jetzig *a.* present, now existing; current.

jetzt *adv.* now, at present; *für* ~, for the present; *von* ~ *an*, henceforth, from this time forward.

Jetzt *n.* the present.

jeweilig *a.* particular; respective.

jeweils *adv.* ~*zwei*, two at a time; ~*am Montag*, each Monday.

jiddisch *a.* Yiddish.

Job *m.* (-s, -s) job.

jobben *v.i.* to do a job.

Joch *n.* (-[e]s, -e) yoke; (*Brücken*~) arch; mountain-ridge.

Jod *n.* (-[e]s, 0) iodine.

jodeln *v.t. & i.* to yodel.

Jodler *m.* (-s, -) yodeller; yodelling song.

Joga *m./n.* yoga.

Jogaübung *f.* yoga exercise.

joggen *v.i.* to jog.

Joghurt *n./m.* yoghurt.

Johannis: ~**beere** *f.* red-currant; ~**würmchen** *n.* glow-worm.

johlen *v.i.* to yell; to howl.

Joint *m.* joint.

Jolle *f.* (-, -n) dinghy.

Jongleur *m.* (-s, -e) juggler, conjurer.

jonglieren *v.i.* to juggle.

Jordanien *n.* (-s, 0) Jordan.

Jordanier *m.*; **Jordanierin** *f.*; **jordanisch** *a.* Jordanian.

Joppe *f.* (-, -n) jacket.

Jota *n.* (-[s], -s) iota.

Journal *n.* (-es, -e) journal, magazine, periodical; (*com.*) day-book.

Journalismus *m.* journalism.

Journalist *m.* (-en, -en) journalist.

jovial *a.* jovial.

Jovialität *f.* joviality.

Jubel *m.* (-s, 0) jubilation; cheering.

Jubelfeier *f.* jubilee.

jubeln *v.i.* to cheer; to jubilate, to exult.

Jubilar *m.* (-s, -e); **Jubilarin** *f.* (-, -nen) aged person or official of long service celebrating his/her

jubilee.
Jubiläum *n.* (-s, Jubiläen) anniversary; jubilee.
jubilieren *v.i.* to jubilate.
Juchtenleder *n.* Russian leather.
juchzen *v.i.* to shout with glee.
Juchzer *m.* shout glee.
jucken *v.i.* to itch.
Judaist *m.*; **Judaistin** *f.* specialist in Jewish studies.
Judaistik *f.* Jewish studies.
Jude *m.* (-n, -n) **Jüdin** *f.* (-, -nen) Jew; *der Ewige* ~ the Wandering Jew.
Judenhaß *m.* anti-Semitism.
Judenhetze *f.* Jew-baiting.
Judenschaft *f.* (-, 0) Jews *pl.* Jewry.
Judenstern *m.* star of David.
Judentum *n.* (-s, 0) Judaism.
Judenverfolgung *f.* persecution of Jews.
Judenviertel *n.* Jewish quarter.
jüdisch *a.* Jewish.
Judo *n.* judo.
Judoka *m.* (-[s], -[s]) judoka.
Jugend *f.* (-, 0) youth; young people.
Jugend: ~**alter** *n.* adolescence; ~**gericht** *n.* juvenile court; ~**herberge** *f.* youth hostel; ~**richter** *m.* juvenile court judge.
jugendlich *a.* youthful, young, juvenile.
Jugendliche *m./f.* juvenile.
Jugendlichkeit *f.* youthfulness.
Jugendstil *m.* art nouveau.
Jugend: ~**sünde** *f.*, ~**torheit** *f.* youthful folly.
Jugendzeit *f.* youth; younger days.
Juli *m.* (-s, -[s]) July.
jung *a.* young; new, recent; (*fig.*) green.
Jungbrunnen *m.* fountain of youth.
Junge *m.* (-n, -n) boy, lad.
Junge *n.* (-n, -n) young one (of animals), cub.
jungenhaft *a.* boyish.
Jungenstreich *m.* boyish prank.
Jünger *m.* (-s, -) disciple.

Jungfer *f.* (-, -n) maid, spinster.
Jungfern: virgin. . .; ~**kranz** *m.* bridal wreath; ~**rede** *f.* maiden speech.
Jungfernschaft *f.* (-, 0) virginity.
Jungfrau *f.* (-, -en) maid, virgin.
jungfräulich *a.* virgin, maidenly, maiden.
Junggesell[e] *m.* bachelor.
Jüngling *m.* (-[e]s, -e) young man, youth.
Jünglingsalter *n.* adolescence.
jüngst *adv.* lately, newly, of late.
jüngst *a.* youngest, last; *der Jüngste Tag,* Doomsday.
Jungsteinzeit *f.* Neolithic period; New Stone Age.
Jungwähler *m.* (-s, -) first-time voter.
Juni *m.* (-[s], -[s]) June.
junior *a.* junior.
Junker *m.* (-s, -) squire.
Junker: ~**ei** *f.*, ~**tum** *n.* squirearchy.
Junktim *n.* (-s, -s) package deal.
Junta *f.* junta.
Jura *pl.* the law; ~ *studieren,* to read for the bar, to study the law.
Jura: ~**student** *m.*; ~**studentin** *f.* law student.
Jurastudium *n.* law studies.
Jurist *m.* (-en, -en); **Juristin** *f.* (-, -nen) jurist, legal practitioner, barrister, lawyer; law-student.
juristisch *a.* legal, juridical; ~*e Person* *f.* legal entity.
Jury *f.* jury.
just *adv.* just, exactly; just now, but just.
justieren *v.t.* to adjust.
Justitiar *m.* **Justitiarin** *f.* company lawyer.
Justiz *f.* (-, 0) justice.
Justiz: ~**beamte[r]** *m.* judicial officer; ~**gebäude** *n.* law-courts *pl.*; ~**gewalt** *f.* judiciary power; ~**minister** *m.* attorney general; Minister of Justice; (*in England*) Lord Chancellor; ~**mord** *m.* judicial murder.
Jute *f.* (-, 0) jute.
Juwel *n.* (-[e]s, -en) jewel, gem.
Juwelier *m.* (-s, -e) jeweler.
Jux *m.* (-es, -e) joke, lark, hoax.

K

K, k *n.* the letter K or k.
Kabale *f.* (-, -n) cabal, intrigue.
Kabarett *n.* (-[e]s, -e) carabet, night-club.
Kabel *n.* (-s, -) *n.* cable; ~**fernsehen** *n.* cable TV.
Kabeljau *m.* (-s, -e) cod(fish).
kabeln *v.t.* to cable.
Kabinett *n.* (-[e]s, -e) cabinet; closet.
Kabinettstück(chen) *n.* tour de force.
Kabine *f.* (-, -n) cabin.
Kabrio *n.* (-s, -s); **Kabriolett** *n.* (-s, -s) convertible.
Kachel *f.* (-, -n) tile.
kacheln *v.t.* to tile.
Kachelofen *m.* tiled stove.
Kacke *f.* (*vulg.*) shit.
kacken *v.i.* (*vulg.*) to shit.
Kadaver *m.* (-s, -) carcass; (*med.*) corpse; ~**gehorsam** *m.* blind obedience.
Kadenz *f.* cadence; cadenza.
Kader *n.* (-s, -) cadre, skeleton staff.
Kadett *m.* (-en, -en) cadet.
Kadetten: ~**anstalt** *f.*, ~**haus** *n.* military college;

~**schiff** *n.* training ship.
Käfer *m.* (-s, -) beetle; chafer.
Kaffee *m.* (-s, -s) coffee.
Kaffee~**bohne** *f.* coffee-bean; ~**geschirr** *n.* coffee-things; ~**haus** *n.* café; ~**kanne** *f.* coffee-pot; ~**mühle** *f.* coffee-mill; ~**satz** *m.* coffee-grounds.
Käfig *m.* (-s, -e) (bird-)cage.
kahl *a.* bald; (*fig.*) bare, naked.
Kahlkopf *m.* bald-head.
kahlköpfig *a.* bald headed.
Kahn *m.* (-[e]s, Kähne) boat, punt.
Kai *m.* (-s, -s) quay.
Kaiman *m.* cayman.
Kaiser *m.* (-s, -) emperor.
Kaiserin *f.* (-, -nen) empress.
kaiserlich *a.* imperial.
Kaiser: ~**reich** *n.* empire; ~**schnitt** *m.* Cæsarean section.
Kaisertum *n.* (-s, 0) imperial dignity.
Kajüte *f.* (-, -n) cabin; *erste* ~, first class saloon; ~**nbett** *n.* berth.
Kakadu *m.* (-[e]s, -s) cockatoo.

Kakao *m.* (-[s], -s) cocoa.
Kakerlake *f.* (-, -n) cockroach.
Kaktus *m.* (-, -teen) cactus.
Kalauer *m.* (-s, -) (*fam.*) joke, pun.
Kalb *n.* (-[e]s, Kälber) calf (*cul.*); veal.
kalben *v.i.* to calve.
Kalb: ~**fell** *n.* calf's skin; (*fig.*) drum; ~**fleisch** *n.* veal.
Kalbs: ~**braten** *m.* roast-veal; ~**haxe** *f.* knuckle of veal; ~**keule** *f.* leg of veal; ~**leder** *n.* calfskin; calf-leather.
Kaldaunen *pl.* tripe; entrails *pl.*
Kaleidoskop *n.* kaleidoscope.
Kalender *m.* (-s, -) calendar, almanac.
Kalesche *f.* (-, -n) light carriage.
kalfatern *v.t.* (*nav.*) to caulk.
Kali *n.* (-s, 0) potash.
Kaliber *n.* (-s, -) calibre; sort.
Kalif *m.* (-en, -en) caliph.
Kalifornien *n.* California.
Kalium *n.* (-s, 0) potassium.
Kalk *m.* (-[e]s, -e) lime; (*gebrannter*) quicklime; (*gelöschter*) slaked lime; (*schwefelsaurer*) carbonate of lime.
Kalk: ~**ablagerung** *f.* deposit of calcium carbonate; ~**boden** *m.* lime soil.
kalken *v.t.* to whitewash.
kalkhaltig *a.* limy, calcareous.
Kalk: ~**erde** *f.* lime, quicklime; ~**mangel** *m.* calcium deficiency; deficiency of lime; ~**ofen** *m.* lime-kiln; ~**stein** *m.* limestone.
Kalkstickstoff *m.* calcium cyanamide.
Kalkül *n./m.* (-s, -e) calculation.
Kalkulation *f.* calculation.
kalkulieren *v.i. & t.* to calculate, to compute; *falsch* ~ to miscalculate.
kalkweiß *a.* chalk-white; deathly pale.
Kalorie *f.* (-, -n) calorie.
kalorien: ~**arm** *a.* low-calorie; ~**reich** *a.* high-calorie.
kalt *a.* cold: frigid, indifferent: ~*es Fieber*, ague; ~*er Brand*, mortification; *das läßt mich* ~, that leaves me unmoved; ~*stellen* to neutralize.
Kaltblüter *m.* cold-blooded animal.
kaltblütig *a.* cool, cool-headed; ~ *adv.* in cold blood.
Kaltblütigkeit *f.* (-, 0) sang-froid.
Kälte *f.* (-, 0) cold; coldness, frigidity.
Kälte: ~**beständig** *a.* cold-resistant; ~**empfindlich** *a.* sensitive to cold.
Kälteperiode *f.* cold spell.
Kaltmiete *f.* rent exclusive of heating charges.
Kaltschale *f.* (-, -n) a cold soup.
kaltschnäuzig *a.* (*fam.*) insensitive.
kaltsinnig *a.* indifferent, cold.
Kaltwasserheilanstalt *f.* hydropathic establishment.
Kaltwasserkur *f.* cold-water cure.
Kalvinismus *m.* calvinism.
Kalzium *n.* calcium.
Kambodscha *n.* (-s, 0) Cambodia.
Kambodschaner *m.*; **Kambodschanerin** *f.*; **kambodschanisch** *a.* Cambodian.
Kamee *f.* (-, -n) cameo.
Kamel *n.* (-[e]s, -e) camel; (*fam.*) blockhead.
Kamelie *f.* (-, -n) camellia.

Kamera *f.* (-, -s) camera.
Kamerad *m.* (-en, -en) **Kameradin** *f.* (-, -nen) companion; comrade; mate.
Kameradschaft *f.* (-, -en) fellowship; comradeship.
kameradschaftlich *a. & adv.* comradely.
Kamera: ~**führung** *f.* camerawork; ~**mann** *m.* cameraman; ~**tasche** *f.* camera case.
Kamerun *n.* Cameroon.
Kameruner *m.*; **Kamerunerin** *f.* Cameroonian.
Kamille *f.* (-, -n) camomile.
Kamin *m.* (-[e]s, -e) chimney; fire-place.
Kamin: ~**feger**, ~**kehrer** *m.* chimneysweep(er); ~**sims** *m.* mantlepiece; ~**vorleger** *m.* hearthrug; ~**vorsetzer** *m.* fender.
Kamm *m.* (-[e]s, Kämme) comb; (*Hahn*) crest; (*eines Berges*) ridge.
kämmen *v.t.* to comb; (*Wolle*) to card.
Kammer *f.* (-, -n) room, chamber; (*Parlament*) chamber.
Kammerdiener *m.* valet.
Kämmerer *m.* treasurer.
Kammer: ~**herr** *m.* gentleman in waiting; ~**jäger** *m.* exterminator; ~**konzert** *n.* chamber concert; ~**musik** *f.* chamber of music; ~**zofe** *f.* lady's maid.
Kammgarn *n.* worsted.
Kampagne *f.* campaign.
Kämpe *m.* (-n, -n) warrior, fighter.
Kampf *m.* (-[e]s, Kämpfe) combat, fight, conflict; struggle; ~ *ums Dasein*, struggle for existence.
Kampf: ~**abstimmung** *f.* crucial vote; ~**bahn** *f.* arena; ring.
kämpfen *v.t.* to combat, to fight; to struggle.
Kampfer *m.* (-s, 0) camphor.
Kämpfer *m.* (-s, -); **Kämpferin** *f.* (-, -nen) combatant; champion.
kämpferisch *a.* fighting (spirit); spirited.
Kämpfernatur *f.* fighter.
Kampf: ~**flugzeug** *n.* bomber (plane); ~**gebiet** *n.* battle arena; combat zone; ~**platz** *m.* battlefield; arena; ~**preis** *m.* prize; ~**richter** *m.* umpire, referee; ~**stoff** *m.* (*mil.*) chemical warfare agent.
kampfunfähig *a.* disabled; out of action.
kampieren *v.i.* to camp, to camp out.
Kanada *n.* (-s, 0) Canada.
Kanadier *m.*; **Kanadierin** *f.*; **kanadisch** *a.* Canadian.
Kanaille *f.* scoundrel.
Kanal *m.* (-s, Kanäle) canal; channel; sewer, drain; the channel; ~**deckel** *m.* manhole cover.
Kanalisation *f.* (-, -en) (*der Stadt*) sewerage; (*Fluß*) canalization.
kanalisieren *v.t.* to channel; to canalize.
Kanapee *n.* (-s, -s) sofa.
Kanaren *pl.* the Canaries.
Kanarienvogel *m.* canary(-bird).
Kanarische Inseln *pl.* the Canary Islands.
Kandare *f.* (-, -n) bit.
Kandelaber *m.* (-s, -) candelabrum; chandelier.
Kandidat *m.* (-en, -en); **Kandidatin** *f.* (-, -nen) candidate.
Kandidatur *f.* candidacy.
kandidieren *v.i.* to be a candidate for; to run; *in einem Wahlkreis* ~, to contest a seat.
kandieren *v.t.* to candy.
Kandis *m.*; **Kandiszucker** *m.* rock candy.

Känguruh *n.* (-s, -s) kangaroo.
Kaninchen *n.* (-s, -) rabbit, cony; ~**stall** *m.* rabbit-hutch.
Kanne *f.* (-, -n) can; tankard; (*Kaffee*~) pot.
kannelieren *v.t.* to channel, to flute.
Kannibale *m.* (-n, -n) cannibal.
Kanonade *f.* (-, -n) bombardment.
Kanon *m.*; (-s, -s) (*mus.*) canon.
Kanone *f.* (-, -n) cannon, gun.
Kanonen: ~**boot** *n.* gun-boat; ~**futter** *n.* cannon fodder; ~**kugel** *f.* cannonball; ~**rohr** *n.* barrel of a cannon; ~**stiefel** *m.pl.* jack-boots *pl.*
Kanonier *m.* (-s, -e) gunner.
kanonieren *v.t.* to cannonade.
kanonisch *a.* canonical.
Kantate *f.* (-, -n) cantata.
Kante *f.* (-, -n) corner, edge; brim; list, border.
kantig *a.* angular, edged.
Kantine *f.* (-, -n) canteen.
Kanton *m.* (-s, -e) canton, district.
kantonal *a.* cantonal.
Kantor *m.* (-s, -en) choirmaster and organist.
Kanu *n.* (-s, -s) canoe.
Kanüle *f.* (-, -n) cannula; needle.
Kanute *m.*; **Kanutin** *f.* canoeist.
Kanzel *f.* (-, -n) pulpit; cockpit.
kanzerogen *a.* carcinogenic.
Kanzlei *f.* (-, -en) office.
Kanzlei: ~**beamter** *m.* clerk; ~**diener** *m.* office attendant.
Kanzler *m.* (-s, -) chancellor; ~**amt** *n.* Chancellery; ~**kandidat** *m* candidate for the chancellorship.
Kap *n.* (-s, -s) cape, promontory.
Kapaun *m.* (-[e]s, -e) capon.
Kapazität *f.* capacity; expert.
Kapelle *f.* (-, -n) chapel; (*Musik*) band.
Kapellmeister *m.* conductor; bandmaster.
Kaper *m.* (-s, -) privateer.
Kaper *f.* (-, -n) (*Beere*) caper.
Kaperei *f.* (-, -en) privateering.
kapern *v.t.* to capture, to seize.
Kaperschiff *n.* privateer.
kapieren *v.t.* (*fam.*) to understand.
kapital *a.* (*fam.*) major, capital.
Kapital *n.* (-es, Kapitalien) capital; principal.
Kapital: ~**abgabe** *f.* capital levy; ~**anlage** *f.* investment; ~**verbrechen** *n.* capital crime.
Kapitalismus *m.* capitalism.
Kapitalist *m.* (-en, -en) capitalist.
kapitalistisch *a.* capitalist(ic).
Kapitän *m.* (-s, -e) captain.
Kapitel *n.* (-s, -) chapter.
Kapitell *n.* (-[e]s, -e) (*arch.*) capital.
kapitulieren *v.i.* to capitulate.
Kaplan *m.* (-es, Kapläne) chaplain.
Kappe *f.* (-, -n) cap, hood.
kappen *v.t.* to cut; to cut back/off.
Kapriole *f.* (-, -n) caper, leap.
kapriziös *a.* capricious.
Kapsel *f.* (-, -n) capsule.
kaputt *a.* broken; out of order; busted.
Kapuze *f.* (-, -n) cowl, hood.
Kapuzinade *f.* (-, -n) Capuchin's sermon.
Kapuziner *m.* (-s, -) Capuchin (friar).
Karabiner *m.* (-s, -) carbine.
Karabinerhaken *m.* snaphook; spring hook;

karabiner.
Karaffe *f.* (-, -n) carafe, decanter.
Karambolage *f.* (-, -n) crash; collision.
Karamel *m.* caramel.
Karamelle *f.* caramel (toffee).
Karat *n.* (-[e]s, -e) carat.
karätig *a.* (*in Zus.*) 22 ~*es Gold*, 22 carat gold.
Karavelle *f.* caravel.
Karawane *f.* (-, -n) caravan.
Karawanserai *f.* (-, -en) caravansary.
Karbid *n.* (-s, -e) (*chem.*) carbide.
Karbolsäure *f.* carbolic acid.
Karbunkel *m.* (-s, -) carbuncle.
Kardinal *m.* (-s, -näle) cardinal.
Kardiogramm *n.* cardiogram.
Karenz *f.*; **Karenzzeit** *f.* waiting period.
Karfreitag *m.* Good Friday.
Karfunkel *m.* (-s, -) carbuncle.
karg *a.* meager; frugal; scant; sparse.
kargen *v.i.* to be niggardly, to stint.
kärglich *a.* sparing, penurious.
Karibik *f.* the Caribbean.
karibisch *a.* Caribbean.
Karies *f.* tooth decay; dental caries.
kariert *a.* checkered; check.
Karikatur *f.* (-, -en) cartoon, caricature; ~**streifen** *m.* comic strip; (*politischer*) **Karikaturist** *m.* cartoonist.
karikieren *v.t.* to caricature.
kariös *a.* decayed.
karitativ *a.* charitable.
Karmeliter *m.* (-s, -) Carmelite.
Karmin *n.* (-[e]s, 0) crimson.
Karneval *m.* (-s, -s *u.* -e) carnival.
Karnickel *n.* (-s, -) (*fam.*) rabbit, bunny.
Kärnten *n.* Carinthia.
Karo *n.* (-[s], -s) square; (*in der Karte*) diamonds *pl.*
Karo: ~**as** *n.* ace of diamonds; ~**bube** *m.* jack of diamonds; ~**dame** *f.* queen of diamonds; ~**könig** *m.* King of diamonds.
Karolinger *m.* Carolingian.
Karosserie *f.* (*mot.*) body work.
Karotin *n.* carotene.
Karotte *f.* (-, -n) carrot.
Karpaten *pl.* the Carpathians.
Karpfen *m.* (-s, -) carp.
Karpfenteich *m.* carp-pond; *er ist Hecht im* ~, he is the wolf in the sheepfold.
Karre *f.* (-, -n) **Karren** *m.* (-s, -) cart.
Karree *n.* (-s, -s) square.
karren *v.t.* to cart.
Karriere *f.* (-, -n) career.
Karrierist *m.*; **Karrieristin** *f.* careerist.
Karsamstag *m.* Holy Saturday.
Karst *m.* (-[e]s, -e) karst.
Kartätsche *f.* (-, -n) canister-shot, grape-shot.
Kartause *f.* (-, -n) Carthusian monastery.
Kartäuser *m.* (-s, -) Carthusian friar.
Karte *f.* (-, -n) card; map; chart; ticket; (*Speise*~) menu; *ein Spiel* ~*n*, a pack of cards; *alles auf eine* ~ *setzen*, to stake everything on one throw.
Kartei *f.* (-, -en) cardfile index.
Kartell *n.* (-s, -e) cartel.
Karten: ~**haus** *n.* house of cards; ~**legerin, ~schlägerin** *f.* fortune-teller; ~**maßstab** *m.* map scale; ~**netz** *n.* grid; ~**spiel** *n.* game at cards; pack

of cards; ~**vorverkauf** *m.* advance booking.

Karthager *m.* Carthaginian.

Karthago *n.* Carthage.

Kartoffel *f.* potato; ~*n in der Schale, Pell* ~*n,* potatoes in jackets; ~**käfer** *m.* Colorado beetle; ~**püree** *n.* mashed potatoes; *Brat* ~*n,* fried potatoes; *Salz* ~*n,* boiled potatoes; *geröstete Kartoffelstreifen (pommes frites),* chipped potatoes; French fries.

Kartograph *m.;* **Kartographin** *f.* cartographer.

Kartographie *f.* cartography.

Karton *m.* (-s, -s) cardboard; cardboard-box.

kartonieren *v.t.* to bind in boards.

Kartothek *f.* (-, -en) card index; filing cabinet.

Karussell *n.* (-[e]s, -s *u.* -e) merry-go-round; carousel.

Karwoche *f.* (-, 0) Holy Week.

Karzer *m.* (-s, -) detention.

karzinogen *a.* carcinogenic.

Karzinom *n.* (-s, -e) carcinoma.

Kaschemme *f.* (*pej.*) dive.

kaschieren *v.t.* to conceal.

Kaschmir *m.* (-s, 0) cashmere.

Käse *m.* (-s, -) cheese.

Käsebrot *n.* bread and cheese.

Kasematte *f.* (-, -n) (*hist.*) casemate.

Käseplatte *f.* assorted cheeses.

Kässerei *f.* cheese factory.

Kaserne *f.* (-, -n) barracks *pl; unter* ~*narrest,* confined to barracks.

käsig *a.* cheesy.

Kasino *n.* (*mil.*) officer's mess; casino.

Kaskade *f.* cascade.

Kaskoversicherung *f.* comprehensive insurance.

Kasper *m.* (-s, -) Punch; clown, fool.

Kasperietheater *n.* Punch and Judy show.

Kaspische Meer *n.* Caspian Sea.

Kasse *f.* (-, -n) cash register; box-office; cash, ready money; *gut, schlecht bei* ~ *sein,* to be flush of money, to be short of cash.

Kassen: ~**arzt** *m.* health-plan doctor; ~**bestand** *m.* cash in hand; ~**patient** *m.* health-plan patient.

Kassette *f.*(-, -n) box; case; cassette.

Kassettenrekorder *m.* cassette recorder.

Kassier[er] *m.* (-s, -); **Kassiererin** *f.* (-, -en) cashier.

kassieren *v.t.* to get in (money); to cashier; (*Urteil*) to quash.

Kastagnette *f.* (-, -n) castanet.

Kastanie *f.* (-, -n) chestnut.

Kästchen *n.* (-s, -) little box.

Kaste *f.* (-, -n) caste; close corporation.

kasteien *v.t.* to chastise; to mortify (the flesh).

Kastell *n.* (-s, -e) fort; castle.

Kasten *m.* (-s, Kästen) chest, case, box.

Kastrat *m.* (-en, -en) eunuch; castrate.

kastrieren *v.t.* to castrate.

Kasus *m.* (-, -) case.

Kasuistik *f.* (-, 0) casuistry.

Katakomben *f.pl.* catacomb.

Katalog *m.* (-[e]s, -e) catalogue.

katalogisieren *v.t.* to catalogue.

Katalysator *m.* (-s, -en) (*chem.*) catalyst.

Katapult *n./m.* catapult.

Katarakt *m.* rapids; cataract.

Katarrh *m.* (-s, -e) catarrh, cold.

Kataster *n.* (-s, -) land register.

Katasteramt *n.* land registry.

katastrophal *a.* catastrophic.

Katastrophe *f.* (-, -n) catastrophe; disaster.

Katasteramt: ~**alarm** *m.* emergency alert; ~**dienst** *m.* emergency service; ~**gebiet** *n.* disaster area.

Katechismus *m.* (-, Katechismen) catechism.

Kategorie *f.* (-, -[e]n) category.

kategorisch *a.* categorical.

kategorisieren *v.t.* to categorize.

Kater *m.* (-s, -) tomcat; hang-over.

Katheder *n.* (-s, -) lectern.

Kathedrale *f.* (-, -n) cathedral.

Katheter *m.* (-s, -) (*med.*) catheter.

Kathode *f.* (-, -n) (*elek.*) cathode; ~*nstrahlen,* cathode-rays.

Katholik *m.* (-en, -en); **Katholikin** *f.* (-, -nen) Roman-Catholic.

katholisch *a.* Roman-Catholic.

Katholizismus *m.* catholicism.

Kattun *n.* (-[e]s, -e) calico, print.

katzbuckeln *v.i.* to cringe.

Katze *f.* (-, -n) cat; *die* ~ *im Sack kaufen,* to buy a pig in a poke.

Katzen: ~**jammer** *m.* hangover; ~**klo** *n.* cat box; ~**sprung** *m. nur einen* ~*sprung entfernt,* just round the corner; ~**streu** *f.* cat litter; ~**wäsche** *f.* (*fig.*) cat's lick.

Kauderwelsch *n.* (-es, *u.* -en, 0) gibberish.

kauen *v.t.* to chew.

kauern *v.i.* to cower, to crouch.

Kauf *m.* (-[e]s, Käufe) purchase, bargain.

kaufen *v.t.* to buy, to purchase.

Käufer *m.* (-s, -) **Käuferin** *f.* (-, -nen) purchaser, buyer.

Kauf: ~**frau** *f.* business women; trader; merchant; ~**haus** *n.* department store; ~**kraft** *f.* purchasing power; ~**leute** *pl.* merchants; shopkeepers.

käuflich *a.* for sale; venal.

Kaufmann *m.* businessman, merchant; shopkeeper.

kaufmännisch *a.* mercantile, commercial.

Kaufvertrag *m.* contract of sale.

Kaugummi: *n.* (-s, -s) chewing gum.

Kaukasus *m.* the Caucasus.

Kaulbarsch *m.* (-es, -e) river-perch, ruff.

Kaulquappe *f.* (-, -n) tadpole.

kaum *adv.* scarcely, hardly.

kausal *a.* causal.

Kausalität *f.* (-, -en) causality.

kaustisch *a.* caustic, sarcastic.

Kautabak *m.* chewing-tobacco.

Kaution *f.* (-, -en) security, bail.

Kautschuk *m.* (-s, -e) rubber.

Kauz *m.* (-es, Käuze) screech-owl; (*fig.*) oddball.

kauzig *a.* odd, queer; funny.

Kavalier *m.* (-es, -e) cavalier, gentleman.

Kavallerie *f.* (-, -[e]n) cavalry.

Kavallerist *m.* (-en, -en) horseman.

Kaviar *m.* (-s, 0) caviar(e).

keck *a.* bold, daring; saucy, pert.

Kegel *m.* (-s, -) cone; ~*pl.* ninepins, skittles *pl.; Kegelschieben,* to play at ninepins *or* skittles; *Kind und* ~, bag and baggage .

Kegelbahn *f.* bowling alley.

kegelförmig *a.* conical, cone-shaped.

kegeln *v.i.* to bowl, to play at ninepins.

Kegelschnitt *m.* conic section.

Kehle *f.* (-, -n) throat, gorge; *aus voller ~*, at the top of one's voice.

kehlig *a.* guttural; throaty.

Kehl: ~**kopf** *m.* larynx; ~**kopfspiegel** *m.* laryngoscope; ~**lant** *m.* guttural sound.

Kehraus *m.* (-, 0) last dance; (*fig.*) end.

Kehre *f.* (-, -n) turn, bend.

kehren *v.t.* to sweep, to brush; to turn; (sich) ~ *v.refl.* (*an etwas*) to mind a thing; *vor seiner eignen Tür ~*, to mind one's own business; *kehrt!* (*mil.*) right about face!

Kehricht *m. & n.* (-s, 0) sweeping *pl.*; garbage.

Kehrreim *m.* refrain.

Kehrseite *f.* reverse, back; seamy side.

kehrtmachen *v.i.* to turn back.

keifen *v.i.* to scold; to nag.

Keil *m.* (-[e]s, -e) wedge; (*mech.*) key.

Keilerei *f.* (-, -en) (*sl.*) free fight, brawl.

keilförmig *a.* wedge-shaped; cuneiform.

Keil: ~**kissen** *n.* wedge-shaped bolster; ~**riemen** *m.* (*mech.*) vee-belt; ~**schrift** *f.* cuneiform characters.

Keim *m.* (-[e]s, -e) germ; bud, sprout; *m. ~ ersticken*, to nip in the bud.

Keim: ~**blatt** *n.* cotyledon; seed leaf; ~**drüse** *f.* gonad.

keimen *v.i.* to germinate, to bud; to sprout.

keimfrei *a.* sterile, aseptic.

Keimling *m.* (-s, -e) embryo.

keimtötend *a.* germicidal; antiseptic.

Keimträger *m.* germ carrier.

Keimzelle *f.* germ cell; (*fig.*) nucleus.

kein (keiner, keine, kein[e]s) *a.* no, no one, not any, none.

keinerlei *a.* no. . . at all; no. . . whatsoever.

keinesfalls *adv.* on no account.

keineswegs *adv.* by no means.

keinmal *adv.* not once, never.

Keks *n.* (-es, -e) biscuit; cookie.

Kelch *m.* (-[e]s, -e) goblet; chalice; (*bot.*) calyx; ~**blatt** *n.* sepal.

Kelle *f.* (-, -n) trowel; ladle; (*rail.*) signalling disk.

Keller *m.* (-s, -) cellar.

Kellerassel *f.* sow bug.

Kellerei *f.* (-, -en) winery.

Kellergeschoß *n.* basement.

Kellner *m.* (-s, -) waiter.

Kellnerin *f.* (-, -nen) waitress.

kellnern *v.i.* to work as waiter/waitress.

Kelte *m.* Celt.

Kelter *f.* (-, -n) wine-press.

keltern *v.t.* to tread (grapes), to press.

keltisch *a.* celtic.

Kenia *n.* (-s, 0) Kenya.

Kenianer *m.*; **Kenianerin** *f.* Kenyan.

kennbar *a.* recognizable, distinct.

kennen *v.i.ir* to know; to be acquainted with; ~**lernen**, to become acquainted with, to get introduced to.

Kenner *m.* (-s, -) connoisseur, expert, authority.

Kennerblick *m.* expert eye.

Kennkarte *f.* identity card.

kenntlich *a.* recognizable.

Kenntlichmachung *f.* labelling.

Kenntnis *f.* -, (-nisse) knowledge; ~ *von etwas nehmen*, to take note *or* cognizance of a thing; *in ~ setzen*, to inform of; *ohne ~ von*, unaware of; *zur Kenntnisnahme*, for information.

kenntnisreich *a.* knowledgable, well-informed, learned.

Kennwort *n.* motto; password.

Kennzeichen *n.* mark, badge, label; characteristic, criterion.

kennzeichen *v.t.* to label, to mark; to characterize.

kentern *v.t.* to capsize.

Keramik *f.* ceramic *pl.*; pottery.

Kerbe *f.* (-, -n) notch.

Kerbel *m.* chervil.

kerben *v.t.* to notch, to indent.

Kerker *m.* (-s, -) prison, jail, dungeon.

Kerl *m.* (-[e]s, -e) fellow; chap.

Kern *m.* (-[e]s, -e) kernel; stone; nucleus; (*fig.*) core.

Kern. . . (*phys.*) nuclear.

kerngesund *a.* thoroughly healthy.

kernig *a.* pithy, solid.

Kernkraft *f.* nuclear power.

Kernkraft: ~**gegner** *m.* opponent of nuclear power; ~**werk** *n.* nuclear power plant.

kernlos *a.* seedless.

Kern: ~**obst** *n.* stone fruit; ~**physik** *f.* nuclear physics; ~**teilung** *f.* (*phys.*) nuclear fission; ~**truppen** *pl.* crack troops.

Kernwaffe *f.* (-, -n) nuclear weapon.

kernwaffenfrei *a.* nuclear-free.

Kerosin *n.* (-s, 0) kerosene.

Kerze *f.* (-, -n) candle.

kerzeng[e]rade *a.* (*fig.*) bolt-upright.

Kerzenhalter *m.* candlestick.

Kerzenlicht *n.* candlelight.

Kerzenständer *m.* candlestick.

kess *a.* pert; jaunty, cheeky.

Kessel *m.* (-s, -) kettle, cauldron; (*Dampf*) boiler; (*mil.*) pocket.

Kesselstein *m.* scale, fur.

Kesseltreiben *n.* hunt; witch-hunt.

ketten *v.t.* to chain, to bind.

Kette *f.* (-, -n) chain; necklace; (*Berg~*) range; (*Weberei*) warp; (*mil., Panzer*) track.

Ketten: ~**brücke** *f.* suspension-bridge ~**glied** *n.* (chain) link; ~**hemd** *n.* coat of chain mail; ~**hund** *m.* watch-dog; ~**rauchen** *n.* chain-smoking.

Ketzer *m.* (-s, -); **Ketzerin** *f.* (-, -nen) heretic.

Ketzerei *f.* (-, -en) heresy.

ketzerisch *a.* heretical.

keuchen *v.i.* to pant, to puff.

Keuchhusten *m.* whooping-cough.

Keule *f.* (-, -n) club; leg (of mutton, etc.).

keusch *a.* chaste, pure.

Keuschheit *f.* (- 0) chastity.

Kibbuz *m.* (-, -im) kibbutz.

Kichererbse *f.* chick-pea.

kichern *v.t.* to giggle.

kicken *v.i.* to kick; to play soccer.

kidnappen *v.t.* to kidnap.

Kiebitz *m.* (-[e]s, -e) lapwing, peewit.

Kiefer *f.* (-, -n) pine (tree); ~ *m.* (-s, -) jawbone.

Kiefernholz *n.* pinewood.

Kiefernzapfen *m.* pine-cone.

Kieferorthopädie *f.* orthodontics.
kieken *v.i.* (*fam.*) to look.
Kiel *m.* (-[e]s, -e) quill; (*nav.*) keel.
Kielwasser *n.* wake.
Kieme *f.* (-, -n) gill.
Kies *m.* (-es, -e) gravel.
Kiesel *m.* (-s, -) flint, pebble.
Kiesgrube *f.* (*fam.*) gravel pit.
kiffen *v.i.* to smoke pot.
kikeriki cock-a-doodle-doo.
killen *v.t.* to do in, to kill.
Kilo... (*in Zus.*) kilo...
Kilo: ~**gramm** *n.* kilogram; ~**hertz** *n.* kilohertz; ~**meter** *m.* kilometer.
Kilometer: ~**geld** *n.* mileage allowance; ~**stand** *m.* mileage reading ~**zähler** *m.* (*mot.*) mileage indicator.
Kind *n.* (-[e]s, -er) child; *kleines* ~, infant, baby.
Kindbett *n.* lying-in; ~**fieber** *n.* puerperal fever.
Kinder: ~**arzt** *m.*, ~**ärztin** *f.* pediatrician; ~**bett** *n.* crib.
Kinderei *f.* (-, -en) childishness; childish prank.
kinderfeindlich *a.* hostile to children; anti-children.
kinderfreundlich *a.* fond of children; suitable for children.
Kinder: ~**fürsorge** *f.* child welfare; ~**garten** *m.* nursery school and kindergarten; ~**gärtnerin** *f.* kindergarten teacher; ~**hort** daycare center; ~**krippe** *f.* daycare for babies; ~**lähmung** *f.* infantile paralysis, polio (myelitis).
kinderleicht *a.* very easy.
kinderlos *a.* childless.
Kinder: ~**mädchen** *n.* nanny; ~**sicherung** *f.* child-proof lock, ~**spiel** *n.* child's play; ~**sterblichkeit** *f.* infant mortality; ~**stube** *f.* nursery; ~**tages-stätte** *f.* day-care center, ~**wagen** *m.* baby carriage ~**zulage** *f.* children's allowance.
Kindes: ~**alter** *n.* childhood, infancy; ~**entführung** *f.* kidnapping, child abduction; ~**mißhandlung** *f.* child abuse; ~**statt** *f. an ~ annehmen,* to adopt; ~**tötung** *f.* infanticide.
kindgemäß *a.* suitable for children.
Kindheit *f.* (-, 0) childhood.
kindisch *a.* childish.
kindlich *a.* infantile; childlike.
Kindskopf *m.* (big) child, silly.
Kindtaufe *f.* christening.
Kinetik *f.* kinetics.
Kinkerlitzchen *pl.* trifles.
Kinn *n.* (-[e]s, -e) chin.
Kinn: ~**backen** *m.* jaw(bone); ~**haken** *m.* uppercut; ~**lade** *f.* jaw.
Kino *n.* (-s, -s) movie theater, cinema.
Kino: ~**karte** *f.* movie ticket; ~**kasse** *f.* movie box-office; ~**programm** *n.* movie guide.
Kippe *f.* (-, 0) stub, butt; dump (garbage).
kippen *v.t.* to tilt, to set atilt.
Kipper *m.* dump truck; dump car.
Kippfenster *n.* tilting window.
Kipp: ~**frequenz** *f.* (*elek.*) sweep frequency; ~**schalter** *m.* (*elek.*) toggle switch.
Kirche *f.* (-, -n) church; divine service.
Kirchen: ~**buch** *n.* parish-register; ~**geschichte** *f.* ecclesiastical history; ~**lied** *n.* hymn; ~**raub** *m.* sacrilege; ~**recht** *n.* canon-law; ~**schiff** *n.* nave;

~**staat** *m.* Papal States *pl.*; ~**steuer** *f.* church tax; ~**stuhl** *m.* pew; ~**vater** *m.* Father (of the church).
kirchlich *a.* ecclesiastical.
Kirch: ~**turm** *m.* steeple; ~**turmspitze** *f.* spire; ~**weih** *f.* wake, fair.
Kirmes *f.* (-, -messen) village-fair.
kirre *a.* jmdn. ~**machen** (*fam.*) to bring s.b. to heel.
Kirsch: ~**baum** *m.* cherry-tree: ~**blüte** *f.* cherry-blossom; ~**branntwein** *m.* cherry-brandy.
Kirsche *f.* (-, -n) cherry; (*saure*) morello, egriot.
Kirschkern *m.* cherry-stone.
Kirschwasser *n.* kirsch.
Kissen *n.* (-s, -) cushion, pillow.
Kissen: ~**bezug** *m.* pillow-case; cushion cover; ~**schlacht** *f.* pillow-fight.
Kiste *f.* (-, -n) box, chest, case.
Kitsch *m.*, (-es, 0) trash, kitsch.
kitschig *a.* kitschy.
Kitt *m.* (-[e]s, -e) putty; glue.
Kittchen *n.* (*fam.*) jail, clink, jug.
Kittel *m.* (-s, -) smock.
kitten *v.t.* to cement; (*fig.*) to patch up.
Kitz *n.* (-es, -e) Reh~ fawn; (*Ziegenn, Gemsen*~) kid.
Kitzel *m.* (-s, 0) tickle, itch; thrill.
kitzeln *v.t.* to tickle.
Kitzler *m.* clitoris.
kitzlig *a.* ticklish; (*fig.*) difficult.
Klacks *m.* dollop; blob.
Kladde *f.* (-, -n) rough copy; scribbling-book; (*com.*) day book.
Kladderadatsch *m.* (-es, 0) crash.
klaffen *v.i.* to gape, to yawn.
kläffen, *v.i.* to yap.
Kläffer *m.* (-s, -) yapping dog; (*fig.*) brawler, wrangler.
Klafter *f.* (-, -n) fathom; (*Holz*) cord of wood.
Klage *f.* (-, -n) complaint; lament; (*gerichtliche*) suit, action; charge.
klagen *v.i.* to complain, to lament; (*law*) to take action, to go to law.
Kläger *m.* (-s, -) **Klägerin** *f.* (-, -nen) plaintiff; prosecuting party; petitioner.
Klageschrift *f.* statement of claim; list of changes; petition.
kläglich *a.* lamentable; pitiful.
Klamauk *m.* fuss, to-do, slapstick.
klamm *a.* numb, clammy.
Klamm *f.* narrow gorge.
Klammer *f.* (-, -n) clip; staple; grip; brace; cramp; peg; bracket, parenthesis; paper-clip, clamp.
klammern *v.t.* to clip; to staple; to peg; (sich) ~ *v.refl.* to cling (to).
klammheimlich *a.* on the quiet.
Klamotte *f.* (-, -n) rags, clobber; junk; slapstick movie.
Klang *m.* (-[e]s, Klänge) sound; ring; tone.
Klangfarbe *f.* timbre.
Klangfülle *f.* sonority.
klanglich *a.* tonal.
klanglos *a.* toneless.
klangvoll *a.* sonorous, rich.
Klappbett *n.* folding bed.
Klappe *f.* (-, -n) flap; valve; (*mus.*) key; (*fig.*) mouth.
klappen *v.i.* to clap, to clatter; (*fig.*) to go well, to

tally.

Klappentext *m.* blurb.

Klapper *f.* (-, -n) rattle.

klapp[e]rig *a.* rattling; shaky.

klappern *v.i.* to clatter, to rattle; (*Zähne*) to chatter.

Klapperschlange *f.* rattle-snake.

Klapp: ~**fenster** *n.* top-hung window; ~**messer** *n.* jackknife; ~**sitz** *m.* folding seat; ~**stuhl** *m.* folding chair; ~**tisch** *m.* folding table; ~**verdeck** *n.* folding top (car).

Klaps *m.* (**Klapses, Klapse** *u.* **Kläpse**) flap, smack.

Klapsmühle *f.* (*sl.*) nut-house.

klar *a.* clear; (*Wasser*) limpid; evident.

Kläranlage *f.* sewage (purification) plant.

Klärbecken *n.* settling basin.

klarblickend clear-sighted.

klären *v.t.* to clear; to clarify; to purify.

klargehen *v.i.st.* to be all right.

Klarheit *f.* (-, -en) clearness; evidence.

Klarinette *f.* (-, -n) clarinet.

klarkommen *v.i.st.* to manage, to cope.

klarsehen *v.i.st.* to understand.

Klarsicht: ~**folie** *f.* transparent film; ~**packung** *f.* transparent pack.

klarspülen *v.i.* to rinse.

Klarstellung *f.* clarification.

klarstellen *v.t.* to clear up.

im Klartext in clear.

Klasse *f.* (-, -n) class, form; order, rank.

Klassen: ~**arbeit** *f.* (class) test; ~**kamerad** *m.* ~**kameradin** *f.* classmate; ~**kampf** *m.* class struggle; ~**lehrer** *m.*, ~**lehrerin** *f.* homeroom teacher.

klassenlos *a.* classless.

klassifizieren *v.t.* to classify, to break down.

Klassifizierung *f.* (-, -en) classification.

Klassik *f.* (*Antike*) classical antiquity; classical period/age.

Klassiker *m.* (-s, -) classic (author).

klassisch *a.* classical.

Klassizismus *m.* classicism.

klassizistisch *a.* classicistic.

klatsch *i.* crack! smack!

Klatsch *m.* (-[e]s, -e) clash; gossip, tittle-tattle.

Klatschbase *f.* gossip, tale-bearer.

klatschen; Beifall ~, to applaud; ~ *v.i.* to clack; to gossip.

Klatscher *m.* (-s, -) clapper; gossip.

Klatscherei *f.* (-, -en) chit-chat, gossip.

klatschhaft *a.* talkative, gossiping.

Klatsch: ~**spalte** *f.* gossip column; ~**tante** *f.*, ~**weib** *n.* (*pej.*) gossip.

klauben *v.t.* to pick, to carp at.

Klaue *f.* (-, -n) claw, talon, paw; clutch.

klauen *v.t.* to pinch.

Klause *f.* (-, -n) cell hermitage.

Klausel *f.* (-, -n) clause, proviso.

Klausner *m.* (-s, -) hermit, recluse.

Klausurarbeit *f.* class exercise; test paper.

Klausurtagung *a.* closed meeting.

Klaviatur *f.* (-, -en) keyboard.

Klavier *n.* (-[e]s, -e) piano.

Klavier: ~**auszug** *m.* piano arrangement; ~**begleitung** *f.* piano accompaniment; ~**hocker** *m.* piano stool; ~**konzert** *n.* piano concerto; piano recital; ~**sonate** *f.* piano sonata; ~**spieler** *m.*, ~**spielerin**

f. pianist; piano player; ~**stimmer** *m.* piano-tuner; ~**stunde** *f.* piano lesson; ~**unterricht** *m.* piano lessons.

Klebe: ~**band** *n.* adhesive tape; ~**folie** *f.* adhesive film.

kleben *v.t.* to paste, to glue, to stick; ~ *v.i.* to adhere, to stick.

kleb[e]rig *a.* sticky, viscous; glutinous.

Kleber *m.* glue.

Kleb: ~**stoff** *m.* adhesive, glue; ~**streifen** *m.* Scotch tape.

kleckern *v.i.* to spill; to drip; to splash.

kleckerweise *adv.* (*fam.*) in dribs and drabs.

Klecks *m.* (-ses, -se) blot, ink-spot, staining, blob.

klecksen *v.t.* to blot, to blotch; to daub.

Klee *m.* (-[e]s, 0) clover.

Kleeblatt *n.* clover leaf (*fig.*) trio.

Kleid *n.* (-[e]s, -er) garment; gown, dress; coat; ~**er** *pl.* clothes *pl.*

kleiden *v.t.* to dress, to clothe; (*passen*) to fit, to become; (sich) ~ *v.refl.* to dress.

Kleider: ~**ablage** *f.* coat rack; ~**bügel** *m.* hanger; ~**bürste** *f.* clothes-brush; ~**größe** *f.* size; ~**schrank** *m.* wardrobe; ~**ständer** *m.* clothes-stand; ~**stange** *f.* clothes rail.

kleidsam *a.* becoming.

Kleidung *f.* (-, -en) clothing, dress, clothes *pl.*

Kleidungsstück *n.* garment; ~**e** *pl.* wearing apparel.

Kleie *f.* (-, -n) bran.

klein *a.* little; small; petty, mean; ~*es Geld*, change; *kurz und* ~, in splinters; (*Gas*) ~ *drehen*, to turn down.

Klein: ~**bahn** *f.* local railway, narrow-gauge railway; ~**buchstabe** *m.* small letter; lower-case letter; ~**bürger**, petty bourgeois; ~**bürgertum** *n.* petite bourgeoisie.

Kleine *m./f.* little boy; little girl.

Klein: ~**familie** *f.* nuclear family; ~**geld** *n.* small change; ~**handel** *m.* retail trade.

Kleinheit *f.* smallness; small size.

Kleinholz *n.* chopped wood.

Kleinigkeit *f.* (-, -en) small matter, trifle, detail.

Kleinigkeitskrämer *m.* pettifogger.

kleinkariert *a.* small-checked; (*fig.*) narrow minded.

Kleinkind *n.* infant.

kleinlaut *a.* subdued, disheartened.

kleinlich *a.* mean, petty, fussy.

kleinmütig *a.* pusillanimous, timid.

Kleinod *n.* (-[e]s, -e *u.* -ien) jewel, treasure, trinkets *pl.*; **Kleinodien** *pl.* insignia of royalty, regalia.

Kleinstaat *m.* small state.

Kleinstädter *m.* provincial.

kleinstädtisch *a.* provincial.

Kleinstlebewesen *n.* microorganism.

kleinstmöglich *a.* smallest possible.

Kleinwagen *m.* small car.

Kleinwüchsig *a.* small, short.

Kleister *m.* (-s, 0) paste.

kleistern *v.t.* to paste.

Klemme *f.* (-, -n) clamp; straits *pl.*, fix, difficulty.

klemmen *v.t.* to pinch; to squeeze; (sich) ~ *v.refl.* to jam one's finger.

Klempner *m.* (-s, -) plumber, tinner.

Klepper *m.* (-s, -) nag, hack.

Kleptomane *m.*; **Kleptomanin** *f.* cleptomaniac.
Kleptomanie *f.* cleptomania.
klerikal *a.* clerical.
Kleriker *m.* (-s, -) clergyman, priest.
Klerus *m.* clergy.
Klette *f.* (-, -n) bur.
klettern *v.i.* to climb, to clamber.
Kletterpflanze *f.* climber, creeper.
Klettverschluß *m.* Velcro.
klicken *v.i.* to click.
Klient *m.* (-en, -en); **Kleintin** *f.* client.
Klima *n.* (-s, -ta *u.* -te) climate.
Klimaanlage *f.* air-conditioning.
Klimakterium *n.* menopause, climacteric.
klimatisch *a.* climatic.
klimatisieren *v.t.* to air condition.
Klimatologie *f.* climatology.
klimmen *v.i.st.* (s) to climb.
Klimmzug *m.* (-s, -züge) pull-up.
klimpern *v.i.* to jingle; to strum.
Klinge *f.* (-, -n) blade; sword.
Klingel *f.* (-, -n) bell, hand-bell.
Klingelbeute *m.* collection-bag.
Klingelknopf *m.* bell push, call button.
klingeln *v.i.* to ring the bell, to tinkle.
Klingelschnur *f.* bell-rope.
klingen *v.i.st.* to ring, to clink, to sound.
Klinik *f.* (-, -en) hospital, clinic.
Klinikum *n.* clinic complex.
klinisch *a.* clinical.
Klinke *f.* (-, -n) latch, door-handle.
Klinker *m.* (-s, -) clinker.
klipp, *adv.* ~*und klar* (*fam.*) quite plainly.
Klippe *f.* (-, -n) reef, rock.
klirren *v.i.* to clink, to clatter, to crash.
Klischee *n.* (-s, -e) cliché; (stereotype) block.
Klistier *n.* (-s, -e) enema; ~**spritze** *f.* enema syringe.
Klitoris *f.* (-, -) clitoris.
klitzeklein *a.* teeny-weeny.
Klo *n.* (*fam.*) toilet, john.
Kloake *f.* (-, -n) sewer.
klobig *a.* coarse, rude, clumsy.
klopfen *v.t.* to knock, to beat, to rap, to tap.
Klopfer *m.* (-s, -) knocker, rapper.
Klöppel *m.* (-s, -) clapper; drum-stick; bobbin, lace-bone.
klöppeln *v.t.* to make bone-lace.
Klöppelspitze *f.* bone-lace.
Klöppler *m.* (-s, -), **Klöpplerin** *f.* (-, -nen) lace maker.
Klops *m.* (-ses, -se) dumpling.
Klosett *n.* ([e]s, -e *u.* -s) toilet.
Kloss *m.* (-es, Klösse) clod; dumpling.
Kloster *n.* (-s, Klöster) cloister; monastery; convent, nunnery.
Klosterbruder *m.* friar.
Klosterfrau *f.* nun.
klösterlich *a.* monastic.
Klosterschule *f.* convent-school.
Klotz *m.* (-es, Klötze) block, log, trunk.
klotzig *a.* log-like; rude; enormous.
Klub *m.* (-s, -s) club.
Kluft *f.* (-, Klüfte) chasm, ravine, gulf.
klug *a.* prudent; intelligent; clever; sharp; *aus etwas nicht* ~ *werden*, to be puzzled by a thing.

klugerweise *adv.* wisely.
Klugheit *f.* (-, 0) prudence, shrewdness.
Klugscheißer *m.* (*vulg.*) smart ass.
Klumpen *m.* (-s, -) lump, clod.
Klumpfuß *m.* club foot.
klumpig *a.* lumpy, clotted.
Klüngel *m.* (-s, 0) clique.
Klunker *m.* (-s, -) (*fam.*) rock (jewels).
knabbern *v.t. & i.* to nibble, to gnaw.
Knabe *m.* (-n, -n) boy, lad.
Knabenalter *n.* boyhood.
knabenhaft *a.* boyish.
Knäckebrot *n.* crispbread.
Knack(s) *m.* (-[e]s, -e *u.* Knackses, -se) crack(ing).
knacken *v.t.* to crack; ~ *v.i.* to break.
Knacker *m.* (-s, -) *alter* ~ (*fam.*) old fogey.
knackig *a.* crisp; crunchy; (*fig.*) delectable.
Knall *m.* (-[e]s, -e *u.* Knälle) clap, crack; bang, detonation; ~ *und Fall*, on a sudden.
Knalt: ~**bonbon** *n.* cracker; ~**affekt** *m.* stage effect.
knallen *v.t.* to crack (a whip); ~ *v.i.* to detonate, to pop.
knallig *a.* loud; gaudy.
Knallkopf *m.* (*fam.*) jerk.
knallrot *a.* glaring red.
knapp *a.* close, tight, narrow; scarce, scanty; (*Stil*) concise; ~ *halten*, to keep (one) short.
Knappe *m.* (-n, -n) esquire; miner.
Knappheit *f.* (-, -en) shortage; scarcity.
knarren *v.i.* to creak, to jar.
Knast *m.* (-s, Knäste) (*fam.*) clink; jug; prison.
Knatsch *m.* (-, 0) trouble.
knattern *v.i.* to rattle, to clatter.
Knäuel *m.* (-s, -) clue, ball of thread; throng.
Knauf *m.* (-[e]s, Knäufe) head, knob.
Knauser *m.* (-s, -) miser, tightwad.
Knauserei *f.* (-, -en) stinginess.
knauserig *a.* stingy, close.
knausern *v.i.* to be stingy.
knautschen *v.t.u.i.* to crumple; to crease; to get creased.
Knebel *m.* (-s, -) gag.
knebeln *v.t.* to gag; to muzzle.
Knecht *m.* (-[e]s, -e) farm-hand; (*fig.*) slave.
knechten *v.t.* to enslave; to oppress.
knechtisch *a.* slavish, servile.
Knechtschaft *f.* (-, 0) servitude, slavery.
kneifen *v.t.st.* to pinch, to nip.
Kneifer *m.* (-s, -) pince-nez.
Kneifzange pincers *pl.*
Kneipe *f.* (-, -n) tavern; pub; bar.
Knete *f.* (-, 0) (*fam.*) money; play dough.
kneten *v.t.* to knead; to massage; to mold.
Knick *m.* (-[e]s, -e) sharp bend; kink; crease.
knicken *v.t.* to snap; to bend; to crease.
Knickerei *f.* (-, -en) niggardliness.
knickerig *a.* niggardly.
knickern *v.i.* to be stingy.
Knicks *m.* (Knickses, Knickse) curtsy.
knicksen *v.i.* to drop a curtsy.
Knie *n.* (-[e]s, -[e]) knee.
Knie: ~**beuge** *f.* kneebend; ~**beugung** *f.* genuflection; ~**kehle** *f.* (-, -n) hollow of the knee.
knie[e]n *v.i.* to kneel.
kniefällig *a.* upon one's knees.

Kniehose *f.* breeches, knickerbockers, plus-fours *pl.*; **~scheibe** *f.* knee-cap.

Kniff *m.* (-[e]s, -e) pinch; trick, dodge.

knifflig *a.* (*fam.*) queer, intricate.

knipsen *v.i.* to snap one's fingers; (*Fahrkarte*) to punch; (*phot.*) to snap.

Knirps *m.* (-es, -e) little guy.

knirschen *v.t.* to grind (one's teeth); ~ *v.i.* to grate.

knistern *v.i.* to crackle.

knitterfrei *a.* non-crease.

knittern *v.i.* to crease; *nicht knitternd*, crease-resisting.

knobeln *v.i.* to play dice/spoof; scissors, paper, stone; to puzzle.

Knoblauch *m.* (-[e]s, 0) m. garlic; **~zehe** *f.* (-, -n) clove of garlic.

Knöchel *m.* (-s, -) knuckle; joint; ankle.

Knochen *m.* (s, -)bone.

Knochen: **~arbeit** *f.* back-breaking work; **~brech** *m.* fracture (of a bone); **~gerüst** *n.* skeleton; **~mark** *n.* (bone) marrow; **~mehl** *n.* bone-dust; **~splitter** *m.* bone splinter.

knöchern *a.* bone. . .; bony.

knochig *a.* bony.

Knödel *m.* (-s, -) dumpling.

Knolle *f.* (-, -n) tuber; bulb.

Knollen *m.* (-s, -) clod, lump; (*fam.*) parking ticket.

Knollenblätterpilz *m.* death cup.

Knollennase *f.* bulbous nose.

knollig *a.* bulbous; knobby.

Knopf *m.* (-es, Knöpfe) button.

knöpfen *v.t.* to button.

Knopfloch *n.* button-hole.

Knorpel *m.* (-s, -) cartilage, gristle.

knorpelig *a.* cartilaginous, gristly.

Knorren *m.* (-s, -) knot, gnarl.

knorrig *a.* gnarled; gruff.

Knospe *f.* (-, -n) bud, eye.

knospen *v.i.* to bud.

knoten *v.t.* to knot.

Knoten *m.* (-s, -) knot; node; (*med.*) lump.

Knotenpunkt *m.* (*rail.*) junction; intersection.

knotig *a.* knobby.

knuffen *v.t.* to poke.

knüllen *v.t.* to rumple, to crumple.

Knüller *m.* (*fam.*) sensation.

knüpfen *v.t.* to tie; to knot, to unite, to connect.

Knüppel *m.* (-s, -) cudgel, stick.

knurren *v.i.* to growl, to snarl; to grumble.

knusp[e]rig *a.* (*Gebäck*) crisp, short, crusty, crunchy.

knuspern *v.t.* to nibble, to munch.

Knute *f.* (-, -n) knout.

knutschen *v.t.* (*fam.*) to smooch with; to neck with; to pet (erotic.).

Knutschfleck *m.* (*fam.*) love bite.

Knüttelvers *m.* doggerel (line).

Koalition *f.* (-, -en) coalition.

Kobalt *m.* (-s, -e) cobalt.

Kobold *m.* (-[e]s, -e) goblin; gnome.

Kobra *f.* cobra.

Koch *m.* (-[e]s, Köche) (male) cook.

Kochbuch *n.* cookbook.

kochen *v.t.* to boil, to cook; ~ *v.i.* to boil; to be cooking.

kochendheiß *a.* boiling hot.

Kocher *m.* (-s, -) cooker.

Köcher *m.* (-s, -) quiver.

kochfertig *a.* ready to cook.

Kochgelegenheit *f.* cooking facility.

Köchin *f.* (-, -nen) (female) cook.

Koch: **~kunst** *f.* culinary art; **~löffel** *m.* wooden spoon; **~nische** *f.* kitchenette; **~rezept** *n.* recipe; **~salz** *n.* table salt; sodium chloride; **~salzlosung** *f.* saline solution; **~topf** *m.* saucepan, cooking-pot, **~wäsche** *f.* boiled wash.

Köder *m.* (-s, -) bait, lure.

ködern *v.t.* to bait, to allure, to decoy.

Kodex *m.* (-, Kodizes) code.

kodieren *v.t.* to code; to encode.

Koeffizient *m.* (-en, -en) coefficient.

Koexistenz *f.* (-, 0) coexistence.

Koffein *n.* caffeine.

koffeinfrei *a.* decaffeinated.

Koffer *m.* (-s, -) suitcase.

Kofferraum *m.* trunk.

Kognak *m.* (-s, -s) brandy, cognac.

Kohl *m.* (-[e]s, 0) cabbage; kale; (*fam.*) twaddle, humbug.

Kohle *f.* (-, -n) charcoal; coal; carbon; (*fam.*) dough (money).

Kohle: **~hydrat** *n.* carbohydrate; **~hydrierung** *f.* hydrogenation; **~kraftwerk** *n.* coal power plant.

kohlen *v.t.* to char, to carbonize; (*nav.*) to coal.

Kohlen: **~bergwerk** *n.* coal mine, colliery; **~dioxyd** *n.* carbon dioxide; **~feld**, **~lager** *n.* coalfield; **~grube** *f.* coalpit, colliery; **~säure** *f.* carbonic acid; **~schiff** *n.* collier; **~schuppen** *m.* coal shed; **~stoff** *m.* carbon; **~stoffhaltig** *a.* carbonaceous; **~wasserstoff** *m.* hydrocarbon.

Kohle: **~papier** *n.* carbon paper; **~tablette** *f.* charcoal tablet; **~zeichnung** *f.* charcoal drawing.

Köhler *m.* (-s, -) charcoal-burner.

Kohlmeise *f.* great tit.

Kohlrabi *m.* (-[e], -[s]) kohl rabi.

Kohlrübe *f.* rutabaga.

Koitus *m.* (-, -) coitus.

Koje *f.* (-, -n) berth, cabin.

Kokain *n.* cocaine.

Kokarde *f.* (-, -n) cockade.

kokett *a.* coquettish.

Kokette *f.* (-, -n) coquette, flirt.

Koketterie *f.* (-, -n) coquetry, flirtation.

kokettieren *v.i.* to flirt.

Kokolores *m.* (*fam.*) rubbish, nonsense.

Kokon *m.* (-s, -s) cocoon.

Kokos: **~flocken** *pl.* shredded coconut; **~nuß** *f.* coconut, **~palme** *f.* coconut tree.

Koks *m.* (-es, 0) coke.

Kolben *m.* (-s, -) butt; piston; flask.

Kolben: **~fresser** *m.* jamming of the piston; **~hub** *m.* piston stroke; **~ring** *m.* piston ring; **~stange** *f.* piston rod.

Kolchose *f.* (-, -n) kolkhoz; collective farm.

Kolibakterie *f.* (-, -n) colibacillus.

Kolibri *m.* (-s, -s) hummingbird.

Kolik *f.* (-, 0) colic.

kollabieren *v.i.* to collapse.

Kollaborateur *m.* (-s, -e) collaborator.

Kollaboration *f.* (-, 0) collaboration.

kollaborierien *v.i.* to collaborate.

Kollaps *m.* collapse.

Kolleg *n.* (-s, -ien) course of lectures.

Kollege *m.* (-s, -n); **Kollegin** *f.* (-, -nen) colleague.

kollegial *a.* cooperative; helpful.

Kollegialität *f.* helpfulness towards colleagues.

Kollegium *n.* (-s, Kollegien); faculty; staff (of teachers).

Kollekte *f.* (-, -n) (church-) collection; (*Gebet*) collect.

Kollektion *f.* collection, range.

kollektiv *a.* collective; *~e Sieherheit f.* collective security.

Kollektivshuld *f.* collective guilt.

Koller *m.* (-s, 0) rage, madness.

kollern *v.t. & i.* to roll.

kollidieren *v.i.* to collide; to clash.

Kollier *n.* necklace.

Kollision *f.* collision; conflict; clash.

Kolloquium *n.* (-s, -quien) colloquium.

Kölnisch-Wasser, Kölnisches Wasser *n.* eau de Cologne.

kolonial *a.* colonial.

Kolonialismus *m.* colonialism.

Kolonie *f.* (-, -[e]n) colony.

Kolonist *m.* (-en, -en) colonist, settler.

kolonisieren *v.t.* to colonize.

Kolonne *f.* (-, -n) column.

Kolophonium *n.* (-s, 0) colophony.

Koloratur *f.* (-, -en) coloratura.

kolorieren *v.t.* to color.

Kolorit *n.* (-s, 0) coloring.

Koloss *m.* (Kolosses, Kolosse) colossus.

kolossal *a.* colossal, huge.

kolportieren *v.t.* to hawk; to spread.

Kolumbianer *m.*; **Kolumbianerin** *f.*; **Kolumbianisch** *a.* Columbian.

Kolumbien *n.* (-s, 0) Columbia.

Kolumne *f.* (-, -n) column (newspaper).

Koma *n.* (-s, -s) coma.

Kombi *m.* station wagon.

Kombination *f.* (-, -en) combination.

kombinieren *v.t.* to combine.

Kombiwagen *m.* station wagon.

Komet *m.* (-en, -en) comet.

kometenhaft *a.* meteroric.

Komfort *m.* (-s, 0) comfort; *mit allem ~*, with all modern conveniences.

komfortabel *a.* comfortable.

Komik *f.* comic effect / element / aspect.

Komiker *m.* (-s, -) comic actor.

komisch *a.* comical; strange, odd, funny.

komischerweise *adv.* strangely enough.

Komitee *n.* (-s, -s) committee.

Komma *n.* (-[s], -ta, *u.* -s) comma.

Kommandant *m.* (-en, -en) commander.

kommandieren *v.t.* to command.

Kommanditgesellschaft *f.* limited company (with shares).

Kommando *n.* (-[s], -s) command; detachment (of soldiers); *~brücke f.* (*nav.*) bridge; *~zentrale f.* control center.

kommen *v.i.st.* (s) to come; to happen; to arrive at, to get to; *woher kommt das?* what is the cause of this? how is it that. .?; *~ lassen*, to send for, to write for; *~ sehen*, to foresee; *abhanden ~ to get lost*, to be mislaid; *einem gleich ~*, to equal one; *zu*

kurz ~, to be a loser; *teuer, hoch zu stehen ~*, to cost a fortune; *wenn es hoch kommt*, at most, in extreme cases; *auf etwas ~* to think of; *ich konnte gestern nicht dazu ~*, I could not find time for it yesterday; *nicht zu Worte ~*, to be unable to put in a word; *um etwas ~*, to lose a thing; *sich etwas zu Schulden ~ lassen*, to be guilty of a thing.

Kommentar *m.* commentary, comment.

Kommentator *m.*; **Kommentatorin** *f.* commentator.

Kommerz *m.* (*pej.*) business interests.

kommerzialisieren *v.t.* to commercialize.

kommerziell *a.* commercial.

kommentieren *v.t. & i.* to comment (upon).

Kommilitone *m.* (-n, -n); **Kommilitonin** *f.* (-, -nen) fellow-student.

Kommissar *m.* (-s, -e) commissioner, captain of police; superintendent.

Kommode *f.* (-, -n) chest of drawers.

kommunal *a.* local; communal, municipal.

Kommunal: *~behörden pl.* local authorities; *~verwaltung f.* local government.

Kommune *f.* (-, -n) local authority, minicipality; commune.

Kommunikation *f.* (-, -en) communication.

Kommunikations: *~mittel pl.* means of communication; *~wissenschaft f.* communication science.

kommunikativ *a.* communicative.

Kommunismus *m.* (-, 0) communism.

Kommunist *m.*; **Kommunistin** *f.* communist.

kommunizieren *v.i.* to communicate.

Komödiant *m.* (-en, -en) **Komödiantin** *f.* (-, -nen) actor, actress, comedian.

Komödie *f.* (-, -nen) comedy; play.

Kompa(g)nie *f.* (-, -en) company.

Kompagnon *m.* (-s, -s) associate; partner.

Komparativ *m.* (-s, -e) comparative.

Komparse *m.*; **Komparsin** *f.* (*film*) extra.

Kompaß *m.* (-es, -e) compass.

kompatibel *a.* compatible.

Kompensation *f.* (-, -en) compensation.

kompensieren *v.t.* to compensate.

kompetent *a.* competent; authorized.

Kompetenz *f.* (-, -en) competence; authority.

komplementär *a.* complementary.

Komplementärfarbe *f.* complementary color.

komplett *a.* complete.

komplettieren *v.t.* to complete.

komplex *a.* complex.

Komplex *m.* (-es, -e) complex.

Komplexität *f.* complexity.

Komplikation *f.* complication.

Kompliment *n.* compliment.

Komplize *m.* (-, -n); **Komplizin** *f.* (-, -nen) accomplice.

kompliziert *a.* complicated.

Komplott *n.* (-s -e) plot; conspiracy.

Komponente *f.* (-, -n) component.

komponieren *v.t.* to compose, to set (to music).

Komponist *m.* (-en, -en); **Komponistin** *f.* (-, -nen) composer.

Komposition *f.* (-, -en) (*mus.*) composition, setting.

Kompositum *n.* (-s, -sita) compound (word).

Komposthaufen *m.* compost heap.

Kompott *n.* (-[e]s, -e *u.* -s) stewed fruit.
Kompresse *f.* compress; pad.
Kompressor *m.* (-s, -en) (*mot.*) compressor, supercharger.
komprimieren *v.t.* to compress.
komprimiert *a.* condensed.
Kompromiß *m.* (-[e]s, -e) compromise.
kompromißlos *a.* uncompromising.
kompromittieren *v.t.* to compromise; *sich ~,* to expose oneself.
kondensierte Milch *f.* condensed milk.
Kondition *f.* condition; trim; shape.
Konditions: ~**schwäche** *f.* lack of fitness; ~**training** *n.* fitness training.
Konditor *m.* (-s, -en) confectioner; pastry cook.
Konditorei *f.* (-, -en) confectioner's(shop); pastry shop.
kondolieren *v.i.* to offer one's condolences.
Kondom *n.* (-s, -e) condom.
Konfekt *n.* (-[e]s, -e) sweets; candy; chocolates.
Konfektion *f.* (-, 0) off-the-rack clothes; garments.
Konferenz *f.* (-, -en) meeting, conference.
konferieren *v.i.* to confer.
Konfession *f.* (-, -en) denomination, religion.
konfessionall *a.* denominational.
konfessionslos *a.* nondenominational.
Konfirmand *m.* (-en, -en); **Konfirmandin** *f.* (-, -nen) confirmand.
konfirmieren *v.t.* to confirm.
konfiszieren *v.t.* to confiscate.
Konfitüre *f.* (-, -n) jam.
Konflikt *m.* (-s, -e) conflict.
Konfliktstoff *m.* (-s, -e) cause of conflict.
Konföderation *f.* (-, -en) confederation.
konform *a.* conforming.
Konformist *m.*; **Konformistin** *f.*; **konformistisch** *a.* conformist.
konfus *a.* confused, scatter-brained.
Kongreß *m.* (-es, -e) congress; Congress.
Kongreßmitglied *n.* Congressman, Congresswoman.
Kongruenz *f.* (-, -en) congruence.
König *m.* (-s, -e) king.
Königin *f.* (-, -nen) queen.
königlich *a.* royal, regal.
Königreich *n.* kingdom.
Königtum *n.* (-[e]s, -tümer) royalty, kingship.
konisch *a.* conical.
Konjugation *f.* conjugation.
konjugieren *v.t.* to conjugate.
Konjunktion *f.* (-, -en) conjunction.
Konjunktiv *m.* (-s, -e) subjunctive.
Konjunktur *f.* (-, -en) economic activity; economy; ~**forschung** *f.* market research.
Konjunktur: ~**abschwächung** *f.* downswing; ~**aufschwung** *m.* upswing; ~**bericht** *m.* economic report; ~**schwankungen** *pl.* cyclical fluctuation.
konkav *a.* concave.
Konkordat *n.* (-[e]s, -e) concordat.
konkret *a.* concrete.
konkretisieren *v.t.* to put s.th. in concrete terms.
Konkubinat *n.* (-[e]s, -e) concubinage.
Konkurrent *m.* (-en, -en) competitor.
Konkurrenz *f.* (-, -en) competition.
konkurrenzfähig *a.* competitive.

konkurrieren *v.i.* to compete.
Konkurs *m.* (-kurses, -kurse) bankruptcy, insolvency; ~ *machen,* to become or go bankrupt.
Konkurs: ~**masse** *f.* bankrupt's assets; ~**ordnung** *f.* bankruptcy law; ~**verfahren** *n.* proceedings in bankruptcy.
können *v.i.ir.* to be able, can, to know, to understand; *ich kann,* I can, I may; *ich kann nichts dafür,* it's no fault of mine, I can't help it.
Können *n.* (-s, 0) ability; skill.
Könner *m.* (-s, -) expert.
konsekutiv *a.* consecutive.
konsequent *a.* consistent, logical.
Konsequenz *f.* (-, -en) consistency; consequence.
konservativ *a.* conservative.
Konservative *m./f.* conservative.
Konservatorium *n.* (-s, -nen) conservatory.
Konserve *f.* (-, -n) canned food.
Konservenbüchse *f.* (-, -n) tin, can; *Konserven...* tinned, canned.
konservieren *v.t.* to preserve, to keep.
Konsistenz *f.* consistency.
konsolidieren *v.t.* to consolidate.
Konsolidierung *f.* consolidation.
Konsonant *m.* (-en, -en) consonant.
Konsorte *n. pl.* (-n, -n) associates.
Konsortium *n.* (-s, Konsortien) group, syndicate.
Konspiration *f.* conspiracy.
konspirativ *a.* conspirational.
konspirieren *v.i.* to conspire; to plot.
konstant *a.* constant.
konstatieren *v.t.* to state, to notice.
Konstellation *f.* combination, constellation.
konsterniert *a.* filled with consternation.
Konsternierung *f.* consternation.
konstituieren *v.t.* to constitute.
Konstitution *f.* (-, -en) constitution.
konstitutionell *a.* constitutional.
konstruieren *v.t.* to construct.
Konstrukteur *m.*; **Konstrukteurin** *f.* designer; design engineer.
Konstruktionsfehler *m.* faulty design.
Konstruktionsbüro *n.* design office.
konstruktiv *a.* constructive; constructional.
Konsul *m.* (-s, -n); **Konsulin** *f.* (-, -nen) consul.
Konsulat *m.* (-s, -e) consulate.
konsultieren *v.t.* to consult.
Konsum *m.* consumption.
Konsum: ~**artikel** *m.* (-s, -) consumer item; ~**güter** *pl.* consumer goods.
Konsument *m.*; **Konsumentin** *f.* consumer.
Konsumgesellschaft *f.* consumer society.
Konsumterror *m.* pressure to buy.
Kontakt *m.* contact.
kontaktfreudig *a.* sociable.
Kontaktlinse *f.* (-, -n) contact lens.
Kontamination *f.* contamination.
kontaminieren *v.t.* to contaminate.
Konter *m.* (-s, -) counter; counter-attack.
Konter: ~**admiral** *m.* rear-admiral; ~**bande** *f.* contraband ~**revolution** *f.* counterrevolution.
Kontext *m.* context.
Kontinent *m.* (-s, -e) continent.
Kontinentalverschiebung *f.* continental drift.
Kontingent *n.* (-[e]s, -e) quota, contingent.
kontinuierlich *a.* steady; continuous.

Kontinuität *f.* continuity.

Konto *n.* (-s, -n, *u.* Konti) account; *Depositen ~,* deposit account; *fiktives ~,* fictitious account; *laufendes ~,* current account; *ein ~ eröffnen,* to open an account; **~auszug** *m.* statement (of account); **~inhaber** *m.* account-holder.

Kontor *n.* (-s, -e) office.

Kontostand *m.* balance (account).

kontra *pr.* contra; against.

Kontra: ~baß *m.* bass-viol.

Kontrahent *m.* (-en, -en) adversary; opponent.

Kontrakt *m.* (-es, -e) contract.

kontraktlich *a. & adv.* by contract, contractual; *~ verpflichtet,* under contract to . . .

Kontrapunkt *m.* (*mus.*) counterpoint.

konträr *a.* contrary, opposite.

Kontrast *m.* contrast.

kontrastieren *v.t.u.i.* to contrast.

Kontrastmittel *n.* radiopaque material.

Kontrollabschnitt *m.* stub.

Kontrolle *f.* (-, 0) control surveillance, check, inspection.

Kontrolleur *m.* (-s, -e) inspector.

kontrollieren *v.t.* to control, to check.

Kontroll: ~kasse *f.* cash register; **~marke** *f.* check; **~punkt** *m.* checkpoint.

kontrovers *a.* conflicting, controversial.

Kontroverse *f.* controversy.

Kontur *f.* (-, -en) outline.

Konvention *f.* convention.

Konventionalstrafe *f.* (*jur.*) liquidated damages.

konventionell *a.* conventional.

Konversation *f.* conversation.

Konversationslexikon *n.* encyclopedia.

Konversion *f.* conversion.

konvertierbar *a.* convertible.

konvertieren *v.t.* to convert.

Konvertit *m.* (-en, -en) convert.

konvex *a.* convex.

Konvoi *m.* convoy.

Konzentrat *n.* (-s, -e) concentrate.

Konzentration *f.* concentration.

Konzentrationslager *n.* concentration camp.

konzentrieren *v.t.* to concentrate, to focus.

konzentriert *a.* concentrated, focused.

Konzept *n.* (-[e]s, -e) (rough) draft, sketch.

Konzeption *f.* central ideal; conception.

konzeptionslos *a.* haphazard; without a clear-plan.

Konzern *m.* (-[e]s, -e) group, combine.

Konzert *n.* (-s, -e) concert, concerto; **~agentur** *f.* concert agency; **~besucher** *m.,* **~besucherin** *f.* concertgoer; **~flügel** *m.* concert grand; **~meister** *m.,* **~meisterin** *f.* concertmaster; **~saal** *m.* concert hall.

Konzession *f.* (-, -en) concession; license; *sich eine ~ beschaffen,* to take out a license; *mit Regierungs~,* under license from the government; **~sinhaber** *m* licensee.

konzessionsbereit *a.* prepared to make concessions.

Konzessivsatz *m.* concessive clause.

Konzil *n.* (-s, -e) council.

Konzil *n.* (-[e]s, -e *u.* -ien) council.

konzipieren *v.t.* to conceive; to draft; *~konzipiert für* designed for.

Kooperation *f.* cooperation.

kooperativ *a.* cooperative.

kooperieren *v.t.* to cooperate.

Koodination *f.* coordination.

koordinieren *v.t.* to coordinate.

Köper *m.* (-s, 0) twill.

Kopf *m.* (-es, Köpfe) head; (*fig.*) mind; (*Pfeifen~*) bowl; *aus dem ~,* from memory; *Hals über ~,* head over heels; *einen vor den ~ stossen,* to offend one; *sich auf den ~ stellen,* to strain every nerve; *sich den ~ über etwas zerbrechen,* to rack one's brains about a thing; *den ~ hängen lassen,* to hang one's head, to be dispirited.

Kopfarbeit *f.* brain-work, intellectual work.

köpfen *v.t.* to behead.

Kopf: ~haut *f.* scalp; **~hörer** *m.* earphone, headphone; **~kissen** *n.* pillow.

kopflos *a.* brainless, silly.

Kopf: ~nicken *n.* nod; **~rechnen** *n.* mental arithmetic; **~salat** *n.* head-lettuce.

kopfscheu *a.* skittish, shy.

Kopf: ~schmerz *m.* headache; **~schmuck** *m.* headdress; **~schuppen** *pl.* dandruff; **~schütteln** *n.* headshake; **~sprung** *m.* header; **~stand** *m.* headstand; **~steinpflaster** *n.* cobblestones; **~steuer** *f.* poll-tax; **~stutze** *f.* headrest; **~tuch** *n.* headscarf.

kopfüber *adv.* head first; (*fig.*) headlong.

Kopf: ~verband *m.* head bandage; **~verletzung** *f.* head injury; **~ wäsche** *f.* hair-wash; shampoo; **~weh** *n.* head-ache; **~zerbrechen** *n.* puzzling of one's head.

Kopie *f.* (-, -[e]n) copy; duplicate; to imitate.

kopieren *v.t.* to copy; (*phot.*) to print.

Kopierer *m.,* **Kopiergerät** *n.* copier; copymachine.

Koppel *f.* (-, -n) paddock.

koppeln *v.t.* to couple, to link; to dock.

Koproduktion *f.* co-production.

Kopulation *f.* copulation.

kopulieren *v.i.* to copulate.

Koralle *f.* (-, -n) coral.

Korb *m.* (-[e]s, Körbe) basket, hamper, crate; *einen ~ bekommen,* to meet with a refusal.

Korbblüter *m.* composite.

Korb: ~flechter, **~macher** *m.* basketmaker; **~flechtwaren** *pl.* wickerwork; **~möbel** *n.* wicker furniture.

Kord *m.* corduroy, cord.

Kordel *f.* cord, string.

Kordsamt *m.* cord velvet.

Korea *n.* (-s, 0) Korea.

Koreaner *m.;* **Koreanerin** *f.;* **koreanisch** *a.* Korean.

Korinthe *f.* currant.

Kork *m.* (-[e]s, -e) **Korken** *m.* (-s, -) cork; stopper; float (fishing).

korken *v.t.* to cork.

Korkenzieher *m.* cork-screw.

Kormoran *m.* (-s, -e) cormorant.

Korn *n.* (-[e]s, Körner) corn; grain.

Korn *m.* wheat liquor.

Kornähre *f.* ear of corn.

Kornblume *f.* cornflower.

körnen *v.t. & i.* to granulate.

Kornfeld *n.* cornfield.

körnig *a.* granulous, granular.
Kornkammer *f.* granary.
Korona *f.* corona: (*fig.*) crowd.
Körper *m.* (-s, -) body; (*toter*) corpse; (*phys.*) solid.
Körper: ~**bau** *m.* physique; ~**beherrschung** *f.* body control; ~**behinderung** *f.* physical handicap; ~**beschädigung** *f.* bodily harm *or* injury; ~**fülle** *f.* corpulence; ~**geruch** *m.* body odor, (*fam.*) BO, ~**haltung** *f.* posture; ~**kontakt** *m.* physical contact; ~**kraft** *f.* physical strength; ~**kultur** *f.* physical culture.
Körperchen *n.* (-s, -) corpuscle.
körperlich *a.* corporal, bodily; physical.
Körperschaft *f.* corporation; ~**ssteuer** *f.* corporation profits tax.
Körpersprache *f.* body language.
Korps (*frz*) *n.* (-, -) corps; body.
Korpulenz *f.* corpulence.
korrekt *a.* correct.
Korrektheit *f.* correctness.
Korrektor *m.* (-s, -en) proof-reader.
Korrektur *f.* (-, -en) correction; proof-reading, revise; ~**bogen** *m.* proof-sheet; ~**fahnen** *pl.* galleys.
Korrelat *n.* (-[e]s, 0) correlate.
Korrespondent *m.* (-en, -en) (*com.*) correspondent.
Korrespondenz *f.* (-, -en) correspondence.
korrespondieren *v.i.* to correspond.
Korridor *m.* (-s, -e) passage, corridor.
korrigieren *v.t.* to correct.
korrumpieren *v.t.* to corrupt.
Korruption *f.* corruption.
Korsar *m.* (-s, -en) corsair, pirate.
Korsett *n.* (-[e]s, -e *u.* -s) corset, straight-jacket.
Kortison *n.* (-s, 0) cortisone.
Koryphäe *m.* (-n, -n) authority.
koscher *a.* kosher.
kosen *v.i.* to caress.
Kosename *m.* pet name.
Kosinus *m.* (*math.*) cosine.
Kosmetik (-, 0) beauty care; cosmetics.
Kosmetiker *m.*; **Kosmetikerin** *f.* cosmetician, beautician.
Kosmetikkoffer *m.* vanity box/case.
Kosmetiksalon *m.* beauty parlor.
Komsetikum *n.* (-s, -ka) cosmetic.
kosmetisch *a.* cosmetic.
kosmetische Chirurgie *f.* cosmetic surgery.
kosmisch *a.* cosmic.
Kosmonaut *m.*; **Kosmonautin** *f.* cosmonaut.
Kosmopolit *m.*; **Kosmopolitin** *f.* cosmopolitan.
kosmopolitisch *a.* cosmopilitan.
Kosmos *m.* (-, 0) cosmos.
Kost *f.* (-, 0) fare, food; board; *in ~ sein bei*, to board with.
kostbar *a.* costly, precious; valuable.
Kostbarkeit *f.* (-, -en) preciousness; valuables *pl.*
kosten *v.t.* to taste; to cost; to require.
Kosten *pl.* cost, costs, charges, expenses *pl.*; *die ~ tragen*, to bear the expenses.
kostenlos *a.* free of charge.
Kostenpunkt *m.* the question of expense.
Kosten-Nutzen-Analyse *f.* cost benefit analysis.
Kostenvoranschlag *m.* (-s, -schläge) estimate.

Kost: ~**gänger** *m.* boarder; ~**geld** *n.* board; allowance; board-wages (*für Dienstboten*).
köstlich *a.* precious; delicious.
Köstlichkeit *f.* (-, -en) delicacy.
Kostprobe *f.* (-, -n) sample, taste.
kostspielig *a.* expensive, costly.
Kostüm *n.* (-s, -e) costume, dress; ~**bildner** *m.*; ~**bildnerin** *f.* costume designer; ~**fest** *n.* fancy-dress ball.
kostümieren *v.t.u.refl.* to dress up.
Kostümprobe *f.* dress rehearsal.
Kostümverleih *m.* costume rental.
Kot *m.* (-[e]s, 0) excrement; feces.
Kotelett *f.* (-s, -s) cutlet, chop.
Koteletten *pl.* sideburns.
Köter *m.* (-s, -) cur.
Kotflügel *m.* mudguard.
Kotze *f.* (-, 0) (*vulg.*) vomit.
kotzen *v.i.* (*vulg.*) to vomit; to puke.
Krabbe *f.* (-, -n) crab; shrimp; prawn.
krabbeln *v.i.* to crawl.
Krach *m.* (-[e]s, -e) noise, crash; quarrel.
krachen *v.i.* to crack, to crash; to creak.
Kracher *m.* banger.
krächzen *v.i.* to croak, to caw.
Kräcker *m.* cracker.
kraft *pr.* by virtue of.
Kraft *f.* (-, Kräfte) strength; (*Natur*) force; (*Macht*) power; vigor, *in ~*, in force; *in ~ setzen*, to put into operation; *außer ~ setzen*, to repeal, to countermand; *in ~ treten*, to come into force; *aus Leibeskräften*, with might and main.
Kraft: ~**akt** *m.* feat of strength; ~**ausdruck** *m.* swearword; ~**brühe** *f.* bouillon, clear soup.
Kräfteverfall *m.* loss of strength.
Kräfteverhältnis *n.* balance of power.
Kräfteverschleiß *m.* waste of energy.
Kraftfahrer *m.* driver; motorist.
Kraftfahrzeug *n.* (-s, -e) motor vehicle; ~**brief** *m.* vehicle registration document; ~**mechaniker** *m.* car mechanic; ~**schein** *m.* vehicle registration document; ~**steuer** *f.* automobile tax.
Kraftfeld *n.* (*phys.*) field of force.
kräftig *a.* strong; powerful; vigorous; nourishing.
kräftigen *v.t.* to strengthen; to fortify; to invigorate.
Kräftigungsmittel *n.* (-s, -) tonic.
kraftlos *a.* weak, feeble; impotent.
Kraft: ~**meier** *m.* (*pej.*) muscleman; ~**probe** *f.* trial of strength; ~**protz** *m.* (*pej.*) muscleman; ~**stoff** *m.* fuel; ~**stoffverbrauch** *m.* fuel consumption.
kraftvoll *a.* vigorous; powerful.
Kraft: ~**wagen** *m.* motor-car; ~**werk** *n.* power station.
Kragen *m.* (-s, -) collar; ~**weite** *f.* collar size.
Krähe *f.* (-, -n) crow.
krähen *v.i.* to crow.
Krake *m.* (-n, -n) octopus; kraken.
krakeelen *v.i.* to kick up a row.
Krakeeler *m.* (-s, -) quarreler, brawler.
Krakel *m.* (-s, -) (*fam.*) scrawl.
krakeln *v.t.u.i.* (*fam.*) to scrawl, to scribble.
Kralle *f.* (-, -n) claw.
krallen *v.t.* to dig one's finger into; *v.refl.* to cling to, to dig one's claws into.
Kram *m.* (-[e]s, Kräme) junk; stuff.

kramen *v.i.* to rummage.

Krämer *m.* (-s, -) shopkeeper, grocer; (*fig.*) stingy person.

Kramladen *m.* (*pej.*) junk shop.

Krampf *m.* (-[e]s, Krämpfe) cramp; spasm, convulsion.

Krampfader *f.* varicose, vein.

krampfhaft *a.* spasmodic, convulsive.

krampflösend *a.* spasmolytic.

Kran *m.* (-[e]s, Kräne) crane; faucet.

Kranich *m.* (-s, -e) crane.

krank *a.* ill, sick; *~werden*, to fall ill; *sich ~ stellen*, to feign illness, to malinger; *~ im Bett liegen*, to be ill in bed; *sich ~ melden*, to call in sick.

Kranke[r] *m./f.* (-n, -n) patient.

kränkeln *v.i.* to be ailing, to be in poor health.

kranken *v.i.* to suffer from.

kränken (sich) *v.t.u.refl.* to vex, to mortify; to injure, to hurt.

Kranken: **~appell** *m.* (*mil.*) sick-call; **~bett** *n.* sickbed; **~blatt** *n.* medical record; **~geld** *n.* sick pay; **~geschichte** *f.* medical history; **~gymnast** *m.*, **~gymnastin** *f.* physiotherapist; **~gymnastik** *f.* physiotherapy; **~haus** *n.* hospital; *ins ~haus überführen*, to hospitalize; **~kasse** *f.* health insurance; **~pflege** *f.* nursing; **~pfleger** *m.*, **~wärter** *m.* male nurse; **~schein** *m.* health insurance certificate; **~schwester** *f.* hospital-nurse; **~träger** *m.* stretcher-bearer; **~urlaub** *m.* sick leave; **~versicherung** *f.* health insurance; **~wagen** *m.* ambulance.

krankhaft *a.* morbid; abnormal; pathological.

Krankheit *f.* (-, -en) disease, sickness; *die englische ~*, the rickets.

Krankheits; **~bild** *n.* clinical picture; **~erreger** *m.* pathogen; **~erscheinung** *f.* symptom; **~fall** *m.* case of illness.

krankheitshalber *adv.* owing to illness.

Krankheits: **~herd** *m.* focus of disease; **~keim** *m.* germ; **~überträger** *m.* carrier.

kränklich *a.* sickly, ailing, poorly.

Krankmeldung *f.* (-, -en) notification of illness.

Kränkung *f.* (-, -en) insult, mortification.

Kranz *m.* (-es, Kränze) wreath, garland.

kränzen *v.t.* to wreathe, to crown.

Krapfen *m.* (-s, -) doughnut.

kraß *a.* coarse, gross; blatant.

Krater *m.* (-s, -) crater.

Kratzbürste *f.* wire brush.

kratzbürstig *a.* (*fig.*) bad-tempered, hostile.

Krätze *f.* (-, 0) scabies.

kratzen *v.t.* to scratch, to scrape; (*Wolle*) to card; *~ v.i.* (*von Federn*) to spurt.

Kratzer *m.* (-s, -) scratch; scraper.

kratzig *a.* scratchy, itchy.

Kraul *n.* (-s, 0) (*sp.*) crawl.

kraulen *v.i.* to crawl.

kraus *a.* curl, frizzy.

Krause *f.* (-, -n) ruff, ruffle; frill, frizziness.

kräuseln *v.t.* to curl, to frizz.

Krauskopf *m.* curly-head.

Kraut *n.* (-[e]s, Kräuter) herb; plant; cabbage.

Krautsalat *m.* coleslaw.

Krawall *m.* (-[e]s, -e) row, riot; **~macher** *m.* rowdy.

Krawatte *f.* (-, -n) (neck-)tie, **~nnadel** *f.* tie pin.

kraxeln *v.i.* (*fam.*) to climb; to clamber.

Kreation *f.* (-, -en) creation (fashion).

kreativ *a.* creative.

Kreativität *f.* creativity.

Kreatur *f.* (-, -en) creature.

Krebs *m.* (Krebses, Krebse) cray-fish; crab; (*med.*) cancer.

krebsartig *a.* cancerous.

krebs: **~erregend** *a.*; **~erzeugend** *a.* carcinogenic.

Krebs: **~forschung** *f.* cancer research; **~gang** *m.* retrogression; **~geschwulst** *f.* cancerous growth/tumor; **~geschwür** *n.* cancerous ulcer; (*fig.*) cancer; **~kranke** *m./f.* cancer patient.

kredenzen *v.t.* to hand (a cup of wine), to serve.

Kredit *m.* (-[e]s, -e) credit; trust; reputation.

Kredit: **~anstalt** *f.* credit institution; **~brief** *m.* letter of credit; **~geber** *m.* lender; **~hai** *m.* (*fam. pej.*) loan shark; **~institut** *n.* credit bank; **~karte** *f.* credit card; **~kauf** *m.* purchase on credit; **~nehmer** *m.* borrower.

kreditfähig *a.* creditworthy, sound.

kreditwürdig *a.* creditworthy.

Kreditwürdigkeit *f.* creditworthiness.

kreditieren *v.t.* to credit.

Kredo *n.* credo.

Kreide *f.* (-, -n) chalk; crayon.

Kreide *f.*, **Kreidezeit** *f.* cretaceous (period).

kreidebleich *a.* as white as a sheet.

kreieren *v.t.* to create.

Kreis *m.* (Kreises, Kreise) circle, cycle; orbit; sphere; county district.

Kreis: **~abschnitt** *m.* segment; **~ausschnitt** *m.* sector; **~bahn** *f.* orbit; **~bogen** *m.* arc of a circle.

kreischen *v.i.* to scream; to shriek.

Kreisel *m.* (-s, -) top; gyroscope.

kreiseln *v.i.* to turn like a top.

kreisen *v.i.* to revolve.

Kreisfläche *f.* circular surface.

kreisförmig *a.* circular.

Kreis: **~lauf** *m.* circulation; cycle; **~laufkollaps** *m.* circulatory collapse; **~laufmittel** *n.* circulatory medicine, **~laufstörungen** *pl.* circulatory trouble; **~linie** *f.* circumference of a circle; **~säge** *f.* circular saw.

kreißen *v.i.* to be in labor.

Kreißsaal *m.* delivery room.

Krematorium *n.* (-s, -rien) crematorium.

Krempe *f.* (-, -n) brim (of a hat).

Krempel *m.* (-s, 0) junk; stuff.

krempen *v.t.* to turn up.

krepieren *v.i.* (*s*) to die a miserable death; (*Geschoß*) to burst, to explode.

Krepp *m.* (-s, 0) crepe.

Kresse *f.* (-, -n) (water-)cress.

Kretin *m.* cretin; imbecile.

Kreuz *n.* (-es, -e) cross, crucifix; (*in der Karte*) club; (*fig.*) cross, tribulation; *kreuz und quer*, right and left, in all directions.

Kreuzband *n.* crucial ligament.

kreuzen *v.t.* to cross; to interbreed; *~ v.i.* (*nav.*) to cruise; *sich ~ v.refl.* to intersect; *die beiden Briefe kreuzten sich*, the two letters crossed.

Kreuzer *m.* (-s, -) (*nav.*) cruiser.

Kreuz: **~fahrer** *m.* crusader; **~fahrt** *f.* crusade **~feuer** *n.* crossfire.

kreuzfidel *a.* very cheerful.

kreuzförmig *a.* cross-shaped; cruciform.
Kreuzgang *m.* cloister.
kreuzigen *v.t.* to crucify.
Kreuzigung *f.* crucifixion.
Kreuz: ~könig *m.* king of clubs; **~otter** *f.* viper; **~schlüssel** *m.* four-way wheel-brace; **~schmerzen** *pl.* lower back pain; **~spinne** *f.* garden spider; **~stich** *m.* cross-stitch;.
Kreuzung *f.* (-, -en) junction; crossroads; cross-breeding.
Kreuz: ~verhör *n.* cross-examination; **~wegstationen** *pl.* stations of the Cross.
kreuzweise *adv.* across, cross-wise.
Kreuzworträtsel *n.* crossword puzzle.
Kreuzzeichen *n.* sign of the cross.
Kreuzzug *m.* crusade.
kribbelig *a.* fidgety, edgy.
kribbeln *v.i.* to tickle, to itch.
Kricket *n.* cricket.
kriechen *v.i.st.* (*h.u.s.*) to creep, to crawl; (*fig.*) to cringe, to fawn, to toady.
Kriecher *m.* (-s, -) (*fig.*) toady; yes-man.
Kriecherei *f.* (-, -en) toadyism, servility.
kriecherisch *a.* crawling, groveling.
Kriech: ~spur *f.* slow/creeper lane; **~strom** *m.* leak current; **~tier** *n.* reptile.
Krieg *m.* (-[e]s, -e) war.
kriegen *v.t.* (*fam.*) to get, to obtain.
Krieger *m.* (-s, -) warrior.
Kriegerdenkmal *n.* war-memorial.
kriegerisch *a.* warlike, martial.
kriegführend *a.* warring; belligerent.
Kriegführung *f.* warfare.
Kriegs: ~artikel *pl.* articles of war; **~ausbruch** *m.* outbreak of war; **~beil** *n.* tomahawk; **~beschädigte[r]** *m.* disabled ex-service man; **~blind** *a.* war-blinded; **~brücke** *f.* military bridge; **~dienst** *m.* military service; **~dienstverweigerer** *m.* conscientious objector; **~einsatz** *m.* war effort; **~entschädigung** *f.* reparations; **~erklärung** *f.* declaration of war; **~fall** *m. im ~* in the event of war; **~flotte** *f.* navy; **~gebiet** *n.* war zone **~gefangene[r]** *m.* prisoner of war; **~gefangenschaft** *f.* captivity; **~gericht** *n.* court martial; **~gewinnler** *m.* war-profiteer; **~gliederung** *f.* order of battle; **~hafen** *m.* naval base; **~hetzer** *m.* war-monger; **~klausel** *f.* war clause; **~list** *f.* stratagem; **~material** *n.* materiel; **~ministerium** *n.* War Office; **~potential** *n.* war potential; **~recht** *n.* military law; **~risiko** *n.* war risk; **~schauplatz** *m.* theater of war; **~schiff** *n.* warship; **~spiel** *n.* (*mil.*) map maneuver; **~verbrechen** *n.* war crime; **~verbrecher** *m.* war criminal; **~wichtiges Ziel** *n.* military target *or* objective; **~wissenschaft** *f.* military science; **~zeit** *f.* wartime; **~zulage** *f.* war bonus.
Krimi *m.* (-[s], -[s]) (*fam.*) crime thriller; detective story.
Kriminalbeamte *m.*; **Kriminalbeamtin** *f.* detective.
Kriminalfilm *m.* crime film; thriller.
kriminalisieren *v.t.* to criminalize.
Kriminalität *f.* (-, 0) criminality; crime rate; delinquency.
Kriminal: ~kommissar *m.*; **~kommissarin** *f.* detective superintendent; **~polizei** *f.* criminal

investigation department; detective police; **~roman** *m.* crime novel; thriller; detective novel.
kriminell *a.* criminal.
Kriminelle *m./f.* criminal.
Kriminologe *m./f.* (-n, -n) criminologist.
Krimskrams *m.* (*fam.*) stuff.
Kringel *m.* (small)ring; round squiggle.
kringeln *v.t.u.refl.* to curl.
Krippe *f.* (-, -n) crib, manger; day nursery; crèche.
Krippenspiel *n.* nativity play.
Krise, Krisis *f.* (-, Krisen) crisis.
kriseln *v.i.imp.* to go through a crisis.
krisenanfälls *a.* crisi-sprone.
krisenfest *a.* stable.
Krisengebiet *n.* crisis area.
krisengeschüttelt *a.* crisis-ridden.
Krisenherd *m.* trouble spot.
Krisenzeit *f.* time of crisis.
Kristall *m.* (-[e]s, -e) crystal.
kristallen *a.* crystalline.
Kristallglas *n.* crystal.
kristallisieren *v.i.* to crystallize.
Kriterium *n.* (-s, -rien) criterion.
Kritik *f.* (-, -en) criticism; critique, review; *unter aller ~,* below contempt.
Kritiker *m.* (-s, -); **Kritikerin** *f.* (-, -nen) critic.
kritiklos *a.* uncritical.
kritisch *a.* critical.
kritisieren *v.t.* to criticize; to review.
Krittelei *f.* (-, -en) fault-finding; carping.
kritteln *v.i.* to find fault; to carp.
Kritzelei *f.* (-, -en) scribbling, doodling.
kritzeln *v.t.* to doodle; to scribble.
Krokodil *n.* (-[e]s, -e) crocodile.
Krokus *m.* crocus.
Krone *f.* (-, -n) crown; coronet; crest.
krönen *v.t.* (*also fig.*) to crown.
Kron: ~leuchter *m.* chandelier; **~prinz** *m.* crown-prince.
Krönung *f.* (-, -en) coronation.
Kronzeuge *m.* chief-witness; *~ werden,* to turn state's evidence.
Kröpf *m.* (-[e]s, Kröpfe) crop; goiter.
kroß *a.* crisp.
Kröte *f.* (-, -n) toad.
Krücke *f.* (-, -n) crutch.
Krückstock *m.* walking stick.
Krug *m.* (-[e]s, Krüge) pitcher; jug; (*Henkel~*) mug.
Krume *f.* (-, -n) crumb; (*Acker*) mold.
Krümel *m.* (-s, -) crumb.
krümelig *a.* crumbling, crumy.
krümeln (sich) *v.i. & refl.* to crumble.
krumm *a.* crooked; curved; bent; *etwas ~ nehmen,* to take a thing (in) ill (part).
krummbeinig *a.* bow-legged.
krümmen *v.t.* to bend, to crook; (sich) ~ *v.refl.* to cringe, to stoop; (*vor Schmerz*) to writhe; (*Fluß*) to bend, to wind; *einem kein Haar ~,* not to hurt a hair of a person's head.
Krummstab *m.* crosier.
Krümmung *f.* (-, -en) curvature; curve.
Krüppel *m.* (-s, -) cripple.
krüppelhaft, krüppelig *a.* crippled, lame.
Kruste *f.* (-, -n) crust.
Krustentier *n.* crustacean.
Kruzifix *n.* (-es, -e) crucifix.

Krypta *f.* (-, Krypten) crypt.
Kübel *m.* (-s, -) tub; pail.
Kubik- (*in Zus.*) cubic.
Kubik: ~**wurzel** *f.* cube root; ~**zahl** *f.* cube (number).
kubisch *a.* cubical; cube-shaped; cubic.
Kubismus *m.* cubism.
Küche *f.* (-, -n) kitchen; cooking, cookery, cuisine; *kalte* ~, cold meal.
Kuchen *m.* (-s, -) cake, pastry.
Küchenabfälle *pl.* kitchen scraps.
Küchenartikel *m.pl.* kitchen utensil.
Kuchenbäcker *m.* pastry-cook.
Kuchenblech *n.* baking sheet.
Küchenchef *m.* chef.
Kuchenform *f.* cake-tin.
Küchengerät *n.* kitchen appliance.
Küchenschabe *f.* cockroach.
Küchlein *n.* (-s, -) chicken.
Kuckuck *m.* (-s, -e) cuckoo.
Kuddelmuddel *m.* (*fam.*) muddle; confusion.
Kufe *f.* (-, -n) skid, runner.
Küfer *m.* (-, -) cooper.
Kugel *f.* (-, -n) ball; (*Flinte*) bullet; (*math.*) sphere, globe; bowl.
kugelfest *a.* bullet-proof.
kugelförmig *a.* spherical.
Kugel: ~**gelenk** *n.* socket joint; (*mech.*) ball and socket; ~**lager** *n.* ball bearing.
kugeln *v.t. & i.* to roll, to bowl.
Kugelschreiber *m.* ballpoint pen.
kugelsicher *a.* bullet-proof.
Kugelstoßen *n.* shotput(ting).
Kugelstoßer *m.*; **Kugelstoßerin** *f.* shot putter.
Kuh *f.* (-, Kühe) cow.
Kuh: ~**dorf** *n.* (*pej.*) one-horse town; ~**fladen** *m.* cow-pat; ~**handel** *m.* (*pej.*) horse-trading; ~**haut** *f.* cowhide.
kühl *a.* cool, fresh.
Kühle *f.* (-, 0) coolness.
kühlen *v.t.* to cool; ~ *v.i.* to grow cool.
Kühler *m.* (-s, -) (*mot.*) radiator; ~**haube** *f.* hood.
Kühlflüssigkeit *f.* (-, -en), **Kühlemittel** *n.* (-s, -) (*mech.*) coolant.
Kühlraum *m.* cold storage.
Kühlschrank *m.* (-s, -schränke) refrigerator.
Kühltasche *f.* (-s, -n) cool box.
Kühltruhe *f.* (chest) freezer.
Kühlung *f.* (-, -en) cooling.
Kühlwagen *m.* refrigerator car (train); refrigerator truck.
Kühlwasser *n.* cooling water.
Kuhmilch *f.* cow's milk.
Kuhmist *m.* cow dung.
kühn *a.* bold, daring, audicious.
Kühnheit *f.* (-, 0) boldness; daringness; audacity.
Kuhstall *m.* cow-shed.
Küken *n.* (-s, -) chicken; (*fam.*) chick.
kulant *a.* (com.) fair.
Kuli *m.* (-s, e) coolie; ballpoint pen.
Kulisse *f.* (-, n); scenery; backdrop; wing, side-scene; *hinter den* ~*n*, behind the scenes.
kullern *v.i.* to roll.
Kult *m.* (-s, -e) cult.
Kult: ~**figur** *f.* cult figure; ~**handlung** *f.* ritual act.
kultisch *a.* ritual, cultic.

kultivieren *v.t.* to cultivate; to culture.
kultiviert *a.* cultivated; cultured; refined; civilized.
Kultstätte *f.* (-, -n) center of worship.
Kultur *f.* (-, -en) culture; civilization; cultivation.
Kultur: ~**banause** *m.*; ~**banausin** *f.* philistine; ~**beutel** *m.* cosmetic bag.
kulturell *a. & adv.* cultural(ly).
Kultur: ~**film** *m.* documentary film; ~**geschichte** *f.* history of civilization; cultural history; ~**gut** *n.* cultural asset(s); ~**hoheit** *f.* autonomy in cultural and educational matters; ~**kreis** *m.* cultural area, ~**politik** *f.* cultural and educational policy.
Kultus *m.* (-, Kulte) (public) worship.
Kultusminister *m.*; **Kultusministerin** *f.* minister of education.
Kümmel *m.* (-s, -) caraway; **Kreuz~** *m.* cumin.
Kummer *m.* (-s, 0) grief, sorrow, distress.
kümmerlich *a.* miserable, scanty.
kümmern (sich) *v.refl.* to care for, to mind.
kummervoll *a.* sorrowful, grievous, afflicted.
Kumpan *m.* (-[e]s, -e); **Kumpanin** *f.* (-, -nen) buddy; companion, pal.
Kumpel *m.* miner; buddy.
kumpelhaft *a.* matey; chummy.
kund *a.* ~ *tun*, to notify, to give notice; **sich** ~**geben**, to manifest oneself.
kündbar *a.* terminable; subject to notice.
Kunde *f.* (-, -n) knowledge; information; ~ *m.* (-n, -n) customer, client.
künden *v.t.* to make known.
Kundgebung *f.* (-, -en) demonstration.
kundig *a.* skilled, versed (in).
kündigen *v.i.*; to give notice; ~*v.t.* to cancel.
Kündigung *f.* (-, -en) notice, cancellation; termination; dismissal; warning; *Geld auf tägliche* ~, call-money; *auf monatliche* ~, at a month's notice; ~**sfrist** *f.* period of notice.
Kündigungs: ~**frist** *f.* period of notice; ~**grund** *m.* grounds for giving notice; ~**schreiben** *n.* letter of notice/dismissal; ~**schutz** *m.* protection against unlawful dismissal.
Kundin *f.* (female) customer, client.
Kundschaft *f.* (-, -en) customers; patronage.
kundschaften *v.i.* to reconnoiter.
Kundschafter *m.* (-s, -) scout; spy.
künftig *a.* future, to be, next; ~ *adv.* in future.
Kunst *f.* (-, Künste) art; skill.
Kunst. . . synthetic *a.*
Kunst: ~**akademie** *f.* academy of fine arts; ~**banause** *m.*; ~**banausin** *f.* philistine; ~**ausstellung** *f.* art exhibition; ~**dünger** *m.* artificial manure.
Künstelei *f.* (-, -en) affectation.
Kunst: ~**fertigkeit** *f.* skill; skilfullness; ~**gegenstand** *m.* work of art.
kunstgerecht *a.* (technically) correct, workmanlike; expert.
Kunst: ~**geschichte** *f.* art history; ~**gewerbe** *n.* arts and crafts; ~**griff** *m.* trick, artifice; ~**händler** *m.* art-dealer; ~**handlung** *f.* fine-art shop; ~**handwerk** *n.* arts and crafts; ~**kenner** *m.* connoisseur; ~**kritik** *f.* art criticism; ~**leder** *n.* imitation leather.
Künstler *m.* (-s, -); **Künstlerin** *f.* (-, -nen) artist.
künstlerisch *a.* artistic.
Künstlername *m.* stage name.

künstlich *a.* artificial; artful.
Kunstliebhaber *m.*; **Kunstliebhaberin** *f.* art lover.
kunstlos *a.* artless, plain.
kunstsinnig *a.* art-loving.
Kunst: ~**richtung** *f.* trend in art; ~**sammlung** *f.* art collection; ~**seide** *f.* artificial silk, rayon; ~**schule** *f.* school of art; ~**springen** *n.* springboard diving; ~**stoff** *m.* synthetic material, plastic; ~**stopferei** *f.* invisible mending; ~**stück** *n.* feat, trick, stunt; ~**tischler** *m.* cabinet-maker; ~**turnen** *n.* gymnastics.
kunst: ~**verständig** *a.* expert; ~**voll** *a.* artistic, elaborate.
Kunstwerk *n.* work of art.
Kunstwissenschaft *f.* aesthetics and art history.
kunterbunt *a. & adv.* colorful; untidy.
Kupfer *n.* (-s, -) copper.
Kupfer: ~**bergwerk** *n.* copper-mine; ~**blech** *n.* sheet-copper; ~**druck** *m.* copper-plate.
Kupfermünze *f.* copper (coin).
kupfern *a.* copper.
Kupferplatte *f.* copper-plate.
kupferrot *a.* copper-colored.
Kupfer: ~**schmied** *m.* coppersmith, brazier; ~**stecher** *m.* engraver (in copper); ~**stich** *m.* engraving, copperplate, print.
Kuppe *f.* (-, -n) curved top, summit; tip (finger).
Kuppel *f.* (-, -n) cupola, dome.
Kuppelbau *m.* domed building.
Kuppelei *f.* (-, -en) procuration, (*pej.*) match making.
kuppeln *v.t.* to couple, to link, to join; ~ *v.i.* to procure.
Kupplung *f.* (- -en) coupling; clutch.
Kuppler *m.* (-s, -) pander, pimp.
Kupplerin *f.* (-, -nen) procuress, bawd.
Kur *f.* (-, -en) cure, medical treatment.
Kür *f.* free program (ice skating); optional exercises (gymnastics).
Kürassier *m.* (-[e]s, -e) cuirassier.
Kuratel *f.* (-, -en) guardianship, trusteeship.
Kurator *m.* (-s, -en) guardian, trustee.
Kuratorium *n.* board of trustees.
Kuraufenthalt *m.* stay at a spa.
Kurbad *n.* spa; health resort.
Kurbel *f.* (-, -n) crank, winder.
kurbeln *v.t.* to crank; (*film*) to reel off.
Kurbelwelle *f.* (*mech.*) crankshaft.
Kürbis *m.* (-bisses, -bisse) gourd, pumpkin.
küren *v.t.* to choose.
Kur: ~**fürst** *m.* elector; ~**fürstentum** *n.* electorate; ~**fürstin** *f.* electress.
kurfürstlich *a.* electoral.
Kur: ~**gast** *m.* visitor at a health-resort/spa, ~**haus** *m.* pump room; casino (of a spa).
Kurie *f.* (-, -n) curia.
Kurier *m.* (-[e]s, -e) courier.
Kurierdienst *m.* messenger service.
kurieren *v.t.* to cure.
kurios *a.* curious, odd, strange.
Kuriosität *f.* (-, -en) strangeness, oddity, peculiarity; curiosity, curio.
Kuriositätenkabinett *n.* gallery of curios.
Kurort *m.* health-resort, spa, watering-place.
Kurpfuscher *m.* quack.

Kurs *m.* (-ses, -se) (rate of) exchange; price; (*nav.*) course; *außer* ~ (*Geld, Briefmarke*), out of circulation.
Kurs: ~**änderung** *f.* change of course; ~**anstieg** *m.* rise in the exchange rate; rise in prices (stock market); ~**buch** *n.* railway-guide, time tables *pl.*
Kürschner *m.* (-s, -); **Kürschnerin** *f.* (-, -nen) furrier, skinner.
kursieren *v.i.* to circulate.
kursiv *a.* ~ *gedruckt*, printed in italics.
Kursivschrift *f.* italics *pl.*
Kurs: ~**korrektur** *f.* course correction; ~**leiter** *m.*, ~**leiterin** *f.* instructor; ~**notierung** *f.* quotation; ~**rückgang** *m.* fall in exchange rates; fall in prices (stock market); ~**schwankung** *f.* fluctuation in prices (stock market); fluctuation in exchange rates; ~**teilnehmer** *m.*, ~**teilnehmerin** *f.* participant.
Kursus *m.* (-, Kurse) course (of lessons); class.
Kurtaxe *f.* visitors' tax at a spa.
Kurve *f.* (-, -n) curve, bent.
kurven *v.i.* to drive/ride around.
Kurvenbild *n.* graph, diagram.
Kurvenlage *f.* cornering stability (car).
kurvenreich *a.* winding, twisting.
Kurverwaltung *f.* administrative offices at a spa.
kurz *a.* short; brief, abrupt; ~ *adv.* in short, briefly; *und gut,* in a word; ~*um,* in short; ~*weg,* briefly, in brief; ~ *und bündig,* concise(ly), terse(ly); *in* ~*em,* shortly, soon; *vor* ~*em,* recently, the other day; *über* ~ *oder lang,* sooner or later; *zu* ~ *kommen,* to get short measure; *den kürzeren ziehen,* to get the worst of it.
Kurzarbeit *f.* part-time work.
Kurzarbeiter *m.*, **Kurzarbeiterin** *f.* part-time worker.
kurzatmig *a.* short-winded.
Kurzbiographie *f.* profile.
Kurze *m.* (*fam.*) short (circuit); schnapps.
Kürze *f.* (-, -n) shortness; brevity.
Kürzel *n.* abbreviation; shorthand symbol.
kürzen *v.t.* to shorten, to curtail; (*Schriftliches*) to abridge.
kurzerhand *adv.* without more ado.
kürzertreten *v.i.st.* to take things easier, to spend less; to cut back.
Kurz: ~**fassung** *f.* shortened/abridged version; ~**film** *m.* short film.
kurzfristig *a.* short term;
Kurzgeschichte *f.* short story.
kürzlich *adv.* lately, recently.
Kurz: ~**schluß** *m.* short circuit; fallacy; ~**schlußhandlung** *f.* sudden irrational act; ~**schrift** *f.* shorthand (writing).
kurzsichtig *a.* near-sighted, short-sighted, narrow-minded.
Kurzstreckenflug *m.* short-haul flight.
Kurzstreckenläufer *m.*; **Kurzstreckenläuferin** *f.* sprinter.
Kürzung *f.* (-, -en) abridgement; curtailment, cut.
Kurzwaren *pl.* notions.
Kurzweil *f.* (-, 0) pastime.
kurzweilig *a.* merry, diverting, amusing.
Kurzwelle *f.* (-, -n) shortwave; radiothermy.
kuschelig *a.* cozy.
kuscheln *v.refl.* to snuggle.

kuschen *v.i.* (*von Hunden*) to crouch, to lie down; *kusch* (*dich*)! lie down!
Kusine *f.* (-, -n) s. **Cousine; cousin.**
Kuß *m.* (Kusses, Küsse) kiss.
küssen *v.t.* to kiss.
Kußhand *f.* blown kiss.
Küste *f.* (-, -n) coast, shore.
Küsten. . . coastal *a.*
Küstenschiffahrt *f.* coastal shipping.
Küstenwache *f.* coastguard.
Küster *m.* (-s, -) sexton, verger.
Kustos *m.* (-, Kustoden) curator, custodian.
Kutschbock *m.* coach-box.
Kutsche *f.* (-, -n) carriage, coach.
Kutscher *m.* (-s, -) coachman, driver.

kutschieren *v.i.* to drive a coach.
Kutte *f.* (-, -n) cowl; monk's habit.
Kutteln *pl.* tripe.
Kutter *m.* (-s, -) (*nav.*) cutter.
Kuvert *n.* (-s, -e) envelope; (*Gedeck*) cover.
Kuvertüre *f.* chocolate coating.
Kux *m.* (-es, -e) mining-share.
Kuwait *n.* (-s, 0) Kuwait.
Kuwaiti *m./f.*; **kuwaitisch** *a.* Kuwaiti.
Kybernetik *f.* (-, 0) cybernetics.
Kybernetiker *m.*; **Kybernetikerin** *f.* cyberneticist.
kybernetisch *a.* cybernetic.
kyrillisch *a.* cyrilic.
KZ-Häftling *m.* concentration camp prisoner.

L

L, l *n.* the letter L or l.
labb(e)rig *a.* (*fam.*) wishy-washy; flopp; limp.
laben *v.t.* to refresh, to comfort; (sich)~ *v.refl.* to refresh oneself.
labern *v.t.* (*fam. pej.*) to babble.
labil *a.* unstable; delicate.
Labilität *f.* delicateness; frailness; instability.
Labor *n.* (-s, -e/s), **Laboratorium** *n.* (-s, -torien) laboratory.
Laborant *m.*, **Laborantin** *f.* lab assistant.
Labsal *n.* (-[e]s, -e) refreshment.
Labyrinth *n.* (-s, -e) maze, labyrinth.
Lachanfall *m.* (-s, -fälle) laughing fit.
Lache *f.* (-, -n) pool, puddle; (*fam.*) laugh.
lächeln *v.i.* to smile.
Lächeln *n.* (-s, 0) smile.
lachen *v.i.* to laugh.
Lachen *n.* (-s, 0) laughter, laugh.
Lacher *m.* (-s, -) laughter.
lächerlich *a.* laughable, ridiculous; ludicrous.
Lächerlichkeit *f.* (-, -en) ridiculous, ludicrousness.
Lachgas *n.* laughing gas.
lachhaft *a.* ridiculous, laughable.
Lachkrampf *m.* convulsive laughter.
Lachs *m.* (-ses, -se) salmon.
Lachsschinken *m.* (-s, -) fillet of smoked ham.
Lack *m.* (-[e]s, -e) gum-lac; varnish, laquer, paint.
Lackaffe *m.* (*fam. pej.*) dandy.
lackieren *v.t.* to varnish, to lacquer, to spray.
Lackmus *n.* (-, 0) litmus.
Lackstiefel *m.* patent-leather boots.
Lade *f.* (-, -n) drawer.
Ladegerät *n.* (*elek.*) charger.
laden *v.t.st.* to load, to charge; to summon, to cite; to invite.
Laden *m.* (-s, -Läden) shop; store.
Laden: ~dieb *m.* shoplifter; **~diebstahl** *f.* shoplifting; **~fenster** *n.* shop-window; **~hüter** *m.* unsaleable article; **~preis** *m.* retail price; (*Bücher*) publication price; **~tisch** *m.* counter.
Lader *m.* (*avi.*) supercharger.
Laderampe *f.* loading ramp.
Laderaum *m.* baggage space; hold.
lädieren *v.t.* to damage; to harm.
Ladung *f.* (-, -en) freight, cargo, shipment; (*Gewehr~*) (*elek.*) charge.

Lage *f.* (-, -n) situation, position; location; condition; layer, stratum; (*mech.*) thickness; **~karte** *f.* (*mil.*) map of the area; **~meldung** *f.* (*mil.*) situation report.
Lager *n.* (-s, -) couch, bed; warehouse; (*von Tieren*) lair; (*Vorrat*) stock; (*Erz*) deposit; (*mil.*) camp.
Lager: ~bier *n.* lager; **~geld** *n.*, **~gebühr** *f.* storage (charge); **~haus** *n.* warehouse.
Lagerist *m.* storekeeper.
lagern *v.t.* to lay, to store, to warehouse; ~ *v.i.* to (en)camp; to be stored; (sich) ~ *v.refl.* to lie down.
Lagerstätte *f.* resting-place; depot.
Lagerung *f.* storage.
Lagune *f.* (-, -n) lagoon.
lahm *a.* lame, halt.
Lahme *m./f.* (-n, -n) cripple.
lahmen *v.i.* to be lame, to halt.
lähmen *v.t.* to lame, to paralyze.
lahmlegen *v.t.* to paralyze.
Lähmung *f.* (-, -en) paralysis.
Laib *m.* (-[e]s, -e) loaf.
Laich *m.* (-[e]s, 0) spawn.
laichen *v.i.* to spawn.
Laie *m.* (-n, -n) layman.
Laienbruder *m.* lay-brother.
Laientheater *n.* (-s, -) amateur theater groups.
Lakai *m.* (en, -en) footman, lackey.
Lake *f.* (-, -n) brine, pickle.
Laken *n.* (-s, -) sheet.
lakonisch *a. & adv.* laconic(ally).
Lakritz *m.* (-es, -e), **Lakritze** *f.* (-, -n) liquorice.
Lakritzenholz *n.* stick-liquorice.
lallen *v.t. & i.* to stammer.
Lama *n.* (-s, -s) llama.
Lamelle *f.* (-, -n) (*elek.*) lamina.
lamentieren *v.i.* to moan, to complain.
Lamm *n.* (-[e]s, Lämmer) lamb.
Lammbraten *m.* roast-lamb.
Lammfell *n.* lambskin.
Lammfleisch *n.* lamb.
Lamm: ~keule *f.* leg of lamb; **~kotelett** *n.* lamb chop.
Lampe *f.* (-, -n) lamp.
Lampen: ~fieber *n.* stage-fright; **~schirm** *m.* lamp-shade.
Lampion *m.* (-s, -s) Chinese lantern.
lancieren *v.t.* (*fig.*) to launch.

Land n. (-[e]s, Länder) or, poet, Lande) land; country; territory; zu ~, by land; auf dem ~, in the country.
Land: ~**adel** m. landed aristocracy; ~**arbeiter** m. farm worker; ~**arzt** m. country doctor.
Landauer m. (-s, -) landau.
Land: ~**besitz** m. landed property; ~**bevölkerung** f. rural population.
Lande: ~**anflug** m. (avi.) approach; ~**bahn** f. runway; ~**erlaubnis** f. permission to land; ~**fähre** f. landing module.
landeinwärts adv. (further) inland.
Landeklappe f. landing flap.
landen v.t. (h) & i. (s) to land; to get ashore, to disembark.
Landenge f. isthmus.
Lande: ~**piste** f. landing strip; ~**platz** m. airstrip; landing pad.
Länderei f. (-, -en) landed property; estate.
Länderkunde f. geography.
Landes. . . regional a.
Landes: ~**farben** pl. national colors; ~**herr** m. sovereign; ~**kirche** f. national or established church; ~**tracht** f. national costume.
landesüblich a. customary, usual.
Landes: ~**verrat** m. treason; ~**verteidigung** f. defense.
Land: ~**friede[n]** m. the king's peace; ~**gericht** n. county court; ~**gut** n. estate, manor; ~**haus** n. country house; ~**karte** f. map; ~**krieg** m. land warfare.
Landmaschine f. agricultural machine.
landläufig a. in current use.
ländlich a. rural.
Landmesser m. surveyor.
Landplage f. plague of the country; (fig.) pest, nuisance.
Landratte f. (fam.) landlubber.
Landschaft f. (-, -en) landscape; scenery; countryside.
landschaftlich a. provincial; scenic.
Landschafts: ~**pflege** f., ~**schutz** m. landscape conservation; ~**schutzgebiet** n. (natural) preserve.
Landsitz m. country-seat.
Lands: ~**knecht** m. hired foot-soldier; ~**mann** m. countryman, compatriot.
Land: ~**straße** f. country road; ~**streicher** m. vagrant, tramp, hobo; ~**streitkräfte** pl. ground forces; ~**strich** m. area ~**tag** m. state parliament; ~**truppen** pl. ground forces.
Landung f. (-, -en) landing, descent.
Landungsbrücke f. landing stage; jetty.
Land: ~**wirt** m. farmer; agriculturist; ~**wirtschaft** f. agriculture, farming.
landwirtschaftlich a. agricultural; ~**er Betriebsleiter** m. farm manager.
Landwirtschafts: ~**minister** m., ~**ministerin** f. Minister of Agriculture; ~**ministerium** n. Ministry of Agriculture.
Landzunge f. promontory.
lang a. long; tall; Tage ~, for days together.
langatmig a. long-winded, lengthy.
lange adv. long; ~ her, long ago.
Länge f. (-, -en) length; tallness; longitude; auf die ~, in the long run; der ~ nach, lengthwise.

langen v.t. to hand, to give, to reach; ~ v.i. to suffice, to be enough.
Längen: ~**grad** m. degree of longitude; ~**kreis** m. longitude; ~**maß** n. long or linear measure.
Langeweile f. (-, 0) boredom.
lang: ~**fristig** a. longterm; ~**jährig** a. of long standing.
Langlauf m. cross-country (skiing).
Langläufer m.; **Langläuferin** f. cross-country skier.
langlebig a. long-lived.
länglich a. oblong.
Langmut f. (-, 0) forbearance.
langmütig a. forbearing.
längs pr. along.
Längsachse f. longitudinal axis.
langsam a. slow; tardy.
Langsamkeit f. slowness.
Langschläfer m.; **Langschläferin** f. late riser.
Langspielplatte f. (-, -n) long playing record, LP.
Längsschnitt m. longitudinal section.
längsseits adv. along side.
längst adv. long since.
längstens adv. at the longest, at latest.
Langstrecke f. long distance; long haul.
Languste f. spiny lobster; langoust.
langweilen v.t. to tire, to bore; (sich) ~ v.refl. to feel dull, to be bored.
Langweiler m. bore.
langweilig a. dull; ~e Person, bore.
Langwelle f. (Radio) long wave.
langwierig a. lengthy, protracted.
Lanze f. (-, -n) lance, spear.
Lanzette f. (-, -n) lancet.
lapidar a. & adv. succinct(ly); terse(ly).
Lappalie f. (-, -n) trifle.
Lappe m.; **Lappin** f. Lapp, Laplander.
Lappen m. (-s, -) rag; patch.
läppisch a. silly, foolish.
Lappland n. (-s, 0) Lapland.
Lärche f. (-, -n) larch.
Larifari n. (fam.) nonsense.
Lärm m. (-[e]s, 0) noise, din; ~**schlagen**, to sound the alarm.
Lärm: ~**bekämpfung** f. noise abatement; ~**belästigung** f. noise pollution.
lärmempfindlich a. sensitive to noise.
lärmen v.i. to make a noise or row.
lärmend a. noisy.
Lärmpegel m. noise level.
Lärmschutz m. protection against noise.
Larve f. (-, -n) mask; larva.
lasch a. limp, lax.
Lasche f. (-, -n) (Kleid) stripe, flap.
Laserstrahl m. laser beam.
lassen v.t.st. to let; to allow, to suffer; to order, to cause; to leave; sein Leben ~, to sacrifice one's life: einen in Ruhe oder zufrieden ~, to leave (let) one alone; kommen ~, to send for, to order; machen ~, to have done; sehen ~, to show; sagen ~, to send word; übrig ~, to leave; sein Tun und Lassen, all his doing; laß das! don't!; das läßt sich hören, it is pleasant to hear; there is something in that.
lässig a. casual; (fam.) cool.
lässlich a. pardonable.
Last f. (-, -n) load, charge, burden; tonnage; zu

Ihren ~en, to your account; *zur ~fallen*, to be a burden on.

lasten *v.i.* to weigh upon, to press.

Laster *n.* (-s, -) vice; crime.

lasterhaft *a.* vicious, profligate.

Lästermaul *n.* slanderer, scandalmonger.

lästern *v.t.* to slander; to blaspheme.

Lästerung *f.* (-, -n) calumny; blasphemy.

lästig *a.* burdensome, troublesome.

Last: *~kraftwagen* *m.* truck; *~tier* *n.* beast of burden; *~*.

Lasur *f.* (-, -en) varnish, glaze.

Latein *n.* (-s, 0) Latin.

Lateinamerika *n.* Latin America.

lateinamerikanisch *a.* Latin American.

lateinisch *a.* Latin.

latent *a.* latent.

Laterne *f.* (-, -n) lantern; (street-)lamp.

Laternenpfahl *m.* lamppost.

Latinum *n.* Latin proficiency certificate.

Latrine *f.* (-, -n) latrine.

Latsche *f.* (-, -n) dwarf pine.

latschen *v.i.* to shuffle along; to slouch; to trudge.

Latte *f.* (-, -n) lath; slat.

Latten: *~rost* *m.* duckboards; slatted frame (bed); *~zaun* *m.* paling fence.

Latz *m.* (-es, Lätze) flap; bib; tucker.

Latzhose *f.* dungarees.

lau *a.* tepid; (*met.*) mild; (*fig.*) lukewarm.

Laub *n.* (-[e]s, 0) leaves *pl.*; foliage.

Laubbaum *m.* deciduous tree.

Laube *f.* (-, -n) arbor, bower.

Laubengang *m.* arcade.

Laubfrosch *m.* treefrog.

laubig *a.* leafy, leaved.

Laubsäge *f.* fret-saw.

Lauch *m.* (-[e]s, -e) leek.

Lauer *f.* (-, 0) lurking-place; ambush; *auf der ~ sein*, to lie in wait.

lauern *v.i.* to lurk, to lie in wait.

Lauf *m.* (-[e]s, Läufe) course; run; race; (*Gewehr~*) barrel; leg (of game); (*mus.*) roulade.

Lauf: *~bahn* *f.* course, career; *~bursche* *m.* errand-boy, messenger boy.

laufen *v.i.st.* (*s*) to run, to flow, to leak.

laufend *a.* running; current; *auf dem ~en sein*, to be well informed; *auf dem ~en halten*, to keep informed; *~e Arbeiten* *pl.* routine work; *~es Band* *n.* conveyor belt; *~e Nummer* *f.* serial number; *~es Wasser* *n.* running water.

laufenlassen *v.t.st.* to let s.b. go.

Läufer *m.* (-s, -) runner, long carpet; (*Schach*) bishop; (*sp.*) halfback.

Lauferei *f.* (-, -en) running around.

Lauffeuer *n.*, *wie ein ~*, like wildfire.

Lauffläche *f.* tread (of tire).

Lauf: *~gitter* *n.* playpen; *~kran* *m.* travelling crane; *~masche* *f.* run (in stocking); *~schritt* *m.* at the double; *~ställchen* *n.* play pen; *~steg* *m.* catwalk; *~zeit* *f.* running time; run; term.

Lauge *f.* (-, -n) lye, suds; (*chem.*) alkaline solution.

Laune *f.* (-, -n) whim, caprice; humor, temper, mood.

launenhaft *a.* temperamental; capricious; fickle.

launig *a.* humorous.

launisch *a.* capricious, wayward.

Laus *f.* (-, Läuse) louse (*pl. lice*).

Lausbub *m.* (-en, -en) scamp.

Lauscher *m.* (-s, -) listener.

lauschig *a.* snug, cozy, quiet.

lausig *a.* lousy, wretched.

Lausjunge, Lausekerl *m.* little rascal.

Laut *m.* (-[e]s, -e) sound.

laut *a.* loud; ~ *adv.* aloud, loud(ly); ~ *pr.* as per, according to.

Laute *f.* (-, -n) lute.

lauten *v.i.* to sound; to run, to read.

läuten *v.i. & t.* to ring.

lauter *a.* clear; pure; mere, none but, nothing but; sincere, ingenuous.

Lauterkeit *f.* (-, 0) purity; integrity.

läutern *v.t.* to purity, to reform.

Läuterung *f.* (-, -en) purification.

Lautgesetz *n.* phonetic law.

lauthals *adv.* at the top of one's voice.

lautlich *a.* phonetic.

lautlos *a.* silent, mute; hushed.

Laut: *~schrift* *f.* phonetic alphabet; *~sprecher* *m.* loudspeaker, speaker; *~sprecherwagen* *m.* loudspeaker van; *~stärke* *f.* (*Radio*) volume; *~stärkeneinstellung* *f.* volume control; *~zeichen* *n.* phonetic symbol.

lauwarm *a.* lukewarm; tepid; warm.

Lava *f.* (-, Laven) lava.

Lavendel *m.* (-s, 0) lavender.

lavieren *v.i.* to maneuver.

Lawine *f.* (-, -n) avalanche.

lax *a.* lax, loose.

Lazarett *n.* (-[e]s, -e) military hospital.

Lazarettschiff *n.* hospital ship; **Lazarettzug** *m.* hospital train.

Leasing *n.* leasing.

Lebemann *m.* man about town; epicure.

leben *v.i.* to live, to be alive; *lebe wohl!* farewell; *hoch ~ lassen*, to cheer.

Leben *n.* (-s, -) life; (*fig.*) animation; *am ~ bleiben*, to live; *ums ~ bringen*, to kill; *ums ~ kommen*, to perish; *sich sein ~ verdienen*, to earn *or* make a living.

lebend *a.* living; alive; *~e Sprachen*, modern languages; *~e Bilder*, tableaux vivants.

lebendig *a.* living, alive; quick, lively.

Lebendigkeit *f.* liveliness.

Lebens: *~abend* *m.* old age, autumn of one's life; *~abschnitt* *m.* period of life; *~alter* *n.* age; *~art* *f.* way of life; manner; *~bedingungen* pl. (living) conditions.

lebensbedrohlich *a.* life-threatening.

Lebens: *~bedürfnisse* pl. necessities of life; *~bejahung* *f.* positive approach to life; *~beschreibung* *f.* biography, life; *~dauer* *f.* (*auch von Dingen*) life-span, *von langer ~dauer*, long-lived; *mutmaßliche ~dauer*, expectation of life; *~erhaltungssystem* *n.* life support system; *~erinnerungen* pl. memoirs; *~erwartung* *f.* life expectancy.

lebensfähig *a.* capable of living, viable.

Lebensfrage *f.* vital question.

Lebensfreude *f.* joy of life.

Lebensgefahr *f.* danger to life.

lebensgefährlich *a.* perilous; ~ *verwundet od. krank*, in critical condition.

Lebens: *~gefährte* *m.*, *~gefährtin* *f.* companion,

partner in life; **~größe** *f.* full length, lifesize; **~haltung** *f.* standard of living; **~haltungskosten** *pl.* cost of living; **~jahr** *n.* year of one's life; **~kampf** *m.* struggle for survival; **~kraft** *f.* vitality, vigor.
lebenslang *a.* lifelong.
lebenslänglich *a.* for life, life-long; **~er Nießbrauch,** (*law*) life-interest.
Lebenslauf *m.* career; curriculum vitae.
lebenslustig *a.* cheery, enjoying life.
Lebensmittel *pl.* provisions, victuals; **~abteilung** *f.* food department; **~geschäft** *n.* grocery store; **~karten** *pl.* ration book; **~vergiftung** *f.* food poisoning.
lebensmüde *a.* weary of life.
lebensunfähig *a.* nonviable.
Lebens: **~unterhalt** *m.* (means of) livelihood; **~versicherung** *f.* life-insurance; **~wandel** *m.* conduct; **~weise** *f.* way of life; **~weisheit** *f.* practical wisdom.
lebenswert *a.* worth living.
lebenswichtig *a.* vital.
Lebens: **~wille** *m.* will to live; **~zeichen** *n.* sign of life; **auf ~zeit,** for life.
Leber *f.* (-, -n) liver.
Leber: **~fleck** *u.* **~flecken** *m.* mole; **~knödel** *m.* (*cul.*) liver dumpling; **~pastete** *f.* (*cul.*) liver pâté; **~tran** *m.* cod-liver oil; **~zirrhose** *f.* cirrhosis of the liver.
Lebewesen *n.* living being; creature; organism.
Lebewohl *n.* (-[e]s, -e *u.* -s) farewell.
lebhaft *a.* vivid, lively, brisk, animated.
Lebhaftigkeit *f.* (-, 0) vivacity, animation.
Lebkuchen *m.* gingerbread.
leblos *a.* lifeless, inanimate; heavy, dull.
Lebzeiten *f.pl.* lifetime.
lechzen *v.i.* to pant, to languish.
leck *a.* leaky; **~ werden,** to spring a leak.
Leck *n.* (-[e]s, -e) leak.
lecken *v.t.* to lick, to lap; **~** *v.i.* to leak.
lecker *a.* tasty; delicious; good.
Leckerbissen *m.* delicacy, tidbit, choice morsel.
Leckerei *f.* (-, -en) dainty; sweet.
Leder *m.* (-s, -) leather.
Lederband *m.* leatherbound book.
ledern *v.t.* to leather.
ledern *a.* leather, leathern; (*fig.*) dull.
Lederzeug *n.* leather straps and belts *pl.*
ledig *a.* unmarried, single.
lediglich *adv.* solely, only.
Lee *n.* (-, 0) (*nav.*) lee-side.
leer *a.* empty, void; vacant.
Leere *f.* (-, 0) emptiness; void, vacuum.
leeren *v.t.* to empty, to clear.
leergefegt *a.* (*fig.*) deserted.
Leerkassette *f.* blank cassette.
Leerlauf *m.* (-[e]s, 0) idle running; neutral gear; freewheel.
leerstehend *a.* unoccupied.
Leertaste *f.* space bar.
Leerung *f.* emptying; **nächste ~** next collection.
Lefzen *pl.* flews.
legal *a. & adv.* legal(ly).
legalisieren *v.t.* to legalize.
Legalität *f.* legality.
Legasthenie *f.* (-, -n) dyslexia; **Legastheniker** *m.*; **Legasthenikerin** *f.* dyslexic.

Legat *n.* (-[e]s, -e) legacy; **~** *m.* (-en, -en) legate.
Legehenne *f.* laying hen.
legen *v.t.* to lay, to put, to place; (sich) **~** *v.refl.* to lie down; (wind) to abate; **Karten ~,** to tell fortunes from cards; **einem das Handwerk ~,** to stop one's little game; **nahe~,** to suggest, to impress upon; **an den Tag ~,** to manifest, to evince; **sich ins Mittel ~,** to step in, to interpose.
legendär *a.* legendary.
Legende *f.* (-, -n) legend.
leger *a.* casual; relaxed.
legieren *v.t.* to alloy.
Legierung *f.* (-, -en) alloy(ing).
Legion *f.* (-, -en) legion.
Legionär *m.* (-s, -e) legionnaire.
Legislative *f.* legislature.
Legislaturperiode *f.* parliamentary term.
legitim *a.* legitimate, lawful.
Legitimationspapier *n.* certificate of identity; **~e** *pl.* identity papers.
legitimieren *v.t.* to legitimate; **sich ~** *v.refl.* to prove one's identity.
Legitimität *f.* (-, 0) legitimacy.
Leh(e)n *n.* (-s, -) fief.
Leh(e)nsrecht *n.* feudal law.
Lehm *m.* (-[e]s, -e) loam, clay.
Lehm: **~boden** *m.* loamy soil; clay soil; **~hütte** *f.* mud hut.
lehmig *a.* loamy, clayey.
Lehmziegel *m.* clay brick.
Lehne *f.* (-, -n) back(rest); arm(rest).
lehnen *v.t. & i. & refl.* (*sich*) to lean (against).
Lehnsessel, -stuhl *m.* arm-chair.
Lehr: **~amt** *n.* teaching position; teaching profession; **~anstalt** *f.* academy, school: **~auftrag** *m.* lectureship; teaching assignment.
lehrbar *a.* teachable.
Lehr: **~beauftragte** *m./f.* lecturer; **~buch** *n.* textbook.
Lehre *f.* (-, -n) doctrine; instruction; precept; moral, warning; lesson; apprenticeship; **in der ~ sein,** to serve one's apprenticeship; gauge (*mech.*).
lehren, *v.t.* to teach, to instruct.
Lehrer *m.* (-s, -) **Lehrerin** *f.* (-, -nen) teacher; tutor.
Lehrer: **~ausbildung** *f.* teacher training; **~kollegium** *n.* teaching faculty; **~konferenz** *f.* faculty meeting; **~zimmer** *n.* teacher's room.
Lehr: **~fach** *n.* subject; **~gang** *m.* course; **film** *m.* instructional film; **~jahre** *n.pl.* apprenticeship.
Lehrkörper *m.* (-s, -) teaching staff; faculty.
Lehrling *m.* (-[e]s, -e) apprentice.
Lehr: **~meister** *m.* instructor; **~mittel** *n.* means of instruction; **~plan** *m.* curriculum; syllabus.
lehrreich *a.* instructive.
Lehr: **~satz** *m.* theorem, maxim; **~stuhl** *m.* (professor's) chair; professorship; **~veranstaltung** *f.* class; lecture, course; **~zeit** *f.* apprenticeship.
Leib *m.* (-[e]s, -er) body; (*Bauch*) belly; **sich vom ~ halten,** to keep at a distance.
Leib: **~ arzt** *m.* private physician; **~binde** *f.* sash, waistband; (*med.*) truss.
Leibchen *n.* (-s, -) bodice.
Leibeigene[r] *m.* (-n, -n) serf.
Leibeigenschaft *f.* serfdom.
Leibes: **~erben** *m.pl.* offspring issue; **~erziehung**

f. physical education; **~frucht** *f.* fetus.
Leibesübung *f.* physical exercise.
Leibgarde *f.* bodyguard.
Leibgericht *n.* favorite dish.
leibhaftig *a.* real.
leiblich *a.* physical, bodily; **~e Eltern** biological parents.
Leib: ~rente *f.* life annuity; **~schmerzen** *m.pl.* stomach-ache; **~wache** *f.* body-guard.
Leiche *f.* (-, -n) corpse, (dead) body.
Leichen: ~begängnis *n.* funeral, burial; **~beschauer** *m.* coroner; **~bestatter** *m.* undertaker; mortician; **~bestattugsinstitut** *n.* funeral home.
leichenblaß *a.* deadly pale.
Leichen: -feier *f.* funeral service; **~gift** *n.* ptomaine; **~halle** *f.* mortuary; **~schauhaus** *n.* morgue; **~starre** *f.* rigor mortis; **~tuch** *n.* shroud; **~verbrennung** *f.* cremation; **~wagen** *m.* hearse.
Leichnam *m.* (-[e]s, -e) corpse; carcass.
leicht *a.* light; easy, slight; mild; ~ *adv.* easily.
Leichtathlet *m.;* **Leichtathletin** *f.* (track and field) athlete.
Leichtathletik *f.* athletics *pl.*
leicht: ~blütig *a.* sanguine; **~fertig** *a.* careless; ill considered; frivolous.
Leichtgewicht *n.* (*sport*) light-weight.
leicht: ~gläubig *a.* gullible; credulous; **~herzig** *a.* light-hearted.
leichthin *adv.* lightly.
Leichtigkeit *f.* (-, -en) ease, facility.
leichtlebig *a.* easygoing.
Leichtmetall *n.* light metal.
Leichtsinn *m.* carelessness, levity, frivolity.
leichtsinnig *a.* careless, frivolous, light-hearted, heedless.
Leid *n.* (-[e]s, 0) grief, sorrow; pain, harm; *einem etwas zu ~e tun,* to harm, to wrong, to hurt one; *es tut mir leid,* I am sorry for (it).
leiden *v.t. & i.st.* to suffer; to endure; to tolerate; *nicht ~ können,* not to be able to stand.
Leiden *n.* (-s, -) suffering; disease.
leidend *a.* ailing, suffering.
Leidenschaft *f.* (-, -en) passion.
leidenschaftlich *a.* passionate, vehement.
Leidensgefährte *m.* , **~gefährtin** *f.;* **~genosse** *m.,* **~genossin** *f.* fellow-sufferer; **~geschichte** *f.* Christ's Passion; sad story; **~miene** *f.* doleful expression.
leider *adv.* unfortunately; ~ *i.* alas!
leidig *a.* tiresome, unpleasant.
leidlich *a.* tolerable; passable.
Leidtragende *m./f.* victim; bereaved; mourner.
leidvoll *a.* sorrowful.
Leidwesen *n.* regret.
Leier *f.* (-, -n) lyre; *die alte ~,* the old story.
Leierkasten *m.* hurdy-gurdy; barrel-organ.
leiern *v.i.* to drone; to reel, to rattle off.
Leihbibliothek *f.* circulating-library.
leihen *v.t.st.* to lend; to borrow.
Leih: ~gabe *f.* loan; **~gebühr** *f.* rental charge; borrowing fee; **~haus** *n.* pawnbroker's shop; **~mutter** *f.* surrogate mother; **~wagen** *m.* rental car.
leihweise *adv.* on loan, by way of loan.
Leim *m.* (-[e]s, -e) glue; *aus dem ~ gehen,* to get out of joint; *auf den ~ gehen,* to fall into the trap.

leimen *v.t.* to glue; (*Papier*) to paste; to take s.b. in.
Leine *f.* (-, -n) line, cord, rope; leash.
leinen *a.* linen.
Leinen *n.* (-s, -) linen (goods) *pl.*
Leinenband *m.* clothbound book.
Lein: ~öl *n.* linseed oil; **~samen** *m.* linseed.
Leinwand *f.* (-, 0) linen; (*Maler~*) canvas; screen.
leise *a.* quiet, low, soft, gentle; ~ *adv.* softly, in a low voice; *~r reden,* to lower one's voice.
Leiste *f.* (-, -n) ridge, ledge; strip; trim; rail.
Leisten *m.* (-s, -) last, form; shoe tree.
leisten *v.t.* to do, to perform; (*Dienst*) to render; (*Eid*) to take; (*Grosses*) to achieve (great things); *Gesellschaft ~,* to keep (someone) company; *ich kann mir das ~,* I can afford it.
Leisten: ~bruch *m.* (*med.*) hernia; **~gegend** *f.* (*med.*) groin.
Leistung *f.* (-, -en) performance; accomplishment.
leistungs: ~berechtig *a.* entitled to claim; **~bezogen** *a.* performance-oriented.
Leistungs: ~denken *n.* performance-oriented outlook; **~druck** *m.* pressure to achieve.
leistungsfähig *a.* efficient; productive.
Leistungsfähigkeit *f.* (-, 0) efficiency; productivity; power, (working) capacity.
Leistungs: ~gesellschaft *f.* performance-oriented society; **~prämie** *f.* productivity bonus.
leistungsschwach *a.* inefficient; low-performance.
Leistungssport *m.* competitive sport(s).
leistungsstark *a.* efficient; high-performance.
Leitartikel *m.* editorial, lead article, leader.
Leitartikler *m.* (-s, -) editorial writer.
Leitbild *n.* model.
leiten *v.t.* to lead, to guide; to conduct; to manage, to direct.
Leiter *m.* (-s, -); **Leiterin** *f.* (-, -nen) manager; leader, conductor; (*elek.*) conductor.
Leiter *f.* (-, -n) ladder; steps.
Leit: ~fähigkeit *f.* (*elek.*) conductivity; **~faden** *m.* (*Buch*) manual; **~gedanke** *m.* central theme; **~hammel** *m.* bellwether; *fig.* leader.
Leit: ~linie *f.* guideline; **~motiv** *n.* (-s, -e) leitmotiv; central theme; **~planke** *f.* crash barrier; guardrail; **~satz** *m.* guiding principle; **~spruch** *m.* motto.
Leitung *f.* (-, -en) guidance; management; direction;(*Röhre*) conduit; (*elek.*) line; *die ~ von etwas haben,* to be in charge of.
Leitungswasser *n.* tap water.
Lektion *f.* (-, -en) lesson; (*fig.*) lecture.
Lektor *m.;* **Lektorin** *f.* editor.
Lektüre *f.* (-, 0) reading; books *pl.*
Lende *f.* (-, -n) loin; haunch, thigh.
Lendenbraten *m.* sirloin; rump of beef.
Lendenschurz *m.* loincloth.
Lendenwirbel *m.* lumbar vertebra.
lenken *v.t.* to guide; to rule; to steer.
Lenker *m.* **Lenkerin** *f.* driver.
Lenker *m.* handlebar.
Lenkrad *n.* steering wheel.
Lenksäule *f.* (*mot.*) steering column.
Lenkstange *f.* (-, -n) handlebar.
Lenkung *f.* control; governing; steering.
Lenz *m.* (-es, -e) spring.
Leopard *m.* (-en, -en) leopard.

Lepra *f.* leprosy.
Lerche *f.* (-, -n) lark, skylark.
lernbar *a.* learnable, acquirable by study.
lernbegierig *a.* eager to learn; keen.
lernbehindert *a.* learning disabled.
Lerneifer *m.* eagerness to learn.
lernen *v.t.* to learn, to study; to train.
Lernende *m./f.* learner.
lernfähig *n.* able to learn.
Lernmittel *n.* (-s, -) teaching-materials.
Lesart *f.* reading, variant.
lesbar *a.* legible; (*fig.*) readable.
Lesbe *f.* (-, -n) Lesbian.
Lesbierin *f.* (-, -nen) Lesbian.
lesbisch *a.* Lesbian.
Lese *f.* (-, -n) grape harvest, vintage.
Lesebrille *f.* reading glasses.
Lesebuch *n.* reader.
Lesegerät *n.* (*comp.*) scanner.
Lesekopf *m.* (*comp.*) reading head.
lesen *v.t. & i.st.* to gather, to glean; to read; to lecture; (*Messe*) to say.
lesenswert *a.* worth reading.
Leser *m.* (-s, -); **Leserin** *f.* (-, -nen) reader; gleaner.
Leseratte *f.* bookworm.
Leserbrief *m.* letter to the editor.
leserlich *a.* legible.
Lesesaal *m.* reading-room.
Leserstift *m.* (*comp.*) scanner.
Lesezeichen *n.* bookmark.
Lesung *f.* (-, -en) reading.
Lethargie *f.* lethargy.
lethargisch *a.* lethargic.
Lette *m.*; **Lettin** *f.* Latvian; Lett.
Letter *f.* (-, -n) letter, type.
lettisch *a.* Latvian; Lettish (language).
Lettland *n.* Latvia.
letzen *v. refl. sich ~ an,* to enjoy, to relish.
letzt *a.* last, final; *~e Ölung,* extreme unction; *zu guter Letzt,* finally.
letztemal *adv.* **das~** last time.
letztere[r] *a.* latter.
letzthin *adv.* lately, to other day.
letztlich *adv.* lastly.
letztwillig *a.* testamentary.
Leuchtbombe *f.* flare (bomb).
Leuchte *f.* (-, -n) lamp, lantern; (*fig.*) shining light.
leuchten *v.i.* to shine; to beam.
leuchtend *a.* shining bright.
Leuchter *m.* (-s, -) candlestick; chandelier.
Leucht: **~farbe** *f.* luminous paint, **~feuer** *n.* beacon; runway light; **~käfer** *m.* glow-worm; **~kugel** *f.* fire-ball; **~pistole** *f.* flare pistol; **~turm** *m.* lighthouse; **~uhr** *f.* luminous watch.
leugnen *v.t.* to deny, to disown.
Leukämie *f.* (-, -n) leukemia.
Leumund *m.* reputation.
Leute *pl.* people, persons *pl.*; servants, *pl.*
Leuteschinder *m.* slave-driver.
Leutnant *m.* (-[e]s, -s) second lieutenant.
leutselig *a.* affable.
Leviten *pl. jm. die ~ lesen* to read s.b. the riot act.
Levkoje *f.* (-, -n) stock, gilly flower.
lexikalisch *a.* lexical.
Lexikographie *f.* lexicography.
Lexikon *n.* (-s, Lexika) encyclopedia.

Liane *f.* (-, -n) liana.
Libanese *m.*; **Libanesin** *f.*; **Libanesisch** *a.* Lebanese.
Libanon *n./m.* Lebanon.
Libelle *f.* (-, -n) dragon-fly.
liberal *a.* liberal; generous, open-handed.
Liberale *m./f.* liberal.
liberalisieren *v.t.* to liberalize.
Liberalisierung *f.* (-, -n) liberalization.
Liberalismus *m.* liberalism.
Libero *m.* sweeper (soccer).
Libyen *n.* Libya.
Libyer *m.*; **Libyerin** *f.*; **Libysch** *a.* Libyan.
Licht *n.* (-[e]s, -er *u.* -e) light; candle; *bei ~e,* (*fig.*) closely; *ungeschütztes ~,* naked light; *einem ein ~ aufstecken,* to open one's eyes; *hinters ~ führen,* to dupe, to impose upon; *ans ~ bringen,* to bring to light; *ins rechte ~ setzen,* to show in its true colors.
licht *a.* light, bright; lucid; clear; **~e Höbe** *f.* overhead clearance.
Licht: **~bild** *n.* photograph; **~bildervortrag** *m.* slide lecture; **~blick** *m.* ray of hope; **~bogen** *m.* electric arc; **~empfindlich** *a.* (*phot.*) sensitive.
lichten *v.t.* (*Wald*) to clear, to thin; *den Anker ~,* to weigh anchor.
lichterloh *a.* blazing.
Licht: **~geschwindigkeit** *f.* speed of light; **~hupe** *f.* (*mot.*) flasher; **~maschine** *f.* dynamo, generator; **~schalter** *m.* light switch.
lichtscheu *a.* shade-loving; (*fig.*) shunning publicity.
Licht: **~spieltheater** *m.* cinema, movies; **~seite** *f.* bright side (of things); **~strahl** *m.* ray of light, beam.
Lichtung *f.* (-, -en) clearing, glade.
lichtvoll *a.* luminous, lucid.
Lid *n.* (-[e]s, -er) eyelid.
Lidschatten *m.* eyeshadow.
lieb *a.* dear, beloved; agreeable.
liebäugeln *v.i.* to have one's eye on s.th.
Liebe *f.* (-, 0) love; (*christliche*) charity.
liebebedürftig *a.* in need of love.
Leibedienerei *f.* (-, -en) servility, obsequiousness.
Liebelei *f.* (-, -en) flirtation.
lieben *v.t.* to love; to like; *~ v.i.* to be in love.
liebend *a.* loving.
Liebende *m./f.* (-n, -n) lover.
liebenswert *a.* lovable; aimiable.
liebenswürdig *a.* amiable, sweet; kind.
liebenswürdigerweise *adv.* kindly.
Liebenswürdigkeit *f.* (-, -en) kindness; winning ways *pl.*
lieber *adv.* rather, sooner.
Liebes: **~dienst** *m.* kindness; **~paar** *n.* couple of lovers; **~roman** *m.* romantic novel.
liebestoll *a.* love crazed.
liebevoll *a.* loving.
liebgewinnen *v.t.st.* to grow fond of.
liebhaben *v.t.st.* to love, to be fond of.
Liebhaber *m.* (-s, -) **Liebhaberin** *f.* (-, -nen) lover; amateur.
Liebhaberei *f.* (-, -en) hobby.
Liebhabertheater *n.* private theatricals *pl.*
liebkosen *v.t.* to caress, to fondle.
lieblich *a.* lovely; charming, sweet.
Liebling *m.* (-[e]s, -e) favorite, pet, darling.

Lieblingsbuch *n.* favorite book.
lieblos *a.* unkind, uncharitable.
liebreich *a.* kind, loving.
Liebreiz *m.* charm, attraction.
liebreizend *a.* charming, lovely.
Liebste *m./f.* (-n, -n) love, sweetheart.
Lied *n.* (-[e]s, -er) song, air; **Kirchen~** hymn.
Liederabend *m.* song recital.
liederlich *a.* loose, dissolute, immoral; messy.
Liedermacher *m.*; **Liedermacherin** *f.* singer-songwriter.
Lieferant *m.* (-n, -en) supplier.
Lieferanteneingang *m.* tradesman's entrance.
lieferbar *a.* available.
Liefer: **~bedingungen** *pl.* terms of delivery; **~frist** *f.* delivery time.
liefern *v.t.* to deliver; to furnish; to supply; *eine Schlacht ~*, to give battle.
Lieferschein *m.* delivery note.
Liefertermin *m.* delivery date.
Lieferung *f.* (-, -en) delivery, supply; number, part (of a book).
Liefervertrag *m.* supply contract.
Lieferwagen *m.* delivery van.
Lieferzeit *f.* term of delivery.
Liege *f.* couch; campbed; sunbed.
Liege: **~geld** *n.* (*nav.*) demurrage; **~kur** rest cure.
liegen *v.i.st.* to lie; to be situated; *vor Anker ~*, to ride at anchor; **~lassen**, to leave (behind); to leave alone, to give up; **~bleiben**, to be left (unfinished, unsettled); *es liegt an mir*, it is my fault; *es liegt nichts daran*, it's of no consequence; *die Sache liegt ganz anders*, the case is different altogether.
Liegenschaften *pl.* real estate, immovables *pl.*
Liege: **~platz** *m.* mooring; **~sitz** *m.* reclining seat; **~stuhl** *f.* deck-chair; **~stütz** *m.*push-up; **~wagen** *m.* couchette car; **~wiese** *f.* lawn (at a pool).
Lift *m.* (-s, -e/s) elevator; lift (ski).
liften *v.t.* **sich ~ lassen** to have a face-lift.
Liga *f.* (-, -gen) league.
liieren *v.refl.* to team up; to start an affair.
Likör *m.* (-[e]s, -e) liqueur.
lila *a.* lilac.
Lilie *f.* (-, -n) lily; (*Wappen*) fleur-de-lis.
Liliputaner *m.*; **Liliputanerin** *f.* dwarf, midget.
Limit *n.* (-s, -s) limit.
limitieren *v.t.* to limit, to restrict.
Limonade *f.* (-, -n), **Limo** *f.* (-, -s) lemonade.
Limone *f.* (-, -n) lime.
Limousine *f.* (-, -n) sedan; limousine.
lind *a. & adv.* soft(ly), mild(ly).
Linde *f.* (-, -n) lime-tree, linden.
lindern *v.t.* to soften, to mitigate; to alleviate.
Linderung *f.* (-, 0) relief; alleviation.
Lineal *n.* (-[e]s, -e) ruler, rule.
Linguist *m.*; **Linguistin** *f.* linguist.
Linguistik *f.* linguistics.
linguistisch *a. & adv.* linguistic; linguistically.
Linie *f.* (-, -n) line; lineage, descent; *in absteigender ~*, in the descending line; *in aufsteigender ~*, in the ascending line; *in gerader ~*, in the direct line.
Linien: **~bus** *m.* regular bus; **~flug** *m.* scheduled flight; **~richter** *m.* (*sp.*) linesman; line judge; touch judge; **~papier** *n.* ruled paper; **~verkehr** *m.* regular services.
linieren *v.t.* to rule.

liniert *a.* ruled, lined.
link *a.* left; left-wing; underhand(ed), shady.
Linke *f.* (-n, 0) left hand *or* side; (*pol.*) left.
Linke *m./f.* left-winger; leftist.
linkisch *a.* awkward.
links *adv.* to the left; on the left-hand side; **~händig** *a.* left-handed; **~ um, kehrt!**, left face!
Linksabbieger *m.* (vehicle) turning left.
Linksaußen *m.* (sp.) left wing; outside left.
Linksextremismus *m.* left-wing extremism.
Linkshänder *m.*; **Linkshänderin** *f.* left hander.
Linksliberale *m./f.* left-wing liberal.
Linksradikalismus *m.* left-wing radicalism.
Linksruck *m.* shift to the left.
Linse *f.* (-, -n) lentil; (*opt.*) lens.
Lippe *f.* (-, -n) lip.
Lippenbekenntnis *n.* empty talk.
Lippenstift *m.* lipstick.
liquidieren *v.t.* to liquidate, to wind up.
lispeln *v.i.* to lisp.
List *f.* (-, -en) cunning, craft; trick, stratagem.
Liste *f.* (-, -n) list, roll; catalogue; *von der ~ streichen*, to strike off the list.
listig *a.* cunning, crafty, sly, artful.
Litanei *f.* (-, -en) litany.
Litauen *n.* (-s, 0) Lithuania.
Litauer *m.*; **Litauerin** *f.*; **Litauisch** *a.* Lithuanian.
Liter *n.* (-s, -) liter (= $\frac{9}{16}$ quart).
Literarhistoriker *m.* literary historian.
literarisch *a.* literary.
Literat *m.* (-en, -en) man of letters.
Literatur *f.* (-, -en) literature, letters *pl.*
Literatur: **~angabe** *f.* reference; **~gattung** *f.* literary genre; **~geschichte** *f.* history of literature; **~kritik** *f.* literary criticism; **~verzeichnis** *n.* list of references; **~wissenschaft** *f.* literary studies.
Litfaßsäule *f.* advertising pillar.
Lithograph *m.* (-en, -en) lithographer.
Lithographie *f.* (-, -n) lithography; lithograph.
Liturgie *f.* (-, -n) liturgy.
Litze *f.* (-, -n) lace, tape, braid; (*elek.*) cord.
Litzenbesatz *m.* piping.
Live-sendung *f.* live program; live broadcast.
Livree *f.* (-, -[e]n) livery.
Lizenz *f.* (-, -en) license; **~ausgabe** *f.* licensed edition; **~gebühr** *f.* royalty.
Lizenz: **~inhaber;** **~träger** *m.* licensee.
LKW-Fahrer *m.* trucker.
Lob *n.* (-[e]s, 0) praise; commendation.
loben *v.t.* to praise to commend.
lobenswert *a.* praiseworthy.
Lobgesang *m.* song of praise.
lobhudeln *v.t.* to flatter, to heap praise on s.b.
löblich *a.* laudable, commendable.
Lobrede *f.* eulogy.
Lobredner *m.* eulogist.
Loch *n.* (-[e]s, Löcher) hole; dungeon.
lochen *v.t.* to perforate, to punch.
Locher *m.* (-s, -) punch.
löcherig *a.* full of holes, in holes.
löchern *v.t.* to pester.
Loch: **~karte** *f.* punch card, **~streifen** *m.* ticker tape.
Locke *f.* (-, -n) curl, ringlet.
locken *v.t.* to lure, to entice.
Lockenwickler *m.* curler.

locker *a.* relaxed, loose; licentious, dissolute.
lockern *v.t.* to loosen; to relax.
Lockerung *f.* loosening; relaxation.
lockig *a.* curled, curly.
Lockmittel *n.* lure, bait.
Lockung *f.* temptation.
Loden *m.* (-s, -) loden.
lodern *v.i.* to blaze; (*fig.*) to glow (with).
Löffel *m.* (-s, -) spoon; (*Schopf*) ladle.
löffeln *v.t.* to spoon (up); to ladle.
löffelweise *adv.* by the spoonful.
Log *n.* (-s, -s) (*nav.*) log.
Logarithmus *m.* (-, men) logarithm.
Loge *f.* (-, -n) box; (*der Freimaurer*) lodge.
Logenschließer *m.* (theater) attendant.
logieren *v.i.* to stay.
Loggia *f.* (-, -gien) balcony.
Logik *f.* (-, 0) logic.
Logiker *m.* (-s, -) logician.
logis *n.* room/rooms (for rent).
logisch *a.* logical.
logischerweise *adv.* logically.
lohen *v.t.* to tan (leather); ~, *v.i.* to blaze.
Lohn *m.* (-[e]s, Löhne), reward; wages *pl.*, pay; salary, fee.
Lohn: ~**abhängige** *m./f.* wage earner, ~**buchhalter** *m.* payroll accountant, ~**empfanger** *m.* wage-earner.
Lohn: ~**erhöhung** *f.* pay raise; ~**schreiber** *m.* literary hack; ~**steuer** *f.* income tax; ~**steuerjahresausgleich** *m.* annual adjustment of income tax; ~**steuerkarte** *f.* income tax card; ~**tarif** *m.* wage scale; ~**tüte** *f.* pay envelope; ~**zettel** *m.* pay-slip.
lohnen *v.t. & i.* to reward, to recompense, to pay; *es lohnt (sich) nicht (der Mühe)*, it is not worth while.
lohnend *a.* rewarding; lucrative.
Loipe *f.* (cross-country) course.
Lok *f.* engine, locomotive.
Lokal *n.* (-[e]s, -e) locality, place, shop, premises *pl.*; (*Gastwirtschaft*) tavern, café.
lokal *a.* local.
Lokalanästhesie *f.* local anaesthesia.
lokalisieren *v.t.* to locate; to prevent from spreading.
Lokal: ~**kolorit** *n.* local color; ~**patriotismus** *m.* local patriotism; ~**termin** *m.* visit to the scene (of the crime); ~**verbot** *n.* to get banned from a bar.
Lokomotive *f.* (-, -n) (locomotive) engine.
Lokomotivführer *m.* engineer.
Lokus *m.* john; ~**papier** *n.* toilet paper.
Lorbeer *m.* (-s, -en) laurel, bay; ~**blatt** *n.* bayleaf; ~**kranz** *m.* laurel wreath.
Lore *f.* (-, -n) lorry, load.
Lorgnette *f.* (-, -n) eye-glass, lorgnette.
Los *n.* (Loses, Lose) lot, destiny, fate; lottery-ticket; *das grosse ~*, the first prize.
los *a.* loose, untied; *was ist los?* what is the matter?; *ich bin es los*, I am rid of it; *etwas ~haben*, to have the knack; *etwas ~kriegen*, to get the hang of a thing.
los let's go!, go!, *Achtung, fertig, ~* ready, set, go.
lösbar *a.* soluble.
losbinden *v.t.st.* to untie.
losbrechen *v.t.st.* to break loose *or* off; ~ *v.i.st.* (*s*) to burst out.

Lösch: ~**blatt** *n.* blotting paper; ~**eimer**, firebucket.
löschen *v.t.* to extinguish; to quench; to slake; to unload.
Lösch; ~**fahrzeug** *n.* fire-engine; ~**papier** *n.* blottingpaper.
lose *a.* loose; dissolute.
Lösegeld *n.* ransom.
losen *v.i.* to cast *or* draw lots.
lösen *v.t.* to loosen, to untie; to free, to deliver; to solve; to buy (a ticket).
Losentscheid *m.* **durch** ~ by drawing lots.
losfahren *v.i.st.* to set off, to drive off.
losgehen *v.i.st.* (*s*) to come off; to get loose; to go off; to rush upon, to fight; to begin, to commence.
loskaufen *v.t.* to redeem, to ransom.
loskommen *v.t.st.* (*s*) to get away.
loslassen *v.t.st.* to let go.
löslich *a.* soluble.
losmachen *v.t.* to disengage, to free.
losplatzen *v.i.* (*s*) to blurt out.
losreissen *v.t.st.* to tear off; to separate; (sich) ~ *v.refl.* to tear oneself away.
lossagen (sich) *v.refl.* to renounce.
losschlagen *v.t.st.* to knock off; (*verkaufen*) to dispose of, to sell off; ~ *v.i.* to begin to fight.
lossprechen *v.t.st.* to absolve.
Lossprechung *f.* (-, -en) absolution.
lossteuern (auf) *v.i.* to make for.
Lostvommel *f.* lottery drum.
Lösung *f.* (-, -en) solving, loosening; solution.
Losung *f.* (-, -en) (*mil.*) password; watchword.
loswerden *v.t.* to get rid of.
loswickeln *v.t.* to reel off.
losziehen *v.i.st.* (*s*) (*fig.*) to set off.
Lot *n.* (-[e]s, -e) plumb line, lead; perpendicular; solder.
loten *v.i.* to take soundings.
löten *v.t.* to solder.
Löt: ~**kolben** *m.* soldering iron; ~**lampe** *f.* blowlamp.
Lotos *m.* lotus.
lotrecht *a.* perpendicular, vertical.
Lötrohr *n.* blowpipe.
Lotse *m.* (-n, -n) pilot; guide.
lotsen *v.t.* to pilot; (*fig.*) to take in tow.
Lotsengebühr *f.* pilotage.
Lotterie *f.* (-[e]n) lottery.
Lotterielos *n.* lottery ticket.
Lotto *n.* national lottery.
Löwe *m.* (-n, -n) lion.
Löwen: ~**anteil** *m.* the lion's share; ~**maul** *n.* (*bot.*) snap-dragon; ~**zahn** *m.* (*bot.*) dandelion.
Löwin *f.* (-, -nen) lioness.
Loyalität *f.* loyalty.
Luchs *m.* (Luchses, Luchse) lynx.
Lücke *f.* (-, -n) gap; (*fig.*) space, void, blank; omission, deficiency, hiatus.
Lückenbüßer *m.* (-s, -) stop-gap.
lückenhaft *a.* defective, fragmentary; sketchy.
lückenlos *a.* without a gap; complete.
Luder *n.* (-s, -) wretch, hussy.
Luft *f.* (-, Lüfte) air; breath; breeze; *frische ~ schöpfen*, to get some air; *in die ~ sprengen*, to blow up.
Luft: ~**angriff** *m.* air raid; ~**aufklärung** *f.* (*mil.*)

air reconnaissance; ~**aufnahme** *f.*, ~**bild** *n.* aerial photograph; ~**brücke** *f.* airlift.

Lüftchen *n* (-s, -) breeze.

luftdicht *a.* air-tight, hermetic.

Luft: ~**druck** *m.* atmospheric pressure; ~**druckbremse** *f.* pneumatic brake.

lüften *v.t.* to air, to ventilate; to raise, to tip (hat).

Luftfahrt *f.* aviation.

Luft: ~**fahrtgesellschaft** *f.* airline; ~**geschwindigkeitsmesser** *m.* airspeed indicator ~**hoheit** *f.* air sovereignty.

luftig *a.* airy; (*dress*) thin; well-ventilated.

Luftkissen: ~**boot** *n.*, ~**fahrzeug** *n.* hovercraft.

luftleer *a.* void of air; ~*er Raum*, vacuum.

Luft: ~**kurort** *m.* health resort; ~**linie** (**nentfernung**) *f.* as the crow flies; ~**loch** *n.* air pocket; ~**pirat** *m.* (aircraft) hijacker; ~**post** *f.* airmail; ~**röhre** *f.* windpipe, trachea; ~**schiff** *n.* airship; ~**schiffahrt** *f.* aeronautics; ~**schloß** *n.* (*fig.*) castle in the air; ~**schraube** *f.* propeller; ~**schraubenblatt** *n.* propeller blade; ~**schutz** *m.* civil air defense; ~**schultzkeller** *m.* air raid shelter; ~**schutzwart** *m.* air raid warden; ~**spiegelung** *f.* mirage; ~**störungen** *pl.* (*Radio*) atmospherics; ~**streitkräfte** *pl.* air force.

Lüftung *f.* (-, -en) airing, ventilation.

Lüftungsklappe *f.* ventilation flap.

Luftveränderung *f.* change of air.

Luft: ~**verpestung** *f.*, ~**verschmutzung** *f.* air pollution; ~**waffe** *f.* air force; ~**weg** *m. auf dem* - by air; ~**zufuhr** *f.* air supply; ~**zug** *m.* breeze; draft.

Lug *m.* (-[e]s, 0) ~**und Trug** lies and deceit.

Lüge *f.* (-, -n) lie, falsehood.

lugen *v.i.* to look out, to peep.

lügen *v.i.st.* to lie, to tell a lie.

lügenhaft *a.* lying, false, mendacious.

Lügner *m.* (-s, -); **Lügnerin** *f.* (-, -nen) liar.

Luke *f.* (-, -n) skylight (roof); trap-door; (*nav.*) hatch(way).

lukrativ *a.* lucrative.

lulatsch *m.* lanky fellow.

lullen *v.t. & i.* to lull (to sleep).

Lümmel *m.* (-s, -) ruffian, lout.

lümmelhaft *a.* loutish.

Lump *m.* (-[e]s, -e) rascal, rogue.

Lumpen *m.* (-s, -) rag, tatter.

Lumpensammler *m.* ragpicker.

Lumperei *f.* (-, -en) trash.

lumpig *a.* (*fig.*) shabby, paltry.

Lunge *f.* (-, -n) lung[s]; lights (of animals) *pl.*

Lungen: ~**entzündung** *f.* pneumonia; ~**flügel** *m.* lobe of the lung; ~**schwindsucht** *f.* tuberculosis.

lungern *v.i.* to idle, to lounge, to skulk.

Lunte *f.* (-, -n) fuse; ~ *riechen* (*fam.*) to smell a rat.

Lupe *f.* (-, -n) magnifying glass.

lupenrein *a.* flawless.

Lupine *f.* (-, -n) (*bot.*) lupin.

Lurch *m.* (-s, -e) amphibian.

Lusche *f.* (-, -n) low card (card game).

Lust *f.* (-, Lüste) joy, delight; inclination; desire, lust; *Keine ~ zu etwas haben*, to have no mind (for to. . .).

Lustbarkeit *f.* (-, -en) amusement, sport.

Lüster *m.* chandelier.

lüstern *a.* greedy (for); lecherous, lascivious, lustful.

lustig *a.* gay, merry, cheerful; funny, droll; *sich über einen ~machen*, to make fun of one, to laugh at one.

Lüstling *m.* lecher.

lustlos *a.* unenthusiastic; listless.

Lust: ~**mord** *m.* murder and rape; ~**schloß** *n.* country-seat; ~**spiel** *n.* comedy.

lustwandelin *v.i.*(*h.u.s.*) to take a walk.

lutherisch *a.* Lutheran.

Luthertum *n.* (-s, 0) Lutheranism.

lutschen *v.i.* to suck.

Lutscher *m.* lollipop.

Luvseite *f.* (*nav.*) windward.

Luxemburg *n.* Luxembourg.

luxuriös *a.* luxurious.

Luxus *m.* (-, 0) luxury.

Luxus. . . de luxe, *a.*

Luxuszug, *m.* luxury train.

Luzerne *f.* (-, -n) (*bot.*) lucern.

Luzifer *m.* Lucifer.

Lymphe *f.* (-, -n) lymph.

Lymph: ~**drüse** *f.*; ~**knoten** *m.* lymph node/gland.

lynchen *v.t.* to lynch.

Lynchjustiz *f.* lynch law.

Lyra *f.* (-, -lyren) lyre.

Lyrik *f.* (-, 0) lyric poetry.

Lyriker *m.* (-s, -) lyric poet.

lyrisch *a.* lyric.

Lysol *n.* (-s, 0) lysol(e).

Lyzeum *n.* (-s, -zeen) high school for girls.

M

M, m *n.* the letter M or m.

Maat *m.* (-[e]s, -e) (*nav.*) (ship)-mate, petty officer.

Machart *f.* (-, -en) style.

Mache *f.* (-, 0) making, workmanship.

machen *v.t.* to make; to do; *was macht das?* how much it is?; *das macht nichts*, that does not matter; *die Rechnung macht so und so viel*, it comes to so much in all; *Licht ~*, to strike a light; *Ernst ~ mit etwas*, to be in earnest about a thing; *zu Gelde ~*, to sell to turn into money; *sich auf den Weg ~*, to set out; *sich daraus nichts ~*, not to care about it.

Machenschaften *pl.* machinations *pl.*

Macher *m.* (*fig.*) doer.

Macho *m.* macho.

Macht *f.* (-, Mächte) power; might; forces.

Macht: ~**befugnis** *f.* power, authority, competence; ~**bereich** *m.* sphere of power; ~**ergreifung** *f.* seizure of power; ~**gier** *f.* craving for power.

Machthaber *m.* (-s, -) potentate, ruler.

mächtig *a.* powerful; mighty.

Machtkampf *m.* power struggle.

machtlos *a.* powerless.

Macht: ~**losigkeit** *f.* impotence; ~**politik** *f.* power politics; ~**probe** *f.* trial of strength; ~**streben** *n.* ambition for power ~**vollkommenheit** *f.* absolute power, authority; ~**wechsel** *m.* change of

government; ~**wort** *n.* word of command.
Machwert *n.* concoction; (*fam.*) lousy job.
Macke *f.* defect; (*fig.*) kink.
Macker *m.* guy; macho.
Mädchen *n.* (-s, -) girl; maid, lass; servant; ~ *für alles*, maid-of-all-work.
mädchenhaft *a.* girlish.
Mädchen: ~**handel** *m.* white slave traffic; ~**name** *m.* (*der Frau*) maiden name; ~**schule** *f.* girls' school.
Made *f.* (-, -n) maggot, larva; mite.
Mädel = **Mädchen** .
Magazin *n.* (-[e]s, -e) store; (*Zietschrift*) magazine.
Magd *f.* (-, Mägde) maid-servant, (*female*) farmhand.
Magen *m.* (-s, -) stomach.
Magen: ~**beschwerden** *pl.* indigestion, dyspepsia; ~**bitter** *m.* bitters; ~**geschwür** *n.* stomach ulcer.
magenleidend *a.* suffering from a disorder of the stomach.
Magen: ~**saft** *m.* gastric juice; ~**saüre** *f.* gastric acid; ~**schmerzen** *pl.* stomach-ache.
mager *a.* lean, thin; meager.
Magerkäse *m.* low-fat cheese.
Magerkeit *f.* thinness; meagerness.
Magermilch *f.* skim milk.
Magie *f.* (-, 0) magic.
Magier *m.* (-s, -) magician.
magisch *a.* magical.
Magistrat *m.* (-[e]s, -e) city council.
Magma *n.* (-s, -men) magma.
Magnat *m.* (-en, -en) magnate.
Magnet *m.* (-[e]s, -e) magnet.
magnetisch *a.* magnetic.
magnetisieren *v.t.* to magnetize.
Magnetismus *m.* (-, 0) magnetism.
Magnetnadel *f.* magnetic needle.
Magnetzünder *m.* (*mot.*) magneto ignition.
Magnolie *f.* magnolia.
Mahagoni *n.* (-s, 0) mahogany.
Mähdrescher *m.* combine harvester.
mähen *v.t.* to mow.
Mahl *n.* (-[e]s, -e *u.* Mähler) meal, repast.
mahlen *v.t.st.* to grind.
Mahlzeit *f.* meal, repast.
Mähmaschine *f.* mower, reaping machine.
Mähne *f.* (-, -n) mane.
mahnen *v.t.* to urge, to remind, to admonish.
Mahn: ~**bescheid** *m.* order to pay; ~**brief** *m.* reminder; ~**gedühr** *f.* reminder fee.
Mahnung *f.* (-, -en) reminder; admonition.
Mähre *f.* (-, -n) mare; (*Schind*~) jade.
Mai *m.* (- *u.* -[e]s, -e) May.
Maibaum *m.* May-pole; birch.
Maid *f.* (-, 0) (*poet.*) maid.
Mai: ~**glöckchen** *n.* lily of the valley; ~**käfer** *m.* May-bug; June-bug; ~**kraut** *n.* woodruff; ~**kundgebung** *f.* May Day rally.
Mais *m.* (- *u.* -ses, 0) corn.
Maiskolben *m.* corncob.
Majestät *f.* (-, -en) majesty.
majestätisch *a.* majestic.
Major *m.* (-[e]s, -e) major.
Majoran *m.* marjoram.
Majorat *n.* (-[e]s, -e) entail(ed estate); primogeniture.

Majorität *f.* (-, 0) majority.
makaber *a.* macabre.
Makel *m.* (-s, -) spot; blemish (*fig.*) stigma.
makellos *a.* unblemished; perfect, immaculate.
mäkeln *v.i.* to find fault (with); to carp.
Make-up *n.* make-up.
Makkaroni *pl.* macaroni.
Makler *m.* (-s, -) broker; realtor; middleman.
Maklergebühr *f.* brokerage charges.
Makrele *f.* (-, -n) mackerel.
makrobiotisch *a.* macrobiotic.
Makrone *f.* (-, -n) macaroon.
Makulatur *f.* (-, -en) wastepaper, trash.
Mal *n.* (-[e]s, -e) time; mark, sign, monument; (on the skin) mole; *einmal*, once; *noch einmal*, once more; *auf einmal*, at once; *ein für allemal*, once for all.
mal *adv.* once, just.
Malachit *m.* (-s, -e) malachite.
Malaie *m.*, **Malaiin** *f.* Malay.
malaiisch *a.* Malayan.
Malaria *f.* malaria.
Malbuch *n.* coloring book.
malen *v.t.* to paint; to portray; *sich ~ lassen*, to sit for one's portrait.
Maler *m.* (-s, -); **Malerin** *f.* (-, -nen) painter, artist.
Malerei *f.* (-, -en) painting; picture.
malerisch *a.* picturesque.
Malermeister *m.* master painter.
Malkasten *m.* paint-box.
malnehmen *v.i.st.* to multiply.
Malpinsel *m.* paintbrush.
malträtieren *v.t* to mistreat.
Malve *f.* mallow.
Malz *n.* (-es, 0) malt.
malzen *v.i.* to malt.
Malzeichen *n.* multiplication sign.
Mälzer *m.* (-s, -) maltster.
Mama *f.* (-, -s) mamma; (*fam.*) ma; mom.
Mammographie *f.* mammography.
Mammon *m.* mammon.
Mammut *n.* (-s, -s) mammoth.
mampfen *v.t.* to munch.
man *pn.* they, people, one.
Management *n.* management.
manager *v.t.* to fix; to organize; to manage.
Manager *m.* (-s, -); **Managerin** *f.* (-, -nen) manager.
Managerkrankheit *f.* executive stress.
mancher, manche, manches *pn.* many a, many a man; **manche** *pl.* some.
mancherlei *a.* various.
manchmal *adv.* sometimes.
Mandant *m.* (-en, -en); **Mandantin** *f.* (-, -nen) (*jur.*) client.
Mandarine *f.* tangerine.
Mandat *n.* (-[e]s, -e) mandate, commission, seat.
Mandel *f.* (-, -n) almond; (*anat.*) tonsil.
Mandelentzündung *f.* tonsilitis.
Mandeloperation *f.* tonsillectomy.
Mandoline *f.* (-, -n) mandolin.
Manege *f.* ring (circus); arena.
Mangan *n.* (-[e]s, 0) manganese.
Mangel *m.* (-s, Mängel) lack; want; deficiency; defect; shortage.
Mangel: ~**beruf** *m.* understaffed profession;

~erscheinung *f.* deficiency symptom.
mangelhaft *a.* incomplete; defective.
mangeln *v.i.* to want, to lack.
mangels *p.* to default of.
Mangelware *f.* goods in short supply *pl.*
Mangrove *f.* (-, -n) mangrove forest.
Manie *f.* (-[e]n) mania.
Manier *f.* (-, -en) manner.
manieriert *a.* affected, mannered.
Manierismus *m.* mannerism.
manierlich *a.* mannerly, polite, civil.
Manifest *n.* (-[e]s, -e) manifesto.
manifestieren *v.i.* to manifest.
Manniküre *f.* manicure; manicurist; ~n *v.t.* to manicure.
Manipulation *f.* (-, -en) manipulation.
manipulierbar *a.* **leicht~** easy to manipulate.
manipulieren *v.t.* to manipulate.
manisch *a.* manic; **~despressiv** *a.* manic-depressive.
Manko *n.* (-s, -s) shortcoming, handicap.
Mann *m.* (-[e]s, Männer) man; husband.
Männchen *n.* (-s, -) (*von Tieren*) male; (*von Vögeln*) cock.
Mannes: **~alter** *n.* manhood; **~kraft** *f.* virility.
mannhaft *a.* manly, manful.
mannigfach, mannigfaltig *a.* manifold; diverse.
Mannigfaltigkeit *f.* (-, 0) variety; diversity.
männlich *a.* male; (*gram.*) masculine; (*fig.*) manly.
Mannschaft *f.* (-, -en) (*Schiffs~*) crew (*Sport*) team.
Mannschaftstransportwagen *m.* (*mil.*) personnel carrier.
mannshoch *a.* as tall as a man.
mannstoll *a.* nymphomaniac.
Mannweib *n.* gynander.
Manöver *n.* (-s, -) maneuvers; exercise.
Manöverkritik *f.* post mortem.
manövrieren *v.i.* to maneuver.
Mansarde *f.* (-, -n) attic, garret; mansard-roof.
manschen *v.i.* to dabble, to paddle; to mix.
Manschette *f.* (-, -n) cuff.
Manschettenknopf *m.* cuff link.
Mantel *m.* (-s, Mäntel) overcoat, mantle; cloak.
manuell *a.* manual.
Manufaktur *f.* (-, -en) manufactory.
Manuskript *n.* (-[e]s, -e) manuscript.
Maoismus *m.* Maoism.
Mäppchen *n.* pencil case.
Mappe *f.* (-, -n) brief-case, portfolio.
Marathon *m.* marathon.
Märchen *n.* (-s, -) (fairy-)tale; fable, fiction; (*Lüge*) fib.
märchenhaft *a.* fabulous, legendary.
Märchenland *n.* fairyland.
Märchenprinz *m.* (*fig.*) prince charming.
Marder *m.* (-s, -) marten.
Margarine *f.* (-, -n) margarine.
Margerite *f.* (-, -n) marguerite.
Marienkäfer *m.* ladybird.
Marihuana *n.* marijuana.
Marinade *f.* marinade; dressing.
Marine *f.* (-, -n) marine, navy.
Marine: **~minister** *m.* Navy Minister. **~offizier** *m.* naval officer; **~stützpunkt** *m.* naval base; **~werft** *f.* navy-yard.
marinierin *v.t.* to marinate; to pickle.

Marionette *f.* (-, -n) (wire-) puppet; marionette.
Marionettentheater *n.* puppet show.
Mark *n.* (-[e]s, 0) marrow, pith; ~ *f.* (-, -en) border, marches *pl.*; district; (*Münze*) Mark.
markant *a.* striking.
Marke *f.* (-, -n) brand; (*Brief~*) (postage-)stamp; (*Spiel~*) counter.
Markenartikel *m.* proprietary article.
Markenzeichen *n.* trade mark.
Marketenderin *f.* (-, -nen) camp follower.
Marketing *n.* marketing.
markieren *v.t.* to mark; (*fig.*) to sham (illness).
markig *a.* pithy, marrowy.
Markise *f.* (-, -n) awning.
Markstein *m.* boundary stone.
Markt *m.* (-e[s], Märkte) market; marketplace; *auf den ~ bringen*, to place on the market; *auf den ~ kommen*, to come into the market.
Marktbericht *m.* market report.
Marktflecken *m.* market town.
marktgängig *a.* current.
marktschreierisch *a.* loud.
Marktwirtschaft *f.* market economy.
Marmelade *f.* (-, -n) jam; (*Apfelsinen~*) marmalade.
Marmor *m.* (-s, 0) marble.
marmoriert *a.* marbled.
marmorn *a.* marble.
marode *a.* rotten, degenerate.
Marodeur *m.* (-s, -e) marauder.
Marokkaner *m.*; **Marokkanerin** *f.*; **marokkanisch** *a.* Moroccan.
Marokko *n.* (-s, 0) Morocco.
Marone *f.* (-, -n) edible chestnut.
Maroquin *m.* (-s, 0) morocco (-leather).
Marotte *f.* (-, -n] fad.
Marquise *f.* (-, -n) marchioness.
Mars *m.* Mars.
Marsbewohner *m.* Martian.
marsch! *i.* march!; be off! get out!.
Marsch *m.* (-es, Märsche) march.
Marsch *f.* (-, -en) (salt-)marsh, fen.
Marschall *m.* (-[e]s, -schälle) marshal.
Marschallsstab *m.* marshal's baton.
Marschbefehl *m.* marching-order.
marschieren *v.i.* (*h u. s*) to march.
Marssegel *n.* topsail.
Marstall *m.* (-[e]s, -ställe) royal stables *pl.*
Marter *f.* (-, -n) torture; (*fig.*) torment.
Marterkammer *f.* torture-chamber.
martern *v.t.* to rack, to torture.
Marterpfahl *m.* stake.
martialisch *a.* martial.
Martinshorn *n.* siren.
Märtyrer *m.* (s, -); **Märtyrerin** *f.* (-, -nen) martyr.
Martyrium *n.* (-s, 0) martyrdom.
Marxismus *m.* Marxism. **Marxistisch** *a.* Marxist.
März *m.* (- u. -en, -e) March.
Marzipan *m.* (-s, -e) marzipan.
Masche *f.* (-, -n) mesh; stitch (in knitting).
Maschendraht *m.* wire netting.
Maschine *f.* (-, -n) machine, engine.
maschinegeschrieben *a.* typed; typewritten.
maschinell *a.* mechanical; machine . . .
Maschinen: **~bau** *m.* mechanical engineer;

~**gewehr** *n.* machine-gun; ~**gewehrnest** *n.* pill-box; ~**pistole** *f.* submachine-gun, tommy-gun, ~**schlosser** *m.* fitter; ~**schrift** *f.* typewriting, typescript.

Maschinerie *f.* (-, -[e]s) machinery.

Maschinist *m.* (-en, -en) machinist.

Masern *pl.* measles *pl.*

masern *v.t.* to vein, to grain.

Maserung *f.* (-, -en) grain; vein; patterning.

Maske *f.* (-, -n) mask; make-up.

Maskenball *m.* masked ball; masquerade.

Maskerade *f.* (-, -n) masquerade; costume.

maskieren (sich) *v.t. & refl.* to mask; to disguise oneself; to dress up.

Maskottchen *n.* (-s, -) mascot.

maskulin *a.* masculine.

Maskulinum *n.* (-s, -lina) masculine noun.

Masochismus *m.* masochism.

Masochist *m.*; **Masochistin** *f.* masochist.

masochistisch *a.* masochistic.

Maß *n.* (-es, -e) measure; (*fig.*) moderation; ~ *halten*, to observe moderation; *nach* ~, to measure; ~ *nehmen*, to take a person's measurement(s).

Maß *f.* (-, -e) quart, pot.

Massage *f.* massage.

Massaker *n.* (-s, -) massacre.

Maßarbeit *f.* made-to-measure; precision work.

Masse *f.* (-, -n) mass, bulk; large quantity, multitude.

Maßeinheit *f.* unit of measurement.

Massen: ~**artikel** *pl.* staple goods; ~**erzeugung** *f.* mass production.

massenhaft *a.* wholesale on a huge/massive scale.

Massenproduktion *f.* mass production.

massenweise *adv.* in large quantities.

Masseur *m.* (-s, -e) masseur.

Masseuse *f.* (-, -n) masseuse.

Maßgabe *f. nach* ~, according to.

maßgearbeitet *a.* made-to-measure; custom-made.

maßgebend *a.* authoritative; standard.

massieren *v.t.* to massage.

massig *a.* massive; bulky.

mäßig *a.* moderate; frugal; ~**e Preise** *pl.* reasonable prices.

mäßigen *v.t.* to moderate; to temper.

Mäßigkeit *f.* (-, 0) temperance, frugality.

Mäßigung *f.* (-, 0) moderation; self-control.

massiv *a.* massive, solid.

Massiv *n.* (-s, -e) massif.

Maßkrug *m.* quart, tankard; stein.

maßlos *a.* immoderate, boundless.

Maßlosigkeit *f.* excessiveness; intemperance.

Maß: ~**nahme** ~**regel** *f.* measure; ~*n treffen*, to take measures; ~**stab** *m.* measure; scale; standard.

maßregeln *v.t.* to take measures against somebody; to discipline.

maßstabsgerecht *a.* (true) to scale.

maßvoll *a.* moderate, measured.

Mast *m.* (-es, -en) mast; (*elec.*) pylon; pole.

Mast *f.* (-, -en) fattening feed.

Mast: ~**baum** *m.* mast; ~**darm** *m.* rectum.

mästen *v.t.* to feed, to fatten.

Mast: ~**korb** *m.* top, masthead, crow's nest; ~**vieh** *n.* beef cattle.

Masturbation *f.* masturbation.

masturbieren *v.i.u.t.* to masturbate.

Matchball *m.* matchpoint.

Material *n.* (-[e]s, -ien) material.

Materialismus *m.* (-, 0) materialism.

Materialist *m.* (-en, -en) materialist.

materialistisch *a.* materialistic.

Materie *f.* (-, -n) matter; subject.

materiell *a.* material; wordly.

Mathematik *f.* (-, 0), **Mathe** mathematics *pl.*.

Mathematiker *m.* (-s, -) mathematician.

mathematisch *a.* mathematical.

Matinée *f.* matinée.

Matratze *f.* (-, -n) mattress.

Mätresse *f.* (-, -n) mistress.

Matriarchat *n.* (-s, -e) matriarchy.

Matrikel *f.* (-, -n) register, roll.

Matrize *f.* (-, -n) matrix.

Matrose *m.* (-n, -n) sailor, mariner.

Matsch *m.* (-[e]s, 0) mud; sludge; mush.

matschig *a.* muddy; slushy.

matt *a.* matt; tired; feeble, languid, faint; (*Gold*) dull; (*Schlach*) (check-)mate; ~ *setzen*, to mate.

Matte *f.* (-, -n) mat; alpine meadow.

Mattglas *n.* frosted glass.

mattherzig *a.* faint-hearted.

Mattigkeit *f.* (-, -0) weakness; weariness.

Mattscheibe *f.* (*fam.*) tube (TV).

Mauer *f.* (-, -n) wall.

Mauerblümchen *n.* wallflower.

mauern *v.t.* to make a wall, to build.

Mauer: ~**segler** *m.* swift; ~**vorsprung** *m.* projecting section of the wall; ~**werk** *n.* stonework; masonry; walls.

Maul *n.* (-[e]s, Mäuler) mouth (animals); gob; *das* ~ *halten*, to hold one's tongue, to shut up.

Maulbeere *f.* mulberry.

maulen *v.i.* to grouse, to moan.

Maulesel *m.* mule; hinny.

Maul: ~**korb** *m.* muzzle; ~**tier** *n.* mule; ~**und Klauenseuche** *f.* foot-and-mouth disease; ~**wurf** mole; ~**wurfshaufen, ~wurfshügel** *m.* mole-hill.

mauhzen *v.i.* to meow plaintively.

Maurer *m.* (-s, -) mason, bricklayer ~**kelle** *f.* brick trowel; ~**meister** *m.* master bricklayer.

Maus *f.* (-, Mäuse) mouse.

mauscheln *v.i.* to engage in shady business.

mäuschenstill *a.* stock still.

Mausefalle *f.* mouse-trap.

mausen *v.t.* to pilfer; ~ *v.i.* to catch mice, to mouse.

mausern (sich) *v.refl.* to moult.

Maut *f.* toll.

Maximal . . . maximum, *a.*

Maxime *f.* (-, -n) maxim.

maximieren *v.t.* to maximize.

Maximierung *f.* maximization.

Mayonnaise *f.* mayonnaise.

Mäzen *m.* (-[e]s, -e) **Mäzenin** *f.* (-, -nen) patron of arts.

Mechanik *f.* (-, -en) mechanics *pl.*; mechanism.

Mechaniker *m.* (-s, -); **Mechanikerin** *f.* (-, -nen) mechanic.

mechanisch *a. & adv,* mechanical(ly); by rote.

Mechanismus *m.* mechanism.

meckern *v.i.* to bleat; (*fig.*) to grumble.

Medaille *f.* (-, -n) medal.

Medaillon *m.* locket; medallion.

Medikament *n.* (-[e]s, -e) medicine.
medikamentös *a.* with drugs (treatment).
Meditation *f.* (-, -en) meditation.
meditieren *v.i.* to meditate.
Medium *n.* (-s, -dien) medium.
Medizin *f.* (-, -en) medicine.
Mediziner *m.* (-s, -) **Medizinerin** *f.* (-, -nen) medical man *or* student.
medizinisch *a.* medical; medicinal; ~**es Gutachten** *n.* medical opinion.
Meer *n.* (-[e]s, -e) sea, ocean; *offenes* ~, main, high sea.
Meer: ~**busen** *m.* bay, gulf; ~**enge** *f.* straits *pl.*
Meeres: ~**biologie** *f.* marine biology; ~**boden** *m.* sea-bed; ~**früchte** *pl.* seafood; ~**klima** *n.* maritime climate; ~**spiegel** *m.* sea level.
Meer: ~**jungfrau** *f.* mermaid; ~**katze** *f.* guenon; ~**rettich** *m.* horse-radish; ~**schaum** *m.* meerschaum; ~**schweinchen** *n.* guinea-pig; ~**wasser** *n.* sea water.
Megahertz *n.* (*elek.*) megacycle; megahertz.
Megaphon *n.* (-s, -e) megaphone.
Mehl *n.* (-[e]s, 0) meal; flour.
Mehlbrei *m.* porridge.
mehlig *a.* mealy.
Mehlspeise *f.* farinaceous food; sweet dish (*Austria*).
mehr *a. & adv.* more; *um so* ~, so much the more; *nicht* ~, no more, no longer; *immer* ~, more and more; *nicht* ~ *als*, not exceeding.
Mehr *n.* (-s, 0) **ein** ~ **an** more of.
Mehr: ~**bedarf** *m.* extra requirement; ~**betrag** *m.* surplus.
mehrdeutig *a.* ambiguous.
Mehreinnahme *f.* increased revenue.
mehren *v.t.* to increase, to augment; (sich) ~ *v.refl.* to multiply.
mehrere *a.pl.* several, various.
mehrfach *a. & adv.* repeated(ly).
Mehrfamilienhaus *n.* multiple dwelling.
Mehrheit *f.* (-, -en) majority, plurality.
mehrheitlich *a.* majority; of the majority.
Mehrheits; ~**entscheidung** *f.* majority decision; ~**wahlrecht** *n.* majority vote system.
mehrjährig *a.* lasting several years; several years.
Mehrkosten *pl.* extra expense.
mehrmalig *a.* repeated.
mehrmals *adv.* several times.
Mehrparteiensystem *n.* multiparty system.
mehrseitig *a.* multilateral.
mehrstimmig *a.* (mus.) arranged for several voices.
Mehrwertsteuer *f.* value added tax; sales tax.
Mehrzahl *f.* plural; majority.
meiden *v.t.st.* to avoid, to shun.
Meile *f.* (-, -n) mile.
Meilenstein *m.* (-s, -e) milestone.
meilenweit *adv.* for miles; miles off.
Meiler *m.* (-s, -) charcoal pile.
mein, meine, mein *pn.* my; mine; ~*esgleichen*, people like me.
Meineid *m.* perjury.
meineidig *a.* perjured.
meinen *v.t.st.* to mean, to think.
meinethalben, meinetwegen *adv.* because of me; as far as I'm concerned.

meinige (*der, die, das*) *a.* mine.
Meinung *f.* (-, -en) opinion; meaning; intention; *nach meiner* ~, in my opinion.
Meinungs: ~**forschung** *f.* opinion research; ~**freiheit** *f.* freedom of opinion; ~**umfrage** *f.* opinion poll; ~**verschiedenheit** *f.* divergence of opinion.
Meise *f.* (-, -n) titmouse.
Meißel *m.* (-s, -) chisel.
meißeln *v.t.* to chisel, to carve.
meist *adv.* most, mostly.
Meistbegünstigungsklausel *f.* most-favored-nation clause.
Meistbietende *m./f.* (-n, -n) highest bidder.
meistens *adv.* mostly, generally.
meistenteils *adv.* for the most part.
Meister *m.* (-s, -) master; master craftsman; (sport) champion.
meisterhaft *a.* masterly.
Meisterin *f.* master craftswoman; champion.
meistern *v.t.* to master; to surpass.
Meisterschaft *f.* (-, 0) mastery, perfection; (sport) championship.
Meister: ~**stück** *n.* masterpiece; ~**werk** *n.* masterly work.
Meistgebot *n.* (-es, -e) highest bid.
Melancholie *f.* (-, 0) melancholy.
melancholisch *a.* melancholy.
Melanom *n.* melanoma.
Melasse *f.* (-, 0) molasses *pl.*
Melde: ~**amt** *n.* police registration office; ~**formular** *n.* report form.
melden *v.t.* to notify, to announce; (sich) ~ *v.refl.* to register; *sich* ~ *lassen*, to send one's name; *sich zu etwas* ~, to enter for.
Meldepflicht *f.* obligatory registration; duty of notification.
meldepflichtig *a.* subject to registration; notifiable.
Meldung *f.* (-, -en) report; mention; announcement, notification; entry.
meliert *a.* mottled.
melken *v.t.st.* to milk.
Melodie *f.* (-, -[e]n) melody; tune; air.
Melodik *f.* melodic features; theory of melody.
melodisch *a.* melodic; melodious, tuneful.
Melone *f.* (-, -n) melon; bowler (hat).
Meltau *m.* (-[e]s, 0) mildew.
Membran *f.* (-, -e) membrane.
Memoiren *pl.* memoirs.
Menagerie *f.* (-, -[e]n) menagerie.
Menge *f.* (-, -n) multitude; quantity; great deal, lots *pl.*; a great many.
mengen *v.t.* to mix, to mingle.
Mengenlehre *f.* set theory.
mengenmässig *a.* quantitative.
Mengenrabatt *m.* bulk discount.
Meningitis *f.* (-, -tiden) meningitis.
Meniskus *m.* (-, -ken) meniscus.
Mennig *m.* (-s, 0) red-lead, minium.
Mensa *f.* (-, -s/-sen) canteen; cafeteria (university).
Mensch *m.* (-en, -en) man, human being.
Menschen: ~**affe** *m.* anthropoid; ~**auflauf** *m.* crowd; ~**feind** *m.* misanthropist; ~**fresser** *m.* cannibal; maneater; ~**freund** *m.* philanthropist.

menschenfreundlich *a.* humane, philanthropic.
Menschen: ~gedenken *n.* memory of man; *seit ~,* time out of mind; **~haß** *m.* misanthropy; **~kenner** *m.* judge of human nature.
menschenleer *a.* deserted.
Menschenliebe *f.* philanthropy, charity.
menschenmöglich *a.* in the power of man.
Menschen: ~opfer *n.* human sacrifice; **~ rechte** *pl.* human rights.
menschenscheu *a.* shy, unsociable.
Menschenschlag *m.* (-s, 0) breed of people.
Menschenverstand *m.* **gesunder ~** common sense.
Menschenwürde *f.* human dignity.
Menschheit *f.* (-, 0) human race, mankind; humanity.
Menschheitsentwicklung *f.* evolution of mankind.
menschlich *a.* human; humane.
Menschlichkeit *f.* (-, 0) humanity.
Menstruation *f.* menstruation.
Mensur *f.* (-, -en) students' fencing match.
Mentalität *f.* (-, -en) mentality.
Menü *n.* (-s, -s) menu (also comp.).
Menuett *n.* (-[e]s, -e) minuet.
Mergel *m.* (-s, -) marl.
Meridian *m.* (-s, -e) meridian.
merkbar *a.* perceptible; noticeable.
Merkblatt *n.* instructional pamphlet, booklet.
merken *v.t.* to notice; to note, to perceive; to remember; **~ lassen,** to betray, to show.
merklich *a.* noticeable.
Merkmal *n.* (-[e]s, -e) mark, sign; feature.
merkwürdig *a.* strange, odd; curious.
Merkwürdigkeit *f.* (-, -en) curiosity.
meschugge *a.* (*fam.*) nuts.
Mesner *m.* (-s, -) sacristan.
Meßband *n.* tape measure.
meßbar *a.* measurable.
Meßbuch *n.* missal.
Messe *f.* (-, -n) mass; fair; (*nav. & mil.*) mess; *stille ~,* low mass; **~ lesen,** to say mass.
Messestand *m.* (-s, -stände) exhibition stand.
messen *v.t.st.* to measure.
Messer *n.* (-s, -) knife; **~ m.** meter.
Messer: ~schmied *m.* cutler; **~stiel** *m.* knife-handle.
Messias *m.* Messiah.
Messing *n.* (-s, 0) brass.
Messung *f.* (-, -en) measurement.
Mestize *m.* mestizo.
Met *m.* (-[e]s, 0) mead.
Metall *n.* (-[e]s, -e) metal.
metallen *a.* (of) metal.
Metaller *m.* (-s, -); **Metallerin** *f.* (-, -nen) metalworker.
Metallfutter *n.* (*mech.*) bush.
metallisch *a.* metallic.
Metallsäge *f.* (*mech.*) hacksaw.
Metallurgie *f.* metallurgy.
Metallverarbeitung *f.* metal processing.
Metallwaren *f. pl.* hardware.
Metamorphose *f.* (-, -n) metamorphosis.
Metapher *f.* (-, -n) metaphor.
Metaphorik *f.* imagery; metaphors.
metaphorisch *a.* metaphorical.

Metaphysik *f.* (-, 0) metaphysics *pl.*
metaphysisch *a.* metaphysical.
Meteor *m.* (-s, -e) meteor.
Meteorit *m.* meteorite.
Meteorologe *m.* (-en, -en); **Meteorologin** *f.* (-, -nen) meteorologist.
Meteorologie *f.* meteorology.
meteorologisch *a.* meteorological.
Meter *n. & m.* (-s, -) meter.
Metermass *n.* tape-measure.
Meterware *f.* fabric/material sold by the meter.
Methode *f.* (-, -n) method.
Methodik *f.* methodology.
methodisch *a.* methodological, methodical.
Metier *n.* (-s, -s) profession.
Metrik *f.* (-, 0) meter; prosody.
metrisch *a.* metrical; **~es System** *n.* metric system.
Metronom *n.* metronome.
Metropole *f.* (-, -n) metropolis.
Metrum *n.* (-s, Metra *u.* Metren) meter.
Mettwurst *f.* smoked sausage.
Metzelei *f.* (-, -en) massacre, butchery.
metzeln *v.t.* to massacre, to butcher.
Metzger *m.* (-s, -) butcher.
Metzgerei *f.* butcher's shop.
Meuchel: ~mord *m.* assassination; **~mörder** *m.* assassin.
meuchlings *adv.* treacherously.
Meute *f.* (-, -n) pack of hounds.
Meuterei *f.* (-, -en) mutiny.
Meuterer *m.* (-s, -) mutineer.
meuterisch *a.* mutinous.
meutern *v.i.* to mutiny, to revolt.
Mexikaner *m.,* **Mexikanerin** *f.;* **mexikanisch** *a.* Mexican.
Mexiko *n.* (-s, 0) Mexico.
miauen *v.i.* to meow.
mich *pn.acc.* me.
mickrig *a.* miserable; measly; puny.
Mieder *n.* (-s, -) bodice.
Miederwaren *pl.* corsetry.
Mief *m.* (*fam.*) stink; stuffy atmosphere.
miefen *v.i.* to stink.
Miene *f.* (-, -en) mien, air, countenance; **~ machen,** to threaten (to do).
Mienenspiel *n.* facial expression.
mies *a.* (*sl.*) bad, rotten.
Miesmacher *m.* (-s, -) defeatist.
Miesmuschel *f.* (-, -n) mussel.
Miete *f.* (-, -n) rent, hire.
mieten *v.t.* to hire, to rent; to take; to charter.
Mieter *m.* (-s, -); **Mieterin** *f.* (-, -nen) tenant, lodger.
mietfrei *a.* rent-free.
Miets: ~flugzeug *n.* charter plane; **~truppen** *pl.* hired troops, mercenaries.
Mietsumme *f.* rental.
mietweise *adv.* on lease.
Miet: ~(s)wohnung *f.* rented apartment; **~zins** *m.* rental (fee).
Mieze *f.* (*fam.*) puss; pussy; chick.
Migräne *f.* (-, 0) migraine.
Mikado *n.* pick-up sticks.
Mikrobe *f.* (-, -n) microbe.
Mikrometer *m.* (-s, -) micrometer.

Mikrophon *n.* (-s, -e) microphone.
Mikroskop *n.* (-[e]s, -e) microscope.
mikroskopisch *a.* microscopic(al).
Mikrowellenherd *m.* microwave oven.
Milbe *f.* (-, -n) mite.
Milch *f.* (-, 0) milk; milt.
Milch: ~**mädchenrechnung** *f.* naive reasoning; ~**straße** *f.* milky way, galaxy; ~**zahn** *m.* milk-tooth.
mild *a.* mild, soft, gentle; liberal, charitable.
Milde *f.* (-, 0) softness, mildness.
mildern *v.t.* to mitigate, to soften.
mildernd *a.* extenuating; ~**e Umstände** *pl.* extenuating circumstances.
Milderung *f.* (-, -en) mitigation.
mildtätig *a.* charitable.
Milieu *n.* milieu; environment.
militant *a.* militant.
Militär *n.* (-[e]s, 0) military, armed forces.
Militär *m.* (-[e]s, -s) military man.
Militär: ~**dienst** *m.* military service; ~**diktatur** *f.* military dictatorship.
militärisch *a.* military.
Militarisierung *f.* militarization.
Militarist *m.* (-en, -en) militarist.
militaristisch *a.* (*pej.*) militarist; militaristic.
Militär: ~**junta** *f.* military junta; ~**regierung** *f.* military government; ~**strafgesetzbuch** *n.* military code.
Miliz *f.* (-, -en) militia.
Milliardär *m.*; **Milliardärin** *f.* billionaire.
Milliarde *f.* (-, -n) billion.
Milligramm *n.* milligram.
Millimeter *m.* millimeter.
Million *f.* (-, -en) million.
Millionär *m.* (-s, -e); **Millionärin** *f.* (-, -nen) millionaire.
Milz *f.* (-, -en) spleen.
mimen *v.t.* to act; to play.
Mimik *f.* mimic art.
Mimikry *f.* mimicry; camouflage.
Mimose *f.* mimosa; (*fig.*) oversensitive person.
minder *a.* less; minor, inferior.
minderbegabt *a.* less gifted.
minderbemittelt *a.* less well-off.
Minderheit *f.* (-, -en) minority.
Minderheitsregierung *f.* minority government.
minderjährig *a.* under age, minor.
mindern *v.t.* to diminish, to lessen, to abate; (sich) ~ *v.refl.* to decrease.
Minderung *f.* (-, -en) diminution, decrease.
minderwertig *a.* (of) inferior (quality).
Minderwertigkeits: ~**gefühl** *n.* feeling of inferiority; ~**komplex** *m.* inferiority complex.
Minderzahl *f.* minority.
mindest *a.* least, lowest; zum ~en, at (the) least, to say the least.
mindestens *adv.* at least.
Mindestmaß, *n.* minimum (size).
Mine *f.* (-, -n) mine.
Minen: -**feld** *n.* minefield; ~**sucher** *m.* minesweeper.
Mineral *n.* (-[e]s, -e *u.* -ien) mineral.
mineralisch *a.* mineral.
Mineralogie *f.* (-, 0) mineralogy.
Mineralquelle *f.* mineral spring.

Miniaturgemälde *n.* miniature.
minieren *v.t.* to (under)mine, to sap.
minimal *a.*, **Minimal. . .** minimal *a.*
Minister *m.* (-s, -) minister (of State).
Minister: ~**präsident** *m.* Prime Minister; ~**rat** *m.* cabinet.
Ministerium *n.* (-s, Ministerien) ministry; department.
Minne *f.* (-, 0) courtly love.
Minnesänger *m.* (-s, -) minnesinger.
minus *pr.* minus.
Minus *n.* (-, 0) deficit; (*fig.*) disadvantage.
Minuspunkt *m.* penalty point.
Minute *f.* (-, -n) minute.
Minutenzeiger *m.* minute-hand.
minuziös *a.* detailed; meticulous.
Minze *f.* (-, 0) mint.
mir *pn.* me, to me.
Misanthrop *m.* (-en, -en) misanthrope.
Mischbrot *n.* bread made from wheat and rye flour.
Mischehe *f.* mixed marriage (between persons of different creeds).
mischen *v.t.* to mix, to blend; (*Karten*) to shuffle.
Mischfarbe *f.* non-primary color.
Mischling *m.* (-s, -e) hybrid, mongrel, half-caste.
Mischmasch *m.* (-es, -e) medley, hotchpotch.
Mischung *f.* (-, -en) mixture, blend.
miserabel *a.* wretched, miserable.
Misere *f.* (-, -n) dreadful state.
Mispel *f.* (-, -n) medlar.
mißachten *v.t.* to disregard, to slight.
Mißachtung *f.* (-, 0) disregard; ~ des Gerichtes, contempt of court.
Mißbehagen *n.* (-s, 0) uneasiness.
Mißbildung *f.* (-, -en) deformity, malformation.
mißbilligen *v.t.* to disapprove (of).
Mißbilligung *f.* (-, 0) disapproval.
Mißbrauch *m.* (-[e]s, -bräuche) abuse; misuse.
mißbrauchen *v.t.* to misuse, to abuse.
mißdeuten *v.t.* to misinterpret.
Mißdeutung *f.* (-, -en) misinterpretation.
missen *v.i.* to miss, to want.
Mißerfolg *m.* (-[e]s, -e) failure.
Mißernte *f.* (-, -n) bad harvest; crop failure.
Missetat *f.* (-, -en) misdeed, crime.
Missetäter *m.* (-s, -) malefactor, criminal.
mißfallen *v.i.st.* to displease.
Mißfallen *n.* (-s, 0) displeasure.
mißfällig *a.* displeasing.
mißgebildet *a.* deformed.
Mißgeburt *f.* (-, -en) monster, freak.
Mißgeschick *n.* (-[e]s, -e) mishap, misfortune.
mißglücken *v.i.* (s) to fail, to miscarry.
mißgönnen *v.t.* to grudge, to envy.
Mißgriff *m.* (-[e]s, -e) mistake, blunder.
Mißgunst *f.* (-, 0) ill-will, grudge, envy.
mißgünstig *a.* envious, jealous.
mißhandeln *v.t.* to ill-treat, to mistreat.
Mißhandlung *f.* ill usage, illtreatment, mistreatment.
Mißheirat *f.* (-, -en) misalliance.
Mißhelligkeit *f.* (-, -en) difference, misunderstanding, dissension.
Mission *f.* (-, -en) mission.
Missionar *m.* (-s, -e) **Missionarin** *f.* (-, -nen)

missionary.

missionarisch *a.* missionary.

missionieren *v.i.* to do missionary work; to convert.

Mißklang *m.* (-[e]s, -Klänge) dissonance.

Mißkredit *m.* (-[e]s, 0) disrepute; discredit.

mißlich *a.* awkward, difficult.

mißliebig *a.* unpopular, objectionable.

mißlingen *v.i.st.* (s) to fail, to miscarry.

Mißmut *m.* (-[e]s) low spirits *pl.*

mißmutig *a.* discouraged, dejected.

mißraten *v.i.st.* (s) turn out badly.

Miß: ~**stand** *m.* (-[e]s, -stände) deplorable state of affairs; ~**stimmung** *f.* (-, -en) bad temper.

Mißton *m.* (-[e]s, -töne) false note; note of discord.

mißtrauen *v.i.* to distrust.

Mißtrauen *n.* (-s, 0) distrust.

Mißtrauensvotum *n.* vote of no confidence.

mißtrauisch *a.* suspicious; distrustful.

mißvergnügt *a.* discontented.

Mißverhältnis *n.* (-nisses, -nisse) disproportion; incongruity.

mißverständlich *a.* unclear; misleading.

Mißverständnis *n.* (-nisses, -nisse) misunderstanding.

mißverstehen *v.t.st.* to misunderstand.

Mißwirtschaft *f.* mismanagement.

Mist *m.* (-es, 0) dung, manure.

Mistel *f.* (-, -n) mistletoe.

misten *v.t.* to manure.

Mist: ~**gabel** *f.* pitchfork; ~**haufen;** *m.* dung heap; ~**käfer** *m.* dung beetle; ~**stück** *n.* (*sl.*) bastard; bitch; ~**wetter** *n.* lousy weather.

mit *pr.* with; by, at; ~ *der Post,* by post; ~ *der Zeit,* in time; ~*einander,* together, jointly; ~ *dabei sein,* to make one (of a party).

Mitangeklagte *m./f.* codefendant.

Mitarbeit *f.* (-, 0) collaboration; assistance; participation.

mitarbeiten *v.i.* to collaborate, to co-operate.

Mitarbeiter *m.* fellow-workers, collaborator, colleague, associate.

mitbekommen *v.t.st.* to get; (*fig.*) to get, to catch.

mitbenutzen *v.t.* to share.

Mitbesitzer *m.* joint owner.

mitbestimmen *v.i.* to have a say in s.th..

Mitbestimmung *f.* (-, 0) participation.

Mitbewerber *m.* competitor.

Mitbewohner *m.;* **Mitbewohnerin** *f.* fellow resident; roommate.

mitbringen *v.t.ir.* to bring (along with one).

Mitbringsel *n.* (-s, -) (*fam.*) present; souvenir.

Mitbrüder *m.* (-s, -brüder) fellow.

Mitbürger *m.* fellow-citizen.

mitdenken *v.i.st.* to follow (the argument, the explanation).

Miteigentümer *m.* (-s, -) joint owner.

miteinander *adv.* together.

Miteinander *n.* togetherness.

mitempfinden *v.t.st.* to sympathize in.

Miterbe *m.;* **Miterbin** *f.,* joint heir.

miterleben *v.t.* to witness.

Mitesser *m.* pimple, blackhead.

mitfahren *v.i.* to ride/to go with.

Mitfahrgelegenheit *f.* lift, ride.

mitfühlen *v.i.* to sympathize (with).

Mitgefühl *n.* sympathy.

mitgehen *v.i.st.* (s) to go along (with), to come (with one).

Mitgift *f.* dowry, portion.

Mitglied *n.* member; fellow.

Mitgliederversammlung *f.* general meeting.

Mitgliedschaft *f.* membership.

Mitglieds: ~**beitrag** *m.* membership subscription; ~**karte** *f.* membership card.

mithalten *v.i.st.* to keep up.

mithelfen *v.i.st.* to lend a hand.

Mithilfe *f.* assistance, co-operation.

mithin *c.* consequently.

Mitinhaber *m.;* **Mitinhaberin** *f.* joint owner.

Mitkämpfer *m.* fellow-combatant.

mitklingen *v.i.st.* to resonate.

Mitläufer *m.* (-s, -) 'fellow-traveller' (*einer Partel*); (*pej.*) hanger on.

Mitlaut[er] *m.* (-s, -) consonant.

Mitleid *n.* compassion, pity.

Mitleidenschaft *f.* sympathy; *in ~ ziehen,* to implicate, involve, affect.

mitleiderregend *a.* pitiful.

mitleidig *a.* compassionate.

mitleidlos *a.* pitiless, ruthless.

mitmachen *v.i.* to take part in.

Mitmensch *m.* fellow human being.

mitmischen *v.i.* (*fam.*) to be involved.

mitnehmen *v.t.st.* to take along with one; (*fig.*) to weaken, to exhaust.

mitrechnen *v.t.* to include in the number.

mitreden *v.i.* to join in the conversation; to have one's say in a matter.

mitreißen *v.t.st.* to sweep away; (*fig.*) to carry away.

mitsamt *pr.* together with.

mitschleppen *v.t.* (*fam.*) to drag along.

mitschreiben *v.i. & t.st.* to take down (a speech, etc.).

Mitschuld *f.* complicity.

Mitschuldige *m./f.* accomplice, accessory.

Mitschüler *m.;* **Mitschülerin** *f.* classmate.

mitspielen *v.i.* to join in a game; *einem übel ~,* to do one an ill turn.

Mitspracherecht *n. ein ~ haben* to have a say.

Mittag *m.* (-s, -e) mid-day, noon; *zu ~ essen, speisen,* to have lunch.

mittags *adv.* at noon.

Mittag(s)essen *n.* (-s, -) lunch.

Mittäter *m.;* **Mittäterin** *f.* accomplice.

Mitte *f.* (-, 0) middle, midst.

mitteilbar *a.* fit to be told *or* printed.

mitteilen *v.t.* to communicate.

mitteilsam *a.* communicative.

Mitteilung *f.* communication, notice.

Mitteilungsbedürfnis *n.* need to talk.

Mittel *n.* (-s, -) medium, average, mean; means, expedient, way; remedy; (*Geld*) means; *sich ins ~ legen,* to step in.

Mittelalter *n.* the Middle Ages *pl.*

mittelalterlich *a.* medieval.

Mittelamerika *n.* Central America.

mittelbar *a.* indirect.

Mittelding *n.* intermediate thing.

Mitteleuropa *n.* Central Europe.

mitteleuropäisch *a.* Central European.

Mittelfinger *m.* middle finger.
mittelgross *a.* middle sized.
Mittelgrösse *f.* medium size.
mittelgut *a.* of second quality.
mittelhochdeutsch *a.* Middle High German.
mittelländisch *a.* Mediterranean; inland.
mittellos *a.* penniless, destitute.
mittelmässig *a.* mediocre.
Mittelmässigkeit *f.* mediocrity.
Mittel: ~**meer** *n.* Mediterranean: ~**ohrentzündung** *f.* inflammation of the middle ear; ear infection; ~**punkt** *m.* center.
mittels, mittelst *pr.* by means of.
Mittelscheitel *m.* middle parting.
Mittelschule *f.* secondary school.
Mittelsmann *m.,* **Mittelsperson** *f.* intermediary.
Mittel: ~**stand** *m.* middle class(es); ~**stürmer** *m.* (sport) center forward; ~**weg** *m.* middle course.
Mittelwelle *f.* (*Radio*) medium wave.
mitten *adv.* midst; ~ *im Winter,* in the depth of winter; ~ *durch,* through the midst; ~ *entzwei,* in twain, broken right in two; ~ *in,* in the middle of.
Mitternacht *f.* (-, -nächte) midnight.
Mittler *m.* (-s, -) mediator.
mittlere[r] *a.* middle, mean.
Mittlerrolle *f.* mediating role.
mittlerweile *adv.* meanwhile.
mittragen *v.t.st.* to bear part of; to share.
Mittsommernacht *f.* Midsummer Night.
mittun *v.t.st.* to join in doing.
Mittwoch *m.* (-s, -e) Wednesday.
mitunter *adv.* now and then.
mitverantwortlich *a.* partly/jointly responsible.
Mitverantwortung *f.* share of the responsibility.
mitversichern *v.t.* to include in one's insurance.
Mitwelt *f.* (-, 0) contemporaries.
mitwirken *v.i.* to co-operate, to concur.
Mitwirkende *m./f.* participant; performer; actor.
Mitwirkung *f.* (-, 0) co-operation.
Mitwisser *m.;* **Mitwisserin** *f.* person who knows about a secret.
mitzählen *v.t.* to count; to include.
Mixbecher *m.* (cocktail) shaker.
Möbel *n.* (-s, -) piece of furniture.
Möbel: ~**händler** *m.* upholsterer, dealer in furniture; ~**magazin** *n.* furniture warehouse; ~**schreiner,** ~**tischler** *m.* cabinetmaker; ~**spedition** *f.* moving firm; ~**wagen** *m.* furniture-van.
mobil *a.* active, quick; ~ *machen,* to mobilize.
Mobiliar *n.* furniture.
Mobilmachung *f.* (-, 0) mobilization.
mobilisieren *v.t.* to mobilize.
möblieren *v.t.* to furnish.
Möchte-gern. . . would-be. . . .
modal *a.* modal.
Modalverb *n.* modal verb.
Mode *f.* (-, -n) mode, fashion.
Modell *n.* (-s, -e) model, pattern; mold.
modellieren *v.t.* to model, to mold.
Modellversuch *n.* pilot project.
modeln *v.t.* to fashion, to form.
Moder *m.* (-s, 0) mold; mud; decay.
Moderator *m.;* **Moderatorin** *f.* moderator.
moderieren *v.t.* to moderate.
moderig *a.* musty, moldy.

modern *v.i.* (s) to molder, to decay.
modern *a.* fashionable; modern.
Moderne *f.* modern age; modern times.
modernisieren *v.t.* to modernize.
Modernisierung *f.* modernization.
Modewaren *n.f.pl.* novelties *pl.*
modifizieren *v.t.* to modify.
modisch *a.* fashionable, stylish.
Modistin *f.* (-, -nen) milliner, dressmaker.
Modus *m.* (-, -Modi) way; method; (*ling.*) mood.
Mogelei *f.* (-, -en) cheating.
mogeln *v.i.* (*sl.*) to cheat (at cards).
mögen *v.i. & t.ir.* to like, to wish; *ich mag,* I may, I can; I like; *ich möchte,* I should like; *ich möchte lieber,* I would rather.
möglich *a.* possible.
möglicherweise *adv.* perhaps; possibly.
Möglichkeit *f.* (-, -en) possibility.
Möglichkeiten *pl.* potentialities.
möglichst *adv.* as much as possible.
Mohammedaner *m.;* **Mohammedanerin** *f.* Muslim.
Mohikaner *m.;* **Mohikanerin** *f.* Mohican.
Mohn *m.* (-[e]s, -e) poppy, poppy-seed.
Mohnsaft *m.* opium.
Mohr *m.* (-en, -en) Moor.
Möhre *f.;* **Mohrrübe** *f.* carrot.
Mohrenkopf *m.* chocolate marshmallow.
mokieren *v.refl.* to mock/scoff at s.th.
Molch *m.* (-es, -e) newt.
Molekül *n.* (-s, -e) molecule.
Molekular. . . molecular *a.*
Molke *f.* (-, -n) **Molken** *pl.* whey.
Molkerei *f.* (-s, -en) dairy.
moll *a.* (*mus.*) minor, flat.
mollig *a.* confortable, snug; plump.
Molltonart *f.* (-, -en) (*mus.*) minor key.
Moment *m.* (-[e]s, -e) moment.
momentan *a.* momentary.
Momentaufnahme *f.* (*phot.*) snapshot.
Monarch *m.* (-en, -en); **Monarchin** *f.* (-, -nen) monarch.
Monarchie *f.* (-, -[e]n) monarchy.
monarchisch *a.* monarchical.
monarchistisch *a.* monarchist; monarchistic.
Monat *m.* (-[e]s, -e) month.
monatelang *a.* lasting for month; *adv.* for months.
monatlich *a. & adv.* monthly.
Monats: ~**binde** *f.* sanitary napkin; ~**blutung** *f.* period; ~**einkommen** *n.* monthly income; ~**gehalt** *n.* month's salary; **dreizehntes** ~**gehalt** *f.* extra month's salary; ~**karte** *f.* monthly ticket; ~**rate** *f.* monthly installment.
Monatsschrift *f.* monthly (magazine).
Mönch *m.* (-e, -e) monk, friar.
mönchisch *a.* monkish; monastic.
Mönchskloster *n.* monastery.
Mond *m.* (-[e]s, -e) moon.
mondän *a.* fashionable.
Mondaufgang *m.* moonrise.
Mondfinsternis *f.* eclipse of the moon.
mondhell *a.* moonlit.
Mond: ~**landefähre** *f.* lunar module; ~**phase** *f.* moon's phase; ~**schein** *m.* moonlight; ~**sichel** *f.* crescent.
mondsüchtig *a.* moonstuck.

Monduntergang *m.* moonset.
Mongole *m.;* **Mongolin** *f.;* **mongolisch** *a.* Mongol(ian).
Mongolei *f.* (-, 0) Mongolia.
Mongolismus *n.* (*med.*) Down's syndrome.
Mongoloid *a.* mongoloid.
monieren *v.t.* to criticize.
monogam *a.* monogamous.
Monogamie *f.* monogamy.
Monogramm *n.* (-s, -e) monogram.
Monographie *f.* (-, -n) monograph.
Monokultur *f.* monoculture.
monolithisch *a.* monolithic.
Monolog *m.* (-s, -e) monologue.
Monopol *n.* (-[e]s, -e) monopoly.
monopolisieren *v.t.* to monopolize.
Monotheismus *m.* monotheism.
monoton *a.* monotonous.
Monotonie *f.* (-, 0) monotony.
Monster *n.* (-s, -stren) monster.
Monster... mammoth *a.*
Monstranz *f.* (-, -en) pyx, monstrance.
monströs *a.* monstrous; hideous.
Monsun *m.* monsoon.
Montag *m.* (-[e]s, -e) Monday.
Montage *f.* assembly; installation; **~band** *n.* assembly line; **~halle** *f.* assembly shop.
montags *adv.* on Monday(s).
Montanaktien *f. pl.* mining shares.
Montanindustrie *f.* mining industry.
Monteur *m.* (-s, -e) mechanic; electrician; fitter.
montieren *v.t.* (*mech.*) to mount, to fit, to assemble.
Montur *f.* outfit; gear.
Monument *n.* (-s, -e) monument.
Moor *n.* (-[e]s, -e) moor, fen, bog.
Moos *n.* (-es, -e) moss.
moosig *a.* mossy.
Mops *m.* (Mopses, Möpse) pug(dog).
mopsen *v.t.* to pinch.
Moral *f.* (-, 0) moral philosophy; morality; (*einer Fabel*) moral; morals *pl*; **doppelte~** double standards.
moralisch *a.* moral; virtuous.
moralisieren *v.i.* to moralize.
Morast *m.* (-es, -e *u.* Moräste) morass; bog; swamp.
morastig *a.* muddy.
Moratorium *n.* (-s, -rien) moratorium.
Morchel *f.*. (-, -n) morel (mushroom).
Mord *m.* (-[e]s, -e) murder, homicide.
morden *v.t. & i.* to murder.
Mörder *m.* (-s, -) murderer.
Mörderin *f.* (-, -nen) murderess.
mörderisch *a.* murderous.
Mordkommission *f.* homicide squad.
Mordskerl *m.* great guy.
mordsmäßig *a.* (*fam.*) tremendous.
Mordtat *f.* murder.
Mordverdacht *m.* suspicion of murder.
Morgen *m.* (-s, -) morning; east; $\frac{5}{8}$ acre (of land).
Morgen *adv.* tomorrow; *heute ~*, this morning; *~ früh*, tomorrow morning.
Morgenland *n.* Orient, East.
Morgen: ~rot *n. u.* **~röte** *f.* dawn, aurora, blush of dawn; **~stern** *m.* morning-star.
morgens *adv.* in the morning.

morgig *a.* of tomorrow, tomorrow's.
Mormone *m.;* **Mormonin** *f.* Mormon.
Morphium *n.* (-s, 0) morphine.
morsch *a.* rotten, decayed.
Morsealphabet *n.* Morse (code).
Mörser *m.* (-s, -) mortar; (*mil.*) howitzer.
Mörserkeule *f.* pestle.
Mortalität *f.* mortality.
Mörtel *m.* (-s, -) mortar, cement.
Mosaik *n.* (-[s], -en) mosaic.
Moschee *f.* (-, -[e]n) mosque.
Moshus *m.* (-, 0) musk.
Moskito *m.* (-s, -s) mosquito.
Moslem *m.* (-s, -s) Muslim.
Most *m.* (-es, -e) mus; (*Apfel~*) cider.
Mostrich *m.* (-s, -) mustard.
Motiv *n.* (-s, -e) motive; (*mus.*) motif.
Motivation *f.* motivation.
motivieren *v.t.* to motivate.
Motodrom *n.* autodrome; speedway.
Motor *m.* (-s, -e) motor, engine.
Motor: ~barkasse *f.* motor launch; **~boot** *n.* motorboat; **~fahrzeug** *n.* motor vehicle; **~haube** *f.* hood; **~rad** *n.* motorcycle; **~unterbau** *m.* engine-bed.
motorisieren *v.t.* to motorize.
Motte *f.* (-, -n) moth; *von ~n zerfressen*, moth-eaten.
Motten: ~frass *m.* damage caused by moths; **~pulver** *n.* moth powder; **~sicher** *a.* moth-proof.
Motto *n.* (-s, -s) motto.
motzen *v.i.* (*fam.*) to grouch.
moussieren *v.i.* to effervesce, to sparkle.
Möwe *f.* (-, -n) seagull.
Mucke *f.* (-, -n) caprice, whim.
Mücke *f.* (-, -n) gnat, midge; mosquito.
mucken *v.i.* to grumble; to mutter.
Mucks *m.* (-es, -er) (*fam.*) murmur.
mucksen *v.refl.* to make a sound.
müde *a.* weary, tired.
Müdigkeit *f.* (-, 0) weariness, fatigue.
Muff *m.* (-[e]s, -e) muff; musty smell.
Muffel *f.* (-, -en) (*chem. and tech.*) muffle; grouch.
Mufflon *m.* (-s, -s) moufflon.
muffig *a.* musty; sulky.
Mühe *f.* (-, -n)trouble, effort; pains *pl.*; *sich ~ geben*, to take pains; *der ~ wert sein*, to be worth while.
mühelos *a.* without trouble, effortless.
mühen (sich) *v. refl.* to trouble oneself.
mühevoll *a.* laborious.
Mühlespiel *n.* (nine men's) morris.
Mühlrad *n.* millwheel.
Mühlstein *m.* millstone.
Mühsal *n.* (-[e]s, -e) *f.* (-, -e) tribulation; hardship.
mühsam *a.* troublesome; toilsome.
mühselig *a.* toilsome; miserable.
Mulatte *m.* (-n, -n); **Mulattin** *f.* (-, -nen) mulatto.
Mulde *f.* (-, -n) hollow
Mull *m.* (-[e]s, 0) gauze, mull.
Müll *m.* (e[e]s, 0) garbage; rubbish.
Müll: ~abfuhr *f.* garbage collection; **~eimer** *m.* garbage can.
Müll: ~halde *f.* refuse dump; **~schlucker** *m.* garbage chute; **~tonne** *f.* garbage can; **~wagen** *m.* garbage truck.
Müller *m.* (-s, -) miller.
mulmig *a.* (*fam.*) uneasy (with fear).

Multiplikation *f.* multiplication.
multiplizieren *v.t.* to multiply.
Mumie *f.* (-, -n) mummy.
mumifizieren *v.t.* to mummify.
Mumm *m.* (*fam.*) guts; drive.
mummeln *v. i. n. t.* (*fam.*) to chew; to nap.
Mund *m.* (-[e]s, -e, *u.* Münder) mouth; *den ~ halten*, to hold one's tongue; *von der Hand in den ~ leben*, to live from hand to mouth.
Mundart *f.* dialect.
mundartlich *a.* dialect.
Munddusche *f.* water pick.
Mündel *n.* (-s, -) ward.
mundgerecht *a.* bite-sized.
munden *v.i.imp* to taste nice.
münden *v.i.* to flow into.
Mundgeruch *m.* bad breath.
Mundharmonika *f.* mouth-organ.
mündig *a.* of age; *~ werden*, to come of age.
Mündigkeit *f.* (-, 0) majority, full age.
mündlich *a.* verbal, oral.
Mundpflege *f.* oral hygiene.
Mundraub *m.* petty theft.
Mundstück *n.* mouth-piece
mundtot *a.* jn *~machen* to silence s.b.
Mündung *f.* (e, -en) mouth; estuary; (*einer Flinte*) muzzle; orifice.
Mund-zu-Mund-Beatmung *f.* mouth-to-mouth resuscitation.
Munition *f.* (e, -en) ammunition.
munkeln *v.i.* to whisper, to mutter.
Münster *n.* or *m.* (-s, -) minster, cathedral.
munter *a.* awake; lively, gay, brisk.
Münzautomat *m.* slotmachine; (telephone) payphone.
Münze *f.* (-, -n) coin; medal; mint; *klingende ~*, hard cash.
Münzeinheit *f.* monetary unit.
münzen *v.t.* to mint; to coin.
Münzkunde *f.* numismatics *pl.*
mürbe *a.* mellow; tender, soft.
Mürbeteig *m.* short pastry.
Murmel *f.* (-, -n) marble.
murmeln *v.t. & i.* to mumble; to murmur; to mutter.
Murmeltier *n.* marmot.
murren *v.i.* to grumble, to growl
mürrisch *a.* morose, surly, peevish.
Mus *n.* (es, -e) pulp, pap; (*Früchte*) jam.
Muschel *f.* (-, -n) shell, mussel.
Muse *f.* (-, -n) muse.
Museum *n.* (-s, Museen) museum.
Musik *f.* (-, 0) music.
Musikalienhandlung *f.* music shop
musikalisch *a.* musical.
Musikalitat *f.* musicality.
Musikant *m.* (en, -en) (inferior) musician.
Musikantenknochen *m.* funny bone
Musikbox *f.* juke box.
Musiker *m.* (-s, -); **Musikerin** *f.* (-, -nen) musician.
Musiklehrer *m.*; **Musiklehrerin** *f.* music teacher.
Musikwissenschaft *f.* musicology.
Musikwissenschaftler *m.*; **Musikwissensch-aftlerin** *f.* musicologist.
musisch *a.* artistic; musically gifted.

musizieren *v.i.* to make music.
Muskat *m.* (-[e]s, -e), **Muskatnuss** *f.* (-, -nüsse) nutmeg
Muskateller *m.* (s, -0) (*Wein*) muscatel.
Muskel *m.* (-s, -n) muscle.
Muskel: *~kater* *m.* sore muscles; *~krampf* *m.* cramp; *~paket* *n.* bulging muscles; *~protz* *m.* muscleman; *~riss* *m.* torn muscle; *~schwund* *m.* muscular atrophy; *~zerrung* *f.* pulled muscle.
Muskete *f.* (-, -n) musket.
Musketier *m.* (-[e]s, -e) musketeer.
Muskulatur *f.* (-, -en) muscular system.
muskulös *a.* muscular.
Müsli *n.* (-s, -s) muesli.
Muß *n.* must.
Musse *f.* (-, 0) leisure; *mit ~*, at leisure.
Musselin *m.* (-[e]s, -e) muslin
müssen *v.i.ir.* to be obliged, to be forced, to be constrained, to have to.
Mussestunde *f.* leisure hour.
müßig *a.* unemployed, idle.
Müßiggang *m.* (-[e]s, 0) idleness, idling.
Müßiggänger *m.* (-s, -) idler, loafer.
Muster *n.* (-s, -) pattern; sample; design; *nach ~*, according to sample.
Muster: *~beispiel* *n.* perfect example; model; *~exemplar* *n.* specimen.
mustergültig *a.* standard; classical.
musterhaft *a.* exemplary, model.
mustern *v.t.* to review, to scrutinize; (*Stoffe*) to examine.
Musterrolle *f.* muster-roll.
Musterschutz *m.* copyright, patent.
Musterung *f.* (-, -en) examination, inspection.
Musterzeichner *m.* designer (of patterns).
Mut *m.* (-[e]s, 0) courage; spirit, mettle.
Mutation *f.* (-, -en) mutation.
mutig *a.* courageous, brave.
mutlos *a.* discouraged, disheartened.
mutmassen *v.t.* to conjecture.
mutmasslich *a.* presumptive.
Mutmassung *f.* conjecture.
Mutter *f.* (-, Mütter) mother; (*Schrauben~*) nut; *werdende~*, expectant mother.
Mutter: *~boden* *m.* top-soil; *~gesellschaft* *f.* parent company; *~komplex* *m.* mother fixation; *~kuchen* *m.* placenta; *~leib* *m.* womb.
mütterlich *a.* motherly; maternal.
mütterlicherseits *adv.* on one's mother's side; maternal (parent).
Mütterlichkeit *f.* motherliness.
Mutter: *~liebe* *f.* motherly love; *~mal* *n.* birth-mark; *~mund* *m.* cervix.
Mutterschaft *f.* (-, 0) motherhood; maternity; *~urlaub* *n.* maternity leave.
Mutter: *~schoss* *m.* womb; *~schwein* *n.* sow.
mutterseelenallein *adv.* all alone.
Mutter: *~söhnchen* *n.* mommy's boy, sissy; *~sprache* *f.* mother-tongue; *~witz* *m.* mother-wit, common-sense.
Mutwille (ns, -0) wilfulness; wantonness.
mutwillig *a.* wilful; wanton.
Mütze *f.* (-, -n) cap.
Myrrhe *f.* (-, -n) myrrh.
Myrte *f.* (-, -n) myrtle.
mysteriös *a.* mysterious.

Mysterium *n.* (-s, -rien) mystery.
mystifizieren *v.t.* to mystify.
Mystik *f.* (-, -e-) mysticism.
Mystiker *m.* (-, -) mystic.
mystisch *a.* mystical.

Mythe *f.* (-, -n) fable, myth.
mythisch *a.* mythical.
Mythologie *f.* (-, -[e]n) mythology.
mythologisch *a.* mythological.
Mythos *m.* (-, -then) myth.

N

N, n *n.* the letter N or n.
na! *i.* well! now!
Nabe *f.* (-, -n) hub.
Nabel *m.* (-s, -) navel.
Nabelschnur *f.* umbilical cord.
nach *pr. & adv.* after, behind; according to; past; to; ~ *und* ~, little by little; ~ *Gewicht*, by weight; ~ *der Reihe*, in turn; ~ *wie vor*, now as before.
nachäffen *v.t. & i.* to ape, to mimic.
nachahmen *v.t.* to imitate; to copy.
nachahmenswert *a.* exemplary.
Nachahmer *m.* (-s, -) imitator.
Nachahmung *f.* (-, -en) imitation.
nacharbeiten *v.t.* to make up missed time; to go over (text).
Nachbar *m.* (-s *u.* -n, -n), **Nachbarin** *f.* (-, -nen) neighbor.
nachbarlich *f.* neighborly.
Nachbarschaft *f.* (-, 0) neighborhood.
nachbarschaftlich *a.* neighborly.
Nachbehandlung *f.* follow-up treatment.
nachbestellen *v.t.* to order again.
Nachbestellung *f.* (-, -en) repeat order.
nachbeten *v.t.* (*fig.*) to echo.
nachbilden *v.t.* to copy, to imitate.
nachblicken *v.i.* to look after.
nachdatieren *v.t.* to postdate.
nachdem *adv.* afterwards, after that; ~ *c.* after; *je* ~, according as.
nachdenken *v.i.ir.* to think; to meditate, to muse.
Nachdenken *n.* (-s, 0) thought; reflection
nachdenklich *a.* thoughtful, pensive.
nachdrängen (*h*) *v.i.,* **nachdringen** (*s*) *v.i.st.* to crowd after, to press in after.
Nachdruck *m.* (-[e]s, -e) energy, emphasis, stress; pirated edition.
nachdrucken *v.t.* to reprint; to pirate.
nachdrücklich *a.* energetic, emphatic.
Nachdrucksrecht *n.* (-s, -e) right of reproduction.
nacheifern *v.i.* to emulate.
Nacheiferung *f.* (-, 0) emulation.
nacheilen *v.i.* (*s*) to hasten after.
nacheinander *adv.* one after another.
nachempfinden *v.t.st.* to empathize with; to feel with.
Nachen *m.* (-s, -) boat, skiff.
nacherzählen *v.t.* to retell.
Nacherzählung *f.* summary.
Nachfahr *m.* (-en, -en); **Nachfahrin** *f.* (-, -nen) descendant
nachfahren *v.i.st.* (*s*) to follow (in a car).
nachfeiern *v.t.* to celebrate at a later date.
Nachfolge *f.* succession; imitation.
nachfolgen *v.i.* (*s*) to succeed; to imitate.
nachfolgend *a.* following, subsequent.
Nachfolger *m.* (-s, -) follower; successor; imitator.
Nachforderung *f.* (-, -en) additional claim *or*

charge
nachforschen *v.i.* to search after; to inquire into, to investigate.
Nachforschung *f.* (-, -en) search, inquiry, investigation.
Nachfrage *f.* demand, request; inquiry.
nachfragen *v.i.* to inquire after.
nachfühlen *v.t.* to feel with someone; to empathize.
nachfüllen *v.t.* to refill.
nachgeben *v.t. & i.s.t.* to give in; to give way.
nachgeboren *a.* posthumous; born later.
Nachgebühr *f.* surcharge for excess postage.
Nachgeburt *f.* afterbirth.
nachgehen *v.i.st.* (*s*) to follow; (*einer Sache*) to investigate; (*Uhr*) to be slow.
nachgelassen *a.* posthumous (writings).
nachgemacht *a.* counterfeit.
nachgerade *adv.* by this time; really.
nachgeraten *v.i.st.* to take after a person.
Nachgeschmack *m.* aftertaste, tang.
nachgiebig *a.* yielding, compliant.
Nachgiebigkeit *f.* compliance, softness.
nachhaken *v.t.* (*fam.*) to follow up.
Nachhall *v.i.* (-s, -e) reverberation.
nachhallen *v.i.* to reverberate.
nachhaltig *a.* lasting, enduring.
Nachhauseweg *m.* (-s, -e) way home.
nachhelfen *v.i.st.* to lend a helping hand.
nachher *adv.* afterwards.
nachherig *a.* subsequent.
Nachhilfe *f.* help, aid; coaching; ~**stunde** (*f.*) private lesson.
nachhinein *adv.* im ~ afterwards; with hindsight.
Nachholbedarf *m.* need to catch up.
nachholen *v.t.* to make up for.
Nachhut *f.* (-, 0) rearguard.
nachjagen *v.i. & t.* (*su.h*) to pursue; to chase after.
Nachklang *m.* resonance; after-effect.
Nachkomme *m./f.* (-n, -n) descendant.
nachkommen *v.i.st.* (*s*) to come after; (*fig.*) to conform to, to obey.
Nachkommenschaft *f.* (-, -en) issue, descendants *pl.*, posterity.
Nachkömmling *m.* much younger child.
Nachkriegs: ~**generation** *f.* post-war generation, ~**zeit** *f.* post-war period.
Nachlaß *m.* (-lasses, -lasse *u.* -lässe) remission; estate, inheritance; ~**steuer** *f.* estate tax.
nachlassen *v.t.st.* to slacken, to relax; (*vom Preise*) to reduce; ~*v.i.st.* to abate, to subside.
nachlässig *a.* negligent, careless.
Nachlässigkeit *f.* (-, -en) negligence.
nachlaufen *v.i.st.* (*s*) to run after.
Nachlese *f.* (-, -n) gleaning.
nachlesen *v.t.st.* to glean; to look up (a passage).
nachliefern *v.t.* to supply later.

Nachlieferung *f.* (-, -en) subsequent delivery.

nachlösen *v.t.* to buy a ticket (on the train).

nachmachen *v.t.* to copy; to counterfeit.

nachmalig *a.* subsequent.

nachmals *adv.* afterwards, subsequently.

nachmessen *v.t.st.* to measure again; to check the measurements.

Nachmittag *m.* afternoon.

nachmittags *adv.* in the afternoon.

Nachnahme *f.* (-, -n)(*com.*) cash on delivery, COD.

Nachname *m.* (-, -n) last name.

nachplappern *v.t. & i.* to repeat (another's words) mechanically.

Nachporto *n.* excess postage.

nachprüfen *v.t.* to verify, to re-examine.

nachrechnen *v.t.* to check (an account).

Nachrede *f.* (-, -n) *üble* ~, slander

nachreden *v.t.* to repeat (another's words).

nachreichen *v.t.* to hand in late.

Nachricht *f.* (-, -en) advice, information, news.

Nachrichten: ~**abteilung** *f.* intelligence department; ~**agentur** *f.* news agency; ~**büro** *n.* news agency; ~**dienst** *m.* intelligence service; ~**sendung** *f.* news broadcast; ~**stelle, zentrale** *f.* (*mil.*) message center, signal center; ~**wesen** *n.* (*mil.*) communications.

nachrücken *v.i.* (*mil.*) to move up.

Nachruf *m.* obituary (notice).

Nachruhm *m.* posthumous fame.

nachrühmen *v.t.* to say to someone's credit.

nachrüsten *v.i.* to close the armament gap; to retrofit (car).

Nachrüstung *f.* rearmament.

nachsagen *v.t.* to repeat of (a person).

Nachsaison *f.* late season.

Nachsatz *m.* postscript; (*gram.*) final clause.

nachschicken *v.t.* to forward.

Nachschlag *m.* (*fam.*) second helping.

Nachschlage: ~**bibliothek** *f.* reference library; ~**buch** *n.* reference book.

nachschlagen *v.t.st.* to look up; to refer to, to consult (a book); ~ *v.i.st.* to take after.

nachschleichen *v.i.st.* (s) to steal after.

Nachschlüssel *m.* duplicate key.

Nachschub *m.* (-[e]s, -schübe) (*mil.*) supply.

nachsehen *v.t. & i.st.* to look after; to pardon, to excuse; to look up (in a book).

Nachsehen *n. das* ~ *haben* to be the loser.

nachsenden *v.t.ir.* (*Briefe*) to forward; *bitte* ~! please forward!

nachsetzen *v.i.* (s) to pursue.

Nachsicht *f.* (-, 0) lenience.

nachsichtig *a.* indulgent, lenient.

Nachsilbe *f.* suffix.

nachsinnen *v.i.st.* to muse.

nachsitzen *v.i.st.* to be in detention (school).

Nachsommer *m.* Indian summer.

Nachspeise *f.* dessert; sweet.

Nachspiel *n.* sequel; epilogue; postlude.

nachspionieren *v.i.* to spy on s.b.

nachsprechen *v.t.st.* to repeat.

nachspüren *v.i.* to trace; to investigate.

nächst *pr.* nearest; next to; ~**beste[r]** *a.* second-best.

Nächste[r] *m.* (-n, -n) neighbor.

nachstehen *v.i.t.* to be inferior to.

nachstehend *a.* following.

nachstellen *v.i.* to persecute; to readjust; ~ *v.t.* (*Uhr*) to put back.

Nachstellung *f.* (-, -en) pursuit; postposition.

Nächstenliebe *f.* charity.

nächstens *adv.* soon, shortly.

nachstreben *v.i.* to strive for; to emulate.

nachsuchen *v.i.* to petition for.

Nacht *f.* (-, Nächte) night; *bei* ~, at night; *über* ~, during the night.

nachtaktir *a.* (*zool.*) nocturnal.

nachtanken *v.t.* to refuel.

Nacht: ~**anzug** *m.* nightclothes; ~**blindheit** *f.* nightblindness.

Nachtdienst *m.* night-duty.

Nachteil *m.* (-[e]s, -e) disadvantage.

nachteilig *a.* disadvantageous; detrimental.

nächtelang *a.* all night; night after night.

Nacht: ~**essen** *n.* supper; ~**eule** *f.* night-owl; ~**falter** *m.* moth; ~**frost** *m.* night frost.

Nachthemd *n.* nightshirt; (*Frauen*~) nightgown.

Nachtigall *f.* (-, -en) nightingale.

nächtigen *v.i.* to pass the night.

Nachtisch *m.* dessert.

nächtlich *a.* nightly, nocturnal.

Nacht: ~**lokal** *n.* nightclub; ~**portier** *m.* night porter.

Nachtrag *m.* (-[e]s, träge) supplement.

nachtragen *v.t.st.* to add, to append; *einem etwas* ~, to bear someone a grudge.

nachtragend *a.* unforgiving.

nachträglich *a.* subsequent, supplementary.

nachtrauern *v.i.* to mourn s.b. (s.th.).

Nachtruhe *f.* sleep.

nachts *adv.* in the night, at night.

Nacht: ~**schatten** *m.* (*bot.*) (deadly) nightshade; ~**tisch** *m.* nighttable; ~**wache** *f.* nightwatch; ~**wächter** *m.* watchman; ~**wandler** *m.* sleepwalker.

Nachuntersuchung *f.* follow-up examination.

nachvollziehbar *a.* comprehensible.

nachwachsen *v.i.st.* (s) to grow again.

Nach: ~**wahl** *f.* special election; ~**wehen** *pl.* afterpains; painful consequences *pl.*

nachweinen *v.i.* to bemoan a loss.

Nachweis *m.* (-weises, -weise) proof.

nachweisen *v.t.st.* to prove.

nachweislich *a.* demonstrable.

Nachwelt *f.* posterity.

nachwirken *v.i.* to have a lasting effect.

Nach: ~**wirkung** *f.* after-effect; ~**wort** *n.* concluding remarks *pl.* afterword; epilog.

Nachwuchs *m.* (-es, 0) offspring; young generation.

nachzahlen *v.t.* to pay later.

nachzählen *v.t.* to count over again.

Nachzahlung *f.* additional payment.

nachzeichnen *v.t.* to copy from, to draw from.

nachziehen *v.i.st.* to follow; to drag; to go over (lips).

Nachzügler *m.* (-s, -) straggler; latecomer.

Nackedei *m.* (-s, -s) naked little thing.

Nacken *m.* (-s, -) nape of the neck.

nackend, nackt *a. & adv.* naked, nude.

Nackt: ~**baden** *n.* nude bathing; ~**badestrand** *m.* nudist beach.

Nackte *m./f.* (-n, -n) naked person.
Nacktheit *f.* nakedness; nudity.
Nadel *f.* (-, -n) needle; pin.
Nadelbaum *m.* coniferous tree.
Nadel: ~**kissen** *n.* pincushion; ~**öhr** *n.* eye of a needle; ~**spitze** *f.* point of a needle *or* pin; ~**stich** *m.* pinprick; ~**wald** *m.* coniferous forest.
Nagel *m.* (-s, Nägel) nail.
Nagel: ~**bürste** *f.* nail-brush; ~**feile** *f.* nail file; ~**häutchen** *n.* cuticle; ~**lack** *m.* nail polish.
nageln *v.t.* to nail.
nagelneu *a.* brand-new.
Nagel: ~**schere** *f.* nail-scissors; ~**schmied** *m.* nailsmith.
nagen *v.t. & i.* to gnaw; (*fig.*) to rankle.
nagend *a.* gnawing; nagging.
Nager *m.* (-s, -), **Nagetier** *n.* rodent.
nah[e] *a.* near, close, nigh; imminent; *das geht mir* ~, that grieves me; *einem zu* ~ *treten,* to hurt someone's feelings.
Nahaufklärüng *f.* (*mil.*) close reconnaissance.
Nahaufnahme *f.* (*Film*) close-up.
Nähe *f.* (-, -n) nearness, proximity; *in der* ~, at hand.
nahebei *adv.* nearby.
nahebringen *v.t.st.* to make s.th. accessible.
nahegehen *v.i.st.* to affect deeply.
nahekommen *v.i.st.* to come close; *v.refl.st.* to become close.
nahen *v.i.* (s) to approach.
nähen *v.t.* to sew, to stitch.
Nähere(s) *n.* details, particulars *pl.*
Näherei *f.* (-, -en) needlework.
Naherholungsgebiet *n.* recreational area close to a city.
Näherin *f.* (-, -nen) seamstress, needlewoman.
nähern (sich) ~ *v. refl.* to draw near.
nahestehen *v.i.st.* to be intimate with.
nahezu *adv.* almost.
Näh: ~**beutel** *m.* workbag; ~**garn** *n.* sewing thread; ~**kästchen** *n.* workbox; ~**korb** *m.* work basket; ~**maschine** *f.* sewing machine; ~**nadal** *f.* sewing needle.
Nähr... nutritive, *a.*; ~**wert** *m.* nutritive value.
Nährboden *m.* breeding ground, hotbed (*also fig.*)
nähren *v.t.* to feed, to nourish; to nurse; (*fig.*) to foster.
nahrhaft *a.* nutritious, nourishing; (*fig.*) profitable, lucrative.
Nahrung *f.* (-, 0) nourishment, food; livelihood, means of subsistence.
Nahrungs: ~**mittel** *n.* (article of) food; *pl.* victuals, provisions *pl.*; ~**sorgen** *pl.* cares for daily bread.
Nährwert *m.* nutritional value.
Nähseide *f.* sewing silk.
Naht *f.* (-, **Nähte**) seam; suture.
nahtlos *a.* seamless.
Nahverkehr *m.* local traffice.
Nähzeug *n.* sewing kit.
Nahziel *n.* short-term goal.
naiv *a.* naive, unsophisticated.
Naivität *f.* (-, -en) naiveté, artlessness.
Name(n), *m.* (-ns, -n) name; title; (*fig.*) reputation, fame; *dem* ~ *nach,* by name only; nominally.
namenlos, *a.* nameless; unspeakable.
namens *adv.* in the name of, on behalf; ~ *N,* of the

name of N.
Namens: ~**liste** *f.* (*mil.*) roster; ~**schild** *n.* nameplate; ~**tag** *m.* name-day; ~**vetter** *m.* name-sake.
namentlich *adv.* by name; particularly.
namhaft *a.* considerable, well-known; ~ *machen,* to name, to specify.
nämlich *a.* the same; ~ *adv.* namely, viz.
Napf *m.* (-[e]s, Näpfe) basin, bowl.
Narbe *f.* (-, -n) scar; stigma.
narbig *a.* scarred.
Narkose *f.* (-, -n) anesthesia; narcosis.
narkotisch *a.* narcotic.
narkotisieren *v.t.* to anesthetize.
Narr *m.* (-en, -en) fool; buffoon, jester; *eiem zum* ~ *en haben,* to fool someone.
narren *v.t.* to make a food of, to chaff.
Narrenfreiheit *f.* fool's license.
narrensicher *a.* foolproof.
Narretei *f.* (-, 0) tomfoolery, buffoonery.
Närrin *f.* (-, -nen) fool.
närrisch *a.* foolish; mad; odd, queer.
Narzisse *f.* (-, -n) narcissus.
Nasal *m.* nasal (sound).
naschen *v.t. & i.* to eat sweets (on the sly).
Nascherei *f.* (-, -en) ~**en** *f. pl* dainties *pl.*
naschhaft *a.* fond of candies.
Nase *f.* (-, -n) nose; (*Tier*~) snout; (*fig.*) reprimand; *die* ~ *rümpfen,* to turn up one's nose (at); *an der* ~ *herumführen,* to lead by the nose.
näseln *v.i.* to talk through the nose.
Nasenbluten *n.* (-s, 0) nosebleed.
Nasen: ~**loch** *m.* nostril; ~**spitze** *f.* tip of the nose.
naseweis *a.* pert, saucy, impertinent.
Nashorn *n.* rhinoceros.
naß *a.* wet, moist.
Nässe *f.* (-, 0) wetness, moisture.
nässen *v.t.* to wet, to moisten.
naßkalt *a.* raw, damp and cold.
Nation *f.* (-, -en) nation.
national *a.* national.
Nationalhymne *f.* (-, -n) national anthem.
nationalisieren *v.t.* to nationalize.
Nationalismus *m.* (-, 0) nationalism.
nationalistisch *a.* nationalist; nationalistic.
Nationalität *f.* (-, -en) nationality.
Natrium *n.* (-s, -0) sodium.
Natron *n.* (-s, 0) soda; *doppeltkohlensaures* ~, (bi)carbonate of soda.
Natter *f.* (-, -n) adder, viper.
Natur *f.* (-, -en) nature; disposition; *von* ~, by nature, naturally.
Naturalien *pl.* natural produce; **in** ~ **bezahlen** to pay in kind.
naturalisieren *v.t.* to naturalize; *sich* ~ *lassen,* to become naturalized.
Naturalismus *m.* naturalism.
naturalistisch *a.* naturalistic; naturalist.
Naturalleistung *f.* payment in kind.
Natur: ~**bursche** *m.*; ~**kind** *n.* child of nature; ~**denkmal** *n.* natural monument.
Naturell *n.* (-[e]s, -e) natural disposition.
Natur: ~**ereignis** *n.* ~**erscheinung** *f.* natural phenomenon; ~**faser** *f.* natural fiber; ~**forscher** *m.*; **Naturforscherin** *f.* scientist, naturalist.
Naturgas *n.* natural gas.

naturgemäß *a. & adv.* natural, normal; in accordance with nature.

Naturgeschichte *f.* nature history.

Naturgesetz *n.* law of nature.

naturgetreu *a.* true to nature *or* life.

Naturgewalt *f.* (-, -en) force of nature.

Naturheilkunde *f.* naturopathy.

Naturkatastrophe *f.* natural disaster.

Naturkunde *f.* science.

Naturlehrpfad *m.* nature trail.

natürlich *a.* natural; innate; unaffected; ~ *adv.* of course.

natürlicherweise *adv.* of course; naturally.

Naturrecht *n.* natural right; law of nature.

naturrein *a.* pure; no artificial ingredients.

Naturschauspiel *n.* natural spectacle.

Naturschutz *m.* conservation.

Naturschutzgebiet *n.* (-s, -e) nature preserve.

Naturtalent *n.* natural talent.

naturverbunden *a.* nature-loving.

Naturvolk *n.* primitive people.

naturwidrig *a.* unnatural.

Naturwissenschaft *f.* (natural) science.

Naturwunder *n.* natural wonder.

Nautik *f.* (-, 0) art of navigation.

Navigation *f.* (-, 0) navigation.

Nazi *m.* (-s, -s) Nazi.

Nazismus *m.* (-, 0) Nazism.

nazistisch *a.* Nazi.

Nazizeit *f.* Nazi period.

Neandertaler *m.* (-s, -) Neanderthal man.

Nebel *m.* (-s, -) mist, fog; (*mil.*) smoke.

nebelhaft *a.* nebulous; misty, hazy.

neb(e)lig *a.* misty, foggy.

Nebel: ~**scheinwerfer** *m.* (*mot.*) fog light; ~**schlußleuchte** *f.* rear fog light.

neben *pr.* near, by, beside; at, next to.

Nebenabsicht *f.* secondary intention.

nebenan *adv.* next door; close by.

Neben: ~**anschluß** *m.* (*tel.*) extension; ~**ausgaben** *pl.* incidentals, sundries; ~**bedentung** *f.* secondary meaning.

nebenbei *adv.* by the way; besides; ~ *bemerkt,* incidentally.

Neben: ~**beschäftigung** *f.* side-line; ~**beruf** *m.* side-line; ~**branche** *f.* side-line; ~**buhler** *m.*; ~**buhlerin** *f.* rival.

nebeneinander *adv.* side by side, abreast.

Nebeneinander *n.* (-s, 0) coexistence.

Nebeneinanderschaltung *f.* (*elek.*) parallel connection.

Neben: ~**eingang** *m.* side entrance; ~**einkünfte** *pl.* extra income; *pl.*; ~**fach** *n.* minor (subject); ~**fluß** *m.* tributary; ~**gebäude** *n.* outbuilding; annex; ~**gleis** *n.* siding; ~**handlung** *f.* subplot.

nebenher *adv.* besides; by the way.

Neben: ~**höhle** *f.* (*anat.*) paranasal sinus; ~**kosten** *pl.* extras; ~**linie** *f.* collateral line; (*rail*) branch-line; ~**mann** *m.* neighbor; ~**person** *f.* inferior *or* secondary character; ~**produkt** *n.* byproduct; ~**rolle** *f.* subordinate part; ~**sache** *f.* matter of secondary importance.

nebensächlich *a.* of secondary importance.

Neben: ~**satz** *m.* subordinate clause; ~**stelle** *f.* extension; branch; ~**tätigkeit** *f.* second job;

~**umstand** *m.* accessory *or* accidental circumstance; ~**verdienst** *m.* extra earnings *pl.*; perquisites, emoluments *pl.*, ~**zimmer** *n.* adjoining room.

nebst *pr.* together with, besides.

Necessaire *n.* (-s, -s) cosmetic kit.

necken *v.t.* to tease.

Neckerei *f.* (-, -en) teasing.

neckisch *a.* playful; saucy.

nee (*fam.*) no; nope

Neffe *m.* (-n, -n) nephew.

Negation *f.* (-, -en) negation.

negativ *a.* negative.

Negativ *n.* (-s, -e) negative.

Neger *m.*; **Negerin** *f;* black; (*fig.*) ghostwriter.

negieren *v.t.* to negate; to deny.

Negligé *n.* (-s, -s) negligee.

nehmen *v.t.st.* to take; *es genau ~,* to be very particular; *es leicht ~,* to take things easy, to make light of.

Neid *m.* (-es, 0) envy, jealousy.

neiden *v.t.* to envy.

Neider *m.* (-s, -) **Neidhammel** (-s, -) envious person.

neidisch *a.* envious.

neidlos *a.* ungrudging, without envy.

neidvoll *a.* envious.

Neige *f.* (-, -n) dregs, *pl. auf die ~ gehen,* to be on the decline; to run short.

neigen *v.t. & i.* to incline; (sich) ~ *v. refl.* to bow, to decline; to feel inclined.

Neigung *f.* (-, -en) inclination; bias, affection; dip, slope, gradient.

Neigungswinkel *m.* angle of inclination.

nein *adv.* no; say.

Nein *n.,* **Neinstimmen** *f.* no vote; vote against.

Nektar *m.* (-s, 0) nectar.

Nektarine *f.* nectarine.

Nelke *f.* (-, -n) carnation.

nennen *v.t. ir.* to name, to call, to mention.

nennenswert *a.* worth mentioning.

Nenner *m.* (-s, -) (*ar.*) denominator.

Nennung *f.* citing; mentioning.

Nenn: ~**wert** *m.* nominal value; denomination; ~**wort** *n.* noun.

Neofaschismus *m.* neo-fascism.

Neon *n.* neon; ~**röhre,** *f.* neon-tube.

Nepp *m.* (*pej.*) rip-off.

neppen *v.t.* (*sl.*) to rook; to rip-off.

Nepplokal *n.* (*fam.*) clip-joint.

Neptun *m.* (-s, 0) Neptune.

Nerv *m.* (-es, -en) nerve; *seine ~en verlieren* to lose one's nerve.

nerven *v.t.* (*fam.*) to get on s.b.'s nerves.

Nervenarzt *m.;* **Nervenärztin** *f.* neurologist.

nervenaufreibend *a.* nerve-racking.

Nerven: ~**belastung** *f.* strain on the nerves; ~**bündel** *n.* (*fam.*) bundle of nerves; ~**fieber** *n.* typhoid fever; ~**heilanstalt,** sanatorium (for nervous diseases); ~**knoten** *m.* ganglion.

nervenkrank, nervenschwach *a.* suffering from a nervous disorder.

Nerven: ~**krankheit** *f.* nervous disease; ~**leiden** *n.* nervous disorder; ~**säge** *f.* (*fam.*) pain in the neck; ~**schmerz** *m.* neuralgia.

nervenstärkend *a.* tonic.

Nervensystem *n.* nervous system.
Nervenzusammenbruch *m.* nervous breakdown.
nervig *a.* nervous; sinewy.
nervlich *a.* nervous.
nervös *a.* nervous; highly strung.
Nervosität *f.* (-, 0) nervousness.
nervtötend *a.* (*fam.*) nerve-shattering.
Nerz *m.* (-es, -e) mink, small otter.
Nessel *m.* untreated cotton fabric.
Nessel *f.* (-, -en) nettle.
Nesselausschlag *m.* nettle-rash.
Nest *n.* (-es, -er) nest; (*fam.*) dump, hole.
Nesthäkchen *n.* youngest child, pet.
nett *a.* neat, fair, nice, pretty.
netterweise *adv.* kindly.
Nettigkeit *f.* kindness; goodness.
netto *adv.* (*vom Preise, Gewichte*) net.
Netto: ~**betrag** *m.* net amount; ~**einnahme** *f.* net receipts *pl.*; ~**ertrag** *m.* net proceeds *pl.*
Netz *n.* (-es, -e) net; network.
Netzanschluß *m.* (*elec.*) mains connection.
netzen *v.t.* to wet; to moisten.
netzförmig *a.* reticular.
Netzhaut *f.* retina.
neu *a.* new, recent; *aufs* ~*e*, *von* ~ *em*, anew, again; ~*e*[*re*] *Zeit*, modern times; ~*ere Sprache*, modern language.
Neuankömmling *m.* newcomer.
Neuanschaffung *f.* new acquisition.
neuartig. *a.* novel.
Neuauflage *f.* new edition, repeat performance.
Neuausgabe *f.* new edition.
Neubau *m.* (-[e]s, ~**bauten**) new building.
Neubearbeitung *f.* (-, -en) revised edition.
neubenennen *v.t. ir.* to redesignate.
Neudruck *m.* reprint.
neuerdings *adv.* lately, recently.
Neuerer *m.* (-s, -) innovator.
Neuerscheinung *f.* (-, -en) new publication; new release.
Neuerung *f.* (-, -en) innovation.
Neuerwerbung *f.* new acquisition.
Neufassung *f.* revised version; remake.
neuformen *v.t.* to reshape.
neugeboren *a.* new-born.
neugestalten *v.t.* to reorganize.
Neugier, Neugierde *f.* (-, 0) curiosity.
neugierig *a.* inquisitive, curious.
Neugliederung *f.* reorganization.
neugotisch *a.* neo-Gothic.
Neugründung *f.* new foundation.
neugültig machen *v.t.* to revalidate.
Neuheit *f.* (-, -en) newness; novelty.
Neuigkeit *f.* (-, -en) news.
Neujahr *n.* (-[e]s, -s) New-Year's Day.
Neuland *m.* new territory; ~**betreten** (*fig.*) to break new ground.
neulich *adv.* recently, the other day.
Neuling *m.* (-[e]s, -e) novice, beginner.
neumodisch *a.* newfangled.
Neumond *m.* new moon.
neun *a.* nine.
Neunauge *n.* lamprey.
neunfach *a.* ninefold.
neunmal *adv.* nine times.
neunzehn *a.* nineteen.

neunzig *a.* ninety.
neunziger *a. die ~ Jahre* the nineties.
Neuordnung *f.* reorganization.
Neuorientierung *f.* reorientation.
Neuphilologe *m.*; **Neuphilologin** *f.* student *or* teacher of modern languages.
Neuralgie *f.* neuralgia.
neuralgisch *a.* neuralgic.
Neuregelung *f.* revision of rules.
neureich *a.* nouveau riche.
Neurologe *m.*; **Neurologin** *f.* neurologist.
Neurose *f.* neurosis.
Neurotiker *m.*; **Neurotikerin** *f.* neurotic.
neurotisch *a.* neurotic.
Neuschnee *m.* fresh snow.
Neuseeland *n.* (-s, 0) New Zealand.
Neuseeländer *m.*; **Neuseeländerin** *f.* New Zealander.
neuseeländisch *a.* New Zealand.
neusprachlich *a.* modern-language.
neutral *a.* neutral.
neutralisieren *v.t.* to neutralize.
Neutralität *f.* (-, 0) neutrality.
Neutron *n.* (-s, -en) neutron.
Neutronenbombe *f.* neutron bomb.
Neutrum *n.* (-s, Neutra) (*gram.*) neuter.
neuvermählt *a.* newly married.
neuwertig *a.* as new.
Neuzeit *f.* modern times, our days *pl.*
Neuzugang *m.* new admission (hospital); new accession (library).
nicht *adv.* not; *auch* ~, not; ~ *einmal*, not even; *durchaus* ~, not at all; *gar* ~, not at all, by no means; *noch* ~, not yet; ~ *mehr*, no more, no longer.
Nichtachtung *f.* disregard.
nichtalkoholische Getränke *pl.* soft drinks.
Nichtangriff *m.* non-aggression.
nichtansässig *a.* non-resident.
Nichtbeachtung, Nichtbefolgung *f.* (-, 0) inattention, noncompliance, nonobservance.
Nichte *f.* (-, -n) niece.
Nichteinmischung *f.* (-, 0) non-intervention.
Nichteisenmetall *n.* non-ferrous metal.
Nichterfüllung *f.* non-fulfilment.
Nichterscheinen *n.* non-attendance.
nichtig *a.* null, void; vain, empty.
Nichtigkeit *f.* (-, -en) invalidity, nullity, futility; vanity, emptiness.
Nichtigkeitsklage *f.* writ of error, plea of nullity.
Nichtkriegführende *m.* non-belligerent.
Nichtmitglied *n.* non-member.
Nichtraucher *m.* non-smoker; ~**abteil** *m.* non-smoking compartment.
nichtrostend *a.* non-rusting; stainless.
nichts *adv.* nothing; ~**als**, nothing but; ~ *weniger als*, anything but this; *mir* ~, *dir* ~, just like that.
Nichts *n.* (-, 0) nothing(ness), void.
nichtsahnend *a.* unsuspecting.
Nichtschwimmer *m.*; **Nichtschwimmerin** *f.* nonswimmer.
nichtsdestotrotz *adv.* **nichtsdestoweniger** *adv.* nevertheless.
Nichtskönner *m.* incompetent.
Nichtsnutz *m.* (-es, -e) good for nothing.
nichtssagend *a.* meaningless, unmeaning.

Nichtstuer *m.* idler, loafer.
Nichtstun *n.* inactivity; idleness.
Nichtswisser *m.* ignoramus.
nichtswürdig *a.* vile, worthless.
Nichtvorhandensein *n.* nonexistence.
Nickel *m.* (-s, -) nickel.
Nickelbrille *f.* metal-rimmed glasses.
nicken *v.t.* to nod; to nap.
Nickerchen *n.* (-s, -) (*fam.*) nap; snooze.
nie *adv.* never.
nieder *a. & adv.* low, lower, nether; down; *auf und* ~, up and down.
niederbeugen *v.t.* to bend down.
niederbrennen *v.t. & i.r.* to burn down.
niederdeutsch *a.* Low-German.
niederdrücken *v.t.* to press down; (*fig.*) to depress, to oppress.
niederfallen *v.i.st.* (*s*) to fall down.
Niedergang *m.* decline.
niedergehen *v.i.st.* to go down.
niedergeschlagen *a.* dejected, downcast.
niederhalten *v.t.st.* to keep down.
niederknie[e]n *v.i.* (*s*) to kneel down.
Niederkunft *f.* (-, 0) delivery.
Niederlage *f.* (-, -n) defeat.
Niederlande *pl.* (-) the Netherlands.
Niederländer *m.* Dutchman, Netherland.
Niederländerin *f.* Dutchwoman, Netherlander.
niederländisch *a.* Dutch, Netherlands.
niederlassen (sich) *v.refl.st.* to establish oneself, to settle down; to set up (in business).
Niederlassung *f.* (-, -en) establishment; settlement.
niederlegen *v.t.* to lay down; to retire from; (*Arbeit*) to strike, to knock off.
niedermachen *v.t.* to kill, to slay.
niedermetzeln *v.t.* to massacre.
niederreißen *v.t.st.* to pull down.
Niedersachsen *n.* Lower Saxony.
Niederschlag *m.* rain; (*chem.*) precipitation.
Niederschlagsmenge *f.* (-, -n) rainfall.
niederschlagen *v.t.st.* to knock down; (*die Augen*) to cast down; (*law*) to quash (a charge); (*chem.*) to precipitate.
niederschmettern *v.t.* to crush.
niederschreiben *v.t.st.* to write down.
niederschreien *v.t.st.* to shout about.
Niederschrift *f.* (-, -en) writing down, copy.
niedersetzen *v.t.* to set *or* put down; (sich) ~ *v. refl.* to sit down.
niederstrecken *v.t.* to fell.
niederträchtig *a.* base, abject, vile.
Niederträchtigkeit *f.* (-, -en) baseness.
niedertreten *v.t.st.* to trample down.
Niederung *f.* (-, -en) lowland.
niederwerfen *v.t.st.* to throw down; (sich) ~ *v.refl.* to prostrate oneself.
niedlich *a.* cute; neat, nice.
niedrig *a.* low; mean, vile, base.
Niedrigkeit *f.* (-, -en) lowness; baseness.
niemals *adv.* never.
niemand *pn.* nobody.
Niemandsland *n.* no man's land.
Niere *f.* (-, -n) kidney; reins *pl.*
Nieren: ~**braten** *m.* roast loin of veal; ~**entzündung** *f.* nephritis; ~**leiden** *n.* kidney disease;

~**stein** *n.* kidney stone; renal calculus.
nieseln *v.i.* to drizzle.
niesen *v.i.* to sneeze.
Nieswurz *f.* (-, 0) hellebore.
Niete *f.* (-, -n) rivet; blank (ticket).
nieten *v.t.* to rivet.
Nihilismus *m.* nihilism.
Nihilist *m.*; **Nihilistin** *f.* nihilist.
nihilistisch *a.* nihilistic.
Nikolaustag *m.* St. Nicholas' Day.
Nikotin *n.* nicotine.
nikotinarm *a.* low-nicotine.
nikotinfrei *a.* nicotine-free.
Nikotinvergiftung *f.* nicotine poisoning.
Nilpferd *n.* hippopotamus.
Nimbus *m.* (-, 0) nimbus, halo; prestige.
nimmer, nimmermehr, *adv.* never, nevermore, no more; by no means, nowise.
Nippel *m.* (-s, -) nipple; valve (inflatables).
nippen *v.t.* to sip.
Nippsachen *pl.* knicknacks *pl.*
nirgend[s] *adv.* nowhere.
Nische *f.* (-, -n) niche.
nisten *v.i.* to nest; to build; to nestle.
Nistkasten *m.* (-s, -kästen) nesting box.
Nitrat *n.* (-s, -e) nitrate.
Nitroglyzerin *n.* nitroglycerine.
Niveau *n.* (-s, -s) level; **ein hohes** ~ high standards.
nivellieren *v.t.* to level.
Nixe *f.* (-, -n) water-fairy, nixie.
nobel *a.* noble; generous; magnificent.
Nobel: ~**herberge** *f.* (*fam.*) high-class hotel ~**kutsche** *f.* flashy car.
Nobel: ~**preis** *m.* Nobel prize; ~**preisträger** *m.*, ~**preisträgerin** *f.* prize-winner.
noch *adv.* still, yet; ~ *einmal,* once more; ~ *etwas,* something more; ~ *immer,* still; ~ *nicht,* not yet.
nochmalig *a.* repeated.
nochmals *adv.* once again.
Nockenwelle *f.* (*mech.*) camshaft.
Nomade *m.* (-n, -n); **Nomadin** *f.* (-, -nen) nomad.
nomadisch *a.* nomadic.
Nomen *n.* (-s, Nomina) noun; substantive.
Nominativ *m.* (-s, -e) nominative (case).
nominell *a.* nominal.
nominieren *v.t.* to nominate; to name.
Nonkonformismus *m.* nonconformism.
nonkonformistisch *a.* nonconformist, unconventional.
Nonne *f.* (-, -n) nun.
Nonnenkloster *n.* nunnery, convent.
Nonsens *m.* nonsense.
Nonstop. . . nonstop.
Noppe *f.* (-, -n) knop; nub; bump; pimple.
Nord(en) *m.* (-s, 0) North.
Nordamerika *m.* North America.
Nordamerikaner *m.*; **Nordamerikanerin** *f.* North American.
norddeutsch *a.* North German.
Norddeutschland *n.* North Germany.
Nordengland *n.* the North of England.
Nordeuropa *n.* Northern Europe.
nordisch *a.* Northern; Nordic.
Nordkap *n.* North Cape.
Nordländer *m.* (-s, -) northerner.

162

nördlich *a.* northerly, northern; arctic; ~*e Breite,* Northern latitude.

Nordlicht *n.* aurora borealis; northern lights.

Nordost *m.* (-ens, 0) north-east.

Nord: ~**pol** *m.* North Pole; ~**polarkreis** *m.* arctic circle.

Nordrhein-Westfalen *n.* North Rhine-Westphalia.

Nordsee *f.* North Sea.

Nordsüd... north-and-south, *a.*

nordwärts *adv.* northward.

Nordwest *m.* (-ens, 0) north-west.

Nordwind *m.* north wind.

nörgeln *v.i.* to grumble, to nag.

Nörgler *m.* (-s, -) moaner; grumbler.

Norm *f.* (-, -en) standard, rule.

normal *a.* normal, standard.

Normalbenzin *n.* regular gasoline.

normalerweise *adv.* normally.

Normalfall *m.* normal case.

normalisieren *v.t.* to normalize.

Normalität *f.* (-, 0) normality.

Normalmass *n.* normal size.

Normalverbraucher *m.* average consumer.

Normalzustand *m.* normal state.

Normandie *f.* Normandy.

normativ *a.* normative.

normen, normieren *v.t.* to standardize.

Normung *f.* standardization.

Norwegen *n.* (-s, 0) Norway.

Norweger *m.;* **Norwegerin** *f.;* **norwegisch** *a.* Norwegian.

Nostalgie *f.* nostalgia.

Not *f.* (-, Nöte) need, misery; necessity, distress, trouble; *zur* ~, if need be; *mit knapper* ~, barely, with great difficulty.

Not... emergency...

Nota *f.* (-, 0) memorandum.

Notar *m.* (-s, -e) notary public.

Notariat *n.* ([e]s, -s) notary's office.

notariell *a.* notarized.

Not: ~**arzt** *m.;* ~**ärztin** *f.* emergency doctor; ~**ausgang** *m.* emergency exit; ~**behelf** *m.* shift, makeshift; ~**bremse** *f.* emergency brake.

Notdurft *f.* (-, 0) *seine* ~ *verrichten,* to ease oneself.

notdürftig *a.* indigent; scant.

Note *f.* (-, -n) note; grade; bill; mark; ~**n** *pl.* music; *ganze* ~, whole note semibreve; *halbe* ~, half note minim.

Noten: ~**bank** *f.* issuing bank; ~**blatt** *n.* sheet of music; ~**linien** *pl.* staff; ~**papier** *n.* music-paper; ~**pult** *n.* music stand; ~**schlüssel** *m.* clef; ~**schrift** *f.* musical notation; ~**ständer** *m.* music stand.

Notfall *m.* case of need, emergency.

notfalls *adv.* if necessary.

notgedrungen *adv.* of necessity.

Notgeld *n.* emergency money.

notieren *v.t.* to note (down); (*com.*) to quote; to be quoted.

nötig *a.* necessary; *etwas* ~ *haben,* to stand in need of, to need.

nötigen *v.t.* to compel, to force, to urge.

nötigenfalls *adv.* in case of need.

Nötigung *f.* (-, -en) intimidation; coercion.

Notiz *f.* (-, -en) notice; memorandum; ~**en** *pl.* notes.

Notizblock *m.* memo pad.

Notlage *f.* predicament, plight.

Notizbuch *n.* notebook.

Notlandung *f.* forced landing.

notleidend *a.* needy.

Notlösung *f.* stopgap.

Notlüge *f.* evasive lie; white lie.

notorisch *a.* notorious.

Not: ~**pfennig** *m.* savings *pl.,* ~**ruf** *m.* emergency call, number; ~**signal** *n.* distress signal; ~**stand** *m.* state of emergency; ~**standsgebiet** *n.* disaster, distressed area; ~**standsarbeiten** *pl.* relief work; ~**verband** *m.* provisional dressing; ~**verbandskasten** *m.* first-aid outfit; ~**verordnung** *f.* emergency decree; ~**wehr** *f.* (-, 0) self-defense.

notwendig *a.* necessary.

notwendigerweise *adv.* necessarily.

Notwendigkeit *f.* (-, 0) necessity.

Notzeit *f.* (-, -en) time of need.

Notzucht *f.* rape, violation.

notzüchtigen *v.t.* to rape.

Novelle *f.* (-, -n) novella; (*jur.*) amendment.

novellieren *v.t.* to amend.

November *m.* (-s, -) November.

Novität *f.* novelty.

Novize *m.* (-n, -n) ; **Novizin** *f.* (-, -nen) novice.

Nu *n.* (-, 0) moment; *in einem* ~, in no time.

Nuance *f.* (-, -n) nuance, shade (*fig.*).

nuancieren *v.t.* to shade, to differentiate.

nüchtern *a.* fasting; sober; (*fig.*) matter-of-fact; dreary, prosaic; *noch* ~ *sein,* not to have eaten anything yet.

nuckeln *v.i.* to suck.

Nudeln *f.pl.* noodles.

Nudist *m.;* **Nudistin** *f.* nudist.

nuklear *a.* nuclear.

Nuklearkrieg *m.* nuclear war.

null *a.* null; ~ *und nichtig,* null and void.

Null *f.* (-, -en) zero.

Nullpunkt *m.* zero, freezing-point.

Nulltarif *m.* free transport; free admission.

Nullwachstum *n.* zero growth.

numerieren *v.t.* to number.

numerisch *a.* numerical.

Numerus *m.* (-, Numeri) number.

Numerus clausus *m.* limited admission (university).

Nummer *f.* (-, -n) number.

Nummernschild *n.* license plate.

nun *adv. & c.* now, at present; therefore; ~? well?

nunmehr *adv.* now, by this time.

Nuntius, Nunzius *m.* (-, -zien) nuncio.

nur *adv.* only, but solely.

nuscheln *v.i.* to mumble.

Nuß *f.* (-, Nüsse) nut; *eine harte* ~, a hard nut to crack.

Nuß: ~**baum** *m.* walnut-tree; ~**holz** *n.* walnut (-wood); ~**knacker** *m.* nutcracker; ~**schale** *f.* nutshell.

Nüster *f.* (-, -n) nostril.

Nutte *f.* (*fam. pej.*) hooker.

Nutz *m.* = **Nutzen:** *sich zu* ~*e machen,* to turn to account.

Nutzanwendung *f.* practical use.

nutzbar *a.* useful; profitable.

nutzbringend *a.* useful, profitable.

nütze *a. zu etwas ~ sein* to be of use, *zu nichts ~ sein* to be of no use.

Nutzeffekt *m.* efficiency.

nutzen, nützen *v.t.* to make use of, to use, to turn to account; *~ v.i.* to be of use, to serve.

Nutzen *m.* (-s, 0) use; profit, benefit.

Nutz: *~fahrzeng n.* commercial vehicle; *~fläche f.* usable floor space.

Nutzholz *n.* timber.

Nutzlast *f.* pay load.

nütlich *a.* useful, profitable; conducive (to).

Nützlichkeit *f.* (-, 0) usefulness, utility.

nutzlos *a.* useless, of no use; futile.

Nutzlosigkeit *f.* uselessness; futility.

Nutznießer *m.* (-s, -); **Nutznießerin** *f.* (-, -nen) beneficiary; usufructuary.

Nutznießung *f.* (-, 0) usufruct.

Nutzung *f.* (-, -en) use; cultivation; exploitation.

Nutzwert *m.* practical value.

Nylon, *n.* nylon.

Nymphe *f.* (-, -n) nymph.

Nymphomanin *f.* (-, -nen) nymphomaniac.

O

O, o *n.* the letter O or o.

o! *i.* o! oh!; *~ weh!* alas! oh dear!

Oase *f.* (-, -n) oasis.

ob *c.* whether; if; *als ~*, as if; *na ~!* (*fam.*) rather!

Obacht *f.* (-, 0) caution, care; *~ geben*, to pay attention.

Obdach *n.* (-[e]s, 0) shelter, lodging.

obdachlos *a.* houseless, homeless.

Obdachlose *m./f.* homeless.

Obdachlosenasyl *n.* homeless shelter.

Obduktion *f.* (-, -en) post-mortem autopsy.

O-Beine *n.pl.* bow legs.

o-beinig *a.* bow legged.

oben *adv.* above; on the surface; upstairs; *von ~ herab*, in a superior way; *von ~ bis unten*, from top to bottom; *diese Seite nach ~*, this side up; *das zweite von ~*, the second down; *~erwähnt a.* above-mentioned.

obenan *adv.* at the top.

obendrauf *adv.* on top.

obendrein *adv.* besides, into the bargain.

obenhin *adv.* superficially.

ober *a.* upper, higher; (*fig.*) chief; *~e rechte Ecke*, top righthand corner.

Ober *m.* (-s, -) (*fam.*)(head-)waiter.

Ober: *~arm m.* upper arm; *~arzt m.* head physician; *~befehl m.* chief command; *~befehlshaber m.* commander-in-chief; *~begriff m.* generic term; *~bett .* duvet; *~bürgermeister m.* *~bürgermeisterin f.* mayor; *~deck n.* upper-deck.

oberdeutsch *a.* Upper German.

Obere[r] *m.* (-n, -n) superior.

Oberfläche *f.* surface.

oberflächlich *a. & adv.* superficial(ly).

Oberflächlichkeit *f.* superficiality.

Obergeschoß *n.* upper floor.

Obergrenze *f.* upper limit, ceiling.

oberhalb *pr.* above.

Ober: *~hand f.* upper hand; *~haupt n.* head, chief; *~haus n.* upper house (of parliament); *~hemd n.* shirt; *~hoheit f.* supremacy.

Oberin *f.* (-, -nen) mother superior; matron.

oberirdisch *a.* overground.

Ober: *~kellner m.* headwaiter; *~kiefer n.* upper jaw; *~klasse f.* upper class; *~kommando n.* high command; *~körper m.* upper part of the body; *~leder n.* uppers *pl.*; *~leitung f.* (*elek.*) overhead wire, overhead cable; *~licht n.* skylight; *~lippe f.* upper lip; *~satz m.* (*Logik*) major term; *~schenkel m.* thigh; *~schicht f.* upper class; *~schwester f.* head nurse; *~seite f.* upper side.

oberst *a.* uppermost; supreme; top.

Oberst *m.* (-en, -en) colonel.

Oberstaatsanwalt *m.*; **Oberstaatsanwältin** *f.* attorney general.

Oberstleutnant *m.* lieutenant-colonel.

Ober: *~studiendirektor m.*, *~studiendirektorin f.* principal; *~studienrat m.*; *~studienrätin f.* senior teacher; *~wasser n.* (*fig.*) *~ bekommen*, to get the upper hand.

obgleich *c.* though, although.

Obhut *f.* (-, 0) protection, care.

obig *a.* above; foregoing.

Objekt *n.* (-s, -e) object; property.

objektiv *a.* objective; impartial.

Objektiv *n.* (-s, -s) objective; lens.

objektivität *f.* objectivity.

Objektsatz *m.* object clause.

Oblate *f.* (-, -n) wafer.

obliegen *v.i.st.* to be incumbent on; to apply onself to; *es liegt mir ob*, it is my duty.

Obliegenheit *f.* (-, -en) duty, obligation.

Obligation *f.* (-, -en) (*com.*) debenture.

obligatorisch *a.* obligatory; compulsory.

Obmann *m.* chairman.

Oboe *f.* (-, -n) oboe.

Obrigkeit *f.* (-, -en) authorities *pl.*, government.

Obrigkeitsstaat *m.* authoritarian state.

obschon *c.* (al)though, albeit.

Observatorium *n.* (-[s], -rien) obsrvatory.

observieren *v.t.* to keep under surveillance; to observe.

obskur *a.* obscure.

Obst *n.* (-es, 0) fruit.

Obst *~baum m.* fruit-tree; *~garten m.* orchard; *~händler m.* fruit seller; *~kern m.* stone, pit; *~saft m.* juice; *~salat m.* fruit salad; *~wasser n.* fruit brandy.

obszön *a.* obscene.

Obszönität *f.* obscenity.

obwalten *v.i.* to prevail.

obwohl *c.* though, although.

Ochs *m.* (Ochsen, Ochsen) ox; bull, bullock; (*fig.*) blockhead.

Ochsen: *~brust f.* brisket of beef; *~schwanzsuppe f.* oxtail soup; *~zunge f.* ox-tongue.

Ochsenfleisch *m.* beef.

Ocker *m.* (-s, 0) ocher.

Ode *f.* (-, -n) ode.

öde *a.* desert, desolate, waste; dull.

Öde *f.* (-, -n) desert, wilderness; wasteland.

Odem *m.* (-s, 0) breath.
oder *c.* or; or else.
Ödland *n.* (-[e]s, -länder) wasteland.
Ofen *m.* (-s, -Öfen) stove, oven; furnace, kiln.
Ofen: ~**kachel** *f.* Dutch tile; ~**loch** *n.* mouth of an oven; ~**röhre** *f.* stove pipe; ~**schirm** *m.* firescreen; ~**setzer** *m.* stove-fitter.
offen *a.* open; (*Stelle*) vacant; (*fig.*) frank; (*Wechsel*) blank check.
offenbar *a.* obvious, evident, manifest.
offenbaren *v.t.* to make known; to disclose, to reveal.
Offenbarung *f.* (-, -en) revelation.
Offenbarungseid *m.* oath of disclosure.
offenbleiben *v.i.st.* to remain open.
offenhalten *v.t.st.* to keep s.th. open; to reserve.
Offenheit *f.* frankness; honesty.
offenherzig *a.* sincere, candid, frank.
offenkundig *a.* notorious, public, obvious.
offensichtlich *a.* obvious.
offensiv *a.* offensive.
Offensive *f.* (-, -n) offensive.
offenstehen *v.i.st.* to be open; to be outstanding.
öffentlich *a.* public; ~**e** Einrichtung *f.* public utility.
Öffentlichkeit *f.* (-, 0) public, publicity; *unter Ausschluss der ~,* (*law*) in camera; in private.
Öffentlichkeitsarbeit *f.* public relations.
öffentlich-rechtlich *a.* under public law.
offerieren *v.t.* to offer.
Offerte *f.* (-, -n) offer, tender.
offiziell *a.* official.
Offizier *m.* (-[e]s, -e) officer.
Offizierkorps *n.* body of officers.
Offiziersanwärter *m.* officer candidate.
Offizierslaufbahn *f.* officer's career.
offiziös *a.* semi-official.
öffnen (sich) *v.t. & refl.* to open.
Öffner *m.* (-s, -) opener.
Öffnung *f.* (-, -en) opening; aperture.
Öffnungszeiten *pl.* opening hours *pl.*
Offsetdruck *m.* offset printing.
oft(mals) *adv.* often, frequently.
öfter *a.* frequent, repeated; ~*adv.* more often.
öfters *adv.* repeatedly.
oftmals *adv.* frequently.
oh! *i.* oh! **oha!** *i.* oho!
Oheim, Ohm *m.* (-s, -e) uncle.
Ohm *n.* (*elek.*)ohm.
ohne *pr.* without; but for, except; ~*e weiteres,* without ceremony, without more ado; *es ist nicht ~,* (*fam.*) it is not to be despised.
ohnedies, ohnehin *adv.* anyhow.
ohneeinander *adv.* without each other.
ohnegleichen *a.* unparalleled.
Ohnmacht *f.* (-[e]s, -en) swoon, fainting fit; weakness.
ohnmächtig *a.* unconscious; powerless; fainting, in a swoon.
Ohr *n.* (-[e]s, -en) ear; *die ~en spitzen,* to prick up one's ears; *einen übers ~hauen,* to make someone pay through the nose; *bis an, bis über die ~en,* head over heels.
Ohr *n.* (-[e]s, Öhre) eye (of a needle).
Ohrenarzt *m.*; **Ohrenärztin** *f.* ear specialist; otologist.

ohrenbetäubend *a.* ear-splitting; deafening.
Ohren: ~**sausen** *n.* ringing/buzzing in the ears; ~**schmalz** *n.* ear-wax; ~**schmerz** *m.* earache; ~**schützer** *pl.* earmuffs; ~**sessel** *m.* wing chair; ~**zeuge** *m.* ear-witness.
Ohrfeige *f.* box on the ear.
ohrfeigen *v.t.* to box a person's ears.
Ohr: ~**läppchen** *n.* ear lobe; ~**muschel** *f.* outer ear, auricle; ~**ring** *m.* earring; ~**stecker** *m.* ear-stud; ~**wurm** *m.* earwig.
Oker = **Ocker.**
okkult *a.* occult.
Okkultismus *m.* (-, 0) occultism.
Ökologe *m.* **Ökologin** *f.* ecologist.
Ökologie *f.* ecology.
ökologisch *a.* ecological.
Ökonom *m.* (-en, -en) economist.
Ökonomie *f.* (-, -[e]n) economy.
ökonomisch *a.* economical.
Ökosystem, *n.* ecozystem.
Oktan *n.* (-s, 0) (*mot.*) octane; ~**zahl** *f.* octane rating.
Oktavband *m.* octavo (volume).
Oktave *f.* (-, -n) (*mus.*) octave.
Oktober *f.* (-s, -) October.
oktroyieren *v.t.* to dictate to, to impose upon.
okulieren *v.t.* (*bot.*) to inoculate, to graft.
ökumenisch *a.* (*eccl.*) ecumenical.
Okzident *m.* (-s, 0) occident.
Öl *n.* (-[e]s, -s) oil; *~ ins Feuer giessen,* (*fig.*) to add fuel to the fire.
Öl: ~**baum** *m.* olive-tree; ~**berg** *m.* Mount of Olives; ~**bild** *n.* oil-painting; ~**druck** *m.* oil pressure; ~**druckbild** *m* chromolithograph.
Oleander *m.* (-s, -) oleander.
ölen *v.t.* to oil; to lubricate.
Öl: ~**farbe** *f.* oil-paint; ~**gemälde** *n.* oil-painting.
ölig *a.* oily.
Oligarchie *f.* (-, -n) oligarchy.
oliv *a.* olive (-green).
Olive *f.* (-, -n) olive.
Olivenbaum *m.* (-s, -bäume) olive tree.
Olivenöl *n.* olive-oil.
Öl: ~**kanne** *f.* oil can; ~**kuchen** *m.* oil-cake; ~**leitung** *f.* oil pipe; ~**malerei** *f.* painting in oil; ~**pest** *f.* oil pollution; ~**raffinerie** *f.* oil refinery; ~**stand** *m.* oil level; ~**standzeiger** *m.* oil gauge; ~**tankschiff** *n.* oil tanker; ~**teppich** *m.* oil slick.
Ölung *f.* (-, -en) oiling; lubrication; *letzte ~,* extreme unction.
Öl: ~**vorkommen** *n.* oil deposit; ~**wanne** *f.* oil sump; ~**wechsel** *m.* oil change; ~**zeug** *n.* oilskins.
Olymp *m.* i(-s, 0) Mount Olympus.
Olympiade *f.* (-, -n) Olympic Games; Olympics.
Olympisch *a.* Olympic.
Ölzweig *m.* olive-branch.
Oma *f.* (*fam.*) granny, grandma.
Omelett *m.* omelet.
ominös *a.* ominous; sinister.
Omnibus *m.* (-sses, -sse) bus.
Omnibushaltestelle *f.* bus stop.
Onanie *f.* (-, 0) onanism; masturbation.
onanieren *v.i.* to masturbate.
ondulieren *v.t.* to wave.
Onkel *m.* (-s, -) uncle.
Opa *m.* (*fam.*) grandad; grandpa.

Opal *m.* (-s, -e) opal.
Oper *f.* (-, -n) opera.
Operateur *f.* (-s, -e) operator.
Operation *f.* (-, -en) operation.
Operationsgebiet *n.* (*mil.*) zone of operations.
Operationssaal *m.* operating room.
operativ *a.* operative.
Operette *f.* (-, -n) operetta, musical comedy.
operieren *v.t. & i.* to operate; *sich ~ lassen* (*med.*) to be operated on.
Opern: ~**arie** *f.* aria; ~**glas** *n.* ~**gucker** *m.* operaglass; ~**haus** *n.* opera-house; ~**sänger**(in) *m.* (*& f.*) opera-singer; ~**text** *m.* libretto, book.
Opfer *n.* (-s, -) offering; sacrifice; victim; *ein ~ bringen,* (*fig.*) to make a sacrifice.
Opfergabe *f.* offering.
Opferlamm *n.* sacrificial lamb.
opfern *v.t.* to sacrifice.
Opferstock *m.* offertory.
Opfertier *n.* sacrificial animal.
Opferung *f.* (-, -en) immolation; sacrifice.
Opiat *n.* (-s, -e) opiate.
Opium *n.* (-s, 0) opium.
Opponent *m.;* **Opponentin** *f.* opponent.
opponieren *v.t.* to oppose.
opportun *a.* appropriate.
Opportunist *m.;* **opportunistisch** *a.* opportunist.
Opposition *f.* opposition.
Oppositions: ~**führer** *m.,* **führerin** *f.* opposition leader; ~**partei** *f.* opposition party.
optieren *v.i.* to opt.
Optik *f.* (-, 0) optics *pl.*
Optiker *m.* (-s, -) optician.
Optimismus *m.* (-, 0) optimism.
Optimist *m.;* **Optimistin** *f.* optimist.
optimistisch *a.* optimistic.
optisch *a.* optical.
Orakel *n.* (-s, -0), **Orakelspruch** *m.* oracle.
orakelhaft, orakelmässig *a.* oracular.
orakeln *v.i.* to speak oracularly.
oral *a. & adv.* oral(ly).
Orange *f.* (-, -n) orange.
orangefarben *a.* orange(-colored).
Orangenbaum *m.* orange-tree.
Orangenschale *f.* orange peel.
Orangerie *f.* (-, -[e]n) orangery; greenhouse.
Orang-Utan *m.* (-s, -e) orangutang.
Oratorium *n.* (-s, -rien) (*mus.*) oratorio.
Orchester *n.* (-s, -) orchestra.
Orchestermusik *f.* orchestral music.
Orchidee *f.* (-, -n) orchid.
Orden *m.* (-s, -) order; decoration, medal.
Ordens: ~**band** *n.* ribbon (of an order); ~**regel** *f.* monastic rule; ~**schwester** *f.* sister, nun.
ordentlich *a.* orderly, tidy; ordinary, usual, regular; ~*er Professor,* (full) professor.
ordentlichkeit *f.* tidiness, neatness.
ordinär *a.* vulgar, mean, low.
Ordinarius *m.* (-, -rien) (full) professor.
ordinieren *v.t.* to ordain; *sich ~ lassen,* to take (holy) orders.
ordnen *v.t.* to put in order; to arrange, to regulate; to classify.
Ordner *m.* file; steward.
Ordnung *f.* (-, -en) order, arrangement; class; *zur ~ rufen,* to call to order; *etwas in ~ bringen,* to

straighten out; *~ schaffen,* to establish order.
ordnungshalber *adv.* as a matter of form.
ordnungsmässig *a.* orderly, regular.
Ordnungsstrafe *f.* (*jur.*) penalty for contempt of court.
ordnungswidrig *a.* irregular, illegal; ~**es Benehmen** *n.* disorderly conduct.
Ordnungszahl *f.* ordinal number.
Organ *n.* (-[e]s, -e) organ; voice.
Organisation *f.* (-, -en) organization.
Organisator *m.;* **Organisatorin** *f.* organizer.
organisatorisch *a.* organizational.
organisch *a.* organic.
organisieren *v.t.* to organize.
Organismus *m.* (-e, -men) organism.
Organist *m.* (-en, -en); **Organistin** *f.* (-, -nen) organist.
Organverpflanzung *f.* organ transplantation.
Orgasmus *m.* (-, -men) orgasm.
Orgel *f.* (-, -n) organ.
Orgelbauer *m.* organ-builder.
Orgel: ~**konzert** *n.* organ concerto; organ recital; ~**pfeife** *f.* organ-pipe; ~**register** *n.* organ stop; ~**spieler** *m.,* ~**spielerin** *f.* organist.
Orgie *f.* (-, -n) orgy.
Orient *m.* (-[e]s, 0) Orient, East(ern countries).
Orientale *m.;* **Orientalin** *f.* Oriental.
orientalisch *a.* oriental.
Orientalist *m.;* **Orientalistin** *f.* specialist in oriental studies.
Orientalistik *f.* oriental studies.
orientieren *v.t.* to orientate, to inform; *~ v. refl.* (*fig.*) to see one's way.
Orientierung *f.* orientation; *zu Ihrer ~,* for your guidance.
orientierungslos *a.* disoriented.
Orientierungssinn *m.* sense of orientation.
Original *n.* (-[e]s, -s) original.
original *a.* original.
Originalfassung *f.* original version.
originalgetreu *a.* faithful (to the original).
Originalität *f.* originality; authenticity.
originell *a.* original, eccentric.
Orkan *m.* (-[e]s, -e) hurricane, tornado.
Ornament *n.* (-s, -e) ornament.
Ornat *n.*(-[e]s, -e) vestments, robes.
Ornithologie *f.* ornithology.
Ort *m.* (-es, -e) place; spot, locality; *on ~ und Stelle,* on the spot.
orten *v.t.* to find the position.
orthodox *a.* orthodox; rigid.
Orthographie *f.* orthography.
orthographisch *a.* orthographic.
Orthopäde *m.;* **Orthopädin** *f.* orthopaedist.
Orthopädie *f.* orthopaedics.
orthopädisch *a.* orthopædic.
örtlich *a.* local.
Örtlichkeit *f.* (-, -en) locality.
Ortsangabe *f.* statement of place.
ortsansässig *a.* **Ortsansässige** *m./f.* resident; local.
Ortschaft *f.* (-, -en) village.
ortsfest *a.* (*mil.*) fixed, static.
Ortsgespräch *n.* (*tel.*) local call.
ortskundig *a.* acquainted with the locality.
Ortsnetzkennzahl *f.* area code.
Ortsverkehr *m.* local traffic.

Ortszeit f. local time.
Öse f. (-, -n) eye (for a hook).
Osmose f. osmosis.
Ost, Osten m. (Ostens, 0) east.
ostdeutsch a. Eastern German.
Ostdeutschland n. Eastern Germany.
ostentativ a. ostentatious; pointed.
Osteoporose f. osteoporosis.
Osterei n. (-s, -er) Easter-egg.
Oster: ~**fest** n. Easter; ~**glocke** f. daffodil; ~**hase** m. Easter bunny; ~**lamm** n. paschal lamb.
österlich a. paschal, Easter. . .
Ostern n. or pl. Easter.
Österreich n. (-s, 0) Austria.
Österreicher m.; **Österreicherin** f.; österreichisch a. Austrian.
Ostertag m. Easter day.
Osterwoche f. week after Easter.
Ostenropa n. Eastern Europe.
Ostküste f. east(ern) coast.

östlich a. eastern, easterly; oriental.
Ostsee f. Baltic Sea.
ostwärts adv. eastward.
Ostwind m. east wind.
Otter f. (-, -n) adder, viper.
Otter m. otter.
Ottomane f. (-, -0) ottoman.
Ouvertüre f. (-, -n) (mus.) overture.
oval a. oval.
Ovation f. (-, -en) ovation.
Ovulation f. ovulation.
Oxyd n. (-[e]s, -e) oxide.
oxydieren v.t.i. to (become) oxidize(d).
Ozean m. (-s, -e) ocean.
Ozeandampfer m. oceanliner.
Ozeanographie f. oceanography.
Ozelot m. (-s, -e) ocelot.
Ozon n. (-s, 0) ozone.
ozonhaltig a. ozoniferous.
Ozon: ~**loch** n. hole in the ozone layer; ~**schicht** f. ozone layer; ~**werte** pl. ozone levels.

P

P, p n. the letter P or p.
Paar n. (-[e]s, -e) pair, couple; brace (of fowl); ein paar, a few.
paaren (sich) v.t. & refl. to pair; to mate; to couple; to copulate.
Paarhufer m. (-s, -) eventoed, ungulate.
Paarlauf m.; **Paarlaufen** n. pair skating.
Paarung f. (-, -en) copulation; pairing.
paarweise adv. by pairs, in twos.
Pacht m. (-[e]s, -e) & f. (-, -en) tenure, lease; rent.
pachten v.t. to rent, to lease.
Pächter m. (-s, -) tenant, leaseholder.
Pacht: ~**geld** m. rental, rent; ~**gut** n. tenant farm, leasehold estate; ~**vertrag** m. lease.
Pachtung f. (-, -en) leaseholding.
pachtweise adv. on lease.
Pack m. ([e]s, -e u. Päcke) pack, bundle, parcel; (fig.) ~ n. rabble.
Päckchen n. (-s, -) small parcel.
Packeis n. (-es, 0) pack ice.
packen v.t. to pack up; to lay hold of, to seize; (ergreifen) to affect; (sich) ~ v. refl. to be gone.
Packen m. (-s, -) pack; bale.
packend a. thrilling.
Pack: ~**esel** m. pack-donkey; ~**papier** n. brown paper; ~**pferd** n. pack-horse; ~**sattel**, m. packsaddle.
Packung f. (-, -en) pack, package.
Pädagoge m. (-en, -en) pedagogue.
Pädagogik f. (-, 0) **Pädagogin** f. (-, -nen) pedagogy; education.
pädagogisch a. educational.
Paddel n. (-s, -) paddle.
Paddelboot n. (-es, -e) canoe.
paddeln v.t. n.i. to paddle.
paffen v.i. to puff; to smoke.
Page m. (-n, -n) page (boy); pellboy.
Pagen: ~**kopf** m. pageboy (hairstyle); ~**streich** m. escapade.
paginieren v.t. to page (a book).
pah! i. pshaw! pooh!

Pair m. (-s, -s) peer.
Paket n. (-[e]s, -e) packet, parcel, pile.
Paketpost f. parcel-post.
Pakezustellung f. parcel delivery.
Pakistan n. (-s, 0) Pakistan.
Pakistani m./f.; **pakistanisch** a. Pakistani.
Pakt m. (-[e]s, -e) agreement, (com)pact.
paktieren v.i. to come to terms, to agree (on).
Palast m. (-[e]s, **Paläste**) palace.
Palästina n. (-s, 0) Palestine.
Palästinenser m.; **Palästinenserin** f.; **palästinensisch** a. Palestinian.
Palaver n. (-s, -) (fam.) palaver.
Palette f. (-, -n) palette.
Palissade f. (-, -n) palisade.
Palme f. (-, -n) palm-tree.
Palmenwedel m. (-s, -) palm frond.
Palmsonntag m. Palm Sunday.
Pampe f. (-, 0) mud; mush.
Pampelmuse f. (-, -n) grapefruit.
pampig a. (fam.) insolent; mushy.
Panama n. (-s, 0) Panama.
Panamese m.; **Panamesin** f.; Panamanian.
Panier n. (-[e]s, -e) banner, standard.
panieren v.t. to roll in crumbs.
Paniermehl n. breadcrumbs.
Panik f. (-, -en) panic.
panisch a. panic; ~er Schrecken, panic.
Panne f. (-, -n) breakdown; flat tire; eine ~ haben, to break down.
Pannendienst m. breakdown service.
panschen v.t. to water down.
Panther m. (-s, -) panther.
Pantoffel m. (-s, -) slipper; (fig.) unter dem ~stehen, to be henpecked.
Pantoffelheld m. henpecked husband.
Pantoffeltierchen n. (biol.) slipper animalcule.
Pantomine f. (-, -n) pantomime.
Panzer m. (-s, -0) armor; (Schiffs~) armorplating.
Panzer: ~**abwehrkanone** f. anti-tank gun; ~**fahrer** m. tank driver; ~**glas** n. bullet-proof glass;

~jäger *pl.* anti-tank troops; **~kreuzer** *m.* armoured cruiser, pocket battleship.

panzern *v.t.* to armor.

Panzer: ~schrank *m.* safe; **~platte** *f.* armor-plate; **~truppen** *pl.* armored troops; **~wagen** *m.* armored car; **~zug** *m.* armored train.

Päonie *f.* (-, -n) peony.

Papa *m.* (-s, -s) ; **Papi** *m.* (-s, -s) papa, dad.

Papagei *m.* (-en, *u.* -[e]s, -en) parrot.

Papier *n.* (-[e]s, -e) paper; *zu ~ bringen,* to commit to paper; *~e pl.* stocks, securities *pl.*

papieren *a.* (of) paper.

Papier: ~deutsch *n.* officialese; **~fabrik** *f.* paper-mill; **~geld** *n.* paper-money; **~handlung** stationery store; *f.* **~korb** *m.* waste-paper basket; **~serviette** *f.* paper napkin.

papistisch *a.* popish, papistical.

Papp: ~arbeit *f.* pasteboard-work; **~band** *m.* (binding in) boards; **~deckel** = **Pappendeckel.**

Pappe *f.* (-, -en) cardboard, pasteboard.

Pappel *f.* (-, -n) poplar.

pappen *v.t.* to paste.

Pappen: ~deckel *m.* cardboard; **~stiel** *m.* (*fig.*) trifle.

Pappschachtel *f.* cardboard box.

Paprika *n.* (-s, -(s)) pepper; paprika.

Papst *m.* (-es, Päpste) pope.

päpstlich *a.* papal; pontifical.

Papsttum *n.* (-, 0) papacy; pontificate.

Parabel *f.* (-, n) parable; (*geom.*) parabola.

Parade *f.* (-, n) parade; (*fig.*) display; (*mil.*) review; (*Fechten*) parry.

Parade: ~anzug *m.* full dress; **beispiel** *n.* perfect example; **~marsch** *m.* ‚arch-past; **~platz** *m.* parade-ground.

paradieren *v.t. & i.* to parade.

Paradies *n.* (-es, -se) paradise.

paradiesisch *a.* paradisiacal.

paradox *a.* paradoxical.

Paradox *n.* paradox.

paradoxerweise *adv.* paradoxically.

Paragraph *m.* (-en, -en) paragraph.

parallel *a.* parallel.

Parallele *f.* (-, -n) parallel, parallel line.

Parallelschaltung *f.* (*elec.*) parallel connection.

Parallelversammlung *f.* overflow meeting.

Paranoia *f.* (-, 0) paranoia.

paranoid *a* paranoid.

Paranuß *f.* Brazil nut.

paraphieren *v.t.* to initial.

Parasit *m.* (-en, -en) parasite.

parasitär *a.* parasitic.

parat *a.* ready.

Paratyphus *m.* (-, 0) paratyphoid (fever).

Parcours *m.* (-, -) course.

Pardon *m.* (-s, 0) pardon.

Parfüm *n.* (-s, -e) perfume, scent.

Parfümerie *f.* perfumery.

parfümieren *v.t.* to perfume.

Pari *n.* (-[s], 0) par (of exchange).

pari *adv.* at par.

parieren *v.t.* to parry; *~ v.i.* to obey.

Parität *f.* (-, -en) parity.

Park *m.* (-[e]s, -e) park.

parken *v.t. & i.* to park; *~ verboten,* no parking!

Parkett *n.* (-[e]s, -e) parquet (floor).

Park: ~gebühr *f.* parking fee; **~haus** *n.* parking garage; **~lücke** *f.* parking space; **~platz** *m.* parking lot; **~scheibe** *f.* parking token; **~uhr** *f.* parking meter.

Parlament *n.* (-[e]s, -e) Parliament.

Parlamentarier *m.* (-, -) parliamentarian; Congressman; **Parlamentarierin** *f.* parliamentarian; Congresswoman.

parlamentarisch *a.* parliamentary.

Parlaments: ~ausschuß *m.* parliamentary committee; **~sitzung** *f.* sitting (of parliament); **~wahl** *f.* parliamentary election.

Parodie *f.* (-, -[e]n) parody.

Parole *f.* (-, -n) motto; password; watchword.

Partei *f.* (-, -en) party, side; *~ ergreifen,* to take sides, to side (with).

Partei: ~apparat *m.* party machine; **~funktionär** *m.* party official; **~gänger** *m.* partisan.

parteiisch, parteilich *a.* partial.

Parteilinie *f.* party line.

parteilos *a.* impartial, neutral.

Parteitag *m.* party conference.

Parteiung *f.* (-, -en) division into parties.

Parterre *n.* (-[s], -s) ground-floor; flowerbed; (*im Theater*) pit.

Partie *f.* (-, -[e]n) parcel, lot; (*Heirat*) match; (*Spiel*) game; (*Ausflug*) excursion.

partiell *a.* partial.

Partikel *f.* (-, -n) particle.

Partisan *m.* (-n, -n) **Partisanin** *f.* (-, -nen) (*mil.*) partisan; guerilla.

Partitur *f.* (-, -en) score.

Partizip *n.* (-s, -zipien) participle.

Partner *m.* (-s, -) **Partnerin** *f.* (-, -nen) partner.

Partnerschaft *f.* (-, -en) partnership.

Partnerstadt *f.* sister city/town.

partout *adv.* at all costs.

Parze *f.* (-, -n) Fate, weird sister.

Parzelle *f.* (-, -n) plot (of land).

parzellieren *v.t.* to parcel out.

Pascha *m.* (-s, -s) pasha.

Pasquill *n.* (-[e]s, -e) lampoon.

Paß *m.* (Passes, Pässe) pass; defile; passport; (*Ritt*) amble.

Passage *f.* (-, -n) arcade; sequence.

Passagier *m.* (-[e]s, -e) passenger; *blinder ~,* stowaway.

Passagierflugzeug *n.* airliner.

Passah *n.* (-s, -s) Passover.

Passant *m.* (-en, -en) passer-by.

Passanten: ~hotel *n.* transient hotel; **~quartier** *n.* transient billets.

Passatwind *m.* tradewind.

passé *a.* (*fam.*) passé; out of date.

passen *v.i.* to fit, so suit, to be convenient; (*im Spiel*) to pass.

passend *a.* fitting, suitable; convenient.

passierbar *a.* passable; navigable.

passieren *v.t.* to pass, to cross; *~ v.i.(s)* to happen.

Passierschein *m.* pass, permit.

passioniert *a.* passionate; ardent.

passiv *a.* passive; indolent, inactive.

Passiv *n.* (-s; -e) passive (voice).

Passiva, Passiven *pl.* liabilities.

Passivhandel *m.* adverse trade.

Passivität *f.* (-, 0) passivity.

Passiv[um] *n.* (-s, -en *u.* -va) passive voice.
Passivposten *m.* liability.
Paste *f.* (-, -n) paste.
Pastell(stift) *m.* (-[e]s, -e) pastel, crayon.
Pastete *f.* (-, -n) pie, pâté.
Pastetenbäcker *m.* pastry-cook.
pasteurisieren *v.t.* to pasteurize.
Pastille *f.* (-, -n) lozenge, pastil.
Pastor *m.* (-s, *u.* -en, -en); **Pastorin** *f.* (-, -nen) pastor, minister.
pastoral *a.* pastoral.
Pate *m.* (-n, -n); **Patin** *f.* (-, -nen) godfather, godmother.
Patenkind *n.* god-child.
Patent *n.* (-[e]s, -e) patent; (*mil.*) commission; *angemeldetes ~,* pending patent.
Patent: ~**amt** *n.* patent office; ~**anmeldung** *f.* application for a patent; ~**anwalt** *f.* patent agent *or* lawyer; ~**beschreibung** *f.* specification; ~**erteilung** *f.* patent-grant.
patentieren *v.* to patent; *sich etwas ~ lassen,* to take out a patent for a thing.
Patent: ~**inhaber** *m.* patentee; ~**inhabergesellschaft** *f.* patent holding company; ~**verlängerung** *f.* renewal of a patent.
Pater *m.* (-s, Patres) Father.
pathetisch *a. & adv.* pathetic(ally); emotional(ly).
Pathologe *m.*; **Pathologin** *f.* pathologist.
Pathologie *f.* pathology.
pathologisch *a.* pathological.
Pathos *n.* emotionalism.
Patient *m.* (-en, -en); **Patientin** *f.* (-, -nen) patient.
patriarchalisch *a.* patriarchal; paternal.
Patriot *m.* (-en, -en); **Patriotin** *f.* (-, -nen) patriot.
patriotisch *a.* patriotic.
Patriotismus *m.* patriotism.
Patrizier *m.* (-s, -); **Patrizierin** *f.* (-, -nen) patrician.
Patron *m.* (-[e]s, -e) patron, protector, supporter.
Patronat *n.* (-[e]s, -e) patronage.
Patrone *f.* (-, -n) pattern; cartridge.
Patronentasche *f.* cartridge-box, pouch.
Patrouille *f.* (-, -) patrol.
patrouillieren *v.i.* to be on patrol.
Patsche *f.* (-, -n) (*fig.*) pickle, mess, fix.
patschen *v.i.* to splash; to slap.
Patt *n.* (-s, -s) stalemate.
patzen *v.i.* (*fam.*) to slip up.
Patzer *m.* (-s, -) (*fam.*) boob.
patzig *a.* (*fam.*) snotty; cheeky.
Pauke *f.* (-, -n) kettle-drum.
pauken *v.i.* to beat the kettle-drums; to bone up; to cram.
pausbackig *a.* chubby(-faced).
pauschal *a.* all inclusive; indiscriminate.
Pauschale *f.* (-, -n) lump sum.
Pauschalreise *f.* package tour.
Pauschalsumme *f.* lump sum.
Pause *f.* (-, -n) pause, stop; (*mus.*) rest; interval, break; traced design.
pausen *v.t.* to trace, to copy.
pausenlos *a.* uninterrupted; continuous.
pausieren *v.i.* to pause.
Pauspapier *n.* tracing paper.
Pavian *m.* (-s, -e) baboon.

Pavillon *m.* (-s, -s) pavilion.
Pazifik *m.* (-, 0) Pacific.
Pazifismus *m.* pacifism.
Pazifist *m.* (-en, -en) pacifist.
pazifistisch *a.* pacifist.
Pech *n.* (-[e]s, -e) pitch; (*fig.*) bad luck.
pechfinster *a.* pitch-dark.
pechschwarz *a.* jet-black, pitch-dark.
Pechvogel *m.* (*fig.*) unlucky person.
Pedal *n.* (-[e]s, -e) pedal.
Pedant *m.* (-en, -en); **Pedantin** *f.* (-, -nen) pedant, prig.
Pedanterie *f.* (-, 0) pedantry.
pedantisch *a.* pedantic; over-punctilious.
Pedell *m.* (-es, *u.* -en, -e[n]) caretaker, janitor.
Pediküre *f.* pedicure.
Pegel *m.* (-s, -) water-gauge.
peilen *v.t.* (*nav.*) to sound, to take soundings, to take the bearings of.
Peilung *f.* (-, -en) direction finding.
Pein *f.* (-, 0) pain, torment.
peinigen *v.t.* to torment, to torture.
peinlich *a.* embarrassing.
Peinlichkeit *f.* embarrassment; meticulousness.
Peitsche *f.* (-, -n) whip, scourge.
peitschen *v.t.* to whip.
pekuniär *a.* pecuniary.
Pelikan *m.* (-[e]s, -e) pelican.
pellen *v.t.* to peel, to skin.
Pellkartoffeln *pl.* potatoes in jackets.
Pelz *m.* (-es, -e) fur, skin; pelt; fur-coat.
Pelzhändler *m.* furrier.
pelzgefüttert *a.* fur-lined.
Pelz: ~**kragen** *m.* fur collar; ~**mantel** *m.* fur coat; ~**mütze** *f.* fur cap.
Pendel *n.* (-s, -) pendulum.
pendeln *v.i.* to oscillate, to swing; to commute.
Pendeltür *f.* swing-door.
Pendelverkehr *m.* shuttle service.
Pendler *m.* (-s, -); **Pendlerin** *f,* (-, -nen) commuter.
penetrant *a.* (*pej.*) penetrating (odor); pushy (person).
penibel *a.* fussy.
Penis *m.* (-, -se) penis.
Penizillin *n.* (-s, 0) penicillin.
Penne *f.* (*fam.*) school; flophouse.
pennen *v.i.* (*fam.*) to sleep.
Penner *m.*; **Pennerin** *f.* (*fam.*) bum; tramp.
Pension *f.* (-, -en) pension; board; boarding-house.
Pensionär *m.* (-[e]s, -e); **Pensionärin** *f.* (-, -nen) pensioner.
Pensionat *n.* (-[e]s, -e) boarding-school.
pensionieren *v.t.* to pension (off); *sich ~ lassen,* to retire.
Pensionierung *f.* (-, -en) retirement.
pensions: ~**berechtigt** *a.* entitled to a pension; ~**fähig** *a.* pensionable.
Pensum *n.* (-s, -sa *u.* -sen) amount of work.
Perfekt *n.* (-s, -e) perfect (tense).
Perfektion *f.* (-, 0) perfection.
perfid *a.* perfidious.
perforieren *v.t.* to perforate.
Pergament *n.* (-[e]s, -e) parchment.
Periode *f.* (-, -n) period.
periodisch *a. & adv.* periodical(ly).

peripher *a.* peripheral.
Peripherie *f.* (-, -[e]n) circumference, periphery.
Perle *f.* (-, -n) pearl; (*Glas*) bead.
perlen *v.i.*(*s*) to sparkle; to drip from.
Perl: ~**graupen** *f. pl.* pearl-barley; ~**huhn** *n.* guinea fowl; ~**mutt** *n.* ~**mutter** *f.* mother-of-pearl.
Perlwein *m.* sparkling wine.
perplex *a.* baffled, puzzled.
Persianer *m.* Persian lamb.
persisch *a.* Persian.
Person *f.* (-, -en) person.
Personal *n.* (-[e]s -e) staff, personnel.
Personal... personnel-; ~**abbau** *m.* reduction of staff; ~**abteilung** *f.* personnel department; ~**akten** *pl.* personnel file; ~**ausweis** *m.* identity card; ~**büro** *n.* personnel office; ~**chef** *m.*; ~**chefin** *f.* personnel manager; ~**computer** *m.* personal computer.
Personalien *pl.* particulars, personal data.
Personal: ~**kosten** *pl.* staff costs; ~**mangel** *m.* staff shortage; ~**pronomen** *n.* personal pronoun.
personell *a.* regarding staff; personnel.
Personen: ~**aufzug** *m.* elevator; ~**beschreibung** *f.* personal description; ~**gedächtnis** *n.* memory for faces; ~**kult** *m.* personality cult; ~**schaden** *m.* personal injury; ~**verkehr** *m.* passenger traffic ~**zug** *m.* (*rail.*) passenger train.
personifizieren *v.t.* to personify.
persönlich *a.* personal; ~**er Wert** *m.* sentimental value; ~ *adv.* in person.
Persönlichkeit *f.* (-, -en) personality.
Perspektive *f.* (-, -n) perspective.
Peru *n.* (-s, 0) Peru.
Peruaner *m.* (-s, -); **Peruanerin** *f.* (-, -nem); **peruanisch** *a.* Peruvian.
Perücke *f.* (-, -n) wig.
pervers *a.* perverse.
Pessimismus *m.* (-, 0) pessimism.
pessimistisch *a.* pessimistic.
Pest *f.* (-, -en) plague, pest(ilence).
Petersilie *f.* (-, 0) parsley.
Petition *f.* (-, -en) petition.
Petroleum *n.* (-s, 0) kerosene.
Petting *n.* (-s, -s) petting.
in petto haben, to have up one's sleeve.
Petze *f.* telltale, sneak.
Pfad *m.* (-es, -e) path.
Pfadfinder *m.* (-s, -) boy scout; ~**in** *f.* girl scout.
Pfaffe *m.* (-n, -n) (*pej.*) parson.
Pfahl *m.* (-[e]s, Pfähle) pile; post, pole.
Pfahlbau *m.* pile dwelling.
Pfand *n.* (-[e]s, Pfänder) pledge, pawn; security; (*Spiel*) forfeit.
pfändbar *a.* distrainable.
Pfandbrief *a.* mortgage bond.
pfänden *v.t.* to distrain, to seize.
Pfänderspiel *n.* game of forfeits.
Pfand: ~**haus** *n.* pawn-shop; ~**leiber** *m.* pawnbroker; ~**schuldner** *m.* pledger.
Pfändung *f.* (-, -en) distraint, seizure; ~**sbefehl** *m.* distress warrant.
Pfanne *f.* (-, -n) pan.
Pfannkuchen *m.* pancake.
Pfarre *f.* (-, -n) rectory, parsonage, vicarage; parish.

Pfarrei *f.* parish.
Pfarrer *m.* (-s, -) minister, pastor, priest, rector.
Pfarr: ~**haus** *n.* parsonage, rectory; ~**kirche** *f.* parish church.
Pfau *m.* (-[e]s *u.* -en, -en) peacock.
Pfauenauge *n.* peacock butterfly.
Pfeffer *m.* (-s, 0) pepper.
Pfefferkuchen *m.* gingerbread.
Pfefferminze *f.* peppermint.
Pfeffermühle *f.* pepper mill.
pfeffern *v.t.* to pepper.
pfeffrig *a.* peppery.
Pfeife *f.* (-, -en) (tobacco-)pipe; whistle; *eine ~ stopfen*, to fill a pipe.
pfeifen *v.i. & i.st.* to pipe; to whistle.
Pfeifenreiniger *m.* pipe cleaner.
Pfeifer *m.* (-s, 0) piper; whistler.
Pfeil *m.* (-[e]s, -e) arrow; bolt, dart.
Pfeiler *m.* (-s, -) pillar; pier.
Pfeilspitze *f.* arrowhead.
Pfennig *m.* (-s, -e) small coin (penny).
Pfennigfuchser *m.* penny-pincher.
Pferch *m.* (-[e]s, -e) fold, pen.
pferchen *v.t.* to pen, to cram.
Pferd *n.* (-[e]s, -s) horse; (*Turnen*) vaulting-horse; *zu ~e*, on horseback.
Pferde: ~**äpfel** *pl.* horse droppings; ~**fuß** *m.* shag; ~**koppel** *f.* paddock; ~**kraft** *f.* horsepower.
Pferde: ~**rennbahn** *f.* racetrack; ~**rennen** *n.* (horse-)race; ~**stall** *m.* stable; ~**stärke (PS)** *f.* horsepower (H.P.); ~**zucht** *f.* breeding of horses.
Pfiff *m.* (-[e]s, -e) whistle; trick.
Pfifferling *m.* (-s, -e) chanterelle.
pfiffig *a.* sly, sharp, smart.
Pfingsten *n. or f. or pl. u.* **Pfingstfest** *n.* Pentecost.
Pfirsich *m.* (-s, -e) peach.
Pflanze *f.* (-, -n) plant.
pflanzen *v.t.* to plant, to set.
Pflanzen: ~**faser** *f.* vegetable fiber; ~**fett** *n.* vegetable fat; ~**fresser** *m.* herbivore; ~**kost**, ~**nahrung** *f.* vegetable diet or food; ~**öl** *n.* vegetable oil; ~**reich** *n.* vegetable kingdom; ~**schädling** *m.* pest; ~**schutzmittel** *n.* pesticide.
Pflanzer *m.* (-s, -) planter.
pflanzlich *a.* plant; vegetable; vegetarian.
Pflanzung *f.* (-, -en) plantation.
Pflaster *n.* (-s, -) plaster; pavement.
pflastern *v.t.* to plaster; to pave.
Pflasterstein *m.* paving-stone.
Pflaume *f.* (-, -n) plum; *getrocknete ~*, prune.
Pflege *f.* (-, 0) care, cultivation.
Pflege: ~**eltern** *f.* foster-parents *pl.*; ~**kind** *n.* foster-child; ~**mutter** *f.* foster-mother.
pflegen *v.t.* to foster, to nurse, to take care of, to attend to; ~ *v.i.* to be accustomed, to use; (sich) ~ *v. refl.* to take care of one's appearance; *Umgang ~*, to see a good deal (of).
Pfleger *m.*; **Pflegerin** *f.* nurse; keeper.
Pflege: ~**sohn** *m.* foster-son; ~**tochter** *f.* foster-daughter; ~**vater** *m.* foster-father.
pfleglich *a.* careful.
Pflegling *m.* (-[e]s, -e) foster-child.
Pflicht *f.* (-, -en) duty; obligation.
pflichtbewußt *a.* conscientious; dutiful.
Pflicht: ~**eifer** *m.* zeal, dutifulness; ~**gefühl** *n.* sense of duty.

plicht: ~**gemäß** *a.* in fulfilment of a duty; ~ *adv.* dutifully; ~**getreu** *a.* dutiful, conscientious; ~**mässig** *a.* prescribed by duty; ~**teil** *m.* lawful portion; ~**vergessen** *a.* undutiful; ~**verletzung** *f.* breach of duty; ~**versäumnis** *f.* neglect of duty.
Pflock *m.* (-[e]s, Pföcke) plug, peg.
pflöcken *v.t.* to peg.
pflücken *v.t.* to pluck; to pick.
Pflug *m.* (-[e]s, Pflüge) plow.
Pflugbagger *m.* bulldozer.
pflügen *v.t.* to plow.
Pflugschar *f.* plowshare.
Pforte *f.* (-, -n) gate; (*nav.*) port-hole.
Pförtner *m.* (-s, -) door-keeper, porter.
Pfosten *m.* (-s, -) post; pale, stake.
Pfote *f.* (-, -n) paw, claw.
Pfriem *m.* (-[e]s, -e), **Pfriemen** *m.* (s, -), **Pfrieme** *f.* (-, -n) awl, punch.
Pfropf *m.* (-[e]s, -e *u.* Pfröpfe), **Pfropfen** *m.* (-s, -) cork, stopper; (*Holz*) plug.
pfropfen *v.t.* to cram; (*Pflanzen*) to graft; to cork.
Pfründe *f.* (-, -n) (*rel.*) benefice; (*fig.*) sinecure.
Pfuhl *m.* (-[e]s, -e) pool, puddle, slough.
pfui! *i.* yuck! shame! ugh!
Pfuiruf *m.* (-s, -e) boo.
Pfund *n.*(-[e]s, -e) pound.
pfündig *a.* (*in Zus.*) of (so many) pounds.
pfundweise *adv.* by the pound.
pfuschen *v.i.* to bungle, to botch; *einem ins Handwerk* ~, (*fig.*) to trespass on another's field.
Pfütze *f.* (-, -n) puddle.
Phänomen *n.* (-s, -e) phenomenon.
Phantasie *f.* (-, -[e]n) fantasy; imagination.
phantasiereich *a.* imaginative.
phantasieren *v.i.* to fantasize; (*med.*) to wander, to rave; (*mus.*) to improvise.
Phantast *m.* (-en, -en) dreamer; visionary.
phantastisch *a.* fantastic, (*fam.*) terrific.
Phantombild *n.* identikit picture.
Pharisäer *m.* (-s, -) Pharisee.
pharisäerhaft, pharisäisch *a.* pharisaical.
Pharmakologie *f.* pharmacology.
Pharmakonzern *m.* pharmaceutical company.
Pharmazeut *m.* (-en, -eu); **Pharmazeutin** *f.* (-, -nen) pharmacist.
Pharmazie *f.* pharmaceutics.
Phase *f.* (-, -n) (*astr.*) phase; stage.
Philanthrop *m.* (-en, -en) philanthropist.
Philharmonie *f.* (-, -n) philharmonic orchestra; philharmonic hall.
Philippinen *pl.* Philippines.
Philister *m.* (-s, -) Philistine.
philisterhaft, philiströs *a.* narrow-minded.
Philologe *m.* (-en, -en); **Philologin** *f.* (-, -nen) philologist.
Philologie *f.* (-, 0) philology.
philologisch *a.* philological.
Philosoph *m.* (-en, -en); **Philosophin** *f.* (-, -nen) philosopher.
Philosophie *f.* (-, -[e]n) philosophy.
philosophieren *v.i.* to philosophize.
philosophisch *a.* philosophical.
Phlegma *n.* (-[s], 0) phlegm.
phlegmatisch *a.* phlegmatic.
Phobie *f.* (-, -n) phobia.
Phonetik *f.* (-, -en) phonetics.

phonetisch *a.* phonetic.
Phosphat *n.* phosphate.
Phosphor *m.* (-s, -e) phosphorus.
phosphoreszieren *v.i.* to phosphoresce.
Phosphorsäure *f.* phosphoric acid.
Photograph *m.* (-en, -en); **Photographin** *f.* (-, -nen) photographer.
Photographie *f.* (-, -[e]n) photograph. (*fam.*) photo; (*Kunst*) photography.
photographieren *v.t.* to photograph.
Photokopie *f.* (-, -n) photostatic copy, photocopy.
Photozelle *f.* photo-electric cell.
Phrase *f.* (-, -n) phrase, idiom.
phrasenhaft *a.* empty, grandiloquent.
pH-Wert *m.* pH(-value).
Physik *f.* (-, 0) physics *pl.*
physikalisch *a.* physics; physical.
Physiker *m.* (-s, 0); **Physikerin** *f.* (-, -nen) physicist.
Physiologie *f.* physiology.
physisch *a.* physical.
Pianist *m.*; **Pianistin** *f.* pianist.
Piano(forte) *n.* (-s, -s) piano.
Picke *f.* (-, -n) pick-axe.
Pickel *m.* (-s, -) stonemason's hammer; pimple.
Pickelhaube *f.* spiked helmet.
picken *v.i.* to peck, to pick.
Picknick *n.* picnic.
piekfein *a.* (*fam.*) classy.
piepen, piepsen *v.i.* to chirp, to squeak; to squeal; to pipe.
piepsig *a.* squeaky.
Pietät *f.* (-, 0) reverence.
pietätvoll *a.* reverent, reverential.
Pietist *m.* (-en, -en) pietist.
Pik *m.* (-[s], -[s]) (*in der Karte*) spade.
pikant *a.* piquant, spicy, pungent; racy.
Pikee *m. & n.* (-s, -s) (*Stoff*) quilting.
Pilger *m.* (-s, -) pilgrim.
Pilgerfahrt *f.* pilgrimage.
pilgern *v.i.* (*s, h*) to go on a pilgrimage.
Pille *f.* (-, -n) pill.
Pilot *pm.* (-en, -en) pilot.
Pilz *m.* (-es, -e) fungus; mushroom; (*giftiger*) toadstool.
Pilzkrankheit *f.* mycosis; fungus (disease).
pingelig *a.* (*fam.*) nitpicking.
Pinguin *m.* penguin.
Pinie *f.* (-, -n) pine.
Pinkel *m.* (*fam. pej.*) feiner~ a stuck-up prig.
pinkeln *v.i.* to pee.
Pinnwand *f.* bulletin board.
Pinscher *m.* (-s, -) pinscher.
Pinsel *m.* (-s, -) (painter's) brush; (*fig.*) simpleton.
pinseln *v.t.* to paint.
Pinzette *f.* (-, -n) tweezers.
Pionier *m.* (*mil.*) engineer; (*fig.*) pioneer.
Pipi *n.* ~**machen** to pee.
Pirat *m.* (-en, -en) pirate.
Piratensender *m.* pirate radio sender.
Pirsch *f.* stalking.
pirschen *v.t.* to go deer-stalking.
pissen *v.i.* to piss.
Pistazie *f.* (-, -n) pistachio.
Piste *f.* (-, -n) piste; ski-run; track.
Pistole *f.* (-, -n) pistol, gun.

pitschnaß *a.* dripping wet.
Pizza *f.* (-, -zen) pizza.
placken *v.t.* to harass, to pester; (sich) ~ *v. refl.* to toil, to drudge.
Plackerei *f.* (-, -en) toil, drudgery; vexation.
plädieren *v.i.* to plead.
Plädoyer *n.* (-s, -s) (*jur.*) final speech.
Plage *f.* (-, -n) plague, torment, bother.
Plagegeist *m.* bore.
plagen *v.t.* to plague, to trouble, to vex; (sich) ~ *v. refl.* to drudge, to slave.
Plagiat *n.* (-[e]s, -e) plagiarism, plagiary.
Plakat *n.* (-[e]s, -e) poster, placard, bill.
Plakatwand *f.* billboard.
Plakette *f.* badge.
Plan *m.* (-[e]s, -e *u.* Pläne) plan; design, scheme.
plan *a.* plain, level.
Plane *f.* (-, -n) tarpaulin.
planen *v.t.* to plan, project.
Planet *m.* (-en, -en) planet.
planieren *v.t.* to level; to plane.
Planierraupe *f.* bulldozer.
Planke *f.* (-, -en) plank, bord.
Plänkelei *f.* (-, -en) skirmishing.
plänkeln *v.i.* (*mil.*) to skirmish.
Plankton *n.* plankton.
planlos *a.* aimless, without a plan; ~ *adv.* at random.
planmäßig *a.* established, scheduled; ~ *adv.* according to plan.
Planschbecken *n.* baby pool.
planschen, plantschen *v.i.* to splash.
Planspiel *n.* (*mil.*) map exercise.
Plantage *f.* (-, -n) plantation.
Planwirtschaft *f.* planned economy.
plappern *v.i.* to prattle, to chatter.
plärren *v.t.* to bawl; to blare.
Plasma *n.* (-s, -men) plasma.
Plastik *f.* (-, 0) plasticity; sculpture.
Plastik *n.* plastic.
plastisch *a.* plastic; ~**e Chirurgie** *f.* plastic surgery.
Platane *f.* (-, -n) plane-tree.
Platin *n.* (-s, 0), platinum.
platschen *v.i.* to splash.
plätschern *v.i.* to splash, to dabble.
platt *a.* flat, level; (*fam.*) amazed.
Plättbrett *n.* ironing-board.
plattdeutsch *a.* Low German.
Platte *f.* (-, -n) plate; bald head, pate; (*Stein*) flag, slab; (*Teller*) tray, silver; (*Tisch*) leaf; (*Grammophon*) record.
Plätteisen *n.* (flat)-iron.
plätten *v.t.* to iron.
Plattenhülle *f.* record sleeve.
Plattenspieler *m.* (Grammophon), record player.
Platt: ~**form** *f.* platform; ~**fuß** *m.* flat foot; ~**fuß-einlage** *f.* arch support, foot support.
plattfüßig *a.* flat-footed.
Plattheit *f.* (-, -en) flatness, platitude.
Platz *m.* (-es, Plätze) place; room space; public place, square; seat; ~ *machen*, to make room; ~ *nehmen*, to take a seat.
Platz: ~**angst** *f.* claustrophobia; agoraphobia; ~**anweiser** *m.*; ~**anweiserin** *f.* usher.
Plätzchen *n.* (-s, -) (chocolate) drop; small cookie.
platzen *v.i.* to burst; to explode.

Platz: ~**patrone** *f.* blank cartridge; ~**regen** *m.* downpour; ~**verweis** *m.* (*sp.*) sending off; ~**vorteil** *m.* (*sp.*) home advantage; ~**wart** *m.* (*sp.*) groundsman; ~**wunde** *f.* lacerated wound.
Plauderei *f.* (-, -en) chat.
plaudern *v.i.* to gossip, to chat.
plausibel *a.* plausible.
Playback *n.* pre-recorded version; backing.
plazieren *v.t.* to place; to position.
Pleite *f.* (-, -n) (*sl.*) bankruptcy; ~ *sein*, ~ *gehen*, to fail, to go bust.
Plenarsitzung *f.* (-, -en) plenary session.
Plenum *n.* (-s, 0) plenary meeting.
Pleuelstange *f.* (-, -n) connecting rod.
Plexiglas *f.* safety glass.
Plissee *n.* (-s, -s) pleating.
Plombe *f.* (-, -n) lead seal; filling.
plombieren *v.t.* to seal with lead; to plug, to fill (a tooth).
plötzlich *a.* sudden; ~ *adv.* suddenly, all of a sudden.
plump *a.* plump; unwieldy, clumsy; coarse.
plumpsen *v.i.* (*s*) (*fam.*) to plump.
Plunder *m.* (-s, 0) junk; trash.
plündern *v.t.* to pillage, to plunder.
Plünderung *f.* (-, -en) plundering, looting.
Plural *m.* (-s, -e) plural (number).
Plüsch *m.* (-es, -e) plush.
Plüschtier *pn.* cuddly toy.
Pluspol *m.* positive pole/terminal.
Plusquamperfekt(um) *n.* (-s, -fekte) pluperfect; past perfect.
Pluszeichen *n.* plus sign.
Po *m.* (-s, -s) bottom.
Pöbel *m.* (-s, 0) mob, rabble, populace.
pöbelhaft *a.* vulgar, low.
pochen *v.t.* to knock; (*vom Herzen*) to beat, to throb; (*fig.*) to boast (of).
Pocken *f. pl.* smallpox.
Pockennarbe *f.* pock mark.
Podest *n./m.* rostrum.
Podium *n.* (-s, -dien) stage; rostrum.
Poesie *f.* (-, -[e]n) poetry, poem.
Poet *m.* (-s, -en); **Poetin** *f.* (-, -nen) poet; bard.
Poetik *f.* (-, -en) poetics.
poetisch *a. & adv.* poetical(ly); poetic.
Pointe *f.* (-, -n) punch line; point; curtain line.
pointiert *a. & adv.* printed(ly).
Pokal *m.* (-[e]s, -e) goblet; (*Sport*) cup.
Pökelfleisch *n.* salt meat.
pökeln *v.t.* to pickle, to salt.
Pol *m.* (-[e]s, -e) pole.
Polar. . . , polar.
Polarkreis *m.* polar circle.
Polarstern *m.* Pole-star.
Pole *m.* (-n, -n); **Polin** *f.* (-, -nen) Pole.
Polemik *f.* (-, 0) controversy.
polemisieren *v.i.* to polemize.
Polen *n.* (-s, 0) Poland.
Police *f.* (-, -n) policy; ~**inhaber** *m.* policy-holder.
Polier *m.* (-[e]s, -e) foreman (of masons).
polieren *v.t.* to polish, to burnish.
Poliklinik *f.* outpatients' clinic.
Politesse *f.* traffic warden.
Politik *f.* (-,0) politics *pl.*, policy.
Politiker *m.* (-s, -); **Politikerin** *f.* (-, -nen)

politician.

politisch *a.* political; **~maßgebende Person** *f.* policy-maker; **~prüfen** *v.t.* to screen.

politisieren *v.t.* to talk politics; to politicize.

Politologe *m.* (-, -n); **Politologin** *f.* (-, -nen) political scientist.

Politur *f.* (-, -en) polish.

Polizei *f.* (-, -en) police; police-office; *sich ~ der stellen,* to give oneself up to the police; **~aufsicht** *f.* police supervision; **~einsatz** *m.* police operation; **~kontrolle** *f.* police check.

polizeilich *a.* of the police.

Polizei: **~präsident** *m.* **~präsidentin** *f.* chief of police; **~präsidium** *n.* police headquarters; **~revier** *n.* precinct; **~streife** *f.* police patrol; **~wache** *f.* police-station.

polizeiwidrig *a.* contrary to the police regulations.

Polizist *m.* (-en, -en) policeman.

Polizistin *f.* policewoman.

Pollen *m.* (-s, -) pollen.

polnisch *a.* Polish.

Polster *n.* (-, -) cushion; bolster.

Polstermöbel *pl.* upholstered furniture.

polstern *v.t.* to upholster; to stuff, to pad.

Polterabend *m.* wedding eve.

poltern *v.i.* to racket, to rattle; to bluster.

Polygamie *f.* polygamy.

Polyp *m.* (-en, -en) polyp(us); (*fam.*) cop.

Polytechnikum *n.* (-[s], -techniken) polytechnic school, engineering college.

Pomade *f.* (-, -n) pomade.

Pomeranze *f.* (-, -n) orange.

Pommern *n.* Pomerania.

Pommes frites *pl.* French fries.

Pomp *m.* (-[e]s, 0) pomp, splendour.

pomphaft *a.* stately, magnificent.

pompös *a.* stately, magnificent.

Ponton *m.* pontoon.

Pony *n.* or *m.* (-s, -s) pony.

Pony *m.* (-s, -s) fringe.

Popanz *m.* (-es, -e) bugbear.

popelig *a.* (*fam.*) crummy; lousy.

Popelin *m.* (-s, -e) poplin.

popeln *v.i.* (*fam.*) to pick one's nose.

Popmusik *f.* popmusic.

Popo *m.* (-s, -s) (*fam.*) backside; bottom.

populär *a.* popular.

Popularität *f.* (-, 0) popularity.

Pore *f.* (-, -n) pore.

Pornographie *f.* (-, -n) pornography.

pornographisch *a.* pornographic.

porös *a.* porous.

Porree *m.* (-s, -s) leek.

Portal *n.* (-[e]s, -e) portal.

Portefeuille *n.* (-[s], -s) portfolio.

Portemonnaie *n.* (-s, -s) purse.

Portier *m.* (-s, -s) porter, janitor; (*Hotel*) hall-porter, desk-clerk.

Portion *f.* (-, -en) portion, ration; *zweite ~,* second helping; *eine ~ Kaffee,* coffee for one.

Porto *n.* (-s, -s *u.* Porti) postage.

portofrei *a.* post free, (pre)paid.

Portospesen *pl.* postal expenses.

Porträt *n.* (-s, -s) portrait.

portraitieren *v.t.* to portray.

Portugal *n.* (-s, 0) Portugal.

Portugiese *m.* (-n, -n); **Portugiesin** *f.* (-, -nen) portugiesisch *a.* Portuguese.

Portwein *m.* (-s, -e) port.

Porzellan *n.* (-[e]s, -e) china, porcelain.

Posaune *f.* (-, -n) trombone.

posaunen *v.t.* (*fig.*) to trumpet.

Pose *f.* (-, -n) pose; attitude.

positiv *a.* positive.

Positur *f.* (-, -en) posture.

Posse *f.* (-, -n) jest; farce, burlesque.

possessiv *a.* possessive.

Possessivpronomen *n.* possessive pronoun.

possierlich *a.* droll, funny.

Post *f.* (-, -en) post, mail; post office; *mit der ~,* by mail; *gewöhnliche ~ (nicht Luftpost),* surface mail; *mit umgehender ~,* postwendend, by return mail.

Postament *n.* (-[e]s, -e) pedestal, base.

Post: **~amt** *n.* post office; **~anweisung** *f.* money order; **~bote** *m.* mailcarrier.

Posten *n.* (-s, -) post, station, place; (*mil.*) outpost; sentry; (*com.*) item, sum; parcel, lot; entry.

Postfach *n.* post-office box.

Postkarte *f.* postcard; *farbige ~,* color postcard.

Postkutsche *f.* stage-coach, mail-coach.

postlagernd *a. & adv.* (*auf Briefen*) to be (kept till) called for, poste restante, general delivery.

Post: **~leitzahl** *f.* zip code; **~ministerium** *n.* Ministry of Post **~paket** *n.* parcel sent by post; **~scheck** *m.* postal check; **~scheckkonto** *n.* postal check(ing) account; **~sparkasse** *f.* post-office savings bank; **~stempel** *m.* postmark.

postum *a. & adv.* posthumous(ly).

Postversandhaus *n.* mail-order house.

postwendend *adv.* by return mail; (*fig.*) right away.

Post: **~wurfsendung** *f.* direct-mail item; **~zustellung** *f.* postal delivery.

potent *a.* potent; strong.

Potentat *m.* (-en, -en) potentate.

Potential *n.* (-s, -e) potential.

potentiell *a. & adv.* potential(ly).

Potenz *f.* (-, -en) potency; (*math.*) power.

potenzieren *v.t.* to raise to a higher power.

Potpourri *n.* (-s, -s) (*mus.*) potpourri, medley.

Präambel *f.* (-, -n) preamble.

Pracht *f.* (-, 0) splendor, pomp, state.

prächtig *a.* magnificent, splendid.

prachtvoll *a.* splendid.

prädestinieren *v.t.* to predestine.

Prädikat *n.* (-[e]s, -e) predicate; title; rating.

prägen *v.t.* to coin, to stamp.

pragmatisch *a.* pragmatic.

prägnant *a.* terse; pithy.

prahlen *v.i.* to boast, to brag.

Prahler *m.* (-s, -) braggart, boaster.

Prahlerei *f.* (-, -en) boasting.

prahlerisch *a.* boastful, ostentatious.

Praktik *f.* (-, -en) practice.

Praktikant *m.* (-en, -en); **Praktikantin** *f.* (-, -nen) trainee, intern.

Praktiker *m.* (-s, -) practical man.

Praktikum *n.* (-s, -ka) internship; practical training.

praktisch *a.* practical; **~e Arzt** *m.* general practitioner.

praktizieren *v.t.* to practise.

Prälat *m.* (-en, -en) prelate.

Praliné *n.* (-s, -s) **Praline** *f.* (-, -n) (filled) chocolate; ~**schachtel** *f.* box of chocolates.

prall *a.* full; firm; tight.

prallen *v.i.* to collide; to crash.

Prämie *f.* (-, -n) premium; prize; bonus.

prämiieren *v.t.* to award a prize.

Prämisse *f.* (-, -n) premiss.

prangen *v.i.* to be clearly visible.

Pranger *m.* (-s, -) pillory.

Pranke *f.* (-, -n) paw.

Präparat *n.* (-[e]s, -e) preparation, mixture.

präparieren *v.t.* to prepare.

Präposition *f.* (-, -en) preposition.

Prärie *f.* (-, -n) prairie.

Präsens *n.* (-, e) present (tense).

präsent *a.* present.

präsentieren *v.t.* to present.

Präsenz *f.* (-, -en) presence; ~**liste** *f.* list of those present; ~**stärke** *f.* actual strength.

Präservativ *n.* (-s, -e) condom.

Präsident *m.* (-en, -en); **Präsidentin** *f.* (-, -nen) president, chairman, chairwoman.

präsidieren *v.t. & i.* to preside over, to be in the chair.

Präsidium *n.* (-s, -dien) chair(man's office), presidency; directorate.

prasseln *v.i.* to crackle.

prassen *v.i.* to feast, to revel.

Prätendent *m.* (-en, -en) pretender.

Präteritum *n.* (-s, -ta) preterite, past tense.

präventiv *a.* preventive.

Praxis *f.* (-, 0) practice; exercise; (*Arzt, Rechtsanwalt*) office.

Präzedenzfall *m.* precedent.

präzis *a.* punctual, exact, precise.

präzisieren *v.t.* to specify.

Präzision *f.* (-, 0) precision; ~**sarbeit** *f.* precision work; ~**swerkzeug** *n.* precision tool.

predigen *v.t.* to preach.

Prediger *m.* (-s, -); **Predigerin** *f.* (-, -nen) preacher.

Predigt *f.* (-, -en) sermon; lecture.

Preis *m.* (-es, -e) (*Belohnung*) prize; (*Wert*) price, rate, cost, figure; (*Lob*) praise, glory; *um keinen ~*, not for the world.

Preis: ~**angabe** *f.* quotation (of price); ~**ausschreiben** *n.* competition.

Preisbindung *f.* price-fixing.

Preiselbeere *f.* (-, -n) cranberry.

preisen *v.t.st.* to praise.

Preis: ~**erhöhung** *f.* price increase; ~**gabe** *f.* abandonment; revelation (secret).

preisgeben *v.t.* to expose; to abandon.

preisgekrönt *a.* prize-winning.

Preis: ~**gericht** *n.* jury; panel of judges; ~**lage** *f.* range of prices; *in niedriger ~lage*, low-priced; ~**richter** *m.* adjudicator; ~**schild** *n.* price tag; ~**träger** *m.*, ~**trägerin** *f.* winner (of a competition); ~**sturz** *m.* sudden fall of prices; ~**überwachung** *f.* price-control.

preiswert *a.* cheap.

prekär *a.* precarious.

Prellbock *m.* buffer.

prellen *v.t.* to cheat.

Prellung *f.* (-, -en) (*med.*) bruise.

Premiere *f.* (-, -n) opening night; premiere.

Premier: ~**minister** *m.*, ~**ministerin** *f.* prime minister.

Presse *f.* (-, -n) press; squeezer.

Presse: ~**agentur** *f.* press agency; ~**bericht** *m.* press report; ~**besprechung** *f.* press conference; ~**empfang** *m.* press reception; ~**erklärung** *f.* press release; ~**freiheit** *f.* freedom of the press; ~**korrespondenz** *f.* press service; ~**tribüne** *f.* press gallery.

pressen *v.t.* to press, to squeeze.

Presse: ~**sprecher** *m.* spokesman, ~**sprecherin** *f.* spokeswoman; ~**zensur** *f.* censorship of the press; ~**zentrum** *n.* press center.

pressieren *v.i.* to be urgent.

Preßluft *f.* compressed air; ~**bohrer** *m.* pneumatic drill; ~**hammer** *m.* pneumatic hammer.

Preßwehen *pl.* bearing-down pains.

Preusse *m.*; **Preussin** *f.*; **preussisch** *n.* Prussian.

preussischblau *a.* Prussian blue.

prickeln *v.t.* to prickle, to itch.

prickelnd *a.* prickling; (*fig.*) thrilling.

Priester *m.* (-s, -) priest.

Priesterin *f.* (-, -nen) priest(ess).

Priesterschaft *f.* clergy; priesthood.

Priestertum *n.* priesthood.

Priesterweihe *f.* ordination of a priest.

Prima *f.* (-, -men) first-class, top grade

prima *a.* (*fam.*) great; fantastic.

primär *a. & adv.* primary; primarily.

Primaten *pl.* primates.

Primel *f.* (-, -n) primrose, cowslip.

primitiv *a.* primitive.

Primzahl *f.* (*ar.*) prime number.

Prinz *m.* (-en, -en) prince.

Prinzessin *f.* (-, -nen) princess.

Prinzip *n.* (-[e]s, -e *u.* -ien) principle.

Prinzipal *m.* (-[e]s, -e) principal, chief.

prinzipiell *a.* in/on principle.

Priorität *f.* (-, -en) priority.

Prise *f.* (-, -n) prize; (*Schnupftabak*) pinch.

Prisma *n.* (-s, -men) prism.

Pritsche *f.* (-, -n) wooden couch, bunk.

privat *a.* private.

Privat: ~**adresse** *f.* home address; ~**angelegenheit** private matter; ~**besitz** *m.* private property.

Privatdozent *m.* university lecturer.

Privatfernsehen *n.* commercial television.

privatim *adv.* privately.

privatisieren *v.i.* to privatize; to live on one's private income.

Privat: ~**klinik** *f.* private clinic; ~**mann** *m.* private person; ~**patient** *m.*, ~**patientin** *f.* private patient; ~**recht** *n.* civil law; ~**wirtschaft** *f.* private sector.

Privileg *n.* (-s, -ien) privilege.

privilegieren *v.t.* to grant s.b. a privilege.

privilegiert *a.* privileged.

pro *pr.* per; ~*Jahr*, per annum.

Pro *n. das ~ und das Kontra* the pros and cons.

Probe *f.* (-, -n) experiment, trial; test; (*Waren ~*) sample; (*Theater*) rehearsal; *auf ~*, on probation; *auf die ~ stellen*, to put to the test.

Probe. . . probationary *a.*

Probe: ~**dienst** *m.* probationary service; ~**exemplar** *n.* specimen copy; ~**fahrt** *f.* trial run; ~**flug** *m.* test flight.
proben *v.t. & i.* to rehearse.
probeweise *adv.* on a trial basis.
Probezeit *f.* term of probation, qualifying period.
probieren *v.t.* to try, to test; to taste.
Problem *n.* (-s, -e) problem, question.
Problematik *f.* problematic nature; problems.
problemlos *a.* problem free.
Produkt *n.* (-s, -e) product.
Produktenbörse *f.* produce exchange.
Produktion *f.* (-, -en) production.
Produktionsmittel *pl.* means of production.
Produktions: ~**prozeß** *m.*, ~**verfahren** *n.* production process.
produktiv *a.* productive.
Produktivität *f.* productivity.
Produzent *m.* (-en, -en) producer.
produzieren *v.t.* to produce.
profan *a.* profane.
profanieren *v.t.* to profane, to desecrate.
Profession *f.* (-, -en) profession; trade.
professionell *a.* professional.
Professor *m.* (-s, -en); **Professorin** *f.* (-, -nen) professor.
Professur *f.* (-, -en) professorship.
Profi *m.* (-s, -s) (*fam.*) pro.
Profil *n.* (-s, -e) profile.
profilieren *v.refl.* to distinguish o.s.
profiliert *a.* distinguished.
Profisport *m.* professional sport.
Profit *m.* (-s, -e) profit; ~**gier** *f.* greed for profit.
profitieren *v.i.* to profit (by).
Profitstreben *n.* profit seeking.
pro forma *adv.* as a matter of form.
profund *a.* profound.
Prognose *f.* (-, -n) prognosis.
Programm *n.* (-[e]s, -e) programe.
programmgemäß *adv. & a.* according to program.
Programmheft *n.* (-s, -e) program.
programmierbar *a.* programmable.
programmieren *v.t.* to program.
Programmierer *m.* (-s, -); **Programmiererin** *f.* (-, -nen) programmer.
Programmiersprache *f.* programming language.
Programmierung *f.* programming.
Programm: ~**vorschau** *f.* program roundup; ~**wahl** *f.* channel selection; ~**zeitschrift** *f.* program guide.
Progression *f.* (-, -en) progression.
progressiv *a.* progressive.
Projekt *n.* (-[e]s, -e) project, scheme.
Projektgruppe *f.* task force.
Projektionsapparat *m.* projector.
Projektionsschirm *m.* screen.
projizieren *v.t.* to project.
proklamieren *v.t.* to proclaim.
Pro-Kopf-Einkommen *n.* per capita income.
Prokura *f.* (-, 0) (power of) procuration; proxy.
Prolet *m.* prole.
Proletariat *n.* (-[e]s, 0) proletariat.
Proletarier *m.* (-s, -) proletarian.
Prolog *m.* (-[e]s, -e) prologue.
Promenade *f.* (-, -n) promenade, walk.
Promille *n.* (-s, -) per mil; alcohol level.

Promillegrenze *f.* legal alcohol limit.
prominent *a.* prominent.
Prominente *m./f.* prominent figure.
Prominenz *f.* (-, -en) celebrities.
Promotion *f.* (-, -en) doctorate.
promovieren *v.i.* to gain a doctorate.
prompt *a.* prompt, quick.
Pronomen *n.* (-s, -mina) pronoun.
propagieren *v.t.* to propagate.
Propeller *m.* (-s, -) propeller.
Prophet *m.* (-en, -en) prophet.
prophetisch *a.* prophetic.
prophezeien *v.t.* to prophesy; to predict.
Prophezeiung *f.* (-, -en) prophecy.
proportional *a.* proportional; *umgekehrt* ~, inversely proportioned.
Proporz *m.* (-es, -e) proportional representation.
Propst *m.* (-es, Pröpste) provost.
Prosa *f.* (-, 0) prose.
prosaisch *a.* prosaic; (*fig.*) prosy.
prosit! *i.* prost! cheers!
Prospekt *m.* (-[e]s, -e) brochure; leaflet.
Prostituierte *m./f.* (-n, -n) prostitute.
protegieren *v.t.* to patronize; to sponsor.
Protein *n.* (-s, -e) protein.
Protektorat *n.* (-es, -e) protectorate.
Protest *n.* (-es, -e) protest; ~ *erheben*, to enter a protest.
Protestant *m.* (-en, -en); **Protestantin** *f.* (-, -nen) Protestant.
protestantisch *a.* Protestant.
protestieren *v.i.* to protest.
Protest: ~**kundgebung** *f.* protest rally; ~**welle** *f.* wave of protest.
Prothese *f.* (-, -n) artificial limb; dentures.
Protokoll *n.* (-[s], -e) minutes *pl.*; ~*führen*, to keep the minutes; *zu* ~ *geben*, to place on record; *zu* ~ *nehmen*, to take down.
protokollieren *v.t.* to write the minutes of.
Protz *m.* (-n, -n) show-off; snob.
protzen *v.i.* to show off.
protzig *a.* showy.
Proviant *m.* (-[e]s, 0) provisions, stores.
Provinz *f.* (-, -en) province.
provinziell *a.* provincial.
Provinzler *m.* provincial.
Provision *f.* (-, -en) commission.
provisorisch *a.* provisional, temporary.
Provokation *f.* provocation.
provokativ *a.* provocative.
provozieren *v.t.* to provoke.
Prozedur *f.* (-, -en) procedure.
Prozent *n.* (-[e]s, -e) per cent.
Prozentsatz *m.* percentage.
Prozeß *m.* (-zesses, -zesse) process; lawsuit (action); proceedings *pl.*; *kurzen* ~ *machen mit*, to make short work of.
Prozeßakten *f.pl.* minutes (*pl.*) of a law case.
prozeßieren *v.i.* to go to court.
Prozession *f.* (-, -en) procession.
Prozeßkosten *f.pl.* legal costs *pl.*
Prozeßverfahren *n.* legal procedure.
prüde *a.* prudish, squeamish.
Prüderie *f.* (-, 0) prudery.
prüfen *v.t.* to try, to test; to examine; to censor; *von der Zensur geprüft*, censored.

Prüfer *m.*; **Prüferin** *f.* tester; inspector; auditor; examiner.

Prüfling *m.* (-s, -e) examinee; candidate.

Prüfstein *m.* touchstone.

Prüfung *f.* (-, -en) trial; examination; *eine ~ machen*, to take an examination *or* test; *sich einer ~ unterziehen*, to sit for an examination *or* test.

Prüfungs: **~angst** *f.* exam nerves; **~kommission** *f.* examination board.

Prügel *m.* (-s, -) stick, cudgel; beating.

Prügelei *f.* (-, -en) fight, row, scuffle.

Prügelknade *m.* (*fam.*) scapegoat.

prügeln *v.t.* to fight; to thrash.

Prügelstrafe *f.* corporal punishment.

Prunk *m.* (-es, 0) ostentation, splendor.

prunken *v.i.* to make a show.

prunkvoll *a.* gorgeous, splendid.

Psalm *m.* (-es, -en) psalm.

Pseudonym *n.* pseudonym; pen name.

pst! *i.* hush!

Psychiater *m.* (-s, -); **Psychiaterin** *f.* (-, -nen) psychiatrist.

psychiatrisch, psychiatric; **~e** *Klinik f.* mental hospital.

psychisch *a.* psychic(al).

Psychoanalyse *f.* psychoanalysis.

Psychoanalytiker *m.*; **Psychoanalytikerin** *f.* psychoanalyst.

psychoanalytisch *a.* psychoanalytical.

Psychologe *m.* (-en, -en); **Psychologin** *f.* (-, -nen) psychologist.

Psychologie *f.* psychology.

psychopathisch *a.* psychopathic.

Psychopharmakon *n.* (-s, -ka) psychochemical.

Psychose *f.* psychosis.

psychosomatisch *a.* psychosomatic.

Psychotherapeut *m.*; **Psychotherapeutin** *f.* psychotherapist.

psychotherapeutisch *a.* psychotherapeutic.

Psychotherapie *f.* psychotherapy.

Pubertät *f.* (-, 0) puberty.

publik *a. etw. ~ machen* to make s.th. public.

Publikum *n.* (-[s], 0) public.

publizieren *v.t.* to publish.

Publizist *m.*; **Publizistin** *f.* publicist; journalist.

Publizistik *f.* journalism.

Pudding *m.* (-s, -s) pudding.

Pudel *m.* (-s, -) poodle.

Puder *m.* (-s, 0) powder.

pudern *v.t.* to powder.

Puderquaste *f.* (powder-)puff.

Puderzucker *m.* confectioners' sugar.

Puff *m.* (e[e]s, -e) cuff, thump; puff; (*Knall*) pop, report; (*fam.*) brothel.

puffen *v.t. & i.* to cuff, to thump.

Puffer *m.* (-s, -) buffer.

Pulk *m.* group; crowd.

Pulle *f.* (*fam.*) bottle.

Pulli *m.*; **Pullover** *m.* sweater.

Puls *m.* (Pulses, Pulse) puls.

Pulsader *f.* artery.

pulsen, pulsieren *v.i.* to pulsate, to throb; (*fig.*) to pulse.

Pult *n.* (-es, -e) desk; lectern.

Pulver *n.* (-s, -) powder; gun-powder.

Pulverfaß *m.* (-es, fässer) barrel of gunpowder; powder-keg.

pulverisieren, pulvern *v.t.* to pulverize.

Pulverkaffee *m.* instant coffee.

Pulverschnee *m.* powder snow.

pummelig *a.* chubby.

Pump *m.* (-[e]s, -e) credit; *auf ~*, on credit.

Pumpe *f.* (-, -n) pump.

pumpen *v.t.* to pump; to lend; to borrow.

Punker *m.* punk (rocker).

Punkt *m.* (-[e]s, -e) point, dot; (*gram.*) full stop; article, item; *Punkt 7 Uhr*, seven o'clock sharp; *der wunde ~*, the sore point *or* spot.

punktieren *v.t.* to point, to dot; to punctuate; (*med.*) to tap.

Punktion *f.* (*med.*) puncture.

pünktlich *a.* punctual; ~ *adv.* punctually.

Punktsieg *m.* (*Boxen*) winning on points.

Punsch *m.* (-es, -e *u. Pünsche*) punch.

Pupille *f.* (-, -n) (*des Auges*) pupil.

Puppe *f.* (-, -n) doll; puppet; chrysalis.

Puppenspiel *n.* puppet-show.

Puppenspieler *m.*; **Puppenspielerin** *f.* puppeteer.

pur *a.* pure, mere.

Püree *n.* (-s, -s) purée.

Puritaner *m.* Puritan.

puritanisch *a.* Puritan; puritanical.

Purpur *m.* (-s, 0) purple; purple robe.

purpurn *a.* purple, crimson.

purpurrot *a.* purple, crimson.

Purzelbaum *m.* somersault.

purzeln *v.i.* (*s*) to tumble.

Puste *f.* (*fam.*) puff; breath.

Pustel *f.* (-, -n) pimple; pustule.

pusten *v.i.* (*s*) to breathe hard, to puff.

Pute, Puthenne *f.* (-, -n) turkey hen.

Puter *m.* (-s, -) turkey cock; turkey (roast).

Putsch *m.* (-es, -e) putsch; coup.

putschen *v.i.* to revolt; to stage a putsch.

Putte *f.* (-, -n) putto.

Putz *m.* (-es, 0) dress, finery, attire; (*Mauer*) roughcast, plaster.

putzen *v.t.* to clean, to polish; (*die Nase*) to blow, to wipe.

Putzfimmel *m.* (-s, -) (*pej.*) mania for cleaning.

Putzfrau *f.* (-, -en) cleaning lady.

putzig *a.* droll, queer.

Putzlappen *m.* (-s, -) cleaning rag.

Putzmacherin *f.* (-, -nen) milliner.

Putzmittel *n.* (-s, -) cleaning agent.

Putzzeug *n.* cleaning utensils *pl.*

Puzzle *n.* (-s, -) jigsaw puzzle.

Pygmäe *m.* (-n, -n) pygmy.

Pyjama *m.* (-s, -s) pyjamas.

Pyramide *f.* (-, -n) pyramid.

pyramidenförmig *a.* pyramidal.

Pyrenäen *pl.* the Pyrenees.

Pyromane *m.* (-n, -n) pyromaniac.

pythagoreisch *a.* Pythagorean; ~*er Lehrsatz*, Pythagorean theorem.

Q

Q, q *n.* the letter Q or q.
Quacksalber *m.* (-s, -) quack.
Quaderstein *m.* square *or* hewn stone.
Quadrat *n.* (-[e]s, -e) square; *im* ~, square.
quadratisch *a.* quadratic, square.
Quadratmeter *m.* squaremeter.
Quadratur *f.* quadrature; *die* ~ *des Kreises,* the squaring of the circle.
Quadratwurzel *f.* square root.
Quadratzahl *f.* square number.
quadrieren *v.t.* to square.
quadrophon *a.* quadrophonic.
quaken *v.i.* to croak; to quack.
quäken *v.i.* to scream, to squawk.
Quäker *m.* (-s, -) Quaker, Friend.
Qual *f.* (-, -en) pain, torment, agony.
quälen *v.t.* to torment, to vex; (sich) ~*v. refl.* to toil, to drudge.
Quälerei *f.* (-, -en) torture; torment; annoyance.
Quälgeist *m.* (*fam.*) pest.
qualifizieren (sich) *v.t. & refl.* to qualify.
Qualität *f.* (-, -en) quality.
qualitativ *a.* qualitative.
Qualitäts. . . quality-.
Qualle *f.* (-, -n) jelly fish.
Qualm *m.* (-[e]s, 0) thick smoke.
qualmen *v.i.* to smoke.
qualvoll *a.* very painful.
Quantität *f.* (-, -en) quantity.
Quantum *n.* (-[e] -ta) quantum; dose; share.
Quarantäne *f.* (-, -n) quarantine.
Quark *m.* (-[e]s, 0) curd cheese; (*sl.*) trifle; trash, rubbish.
Quarkkäse *m.* white cheese.
Quart *n.* (-[e]s, -e) quart; *in* ~, in quarto.
Quarta *f.* (-, -ten) (lower) fourth form.
Quartal *n.* (-s, -s) a quarter of a year.
Quart: ~band *m.* quarto volume; **~blatt** *n.* quarter of a sheet.
Quart[e] *f.* (-, -n) (*mus.*) fourth.
Quartett *n.* (-[e]s, -e) quartet(te).
Quartier *n.* (-[e]s, -e) quarters *pl.*
Quartiermeister *m.* (*mil.*) quartermaster.
Quarz *m.* (-es, -e) quartz.
quasseln *v.t.* to prate, to twaddle.
Quasselstrippe *f.* chatterbox.
Quast *m.* (-es, -en), **Quaste** *f.* (-, -n) tassel, tuft; puff; mop, brush.

Quatsch *m.* (-es, 0) foolish talk, rubbish; nonsense.
quatschen *v.i.* to talk nonsense.
Quatschkopf *m.* silly goose.
Quecksilber *n.* quicksilver, mercury.
Quell *m.* (-s, 0) **Quelle** *f.* (-, -n) well, spring, source.
quellen *v.t.* to soak, to swell; ~ *v.i.st.* (*s*) to spring, to gush, to flow; to swell.
quengelig *a.* whining; fretful.
quengeln *v.i.* to whine; to carp.
quer *a.* cross; oblique, transverse; ~ *adv.* across, diagonally.
Querbalken *m.* cross-beam.
querdurch *adv.* straight across.
Quere *f.* (-, 0) oblique direction; *der* ~ *nach,* crosswise; *in die* ~ *kommen,* to thwart.
querfeldein *adv.* across country.
Quer: ~flöte *f.* transverse flute; **~format** *n.* horizontal format; **~linie** *f.* cross-line; **~schiff**, *n.* transept; **~schnitt** *m.* cross-section; **~schnittslähmung** *f.* paraplegia; **~strasse** *f.* intersection; **~stück** *n.* (*mech.*) traverse; **~summe** *f.* sum of the digits; **~treiber** *m.* (*fam.*) obstructionist.
querüber *adv.* over against, athwart.
Querulant *m.* (-en, -en) litigious person; grumbler.
Querverbindung *f.* cross connection; **~verweis** *m.* cross reference.
quetschen *v.t.* to squeeze, to squash, to bruise.
Quetschung *f.* (-, -en) contusion, bruise.
Queue *n.* (-s, -s) cue, billiard-stick.
quicklebendig *a.* lively, brisk.
quieken, quietschen *v.i.* to squeak.
quietschfidel *a.* chipper.
Quinta *f.* (-, -ten) fifth grade.
Quinte *f.* (-, -n) (*mus.*) fifth.
Quintessenz *f.* (-, -en) quintessence, gist.
Quintett *n.* (-[e]s, -e) quintet(te).
Quirl *m.* hand blender; beater.
quirlen *v.t.* to whisk.
quirlig *a.* lively.
quitt *adv.* quits, even; rid, free.
quittieren *v.t.* to receipt (a bill); to quit.
Quittung *f.* (-, -en) receipt.
Quittungsmarke *f.* **Quittungsstempel** *m.* receipt-stamp.
Quote *f.* (-, -n) quota, share.
Quotient *m.* (-en, -en) (*ar.*) quotient.

R

R, r *n.* the letter R or r.
Rabatt *m.* (-[e]s, 0) abatement, discount.
Rabatte *m.* border (flowers).
Rabatz *m.* racket; din.
Rabanke *m.* (*fam.*) roughneck.
Rabbi, Rabbiner *m.* (-s, -) rabbi.
Rabe *m.* (-n, -n) raven.
Rabeneltern *pl.* uncaring parents.
rabenschwarz *a.* jet black.
rabiat *a.* violent.

Rache *f.* (-, 0) revenge, vengeance.
Rachen *m.* (-s, -) mouth (of an animal), jaws *pl.*; pharynx; (*fig.*) abyss.
rächen *v.t.* to avenge, to revenge; (sich) ~ *v. refl.* to take vengeance.
Rächer *m.* (-s, -) avenger.
Rachitis *f.* (-, 0) rickets *pl.*
Rachsucht *f.* vindictiveness.
rachsüchtig *a.* vindictive.
Rad *n.* (-[e]s, Räder) wheel; bicycle; *fünftes* ~ *am*

Wagen sein, to be superfluous.
Radachse *f.* axle.
Radar *n./m.* radar; **~falle** *f.* speed trap; **~kontrolle** *f.* speed check.
Radau *m.* (-[e]s, 0) (*sl.*) noise, row.
Raddampfer *m.* paddle-steamer.
radebrechen *v.t.* to manage (a language).
radeln *v.i.* to cycle, to bike.
Rädelsführer *m.* ringleader.
rädern *v.t.* to break on the wheel.
Räderwerk *n.* gearing.
radfahren *v.i.* to cycle, to wheel.
Radfahrer *m.* (-s, -) cyclist.
Radfahrweg *m.* cyclists' path.
radieren *v.t.* to erase; (*Kunst*) to etch.
Radiergummi *n.* eraser.
Radierung *f.* (-, -en) erasure; etching.
Radieschen *n.* (-s, -) radish.
radikal *a.* radical; drastic.
Radikale *m./f.* (-n, -n) radical.
Radikalismus *m.* radicalism.
Radikalität *f.* radicalness.
Radio *n.* (-s, 0) radio, wireless; **~apparat** *m.* wireless set.
radioaktiv *a.* radioactive; **~er Niederschlag** *m.* fallout.
Radioaktivität *f.* radioactivity.
Radiosender *m.* radiostation.
Radiotherapie *f.* radiotherapeutics.
Radium *n.* radium.
Radius *m.* (-, -dien) radius.
Rad: ~kappe *f.* hubcap; **~lager** *n.* wheel bearing; **~rennen** *n.* cycle racing.
radschlagen *v.i.* to do a cartwheel.
Radweg *m.* cycle path/track.
raffen *v.t.* to snatch up; to gather.
Raffinerie *f.* refinery.
Raffinesse *f.* cleverness; subtleness.
raffinieren *v.t.* to refine.
raffiniert *p. & a.* refined; (*fig.*) ingenious, crafty, wily; exquisite.
Rage *f.* fury; rage.
ragen *v.i.* to project, to be prominent.
Ragout *m.* (-s, -s) stew, ragout.
Rahm *m.* (-[e]s, 0) cream.
Rahmen *m.* (-s, -) frame; *im ~ von,* within the framework of.
rahmen *v.t.* to frame.
Rahmkäse *m.* cream-cheese.
Rakete *f.* (-, -n) rocket; missile.
Raketenwurfmaschine *f.* (*mil.*) rocket launcher.
rammen *v.t.* to ram, to drive in.
Rampe *f.* (-, -n) ramp, sloping drive.
Rampenlicht *n.* footlights *pl.; im ~ stehen* to be in the limelight.
ramponieren *v.t.* to knock about, to batter.
Ramsch *m.* (-es, -e) trash; rubbish.
Ramschverkauf *m.* rummage sale.
Rand *m.* (-es, Ränder) edge; (*Hut*) brim; (*Buch*) margin; (*Teller*) rim; (*Wunde*) lip; (*fig.*) brink, verge; border.
Randale *f.* (*fam.*) riot.
randalieren *v.i.* to riot.
Randalierer *m.* (-s, -) hooligan, rioter.

Rand: ~bemerkung *f.* marginal note; **~erscheinung** *f.* peripheral phenomenon; **~gebiet** *n.* borderland; outskirts; (*fig.*) fringe area; **~gruppe** *f.* marginal group; **~problem** *n.* side issue; **~streifen** *m.* shoulder (street).
Rang *m.* (-[e]s, Ränge) rank, order; quality, rate; (*Theater*) circle, row, tier; *erster ~,* dress circle; *zweiter ~,* upper circle.
Range *m.* (-n, -n) ~ *f.* (-, -n) naughty boy; romp; tomboy.
Rangfolge *f.* order of precedence.
Rangierbahnhof *m.* switch yard.
rangieren *v.i.* (*rail.*) to switch; ~ *v.i.* to rank.
Rangiergleis *n.* siding.
Rang: ~liste *f.* ranking list; **~ordnung** *f.* (order of) precedence; pecking order; **~stufe** *f.* degree, order.
Ranke *f.* (-, -n) tendril, creeper.
Ränke *m.pl.* intrigues.
ranken (sich) *v.refl.* to climb, to creep.
Ränkeschmied *m.* intriguer, trickster.
Ränzel *n.* (-s, -) **Ranzen** *m.* (-s, -) knapsack, satchel.
ranzig *a.* rancid.
Rappe *m.* (-n, -n) black horse.
Rappel *m.* (*fam.*) crazy mood.
Rapport *m.* (-[e]s, -e) report.
Raps *m.* (-ses, 0) rape-seed, colza.
rar *a.* rare; exquisite; scarce.
Rarität *f.* (-, -en) curio; rarity.
rasant *a.* fast; dynamic; dashing.
rasch *a.* speedy, swift; brisk, prompt.
rascheln *v.i.* to rustle.
Rasen *m.* (-s, -) turf, lawn.
rasen *v.i.* to rave, to rage; to rush.
Rasen: ~mähmaschine *f.* lawn-mower; **~platz** *m.* grass-plot, lawn, green; **~stück** *n.* sod.
rasend *a.* furious, frantic.
Rasenmäher *m.* lawn mower; **~platz** *m.* pitch (soccer), grass court (tennis).
Raserei *f.* (-, -en) delirium, frenzy.
Rasierapparat *m.* (-es, -e) electric shaver.
rasieren *v.t.* to shave.
Rasier: ~klinge *f.* razor blade; **~messer** *n.* razor; **~seife** *f.* shaving soap, shaving-stick; **~zeug** *n.* shaving things *or* tackle.
Raspel *f.* (-, -n) rasp; grater.
raspeln *v.t.* to grate.
Rasse *f.* (-, -n) breed, race; *von reiner ~,* thoroughbred.
Rassehund *m.* pedigree-dog.
Rassel *f.* rattle.
rasseln *v.i.* to rattle.
Rassen... racial, *a.;* **~krawall** *m.* race riot; **~schranke** *f.* color bar; **~trennung** *f.* segregation; **~unruhen** *pl.* race riots.
Rassepferd *n.* thoroughbred.
rassig *a.* racy.
Rassismus *m.* (-, 0) racism.
Rassist *m.* (-en, -en); **Rassistin** *f.* (-, -nen) racist.
rassistisch *a.* racist.
Rast *f.* (-, 0) rest; halt.
rasten *v.i.* to rest, to repose; to halt.
Raster *n.* (-s, -) grid; screen; framework.
Rasthaus *n.* road restaurant.
rastlos *a. & adv.* restless(ly).

Rastplatz *m.* reststop.
Raststätte *f.* service area.
Rasttag *m.* day of rest.
Rasur *f.* (-, -nen) shave.
Rat *m.* (-[e]s, Räte) counsel, advice; consultation; council, board; (*Person*) councillor; *zu ~e ziehen*, to consult; *mit sich zu ~e gehen*, to take counsel with oneself; *um ~ fragen*, to ask advice of; *mit ~ und Tat*, with advice and assistance.
Rate *f.* (-, -n) (*com.*) installment; (*Statistik*) rate; *in ~n, ratenweise*, by installments.
raten *v.t.st.* to guess, to divine; to counsel, to advise.
Ratenzahlung *f.* payment by installments.
Ratespiel *n.* guessing game.
Rat: ~geber *m.* adviser; **~haus** *n.* town-hall.
Ratifikation *f.*, **Ratifizierung** *f.* ratification.
ratifizieren *v.t.* to ratify.
Ration *f.* (-, en) ration, allowance.
rational *a.* rational.
rationalisieren *v.i.* to rationize.
rationell *a. & adv.* efficient(ly); economic(ally).
rationieren *v.t.* to ration; *nicht mehr rationiert sein*, to come off the ration; *rationiert werden*, to go on rations.
Rationierung *f.* (-, -en) rationing; *von der ~befreien*, to de-ration.
ratlos *a.* perplexed, helpless, at a loss.
ratsam *a.* advisable, expedient.
Ratschlag *m.* advice, counsel.
ratschlagen *v.i.* to consult, to deliberate.
Ratschluß *m.* decree, resolution.
Rätsel *n.* (-s, -) riddle engima; mystery; problem.
rätselhaft *a.* enigmatical, mysterious.
Ratte *f.* (-, -n) rat.
Ratten: ~fänger *m.* rat-catcher; **~gift** *m.* rat poison.
rattern *v.i.* to clatter, to rattle.
Raub *m.* (-[e]s, 0) robbery, piracy; prey.
rauben *v.t.* to rob; (*Kinder*) to kidnap.
Räuber *m.* (-s, -) robber.
Räuberbande *f.* gang of robbers.
Räuberei *f.* (-, -en) robbery.
räuberisch *a.* rapacious, predatory.
Raub: ~fisch *m.* predatory fish; **~gier** *f.* rapacity; **~mord** *m.* murder with robbery; **~ritter** *m.* robber baron; **~tier** *n.* beast of prey; **~überfall** *m.* armed robbery; hold-up; **~vogel** *m.* bird of prey; **~zug** *m.* raid.
Rauch *m.* (-[e]s, 0) smoke, fume.
rauchen *v.t. & i.* to smoke; *Rauchen verboten*, no smoking!
Raucher *m.* (-s, -) smoker; *starker ~*, heavy smoker.
Räucheraal *m.* smoked eel.
Raucherabteil *n.* smoking compartment.
Räucherhering *m.* smoked herring.
räuchern *v.t.* to perfume; to cure, to smoke (dry); to fumigate.
Rauchfang *m.* chimney; flue.
rauchig *a.* smoky; husky (voice).
Rauch: ~tabak *m.* smoking tobacco; **~waren** *f.pl.* furs *pl.*; **~zimmer** *n.* smoking-room.
Räude *f.* (-, 0) mange, scab.
räudig *a.* scabbed, mangy.
Raufbold *m.* brawler; bully.
raufen *v.t.* to pluck; (sich) *~v. refl.* to scuffle, to

fight.
Rauferei *f.* (-, -en) fight; brawl, scuffle.
rauh *a.* rough, rugged; boisterous; (*Wetter*) raw; (*im Halse*) hoarse;(*fig.*) harsh, rude.
Rauhhaardackel *m.*, wire-haired dachshund.
Rauhreif *m.* (-[e]s, 0) hoar-frost.
Raum *m.* (-[e]s, Räume) room, space, place; (*Schiff*) hold; *leerer ~*, vacuum; (*der Hoffnung*) to indulge in; (*dem Gedanken*) to give way to; (*der Bitte*) to grant.
räumen *v.t.* to clear away, to remove; (*Platz*) to evacuate; *aus dem Wege ~*, to put out of the way.
Raum: ~fahrer *m.*, **~fahrerin** *f.* astronaut, cosmonaut; **~fahrt** *f.* space travel, space...; **~fahrzeug** *n.* spacecraft.
Räumfahrzeug *n.* snow plow.
Raum: ~gehalt *m.* tonnage; **~inhalt** *m.* volume, capacity; **~kunst** *f.* interior decoration.
räumlich *a.* relating to space.
Raumpfleger *m.;* **Raumpflegerin** *f.* cleaner.
Raumschiff *n.* spacecraft.
Raumstation *f.* space station.
Räumung *f.* (-, -en) clearing; removal; evacuation.
Räumungsausverkauf *m.* clearance sale.
raunen *v.t. & i.* to whisper.
Raupe *f.* (-, -n) caterpillar.
Raupenfahrzeuge *pl.* caterpillar (truck).
Rausch *m.* (-es, Räusche) drunkenness, intoxication; (*fig.*) frenzy (of love, etc.).
rauschen *v.i.* to rustle, to rust.
Rauschgift *m.* (-[e]s, -e) drug, narcotic; **~handel** *m.* drug traffic; **~händler** *m.*, **~händlerin** *f.* drug trafficker, dealer; **~sucht** *f.* drug addiction; **~süchtige** *m./f.* drug addict.
räuspern (sich) *v.refl.* to clear one's throat, to hem and haw.
Rausschmeißer *m.* (*fam.*) bouncer.
Raute *f.* (-, -n) rhombus.
rautenförmig *a.* rhombic.
Razzia *f.* (-, Razzien) raid.
Reagenzglas *n.* test-tube.
reagieren *v.i.* to react (upon).
reaktionär *a.* reactionary.
Reaktionär *m.* (-[e]s, -e); **Reaktionärin** *f.* (-, -nen) reactionary.
Reaktionsfähigkeit *f.* ability to react.
reaktionsschnell *a.* with quick reactions.
Reaktionszeit *f.* reaction time.
real *a.* real.
realisierbar *a.* realizable.
Realisierbarkeit *f.* practicability.
realisieren *v.t.* to realize; to turn into money.
Realismus *m.* realism.
Realist *m.;* **Realistin** *f.* realist.
realistisch *a.* realistic.
Realität *f.* reality.
Realschule *f.* non-classical secondary school.
Rebe *f.* (-, -n) vine, vine-branch.
Rebell *m.* (-en, -en); **Rebellin** *f.* (-, -nen) rebel, mutineer.
rebellieren *v.i.* to rebel, to mutiny.
Rebellion *f.* (-, -en) rebellion.
rebellisch *a.* rebellious.
Reb: ~huhn *n.* partridge; **~laus** *f.* phylloxera; **~stock** *m.* vine.
Rechen *m.* (-s, -) rake.

rechen *v.i.* to rake.

Rechen: ~**art** *f.* type of arithmetical operation; ~**aufgabe** *f.* sum, mathematical problem; ~**buch** *n.* arithmetic-book; ~**exempel** *n.* sum, arithmetical problem; ~**fehler** *m.* miscalculation; ~**kunst** *f.* arithmetic; ~**maschine** *f.* calculator.

Rechenschaft *f.* (-, 0) account; ~ *ablegen,* to give an account; *zur* ~ *ziehen,* to call to account.

Rechenschieber *m.* slide rule.

recherchieren *v.i.u.t.* to investigate.

rechnen *v.t. & i.* to count, to reckon, to compute, to calculate; *auf einen* ~, to depend, to rely, to count on one; ~ *zu,* to class with.

Rechner *m.* calculator; computer; *ein guter* ~ *sein* to be good at arithmetic.

Rechnung *f.* (-, -en) reckoning, calculation, computation; *(Nota)* bill, account; *die* ~ *stimmt, trifft zu,* the account squares, is correct; *auf die* ~ *setzen,* to add to the bill; *in* ~ *stellen,* to carry to account; *auf* ~ *bestellen,* to order on account; *auf eigene, fremde* ~, on one's own account, for account of another; *einen Strich durch die* ~ *machen,* to thwart one's plans; *den Umständen* ~ *tragen,* to accommodate oneself to circumstances.

Rechnungs: ~**abschluß** *m.* balance of account; ~**jahr** *n.* business year; ~**prüfer** *m.* auditor; ~**wesen** *n.* bookkeeping, accounts *pl.*

recht *a.* right, just; convenient, fitting; correct, proper; ~ *adv.* right, fairly; well; *ein* ~*er Winkel,* a right angle; ~*e Seite* right-hand side; *zur* ~*en Zeit,* in time; ~ *haben,* to be right; **rechts** *adv.* on the right hand.

Recht *n.* (-[e]s, -e) right; justice; title, claim; law, jurisprudence; *mit Fug und* ~, with good reason, in all conscience; ~ *sprechen,* to administer justice; *die* ~*e studieren,* to study law, to read for the bar; *von* ~*s wegen,* by right, according to law.

Rechte *f.* (-n, -n) right hand.

Rechteck *n.* (-s, -e) rectangle.

rechteckig *a.* rectangular.

rechten *v.i.* to contest, to dispute.

rechtfertigen *v.i.* to justify, to vindicate.

Rechtfertigung *f.* (-, -en) justification.

rechtgläubig *a.* orthodox.

Rechtgläubigkeit *f.* (-, 0) orthodoxy.

Rechthaberei *f.* (-, -en) self-opinionatedness.

rechthaberisch *a.* self-opinionated, dogmatic, obstinate.

rechtlich *a.* legal, lawful.

rechtlos *a.* illegal; outlaw.

Rechtlosigkeit *f.* (-, 0) lack of rights.

rechtmässig *a.* lawful, legitimate, rightful.

Rechtmässigkeit *f.* (-, 0) legitimacy, legality.

rechts *adv.* on the right to the right; ~*um, kehrt!* right, face!

Rechts: ~**anwalt** *m.,* ~**anwältin** *f.* lawyer, attorney; *als* ~*anwalt praktizieren,* to practice at the bar; ~**beistand** *m.* counsel, legal adviser; ~**beugung** *f.* miscarriage of justice.

rechtschaffen *a.* righteous, honest.

Rechtschreibfehler *m.* spelling mistake.

Rechtschreibung *f.* spelling, orthography.

Rechts: ~**extremismus** *m.* right-wing extremism; ~**extremist** *m.,* ~**extremistin** *f.* right-wing extremist; ~**frage** *f.* legal question/issue; ~**fall** *m.* case (at law); ~**gelehrter** *m.* jurist; ~**grund** *m.* legal argument; ~**grundsatz** *m.* legal principle.

rechtsgültig *a.* legal, valid.

Rechts: ~**händer** *m.,* ~**händerin** *f.* right-hander; ~**hilfe** *f.* legal aid; ~**kraft** *f.* force of law.

rechtskräftig *a.* legal, valid.

Rechts: ~**lage** *f.* legal situation; ~**lehrer** *m.* professor of jurisprudence; ~**mittel** *n.* legal remedy, appeal; ~**pflege** *f.* administration of justice; ~**radikalismus** *m.* right-wing radicalism; ~**ruck** *m.* shift to the right; ~**sache** *f.* lawsuit, case; ~**schutz** *m.* legal protection.

Rechtsprechung *f.* administration of justice.

Rechts: ~**spruch** *m.* legal decision; ~**staat** *m.* constitutional state; ~**staatlichkeit** *f.* rule of law; ~**stellung** *f.* legal status; ~**titel** *m.* (legal) title.

rechtswidrig *a.* contrary to law, illegal.

Rechtswissenschaft *f.* jurisprudence.

recht: ~**wink[e]lig** *a.* rectangular; ~**zeitig** *a.* well-timed; ~ *adv.* in due time.

Reck *n.* (-[e]s, -e) horizontal bar; high bar.

Recke *m.* (-n, -n) hero, warrior.

recken *v.t.* to extend, to stretch, to rack; *(Hals)* to crane.

Redakteur *m.* (-[e]s, -e); **Redakteurin** *f.* (-, -nen) editor.

Redaktion *f.* (-, -en) editorship; editor's office; editorial staff; editing.

redaktionell *a.* editorial.

Rede *f.* (-, -n) speech; oration, address, *eine* ~ *halten,* to make a speech; *in die* ~ *fallen,* to interrupt; *zur* ~ *stellen,* to call to account; ~ *stehen,* to give an account; *nicht der* ~ *wert,* not worth mentioning.

Rede: ~**freiheit** *f.* freedom of speech; ~**gewandtheit** *f.* eloquence; ~**kunst** *f.* rhetoric; oratory.

reden *v.t. & i.* to speak, to talk.

Redensart *f.* phrase; expression; saying; **Redensarten** *pl.* empty phrases.

Redewendung *f.* idiom; idiomatic expression.

redigieren *v.t.* to edit.

redlich *a.* honest, just, candid.

Redlichkeit *f.* honesty.

Redner *m.* (-s, -); **Rednerin** *f.* (-, -nen) orator, speaker; lecturer.

Rednerbühne *f.* platform.

rednerisch *a.* oratorical, rhetorical.

Redoute *f.* (-, -n) masquerade.

redselig *a.* talkative.

Reduktion *f.* (-, -en) reduction.

reduzieren *v.t.* to reduce, to diminish.

Reeder *m.* (-s, -) shipowner.

Reederei *f.* (-, -en) shipping company.

reell *a.* honest, respectable, solid.

Reet *n.* (-s, 0) reeds.

reetgedeckt *a.* thatched.

Referat *n.* (-s, -e) paper; report; department.

Referendar *m.* (-s, -e); **Referendarin** *f.* (-, -nen) candidate for the higher civil service.

Referenz *f.* (-, -en) reference.

referieren *v.t.* to report.

reffen *v.t.* to reef (the sails).

reflektieren *v.t. & i.* to reflect.

Reflex *m.* (-es, -e) reflex.

Reflexion *f.* (-, -en) reflection.

reflexiv *a.* reflexive.

Reflexivpronomen *n.* (-s, -) reflexive pronoun.

Reform *f.* (-, -en) reform.

Reformation *f.* reformation.
reformbedürftig *a.* in need of reform.
Reformhaus *n.* health food store.
reformieren *v.t.* to reform.
Refrain *m.* (-s, -s) refrain.
Regal *n.* (-[e]s, -e) shelf, shelves *pl.*
Regatta *f.* (-, -ten) boat race, regatta.
rege *a.* stirring, brisk; active.
Regel *f.* (-, -en) rule, regulation; (*med.*) menses; *in der ~,* as a rule, generally.
regel: ~**los** *a.* irregular; ~**mäßig** *a.* regular.
Regelmäßigkeit *f.* (-, -en) regularity.
regeln *v.t.* to regulate; to settle.
regelrecht *a.* regular, correct.
Regelung *f.* (-, -en) regulation, settlement.
regelwidrig *a.* contrary to rule.
regen (sich) *v.refl.* to stir.
Regen *m.* (-s, 0) rain; (*fig.*) shower.
regenarm *a.* with low rainfall.
Regen: ~**bogen** *m.* rainbow; ~**bogenfarben** *f.pl.* prismatic colors *pl.*; ~**bogenhaut** *f.* iris (eye); ~**dach** *n.* eaves *pl.*
Regeneration *f.* regeneration; ~**sfähigkeit** *f.* regenerative power.
regenerieren *v.i.* to regenerate.
Regen: ~**fälle** *pl.* rain(fall); ~**guss** *m.* downpour; ~**mantel** *m.* raincoat; ~**messer** *m.* rain-gauge; ~**schauer** *m.* shower; ~**schirm** *m.* umbrella; ~**schirmständer** *m.* umbrella stand.
Regent *m.* (-en, -en); **Regentin** *f.* (-, -nen) regent.
Regentonne *f.* water butt.
Regentschaft *f.* (-, 0) regency.
Regen: ~**wetter** *n.* rainy weather; ~**wurm** *m.* earthworm; ~**zeit** *f.* rainy season.
Regie *f.* (-, -[e]n) direction (performing arts); management.
regieren *v.i.* to rule, to reign; ~ *v.t.* to govern, to rule.
Regierung *f.* (-, -en) government; reign.
Regierungs: ~**antritt** *m.* accession; ~**bezirk** *m.* administrative district; ~**chef** *m.*, ~**chefin** *f.* head of government; ~**erklärung** *f.* government declaration; ~**sprecher** *m.*, ~**sprecherin** *f.* government spokesman/woman; ~**umbildung** *f.* government reshuffle; ~**wechsel** *m.* change of government; ~**zeit** *f.* reign; term of office.
Regime *n.* (-s, -) regime.
Regimegegner *m.*; **Regimegegnerin** *f.* dissident.
Regiment *n.* (-[e]s, -er) regiment.
Region *f.* (-, -en) region.
regional *a.* regional.
Regisseur *m.* (-s, -e); **Regisseurin** *f.* (-, -nen) director; producer.
Register *n.* (-s, -) register; index; (*Orgel*) stop.
registrieren *v.t.* to register.
Registrierung *f.* registration.
reglementieren *v.t.* to regulate.
Regler *m.* (-s, -) (*elek.*) regulator.
reglos *a.* motionless.
regnen *v.i.* to rain; *fein ~,* to drizzle.
regnerisch *a.* rainy.
Regress *m.* (-es, -e) recourse; ~ *nehmen,* to have recourse, to seek recovery; ~**pflichtige** *m./f.* person liable to recourse.
regsam *a.* quick, agile, active.
regulär *a.* regular.

regulieren *v.t.* to regulate, to adjust; *die Uhr ~,* to set a watch.
Regung *f.* (-, -en) impulse.
regungslos *a.* motionless.
Reh *n.* ([e]s, -e) roe-deer.
Reh: ~**bock** *m.* roebuck; ~**braten** *m.* venison; ~**keule** *f.* haunch of venison.
rehabilitieren *v.t.* to rehabilitate.
Reibach *m.* (-s, 0) (*fam.*) *einen ~ machen,* to make a killing.
Reibeisen *n.* grater.
reiben *v.t.st.* to rub; to grate; to grind; *wund ~,* to gall, to chafe.
Reiberei *f.* (-, -en) provocation; friction.
Reibung *f.* (-, -en) friction.
Reibungsfläche *f.* friction surface.
reibungslos *a. & adv.* smooth(ly).
reich *a.* rich, opulent, wealthy; copious.
Reich *n.* (-[e]s, -e) empire, kindom.
reichen *v.t.* to reach; to pass, to hand; ~ *v.i.* to reach, to extend (to); to suffice.
reichhaltig *a.* copious, comprehensive.
reichlich *a.* copious, plentiful.
Reichtum *m.* (-s, tümer) riches, wealth; abundance.
Reichweite *f.* reach; range.
reif *a.* ripe; mature; *in reiferen Jahren,* advanced in years; ~ *zu, für,* ripe for.
Reif *m.* ([e]s, 0) frost.
Reife *f.* (-, 0) maturity, ripeness.
reifen *v.t.* to mature; ~ *v.i.* to ripen, to grow ripe.
Reifen *m.* (-s, -) hoop, ring; tire; ~**panne** *f.* flat tire.
Reife: ~**prüfung** *f.* school certificate examination (*Gymnasium*); ~**zeugnis** *n.* school certificate (*Abitur*).
Reifglätte *f.* slippery frost on the road.
reiflich *a.* careful, mature; ~ *adv.* maturely, thoroughly.
Reigen *m.* (-s, -) round dance.
Reihe *f.* (-, -n) row, line; rank, range; series; turn; *in Reih und Glied,* with closed ranks; *er ist an der ~, er kommt an die ~, die ~ ist an ihm,* it is his turn; *nach der ~,* by turns.
reihen *v.t.* to range, to rank; to string.
Reihen *m.* (-s, -) round dance.
Reihenfolge *f.* succession, sequence, order.
Reihengeschäft *n.* chain-store.
Reihenschaltung *f.* (*elek.*) series connection.
reihenweise *adv.* in rows; by files.
Reiher *ni.* (-s, -) heron.
reihum *adv.* by turns.
Reim *m.* (-[e]s, -e) rhyme.
reimen *v.t.* to rhyme; (sich) ~ *v. refl.* (*fig.*) to rhyme.
reimlos *a.* blank, unrhymed.
rein *a.* clean, pure; clear; *der ~e Zufall,* pure coincidence; *ins ~e schreiben,* to make a fair copy; *ins ~e bringen,* to settle, to arrange.
Rein: ~**ertrag** *m.* net proceeds *pl.* ~**fall** (*sl.*) washout; flop; ~**gewinn** *m.* net profit.
Reinheit *f.* (-, 0) cleanness, purity.
reinigen *v.t.* to clean, to purify.
Reinigung *f.* dry-cleaning; dry-cleaners.
reinlich *a.* cleanly, neat; ~ *adv.* cleanly.
Reinlichkeit *f.* (-, 0) cleanliness.

Reinschrift f. fair copy.
reinweg adv. clean, flatly.
Reis n. (Reises, Reiser) scion; sprig.
Reis m. (Reises, 0) rice.
Reise f. (-, -n) trip, journey, tour; (See) voyage; travels pl.; eine ~ antreten, to go on a trip; auf ~n sein, to be traveling.
Reise: ~**agent** m. tourist agent; ~**agentur** f. travel agency; ~**andenken** n. souvenir; ~**artikel** pl. travel goods; ~**büro** n. travel agency.
reisefertig a. ready to start.
Reise: ~**führer** m. guide(-book); ~**gepäck** n. baggage; ~**gruppe** f. tourist party; ~**handbuch** n. guide (-book); ~**leiter** m., ~**leiterin** f. courier.
reisen v.i. (h) to travel, to journey; (s) to go (to).
Reisende m./f. (-n, -n) traveler.
Reise: ~**omnibus** m. coach; ~**pass** m. passport; ~**route** f. itinerary; ~**scheck** m. traveler's check; ~**tasche** f. traveling bag; ~**veranstalter** m. tour operator; ~**zeit** f. holiday season; ~**ziel** n. destination; ~**zuschuß** m. travel allowance.
Reisfeld n. paddy field.
Reisig n. (-s, 0) brushwood.
Reißaus nehmen v.i. to take to one's heels.
Reißbrett n. drawing-board.
reißen v.t.st. to tear, to rend, to pull; ~ v.st. to burst; to split; entzwei, to tear to pieces; Witze ~, to crack jokes; an sich ~, to take hold of; sich um einen oder etwas ~, to scramble for, to fight for; das reißt in den Geldbeutel, that runs into money; mir reißt die Geduld, I am losing patience; wenn alle Stränge ~, if the worst comes to the worst.
Reißen n. (-s, 0) rheumatism, ache.
reißend a. rapid; rapacious (animal).
Reißer m. (-s, -) (Buch) best-seller.
reißerisch a. sensational; lurid.
Reiß: ~**feder** f. drawing pen; ~**nagel** m.; ~**zwecke** f. drawing pin, thumb-tack; ~**verschluß** m. zipper; ~**zahn** m. fang, canine tooth; ~**zeug** n. case of mathematical instruments.
Reitbahn f. riding arna, manège.
reiten v.t. & i.st. (s & h) to ride, to go on horseback; auf etwas immer herum~, to be always harping on the same string.
Reiter m. (-s, -) rider, horseman.
Reiterei f. (-, -en) cavalry.
Reiterin f. (-, -nen) horsewoman.
Reit: ~**gerte**, ~**peitsche** f. riding-whip; ~**hose** f. riding breeches; ~**kleid** n. riding habit; ~**knecht** m. groom; ~**kunst** f. horsemanship; ~**pferd** n. saddle-horse; ~**schule** f. riding-school; ~**stiefel** m.pl. boots; ~**turnier** n. riding event; ~**weg** m. bridlepath; ~**zeug** n. riding equipment.
Reiz m. (-es, -e) charm, attraction; incentive, stimulus; irritation.
reizbar a. sensitive; irritable.
Reizbarkeit f. irritability.
reizen v.t. to stimulate; to charm; to irritate, to annoy.
reizend a. charming.
Reizhusten m. dry cough.
reizlos a. unattractive.
Reizmittel n. incentive; (med.) stimulant.
Reizung f. irritability.
reizvoll a. attractive.
Reizwort n. emotive word.

rekapitulieren v.t. to recapitulate.
rekeln v. refl. to lounge around.
Reklamation f. (-, -en) complaint.
Reklame f. (-, -en) advertisement; publicity; ~ machen, to advertise; ~**wirkung** f. appeal.
reklamieren v.t. to claim; ~ v.i. to protest.
rekonstruieren v.t. to reconstruct.
Rekonstruktion f. reconstruction.
Rekonvaleszent m. (-en, -en); **Rekonvaleszentin** f. convalescent.
Rekord m. (-[e]s, -e) record.
Rekrut m. (-en, -en) recruit.
rekrutieren v.t. to recruit.
Rektor m. (-s, -toren); **Rektorin** f. rector; head (-master); principal (of a college).
Rektorat n. (-[e]s, -e) rectorship.
Relais n. relay.
relativ a. relative.
relativieren v.t. to relativize.
Relativität f. (-, -en) relativity.
Relativitätstheorie f. theory of relativity.
Relativpronomen n. relative pronoun.
Relativsatz m. relative clause.
Relief n. (-s, -s) relief.
Religion f. (-, -en) religion.
Religions: ~**freiheit** f. freedom of worship; ~**gemeinschaft** f. religious community; confession; ~**zugehörigkeit** f. religion, religious confession.
religiös a. religious.
Relikt n. (-[e]s, -e) relic; (biol.) relict.
Reling f. (-, -s/e) rail.
Reliquie f. (-, -n) (rel.) relic.
Remis n. (-, -) draw(chess).
rempeln v.t. (fam.) to push; to jostle.
Renaissance f. (-, -n) Renaissance; (fig.) revival.
Renegat m. (-en, -en) renegade.
renitent a. refractory.
Rennbahn f. race-course; racetrack.
rennen v.i.ir. (s) to run hard; to race.
Rennen n. (-s, -) race; run; heat.
Renner m. (-s, -) (fam.) big seller.
Rennpferd n. racehorse.
Renn: ~**platz** m. race-course; ~**sport** m. racing, the turf; ~**stall** m. racing stable.
Renommee n. (-s, -s) reputation.
renommieren v.i. to brag, to show off.
renommiert a. well-known, renowned.
renovieren v.t. to renovate.
Renovierung f. renovation.
rentabel a. profitable, economic.
Rentabilität f. (-, 0) profitableness.
Rente f. (-, -n) annuity; pension.
Rentier n. (-s, -e) reindeer.
rentieren (sich) v. refl. to pay.
Rentner n. (-s, -); **Rentnerin** f. (-, -nen) pensioner.
reparabel a. repairable.
Reparatur f. (-, -en) repair; ~**werkstatt** f. repair shop.
reparieren v.t. to repair.
Repertoire n. (-s, -s) (theat.) stock, repertoire, repertory.
repetieren v.t. to repeat.
Replik f. (-, -en) replica; reply.
Report m. (-s, -e) report.

Reporter *m.*; **Reporterin** *f.* reporter.
Repräsentant *m.* (-en, -en); **Repräsentantin** *f.* (-, -nen) representative.
Repräsentantenhaus *f.* House of Representatives.
Repräsentativumfrage *f.* representative survey.
repräsentieren *v.t.* to represent.
Repressalien *pl.* reprisals *pl.*
repressiv *a.* repressive.
Reproduktion *f.* reproduction.
reproduzieren *v.t.* to reproduce.
Reptil *n.* (-s, -ien) reptile.
Republik *f.* (-, -en) republic.
Republikaner *m.* (-s, -); **Republikanerin** *f.* (-, -nen) republican.
republikanisch *a.* republican.
requirieren *v.t.* (*mil.*) to requisition.
Requisit *n.* (-s, -en) prop; property.
Reservat *n.* (-s, -e) reservation; reserve.
Reserve *f.* (-, -n) reserve.
Reserve: ~**bank** *f.* substitutes' bench; ~**rad** *n.* spare wheel; ~**reifen** *m.* spare tire; ~**tank** *m.* reserve tank.
reservieren *v.t.* to reserve.
Reservist *m.* (-en, -en) reservist.
Residenz *f.* (-, -en) (monarch's) residence.
residieren *v.i.* to reside.
resignieren *v.i.* to give up.
resistent *a.* resistant.
resolut *a.* resolute.
Resolution *f.* (-, -en) resolution.
Resonanzboden *m.* sounding-board.
resozialisieren *v.t.* to reintegrate into society.
Resozialisierung *f.* reintegration into society.
Respekt *m.* (-[e]s, 0) respect, regard.
respektabel *a.* respectable.
respektieren *v.t.* to respect, to honour.
respektlos *a.* without respect.
Respektlosigkeit *f.* (-, -en) disrespect.
respektvoll *a.* respectful.
Ressentiment *n.* (-s, -s) antipathy.
Ressort *n.* (-s, -s) department.
Rest *m.* (-[e]s, -e) rest, residue, remainder; remnant; leftovers.
Restaurant *n.* restaurant; ~*mit Selbstbedienung f.* cafeteria.
Restaurateur *m.* (-[e]s, -e) inn-keeper.
Restauration *f.* (-, -en) restoration; restaurant.
restaurieren *v.t.* to restore, to renovate (a building, etc.).
Restbestand *m.* remainder; residue.
restlich *a.* remaining.
restlos *a. & adv.* complete(ly).
Restbestand *m.* remaining stock.
Restbetrag *m.,* **Restsumme** *f.* balance.
Resultat *n.* (-[e]s, -e) result; (*Rechnung*) answer.
resultieren *v.i.* to result.
Resümee *n.* (-s, -s) summary.
resümieren *v.t.* to summarize.
Retorte *f.* (-, -n) retort, alembic.
retour *adv.* back.
Retrospektive *f.* (-, -n) retrospective (view).
retten *v.t. & refl.* (*sich*) to save, to rescue, to preserve; to save oneself.
Retter *m.* (-s, -); **Retterin** *f.* (-, -nen) rescuer; savior.
Rettich *m.* (-[e]s, -e) radish.

Rettung *f.* (-, -en) rescue; salvation.
Rettungs: ~**boot** *n.* life-boat; ~**dienst** *m.* ambulance service; rescue service; ~**gürtel** *m.* life-belt.
rettungslos *adv.* hopeless.
Rettungs: ~**ring** *m.* lifebelt; ~**schwimmer** *m.*, ~**schwimmerin** *f.* life saver; life guard; ~**wagen** *m.* ambulance.
retuschieren *v.t.* to retouch.
Reue *f.* (-, 0) remorse; repentance.
reuelos *a.* simpenitent; unrepentant.
reuen *v.t.imp. es reut mich,* I repent (of it).
reuig, reumütig *a.* repentant.
reuvoll *a.* repentant.
Revanche *f.* (-, -n) revenge; (*sp.*) return match/fight.
revanchieren (sich) *v.refl.* to return (a service, etc.); to take one's revenge.
Reverenz (-, -en) curtsy, bow.
revidieren *v.t.* to revise; to check.
Revier *n.* (-[e]s, -e) (hunting-)district; quarter, district; beat; (*mil.*) sick-bay, sickward, infirmary.
Revision *f.* (-, -en) revision; inspection; (*law*) review.
Revolte *f.* (-, -n) revolt.
revoltieren *v.i.* to revolt.
Revolution *f.* (-, -en) revolution.
revolutionär *a.* revolutionary.
Revolutionär *m.* (-[e]s, -e); **Revolutionärin** *f.* (-, -nen) revolutionist.
revolutionieren *v.t.* to revolutionize.
Revolver *n.* (-s, -) revolver.
Revolverheld *m.* gunslinger.
Revue *f.* (-, -n) review; revue.
Rezensent *m.* (-en, -en) reviewer, critic.
rezensieren *v.t.* to review.
Rezension *f.* (-, -en) review.
Rezept *n.* (-es, -e) prescription; recipe.
rezeptfrei *a.* obtainable without a prescription.
Rezeption *f.* i(-, -en) reception.
rezeptpflichtig *a.* obtainable only on prescription.
Rezession *f.* (-, -en) recession.
Rezitativ *n.* (-s, -e) recitative.
rezitieren *v.t.* to recite.
R-Gespräch *n.* collect call.
Rhabarber *m.* (-s, 0) rhubarb.
Rhapsodie *f.* (-, -n) rhapsody.
Rhein *m.* (-s) Rhine.
rheinisch *a.* Rhenish.
Rheinland-Pfalz *n.* Rhineland-Palatinate.
Rhesusfaktor *m.* rhesus factor, Rh factor.
Rhetorik *f.* (-, 0) rhetoric.
rhetorisch *a.* rhetorical.
Rheuma *n.* (-s, 0) (*fam.*) rheumatism.
rheumatisch *a.* rheumatic.
Rheumatismus *m.* (-, 0) rheumatism.
Rhinozeros *n.* (-ses, -se) rhinoceros.
rhombisch *a.* rhombic.
rhythmisch *a.* rhythmical.
Rhythmus *m.* (-, -men) rhythm.
richten *v.t.* to direct; to judge; *sich ~ nach,* to be determined by; *eine Bitte an einen ~,* to make a request of one; *zu Grunde ~,* to ruin, to destroy.
Richter *m.* (-, -); **Richterin** *f.* (-, -nen) judge.
richterlich *a.* judicial.
Richterspruch *m.* sentence.
Richtfest *n.* housewarming.

Richtgeschwindigkeit *f.* recommended speed.
richtig *a. & adv.* right(ly), exact(ly); correct(ly); *die Uhr geht nicht ~,* the watch does not go right.
Richtige *m./f./n.* the right one.
Richtigkeit *f.* (-, 0) accuracy; correctness.
richtigstellen *v.t.* to rectify.
Richtlinie *f.* guideline, directive.
Richtschnur *f.* guiding principle.
Richtung *f.* (-, -en) direction.
richtungweisend *a.* trendsetting.
riechen *v.t. & i.st.* to smell; to scent; *~ nach,* to smell of.
Riegel *m.* (-s, -) bar, bolt.
Riemen *m.* (-s, -) strap, belt, thong; *(nav.)* oar.
Riese *m.* (-n, -n) giant.
Rieselfeld *n.* field irrigated with sewage.
rieseln *v.i.* to trickle; to fall slightly.
riesengross, riesenhaft, riesig *a.* gigantic.
Riesen: *~rad n.* Ferris wheel; *~schlange f.* boa constrictor; *~schritt m.* giant-stride.
Riff *n.* (-[e]s, -e) reef, ridge.
rigoros *a.* rigorous.
Rille *f.* (-, -n) small groove.
Rind *n.* (-[e]s, -er) cow, cattle; beef; bovine.
Rinde *f.* (-, -n) bark, rind; *(des Brotes)* crust.
Rinder: *~braten m.* roast-beef; *~pest, ~seuche f.* cattle-plague.
Rindfleisch *n.* beef.
Rindvieh *n.* horned cattle; *(sl.)* blockhead.
Ring *m.* (-[e]s, -e) ring; circle; link.
Ringelblume *f.* marigold.
Ringellocke *f.* ringlet.
ringeln *v.t. & refl. (sich)* to curl.
Ringelnatter *f.* grass snake.
ringen *v.t.st.* to wring, to wrest; to struggle, to wrestle; to strive (after).
Ringer *m.* (-s, -) wrestler.
ringförmig *a.* circular; ring shaped.
Ringkampf *m.* wrestling-match.
rings *adv.* around.
ringsum(her) *adv.* all around.
Rinne *f.* (-, -n) groove, channel; gutter.
rinnen *v.i.* (s, h) to run; to leak.
Rinnsal *n.* (-[e]s, -e), **Rinnsel** *n.* (-s, -) rivulet.
Rinnstein *m.* gutter(-stone), sink.
Rippe *f.* (-, -n) rib; *(arch.)* groin.
Rippen: *~fell n.* pleura; *~fellentzündung f.* pleurisy.
Risiko *n.* (-s, -s) risk.
riskant *a.* hazardous, risky.
riskieren *v.t.* to risk.
Riß *m.* (Risses, Risse) crevice, chink, cleft; rent, tear; breach, schism.
rissig *a.* cracked; chapped.
Rist *m.* (-es, -e) instep; *(Hand)* wrist; *(eines Pferdes)* withers *pl.*
Ritt *m.* (-[e]s, -) ride.
Ritter *m.* (-s, -) knight, cavalier.
Ritter: *~gut n.* estate, manor; *~gutsbesitzer m.* landed gentleman.
ritterlich *a.* chivalrous, knightly.
Ritter: *~schlag m.* knightly accolade; *~sporn m.* larkspur.
rittlings *adv.* astride, astraddle.
Rittmeister *m.* cavalry captain.
rituell *a.* ceremonial.

Ritus *m.* (-, *-u.* Riten) rite.
Ritz *m.* (-es, -e) scratch.
Ritze *f.* (-, -n) chink.
ritzen *v.t.* to scratch.
Rivale *m.* (-n, -n); **Rivalin** *f.* (-, -nen) rival.
rivalisieren *v.i.* to rival.
Rivalität *f.* (-, -en) rivalry.
Rizinusöl *n.* castor oil.
Robbe *f.* (-, -n) seal.
robben *v.i.* to crawl.
Robe *f.* (-, -n) gown.
Roboter *m.* (-s, -) robot.
Rochade *f.* castling (chess).
röcheln *v.i.* to rattle in the throat.
Rochen *m.* ray.
Rock *m.* (-[e]s, Röcke), coat; petticoat; skirt; rock (music).
rodeln *v.i.* to toboggan.
Rodel: *~bahn f.* tobogganing course; *~schlitten m.* toboggan; *(mit Steuerung)* bobsled; luge.
roden *v.t.* to root out; to clear (for cultivation).
Rodung *f.* (-, -en) clearing, cleared land.
Rogen *m.* (-s, -) roe, spawn.
Roggen *m.* (-s, 0) rye.
roh *a.* raw, crude, rude.
Roheit *f.* roughness; brutality.
Roh: *~fassung f.* rough draft; *~gewinn m.* gross profit; *~gummi m.* crude rubber; *~kost f.* raw fruit and vegetables; *~material n.* raw material; *~öl n.* crude oil.
Rohr *n.* (-[e]s, -e) reed, cane; pipe; tube; barrel.
Rohrbruch *m.* burst pipe.
Röhre *f.* (-, -n) tube, pipe; funnel; conduit; *(radio)* tube.
röhrenförmig *a.* tubular.
Röhrenleitung *f.* conduit-pipes *pl.*
Röhricht *n.* (-[e]s, -e) reed-bank.
Rohr: *~leitung f.* pipeline; *~post f.* pneumatic post; *~stuhl m.* cane-bottomed chair; *~zucker m.* cane-sugar.
Roh: *~seide f.* raw silk; *~stoff m.* raw material.
Rokoko *n.* (-(s), 0) rococo (period).
Rolladen *m.* (-s, -) roller shutters.
Rollbahn *f.* (-, -n) runway.
Rolle *f.* (-, -n) reel; roll, roller; register; *(theat. und fig.)* role; part; *Geld spielt keine ~,* money is no object.
rollen *v.t. & i.* to roll, to rumble.
Rollenbesetzung *f.* cast.
Rollenlager *n.* *(mech.)* roller-bearing.
Rollen: *~spiel n.* role-playing; *~tausch m.* reversal of roles; *~verteilung f.* casting.
Roll: *~feld n.* landing field; *~holz n.* rolling pin; *~kragen m.* turtle neck; *~schuh m.* roller-skate; *~stuhl m.* wheelchair; *~treppe f.* escalator.
Roman *m.* (-[e]s, -e) novel; romance.
Romanfigur *f.* (-, -en) character from a novel.
Romanik *f.* (-, 0) Romanesque (period).
romanisch *a.* Romanic, Romance, *(language and lit.)* Romanesque.
Romanistik *f.* Romance studies; Romance languages and literatures.
Romanschreiber *m.* novelist.
Romantik *f.* romanticism; Romanticism.
romantisch *a.* romantic.
Romanze *f.* (-, -n) romance.

Römer *m.* (-s, -); **Römerin** *f.* (-, -nen) Roman.

römisch *a.* Roman.

römisch-katholisch *a.* Roman Catholic.

römische Zahl *f.* Roman numeral.

Rommé *n.* rummy.

Röntgen: ~**bild** *n.* radiograph; ~**röhre** *f.* X-ray tube; ~**strahlen** *pl.* X-rays *pl.*

rosa *a.* pink.

Rose *f.* (-, -n) rose.

rosenfarben *a.* rose-colored, rosy.

Rosen: ~**beet** *n.* rose-bed; ~**kohl** *m.* Brussels sprouts *pl.* ~**kranz** *m.* rosary; ~**montag** *m.* Monday before Lent.

rosenrot *a.* rose-colored.

Rosenstock *m.* rose-tree.

Rosette *f.* (-, -n) rose-window; rosette.

rosig *a.* rosy, roseate.

Rosine *f.* (-, -n) raisin; (*kleine*) currant.

Rosmarin *n.* rosemary.

Ross *n.* (Rosses, Rosse) horse.

Ross: ~**haar** *n.* horsehair; ~**kastanie** *f.* horse-chestnut; ~**kur** *f.* drastic cure.

Rost *m.* (-[e]s, -e) rust; gridiron, grate.

Rostbraten *m.* roast-meat, roast-beef.

rosten *v.i.* to rust, to get rusty.

rösten *v.t.* to roast, to grill; (*Brot*) to toast.

Rostfleck *m.* rust stain.

rostfrei *a.* (*Stahl*) stainless.

rostig *a.* rusty.

rot *a.* red.

Rot *n.* (-es, 0) red color.

Rotationsmaschine *f.* rotary press.

rotbäckig *a.* red-cheeked.

rotbraun *a.* reddish-brown, ruddy; bay.

Rot: ~**buche** *f.* copper-beech; ~**dorn** *m.* pink hawthorn.

Röte *f.* (-, 0) redness; blush.

Röteln *pl.* German measles *pl.*

röten *v.t.* to redden.

rote Rühe *f.* red beet.

Rotes Kreuz *n.* Red Cross.

Rotfuchs *m.* sorrel *or* chestnut; red fox.

rotgelb *a.* orange-colored, flame-colored.

rotglühend *a.* red-hot.

Rotglut *f.* red-heat.

rothaarig . red-haired, carroty.

Rot: ~**haut** *f.* redskin; ~**hirsch** *m.* red deer.

rotieren *v.i.* to rotate; to get into a flap.

Rot: ~**käppchen** *n.* Little Red Riding Hood; ~**kehlchen** *n.* robin red-breast; ~**kohl** *n.*, ~**kraut** *n.* red cabbage.

rötlich *a.* reddish.

Rot: ~**stift** *m.* red pencil.

Rotte *f.* (-, -n) band, gang; (*mil.*) troop.

Rotwild *n.* red deer.

Rotz *m.* (-es, 0) mucus; (*vulg.*) snot; (*der Pferde*) glanders *pl.*

rotzfrech *a.* insolent, snotty.

rotzig *a.* (*fam.*) snotty.

Rotznase *f.* snotty nose.

Roulade *f.* roulade; roll.

Rouleau *n.* (-[s], -s, -*u.* -x) (roller-)blind.

Route *f.* route.

Routine *f.* experience; expertise; routine.

routiniert *a.* experienced; smart.

Rowdy *m.* (-s, -s) hooligan.

rubbeln *v.i.* (*fam.*) to rub.

Rübe *f.* (-, -n) (*weisse*) turnip; (*gelbe*) carrot; (*rote*) red beet.

Rubel *m.* (-s, -) rouble.

Rübenzucker *m.* beet sugar.

rüber *adv.* (*fam.*) over.

Rubin *m.* (-[e]s, -e) ruby.

Rubrik *f.* (-, -en) column.

rubrizieren *v.t.* to distribute in columns.

ruchbar *a.* notorious, rumoured.

ruchlos *a.* profligate, reprobate.

Ruck *m.* (-[e]s, -e) jolt, jerk, start.

ruckartig *a.* jerky; *adv.* with a jerk.

Rück: ~**anschrift** *f.* return address; ~**antwort** *f.* reply; ~**blick** *m.* retrospect.

rückblickend *a. & adv.* retrospective(ly).

rücken *v.t.* to move, to push; ~ *v.i.* (*s*) to move, to budge; *näher* ~, to draw near; *ins Feld* ~, to take the field.

Rücken *m.* (-s, -) back, ridge; (*mil.*) rear; *einem den* ~ *kehrend,* to turn one's back on one.

Rücken: ~**deckung** *f.* (*mil.*) rear cover; ~**flosse** *f.* dorsal fin; ~**lehne** *f.* back (of a chair); ~**mark** *n.* spinal marrow cord; ~**schmerz** *m.* backache; ~**schwimmen** *n.* back stroke; ~**stück** *n.* sirloin; ~**wind** *m.* following wind; ~**wirbel** *m.* vertebra.

Rück: ~**erstattung** *f.* refund; ~**fahrkarte** *f.* return ticket; ~**fahrt** *f.* return; ~**fall** *m.* relapse.

rückfällig *a.* relapsing; revertible.

Rückfracht *f.* freight back; return cargo.

Rückfrage *f.* further inquiry,

Rückführung *f.* repatriation.

Rückgabe *f.* restitution, return.

Rückgang *m.* drop, decline.

rückgängig *a.* ~ *machen,* to annul, to cancel.

Rückgrat *n.* backbone, spine; ~**los** *a.* spineless.

Rückhalt *m.* reserve; support.

rückhaltlos *a. & adv.* unreserved(ly).

Rückkauf *m.* redemption, buying back.

Rückkehr, Rückkunft *f.* (-, 0) return.

Rücklage *f.* i(-, -n) savings.

Rücklauf *m.o* (-s, -läufe) rewinding; return flow.

rückläufig *a.* decreasing; declining.

rücklings *adv.* backwards; from behind.

Rückmarsch *m.* march back; return, retreat.

Rückporto *n.* return postage.

Rückreise *f.* return journey; *auf der* ~, homeward bound.

Rückruf *m.* return call.

Rucksack *m.* backpack, rucksack.

Rückschau *f.* review.

Rückschlag *m.* set-back.

Rückschluß *m.* inference, conclusion.

Rückschreiben *n.* reply, letter.

Rückschritt *m.* step backward.

rückschrittlich *a.* reactionary.

Rückseite *f.* back, reverse.

Rücksicht *f.* (-, -en) regard, consideration, respect; *in* ~ *auf,* in consideration of, with regard to; ~ *neh-men auf,* to take notice of; to make allowance for.

rücksichtslos *a.* inconsiderate, reckless.

Rücksichtslosigkeit *f.* (-, -en) lack of consideration; recklessness.

rücksichtsvoll *a.* considerate.

Rücksitz *m.* back-seat.

Rückspiegel *m.* (s, -) rearview mirror.

Rückspiel *n.* (-s, -e) return match.
Rücksprache *f.* consultation; ~ *nehmen mit,* to confer with.
Rückstand *m.* arrears *pl.*; residue; backlog.
rückständig *a.* overdue; in arrears; backward.
Rückständigkeit *f.* backwardness.
Rückstau *m.* (-s, -s) build-up; backup.
Rückstoß *m.* recoil; repulsion.
Rückstrahler *m.* reflector.
Rücktritt *m.* withdrawal, resignation; ~**bremse** *f.* back pedal brake.
Rücktritts: ~**gesuch** *n.* (letter of) resignation; ~**recht** *n.* right to rescind.
Rückübersetzung *f.* retranslation.
Rückvergütung *f.* refund.
Rückversicherung *f.* reinsurance.
rückwärtig *a.* rear; ~*es Gebiet n.* rear area.
rückwärts *adv.* backwards; reverse; ~**gang** *m.* reverse gear.
Rückweg *m.* way back, return.
ruckweise *a. & adv.* jerky; jerkily.
rückwirkend *a.* retroactive; *mit ~er Kraft,* with retroactive effect.
Rückwirkung *f.* reaction, repercussion.
Rückzahlung *f.* repayment.
Rückzug *m.* retreat.
rüde *a.* rude, coarse.
Rudel *n.* (-s, -) pack; herd.
Ruder *n.* (-s, -) oar; rudder; (*fig.*) helm.
Ruderboot *n.* rowing boat.
Ruderer *m.* (-s, -) rower, oarsman.
rudern *v.t. & i.* to row.
rudimentär *a.* rudimentary.
Ruf *m.* (-[e]s, -e) call; shout; vocation; report; reputation; (*com.*) credit, standing; *in gutem ~e stehen,* to have a good reputation.
rufen *v.i. & t.st.* to call; to cry, to shout; *um Hilfe rufen,* to cry for help; *etwas ins Leben ~,* to start a thing; *~ lassen,* to send for, to summon.
Rüffel *m.* (-s, -) (*fam.*) tongue-lashing.
Rufmord *m.* (-s, -e) character assassination.
Rufname *m.* (-ns, -n) first name (by which one is called).
Rufnummer *f.* (-, -n) telephone number.
Rufweite *f. in ~,* within call.
Rufzeichen *n.* exclamation mark.
Rüge *f.* (-, -n) censure, blame, reprimand.
rügen *v.t.* to censure, to reprimand.
Ruhe *f.* (-, 0) silence, rest, repose; quiet, tranquility; *sich zur ~ setzen,* to retire from business (office, active life); *~ stiften,* to make peace; *~!* hush! be quiet!; *in ~ lassen,* to let alone.
ruhebedürftig *a.* in need of rest.
ruhelos *a.* restless.
ruhen *v.i.* to rest, to repose; *ein Verdacht ruht auf ihm,* he is under suspicion (of).
Ruhe: ~**pause** *f.* break; ~**stand** *m.* retirement; *im ~stand,* retired; *in den ~stand versetzen,* to retire, to put on the retired list; ~**störung** *f.* disturbance; ~**tag** *m.* day off.
ruhig *a.* quiet; calm; silent.
Ruhm *m.* (-[e]s, 0) fame, glory, renown.
rühmen *v.t.* to praise, to extol; (sich) ~ *v. refl.* to boast of, to glory (in).
rühmlich *a.* inglorious.
ruhmreich *a.* glorious; celebrated.

Ruhr *f.* (-, 0) dysentery.
Rührei *n.* scrambled *or* buttered eggs *pl.*
rühren *v.t. & i.* to stir; to beat (the drum, eggs); (sich) ~ *v. refl.* to stir, to bestir oneself; *sich nicht vom Flecke ~,* not to budge; *rührt euch!* (*mil.*) stand at ease; *rührende Worte,* touching words; *ich bin ganz gerührt,* I am deeply affected.
rührend *a.* touching.
rührig *a.* active, stirring, bustling.
rührselig *a.* sentimental.
Rührung *f.* (-, -en) emotion.
Ruin *m.* (-[e]s, 0) ruin.
Ruine *f.* (-, -n) ruins *pl.*
ruinieren *v.t.* to ruin, to spoil; (*einen*) to undo (one).
rülpsen *v.i.* to belch, to burp.
Rum *m.* (-s, -s) rum.
Rumäne *m.*; **Rumänin** *f.*; **rumänisch** *a.* Romanian.
Rumänien *n.* (-s, 0) Romania.
Rummel *m.* (-s, 0) commotion; fair.
rumoren *v.i.* to make a noise *or* row.
Rumpelkammer *f.* junk room.
Rumpf *m.* (-[e]s, Rümpfe) trunk; torso; (*Schiffs~*) hull; (*Flugzeug*) fuselage.
rümpfen *v.t. die Nase ~,* to turn up one's nose.
rund *a.* round; plain; ~**e Summe** *f.* round sum.
Rund: ~**blick** *m.* panorama; ~**brief** *m.* circular (letter).
Rundbogen *m.* Roman arch.
Runde *f.* (-, -n) round.
Rund: ~**erlaß** *m.* circular (notice); ~**fahrt** *f.* tour.
Rundfunk *m.* broadcasting; ~**anstalt** *f.* radio corporation; ~**gebühren** *pl.* radio license fees; ~**gerät** *n.* radio set; ~**sender** *m.* radio station; ~**sendung** *f.* radio program; ~**sprecher** *m.*, ~**sprecherin** *f.* radio announcer; ~**übertragung** *f.* radio broadcast.
Rundgang *m.* round.
rundheraus *adv.* straight out; bluntly.
rundherum *adv.* all around.
rundlich *a.* roundish; chubby.
Rund: ~**reise** *f.* (circular) tour; ~**reisekarte** *n.* roundtrip ticket; ~**schreiben** *n.* circular.
Rundung *f.* curve; bulge.
rundweg *adv.* flatly, plainly.
Rundweg *m.* circular path/walk.
Rune *f.* (-, -n) Rune, Runic character.
Runkelrübe *f.* red beet.
runter *adv.* (*fam.*) off; down.
Runzel *f.* (-, -n) wrinkle; (*um die Augen*) crow's feet *pl.*
runz(e)lig *a.* wrinkled.
runzeln *v.t.* to wrinkle; *die Stern ~,* to knit one's brows.
Rüpel *m.* (-s, -) lout, boor.
Rüpelei *f.* (-, -en) insolence.
rüpelhaft *a.* loutish; unmannerly.
rupfen *v.t.* to pluck; (*fig.*) to fleece.
Rupie *f.* (-, -n) rupee.
ruppig *a.* gruff; shabby; rude.
Ruß *m.* (-es, 0) soot.
Russe *m.* (-n, -n); **Russin** *f.* (-, -nen); **russisch** *a.* Russian.
Rüssel *m.* (-s, -) snout, trunk, proboscis.
rußen *v.i.* to smoke; to blacken.

rußig *a.* sooty.
Rußland *n.* (-s, 0) Russia.
rüsten *v.t.* to arm; to prepare; ~ *v.i.* to prepare for war.
rüstig *a.* vigorous, robust, strong.
rustikal *a.* country-style; rustic.
Rüstung *f.* (-, -en) armament; armour.
Rüstungs: ~**ausgaben** *pl.* defense expenditure; ~**begrenzung** *f.* arms limitation; ~**industrie** *f.* defense industry; ~**kontrolle** *f.* arms control;

~**stopp** *m.* arms freeze; ~**wettlauf** *m.* arms race.
Rüstzeug *n.* equipment.
Rute *f.* (-, -n) rod, wand, twig, switch; (*Mass*) perch (=12 feet).
Rutsch *m.* (-es, -e) slide, landslip.
Rutschbahn *f.* slide.
Rutsche *f.* slide; chute
rutschen *v.i.* (*s*) to slide; to skid.
rutschig *a.* slippery.
rutschsicher *a.* nonslip; nonskid.
rütteln *v.t.* to shake, to jolt; to vibrate.

S

S, s *n.* the letter S or s.
Saal *m.* (-[e]s, Säle) hall, (large) room.
Saarland *n.* (-s, 0) Saarland.
Saat *f.* (-, -en) seed; standing corn; sowing.
Saatkorn *n.* seed-corn.
Sabbat *m.* (-[e]s, -e) Sabbath.
sabbern *v.i.* to slobber; to dribble.
Säbel *m.* (-s, -) sabre, sword.
Säbelrasseln *n.* sabre-rattling.
Sabotage *f.* (-, -n) sabotage.
sabotieren *v.t.* to sabotage.
Sacharin *n.* (-s, 0) saccharine.
Sachbeschädigung *f.* damage to property.
Sachbuch *n.* nonfiction book.
Sache *f.* (-, -n) thing, matter; affair, business; cause; (*Prozeß*) case; *es ist seine ~*, it is up to him; *das gehört nicht zur ~*, that is beside the question; *bei der ~ bleiben*, to stick to the point; *nicht bei der ~*, inattentive, absent-minded; *gemeinschaftliche ~ mit einem machen*, to make common cause with; ~**nrecht** *n.* law of property.
sachgemäß *a.* appropriate; relevant.
sachgerecht *a.* proper, correct.
Sach: ~**kenner** *m.*, ~**kennerin** *f.* expert; ~**kenntnis** *f.* knowledge of a subject, experience.
sachkundig *a.* expert.
Sachleistung *f.* payment in kind.
Sachlage *f.* (-, 0) state of affairs.
sachlich *a.* real, to the point; material (not formal); impartial, objective.
sächlich *a.* (*gram.*) neuter.
Sachlichkeit *f.* (-, 0) objectivity; functionalism.
Sachregister *n.* subject-index.
Sachschaden *m.* (-s, -schäden) material damage.
Sachse *m.*; **Sächsin** *f.*; **sächsisch** *a.* Saxon.
Sachspende *f.* (-, -n) donation in kind.
sacht *a. & adv.* soft(ly), gentle(ly).
Sachverhalt *m.* (-[e]s, 0) facts *or* bearings (of a case) *pl.*
sachverständig *a.* expert.
Sachverständige *m./f.* (-n, -n) expert.
Sachwalter *m.* (-s, -) advocate.
Sachwert *m.* real value.
Sachzwang *m.* (-s, -zwänge) (factual *or* material) constraints.
Sack *m.* (-[e]s, Säcke) bag, sack; *mit ~ und Pack*, bag and baggage.
Säckel *m.* (-s, -) (*fam. fig.*) purse.
sacken *v.i.* to sink to slump; to plummet.
Sackgasse *f.* dead end.
Sackhüpfen *n.* sack race.

Sadismus *m.* (-, 0) sadism.
Sadist *m.*; **Sadistin** *f.* sadist.
sadistisch *a.* sadistic.
Sä[e]: ~**mann** *m.* sower; ~**maschine** *f.* sowing-machine.
säen *v.t.* to sow.
Safran *m.* (-s, 0) saffron.
safrangelb *a.* saffron-colored.
Saft *m.* (-[e]s, Säfte) juice; (*der Bäume*) sap.
saftig *a.* juicy, sappy, succulent.
saftlos *a.* sapless; (*fig.*) insipid, stale, dry.
Saftpresse *f.* squeezer; juice extractor.
Sage *f.* (-, -n) myth; saga; tale, legend; *die ~ geht*, it is rumoured.
Säge *f.* (-, -n) saw.
Säge: ~**blatt** *n.* saw blade; ~**bock** *m.* sawhorse; ~**mehl** *n.* sawdust; ~**mühle** *f.* saw-mill.
sagen *v.t.* to say, to tell; ~ *lassen*, to send word; *er läßt sich nichts ~*, he will not listen to reason; *das hat nichts zu ~*, that does not matter; *das will nicht viel ~*, there is not much in that; *so zu ~*, as it were; *Dank ~*, to return thanks.
sägen *v.i.u.t.* to saw.
sagenhaft *a.* fabulous, legendary.
Sägespäne *m.pl.* wood shavings.
Sägewerk *n.* sawmill.
Sahne *f.* (-, 0) cream.
Saison *f.* (-, -s) season.
Saisonarbeit *f.* (-, -en) seasonal work.
saisonbedingt *a.* seasonal.
Saite *f.* (-, -n) string, chord.
Saiteninstrument *n.* stringed instrument.
Saitenspiel *n.* string-music; lyre.
Sakko *m.* (-s, -s) jacket.
Sakrament *n.* (-[e]s, -e) sacrament.
Sakristan *m.* (-[e]s, -e) sacristan, sexton.
Sakristei *f.o* (-, -en) vestry, sacristy.
säkularisieren *v.t.* to secularize.
Salamander *m.* (-s, -) salamander.
Salat *m.* (-[e]s, -e) salad; lettuce.
Salatsoße *f.* salad dressing.
salbadern *v.i.* to talk nonsense.
Salbe *f.* (-, -n) ointment.
Salbei *m.* (-s, -e) *f.* (-, -en) sage.
salben *v.t.* to anoint.
Salböl *n.* consecrated oil.
Salbung *f.* (-, -en) unction.
salbungsvoll *a.* unctuous.
Saldo *m.* (-[e]s, -s *u.* -di) balance; *den ~ ziehen*, to strike a balance; *per ~ quittieren*, to receipt in full.
Saldobetrag *m.* (amount of) balance.

Saline f. (-, -n) salt-works pl.
Salizylsäure f. salicylic acid.
Salm m. (-[e]s, -e) salmon.
Salmiak m. (-s, 0) ammonium chloride.
Salmiakgeist m. ammonia.
Salon m. (-s, -s) drawing-room; parlor.
salonfähig a. presentable; respectable.
salopp a. casual.
Salpeter m. (-s, 0) saltpeter.
salpetrig a. nitrous; ~e Säure, nitric acid.
Salut m. (-[e]s, -e) salute.
Salve f. (-, -n) volley; salvo.
Salz n. (-es, -e) (also fig.) salt.
salzarm a. low in salt.
Salzbrühe f. pickle, brine.
salzen v.t. to salt; **gesalzen** a. (fig.) biting, smart.
Salz: ~**faß** n. saltshaker; ~**kartoffeln** pl. boiled potatoes.
salzig a. salt(y), briny.
salzlos a. saltfree.
Salzsäure f. hydrochloric acid.
Salzstreuer m. salt shaker.
Samen, m. (-ns, -n) seed; sperm, semen.
Samen: ~**bank** f. sperm bank; ~**erguß** m. ejaculation; ~**faden** m. spermatozoon; ~**leiter** m. vas deferens; ~**spender** m. (sperm) donor; ~**strang** m. spermatic cord.
Sämerei f. (-, -en) seeds (of plants) pl.
Sammel: ~**band** m. anthology; ~**becken** n. reservoir; (fig.) gathering place; ~**bestellung** f. joint order; ~**büchse** f. collecting-box.
sammeln v.t. to gather, to collect; (sich) ~ v.refl. to assemble; (fig.) to collect oneself.
Sammel: ~**platz** m. meeting-place; ~**punkt** m. rallying-point.
Sammelsurium n. (-[s], -surien) omnium-gatherum.
Sammet, Samt m. (-[e]s, -e) velvet.
Sammler m. (-s, -); **Sammlerin** f. (-, -nen) collector, gatherer.
Sammlung f. (-, -en) collection; composure.
Samstag m. Saturday.
samstags adv. on Saturdays.
samt pr. & adv. together with; ~ und sonders, each and all.
Samt m. (-s, -e) velvet; velveteen.
samtartig a. velvety.
samtig a. velvety.
sämtlich a. all, entire, complete.
Sand m. (-[e]s, 0) sand; einem ~ in die Augen streuen, to throw dust in a person's eyes.
Sandale f. (-, -n) sandal.
sandalette f. (-, -n) high-heeled sandals.
Sand: ~**bank** f. sand-bank, sands pl.; ~**burg** f. sandcastle.
Sanddorn m. buckthorn.
sandig a. sandy.
Sand: ~**kasten** m. sandbox; ~**männchen** n. sandman; ~**papier** n. sandpaper; ~**sack** m. sandbag; ~**stein** m. sandstone; ~**uhr** f. hourglass.
sanft a. soft, gentle, mild; meek.
Sänfte f. (-, -n) sedan-chair, litter.
Sanftmut f. (-,0) meekness.
sanftmütig a. gentle, mild.
Sang m. (-[e]s, Sänge) song; ohne ~ und Klang, quietly.

Sänger m. (-s, -) singer.
Sängerin f. (-, -nen) singer.
Sanguiniker m. (-s, -) sanguine person.
sanguinisch a. sanguine.
sanieren v.t. to redevelop; to restore, to reorganize.
Sanitäter m. first-aid man; ambulance man.
Sanitäts: ~**behörde** f. Public Health Department; ~**dienst** m. medical service; ~**wache** f. ambulance station.
Sanktion f. (-, -en) sanction.
sanktionieren v.t. to sanction.
Saphir m. (-s, -e) sapphire.
Sardelle f. (-, -n) anchovy.
Sardine f. (-, -n) sardine.
Sarg n. (-[e]s, Särge) coffin.
Sarkasmus m. (-, 0) sarcasm.
sarkastisch a. sarcastic.
Sarkophag m. (-s, -e) sarcophagus.
Satan m. (-s, -) Satan.
satanisch a. satanic.
Satellit m. (-en, -en) satellite.
Satelliten: ~**bild** n., ~**foto** n. satellite picture; ~**übertragung** f. (TV) satellite transmission.
Satin m. (-s, -s) satin; sateen.
Satire f. (-, -n) satire.
Satiriker m. (-s, -); **Satirikerin** f. (-, -nen) satirist.
satt a. satisfied, full; etwas ~ haben, to be sick of a thing; es ~ bekommen, to get sick of a thing.
Sattel m. (-s, Sättel) saddle.
Satteldecke f. saddle-cloth.
sattelfest a. (fig.) experienced.
satteln v.t. to saddle.
sättigen v.t. to satiate, to fill; (chem.) to saturate.
sättigend a. filling.
Sättigung f. (-, -en) (chem.) saturation.
Sattler m. (-s, -) saddler.
sattsam adv. sufficiently, enough.
Satz m. (-es, Sätze) leap, jump; (Boden~) sediment, dregs pl.; (gram.) sentence, clause; (mus.) movement; (log.) proposition; (Druck) composition; (gleichartige Dinge) set; (Verhältnis) rate.
Satz: ~**aussage** f. predicate; ~**ergänzung** f. complement; ~**gefüge** n. complex sentence; ~**gegenstand** m. subject; ~**glied** n. component part (of a sentence); ~**lehre** f. syntax; ~**teil** m. part of a sentence.
Satzung f. (-, -en) statute, regulation.
satzungsgemäß a. statutory.
Satzzeichen n. (-s, -) punctuation mark.
Sau f. (-, -en) sow, hog; (fig. vulg.) slut.
sauber a. clean, neat; fine, pretty.
sauberhalten v.t.st. to keep clean.
Sauberkeit f. (-, 0) cleanliness; neatness.
säuberlich a. & adv. neatly; properly.
saubermachen v.t.u.i. to clean.
säubern v.t. to clean, to cleanse, to purge, (mil.) to mop up.
Säuberung f. (-, -en) cleaning; (pol.) purge.
Saubohne f. broad bean.
Sauce f. (-, -n) gravy; sauce.
Sauciere f. (-, -n) gravy boat.
Saudi m., **Saudiaraber** m.; **Saudiaraberin** f. Saudi.
Saudi-Arabien n. (-s, 0) Saudi Arabia.
Saudiarabisch a. Saudi Arabian.
saudumm a. (fam.) damned stupid.

sauer *a.* sour; acid; morose; ~ *werden,* to go sour;
saurer Regen *m.* acid rain.
Sauerampfer *m.* sorrel.
Sauerei *f.* (-, -en) mess, filth; obscenity, scandal.
Sauerkirsche *f.* (-,-n) sour cherry.
Sauerkraut *n.* pickled cabbage, sauerkraut.
säuerlich *a.* sour; acidulous.
Sauermilch *f.* curdled milk.
Sauer: ~**stoff** *m.* oxygen; ~**teig** *m.* sour dough;
leaven.
Sauerstoffgerät *n.* oxygen apparatus.
saufen *v.t. & i.st.* to drink to excess.
Säufer *m.* (-s, -); **Säuferin** *f.* (-, -nen) alcoholic;
boozer.
Sauferei *f.* (-, -en) drinking-bout, boozing.
Säuferwahnsinn *m.* delirium tremens.
Saufgelage *n.* drinking-bout.
saugen *v.t. i.st.* to suck; to vacuum.
säugen *v.t.* to suckle, to nurse.
Sauger *m.* i(-s, -) sucker; teat; siphon.
Säuger *m.,* **Säugetier** *n.* mammal.
saugfähig *a.* absorbent.
Saugflasche *f.* feeding-bottle.
Säugling *m.* (-s, -e) baby, infant.
Säuglings: ~**alter** *n.* infancy; ~**nahrung** *f.* baby
food; ~**pflege** *f.* baby care; ~**schwester** *f.* baby
nurse; ~**sterblichkeit** *f.* infant mortality.
Saugnapf *m.* (-s, -näpfe) sucker.
saukalt *a.* bloody cold.
Säule *f.* (-, -n) pillar, column; (galvanic) pile.
Säulen: ~**gang** *m.* colonnade; ~**halle** *f.* portico;
~**schaft** *m.* shaft of a column.
Saum *m.* (-[e]s, Säume) border, edge; seam, hem.
Saumagen *m.* (*cul.*) stuffed pig's stomach.
saumäßig *a.* lousy; damned.
säumen *v.t.* to hem; ~ *v.i.* to delay, to tarry.
säumig *a.* tardy, late.
saumselig *a.* tardy, dilatory; negligent.
Säure *f.* (-, -n) (*chem.*) acid; tartness; sourness.
säurearm *a.* low in acid.
säurebeständig *a.* acid-proof.
Sauregurkenzeit *f.* silly season.
Saurier *m.* (-s, -) saurian.
Saus *m.* (-ses, 0) ~ *und Braus,* riot and revelry.
säuseln *v.i.* to rustle; to whisper; to murmur.
sausen *v.i.* to whistle; to whiz; to buzz; to rush; to
roar.
Saustall *m.* pigsty (*fig.*) mess.
Sauwetter *n.* (*fam.*) lousy weather.
sauwohl *a.* sich ~ *fühlen* to feel great.
Savanne *f.* (-, -n) savannah.
Saxophon *n.* (-s, -e) saxophone.
S-Bahn *f.* city and suburban railroad.
Schabe *f.* (-, -n) cockroach.
Schabefleisch *n.* ground meat.
schaben *v.t.* to scrape; to rub.
Schabernack *m.* (-[e]s, -e) hoax; practical joke.
schäbig *a.* shabby; mean.
Schäbigkeit *f.* shabbiness; paltriness.
Schablone *f.* (-, -n) pattern; template; cliché.
Schach *n.* (-s, 0) chess; check!; ~ *bieten,* to give
check; *einem im* ~ *halten,* to keep one in check.
Schacher *m.* (-s, 0) mean or unfair traffic, petty
trade.
schachern *v.t.* to bargain; to haggle.
Schach: ~**brett** *n.* chessboard; ~**feld** *n.* square;

~**figur** *f.* chessman.
schachmatt *a.* checkmate.
Schacht *m.* (-[e]s, Schächte) pit, shaft.
Schachtel *f.* (-, -n) box; bandbox; (*fig. pej.*) *alte* ~,
old bag.
schächten *v.t.* to slaughter in the Jewish fashion.
Schachzug *m.* move.
schade *es ist* ~, it is a pity.
Schädel *m.* (-s, -) skull.
Schädelbruch *m.* fracture of the skull.
Schaden *m.* (-s, Schäden) damage, hurt; ~*n leiden,*
nehmen, zu ~*n kommen,* to come to grief, to be hurt.
schaden *v.i.* to hurt, to injure, to damage; *es schadet*
nichts, it does not matter.
Schaden: ~**ersatz** *m.* indemnification; damages *pl.,*
compensation; ~**freude** *f.* malicious joy.
schadhaft *a.* damaged, defective, faulty.
schädigen *v.t.* to damage, to injure.
schädlich *a.* hurtful, detrimental.
Schädlichkeit *f.* harmfulness.
Schädling *m.* (-s, -e) (insect) pest; noxious
creature.
Schädlings: ~**bekämpfung** *f.* pest control;
~**bekämpfungsmittel** *n.* pesticide.
schädlos *a.* sich ~ *halten,* to recover one's losses.
Schadstoff *m.* harmful substance; pollutant.
schadstoffarm *a.* low in harmful substances.
Schaf *n.* (-[e]s, -e) sheep; (*fig.*) simpleton;
schwarzes ~ black sheep; (*fig.*) ninny.
Schafbock *m.* ram.
Schäfchen *n.* (-s, -) lamb.
Schäfer *m.* (-s, -) shepherd.
Schäferhund *m.* German shepherd.
Schäferin *f.* shepherdess.
Schäferstündchen *n.* lovers' tryst.
Schaffell *n.* sheepskin.
schaffen *v.t.st.* to create; ~ *v.t.* to afford, to procure;
to convey; ~ *v.i.* to be active, to work, to do; *aus*
dem Wege ~, to remove; *sich vom Halse* ~, to rid
oneself of; *zu* ~ *machen,* to give trouble; *sich zu* ~
machen, to busy oneself.
Schaffen *n.* (creative) work; ~**skraft** *f.* creative
power.
Schaffner *m.* (-s, -); **Schaffnerin** *f.* (-, -nen) (*rail.*)
conductor.
Schaffleisch *n.* mutton.
Schaffung *f.* creation.
Schaf: ~**garbe** *f.* yarrow; ~**herde** *f.* flock of sheep;
~**hirt** *m.* shepherd.
Schafott *n.* (-[e]s, -e) scaffold.
Schafschur *f.* sheep-shearing.
Schaf(s)kopf *m.* blockhead.
Schaft *m.* (-[e]s, Schäfte) shaft; leg (of a boot);
(*Baum*) trunk; (*Blumen*) stalk; (*tech.*) shank.
Schaftstiefel *m.* high boot.
Schaf: ~**weide** *f.* sheep pasture; ~**zucht** *f.* sheep-
farming.
Schakal *m.* (-s, -e) jackal.
schäkern *v.i.* to fool about; to flirt.
schal *a.* stale, flat, inspid.
Schal *m.* (-s, -s) scarf.
Schale *f.* (-, -n) shell; peel; husk; pod; dish; bowl;
saucer; (*Wage*) scale; (*fig.*) outside.
schälen *v.t.o* to shell; to peel, to pare; to husk; to
bark; (sich) ~ *v.refl.* to peel off, to come off.
Schalk *m.* (-[e]s, -e) rogue; prankster.

schalkhaft *a.* waggish, roguish.
Schall *m.* (-[e]s, -e) sound.
schalldämpfend *a.* sound-deadening.
Schalldämpfer *m.* sound absorber; silencer.
Schalldämpfung *f.* sound insulation.
schalldicht *a.* sound-proof.
schallen *v.i.* to sound, to ring.
Schall: ~**geschwindigkeit** *f.* sonic speed; ~**mauer** *f.* sound/sonic barrier.
Schallplatte *f.* record.
Schallwelle *f.* sound-wave.
Schalotte *f.* shallot.
Schaltbrett *n.* instrument panel.
schalten *v.i.* to act, to command; to switch; ~ *und walten,* to manage.
Schalter *m.* (-s, -) ticket window; counter; (*elek.*) switch.
Schaltgetriebe *n.* gear box.
Schalthebel *m.* control *or* gear lever.
Schaltjahr *m.* leap year.
Schalt: ~**kasten** *m.* switch box; ~**knopf** *m.* button; ~**kreis** *m.* circuit; ~**plan** *m.* wiring diagram; ~**pult** *n.* control desk.
Schalttag *m.* intercalary day.
Schaltung *f.* (-, -en) (*elek.*) connection; manual gear change; circuit.
Schaluppe *f.* (-, -n) sloop; yawl.
Scham *f.* (-, 0) shame; genitals *pl.*
schämen (sich) *v.refl.* to be ashamed.
Schamgefühl *n.* sense of shame.
Schamhaare *pl.* pubic hair.
schamhaft *a.* bashful, shamefaced.
Schamlippen *pl.* labia.
schamlos *a.* shameless; indecent.
Schamlosigkeit *f.* shamelessness.
Schamotte *f.* (-, -) fire-clay.
schamponieren *v.t.* to shampoo.
schamrot *a.* red with shame.
Scham: ~**röte** *f.* blush; ~**teile** *m.pl.* genitals *pl.*
schandbar *a.* shameful; indecent.
Schande *f.* (-, 0) shame; disgrace; *zu* ~*n machen,* to destroy, to ruin.
schänden *v.t.* to violate, to rape, to defile.
Schandfleck, *m.* stain, blemish.
schändlich . disgraceful, shameful.
Schändlichkeit *f.* shamefulness; shameful action.
Schandtat *f.* disgraceful deed.
Schankwirtschaft *f.* public bar.
Schanze *f.* (-, -n) ski-jump.
Schar *f.* (-, -en) crowd; horde.
Scharade *f.* (-, -n) charade.
scharen (sich) *v.refl.* to assemble, to collect, to flock together, to rally.
scharenweise *adv.* in swarms/hordes.
scharf *a.* sharp, keen; (*spitz*) acute; hot, acrid, pungent.
Scharfblick *m.* (-[e]s, 0) perspicacity.
Schärfe *f.* (-, -n) sharpness; acuteness; pungency; acrimony; severity; edge.
Scharfeinstellung *f.* focusing.
schärfen *v.t.* to sharpen; *Minen~,* to fuse mines.
Schärfentiefe *f.* depth of focus.
Scharf: ~**macher** *m.* firebrand; ~**richter** *m.* execution; ~**schütze** *m.* marksman.
scharfsichtig *a.* sharp-sighted; perspicacious.
Scharfsinn *m.* (-[e]s, 0) acumen, acuteness.

scharfsinnig *a.* sagacious, shrewd.
scharfzüngig *a.* sharp tongued.
Scharlach *m.* (-[e]s, 0) scarlet.
Scharlachfieber, *n.* scarlet-fever.
Scharlatan *m.* (-s, -e) charlatan, quack.
Scharmützel *n.* (-s, -) skirmish.
Scharnier *n.* (-[e]s, -e) hinge, joint.
Schärpe *f.* (-, -n) sash, sling.
scharren *v.t. & i.* to scrape, to scratch.
Scharte *f.* (-, -n) nick, notch.
schartig *a.* jagged.
Schatten *m.* (-s, -) shade, shadow; *in* ~ *stellen,* (*fig.*) to throw into the shade.
Schatten: ~**bild** *n.* shade, phantom; ~**morelle** *f.* morello cherry; ~**riß** *m.* silhouette; ~**seite** *f.* shady side; (*fig.*) drawback.
schattieren *v.t.* to shade.
Schattierung *f.* (-, -en) shade, nuance.
schattig *a.* shady, shadowy.
Schatulle *f.* (-, -n) casket.
Schatz *m.* (-es, Schätze) treasure; (*fig.*) darling, love.
Schatzamt *n.* Treasury.
Schatzanweisung *f.* (-, -en) treasury bond.
schätzbar *a.* valuable, estimable.
schätzen *v.t.* to value, to esteem; to estimate; *geschätzt auf,* valued at.
schätzenlernen *v.t.* to come to appreciate.
schätzenswert *a.* estimable.
Schätzer *m.* (-s, -) appraiser, valuer.
Schatz: ~**gräber,** *m.* treasure-hunter; ~**kammer** *f.* treasury; ~**meister** *m.,* ~**meisterin** *f.* treasurer; ~**suche** *f.* treasure hunt.
Schätzung *f.* (-, -en) valuation; estimate.
Schau *f.* (-, 0) view; show; *zur* ~ *stellen,* to exhibit, to display; *zur* ~ *tragen,* to parade, to sport; to boast of.
Schau: ~**bild** *n.* chart; ~**bude** *f.* show-booth.
Schauder *m.* (-s, -) shudder; horror.
schauderhaft, schaudervoll *a.* horrible, dreadful, shocking.
schaudern *v.i.* to shudder, to shiver.
schauen *v.t. & i.* to look, to view, to gaze.
Schauer *m.* (-s, -) shivering fit; horror, awe; (*Regen~*) shower.
schauerlich *a.* awful, horrifying.
Schaufel *f.* (-, -n) hovel; ladle; paddle; dustpan.
schaufeln *v.t.* to shovel, to dig.
Schaufelrad *n.* paddle-wheel.
Schaufenster *n.* shop-window; ~**dekorateur** *m.* window-dresser.
Schaukasten *m.* showcase.
Schaukel *f.* (-, -n) swing.
schaukeln *v.t. & i.* to swing, to rock.
Schaukelpferd *n.* rocking-horse.
Schankelstuhl *m.* rocking chair.
schaulustig *a.* curious.
Schaulustige *m./f.* (-n -n) curious onlooker.
Schaum *m.* (-[e]s, Schäume) foam, froth.
Schaumbad *n.* bubble bath.
schäumen *v.i.* to foam, to froth.
Schaumgummi *n.* foam rubber.
schaumig *a.* foamy, foaming.
Schaumstoff *m.* (plastic) foam.
Schaumwein *m.* sparkling wine.
Schauplatz *m.* scene; (*fig.*) theater.

schaurig *a.* awful, horrid.

Schau: ~**spiel** *n.* spectacle, sight; play, drama; ~**spieldirektor** *m.* manager of a theater; ~**spieler** *m*; actor, player; ~**spielerei** *f.* hypocrisy; ~**spielerin** *f.* actress.

schauspielerisch *a.* stagey, theatrical.

Schau: ~**spielhaus** *n.* theater; ~**spielkunst** *f.* dramatic art.

Scheck *m.* check; *einen* ~ *sperren*, to stop payment on a check.

Scheck: ~**buch** *n.*, ~**heft** *n.* checkbook; ~**karte** *f.* check card.

scheckig *a.* piebald, dapple.

scheel *a.* squint-eyed; envious; ~ *adv.* askance.

Scheffel *m.* (-s, -) bushel.

scheffeln *v.t.* to rake in; to pile up.

scheffelweise *a. & adv.* by the bushel.

Scheibe *f.* (-, -n) disk, puck; target; (*Glas*~) pane; (*Schnitte*) cut, slice.

Scheibenschießen *n.* target-practice.

Scheibenwischer *m.* (*mot.*) windshield wiper.

Scheich *m.* (-s, -s) sheikh.

Scheide *f.* (-, -n) sheath; (*anat.*) vagina.

scheiden *v.t.st.* to divide; to separate; to divorce; ~ *v.i.* to depart, to part, to leave.

Scheidewand *f.* partition; (*fig.*) barrier.

Scheidung *f.* (-, -en) separation; divorce.

Scheidungsklage *f.* divorce-suit.

Schein *m.* (-[e]s, -e) shine; luster, splendor; appearance; pretext; certificate, bill; *zum* ~, seemingly.

Scheinangriff *m.* (*mil.*) feint attack.

scheinbar *a.* apparent, ostensible.

Scheinbeweis *m.* sophism.

Scheinehe *f.* sham marriage.

scheinen *v.t.st.* to shine; to see, to appear.

Scheingeschäft *n.* fictitious transaction.

scheinheilig *a.* hypocritical; sanctimonious.

Schein: ~**heiligkeit** *f.* hypocrisy; ~**tod**, *m.* apparent death, catalepsy; ~**werfer** *m.* searchlight; *mit* ~*werfer beleuchten*, to floodlight; ~**werferlicht** *n.* spotlight; (*mot.*) headlights.

Scheiß (*vulg.*) . . . fucking.

Scheiße *f.* (-, 0) (*vulg.*) shit; crap.

scheißen *v.i.* (*vulg.*) to shit.

Scheit *n.* (-[e]s, -e) piece of wood, billet.

Scheitel *m.* (-s, -) (*Haar*~) parting.

Scheiterhaufen *m.* funeral pyre, stake.

scheitern *v.i.* to be wrecked; (*fig.*) to fail.

Schellack *m.* (-[e]s -e) shellac.

Schelle *f.* (-, -n) (small) bell.

schellen *v.i.* to ring the bell.

Schellfisch *m.* haddock.

Schelm *m.* (-[e]s, -e) rogue, rascal.

schelmisch *a.* roguish.

Schelte *f.* (-, -n) scolding.

schelten *v.t. & i.st.* to scold, to moan about.

Schema *n.* (-s, -s *u.* -mata) pattern; diagram.

schematisch *a.* mechanical; *adv.* in diagram form.

Schemel *m.*, **Schemen** *m.* (-s, -) stool; foot-stool.

Schenke *f.* (-, -n) inn, public-house.

Schenkel *m.* (-s, -) thigh, shank; leg; (*des Winkels*) side.

schenken *v.t.* to make a present of, to give, to grant; *die Strafe* ~, to remit a punishment.

Schenker *m.* (-s, -) donor.

Schenkung *f.* (-, -en) donation.

Schenkungsurkunde *f.* deed of gift.

Scherbe *f.* (-, -n), **Scherben** *m.* (-s, -) broken piece; fragment.

Schere *f.* (-, -n) scissors; (*grosse*) pair of shears *pl.*; (*Hummer*~) claw.

scheren *v.t.st.* to shear, to clip; to fleece, to cheat; *sich um etwas* ~, to trouble oneself about a thing; *sich zum Teufel* ~, to go to the devil; *das schert mich nichts*, that doesn't worry me.

Scherenschleifer *m.* knife-grinder.

Schererei *f.* (-, -en) trouble.

Scherflein *n.* (-s, -) mite.

Scherz *m.* (-es, -) joke; ~ *beiseite*, joking apart.

scherzen *v.i.* to jest, to joke; ~ *über*, to make fun of.

scherzhaft *a.* jocular; playful, funny.

scherzweise *adv.* jestingly, in fun.

scheu *a.* shy; timid, bashful.

Scheu *f.* (-, 0) shyness; aversion; awe.

scheuchen *v.t.* to frighten away; to scare.

scheuen *v.t.* to shun, to avoid; ~ *v.i.* to shy (at); (sich) ~ *v.refl.* to be shy; to fight shy (of).

Scheuer *f.* (-, -n) shed, barn.

scheuern *v.t.* to scour; to scrub.

Scheuklappe *f.*, **Scheuleder** *n.* blinker.

Scheune *f.* (-, -n) barn, shed.

Scheusal *n.* (-[e]s, -e) monster.

scheußlich *a.* frightful, hideous.

Schicht *f.* (-, -en) layer, bed, stratum; (*Gesellschafts*~) class, rank; shift, task.

Schichtarbeiter *m.* shift worker.

schichten *v.t.* to dispose in layers, to pile up; to arrange.

Schichtwechsel *m.* change of shifts.

schichtweise *a. & adv.* in layers.

Schick *m.* (-[e]s, 0) style.

schick *a.* stylish, smart.

schicken *v.t.* to send, to dispatch; (sich) ~ *v.refl.* to be suitable, to be proper.

Schickeria *f.* the chic set; the trendies.

Schickimicki *m.* (*fam.*) trendy type.

schicklich *a.* suitable, decent, proper.

Schicksal *n.* (-[e]s, -e) fate; destiny.

schicksalhaft *a.* fateful.

Schicksalsfrage *f.* vital question.

Schicksalsgenoße *m.*; **Schicksalsgenoßin** *f.* companion in distress.

Schicksalsschlag *m.* (bad) blow.

Schiebedach *n.* sunroof.

Schiebefenster *n.* sash window.

schieben *v.t.st.* to shove, to push; (*fig.*) to act corruptly; *Kegel* ~, to bowl; *einem etwas in die Schuhe* ~, to lay a fault at someone's door.

Schieber *m.* (-s, -) bolt, slide; slide-valve; (*am Ofen*) damper, register; profiteer.

Schiebe: ~**tür** *f.* sliding door; ~**ventil** *n.* slide-valve.

Schiebung *f.* (-, -en) shady deal; rigging; fixing.

Schieds: ~**gericht** *n.* court of arbitration; jury; ~**richter** *m.* arbitrator, umpire, referee; ~**spruch** *m.* award; arbitration.

schief *a.* oblique, wry, crooked; ~ *adv.* askew, awry; ~*gehen* (*fig.*) to go wrong; ~*e Ebene*, inclined plane.

Schiefer *m.* (-s, -) slate; splinter.

Schiefer: ~**dach** n. slated roof; ~**decker** m. slater; ~**platte** f. slab of slate; ~**tafel** f. (school) slate.

schielen v.i. to squint; to leer (at).

schielend a. squint-eyed, squinting.

Schienbein n. shin(-bone).

Schiene f. i(-, -n) splint; (rail.) rail.

schienen v.t. to splint.

Schienen: ~**bus** m. rail bus; ~**fahrzeug** n. rail vehicle; ~**netz** n. railroad system; ~**verkehr** m. rail traffic.

schier adv. sheer, pure; (adv.) almost.

Schierling m. (-[e]s, -e) hemlock.

Schieß: ~**befehl** m. order to fire; ~**bude** f. shooting gallery; ~**eisen** n. (fam.) shooting-iron.

schießen v.t. & i.st. to shoot, to discharge, to fire; (football, Tor ~) to score; to rush; die Zügel ~ lassen, to let go the reins; einen Bock ~, (fam.) to make a blunder.

Schießerei f. gunfight; shooting.

Schießfertigkeit f. marksmanship.

Schieß: ~**gewehr** n. fire-arm; ~**pulver** n. gunpowder; ~**scharte** f. embrasure, loop-hole; ~**scheibe** f. target; ~**stand** m. shooting range.

Schiff n. (-[e]s, -e) ship, vessel, boat; (Kirchen~) nave; (Weber) shuttle.

Schiffahrt f. (-, 0) navigation.

Schiffahrts: ~**linie** f. shipping line; ~**weg** m. shipping route.

schiffbar a. navigable.

Schiff: ~**bau** m. shipbuilding; ~**bruch** m. shipwreck; ~bruch leiden, to be shipwrecked.

schiffbrüchig a. shipwrecked.

schiffen v.i. to navigate, to sail.

Schiffer m. (-s, -) boatman; skipper.

Schiffs: ~**brücke** f. pontoon bridge; ~**junge** m. cabin-boy; ~**raum** m. shipping space; ~**schraube** f. ship's screw; ~**spediteur** m. shipping-agent; ~**verkehr** n. shipping traffic; ~**werft** f. shipyard.

Schiite pm. (-n, -n) Shiite.

Schikane f. chicanery, trickery.

schikanieren v.t. to harass, to vex.

schikanös a. harassing; vexatious.

schilaufen v.i. to ski.

Schild m. (-es, -e) shield, buckler.

Schild n. (-es, -er) road sign; sign-board; door-plate; label.

Schildbürger m. (-s, -) simpleton.

Schilddrüse f. thyroid gland.

schildern v.t. to describe, to picture.

Schilderung f. (-, -en) description.

Schild: ~**kröte** f. turtle, tortoise; ~**laus** f. cochineal kermes; ~**wache** f. sentinel, sentry.

Schilf n. (-[e]s, -e) reed, rush; sedge.

Schilfgras n. reed-grass, sedge.

Schilfrohr n. reed.

schillern v.i. to be iridescent, to glitter.

schillernd a. glistening, irridescent.

Schilling m. (-s, -e) (Münze) shilling.

Schimäre f. (-, -n) chimera, bogy.

Schimmel m. (-s, -) mold, mustiness; white horse.

schimm[e]lig a. moldy, musty.

schimmeln v.i. to get moldy, to mold.

Schimmelpilz m. mold.

Schimmer m. (-s, -) glitter, gleam, glimmer; (fig.) idea; keinen ~, not the faintest notion.

schimmern v.i. to glitter, to glisten; to glean.

Schimpanse m. (-n, -n) chimpanzee.

Schimpf m. (-[e]s, -e) affront, insult; disgrace.

schimpfen v.t. to scold; to grumble; to moan.

schimpflich a. disgraceful.

Schimpfwort n. invective, insult; swearword.

Schindel f. (-s, -n) shingle.

Schindeldach n. shingle-roof.

schinden v.t.st. to mistreat; (fig.) to oppress, to grind; sich ~, to slave.

Schinderei f. (-, -en) drudgery.

Schinken m. (-s, -) ham.

Schinkenspeck m. bacon.

Schirm m. i(-[e]s, -e) screen; shade; (Regen~) umbrella; (Sonnen~) parasol; (Mützen~) peak; (fig.) shelter, protection.

schirmen v.t. to shelter, to protect.

Schirm: ~**herr** m. patron; ~**herrin** f. patroness; ~**herrschaft** f. patronage; ~**mütze** f, peaked cap; ~**ständer** m. umbrella stand.

Schisma n. (-s, -s u. -mata) schism.

schismatisch a. schismatic.

Schiß m. (-s, 0) (vulg.) ~**haben** to be scared stiff.

schizophren a. schizophrenic.

Schizophrenie f. (-, -n) schizophrenia.

Schlacht f. (-, -en) battle; eine ~ liefern, to fight a battle.

Schlachtbank f. shambles pl.

schlachten v.t. to slaughter, to kill.

Schlachtenbummler m. (sp.) fan; supporter.

Schlachter m., **Schlächter** m. i(-s, -) butcher.

Schlacht: ~**feld** n. battle-field; ~**kreuzer** m. battle-cruiser; ~**ruf** n. war-cry; ~**schiff** n. battleship.

Schlacke f. (-, -n) dross, slag, cinders.

schlackern v.i. to flap; to dangle; to be baggy (pants).

Schlaf m. (-[e]s, 0) sleep; im ~e, asleep.

Schlafanzug m. pajamas.

Schläfe f. (-, -n) temple.

schlafen v.i.st. to sleep.

Schlafenszeit f. bedtime.

Schläfer m. (-s, -); **Schläferin** f. (-, -nen) sleeper.

schlaff a. limp, slack, flabby; indolent.

Schlaffheit f. (-, 0) slackness, indolence.

Schlaf: ~**gast** m. overnight guest; ~**gelegenheit** f. place to sleep; ~**krankheit** f. sleeping sickness; ~**lied** n. lullaby.

schlaflos a. sleepless.

Schlaf: ~**losigkeit** f. sleeplessness; insomnia.

Schlaf: ~**mittel** n. soporific; ~**mütze** f. nightcap; (fig.) sleepyhead.

schläfrig a. sleepy, drowsy; sluggish.

Schlaf: ~**rock** m. dressing-gown; ~**saal** m. dormitory; ~**sack** m. sleeping bag; ~**tablette** f. sleeping pill.

schlaftrunken a. drowsy.

Schlaf: ~**wagen** n. sleeping-car, sleeper; ~**wagenschaffner** m. sleeping-car attendant; ~**wandler** m., ~**wandlerin** f. sleep-walker; ~**zimmer** n. bedroom.

Schlag m. i(-[e]s, Schläge) stroke, blow; (elek.) shock; apoplexy, fit; (fig.) kind, sort; (Donner~) clap; (Puls~) beat; ~ auf ~, in rapid succession, as thick as hail; ~ zwölf Uhr, at twelve o'clock sharp.

Schlag: ~**ader** f. artery; ~**anfall** m. stroke; ~**baum** n. barrier.

schlagen v.t.st. to beat, to strike; (den Feind) to

defeat; (*Eier*) to beat; *Holz* ~, to fell wood; *eine Brücke* ~, to build a bridge; *Geld* ~, to coin money; *ein Kreuz* ~, to make the sign of the Cross; *Alarm* ~, to sound the alarm; *ans Kreuz* ~, to crucify; *zum Ritter* ~, to knight; ~ *v.i.* (*Uhr*) to strike; *es schlägt 12 Uhr*, it strikes 12; ~ *v.refl. sich schlagen*, to fight.

schlagend *a.* cogent; conclusive.

Schlager *m.* (-s, -) (*theat.*) hit, pop song; best-seller.

Schläger *m.* (-s, -) (*Tennis*) racket, (*Kricket*) bat.

Schlägerei *f.* (-, -en) brawl; row.

schlagfertig *a.* quick at repartee.

Schlag: ~**instrument** *n.* percussion instrument; ~**kraft** *f.* striking power; ~**loch** *n.* pothole; ~**obers** *m.*, ~**rahm** *m.*, ~**sahne** *f.* whipped cream; ~**stock** *m.* truncheon; cudgel; ~**weite** *f.* striking distance; ~**wetter** *n.* firedamp; ~**wort** *n.* catchword; slogan; ~**zeile** *f.* headline; ~**zeug** *n.* drums; ~**zeuger** *m.*, ~**zeugerin** *f.* drummer.

Schlaksig *a.* gangling, lanky.

Schlamassel *n.* (-s, -) mess.

Schlamm *m.* (-[e]s, 0) mud.

schlammig *a.* muddy.

Schlampe *f.* (-, -n) slut.

schlampen *v.i.* to be sloppy.

Schlamperei *f.* sloppiness.

schlampig *a.* slovenly, sloppy.

Schlange *f.* (-, -n) snake, serpent; coil; (*Reihe*) line, queue.

schlängeln (sich) *v.refl.* to wind; to snake; to meander.

schlangenförmig *a.* serpentine.

Schlangenlinie *f.* wavy line.

schlank *a.* slender, slim.

Schlankheit *f.* slimness; ~**skur** slimming diet.

schlankweg *adv.* right away.

schlapp *a.* worn out; feeble; slack.

Schlappe *f.* (-, -n) setback.

schlappen *v.i.* to shuffle.

Schlapphut *m.* slouched hat.

schlappmachen *v.i.* to give up; to wilt.

Schlappschwanz *m.* (*fam.*) wimp.

Schlaraffenland *n.* Land of Cockaigne.

schlau *a. & adv.* sly (silly); cunning(ly), crafty(ily).

Schlauberger, **Schlaukopf**, **Schlaumeier**, *m.* (*fam.*) smartie.

Schlauch *m.* (-[e]s, Schläuche) hose; (*Fahrrad*) tube.

Schlauch: ~**boot** *n.* rubber dinghy; ~**mantel** *m.* cover of a tire.

schlauchen *v.t.u.i.* (*fig.*) to drain.

Schläue *f.* (-, 0) shrewdness; astuteness.

Schlauheit *f.* (-, -en) cunning, slyness.

Schlaufe *f.* (-, -n) loop; strap.

schlecht *a.* mean, base, bad, wicked; (*Geld*) base; vile; ill; *mir ist* or *wird* ~, I feel ill; *es* ~ *haben*, to have a bad time; *es geht ihm* ~, he is unwell or badly off.

schlechtgelaunt *a.* bad-tempered.

schlechtgesinnt *a.* evil-minded.

schlechterdings *adv.* absolutely.

schlechthin *adv.* plainly; positively.

Schlechtigkeit *f.* (-, -en) meanness, baseness, badness.

schlechtmachen *v.t.* to run s.o./s.th. down

schlectweg *adv.* plainly, simply.

schlecken *v.t. & i.* to lick.

Schleckerei *f.* (-, -en) sweets, dainties *pl.*

Schlegel *m.* (-s, -) mallet; leg (of mutton, etc.); drumstick.

Schlehdorn *m.* blackthorn.

Schlehe *f.* (-, -n) sloe.

schleichen *v.i.st.* (*s*) to sneak, to steal, to glide, to slink; *sich fort~*, to steal away, to sneak off.

schleichend *a.* sneaking; insiduous (disease); (*fig.*) lingering.

Schleich: ~**handel** *m.* black market; ~**händler** *m.* black marketeer; ~**weg** *m.* (*fig.*) secret path.

Schleie *f.* (-, -n) (*Fisch*) tench.

Schleier *n.* (-s, -) veil.

schleierhaft *a.* (*fig.*) mysterious; *das ist mir* ~, I don't know what to make of it.

Schleife *f.* (-, -n) loop; knot, bow; sledge, drag.

schleifen *v.t. & i.* to drag, to trail; to raze; to glide, to slide; ~ *v.t.st.* to grind, to polish; to cut (glass).

Schleifer *m.* (-s, -) grinder, polisher; (*Edelstein~*) cutter.

Schleifmittel *n.* abrasive.

Schleifstein *m.* whetstone, grindstone.

Schleim *m.* (-[e]s, -e) slime; phlegm; mucous; gruel.

Schleimhaut *f.* mucous membrane.

schleimig *a.* slimy, mucous.

schlemmen *v.i.* to feast, to revel.

Schlemmer *m.* (-s, -) gourmet.

Schlemmerei *f.* feasting.

Schlemmerlokal *n.* gourmet restaurant.

schlendern *v.i.* (*s*) to stroll.

Schlendrian *m.* (-s, 0) dawdling; rut.

schlenkern *v.t. & i.* to swing; to dangle.

Schleppdampfer *m.* steam-tug.

Schleppe *f.* (-, -n) train (of a dress).

schleppen *v.t. & i.* to drag; to trail; (*nav.*) to tow, to tug.

schleppend *a.* flagging, lengthy, heavy.

Schlepper *m.* (-s, -) tug.

Schlepp: ~**lift** *m.* ski tow; ~**kleid** *n.* dress with a train; ~**tau** *n.* tow-rope; *ins* ~ *nehmen*, to take in tow.

Schlesien *n.* (-s, 0) Silesia.

Schlesier *m.*; **Schlesierin** *f.* Silesian.

Schleuder *f.* (-, -n) sling; slingshot.

schleudern *v.t.* to sling; to throw; ~ *v.i* to swing.

Schleuderpreis *m.* knock-down price.

Schleudersitz *m.* (-es, -e) ejector seat.

schleunig *a.* quick, speedy.

Schleuse *f.* (-, -n) sluice, lock, flood-gate.

Schlich *m.* (-[e]s, -e) trick, dodge; *hinter die* ~*e kommen*, to be up to one's dodges or tricks.

schlicht *a.* plain; sleek, smooth.

schlichten *v.t.* to smooth; (*fig.*) to settle, to arrange, to adjust.

Schlichter *m.* (-s, -) arbitrator.

Schlichtheit *f.* simplicity; plainness.

Schlichtung *f.* (-, 0) settling (of differences); ~**samt** *n.* conciliation board; ~**sausschuß** *m.* court of arbitration.

Schlick *m.* slit.

Schließe *f.* (-, -n) buckle; clasp.

schließen *v.t. & i.st.* to shut, to close, to bolt; to conclude; (*Ehe*) to contract; *in sich* ~, to include.

Schließfaß *n.* post-office box; safe deposit box; locker.

schließlich *adv.* lastly, finally.
Schließmuskel *m.* sphincter.
Schließung *f.* (-, -en) closure.
Schliff *m.* (-[e]s, -e) (*fig.*) polish; cutting; sharpening.
schlimm *a.* bad, evil, serious.
schlimmstenfalls *adv.* if the worst comes to the worst.
Schlinge *f.* (-, -n) noose, knot; loop, snare; (*med.*) sling.
Schlingel *m.* (-s, -) rascal; naughty boy.
schlingen *v.t. & i.st.* to swallow, to gulp (down); to twist, to entwine; (sich) ~ *v.refl.st.* to wind, to twine (round).
schlingern *v.i.* (*nav.*) to roll.
Schlingpflanze *f.* creeper.
Schlips *m.* (-es, -e) (neck-)tie.
Schlipsnadel *f.* tie-pin.
Schlitten *m.* (-s, -) sledge, sleigh; (*kleiner*) toboggan; (*mech.*) slide, carriage.
Schlittenfahrt *f.* sleigh ride.
schlittern *v.i.* to slide; to slip; to skid.
Schlittschuh *m.* skate; ~ *laufen,* to skate.
Schlittschuhläufer *m.*; **Schlittschuhläuferin** *f.* skater.
Schlitz *m.* (-es, -e) slit, slash; fissure; slot.
Schlitz: ~**auge** *n.* slit eye; ~**ohr** *n.* (*fig.*) crafty devil.
schlitzen *v.t.* to slit, to slash.
Schloß *n.* (Schlosses, Schlösser) lock; castle; palace; *unter* ~ *und Riegel,* under lock and key.
Schlosser *m.* (-s, -) locksmith; metal worker; fitter.
Schlot *m.* (-[e]s, -e *u.* Schlöte) chimney.
schlotterig *a.* wobbling.
schlottern *v.i.* to wobble, to hang loose.
Schlucht *f.* (-, -en) cleft, ravine.
schluchzen *v.i.* to sob.
Schluchzer *m.* sob.
Schluck *m.* (-[e]s, Schlucke) swallow; mouthful; gulp, drink.
Schluckauf *m.* (-s, 0) hiccups.
schlucken *v.i. & t.* to gulp (down), to swallow; (*fig.*) to swallow.
Schlucker *m.* (-s, -) hiccup; *armer* ~, poor wretch.
Schluckimpfung *f.* oral vaccination.
schludern *v.i.* to work sloppily.
schludrig *a.& adv.* sloppy; sloppily.
Schlummer *m.* (-s, 0) slumber; doze.
schlummern *v.i.* to slumber, to doze.
Schlund *m.* (-[e]s, Schlünde) throat, gullet; gulf, abyss.
schlüpfen *v.i.* (*s*) to slip, to slide.
Schlüpfer *m.* (-s, -) panties.
Schlupf: ~**loch** *n.* loop-hole; hiding place; ~**winkel** *m.* hiding place.
schlüpfrig *a.* slippery; prurient, obscene.
schlurfen *v.i.* to shuffle.
schlürfen *v.t.* to sip, to slurp.
Schluß *m.* (Schlusses, Schlüsse) conclusion, end; (*log.*) inference; closure.
Schluß: ~**abstimmung** *f.* final vote; ~**akkord** *m.* final chord; ~**akte** *f.* final communiqué.
Schlüssel *m.* (-s, -) key; (*mus.*) key.
Schlüssel: ~**anhänger** *m.* key-fob; ~**bein** *n.* collarbone; ~**blume** *f.* cowslip, primrose; ~**bund** *m.* bunch of keys; ~**erlebnis** *n.* crucial experience;

~**figur** *f.* key figure; ~**kind** *n.* latchkey child; ~**loch** *n.* keyhole; ~**ring** *m.* keyring; ~**roman** *m.* roman à clef; ~**stellung** *f.* key position; ~**wort** *n.* keyword; (*comp.*) password.
Schluß: ~**examen** *m.* final examination; ~**feier** *f.* (*Schule*) commencement; speech day; ~**folgerung** *f.* inference, conclusion.
schlüssig *a.* conclusive; *sich* ~ *werden,* to make up one's mind.
Schluß: ~**licht** *n.* rear lamp *or* light; (*fig.*) last one; ~**notierung** *f.* closing price; ~**satz** *m.* concluding sentence; (*mus.*) finale; ~**stein** *m.* keystone; ~**verkauf** *m.* (end of season) sale.
Schmach *f.* (-, 0) ignominy; insult.
schmachten *v.i.* to languish, to long for, to pine.
schmachtend *a.* soulful.
schmächtig *a.* slight; thin.
schmachvoll *a.* ignominious; disgraceful.
schmackhaft *a.* savory, tasty.
schmähen *v.t.* to revile.
schmählich *a.* shameful; despicable.
Schmähschrift *f.* libel, lampoon.
Schmähung *f.* (-, -en) abuse, invective.
schmal *a.* narrow; small; scanty; slim.
schmälern *v.t.* to lessen; to belittle.
Schmalspur *f.* narrow gauge; (*fig.*) light weight.
Schmalz *m.* (-es, 0) lard.
Schmalz *n.* (*pej.*) schmaltz.
schmalzig *a.* greasy; (*fig.*) sentimental.
schmarotzen *v.i.* to sponge (on others).
Schmarotzer *m.* (-s, -) parasite; (*fig.*) sponger.
schmatzen *v.t. & i.* to smack one's lips.
Schmaus *m.* (-ses, Schmäuse) feast, treat.
schmausen *v.i.* to feast, to banquet.
schmecken *v.t. & i.* to taste (*nach,* of); to savor; to taste well; *wie schmeckt dir...?* how do you like?
Schmeichelei *f.* (-, -en) flattery.
schmeichelhaft *a.* flattering.
schmeicheln *v.i.* to flatter.
Schmeichler *m.*; **Schmeichlerin** *f.* flatterer.
schmeichlerisch *a.* flattering, fawning.
schmeißen *v.t.st.* to chuck, to fling.
Schmeißfliege *f.* (-, -n) bluebottle; blowfly.
Schmelz *m.* (-es, -e) enamel; (*fig.*) mellowness.
Schmelze *f.* (-, -n) melting.
schmelzen *v.t.st.* to melt; (*Erze*) to smelt; to fuse; ~ *v.i.st.* to melt (away).
schmelzend *a.* melodious; languishing.
Schmelz: ~**käse** *m.* soft cheese; ~**punkt** *m.* melting point; ~**tiegel** *m.* crucible; (*fig.*) melting pot.
Schmerbauch *m.* paunch.
Schmerle *f.* (-, -n) loach.
Schmerz *m.* (-es, -en) pain, ache; grief.
schmerzempfindlich *a.* sensitive to pain.
schmerzen *v.t.* to hurt, to grieve.
Schmerzensgeld *n.* compensation; punitive damages.
schmerzfrei *a.* painless.
schmerzhaft *a.* painful, grievous.
schmerzlich *a.* painful.
schmerzlos *a.* painless.
schmerzstillend *a.* anodyne; soothing, pain-killing.
Schmerztablette *f.* pain-killer; analgesic tablet.
schmerzverzerrt *a.* distorted with pain.
Schmetterling *m.* (-[e]s, -e) butterfly.

schmettern *v.i.* (*von Trompeten*) to bray, to blare; (*von Singvögeln*) to warble.

Schmetterschlag *m.* smash.

Schmied *m.* (-[e]s, -e) (black-)smith.

Schmiede *f.* (-, -n) forge, smithy.

Schmiede: ~**eisen** *n.* wrought iron; ~**hammer** *m.* sledge(-hammer).

schmieden *v.t.* to forge; (*fig.*) to plan, to frame, to concoct.

schmiegen (sich) *v.refl.* to nestle, to snuggle.

schmiegsam *a.* (*fig.*) pliant, supple.

Schmiere *f.* (-,-n) grease; salve; (*sl.*) low theater.

schmieren *v.t. & i.* to grease, to lubricate; (*Butter*) to spread; (*sudeln*) to scrawl; (*fig.*) to bribe; *es geht wie geschmiert*, things go like clockwork.

Schmierenkomödiant *m.* ham actor.

Schmiereren *f.* scrawling, scribbling.

Schmierfink *m.* (*fam.*) dirty fellow.

Schmierheft *n.* rough book.

schmierig *a.* greasy; dirty; (*fig.*) sordid.

Schmier: ~**mittel** *n.* lubricant; ~**papier** *n.* scrap paper; ~**seife** *f.* soft-soap.

Schminkdose *f.*, **Schminktopf** *m.* rouge-pot.

Schminke *f.* (-, -n) paint, rouge, make-up.

schminken *v.t.* to paint; ~*v.refl.* to put on make up.

schmirgeln *v.t.* to rub down; to sand.

Schmirgel *m.* (-s, 0) emery paper; sandpaper.

Schmiß *m.* (Schmisses, Schmisse) stroke, blow; cut, slash; (*fig.*) smartness.

schmissig *a.* snappy.

Schmöker *m.* (-s, -) (*fam.*) old book; light novel.

schmollen *v.i.* to pout, to sulk.

Schmorbraten *m.* braised beef.

schmoren *v.t. & i.* to braise, to stew.

Schmu *m.* (-s, 0) (*fam.*) unfair gain.

Schmuck *m.* (-[e]s, 0) ornament, jewels *pl.*

schmuck *a.* neat, spruce, trim, natty.

schmücken *v.t.* to adorn; to trim; to decorate; ~*v.refl.* to dress up.

Schmuckkasten *m.* jewelry box.

schmucklos *a.* plain, unadorned.

Schmucksachen *f.pl.* jewelry.

Schmuckstück *n.* ornament; piece of jewelry.

schmuddelig *a.* (*fam.*) messy; grubby.

Schmuggel *m.* (-s, 0) smuggling.

schmuggeln *v.t.* to smuggle.

Schmuggelware *f.* contraband.

Schmuggler *m.*; **Schmugglerin** *f.* smuggler.

schmunzeln *v.i.* to smile to oneself.

Schmus *m.* (-es, 0) (*fam.*) soft soap.

schmusen *v.i.* (*fam.*) to cuddle.

Schmutz *m.* (-s, 0) dirt, soil, filth.

schmutzen *v.t. & i.* to soil; to get dirty.

Schmutz: ~**fink** *m.* (*fam.*) pig; ~**fleck** *m.* stain; (*fig.*) blot.

schmutzig *a.* dirty, filthy; sordid; obscene.

Schnabel *m.* (-s, Schnäbel) bill, beak; gob.

Schnake *f.* (-, -n) mosquito.

Schnakenstich *m.* (*fig.*) mosquito bite.

Schnalle *f.* (-, -n) buckle.

schnallen *v.t.* to buckle.

schnalzen *v.i.* to smack; to snap; to crack (a whip).

schnappen *v.i.* to snap, to snatch; *nach Luft* ~, to gasp for breath.

Schnappschloß *n.* spring-lock.

Schnaps *m.* (Schnapses, Schnäpse) strong liquor; dram.

Schnapsidee *f.* (*fig.*) crazy idea.

schnarchen *v.i.* to snore.

Schnarcher *m.*; **Schnarcherin** *f.* snorer.

Schnarre *f.* (-, -n) rattle.

schnarren *v.i.* to rattle; to buzz.

schnattern *v.i.* to cackle; chatter.

schnauben *v..i.* to snort.

schnaufen *v.i.* to puff; to pant.

Schnauzbart *m.* moustache.

Schnauze *f.* (-, -n) snout, muzzle.

schnauzen *v.t.u.i.* to bark; to snarl.

Schnauzer *m.* schnauzer; moustache.

Schnecke *f.* (-, -n) snail; slug; (*Gebäck*) sweet-roll.

schneckenförmig *a.* spiral, helical.

Schnecken: ~**haus** *n.* snail-shell; ~**temp** *n.* snail's pace.

Schnee *m.* (-[e]s, 0) snow.

Schneeball *m.* snowball.

Schneeballschlacht *f.* snowball fight.

Schneebesen *m.* whisk.

Schneeblind *a.* snow-blind.

Schnee: ~**brille** *f.* goggles *pl.*; ~**flocke** *f.* snow-flake; ~**gestöber** *n.* snow flurry; ~**glätte** *f.* packed snow; ~**glöckchen** *n.* snowdrop; ~**grenze** *f.* snowline; ~**kette** *f.* snow-chain; ~**mann** *m.* snow-man; ~**matsch** *m.* slush; ~**pflug** *m.* snow-plow; ~**schmelze** *f.* thaw; ~**treiben** *n.* snow flurry; ~**verwehungen** *pl.* snow-drifts; ~**wetter** *n.* snowy weather.

Schneewittchen *n.* snow white.

Schneid *m.* (-s, 0) guts.

Schneide *f.* (-, -n) (cutting) edge; blade.

schneiden *v.t.st.* to cut; to carve; to saw; to reap; to pull (faces); (sich) ~ *v.refl.* (*math.*) to intersect.

schneidend *a.* cutting, caustic, trenchant.

Schneider *m.* (-s, -), **Schneiderin** *f.* (-, -nen) tailor, dressmaker.

schneidern *v.i.* to make clothes, to tailor.

Schneider: ~**puppe** *f.* tailor's dummy; ~**sitz** *m.* cross-legged position.

Schneidezahn *m.* incisor.

schneidig *a.* plucky, dashing.

schneien *v.i.* to snow.

Schneise *f.* (-, -n) aisle (forest); air corridor.

schnell *a.* quick, swift, speedy, fast; rapid; prompt.

Schnellbahn *f.* municipal railroad.

Schnellboot *n.* speedboat.

schnellen *v.t.* to let fly, to jerk, to toss; ~ *v.i.* (*s*) spring.

Schnell: ~**feuer** *n.* rapid fire; ~**feuergeschütz** *n.* quick-firing gun; ~**gang** *m.* (*mot.*) overdrive; ~**gericht** *n.* court of summary jurisdiction; quick meal.

Schnelligkeit *f.* (-, 0) quickness, velocity, rapidity, speed.

Schnell: ~**imbiß** *m.* snack; ~**kraft** *f.* elasticity; ~**verfahren** *n.* (*law*) summary proceeding; ~**wirkend**, *a.* fast-acting; ~**zug** *m.* fast train, express.

Schnepfe *f.* (-, -n) snipe; woodcock.

schneuzen (sich) *v.refl.* to blow one's nose.

schnetzeln *v.t.* to cut into thin strips.

Schnickschnack *m.* (*fam.*) trinkets; frills; drivel.

schniefen *v.i.* to sniffle.

schniegeln *v. refl.* to spruce oneself up.

Schnippchen *n.* (-s, -) *ein ~ schlagen*, to trick.

schnippeln *v.t.u.i.* to snip.

schnippen *v.i.* to snap (fingers); to flap.

schnippisch *a.* pert.

Schnipsel *m./n.* scrap; shred.

Schnitt *m.* (-[e]s, -e) cut; incision; (*Buch~*) edge; fashion, pattern; section.

Schnittchen *n.* open sandwich.

Schnitte *f.* (-, -n) slice, steak, cut.

Schnitter *m.* (-s, -) reaper.

schnittfest *a.* firm.

schnittig *a.* stylish; racy.

Schnitt: ~**lauch** *m.* chives *pl.*; ~**muster** *n.* pattern; ~**punkt** *m.* intersection; ~**wunde** *f.* cut; gash.

Schnitzel *n.* (-s, -) chip, shred; escalope; cutlet.

Schnitzeljagd *f.* paper chase.

schnitzen *v.t.* to carve, to cut.

Schnitzer *m.* (-s, -) carver; blunder.

Schnitzerei *f.* (-, -en) carved work.

schnoddrig *a.* snotty; brash.

schnöde *a.* scornful; base, vile.

Schnorchel *m.* snorkel.

Schnörkel *m.* (-s, -) (*arch.*) scroll; flourish.

schnorren *v.t.* to scrounge.

Schnorrer *m.* scrounger.

Schnösel *m.* snot-nose.

schnucklig *a.* (*fam.*) cuddly.

schnüffeln *v.i.* to sniff; to pry.

Schnüffler *m.* (-s, -) spy.

Schnuller *m.* pacifier.

Schnulze *f.* tear-jerker.

schnupfen *v.t.* & *i.* to take snuff; to sniff.

Schnupfen *m.* (-s, 0) cold (in the head); *sich den ~ holen*, to catch cold.

Schnupf: ~**tabak** *m.* snuff; ~**tabaksdose** *f.* snuffbox; ~**tuch** *n.* (pocket-)handkerchief.

schnuppern *v.i.* to sniff, to snuffle.

Schnur *f.* (-, Schnüre) string, cord.

Schnürchen *n.* (-s, -) *wie am ~*, like clockwork.

schnüren *v.t.* to lace; to cord, to tie up.

schnurgerade *a.* straight.

Schnurrbart *m.* moustache.

schnurren *v.i.* to hum, to whiz, to whir; (*von Katzen*) to purr.

schnurrig *a.* droll, funny.

Schnurrhaar *n.* whiskers.

Schnür: ~**senkel** *m.* boot-lace; ~**schuh**, ~**stiefel** *m.* lace-boot.

schnurstracks *adv.* directly.

Schnute *f.* (-, -n) mouth; gob.

Schober *m.* (-s, -) stack, rick; open-sided barn.

Schock *m.* (-s, -s) shock.

schocken *v.t.* (*fam.*) to shock.

schockieren *v.t.* to shock.

schofel *a.* mean, paltry.

Schöffe *m.* (-n, -n) juror, juryman, lay-judge.

Schöffengericht *n.* lowest court of law.

Schokolade *f.* (-, -n) chocolate.

Schokoladeneis *n.* chocolate icing.

Scholle *f.* (-, -n) clod, glebe; (*Fisch*) plaice.

schon *adv.* already; surely.

schön *a.* fine, fair, beautiful, handsome; ~**e Künste** *pl.* fine arts.

schonen *v.t.* to spare, to save; (sich) ~ *v.refl.* to take great care of oneself.

Schoner *m.* (-s, -) schooner.

Schönfärberei *f.* (-, -en) (*fig.*) embellishment,

glossing over the facts.

Schonfrist *f.* period of grace; period of convalescence.

Schöngeist *m.* wit, aesthete.

schöngeistig *a.* aesthetic.

Schönheit *f.* (-, -en) beauty.

Schönheits: ~**chirurgie** *f.* cosmetic surgery; ~**fehler** *m.* blemish; flaw; ~**salon** *m.* beauty parlor; ~**wettbewerb** *m.* beauty contest.

Schnonkost *f.* light diet.

Schonung *f.* (-, -en) forbearance, indulgence; rest; protection; sparing; nursery for young trees.

schonungslos *a.* unsparing, relentless.

Schonzeit *f.* close time *or* season.

Schopf *m.* (-[e], Schöpfe) shock of hair.

schöpfen *v.t.* to draw (water); to obtain, to get; *Luft ~*, to get some air; *Verdacht ~*, to conceive a suspicion; *Hoffnung ~*, to be reanimated by hope.

Schöpfer *m.* (-s, -); **Schöpferin** *f.* (-, -nen) creator; author.

schöpferisch *a.* creative, productive.

Schöpferkraft *f.* creative power.

Schöpf: ~**kelle** *f.*, ~**löffel** *m.* ladle, scoop.

Schöpfung *f.* (-, -en) creation; work.

Schoppen *m.* (-s, -) pint.

Schorf *m.* (-[e]s, -e) scab.

schorfig *a.* scabby.

Schorle *m.* (-, -n) wine/applejuice with mineral water.

Schornstein *m.* chimney; funnel; smokestack.

Schornsteinfeger *m.* chimney-sweep.

Schoß *m.* (-es, Schösse) lap; (*fig.*) womb; (*Rock~*) flap, skirt, coat-tail; *die Hände in den ~ legen*, to sit with folded hands.

Schoß: ~**hund** *m.* lapdog; ~**kind** *n.* darling, pet child.

Schößling *m.* (-[e]s, -e) shoot, sprout.

Schote *f.* (-, -n) husk; pod.

Schott *n.* (-[e]s, -e) (*nav.*) bulkhead.

Schotte *m.* (-n, -n) Scotsman, Scot.

Schottenrock *m.* tartan skirt; kilt.

Schotter *m.* (-s, -) gravel; metal.

Schottin *f.* (-, -nen) Scotswoman, Scot.

Schottisch *a.* Scottish; ~**er Whisky** *m.* Scotch whiskey.

Schottland *n.* (-s, 0) Scotland.

schraffieren *v.t.* to hatch.

schräg *a.* oblique, slanting; tilted; ~**er Anschnitt** *m.* (*mech.*) bevel.

Schräge *f.* (-, 0) slant; slope.

Schramme *f.* (-, -n) scratch, slight wound.

schrammen *v.t.* to scratch, to graze.

Schrank *m.* (-[e]s, Schränke) cupboard; wardrobe; cabinet; closet.

Schranke *f.* (-, -n) bar, barrier, bound, limit; (*Eisenbahn*) gate.

schrankenlos *a.* boundless.

Schrankenwärter *m.* gatekeeper.

Schraube *f.* (-, -n) screw; bolt; (*Dampfer~*) propeller.

schrauben *v.t.* to screw.

Schrauben: ~**gewinde** *n.* thread of a screw; ~**mutter** *f.* nut; ~**schlüssel** *m.* wrench; ~**zieher** *m.* screwdriver.

Schraubstock *m.* vise.

Schrebergarten *m.* allotment (garden).

Schreck *m.* (-[e]s, -) fright, terror.
Schreckbild *n.* bugbear, fright.
schrecken *v.t.* to frighten.
Schrecken *m.* (-s, -) fright, terror; *ein blinder ~*, a false alarm.
schreckenerregend *a.* horrific.
Schreckensherrschaft *f.* reign of terror, terrorism.
schreckhaft *a.* easily frightened.
schrecklich *a.* awful, dreadful, terrible.
Schreckschuß *m.* warning shot.
Schrei *m.* (-[e]s, -e) cry, shriek, scream.
schreibarbeit *f.* paperwork.
Schreibblock *m.* writing-pad, writing-tablet.
schreiben *v.t.st.* to write; to type(write); *ins Reine ~*, to copy out; *einem auf die Rechnung ~*, to put down to one's account.
Schreiben *n.* (-s, -) letter, epistle; (art of) writing.
Schreiber *m.* (-s, -); **Schreiberin** *f.* (-, -nen) writer; clerk, copyist.
Schreib: ~**feder** *f.* pen; ~**fehler** *m.* slip of the pen, spelling mistake; ~**heft** *n.* exercise-book; ~**kraft** *f.* typist; ~**maschine** *f.* typewriter; ~**papier** *n.* writing-paper; ~**pult** *n.* writing desk; ~**stube** *f.* (*mil.*) orderly room; ~**tisch** *m.* desk; writing table; ~**waren** *f.pl.* stationery; ~**warenhändler** *m.* stationer; ~**weise** *f.* spelling; ~**zeug** *n.* writing things.
schreien *v.t.* & *i.st.* to cry, to scream; to yell; to screech.
schreiend *a.* loud; blatant; glaring.
Schreier *m.* (-s, -), **Schreihals** *m.* crier; bawler; squalling child.
Schrein *m.* (-[e]s, -e) shrine.
Schreiner *m.* (-s, -) joiner, cabinet-maker; carpenter.
schreiten *v.i.st.* (*s*) to stride, to step.
Schrift *f.* (-, -en) writing; handwriting; script; type; book; Scripture, Bible.
schriftdeutsch *a.* written German.
Schrift: ~**führer** *m.* secretary; ~**giesserei** *f.* typefoundry; ~**leiter** *m.* editor.
schriftlich *a.* written; ~ *bewußt.* in writing, by letter; ~**er Lehrkurs** *m.* correspondence course.
Schrift: ~**satz** *m.* (*law*) written statement; ~**setzer** *m.* typesetter; ~**sprache** *f.* written language; ~**stelle** *f.* Scripture text; ~**steller** *m.*, ~**stellerin** *f.* writer, author; ~**stellerei** *f.* authorship; ~**stellername** *m.* penname.
schriftstellerisch *a.* literary.
Schrift: ~**stück** *n.* document, letter; ~**wechsel** *m.* exchange of letters; ~**zeichen** *n.* character.
schrill *a.* shrill, piercing.
Schritt *m.* (-[e]s, -e) step, stride, pace; gait; demarche; ~ *vor* (*für*) ~, step by step; *für einen ~e tun*, to take steps in behalf of one; *im ~ gehen*, to walk, to pace; ~ *mit einem halten*, to keep pace with one; *aus dem ~ kommen*, to fall out of time; ~ *reiten*, *fahren*, to pace, to walk.
Schrittempo *n.* walking pace.
Schrittmacher *m.* pace-maker.
schrittweise *adv.* step by step.
schroff *a.* steep, rugged; (*fig.*) gruff.
schröpfen *v.t.* to cup; (*fig.*) to fleece.
Schrot *n.* (-[e]s, -e) due weight (of a coin); small shot; whole grain.
Schrotflinte *f.* shotgun.

Schrotkugel *f.* pellet.
Schrott *m.* (-, 0) scrap(iron); ~**platz** *m.* scrap yard; ~**wert** *m.* scrap value.
schrubben *v.t.* to scrub.
Schrulle *f.* (-, -n) cranky idea; whim.
schrullenhaft *a.* whimsical.
schrullig *a.* cranky.
schrumpelig *a.* (*fam.*) wrinkled.
schrumpeln *v.i.* (*fam.*) to wrinkle.
schrumpfen *v.i.* (*s*) to shrink, to shrivel.
Schrumpfkopf *m.* shrunken head.
Schub *m.* (-[e]s, Schübe) shove, push; thrust; phase.
Schub: ~**fach** *n.* drawer; ~**fenster** *n.* sash-window; ~**karren** *m.* wheel-barrow; ~**lade** *f.* drawer.
Schubs *m.* (*fam.*) push, shove.
schubsen *v.t.* (*fam.*) to push, to shove.
schubweise *adv.* in batches.
schüchtern *a.* shy, coy, bashful.
Schüchternheit *f.* shyness.
Schuft *m.* (-[e]s, -e) blackguard, scoundrel.
schuften *v.i.* (*sl.*) to slave.
schuftig *a.* base, abject.
Schuh *m.* (-[e]s, -e) shoe; (*fig.*) *einem etwas in die ~e schieben*, to lay a fault at one's door.
Schuh: ~**band** *n.* shoe-lace; ~**einlage** *f.* insole, sock; ~**flicker** *m.* cobbler; ~**leisten** *m.* shoe-tree; ~**litze** *f.* shoe-lace; ~**löffel** *m.* shoehorn; ~**macher** *m.* shoemaker; ~**putzer** *m.* boot-black; ~**riemen** *m.* bootlace; ~**sohle** *f.* sole; ~**wichse** *f.* shoe polish.
Schul: ~**abgänger** *m.*, ~**abgängerin** *f.* school lever; ~**abschluß** *m.* school leaving certification; ~**alter** *n.* school age; ~**behörde** *f.* education authority; ~**beispiel** *n.* textbook example; ~**besuch** *m.* school attendance; ~**bildung** *f.* education; ~**buchverlag** *m.* educational publisher.
Schuld *f.* (-, -en) guilt, fault; debt; *einem ~ geben*, to blame; *sich etwas zu ~en kommen lassen*, to be guilty of a thing; *ich bin daran ~*, it is my fault; *eine ~ abtragen*, to pay off a debt.
Schuldbekenntnis *n.* confession (of guilt).
schuldbewußt *a.* guilty.
schulden *v.t.* to owe, to be indebted to.
Schulden *f.pl.* debts; ~ *eingehen*, *machen*, to contract *or* incur debts.
schuldenfrei *a.* debt-free; unmortgaged.
Schuldentilgung *f.* liquidation of debts.
Schuldforderung *f.* claim, demand.
Schuldgefühl *n.* feeling of guilt.
Schuldirektor *m.*; **Schuldirektorin** *f.* principal.
schuldig *a.* guilty, culpable; due; indebted, owing; *etwas ~ bleiben*, to remain one's debtor for a thing; *einen ~ sprechen*, to find a person guilty.
Schuldige *m./f.* guilty person; guilty party.
Schuldigerklärung *f.* (*law*) conviction.
Schuldigkeit *f.* (-, 0) obligation, duty.
Schuldklage *f.* action for debt.
schuldlos *a.* guiltless; innocent.
Schuldner *m.* (-s, -) debtor.
Schuld: ~**schein** *m.*, ~**verschreibung** *f.* promissory note, I.O.U. (I owe you); ~**spruch** *m.* verdict of guilt.
Schule *f.* (-, -n) school; school-house; *eine ~ besuchen*, *in die ~ gehen*, *auf der ~ sein*, to go to school, to be at school.
schulen *v.t.* to school; to train.

Schulentlassungsalter *n.* school-leaving age.

Schüler *m.* (-s, -), **Schülerin** *f.* (-, -nen) student, schoolboy, schoolgirl; pupil.

Schüleraustausch *m.* school exchange.

Schülerlotse *m.* student acting as a school crossing warden.

Schülermitverwaltung *f.* student participation in school organization.

Schülerzeitung *f.* school magazine.

Schul: ~**fach** *n.* school subject; ~**fall** *m.* test case; ~**feier** *f.* speech day.

Schulfrei *a.* (day) off school.

Schul: ~**freund** *m.*, ~**freundin** *f.* schoolmate; ~**gelände** *n.* premises; campus; ~**geld** *n.* school-fees *pl.*, schooling; ~**heft** *n.* exercise book; ~**hof** *m.* school yard.

schulisch *a.* at school; school.

Schul: ~**jahr** *n.* session, scholastic year; ~**kamerad** *m.* schoolfellow; ~**leiter** *m.*, ~**leiterin** *f.* principal; ~**mappe** *f.* schoolbag; satchel.

schulmeistern *v.t.* to censure.

Schulordnung *f.* school rule.

Schulpflicht *f.* required school attendance.

schulpflichtig *a.* required to attend school; ~*es Alter*, school age.

Schulschiff *n.* training ship.

Schul: ~**schluß** *m.* end of school; ~**schwänzer** *m.* truant; ~**sprecher** *m.*, ~**sprecherin** *f.* students' representative; ~**stunde** *f.* period; ~**tasche** *f.* school-bag.

Schulter *f.* (-, -n) shoulder.

Schulterblatt *n.* shoulder-blade.

schulterfrei *a.* off-the-shoulder.

schultern *v.t.* to shoulder.

Schultertasche *f.* (*für Damen*) shoulder-bag.

Schulung *f.* (-, -en) training, practice.

Schul: ~**unterricht** *m.* lessons, classes; ~**weg** *m.* way to school; ~**wesen** *n.* school system; ~**zeit** *f.* school-days; ~**zeugnis** *n.* report; ~**zwang** *nm.* compulsory education.

schummeln *v.i.* to cheat.

schummerig *a.* (*fam.*) dim.

Schund *m.* (-[e]s, 0) trash, rubbish.

Schunkeln *v.i.* to rock; to sway.

Schuppe *f.* (-, -n) scale; dandruff.

schuppen, (sich) ~ *v.refl.* to scale off.

Schuppen *m.* (-s, -) shed; (*fam.*) joint (restaurant).

schuppig *a.* scaly.

Schur *f.* (-, -en) shearing; fleece.

schüren *v.t.* to stoke; (*fig.*) to stir up.

schürfen *v.t.* to scratch, to cut; to prospect (*nach*, for); to open a mine.

Schürfwunde *f.* (-, -n) graze, abrasion.

Schurke *m.* (-n, -n) rogue, rascal, villain.

Schurkenstreich *m.* villainy.

schurkisch *a.* knavish, rascally.

Schurwolle *f.* virgin wool.

Schurz *m.* (-es, -e) apron.

Schürze *f.* (-, -n) apron.

schürzen *v.t.* to tuck up; to purse (lips).

Schürzenjäger *m.* womanizer.

Schuß *m.* (Schusses, Schüsse) shot.

Schüssel *f.* (-, -n) dish, platter.

Schußfeld *n.* range.

Schuß: ~**waffe** *f.* fire-arm; ~**weite** *f.* range; ~**wunde** *f.* gunshot wound.

Schuster *m.* (-s, -) shoemaker.

schustern *v.i.* to cobble.

Schutt *m.* (-[e]s, 0) rubble.

Schüttelfrost *m.* shivering fit.

schütteln *v.t.* to shake, to toss; *einem die Hand ~*, to shake hands with a person; *aus dem Ärmel ~*, to produce offhand.

schütten *v.t. & i.* to shed, to pour; to heap.

Schutz *m.* (-es, 0) protection, shelter; *in ~ nehmen*, to take under one's protection.

Schutz: ~**befohlene** *m./f.* protégé, client; ~**blech** *n.* mudguard; ~**brille** *f.* goggles.

Schütze *m.* (-n, -n) shot, marksman; (*mil.*) rifleman.

schützen *v.t.* to protect, to guard, shelter.

Schützengraben *m.* trench, rifle-pit.

Schutzengel *m.* guardian angel.

Schützenregiment *m.* rifle regiment.

Schutz: ~**frist** *f.* term of copyright; ~**haft** *f.* protective custody; ~**helm** *m.* helmet; ~**herr** *m.* patron, protector; ~**impfung** *f.* immunization.

Schützling *m.* (-[e]s, -e) protégé.

schutzlos *a.* defenseless, unprotected.

Schutz: ~**mann** *m.* policeman, constable; ~**marke** *f.* trade-mark; ~**raum** *m.* (*Luftschutz*) shelter; ~**rücken** *m.* (*Buch*) cover; ~**umschlag** *m.* (publisher's) jacket, dust-cover; ~**zoll** *m.* protection; ~**zöllner** *m.* protectionist.

schwäbeln *v.i.* (*fam.*) to speak like a Swabian.

schwabbelig *a.* (*fam.*) flabby; wobbly.

schwabbeln *v.i.* (*fam.*) to wobble.

Schwabe *m.*; **Schwäbin** *f.*; **schwäbisch** *a.* Swabian.

Schwaben *n.* Swabia.

schwach *a.* weak, feeble, infirm; *mir wird ~*, I feel faint.

Schwäche *f.* (-, -) weakness, feebleness.

schwächen *v.t.* to weaken, to enfeeble.

Schwachheit *f.* (-, -en) weakness, frailty, infirmity.

Schwachkopf *m.* simpleton, idiot.

schwachköpfig *a.* weak-headed, idiotic.

schwächlich *a.* infirm, feeble, sickly.

Schwächling *m.* (-s, -e) weakling.

Schwachsinn *m.* mental deficiency.

schwachsinnig *a.* feeble-minded, mentally deficient *or* defective.

Schwachstrom *m.* low-voltage.

Schwächung *f.* (-, -en) weakening.

Schwaden *m.* (-s, 0) cloud; vapor, steam.

Schwadron *f.* (-, -en) squadron, squad.

schwadronieren *v.i.* to bluster.

Schwafelei: *f.* (-, -en) nonsense, gibberish.

Schwafeln *v.i.* (*fam.*) to talk nonsense, to babble.

Schwager *m.* (-s, Schwäger) brother-in-law.

Schwägerin *f.* (-, -nen) sister-in-law.

Schwalbe *f.* (-, -n) swallow.

Schwall *m.* (-[e]s, 0) gush, flood.

Schwamm *m.* (-[e]s, Schwämme) sponge; mushroom, fungus; *Haus~*, dry rot.

schwammig *a.* spongy; bloated; woolly; *adv.* vaguely.

Schwan *m.* (-[e]s, Schwäne) swan.

schwanen *v.i. & imp.* to sense something.

Schwanengesang *m.* swan's song.

schwanger *a.* pregnant.

Schwangere f. (-n, -n) pregnant woman.
schwängern v.t. to make pregnant; (fig.) to impregnate.
Schwangerschaft f. (-, -en) pregnancy.
Schwangerschaftsunterbrechung f. abortion, termination of pregnancy.
Schwank m. (-[e]s, Schwänke) merry tale; (theatr.) farce.
schwanken v.i. to totter, to stagger; (fig.) to waver; to fluctuate; to hesitate.
Schwanz m. (-es, Schwänze) tail.
Schwankung f. (-, -en) fluctuation
schwänzeln v.i. to wag its tail.
schwänzen v.t. (die Schule, etc.) to play hooky.
Schwanzflosse f. tail fin.
schwappen v.i. to splash; to slosh.
Schwäre f. abscess, ulcer.
schwären v.i. to fester, to suppurate.
Schwarm m. (-[e]s, Schwärme) swarm.
schwärmen v.i. to swarm; to riot, to revel; ~ für, to be mad about.
Schwärmer m. (-s, -) dreamer; enthusiast.
Schwärmerei f. (-, -en) enthusiasm.
schwärmerisch a. enthusiastic, fanatic.
Schwarte f. (-, -n) rind (bacon).
schwarz a. black; es wird einem ~ vor den Augen, his head begins to swim; ins Schwarze treffend, to hit the mark; ~ auf weiß, in black and white; ~e Liste, black list; ~es Brett n. notice board, bulletin board.
Schwarz n. (-es, 0) black color.
Schwarz: ~arbeit f. moonlighting; ~brot f. rye bread; ~dorn m. blackthorn.
Schwarze m./f. black.
Schwarze n. bull's eye (target).
Schwärze f. (-, -n) blacking; (printer's) ink.
schwärzen v.t. to black(en); to black out.
Schwarzfahrer m.; **Schwarzfahrerin** f. fare-dodger.
Schwarzhandel m. black marketeering.
schwärzlich a. blackish.
Schwarz: ~markt m. black market; ~seher m. pessimist; ~wald m. the Black Forest.
schwarzweiß a. black-and-white.
Schwarzwurzel f. black salsify.
Schwatz m. chat; natter.
schwatzen, schwätzen v.i. to chatter, to talk idly.
Schwätzer m. (-s, -); **Schwätzerin** f. chatterbox, blabber.
schwatzhaft a. talkative, garrulous.
Schwebe f. (-, 0) suspense; in der ~, undecided, trembling in the balance.
Schwebebahn f. suspension railway.
Schwebebalken m. (s-, -) balance beam.
schweben v.i. to hover, to float; to be pending; in Gefahr ~, to be in danger; die Sache schwebt noch, the matter is still pending.
Schwede m.; **Schwedin** f. Swede.
Schweden n. (-s, 0) Sweden.
Schwedisch a. Swedish.
Schwefel m. (-s, -) sulfur.
schwefelig s. sulfurous.
schwefeln v.t. to sulphurize.
Schwefelsäure f. sulphuric acid.
Schwefelwasserstoff m. hydrogen sulfide.
Schweif m. (-[e]s, -e) tail; train.
schweifen v.i. to roam, to stray.

Schweigegeld n. hush-money.
Schweigemarsch m. silent march.
Schweigeminute f. minute's silence.
schweigen v.i.st. to be silent, to hold one's tongue.
Schweigen n. (-s, 0) silence.
schweigsam a. taciturn, silent; quiet.
Schwein n. (-[e], -e) pig, hog, swine; pork; (fam.) luck.
Schweine: ~braten m. roast pork; ~fett n. lard; ~fleisch n. pork; ~hirt m. swineherd.
Schweinehund m. (pej.) bastard.
Schweinerei f. (-, -en) filth, mess; (fig.) obscenity.
Schweinestall m. pigsty, pigpen.
schweinisch a. swinish, filthy.
Schweins: ~borste f. hog's bristle; ~hachse ~haxe f. knuckle of pork; ~keule f. leg of pork; ~leder n. pig-skin.
Schweiß m. (-es, 0) sweat; perspiration.
schweißen v.t. to weld.
Schweißer m. (-s, -); **Schweißerin** f. (-, -nen) (mech.) welder.
schweißtreibend a. sudorific.
Schweiz f. (-, 0) Switzerland.
Schweizer m. (-s, -); **Schweizerin** f. (-, -nen); **schweizerisch** a. Swiss.
schweizerdeutsch a. Swiss German.
Schweizer Käse m. Swiss cheese.
Schwelbrand m. smoldering fire.
schwelen v.i. to smolder.
schwelgen v.i. to revel, to feast.
schwelgerisch a. luxuriant; sumptuous.
Schwelle f. (-, -n) threshold, sill; (rail.) sleeper.
schwellen v.i. (s) to swell.
Schwellenangst f. fear of entering a place.
Schwellung f. (-, -en) swelling, to become swollen.
Schwemme f. (-, -n) glut; watering place.
schwemmen v.t. to wash.
Schwemmland n. alluvial place.
Schwengel m. (-s, -) (Glocken~) clapper; (Pumpen~) handle.
Schwenk m. (-s, -s) swing; pan (film).
schwenken v.t. to swing; to wave; to pan; ~ v.i. to wheel.
schwer a. heavy, weighty; difficult, hard; (Wein) strong; grave; grievous; ~e Artillerie f. medium artillery; ein Pfund ~, weighing one pound; es fällt mir ~, I find it hard.
Schwer: ~arbeit f. heavy work; ~behinderte m./f. severely handicapped person; ~beschädigter m. seriously disabled ex-service man.
schwerbewaffnet a. heavily armed.
Schwere f. (-, 0) gravity; heaviness.
schwerelos a. weightless.
Schwerelosigkeit f. weightlessness.
Schwerenöter m. (-s, -) ladykiller.
schwerfällig, a. ponderous; unwieldy; clumsy.
Schwergewicht n. weight; (Boxer) heavyweight.
schwerhörig a. hard of hearing.
Schwer: ~kraft f. gravitation; ~industrie f. heavy industries.
schwerlich adv. hardly, scarcely.
Schwermut f. melancholy.
schwermütig a. melancholic.
Schwerpunkt m. center of gravity.
schwerste Artillerie f. heavy artillery.

Schwert n. (-[e]s, -er) sword; ~**fisch** m. swordfish; ~**lilie** f. iris.

Schwerverbrecher m. serious offender.

schwerverdaulich a. hard to digest.

schwerverletzt a. seriously injured.

schwer: ~**verständlich** a. hard to understand, abstruse; ~**verwundet** a. severely wounded.

Schwester f. (-, -n) sister; nun; nurse.

schwesterlich a. sisterly.

Schlwieger: ~**eltern** pl. parents-in-law pl.; ~**mutter** f. mother-in-law; ~**sohn** m. son-in-law; ~**tochter** f. daughter-in-law; ~**vater** m. father-in-law.

Schwiele f. (-, -n) callus.

schwielig a. callused, horny.

schwierig a. hard, difficult.

Schwierigkeit f. (-, -en) difficulty.

Schwierigkeitsgrad m. degree of difficulty.

Schwimm: ~**anzug** m. swimsuit; ~**bad** n. swimming pool; ~**dock** n. floating dock.

schwimmen v.i.st. to swim; to float.

Schwimmen n. (-s, 0) swimming.

Schwimmer m. (-s, -) swimmer; float.

Schwimmerin f. (-s, -nen) swimmer.

Schwimm: ~**flosse** f. flipper; fin; ~**gestell** n. (avi.) float; ~**gürtel** m. life-belt; ~**vogel** m. web-footed bird; ~**weste** f. life jacket.

Schwindel m. (-s, 0) giddiness, dizziness, vertigo; swindle, cheat, humbug, bubble.

Schwindelei f. swindle, fraud; (Lüge) fib.

Schwindelerregend a. vertiginous; meteoric.

schwindelfrei a. not suffering from vertigo; free from giddiness.

schwindelhaft a. fraudulent.

schwind(e)lig a. dizzy, giddy.

schwindeln v.i. to swindle, to cheat, ~v.imp. to be giddy.

Schwindelpreis m. extortionate price.

schwinden v.t.st. (s) to disappear, to vanish; (Radio) to fade.

Schwindler m. (-s, -) swindler, cheat.

schwindlerisch a. swindling.

Schwindsucht f. consumption, tuberculosis.

schwindsüchtig a. consumptive, tubercular.

Schwinge f. (-, -n) wing.

schwingen v.t. & i.st. to brandish; to swing; to vibrate, to oscillate.

Schwingtür f. swing door.

Schwingung f. (-, -en) vibration, oscillation.

Schwips m. (Schwipses, Schwipse) einen ~ haben, to be tipsy.

schwirren v.i. to whir; to buzz.

Schwitzbad n. steam-bath, Turkish bath.

schwitzen v.i. to sweat, to perspire.

Schwitzkur f. sweating-cure.

schwitzig a. sweaty.

schwören v.t.st. to swear; einen Eid ~, to take an oath; auf etwas ~, bei etwas ~, to swear by; falsch ~, to swear false.

schwul a. gay, homosexual.

schwül a. sultry.

Schwule m. (-n, -n) (fam.) gay man.

Schwüle f. (-, 0) sultriness.

Schwulst m. (-es, 0) bombast.

schwülstig a. bombastic, inflated.

Schwund m. (-[e]s, 0) decrease, decline; fading; atrophy.

Schwung m. (-[e]s, Schwünge) swing, vibration; momentum; flight, strain; rapture; etwas ist im ~, kommt in ~, a thing is in full swing, is getting into vogue.

schwunghaft a. flourishing, spirited; thriving.

schwunglos a. spiritless, lifeless.

Schwungrad m. flywheel.

schwungvoll a. full of fire.

Schwur m. (-[e]s, Schwüre) oath.

Schwurgericht n. jury court; ~**sverhandlung,** f. trial by jury.

sechs a. six.

Sechs f. (-, 0) number six; worst grade (in German school).

Sechsachteltakt m. six-eight time.

Sechseck n. (-[e]s, -e) hexagon.

sechserlei a. of six kinds.

sechsfach a. sixfold.

sechsmal adv. six times.

sechsmonatlich a. half-yearly.

sechsseitig a. hexagonal.

sechstens adv. sixthly.

sechzehn a. sixteen.

Sechzehntel n. (-s, -) sixteenth part; note, f. (mus.) sixteenth note.

sechzig a. sixty; ein Mann in den ~ern, ein Sechziger, a sexagenarian.

See m. (-[e]s, -[e]n) lake; ~ f. (-, 0) sea; zur ~, at sea; hohe (offene) ~, main or open sea; in ~ gehen, to put to sea.

See: ~**adler** m. sea eagle; ~**bad** n. seaside resort; ~**fahrt** f. voyage, cruise; navigation.

seefest a. seaworthy; ~ sein, to be a good sailor.

See: ~**Gang** m. motion of the sea; ~**gefecht** n. naval battle; ~**gras** n. seaweed; ~**hafen** m. seaport; ~**handel** m. maritime trade; ~**herrschaft** f. naval supremacy; ~**hund** m. seal; ~**igel** m. sea urchin; ~**kadett** m. naval cadet; ~**karte** f. chart; ~**klima** n. maritime climate.

seekrank a. seasick.

See: ~**krankheit** f. seasickness; ~**krieg** m. naval war; ~**küste** f. sea-coast, ~**lachs** m. pollack.

Seele f. (-, -n) soul; mind; mit Leib und ~, body and soul.

Seelenamt n. office for the dead.

Seelenfriede m. peace of mind.

seelenfroh a. heartily glad.

Seelen: ~**größe** f. magnanimity; ~**heil** n. spiritual welfare; ~**hirt** m. pastor; ~**messe** f. requiem; ~**ruhe** f. composure, calmness.

seelenruhig a. calm; unruffled.

seelenvergnügt a. thoroughly happy.

Seelenwanderung f. transmigration of souls.

Seeleute pl. seamen, mariners pl.

seelisch a. mental; psychological.

Seelöwe m. sealion.

Seel: ~**sorge** f. pastoral care; ~**sorger** m. pastor.

Seeluft f. sea-air.

See: ~**macht** f. maritime power; ~**mann** m. sailor, mariner; ~**meile** f. nautical mile, knot; ~**not** f. distress; ~**offizier** m. naval officer; ~**pferd** n. sea horse; ~**räuber** m. pirate, corsair; ~**räuberei** f. piracy; ~**recht** n. maritime law; ~**reise** f. voyage, cruise; ~**rose** f. water-lily; ~**schiffahrt** f. ocean navigation; ~**schlacht** f. naval battle; ~**sieg** m.

naval victory; ~**soldat** *m.* marine.
seetüchtig *a.* seaworthy.
See: ~**ufer** *n.* shore, beach; ~**warte** *f.* naval observatory.
seewärts *adv.* seaward, outward.
See: ~**weg** *m.* sea-route; *auf dem ~e,* by sea; ~**wesen** *n.* naval affairs *pl.*; ~**zunge** *f.* (*Fisch*) sole.
Segel *m.* (-s, -) sail; ~ *setzen,* to set sail; ~ *streichen,* to strike sail.
Segelboot *n.* sailing-boat.
Segel: ~**flug** *m.* gliding; ~**flieger** *m.* glider; ~**jacht** *f.* sailing yacht.
segeln *v.i.* (*s, h*) to sail.
Segel: ~**regatta** *f.* sailing regatta; ~**schiff** *n.* sailing-vessel; ~**tuch** *n.* canvas, sail-cloth.
Segen *m.* (-s, -0) blessing, benediction; abundance.
segensreich *a.* blessed.
segensvoll . blessed, fruit-bearing.
Segenswunsch *m.* blessing, kind wishes *pl.*
Segler *m.* (-s, -) yachtsman.
Seglerin *f.* (-, -nen) yachtswoman.
segnen *v.t.* to bless.
Segnung *f.* (-, -en) blessing, benediction.
sehen *v.i. & t.st.* to see, to look, to behold; *einem auf die Finger ~,* to watch one closely; *durch die Finger ~,* to connive at, to wink at; *ungern ~,* to dislike; *ähnlich ~,* to look like, to resemble; ~ *nach,* to look for; (*sorgen*) to look after; *vom ~,* by sight.
sehenswert *a.* worth seeing.
Sehenswürdigkeit *f.* (-, -en) sight, place of interest.
Seher *m.* (-s, -) seer, prophet.
Sehergabe *f.* gift of prophecy.
Seherin *f.* (-, -nen) seer, prophetess.
Seh: ~**fehler** *m.* eye defect; ~**feld** *n.* range of vision; ~**kraft** *f.* visual faculty, eyesight.
Sehne *f.* (-, -n) sinew, tendon; (*Bogen~*) string; (*math.*) chord.
sehnen (sich) *v.refl.* to long (for); to yearn.
Sehnenzerrung *f.* pulled tendon.
Sehnerv *m.* optic nerve.
sehnig *a.* sinewy; wiry; stringy (meat).
sehnlich *a.* ardent, fervent; ~ *adv.* eagerly, ardently.
Sehnsucht *f.* (-, 0) intense longing; yearning.
sehnsüchtig *a.* longing, yearning.
sehr *adv.* very, much, greatly.
Sehschärfe *f.* visual power, (eye) sight.
Sehschwäche *f.* poor (eye) sight.
Sehstörung *f.* impaired vision.
Sehtest *m.* eye test.
seicht *a.* shallow, flat, superficial.
Seide *f.* (-, 0) silk.
Seidel *m.* (-s, -) beer mug (pint).
seiden *a.* silk(en).
Seiden: ~**händler** *m.* silk-merchant; ~**papier** *n.* tissue-paper; ~**raupe** *f.* silk-worm.
seidenweich *a.* silky.
seidig *a.* silky.
Seife *f.* (-, -n) soap.
seifen *v.t.* to soap.
Seifen: ~**blase** *f.* soap-bubble; ~**lauge** *f.* soapsuds; ~**pulver** *n.* soap powder; ~**schale** *f.* soap dish; ~**schaum** *m.* lather.
seifig *a.* soapy.
seihen *v.t.* to strain, to filter.

Seiher *m.* (-s, -) strainer.
Seihtuch *n.* straining-cloth.
Seil *n.* (-[e]s, -e) rope, cord, line.
Seilbahn *f.* cableway.
Seiltänzer *m.*, **Seiltänzerin** *f.* tightrope walker.
sein *pn.* his, of him; its, of it; *das Seine,* his property; *die Seinen,* his people.
sein *v.i.ir.* (*s*) to be, to exist.
Sein *n.* (-s, 0) being, existence.
seinerseits *adv.* on his part.
seinerzeit *adv.* in its time, in those days.
seinethalben, seinetwegen, um seinetwillen *adv.* on his account, for his sake.
Seinige *n.* (-n, 0) his; **die ~n** *pl.* his family.
Seismograph *m.* seismograph; **Seismologe** *m.*, **Seismologin** *f.* seismologist.
seit *pr. & c.* since; for.
seitdem *adv.* since then.
Seite *f.* (-, -n) side, part, flank; page; party; *schwache ~,* foible; *bei ~,* aside; *sich auf eines ~ stellen,* to side with one; *bei ~ schaffen,* to put out of the way, to make away with; *auf eines ~ stehen,* to take one's part.
Seiten: ~**angriff** *m.* flank-attack; ~**ansicht** *f.* profile, side-view; ~**ausgang** *m.* side exit; ~**blick** *m.* sidelong glance; ~**eingang** *f.* side entrance; ~**flügel** *m.* side-aisle, wing; ~**hieb** *m.* (*fig.*) side swipe.
seitenlang *a.* of many pages; ~ *adv.* for pages and pages.
Seiten: ~**linie** *f.* collateral line; sideline; touchline; ~**loge** *f.* side box; ~**schiff** *n.* aisle; ~**sprung** *f.* escapade; ~**stechen** *n.* pain in the side, stitch; ~**steuer** *n.* (*avi.*) rudder; ~**streifen** *m.* shoulder (highway); ~**tür** *f.* side-door; ~**verwandte** *m./f.* collateral relation.
seitens *pr. von Seiten,* at the hands of.
seither *adv.* since (that time)
seitlich *a.* lateral, collateral.
seitwärts *adv.* sideways, aside.
Sekret *n.* (-s, -e) secretion.
Sekretär *m.* (-s, -e); **Sekretärin** *f.* (-, -nen) (secretary's) office.
Sekt *m.* (-[e]s, -e) sparkling wine; champagne.
Sekte *f.* (-, -n) sect.
Sektierer *m.* (-s, -) sectarian.
Sektion *f.* (-, -en) section; post-mortem (examination).
Sektor *n.* (-s, -en) field; sector.
Sekunda . (-, -den) second grade.
Sekundant *m.* (-en, -en) second.
sekundär *a.* secondary.
Sekunde *f.* (-, -n) second; *Bruchteil einer ~,* split-second.
Sekundenschnelle *f.* **in ~** in a matter of seconds.
Sekundenzeiger *m.* second-hand (of a watch).
selber *pn.* myself, himself, etc., personally (*cp.* **derselbe**).
selbst *pn.* self; myself, etc.; ~ *adv.* even.
Selbstachtung *f.* self-respect.
selbständig *a.* independent.
Selbständigkeit *f.* (-, 0) independence.
Selbst: ~**auslöser** *m.* selftimer; ~**bedienung** *f.* self service; ~**befriedigung** *f.* masturbation; ~**behauptung** *f.* self assertion; ~**beherrschung** *f.* self-control; ~**bestimmung** *f.* self-determination; ~**betrug** *m.* self-deception.

selbstbewußt *a.* self-confident.

Selbst: ~**bewußtsein** *n.* self-confidence; ~**erhaltung** *f.* self-preservation; ~**erkenntnis** *f.* self-knowledge.

selbstgefällig *a.* smug, self-complacent.

Selbstgefälligkeit *f.* complacency.

selbst: ~**genügsam** *a.* self-sufficient; ~**gerecht** *a.* self-righteous.

Selbst: ~**gespräch** *n.* monologue, soliloquy; *ein ~ führen*, to talk to oneself; ~**hilfe** *f.* self-help.

selbstherrlich *a. & adv.* high-handed(ly).

Selbst: ~**justiz** *f.* self-administered justice; ~**klebefolie** *f.* self-adhesive plastic sheeting; ~**kostenpreis** *m.* cost-price; ~**kritik** *f.* self-criticism; ~**laut** *m.* vowel.

selbstlos *a.* unselfish, disinterested.

Selbstlosigkeit *f.* unselfishness, altruism.

Selbst: ~**mord** *m.* suicide; ~*mord begehen*, to commit suicide; ~**mörder** *m.* suicide.

selbstmörderisch *a.* suicidal.

selbstredend *a.* self-evident; (*adv.*) of course.

Selbstchuß *m.* spring-gun.

selbstsicher *a.* self-confident.

Selbstsucht *f.* (-, 0) selfishness.

selbstsüchtig *a.* selfish, self-seeking.

selbsttätig *a.* spontaneous; automatic.

Selbsttäuschung *f.* self-delusion.

Selbst: ~**überwindung** *f.* self-conquest; ~**verleugnung** *f.* self-denial.

selbstverständlich *a.* self-evident; (*adv.*) of course; needless to say, obviously, it goes without saying.

Selbst: ~**vertrauen** *m.* self-confidence, self-reliance; ~**verwaltung,** *f.* self-government; ~**zufriedenheit** *f.* self-satisfaction; ~**zweck** *m.* end in itself.

Selen *n.* (-s, 0) selenium.

selig *a.* blessed, blissful; deceased, late; ~**sprechen,** to beatify; *~ werden*, to be saved.

Seligkeit *f.* (-, -en) salvation; perfect happiness.

seligmachend *a.* beatific; saving.

Seligsprechung *f.* (-, -en) beatification.

Sellerie *m.* (-s, -s) celery.

selten *a.* rare, scarce; *adv.* seldom, rarely.

Seltenheit *f.* (-, -en) rarity, scarcity; curiosity, curio.

Selterswasser *n.* seltzer (water).

seltsam *a.* singular, strange, odd.

seltsamerweise *adv.* strangely enough.

Semantik *f.* (-, 0) semantics.

semantisch *a.* semantic; *adv.* semantically.

Semester *m.* (-s, -) academic term; semester.

Seminar *n.* (-s, -e) training college; seminary.

Seminar: ~**arbeit** *f.* seminar paper; ~**schein** *m.* credits for a seminar.

Semit *m.* (-en, -en); **Semitin** *f.* (-, -nen) semite.

semitisch *a.* semitic.

Semmel *f.* (-, -n) roll; ~**brösel** *pl.* bread crumbs; ~**knödel** *m.* bread dumpling.

Senat *m.* (-s, -e) senate.

Sendbote *m.* emissary.

Sendebereich *m.* transmitting area.

senden *v.t.ir.* to send, to dispatch; *nach einem ~,* to send for one; *Waren mit der Post ~,* to send things through the post; to broadcast.

Sender *m.* (-s, -) transmitter; broadcasting station.

Senderaum *m.* (*Radio*) studio.

Sendestation *f.* radio *or* broadcasting station.

Sendung *f.* (-, -en) mission; consignment, parcel; broadcast.

Senf *m.* (-[e]s, -e) mustard.

Senfkorn *n.* mustard-seed.

sengen *v.t.* to singe, to scorch; to scald; *~ und brennen,* to lay waste by fire.

senil *a.* senile.

Senilität *f.* senility.

Senior *m.*; **Seniorin** *f.* senior; senior partner; senior citizen.

Seniorenheim *n.* home for the elderly.

Senkblei *n.* plumb.

senken *v.t.* to let down, to lower; (sich) ~ *v.refl.* to sink.

Senkgrube *f.* cesspit.

senkrecht *a.* perpendicular; vertical.

Senkrechtstarter *m.* vertical takeoff aircraft; (*fig.*) whiz-kid.

Senkung *f.* (-, -en) sinking; depression; (*Preise*) reduction; lowering; unstressed syllable.

Senner *m.* (-s, -) (Alpine) herdsman and dairyman.

Sennerei (-, -en), **Sennhütte** *f.* Alpine cheese-dairy.

Sennerin *f.* (-, -nen) (Alpine) dairymaid.

Sensation *f.* sensation.

sensationell *a.* sensational.

Sense *f.* (-, -n) scythe.

sensibel *a.* sensitive.

Sensibilität *f.* sensitivity.

Sensor *m.* (-s, -en) sensor.

sentimental *a.* sentimental.

Sentimentalität *f.* sentimentality.

separat *a.* separate.

Separatismus *m.* separation.

September *m.* (-s, -) September.

Septime *f.* seventh (music).

sequestrieren *v.t.* to sequestrate.

Serail *m. n.* (-s, -s) seraglio.

Serbe *m.*; **Serbin** *f.* Serb.

Serbien *n.* Serbia.

serbisch *a.* Serbian.

Serenade *f.* serenade.

Sergeant *m.* (-en, -en) sergeant.

Serie *f.* (-, -n) series.

serienmäßig *a.* standard; fitted as standard.

Serienproduktion *f.* series production.

seriös *a.* respectable; trustworthy.

Serum *n.* (-s, -ra, -ren) serum.

Service, *n.* service, set.

service *m.* service; serve (tennis).

servieren *v.t.* to serve.

Serviererin *f.* waitress.

servierfertig, *a.* ready-to-serve.

Serviette *f.* (-, -n) serviette, (table)-napkin.

Sessel *m.* (-s, -) easy chair, arm chair.

Sessellift *m.* chair-lift.

seßhaft *a.* settled; sedentary resident.

Setzei *n.* fried-egg.

setzen *v.t.* to set, to put, to place; to stake; to compose; *~ v.i.* to leap; (sich) ~ *v.refl.* to sit down; to settle; *alles auf eine Karte ~,* to stake everything on one card; *aufs Spiel ~,* to stake, to risk; *instand ~,* to enable; to repair; *in Schrecken ~,* to frighten; *unter*

Wasser ~, to inundate; *alles daran* ~, to risk everything; *sich zur Ruhe* ~, to retire into private life; *sich zur Wehr* ~, to offer resistance; *über den Fluß* ~, to cross the river; *gesetzt den Fall*, put the case, suppose.

Setzer *m.* (-s, -); **Setzerin** *f.* (-, -nen) typesetter.

Setzling *m.* (-s, -e) seedling.

Seuche *f.* (-, -n) epidemic; pestilence.

seuchenartig *a.* epidemic, contagious.

Seuchenbekämpfung *f.* epidemic control.

seufzen *v.i.* to sigh, to groan.

Seufzer *m.* (-s, -) sigh, groan; ~ *ausstossen*, to heave sighs, to utter groans.

Sex *m.* (-es, 0) sex.

Sexismus *m.* sexism.

sexistisch *a.* sexist.

Sexta *f.* (-, -ten) sixth grade.

Sextett *n.* (-[e]s, -e) sextet(te).

Sexual: ~**erziehung** *f.* sex education; ~**hormon** *n.* sex hormone.

Sexualität *f.* sexuality.

sexuell *a.* sexual.

Sezessionskrieg *m.* American Civil War.

sezieren *v.t.* to dissect.

Seziermesser *n.* dissecting-knife.

Show *f.* (-, -s) show.

Siam *n.* Siam.

Siamese *m.*; **Siamesin** *f.* Siamese.

Sibirien *n.* Siberia.

Sibylle *f.* (-, -n) Sibyl, prophetess.

sich *pn.* oneself, himself, etc.; each other; *an und für* ~, in itself; *wieder zu* ~ *kommen*, to come to, to recover consciousness; *es hat nichts auf* ~, it is of no consequence.

Sichel *f.* (-, -n) sickle; (*Mond*~) crescent.

sicher *a.* sure, certain; secure, safe; ~ *adv.* for sure, for certain; ~ *wissen*, to be sure; *~e Hand*, steady hand; *~es Geleit*, safe-conduct; (*sich*) ~ *stellen*, to secure (oneself).

Sicherheit *f.* (-, -en) security; surety, safety; *in* ~ *bringen*, to secure; ~ *leisten*, to go bail, to give security; *in* ~, in (a place of) safety.

Sicherheits: ~**abstand** *m.* safe distance; ~**glas** *n.* shatter-proof glass, safety-glass.

sicherheitshalber *adv.* as a precaution.

Sicherheits: ~**kontrolle** *f.* security check; ~**lampe** *f.* safety-lamp; ~**maßregeln** *pl.* precautions; ~**nadel** *f.* safety-pin; ~**rat** *m.* Security Council; ~**schloß** *n.* safety-lock; ~**ventil** *n.* safety-valve; ~**zündholz** *m.* safety-match.

sicherlich *adv.* surely, certainly.

sichern *v.t.* to secure.

Sicherung *f.* (-, -en) (*am Gewehr*) safety bolt; (*elek.*) fuse.

Sicherungskasten *m.* fusebox.

Sicht *f.* (-, 0) sight; *auf* ~, at *or* on sight; *nach* ~, after sight; *auf kurze* ~, at short date; *auf 8 Tage* ~, seven days after sight; *auf 2 Monate* ~, at two months' sight; *ausser* ~ *sein*, to be out of sight.

sichtbar *a.* visible; (*fig.*) evident.

sichten *pv.t.* to sift; (*nav.*) to sight.

sichtlich *a.* obvious, perceptible.

Sichtverhältnisse *pl.* visibility.

Sichtvermerk *m.* (-s, -e) visa.

Sichtweite *f.* visual range.

sickern *v.i.* to trickle, to ooze.

sie *pn.* she, her; they, them.

Sie *pn.* you.

Sieb *n.* (-[e]s, -e) sieve; strainer.

sieben *v.t.* to sift, to strain.

sieben *a.* seven, *es ist halb* ~, it is half-past six.

siebenerlei *a.* of seven kinds.

siebenfach, siebenfältig *a.* sevenfold.

siebenmal *dv.* seven times.

Siebenmeilenstiefel *pl.* seven-league boots *pl.*

Siebensachen *pl.* one's belongings.

siebzehn *a.* seventeen.

siebzig *a.* seventy.

Siebziger *m.* (-s, -) septuagenarian.

siech *a.* sick, sickly, infirm.

Siechbett *n.* sick-bed.

siechen *v.i.* to be sickly; to pine away.

Siechtum (-s, 0) *n.* protracted sickness.

siede(nd)heiß *a.* scalding hot.

Siedehitze *f.* boiling heat.

siedeln *v.i. & t.* to colonize, to settle.

sieden *v.t. & i.st.* to seethe, to boil; to simmer.

Siedepunkt *m.* boiling-point.

Siedler *m.* (-s, -); **Siedlerin** *f.* (-, -nen) settler.

Siedlung *f.* (-, -en) settlement.

Sieg *m.* (-[e]s, -e) victory; triumph.

Siegel *n.* (-s, -) seal; *sein* ~ *drauf drücken*, to set one's seal to it.

Siegel: ~**abdruck** *m.* imprint (of a seal); ~**lack** *m.* sealing-wax.

siegeln *v.t.* to seal.

Siegelring *m.* signet-ring.

siegen *v.i.* to conquer, to win, to be victorious (over).

Sieger *m.* (-s, -); **Siegerin** *f.* (-, -nen) conqueror, victor; (*Sport*) winner.

siegreich *a.* victorious, triumphant.

sieh! *i.* see! lo!; ~ *einmal!* ~ *da!* look there!

siezen *v.t.* to use the polite 'Sie'.

Signal *n.* (-[e]s, -e) signal.

signalisieren *v.t.* to signal.

Signalwächter *m.* (*rail.*) signalman.

Signatur *f.* (-, -en) initials; abbreviated signature; autograph; mark, brand; (*fig.*) stamp.

signieren *v.t.* to sign; to autograph.

Silbe *f.* (-, -n) syllable.

Silben: ~**schrift** *f.* syllabic writing; ~**teilung** *f.* syllabication.

Silber *n.* (-s, 0) silver; *gediegenes* ~ solid silver.

Silber: ~**barre** *f.*, ~**barren** *m.* ingot of silver; ~**geschirr** *n.* (silver-)plate, silverware.

silbern *a.* (of) silver; *~e Hochzeit*, silver wedding.

Silber: ~**pappel** *f.* white poplar; ~**streifen** *m.* silver lining; ~**währung** *f.* silver standard; ~**waren** *pl.* silver ware, plate.

Silberzeug *n.* silver-plate.

Silentium! *i.* silence!

Silhouette *f.* (-, -n) silhouette.

Silikat *n.* silicate.

Silikon *n.* silicone.

Silvesterabend *m.* New Year's Eve.

Simbabwe *n.* (-s, 0) Zimbabwe.

simpel *a.* simple, plain.

Simpel *m.* (-s, -) simpleton.

Sims *m. & n.* (-es, -e) ledge; sill; mantelpiece.

Simulant *m.* (-en, -en); **Simulantin** *f.* (-, -nen) malingerer.

simulieren *v.t.* to malinger, to simulate (illness).
Simultan: ~**dolmetscher** *m.*, ~**dolmetscherin** *f.* simultaneous interpreter.
Sinaihalbinsel *f.* Sinai Peninsula.
Sinekure *f.* (-, -n) sinecure.
Sinfonie *f.* (-, -n) symphony.
Sinfonieorchester *n.* symphony orchestra.
sinfonisch *a.* symphonic.
singen *v.i.* & *t.st.* to sing; *vom Blatt* ~ to sing at sight; *nach Noten* ~, to sing from notes.
Single *f.* single (record).
Single *m.* single (person).
Single *n.* singles (tennis etc.).
Sing: ~**sang** *m.* sing-song; ~**spiel** *n.* Singspiel; ~**stimme** *f.* vocal part.
Singular *m.* singular.
Sing: ~**vogel** *m.* singing-bird; ~**weise** *f.* melody, tune.
sinken *v.i.st* (*s*) to sink, to decline; *den Mut* ~ *lassen,* to get discouraged.
Sinn *m.* (-[e]s, -e) sense; mind; liking, taste (for, *für*); meaning; *im* ~ *haben,* to intend; *nicht nach meinem* ~, not to my mind; *die fünf* ~*e,* the five senses; *bei* ~*en sein,* to have one's wits about one.
Sinnbild *n.* symbol, emblem; allegory.
sinnbildlich *a.* symolic(al), emblematic.
sinnen *v.i.st.* to meditate, to reflect, to muse; *anders gesinnt sein,* to be otherwise inclined; *nicht gesonnen sein,* to feel disinclined; *all sein Sinnen und Trachten,* all his thoughts and aspirations.
Sinnen: ~**genuß** *m.* sensual pleasure; ~**lust** *f.* sensuality.
sinnentstellend *a.* distorting (meaning).
sinnentstellt *a.* distorted.
Sinnenwelt *f.* external world.
Sinnes: ~**änderung** *f.* change of mind; ~**art** *f.* disposition, character; ~**eindruck** *m.* sensation; ~**organ** *n.* sense-organ, sensory organ; täuschung *f.* illusion; hallucination; delusion; ~**wandel** *m.* change of mind; ~**werkzeug** *n.* sense organ.
Sinngedicht *n.* epigram.
Sinngemäß *a.* conveying the general meaning.
sinnig *a.* thoughtful; sensible.
sinnlich *a.* sensual; sensuous, material.
Sinnlichkeit *f.* (-, 0) sensuality.
sinnlos *a.* senseless; irrational; useless.
Sinnlosigkeit *f.* senselessness; pointlessness.
sinnreich *a.* ingenious; clever.
Sinnspruch *m.* maxim, motto, device.
sinnverwandt *a.* synonymous.
sinnvoll *a.* sensible; meaningful.
sinnwidrig *a.* nonsensical.
Sintflut *f.* (great) Flood, Deluge.
sintflutartig *a.* torrential; *adv.* in torrents.
Sinus *m.* (-, -) sine.
Sippe *f.* (-, -n) **Sippschaft** *f.* clan; tribe, family.
Sirene *f.* (-, -n) siren.
Sirenengeheul *n.* wail of sirens.
Sirup *m.* (-s, -e) treacle; syrup.
Sitte *f.* (-, -n) custom, usage, fashion.
Sitten *n.pl.* manners; morals *pl.*
Sitten: ~**dezernat** *n.* vice squad; ~**geschichte** *f.* history of life and customs; ~**gesetz** *n.* moral law; ~**lehre** *f.* moral philosophy, ethics *pl.*
sittenlos *a.* immoral.
Sittenlosigkeit *f.* (-, 0) immorality.

sittenrein *a.* (morally) pure.
Sittenstrenge *f.* austerity.
sittlich *a.* moral.
Sittlichkeit *f.* (-, 0) morality.
Sittlichkeits: ~**verbrechen** *n.* sex crime; ~**verbrecher** *m.* sex offender.
Sittlichkeitsvergehen *n.* indecent assault.
sittsam *a.* modest; demure.
Situation *f.* (-, -en) situation.
situiert *a. gut* ~, well off.
Sitz *m.* (-es, -e) seat; residence; chair.
Sitzbad *n.* hip-bath, sitz-bath.
sitzen *v.i.st.* to sit; to fit; to be imprisoned; *gut* ~, to fit well; *auf sich* ~ *lassen,* to pocket; *ein Mädchen* ~*lassen,* to jilt a girl; ~*bleiben,* to remain a spinster; (*in der Schule*) to be held back; *das Kleid sitzt gut,* the dress is an excellent fit; *sitzende Lebensweise,* sedentary life.
Sitz: ~**fleisch** *n.* (*fig.*) steadiness; ~**gelegenheit** *f.* seating accommodation; ~**platz** *m.* seat; ~**streik** *m.* sit-down strike.
Sitzung *f.* (-, -en) meeting, conference; sitting, session.
Sitzungsbericht *m.* minutes, (report of) proceedings *pl.*
Sitzungssaal *m.* (-s, -säle) conference hall; court room.
Sizilianer *m.*; **Sizilianerin** *f.* Sicilian.
Sizilien *n.* Sicily.
Skala *f.* (-, -len) scale; range.
Skalp *n.* (-s, -s) scalp.
Skalpell *n.* (-s, -s) scalpel.
skalpieren *v.t.* to scalp.
Skandal *m.* (-[e]s, -e) scandal; row.
skandalös *a.* scandalous.
skandieren *v.t.* to scan; to chant.
Skat *m.* (-[e]s, -e) a German national card-game.
Skelett *n.* (-[e]s, -e) skeleton.
Skepsis *f.* scepticism.
Skeptiker *m.* (-s, -); **Skeptikerin** *f.* (-, -nen) sceptic.
skeptisch *a.* sceptical.
Ski *m.* (-s, -er) ski.
Ski: ~**bindung** *f.* ski binding; ~**lauf** *m.*, ~**laufen** *n.* skiing; ~**läufer** *m.*, ~**läuferin** *f.* skier; ~**stock** *m.* ski pole.
Skizze *f.* (-, -n) sketch; outline.
Skizzenbuch *n.* sketch-book.
skizzieren *v.t.* to sketch.
Sklave *m.* (-n, -n); **Sklavin** *f.* (-, -nen) slave.
Sklaven: ~**halter** *m.* slave-owner; ~**handel** *m.* slave-trade; ~**händler** *m.* slave-trader.
Sklaverei *f.* (-, 0) slavery.
sklavisch *a.* slavish, servile.
Sklerose *f.* sclerosis.
Skonto *m.* (-[s], 0) discount.
Skorbut *m.* (-[e]s, 0) scurvy.
Skorpion *m.* (-[e]s, -e) scorpion; Scorpio (astrology).
Skrupeln *pl.* scruples *pl.*; *sich keine* ~ *machen,* to have no scruples.
skrupelös *a.* scrupulous.
skrupellos *a.* unscrupulous.
Skulptur *f.* (-, -en) sculpture.
skurril *a.* absurd; bizarre.
S-Kurve *f.* (-, -n) hairpin-bend.

Slalom *m.* (-s, -s) slalom.
Slawe *m.* (-n, -n); **Slawin** *f.* (-, -nen) Slav.
slawisch *a.* Slav; Slavonic.
slip *m.* (-s, -s) briefs.
Slogan *m.* (-s, -s) slogan.
Slowake *m.* (-n, -n); **Slowakin** *f.* (-, -nen) Slovak.
Slowakei *f.* (-, 0) Slovakia.
slowakisch *a.* Slovak; Slovakian.
Slowene *m.* (-n, -n); **Slowenin** *f.* (-, -nen) Slovene, Slovenian.
Slowenien *n.* (-s, 0) Slovenia.
slowenisch *a.* Slovene; Slovenian.
Slum *m.* (-, -s) slum.
Smaragd *m.* (-[e]s, -e)u emerald.
Smog *m.* (-s, -s) smog; ~**alarm** *m.* smog warning.
Smoking *m.* (-s, -s) tuxedo; dinner-jacket.
Snob *n.* (-s, -s) snob.
Snobismus *m.* snobbery; snobbishness.
snobistisch *a.* snobbish.
so *adv. & c.* so, thus, in such a manner, like this; *sobald als,* as soon as; *sowohl. . ., als auch,* as well as; *~ und ~ viel,* so and so much; *~ reich er auch ist,* rich as he may be; *~ sehr auch, wenn auch noch ~ sehr,* however much, if. . . ever so much; *~ ein Mann,* such a man; *~ etwas,* such a thing; *um ~ besser,* so much the better; *zweimal soviel,* twice as much? *wieso?* how so? how do you mean?
sobald *c.* as soon as.
Socke *f.* (-, -n) sock.
Sockel *m.* (-s, -) plinth; base.
Sockenhalter *m.* garter.
Soda *f.* (-, 0) soda.
sodann *adv.* then.
Sodawasser *n.* soda(-water).
Sodbrennen *n.* heartburn; pyrosis.
soeben *adv.* just now, this minute.
Sofa *n.* (-s, -s) sofa.
sofern *c.,* if; inasmuch as, so far as.
sofort *adv.* at once, immediately.
Sofortbildkamera *f.* instant (picture) camera.
Soforthilfe *f.* immediate aid.
sofortig *a.* immediate, instantaneous.
Sofortmassnahme *f.* immediate measure.
Soft-Eis *n.* soft ice-cream.
Software *f.* (-, -s) software.
Sog *m.* (-[e]s, -e) suction; current; wake (ship); slipstream (plane).
sogar *adv.* even.
sogenannt *a.* so-called; pretended.
sogleich *adv.* immediately, directly.
Sohle *f.* (-, -n) sole.
sohlen *v.t.* to sole.
Sohn *m.* (-[e]s, Söhne) son; *der verlorene ~,* the prodigal son.
Soja: ~**bohne** *f.* soy bean; ~**soße** *f.* soy sauce.
solange, als, as long as.
solar *a.* solar.
Solarium *n.* (-s, -rien) solarium.
Solar: ~**technik** *f.* solar technology; ~**zelle** *f.* solar cell.
solcher, solche, solch[es] *pn.* such; the same.
solchergestalt *a.* thus, in such manner.
solcherlei *a.* of such a kind.
Sold *m.* (-[e]s, 0) (military) pay; (*fig.*) wages; *in ~ stehen,* to be the hireling of. . .
Soldat *m.* (-en, -en); **Soldatin** *f.* (-, -nen) soldier;

~ *werden,* to enlist.
Soldatenfriedhof *m.* war cemetery.
Soldateska *f.* (-, 0) (brutal) soldiery.
soldatisch *a.* soldier-like, military.
Söldner *m.* (-s, -) mercenary, hireling.
Soldliste *f.* (*mil.*) pay-roll.
Sole *f.* (-, -n) salt-water, brine.
solidarisch *a.* united.
Solidarität *f.* (-, 0) solidarity.
solide *a.* solid, strong; (*fig.*) respectable, steady, safe, solvent.
Solidität *f.* (-, 0) solidity; (*com.*) respectability, acknowledged standing.
Solist *m.* (-en, -en); **Solistin** *f.* (-, -nen) soloist.
Soll *n.* (-[e]s, -[s]) debit; ~ *und Haben,* debit and credit.
sollen *v.i.ir.* shall, to be to; to be said, be supposed to; *was soll das?* what does this mean?
Solo *n.* (-s, -s *u.* Soli) solo.
Solquelle *f.* saline-spring.
somatisch *a.* somatic.
somit *adv.* therefore; consequently.
Sommer *m.* (-s, -) summer.
Sommer: ~**anfang** *f.* beginning of the Summer; ~**aufenthalt** *m.* summer-resort; ~**fahrplan** *m.* summer-service timetables; ~**fäden** *m.pl.* gossamer; ~**frische** *f.* summer-resort; ~**gäste** *pl.* visitors.
sommerlich *a.* summerlike.
Sommerschlußverkauf *m.* summer sale.
Sommersemester *n.* (-s, -) summer term/semester.
Sommersprosse *f.* freckle.
sommersprossig *a.* freckled.
Sommerzeit *f.* summertime.
somnambul *a.* somnambulistic.
sonach *adv.* therefore, accordingly.
Sonate *f.* (-, -n) sonata.
Sonde *f.* +(-, -n) (*med.*) probe; sonde.
Sonderangebot *n.* (-s, -e) special offer.
Sonderausgabe *f.* special edition.
sonderbar *a.* strange, singular, odd.
Sonderberichterstatter *m.* special correspondent.
Sonderfall *m.* special case; exception.
sondergleichen *a.& adv.* without equals.
Sonderinteresse *n.* special interest.
sonderlich *a.* special, particular; important.
Sonderling *m.* (-[e]s, -e) odd character.
sondern *v.t.* to separate, to sever; ~ *c.* but; *nicht nur. . ., ~ auch,* not only. . . but also.
Sonder: ~**nummer** *f.* special edition/issue; ~**recht** *n.* privilege; ~**stellung** *f.* unique *or* exceptional position; ~**zug** *m.* special train.
sondieren *v.t.* (*med.*) to probe; to sound; (*fig.*) to explore, to feel one's way.
Sonett *n.* (-[e]s, -e) sonnet.
Sonnabend *m.* (-s, -e) Saturday.
Sonne *f.* (-, -n) sun.
sonnen (sich) ~ *v.refl.* to sunbathe.
Sonnen: ~**aufgang** *m.* sunrise; ~**bad** *n.* sun-bath; ~**blume** *f.* sunflower; ~**brand** *m.* sunburn; ~**brille** *f.* sun-glasses; ~**energie** *f.* solar energy; ~**finsternis** *f.* solar eclipse; ~**fleck** *m.* sun-spot.
Sonnenjahr *n.* solar year.
sonnenklar *a.* as clear as daylight.
Sonnen: ~**kollektor** *m.* solar collector; ~**licht** *n.*

sunlight; ~**schein** *m.* sunshine; ~**schirm** *m.* parasol, sunshade; ~**spektrum** *n.* solar spectrum; ~**stich** *m.* sunstroke; ~**strahl** *m.* sunbeam; ~**system** *n.* solar system; ~**uhr** *f.* sundial.
Sonnenuntergang *m.* sunset, sundown.
sonnenverbrannt *a.* sunburnt.
Sonnenwende *f.* solstice.
sonnig *a.* sunny, sunshiny.
Sonntag *m.* (-s, -e) Sunday.
sonntäglich *a.* Sunday.
sonntags *adv.* on Sunday(s).
sonst *adv.* else, otherwise; besides; formerly; ~ *etwas,* anything else; ~ *jemand,* anybody else; ~ *nichts,* nothing else; ~ *nirgends,* nowhere else; ~ *wo,* elsewhere.
sonstig *a.* other, remaining; former.
Sophistik *f.* (-, 0) sophistry.
sophistisch *a.* sophistic(al).
Sopran *m.* (-[e]s, -e) soprano, treble.
Sopranist *m.* (-en, -en); **Sopranistin** *f.* (-, -nen) soprano.
Sorge *f.* (-, -n) care; worries *pl.; sich ~ machen um,* to be concerned about. . .
sorgen *v.i.* to worry; to care, provide; *sich um etwas ~,* to be concerned about a thing; *~ für,* to provide for, to see to it, to look after, to take care of.
sorgenfrei, sorgenlos *a.* carefree.
Sorgenkind *n.* problem child.
sorgenschwer *a.* anxious, uneasy.
sorgenvoll *a.* anxious, uneasy.
Sorgfalt *f.* (-, 0) care(fulness).
sorgfältig *a.* careful, heedful.
Sorgfältigkeit *f.* carefulness.
sorglos *a.* careless, thoughtless.
sorgsam *a.* careful.
Sorte *f.* (-, -n) sort, kind.
sortieren *v.t.* to (as)sort.
Sortierer *m.* (-s, -0) sorter.
Sortimenter *m.* (-s, -), **Sortimentsbuchhändler** *m.* retail bookseller.
sosehr *konj.* however much.
Soße *f.* (-, -n) sauce; gravy; dressing.
Souffleur *m.* (-[e]s, -e); **Souffleuse** *f.* (-, -n) prompter.
Souffleurkasten *m.* prompter's box.
soufflieren *v.i.* to prompt.
Souterrain *n.* (-[e]s, -s) basement.
Souvenir *n.* (-s, -s) souvenir.
souverän *a.* sovereign.
Souverän *m.* (-[e]s, -e) sovereign.
Souveränität *f.* (-, 0) sovereignty.
soviel *c.* as far as; as soon as.
soweit *c.* as far as.
sowenig *c.* however; (*indefinite*) *n. ~ wie möglich* as little as possible.
sowie *c.* as well as; as soon as.
sowieso *adv.* anyhow, anyway.
sowohl *c. ~ . . . als/wie. . . . . .* as well as. . .
sozial *a.* social.
Sozial: ~**abgaben** *pl.* social contributions; ~**amt** *n.* social welfare office; ~**arbeiter** *m.,* ~**arbeiterin** *f.* social worker.
Sozialdemokrat *m.* (-en, -en); **Sozialdemokratin** *f.* (-, -nen) Social Democrat.
Sozialdemokratie *f.* social democracy.
sozialdemokratisch *a.* social-democratic.

Sozialhilfe *f.* social welfare.
sozialisieren *v.t.* to socialize.
Sozialismus *m.* (-, 0) socialism.
Sozialist *m.;* **Sozialistin** *f.* socialist.
sozialistisch *a.* Socialist.
Sozialkunde *f.* social studies.
Sozialleistungen *pl.* social welfare benefits.
Sozial: ~**politik** *f.* social policy; ~**prestige** *f.* social status; ~**produkt** *n.* national product; ~**staat** *m.* welfare state; ~**versicherung** *f.* social security; ~**wissenschaft** *f.* sociology; ~**wohnung** *f.* municipal housing unit.
Soziologie *f.* (-, 0) social science, sociology.
soziologisch *a.* sociological.
Sozius *m.* (-, Sozii) (*com.*) partner.
sozusagen *adv.* as it were, so to speak.
Spachtel *m.* putty knife; paint-scraper.
Spachtelmasse *f.* filler.
spachteln *v.t.* to fill; to smooth over.
Spagat *m.* (-[e]s, -e) splits.
spähen *v.i. & t.* to spy, to peer.
Späher *m.* (-s, -) spy, scout.
Spähtrupp *m.* patrol; ~**tätigkeit** *f.* patrol activity.
Spalier *n.* (-[e]s, -e) espalier, trellis; (*fig.*) lane.
Spalierobst *n.* wall-fruit.
Spalt *m.* (-[e]s, -e), **Spalte** *f.* (-, -n) opening; crack, crevice, fissure; *Spalte* (newspaper) column.
spalten *v.t.* to split, to cleave, to slit; (sich) ~ *v.refl.* to divide; to bifurcate.
spaltig *a.* fissured, cracked.
Spaltung *f.* (-, -en) division, cleavage, schism; (*Atomkern, Zelle*) fission.
Span *m.* (-[e]s, Späne) chip, splinter; *Späne pl.* shavings, chips *pl.*
Spanferkel *n.* sucking-pig.
Spange *f.* (-, -n) buckle, clasp; bracelet.
Spaniel *m.* spaniel.
Spanien *n.* (-s, 0) Spain.
Spanier *m.* (-s, -); **Spanieren** *f.* (-, -nen) Spaniard.
spanisch *a.* Spanish; ~**e Wand** *f.* folding screen.
Spankorb *m.* wire or wood basket.
Spann *m.* (-[e]s, -e) instep.
Spanne *f.* (-, -n) span; (*fig.*) short space; (*com.*) margin.
spannen *v.t.* to stretch, to strain; to extend; to span; (*den Bogen*) to bend; (*das Gewehr*) to cock; *seine Forderungen zu hoch ~,* to set one's stakes too high; *einen auf die Folter ~,* to keep s.b. in suspense.
spannend *a.* exciting; deeply interesting, thrilling.
Spanner *m.* (-s, -) press; shoe-tree; (*fig.*) peeping Tom.
Spann: ~**feder** *f.* spring; ~**kraft** *f.* elasticity.
Spannung *f.* (-, -en) tension; (*elek.*) voltage; strained relations *pl.*
Spannungsgebiet *n.* area of pol. tensions.
spannungsgeladen *a.* tense.
spannungslos *a.* (*elek.*) dead.
Spannweite *f.* spread; span.
Spanplatte *f.* chipboard.
Spar: ~**buch** *n.* savings book; ~**büchse** *f.* money-box; ~**einlage** *f.* savings deposit.
sparen *v.t.* to save, to spare; to economize.
Spargel *m.* (-s, -) asparagus.
Sparkasse *f.* savings-bank.
spärlich *a.* scanty, meagre, frugal.
Sparmaßnahmen *pl.* economy measures.

Sparren *m.* (-s, -) rafter.
sparsam *a.* economical, thrifty.
Sparsamkeit *f.* (-, 0) thrift, economy.
Sparschein *m.* savings certificate.
Sparschwein *n.* piggy bank.
spartanisch *a.* Spartan.
Sparte *f.* (-, -n) department, branch.
Spaß *m.* (-es, Spässe) jest, joke, sport; *das macht mir ~*, it amuses me; *das ist kein ~*, this is no laughing matter; *zum ~*, for fun.
spaßen *v.i.* to jest, to joke.
spaßeshalber *adv.* for the fun of it.
spaßhaft *a.* waggish, funny, jocular.
spaßig *a.* funny, amusing.
Spaßmacher, Spaßvogel *m.* comedian, clown.
spastisch *a.* spastic.
Spat *m.* (-[e], -e) (*Mineral*) spar.
spät *a.& adv.* late; *wie ~ ist es?* what is the time? *früher oder später*, sooner or later; *~ am Tage, im Jahre*, late in the day, in the year.
Spaten *m.* i(-s, -) spade.
späterhin *adv.* later on.
spätestens *adv.* at the latest.
Spät: *~herbst* *m.* late autumn; *~lese* *f.* late vintage; *~obst* *n.* late fruit; *~schicht* *f.* late shift; *~sommer* *m.* late summer.
Spatz *m.* (-en, -en) sparrow.
spazieren *v.i.* (*s*) to take a walk, to stroll; *~gehen* to go for a walk.
Spazier: *~fahrt* *f.* drive, ride; *~gang* *m.* walk, stroll; promenade; *~stock* *m.* walking-stick; *~weg* *m.* walk, promenade.
Specht *m.* (-[e]s, -e) woodpecker.
Speck *m.* (-[e]s, 0) bacon; blubber (whales); (*fam.*) fat.
speckig *a.* greasy.
Speck: *~schwarte* *f.* rind, skin of bacon; *~seite* *f.* side of bacon; *~stein* *m.* (mineral) soapstone.
spedieren *v.t.* to dispatch, to forward.
Spediteur *m.* (-s, -) forwarding agent, carrier; furniture remover.
Speditionsfirma *f.* forwarding/shipping company; moving company.
Speditionskosten *pl.* transport *or* forwarding charges.
Speer *m.* (-[e]s, -e) spear; javelin.
Speiche *f.* (-, -n) spoke.
Speichel *m.* (-s, 0) spittle, saliva.
Speichellecker *m.* lick-spittle, toady.
Speicher *m.* (-s, -) granary; warehouse; attic.
speichern *v.t.* to store.
speien *v.t. & t.st.* to spit; to vomit.
Speise *f.* (-, -n) food, meat; dish.
Speise: *~gaststätte* *f.* restaurant; *~kammer* *f.* larder, pantry; *~karte* *f.* bill of fare, menu.
speisen *v.t.* to feed; *~ v.i.* to eat; to dine.
Speise: *~öl* *n.* salad-oil; *~röhre* *f.* gullet, esophagus; *~saal* *m.* dining-room; *~wagen* *m.* dining-car; *~wagenschaffner* *m.* dining-car attendant; *~zimmer* *n.* dining-room.
Spektakel *m. & n.* (-s, -) noise, row.
spektakulär *a.* spectacular.
Spektralanalyse *f.* spectral-analysis.
Spektrum *n.* (-s, -tren) spectrum.
Spekulant *m.* (-en, -en) speculator.
Spekulation *f.* (-, -en) speculation.

spekulieren *v.i.* to speculate (in, on).
Spelunke *f.* (-, -n) (*fam.*) dive.
Spelze *f.* (-, -n) husk.
spendabel *a.* generous.
Spende *f.* (-, -n) donation.
spenden *v.t.* to contribute (to), to donate.
Spender *m.* (-s, -); **Spenderin** *f.* (-, -nen) donor.
spendieren *v.t.* to give liberally.
Spengler *m.* (-s, -) plumber.
Sperber *m.* (-s, -) sparrow-hawk.
Sperling *m.* (-s, -e) sparrow.
Sperma *n.* (-s, -men) sperm; semen.
sperrangelweit *a.* wide open.
Sperrbezirk *m.* restricted area.
Sperrdruck *m.* spaced-out type.
Sperre *f.* (-, -n) bar, barrier; (*nav.*) embargo, blockade; (*Straßen~*) block.
sperren *v.t.* to shut up, to bar, to stop; (*Druck*) to space; (*Straße*) to block; (sich) *~ v.refl.* to turn restive.
Sperr: *~feuer* *n.* barrage; *~holz* *n.* plywood; *~konto* *n.* blocked account; *~rad* *n.* ratchet(--wheel); *~sitz* *m.* (*theat.*) orchestra seat.
Sperrung *f.* (-, -en) closing (off); disconnection; embargo, blockade.
Spesen *f.pl.* charges, expenses *pl.*
Spezerei *f.* (-, -en) grocery; spices *pl.*
Spezialarzt *m.* specialist.
spezialisieren *v.t.* to specialize, to detail.
Spezialist *m.* (-en, -en); **Spezialistin** *f.* (-, -nen) specialist.
Spezialität *f.* (-, -en) specialty; special line.
speziell *a.* specific, special.
spezifisch *a.* specific; *~es Gewicht*, specific gravity.
spezifizieren *v.t.* to specify.
Sphäre *f.* (-, -n) sphere; province, range.
sphärisch *a.* spherical.
spicken *v.t.* to lard.
Spickzettel *m.* (*fam.*) crib, pony.
Spiegel *m.* (-s, -) mirror.
Spiegelbild *n.* reflected image.
Spiegel: *~ei* *n.* fried egg; *~fechterei* *f.* shadow boxing; *~fläche* *f.* smooth surface; *~glas* *n.* mirror-glass.
spiegelglatt *a.* smooth as a mirror.
spiegeln *v.i.* to glitter, to shine; *~ v.t.* to reflect; (sich) *~ v.refl.* to be reflected.
Spiegel: *~reflexkamera* *f.* reflex camera; *~schrift* *f.* mirror writing.
Spiegelung *f.* (-, -en) reflection; mirage.
Spiel *n.* (-[e]s, -e) play; game; *auf dem ~e stehen*, to be at stake; *aufs ~ setzen*, to risk, to stake; *etwas anderes ist dabei im ~*, there is something else in the case; *die Hand dabei im ~ haben*, to have a finger in the pie; *einen aus dem ~ lassen*, to let one alone.
Spiel: *~art* *f.* variety; (*Biol.*) sport; *~ball* *m.* (*fig.*) sport, plaything; *~bank* *f.* casino.
spielen *v.t. & i.* to play; to gamble; to act, to perform; *falsch ~*, to cheat at play; *vom Blatte ~*, to play at sight; *jm einen Streich ~*, to play a trick on s.b.
spielend *a. & adv.* (*fig.*) easy; easily.
Spieler *m.* (-s, -); **Spielerin** *f.* (-, -nen) player; gambler.
Spielerei *f.* (-, -en) child's play, sport.
spielerisch *a.* playful, sportive.

Spiel: ~**film** *m.* (feature) film; ~**hölle** *f.* gambling-den; ~**karte** *f.* playing-card; ~**leiter** *m.* stage manager; ~**plan** *m.* (*theat.*) program; ~**platz** *m.* playground; ~**raum** *m.* elbow-room, play, scope; ~**regel** *f.* rule of a game; ~**sache** *f.* plaything, toy; ~**verderber** *m.* spoil sport; ~**zeug** *n.* plaything(s), toy(s *pl.*).

Spieß *m.* (-es, -e) spear, pike; (*Brat*~) spit, skewer; *den ~ umkehren,* (*fig.*) to turn the tables (upon).

Spießbürger *m.* petty bourgeois; Philistine.

spießbürgerlich *a.* petty bourgeois; humdrum, Philistine.

Spießer *m.* (-s, -) = **Spießbürger.**

spießig *a.* = **spießbürgerlich.**

Spieß: ~**geselle** *m.* accomplice; ~**ruten** *f.pl.* ~ *laufen,* to run the gauntlet (of).

Spike *m.* (-s, -s) spike; stud (tyre).

Spill *n.* (-s, -e) capstan.

Spinat *m.* (-[e]s, 0) spinach.

Spind *n.* (-es, -e) locker.

Spindel *f.* (-, -n) spindle; distaff; (*mech.*) mandrel.

spindeldürr *a.* skinny.

Spinett *n.* (-[e]s, -e) spinet, harpsichord.

Spinne *f.* (-, -n) spider.

spinnen *v.i. & t.st.* to spin; (*fam.*) to be crazy.

Spinnennetz *n.* spider's web.

Spinner *m.*; **Spinnerin** *f.* spinner; (*fam.*) idiot.

Spinnerei *f.* (-, -en) spinning-mill.

Spinn: ~**maschine** *f.* spinning-jenny; ~**rad** *n.* spinning-wheel.

Spinnwebe *f.* cobweb.

Spion *m.* (-[e]s, -e); **Spionin** *f.* (-, -nen) spy.

Spionage *f.* (-, 0) espionage.

Spionageabwehr *f.* counter-espionage; counter-intelligence.

spionieren *v.i.* to spy.

Spirale *f.* (-, -n) spiral (line); coil (contraceptive).

Spiralfeder *f.* spiral spring.

spiralförmig *a.* spiral.

Spiritismus *m.* (-, 0) spiritualism.

Spiritist *m.* (-en, -en); **Spiritistin** *f.* (-, -nen) spiritualist.

Spirituosen *pl.* spirits *pl.*

Spiritus *m.* (-, -u. -tusse) spirit, alcohol.

Spiritusbrennerei *f.* distillery.

Spital *n.* (-[e]s, -täler), **Spittel** *m. & n.* (-s, -) hospital.

spitz *a.* pointed; (*math.*) acute; (*fig.*) sharp, shrill; cutting; ~ *zulaufen,* to taper.

Spitz *m.* (-es, -e) Pomeranian dog.

Spitz: ~**bart** *n.* goatee; pointed beard; ~**bogen** *m.* (*arch.*) pointed *or* Gothic arch; ~**bube** *m.* scoundrel; rascal.

spitzbübisch *a.* mischievous.

Spitze *f.* (-, -n) point; top; (*Gewebe*) lace; (*Feder*~) tip; (*mil.*) spearhead; *auf die ~ treiben,* to carry to extremes; *an der ~ stehen,* to be at the head (of).

Spitzel *m.* (-s, -) police-spy, informer.

spitzen *v.t.* to point; to sharpen; *die Ohren* ~, to prick up one' ears.

Spitzen: ~**geschwindigkeit** *f.* top speed; ~**kandidat** *m.*, ~**kandidatin** *f.* frontrunner.

Spitzenklöppel, *m.* lace-bobbin.

Spitzentechnologie *f.* state-of-the-art technology.

Spitzer *m.* (pencil) sharpener.

spitzfindig *a.* subtle; shrewd; cavilling.

Spitzfindigkeit *f.* (-, -en) subtlety, sophistry.

Spitzhacke *f.* pick-axe.

spitzig *a.* pointed, sharp; poignant.

Spitzname *m.* nickname.

Spitzwegerich *m.* ribwort.

spitzwinklig *a.* acute-angled.

spitzzüngig *a.* sharp-tongued.

Spleen *m.* (-s, -e) (*fam.*) tic; quirk.

spleißen *v.t. & t.st.* to splice.

splitten *v.t.* to split.

Splitter *m.* (-s, -) splinter, chip.

Splitterbruch *m.* chip fracture.

Splittergruppe *f.* splinter group.

splittern *v.i.* to splinter, to shatter.

splitternackt *a.* stark naked.

Splitterpartei *f.* splinter party.

splittersicher *a.* splinter-proof.

sponsern *v.t.* to sponsor.

Sponsor *m.* (-s, -en); **Sponsorin** *f.* (-, -nen) Sponsor.

spontan *a.* spontaneous.

sporadisch *a. & adv.* sporadic(ally).

Spore *f.* (-, -n) (*bot.*) spore.

Sporenpflanze *f.* cryptogam.

Sporentierchen *n.* sporozoan.

Sporn *m.* (-[e]s, Sporen) spur.

spornen *v.t.* to spur.

spornstreichs *adv.* directly.

Sport *m.* (-s, -e) sport; physical education.

Sportanlage *f.* sports complex.

Sportkleidung *f.* sportswear.

Sportler *m.* (-s, -); **Sportlerin** *f.* (-, -nen) athlete.

sportlich, sportsmäßig *a.* sporting, sporty, sportsmanlike.

Spott *m.* (-[e], 0) derision, ridicule, mockery; scorn; laughing-stock.

spottbillig *a.* dirt cheap.

Spöttelei *f.* (-, -en) sneer, taunt, gibe.

spötteln *v.i.* to mock, to sneer at.

spotten *v.i.* to mock, to deride; *das spottet aller Beschreibung,* it beggars description.

Spötter *m.* (-s, -) mocker, scoffer.

spöttisch *a.* satirical, ironical, scoffing.

Sprachbegabung *f.* gift for languages.

Sprache *f.* (-, -n) language, tongue; speech, voice; *zur ~ bringen,* to bring s.th. up; *zur ~ kommen,* to be mentioned.

Sprach[en]kunde *f.* linguistics *pl.*

Sprach: ~**fehler** *m.* speech defect/impediment; ~**forscher** *m.* linguist, philologist; ~**forschung** *f.* linguistics; philology; ~**führer** *m.* phrase-book; ~**gebrauch** *m.* usage (in language); ~**lehre** *f.* grammar.

sprachlich *a.* linguistic.

sprachlos *a.* speechless; (*fig.*) dumb.

Sprachrohr *n.* speaking tube; (*fig.*) mouth-piece.

sprachwidrig *a.* ungrammatical.

Sprachwissenschaft *f.* linguistics.

sprechen *v.t. & i.st.* to speak; to talk; *er ist nicht zu* ~, you cannot see him now.

sprechend *a. & adv.* striking(ly); ~**ähnlich** *a.* (of a) speaking likeness.

Sprecher *m.* (-s, -); **Sprecherin** *f.* (-, -nen) spokesman/spokeswoman; announcer.

Sprech: ~**film** *m.* talking film, talkie; ~**stunden** *pl.* office hours, (*Stellen*) interviewing hours;

~zimmer *n.* consulting room.
spreizen *v.t.* to spread open, to stretch, to straddle.
Spreizfuß *m.* splayfoot.
Sprengel *m.* (-s, -) diocese; parish.
sprengen *v.t. & i.* to sprinkle, to water; to burst open; (*Bank*) to break; to blow up, to blast; to gallop.
Spreng: ~geschoß *n.* explosive, shell; **~kapsel** *f.* detonator; **~kraft** *f.* explosive power; **~ladung** *f.* explosive charge; **~stoff** *m.* high explosive.
Sprenkel *m.* (-s, -) spot; dot; speckle.
sprenkeln *v.t.* to sprinkle.
Spreu *f.* (-, 0) chaff.
Sprichwort *n.* proverb.
sprichwörtlich *a. & adv.* proverbial(ly).
sprießen *v.i.st.* (*s, h*) to sprout, to shoot.
Spring: ~brett *n.* spring board; **~brunnen** *m.* fountain, jet.
springen *v.i.st.* (s, h) to spring; to leap, to jump; to crack, to burst; *entzwei ~*, to burst asunder; *in die Augen ~*, to be obvious.
Springer *m.* (-s, -) (*im Schachspiel*) knight.
Spring: ~feder *f.* spring; **~federmatratze** *f.* spring mattress; **~flut** *f.* spring tide; **~kraft** *f.* elasticity; **~quelle** *f.* spring, fountain.
Sprint *m.* sprint.
sprinten *v.i.* to sprint.
Sprinter *m.*; **Sprinterin** *f.* sprinter.
Sprit *m.* (-s, 0) alcohol; gas.
Spritze *f.* (-, -n) syringe; injection; spray; fire-engine.
spritzen *v.t.* to spray; to water; to spout, to squirt.
Spritzer *m.* (-s, -) splash; drop.
spritzig *a.* sparkling; peppy.
Spritzmittel *n.* spray.
Spritzpistole *f.* spray gun.
Spritztour *f.* (-, -en) spin (car).
spröde *a.* brittle; (*Haut*) rough; (*fig.*) coy, reserved, prim.
Sprödigkeit *f.* (-, 0) brittleness; coyness.
Sproß (Sprosses, Sprossen) shoot, sprout; scion, offspring.
Sprosse *f.* (-, -n) step, round, rung.
Sprossenwand *f.* wall bars.
Sprößling *m.* (-[e]s, -e) sprout, shoot, (*fig.*) offspring.
Sprotte *f.* (-, -n) sprat.
Spruch *m.* (-[e]s, Sprüche) maxim, saying; (*Bibel~*) text.
Sprücheklopfer *m.* (-s, -) big mouth.
spruchreif *a. etwas ist noch nicht ~*, something isn't decided yet.
Sprudel *m.* (-s, -) sparkling mineral water.
sprudeln *v.i.* to bubble; to sputter.
Sprühdose *f.* spray can.
sprühen *v.t.* to spray; to sprinkle; to emit; *~ v.i.* to emit sparks, to scintillate.
Sprühregen *m.* drizzle.
Sprung *m.* (-[e]s, Sprünge) spring; leap jump; dive; chink, crack, fissure; *auf dem ~e sein, stehen*, to be on the point of.
Sprung: ~brett *n.* springboard; **~feder** *f.* (coil) spring.
sprunghaft *a.* erratic; disjointed.
Sprung: ~rahmen *m.* spring bed frame; **~schanze** *f.* ski jump; **~tuch** *n.* safety blanket; **~turm** *m.*

diving platform.
sprungweise *adv.* by leaps.
Spucke *f.* (-, 0) spittle.
spucken *v.i.* to spit.
Spucknapf *m.* spittoon.
Spuk *m.* (-[e]s, -e) apparition, specter.
spuken *v.i.* to haunt; to be haunted.
Spukgeschichte *f.* ghost-story.
Spülbecken *n.* sink.
Spule *f.* (-, -en) spool, bobbin; (*Feder*) quill; (*elek.*) coil.
spulen *v.t.* to spool, to reel.
spülen *v.t.* to rinse; to wash.
Spül: ~maschine *f.* dishwasher; **~mittel** *n.* dishwashing liquid.
Spülung *f.* rinse; irrigation; douche; flush.
Spülwasser *n.* dish-water.
Spulwurm *m.* roundworm.
Spund *m.* (-[e]s, Spünde) bung, stopper.
Spundloch *n.* bung-hole.
Spur *f.* (-, -en) track, trace; vestige; (*Wagen~*) rut; *keine ~ von*, not an idea *or* inkling of.
spürbar *a.* noticeble; perceptible; evident.
spüren *v.t.* to track, to trace; to perceive, to feel.
Spürhund *m.* tracker dog; (*fig.*) spy.
spurlos *adv.* without leaving a trace.
Spürnase *f.* **Spürsinn** *m.* good nose.
sputen (sich) *v.refl.* to hurry.
Staat *m.* (-es, -en) state; pomp, show.
Staattenbund *m.* confederation.
staatlich *a.* state-. . ., public; politic(al).
staatlich unterstützt, state-subidized.
Staats: ~amt *n.* public office; **~angehörige** *m./f.* national, subject; **~angehörigkiet** *f.* nationality; citizenship; **~anleihe** *f.* government-loan; **~anwalt** *m.* public prosecutor; **~anwaltschaft** *f.* public prosecutor's office; **~anzeiger** *m.* official gazette; **~beamte** *m./f.* civil servant.
Staats: im Staatsbesitz, state-owned; **~bürger** *m.* subject, citizen; **~dienst** *m.* public *or* civil service; **~einkünfte** *pl.* revenue; **~gesetz** *n.* law of the land, statute law; **~gewalt** *f.* supreme *or* executive power; **~haushalt** *m.* budget; **~kirche** *f.* established church; **~kunst** *f.* statesmanship; **~mann** *m.* (-[e]s, männer) statesman.
staatsmännisch *a.* statesmanlike.
Staats: ~minister *m.* minister of state; **~oberhaupt** *n.* head of state; **~papiere** *n.pl.* stocks, public funds *pl.*; **~recht** *n.* public law; **~schuld** *f.* national debt; **~sekretär** *m.* Secretary of state; **~streich** *m.* coup d'état; **~verfassung** *f.* constitution; **~verwaltung** *f.* government, public administration; **~wesen** *n.* state-affairs, *pl.* politics; **~wissenschaft** *f.* political science, politics *pl.*
Stab *m.* (-[e]s, Stäbe) staff, stick; bar; rod.
Stabhochspringer *m.* pole vaulter.
Stabhochsprung *m.* pole vaulting.
stabil *a.* stable; sturdy.
stabilisieren *v.t.* to stabilize.
Stabilität *m.* stability; sturdiness.
Stabreim *m.* alliteration.
Stabs: ~arzt *m.* medical officer; **~offizier** *m.* field officer.
Stachel *m.* (-s, -u) (*Insekten~*) spine; sting; prickle, thorn.
Stachel: ~beere *f.* gooseberry; **~draht** *m.* barbed

wire.
stach(e)lig *a.* prickly, thorny.
Stachelschwein pn. porcupine.
Stadion *n.* (-s, -dien) stadium.
Stadium *m.* (-[s], -dien *u.* -dia) stage.
Stadt *f.* (-, Städte) town; city.
Stadt: ~**amt** *n.* municipal office; ~**bahn** *f.* municipal railroad.
Städtebau *m.* town-planning.
Städtepartnerschaft *f.* sistercity relation.
Städter *m.* (-s, -); **Städterin** *f.* (-, -nen) city dweller; town dweller.
Stadtgespräch *n.* talk of the town; (*tel.*) local call.
städtisch *a.* municipal; urban.
Stadt: ~**kämmerer** *m.* city-treasurer; ~**mauer** *f.* city wall; ~**rat** *m.* municipal council; town-councillor; ~**verordnete[r]** *m.* town-councillor; ~**viertel** *n.* quarter (of a town).
Staffel *f.* (-, -n) step, rung; degree; (*Sport*) relay; (*mil.*) echelon; (*avi.*) squadron.
Staffelei *f.* (-, -en) easel.
Staffel: ~**kapitän** *m.* squadron-leader; ~**lauf** *m.* relay race.
staffeln *v.t.* to grade; to stagger; *gestaffelte Ferien, pl.* staggered holidays.
Staffelung *f.* staggering; progressive rates.
Stagnation *f.* stagnation.
stagnieren *v.n.* to stagnate.
Stahl *m.* (-[e]s, Stähle) steel; (*mech.*) tool.
Stahl: ~**bau** *m.* steel construction; ~**beton** *m.* reinforced concrete; ~**blech** *n.* sheet steel.
stählen *v.t.* to temper, to harden.
stählern *a.* (of) steel; steely.
Stahl: ~**helm** *m.* steel hlemet, ~**werk** *n.* steelworks *pl.*; ~**wolle** *f.* steel-wool.
staken *v.t.* to pole, to punt.
Stalagmit *m.* stalagmite.
Stalaktit *m.* stalactite.
Stall *m.* (-[e]s, Ställe) stable.
Stallbursche *m.* groom.
Stallung *f.* (-, -en) stable; cowshed; pigsty.
Stamm *m.* (-[e]s, Stämme) stem, stalk; trunk, body; stock, race, family, tribe; (*gram.*) root.
Stamm: ~**aktie** *f.* common stock; ~**baum** *m.* family tree; pedigree; ~**buch** *n.* album.
stammeln *v.t. & i.* to stammer, to stutter.
Stammeltern *pl.* progenitors *pl.*
stammen *v.i.* (*s*) to originate, to proceed; to descend from; to be derived.
Stammes: ~**geschichte** *f.* phylogenesis; ~**häuptling** *m.* tribal chief.
Stamm: ~**gast** *m.* regular customer; ~**halter** *m.* son and heir.
stämmig *a.* stout, strong.
Stammkapital *n.* nominal capital.
Stammler *m.* (-s, -) stammerer, stutterer.
Stamm: ~**personal;** *n.* regular staff; ~**tisch** *m.* table reserved for regular customers; ~**vater** *m.* ancestor.
stampfen *v.i. & t.* to stamp; to pound.
Stand *m.* (-[e]s, Stände) state, condition; (*Verkaufs*~) stand, stall; station, situation; rank, profession, order, class; (*im Stall*) stall; (*Barometer, etc.*) reading; *neu in ~ setzen*, to recondition.
Standard *m.* (-s, -s) standard.
standardisieren *v.t.* to standardize.

Standardisierung *f.* standardization.
Standarte *f.* (-, -n) standard.
Standbild *n.* statue.
Ständchen *n.* (-s, -) serenade.
Stände *m.pl.* estates (*pl.*) of the realm.
Ständer *m.* (-s, -) stand, upright; (*elek.*) stator.
Standesamt *n.* registry office.
standesamtlich *a.* before the registrar.
Standesbeamte[r] *m.* registrar.
standesgemäß *a.* in accordance with one's rank.
standhaft *a.* firm, steady, steadfat; constant.
Standhaftigkeit *f.* (-, 0) constancy, steadfastness.
ständig *a.* permanent, constant.
ständisch *a.* corporate.
standhalten *v.i.st.* to hold one's ground.
Stand: ~**licht** *n.* sidelights; ~**ort** *m.* location; ~**punkt** *m.* point of view; standpoint; ~**recht** *n.* martial law.
standrechtlich *a.* according to martial law.
Standspur *f.* hard shoulder (street).
Stange *f.* (-, -n) pole, perch; bar; stick; ~**bohne** *f.* string bean.
Stänkerei *f.* (-, -en) quarrel, row.
stänkern *v.i.* (*fig.*) to quarrel, to pick quarrels; to find fault.
Stanniol *n.* (-[e]s, 0) tinfoil.
stanzen *v.t.* to stamp, to punch.
Stapel *m.* (-s, -) heap, pile; staple, emporium; *vom ~ lassen,* to launch (a ship, an enterprise).
Stapellauf *m.* launching.
stapeln *v.t.* to pile up.
stapfen *v.i.* to trudge.
Star *m.* (-[e]s, -e) star (celebrity); starling; (*med.*) *grauer* ~ cataract; *grüner* ~, glaucoma.
stark *a.* strong, robust; stout, fat; intense; ~*e Seite,* strong point.
starkbesetzt *a.* well attended, crowded.
Stärke *f.* (-, 0) strength, force, vigor; starch; thickness.
stärkehaltig *a.* containing starch.
Stärkemehl *n.* cornstarch.
stärken *v.t.* to strengthen; to corroborate; to comfort; to starch.
stärkend *a.* strengthening, invigorating.
Starkstrom *m.* high voltage current.
Stärkung *f.* (-, -en) strengthening; consolation; refreshment, food.
Stärkungsmittel *n.* tonic.
starr *a.* stiff, rigid; fixed; ~ *sein vor Erstaunen,* to be dumb with astonishment.
starren *v.i.* to stare; *von Schmutz* ~, to be stiff with dirt; (*von Fehlern, etc.*) to bristle with.
Starrheit *f.* stiffness, rigidity; obstinacy.
Starrkopf *m.* stubborn fellow.
starrköpfig *a.* stubborn, headstrong.
Starr: ~**krampf** *m.* tetanus; ~**sinn** *m.* stubbornness.
starrsinnig *a.* stubborn, headstrong.
Start *m.* start.
Startbahn *f.* (*avi.*) runway.
starten *v.i.u.t.* to start.
Startplatz *m.* starting place.
Startrampe *f.* launching pad.
Statik *f.* (-, 0) statics.
Station *f.* (-, -en) station; stopping-place, stage.
stationär *a.* in hospital; as an inpatient.

stationieren *v.t.* (*mil.*) to station; to deploy.
Stations: ~**arzt** *m.*, ~**ärztin** *f.* ward doctor; ~**schwester** *f.* floor nurse; ~**vorsteher** *m.* station-master.
statisch *a.* static.
Statist *m.* (-en, -en), **Statistin** *f.* (-, -nen) (*theat.*) extra.
Statistik *f.* (-, -en) statistics.
statistisch *a.* statistic(al).
Stativ *n.* (-s, -e) stand; (*phot.*) tripod.
Statte *f.* (-, 0) place, stead; *an meiner* ~, in my place; *an Kindes* ~ *annehmen*, to adopt.
statt *pr.* instead of, in lieu of; ~ *dessen*, instead of this.
Stätte *f.* (-, -n) place, site.
stattfinden *v.i.st.* to take place.
stattgeben *v.i.st.* to grant.
statthaben *v.i.st.* to take place.
statthaft *a.* admissible, allowable, lawful.
Statthalter *m.* governor.
stattlich *a.* considerable; imposing; impressive.
Statue *f.* (-, -n) statue.
Statuette *f.* (-, -n) statuette.
Statur *f.* (-, -en) stature, size.
Status *m.* (-, -) status.
Statut *n.* (-[e]s, -e) statute, regulation.
statutenmäßig *a.* statutory.
Stau *m.* (-s, -s) accumulation; congestion; traffic jam.
Staub *m.* (-[e]s, 0) dust; powder; *sich aus dem* ~*e machen*, to make off, to abscond.
Stäubchen *n.* (-s, -) speck of dust.
stauben *v.i.* to give off dust, to be dusty.
staubig *a.* dusty.
Staubsauger *m.* vacuum cleaner.
Staubtuch *n.* duster.
Staubwedel *m.* feather duster.
Staudamm *m.* dam.
Staude *f.* (-, -n) shrub; bush.
stauen *v.t.* to dam up, to bank up; *das Wasser staut sich*, the water is dammed up.
Staumauer *f.* dam (wall).
staunen *v.i.* to be astonished, to be surprised, to be amazed.
Staunen *n.* amazement; astonishment.
staunenswert *a.* amazing, marvellous.
Staupe *f.* (-, 0) (*Hunde~*) distemper.
Stausee *m.* reservoir.
stechen *v.t.st.* to sting, to prick; to stab; (*Torf*) to cut; ~ *v.i.st.* (*Sonne*) to burn; *in die Augen* ~, to catch one's eye; *in See* ~, to put to sea, to set sail.
stechend *a.* penetrating; piercing.
Stech: ~**karte** *f.* timecard; ~**mücke** *f.* mosquito; ~**palme** *f.* holly; ~**schritt** *m.* goose-step; ~**uhr** *f.* time clock; ~**zirkel** *m.* dividers.
Steckbrief *m.* 'wanted' poster.
steckbrieflich *a. & adv. einen* ~ *verfolgen*, to issue a warrant against someone.
Steckdose *f.* socket.
stecken *v.t.* to stick; ~ *v.i.st.* to stick, to be fixed; ~**bleiben**, to stick fast; *was steckt dahinter?* what can be at the bottom of it? *Geld in ein Unternehmen* ~, to invest money in an undertaking; *mit einem unter einer Decke* ~, to play into each other's hands.
Stecken *m.* (-s, -) stick, staff.

Steckenpferd *n.* hobby-horse; (*fig.*) hobby, fad.
Stecker *m.* (-s, -) plug.
Steckling *m.* (-s, -e) cutting.
Steck: ~**nadel** *f.* pin; ~**nadelkopf** *m.* pinhead; ~**rübe** *f.* turnip.
Steg *m.* (-[e]s, -e) path; small bridge; (*Geigen~*) bridge.
Stegreif *m. aus dem* ~*e*, extempore, offhand; *aus dem* ~ *sprechen*, to extemporize.
Stehaufmännchen *n.* tumbling figure.
stehen *v.i.st.* to stand; to suit (well, ill); to be; *es steht fest*, it is beyond doubt that; *frei* ~, to be permitted; *es steht Ihnen frei*, you are at liberty to; *es steht in der Zeitung*, it's in the paper; *Modell* ~, to serve as model (to); *wie steht's?* how are you? *sich gut* ~, to be well off; *die Aktien* ~ *auf...*, the shares stand at...; *seinen Mann* ~, to hold one's own; ~**bleiben**, to stop, to pause; *Geld bei einem* ~ *haben*, to have deposited money with one; *sich den Bart* ~ *lassen*, to let one's beard grow; *es steht zu erwarten*, it is to be expected; *zum* ~ *bringen*, to bring to a stand.
stehend *a.* standing; ~*es Heer*, standing army; ~*e Redensart*, stock phrase.
Stehkragen *m.* stand-up collar.
Stehlampe *f.* floor lamp.
stehlen *v.t.st.* to steal; to pilfer; *sich aus dem Hause* ~, to steal out of the house.
Steh: ~**platz** *m.* standing-room; ~**pult** *n.* standing-desk.
steif *a.* stiff; rigid; awkward, formal; ~ *werden*, to stiffen; ~ *und fest behaupten*, to maintain obstinately; ~*er Grog*, strong grog.
Steifheit *f.* (-, -en) stiffness; (*fig.*) formality, pedantry.
Steig *m.* (-[e]s, -e) path.
Steigbügel *m.* (-s, -) stirrup.
steigen *v.i.st.* (*s*) to mount, to ascend, to rise; to increase; to climb; *die Haare* ~ *mir zu Berge*, my hair stands on end; *die Aktien* ~, the shares are going up.
Steiger *m.* (-s, -) foreman of miners.
steigern *v.t.* to raise (the price), to enhance, to increase.
Steigerung *f.* (-, -en) rise, increase, gradation; (*gram.*) comparison.
Steigerungsgrad *m.* (*gram.*) degree of comparison.
Steigerungsform *f.* comparative form.
Steigung *f.* (-, -en) rising, ascent; (*rail.*) gradient; (*mot.*) steep hill (up).
steil *a.* steep, stiff.
Steil: ~**hang** *m.* steep slope; ~**küste** *f.* cliffs.
Stein *m.* (-[e]s, -e) stone; (*im Schachspiele*), piece; ~ *des Anstosses*, stumbling-block; ~ *der Weisen*, philosophers' stone; *es fällt mir ein* ~ *vom Herzen*, a great weight is taken off my mind; *wie ein Tropfen auf einen heißen* ~, altogether insufficient.
Stein: ~**bild** *n.* statue; ~**bock** *m.* ibex; (*Sternbild*) Capricorn; ~**bruch** *m.* quarry; ~**butt** *m.*, ~**butte** *f.* turbot; ~**druck** *m.* lithography.
steinern *a.* (of) stone; (*fig.*) stony.
Steingut *n.* earthenware, crockery.
steinhart *a.* hard as stone, stony.
steinig *a.* stony, rocky.
steinigen *v.t.* to stone.
Steinigung *f.* (-, -en) stoning.

Stein: ~**kohle** f. hard coal; ~**metz** m. stone-mason; ~**obst** n. stone-fruit; ~**öl** n. petroleum; ~**pilz** m. cep; ~**platte** f. slab, flagstone.

steinreich a. enormously rich.

Stein: ~**schlag** m. falling rocks; ~**setzer** m. pavior; ~**wurf** m. stone's throw; ~**zeit** f. Stone Age.

Steiß m. (-[e]s, -e) backside, rump, buttocks pl.

Steißbein n. rump-bone, coccyx.

Stelldichein n. (-[e]s, -) rendezvous.

Stelle f. (-, -n) place, spot; situation, office; (Buch~) passage; an höchster ~, on top level; auf der ~ treten, to mark time; nicht von der ~ kommen, not to get anywhere; sich nicht von der ~ rühren, not to move an inch; an Ort und ~ sein, to be on the spot; an ~ von, in lieu of; sich zu einer ~ melden, to apply for a situation; auf der ~, at once, on the spot.

stellen v.t. to put, to place, to set; to regulate; (sich) ~ v.refl. to step, to stand; (Preis) to amount to; to dissemble, to make believe; bereit ~, to place in readiness; sich krank ~, to feign sickness; sich ~ als ob, to pretend, to make believe; eine Uhr richtig ~, to set a watch; einem ein Bein ~, to trip someone up; nach dem Leben ~, to attempt one's life; einen Antrag ~, to move.

Stellen: ~**angebot** n. job offer; ~**besetzung** f. placement; ~**gesuch** n. (Zeitung) situation wanted; ~**suche** f. job hunting, search for a job.

Stellenvermittlungsbüro n. employment agency.

stellenweise a. sporadically, in parts.

Stellung f. (-, -en) position; situation; (Körper~) posture.

Stellungnahme f. comment(s); statement.

Stellungskrieg n. trench warfare.

stellungslos a. unemployed.

stellvertretend a. acting; deputy.

Stellvertreter m. deputy; subtitute.

Stellwerk n. signal box; switch-tower.

Stelze f. (-, -n) stilt.

stelzen v.i. to stalk; to strut.

Stelzfuß m. wooden leg.

Stemmeisen n. chisel.

stemmen v.t. (Flut, usw.) to stem; (sich) ~ v.refl. to lean (against); to resist; die Hände in die Seiten ~, to set one' arms akimbo; sich gegen etwas ~, to press against; to resist.

Stempel m. (-s, -) stamp; (bot.) pistil; post-mark.

Stempel: ~**kissen** n. stamp-pad; ~**marke** f. stamp.

stempeln v.t. to stamp, to mark; ~**gehen** v.i. to be on welfare.

Stengel m. (-s, -) stalk, stem.

Steno f., **Stenographie** (-, -en) shorthand.

stenographieren v.t. & i. to write (in) shorthand.

Stenotypistin f. (-n, -nen) shorthand typist.

Steppdecke f. quilt, eiderdown.

Steppe f. (-, -n) steppe.

steppen v.t. & i. to backstitch; to tapdance.

Steptanz m. tapdance.

Sterbe: ~**bett** n. deathbed; ~**fall** m. (case of) death; ~**hilfe** f. euthanasia.

sterben v.i.st. (s) to die; eines natürlichen Todes ~, to die a natural death; Hungers ~, to die of hunger.

Sterben n. (-s, -) dying; epidemic; im ~ liegen, to be dying.

sterbenskrank a. mortally ill.

Sterbenswörtchen n. a single word, a syllable.

Sterbesakramente pl. the last rites.

sterblich a. mortal; ~ verliebt, desperately in love.

Sterblichkeit f. (-, 0) mortality; ~**ziffer** f. death rate, mortality.

Stereo: ~**anlage** f. stereo system; ~**aufnahme** f. stereo recording; ~**ton** m. stereo sound.

stereotyp a. stereotyped.

stereotypieren v.t. to stereotype.

steril a. sterile.

sterilisieren v.t. to sterilize.

Stern m. (-[e]s, -e) star; (im Druck) asterisk.

Sternbild n. constellation.

Sternchen n. (-s, -) little star; asterisk.

Sterndeuter m. (-s, -) astrologer.

Sternen: ~**banner** n. stars and stripes; ~**himmel** m. starry sky; ~**licht** n. starlight.

Sternfahrt f. (mot.) motor rally.

sternförmig a. star-shaped.

sternhell a. starlight, starry.

Stern: ~**himmel** m. firmament, starry sky; ~**kunde** f. astronomy; ~**schnuppe** f. shooting star; ~**warte** f. observatory; ~**zeichen** n. zodiac sign.

Sterz m. (-es, -e) tail.

stet a. steady, constant, continued.

Stethoskop n. (-s, -e) stethoscope.

stetig a. steady, contintual, continuous.

Stetigkeit f. (-, 0) continuity, constancy, stability.

stets adv. continually, always, ever.

Steuer n. (-s, -) wheel; rudder.

Steuer f. (-, -n) (Staats~) tax; (Gemeinde~) rate; (Zoll) duty.

steuerbar a. assessable, liable to duty.

Steuer: ~**beamter** m. tax-collector, revenue officer; ~**behörde** f. board of inland revenue; ~**bord** n. starboard; ~**einnehmer** m. tax-collector; ~**erklärung** f. income-tax return; ~**erlaß** m. tax remission.

steuerfrei a. exempt from taxes, duty-free.

Steuer: ~**freibetrag** m. tax allowance; ~**freiheit** f. exemption from taxes; ~**hinterziehung** f. evasion of taxes; ~**klasse** f. tax category; ~**knüppel** m. control lever; joystick.

steuerlich a. tax.

Steuer: ~**mann** m. helmsman; steersman; ~**marke** f. revenue stamp.

steuern v.t. to steer; to pilot; ~ v.i. to steer; (einem Dinge) to check, to repress.

Steuern hinterziehen, to evade taxes.

Steuer: ~**nachlaß** m. tax remission; ~**pflichtig** a. dutiable, subject to taxation; ~**politik** f. fiscal policy; ~**rad** n. (mot.) steering wheel; ~**rückvergütung** f. tax refund; ~**ruder** n. helm, rudder; ~**satz** m. rate of assessment; ~**schuld** f. tax arrears; ~**senkung** f. tax cut, tax reduction.

Steuerung f. (-, -en) (mech.) control.

Steuer: ~**veranschlagung** f. assessment; ~**zahler** m. tax-payer.

Steven m. (-s, -) (nav.) posts at bow or stern.

stibitzen v.t. (fam.) to pinch.

Stich m. (-[e]s, -e) puncture; stab; (Nadel) prick; sting; (Näh~) stitch; engraving; ~ halten, to hold good; im ~ lasssen, to leave in the lurch.

Stichelei f. (-, -en) taunt, raillery, sneer.

sticheln v.i. (auf einen), to taunt.

Stichflamme f. (-, -n) jet of flame.

stichhaltig a. valid, sound.

Stichprobe *f.* (-, -n) spotcheck; *~machen*, to spotcheck.
Stichtag *m.* deadline.
Stichwahl *f.* second ballot.
Stichwort *n.* cue; headword; catchword.
sticken *v.t.* to embroider.
Stickerei *f.* (-, -en) embroidery.
Stickerin *f.* -, -nen) embroideress.
stickig *a.* stuffy.
Stick: **~luft** *f.* stuffy air; **~muster** *n.* pattern for embroidering, sampler; **~rahmen** *m.* embroidery-frame; **~stoff**, *m.* nitrogen.
stickstoffhaltig *a.* nitrogenous.
Stickstoffverbindung *f.* nitrous compound.
Stiefbruder *m.* step-brother, half-brother.
Stiefel *m.* (-s, -) boot.
Stiefelknecht *m.* bootjack.
Stiefelputzer *n.* bootblack.
Stiefeltern *pl.* step-parents *pl.*
Stief: **~geschwister** *pl.* step-brother[s] and sister[s]; **~kind** *n.* step-child; **~mutter** *f.* step-mother; **~mütterchen** *n.* (*bot.*) pansy.
stiefmütterlich *a.* **~behandeln** to treat badly.
Stief: **~schwester** *f.* step-sister; **~sohn** *m.* step-son; **~tochter** *f.* step-daughter; **~vater** *m.* step-father.
Stiege *f.* (-, -n) staircase, stairway.
Stieglitz *m.* (-es, -e) goldfinch.
Stiel *m.* (-[e]s, -e) handle, helve; (*bot.*) stem, stalk, pedicle; *mit Stumpf und ~*, root and branch.
Stier *m.* (-[e]s, -e) bull; (*astrol.*) Taurus.
stieren *v.i.* to stare.
Stier: **~kampf** *m.* bullfight; **~kämpfer** *m.*; **~kämpferin** *f.* bullfighter.
stiernackig *a.* bullnecked.
Stift *m.* (-[e]s, -e) peg; pencil, crayon; (*fam.*) office boy.
Stift *n.* (-[e]s, -e *u.* -er) (charitable) foundation; home for old people; chapterhouse; college.
stiften *v.t.* to establish; to found; *Gutes, Nutzen ~*, to do good, to be useful.
Stifter *m.* (-s, -); **Stifterin** *f.* (-, -nen) founder, donor.
Stiftung *f.* (-, -en) foundation; endowment; institution.
Stiftungsfest *n.* founder's day.
Stil *m.* (-[e]s, -e) style; manner.
Stilblüte *f.* howler.
Stilebene *f.* level of style.
stilecht *a.* in period.
Stilett *n.* stiletto.
stilisieren *v.t.* to stylize.
Stilistik *f.* (-, -en) theory of style; stylistics.
stilistisch *a.* relating to style.
still *a.* still, silent; calm, quiet, tranquil; *~!* hush!; *im ~en*, quietly; *~halten*, to keep still; *~schweigen*, to be silent, to keep silence; *~sein*, to be quiet; *~stehen*, to stand still; *der ~e Ozean*, the Pacific; **~er Teilhaber** *m.* silent partner.
Stille *f.* (-, 0) silence, tranquillity; *in aller ~*, secretly.
Stilleben *n.* still life.
stillegen *v.t.* to close down.
Stillegung *f.* (-, -en) shut down.
stillen *v.t.* to quiet, to appease, to quench; (*Blut*) to staunch; (*Begierden*) to gratify; (*ein Kind*) to feed, to nurse.

stillgestanden! (*mil.*) attention.
stilliegend *a.* *~e Fabrik*, idle factory.
stillos *a.* lacking in style.
Stillchweigen *n.* silence.
stillschweigend *a.* silent, tacit.
Stillstand *m.* standstill, stop, deadlock.
stillstehen *v.i.* to stand still.
Stillzeit *f.* lactation period.
Stilmittel *n.* (-s, -) stylistic device.
Stilmöbel *n.pl.* period furniture.
stilvoll *a.* in style; stylish.
Stimmband *n.* vocal chord.
stimmberechtigt *a.* entitled to vote.
Stimmbruch *m.* breaking of the voice.
Stimme *f.* (-, -n) voice; (*Wahl~*) vote; (*mus.*) part; *sine ~ abgeben*, to cast one's vote.
stimmen *v.t.* to tune; (*fig.*) to dipose; *das stimmt!* that's true enough; *~ v.t.* to vote; *das Rechnung stimmt*, the account is square *or* correct; *er ist heute schlecht gestimmt*, he is in a bad mood today.
Stimm(en)abgabe *f.* voting.
Stimmenthaltung *f.* (-, -en) abstention.
Stimmen: **~gleichheit** *f.* equality of votes, tie; **~mehrheit** *f.* majority of votes.
Stimmer *n.* (-s, -) tuner.
stimmfähig *a.* entitled to vote.
Stimmgabel *f.* tuning-fork.
stimmhaft *a.* voiced.
stimmlos *a.* voiceless.
Stimmrecht *n.* right to vote; **allgemeines ~** universal suffrage.
Stimmung *f.* (-, -en) mood, humour, disposition; (*mil.*) morale, general feeling.
Stimmwechsel *m.* breaking of the voice.
Stimmzettel *m.* paper ballot.
stinken *v.i.st.* to stink (of).
Stipendiat *m.* (-en, -en) **Stipendiatin** *f.* (-, -nen) person receiving a scholarship.
Stipendium *n.* (-[e]s, -dien) scholarship, exhibition.
stippen *v.t.* to dip, to steep.
Stirn *f.* (-, -en) forehead; front; (*fig.*) insolence; *einem die ~ bieten*, to defy someone.
Stirn: **~band** *n.* headband; **~runzeln** *n.* frown(ing).
stöbern *v.i.* (*nach*) to rummage (for).
stochern *v.t.* to poke, to stir.
Stock *m.* (-[e]s, Stöcke) stick; staff; cane; log, block, trunk; (*Stockwerk*) story, floor.
stockdumm *a.* utterly stupid.
stockdunkel *a.* pitch-dark.
Stöckelschuh *m.* (-s, -e) high-heeled shoe.
stocken *v.i.* to stop; (*gerinnen*) to curdle; (*fig.*) to hesitate; *die Geschäfte ~*, business is at a standstill.
Stocken *n.* (-s, 0) *ins ~ geraten*, to come to a standstill.
stockfinster *a.* pitch-dark.
Stockfisch *m.* dried cod.
stocksteif *a.* stiff as a poker.
stocktaub *a.* stone-deaf, deaf as a post.
Stockung *f.* (-, -en) stagnation; interruption; block; (*med.*) congestion.
Stockwerk *n.* floor, story.
Stoff *m.* (-[e]s, -e) stuff, material, fabric; matter; subject.
stofflich *a.* material.

Stoffwechsel *m.* (*med.*) metabolism.
stöhnen *v.i.* to groan.
Stoiker *m.* (-s, -) stoic.
stoisch *a.* stoic(al).
Stoizismus *m.* (-, 0) stoicism.
Stola *f.* (-, -en) stole.
Stollen *m.* (-s, -) (mining) adit, gallery.
stolpern *v.i.* (*s*) to stumble, to trip.
stolz *a.* proud; stately.
Stolz *m.* (-es, 0) pride; *seinen ~ in etwas setzen*, to take pride in a thing.
stolzieren *v.i.* (*s*) to flaunt, to strut.
stopfen *v.t.* to stop; to stuff, to cram; to fill (a pipe); to obstruct; (*mit Garn*) to darn; (*med.*) to constipate.
Stoppel *f.* (-, -n) stubble.
Stoppel: **~bart** *m.* stubble; **~feld** *n.* stubble field.
stopp(e)lig *a.* stubbly.
stoppen *v.t.* (*nav.*) to stop.
Stopper *m.* (-s, -) center-half (soccer).
Stoppschild *n.* stop sign.
Stoppuhr *f.* stop-watch.
Stöpsel *m.* (-s, -) plug; stopper, cork.
stöpseln *v.t.* to cork, to plug.
Stör *m.* (-[e]s, -e) sturgeon.
Storch *m.* (-[e]s, Störche) stork.
stören *v.t.* to disturb, to trouble; (*Radio*) to jam; ~ *v.i.* to be in the way.
Störenfried *m.* (-[e]s, -e) troublemaker.
stornieren *v.t.* to cancel; to reverse.
Stornierung *f.*, **Storno** *n.* cancellation; reversal.
störrisch *a.* stubborn, refractory.
Störsender *m.* jamming station.
Störung *f.* (-, -en) disturbance, interruption; **~en**, (*Radio*) atmospherics *pl.*
Stoß *m.* (-es, Stösse) thrust, push; shock; punch; (*Fuß*) kick; jolt; (*phys.*) impact; (*Billiard*) stroke; (*Haufen*) pile, heap; (*Akten~*) file, bundle.
Stoßdämpfer *m.* shock absorber (car).
Stößel *m.* (-s, 0) pestle.
stoßempfindlich *a.* sensitive to shock.
stoßen *v.t.* to thrust, to push; to kick, to knock; (*im Mörser*) to pound; ~ *v.i.st.* (*Wagen*) to jolt; to butt; (*an etwas*) to border (on); to strike against; (*auf etwas*) to come across; (sich) ~ *v.refl.* to knock against; to hurt oneself; *einen vor den Kopf ~*, to offend one; *über den Haufen ~*, to overturn; *sich an etwas ~*, to take offense at.
Stoß: **~seufzer** *m.* deep sigh; **~stange** *f.* bumper; **~verkehr** *m.* rush-hour traffic.
stoßweise *adv.* by fits and starts; intermittently.
Stoßzahn *n.* tusk.
Stoßzeit *f.* rush hour.
stottern *v.i.* to stutter, to stammer.
stracks *adv.* straightaway, immediately.
Straf... punitive *a.*
Staf: **~anstalt** *f.* prison; **~antrag** *m.* (*jur.*) demand for punishment; **~arbeit** *f.* extra work; **~bank** *f.* (*sp.*) penalty bench.
strafbar *a.* punishable; ~ *sein*, to be liable to prosecution.
Straf: **~befugnis** *f.* right to impose penalties; **~betimmung** *f.* clause in penal code; **~buch** *n.* book of fines.
Strafe *f.* (-, -n) punishment; (*Geld*) fine, penalty; *seine ~ erleiden*, to undergo one's punishment; *es ist*

bei ~ verboten, it is forbidden on pain of (the law, a fine, etc.); *seine ~ absitzen*, to serve one's sentence.
strafen *v.t.* to punish, to chastise; (*an Geld*) to fine; *einen Lügen ~*, to give someone the lie.
Strafentlassene *m./f.* ex-convict.
Straferlaß *m.* remission; amnesty.
straff *a.* tight, tense; (*nav.*) taut.
straffällig *a.* **~werden** to commit an offense.
straffen (sich) *v.t.* & *refl.* to tighten; to tauten.
Straffrei *a.* unpunished.
Straf: **~freiheit** *f.* immunity from prosecution; **~gefangene** *m./f.* convict; **~gericht** *n.* judgment; **~gesetz** *n.* penal law; **~gesetzbuch** *n.* penal code; **~kolonie** *f.* penal settlement.
sträflich *a.* criminal.
Sträfling, *m.* (-[e]s, -e) convict; prisoner.
straflos *adv.* unpunished.
Straf: **~mandat** *n.* ticket; **~maß** *n.* sentence; **~porto** *n.* surcharge; **~predigt** *f.* lecture, reprimand; **~prozeß** *m.* criminal case; criminal procedure; **~prozeßordnung** *f.* code of criminal procedure; **~punkt** *m.* (*Sport*) penalty; **~recht** *n.* criminal law; **~rechtspflege** *f.* criminal justice; **~rechtsreform** *f.* penal reform; **~rechtlich** *a.* criminal, penal; **~register** *n.* criminal register; **~richter** *m.* criminal judge; **~sache** *f.* criminal case; **~summe** *f.* penalty, fine; **~tat** *f.* criminal offense; **~umwandlung** *f.* commutation of sentence; **~urteil** *n.* sentence; **~verfahren** *n.* criminal proceedings; **~versetzung** *f.* disciplinary transfer; **~vollstreckung** *f.*, **~vollzug** *m.* penal administration; **~stafwürdig** *a.* punishable; **~zeit** *f.* prison term; **~zettel** *m.* ticket.
Strahl *m.* (-[e]s, -en) beam, ray flash; (*Wasser~*) jet.
strahlen *v.t.* & *i.* to radiate, to beam; to shine.
Strahlenbelastung *f.* radioactive contamination.
Strahlenbrechung *f.* refraction.
strahlend *a.* radiant, shining.
Strahlendosis *f.* radiation dose.
strahlenförmig *a.* radial.
Strahlentherapie *f.* radiotherapy.
Strahlenunfall *m.* radiation accident.
Strahlung *f.* radiation.
Strähne *f.* (-, -n) strand; streak.
strähnig *a.* straggly.
stramm *a.* tight; sturdy, strapping; erect; (*im Dienst*) strict.
strammstehen *v.i.* to stand at attention.
Strampelhöschen *n.* rompers.
strampeln *v.i.* to kick, to struggle.
Strand *m.* (-[e]s, -e) strand, shore, beach; *auf den ~ laufen*, to run ashore.
stranden *v.i.* (*s*) to strand, to be stranded.
Strand: **~gut** *n.* jetsam, flotsam; **~korb** *m.* wicker chair for the beach.
Strang *m.* (-[e]s, Stränge) rope; (*Galgen~*) noose; (*Schienen~*) track.
strangulieren *v.t.* to strangle.
Strapaze *f.* (-, -n) strain; fatigue, over-exertion.
strapazieren *v.t.* to strain, to exhaust, to be hard on.
Strapazierfähigkeit *f.* resistance to wear.
strapaziös *a.* wearing.
Straße *f.* (-, -n) road, highway; street; (*Meeresenge*) straits *pl.*
Straßen: **~bahn** *f.* streetcar; **~bahnwagen** *m.*

streetcar, trolley; ~**bau** *m.* road construction; ~**gabel** *f.* road-junction; ~**karte** *f.* road map; ~**kreuzung** *f.* intersection, crossing, cross-roads; ~**laterne** *f.* street lamp; ~**pflaster** *n.* pavement; ~**raub** *m.* highway-robbery; ~**schild** *n.* streetname sign; ~**sperre** *f.* (*mil.*) roadblock; ~**unterbau** *m.* road-bed; ~**verkehrsordnung** *f.* rule of the road; ~**verkäufer** *m.* street vendor.

Stratege *m.* (-en, -en) strategist.

Strategie *f.* (-, 0) strategy.

strategisch *a.* strategic(al).

sträuben (sich) *v.t.* to bristle; ~ *v.refl.* to struggle.

Strauch *m.* (-[e]s, Sträuche[r]) bush, shrub.

straucheln *v.i.* (*s*) to stumble.

Strauß *m.* (-e,s -e) ostrich; (*pl. Sträuße*) bunch, bouquet.

streben *v.i.* to strive, to aspire.

Streben *n.* (-s, 0) effort, endeavour.

Strebepfeiler *m.* buttress.

Streber *m.* (-s, -) grind.

strebsam *a.* active, industrious.

Strebsamkeit *f.* industriousness.

Strecke *f.* (-, -n) extent, distance; (*rail.*) section.

strecken *v.i.* to stretch; to extend; *die Waffen ~,* to lay down one's arms; *zu Boden ~,* to fell.

Streckennetz *n.* railroad network.

streckenweise *adv.* in sections; at times.

Streich *m.* (-[e]s, -e) stroke, blow, lash; trick; *auf einen ~,* at one blow; *einem einen ~ spielen,* to play someone a trick; *ein dummer ~,* a foolish trick; *ein lustiger ~,* a prank.

streicheln *v.t.* to stroke, to caress.

streichen *v.t.st.* to rub; (*Butter*) to spread; (*die Flagge*) to strike; (*Segel*) to lower; (*ausstreichen*) to strike out, to erase; ~ *v.i.* (*s*) to rove, to stroll.

Streicher *pl.* (*mus.*) the strings.

Streich: ~**holz,** ~**hölzchen** *n.* match; ~**holzschachtel** *f.* matchbox; ~**instrument** *n.* string instrument; ~**music** *f.* string music; ~**riemen** *m.* razor-strop.

Streichquartett *n.* string quartet.

Streichung *f.* (-, -en) cut, deleted passage.

Streife *f.* (-, -n) patrol.

streifen *v.t.* to graze, to touch slightly, to brush; to stripe, to streak; ~ *v.i.* (*s*) to ramble, to rove; (*h*) (*an etwas*) to border *or* verge (upon); *in die Höhe ~,* to tuck up (one's sleeves).

Streifen *m.* (-s, -) stripe, streak; strip.

Streifen: ~**dienst** *m.* patrol duty; ~**wagen** *m.* patrol car.

streifig *a.* striped; streaky (bacon).

Streif: ~**schuß** *m.* grazing shot; ~**zug** *m.* expedition; prowl (animals).

Streik *m.* (-s, -e) strike (of workmen).

Streikbrecher *m.* (-s, -) strike breaker.

streiken *v.i.* to strike.

streikend *a.* on strike.

Streikende *m./f.* striker.

Streik: ~**kasse** *f.* strike-fund; ~**posten** *m.* picket.

Streit *m.* (-[e]s, -e) fight; contest, dispute, quarrel; conflict; *in ~ geraten,* to fall out, to get into a quarrel.

Streitaxt *f.* battleaxe.

streitbar *a.* valiant.

streiten *v.i.st.* to fight; to dispute, to quarrel; to disagree; *darüber lässt sich ~,* that is a matter of opinion; *die streitenden Parteien,* the contending parties.

Streit: ~**frage** *f.* moot point, controversial question; ~**gegenstand** *m.* (*law*) matter in controversy; ~**handel** *m.* dispute.

streitig *a.* contested, controversial; *einem etwas ~ machen,* to contest one's right to a thing.

Streitigkeit *f.* (-, -en) contention; controversy; quarrel.

Streit: ~**kräfte** *pl.* (military) forces; ~**lust** *f.* quarrelsome disposition.

streitlustig *a.* contentious, litigious.

Streit: ~**punkt** *m.* point at issue; ~**schrift** *f.* polemic treatise; ~**sucht** *pf.* contentiousness.

streitsüchtig *a.* litigious, quarrelsome.

streng *a.* severe, stern; (*Charakter*) austere; strict, stringent.

Strenge *f.* (-, 0) severity; austerity; rigor (of climate).

strenggenommen *adv.* strictly speaking.

strenggläubig *a.* strict.

Streß *m.* (-es, -e) stress.

stressen *v.t.* (*fam.*) to put s.b. under stress.

stressig *a.* (*fam.*) stressful.

Streu *f.* (-, -en) litter.

Streubüchse *f.* shaker (salt, sugar).

streuen *v.t.* to strew; to scatter, to spread; to sprinkle.

streunen *v.i.* to roam around; ~**de Hunde** stray dogs.

Streuzucker *m.* confectioners' sugar.

Strich *m.* (-[e]s, -e) stroke, line, dash; (*Land~*) tract; *in einem ~,* at a stretch; *das macht einen ~ durch die Rechnung,* that upsets the whole plan; *gegen oder wider den ~,* against the grain.

stricheln *v.i.* to sketch in; to hatch; **eine gestrichelte Linie** a broken line.

Strich: ~**junge** *m.* young male prostitute; ~**mädchen** *n.* hooker.

Strichpunkt *m.* semicolon.

strichweise *adv.* here and there.

Strick *m.* (-[e]s, -e) cord, rope.

Strickbeutel *m.* knitting-bag.

stricken *v.t.* to knit.

Strickerei *f.* (-, -en) knitting.

Strick: ~**jacke** *f.* cardigan; ~**leiter** *f.* rope-ladder; ~**nadel** *f.* knitting-needle; ~**waren** *pl.* knitwear.

Striegel *m.* (-s, -) curry-comb.

striegeln *v.t.* to groom.

Striemen *m.* (-s, -), **Strieme** *f.* (-, -n) stripe, weal.

strikt *a.* strict.

Strippe *f.* (-, -n) string; strap, band.

strippen *v.i.* to strip; to do a strip-tease.

Striptease *n./n.* (-, 0) strip-tease.

strittig *a.* contentious; disputed.

Stroh *n.* (-[e]s, 0) straw.

Strohdach *n.* thatch.

Stroh: ~**halm** *m.* straw; ~**hut** *m.* strawhat; ~**hütte** *f.* thatched hut; ~**sack** *m.* straw-mattress; palliasse; ~**witwe** *f.* grass-widow; ~**witwer** *m.* grass-widower.

Strolch *m.* (-[e]s, -e) tramp.

strolchen *v.i.* (*s*) to loaf *or* prowl about.

Strom *m.* (-[e]s, Ströme) large river; (*elek. usw.*)

current; (*fig.*) torrent, flood; *gegen den ~, mit dem ~ schwimmen*, to swim against, with the stream *or* the tide.

stromabwärts *adv.* downstream.

stromaufwärts *adv.* upstream.

strömen *v.i.* (*s*) to stream, to flow; to pour.

Stromer *n.* (-s, -) vagabond, tramp.

Strom: ~**kreis** *m.* circuit; ~**linienförmig**, streamlined, *a.*; ~**schnelle** *f.* rapid; ~**stärke** *f.* amperage.

Strömung *f.* (-, -en) current, drift.

Stromverbrauch *m.* power consumption.

Stromversorgung *f.* power supply.

Stromzähler *m.* electric meter.

Strophe *f.* (-, -n) stanza, verse; strophe.

strophisch *a.* strophic, in stanzas.

strotzen *v.i.* to be full of.

Strudel *m.* (-s, -) whirlpool.

Struktur *f.* (-, -en) structure.

strukturell *a.* structural.

strukturieren *v.t.* to structure.

Strumpf *m.* (-[e]s, Strümpfe) stocking; (*Glüh~*), mantle.

Strumpf: ~**band** *n.* garter; ~**halter** *m.* garter; ~**hose** *f.* pantyhose; ~**ware** *f.* hosiery.

Strunk *m.* (-s, Strünke) stalk.

struppig *a.* touseled, shaggy (dog).

Struwwelkopf *m.* tousle-head.

Strychnin (*Strich~*), *m.* (-[e]s, 0) strychnine.

Stube *f.* (-, -n) (living) room, chamber.

Stuben: ~**arrest** *m.* confinement in one's own room; ~**hocker** *m.* stay-at-home; ~**mädchen** *n.* chamber-maid.

stubenrein *a.* clean; housebroken.

Stuck *m.* (-[e]s, 0) stucco(-work).

Stück *n.* (-[e]s, -e) piece, bit, morsel; fragment; (*Theater*) piece, play; (*Zucker*) lump; *~ für ~*, piece by piece; *im ~*, by the piece; *grosse -e auf einen halten*, to think much of someone; *aus freien ~en*, of one's own accord; *in allen ~en*, in every respect.

Stückeschreiber *m.* playwright.

Stücklohn *m.* piece rate.

Stückpreis *m.* unit price.

stückweis *adv.* by the piece, piecemeal.

Stückzucker *m.* lump-sugar.

Student *m.* (-en, -en); **Studentin** *f.* (-, -nen) student, undergraduate.

Studentenverbindung *f.* fraternity.

Studentenschaft *f.* (-, 0) students.

studentisch *a.* student-like, student.

Studie *f.* (-, -n) (*Maler~*) (painter's) study; essay, sketch.

Studien: ~**aufenthalt** *m.* study visit; ~**direktor** *m.* principal (of a secondary school); ~**fach** *n.* subject; ~**gang** *m.* course of study; ~**gebühr** *f.* tuition fee; ~**kopf** *m.* study of a head; ~**rat** *m.*, ~**rätin** *f.* tenured teacher at secondary school.

studieren *v.t. & i.* to study; to read.

Studierende *m./f.* (n, -n) = **Student.**

Studier: ~**lampe** *f.* reading-lamp; ~**stube** *f.* study.

Studio *n.* studio.

Studiobühne *f.* studio theater.

Studiosus *m.* (-, -sen, *u.* -s) student, undergraduate.

Studium *n.* (-s, Studien) study.

Stufe *f.* (-, -n) step; stair; degree.

stufenartig *a.* gradual, graduated.

Stufen: ~**barren** *m.* asymmetric bars; ~**leiter** *f.* scale; (*fig.*) gradation.

stufenweise *dv.* gradually, by degrees.

stufig *a.* layered.

Stuhl *m.* (-[e]s, Stühle) chair, seat; (*ohne Lehne*) stool; (*Kirchen~*) pew; *der apostoliche ~*, the Holy See; *sich zwischen zwei Stühle setzen*, (*fig.*) to fall between two stools.

Stuhl: ~**bein** *n.* leg of a chair; ~**drang** *m.* need of relieving the bowels; ~**gang** *m.* bowel movement, (*med.*) stool; ~**lehne** *f.* back of a chair.

Stukkateur *m.* (-s, -e) stucco-worker.

Stukkatur *f.* (-, -en) stucco(-work).

Stulle *f.* (-, -n) slice of bread and butter.

stülpen *v.t.* to cock (a hat); to tilt, to turn up; to put over.

Stulp[en]stiefel *m.* top-boot.

stumm *a.* dumb, mute, silen; *~er Film m.* silent film.

Stumme *m./f.* mute.

Stummel *m.* (-s, -) stump, cigar butt; stub (pencil).

Stümper *m.* (-s, -) botcher; bungler.

Stümperei *f.* (-, -en) botching; bungling.

stümperhaft *a.* bungling.

stümpern *v.t.* to bungle, to botch.

stumpf *a.* obtuse; blunt; dull; *~er Winkel*, obtuse angle.

Stumpf *m.* (-[e]s, Stümpfe) stump, trunk.

Stumpfsinn *m.* dullness; apathy.

stumpfsinnig *a.* stupid, dull.

Stunde *f.* (-, -n) hour; lesson.

stunden *v.t.* to grant a delay for sth.

Stunden: ~**geld** *n.* fee for a lesson; ~**glas** *n.* hour-glass.

stundenlang *a.* lasting for hours.

Stunden: ~**plan** *m.* time-table; ~**zeiger** *m.* hour-hand.

stündlich *a. & adv.* hourly; every hour.

Stundung *f.* (-, -en) delay (of payment), respite.

Stundungsfrist *f.* (*com.*) days of grace.

stupide *a.* dull; moronic.

Stups *m.* (-es, -e) (*fam.*) push; shove.

stupsen *v.t.* (*fam.*) to push; to shove.

Stupsnase *f.* snubnose.

stur *a.* stubborn; obstinate.

Sturheit *f.* stubbornnes; obstinacy.

Sturm *m.* (-[e]s, Stürme) gale, storm; tempest; (*mil.*) assault.

Sturm: ~**angriff** *m.* assault; ~**warnung** *f.* gale warning.

stürmen *v.t. & i.* to storm; to rush; to assault.

Stürmer (-s, -) (*Fußball*) forward.

Sturmflut *f.* storm tide.

stürmisch *a.* stormy, tempestuous.

Sturmwind *m.* heavy gale.

Sturz *m.* (-es, Stürze) rush; fall, ruin; plunge; (*fig.*) overthrow.

Sturzbach *m.* torrent.

stürzen *v.t.* to plunge; to plummet; to shoot; (*fig.*) to overthrow, to ruin; *~ v.i.* (*s*) to fall; to tumble down; to rush; *sich in Gefahren ~*, to rush into dangers; *sich in Schulden, Kosten ~*, to plunge into debt, to incur heavy expenses; *ins Elend ~*, to plunge s.b. into misery; *ins Verderben ~*, to undo, to ruin.

Sturzflug *m.* (*avi.*) nose-dive.

Sturzhelm *m.* (-s, -e) crash helmet.

Stute *f.* (-, -n) mare.
Stütze *f.* (-, -n) prop, stay; support.
stutzen *v.t.* to curtail; to prune; to crop (ears); to clip, to lop, to trim; ~ *v.i.* to be startled; to stop short.
stützen *v.t.* to prop, to support; to base on; (sich) ~ *v.refl.* to rely upon, to lean against; to refer to.
Stutzer *m.* (-s, -) dandy.
stutzerhaft *a.* dandified.
Stutzflügel *m.* baby grand (piano).
stutzig *a.* ~ *machen*, to startle.
Stützpunkt *m.* point of support; (*des Hebels*) fulcrum; (*mil.*) base.
Stutzschwanz *m.* bob-tail.
subaltern *a.* subaltern, inferior.
Subdominante *f.* subdominant.
Subjekt *n.* (-[e]s, -e) subject; (*fam.*) person, fellow.
subjektiv *a.* subjective.
Subjektivität *f.* subjectivity.
Subjektsatz *m.* subject clause.
Subkultur *f.* (-, -en) subculture.
subordinieren *v.t.* to subordinate.
Subsidiengelder *pl.* subsidies.
subskribieren *v.t.* to subscribe (to).
Subskription *f.* (-, -en) subscription.
Substantiv *n.* (-s, -e) noun.
Substanz *f.* (-, -en) substance.
Substrat *n.* (-[e]s, -e) substratum.
subtil *a.* subtle.
subtrahieren *v.t.* to subtract.
Subtraktion *f.* subtraction.
subtropisch *a.* subtropic(al).
subventionieren *v.t.* to subsidize.
Subventionierung *f.* (-, -en) subsidy.
Suche *f.* (-, -n) search; *auf der ~ sein*, to be in search (of).
suchen *v.t.* to seek, to look for; (*versuchen*) to endeavour, to try; *er hat hier nichts zu ~*, he has no business here; *gesucht*, wanted; affected; far-fetched.
Sucher *m.* (-s, -) (*phot.*) viewfinder.
Suchhund *m.* tracker dog.
Sucht *f.* (-, 0) addiction.
süchtig *a.* addicted.
Süchtige *m./f.*, **Suchtkranke** *m./f.* addict.
Südafrika *n.* South Africa.
Südafrikaner *m.*; **Südafrikanerin** *f.*; **südafrikanisch** *a.* South African.
Südamerika *n.* South America.
Sudan *m./n.* Sudan.
süddeutsch *a.* South German.
Süden *m.* (-s, 0) south.
Sudelei *f.* (-, -en) mess.
sudeln *v.t.* to make a mess.
Südfrüchte *pl.* fruits grown in the south.
Südküste *f.* south coast.
südlich *a.* south(ern).
Südost[en], *m.* south-east.
südöstlich *a.* south-east(ern).
Süd: ~**pol** *m.* South-Pole; ~**see** *f.* South-Sea; ~**seite** *f.* south side.
südwärts *adv.* southward.
südwestlich *a.* south-west(ern).
Südwind *m.* south/southerly wind.
Suff *m.* (-[e]s, 0) (*vulg.*) boozing.

süffig *a.* drinkable.
süfisant *a.* smug.
suggerieren *v.t.* to suggest.
suggestiv *a.* suggestive.
suhlen *v.refl.* to wallow.
Sühne *f.* (-, -n) expiation, atonement.
sühnen *v.t.* to expiate, to atone for.
Suite *f.* (-, -n) retinue; set of things.
sukzessiv *a.* gradual.
Sulfat *n.* sulfate.
Sulfonamid *n.* sulfonamide.
Sultan *m.* (-[e]s, -e) sultan.
Sultanine *f.* (-, -n) sultana (raisin).
Sülze *f.* (-,-n) brawn; aspic.
Summa *f.* (-, Summen) sum (total).
summarisch *a.* summary.
Summe *f.* (-, -n) sum; sum-total.
summen *v.i.* to buzz, to hum.
summieren (sich) *v.t. & refl.* to add up (to).
Sumpf *m.* (-[e]s, Sümpfe) marsh, swamp, (*fig.*) morass.
sumpfig *a.* marshy, swampy.
Sumpfhuhn *n.* moor-hen.
Sund *m.* (-[e], -e) straits *pl.*, sound.
Sünde *f.* (-, -n) sin.
Sünden: ~**bock** *m.* scapegoat; ~**fall** *m.* fall (of man); ~**vergebung** *f.* remission of sins.
Sünder *m.* (-s, -), **Sünderin** *f.* (-, -nen) sinner.
sündhaft *a.* sinful.
sündig *a.* sinful.
sündigen *v.i.* to sin.
sündlos *a.* sinless.
Super *n.* premium (gas).
superklug *a.* (*fam.*) overwise.
Superlativ *m.* (-s, -e) superlative.
Supermarkt *m.* supermarket.
Suppe *f.* (-, -n) soup; *jm. eine ~ einbrocken*, to do s.b. a bad turn.
Suppen: ~**fleisch** *n.* meat for soup; ~**löffel** *m.* table-spoon, soup-ladle; ~**schüssel** *f.* soup tureen; ~**würfel** *m.* bouillon cube.
Surfbrett *n.* surfboard.
surfen *v.i.* to surf.
Surrealismus *m.* surrealism.
surrealistisch *a.* surrealist; surrealistic.
surren *v.i.* to hum, to buzz.
Surrogat *n.* (-[e]s, -e) substitute.
suspekt *a.* suspicious.
suspendieren *v.t.* to suspend; to dismiss.
süß *a.* sweet.
Süße *f.* (-, 0) sweetness.
süßen *v.t.* to sweeten.
Süßigkeit *f.* (-, -en) sweet; sweetness; *Süßigkeiten f.pl.* sweets, lollipops *pl.*
süßlich *a.* sweetish; on the sweet side; mawkish.
Süßwasser *n.* fresh water.
Sylphe *f.* (-, -n) sylph.
Syllogismus *m.* (-, -gismen) syllogism.
Sylvester[abend] *m.* New Year's Eve.
Symbol *n.* (-[e]s, -e) symbol.
symbolhaft *a. & adv.* symbolic(ally).
Symbolik *f.* (-, 0) symbolism.
symbolisch *a.* symbolic.
symbolisieren *v.t.* to symbolize.
Symbolismus *m.* symbolism; Symbolism (art).
Symmetrie *f.* (-, -[e]n) symmetry.

symmetrisch a. symmetrical.
Sympathie f. (-, -[e]n) sympathy.
Sympathisant m. (-en, -en); **Sympathisantin** f. (-, -nen) sympathizer.
sympathisch a. congenial, likeable; nice.
sympathisieren v.i. to sympathize (with).
Symphonie f. (-, -[e]n) symphony.
Symptom n. (-[e]s, -e) symptom.
symptomatisch a. symptomatic (of).
Synagoge f. (-, -n) synagogue.
synchronisieren v.t. to dub; to synchronize.
Syndikat n. (-es, -e) syndicate.
Syndikus m. (-, -dizi u. -diken) company lawyer.
Syndrom n. (-s, -e) syndrome.
Synkope f. (-, -n) syncopation.
synkopieren v.t. to syncopate.

Synode f. (-, -n) synod.
synonym a. synonymous.
Synonym n. synonym.
syntaktisch a. syntactic.
Syntax f. (-, 0) syntax.
Synthese f. (-, -n) synthesis.
synthetisch a. synthetic.
Syphilis f. (-, 0) syphilis.
Syrer m.; **Syrerin** f.; **syrisch** a. Syrian.
Syrien n. (-s, 0) Syria.
Syrup m. (-s, 0) syrup, molasses.
System n. (-[e]s, -e) system.
systematisch a. systematic.
Szenario n. (-, -s) scenario.
Szene f. (-, -n) scene.
Szenerie f. (-, -en) scenery; setting.
Szepter n. = **Zepter.**

T

T, t n. the letter T or t.
Tabak m. (-[e]s, -e) tobacco.
Tabaks: ~**beutel** m. tobacco-pouch; ~**dose** f. snuff-box.
tabellarisch a. tabular, tabulated.
Tabelle f. (-, -n) table(s), schedule.
Tabellenführer m. top team/player.
Tablett n. (-s, -e) tray.
Tablette f. (-, -n) tablet.
Tacho m. (fam.), **Tachometer** n. (-s, -) speedometer.
Tadel m. (-s, -) blame, censure; fault, blemish.
tadelhaft a. blameable.
tadellos a. impeccable; blameless, faultless, perfect.
tadeln v.t. to rebuke; to blame.
tadelnswert a. reprehensible.
Tadler m. (-s, -) fault-finder.
Tafel f. (-, -n) (dining-)table; (Wand~) black-board; (Stein~) slab; plate; slate; bar (of chocolate); dinner.
tafelfertig a. ready to serve.
tafelförmig a. tabular, table-shaped.
Tafelgeschirr n. dinner-service.
tafeln v.i. to dine, to feast.
täfeln v.t. to panel.
Täfelung f. (-, -en) panelling.
Tafelwasser n. mineral water.
Tafelwein m. table wine.
Taft m. (-[e]s, -e) taffeta.
Tag m. (-[e]s, -e) day; light; es ist heller ~, it is broad day; an den ~ kommen, to come to light; bei Tage, in the daytime; heute über acht ~e, a week from today; in den ~ hinein, thoughtlessly.
tagaus adv. ~, **tagein** day in, day out.
Tage: ~**bau** m. stripmining; ~**buch** n. diary, journal; (com.) day-book; ~**geld** n. per diem allowance.
tagelang a. & adv. for days together.
Tage: ~**lohn** m. daily wages pl.; ~**löhner** m. day-laborer.
tagen v.imp. to dawn; ~ v.i. (of assemblies) to meet, to sit.
Tagereise f. day's journey.
Tages: ~**ablauf** m. day; daily; ~**anbruch** m. daybreak; ~**angriff** m. (avi.) daylight attack; ~**befehl**

m. (mil.) order of the day; routine; ~**gespräch** n. topic of the day; ~**licht** n. daylight; ans ~licht kommen, to come to light; ~**ordnung** f. agenda, order of the day; ~**zeit** f. time of day.
tageweise adv. by the day.
Tagewerk n. day's work, day's task.
taghell a. light as day.
täglich a. daily; ~es Geld n. call money.
tags adv. by day; ~**zuvor** the day before; ~**darauf** the day after.
Tagschicht f. day shift.
tagtäglich adv. every day.
Tagträumer m. daydreamer.
Tag- und Nachtgleiche f. equinox.
Tagung f. (-, -en) conference, rally, session.
Tagungsort m. conference venue.
Taifun m. (-s, -e) typhoon.
Taille f. (-, -n) waist; waistline.
tailliert a. waisted.
Takel n. (-s, -) (nav.) tackle.
Takelage f. rigging.
takeln v.t. to tackle, to rig.
Takelwerk n. rigging.
Takt m. (-es, -e) time, measure; bar; (fig.) tact; ~ halten, to keep time; ~ schlagen, to beat time; im ~, in time.
Taktgefühl n. sense of tact.
Taktik f. (-, -en) tactics pl.
Taktiker m. (-s, -); **Taktikerin** f. (-, -nen) tactician.
taktisch a. tactical.
taktlos a. tactless.
Taktlosigkeit f. (-, -en) tactlessness.
Takt[ier]stock m. baton; ~**strich** m. (mus.) bar.
taktvoll a. tactful; discreet.
Tal n. (-[e]s, Täler) valley, dale, glen.
Talar m. (-[e]s, -e) robe.
Talent n. (-[e]s, -e) talent; gift, aptitude.
talentiert a. talented.
talentvoll a. talented, gifted.
Talg m. (-[e]s, 0) tallow, suet.
Talglicht n. tallow-candle.
Talisman m. talisman; mascot.
Talsohle f. valley floor; (fig.) depression.
Talsperre f. dam; reservoir.

Talstation *f.* valley station.

Tambour *m.* (-s, -e *u.* -s) drummer.

Tamburin *n.* (-[e]s, -e *u.* -s) tambourine.

Tampon *n.* (-s, -s) tampon; plug.

Tand *m.* (-[e]s, 0) knicknacks *pl* toy(s).

tändeln *v.t.* to trifle, to toy, to dandle.

Tang *m.* (-[e]s, -e) sea-weed.

Tangens *m.* (-, -) tangent.

Tangente *f.* (-, -n) tangent.

tangieren *v.t.* to affect; (*math.*) to be tangent to.

Tank *m.* (-[e]s, -s) tank; **~dampfer** *m.* tanker.

tanken *v.i.* to fill up; to refuel.

Tankstelle *f.* (-, -n) gas station.

Tankwart *m.* gas station attendant.

Tanne *f.* (-, -n) fir(-tree), silver-fir.

Tannennadel *f.* fir needle.

Tannenzapfen *m.* pine-cone, fir-cone.

Tannin *m.* (-[e]s, 0) tannic acid, tannin.

Tante *f.* (-, -n) aunt.

Tantieme *f.* (-, -n) royalty.

Tanz *m.* (-es, Tänze) dance.

tänzeln *v.i.* to prance; to skip.

tanzen *v.i.* to dance.

Tänzer *m.* (-s, -); **Tänzerin** *f.* (-, -nen) dancer.

Tanz: **~lehrer**, **~lehrerin** dancing-instructor; **~sport** *m.* ballroom dancing; **~stunde** *f.* dancing-lesson.

Tapet *n.* (-[e]s, -e) (*obs.*) *aufs ~ bringen*, to broach *or* to introduce (a subject).

Tapete *f.* (-, -n) wall-paper.

tapezieren *v.t.* to paper; to hang with tapestry.

Tapezier[er] *m.* (-s, -) paper-hanger, upholsterer.

tapfer *a.* brave, valiant.

Tapferkeit *f.* (-, 0) valor, bravery.

tappen *v.i.* to grope; to patter.

täppisch *a.* awkward, clumsy.

tapsen *v.i.* to lurch along.

tapsig *a.* awkward, clumsy.

Tara *f.* (-, 0) (*Gewicht*) (*com.*) tare.

Tarantel *f.* (-, -n) tarantula; *wie von der ~ gestochen*, like one possessed.

Tarif *m.* (-s, -e) tariff; scale of wages; railway rate.

Tarif: **~gruppe** *f.* wage group; salary group; **~lohn** *m.* standard wage; **~vertrag** *m.* collective agreement.

tarnen *v.i.* (*mil.*) to camouflage.

Tarnung *f.* (-, -en) camouflage.

Tarock *m. & n.* (-s, 0) taroc.

Tasche *f.* (-, -n) pocket; bag; (*Schul~*) satchel.

Taschen: **~ausgabe** *f.* pocket edition; **~buch** *n.* paperback; **~dieb** *m.* pickpocket; **~format** *n.* pocket-size; **~geld** *n.* pocket-money; **~krebs** *m.* crab; **~lampe** *f.* flashlight; **~messer** *n.* pocket-knife; **~spiel** *n.* juggling, sleight-of-hand; **~spieler** *m.* conjurer, juggler; **~tuch** *n.* handkerchief; **~uhr** *f.* pocket watch.

Tasse *f.* (-, -n) cup.

Tastatur *f.* (-, -en) (*mus.*) key-board, keys *pl.*

Taste *f.* (-, -n) (*mus.*) key.

tasten *v.t. & i.* to grope, to feel, to touch.

Tasten: **~instrument** *n.* keyboard instrument; **~telefon** *n.* push-button telephone.

Taster *m.* (-s, -) feeler, antenna.

Tastsinn *m.* (sense of) touch, feeling.

Tat *f.* (-, -en) action, deed, fact, act; *in der ~*, indeed, as a matter of fact; *auf frischer ~*, in the very act;

mit Rat und ~, by word and deed.

Tatbestand *m.* facts of the case *pl.*

Tatendrang, Tatendurst *m.* desire for action.

tatenlos *a.* inactive.

Täter *m.* (-s, -); **Täterin** *f.* (-, -nen) culprit; offender.

tätig *a.* active; busy, industrious.

tätigen *v.t.* to effect, to carry out.

Tätigkeit *f.* (-, -en) activity; *außer ~ setzen*, to suspend.

Tatkraft *f.* energy.

tatkräftig *a.* energetic.

tätlich *a.* *~werden*, to become violent; *~e Beleidigung*, assault and battery.

Tatort *m.* crime scene.

tätowieren *v.t.* to tattoo.

Tatsache *f.* (-, -n) fact.

tatsächlich *a. & adv.* actual(ly), as a matter of fact, in point of fact.

tätscheln *v.t.* to pat.

tatte(e)rig *a.* shaky.

tatverdächtig *a.* suspected.

Tatze *f.* (-, -n) paw, claw.

Tau *n.* (-[e]s, -e) cable rope.

Tau *m.* (-[e]s, 0) dew.

taub *a.* deaf.

Taube *f.* (-, -n) pigeon, dove.

Taube *m./f.* deaf person.

Taubenschlag *m.* pigeon-loft.

Taubheit *f.* (-, 0) deafness.

Taubnessel *f.* deadnettle.

taubstumm *a.* deaf-and-dumb.

Taubstumme *m./f.* deaf mute.

tauchen *v.t.* to dip, to steep, to duck; *~ v.i.* to dive, to plunge.

Taucher *m.* (-s,-); **Taucherin** *f.* (-, -nen) diver; skin diver.

Taucher: **~anzug** *m.* diving suit; **~brille** *f.* diving goggles; **~glocke** *f.* diving-bell; **~maske** *f.* diving mask.

Tauchsieder *m.* immersion heater.

tauen *v.i.imp.* to thaw; to melt.

Tauf: **~becken** *n.* (baptismal) font; **~buch** *n.* parish-register.

Taufe *f.* (-, -n) baptism, christening.

taufen *v.t.* to christen, to baptize.

Täufer *m.* (-s, -) *Johannes der ~*, St. John the Baptist.

Täufling *m.* (-[e]s, -e) child (*or* person) to be baptized.

Tauf: **~name** *m.* Christian name; **~pate** *m.* godfather; **~patin** *f.* godmother; **~schein** *m.* certificate of baptism.

taugen *v.i.* to be good *or* fit for; *nichts ~*, to be good for nothing.

Taugenichts *m.* (-, -nichtse) good-for-nothing.

tauglich *a.* fit, able, qualified; (*mil.*) able-bodied.

Taumel *m.* (-s, 0) dizziness; ecstasy, passion.

taumeln *v.i.* (*s*) to reel, to stagger.

Tausch *m.* (-es, -e) exchange, barter.

tauschen *v.t.* to exchange, to barter.

täuschen *v.t.* to deceive, to delude; (sich) *~ v.refl.* to be deceived; *sich durch etwas ~ lassen*, to be deceived by a thing.

täuschend *a.* deceptive; striking.

Tauschhandel *m.* barter; *~ treiben*, to barter.

Täuschung *f.* (-, -en) deception; delusion, illusion; *optische ~,* optical illusion.

tauschweise *adv.* by way of exchange.

tausend *a.* thousand; *zu Tausenden,* by thousands, in the thousands.

Tausend *n.* (-s, -e) thousand.

Tausender *m.* (-s, -) thousand, figure denoting the thousand.

tausenderlei *a.* of a thousand kinds.

tausendfach, tausendfältig *a.* thousand-fold.

Tausendfüßler *m.* centipede, millipede.

tausendjährig *a.* millennial.

tausendmal *adv.* a thousand times.

Tautropfen *m.* dewdrop.

Tauwetter *n.* thaw.

Tauzieben *n.* tug-of-war.

Taxe *f.* (-, -n) fee, fixed scale of charges; taxi.

Taxi *n.* (-s, -s) taxi.

taxieren *v.t.* to estimate; to value.

Taxi: ~**fahrer** *m.;* ~**fahrerin** *f.* taxi-driver; ~**stand** *m.* taxi-stand.

Taxushecke *f.* yew hedge.

Taxwert *m.* estimated value.

Tb-Kranke *m./f.* TB patient.

Team *n.* i(-s, -s) team; ~**arbeit** *f.,* ~**work** *n.* team work.

Technik *f.* (-, 0) technology; *(in der Kunst)* technique, execution.

Techniker *m.* (-s, -); **Technikerin** *f.* (-, -nen) technical expert.

Technikum *n.* (-s, -ken) technical school.

technisch *a.* technical.

technischer Berater *m.* consulting engineer.

Technokrat *m.* (-en, -en); **Technokratin** *f.* (-, -nen) technocrat.

Technologie *f.* technology.

technologisch *a.* technological.

Teckel *m.* (-s, -) dachshund.

Tedeum *n.* (-[e]s, -[e]s) Te Deum.

Tee (-s, -e *u.* -s) tea.

Tee: ~**beutel** *m.* tea-bag; ~**gesellschaft** *f.* tea-party; ~**kanne** *f.* teapot; ~**kessel** *m.* tea-kettle; ~**löffel** *m.* teaspoon.

Teenager *m.* (-s, -); **Teenagerin** *f.* (-, -nen) teenager.

Teer *m.* (-[e]s, -e) tar.

teeren *v.t.* to tar.

Tee: ~**sieb** *n.* strainer; ~**stube** *f.* tearoom; ~**tasse** *f.* teacup.

Teich *m.* (-[e]s, -e) pond.

Teig *m.* (-[e]s, -e) dough, pastry; batter.

Teigwaren *pl.* pasta.

Teil *m./n.* (-[e]s, -e) share, part, portion; division; *teilhaben an,* to participate; ~*nehmen an,* to take part in; *beide ~e,* both parties; *zu gleichen ~en,* in equal shares; *ich für meinen ~,* I, for one; for my part; *zum ~,* partly.

teilbar *a.* divisible.

Teilchen *n.* (-s, -) particle.

teilen *v.t.* to divide; to share.

Teiler *m.* (-s, -) *(ar.)* divisor.

teilhaben *v.i.* to share.

Teilhaber *m.* (-s, -); **Teilhaberin** *f.* (-, -nen) partner.

Teilhaberschaft *f.* partnership.

teilhaft(ig) *a.* participating in; ~ *werden,* to partake

of, to share.

Teilkaskoversicherung *f.* insurance with partial coverage.

Teilnahme *f.* (-, 0) participation; interest, sympathy.

teilnahms: ~**los** indifferent; ~**voll** compassionate.

Teilnahmslosigkeit *f.* (-, 0) indifference.

teilnehmend *a.* sympathetic.

Teilnehmer *m.* (-s, -); **Teilnehmerin** *f.* (-, -nen) participant, contestant; *(tel.)* subscriber.

teils *adv.* partly.

Teil: ~**strecke** *f.* stretch; stage; ~**stück** *n.* piece, section.

Teilung *f.* (-, -en) division, partition.

teilweise *adv.* in part(s), partially.

Teilzahlung *f.* part-payment, installment.

Teilzeitarbeit *f.* part-time work.

Teint *m.* (-s, -s) complexion.

Telefon *n.* (-s, -e) telephone.

Telefon: ~**anruf** *m.* (tele)phone call; ~**apparat** *m.* telephone.

Telfonat *n.* (-s, -e) telephone call.

Telefon: ~**buch** *n.* directory; ~**gebühr** *f.* telephone charge; ~**hörer** *m.* receiver.

telefonieren *v.i.* to make a phone call; *mit jm.* ~ to talk to s.b. over the phone.

Telefonist *m.* (-en, -en)u; **Telefonistin** *f.* (-, -nen) switchboard operator.

Telefon: ~**karte** *f.* phonecard; ~**nummer** *f.* phone number; ~**zelle** *f.* (tele)phone booth.

Telegraf *m.* (-en, -en) telegraph.

Telegrafen: ~**leitung** *f.* telegraph wire *or* line; ~**linie** *f.* telegraph line; ~**stange** *f.* telegraph pole.

Telegrafie *f.* (-, 0) telegraphy; *drahtlose ~,* wireless (telegraphy).

telegrafieren *v.t.* to telegraph, to wire; to cable.

telegrafisch *a. & adv.* telegraphic; by wire, by telegram.

Telegramm *n.* (-s, -e) telegram, wire.

Telegrammadresse *f.* telegraphic address.

Teleobjektiv *n.* telephoto lens.

Telepathie *f.* telepathy.

Teleskop *n.* (-s, -e) telescope.

Teller *m.* (-s, -) plate.

Tempel *m.* (-s, -) temple.

Temperafarbe *f.* distemper; tempera.

Temperament *n.* (-[e]s, -e) temper.

temperamentlos *a.* spiritless; lifeless.

temperamentvoll *a.* fiery, spirited; lively.

Temperatur *f.* (-, -en) temperature; ~ *nehmen,* to take the temperature.

Temperatur: ~**anstieg** *m.* rise in temperature; ~**rückgang** *m.* drop in temperature; ~**sturz** *m.* sudden drop in temperature.

temperieren *v.t.* to temper.

Tempo *n.* (-s, -s *u.* -pi) *(mus.)* time; movement; pace; speed.

Tempolimit *n.* speed limit.

temporär *a.* temporary.

Tempus *n.* (-, Tempora) *(gram.)* tense.

Tendenz *f.* (-, -en) tendency; bias; slant.

tendenziös *a.* biased, tendentious.

Tender *m.* (-s, -) (engine-)tender.

tendieren *v.i.* to tend.

Tenne *f.* (-, -n) threshing-floor.

Tennis *n.* (-, 0) tennis; ~**platz** *m.* tennis court;

~schläger *m.* racket.
Tenor *m.* (-[e]s, -e *u.* -nöre) tenor (voice).
Teppich *m.* (-[e]s, -e) rug; carpet.
Teppich: ~boden wall-to-wall carpeting; **~fliese** *f.* carpet tile; **~kehrer** *m.* carpet sweeper; **~klopfer** *m.* carpet beater.
Termin *n.* (-[e]s, -e) term, time-limit, deadline; *einen ~ anberaumen*, *(law)* to fix a hearing.
Termindruck *m.* time pressure.
termingemäß *a.* & *adv.* on schedule.
Termingeschäft *n.* futures trading.
Terminkalender *m.* appointment calendar.
Terminologie *f.* (-, -[e]n) terminology.
Termite *f.* (-, -n) termite.
Terpentin *m. or n.* (-s, 0)u turpentine.
Terrain *n.* (-s, -s) ground.
Terrarium *n.* (-s, -rien) terrarium.
Terrasse *f.* (-, -n) terrace.
terrassenförmig *a.* terraced.
Terrine *f.* (-, -n) tureen.
Territorium *n.* (-[s], -rien) territory.
Terror *m.* (-s, 0) terror.
Terroranschlag *m.* terrorist attack.
terrorisieren *v.t.* to terrorize.
Terrorismus *m.* terrorism.
Terrorist *m.* (-en, -en); **Terroristin** *f.* (-, -nen) terrorist.
Tertia *f.* (-, -tien) third grade.
Terz *f.* (-, -en) *(mus.)* third; *grosse ~*, major third; (fencing) tierce.
Terzett *n.* (-[e]s, -e) terzetto, trio.
Test *m.* (-s, -s/e) test.
Testament *n.* (-[e]s, -e) testament, will.
testamentarisch, testamentlich *a.* testamentary, by will.
Testamentsvollstrecker *m.* executor.
testen *v.t.* to test.
testieren *v.i.* to make a will; to bequeath; to testify.
Tetanus *m.* (-, 0) tetanus.
teuer *a.* expensive; *wie ~ ist das?* how much is this?
Teuerung *f.* (-, -en) rise in prices.
Teufel *m.* (-s, -) devil.
teuflisch *a.* devilish, diabolical.
Text *m.* (-es, -e) text; context; *(Lied~)* words; *(Opern~)* libretto.
Textbuch *n.* libretto, words *pl.*
texten *v.t.* to write.
Texter *m.* (-s, -)u writer; copy-writer (advertising).
Textilbranche *f.* textile industry.
Textilien *pl.* textiles.
Textilindustrie *f.* textile industry.
Text: ~stelle *f.* passage of a text; **~verarbeitung** *f.* word processing; **~verarbeitungssystem** *n.* word processor.
Thailand *n.* Thailand.
Thailänder *m.*, **Thailänderin** *f.* Thai.
Theater *n.* (-s, -) theater; stage.
Theater: ~besucher *m.*, **~besucherin** *f.* theater goer; **~dichter** *m.* dramatist, playwright; **~direktor** *m.* theatrical manager; **~kasse** *f.* box-office; **~loge** *f.* box; **~stück** *n.* play; **~zettel** *m.* play-bill.
theatralisch *a.* theatrical, stagey.
Theismus *m.* (-, 0) theism.
Theist *m.* (-en, -en) theist.
Theke *f.* counter.
Thema *n.* (-s, -ta *u.* -men *u.* -s) theme, subject,

topic.
Thematik *f.* complex theme.
thematisch *a.* thematic.
Theologe; *m.* **Theologin** *f.* theologian; divinity student.
Theologie *f.* (-, -[e]n) theology, divinity.
theologisch *a.* theological.
Theoretiker *m.* (-s, -) theorist; theoretician.
theoretisch *a.* theoretical.
Theosophie *f.* theosophy.
Theorie *f.* (-, -[e]n) theory.
Therapeut *m.*; **Therapeutin** *f.* therapist.
therapeutisch *a.* therapeutic.
Therapie *f.* (-, -en) therapy.
Thermalbad *n.* (-s, -bäder) thermal spa.
Thermik *f.* thermionics.
Thermodynamik *f.* thermodynamics.
Thermometer *n.* (*m.*) (-s, -) thermometer.
Thermosflache *f.* thermos *or* vacuum flask.
These *f.* (-, -n) thesis.
Thron *m.* (-[e]s, -e) throne.
thronen *v.i.* to sit enthroned; to reign.
Thron: ~erbe *m.*, **~erbin** *f.*; **~folger** *m.*, **~folgerin** *f.* heir to the throne; **~rede** *f.* King's speech.
Thunfisch *m.* tuna.
Thüringen *n.* (-s, 0) Thuringia.
Thymian *m.* (-s, 0) thyme.
Tiara *f.* (-, Tiaren) tiara, triple crown.
Tibet *n.* Tibet.
Tibeter *m.*; **Tibeterin** *f.*; **tibetisch** *a.* Tibetan.
Tick *m.* (-[e]s, -e) quirk; tic.
ticken *v.i.* *(von Uhren)* to tick.
tief *a.* deep; profound; low; *(von Farben)* dark.
Tief *n.* (-[e]s, -e) *(Wetterkunde)* low.
Tief: ~bau *m.* deep mining; underground constructions *pl.*; road construction; **~blick** *m.* keen insight.
tiefblickend *a.* deep-sighted.
Tiefdruck *m.* low pressure.
Tiefe *f.* (-, -n) depth; profundity.
Tiefebene *f.* lowlands.
Tiefgang *m.* draft (of a ship), depth.
Tiefgarage *f.* underground garage.
tiefgreifend *a.* profound; far-reaching.
tiefgründig *a.* profound.
tiefkühlen *v.t.* to deep freeze.
Tiefkühl: ~kost *f.* frozen food; **~schrank** *m.* freezer.
Tiefland *n.* lowlands.
tiefliegend *a.* deep-set, sunken.
Tief: ~punkt *m.* nadir; **~sinn** *m.* melancholy; profoundness.
tiefsinnig *a.* thoughtful, pensive; profound.
Tiefstand *m.* low level.
Tiegel *m.* (-s, -) crucible; saucepan.
Tier *n.* (-[e]s, -e) animal; **Haus~** pet.
Tier: ~art *f.* animal species; **~arzt** *m.* veterinarian vet; **~garten** *m.* Zoological Gardens, Zoo; **~handlung** *f.* pet shop.
tierisch *a.* animal; brutish, bestial.
Tier: ~kreis *m.* zodiac; **~liebe** *f.* love of animals; **~quälerei** *f.* cruelty to animals; **~reich** *n.* animal kingdom; **~schutzverein** *m.* society for the prevention of cruelty to animals.
Tiger *m.* (-s, -) tiger.
Tigerin *f.* tigress.

Tilde *f.* (-, -n) tilde.

tilgbar *a.* redeemable.

tilgen *v.t.* to extinguish, to annul, to cancel; (*eine Schuld*) to repay.

Tilgung *f.* i(-, -en) cancelling, repayment.

timen *v.t.* to time.

Tinktur *f.* (-, -en) tincture.

Tinte *f.* (-, -n) ink; *in der ~ sitzen*, to be in a nice pickle.

Tinten: **~faß** *n.* inkstand; **~fisch** *m.* cuttle-fish, sepia; **~fleck, ~klecks** *m.* blot, ink-spot; **~stift** *m.* indelible pencil.

Tip *m.* (-[e]s, -e) tip.

tippen *v.t.* to touch gently, to tap; to type.

Tirade *f.* (-, -n) flourish, tirade.

Tirol *n.* (-s, 0) Tyrol.

Tisch *m.* (-es, -e) table; board; (*fig.*) dinner; *bei ~e*, at table; *zu ~e*, to dinner; *den ~ decken*, to lay the table; *reinen ~ machen*, to make a clean slate.

Tisch: **~decke** *f.* table-cloth; table-cover; **~gebet** *n.* grace; **~gesellschaft** *f.* dinner-party.

Tischler *m.* (-s, -) joiner, cabinet-maker.

Tischlerei *f.* (-, -en) joinery.

tischlern *v.i.* to do woodwork.

Tisch: **~manieren** *pl.* table manners; **~platte** *f.* table top; **~rücken** *n.* table-turning; **~tennis** *n.* table tennis; **~tuch** *n.* table-coth; **~zeug** *n.* table-linen.

titanenhaft, titanisch *a.* titanic.

Titel *m.* (-s, -) title; style.

Titel: **~anwärter** *m.*, **~anwärterin** *f.* title contender; **~bild** *n.* frontispiece; **~blatt** *n.* title-page; **~kampf** *m.* final; **~rolle** *f.* title role; **~verteidiger** *m.*, **~verteidigerin** *f.* title holder.

titulieren *v.t.* to call, to title.

Toast *m.* (-es, -e) toast; *einen ~ ausbringen*, to drink someone's health.

toasten *v.t.* to toast.

toben *v.i.* to rage, to storm.

Tobsucht *f.* raving madness, frenzy.

Tochter *f.* (-, Töchter) daughter.

Tochtergesellschaft *f.* subsidiary (company).

Tod *m.* (-[e]s, Todesfälle) death, decease.

todbringend *a.* deadly, lethal; fatal.

Todes: **~angst** *f.* agony, mortal fear; **~anzeige** *f.* obituary (notice); **~art** *f.* manner of death; **~fall** *m.* death, decease; (*mil.*) fatal casualty; **~kampf** *m.* agony; **~stoß** *m.* death-blow; **~strafe** *f.* capital punishment; *bei ~*, on pain of death; **~urteil** *n.* death sentence.

Todfeind *m.* deadly enemy.

todkrank *a.* fatally ill.

tödlich *a.* mortal, deadly.

todmüde *a.* dead-tired.

Todsünde *f.* mortal sin.

Toilette *f.* (-, -n) toilet, lavatory; **~ngarnitur** *f.* toilet-set; **~nseife** *f.* toilet soap.

tolerant *a.* tolerant.

Toleranz *f.* (-, 0) tolerance.

toll *a.* great, fantastic, mad, frantic.

tollen *v.i.* (*fam.*) to romp, to fool about.

Toll: **~haus** *n.* madhouse, bedlam.

Tollheit *f.* (-, -en) madness.

Tollkirsche *f.* deadly nightshade.

tollkühn *a.* foolhardy.

Tollwut *f.* rabies.

Tolpatsch *m.* (-es, -e) awkward fellow.

Tölpel *m.* (-s, -) awkward fellow.

tölpelhaft, tölpisch *a.* clumsy, awkward.

Tomate *pf.* (-, -n) tomato.

Tombola *f.* (-, -s) raffle.

Ton *m.* (-[e]s, Töne) sound; tone; note; key; stress, accent; shade, tint; *güter, feiner ~;* 'good form'; *einen andern ~ anschlagen,* (*fig.*) to change one's tune; *den ~ angeben,* to set the fashion.

Ton *m.* (-[e]s, -e) clay, potter's earth.

tonangebend *a.* setting the tone; predominant.

Ton: **~art** *f.* (*mus.*) key; **~band** *n.* tape; **~bandaufnahme** *f.* tape recording; **~bandgerät** *n.* tape recorder; **~dichter** *m.* musical composer.

tönen *v.t.* to sound; to resound; to tint.

tönern *a.* (of) clay, earthern.

Ton: **~erde** *f.* clay; **~fall** *m.* tone; intonation; **~film** *m.* sound film, talkie; **~kunst** *f.* music, musical art; **~leiter** *f.* scale.

tonlos *a.* toneless, feeble; unaccented (syllable).

Tonne *f.* (-, -n) (*Schiffs~*) ton; barrel, tun.

Tonnen: **~gehalt** *n.* tonnage; **~gewölbe** *n.* barrel-vault.

Tonspur *f.* (*Film*) sound-track.

Tonsur *f.* (-, -en) tonsure.

Tontechniker *m.* sound technician.

Tönung *f.* (-, -en) tint, shading.

Topas *m.* (Topases, Topase) topaz.

Topf *m.* (-[e]s, Töpfe) pot, saucepan; *alles in einen ~ werfen,* (*fig.*) to treat all alike.

Töpfer *m.* (-s, -); **Töpferin** *f.* (-, -nen) potter.

Töpferei *f.* pottery.

töpfern *v.i.u.t.* to make pottery.

Töpferscheibe *f.* potter's wheel.

Tor *n.* (-[e]s, -e) gate; (*Fußball*) goal.

Tor *m.* (-n, -en) fool.

Torf *m.* (-[e]s, -e *u.* Törfe) peat.

Torheit *f.* folly, foolishness.

Torhüter *m.* goalkeeper; goalie.

töricht *a.* foolish, silly.

torkeln *v.i.* (*s*) to stagger, to reel.

Tormann *m.* goalkeeper.

Tornister *m.* (-s, -) knapsack, pack.

Torpedo *m.* (-[e]s, -e), torpedo.

Torpedo: **~boot** *n.* torpedo-boat.

Torso *m.* (-s, -s) torso, trunk.

Torte *f.* (-, -n) layer cake; fruit tart.

Tortur *f.* (-, -en) torture, rack.

Tor: **~wächter** *m.*, **~wart** *m.* (*Fussball*) goalkeeper; **~weg** *m.* gateway.

tosen *v.i.* to roar, to rage.

tot *a.* dead, deceased; **~es** *Kapital,* idle capital; **~schlagen,** to slay; to kill (time); **~schießen,** to shoot dead; **~schweigen,** to hush up (an affair); *sich ~lachen,* to die laughing **~geboren,** stillborn.

total *a.* total.

Total: **~ausfall** *m.* total loss; **~betrag** *m.* aggregate amount.

Totalschaden *m.* (-s, -schäden) write-off.

Tote *m./f.* (-n, -n) dead person, dead man/woman; *die ~n,* the dead.

töten *v.t.* to kill; (*Nerv*) to deaden.

Toten: **~amt** *n.* requiem; **~bahre** *f.* bier.

totenblaß, totenbleich *a.* deadly pale.

Toten: **~feier** *f.* funeral service; **~gedenktag** *m.* memorial day; **~gräber** *m.* gravedigger; **~hemd** *n.*

shroud; **~kopf** *m*. skull; death's head; **~messe** *f*. requiem, mass for the dead; **~schein** *m*. death certificate.

totenstill *a*. silent as the grave.

Totenstille *f*. deathly silence.

Totgeburt *f*. stillbirth.

Toto *n./m* lottery; **~schein** *m*.lottery ticket.

Totschlag *m*. manslaughter.

totschlagen *v.t.st*. to beat to death.

totschweigen *v.t.st*. to hush up; to leave unmentioned.

totsicher *a*. cocksure.

totstellen *v.refl*. to play dead.

tottroten *v.t.st*. to trample to death.

Tötung *f*. (-, -n) killing, slaying.

Toupet *n*. (-s, -s) toupee.

toupieren *v.t*. to back-comb.

Tour *f*. (-, -en) tour, trip.

Tourismus *m*. tourism.

Tourist *m*. (-en, -en); **Touristin** *f*. (-, -nen) tourist.

Tournee *f*. (-, -n) tour.

Trab *m*. (-[e]s, 0) trot; *~ reiten*, to trot.

Trabant *m*. (-en, -en) satellite.

traben *v.i*. (*s*) to trot.

Trabrennen *n*. trotting race.

Tracht *f*. (-, -en) fashion, costume; *eine ~ Prügel*, a thrashing.

trachten *v.i*. to strive.

trächtig *a*. pregnant (animals).

Tradition *f*. (-, -en) tradition.

traditionell *a*. traditional.

Trag: **~bahre** *f*. stretcher, litter; **~balken** *m*. beam, transom.

tragbar *a*. portable; tolerable.

Trage *f*. (-, -n) stretcher, litter.

träge *a*. lazy, inert, idol, indolent.

tragen *v.t.st*. to bear; to carry; (*Kleider*) to wear; (sich) *~ v.refl*. to wear (well, etc.); *bei sich ~*, to carry on the person; *kein Bedenken ~*, not to hesitate; *die Kosten ~*, to bear the expense; *sich mit etwas ~*, to have one's mind occupied with.

tragend *a*. supporting; basic; leading.

Träger *m*. (-s, -) bearer; carrier, porter; wearer; (*arch*.) beam, girder.

Tragetasche *f*. carrier bag.

Tragfähigkeit *f*. capacity.

tragfertig *a*. ready-to-wear.

Tragfläche *f*. (*avi*.) wing.

Trägheit *f*. (-, 0) laziness; (*phys*.) inertia.

Tragik *f*. tragedy.

Tragiker *m*. (-s, -) tragic poet; tragedian.

tragikomisch *a*. tragicomic(al).

Tragikomödie *f*. tragicomedy.

tragisch *a*. tragic; *~ adv*. tragically.

Tragkraft *f*. load.

Tragöde *m*. (-n, -n) tragic actor.

Tragödie *f*. (-, -n) tragedy.

Trag: **~riemen** *m*. sling, strap; **~weite** *f*. range; (*fig*.) bearing, significance.

Trainer *m*. (-s, -); **Trainerin** *f*. (-, -nen) coach.

trainieren *v.t*. to train, to practice; to coach.

Training *n*. (-s, -s) training, practice.

Trainingsanzug *m*. track suit.

Trakt *m*. (-s, -e) section; wing.

Traktat *m. or n*. (-[e]s, -e) treatise.

Traktor *m*. (-s, -en) tractor.

trällern *v.t*. to warble.

Trambahn *f*. tramway.

trampeln *v.i*. to trample.

trampen *v.i*. to hitch-hike.

Tramper *m*.; **Tramperin** *f*. hitch-hiker.

Trampolin *n*. trampoline.

Tran *m*. (-[e]s, -e) trail-oil; blubber.

tranchieren *v.t*. to carve meat.

Tranchieremesser *n*. carving-knife.

Träne *f*. i(-, -n) tear.

tränen *v.i*. to water.

Tränen: **~drüse** *f*. tear-gland; **~gas** *n*. tear-gas.

tränenlos *a*. tearless.

Trank *m*. (-[e]s, Tränke) drink, beverage; potion, decoction.

Tränke *f*. (-, -n) watering-place (for animals).

tränken *v.t*. to water (cattle), to give to drink; to soak.

Transaktion *f*. (-, -en) transaction.

transatlantisch *a*. transatlantic.

Transformator *m*. (-s, -en) (*elek*.) transformer; adapter.

Transit: **~handel** *m*. transit-trade.

transitiv *a*. transitive.

Transitverkehr *m*. transit-traffic.

Transmission *f*. (-, -en) transmission.

Transparent *n*. (-[e]s, -s) banner; transparency.

Transparenz *f*. transparency.

transpirieren *v.i*. to perspire.

Transplantation *f*. (-, -en) transplant; graft (skin).

Transport *m*. (-[e]s, -e) transport, haulage; *auf ~*, in transit.

transportfähig *a*. transportable.

transportieren *v.t*. to transport.

Transport(mittel), *n*. transportation.

Transporteur *m*. (-s, -e) carrier.

Transportunternehmer *m*. haulage contractor.

Transvestit *m*. (-en, -ent) transvestite.

transzendental *a*. transcendental.

Transzendenz *f*. (-, 0) transcendency; transcendence.

Trapez *n*. (-es, -e) (*math*.) trapezium; (*Gymnastik*) trapeze.

Trasse *f*. route, line.

trassieren *v.i*. to draw.

Tratsch *m*. (-(e)s, 0) (*fam*.) gossip.

tratschen *v.i*. to gossip.

Traualtar *m*. (marriage-)altar.

Traube *f*. (-, -n) bunch of grapes; cluster.

Traubenzucker *m*. glucose.

trauen *v.t*. to marry, to join in wedlock; *~ v.i*. to trust, to confide in; (sich) *~ v.refl*. to venture, to dare; *sich ~ lassen*, to get married.

Trauer *f*. (-, 0) mourning; mourning-dress; affliction; *~ haben um*, to be in mourning for.

Trauer: **~fall** *m*. death, mournful event; **~flor** *m*. mourning band; **~geleit** *n*. funeral procession; **~kleid** *n*. mourning (dress); **~marsch** *m*. funeral march.

trauern *v.i*. to mourn; to be in mourning (for).

Trauer: **~spiel** *n*. tragedy; **~weide** *f*. weeping willow; **~zug** *m*. funeral procession.

Traufe *f*. (-, -n) eaves *pl*.; gutter; water dripping from the eaves; *aus dem Regen in die ~ kommen*, to drop from the frying pan into the fire.

träufeln *v.t. & i*. to drip, to trickle.

traulich *a.* cordial, intimate; cozy.

Traum *m.* (-[e]s, Träume) dream.

Trauma *n.* (-s, -men) trauma.

träumen *v.t. & i.* to dream.

Träumer *m.* (-s, -); **Träumerin** *f.* (-, -nen) dreamer.

Träumerei *f.* (-, -en) reverie; day dream.

träumerisch *a.* dreamy; wistful.

traumhaft *a.* dreamlike.

traurig *a.* mournful, sad, dismal.

Traurigkeit *f.* sadness; sorrow.

Trau: ~**ring** *m.* wedding-ring; ~**schein** *m.* marriage certificate.

Trauung *f.* (-, -en) wedding ceremony.

Trauzeuge *m.*; **Trauzeugin** *f.* witness to a marriage.

Travestie *f.* (-, -n) travesty.

Treff *n.* (-s, 0) meeting place; (*Kartenspiel*) club.

treffen *v.t.st.* to hit; to meet (with); to befall; *ihn trifft die Schuld*, it is his fault; *sein Bild ist gut getroffen*, his portrait is a good likeness; *es trifft sich gut*, it is lucky; *Anstalten, Vorkehrungen ~*, to take measures, precautions; *sich ~*, to happen; to meet.

Treffen *n.* (-s, -) encounter; meeting.

treffend *a.* apt.

Treffer *m.* (-s, -) hit; blow; goad; prize (in a lottery).

trefflich *a.* excellent, exquisite.

Treffpunkt *m.* meeting place, venue.

Treibeis *n.* drift ice.

treiben *v.t.st.* to drive, to propel; (*fig.*) to urge, to impel, to incite; (*Gewerbe*) to carry on, to do, to exercise; (*Blätter*) to put forth; *~ v.i.st.* to float, to drift; *auf die Spitze, aufs Äußerste ~*, to carry to excess; *in die Enge ~*, to drive into a corner; *die Preise in die Höhe ~*, to send *or* force the prices up; *Musik ~* to study *or* practise music; *alte Sprachen ~*, to work at Latin and Greek; *Aufwand ~*, to live in great style; *sein Wesen ~*, to be at it (again).

Treibhaus *n.* hothouse, greenhouse; ~**effekt** *m.* greenhouse effect.

Treib: ~**holz** *n.* drift-wood; ~**jagd** *f.* drive, roundup; (*fig.*) witch hunt; ~**rad** *n.* driving-wheel; ~**riemen** *m.* driving-belt; ~**sand**, **Triebsand** *m.* quicksand *pl.*; ~**stoff** *m.* fuel.

tremulieren *v.t.* to quaver, to trill.

Trend *m.* (-s, -s) trend.

trennbar *a.* separable.

trennen *v.t.* to separate, to sever; to disunite; (sich) *~ v.refl.* to part.

Trennung *f.* (-, -en) separation; parting.

Trennungs: ~**linie** *m.* dividing line; ~**strich** *m.* hyphen.

trepanieren *v.t.* to trepan.

Treppe *f.* (-, -n) staircase, stairway; stairs; flight of stairs; *treppauf, treppab*, up and down the stairs; *eine, zwei ~n hoch wohnen*, to live on the first, second floor.

Treppen: ~**absatz** *m.* landing; ~**geländer**, *n.* bannisters *pl.*; ~**haus** *n.* staircase; ~**stufe** *f.* stair; step.

Tresen *m.* bar; counter.

Tresor *m.* (-s, -s) safe, vault.

treten *v.i. & i.st.* to tread; to step; to trample (upon); *einem zu nahe ~*, to hurt someone's feelings; *an die Spitze ~*, to take the lead; *an die Stelle eines ~*, to take another's place; *aus den Ufern ~*, to

overflow its banks; *in den Vordergrund ~*, to come to the front.

Tretmühle *f.* tread-mill.

treu *a.* faithful, true; *zu ~en Händen*, in trust.

Treubruch *m.* breach of faith.

treubrüchig *a.* faithless, perfidious.

Treue *f.* (-, 0) faithfulness, fidelity; allegiance, loyalty; *auf Treu und Glauben*, on trust.

Treuied schwören, to swear allegiance.

Treuhand *f.* trust; ~**gesellschaft** *f.* trust company.

Treuhänder *m.* trustee.

treuherzig *a.* naive, artless.

treulos *a.* faithless, perfidious.

Treulosigkeit *f.* infidelity; disloyalty; faithlessness.

Triangel *m.* (-s, -) triangle.

Tribunal *n.* (-[e]s, -e) tribunal.

Tribüne *f.* (-, -n) platform; (grand-) stand (at races).

Tribut *m.* (-[e]s, -e) tribute; *seinen ~ entrichten, zollen*, to pay one's tribute.

tributpflichtig *a.* tributary.

Trichine *f.* (-, -n) trichina.

Trichter *m.* (-s, -) funnel; (*Granat~*) crater.

Trick *pm.* (-s, -s) trick, dodge.

Trickfilm *m.* cartoon film.

Trieb *m.* (-[e]s, -e) sprout, shoot; impulse, bent, instinct.

Trieb: ~**feder** *f.* motive; ~**rad** *n.* driving-wheel; ~**wagen** *m.* (*rail.*) rail car; ~**werk** *n.* engine.

triefen *v.i. & st.* to drip, to trickle; *seine Augen ~*, his eyes run.

triefnaß *a.* dripping wet.

Triennium *n.* (-[e]s, -nien) period of three years.

triftig *a.* weighty, cogent, forcible.

Trikot *m.* (-s, -s) tights, leotard.

Trikotagen *pl.* knitted goods.

Triller *m.* (-s, -) trill; quaver; shake.

trillern *v.i.* to trill, to quaver; (*Vogel*) to warble.

Trillion *f.* (-, -en) quadrillion.

Trilogie *f.* (-, -n) trilogy.

Trimester *n.* term.

Trimm-dich-Pfad *m.* fitness trail.

trimmen *v.t.* to trim; to train; *v.refl.* to keep fit.

Trinität *f.* (-,0) Trinity.

trinkbar *a.* drinkable, potable.

Trinkbecher *m.* mug.

trinken *v.t. & i.st.* to drink; to imbibe; *er trinkt*, he is a drunkard.

Trinker *m.* (-s, -); **Trinkerin** *f.* (-, -nen) alcoholic; drunkard.

Trink: ~**gelage** *n.* drinking-bout; ~**geld** *n.* gratuity, tip; ~**halm** *m.* drinking straw; ~**wasser** *n.* drinking water.

Trio *n.* (-[e]s, -e) trio.

trippeln *v.i.* to trip; to patter; to mince.

Tripper *m.* (-s, -) (*med.*) gonorrhœa.

Triptychon *n.* triptych.

trist *a.* dreary; sad.

Tritt *m.* (-[e]s, -e) tread, step, pace; kick; (*Spur*) footstep; steps; *~ halten*, to keep pace; *im ~*, in step.

Tritt: ~**brett**, *n.* step; (*mot.*) running-board; ~**leiter** *f.* stepladder.

Triumph *m.* (-[]es, -e) triumph.

Triumphbogen *m.* triumphal arch.

triumphieren *v.i.* to triumph.

Triumphzug *m.* triumphal procession.

Triumvirat *n.* (-[e]s, -e) triumvirate.

trivial *a. & adv.* trite, trivial(ly).

Trivialität *f.* (-, -en) triviality, triteness; (*konkret*) banality.

Trochäus *m.* (-, chäen) trochee.

trocken *a.* dry, arid; barren; (*fig.*) plain; prosy; *auf dem Trocknen sitzen*, to be stuck.

Trocken: ~**dock** *n.* dry dock; ~**gebiet** *n.* arid region; ~**haube** *f.* hairdrier.

Trockenheit *f.* (-, 0) dryness; drought; (*fig.*) barrenness, aridity, dullness.

trockenlegen *v.t.* to change the diapers; to drain.

Trockenlegung *f.* drainage, draining.

Trockenzeit *f.* dry season.

trocknen *v.t. & i.o* to dry, to dry up.

Troddel *f.* (-, -n) tassel.

Trödel *m.* (-s, 0) lumber, junk.

Trödelei *f.* (-, -en) (*fig.*) dawdling.

Trödel: ~**laden** *m.* junk shop; ~**markt** *m.* flea market.

trödeln *v.i.* to dawdle.

Trödler: *m.*; **Trödlerin** *f.* junk dealer; dawdler.

Trog *m.* (-[e]s, Tröge) trough.

trollen (sich) *v.refl.* to go off.

Trommel *f.* (-, -n) drum.

Trommel: ~**fell** *m.* (*Ohr*) eardrum; drumskin; ~**feuer** *n.* barrage.

trommeln *v.i.* to drum, to beat the drum.

Trommel: ~**schlag** *m.* drumbeat; ~**schlegel** *m.* drumstick; ~**wirbel** *m.* drum roll.

Trommler *m.* (-s, -); **Trommlerin** *f.* (-, -nen) drummer.

Trompete *f.* (-, -n) trumpet.

trompeten *v.i.* to (sound the) trumpet.

Trompeter *m.* (-s, -); **Trompeterin** *f.* (-, -nen) trumpeter.

Tropen *pl.* tropics *pl.*; ~**helm** *m.* sun helmet.

Tropf *m.* (-[e]s, Tröpfe) simpleton, dunce; (*med.*) intravenous feeding, *am ~ hängen* to be on intravenous.

tröpfeln, tropfen *v.t. & i.* to drop; to trickle, to drip.

Tropfen *m.* (-s, -) drop; bead (of perspiration).

tropfenweise *adv.* by drops.

tropfnaß *a.* dripping wet.

Tropfstein *m.* stalactite; stalagmite.

Trophäe *f.* (-, -n) trophy.

tropisch *a.* tropical.

Troposphäre *f.* troposphere.

Troß *m.* (Trosses, Trosse) baggage-(train); retinue.

Trosse *f.* (-, -n) cable, hawser.

Trost *m.* (-es, 0) consolation, comfort; *schwacher ~*, cold comfort; *nicht recht bei ~e sein*, to be not all there.

trost: ~**bedürftig** *a.* in need of consolation; ~**bringend** *a.* consolatory.

trösten *v.t.* to console; *sich über etwas ~*, to get reconciled to a thing.

tröstlich *a.* conforting, consoling.

trostlos *a.* inconsolable, hopeless.

trostreich *a.* comforting, consoling.

Tröstung *f.* (-, -en) consolation.

Trott *m.* (-[e]s, 0) trot; routine.

Trottel *m.* (-s, 0) fool, idiot.

trotten *v.i.* (*s*) to trot, to trudge.

Trottoir *n.* (-[e]s, -e *u.* -s) (foot-) pavement, sidewalk.

Trotz *m.* (-es, 0) defiance.

trotz *pr.* in spite of; ~**dem** *adv.* nevertheless; ~**alledem**, for all that; ~**dem** (*daß*), although.

trotzen *v.i.* to brave, to defy.

trotzig *a.* defiant; pig-headed; sulky.

trüb(e) *a.* troubled, murky, muddy, thick; dim, dull; *im trüben fischen*, (*fig.*) to fish in troubled waters.

Trubel *m.* (-s, 0) hubbub, bustle.

trüben *v.t.* to trouble, to dim.

Trübsal *f.* (-, -e) afflication, calamity.

trübselig *a.* woeful, doleful.

Trübsinn *m.* melancholy; dejection.

Trüffel *f.* (-, -n) truffle.

Trug *m.* (-[e]s, 0) deceit, fraud; delusion.

Trugbild *n.* phantom.

trügen *v.t. & i.st.* to deceive, to delude.

trügerisch, trüglich *a.* deceptive, deceitful, illusory.

Trugschluß *m.* logical fallacy, non sequitur.

Truhe *f.* (-, -n) chest, trunk.

Trümmer *pl.* fragments; ruins *pl.*; rubble.

Trümmer: ~**feld** *n.* expanse of rubble; ~**haufen** *m.* heap of rubble.

Trumpf *m.* (-[e]s, Trümpfe) trump.

trumpfen *v.t.* to trump.

Trumpfkarte *f.* trump card.

Trunk *m.* (-[e]s, Trünke) potion; drink.

trunken *a.* drunken; tipsy.

Trunkenbold *m.* (-[e]s, -e) drunkard.

Trunkenheit *f.* drunkenness.

Trunksucht *f.* alcoholism.

Trupp *m.* (-[e]s, -s) troop, band; flock.

Truppe *f.* (-, -n) troop.

Truppen *f.pl.* troops, forces *pl.*

Truppen: ~**gattung** *f.* arm *or* branch of service; ~**parade** *f.* military parade; ~**übungsplatz** *m.* troop training ground.

truppweise *dv.* in troops, in flocks.

Truthahn *m.* turkey(-cock).

Trutz *m.* (-es, 0) defiance, attack.

Tschako *m.* (-s, -s) shako.

Tscheche *m.* (-n, -n); **Tschechin** *f.* (-, -nen); **tschechisch** *a.* Czech.

Tschechische Republik *f.* Czech Republic.

tschilpen *v.i.* to chirp.

tschüs (*fam.*) bye.

Tuba *f.* (-, -ben) tuba.

Tube *f.* (-, -n) tube.

tuberkulös *a.* tubercular, tuberculous.

Tuberkulose *f.* (-, 0) tuberculosis.

Tuch *n.* (-[e]s, Tücher) cloth; shawl.

Tuch: ~**händler** *m.* cloth-merchant, draper; ~**muster** *n.* swatch.

tüchtig *a.* able, apt, fit; excellent; ~ *adv.* thoroughly.

Tüchtigkeit *f.* industry; ability.

Tücke *f.* (-, -n) deceit; treachery.

tückisch *a.* deceitful; treacherous.

Tuff *m.* (-[e]s, -e), **Tuffstein** *m.* tufa, tuff.

tüfteln *v.i.* to fiddle; to puzzle.

Tugend *f.* (-, -en) virtue.

tugendhaft *a.* virtuous.

tugendsam *a.* virtuous.

Tüll *m.* (-[e]s, -e) tulle.

Tulpe *f.* (-, -n) tulip.
Tulpenzwiebel *f.* tulip bulb.
tummeln (sich) ~ *v.refl.* to bestir oneself.
Tummelplatz *m.* playground.
Tumor *m.* (-s, -en) tumor.
Tümpel *m.* (-s, -) pool, puddle.
Tumult *m.* (-[e]s, -e) tumult, riot.
tumultuarisch *a.* tumultuous, riotous.
tun *v.t. & i.st.* to do, to make; to perform, to act; ~ *als ob*, to make as if, to pretend...; *mit einem schön~*, to cajole; *er tut nur so*, it's all a sham, it's all make-believe; *es tut nichts*, it does not matter; *es tut mir leid*, I am sorry (for); *ich kann nichts dazu ~*, I cannot help it; *das hat damit nichts zu ~*, that has nothing to do with it; *es ist mir sehr darum zu ~*, I feel very anxious about it.
Tun *n.* (-s, 0) doing; activity.
Tünche *f.* (-, -n) distemper; whitewash.
tünchen *v.t.* to distemper; whitewash.
Tunesien *n.* (-s, 0) Tunisia.
Tunesier *m.*; **Tunesierin** *f.*; **tunesisch** *a.* Tunisian.
Tunichtgut *m.* (-s, -es) ne'er-do-well.
Tunke *f.* (-, -n) gravy; sauce.
tunken *v.t.* to dip, to steep.
tunlichst *adv.* as far as possible.
Tunnel *m.* (-s, -[s]) tunnel.
Tüpfelchen *n.* dot.
tüpfeln *v.t.* to dot.
tupfen *v.t.* to swab; to dot.
Tür *f.* (-, Türen) door.
Türangel *f.* door hinge.
Turban *m.* (-[e]s, -e) turban.
Turbine *f.* (-, -n) turbine.
Tür: **~flügel** *m.* leaf of a door; **~füllung** *f.* door-panel; **~hüter** *m.* doorkeeper.
Türke *m.* (-n, -n); **Türkin** *f.* (-, -nen) Turk.
Türkei *f.* Turkey.
Türkis *m.* (-kises, -kise) turquoise.
türkisch *a.* Turkish; *~er Weizen*, maize, Indian corn.

Tür: **~klinke** *f.* latch, door handle; **~klopfer** *m.* knocker.
Turm *m.* (-[e]s, Türme) tower; turret; (*im Schach*) rook; castle.
türmen *v.t.* to run away; (sich) ~ *v.refl.* to pile up; to stack up.
turmhoch *a.* towering, very high.
Turnanstalt *f.* gymnasium.
turnen *v.t. & i.* to practise gymnastics *or* athletics.
Turnen *n.* (-s, 0) gymnastics.
Turner *m.* (-s, -); **Turnerin** *f.* (-, -nen) gymnast.
Turn: **~halle** *f.* (covered) gymnasium; **~hose** *f.* shorts *pl.*
Turnier *n.* (-[e]s, -e) tournament, joust.
turnieren *v.i.* to joust, to tilt.
Turnierplatz *m.* the lists *pl.*
Turn: **~schuh** *m.* gymshoe; **~übung** *f.* gymnastic exercise; gymnastics.
Tür: **pfosten** *m.* door post; **~rahmen** *m.* door frame; **~schild** *n.* door-plate; **~schwelle** *f.* threshold.
Turteltaube *f.* turtle-dove.
Türvorleger *m.* doormat.
Tusch *m.* (-es, -e) fanfare.
Tusche *f.* (-, -n) India ink.
tuscheln *v.i.* to whisper secretly.
tuschen *v.t.* **die Wimpern** ~ to put mascara on.
Tüte *f.* (-, -n) paper-bag.
tuten *v.t. & i.* to toot; (*mot.*) to honk.
Typ *m.* (-s, -en), **Type** *f.* (-, -n) type.
Typhus *m.* (-, 0) typhoid.
typisch *a.* typical.
Typographie *f.* typography.
typographisch *a.* typographical.
Typus *m.* (-, Typen) type.
Tyrann *m.* (-en, -en) tyrant.
Tyrannei *f.* (-, -en) tyranny.
tyrannisch . tyrannic(al).
tyrannisieren *v.t.* to tyrannize, to oppress; to bully.

U

U, u the letter U or u; *einem ein X für ein ~ machen*; to bamboozle, to hoodwink someone.
U-Bahn *f.* subway.
U-Bahnhof *m.*, **U-Bahn-Station** *f.* subway station.
übel *a.* evil, bad; sick; ~ *adv.* ill, badly; *wohl oder ~*, willy-nilly; *~nehmen*, to take ill *or* amiss; ~ *daran sein*, to be in a sad plight; *mir wird ~*, I feel sick.
Übel *n.* (-s, -) evil; disease; injury.
übel: **~gelaunt** *a.* bad-tempered; **~gesinnt** *a.* evil-minded; hostile.
Übelkeit *f.* (-, -en) sickness, nausea.
übellaunig *a.* ill-humored, cross.
übelnehmen *v.t.* to take offense.
übelriechend *a.* foul-smelling.
Übel: **~stand** *m.* inconvenience, nuisance; drawback; **~tat** *f.* misdeed, crime; **~täter** *m.* wrong doer; criminal.
übelwollend *a.* malevolent.
üben *v.t.* to exercise; to practise; (*mil.*) to drill, to train; *geübt sein in*, to be versed in.

über *pr.* over, above; about; across, beyond; by, on, upon; more than; ~ *und* ~, all over; ~ *Berlin reisen*, to travel via Berlin; *Fehler ~ Fehler* blunder upon blunder; *~dies*, besides, moreover; *heute ~ 8 Tage*, a week from today; *~ zwanzig*, more than twenty; *10 Minuten ~ 4 Uhr*, ten minutes past four; ~ *kurz oder lang*, sooner or later; *~Nacht*, over night; *tags~*, during daytime; *einem ~ sein*, to surpass someone.
überall *adv.* everywhere, throughout; *von ~her*, from everywhere; *~hin*, in all directions.
Überangebot *n.* excessive supply.
überängstlich *a.* overanxious.
überanstrengen *v.t.* to strain; (sich) ~ *v.refl.* to over-exert oneself.
Überanstrengung *f.* over-exertion.
überarbeiten *v.t.* to revise; to rework; (sich) ~ *v.refl.* to over-work oneself.
Überarbeitung *f.* revision; reworking.
überaus *adv.* extremely.
überbacken *v.t.st.* to brown s.th. in the oven.
Überbau *m.* superstructure.
überbeanspruchen *v.t.* to strain; to overburden;

to overload.
überbelegt *a.* overcrowded.
überbelichten *v.t.* (*phot.*) to overexpose.
Überbeschäftigung *f.* overemployment.
überbesetzt *a.* overstuffed.
überbewerten *v.t.* to overvalue.
überbieten *v.t.st.* to outbid; to outdo.
Überbleibsel *n.* (-s, -) remnant; relic.
Überblick *m.* general view; survey.
überblicken *v.t.* to survey.
überbringen *v.t.st.* to deliver, to bring.
Überbringer *m.* bearer.
überbrücken *v.t.* to bridge.
Überbrückungskredit *m.* (*com.*) short term credit, bridging loan.
überbuchen *v.t.* to overbook.
überdachen *v.t.* to roof in.
überdauern *v.t.* to outlast.
überdenken *v.t.* to think s.th. over.
überdies *adv.* besides, moreover.
überdosieren *v.t.* to overdose.
Überdosis *f.* overdose.
überdreht *a.* (*fam.*) wound up; crazy.
Überdruck *m.* over-pressure.
Überdruß *m.* (-drusses, 0) disgust.
überdrüssig *a.* disgusted with.
überdurchschnittlich *a.* above average.
übereignen *v.t.* to make s.th. over to s.b.
übereilen *v.t.* to precipitate; (sich) ~ *v.refl.* to be over-hasty.
übereilt *a.* precipitate, over hasty.
Übereilung *f.* (-, -en) precipitation, rush.
übereinander *adv.* one upon another.
übereinkommen *v.i.st.* (*s*) to agree.
Übereinkommen *n.* (-s, -) agreement; *ein ~ treffen,* to make an agreement.
Übereinkunft *f.* (-, -künfte) agreement.
übereinstimmen *v.t.* to agree.
übereinstimmend *a.* in conformity with.
Übereinstimmung *f.* (-, -en) agreement.
überempfindlich *a.* oversensitive; (*med.*) hypersensitive.
übereßen (sich) *v.refl.* to overeat.
überfahren *v.t.* to run over.
Über: ~**fahrt** *f.* crossing; passage; ~**fall** *m.* sudden attack; raid.
überfallen *v.t.st.* to surprise, to attack suddenly; (*Nacht*) to overtake.
überfällig *a.* overdue.
Überfallkommando *n.* flying squad.
überfein *a.* over-refined, fastidious.
überfliegen *v.t.* to fly over; to glance over (a book).
überfließen *v.i.st.* (*s*) to overflow.
überflügeln *v.t.* to outstrip.
Überfluß *m.* abundance, profusion.
überflüssig *a.* superfluous, needless.
überfluten *v.t.* to flood; to overflow.
überfordern *v.t.* to overcharge; to demand too much.
überführen *v.t.* to convict.
Überführung *f.* (-, -en) conviction.
Überfülle *f.* superabundance.
überfüllen *v.t.* to cram, to glut.
überfüllt *a.* overcrowded.
Überfüllung *f.* overcrowding, congestion; repletion.

überfüttern *v.t.* to overfeed.
Übergabe *f.* handing over; delivery; surrender.
Übergang *m.* passage; change, transition; crossing; ~ *für Fahrzeuge,* vehicle crossing: ~ *für Fußgänger,* pedestrian crossing.
Übergangs: ~**bestimmungen** *pl.* temporary regulations *pl*; ~**zeit** *f.* period of transition, transition stage.
übergeben *v.t.st.* to deliver (up), to hand over, to turn over, (*mil.*) to surrender; (sich) ~ *v.refl.* to vomit; to surrender.
übergehen *v.t.st.* to pass over; to omit; to skip, to revise; *mit Stillschweigen ~,* to pass over in silence; ~ *v.i.* (*s*) (*mil.*)to go over.
übergenau *a.* overmeticulous.
Übergewicht *n.* over-weight, excess weight; preponderance.
überglücklich *a.* overjoyed.
übergreifen *v.i.* to spread.
Übergriff *m.* encroachment.
übergroß *a.* huge, oversized.
Überguß *m.* icing.
überhand *adv.* ~ *nehmen,* to gain too much ground.
überhäufen *v.t.* to overload.
überhaupt *adv.* in general; at all.
überheben *v.t.st.* to lift over; (sich) ~ *v.refl.st.* to be overbearing.
überheblich *a.* arrogant.
Überheblichkeit *f.* arrogance.
überheizen *v.t.* to overheat.
überhin *adv.* superficially.
überhitzen *v.t.* to overheat.
überhöht *a.* excessive.
überholen *v.t.* to overhaul; to overtake, to pass (*Verkehr*).
Überhol: ~**manöver** *n.* passing maneuver; ~**spur** *f.* passing lane; ~**verbot** *n.* No Passing.
überhören *v.t.* to miss a word; to overhear.
überirdisch *a.* celestial; supernatural.
überkandidelt *a.* (*fam.*) affected.
überkippen *v.i.* (*s*) to tilt over.
überkleben *v.t* to paste over.
Überkleid *n.* outer garment; overall.
überklug *a.* overwise, conceited.
überkochen *v.i.* (*s*) to boil over.
überkommen *v.t.st. die Angst überkam ihn,* he was overcome by fear.
überladen *v.t.st.* to overload.
überlagern *v.t.* to superimpose; to overlap.
Überlandreise *f.* overland journey.
überlappen *v.t.* to overlap.
überlassen *v.t.st.* to cede; (sich) ~ *v.refl.st.* to give oneself up to.
Überlassung *f.* (-. -en) cession, abandonment.
überlasten *v.t.* to overburden; to overwork.
überlaufen *v.t.st.* to overrun; to importune; *es überläuft mich,* I shudder; ~ *v.i.st.* (*s*) to go over.
überlaufen *a.* overcrowded.
Überläufer *m.* defector.
überlaut *a.* too *or* very loud, noisy.
überleben *v.t.* to outlive, to survive; *diese Sache hat sich überlebt,* the thing is out of date altogether.
Überlebende *m./f.* survivor.
überlebensgroß *a.* more than lifesize.
überlegen *v.t. & refl.* (*sich ~*) to reflect upon, to consider, to think over; **überlegen** *a.* superior.

Überlegenheit *f.* (-, 0) superiority.
überlegt *a.* carefully considered.
Überlegung *f.* (-, -en) reflection; consideration.
überleiten *v.t.* lead over.
Überleitung *f.* (-, -en) transition.
überlesen *v.t.st.* to read over; to overlook.
überliefern *v.t.* to surrender; to hand down (to posterity, etc.)
Überlieferung *f.* tradition.
überlisten *v.t.* to outwit, to dupe.
Übermacht *f.* superiority; superior force.
übermächtig *a.* overpowering; superior.
übermalen *v.t.* to paint over.
übermannen *v.t.* overpower.
Übermaß *n.* excess.
übermäßig *a.* exorbitant, excessive.
Übermensch *m.* superman.
übermenschlisch *a.* superhuman.
übermitteln *v.t.* to transmit.
übermorgen *adv.* the day after tomorrow.
Übermüdung *f.* (-, 0) over-fatigue.
Übermut *m.* high spirits.
übermütig *a.* high-spirited; in high spirits.
übernachten *v.i.* to pass the night.
übernächtigt *a.* overtired; worn out.
Übernachtung *f.* overnight stay; ~ **und Frühstück** bed and breakfast.
Übernachtungsmöglichkeit *f.* overnight accommodation.
Übernahme *f.* (-, 0) taking possession of, taking charge of.
übernatürlich *a.* supernatural.
übernehmen *v.t.st.* to take possesion of, to take upon oneself; (sich) ~ *v.refl.* to overdo; to overwork.
überordnen *v.t.* to place *or* set over.
Überproduktion *f.* overproduction.
überprüfen *v.t.* to check; to inspect; to examine.
Überprüfung *f.* check up; examination.
überquellen *v.i.st.* to spill over.
überqueren *v.t.* to cross.
überragen *v.t.* to surpass; to outclass.
überragend *a.* outstanding.
überraschen *v.t.* to surprise.
überraschend *a.* surprising, unexpected.
Überraschung *f.* (-, -en) surprise.
überreden *v.t.* to persuade.
Überredung *f.* (-, -en) persuasion.
überreich *a.* abundant; lavish.
überreichen *v.t.* to hand over, to present.
überreif *a.* over-ripe.
überreizen *v.t.* to over-excite; to strain.
überrennen *v.t.* to overrun.
Überrest *m.* remains, residue, remnant.
überrumpeln *v.t.* to (take by) surprise.
überrunden *v.t.* to lap; to outstrip.
übers = **über das.**
übersät *a.* covered.
übersättigen *v.t.* oversaturate.
Überschall *m.* supersonic.
überschatten *v.t.* to overshadow.
überschätzen *v.t.* to overrate; to overestimate.
Überschau *f.* (-, 0) review, survey.
überschauen *v.t.* to survey, to overlook.
überschäumen *v.i.* (h, s) to froth over.
Überschlag *m.* estimate, rough calculation; (*am*

Rock) facing; somersault, handspring.
überschlagen *v.t.st.* to estimate.
überschnappen *v.i.* (*s.*) to squeak; (*fig.*) to turn crazy.
überschneiden (sich) *v.refl.* to overlap partially; to cross.
überschreiben *v.t.st.* to transfer; to entitle.
Überschreibung *f.* transfer.
überschreien *v.s.st.* to cry down; (sich) ~ *v.refl.st.* to overstrain one's voice.
überschreiten *v.t.st.* to pass, to exceed; to go beyond; to cross.
Über: ~schrift *f.* heading; title; headline; **~schuh** *m.* goloshes *pl.*
überschuldet *a.* overburdened with debt.
Überschuß *m.* surplus, excess.
überschüssig *a.* surplus (money, etc.).
überschütten *v.t.* to cover (with).
Überschwang *m.* exuberance.
überschwappen *v.i.* to slop over.
überschwemmen *v.t.* to flood, to inundate, to submerge.
Überschwemmung *f.* inundation, flood.
überschwenglich *a.* exuberant; effusive.
Übersee *n.* oversea(s).
überseeisch *a.* transatlantic, overseas.
übersehbar *a.* assessable.
übersehen *v.t.st.* to omit; to overlook; to disregard; to let pass; to survey.
übersein *v.ir.* (*fam.*) *das ist mir über,* I am sick of it; *er ist dir über,* he has the better of you.
übersenden *v.t.st.* to send.
Übersendung *f.* transmission.
übersetzen *v.t.* to ferry across; to translate; ~ *v.i.* (*s*) to leap over; to pass over, to cross.
Übersetzer *m.;* **Übersetzerin** *f.* translator.
Übersetzung *f.* (-, -en) translation, version; (*Fahrrad*) gear; *grosse ~,* high gear; *kleine ~,* low gear.
Übersicht *f.* (-, -en) survey; summary; overall view.
übersichtlich *a.* well arranged; open.
Übersichtstafel *f.* chart.
übersiedeln *v.i.* (*s*) to move (to).
übersinnlich *a.* supernatural.
überspannen *v.t.* to span; to overstrain; (*fig.*) to exaggerate.
überspannt *a.* (*fig.*) eccentric.
überspielen *v.t.* to cover up; to smooth over.
überspitzen *v.t.* to push s.th. too far.
überspringen *v.t.st.* to leap over; (*fig.*) to skip.
übersprudeln *v.i.* to bubble over.
überstehen *v.t.st.* to get over; to survive; (*einen Sturm*) to weather, to ride out.
übersteigen *v.t.st.* to surmount; to surpass; to exceed.
überstellen *v.t.* to hand over.
übersteuern *v.t.* to oversteer; to overmodulate.
überstimmen *v.t.* to outvote.
überstrahlen *v.t.* to outshine; to shine upon.
überströmen *v.t.* to flood, to overwhelm; ~ *v.i.* (*s*) to overflow; to abound.
Überstunden *pl.* overtime; ~ *machen,* to work overtime.
überstürzen *v.t.* to hasten, to precipitate; (sich) ~ *v.refl.* to act rashly.

überstürzt *a.* hurried; over-hasty.
übertäuben *v.t.* to stun, to deafen.
überteuert *a.* overpriced.
übertölpeln *v.t.* to dupe, to take in.
übertönen *v.t.* to drown out.
Übertrag *m.* (-[e]s, -träge) sum carried over; carry over.
übertragbar *a.* transferable; negotiable; (*med.*) infectious.
übertragen *v.t.st.* to translate; to transfer; to carry over; to confer (an office upon one); (*Befugnis*) to delegate; (*Schrift*) to transcribe; (*Blut*) to transfuse. *a.* figurative, metaphorical.
Übertragung *f.* (-, -en) transfer, cession; translation; (*tech.*) transmission.
Übertragungswagen *m.* outside broadcasting van.
übertreffen *v.t.st.* to surpass, to excel.
übertreiben *v.t.st.* to exaggerate; to overdo, to overact.
Übertreibung *f.* (-, -en) exaggeration.
übertreten *v.t.st.* to transgress, to trespass (against), to infringe; ~ *v.i.st.* (*s*) to go over.
Übertretung *f.* (-, -en) violation, transgression.
übertrieben *a.* excessive, exaggerated.
Übertritt *m.* (*Kirche*) conversion; change.
übertrumpfen *v.t.* to outdo.
übertünchen *v.t.* to whitewash.
übervölkern *v.t.* to overpopulate.
Übervölkerung *f.* (-, 0) overpopulation.
übervoll *a.* overfull.
übervorteilen *v.t.* to cheat.
überwachen *v.t.* to keep under surveillance; to supervise.
Überwachung *f.* supervision, control, surveillance.
überwältigen *v.t.* to overpower; to overwhelm.
überwältigend *a.* overwhelming; stunning.
überwechseln *v.i.* to cross over; to change (sides; lanes).
überweisen *v.t.st.* to refer, to transfer.
Überweisung *f.* transfer, remittance.
überwerfen *v.t.st.* to slip on (clothing); sich ~ *v.refl.st.* to fall out (with).
überwiegen *v.t.st.* to predominate (over).
überwiegend *a.* predominant.
überwinden *v.t.st.* to overcome, to vanquish; (sich) ~ *v.ref.st.* to prevail on oneself.
Überwindung *f.* (-, -en) conquest; effort; (*Selbst~*) willpower.
überwintern *v.i.* to spend the winter; to hibernate (animals).
überwölken (sich) *v.refl. imp.* to get overcast.
überwuchern *v.t.* to overgrow luxuriantly.
Überwurf *m.* shawl.
Überzahl *f.* (-, 0) numerical superiority.
überzählig *a.* surplus.
überzeugen *v.t.* to convince (of).
überzeugend *a.* convincing, conclusive.
Überzeugung *f.* (-, -en) conviction.
überziehen *v.t.st.* to cover; (*Bett*) to put fresh sheets on; (account) to overdraw; (sich) ~ *v. refl.imp.st.* to become overcast.
Überzieher *m.* (-s, -) overcoat, top-coat.
überzüchtet *a.* overbred.
überzuckern *v.t.* to candy, to ice.
Überzug *m.* cover, coat(ing); pillowcase.
üblich *a.* usual, customary, in use.

U-Boot *n.* submarine; **U-Boot Bunker** *m.* submarine pen.
übrig *a.* remaining, left; ~*bleiben*, to be left: *im übrigen*, for the rest; ~*sein*, to be left; ~*behalten*, to keep, to spare; ~*haben*, to have . . . left *or* to spare; ~*lassen*, to leave; *das Übrige, die Übrigen*, the rest.
übrigens *adv.* by the way.
übriglassen *v.t.st.* to leave.
Übung *f.* (-, -en) exercise, practice; (*mil.*) drill(ing); *aus der ~*, out of practice.
Ufer *n.* (-s, -) (*Fluß~*) bank; (*See~*) shore, beach; ~*böschung* *f.* embankment.
uferlos *a.* boundless.
UFO, Ufo *n.* (-(s), -s) UFO.
Uganda *n.* (-s, 0) Uganda.
Ugander *m.*; **Uganderin** *f.* Ugandan.
Uhr *f.* (-, -en) clock; (*Taschen~*) watch; *weiviel ~ ist es?* what time is it?; *es ist halb drei* (~), it is half past two; *eine ~ aufziehen*, to wind up a watch; *eine ~ stellen*, to set a clock *or* watch; *die ~ ist abgelaufen*, the watch has stopped.
Uhr: ~**band** (Leder) *n.* watch-strap; ~**blatt** *n.* face.
Uhrenarmband *n.* watchband.
Uhr: ~**gehäuse** *n.* watch-case; ~**macher** *m.* watchmaker, clockmaker; ~**werk** *n.* clock-work.
Uhrzeiger *m.* hand; *im* ~*sinn*, clockwise; *entegegen dem* ~*sinn*, counterclockwise.
Uhu *m.* (-s, -e *u.* -s) eagle owl.
Ukraine *f.* (-, 0) Ukraine.
Ukrainer *m.*; **Ukrainerin** *f.*; **ukrainisch** *a.* Ukrainian.
UKW-sender *m.* FM station.
Ulk *m.* (-[3]s, -e) (*fam.*) spree, lark, hoax.
ulkig *a.* funny.
Ulme *f.* (-, -en) elm.
Ultimatum *n.* (-s, -ten) ultimatum.
Ultimo *m.* (-[s], -s *u.* -tims) last day of the month.
Ultrakurzwelle *f.* (*Radio*) ultra-short wave; very high frequency VHF.
Ultraschall *m.* ultrasound.
ultraviolett *a.* ultra-violet.
um *pr.* about, round; at; by; for; ~ 3 *Uhr*, at three (o'clock); *es ist gerade* ~, it is just past; ~ *so besser*, all the better; ~ *etwas kommen*, to lose a thing; ~ *zu*, in order to.
umackern *v.t.* to plow up.
umadressieren *v.t.* to redirect
umändern *v.t.* to change, to alter.
Umänderung *f.* change, alteration.
umarbeiten *v.t.* to rework, to remodel.
umarmen *v.t.* to embrace, to hug.
Umarmung *f.* (-, -en) embrace.
umbauen *v.t.* to rebuild; to alter; to change.
umbehalten *v.t.st.* to keep s.th. on.
umbenennen *v.t.* to change the name; to rename.
umbiegen *v.t.st.* to bend, to double up.
umbilden *v.t.* to transform; to reshuffle.
Umbildung *f.* transformation; reshuffle.
umbinden *v.t.st.* to tie round, to put on.
umblättern *v.t.* to turn over (a page).
umblicken (sich) ~ *v.refl.* to look around.
umbringen *v.t.ir.* to kill.
Umbruch *m.* (*typ.*) page-proof; radical change.
umbuchen *v.t.* to transfer (money); to change (flight).
umdenken *v.i.st.* to have to do some rethinking.

umdisponieren *v.i.* to change arrangements.
umdrehen *v.t.* to turn, to twist, to wring; (sich) ~ *v.refl.* to turn round; to rotate, to revolve.
Umdrehung *f.* turn; rotation; (*mech.*) revolution.
umfahren *v.t.st.* to run down; to circumnavigate.
umfallen *v.i.st.* to fall over.
Umfang *m.* (-[e]s, -fänge) circumference, size; compass, extent.
umfangen *v.t.st.* to encircle; to embrace; to encompass.
umfangreich *a.* extensive; voluminous.
umfassen *v.t.* to grasp; to comprise, to include, to embrace; (*mil.*) to envelop.
umfassend *a.* comprehensive.
Umfassung *f.* enclosure; embrace, grasp.
Umfeld *n.* milieu.
umfliegen *v.t.st.* to circle round.
umformen *v.t.* to remodel, to recast; to transform.
Umformer *m.* (*elek.*) converter.
Umfrage *f.* survey.
umfrieden *v.t.* to fence, to hedge in.
umfüllen *v.t.* to transfuse; to decant.
Umgang *m.* contact; dealings; handling.
umgänglich *a.* sociable, conversable.
Umgangssprache *f.* colloquial speech.
umgarnen *v.t.* (*fig.*) to ensnare.
umgeben *v.t.st.* to surround.
Umgebung *f.* (-, -en) environs, surroundings *pl.*; environment; (*Personen*) entourage.
Umgegend *f.* (-, 0) neighborhood; surroundings.
umgehen *v.t.st.* to evade, to elude, to bypass; ~ *v.i.st.* (*s*) to associate (with); *es geht in dem Schlosse um*, the castle is haunted; *mit einem umzugehen wissen*, to know how to deal with someone; *umgehend antworten*, to answer immediately.
Umgehung *f.* (*Gesetz*) evasion.
Umgehungsstraße *f.* bypass road.
umgekehrt *a.* opposite, contrary, reverse; inverse; the other way round.
umgestalten *v.t.* to transform, to recast.
umgraben *v.t.st.* to dig (up).
umgrenzen *v.t.* to circumscribe.
umgruppieren *v.t.* to regroup, to realign.
Umgruppierung *f.* (*mil.*) regrouping.
umgucken (sich) ~ *v.refl.* to look round.
umgürten *v.t.* to buckle on (a sword); (*fig.*) to encircle.
umhaben *v.i.ir.* to have on *or* about one.
Umhang *m.* (-[e]s, -hänge) cape.
umhängen *v.t.* to put on.
umhauen *v.t.st.* to fell, to cut down.
umher *adv.* around, (round) about.
umherschweifen *v.t.* (*s*) to rove, to wander.
umherziehend *a.* ambulatory; vagrant.
umhin *adv. ich kann nicht* ~ , I cannot help.
umhören *v.refl.* to ask around.
umhüllen *v.t.* to wrap (up), to shroud.
Umhüllung *f.* (-, -en) cover, wrapping, veil.
Umkehr *f.* (-, 0) return; complete change, revulsion (of feeling).
umkehren *v.t.* to turn (round), to invert; (*mech.*) to reverse; ~ *v.i.* (*s*) to turn back; *in umgekehrtem Verhältnis stehen*, to be in inverse ratio (to).
Umkehrung *f.* (-, -en) reversal.
umkippen *v.i.* (*s*) to tilt over; ~ *v.t.* to upset, to overturn.

umklammern *v.t.* to clasp, to cling to; to clutch.
umkleiden (sich) *v.refl.* to change one's clothes.
Umkleide: ~**kabine** *f.* changing cubicle; ~**raum** *m.* changing room; (*sp.*) locker room.
umknicken *v.i.* to sprain one's ankle; *v.t.* to fold over (paper); to break (flower).
umkommen *v.i.st.* (*s*) to perish; to die; to get killed.
Umkreis *m.* (-kreises, -kreise) compass, circle; circumference; *im ~ von*, within a radius of . . .
umkreisen *v.t.* to circle, to orbit, to revolve.
umkrempeln *v.t.* to tuck up; to turn inside out.
umladen *v.t.st.* to reload.
Umlagen *pl.* utilities.
umlagern *v.t.* to besiege.
Umlauf *m.* (-[e]s, -läufer) circulation (of coins, words); *in ~ bringen, setzen*, to circulate; to issue; *im ~ sein*, to circulate.
Umlaut *m.* umlaut, mutation.
umlegen *v.t.* to put round *or* on; to fell; to fold down; (*fam.*) to kill.
umleiten *v.t.* (*Verkehr*) to divert.
Umleitung *f.* diversion; detour; ~**sschild** *n.* detour sign.
umlenken *v.t.* to divert.
umlernen *v.t.* to readjust one's views.
umliegend *a.* surrounding, neighboring.
ummauern *v.t.* to wall in.
umnachten *v.t.* to wrap in darkness.
Umnachtung *f.* derangement.
umnebeln *v.t.* to dim.
umpacken *v.t.* to repack.
umpflanzen *v.t.* to transplant.
umpflügen *v.t.* to plow up.
umprägen *v.t.* to recoin.
umquartieren *v.t.* to reaccommodate; to remove to other quarters.
umrahmen *v.t.* to frame, to encircle.
umrändern *v.t.* to border, to edge.
umranken *v.t.* to twine around.
umräumen *v.t.* to rearrange.
umrechnen *v.t.* to convert.
Umrechnungskurs *m.* exchange rate.
umreißen *v.t.st.* to pull down; to sketch the outlines of; to outline.
umrennen *v.t.ir.* to run down *or* over.
umringen *v.t.* to encircle, to surround.
Umriß *m.* (-risses, -risse) sketch, outline, contour.
umrühren *v.t.* to stir.
umrüsten *v.t.* to convert; to reequip (army).
ums = **um das**
umsatteln *v.i.* (*fig.*) to change one's profession.
Umsatz *m.* (-es, 0) turnover; ~**steuer** *f.* turnover tax.
umsäumen *v.t.* to hem; (*fig.*) to surround.
umschalten *v.t.* to switch (on), to reverse (the current).
Umschalter *m.* switch, commutator.
umschatten *v.t.* to shade.
Umschau *f.* (-, 0) survey; ~ *halten* , to look round.
umschauen (sich) *v.refl.* to look back *or* round.
umschiffen *v.t.* to circumnavigate.
Umschlag *m.* (-[e]s, -schläge) envelope, wrapper; poultice, compress; sudden change, turn; (*Ärmel*) cuff, tuck; (*Waren*) transhipment.
umschlagen *v.t.st.* (*Saum*) to turn up; (*Kragen*) to

turn down; (*Blatt*) to turn over; (*Ärmel*) to tuck up; to wrap round; to buy and sell; ~ *v.i.st.* (*s*) to capsize; to change suddenly; to turn sour; (*Stimme*) to break.

umschleichen *v.t.st.* to prowl round.

umschließen *v.t.st.* to enclose.

umschlingen *v.t.st.* to embrace.

umschmeißen *v.t.st.* to overturn.

umschnallen *v.t.* to buckle on.

umschreiben *v.t.st.* to transcribe; to transfer; (*Wechsel*) to reindorse; (*mit Worten*) to paraphrase; (*math.*) to circumscribe.

Umschreibung *f.* (-, -en) paraphrase; description; definition.

Umschrift *f.* (-, -en) (*phonetische* ~), phonetic transcription.

umschulen *v.t.* to retrain; to transfer to another school.

Umschulung *f.* retraining.

Umschuldung *f.* debt-conversion.

umschütten *v.t.* to spill, to pour (into another container).

umschwärmen *v.t.* to idolize; to adore.

Umschweif *m* (-[e]s, -e) digression; **ohne ~e** without beating about the bush.

umschwenken *v.i.* (*h. s*) to wheel round.

Umschwung *m.* (-[e]s, -schwünge) revolution; reversal, the turning of the tide.

umsehen (sich) *v.refl.st.* to look round *or* back; (*nach*) to look out for; (*in*) to become acquainted (with).

um sein *v.i.ir.* (*s*) to be over.

umseitig *adv.* overleaf; *Fortsetzung* ~, continued over.

umsetzen *v.t.* (*Pflanzen*) to transplant; to turn over; *in Taten* ~, to translate into deeds.

Umsichgreifen *n.* (-s, 0) spread, proliferation.

Umsicht *f.* (-, 0) circumspection.

umsichtig *a.* circumspect.

umsiedeln *v.t.* to resettle.

Umsiedlung *f.* (-, -en) resettlement.

umsinken *v.i.st.* (*s*) to drop, to faint.

umsonst *adv.* gratis, for nothing; in vain; *nicht* ~, not without good reason.

umspannen *v.i.* to span, to encompass.

umspringen *v.i.st.* (*s*) to veer (round), to turn; ~ *mit* to manage, to handle.

Umstand *m.* (-[e]s, -stände) circumstance; **Umstände** *pl.* ceremonies, fuss; particulars *pl.*; *in anderen Umständen sein* (*von Frauen*), to be in the family way; to be expecting.

umständlich *a.* involved, awkward.

Umstandskleid *n.* maternity dress.

Umstandswort *n.* adverb.

umstehend *a.* next (page); standing round.

Umstehende[n] *m.pl.* bystanders *pl.*

umsteigen *v.i.st.* (*s*) to change (trains, etc.).

umstellen *v.t.* to transpose; to surround.

Umstellung *f.* (-, -en) inversion; changeover.

umstimmen *v.t.* to bring (one) round.

umstoßen *v.t.st.* to knock down.

umstricken *v.t.* (*fig.*) to ensnare.

umstritten *a.* controversial; disputed.

umstrukturieren *v.t.* to restructure.

umstülpen *v.t.* to turn inside out.

Umsturz *m.* (-es, -stürze) overthrow; revolution; coup.

umstürzen *v.t.* to throw down, to overturn; ~ *v.i.* (*s*) to be upset.

Umstürzler *m.* (-s, -) revolutionary.

Umsturzversuch *m.* attempted coup.

umtaufen *v.t.* to give another name.

Umtausch *m.* (-[e]s, 0) exchange, barter.

umtauschen *v.t.* to exchange.

Umtrieb *m.* (-[e]s, -e) intrigue.

umtun *v.t.st.* to put on; *sich nach etwas* ~, to look for.

U-Musik *f.* (*Unterhaltungsmusik*) light music.

umwälzen *v.t.* to revolutionize; to circulate.

Umwälzung *f.* (-, -en) revolution.

umwandeln *v.t.* to change, to convert (into); to commute (sentence).

Umwandlung *f.* (-, -en) change, transformation; conversion; commutation (sentence).

umwechseln *v.t.* to (ex)change.

Umweg *m.* (-[e]s, -e) detour.

umwehen *v.t.* to blow down.

Umwelt *f.* (-, 0) environment.

Umwelt: ~belastung *f.* environmental pollution; **~forschung** *f.* ecology

umweltfreundlich *a.* environment-friendly; non-polluting; biodegradable.

Umwelt: ~katastrophe *f.* catastrophe for the environment; **~kriminalität** *f.* environmental crime; **~ministerium** *n.* Department of the Environment; **~schäden** *pl.* environmental damage.

umweltschädlich *a.* polluting; harmful to the environment.

Umwelt: ~schutz *m.* environmental protection; **~verschmutzung** *f.* pollution (of the environment); **~zerstörung** *f.* destruction of the environment.

umwenden *v.t.ir.* to turn round.

umwerben *v.t.st.* to court.

umwerfen *v.t.st.* to overthrow; to knock over.

Umwertung *f.* (-, -en) revaluation.

umwickeln *v.t.* to wrap up.

umwölken (sich) *v.refl.* to get cloudy; (*fig.*) to darken.

umworben *a.* sought in marriage, courted.

umzäunen *v.t.* to hedge, to fence.

Umzäunung *f.* (-, -en) enclosure, fence.

umziehen *v.i.st.* (*s*) to move, to relocate, *v.t.st.*(*h*) *jn.* ~, to change somebody's clothes; (sich) ~ *v.refl.st.* to change (one's clothes).

umzingeln *v.t.* to encircle, to surround.

Umzug *m.* (-[e]s, -züge) procession; (*Wohnungswechsel*) move.

unabänderlich *a.* irrevocable.

unabdingbar *a.* indispensable.

unabhängig *a.* independent.

Unabhängigkeit *f.* (-, 0) independence.

unabkömmlich *a.* indispensable.

unablässig *a.* incessant; unremitting.

unabsehbar *a.* immeasurable, unbounded.

unabsichtlich *a.* unintentional.

unabwendbar *a.* inevitable.

unachtsam *a.* inadvertent; careless.

Unachtsamkeit *f.* (-, -en) inadvertency.

unähnlich *a.* unlike, dissimilar.

unanfechtbar *a.* incontestable.

unangebracht *a.* inappropriate; out of place.
unangefochten *a.* unchallenged; unmolested.
unangekündigt *a.* unannounced.
unangemeldet *a. & adv.* without (previous) notice; unannounced.
unangemessen *a.* inadequate, unsuitable.
unangenehm *a.* disagreeable, unpleasant.
unangetastet *a.* untouched.
unangreifbar *a.* unassailable.
unannehmbar *a.* unacceptable.
Unannehmlichkeit *f.* (-, -en) inconvenience.
unansehnlich *a.* unsightly, poor-looking; plain.
unanständig *a.* indecent; improper.
unantastbar *a.* inviolable.
unappetitlich *a.* unsavory, unappetizing.
Unart *f.* (-, -en) bad habit.
unartig *a.* naughty, rude.
unartikuliert *a.* inarticulate.
unästhetisch *a.* unpleasant, disgusting.
unauffällig *a.* inconspicuous; discreet.
unauffindbar *a.* undiscoverable.
unaufgefordert *a.* unasked; ~ *eingesandte Manuskripte,* unsolicited manuscripts.
unaufhaltsam *a.* irresistible.
unaufhörlich *a.* incessant.
unauflöslich *a.* indissoluble.
unaufmerksam *a.* inattentive.
unaufrichtig *a.* insincere.
unaufschiebbar *a.* urgent, pressing.
unaufspürbar *a.* untraceable.
unausbleiblich *a.* inevitable.
unausführbar *a.* impracticable.
unausgeglichen *a.* unstable; unsettled.
unausgesetzt *a.* uninterrupted.
unauslöschlich *a.* indelible.
unaussprechlich *a.* unpronounceable; (*fig.*) unspeakable.
unausstehlich *a.* insufferable.
unausweichlich *a.* inevitable.
unbändig *a.* boisterous; unbridled.
unbarmherzig *a.* merciless.
unbeabsichtigt *a.* unintentional.
unbeachtet *a.* unnoticed.
unbeanstandet *a.* approved.
unbeaufsichtigt *a.* unattended.
unbedacht, unbedächtig, unbedachtsam *a.* inconsiderate, rash.
unbedenklich *a.* unhesitating; unobjectionable; ~ *adv.* without hesitation.
unbedeutend *a.* insignificant, trifling.
unbedingt *a.* unconditional, absolute; implicit; ~ *adv.* by all means.
unbeeinflust *a.* uninfluenced.
unbefangen *a.* unprejudiced; unembarrassed; candid, natural.
unbefleckt *a.* immaculate, pure.
unbefriedigend *a.* unsatisfactory.
unbefriedigt *a.* unsatisfied.
unbefristet *a.* indefinite; unlimited.
unbefugt *a.* unauthorized; incompetent.
unbegreiflich *a.* incomprehensible, inconceivable.
unbegreiflicherweise *adv.* inexplicably.
unbegrenzt *a.* unbounded, unlimited.
unbegründet *a.* unfounded, groundless.
unbegütert *a.* not rich, without landed property.
Unbehagen *n.* uneasiness, discomfort.

unbehaglich *a.* uneasy, uncomfortable.
Unbehaglichkeit *f.* discomfort.
unbehelligt *a.* unmolested.
unbeherrscht *a.* uncontrolled.
Unbeherrschtheit *f.* lack of self-control.
unbehindert *a.* unrestrained, unhindered.
unbeholfen *a.* awkward, clumsy.
unbekannt *a.* unknown.
Unbekannte *m./f.* unknown/unindentified person.
unbekehrbar *a.* inconvertible.
unbekümmert *a.* unconcerned (about).
unbelebt *a.* inanimate; lifeless, dull.
unbeleckt *a.* untouched, untainted.
unbeleuchtet *a.* unlit.
unbeliebt *a.* unpopular.
unbemerkt *a.* unnoticed, unperceived.
unbemittelt *a.* poor, without means.
unbenannt *a.* anonymous.
unbenommen *a. es bleibt dir ~,* you are quite free to . . .
unbenutzt *a.* unused.
unbeobachtet *a.* unobserved.
unbequem *a.* uncomfortable.
unberechenbar *a.* unpredictable; incalculable.
unberechtigt *a.* unauthorized; unlawful.
unberichtigt *a.* uncorrected; (*Rechnung*) unpaid.
unberücksichtigt *a.* unconsidered.
unberührt *a.* untouched.
unbeschadet *adv.* without prejudice to.
unbeschädigt *a.* unhurt, uninjured.
unbescheiden *a.* immodest; presumptuous.
unbescholten *a.* blameless.
Unbescholtenheit *f.* blameless reputation.
unbeschränkt *a.* unlimited.
unbeschreiblich *a.* indescribable.
unbeschrieben *a.* blank; empty.
unbeschwert *a.* carefree; light.
unbeseelt *a.* inanimate.
unbesehen *a.* unseen, unexamined; ~ *adv.* without hesitation.
unbesetzt *a.* unoccupied, vacant.
unbesiegbar *a.* invincible.
unbesiegt *a.* unbeaten.
umbesoldet *a.* unsalaried, unpaid.
unbesonnen *a.* thoughtless, rash; impulsive.
unbesorgt *a.* unconcerned; easy.
unbeständig *a.* inconstant, fickle.
Unbeständigkeit *f.* instability, fickleness.
unbestätigt *a.* unconfirmed.
unbestechlich *a.* incorruptible.
unbestellbar *a.* not deliverable.
unbestimmt *a.* indeterminate.
unbestreitbar *a.* indisputable.
unbestritten *a.* uncontested.
unbeteiligt *a.* not concerned (in).
unbetont *a.* unstressed.
unbeträchtlich *a.* inconsiderable.
unbeugsam *a.* inflexible.
unbewacht *a.* unguarded; unwatched.
unbewaffnet *a.* unarmed; *mit unbewaffnetem Auge,* with the naked eye.
unbewältigt *a.* unmastered; uncompleted.
unbewandert *a.* unversed in.
unbeweglich *a.* motionless; immovable; real (property); (*fig.*) inflexible.

Umbeweglichkeit *f.* immobility.
unbewiesen *a.* unproved.
unbewohnbar *a.* uninhabitable.
unbewohnt *a.* uninhabited.
unbewußt *a.* unconscious (of); unknown.
unbezahlbar *a.* priceless.
unbezahlt *a.* unpaid.
unbezähmbar *a.* indomitable.
unbezeugt *a.* unattested, not proved.
unbezweifelt *a.* undoubted.
unbezwingbar *a.* invincible, impregnable.
unbiegsam *a.* not pliant; inflexible.
Unbill *f.* (i, -bilden) injury, wrong; (*des Wetters*) inclemency.
unblutig *a.* bloodless.
unbotmässig *a.* unruly, refractory.
unbrauchbar *a.* useless, unusable.
unbußfertig *a.* impenitent.
und *c.* and; ~ *wenn*, even if; ~ *so weiter*, and so on; etc.; *der* ~ *der*, so and so.
Undank *m.* (-[e]s, 0) ingratitude.
undankbar *a.* ungrateful; thankless.
undatiert *a.* undated.
undefinierbar *a.* undefinable.
undenkbar *a.* inconceivable.
undenklich *a.* immemorial.
undeutlich *a.* indistinct; inarticulate.
undicht *a.* not tight, leaking.
Unding *n.* absurdity.
undiszipliniert *a.* undisciplined.
unduldsam *a.* intolerant.
undurchdringlich *a.* impenetrable.
undurchführbar *a.* impracticable.
undurchlässig *a.* impermeable; waterproof.
undurchsichtig *a.* opaque.
Undurchsichtigkeit *f.* opacity.
uneben *a.* uneven, rugged.
unecht *a.* not genuine; spurious, counterfeit, sham.
unehelich *a.* illegitimate.
unehrenhaft *a.* dishonorable.
unehrerbietig *a.* irreverent, disrespectful.
unehrlich *a.* dishonest.
uneigennützig *a.* disinterested.
uneingeschränkt *a.* unrestricted.
uneingeweiht *a.* uninitiated.
uneinig *a.* discordant, divided.
Uneinigkeit *f.* disagreement, discord.
uneinnehmbar *a.* impregnable.
uneins *a.* divided; ~ **sein** to be at variance.
uneinträglich *a.* unprofitable, barren.
unempfänglich *a.* unreceptive.
unempfindlich *a.* insensitive, indifferent.
unendlich *a.* endless, infinite.
Unendlichkeit *f.* infinity; infinite space.
unentbehrlich *a.* indispensable.
unentgeltlich *a.* gratuitous; free (of charge); ~ *adv.* gratis.
unenthaltsam *a.* incontinent.
unentrinnbar *a.* inevitable, unavoidable.
unentschieden *a.* undecided; irresolute.
Unentschieden *n.* (-, -) (*sport*) draw.
unentschlossen *a.* undecided; irresolute.
Unentschlossenheit *f.* indecision; irresolution.
unentschuldbar *a.* inexcusable.
unentwegt *a.* steady.

unentwickelt *a.* undeveloped.
unentwirrbar *a.* inextricable.
unerbittlich *a.* inexorable.
unerfahren *a.* inexperienced.
Unerfahrenheit *f.* (-, 0) inexperience.
unerfindlich *a.* inexplicable.
unerforschlich *a.* inscrutable.
unerfreulich *a.* unpleasant.
unerfüllbar *a.* not to be fulfilled *or* complied with, unrealizable.
unergiebig *a.* unproductive.
unergründlich *a.* unfathomable.
unerheblich *a.* inconsiderable; irrelevant.
unerhört *a.* unheard of, unprecedented.
unerkannt *a.* unrecognized.
unerkennbar *a.* unrecognizable.
unerkenntlich *a.* ungrateful.
unerklärlich *a.* inexplicable.
unerläßlich *a.* indispensable.
unerlaubt *a.* illicit, unlawful.
unerledigt *a.* unattended, not dispatched.
unermeßlich *a.* immeasurable; immense.
Unermeßlichkeit *f.* (-, 0) immensity.
unermüdlich *a.* untiring, tireless.
unerörtert *a.* undiscussed; undecided.
unerquicklich *a.* unpleasant, unedifying.
unerreichbar *a.* unattainable.
unerreicht *a.* unequalled.
unersättlich *a.* insatiable.
unerschlossen *a.* undeveloped.
unerschöpflich *a.* inexhaustible.
unerschrocken *a.* intrepid, undaunted.
unerschütterlich *a.* unshakable, imperturbable, firm, unshaken.
unerschwinglich *a.* beyond one's means; ~*er Preis*, prohibitive price.
unersetzlich *a.* irreparable; irreplaceable.
unersprießlich *a.* unprofitable.
unerträglich *a.* intolerable.
unerwähnt *a.* unmentioned; ~ *lassen*, to pass over (in silence).
unerwartet *a.* unexpected.
unerwidert *a.* unanswered; unreturned.
unerwiesen *a.* not proved.
unerwünscht *a.* undesirable.
unerzogen *a.* naughty.
unfähig *a.* incapable, inefficient.
Unfähigkeit *f.* incompetence; inability.
Unfall *m.* accident; mischance.
Unfall: ~station *f.* ambulance station; ~**versicherung** *f.* accident insurance; ~**wagen** *f.* ambulance.
unfaßbar *a.* inconceivable.
unfehlbar *a.* infallible.
Unfehlbarkeit *f.* (-, 0) infallibility.
unfein *a.* ill mannered; coarse.
unfern *adv.* not far off; ~ *pr.* near, not far from.
unfertig *a.* unfinished, not ready.
unflätig *a.* filthy; obscene.
unfolgsam *a.* disobedient.
Unfolgsamkeit *f.* disobedience.
unförmig *a.* shapeless.
unfrankiert *a.* unstamped.
unfrei *a.* not free.
unfreiwillig *a.* involuntary; compulsory.
unfreundlich *a.* unfriendly; unkind; harsh.

Unfreundlichkeit *f.* unfriendliness; unkindness.
Unfriede *m.* discord, dissension.
unfruchtbar *a.* infertile; barren, sterile.
Unfruchtbarkeit *f.* infertility; sterility, barrenness.
Unfug *m.* (-[e]s, 0) mischief, nuisance, *grober ~*, gross misdemeanor.
unfügsam *a.* uncomplying, intractable.
ungangbar *a.* (*Weg*) impassable.
Ungar *m.* (-n, -n); **Ungarin** *f.* (-, -nen); **ungarisch** *a.* Hungarian.
Ungarn *n.* (-s, 0) Hungary.
ungastlich *a.* inhospitable.
ungeachtet *pr.* notwithstanding.
ungeahnt *a.* unexpected, unthought-of.
ungebändigt *a.* untamed, unsubdued.
ungebärdig *a.* unruly.
ungebeten *a.* uninvited.
ungebildet *a.* uneducated, uncultured.
ungebleicht *a.* unbleached.
ungeboren *a.* unborn.
ungebräuchlich *a.* unusual; obsolete.
ungebraucht *a.* unused; new.
ungebrochen *a.* unbroken.
ungebührlich *a.* improper, unmannerly.
ungebunden *a.* unbound; (*Bücher*) in sheets; (*fig.*) loose, licentious; *~e Rede*, prose; *~es Wesen*, dissolute ways *pl.*
ungedeckt *a.* uncovered; (*com.*) unpaid; *~er Kredit*, unsecured credit.
ungedruckt *a.* unprinted.
Ungeduld *f.* impatience.
ungeduldig *a.* impatient.
ungeeignet unsuitable (for).
ungefähr *a.* approximate; *~ adv.* about, nearly; *von ~*, by chance.
ungehährlich *a.* harmless, safe.
ungefärbt *a.* undyed, uncolored.
ungefüttert *a.* unlined.
ungehalten *a.* angry, indignant.
ungeheißen *a.* spontaneous, unbidden.
ungeheizt *a.* unheated.
ungehemmt *a.* unchecked, uninhibited.
ungeheuchelt *a.* unfeigned.
ungeheuer *a.* immense, prodigious, huge.
Ungeheuer *n.* (-s, -) monster.
ungeheuerlich *a.* monstrous.
Ungeheuerlichkeit *f.* (-, -en) monstrosity.
ungehindert *a.* unimpeded.
ungehobelt *a.* unplaned; (*fig.*) coarse.
ungehörig *a.* improper; unsuitable.
ungehorsam *a.* disobedient.
Ungehorsam *m.* disobedience.
ungeimpft *a.* unvaccinated.
ungekämmt *a.* uncombed, unkempt.
ungeklärt *a.* unsolved; unknown.
ungekünstelt *a.* unaffected.
ungekürzt *a.* unabridged.
ungeladen *a.* uninvited; unloaded.
ungeläufig *a.* unfamiliar.
ungelegen *a.* inconvenient, inopportune.
Ungelegenheit *f.* inconvenience, trouble.
ungelehrig *a.* indocile, not docile.
ungelehrt *a.* unlettered, unlearned.
ungelenk *a.* stiff; clumsy, awkward.
ungelernt *a.* unskilled.
Ungemach *n.* (-[e]s, -e) discomfort, adversity; trouble, hardship.

ungemein *a.* uncommon; extraordinary.
ungemildert *a.* unmitigated.
ungemütlich *a.* uncomfortable.
ungenannt *a.* unnamed.
ungenau *a.* inaccurate, inexact.
Ungenauigkeit *f.* inaccuracy.
ungeniert *a.* uninhibited.
ungenießbar *a.* unpalatable.
ungenügend *a/* insufficient; inadequate.
ungenutzt *a.* unused, unemployed.
ungeöffnet *a.* unopened.
ungeordnet *a.* unarranged; unsettled.
ungerade *a.* (*Zahl*) odd; uneven.
ungeraten *a.* (*Kind*) spoiled.
ungerecht *a.* unjust.
Ungerechtigkeit *f.* injustice.
ungereimt *a.* (*Vers*) unrhymed; blank; (*fig.*) absurd, preposterous.
Ungereimtheit *f.* (-, -en) (*fig.*) absurdity.
ungern *adv.* unwillingly, reluctantly.
ungerufen *a.* uncalled.
ungerügt *a.* uncensured, unpunished.
ungesagt *a.* unsaid.
ungesalzen *a.* unsalted; fresh.
ungeschehen *~ machen*, to undo.
Ungeschicklichkeit, Ungeschicktheit *f.* awkwardness, ineptitude.
ungeschickt *a.* awkward, clumsy.
ungeschliffen *a.* (*von Edelsteinen*) rough; (*fig.*) unpolished, rude, unmannerly.
ungeschmälert *a.* undiminished.
ungeschminkt *a.* unvarnished.
ungeschoren *a.* unshorn; undisturbed.
ungesellig *a.* unsociable.
ungesetzlich *a.* illegal.
Ungesetzlichkeit *f.* illegality.
ungesetzmäßig *a.* illegal, unlawful.
ungesittet *a.* unmannerly.
ungestalt(et) *a.* ill-shaped, misshapen.
ungestillt *a.* unquenched, unslaked.
ungestört *a.* undisturbed.
ungestraft *a.* unpunished; *~ adv.* with impunity.
ungestüm *a.* impetuous.
Ungestüm *n.* (-[e]s, 0) impetuosity.
ungesund *a.* unwholesome; unhealthy.
ungeteilt *a.* undivided.
ungetreu *a.* faithless.
ungetrübt *a.* cloudless, untroubled.
Ungetüm *m.* (-[e]s, -e) monster.
ungeübt *a.* unpractised.
ungewiß *a.* uncertain.
Ungewißheit *f.* uncertainty.
ungewöhnlich *a.* unusual, uncommon.
ungewohnt *a.* unaccustomed, unfamiliar.
ungewollt *a.* unwanted; unintentional.
ungezählt *a.* unnumbered, untold.
ungezähmt *a.* untamed; (*fig.*) uncurbed.
Ungeziefer *n.* vermin.
ungezogen *a.* ill-bred, rude; naughty.
ungezügelt *a.* unbridled.
ungezwungen *a.* unaffected, easy.
Unglaube *m.* disbelief, (*kirchlich*)) unbelief.
unglaubhaft *a.* unbelievable.
ungläubig *a.* unbelieving, infidel.
Ungläubige[r] *m.* infidel, unbeliever.

unglaublich *a.* incredible.
unglaubwürdig *a.* unworthy of belief.
ungleich *a.* unequal; unlike, dissimilar, uneven; odd; ~ *adv.* (by) far, much.
ungleichartig *a.* heterogeneous.
ungleichförmig *a.* not uniform.
Ungleichheit *f.* inequality, dissimilarity.
ungleichmäßig *a.* uneven.
Unglück *n.* misfortune; adversity; ill-luck.
unglücklich *a.* unlucky, unhappy, unfortunate.
unglücklicherweise *a.* unfortunately.
unglückselig *a.* miserable; disastrous.
Unglücks(fall) *m.* misfortune; accident; ~vogel *m.* poor devil.
Ungnade *f.* disgrace, disfavor.
ungnädig *a.* ungracious, unkind, angry.
ungrammatisch *a.* ungrammatical.
ungültig *a.* invalid, void: (*Fahrkarte*) not available; *für ~erklären, ~ machen,* to annul, to invalidate, to void.
Ungunst *f.* disfavor; (*Wetter*) inclemency.
ungünstig *a.* unfavorable.
ungut, *nights für ~!* no offence!
unhaltbar *a.* untenable.
Unheil *m.* (-[e]s, 0) harm; calamity.
unheilbar *a.* incurable.
unheilig *a.* unholy, profane, unhallowed.
unheilvoll *a.* calamitous, disastrous.
unheimlich *a.* uncanny; eerie.
unhistorisch *a.* unhistoric.
unhöflich *a.* uncivil, rude.
Unhöflichkeit *f.* rudeness, incivility.
Unhold *m.* (-[e]s, -e) monster; fiend.
unhörbar *a.* inaudible.
unhygienisch *a.* insanitary; unhygienic.
Uniform *f.* (-, -en) uniform.
Unikum *n.* (-[e]s, -ka) unique object.
uninteressant *a.* uninteresting.
uninteressiert *a.* uninterested.
Union *f.* (-, -en) union.
universal *a.* universal.
Universalerbe *m.* sole heir.
Universität *f.* (-, -en) university.
Universum *n.* (-[s], 0) universe.
unkenntlich *a.* unrecognizable.
Unkenntnis *f.* (-, 0) ignorance.
unkeusch *a.* unchaste.
unklar *a.* confused, unintelligible; *im unklaren sein,* to be in the dark (about).
unklug *a.* imprudent, indiscreet.
unkompliziert *a.* uncomplicated.
unkontrollierbar *a.* uncontrollable.
unkontrolliert *a.* uncontrolled.
Unkosten *pl.* charges, expenses *pl.; laufende ~,* overhead expenses.
Unkraut *n.* (-[e]s, 0) weeds.
unkritisch *a.* uncritical.
unkultiviert *a.* uncultivated.
Unkultur *f.* (-, 0) lack of civilization.
unkündbar *a.* permanent (position).
unkundig *a.* ignorant (of).
unlängst *adv.* lately; the other day.
unlauter *a.* dishonest; unfair; *~er Wettbewerb,* unfair competition.
unleidlich *a.* intolerable.
unlenksam *a.* unmanageable, unruly.

unlesbar *a.* unreadable.
unleserlich *a.* illegible.
unleugbar *a.* undeniable.
unlieb *a.* disagreeable.
unliebsam *a.* unpleasant.
unlogisch *a.* illogical.
unlösbar *a.* unsolvable.
unlöslich *a.* insoluble.
Unlust *f.* (-, 0) disinclination.
unmanierlich *a.* unmannerly.
Unmasse *f.* (*fam.*) vast quantity.
unmaßgeblich *a.* without authority.
unmäßig *a.* immoderate; intemperate.
Unmäßigkeit *f.* intemperance; excess.
Unmenge *f.* vast quantity *or* number.
Unmensch *m.* monster, brute.
unmenschlich *a.* inhuman, cruel.
Unmenschlichkeit *f.* inhumanity, cruelty.
unmerklich *a.* imperceptible.
unmethodisch *a.* unmethodical.
unmittelbar *a.* immediate, direct.
unmöbliert *a.* unfurnished.
unmodern *a.* old-fashioned; outmoded.
unmöglich *a.* impossible.
Unmöglichkeit *f.* impossibility.
unmoralisch *a.* immoral.
unmotiviert *a.* without any motive.
unmündig *a.* under age.
Unmündigkeit *f.* (*jur.*) minority.
unmusikalisch *a.* unmusical.
Unmut *m.* ill-humor, discontent.
unmutig *a.* ill-humoured.
unnachahmlich *a.* inimitable.
unnachgiebig *a.* intransigent; unyielding.
unnachsichtlich *a.* unrelenting.
unnahbar *a.* unapproachable.
Unnatur *f.* unnaturalness, affectation.
unnatürlich *a.* unnatural; affected.
unnennbar *a.* ineffable, unutterable.
unnötig *a.* unnecessary, needless.
unnütz *a.* useless, unprofitable.
unordentlich *a.* disorderly, untidy.
Unordnung *f.* disorder, untidiness.
unparteiisch, unparteilich *a.* impartial.
Unparteiische *m./f.* umpire.
Unparteilichkeit *f.* impartiality.
unpassend *a.* unbecoming; improper.
unpäßlich *a.* indisposed, unwell.
Unpäßlichkeit *f.* (-, 0) indisposition.
unpatriotisch *a.* unpatriotic.
unpersönlich *a.* impersonal.
unpolitisch *a.* apolitical.
unpopulär *a.* unpopular.
unpraktisch *a.* unpractical.
unproduktiv *a.* unproductive.
unpünktlich *a.* unpunctual.
unqualifiziert *a.* unqualified.
unrasiert *a.* unshaven.
Unrast *f.* (-, 0) restlessness.
Unrat *m.* (-[e]s, 0) dirt, rubbish.
unratsam *a.* inadvisable.
unrecht *a.* wrong; unjust; *an den Unrechten kommen,* to catch a Tartar.
Unrecht *n.* wrong, injustice, injury; *~ haben,* to be wrong; *ins ~ setzen,* to put in the wrong.
unrechtmäßig *a.* unlawful, illegal.

unredlich *a.* dishonest.
Unredlichkeit *f.* dishonesty.
unregelmäßig *a.* irregular.
unreif *a.* unripe; (*fig.*) immature.
Unreife *f.* (-, 0) immaturity; unripeness.
unrein *a.* unclean, impure.
unreinlich *a.* unclean.
unrentabel *a.* unprofitable.
unrettbar *a.* past help, past recovery; ~ *verloren sein*, to be irretrievably lost.
unrichtig *a.* wrong, incorrect.
unritterlich *a.* unchivalrous.
Unruhe *f.* disquiet, trouble; disturbance; alarm; noise; restlessness.
unruhig *a.* restless; uneasy; turbulent.
unrühmlich *a.* inglorious.
uns *pn.* us, to us; ourselves.
unsachgemäß *a.* improper.
unsachlich *a.* unobjective.
unsäglich *a.* unspeakable.
unsanft *a.* hard, harsh, rough.
unsauber *a.* unclean, slovenly; shady, unfair.
unschädlich *a.* harmless, innocuous.
unschätzbar *a.* inestimable, invaluable.
unscheinbar *a.* inconspicuous.
unschicklich *a.* improper, unseemly.
unschlüssig *a.* undecided; irresolute; ~ *sein*, to hesitate.
unschön *a.* plain, homely, not nice.
Unschuld *f.* innocence.
unschuldig *a.* innocent.
unschwer *adv.* easily.
unselbständig *a.* dependent, unable to act *or* judge by oneself.
unselig *a.* luckless, unfortunate, fatal.
unser *pn.* our, ours; ~*einer*, ~*eins*, the likes of us.
unsrige (der, die, das) *pn.* ours.
unseretwegen *adv.* for our sake; as far as we are concerned.
unsicher *a.* unsafe; uncertain, dubious.
Unsicherheit *f.* insecurity; uncertainty.
Unsicherheitsfaktor *m.* element of uncertainty.
unsichtbar *a.* invisible.
unsigniert *a.* unsigned.
Unsinn *m.* (-[e]s, 0) nonsense.
unsinnig *a.* nonsensical, absurd.
Unsitte *f.* bad habit.
unsittlich *a.* indecent.
unsolide *a.* dissipated, loose; unreliable.
unsozial *a.* antisocial.
unstatthaft *a.* inadmissible; illicit.
unsterblich *a.* immortal.
Unsterblichkeit *f.* (-, 0) immortality.
Unstern *m.* (-[e]s, 0) evil star, ill-luck.
unstet *a.* unsteady, unsettled.
unstillbar *a.* unquenchable.
Unstimmigkeit *f.* inconsistency; discrepancy.
unstreitig *a.* unquestionable.
Unsumme *f.* (*fam.*) immense number.
unsymmetrisch *a.* unsymmetrical.
unsympatisch *a.* disagreeable; unpleasant; *mir ist es* ~, I do not like.
untadelhaft, untadelig *a.* blameless.
Untat *f.* crime, misdeed.
untätig *a.* inactive; idle.
Untätigkeit *f.* (-, 0) inactivity.

untauglich *a.* unsuitable; unfit; *für* ~ *erklären*, to condemn.
unteilbar *a.* indivisible.
unten *adv.* below; downstairs; at the bottom; *nach* ~, down(wards); *von oben bis* ~, from to to bottom; *weiter* ~, lower down; *der zweite von* ~, the second up.
untendrunter *adv.* (*fam.*) underneath.
unter *pr.* under, below; among, between; beneath; during; ~ *uns*, among ourselves; ~ *uns gesagt*, between you and me.
unter *a.* inferior, lower.
Unter: ~**abteilung** *f.* subdivision ~**arm** *m.* forearm; ~**art** *f.* subspecies; ~**bau** *m.* foundation, groundwork; (*rail.*) sub-structure.
unterbelichten *v.t.* to underexpose.
unterbeschäftigt *a.* underemployed.
unterbesetzt *a.* understaffed.
unterbewerten *v.t.* to undervalue; to underrate.
unterbewußt *a.* subconscious.
Unterbewußtein *n.* subconscious; *im* ~, subconsciously.
unterbieten *v.t.st.* to undercut.
unterbinden *v.t.st.* to ligature (an artery); to stop; to cut off (supplies, etc.).
unterbleiben *v.i.st.* (*s*) to be left undone; not to take place.
unterbrechen *v.t.st.* to interrupt.
Unterbrechung *f.* (-, -en) interruption.
unterbreiten *v.t.* to submit (to).
unterbringen *v.t.ir.* to put up, to accommodate; to provide for; (*Waren*) to dispose of; to place (a loan); (*Wechsel*) to negotiate.
unterdes, unterdessen *adv.* meanwhile, in the meantime.
unterdrücken *v.t.* to oppress; to suppress, to crush.
Unterdrücker *m.* (-s, -) oppressor.
Unterdrückung *f.* (-s, -en) oppression; suppression.
unterdurchschnittlich *a.* below average.
untereinander *adv.* one below the other; among one another.
unterentwickelt *a.* underdeveloped.
unterernährt *a.* underfed.
Unterernährung *f.* malnutrition.
Unterfangen *n.* (-s, 0) venture; undertaking.
Unterführung *f.* underpass.
Untergang *m.* (-[e]s, 0) decline; fall, ruin, destruction.
untergeben *a.* inferior (to).
Untergebene *m./f.* (-n, -n) subaltern, subordinate.
untergehen *v.i.st.* (*s*) to go down, to set; to sink; to drown.
untergeordnet *a.* subordinate, inferior.
Untergeschoß *n.* basement.
Untergestell *n.* truck, frame.
untergliedern *v.t.* to subdivide.
untergraben *v.t.st.* to undermine, to sap.
Untergrund *m.* subsoil; foundation; underground. ~**bahn** *f.* subway.
unterhalb *pr.* below.
Unterhalt *m.* (-[e]s, 0) maintenance; livelihood; living.
unterhalten *v.t.st.* to maintain, to support, to keep (up); to amuse, to entertain; (sich) ~ *v.refl.st.* to

converse, to talk; to enjoy oneself.

unterhaltend *a.* **unterhaltsam** *a.* entertaining, amusing.

Unterhaltung *f.* (-en, -en) entertainment; maintenance; conversation.

Unterhaltungs: ~**brauche** *f.* entertainment industry; ~**literatur** *f.* light fiction; ~**musik** *f.* light music; ~**wert** *m.* entertainment value.

Unterhändler *m.* negotiator, agent.

Unterhaus *n.* lower house of parliament.

Unterhemd *n.* undershirt.

unterhöhlen *v.t.* to hollow out; to erode.

Unter: ~**holz** *n.* undergrowth; ~**hose** *f.* underpants; panties.

unterirdisch *a.* underground; subterranean.

unterjochen *v.t.* to subjugate, to subdue.

Unterkiefer *m.* lower jaw.

unterkommen *v.i.st.* (s) to find lodgings, employment, etc.

Unterkommen *n.* (-s, 0) shelter, accommodation, lodging; place, employment.

unterkriegen *v.t.* (*fam.*) to get the better of s.b.

Unterkühlung *f.* hypothermia.

Unterkunft *f.* (-, 0) accommodation; shelter, (*mil.*) quarters.

Unterlage *f.* deskpad, mat; padding; (*Beweis*) evidence; ~**n** *pl.* documentation.

Unterlaß *m* (-lasses, 0) intermission.

unterlassen *v.t.st.* to refrain from; to fail to do sth.

Unterlassung *f.* (-, -en) omission.

Unterlauf *m.* lower course (of a river).

unterlaufen *v.i.st.* to occur; to evade; *mir ist ein Fehler ~,* I made a mistake.

unterlegen *v.t.* to lay *or* put under; (*fig.*) to put (a construction) upon; *einer Melodie einen Text, Worte ~,* to adapt words to a melody.

unterlegen *a.* inferior.

Unterleib *m.* lower abdomen.

unterliegen *v.i.st.* (s) to succumb; to be defeated; to admit of (doubt).

Unterlippe *f.* lower-lip.

unterm = **unter dem**

Untermalung *f.* accompaniment; background music.

untermauern *v.t.* to underpin; to support.

untermengen *v.t.* to mix in; to mingle.

Untermiete *f.* subtenancy; sublease.

Untermieter *m.* subtenant.

unterminieren *v.t.* to undermine.

untern = **under den**

unternehmen *v.t.st.* to undertake, to take upon oneself.

Unternehmen *n.* (-s, -) enterprise; (*mil.*) operation.

unternehmend *a.* enterprising, bold.

Unternehmer *m.* (-s, -) contractor; employer; entrepreneur.

Unternehmung *f.* (-, -en) enterprise.

unternehmungslustig *a.* active; enterprising.

unternormal *a.* subnormal.

Unteroffizier *m.* non-commissioned officer, corporal.

unterordnen *v.t.* to subordinate.

Unter: ~**ordnung** *f.* subordination; ~**pfand** *n.* pledge; pawn, mortgage.

Unterproduktion *f.* underproduction.

unterreden (sich) *v.refl.* to converse.

Unterredung *f.* conversation; conference.

Unterricht *m.* (-[e]s, 0) instruction, teaching, lessons *pl.*

unterrichten *v.t.* to instruct, to teach; to inform.

Unterrichts: ~**fach** *n.* subject; ~**ministerium** *n.* Department of Education.

unterrühren *v.t.* to stir in.

unters = **unter das.**

untersagen *v.t.* to forbid, to prohibit.

Untersatz *m.* stand, support.

unterschätzen *v.t.* to underrate, to underestimate.

Unterschätzung *f.* (-, 0) undervaluation.

unterscheiden *v.t. & i.st.* to distinguish, to discern; to discriminate; **sich** ~ *v.refl.* to differ.

unterscheidend *a.* distinctive.

Unterscheidung *f.* distinction.

Unterschenkel *m.* shank, lower leg.

unterschieben *v.t.st.* to push under; (*fig.*) to accuse falsely.

Unterschiebung *f.* (-, -en) false accusation.

Unterschied *m.* (-[e]s, -e) difference.

unterschiedlich *a.* distinct, various.

unterschiedslos *a.* indiscriminate.

unterschlagen *v.t.st.* (*Geld*) to embezzle; to intercept; to misappropriate.

Unterschlagung *f.* (-, -en) embezzlement; interception (of letters); misappropriation.

Unterschlupf *m.* shelter; hide-out.

unterschreiben *v.t.st.* to subscribe; to sign.

unterschreiten *v.t.st.* to fall below.

Unterschrift *f.* signature.

unterschwellig *a.* subliminal.

Unterseeboot *n.* submarine.

unterseeisch *a.* submarine.

Unterseekabel *n.* submarine cable.

untersetzt *a.* stocky.

Untersetzer *m.* mat; coaster (glass).

untersinken *v.i.st.* (s) to go down, to sink.

unterspülen *v.t.* to wash away.

Unterspülung *f.* washout.

unterst *a.* lowest, undermost.

Unterstaatssekretär *m.* Under-Secretary of State.

Unterstand *m.* (*mil.*) dug-out.

unterstehen (sich) *v.refl.st.* to dare, to venture; *einem ~,* to be under another's orders.

unterstellen *v.t.* to place *or* put under; to insinuate, to impute; (sich) ~ *v.refl.* to take shelter.

Unterstellung *f.* (-, -en) insinuation; allegation.

unterstreichen *v.t.st.* to underline; to emphasize.

Unterströmung *f.* undercurrent.

unterstützen *v.t.* to support; to assist.

Unterstützung *f.* (-, -en) aid, support; assistance, relief.

untersuchen *v.t.* to search; to examine, to investigate.

Untersuchung *f.* (-, -en) inquiry, examination, investigation; (*chem.*) analysis.

Untersuchungs: ~**haft** *f.* pretrial detention; *in ~ nehmen,* to commit for trial; *~ anrechnen,* to make allowance for the period of custody; ~**richter** *m.* examining magistrate.

untertags *adv.* by day.

untertan *a.* subject, obedient.

Untertan *m.* (-s, *u.* -en, -en) subject.

untertänig *a.* subservient; submissive.

Untertasse *f.* saucer.
untertauchen *v.t. & i.* (*s*) to dip, to immerse, to duck; to dive.
Unterteil *n. & m.* lower part.
unterteilen *v.t.* to subdivide.
Unterteilung *f.* (-, -en) subdivision.
Untertitel *m.* (-s, -) subtitle
Unterton *m.* undertone.
untertreiben *v.i.st.* to understate.
Untertreibung *f.* (-, -en) understatement.
untervermieten *v.t.u.i.* to sublet.
Untervermietung *f.* subletting.
unterwandern *v.t.* to infiltrate.
Unterwäsche *f.* underwear.
unterwegs *adv.* on the way; in transit, en route.
unterweisen *v.t.st.* to instruct, to teach.
Unterweisung *f.* (-, -en) instruction.
Unterwelt *f.* underworld.
unterwerfen *v.t.st.* to subject; to subjugate, to subdue; (sich) ~ *v.refl.st.* to submit.
Unterwerfung *f.* (-, 0) subjection; submission; resignation (to).
unterwühlen *v.t.* to undermine.
unterwürfig *a.* submissive.
unterzeichnen *v.t.* to subscribe; to sign.
Unterzeichner *m.* (-s, -) signatory.
Unterzeichnete *m./f.* (-n, -n) undersigned.
Unterzeichnung *f.* (-, -en) signing; ratification (of a treaty).
unterziehen (sich) *v.refl.st.* to undergo; *v.t.st.* to put on underneath.
Untiefe *f.* shallow place, shoal.
Untier *n.* monster.
untilgbar *a.* (*Schuld*) irredeemable.
untragbar *a.* unbearable.
untrennbar *a.* inseparable.
untreu *a.* unfaithful; disloyal.
Untreue *f.* unfaithfulness; disloyalty.
untröstlich *a.* disconsolate, inconsolable.
untrüglich *a.* infallible, unmistakable.
untüchtig *a.* unfit, incapable.
Untugend *f.* vice; bad habit.
unüberlegt *a.* rash, inconsiderate.
unübersehbar *a.* vast, immense; obvious.
unübersichtlich *a.* badly arranged; confusing.
unübertrefflich *a.* unequalled, unrivalled.
unübertroffen *a.* unbeaten, unsurpassed.
unüberwindlich *a.* invincible; insurmountable.
unumgänglich *a.* indispensable; *adv.* absolutely.
unumschränkt *a.* unlimited, absolute.
unumstößlich *a.* irrefutable; irrevocable.
unumwunden *a.* frank, plain.
ununterbrochen *a.* uninterrupted; ~ *adv.* without interruption.
unveränderlich *a.* unchangeable; unchanging.
unverändert *a.* unaltered, unchanged.
unverantwortlich *a.* irresponsible.
unveräußerlich *a.* inalienable.
unverbesserlich *a.* incorrigible.
unverbindlich *a.* not binding; *adv.* without any commitment.
unverblümt *a.* plain, frank, blunt.
unverbrüchlich *a.* inviolable.
unverbürgt *a.* unconfirmed.
unverdächtig *a.* unsuspicious.
unverdaulich *a.* indigestible.

unvereinbar *a.* incompatible.
unverdaut *a.* undigested.
unverdient *a.* underserved, unmerited.
unverdorben *a.* uncorrupted, unspoilt.
unverdrossen *a.* indefatigable.
unvereidigt *a.* unsworn.
unvereinbar *a.* incompatible (with).
unverfälscht *a.* unadulterated, genuine.
unverfänglich *a.* innocuous, harmless.
unverfroren *a.* (*fam.*) impudent, insolent.
unvergänglich *a.* imperishable; immortal.
unvergessen *a.* unforgotten.
unvergeßlich *a.* unforgettable.
unvergleichlich *a.* incomparable.
unverhältnismäßig *a.* disproportionate.
unverheiratet *a.* unmarried.
unverhofft *a.* unexpected.
unverhohlen *a.* unconcealed, open.
unverkäuflich *a.* unsal(e)able.
unverkauft *a.* sold.
unverkennbar *a.* unmistakable.
unverletzbar, unverletzlich *a.* inviolable.
unverletzt *a.* intact, uninjured.
unvermeidlich *a.* inevitable.
unvermindert *a.* undiminished, unabated.
unvermittelt *a.* sudden, abrupt.
Unvermögen *n.* inability; impotence.
unvermögend *a.* unable; penniless.
unvermutet *a.* unexpected.
unvernehmlich *a.* inaudible, indistinct.
Unvernunft *f.* unreasonableness.
unvernünftig *a.* unreasonable; irrational.
unveröffentlicht *a.* unpublished.
unverrichtet *a.* unperformed; ~*er Sache*, unsuccessfully; with empty hands.
unverschämt *a.* impudent; impertinent.
Unverschämtheit *f.* impudence; impertinence.
unversehens *adv.* unexpectedly.
unversehrt *a.* safe, uninjured, intact.
unversiegbar *a.* inexhaustible, perennial.
unversiegelt *a.* unsealed.
unversöhnlich *a.* irreconcilable.
unversorgt *a.* unprovided for.
Unverstand *m.* folly.
unverständig *a.* ignorant; unable to understand.
unverständlich *a.* unintelligible.
Unverständnis *f.* (-nisses, 0) incomprehension.
unversucht *a.* untried.
unverträglich *a.* unsuitable; quarrelsome; incompatible.
unvertretbar *a.* unjustifiable.
unverwandt *a.* steadfast, fixed.
unverwechselbar *a.* unmistakable.
unverwehrt *a.* *es ist dir ~ zu . . .*, you are quite free to . . .
unverweilt *adv.* without delay.
unverwundbar *a.* invulnerable.
unverwüstlich *a.* indestructible.
unverzagt *a.* intrepid, undaunted.
unverzeihlich *a.* unpardonable; inexcusable.
unverzinslich *a. & adv.* non-interest-bearing.
unverzollt *a.* duty unpaid.
unverzüglich *a. & adv.* immediate; without delay, immediately.
unvollendet *a.* unfinished.
unvollkommen *a.* imperfect.

Unvollkommenheit *f.* imperfection.
unvollständig *a.* incomplete.
unvollzählig *a.* incomplete number.
unvorbereitet *a.* unprepared.
unvorhergesehen *a.* unforeseen.
unvorhersehbar *a.* unforeseeable.
unvorsichtig *a.* careless, heedless.
Unvorsichtigkeit *f.* (-, -en) imprudence.
unvorstellbar *a.* inconceivable.
unvorteilhaft *a.* unattractive; unprofitable.
unwahr *a.* untrue, false, feigned.
Unwahrheit *f.* (-, -en) untruth, falsehood.
Unwahrscheinlichkeit *f.* (-, -en) improbability.
unwandelbar *a.* immutable, invariable.
unwegsam *a.* impassable.
unweigerlich *a. & adv.* inevitab(ly).
unweit *pr.* not far from, near.
unwert *a.* unworthy.
Unwesen *n.* (-s, 0) nuisance; *sein ~ treiben,* to be up to one's tricks.
unwesentlich *a.* immaterial, irrelevant.
Unwetter *n.* storm.
unwichtig *a.* unimportant.
unwiderlegbar, unwiderleglich *a.* irrefutable.
unwiderufflich *a.* irrevocable.
unwidersprochen *a.* unchallenged.
unwiderstehlich *a.* irresistible.
unwiederbringlich *a.* irretrievble.
Unwille *m.* displeasure, indignation.
unwillig *a. & adv.* indignant(ly), reluctant(ly).
unwillkommen *a.* unwelcome.
unwillkürlich *a.* involuntary; spontaneous.
unwirklich *a.* unreal.
unwirksam *a.* ineffective.
unwirsch *a.* harsh.
unwirtlich *a.* inhospitable.
unwirtschaftlich *a.* uneconomical.
Unwissen *n.* ignorance.
unwissend *a.* ignorant.
Unwissenheit *f.* (-, 0) ignorance.
unwissenschaftlich *a.* unscientific.
unwissentlich *adv.* unknowingly.
unwohl *a.* indisposed, unwell; *sich ~ fühlen,* to feel unwell.
Unwohlsein *n.* (-s, 0) indisposition.
unwohnlich *a.* uninhabitable.
unwürdig *a.* (-, 0) unworthy; undeserving.
Unzahl *f.* (-, 0) immense number.
unzählbar, unzählig *a.* innumerable, uncountable; countless.
unzähmbar *a.* untameable.
unzart *a.* (-, -en) indelicate, rude.
Unze *f.* (-, -n) ounce.
Unzeit *f. zur ~,* inopportunely.
unzeitgemäß *a.* old-fashioned.
unzeitig *a.* untimely, unseasonable.
unzensiert *a.* uncensored.
unzerbrechlich *a.* unbreakable.
unzerreißbar *a.* untearable; (*fig.*) indisoluble.
unzerstörbar *a.* indestructible.
unzertrennlich *a.* inseparable.
unzivilisiert *a.* uncivilized, uncultured.
Unzucht *f.* (-, 0) sexual offense.
unzüchtig *a.* obscene; indecent.
unzufreiden *a.* discontented, dissatisfied.
Unzufreidene *m./f.* (-n. -n) malcontent.

Unzufriedenheit *f.* discontent, dissatisfaction.
unzugänglich *a.* inaccessible.
unzulänglich *a.* insufficient, inadequate.
Unzulänglichkeit *f.* (-, -en) insufficiency, inadequacy.
unzulässig *a.* inadmissible.
unzumutbar *a.* unreasonable.
unzurechnungsfähig *a.* not responsible for one's actions.
unzureichend *a.* insufficient.
unzusammenhängend *a.* incoherent.
unzuständig *a.* not competent.
unzuträglich *a.* disadvantageous; unhealthy; bad for.
unzutreffend *a.* inappropriate; incorrect.
unzuverlässig *a.* unreliable.
Unzuverlässigkeit *f.* unreliability.
unzweckmässig *a.* unsuitable.
unzweideutig *a.* unequivocal.
unzweifelhaft *a.* undoubted; indubitable; *~ adv.* doubtless, without doubt, indubitably.
üppig *a.* luxurious; luxuriant, opulent, sumptuous.
Üppigkeit *f.* (-, -en) lushness; luxuriance.
Ur *m.* (-[e]s, -en) aurochs.
Urabstimmung *f.* strike ballot.
Urahn *m.* ancestor.
uralt *a.* very old, very ancient.
Uran *n.* uranium.
Uraufführung *f.* (-, -en) première, first night.
urbar *a.* arable; *~ machen,* to bring under cultivation.
Urbeginn *m.* first beginning.
Urbevölkerung *f.* native population.
Urbild *a.* prototype.
Urchristentum *n.* primitive Christianity.
ureigen *a.* very own; original.
Ureinwohner *m.* original inhabitant.
Urelten *pl.* ancestors.
Urenkel *m.* great-grandson.
Urenkelin *f.* great-granddaughter.
Urform *f.* archetype.
Urgeschichte *f.* primitive history.
Urgestalt *f.* archetype, prototype.
Urgroßmutter *f.* great-grandmother.
Urgroßvater *m.* great-grandfather.
Urheber *m.* (-s, -) author, originator.
Urheberrecht *n.* copyright.
Urheberschaft *f.* (-, 0) authorship.
Urin *m.* (-[e]s, 0) urine; *~lassen,* to urinate.
urinieren *v.i.* to urinate.
Urinprobe *f.* urine specimen.
urkomisch *a.* irresistibly ludicrous.
Urknall *m.* big bang.
Urkunde (-, -n) record, document.
Urkundenbeweis *m.* documentary evidence.
urkundlich *a.* authentic; documentary.
Urlaub *m.* (-[e]s, -e) vacation; holiday; leave (of absence).
Urlauber *m.* (-s, -); **Urlauberin** *f.* (-, -nen) vacationer.
Urmensch *m.* primitive man.
Urne *f.* (-, -n) urn.
Urologe *m.;* **Urologin** *f.* urologist.
urplötzlich *a.* very sudden.
Ursache *f.* (-, -en) cause; reason; motive.
ursächlich *a.* causal; causative.

Urschrei *m.* primal scream.
Urschrift *f.* original (text).
Ursprung *m.* (-[e]s, -sprünge) source, origin; *seinen*
~ *haben* or *nehmen von,* to originate in.
ursprünglich *a.* original, primitive.
Ursprungsland *n.* country of origin.
Urteil *n.* (-[e]s, -e) judgment; sentence, verdict;
einem das ~ *sprechen,* to pass sentence upon
someone.
urteilen *v.t. & i.* judge.
Urteilsbegründung *f.* reasons for the verdict.
Urteilskraft *f.* (power of) judgment.
Urteilsspruch *m.* sentence.
Urtext *m.* original (text).
Ururgroßmutter *f.* great-great grandmother.

Ururgroßvater *m.* great-great grandfather.
Urwald *m.* primeval forest; jungle
urweltlich *a.* primeval.
urwüchsig *a.* original, native; rough.
Urzeit *f.* primeval times.
Urzustand *m.* original state.
Usurpator *m.* (-s, -storen) usurper.
Usus *m.* (-, 0) usage, custom.
Utensilien *pl.* utensils, implements *pl.*
Utilitarier *m.* (-s, -) utilitarian.
Utopie *f.* (-, -n) utopia, utopian scheme.
utopisch *a.* utopian.
UV-strahlen *pl.* UV rays.
Ü-Wagen *m.* outside broadcast van.
uzen *v.t.* to tease, to chaff, to mock.

V

v *n.* the letter V or v.
vag *a.* vague, loose.
Vagabond *m.* (-en, -en) vagabond.
vagabundieren *v.i.* to tramp (about).
vage *a.* vague.
Vagina *f.* (-, -nen) vagina.
vakant *a.* vacant.
Vakanz *f.* (-, -en) vacancy.
Vakuum *n.* (-s, -kuen) vacuum.
Valuta *f.* (-, -uten) currency.
Vamp *m.* (-s, -s) vamp.
Vampir *m.* (-[e]s, -e) vampire.
Vandalismus *m.* (-, 0) vandalism.
Vanille *f.* (-, -n) vanilla.
variabel *a.* variable.
Variable *f.* variable.
Variante *f.* (-, -n) variant; variation.
Varieté *n.* (-s, -s) music hall, vaudeville (theater).
variieren *v.t. & i.* to vary; to fluctuate.
Vasall *m.* (-en, -en) vassal.
Vasallenstaat *m.* satellite state.
Vase *f.* (-, -en) vase.
Vaselin *n.* (-s, -e) vaseline.
Vater *m.* (-s, **Väter**) father.
Vater: ~**haus** *n.* parental house, home; ~**land** *n.*
native country, fatherland.
vaterländisch *a.* patriotic.
Vaterlandsliebe *f.* patriotism.
väterlich *a.* fatherly; paternal.
Vater: ~**mord** *m.* patricide; ~**mörder** *m.* patricide.
Vaterschaft *f.* (-, 0) paternity; fatherhood;
~**sklage** *f.* paternity suit.
Vaterstadt *f.* native town.
Vaterunser *n.* (-s, -) Lord's prayer.
Vegetarier *m.* (-s, -); **Vegetarierin** *f.* (-, -nen)
vegetarian.
vegetarisch *a.* vegetarian.
Vegetation *f.* (-, -en) vegetation.
vegetieren *v.i.* to vegetate.
vehement *a. & adv.* vehement(ly).
Veilchen *n.* (-s, -) violet.
veilchenblau *a.* violet(-colored).
Veitstanz *m.* St. Vitus' dance.
Vektor *m.* (-s, -en) vector.
Vene *f.* (-, -n) vein.
Venenentzündung *f.* (*med.*) phlebitis.
venerisch *a.* venereal.

Ventil *n.* (-[e]s, -e) valve
Ventilaton *f.* (-, -en) ventilation.
Ventilator *m.* (-s, -en) ventilator, fan.
ventilieren *v.t.* to ventilate.
Venus *f.* Venus.
verabfolgen *v.t. & t.* to deliver.
verabreden *v.t.*, (sich) ~ *v.refl.* to agree upon; to
make an appointment.
Verabredung *f.* (-, -en) appointment; *nach* ~, by
appointment; *eine Verabredung treffen,* to make an
appointment.
verabreichen *v.t.* to administer, to give.
verabsäumen *v.t.* to neglect, to omit.
verabscheuen *v.t.* detest.
verabscheuungswürdig *a.* detestable; abominable.
verabschieden *v.t.* to say goodbye; to discharge; to
adopt (plan); to pass (law); (sich) ~ *v.refl.* to say
goodbye.
Verabschiedung *f.* (-en) leave-taking; retirement;
adoption (plan); passing (law).
verachten *v.t.* to despise, to scorn, to disdain.
Verächter *m.* (-s, -) opponent.
verächtlich *a.* contemptible, despicable; (*verachtend*) contemptuous.
Verachtung *f.* (-, 0) contempt, scorn.
veralbern *v.t.* to make fun of.
verallgemeinern *v.t.* to generalize.
Verallgemeinerung *f.* generalization.
veralten *v.i.* (*s*) to become obsolete.
veraltet *a.* obsolete, antiquated.
Veranda *f.* (-, -den) porch; veranda.
veränderlich *a.* variable; changeable.
Veränderlichkeit *f.* changeability; variability.
verändern *v.t.* to alter; to change.
Veränderung *f.* (-, -en) change, alteration.
verängstigen *v.t.* to frighten; to scare.
verankern *v.t.* (*nav.*) to anchor; (*fig.*) to establish
firmly; (*mech.*) to stay.
veranlagen *v.t.* to assess (taxes); *gut veranlagt,*
gifted, clever.
Veranlagung *f.* (-, -en) disposition; assessment;
talent, aptitude (for).
veranlassen *v.t.* to occasion; to cause; to induce
(one to do something).
Veranlassung *f.* (-, -en) occasion.
veranschaulichen *v.t.* to illustrate.

Veranschaulichung *f.* (-. -en) illustration.
veranschlagen *v.t.* to estimate (at).
veranstalten *v.t.* to arrange, to organize.
Veranstaltung *f.* (-, -en) function; (*Sport*) event.
verantworten *v.t.* to answer for; to take responsibility; (sich) ~ *v.refl.* to justify *or* defend oneself.
verantwortlich *a.* responsible, accountable.
Verantwortung *f.* (-, 0) responsibility; *zur ~ ziehen,* to call to account.
verantwortungsbewußt *a.* responsible.
Verantwortungsgefühl *n.* sense of responsibility.
verantwortungsvoll *a.* involving great responsibility, responsible.
verarbeiten *v.t.* to process, to digest; to assimilate (film); to come to terms with.
verargen *v.t.* to blame (one) for.
verärgert *a.* annoyed.
verarmen *v.i.* (s) to become poor.
verarmt *a.* impoverished.
verästeln (sich) ~ *v.refl.* to ramify.
Verästelung *f.* (-, -en) ramification.
verausgaben *v.t.* to pay away, to spend (in, on); (sich) ~ (*v.refl.*) to run out of money; to exhaust oneself.
veräußern *v.t.* to dispose of; to sell.
Verb *n.* (-s, -en) verb.
verbal *a. & adv.* verbal(ly).
verballhornen *v.t.* to corrupt, distort.
Verband *m.* (-[e]s, -bände) association, federation, union; (*einer Wunde*) dressing, bandage.
Verbandplatz *m.* first-aid station.
Verbandskasten *m.* first-aid kit.
Verbandzeug *n.* first aid.
verbannen *v.t.* to banish.
Verbannte *m./f.* (-n, -n) exile.
Verbannung *f.* (-, 0) banishment, exile.
verbarrikadieren *v.t.* to barricade.
verbauen *v.t.* (*fig.*) to obstruct.
verbeißen *v.t.st.* (*fig.*) to suppress by an effort.
verbergen *v.t.st.* to conceal, to hide.
verbessern *v.t.* to correct; to improve.
Verbesserung *f.* improvement.
verbesserungsfähig *a.* capable of improvement.
verbeugen (sich) *v.refl.* to bow (to).
Verbeugung *f.* (-, -en) bow.
verbeulen *v.t.* to dent.
verbiegen *v.t.st.* to bend out of shape.
verbieten *v.t.st.* to forbid, to prohibit, to ban.
verbilligen *v.t.* to lower the prices.
verbinden *v.t.st.* to dress (a wound); to join; to connect; (*Telephon*) to put through; (sich) ~ *v.refl.* to unite oneself (with), to join.
verbindlich *a.* obliging; obligatory, binding.
Verbindlichkeit *f.* (-, -en) obligation, liability, engagement; civility, obligingness.
Verbindung *f.* (-, -en) connection; union, alliance; junction; society, club; communication; (*chem.*) compound; *mit einem in ~ stehen,* to be in touch with one; *in ~ bleiben,* to keep in touch; *sich in ~ setzen,* to get in touch.
Verbindungs: ~**glied** *n.* connecting link; ~**linie** *f.* line of communication; ~**offizier** *m.* liaison officer.
verbissen *a.* dogged, obstinate.
verbitten (sich) *v.refl.st.* to deprecate.
verbittern *v.t.* to embitter, to exasperate.

verblassen *v.i.* (s) to fade; to turn pale.
Verbleib *m.* (-[e]s, 0) whereabouts; staying.
verbleiben *v.i.st.* (s) to remain.
verblenden *v.t.* to delude; to blind.
Verblendung *f.* (-. 0) infatuation.
verblichen *a.* faded; deceased.
verblüffen *v.t.* to amaze; to baffle.
verblühen *v.i.* (s) to wither, to fade.
verblümt *a.* allusive; ~ *adv.* by innuendo.
verbluten *v.refl.* to bleed to death.
verbohren *v.t. sich in etwas ~,* to become obsessed; *ein verbohrter Mensch,* a crank, a faddist.
verborgen *a.* concealed, secret.
Verbot *n.* (-[e]s, -e) prohibition; (*amtlich*) ban.
verbrämen *v.t.* to border, to trim.
verbrannte Erde (mil.) scorched earth.
Verbrauch *m.* (-[e]s, 0) consumption, use; (*mil. Munitions~*) expenditure.
verbrauchen *v.t.* to consume.
Verbraucher *m.* (-s, -); **Verbraucherin** *f.* (-, -nen) consumer.
Verbraucher: ~**schutz** *m.* consumer protection; ~**umfrage** *f.* consumer survey.
Verbrauchsgüter *pl.* consumer goods.
Verbrauchsteuer *f.* excise duty.
verbraucht *a.* used.
Verbrechen *n.* (-s, -) crime, offence.
verbrechen *v.t.st.* to commit, (ironically) to perpetrate.
Verbrecher *m.* (-s, -); **Verbrecherin** *f.* (-, -nen) criminal, convict.
verbrecherisch *a.* criminal.
verbreiten *v.t.* to spread, to diffuse, to disseminate; (sich) ~ *v.refl.* to spread; (*fig.*) to enlarge upon.
verbreitern *v.t.* to widen.
Verbreitung *f.* (-, 0) propagation; diffusion.
verbrennbar *a.* combustible.
verbrennen *v.t.ir.* to burn; ~ *v.i.ir.* (s) to be burnt (down); (sich) ~ *v.refl.* to burn *or* scald oneself.
Verbrennung *f.* (-, 0) burning; incineration; combustion.
verbriefen *v.t.* to document, guarantee; *verbriefte Rechte pl.* vested rights *pl.*
verbringen *v.t.st.* to pass, to spend.
verbrüdern (sich) *v.refl.* to fraternize.
Verbrüderung *f.* (-, -en) fraternization.
verbrühen *v.t.* to scald.
verbuchen *v.t.* to book.
verbummeln *v.t.* (*fam.*) to idle away; to forget.
verbunden *a.* obliged; connected.
verbünden (sich) *v.refl.* to ally oneself (to *or* with).
Verbündete *m./f.* (-n, -n) ally.
verbürgen *v.t.* to warrant; *sich ~ für,* to vouch for, to guarantee.
verbüssen *v.t.* to serve one's time.
verchromt *a.* chromium-plated.
Verdacht *m.* (-[e]s, 0) suspision; *über allen ~ erhaben,* above suspicion.
verdächtig *a.* suspect, suspicious.
verdächtigen *v.t.* to suspect; to cast suspicion on.
Verdächtigung *f.* (-, -en) suspicion; insinuation.
Verdachtsperson *f.*, **Verdächtiger** *m.* suspect.
verdammen *v.t.* to condemn; to damn.
verdammlich *a.* damnable.
Verdammnis *f.* (-, 0) damnation.
verdammt *adv.* damned.

Verdammung f. (-, -en) damnation; condemnation.

verdampfen v.i. (s) to evaporate.

verdanken v.t. to owe, to be indebted for (a thing to one).

verdauen v.t. to digest.

verdaulich a. digestible.

Verdauung f. (-, 0) digestion.

Verdauungs: ~**beschwerden** pl. indigestion; ~**kanal** m. digestive tract; ~**system** n. digestive system.

Verdeck n. (-[e]s, -e) top; hood (car).

verdecken v.t. to cover, to hide.

verdenken v.t.ir. ich kann es ihr nicht ~ I can't blame her.

verderben v.t.st. to spoil; to corrupt; ~ v.i.st. (s) to be spoiled, to go bad; sich den Magen ~, to upset one's stomach; es mit einem nicht ~ wollen, not want to quarrel with s.b.

Verderben n. (-s, 0) ruin; downfall.

verderblich a. pernicious; (Waren) perishable; fatal.

Verderbnis n. (-nisses, -nisse) corruption; decay.

verdeutlichen v.t. to make plain.

verdeutschen v.t. to translate into German.

verdichten v.t. to condense.

verdicken v.t. u.refl. to thicken.

verdienen v.t. to gain, to earn; to deserve, to merit; sich verdient machen um, to deserve well of.

Verdienst m. (-es, 0) gain, profit; earnings pl.

Verdienst n. (-es, -e) merit, desert.

Verdienstausfall m. lost earnings.

verdienstvoll a. deserving, able.

verdient a. deserving, meritorious; (Strafe) deserved.

Verdikt n. (-[e]s, -e) verdict.

verdingen v.t.r. & st. to hire (out).

verdolmetschen v.t. to interpret.

verdonnern v.t. (fam.) to sentence.

verdoppeln v.t. to double.

verdorben a. spoiled; depraved; ~er Magen, upset stomach.

verdorren v.i. (s) to dry up, to wither.

verdrängen v.t. to displace.

Verdrängung f. displacement; repression, suppression; inhibition.

verdrehen v.t. to twist; (fig.) to misrepresent, to distort.

verdreht a. distorted; (fig.) cracked, flighty.

Verdrehung f. (-, -en) distortion.

verdreifachen v.t. to treble.

verdreschen v.t.st. to thrash.

verdrießen v.t.imp.st. to vex, to annoy, to grieve.

verdrießlich a. tiresome, annoying; vexed; peevish, morose.

verdrossen a. sullen, unwilling.

Verdrossenheit f. moroseness; sullenness.

verdrücken v.t. (fam.) to polish off; to crumple (fabric); v.refl. to slip away.

Verdruß m. (-drusses, 0) annoyance, trouble.

verduften v.i. (fam.) to slip away; to clear off.

verdummen v.t. to make stupid; to stultify; ~ v.i. (s) to become stupid.

verdunkeln v.t. to darken; to obscure; (fig.) to eclipse.

Verdunkelung f. (-, -en) darkening; (Luftschutz) blackout.

verdünnen v.t. to dilute.

Verdünnung f. dilution.

verdunsten v.i. (s) to evaporate.

verdursten v.i. (s) to die of thirst.

verdüstern v.refl. to darken.

verdüstert a. (fig.) gloomy.

verdutzt a. baffled; nonplussed.

veredeln v.t. to improve, to refine.

verehelichen v.t. & refl. (sich) to marry.

verehren v.t. to venerate, to revere; to worship, to adore.

Verehrer m. (-s, -) ; **Verehrerin** f. (-, -en) worshipper; admirer.

Verehrung f. (-, 0) veneration; worship.

verehrungswürdig a. venerable.

vereidigen v.t. to administer an oath to; to swear (in).

Vereidigung f. (-, -en) swearing in.

Verein m. (-s, -e) union, society, club; im ~ mit meinem Freunde, jointly with my friend.

vereinbar a. compatible, consistent.

vereinbaren v.t. to agree; to arrange.

Vereinbarung f. (-, -en) agreement.

vereinen v.t. to unite; to reconcile; (sich) ~ v.refl. to unite; die Vereinigten Staaten, the United States.

vereinfachen v.t. to simplify.

vereinheitlichen v.t. to standardize.

vereinigen v.t. to unite; to merge, to combine.

vereinigt a. united.

Vereinigung f. (-, -en) association; organization.

vereinnahmen v.t. to receive, to take.

vereinsamen v.i. to become lonely.

vereinzelt a. sporadic; occasional.

Vereinzelung f. (-, 0) isolation.

vereisen v.i. to freeze over; to ice over.

vereiteln v.t. to frustrate; to prevent.

vereitert a. septic.

verekeln v.t. to render loathsome.

verenden v.i. (s) to die.

verengen v.t. to narrow, to contract.

vererbbar a. inheritable.

vererben v.t. to bequeath, to leave; to transmit (disease); (sich) ~ v.refl. to be hereditary, to run in the family.

Vererbung f. (-, 0) heredity; hereditary transmission.

verewigen v.t. to immortalize.

verfahren v.i.s.t. (s) to proceed, to go to work, to act; ~ v.t.st. to bungle; v.refl.st. to lose one's way.

verfahren a. muddled.

Verfahren n. (-s, -) method, procedure; (chem.) process; (law) proceedings; beschleunigtes ~, summary proceedings.

Verfahrensfrage f. procedural question.

Verfall m. (-[e]s, 0) decay, decline, ruin; forfeiture; (eines Wechsels) maturity.

verfallen v.i.st. (s) to decay; to decline; (von Wechseln) to fall due; (Rechte) to lapse; to expire; auf einen Gedanken ~, to hit upon an idea; das Pfand ist ~, the pledge is forfeited.

Verfalltag m. day of maturity.

verfälschen v.t. to falsify; to adulterate.

verfangen v.i.st. to take effect, to tell; das verfängt bei mir nicht, you need not try that with me; (sich) ~ v.refl. to get entangled.

verfänglich *a.* risky, awkward.
verfärben (sich) *v.refl.* to change color; to discolor.
verfassen *v.t.* to compose, to write.
Verfasser *m.* (-s, -), **Verfasserin** *f.* (-, -nen) author; writer.
Verfassung *f.* (-, -en) constitution; state.
verfassunggebend *a.* constituent.
verfassungsmäßig *a.* constitutional.
Verassungsrecht *n.* constitutional law.
verfassungswidrig *a.* unconstitutional.
verfaulen *v.i.* (*s*) to rot, to putrify.
verfechten *v.t.st.* to advocate; to champion.
verfehlen *v.t.* to miss.
Verfehlung *f.* (-, -en) misdemeanour.
verfehlt *a.* unsuccessful, abortive.
verfeinden *v.t.* to set (one) against (another); (sich) ~ *v.refl.* to fall out with.
verfeinern *v.t.* to refine, to polish.
verfertigen *v.t.* to make, to manufacture.
verfestigen *v.t. u.refl.* to harden.
Verfettung *f.* (-, 0) adiposis.
verfilmen *v.t.* to film, to make a film of.
verfilzen *v.i.* to become felted/matted.
verfinstern *v.t. u.refl.* to darken; to eclipse.
Verfinsterung *f.* (-, -en) eclipse.
verflachen *v.t.* to flatten, to level.
verflechten *v.t.st.* to interlace; to entangle in.
verfliegen *v.i.st.* (*s*) to evaporate, to vanish.
verflossen *a.* (*fam.*) former.
verfluchen *v.t.* to curse, to execrate.
verflucht *a.* damned; cursed.
verflüchtigen *v.i.* (*s*) (sich) ~ *v.refl.* to evaporate, to vanish.
verfolgen *v.t.* to pursue; to persecute; (eine Sache) to follow up; *gerichtlich* ~, to prosecute at law.
Verfolger *m.* (-s, -); **Verfolgerin** *f.* (-, -nen) pursuer.
Verfolgte *m./f.* victim of persecution; **politisch** ~ victim of political persecution.
Verfolgung *f.* (-, -en) pursuit; persecution; **strafrechtliche** ~ prosecution.
Verfolgungswahn *m.* persecution mania.
verfrachten *v.t.* to freight; to load; to ship.
verfressen *a.* greedy.
verfroren *a.* sensitive to the cold.
verfrüht *a.* premature.
verfügbar *a.* available.
verfügen *v.t.* to order; ~ *v.i.* to dispose (of).
Verfügung *f.* (-, -en) disposition, disposal; order, decree, injunction; (*gerichtlich*) rule; ~**srecht** *n.* power of disposal.
verführen *v.t.* to tempt; to seduce.
Verführer *m.* (-s, -) seducer.
Verführerin *f.* (-, -nen) seductress.
verführerisch *a.* tempting, seductive.
Verführung *f.* (-, -en) temptation; seduction.
verfüttern *v.t.* to feed; to use as animal food.
vergällen *v.t.* (*fig.*) to spoil.
vergammeln *v.i.* (*fam.*) to rot; *v.t.* to waste (time).
vergammelt *a.* (*fam.*) scruffy; rotten.
vergangen *a.* past, last, bygone.
Vergangenheit *f.* (-, 0) the past, time past; (*gram.*) past tense.
vergänglich *a.* transient; transitory; ephemeral.
Vergänglichkeit *f.* transience; transitoriness.
Vergaser *m.* (-s, -) carburetor.

vergeben *v.t.st.* to forgive, to pardon; to give away, to dispose of; *seiner Ehre etwas* ~, to compromise one's honor.
vergebens *adv.* in vain, vainly.
vergeblich *a.* futile; vain, fruitless.
Vergeblichkeit *f.* futility.
Vergebung *f.* (-, 0) forgiveness, pardon.
vergegenwärtigen *v.refl.* to figure, to represent, to visualize; to realize.
vergehen *v.i.st.* (*s*) to pass away, to elapse; to vanish; *sich* ~, to offend; to violate.
Vergehen *n.* (-s, -) fault, offense; misdemeanor.
vergeistigen *v.t.* to spiritualize.
vergelten *v.t.st.* to requite, to return, to repay.
Vergeltung *f.* (-, 0) repayment; (*feindliche*) retaliation, reprisal.
vergessen *v.t.st.* to forget; (sich) ~ *v.refl.* to forget oneself.
Vergessenheit *f.* (-, 0) oblivion.
vergeßlich *a.* forgetful.
Vergeßlichkeit *f.* forgetfulness.
vergeuden *v.t.* to squander, to waste.
Vergeudung *f.* (-, -en) squandering; waste.
vergewaltigen *v.t.* to violate; to rape; to oppress.
Vergewaltigung *f.* (-, -en) rape; violation.
vergiwissern (sich) ~ *v.refl.* to ascertain, to make sure of.
Vergewisserung *f.* (-, 0) confirmation.
vergießen *v.t.st.* to spill; to shed.
vergiften *v.t.* to poison; (*fig.*) to envenom, to embitter.
Vergiftung *f.* (-, -en) poisoning.
vergilbt *a.* yellowed.
Vergißmeinnicht *n.* (-s, -) forget-me-not.
vergittern *v.t.* to bar, to lattice.
verglassen *v.t.* to glaze; to vitrify.
Vergleich *m.* (-[e]s, -e) comparison; arrangement, compromise, agreement.
vergleichbar *a.* comparable.
vergleichen *v.t.st.* to compare; *sich* ~ *mit*, to compete with.
vergleichsweise *adv.* comparatively.
vergnügen *v.t.* to amuse; (sich) ~ *v.refl.* to enjoy oneself, to take pleasure in.
Vergnügen *n.* (-s, -) pleasure; diversion; ~ *finden an*, to delight in.
vergnüglich *a.* amusing; entertaining.
vergnügt *a.* pleased, cheerful.
Vergnügung *f.* pleasure, amusement.
Vergnügungspark *m.* amusement park.
Vergnügungsteuer *f.* entertainment tax.
Vergnügungsviertel *n.* night-life district.
vergolden *v.t.* to gild.
vergönnen *v.t.* to grant, to allow; not to grudge.
vergöttern *v.t.* to deify; (*fig.*) to idolize.
Vergötterung *f.* (-, -en) deification.
vergraben *v.t.st.* to bury.
vergrämt *a.* careworn.
vergraulen *v.t.* (*fam.*) to scare off.
vergreifen (sich) *v.refl.st.* to make a mistake; (*an Geld*) to embezzle.
vergriffen *a.* sold out; out of print.
vergrössern *v.t.* to magnify; (*phot.*) to enlarge; to extend; to increase.
Vergrösserung *f.* (-, -en) (*Mikroskop, etc.*) magnification; (*phot.*) enlargement; extension; increase.

Vergrösserungglas *n.* magnifying-glass.

Vergünstigung *f.* (-, -en) favor, privilege.

vergüten *v.t.* to compensate; (*Auslagen*) to reimburse.

Vergütung *f.* (-, -en) remuneration; reimbursement.

verhaften *v.t.* to arrest.

Verhaftete *m./f.* person under arrest.

Verhaftung *f.* (-, -en) arrest.

verhallen *v.i.* (s) to die away.

verhalten *v.t.st.* to retain, to keep back; (*das Lachen*) to restrain; (sich) ~ *v.refl.* to stand; to behave; *wie verhält sich die Sache?* how does the matter stand?; *sich ruhig* ~, to keep quiet.

verhalten *a.* restrained.

Verhalten *n.* (-s, 0) conduct, behaviour.

Verhaltensmaßregel *f.* rule of conduct.

Verhaltensweise *f.* (-, -n) behavior.

Verhältnis *n.* (-nisses, -nisse) proportion, rate, ratio; circumstance; state, condition; relationship, love affair; *im* ~ *zu*, in proportion to.

verhältnismäßig *adv.* relatively.

verhältniswidrig *a.* disproportionate.

Verhältniswahl *f.* proportional representation.

Verhältniswort *n.* preposition.

verhandeln *v.t. & i.* to negotiate, to treat; *gerichtlich* ~, to try, to hear a case; *erneut* ~, to retry.

Verhandlung *f.* (-, -en) negotiation; (*law*) trial, hearing; *nochmalige Verhandlung*, rehearing, retrial; *~en aufnehmen*, to enter into negotiations.

verhängen *v.t.* (*Strafe*) to inflict.

Verhängnis *n.* (-nisses, -nisse) fate, destiny.

verhängnisvoll *a.* fatal, fateful.

verhärmt *a.* careworn.

verharren *v.i.* to persist (in); to remain.

verhärten *v.t.* (h), *v.i.* (s) & (sich) ~ *v.refl.* to harden.

verhaßt *a.* hated, odious.

verhätscheln *v.t.* to pamper, to spoil.

verhauen *v.t.st.* (*fam.*) to thrash; (sich) ~ *s.refl.st.* to plunder.

verheddern *v.refl.* to tangle.

verheeren *v.t.* to devastate, to lay waste.

verheerend *a.* devastating; disastrous.

Verheerung *f.* (-, -en) devastation.

verhehlen *v.t.* to conceal, to hide.

verheilen *v.i.* (s) to heal up.

verheimlichen *v.t.* to keep (a thing) a secret; to conceal.

Verheimlichung *f.* (-, -en) concealment.

verheiraten *v.t.* to give in marriage; (sich) ~ *v.refl.* to marry, to get married.

verheißen *v.t.st.* to promise.

Verheißung *f.* (-, -en) promise.

verheißungsvoll *a.* promising.

verheizen *v.t.* to burn; to use as fuel.

verhelfen *v.i.st.* to help to.

verherrlichen *v.t.* to glorify; to extol.

Verherrlichung *f.* (-, -en) glorification.

verhetzen *v.t.* to instigate, to set (against).

Verhetzung *f.* (-, -en) instigation.

verhexen *v.t.* to bewitch.

verhindern *v.t.* to prevent.

Verhinderung *f.* (-, -en) prevention.

verhohlen *a. & adv.* secret(ly).

verhöhnen *v.t.* to mock; to ridicule; to deride.

Verhöhnung *f.* (-, -en) derision, mockery.

Verhör *n.* (-[e]s, -e) trial; cross-examination; *ins ~nehmen*, to cross-examine.

verhören *v.t.* to question, to interrogate; (sich) ~ *v.refl.* to mishear.

verhüllen *v.t.* to wrap up, to veil.

Verhüllung *f.* (-, -en) disguise.

verhundertfachen (sich) *v.i. & refl.* to increase a hundredfold; to centuple.

verhungern *v.i.* (s) to starve.

verhunzen *v.t.* to spoil.

verhüten *v.t.* to prevent, to avert.

Verhütung *f.* (-, 0) prevention; **Empfängnis~** *f.* contraception.

verirren (sich) *v.refl.* to get lost; to lose one's way.

verirrt *a.* stray(ing), erring; misled.

Verirrung *f.* (-, -en) aberration.

verjagen *v.t.* to chase away.

verjähren *v.i.* (s) to come under the statute of limitations.

verjährt *a.* cancelled by the statute of limitations; (*Schulden*) superannuated.

Verjährung *f.* (-, -en) prescription, limitation; **~sfrist** *f.* period of limitation.

verjüngen *v.t.* to rejuvenate; to reduce in size; (sich) ~ *v.refl.* to grow young again; to taper.

Verjüngung *f.* (-, -en) rejuvenation; tapering.

verkabeln *v.t.* to connect by cable (TV).

verkalken *v.i.* to calcify; to become calcified/hardened; to become senile.

Verkalkung *f.* (-, -en) calcification; hardening; senility.

verkannt *a.* misjudged, misunderstood.

verkappt *a.* disguised.

verkatert *a.* (*fam.*) hung-over.

Verkauf *m.* (-[e]s, -käufe) sale.

verkaufen *v.t.* to sell, to dispose of.

Verkäufer *m.* (-s, -) seller, (*law*) vendor; salesman, sales assistant, sales-clerk; **~in** *f.* saleswoman.

verkäuflich *a.* sal(e)able; marketable.

Verkaufpreis *m.* retail price.

Verkaufssteuer *f.* sales-tax.

Verkehr *m.* (-s, 0) traffic; contact; intercourse; *starker* ~, heavy traffic.

verkehren *v.t.* to invert; (*fig.*) to pervert; ~ *v.i.* to associate (with); to frequent (a place).

Verkehrs-: ~ampel *f.* traffic light; **~amt** *n.* tourist office; **~aufkommen** *n.* volume of traffic; **~delikt** *f.* traffic offense; **~flugzeug** *n.* commercial or passenger plane; **~insel** *f.* traffic island; **~minister** *m.* Minister of Transport; **~mittel** *f.* means of transport; **~ordnung** *f.* traffic regulations; **~regeln** *pl.* traffic code; **~regelung** *f.* traffic regulation; **~schild** *n.* traffic sign; road-sign; **~schutzmann** *m.* traffic cop; **~stau** *f.* traffic jam; **~störung** *f.* traffic hold-up; **~zeichen** *n.* traffic sign.

verkehrt *a.* inverted, upside down; wrong.

verkennen *v.t.ir.* to misjudge; to undervalue; to deny, to disbelieve.

Verkennung *f.* (-, -en) misjudgment, underestimation.

verketten *v.t.* to link together.

Verkettung *f.* (-, -en) chain; concatenation.

verkitten *v.t.* to cement.

verklagen *v.t.* to sue, to bring an action against; to

accuse.

verklären *v.t.* to glorify, to transfigure.

Verklärung *f.* (-, -en) transfiguration.

verklauseln, verklausulieren *v.t.* to limit by provisos, (*fig.*) to express in a roundabout way.

verkleben *v.a.* to paste up *or* over.

verkleiden *v.t.* to line; to disguise; (*arch.*) to face.

Verkleidung *f.* (-, -en) disguise.

verkleinern *v.t.* to diminish; to reduce; (*fig.*) to belittle, to derogate from.

Verkleinerung *f.* (-, -en) (*phot.*) reduction.

Verkleinerungsform *f.* diminutive form.

verkleistern *v.t.* to paste up, to glue up.

verklingen *v.i.st.* (*s*) to die away.

Verknappung *f.* (-, 0) shortage.

verkneifen, sich etwas ~ *v.refl.st.* (*sl.*) to do without.

verknöchern *v.i.* to ossify.

verknüpfen *v.t.* to connect; to join, to combine.

Verknüpfung *f.* (-, -en) connection.

verkommen *v.i.st.* (*s*) to be neglected, to perish, to decay.

verkörpern *v.t.* to embody.

Verkörperung *f.* (-, -en) embodiment.

verkorksen *v.t.* to mess up.

verköstigen *v.t.* to board, to feed.

verkrachen *v.refl.* to fall out.

verkrampfen *v.refl.* to cramp; to tense up (person).

verkriechen (sich) *v.refl.st.* to hide.

verkrümmt *a.* crooked.

verkrüppeln *v.t.* to cripple, to stunt.

verkrusten *v.i.* to form a crust/scab.

verkümmern *v.i.* (*s*) to pine away, to fail away; to atrophy; to be stunted, to starve.

verkünden *v.t.* to announce; to pronounce; to promulgate (law).

verkündigen *v.t.* to preach; to announce, to proclaim.

Verkündigung *f.* (-, -en) preaching; announcement, proclamation; ~ *Maria,* Annunciation Day.

Verkündung *f.* announcement; pronouncement; promulgation.

verkuppeln *v.t.* to pair off.

verkürzen *v.t.* to shorten; to abridge.

Verkürzung *f.* (-, -en) shortening.

verlachen *v.t.* to deride, to laugh at.

verladen *v.t.st.* to load; to ship; to embark.

Verladung *f.* loading.

Verlag *m.* (-[e]s, -lage) publishing house.

verlagern *v.t.* to shift.

Verlagerung *f.* shifting.

Verlags: ~**buchhändler** *m.* publisher; ~**buchhandlung** *f.* publishing house; ~**recht** *n.* copyright.

verlangen *v.t.* to demand; to desire.

Verlangen *n.* (-s, 0) desire; request, demand.

verlängern *v.t.* to lengthen, to prolong; (sich) ~ *v.refl.* to be extended.

Verlängerung *f.* (-, -en) prolongation.

verlangsamen *v.t.* to slow down.

Verlangsamung *f.* (-, -en) slow-down.

Verlaß *m. es ist auf ihn kein* ~, he is not to be relied on.

verlassen *v.t.st.* to leave; to desert; (sich) ~ **auf** *v.refl.st.* to rely *or* depend (on); ~ *a.* deserted.

Verlassenheit *f.* (-, 0) loneliness.

verläßlich *a.* reliable.

Verläßlichkeit *f.* reliability.

Verlauf *m.* (-[e]s, 0) course; lapse.

verlaufen *v.i.st.* (*s*) to elapse; (sich) ~ *v.refl.st.* to lose one's way; *wie ist die Sache* ~? how has the matter turned out?

verlautbaren *v.t.* to make known; ~ *v.imp.* to be divulged.

Verlautbarung *f.* (-, -en) announcement.

verlauten *v.imp.* to be reported.

verleben *v.t.* to spend, to pass.

verlebt *a.* dissipated.

verlegen *v.t.* to remove; to mislay; (*Weg*) to bar; (*aufschieben*) to put off; (*Buch*) to publish, to bring out; *sich* ~ *auf,* to go in for, to apply oneself to.

verlegen *a.* embarrassed.

Verlegenheit *f.* (-, -en) self-consciousness, embarrassment, dilemma.

Verleger *m.* (-s, -) publisher.

Verlegung *f.* (-, -en) removal, transfer; postponement.

verleiden *v.t.* to spoil sth. for s.b.

Verleih *m.* hiring out; distribution (film).

verleihen *v.t.st.* to lend, to let out; to confer upon, to grant; to invest with.

verleiten *v.t.* to induce/entice s.b. to do s.th.

verlernen *v.t.* to unlearn, to forget.

verlesen *v.t.st.* to read out; (sich) ~ *v.refl.* to read wrong.

verletzbar, verletzlich *a.* vulnerable.

verletzen *v.t.* to injure; to violate; to infringe; to offend.

verletzlich *a.* vulnerable.

verletzlichkeit *f.* vulnerability.

Verletzte *m./f.* injured person.

Verletzung *f.* (-, -en) hurt, injury; (*med.*) lesion; violation, infraction.

verleugnen *v.t.* to deny, to disown.

Verleugnung *f.* (-, 0) denial; abnegation.

verleumden *v.t.* to slander; to libel; to calumniate.

Verleumder *m.* (-s, -); **Verleumderin** *f.* (-, -nen) slanderer; libeler.

verleumderisch *a.* slanderous.

Verleumdung *f.* (-, -en) calumny, slander.

verlieben (sich) *v.refl.* to fall in love (with).

verliebt *a.* in love, enamored; amorous.

Verliebte *m./f.* lover.

Verliebtheit *f.* being in love.

verlieren *v.t.st.* to lose; *aus den Augen* ~, to lose sight of; ~ *v.i.* to be a loser; (sich) ~ *v.refl.* to lose one's way; to disappear gradually.

Verlierer *m.* (-s, -); **Verliererin** *f.* (-, -nen) loser.

Verlies *n.* (-es, -e) dungeon.

verloben *v.t.* to betroth; (sich) ~ *v.refl.* to become engaged (to).

Verlöbnis *n.* (-nisses, -nisse) betrothal, engagement.

verlobt *a.* engaged (to be married).

Verlobte *m.* (-n, -n) fiancé.

Verlobte *f.* (-n, -n) fiancée.

Verlobung *f.* (-, -en) engagement; *die* ~ *auflösen,* to break off the engagement.

Verlobungsring *m.* engagement ring.

verlocken *v.t.* to entice, to allure.

verlockend *a.* tempting; enticing.

Verlockung *f.* temptation; enticement.

verlogen *a.* given to lying, mendacious.

Verlogenheit *f.* falseness; mendacity; lying.

verlohnen *v.t. es verlohnt sich der Mühe*, it is worth while.

verloren *a. & p.* lost.

verlöschen *v.t.* to extinguish; ~ *v.i.st.* (*s*) to go out.

verlosen *v.t.* to raffle.

Verlosung *f.* (-, -en) lottery, raffle.

verlottern *v.i.* (*s*) to go downhill.

Verlust *m.* (-es, -e) loss; ~ **und Gewinnkonto** *n.* profit and loss account.

verlustig *a.* ~ *gehen*, to lose.

Verlustliste *f.* list of casualties.

vermachen *v.t.* to bequeath.

Vermächtnis *n.* (-nisses, -nisse) legacy, bequest.

vermählen (sich) *v.refl.* to marry, to get married.

Vermählung *f.* (-, -en) marriage; wedding.

vermauern *v.t.* to wall up; to close.

vermehren *v.t.* to augment, to increase; (sich) ~ *v.refl.* to multiply.

Vermehrung *f.* (-, -en) increase; (*bio.*) reproduction.

vermeidbar *a.* avoidable.

vermeiden *v.t.st.* to avoid, to shun.

vermeidlich *a.* avoidable.

Vermeidung *f.* (-, 0) avoidance.

vermeinen *v.t.* to suppose, to think.

vermeintlich *a.* supposed, pretended.

vermengen *v.t.* to mix, to intermingle; to confound.

Vermengung *f.* (-, -en) mingling; mixture, medley; confusion, mistake.

Vermerk *m.* (-[e]s. -e) entry, note.

vermerken *v.t.* to make a note of.

vermessen *v.t.st.* to measure; to survey; ~ *a.* audacious, presumptuous.

Vermessenheit *f.* (-, -en) presumption.

Vermessung *f.* (-, -en) measuring; survey.

vermieten *v.t.* to let (out), to lease; *zu* ~, for rent.

Vermieter *m.* (-s, -) landlord; (*law*) lessor.

Vermieterin *f.* landlady.

Vermietung *f.* renting (out); hiring (out).

vermindern *v.t.* to diminish; to reduce; (sich) ~ *v.refl.* to decrease.

vermindert *a.* diminished; ~*e Zurechnungsfähigkeit f.* diminished responsibility.

Verminderung *f.* (-, -en) diminution.

vermischen *v.t.* to (inter)mix, to mingle.

Vermischung *f.* (-, -en) mixture.

vermissen *v.t.* to miss.

Vermißte *m./f.* (-ten, -ten) missing person.

vermitteln *v.t.* to mediate; (*Zwist*) to make up; (*Frieden, Anleihen*) to negotiate.

Vermittler *m.* (-s, -) mediator.

Vermittlung *f.* (-, -en) mediation.

vermodern *v.i.* (*s*) to molder, to rot.

vermögen *v.t.ir.* to be able to do.

Vermögen *n.* (-s, -) ability, faculty; power; fortune, property; *über mein* ~, beyond my power *or* reach.

vermögend *a.* rich, wealthy.

Vermögens: ~**abgabe** *f.* capital levy; ~**bestand** *m.* assets *pl.*; ~**einkommen** *n.* unearned income; ~**steuer** *f.* property tax; ~**umstände** *pl.*, ~**verhältnisse** *n.pl.* financial circumstances.

vermummen *v.t.* to mask; to wrap up.

vermuten *v.t.* to conjecture, to suspect.

vermutlich *a.* presumable; presumptive.

Vermutung *f.* (-, -en) supposition; conjecture.

vernachlässigen *v.t.* to neglect.

Vernachlässigung *f.* (-, -en) neglect.

vernähen *v.t.* to sew up.

vernarben *v.i.* to scar; to heal.

vernarrt *a.* infatuated (with).

vernebeln *v.t.* to shroud in fog.

vernehmbar *a.* audible.

vernehmen *v.t.st.* to understand, to hear; to interrogate, to examine.

vernehmlich *a.* audible, distinct.

Vernehmung *f.* (-, -en) interrogation, examination.

vernehmungsfähig *a.* fit to be questioned.

verneigen (sich) *v.refl.* to bow.

Verneigung *f.* (-, -en) bow, curtsy.

verneinen *v.t.* to answer in the negative.

verneinend *a.* negative; ~ *antworten*, to answer in the negative.

Verneinung *f.* (-, -en) negation; denial.

vernichten *v.t.* to annihilate, to destroy; (*mil.*) to wipe out.

Vernichtung *f.* (-, 0) destruction; annihilation.

verniedlichen *v.t.* to trivialize; to play down.

Vernunft *f.* (-, 0) reason; sense, judgment.

vernunftbegabt *a.* endowed with reason; rational.

Vernunftehe *f.* marriage of convenience.

vernunftgemäß *a.* reasonable, rational.

vernünftig *a.* reasonable; rational; sensible.

Vernunftmensch *m.* rational person.

vernunftwidrig *a.* irrational.

veröden *v.i.* (*s*) to become deserted.

veröffentlichen *v.t.* to publish.

Veröffentlichung *f.* (-, -en) publication.

verordnen *v.t.* to decree, to ordain; (*med.*) to prescribe.

Verordnung *f.* (-, -en) decree; ordinance, regulations *pl.*; (*med.*) prescription.

verpachten *v.t.* to lease (land).

verpacken *v.t.* to pack; to wrap up.

Verpackung *f.* (-, -en) wrapping; packing.

verpäppeln *v.t.* to pamper.

verpassen *v.t.* to miss (bus, etc.).

verpesten *v.t.* to infect, to pollute.

verpfänden *v.t.* to pawn, to pledge; to mortgage.

verpflanzen *v.t.* to transplant.

Verpflanzung *f.* (-, 0) transplantation.

verpflegen *v.t.* to feed, to board.

Verpflegung *f.* (-, -en) catering; maintenance; (*mil.*) provisioning; *volle* ~, full board; *teilweise* ~, partial board; ~**sgeld** *n.* subsistence allowance.

verpflichten *v.t.* to oblige, to engage, to obligate; (sich) ~ *v.refl.* to pledge oneself; to undertake; *einen eidlich* ~, to bind one by oath; *zu Dank* ~, to lay under an obligation.

verpflichtend *a.* obligatory.

Verpflichtung *f.* (-, -en) obligation, engagement; (*Diplomatie*) commitment; (*Geld*) liability; *seinen* ~*en nachkommen*, to meet one's obligations; *eine* ~ *eingehen*, to incur an obligation.

verpfuschen *v.t.* to make a mess of.

verplanen *v.t.* to book up (time); to commit (money).

verplappern (sich) *v.refl.* to blab.
verplempern *v.t.* (*fam.*) to waste.
verpönt *a.* scorned; taboo.
verprassen *v.t.* to squander.
verprügeln *v.t.* to beat up, to thrash.
verpuffen *v.i.* (*s*) (*fig.*) to fizzle out; to blow up.
verpuppen (sich) *v.refl.* to pupate.
Verputz *m.* (-es, 0) plaster.
verputzen *v.t.* to plaster (walls).
verquer *a.* crooked; angled; weird.
verquicken *v.t.* to amalgamate.
verrammeln *v.t.* to barricade, to bar.
verrannt *a.* obsessed.
Verrat *m.* (-[e]s, 0) treason; treachery; betrayal.
verraten *v.t.st.* to betray; to disclose.
Verräter *m.* (-s, -); **Verräterin** *f.* traitor.
verräterisch *a.* treacherous; traitorous.
verrauchen *v.i.* (*s*) to go up in smoke, to evaporate; (*fig.*) to cool, to pass away.
verräuchern *v.t.* to fill with smoke.
verraucht *a.* smoke-filled; smoky.
verrauschen *v.i.* (*s*) to pass away, to die away, (music; festivity).
verrechnen *v.t.* to take into account; to credit to another account; (sich) ~ *v.refl.* to miscalculate; to be mistaken.
Verrechnung *f.* (-, -en) settlement; *nur zur ~,* (*Scheck*) not negotiable; **~sscheck** *m.* non-negotiable check.
verrecken *v.i.* (*s*) (*von Tieren*) to die; (*vulg.*) to kick the bucket.
verregnen *v.t.* (*s*) to spoil by rain.
verreisen *v.i.* (*s*) to go on a journey.
verreist *a.* away on travel.
verreissen *v.t.* to tear into pieces.
verrenken *v.t.* to dislocate, to sprain.
Verrenkung *f.* (-, -en) dislocation.
verrennen *v. refl. ir. sich ~ in,* (*fig.*) to become obsessed with.
verrichten *v.t.* to do, to perform, to execute, to achieve; *seine Notdurft ~,* to ease oneself; *sein Gebet ~,* to say one's prayers.
Verrichtung *f.* (-, -en) carrying out; performance.
verriegeln *v.t.* to bolt, to bar.
verringern *v.t. & refl.* to diminish, to lessen.
verrinnen *v.i.st.* (*s*) to run off *or* out.
verrohen *v.t. & i.* to brutalize; to grow brutal.
verrosten *v.i.* (*s*) to rust (all over).
verrostet *a.* rusty.
verrottet *a.* rotten.
verrucht *a.* infamous.
verrücken *v.t.* to displace, to remove.
verrückt *a.* deranged, crazy, mad.
Verrückte *m./f.* lunatic, madman, madwoman.
Verrücktheit *f.* (-, -en) craziness; madness.
Verruf *m.* (-[e]s, 0) *in ~ kommen,* to fall into disrepute.
verrufen *a.* ill reputed; disreputable.
verrühren *v.t.* to stir together.
verrußt *a.* sooted up.
verrutschen *v.i.* to slip.
Vers *m.* (**Verses, Verse**) verse.
versagen *v.t. & i.* to deny, to refuse; ~ *v.i.* to misfire; (*Stimme*) to fail.
Versager *m.;* **Versagerin** *f.* failure.
versalzen *v.t.* to oversalt.

versammeln *v.t.* to gather; to assemble; (sich) ~ *v.refl.* to assemble, to congregate, to meet.
Versammlung *f.* (-, -en) assembly, meeting; *eine ~ auf 10 Uhr einberufen,* to call a meeting for 10 o'clock.
Versand *m.* (-[e]s, 0) dispatch
versanden *v.i.* to silt up; (*fig.*) to peter out.
Versandhaus *n.* mail-order firm.
versauen *v.t.* (*sl.*) to make a mess of.
versauern *v.t.* to embitter.
versaufen *v.t.st.* to waste in drink.
versäumen *v.t.* to miss, to neglect.
Versäumnis *f.* (-, -nisse) omission; **~urteil** *n.* judgment by default.
verschaffen *v.t.* to procure, to provide; (sich) ~ *v.refl.* to procure, to secure, to acquire.
verschalen *v.t.* to board over.
Verschalung *f.* (-, -en) wooden covering.
verschämt *a.* bashful, shamefaced.
verschandeln *v.t.* to disfigure, to spoil.
verschanzen *v.t.* to entrench, to fortify.
Verschanzung *f.* (-, -en) fortification.
verschärfen *v.t.* to intensify; to increase; to aggravate.
verscharren *v.t.* to bury (without ceremony).
verscheiden *v.i.st.* (*s*) to expire, to die.
verschenken *v.t.* to give away.
verscherzen *v.t.* to forfeit, to lose.
verscheuchen *v.t.* to scare away.
verschicken *v.t.* to dispatch.
verschieben *v.t.st.* to shift, to displace; to delay, to put off, to postpone.
verschieden *a.* different; various; diverse; deceased.
verschiedenartig *a.* various, heterogeneous.
verschiedenerlei *a.* of various kinds.
verschiedenfarbig *a.* in different colors.
Verschiedenheit *f.* (-, -en) diversity.
verschiedentlich *adv.* on various occasions.
verschießen *v.t.st.* to shoot.
verschiffen *v.t.* to ship; to export.
verschimmeln *v.i.* (*s*) to go moldy.
verschimmelt *a.* moldy.
verschlafen *v.t.st.* to sleep away; to oversleep.
verschlafen *a.* half-asleep; sleepy.
Verschlag *m.* (-[e]s, -schläge) shed; hutch.
verschlagen *v.t.st.* to mishit (tennis); *es hat mir den Atem ~,* it took my breath away.
verschlagen *a.* cunning, sly, crafty.
Verschlagenheit *f.* (-, 0) cunning; slyness.
verschlechtern *v.t.* to impair; (sich) ~*v.refl.* to deteriorate.
Verschlechterung *f.* deterioration, worsening.
verschleiern *v.t.* to veil; to screen.
verschleiert *a.* veiled; misty.
Verschleierung *f.* veiling; covering up.
Verschleimung *f.* (-, -en) mucus congestion.
Verschleiß *m.* (-es, -e) wear and tear.
verschleißen *v.t.st.* to wear out.
verschleppen *v.t.* to mislay; to abduct; (*Krankheiten*) to spread; (*fig.*) to protract, to put off, to delay.
Verschleppung *f.* (-, -en) protraction; kidnapping; delaying.
verschleudern *v.t.* to waste; to sell dirt cheap.
verschließbar *a.* closable; lockable; *luftdich ~*

sealable.

verschließen *v.t.st.* to shut, to close; to lock; (sich) ~ *v.refl.st.* to lock oneself off *or* up.

verschlimmern *v.t.* to make worse; to aggravate; (sich) ~ *v.refl.* to get worse, to worsen; to deteriorate.

Verschlimmerung *f.* (-, 0) change for the worse; worsening.

verschlingen *v.t.st.* to (inter)twine; to interlace; to swallow (up), to devour.

verschlossen *a. & p.* locked up, shut; (*fig.*) reticent, reserved, close.

Verschlossenheit *f.* (-, 0) (*fig.*) reserve.

verschlucken *v.t.* to swallow; (sich) ~ *v.refl.* to choke, to swallow the wrong way.

Verschluß *m.* (-schlusses, -schlüsse) lock; (*phot.*) shutter; *unter ~,* under lock and key.

verschlüsseln *v.t.* to encode.

verschmachten *v.i.* (*s*) to pine away.

verschmähen *v.t.* to disdain, to scorn.

verschmelzen *v.t.st.* to blend; ~ *v.i.st.* (*s*) to be blended.

verschmerzen *v.t.* to get over (a loss).

verschmieren *v.t.* to smear; to smudge, to blur.

verschmitzt *a.* cunning, sly, artful.

verschmutzen *v.t.* to dirty, to soil; *v.i.*(*s*) to get dirty.

Verschmutzung *f.* (-, -en) pollution; soiling.

verschnaufen (sich) *v.refl.* to have/take a breather.

Verschnaufpause *f.* rest; breather.

verschneiden *v.t.st.* to adulterate (wine).

verschneit *a.* snow-covered.

Verschnitt *m.* (-es, -e) blend.

verschnörkelt *a.* ornate.

verschnupfen *v.t.imp.* to offend; *verschnupft sein,* to have a cold in one's head; (*fig.*) to feel offended.

verschnüren *v.t.* to tie up.

verschollen *a.* forgotten; presumed dead *or* lost.

verschonen *v.t.* to spare.

verschönern *v.t.* to embellish.

verschossen *a.* faded, discolored.

verschränken *v.t.* to cross (one's arms); to interlace, to entwine.

verschreiben *v.t.st.* (*med.*) to prescribe; (sich) ~ *v.refl.st.* to make a slip of the pen.

Verschreibung *f.* (-, -en) prescription.

verschreibungspflichtig *a.* available only on prescription.

verschroben *a.* eccentric, queer.

verschroten *v.t.* to grind (up).

verschrotten *v.t.* to scrap.

verschrumpeln *v.i.* (*fam.*) to shrivel (up).

verschüchtern *v.t.* to intimidate.

verschulden *v.t.* to be guilty of, to commit; to involve in debt.

Verschulden *n.* (-, 0) fault, guilt.

Verschuldung *f.* (-, -en) indebtedness; offense, fault.

verschütten *v.t.* to spill; *verschüttet werden,* to be buried under (falling) earth or stones.

verschwägert *a.* related by marriage.

verschweigen *v.t.st.* to keep (a thing) a secret, to conceal; to suppress.

verschwenden *v.t.* to squander, to dissipate, to waste.

Verschwender *m.;* **Verschwenderin** *f.* spendthrift; squanderer.

verschwenderisch *a.* wasteful, lavish; (*reichlich*) profuse.

Verschwendung *f.* (-, -en) waste; extravagance.

verschwiegen *a.* close, discreet, reticent.

Verschwiegenheit *f.* (-, 0) discretion.

verschwimmen *v.i.st.* (*s*) to become indistinct *or* blurred.

verschwinden *v.i.st.* (*s*) to disappear, to vanish.

verschwistert *a.* ~ *sein* to be brother and sister.

verschwitzen *v.t.* to make (clothing) sweaty; (*fam.*) to forget.

verschwitzt *a.* sweaty.

verschwollen *a.* swollen.

verschwommen *a.* indistinct, blurred.

verschwören (sich) ~ *v.refl.st.* to plot, to conspire.

Verschwörer *m.* (-s, -); **Verschwörerin** *f.* (-, -nen) conspirator.

Verschwörung *f.* (-, -en) conspiracy, plot.

versehen *v.t.* to provide, to supply; (*Dienst*) to perform; (sich) ~ *v.refl.* to make a mistake; *ehe ich mir's versehe,* before I am aware of it.

Versehen *n.* (-s, -) oversight; slip; *aus ~,* inadvertently.

versehentlich *adv.* by mistake; inadvertently.

versehrt *a.* disabled.

Versehrte *m./f.* (-n, -n) disabled person.

verselbständigen *v.refl.* to become independent.

versenden *v.t.ir.* to dispatch, to ship.

Versendung *f.* (-, -en) dispatch; sending.

versengen *v.t.* to singe, to scorch.

versenken *v.t.* to sink, to submerge.

Versenkung *f.* sinking; lowering; *in der ~ verschwinden* to vanish from the scene.

versessen *a.* ~ *sein auf* to be crazy about.

versetzen *v.t.* to displace; to transplant; to pawn; to promote (to a higher form); to mix, to alloy; ~ *v.i.* to reply, to rejoin; *in die Notwendigkeit ~,* to lay under the necessity of; *einem einen Schlag, Hieb ~,* to deal someone a blow, a cut.

Versetzung *f.* (-, -en) transfer (*eines Beamten*); removal; promotion (school, etc.); transplanting.

Versetzungszeugnis *n.* end-of-year report.

verseuchen *v.t.* to contaminate.

Verfuß *m.* (metrical) foot, meter.

Versicherer *m.* insurer.

versichern *v.t.* to assure, to affirm; to insure; *das Leben seiner Frau ~,* to take out a policy on the life of one's wife; (sich) ~ *v.refl.* to make sure of, to ascertain; to secure.

Versicherte *m./f.* (-n, -n) insured (person).

Versicherung *f.* (-, -en) assurance, affirmation; insurance; *eine ~ abschließen,* to take out insurance.

Versicherungs: **~anspruch** *m.* insurance claim; **~beitrag** *m.* premium; **~fähig** *a.* insurable; **~makler** *m.* insurance broker; **~nehmer** *m.* policy holder; **~police,** insurance policy; **~prämie** *f.* insurance premium.

versickern *v.i.* to drain away.

versiegeln *v.t.* to seal (up).

Versiegelung *f.* seal; sealing.

versiegen *v.i.* (*s*) to dry up, to be drained.

versilbern *v.t.* to (silver)-plate; (*fig.*) to convert into money.

Versilberung *f.* (-, -en) silver-plating; conversion.

versinken *v.i.st.* (*s*) to sink; (*fig.*) ~ *in* to become immersed.

versinnbildlichen *v.t.* to symbolize.

Version *f.* (-, -en) version.

versklaven *v.t.* to enslave.

Versmaß *n.* meter.

versoffen *a.* drunken.

versöhnen *v.t.* to reconcile.

versöhnlich *a.* placable, conciliatory.

Versöhnung *f.* (-, -en) reconciliation.

versonnen *a.* dreamy; lost in thought.

versorgen *v.t.* to provide with, to supply; to provide for, to take care of, to maintain.

Versorger *m.* (-s, -); **Versorgerin** *f.* (-, -nen) provider; breadwinner (for).

Versorgung *f.* (-, -en) provision; supply(ing).

verspannen *v.refl.* to tense up.

verspannt *a.* tense; cramped.

verspäten *v.t.* (*sich*) *v.refl.* to be late.

verspätet *a.* late.

Verspätung *f.* (-, -en) delay, lateness.

verspeisen *v.t.* to consume.

verspekulieren *v.t.* to lose by speculation.

versperren *v.t.* to block up, to obstruct.

verspielen *v.t.* to gamble away.

verspielt *a.* playful; fanciful.

versponnen *a.* eccentric; odd.

verspotten *v.t.* to mock; to ridicule.

Verspottung *f.* (-, -en) mockery, derision.

versprechen *v.t.st.* to promise; (sich) ~ *v.refl.st.* to make a slip of the tongue.

Versprechen *n.* (-s, -) promise.

Versprecher *m.* (-s, -) slip of the tongue.

Versprechung *f.* (-, -en) promise.

versprengen *v.t.* to disperse; to sprinkle.

versprühen *v.t.* to spray.

verspüren *v.t.* to perceive, to feel.

verstaatlichen *v.t.* to nationalize.

verstädtern *v.i.* to become urbanized.

Verstädterung *f.* urbanization.

Verstand *m.* (-[e]s, 0) understanding, intellect; (good) sense; *gesunder* ~, common sense; *den ~ verlieren*, to go out of one's mind.

verstandesmäßig *a.* intellectual, rational.

verständig *a.* intelligent, sensible.

verständigen *v.t.* to inform; to notify; *sich mit einem* ~, to come to an understanding with someone.

Verständigung *f.* (-, -en) arrangement, agreement; information; communication.

verständlich *a.* intelligible; *allgemein* ~, popular, within the reach (comprehension) of everyone.

verständlicherweise *adv.* understandably.

Verständnis *n.* (-nisses, -nisse) comprehension; understanding.

verständnislos *a.* uncomprehending.

Verständnislosigkeit *f.* (-, 0) lack of understanding; incomprehension.

verständnisvoll *a.* understanding.

verstärken *v.t.* to strengthen, to reinforce; to intensify; (*radio*) to amplify.

Verstärker *m.* amplifier.

verstärkt *a.* increased; reinforced.

Verstärkung *f.* (-, -en) reinforcement, strengthening.

verstauben *v.i.* (*s*) to get dusty.

verstaubt *a.* dusty; (*fig.*) old-fashioned.

verstauchen *v.t.* to sprain; to dislocate.

Verstauchung *f.* (-, -en) spraining; dislocation.

Versteck *m.* (-[e]s, -e) hiding-place; ~*en spielen*, to play at hide-and-seek.

verstecken *v.t.* to hide, to conceal.

versteckt *a.* hidden; concealed; veiled.

verstehen *v.t.st.* to understand; to comprehend; to know (how); to mean; *falsch* ~, to misunderstand.

versteifen *v.t.* to stiffen; (sich) ~ *v.refl.* to harden. (*Börse*); (*fig.*) to insist upon.

versteigen (sich) *v.refl.st.* *sich zu einer Behauptung* ~, to go as far as to maintain that. . .

versteigern *v.t.* to auction.

Versteigerung *f.* (-, -en) auction, public sale.

versteinert *a.* petrified.

Versteinerung *f.* (-, -en) petrifaction, fossil.

verstellbar *a.* adjustable.

verstellen *v.t.* to misplace; to shift; (*den Weg*) to bar; (sich) ~ *v.refl.* to dissemble, to feign.

Verstellung *f.* (-, -en) pretense; disguising.

versterben *v.i.st.* to die; to pass away.

versteuern *v.t.* to pay excise or duty on.

verstiegen *a.* high-flown, extravagant.

verstimmen *v.t.* to put in a bad mood.

verstimmt *a.* out of tune; (*fig.*) out of humor, put out.

Verstimmtheit, Verstimmung *f.* (-, -en) (*fig.*) bad humor, ill-humor, ill-feeling.

verstocken *v.t.* to harden.

verstockt *a.* obdurate, hardened.

Verstocktheit *f.* obduracy; stubbornness.

verstohlen *a.* surreptitious, stealthy.

verstopfen *v.t.* to block, to stop; (*med.*) to constipate.

Verstopfung *f.* (-, -en) stopping, obstruction; constipation.

verstorben *a.* deceased, defunct; *mein* ~*er Mann*, my late husband

verstört *a.* distraught; troubled, haggard.

Verstoß *m.* (-es, -stösse) violation; fault, offense, mistake.

verstossen *v.t.st.* to cast off, to expel; ~ *v.i.st.* ~ *gegen*, to offend against, to transgress.

verstrahlen *v.t.* to radiate; to contaminate with radiation.

verstreichen *v.i.st.* (*s*) to elapse.

verstreuen *v.t.* to scatter, to disperse.

verstricken *v.t.* (*fig.*) to entangle, to ensnare; *v.refl.* to become involved.

Verstrickung *f.* involvement.

verstümmeln *v.t.* to mutilate, to mangle.

Verstümmelung *f.* (-, -en) mutilation.

verstummen *v.i.* (*s*) to fall silent; to fade away.

Versuch *m.* (-[e]s, -e) experiment; trial, attempt; test.

versuchen *v.t.* to try, to attempt; to taste.

Versucherin *f.* (-, -nen) temptress.

Versuchs- ~**anordnung** *f.* set-up for an experiment; ~**ballon** *m.* trial balloon; ~**fabrik** *f.* pilot plant; ~**kaninchen** *n.* guinea pig; ~**objekt** *n.* test object; ~**person** *f.* test person; ~**reihe** *f.* series of tests; ~**tier** *n.* laboratory animal.

versuchsweise *adv.* by way of experiment.

Versuchung *f.* (-, -en) temptation.

versündigen (sich) *v.refl.* to sin (against).

Versündigung *f.* (-, -en) grave offense.

Versunkenheit *f.* (-, 0) absorption; contemplation.

versüßen *v.t.* to sweeten.

vertagen *v.t.* to adjourn; (sich) ~ *v.refl.* to adjourn.

Vertagung *f.* (-, -en) adjournment.

vertändeln *v.t.* to trifle away.

vertauschen *v.t.* to exchange.

Vertauschung *f.* (-, -en) exchange, reversal; switching.

verteidigen *v.t.* to defend.

Verteidiger *m.* (-s, -); **Verteidigerin** *f.* (-, -nen) defender; (*law*) counsel for the defense; (*Fußball*) back.

Verteidigung *f.* (-, -en) defense.

verteilen *v.t.* to distribute, to apportion.

Verteiler *m.* (-s, -) (*auf Akten*) distribution list.

Verteilung *f.* (-, -en) distribution.

verteuern *v.t.* to make more expensive.

verteufeln *v.t.* to condemn.

verteufelt *a.* (*fam.*) devilish.

vertiefen *v.t.* to deepen; (sich) ~ *v.refl.* to be absorbed in.

Vertiefung *f.* (-, -en) deepening; strengthening; hollow.

vertikal *a.* vertical.

Vertikale *f.* (-, -n) vertical (line).

vertilgen *v.t.* to exterminate; to consume.

vertippen *v.refl.* to make a typing mistake; to get it wrong (lotto); *v.t.* to mistype.

vertonen *v.t.* to set to music.

Vertonung *f.* (-, -en) setting to music.

vertrackt *a.* odd, strange; confounded, intricate.

Vertrag *m.* (-[e]s, -träge) contract, agreement; (*Staats~*) treaty; *mündlicher ~ m.* verbal agreement.

vertragen *v.t.st.* to bear, to stand, to endure; to digest; *ich kann kein Bier ~,* beer does not agree with me; (sich) ~ *v.refl.* to get along well (together).

vertraglich *a.* contractual.

verträglich *a.* digestible; social, peaceable; compatible.

Verträglichkeit *f.* digestibility; good nature.

Vertrags: ~**abschluß** *m.* conclusion of a contract; ~**bedingungen** *pl.* terms of the contract; ~**bruch** *m.* breach of contract; ~**entwurf** *m.* draft contract; ~**partei** *f.* contracting party; ~**recht** *n.* contract law.

vertragswidrig *a.* contrary to a contract *or* treaty.

vertrauen *v.t.* to entrust, to confide; ~ *v.i.* to confide, to rely upon.

Vertrauen *n.* (-s, 0) confidence; trust; *im ~,* privately, confidentially.

vertrauenerwechend *a.* inspiring confidence.

Vertrauensbruch *m.* breach of trust.

Vertrauensstellung *f.* position of trust.

vertrauens: ~**selig** *a.* too confiding; gullible; rashly trustful; ~**voll** *a.* confiding, trusting, trustful; ~**würdig** *a.* trustworthy.

vertraulich *a.* confidential, intimate.

Vertraulichkeit *f.* (-, -en) familiarity, intimacy.

verträumen *v.t.* to dream away.

verträumt *a.* dreamy.

vertraut *a.* intimate, familiar; conversant (with), versed (in); *auf ~em Fuss stehen,* to be on terms of intimacy.

Vertraute *m./f.* (-n, -n) confidant; close friends.

Vertrautheit *f.* (-, 0) familiarity.

vertreiben *v.t.st.* to drive away, to expel, to banish; to sell; to pass (time).

Vertreibung *f.* (-, -en) expulsion.

vertretbar *a.* defensible; tenable; justifiable.

vertreten *v.t.st.* to represent.

Vertreter *m.* (-s, -); **Vertreterin** *f.* (-, -nen) representative.

Vertretung *f.* (-, -en) representation; substitution; *in ~ von,* acting for *or* as representative of; by proxy.

Vertrieb *m.* (-[e]s, 0) sale, distribution.

Vertriebene *m./f.* (-n, -n) exile.

vertrinken *v.t.st.* to spend on drink.

vertrocknen *v.i.* to dry up, to wither.

vertrödeln *v.t.* to trifle away; to waste time.

vertrösten *v.t.* to put off (with fine words).

vertun *v.t.st.* to waste, to squander.

vertuschen *v.t.* to hush up; to suppress (news).

verübeln *v.t.* to take amiss.

verüben *v.t.* to commit, to perpetrate.

verulken *v.t.* to make fun of.

verunglimpfen *v.t.* to denigrate; to revile.

verunglücken *v.i.* (*s*) to be involved in an accident.

verunreinigen *v.t.* to soil, to contaminate; (*Wasser*) to pollute; (*Lust*) to infect; (*fig.*) to defile.

Verunreinigung *f.* (-, -en) defilement, contamination.

verunsichern *v.t.* to make s.b. feel unsure/ uncertain.

Verunsicherung *f.* felling of insecurity.

verunstalten *v.t.* to disfigure, to deface.

Verunstaltung *f.* (-, -en) disfigurement.

veruntreuen *v.t.* to embezzle.

Veruntreuung *f.* (-, -en) embezzlement.

verunzieren *v.t.* to disfigure, to mar.

verursachen *v.t.* to cause; to occasion.

Verursacher *m.* (-s, -) person responsible; cause.

verurteilen *v.t.* to condemn; to convict, to sentence.

Verurteilte *m./f.* convicted person.

Verurteilung *f.* (-, -en) condemnation.

vervielfältigen *v.t.* to multiply; to duplicate.

Vervielfältigung *f.* (-, -en) reproduction; duplication; copying.

vervierfachen *v.t.* to quadruple.

vervollkommen *v.t.* to perfect.

vervollständigen *v.t.* to complete, to complement.

Vervollständigung *f.* completion.

verwachsen *v.i.st.* (*s*) to grow together.

verwachsen *a.* deformed, crippled.

verwählen *v.refl.* to dial the wrong number.

verwahren *v.t.* to keep; *sich gegen etwas ~,* to protest against.

verwahrlost *a.* neglected, unkempt.

Verwahrlosung *f.* (-, -en) neglect.

Verwahrung *f.* (-, -en) keeping, custody; protest; *in ~ nehmen,* to take into custody.

verwaisen *v.i.* (*s*) to become an orphan.

verwaist *a.* orphaned; (*fig.*) deserted.

verwalten *v.t.* to administer.

Verwalter *m.* (-s, -); **Verwalterin** *f.* (-, -nen) administrator.

Verwaltung *f.* (-, -en) administration, management.

Verwaltungs: ~**gericht** *n.* administrative court; ~**recht** *n.* administrative law.

verwandelbar *a.* convertible.

verwandeln *v.t.* to change, to transform, to convert, to turn; (*Strafe*) to commute; (sich) ~ *v.refl.* to be changed.

Verwandlung *f.* (-, -en) change, transformation; changing, turning.

verwandt *a.* related, akin to; (*Begriffe*) cognate.

Verwandte *m./f.* (-n, -n) relation, relative, kinsman, kinswoman; *nächste* ~, next-of-kin.

Verwandtschaft *f.* (-, -en) relationship; relations *pl.*; (*fig.*) affinity.

verwandtschaftlich *a.* relational.

verwarnen *v.t.* warn; to caution.

verwaschen *a.* washed-out, faded.

verwässern *v.t.* to dilute, to drown.

verweben *v.t.* to interweave.

verwechselbar *a.* mistakable.

verwechseln *v.t.* to mistake (for), confuse.

Verwechslung *f.* (-, -en) mistake, confusion.

verwegen *a.* audacious, daring, bold.

Verwegenheit *f.* audacity; daring.

verwehen *v.t.* to blow away.

verwehren *v.t.* to hinder, to prohibit.

verweichlichen *v.t.* to make s.b. soft; to render effeminate.

verweigern *v.t.* to refuse.

Verweigerung *f.* (-, -en) denial, refusal.

verweilen *v.i.* to stay; to sojourn; (*fig.*) to dwell (on).

verweint *a.* red with tears; tearstained.

Verweis *m.* (-es, -e) rebuke, reprimand; (*im Buch*) (cross) reference.

verweisen *v.t.st.* to refer (one) to; *einen des Landes oder aus dem Lande* ~, to exile, to banish someone; (*einem etwas* ~), to rebuke someone for, to have someone up for.

Verweisung *f.* (-, -en) reference; banishment, exile; ~**szeichen**, reference.

verwelken *v.i.* (s) to wither, to fade.

verweltlichen *v.t.* to secularize.

verwendbar *a.* usable; applicable.

Verwendbarkeit *f.* usability.

verwenden *v.t.ir.* to use; to apply (to), to spend (on), to employ (in); *sich* ~ *für*, to intercede on behalf of.

Verwendung *f.* (-, -en) application, use, employment.

verwendungsunfähig *a.* unemployable.

verwerfen *v.t.st.* to reject; to quash; to condemn.

verwerflich *a.* reprehensible.

Verwerfung *f.* (-, -en) rejection; condemnation.

verwertbar *a.* utilizable; usable.

Verwertbarkeit *f.* usability.

verwerten *v.t.* utilize.

Verwertung *f.* utilization; exploitation.

verwesen *v.t.* to administer; ~ *v.i.* (s) to rot, to decay; to decompose.

verweslich *a.* perishable.

Verwesung *f.* (-, -en) decomposition.

verwickeln *v.t.* to entangle; to complicate, to implicate; to involve; (sich) ~ *v.refl.* to become complicated; to get involved.

verwickelt *a.* complicated, intricate.

Verwicklung *f.* (-, -en) entanglement, complication; plot (of a play).

verwildern *v.i.* (s) to become overgrown (garden); to go wild.

verwildert *a.* overgrown (garden); wild; which has gone wild.

verwirken *v.t.* to forfeit.

verwirklichen *v.t.* to realize; (sich) ~, to be or become realized, to materialize.

Verwirklichung *f.* (-, -en) realization.

verwirren *v.t.* to entangle; to embarrass, to perplex.

verwirrt *a.* confused; embarrassed.

Verwirrung *f.* (-, -en) confusion.

verwirtschaften *v.t.* to waste (by mismanagement).

verwischen *v.t.* to wipe out, to blot out; (*fig.*) to become blurred.

verwittern *v.i.* (s) to become disintegrated, dilapidated.

verwittert *a.* weather-beaten.

verwitwet *a.* widowed.

verwöhnen *v.t.* to spoil, to pamper.

verworfen *a.* abandoned, depraved; (*fig.*) immoral.

verworren *a.* intricate, confused.

verwundbar *a.* vulnerable.

Verwundbarkeit *f.* vulnerability.

verwunden *v.t.* to wound, to hurt.

verwunderlich *a.* strange, odd.

verwundern (sich) *v.refl.* to be surprised.

verwundert *a.* astonished, surprised.

Verwunderung *f.* surprise; astonishment.

verwundet *a.* wounded, injured.

Verwundete *m./f.* wounded person; casualty.

Verwundung *f.* (-, -en) wound; injury.

verwunschen *a.* enchanted.

verwünschen *v.t.* to curse, to execrate.

Verwünschung *f.* (-, -en) curse.

verwüsten *v.t.* to devastate, to lay waste.

Verwüstung *f.* (-, -en) devastation.

verzagen *v.i.* to lose courage, to despair.

verzagt *a.* discouraged, despondent.

verzählen (sich) *v.refl.* to count wrong; to miscount.

Verzahnung *f.* (-, -en) (*Holz*) dovetailing.

verzärteln *v.t.* to coddle, to pamper.

verzaubern *v.t.* to bewitch, to enchant; to cast a spell.

Verzauberung *f.* (-, -en) enchantment; the spell.

Verzehr *m.* (-s, 0) consumption.

verzehren *v.t.* to consume; to eat.

verzeichnen *v.t.* to list; to note down; to specify.

Verzeichnis *n.* (-nisses, -nisse) list, catalogue; index.

verzeihen *v.i.st.* to pardon, to forgive.

verzeihlich *a.* pardonable; excusable; forgivable.

Verzeihung *f.* (-, 0) pardon; forgiveness; *um* ~ *bitten*, to beg pardon.

verzerren *v.t.* to distort.

verzetteln *v.t.* to fritter away.

Verzicht *m.* (-[e]s, -e) renunciation; ~ *leisten auf*, to renounce.

verzichten *v.i.* to renounce, to resign.

Verzichtleistung *f.* renunciation.

verziehen *v.t.st.* to distort; ~ *v.i. ein Kind* ~, to spoil a child; *in die Stadt* ~, to move into town; (sich) ~ *v.refl.* to go out of shape; to disperse.

verzieren *v.t.* to decorate, to adorn.

Verzierung *f.* (-, -en) decoration, ornament.

verzinsen *v.t.* to pay interest on; (sich) ~ *v.refl.* to bear *or* yield interest.

verzinslich *a.* bearing interest.

verzogen *a.* spoilt (child); removed (into another house).

verzögern *v.t.* to delay, to protract.

Verzögerung *f.* (-, -en) delay; ~**staktik** *f.* delaying tactics.

verzollbar *a.* liable to pay duty.

verzollen *v.t.* to pay duty on.

verzuckern *v.t.* to sugar over; to put too much sugar in.

verzückt *a.* enraptured; ecstatic.

Verzückung *f.* (-, -en) rapture; ecstasy.

Verzug *m.* (-[e]s, 0) delay.

verzweifeln *v.i.* (*s*) to despair (of/at).

verzweifelt *a.* desperate; despairing.

Verzweiflung *f.* (-, 0) despair, desperation.

verzweigen (sich) *v.refl.* to branch out; to ramify.

verzweigt *a.* branching.

verzwickt *a.* odd, strange; intricate.

Vesper *f.* (-, -n) vespers *pl.*

vespern *v.i.* to have one's tea or supper.

Vestalin *f.* (-n -nen) vestal.

Veteran *m.* (-en, -en) veteran.

Veterinär *m.* (-s, -e) veterinary surgeon.

Veto *n.* (-[s], -s) veto.

Vetter *m.* (-s, -n) (male) cousin; ~ *zweiten Grades*, second cousin.

Vetternwirtschaft *f.* nepotism.

vexieren *v.t.* to tease, to banter; to quiz, to puzzle, to mystify.

via *pr.* via, by way (of).

Viadukt *m.* (-[e]s, -e) viaduct.

Vibration *n.* (-, -en) vibration.

vibrieren *v.i.* to vibrate.

Video *n.* (-s, -s) video.

Video: ~**band** *n.* videotape; ~**gerät** *n.* video recorder; ~**kassette** *f.* video cassette; ~**recorder** *m.* video recorder; ~**spiel** *n.* video game; ~**text** *m.* teletext.

Videothek *f.* (-, -en) video tape library.

Vieh *n.* (-[e]s, 0) beast; cattle; livestock.

Vieh: ~**futter** *n.* fodder, provender; ~**händler** *m.* cattle dealer.

viehisch *a.* beastly, brutal, bestial.

Vieh: ~**seuche** *f.* cattle-plague, rinderpest; foot-and-mouth disease; ~**zucht** *f.* cattle-breeding; ~**züchter** *m.* stock-farmer, cattle-breeder.

viel *a. & adv.* a lot; plenty; much, a great deal; ~**e** *pl.* many; *gleich viel*, as many *or* much; no matter; just the same.

vielbändig *a.* in many volumes.

vielbeschäftigt *a.* busy, much occupied.

vieldeutig *a.* ambiguous.

vieldiskutiert *a.* much-discussed.

Vieleck *n.* (-[e]s, -e) polygon.

vielerlei *a.* different, various.

vielfach, vielfältig *a. & adv.* manifold, multiple; multifarious; repeatedly.

Vielfraß *m.* (-es, -e) glutton.

vielgeliebt *a.* much-loved.

vielgepriesen *a.* much-vaunted.

vielgestaltig *a.* multiform.

Vielgötterei *f.* (-, 0) polytheism.

Veilheit *f.* (-, -en) multitude; plurality.

vielköpfig *a.* many-headed.

vielleicht *adv.* perhaps, maybe.

vielmals *adv.* many times, frequently.

vielmalig *a.* repeated, frequent.

vielmehr *adv.* rather; on the contrary.

vielsagend *a.* significant, expressive; meaningful.

vielseitig *a.* multilateral; (*fig.*) many-sided; versatile.

Vielseitigkeit *f.* (-, 0) versatility.

vielsilbig *a.* polysyllabic.

vielsprachig *a.* polyglot.

vielstimmig *a.* (*mus.*) polyphonic; for many voices; many-voiced.

vielverheissend *a.* promising.

Vielvölkerstaat *m.* multiethnic state.

Vielweiberei *f.* (-, 0) polygamy.

vier *a.* four; *auf allen* ~**en**, on all fours; *unter* ~ *Augen*, in private, between you and me.

Vier *f.* (-, -en) the number/figure/grade four.

vierbeinig *a.* four-footed, four-legged.

vierblättrig *a.* four-leaved.

Viereck *n.* (-[e]s, -e) square, quadrangle.

viereckig *a.* quadrangular, square.

viererlei *a.* of four sorts.

vierfach, vierfältig *a.* fourfold.

vierfüßig *a.* four-footed.

Vierfüßler *m.* (-s, -) quadruped.

vierhändig *a.* four-handed; ~ (*Klavier*) **spielen**, to play four-handed.

vierhundert *a.* four hundred.

vierjährig *a.* four years old.

Vierlinge *pl.* quadruplets.

viermal *adv.* four times; ~ *so viel*, four times as much, four times the number.

Viermächte. . . quadripartite *a.*

viermalig *a.* four times repeated.

viermotorig *a.* four-engined(d).

Vierradbremse *f.* four-wheel brake.

vierrädrig *a.* four-wheeled.

vierschrötig *a.* square-built, robust.

vierseitig *a.* four-sided; quadrilateral.

Viersitzer *m.* four-seater.

viersitzig *a.* four-seated.

vierspännig *a.* four-horse(d).

vierstimmig *a.* for four voices *or* parts.

vierteilen *v.t.* to quarter.

Viertel *n.* (-s, -) fourth part; quarter; (*Stadt*) quarter; (*Villen*~) residential quarter.

Vierteljahr *n.* quarter.

vierteljährig *a.* quarterly.

vierteljährlich *adv.* every three months, quarterly.

Vierteljahrsschrift *f.* quarterly (journal).

Viertel: ~**note** *f.* quarter note; ~**stunde** *f.* quarter of an hour.

viertelstündlich *a.* every quarter of an hour.

viertens *adv.* fourthly, in the fourth place.

Vierviertaktakt *m.* (*mus.*) common time.

vierzehn *a.* fourteen; ~ *Tage*, a fortnight; fourteen days.

vierzig *a.* forty.

Vierziger *m.* (-s, -), **-in,** *f.* (-, -nen) quadraganarian; forty-year-old; *in den vierziger Jahren,* in the forties.
Vietnam *n.* (-s, 0) Vietnam.
Vietnamese *m.* (-n, -n); **Vietnamesin** *f.* (-, -nen); **vietnamesisch** *a.* Vietnamese.
Vietnamkrieg *m.* Vietnam War.
Vikar *m.* (-s, -e) curate, assistant.
viktorianisch *a.* Victorian.
Viktualien *pl.* victuals, eatables *pl.*
Villa *f.* (-, Villen) residence; country-house, country-box.
Villenviertel *n.* residential area.
Viola *f.* (-, -len) viola.
violett *a.* purple; violet.
Violinbogen *m.* bow.
Violine *f.* (-, -n) violin.
Violinist *m.* (-en, -en); **Violinistin** *f.* (-, -nen); **Violinspieler** *m.*; **Violinspielerin** *f.* violinist.
Violin: ~**konzert** *n.* violin concerto; ~**saite** *f.* string; ~**schlüssel** *m.* treble-clef.
Violon *n.* (-s, -s) bass-viol.
Violoncello *n.* (-[s], -cellos *u.* -celli) cello, violoncello.
Viper *f.* (-, -n) viper.
Virtuose *m.* (-n, -n); **Virtuosin** *f.* (-, -nen) virtuoso.
Virtuosität *f.* (-, -en) virtuosity.
Virus *n./m.* (-, Viren) virus.
Visier *n.* (-[e]s, -e) visor; (*am Gewehr*) back sight.
visieren *v.t.* to aim; to gauge.
Vision *f.* (-, -en) vision.
visionär *a.* visionary.
Visite *f.* (-, -n) doctor's round.
Visitenkarte *f.* (visiting)-card.
visuell *a.* visual.
Visum *n.* (-s, -sa) visa.
vital *a.* vital; energetic.
Vitalität *f.* vitality.
Vitamin *n.* (-s, -e) vitamin.
Vitaminarm *a.* low in vitamins.
Vitaminmangel *m.* vitamin deficiency.
vitaminreich *a.* rich in vitamins.
Vitrine *f.* (-, -n) display case; glass cupboard.
Vize: vice. . .; **Vizekönig** *m.* viceroy.
Vogel *m.* (-s, Vögel) bird; (*Huhn*) fowl; *einen ~ haben,* (*fig.*) to have a bee in one's bonnet; *den ~ abschiessen,* to carry off the prize.
Vogel: ~**bauer** *m.* bird-cage.
vogelfrei *a.* outlawed.
Vogel: ~**haus** *n.* aviary; ~**kunde** *f.* ornithology; ~**perspektive** *f.* bird's-eye view; ~**schau** *f.* bird's-eye view; *aus der ~,* a bird's-eye view of; ~**scheuche** *f.* scarecrow; ~**warte** *f.* ornithological station.
Vöglein *n.* (-s, -) little bird.
Vogt *m.* (-[e]s, Vögte) steward; bailiff.
Vokabel *f.* (-, -n) word.
Vokal *m.* (-[e]s, -e) vowel.
Vokalmusik *f.* vocal music, singing.
Vokativ *m.* (-s, -e) vocative.
Volk *n.* (-[e]s, Völker) people, nation.
Völker: ~**bund** *m.* League of Nations; ~**kunde** *f.* ethnology; ~**mord** *m.* genocide; ~**recht** *n.* international law.
völkerrechtlich *a.* relating to international law.
Völkerschaft *f.* (-, -en) tribe, people.

Völkerwanderung *f.* migration of nations.
volkreich *a.* populous.
Volks. . . ethnic *a.*
Volks: ~**abstimmung** *f.* plebiscite, referendum; ~**bibliothek** *f.* public library; ~**charakter** *m.* national character; ~**entscheid** (über) *m.* referendum (on); ~**fest** *n.* public festival; ~**hochschule** *f.* adult education center; ~**kunde** *f.* folklore; ~**lied** *n.* popular song, folk-song.
Volks: ~**menge** *f.* multitude, throng; ~**partei** *f.* people's party; ~**redner** *m.* popular speaker, stump-orator; ~**schule** *f.* elementary school; ~**schullehrer** *m.* elementary teacher; ~**schulwesen** *n.* system of national education; ~**stamm** *m.* tribe; ~**tracht** *f.* national dress *or* costume.
Volkstum *n.* (-s, 0) nation(ality); national character.
volkstümlich *a.* popular; national.
Volks: ~**unterricht** *m.* public instruction; ~**versammlung** *f.* public meeting; ~**vertreter** *m.* representative of the people; ~**vertretung** *f.* popular representation; national assembly, parliament; ~**wirtschaft** *f.* national economy; economics.
volkswirtschaftlich *a.* economic.
Volkszählung *f.* census.
voll *a.* full; entire; (*vulg.*) drunk; *es war ~ im Theater,* the house was crowded; *nicht für ~ ansehen,* not to take seriously; *das Maß ~machen,* to fill up the measure, to crown all; *um das Unglück ~zumachen,* to make things worse; ~*pfropfen,* to cram, to stuff.
vollauf *adv.* completely; fully.
voll ausgeschrieben *a.* in full.
vollautomatisch *a.* fully automatic.
Vollbart *m.* beard.
Vollbesitz *m.* full possession.
Vollblut, Vollblutpferd *n.* thoroughbred (horse).
vollbringen *v.t.st.* to accomplish.
Volldampf *m.* full steam.
Völlgefühl *n.* feeling of fullness.
vollenden *v.t.* to finish; to accomplish.
vollendet *a.* perfect.
vollends *adv.* altogether, wholly; finally.
Vollendung *f.* (-, 0) completion, perfection.
Völlerei *f.* (-, 0) gluttony.
vollführen *v.t.* to execute, to accomplish.
Vollgehalt *m.* full *or* entire contents *pl.*
Vollgenuß *m.* full enjoyment.
vollgepfropft, vollgerüttelt *a.* crammed (with), chockfull.
vollgültig *a.* full value.
völlig *a.* entire, whole; *~ adv.* fully.
volljährig *a.* of age.
Volljährigkeit *f.* (-, 0) full age, majority.
vollkommen *a.* perfect; consummate.
Vollkommenheit *f.* (-, -en) perfection.
Vollkraft *f.* (-, 0) full vigour, energy.
Vollmacht *f.* (-, -en) full power; power of attorney; letter of attorney.
Vollmatrose *m.* able-bodied seaman.
Vollmilch *f.* unskimmed milk; whole milk.
Vollmond *m.* full moon.
Vollpension *f.* (full) board and lodging.
vollständig *a.* complete, full, integral; *~ adv.* completely, in full.
Vollständigkeit *f.* completeness.
vollstreckbar *a.* executable; (*law*) enforceable.

vollstrecken *v.t.* to execute, to carry out.
Vollstreckung *f.* execution.
Vollstreckungsbefehl *m.* writ of execution.
volltanken *v.t.* to fill up.
volltönend *a.* sonorous, full-toned.
Volltreffer *m.* direct hit.
Vollversammlung *f.* general assembly.
vollwertig *a.* of full value.
Vollwertkost *f.* macrobiotic food.
vollzählig *a.* complete (in number).
vollziehen *v.t.st.* to execute; to carry out; to consummate (marriage); (*Testament*) to administer; *~de Gewalt*, executive (power).
Vollziehung *f.* (-, -en) **Vollzug** *m.* (-[e]s, 0) execution, consummation.
Volontär *m.* (-s, -s); **Volontärin** *f.* (-, -nen) unpaid trainee.
Volontariat *n.* (-s, -e) period of training; traineeship.
Volt *n.* (-s, -) volt.
Voltmeter *n.* (-s, -) volt-meter.
Volumen *n.* (-s, -mina) volume.
vom = **von dem.**
von *pr.* of; from; by; upon; on; *~... an*, since, from... upwards (downwards, forward); *~... her*, from; *~...herab*, from; *~ selbst*, of itself, of its own accord, automatically.
voneinander *a.* from each other.
vonnöten *a.* necessary.
vonstatten gehen *v.i.* to proceed.
vor *pr.* before, in front of; above; prior to; since, ago; *~ adv.* before; *nach wie ~*, now as before; *~ allem*, above all; *vor 8 Tagen*, a week ago; 10 *Minuten vor 8 Uhr*, ten minutes to eight; *Gnade ~ Recht ergehen lassen*, to let mercy overrule justice.
vorab *adv.* beforehand.
Vorabend *m.* eve.
Vorahnung *f.* premonition; presentiment.
voran *adv.* before, in front; on, ahead.
vorangehen *v.i.* (*s*) to go before, to lead the way; to precede; *mit gutem Beispiel ~*, to set the example.
Vorankündigung *f.* advance announcement.
Voranschlag *m.* previous estimate.
Vorarbeit *f.* preliminary work.
vorarbeiten *v.i.* to prepare the ground (for).
Vorarbeiter *m.* foreman.
voraus *adv.* before; beforehand, in advance; ahead of; *im (zum) voraus*, beforehand, in anticipation.
vorausahnen *v.t.* to anticipate.
vorausbestellbar *a.* bookable in advance.
vorausbestellen *v.t.* to order in advance.
Vorausbestellung *f.* booking.
vorausbezahlen *v.t.* to pay in advance, to prepay.
vorauseilen *v.i.* to hurry on in advance.
vorausgehen *v.i.st.* to lead the way.
voraushaben *v.t.ir.* to have an advantage over; to have in advance.
vorausnehmen *v.t.st.* to anticipate.
voraussagen *v.t.* to foretell, to predict.
vorausschicken *v.t.* to send before *or* in advance; (*fig.*) to premise.
voraussehen *v.t.st.* to foresee.
voraussetzen *v.t.* to suppose, to presuppose, to presume; to take for granted.
Voraussetzung *f.* (-, -en) prerequisite; supposition; *unter der ~ daß*, on the understanding that.

Voraussicht *f.* foresight, prudence.
voraussichtlich *a.* prospective; *~ adv.* probably, presumably.
Vorauszahlung *f.* advance payment.
Vorbau *m.* (-s, -ten) porch; front part.
vorbauen *v.i.* (*fig.*) to prevent, to preclude, to guard against.
vorbedacht *a.* premeditated.
Vorbedacht *m.* (-[e]s, 0) premeditation; *mit Vorbedacht*, intentionally; deliberately.
Vorbedeutung *f.* omen, portent.
Vorbedingung *f.* (-, -en) precondition.
Vorbehalt *m.* (-[e]s, -e) reservation; *unter ~*, with the proviso that.
vorbehalten *v.t.st.* to reserve; *alle Rechte ~*, all rights reserved; (sich) *~ v.refl.* to reserve to oneself.
vorbehaltlich *a.* conditional; *~ pr. & adv.* with the proviso that (of), subject to.
vorbehaltlos *a.* unreserved.
vorbehandeln *v.t.* to pretreat.
vorbei *adv.* by, past; over; finished.
vorbeifahren *v.i.st.* to drive past.
vorbeigehen *v.i.st.* (*s*) to pass by.
vorbeilassen *v.t.st.* to let pass.
vorbeischießen *v.i.st.* to miss (one's mark); (*s*) shoot past, to rush past.
vorbelastet *a.* handicapped.
Vorbemerkung *f.* preliminary remark.
vorbereiten *v.t.* to prepare.
vorbereitend *a.* preparatory.
Vorbereitung *f.* (-, -en) preparation.
Vorbesitzer *m.*; **Verbesitzerin** *f.* previous owner.
vorbestellen *v.t.* to order in advance.
Vorbestellung *f.* (-, -en) reservation.
vorbestraft *a.* previously convicted; *nicht ~*, no criminal record; *nicht ~er Verbrecher*, first offender.
vorbeten *v.t. & i.* to lead prayers.
vorbeugen *v.i.* (*fig.*) to prevent, to preclude, to guard against; (sich) *~ v.refl.* to bend forward.
Vorbeugung *f.* prevention, preventing.
Vorbild *n.* model, standard; (proto-)type.
vorbildlich *a.* exemplary; model.
Vorbildung *f.* (-, 0) previous training.
Vorbote *m.* harbinger; forerunner.
vorbringen *v.t.ir.* to bring forward, to advance; to utter.
vorchristlich *a.* pre-Christian.
Vordach *n.* canopy.
vordatieren *v.t.* to antedate.
vordem *adv.* formerly.
vordemonstrieren *v.t.* to demonstrate.
vorder *a.* anterior, fore-, front-.
Vorder: *~achse f.* front axle; *~ansicht f.* frontview; *~arm m.* fore-arm; *~fuß m.* fore-foot; *~gebäude n.* front building; *~grund m.* foreground.
vorderhand *adv.* for the present.
Vorder: *~mann m.* man in front; *~rad n.* frontwheel; *~radantrieb m.* front-wheel drive; *~seite f.* front (face); *~sitz m.* front-seat.
vorderst *a.* foremost.
Vorder: *~teil n.* forepart; *~tür f.* front door.
vordrängen *v.t.* (sich) *~ v.refl.* to press *or* push forward.
vordringen *v.i.st.* (*s*) to advance.
vordringlich *a.* urgent.

Vordruck *m.* printed form.
vorehelich *a.* premarital.
voreilig *a.* hasty, forward, rash.
voreinander *adv.* one in front of the other.
voreingenommen *a.* prejudiced, biased.
Voreingenommenheit *f.* (-, 0) bias.
vorenthalten *v.t.st.* to withhold (from).
Vorentscheidung *f.* preliminary decision.
vorerst *adv.* for the time being.
vorerwähnt *a.* aforementioned.
Vorfahr[e] *m.* (-s *u.* -en, -en) ancestor.
vorfahren *v.i.st.* (*s*) to drive up to a house; (*Verkehr*) to pass; to move foreward.
Vorfahrt *f.* priority; right of way.
Vorfall *m.* occurrence, incident; (*med.*) prolapse.
vorfallen *v.i.st.* (*s*) to occur, to happen.
vorfinden *v.t.st.* to find, to meet with.
Vorfrage *f.* preliminary question.
Vorfreude *f.* anticipated joy.
Vorfrühling *m.* early spring.
vorfühlen *v.t.* to sound s.b. out.
vorführen *v.t.* to show; to present; to perform.
Vorführraum *m.* (*Lichtbilder, etc.*) projection room.
Vorführung *f.* (-, -en) performance; presentation; demonstration; (~ *vor Gericht*) arraignment.
Vorführwagen *n.* demonstration car.
Vorgabe *f.* (-, -en) handicap.
Vorgang *m.* occurrence, incident.
Vorgänger *m.* (-s, 0); **Vorgängerin** *f.* (-, -nen) predecessor.
Vorgarten *m.* front garden.
vorgaukeln *v.t.* einem etwas ~, to deceive one by false promises.
vorgeben *v.t.st.* to pretend.
Vorgebirge *n.* promontory; foothills.
vorgeburtlich *a.* prenatal.
vorgefaßt *a.* preconceived.
vorgefertigt *a.* prefabricated.
Vorgefühl *n.* presentiment, misgiving.
vorgehen *v.i.st.* (*s*) to go before; (*Uhr*) to be fast; to proceed, to act; to occur, to happen.
Vorgehen *n.* proceedings *pl.*
vorgenannt *a.* aforementioned.
Vorgeschichte *f.* prehistory.
vorgeschichtlich *a.* prehistoric.
Vorgeschmack *m.* forestaste.
Vorgesetzte *m./f.* (-n, -n) superior.
vorgesetzte Stelle *or* **Behörde** *f.* superior authority, headquarters.
vorgestern *adv.* the day before yesterday.
vorgreifen *v.i.st.* to anticipate.
Vorgriff *m.* im ~ **auf** in anticipation of.
vorhaben *v.t.ir.* to intend, to plan.
Vorhaben *n.* (-s, -) design, intention.
Vorhalle *f.* entrance-hall.
vorhalten *v.t.st.* to reproach with, to rebuke; ~ *v.i.* to last, to hold out.
Vorhaltung *f.* reproach.
vorhanden *a.* at hand; on hand, in stock; ~ *sein*, to exist; to be at hand.
Vorhand *f.* forehand.
Vorhang *m.* (-[e]s, -hänge) curtain; den ~ zuziehen, to draw the curtain.
Vorhängeschloß *n.* padlock.
Vorhangstange *f.* curtain-rail.
Vorhaut *f.* prepuce, foreskin.

vorher *adv.* before(hand), previously.
vorherbestimmen *v.t.* to predestine; to predetermine.
Vorherbestimmung *f.* predestination.
vorhergehen *v.i.st.* (*s*) to go before, to precede.
vorhergehend *a.* preceding, previous.
vorherig *a.* prior; preceding.
Vorherrschaft *f.* supremacy; dominance.
vorherrschen *v.i.* to predominate.
Vorhersage *f.* prediction; (weather) forecast.
vorhersagen *v.t.* to forecast, to predict.
vorhersehen *v.t.st.* to foresee.
vorhin *adv.* before; a short time ago.
Vorhof *m.* (outer-)court, entry.
Vorhut *f.* (-, 0) vanguard.
vorig *a.* former, preceding, last; ~ *Woche*, last week.
Vorjahr *n.* preceding year.
vorjährig *a.* of last year.
Vorkämpfer *m.* pioneer.
vorkauen *v.t.* (*fig.*) to repeat over and over again.
Vorkaufsrecht *n.* first refusal.
Vorkehrung *f.* (-, -en) preventive measure, precaution; preparation; ~*en treffen*, to make provisions.
Vorkenntnisse *f.pl.* preliminary knowledge.
vorklassisch *a.* pre-classical.
vorkommen *v.i.st.* (*s*) to occur, to happen; to seem, to appear.
Vorkommen *n.* (-s, -) occurrence; deposit.
Vorkommnis *n.* (-nisses, -nisse) occurrence; incident.
Vorkriegs... .pre-war.
vorladen *v.t.st.* to cite, to summon.
Vorladung *f.* citation, summons.
Vorladungsschreiben *n.* writ of summons, subpœna.
Vorlage *f.* draft, bill; model, pattern (for drawing *or* writing).
Vorläufer *m.* forerunner, precursor.
vorläufig *a.* provisional, preliminary; temporary.
vorlaut *a.* pert, forward.
Vorleben *n.* (-s, -) former life; gutes, schlechtes ~, good, bad record.
Vorlegemesser *n.* carving-knife.
vorlegen *v.t.* to lay before, to present; to produce, to exhibit; to propose, to submit (a plan).
Vorleger *m.* (-s, -) mat; rug.
Vorlegeschloß *n.* padlock.
vorlesen *v.t.st.* to read (to); to read aloud.
Vorlesung *f.* (-, -en) lecture; course of lectures; ~*en halten*, to lecture.
Vorlesungsraum *m.* lecture-room.
Vorlesungsverzeichnis *f.* course catalogue.
vorletzt *a.* last but one, penultimate.
vorleuchten *v.i.* to shine before.
Vorliebe *f.* predilection.
vorliebnehmen *v.i.* to put up with.
vorliegen *v.i.st.* to lie before.
vorliegend *a.* in question; present.
vorlügen *v.t.st.* (einem etwas) to tell lies *or* stories (to one).
vormachen *v.t.* to show how a thing is done; einem etwas oder blauen Dunst ~, to deceive someone.
Vormacht *f.* leading power; supremacy.
Vormachtstellung *f.* position of supremacy.
vormalig *a.* former.

vormals *adv.* formerly, heretofore.
Vormarsch *m.* advance.
vormerken *v.t.* to book.
vormilitärisch *a.* premilitary.
Vormittag *m.* morning.
vormittägig *a.* in the morning.
vormittags *adv.* in the morning; a.m. (*ante meridiem*)
Vormund *m.* (-[e]s, -e *u.* -münder) guardian.
Vormundschaft *f.* guardianship; *unter ~ stellen*, to place under the care of a guardian.
vormundschaftlich *a.* custodial.
Vormundschaftsgericht *n.* Surrogate Court.
vorn *adv.* before, in front; (*nav.*) fore; *von ~*, facing, head . . .; from the beginning over again, anew; *von vornherein*, from the first.
Vorname *m.* Christian name, first name.
vornehm *a.* distinguished.
vornehmen *v.t.st.* to take in hand; to examine; (sich) *~ v.refl.* to resolve on, to intend.
Vornehmen *n.* (-s, 0) intention.
Vornehmheit *f.* (-, 0) rank, distinction.
vornehmlich *adv.* chiefly, principally.
vornherein, von *~* from the first.
Vorort *m.* suburb.
Vorortszug *m.* commuter train.
Vorplatz *m.* forecourt; hall; vestibule.
Vorposten *m.* outpost.
vorpredigen *v.t.* to preach to.
vorpreschen *v.i.* (*fig.*) to rush ahead.
Vorprogramm *n.* supporting program.
vorprogrammieren *v.t.* to preprogram.
Vorprüfung *f.* preliminary examination.
Vorrang *m.* (-s, 0) precedence, priority.
vorrangig *a.* priority.
Vorrat *m.* (-[e]s, -räte) store, stock, provision, supply; stockpile; (*Erz*) resources.
vorrätig *a.* in stock, on hand.
Vorratskammer *f.* pantry; larder.
Vorraum *m.* anteroom.
vorrechnen *v.t.* to calculate s.th. (for demonstration).
Vorrecht *n.* prerogative, privilege.
Vorrede *f.* preface, foreword; prologue.
Vorredner *m.*; **Vorrednerin** *f.* previous speaker.
Vorrichtung *f.* (-, -en) device.
vorrücken *v.t.* to advance; *~ v.i.* (*s*) to march on, to advance.
Vorrücken *n.* (-s, 0) advance.
Vorruhestand *m.* early retirement.
Vorrunde *f.* qualifying round.
vorsagen *v.t.* to prompt; to tell s.b. the answer.
Vorsaison *f.* early season.
Vorsänger *m.*; **Vorsängerin** *f.* leader of a choir.
Vorsatz *m.* (-es, -sätze) purpose, design, intention; *mit ~*, intentionally, on purpose.
vorsätzlich *a.* premeditated, wilful; *~ adv.* on purpose.
Vorschau *f.* (-, -en) preview.
Vorschein *m. zum ~ kommen*, to come forth, to appear.
vorschicken *v.t.* to send forward.
vorschieben *v.t.st.* to shove *or* push forward; to plead as an excuse; to slip (a bolt).
vorschießen *v.t.st.* to advance (money).
Vorschlag *m.* proposal, offer.

vorschlagen *v.t.st.* to propose.
Vorschlaghammer *m.* sledgehammer.
vorschnell *a.* precipitate, hasty, rash.
vorschreiben *v.t.st.* to prescribe.
Vorschrift *f.* direction, instruction.
vorschriftsmäßig *a.* according to rule; regulation; *~es Verfahren n.* (*mil.*) standard operating procedure (SOP).
Vorschub *m.* (-[e]s, 0) *~ leisten*, to promote; to support.
Vorschule *f.* kindergarten; preschool.
Vorschuß *m.* payment in advance.
vorschützen *v.t.* (*fig.*) to pretend.
vorschweben *v.i.* to be (vaguely) before one's mind.
vorsehen (sich) *v.refl.st.* to take care, to guard (against).
Vorsehung *f.* (-, 0) Providence.
vorsetzen *v.t.* to put before.
Vorsicht *f.* (-, 0) caution; *~! (auf Kisten)* with care!
vorsichtig *a.* cautious, careful; *~e Schätzung*, conservative estimate.
vorsichthalber *adv.* as a precaution.
Vorsichtsmaßnahme *f.* precaution; *~n treffen*, to take precautions.
Vorsilbe *f.* prefix.
vorsingen *v.i.st.* to sing to; to audition.
vorsintflutlich *a.* antediluvian.
Vorsitz *m.* (-es, 0) chair, chairmanship; *den ~ führen*, to be in the chair.
vorsitzen *v.i.st.* to be in the chair.
Vorsitzender *m.* (-n, -n) chairman; *stellvertretender ~*, vice-chairman.
Vorsorge *f.* foresight; precaution; *~untersuchung f.* (preventive) medical checkup.
vorsorgen *v.i.* to make provisions.
vorsorglich *a.* careful; provident.
Vorspann *m.* opening credits (film, TV).
Vorspeise *f.* hors d'œuvre.
vorspiegeln *v.t.* to make a false show of.
Vorspiegelung *f.* (-, -en) pretence; *~ falscher Tatsachen*, false pretences.
Vorspiel *n.* prelude; prologue; foreplay.
vorspielen *v.t.* to play to; to audition (theater).
vorsprechen *v.i.st.* to call on; to audition (theater).
vorspringen *v.i.st.* (*s*) to project.
Vorsprung *m.* (-[e]s, -sprünge) advantage, start, lead.
Vorstadt *f.* suburb.
vorstädtisch *a.* suburban.
Vorstand *m.* (-[e]s, -stände) (*Firma*) executive committee *or* board, management; (*Krankenhaus, etc.*) governing body; principal, head.
Vorstandsmitglied *n.* board member.
Vorstandssitzung *f.* board meeting.
vorstehen *v.i.st.* to preside over.
vorstehend *a.* preceding; *~ adv.* above.
Vorsteher *m.* (-s, -), **Vorsteherin** *f.* (-, -nen) head; chairman.
Vorsteherdrüse *f.* prostate (gland).
vorstellbar *a.* imaginable.
vorstellen *v.t.* to introduce; to represent; to act; (*eine Uhr*) to put forward; (sich) (*Dativ*) *~ v.refl.* to imagine.
Vorstellung *f.* (-, -en) introduction, presentation; performance; conception, idea; expostulation.

Vorstellungs: ~**gespräch** *n.* (job) interview; ~**kraft** *f.*, ~**vermögen** *n.* powers of imagination.
Vorstoß *m.* advance.
vorstoßen *v.t.st.* to push forward.
Vorstrafe *f.* previous conviction.
Vorstrafenregister *n.* criminal records.
vorstrecken *v.t.* to stretch forward, to thrust *or* poke out; (*fig.*) to advance, to lend (money).
Vorstufe *f.* preliminary stage.
Vortag *n.* day before.
vortanzen *v.t.* to demonstrate; *v.i.* to audition (ballet).
vortäuschen *v.t.* to feign.
Vorteil *m.* (-[e]s, -e) advantage, profit.
vorteilhaft *a.* advantageous, profitable.
Vortrag *m.* (-[e]s, -träge) elocution; recitation; lecture; (*Musik*) recital; (*com.*) balance carried forward; *einen* ~ *halten* to deliver a lecture, to read a paper.
vortragen *v.t.st.* to carry forward; to recite; to declaim; to lecture (on), to deliver (a speech); (*mus.*) to execute.
Vortragende *m./f.* speaker; lecturer.
Vortragskunst *f.* elocution.
Vortragsreihe *f.* series of lectures/talks.
Vortragsreise *f.* lecture tour.
vortrefflich *a.* excellent, superior.
vortreten *v.i.st.* (*s*) to step forward.
Vortritt *m.* (-[e]s, 0) precedence.
vorüber *adv.* by; past, over, finished.
vorübergehen *v.t.st.* (*s*) to pass by.
vorübergehend *a.* transitory, temporary.
Vorübergehende *m./f.* passer-by.
Vorübung *f.* preliminary exercise.
Voruntersuchung *f.* preliminary examination.
Vorurteil *n.* prejudice.
vorurteilslos *a.* unprejudiced.
Vorvergangenheit *f.* past perfect; pluperfect.
Vorverhör *n.* preliminary examination.
Vorverkauf *m.* (*theat.*) booking in advance; advance sale.
vorverlegen *v.t.* to move up (appointment).

Vorwahl *f.* preliminary election; primary; area code.
Vorwand *m.* (-[e]s, -wände) pretence, pretext.
vorwärmen *v.t.* to preheat.
vorwärts *adv.* ahead, forward(s), on; ~ *marsch!* quick march!; ~ *kommen*, to get on, to make one's way.
Vorwäsche *f.* prewash.
vorweg *adv.* before(hand).
vorwegnehmen *v.t.st.* to anticipate.
vorweisen *v.t.st.* to produce.
vorwerfen *v.t.st.* (*einem etwas*) to accuse s.b. of; to reproach with.
vorwiegen *v.i.* to prevail.
verwiegend *adv.* mainly.
Vorwissen *n.* (-s, 0) preliminary knowledge.
vorwitzig *a.* impertinent; prying.
Vorwort *n.* (-[e]s, -worte) foreword, preface.
Vorwurf *m.* (-[e]s, -würfe) reproach; accusation.
vorwurfsfrei, vorwurfslos *a.* irreproachable.
vorwurfsvoll *a.* reproachful.
Vorzeichen *n.* omen, token, portent; (*mus.*) signature; (*math.*) sign.
vorzeichnen *v.t.* to trace out, to sketch (a plan).
vorzeigen *v.t.* to produce; to show.
Vorzeit *f.* (-, 0) prehistory.
vorzeitig *a.* premature; precocious.
vorziehen *v.t.st.* to prefer.
Vorzimmer *n.* anteroom, antechamber.
Vorzug *m.* preference; advantage, privilege.
vorzüglich *a.* superior, excellent, exquisite; ~ *adv.* chiefly, especially.
Vorzüglichkeit *f.* (-, -en) superiority, excellence.
Vorzugs. . . preferential *a.*
Vorzugs: ~**aktie** *f.* preferred stock; ~**behandlung** *f.* preferential treatment; ~**tarif** *m.* preference.
vorzugsweise *adv.* preferably.
votieren *v.t. & i.* to vote.
Votum *n.* (-[s], -ta *u.* -ten) vote, suffrage.
vulgär *a.* vulgar.
Vulkan *m.* (-[e]s, -e) volcano.
vulkanisch *a.* volcanic.
vulkanisieren *v.t.* to vulcanize.

W

W, w *n.* the letter W or w.
Waage *f.* (-, -n) scales; balance.
waagerecht *a.* horizontal.
Waagschale *f.* (-, -n) scale; *in die* ~ *werfen*, to bring s.th. to bear.
wabb(e)lig *a.* flabby.
wabbeln *v.i.* to wobble.
Wabe *f.* (-, -n) honey-comb.
wach *a.* awake, alert.
Wachablösung *f.* changing of the guard; (*fig.*) transfer of power.
Wachdienst *m.* guard-duty.
Wache *f.* (-, -en) guard, watch; guard-room; sentry; *auf* ~ *sein*, to be on guard.
wachen *v.i.* to be awake; to watch over.
wachhabend *a.* on duty, on guard.
wachhalten *v.t.* (*fig.*) to keep s.th. alive.
Wachhund *m.* watchdog.
Wacholder *m.* (-s, -) juniper.

Wacholderbranntwein *m.* gin.
Wachs *n.* (-es, -e) wax.
wachsam *a.* watchful, vigilant.
Wachsamkeit *f.* vigilance.
wachsen *v.i.st.* (*s*) to grow; *einem gewachsen sein*, to be a match for someone; *eine Sache gewachsen sein*, to be equal to a task; *v.t.* to wax.
wächsern *a.* waxen, made of wax.
Wachs: ~**figurenkabinett** *n.* wax-works *pl.*; ~**leinwand** *f.* oil-cloth; ~**tuch** *m.* oil-cloth.
Wachstum *n.* (-[e]s, 0) growth; increase.
wachstums: ~**fördernd** *a.* growth-inducing; ~**hemmend** *a.* growth-retarding.
Wacht *f.* (-, -en) guard, watch.
Wachtel *f.* (-, -n) quail.
Wächter *m.* (-s, -) watchman; keeper.
Wachtposten *m.* post, sentinel, sentry.
wack(e)lig *a.* shaky, rickety, tottering.
wackeln *v.i.* to wobble, to totter.

wacker *a.* stout, gallant, brave, valiant.

Wade *f.* (-, -en) calf (of the leg).

Waffe *f.* (-, -n) weapon; arm.

Waffel *f.* (-, -n) waffle, wafer.

Waffeleisen *n.* waffle iron.

Waffengattung *f.* branch of the service, arm; ~**besitz** *m.* possession of firearms; ~**fabrik** *f.* arms factory; ~**gewalt** *f. mit* ~, by force of arms; ~**handel** *m.* arms trade; ~**kammer** *f.* armory.

waffenlos *a.* unarmed.

Waffen: ~**ruhe** *f.* cease-fire; ~**schein** *m.* gun license; ~**schmied** *m.* armorer; ~**schmuggel** *m.* gun-running; ~**stillstand** *m.* armistice; cease-fire; truce.

wägbar *a.* ponderable.

Wagehals *m.* dare-devil.

wagen *v.t.* to venture, to dare, to risk; *sich* ~, to venture.

Wagen *m.* (-s. -) vehicle; car; (*Last*~) wagon, cart, carriage, coach.

wägen *v.t.st.* to weigh.

Wagen ~**heber** *m.* jack; ~**ladung** *f.* cart-load, wagon-load; ~**pflege** *f.* car maintenance; ~**typ** *m.* model.

Waggon *m.* (-s, -s) railway-carriage; (*Güter*~) truck, van.

waghalsig *a.* foolhardy, rash.

Wagnis *n.* (-nisses, -nisse) venture.

Wahl *f.* (-, -en) choice, selection, option; (*politisch*) election.

wählbar *a.* eligible.

Wählbarkeit *f.* (-, 0) eligibility.

wahlberechtigt *a.* entitled to vote.

Wahlbeteiligung *f.* (voter) turnout.

Wahlbezirk *m.* electoral district.

wählen *v.t.* to choose; to select; (*politisch*) to elect; ~ *v.i.* (*politisch*) to vote; (*Telephon*) to dial.

Wähler *m.* (-s, -); **Wählerin** *f.* (-, -nen) voter, constituent, elector.

Wahlergebnis *n.* election returns *or* result.

wählerisch *a.* particular, fastidious.

Wählerschaft *f.* (-, 0) electorate; constituency.

wahlfähig *a.* eligible; entitled to vote.

wahlfrei *a.* optional.

Wahl: ~**gang** *f.* ballot; ~**heimat** *f.* adopted country; ~**kampf** *m.* election campaign; ~**kreis** *m.* constituency; ~**lokal** *n.* polling station; ~**recht** *n.* right to vote, franchise; (*allgemeines*) universal suffrage; ~**spruch** *m.* motto; ~**urne** *f.* ballot-box; ~**zettel** *m.* paper ballot.

Wählscheide *f.* dial.

Wahn *m.* (-[e]s, 0) illusion, error.

Wahnbild *n.* phantasm, delusion.

wähnen *v.t.* to imagine.

Wahnsinn *m.* -, 0 madness, frenzy.

wahnsinning *a.* insane, mad, frantic.

Wahnsinnige *m./f.* maniac; madman, madwoman; lunatic.

wahnwitzig *a.* insane, mad, frantic.

wahr *a.* true; real; genuine; *so* ~ *ich lebe!* as sure as I live!; ~ *machen*, to bear out; to prove, to fulfil; *nicht* ~? isn't it? don't you think so?

wahren *v.t.* to guard; *das Gesicht wahren*, to save face.

währen *v.i.* to last.

während *pr.* during; ~ *c.* while.

währenddessen *adv.* in the meantime; meanwhile.

wahrhaft *a.* true, veracious, truthful, real.

wahrhaftig *a.* genuine; ~ *adv.* truly.

Wahrhaftigkeit *f.* (-, 0) veracity.

Wahrheit *f.* (-, -en) truth; *einem die* ~ *sagen*, to tell a person off.

wahrheits: ~**gemäß** *a.* veracious; ~**getreu** *a.* truthful.

Wahrheitsliebe *f.* love of truth.

wahrlich *adv.* truly, verily.

wahrnehmbar *a.* perceptible.

wahrnehmen *v.t.st.* to perceive, to observe.

Wahrnehmung *f.* (-, -en) perception, observation; care (of).

wahrsagen *v.i.* to tell fortunes.

Wahrsager *m.* (-s, -); **Wahrsagerin** *f.* (-, -nen) fortune-teller, soothsayer.

wahrscheinlich *a.* likely, probable.

Wahrscheinlichkeit *f.* (-, -en) likelihood, probability.

Wahrung *f.* (-, 0) preservation; maintenance.

Währung *f.* (-, -en) currency.

Währungsausgleichfonds *m.* exchange stabilization fund.

Wahrzeichen *n.* symbol; landmark (city).

Waise *f.* (-, -n) orphan(-child).

Waisenhaus *n.* orphanage.

Wal *m.* (-[e]s, -e) whale.

Wald *m.* (-[e]s, **Wälder**) wood, forest.

Wald: ~**arbeiter** *m.* forestry worker; ~**brand** *m.* forest-fire; ~**gebiet** *n.*, ~**gegend** *f.* wooded area, woodland; ~**horn** *n.* bugle-horn, French-horn.

waldig *a.* wooded, woody.

Waldmeister *m.* (*bot.*) woodruff.

waldreich *a.* wooded.

Waldsterben *n.* dying of the forest.

Waldung *f.* (-, -en) woodland; forest.

Waldweg *m.* wood-path.

Walfang *m.* whaling.

Walfänger *m.* (-s, -) whaler.

Walfisch *m.* whale.

Waliser *m.* (-s, -) Welshman.

Waliserin *f.* (-, -nen) Welshwoman.

walisisch *a.* Welsh.

Walküre *f.* (-, -n) Valkyrie.

Wall *m.* (-[e]s, **Wälle**) rampart; mound.

Wallach *m.* (-[e]s *u.* -en, -e *u.* -en) gelding.

wallen *v.i.* to boil (up), to bubble.

wallfahren *v.i.* to go on a pilgrimage.

Wallfahrer *m.* (-s. -) pilgrim.

Wallfahrt *f.* pilgrimage.

Wallung *f.* (-, -en) ebullition; agitation.

Walnuß *f.* walnut.

Walroß *n.* (-rosses, -rosse) walrus.

walten *v.i.* to rule, to manage; *seines Amtes* ~, to perform the duties of one's office, to officiate.

Walze *f.* (-, -n) roller, cylinder; (*Schreib*-) platen.

walzen *v.t.* to roll; ~ *v.i.* to waltz.

wälzen *v.t.* to roll, to turn about; (sich) ~ *v.refl.* to wallow, to welter.

walzenförmig *a.* cylindrical.

Walzer *m.* (-s, -) waltz.

Walzwerk *n.* rolling-mill.

Wampe *f.* (-, -n) (*fam.*) pot belly.

Wand *f.* (-, **Wände**) wall, partition; *spanische* ~, folding-screen.

Wandalismus *m.* vandalism.

Wandel *m.* (-s, 0) changed.

wandelbar *a.* variable.

Wandehalle *f.* lobby.

wandeln (sich) *v.refl.* to change; *v.i.* to stroll.

Wander: ~**ausstellung** *f.* touring exhibition; ~**bühne** *f.* touring company; ~**düne** *f.* shifting sand dune.

Wanderer *m.* (-s, -); **Wanderin** *f.* (-, -nen) wanderer, hiker.

Wandergewerbe *f.* itinerant trade.

Wanderhenschrecke *f.* migratory locust.

wandern *v.t.* (*s*) to wander, to hike; to ramble.

Wanderpokal *m.* challenge cup.

Wanderschaft *f.* (-, 0) *auf der ~ sein*, to be traveling.

Wanderung *f.* (-, -n) walking tour.

Wanderweg *m.* foot path.

Wand: ~**gemälde** *n.* wall-painting, mural; ~**karte** *f.* wall-map; ~**schirm** *m.* folding-screen; ~**tafel** *f.* blackboard; ~**uhr** *f.* clock.

Wandlung *f.* (-, -en) change; (*Religion*) transubstantiation.

wandlungsfähig *a.* flexible; versatile.

Wange *f.* (-n -n) cheek; side-piece.

Wankelmut *m.* fickleness.

wankelmütig *a.* fickle, inconstant.

wanken *v.i.* to totter, to stagger; to waver.

wann *adv.* when; *dann und ~*, now and then, occasionally.

Wanne *f.* (-, -en) bath tub, bath; tub.

Wanst *m.* (-es, Wänste) belly, paunch.

Wanze *f.* (-, -n) bug, bedbug.

Wappen *m.* (-s, -) (coat of) arms.

wappnen *v.t.* to arm.

Ware *f.* (-, -n) merchandise, ware, goods *pl.*, commodity.

Waren: ~**haus** *n.* department store; ~**lager** *n.* warehouse, stock-in-trade; ~**probe** *f.* sample; ~**sendung** *f.* shipment, consignment; ~**zeichen** *n.* trademark.

warm *a.* warm; hot.

warmblütig *a.* warm-blooded.

Wärme *f.* warmth, heat; *Blutwärme, Körperwärme* , etc., blood heat, body heat.

wärmbeständig *a.* heat-resistant.

Warme: ~**dämmung** *f.* heat insulation; ~**kraftwerk** *n.* thermoelectric powerplant; ~**lehre** *f.* thermodynamics.

wärmen *v.t.* to warm, to heat.

Wärmepumpe *f.* heat pump.

wärmesicher *a.* heatproof.

Wärmflasche *f.* hot-water bottle.

warmherzig *a.* warm hearted.

Warnanlage *f.* warning device.

warnen *v.t.* to warn.

Warn: ~**schild** *n.* warning sign; ~**schuß** *m.* warning shot; ~**signal** *n.* warning signal; ~**streik** *m.* token strike.

Warnung *f.* (-, -en) warning, caution.

Warnzeichen *n.* warning sign.

Warte *f.* (-, -n) watch-tower; observatry.

Warteliste *f.* waiting list.

warten *v.t.* to tend, to nurse; ~ *v.i.* to wait, to stay; to attend to; ~*lassen*, to keep waiting.

Wärter *m.* (-s. -) attendant; keeper.

Wärterin *f.* (-, -nen) nurse; attendant.

Warte: ~**saal** *m.* waiting-room (at a station); ~**zimmer** *n.* (physician's) waiting-room.

Wartung *f.* (-, -en) service; attendance; (*Wagen*) maintenance.

warum *adv.* why.

Warze *f.* (-, -n) wart; (*Brust~*) nipple.

was *pn.* what; which; something; ~ *immer*, whatever; ~ *für ein*, what (kind of).

Wasch: ~**anstalt** *f.* laundry; ~**bär** *m.* racoon; ~**becken** *n.* wash-(*or* hand)basin.

waschbar *a.* washable.

Wäsche *f.* (-, -n) washing, linen; laundry; *schmutzige ~*, soiled, dirty linen.

waschecht *a.* fast (colors); (*fig.*) genuine.

Wäsche: ~**klammer** *f.* clothes-pin; ~**korb** *m.* linen-basket; ~**leine** *f.* clothes-line.

waschen *v.t. & i.*, (sich) ~ *v.refl.* to wash; (*Wäsche*) to launder.

Wäscherei *f.* (-, -en) laundry.

Wäsche: ~**schleuder** *f.* spin drier; ~**ständer** *m.* drying rack; ~**trockner** *m.* drier.

Wasch: ~**gelegenheit** *f.* washing facilities; ~**lappen** *m.* flannel, washcloth; ~**maschine** *f.* washing machine; ~**mittel** *n.* detergent; ~**salon** *m.* laundromat; ~**seife** *f.* laundry soap; ~**straße** *f.* car wash; ~**tag** *m.* washday; ~**tisch** *m.* washing-stand.

Wasser *n.* (-s, -) water; ~**abschlagen**, to make water; *fliessendes ~*, running water; *unter ~ setzen*, to submerge, to flood; *zu ~ und zu Lande*, by sea and land.

wasserabstoßend *a.* water-repellent.

wasserarm *a.* dry, arid.

Wasseraufbereitungsanlage *f.* water treatment plant.

wasserblau *a.* marine-blue, light-blue.

Wasserdampf *m.* steam.

wasserdicht *a.* waterproof, tight.

Wasser: ~**fahrzeug** *n.* watercraft; vessel; ~**fall** *m.* waterfall, cataract, cascade; ~**farbe** *f.* water-color; ~**glas** *n.* water-glass; ~**graben** *m.* ditch, moat; ~**hahn** *m.* faucet.

wäss(e)rig *a.* watery; (*fig.*) insipid, flat.

Wasser: ~**kessel** *m.* kettle; ~**kopf** *m.* hydrocephalus; ~**kraft** *f.* water-power; ~**kraftwerk** *n.* hydroelectric station; ~**leitung** *f.* water pipe; water-main; ~**mann** *m.* (*als Sternbild*) Aquarius; ~**melone** *f.* melon.

wässern *v.t.* to water, to irrigate.

Wasserpflanze *f.* aquatic plant.

wasserreich *a.* abounding in water.

Wasser: ~**röhre** *f.* water-pipe; ~**scheide** *f.* watershed.

wasserscheu *a.* afraid of water.

Wasser: ~**spiegel** *m.* surface of the water, water-level; ~**sport** *m.* aquatic sports *pl.*; ~**spülung** *f.* flush; ~**stand** *m.* water level; ~**standmesser** *m.* water-gauge; ~**stelle** *f.* watering place; ~**stoff** *m.* hydrogen.

Wasserstoffsuperoxyd *n.* hydrogen peroxide.

Wasser: ~**strahl** *m.* jet of water; ~**straße** *f.* waterway; ~**sucht** *f.* dropsy.

Wasser: ~**tier** *n*. aquatic animal; ~**turm** *m*. water-tower; ~**verschmutzung** *f*. water pollution; ~**versorgung** *f*. water-supply; ~**waage** *f*. level; ~**werk** *n*. water-works; ~**zeichen** *n*. watermark.

waten *v.i.* (*s*) to wade.

watscheln *v.i.* (*s*) to waddle.

Watt *n*. (-[e]s, -e) mud flats; (*elek.*) watt.

Watte *f*. (-, -n) (absorbent) cotton.

wattieren *v.t.* to wad, to pad.

wauwau! *i.* bow-wow!

weben *v.t.st.* to weave.

Weber *m*. (-s, -); **Weberin** *f*. (-, -nen) weaver.

Weberei *f*. weaving mill; weaving (product).

Webstuhl *m*. weaver's loom, frame.

Wechsel *m*. (-s. -) change, vicissitude; exchange; bill of exchange; (*auf Sicht*) bill payable at sight; (*gezogener*) draft; *auf einen einen ~ ziehen*, to draw on a person.

Wechsel: ~**balg** *m*. changeling; ~**beziehung** *f*. mutual relation, correlation; ~**fall** *m*. vicissitudes *pl.*; ~**geld** *n*. bank-money; change; ~**geschäft** *n*. exchange office, banking business; ~**gläubiger** *m*. holder *or* bearer of a bill of exchange; ~**inhaber** *m*. holder of a bill of exchange; ~**jahre** *pl.* menopause; ~**klage** *f*. action on *or* about a bill of exchange; ~**konto** *n*. account of exchange, bill-account; ~**kredit** *m*. discount credit; ~**kurs** *m*. rate of exchange; ~**makler** *m*. exchange-broker.

wechseln *v.t.* to change, to exchange; ~ *v.i.* to alternate; *Briefe ~*, to correspond.

wechselnd *a*. alternating.

wechselseitig *a*. reciprocal, mutual.

Wechselseitigkeit *f*. reciprocity.

Wechsel: ~**strom** *m*. alternating current; ~**verhältnis** *n*. reciprocal relation *or* proportion.

wechsel: ~**voll** *a*. changeable, varied; ~**weise** *adv.* alternately; mutually.

Wechselwirkung *f*. interaction.

wecken *v.t.* to wake, to awaken, to rouse.

Wecken *n*. (-s, 0) waking, awaking; ~ *m*. (-s, 0) small loaf.

Wecker *m*. (-s. -) alarm clock.

wedeln *v.i.* to wag (the tail); to fan.

weder *c*. neither; ~..., *noch*..., neither..., nor...

weg *adv.* away; gone; off; *das Buch ist ~*, the book is gone, missing; *über etwas ~* (*hinweg*) *sein*, to be above a thing; *in einem ~*, at a stretch, at a sitting; *kurzweg*, briefly, curtly; *schlechtweg*, simply, unceremoniously.

Weg *m*. (-[e]s, -e) way, path; (*Gang*) road; course; errand; (*fig.*) manner, means; *auf gütlichem ~*, amicably; *auf halbem ~e*, halfway, midway; *verbotener ~!* no thoroughfare!; *sich auf den ~ machen*, to set out, to start; *auf bestem ~ sein*, to be in a fair way to; *im ~e sein, stehen*, to be in the way.

wegbegeben (sich) *v.refl.st.* to go away.

Wegbereiter *m.*; **Wegbereiterin** *f*. forerunner.

wegblasen *v.t.st.* to blow away.

wegbleiben *v.i.st.* (*s*) to stay away *or* out; to be omitted.

wegbringen *v.t.ir.* to remove.

wegdenken *v.t.ir.* *etw. ~*, to imagine s.th. is not there.

wegdürfen *v.i.ir.* to be permitted to go.

wegeilen *v.i.* (*s*) to hasten away.

Wegelagerer *m*. (-s, -) highwayman.

wegen *pr.* on account of, because of; *von Rechts ~*, by right.

Wegerecht *n*. right of way.

Wegerich *m*. plantain.

wegessen *v.t.st.* to eat away, to eat up.

wegfahren *v.t.st.* to carry away; ~ *v.i.st.* (*s*) to drive off, to start.

Wegfall *m*. omission; *in ~ kommen*, to be abolished *or* omitted, to cease.

wegfallen *v.i.st.* (*s*) to be omitted.

wegfangen *v.t.st.* to catch (away).

wegfliegen *v.i.st.* (*s*) to fly away *or* off.

wegführen *v.t.* to lead *or* carry away.

Weggang *m*. (-[e]s, 0) departure.

weggeben *v.t.st.* to give away.

weggehen *v.i.st.* (*s*) to go away, to leave; *über etwas ~*, to pass over.

weggetreten! dismissed!

weggießen *v.t.st.* to pour away.

weghaben *v.t.ir. sein Teil ~*, to have got one's share.

weghelfen *v.t.st.* to help to get away.

wegholen *v.t.* to take *or* carry away.

wegjagen *v.t.* to chase away.

wegkommen *v.i.st.* (*s*) to get away; to come off.

wegkönnen *v.i.ir.* to be able to go *or* get away.

weglassen *v.t.st.* to let go; to leave out, to omit.

weglaufen *v.i.st.* (*s*) to run off *or* away.

weglegen *v.t.* to put away, to lay aside.

wegleugnen *v.t.* to deny flatly.

weglocken *v.t.* to entice away.

wegmachen (sich) *v.refl.* (*fam.*) to go away; *v.t.* to remove.

wegmüssen *v.i.ir.* to be obliged to leave.

Wegnahme *f*. (-, 0) seizure; capture.

wegnehmen *v.t.st.* to take away, to seize.

wegraffen *v.t.* to sweep off.

wegräumen *v.t.* to clear away.

wegreisen *v.i.* (*s*) to depart.

wegreißen *v.t.st.* to tear *or* snatch away.

wegrücken *v.t.* to remove; ~ *v.i.* (*s*) to move aside.

wegrufen *v.t.st.* to call away.

wegschaffen *v.t.* to remove.

wegschenken *v.t.* to give away.

wegscheuchen *v.t.* to frighten away.

wegschicken *v.t.* to send away *or* off.

wegschieben *v.t.st.* to shove away.

wegschleichen (sich) *v.refl.st.* to steal *or* sneak away.

wegschleppen *v.t.* to drag *or* force away.

wegschmeißen *v.t.st.* to chuck away.

wegschnappen *v.t.* to snatch away.

wegschneiden *v.t.st.* to cut away *or* off.

wegsehen *v.i.st.* to look away; (*über etwas*) to overlook.

wegsehnen (sich) *v.refl.* to wish oneself away.

weg sein *v.i.ir.* (*s*) to be gone, to be absent; to be lost; *über etwas ~*, to be above (minding) a thing; *ganz ~*, to be enraptured with.

wegsenden *v.t.ir.* to send away.

wegsetzen *v.i.* (*s*) (*über etwas*) to leap (over), to clear; *sich über etwas ~*, not to mind a thing.

wegspringen *v.i.st.* (*s*) to leap away; to run away, to escape.

wegspülen *v.t.* to wash away.

wegstehlen *v.t.st.* (sich) *v.refl.* to steal away.

wegstellen *v.t.* to put away *or* aside.

wegsterben *v.i.st.* (s) to die off.

wegstoßen *v.t.st.* to push away.

wegstreichen *v.t.st.* to strike out.

wegtragen *v.t.st.* to bear *or* carry away.

webtreiben *v.t.st.* to drive away.

wegtreten *v.i.st.* to step aside.

wegtun *v.t.st.* to put away, to remove.

wegwälzen *v.t.* to roll away.

Wegweiser *m.* (-s, -) road-sign.

wegwerfen *v.t.st.* to throw *or* cast away; (sich) ~ *v.refl.* to degrade oneself.

wegwerfend *a.* disparaging.

Wegwerf: **~flasche** *f.* disposable bottle; **~gesellschaft** *f.* throwaway society.

wegwollen *v.i.ir.* to want to go.

wegwünschen *v.t.* to wish away.

wegzaubern *v.t.* to spirit away.

wegziehen *v.t.st.* to pull away; ~ *v.i.st.* (s) to march away; *(aus einer Wohnung)* to move.

weh, wehe *i.* wo! woe!

weh *a.* painful, sore; *~tun,* to cause pain; *sich ~tun,* to hurt oneself.

Weh *n.* (-[e]s, 0) woe, pain, grief; *Wohl und ~,* weal and woe.

Wehe *f.* drift.

Wehen *f.pl.* labor-pains.

wehen *v.t. & i.* to blow.

Wehgeschrei *n.* lamentations, wailings *pl.*

Wehklage *f.* lamentation, wailing.

wehklagen *v.i.* to lament, to wail.

wehleidig *a.* plaintive; whining.

Wehmut *f.* sadness, *(sweet)* melancholy.

wehmütig *a.* sad, melancholy; nostalgic.

Wehr *f.* (-, -en) defense; *sich zur ~ setzen,* to offer resistance.

Wehr *n.* (-[e]s, -e) weir; dam, dike.

Wehrdienst *m.* military service.

Wehrdienstverweigerer *m.* conscientious objector.

wehren *v.t. & i.* to restrain; to hinder; (sich) ~ *v.refl.* to defend oneself.

Wehrersatzdienst *m.* obligatory service for conscientious objectors.

wehrfähig *a.* fit for military service.

wehrhaft *a.* ready to defend o.s.; fortified.

wehrlos *a.* defenseless, weak.

Wehrlosigkeit *f.* defenselessness.

Wehr: **~paß** *m.* service record; **~pflicht** *f.* compulsory military service, conscription.

wehrpflichtig *a.* liable to military service.

Weib *n.* (-es, -er) woman, female; wife.

Weibchen *n.* (-s, -) *(pej.)* little woman; *(von Tieren)* female.

Weiberfeind *m.* woman-hater, misogynist.

weiberhaft *a.* womanlike, womanish.

Weiberheld *m.* lady-killer.

weibisch *a.* womanish; effeminate.

weiblich *a.* female; womanly, feminine.

Weiblichkeit *f.* (-, 0) femininity.

Weibsbild *n.* *(fam. pej.)* female, wench, hussy.

weich *a.* soft, mellow; tender(-hearted).

Weiche *f.* (-, -n) softness; side; flank; *(rail.)* points *pl.*; *(elek.)* switch, shunt.

weichen *v.t.* to steep, to soak, to soften; ~ *v.i.* (s) to soak, to soften.

weichen *v.i.st.* (s) to give way, to yield; *von der*

Stelle ~, to budge, to stir.

weichgekocht *a.* soft-boiled.

weichherzig *a.* tender-hearted.

weichlich *a.* soft; weak, effeminate.

Weichling *m.* (-[e]s, -e) weakling.

Weich: **~macher** *m.* softener; **~spüler** *m.* (fabric) softener; **~teile** *pl.* soft parts; **~tier** *n.* mollusc.

Weide *f.* (-, -n) pasture(-ground); pasturage; *(Baum)* willow.

Weideland *n.* pasture-land.

weiden *v.t.* to feed, to tend; ~ *v.i.* to pasture, to graze; *sich ~ (an etwas),* to delight (in), to gloat (over).

Weidengeflecht *n.* wicker-work.

weidlich *adv.* thoroughly.

Weidmann *m.* huntsman.

weidmännisch *a.* huntsmanlike.

weigern (sich) *v.refl.* to refuse.

Weigerung *f.* (-, -en) refusal, denial.

Weih: **~becken** *n.* holy-water font; **~bischof** *m.* suffragan bishop.

Weihe *f.* (-, -n) consecration; ordination.

weihen *v.t.* to consecrate, to ordain; *(fig.)* to dedicate, to devote; *sich ~lassen,* to take (holy) orders.

Weiher *m.* (-s, -) (fish-)pond.

weihevoll *a.* sacred, hallowed, solemn.

Weihnachten *f.pl.* Christmas, Xmas.

Weihnachts: **~abend** *m.* Christmas eve; **~baum** *m.* Christmas-tree; **~(feier)tag** *m.* Christmas-day; **~lied** *n.* Christmas carol *or* hymn; **~mann** *m.* Father Christmas, Santa Claus.

Weihrauch *m.* (-[e]s, 0) incense.

Weihrauchfaß *n.* censer.

Weihwasser *n.* holy-water.

weil *c.* because, since, as.

weiland *adv.* formerly; late, deceased.

Weilchen *n.* (-s, 0) little while.

Weile *f.* (-, 0) while, time; leisure; *eine ~,* for a while.

weilen *v.i.* to tarry, to stay.

Weiler *m.* (-s, -) hamlet.

Wein *m.* (-[e]s, -e) wine; *(bot.)* vine; *einem reinen ~ einschenken,* to tell one the plain truth, not to mince matters; *wilder ~,* Virginia creeper.

Wein: **~bau** *m.* viticulture; **~bauer** *m.*; **~bäuerin** *f.* wine grower; **~berg** *m.* vineyard; **~brand** *m.* brandy.

weinen *v.i.* to weep (for, at, over), to cry.

weinerlich *a.* tearful; weepy; whining.

Wein: **~essig** *m.* (wine-)vinegar; **~geist** *m.* spirit of wine; **~handel** *m.* wine-trade; **~händler** *m.* wine-merchant; **~jahr** *n. gutes ~,* good vintage; **~karte** *f.* wine-list; **~keller** *m.* wine-cellar; **~kenner** *m.* connoisseur of wine; **~lese** *f.* grape harvest; **~säure** *f.* acidity of wine, tartaric acid; **~stein** *m.* tartar; **~stock** *m.* vine; **~stube** *f.* wine tavern; **~traube** *f.* (bunch of) grapes.

weise *a.* wise.

Weise *m./f.* (-n, -n) sage, philsopher, wise man or woman; *Stein der ~n,* philosopher's stone.

Weise *f.* (-, -n) manner, way; method, fashion; habit; tune, melody; *auf keine ~,* no ways, by no means.

weisen *v.t.st.* to point out, to show, to direct; *an einem ~,* to refer to one; *von sich ~,* to reject, to refuse; to repudiate; *etwas von der Hand ~,* to dismiss.

Weisheit *f.* (-, -en) wisdom, prudence.

Weisheitszahn *m.* wisdom-tooth.

weislich *adv.* wisely, prudently.

weismachen *v.t.* to make one believe a thing.

weiß *a.* white; clean.

Weiß *n.* (-es, 0) white color.

weissagen *v.t.* to prophesy, to foretell.

Weissager *m.* (-s, -) fortune-teller, prophet.

Weissagerin *f.* (-, -nen) prophetess; fortune-teller.

Weissagung *f.* (-, -en) prophecy.

Weiß: ~**blech** *n.* tin-plate, white metal; ~**brot** *n.* white bread; ~**dorn** *m.* hawthorn.

Weiße *f.* (-, 0) whiteness, white; (*fam.*) glass of Berlin pale beer.

Weiße *m./f.* white man/woman.

weißen *v.t.* to whiten; to whitewash.

Weißfisch *m.* whiting; whitebait.

weißglühend *a.* at a white heat.

Weißglut *f.* white heat.

Weißherbst *m.* rosé wine.

Weißkohl *m.*, **Weißkraut** *n.* common cabbage.

weißlich *a.* whitish.

Weißmetall *n.* white metal.

Weiß: ~**näherin** *f.* seamstress; ~**wein** *m.* white wine; ~**wurst** *f.* veal sausage; ~**zeug** *n.* linen.

Weisung *f.* (-, -en) direction, instruction.

weit *a.* distant, remote, far, far off, wide; large; ~ *adv.* far; widely; *zwei Meilen* ~, two miles off; *bei* ~*em*, by far; *von* ~*em*, from afar; ~ *und breit*, far and wide; *nicht* ~ *kommen*, to make no great progress; *mit etwas* ~ *sein*, to have got well into a thing; *die Sache ist noch lange nicht soweit*, the matter has not got nearly so far as that; *nicht* ~ *her sein*, (*fam.*) not much to speak of; *es* ~ *bringen*, to get on in the world; *das geht zu* ~, that is going too far; *es zu* ~ *treiben*, to carry things too far; *einen* ~ *übertreffen*, far to surpass someone; ~ *gefehlt!*, very wide of the mark!; (*in*)-*soweit*, so far; *soweit* (*als*), so far as; *des Weiten und Breiten erzählen*, to spin a long yarn about.

weitaus *adv.* by far.

weitblickend *a.* (*fig.*) far-sighted.

Weite *f.* (-, -n) width; distance; capacity.

weiten *v.t.* to widen; (sich) ~ *v.refl.* to widen, to expand.

weiter *adv.* further; forward, on; *und so* ~, and so on, etc.; ~ *nichts*, nothing else; ~! *i.* go on! proceed!; ~ *niemand*, no one else *or* besides; ~**lesen**, to go on reading; ~**kommen**, to get on, to proceed; *bis auf* ~*es*, until further notice, advice *or* orders; *ohne* ~*es*, without much ado.

Weiterbeförderung *f.* forwarding; *zur* ~ *an*, to be forwarded *or* sent on to. . .

Weiterbestand *m.* continued existence.

weiterentwickeln *v.t. u.refl.* to develop further.

weitergeben *v.t.st.* to pass on.

weitergehen *v.i.st.* (*s*) to proceed.

weiterhin *adv.* further.

weiterleiten *v.t.* to pass on.

Weiterreise *f.* journey onwards.

weiterverarbeiten *v.t.* to process.

weiterverfolgen *v.t.* to follow up.

weiterziehen *v.i.st.* to move on.

weitgehend *a.* far-reaching; extensive.

weitgereist *a.* widely traveled.

weitgreifend *a.* far-reaching.

weither *adv.* from afar; ~ *geholt*, far-fetched.

weitherzig *a.* generous.

weithin *adv.* to a great distance, far off.

weitläufig *a.* ample, spacious; detailed; *sie sind* ~ *verwandt*, they are distantly related.

weit: ~**maschig** *a.* wide meshed; ~**reichend** *a.* far-reaching: ~**schweifig** *a.* prolix, lengthy, tedious.

weitsichtig *a.* long-sighted; (*fig.*) far-sighted.

Weitsprung *m.* broad jump.

weittragend *a.* far-reaching, portentous; ~**verzweigt** *a.* extensive; with many branches.

Weitwinkelobjektiv *a.* wide-angle lense.

Weizen *m.* (-s, -) wheat.

welcher, welche, welches *pn.* who, which, that; some, any.

welk *a.* withered, faded, flabby.

welken *v.i.* (*s*) to wither, to fade.

Wellblech *n.* corrugated iron.

Welle *f.* (-, -n) wave, billow; shaft, axle-tree.

wellen *v.t.* (*Haar*) to wave.

Wellen: ~**band** *n.* (*Radio*) waveband; ~**brecher** *n.* breakwater.

wellenförmig *a.* wavy, undulating.

Wellenlänge *f.* wavelength.

Wellenlinie *f.* wavy line.

Wellenreiten *n.* surfing.

wellig *a.* wavy.

Wellpappe *f.* corrugated cardboard.

Welpe *m.* (-n, -n) whelp; pup; cub.

Wels *m.* (**Welses, Welse**) cat-fish.

Welsche *m.* (-n, -n) Italian; Frenchman.

Welt *f.* (-, -en) world; universe; people; *alle* ~, all the world, everybody; *zur* ~ *bringen*, to give birth to; *aus der* ~ *schaffen*, to do away with; *um alles in der* ~ *nicht*, not for the world.

Weltall, Weltenall *n.* (-s, 0) universe.

Welt: ~**anschaulich** *a.* ideological; ~**anschauung** *f.* world-view; ~**ausstellung** *f.* international exhibition.

welt: ~**bekannt** *a.*, ~**berühmt** *a.* world-famous.

Weltbürger *m.*; **Weltbürgerin** *f.* cosmopolitan.

Weltenbummler *m.* (-s, -) globetrotter.

welterfahren *a.* experienced.

welterschütternd *a.* world-shaking.

weltfremd *a.* unworldly; naive.

Welt: ~**frieden** *m.* universal peace; ~**geschichte** *f.* universal history.

weltgeschichtlich, welthistorisch *a.* historical.

weltgewandt *a.* experienced in the world.

Welt: ~**handel** *m.* international trade; ~**herrschaft** *f.* world supremacy; ~**karte** *f.* map of the world; ~**kenntnis** *f.* knowledge of the world; ~**krieg** *m.* world war; ~**lage** *f.* international situation; ~**lauf** *m.* course of the world.

weltlich *a.* worldly, mundane; temporal, secular.

Welt: ~**literatur** *f.* literature of the world; ~**macht** *f.* world power *or* empire.

weltmännisch *a.* characteristic of a man of the world, gentlemanly.

Welt: ~**markt** *m.* international market; ~**meister** *m.* world-champion; ~**meisterschaft** *f.* world-championship.

Welt: ~**raum** *m.* space; ~**reich** *n.* great empire; ~**schmerz** *m.* weariness of life, pessimistic melancholy; ~**sprache** *f.* universal language; ~**stadt** *f.* cosmopolitan city; ~**stellung** *f.* position in the world; ~**teil** *m.* part of the world; ~**untergang** *m.* end of the world; ~**verkehr** *m.* international trade.

wem *pn.* to whom; he to whom.

Wemfall *m.* dative (case).

wen *pn.* whom; he whom.

Wende *f.* (-, -n) turn, turning point.

Wendekreis *m.* tropic.

Wendeltreppe *f.* winding-stairs *pl.*, spiral staircase.

wenden *v.t. & ir. & reg.* to turn; (sich) ~ *v.refl.* to turn; (*an einen*) to address, to apply to; *bitte* ~! please turn over!

Wendepunkt *m.* turning-point.

Wendung *f.* (-, -en) turn; *eine* ~ *zum Schlimmeren*, a change for the worse.

wendig *a.* nimble; easy to steer.

Wenfall *m.* accusative (case).

wenig *a. & adv.* little; some; ~*e*, few; *ein* ~, a little.

weniger *a.* less; fewer.

Wenigkeit *a.* (-, 0) small quantity, trifle; *meine* ~, yours truly.

wenigstens *adv.* at least.

wenn *c.* when; if; ~ *anders*, ~*nur*, provided that; *es ist als* ~, it is as if; *außer* ~, unless, except when (if); ~ *auch*, though, although; *selbst* ~, *und* ~, even when (if); ~ *anders*, if. . .at all, if really; ~ *schon, denn schon*, (*fam.*) in for a penny, in for a pound; ~ *auch noch so*, if. . .ever so.

wenngleich, wennschon *c.* though, although, albeit.

wer *pn.* who; he who; which; whoever, whosoever; ~ *da*? who goes there?

Werbe. . . (*in Zus.*), advertising. . .

Werbe: ~**abteilung** *f.* advertising department; ~**agentur** *f.* advertising agency; ~**fachmann** *m.* publicity agent; ~**fernsehen** *n.* commercial TV; ~**geschenk** *n.* free gift.

werben *v.i.st.* to apply for, to sue, to court; to canvass, to make propaganda; ~ *v.t.st.* to recruit, to enlist; ~ *um*, to court, to woo (a girl), to sue for.

Werber *m.* (-s, -) wooer, suitor.

Werbe: ~**slogan** *m.* advertising slogan; ~**spot** *m.* commercial.

Werbung *f.* (-, -en) recruiting; courtship; (*com.*) advertising, public relations.

Werdegang *m.* career.

werden *v.i.ir.* (*s*) to become; to grow, to turn, to get; *zuteil* ~, to fall to one's share; *was soll aus ihm* ~? what is to become of him?; *die Sache wird*, the matter is in a fair way; *es wird schon!*, we are getting on well!; *wird's bald*? will you soon have done?

Werden *n.* (-s, 0) genesis; *im* ~ *sein*, to be in progress, to be in the making.

werfen *v.t.st.* to throw, to cast, to fling; (*von Tieren*) to bring forth; (sich) ~ *v.refl.st.* (*Holz*) to warp; *Verdacht* ~ *auf*, to cast suspicions on.

Werft *m.* (-[e]s, -e) shipyard, dockyard.

Werg *n.* (-es, 0) tow.

Werk *n.* (-[e]s, -e) work; action, deed; clockwork; mechanism; *ins* ~ *setzen*, to set going; *im* ~*e sein*, to be going on; *ans* ~ *gehen*, to go to work; *Hand ans* ~ *legen*, to set to work; *sich ans* ~ *machen*, to begin work; *zu* ~*e gehen*, to set about (a thing), to go (the right way) to work.

Werkbank *f.* work-bench, shop-counter.

Werk: ~**führer** *m.* foreman; ~**führerin** *f.* forewoman; ~**meister** *m.* foreman; ~**schutz** *m.* factory guard; ~**statt, ~stätte** *f.* workshop; ~**stattauftrag** *m.* work-order; ~**stoff** *m.* material; ~**student** *m.* working student; ~**tag** *m.* working-day.

werktäglich *a.* workaday, every-day.

werktags *adv.* on weekdays.

werktätig *a.* active, industrious.

Werk: ~**zeug** *n.* instrument, tool; ~**zeugkasten** *m.* tool box; ~**zeugmaschine** *f.* machine tool.

Wermut *m.* (-[e]s, 0) wormwood; vermouth.

wert *a.* worth, worthy; valuable; dear; *der Mühe* ~, worth (our) while; ~**achten**, ~**schätzen**, to hold dear, to prize highly.

Wert *m.* (-[e]s, -e) value, worth; rate, price; ~ *auf etwas legen*, to attach value to.

Wert: ~**angabe** *f.* declaration of value; ~**arbeit** *f.* high-quality workmanship.

wertbeständig *a.* of fixed value.

Wert: ~**bestimmung** *f.* valuation; ~**betrag** *m.* value in money; ~**brief** *m.* insured letter.

Wertgegenstand *m.* valuable.

Wertigkeit *f.* (*chem.*) valency; significance.

wertlos *a.* worthless.

Wert: ~**maßstab** *m.* standard of value; ~**paket** *n.* insured package; ~**papiere** *n.pl.* securities *pl.*; ~**sachen** *pl.* valuables.

wertschätzen *v.t.* to esteem highly.

Wertschätzung *f.* (-, 0) esteem, regard.

Wertsendung *f.* parcel containing money *or* valuables.

Wertsteigerung *f.* increase in value.

Werturteil *n.* value judgment.

wertvoll *a.* valuable; precious.

Wertzuwachs *m.* increment value; ~**steuer** *f.* increment value duty.

Werwolf *m.* (-[e]s, -wölfe) wer(e)wolf.

wes *pn* whose (*obs. poet.*).

Wesen *n.* (-s, -) being, entity; essence; substance, nature, character; ado, hubbub, noise; *sein* ~ *treiben*, to be at it (again); *viel* ~*s aus etwas machen*, to make a good deal of fuss *or* much ado about a thing; . . .*wesen*, (*in Zus.*) affairs, concerns *pl.*; *Finanzwesen*, finances; *Kriegswesen*, military affairs; *Schulwesen*, educational affairs.

Wesenheit *f.* (-, 0) essence, nature.

wesenlos *a.* unsubstantial, unreal.

Wesens: ~**art** *f.* nature, character; ~**zug** *m.* characteristic.

wesentlich *a.* fundamental, essential; substantial.

Wesfall *m.* genitive (case).

weshalb, weswegen *adv.* wherefore, why.

Wespe *f.* (-, -n) wasp; yellow jacket.

Wespenstich *m.* wasp sting.

wessen *pn.* whose.

West (without article) west; West.

westdeutsch *a.*; **Westdeutsche** *m./f.* West German.

Weste *f.* (-, -n) vest.

Westen *m.* (-s, 0) west, Occident.

Westentasche *f.* vest pocket.

Westindien *n.* the West Indies.

westlich *a.* western, westerly.

Westmächte *pl.* Western Powers.

Westseite *f.* western side.
westwärts *adv.* westward.
Westwind *m.* west wind.
wett *a.* equal, (*fam.*) quits; *etwas ~ machen,* to even scores.
Wettbewerb *m.* competition; contest.
Wettbewerber *m.* competitor.
Wettbüro *n.* betting office.
Wette *f.* (-n -n) bet, wager; *um die ~ laufen,* to race one another; *eine ~ eingehen, machen,* to lay a wager, to make a bet.
Wetteifer *m.* competition; rivalry.
wetteifern *v.i.* to vie, to contend with.
wetten *v.t.* to wager, to bet, to lay a wager; *es läßt sich* 100 *gegen eins ~,* you may bet *or* lay 100 to one; *auf etwas ~,* to back (a horse).
Wetter *n.* (-s, -) weather; *schlechtes ~,* bad weather; *schönes ~,* fine *or* fair weather; *bei gutem ~,* weather permitting.
Wetter: ~amt *n.* meteorological office; **~aussichten** *pl.* weather outlook; **~bericht** *m.* weather report; **~dienst** *m.* meteorological service; **~fahne** *f.* weather-cock, vane; (*fig.*) turn-coat.
wetterfest *a.* weather-proof.
Wetter: ~karte *f.* meteorological chart; **~kunde** *f.* meteorology.
Wetterlage *f.* weather conditions.
Wetterleuchten *n.* summer lightning.
wettern *v.i.* to storm, to swear.
Wetter: ~vorhersage *f.* weather forecast; **~warte** *f.* weather bureau.
wetterwendisch *a.* changeable, fickle.
Wetterwolke *f.* thunder cloud.
Wett: ~kampf *m.* contest; prize fight, match; **~lauf** *m.* race, running-match.
wettlaufen *v.i.st.* (*s*) to run a race; *~ gegen einen,* to race against one.
Wett: ~läufer *m.* prize runner; **~rennen** *n.* horse race; racing; **~rudern** *n.* boat race; **~streit** *m.* contest, contention, match.
wetzen *v.t.* to whet, to sharpen.
Wetzstein *m.* whetstone.
Whiskey *m.;* **Whisky** *m.* whiskey, whisky.
Wichse *f.* (-, -en) blacking, polish.
wichsen *v.t.* to black, to polish; *v.i.* (*vulg.*) to wank; to jerk off.
Wicht *m.* (-[e]s, -e) little imp; creature.
Wichtel *m.* (-s, -) gnome; goblin.
wichtig *a.* important.
Wichtigkeit *f.* (-, 0) importance.
Wichtigtuer *m.* pompous ass.
wichtigtuerisch *a.* pompous; self-important.
Wicke *f.* vetch, sweet pea.
Wickel *m.* (-s, -) compress.
Wickel: ~kind *n.* child in swaddling clothes, baby; **~kommode** *f.* changing table.
wickeln *v.t.* to wind (up); to wrap up; to roll, to curl; to swathe, to swaddle; *auseinander ~,* to unwrap, to undo, to unfold.
Wicklung *f.* (-, -en) (*elek.*) winding.
Widder *m.* (-s, -) ram; (*Sternbild*) Aries.
wider *pr.* against, contrary to; versus; *~ Willen,* unwillingly; *das Für und Wider,* the pros and cons.
widerborstig *a.* unruly; rebellious.
widerfahren *v.i.st.* (*s*) to happen to, to befall; *einem Gerechtigkeit ~ lassen,* to do one justice.

Widerhaken *m.* barbed hook; barb (of an arrow *or* hook).
Widerhall *m.* (-[e]s, -e) echo.
widerhallen *v.i.* to (re-)echo.
widerlegen *v.t.* to refute, to disprove.
Widerlegung *f.* (-, -en) refutation.
widerlich *a.* disgusting, repulsive.
widernatürlich *a.* contrary to nature.
Widerpart *m.* (-[e]s, -e) opponent.
widerraten *v.t.st.* to dissuade (from).
widerrechtlich *a.* unlawful.
Widerrede *f.* contradiction.
Widerruf *m.* revocation; recantation.
widerrufen *v.t.st.* to revoke; to recant, to retract.
widerruflich *a.* revocable; *~ adv.* on probation.
Widerrufung *f.* (-, -en) revocation.
Widersacher *m.* (-s, -); **Widersacherin** *f.* (-, -nen) adversary.
Widerschein *m.* reflection, reflex.
widersetzen (sich) *v.refl.* to resist.
widersetzlich *a.* refractory.
Widersinn *m.* nonsense, absurdity.
widersinnig *a.* nonsensical, absurd.
widerspenstig *a.* refractory, obstinate.
widerspiegeln *v.t.* to reflect.
widersprechen *v.i.st.* to contradict, to gainsay; (sich) *~ v.refl.* to contradict oneself; *sich ~d,* contradictory.
Widerspruch *m.* contradiction.
widersprüchlich *a.* contradictory.
widerspruchslos *a.* unprotesting, uncontradicting.
Widerstand *m.* resistance, opposition; (*elek.*) resistance; *~ leisten,* to offer resistance; **~sbewegung** *f.* resistance; underground movement.
widerstandsfähig *a.* robust; capable of resistance.
Widerstandkämpfer *m.* resistance fighter.
Widerstandskraft *f.* resistance.
widerstandslos *a.* without resistance.
widerstehen *v.i.st.* to resist, to withstand; to be repugnant (to).
widerstreben *v.i.* to oppose, to resist; *das widerstrebt mir,* the thing jars upon me.
Widerstreben *n.* reluctance.
widerstrebend *a. & adv.* reluctant(ly).
Widerstreit *m.* conflict, clash.
widerstreiten *v.i.* to conflict with.
widerstreitend *a.* conflicting.
widerwärtig *a.* repulsive, revolting; offensive.
Widerwille *m.* aversion, repugnance.
widerwillig *a.* reluctant, unwilling.
widmen *v.t.* to dedicate, to inscribe; to devote.
Widmung *f.* (-, -en) dedication.
widrig *a.* contrary; adverse; offensive.
Widrigkeit *f.* (-, -en) adversity.
wie *adv.* how; *~ c.* as, like; *~so?* how do you mean?; *~ wenn,* as if, as though; *~ glücklich er auch sein mag,* however happy he may be; *~dem auch sei,* be that as it may.
wieder *adv.* again, anew, afresh; back, in return; *hin und ~,* now and then; *~ gut machen,* to redress.
wiederabdrucken *v.t.* to reprint.
Wiederaufbau *m.* reconstruction.
wiederaufbauen *v.t.* to rebuild.
Wiederaufbereitung *f.* reprocessing; **~sanlage** *f.* reprocessing plant; recycling plant.

wiederaufleben *v.i.* (*s*) to revive.
Wiederaufnahme *f.* resumption.
Wiederaufnahmeverfahren *n.* (*law*) retrial.
wiederaufnehmen *v.t.st.* to resume.
wiederauftauchen *v.i.* to turn up again.
Wiederbeginn *m.* recommencement; resumption.
wiederbekommen *v.t.st.* to get back.
wiederbeleben *v.t.* to revive, to resuscitate.
Wiederbelebungsversuch *m.* attempt to revive.
wiederbringen *v.t.ir.* to return.
wiedereinführen *v.t.* to reintroduce, to reimport.
wiedereinlösen *v.t.* to redeem.
Wiedereinreiseerlaubnis *f.* reentry permit.
wiedereinsetzen *v.t.* to reinstate.
wiederentdecken *v.t.* to rediscover.
wiedererkennen *v.t.ir.* to recognize.
wiedererlangen *v.t.* to recover.
wiedererobern *v.t.* to reconquer.
wiedereröfnen *v.t.* to reopen.
Wiedererstattung *f.* repayment.
wiedererzählen *v.t.* to recount.
wiederfinden *v.t.st.* to find again.
Wiedergabe *f.* reproduction, rendering.
wiedergeben *v.t.st.* to give back; to reproduce, to render; interpret (music, etc.).
Wiedergeburt *f.* regeneration, new birth.
wiedergenesen *v.i.st.* (*s*) to recover (one's health).
wiedergewinnen *v.t.st.* to regain.
Wiedergutmachung *f.* reparation.
wiederhaben *v.t.ir.* to have (got) back.
wiederherstellen *v.t.* to restore; to cure.
Wiederherstellung *f.* restoration.
wiederholen *v.t.* to repeat, to reiterate.
Widerholung *f.* (-, -en) repetition.
Wiederholungsaufführung *f.* repeat performance.
Wiederholungskurs *m.* refresher course.
wiederkäuen *v.i. & t.* (*auch fig.*) to ruminate, to chew the cud.
Wiederkäuer *m.* ruminant.
Wiederkehr *f.* (-, 0) return.
wiederkehren *v.i.* (*s*) to return.
wiederkommen *v.i.st.* (*s*) to come again *or* back, to return.
wiedersehen *v.t.st.* to see *or* meet again.
Wiedersehen *n.* (-s, 0) meeting after a separation; *aus ~!* so long!, I'll be seeing you.
Wiedertäufer *m.* anabaptist.
wiederum *adv.* again, anew, afresh.
wiedervereinigen *v.t.* to reunite.
Wiedervereinigung *f.* reunion.
wiederverheiraten *v.t.* remarry.
Wiederverheiratung *f.* remarriage.
Wiederverkauf *m.* resale.
Wiederwahl *f.* re-election.
wiederwählbar *a.* re-eligible.
wiederwählen *v.t.* to re-elect.
Wiederzulassung *f.* readmission; relicensing (car).
Wiege *f.* (-, -n) cradle.
wiegen *v.t.* to rock; to mince; ~ *v.t. & i.st.* to weigh; *sich ~ in*, lull oneself into.
Wiegen: ~**fest** *n.* birthday; ~**lied** *n.* lullaby.
wiehern *v.i.* to whinny; to neigh.
Wiener *f.* (-, -) wiener (wurst).
wienerisch *a.* Viennese.
wienern *v.t.* to polish.

Wiese *f.* (-, -n) meadow.
Wiesel *n.* (-s, -) weasel.
wieso *adv.* why.
wieviel *interrogativ pn.* how much; how many.
wievielmal *adv.* how many times.
wievielte *a.* which of the number; *der ~?* what day of the month?
wieweit *adv.* to what extent.
wiewohl *c.* though, although.
Wikinger *m.* (-s, -) Viking.
wild *a.* wild; savage, uncultivated; fierce, ferocious; turbulent; unmanageable.
Wild *n.* (-[e]s, 0) game, deer.
Wild: ~**bret** *n.* venison, game; ~**dieb** *m.* poacher.
Wilde *m./f.* (-n, -n) savage.
Wilderei *f.* poaching.
Wilderer *m.* (-s, -) poacher.
wildern *v.i.* to poach.
Wildfang *m.* (-[e]s, -fänge) romp.
wildfremd *a.* completely strange.
Wildheit *f.* (-, 0) wildness, savageness.
Wildleder *n.* suede.
Wildnis *f.* (-, -nisse) wilderness.
Wildpark *m.* deer park.
Wildschwein *n.* wild boar.
wildwachsend *a.* growing wild.
Wildwechsel *m.* game path; game crossing.
Wille *m.* (-ns, 0) will; mind, wish; design, intention, purpose; *letzter ~*, last will; *um. . .willen*, for the sale of; *~s sein*, to intend, to have a mind; *einem zu Willen sein*, to be someone's will *or* pleasure; *aus freiem Willen*, of one's own accord, voluntarily; *wider Willen*, unwillingly.
willenlos *a.* irresolute, weak.
Willensfreiheit *f.* freedom of will.
Willenskraft *f.* will-power.
willensschwach *a.* weak-willed.
willensstark *a.* strong-willed.
willfährig *a.* compliant, complaisant.
willig *a.* willing, docile, co-operative.
willkommen *a. & i.* welcome; *~ heißen*, to welcome.
Willkomm(en) *m.* (-s, 0) welcome.
Willkür *f.* (-, 0) arbitrariness; (*Belieben*) discretion; *nach ~*, at one's pleasure; ~**akt** *m.* arbitrary act; ~**herrschaft** *f.* tyranny.
willkürlich *a.* arbitrary.
wimmeln *v.i.* to swarm (with).
wimmern *v.i.* to whimper, to whine.
Wimpel *f.* (-, -n) pennant.
Wimper *f.* (-, -n) eyelash.
Wimperntusche *f.* mascara.
Wind *m.* (-[e]s, -e) wind, breeze.
Windbeutel *m.* (*Backwerk*) cream puff; (*fig.*) swaggerer, windbag.
Windbö(e) *f.* (-, -n) gust of wind.
Winde *f.* (-, -n) winch; (*bot.*) bindweed.
Windel *f.* (-, -n) diaper.
windelweich *a. einen ~ schlagen*, to beat someone to a pulp.
winden *v.t.st.* to wind; to twist; (sich) ~ *v.refl.* to wind, to meander; to writhe.
Windeseile *f. mit ~*, in no time.
Wind: ~**fahne** *f.* vane; ~**hose** *f.* water spout; ~**hund** *m.* greyhound.
windig *a.* windy; doubtful, shaky.

Wind: ~**jacke** *f.* wind breaker; ~**mühle** *f.* windmill; ~**pocken** *pl.* chicken-pox; ~**rose** *f.* compass-card.

Windschutzscheibe *f.* (*mot.*) windshield.

windschief *a.* crooked.

windstill *a.* calm.

Wind: ~**stille** *f.* calm; ~**stoß** *m.* gust, squall.

Windsurfen *n.* windsurfing.

Windung *f.* (-, -en) winding, coil; spire, whorl (of a shell); worm (of a screw).

Wink *m.* (-[e]s, -e) sign, nod; (*fig.*) hint; tip; ~ *mit einem Zaunpfahl*, broad hint.

Winkel *m.* (-s, -) angle; corner; nook.

Winkeladvokat *m.* (*fam.*) shyster.

winkelförmig *a.* angular.

wink(e)lig *a.* angular; crooked.

Winkelmaß *n.* (carpenter's) square, iron rule.

Winkelmesser *m.* protractor.

Winkelzug *m.* shady trick/move.

winken *v.i.* to beckon to, to nod; *mit den Augen ~,* to wink.

winseln *v.i.* to whimper, to whine.

Winter *m.* (-s, -) winter.

Winterhalbjahr *n.* winter-term.

winterlich *a.* wintry.

Winterschlaf *m.* hibernation.

Winterzeit *f.* wintertime.

Winzer *m.* (-s, -) wine-grower.

winzig *a.* tiny.

Wipfel *m.* (-s, -) treetop.

Wippe *f.* (-, -n) see-saw.

wippen *v.i.* to see-saw; to bob.

wir *pn.* we.

Wirbel *m.* (-s, -) whirl, eddy, whirlpool; (*phys.*) vortex; crown (of the head); vertebra; (drum) roll.

wirbellos *a.* invertebrate.

wirbeln *v.i.* to whirl, to eddy; *mir wirbelt der Kopf,* my head is swimming.

Wirbel: ~**säule** *f.* spine, spinal column; ~**sturm** *m.* cyclone, tornado; ~**tier** *n.* vertebrate; ~**wind** *m.* whirlwind; tornado.

wirken *v.t.* to weave; to effect; to work, to produce; ~ *v.i.* to act (upon), to operate, to influence.

wirkend *a.* active, efficient, operative.

wirklich *a.* real, actual; effective; ~ *adv.* really, actually, positively; ~?, indeed?

Wirlichkeit *f.* (-, -en) reality.

wirksam *a.* efficient, effective; (*med*) operative; ~ *werden* (*law*), to take effect.

Wirksamkeit *f.* (-, 0) effectiveness; efficiency; (*eines Gesetzes*) operation.

Wirkstoff *m.* (-s, -e) active agent.

Wirkstuhl *m.* loom.

Wirkung *f.* (-, -en) effect, operation, action; *mit sofortiger ~,* effective immediately; *mit ~ vom 1 Juni,* effective 1 June.

Wirkungs: ~**kraft** *f.* efficiency; efficacy; ~**kreis** *m.* sphere of activity.

wirkungslos *a.* ineffective.

wirkungsvoll *a.* effective.

Wirkungsweise *f.* operation; function; action.

wirr *a.* confused; ~*es Haar,* dishevelled hair.

Wirren *f.pl.* turmoil.

wirrköpfig *a.* muddle-headed.

Wirrnis *f.* (-nisses, -nisse), **Wirrsal** *n.* (-[e]s, -e) confusion, jumble.

Wirrwarr *m.* (-s, 0) confusion, jumble.

Wirsing *m.* (-s, 0), **Wirsingkohl** *m.* savoy (cabbage).

Wirt *m.* (-[e]s, -e) host, landlord, innkeeper.

Wirtin *f.* (-, -nen) hostess, landlady.

Wirtschaft *f.* (-, -en) economy; public house, inn; *freie ~,* private enterprise.

wirtschaften *v.i.* to manage, to keep house; to economize.

Wirtschafterin *f.* (-m -nen) housekeeper.

wirtschaftlich *a.* economic(al), thrifty.

Wirtschaftlichkeit *f.* profitability; economic efficiency.

Wirtschafts: ~**betrieb** *m.* management (of household, inn, etc.); ~**gebäude** *pl.* domestic quarters; ~**geld** *n.* housekeeping money; ~**krieg** *m.* economic warfare; ~**krise** *f.* economic crisis; ~**politik** *f.* economic policy; ~**minister** *m.,* ~**ministerin** *f.* minister for economic affairs; ~**ministerium** *n.* Ministry of economics, (*in Eng.*) Board of Trade; ~**wissenschaft** *f.* economics; ~**wissenschaftler** *m.,* ~**wissenschaftlerin** *f.* economist; ~**zeitung** *f.* financial newspaper; ~**zweig** *m.* economic sector.

Wirtshaus *n.* inn; tavern.

Wirts: ~**leute** *pl.* host and hostess; ~**stube** *f.* inn parlor; common room.

Wisch *m.* (-es, -e) piece of paper.

wischen *v.t.* to wipe, to rub.

Wischer *m.* (-s, -) wiper.

Wischlappen *m.* dish cloth; duster.

Wisent *m.* (-s, -e) bison.

Mismut *m.* (-[e]s, 0) bismuth.

wispern *v.i.* to whisper.

Wißbegierde *f.* thirst for knowledge.

wißbegierig *a.* eager for knowledge; curious.

wissen *v.t. & i.ir.* to know; to be aware of; *einem Dank ~,* to owe, to feel indebted to a person for; *er will von uns nichts ~,* he will have nothing to do with us.

Wissen *n.* (-s, 0) knowledge; learning; *meines ~s,* as far as I know, to my knowledge; *nach bestem ~ und Gewissen,* to the best of my knowledge and belief.

wissend *a.* knowing.

Wissenschaft *f.* (-, -en) knowledge; science; learning; *die schönen ~en,* belles-lettres, the humanities.

Wissenschaftler *m.;* **Wissenschaftlerin** *f.* scholar, scientist.

wissenschaftlich *a.* scientific, scholarly; learned.

Wissensdrang, Wissensdurst, Wissenstrieb *m.* desire for knowledge.

wissenswert *a.* worth knowing.

wissentlich *a.* knowing, willful.

wittern *v.t.* to scent, to smell.

Witterung *f.* (-, -en) weather; scent.

Witwe *f.* (-, -en) widow.

Witwer *m.* (-s, -) widower.

Witz *m.* (-es, -e) joke, witticism.

Witzblatt *n.* comic paper.

Witzbold *m.* (-[e]s, -e) joker.

Witzelei *f.* (-, -en) teasing; jokes.

witzeln *v.i.* to joke.

witzig *a.* funny; amusing; witty; ~*er Einfall,* flash of wit.

wo *adv.* where; somewhere; when; ~ *nicht,* unless; ~ *nur,* wherever.

woanders *adv.* somewhere else.

wobei *adv.* at, by, in, with, which *or* what, in

Woche *f.* (-, -n) week.
Wochen *pl.* childbed.
Wochen: ~**bett** *n.* childbed; ~**ende** *n.* week-end; ~**schau** *f.* (*Film*) newsreel; ~**schrift** *f.* weekly; ~**tag** *m.* week-day.
wochenlang *a. & adv.* for weeks together.
wochentags *adv.* on weekdays.
wöchentlich *a. & adv.* weekly.
Wöcherin *f.* (-n -nen) woman lying-in.
wodurch *adv.* by which, through what *or* which.
wofür *adv.* for what *or* which.
Woge *f.* (-, -n) wave.
wogegen *adv.* against what *or* which; (in return) for what *or* which.
wogen *v.i.* to wave; to fluctuate; to heave; to surge.
woher *adv.* where from, from what place.
wohin *adv.* where to.
wohingegen *c.* whereas.
wohl *adv.* well; indeed; possibly, probably; *wieder* ~ *sein*, to be all right again; ~ *oder übel*, willy-nilly, 'whether or no'; *mir ist* ~, I feel comfortable.
Wohl *n.* (-[e]s, 0) welfare, good, benefit.
wohlan! *i.* now then! well!
wohlauf! *i.* now then! up!; *er ist* ~, he is in good health.
wohlbedacht *a.* well-considered, well-advised.
Wohl: ~**befinden** *n.* good health; ~**behagen** *n.* comfort, ease.
wohl: ~**behalten** *a.* safe (and sound); ~**bekannt** *a.* well-known; ~**beliebt** *a.* corpulent, stout; ~**beschaffen** *a.* in good condition; ~**besetzt** *a.* well-filled, well-stored; ~**betagt** *a.* stricken in years; ~**bewandert** *a.* well-versed, well up (in).
wohlerfahren *a.* experienced, well skilled.
Wohlergehen *n.* (-s, 0) welfare.
wohl: ~**erhalten** *a.* in good condition, well-preserved, safe; ~**erwogen** *a.* well-considered; ~**erworben** *a.* duly acquired; ~**erzogen** *a.* well-bred.
Wohlfahrt *f.* welfare.
Wohlfahrtspflege *f.* welfare work.
wohlfeil *a.* cheap.
wohl: ~**gebildet** *a.* well-formed, well-shaped.
Wohlgefallen *n.* pleasure, delight; *sein* ~ *haben an*, to take delight in; *sich in* ~ *auflösen*, to end satisfactorily.
wohlgefällig *a.* pleasant; pleased, complacent.
wohl: ~**gelitten** *a.* well-liked; ~**gemeint** *a.* well-meant; ~**gemut** *a.* cheerful, merry; ~**genährt** *a.* well-fed; ~**geordnet** *a.* well-ordered; ~**geraten** *a.* fine; successful.
Wohl: ~**geruch** *m.* perfume, fragrance; ~**geschmack** *m.* flavor, relish.
wohl: ~**gesinnt** *a.* well-meaning; ~**gesittet** *a.* well-mannered.
wohl: ~**gestaltet** *a.* well-shaped; ~**gewogen** *a.* kind.
wohlhabend *a.* well off, well-to-do.
Wohlhabenheit *f.* (-, 0) wealth, affluence.
wohlig *a.* comfortable, snug, cozy.
Wohlklang, Wohllaut *m.* euphony, harmony; harmonious sound.
wohlklingend *a.* sweet(-sounding), harmonious, euphonious.
Wohlleben *n.* life of luxury.

wohlmeinend *a.* well-meaning.
wohl: ~**riechend** *a.* sweet-scented, fragrant; ~**schmeckend** *a.* tasty.
Wohl: ~**sein** *n.* good health; ~**stand** *m.* prosperity, comfort; ~**tat** *f.* benefit; kindness, good action; ~**täter** *m.* benefactor; ~**täterin** *f.* benefactress.
wohltätig *a.* charitable, salutary.
Wohl: ~**tätigkeit** *f.* charity, benevolence; ~**tätigkeitsverein** *m.* charitable society.
wohltuend *a.* beneficial, salutary.
wohltun *v.i.st.* to do good, to benefit.
wohlverbürgt *a.* well authenticated.
wohlverdient *a.* well-deserved; deserving.
Wohlverhalten *n.* good conduct.
wohlverstanden *a.* well understood.
wohlweislich *adv.* prudently.
wohlwollen *v.i.ir.* to wish (one) well.
Wohlwollen *n.* good-will, kindness.
wohlwollend *a.* benevolent, kind.
Wohn. . . residential, *a.*
wohnen *v.i.* to dwell, to live, to reside; to lodge, to stay.
Wohnbegäude *n.* residential building.
wohnhaft *a.* resident.
Wohnhaus *n.* residential building.
wohnlich *a.* comfortable.
Wohn: ~**ort,** ~**platz,** ~**sitz** *m.* place of residence.
Wohnung *f.* (-, -en) apartment.
Wohnungs: ~**amt** *n.* housing office; ~**mangel** *m.,* ~**not** *f.* housing shortage; ~**wechsel** *m.* change of residence.
Wohn: ~**viertel** *n.* residential district; ~**wagen** *m.* trailer, mobile home; ~**zimmer** *n.* living room
wölben *v.t.* to vault, to arch.
Wölbung *f.* (-, -en) vault(ing).
Wolf *m.* (-[e]s, Wölfe) wolf.
wölfisch *a.* wolfish.
Wolfram *m.* (-s, 0) tungsten; ~**erz** *n.* wolfram.
Wolfs: ~**hund** *m.* German shepherd; ~**hunger** *m.* ravenous appetite.
Wolke *f.* (-, -n) cloud.
Wolkenbruch *m.* cloudburst.
Wolkenkratzer *m.* skyscraper.
wolkenlos *a.* cloudless, serene.
wolkig *a.* cloudy, clouded.
Wolldecke *f.* (woollen) blanket.
Wolle *f.* (-, -n) wool.
wollen *a.* woolen; worsted; *v.i.ir.* to be willing, to intend, to wish, to want; *ich will,* I will; *lieber* ~, to prefer.
Wollen *n.* will; volition (*phil.*).
Wollgarn *n.* worsted.
wollig *a.* woolly.
Woll: ~**jacke** *f.* woolen cardigan; ~**kleid** *n.* woolen dress; ~**knäuel** *n.* ball of wool; ~**stoff** *m.* woolen cloth.
Wollust *f.* (-, -lüste) lust, voluptuousness, sensuality.
wollüstig *a.* voluptuous; lustful; sensual.
Wollüstig *m.* (-[e]s, -) lecher.
womit *adv.* with which *or* what.
womöglich *adv.* possibly.
wonach *adv.* after what *or* which.
Wonne *f.* (-, -n) delight, bliss, rapture.
wonnetrunken *a.* enraptured.
wonnig *a.* delightful, blissful; lovely.

woran *adv.* on what *or* which; ~ *liegt es?* how is it that?

worauf *adv.* whereupon.

woraus *adv.* wherefrom.

worein *adv.* in(to) what *or* which.

worin *adv.* wherein, in which *or* what.

Wort *n.* (-[e]s, Worte *u.* Wörter) word, term; *mit anderen ~en,* in other words; *ich bitte ums Wort,* I request permission to speak; *sein ~ brechen, halten,* to break, keep one's word; *das ~ haben,* to have the floor; *ins ~ fallen,* to interrupt.

Wortbildung *f.* word formation.

Wortbruch *m.* breach of faith.

wortbrüchig *a.* ~*werden* to break one's word.

Wörterbuch *n.* dictionary.

Wortführer *m.* spokesman.

Wortführerin *f.* spokeswoman.

wortgetreu *a.* literal.

Wortklauberei *f.* hairsplitting.

wortkarg *a.* laconic; taciturn.

Wortlaut *m.* wording, text.

wörtlich *a.* verbal, literal; ~ *adv.* literally, word for word, verbatim.

wortlos *a.* wordless; unspoken.

wortreich *a.* verbose, wordy, voluble.

Wort: ~**schatz** *m.* vocabulary; ~**schöpfung** *f.* coinage; neologism; ~**schwall** *m.* bombast; volley of words; ~**sinn** *m.* literal sense; ~**spiel** *n.* pun; ~**stellung** *f.* order of words; ~**streit** *m.* dispute (about words) quarrel; ~**wechsel** *m.* dispute, argument; ~**witz** *m.* pun.

worüber *adv.* over what.

worum *adv.* about what *or* which.

worunter *adv.* under *or* among which *or* what.

wovon *adv.* from where; ~ *level sie?* what do they live on?

wovor *adv.* before, of what *or* which.

wozu *adv.* to what; what for.

Wrack *n.* (-[e]s, -e) wreck.

wringen *v.t.st.* to wring (out).

Wucher *m.* (-s, 0) usury, profiteering.

Wucherer *m.* (-s, -) usurer.

wucherhaft, wucherisch *a.* usurious.

wuchern *v.i.* (*von Pflanzen*) to proliferate.

Wucherpreis *m.* extortionate price.

Wucherung *f.* (-, -en) growth.

Wuchs *m.* (-es, Wüchse) growth; figure, stature, shape, size.

Wucht *f.* (-, 0) weight; force, impact.

wuchten *v.t.* to heave.

wuchtig *a.* heavy, ponderous.

Wühlarbeit *f.* subversive activities *pl.*

wühlen *v.i. & t.* to dig (up); (*fig.*) to agitate, to stir up; to wallow.

Wulst *m.* (-s, Wülste) roll; pad.

wulstig *a.* bulging; thick (lip).

wund *a.* sore, wounded; *ein ~er Punkt,* a sore spot.

Wundbrand *m.* gangrene.

Wunde *f.* (-, -n) wound, cut.

Wunder *n.* (-s, -) wonder, marvel; miracle; *es nimmt mich wunder,* I wonder at it.

wunderbar *a.* wonderful, miraculous, marvelous, strange.

Wunder: ~**ding** *n.* wonderous thing, prodigy; ~**doktor** *m.* miracle doctor.

wunderhübsch *a.* simply lovely.

Wunder: ~**kind** *n.* child prodigy; ~**kraft** *f.* miraculous power; ~**kur** *f.* miraculous cure.

wunderlich *a.* strange, odd, peculiar.

wundern (sich) *v.refl.* to wonder, to be amazed; *es wundert mich,* I wonder at it, I am surprised.

wunderschön *a.* wonderful, beautiful.

Wundertäter *m.*; **Wundertäterin** *f.* miracle worker.

wundervoll *a.* wonderful, marvellous.

Wunderwerk *n.* marvel.

Wundfieber *n.* wound fever.

wundgelaufen *a.* footsore.

wundliegen *v.refl.st.* to get bedsores.

Wundmal *n.* scar, cicatrice; stigma.

Wundstarrkrampf *m.* tetanus.

Wunsch *m.* (-es, Wünsche) wish, desire; *auf ~,* at the request of; *nach ~* according to one's wish; *ein frommer ~,* a vain desire *or* wish.

Wunschdenken *n.* wishful thinking.

Wünschelrute *f.* divining-rod.

Wünschelrutengänger *m.* dowser; diviner.

wünschen *v.t.* to wish (for); to desire, to long for; *Glück ~,* to congratulate.

wünschenswert *a.* desirable.

wunschgemäß *adv.* as desired.

Wunschkind *n.* wanted child.

Wunschkonzert *n.* request program.

wunschlos *a.* contented.

Wunschtraum *m.* pipe-dream.

Wunschzettel *m.* list of presents.

Würde *f.* (-, -n) dignity; honor; office.

würdelos *a.* undignified.

Würdenträger *m.* dignitary.

würdevoll *a.* dignified, grave.

würdig *a.* worthy; deserving (of).

würdigen *v.t.* to appreciate, to value.

Würdigung *f.* (-, -en) appreciation.

Wurf *m.* (-[e]s, Würfe) cast, throw; litter, brood.

Würfel *m.* (-s, -) die; (*math.*) cube.

Würfelbecher *m.* dice-box.

würfelförmig *a.* cubic(al).

würfeln *v.i.* to throw the dice; to play dice; to dice (vegetables).

Würfel: ~**spiel** *n.* game of dice; ~**zucker** *m.* cube-sugar.

Wurf: ~**geschoß** *n.* missile, projection; ~**linie** *f.* trajectory; ~**maschine** *f.* catapult; ~**speer,** ~**spieß** *m.* javelin.

würgen *v.t.* to strangle, to throttle; to retch; to choke on.

Würger *m.* (-s, -) murderer, cut-throat.

Wurm *m.* (-[e]s, Würmer) worm.

Wurm *n.* little mite.

wurmartig *a.* vermicular, worm-like.

wurmen *v.t.* to vex, to annoy.

Wurmfortsatz *m.* (*med.*) appendix.

wurmig *a.* wormy; worm-eaten.

Wurst *f.* (-, würste) sausage; *das ist mir (ganz) ~,* I couldn't care less.

Wursthändler *m.* pork-butcher.

Wurstigkeit *f.* (-, 0) (*sl.*) to-hell-with-it attitude.

Würze *f.* (-, -n) spice, seasoning.

Wurzel *f.* (-, -n) root; carrot; ~ *fassen* (*schlagen*), to take root.

wurzeln *v.t.* to root, to be rooted.

Wurzelwerk *n.* roots.

Wurzelzeichen *n.* (*math.*) radical sign.
würzen *v.t.* to season, to spice.
würzhaft, würzig *a.* aromatic, spicy.
wuschelig *a.* frizzy; fuzzy.
Wuschelkopf *m.* shock of frizzy/fuzzy hair.
Wust *m.* (-es, -e) chaos; jumble
wüst *a.* waste, desert, wilderness.
Wüste *f.* (-, -en) desert, wilderness.
Wüstenei *f.* (-, -en) desert, wasteland.

Wüstling *m.* (-[e]s, -e) libertine, rake.
Wut *f.* (-, 0) rage, fury.
Wutanfall *m.* fit of rage.
wüten *v.i.* to rage, to rave.
wütend, wutentbrannt *a.* furious, enraged.
Wüterich *m.* (-s, -e) brute.
wütig *a.* enraged, furious.
wutschnaubend *a.* infuriated.

X

X, x *n.* the letter X or x.
X *n. einem ein X für ein U (vor-)machen*, to fool s.b.; to dupe s.b.
Xanthippe *f.* (*pej.*) shrew; battle axe.
X-Beine *n.pl.* knock-knees *pl.*
x-beinig *a.* knock-kneed.

x-beliebig *a.* any...(you like).
X-Chromosom *n.* X chromosome.
x-fach *adv.* x times.
x-mal *adv.* ever so many times.
Xylophon *n.* (-s, -e) xylophone.

Y

Y, y *n.* the letter Y or y.
Yacht *f.* (-, -en) yacht.
Y-Chromosom *n.* Y chromosome.

Yoga *m./n.* yoga.
Ypsilon *n.* y Y; upsilon in the Greek alphabet.

Z

Z, z *n.* the letter Z or z.
Z *n. von A bis Z*, from beginning to end.
Zack *auf ~ sein*, to be on the ball.
Zacke *f.* (-, -n), **Zacken** *m.* -s, - tooth, spike, prong; (*Felsen~*) jag.
zacken *v.t.* to tooth, to indent.
zackig *a.* pronged, indented; jagged.
zagen *v.i.* to hesitate; to be afraid.
zaghaft *a.* timid; hesitant; cautious.
zäh *a.* tough; sticky; tenacious.
Zäheit *f.* toughness; heaviness; viscosity.
zähflüssig *a.* viscous; heavy.
Zäflüssigkeit *f.* (-, 0) viscosity.
Zähigkeit *f.* toughness.
Zahl *f.* (-, -en) number; figure, digit.
Zählapparat *m.* counter; meter (gas).
zahlbar *a.* payable, due.
zählbar *a.* numerable, countable.
zahlen *v.t.* to pay; *Kellner ~!* the check, please!
zählen *v.t.* to count, to number.
zahlender Gast *m.* paying guest.
zahlenmäßig *a.* numerical.
Zahlenschloß *n.* combination lock.
Zahlenwert *m.* numerical value.
Zahler *m.* (-s, -) payer.
Zähler *m.* (-s, -) (*math.*) numerator; (*gas, elek.*) meter.
zahllos *a.* numberless, innumerable.
Zahlmeister *m.* paymaster.
zahlreich *a.* numerous.
Zahl: *~stelle f.* pay-office; *~tag m.* pay-day.
Zahlung *f.* (-, -en) payment; *als ~*, in settlement;

~en einstellen, to stop *or* suspend payment.
Zahlungs: *~anweisung f.* money order; *~bedingungen pl.* terms of payment; *~befehl m.* payment order; *~einstellung f.* suspension of payment; *~empfänger m.* payee.
zahlungsfähig *a.* solvent, capable to pay.
Zahlungs: *~fähigkeit f.* solvency; *~frist f.* time *or* respite of payment; *~mittel n.* (legal) tender; *~ort m.* place of payment; *~termin m.* date of payment.
zahlungsunfähig *a.* insolvent.
Zahlungs: *~unfähigkeit f.* insolvency; *~verbindlichkeit f.* liability (to pay).
Zahl: *~wort n.* numeral; *~zeichen n.* numeral; figure; digit (0-9).
zahm *a.* tame, domesticated; (*fig.*) gentle.
zähmen *v.t.* to tame, to domesticate.
Zahn *m.* (-[e]s, Zähne) tooth; cog (of a wheel); *Haare auf den Zähnen haben*, to know what's what; to be a Tartar; an awkward customer to deal with.
Zahnarzt *m.* dentist.
Zahnbeleg *m.* plaque.
Zahnbürste *f.* toothbrush.
Zahncreme *f.* toothpaste.
Zähnefletschen *n.* (-s, 0) showing one's teeth.
Zähn(e)klappern *n.* (-s. 0) chattering of teeth.
Zähn(e)knirschen *n.* gnashing of teeth.
zahnen *v.i.* to teethe, to cut one's teeth;
zähnen *v.t.* to indent, to tooth, to notch.
Zahn: *~ersatz m.* dentures; *~fäule f.* tooth decay; caries; *~fleisch n.* gums *pl.*; *~füllung f.* filling; *~heilkunde f.* dentistry; *~krone f.* crown; *~laut*

m. dental (sound).

zahnlos *a.* toothless.

Zahnlücke *f.* gap between two teeth.

Zahn: ~**medizin** *f.* dentistry; ~**paste** *f.* tooth-paste; ~**pflege** *f.* dental hygiene; ~**prothese** *f.* dentures; ~**pulver** *n.* tooth-powder; ~**rad** *n.* gear, pinion, cog-wheel; ~**radbahn** *f.* cog railroad; ~**schmerzen** *m.* toothache; ~**seide** *f.* dental floss; ~**stein** *m.* tartar; ~**stocher** *m.* toothpick; ~**techniker** *m.* dental technician; ~**weh** *n.* toothache.

Zaire *n.* (-s, 0) Zaire.

Zange *f.* (-, -en) pincers; tongs; pliers *pl.*

Zank *m.* (-[e]s, 0) quarrel, squabble.

Zankapfel *m.* (*fig.*) bone of contention.

zanken *v.i.* to quarrel, to wrangle; (sich) ~ *v.refl.* to quarrel, to dispute.

zänkisch *a.* quarrelsome.

Zank: ~**lust,** ~**sucht** *f.* quarrelsomeness.

zanksüchtig *a.* quarrelsome.

Zäpfchen *n.* (-s, -) (*anat.*) uvula; (*med.*) suppository.

Zapfen *m.* (-s, -) cone, pin, peg; (*Faß*) tap.

zapfen *v.t.* to draw, to tap; to mortise.

Zapfenstreich *m.* taps; *der Grosse* ~, tattoo.

Zapfhahn *m.* tap.

Zapfsäule *f.* gasoline pump.

zapp(e)lig *a.* fidgety, restless, fussy.

zappeln *v.i.* to sprawl, to kick, to struggle, to flounder; to fidget.

Zar *m.* (-en, -e) czar, tsar.

Zarin *f.* czarina, tsarina.

zart *a.* tender; delicate; frail.

zartbesaitet *a.* highly sensitive.

zartbitter *a.* bittersweet.

zartfühlend *a.* considerate, sensitive.

Zartgefühl *n.* delicacy of feeling.

Zartheit *f.* (-, -en) tenderness; delicacy.

zärtlich *a.* tender, delicate, fond.

Zärtlichkeit *f.* (-, -en) tenderness; fondness; ~**en** *pl.* caresses *pl.*

Zartsinn *m.* delicacy.

Zäsur *f.* (-, -en) caesura.

Zauber *m.* (-s, -) magic, charm, enchantment, spell, fascination.

Zauberei *f.* (-, -en) magic, witchcraft.

Zauberer *m.* (-s, -) magician, sorcerer.

Zauberformel *f.* magic spell; magic formula.

zauberhaft *a.* magical, enchanting.

Zauberin *f.* (-, -nen) sorceress, witch.

zauberisch *a.* magical; enchanting.

Zauberkraft *f.* magic power.

Zauberkunst *f.* magic.

Zauberkünstler *m.* magician, conjurer.

zaubern *v.i.* to practise magic, to conjure.

Zauberstab *m.* magic wand.

Zaubertrick *m.* conjuring trick.

zaudern *v.i.* to hesitate, to waver.

Zaum *m.* (-[e]s, Zäume) bridle; *im* ~*e halten,* to bridle, to check.

zäumen *v.t.* to bridle; (*fig.*) to restrain.

Zaumzeug *n.* horse's headgear.

Zaun *m.* (-[e]s, Zäune) hedge, fence.

Zaungast *m.* onlooker.

Zaunkönig *m.* wren.

Zaunpfahl *m.* fence post; *ein Wink mit dem* ~, a broad hint.

Zebra *n.* (-[s], -s) zebra.

Zebrastreifen *m.* pedestrian crossing.

Zechbruder *m.* (*sl.*) boozer.

Zeche *f.* (-, -n) tab (in a bar); (*Berkwerk*) mine, colliery; *die* ~ *bezahlen* (*fig.*) to pick up the tab.

zechen *v.i.* to tipple, to drink hard, to carouse.

Zechgelage *n.* drinking-bout.

Zechkumpan *m.* drinking companion.

Zech: ~**preller** *m.* cheat, swindler.

Zecke *f.* (-, -n) tick.

Zeder *f.* (-, -n) cedar.

zedieren *v.t.* to cede, to surrender.

Zehe *f.* (-, -n) **Zeh** *m.* (-en, -en) toe; *die grosse* ~, the big toe; *auf den* ~*n gehen,* to walk on tiptoe.

Zehennagel *m.* toenail.

Zehenspitze *f.* tiptoe; point of the toe.

zehn *a.* ten.

Zehner *m.* (-s, -) ten.

zehnerlei *a.* of ten sorts.

zehnfach, zehnfältig *a.* tenfold.

zehnjährig *a.* ten years old, of ten years.

Zehnkampf *m.* decathlon.

Zehnkämpfer *m.* decathlete.

zehnmal *adv.* ten times.

Zehnmarkschein *m.* ten-mark bill.

Zehnpfennigbriefmarke *f.* ten-pfennig stamp

Zehnpfennigstück *n.* ten-pfennig piece.

zehnt *a.* tenth.

Zehnte *m.* (-n, -n) tithe.

Zehntel *n.* (-s, -) tenth.

zehntens *adv.* tenthly.

zehren *v.i.* (*an, von*) to live on, to fed on.

Zeichen *n.* (-s, -) sign, token, mark; (*com.*) reference(-number); *seines* ~*s ist er Schuster,* he is a shoemaker by trade.

Zeichen: ~**block** *m.* sketch-pad; ~**brett** *n.* drawing-board; ~**erklärung** *f.* legend; ~**setzung** *f.* punctuation; ~**sprache** *f.* sign-language; ~**tinte** *f.* marking ink; ~**trickfilm** *m.* animated cartoon.

zeichnen *v.t.* to draw, to design; to mark; to sign, to subscribe; (*Anleihe*) to subscribe for.

Zeichner *m.* (-s, -) graphic artist; draftsman; subscriber.

Zeichnung *f.* (-, -en) drawing, design, sketch, diagram; subscription.

zeichnungsberechtigt *a.* authorized to sign.

Zeichnungsliste *f.* subscription list.

Zeigerfinger *m.* forefinger, index.

zeigen *v.t.* to show, to point out, to demonstrate; (sich) ~ *v.refl.* to appear; *es muß sich zeigen,* it remains to be seen.

Zeiger *m.* (-s, -) hand (of a clock); pointer.

Zeigerstock *m.* pointer.

zeihen *v.t.st.* to accuse (of).

Zeile *f.* (-, -n) line; **einzeilig** *a.* single-spaced; **zweizeilig** *a.* double-spaced.

Zeilen: ~**abstand** *m.* spacing; ~**anzeige** *f.* line display; ~**drucker** *n.* (*comp.*) line printer.

Zeisig *m.* (-[e]s, -e) siskin.

Zeit *f.* (-, -en) time; season; age; era, period; tide; *zur* ~, at present; *mit der* ~, in the course of time; *vor* ~*en,* in former times; *in rechter* ~, *zur rechten* ~, in (good) time; *zu* ~*en, eine* ~*lang,* for a while, for some time; ~ (*seines*) *Lebens,* (in) (all) his life; *sich* ~ *lassen,* to take (one's) time; *sich die* ~ *vertreiben,* to pass the time with.

Zeit: ~**ablauf** *m.* lapse of time; ~**abschnitt** *m.* epoch, period; ~**alter** *n.* age, era; ~**bombe** *f.* time-bomb; ~**dauer** *f.* duration, lapse of time; ~**form** *f.* (*gram.*) tense; ~**geist** *m.* spirit of the age.
zeitgemäß *a.* modern.
Zeitgenosse *m.*; **Zeitgenossin** *f.* contemporary.
zeitgenössisch *a.* contemporary.
Zeitgeschehen *n.* current events.
zeitgleich *a.* simultaneous.
zeitig *a.* early, timely; ripe; ~ *adv.* early, in (due) time.
zeitigen *v.t.* to produce; to yield; to provoke.
Zeitkarte *f.* commutation ticket.
Zeitlang *eine* ~, for a while.
zeitlebens *adv.* for life; during life.
zeitlich *a.* temporal, temporary, earthly.
Zeitlichkeit *f.* (-, 0) earthly life.
Zeit: ~**lupe** *f.* slow motion; ~**lupenaufnahme** *f.* slow-motion picture; ~**punkt** *f.* moment; ~**raffer** *m.* time lapse; quick motion.
zeitraubend *a.* time consuming.
Zeit: ~**raum** *m.* space of time, period; ~**rechnung** *f.* chronology; era; ~**schrift** *f.* periodical, journal, magazine.
Zeitung *f.* (-, -en) newspaper, gazette.
Zeitungs: ~**anzeige** *f.* advertisement; ~**ausschnitt** *m.* newspaper cutting *or* clipping; ~**ente** *f.* canard; ~**inserat** *n.* advertisement; ~**kiosk** *m.* news-stall; ~**papier** *n.* newsprint; ~**verkäufer** *m.* newsvendor; ~**wesen** *n.* journalism, the press.
Zeitvergeudung *f.* waste of time.
Zeit: ~**verhältnisse** *ol.* circumstances; ~**verlauf** *m.* lapse of time; ~**verschwendung** *f.* waste of time; ~**vertreib** *m.* pastime, diversion.
zeitvertreibend *a.* diverting, amusing.
zeitweilig *a.* temporary; ~*er Dienst*, (*mil.*) temporary duty.
zeitweise *adv.* at times.
Zeit: ~**wort** *n.* verb; ~**zeichen** *n.* (*Radio*) time signal.
Zeitzünder *m.* time-fuse.
zelebrieren *v.t.* to celebrate.
Zelle *f.* (-, -n) cell.
Zellgewebe *n.* cell tissue.
Zellkern *m.* nucleus.
Zellophan *n.* (-s, 0) cellophane.
Zellstoff *m.* cellulose; pulp.
zellular *a.* cellular.
Zellulitis *f.* cellulitis.
Zelluloid *n.* (-s, 0) celluloid.
Zellulose *f.* (-, 0) cellulose; pulp.
Zellwolle *f.* rayon.
Zelot *m.* (-en, -en) zealot.
Zelt *n.* (-[e]s, -e) tent, awning; pavilion.
Zeltdach *n.*, **Zeltdecke** *f.* marquee.
zelten *v.i.* to camp.
Zelter *m.* (-s, -) ambler, palfrey (horse).
Zeltlager *n.* tent camp.
Zeltplane *f.* tarpaulin.
Zeltplatz *m.* campsite.
Zement *m.* (-es, -) cement.
Zementboden *m.* concrete floor.
zementieren *v.t.* to cement.
Zenit *m.* (-[e]s, 0) zenith.
zensieren *v.t.* to mark; to criticize; to censure.
Zensor *m.* (-s, -en) censor.

Zensur *f.* censorship; (school-)report, mark, grade.
Zensus *m.* (-, 0) census.
Zentigramm *n.* centigram.
Zentimeter *m.* or *n.* (-n) centimeter.
Zentner *m.* (-s, -) hundredweight; centner.
Zentnerlast *f.* heavy burden.
zentnerschwer *a.* very heavy, ponderous, oppressive.
zentral *a.* central.
Zentrale *f.* (-, -n) central office *or* station; headquarters.
Zentralheizung *f.* central heating; *mit* ~, centrally heated.
zentralisieren *v.t.* to centralize.
Zentralismus *m.* centralism.
Zentralverriegelung *f.* central locking system (car).
zentrieren *v.t.* to center.
Zentrifugalkraft *f.* centrifugal force.
Zentripetalkraft *f.* centripetal force.
zentrisch *a.* centric.
Zentrum *n.* (-s, -tren) center; bull's eye; ~ *der Stadt*, downtown.
Zepter *n.* & *m.* (-s, -) sceptre; mace.
zerbeißen *v.t.st.* to bite into pieces.
zerbersten *v.i.st.* (*s*) to burst asunder.
zerbrechen *v.t.st.* to break (to pieces); *sich den Kopf* ~, to rack one's brains; ~ *v.i.st.* (*s*) to break.
zerbrechlich *a.* fragile, brittle.
zerbröckeln *v.i.* (*s*) to crumble.
zerdrücken *v.t.* to crush; to bruise.
Zeremonie *f.* (-, -n) ceremony.
zeremoniell *n.* (-s, -e) ceremonial.
zeremoniös *a.* ceremonious.
zerfahren *a.* thoughtless, incoherent.
Zerfall *m.* (-[e]s, 0) ruin, decay, disintegration; decomposition.
zerfallen *v.i.st.* (*s*) to fall to pieces; to decay; (*fig.*) to fall out (with one).
Zerfalls: ~**produkt** *n.* decomposition product; ~**zeit** *f.* decomposition period.
zerfasern *v.t.* to ravel out.
zerfetzen *v.t.* to slash, to tatter.
zerfleischen *v.t.* to tear to pieces; to mangle.
zerfließen *v.i.st.* (*s*) to dissolve, to melt.
zerfressen *v.t.st.* to corrode.
zergehen *v.i.st.* (*s*) to dissolve.
zergliedern *v.t.* to dissect, to dismember.
Zergliederung *f.* (-, -en) dissection; (*fig.*) analysis.
zerhacken *v.t.* to chop, to mince.
zerhauen *v.t.st.* to chop up; to cut up, to slash.
zerkauen *v.t.* to chew.
zerkleinern *v.t.* to chop (wood).
zerklüftet *a.* fissured; craggy.
zerknirscht *a.* contrite.
Zerknirschung *f.* (-, 0) contrition.
zerknittern, zerknüllen *v.t.* to crumple.
zerkratzen *v.t.* to scratch.
zerkrümeln *v.t.* to crumble.
zerlassen *v.t.st.* to dissolve, to melt.
zerlegbar *a.* dissectible.
zerlegen *v.t.* to take to pieces; to carve.
zerlumpt *a.* ragged, tattered.
zermahlen *v.t.st.* to grind (to powder).
zermalmen *v.t.* to bruise, to crush.
zermürben *v.t.* to wear down.

zerhagen *v.t.* to gnaw to pieces.
zerpflücken *v.t.* to pick to pieces.
zerplatzen *v.i.* (*s*) to burst.
zerquetschen *v.t.* to crush, to squash.
Zerrbild *n.* caricature; distorted picture.
zerreiben *v.t.st.* to grind to powder.
zerreißbar *a.* tearable.
zerreißen *v.t.st.* to tear, to rend; ~ *v.i.st.* (*s*) to be torn.
zerren *v.t.* to pull, to tug.
zerrinnen *v.i.st.* (*s*) to dissolve, to melt.
Zerrissenheit *f.* (-, 0) *innere* ~, inner conflicts.
Zerrung *f.* strain.
zerrütten *v.t.* to unsettle, to ruin, to shatter; (*den Geist*) to unhinge.
Zerrüttung *f.* (-, -en) disorder, ruin; (*Geistes~*) derangement.
zersägen *v.t.* to saw to pieces.
zerschellen *v.i.* (*s*) to be dashed to pieces.
zerschlagen *v.t.st.* to shatter, to smash, to break (by striking); (sich) ~ *v.refl.* to come to nothing; ~ *a.* shattered.
zerschmettern *v.t.* to crush, to shatter.
zerschneiden *v.t.st.* to cut to pieces.
zersetzen *v.t.* to decompose.
zersetzend *a.* submersive.
Zersetzung *f.* (-, -en) decomposition.
zerspalten *v.t.* to cleave, to split.
zersplittern *v.t.* to split, to shiver; to fritter away.
zersprengen *v.t.* to disperse, to scatter.
zerspringen *v.i.st.* (*s*) to burst; (*Glas*) to crack; (*Kopf*) to split.
zerstäuben *v.t.* to spray.
zerstechen *v.t.st.* to sting all over; to puncture.
zerstieben *v.i.st.* (*s*) to vanish, to fly asunder.
zerstörbar *a.* destructible.
zerstören *v.t.* to destroy, to ruin.
Zerstörer *m.* (-s, -) (*nav.*) destroyer.
zerstörerisch *a.* destructive.
Zerstörung *f.* (-, -en) destruction.
zerstossen *v.t.st.* to pound, to triturate.
zerstreuen *v.t.* to scatter, to disperse; to dispel; (sich) ~ *v.refl.* to divert oneself, to seek diversion.
zerstreut *a.* (*fig.*) absent-minded; (*Licht*) diffused.
Zerstreutheit *f.* (-, 0) absentmindedness.
Zerstreuung *f.* (-, -en) dispersion; diversion.
zerstückeln *v.t.* to dismember; to cut up, to parcel out.
Zerstück[e]lung *f.* (-, -en) dismemberment, parcelling (out).
zerteilbar *a.* divisible.
zerteilen *v.t.* to divide, to disperse, to dismember; (*math.*) to resolve (into factors).
zertrennen *v.t.* to take apart; to rip up.
zertreten *v.t.st.* to crush.
zertrümmern *v.t.* to destroy, to wreck.
Zervelatwurst *f.* salami.
zerwühlen *v.t.* to churn up; to make a mess of.
Zerwürfnis *n.* (-nisses, -nisse) difference, discord, quarrel, dissension.
zerzausen *v.t.* to ruffle, to tousle.
Zeter *n.* ~ *über einen schreien*, raise a hue and cry after s.b.
zetern *v.i.* to wail; to nag.
Zettel *m.* (-s, -) slip of paper, note; label; poster.
Zeug *n.* (-[e]s, -e) stuff; matter; cloth; rubbish,

trash; *das* ~ *haben zu etwas*, (*fig.*) to have the makings of; *sich ins* ~ *legen*, to launch out; *dummes* ~, stuff and nonsense.
Zeuge *m.* (-n, -n) witness; *einen* ~*n beibringen*, to produce a witness.
zeugen *v.t.* to father; ~ *v.i.* to witness, to testify, to depose.
Zeugen: ~**aussage** *f.* testimony; ~**beweis** *n.* evidence; ~**bank** *f.* witness-box; ~**stand** *m.* witness stand; ~**verhör** *n.*, ~**vernehmung** *f.* examination of witnesses; ~**vorladung** *f.* witness summons.
Zeughaus *n.* arsenal.
Zeugin *f.* (female) witness.
Zeugnis *n.* (-nisses, -nisse) testimony, evidence; character, certificate; (*Schul~*) report; ~ *ablegen*, to give evidence; to bear witness.
Zeugung *f.* (-, -en) fathering, procreation, generation.
zeugungsfähig *a.* fertile.
zeugungsunfähig *a.* impotent, sterile.
Zichorie *f.* (-, -n) chicory.
Zicke *f.*, **Zicklein** *n.* (-s, -) kid.
zickig *a.* prim; prudish.
Zickzack *m.* (-[e]s, -e) zigzag.
Ziege *f.* (-, -n) goat, she-goat.
Ziegel *m.* (-s, -) tile; brick.
Ziegelbrenner *m.* brickmaker.
Ziegelbrennerei *f.* brickworks *pl.*
Ziegel: ~**dach** *n.* tiled roof; ~**decker** *m.* tiler.
Ziegelei *f.* (-, -en) brickworks.
Ziegelstein *m.* brick.
Ziegen: ~**bock** *m.* he-goat; ~**fell** *n.* goatskin; ~**hirt** *m.* goatherd; ~**leder** *n.* goatskin.
Ziegenpeter *m.* (-s, -) (*fam.*) mumps *pl.*
Ziehbrunnen *m.* well.
ziehen *v.t.st.* to draw; to pull; to cultivate, to grow, to breed; (*Schiff*) to tow; to extract (a tooth, a root of a nubmer); (sich) ~ *v.refl.* to extend; (*Holz*) to warp; ~ *v.i.* (*h*) (*im Schach*) to move; (*aus der Wohnung*) to move, to remove; *die Bilanz* ~, to draw up the balance-sheet; *Nutzen aus etwas* ~, to derive profit from; *in den Schmutz* ~, (*fig.*) to blacken, to asperse; *in Betracht, in Erwähung* ~, to take into consideration, to consider; *ins Geheimnis, ins Vertrauen* ~, to take (a person) into the secret, into one's confidence; *Gesichter* ~, to pull faces; *den kürzeren* ~, to get the worst of it; *in die Länge* ~, to spin out; *in Zweifel* ~, to (call in) question, to doubt; *Folgen nach sich* ~, to entail consequences; *das Stück zieht*, the play draws large audiences; *der Tee muß noch* ~, the tea hasn't brewed yet; *es zieht hier*, there's a draft here.
Zieh: ~**harmonika** *f.* accordion, concertina; ~**kind** *n.* foster-child.
Ziehung *f.* (-, -en) drawing (of the lottery).
Ziel *n.* (-[e]s, -e) aim, goal, mark; (*Luftkrieg*) target, objective; (*Reise*) destination; *ein* ~ *setzen*, to aim at.
zielbewußt *a.* purposeful; determined.
zielen *v.i.* to aim, to take aim, to sight; (*fig.*) to drive at.
Zielgerade *f.* home stretch.
zielgerichtet *a.* goal directed.
Zielgruppe *f.* target group.
Ziellinie *f.* finishing line.
zielen *v.i.* to aim, to take aim, to sight; (*fig.*) to

drive at.

ziellos *a.* aimless.

Zielscheibe *f.* target.

Zielsetzung *f.* objective; target.

zielsicher *a.* unerring.

Zielsprache *f.* target language.

zielstrebig *a.* purposeful, determined.

Zielstrebigkeit *f.* determination.

ziemen *v.i.* to become, to be suitable.

ziemlich *a.* suitable, fit; fair, moderate, passable, middling; *adv.* rather; quite.

Zier *f.* (-, -en) ornament, decoration.

Zierat *m.* (-[e]s, -en) ornament; decoration.

Zierde *f.* (-, -n) ornament; decoration.

zieren *v.t.* to adorn, to decorate; (sich) ~ *v.refl.* to be coy; to need some pressing.

zierlich *a.* delicate; neat.

Ziffer *f.* (-, -n) figure; digit; cipher; numeral.

Zifferblatt *n.* dial, (clock-) face.

ziffer(n)mäßig *a.* by figures, in number.

Zigarette *f.* (-, -n) cigarette.

Zigaretten: ~**etui** *n.* cigarette-case; ~**stummel** *m.* cigarette butt.

Zigarre *f.* (-, -n) cigar.

Zigarren: ~**spitze** *f.* cigar-holder; tip (of a cigar); ~**tasche** *f.* cigar-case.

Zigeuner *m.* (-s, -) ~**in** *f.* (-, -nen) gipsy.

Zikade *f.* (-, -n) cicada, cigala.

Zimbel *f.* (-, -n) cymbal.

Zimmer *n.* (-s, -) room, chamber.

Zimmer: ~**kellner** *m.* room waiter; ~**mädchen** *n.* chambermaid; ~**mann** *m.* carpenter.

zimmern *v.t.* to construct (of wood); to do carpentry.

Zimmervermieter(in) *f. m.* landlord.

Zimt *m.* (-[e]s, -e) cinnamon.

zimperlich *a.* prim, prudish, mincing.

Zink *n.* (-[e]s, 0) zinc; spelter.

Zinke *f.* (-, -n) prong; (*mus.*) cornet.

Zinkgießer *m.* zinc-founder.

Zinn *n.* (-[e]s, 0) tin; (*für Geräte*) pewter.

Zinnbergwerk *n.* tin-mine, stannary.

Zinne *f.* (-, -n) battlement; pinnacle.

Zinngeschirr *n.* pewter(-utensils *pl.*).

Zinngießer *m.* pewterer.

Zinnober *m.* (-s, 0) cinnabar, vermilion; (*fam. fig.*) rubbish, fuss.

zinnoberrot *a.* vermilion.

Zins *m.* (-es, -en) rent; interest.

zinsbringend *a.* bearing interest.

Zinsen *f.pl.* interest; ~ *tragen*, to bear interest.

Zinseszins *m.* compound interest.

zinsfrei *a.* rent-free.

Zinsfuß *m.* interest rate.

Zinssatz *m.* interest rate.

Zionismus *m.* zionism.

Zipfel *m.* (-s, -) tip, corner.

Zipfelmütze *f.* tasselled cap.

Zipperlein *n.* (-s, 0) gout.

zirka *adv.* approximately.

Zirkel *m.* (-s, -) circle (of people); pair of compasses *or* dividers.

zirkulieren *v.t. & i.* to circulate.

Zirkumflex *m.* (-es, -e) circumflex (accent).

Zirkus *m.* (-, - *u.* -kusse) circus.

zirpen *v.i.* to chirp.

zischeln *v.i.* to whisper.

zischen *v.i.* to hiss; to whiz.

Zischlaut *m.* hissing sound; sibilant.

ziselieren *v.t.* to chase, to enchase.

Zisterne *f.* (-, -n) cistern.

Zitadelle *f.* (-, -n) citadel.

Zitat *n.* (-[e]s, -e) quotation.

Zither *f.* (-, -n) zither.

zitieren *v.t.* to cite; to quote.

Zitronat *n.* candied lemon peel.

Zitrone *f.* (-, -n) lemon.

zitronengelb *a.* lemon-colored.

Zitronen: ~**saft** *m.* lemon-juice; ~**säure** *f.* citric acid; ~**schale** *f.* lemon peel; ~**wasser** *n.* lemonade.

zittern *v.i.* to tremble, to quake, to shiver.

zittrig *a.* shaky; doddery.

Zitze *f.* (-, -n) teat, nipple.

zivil *a.* civil; **Zivil** *n.* (-s, 0) civilian clothes; *in* ~, in plain clothes, in mufti.

Zivil: ~**bevölkerung** *f.* civilian population; ~**courage** *f.* courage of one's convictions; ~**dienst** *m.* alternative service for consientious objectors; ~**dienstleistende** *m.* conscientious objectors doing alternative service.

Zivilehe *f.* civil marriage.

Zivilisation *f.* (-, -en) civilization.

Zivilisationskrankheit *f.* disease of modern civilization.

zivilisatorisch *a.* civilizing.

zivilisieren *v.t.* to civilize.

Zivilist *m.* (-en, -en) civilian.

Zivil: ~**klage** *f.* (*law*) civil action; ~**prozeßordnung** *f.* civil law; ~**sache** *f.* civil case.

Zobel *m.* (-s, -) sable.

Zofe *f.* (-, -n) (lady's) maid.

Zoff *m.* (*fam.*) trouble.

zögerlich *a.* hesitant, tentative.

zögern *v.i.* to hesitate, to delay.

Zögling *m.* (-[e]s, -e) pupil.

Zölibat *n.* (-es, 0) celibacy.

Zoll *m.* (-[e]s, -) inch; (*pl.* Zölle) duty, tariff, customs; (*fig.*) tribute.

Zollabfertigung *f.* customs clearance.

Zollamt *n.* customs house; customs station.

Zollbeamte *m./f.* customs officer.

zollen *v.t.* to pay, to give.

Zolleinnehmer *m.* customs agent.

Zollerklärung *f.* customs declaration.

zollfrei *a.* duty-free.

Zoll: ~**grenze** *f.* customs-frontier; ~**haus** *n.* customs-house; ~**kontrolle** *f.* customs check.

zollpflichtig *a.* liable to duty.

Zollrevision *f.* customs examination *or* inspection.

Zollschranke *f.* customs barrier.

Zollstock *m.* folding rule.

Zoll: ~**tarif** *m.* tariff; ~**verband**, ~**verein** *m.* customs-union; ~**verschluß** *m.* customs-seal; *unter* ~, in bond.

zollweise *adv.* by inches.

Zone *f.* (-, -n) zone.

Zonen... zonal, *a.*

Zonentarif *m.* zone-tariff.

Zoo *m.* zoo.

Zoohandlung *f.* pet shop.

Zoologe *m.* (-n, -n); **Zoologin** *f.* (-, -nen) zoologist.

Zoologie *f.* (-, 0) zoology.
zoologisch *a.* zoological.
Zoowärter *m.* zookeeper.
Zopf *m.* (-[e]s, Zöpfe) pigtail; (*Mädchen~*) plait.
Zorn *m.* (-[e]s, 0) wrath, anger, ire.
Zornausbruch *m.* fit *or* burst of anger.
zornentbrannt *a.* angry.
zornig *a.* furious; wrathful, angry.
Zote *f.* (-, -n) dirty joke; obscenity.
zotenhaft, zotig *a.* smutty, obscene.
Zotte, Zottel *f.* (-, -n) tuft, lock; *pl.* straggly hair.
zottig *a.* shaggy, ragged; matted.
zu *pr.* to, at, by, in, on, for; ~ *adv.* too; shut; ~ *Land*, by land, on (dry) land; *zur See*, by sea; *zum Beispiel*, for instance; *zur Not*, if need be; ~ *zweien*, two of us (them, etc.); ~ *Hunderten*, by hundreds, in the hundreds; ~ *dritt*, three of them (us, etc.); *Tür ~!*, shut the door, please.
zuallererst *adv.* first of all.
zuallerletzt *adv.* last of all.
zubauen *v.t.* to block; to obstruct.
Zubehör *n.* accessories; attachments.
Zubehörteile *pl.* accessories.
zubeißen *v.i.st.* to bite *or* snap (at a thing).
Zuber *m.* (-s, -) (two-handled) tub.
zubereiten *v.t.* to prepare, to cook.
Zubereitung *f.* preparation; cooking.
zubilligen *v.t.* to grant.
zubinden *v.t.st.* to tie up; (*die Augen*) to blindfold.
zubleiben *v.i.st.* to remain closed.
zublinzeln *v.i.* to wink.
zubringen *v.t.ir.* to pass, to spend (time).
Zubringen *m.* access road; shuttle.
Zubrot *n.* (*sl.*) bit on the side.
zubuttern *v.t.u.i.* (*fam.*) to chip in.
Zucht *f.* (-, 0) breeding, breed; discipline, education; modesty.
Zuchtbuch *n.* stud-book.
züchten *v.t.* to breed; to grow, to cultivate; to train.
Züchter *m.* (-s, -) breeder (of animals); grower (of plants).
Zuchthaus *n.* penitentiary; (*Strafe*) penal servitude; *lebenslängliches ~*, penal servitude for life.
züchtig *a.* modest, chaste.
züchtigen *v.t.* to punish; to beat.
Züchtigung *f.* (-, -en) punishment.
zuchtlos *a.* undisciplined; disorderly.
Zuchtlosigkeit *f.* indiscipline.
Zuchtperle *f.* cultured pearl.
Zuchtpferd *n.* pedigree horse.
Züchtung *f.* (-, -en) breeding; (*von Pflanzen*) cultivation; training.
Zucht: ~**vieh** *n.* breeding cattle.
zucken *v.i.* to twitch; to wince; ~ *v.t.* to shrug (one's shoulders).
zücken *v.t.* to draw, to pull out (a sword).
Zucker *m.* (-s, 0) sugar.
Zucker: ~**bäcker** *m.* confectioner; ~**bäckerei** *f.* confectioner's shop; ~**dose** *f.* sugar bowl; ~**fabrik** *f.* refinery; ~**guß** *m.* (sugar) icing, frosting; ~**hut** *m.* sugar loaf; ~**kranker** *m.* diabetic; ~**krankheit** *f.* diabetes.
zuckern *v.t.* to sugar (over).
Zucker: ~**rohr** *n.* sugar cane; ~**rübe** *f.* sugar beet.
zuckersüß *a.* as sweet as sugar.
Zucker: ~**watte** *f.* cotton candy; ~**werk** *n.* sweets

pl., confectionery; ~**zange** *f.* sugar-tongs *pl.*
Zuckung *f.* (-, -en) convulsion.
zudecken *v.t.* to cover (up).
zudem *adv.* besides, moreover.
Zudrang *m.* (-[e]s, 0) rush, run (on).
zudrehen *v.t.* to shut off, to turn off; *einem den Rücken ~*, to turn one's back upon one.
zudringlich *a.* obtrusive; importunate; pushy.
zudrücken *v.t.* to close (by pressure); *ein Auge bei etwas ~*, to connive *or* wink at a thing.
zueignen *v.t.* to dedicate.
Zueignung *f.* (-, -en) dedication.
zueilen *v.i.* (*s*) to hasten (up) to.
zueinander *adv.* to each other; to one another.
zuerkennen *v.t.ir.* to award, to adjudicate; to sentence (one) to.
zuerst *adv.* first, at first.
zufahren *v.i.st. auf eine, ~*, to head towards.
Zufahrt *f.* access; driveway.
Zufahrtsstraße *f.* access road.
Zufall *m.* chance, hazard, accident.
zufallen *v.i.st.* (*s*) to shut by itself, to close; *jm. ~* to fall to s.b.
zufällig *a.* casual, accidental.
zufälligerweise *adv.* by chance.
Zufalls: ~**auswahl** *f.* random selection; ~**bekanntschaft** *f.* chance acquaintance; ~**treffer** *m.* lucky hit.
zufassen *v.i.* to grab.
zufliegen *v.i.st.* (*s*) to fly to *or* towards; (*Tür*) to slam.
zufließen *v.i.st.* (*s*) to flow to *or* towards; *einem etwas ~ lassen*, to make a thing come somebody's way.
Zuflucht *f.* (-, 0) refuge; recourse; *seine ~ nehmen zu*, to have recourse to.
Zufluchtsort *m.* **Zufluchtsstätte** *f.* place of refuge, asylum.
Zufluß *m.* (-flusses, -flüsse) influx; inflow; supply; tributary.
zuflüstern *v.t.* to whisper to.
zufolge *pr.* according to.
zufrieden *a.* content(ed), satisfied; ~*stellen*, to satisfy, to content.
zufriedengeben *v.refl.st.* to content o.s.
Zufriedenheit *f.* (-, 0) contentment; satisfaction.
zufriedenstellen *v.t.* to satisfy.
zufriedenstellend *a.* satisfactory.
zufrieren *v.i.st.* (*s*) to freeze over *or* up.
zufügen *v.t.* to do, to inflict, to cause.
Zufuhr *f.* (-, -en) (*mil.*) provisions *pl.*, supply.
zuführen *v.t.* to lead to, to bring to; to introduce; to import, to supply; (*mech.*) to feed.
Zug *m.* (-[e]s, Züge) pull; draft, current (of air); procession; (*im Schach*) move; (*Eisenbahn~*) stroke; (*Neigung*) bent, impulse; (*mil.*) platoon; ~ *Pferde*, team of horses; (*Gebirgs~*) mountain range; *der Ofen hat keinen guten ~*, the stove draws badly; *in einem ~, auf einen ~*, at one stroke; *in den letzten Zügen liegen*, to be breathing one's last.
Zugabe *f.* addition, adjunct; (*theat.*) encore.
Zugang *m.* access, approach; entrance.
zugänglich *a.* accessible; (*fig.*) affable.
Zuganschluß *m.* (train) connection.
Zugbrücke *f.* drawbridge.
zugeben *v.t.st.* to add; to permit; to admit, to grant.

zugegebenermassen *adv.* admittedly.
zugegen *a.* present.
zugehen *v.i.st.* (*s*) to shut; to go up to, to move towards; to come to hand; to come to pass, to happen; *einem etwas ~ lassen*, to send, to foward, to transmit a thing to someone.
zugehören *v.i.* to belong to.
zugehörig *a.* belonging to.
Zugehörigkeit *f.* (-, 0) membership (of a company, union, club, etc.).
zugeknöpft *a.* buttoned up; (*fig.*) tight-lipped.
Zügel *m.* (-s, -) rein, bridle.
zügellos *a.* (*fig.*) unbridled.
zügeln *v.t.* to bridle; to curb, to check.
zugesellen *v.t.* to associate, to unite.
Zugeständnis *n.* concession.
zugestehen *v.t.st.* to concede, to grant, to admit.
zugetan *a.* attached.
Zugewinn *m.* gain.
Zugfestigkeit *f.* tensile strength.
zugießen *v.t.st.* to pour more on, to add.
zugig *a.* drafty; windy.
Zugkraft *f.* power of traction; (*fig.*) attractiveness.
zugkräftig *a.* attractive.
zugleich *adv.* at the same time, together.
Zugluft *f.* draft (of air).
zugreifen *v.i.st.* to seize, to help oneself (at table).
Zugriff *m.* grasp; access.
zugrunde *adv.* ~ *gehen*, to perish; ~ *richten*, to ruin.
zugucken *v.i.* to look on.
Zugunglück *n.* train crash.
zugunsten *adv.* in favor of.
zugute *adv.* ~ *halten*, to make allowances for; ~ *kommen lassen*, to give the benefit of; *sich etwas auf eine Sache ~ tun*, to be proud of a thing.
zuguterletzt *adv.* finally, ultimately.
Zug: ~**verbindung** *f.* railroad service; ~**verkehr** *m.* train services; ~**vieh** *n.* draft-cattle; ~**vogel** *m.* bird of passage.
Zugzwang *m.* *in ~ geraten*, to be forced to act.
zuhaben *v.i.* to be closed.
zuhalten *v.t.st.* to keep closed, to stop.
Zuhälter *m.* (-s, -) pimp.
zuhängen *v.t.st.* to hang (curtain) over or in front of.
zuhauen *v.t.st.* to rough-hew, to shape; ~ *v.i.st.* to shut; to slam; to strike.
Zuhause *n.* home.
zuheilen *v.i.* (*s*) to heal up, to close.
Zuhilfenahme *f.* (-, 0) *unter oder mit ~ von*, with the aid of.
zuhinterest *adv.* at the very end.
zuhorchen *v.i.* to listen to.
zuhören *v.i.* to give ear to, to listen.
Zuhörer *m.* (-s, -); **Zuhörerin** *f.* (-, -nen) listener.
Zuhörerraum *m.* lecture room, auditorium.
Zuhörerschaft *f.* (-, 0) audience.
zujauchzen, zujubeln *v.i.* to cheer.
zukehren *v.t.* to turn (towards).
zuklappen *v.t.u.i.* to close; to fold; to shut.
zukleben, zukleistern *v.t.* to glue or paste up.
zuknallen *v.t.* to slam.
zukneifen *v.t.st.* to squeeze; to shut tight.
zuknöpfen *v.t.* to button up.
zukommen *v.i.st.* (*s*) to come to hand; to belong to; to befit, to be due or suitable; to fall to one's

share; *einem etwas ~ lassen*, to let. . . have.
Zukunft *f.* (-, 0) future, time to come; *in ~*, in future.
zukünftig *a.* future; next; intended.
Zukünftige *m./f.* (*fam.*) *mein ~r/meine ~*, my husband/wife to be.
Zukunfts: ~**anssichten** *pl.* future prospects; ~**forschung** *f.* futurology.
zukunftsorientiert *a.* future-oriented.
Zukunftsroman *m.* science fiction novel.
zukunftsweisend *a.* advanced.
zulächeln *v.i.* to smile at.
Zulage *f.* (-, -n) extra pay, allowance.
zulangen *v.i.* to help oneself.
zulänglich *a.* sufficient.
zulassen *v.t.st.* to permit; to admit.
zulässig *a.* admissible, allowable.
Zulassung *f.* (-, 0) admission, admittance; permission; registration (car).
Zulauf *m.* (-[e]s, 0) run (of customers); *grossen ~ haben*, to be in vogue.
zulaufen *v.i.st.* (*s*) to run on; to run to; *spitz ~*, to taper.
zulegen *v.t.* to add, to increase; *sich etwas ~*, to provide oneself with.
zuleide *adv.* ~ *tun*, to do hrm.
zuleiten *v.t.* to direct to; to supply; to send.
zulernen *v.i. & t.* to enlarge one's knowledge, to live and learn.
zuletzt *adv.* (at) last, finally, after all.
zuliebe *adv.* for the sake.
zumachen *v.t.* to shut, to close, to fasten.
zumal *adv.* especially, chiefly; *c.* especially as.
zumauern *v.t.* to wall or brick up.
zumeist *adv.* for the most part, mostly.
zumindest *adv* at least.
zumutbar *a.* reasonable.
Zumutbarkeit *f.* reasonableness.
zumute *a.* ~ *sein*, to feel.
zumuten *v.t.* to expect of a person.
Zumutung *f.* (-, -en) (unreasonable) demand; imposition.
zunächst *adv.* first, above all.
zunageln *v.t.* to nail up.
zunähen *v.t.* to sew up.
Zunahme *f.* (-, 0) increase, growth.
Zuname *m.* surname, family name.
zündeln *v.i.* to play with fire.
zünden *v.i.* to catch fire; (*fig.*) to take, to catch on; ~ *v.t.* to kindle.
zündend *a.* stirring (speech).
Zunder *m.* (-, 0) tinder.
Zünder *m.* (-s, -) fuse, match, igniter.
Zünd: ~**holz** *n.* match; *ein ~holz anzünden*, to strike a match; ~**kerze** *f.* spark plug; ~**schnur** *f.* fuse.
Zündung *f.* (-, -en) ignition.
zunehmen *v.i.st.* to increase, to grow; to put on weight.
zuneigen *v.t.* to bend or incline (towards).
Zuneigung *f.* inclination, affection.
Zunft *f.* (-, Zünfte) guild.
zünftig *a.* proper; competent.
Zunge *f.* (-, -n) tongue.
züngeln *v.t.* (*von Flammen*) to flicker; to dart.
Zungen: ~**belag** *m.* coating of the tongue; ~**brecher** *m.* tongue twister.

zungenfertig *a.* glib.

Zungen: ~kuß *m.* French kiss; **~spitze** *f.* tip of the tongue.

zunichte *adv.* undone, ruined.

zunicken *v.i.* to nod to.

zunutzemachen *v.t.* to make use of s.th.

zuoberst *adv.* at the top, uppermost.

zuordnen *v.t.* to classify with.

zupfen *v.t.* to pull, to tug, to pluck, to pick.

zupflastern *v.t.* to pave or plaster over.

zuprosten *v.i.* raise one's glass to.

zuraten *v.t.st.* to advise.

zuraunen *v.t.* to whisper (into one's ear).

zurechnen *v.t.* to attribute.

zurechnungsfähig *a.* of sound mind.

Zurechnungsfähigkeit *f.* soundness of mind; (*jur.*) responsibility.

zurecht *adv.* in time; ready.

zurechtbringen *v.t.ir.* to put to rights, to restore, to adjust.

zurechtfinden (sich) *v.refl.st.* to find *or* see one's way.

zurechtkommen *v.i.st.* (*s*) to succeed, to get on well; (*mit einem*) to get on (with), to agree (with); (*der Zeit nach*) to arrive in (the nick of) time.

zurechtlegen *v.t.* to arrange, to lay out in order; *sich ~,* to explain to oneself.

zurechtmachen *v.t.* to prepare; (sich) ~ *v.refl.* to get ready.

zurechtschneiden *v.t.st.* to trim.

zurechtsetzen *v.t.* to set *or* put right.

zurechtweisen *v.t.st.* to reprimand.

Zurechtweisung *f.* reprimand; rebuke.

zureden *v.i.* to persuade, to encourage.

zureichend *a.* sufficient.

zureiten *v.t.st.* to break in (a horse).

zurichten *v.t.* (*fam.*) to injure; to make a mess.

zuriegeln *v.t.* to bolt.

zürnen *v.i.* to be angry.

Zurschaustellung *f.* exhibition, display.

zurück *adv.* back, backwards; ~ *sein* (*fig.*) to be back/behind; ~*!* stand back!; *ich werde bald ~ sein,* I shan't be long.

zurückbegeben (sich) *v.refl.st.* to go back, to return.

zurückbehalten *v.t.st.* to keep back.

zurückbekommen *v.t.st.* to get back.

zurückberufen *v.t.st.* to recall.

zurückbezahlen *v.t.* to repay, to reimburse.

zurückbleiben *v.i.st.* (*s*) to remain behind; to lag behind.

zurückblicken *v.i.* to look back.

zurückbringen *v.t.ir.* to bring back, to return.

zurückdatieren *v.t.* to antedate; ~ *v.i.* to date back.

zurückdenken *v.i.st.* (*an*) to think back.

zurückdrängen *v.t.* to repress.

zurückerhalten *v.t.st.* to get back.

zurückerstatten *v.t.* to give back, to return.

zurückfahren *v.i.st.* to drive back; (*fig.*) to recoil.

zurückfinden (sich) *v.refl.* to find one's way back.

zurückfordern *v.t.* to demand back.

Zurückforderung *f.* reclamation.

zurückführen *v.t.* to lead back; (*ar.*) to reduce (to); to trace (back) (to).

zurückgeben *v.t.st.* to give back, to return, to restore.

zurückgehen *v.i.st.* (*s*) to go back; to decrease; (*Preis*) to decline.

zurückgezogen *a.* retired; secluded.

Zurückgezogenheit *f.* (-, 0) retirement; seclusion.

zurückgreifen *v.i.st.* (*auf*) to fall back (on).

zurückhaben *v.t.ir.* to have back.

zurückhalten *v.t.st.* to hold back, to restrain; *mit etwas ~,* to be reserved concerning sth.

zurückhaltend *a.* reserved; cautious.

Zurückhaltung *f.* (-, 0) reserve.

zurückkaufen *v.t.* to buy back, to buy in.

zurückkehren *v.i.* (*s*) to return.

zurückkommen *v.i.st.* (*s*) to come back, to return.

zurückkönnen *v.i.ir.* to be able to return.

zurücklassen *v.t.st.* to leave (behind).

zurücklegen *v.t.* to put by, to save; (*Weg*) to travel.

Zurücknahme *f.* revocation, withdrawal.

zurücknehmen *v.t.st.* to take back; to withdraw, to retract.

zurückprallen *v.i.* (*s*) to rebound.

zurückrufen *v.t.st.* to call back.

zurückschaudern *v.i.* (*s*) to recoil (from).

zurückschlagen *v.t.st.* to beat back, to repulse.

zurückschrecken *v.t.st.* (*s*) to recoil; to start back.

zurücksehnen *v.refl.* to long to be back.

zurücksetzen *v.t.* to put back; to reduce the price of; to slight, to neglect.

Zurücksetzung *f.* (-, -en) neglect, slight.

zurücksinken *v.i.st.* (*s*) to relapse (into).

zurückspringen *v.i.st.* (*s*) to rebound.

zurückstehen *v.i.st.* to be inferior (to).

zurückstellen *v.t.* to put back; to shelve; (*mil.*) to defer.

Zurückstellung *f.* (-, -en) (*mil.*) deferment.

zurückstrahlen *v.t.* to reflect, to throw back.

zurücktreiben *v.t.st.* to drive back, to thrust back, to repulse, to repel.

zurücktreten *v.i.st.* (*s*) to step back; (*vom Amt*) to resign office.

zurückübersetzen *v.t.* to retranslate.

zurückverlangen *v.t.* to demand *or* ask back; ~ *v.i.* to desire to go back (to).

zurückversetzen *sich in eine Zeit ~,* to go back to a time.

zurückweichen *v.i.st.* (*s*) to fall back, to recede, to give away, to yield.

zurückweisen *v.t.st.* to reject, to repel, to decline.

Zurückweisung *f.* (-, -en) repulse, repudiation.

zurückwerfen *v.t.st.* to throw back.

zurückzahlen *v.t.* to pay back, to repay.

zurückziehen *v.t.st.* to withdraw; (sich) ~ *v.refl.* to withdraw (from); to retreat; to retire.

Zuruf *m.* (-[e]s, -e) acclamation; call.

zurufen *v.i.st.* to call to, to shout to; *Beifall ~,* to cheer, to applaud.

zurzeit *adv.* for the time being.

Zusage *f.* (-, -n) promise; assent; acceptance.

zusagen *v.t.* to promise; ~ *v.i.* to promise to come; to suit, to please.

zusammen *adv.* together; jointly.

zusammenarbeiten *v.i.* to collaborate, to co-operate.

Zusammenarbeit *f.* co-operation.

zusammenballen *v.t.* to conglomerate.

zusammenbeißen *v.t.st.* to clench (one's teeth).

zusammenbinden *v.t.st.* to bind *or* tie together.

zusammenbleiben *v.i.st.* to stay together.

zusammenbrechen *v.i.st.* (*s*) to break down, to collapse.

zusammenbringen *v.t.ir.* to bring together; to collect.

Zusammenbruch *m.* collapse.

zusammendrängen *v.t.* to compress; to condense; (sich) ~ *v.refl.* to crowd together.

zusammendrücken *v.t.* to compress.

zusammenfahren *v.i.st.* (*s*) to start, to wince.

zusammenfallen *v.i.st.* (*s*) to collapse; to coincide.

zusammenfalten *v.t.* to fold (together, up), to double up.

zusammenfassen *v.t.* to collect; to sum up, to summarize.

Zusammenfassung *f.* summary.

zusammenfinden (sich) *v.refl.st.* to meet.

zusammenflicken *v.t.* to patch together, to botch up.

Zusammenfluß *m.* (-flusse, -flüsse) confluence; concourse, crowd.

zusammenfügen *v.t.* to join, to unite.

zusammengehen *v.i.st.* (*s*) to coincide; to cooperate; to match.

zusammengehören *v.i.* to belong together, to be of the same kind.

zusammengesetzt *a.* composed, compound; composite.

Zusammenhalt *m.* (-[e]s, 0) cohesion.

zusammenhalten *v.t.st.* to hold together; ~ *v.i.st.* to assist one another.

Zusammenhang *m.* (-[e]s, -hänge) connection, coherence; *ohne* ~, incoherent; *aus dem* ~, out of context.

zusammenhängen *v.i.st.* to cohere; to be connected (with).

zusammenhangslos *a.* incoherent.

zusammenkauern (sich) *v.refl.* to huddle up.

zusammenketten *v.t.* to chain together.

zusammenkitten *v.t.* to cement together.

Zusammenklang *m.* accord, harmony.

zusammenklappen *v.t.* to fold together, to shut; ~ *v.i.* (*fig.*) to break down.

zusammenkommen *v.i.st.* (*s*) to meet.

Zusammenkunft *f.* (-, -künfte) meeting.

zusammenlaufen *v.i.st.* (*s*) to flock together; to shrink; to curdle; (*math.*) to converge.

Zusammenleben *n.* (-s, 0) social life; (*eheliches*) cohabitation.

zusammenleben *v.i.* to live together.

zusammenlegbar *a.* folding, collapsible.

zusammenlegen *v.t.* to lay together, to fold up; (*Geld*) to club together.

zusammenleimen *v.t.* to stick together.

zusammennehmen *v.t.st.* to summon; ~(*sich*) *v.refl.st.* to pull oneself together; *seine Gedanken gehörig* ~, to collect one's thoughts.

zusammenpacken *v.t.* to pack up.

zusammenpassen *v.i.* to go together; to be well matched.

zusammenpferchen *v.t.* to herd together.

zusammenprallen *v.i.* to collide, to clash.

zusammenpressen *v.t.* to squeeze/press together.

zusammenraffen *v.t.* to collect hurriedly; (sich) ~ *v.refl.* to muster courage; *seine Kräfte* ~, to collect all one's strength.

zusammenrechnen *v.t.* to add up.

zusammenreißen *v.refl.st.* to pull o.s. together.

zusammenrotten (sich) *v.refl.* to band together; to gang up; to form a mob.

zusammenrücken *v.t.* to join together, to put close together; ~ *v.i.* (*s*) to draw together.

zusammenscharen *v.refl.* to flock together.

zusammenschießen *v.t.st.* to put a bullet through s.b.

zusammenschlagen *v.t.st.* to beat up; to smash; *die Hände über dem Kopf* ~, to throw up one's arms in astonishment; ~ *v.i.* (*s*) *die Wogen schlugen über ihm zusammen*, the waves closed over him.

zusammenschließen *v.t.st.* to lock together; to unite; (sich) ~ *v.refl.st.* to merge; to line up (against).

Zusammenschluß *m.* union, fusion, merger.

zusammenschnüren *v.t.* to tie up.

zusammenschrecken *v.i.* (*s*) to startle.

zusammenschrumpfen *v.i.* (*s*) to shrivel up, to dwindle; to wrinkle.

zusammensetzen *v.t.* to compose; (*mech.*) to assemble; (sich) ~ *v.refl.* to consist of.

Zusammensetzung *f.* (-, -en) composition.

zusammensinken *v.i.st.* (*s*) to collapse.

Zusammenspiel *n.* (-[e]s, -e) (*sport*) team work.

zusammenstellen *v.t.* to put together; to make up, to compile.

Zusammenstellung *f.* (-, -en) combination; (*fig.*) compilation.

zusammenstimmen *v.t.* to accord, to chime in, to agree; to harmonize.

zusammenstoppeln *v.t.* to piece together.

Zusammenstoß *m.* (-es, -stösse) collision; (*mil.*) encounter; (*fig.*) clash, conflict.

zusammenstossen *v.i.st.* (*s*) to collide; to adjoin each other; ~ *v.t.* to knock together; (*Gläser*) to clink.

zusammenströmen *v.i.* (*s*) to flock together.

zusammenstürzen *v.i.* (*s*) to tumble down; to collapse.

zusammentreffen *v.i.st.* (*s*) to meet; to coincide; to clash; to encounter.

zusammentreten *v.i.st.* (*s*) to meet.

zusammentrommeln *v.t.* (*fam.*) to drum up; (*Geld*) to raise by hook and by crook.

zusammentun *v.refl.* to combine.

zusammenwachsen *v.i.st.* (*s*) to grow together.

zusammenwerfen *v.t.st.* to jumble *or* throw together, to pool, to confound.

zusammenwürfeln *v.t.* to mix up confusedly.

zusammenwirken *v.i.* to collaborate, cooperate.

zusammenzählen *v.t.* to add up.

zusammenziehen *v.t.st.* to draw together, to contract; to gather, to concentrate; to abridge; (sich) ~ *v.refl.* to shrink up; to gather.

zusammenziehend *a.* astringent.

Zusatz *m.* (-es, -sätze) addition, supplement; alloy, admixture; codicil; postscript.

zusätzlich *a.* additional.

zuschanzen *v.t.* (*fam.*) *einem etwas* ~, to make a thing come somebody's way.

zuschauen *v.i.* to look on.

Zuschauer *m.* (-s, -); **Zuschauerin** *f.* (-, -nen) spectator, looker-on.

Zuschauerraum *m.* auditorium.

zuschicken *v.t.* to send (to).

zuschieben *v.t.st.* to push towards; shut gently.

zuschießen *v.t.st.* to contribute.

Zuschlag *m.* (-[e]s, -schläge) knocking down (to the highest bidder); extra-payment; excess fare; (*Steuer*) surtax; *Teuerungs~*, bonus.

zuschlagen *v.t.st.* to slam (a door); to knock down (to a bidder); ~ *v.i.st.* to strike hard, to hit away.

Zuschlagporto *n.* surcharge.

zuschließen *v.t.st.* to lock (up).

zuschmeißen *v.t.st.* (*fam.*) to bang.

zuschneiden *v.t.st.* to cut out.

Zuschneider *m.* (-s, -) cutter.

Zuschnitt *m.* (-[e]s, -e) cut; style.

zuschnüren *v.t.* to lace; to tie up.

zuschrauben *v.t.* to screw on.

zuschreiben *v.t.st.* to ascribe, to impute; (*com.*) to put to one's credit.

zuschreiten *v.i.st.* (s) to step up to.

Zuschrift *f.* (-, -en) letter.

Zuschuß *m.* (-schusses, -schüsse) additional allowance; grant.

zuschütten *v.t.* to fill up; to pour on.

zusehen *v.i.st.* to look on; to suffer; to see to, to take care.

zusehends *adv.* visibly.

zusein *v.i.st.* to be shut.

zusenden *v.t.ir.* to send (to).

Zusendung *f.* sending.

zusetzen *v.t.* to add; ~ *v.i.* (*einem*) to press hard.

zusichern *v.t.* to promise.

Zusicherung *f.* (-, -en) assurance.

zusperren *v.t.* to lock, to bar.

Zuspiel *n.* passing; pass.

zuspielen *v.t.* to pass (the ball).

zuspitzen *v.t.* to point; (sich) ~ *v.refl.* to taper; (*fig.*) to come to a crisis.

Zusprache *f.* (-, -n) encouragement.

zusprechen *v.i.st.* to exhort; to comfort, to encourage; ~ *v.t.st.* to award, to adjudge; to do justice to (a dish).

Zuspruch *m.* (-[e]s, -sprüche) encouragement; run of customers.

Zustand *m.* (-[e]s, -stände) condition, situation, state (of affairs).

zustande *adv.* ~ *bringen*, to accomplish, to bring about; ~ *kommen*, to come about, to be realized.

zuständig *a.* competent; responsible.

Zuständigkeit *f.* (-, 0) competence; responsibility.

zustatten kommen *v.i.* to prove useful.

zustecken *v.t.* to pin up; *einem etwas ~*, to convey a thing secretly to one.

zustehen *v.i.st.* to be due; to belong; (*law*) to be vested in; *das steht mir zu*, I'm entitled to it.

zustellen *v.t.* to deliver, to hand to.

Zustellung *f.* service; delivery.

zustimmen *v.t.* to agree to.

Zustimmung *f.* (-, -en) consent, approval.

zustopfen *v.t.* to plug; to darn.

zustoßen *v.i.st.* (s) to happen, to befall.

zuströmen *v.i.* (s) to flow towards; to crowd in (upon one).

zustutzen *v.t.* to trim, to fashion.

zutage *adv.* to light; to the surface.

Zutat *f.* (-, -en) ingredient, addition; (*Schneiderei*) trimmings *pl.*

zuteilen *v.t.* to allot, to assign.

zuteil *adv.* ~ *werden*, to fall to one's share; ~ *werden lassen*, to allot to.

Zuteilung *f.* (-, -en) quota, allowance.

Zuteilungsperiode *f.* ration period.

zutragen *v.t.st.* to carry to; to report; (sich) ~, *v.refl.* to happen.

zuträglich *a.* wholesome; conducive (to).

zutrauen *v.t.* (*einem etwas*) to believe someone capable of.

Zutrauen *n.* (-s, 0) trust, confidence, faith.

zutraulich *a.* confiding, trustful.

zutreffen *v.i.st.* to prove right; to come true.

zutreffend *a.* correct, applicable.

zutreiben *v.t.st.* to drive towards; ~ *v.i.st.* (s) to drift towards.

zutrinken *v.i.st.* to drink to, to pledge.

Zutritt *m.* (-[e]s, -e) access, admission; ~ *verboten*, no entrance, no entry; *Unbeschäftigten ~ verboten*, no admittance except on business.

Zutun *n.* (-s, 0) aid, interference.

zuungunsten *pr.* to the disadvantage of.

zuunterst *adv.* at the (very) bottom.

zuverlässig *adv.* reliable, trustworthy, dependable.

Zuverlässigkeit *f.* (-, 0) reliability.

Zuversicht *f.* (-, 0) confidence, trust.

zuversichtlich *a.* confident.

zuviel *indef.pn.* too much.

zuvor *adv.* before(hand), previously.

zuvorkommen *v.i.st.* (s) to get the start of; to prevent; to anticipate.

zuvorkommend *a.* obliging; courteous.

Zuvorkommenheit *f.* courteousness; courtesy.

zuvortun *v.t.st. es einem ~*, to outdo.

Zuwachs *m.* (-wachses, 0) increase.

zuwachsen *v.i.st.* to become overgrown.

Zuwanderung *f.* (-, -en) immigration.

zuwarten *v.t.* to wait.

zuwege bringen *v.t.ir.* to bring s.th. off; to achieve.

zuweilen *adv.* sometimes.

zuweisen *v.t.st.* to assign to.

zuwenden *v.t.ir.* to turn or direct towards; to procure (for).

Zuwendung *f.* grant; allowance; love; loving care; attention.

zuwenig *indef.pn.* too little.

zuwider *a.* repugnant, odious.

zuwiderhandeln *v.i.* to contravene.

Zuwiderhandelnde *m./f.* (-n, -n) offender.

Zuwiderhandlung *f.* (-, 0) non-compliance.

zuwiderlaufen *v.i.st.* (s) to run counter to.

zuwinken *v.i.* to wave to.

zuzahlen *v.t.* to pay extra.

zuziehen *v.t.st.* to pull shut; to draw together or tight; to draw (a curtain); to call in (another physician); (sich) ~ *v.refl.* to incur; to catch.

Zuzug *m.* (-[e]s, -züge) influx.

zuzüglich *pr.* plus.

zuzwinkern *v.i.* to wink at.

Zwang *m.* (-[e]s, 0) constraint, compulsion, coercion; force.

zwängen *v.t.* to force, to press (into).

zwanglos *a.* unconstrained; informal.

Zwangs: *~anleihe* *f.* forced loan; *~arbeit* *f.* forced or hard labour; *~jacke* *f.* straitjacket; *~läufig* *n.*

automatic; **~maßnahme** f. **~mittel** n. coercive measure; **~verkauf** m. forced sale; **~verschleppter** m. displaced person (DP); **~versteigerung** f. forced sale; **~verwaltung** f. sequestration; **~vollstreckung** f. (law) execution; **~wirtschaft** f. government control.

zwangsweise adv. by compulsion or force.

zwanzig a. twenty; a score; in den Zwanzigern sein, stehen, to be between twenty and thirty (years of age).

zwar adv. it is true, no doubt.

Zweck m. (-[e]s, -e) aim, purpose, object, end; es hat keinen ~, there is no point in.

zweckdienlich a. relevent; useful.

Zwecke f. (-, -n) hob-nail, tack.

zweckentfremden v.t. to use for another purpose.

zweckenstsprechend a. suitable.

zwecklos a. useless; purposeless, aimless.

zweckmäßig a. expedient, suitable.

zwecks pr. for the purpose of.

zweckwidrig a. unsuitable, inexpedient.

zwei a. two.

Zwei f. (-, -en) number or figure of two; (im Spiel) deuce.

zwei: **~armig** a. two-armed; **~beinig** a. two-legged.

Zweibettzimmer n. double room.

zweideutig a. ambiguous, equivocal.

Zweideutigkeit f. (-, -en) ambiguity.

zweierlei a. of two sorts; different.

zweifach a. double, twofold; in ~er Ausfertigung, in duplicate.

Zweifel m. (-s, -) doubt.

zweifelhaft a. doubtful; dubious.

zweifellos a. undoubtedly; doubtless.

zweifeln v.i. to doubt, to question.

Zweifelsfall m. case of doubt; im ~ zu eines Gunsten entscheiden, to give a person the benefit of the doubt.

zweifelsohne adv. doubtless.

Zweifler m. (-s, -); **Zweiflerin** f. (-, -nen) sceptic, doubter.

zweifüßig a. two-footed, biped.

Zweig m. (-[e]s, -e) branch, bough; twig.

Zweigespann n. team of two (horses).

Zweiggeschäft n. branch (establishment).

zweigleisig a. double track (rail.).

zweihändig a. two handed.

zweijährig a. two years old, of two years.

Zweikammersystem n. two-chamber system of government.

Zweikampf m. single combat, duel.

zweimal adv. twice.

zweimalig a. done twice.

zweimonatlich a. bimonthly.

zweimotorig a. (avi.) twin engined.

Zweirad n. bicycle; (sl.) bike.

zweirädrig a. two wheeled.

zweireihig a. double-breasted (coat).

zweischneidig a. double edged.

zweiseitig a. two-sided, bilateral.

zweisilbig a. dissyllabic.

zweisitzig a. having two seats.

zweispaltig a. in double columns.

zweispännig a. drawn by two horses.

zweisprachig a. bilingual.

zweistimmig a. for two voices.

zweistündig a. (lasting) two hours.

zweite[r] a. second; jeden zweiten Tag, every other day; ~s Gesicht, second sight; der zweitbeste, the second-best; der zweitletzte, the last but one.

zweiteilig a. two-part ~er Anzug, two-piece suit.

zweitens adv. secondly.

zweitjüngst a. youngest but one.

Zweiunddreißigstelnote f. thirty-second note.

zweiwöchentlich a. biweekly.

Zwerchfell n. diaphragm.

Zwerg m. (-[e]s, -e) dwarf, pygmy, midget.

zwergartig, zwerghaft a. dwarfish.

Zwetsche, Zwetschge f. (-, -n) plum.

Zwickel m. (-s, -) clock (of a stocking); gusset (of a shirt); (arch.) spandrel.

zwicken v.t. to pinch, to nip.

Zwicker m. (-s, -) pince-nez.

Zwickmühle f. Spiel double-mill; (fig.) dilemma.

Zwieback n. (-[e]s, -e) biscuit, rusk.

Zwiebel f. (-, -n) onion; (Blumen~) bulb.

zwiefach, zwiefältig a. twofold.

Zwiegespräch n. dialogue.

Zwielicht n. twilight.

zwielichtig a. shady, dubious.

Zwiespalt m. (-[e]s, -e) inner conflict, dissension, discord.

zwiespältig a. (fig.) conflicting, discordant.

Zwietracht f. (-, 0) discord.

Zwilling m. (-[e]s, -e) twin.

zwingen v.t.st. to constrain, to compel, to force; gezwungen, forced, constrained.

zwingend a. compelling; imperative; urgent.

Zwinger m. (-s, -) kennel; dungeon.

Zwingherrschaft f. despotism, tyranny.

zwinkern v.i. to twinkle, to blink.

Zwirn m. (-[e]s, -e) thread; twine.

Zwirnfaden m. thread.

zwischen pr. between.

Zwischen: **~akt** m. intermission. **~bemerkung** f. incidental remark; digression; **~ding** n. cross.

zwischendurch adv. at intervals, in between.

Zwischen: **~fall** m. incident, episode; **~glied** n. connecting link; **~handel** m. commission business; **~händler** m. middleman; **~landung** f. stopover.

zwischenliegend a. intermediate.

Zwischen: **~lösung** f. interim solution; **~raum** m. interval, interstice, intermediate space; **~ruf** m. interruption; **~rufer** m. heckler; **~satz** m. parenthesis; **~spiel** n. interlude; **~zeit** f. intervening time, meantime.

Zwischenzonen. . .interzonal, a.

Zwist m. (-[e]s, -e) dispute, quarrel.

Zwistigkeit f. (-, -en) discord, quarrel.

zwitschern v.i. to chirp, to twitter.

Zwitter m. (-s, -) hermaphrodite; (bot.) hybrid.

zwo a. two.

zwölf a. twelve.

zwölferlei a. of twelve sorts.

Zwölffingerdarm m. duodenum.

zwölfjährig a. twelve years old.

zwölftens adv. twelfthly.

Zyankali n. (-s, -) cyanide of potassium.

zyklisch a. cylindrical.

Zyklon m. (-s, -e) cyclone.

Zyklus *m.* (-, -len) cycle.
Zylinder *m.* (-s, -) cylinder; (*Hut*) silk hat, top hat.
zylindrisch *a.* cylindrical.
Zyniker *m.*; **Zynikerin** *f.* cynic.
zynisch *a.* cynical.

Zynismus *m.* (-, -men) cynicism.
Zypern *n.* (-s, 0) Cyprus.
Zypresse *f.* (-, -n) cypress.
Zypriot *m.*; **Zypriotin** *f.*; **zypriotisch** *a.* Cypriot.
Zyste *f.* (-, -n) cyst.

Geographical Names*

Aachen *n.* Aix-la-Chapelle.
Abessinien *n.* Abyssinia.
Abruzzen *pl.* Abruzzi.
Admiralitätsinseln *f.pl.* the Admiralty Islands.
Adrianopel *n.* Adrianople.
Adriatische(s) Meer *n.* Adriatic (Sea).
Afrika *n.* Africa.
Afrikaner(in) *m.* (& *f.*), **afrikanisch** *a.* African.
Ägäische(s) Meer *n.* Ægean Sea.
Ägypten *n.* Egypt.
Ägypter(in) *m.* (& *f.*), ägyptisch, *a.* Egyptian
Akko *n.* Acre.
Albanese *m.* Albanian.
Albanien *n.* Albania.
Algier *n.* Algeria (*Land*); Algiers (*Stadt*).
Alpen *pl.* Alps.
Alpen . . . *a.* Alpine.
Amazonenstrom *m.* Amazon (river).
Amerika *n.* America.
Amerikaner(in) *m.* (& *f.*), **amerikanisch** *a.* American.
Anatolien *n.* Anatolia.
Andalusien *n.* Andalusia.
Andalusier(in) *m.* (& *f.*), **andalusisch** *a.* Andalusian.
Anden *pl.* Andes.
Angelsachse *m.* Anglo-Saxon.
Ansbach *n.* Anspach.
Antillen *pl.* Antilles.
Antwerpen *n.* Antwerp.

Apenninen *pl.* Apennines.
Apulien *n.* Apulia.
Araber(in) *m.* (& *f.*) Arab.
Arabien *n.* Arabia.
Aragonien *n.* Aragon.
Aragonier(in) *m.* (& *f.*), **aragonisch** *a.* Aragonese.
Ardennen *pl.* Ardennes.
Arktis *f.* Arctic.
Armenien *n.* Armenia.
Armenier(in) *m.* (& *f.*), **armenisch** *a.* Armenian.
Asiat(in) *m.* (& *f.*), **asiatisch** *a.* Asiatic.
Asien *n.* Asia.
Asowsche(s) Meer *n.* Sea of Azov.
Athen *n.* Athens.
Athener(in) *m.* (& *f.*), **athenisch** *a.* Athenian.
Äthiopien *n.* Ethiopia.
Atlantische(s) Meer *n.* Atlantic.
Ätna (der) Mount Etna.
Australien *n.* Australia.
Azoren, (die) *pl.* Azores.

Balkanstaaten(die) *pl.* Balkan States.
Balte *m.*, **Baltin** *f.* native of the Baltic States.
baltisch *a.* Baltic.
Baltische(s) Meer *n.* the Baltic.
Balearen *pl.* the Balearic Isles.
Basel *n.* Basle, Bâle.
Baske *m.* **Baskin** *f.*, **baskisch** *a.* Basque.

---

* Names of countries, places and peoples in -er, generally take -es (or -[e]s) in the Gen. Sing. [*Asien, Asiens, Athen, Athens; Afrika, Afrikas; Gent, Gents; Rußland, Rußlands; Hessen, Hessens;* also: *der Holländer, des Holländers*] (Nom. Sing. and Plur. always alike). Names of peoples in -e take -n in the Gen. Sing. and Nom. Plur.; feminine names in -in take -nen in the Nom. Plur. [*der Pole,* Gen. Sing. *des Polen* Nom. Plur. *die Polen; die Polin, die Polinnen*] (Masc. Gen. Sing. always like the Nom. Plur.).

Bayer(in) *m.* (& *f.*) (-n, -n), **bayrisch** *a.* Bavarian.
Bayern *n.* Bavaria.
Beduine *m.* Bedouin.
Behringstraße *f.* Bering Strait.
Belgien *n.* Belgium.
Belgier(in) *m.* (& *f.*), **belgisch** *a.* Belgian.
Belgrad *n.* Belgrade.
Bengale *m.*, **Bengalin** *f.*, **bengalisch** *a.* Bengali.
Bengalen *n.* Bengal.
Berberei *f.* (-) Barbary States *pl.*
Bessarabien *n.* Bessarabia.
Birma *n.* Burma; **Birmane** *m.*, **birmanisch** *a.* Burmese.
Biskaya, Biscay.
Blindheim *n.* Blenheim.
Bodensee *m.* (-s) Lake Constance.
Böhme *m.*, **Böhmin** *f.*, **böhmisch** *a.* Bohemian.
Böhmen *n.* Bohemia.
Böotien *n.* Bœotia.
Bosnien *n.* Bosnia.
Bosporus *m.* (-) Bosphorus.
Bottnischer Meerbusen *m.* Gulf of Bothnia.
Brasilier(in) *m.* (& *f.*), **brasilianisch** *a.* Brazilian.
Brasilien *n.* Brazil.
Braunschweig *n.* Brunswick.
Bretagne *f.* Brittany.
Britannien *n.* Britain.
britisch *a.* British.
Brite *m.*, **Britin** *f.* Briton.
Brügge *n.* Bruges.
Brüssel *n.* Brussels.
Bukarest *n.* Bucharest.
Bulgare *m.*, **Bulgarin** *f.*, **bulgarisch** *a.* Bulgarian.
Bulgarien *n.* Bulgaria.
Bundesrepublik Deutschland *f.* Federal Republic of Germany.
Burgund *n.* Burgundy.
Burgunder(in) *m.* (& *f.*), **burgundisch** *a.* Burgundian.

Byzanz *n.* Byzantium.

Cadix *n.* Cadiz.
Chaldäer *m.*, **chaldäisch** *a.* Chaldean.
Chilene *m.*, **Chilenin** *f.* Chilian.
Chinese *m.*, **Chinesin** *f.*, **chinesisch** *a.* Chinese.

Dahome *n.* Dahomey.
Dalmatien *n.* Dalmatia.
Dalmatiner(in) *m.* (& *f.*), **dalmatinisch** *a.* Dalmatian.
Däne *m.*, **Dänin** *f.* Dane.
Dänemark *n.* Denmark.
dänisch *a.* Danish.
Danzig *n.* Dantzig, Danzig.
Dardanellenstraße *f.* (Straits of) the Dardanelles.
Dauphiné *f.* (-) Dauphiny.
Delphi *n.* Delphos.
Den Haag *m.* The Hague.
deutsch *a.*, **Deutsche[r]** *m.* & *f.* German.
Deutschland *n.* Germany.
Dnjeper *m.* Nieper, Dnieper.
Dnjester *m.* Niester, Dniester.
Donau *f.* (-) Danube.
Drau *f.* River Drave.
Düna *f.* River Dwina.
Dünkirchen *n.* Dunkirk.

Eismeer *n.* Polar Sea; *Nördliches* ~, Arctic Sea; *Südiches* ~, Antarctic Sea.
Elsaß *n.* Alsace.
Elsässer(in) *m.* (& *f.*), **elsässisch** *a.* Alsatian.
Engländer(in) *m.* (& *f.*) Englishman; Englishwoman.
englisch *a.* English.
Epirus *m.* (-) Epiros.
Estland *n.* Estonia.
Etsch *f.* (-) Adige.
Euphrat *m.* Euphrates.

Europa *n.* Europe.
Europäer(in) *m.* (& *f.*), **europäisch** *a.* European.

Felsengebirge *n.* Rocky Mountains *pl.*
Ferne Osten, der, Fernost *m.* Far East.
Feuerland *n.* Tierra del Fuego.
Fidschiinseln *pl.* Fiji Islands.
Finnland *n.* Finland.
Finnländer(in), Finne *m.* (& *f.*) Finlander.
Flame *m.*, **Flamin** *f.* Fleming; **flämisch** *a.* Flemish.
Flandern *n.* Flanders.
Florentiner(in) *m.* (& *f.*), **florentinisch** *a.* Florentine.
Florenz *n.* Florence.
Franke *m.*, **fränkisch** *a.* Franconian, Frank.
Franken *n.* Franconia.
Frankfurt *n.* Frankfort.
Frankreich *n.* France.
Franzose *m.* Frenchman; *die ~n*, the French.
Französin *f.* Frenchwoman.
französisch *a.* French.
Freiburg *n.* Friburg.
Freundschaftsinseln *pl.* Tonga (or Friendly Islands).
Friese *m.*, **Friesin** *f.*, **Friesländer(in)** *m.* (& *f.*) Frisian; **friesisch** *a.* Frisian.

Galiläa *n.* Galilee.
gälisch *a.* Gaelic.
Galizien *n.* Galicia.
Gallen, St. *n.* St. Gall.
Gascogne *f.* (-) Gascony.
Genf *n.* Geneva.
Genfer(in) *m.* (& *f.*), **genferisch** *a.* Genevese.
Gent *n.* Ghent.
Genua *n.* Genoa.
Genuese(rin) *m.* (& *f.*), **genuesisch** *a.* Genoese.

Germane *m.* Teuton; **Germanin** *f.* Teuton woman; **germanisch**, Germanic, Teutonic.
Golanhöhen *f.* Golan Height.
Gote *m.* Goth; **gotisch** *a.* Gothic.
Graubünden *n.* the Grisons *pl.*
Grieche *m.*, **Griechin** *f.* Greek; **griechisch** *a.* Greek, Hellenic.
Griechenland *n.* Greece.
Grönland *n.* Greenland.
Grönländer(in) *m.* (& *f.*) Greenlander.
Grossbritannien *n.* Great Britain.
Grosser[r] Ozean *m.* Pacific (Ocean).

Haag *m.* The Hague.
Hamelin *n.* Hamelin.
Hannover *n.* Hanover.
Hansastädte *pl.* Hanse Towns, Hanseatic Towns *pl.*
Harz *m.* (-es) Hartz Mountains *pl.*
Havanna *n.* Havana.
Hebräer *m.*, **hebräisch** *a.* Hebrew.
Hebriden *pl. Hebrides.*
Helgoland *n.* Heligoland.
Helsingör *n.* Elsinore.
Hennegau *m.* Hainault.
Herzegowina Herzegovina.
Hesse *m.*, **Hessin** *f.*, **hessisch** *a.* Hessian.
Hessen *n.* Hesse.
Hinterindien *n.* Indo-China.
Hochland, schottische(s) *n.* the Highlands *pl.*
Holländer(in) *m.* (& *f.*) Dutchman; Dutchwoman.
holländisch *a.* Dutch.

Iberische Halbinsel *f.* Iberian Peninsula.
Illyrien *n.* Illyria.
Inder(in) *m.* (& *f.*) Indian.

Indianer(in) *m.* (& *f.*) Indian, Native American.
Indien *n.* India.
indisch *a.* Indian.
indo: **~europäisch** *a.* Indo-European; **~germanisch** *a.* Indo-Germanic.
ionisch *a.* Ionian.
Irak *m.* Iraq.
irisch, irländisch *a.* Irish.
Irland *n.* Ireland.
Irländer(in) *m.* (& *f.*) Irishman; Irishwoman.
Island *n.* Iceland.
Isländer(in) *m.* (& *f.*) Icelander; **isländisch** *a.* Icelandic.
Istrien *n.* Istria.
Italien *n.* Italy.
Italiener(in) *m.* (& *f.*), **italienisch** *a.* Italian.

Japaner *m.*, **Japanerin** *f.*, **japan[es]isch,** Japanese.
Joppe *n.* Jaffa.
Jugoslavien *n.* Yugoslavia.

Kalabrien *n.* Calabria.
Kalifornien *n.* California.
Kalvarienberg *m.* Mount Calvary.
Kamerun *n.* Cameroon
Kanada *n.* Canada.
Kanadier(in) *m.*(*f.*), **kanadisch** *a.* Canadian.
Kanal *m.* the Channel.
Kanarische(n) Inseln *f.pl.* Canaries *pl.*
Kap der guten Hoffnung *n.* Cape of Good Hope.
Kärnten *n.* Carinthia.
Karpaten *pl.* Carpathians.
Kaschmir *n.* Kashmir.
Kaspische(s) Meer *n.* Caspian Sea.
Kastilien *n.* Castile.
Kaukasus *m.* (-s) Caucasus.
Kelte *m.* Celt; **keltisch** *a.* Celtic.

Kleinasien *n.* Asia Minor.
Kleve *n.* Cleves.
Köln *n.* Cologne.
Korse *m.*, **Korsin** *f.*, **korsisch** *a.* Corsican.
Kosak *m.* (-en, -en) Cossack.
Krakau *n.* Cracow.
Kreta *n.* Crete.
Krim *f.* (-) the Crimea.
Kroate *m.*, **Kroatin** *f.*, **kroatisch** *a.* Croatian.
Kroatien *n.* Croatia.

Lakedämon *n.* Lacedæmonian.
Lakedämonier(in), *m.* (& *f.*), **lakedämonisch** *a.* Lacedæmonian.
Lappe, Lappländer(in) *m.* (& *f.*) Laplander; **lappländisch** *a.* Lapp.
Lausitz *f.* Lusatia.
Lausitzer(in) *m.* (& *f.*), **lausitzisch** *a.* Lusatian.
Levante *f.* Levant.
Libanon *m.* Lebanon.
libysch *a.* Libyan.
Lille *n.* Lisle.
Liparische Inseln *pl.* Lipari Islands.
Lissabon *n.* Lisbon.
Litauen *n.* Lithuania.
Litauer(in) *m.* (& *f.*), **litauisch** *a.* Lithuanian.
Livland *n.* Livonia.
Livländer(in) *m.* (& *f.*), **livländisch** *a.* Livonian.
Livorno *n.* Leghorn.
Lofoten *pl.* Lofoden Islands.
Lombardo *m.* **Lombardin** *f.*, **lombardisch** *a.* Lombard.
Lombardei *f.* (-) Lombardy.
Lothringen *n.* Lorraine.
Löwen *n.* Louvain.
Ludwigsburg *n.* Lewisburg.
Luganer See *m.* Lake Lugano.
Lüttich *n.* Liège.
Luzern *n.* Lucerne.
Lyon *n.* Lyons.

Maas *f.* Meuse.
Mähre *m.*, **Mährin** *f.*, **mährisch** *a.* Moravian.
Mähren *n.* Moravia.
Mailand *n.* Milan.
Malaie *m.* Malay; **malaiisch** *a.* Malayan.
Malteser(in) *m.* (& *f.*) **maltesisch** *a.* Maltese.
Mandschurei *f.* Manchuria.
Mark *f.* (-) the March.
Marmarameer *n.* Sea of Marmara.
Marokko *n.* Morocco.
Marseille *n.* Marseilles.
Maure *m.* Moor.
maurisch *a.* Moorish.
Mazedonien *n.* Macedonian.
Mazedonier(in) *m.* (& *f.*), **mazedonisch** *a.* Macedonian.
Mecheln *n.* Malines.
Meerbusen: der Arabische ~, the gulf of Arabia; *der Bengalische ~,* the bay of Bangal; *der Finnische ~,* the gulf of Finland; *der Persische ~,* the Persian gulf.
Mittel . . ., Central . . .
Mittelamerika *n.* Central America.
Mittelmeer *n.* Mediterranean.
Mittlere Osten, der *m.* Middle East.
Moldau *f.*(-) (*Land*) Moldavia.
Molukken, molukkische(n) Inseln (die) *pl.* the Moluccas.
Mongole *m.*, **Mongolin** *f.*, **mongolisch,** Mongol.
Mongolei *f.* (-) *n.* Mongolia.
Mosel *f.* (-) Moselle.
Moskau *n.* Moscow.
Mülhausen *n.* Mulhouse.
München *n.* Munich.

Neapel *n.* Naples.
Neapolitaner(in) *m.* (& *f.*),
neapolitanisch *a.* Neapolitan.
Neufundland *n.* Newfoundland.
Neuschottland *n.* Nova Scotia.
Neuseeland *n.* New Zealand.
Niederlande *pl.* the Netherlands.
Niederländer(in) *m.* (& *f.*) Dutchman; Dutchwoman.
niederländisch *a.* Dutch.
Niederrhein *m.* Lower Rhine.
Nil *m.* Nile.
Nimwegen *n.* Nijmegen.
Nizza *n.* Nice.
Nordafrika *n.* North Africa.
Nordamerika *n.* North America.
nordisch *a.* Norse; Nordic.
Nordsee *f.* North Sea.
Normandie *f.* (-) Normandy.
Normanne *m.*, **normannisch** *a.* Norman.
Norwegen *n.* Norway.
Norweger(in) *m.* (& *f.*), **norwegisch** *a.* Norwegian.
Nubien *n.* Nubia.
Nubier(in), *m.* (& *f.*), **nubisch** *a.* Nubian.
Nürnberg *n.* Nuremberg.

Ober..., Upper...
Olymp *m.* Olympus.
Oranien *n.* Orange.
Oranjefreistaat *m.* Orange Free State.
Orkaden (*Inseln*) *pl.* the Orkneys.
Osmanische(s) Reich *n.* Ottoman Empire.
Ostasien *n.* Eastern Asia, Far East.
Osteuropa *n.* Eastern Europe.
Ostende *n.* Ostend.
Ostfriesland *n.* East Frisia.
Ostindien *n.* the East Indies *pl.*
Ostindische(r) Archipel *m.* the Malay Archipelago.

Österreich *n.* Austria.
Österreicher(in) *m.* (& *f.*), **österreichisch** *a.* Austrian.
Ostsee *f.* Baltic (Sea).
Ozeanien *n.* Oceania.

Palästina *n.* Palestine.
Parnaß *m.* (**-nasses**) Parnassus.
Peloponnes *m.* (-) Peloponnese.
Perser(in) *m.*(& *f.*), **persisch** *a.* Persian.
Persien *n.* Persia.
Persische Golf *m.* Persian Gulf.
Pfalz *f.* (-) the Palatinate.
Pfälzer(in) *m.* (& *f.*), **pfälzisch** *a.* Palatine.
Philippinen *pl.* Philippines.
Piemont *n.* Piedmont.
Piemontese(rin) *m.* (& *f.*), **piemontesisch** *a.* Piedmontese.
Polen *n.* Poland.
polnisch *a.* Polish.
Pommern *n.* Pomerania.
Portugiese *m.*, **Portugiesin** *f.*, **portugiesisch** *a.* Portuguese.
Prag *n.* Prague.
Preuße *m.*, **Preußin** *f.*, **preußich** *a.* Prussian.
Preußen *n.* Prussia.
Pyrenäen *pl.* the Pyrenees.

Regensburg *n.* Ratisbon.
Rhein *m.* Rhine.
rheinisch, rheinländisch *a.* Rhenish.
Rhodier(in) *m.* (& *f.*), Rhodian.
Rhodus *n.* Rhodes.
Rom *n.* Rome.
Römer(in) *m.* (& *f.*), **römisch** *a.* Roman.
Rumänien *n.* Rumania.
Rumänier(in) *m.* (& *f.*), **rumänisch** *a.* Rumanian.
Rumelien *n.* Roumelia.
Russe *m.*, **Russin** *f.*, **russisch** *a.* Russian.

Rußland *n.* Russia.

Sachse *m.*, **Sächsin** *f.*, **Sächsisch** *a.* Saxon.
Sachsen *n.* Saxony.
Saloniki *n.* Thessalonica.
Sambia, Zambia.
Sansibar *n.* Zanzibar.
Sarde *m.*, **Sardinier(in)** *m.* (& *f.*), **sardinisch** *a.* Sardinian.
Sardinien *n.* Sardinia.
Sauerland *n.* Southern Westphalia.
Savoyarde *m.*, **Savoyer(in)** *m.* (& *f.*), **savoyisch** *a.* Savoyard.
Savoyen *n.* Savoy.
Schelde *f.* Scheldt.
Schlesien *n.* Silesia.
Schlesier(in) *m.* (& *f.*), **schlesisch** *a.* Silesian.
Schotte *m.* **Schottin** *f.*, Scotsman; Scotswoman.
schottisch *a.* Scottish.
Schottland *n.* Scotland.
Schwabe *m.*, **Schwäbin** *f.*, **schwäbisch** *a.* Swabian.
Schwaben *n.* Swabia.
Schwarze(s) Meer *n.* Black Sea.
Schwarzwald *m.* Black Forest.
Schwede *m.* **Schwedin** *f.* Swede.
Schweden *n.* Sweden.
schwedisch *a.* Swedish.
Schweiz *f.* Switzerland.
Schweizer(in) *m.* (& *f.*), **schweizerisch** *a.* Swiss.
Seeland *n.* Zealand.
Serbe *m.*, **Serbin** *f.*, **serbisch** *a.* Serb.
Serbien *n.* Serbia.
Sevilla *n.* Seville.
Sirbien *n.* Siberia.
sibirisch *a.* Siberian.
Siebenbürgen *n.* Transylvania.
Simbabwe Zimbabwe.

Sizili[an]er(in) *m.* (& *f.*), **sizil[-ian]isch** *a.* Sicilian.
Sizilien *n.* Sicily.
Skandinavien *n.* Scandinavia.
Slave *m.*, **Slavin** *f.* Slav.
slavisch *a.* Slavonic, Slav.
Slavonien *n.* Slavonia.
Slavonier(in), **Slavone** *m.* (& *f.*), **slavonisch** *a.* Slavonian.
Slowake *m.*, **Slowakin** *f.*, **slowakisch** *a.* Slovak.
Slowene *m.*, **Slowenin** *f.*, **slowenisch** *a.* Slovenian.
Sowjets *pl.* Soviets.
Spanien *n.* Spain.
Spanjer(in) *m.* (& *f.*) Spaniard.
spanisch *a.* Spanish.
Stambul *n.* Istanbul.
Steiermark *f.* Styria.
Steiermärker(in) *m.* (& *f.*), **steiermärkisch, steirisch** *a.* Styrian.
Stille(r) Ozean *m.* Pacific.
Südafrika *n.* South Africa.
Südamerika *n.* South America.
Sudeten *pl.* Sudetes.
Südsee *f.* South Sea.
Sund *m.* The Sound.
Syrakus *n.* Syracuse.
Syrien *n.* Syria, **syrisch** *a.* Syrian.

Tafelberg *m.* Table Mountain.
Tajo *m.* Tagus.
Tanger *n.* Tangier.
Tartare *m.*, **tartarisch** *a.* Tartar.
Tartarei *f.* Tartary.
Taurien, Tauris *n.* Taurie Chersonese.
Themse *n.* Thames.
Thermopylen *pl.* Thermopylæ.
Thessalien *n.* Thessaly.
Thessal(i)er(in) *m.* (& *f.*), **thessalisch** *a.* Thessalian.
Thrazien *n.* Thrace.
Thüringen *n.* Thuringia.

Thüringer(in) *m.* (& *f.*) **thüringisch** *a.* Thuringian.
Thüringer Wald *m.* Thuringian Forest.
Tirol *n.* the Tyrol.
Tiroler(in) *m.* (& *f.*), **tirolisch** *a.* Tyrolese.
Toskana *n.* Tuscany.
Tote(s) Meer *n.* Dead Sea.
Trient *n.* Trento.
Trier *n.* Treves.
Tripolis *n.* Tripoli.
Troja *n.* Troy.
Trojaner(in) *m.* (& *f.*), **trojanisch** *a.* Trojan.
Tschad *m.* Chad.
Tschece *m.*, **tschechisch** *a.* Czech.
Tschechien Czech Republic.
Tschechoslovakei *f.* Czechoslovakia.
Türke *m.*, **Türkin** *f.* Turk.
Türkei *f.* (-) Turkey.
türkisch *a.* Turkish.
Tyrrhenische(s) Meer *n.* Tyrrhenian Sea.

Ungar(in) *m.* (& *f.*), **ungarisch** *a.* Hungarian.
Ungarn *n.* Hungary.

Venedig *n.* Venice.
Venetianer(in) *m.* (& *f.*) **venetianisch** *a.* Venetian.
Vereinigte Arabische Emirate United Arab Emirates.
Vereinigte Staaten *pl.* United States.
Vesuv *m.* Vesuvius.
Vierwaldstätter See *m.* Lake Lucerne.
Vogesen *pl.* Vosges.
Voralpen *pl.* Lower Alps.
Vorderasien *n.* Middle East.
Vorderindien *n.* India.

Walachei *f.* Wallachia.
Wallis *n.* Valais.

Waliser *m.* Welshman.
walisisch *a.* Welsh.
Wallone *m.* Walloon.
Warschau *n.* Warsaw.
Wasgau, Wasgenwald *m.* the Vosges *pl.*
Weichsel *f.* (-) Vistula.
Weißrußland *n.* Belarus, Belorussia.
Westeuropa *n.* Western Europe.
Westfalen *n.* Westphalia; **Westfale** *m.*, **westfälisch** *a.*

Westphalian.
Westindien *n.* West Indies *pl.*
Wien *n.* Vienna.
Wiener(in) *m.* (& *f.*), **wienerisch** *a.* Viennese.
Württemberg *n.* Würtemberg.

Zentralafrikanische Republik *f.* Central African Republic.
Zürich *n.* Zurich.
Zweibrücken *n.* Deux-Ponts.
Zypern *n.* Cyprus; **zyprisch** *a.* Cyprian.

Table of German Strong and Irregular Verbs
Forms in parentheses are less common but acceptable.

Infinitive	Indicative Present	Preterite	Participle Past
backen	ich backe, du bäckst (backst), er bäckt (backt)	ich buk*	gebacken
befehlen	ih befehle, du befiehlst, er befiehlt	ich befahl	befohlen
beginnen	ich beginne	ich begann	begonnen
beißen	ich beisse, du beißt, er beißt etc.	ich biß	gebissen
bergen	ich berge, du birgst, er birgt	ich barg	geborgen
bersten	ich berste, du berstest u. birst, er birst (berstet)	ich barst	geborsten
besinnen sich	ich besinne mich	ich besann mich	besonnen
besitzen	ich besitze, du besitzest u. besitzt	ich besaß	besessen
betrügen	ich betrüge	ich betrog	betrogen
bewegen†	ich bewege	ich bewog	bewogen
biegen	ich biege	ich bog	gebogen
bieten	ich biete	ich bot	geboten
binden	ich binde	ich band, du band(e)st	gebunden
bitten	ich bitte	ich bat, du bat(e)st	gebeten
blasen	ich blase, du bläst, er bläst	ich blies, du bliesest	geblasen
bleiben	ich bleibe	ich blieb, du bliebst	geblieben
braten	ich brate, du brätst, er brät	ich briet	gebraten
brechen	ich breche, du brichst, er bricht	ich brach	gebrochen
brennen	ich brenne	ich brannte	gebrannt
bringen	ich bringe	ich brachte	gebracht
denken	ich denke	ich dachte	gedacht
dingen	ich dinge	ich dang	gedungen
dreschen	ich dresche, du drischst, er drischt	ich drosch (drasch)	gedroschen
dringen	ich dringe	ich drang	gedrungen
dünken	mich dünkt, deucht	mich deuchte, dünkte	gedeucht
dürfen**	ich darf, du darfst, er darf; wir dürfen	ich durfte	gedurft (dürfen)
empfangen	ich empfange, du empfängst, er empfängt	ich empfing	empfangen
empfehlen	ich empfehle, du empfiehlst, er empfiehlt	ich empfahl	empfohlen
empfinden	ich empfinde	ich empfand	empfunden
erbleichen	ich erbleiche	ich erblich	erblichen
erfrieren	ich erfriere	ich erfror	erfroren
erlöschen	ich erlösche, du erlischst, er erlischt	ich erlosch	erloschen
erscheinen	ich erscheine	ich erschien	erschienen
erschreck-en††	ich erschrecke, du erschrickst, er erschrickt	ich erschrak	erschrocken
ertrinken	ich ertrinke	ich ertrank	ertrunken

* The German verbs and tenses marked by one asterisk (*) are more commonly used in their regular form.

** The past participle of a modal auxiliary verb (*dürfen, können, mögen, müssen, sollen, wollen*) is replaced by its infinitive in the perfect tenses when it is immediately preceded by a dependent infinitive (e.g., *Ich habe in die Stadt gehen müssen*). This principle also applies to the following verbs when used as auxiliaries with dependent infinitives: *heißen, helfen, hören, lassen, lehren, lernen,* and *sehen.*

† The verb *'bewegen'* 'to move' is regular, 'to induce' strong.

†† The verb *'erschrecken'* in its transitive sense *'einen erschrecken'* is regular.

Infinitive	Indicative Present	Preterite	Participle Past
erwägen	ich erwäge	ich erwog	erwogen
essen	ich esse, du ißt, er ißt	ich aß	gegessen
fahren	ich fahre, du fährst, er fährt	ich fuhr, du fuhrst	gefahren
fallen	ich falle, du fällst, er fällt	ich fiel	gefallen
fangen	ich fange, du fängst, er fängt	ich fing	gefangen
fechten	ich fechte, du fichtst, er ficht	ich focht	gefochten
finden	ich finde	ich fand	gefunden
flechten	ich flechte, du flichtst*, er flicht*	ich flocht	geflochten
fliegen	ich fliege	ich flog	geflogen
fliehen	ich fliehe	ich floh	geflohen
fließen	ich fliesse	ich floß	geflossen
fragen	ich frage, du fragst, er fragt	ich fragte	gefragt
fressen	ich fresse, du frißt, er frißt	ich fraß	gefressen
frieren	ich friere	ich fror	gefroren
gären	ich gäre	ich gor u. gärte	gegoren, gegärt
gebären	ich gebäre, du gebierst, sie gebiert	ich gebar	geboren
geben	ich gebe, du gibst, er gibt	ich gab	gegeben
gebieten	ich gebiete	ich gebot	geboten
gedeihen	ich gedeihe	ich gedieh	gediehen
gefallen	ich gefalle, du gefällst, er gefällt	ich gefiel	gefallen
gehen	ich gehe, du gehst	ich ging	gegangen
gelingen	es gelingt	es gelang	gelungen
gelten	ich gelte, du giltst, er gilt	ich galt, du galt(e)st	gegolten
genesen	ich genese, du genesest u. genest, er genest	ich genas, du genasest	genesen
genießen	ich geniesse	ich genoß	genossen
geraten	ich gerate, du gerätst, er gerät	ich geriet	geraten
geschehen	es geschieht, sie geschehen	es geschah	geschehen
gewinnen	ich gewinne	ich gewann, du gewannst	gewonnen
gießen	ich giesse, du gießt	ich goß	gegossen
gleichen	ich gleiche	ich glich, du glichst	geglichen
gleiten	ich gleite	ich glitt	geglitten
glimmen	ich glimme	ich glomm*	geglommen*
graben	ich grabe, du gräbst, er gräbt	ich grub, du grubst	gegraben
greifen	ich greife	ich griff, du griffst	gegriffen
haben	ich habe, du hast, er hat, wir haben, ihr habt, sie haben	ich hatte	gehabt
halten	ich halte, du hältst, er hält	ich hielt	gehalten
hängen†	ich hänge, du hängst, er hängt	ich hing, du hing(e)st	gehangen*
hauen	ich haue, du haust	ich hieb, (haute) du hiebst	gehauen
heben	ich hebe	ich hob	gehoben
heißen**	ich heisse, du heißt, er heißt	ich hieß	geheissen
helfen**	ich helfe, du hilfst, er hilft	ich half	geholfen
kennen	ich kenne	ich kannte	gekannt
klimmen	ich klimme	ich klomm*	geklommen
klingen	es klingt	es klang	geklungen
kneifen	ich kneife	ich kniff	gekniffen
kommen	ich komme	ich kam	gekommen

† **hängen** *v.i.* is regular.

Table of German Strong and Irregular Verbs—*continued*

Infinitive	Indicative Present	Preterite	Participle Past
können**	ich kann, du kannst, er kann	ich konnte	gekonnt (können)
kriechen	ich krieche	ich kroch	gekrochen
laden	ich lade, du lädst, er lädt	ich lud	geladen
lassen**	ich lasse, du läßt, er läßt	ich ließ	gelassen (lassen)
laufen	ich laufe, du läufst, er läuft	ich lief	gelaufen
leiden	ich leide	ich litt	gelitten
leihen	ich leihe	ich lieh	geliehen
lesen	ich lese, du liest, er liest	ich las	gelesen
liegen	ich liege	ich lag	gelegen
lügen	ich lüge	ich log	gelogen
mahlen	ich mahle	ich mahlte	gemahlen
meiden	ich meide	ich mied	gemieden
melken	ich melke	ich molk*	gemolken
messen	ich messe, du [missest] u. mißt, er mißt	ich maß	gemessen
mißfallen	ich mißfalle, du mißfällst, er mißfällt	ich mißfiel	mißfallen
mögen**	ich mag, du magst, er mag, wir mögen, ihr mög(e)t, sie mögen	ich mochte	gemocht (mögen)
müssen**	ich muß, du mußt, er muß; wir müssen, ihr müßt, sie müssen	ich mußte	gemußt (müssen)
nehmen	ich nehme, du nimmst, er nimmt	ich nahm	genommen
nennen	ich nenne	ich nannte	genannt
pfeifen	ich pfeife	ich pfiff	gepfiffen
pflegen†	ich pflege	ich pflog*	gepflogen*
preisen	ich preise	ich pries	gepriesen
quellen	ich quelle, du quillst, er quillt	ich quoll	gequollen
raten	ich rate, du rätst, er rät	ich riet	geraten
reiben	ich reibe	ich rieb	gerieben
reißen	ich reisse	ich riss	gerissen
reiten	ich reite	ich ritt	geritten
rennen	ich renne	ich rannte	gerannt
riechen	ich rieche	ich roch	gerochen
ringen	ich ringe	ich rang	gerungen
rinnen	ich rinne	ich rann	geronnen
rufen	ich rufe	ich rief	gerufen
salzen	ich salze	ich salzte	gesalzen, gesalzt††
saufen	ich saufe, du säufst, er säuft	ich soff	gesoffen
saugen	ich sauge	ich sog*	gesogen (gesaugt)
schaffen†††	ich schaffe	ich schuf, du schufst	geschaffen
schallen	es schallt	schallte u. scholl	geschallt
scheiden	ich scheide	ich schied	geschieden
scheinen	ich scheine	ich schien	geschienen
scheißen	ich scheisse	ich schiß	geschissen
schelten	ich schelte, du schiltst, er schilt	ich schalt, du schalt(e)st	gescholten
scheren	ich schere, du scherst, u. schierst, er schert u. schiert	ich schor*	geschoren
schieben	ich schiebe	ich schob	geschoben
schießen	ich schiesse, du schiessest u. schießt	ich schoß, du schossest	geschossen

† The verb '*pflegen*' in the sense of *to nurse, to attend to*, is regular.
†† In compounds and fig. use only (*ge*)*salzen*.
††† '*schaffen*' when used in the sense of *arbeiten* is regular.

Table of German Strong and Irregular Verbs—*continued*

Infinitive	Indicative Present	Preterite	Participle Past
schinden	ich schinde	ich schund*, du schund(e)st*	geschunden
schlafen	ich schlafe, du schläfst, er schläft	ich schlief	geschlafen
schlagen	ich schlage, du schlägst, er schlägt	ich schlug	geschlagen
schleichen	ich schleiche	ich schlich	geschlichen
schleifen	ich schleife	ich schliff	geschliffen
schließen	ich schliesse, du schliessest u. schließt	ich schloß	geschlossen
schlingen	ich schlinge	ich schlang	geschlungen
schmeißen	ich schmeisse, du schmeißt	ich schmiß	geschmissen
schmelzen†	ich schmelze, du schmilzt, er schmilzt	ich schmolz, du schmolzest	geschmolzen
schnauben	ich schnaube	ich schnob*	geschnoben
schneiden	ich schneide	ich schnitt	geschnitten
schrecken	ich schrecke	ich schrak	geschreckt
schreiben	ich schreibe	ich schrieb	geschrieben
schreien	ich schreie	ich schrie	geschrie[e]n
schreiten	ich schreite	ich schritt	geschritten
schweigen	ich schweige	ich schwieg	geschwiegen
schwellen	ich schwelle, du schwillst, er schwillt	ich schwoll	geschwollen
schwimmen	ich schwimme	ich schwamm	geschwommen
schwinden	ich schwinde	ich schwand	geschwunden
schwingen	ich schwinge	ich schwang	geschwungen
schwören	ich schwöre	ich schwor	geschworen
sehen**	ich sehe, du siehst, er sieht	ich sah	gesehen
sein	ich bin, du bist, er ist; wir sind, ihr seid, sie sind. *Subjunctive* ich sei, du seist, er sei; wir seien, ihr seiet, sie seien	ich war	gewesen
senden	ich sende	ich sandte*	gesandt (gesendet)
sieden	ich siede	ich sott*	gesotten
singen	ich singe	ich sang	gesungen
sinken	ich sinke	ich sank	gesunken
sinnen	ich sinne	ich sann	gesonnen
sitzen	ich sitze	ich saß	gesessen
sollen**	ich soll, du sollst, er soll	ich sollte	gesollt (sollen)
spalten	ich spalte, du spaltest	ich spaltete	gespalten, gespaltet
speien	ich speie	ich spie	gespie(e)n
spinnen	ich spinne	ich spann	gesponnen
sprechen	ich spreche, du sprichst, er spricht	ich sprach	gesprochen
sprießen	ich spriesse, du spriessest u. sprießt	ich sproß	gesprossen
springen	ich springe	ich sprang	gesprungen
stechen	ich steche, du stichst, er sticht	ich stach	gestochen
stecken††	ich stecke	ich stak u. steckte	gesteckt
stehen	ich stehe, du stehst	ich stand, du standst	gestanden
stehlen	ich stehle, du stiehlst, er stiehlt	ich stahl	gestohlen
steigen	ich steige	ich stieg	gestiegen
sterben	ich sterbe, du stirbst, er stirbt	ich starb	gestorben
stieben	ich stiebe	ich stob	gestoben

† The verb '*schmelzen*' is regular in its transitive sense.
†† The verb '*stecken*' meaning *to put to, to fix*, is regular and transitive.

Infinitive	Indicative Present	Preterite	Participle Past
stinken	ich stinke	ich stank	gestunken
stoßen	ich stosse, du stößt, er stößt	ich stieß, du stiessest	gestossen
streichen	ich streiche	ich strich	gestrichen
streiten	ich streite	ich stritt	gestritten
tragen	ich trage, du trägst, er trägt	ich trug	getragen
treffen	ich treffe, du triffst, er trifft	ich traf	getroffen
treiben	ich treibe	ich trieb	getrieben
treten	ich trete, du trittst, er tritt	ich trat	getreten
triefen	ich triefe, du triefst	ich troff*	getroffen, getrieft
trinken	ich trinke	ich trank	getrunken
trügen	ich trüge	ich trog	getrogen
tun	ich tue, du tust, er tut	ich tat	getan
verbergen	ich verberge, du verbirgst er verbirgt	ich verbarg	verborgen
verbieten	ich verbiete	ich verbot	verboten
verbleiben	ich verbleibe	ich verblieb	verblieben
verbleichen	ich verbleiche	ich verblich	verblichen
verderben†	ich verderbe, du verdirbst, er verdirbt	ich verdarb	verdorben
verdrießen	es verdrießt	es verdroß	verdrossen
vergessen	ich vergesse, du vergißt, er vergißt	ich vergaß	vergessen
verlieren	ich verliere	ich verlor	verloren
verlöschen	ich verlösche, du verlischt, er verlischt	ich verlosch*	verloschen*
verschallen	verschallt	verschallte, verscholl	verschollen
verschleißen	ich verschleisse	ich verschliß	verschlissen
verschwinden	ich verschwinde	ich verschwand	verschwunden
verzeihen	ich verzeihe	ich verzieh	verziehen
wachsen	ich wachse, du wächst, er wächst	ich wuchs	gewachsen
wägen	ich wäge, du wägst, er wägt	ich wog	gewogen
waschen	ich wasche, du wäsch(e)st, er wäscht	ich wusch	gewaschen
weben	ich webe, du webst	ich webte (wob)	gewebt (gewoben)
weichen††	ich weiche	ich wich	gewichen
weisen	ich weise, du weist	ich wies, du wiesest	gewiesen
wenden	ich wende	ich wandte*	gewandt*
werben	ich werbe, du wirbst, er wirbt	ich warb	geworben
werden	ich werde, du wirst, er wird	ich wurde u. ward, du wurdest u. wardst, er wurde u. ward	geworden (worden)
werfen	ich werfe, du wirfst, er wirft	ich warf	geworfen
wiegen†††	ich wiege, du wiegst, er wiegt	ich wog	gewogen
winden	ich winde	ich wand	gewunden
wissen	ich weiß, du weißt, er weiß, wir (sie) wissen, ihr wißt	ich wußte	gewußt
wollen**	ich will, du willst, er will	ich wollte	gewollt (wollen)
zeihen	ich zeihe	ich zieh	geziehen
ziehen	ich ziehe	ich zog	gezogen
zwingen	ich zwinge	ich zwang	gezwungen

† The verb '*verderben*' is irregular in the sense of *to spoil*, but its participle is regular when used in the sense of *to corrupt*.
†† Compounds meaning *to soften*, *to mollify*, are regular.
††† '*Wiegen*' in the sense of *to rock a cradle or to mince*, is regular.

List of German Abbreviations

AA, *Auswärtiges Amt,* Foreign Office; *Anonyme Alkoholiker,* Alcoholics Anonymous.

a.a.O., *am angeführten Orte,* in the above-mentioned place.

Abb., *Abbildung,* illustration, ill.

Abf., *Abfahrt,* departure, dep.

Abh., *Abhandlung,* treatise.

Abk., *Abkürzung,* abbreviation, abbr.

Abo., *Abonnement,* subscription.

Abs., *Absatz,* paragraph, par.; *Absender,* sender.

Abt., *Abteilung,* department, dept.

a.Ch., *ante Christum,* before Christ, B.C.

a.D., *außer Dienst,* retired.

Adr., *Adresse,* address.

A.G., *Aktien-Gesellschaft,* stock corporation.

ahd., *althochdeutsch,* Old High German, O.H.G.

a.d.L., *an der Lahn,* on the Lahn.

AKW, *Atomkraftwerk,* nuclear power plant.

allg., *allgemein,* general, gen.

a.M., *am Main,* on the Main.

amtl., *amtlich,* official, off.

Anh., *Anhang,* appendix, app.

Ank., *Ankunft,* arrival, arr.

Anl., *Anlage,* enclosure, encl.

Anm., *Anmerkung,* note.

a.d.O., *an der Oder,* on the Oder.

Apr., *April,* April, Apr.

a.Rh., *am Rhein,* on the Rhein.

Art., *Artikel,* article, art.

a.d.S., *an der Saale,* on the Saale.

A.T., *Altes Testament,* Old Testament.

Aufl., *Auflage,* edition, ed.

Aug., *August,* August, Aug.

Az., *Aktenzeichen,* file number.

b., *bei,* near.

B., *Bundestraße,* major road.

BAT, *Bundesangestelltentarif,* salary scale for public employees.

Bd., *Band,* volume, vol.

Bde., *Bände,* volumes, vols.

BE., *Broteinheit,* bread unit.

beil., *beiliegend,* enclosed, encl.

bes., *besonders,* especially, esp.

Best.-Nr., *Bestellnummer,* order number, ord. no.

Betr., *Betreff, betrifft,* regarding, re.

Bev., *Bevölkerung,* population, pop.

Bez., *Bezeichnung,* designation; *Bezirk,* district, dist.

bez., *bezüglich,* with reference to.

bezw., bzw., *beziehungsweise,* respectively.

B.G.B., *Bürgerliches Gesetzbuch,* Civil Code.

BGH, *Bundesgerichtshof,* Federal Supreme Court.

Bhf., *Bahnhof,* station.

BLZ, *Bankleitzahl,* bank code.

BND, *Bundesnachrichtendienst,* Federal Intelligence Service.

Bq., *Becquerel,* becquerel, bq.

BRD., *Bundesrepublik Deutschland,* Federal Republic of Germany, FRG.

bsd., *besonders,* especially, esp.

Btx., *Bildschirmtext,* view data.

Bw., *Bundeswehr,* Federal Armed Forces.

b.w., *bitte wenden,* please turn over, p.t.o.

bzgl., *bezüglich,* with reference to.

bzw., *beziehungsweise,* respectively, resp.

C., *Celsius,* Celsius, centigrade C.
ca., *circa,* about, ca.
CDU, *Christlich-Demokratische Union,* Christian Democratic Union.
Chr., Christus.
cm, *zentimeter,* centimeter.
Co., *Compagnie,* company, co.
CSU, *Christlich-Soziale Union,* Christian Social Union.
CVJM, *Christlicher Verein Junger Männer,* Young Men's Christian Association, YMCA.

d.Ä., *der Ältere,* senior, Sen., Snr., Sr.
DAAD, *Deutscher Akademischer Austauschdienst;* German Academic Exchange Service.
DAG, *Deutsche Angestelltengewerkschaft,* Trade Union of German Employees.
DB, *Deutsche Bundesbahn,* German Federal Railway.
DBP, *Deutsche Bundespost,* German Federal Postal Services.
Dez., *Dezember,* December, Dec.
DFB, *Deutscher Fußballbund,* German Football Association.
DGB, *Deutscher Gewerkschaftsbund,* Federation of German Trade Unions.
dgl., *dergleichen, desgleichen,* the like.
d.Gr., *der Grosse,* the Great.
d.h., *das heißt,* that is, i.e.
d.i., *das ist,* that is, i.e.
Di., *Dienstag,* Tuesday, Tues.
DIN, *Deutsches Institut für Normung,* German Institute for Standardization.
Dipl., *Diplom,* diploma, Dip., Dipl.
Dir., *Direktor,* director, dir.
d.J., *dieses Jahres,* of this year; *der Jüngere,* Junior, Jun., Jr.
DJH, *Deutsches Jugendherbergswerk,* German Youth Hostel Association.
DKP, *Deutsche Kommunistische Partei,* German Communist Party.
DM, *Deutsche Mark,* German mark.
d.M., *dieses Monats,* of this month, inst.
d.O., *der Obige,* the above.
do., *ditto,* ditto, do.
Do., *Donnerstag,* Thurs., Thursday.
Doz., *Dozent(in),* lecturer.
dpa, *Deutsche Presse-Agentur,* German Press Agency.
Dr. jur., *Doktor der Rechte,* Doctor of Laws, LLD.
Dr. med., *Doktor der Medizin,* Doctor of Medicine, MD.
Dr. phil., *Doktor der Philosophic,* Doctor of Philosophy, Ph.D.
Dr. rer. nat., *Doktor der Naturwissenschaften,* Doctor of Science, Sc.D, D.Sc.
Dr. theol., *Doktor der Theologie,* Doctor of Theology, Th.D.
dt., *deutsch,* German.
Dtz., *Dutzend,* dozen.
d.Vf., *der Verfasser,* the author.
DZ, *Doppelzimmer,* double room.
D-Zug., *Durchgangszug,* corridor train.

E, *Eilzug,* fast train; *Europastraße,* European Highway.
ebd., *ebenda,* in the same place, ibid.
Ed., *Edition, Ausgabe,* edition, ed.
EDV, *elektronische Datenverarbeitung,* electronic data processing, EDP.
EEG, *Elektroenzephalogramm,* electroencephalogram, EEG.
e.G., *eingetragene Gesellschaft,* incorporated company.
EG, *Europäische Gemeinschaft,* European Community, EC.

eig., eigtl., *eigentlich,* properly.
einschl., *einschließlich,* inclusive, incl.
EKG, *Elektrokardiogramm,* electrocardiogram, EKG, ECG.
engl., *englisch,* English.
entspr., *entsprechend,* corresponding.
erb., *erbaut,* built.
Erw., *Erwachsene,* adults.
ev., *evangelisch,* Protestant, Prot.
e.V., *eingetragener Verein,* registered society, incorporated, inc.
evtl., *eventuell,* possibly, poss.
EWS, *Europäisches Währungssystem,* European Monetary System, EMS.
exkl., *exklusive,* not included.
EZ, *Einzelzimmer,* single room.

Fa., *Firma,* firm.
Fam., *Familie,* family.
FCKW, *Fluorchlorkohlenwasserstoff,* chlorofluorocarbon, CFC.
F.D.P., *Freie Demokratische Partei,* Liberal Democratic Party.
Feb(r)., *Februar,* February, Feb.
ff., *folgende,* following.
FF, *Französischer Franc,* French franc, FF.
FH, *Fachhochschule,* technical college.
Fig., *Figur,* figure, fig.
FKK, *Freikörperkultur,* nudism.
Fol., fol., *Folio,* page, folio.
Forts., *Fortsetzung,* continuation.
Fr., *Frau,* Mrs., Ms.; *Freitag,* Friday, Fri.
Frl., *Fraülein,* Miss, Ms.
frz., *französisch,* French, Fr.

g., *Gramm,* gram.
GAU, *größter anzunehmender Unfall,* maximum credible accident, MCA.
geb., *geboren,* born, b.
Gebr., *Gebrüder,* Brothers, Bros.

gegr., *gegründet,* established, est.
gek., *gekürzt,* abridged, abr.
Ges., *Gesellschaft,* company, co., society, soc.
gesch., *geschieden,* divorced, div.
gest., *gestorben,* died, d.
gez., *gezeichnet,* signed.
GG, *Grundgesetz,* constitution.
ggf(s)., *gegebenenfalls,* if necessary, if applicable.
G.m.b.H., *Gesellschaft mit beschränkter Haftung,* limited liability company, Ltd.
GUS, *Gemeinschaft unabhängiger Staaten,* Commonwealth of Independent States, CIS.

ha, *Hektar,* hectare.
Hbf., *Hauptbahnhof,* main station, main sta.
h.c., *honoris causa, ehrenhalber,* honorary, hon.
HGB, *Handelsgesetzbuch,* Commercial Code.
Hj., *Halbjahr,* half-year.
hl, *hektoliter,* hectoliter.
hl., *heilig,* holy.
hd., *hochdeutsch,* High German, H.G.
holl., *holländisch,* Dutch.
HP, *Halbpension,* half board.
Hr., *Herr,* Mr.
h(rs)g., *herausgegeben,* edited.
H(rs)g., *Herausgeber,* editor, ed.
Hs., *Handschrift,* manuscript, MS.; **Hss.,** *Handschriften,* MSS.
Hz, *Hertz,* hertz, Hz.

i., *im, in* in.
i.A., *im Auftrag,* per procurationem, p.p., by proxy.
i. allg., *im allgemeinen,* in general, gen.
i.b., *im besonderen,* in particular.
IC, *Intercity(-Zug),* inter-city (train).
ICE, *Intercity-Expreßzug,* intercity express (train).

i.D., *im Dienst,* on duty; *im Durchschnitt,* on average, on av.

i.e., *im einzelnen,* in detail.

IFO, *Institut für Wirtschaftsforschung,* Institute for Economic Research

IG, *Industriegewerkschaft,* industrial union.

IHK, *Industrie-und Handelskammer,* Chamber of Industry and Commerce.

i.J., *im Jahre,* in the year.

i.M., *im Monat,* in the month.

Ing., *Ingenieur,* engineer, eng.

Inh., *Inhaber,* proprietor, prop.; *Inhalt,* contents, cont.

inkl., *inklusive,* included, incl.

IQ, *Intelligenz quotient,* intelligence quotient, IQ.

i.R., *im Ruhestand,* retired, ret.

IRK, *Internationales Rotes Kreuz,* International Red Cross, IRC.

ISBN, *Internationale Standardbuchnummer,* international standard book number, ISBN.

i.V., *in Vertretung,* on behalf of, by proxy, p.p.; *in Vorbereitung,* in preparation, in prep.

IWF, *Internationaler Währungsfonds,* International Monetary Fund, IMF.

J, *Joule,* joule.

Jan., *Januar,* January, Jan.

JH, *Jugendherberge,* youth hostel, Y.H.

Jh., *Jahrhundert,* century, c., cent.

jhrl., *jährlich,* yearly, annual(ly), ann.

jr., jun., *junior,* junior, Jun., jun., Jr.

Jul., *Juli,* July, Jul.

Jun., *Juni,* June, Jun.

Kap., *Kapitel,* chapter, ch.

kath., *katholisch,* Catholic, C(ath).

KB, *Kilobyte,* kilobyte, KB.

Kffr., *Kauffrau,* businesswoman.

Kfm., *Kaufmann,* businessman.

Kfz, *Kraftfahrzeug,* motor vehicle.

kg, *Kilogramm,* kilogramme, kg.

KG, *Kommanditgesellschaft,* limited partnership.

kgl., *königlich,* royal.

k.k., *kaiserlich-königlich,* imperial and royal.

KKW, *Kernkraftwerk,* nuclear power station.

Kl., *Klasse,* class, cl.

km, *Kilometer,* kilometer, km.

KSZE, *Konferenz über Sicherheit und Zusammenarbeit in Europa,* Conference on security and cooperation in Europe, CSCE.

Kto., *Konto,* account, acct, a/c.

kW, *Kilowatt,* kilowatt.

kWh, *Kilowattstunde,* kilowatt-hour.

KZ, *Konzentrationslager,* concentration camp.

l, *Liter,* liter.

l., *links,* left, l.

l.c., *loco citato,* in the place quoted.

led., *ledig,* single, unmarried.

lfd., *laufend,* current, running.

Lfrg., *Lieferung,* delivery; part.

Lkw, *Lastkraftwagen,* truck.

lt., *laut,* according to, acc. to.

luth., *lutherisch,* Lutheran, Luth.

LZB, *Landeszentralbank,* State Central Bank.

m, *Meter,* meter.

MAD, *Militärischer Abschirmdienst,* Military Counter-Intelligence Service.

m.a.W., *mit anderen Worten,* in other words.

MB, *Megabyte,* megabyte, mb.

mbH, *mit beschränkter Haftung,*

with limited liability.

MdB, *Mitglied des Bundestages,* Member of the Bundestag.

MdL, *Mitglied des Landtags,* Member of the Landtag.

mdl., *mündlich,* verbal, oral.

m.E., *meines Erachtens,* in my opinion.

M.E.Z., *Mitteleuropäische Zeit,* Central European Time, CET.

mg, *Milligramm,* milligram.

mhd., *mittelhochdeutsch,* Middle High German, M.H.G.

Mi., *Mittwoch,* Wednesday, Wed.

Mill., Mio., *Million,* million, m.

Mitw., *Mitwirkung,* assistance, participation.

mm, *Millimeter,* millimeter.

Mo., *Montag,* Monday, Mon.

möbl., *möbliert,* furnished, furn.

Mrd., *Milliarde,* billion, bn.

MS, Ms., *Manuskript,* manuscript, MS, ms.

MT, *Megatonne,* megaton.

mtl., *monatlich,* monthly.

m.ü.M., *Meter über dem Meeresspiegel,* meters above sea level.

MWSt., *Mehrwertsteuer,* value-added tax, VAT.

N, *Nord(en),* north, N.

n., *nach,* after.

nachm., *nachmittags,* in the afternoon, P.M.

näml., *nämlich,* that is to say, viz.

NATO, *Nordatlantikpakt-Organisation,* North Atlantic Treaty Organization, NATO.

n.Br., *nördliche Breite,* northern latitude.

n.Chr., *nach Christus,* after Christ, A.D.

nhd., *neuhochdeutsch,* New High German, N.H.G.

N.N., *nomen nominandum,* name to be announced.

NO, *Nordost(en),* northeast, NE.

No., Nr., *Numero,* number, no.

Nov., *November,* November, Nov.

NPD, *Nationaldemokratische Partei Deutschlands,* National-Democratic Party of Germany.

N.T., *Neues Testament,* New Testament.

NW, *Nordwest(en),* northwest, NW.

O, *Ost(en),* east, E.

o., *oben,* above; *oder,* or; *ohne,* without, w/o.

o.a., *oben angeführt,* above (-mentioned).

o.ä., *oder ähnliche,* or the like.

OB, *Oberbürgermeister,* mayor.

o.B., *ohne Befund,* results negative.

ÖBB, *Österreichische Bundesbahn,* Austrian Federal Railways.

od., *oder,* or.

o.J., *ohne Jahr,* no date, n.d..

Okt., *Oktober,* October, Oct.

ö.L., *östliche Länge,* east longitude.

OLG, *Oberlandesgericht,* Higher Regional Court.

o.O., *ohne Ort,* no place (of publication), n.p.

OP, *Operationssaal,* operating room, OR.

o.Prof., *ordentlicher Professor,* full professor, prof.

orth., *Orthodox,* Orthodox, Orth.

ÖVP, *Österreichische Volkspartei,* Austrian People's Party.

p., *per,* per, by.

p.A., p.Adr., *per Adresse,* care of, c/o.

PDS *Partei des Demokratischen Sozialismus,* Party of Democratic Socialism.

Pf., *Pfennig(e),* pfennig.

Pfd., *Pfund,* German pound.

PH, *Pädagogische Hochschule,* teachers' college.

Pkw, *Personenkraftwagen,* (motor) car.

Pl., *Platz,* Square, Sq.; *Plural,* plural, pl.

PLZ, *Postleitzahl,* zip code.

Priv.-Doz., *Privatdozent,* university lecturer.

Prof. Ord., *Professor Ordinarius,* Professor.

P.S., *Pferdestärke f.* horse-power, hp; *Nachschrift,* postscript, P.S.

qkm, *Quadratkilometer,* square kilometer.

qm, *Quadratmeter,* square meter.

r., *rechts,* right, r.

RA, *Rechtsanwalt,* lawyer, attorney, att.

rd., *rund,* roughly.

Ref., *Referent,* referee.

Reg.-Bez., *Regierungsbezirk,* administrative district.

Rel., *Religion,* religion, rel.

Rep., *Republik,* Republic, Rep.

resp., *respektive,* respectively.

Rh., *Rhein,* the Rhine.

rk, *r.-k., römisch-katholisch,* Roman Catholic, RC.

röm., *römisch,* Roman, Rom.

S, *Süd(en),* south, S; *Schilling,* shilling, s.

S., *Seite,* page, p.

s., *siehe,* see.

Sa., *Samstag,* Saturday, Sat.

s.d., *siehe dort,* see above *or* there.

SB-, *Selbstbedienungs-,* self-service . . .

Sek., sek., *sekunde,* second, sec., s.

sen., *senior,* senior, Sen., Sr.

Sept., *September,* September, Sept.

SFr., *sfr, Schweizer Franken,* Swiss Franc, SF, sfr.

Sg., *Singular,* singular, sing.

sg., sog., *sogenannt,* so-called.

SO, *Südost(en),* southeast, SE.

So, *Sonntag,* Sunday, Sun.

SPD, *Sozialdemokratische Partei Deutschlands,* Social Democratic Party of Germany.

SPÖ, *Sozialistische Partei Österreichs,* Austrian Socialist Party.

s.o., *siehe oben,* see above.

s.R., *siehe Rückseite,* see overleaf.

SS, *Sommersemester,* summer term.

St., *Sankt,* Saint, St.; *Stück,* piece.

Std., *Stunde,* hour, hr., h.

stdl., *stündlich,* hourly.

StGB, *Strafgesetzbuch,* criminal code.

StPO, *Strafprozeßordnung,* Code of Criminal Procedure.

Str., *Straße,* street, st.

StVO, *Straßenverkehrsordnung,* traffic regulations.

s.u., *siehe unten,* see below.

SW, *südwest(en),* southwest, SW.

t., *Tonne,* ton.

tgl., *täglich,* daily.

Tb, *Tuberkulose,* TB, tuberculosis.

teilw., *teilweise,* partly.

Tel., *Telefon,* telephone, tel.

TH, *Technische Hochschule,* school of technology.

TU, *Technische Universität,* Technical University.

TÜV, *Technischer Überwachungsverein,* Technical Control Board.

u., *und,* and.

u.a., *unter anderm,* among other things; *und andere,* and others.

u.ä., *und ähnliche(s),* and the like.

u.A.w.g., *um Antwort wird gebeten,* R.S.V.P.

U-Bahn, *Untergrundbahn,* subway.

u.dergl.m., *und dergleichen mehr,* and more of the kind.

u.d.M., *unter dem Meeresspiegel,* below sea level.

ü.d.M., *über dem Meeresspiegel,* above sea level.

UFO, *unbekanntes Flugobjekt,* unidentified flying object, UFO.

U-Haft, *Untersuchungshaft,* custody.

UKW, *Ultrakurzwelle,* frequency modulation, FM.

U/min, *Umdrehungen pro Minute,* revolutions per minute, r.p.m.

U-Musik, *Unterhaltungsmusik,* light music.

unbek., *unbekannt,* unknown.

unbez., *unbezahlt,* unpaid.

unverb., *unverbindlich,* not binding.

unvollst., *unvollständig,* incomplete.

urspr., *ursprünglich,* originally.

USA, *Vereinigte Staaten (von Amerika),* United States (of America), US(A).

usf., usw., *und so fort, und so weiter,* and so forth, etc.

u.U., *unter Umständen,* perhaps, perh.; if need be.

UV, *Ultraviolett,* ultraviolet, UV.

V, *Volt,* volt, V.

V., *Vers,* verse, v.

v., *von,* of, from; *versus,* versus, v., vs.

VB, *Verhandlungsbasis,* or nearest offer, o.n.o.

v. Chr., *vor Christus,* before Christ, B.C.

v.D., *vom Dienst,* on duty.

Verf., Vf., *Verfasser,* author.

vergr., *vergriffen,* out of print.

verh., *verheiratet,* married, mar.

Verl., *Verlag,* publishing house.

Verw., *Verwaltung,* administration, adm.

vgl., *vergleiche,* compare, cf.

v.H., *vom Hundert,* per cent.

v.J., *vorigen Jahres,* of last year.

v.M., *vorigen Monats,* of last month.

v.o., *von oben,* from the top.

Vorm., *Vormittag,* forenoon, A.M.

Vors., *Vorsitzende(r),* chairperson.

VP, *Vollpension,* full board.

v.T., *vom Tausend,* per thousand.

v.u., *von unten,* from the bottom.

W, *West(en),* west, W; *Watt,* watt, w.

w., *wenden,* turn over, T.O.

WAA, *Wiederaufbereitungsanlage,* reprocessing plant.

wbl., *weiblich,* female, fem.

WC, *Wasserklosett,* toilet, WC.

Wdh., *Wiederholung,* repetition, repeat.

Werkt., *Werktags,* weekdays.

westl., *westlich,* western.

WEZ, *Westeuropäische Zeit,* Greenwich Mean Time, GMT.

WG, *Wohngemeinschaft,* people sharing an apartment.

Whg., *Wohnung,* apartment.

wiss., *wissenschaftlich,* academic.

w.L., *westliche Länge,* Western longitude, W long.

w.o., *wie oben,* as above.

wö., *wöchentlich, weekly.*

WS, *Wintersemester,* winter term.

Wz., *Warenzeichen,* trademark, TM.

Z., *Zeile,* line; *Zoll,* inch.

z., *zu, zum, zur,* to, at.

z.B., *zum Beispiel,* for instance.

zeitgen., *zeitgenössisch,* contemporary.

ZH, *Zentralheizung,* central heating, centr. heat.

z.H., *zu Händen,* at *or* on hand; care of.

Zi., *Zimmer,* room, rm; *Ziffer,* figure, fig., number, no.

Zlg., *Zahlung,* payment.

z.T., *zum Teil,* partly.

Ztr., *Zentner,* German hundredweight, cwt.

Ztschr., *Zeitschrift,* periodical.

Zub., *Zubehör,* accessories.

zul., *zulässig,* permissible.

zur., *zurück,* back.

zus., *zusammen,* together, tog.

zzgl., *zuzüglich,* plus.

zw., *zwischen,* between, bet.

Zwgst., *Zweigstelle,* branch.

z.Z., *zur Zeit,* at the moment.

English–German
Dictionary

A

A, a *s.* der Buchstabe A oder a *n.*; (*mus.*) **A, a, A-sharp** Ais, ais, **A-flat** As, as.

a(n) *art.* ein, eine, ein.

A 1 *a. & adv.* (*fam.*) erster Klasse, vorzüglich.

aback *adv.*; *taken* ~, bestürzt, verblüfft.

abandon *v.t.* aufgeben; verlassen, preisgeben.

abandoned *p. & a.* verlassen; liederlich.

abandonment *s.* Aufgeben *n.*; Verlassenheit *f.*; Hingabe *f.*

abase *v.t.* erniedrigen.

abasement *s.* Erniedrigung *f.*

abash *v.t.* beschämen, verlegen machen.

abashed *a.* beschämt, verlegen.

abate *v.t. & i.* vermindern, herabsetzen; nachlassen; fallen (vom Preise).

abatement *s.* Verminderung *f.*; Abnahme *f.*; Rabatt *m.*, Abzug *m.*

abbess *s.* Äbtissin *f.*

abbey *s.* Abtei *f.*

abbot *s.* Abt *m.*

abbreviate *v.t.* abkürzen.

abbreviation *s.* Abkürzung *f.*

abdicate *v.t. & i.* aufgeben; abdanken.

abdication *s.* Abdankung *f.*

abdomen *s.* Unterleib *m.*; Bauch *m.*

abdominal *a.* Unterleibs-, Bauch-.

abduct *v.t.* entführen, wegführen.

abduction *s.* Wegführung, Entführung *f.*

aberration *s.* Abweichung *f.*; geistige Verwirrung *f.*, (*phys.*) Aberration *f.*

abet *v.t.* unterstützen.

abettor *s.* Anstifter *m.*, Mitschuldige *m./f.*

abeyance *s.* *to fall into* ~, außer Kraft treten, außer Gebrauch kommen.

abhor *v.t.* verabscheuen.

abhorrence *s.* Abscheu *m.*

abhorrent *a.* widerlich; abscheulich.

abide *v.t. & i.st.* bleiben, warten; aushalten; *to* ~ *by*, befolgen (Gesetze).

abiding *a.* dauernd.

ability *s.* Fähigkeit *f.*; abilities *pl.* Geisteskräfte *f. pl.*; *to the best of one's* ~, nach bestem Vermögen.

abject *a.*, ~ly *adv.* elend, erbärmlich; demütig.

abjuration *s.* Abschwörung *f.*

abjure *v.t.* abschwören; entsagen.

ablative *s.* Ablativ *m.*

ablaze *adv.* lodernd.

able *a.* fähig, geschickt; *to be* ~, imstande sein; ~-**bodied**, rüstig, dienstfähig.

able(-bodied) seaman *s.* Vollmatrose *m.*

ablution *s.* Abwaschung *f.*

abnegate *v.t.* ableugnen.

abnegation *s.* Selbstverleugnung *f.*

abnormal *a.* abnorm, anormal.

abnormally *adv.* ungewöhnlich.

abnormity *s.* Abnormität *f.*

aboard *pr. & adv.* an Bord.

abode *s.* Wohnort *m.*; Aufenthalt *m.*

abolish *v.t.* abschaffen, vernichten

abolition *s.* Abschaffung *f.*

A-bomb *s.* Atombombe *f.*

abominable *a.*, ~bly *adv.* abscheulich.

abominate *v.t.* verabscheuen.

abomination *s.* Abscheu *f.*; Greuel *m.*; *to hold in* ~, verabscheuen.

aboriginal *a.* ursprünglich.

Aborigine *s.* Ureinwohner(in) *m.(f.)*

abort *v.t.* abbrechen; abtreiben; *v.i.* Fehlgeburt haben.

abortion *s.* Fehlgeburt *f.*; Mißgeburt *f.*; Abtreibung *f.*; *to have an* ~, abtreiben.

abortive *a.*,~ly *adv.* fehlgeschlagen; mißlungen.

abound *v.i.* Überfluß haben an, reichlich vorhanden sein.

about *pr. & adv.* um, herum; (*fig.*) über; etwa, ungefähr, bei, an, auf; wegen; *to be* ~, im Begriffe sein; *round* ~, ringsumher; *to see* ~ *a thing*, eine Sache erledigen; ~ *turn*, ~ *face*, linksum kehrt; *right* ~ *turn*, rechtsum kehrt.

above *pr. & adv.* oben, über, mehr als; ~ *all*, vor allem; ~ *board*, frank und frei, ehrlich; ~-**mentioned**, obenerwähnt; *over and* ~, außer, über, obendrein.

abrasion *s.* Abschabung *f.*

abrasive *s.* Scheuermittel *n.*

abreast *adv.* nebeneinander.

abridge *v.t.* (ab)kürzen.

abridgment *s.* Abkürzung *f.*, Kürzung *f.*

abroad *adv.* draußen; im Ausland; *from abroad*, vom Ausland.

abrogate *v.t.* abschaffen; aufheben (Gesetz).

abrupt *a.*, ~ly *adv.* jäh; barsch.

abscess *s.* Abszeß *m.*

abscond *v.i.* durchbrennen; sich verstecken.

absence *s.* Abwesenheit *f.*; ~ *of mind*, Zerstreutheit *f.*; *leave of* ~, Urlaub *m.*

absent *a.* abwesend; ~ *without leave*, abwesend ohne Urlaub; ~-**minded**, geistesabwesend, zerstreut; ~ *v. refl.* sich entfernen, fernbleiben.

absentee *s.* Abwesende *m./f.* (bes. von der Arbeit).

absolute *a.*, ~ly *adv.* unbeschränkt, unbedingt; schlechthin.

absolution *s.* Lossprechung *f.*

absolutism *s.* Absolutismus *m.*

absolve *v.t.* freisprechen.

absorb *v.t.* einsaugen; in Anspruch nehmen.

absorbent *a.* einsaugend; ~ *s.* aufsaugendes Mittel *n.*

absorption *s.* Aufsaugen *n.*

abstain *v.i.* sich enthalten.

abstemious *a.*, ~ly *adv.* enthaltsam.

abstention *s.* Enthaltung *f.*

abstinence *s.* Enthaltsamkeit *f.*; *day of* ~, Fasttag *m.*

abstinent *a.*, ~ly *adv.* enthaltsam, mäßig.

abstract *v.t.* abziehen; wegnehmen.

abstract *a.* abstrakt; abgesondert; ~ *s.* Zusammenfassung *f.*, Inhaltsangabe *f.*, Auszug *m.*; *in the* ~, theoretisch.

abstraction *s.* Abstraktion *f.*; abstrakter Begriff *m.*; Zerstreutheit *f.*

abstruse *a.*, ~ly *adv.* dunkel.

absurd *a.*, ~ly *adv.* vernunftwidrig.

absurdity *s.* Ungereimtheit *f.*

abundance *s.* Überfluß *m.*, Menge *f.*

abundant *a.*, ~ly *adv.* überflüssig, reichlich.

abuse *v.t.* mißbrauchen; betrügen; schmähen; schänden, verführen; ~ *s.* Mißbrauch *m.*; Beschimpfung *f.*

abusive *a.*, ~ly *adv.* mißbräuchlich; schimpfend.

abut *v.i.* ~ *on* grenzen an; stoßen an.

abutment *s.* Strebe-, Stützpfeiler *m.*

abysmal *a.*, abgrundtief; katastrophal.

abyss *s.* Abgrund *m.*

acacia *s.* Akazie *f.*

academic(al) *a.*, ~ly *adv.* akademisch.

academy *s.* Akademie *f.*

accede *v.i.* beitreten, beipflichten.

accelerate *v.t.* beschleunigen.

acceleration *s.* Beschleunigung *f.*

accelerator *s.* (*mot.*) Gasfußhebel *m.*, Gaspedal *n.*

accent *s.* Betonung *f.*; Tonzeichen *n.*; Nachdruck *m.*, Aussprache *f.*; ~ *v.t.* betonen, hervorheben.

accentuate *v.t.* betonen.

accept *v.t.* annehmen; (einen Wechsel) akzeptieren.

acceptability *s.* Angemessenheit *f.*; Annehmbarkeit *f.*

acceptable *a.*, ~bly *adv.* annehmbar.

acceptance *s.* Annahme *f.*; Akzept (eines Wechsels) *n.*; Abnahme (von Maschinen) *f.*

accepted *a.* allgemein anerkannt.

access *s.* Zugang *m.*; Zuwachs, *m.*; *easy* ~, leicht zugänglich.

accessible *a.* zugänglich.

accession *s.* Amtsantritt *m.*; Thronbesteigung *f.*

accessory *a.* hinzukommend; Neben-; ~ *s.* Mitschuldige *m./f.*; *accessories pl.* Beiwerk, Zubehör *n.*

access road *s.* Zufahrtstraße *f.*

accident *s.* Unfall *m.*; Zufall *m.*; *by* ~, zufällig; ~ *insurance*, Unfallversicherung *f.* ~-**prone** *a.* unfallgefährdet.

accidental *a.*, ~ly *adv.* zufällig; Neben-.

acclaim *v.t.* feiern.

acclamation *s.* Zuruf, Beifall *m.*

acclimatization *s.* Akklimatisierung *f.*

acclimatize *v.t.* akklimatisieren.

accommodate *v.t.* schlichten; unterbringen, versorgen; Geld leihen.

accommodating *a.* gefällig.

accommodation *s.* Anpassung *f.*; Vergleich *m.*; Unterkommen (für die Nacht) *n.*, Unterkunft *f.*; ~-**bill** *s.* Gefälligkeitswechsel *m.*

accompaniment *s.* (*mus.*) Begleitung *f.*

accompanist *s.* (*mus.*) Begleiter *m.*

accompany *v.t.* begleiten; mitspielen.

accomplice *s.* Mitschuldige *m./f.*, Komplize *m.*, Komplizin *f.*

accomplish *v.t.* vollenden, erreichen.

accomplished *a.* fähig.

accomplishment *s.* Ausführung *f.*; Fertigkeit *f.*; Vollendung *f.*, Leistung *f.*; ~**s** *pl.* Talente *n. pl.*

accord *s.* Eintracht *f.*; Vergleich *m.*; ~*v.t. & i.* übereinstimmen.

accordance *s.* Übereinstimmung *f.*

according (to) *pr.* gemäß.

accordingly *adv.* demgemäß, folglich; entsprechend.

accordion *s.* Akkordeon *n.*, Ziehharmonika *f.*

accost *v.t.* ansprechen.

account *s.* Rechnung *f.*; Rechenschaft *f.*; Bericht *m.*; Rücksicht *f.*; Konto *n.*; ~-**book**, Kontobuch *n.*; ~-**holder**, Kontoinhaber *m.*; *current* ~, laufende Rechnung *f.*, laufendes Konto *n.*; *deposit* ~, Depositenkonto *n.*; *fictitious* ~, fiktives Konto *n.*; *on* ~, auf Rechnung; *on* ~ *of*, wegen; *to call to* ~, zur Rechenschaft ziehen; *to keep* ~, Buch führen; *to open an* ~, ein Konto eröffnen; ~ *v.t.* schätzen, halten für; *to* ~ *for*, Rechenschaft ablegen von; erklären.

accountable *a.* verantwortlich; *to hold s.o.* ~ *jn.* verantwortlich machen.

accountant *s.* Buchhalter(in) *m.(f.)*; Steuerberater(in) *m.(f.)*

accounting *s.* Buchführung *f.*

accredit *v.t.* beglaubigen.

accrue *v.i.* auflaufen, zufallen; *accrued interest*, angefallene Zinsen *m. pl.*

accumulate *v.t. & i.* sammeln; aufhäufen; sich häufen; *accumulated interest*, aufgelaufene Zinsen *m. pl.*

accumulation *s.* Ansammeln *n.*, Anhäufung *f.*

accumulative *a.* sich anhäufend.

accumulator *s.* Akkumulator *m.*

accuracy *s.* Genauigkeit, Pünktlichkeit *f.*

accurate *a.*, ~ly *adv.* genau, sorgfältig.

accursed *p. & a.* verflucht, verwünscht.

accusation *s.* Anklage, Beschuldigung *f.*

accusative *s.* Akkusativ *m.*

accuse *v.t.* anklagen; beschuldigen.

accused *s.* (*law*) Angeklagte *m./f.*

accustom *v.t.* gewöhnen.

accustomed *a.* gewohnt.

ace *s.* As, *n.*; Eins (auf Würfeln) *f.*; (*avi.*) Fliegerheld.

acetylene *s.* Azetylen *n.*

ache *s.* Schmerz *m.*; ~ *v.i.* schmerzen.

achieve *v.t.* zustande bringen; erwerben.

achievement *s.* Vollendung *f.*; Leistung *f.*

acid *a.*, sauer; ~ *s.* Säure *f.*; ~-**proof**, säurefest; ~-**rain** *s.* Sauerregen *m.*

acidic *a.* säuerlich.

acidity *s.* Säure, Schärfe *f.*

acknowledge *v.t.* anerkennen; bestätigen; *to* ~ *receipt*, den Empfang bestätigen.

acknowledgment *s.* Anerkennung *f.*; Empfangsbestätigung *f.*

acme *s.* Gipfel, höchster Punkt *m.*

acne *s.* Akne *f.*

acorn *s.* Eichel *f.*

acoustic *a.* akustisch; ~ **guitar** *s.* Konzertgitarre *f.*; ~ **nerve** *s.* Gehörnerv *m.*

acoustics *s. pl.* Schallehre, Akustik *f.*

acquaint *v.t.* bekannt machen, *to be* ~ed *with s.b.* mit jm. bekanntsein.

acquaintance *s.* Bekanntschaft *f.*; Bekannte *m./f.*

acquiesce *v.i.* sich beruhigen, einwilligen.

acquiescence *s.* Einwilligung, Fügung *f.*

acquiescent *a.* fügsam; ergeben.

acquire *v.t.* erwerben, erlangen.
acquirement *s.* Erwerbung *f.*; Fertigkeit *f.*; ~s *pl.* Kenntnisse *f. pl.*
acquisition *s.* Erwerbung *f.*; Errungenschaft *f.*
acquisitive *a.*, ~ly *adv.* habsüchtig.
acquit *v.t.* freisprechen; quittieren; *refl.* (gut, schlecht) machen.
acquittal *s.* Freisprechung *f.*
acre *s.* Morgen (Land) *m.*, Acker *m.*
acreage *s.* Ackerfläche *f.*
acrimonious *a.*, ~ly *adv.* scharf, beißend.
acrimony *s.* Schärfe *f.*
acrobat *s.* Akrobat(in) *m.*(*f.*)
acrobatic *a.* akrobatisch.
acrobatics *s.* Akrobatik *f.*
across *adv.* kreuzweise; ~ *pr.* quer durch, quer hinüber; *to come* ~, zufällig finden, begegnen.
act *v.t.* spielen, darstellen; ~ *v.i.* handeln; ~ *s.* Handlung, Tat *f.*; (*theat.*) Aufzug, Akt *m.*; Gesetz *n.*; *Act of God*, höhere Gewalt *f.*; *Act of Parliament*, Parlamentsakte *f.*; *in the very* ~, auf frischer Tat; *Acts of the Apostles*, Apostelgeschichte *f.*
acting *p. & a.* stellvertretend; ~ *s.* Schauspielerei.
action *s.* Handlung, Wirkung *f.*; Klage *f.*; Gefecht *n.*; *to bring an* ~ *against a person*, gegen einen eine Klage anstrengen, einen verklagen; *to put out of* ~, (*mil.*) außer Gefecht setzen; (*mech.*) außer Betrieb setzen; *to take* ~, Maßnahmen ergreifen; (*law*) klagen.
activate *v.t.* in Gang setzen; aktivieren.
active *a.*, ~ly *adv.* tätig, wirksam, lebhaft, rührig; (*com.*) gesucht, belebt; (*mil.*) aktiv; ~ *voice*, (*gram.*) Aktiv *n.*
activity *s.* Aktivität *f.*; Lebhaftigkeit *f.*
actor *s.* Schauspieler *m.*
actress *s.* Schauspielerin *f.*
actual *a.*, ~ly *adv.* wirklich; faktisch; ~ *stock*, Ist-Bestand *m.*; ~ *strength*, (*mil.*) Ist-Stärke.
actuate *v.t.* antreiben; auslösen.
acumen *s.* Scharfsinn *m.*
acupuncture *s.* Akupunktur *f.*; ~ *v.t.* akupunktieren.
acute *a.*, ~ly *adv.* scharf, spitz; scharfsinnig; (*med.*) akut, hitzig; ~-**angled,** spitzwink[e]lig.
ad *s.* (*fam.*) Annonce Anzeige *f.*
adamant *a.*, ~ly *adv.* fest, unerbittlich.
Adam's apple *s.* Adamsapfel *m.*
adapt *v.t.* anpassen; adaptieren.
adaptability *s.* Anpassungsfähigkeit *f.*
adaptable *a.* anpassungsfähig.
adaptation *s.* Anpassung *f.*
adapter, adaptor *s.* Adapter *m.*
add *v.t. & i.* hinzutun; addieren.
addendum *s.* Nachtrag *m.*
adder *s.* Natter *f.*
addict *s.* Süchtige *m./f.*; *drug* ~, Rauschgiftsüchtige *m./f.*
addicted *s.* süchtig.
addiction *s.* Sucht *f.*
addictive *a. to be* ~ süchtig machen.
adding machine *s.* Rechenmaschine *f.*
addition *s.* Hinzusetzung *f.*; (*ar.*) Addition *f.*; Zusatz *m.*; *sign of* ~, Additionszeichen *n.*
additional *a.* weiter; zusätzlich; Neben-, Zusatz-; ~ *claim*, ~ *charge*, Nachforderung *f.*
additive *s.* Zusatz *m.*

address *s.* Anrede *f.*; Adresse *f.*; Bittschrift *f.*; Geschicklichkeit *f.*; ~ *v.t.* anreden; richten, adressieren; *to* ~ *oneself to a person*, sich an einen wenden.
address book *s.* Adreßbuch *n.*
addressee *s.* Adressat(in), Empfänger(in) *m./f.*
address label *s.* Adressenaufkleber *m.*
adept *a.* erfahren; ~ *s.* erfahrener Mann *m.*; Eingeweihter *m.*
adequacy *s.* Angemessenheit *f.*
adequate *a.*, ~ly *adv.* angemessen; adäquat.
adhere *v.i.* anhängen; ankleben.
adherence *s.* Anhänglichkeit *f.*
adherent *a.*, ~ly *adv.* anhängend; ~ *s.* Anhänger(in) *m./f.*
adhesion *s.* Anhaften *n.*
adhesive *a.*, ~ly *adv.* anhaftend; klebrig; ~ *dressing*, Heftverband *m.*; ~ *envelopes* *s. pl.* gummierte Briefumschläge; ~ *plaster* *s.* Heftpflaster *n.*; Klebstoff *m.*, Klebemittel *n.*
adjacent *a.* anliegend, angrenzend.
adjective *s.* Eigenschaftswort *n.*
adjoin *v.t.* anfügen; ~ *i.* angrenzen.
adjourn *v.t. & i.* vertagen; sich vertagen; unterbrechen.
adjournment *s.* Vertagung *f.* Unterbrechung *f.*
adjudge *v.t. to* ~ *s.b. to be s.th.* jn. für etw. erklären.
adjudication *s.* Beurteilung *f.*; Entscheidung *f.*
adjudicator *s.* Preisrichter *m.*
adjunct *s.* Zusatz *m.*; Attribut *n.*; ~ **position** stundenweise Anstellung an Universitäten.
adjure *v.t.* beschwören.
adjust *v.t.* ordnen; berichtigen; einstellen; ausgleichen; eichen.
adjustable *a.* einstellbar, verstellbar, anpaßbar.
adjustment *s.* Ausgleich *m.*; Beilegung *f.*; Anpassung *f.*
adjutant *s.* Adjutant *m.*
ad-lib *a.* aus dem Stegreif.
adman *s.* Werbefachmann *m.*; Reklametexter *m.*
administer *v.t.* verwalten; darreichen; (Verweis) erteilen; *to* ~ *an oath*, (einem) einen Eid abnehmen; *to* ~ *a will*, ein Testament vollziehen.
administration *s.* Verwaltung, Regierung *f.*; Austeilung (der Sakramente); ~ *of justice*, Rechtspflege *f.*
administrative *a.* verwaltend; ~ *court*, Verwaltungsgericht *n.*; ~ *law*, Verwaltungsrecht *n.*
administrator *s.* Verwalter *m.*; Testamentsvollstrecker *m.*
admirable *a.* bewunderungswürdig.
admiral *s.* Admiral *m.*; *rear* ~, Konteradmiral *m.*
admiralty *s.* Marineministerium *n.*
admiration *s.* Bewunderung *f.*
admire *v.t.* bewundern.
admirer *s.* Bewunderer *m.*, Bewunderin *f.*
admissible *a.*, ~bly *adv.* zulässig.
admission *s.* Zulassung *f.*, Eintritt *m.*; Zugeständnis *n.*; ~ *ticket*, Eintrittskarte *f.*
admit *v.t.* zulassen, zugeben.
admittance *s.* Zulassung *f.*; *no* ~! zutritt verboten
admittedly *adv.* zugestandenermaßen.
admixture *s.* Beimischung *f.*
admonish *v.t.* ermahnen, warnen.
admonition *s.* Erinnerung, Warnung *f.*
ad nauseam *adv.* bis zum Überdruß.

ado *s.* Getue *n.*; Aufheben *n.*
adobe *s.* Backstein *m.*
adolescence *s.* judgendliches Alter *n.*
adolescent *a.* heranwachsend; ~ *s.* Heranwachsende *m./f.*
adopt *v.t.* annehmen; adoptieren.
adoption *s.* Adoption *f.*; Annahme *f.*
adoptive *a.* adoptiert.
adorable *a.*, **~bly** *adv.* anbetungswürdig; bezaubernd.
adoration *s.* Anbetung *f.*
adore *v.t.* anbeten; innig lieben.
adorn *v.t.* schmücken.
adornment *s.* Verschönerung *f.*, Verzierung *f.*
Adriatic *s.* Adria.
adrift *adv.* treibend, schwimmend; *cast ~*, in die weite Welt gestoßen.
adroit *a.*, **~ly** *adv.* gewandt.
adulate *v.t.* schmeicheln.
adulation *s.* Schmeichelei *f.*
adulator *s.* Schmeichler(in) *m.(f.)*
adulatory *a.* schmeichlerisch.
adult *a.* erwachsen; ~ *s.* Erwachsene *m./f.*
adulterate *v.t.* verfälschen.
adulterer *s.* Ehebrecher *m.*
adulteress *s.* Ehebrecherin *f.*
adulterous *a.* ehebrecherisch.
adultery *s.* Ehebruch *m.*
adulthood *s.* Erwachsenenalter.
adumbrate, flüchtig skizzieren; hindeuten auf.
advance *s.* Fortschritt *m.*; Vorschuß *m.*; Steigen (der Preise), *n.*; *in ~,* im voraus; **~s** *pl.* Auslagen *f. pl*; ~ *v.t. & i.* vorrücken; befördern; vorschießen; Fortschritte machen; im Preise steigen; *to ~ a claim,* eine Forderung geltend machen; *to ~ an opinion,* eine Meinung vorbringen.
advanced *a.* fortgeschritten.
advancement *s.* Beförderung, Verbesserung *f.*
advantage *s.* Vorteil, Vorzug *m.*; Überlegenheit *f.*; *to take ~ of,* sich etwas zunutze machen; betrügen.
advantageous *a.*, **~ly** *adv.* vorteilhaft.
advent *s.* Advent *m.*; (*poet.*) Herannahen *n.*
adventitious *a.*, **~ly** *adv.* zufällig.
adventure *s.* Abenteuer *n.*; ~ *v.t. & i.* wagen.
adventurer *s.* Abenteurer *m.*
adventuress *s.* Abenteuerin *f.*
adventurous *a.*, **~ly** *adv.* abenteuerlich.
adverb *s.* Umstandswort *n.*, Adverb *n.*
adverbial *a.* adverbial.
adversary *s.* Gegner *m.*; Widersacher(in) *m.(f.)*
adverse *a.*, **~ly** *adv.* widrig; (Bilanz) passiv.
adversity *s.* Not *f.*, Widrigkeit *f.*
advertise *v.t.* inserieren, annoncieren.
advertisement *s.* Anzeige *f.*; Reklame *f.*; Inserat *n.*
advertiser *s.* Inserent(in) *m.(f.)*, Auftraggeber(in) *m.(f.).*
advertising *s.* Werbung *f.*; **– agency** *s.* Werbeagentur *f.*
advice *s.* Rat *m.*; Bericht *m.*
advisable *a.* ratsam.
advise *v.t.* raten; benachrichtigen; ~ *v.i.* sich beraten.
advisedly *adv.* bewußt.
adviser *s.* Ratgeber(in) *m.(f.)*
advisory board, ~ council s. Beirat *m.*
advocacy *s.* Befürwortung *f.*

advocate *s.* Verteidiger, Anwalt *m.*; ~ *v.t.* verteidigen; befürworten.
Aegean *s.* Ägäis *f.*
aegis *s.* Schirmherrschaft *f.*
aerial *a.* luftig; Luft . . . ; ~ *s.* (*radio*) Antenne *f.*; ~ *photograph,* Luftbild *n.*, Luftaufnahme *f.*
aerobics *s.* Aerobic *n.*
aerodrome *s.* Flugplatz *m.*
aerodynamic *a.* aerodynamisch.
aeronautics *s.* Aeronautik *f.*
aerosol *s.* Spray *m.*, *n.*
aerospace *s.* Weltraum *m.*
aesthetic *a.*, **~ally** *adv.* ästhetisch.
aesthetics *s.* Ästhetik *f.*
afar *adv.* fern, von fern.
affability *s.* Leutseligkeit.
affable *a.*, **~ly** *adv.* leutselig, gesprächig; freundlich.
affair *s.* Geschäft *n.*; Angelegenheit *f.*
affect *v.t.* betreffen; begehren; affektieren.
affectation *s.* Ziererei *f.*; Affektiertheit *f.*
affected *p. & a.* gerührt; geziert.
affecting *a.* rührend, ergreifend.
affection *s.* Gemütsbewegung *f.*; Zuneigung *f.*
affectionate *a.* liebend zugetan; liebevoll.
affidavit *s.* beeidigte Erklärung *f.*; *to make an ~,* eine eidliche Versicherung abgeben.
affiliate *v.t. to be ~d with* angegliedert sein an; verbunden sein mit.
affiliation *s.* Angliederung *f.*
affinity *s.* Verschwägerung, Verwandtschaft *f.*; (*chem.*) Affinität *f.*
affirm *v.t.* bestätigen, behaupten.
affirmation *s.* Bekräftigung *f.*
affirmative *a.*, **~ly** *adv.* bejahend; ~ *s.* Bejahung *f.*; *in the ~,* bejahend.
affix *v.t.* anheften; ~ *s.* Affix.
afflict *v.t.* betrüben; plagen; heimsuchen.
affliction *s.* Kummer *m.*, Mißgeschick *n.*
affluence *s.* Reichtum *m.*; Überfluß *m.*
affluent *a.*, **~ly** *adv.* reich.
afflux *s.* Zufluß *m.*
afford *v.t.* sich leisten können; liefern.
affordable *a.* erschwinglich.
afforest *v.t.* aufforsten.
afforestation *s.* Aufforstung *f.*
affray *s.* Schlägerei *f.*; Auflauf *m.*
affront *v.t.* beleidigen; ~ *s.* Affront *m.* Beleidigung *f.*, Schimpf *m.*
Afghan *a.* afghanisch; ~ *s.* Afghane *m.*, Afghanin *f.*
Afghanistan *s.* Afghanistan *n.*
afield *adv.* in der Ferne.
aflame *adv.* in Flammen.
afloat *adv.* schwimmend, flott.
afoot *adv.* zu Fuß; im Gange.
aforementioned *a.* vorerwähnt.
aforesaid *a.* vorerwähnt.
afraid *a.* besorgt, bange.
afresh *adv.* von neuem.
Africa *s.* Afrika *n.*
African *a.* afrikanisch; Afrikaner(in) *m.(f.)*
after *pr.* nach, hinter; zufolge; ~ *all,* am Ende, alles wohl erwogen, schließlich; ~ *adv.* hinterher, darauf; ~ *c.* nachdem.
after-birth *s.* Nachgeburt *f.*
after-care *s.* Nachbehandlung *f.*, Nachsorge *f.*; Resozialisierungshilfe *f.*
after-dinner speech *s.* Tischrede *f.*

after-effect *s.* Nachwirkung *f.*
after-life *s.* Leben nach dem Tode.
aftermath *s.* Nachwirkungen *f. pl.*
afternoon *s.* Nachmittag *m.*
aftertaste *s.* Nachgeschmack *m.*
afterthought *s.* nachträglicher Einfall *m.*
afterwards *adv.* nachher.
again *adv.* wieder, zurück; ~ *and* ~, immer wieder.
against *pr.* wider, gegen.
agape *adv.* gaffend.
agate *s.* Achat *m.*
age *s.* Alter *n.*; Zeitalter *n.*; *to be of* ~, mündig sein; **~-class**, **~-group** Altersklasse *f.*; **~-limit**, Altersgrenze *f.*; *old* ~, Greisenalter *n.*; *under* ~, unmündig; *not seen for ages*, seit einer Ewigkeit nicht gesehen; ~ *v.i.* altern, alt werden.
aged *a.* bejahrt; ~ *9 years*, neun Jahre alt.
agency *s.* Wirkung *f.*; Vermittelung *f.*; Agentur *f.*; Dienststelle *f.*
agenda *s. pl.* Tagesordnung *f.*
agent *s.* Agent *m.*; Mittel *n.*
age-old *a.* uralt.
agglomerate *v.i.* sich klumpen.
agglutinate *v.t.* zusammenkleben; agglutinieren.
aggrandizement *s.* Vergrößerung *f.*
aggravate *v.t.* erschweren; ärgern.
aggravating *a.* ärgerlich; ~ *circumstances*, (*law*) erschwerende Umstände *m. pl.*
aggravation *s.* Verschlimmerung *f.*; Ärger *m.*
aggregate *s.* Haufen *m.*; Ganze *n.*; Aggregat *n.*; ~ *a.*, **~ly** *adv.* gehäuft; ~ *amount*, aufgelaufene Summe *f.* ~ *v.t.* verbinden, ansammeln.
aggregation *s.* Ansammlung *f.*; Aggregation *f.*
aggression *s.* Angriff, Anfall *m.*
aggressive *a.* angreifend; ~ *war*, Angriffskrieg *m.*
aggressiveness *s.* Aggressivität.
aggressor *s.* Angreifer *m.*
aggrieve *v.t.* kränken.
aggrieved *a.* verärgert; gekränkt.
aghast *a.* erschrocken, bestürzt.
agile *a.* behend, flink.
agility *s.* Beweglichkeit, Behendigkeit *f.*
agitate *v.t.* aufregen, beunruhigen.
agitation *s.* Bewegung, Hetzerei *f.*
agitator *s.* Volksaufwiegler *m.*
aglow *a. & adv.* glühend.
agnostic *s.* Agnostiker(in) *m.(f.)*; ~ *a.* agnostisch.
ago *adv.* vor; *a year* ~, vor einem Jahre; *long* ~, lange her.
agog, *a. & adv., all* ~, ganz erpicht.
agonize *v.t.* martern, quälen, mit dem Tode ringen.
agony *s.* Qual *f.*; Seelenangst *f.*; Pein *f.*
agrarian *s.* Agrarier *m.*; ~ *a.* agrarisch.
agree *v.i.* übereinstimmen; sich vergleichen; vereinbaren; zuträglich, sein; zustimmen; *that does not* ~ *with me*, das bekommt mir nicht.
agreeable *a.* angenehm; erfreulich; einverstanden.
agreed *a.* einig, vereinbart.
agreement *s.* Übereinstimmung *f.*; Vergleich *m.*; Vertrag *m.*; *to come to an* ~, sich verständigen, sich vergleichen; *to enter into an* ~, *to make an* ~, ein Übereinkommen treffen.
agricultural *a.* landwirtschaftlich.
agriculture *s.* Landwirtschaft *f.*
aground *adv.* gestrandet; *to go* ~, *to run* ~, auf

Grund laufen.
ague *s.* kaltes Fieber *n.*
ahead *adv.* voran; *go* ~! vorwärts!
aid *v.t.* helfen; *to* ~ *and abet*, (*law*) Beihilfe leisten; ~ *s.* Hilfe *f.*
aide *s.* Berater(in) *m.(f.)*
aide-de-camp (*frz.*) Adjutant *m.*
AIDS *s.* Aids *n.* (acquired immune deficiency syndrome).
ail *v.t.* plagen; *what* ~*s you?* Was fehlt dir?
ailing *a.* kränklich.
ailment *s.* Unpäßlichkeit *f*; Gebrechen *n.*
aim *v.i. & t.* zielen, trachten; richten; ~ *s.* Ziel *n.*, Richtung *f.*; Absicht *f.*
aimless *a.*, **~ly** *adv.* ziellos.
ain't (*sl.*) = **is not, am not, are not.**
air *v.t.* lüften; ~ *s.* Luft *f.*; Luftzug, Wind *m.*; Melodie *f.*; Miene *f.*; Schein *m.*; *by* ~, auf dem Luftwege; *open* ~, freie Luft.
airbase *s.* Luftwaffenstützpunkt.
airborne troops *s. pl.* (*mil.*) Luftlandetruppen *f. pl.*
aircraft *s.* Flugzeug *n.*; ~ *carrier* (*nav.*) Flugzeugträger *m.*
airfield *s.* Flugplatz *m.*
air-gun *s.* Luftgewehr.
airing *s.*, *to take an* ~, frische Luft schöpfen.
airless *a.* stickig; windstill.
airlift *s.* Luftbrücke.
airline *s.* Flugverkehrsgesellschaft *f.*
airliner *s.* Verkehrs-, Linienflugzeug *n.*
air-mail *s.* Luftpost; *by* ~, mit Luftpost.
airman *s.* Flieger *m.*
airplane *s.* Flugzeug *n.*
airpocket *s.* (*avi.*) Luftloch *n.*
air pollution *s.* Luftverschmutzung *f.*
airport *s.* Flughafen *m.*
air-raid *s.* Luftangriff *m.*
air-raid protection (ARP) *s.* Luftschutz *m.*
air-raid warning *s.* Fliegeralarm *m.*
air-reconnaissance *s.* (*mil.*) Luftaufklärung *f.*
airship *s.* Luftschiff *n.*
air-speed indicator *s.* (*avi.*) (Luft-) Geschwindigkeitsmesser *m.*
airtight *a.* luftdicht.
air traffic *s.* Flugverkehr *m.*; ~ **control** *s.* Flugsicherung *f.*
airworthy *a.* flugtüchtig.
airy *a.* luftig; leicht, flüchtig, lebhaft.
aisle *s.* Gang *m.*; Seitenschiff *n.*; Chorgang *m.*
ajar *adv.* halb offen, angelehnt.
akimbo *adv.* mit eingestemmten Armen.
akin *a.* verwandt.
alabaster *s.* Alabaster *m.*
alacrity *s.* Bereitwilligkeit *f.*
alarm *v.t.* alarmieren; beunruhigen; ~ *s.* Alarm, Lärm, Aufruhr *m.*; Besorgnis *f.*
alarmclock *s.* Weckuhr *f.*
alarming *a.* alarmierend.
alarmist *s.* Panikmacher *m.*; Bangemacher *m.*
alas *i.* ach! o weh! leider!
Albania *s.* Albanien.
Albanian *a.* albanisch; ~ *s.* Albanier(in) *m.(f.)*
albatross *s.* Albatros *m.*
albeit *c.* obschon.
albino *s.* Albino *m.*
album *s.* Album *n.*

albumen s. Eiweiß n.
alchemy s. Alchimie f.
alcohol s. Alkohol m.
alcoholic a. alkoholisch, spiritusartig.
alcoholism s. Alkoholismus m., Trunksucht f.
alcove s. Alkoven m.; Nische f.
alder s. Erle f.
alderman s. Ratsherr m., Stadtrat m.
ale s. helles englisches Bier n.
alert a., **~ly** adv. wachsam, flink; on the ~, auf der Hut, wach.
alga s. -e pl. Alge f.
algebra s. Algebra f.
algebraic a. algebraisch.
Algeria s. Algerien n.
Algerian a. algerisch; ~ s. Algerier(in) m.(f.)
algorithm s. Algorithmus.
alias s. alias; falscher Name m.
alibi s. (law) Alibi n.; to prove one's ~, sein Alibi nachweisen.
alien a. fremd; ~ s. Ausländer(in) m.(f.).
alienate v.t. entfremden, veräußern.
alienation s. Entfremdung.
alight v.i. sich niederlassen; aussteigen; ~ a. brennend, angezündet.
align v.t. in eine Linie bringen, richten.
alignment s. Aufstellung in einer Linie f.; Richtung f.
alike a. & adv. gleich, ähnlich; ebenso.
alimentary a. Nahrungs . . . , nahrhaft.
alimony s. Unterhaltszahlung f.
alive a. lebendig; (fig.) munter; (elek.) geladen.
alkali s. Laugensalz n.; Alkali n.
alkaline a. laugensalzig; alkalisch.
all a. aller, alle, alles; ~ adv. gänzlich; at ~, überhaupt; ~ at once, auf einmal; ~ but, fast; by ~ means, auf jeden Fall; on ~ fours, auf allen Vieren; not at ~, ganz und gar nicht; once for ~, ein für allemal; ~ the better, desto besser; ~ the same, trotzdem, doch; ~ right!, ganz recht! in Ordnung; ~ of a sudden, urplötzlich; ~ along, die ganze Zeit.
all-around a. vielseitig; Allround . . .
allay v.t. lindern, beruhigen.
all-clear signal s. (mil.) Entwarnung f.
allegation s. Angabe f.; Behauptung f.
allege v.t. behaupten.
alleged a. angeblich.
allegiance s. Loyalität f.; Gehorsam m.; to swear ~, den Treueid schwören.
allegoric(al) a. sinnbildlich; allegorisch.
allegory s. bildliche Rede f.; Allegorie f.
all-embracing a. alles umfassend.
allergic a. allergisch.
allergy s. Allergie.
alleviate v.t. erleichtern.
alley s. Gäßchen n.
alliance s. Bündnis n; Allianz f.
allied a. verbündet; verwandt.
alligator s. Alligator.
alliteration s. Stabreim m.
allocate v.t. zuteilen; anweisen.
allocation s. Anweisung, Zuteilung f.
allot v.t. zuteilen, zuerkennen.
allotment s. Anteil m.; Zuteilung f.; Landparzelle f.; Schrebergarten m.
all-out a. mit allen Mitteln; kompromißlos.

allow v.t. erlauben, bewilligen; zugestehen; vergüten; abrechnen.
allowable a. zuläßig.
allowance s. Erlaubnis f.; Taschengeld, Kostgeld n.; Ration f.; Nachsicht f.; Abzug m.; Zulage f.; family ~, Familienzulage f.
alloy s. Legierung f.; to ~ v.t. (Metalle) vermischen, legieren.
all-powerful a. allmächtig.
all-purpose a. Allzweck . . .
All Saints' Day s. Allerheiligen n.
all-time a. beispiellos; unerreicht.
allude (to) v.i. anspielen (auf).
allure v.t. anlocken; faszinieren; ~ s Verlockung f.
allusion a. Anspielung f.
allusive a. anspielend.
alluvial a. angeschwemmt.
all-weather a. Allwetter . . .
all-wool a. Ganzwolle . . .
ally s. Bundesgenosse m.; ~ v.t. verbünden; verbinden (mit).
almanac s. Almanach m.; Kalender m.
almighty a. allmächtig.
almond s. Mandel f.
almost adv. beinahe, fast.
alms s.pl. Almosen n.
aloe s. Aloë f.
aloft adv. hoch, erhaben.
alone a. & adv. allein; to let ~, in Ruhe lassen.
along pr. längs, an . . . entlang; adv. entlang; weiter.
alongside adv. daneben; längsseits, Bord an Bord.
aloof adv. weit ab; to keep ~ from, sich fernhalten von.
aloofness s. Zurückhaltung f.
aloud adv. laut.
alphabet s. Alphabet n; Abc n.
alphabetical a. alphabetisch.
Alpine a. von den Alpen, alpinisch.
Alps s.pl. Alpen pl.
already adv. schon, bereits.
Alsace s. Elsaß n.
Alsatian a. elsässisch; ~ s. Elsässer(in) m.(f.); ~ dog Schäferhund m.
also adv. auch, ebenfalls.
altar s. Altar m.
altar-cloth s. Altardecke f.
altar-piece s. Altargemälde n.
alter v.t. & i. ändern; sich ändern.
alterable a. veränderlich.
alteration s. Änderung f.
altercate v.i. streiten.
altercation s. Zank m.; Auseinadersetzung f.
alternate v.t. & i. abwechseln; ~ a., **~ly** adv. abwechselnd.
alternative s. Alternative f.; ~ a. abwechselnd; alternativ.
alternator s. Wechselstrom generator m.
although c. obgleich.
altimeter s. (avi.) Höhenmesser m.
altitude s. Höhe (Luft, geographisch).
alto s. Alt m.; Altist(in) m.(f.).
altogether adv. völlig; gänzlich, ganz und gar.
altruism s. Altruismus m.; Uneigennützigkeit f.
altruistic a. altruistisch, uneigennützig.
alum s. Alaun f.
aluminum s. Aluminium n.

aluminum acetate *s.* essigsaure Tonerde *f.*
always *adv.* immer.
a.m. (=ante meridiem), vormittags.
amalgam *s.* Amalgam *n.*
amalgamate *v.t. & i.* verschmelzen; vereinigen.
amalgamation *s.* Vereinigung, Fusion *f.*
amass *v.t.* anhäufen.
amateur *s.* Amateur, Liebhaber, Dilettant *m.*
amateurish *a.* (*pej.*) amateurhaft, laienhaft.
amaze *v.t.* in Erstaunen setzen; verwundern.
amazement *s.* Erstaunen *n.* Verwunderung *f.*
amazing *a.,* ~ly *adv.* erstaunlich.
Amazon *s.* Amazone *f.; the* ~ der Amazonas.
ambassador *s.* Botschafter(in) *m.*(*f.*)
amber *s.* Bernstein *m.*
ambidextrous *a.* beidhändig.
ambience *s.* Ambiente *n.*
ambient *a.* umliegend.
ambiguity *s.* Zweideutigkeit *f.*
ambiguous *a.,* ~ly *adv.* zweideutig.
ambiguousness *s.* Zweideutigkeit.
ambition *s.* Ehrgeiz *m.,* Ambition *f.*
ambitious *a.,* ~ly *adv.* ehrgeizig, begierig.
ambivalent *a.* ambivalent.
amble *s.* Paßgang *m.;* ~ *v.i.* paßgehen; schlendern.
ambrosia *s.* Götterspeise *f.*
ambulance *s.* Krankenwagen.
ambulatory *a.* herumziehend.
ambuscade, ambush *s.* Hinterhalt *m.*
ambush *v.t.* im Hinterhalt auflauern.
ameliorate *v.t.* verbessern.
amen *adv.* amen; *s.* Amen *n.*
amenable *a.* zugänglich; verantwortlich.
amend *v.t. & i.* bessern; (Gesetzentwurf) ändern od. ergänzen; sich bessern.
amendment *s.* Verbesserung *f.;* Verbesserungsantrag *m.*
amends *s.pl.* Ersatz *m.*
amenity *s.* Annehmlichkeit *f.* Attraktivität *f.;* Reiz *m.*
America *s.* Amerika *n.*
American *a.* amerikanisch; ~ *s.* Amerikaner(in) *m.*(*f.*)
American Indian *s.* Indianer(in) *m.*(*f.*)
Americanism *s.* Amerikanismus *m.*
Americanize *v.t.* amerikanisieren.
amiability *s.* Liebenswürdigkeit *f.*
amiable *a.,* ~bly *adv.* liebenswürdig.
amicable *a.,* ~bly *adv.* freundschaftlich.
amid(st) *pr.* mitten in, mitten unter.
amidships *adv.* mittschiffs.
amino acid *s.* Aminosäure *f.*
amiss *adv.* unrecht, verkehrt, fehlerhaft; *to take* ~, übelnehmen.
amity *s.* gutes Einvernehmen *n.*
ammeter *s.* (*elek.*) Strommesser, Amperemeter *m.*
ammonia *s.* Ammoniak; *liquid* ~, Salmiakgeist *m.*
ammonite *s.* Ammonshorn *n.*
ammunition *s.* Munition *f.,* Kriegsvorrat *m.*
amnesia *s.* Amnesie *f.*
amnesty *s.* Amnestie *f.;* ~ *v.t.* begnadigen.
amoeba *s.* Amöbe *f.*
among(st) *pr.* unter, zwischen.
amoral *a.* amoralisch.
amorous *a.,* ~ly *adv.* verliebt.
amorphous *a.* amorph, gestaltlos.

amortization *s.* Tilgung (einer Schuld) *f.*
amortize *v.t.* tilgen, amortisieren.
amount *s.* Betrag *m.;* ~ *v.i.* sich belaufen (auf).
ampere *s.* (*elek.*) Ampere *n.; ampere-hour,* Amperestunde *f.*
amphetamine *s.* Amphetamin *f.*
amphibian, amphibious *a.* amphibisch; ~ *s.* Amphibie *f.;* ~ *tank,* (*mil.*) Schwimmpanzer *m.*
amphitheater *s.* Amphitheater *n.*
ample *a.* groß, weit; reichlich.
amplification *s.* Verstärkung, Erweiterung *f.*
amplifier *s.* (*radio, elek.*) Verstärker *m.*
amplify *v.t.* verstärken; erweitern.
amplitude *s.* Umfang *m.*
amply *adv.* ausreichend; reichlich.
ampoule *s.* Ampulle *f.*
amputate *v.t.* amputieren.
amputation *s.* Amputation *f.*
amputee *s.* Amputierte *m./f.*
amuck *adv., to run* ~ (*against or at*), Amok laufen.
amulet *s.* Amulett *n.*
amuse *v.t.* unterhalten, ergötzen.
amusement *s.* Unterhaltung *f.*
amusing *a.,* ~ly *adv.* unterhaltsam.
an *art.* ein, eine, ein.
anabaptist *s.* Wiedertäufer *m.*
anachronism *s.* Anachronismus *m.*
anagram *s.* Anagramm *n.*
analogous *a.,* ~ly *adv.* ähnlich.
analogy *s.* Ähnlichkeit *f.*
analysis *s.* Analyse, Auflösung *f.*
analyst *s.* Analytiker(in) *m.*(*f.*)
analytic(al), ~ly *adv.* analytisch.
analyze *v.t.* analysieren.
anarchic(al) *a.* anarchisch.
anarchist *s.* Anarchist *m.*
anarchy *s.* Anarchie *f.,* Gesetzlosigkeit *f.*
anathema *s. to be* ~ *to s.b.* jm. verhaßt sein.
anatomical *a.* anatomisch.
anatomist *s.* Anatom *m.*
anatomize *v.t.* zergliedern.
anatomy *s.* Anatomie *f.*
ancestor *s.* Ahn(in) *m.*(*f.*); Vorfahre *m.*(*f.*)
ancestral *a.* ererbt, angestammt.
ancestry *s.* Abstammung *f.;* Herkunft *f.;* Ahnen *m. pl.*
anchor *s.* Anker *m.;* (Radio, TV) Moderator(in) *m.*(*f.*); *to cast* ~, vor Anker gehen; *to weigh* ~, Anker lichten; ~ *v.t. & i.* vor Anker legen; vor Anker liegen; (Radio, TV) moderieren.
anchorage *s.* Ankerplatz *m.*
anchovy *s.* Sardelle, Anchovis *f.*
ancient *a.* alt; ~ly *adv.* vor alters; *the ancients,* die Alten.
ancillary *a.* dienstbar, untergeordnet.
and *c.* und.
Andes *pl.* die Anden.
anecdotal *a.* anekdotisch; anekdotenhaft.
anecdote *s.* Anekdote *f.*
anemia *s.* Anämie, Blutarmut *f.*
anemic *a.* anämisch, blutarm.
anemone *s.* Anemone *f.*
anesthesia *s.* Anästhesie *f.,* Betäubung *f.*
anesthetic *a.* (*med.*) (Schmerz) betäubend; ~ *s.* Betäubungsmittel *n.*
anesthetist *s.* Anesthetist(in) *m.*(*f.*); Narkosearzt

m., Narkoseärztin *f.*
anesthetize *v.t.* betäuben.
anew *adv.* von neuem.
angel *s.* Engel *m.*
angelic *a.* engelgleich.
anger *v.t.* erzürnen, ärgern; ~ *s.* Zorn, Ärger *m.*
angina *s.* Angina *f.*, Halsentzündung *f.*
angle *s.* Winkel *m.*; *right* ~, rechter Winkel *m.*; ~ *v.i.* angeln.
Anglican *a.* anglikanisch.
Anglicize *v.t.* anglisieren.
Anglicism *s.* englische Spracheigenheit *f.*
Anglo-American *s.* Angloamerikaner(in) *m.*(*f.*); ~ *a.* angloamerikanisch.
anglophile *s.* Englandfreund *m.*
anglophobe *s.* Englandfeind *m.*
Anglo-Saxon *s.* Angelsachse *m.*; ~ *a.* angelsächsisch.
angry *a.* zornig.
anguish *s.* Seelenangst *f.*; Qual *f.*
angular *a.*, ~**ly** *adv.* winkelig, eckig.
aniline *s.* Anilin *n.*
animal *s.* Tier *n.*; ~ *a.* animalisch, tierisch; ~ *fat*, tierisches Fett *n.*; ~ *lover* *s.* Tierfreund(in) *m.*(*f.*)
animate *v.t.* beseelen; beleben; ~ *a.* beseelt.
animated *a.* lebhaft; ~ **cartoon** *s.* Zeichentrickfilm *m.*
animation *s.* Lebhaftigkeit *f.*
animosity *s.* Feindseligkeit *f.*
aniseed *s.* Aniskorn *n.*
ankle *s.* Fußknöchel *m.*, Fußgelenk *n.*
annals *s.pl.* Jahrbücher *n.pl.*; Annalen *pl.*
anneal *v.t.* ausglühen; kühlen (Glas).
annex *v.t.* anhängen; annektieren; ~ *s.* Anhang *m.*; Nebengebäude *n.*
annexation *s.* Einverleibung, Annexion *f.*
annihilate *v.t.* vernichten, zerstören.
annihilation *s.* Vernichtung, Zerstörung *f.*
anniversary *s.* Jahrestag *m.*; Jubiläum *n.*; **wedding** ~ Hochzeitstag.
annotate *v.t.* mit Anmerkungen versehen.
annotation *s.* Anmerkung *f.*; Kommentar *m.*
announce *v.t.* ankündigen.
announcement *s.* Ankündigung *f.*
announcer *s.* Ansager *m.*
annoy *v.t.* ärgern, belästigen.
annoyance *s.* Plage *f.*; Verdruß *m.*
annoyed *a.* ärgerlich; verärgert.
annoying *a.* ärgerlich; lästig.
annual *a.*, ~**ly** *adv.* jährlich; ~ *leave*, Jahresurlaub *m.*; ~ *report*, Jahresbericht *m.*
annuity *s.* Jahresrente *f.*
annul *v.t.* annullieren, aufgeben.
annular *a.* ringförmig.
annulment *s.* Annullierung *f.*
Annunciation *s.* Verkündigung *f.*; Mariä Verkündigung *f.*
anode *s.* Anode *f.*
anodyne *a.* schmerzstillend; ~ *s.* (*med.*) schmerzstillendes Mittel, (*fig.*) Linderungsmittel *n.*
anoint *v.t.* salben.
anointment *s.* Salbung *f.*
anomalous *s.* abweichend, unregelmäßig.; anomal.
anomaly *s.* Anomalie *f.*
anon *adv.* sogleich.

anonymity *s.* Anonymität *f.*
anonymous *a.*, ~**ly** *adv.* anonym.
anorak *s.* Anorak *m.*
anorexia *s.* Anorexie *f.*
another *a.* ein anderer; *one another*, einander.
answer *s.* Antwort *f.*; Resultat (einer Rechnung), *n.*; ~ *v.t.* & *i.* antworten; verantwortlich sein für; entsprechen; (*com.*) sich rentieren; *to ~ for*, bürgen; *to ~ the bell* (*door*), nach der Tür sehen; *to ~ the telephone*, ans Telephon gehen; *to ~ to a name*, auf einen Namen hören.
answerable *a.* verantwortlich.
answering machine *s.* Anrufbeantworter *m.*
ant *s.* Ameise *f.*
antagonism *s.* Widerstreit *m.*
antagonist *s.* Gegner *m.*
antagonistic *a.* feindlich; gegensätzlich; antagonistisch.
antagonize *v.t.* sich einen zum Gegner machen.
antarctic *a.* antarktisch.
Antarctic *s.* Antarktis *f.*
Antarctica *s.* die Antarktis *f.*
anteater *s.* Ameisenfresser.
antecedent *a.*, ~**ly** *adv.* vorhergehend; ~ *s.* Vorhergehender *m.*; **antecedents** *pl.* frühere Lebensumstände.
antechamber *s.* Vorzimmer *n.*
antedate *v.t.* vordatieren; ~ *s.* Vordatierung *f.*
antediluvian *a.* vorsintflutlich.
antelope *s.* Antilope *f.*
antenatal *a.* vorgeburtlich; ~ *care* *s.* Schwangerenfürsorge *f.*
antenna *s.* (*radio*) Antenne *f.*
anterior *a.* vorherig; älter.
anthem *s.* Hymne *f.*
anthill *s.* Ameisenhaufen *m.*
anthology *s.* Anthologie *f.*; Auslese *f.*
anthracite *s.* Anthrazit *m.*
anthrax *s.* Milzbrand *m.*
anthropoid *s.* Anthropoid *m.*; Menschenaffe *m.*
anthropological *a.* anthropologisch.
anthropologist *s.* Anthropologe *m.*
anthropology *s.* Anthropologie *f.*
anti *a.* (in Zus.) gegen . . .
anti-aircraft *a.* Fliegerabwehr . . .
antibiotic *s.* Antibiotikum *n.*
antibody *s.* Antikörper *m.*
antic *a.*, ~**ly** *adv.* lächerlich; ~ *s.* Posse *f.*; Possenreißer *m.*
anticipate *v.t.* vorwegnehmen; zuvorkommen; voraussehen.
anticipation *s.* Vorwegnahme *f.*; Erwartung *f.*; Vorgeschmack *m.*
anticlimax *s.* Abstieg *m.*, Abfall *m.*; Antiklimax *f.*
anticlockwise *adv.* gegen die Richtung des Uhrzeigers.
anticyclone *s.* Hochdruckgebiet *n.*; Antizyklone *f.*
antidote *s.* Gegengift *m.*
antifreeze *s.* Frostschutzmittel *n.*
anti-nuclear *a.* Anti-Atomkraft . . .
antipathetic *a.* antipathisch, zuwider.
antipathy *s.* natürliche Abneigung *f.*
antipodes *s.pl.* Gegenfüßler *m.* *pl.*
antiquarian *a.* antiquarisch.
antiquary *s.* Altertumsforscher *m.*
antiquated *a.* veraltet.

antique *a.* antik; altertümlich; ~ *s.* Antiquität *f.*; **~-dealer,** Antiquitätenhändler *m.*; ~ *furniture,* antike Möbel.

antiquity *s.* Vorzeit *f.*, Altertum *n.*

anti-Semite *s.* Antisemit *m.*

anti-Semitic *a.* antisemitisch.

antiseptic *a.* antiseptisch; ~ *s.* Antiseptikum.

antisocial *a.* asozial.

antitank *a.* Antitank . . .; ~ **ditch,** Panzergraben *m.*; **~-gun,** Panzerabwehrkanone; **~-troops,** Panzerjäger *m. pl.*

antithesis *s.* Antithese *f.*; Entgegenstellung *f.*

antithetic, antithetic(al) *a.* antithetisch; gegensätzlich.

antitoxin *s.* Gegengift *n.*

antler *s.* Geweih *n.*; Sprosse *f.* (am Hirschgeweih).

antonym *s.* Antonym *n.*

anus *s.* After *m.*

anvil *s.* Amboß *m.*

anxiety *s.* Angst *f.*; Beklemmung *f.*

anxious *a.*, **~ly** *adv.* ängstlich; begierig.

any *a.* jeder, jede; irgendein, -eine, -ein; *anybody,* ~ *one,* irgend jemand; *anything,* etwas, irgend etwas; *anyhow,* irgendwie, immerhin; jedenfalls; *anywhere,* irgendwo.

aorta *s.* Aorta *f.*; Hauptschlagader *f.*

apace *adv.* hurtig, zusehends.

apart *adv.* beiseite, für sich; ~ *from,* abgesehen von.

apartment *s.* Wohnung *f.*

apathetic *a.* apathisch, stumpf.

apathy *s.* Gleichgültigkeit *f.*, Apathie *f.*

ape *s.* Menschenaffe *m.*; Nachäffer *m.*; ~ *v.t.* nachäffen.

aperient *a.* (*med.*) abführend; ~ *s.* Abführmittel *n.*

aperture *s.* Öffnung *f.*

apex s. Spitze *f.*, Gipfel *m.*

aphorism *s.* Aphorismus *m.*

apiece *adv.* für das Stück.

apish *a.*, **~ly** *adv.* affenartig.

aplomb *s.* Aplomb *m.*; Fassung *f.*

apocalypse *s.* Apokalypse *f.*

apocalyptic *a.* apokalyptisch.

apocryphal *a.* apokryph.

apodictic(al) *a.*, **~ly** *adv.* apodiktisch.

apolitical *a.* apolitisch.

apologetic(al) *a.*, **~ly** *adv.* entschuldigend.

apologize *v.i.* sich entschuldigen.

apology *s.* Verteidigung *f.*; Entschuldigung *f.*

apoplectic(al) *a.* apoplektisch.

apoplexy *s.* Schlaganfall *m.*

apostasy *s.* Abtrünnigkeit *f.*

apostate *a.* abtrünnig.

apostatize *v.i.* abtrünnig werden.

apostle *s.* Apostel *m.*

apostrophe *s.* Anrede *f.*; Apostroph *m.*

apothecary *s.* Apotheker *m.*

apotheosis *s.* Vergötterung, Apotheose *f.*

appal *v.t.* erschrecken.

appalling *a.* schrecklich, entsetzlich.

apparatus *s.* Gerät *n.*; Apparat *m.*

apparel *s.* Kleidung *f.*; ~ *v.t.* ankleiden.

apparent *a.*, **~ly** *adv.* augenscheinlich; *heir* ~, rechtmäßiger Thronerbe *m.*

apparently *adv.* offensichtlich; scheinbar.

apparition *s.* Erscheinung *f.*; Gespenst *n.*

appeal *v.i.* appellieren, Berufung einlegen; gefallen; ~ *v.t.* anrufen; ~ *s.* Ruf *m.*, Bitte *f.*; Anziehungskraft *f.*; Reklamewirkung *f.*; (*law*) Berufung *f.*, Rechtsmittel *n.*; *court of* ~, Berufungsgericht *n.*; *to allow an* ~, einer Berufung stattgeben; *to dismiss an* ~, eine Berufung zurückweisen; *to lodge an* ~, Berufung einlegen.

appealing *a.* flehend, ansprechend, verlockend.

appear *v.i.* erscheinen, scheinen.

appearance *s.* Erscheinung *f.*; Anschein *m.*; *to keep up* ~*s,* den Schein wahren; *to put in an* ~, sich blicken lassen; *outward* ~ äußere Erscheinung; *~s Äußerlichkeiten f. pl.*; *to judge by* ~*s* allem Anschein nach.

appease *v.t.* besänftigen.

appeasement *s.* Besänftigung *f.*; Beruhigung *f.*

appellant *s.* Berufungskläger *m.*

appendage *s.* Anhang *m.*, Zubehör. *n.*, *m.*

appendicitis *s.* Blinddarmentzündung *f.*

appendix *s.* Anhang *m.*; Blinddarm *m.*

appertain *v.i.* gehören.

appetite *s.* Appetit *m.*; Eßlust *f.*, Verlangen *n.*

appetizer *s.* Appetitanreger *m.*

appetizing *a.* appetitlich.

applaud *v.t.* Beifall spenden.

applause *s.* Beifall *m.*

apple *s.* Apfel *m.*

apple-pie *s.* Apfelpastete *f.*

apple-sauce *s.* Apfelmus *n.*

appliance *s.* Vorrichtung, Anwendung *f.*; Gerät *n.*

applicable *a.* anwendbar; geeignet.

applicant *s.* Bewerber(in) *m.*(*f.*)

application *s.* Bewerbung *f.*; Anwendung *f.*; Gesuch *n.*; (*med.*) Verband *m.*; Fleiß *m.*; Aufmerksamkeit *f.*; *to make an* ~, ein Gesuch einreichen; *to grant an* ~, ein Gesuch bewilligen; ~ *form,* Antragsformular *n.*

apply *v.t. & i.* anwenden; sich auf etwas verlegen; sich bewerben um; sich wenden an; *for particulars* ~ *to* . . ., Näheres zu erfragen bei . . .

appoint *v.t.* bestimmen, ernennen; *at the appointed time,* zur verabredeten Zeit, zur festgesetzten Zeit.

appointment *s.* Festsetzung *f.*; Verabredung *f.*; Ernennung *f.*; *by* ~, nach Verabredung; *to make an* ~, eine Verabredung treffen.

apportion *v.t.* einverteilen, zuteilen.

apposite *a.* passend; treffend.

apposition *s.* Zusatz *m.*; Apposition *f.*

appraisal *s.* Beurteilung *f.*

appraise *v.t.* abschätzen, bewerten.

appreciable *a.* nennenswert.

appreciate *v.t.* schätzen, zu würdigen wissen.

appreciation *s.* Würdigung, Schätzung *f.*

apprehend *v.t.* ergreifen; begreifen; fürchten.

apprehensible *a.* begreiflich.

apprehension *s.* Verhaftung *f.*; Besorgnis *f.*; Auffassung *f.*; Ansicht *f.*

apprehensive *a.*, **~ly** *adv.* besorgt.

apprentice *s.* Lehrling *m.* Auszubildende *m./f.*; ~ *v.t.* in die Lehre geben.

apprenticeship *s.* Lehrzeit *f.*

approach *v.t. & i.* nähern; sich nähern; sich wenden an; ~ *s.* Annäherung *f.*; Zutritt *m.*; Auffahrt *f*; Ansatz *m.*

approbation *s.* Billigung *f.*, Beifall *m.* Zustimmung *f.*

appropriate *v.t.* sich aneignen; zu einem Zwecke bestimmen; *appropriated funds*, bewilligte Gelder; ~ *a.* angemessen.

appropriation *s.* Aneignung *f.*; Bewilligung (von Geldern) *f.*; ~s *s. pl.* bewilligte Gelder *n. pl.*

approval *s.* Billigung *f*; Genehmigung *f.*

approve *v.t.* billigen, genehmigen.

approving *a.* zustimmend; beipflichtend.

approximate *v.t. & i.* nahe bringen; sich nahen; *a.* annähernd.

approximation *s.* Annäherung *f.*

appurtenance *s.* Zubehör *n.*

apricot *s.* Aprikose *f.*

April *s.* April *m.*; ~ *Fool's Day* der 1. April.

apron *s.* Schürze *f.*; Schurzfell *n.*

apron-string *s.* Schürzenband *n.*

apropos *adv.* beiläufig.

apse, apsis *s.* (*arch.*) Apsis *f.*

apt *a.*, ~**ly** *adv.* geschickt; geneigt; fähig.

aptitude, aptness *s.* Begabung *f.*; Tauglichkeit *f.*

aquarelle *s.* Aquarell *n.*

aquarium *s.* Aquarium *n.*

Aquarius *s.* Wassermann *m.*

aquatic *a.* Wasser...; ~s *s. pl.* Wassersport *m.*

aqueduct *s.* Wasserleitung *f.*

aquiline *a.* adlerartig.

Arab *s.* Araber(in) *m.*(*f.*); *a.* arabisch.

Arabia *s.* Arabien *n.*

Arabian *a.* arabisch.

Arabic *a.* arabisch, ~**numeral** *s.* arabische Ziffer *f.*

arable *a.* kultivierbar.

arbiter *s.* (Schieds)richter *m.*

arbitrariness *s.* Willkür *f.*

arbitrary *a.*, ~**ily** *adv.* willkürlich.

arbitrate *v.t. & i.* schlichten.

arbitration *s.* Schiedsspruch *m.*; (*com.*) Arbitrage *f.*; *court of* ~, Schiedsgericht *n.*, Schlichtungsausschuß *m.*

arbitrator *s.* Schiedsrichter *m.*; ~'s *award*, Schiedsspruch *m.*

arbor *s.* Laube *f.*

arc *s.* (*geom.*) Bogen *m.*; ~~**lamp**, Bogenlampe; ~~**welding**, Lichtbogenschweißung *f.*

arcade *s.* Bogengang *m.*

Arcadian *a.* idyllisch, ländlich, einfach.

arcane *a.* geheimnisvoll.

arch *a.*, ~**ly** *adv.* schlau; schalkhaft; ~ *a.* (in Zus.) Erz...; ~ *v.t.* wölben; ~ *s.* Bogen *m.*; Gewölbe *n.*; ~~**support**, Plattfußeinlage *f.*

archaeologic(al) *a.* archäologisch.

archaeologist *s.* Altertumsforscher *m.* Archäologe *m.*, Archäologin *f.*

archaeology *s.* Altertumskunde, Archäologie, *f.*

archaic *a.* veraltet; altertümlich.

archaism *s.* veraltete Sprachwendung *f.*; Archaismus.

archangel *s.* Erzengel *m.*

archbishop *s.* Erzbischof *m.*

archduchess *s.* Erzherzogin *f.*

archduchy *s.* Erzherzogtum *f.*

archduke *s.* Erzherzog *m.*

archer *s.* Bogenschütze *m.*

archery *s.* Bogenschießen *n.*

archetypal *a.* archetypisch; typisch.

archetype *s.* Archetyp *m* ; Prototyp *m.*

archiepiscopal *a.* erzbischöflich.

archipelago *s.* Archipel *m.*, Inselmeer *n.*

architect *a.* Baumeister *m.*

architecture *s.* Baukunst *f.*

archives *s. pl.* Archiv *n.*

archway *s.* Bogengang *m.*

arctic *a.* arktisch, nördlich, Polar...

Arctic *s.* die Arktis *f.*

ardent *a.*, ~**ly** *adv.* heiß; inbrünstig.

ardor *s.* Hitze *f.* Eifer *m.*

arduous *a.* anstrengend; schwierig; steil.

area *s.* Fläche *f.*, Flächenraum *m.*; Bezirk *m.*

arena *s.* Kampfplatz *m.*, Arena *f.*

Argentina *s.* Argentinien.

Argentine *a.* argentinisch.

Argentinian *a.* argentinisch; Argentinier(in) *m.*(*f.*)

arguable *a.* fragwürdig.

arguably *adv.* möglicherweise.

argue *v.i.* Gründe anführen; streiten; ~ *v.t.* beweisen.

argument *s.* Beweisgrund *m.*; Streitfrage *f.*; Inhalt *m.*

argumentation *s.* Beweisführung *f.*

argumentative *a.* beweisend; streitsüchtig.

aria *s.* Arie *f.*

arid, *a.* dürr.

aridity *s.* Trockenheit *f.*

Aries *s.* Widder.

aright *adv.* gerade, richtig.

arise *v.i.st.* aufsteigen; entstehen.

aristocracy *s.* Aristokratie *f.*

aristocrat *s.* Aristokrat(in) *m.*(*f.*)

aristocratic *a.*, ~**ally** *adv.* aristokratisch.

arithmetic *s.* Rechenkunst *f.*; *mental* ~, Kopfrechnen *n.*

arithmetical *a.*, ~**ly** *adv.* arithmetisch.

ark *s.* Arche *f.*

arm *s.* Arm *m.*; *to keep at arm's length*, in gehöriger Entfernung halten; ~ *v.t. & i.* bewaffnen; sich rüsten.

armadillo *s.* Gürteltier *n.*

armament *s.* Rüstung *f.*

armature *s.* Rüstung *f.*; Armatur *f.*; Anker (*elek.*) *m.*

arm-chair *s.* Lehnsessel *m.*

armed *a.* bewaffnet; ~ *conflict s.* bewaffnete Auseinandersetzung *f.*; ~ *forces s.* Streitkräfte *f.*

armful *s.* Armvoll *m.*

armistice *s.* Waffenstillstand *m.*

armor *s.* Rüstung *f.*; Panzer *m.*

armored *a.* Panzer...; ~ *troops*, Panzertruppen *f. pl.*

armorer *s.* Waffenschmied *m.*

armorial *a.* Wappen...

armory *s.* Waffenfabrik *f.*

arm-pit *s.* Achselgrube *f.*

arms *s. pl.* Waffen *f. pl.*; Wappen *n.*; *small* ~, Handwaffen *pl.*; *under* ~, gerüstet.

army *s.* Heer *n.*

army-list *s.* Rangliste der Offiziere *f.*

aroma *s.* Wohlgeruch *m.*

aromatic(al) *a.* würzig.

around *adv.* ringsherum.

arousal *s.* Aufwachen *n.*; Erregung *f.*

arouse *v.t.* wecken, aufwecken; erregen.

arrack *s.* Reisbranntwein *m.*; Arrak *m.*

arraign *v.t.* anklagen, vor Gericht stellen.
arraignment *s.* (*law*) öffentliche Anklage *f.*, Vorführung vor Gericht *f.*
arrange *v.t.* ordnen, einrichten; anordnen (Stühle usw.); schlichten.
arrangement *s.* Beilegung *f.*, Vergleich *m.*; Anordnung *f.*
array *s.* Reihe *f.*; Anzug *m.*; ~ *v.t.* anordnen; ankleiden.
arrear *s.* (Zahlungs-)Rückstand *m.*; *in arrears*, rückständig; *interest on arrears*, Verzugszinsen *m.pl.*
arrest *s.* Verhaftung *f.*; Festnahme *f.*; *under ~*, in Verhaft, in Gewahrsam; ~ *v.t.* hemmen; verhaften; (*fig.*) fesseln.
arrival *s.* Ankunft *f.*; Ankömmling *m.*
arrive *v.t.* ankommen; gelangen
arrogance *s.* Überheblichkeit *f.*; Arroganz *f.*
arrogant *a.*, **~ly** *adv.* anmaßend.
arrogate *v.t.* sich anmassen.
arrow *s.* Pfeil *m.*; **~-head** *s.* Pfeilspitze *f.*
arse *s.* (*vulg.*) Arsch *m.*
arsenal *s.* Zeughaus *n.*
arsenic *s.* Arsenik *n.*
arson *s.* Brandstiftung *f.*
arsonist *s.* Brandstifter(in) *m.(f.)*
art *s.* Kunst *f.*; List *f.*; **~-dealer**, Kunsthändler *m.*
arterial *a.* Pulsader...; ~ *road*, Hauptverkehrsstraße *f.*
artery *s.* Pulsader *f.*
artesian *a.* artesisch.
art-form *s.* Kunstgattung *f.*, Kunstform *f.*
artful *a.*, **~ly** *adv.* schlau, listig; künstlich.
art gallery *s.* Kunstgallerie *f.*
arthritis Gelenkentzündung *f.*
artichoke *a.* Artischocke *f.*
article *s.* Artikel *m.*
articulation *s.* Aussprache *f.*; Artikulation *f.*
articulate *a.*, **~ly** *adv.* gegliedert; vernehmlich; ~ *v.t.* artikulieren; zusammenfügen.
artifice *s.* Kunstgriff *m.*; List *f.*
artificial *a.*, **~ly** *adv.* künstlich,; ~ *insemination s.* künstliche Befruchtung *f.*; ~ *intelligence s.* künstliche Intelligenz.
artificiality *s.* Künstlichkeit *f.*
artificial respiration *s.* künstliche Beatmung.
artillery *s.* Artillerie *f.*; *long-range* ~ Fernkampfartillerie *f.*
artillery-man *s.* Artillerist, Kanonier *m.*
artisan *s.* Handwerker *m.*
artist *s.* Künstler(in) *m.(f.)*
artiste *s.* Artist(in) *m.(f.)*
artistic *a.* künstlerisch.
artless *a.* kunstlos; naiv.
art nouveau *s.* Jugendstil *m.*
as *c.* als, da, so, sowie, sofern, wenn; wie; weil; indem; ~ . . . ~ . . ., (eben) so . . . wie; ~ *for*, ~ *to*, was betrifft; ~ *it were*, sozusagen; *as if, as though*, als ob, wie wenn; ~ *far* ~ soweit als; ~ *long* ~, solange; ~ *soon* ~, sobald (als); ~ *yet*, noch, bisher.
asbestos *s.* Asbest *m.*
ascend *v.t. & i.* hinaufsteigen; ersteigen.
ascendancy *s.* Vorherrschaft *f.*; Überlegenheit *f.*
ascendant *a.* aufsteigend; überlegen,; *s.* Aszendent *m.*
ascension *s.* Aufsteigen *n.*, Besteigung *f.*; *s.* Himmelfahrtstag *m.*

ascent *s.* Aufstieg *m.*
ascertain *v.t.* feststellen, ermitteln.
ascertainable *a.* feststellbar.
ascetic *a.* asketisch; ~ *s.* Asket(in) *m.(f.)*
asceticism *s.* Askese *f.*
ascribe *v.f.* zuschreiben.
aseptic *a.* keimfrei, aseptisch.
asexual *a.* asexuell.
ash *s.* Esche *f.*; Asche *f.*
ashamed *a.* beschämt.
ash-can *s.* Müllkasten *m.*
ashen *a.* aschfarben; aschfahl.
ashes *s.pl.* Asche *f.*
ashore *adv.* am Ufer; *to get* ~ landen.
ashtray *s.* Aschenbecher *m.*
Ash-Wednesday *s.* Aschermittwoch *m.*
Asia *s.* Asien *n.*; ~ **Minor** Kleinasien *n.*
Asian *a.* asiatisch; *s.* Asiat(in) *m.(f.)*
aside *adv.* beiseite, abseits; ~ *s.* beiseite gesprochene Worte *n.pl.*
asinine *a.* eselhaft; Esel. . .
ask *v.t. & i.* fordern, fragen, bitten; *to be had for the asking*, umsonst zu bekommen.
askance *adv. to look* ~ *at*, schief, schräg ansehen.
askew *adv.* schief; *to go* ~, schiefgehen.
aslant *adv.* schräg, quer.
asleep *adv.* schlafend; *to fall* ~, einschlafen.
asparagus *s.* Spargel *m.*
aspect *s.* Anblick *m.*; Aussicht *f.*
aspen *s.* Espe *f.*
asperity *s.* Rauheit *f.*
asperse *v.f.* besprengen; verleumden.
aspersion *s.* Verleumdung *f.*
asphalt *s.* Asphalt *m.*
asphyxiate *v.t.* ersticken.
asphyxiation *s.* Erstickung *f.*
aspirant *s.* Bewerber(in) *m.(f.)*; *a.* aufstrebend.
aspirate *v.t.* aspirieren.
aspiration *s.* Streben *n.*; Sehnsucht *f.*
aspire *v.i.* streben, heftig verlangen.
aspirin *s.* Aspirin *n.*
aspiring *a.* aufstrebend.
ass *s.* Esel *m.*; (*vulg.*) Arsch *m.*
assail *v.t.* anfallen, angreifen.
assailant *s.* Angreifer *m.*
assassin *s.* Mörder(in) *m.(f.)*
assassinate *v.t.* meuchlings ermorden.
assassination *s.* Mord *m.*, Attentat *n.*
assault *s.* Angriff, Sturm *m.*; (*law*) tätliche Beleidigung *f.*; ~ *and battery*, schwere tätliche Beleidigung *f.*; *indecent* ~, Sittlichkeitsvergehen *n.*;~ *v.t.* angreifen, anfallen.
assay *s.* Probe *f.*, Prüfung *f.*; *v.t.* prüfen, probieren.
assemblage *s.* Zusammenkunft *f.*; Zusammensetzen *n.*
assemble *v.t. & i.* sammeln; sich versammeln; (*mech.*) zusammensetzen, montieren.
assembly *s.* Versammlung *f.*; **~-plant** *s.* Montagewerkstatt *f.*; **~-line** Montagefließband *n.*
assent *s.* Genehmigung *f.*; ~ *v.i.* beipflichten.
assert *v.t.* behaupten, verfechten.
assertion *s.* Behauptung *f.*
assertive *a.* energisch; bestimmt.
assess *v.t.* abschätzen, besteuern.
assessable *a.* steuerbar.
assessment *s.* Einschätzung *f.*

asset *s.* Aktivposten *m.*; (*fig.*) Vorteil *m.*; ~**s** *pl.* (*com.*) Activa *pl.* Vermögen *n.*

asseveration *s.* Beteuerung *f.*

assiduity *s.* Emsigkeit *f.*

assiduous *a.*, ~**ly** *adv.* emsig.

assign *v.t.* anweisen; abtreten; *to* ~ *to a unit,* (*mil.*) einer Einheit unterstellen.

assignment *s.* Anweisung *f.*; (*mil.*) Auftrag *m.*

assimilate *v.t.* angleichen; in sich aufnehmen; ~ *v.i.* ähnlich werden.

assimilation *s.* Angleichung *f.*

assist *v.t.* beistehen; ~ *v.i.* zugegensein, teilnehmen (an).

assistance *s.* Beistand *m.*

assistant *a.* behilflich; ~ *s.* Helfer(in) *m.*(*f.*); Gehilfe *m.*; Assistent(in) *m.*(*f.*); ~ *master,* Studienrat *m.*

associate *s.* Genosse *m.*; Teilhaber *m.*; Mitarbeiter *m.*; ~ *v.t. & i.* zugesellen; umgehen mit.

association *s.* Vereinigung *f.*, Verband *m.*

assort *v.t.* aussuchen, sortieren; ~ *v.i.* übereinstimmen.

assorted *a.* gemischt; sortiert.

assortment *s.* Auswahl *f.*; Sortiment *n.*

assuage *v.t.* besänftigen.

assume *v.t.* annehmen, sich anmaßen; *to* ~ *duty,* Dienst antreten.

assumption *s.* Annahme *f.*; (*law*) ~ *of authority,* Dienstanmaßung *f.*

assurance *s.* Vertrauen *n.*; Selbstsicherheit *f.*; Versicherung *f.*

assure *v.t.* versichern, sicher stellen.

assured *a.*, ~**ly** *adv.* gewiß.

asterisk *s.* Sternchen *n.*

astern *adv.* achtern; achteraus.

asthma *s.* (*med.*) Asthma *n.*

asthmatic(al) *a.* asthmatisch.

astir *adv.* rege, wach.

astonish *v.t.* in Erstaunen setzen.

astonishing *a.* ~**ly** *adv.* erstaunlich.

astonishment *s.* Erstaunen *n.*

astound *v.t.* in Staunen versetzen; verblüffen.

astounding *a.* erstaunlich.

astraddle *adv.* rittlings.

astray *adv.* in der Irre; *to go* ~, irregehen.

astride *adv.* sperrbeinig, rittlings.

astringent *a.* (*med.*) zusammenziehend; adstringent, blutstillend.

astrologer *s.* Astrologe *m.*, Astrologin *f.*

astrological *a.* astrologisch.

astrology *s.* Astrologie.

astronaut *s.* Astronaut(in) *m.*(*f.*)

astronautical *a.* astronautisch.

astronautics *s.* Raumfahrt *f.*

astronomer *s.* Astronom(in) *m.*(*f.*)

astronomical *a.* astronomisch.

astronomy *s.* Sternkunde *f.*; Astronomie *f.*

astute *a.* schlau; scharfsinnig.

astuteness *s.* Scharfsinnigkeit *f.*

asunder *adv.* auseinander, entzwei.

asylum *s.* Zufluchtsort *m.*; *lunatic* ~ *s.* Irrenhaus *n.*

asymmetric, asymmetrical *a.* asymmetrisch.

asymmetry *s.* Asymmetrie *f.*

at *pr.* an, zu, bei, auf, in, gegen; ~ *first,* zuerst; ~ *last,* endlich; ~ *least,* wenigstens; ~ *length,* schließlich; ~ *once,* auf einmal.

athesism *s.* Gottesleugnung *f.*

atheist *s.* Atheist(in) *m.*(*f.*)

athlete *s.* Athlet(in) *m.*(*f.*)

athletic *a.* athletisch; kraftvoll.

athletics *s.pl.* Leichtathletik *f.*

athwart *pr.* querüber.

Atlantic *a.* atlantisch; ~ **Ocean** *s.* Atlantik *m.*, Atlantischer Ozean *m.*

atlas *s.* Atlas *m.*

atmosphere *s.* Atmosphäre *f.*

atmospheric(al) *a.* atmosphärisch, Luft . . .; ~ *pressure,* Luftdruck *m.*

atmospherics *s.pl.* (*radio*) Luftstörungen *f.pl.*

atoll *s.* Atoll *n.*

atom *s.* Atom *n.*

atomic *a.* Atom . . ., atomar; ~ **bomb** *s.* Atombombe *f.* ~ **energy** *s.* Atomenergie *f.*; ~ **power** *s.* Atomkraft; ~ **waste** *s.* Atommüll *m.*

atomizer *s.* Zerstäuber *m.*

atone *v.i.* sühnen; büßen.

atonement *s.* Sühne *f.*; Buße.

atop *adv.* obenauf.

atrocious *a.*, ~**ly** *adv.* abscheulich.

atrocity *s.* Abscheulichkeit, Gräßlichkeit *f.*; Greueltat *f.*

atrophy *s.* Abzehrung, Verkümmerung *f.*

attach *v.t.* anhängen, anheften; beilegen; fesseln; verhaften; ~ *v.i.* verknüpft sein mit.

attaché *s.* Attaché *m.*; ~**-case** *s.* Aktentasche *f.*

attached *a.* beiliegend, angeschlossen.

attachment *s.* Anhänglichkeit, Ergebenheit *f.*; Anhängsel *n.*

attack *v.t.* angreifen; ~ *s.* Angriff *m.*; Anfall *m.*

attain *v.t. & i.* erreichen, erlangen.

attainable *a.* erreichbar.

attainment *s.* Erreichung; Verwirklichung; Leistung *f.*

attempt *s.* Versuch *m.*; Angriff *m.*; Attentat *n.*; ~ *v.t.* versuchen; angreifen.

attend *v.t.* begleiten; aufmerken; aufwarten; pflegen; ~ *v.i.* achthaben; besorgen; zugegen sein; besuchen; *to* ~ *to,* bearbeiten (Angelegenheit).

attendance *s.* Bedienung *f.*; Gefolge *n.*

attendant *a.* begleitend; ~ *s.* Diener *m.*; Aufwärter *m.*

attention *s.* Aufmerksamkeit *f.*; *to call* (*draw*) *a person's* ~ *to a thing,* einen auf etwas aufmerksam machen; *attention Mr. Smith,* zu Händen Herrn Smith; *attention!,* stillgestanden!; *to stand to* ~, stramm stehen.

attentive *a.*, ~**ly** *adv.* aufmerksam.

attentiveness *s.* Aufmerksamkeit *f.*

attenuate *v.t.* verdünnen, vermindern.

attest *v.t.* bezeugen; beglaubigen.

attestation *s.* Beglaubigung; Bescheinigung *f.*

attic *s.* Dachstube *f.*; Dachgeschoß *n.*

attire *s.* Anzug, Putz *m.*; ~ *v.t.* ankleiden, putzen.

attitude *s.* Stellung *f.*, Haltung *f.*

attorney *s.* Bevollmächtigter, Anwalt *m.*; *power of* ~, schriftliche Vollmacht *f.*; ~**-general** *s.* Oberstaatsanwalt *m.*

attract *v.t.* anziehen, reizen.

attraction *s.* Anziehung *f.*; Reiz *m.*

attractive *a.*, ~**ly** *adv.* anziehend.

attribute *v.t.* beilegen, beimessen; ~ *s.* Abzeichen *n.*; Merkmal *n.*

attribution *s.* Zuordnung *f.* Zurückführung *f.*

attributive *a.* zueignend.
attrition *s.* Zermürbung *f.*; Zerknirschung *f.*; Reduzierung (Personal) *f.*
attune *v.t.* gewöhnen.
auburn *a.* nußbraun, kastanienbraun.
auction *s.* Versteigerung *f.*; Auktion *f.*; *to sell by ~* versteigern; *~ v.t.* versteigern.
auctioneer *s.* Auktionator(in) *m.(f.)*
audacious *a.*, *~ly adv.* kühn.
audacity *s.* Kühnheit *f.*
audibility *s.* Hörbarkeit *f.*
audible *a.*, *~bly adv.* hörbar.
audience *s.* Publikum *n.*, Audienz *f.*; Zuhörer *m.pl.*
audio-visual *a.* audio visuell.
audit *s.* Rechnungsprüfung *f.*; *~ v.t.* Rechnungen prüfen.
audition *s.* Hörvermögen *n.*, Gehör *n.*; Vorspielen, *n.*, Vorsingen *n.*, Vorsprechen *n.*, Vortanzen *n. v.t. & i.* vorsingen, vorsprechen, vorspielen, vortanzen.
auditor *s.* Buchprüfer(in) *m.(f.).*
auditorium *s.* Zuhörerraum, *m.* Vortragssaal *m.*, Konzerthalle *f.*
aught *pn.* irgend etwas.
augment *v.t.* vermehren.
augmentation *s.* Vermehrung.
augur *v.t.* vorhersagen; weissagen.
augury *s.* Wahrsagung *f.*; Vorzeichen *n.*
august *a.* erhaben, hehr.
August *s.* August (Monat) *m.*
aunt *s.* Tante *f.*
aura *s.* Fluidum *n.*
auricle *s.* Ohrmuschel *f.*
auricular *a.*, *~ly adv.* Ohren . . .; *~ confession s.* Ohrenbeichte *f.*
aurora *s.* Morgenröte *f.*; *~ borealis,* Nordlicht *n.*
auspices *s.* Vorbedeutung *f.*; (*fig.*) Schutz *m.*
auspicious *a.*, *~ly adv.* günstig.
austere *a.*, *~ly adv.* herb, streng.
austerity *s.* Strenge *f.*
Australia *s.* Australien *n.*
Australian *a.* australisch; *s.* Australier(in) *m.(f.)*
Austria *s.* Österreich *n.*
Austrian *a.* österreichisch; *~ s.* Österreicher(in) *m.(f.)*
authentic(al) *a.*, *~ly adv.* glaubwürdig, echt.
authenticate *v.t.* beurkunden.
authentication *s.* Bestätigung *f.*
authenticity *s.* Echtheit *f.*
author *s.* Verfasser(in) *m.(f.)*, Urheber(in) *m.(f.)*, Schriftsteller(in) *m.(f.)*, Autor(in) *m.(f.)*
authoritarian *a.* autoritär.
authoritative *a.*, *~ly adv.* gebieterisch; bevollmächtigt; maßgebend.
authority *s.* Ansehen *n.*; Glaubwürdigkeit *f.*; Gewährsmann *m.*, Autorität *f.*; Befugnis, Vollmacht *f.*; **authorities** *pl.* Behörden *f.pl.*
authorization *s.* Bevollmächtigung *f.*; Genehmigung *f.*
authorize *v.t.* bevollmächtigen; ermächtigen.
authorship *s.* Autorschaft *f.*
autistic *a.* autistisch.
autobiographic(al) *a.* autobiographisch.
autobiography *s.* Selbstbiographie *f.*
autocracy *s.* Selbstherrschaft *f.*; Autokratie *f.*
autocrat *s.* Selbstherrscher *m.*; Autokrat *m.*

autocratic(al) *a.* selbstherrlich.
autograph *s.* Handschrift *f.*, Autograph *n.*; Autogramm *n.*; *~ v.t.* signieren.
autographic *a.* eigenhändig.
automat *s.* Automat *m.*
automate *v.t.* automatisieren.
automatic *a.* automatisch, selbsttätig.
automation *s.* Automation *f.*; Automatisierung *f.*
automaton *s.* Automat *m.*
automobile *s.* Automobil *n.*
automotive *a.* Kraftfahrzeug. . .; *~ industry s.* Automobilindustrie *f.*
autonomous *a.* autonom.
autonomy *s.* Selbstregierung, Autonomie *f.*
autopsy *s.* Autopsie *f.*, Obduktion *f.*
autumn *s.* Herbst *m.*
autumnal *a.* herbstlich.
auxiliaries *s.pl.* Hilfstruppen *f.pl.*
auxiliary *a.* Hilfs . . . ; *s.* Hilfsverb.
avail *s.* Vorteil *m.*; *of no ~,* vergeblich; *~ v.t. & i.* helfen, nützen; *to ~ oneself of a thing,* sich etwas zunutze machen.
availability *s.* Verfügbarkeit *f.*
available *a.* verfügbar.
avalanche *s.* Lawine *f.*
avarice *s.* Geiz *m.*, Habsucht *f.*
avaricious *a.*, *~ly adv.* geizig, habsüchtig.
avenge *v.t.* rächen.
avenger *s.* Rächer(in) *m.(f.)*
avenue *s.* Allee *f.*; Zugang *m.*
aver *v.t.* behaupten.
average *s.* Durchschnitt *m.*; Havarie *f.*; *on an ~,* durchschnittlich; *~ v.t. & i.* durchschnittlich fertig bringen, liefern, betragen.
averse *a.*, *~ly adv.* abgeneigt.
aversion *s.* Widerwille *m.*, Abneigung *f.*
avert *v.t.* abwenden, wegwenden.
aviary *s.* Vogelhaus *n.*
aviation *s.* Fliegen *n.*; Flugwesen *n.*
aviator *s.* Flieger(in) *m.(f.)*
avid *a.* begeistert; passioniert.
avoid *v.t.* vermeiden.
avoidable *a.* vermeidlich.
avoidance *s.* Vermeidung *f.*
avoirdupois weight *s.* Handelsgewicht *n.* (*pound* = 16 Unzen).
avouch *v.t.* behaupten, bekräftigen.
avow *v.t.* anerkennen, eingestehen.
avowal *s.* Geständnis *n.*
avowedly *adv.* eingestandenermaßen.
avuncular *a.* onkelhaft.
await *v.t.* erwarten.
awake *v.t.st.* aufwecken; *~ v.i.st.* aufwachen; *~ a.* wach.
awaken *v.t.* erwecken.
awakening *s.* Erwachen *n.*; *a rude ~,* ein böses Erwachen.
award *s.* Urteil *n.*; Spruch *m.*; Auszeichnung *f.*, Preis *m.*; Stipendium *n.*; *~ v.t.* zuerkennen; gewähren.
award-winning *a.* preisgekrönt.
aware *a.* gewahr, bewußt; *I am ~ of it,* ich weiß es.
awareness *s.* Bewußtsein *n.*; Kenntnis *f.*
away *adv.* weg, fort; abwesend.
awe *s.* Ehrfurcht *f.*; Scheu *f.*; *~ v.t.* in Furcht halten; Ehrfurcht einflößen.

awe-inspiring *a.* ehrfurchtgebietend.
awesome *a.* überwältigend.
awe-struck *a.* von Ehrfurcht ergriffen.
awful *a.*, **~ly** *adv.* (*fam.*) schrecklich.
awhile *adv.* eine Zeitlang.
awkward *a.*, **~ly** *adv.* linkisch; ungelegen.
awkwardness *s.* Unbeholfenheit *f.*; Peinlichkeit *f.*
awl *s.* Ahle *f.*, Pfriem *m.*
awning *s.* Markise *f.*; Zeltdecke *f.*

awry *adv.* schief; verkehrt.
axe *s.* Axt *f.*; Beil *n.*
axiom *s.* Axiom *n.*, Grundsatz *m.*
axiomatic(al) *a.* axiomatisch, unumstößlich.
axis *s.* (*math.*) Achse *f.*
axle *s.* Achse *f.*; **~-tree** *s.* Radachse *f.*
ay *s.* Jastimme *f.*
azalea *s.* (*bot.*) Azalee *f.*
azure *a.* himmelblau.

B

B, b *s.* der Buchstabe B oder b *n.*; (*mus.*) H, h; **B flat** b.
babble *v.i.* schwatzen; ~ *s.* Geschwätz *n.*
baboon *s.* Pavian *m.*
baby *s.* Baby *n.*, kleines Kind *n.*
baby-carriage *s.* Kinderwagen *m.*
babyfood *s.* Babynahrung *f.*
baby grand (*piano*) *s.* Stutzflügel *m.*
babyhood *s.* Säulingsalter *n.*
babyish *a.* kindisch; kindlich.
baby-sit *v.i.* babysitten.
baby-sitter *s.* Babysitter(in) *m.*(*f.*)
baby-snatcher *s.* Kindesentführer(in) *m.*(*f.*)
baby-talk *s.* Babysprache *f.*
bachelor *s.* Junggeselle *m.*; ~ *of Arts*, Bakkalaureus Artium (erster akademischer Grad) *m.*
bachelorhood *s.* Junggesellentum *n.*
bacillus *s.* Bacillus *m.*
back *s.* Rücken *m.*; Rückseite *f.*; Rücksitz (Wagen) *m.*; (Fußball) Verteidiger *m.*; ~ *of*, hinter; ~*v.t.* unterstützen; ~ *up*, zurückfahren; *to ~ a horse*, auf ein Rennpferd wetten; *gold-backing*, Golddeckung *f.*; *dollar-backed instruments*, Zahlungsmittel mit Dollardeckung; ~ *adv.* hinterwärts, zurück.
backache *s.* Rückenschmerzen *m. pl.*
backbite *v.t.st.* lästern; verleumden.
backbone *s.* Rückgrat *n.*
back-breaking *a.* äußerst mühsam; anstrengend.
backdate *v.t.* zurückdatieren.
backdoor *s.* Hintertür *f.*
backer *s.* Unterstützer *m.*
backfire *v.i.* fehlzünden, fehlschlagen.
backgammon *s.* Tricktrack *n.*
background *s.* Hintergrund *m.*
backhander *s.* Rückhandschlag *m.*
backlash *s.* Rückstoß *m.*; Gegenreaktion *f.*
backless *a.* rückenfrei.
backlog *s.* Rückstand *m.*
back-number *s.* frühere Nummer (*f.*) einer Zeitschrift oder Zeitung.
backpack *s.* Rucksack *m.*
backpedal *v.i.* rückwärts treten.
backside *s.* Rückseite *f.*; Hintere *m.*
backslide *v.i.* rückfällig werden.
backstage *s.* hinter den Kulissen.
backstairs *s.pl.* Hintertreppe *f.*
backstitch *s.* Steppstich *m.*
backstroke *s.* Rückenschwimmen *n.*
backtrack *v.i.* wieder zurückgehen; eine Kehrtwendung machen.
backward *adv.* zurück, rücklings; ~ *a.*, **~ly** *adv.* langsam; rückständig; spät.

backwardness *s.* Zurückhaltung *f.*; Rückständigkeit *f.*
backwards *adv.* nach hinten.
backwash *s.* Rückströmung *f.*; (*fig.*) Auswirkungen *pl.*
backwater *s.* Stauwasser *n.*; totes Wasser *n.*
backwoodsman *s.* Hinterwäldler *m.*
backyard *s.* Garten *m.*; Hinterhof *m.*
bacon *s.* Speck *m.*
bacterial *a.* bakteriell.
bacteriological *a.* bakteriologisch, Baktieren...
bacterium *s.* Bakterie *f.*
bad *a.*, **~ly** *adv.* schlecht; böse; schlimm; *to be badly off*, übel daran sein.
badge *s.* Abzeichen, Ehrenzeichen *n.*
badger *s.* Dachs *m.*; ~*v.t.* hetzen.
bad-tempered *a.* griesgrämig, schlechtgelaunt.
baffle *v.t.* vereiteln; verwirren; vor ein Rätsel stellen.
bafflement *s.* Verwirrung *f.*
baffling *a.* rätselhaft.
bag *s.* Sack, Beutel *m.*; Handtasche *f.*; ~ *v.t.* einsacken; ~ *v.i.* bauschen.
bagatelle *s.* Kleinigkeit, Lappalie *f.*
baggage *s.* Gepäck *n.*; ~ **allowance** *s.* Freigepäck *n.*; ~ **car** *s.* Gepäckwagen *m.*; **~check** *m.* Gepäckschein *m.* **~insurance** *s.* Reisegepäckversicherung *f.*
baggy *a.* bauschig, ausgebeult.
bagsnatcher *s.* Handtaschendieb(in) *m.*(*f.*).
bagpipe *s.* Dudelsack *m.*
bail *s.* Kaution *f.*; Bürgschaft *f.*; Bürge *m.*; *to allow* ~, Bürgschaft zulassen; *to give* ~, einen Bürgen stellen; *to release on* ~, gegen Bürgschaft freilassen; ~ *v.t.* sich verbürgen für; freibürgen; *to bail out v.i.* (*avi.*) mit Fallschirm abspringen.
bailable *a.* bürgschaftsfähig.
bailiff *s.* Gerichtsvollzieher *m.*
bairn *s.* Kind *n.*
bait *s.* Köder *m.*; ~ *v.t. & i.* ködern; hetzen.
baiting *s.* Hetze *f.*
bake *v.t. & i.* backen (im Ofen).
baker *s.* Bäcker(in) *m.*(*f.*).
bakery *s.* Bäckerei *f.*
baking: ~ **dish** *s.* Auflaufform *f.*; ~ **powder** *s.* Backpulver *n.*; ~ **sheet** *s.* Backblech *n.*; ~ **soda** *s.* Natron *m.*
balance *s.* Wage *f.*; Gleichgewicht *n.*; Bilanz *f.*; Bankguthaben *n.*; Rest *m.*; Saldo *m.*; (*fig.*) Unschlüssigkeit *f.*; Unruhe (in der Uhr) *f.*; ~ *of power* s. politisches Gleichgewicht der Mächte; ~ *of trade* s. Handelsbilanz *f.*; **~sheet** *s.* Bilanz *f.*; ~ *v.t.* wägen, wiegen; balanzieren; erwägen; ~ *v.i.* sich

ausgleichen, sich balanzieren.
balcony *s.* Balkon, Altan *m.*
bald *a.*, **~ly** *adv.* kahl.
balderdash *s.* dummes Zeug *n.*
bald-headed *a.* glatzköpfig.
balding *a.* mit beginnender Glatze.
baldly *adv.* offen; direkt; umverblümt.
baldness *s.* Kahlheit *f.*, Knappheit *f.*
bale *s.* Ballen *m.*
baleful *a.*, **~ly** *adv.* unheilvoll.
balk *s.* Balken *m.*; (*fig.*) Querstrich *m.*; ~ *v.t.* vereiteln; ~ *v.i.* scheuen (vor).
Balkan *s.* Balkan *m.*
ball *s.* Ball *m.*; Kugel *f.*; **~-joint**, ~ *and socket joint s.* Kugelgelenk *n.*; ~ *of wool s.* Wollknäuel *m.*; ~ *v.i.* sich ballen; ~ *v.t.* zusammenballen.
ball *s.* (dance) Ball *m.*; *to have a* ~, sich riesig amüsieren.
ballad *s.* Ballade *f.*, Volkslied *n.*
ballast *s.* Ballast *m.*; Schotter *m.*
ball-bearing *s.* Kugellager *n.*
ballet *s.* Ballett *n.*
ballistics *s.* Ballistik.
balloon *s.* Luftballon *m.*; **hot-air** ~, Heißluftballon.
ballot *s.* Abstimmung *f.*; Wahl durch Stimmzettel; ~ *v.t. & i.* abstimmen.
ballot-box *s.* Wahlurne *f.*
ballot-paper *s.* Stimmzettel *m.*
ball-point (pen) *s.* Kugelschreiber *m.*
ballroom *s.* Ballsaal *m.* ~ **dancing** *s.* Gesellschaftstanz *m.*
ballyhoo *s.* Wirbel *m.*; Tamtam *s.*
balm *s.* Balsam *m.*; Salböl *n.*; ~ *v.t.* balsamieren.
baloney *s.* (*fam.*) Quatsch *m.*
balsam *s.* Balsam *m.*
balsamic *a.* balsamisch.
Baltic *s.* Ostsee *f.*; ~ *a.* baltisch; *the* ~ *Sea s.* Ostsee *f.*; *the* ~ *States,* Baltikum *n.*
baluster *s.* Geländerpfosten *m.*
balustrade *s.* Geländer *n.*
bamboo *s.* Bambus *m.*
bamboozle *v.t.* hintergehen.; verwirren; verblüffen.
ban *s.* öffentliche Ächtung *f.*; Bann *m.*; amtliches Verbot *n.*; ~ *v.t.* in den Bann tun, verbieten.
banality *s.* Trivialität *f.*
banana *s.* Banane *f.*
band *s.* Band *n*; Binde *f.*; Bande *f.*; Musikkapelle *f.*; ~ *v.t.* binden, sich verbinden.
bandage *s.* Verband *m.*
band-aid *s.* Heftpflaster *n.*
bandit *s.* Bandit *m.*
bandy *v.t.* (den Ball) schlagen; wechseln; *to* ~ *about,* (Gerücht) verbreiten; ~ *v.i.* wettstreiten.; ~ *a.* krumm.
bandy-legs *s.pl.* O-Beine *n.pl.*; **~-legged** *a.* obeinig.
bane *s.* Verderben *n.*; Ruin *m.*
bang *s.* Schlag, Stoß, Knall *m.*; **big bang** *s.* Urknall *m.*; *i.* bums!; *to go* ~, explodieren, zuschlagen; ~ *v.t.* knallen, schlagen; zuschlagen.
bangle *s.* Armreif *m.*
banish *v.t.* verbannen.
banishment *s.* Verbannung *f.*
banister *s.* Geländer *n.*
banjo. *s.* Banjo *n.*
bank *s.* Ufer *n.*; Damm *m.*; Bank *f.*; ~ **account** *s.*

Bankkonto *n.*; ~ **balance** *s.* Kontostand *m.*; ~ **card** *s.* Scheckkarte *f.*; ~ *v.t.* eindämmen.
banker *s.* Bankier *m.*
bank: ~ **hold-up** *s.* Banküberfall *m.*; ~ **holiday** *s.* bürgerlicher Feiertag *m.*
banking *s.* Bankwesen *n.*
bank: ~ **manager** *s.* Zweigstellenleiter(in) *m.*(*f.*); **~note** *s.* Banknote *f.*; ~ **rate** *s.* Bankdiskont *m.*; ~ **robber** *s.* Bankräuber; **~robbery** *s.* Bankraub *m.*
bankrupt *a.* bankrott; *to go* ~, *become* ~, Konkurs machen; ~ *s.* Bankrotteur *m.*; **~'s estate** *s.* Konkursmasse *f.*; ~ *v.t.* (einen) bankrott machen.
bankruptcy *s.* Bankrott *m.*; *fraudulent* ~, betrügerischer Bankrott.
bank statement *s.* Kontoauszug *m.*
banner *s.* Standarte *f.*; Banner *n.*; Spruchband *n.*
banns *s.pl.* Aufgebot (vor der Heirat) *n.*
banquet *s.* Festmahl *n.*; Bankett *n.*
bantam *s.* Zwerghuhn *n.*; **~-weight** *s.* Bantamgewicht (Boxen).
banter *v.t.* zum besten haben; ~ *s.* Scherz, Spott *m.*
baptism *s.* Taufe *f.*; *certificate of* ~, Taufschein *m.*
baptismal *a.*, **~font,** Taufstein *m.*
baptize *v.t.* taufen.
bar *s.* Barre, Stange *f.*; Riegel, Balken, Schlagbaum *m.*; Schranken *f.pl.*; Schenktisch *m.*; Gericht *m.*; Anwaltschaft *f.*; Taktstrich *m.*; Takt (eines Musikstücks) *m.*; *to practice at the* ~, als Anwalt tätig sein; *to call to the* ~, zum Anwalt berufen; ~ *v.t.* verriegeln; hindern, schließen.
barb *s.* Widerhaken *m.*
barbarian *a.* barbarisch; ~ *s.* Barbar *m.*
barbaric *a.* barbarisch.
barbarism *s.* Barbarei *f.*
barbarity *s.* Grausamkeit *f.*
barbarous *a.*, **~ly** *adv.* roh, grausam.
barbecue *s.* Grill *m.*; Grillfest *n.*; Barbecue *m.*; ~ *v.t.* grillen; auf dem Rost braten.
barbed *a.* **~wire** *s.* Stacheldraht *m.*
barber *s.* Barbier *m.*
barbiturate *s.* Barbiturat *n.*
bard *s.* Barde, Dichter *m.*
bare *a.* bloß; nackt; ~ *v.t.* entblößen.
bareback *a.* ungesattelt; ohne Sattel.
barefaced *a.* (*fig.*) unverschämt.
barefoot(ed) *a.* barfüßig.
bareheaded *a.* barhäuptig.
barely *adv.* kaum; knapp; spärlich.
bargain *s.* Handel *m.*; Kauf *m.*; Gelegenheitskauf *m.*; *into the* ~, obendrein.
bargain *v.t.& i.* handeln, feilschen.
bargaining *s.* Handel *n.*; Verhandlungen *f. pl.*
barge *s.* Barke *f.*; Boot *m.*
baritone *s.* Bariton *m.*; Baritonstimme *f.*
bark *s.* Baumrinde *f.*; Borke *f.*; (Schiff) Barke *f.*; ~ *v.t.* abrinden; ~ *v.i.* bellen; ~ *s.* Bellen *n.*
barley *s.* Gerste *f.*
barley-corn *s.* Gerstenkorn *n.*
barmaid *s.* Bardame *f.*
barman *s.* Barmann *m.*
barmy *a.* hefig; blödsinnig, verdreht.
barn *s.* Scheune *f.*
barn-floor *s.* Dreschtenne *f.*
barn-owl *s.* Schleiereule *f.*
barnyard *s.* Wirtschaftshof *m.*
barometer *s.* Barometer *m.*

barometric *a.* barometrisch; ~ *pressure* Luftdruck *m.*

baron *s.* Freiherr, Baron *m.*; **press** ~ Pressezar *m.*

baroness *s.* Baronin *f.*; Freifrau *f.*

baronet *s.* Baronet *m.*

baronetcy *s.* Baronetswürde *f.*

baroque *s.* (*Kunst*) Barock *m.*; *a.* barock.

barrack *s.* Hütte *f.*; ~**s** *pl.* Kaserne *f.*

barrage *s.* Talsperre *f.*; Damm *m.*, Wehr *n.*; (*mil.*) Sperrfeuer *n.*

barrel *s.* Faß *n.*; Flintenlauf *m.*

barrel-organ *s.* Drehorgel *f.*

barren *a.*, ~**ly** *adv.* unfruchtbar.

barrette *s.* Haarspange *f.*

barricade *s.* Barrikade *f.*; ~ *v.t.* verrammeln; hindern.

barrier *s.* Schlagbaum *m.*; Barriere *f.*; Grenze *f.*; (*fig.*) Hindernis *n.*; ~**s** *pl.* Schranken *f.pl.*

barring *pr.* ausgenommen; außer im Fall.

barrister *s.* (vor Gericht auftretender) Rechtsanwalt *m.*

bar-room *s.* Bar *f.*

barrow *s.* Trage *f.*; Schiebkarren *m.*

bartender *s.* Barkeeper *m.*

barter *v.t.* & *i.* tauschen; ~ *s.* Tauschhandel *m.*

basalt *s.* Basalt *m.*

base *a.*, ~**ly** *adv.* niedrig; verächtlich; (von Metallen) unedel; ~ *s.* Grundfläche *f.*; Grundlinie (des Dreiecks), *f.*; Grund *m.*; Fußgestell *n.*; (*mil.*) Stützpunkt *m.*; (*mus.*) Basis *f.*; (*chem.*) Basis *f.*

baseball *s.* Grundballspiel *n.*

baseboard *s.* Fußleiste *f.*

baseless *a.* grundlos.

basement *s.* Kellergeschoß *n.*

base pay *s.* Grundgehalt *n.*

bash *v.t.* verprügeln; schlagen; ~ *s.* Party *f.*

bashful *a.*, ~**ly** *adv.* schamhaft.

basic *a.* grundlegend; (*geol.*) basisch-; ~ **salary** *s.* Grundgehalt *n.*

basically *adv.* im Grunde.

basics *s.* Grundlagen *pl.*, Wesentliches *n.*

basil *s.* Basilikum *n.*

basilica *s.* Basilika *f.*

basin *s.* Becken *n.*; Schale *f.*

basis *s.* Grundlage *f.*; Basis *f.*; Grundbestandteil *m.*

bask *v.t.* & *i.* sonnnen; sich sonnen.

basket *s.* Korb *m.*

basque *s.* Baske *m.*; Baskin *f.*; ~ *a.* baskisch.

bas-relief *s.* Basrelief *n.*

bass *s.* (*mus.*) Baß *m.*; (fish) Barsch *m.*

bassoon *s.* Fagott *n.*

bast *s.* Bast *m.*

bastard *s.* Bastard *m.*

baste *v.t.* mit Fett begießen.

bastion *s.* Bollwerk *n.*

bat *s.* Fledermaus *f.*; Knüttel *m.*; Schlagholz *n.*, Schläger (im Baseball) *m.*

bate *v.t.* (Preis) ablassen, verringern; *with* ~*d breath* mit angehaltenem Atem.

bath *s.* Bad *n.*; Badewanne *f.*; ~**chair** *s.* Rollstuhl *m.*

bathe *v.t.* baden; ~ *v.i.* ein Bad nehmen; ~ *s.* Bad (Handlung) *n.*

bathing cap *s.* Badehaube *f.*

bathing suit *s.* Badeanzug *m.*

bath: ~**mat** *s.* Badematte *f.*; ~**robe** *s.* Bademantel *m.*, ~**room** *s.* Badezimmer *n.*; Toilette *f.*; ~**salts** *s.pl.* Badesalz *n.*; ~**towel** *s.* Badetuch *n.*; ~**tub** *s.* Badewanne *f.*

batiste *s.* Batist *m.*

baton *s.* Taktstock *m.*, Stab *m.*

batsman *s.* Schläger *m.*, Schlagmann *m.*

battalion *s.* Bataillon *n.*

batten *s.* Latte *f.*, Leiste *f.*

batter *v.t.* schlagen, zerschlagen, mißhandeln.

batter *s.* Backteig *m.*; Eierkuchenteig *m.*

battery *s.* Angriff *m.*; Batterie *f.*; eine ganze Reihe.

battery: ~**-charger** *s.* Aufladegerät *n.*; ~**-operated** *a.* batteriebetrieben.

battle *s.* Schlacht *f.*; Schlägerei *f.*; ~ *v.i.* kämpfen, fechten.

battleaxe *s.* Streitaxt *f.*; (*pej.*) Schreckschraube *f.*

battle-cruiser *s.* (*nav.*) Schlachtkreuzer *m.*

battlefield *s.* Schlachtfeld *n.*

battlement *s.* Zinne *f.*

battleship *s.* (*nav.*) Schlachtschiff *n.*

battue *s.* Treibjagd *f.*

bauble *s.* Spielzeug *n.*; Tand *m.*

bauxite *s.* Bauxit *m.*

Bavaria *s.* Bayern *n.*

Bavarian *a.* bayrisch; ~ *s.* Bayer(in) *m.*(*f.*)

bawdy *a.* zweideutig; obszön.

bawl *v.t.* & *i.* laut schreien; ausrufen.

bay *a.* rotbraun; ~**horse** *s.* Braune *m.*; ~ **window** *s.* Erkerfenster *n.*; ~ *s.* Bucht *f.*; Fach *m.*; Nische, Abteilung *f.*, Erker *m.*; Lorbeer *m.*; *to stand at* ~, gestellt sein, in Bedrängnis; ~ *v.i.* bellen; blöken; ~ *v.t.* jagen.

bayleaf *s.* Lorbeerblatt *n.*

bayonet *s.* Bajonett *n.*; ~ *v.t.* mit dem Bajonett erstechen.

bazaar *s.* Basar *m.*

be *v.i.ir.* sein; (*pass.*) werden; *to* ~ *off,* sich fortmachen; *to* ~ *in,* zuhause sein.

beach *s.* Strand *m.*; Gestade *n.*; ~ *v.t.* auf den Strand setzen.

beach ball *s.* Wasserball *m.*

beachhead *s.* (*mil.*) Brückenkopf *m.*

beacon *s.* Leuchtfeuer *n.*; Bake *f.*

bead *s.* Kügelchen *n.*; Pearle *f.*

beadle *s.* Pedell *m.*; Büttel *m.*

beak *s.* Schnabel *m.*; Tulle *f.*; Hakennase *f.*

beaker *s.* Becher *m.*

beam *s.* Balken *m.*; Strahl *m.*; Deichsel *f.*; ~ *v.i.* strahlen.

beam-ends *s.pl. to be on one's* ~, (finanziell) ruiniert sein.

beaming *a.* strahlend.

bean *s.* Bohne *f.*; *French* ~, grüne Bohne *f.*; *broad* ~, Saubohne *f.*

bean: ~**bag** *s.* Knautschsessel *m.*; ~**pole** *s.* Bohnenstange; ~**sprout** *s.* Sojabohnenkeim *m.*; ~**stalk** *s.* Bohnenstengel *m.*

bear *s.* Bär *m.*; ~ *v.t.* & *i.st.* tragen, bringen; dulden; gebären; *to* ~ *company,* Gesellschaft leisten; *to* ~ *in mind,* nicht vergessen; *to* ~ *on,* Bezug haben, wirken auf; *to* ~ *out,* bestätigen; *to* ~ *witness,* Zeugnis ablegen.

bearable *a.* erträglich.

beard *s.* Bart *m.*

bearded *a.* bärtig.

beardless *a.* bartlos.
bearer *s.* Träger *m.*; Wechselinhaber *m.*
bearing *s.* Tragweite *f.*; Lage, Haltung *f.*; Stütze, Höhe *f.*; Peilung *f.*; *to take one's ~s*, sich orientieren.
bearish *a.* bärenhaft.
bearpaw *s.* Radkralle *f.*
bear market *s.* Markt mit fallenden Preisen.
bearskin *s.* Bärenfell *n.*
beast *s.* Vieh, Tier *n.*; Bestie *f.*; Biest *n.*
beastly *a.* viehisch; (*fig.*) scheußlich, niederträchtig.
beat *v.t. & i.st.* schlagen; zertossen; besiegen; klopfen; *to ~ off,* zurückschlagen; *to ~ time,* den Takt schlagen; *to ~ up,* verprügeln; *~ s.* Schlag *m.*; Revier *n.*, Runde *f.*
beatification *s.* Seligsprechung *f.*
beatify *v.t.* seligsprechen.
beating *s.* Schläge *pl.*; Prügel *pl.*
beatitude *s.* Seligkeit *f.*
beau *s.* Stutzer *m.*; Verehrer *m.*
beautician *s.* Kosmetiker(in) *m.(f.)*
beautiful *a.*, **~ly** *adv.* schön.
beautify *v.t.* verschönern.
beauty *s.* Schönheit *f.*
beauty: ~ contest *s.* Schönheitswettbewerb *m.*; **~ parlor, ~ salon** *s.* Schönheitssalon.
beaver *s.* Biber *m.*
becalm *v.t.* besänftigen.
because *c.* weil; *~ of,* wegen.
beck *s. at a person's ~ and call,* jm. zur Verfügung stehen.
beckon *v.t. & i.* winken; locken.
becloud *v.t.* umwölken.
become *v.i. & t.st.* werden; sich schicken; anstehen.
becoming *a.*, **~ly** *adv.* anständig.; vorteilhaft.
bed *s.* Bett *n.*; Beet *n.*; Schicht *f.* (*mech.*) Bett *n.*, Unterbau *m.*; *~ v.t.* betten.
bedaub *v.t.* besudeln.
bedbug *s.* Wanze *f.*
bedclothes *s.* Bettzeug *n.*
bedding *s.* Bettzeug *n.*; **~ plant** *s.* Freilandpflanze *f.*
bedeck *v.t.* schmücken.
bedevil *v.t.* durcheinanderbringen.
bedfellow *s.* Schlafkamerad *m.*
bedjacket *s.* Bettjacke *f.*
bedlam *s.* Tollhaus *n.*
bedlinen *s.* Bettwäsche *f.*
bedouin *s.* Beduine *f.*; Beduinin *f.*
bed: ~pan *s.* Bettpfanne *f.*; **~post** *s.* Bettpfosten *m.*
bedraggled *a.* verschmutzt.
bedridden *a.* bettlägerig.
bedrock *s.* Felssohle *f.*; Basis *f.*
bedroom *s.* Schlafzimmer *n.*
bedsore *s.* wundgelegene Stelle.
bedspread *s.*, Tagesdecke *f.*
bedstead *s.* Bettstelle *f.*
bedtime *s.* Schlafenszeit *f.*
bee *s.* Biene *f.*
beech *s.* Buche *f.*
beechen *a.* buchen.
beech-nut *s.* Buchecker *f.*
beef *s.* Rindfleisch *n.*; Rind *n.*; **~~cattle,** Mastvieh *n.*
beefsteak *s.* Beefsteak *n.*
beefy *a.* muskulös; bullig.

beehive *s.* Bienenstock *m.*
beekeeper *s.* Imker *m.*
beep *s.* Piepton *m.*; *~ v.i.* piepen.
beeper *s.* Funkrufempfänger *m.*
beer *s.*, Bier *n.*; *small ~,* Kleinigkeiten *pl.*
beeswax *s.* Bienenwachs *n.*
beet *s.* (rote) Rübe *f.*
beetle *s.* Käfer *m.*
beet: ~root *s.* Runkelrübe *f.*; **~ sugar,** Rübenzucker *m.*
befall *v.t.st.* zustoßen, widerfahren; *~ v.i.* sich ereignen.
befit *v.t.* sich schicken.
before *pr.* vor; *~ c.* bevor, ehe; *~ adv.* vorn; früher; schon einmal.
beforehand *adv.* voraus, im voraus.
befoul *v.t.* besudeln.
befriend *v.t.* sich anfreunden mit; sich annehmen.
beg *v.t.* bitten, betteln; *to ~ the question,* die Streitfrage als bewiesen voraussetzen; *I ~ your pardon?,* Verzeihung, entschuldigen Sie, bitte!; *~ v.i.* betteln gehen; sich erlauben.
beget *v.t.st.* zeugen, erzeugen.
beggar *s.* Bettler *m.*; Lump *m.*; *~ v.t.* zum Bettler machen.
beggarly *a.* bettelhaft; ärmlich.
beggary *s.* Bettelei *f.*; *to reduce to ~,* an den Bettelstab bringen.
begin *v.t. & i.st.* anfangen.
beginner *s.* Anfänger(in) *m.(f.)*
beginning *s.* Anfang *m.*; **~s** *pl.* Anfangsgründe *m.pl.*
begone *i.* fort! packe dich!
begonia *s.* Begonie *f.*, Schiefblatt *s.*
begrudge *v.t.* mißgönnen.
beguile *v.t.* betören; verführen; betrügen.
behalf *s. on ~,* im Namen, behufs, wegen; *in ~ of,* im Interesse von, für.
behave *v.i.* sich betragen.
behavior *s.* Betragen *n.*
behaviorism *s.* Behaviorismus.
behead, *v.t.* enthaupten.
behest *s.* Befehl *m.*
behind *pr. & adv.* hinter, zurück; *~ s.* Hintern *m.*
behindhand *a.* im Rückstande.
behold *v.t.st.* erblicken, betrachten.
beholden *a.* verpflichtet.
behoove *v.i.* sich ziemen.
being *s.* Dasein *n.*; Wesen, Geschöpf *n.*
belabor *v.t.* jn. bearbeiten; jm. zusetzen.
Belarus *s.* Weißrußland *n.*
belated *a.* verspätet.
belch *v.i. & t.* rülpsen; *~ s.* Rülpser *m.*
beleaguer *v.t.* belagern.
belfry *s.* Glockenturm. *m.*
Belgian *s.* Belgier(in) *m.(f.)*; *a.* belgisch.
Belgium *s.* Belgien *n.*
belie *v.t.* Lügen strafen; enttäuschen; widersprechen.
belief *s.* Glaube *m.*
believable *a.* glaubhaft; glaubwürdig.
believe *v.t. & i.* glauben, vertrauen; *to ~ in,* glauben an.
believer *s.* Gläubige *m./f.*
belittle *v.t.* herabsetzen, (boshaft) verkleinern.
bell *s.* Glocke *f.*; Klingel *f.*; *to ring the ~,* klingeln; *to answer the ~,* auf vorheriges Klingeln öffnen.

bell-circuit s. (elek.) Klingelleitung f.
bell-founder s. Glockengießer m.
bell-foundry s. Glockengießerei f.
bellicose a. kriegerisch.
belligerent a. kriegführend; kriegerisch; aggressiv.
bellow v.i. brüllen.
bellows s.pl. Blasebalg m.
bell push s. Klingel(knopf) f.(m.)
bell-rope s. Klingelzug m.
bell-tower s. Glockenturm m.
bellwether s. Leithammel m.
belly s. Bauch m.; ~ v.t. schwellen.
belly: ~ache s. Bauchschmerzen m. pl.; ~ button s. Nabel m.; ~ dancer s. Bauchtänzerin f.; ~landing s. Bauchlandung f.
belong v.i. gehören; betreffen.
belongings s.pl. Habe f.
Belorussia s. Weißrußland n.
Belorussian s. Weißrusse m.; Weißrussin f.; ~ a. weißrussisch.
beloved a. geliebt.
below pr. unter; ~ adv. unten.
belt s. Gürtel m.; Gehenk n.; Treibriemen m.; ~ v.t. umgürten.
bemoan v.t. beklagen, beweinen.
bemused a. verwirrt; gedankenverloren.
bench s. Bank f.; Richterbank f.; Werkbank.
benchmark s. Maßstab m.
bend v.t.ir biegen; ~ v.i. sich biegen; ~ s. Biegung f.; Kurve f.
beneath pr. unter; ~adv. unten.
benediction s. Segen m.
benefactor s. Wohltäter m.
benefactress s. Wohltäterin f.
benefice s. Pfründe f.
beneficence s. Wohltätigkeit f.
beneficent a. wohltätig.
beneficial a., ~ly adv. heilsam; wohltuend; vorteilhaft.
beneficiary s. Nutznießer.
benefit s. Wohltat f.; Vorteil m.; Benefizvorstellung f.; Vorrecht m.; (Versicherung) Unterstützung f.; Geld n.; ~ v.t. & i. Vorteil bringen; heilsam sein; to ~ by, Nutzen ziehen von.
benevolence s. Wohlwollen n.; Gunst f.
benevolent a., ~ly adv. wohlwollend.
benign a., ~ly adv. gütig, mild; (med.) gutartig.
benignant a. gütig, wohltätig.
bent a. gebogen; ~ on, versessen auf; ~ s. Biegung f.; Neigung f.
benumb v.t. betäuben, erstarren.
benzene (-ine) s. Benzin n.
benzole (-line) s. Benzol n.
bequeath v.t. vermachen.
bequest s. Vermächtnis n.
bereave v.t.st. & r. berauben.
bereavement s. Verlust m.; Trauerfall m.
bereft a. to be ~ of, etw. verloren haben.
beret s. Baskenmutze f.
bergamot s. Bergamotte (Birne) f.
berry s. Beere f.; (Kaffee)bohne f.
berserk a. rasend; to go ~ durchdrehen.
berth s. Ankerplatz m.; (nav.) Koje f., Schiffsbett n., Kajütenbett n.; Posten m.
beseech v.t.ir. bitten, anflehen.
beseechingly adv. flehentlich.

beseem v.t. sich schicken.
beset v.t.st. heimsuchen; plagen.
besetting sin Gewohnheitssünde f.
beside pr. neben; ~ onself, außer sich; ~ the mark, weit vom Ziel.
besides pr. außer; ~ adv. außerdem.
besiege v.t. belagern.
besmear v.t. beschmieren.
besmirch v.t. besudeln.
bespectacled a. bebrillt.
bespoke tailor s. Maßschneider m.
best a. & adv. best; aufs beste; am besten; ~ s. Beste n.; to make the ~ of, mit etwas tun was man kann; to do one's ~, tun was man kann; as ~ he could, so gut er konnte; to the ~ of one's abilities, nach besten Kräften.
bestial a., ~ly adv. tierisch; barbarisch; bestialisch.
bestiality s. viehisches Wesen n.
bestir v.refl. sich rühren, sich regen.
best man s. Trauzeuge m.
bestow v.t. verleihen.
bestowal s. Verleihung f.
bestseller s. Reißer (Buch) m.; Bestseller m.
bet s. Wette f.; ~ v.t. wetten um.
betray v.t. verraten; verführen.
betrayal s. Verrat m.
betroth v.t. verloben.
betrothal s. Verlobung f.
better a. & adv. besser; lieber; mehr; so much the ~, desto besser; you had ~ go, Sie tun wohl am besten, hinzugehen; to think ~ of it, sich eines Bessern besinnen; ~ s. Vorteil; to get the ~ of a person, einem den Vorteil abgewinnen; ~s pl. Vorgesetzte m.pl.; ~ v.t. & i. verbessern; besser werden.
betterment s. Verbesserung f.
betting s. Wetten n.
between, betwixt pr. zwischen; they did it ~ them, sie taten es zusammen; ~ you and me, unter uns.
bevel a. schräg, schief; ~ s. Schräge f., schräger Anschnitt m., (mech.) Fase f.; ~gear s. (mech.) Kegelrad n.; ~ v.t. abschrägen, facettieren.
beverage s. Getränk n.
bevy s. Schar f.; Gesellschaft f.
bewail v.t. betrauern; beklagen.
beware v.i. sich hüten.
bewilder v.t. verwirren, bestürzt machen.
bewildering a. verwirrend.
bewilderment s. Verwirrung.
bewitch v.t. behexen, bezaubern; verzaubern.
bewitching a. bezaubernd.
beyond pr. über, jenseits; ~adv. darüber hinaus.
bias s. Neigung m.; Vorurteil n.; ~ v.t. auf eine Seite neigen.
bib s. Lätzchen n.
Bible s. Bibel f.
biblical a. biblisch.
bibliographer s. Bibliograph(in) m.(f.)
bibliography s. Bibliographie f.
bibliophile s. Bücherfreund m.
bicarbonate, ~ of soda, Natronbikarbonat n.
bicker v.i. streiten, zanken; glitzern.
bickerings s.pl. Gezänk n.
bicycle s. Fahrrad n., Zweirad n.
bid v.t.ir. befehlen; einladen; wünschen, bieten; (Kartenspiel) ansagen; to ~ fair, Aussicht geben auf; ~ s. (Auktions-)Gebot n.; no ~, ich passe

(Kartenspiel).

bidder *s.* Bieter *m.*; *highest ~ s.* Meistbietender *m.*

bidding *s.* Befehl *m.*; *(com.)* Gebot *n.*

bide *v.t.* ertragen; *~ v.i.* abwarten.

biennial *a.* zweijährig.

bier *d.* Bahre *f.*

biff *s.* Klapps *m.*; *v.t.* hauen.

bifocal *a.* Bifokal-; *~ s. pl.* Bifokalgläser *pl.*

bifurcated *a.* gabelförmig gespalten.

big *a.* groß, stark, dick; *to talk ~*, prahlen.

bigamist *s.* Bigamist *m.*; Bigamistin *f.*

bigamy *s.* Bigamie *f.*, Doppelehe *f.*

big: *~bang s.* Urknall *m.*; *~-circulation a.* auflagenstark (Zeitung); *~-headed a.* eingebildet; *~-hearted a.* großherzig; *~mouth s.* Großmaul *n.*

bight *s.* Bai, Bucht *f.*

bigot *s.* blinder Anhänger; Frömmler *m.*

bigoted *a.* bigott; eifernd.

bigotry *s.* Frömmelei *f.*

big top *s.* Zirkuszelt *n.*

big-wig *s.* (*fig.*) großes Tier n.

bike *s.* Fahrrad *n.*

bilateral *a.* zweiseitig; bilateral.

bilberry *s.* Heidelbeere *f.*

bile *s.* Galle *f.*

bilingual *a.* zweisprachig.

bilious *a.* gallig.

bilk *v.t.* beschwindeln, betrügen.

bill *s.* Schnabel *m.*; Hippe *f.*; Rechnung *f.*; Wechsel *m.*; Zettel *m.*; Gesetzentwurf *m.*; *~ of exchange*, Wechsel *m.*; *~ of lading*, Konnossement *n.*, Frachtbrief *m.*

billboard *s.* Reklametafel *f.*

billet *s.* Quartierzettel *n.*; Quartier n.; Schein *m.*; *~ v.t.* einquartieren.

billfold *s.* Brieftasche *f.*

billiard-cue *s.* Queue (n).

billiards *s.pl.* Billiard(spiel) *n.*

billiard-table *s.* Billiardtisch *m.*

billow *s.* Welle *f.*; *~ v.i.* anschwellen.

billy-goat *s.* Ziegenbock *m.*

bimonthly *a.* zweimonatlich.

bin *s.* Behälter *m.*, Kasten *m.*

bind *v.t.* binden; verpflichten; *to ~ over,* (*law*) durch Gerichtsbeschluß verpflichten; *to be bound over for two years,* zwei Jahre Bewährungsfrist erhalten; *clothbound a.* in Leinen (Kaliko) gebunden (Buch); *leatherbound a.* in Leder gebunden.

binder *s.* (Buch)Binder *m.*, Binde *f.*

binding *s.* Einband *m.*; *~ a.* bindend.

bindweed *s.* (*bot.*) Winde *f.*

binge *s.* Gelage *n.*

binocular *a.* für beide Augen; *~s s.pl.*, Fernglas *n.*

biochemical *a.* biochemisch.

biochemist *s.* Biochemiker(in) *m.*(*f.*)

biochemistry *s.* Biochemie *f.*

biographer *s.* Biograph(in) *m.*(*f.*)

biographical *a.* biographisch.

biography *s.* Biographie *f.*, Lebensbeschreibung *f.*

biological *a.* biologisch; *~warfare s.* biologische Kriegsführung. *f.*

biologist *s.* Biologe *m.*, Biologin *f.*

biology *s.* Biologie *f.*

biotechnology *s.* Biotechnologie *f.*

bipartite *a.* zweiteilig; Zweimächte. . .

biplane *s.* Doppeldecker *m.*

birch *s.* Birke *f.*; Rute *f.*

bird *s.* Vogel *m.*; *~ of passage*, Zugvogel *m.*; *~ of prey*, Raubvogel *m.*

bird-cage *s.* Vogelbauer *m.*; Vogelkäfig *m.*

bird-house *s.* Nistkasten *m.*

birdie *s.* Vögelchen *n.*

bird-sanctuary *s.* Vogelschutzgebiet *n.*

bird's eye *s.* aus der Vogelschau gesehen; *~ view s.* Vogelperspektive *f.*

bird's nest *s.* Vogelnest *n.*

bird-watcher *s.* Vogelbeobachter(in) *m.*(*f.*)

birth *s.* Geburt *f.*

birth-certificate *s.* Geburtsurkunde *f.*

birth-control *s.* Geburtenkontrolle, Geburtenbeschränkung *f.*

birthday *s.* Geburtstag *m.*

birthmark *s.* Muttermal *n.*

birthplace *s.* Geburtsort *m.*

birth rate *s.* Geburtenziffer *f.*

biscuit *s.* Keks *m.*; kleines Brötchen *n.*

bisect *v.t.* halbieren.

bisexual *a.* bisexuell.

bison *s.* Bison *m.*; Wisent *n.*

bishop *s.* Bischof *m.*; Läufer (im Schach) *m.*

bishopric *s.* Bistum *n.*

bismuth *s.* Wismut *m.*

bit *s.* Bißchen *n.*; Stückchen *n.* Pferdegebiß *n.*; Schlüsselbart *m.*; (*comp.*) Bit *n.*

bitch *s.* Hündin *f.*; (*pej.*) Miststück *n.*

bite *v.t.st.* beißen; *~ v.i.st.* greifen; *~ s.* Biß *m.*

biting *a.* beißend; bissig.

bitter *a.*, *~ly adv.* bitter; erbittert.

bitterness *s.* Bitterkeit *f.*; Gram *m.*

bitumen *s.* Bitumen *f.*

bituminous *a.* bituminös.

bivouac *s.* Biwak *n.*, Beiwacht *f.*; *~ v.i.* biwakieren.

biweekly *a.* zweiwöchentlich.

bizarre *a.* bizarr.

blab *v.t.& i.* ausschwatzen.

black *a.* schwarz, dunkel; finster; *~ s.* Schwärze *f.*; Trauer *f.*; Schwarze *m./f.*; *~ v.t.* schwärzen; (Stiefel) wichsen.

blackball *s.* schwarze Wahlkugel *f.*; *~ v.t.* hinausballotieren.

blackberry *s.* Brombeere *f.*; *~ v.t.* Brombeeren pflücken.

blackbird *s.* Amsel *f.*

blackboard *s.* Wandtafel *f.*

blacken *v.t. & i.* schwärzen; schwarz werden.

blackhead *s.* Mitesser *m.*

black hole *s.* schwarzes Loch.

blackish *a.* schwärzlich.

blackleg *s.* Gauner *m.*; Streikbrecher *m.*

blacklist *s.* schwarze Liste; *~ v.t.* auf die schwarze Liste setzen.

blackmail *s.* Erpressung *f.*; *~ v.t.* Geld erpressen von.

black market *s.* schwarzer Markt *m.*

blackness *s.* Schwärze *f.*; Finsternis *f.*

blackout *s.* (Luftschutz) Verdunkelung *f.*

black-pudding *s.* Blutwurst *f.*

blacksmith *s.* Schmied *m.*

blackthorn *s.* Schlehdorn *m.*

black tie *s.* schwarze Fliege (zum Smoking).

black widow *s.* schwarze Witwe.

bladder *s.* Blase *f.*

blade *s.* Blatt, Halm *m.*; Klinge *f.*
blame *v.t.* tadeln; ~ *s.* Tadel *m.*; Schuld *f.*
blameable *a.*, **~bly** *adv.* tadelhaft.
blameless *a.*, **~ly** *adv.* untadelhaft.
blameworthy *a.* tadelnswürdig.
blanch *v.t.* weiß machen, bleichen.
blancmange *s.* Flammeri *m.*
bland *a.* sanft, gütig; glattzüngig.
blandishment *s.* Schmeichelei.
blandness *s.* Verbindlichkeit *f.*; Freundlichkeit *f.*
blank *a.*, **~ly** *adv.* weiß; unbeschrieben, leer; verwirrt; reimlos; (*com.*) Blanko; ~ *s.* Weiße *n.*; leeres Blatt *n.*; leerer Raum *m.*; Niete *f.*; ~ *cartridge*, Platzpatrone *f.*; ~ *check*, Blankoscheck *m.*; ~ *verse*, reimloser Vers *m.*
blanket *s.* Decke *f.*; ~ *v.t.* bedecken.
blankly *a.* verdutzt.
blare *v.i.* blöken, brüllen; schmettern.
blasé *a.* blasiert.
blaspheme *v.t.* (Gott) lästern.
blasphemous *a.*, **~ly** *adv.* gotteslästerlich.
blasphemy *s.* Gotteslästerung *f.*
blast *s.* Windstoß *m.*; Schall, Trompetenstoß *m.*; Explosion *f.*; ~ *v.t.* sprengen; versengen; zerstören.
blast-furnace *s.* Hochofen *m.*
blast-off *s.* Abheben *n.*
blast-pipe *s.* Dampfauslaßrohr (der Lokomotive) *n.*
blatant *a.* offensichtlich, unverhohlen.
blaze *s.* Lichtstrahl *m.*; Flamme *f.*; weißer Fleck, Blesse *f.*; ~ *v.i.* flammen, leuchten; ~ *v.t.* ausposaunen.
blazer *s.* farbige Flanelljacke *f.*
blazon *s.* Wappenschild *n.*; ~ *v.t.* schildern; ausposaunen.
blazonry *s.* Wappenkunde *f.*; Zurschaustellung *f.*
bleach *v.t. & i.* bleichen; weiß werden.
bleak *a.*, **~ly** *adv.* öde; rauh, kalt.
bleary *a.* trübe.
blear-eyed *a.* triefäugig.
bleat *v.i.* blöken; ~ *s.* Blöken *n.*
bleed *v.i.ir.* bluten; ~ *v.t.st.* zur Ader lassen.
bleeding *s.* Blutung *f.*
bleep *s.* Piepen *n.*; ~ *v.t.* piepen.
blemish *s.* Schandfleck *m.*; Schande *f.*; ~ *v.t.* verunstalten, entehren.
blend *v.t. & i.* vermischen; sich mischen; ~ *s.* Mischung (*f.*) von Tee, Kaffee, Tabaken, etc.
blender *s.* Mixer *m.*; Mixgerät *n.*
bless *v.t.* segnen, beglücken.
blessed *a.* gesegnet, selig; verwünscht.
blessing *s.* Segen *m.*
blight *s.* Melhtau *m.*; Fäule *f.*, Schandfleck *m.*; ~ *v.t.* verderben.
blind *a.* blind; ~ *alley*, Sackgasse *f.*; ~ *s.* Blende *f.*; Vorwand *m.*; Rouleau *n.*; Venetian ~ *s.* Jalousie *f.*; ~ *v.t.* blind machen; blenden.
blindfold *a. & adv.* blindlings; ~ *v.t.* die Augen verbinden.
blinding *a.* blendend; grell.
blindman's-buff *s.* Blindekuh(spiel) *n.*
blindness *s.* Blindheit *f.*
blindworm *s.* Blindschleiche *f.*
blink *s.* Blinken *n.*; ~ *v.i.* blinzeln; ~ *v.t.* nicht sehen wollen.
blinker *s.* Scheuklappen *f. pl.*

bliss *s.* Wonne, Seligkeit *f.*
blissful *a.*, **~ly** *adv.* wonnevoll, selig.
blister *s.* Blase *f.*; Bläschen *f.*; ~ *v.t. & i.* Blasen bekommen.
blistering *a.* ätzend; vernichtend (Kritik).
blithe *a.*, **~ly** *adv.* munter, lustig.
blitz *s.* Luftangriff *m.*; Blitzkrieg *m.*; ~ *v.t.* bombardieren.
blizzard *s.* Schneesturm *m.*
bloat *v.t. & i.* aufschwellen.
bloated *a.* aufgedunsen; (*fig.*) aufgeblasen.
blob *s.* Tropfen *m.*; Klecks *m.*
bloc *s.* (*pol.*) Block *m.*
block *s.* Block, Klotz *m.*; Häuserviereck *n.*; Versperrung, Stockung *f.*; ~ *v.t.* versperren, blockieren, verstopfen; *blocked account*, Sperrkonto *n.*
blockade *s.* Blockade *f.*; *to run the* ~, die Blockade brechen; **~runner** *s.* Blockadebrecher *m.*; ~ *v.t.* blockieren.
blockage *s.* Block *m.*; (Röhre) Verstopfung *f.*
block: ~buster *s.* Knüller *m.*; **~capital** *s.* Blockbuchstabe; **~head** *s.* Dummkopf *m.*
blockish *a.*, **~ly** *adv.* tölpisch.
block letters *s.pl.* Blockschrift *f.*
bloke *s.* (*fam.*) Kerl *m.*
blond(e) *a.* blond; ~ *s.* Blondine *f.*
blood *s.* Blut *n.*; *related by* ~, blutsverwandt.
blood: ~bank *s.* Blutbank *f.*; **~-bath** *s.* Blutbad *n.*; **~cell** *s.* Blutkörperchen *n.*; **~clot** *s.* Blutgerinnsel *n.*; **~count** *s.* Blutsenkung *f.*
bloodcurdling *a.* grauenerregend.
blood donor *s.* Blutspender *m.*
blood group *s.* (*med.*) Blutgruppe *f.*
bloodhorse *s.* Vollblutpferd *n.*
bloodhound *s.* Bluthund *m.*
bloodless *a.* blutlos; unblutig.
blood-orange *s.* Blutorange *f.*
blood poisoning *s.* Blutvergiftung *f.*
blood pressure *s.* Blutdruck *m.*
blood pudding *s.* Blutwurst *f.*
blood-relation *s.* Blutsverwandter *m.*
blood-relationship *s.* Blutsverwandtschaft *f.*
bloodshed *s.* Blutvergießen *n.*
bloodshot *a.* blutunterlaufen (Augen).
bloodthirsty *a.* blutdürstig.
blood transfusion *s.* Blutübertragung, Bluttransfusion *f.*
blood vessel *s.* Blutgefäß *n.*
bloody *a.* blutig; blutdürstig; (*sl.*) verdammt!
bloom *s.* Blüte, Blume *f.*; ~ *v.i.* blühen.
bloomer *s.* (*sl.*) Schnitzer, Fehler *m.*
blooming *a.* blühend; verfixt.
blossom *s.* Blüte *f.*; *to be in* ~, in Blüte sein, blühen; ~ *v.i.* blühen.
blot *s.* Klecks *m.*; Schandfleck *m.*; ~ *v.t.* klecksen; *to* ~ *out*, auslöschen.
blotch *s.* Fleck *m.*; Hautfleck *m.*; ~ *v.t.* beklecksen.
blotter *s.* Schreibunterlage *f.*
blotting pad *s.* Löscher *m.*
blotting paper *s.* Löschpapier *n.*
blouse *s.* Bluse *f.*
blow *s.* Schlag, Stoß *m.*; Hieb *m.*; ~ *v.i.st.* wehen; schnauben; schallen; blühen; ~ *v.t.* blasen, hauchen; *to* ~ *one's nose*, sich schneuzen; *to* ~ *over*, vorübergehen, sich legen; *to* ~ *up*, sprengen; *to* ~ *a kiss*, eine Kußhand zuwerfen.

blower *s.* Gebläse *n.*
blowgun *s.* Spritzpistole *f.*
blowlamp *s.* Lötlampe *f.*
blowpipe *s.* Blasrohr, Lötrohr *n.*
blowy *a.* windig.
blowzy *a.* rotbäckig, pausbäckig; schlampig.
blubber *s.* Wallfischspeck *m.*; ~ *v.i.* plärren, schluchzen.
bludgeon *s.* Knüppel *m.*
blue *a.* blau; ~ *s.* Blau *m.*; *the blues s.pl.* Trübsinn *m.*; *out of the ~,* aus heiterem Himmel; ~ *v.t.* blau färben.
blueberry *s.* Blaubeere *f.*
blue: ~**bottle** *s.* Schmeißfliege *f.*; ~**cheese** *s.* Blauschimmelkäse *m.*; ~**collar (worker)** *s.* Arbeiter(in) *m.(f.)*
bluedevils *s.pl.* Trübsinn *m.*
bluejacket *s.* Blaujacke *f.,* Matrose *m.*
blueness *s.* Bläue *f.*
blue pencil *s.* Blaustift.
blueprint *s.* Entwurf *m.*; Blaupause *f.,* technische Zeichnung *f.*
bluestocking *s.* (*fig.*) Blaustrumpf *m.*
bluff *a.* grob; steil; barsch; ~ *s.* Irreführung *f.*; Täuschungsmanöver *n.,* ~ *v.t.* irreführen.
bluish *a.* bläulich.
blunder *s.* Fehler *m.*; Schnitzer *m.*; ~ *v.i.* einen Schnitzer machen.
blunt *a.,* ~**ly** *adv.* stumpf; grob, plump; ~ *v.t.* abstumpfen.
bluntness *s.* Stumpfheit *f.*; Unverblümtheit *f.*; Direktheit *f.*
blur *s.* Klecks, Flecken *m.*; ~ *v.t.* besudeln; verwischen.
blurb *s.* Klappentext *m.*; Waschzettel *m.*
blurt *v.t.* (*out*) unbesonnen heraussagen.
blush *v.i.* erröten; ~ *s.* Schamröte *f.*
bluster *v.i.* toben; großtun; ~ *s.* Ungestüm *n.*; Prahlerei *f.*
blustery *a.* stürmisch.
boa *s.* Riesenschlange *f.*; Pelzboa *f.*
boar *s.* Eber *m.,* Keiler *m.*
board *s.* Brett *n.*; Bohle *f.*; Bord *m.*; Tafel, Kost *f.*; Behörde *f.*; Direktorium *n.*; Kostgeld *n.*; *full* ~, volle Verpflegung *f.*; *partial* ~, teilweise Verpflegung *f.*; ~ *of directors,* Aufsichtsrat *m.*; ~ *of Trade,* Handelsministerium *n.*; ~ *v.t.* dielen; in die Kost tun, beköstigen; entern; *to* ~ *up,* mit Brettern verschlagen; ~ *v.i.* in der Kost sein.
boarder *s.* Kostgänger *m.*; Enterer *m.*
board game *s.* Brettspiel *n.*
boarding: ~ **pass** *s.* Bordkarte *f.*; ~ **house** *s.* Pension *f.*; ~ **school** *s.* Internat *n.*
board: ~**meeting** *s.* Aufsichtsratsitzung *f.*; Vorstandssitzung *f.*; ~**room** *s.* Sitzungssaal *m.*
boast *v.i. & t.* prahlen; stolz sein auf.
boastful *a.* prahlerisch.
boat *s.* Boot *n.*; Schiff *n.*; Dampfer *m.*
boater *s.* Bootsfahrer(in) *m.(f.)*
boatswain *s.* (Hoch)bootsmann *m.*
bob *s.* Gehänge *n.*; Ruck *m.*; Büschel *n.*; ~ *v.i.* baumeln; mit dem Kopfe nicken; ~ *v.t.* stutzen; *bobbed hair,* Bubikopf *m.*
bobbin *s.* Spule *f.*; Klöppel *m.*
bobby *s.* (*sl.*) Polizist *m*; ~**pin** *s.* Haarsprange *f.*
bobsled *s.* Rennschlitten *m.*; Bob *m.*

bobtail *s.* Stutzschwanz *m.*
bode *v.t.* vorbedeuten, ahnen.
bodice *s.* Oberteil, Mieder *n.*
bodiless *a.* unkörperlich.
bodily *a.* körperlich; wirklich, ganz und gar; ~ *harm,* ~ *injury,* Körperverletzung *f.*
body *s.* Leib, Körper *m.*; Körperschaft *f.*; Wagenkasten *m.,* (*mot.*) Karosserie *f.*; (*mil.*) Abteilung *f.*; ~ *corporate,* juristische Person *f.*; *in a* ~, geschlossen, sämtlich; ~ *v.t.* formen; verkörpern.
bodyguard *s.* Leibwächter *m.*; Leibgarde *f.*
body language *s.* Körpersprache *f.*
body odor *s.* Körpergeruch *m.*
bodywork *s.* Karosserie *f.*
bog *s.* Sumpf *m.* Moor *m.*
boggle *v.i.* sprachlos/fassungslos werden.
boggy *a.* sumpfig.
bogus *a.* unecht, falsch; Schwindel. . .
bogy *s.* Kobold *m.,* Popanz *m.*
Bohemia *s.* Böhmen *n.*
Bohemian *s.* Böhme *m.*; ~ *a.* böhmisch.
boil *s.* Furunkel, *m.*; Geschwür *n.*; ~ *v.t. & i.* kochen, wallen; *boiled beef,* Suppenfleisch *n.*; *boiled egg,* gekochtes Ei *n.* (*hard-boiled,* hartgekocht; *soft-boiled,* weichgekocht); *boiled shirt,* Hemd mit steifem Einsatz.
boiler *s.* Kochkessel *m.*; Dampfkessel *m.*
boiler-maker *s.* Kesselschmied *m.*
boiling-point *s.* Siedepunkt *m.*
boisterous *a.,* ~**ly** *adv.* ungestüm, heftig.
bold *a.,* ~**ly** *adv.* kühn; dreist; *to make* ~, sich erkühnen.
boldface *s.* (*typ.*) Fettdruck *m.*
boldness *s.* Kühnheit *f.*; Dreistigkeit *f.*
Bolivia *s.* Bolivien *n.*
Bolivian *s.* Bolivianer(in) *m.(f.)*; ~ *a.* bolivianisch.
bolster *s.* Polster *n.*; Kompresse *f.*; ~ *v.t.* polstern; unterstützen.
bolt *s.* Bolzen *m.*; Pfeil *m.*; Riegel *m.*; Blitzstrahl *m.*; ~ *v.t.* verriegeln; beuteln, sieben; gierig hinunterschlingen; ~ *v.i.* davonlaufen, durchgehen.
bolt-hole *s.* Schlupfloch *n.*
bomb *s.* Bombe *f.*; ~ *v.t.* mit Bomben belegen; bombardieren.
bombard *v.t.* bombardieren.
bombardment *s.* Bombardieren *n.*
bombast *s.* Schwulst *m.*
bombastic *a.* schwülstig.
bomber *s.* Bombenflugzeug *m.,* Kampfflugzeug *n.*
bombing *s.* Bombardierung *f.*
bomb-proof *a.* bombenfest.
bombshell *s.* Bombe *f.*
bona fide (*law*) in gutem Glauben, gutgläubig.
bond *s.* Band, Seil *n.*; Fessel *f.*; Schuldverschreibung; *in* ~, unter Zollverschluß.
bondage *s.* Knechtschaft *f.*
bonded goods *s.pl.* Güter under Zollverschluß *n.pl.*
bonded warehouse *s.* Zollspeicher *m.*
bone *s.* Knochen *m.*; Gräte *f.*; ~ *v.t.* entknochen, entgräten; (*med.*) ~**grafting,** Knochenübertragung *f.*
bonelace *s.* Spitzen *f.pl.*
bonelazy *a.* stinkfaul.
bonemeal *s.* Knochenmehl *n.*
bonfire *s.* Freudenfeuer *n.*; Feuer im Freien.

bonkers *a.* (*fam.*) übergeschnappt.
bonnet *s.* Mütze *f.*; Barett *n.*; Frauenhut *m.*; *to have a bee in one's ~,* einen Vogel haben.
bonny *a.*, munter; hübsch.
bonus *s.* Zulage *f.*; Zuschlag *m.*; Bonus *m.*
bony *a.* knochig.
boo *i.* buh; ~ *s.* Buhruf *m.*; ~ *v.t.* ausbuhen.
booby *s.* Töpel *m.*
book *s.* Buch *n.*; Heft *n.*; *to keep the ~ s,* the Bücher führen; ~ *v.t.* eintragen, buchen; ~ *v.i.* (einen Platz) bestellen; eine Fahrkarte lösen (auf der Eisenbahn); *bookable in advance,* vorausbestellbar.
bookbinder *s.* Buchbinder *m.*
bookcase *s.* Bücherschrank *m.*
book club *s.* Buchclub *m.*
book end *s.* Bücherstütze *f.*
bookie *s.* Buchmacher *m.*
booking *s.* Buchung *f.*; Vorbestellung *f.*
booking-office *s.* Fahrkartenschalter *m.*; Kasse *f.*
bookish *a.* belesen; papieren (Stil).
bookkeeper *s.* Buchhalter *m.*
bookkeeping *s.* Buchführung *f.*; ~ *by double (single) entry,* doppelte (einfache) Buchführung *f.*
booklet *s.* Broschüre *f.*
bookmaker *s.* Buchmacher (Sport) *m.*
bookmark *s.* Buchzeichen *n.*
book review *s.* Buchbesprechung *f.*
bookseller *s.* Buchhändler *m.*
bookshelf *s.* Regal, Bücherbrett *n.*
bookstall *s.* Bücherstand (an Bahnhöfen) *m.*
bookstore *s.* Buchhandlung *f.*
booktrade *s.* Buchhandel *m.*
bookworm *s.* Bücherwurm *m.*
boom *s.* Ausleger *m.*; Stange *f.*; Aufschwung *m.*, (Börse) Hausse *f.*; ~ *v.i.* dumpf dröhnen; in die Höhe treiben; anpreisen.
boomerang *s.* Bumerang *m.* (australische Schleuder).
boon *s.* Gabe, Wohltat *f.*; ~**companion** *m.* Zechkumpan *m.*
boor *s.* Lümmel *m.*
boorish *a.*, ~**ly** *adv.* bäuerisch, rüpelhaft.
boost *v.t.* ankurbeln; steigern; erhöhen; ~ *s.* Auftrieb *m.*; Erhöhung *f.*
boot *s.* Stiefel *m.*; ~ *v.t.* treten, kicken; (*comp.*) laden.
boot-black *s.* Stiefelputzer *m.*
booted *a.* gestiefelt.
booth *s.* Bude *f.*; Telefonzelle *f.*; Kabine *f.*
boot-jack *s.* Stiefelknecht *m.*
bootlegger *s.* Alkoholschmuggler *m.*
bootless *a.* unnütz, vergeblich.
boots *s.* Hausknecht *m.*
boot-tree *s.* Leisten *m.*
booty *s.* Beute *f.*
booze *v.t.* zechen.; ~ *s.* Sauferei *f.*
boozy *a.* versoffen.
borax *s.* (*chem.*) Borax *m.*
border *s.* Rand, Saum *m.*; Grenze *f.*; ~ *v.i.* grenzen; ~ *v.t.* einfassen.
borderer *s.* Grenzbewohner *m.*
borderland *s.* Grenzgebiet *n.*
borderline case *s.* Grenzfall *m.*
bore *v.t.* bohren, eindringen; langweilen; ~ *s.* Bohrer *m.*; Bohrloch *n.*; Kaliber *n.*; langweilige Person *f.*

boredom *s.* Langeweile *f.*
borehole *s.* Bohrloch *n.*
boring *s.* langweilig.
born *p.* & *a.* geboren.
borough *s.* Stadtgemeinde *f.*; Stadt *f.*
borrow *v.t.* borgen; leihen.
borrower *s.* Kreditnehmer(in) *m.*(*f.*).
borrowing *s.* Kreditaufnahme *f.*
bosh *s.* Unsinn *m.*
bosom *s.* Busen *m.*; (*fig.*) Schoß *m.*
boss *s.* Buckel, Knopf *m.*; Meister, Herr, Prinzipal, Chef *m.*; ~ *v.t. to ~ around* herumkommandieren.
bossy *a.* (*fam.*) herrisch.
botanical *a.* botanisch.
botanist *s.* Botaniker *m.*
botany *s.* Botanik *f.*
botch *v.t.* flicken; verpfuschen; ~ *s.* Flickwerk *n.*; Pfuscherei *f.*
botcher *s.* Flickschneider *m.*; Pfuscher *m.*
both *a.* beide; beides; *both. . . and c.* sowohl. . . als auch.
bother *v.t.* plagen, quälen; ~ *s.* Last, Plage *f.*
bottle *s.* Flasche *f.*; ~ *v.t.* in Flaschen abfüllen; *bottled beer,* Flaschenbier *n.*
bottleneck *s.* Flaschenhals *m.*; (*fig.*) Engpaß *m.*
bottleopener *s.* Flaschenöffner *m.*
bottom *s.* Boden *m.*; Grund *m.*; Schiff *n.*; Ende *n.*; Steiß *m.*; *at the ~,* unten, am unteren Ende, im Grunde; ~ *a.* untere.
bottomless *a.* bodenlos.
bottomline *s.* Fazit *n.*; Endergebnis *n.*
bough *s.* Ast *m.*
bouillon cube *s.* Bouillonwürfel *m.*
boulder *s.* Felsbrocken *m.*
bounce *s.* Knall *m.*; Rückprall *m.*; Prahlerei *f.*; ~ *v.i.* aufspringen; anprallen; prahlen.
bouncer *s.* (*fam.*) Rausschmeißer *m.*
bouncing *a.* stramm.
bound *s.* Sprung *m.*; Prall *m.*; ~ *v.i.* springen, prallen; ~ *s.* Grenze *f.*; *out of ~ s,* gesperrt, Zutritt verboten; ~ *v.t.* begrenzen, einschränken; ~ *a.* bestimmt, auf der Reise (nach); *north-bound,* in nördlicher Richtung fahrend.
boundary *s.* Grenze *f.*
boundless *a.* grenzenlos.
bountiful *a.* freigebig, großzügig.
bounty *s.* Prämie *f.*
bouquet *s.* Strauß *m.*, Blume (des Weins) *f.*
bourbon *s.* Bourbon *m.*
bourgeois *s.* Bürger(in) *m.*(*f.*); Spießer(in) *m.*(*f.*); ~ *a.* bürgerlich.
bourgeoisie *s.* Bürgertum *n.*; Bourgeoisie *f.*
bout *s.* Gelage *n.*; (*fencing*) Gang *m.*; Anfall *m.*
bovine *a.* zum Rind gehörig, Rind. . .; (*fig.*) träge.
bow *v.t.* & *i.* biegen, bücken; sich verbeugen; ~ *s.* Verbeugung *f.*
bow *s.* Bogen *m.*; Schleife *f.*; (*nau.*) Bug *m.*
bowdlerize *v.t.* Buchtext verstümmeln.
bowel *s.* Darm *m.*; Innere *n.*
bowels *s.pl.* Eingeweide *n.pl.*
bowl *s.* Becken *n.*; Pfeifenkopf *m.*; Schüssel *f.*; Kugel *f.*; *to play at ~ s,* Kegel schieben; ~ *v.i.* kegeln, rollen.
bow-legs *s.pl.* O-Beine *n.pl.*
bowler *s.* Bowlingspieler(in) *m.*(*f.*)
bowler hat *s.* neidriger steifer Filzhut.

bowling s. Bowling n.; **~-alley** s. Kegelbahn f.
bowsprit s. (nav.) Bugspriet n.
bow-string s. Bogensehne f.
bow-tie s. Fliege f.; Schleife f.
bow-window s. Bogenfenster, vorspringendes Fenster n.
bow-wow s. Wauwau m.
box s. Büchse f.; Kasten m.; Schachtel f.; Verschlag m.; Schließfach n.; Kutschersitz, Bock m.; Loge f.; Koffer m.; Buchsbaum m.; Schlag m.; ~ on the ear, Ohrfeige f.
box v.t. ohrfeigen; ~ v.i. boxen.
box-car s. (rail.) Güterwagen m.
boxer s. Boxer m.
boxing s. Boxen n.; **~gloves** pl. Boxhandschuhe m.pl.; **~match** s. Boxkampf m.
box-office s. Kartenausgabe f., Kasse f.
box-wood s. Buchsbaumholz n.
boy s. Knabe m., Junge m.
boycott v.t. boykottieren, in Verruf erklären; ~ s. Boykott m.
boyfriend s. Freund m.
boyhood s. Knabenalter n.
boyish a., **~ly** adv. knabenhaft, kindisch.
bra s. BH m.; Büstenhalter m.
brace s. Schnalle f.; Strebe f.; Klammer f.; Stütze f.; (nav.) Brasse; (Federwild) Paar n.; (mus.) Ligaturbogen m.; ~ v.t. schnüren, spannen, anschnallen; erfrischen.
bracelet s. Armband n.
brachial a. Arm...
bracing a. stärkend, gesund.
bracken s. Farnkraut n.
bracket s. Klammer f.; Wandarm m.; Gasarm m.; (arch.) Träger m.; in the lower brackets, in den unteren Einkommensklassen.
bracket v.t. einklammern.
brackish a. salzig (vom Wasser); brackig.
brag v.i. prahlen; ~ s. Prahlerei f.
braggart s. Prahler m.; ~ a. prahlerisch.
Brahman s. Brahmane m.; Brahmanin f.
braid v.t. flechten; ~ s. Flechte f.; Litze f.
Braille s. Blindenschrift f.
brain s. Gehirn n.; ~ s. Verstand m.
brain: **~child** s. Geistesprodukt n.; ~ **death** s. Hirntod m.; ~ **drain** s. Abwanderung f. (von Wissenschaftlern).
brainless a. unbesonnen; hirnlos.
brain: **~storm** s. Anfall geistiger Umnachtung; **~storming** s. Brainstorming n.; **~washing** s. Gehirnwäsche f.
brainwave s. Eingebung f., Geistesblitz m.
brainy a. gescheit.
braise v.t. schmoren.
brake s. Bremse f.; ~ v.t. brechen (Flachs); bremsen.
brake: **~drum** s. Bremstrommel f.; **~fluid** s. Bremsflüssigkeit f.; **~light** s. Bremslicht n.
bramble s. Brombeerstrauch m.
bran s. Kleie f.
branch s. Zweig m.; Abschnitt m.; Fach n.; Filiale f., Zweigstelle f.
branch v.t. in Zweige teilen; ~v.i. Zweige treiben; abzweigen.
branch-line s. Nebenstrecke f.
brand s. Brandmal n.; Sorte f.; Handelsmarke f.; ~

v.t. brandmarken.
brandish v.t. schwingen; schwenken.
brandname s. Markenname.
brand-new a. funkelnagelneu.
brandy s. Weinbrand m.
brash a. dreist; auffällig.
brass s. Messing n.; Unverschämtheit f.; the ~ (mus.) das Blech; die Blechbläser; (fam.) Knete f. (Geld).
brass band s. Blasorchester n.
brassiere s. Büstenhalter m.
brassplate s. Messingschild n.
brat s. Balg m., Kind n.
bravado s. Mut m.
brave a. tapfer, edel; stattlich; ~ v.t. herausfordern, trotzen.
bravery s. Tapferkeit f.; Pracht f.
bravo s. Bandit m.; bravo.
brawl v.i. schlagen; zanken; ~ s. Schlägerei f., Zank m.
brawn s. Muskelstärke f.; Preßsülze f.
brawny a. fleischig; muskelstark.
bray s. Eselsgeschrei n.; ~ v.i. schreien, schmettern.
brazen a., **~ly** adv. ehern; unverschämt.
brazen-faced a. unverschämt.
brazier s. Kupferschmied m.; Kohlenbecken n.
Brazil s. Brasilien n.
Brazilian s. Brasilianer(in) m.(f.); ~ a. brasilianisch.
Brazil nut s. Paranuß f.
breach s. Verstoß m.; Bruch m.; Bresche f.; Uneinigkeit f.; ~ of promise, Bruch des Eheversprechens m.
bread s. Brot n.; ~ and butter Butterbrot n.; ~ and cheese, Käsebrot n.
breadcrumb s. Brotkrume f.; pl. Paniermehl n.
breadspread s. Brotaufstrich m.
breadth s. Breit f.; Weite f.
breadwinner s. Ernährer(in) m.(f.).
break v.t. & i. brechen; bersten; anbrechen; vernichten; bankrott werden; umschlagen (Wetter); (ein Pferd) zureiten; to ~ down, zusammenbrechen, versagen, nicht funktionieren (Maschine), eine Panne haben (Motor); klassifizieren; to ~ in, anlernen; to ~ off, abbrechen; to ~ out, ausbrechen; to ~ up, (bes. mil.) zersprengen, sich auflösen, auseinandergehen; ~ s. Bruch m.; Lücke f.; Absatz m.; Pause f.; Anbruch m.; ~ in the weather, Witterungsumschlag m.; breaking of the voice, Stimmbruch m.
breakable a. zerbrechlich.
breakage s. Bruch (der Waren) m.
breakdown s. Zusammenbruch m.; (Betriebs)störung, f.; Panne f.; Klassifizierung f.
breaker s. Brecher m.
breakfast v.i. frühstücken; ~ s. Frühstück n.; to lay ~, das Frühstück anrichten.
breakfast cereal s. Frühstücksflocken f.pl.
break-in s. Einbruch m.
breaking-point s. Belastungsgrenze f.
breakneck a. halsbrecherisch.
breakthrough s. (mil.) Durchbruch m.
break-up s. Auflösung f., Bruch m.; Trennung f.
breakwater s. Wellenbrecher m.
breast s. Brust f.; Busen m.; ~ v.t. die Stirn bieten; **~bone** s. Brustbein n.; ~ **cancer** s. Brustkrebs; **~-feed** v.t. & i. stillen.

breast pin *s.* Anstecknadel *f.*

breaststroke *s.* Brustschwimmen *m.*

breast-work *s.* Brustwehr *f.*

breath *s.* Atem *m.;* Hauch *m.; to hold one's ~,* den Atem anhalten; *out of ~,* außer Atem.

breathalyzer *s.* Alcotest-Röhrchen *n.*

breathe *v.t. & i.* atmen; äußern.

breather *s.* (*fam.*) Atem-, Verschnaufpause *f.*

breathing *s.* Atmen *n.; ~* **apparatus** *s.* Beatmungsgerät *n.; ~* **space** *s.* Atempause *f.*

breathless *s.* atemlos.

breathlessness *s.* Atemlosigkeit *f.*

breathtaking *a.* atemberaubend.

breeches *s.pl.* Kniehosen *f.pl.*

breed *v.t. & i.* zeugen; züchten; *~ s.* Zucht *f.;* Schlag *m.;* Tierrasse *f.;* **~-dog,** Rassehund *m.*

breeder *s.* Erzeuger *m.;* Züchter *m.*

breeding *s.* Züchten *n.;* Erziehung *f.*

breeze *s.* frischer Wind *m.;* Brise *f.*

breezy *a.* windig, luftig; jovial.

brethren *s.pl.* (*Bibl.*) Brüder *m.pl.*

breviary *s.* Brevier *n.*

brevity *s.* Kürze *f.*

brew *v.t.* brauen; mischen; *~ s.* Gebräu *n.*

brewer *s.* Brauer *m.*

brewery *s.* Brauerei *f.*

briar = **brier.**

bribable *a.* bestechlich.

bribe *s.* Bestechung *f.; ~ v.t.* bestechen.

bribery *s.* Bestechung *f.*

bric-à-brac *s.* Nippsachen *f.pl.*

brick *s.* Backstein *m.; ~ v.t.* mit Ziegelsteinen mauern; *to ~ up,* zumauern.

bricklayer *s.* Maurer *m.*

bridal *a.* hochzeitlich, bräutlich.

bride *s.* Braut (am Hochzeitstag) *f.*

bridegroom *s.* Bräutigam *m.*

bridesmaid *s.* Brautjungfer *f.*

bridesman *s.* Brautführer *m.*

bridge *s.* Brücke *f.* (auch Zahnbrücke); Steg *m.* (der Geige); Bridge *n.; ~ v.t.* überbrücken.

bridgehead *s.* (*mil.*) Brückenkopf *m.*

bridging loan *s.* Überbrückungskredit *m.*

bridle *s.* Zaum *m.; ~ v.t.* aufzäumen; bändigen.

bridle path *s.* Reitweg *m.*

brief *a.,* **~ly** *adv.* kurz; knapp; *~ s.* Aktenauszug *m.;* schriftlicher Auftrag *m.;* (*law*) Schriftsatz *m.*

brief-case *s.* Aktentasche *f.*

briefing *s.* (*mil.*) Befehlsausgabe *f.*

briefs *s.pl.* Slip *m.*

brier *s.* Dornstrauch *m.,* wilde Rose *f.*

brig *s.* (*nau.*) Zweimaster *m.,* Brigg *f.*

brigade *s.* Brigade *f.*

brigadier *s.* Brigadeführer *m.*

brigand *s.* Straßenräuber *m.*

brigandage *s.* Räuberwesen *n.,* Räuberei *f.*

bright *a.,* **~ly** *adv.* hell; gescheit.

brighten *v.i.* hell werden, glänzen; *~ v.t.* glänzend machen; aufheitern.

brightness *s.* Glanz *m.;* Scharfsinn *m.*

brilliance, brilliancy *s.* Glanz *m.*

brilliant *a.,* **~ly** *adv.* glänzend; hervorstehend; *~ s.* Brilliant *m.*

brim *s.* Rand *m.;* Krempe *f.; ~ v.t.* bis an den Rand füllen; *~ v.i.* voll sein.

brimful *a.,* **~ly** *adv.* ganz voll.

brimstone *s.* Schwefel *m.*

brindled *a.* scheckig, gestreift.

brine *s.* Salzwasser *n.;* Sole *f.*

bring *v.t. ir.* bringen; *to ~ about,* zustande bringen; *to ~ forth,* hervorbringen, gebären; *to ~ round,* wieder zu sich bringen; *to ~ to bear,* anwenden, zur Wirkung bringen; *to ~ up,* erziehen, aufziehen; (*mil.*) heranführen; *to ~ up the subject,* den Gegenstand zur Sprache bringen.

brink *s.* Rand *m.*

briny *a.* salzig.

briquette, briquet *s.* Preßkohle *f.,* Brikett *n.*

brisk *a.,* **~ly** *adv.* frisch, lebhaft, feurig, stark; *~ v.t.* (*up*), aufmuntern.

brisket *s.* Bruststück (Speise) *n.*

bristle *s.* Borste *f.; ~ v.t.* (die Borsten) aufrichten; *~ v.i.* starren.

bristly *a.* borstig; stoppelig.

Brit *s.* Brite *m.;* Britin *f.*

Britain *s.* Britannien *n.*

British *s.* Brite *m.;* Britin *f.; ~ a.* britisch.

Britisher *s.* (*fam.*) Brite *m.*

British Isles *pl.* Britische Inseln *pl.*

Briton *s.* Brite *m.,* Britin *f.*

Britanny *s.* Bretagne *f.*

brittle *a.* zerbrechlich; spröde.

broach *s. ~ v.t.* anspießen; (ein Faß) anzapfen; (*fig.*) vorbringen; anfangen.

broad *a.,* **~ly** *adv.* breit, groß; grob; schlüpfrig; derb; *~ day,* heller Tag *m.*

broad bean *s.* Saubohne *f.*

broadcast *v.t.* rundfunken; **broadcasting** *s.* Rundfunk *m.*

broad-cloth *s.* feines Tuch *n.*

broaden *v.t.* weiten; verbreitern.

broadly *a.* dentlich; allgemein.

broad-minded *a.* tolerant; großzügig.

broadside *s.* (*nav.*) Breitseite, volle Lage *f.*

broad-sword *s.* Säbel *m.*

brocade *s.* Brokat *m.*

broccoli *s.* Brokkoli *m.*

brochure *s.* Broschüre (eines Hotels u.dgl.) *f.*

brogue *s.* starker Schuh *m;* irländische Aussprache *f.*

broil *s.* Lärm, Aufruhr *m.; ~ v.t. & i.* vor dem Feuer rösten.

broke *a.* (*fam.*) pleite.

broken *p. & a.* gebrochen (auch *fig.*); zerrissen; unterbrochen; *~* **stones** *s.* Schotter *m.; ~* **ground** *s.* unebenes Gelände *f.;* **~-hearted** gebrochenen Herzens, gramvoll.

broker *s.* Makler *m.;* Trödler *m.*

brokerage *s.* Maklergebühr *f.*

bromide *s.* Bromsalz *n.;* Bromid *n.*

bromine *s.* Brom *n.*

bronchial *a.* bronchial; Bronchial. . .; zur Luftröhre gehörig; *~* **tube** *s.* Luftröhre *f.*

bronchitis *s.* Luftröhrenentzündung *f.*

bronze *s.* Bronze *f.; ~ v.t.* bronzieren.

brooch *s.* Brosche *f.*

brood *v.i.* brüten; *~ v.t.* ausbrüten; *~ s.* Brut *f.*

brook *s.* Bach *m.; ~ v.t.* ertragen.

broom *s.* Ginster *m.;* Besen *m.*

broth *s.* Fleischbrühe *f.*

broomstick *s.* Besenstiel *m.*

brothel *s.* Bordell *n.*

brother *s.* Bruder *m.*
brotherhood *s.* Brüderschaft *f.*
brother-in-law *s.* Schwager *m.*
brotherly *a.* brüderlich.
brow *s.* Augenbraue *f.*; Stirn *f.*
browbeat *v.t. st.* einschüchtern.
brown *a.* braun.; *v.i.* (*cul.*) bräunen; braun werden.
browned off *a.* (*fam.*) restlos bedient.
brownie *s.* Heinzelmännchen *n.* kleiner Schokoladenkuchen.
brownish *a.* bräunlich.
brown-paper *s.* Packpapier *n.*
browse *s.* junger Sproß *m.*; ~ *v.t.* abweiden; ~ *v.i.* weiden; flüchtig lesen.
bruise *v.t.* quetschen, zerstoßen; ~ *s.* blauer Fleck *m.*, Druckstelle *f.*
brunch *s.* spätes Frühstück *n.*
brunette *a.* brünett; ~ *s.* Brünette *f.*
brunt *s. to bear the* ~ die Hauptlast tragen.
brush *s.* Bürste *f.*; Pinsel *m.*; Schwanz (*m.*) des Fuchses; ~ *v.t.* bürsten; fegen; streifen; *to* ~ *up, v.t.* auffrischen; zusammenfegen.
brush: ~ *off s.* Abfuhr *f.*; ~**stroke** *s.* Pinselstrich *m.*
brushwood *s.* Gestrüpp, Buschholz *n.*
brusque *a.* barsch, trotzig.
Brussels sprouts *s.pl.* Rosenkohl *m.*
brutal *a.*, ~**ly** *adv.* viehisch; roh; brutal.
brutalize *v.t.* verrohen.
brutality *s.* rohes Wesen *n.*, Brutalität *f.*
brute *a.* tierisch, wild; ~ *s.* Vieh *n.*; roher Kerl *m.*, (*fam.*) Scheusal *n.*
brutish *a.*, ~**ly** *adv.* viehisch, grob.
bubble *s.* Blase *f.*; Seifenblase *f.* Wasserblase *f.*; leerer Schein *m.*; Betrug, Schwindel *m*; ~ *v.i.* sprudeln; *to* ~ *over v.i.* überschäumen.
bubble bath *s.* Schaumbad *n.*
bubbly *a.* sprudelnd, schäumend.
buccaneer *s.* Seeräuber *m.*
buck *s.* Bock *m.*; männliches Tier *n.*; Stutzer *m.*; (*fam.*) Dollar *m.*; *to pass the* ~ einem andern die Schuld zuschieben; ~ *v.i.* bocken; *to* ~ *up,* Mut machen, anfeuern.
bucket *s.* Eimer *m.*
bucketful *s.* ein Eimer voll *m.*
buckle *s.* Schnalle *f.*; Spange *f.*; ~ *v.t.* schnallen; sich biegen; *to* ~ *up* sich anschnallen.
buckram *s.* Steifleinwand *f.*
buckskin *s.* Hirschleder *n.*; (Stoff) Buckskin *m.*
bucktooth *s.* vorstehender Zahn *m.*; Raffzahn *m.*
buckwheat *s.* Buchweizen *m.*
bucolic *a.* hirtenmäßig, Hirten . . .
bud *s.* Knospe *f.*; ~ *v.i.* sprossen, blühen; ~ *v.t.* pfropfen.
Buddhism *s.* Buddhismus *m.*
Buddhist *s.* Buddhist *m.*, Buddhistin *f.*; ~ *a.* buddhistisch.
buddy *s.* (*fam.*) Kumpel *m.*
budge *v.i.* sich regen.
budget *s.* Budget *n.*; Haushaltsplan *m.*, Etat *m.*; ~ *estimate,* Haushaltsvoranschlag *m.*
buff *a.* mattgelb; ~ *v.t.* polieren; putzen.
buffalo *s.* Büffel *m.*
buffer *s.*, Puffer *m.*, Stoßkissen *n.*; Prellbock *m.*
buffet *s.* Anrichte(tisch) *f.*; Schenktisch *m.*; Wirtschaftsbetrieb *m.*, Buffet *n.*; ~ *v.t.* puffen, schlagen.
buffoon *s.* Possenreißer *m.*

buffoonery *s.* Possen *f.pl.*
bug *s.* Wanze *f.*; Insekt *n.*, Käfer *m.*; Bazillus *m.*; ~ *v.t.* abhören; (*fam.*) nerven; beunruhigen.
bugbear *s.* Popanz *m.*
buggy *s.* leichter, zweirädriger Wagen *m.*
bugle *s.* Wald-, Signalhorn *n.*
bugs *s.pl.* Ungeziefer *n.*
build *v.t. & i.* bauen; ~ *s.* Bauart *f.*
builder *s.* Bauunternehmer *m.*; Erbauer *m.*
building *s.* Bauen *n.*; Gebäude *n.*
building contractor *s.* Bauunternehmer *m.*
building society *s.* Bausparkasse *f.*
built-up *a.* bebaut.
bulb *s.* Zwiebel *f.*; Thermometerkugel *f.*; *light* ~, Glühlampe, Birne *f.*
Bulgaria *s.* Bulgarien *n.*
Bulgarian *s.* Bulgare *m.*, Bulgarin *f.*; ~ *a.* bulgarisch.
bulge *s.* Ausbeulung *f.*; ~ *v.i.* anschwellen, vorragen.
bulk *s.* Umfang *m.*; Masse *f.*; Hauptteil *m.*; ~ *v.i.* vorragen.
bulkhead *s.* (*nav.*) Schott *n.*
bulk-purchase *s.* Großeinkauf *m.*
bulky *a.* groß, schwer; sperrig.
bull *s.* Bulle, Stier *m.*; Schnitzer *m.*; Haussier *m.*; päpstliche Bulle *f.*
bulldog *s.* Bullenbeißer *m.*, Bulldogge *f.*
bulldozer *s.* Planierraupe *f.*
bullet *s.* Kugel *f.*
bullet-hole *s.* Einschuß *m.*, Einschußloch *n.*
bulletin *s.* Tagesbericht *m.*; ~**-board** *s.* schwarzes Brett *n.*
bullet-proof *a.* kugelfest; ~ *glass* *s.* Panzerglas *n.*
bull fight *s.* Stierkampf *m.*
bullfighter *s.* Stierkämpfer *m.*
bull frog *s.* Ochsenfrosch, Brüllfrosch *m.*
bullion *s.* Gold- oder Silberbarren *m.*
bull market *s.* Haussemarkt *m.*
bullock *s.* Ochse *m.*
bullring *s.* Stierkampfarena *f.*
bull's-eye *s.* Schwarze (in der Scheibe) *n.*
bullshit *s.* (*vulg.*) Scheiße *f.*
bully *s.* (feige) Tyrann *m.*; grober Flegel *m.*; ~ *v.t.* einschüchtern; tyrannisieren.
bulrush *s.* glatte Binse *f.*
bulwark *s.* Bollwerk *n.*
bum *s.* Penner, Gammler *m.*
bumble-bee *s.* Hummel *f.*
bump *s.* Schlag *m.*; Beule *f.*; ~ *v.t.* puffen, (*boat*) überholen; *to* ~ *into* zufällig treffen.
bumper *s.* Stoßstange *f.*; Puffer *m.*
bumper car *s.* Autoskooter *m.*
bumpkin *s.* Tölpel *m.*
bumptious *a.* aufgeblasen, anmaßend.
bumpy *a.* holperig; uneben.
bun *s.* süßes Bröchen *n.*
bunch *s.* Bündel *n.*; Büschel *n.*; Strauß *m.*; ~ *of grapes,* Weintraube *f.*; ~ *of keys,* Schlüsselbund *m.*; ~ *v.i.* schwellen, strotzen.
bundle *s.* Bündel *n.*; (*fig.*) Bürde *f.*; ~ (*up*), *v.t.* einpacken.
bung *s.* Spund *m.*; ~ *v.t.* zuspunden.
bungalow *s.* Bungalow *m.*
bungle *v.t. & i.* verpfuschen; stümpern.
bungler *s.* Stümper *m.*

bungling *a.* stümperhaft.
bunion *s.* Schwellung (am Fuß) *f.*
bunk *s.* (*nav.*) Bettgestell *n.*; Blech *n.*, Unsinn *m.*
bunk-bed *s.* Etagenbett *n.*
bunker *s.* (*nav.*) Bunker *m.*, Kohlenbehälter *m.*
bunny *s.* Häschen *n.*
bunting *s.* Flaggentuch *n.*; Wimpel *m.*
buoy *s.* Boje, Bake *f.*; ~ *v.t. & i.* schwimmen; über Wasser halten.
buoyancy *s.* Auftrieb *m.*; (*fig.*) Schwungkraft *f.*
buoyant *a.* schwimmend; (*fig.*) leicht, heiter.
bur *s.* Klette *f.*
burble *v.i.* quasseln, drummeln.
burden *s.* Bürde *f.*; Ladung *f.*; (*fig.*) Last *f.*; Refrain *m.*, Kehrreim *m.*; ~ *of proof,* (*law*) Beweislast *f.*; ~ *v.t.* aufbürden.
burdensome *a.* beschwerlich.
bureau *s.* Büro *n.*, Geschäftszimmer *f.*; Schreibtisch *m.*; Kommode *f.*
bureaucracy *s.* Bürokratie *f.*
bureaucrat *s.* Bürokrat(in) *m.*(*f.*).
bureaucratic *a.* bürokratisch.
burgeon *s.* Knospe *f.*; ~ *v.i.* knospen.
burgher *s.* Bürger *m.*
burglar *s.* Einbrecher *m.*
burglar alarm *s.* Alarmanlage *f.*
burglarize *v.t.* einbrechen.
burglary *s.* Einbruch *m.*
Burgundy *s.* Burgunder *m.*
burial *s.* Begräbnis *n.*
burlesque *a.* possenhaft; ~ *s.* Burleske *f.*
burly *a.* stämmig.
Burma *s.* Birma *n.*
Burmese *s.* Birmane *m.*, Birmanin *f.*; ~ *a.* birmanisch.
burn *v.t. & i.ir.* brennen; strahlen; ~ *s.* Brand, Brandschaden *m.*
burner *s.* Brenner *m.*
burnish *v.a.* polieren; ~ *s.* Glanz *m.*
burnous *s.* Burnus *m.*
burr *s.* (*mech.*) Grat *m.*; gerolltes R *n.*
burrow *s.* Kaninchenbau *m.*; ~ *v.i.* sich eingraben, wühlen.
bursar *s.* Kassenwart *m.*; Stipendiat *m.*
bursary *s.* Kasse *f.*; Stipendium *n.*
burst *v.i.* bersten; ~ *v.t.* sprengen; ~ *s.* Riß *m.*; Ausbruch *m.*
bury *v.t.* begraben; vergraben.
bus *s.* Omnibus *m.*, Bus *m.*
bush *s.* Busch *m.*, Strauch *m.*; (*mech.*) Metallfutter *n.*
bushel *s.* Bushel *m.* (36 Liter).
bushey *a.* buschig.
business *s.* Geschäft *n.*; Handel *m.*; (*fam.*) Geschichte *f.*; *small* ~, Kleingeschäft *n.*; Kleingewerbe *n.*; *line of* ~, Geschäftszweig *m.*; *to do* (*transact*) ~ *with*, in geschäftlicher Verbindung stehen mit; *to go into* ~, Kaufmann werden; *mind your own* ~,

kümmere dich um deine eigenen Angelegenheiten; *what* ~ *have you to...*, wie kommst du dazu...?; ~**like** *a.* geschäftsmäßig.
businessman *s.* Geschäftsmann *m.*
businesswoman *s.* Geschäftsfrau *f.*
buskin *s.* Kothurn *m.*, Halbstiefel *m.*
bus-stop *s.* Haltestelle *f.*
bust *s.* Büste *f.*
bustle *s.* Lärm, Auflauf *m.*; ~ *v.i.* sich rühren, geschäftig sein.
bustling *a.* belebt, geschäftig.
busy *a.* geschäftig; unruhig; ~ *v.t.* beschäftigen; *to be* ~, zu tun haben; *the line is busy*, (*tel.*) die Verbindung ist besetzt.
busybody *s.* Wichtigtuer *m.*
but *c.* aber, sondern; doch; nur; als; wenn nur; ~ *pr.* außer.
butcher *s.* Fleischer *m.*; ~ *v.t.* schlachten.
butchery *s.* Metzelei *f.*
butler *s.* Diener *m.*
butt *s.* dickes Ende *n.*; Stoß *m.*; Zielscheibe *f.*; Faß *n.*; Tonne *f.*; (*sl.*) Hintern *m.* ~ *v.t.* stoßen.
butter *s.* Butter *f.*; ~ *v.t.* buttern.
buttercup *s.* Butterblume *f.*
butterdish *s.* Butterdose *f.*
butter-fingers *s.* Tolpatsch *m.*
butterfly *s.* Schmetterling *m.*; ~ **stroke** *s.* Schmetterlingsstil *m.*
butter-milk *s.* Buttermilch *f.*
buttock *s.* Hinterteil *m.*
button *s.* Knopf *m.*; ~ *v.t.* zuknöpfen.
button-hole *s.* Knopfloch *n.*; Sträußchen (fürs Knopfloch) *n.*; ~ *v.t* (*fig.*) zu fassen kriegen.
buttress *s.* Strebepfeiler *m.*
buxom *a.*, ~**ly** *adv.* drall; kräftig.
buy *v.t.ir.* kaufen.
buyer *s.* Käufer(in) *m.*(*f.*).
buzz *v.i.* summen, flüstern; ~ *s.* Gesumse, Geflüster *n.*
buzzard *s.* Bussard *m.*
buzzer *s.* summer *m.*
buzzword *s.* Modewort *n.*
by *pr.* von, zu, nach, auf, neben, bei; ~ *adv.* nahe, vorbei; ~ *and* ~, nach und nach; ~ *no means*, keinesfalls, keineswegs; ~ *all means*, freilich, auf jeden Fall; ~ *myself,* ~ *yourself, etc.*, allein; ~ *nine o'clock*, bis neun Uhr; ~ *that time*, bis dahin.
by-election *s.* Nachwahl *f.*
bygone *a.* vergangen.
by-law *s.* Ortstatut *n.*; Verordnung *f.*
by-name *s.* Beiname, Spitzname *m.*
by-pass *s.* Entlastungs-, Umgehungsstraße *f.*; Bypass *m.*; ~ *v.t.* umgehen.
by-product *s.* Nebenprodukt *n.*
bystander *s.* Zuschauer *m.*
byte *s.* Byte *n*
byway *s.* Nebenweg, Umweg *m.*
byword *s.* Inbegriff *m.*
Byzantine *a.* byzantinisch.

C

C, c der Buchstabe C oder c, *n.*; (*mus.*) C, c, **C-sharp** Cis, cis, **C-flat** Ces, ces.
cab *s.* Taxi *n.*; Fahrerhaus *n.*; (*rail.*) Führerstand *m.*
cabaret *s.* Kabarett *n.*; Variété *n.*

cabbage *s.* Kohl *m.*
cabby, cabbie, cab-driver *s.* Taxifahrer(in) *m.*(*f.*)
cabin *s.* Kajüte *f.*; Hütte *f.*; Kabine *f.*; ~ *v.t.* einsperren.

cabin-boy s. Kabinensteward m.
cabin-cruiser s. Kabinenkreuzer m.
cabinet s. Kabinett n.; Schrank m.
cabinet-maker s. Kunsttischler m.
cable s. Kabel n.; ~ v.t. kabeln.
cable: ~ **car** s. Kabine f. (Seilbahn); ~ **television** s. Kabelfernsehen n.
caboodle s. the whole ~ der ganze Kram.
cab-stand s. Taxistand m.
cacao s. Kakaobaum m.
cache s. geheimes Vorrats-, Schatzlager n.
cackle v.i. gackern; kichern; ~ s. Geschnatter n.
cacophony s. Kakophonie f.; Mißklang m.
cactus s. Kaktus m.
cad s. gemeine Kerl, Knote m.
cadaver s. Kadaver m.
caddie s. Junge (beim Golfspiel) m.
caddy s. Teekästchen n., Büchse f.
cadence s. Tonfall m.
cadet s. Kadett m.
café a. Kaffeehaus n.
cafeteria s. Imbißraum mit Selbstbedienung m., Cafeteria f.; Mensa f.
caffeine s. Koffein n.
cage s. Käfig m.; ~ v.t. einsperren.
cagey a. vorsichtig, schlau.
caginess s. Vorsicht f.
cajole v.t. liebkosen.
cajolery s. Liebkosung f.; Schmeichelei f.
cake s. Kuchen m.; ~ of soap, Stück Seife n.; ~ v.t. zusammenbacken.
calamitous a. unheilvoll.
calamity s. Unglück n.; Trübsal f.
calcareous a. kalkartig; kalkig.
calciferous a. kalkhaltig.
calcify v.i. verkalken.
calcium s. Kalzium n.
calculable a. berechenbar.
calculate v.t. berechnen; ~ v.i. rechnen.
calculated a. vorsätzlich; bewußt.
calculation s. Berechnung f.
calculator s. Rechner m.
calculus s. (math.) Rechnung f.
calendar s. Kalender m.
calender s. Tuchpresse f.; ~ v.t. warm pressen.
calf s. **calves** pl. Kalb n.; Kalbleder n.; Wade f.; in ~, trächtig (Kuh).
caliber s. Kaliber n.; Beschaffenheit f.; Befähigung f.; Format n.
calibrate v.t. kalibrieren, eichen.
calico s. Kattun m.
California s. Kalifornien n.
caliph s. Kalif m.
call v.t. & i. rufen, nennen; wecken; (tel.) anrufen; anlegen (Schiff); heißen; besuchen; to ~ for, abholen; erfordern; to ~ to account, zur Rechenschaft ziehen; to ~ to mind, sich erinnern; to ~ off absagen; to ~ up, anrufen (tel.); ~ s. Ruf m.; Aufforderung f.; Besuch m.; Telephongespräch n.; local ~, Ortsgespräch n., long-distance ~, Ferngespräch n.; on ~, auf Abruf, auf tägliche Kündigung.
call-box s. Telephonzelle f.
caller s. Besucher(in) m.(f.), Anrufer(in) m.(f.).
calligraphy s. Schönschreiben n.
calling s. Rufen n.; Beruf, Stand m.
callipers s.pl. (mech.) Kaliberzirkel, Tastzirkel m.pl.

call-money s. tägliches Geld n., Geld auf Abruf n.
callosity s. Schwiele f., Hautverhärtung f.
callous a. schwielig; (fig.) unempfindlich.
callow a. nicht flügge; (fig.) gefühllos, gleichgültig.
call-up s. Einberufung f.
calm a., ~ly adv. ruhig; ~ s. Windstille, Ruhe f.; ~ v.t. besänftigen.
calmness s. Ruhe f., Stille f.
calorie s. Wärmeeinheit f., Kalorie f.
calorific a. wärmeerzeugend.
calumniate v.t. verleumden.
calumny s. Verleumdung f.
calve v.i. kalben.
cam s. (mech.) Nocken m.
camber v.t. & i. wölben; ~ s. Wölbung.
cambric s. Batist m.
camcorder s. Videokamera f.
camel s. Kamel n.
cameo s. Kamee f.
camera s. Kamera f., Photoapparat m.; (law) in ~, unter Ausschluß der Öffentlichkeit.
cameraman s. Kameramann m.
Cameroon s. Kamerun n.
camomile s. Kamille f.; ~ **tea** s. Kamillentee m.
camouflage s. (mil.) Tarnung f.; ~ v.t. tarnen.
camp s. Lager n.; ~ v.i. kampieren.
campaign s. Feldzug m.; Kampagne f.
campaigner s. Vorkämpfer(in) m.(f.); Veteran m.; alter Kämpfer m.
camp-bed s. Feldbett n.; ~-**stool** s. Klappstuhl m.
camp-fire s. Lagerfeuer n.
camp-followers s.pl. Troßpersonen f.pl.
camp-ground s. Lagerplatz m.; Zeltplatz m.; Campingplatz m.
camp-site s. Campingplatz m.
camphor s. Kampfer m.
campus s. Campus m.; Hochschulgelände n.
camshaft s. Nockenwelle f.
can s. Kanne f.; Konservenbüchse f.; Dose f.; ~ v.t. in Büchsen einmachen.
can v.i.ir. können.
Canada s. Kanada n.
Canadian s. Kanadier(in) m.(f.); ~ a. kanadisch.
canal s. Kanal m.; Rinne f.
canalization s. Kanalisierung f.
canalize v.t. kanalisieren.
canard s. Zeitungsente f.
canary s. Kanarienvogel m.
Canary Islands pl. Kanarische Inseln f.pl.
cancel v.t. absagen, ausstreichen, tilgen; ungültig machen; widerrufen.
cancellation s. Absage, Aufhebung f.; Widerruf m.; Tilgung f.
cancer s. Krebs m.
cancerous a. krebsartig.
candelabra, candelabrum s. Armleuchter m., Kandelaber m.
candid a., ~ly adv. aufrichtig, offen.
candidacy s. Kandidatur f.; Bewerbung f.
candidate s. Kandidat m.; Bewerber m.
candle s. Licht n.; Kerze f.; ~**light** s. Kerzenlicht n.
candlestick s. Leuchter m.
candor s. Redlichkeit, Offenheit f.
candy v.t. überzuckern; kandieren; ~ s. Süßigkeiten f.pl.; Bonbon n.
cane s. Rohr n.; Stock m.; ~ v.t. durchprügeln.

cane chair s. Rohrstuhl m.
cane-sugar s. Rohrzucker m.
canine a. hündisch; Hunds...
canister s. Büchse f., Dose f.; Kanister m.
canker s. Lippengeschwür n.
cannabis s. Cannabis m.; Haschisch n.
cannibal s. Menschenfresser m.; Kannibale m.; ~ a. kannibalisch.
cannibalism s. Kannibalismus m.
cannibalize v.t. ausschlachten (Auto).
cannily adv. schlau, vorsichtig.
cannon s. Kanone f.
cannonade s. Kanonade f.
cannon-ball s. Kanonenkugel f.
cannon-fodder s. Kanonenfutter n.
cannot = can not.
canny a. schlau, vorsichtig.
canoe s. Paddelboot n.
canoeing s. Paddeln n.; Kanusport m.
canoeist s. Kanute m.; Kanutin f.; Paddelbootfahrer(in) m.(f.).
canon s. Regel f.; Kanon m.; Domherr m.
canonical a. kanonisch, kirchlich.
canonize v.t. heiligsprechen.
canon-law s. kanonisches Recht n.
can-opener s. Dosenöffner m.
canopy s. Traghimmel m.; Baldachin m.; Vordach n.; ~ v.t. mit einem Baldachin bedecken.
cant s. Schrägung f.; Zunftsprache f.; Heuchelei f.; ~ v.i. kanten; kauderwelschen; scheinheilig reden.
can't = can not.
cantankerous a. rechthaberisch.; streitsüchtig.
cantata s. Kantate f.
canteen s. Feldflasche f.; Kantine f.; ~ of cutlery, Messerwarenkoffer m.
canter s. kurzer Galopp m.; Kanter m.; ~ v.i. im kurzen Galopp reiten.
cantilever s. (arch.) Dielenkopf m.; Konsole f.; Träger m.
canto s. Gesang m.
canton s. Kanton m.
canvas s. Kanevas m.; Leinwand f.; Segeltuch n.; Gemälde n.; under ~, in Zelten.
canvass s. Bewerbung (um Wahlstimmen) f.; ~ v.t. prüfen, erörtern; ~ v.i. sich bewerben, Stimmen sammeln.
canyon s. Felsental n., Klamm f.; Cañon m.
caoutchouc s. Kautschuk m. or n.
cap s. Mütze f., Kappe f.; Deckel m.; ~ v.t. mit einer Kappe bedecken; übertreffen.
capability s. Fähigkeit f.
capable a. fähig; ~ of work, arbeitsfähig.
capacious a., ~ly adv. geräumig.
capacitate v.t. befähigen.
capacitor s. Kondensator m.
capacity s. Umfang m.; Fähigkeit f.; Eigenschaft f.; Inhalt m.; Leistungsfähigkeit f.; Aufnahmefähigkeit f.; legal ~, Rechtsfähigkeit, Geschäftsfähigkeit f.; ~ measures, Hohlmaße n.pl.
caparison s. Pferdedecke f.
cape s. Kap n.; Umhang m.; Cape n.
caper s. Kaper f.; Luftsprung m.; ~ v.i. Luftsprünge machen.
capful s. Inhalt einer Verschlußkappe.
capillary a. haarfein.; Kapillar...; s. Kapillare f.
capital a., ~ly adv. Haupt...; vorzüglich; ~ s.

Hauptstadt f.; Kapital n.; Kapitäl n.; großer Buchstabe m.
capital assets s.pl. Kapitalvermögen n.
capital gains tax s. Kapitalgewinnsteuer f.
capital letter s. Großbuchstabe m.
capital punishment s. Todesstrafe f.
capitalism s. Kapitalismus m.
capitalist s. Kapitalist(in) m.(f.)
capitalize v.t. kapitalisieren; mit großen Buchstaben schreiben.
capitulate v.i. kapitulieren.
capon s. Kapaun m.; ~ v.t. verschneiden.
caprice s. Grille f.; Eigensinn m.
capricious a., ~ly adv. launenhaft.
Capricorn s. (astr.) Steinbock m.
capriole s. Luftsprung, Gaukelsprung m.
capsize v.t. (nav.) zum Kentern bringen; ~ v.i. kentern.
capstan s. (nav.) Winde f., Gangspill n.
capsule s. Kapsel f.
captain s. Hauptmann m.; (Schiffs-)kapitän m.; Kapitän m.
captaincy, s. Hauptmanns-, Kapitänsstelle f.
caption s. Überschrift f.
captious a., ~ly adv. trügerisch, spitzfindig; tadelsüchtig.
captivate v.t. (fig.) einnehmen, fesseln.
captive a. gefangen; ~ balloon, Fesselballon m.; ~ s. Gefangene m./f.
captivity s. Gefangenschaft f.
captor s. Eroberer m.; Fänger m.
capture s. Festnahme f.; Fang m.; Prise f.; ~ v.t. erbeuten; kapern.
capuchin s. Kapuziner m.
car s. Auto n.; Karren m.; Wagen m.; Eisenbahnwagen m.
caracole s. (mil.) halbe Schwenkung f.; ~ v.i. schwenken.
carafe s. Karaffe f.; Wasserflasche f.
caramel s. gebrannter Zucker m.; Karamelle f.
carat s. Karat n.
caravan s. Karawane f.; (großer) Wohnwagen m.
caraway s. Kümmel (Pflanze) m.
carbide s. Karbid n.
carbine s. Karabiner m.
carbohydrate s. Kohlehydrat n.
carbolic acid s. Kohlsäure f.
car bomb s. Autobombe f.
carbon s. Kohlenstoff m.; Durchschlag m.
carbonaceous a. kohlenstoffhaltig, kohleführend.
carbonate s. kohlensaures Salz n.
carbon-copy s. Durchschlag m.; ~-**paper** s. Kohlepapier n.
carbon dioxide s. Kohlendioxid n.
carbonic acid s. Kohlensäure f.
carbonize v.t. verkohlen.
carbuncle s. Karfunkel m.; (med.) Karbunkel m.
carburetor s. Vergaser m.
carcass s. Gerippe n.; toter Körper m.
carcinogen s. Karzinogen n.; Krebserreger m.
carcinogenic a. karzinogen; krebserregend.
car crash s. Autounfall m.
card s. Karte f.; Visitenkarte f.; Seekarte f.; Wollkratze f.; ~ v.t. krempeln, aufkratzen; house of ~s, Kartenhaus n.
cardboard s. Pappendeckel m., Pappe f.

card game s. Kartenspiel n.

cardiac a. Herz. . .; ~ **arrest** s. Herzstillstand m.

cardigan s. Wollweste f.

cardinal a. vornehmst, Haupt. . .; hochrot; ~ s. Kardinal m.

cardinal numbers s.pl. Grundzahlen f.pl.

card-index s. Kartei f.

cardiogram s. Kardiogramm.

cardiology s. Kardiologie f.

card-party s. Spielgesellschaft f.

card-sharper s. Betrüger im Kartenspiel m.

card-table s. Spieltisch m.

care s. Sorge f.; Vorsicht, Pflege f.; ~ of (c/o) Mrs. S., (auf Briefen) per Adresse, bei; to take ~ (to), dafür sorgen, daß; to take ~ (of), sich einer Sache oder Person annehmen; ~ v.i. sorgen; to ~ for, gern haben.

career s. Laufbahn f.; Lauf m.; Beruf m.; ~ v.i. rennen.

career-diplomat s. Berufsdiplomat m.

career adviser s. Berufsberater(in) m.(f.).

carefree a. sorgenfrei; pflegeleicht.

careful a., ~**ly** adv. besorgt, sorgfältig; vorsichtig; to be ~, sich in Acht nehmen.

careless a., ~**ly** adv. sorglos; unvorsichtig; nachlässig; gedankenlos.

carelessness s. Nachlässigkeit f.; Gedankenlosigkeit f.

caress v.t. liebkosen; ~ s. Liebkosung f.

caretaker s. Hausmeister(in) m.(f.); Verwalter(in) m.(f.).

careworn a. abgehärmt.

car ferry s. Autofähre f.

cargo s. Schiffsladung f.; ~ **boat** s. Frachtschiff; ~ **steamer** s. Frachtdampfer m.

Caribbean s. Karibik f.; ~ a. karibisch.

caribou s. Karibu m.

caricature s. Karikatur f.; Zerrbild n.; ~ v.t. lächerlich darstellen, karikieren.

caricaturist s. Karikaturist(in) m.(f.).

caries s. Karies f.; Knochenfraß m.

carillon s. Glockenspiel n.

carious a. kariös.

carjack s. Wagenheber m.

carjacking s. Autodiebstahl m.

carload s. Wagenladung f.

carmelite s. Karmeliter m.

carmine s. Karmin m.

carnage s. Blutbad n.; Gemetzel n.

carnal a., ~**ly** adv. fleischlich.

carnation s. Gartennelke f.

carnival s. Karneval, Fasching m.

carnivore s. Fleischfresser m.; fleischfressende Pflanze f.

carnivorous a. fleischfressend.

carol s. Lobgesang m.; Weihnachtslied n.; ~ v.t. & i. lobsingen, jubeln.

carotid a., ~ **artery** s. Halsschlagader f.

carousal s. Gelage n., Fest n.

carouse v.i. zechen; ~ s. Gelage n.

carousel s. Karussel n.

carp s. Karpfen m.; ~ v.i. bekritteln; herumnörgeln.

carpenter s. Zimmermann m.

carpentry s. Zimmerhandwerk n.

carpet s. Teppich m.; Teppichboden m.

carpet-sweeper s. Teppichkehrmaschine f.

carphone s. Autotelefon n.

carpool s. Fahrgemeinschaft f.

carport s. Einstellplatz m.

carriage s. Kutsche f.; Fuhre f.; Fracht f.; Wagen m.; Eisenbahnwagen m.; (mech.) Schlitten m.; Fuhrlohn m.; Frachtkosten f.pl.; Haltung f.

carriage-free, carriage-paid a. frachtfrei.

carrier s. Transportunternehmen n.; Überbringer m.; Träger m.; Gepäckhalter (Fahrrad) m.

carrier-pigeon s. Brieftaube f.

carrier-wave s. (radio) Trägerwelle f.

carrion s. Aas n.

carrot s. gelbe Rübe, Möhre f.

carry v.t. & i. führen, fahren, fortbringen; befördern; tragen; sich betragen; to ~ forward, (com.) übertragen; to ~ a motion, einen Antrag durchbringen; to ~ on, treiben, weiterführen; to ~ on one's person, bei sich tragen; to ~ out, ausführen, durchführen; to ~ through, durchführen; to ~ on v.i. sein Wesen treiben, fortfahren.

carsick a. übel (vom Autofahren).

carsickness s. Übelkeit beim Autofahren f.

cart s. Wagen, Karren m.; ~ v.t. karren, auf dem Karren fahren.

cartage s. Fuhrlohn m.; Fahren n.

carte blanche s. unbeschränkte Vollmacht f.

cartel s. Kartell n.

cart-horse s. Zugpferd n.

Carthusian s. Kartäusermönch m.

cartilage s. Knorpel m.

cart-load s. Fuhre, f. Karrenladung f.

carton s. Kartonschachtel f.

cartoon s. Cartoon m.; politische Karikatur f.; Zeichentrickfilm m.

cartoonist s. Karikaturist(in) m.(f.); Cartoonist(in) m.(f.)

cartridge s. Patrone f.; Kassette f; ~ **box** Patronentasche f.

cartwheel s. Wagenrad n.; to do ~s radschlagen.

carve v.t. tranchieren; aushauen; in Kupfer stechen; schnitzen; vorschneiden.

carving s. Schnitzerei f., Schnitzwerk n.; Stich m.

cascade s. Wasserfall m.; Kaskade f.

case s. Fall m.; Futteral, Gehäuse n.; Kiste f.; Schriftkasten m.; Rechtsfall m.; (gram.) Fall m.; Koffer m.; Aktentasche f.; glass ~, Glaskasten m.; civil ~, (law) Zivilsache f.; criminal ~, Strafsache f.; the ~ for, die Argumente zu Gunsten; in ~, im Falle, falls; in any case, auf jeden Fall.

case-harden v.t. (mech.) einsatzhärten, oberflächenhärten.

case-history s. Krankengeschichte f.; (jur.) Vorgeschichte f.

casement s. Fensterflügel m.

casestudy s. Fallstudie f.

caseworker s. (mit Einzelnen arbeitender) Sozialarbeiter(in) m.(f.)

cash s. Kasse f.; Bargeld n.; for ~, gegen bar; ~ on delivery, per Nachnahme; ~ v.t. einlösen (Scheck); einkassieren; ~ **register** s. Kasse f.

cash dispenser s. Geldautomat m.

cashier s. Kassierer(in) m.(f.); ~ v.t. absetzen; kassieren.

cashmere a. Kaschmir. . . .

casing s. Futteral n., Gehäuse n.

cask s. Faß n.

casket s. Schmuckkästchen n., Sarg m.
Caspian Sea s. Kaspisches Meer n.
casserole s. kleiner Kochtopf m., Kasserolle f.
cassette s. Kassette f.
cassette; ~ **deck** s. Kassettendeck n.; ~ **recorder** s. Kassettenrekorder m.
cassia s. Kassia f., Zimt m.
cassock s. Soutane f.
cast v.t.ir. (aus-, ent-, weg-)werfen; ausrechnen; gießen; (Rollen) verteilen; to ~ up, addieren; to ~ one's skin, sich häuten; to ~ a vote, eine Stimme abgeben; ~ down a. niedergeschlagen; ~ s. Wurf, Guß m.; Form f.; Gattung f.; Probe f.; angeborene Manier f.; Blick m.; Rollenverteilung f., Rollenbesetzung f.
castanet s. Kastagnette f.
castaway a. weggeworfen; ~ s. Schiffbrüchiger m.
caste s. (in Indien) Kaste f.; to lose ~, seinen gesellschaftlichen Rang verlieren.
castigate v.t. züchtigen.
castigation s. Züchtigung f.
casting s. Guß(stück n.) m.; Rollenbesetzung f.
casting vote s. entscheidende Stimme f.
cast iron s. Gußeisen n.
castle s. Burg f.; Schloß n.; Turm (im Schach) m.
cast-off a. abgeworfen, abgelegt.
castor s. Biber m.; Kastorhut m.; Streubüchse; ~-**oil**, Rizinusöl n.
castor sugar s. Streuzucker m.
castrate v.t. kastrieren; entmannen.
castration s. Kastration f.
casual a., ~**ly** adv. ungezwungen; lässig; flüchtig; zufällig; ~ laborer, Gelegenheitsarbeiter m.
casualty s. Verletzter m.; Tote(s) m.; (mil.) Verlust m.
casuistic a. kasuistisch.
casuistry s. Kasuistik f.
cat s. Katze f.; ~ burglar, Fassadenkletterer m.
cataclysm s. (Natur)katastrophe f.
cataclysmic a. katastrophal, verheerend.
catacomb s. Katakombe f.
catalepsy s. (med.) Katalepsie, Starrsucht f.
cataleptic a. starrsüchtig.
catalog s. Katalog m.; Verzeichnis n.; ~ v.t. katalogisieren.
catalyst s. (chem.) Katalysator m.
catapult s. Katapult n.
cataract s. Wasserfall m.; grauer Star (im Auge) m.
catarrh s. Schnupfen m.; Katarrh m.
catastrophe s. Katastrophe f.
catastrophic a. katastrophal.
cat call s. schrilles Pfeifen (als Mißbilligung) n.; Pfiff m.
catch v.t. & i.ir. fangen; überfallen; einnehmen; anstecken; to ~ a cold, sich erkälten; to ~ the train, den Zug erreichen; to ~ up with, aufholen.
catch s. Fang m.; Beute f.; Rundgesang m.; Kniff m.
catching a. ansteckend; packend.
catchment s. Reservoir n.
catchphrase s. Slogan m.
catchword s. Schlagwort n.
catchy a. eingängig.
catechism s. Katechismus m.
catechize v.t. katechisieren.
categorical a., ~**ly** adv. kategorisch.
category s. Kategorie f.; Klasse f.

cater v.i. Speisen und Getränke liefern.
caterer s. Lieferant m., Einkäufer m., Caterer m.
caterpillar s. Raupe f.
caterwaul v.i. miauen; ~ s. Katzengeschrei n.
catgut s. Darmsaite f.
cathedral a. Dom...; ~ s. Dom(kirche f.) m.
catheter s. (med.) Katheter m.
cathode s. Kathode f.; ~-**rays** s.pl. Kathodenstrahlen m.pl.; ~-**ray tube** s. Braunsche Röhre f.
catholic a. katholisch; ~ s. Katholik m.
Catholicism s. katholischer Glaube m.
catkin s. (bot.) Kätzchen n.
cattle s. Vieh, Rindvieh n.
cattle-breeding s. Rinderzucht f.
cattle-dealer s. Viehhändler m.
cattle-plague s. Rinderpest f.
cattle-show s. Tierschau f.
catwalk s. Laufsteg m.
cauldron s. Kessel m.
cauliflower s. Blumenkohl m.
causal a., ~**ly** adv. ursächlich, kausal.
causation s. Verursachung f.
cause s. Ursache f.; Rechtssache f.; Sache f., Umstand m.; ~ v.t. verursachen.
causeless a., ~**ly** adv. grundlos.
causeway s. Dammweg m.
caustic a. ätzend; beißend; ~ s. Ätzmittel n.
cauterize v.t. ätzen, ausbrennen.
cautery s. Brenneisen n.
caution s. Vorsicht f.; Behutsamkeit f.; Warnung f.; ~ v.t. warnen.
cautionary a. warnend.
cautious a., ~**ly** adv. vorsichtig.
cavalcade s. Reiterzug m.
cavalier s. Reiter m.; Ritter m.
cavalry s. Reiterei f.
cave s. Höhle f.; ~ v.i. (in) einsinken.
cave-dweller s. Höhlenbewohner(in) m.(f.)
cavern s. Höhle f.
cavernous a. höhlenartig.
caviar s. Kaviar m.
cavil v.i. spitzfindig tadeln; ~ s. Spitzfindigkeit, Schikane f.
cavity s. Höhlung, Höhle f.; Zahnloch n.
cavort v.i. (fam.) herumtollen.
caw v.i. krächzen, schreien.
cayenne-pepper s. Cayenne Pfeffer m.
CD s. Compact Disc, CD f.
CD player s. CD-Spieler m.
cease v.i. aufhören, nachlassen; ~ v.t. aufhören machen, einstellen.
cease-fire s. (mil.) Waffenruhe f.
ceaseless a. unaufhörlich.
cedar s. Zedar f.
cede v.t. & i. abtreten; nachgeben.
ceiling s. Zimmerdecke f.; Höchstgrenze f.
celebrate v.t. preisen; feiern.
celebrated a. berühmt.
celebration s. Feier f.
celebrity s. Berühmtheit f.
celery s. Stangensellerie m. & f.
celestial a., ~**ly** adv. himmlisch.
celibacy s. eheloser Stand m.; Zölibat m.
celibate a. unverheiratet.
cell s. (elek.) Element n.; Zelle f.
cellar s. Keller m.

cellist *s.* Cellist(in) *m.(f.)*.
cello *s.* Cello *n.*
cellophane *s.* Zellophanpapier *n.*
cell therapy *s.* Zelltherapie *f.*
cellular *a.* zellular; porös; luft durchlässig; ~
phone *s.* Mobiltelefon *n.*
celluloid *s.* Zelluloid *n.*
cellulose *s.* Zellstoff *m.*; ~ **wool** *s.* Zellwolle *f.*
Celt *s.* Kelte *m.*; Keltin *f.*
Celtic *a.* keltisch.
cement *s.* Zement *m.*; Kitt *m.*; (*fig.*) Band *n.*; ~ *v.t.*
  & *i.* verkitten.
cemetery *s.* Friedhof *m.*
cenotaph *s.* Ehren(grab)mal *n.*
censer *s.* Weihrauchfaß *n.*
censor *s.* Zensor *m.*; ~ *v.t.* der Zensur unterwerfen,
  prüfen; **-ed** *a.* geprüft.
censorious *a.*, **-ly** *adv.* tadelsüchtig.
censorship *s.* Zensur *f.*
censure *s.* Verweis *m.*; Tadel *m.*; *vote of ~*,
  Mißtrauensantrag *m.*; ~ *v.t.* tadeln, verurteilen.
census *s.* Volkszählung *f.*; Schätzung *f.*
cent *s.* Cent *m.*; *per ~*, Prozent *n.*
centaur *s.* Kentaur *m.*
centenarian *s.* Hundertjähriger *m./f.*
centenary *s.* Hundertjahrfeier *f.*
centennial *a.* hundertjährig.
center *s.* Zentrum *n.*; Mittelpunkt *m.*; *~ of gravity*,
  Schwerpunkt *m.*; ~ *v.t.* in den Mittelpunkt stellen;
  ~ *v.i.* im Mittelpunkte zusammenlaufen.
centerpiece *s.* Tafelschmuck *m.*; Kernstück *n.*
centigrade *a.* Celsius *n.*
centimeter *s.* Zentimeter *m.* or *n.*
centipede *s.* Tausendfüßler *m.*
central *a.*, **-ly** *adv.* im Mittelpunkte befindlich.
Central: America *s.* Zentralamerika *n.*; ~ **Europe**
  s. Mitteleuropa *n.*
central heating *s.* Zentralheizung *f.*; *centrally
  heated*, mit Zentralheizung.
centralize *v.t.* zentralisieren.
central: -locking *s.* Zentralverriegelung *f.*; ~ **nervous system** *s.* Zentralnervensystem *n.*; ~
  station *s.* Hauptbahnhof *m.*
centric(al) *a.* im Mittelpunkte befindlich.
centrifugal *a.* vom Mittelpunkte wegstrebend;
  zentrifugal.
centrifuge *s.* Zentrifuge *f.*
centripetal *a.* zum Mittelpunkte hinstrebend;
  zentripetal.
centurion *s.* Zenturio *m.*
centuple *a.* hundertfältig.
century *s.* Jahrhundert *n.*; Hundert *n.*
ceramic *a.* Töpfer. . ., keramisch.
ceramics *s.* Keramik *f.*
cereal *a.* Getreide. . .; **-s** *s.pl.* Getreidearten *pl.* Ge-
  treideflocken *pl.*
cerebral *a.* Gehirn. . .; zerebral.
ceremonial *a.*, **-ly** *adv.* förmlich, umständlich; ~ *s.*
  Zeremoniell *n.*
ceremonious *a.*, **-ly** *adv.* feierlich; förmlich.
ceremony *s.* Feierlichkeit *f.*
certain *a.* gewiß, zuverlässig; *for ~*, bestimmt.
certainly *adv.* gewiß, allerdings, freilich.
certainty *s.* Gewißheit *f.*
certifiable *a.* nachweislich; überprüfbar.
certificate *s.* Bescheinigung *f.*; Zeugnis *n.*; ~ *of good*

conduct, Führungszeugnis *n.*; ~ *v.t.* ein Zeugnis
  ausstellen; bescheinigen.
certify *v.t.* bescheinigen; **certified** *a.* staatlich
  anerkannt od. geprüft; *certified true copy*, die Richtigkeit der Abschrift wird bezeugt.
certitude *s.* Gewißheit *f.*
cerulean *a.* nachtblau.
cervical *a.* Hals. . ., Nacken. . .
cervix *s.* Gebärmutterhals *m.*
Cesarean section *s.* (*med.*) Kaiserschnitt *m.*
cessation *s.* Aufhören *n.*
cession *a.* Abtretung *f.*
cesspool *s.* Senkgrube *f.*
chafe *v.t.* wund reiben; ärgern; ~ *v.i.* sich ärgern.
chaff *s.* Spreu *f.*; Neckerei *f.*; ~ *v.t.* necken, foppen.
chaffinch *s.* Buchfink *m.*
chagrin *s.* Verdruß, Ärger *m.*
chain *s.* Kette *f.*; Kettenglied *n.*; ~ *of command*, (*mil.*)
  Befehlsweg *m.*; ~ *of reasoning*, Schlußkette *f.*; ~ *v.t.*
  anketten.
chain reaction *s.* Kettenreaktion *f.*
chain smoker *s.* Kettenraucher(in) *m.(f.)*.
chain-store *s.* Kettenladen *m.*
chair *s.* Stuhl *m.*; Lehrstuhl *m.*; Vorsitz *m.*; *to take
  the ~*, die Sitzung eröffnen; *to be in the ~*, den Vorsitz führen (in einer Versammlung).
chair bottom *s.* Stuhlsitz *m.*
chairman *s.* Vorsitzender *m.*
chairmanship *s.* Vorsitz *m.*
chairperson *s.* Vorsitzender *m./f.*
chairwoman *s.* Vorsitzende *f.*
chalice *s.* Kelch *m.*
chalk *s.* Kreide *f.*; ~ **out** *v.t.* entwerfen.
challenge *v.t.* herausfordern; ablehnen (Richter
  od. Geschworene); ~ *s.* Herausforderung *f.*; (*mil.*)
  Anruf *m.*; Verwerfung, Ablehnung (von Richtern
  od. Geschworenen) *f.*
challenger *s.* Herausforderer *m.*, Herausforderin *f.*
challenging *a.* herausfordernd, faszinierend.
chamber *s.* Zimmer *n.*; Kammer *f.*
chamber of commerce *s.* Handelskammer *f.*
chamber-concert *s.* Kammerkonzert *n.*; **-maid** *s.*
  Zimmermädchen *n.* **--music** *s.* Kammermusik *f.*
chameleon *s.* Chamäleon *n.*
chamois *s.* Gemse *f.*; Gemsleder *n.*
champ *v.t.* & *i.* kauen; verschlingen.
champagne *s.* Champagner *m.*; Sekt *m.*
champion *s.* Kämpe, Vorkämpfer *m.*; (Sport) Meister *m.*; preisgekröntes Rassetier *n.*; ~ *v.t.* verteidigen; verfechten.
championship *s.* (Sport) Meisterschaft *f.*
chance *s.* Zufall *m.*; Schicksal *n.*; Glück *n.*; Aussicht
  f.; Chance *f.*; Gelegenheit *f.*; *by ~*, von ungefähr; *to
  give a person a ~*, jm. eine Chance geben; *to take a
  ~*, es darauf ankommen lassen; *to take no ~s*, es
  nicht darauf ankommen lassen; **-v.i.** sich
  zutragen.
chancellery *s.* Kanzlei *f.*
chancellor *s.* Kanzler *f.*; ~ *of the Exchequer*, bri-
  tischer Finanzminister *m.*
chancy *a.* gewagt, riskant.
chandelier *s.* Armleuchter *m.*
change *v.t.* ändern, wechseln, tauschen; herausgeben (auf); ~ *v.i.* sich ändern; sich umziehen;
  (Eisenbahn) umsteigen; ~ *s.* Veränderung *f.*;
  Tausch, Wechsel *m.*; Kleingeld *n.*; Agio *n.*; Börse *f.*;

~ *of clothes* (*linen*), Anzug (Wäsche) zum Wechseln; *small* ~, Kleingeld *n.*; *a* ~ *for the worse*, eine
Wendung zum Schlimmeren *f.*; *for a* ~, zur
Abwechslung.
changeable *a.*, **-ly** *adv.* veränderlich.
changeless *a.* unveränderlich.
changeover *s.* Umstellung *f.*
changing *a.* wechselnd; sich ändernd.
changing-room *s.* Umkleideraum *m.*; Umkleideka-
bine *f.*
channel *s.* Kanal *m.*; Rinne *f.*; Flußbett *n.*; (*fig.*)
Weg *m.*; *through official* ~s, im Instanzenweg; ~ *v.t.*
aushöhlen, in Kanäle leiten.
chant *s.* Gesang *m.*; ~ *v.t.* singen.
chaos *s.* Chaos *n.*; Wirrwarr *m.*
chaotic *a.* chaotisch.
chap *s.* Spalte *f.*; Riß *m.*; Kinnbacken von Tieren
m.; Kerl, Bursche *m.*
chapel *s.* Kapelle *f.*
chaperon *s.* Anstandsdame *f.*; Aufsichtsperson *f.*; ~
v.t. begleiten.
chaplain *s.* Kaplan *m.*, Feldprediger *m.*
chaplet *s.* Kranz *m.*; Rosenkranz *m.*
chapter *s.* Kapitel *n.*; Domkapitel *n.*
char *v.t.* verkohlen; ~*v.i.* um Tagelohn dienen; ~ *s.*
Tagearbeit *f.*
char-a-banc *s.* Gesellschaftswagen *m.*
character *s.* Merkmal *n.*; Schriftzug *m.*; Charakter
m.; Original *n.*; Sonderling *m.*; Stand *m.*; Rolle *f.*;
Zeugnis *n.*; *the characters*, die handelnden Personen (in einem Stück oder Roman).
characterize *v.t.* charakterisieren.
characteristic *a*, charakteristisch; ~ *s.* Kennzeichen *n.*
charade *s.* Silbenrätsel *n.*
charcoal *s.* Holzkohle *f.*; Zeichenkohle *f.*
charge *v.t.* laden, beladen; beauftragen; beschuldigen; angreifen; anrechnen; debitieren; einschärfen; ~ *s.* Last *f.*; Ladung *f.*; Auftrag *m.*;
Beschwerde *f.*; Aufsicht *f.*; Amt *n.*; Kosten *f. pl.*;
Mündel *n.*; Ermahnung *f.*; Beschuldigung, Anklage *f.*; Angriff *m.*; *to be in* ~ *of*, die Leitung von
etwas haben; *to take* ~ *of*, die Sorge für etwas übernehmen; *free of* ~, kostenfrei; ~**s** *pl.* Spesen *pl.*
chargeable *a.*, *to be* ~ *to sb.* auf jemandes Kosten
gehen.
chargé d'affaires, Geschäftsträger *m.*
charger *s.* Schlachtroß *n.*; Ladegerät *n.*
chariot *s.* (Triumph-, Kriegs-)wagen *m.*
charisma *s.* Charisma *n.*
charismatic *a.* charismatisch.
charitable *a.*, **-bly** *adv.* wohltätig.
charity *s.* christliche Liebe *f.*; Mildtätigkeit *f.*;
Wohltätigkeitseinrichtung *f.*; milde Gabe *f.*;
Almosen *n.*
charlatan *s.* Scharlatan *m.*; Marktschreier *m.*
charm *v.t.* bezaubern; ~ *s.* Zauber, Charme *m.*
charming *a.* bezaubernd, reizend.
charnel house *s.* Beinhaus *n.*
chart *s.* Seekarte *f.*; Tabelle *f.*; Übersichtstafel *f.*
charter *s.* Charta *f.*; Gründungsbrief *m.*; Urkunde
f.; ~ *v.t.* (ein Schiff) mieten, chartern.
chartered accountant *s.* beeidigter Bücherrevisor
m.; Wirtschaftsprüfer *m.*
charwoman *s.* Scheuerfrau *f.*
chary *a.* sorgsam; karg; vorsichtig.

chase *v.t.* jagen, verfolgen; ziselieren; einfassen; ~
s. Jagd *f.*; *to give* ~, Jagd machen.
chasm *s.* Kluft *f.*; Schlund *m.*
chassis *s.* Rahmen (eines Wagens) *m.*
chaste *a.*, **-ly** *adv.* keusch.
chasten *v.t.* züchtigen, läutern; demütigen.
chastening *a.* ernüchternd.
chastise *v.t.* züchtigen; bestrafen.
chastisement *s.* Züchtigung *f.*
chastity *s.* Keuschheit *f.*
chat *s.* Plauderei *f.*; ~ *v.i.* plaudern.
chattels *s.pl.* bewegliche Habe *f.*
chatter *v.i.* plaudern; klappern; ~ *s.* Geschnatter *n.*;
Gezwitscher *n.*
chatterbox *s.* Quasselstrippe *f.*, Plappermaul *n.*
chatty *a.* gesprächig.
chauffeur *s.* Chauffeur, Führer *m.*
chauvinism *s.* Chauvinismus *m.*
chauvinist *s.* Chauvinist, Chauvi *m.*; Chauvinistin
f.
chauvinistic *a.* chauvinistisch.
cheap *a.*, **-ly** *adv.* wohlfeil, billig.; (*fig.*) schäbig.
cheapen *v.t.* verbilligen.
cheapness *s.* Billigkeit *f.*
cheat *s.* Betrug *m.*; Betrüger(in) *m.*(*f.*); ~ *v.t.*
betrügen.
check *s.* Anstoß *m.*; Einhalt *m.*; Hindernis *n.*; Kontrolle *f.*; Gepäckschein *m.*; Kontrollmarke *f.*;
Scheck *m.*; Rechnung *f.*; ~ *v.t.* zurückhalten, hemmen; kontrollieren; nachprüfen; ~ *v.i.* Schach
bieten; *to* ~ *out*, Hotel verlassen, (Buch) ausleihen;
~ *room* Gepäckaufbewahrung *f.*
checkbook *s.* Scheckbuch *n.*
checked *a.* kariert.
checker *s.* Damestein *m.*; Kassierer(in) *m.*(*f.*).
checkerboard *s.* Schachbrett *n.*
checkers *s.pl.* Damespiel *n.*
check-in *s.* Anmeldung *f.*; Einchecken *n.*
checking-account *s.* Girokonto *n.*
checklist *s.* Checkliste *f.*, Kontrolliste *f.*
checkmate *s.* Schachmatt *n.*; ~ *v.t.* matt setzen.
checkpoint *s.* Kontrollpunkt *m.*
check-up *s.* Untersuchung *f.*; Überprüfung *f.*
cheek *s.* Backe, Wange *f.*; (*fam.*) Unverschämtheit
f.
cheek bone *s.* Backenknochen *m.*
cheeky *a.* frech.
cheep *v.i.* piepsen.
cheer *s.* Bewirtung *f.*; Frohsinn *m.*; Beifallsruf *m.*;
of good ~, guter Laune; ~ *v.t. & i.* erheitern; mit
lautem Ruf begrüßen.
cheerful *a.*, **-ly** *adv.* fröhlich.
cheerfulness, cheeriness *s.* Heiterkeit *f.*
cheerily *adv.* fröhlich.
cheering *a.* jubelnd; fröhlich stimmend.
cheerless *a.* mutlos; freudlos.
cheery *a.* heiter, lustig.
cheese *s.* Käse *m.*
cheese: ~ **board** *s.* Käseplatte *f.*; ~**cake** *s.* Käse-
kuchen *m.*; ~**cloth** *s.* Baumwollstoff *m.*
cheesy *a.* käsig.
cheetah *s.* Gepard *m.*
chef *s.* Küchenchef, Koch, *m.*
chemical *a.* chemisch; ~ *action*, chemische Wirkung *f.*; (*mil.*) ~ *warfare*, Gaskrieg *m.*, chemischer
Krieg *m.*; ~ *warfare agent*, Kampfstoff *m.*; ~**s** *s.pl.*

Chemikalien *f.pl.*
chemise *s.* (Frauen-)hemd *n.*
chemist *s.* Drogist *m.*; Chemiker *m.*
chemistry *s.* Chemie *f.*
chemotherapy *s.* Chemotherapie *f.*
cheque *s.* (*Brit.*) Scheck, Bankschein *m.*
cherish *v.t.* pflegen, hegen; liebkosen.
cherry *s.* Kirsche *f.*
cherry brandy *s.* Kirschlikör *n.*
cherry pit *s.* Kirschkern *m.*
cherub *s.* Cherub *m.*
chess *s.* Schach(spiel) *n.*
chess board *s.* Schachbrett *n.*
chess man *s.* Schachfigur *f.*
chess player *s.* Schachspieler(in) *m.*(*f.*)
chest *s.* Lade, Kiste *f.*; Brust *f.*; ~ *of drawers*, Kommode *f.*
chestnut *s.* Kastanie *f.*; ~ *a.* kastanienbraun.
chew *v.t. & i.* kauen; (*fig.*) überlegen.
chewing gum *s.* Kaugummi *m.*
chewing tobacco *s.* Kautabak *m.*
chewy *a.* zäh.
chic *s.* Eleganz *f.*; Schick *m.*; ~ *a.* schick, elegant.
chicane *s.* Schikane *f.*; ~ *v.t.* schikanieren.
chicanery *s.* Schikane *f.*
chick *s.* Küken *n.*
chicken *s.* (junges) Huhn *n.*, Hähnchen *n.*
chickenhearted *a.* feig.
chicken-house *s.* Hühnerstall *m.*
chicken-pox *s.* Windpocken *pl.*
chicory *s.* Zichorie *f.*; Endiviensalat *m.*
chide *v.t. & i.st.* schelten.
chief *a.*, ~**ly** *adv.* vornehmst; hauptsächlich; ~ *s.* Erste *m.*; Oberhaupt *n.*; ~ *of staff,* Generalstabschef *m.*
chiefly *adv.* hauptsächlich; vor allem.
chieftain *s.* Anführer, Häuptling *m.*
chiffon *s.* Chiffon *m.*
chilblain *s.* Frostbeule *f.*
child *s.* Kind *n.*
childbed *s.* Wochenbett *n.*
childbirth *s.* Geburt *f.*, Gebären *n.*
childhood *s.* Kindheit *f.*
childish *a.*, ~**ly** *adv.* kindisch; kindlich.
childishness *s.* kindisches Benehmen *n.*
childless *a.* kinderlos.
childlike *a.* kindlich.
child prodigy *s.* Wunderkind *n.*
child-proof *a.* kindersicher.
children *pl.* of child.
Chile *s.* Chile *n.*
Chilean *a.* chilenisch; ~ *s.* Chilene *m.*; Chilenin *f.*
chill *a.* frostig; ~ *s.* Kälte *f.*; Verkühlung *f.*; *to take the* ~ *off,* leicht anwärmen; ~ *v.t.* kühlen; mutlos machen.
chilling *a.* ernüchternd; frostig.
chilly *a.* etwas kalt, frostig, kühl.
chime *s.* Glockenspiel *n.*; ~ *v.t.* Glocken läuten; ~ *v.i.* einstimmig sein.
chimera *s.* Hirngespinst *n.*
chimerical *a.*, ~**ly** *adv.* schimärisch.
chimney *s.* Schornstein *m.*; Kamin *m.*
chimney-piece *s.* Kaminsims *m.*
chimney-sweep(er) *s.* Schornsteinfeger *m.*
chimpanzee *s.* Schimpanse *m.*
chin *s.* Kinn *n.*

china *s.* Porzellan *n.*
China *s.* China *n.*
Chinese *a.* chinesisch; ~ *s.* Chinese *m.*, Chinesin *f.*; ~ **lantern** *s.* Lampion *m.*
chink *s.* Ritze *f.*; Spalt *m.*; ~ *v.t. & i.* klimpern; sich spalten.
chintz *s.* Chintz *m.*, Möbelkattun *m.*
chip *v.t.* schnitzeln; abraspeln; ~ *s.* Span *m.*; Schnitzel *n.*
chipboard *s.* Spanplatte *f.*
chipmunk *s.* Chipmunk *n.*, Streifenhörnchen *n.*
chippings *s. pl.* Splitt *m.*
chiropodist *s.* Fußpfleger(in) *m.*(*f.*)
chiropractor *s.* Chiropraktiker(in) *m.*(*f.*)
chirp *v.i.* zwitschern; ~ *s.* Gezwitscher *n.*
chirrup *s.* Zwitschern *n.*
chisel *s.* Meißel *m.*; ~ *v.t.* meißeln.
chit *s.* Schein *m.*, Schriftstück *n.*; Notiz *f.*
chitchat *s.* Plauderei *f.*
chivalrous *a.* ritterlich.
chivalry *s.* Ritterlichkeit *f.*; Rittertum *n.*
chive *s.* Schnittlauch *m.*
chloride *s.* Chlorid *n.*
chlorinate *v.t.* chloren.
chlorine *s.* Chlor *n.*
chloroform *s.* Chloroform *n.*; ~ *v.t.* chloroformieren.
chlorophyll *s.* Chlorophyll *n.*
chock *s.* Bremsklotz *m.*; ~ *v.t.* festkeilen.
chock-full *a.* gestopft voll.
chocolate *s.* Schokolade *f.*; ~**s** ~ *s.pl.* Pralinen *f.pl.*; *box of* ~*s* ~*s.* Pralinenschachtel *f.*
choice *s.* Wahl *f.*; Auswahl *f.*; ~ *a.*, auserlesen, sehr schön.
choir *s.* Chor *m.*
choke *v.t.* ersticken; verstopfen.
choking *a.* stickig; erstickt.
cholera *s.* Cholera *f.*
choleric *a.* cholerisch; hitzig.
choose *v.t. & i.st.* wählen, aussuchen.
choosy *a.* (*fam.*) wählerisch.
chop *v.t. & i.* spalten; ~ *s.* Hieb *m.*; Röstrippchen, Kotelett *n.*
chopper *s.* Hackbeil *n.*; (*fam.*) Hubschrauber *m.*
chopping-block *s.* Hackblock *m.*
chopping-knife *s.* Hackmesser *n.*
choppy *a.* unstet; hohl (sea).
chopstick *s.* Eßstäbchen *n.*
choral *a.* chorartig, Chor. . .; ~ *s.* Choral *m.*
chord *s.* Saite *f.*; Akkord *m.*
chore *s.* Hausarbeit *f.*
choreographer *s.* Choreograph(in) *m.*(*f.*).
choreography *s.* Choreographie *f.*
chorister *s.* Chorsänger *m.*
chorus *s.* Chor *m.*
chorus girl *s.* Revuegirl *n.*
chowder *s.* dicke Suppe mit Kartoffeln u. Milch.
christen *v.t.* taufen.
Christendom *s.* Christenheit *f.*
christening *s.* Taufe *f.*
Christian *a.*, ~**ly** *adv.* christlich; ~ *s.* Christ *m.*; Christin *f.*; ~ **name** *s.* Vorname *m.*
Christianity *s.* Christentum *n.*
christianize *v.t.* christianisieren.
Christmas (Xmas) *s.* Weihnachten *n.*
Christmas carol *s.* Weihnachtslied *n.*

chromatic *a.* chromatisch.
chrome *a.* chromgelb.
chromium *s.* Chrom *n.*; **~-plated** *a.* verchromt.
chromosome *s.* Chromosom *n.*
chronic *a.* chronisch; langwierig.
chronicle *s.* Chronik *f.*; ~ *v.t.* aufzeichnen.
chronicler *s.* Chronist *m.*
chronological *a.*, **~ly** *adv.* chronologisch.
chronology *s.* Zeitrechnung *f.*; Chronologie *f.*
chrysalis *s.* (Insekten) Puppe *f.*
chrysanth, chrysanthemum *s.* Chrysantheme *f.*
chubby *a.* pummelig; pausbäckig.
chuck *v.i.* glucken; sanft stoßen; (*fam.*) wegwerfen; ~ *s.* Glucken *n.*; (*mech.*) Spannfutter *n.*
chuckle *v.i.* schmunzeln, kichern.
chug *s.* Tuckern *n.*; ~ *v.i.* tuckern.
chum *s.* Stubengenosse *m.*; Kamerad *m.*
chump *s.* Klotz *m.*
chunk *s.* Kloben, Klumpen *m.*
church *s.* Kirche *f.*; ~ **attendance,** Kirchenbesuch *m.*
churchwarden *s.* Kirchenvorsteher *m.*
churchyard *s.* Kirchhof *m.*
churl *s.* Bauer *m.*; Grobian *m.*
churlish *a.*, **~ly** *adv.* grob; mürrisch.
churn *v.i.* buttern; ~ *s.* Butterfaß *n.*
chute *s.* Schütte *f.*; Rutsche *f.*
cicada *s.* Zikade, Baumgrille *f.*
cider *s.* Apfelwein *m.*
cigar *s.* Zigarre *f.*
cigar-case *s.* Zigarrentasche *f.*
cigarette *s.* Zigarette *f.*; **~-case** *s.* Zigarettenetui *n.*; **~-butt,** *s.* Zigarettenstummel *m.*; **~-lighter** *s.* Feuerzeug *n.*
cigar-holder *s.* Zigarrenspitze *f.*
cinch *s.* Klacks *m.*; Kinderspiel *n.*
cinder *s.* Löschkohle *f.*; Schlacke *f.*
Cinderella *s.* Aschenbrödel *n.*
cinder-track *s.* Aschenbahn *f.*
cinema *s.* Kino *n.*
cinematography *s.* Kinematographie *f.*
cinnamon *s.* Zimt *m.*
cipher *s.* Ziffer *f.*; Null *f.*; Geheimschrift *f.*; ~ *v.i.* rechnen; ~ *v.t.* mit Chiffern schreiben.
circa *pr.* zirka.
circle *s.* Kreis *m.*; Kreislinie *f.*; ~ *v.t.* einschließen; ~ *v.i.* umkreisen.
circuit *s.* Umkreis *m.*; (*elek.*) Stromkreis *m.*; **short ~,** Kurzschluß *m.*; Bezirk *m.*; Rundreise der Richter *f.*
circuitous *a.* weitschweifig, Um. . .
circular *a.*, **~ly** *adv.* kreisförmig; ~ *s.* Rundschreiben *n.*
circularize *v.t.* Zirkulare herumschicken an.
circulate *v.t.* in Umlauf bringen; ~ *v.i.* umlaufen; *circulating library s.* Leihbibliothek *f.*
circulation *s.* Kreislauf, Umlauf *m.*; Auflage (einer Zeitung) *f.*
circulatory *a.* Kreislauf. . .
circumcise *v.t.* beschneiden.
circumcision *s.* Beschneidung *f.*
circumference *s.* Umfang *m.*
circumflex *s.* Zirkumflex (Akzent) *m.*
circumlocution *s.* Umschreibung *f.*; Umschweif *m.*
circumnavigate *v.t.* umschiffen.
circumscribe *v.t.* umschreiben; einschränken.
circumscription *s.* Begrenzung *f.*

circumspect *a.*, **~ly** *adv.* umsichtig.
circumspection *s.* Umsicht, Vorsicht *f.*
circumstance *s.* Umstand, Zufall *m.*
circumstanced *a.* beschaffen.
circumstantial *a.*, **~ly** *adv.* zufällig; eingehend; ~ **evidence** *s.* (*law*) Indizienbeweis *m.*
circumvent *v.t.* umgehen; überlisten.
circus *s.* Zirkus *m.*
cirrus *s.* Federwolke *f.*; Zirruswolke *f.*
Cistercian *a.* zisteriensisch.
cistern *s.* Wasserbehälter *m.*; Zisterne *f.*
citadel *s.* Festung *f.*; Zitadelle *f.*
citation *s.* Vorladung *f.*; Zitat *n.*
cite *v.t.* vorladen; (Stellen) anführen; zitieren.
citizen *s.* Bürger(in) *m.*(*f.*).
citizenship *s.* Staatsbürgerschaft *f.*
citric *a.*, ~ **acid** *s.* Zitronensäure *f.*
citrus *s.* Zitrusgewächs *n.*
city *s.* (große) Stadt *f.*
civic *a.* bürgerlich.
civil *a.*, **~ly** *adv.* bürgerlich; höflich; ~ **action** *s.* (*law*) Zivilklage *f.*; ~ **code** *s.* bürgerliches Gesetzbuch *n.*
civilian *s.* Zivilist, Bürger *m.*
civility *s.* Höflichkeit *f.*
civilization *s.* Kultur, Zivilisation *f.*
civilize *v.t.* zivilisieren; verfeinern.
civilized *a.* zivilisiert, buttiviert.
civil: ~law *s.* Zivilrecht *n.*; **~rights** *s.pl.* Bürgerrechte *n.pl.*; ~ **servant** *s.* Staatsbeamter *m.*; ~ **service** *s.* Staatsdienst *m.*; ~ **war** *s.* Bürgerkrieg *m.*
clack *s.* Geklapper *n.*; Geplauder *n.*; ~ *v.i.* klappern; plaudern.
clad *p.* gekleidet.
claim *v.t.* Anspruch machen, fordern; ~ *s.* Anspruch *m.*; Forderung *f.*
claimant *s.* Antragsteller(in) *m.*(*f.*); Forderer *m.*
clairvoyant *s.* Hellseher(in) *m.*(*f.*).
clam *s.* eßbare Muschel *f.*
clamber *v.i.* klettern.
clammy *a.* klamm.
clamor *s.* lautes Geschrei *n.*, Lärm *m.*
clamorous *a.* schreiend, tobend.
clamp *s.* Schraubzwinge *f.*; Klammer *f.*; ~ *v.t.* verklammern, verzapfen.
clan *s.* Stamm *m.*; Sippschaft *f.*
clandestine *a.*, **~ly** *adv.* heimlich.
clang *s.* Schall *m.*; ~ *v.i.* schallen.
clank *s.* Geklirr *n.*; ~ *v.i.* klirren.
clap *v.t.* klappern; beklatschen; ~ *v.i.* zusammenschlagen; ~ *s.* Klaps, Schlag *m.*; Klatschen *n.*
clapper *s.* Klöppel (Glocke) *m.*; Schwengel *m.*
clapping *s.* Beifall *m.*; Applaus *m.*
claptrap *s.* Phrasen *f.pl.*; Getue *n.*
claret *s.* Rotwein, Bordeaux *m.*
clarification *s.* Abklärung *f.*
clarify *v.t.* abklären; aufhellen; ~ *v.i.* sich aufklären.
clarinet *s.* Klarinette *f.*
clarion *s.* Trompete *f.*
clash *v.t. & i.* zusammenstoßen; rasseln; widerstreiten; ~ *s.* Stoß *m.*; Geklirr *n.*; Widerspruch *m.*; (*mil.*) Zusammenstoß *m.*
clasp *s.* Haken *m.*; Schnalle *f.*; Spange *f.*; Umarmung *f.*; ~ *v.t.* zuhaken; sich anklammern, umarmen.
class *s.* Klasse *f.*; Gesellschaftsschicht *f.*; Seminar *n.*

~ *v.t.* klassifizieren.

class-conscious *a.* klassenbewußt.

class-consciousness *s.* Klassenbewußtsein *n.*

classic(al) *a.* mustergültig, klassisch; ~ *s.* Klassiker *m.*

classicist *s.* Altphilologe *m.*, Altphilologin *f.*

classifiable *a.* klassifizierbar.

classification *s.* Einteilung in Klassen *f.*

classified *a.* gegliedert, unterteilt; ~ **advertisement** *s.* Kleinanzeige *f.*

classify *v.t.* klassifizieren, einordnen.

classless *a.* klassenlos.

classmate *s.* Klassenkamerad(in) *m.(f.)*

classroom *s.* Klassenzimmer *n.*

class struggle, class war *s.* Klassenkampf *m.*

clatter *v.t. & i.* klappern; ~ *s.* Getöse *n.*

clause *s.* Klausel *f.*; *(gram.)* Satzglied *n.*, (Neben-)satz *m.*

claustrophobia *s.* Klaustrophobie *f.*

clavicle *s.* Schlüsselbein *n.*

claw *s.* Klaue, Pfote *f.*; ~ *v.t.* kratzen.

clay *s.* Ton, Lehm *m.*; ~ *v.t.* mit Tonerde mischen, düngen.

clayey, clayish *a.* tonig, lehmig.

clean *a.* rein, sauber, blank; **~ly** *adv.* gänzlich; ~ *v.t.* reinigen.

clean-cut *a.* klar (umrissen).

cleaner *s.* Raumpfleger(in) *m.(f.)*; Reinigungsmittel *n.*

cleanliness *s.* Sauberkeit *f.*

cleanly *a.* rein, sauber; ~ *adv.* reinlich.

cleanness *s.* Sauberkeit *f.*

cleanse *v.t.* reinigen, scheuern.

cleanser *s.* Reinigungsmittel *n.*; Reinigungscreme *f.*

clean-shaven *a.* glattrasiert.

cleansing cream *s.* Reinigungscreme *f.*

clear *a.*, **~ly** *adv.* klar, rein, hell; deutlich; schuldlos; *in the ~*, vom Verdacht gereinigt; frei; ~ *v.t.* reinigen; aufklären; befreien; abräumen; springen über; ~ *v.i.* hell, frei werden.

clearance *s.* Freilegung, Räumung *f.*; Abfertigung *f.*; Spielraum *m.*; ~ **order** *s.* Räumungsbefehl *m.* ~ **sale,** Ausverkauf *m.*

clear-cut *a.* klar umrissen; scharf.

clear-headed *a.* klardenkend.

clearing *s.* Lichtung *f.*; Abrechnung *f.*

clear-sighted *a.* scharfsichtig.

cleat *s.* Klampe *f.*

cleavage *s.* Spaltung *f.*

cleave *v.i.st.* ankleben; ~*v.t.st.* spalten.

clef *s.* *(mus.)* Schlüssel *m.*

cleft *s.* Spalte *f.*; Kluft *f.*; ~ **palate** *s.* Wolfsrachen *m.*

clemency *s.* Gnade, Milde *f.*; ~ *plea, petition for ~, (law)* Gnadengesuch *n.*

clement *a.* sanft, mild.

clench *v.t.* zusammenpressen; umklammern.

clergy *s.* Geistlichkeit *f.*

clergyman *s.* Geistlicher *m.*

cleric *s.* Kleriker *m.*

clerical error *s.* Schreibfehler *m.*; **clerical staff** *s.* Büropersonal *n.*

clerk *s.* Angestellter *m.*; Angestellte *f.*

clerkship *s.* Schreiberstelle *f.*

clever *a.*, **~ly** *adv.* gewandt, gescheit.

clew *s.* Knäuel *m.*

cliché *s.* Klischee *n.*; Gemeinplatz *m.*; abgedroschene Redewendung *f.*

click *s.* Ticken (einer Uhr) *m.*; Türklinke *f.*; ~ *v.i.* ticken.

client *s.* Klient(in) *m.(f.)*, Kunde *m.*, Kundin *f.*; *(law)* Mandant(in) *m.(f.)*

clientele *s.* Klientel *f.*, Kundschaft *f.*

cliff *s.* Klippe *f.*

climacteric *a.* klimakterisch; ~ *s.* Wechseljahre *pl.*; Klimakterium *n.*

climate *s.* Klima *n.*

climatic *a.* klimatisch.

climax *s.* Höhepunkt *m.*; Orgasmus *m.*

climb *v.i.* klettern; ~ *v.t.* ersteigen.

climber *s.* Bergsteiger(in) *m.(f.)*; Kletterpflanze *f.*

clinch *v.t.* anpacken; (die Faust) ballen; nieten; befestigen; entscheiden, erledigen; ~ *s.* Vernietung *f.*; Klinke *f.*

cling *v.i.st.* anklammern, ankleben.

clinic *s.* Klinik *f.*

clinical *a.* klinisch.

clink *v.i. & t.* klingen, klirren; (Gläser) anstoßen; ~ *s.* Geklirr *n.*, Klirren *n.*

clip *v.t.* beschneiden; (Billette) lochen; klammern; ~ *s.* Zwicke *f.*; Hosenklammer *f.*

clipped *a.* abgehackt.

clipper *s.* Schnellsegler *m.*

clipping *s.* Schnipsel *m.*, Ausschnitt *m.*

clique *s.* Clique *f.*, Klüngel *m.*

clitoris *s.* Kitzler *m.*, Klitoris *f.*

cloak *s.* Mantel *m.*; *(fig.)* Deckmantel *m.*; **~-room** *s.* (Eisenbahn) Gepäckaufbewahrung *f.*; Garderobe *f.*; ~ *v.t.* einhüllen; bemänteln.

clock *s.* Uhr *f.*; Schlaguhr *f.*; Wanduhr *f.*; ~ **face** Zifferblatt *n.*; ~ **tower** *s.* Uhrturm *m.*

clockwise *adv.* im Uhrzeigersinn.

clockwork *s.* Uhrwerk *n.*

clod *s.* Erdkloß, Klumpen *m.*

clog *v.t.* verstopfen, blockieren, hemmen; ~ *v.i.* gerinnen; ~ *s.* Hindernis *n.*; Klotz *m.*; Holzschuh *m.*

cloister *s.* Kloster *n.*; Kreuzgang *m.*

clone *s.* Klon *m.*; Kopie *f.*; ~ *v.t.* klonen.

close *v.t.* verschließen; beschließen; vereinigen; *to ~ up,* abschließen; *to ~ down,* (Betrieb) einstellen, stillegen; ~ *v.i.* sich schließen; übereinkommen; ~ *s.* Einzäunung *f.*; Schluß, Beschluß, *m.*; Ruhepunkt *m.*; ~ *a.* verschlossen; verschwiegen; knapp; dicht, steif; bündig; trübe; drückend (Luft); einsam; geizig; ~ *prisoner,* strengbewachter Gefangener *m.*; ~ *quarters,* Handgemenge *n.*; ~ *season,* Schonzeit (Jagd) *f.*

closely *adv.* geschlossen; genau, streng; verborgen; sparsam.

closeness *s.* Nähe, Enge *f.*

close season *s.* Schonzeit *f.*

closet *s.* Schrank *m.*; Kabinett *n.*; Verschlag *m.*; **water** ~ Klosett *n.* (W.C. = water closet); ~ *v.t.* einschließen.

close-up *s.* *(film)* Nahaufnahme *f.*; Großaufnahme *f.*

closing *s.* Vertragsabschluß (Hauskauf) *m.*; ~ **date** *s.* Einsendeschluß *m.*; Meldefrist *f.*

closure *s.* Einschließung *f.*; Schließung *f.*; Schluß der Debatte *m.*

clot *a.* Klumpen *m.*; ~ *v.i.* gerinnen; klumpen; *blood ~ s.* Blutgerinnsel *n.*

cloth s. Zeug, Tuch n.; Tischtuch n.; Leinwand f.; bound in ~, in Leinwand gebunden.
clothe v.t. bekleiden; ~ v.i. sich kleiden.
clothes s.pl. Kleider n.pl; Wäsche f.
clothes-basket s. Wäschekorb m.
clothes-brush s. Kleiderbürste f.
clothes-line s. Wäscheleine f.
clothes-peg s. **clothes-pin** s. Wäscheklammer f.
clothing s. Kleidung f.
cloth worker s. Tuchwirker m.
cloud s. Wolke f.; (fig.) Gewühl n.; ~ v.t. bewölken, verdunkeln; ~ v.i. sich umwölken.
cloudburst s. Wolkenbruch m.
cloudless a. unbewölkt.
cloudy a., **~ily** adv. wolkig.
clout s. Schlag m.; (fig.) Einfluß m.
clove s. Gewürznelke f.; ~ of garlic s. Knoblauchzehe f.
cloven a. gespalten.
clover s. Klee m.; (fig.) in ~, üppig.
clown s. Clown, Hanswurst m.
clownish a., **~ly** adv. bäuerisch, grob.
cloy v.t. überladen; sättigen.
club s. Keule f.; Kreuz, Treff (der Karte) n.; Klub m.; Verein m.; ~v.t. & i. beitragen; sich vereinigen.
club-foot s. Klumpfuß m.
club-law s. Faustrecht n.
cluck v.i. glucken.
clue s. Leitfaden m.; (fig.) Schlüssel m.; Anhaltspunkt m.
clump s. Klumpen m.; Gruppe f.
clumsy a., **~ily** adv. plump, ungeschickt.
cluster s. Büschel m.; Traube f.; Haufen m.; ~ v.t. häufen; ~ v.i. in Büscheln wachsen.
clutch v.t. greifen; packen; umspannen; ~ s. Griff m.; Kupplung f.
clutter s. Verwirrung f.; ~ v.i. verworren rennen.
coach s. Kutsche f.; Eisenbahnwagen m.; Überlandomnibus m.; (pers.) Einpauker m.; (Sport) Trainer m.; a ~ and four, vierspännige Kutsche f.; ~ v.t. einpauken; trainieren.
coachman s. Kutscher m.
coachtour s. Omnibusreise f.
coadjutor s. Mitgehilfe m.
coagulate v.t. gerinnen machen; ~ v.i. gerinnen.
coal s. Kohle f.; ~ v.i. zu Kohle werden; Kohlen einnehmen.
coal dust s. Kohlenstaub m.
coalesce v.i. verschmelzen.
coalfield s. Kohlenlager n.; Kohlenfeld n.
coalition s. Vereinigung f.
coal mine, coal pit s. Kohlengrube f.
coarse a., **~ly** adv. grob, gemein.
coast s. Küste f.; ~ v.i. längs der Küste hinfahren; einen Abhang hinabfahren.
coastal a. Küsten. . .
coaster s. Untersetzer m.; **roller** ~ s. Achterbahn f.
coat s. Mantel, Rock m.; Fell, n.; Schicht f.; ~ of arms, Wappenschild n.; ~ of mail, Panzerhemd n.; ~ v.t. bekleiden.
coated a. überzogen, bedeckt; belegt (Zunge).
coating s. Schicht f.; Anstrich m.
co-author s. Mitautor(in) m.(f.)
coax v.t. überreden, beschwatzen.
cob s. Kolben m.
cobalt s. Kobalt m.

cobble s. Kopfstein, Pflasterstein m.; ~ v.t., flicken; pflastern.
cobbler s. Schuster m.
cobra s. Kobra f.
cobweb s. Spinngewebe n.
cocaine s. Kokain n.
cock s. Hahn m.; Männchen n.; (vulg.) Penis m.; ~ v.t. (den Hahn) spannen; aufstellen; ~ v.i. stolzieren.
cockade s. Kokarde f.
cock-a-doodle-doo kikeriki!
Cockaigne s. Schlaraffenland n.
cockatoo s. Kakadu m.
cockatrice s. Basilisk m.
cockchafer s. Maikäfer m.
cocked a. ~ **hat** s. dreieckiger Hut m.
cockerel s. junger Hahn m.
cock-eyed a. schief.
cockfight s. Hahnenkampf m.
cockle v.t. runzeln; ~ s. Herzmuschel f.
cockney s. Londoner m.
cockpit s. (avi.) Führersitz m., Cockpit n.
cockroach s. Schabe f.
cocksure a. todsicher.
coco s. Kokospalme f.
cocoa s. Kakao m.
cocktail s. Parvenü m.; Cocktail m.
coconut s. Kokosnuß f.
cocoon s. Seidenraupenpuppe f., Kokon m.
cod s. Kabeljau m.; ~-liver oil, Lebertran m.
coddle v.t. verhätscheln.
code s. Gesetzbuch n.; (Telegramm) Schlüssel m.; Chiffre f.;~ of civil procedure, Zivilprozeßordnung f.; ~ of criminal procedure, Strafprozeßordnung f.; commercial ~, Handelsgesetzbuch n.; ~ **name** s. Deckname m.; ~ v.t. chiffrieren.
codicil s. Kodizill n.
codification s. Kodifizierung f.
codify v.t. kodifizieren.
coeducation s. gemeinsame Erziehung (f.) der Knaben und Mädchen; Koedukation f.
coefficient a. mitwirkend; ~ s. Koeffizient m.
coerce v.t. zwingen.
coercion s. Zwang m.
coercive a. zwingend, Zwangs. . .
coeval a. gleichalt, gleichzeitig.
coexist v.i. zugleich da sein; koexistieren.
coexistent a. gleichzeitig.
coffee s. Kaffee m.
coffee-bean s. Kaffeebohne f.
coffee-grinder s. Kaffeemühle.
coffee-grounds s.pl. Kaffeesatz m.
coffee-pot s. Kaffeekanne f.
coffee-roaster s. Kaffeebrenner f.
coffee-shop s. Imbißraum m.
coffee-table s. Couchtisch m.
coffin s. Sarg m.
cog s. Zahn (am Rad) m.
cogency s. zwingende Kraft f.
cogent a., **~ly** adv. zwingend, triftig.
cogitate v.i. denken, erwägen.
cognate a. verwandt.
cognition s. (Er)kenntnis, Kunde f.
cognizance s. Kenntnis f.
cognizant a. wissend.
cogwheel s. Zahnrad, Kammrad n.

cohabit *v.i.* bei(sammen)wohnen.
cohabitation *s.* (eheliche) Beiwohnung *f.*; Beisammenwohnen *n.*
co-heir *s.* Miterbe *m.*
co-heiress *s.* Miterbin *f.*
cohere *v.i.* zusammenhängen; zusammenhalten.
coherence *s.* Zusammenhang *m.*
coherent *s.* zusammenhängend.
cohesion *s.* Kohäsion *f.*; Zusammenhang *m.*
cohesive *a.* zusammenhaltend.
cohort *s.* Kohorte *f.*
coil *v.t.* aufwickeln; ~ *s.* (Draht) Rolle, *f.*; Windung *f.*; Schlinge *f.*
coin *s.* Münze *f.*; *false* ~, falsches Geld *n.*; ~ *v.t.* münzen; erdichten; prägen.
coinage *s.* Geld *n.*; Gepräge *n.*
coincide *v.i.* zusammentreffen.
coincidence *s.* Zusammentreffen *n.*; Zufall *m.*
coincident *a.* übereinstimmend; zusammentreffend.
coincidental *a.* zufällig.
coincidentally *adv.* zufälligerweise.
coitus *s.* Koitus *m.*, Beischlaf *m.*
coke *s.* Koks *m.*
colander *s.* Sieb *n.*
cold *a.*, **-ly** *adv.* kalt; ~ *s.* Kälte, Erkältung *f.*; *to catch a* ~, sich erkälten, einen Schnupfen bekommen.
coldness *s.* Kälte *f.*
cold storage *s.* Kühlraum *m.*
coleslaw *s.* Krautsalat *m.*
colic *s.* Bauchkrampf *m.*, Kolik *f.*
collaborate *v.i.* zusammenarbeiten.
collaboration *s.* Mitarbeiterschaft *f.*
collaborator *s.* Mitarbeiter(in) *m.(f.).*
collapse *v.i.* zusammenfallen; ~ *s.* Zusammenbruch *m.*
collapsible *a.* zusammenlegbar, zusammenklappbar; ~ **boat** *s.* Faltboot *n.*
collar *s.* Halsband *n.*; Kragen *m.*; ~ **bone** *s.* Schlüsselbein *n.*; ~ *v.t.* beim Kragen fassen.
collate *v.t.* vergleichen; verleihen; zusammenstellen (Daten).
collateral *a.*, **-ly** *adv.* Seiten..., neben; gleichlaufend; *s.* Sicherheiten (Anleihe) *pl.*; **~s** *s.pl.* Seitenverwandte *m.f.pl.*
colleague *s.* Kollege *m.*, Kollegin *f.*
collect *v.t.* sammeln; einkassieren; ~ *s.* Kollekte *f.*
collected *a.* ruhig, gefaßt.
collection *s.* Sammlung *f.*; Abholung *f.*; Leerung der Briefkästen *f.*
collective *a.* gesammelt; Kollektiv...; ~ *agreement*, Tarifvertrag *m.*; ~ *security*, kollektive Sicherheit *f.*
collector *s.* Sammler *m.*
college *s.* Kollegium *n.*; höhere Lehranstalt *f.*, College *n.*
collide *v.i.* zusammenstoßen (von Schiffen etc.).
collier *s.* Kohlenarbeiter *m.*; Kohlenschiff *n.*
colliery *s.* Kohlenbergwerk *n.*; Zeche *f.*
collision *s.* Zusammenstoß *m.*
collocation *s.* Stellung, Ordnung *f.*
colloquial *a.* umgangssprachlich; in der Umgangssprache üblich.
colloquialism *s.* Ausdruck der Umgangssprache *m.*
colloquy *s.* Gespräch *n.*; Kolloquium *n.*
collusion *s.* heimliches Einverständnis *n.*; Verdunkelung *f.*

Colombia *s.* Kolumbien *n.*
Colombian *a.* kolumbianisch; ~ *s.* Kolumbianer(in) *m.(f.).*
colon *s.* Doppelpunkt *m.*; (*anat.*) Dickdarm *m.*
colonel *s.* Oberst *m.*
colonelcy *s.* Oberstenstelle *f.*
colonial *a.* Kolonial...; kolonial.
colonialism *s.* Kolonialismus *m.*
colonist *s.* Kolonist(in), Siedler(in) *m.(f.).*
colonization *s.* Kolonisierung *f.*
colonize *v.t.* besiedeln, kolonisieren.
colonnade *s.* Säulengang *m.*
colony *s.* Kolonie *f.*
colophony *s.* Geigenharz *n.*
color *s.* Farbe *f.*; Schein *m.*; Vorwand *m.*; **~s** *pl.* Fahne *f.*; *to show a person in his true* ~*s*, jemand nach dem Leben malen; ~ *v.t.* färben; beschönigen; ~ *v.i.* erröten.
coloration *s.* Färbung *f.*
color-blind *a.* farbenblind.
color-box *s.* Malkasten *m.*
coloring *s.* Färben, Beschönigen *n.*
colorless *a.* farblos.
colors *s.pl.* Fahne *f.*; *with the* ~*s*, bei der Wehrmacht.
colossal *a.* kolossal, riesig.
colossus *s.* Koloß *m.*
colt *s.* Füllen *n.*; (*fig.*) Wildfang *m.*
columbine *s.* (*bot.*) Akelei *f.*
column *s.* Säule *f.*; (*print.*) Spalte *f.*; Kolonne *f.*
columnar *a.* säulenförmig.
columnist *s.* Kommentator(in) (in der Presse) *m.(f.);* Kolumnist(in) *m.(f.).*
coma *s.* Koma *n.*
comb *s.* Kamm *m.*; Striegel *m.*; ~ *v.t.* kämmen, striegeln.
combat *s.* Kampf *m.*; Gefecht *n.*; *single* ~, Zweikampf *m.*; ~ *v.i.* kämpfen; ~ *v.t.* bekämpfen.
combatant *s.* Kombattant *m.*; Kämpfer *m.*
combative *a.* streitsüchtig.
combed *a.* gekämmt.
combination *s.* Verbindung *f.*
combine *v.t.* verbinden; (*mil.*) *combined operations*, Operationen der verbundenen Waffen; ~ *v.i.* sich verbinden; ~ *s.* Zusammenschluß, Verband, Konzern *m.*; Mähdrescher *m.*
combined *a.* vereint.
combustible *a.* brennbar; ~ *s.* Brennmaterial *n.*
combustion *s.* Verbrennung *f.*
come *v.i.st.* kommen; werden; *to* ~ *about*, sich wenden; sich zutragen; *to* ~ *by*, etwas bekommen; vorbeikommen; *to* ~ *for*, holen kommen, kommen um...; *to* ~ *off*, zustande kommen; davonkommen; loskommen; *to* ~ *of age*, mündig werden; *to* ~ *round*, sich anders besinnen; sich erholen; *to* ~ *to pass*, geschehen, sich ereignen.
comeback *s.* Comeback *n.*
comedian *s.* Komödiant *m.*
comedienne *s.* Komikerin *f.*
comedown *s.* Abstieg *m.*
comedy *s.* Komödie *f.*, Lustspiel *n.*
comely *a.* hübsch; artig.
comestibles *pl.* Nahrungsmittel *n.pl.*
comet *s.* Komet *m.*
comfort *v.t.* trösten; erquicken; ~ *s.* Trost *m.*; Erquickung *f.*; Bequemlichkeit *f.*; Behaglichkeit *f.*;

cold ~, schwacher Trost *m*.
comfortable *a*., **~bly** *adv*. tröstlich, erfreulich; bequem, behaglich.
comforter *s*. Halstuch *m*.; Steppdecke *f*.
comforting *a*. beruhigend; tröstend.
comfortless *a*. trostlos; unbequem.
comic(al) *a*., **~ly** *adv*. komisch; ~ **strip** *s*., **comics** *s.pl*. Comics *pl*.
comma *s*. Komma *n*.; *inverted ~*, Anführungszeichen *n*.
command *v.t. & i*. befehlen; anführen, herrschen; bestellen; ~ *s*. Befehl *m*.; Beherrschung *f*.; Herrschaft *f*.; Bestellung *f*.
commandant *s*. Befehlshaber *m*.
commandeer *v.t*. requirieren.
commander *s*. Befehlshaber *m*.; (*nav*.) Fregattenkapitän *m*.; Handramme *f*.; *~-in-chief*, Oberbefehlshaber *m*.
commanding *a*. gebieterisch, imposant.
commandment *s*. Befehl *m*.; Gebot *n*.
commando *s*. Kommando *n*.; Kommandotrupp *m*.
commemorate *v.t*. feiern, gedenken.
commemoration *s*. Gedächtnisfeier *f*.
commemorative *a*. erinnernd, Erinnerungs. . .
commence *v.t. & i*. anfangen; beginnen.
commencement *s*. Anfang *m*.
commend *v.t*. empfehlen, loben.
commendable *a*., **~bly** *adv*. empfehlenswert.
commendation *s*. Lob *n*.; Belobigung *f*.; Auszeichnung *f*.
commendatory *a*. empfehlend.
commensurable *a*. kommensurabel.
commensurate *a*., **~ly** *adv*. entsprechend; angemessen.
comment *v.i*. erläutern, auslegen; ~ *s*. Auslegung *f*.; **~s** *s.pl*. Bemerkungen *f.pl*.; Stellungnahme *f*.
commentary *s*. Kommentar *m*.
commentate *v.i*. kommentieren.
commentator *s*. Kommentator(in), Reporter(in) *m*.(*f*.)
commerce *s*. Handel, Verkehr *m*.; Gewerbe *n*.
commercial *a*. kaufmännisch, Handels. . .; ~ *directory*, Handelsadreßbuch *n*.; ~ *law*, Handelsrecht *n*.; ~ **papers** *s.pl*. Geschäftspapiere *n.pl*. (Post); ~ *traveler*, Handlungsreisender *m*.; ~ *treaty*, Handelsvertrag *m*.
commercialize *v.t*. kommerzialisieren.
commingle *v.t. & i*. vermischen.
commiserate *v.t*. bemitleiden.
commiseration *s*. Mitgefühl *n*.; Teilnahme *f*.
commission *s*. Auftrag *m*.; Vollmacht *f*.; Ausschuß *m*.; Begehung (von Sünden) *f*. Offizierspatent *n*.; Provision *f*.; ~ *v.t*. einen Auftrag geben, bevollmächtigen; in Dienst stellen.
commissioner *s*. Bevollmächtigter, Kommissar *m*., Kommissionsmitglied *n*.
commit *v.t*. übergeben, anvertrauen; verüben; verpflichten, festlegen; (*mil*.) einsetzen (Truppen); *to ~ oneself*, sich binden; *to ~ to prison*, einsperren.
commitment *s*. Verpflichtung *f*.; (*mil*.) Einsatz *m*.; *without any ~*, unverbindlich.
committee *s*. Ausschuß *m*.; *to be on the ~*, dem Ausschuß angehören.
commodity *s*. Ware *f*.
commodore *s*. Kommodore *m*.

common *a*., **~ly** *adv*. gemein, gewöhnlich; gemeinschaftlich; ~ *law*, Gewohnheitsrecht *n*.; ~ *room*, Konversationszimmer *m*.; ~ *time* *s*. (*mus*.) gerader Takt *m*.; ~ *s*. Gemeindeweide *f*.; **~s** *pl*. Gemeinen *m.pl*.; Volk *n*.; Kost *f*.; *House of Commons*, Unterhaus (in England) *n*.
commoner *s*. Bürgerliche *m*.
commonplace *a*. gewöhnlich.
common sense *s*. gesunder Menschenverstand *m*.
common stock *s*. Stammaktien *f.pl*.
Commonwealth *s*. Commonwealth *m*.
commotion *s*. Erschütterung *f*.; Aufruhr *m*.
communal *a*. Gemeinde. . .
commune *s*. Gemeinde *f*.; Kommune *f*.
communicable *a*. mitteilbar.
communicate *v.t*. mitteilen; ~ *v.i*. Gemeinschaft haben; kommunizieren.
communication *s*. Mitteilung *f*.; Umgang *m*.; Verbindung *f*.; **~s** *satellite* *s*. Nachrichtensatellit *m*.
communicative *s*. mitteilsam.
communion *s*. Gemeinschaft *f*.; Umgang *m*.; Abendmahl *n*.
communiqué *s*. Kommuniqué *n*.
communism *s*. Kommunismus *m*.
communist *s*. Kommunist *m*.
community *s*. Gemeinschaft, Gemeinde *f*.; Allgemeinheit *f*.; Staat *m*.; ~ *of goods*, (*law*) Gütergemeinschaft *f*.
community center *s*. Gemeinschaftszentrum *n*.
community service *s*. (freiwilliger) sozialer Dienst.
commutable *a*. vertauschbar.
commutation *s*. Vertauschung *f*.; Auswechslung *f*.; ~ *of a sentence*, (*law*) Strafumwandlung *f*.
commute *v.t*. umtauschen, auswechseln; ersetzen; (*law*) (Strafe) umwandeln od. mildern; täglich in die Stadt fahren, pendeln.
commuter *s*. Pendler(in) *m*.(*f*.)
compact *s*. Vertrag *m*.; ~ *a*., **~ly** *adv*. dicht, gedrängt, bündig; ~ *v.t*. festverbinden.
compact disk *s*. Compact Disc *f*.; Kompaktschallplatte *f*.
companion *s*. Gefährte *m*.; Gefährtin *f*.
companionable *a*., **~bly** *adv*. gesellig, umgänglich.
companionship *s*. Gesellschaft *f*.
company *s*. Gesellschaft *f*.; (*mil*.) Kompanie; Zunft *f*.; Trupp *m*.
comparable *a*., **~bly** *adv*. vergleichbar; vergleichsweise.
comparative *a*., **~ly** *adv*. vergleichend; verhältnismäßig; ~ *s*. (*gram*.) Komparativ *m*.
compare *v.t*. vergleichen.
comparison *s*. Vergleich *m*.
compartment *s*. Abteilung *f*.; Fach *n*.; (*rail*.) Abteil *n*.
compass *v.t*. umgeben, einschließen; erreichen; ~ *s*. Bereich *m*.; Umfang *m*.; Kompaß *m*.; (*pair of*) *compasses* *pl*. Zirkel *m*.
compassion *s*. Mitleid *n*.
compassionate *a*. mitfühlend; ~ **leave** *s*. Familienurlaub *m*.
compatibility *s*. Vereinbarkeit *f*.
compatible *a*., **~bly** *adv*. vereinbar.
compatriot *s*. Landsmann *m*., Landsmännin *f*.
compeer *s*. Genosse, Gevatter *m*.
compel *v.t*. zwingen, nötigen.

compelling *a.* bezwingend.
compendium *s.* Auszug *m.*; Kompendium *n.*
compensate *v.t.* ersetzen, entschädigen.
compensation *s.* Ersatz *m.*; Entschädigung *f.*; *(elek.)* Ausgleich *m.*; *to make ~ for,* Entschädigung leisten für. . .
compensatory *a.* ausgleichend.
compete *v.i.* sich mitbewerben, konkurrieren.
competence, competency *s.* behagliches Auskommen *n.*; Befugnis, Kompetenz *f.*; Befähigung *f.*
competent *a.* hinlänglich; kompetent.
competition *s.* Mitbewerbung, Konkurrenz *f.*; Preisausschreiben *n.*; Wettbewerb *m.*; *unfair ~,* unlauterer Wettbewerb *m.*
competitive *a.* wetteifernd; Konkurrenz. . .; *~ price,* konkurrenzfähiger Preis *m.*
competitor *s.* Mitbewerber(in), Konkurrent(in) *m.(f.).*
compilation s. Zusammenstellung *f.*
compile *v.t.* zusammentragen; zusammenstellen.
compiler *s.* Kompilator(in) *m.(f.).*
complacence, complacency *s.* Wohlgefallen *n.*; Sebstgefälligkeit *f.*
complacent *a.* gefällig, selbstzufrieden.
complain *v.i.* sich beklagen.
complainant *s.* Beschwerdeführer(in) *m.(f.)*
complaint *s.* Beschwerde *f.*; Klage *f.*; *to lodge a ~,* eine Beschwerde einlegen.
complaisance *s.* Nachgiebigkeit *f.*
complaisant *a.* gefällig, höflich.
complement *s.* Ergänzung *f.*; volle Zahl *f.*, volle Besetzung *f.*; *~ v.t.* vervollständigen.
complementary *a.* ergänzend.
complete *a.*, **~ly** *adv.* vollständig, vollendet; gänzlich; *~ v.t.* vervollständigen, ergänzen; *to ~ a form,* ein Formular ausfüllen.
completion *s.* Ergänzung *f.*; Vollendung *f.*
complex s. Komplex *m.*; *a.*, **~ly** *adv.* zusammengesetzt, verwickelt.
complexion *s.* Aussehen *n.*; Gesichtsfarbe *f.*
complexity *s.* Verwickeltheit, Kompliziertheit *f.*
compliance *s.* Willfährigkeit *f.*; Einwilligung *f.*; Unterwürfigkeit *f.*
compliant *a.*, **~ly** *adv.* willfährig; unterwürfig.
complicate *v.t.* verwickeln.
complicated *a.* kompliziert, verwickelt.
complication *s.* Verwicklung *f.*
complicity *s.* Mitschuld *f.*
compliment *s.* Kompliment *n.*; **~s** *pl.* Gruß *m.*; *~ v.t.* grüßen; beglückwünschen; einem Komplimente machen.
complimentary *a.* höflich; Frei. . . *~ dinner,* Festessen *n.*
comply *v.i.* sich fügen; *to ~ with* (Gesetze) befolgen.
component *s.* Bestandteil *m.*; *~ a.* Teil. . .
compose *v.t.* zusammensetzen, verfassen; komponieren; (*print.*) setzen; beruhigen, ordnen; schlichten, beilegen; *to ~ oneself,* sich fassen, sich beruhigen.
composed *a.*, **~ly** *adv.* ruhig, gesetzt.
composer *s.* Komponist(in) *m.(f.).*
composite *a.* zusammengesetzt.
composition *s.* Zusammensetzung *f.*; Aufsatz *m.*; Schriftsatz *m.*; Tonsatz *m.*; Komposition *f.*
compositor *s.* Schriftsetzer(in) *m.(f.)*

compost *s.* Dünger *m.*; *~ v.t.* düngen; *~* **heap,** *~* **pile** *s.* Komposthaufen *m.*
composure *s.* Gemütsruhe, Fassung *f.*
compote *s.* Kompott *n.*
compound *v.t.* zusammensetzen; beilegen; *~ v.i.* sich vergleichen; *~ a.* zusammengesetzt; *~* **eye** *s.* Facettenauge *n.*; *~* **interest** *s.* Zinseszins *m.*; *~* **fraction** *s.* (*math.*) Doppelbruch *m.*; (*med.*) *~* **fracture** *s.* komplizierter Bruch *m.*; *~* **word** *s.* zusammengesetztes Wort *n.*; *~ s.* Mischung *f.*; (*chem.*) Verbindung *f.*; Zusammensetzung *f.*; Einzäunung *f.*, Gelände *n.*
comprehend *v.t.* zusammenfassen; begreifen.
comprehensible *a.*, **~bly** *adv.* begreiflich, verständlich.
comprehension *s.* Verständnis *n.*; Fassungskraft *f.*; Umfang *m.*
comprehensive *a.*, **~ly** *adv.* umfassend; gedrängt.
compress *v.t.* zusammendrücken.
compressed air *s.* Druck-, Preßluft *f.*
compressible *a.* zusammendrückbar.
compression *s.* Zusammendrückung *f.*, Kompression *f.*
compressor *s.* (*mot.*) Kompressor, Verdichter *m.*
comprise *v.t.* in sich fassen, enthalten.
compromise *s.* Kompromiß *m.*; *~ v.t.* durch Vergleich beilegen; *to ~ oneself,* sich kompromittieren.
compulsion *s.* Zwang *m.*
compulsory *a.*, **~ily** *adv.* Zwangs. . .
compunction *s.* Gewissensangst *f.*
computation *s.* Berechnung *f.*
compute *v.t.* rechnen, berechnen.
computer *s.* Computer *m.*
computerize *v.t.* computerisieren.
computer: ~-operated *a.* computergesteuert; *~* **program** *s.* Computerprogramm *n.*; *~* **programmer** *s.* Programmierer(in) *m.(f.).*
comrade *s.* Gefährte *m.*; Gefährtin *f.*; Kamerad(in) *m.(f.).*
comradeship *s.* Kameradschaft *f.*
con *v.t.* auswendig lernen, wiederholen; *~ adv.* pro *and ~,* für und wider; *~ s.* Gegenstimme *f.*; *~* **man** Hochstapler(in) *m.(f.).* Betrüger(in) *m.(f.).*
concatenation *s.* Verkettung *f.*
concave *a.*, **~ly** *adv.* hohlrund, konkav.
concavity *s.* Hohlrundung *f.*
conceal *v.t.* verhehlen.
concealed *a.* verdeckt; *~* **lighting** indirekte Beleuchtung *f.*
concealment *s.* Verheimlichung *f.*; Verbergen *n.*
concede *v.t.* einräumen, gestatten.
conceit *s.* Einbildung *f.*, Dünkel *m.*; Witzelei *f.*
conceited *a.* eingebildet, dünkelhaft.
conceivable *a.*, **~bly** *adv.* denkbar.
conceive *v.t. & i.* begreifen; erdenken; meinen; empfangen, schwanger werden.
concentrate *v.t.* zusammenziehen, konzentrieren.
concentration *s.* Zusammenziehung, Konzentrierung *f.*; **~-camp** Konzentrationslager *n.*
concentric *a.* konzentrisch.
concept *s.* Begriff *m.*
conception *s.* Empfängnis *f.*; Auffassung *f.*; Begriff *m.*; Meinung *f.*
conceptual *a.* begrifflich.
concern *v.t.* betreffen; beunruhigen; *to ~ oneself about,* sich kümmern um; *~ s.* Angelegenheit *f.*;

Belang *m.*; Unternehmen *n.*; Anteil *m.*; Unruhe *f.*; Geschäft *n.*

concerned *p. & a.* bekümmert; interessiert; *those ~,* die Beteiligten *m.pl.*

concerning *pr.* betreffend.

concert *s.* Einverständnis *n.*; (*mus.*) Konzert *n.*; *in ~* gemeinsam, zusammen.

concerted *a.* gemeinsam; *~ action s.* gemeinsames Vorgehen *n.*; konzertierte Aktion *f.*

concert-goer *s.* Konzertbesucher(in) *m.*(*f.*)

concert-hall *s.* Konzertsaal *m.*

concertina *s.* Ziehharmonika *f.*

concerto *s.* **concerti** *pl.* (*mus.*) Konzert *n.*

concert pianist *s.* Konzertpianist(in) *m.*(*f.*)

concert pitch *s.* Kammerton *m.*

concession *s.* Zugeständnis *n.*; Konzession *f.*

concessionnaire *s.* Inhaber einer Konzession *m.*

conciliate *v.t.* versöhnen; ausgleichen.

conciliation *s.* Versöhnung *f.*; **~-board,** Schlichtungsamt *n.*; **~-proceedings** *s.pl.* (*law*) Sühneverfahren *n.*

conciliator *s.* Vermittler *m.*

conciliatory *a.* vermittelnd, versöhnlich.

concise *a.*, **~ly** *adv.* kurz, gedrängt.

conclave *s.* Konklave *n.*; geheime Beratung *f.*

conclude *v.t. & i.* folgern, schließen; sich entschließen; beschließen.

conclusion *s.* Schluß *m.*; Beschluß *m.*; Ende *n.*; Folgerung *f.*; Abschluß (eines Vertrags) *m.*

conclusive *a.*, **~ly** *adv.* entscheidend; endgültig; schlüssig, überzeugend.

concoct *v.t.* schmieden, anzetteln.

concoction *s.* Gebräu *n.*; Ausbrütung *f.*

concomitant *a.*, **~ly** *adv.* begleitend.

concord *s.* Eintracht *f.*; (*gram.*) Übereinstimmung *f.*

concordance *s.* Übereinstimmung *f.*; Konkordanz *f.*

concordant *a.* übereinstimmend.

concordat *s.* Konkordat *n.*

concourse *s.* Zusammenfluß *m.*; Menge *f.*, Auflauf *m.*

concrete *v.i.* sich verdichten; **~ly** *adv.* konkret, bestimmt; *~ s.* Beton *m.*

concubine *s.* Konkubine *n.*

concupiscence *s.* Begierde, Wollust *f.*

concur *v.i.* zusammentreffen; übereinstimmen; mitwirken.

concurrence *s.* Zusammentreffen *n.*; Mitwirkung *f.*; Einverständnis *n.*

concurrent *a.* mitwirkend; begleitend; übereinstimmend.

concuss *v.t. to be ~ed* eine Gehirnerschütterung haben.

concussion *s.* Erschütterung *f.*; (*med.*) Prellung *f.*; Quetschung *f.*

condemn *v.t.* verdammen, verurteilen; tadeln; verwerfen; (Ware) beschlagnahmen, (Ware) für untauglich erklären.

condemnation *s.* Verurteilung *f.*

condemnatory *a.* verdammend.

condensation *s.* Verdichtung *f.*; Kurzfassung *f.*; Kondensation *f.*

condense *v.t.* verdichten; einen Auszug machen von; *~ v.i.* sich verdichten.

condensed milk *s.* kondensierte Milch *f.*

condenser *s.* Kondensator (Dampfmaschine od. elek.) *m.*

condescend *v.t.* sich herablassen; **~ingly** *adv.* herablassend, gefällig.

condescension *s.* Herablassung *f.*

condign *a.* gehörig, verdient.

condiment *s.* Gewürz *n.*

condition *s.* Zustand *m.*; Beschaffenheit *f.*; Bedingung *f.*; Stand *m.*; Stellung *f.*; *~ v.t.* bedingen; (*mech.*) in guten Zustand bringen (Maschinen usw.).

conditional (on) *a.* bedingt (durch).

conditionally *adv.* bedingungsweise, unter Bedingungen.

conditioned *a.* bedingt; abhängig; konditioniert.

condole *v.t. & i.* Beileid bezeigen.

condolence *s.* Beileid *n.*

condom *s.* Kondom *n.*

condominium *s.* Appartementhaus *n.*; Eigentumswohnung *f.*

condone *v.t.* vergeben, verzeihen.

conduce *v.i.* dienlich sein, fördern.

conducive *a.* förderlich, behilflich.

conduct *s.* Führung *f.*; Geleit *n.*; Aufführung *f.*; Verwaltung *f.*; *~ v.t.* führen; verwalten; (*mus.*) dirigieren; (*phys.*) leiten; *to ~ onself,* sich aufführen; *conducted tour s.* Gesellschaftsreise *f.*

conductivity *s.* (*elek.*) Leitfähigkeit *f.*

conductor *s.* Schaffner, Kondukteur *m.*; Leiter *m.*; (*mus.*) Dirigent *m.*

conduit *s.* Röhre *f.*; Wasserleitung *f.*

cone *s.* Kegel *m.*; Tannenzapfen *m.*

confabulation *s.* vertrauliches Gespräch *n.*

confection *s.* Zuckerwerk *n.*; Konfekt *n.*

confectioner *s.* Konditor *m.*

confectionary *s.* Zuckerwerk *n.*; Konditorei *f.*

confederacy *s.* Bündnis *n.*

confederate *v.t. & i.* (sich) verbünden; *~ a.* verbündet; *~ s.* Bundesgenosse *m.*

confederation *s.* Bündnis *n.*; Bund *m.*

confer *v.t.* vergleichen; verleihen; *~ v.i.* verhandeln.

conference *s.* Verhandlung, Beratschlagung *f.*; Konferenz *f.*

confess *v.t. & i.* bekennen, gestehen; beichten; kundgeben.

confession *s.* Geständnis *n.*; Bekenntnis *n.*; Beichte *f.*

confessional *s.* Beichtstuhl *m.*

confessor *s.* Bekenner *m.*; Beichtvater *m.*

confidant *s.* Vertraute *m.*/*f.*

confide *v.t. & i.* anvertrauen; vertrauen.

confidence *s.* Vertrauen *n.*; Zuversicht *f.*; **~ game** *s.* Trickbetrug *m.*; **~-trickster** *s.* Hochstapler *m.*

confident *a.*, **~ly** *adv.* vertrauend.

confidential *a.*, **~ly** *adv.* vertraulich.

confidentiality *s.* Vertraulichkeit *f.*

configuration *s.* Gestaltung, Bildung *f.*

confine *s.* Grenze *f.*; *~ v.t.* begrenzen; beschränken; einsperren; *to be confined,* in den Wochen liegen; *confined to barracks,* unter Kasernenarrest.

confinement *s.* Haft *f.*; Wochenbett *n.*; Niederkunft *f.*; *solitary ~,* Einzelhaft *f.*

confirm *v.t.* bestätigen, bewähren; einsegnen, konfirmieren.

confirmation *s.* Bestätigung *f.*; Konfirmation *f.*;

Firmung *f.*
confirmatory *a.* bekräftigend.
confirmed *a.* unverbesserlich; eingefleischt.
confiscate *v.t.* einziehen; ~ *a.* verfallen.
confiscation *s.* Beschlagnahme *f.*
conflict *s.* Kampf *m.*, Streit *m.*, Konflikt *m.*; ~ *v.i.* kämpfen; widerstreiten.
conflicting *a.* widersprüchlich.
confluence *s.* Zusammenfluß *m.*
confluent *a.* zusammenfließend.
conform *v.t.* gleichförmig machen; ~ *v.i.* sich richten.
conformable *a.*, **~bly** *adv.* übereinstimmend.
conformism *s.* Konformismus *m.*
conformist *s.* Konformist(in) *m.* (*f.*).
conformity *s.* Übereinstimmung *f.*; Konformität *f.*; *in* ~ *with,* gemäß; gleichlaufend.
confound *v.t.* verwirren; verwechseln; zerstören; ~ *it!* verwünscht!
confounded *a.* bestürzt; verwünscht.
confront *v.t. & i.* gegenüberstellen; gegenüberstehen.
confrontation *s.* Gegenüberstellung *f.*; Konfrontation *f.*
confuse *v.t.* verwirren; verwechseln.
confused *a.*, **~ly** *adv.* verworren.
confusion *s.* Verwirrung *f.*; Verwechslung *f.*
confutation *s.* Wilderlegung *f.*
confute *v.t.* widerlegen.
congeal *v.t.* zum Gefrieren bringen; gerinnen lassen; ~ *v.i.* gefrieren.
congenial *a.* sympathisch, zusagend; geistesverwandt.
congenital *a.* angeboren.
congeries *s.* Masse *f.*; Gemenge *n.*
congest *v.t.* verstopfen.
congested *a.* überfüllt (Straßenverkehr, Bevölkerung); (*med.*) mit Blut überfüllt.
congestion *s.* Überfüllung *f.*; Blutandrang *m.*; Stauung *f.*
conglomeration *s.* Zusammenhäufung *f.*
congratulate (on) *v.t. & i.* gratulieren, Glück wünschen (zu).
congratulations *s.* Glückwunsch *m.*
congratulatory *a.* beglückwünschend.
congregate *v.t. & i.* (sich) versammeln.
congregation *s.* Gemeinde *f.*
congress *s.* Kongreß *m.*
congressional *a.* Kongress . . .
congressman *s.* Kongreßabgeordneter *m.*
congresswoman *s.* Kongreßabgeordnete *f.*
congruence *s.* Übereinstimmung *f.*
congruent *a.* übereinstimmend.
congruity *s.* Übereinstimmung *f.*
congruous *a.*, **~ly** *adv.* übereinstimmend, angemessen.
conic(al), *a.*, **~ly** *adv.* konisch; kegelförmig; ~ *section s.* Kegelschnitt *m.*
conifer *s.* Nadelbaum *m.*
coniferous *a.* Nadelholz. . .
conjectural *a.*, **~ly** *adv.* mutmaßlich.
conjecture *s.* Mutmaßung *f.*; ~ *v.t.* mutmaßen.
conjoin *v.t. & i.* verbinden.
conjoint *a.*, **~ly** *adv.* vereinigt.
conjugal *a.*, **~ly** *adv.* ehelich.
conjugate *v.t.* konjugieren.

conjugation *s.* Konjugation *f.*
conjunction *s.* Verbindung *f.*; Bindewort *n.*; Konjunktion *f.*
conjunctiva *s.* Bindehaut *f.*
conjunctive *a.*, **~ly** *adv.* verbindend; ~ *s.* (*gram.*) Konjunktiv *m.*
conjunctivitis *s.* Bindehautentzündung *f.*
conjuncture *s.* Zusammentreffen *n.*
conjuration *s.* Beschwörung *f.*
conjure *v.t. & i.* beschwören; bezaubern; zaubern; bannen.
conjurer *s.* Zauberer *m.*; Taschenspieler *m.*
connect *v.t.* verbinden, verknüpfen; ~ *v.i.* verbunden sein; *well-connected a.* mit guten Beziehungen.
connecting-rod *s.* (*mech.*) Pleuelstange *f.*
connection, *s.* Zusammenhang *m.*; Verbindung *f.*; (*rail.*) Anschluß *m.*; (*tel.*) Anschluß *m.*; Praxis (Arzt, Rechtsanwalt) *f.*; (*elek.*) Schaltung *f.*; Anschluß *m.*; ~ *box* (*elek.*) Anschlußdose *f.*
conning tower *s.* Kommandoturm *m.*
connivance *s.* Nachsicht *f.*; stillschweigende Einwilligung *f.*
connive (at) *v.i.* stillschweigend dulden.
connoisseur *s.* Kenner *m.*
connotation *s.* Mitbezeichnung *f.*; Konnotation *f.*
connote *v.t.* mitbezeichnen.
conquer *v.t. & i.* erobern, (be)siegen.
conqueror *s.* Eroberer, Sieger *m.*
conquest *s.* Eroberung *f.*; Sieg *m.*
consanguineous *a.* blutsverwandt.
consanguinity *s.* Blutsverwandtschaft *f.*
conscience *s.* Gewissen *n.*
conscientious *a.*, **~ly** *adv.* gewissenhaft.
conscientious objector *s.* Kriegsdienstverweigerer *m.*
conscientiousness *s.* Gewissenhaftigkeit *f.*
conscious *a.*, **~ly** *adv.* bewußt; wissentlich.
consciousness *s.* Bewußtsein *n.*
conscript *s.* ausgehobener Rekrut *m.*; Einberufene *m./f.*; ~ *a.* ausgehoben; einberufen.
conscription *s.* Einberufung *f.*; Aushebung *f.*; allgemeine Wehrpflicht *f.*
consecrate *v.t.* weihen; einsegnen.
consecration *s.* Einsegnung.
consecutive *a.*, **~ly** *adv.* aufeinander folgend; folglich; konsekutiv.
consensus *s.* Übereinstimmung *f.*
consent *s.* Einwilligung *f.*; *age of* ~ ,(*law*) Mündigkeitsalter *n.*; ~ *v.i.* einwilligen, einstimmen.
consequence *s.* Folge *f.*; Einfluß *m.*; Wichtigkeit *f.*
consequent *a.*, **~ly** *adv.* folgend; folglich; konsequent.
consequential *a.* konsequent.
conservation *s.* Erhaltung *f.*
conservation area *s.* Landschaftsschutzgebiet *n.*
conservationist *s.* Naturschützer(in) *m.*(*f.*)
conservatism *s.* Konservati(vi)smus *m.*
conservative *a.* erhaltend; konservativ; ~ *estimate,* vorsichtige Schätzung *f.*
conservator *s.* Erhalter, Konservator *m.*
conservatory *a.* erhaltend; ~ *s.* Gewächshaus *n.*; Konservatorium *n.*
conserve *v.t.* erhalten.
consider *v.t. & i.* betrachten; überlegen; achten.
considerable *a.*, **~bly** *adv.* ansehnlich.

considerate *a.*, **~ly** *adv.* bedächtig; rücksichtsvoll.
consideration *s.* Betrachtung, Überlegung *f.*; Rücksicht *f.*; Preis *m.*
considering *pr.* in Erwägung (daß); in Betracht auf.
consign *v.t.* übertragen; zusenden.
consignee *s.* Warenempfänger *m.*
consignment *s.* Übersendung *f.*; Warensendung, Konsignation *f.*
consignor *s.* Warenabsender *m.*
consist *v.i.* bestehen.
consistence, consistency *s.* Festigkeit *f.*; Folgerichtigkeit *f.*
consistent *a.*, **~ly** *adv.* dicht, fest; übereinstimmend; konsequent.
consistory *s.* Konsistorium *n.*
consolation *s.* Trost *m.*
consolatory *a.* tröstlich.
console *v.t.* Trösten; ~ *s.* Tragstein, *m.*; Konsole *f.*
consolidate *v.t.* befestigen; ~ *v.i.* sich verbinden; zuheilen; sich befestigen.
consolidation *s.* Verdichtung *f.*; Verbindung *f.*; Zusammenlegung *f.*
consoling *a.* tröstlich.
consommé *a.* Kraftbrühe *f.*
consonance *s.* Einklang *m.*
consonant *a.*, **~ly** *adv.* übereinstimmend. ~ *s.* Konsonant *m.*
consort *s.* Gefährte *m.*; Gatte *m.*; Gattin *f.*; ~ *v.i.* sich gesellen, umgehen; übereinstimmen.
consortium *s.* Konsortium *n.*
conspicuous *a.*, **~ly** *adv.* sichtbar, auffallend; hervorragend.
conspiracy *s.* Verschwörung *f.*
conspirator *s.* Verschwörer(in) *m.*(*f.*).
conspiratorial *a.* verschwörerisch.
conspire *v.i.* sich verschwören.
constable *s.* Polizist, Schutzmann *m.*; **Chief ~**, Polizeipräsident *m.*
constabulary *s.* Schutzpolizei, Schupo *f.*
constancy *s.* Beständigkeit.
constant *a.*, **~ly** *adv.* standhaft, zuverlässig; dauernd; ~ *hot water*, fließendes warmes Wasser *n.*
constellation *s.* Sternbild *n.*
consternation *s.* Bestürzung *f.*
constipate *v.t.* verdichten, verstopfen.
constipation *s.* Verstopfung *f.*
constituency *s.* Wahlkreis *m.*; Wählerschaft *f.*
constituent *a.* ausmachend, wesentlich; Wahl...; verfassunggebend; ~ *body*, Wählerschaft *f.*; ~ *s.* Vollmachtgeber *m.*; Bestandteil *m.*; Wähler *m.*
constitute *v.t.* ausmachen; bilden, errichten; gründen.
constitution *s.* Einrichtung *f.*; Verfassung *f.*; Körperbeschaffenheit *f.*
constitutional *a.*, **~ly** *adv.* verfassungsmäßig; ~ *s.* Spaziergang zur Verdauung *m.*
constitutional law *s.* Verfassungsrecht *n.*
constitutive *a.* verordnend; wesentlich.
constrain *v.t.* zwingen.
constraint *s.* Zwang *m.*; Nötigung *f.*
constrict *v.t.* zusammenziehen.
constriction *s.* Zusammenziehung *f.*
constrictor *s.* boa ~, Riesenschlange *f.*
constringent *a.* zusammenziehend.
construct *v.t.* errichten, bauen; konstruieren;

ersinnen.
construction *s.* Zusammensetzung *f.*; Bau *m.*; Deutung *f.*; *under* ~, im Bau; ~ **battalion** (*mil.*) Baubataillon *n.*
constructive *a.* Bau...; aufbauend.; konstruktiv.
construe *v.t.* konstruieren; auslegen.
consul *s.* Konsul *m.*; ~ *General*, Generalkonsul *m.*
consular *a.* konsularisch.
consulate, consulship *s.* Konsulat *n.*
consult *v.i.* sich beraten; ~ *v.t.* um Rat fragen.
consultant *s.* Berater(in) *m.*(*f.*)
consultation *s.* Beratung, Beratschlagung *f.*; Rücksprache *f.*
consulting *a.* beratend.
consulting engineer *s.* technischer Berater *m.*
consulting hours *s.pl.* Sprechstunden (Arzt) *f.pl.*
consume *v.t.* verzehren; verbrauchen.
consumer *s.* Verbraucher(in), Konsument(in), *m.* (*f.*). Abnehmer(in) *m.*(*f.*); ~ **goods** Verbrauchsgüter *n.pl.*; ~ **protection** *s.* Verbraucherschutz *m.*
consummate *a.* vollendet.; *v.t.* vollenden; vollziehen.
consummation *s.* Vollendung *f.*; Vollzug *m.*
consumption *s.* Verzehrung *f.*; Verbrauch *m.*; Schwindsucht *f.*
consumptive *a.* schwindsüchtig.
contact *s.* Berührung *f.*; (*elek.*) Kontakt *m.*; ~ *v.t.* sich in Verbindung setzen mit.
contact lens *s.* Kontaktlinse *f.*
contagion *s.* Ansteckung, Seuche *f.*
contagious *a.* ansteckend.
contain *v.t.* in sich fassen, enthalten; (*mil.*) Kräfte binden; *to* ~ *oneself*, sich beherrschen.
container *s.* Behälter *m.*; Container *m.*
contaminate *v.t.* verseuchen, verunreinigen, infizieren.
contamination *s.* Verunreinigung *f.*; Infizierung *f.*
contemplate *v.t.* betrachten; beabsichtigen; ~ *v.i.* nachdenken.
contemplation *s.* Betrachtung *f.*
contemplative *a.*, **~ly** *adv.* beschaulich.
contemporaneous *a.* gleichzeitig.
contemporary *a.* gleichzeitig, zeitgenössisch; ~ *s.* Zeitgenosse *m.*; Zeitgenossin *f.*
contempt *s.* Verachtung *f.*; ~ *of court*, (*law*) Missachtung des Gerichts *f.*
contemptible *a.*, **~bly** *adv.* verächtlich.
contemptuous *a.*, **~ly** *adv.* verachtend; überheblich.
contend *v.i.* streiten; streben; behaupten.
contender *s.* Bewerber(in) *m.*(*f.*)
content *a.* zufrieden; ~ *s.* Zufriedenheit *f.*; Inhalt *m.*; Zusammensetzung *f.*; ~ *v.t.* befriedigen.
contented *a.*, **~ly** *adv.* zufrieden.
contention *s.* Streit *m.*; Wetteifer *m.*; Behauptung *f.*; Argument *n.*
contentious *a.*, **~ly** *adv.* strittig; umstritten.
contentment *a.* Zufriedenheit *f.*
contest *v.t.* streiten; bestreiten, anfechten; *to* ~ *a seat*, in einem Wahlkreis kandidieren; ~ *v.i.* wetteifern; ~ *s.* Streit *m.*; Wettbewerb, Wettkampf *m.*
contestable *a.* anfechtbar, streitig.
contestant *s.* (Wett)bewerber(in) *m.*(*f.*), Wettkämpfer(in) *m.*(*f.*)
context *s.* Zusammenhang *m.*
contexture *s.* Bau *m.*; Gewebe *n.*

contiguity s. Aneinanderstoßen n.
contiguous a., **~ly** adv. anstoßend, nahe.
continence s. Enthaltsamkeit f.
continent a., **~ly** adv. enthaltsam, mäßig; ~ s. Festland n.; Kontinent m.
continental a. festländisch; kontinental.
contingency s. Zufall m.; Möglichkeit f.
contingent a. möglich; abhängig von; (mil.) Kontingent n.
continual a., **~ly** adv. fortwährend; ständig.
continuance s. Fortdauer f.
continuation s. Fortsetzung f.; ~ school, Fortbildungsschule f.
continue v.t. & i. fortsetzen; fortdauern, beharren.
continuity s. Zusammenhang m.; Kontinuität f.
continuous a. zusammenhängend; durchgehend.
continuum s. Kontinuum n.
contort v.t. verdrehen; verzerren.
contortion s. Verdrehung, Verzerrung f.
contour s. Umriß m.
contra pr. gegen, wider.
contraband a. Schmuggel. . .; ~ s. Schmuggelware f.
contraception s. Empfängnisverhütung f.
contraceptive a. empfängnisverhütend; ~ s. empfängnisverhütendes Mittel n.
contract s. Vertrag m.; Akkord m.; law of ~, Vertragsrecht n.; to make a ~, einen Vertrag eingehen; under ~ to, einem kontraktlich verpflichtet; ~ v.t. zusammenziehen; sich zuziehen; erlangen; to ~ debts, Schulden eingehen; ~ v.i. einschrumpfen; einen Vertrag schließen; sich verpflichten; contracting party, Vertragspartei f.
contraction s. Zusammenziehung f.; Krampf m.; Wehe f.
contractor s. Lieferant m.; Unternehmer m.
contractual a. vertragsmäßig; vertraglich.
contradict v.t. widersprechen.
contradiction s. Widerspruch m.
contradictory a., **~ily** adv. widersprechend.
contralto s. tiefe Altstimme f.; Kontraalt m.
contrariwise adv. umgekehrt.
contrary a. entgegengesetzt, zuwider; widerspenstig; ~ s. Gegenteil n.; ~ to, im Gegensatz zu; on the ~, im Gegenteil.
contrast s. Kontrast m.; Gegensatz m.
contrast v.t. & i. gegenüberstellen; abstechen von.
contrasting a. gegensätzlich, kontrastierend.
contravene v.t. zuwiderhandeln.
contravention s. Übertretung f.
contribute v.t. & i. beitragen.
contribution s. Beitrag m., Beisteuer f.
contributor s. Beitragender m.; Mitarbeiter (an einer Zeitung) m.
contributory a. beitragend.
contrite a., **~ly** adv. zerknirscht.
contrition s. Zerknirschung f.
contrivance s. Vorrichtung f.; Kunstgriff m.
contrive v.t. & i. ersinnen; veranstalten, fertigbringen; darauf ausgehen.
control s. Einschränkung f.; Aufsicht f.; Gewalt f.; Kontrolle f.; Überwachung f.; (mech.) Steuerung, Kontrollvorrichtung f.; ~ **center** s. Kontrollzentrum n.; ~ **desk** s. Schaltpult n.; ~**-office** Überwachungsstelle f.; ~ **room** s. Kontrollraum m.; ~ v.t.

beaufsichtigen, überwachen; beherrschen; kontrollieren.
controllable a. kontrollierbar.
controller s. Kontrolleur m., Aufseher m., Leiter m.; Rechnungsprüfer m.
controversial a. strittig, streitsüchtig.
controversy s. Streitfrage f.; Streit m.; Kontroverse f.; matter in ~, (law) Streitgegenstand m.
controvert v.t. bestreiten.
controvertible a. bestreitbar, streitig.
contumacious a., **~ly** adv. widerspenstig.
contumacy s. Widerspenstigkeit f.
contuse v.t. quetschen.
contusion s. Quetschung f.
conundrum s. Wortspiel n., Scherzrätsel n.
conurbation s. Ballungszentrum n.
convalesce v.i. genesen, rekonvaleszieren.
convalescence s. Genesung f.
convalescent a. genesend; **~-home,** Genesungsheim n.
convene v.t. zusammenberufen; vorladen; ~ v.i. zusammenkommen.
convenience s. Schicklichkeit, Gelegenheit, Bequemlichkeit f.; at your earliest ~, umgehend; with all modern ~s, mit allem Komfort.
convenient a., **~ly** adv. bequem.
convent s. (Nonnen-)Kloster n.
conventicle s. Zusammenkunft f.
convention s. Zusammenkunft f., Versammlung f.; Vergleich m.; Bund m.; Tagung f.; Kongreß m.
conventional a. verabredet, vertragsmäßig; herkömmlich.
converge v.i. zusammenlaufen.
convergence s. Zusammenlaufen.
convergent a. konvergierend.
conversant a. vertraut, bewandert.
conversation s. Unterhaltung f.; Umgang m.
conversational a. Unterhaltungs. . .; gesprächig.
converse a. umgekehrt; ~ v.i. Umgang haben, sich unterhalten.
conversely adv. umgekehrt.
conversion s. Umwandlung f.; Bekehrung f.; Schwenkung f.; Konvertierung (von Staatspapieren) f.; Versilberung f.; fraudulent ~, (law) betrügerische Verwendung anvertrauten Geldes.
convert s. Bekehrter m.; ~ v.t. umändern; bekehren, umkehren; ~ v.i. sich verwandeln.
converter s. (elek.) Umformer m.
convertible a. umwandelbar; umsetzbar, vertauschbar; (com.) konvertierbar; ~ s. Kabriolett n.
convex a. konvex.
convexity s. Konvexheit f.
convey v.t. führen; befördern; übertragen; übermitteln; vermitteln.
conveyance s. Beförderung f.; Abtretung f.
conveyor belt s. Förderband n.
convict v.t. für schuldig erklären; überführen; ~ s. Strafgefangene m., Verbrecher m.
conviction s. Überzeugung f.; Überführung f.; (law) Schuldigerklärung f.
convince v.t. überzeugen.
convincing a. überzeugend.
convivial a. gastlich, festlich.
convocation s. Zusammenberufung f.; Versammlung, Synode f.
convoke v.t. zusammenberufen.

convoluted *a.* verschlungen.
convoy *v.t.* geleiten; ~ *s.* Geleit *n.*; Bedeckung *f.*; (*nav.*) Geleitzug *m.*
convulse *v.t.* in Zuckungen versetzen; *to be ~d* von Krämpfen geschüttelt werden.
convulsion *s.* Zuckung *f.*; Krampf *m.*
convulsive *a.* zuckend, krampfhaft.
coo *v.i.* gurren.
cook *s.* Koch *m.*; Köchin *f.*; ~ *v.t.* kochen; *what's ~ing? was gibt's?*
cookbook *s.* Kochbuch *n.*
cooker *s.* Kochapparat, Kochherd *m.*
cookery *s.* Kochkunst *f.*
cookie *s.* Plätzchen *n.*; Keks *m.*
cooking *s.* Kochen *n.*
cool *a.* kühl; kaltblütig; unverfroren; (*fam.*) spitze, cool; ~ *v.t.* kühlen, erfrischen; besänftigen; ~ *v.i.* erkalten.
coolant *s.* (*mech.*) Kühlflüssigkeit *f.*
cooler *s.* (Wein)kühler *m.*
coolie *s.* Kuli *m.*
coolly *adv.* kaltblütig; kühl; ruhig.
coolness *s.* Kühle *f.*; Kaltblütigkeit *f.*
cooper *s.* Böttcher *m.*; Küfer *m.*
cooperate *v.i.* mitwirken, teilnehmen.
cooperation *s.* Mitwirkung *f.*
cooperative *a.* mitwirkend; zur Mitarbeit bereit, willig; ~ **society** *s.* Konsumverein *m.*
cooperator *s.* Mitarbeiter *m.*
coopt *v.t.* kooptieren.
coordinate *a.*, **-ly** *adv.* beigeordnet; koordiniert; ~ *v.t.* beiordnen; gleichordnen; koordinieren.
coordination *s.* Koordinierung *f.*; Koordination *f.*; Abstimmung.
cop *s.* (*fam.*) Polizist, Bulle *m.*
copartner *s.* Teilhaber *m.*
cope *s.* Decke, Kuppel *f.*; Chorrock *m.*; ~ *v.t.* bedecken; ~ *v.i. to ~ with,* es mit einem aufnehmen, einer Sache gewachsen sein.
copier *s.* Kopierer *m.*; Kopiergerät *n.*
copilot *s.* Kopilot(in) *m.* (*f.*)
coping *s.* Sims *m.*; ~ *stone,* Deckstein *m.*
copious *a.*, **-ly** *adv.* reichlich.
cop-out *s.* Drückebergerei *f.*
copper *s.* Kupfer *n.*; Kupfergeschirr *n.*; Kupfermünze *f.*; ~ *a.* kupfern.
copperplate *s.* Kupferplatte *f.*; Kupferstich *m.*
coppice, copse *s.* Unterholz *n.*
copula *s.* (*ling.*) Kopula *n.*
copulate *v.i.* kopulieren, sich begatten.
copulation *s.* Begattung *f.*
copulative *a.* verbindend, Binde...
copy *s.* Abschrift *f.*; Abdruck *m.*; Durchschlag *m.*; Exemplar *n.*; Nachahmung *f.*; *fair ~, clean ~,* Reinschrift *f.*; *rough ~,* Konzept *n.*; ~ *v.t.* kopieren; nachzeichnen, nachahmen; *to ~ out,* ins Reine schreiben.
copyist *s.* Abschreiber, Kopist *m.*
copyright *s.* Verlagsrecht, Urheberrecht *n.*; ~ *in designs,* Musterschutz *m.*
coquette, coquettish *a.* gefallsüchtig, kokett.
coral *s.* Koralle *f.*
cord *s.* Strick *m.*; Schnur *f.*; Tau *n.*; gerippter Stoff *m.*; ~ *v.t.* mit Stricken befestigen.
cordial *a.*, **-ly** *adv.* herzlich; ~ *s.* Herzstärkung *f.*; Magenlikör *m.*

cordiality *s.* Herzlichkeit *f.*
cordon *s.* Truppenkette *f.*; *to ~ off v.t.* (polizeilich) absperren.
corduroy *s.* gerippter Stoff *m.*; Kordsamt *m.*
core *s.* Mark *n.*; Herz *n.*; Kern *m.*
co-respondent *m.* Mitbeklagter im Scheidungsprozeß *m.*
coriander *s.* Koriander *m.*
cork *s.* Kork *m.*; ~ *v.t.* verkorken; *the wine is ~ed,* der Wein schmeckt nach dem Kork.
corkscrew *s.* Korkzieher *m.*
cork-tree *s.* Korkeiche *f.*
cormorant *s.* Kormoran *m.*; Scharbe *f.*
corn *s.* Korn *n.*; Getreide *n.*; Mais *m.*; Hühnerauge *n.*; ~ed beef, Büchsenrindfleisch *n.*; ~-cob *s.* Maiskolben *m.*
cornea *s.* Hornhaut (Auge) *f.*; Cornea *f.*
corner *s.* Winkel *m.*; Ecke *f.*; ~-stone, Eckstein *m.*; (*fig.*) Eckpfeiler *m.*; ~ *v.t.* in eine Ecke treiben.
cornet *s.* (Eis)Tüte *f.*; Eishörnchen *n.*; (*mus.*) Kornett *n.*
cornflower *s.* Kornblume *f.*
cornice *s.* Karnies *n.*; Fries *m.*
cornstarch *s.* Maismehl *n.*; Stärkemehl *n.*
cornucopia *s.* Füllhorn *n.*
corny *a.* altmodisch; abgedroschen.
corollary *s.* Folgesatz *m.*; Korrollar(ium) *n.*
coronary *a.* (*med.*) Koronar...; ~ **vessel** *s.* Herzkranzgefäß *n.*
coronation *s.* Krönung *f.*
coroner *s.* Leichenbeschauer (bei gewaltsamem od. rätselhaftem Tode); ~'s *inquest,* gerichtliche Leichenschau *f.*
coronet *s.* Adelskrone *f.*
corporal *a.*, **-ly** *adv.* körperlich, leiblich; ~ *s.* Korporal *m.*
corporal punishment *s.* Prügelstrafe *f.*
corporate *a.*, **-ly** *adv.* körperschaftlich, Gesellschafts...
corporation *s.* Gemeinde, Innung, Körperschaft *f.*; ~ *profits tax,* Körperschaftssteuer *f.*
corporeal *a.* körperlich.
corps *s.* Armeekorps *n.*
corpse *s.* Leichnam *m.*
corpulence *s.* Wohlbeleibtheit *f.*
corpulent *a.* wohlbeleibt.
Corpus Christi *s.* Fronleichnamsfest *n.*
corpuscle *s.* Blutkörperchen *n.*
corral *s.* Pferch *m.*; *v.t.* einpferchen.
correct *v.t.* verbessern; tadeln; strafen; (Zahlen) abrunden; ~ *a.*, **-ly** *adv.* fehlerfrei, richtig.
correction *s.* Verbesserung *f.*; Berichtigung *f.*; Bestrafung *f.*; *house of ~,* Besserungsanstalt *f.*; ~ *of the press,* Korrektur *f.*
corrective *a.* verbessernd; ~ *s.* Besserungsmittel *m.*
correctness *s.* Korrektheit *f.*; Richtigkeit *f.*
correlate *v.t. & i.* in Wechselwirkung bringen od. stehen.
correlation *s.* Wechselbeziehung *f.*, Korrelation *f.*
correlative *a.* in Wechselbeziehung stehend, korrelativ.
correspond *v.i.* in Briefwechsel stehen; entsprechen.
correspondence *s.* Briefwechsel *m.*; Übereinstimmung *f.*; ~ **course,** schriftlicher Lehrkurs *m.*
correspondent *s.* Korrespondent(in) *m.* (*f.*).

corresponding *a.*, **~ly** *adv.* entsprechend.
corridor *s.* Gang *m.*; ~ *train*, D-Zug (Durchgangszug) *m.*
corroborate *v.t.* stärken; bestätigen.
corroboration *s.* Bestätigung *f.*
corroborative *a.* bestätigend.
corrode *v.t.* zernagen, zerfressen, korrodieren.
corrosion *s.* Zerfressung *f.*; Korrosion *f.*
corrosive *a.*, **~ly** *adv.* zerfressend, ätzend; ~ *s.* Ätzmittel *n.*
corrugate *v.t.* zerfurchen.
corrugated *a.* gewellt; ~ *iron*, Wellblech *n.*
corrugation *s.* Zerfurchung *f.*; Furche *f.*
corrupt *v.t.* verderben; verführen; bestechen; korrumpieren. ~ *v.i.* verderben; verfaulen; ~ *a.*, **~ly** *adv.* verfault; lasterhaft; verderbt; bestechlich, korrupt.
corruption *s.* Verdorbenheit, Fäulnis *f.*; Bestechung *f.*, Korruption *f.*
corsair *s.* Seeräuber *m.*; Raubschiff *n.*
corset *s.* Schnürleib *m.*, Korsett *n.*
cortisone *s.* Kortison *n.*
coruscate *v.t.* schimmern.
coruscation *s.* Schimmern *n.*, Lichtglanz *m.*
corvette *s.* Korvette *f.*
cosh *s.* Totschläger *m.*
cosine *s.* (*math.*) Kosinus *m.*
cosmetic *a.* kosmetisch; ~ *s.* Schönheitsmittel *n.*
cosmic(al) *a.* kosmisch, Welt...; ~ **radiation** *s.* kosmische Strahlung *f.*
cosmonaut *s.* Kosmonaut(in) *m.*(*f.*).
cosmopolitan, cosmopolite *s.* Weltbürger(in) *m.*(*f.*); ~ *a.* weltbürgerlich, kosmopolitisch.
Cosmos *s.* Kosmos *m.*
Cossack *s.* Kosak *m.*
cosset *v.t.* verhätscheln.
cost *s.* Kosten, Unkosten *f.pl.*; Preis *m.*; Aufwand *m.*; Schaden *m.*; *cost of living*, Lebenshaltungskosten *pl.*; **~s** *pl.* Gerichtskosten *pl.*; *to dismiss with* ~ (*law*) kostenpflichtig abweisen; ~ *v.i.* kosten, zustehen kommen.
cost-effective *a.* kostensparend.
costly *a.* kostspielig, kostbar.
cost price *s.* Selbstkostenpreis *m.*
costume *s.* Kostüm *n.*
cot *s.* Hütte *f.*; Kinderbett *n.*
coterie *a.* Clique, Sippschaft *f.*
cottage *s.* Hütte *f.*; Landhäuschen *n.*
cotton *s.* Baumwolle *f.*; Kattun *m.*; Garn *n.*; (*absorbent*) ~, Watte *f.*; ~ *v.t.* in Baumwolle packen; ~ *v.i.* sich vertragen, anpassen.
cotton-mill *s.* Baumwollspinnerei *f.*
cotton-wool *s.* rohe Baumwolle, Watte *f.*
couch *s.* Liegesofa *n.*; Couch *f.*; ~ *v.t.* (in Worte) fassen.
cough *s.* Husten *m.*; ~ *v.i.* husten.
coughing *s.* Husten *m.*; Gehuste *n.*
cough medicine *s.* Hustenmittel *n.*
council *s.* Ratsversammlung *f.*; Rat *m.*; *Common* ~, Stadtrat *m.*
councillor *s.* Ratsmitglied *n.*, Ratsherr *m.*; Stadtverordneter *m.*
counsel *s.* Rat *m.*; Beratschlagung *f.*; Vorhaben *n.*; Anwalt *m.*; die juristischen Berater im Prozeß, *m.pl.*; ~ *for the defense*, Verteidiger; ~ *for the prosecution*, Staatsanwalt *m.*, Staatsanwaltschaft *f.*,

Anklagevetreter *m.*; *to keep one's* ~, seine Gedanken bei sich behalten; ~ *v.t.* raten.
counseling *s.* Beratung *f.*
counselor *s.* Ratgeber; ~ *of legation*, Gesandtschaftsrat *m.*
count *s.* Graf *m.*; Zählung *f.*; Rechnung *f.*; Anklagepunkt *m.*; ~ *v.t.* zählen, rechnen; dafür halten; ~ *v.i.* rechnen, sich verlassen; gelten.
countenance *s.* Antlitz *n.*; Miene *f.*; Fassung *f.*
counter *s.* Spielmarke *f.*; Zahltisch *m.*; Ladentisch *m.*; ~ *v.t.* entgegenwirken; ~ *adv.* zuwider; entgegen.
counteract *v.t.* entgegenwirken.
counteraction *s.* Gegenwirkung *f.*
counter-attack *s.* Gegenangriff *m.*
counterbalance *s.* Gegengewicht *n.*; ~ *v.t.* aufwiegen, ausgleichen.
counter-charge *s.* Gegenbeschuldigung *f.*
counter-claim *s.* Gegenforderung *f.*
counterclockwise *adv.* gegen den Uhrzeigersinn.
counter-espionage *s.* Spionageabwehr *f.*
counterfeit *s.* nachgemachte Sache *f.*; Fälschung *f.*; Falschgeld *n.*; ~ *a.* nachgemacht; falsch, gefälscht; ~ *v.t.* fälschen.
counterfeiter *s.* Fälscher(in) *m.*(*f.*)
counterfoil *s.* Kontrollabschnitt *m.*
counter-intelligence *s.* (*mil.*) Abwehr *f.*
countermand *v.t.* abbestellen, widerrufen.
countermeasure *s.* Gegenmaßnahme *f.*
countermove *s.* Gegenschlag *m.*
counteroffensive *s.* Gegenoffensive *f.*
counter-order *s.* Gegenbefehl *m.*
counterpart *s.* Gegenstück *n.*
counterpoint *s.* Kontrapunkt *m.*
counterpoise *s.* Gegengewicht *n.*; ~ *v.t.* das Gleichgewicht halten.
counterproductive *a.* kontraproduktiv.
counterproposal *s.* Gegenvorschlag *m.*
counterrevolution *s.* Gegenrevolution *f.*
countersign *v.t.* gegenzeichnen.
countersink *v.t.* (*mech.*) versenken; *countersunk screw*, Senkschraube *f.*
countertenor *s.* Kontratenor *m.*
countervail *v.t.* ausgleichen, aufwiegen.
counterweight *s.* Gegengewicht *n.*
countess *s.* Gräfin *f.*
countless *a.* unzählbar.
country *s.* Land *n.*; Gegend, Landschaft *f.*; Vaterland *n.*; ~ *a.* ländlich, Land...
country-dance *s.* Volkstanz *m.*
country-house *s.* Landhaus *n.*
countryman *s.* Landsmann *m.*; Landmann *m.*
country-seat *s.* Landsitz *m.*
countryside *s.* Gegend *f.*; Landschaft *f.*
countrywide *a.* landesweit.
countrywoman *s.* Landsmännin *f.*; Landbewohnerin *f.*
county *s.* Grafschaft *f.*; (Land)kreis *m.*
coup *s.* Schlag, Streich *m.*
coup d'état *s.* Staatsstreich *m.*
couple *s.* Paar *n.*; ~ *v.t.* koppeln.
couplet *s.* Verspaar *n.*
coupling *s.* Kuppelung *f.*
coupon *s.* Coupon, Gutschein *m.*
courage *s.* Mut *m.*; Tapferkeit *f.*
courageous *a.*, **~ly** *adv.* mutig, tapfer.

courier *s.* Kurier, Eilbote *m.*
course *s.* Lauf, Gang *m.*; Fahrt *f.*; Kurs *m.*; Gang (beim Essen) *m.*; *a ~ of bricks,* eine Lage Ziegel; *in due ~,* zur gehörigen Zeit; *in (the) ~ of time,* mit der Zeit, nach und nach; *the fever has run its ~,* das Fieber hat seinen Verlauf gehabt; *of ~,* natürlich, versteht sich; *~ v.i.* laufen, rennen; *~ v.t.* jagen, hetzen.
court *s.* Hof *m.*; Gerichtshof *m.*; *criminal ~,* Strafgericht *n.*; *commercial ~,* Handelsgericht *n.*; *~-house,* Gerichtsgebäude *n.*; *~-room,* Gerichtssaal *m.*; *out of ~,* außergerichtlich; *~ v.t.* den Hof machen; freien; huldigen; sich bewerben um.
courteous *a.,* *~ly adv.* höflich, gefällig.
courtesy *s.* Artigkeit, Höflichkeit *f.*; *by ~ of,* mit freundlicher Genehmigung von; *~ v.i.* sich verneigen.
courtier *s.* Höfling *m.*
court-martial *s.* Kriegsgericht *n.*; *~ v.t.* vor ein Kriegsgericht stellen.
courtship *s.* Freien *n.*; Werben *n.*
courtyard *s.* Hof, Hofraum *m.*
cousin *s.* Vetter *m.*; Base, Kusine *f.*; *first ~,* Vetter ersten Grades; *second ~,* Vetter zweiten Grades.
cove *s.* Bucht *f.*; Wölbung *f.*
covenant *s.* Vertrag *m.*; Bündnis *n.*; *~ v.i.* übereinkommen; geloben.
cover *v.t.* decken, bedecken; bemänteln; schützen; (Weg) zurücklegen; (Gelände) bestreichen; brüten; *~ s.* Decke *f.*; Deckel *m.*; Umschlag *m.*; Kuvert *n.*; Schutzrücken (eines Buches) *m.*; Gehege *n.*; Dickicht *n.*; Schutz *m.*; *(mil.)* Deckung *f.*; *~ of a tire,* Schlauchmantel *m.*; *~(ing) letter,* Begleitbrief *m.*; *~ address,* Deckadresse *f.*
coverage *s.* Berichterstattung *f.*
coverall *s.* Overall *m.*
cover charge *s.* (Preis für das) Gedeck *n.*
cover girl *s.* Covergirl *n.*
covering *s.* Deckschicht *f.*; *~ letter s.* Begleitbrief *m.*
covert *s.* Dickicht *n.*; *~ a.* bedeckt, verborgen; *~ly adv.* heimlich.
cover-up *s.* Verschleierung *f.*
covet *v.t.* begehren, gelüsten.
covetous *a.,* *~ly adv.* habsüchtig.
cow *s.* Kuh *f.*; *~ v.t.* einschüchtern.
coward *s.* Feigling *m.*; *~ a.* feig.
cowardice *s.* Feigheit *f.*
cowardly *a. & adv.* feig(e).
cowboy *s.* Rinderhirt *m.*
cower *v.i.* niederkauern.
cowherd *s.* Kuhhirt *m.*
cowhide *s.* Ochsenziemer *m.*
cowl *s.* Kapuze *f.*, Kutte *f.*
co-worker *s.* Kollege *m.*, Kollegin *f.*
cowpox *s.* Kuhpocken *f.pl.*
cowslip *s.* (wilde) Schlüsselblume *f.*
coxcomb *s.* Stutzer, Narr *m.*
coxswain *s.* Bootführer *m.*
coy *a.,* *~ly adv.* schüchtern; spröde.
coyote *s.* Kojote *m.*
cozen *v.t.* täuschen; prellen.
cozenage *s.* Betrug.
cozily *adv.* bequem; gemütlich.
cozy *a.* gemütlich.
crab *s.* Taschenkrebs *m.*; Krabbe *f.*; Nörgler(in)

m.(f.); *~ v.t.* nörgeln; verpatzen.
crabbed *a.,* *~ly adv.* herb; mürrisch, schwierig; unleserlich.
crack *s.* Knall *m.*; Riß *m.*; Spalte *f.*; (Rauschgift) Crack *m.*; *~ v.t.* sprengen, aufbrechen, zerreißen; knallen; *~ v.i.* krachen, bersten, springen, zerplatzen.
cracked *a.* geborsten; nicht recht gescheit.
cracker *s.* knuspriger Keks *m.*; Knallbonbon *m.*
crackle *v.i.* krachen; knistern.
crackling *s.* Geknister *n.*; Kruste (*f.*) des Schweinebratens.
crackpot *s.* verschrobener Mensch *m.*
cradle *s.* Wiege *f.*; *~ v.t.* einwiegen.
craft *s.* Fertigkeit *f.*; Gewerbe, Handwerk *n.*; List *f.*; Schiff *n.*
craftsman *s.* (Kunst-)Handwerker *m.*
craftsmanship *s.* fachmännische Arbeit *f.*
crafty *a.,* *~ily adv.* listig.
crag *s.* Klippe *f.*; Fels *m.*
craggy *a.* schroff, felsig.
cram *v.t. & i.* stopfen, nudeln; mästen; einpauken.
cramp *s.* Krampf *m.*; Klammer *f.*; *~ v.i.* verklammern; verzerren.
cramped *a.* eng, gedrängt.
cranberry *s.* Preiselbeere *f.*
crane *s.* Kranich *m.*; Kran *m.*; *~ v.t.* aufwinden.
cranial *s.* Schädel. . .
cranium *s.* Hirnschale *f.*
crank *s.* Kurbel *f.*; Krummzapfen *m.*; grillenhafter Mensch *m.*
crankiness *s.* Verdrehtheit *f.*
crankshaft *s.* *(mech.)* Kurbelwelle *f.*
cranky *a.* reizbar, schlecht gelaunt.
cranny *s.* Riß, Spalt *m.*
crap *s.* (*fam.*) Mist *m.*; Quatsch *m.*; Schrott *m.*
crape *s.* Flor *m.*; Krepp *m.*
crash *v.i.* krachen, platzen; *~ s.* Bruch *m.*; Krach *m.*; *(avi.)* Absturz *m.*
crash: ~ barrier *s.* Leitplanke *f.*; *~ course s.* Intensivkurs *m.*; *~ landing s.* Bruchlandung *f.*; *~ test s.* Crashtest *m.*
crass *a.* dick, kraß; dumm.
crate *s.* Kiste *f.*
crater *s.* Krater *m.*
crave *v.t.* dringend bitten, verlangen.
craving *s.* Begierde *f.*; Verlangen *n.*; *~ a.* begehrlich, gierig.
crawl *v.i.* kriechen, schleichen; kraulen (schwimmen); *to ~ with,* wimmeln von.
crayfish *s.* Flußkrebs *m.*
crayon *s.* Farbstift *m.*
craze *v.t.* verrückt machen; *~ s.* Grille *f.*, Manie *f.*
crazy *a.* wahnsinnig; verrückt.
creak *v.n.* knarren.
cream *s.* Rahm *m.*; Sahne *f.*; (*fig.*) Beste *n.*; *~ v.t.* abrahmen.
creamery *s.* Butterei *f.*; Milchgeschäft *n.*
cream cheese *s.* Frischkäse *n.*
crease *s.* Falte, Bügelfalte *f.*; Eselsohr (im Buch) *n.*; *~-resisting,* nicht knitternd; *~ v.t.* umbiegen, kniffen; *~ v.i.* knittern.
create *v.t.* erschaffen; ernennen.
creation *s.* Schöpfung *f.*; Ernennung *f.*
creative *a.* schöpferisch.
creator *s.* Schöpfer *m.*

creature *s.* Geschöpf *n.*; Wesen *n.*

credentials *s.pl.* Beglaubigungsschreiben *n.*

credibility *s.* Glaubwürdigkeit *f.*

credible *a.*, **~bly** *adv.* glaubwürdig.

credit *s.* Glaube *m.*; Glaubwürdigkeit *f.*; Zeugnis *n.*; Einfluß *m.*; Ehre *f.*; Kredit *m.*; *to his* ~, zu seinen Gunsten; *open* ~, Blankokredit *f.*; *letter of* ~, Kreditbrief *m.*; **~-balance,** Guthaben *n.*; **~-restriction,** Kreditbeschränkung *f.*; **~-voucher,** Kreditkassenschein *m.*; *on* ~, auf Kredit; *to enter to a person's* ~, einem gutschreiben; ~ *v.t.* glaubentrauen; kreditieren, gutschreiben.

creditable *a.*, **~bly** *adv.* anerkennenswert.

credit card *s.* Kreditkarte *f.*

creditor *s.* Gläubiger *m.*

creditworthy *a.* kreditwürdig.

credulity *s.* Leichtgläubigkeit *f.*

credulous *a.* leichtgläubig.

creed *s.* Glaubensbekenntnis *n.*

creek *s.* kleine Bucht *f.*; kleiner Fluß *m.*, Flüßchen *n.*

creep *v.i.* kriechen, schleichen; *my flesh creeps,* mich überläuft eine Gänsehaut.

creeper *s.* Schlingpflanze *f.*; Kletterpflanze *f.*

creepy *a.* gruselig.; unheimlich.

cremate *v.t.* einäschern.

cremation *s.* Einäscherung *f.*; Leichenverbrennung *f.*

crematorium, crematory *s.* Krematorium *n.*

crenellated *a.* mit Zinnen gezackt.

creosote *s.* Kreosot *n.*

crêpe *s.* Krepp *m.*

crescendo *s.* (*mus.*) Crescendo *n.*; (*fig.*) Zunahme *f.*

crescent *s.* zunehmender Mond *m.*; Halbmond *m.*; ~ *a.* halbmondförmig; ~ *s.* halbmondförmige Straße *f.*

cress *s.* Kresse *f.*

crest *s.* Kamm *m.*; Mähne *f.*; Bergrücken *m.*; Helmschmuck (im Wappen) *m.*

crestfallen *a.* niedergeschlagen.

cretin *a.* Kretin *m.*

crevasse *s.* Gletscherspalte *f.*

crevice *s.* Riß *m.*

crew *s.* Besatzung (Schiff, Panzer) *f.*; Mannschaft *f.*; Personal *n.*

crib *s.* Krippe *f.*; Kinderbettchen *n.*; (*fig.*) Eselsbrücke *f.*; ~ *v.t.* abschreiben.

cricket *s.* Grille *f.*; Heimchen *n.*; Kricket, Schlagballspiel *n.*

crier *s.* Ausrufer *m.*

crime *s.* Verbrechen *n.*; *capital* ~, Kapitalverbrechen *n.*

crime rate *s.* Kriminalitätsrate *f.*

criminal *a.*, **~ly** *adv.* verbrecherisch; Straff...; ~ *code,* Strafgesetzbuch *n.*; ~ *investigation department,* Kriminalabteilung *f.*; ~ *justice,* Strafrechtspflege *f.*; ~ *law* s. Strafrecht *n.*; ~ *procedure,* Strafprozeß *m.*; ~ *record,* Strafregister *n.*; ~ *s.* Verbrecher *m.*; *habitual* ~, Gewohnheitsverbrecher *m.*

criminally *a.* kriminell; strafrechtlich.

criminologist *s.* Kriminologe *m.*

criminology *s.* Kriminologie *f.*

crimson *s.* Karmesin *n.*; ~ *a.* karmesinrot; ~ *v.t.* rot färben.

cringe *v.i.* sich krümmen; kriechen.; zusammenzucken.

cringing *a.* kriecherisch.

crinkle *v.i.* knittern, zerknittern; kranseln; ~ *s.* Kränsel *m.*; Knitterfalte *f.*

crinoline *s.* Krinoline *f.*

cripple *s.* Krüppel *m.*; ~ *a.* krüpplig; ~ *v.t.* verstümmeln; lähmen.

crippled *a.* verkrüppelt.

crisis *s.* Krise *f.*; Wendepunkt *m.*

crisp *a.* kraus; knusperig; frisch; ~ *v.t.* kräuseln; braun rösten.

crispbread *s.* Knäckebrot *n.*

crispy *a.* knusprig, knackig.

criss-cross *s.* Gewirr (von Straßen, Kanälen, usw.) *n.*

criterion *s.* Kriterium, Merkmal *n.*

critic *s.* Kritiker(in) *m.*(*f.*).

critical *a.* kritisch; bedenklich; entscheidend; *in a* ~ *condition,* lebensgefährlich verwundet od. krank; ~ *goods* *s.pl.* Mangelware *f.*

critically *adv.* kritisch.

criticize *v.t. & i.* beurteilen, tadeln.

criticism *s.* Kritik *f.*; *open to* ~, anfechtbar.

critique *s.* Kritik *f.*

croak *v.i.* quaken, krächzen.

croaker *s.* Unglücksprophet *m.*

crochet *s.* Häkelarbeit *f.*; ~ *v.i.* häkeln.

crock *s.* Krug, Topf *m.*

crockery *s.* Töpferware *f.*

crocodile *s.* Krokodil *n.*; ~ *tears* Krokodilstränen *pl.*

crocus *s.* Krokus *m.*

croissant *s.* Hörnchen *n.*

crone *s.* alte Frau *f.*; Hexe *f.*

crony *s.* alte Bekannte *m.*/*f.*

crook *s.* Haken *m.*; Schwindler *m.*; ~ *v.t.* krümmen.

crooked *a.*, **~ly** *adv.* krumm, verdreht, schief; betrügerisch.

croon *v.i.* leise singen; smachtend singen.

crooner *s.* Schnulzensänger *m.*

crop *s.* Kropf (der Vögel) *m.*; Ernte *f.*; kurzes Haar *n.*; Jagdpeitsche, Reitgerte *f.*; ~ *v.t.* stutzen, verschneiden; abpflücken, einsammeln, ernten; ~(*up*) *v.i.* auftauchen.

cropper *s.* schwerer Sturz *m.*

croquet *s.* Krocket, Kugelschlagspiel *n.*

crosier *s.* Bischofsstab *m.*

cross *s.* Kreuz *n.*; Leiden *n.*; (Rassen-)Kreuzung *f.*; ~ *a. & adv.* kreuzweise; zuwider, widrig; störrisch, mürrisch; böse; querdurch; ~ *v.t.* kreuzen; überschreiten, gehen über; widersprechen, widerstehen; ~ *v.i.* sich kreuzen; *to* ~ *out,* ausstreichen; *your letter crossed mine,* unsere Briefe haben sich gekreuzt; *crossed check,* Verrechnungsscheck *m.*

cross-bar *s.* Querholz *n.*; Fahrradstange *f.*

crossbow *s.* Armbrust *f.*

cross-bred *a.*, ~ *horse* s. Halbblut *n.*

cross-check *s.* Gegenprobe *f.*

cross-country *a.* querfeldein...

cross-dressing *s.* Transvestismus *m.*

crossed *a.* gekreuzt.

cross-examination *s.* Kreuzverhör *n.*

cross-examine *v.t.* einem Kreuzverhör unterziehen.

crossing *s.* Übergang (auf der Straße) *m.*; Kreuzung

f.; Überfahrt *f.*; *pedestrian ~*, Übergang für Fußgänger; *vehicle ~*, Übergang für Fahrzeuge.

cross-legged *a.* mit gekreuzten Beinen.

crossly *a.* verärgert.

cross-over *s.* Überführung (Straße) *f.*

cross-purpose *s.* Mißverständnis *n.*

cross-reference *s.* Verweis (im Buch) *m.*

cross-roads *s.pl.* Straßenkreuzung *f.*

cross-section *s.* Querschnitt *n.*

crosswalk *s.* Fußgängerübergang *m.*

crosswise *adv.* kreuzweise.

crossword (puzzle) *s.* Kreuzworträtsel *n.*

crotchet *s.* Viertelnote *f.*

crouch *v.i.* kriechen, sich zusammenkauern; *s.* Hocke *f.*

crow *s.* Krähe *f.*; *distance as the ~ flies*, Luftlinie *f.*, Kartenentfernung *f.*; *~ bar s.* Brecheisen *n.*, Hebestange *f.*; *~ v.i.* krähen.

crowd *s.* Menschenmenge *f.*; Gedränge *n.*; *~ v.t.* drängen; vollstopfen; *~ v.i.* sich drängen.

crowded *a.* überfüllt.

crown *s.* Krone *f.*; Kranz *m.*; Scheitel, Gipfel *m.*; Kopf (des Hutes) *m.*; *~ v.t.* krönen.

crown-prince *s.* Kronprinz *m.*

crown-princess *s.* Kronprinzessin *f.*

crown-witness *s.* Kronzeuge *m.*, Kronzeugin *f.*

crow's nest *s.* Krähennest *n.*; Mastkorb *m.*

crucial *a.* entscheidend; kritisch.

crucible *s.* Schmelztiegel *m.*

crucifix *s.* Kruzifix *n.*

crucifixion *s.* Kreuzigung *f.*

cruciform *a.* kreuzförmig.

crucify *v.t.* kreuzigen.

crude *a.*, **~ly** *adv.* roh, unreif; *~ oil s.* Rohöl *n.*; *~ rubber s.* Rohgummi *m.*

crudity *s.* Roheit, Unreife *f.*

cruel *a.*, **~ly** *adv.* grausam.

cruelty *s.* Grausamkeit *f.*; *~ to animals*, Tierquälerei *f.*

cruise *v.n.* hin- und herfahren; mit Reisegeschwindigkeit fliegen; mit Dauergeschwindigkeit fahren. *~ s.* Kreuzen *n.*; Seefahrt *f.*

cruise missile *s.* Marschflugkörper *m.*

cruiser *s.* (*nav.*) Kreuzer *m.*

crumb *s.* Krume *f.*; Brösel *m.*, Krümel *m.*

crumble *v.i.* zerbröckeln; krümeln.

crumbly *a.* krümelig; bröckelig.

crumple *v.t.* zerknittern; *~ v.i.* einschrumpfen.

crunch *v.t. & i.* knirschen; zerkauen.

crunchy *a.* knusprig; knackig.

crusade *s.* Kreuzzug *m.*

crusader *s.* Kreuzfahrer *m.*

crush *s.* Gedränge *n.*, Gewühl *n.*; Schwärmerei *f.*; *~ v.t.* quetschen; unterdrücken; vernichten.

crust *s.* Rinde *f.*; Schale *f.*; Brotkruste *f.*; *~ v.t.* mit einer Kruste überziehen.

crustacean *s.* Krebstier *n.*; Krustentier *n.*

crusty *s.*, **~ily** *adv.* krustig, rindig; mürrisch.

crutch *s.* Krücke *f.*

crux *s.* Crux *f.*; Kernpunkt *m.*

cry *v.i. & t.* schreien; weinen; rufen; *~ s.* Geschrei *n.*; Zuruf *m.*

crypt *s.* Gruft, Krypta *f.*

cryptic *a.* geheim, undurchsichtig.

crystal *s.* Kristall *m.*; *~ a.* kristallen.

crystal-gazing *s.* Hellseherei *f.*

crystalline *a.* kristallen.

crystallize *v.t. & i.* kristallisieren.

cub *s.* Junge *n.*; *~ v.t.* Junge werfen.

Cuba *s.* Kuba *n.*

Cuban *a.* kubanisch; *~ s.* Kubaner(in) *m.(f.)*

cubby *s.* Spint *m.*; Kämmerchen *n.*

cube *s.* Kubus *m.*; Würfel *m.*; *~ (-number) s.* Kubikzahl *f.*; *~ root s.* Kubikwurzel *f.*

cubic *a.* kubisch; *~ meter*, Kubikmeter *m.*

cubicle *s.* Bettnische *f.*; Kabine *f.*

cubit *s.* Unterarm *m.*; Elle *f.* ($1\frac{1}{2}$ Fuß).

cuckold *s.* Hahnrei *m.*

cuckoo *s.* Kuckuck *m.*

cucumber *s.* Gurke *f.*; *pickled ~*, saure Gurke *f.*

cud *s.* Futter (*n.*) im Vormagen der Tiere; *to chew the ~*, wiederkäuen.

cuddle *v.t.* hätscheln, umarmen; *~ s.* Liebkosung *f.*

cuddly *a.* verschmust.

cudgel *s.* Prügel *m.*; *~ v.t.* prügeln.

cue *m.* Queue *n.*, Billardstock *m.*; Stichwort *n.*; Wink *m.*

cuff *s.* Puff *m.*; Manschette *f.*; Hosenaufschlag *m.*; *~ v.t. & i.* puffen; sich schlagen.

cuisine *s.* Küche (Art zu kochen) *f.*

culinary *a.* zur Küche gehörig.

cull *v.t.* aussuchen; auslesen.

culminate *v.i.* kulminieren; gipfeln.

culmination *s.* Gipfelpunkt *m.*

culpability *s.* Strafbarkeit, Schuld *f.*

culpable *a.*, **~bly** *adv.* strafbar, schuldig.

culprit *s.* Schuldiger *m.*; Verbrecher *m.*

cult *s.* Kult *m.*

cultivate *v.t.* anbauen; (Pflanzen, Pilze) züchten; ausbilden; pflegen.

cultivation *s.* Anbau *m.*; Pflege *f.*

cultivator *s.* Pflanzer *m.*

cultural *a.* kulturell.

culture *s.* Anbau *m.*; Bildung *f.*; Kultur *f.*; *cultured pearl* Zuchtperle *f.*

cumber *v.t.* überhäufen; hindern.

cumbersome *a.*, **~ly** *adv.* lästig, hinderlich; unbehilflich.

cumulative *a.* aufhäufend.

cuneiform *a.* keilförmig; Keilschrift. . .

cunning *a.*, **~ly** *adv.* listig; kundig; *~ s.* List *f.*; Geschicklichkeit *f.*

cup *s.* Becher *m.*; Tasse *f.*; Schröpfkopf *m.*; *~ v.t.* schröpfen.

cupboard *s.* Schrank *m.*

cupful *s.* Tasse *f.*

cupidity *s.* Begierde *f.*, Habgier *f.*

cupola *s.* Kuppel *f.*

cur *s.* Köter *m.*; Schurke *m.*

curable *a.* heilbar.

curate *s.* Hilfsgeistlicher *m.*

curative *a.* heilend.

curator *s.* Kurator(in) *m.(f.)*; Direktor(in) *m.(f.)*

curb *s.* Kandare *f.*; Bordstein, Randstein *m.*; *~ v.t.* bändigen; zügeln.

curd *s.* Quark *m.*; dicke Milch *f.*

curdle *v.t. & i.* gerinnen machen; gerinnen; erstarren.

cure *s.* Kur *f.*; *~ of souls*, Seelsorge *f.*; *~ v.t.* heilen; einpökeln; räuchern.

curfew *s.* Ausgehverbot *n.*; Ausgangssperre *f.*; *to lift the ~*, das Ausgehverbot aufheben.

curio s. Rarität f.
curiosity s. Neugierde f.; Kuriostät f.
curious a., **~ly** adv. neugierig; sorgfältig; zierlich; seltsam.
curl s. Locke f.; Wallung f. ~ v.t. kräuseln; winden; ~ v.i. sich locken.
curler s. Lockenwickler m.
curling s. Eisstockschießen n.
curling-iron s. Brenneisen n.
curly a. gekräuselt.
curmudgeon s. Geizhals, Knicker m.
currant s. Korinthe f.; Johannisbeere f.
currency s. Lauf, Umlauf m.; Währung f.; Kurs m.; Umlaufsmittel n.; hard ~, feste Währung; soft ~, unstabile Währung.
current a., **~ly** adv. (um)laufend; gangbar; geläufig; ~ s. Lauf, Strom m.; Zug m.; elektrischer Strom m.; alternating ~ (AC), Wechselstrom m.; direct ~ (DC), Gleichstrom m.
current: ~ **account** s. Girokonto n.; ~ **events** pl. Tagesereignisse pl.; ~ **meter** s. Stromzähler m.
curriculum s. Lehrplan m.; ~ **vitae** s. Lebenslauf m.
curry v.t. striegeln; prügeln; to ~ favor, die Gunst erschleichen; ~ s. Curry m. (ostindisches Mischgewürz).
currycomb s. Pferdestriegel m.
curse s. Fluch m.; Verwünschung f.; ~ v.i. & t. fluchen; verwünschen.
cursed a. verflucht.
cursive a. laufend, Kursiv...
cursor s. Läufer m.; Cursor m.
cursory a. flüchtig, oberflächlich.
curt a., **~ly** adv. kurz, kurz angebunden.
curtail v.t. stutzen, abkürzen; verstümmeln; (fig.) einschränken.
curtailment s. Beschränkung, Kürzung f.
curtain s. Vorhang m.; (mil.) Zwischenwall m.; to draw the ~, den Vorhang zuziehen; ~ v.t. mit Vorhängen versehen, verhüllen.
curtain-fire s. (mil.) Sperrfeuer n.
curtain-rod s. Vorhangstange f.
curtsy s. Knicks m.; ~ v.i. knicksen.
curvaceous a. kurvenreich.
curvature s. Krümmung f.
curve s. Krümmung f.; ~ v.t. krümmen, biegen.
curved a. krumm, gebogen.
cushion s. Kissen n.; Polster m.
cushy a. bequem.
cuss s. Fluch m.; Kerl m.
cussed a. stur.
cussedness s. Sturheit f.
custard s. Vanille pudding m.; Vanillesoße f.
custodial a. vormundschaftlich.
custodian s. Hüter(in) m. (f.); Wächter(in) m.(f.); Kustos m.

custody s. Verwahrung f.; Haft f.; Aufsicht f.; Obhut f.; protective ~, Schutzhaft f.; to take into ~, verhaften.
custom s. Gebrauch m.; Gewohnheit f.; Kundschaft f.; Zoll m.
customary a., **~ily** adv. gebräulich.
customer s. Kunde m.; Kundin f.; regular ~, Stammkunde, Stammgast m.
customhouse s. Zollamt n.
custom-made a. spezialgefertigt; maßgeschneidert.
customs s.pl. Zoll m.; **~-clearance,** Zollabfertigung f.; **~-declaration,** Zollerklärung f.; **~-examination,** Zollrevision f.; **~-officer** s. Zollbeamter m.; **~-station** Zollamt n.
cut v.t. & i.ir. schneiden, hauen; schnitzen; spalten; verstümmeln; kürzen; abheben (Karten); to ~ a person, einen nicht sehen wollen, schneiden; to ~ out, (mech.) ausschalten; (com.) unterbieten; to ~ prices, Preise herabsetzen; to ~ teeth, Zähne bekommen; ~ and dried, fix und fertig; ~ s. Schnitt, Einschnitt m.; Stich, Hieb m.; Kürzung f.; short ~, Abkürzungsweg m.
cutaneous a. zur Haut gehörig.
cut-back s. Kürzung f.
cute a. (fam.) schlau.
cut-glass s. Kristallglas n.
cuticle s. Oberhaut f., Häutchen n.
cutlery s. Messerwaren f.pl.
cutlet s. Schnitzel n.
cutter s. Steinschneider m.; Schneidezeug n.; Zuschneider m.; (mech.) Schneider m.; Kutter (Schiff) m.; Cutter(in) m.(f.).
cut-throat s. Meuchelmörder m.; ~ a. mörderisch, gnadenlos.
cutting s. Einschnitt m.; Zeitungsausschnitt m.; ~ a. schneidend, scharf.
cuttle s. Tintenfisch m.
cyanide s. Cyanid n.
cyclamen s. Alpenveilchen n.
cycle s. Kreis m.; Fahrrad n.; Zyklus m.
cycler s. Radfahrer(in) m.(f.)
cycling s. Radfahren n.
cyclist s. Radfahrer m.; ~'s path, Radfahrweg m.
cyclone s. Wirbelsturm m.
cygnet s. junger Schwan m.
cylinder s. Zylinder m.; Walze f.
cylindrical a. zylindrisch.
cymbal s. Schallbecken n., Zimbel f.
cynic a. zynisch; schamlos; ~ s. Zyniker(in) m.(f.)
cynicism s. Zynismus m.
cypress s. Zypresse f.
cyst s. Blase f.; Eitersack m.
czar s. Zar m.
Czech a. tschechisch; ~ s. Tscheche m., Tschechin f.
Czech Republic s. Tschechische Republik f.

D

D, d der Buchstabe D oder d n.; (mus.) D, d; **D-sharp** Dis, dis; **D-flat** Des, des.
dab v.t. betupfen; besudeln; ~ s. Tupfer m.; Klecks m.
dabble v.i. planschen; stümpern; ~ v.t. bespritzen.
dachshund s. Dachshund m., Dackel m.

dad, daddy s. Papa, Vater m.; ~ **longlegs** s. langbeinige Mücke f.; Weberknecht m.
daffodil s. gelbe Narzisse f.
daft a. doof; blöd.
dagger s. Dolch m.
dahlia s. Dahlie f.

daily *a. & adv.* täglich; ~ *s.* Tageszeitung *f.*

dainty *a.,* **~ily** *adv.* lecker; niedlich; zierlich, fein; geziert; heikel; ~ *s.* Leckerbissen *m.,* Naschwerk *n.*

dairy *s.* Molkerei *f.;* Milchwirtschaft *f.;* **~-farm** Meierei *f.*

dairy produce *s.* **products** *s.pl.* Molkereiprodukte *n.pl.*

dais *s.* Podium *n.*

daisy *s.* Gänseblümchen *n.;* Margerite *f.*

dale *s.* Tal *n.*

dalliance *s.* Tändelei *f.;* Trödelei *f.;* Verzögerung *f.*

dally *v.i.* tändeln, trödeln.

dam *s.* Damm *m.;* Talsperre *f.;* Muttertier *f.;* ~ *v.t.* dämmen.

damage *s.* Schaden, Verlust *m.;* Beschädigung *f.;* ~ *to property,* Sachbeschädigung *f.;* ~ *v.t.* beschädigen.

damageable *a.* leicht zu beschädigen.

damages *s.pl.* Schadenersatz *m.*

damaging *a.* schädlich.

damask *s.* Damast *m.;* ~ *a.* damasten.

dame *s.* Dame *f.* (Adelstitel); (*fam.*) Weid *n.*

damn *v.t.* verdammen; verwerfen.

damnation *s.* Verdammung *f.*

damned *a.* verdammt, verflucht.

damning *a.* vernichtend; belastend.

damp *a.* feucht, dumpfig; ~ *s.* Feuchtigkeit *f.;* Schwaden *m.;* ~ *v.t.* befeuchten; dämpfen.

damper *s.* Dämpfer *m.*

dampness *s.* Feuchtigkeit *f.*

damp-proof *a.* feuchtigkeitssicher.

damsel *s.* Mädchen *n.;* Jungfer *f.*

dance *s.* Tanz *m.;* ~ *v.i.* tanzen; *ballroom dancing,* Gesellschaftstanz *m.*

dance master *s.* Tanzlehrer *m.*

dancer *s.* Tänzer *m.,* Tänzerin *f.*

dandelion *s.* (*bot.*) Löwenzahn *m.*

dandle *v.t.* schaukeln, hätscheln.

dandruff *s.* Kopfschuppen *f.pl.*

dandy *s.* Stutzer *m.,* Dandy *m.*

Dane *s.* Däne *m.;* Dänin *f.*

danger *s.* Gefahr *f.* ~ **signal** *s.* Warnzeichen.

dangerous *a.,* **~ly** *adv.* gefährlich.

dangle *v.i.* baumeln; anhängen.

Danish *a.* dänisch; ~ *s.* Däne *m.,* Dänin *f.*

dank *a.* unangenehm feucht.

Danube *s.* Donau *f.*

dapper *a.* flink, gewandt; nett.

dapple *a.* gefleckt, scheckig; ~ *v.t.* sprenkeln.

dare *v.i.* dürfen; wagen; *I* ~ *say,* ich denke; ~ *v.t.* trotzen.

daredevil *a.* waghalsig; ~ *s.* Draufgänger(in) *m.*(*f.*); Teufelskerl *m.*

daring *a.,* **~ly** *adv.* vermessen, verwegen; ~ *s.* Kühnheit *f.*

dark *a.* dunkel, trübe; *Dark Ages pl.* finsteres Mittelalter *n.;* ~ **room** *s.* Dunkelkammer *f.; after* ~, nach Eintritt der Dunkelheit; ~ *s.* Finsternis *f.*

darken *v.t. & i.* verdunkeln; dunkel werden.

darkish *a.* etwas dunkel.

darkness *s.* Dunkelheit *f.;* Verborgenheit *f.;* Unwissenheit *f.*

darling *a.* teuer; ~ *s.* Liebling *m.*

darn *v.t.* stopfen, ausbessern.

darned *a. adv.* verflixt.

darning *s.* Stopfen *n.;* ~ **needle** *s.* Stopfnadel *f.*

dart *s.* Wurfgeschoß *n.;* Pfeil *m.;* ~ *v.t.* werfen, schießen; ~ *v.i.* hinschießen, stürzen; **darts** *s.pl.* Pfeilwurfspiel *n.*

dash *v.t.* schmeißen, stoßen; vermischen; zerschmettern; vereiteln; ~ *v.i.* stoßen; stürmen, stürzen, jagen; dahinrauschen; scheitern; ~ *it!,* verwünscht!; ~ *s.* Klatsch, Schlag, Stoß *m.;* Federzug *m.;* Gedankenstrich *m.;* Aufguß *m.;* Stückchen, Bißchen *n.;* Wagemut *m.,* Schneid *f.*

dashboard *s.* Armaturenbrett *n.*

dashing *a.* schneidig, flott.

dastard *s.* feige Memme *f.;* ~ *a.,* **~ly** *adv.* feig; abscheulich.

data *s.pl.* Daten; **~bank** *s.* Datenbank *f.;* ~ **processing** Datenverarbeitung *f.;* ~ **transmission** *s.* Datenübertragung *f.*

date *s.* Datum *n.;* Frist *f.;* Dattel *f.; what is the* ~?, den wievielten haben wir?; *up-to-*~, zeitgemäß, modern; *out of* ~, aus der Mode; ~ *v.t.* datieren; mit jemandem ausgehen.

dated *a.* altmodisch.

date-palm *s.* Dattelpalme *f.*

dative *s.* (*gram.*) Dativ *m.*

daub *v.t.* überschmieren, sudeln.

daughter *s.* Tochter *f.;* **~-in-law,** Schwiegertochter *f.*

daunt *v.t.* entmutigen.

dauntless *a.* unerschrocken.

davit *s.* Jütte *f.,* Davit *m.*

dawdle *v.i.* trödeln; schlendern.

dawdler *s.* Tagedieb *m.*

dawn *v.i.* dämmern, tagen; ~ *s.* Dämmerung *f.*

day *s.* Tag *m.; by* ~, untertags; *the other* ~, neulich; ~*s of grace pl.* Verzugstage *m.pl.*

daybreak *s.* Tagesanbruch *m.*

day care *s.* Kinderbetreuung *f.*

daydream *s.* Tagtraum *m.*

daylight *s.* Tageslicht *f.;* (*avi.*) **~-attack,** Tagesangriff *m.*

day-nursery *s.* Kinderhort *m.*

day shift *s.* Tagesschicht *f.*

day-time *s.* Tageszeit *f.; in the* ~, bei Tag.

day trip *s.* Tagesausflug *m.*

daze *v.t.* benommen machen; ~ *s.* Benommenheit *f.*

dazzle *v.t.* blenden.

deacon *s.* Diakon *m.*

dead *a.* tot; dumpf, schal; (*elek.*) spannungslos; ~ *against,* gerade entgegen; ~ *bargain,* Spottpreis *m.;* **~-wall** *s.* blinde Mauer *f.;* **~-letter** *s.* unzustellbarer Brief *m.;* ~ *adv.* ganz, völlig; ~ **silence** *s.* Totenstille *f.; the* ~, die Toten *pl.*

deaden *v.t.* abstumpfen, schwächen.

dead end *s.* Sackgasse *f.*

deadline *s.* Termin *m.*

deadlock *s.* Stockung *f.,* Stillstand *m.*

deadly *a. & adv.* tödlich.

deaf *a.,* **~ly** *adv.* taub; dumpf; ~ *and dumb,* taubstumm.

deafen *v.t.* taub machen.

deafening *a.* ohrenbetäubend.

deaf-mute *s.* Taubstummer *m.;* ~ *a.* taubstumm.

deafness *s.* Taubheit *f.*

deal *s.* Teil *m.;* Anzahl *f.;* Geschäft *f.;* Kartengeben *n.;* Fichtenholz, Brett *n.; a good* ~, *a great* ~, viel, sehr; ~ *v.t.* austeilen, ausstreuen; Karten geben; ~

v.i. handeln, verfahren; vermitteln; *to ~ with,* behandeln.
dealer *s.* Händler *m.*; Kartengeber *m.*
dealing *s.* Verfahren *n.*; Austeilen *n.*; Umgang *m.*; *to have ~s with,* mit einem zu tun haben.
dean *s.* Dechant, Dekan *m.*
dear *a.* teuer, wert; innig; *~ s.* Geliebter *m.*, Geliebte *f.*; *~ me!,* meine liebe Güte!
dearth *s.* Teuerung *f.*; Mangel *m.*
death *s.* Tod *m.*; Todesfall *m.*; *to put to ~,* hinrichten.
deathbed *s.* Sterbebett *n.*
death certificate *s.* Totenschein *m.*
death blow *s.* Todesstoß *m.*
deathless *a.* unsterblich.
deathly *a.* tödlich, Todes. . .
deathpenalty *s.* Todesstrafe *f.*
deathrate *s.* Sterblichkeitsziffer *f.*
death's-head *s.* Totenkopf *m.*
death toll *s.* Zahl der Todesopfer *f.*
death warrant *s.* Todesurteil *n.*
debacle *s.* Debakel *n.*
debar *v.t.* ausschließen; verhindern.
debase *v.t.* erniedrigen; verfälschen.
debasement *s.* Erniedrigung *f.*
debatable *a.* streitig.
debate *s.* Debatte *f.*; *~ v.t.* bestreiten, erörtern.
debauch *v.t.* verführen, verderben.
debauchee *s.* Schwelger, Wüstling *m.*
debauchery *s.* Ausschweifung *f.*
debenture *s.* Schuldschein *m.*; *(com.)* Obligation *f.*
debilitate *v.t.* schwächen, entkräften.
debilitation *s.* Schwächung *f.*; Entkräftung *f.*
debility *s.* Schwachheit.
debit *v.t.* belasten, debitieren; *~ s.* Soll *n.*; Lasten *f.pl.*
debonair *a.* gefällig, höflich.
debouch *v.i.* hervorbrechen; einmünden.
debris *s.* Trümmer *pl.*
debt *s.* Schuld *f.*; *to run into ~,* in Schulden geraten.
debtor *s.* Schuldner(in) *m.(f.)*
debug *v.t.* *(fam.)* entwanzen (Abhörgeräte entfernen); Fehler beheben.
debut *s.* Debüt *n.*
debutante *s.* Debütantin *f.*
decade *s.* Jahrzehnt *n.*
decadence *s.* Verfall *m.*
decadent *a.* dekadent.
Decalogue *s.* die zehn Gebote *n.pl.*
decamp *v.i.* aufbrechen, ausreißen.
decant *v.t.* abgießen; umfüllen.
decanter *s.* Karaffe *f.*
decapitate *v.t.* köpfen.
decathlon *s.* Zehnkampf *m.*
decay *v.i.* verfallen; verwelken; *~ s.* Verfall *m.*; Abnahme *f.*
decease *s.* Ableben *n.*; *~ v.i.* sterben, verscheiden.
deceased *a.* verstorben; *~ s.* Verstorbene *m.*
deceit *s.* Betrug *m.*; List *f.*
deceitful *a.*, **~ly** *adv.* betrügerisch.
deceitfulness *s.* Falschheit *f.*; Hinterlistigkeit *f.*
deceive *v.t.* betrügen, täuschen.
December *s.* Dezember *m.*
decency *s.* Anstand *m.*; Schicklichkeit *f.*
decennial *a.* zehnjährig.
decent *a.*, **~ly** *adv.* sittsam, anständig.
decentralize *v.t.* dezentralisieren.

decentralization *s.* Dezentralisierung *f.*
deception *s.* Betrug *m.*
deceptive *a.* trügerisch.
decibel *s.* Dezibel *n.*
decide *v.t.* entscheiden, bestimmen.
decided *a.* & *adv.* entschieden, bestimmt.
deciduous *a.* *~ tree* laubwerfender Baum, Laubbaum *m.*
decimal *a.* dezimal; *~ s.* Dezimale.
decimate *v.t.* zehnten, dezimieren.
decipher *v.t.* entziffern.
decision *s.* Entscheidung *f.*; Entschlossenheit *f.*
decisive *a.*, **~ly** *adv.* entscheidend.
deck *s.* Deck, Verdeck *n.*; *~ v.t.* bekleiden; schmücken.
deck-chair *s.* Liegestuhl *m.*
declaim *v.t.* deklamieren; eifern.
declamation *s.* Deklamation *f.*
declamatory *a.* deklamatorisch.
declaration *s.* Erklärung *f.*
declare *v.t.* erklären, behaupten; (Zoll) deklarieren; *~ v.i.* sich erklären.
declassify *v.t.* freigeben (Dokument).
declension *s.* *(gram.)* Deklination *f.*
declination *s.* Abweichung *f.*; Abnahme *f.*; Deklination *f.*
decline *v.i.* abweichen; abnehmen; sich weigern; fallen (im Preise); *~ v.t.* ablehnen; deklinieren; *~ s.* Abnahme *f.*; Verfall *m.*
declivity *s.* Abhang *m.*
declutch *v.t.* auskuppeln.
decoction *s.* Absud *m.*, Absieden *n.*
decode *v.t.* entziffern.
decompose *v.t.* zerlegen.; *~ v.i.* zersetzen.
decomposition *s.* Zersetzung *f.*
decompression *s.* Dekompression *f.*
decontaminate *v.t.* dekontaminieren, entseuchen.
decontamination *s.* Dekontamination *f.*; Entseuchung *f.*
decontrol *v.t.* freigeben.
decor *s.* Ausstattung *f.*
decorate *v.t.* verzieren, schmücken.
decoration *s.* Dekoration *f.*, Schmuck *m.*; Ordenszeichen *n.*
decorative *a.* schmückend.
decorator *s.* Dekorateur(in) *m.(f.)*; *Tapezierer(in) m.(f.)*
decorous *a.*, **~ly** *adv.* anständig, schicklich.
decorum *s.* Anstand *m.*, Schicklichkeit *f.*
decoy *v.t.* locken, ködern; *~ s.* Köder *m.*
decrease *v.t.* vermindern; *~ v.i.* abnehmen; *~ s.* Abnahme *f.*
decree *v.t.* beschließen; verfügen; *~ s.* Beschluß *m.*, Verordnung *f.*
decrepit *a.* altersschwach, heruntergekommen.
decrepitude *s.* Altersschwäche *f.*
decry *v.t.* herabsetzen; schlechtmachen.
dedicate *v.t.* widmen, zueignen.
dedication *s.* Widmung, Zueignung *f.*
dedicatory *a.* Widmungs. . .
deduce *v.t.* ableiten; schließen, folgern.
deducible *a.* ableitbar.
deduct *v.t.* abziehen, abrechnen.
deduction *s.* Abzug, Rabatt *m.*; Schlußfolge *f.*
deductive *a.*, **~ly** *adv.* deduktiv, folgernd.
deed *s.* Tat, Handlung *f.*; Urkunde *f.*; *~ of gift,*

deem

Schenkungsurkunde *f.*; ~ *of partnership*, Gesellschaftsvertrag *m.*; ~ *of sale*, Kaufkontrakt *m.*

deem *v.t.* halten für, erachten.

deep *a.*, **~ly** *adv.* tief; geheim; schlau; ~ *s.* Tiefe *f.*; Meer *n.*

deepen *v.t.* vertiefen; ~ *v.i.* sich vertiefen; stärker werden.

deep-freeze *s.* Tiefkühlgerät *n.*; *v.t.* tiefkühlen, einfrieren.

deep-fry *v.t.* fritieren.

deep-rooted *a.* tiefverwurzelt.

deer *s.* Rotwild *n.*; Hirsch *m.*

deerskin *s.* Wildleder *n.*

deer stalking *s.* Pirschen *n.*

deface *v.t.* verunstalten, entstellen.

defalcate *v.i.* (Geld) unterschlagen.

defamation *s.* Verleumdung *f.*; Diffamierung *f.*

defamatory *a.* verleumderisch.

defame *v.t.* verleumden; verlästern.

default *s.* Versäumnis *n.*; Zahlungseinstellung *f.*; Nichterscheinen *n.*; *in* ~ *of*, mangels; *judgment by* ~, (*law*) Versäumnisurteil *n.*; ~ *v.i.* unterlassen; fehlen; im Verzug sein, Verpflichtungen nicht erfüllen.

defaulter *s.* säumiger Zahler *m.*; zum Termin nicht Erscheinender *m.*

defeat *v.t.* besiegen; schlagen; vereiteln; ~ *s.* Niederlage, Vereitelung *f.*

defeatism *s.* Miesmacherei *f.*, Defätismus *m.*

defeatist *s.* Defätist *m.*; ~ *a.* defätistisch.

defecate *v.i.* Kot ausscheiden, defäkieren.

defect *s.* Mangel *m.*; Gebrechen *n.*; ~ *of speech*, Sprachfehler *m.*

defection *s.* Mangel *m.*; Abtrünnigkeit *f.*; Abfall *m.*

defective *a.* mangelhaft, unvollständig.

defector *s.* Überläufer(in) *m.*(*f.*); Abtrünnige *m.*/*f.*

defend *v.t.* verteidigen.

defendant *s.* Verteidiger *m.*; (*law*) Angeklagter, Beklagter *m.*

defender *s.* Verteidiger(in) *m.*(*f.*).

defense *s.* Verteidigung (auch *law*) *f.*; (*mil.*) Widerstand *m.*; *witness for the* ~, Entlastungszeuge *m.*

defenseless *a.*, **~ly** *adv.* wehrlos.

defense mechanism *s.* Abwehrmechanismus *m.*

defensible *a.* zu verteidigen, haltbar.

defensive *a.*, **~ly** *adv.* Verteidigungs. . .; ~ *s.* (*mil.*) Defensive *f.*; *to be on the* ~, in der Defensive sein.

defer *v.t.* aufschieben, vorenthalten; (*mil.*) zurückstellen; *~red shares*, Verzugsaktien *f.pl.*; ~ *v.i.* sich beugen, nachgeben.

deference *s.* Ehrerbietung *f.*; Nachgiebigkeit *f.*

deferential *a.*, **~ly** *adv.* ehrerbietig.

deferment *s.* (*mil.*) Aufschub *m.*; Zurückstellung *f.*

defiance *s.* Herausforderung *f.*; Trotz *m.*

defiant *a.* herausfordernd, trotzig.

deficiency *s.* Mangel *m.*

deficient *a.* unzulänglich, mangelhaft.

deficit *s.* Fehlbetrag *m.*, Defizit *n.*

defile *v.t.* beflecken; ~ *v.i.* defilieren; ~ *s.* Engpaß *m.*

defilement *s.* Befleckung *f.*

define *v.t.* festsetzen; definieren.

definite *a.* festgesetzt, bestimmt.

definitely *adv.* eindeutig; endgültig.

definition *s.* Begriffsbestimmung *f.*, Definition *f.*; (*TV*) Schärfe *f.*

deliver

definitive *a.*, **~ly** *adv.* endgültig.

deflate *v.t.* Luft rauslassen (aus Reifen), ernüchtern.

deflation *s.* Entleerung *f.*; Deflation *f.*

deflationary *a.* deflationär.

deflect *v.t. & i.* ablenken; abweichen.

deflection *s.* Abweichung *f.*

deform *v.t.* verunstalten, entstellen.

deformity *s.* Ungestaltheit *f.*, Gebrechen *n.*

defraud *v.t.* betrügen; *to* ~ *the revenue*, Steuern hinterziehen.

defray *v.t.* bestreiten, bezahlen.

defrost *v.t.* auftauen; enteisen.

deft *a.*, **~ly** *adv.* geschickt, gewandt.

defunct *a.* verstorben; defekt; veraltet.

defuse *v.t.* entschärfen.

defy *v.t.* herausfordern, trotzen.

degeneracy *s.* Entartung *f.*

degenerate *v.i.* entarten ~ *a.*, **~ly** *adv.* ausgeartet, schlecht, entartet.

degeneration *s.* Degeneration *f.*

degradation *s.* Erniedrigung *f.*

degrade *v.t.* herabsetzen, erniedrigen, herabwürdigen; vermindern.

degrading *a.* entwürdigend.

degree *s.* Grad *m.*; Stufe *f.*; Diplom *n.*

dehydrate *v.t.* Wasser entziehen, **~d** *a.* dehydratisiert; ~ *food*, Trockennahrung *f.*

de-ice *v.t.* enteisen.

deify *v.t.* vergöttern.

deign *v.t.* geruhen; belieben.

deity *s.* Gottheit *f.*

deject *v.t.* entmutigen.

dejected *a.* niedergeschlagen.

dejection *s.* Niedergeschlagenheit *f.*

delay *v.t.* aufschieben, hinhalten; hindern; *~ed action*, (mit) Verzug *m.*; ~ *v.i.* zaudern; ~ *s.* Aufschub *m.*, Verzug *m.*

delectable *a.*, **~bly** *adv.* angenehm.

delegacy *s.* Abordnung *f.*

delegate *v.t.* abordnen; übertragen; *to* ~ *authority*, Befugnis übertragen; ~ *s.* Abgeordneter *m.*

delegation *s.* Abordnung *f.*

delete *v.t.* auslöschen, tilgen.

deleterious *a.* schädlich.

deletion *s.* (*comp.*) Streichung *f.*; Löschung *f.*

deliberate *v.i.* beratschlagen; ~ *a.* absichtlich.

deliberation *s.* Beratschlagung *f.*

deliberative *a.* beratschlagend.

delicacy *s.* Schmackhaftigkeit *f.*; Leckerbissen *m.*; Zartheit *f.*

delicate *a.*, **~ly** *adv.* zart; fein; heikel.

delicatessen *pl.* Feinkostgeschäft *n.*

delicious *a.*, köstlich.

delight *s.* Vergnügen *n.*; Wonne *f.*; ~ *v.t.* ergötzen, vergnügen; ~ *v.i.* Vergnügen finden.

delighted *a.* hocherfreut.

delightful *a.*, **~ly** *adv.* entzückend.

delimit *v.t.* abgrenzen; begrenzen.

delimitation *s.* Abgrenzung *f.*

delineate *v.t.* zeichnen, entwerfen.

delinquency *s.* Vergehen *n.*; Kriminalität *f.*

delinquent *s.* Delinquent(in) *m.*(*f.*); Straffällige *m.*

delirious *a.* wahnsinnig.

delirium *s.* (Fieber-) Wahnsinn *m.*

deliver *v.t.* überliefern; befreien; vortragen;

entbinden; abliefern; (Angriff) ausführen.
deliverance *s.* Befreiung *f.*; Erlösung *f.*
delivery *s.* Lieferung *f.*; Befreiung *f.*; Vortrag *m.*; Entbindung *f.*; Briefbestellung *f.*
delivery-note *s.* Lieferschein *m.*
delta *s.* Delta *n.*
delude *v.t.* betrügen, täuschen.
deluge *s.* Überschwemmung *f.*; Sintflut *f.*; ~ *v.t.* überschwemmen.
delusion *s.* Täuschung *f.*; Wahn *m.*
delusive *a.*, **~ly** *adv.* täuschend.
deluxe *a.* Luxus. . .
delve *v.t.* graben.
demagogic *a.* demagogisch.
demagogue *s.* Aufwiegler(in) *m.*(*f.*); Demagoge *m.*, Demagogin *f.*
demand *v.t.* fordern; fragen; verlangen; ~ *s.* Forderung *f.*; Frage *f.*; Anspruch *m.*; Nachfrage *f.*
demanding *a.* anspruchsvoll.
demarcate *v.t.* abgrenzen.
demarcation *s.* Grenzlinie *f.*
demean *v.t.* ~ *o.s.* sich erniedrigen.
demeaning *a.* erniedrigend.
demeanor *s.* Betragen *n.*
demented *a.* toll, verrückt.
démenti *s.* Dementi *n.*
demi- (*prefix*) halb.
demigod *s.* Halbgott *m.*
demilitarize *v.t.* entmilitarisieren.
demise *s.* Übertragung *f.*; Ableben *n.*; ~ *v.t.* vermachen; verpachten.
demobilize *v.t.* abrüsten, demobilisieren.
democracy *s.* Demokratie *f.*
democrat *s.* Demokrat(in) *m.*(*f.*)
democratic *a.* demokratisch.
democratically *adv.* demokratisch.
demolish *v.t.* niederreißen, abtragen; abreißen.
demolition *s.* Niederreißen *n.*; Abriß *m.*; Zerstörung *f.*
demon *s.* Dämon *m.*; Teufel *m.*
demoniac *a.* dämonisch.
demonstrable *a.*, **~bly** *adv.* beweisbar.
demonstrate *v.t.* beweisen.
demonstration *s.* Beweis *m.*; Äußerung (des Gefühls) *f.*; Vorführung *f.*; Demonstration *f.*
demonstrative *a.*, **~ly** *adv.* beweisend; auffällig; (*gram.*) hinweisend.
demonstrator *s.* Demonstrant(in) *m.*(*f.*)
demoralization *s.* Demoralisierung *f.*
demoralize *v.t.* demoralisieren.
demotivate *v.t.* demotivieren.
demur *v.i.* Einwände erheben.
demure *a.*, **~ly** *adv.* betont zurückhaltend, gesetzt.
demurrer *s.* Rechtseinwand *m.*
den *s.* Höhle, Grube *f.*; (*slang*) Bude *f.*
denial *s.* Verneinung, Verweigerung *f.*
denigrate *v.t.* verunglimpfen.
denizen *s.* Bewohner *m.*
Denmark *s.* Dänemark *n.*
denomination *s.* Benennung *f.*; Klasse *f.*; Nennwert (Banknote, Scheck) *m.*; Konfession *f.*
denominational *a.* konfessionell.
denominative *a.* benennend.
denominator *a.* (*ar.*) Nenner *m.*
denote *v.t.* bezeichnen, bedeuten.
denounce *v.t.* verklagen, anklagen; denunzieren.

dense *a.* dicht, fest; dumm.
denseness *s.* Dichte *f.*; (*fig.*) Begriffsstutzigkeit *f.*
density *s.* Dichtheit *f.*
dent *s.* Kerbe *f.*, Einschnitt *m.*; Beule *f.*; ~ *v.t.* einbeulen.
dental *a.* Zahn. . .
dental surgeon *s.* Zahnarzt *m.*, Zahnärztin *f.*
dentifrice *s.* Zahnpulver *n.*
dentist *s.* Zahnarzt *m.*, Zahnärztin *f.*
dentistry *s.* Zahnheilkunde *f.*
denture *s.* künstliches Gebiß *n.*
denude *v.t.* entblößen.
denunciate *v.t.* denunzieren.
denunciation *s.* Anzeige; Anklage *f.*
deny *v.t.* verneinen; abschlagen; (ver)leugnen.
deodorant *s.* Deodorant *n.*
deodorize *v.t.* geruchlos machen.
depart *v.i.* abreisen; weggehen; abweichen.
department *s.* Abteilung *f.*; Bezirk *m.*; Geschäftskreis *m.*; Behörde *f.*; Ministerium *n.*
department store *s.* Kaufhaus *n.*
departure *s.* Abreise *f.*; Abweichung *f.*; (*fig.*) Tod *m.*; *a new* ~, eine neuer Anfang *m.*
depend *v.i.* abhängen; *to ~ on*, sich verlassen auf; *it ~s*, das kommt darauf an; je nachdem.
dependable *a.* zuverlässig.
dependant *s.* Abhängige *m.*/*f.*
dependence *s.* Abhängigkeit *f.*
dependency *s.* Besitzung, Kolonie *f.*
dependent *a.* abhängig.
depict *v.t.* darstellen.
depilatory *s.* Enthaarungsmittel *n.*
deplete *v.t.* entleeren; erschöpfen.
depletion *s.* Entleerung *f.*
deplorable *a.*, **~bly** *adv.* beklagenswert.
deplore *v.t.* beklagen, beweinen.
deploy *v.t.* aufmarschieren, Truppen einsetzen.
deployment *s.* Aufmarsch *m.*; Einsatz *m.*
deponent *s.* vereidigter Zeuge *m.*
depopulate *v.t.* entvölkern.
deport *v.t.* fortschaffen, deportieren.
deportation *s.* Deportation *f.*
deportee *s.* Deportierter *m.*
depose *v.t. & i.* niedersetzen; absetzen.
deposit *v.t.* niederlegen; ablegen; deponieren; ausleihen; ablagern; ~ *s.* Unterpfand, Pfand *n.*; Kaution *f.*; Einlage *f.*; Depot *n.*, Einzahlung *f.*, Depositum *n.*; anvertrautes Gut *n.*; Niederschlag *m.*; (Erz-)lager *n.*
depositary *s.* Verwahrer *m.*
deposition *s.* Absetzung *f.*; Zeugenaussage *f.*
depositor *s.* Einzahler, Hinterleger *m.*
depository *s.* Gewahrsam *m.*; Niederlage *f.*; Verwahrungsort *m.*
depot *s.* Lagerhaus *n.*
deprave *v.t.* verderben.
deprecate *v.t.* mißbilligen.
deprecatory *a.* mißbilligend.
depreciate *v.t.* herabsetzen, verkleinern; entwerten; abschreiben.
depreciation *s.* Wertverlust *m.*; Abschreibung *f.*
depredation *s.* Plünderung *f.*; Räuberei *f.*
depress *v.t.* niederdrücken, deprimieren.
depressant *s.* Beruhigungsmittel *n.*
depressed *a.* deprimiert.
depressed area *a.* Notstandsgebiet *n.*

depression *s.* Tief *n.*; Niedergeschlagenheit *f.*; Erniedrigung *f.*; Sinken (im Preis) *n.*

depressive *a.* deprimiert, depressiv.

deprivation *s.* Entzug *m.*; Aberkennung *f.*

deprive *v.t.* berauben; entziehen.

deprived *a.* benachteiligt.

depth *s.* Tiefe *f.*; ~ *charge*, Unterwasserbombe *f.*

deputation *s.* Abordnung *f.*; Delegation *f.*

depute *v.t.* abordnen.

deputy *s.* Abgeordnete *m.*; Stellvertreter(in) *m.*(*f.*)

derail *v.t. & i* entgleisen (lassen).

derailment *s.* Entgleisung *f.*

derange *v.t.* zerrütten.

deranged *a.* geistesgestört.

derangement *s.* Unordnung *f.*; Geisteszerrüttung *f.*

derelict *a.* verlassen, herrenlos; ~ *s.* Obdachlose *m.*

dereliction *s.* Vernachlässigung *f.*; ~ *of duty*, Pflichtvergessenheit *f.*

deride *v.t.* verlachen.

derision *s.* Verspottung *f.*; Spott *m.*

derisive *a.* spöttisch, höhnisch.

derisory *a.* lächerlich; spöttisch.

derivation *s.* Ableitung, Herleitung *f.*

derivative *a.*, **~ly** *adv.* hergeleitet; abgeleitet; ~ *s.* abgeleitetes Wort *n.*, Ableitung *f.*; (*chem.*) Derivat *n.*

derive *v.t.* ableiten; herleiten.

dermatitis *s.* Hautentzündung *f.*

dermatologist *s.* Dermatologe *m.*, Dermatologin *f.*; Hautarzt *m.*, Hautärztin *f.*

derogate *v.i.* Abbruch tun.

derogation *s.* Schmälerung *f.*

derogatory *a.* verletzend; abfällig.

derrick *s.* Hebekran *m.*

descant *s.* Diskantstimme *f.*

descend *v.i. & t.* herabsteigen; sich senken; landen; abstammen.

descendant *s.* Nachkomme *m.*/*f.*

descent *s.* Herabsteigen *n.*; Abstieg *m.*; Senkung *f.*; Abstammung *f.*

describe *v.t.* beschreiben, schildern.

description *s.* Beschreibung *f.*; Sorte *f.*

descriptive *a.* beschreibend.

descry *v.t.* ausspähen, entdecken.

desecrate *v.t.* entweihen.

desegregate *v.t.* die Rassentrennung aufheben.

desegregation *s.* Aufhebung der Rassentrennung.

desert *a.* öde, wild; ~ *s.* Wüste *f.*; ~ *v.t. & i.* verlassen, entlaufen, desertieren.

deserted *a.* verlassen.

deserter *s.* Fahnenflüchtige *m.*/*f.*, Deserteur *m.*

desertion *s.* Fahnenflucht *f.*

deserve *v.t.* verdienen.

deservedly *adv.* verdientermaßen.

deserving *a.*, **~ly** *adv.* verdienstvoll.

desiccated *a.* getrocknet.

desideratum *s.* Wünschenswertes *n.*

design *v.t. & i.* bestimmen; entwerfen, zeichnen; planen; ~ *s.* Absicht *f.*; Entwurf *m.*; Zeichnung *f.*; Muster *n.*

designate *v.t.* bezeichnen; ernennen.

designation *s.* Bezeichnung, Bestimmung *f.*

designer *s.* Musterzeichner(in) *m.*(*f.*); Designer(in) *m.*(*f.*).

designing *a.* hinterlistig.

desirable *a.* wünschenswert.

desire *s.* Verlangen *n.*; Wunsch *m.*; ~ *v.t.* wünschen, verlangen; bitten.

desirous *a.*, **~ly** *adv.* wünschend, begierig.

desist *v.i.* ablassen.

desk *s.* Pult *n.*; Schreibtisch *m.*

desk clerk *s.* Empfangschef *m.*, Empfangsdame *f.*

desolate *a.*, **~ly** *adv.* öde; wüst; betrübt; ~ *v.t.* verwüsten.

desolation *s.* Verwüstung, Einöde *f.*

despair *s.* Verzweiflung *f.*; ~ *v.i.* verzweifeln.

desperate *a.*, **~ly** *adv.* verzweifelt; verwegen.

desperation *s.* Verzweiflung *f.*

despicable *a.*, **~bly** *adv.* verachtenswert; verabscheuungswürdig.

despise *v.t.* verachten, verschmähen.

despite *pr.* trotz.

despoil *v.t.* plündern.

despondency *s.* Kleinmut *m.*; Niedergeschlagenheit *f.*

despondent *a.* verzagend, niedergeschlagen.

despot *s.* Gewaltherrscher, Despot *m.*

despotic *a.*, **~ly** *adv.* despotisch.

despotism *s.* Gewaltherrschaft *f.*

dessert *s.* Nachtisch *m.*

destination *s.* Bestimmung *f.*; Ziel *n.*

destine *v.t.* bestimmen.

destiny *s.* Schicksal, Verhängnis *n.*

destitute *a.* mittellos; verlassen, hilflos.

destitution *s.* Hilflosigkeit, Not *f.*

destroy *v.t.* zerstören, verwüsten.

destroyer *s.* Zerstörer (auch Schiff) *m.*

destruction *s.* Zerstörung *f.*

destructive *a.*, **~ly** *adv.* zerstörend.

desultory *a.* sprunghaft; oberflächlich.

detach *v.t.* entfernen, ablösen.

detachable *a.* abtrennbar.

detachment *s.* Ablösung *f.*; Detachement, Absonderung *f.*; (*mil.*) Abteilung *f.*, Trupp *m.*

detail *v.t.* einzeln aufführen; (*mil.*) abordnen; ~ *s.* Einzelheit *f.*; Detail *n.*; *in* ~, ausführlich; **~ed** *a.* ausführlich, genau, eingehend.

detain *v.t.* zurückhalten; abhalten; in Haft halten.

detainee *s.* Verhaftete *m.*/*f.*

detect *v.t.* entdecken, aufdecken.

detectable *a.* feststellbar, wahrnehmbar.

detection *s.* Entdeckung *f.*

detective *s.* Geheimpolizist, Detektiv *m.*

detector *a.* (*radio*) Detektor.

detente *s.* Entspannung.

detention *s.* Haft *m.*; Festnahme *f.*

deter *v.t.* abschrecken.

detergent *s.* Reinigungsmittel *n.*

deteriorate *v.t.* verschlimmern.

deterioration *s.* Verschlimmerung.

determinate *a.*, **~ly** *adv.* bestimmt.

determination *s.* Bestimmung; Entschlossenheit *f.*; Beschluß *m.*

determinative *a.*, **~ly** *adv.* bestimmend.

determine *v.t.* festsetzen; feststellen; beendigen; ~ *v.i.* sich entschließen.

determined *a.* entschlossen.

deterrence *s.* Abschreckung *f.*

deterrent *s.* Abschreckungsmittel *n.*

detest *v.t.* verabscheuen.

detestable *a.*, **~bly** *adv.* abscheulich.
detestation *s.* Abscheu *m.*
dethrone *v.t.* entthronen.
dethronement *s.* Entthronung *f.*
detonate *v.i.* explodieren, zur Explosion bringen.
detonation *s.* Knall *m.*, Denotation *f.*
detonator *s.* Zünder *m.*; Sprengkapsel *f.*
detour *s.* Umweg *m.*, ~ *v.t.* umleiten.
detract *v.t.* schmälern; ablenken.
detraction *s.* Verleumdung, Beeinträchtigung *f.*
detriment *s.* Schaden, Nachteil *m.*
detrimental *a.*, **~ly** *adv.* nachteilig.
detritus *s.* Überbleibsel *n.*
deuce *s.* Zwei *f.*; Einstand *m.*
devaluation *s.* Abwertung *f.*
devalue *v.t.* abwerten.
devastate *v.t.* verwüsten.
devastating *a.* verheerend, vernichtend.
devastation *s.* Verwüstung *f.*
develop *v.t.* entwickeln, enthüllen.
developer *s.* (*phot.*) Entwickler *m.*; Bauunternehmer(in) *m.*(*f.*)
developing country *s.* Entwicklungsland *n.*
development *s.* Entwicklung *f.*
deviant *a.* abweichend.
deviate *v.i.* abweichen.
deviation *s.* Abweichung, Verirrung *f.*
device *s.* Kunstgriff *m.*; Vorrichtung *f.*; Wahlspruch *m.*
devil *s.* Teufel *m.*
devilish *a.* teuflisch.
devil-may-care *a.* sorglos, unbekümmert.
devilry *s.* Teufelei *f.*
devious *a.* abwegig.
devise *v.i.* ersinnen; (*by will*) vermachen.
devoid *a.* bar, frei; ~ *of*, ohne.
devolution *s.* Dezentralisierung *f.*; Übertragung von Aufgaben *f.*
devolve *v.t.* (*fig.*) übertragen; ~ (*upon*) *v.i.* zufallen, heimfallen.
devote *v.t.* widmen; aufopfern.
devoted *a.*, **~ly** *adv.* ergeben, fromm.
devotee *s.* Verehrer(in) *m.*(*f.*); Anhänger(in) *m.* (*f.*).
devotion *s.* Aufopferung, Hingabe *f.*; Widmung *f.*; Andacht *f.*
devotional *a.*, **~ly** *adv.* andächtig.
devour *v.t.* verschlingen.
devout *a.*, **~ly** *adv.* andächtig.
dew *s.* Tau *m.*; ~ *v.t.* betauen.
dewy *a.* taufeucht; taufrisch.
dexterity *s.* Gewandtheit, Fertigkeit *f.*
dexterous *a.*, **~ly** *adv.* gewandt, geschickt.
dextrose *s.* Traubenzucker *m.*
diabetes *s.* (*med.*) Zuckerkrankheit *f.*
diabetic *a.* zuckerkrank; ~ *s.* Zuckerkranker *m.*/*f.*, Diabetiker(in) *m.*(*f.*).
diabolic(al) *a.*, **~ly** *adv.* teuflisch.
diagnose *v.t.* diagnostizieren.
diagnosis *s.* Diagnose *f.*
diagnostic *a.* diagnostisch.
diagonal *a.*, **~ly** *adv.* schräg; diagonal; ~ *s.* Diagonale *f.*
diagram *s.* (*geom.*) Riß *m.*; Figur *f.*; graphische Darstellung *f.*
dial *s.* Zifferblatt *n.*; Wählscheibe *f.*; ~ *v.t.* (*tel.*)

wählen.
dialect *s.* Mundart *f.*, Dialekt *m.*
dialectical *a.*, **~ly** *adv.* dialektisch.
dialectics *s.* Dialektik *f.*
dialogue *s.* Zwiegespräch *n.*
dial tone *s.* Freizeichen *n.*
dialysis *s.* Dialyse *f.*
diameter *s.* Durchmesser *m.*
diametrical *a.*, **~ly** *adv.* diametral; ~ *opposed*, gerade entgegengesetzt.
diamond *s.* Diamant *m.*; Karo, Rot (Karte) *n.*
diapason *s.* (*mus.*) Zusammenklang *m.*; Mensur (Orgel) *f.*
diaper *s.* Windel *f.*
diaphragm *s.* Zwerchfell *n.*; (*tel.*) Membrane *f.*; (*optics*) Blende *f.*
diarrhea *s.* Durchfall *m.*
diary *s.* Tagebuch *n.*; Terminkalender *m.*
diatribe *s.* heftiger Angriff, Tadel *m.*
dice *s.* (*pl.* von *die*) Würfel *m.pl.*; ~ *v.i.* würfeln.
dice cup *s.* Würfelbecher *m.*
dicey *a.* riskant; heikel.
dichotomy *s.* Dichotomie *f.*
dick *s.* (*fam.*) Schnüffler *m.*; (*vulg.*) Schwanz *m.*
dickens *s.* *what the* ~*!* was zum Kuckuck!
dick(e)y *a.* (*fam.*) schwach, klapprig.
dictate *v.t.* diktieren; ~ *s.* Vorschrift *f.*
dictation *s.* Diktat *n.*; Geheiß *n.*
dictator *s.* Diktator(in) *m.*(*f.*)
dictatorial *a.* gebieterisch.
dictatorship *s.* Diktatur *f.*
diction *s.* Sprechweise *f.*, Stil *m.*, Diktion *f.*
dictionary *s.* Wörterbuch *n.*
didactic *a.* didaktisch, lehrhaft; Lehr...
diddle *v.t.* beschwindeln.
die *s.* Würfel *m.*; Stempel *m.*; Matrize *f.*; ~ *v.i.* sterben; umkommen; verwelken; sich verlieren.
diehard *s.* Unentwegter *m.*
diesel *s.* Diesel *m.*
diet *s.* Diät *f.*; Kost *f.*; ~ *v.t.* eine Diät machen.
dietary *a.* diätetisch.
diatetics *s.pl.* Ernährungswissenschaft *f.*, Diätetik *f.*
dietitian *s.* Diätassistent(in) *m.*(*f.*).
differ *v.i.* verschieden sein, abweichen; streiten; sich unterscheiden.
difference *s.* Unterschied *m.*; Streit *m.*
different *a.*, **~ly** *adv.* verschieden, anders.
differential tariff *s.* Staffeltarif *m.*
differentiate *v.t. & i.* (sich) unterscheiden; differenzieren.
differing *a.* unterschiedlich.
difficult *a.* schwierig.
difficulty *s.* Schwierigkeit *f.*
diffidence *s.* Schüchternheit *f.*, Mangel an Selbstvertrauen.
diffident *a.*, **~ly** *adv.* schüchtern.; zurückhaltend.
diffuse *v.t.* ausgießen; verbreiten; zerstreuen; ~ *a.* weitläufig.
diffusion *s.* Verbreitung *f.*
dig *v.t. & i.st.* graben; bohren.
digest *v.t.* verdauen; überdenken; ertragen; ~ *s.* Auszug, Abriß *m.*; Übersicht *f.*; Gesetzessammlung *f.*
digestible *a.* verdaulich.
digestion *s.* Verdauung *f.*; Überlegung *f.*

digestive system *s.* Verdauungssystem *n.*
digger *s.* Gräber *m.*; Bagger *m.*
digging *s.* Graben *n.*
digit *s.* Finger *m.*; Zehe *f.*; Ziffer *f.* (unter Zehn).
digital *a.* digital.
dignified *a.* würdevoll.
dignitary *s.* Würdenträger *m.*
dignity *s.* Würde *f.*; Rang *m.*
digress *v.t.* abschweifen.
digression *s.* Abschweifung *f.*
digressive *a.* abweichend, abschweifend.
dike *s.* Deich *m.*; Graben *m.*; Damm *m.*
dilapidate *v.t.* niederreißen; zerstören.
dilapidated *a.* baufällig; verfallen.
dilapidation *s.* Verfall *m.*
dilate *v.t.* erweitern, ausdehnen.
dilation *s.* Dilation *f.*, Ausdehnung *f.*; Erweiterung *f.*
dilatory *a.*, **~ily** *adv.* aufschiebend.
dilemma *s.* Dilemma *n.*
dilettante *s.* Dilettant(in) *m.*(*f.*)
diligence *s.* Fleiß *m.*; Sorgfalt *f.*
diligent *a.*, **~ly** *adv.* fleißig, emsig.
dill *s.* (*bot.*) Dille *f.*, Dill *m.*
dilly-dally *v.i.* trödeln.
dilute *v.t.* verdünnen; mildern.
dilution *s.* Verdünnung *f.*
dim *a.*, **~ly** *adv.* dunkel, trübe, matt; ~ *v.t.* verdunkeln, trüben; (*mot.*) abblenden.
dime *a.* Münze von zehn Cents *f.*
dimension *s.* Ausdehnung *f.*; Maß *n.*
diminish *v.t.* vermindern; ~ *v.i.* abnehmen.
diminution *s.* Verkleinerung *f.*; Abnahme *f.*
diminutive *a.*, **~ly** *adv.* vermindernd; winzig; ~ *s.* Verkleinerungsform *f.*
dimple *s.* Grübchen *n.*
din *s.* Gerassel, Getöse *n.*; ~ *v.t.* & *i.* schallen; rasseln; betäuben.
dine *v.i.* zu Mittag/Abend essen.
diner *s.* Gast (beim Essen) *m.*
ding-dong *s.* Klingklang *m.*; ~ *fight*, schwankender heißumstrittener Kampf *m.*
dinghy *s.* flaches Boot *n.*
dingy *a.* schmutzig.
dining-car *s.* Speisewagen *m.*; ~ **attendant** *s.* Speisewagenschaffner *m.*
dining-room *s.* Speisesaal *m.*; Eßzimmer *n.*
dining-table *s.* Eßtisch *m.*
dinner *s.* Hauptmahlzeit *f.*; **~-jacket**, Smoking *m.*; **~-set** Eß-Service *n.*
dinosaur *s.* Dinosaurier *m.*
dint, *by* ~ *of*, mittels, kraft.
diocese *s.* Diözese *f.*
dioxin *s.* Dioxin *n.*
dip *v.t.* eintauchen; ~ *v.i.* sich senken; ~ *s.* Eintauchen *n.*; Neigung *f.*; Dip *m.*
diphtheria *s.* Diphtherie *f.*
diphthong *s.* Diphthong *m.*
diploma *s.* Diplom *n.*
diplomacy *s.* Diplomatie *f.*
diplomat *s.* Diplomat(in) *m.*(*f.*)
diplomatic(al) *a.* diplomatisch.
dipsomania *s.* Trunksucht *f.*
dipstick *s.* Meßstab *m.*
dire *a.* gräßlich.
direct *a.* gerade, unmittelbar; ausdrücklich; **~ly**

adv. geradezu, sogleich, direkt; ~ *v.t.* richten, anweisen; adressieren.
direction *s.* Richtung *f.*; Leitung, Anordnung *f.*; Adresse *f.*
directions for use *pl.* Gebrauchsanweisung *f.*
directive *s.* Anweisung *f.*; **~s** *pl.* Richtlinien *f.pl.*
directness *s.* Direktheit *f.*; Geradheit *f.*
director *s.* Direktor(in) *m.*(*f.*), Leiter(in) *m.*(*f.*)
directorate *s.* Präsidium *n.*
directory *s.* Adreßbuch *n.*; Telfonbuch *n.*; Branchenverzeichnis *n.*
dirge *s.* Trauergesang *m.*
dirk *s.* Dolch *m.*
dirt *s.* Kot, Schmutz *m.*; **~-cheap**, spottbillig.
dirty *a.* schmutzig; ~ *v.t.* besudeln.
dirty word *s.* unanständige Wort *n.*; Schimpfwort *n.*
disability *s.* Unvermögen *n.*; Unfähigkeit *f.*
disable *v.t.* unfähig machen.
disabled *a.* unfähig, untauglich; invalid.
disablement *s.* Behinderung *f.*
disabuse *v.t.* aufklären.
disadvantage *s.* Nachteil *m.*
disadvantageous *a.*, **~ly** *adv.* nachteilig.
disaffected *a.* unzufrieden.
disaffection *s.* Abneigung *f.*; Unzufriedenheit *f.*
disagree *v.i.* nicht übereinstimmen; nicht gut bekommen (von Speisen).
disagreeable *a.*, **~bly** *adv.* unangenehm.
disagreement *s.* Meinungsverschiedenheit *f.*
disallow *v.t.* & *i.* nicht gestatten; in Abrede stellen.
disappear *v.i.* verschwinden.
disappearance *s.* Verschwinden *n.*
disappoint *v.t.* vereiteln, enttäuschen.
disappointing *a.* enttäuschend.
disappointment *s.* Enttäuschung *f.*
disapprobation, disapproval *s.* Mißbilligung *f.*
disapprove *v.t.* & *i.* mißbilligen.
disapproving *a.* mißbilligend.
disarm *v.t.* entwaffnen; ~ *v.i.* abrüsten.
disarmament *s.* Abrüstung *f.*
disarming *a.* entwaffnend.
disarrange *v.t.* verwirren.
disarray *v.t.* in Unordnung bringen; ~ *s.* Verwirrung *f.*
disaster *s.* Unglück *n.*, Unfall *m.*, Katastrophe *f.*; ~ **area** *s.* Katastrophengebiet *n.*
disastrous *a.*, **~ly** *adv.* unheilvoll.
disavow *v.t.* nicht anerkennen.
disband *v.t.* verabschieden; (*mil.*) (Einheit) auflösen; ~ *v.i.* sich auflösen.
disbelief *s.* Unglaube, Zweifel *m.*
disbelieve *v.t.* nicht glauben.
disburse *v.t.* auszahlen, verschießen.
disbursement *s.* Auszahlung *f.*
discard *v.t.* entfernen; verabschieden, abdanken; abwerfen (eine Karte); ablegen (Kleider); wegwerfen.
discern *v.t.* & *i.* unterscheiden, erkennen.
discernible *a.*, **~bly** *adv.* unterscheidbar; erkennbar.
discerning *a.* scharf; kritisch; fein; urteilsfähig.
discharge *v.t.* ausladen, löschen; abfeuern; loslassen; entlassen; entlasten; freisprechen ~ *v.i.* sich entladen; eitern; ~ *s.* Entladung *f.*; Entlassung, Befreiung *f.*; Entlastung *f.*; Abfeuern *n.*; Abfluß *m.*;

(*med.*) Ausfluß *m.*

disciple *s.* Schüler, Jünger *m.*, Anhänger(in) *m.*(*f.*)

disciplinarian *s.* Zuchtmeister *m.*

disciplinary *a.* disziplinarisch; ~ *action*, Disziplinarverfahren *n.*; ~ *power*, Disziplinargewalt *f.*; ~ *proceedings pl.* Disziplinarverfahren *n.*

discipline *s.* Unterweisung, Zucht *f.*; Disziplin *f.* ~ *v.t.* züchtigen.

disciplined *a.* diszipliniert.

disc jockey *s.* Diskjockey *m.*

disclaim *v.t.* leugnen; abstreiten.

disclaimer *s.* Verzicht *m.*; Widerruf *m.*

disclose *v.t.* enthüllen; offenbaren.

disclosure *s.* Enthüllung, Mitteilung *f.*

discolor *v.t.* entfärben; entstellen.

discoloration *s.* Verfärbung *f.*; Verschießen *n.*

discomfit *v.t.* verunsichern.

discomfiture *s.* Verunsicherung.

discomfort *s.* Mißbehagen *n.*

discompose *v.t.* beunruhigen; verwirren.

discomposure *s.* Verwirrung, Verlegenheit *f.*; Verdrießlichkeit *f.*

disconcert *v.t.* außer Fassung bringen.

disconnect *v.t.* trennen; (*mech.*) entkuppeln, ausschalten.

disconnected *a.* zusammenhangslos.

disconsolate *a.*, **~ly** *adv.* trostlos, betrübt.

discontent *a.* mißvergnügt; ~ *s.* Unzufriedenheit *f.*; ~ *v.t.* mißvergnügt machen.

discontinuance *s.* Unterbrechung *f.*; Aufhören *n.*; Trennung *f.*

discontinue *v.t.* unterbrechen; abbestellen; ~ *v.i.* aufhören.

discord *s.* Mißklang *m.*; Zwietracht *f.*

discordance *s.* Uneinigkeit *f.*

discordant *a.* mißklingend; verschieden; mißhellig.

discotheque *s.* Diskothek *f.*

discount *v.t.* abziehen, diskontieren; ~ *s.* Abzug *m.*; Diskonto *n.*

discountenance *v.t.* außer Fassung bringen, entmutigen; mißbilligen.

discourage *v.t.* entmutigen; abraten.

discouragement *s.* Entmutigung *f.*

discourse *s.* Diskurs *m.*; Gespräch *n.*; Vortrag *m.*; Abhandlung *f.*; ~ *v.i.* sich unterreden; sprechen.

discourteous *a.* unhöflich.

discourtesy *s.* Unhöflichkeit *f.*

discover *v.t.* entdecken, offenbaren.

discoverer *s.* Entdecker(in) *m.*(*f.*)

discovery *s.* Entdeckung *f.*

discredit *s.* Mißkredit *m.*; übler Ruf *m.*; ~ *v.t.* in schlechten Ruf bringen; bezweifeln.

discreditable *a.*, **~bly** *adv.* schimpflich.

discreet *a.*, **~ly** *adv.* vorsichtig; klug; verschwiegen.

discrepancy *s.* Widerspruch *m.*; Diskrepanz *f.*

discrepant *a.* widersprechend.

discretion *s.* Besonnenheit, Klugheit, Verschwiegenheit *f.*; Takt *m.*; Belieben *n.*; *to surrender at* ~, sich auf Gnade und Ungnade ergeben.

discriminate *v.t.* unterscheiden; unterschiedlich behandeln; diskriminieren; ~ *a.*, **~ly** *adv.* unterschieden; genau, deutlich.

discriminating *a.* diskriminierend; kritisch, fein.

discrimination *s.* Unterscheidung *f.*; Unterschied *m.*; Scharfsinn *m.*

discriminative *a.* unterscheidend.

discursive *a.* weitschweifend.

discuss *v.t.* erörtern; verzehren.

discussion *s.* Erörterung *f.*; Diskussion *f.*

disdain *s.* Verachtung *f.*; ~ *v.t.* verschmähen, verächtlich herabsetzen.

disdainful *a.*, **~ly** *adv.* geringschätzig.

disease *s.* Krankheit *f.*

diseased *a.* krank.

disembark *v.t. & i.* ausschiffen, landen.

disembarkation *s.* Ausschiffung *f.*

disembarrass *v.t.* aus der Verlegenheit bringen.

disembodied *a.* körperlos; geisterhaft.

disembowl *v.t.* ausweiden.

disenchant *v.t.* entzaubern; ernüchtern.

disenchantment *s.* Ernüchterung *f.*

disencumber *v.t.* befreien; entbinden.

disengage *v.t.* losmachen; befreien; ~ *v.i.* (*mil.*) sich absetzen.

disengaged *a.* frei, unbeschäftigt.

disengagement *s.* Entbindung *f.*; (*mil.*) Absetzungsbewegung *f.*

disentangle *v.t.* entwirren, losmachen.

disfavor *s.* Ungnade *f.*; Mißfallen *n.*; ~ *v.t.* nicht begünstigen.

disfigure *v.t.* entstellen.

disfigurement *s.* Entstellung *f.*

disfranchise *v.t.* das Wahlrecht entziehen.

disgorge *v.t.* ausspucken, ausspeien.

disgrace *s.* Ungnade *f.*; Schande *f.*; ~ *v.t.* die Gunst entziehen; entehren.

disgraceful *a.*, **~ly** *adv.* schimpflich.; erbärmlich.

disgruntled *a.* unzufrieden.

disguise *v.t.* vermummen; verbergen; verkleiden; ~ *s.* Verkleidung, Verstellung *f.*

disgust *s.* Ekel, Widerwille *m.*; ~ *v.t.* anwidern; Ekel verursachen; verdrießen.

disgusting *a.* ekelhaft, widerlich.

dish *s.* Schüssel *f.*; Napf *m.*; Gericht *n.*; ~ *v.t.* (*up*) anrichten, auftragen.

dishearten *v.t.* verzagt machen; entmutigen.

disheartening *a.* entmutigend.

dishevel *v.t.* zerzausen.

disheveled *a.* zerzaust; unordentlich.

dishonest *a.*, **~ly** *adv.* unehrlich; unaufrichtig.

dishonesty *s.* Unredlichkeit *f.*; Unaufrichtigkeit *f.*

dishonor *s.* Schande *f.*; ~ *v.t.* beleidigen; nicht honorieren (Wechsel).

dishonorable *a.*, **~bly** *adv.* ehrlos.

dish: **~-rack** *s.* Abtropfgestell *n.*; **~-towel** *s.* Geschirrtuch *n.*; **~washer** *s.* Geschirrspüler *m.*; **~-water** *s.* Spülwasser *n.*

disillusion *s.* Ernüchterung *f.*; ~ *v.t.* ernüchtern.

disillusioned *a.* desillusioniert.

disillusionment *s.* Desillusionierung *f.*

disincentive *s.* Hemmnis *n.*

disinclination *s.* Abneigung *f.*

disincline *v.t.* abgeneigt machen.

disinclined *a.* abgeneigt.

disinfect *v.t.* desinfizieren.

disinfectant *s.* Desinfizierungsmittel *n.*; ~*a.* desinfizierend.

disinfection *s.* Desinfizierung *f.*

disingenuous *a.* unaufrichtig; hinterhältig.

disinherit *v.t.* enterben.

disintegrate *v.t. & i.* (sich) (in Bestandteile)

auflösen.

disintegration *s.* Zerfall *m.*; Auflösung *f.*

disinter *v.t.* wieder ausgraben.

disinterested *a.*, **~ly** *adv.* uneigennützig; unvoreingenommen.

disjoin *v.t.* trennen.

disjoint *v.t.* zerlegen.

disk *s.* Scheibe *f.*; (Schall)Platte *f.*; **compact ~** *s.* Compact Disk; **hard ~** *s.* Festplatte *f.*

disk drive *s.* Diskettenlaufwerk *n.*

diskette *s.* Diskette *f.*

dislike *s.* Abneigung *f.*; Mißfallen *n.*; **~** *v.t.* mißbilligen, nicht mögen.

dislocate *v.t.* verrenken.

dislocation *s.* Verrenkung *f.*; Störung *f.*

dislodge *v.t.* vertreiben.

disloyal *a.*, **~ly** *adv.* ungetreu, treulos.

disloyalty *s.* Treulosigkeit *f.*

dismal *a.* trübe; schrecklich; traurig.

dismantle *v.t.* entblößen; niederreißen; demontieren; abtakeln.

dismantling *s.* Demontage *f.*

dismay *v.t.* erschrecken; **~** *s.* Bangigkeit *f.* Bestürzung *f.*

dismember *v.t.* zerstückeln.

dismiss *v.t.* entlassen; abweisen; **~ed!** (*mil.*) weggetreten!

dismissal *s.* Entlassung, Abdankung *f.*

dismount *v.i.* absitzen.; absteigen (Reiter).

disobedience *s.* Ungehorsam *m.*

disobedient *a.*, **~ly** *adv.* ungehorsam.

disobey *v.i.* nicht gehorchen.

disoblige *v.t.* ungefällig begegnen.

disobliging *a.* ungefällig.

disorder *s.* Unordnung *f.*; Störung *f.*; Unpäßlichkeit *f.*

disordered *p. & a.*, **~ly** *adv.* unordentlich; liederlich.

disorderly *a.* gesetzwidrig; liederlich; **~ conduct,** ordnungswidriges Betragen *n.*

disorganization *s.* Desorganisation *f.*

disorganize *v.t.* auflösen, zerrütten.

disorganized *a.* desorganisiert, chaotisch.

disorient *v.t.* desorientieren.

disoriented *a.* desorientiert.

disown *v.t.* verleugnen, verwerfen.

disparage *v.t.* herabsetzen, schmälern.

disparagement *s.* Herabsetzung *f.*; Beeinträchtigung *f.*

disparaging *a.* abschätzig.

disparate *a.* verschieden, disparat.

disparity *s.* Ungleichheit *f.*; Unterschied *m.*

dispassionate *a.*, **~ly** *adv.* leidenschaftslos.

dispatch *v.t.* schicken; abfertigen; befördern; erledigen; **~** *s.* Abfertigung *f.*; Absendung *f.*; Eile *f.*; Depesche *f.*; **~-box** Depeschenmappe *f.*

dispel *v.t.* vertreiben.

dispensable *a.* entbehrlich.

dispensary *s.* Apotheke *f.*

dispensation *s.* Austeilung *f.*; Erlassung *f.*; Dispens *f.*

dispense *v.t.* austeilen; dispensieren; *to* **~** *with,* erlassen; entbehren können, nicht missen.

dispersal *s.* Zerstreuung *f.*; **~** *of industry,* Industrieauslagerung *f.*

disperse *v.t.* zerstreuen; verteilen; **~** *v.i.* sich

zerstreuen.

dispersion *s.* Zerstreuung *f.*

dispirit *v.t.* entmutigen.

dispirited *a.* entmutigt.

dispiriting *a.* entmutigend.

displace *v.t.* verschieben; absetzen; verdrängen.

displaced person *s.* Zwangsverschleppte *m.*

displacement *s.* Verschiebung *f.*; Verrückung *f.*; Absetzung *f.*; Verdrängung *f.*

display *v.t.* entfalten; zur Schau stellen; **~** *s.* Schaustellung *f.*; Darstellung *f.*; Pomp *m.*; *on* **~,** ausliegend.

displease *v.t. & i.* mißfallen.

displeased *p. & a.* ungehalten.

displeasure *s.* Mißfallen *n.*; Verdruß *m.*

disposable *a.* Wegwerf. . .; Einweg. . .

disposal *s.* Verfügung *f.*; Beseitigung *f.*; Entsorgung *f.*

dispose *v.t.* anordnen, einrichten, anwenden; geneigt, bereit machen; verfügen; **~** *of,* beseitigen; absetzen.

disposed *p. & a.* gesinnt; gelaunt.

disposition *s.* Einrichtung, Anordnung *f.*; Zustand *m.*; Neigung, Gemütsart *f.*; (*mil.*) Aufstellung *f.*

dispossess *v.t.* jmdm. etwas rauben; enteignen.

disproportion *s.* Mißverhältnis *n.*

disproportionate *a.*, **~ly** *adv.* unverhältnismäßig.

disprove *v.t.* widerlegen.

disputable *a.* strittig.

disputant *s.* Streiter, Gegner *m.*

disputation *s.* gelehrter Streit *m.*

dispute *v.i.* streiten, disputieren; **~** *v.t.* bestreiten; **~** *s.* Streit *m.*

disqualification *s.* Disqualifikation *f.*

disqualify *v.t.* disqualifizieren; untauglich machen; unfähig erklären; aus der Liste streichen.

disquiet *s.* Unruhe *f.*; **~** *v.t.* beunruhigen.

disregard *s.* Mißachtung *f.*; **~** *v.t.* unbeachtet lassen.

disrepair *s.* Baufälligkeit *f.*

disreputable *a.* verrufen; schimpflich.

disrepute *s.* übler Ruf *m.*; Ehrlosigkeit *f.*

disrespect *s.* Geringschätzung, Unehrerbietigkeit *f.*

disrespectful *a.* unehrerbietig, unhöflich.

disrupt *v.t.* unterbrechen; stören (Unterricht).

disruption *s.* Unterbrechung *f.*; Störung *f.*

disruptive *a.* störend.

dissatisfaction *s.* Unzufriedenheit *f.*

dissatisfied *a.* unzufrieden.

dissatisfy *v.t.* nicht befriedigen.

dissect *v.t.* zerlegen; sezieren.

dissection *s.* Zerlegung *f.*; Präparation *f.*

dissemble *v.i.* sich verstellen, heucheln; **~** *v.t.* verhehlen.

disseminate *v.t.* aussäen, ausstreuen.

dissension *s.* Uneinigkeit *f.*, Zwist *m.*; Dissens *m.*

dissent *v.i.* anderer Meinung sein; **~ing** *opinion,* (*law*) abweichende Meinung *f.*; **~** *s.* Abweichung *f.*

dissenter *s.* Andersdenkende *m./f.*

dissertation *s.* Abhandlung *f.*; Dissertation *f.*

disservice *s.* schlechter Dienst *m.*

dissever *v.t.* absondern, trennen.

dissidence *s.* Uneinigkeit *f.*

dissident *a.* verschieden; *s.* Andersdenkende *m./f.*; Dissident(in) *m.(f.)*

dissimilar *a.* ungleichartig.

dissimilarity *s.* Ungleichheit.
dissimulate *v.i.* sich verstellen.
dissipate *v.t.* zerstreuen; verschwenden.
dissipated *a.* ausschweifend.
dissipation *s.* Zerstreuung *f.*; Ausschweifung *f.*
dissociate *v.t.* trennen.
dissolute *a.*, ~**ly** *adv.* ausschweifend.
dissolution *s.* Auflösung *f.*
dissolve *v.t.* auflösen, schmelzen; ~ *v.t.* zergehen.
dissonance *s.* Mißklang *m.*; Dissonanz *f.*
dissuade *v.t.* abraten.
dissuasion *s.* Abraten *n.*
dissuasive *a.*, ~**ly** *adv.* abratend.
distance *s.* Entfernung, Weite *f.*; Abstand *m.*; Entfremdung, Kälte *f.*; ~ *v.t.* hinter sich lassen.
distant *a.* entfernt; zurückhaltend, kalt.
distaste *s.* Widerwille *m.*; Abneigung *f.*
distasteful *a.*, ~**ly** *adv.* ärgerlich, widrig.
distemper *s.* Stumpe *f.* (Hunde); Temperafarbe *f.*
distend *v.t.* ausdehnen, ausstrecken.
distil *v.i.* & *a.* destillieren.
distillation *s.* Destillation *f.*; Destillat *n.*
distillery *s.* (Branntwein-) Brennerei *f.*
distinct *a.*, ~**ly** *adv.* verschieden; unterschieden; deutlich.
distinction *s.* Unterscheidung *f.*; Unterschied *m.*; Auszeichnung *f.*
distinctive *a.* unterscheidend; ~**ly** *adv.* deutlich.
distinguish *v.t.* unterscheiden; auszeichnen.
distinguishable *a.* unterscheidbar.
distinguished *a.* namhaft; angesehen.
distort *v.t.* verdrehen; verzerren.
distortion *s.* Verdrehung *f.*; Verzerrung *f.*
distract *v.t.* ablenken, zerstreuen; beunruhigen, stören, zerrütten.
distraction *s.* Zerstreuung *f.*; Kummer *m.*; Zerrüttung *f.*; Wahnsinn *m.*
distraught *a.* verstört.
distress *s.* Elend *n.*, Not *f.*; Seenot *f.*; Beschlagnahme, Pfändung *f.*; ~**-signal** (*nav.*) Notzeichen *n.*; ~**-warrant,** Pfändungsbefehl *m.*; ~ *v.t.* auspfänden; in Verlegenheit, in Not bringen.
distressed *a.* leidvoll; betrübt.
distressing *a.* erschütternd.
distribute *v.t.* verteilen, austeilen.
distribution *s.* Verteilung *f.*; ~**-list,** Verteiler (auf Akten) *m.*
distributor *s.* Verteiler(in) *m.*(*f.*); Vertrieb *m.*
district *s.* Bezirk *m.*; Landstrich *m.*; Wahlkreis *m.*; ~ **attorney** *s.* Bezirksstaatsanwalt *m.*
distrust *v.t.* mißtrauen; ~ *s.* Mißtrauen *n.*
distrustful *a.*, ~**ly** *adv.* mißtrauisch.
disturb *v.t.* stören.
disturbance *s.* Störung, Verwirrung *f.*; Aufruhr *m.*
disturbed *a.* besorgt; geistesgestört.
disunite *v.t.* trennen, entzweien.
disuse *s.* Nichtgebrauch *m.*
disused *a.* stillgelegt; leerstehend.
ditch *s.* Graben *m.*; ~ *v.t.* (*fam.*) sitzenlassen.
dither *v.t.* schwanken.
ditto *adv.* desgleichen.
ditty *s.* Liedchen *n.*, Gesang *m.*
diurnal *a.* täglich.
divan *s.* Diwan *m.*
dive *v.i.* (unter)tauchen; eindringen.
divebomber *s.* Sturzkampfflieger *m.*

diver *s.* Taucher(in) *m.*(*f.*); Kunstspringer(in) *m.*(*f.*)
diverge *v.i.* auseinanderlaufen; abweichen.
divergence *s.* Abweichen *n.*
divergent *a.* divergierend, abweichend.
diverse *a.*, ~**ly** *adv.* verschieden, mannigfaltig.
diversify *v.t.* verschieden machen.
diversion *s.* Ablenkung *f.*; Zeitvertreib *m.*
diversity *s.* Verschiedenheit *f.*; Mannigfaltigkeit *f.*
divert *v.t.* umleiten; ablenken; belustigen.
diverting *a.* unterhaltsam.
divest *v.t.* berauben.
divide *v.t.* teilen, trennen; dividieren; ~ *v.i.* sich trennen; namentlich abstimmen.
dividend *s.* (*com.*) Dividende *f.*; (*ar.*) Dividend *m.*
divider *s.* Trennwand *f.*
dividers *s.pl.* Zirkel *m.*
divine *v.t.* weissagen, erraten; ahnen; ~ *a.* ~**ly** *adv.* göttlich; ~ *s.* Geistliche *m.*
diving *s.* Kunstspringen *n.*
diving: ~ **bell** *s.* Taucherglocke *f.*; ~ **board** *s.* Sprungbrett *n.*; ~ **suit** *s.* Taucheranzug *m.*
divining rod *s.* Wünschelrute *f.*
divinity *s.* Gottheit *f.*; Theologie *f.*
divisible *a.* teilbar.
division *s.* Teilung *f.*; Trennung *f.*; Abteilung *f.*; Division *f.*; Abstimmung (durch Hammelsprung) *f.*
divisor *s.* (*ar.*) Divisor *m.*; Teiler *m.*
divorce *s.* Ehescheidung *f.*; ~ *v.t.* scheiden; verstossen.
divorcee *s.* Geschiedene *m.*/*f.*
divulge *v.t.* verbreiten; ausschwatzen.
dizzy *a.* schwindlig; unbesonnen; ~ *v.t.* schwindlig machen.
do *v.t.* & *i.st.* tun, machen; ausführen; *that will* ~, das genügt; *that won't* ~, das geht nicht; *I cannot* ~ *without it,* ich kann es nicht entbehren; *to* ~ *away with,* abschaffen; *to* ~ *up,* instand setzen; einpacken; *to* ~ *ill,* schlecht fortkommen; *to* ~ *well,* gut fortkommen.
docile *a.* sanft; unterwürfig.
dock *s.* (*nav.*) Dock *n.*; Stutzschwanz *m.*; Anklagebank *f.*; ~ *v.t.* stutzen; in ein Dock bringen; docken.
docker *s.* Hafenarbeiter *m.*
docket *s.* Liste *f.*; Zettel *m.*
dockyard *s.* Schiffswerft *n.* & *f.*
doctor *s.* Doktor *m.*; Arzt *m.*; ~ *v.t.* ärztlich behandeln; zustutzen; fälschen; (Tier) kastrieren.
doctorate *s.* Doktorwürde *f.*
doctrinaire *a.* doktrinär.
doctrine *s.* Lehre *f.*; Doktrin *f.*
document *s.* Urkunde *f.*, Dokument *n.*
documentary *a.* urkundlich; ~ *evidence,* Urkundenbeweis *m.*; ~ *film,* Dokumentarfilm *m.*
documentation *s.* Urkundenbelege *m.pl.*; Dokumentation *f.*
dodder *v.i.* zittern; schlottern.
doddering *a.* tatterig.
dodge *v.i.* ausweichen; ~*s.* Kniff, Schlich *m.*
doe *s.* Reh *n.*
doeskin *s.* Rehleder *n.*
doff *v.t.* lüften, ziehen.
dog *s.* Hund *m.*; Gestell *n.*; Kerl *m.*
dogdays *s.pl.* Hundstage *m.pl.*

dogfight *s.* Handgemenge *n.*; (*avi.*) Kurvenkampf *m.*

dogged *a.*, **~ly** *adv.* verbissen.

doggerel *s.* Knittelvers *m.*

doghouse *s.* Hundehütte *f.*

dogma *s.* Glaubenssatz, Lehrsatz *m.*

dogmatic *a.*, **~ally** *adv.* dogmatisch.

dogmatize *v.i.* Behauptungen aufstellen.

dogmatism *s.* Dogmatismus *m.*

dog-rose *s.* Heckenrose, wilde Rose *f.*

dog's ear *s.* Eselsohr (im Buche) *n.*

doing *s.* Begebenheit *f.*; Tätigkeit *f.*; Treiben *n.*

do-it-yourself *s.* Heimwerken *n.*

doldrums *s.pl.* *in the* ~ niedergeschlagen; in einer Flaute.

dole *s.* Spende *f.*; Erwerbslosenunterstützung *f.*; ~ *v.t.* spenden.

doleful *a.*, **~ly** *adv.* kummervoll, kläglich.

doll *s.* Puppe *f.*

dollhouse *s.* Puppenhaus *n.*

dolomite *s.* Dolomit, Bitterspat *m.*

Dolomites *s.pl.* Dolomiten *pl.*

dolorous *a.* schmerzhaft.

dolphin *s.* Delphin *m.*

dolt *s.* Tölpel *m.*

doltish *a.*, **~ly** *adv.* tölpisch, plump.

domain *s.* Gebiet *n.*; Staatsgut *n.*

dome *s.* Kuppel *f.*; Wölbung *f.*

domestic *a.* häuslich; inländisch; zahm, ~ *fuel*, Hausbrand *m.*; ~ *politics*, Innenpolitik *f.*; ~ *subjects pl.* Haushaltskunde *f.*; ~ *s.* Dienstbote *m.*

domesticate *v.t.* heimisch machen; zähmen; domestizieren.

domesticated *a.* domestiziert.

domesticity *s.* Häuslichkeit *f.*

domicile *s.* Wohnsitz *m.*

domiciled *a.* wohnhaft.

dominance *s.* Dominanz *f.*; Vorherrschaft *f.*

dominant *a.* herrschend.; beherrschend; dominierend.

dominate *v.t. & i.* (be)herrschen.

domination *s.* Herrschaft *f.*

domineering *a.* herrisch; herrschsüchtig.

Dominican *s.* Dominikaner *m.*

dominion *s.* Herrschaft *f.*; Dominium (Kolonie (*f.*) mit Selbstverwaltung) *m.*

domino *s.* Domino *m.*

dominoes *s.* Domino(spiel) *n.*

don *s.* Universtätsdozent(in) *m.*(*f.*); ~ *v.t.* anziehen; aufsetzen.

donate *v.t.* spenden; stiften.

donation *s.* Schenkung *f.*; Stiftung *f.*

donkey *s.* Esel *m.*

donor *s.* Schenker(in) *m.*(*f.*)

doom *s.* Urteilsspruch *m.*; Schicksal *n.*; Verderben *n.*; ~ *v.t.* verurteilen.

doomsday *s.* Jüngster Tag *m.*

door *s.* Tür *f.*; *within* ~*s*, im Hause; *out of* ~*s*, draußen, im Freien.

door-keeper *s.* Pförtner *m.*

door-plate *s.* Türschild *n.*

doorpost *s.* Türpfosten *m.*

doorway *s.* Eingang *m.*, Türöffnung *f.*

dope *s.* Dopingmittel *n.*; Rauschgift *n.*; Betäubungs-strank *m.*; ~ *v.t.* betäuben.

dopey *a.* benebelt.

dormant *a.* schlafend; unbenutzt.

dormer *s.* Dachfenster *n.*

dormitory *s.* Schlafsaal *m.*

dormouse *s.* Haselmaus *f.*

dorsal *a.* Rücken. . .

dosage *s.* Dosierung *f.*

dose *s.* Dosis *f.*; ~ *v.t.* eingeben.

dossier *s.* Akte, Personalakte *f.*

dot *s.* Punkt *m.*; ~ *v.t.* punktieren.

dotage *s.* *to be in one's* ~ senil sein.

dote *v.i.* kindisch werden; vernarrt sein; abgöttisch lieben.

double *a. & adv.* doppelt; **~-barrelled gun** *s.* Dop-pelflinte *f.*; **~-breasted coat** *s.* zweireihiger lieben. Rock *m.*; ~ *room*, zweitbettiges Zimmer *n.*; ~ *time*, Laufschritt *m.*; **~-track** *a.* zweigleisig; ~ *window*, Doppelfenster *n.*; ~ *s.* Doppelte *n.*; Dop-pelgänger *m.*; ~ *v.t.* verdoppeln; (Faust) ballen; umschiffen; ~ *up*, zusammenklappen, zusammen-falten; ~ *v.i.* sich verdoppeln.

doublecross *v.t.* betrügen.

double-dealer *s.* Betrüger *m.*

double-quick *a.* im Laufschritt.

double room *s.* Doppelzimmer *n.*

double-spaced *a.* zweizeilig.

doubly *adv.* doppelt.

doubt *v.t. & i.* (be)zwiefeln; ~ *s.* Zweifel *m.*; *to give a person the benefit of the* ~, im Zweifelsfall zu je-mandes Gunsten entscheiden.

doubter *s.* Zweifler(in) *m.*(*f.*)

doubtful *a.*, **~ly** *adv.* zweifelhaft.

doubtless *a. & adv.* ohne Zweifel, gewiß.

dough *s.* Teig *m.*

doughnut *s.* Krapfen *m.*

doughty *a.*, **~ily** *adv.* beherzt, tapfer.

dour *a.* hartnäckig; mürrisch.

dove *s.* Taube *f.*

dove-cote *s.* Taubenschlag *m.*

dovelike *a.* sanft (wie eine Taube).

dovetail *v.t.* keilförmig befestigen; innig ver-binden; ~ *s.* Schwalbenschwanz *m.*

dowager *s.* Witwe von Stand *f.*

dowdy *a.* schlampig; ~ *s.* Schlampe *f.*

dowel *s.* Dübel *m.*

dower *s.* Ausstattung, Mitgift *f.*

down *s.* Flaum *m.*, Daune *f.*; Düne *f.*; ~ *pr. & adv.* nieder, hinab, herunter, zu Boden; *the second* ~, der zweite von oben; ~ *under*, bei den Antiopden; ~ *a.* niedergeschlagen; **to** ~ *v.t.* niederlegen.

down-cast *a.* niedergeschlagen.

downfall *s.* Sturz, Untergang *m.*

downgrade *v.t.* im Rang herabsetzen; *on the* ~, im Niedergang begriffen.

downhearted *a.* mutlos.

down-hill *a.* bergab.

down-payment *s.* Anzahlung *f.*

downpour *s.* Regenguß *m.*

downright *a.* offen, bieder; ~ *adv.* geradezu; gänzlich.

down-stairs *adv.* treppab; unten, (die Treppe) hinunter.

downstream *adv.* stromabwärts.

down-to-earth *a.* nüchtern; realistisch.

downtown *a. & adv.* im Stadtzentrum; in der Innenstadt; ~ *s.* Innenstadt *f.*; City *f.*

down under *adv.* nach Neuseeland; nach Australien; ~ *s.* Neuseeland *n.*; Australien *n.*

downward(s) *adv.* abwärts, hinab.

downwind *a.* mit dem Wind, vor dem Wind.

dowry *s.* Mitgift *f.*; Aussteuer *f.*

dowser *m.* Wünschelrutengänger *m.*

dowsing rod *s.* Wünschelrute *f.*

doze *v.i.* schläfrig sein; schlummern, dösen.

dozen *s.* Dutzend *n.*

drab *s.* graubraun; düster; langweilig.

draft *s.* Skizze *f.*; Zeichnung *f.*; Entwurf *m.*; Aushebung *f.*; Zug *m.*; Luftzug *m.*; (Schiff) Tiefgang *m.*; Schluck *m.*; Rinne *f.*; Wehrpflicht *f.* beer on ~ Bier vom Faß; ~ *a.* zum Ziehen bestimmt; ~ *v.t.* zeichnen, entwerfen; detachieren.

draftsman *s.* Zeichner *m.*

draft-horse *s.* Zugpferd *n.*

drafty *a.* zügig.

drag *v.t. & i.* ziehen; schleppen ~ *s.* Schleife *f.*; Hemmung *f.*

dragnet *s.* Schleppnetz *n.*; Netz *n.*

dragon *s.* Drache *m.*; ~-**fly,** Libelle *f.*

dragoon *s.* Dragoner *m.*

drain *v.t.* ablassen; austrocknen; ~ *s.* Abzugsgraben *m.*

drainage *s.* Entwässerung *f.*

drainpipe *s.* Regen(fall)rohr *n.*; Abflußrohr *n.*

drake *s.* Enterich *m.*

dram *s.* Quentchen *n.*; Schluck *m.*

drama *s.* Schauspiel *n.*, Drama *n.*

dramatic *a.*, ~**ally** *adv.* dramatisch.

dramatist *s.* Dramatiker(in) *m.(f.)*

dramatize *v.t.* dramatisieren.

drape *v.t.* drapieren, einhüllen; ~ *s.* Tuch *n.*; Vorhang *m.*

draper *s.* Tuchhändler *m.*

drapery *s.* Tuchhandel *m.*; Draperie *f.*; Faltenwurf *m.*

drastic *a.* wirksam, durchschlagend.

draw *v.t. & i.st.* ziehen; spannen; abzapfen; zeichnen; trassieren; herleiten; locken; (Pension, Lohn) beziehen; (Geld) abheben; *to ~ up,* anhalten; aufsetzen, entwerfen, abfassen; *to ~ on a person,* sechs Fuß Tiefgang haben; *to ~ on a person,* einen Wechsel auf einen ziehen; ~ *s.* Ziehen *n.*; Los *n.*; unentschiedenes Spiel *n.*; ~ *s.* Zugstück *n.*

drawback *s.* Nachteil *m.*; Schattenseite *f.*

drawbridge *s.* Zugbrücke *f.*

drawer *s.* Schublade *f.*

drawing *s.* Ziehen *n.*; Zeichnung *f.*

drawing-board *s.* Reißbrett *n.*

drawing-office *s.* Konstruktionsbüro *n.*

drawing-pin *s.* Reißnagel *m.*

drawing-room *s.* Gesellschaftszimmer *n.*

drawl *v.i.* dehnen; (die Worte)schleppen.

drawn *s.* unentschieden, verzogen (Gesicht).

dread *s.* Schrecken *m.*; ~ *a.* schrecklich; ~ *v.t.* erschrecken; ~ *v.i.* sich fürchten.

dreadful *a.* schrecklich.

dream *s.* Traum *m.*; ~ *v.i.r. & ir.* träumen.

dreamer *s.* Träumer(in) *m.(f.)*

dream reader *s.* Traumdeuter(in) *m.(f.)*

dreamy *a.* träumerisch; verträumt.

dreary *a.*, ~**ily** *adv.* öde; traurig.

dredge *s.* Bagger *m.*; ~ *v.t.* ausbaggern; bestreuen (Mehl).

dregs *s.pl.* Bodensatz *m.*

drench *v.t.* tränken; durchnässen.

dress *s.* Anzug *m.*; Kleidung *f.*; Kleid *n.*; ~-**boots,** Lackstiefel *m.pl.*; ~-**circle,** erster Rang (im Theater) *m.*; ~-**rehearsal,** *s.* Hauptprobe *f.*; ~-**shirt,** Frackhemd *n.*; ~ *v.t.* ankleiden; putzen; zurichten; anrichten; verbinden; ~ *v.i.* sich ankleiden; (mil.) sich richten; ~ *left,* ~!, nach links, richt euch!; ~ *right,* ~!, richt euch!

dresser *s.* Anrichtetisch *m.*; (Theater) Kostümier *m.*

dressing *s.* Ankleiden *n.*; Anzug *m.*; Verband *m.*; Füllung (Braten) *f.*; Haarsalbe *f.*; *salad* ~, Salatsoße *f.*

dressing-gown *s.* Bademantel *m.*

dressing-station *s.* Verbandplatz *m.*; Verbandstelle *f.*

dressing-table *s.* Frisiertisch *m.*

dressmaker *s.* Schneider(in) *m.(f.)*

dribble *v.t. & i.* tröpfeln, geifern; sabbern.

dribs and drabs *s.pl. in* ~ kleckerweise.

dried *a.* Dörr. . ., getrocknet.

drier *s.* (Wäsche)trockner *m.*; Haartrockner *m.*

drift *s.* Trieb, Antrieb *m.*; Tendenz *f.*; Schneewehe *f.*; ~ *v.i.* sich aufhäufen; ~**wood** *s.* Treibholz *n.*

drill *s.* Drillbohrer *m.*; Exerzieren *n.*; Furch *f.*; Drillich *m.*; ~ *v.t. & i.* drillen, bohren; einexerzieren.

drink *s.* Getränk *n.*; ~ *v.t.st.* trinken.

drinkable *a.* trinkbar.

drinker *s.* Trinker(in) *m.(f.)*

drinking straw *s.* Trinkhalm *m.*

drinking water *s.* Trinkwasser *n.*

drip *v.t. & i.* tröpfeln; ~ *s.* Traufe *f.*

dripping *s.* Bratenfett *n.*; Schmalz *n.*

dripping wet *a.* tropfnaß.

drive *v.t.st.* treiben; fahren; ~ *v.i.* fahren; *what he is driving at,* worauf er hinauswill; *driving-belt,* (*mech.*) Treibriemen *m.*; *driving-license,* Führerschein *m.*; *driving-test,* Führerprüfung *f.*; ~ *s.* (*tennis*) Treibschlag *m.*; Spazierfahrt *f.*; Fahrweg *m.*; Schwung *m.*; Energie *f.*; Aktion *f.*

drivel *v.i.* geifern; faseln; ~ *s.* Geifer *m.*; Gefasel *n.*

driver *s.* Kutscher *m.*; Lokomotivführer *m.*; Chauffeur *m.*; ~'s **license** *s.* Führerschein *m.*

driveway *s.* Zufahrt(straße) *f.*; Auffahrt *f.*

driving: ~-**instructor** *s.* Fahrlehrer(in) *m.(f.)*; ~-**lesson** *s.* Fahrstunde *f.*

drizzle *s.* Sprühregen *m.*; Nieseln *n.*; Nieselregen *m.*

droll possierlich, drollig.

drollery *s.* Posse, Schnurre *f.*

dromedary *s.* Dromedar *n.*

drone *s.* Drohne *f.*; Brummen *n.*; ~ *v.i.* summen.

droop *v.t.* sinken lassen; ~*v.i.* niederhängen; den Kopf hängen lassen.

drop *s.* Tropfen *m.*; Rückgang, Fall *m.*; ~ *v.i.* tropfen; fallen; sinken; ~ *v.t.* tropfen; fallen lassen; fahren lassen.

droplet *s.* Tröpfchen *n.*

drop-out *s.* Aussteiger(in) *m.(f.)*; (Schul-, Studien) Abbrecher(in) *m.(f.)*

droppings *s.pl.* Mist *m.*, tierischer Kot *m.*

drop-shot *s.* Stoppball *m.*

dropsy *s.* Wassersucht *f.*

drought *s.* Trockenheit, Dürre *f.*

drove *s.* Herde *f.*; Schar *f.*

drown *v.t.* ertränken; überschwemmen; *he was*

~ed, er ertrank.
drowse *v.i.* dösen.
drowsy *a.,* **~ily** *adv.* schläfrig.
drudge *s.* Arbeitstier *n.;* Kuli *m.;* Knecht *m.;* ~ *v.i.* schwere Arbeit verrichten, sich placken.
drudgery *s.* Plackerei *f.*
drug *s.* Droge, Medikament *n.;* Rauschgift *n.;* Ladenhüter *f.;* ~ *v.i.* mit Arznei versetzen, Arznei eingeben, vergiften.
drug: ~ **addict** *s.* Drogensüchtige *m./f.;* ~ **addiction** *s.* Drogensucht; ~ **dealer** *s.* Drogenhändler(in) *m.(f.)*
druggist *s.* Drogist *m.*
drugstore *s.* Drugstore *m.*
drum *s.* Trommel *f.;* ~ *v.t.* trommeln.
drum: **~-fire,** Trommelfeuer *n.;* **~-head** *s.* Fell der Trommel *n.;* **~-stick** *s.* Trommelstock *m.*
drummer *s.* Schlagzeuger(in) *m.(f.)*
drunk *a.* betrunken.
drunkard *s.* Trinker(in) *m.(f.)*
drunkenness *s.* Trunkenheit *f.*
dry *a.* trocken, dürr; durstig; (Wein) herb; ~ *v.t.* trocknen; ~ *v.i.* dürr werden.
dry cell *s.* Trockenbatterie *f.*
dry cleaning *s.* chemische Reinigung *f.*
dry dock *s.* Trockendock *n.*
dryness *s.* Trockenheit *f.*
dry run *s.* (*fam.*) Probelauf *m.*
dual *a.* Zwei. . ., doppelt.
dub *v.t.* synchronisieren.
dubious *a.,* **~ly** *adv.* zweifelhaft.
ducal *a.* herzoglich.
duchess *s.* Herzogin *f.*
duchy *s.* Herzogtum *n.*
duck *s.* Ente *f.;* ~ *v.t.* untertauchen; ~ *v.i.* sich ducken.
duckling *s.* junge Ente *f.;* Entenküken *n.*
duck-pond *s.* Ententeich *m.*
duct *s.* Gang *m.;* Röhre *f.*
ductile *a.* dehnbar.; (*fig.*) fügsam.
dud *s.* Blindgänger (Granate, Bombe) *m.;* (*fig.*) Niete *f.*
dude *s.* (*fam.*) Stadtmensch *m.*
dudgeon *s.* Groll, Unwille *m.*
due *a. & adv.* schuldig, gebührend; fällig; recht, pünktlich; *to become* ~, fällig werden (Wechsel, etc); *in* ~ *course,* zur gehörigen Zeit; ~ *s.* Gebühr, Pflicht *f.;* Gerechtsame *f.;* Abgabe *f.*
duel *s.* Zweikampf *m.* ~ *v.i.* sich duellieren.
duellist *s.* Duellant *m.*
duet *s.* Duett *n.*
dug-out *s.* Unterstand *m.* (*mil.*) Einbaum *m.*
duke *s.* Herzog *m.*
dukedom *s.* Herzogtum *n.;* Herzogwürde *f.*
dull *a.* matt; stumpf; einfältig, dumm; plump, langweilig, dumpf; (*com.*) flau; ~ *v.t.* abstumpfen; dumm machen.
dullness *s.* Stumpfheit, Stumpfsinnigkeit *f.;* Flauheit *f.*
duly *adv.* gehörig, richtig.
dumb *a.,* **~ly** *adv.* stumm; dumm.
dumb bells *s.pl.* Hanteln *f.pl.*
dumbfound *v.t.* sprachlos machen; verblüffen.
dumbfounded *a.* sprachlos; verblüfft.
dumb show *s.* Gebärdenspiel *n.*
dumbwaiter *s.* Serviertisch *m.*

dummy *s.* Attrappe *f.;* (*mil.*) Blindgänger *m.;* Strohmann (im Kartenspiele) *m.;* Schein. . ., Schwindel. . .
dump *s.* Müllkippe *f.;* Müllhalde *f.;* Munitionslager *n.;* ~ *v.t.* hinwerfen; umkippen, (Waren) verschleudern.
dumping *s.* Schleuderausfuhr *f.*
dumping-ground *s.* (Schutt-)abladeplatz *m.*
dumpling *s.* Kloß *m.;* Knödel *m.*
dumps *s.pl.* (*fam.*) *in the* ~, niedergeschlagen.
dumpy *a.* kurz und dick.
dun *a.* graubraun; dunkel; ~ *v.t.* mahnen.
dunce *s.* Dummkopf *m.*
dune *s.* Düne *f.*
dung *s.* Mist, Dünger *m.;* ~ *v.t.* düngen.
dungarees *s.pl.* Latzhose *f.*
dungeon *s.* Kerker *m.*
dungfork *s.* Mistgabel *f.*
dunghill *s.* Misthaufen *m.*
dunk *v.t.* eintunken, stippen.
duodenal *a.* duodenal; Zwölffingerdarm. . .
duodenum *s.* Duodenum *n.;* Zwölffingerdarm *m.*
dupe *s.* Geprellte *f./m.;* Narr *m.;* ~ *v.t.* prellen.
duplex *a.* zweistöckig; doppelt, Doppel. . .
duplicate *a.* doppelt; ~ *s.* Duplikat *n.;* ~ *v.t.* verdoppeln; vervielfältigen.
duplication *s.* Verdoppelung *f.;* Wiederholung *f.*
duplicity *s.* Falschheit, Zweideutigkeit *f.*
durability *s.* Dauerhaftigkeit *f.*
durable *a.,* **~bly** *adv.* dauerhaft.
duration *s.* Dauer *f.*
duress *s.* Zwang *m.;* Haft *f.; under* ~, (*law*) durch Nötigung.
during *pr.* während.
dusk *a.* dämmerig, dunkel; ~ *s.* Dämmerung, Dunkelheit *f.*
dust *s.* Staub *m.;* ~ *v.t* abstauben.
dustbin *s.* Müll-, Kehrichtkasten *m.*
dust-cart *s.* Müll-, Kehrichtwagen *m.*
dust-cover *s.* Schutzumschlag (Buch) *m.;* Abdeckhaube *f.*
duster *s.* Wischlappen *m.;* Staubbesen *f.*
dustman *s.* Müllmann *m.*
dustpan *s.* Kehrschaufel *f.*
dusty *a.* staubig; verstaubt.
Dutch *a.* holländisch.; ~ *s.* Holländer(in) *m.(f.)*
duteous, dutiful *a.,* **~ly** *adv.* pflichttreu.
dutiable *a.* zollpflichtig, steuerpflichtig.
duty *s.* Pflicht, Schuldigkeit *f.;* Abgabe *f.;* Zoll *m.;* Dienst *m.;* *free of* ~, zollfrei; *on* ~, im Dienst; *off* ~, außer Dienst; **~-hours** *pl.* Dienststunden *f.pl.; breach of* ~, Pflichtverletzung *f.*
dwarf *s.* Zwerg *m.;* ~ *v.t.* am Wachstum hindern.
dwarfish *a.,* **~ly** *adv.* zwergartig.
dwell *v.i.r. & ir.* wohnen; verweilen.
dwelling *s.* Wohnort, Aufenthalt *m.*
dwindle *v.i.* einschrumpfen, abnehmen.
dye *s.* Farbstoff *m.;* **~-works** *s.pl.* Farbwerke *n.pl.;* **~-stuff,** Farbstoff *m.;* ~ *v.t.* färben.
dyer *s.* Färber *m.*
dying *a.* sterbend.
dynamic(al) *a.* dynamisch.
dynamics *s.pl.* Dynamik *f.*
dynamite *s.* Dynamit *n.*
dynamo *s.* Dynamo(maschine *f.*) *m.*
dynastic *a.* dynastisch.

dynasty s. Dynastie f.
dysentery s. Ruhr f.; Dysenterie f.
dyslexia s. Dyslexie f.; Lesestörung f.

dysfunction s. Funktionsstörung f.
dyspepsia s. Verdauungsstörung f.; Dyspepsie f.

E

E, e der Buchstabe E oder e n.; (mus.) E, e; **E-sharp** Eis; **E-flat** Es.
each pn. jeder, jede, jedes; ~ other, einander.
eager a., **-ly** adv. eifrig; erpicht.
eagerness s. Eifer m.; Begierde f.
eagle s. Adler m.
eaglet s. junger Adler m.
ear s. Ohr n.; Gehör n.; Öhr n.; Henkel m.; Ähre f.; ~ **ache** s. Ohrenschmerzen; **--drum** s. Ohrentrommel f.
earl s. (englischer) Graf m.
earlobe s. Ohrläppchen n.
earldom s. Grafenwürde f.
early a. & adv. früh, zeitig.
ear-mark s. Ohrenzeichen (bei Schafen) n.; ~ v.t. vormerken.
ear-muffs s.pl. Ohrenschützer pl.
earn v.t. verdienen, erwerben, gewinnen.
earnest a., **-ly** adv. ernstlich; dringend; ~ s. Ernst m.; Eifer m.; Handgeld n.; Unterpfand n.; in good ~, in vollem Ernste.
earnings s.pl. Verdienst, Lohn m.
earphones s.pl. Kopfhörer m.
ear-ring s. Ohrring m.
ear-shot s. Hörweite f.
ear-splitting a. ohrenbetäubend.
earth s. Erde f.; (radio) Erdung f.; ~ v.t. (radio) erden.
earthen a. irden.
earthenware s. Steingut n.
earthly a. irdisch, sinnlich.
earthquake s. Erdbeben n.
earthworm s. Regenwurm m.
earthy a. erdig; derb.
ear-trumpet s. Hörrohr n.
ear-wax s. Ohrenschmalz n.
earwig s. Ohrwurm m.
ear-witness s. Ohrenzeuge m.
ease s. Ruhe, Gemächlichkeit f.; Erleichterung f.; at ~, gemächlich; stand at ~, (mil.) rührt euch!; ~ v.t. erleichtern; beruhigen; lindern.
easel s. Staffelei f.
easiness s. Leichtigkeit f.
east s. Osten m.; Orient m.; ~ a. östlich.
Easter s. Ostern n. or pl.; **--day,** Ostersonntag m.; ~ **egg** s. Osterei n.
easterly a. & adv. östlich.
eastern a. östlich; morgenländisch.
eastward adv. ostwärts.
easy a., **-ly** adv. leicht, bequem, frei; willig, gefällig.
easy-chair s. Lehnstuhl m.
easy-going a. lässig, gemütlich.
eat v.t. & i.st. essen; fressen; zerfressen.
eatable a. eßbar; **-s** pl. Eßwaren f.pl.
eater s. Esser(in) m.(f.)
eating-apple s. Eßapfel m.
eating-house s. Speisehaus n.
eaves s.pl. Dachtraufe f.
eavesdropper s. Horcher m.

ebb s. Ebbe f.; ~ v.i. abfließen.
ebony s. Ebenholz n.
ebullient a. sprudelnd; überschwenglich.
ebullition s. Aufwallung f.
eccentric a. exzentrisch; überspannt.
ecclesiastic(al) a. kirchlich, geistlich; ~ s. Geistliche m.
echelon s. Staffelung f.; in ~ formation, (mil.) gestaffelt.
echo s. Widerhall m.; Echo n.; ~ v.i. & t. widerhallen; wiederholen.
eclectic a. eklektisch, auswählend.
eclecticism s. Eklektizismus m.
eclipse s. Finsternis f.; ~ v.t. verfinstern, verdunkeln.
ecological a. ökologisch.
ecology s. Ökologie.
economic(al) a. wirtschaftlich; sparsam.
economic warfare s. Wirtschaftskrieg m.
economist s. Nationalökonom(in) m.(f.); Wirtschaftswissenschaftler(in) m.(f.)
economics s.pl. Volkswirtschaftslehre f.
economize v.t. haushälterisch verwalten; sparen.
economy s. Sparsamkeit f.; Anordnung f., Bau m.; Haushaltung f.; Wirtschaft, Volkswirtschaft f.; **--measures** pl. Sparmaßnahmen f.pl.; planned ~, Planwirtschaft f.; political ~, Volkswirtschaft, Nationalökonomie f.
ecstasy s. Verzückung f.; Ekstase f.
ecstatic a. verzückt; ekstatisch.
Ecuador s. Ekuador n.
Ecuadorian s. Ekuadorianer(in) m.(f.); a. ekuadorianisch.
ecumenical a. ökumenisch.
eczema s. Hautausschlag m.; Ekzem n.
eddy s. Wirbel m.; ~ v.i. wirbeln.
edge s. Schärfe, Schneide f.; Ecke f.; Kante f.; Rand m.; on ~, hochkant; to be on ~ over, nervös sein über; **cutting--** s. Schneide f.; ~ v.t. schärfen; säumen, einfassen; drängen; ~ v.i. vordringen.
edgeways, edgewise adv. hochkantig.
edging s. Saum m., Einfassung f.
edible a. eßbar; **-s**, Eßwaren f.pl.
edict s. Verordnung f.
edification s. (fig.) Erbauung f.
edifice s. Gebäude n.
edify v.t. (fig.) erbauen.
edit v.t. herausgeben (ein Buch); edieren; redigieren; bearbeiten.
edition s. Ausgabe, Auflage f.
editor s. Herausgeber(in) m.(f.); Redakteur(in) m.(f.); **--in-chief,** Chefredakteur(in) m.(f.)
editorial s. Leitartikel m.; ~ a. Redaktions. . .
editorialist s. Leitartikler m.
educate v.t. erziehen.
educated a. gebildet.
education s. Erziehung f.
educational a. Erziehungs. . .
educator s. Erzieher(in) m.(f.)

eel *s.* Aal *m.*
eerie *a.* gespenstisch, unheimlich.
efface *v.t.* auslöschen, ausstreichen; in den Schatten stellen.
effect *s.* Wirkung *f.*; *in* ~, in Wirklichkeit; *to take* ~, *to go into* ~, wirksam werden (Verordnung etc.); *with* ~ *from*, mit Wirkung von; *to the* ~ *that*, des Inhaltsdaß; ~ *v.t.* ausführen, bewirken; *to* ~ *a policy*, eine Versicherung abschließen.
effective *a.*, **~ly** *adv.* wirksam, kräftig; wirklich vorhanden; ~ *1 June*, mit Wirkung vom 1. Juni; ~ *immediately*, mit sofortiger Wirksamkeit.
effectiveness *s.* Wirksamkeit *f.*
effectual *a.*, **~ly** *adv.* wirklich, wirksam.
effectuate *v.t.* bewerkstelligen.
effeminacy *s.* Verweichlichung *f.*
effeminate *a.*, **~ly** *adv.* effeminiert, weichlich; üppig; ~ *v.t.* verweichlichen; ~ *v.i.* sich verweichlichen.
effervesce *v.i.* sprudeln; ~ **powder** *s.* Brausepulver *n.*
effervescence *s.* Sprudeln *n.*; Überschaumen *n.*
effete *a.* entkräftet; abgenutzt.
efficacious *a.*, **~ly** *adv.* wirksam.
efficacy *s.* Wirksamkeit *f.*
efficiency *s.* Wirksamkeit *f.*; (*mech.*) Nutzeffekt *m.*; Tüchtigkeit, Brauchbarkeit, Leistungsfähigkeit *f.*; **~-rating,** (*mil.*) Beurteilung *f.*
efficient *a.*, **~ly** *adv.* wirksam, leistungsfähig; tüchtig, brauchbar.
effigy *s.* Bildnis *n.*
effort *s.* Anstrengung *f.*
effortless *a.* mühelos.
effuse *v.t.* ausgießen.
effusion *s.* Verschwendung *f.*; (*fig.*) Erguß *f.*
effusive *a.* überschwenglich.
egg *s.* Ei *n.*; *dried* ~, Trockenei *n.*; *newlaid* ~, frisch gelegtes Ei *n.*; *bad* ~, übler Bursche *m.*; ~ *on*, *v.t.* anhetzen.
egg-cup *s.* Eierbecher *n.*
egg plant *s.* Aubergine *f.*
egg-shell *s.* Eierschale *f.*
egg whisk *s.* Schneebesen *m.*
egg white *s.* Eiweiß *n.*
egg yolk *s.* Eigelb *n.*
ego *s.* Ego *n.*; Ich *n.*
egoism *s.* Egoismus *m.*, Selbstsucht *f.*
egoist *s.* Egoist(in) *m.*(*f.*)
egotism *s.* Selbstsucht *f.*
egotist *s.* Egotist(in) *m.*(*f.*)
egotistic(al) *a.* egoistisch, selbstbezogen.
Egypt *s.* Ägypten *n.*
Egyptian *s.* Ägypter(in) *m.*(*f.*); *a.* ägyptisch.
eh *i.* he? hoho!
eiderdown *s.* Daunendecke *f.*
eight *a.* acht.
eighteen *a.* achtzehn.
eighteenth *a.* achtzehnt. . .
eightfold *a.* achtfach.
eighth *a.* acht. . .; **~-note** *s.* Achtelnote.
eightieth *a.* achtzigst. . .
eighty *a.* achtzig.
either *pn.* einer von beiden; beide; ~ *s.* entweder. . .; *not*. . .*either*, auch nicht; *nor*. . .*either*, und. . .auch nicht.
ejaculate *v.t.* ausstoßen; ejakulieren.

ejaculation *s.* Ausstoßen *n.*; Stosseufzer *m.*; Ejakulation *f.*, Samenerguß *m.*
eject *v.t.* hinauswerfen, ausstoßen, vertreiben.
ejection *s.* Vertreibung *f.*; Ausstoßung *f.*
eke *v.t.* *to* ~ *out*, dehnen, verlängern; ergänzen; sich durchhelfen.
elaborate *v.t.* ausarbeiten; verfeinern; ~ *a.*, **~ly** *adv.* ausgearbeitet; verfeinert, umständlich; kunstvoll.
elapse *v.i.* verfließen, verlaufen.
elastic *a.* elastisch; ~ *s.* Gummiband *n.*
elasticity *s.* Spring-, Federkraft *f.*
elated *a.* freudig erregt.
elation *s.* gehobene Stimmung *f.*; Stolz *m.*
elbow *s.* Ellbogen *m.*; (*mech.*) Knie *n.*; ~ *v.t.* wegstoßen; verdrängen.
elbow-room *s.* Spielraum *m.*; Ellbogenfreiheit *f.*
elder *a.* älter; ~ *s.* Kirchenälteste *m.*; ~ *s.* Holunder *m.* **~berry** *s.* Holunderbeere *f.*
elderly *a.* älter, bejahrt. ~ *s. pl.* ältere Menschen *pl.*
eldest *a.* älteste.
elect *v.t.* (er)wählen; ~ *a.* erwählt.
election *s.* Erwählung *f.*, Wahl *f.*;~ **campaign** *s.* Wahlkampf *m.*
electioneering *a.* Wahl. . .; ~ *s.* Wahlarbeit *f.*
elective *a.*, **~ly** *adv.* wählend; Wahl. . .
elector *s.* Wähler (in) *m.*(*f.*)
electoral *a.* Wahl. . .
electoral district *s.* Wahlbezirk *m.*
electorate *s.* Wählerschaft *f.*; Kurfürstentum *n.*
electric *a.* elektrisch; ~ **arc** *s.* Lichtbogen *m.*; ~ **heater** *s.* elektrische Heizvorrichtung *f.*
electrical *a.*, ~ *adv.* elektrisch; ~ *engineer*, Elektroingenieur (in) *m.*(*f.*)
electricity *s.* Elektrizität *f.*
electric shock *s.* Stromschlag *m.*
electrify *v.t.* elektrisieren; elektrifizieren.
electrocute *v.t.* durch Stromschlag töten.
electrode *s.* Elektrode *f.*
electrolysis *s.* Elektrolyse *f.*
electrolyte *s.* Elektrolyt *m.*
electromagnetic *a.* elektromagnetisch.
electron *s.* Elektron *n.*
electronic *a.* elektronisch.
electronics *s.* Elektronik *f.*
electroplate *v.t.* galvanisieren.
elegance *s.* Eleganz *f.*
elegant *a.*, **~ly** *adv.* zierlich; geschmackvoll; elegant.
elegiac *a.* elegisch.
elegy *s.* Elegie *f.*, Trauergedicht *n.*
element *s.* Urstoff *m.*; Bestandteil *m.*, Element *n.*; **~s** *pl.* Anfangsgründe *m.pl.*
elementary *a.* elementar, Anfangs. . .
elementary school *s.* Grundschule *f.*
elephant *s.* Elefant *m.*
elephantine *a.* elefantenartig.
elevate *v.t.* erhöhen, erheben.
elevated *p.* & *a.* hoch, erhaben; stolz.
elevation *s.* Erhöhung, Erhabenheit *f.*; Höhe *f.*; Polhöhe *f.*; Aufriß *m.*
elevator *s.* Aufzug *m.*
eleven *a.* elf.
elf *s.* Elf(e) *m.*(*f.*), Kobold *m.*
elicit *v.t.* entlocken, hervorlocken.
eligibility *s.* Wählbarkeit *f.*
eligible *a.* wählbar; wünschenswert.

eliminate *v.t.* ausscheiden, entfernen.
elimination *s.* Beseitigung *f.*
elite *s.* Elite *f.*
Elizabethan *a.* elisabethanisch.
elk *s.* Elch *m.*
ell *s.* Elle *f.*
ellipse *s.* Ellipse *f.*
ellipsis *s.* (*ling.*) Ellipse *f.*
elliptical *a.* elliptisch.
elm *s.* Ulme *f.*
elocution *s.* Vortragsweise *f.*; Vortragskunst *f.*
elongate *v.t.* verlängern.
elope *v.i.* (*fam.*) durchbrennen.
elopement *s.* (*fam.*) Durchbrennen *n.*
eloquence *s.* Beredsamkeit *f.*
eloquent *a.*, **~ly** *adv.* beredt.
else *adv.* anders, sonst, außerdem.
elsewhere *adv.* anderswo.
elucidate *v.t.* erläutern.
elude *v.t.* entwischen, ausweichen; entgehen; (Gesetz) umgehen.
elusive *a.* ausweichend; flüchtig.
emaciate *v.t.* ausmergeln, abmagern.
emaciated *a.* abgezehrt.
emanate *v.i.* ausströmen; herrühren.
emancipate *v.t.* emanzipieren.
emancipated *a.* emanzipiert.
emancipation *s.* Emanzipation *f.*
emasculate *v.t.* entmannen.
embalm *v.t.* einbalsamieren.
embank *v.t.* eindeichen, dämmen.
embankment *s.* Eindämmung *f.*; (*rail.*) Damm *m.*; Kai *m.*; Ufereinfassung *f.*
embargo *s.* Embargo *n.*, Handelsverbot *n.*
embark *v.t.* einschiffen; **~** *v.i.* (*fig.*) sich einlassen (auf).
embarkation *s.* Einschiffung *f.*
embarrass *v.t.* verwirren; verlegen machen.
embarrassed *a.* verlegen.
embarrassing *a.* peinlich; unangenehm.
embarrassment *s.* Verlegenheit *f.*
embassy *s.* Botschaft *f.*
embed *v.t.* betten, lagern, legen.
embellish *v.t.* verschönern.
embellishment *s.* Verschönerung *f.*
embers *s.pl.* glühende Kohle, Glut *f.*
embezzle *v.t.* unterschlagen, veruntreuen.
embezzlement *s.* Unterschlagung *f.*
embitter *v.t.* verbittern.
emblem *s.* Sinnbild *n.*; Symbol *n.*
emblematic *a.*, **~ally** *adv.* sinnbildlich; symbolisch *a.*
embodiment *s.* Verkörperung *f.*
embody *v.t.* verkörpern; enthalten.
embolden *v.t.* anfeuern, kühn machen.
emboss *v.t.* prägen.
embrace *v.t.* umarmen; enthalten; ergreifen; **~** *s.* Umarmung *f.*
embrasure *s.* Schießscharte *f.*
embroider *v.t.* sticken; ausschmücken.
embroidery *s.* Stickerei *f.*
embroil *v.t.* verwirren, verwickeln.
embryo *s.* Embryo *m.*
embryonic *a.* Embryonal . . .
emend *v.t.* emendieren; berichtigen.
emendation *s.* Verbesserung *f.*

emerald *s.* Smaragd *m.*
emerge *v.i.* auftauchen, emporkommen.
emergence *s.* Auftauchen *n.*; Hervortreten *n.*
emergency *s.* unerwartetes Ereignis *n.*; Notfall *m.*; Not. . .; **~-exit** Notausgang *m.*
emergent *a.* aufstrebend, auftauchend.
emery *s.* Schmirgel. . .
emetic *s.* Brechmittel *n.*
emigrant *s.* Auswanderer *m.*, Auswanderin *f.*
emigrate *v.i.* auswandern.
emigration *s.* Auswanderung *f.*
eminence *s.* Höhe, Anhöhe *f.*; Auszeichnung *f.*; Eminenz (Titel) *f.*
eminent *a.*, **~ly** *adv.* hervorragend; bedeutend.
emissary *s.* Kundschafter (in) *m.*(*f.*), Abgesandte *m./f.*
emission *s.* Aussendung *f.*; Ausgabe *f.*
emit *v.t.* aussenden; äußern; ausgeben.
emotion *s.* Gefühl *n.*, Emotion *f.*, Gemütsbewegung *f.*
emotional *a.* gefühlsmäßig; gefühlvoll erregbar.
emotionally *adv.* emotional.
emotive *a.* emotional, gefühlsbetont.
empathy *s.* Empathie *f.*; Einfühlung *f.*
emperor *s.* Kaiser *m.*
emphasis *s.* Betonung *f.*, Nachdruck *m.*; **~ added**, Unterstreichung zugefügt.
emphasize *v.t.* betonen, hervorheben.
emphatic(al) *a.*, **~ly** *adv.* nachdrücklich.
empire *s.* Reich *n.*
empiric *s.* Empiriker; Quacksalber *m.*
empirical *a.* erfahrungsmäßig.
employ *v.t.* anstellen; beschäftigen.
employe *s.* Arbeitnehmer(in) *m.*(*f.*)
employer *s.* Arbeitgeber(in) *m.*(*f.*)
employment *s.* Arbeit *f.*; Beschäftigung *f.*; **~ agency** *s.* Arbeitsamt *n.*; *creation of* **~**, Arbeitsbeschaffung *f.*
empower *v.t.* ermächtigen.
empress *s.* Kaiserin *f.*
emptiness *s.* Leere *f.*
empty *a.* leer; **~-handed** *a.* mit leeren Händen; **~** *v.t.* ausleeren.
emulate *v.t.* nacheifern; wetteifern mit.
emulation *s.* Nacheiferung *f.*; Wetteifer *m.*
emulous *a.*, **~ly** *adv.* nacheifernd.
enable *v.t.* fähig machen, ermöglichen.
enabling act *s.* Ermächtigungsgesetz *n.*
enact *v.t.* verordnen, verfügen; (Gesetz) erlassen.; aufführen, spielen.
enactment *s.* Verordnung, Verfügung *f.*
enamel *s.* Emaille *f.*; Schmelzglas *n.*; Zahnschmelz *m.*; **~** *v.t.* emaillieren.
enamored *a.* verliebt.
encamp *v.t. & i.* (sich) lagern.
encampment *s.* Lagern *n.*; Lager *n.*
encase *v.t.* einschließen.
enchant *v.t.* bezaubern, verzaubern.
enchanter *s.* Zauberer *m.*
enchanting *a.* entzückend, bezaubernd.
enchantment *s.* Entzücken *n.*
enchantress *s.* Zauberin *f.*
encircle *v.t.* umringen; umgeben.
enclave *s.* Enklave *f.*
enclose *v.t.* einhegen; einschließen; enthalten; (einem Brief) beilegen.

enclosure *s.* Einhegung *f.*; Einlage, Anlage (in Briefen) *f.*

encode *v.t.* verschlüsseln.

encompass *v.t.* umgeben.

encore *s.* Zugabe *f.*

encounter *s.* Zusammentreffen *n.*; Gefecht *n.*; ~ *v.t.* zusammentreffen mit; ~ *v.i.* sich begegnen.

encourage *v.t.* ermutigen; fördern.

encouragement *s.* Ermutigung *f.*; Unterstützung *f.*

encouraging *a.* ermutigend.

encroach *v.i.* Eingriff tun; übergreifen.

encroachment *s.* Eingriff, Übergriff *m.*

encumber *v.t.* verwickeln; belasten.

encumbrance *s.* Beschwerde, Last *f.*; Hindernis *n.*

encyclic(al) *s.* Enzyklika *f.*

encyclopedia *s.* Enzyklopädie *f.*

end *s.* Ende, Ziel *n.*; Absicht *f.*; Stückchen *n.*; *at an* ~, am Ende; *no ~ of . . .*, eine Unzahl von . . .; *on* ~, aufrechtstehend, hochkant; ~ *in itself,* Selbstzweck *m.*; ~ *v.t.* beendigen; ~ *v.i.* aufhören.

endanger *v.t.* gefährden, *~ed species s.* vom Aussterben bedrohte Art *f.*

endear *v.t.* wert machen, teuer machen.

endearment *s.* Zärtlichkeit *f.*

endeavor *s.* Bestreben *n.*, Bemühen *n.*; ~ *v.i.* sich bemühen.

endemic *a.* endemisch, verbreitet.

ending *s.* Ende *n.*; Schluß *m.*; Endung *f.*

endive *s.* Chicorée *f.*

endless *a.*, *~ly adv.* unendlich, endlos.

endorse *v.t.* indossieren; gutheißen.

endorsement *s.* Indossament *n.*; Unterstützung *f.*; Billigung *f.*

endow *v.t.* ausstatten; finanzieren.

endowment *s.* Begabung; Stiftung; Ausstattung *f.*; **~-policy** *s.* abgekürzte Lebensversicherung *s.*

end-product *s.* Endprodukt *n.*, Resultat *n.*

endurable *a.* erträglich.

endurance *s.* Beharrlichkeit *f.*; Widerstandskraft *f.*; Ausdauer *f.*; **~test** *s.* Belastungsprobe *f.*

endure *v.t. & i.* ertragen; erdulden; dauern.

enduring *a.* dauerhaft; beständig.

enema *s.* Einlauf *m.*; Klistierspritze *f.*

enemy *s.* Feind *m.*; ~ *alien,* feindlicher Ausländer *m.*

energetic *a.* kräftig, nachdrücklich.

energetically *adv.* schwungvoll; entschieden.

energy *s.* Tatkraft *f.*, Energie *f.*

energy: ~crisis *s.* Energiekrise *f.*; **~-giving** *a.* energiespendend; **~-saving** *a.* energiesparend.

enervate *v.t.* entnerven; schwächen.

enfeeble *v.t.* schwächen.

enforce *v.t.* erzwingen; durchsetzen.

enforceable *a.* durchsetzbar.

enforcement *s.* Durchsetzung *f.*

enfranchise *v.t.* das Stimmrecht verleihen.

engage *v.t.* verpflichten; anwerben; beschäftigen; angreifen; ~ *v.i.* fechten; sich einlassen; sich verloben.

engaged *p. & a.* verlobt; bestellt, besetzt; beschäftigt.

engagement *s.* Verabredung *f.*; Verpflichtung *f.*; Verbindlichkeit *f.*; Beschäftigung *f.*; Verlobung *f.*; Einladung *f.*; Gefecht *n.*; *to meet one's engagements,* seinen Verpflichtungen nachkommen; *to break off the ~,* die Verlobung auflösen.

engaging *a.* verbindlich, einnehmend; bezaubernd.

engender *v.t.* erzeugen.

engine *s.* Maschine *f.*; Motor *m.*; Lokomotive *f.*; Feuerspritze *f.*

engine-drive *s.* Lokomotivführer *m.*

engineer *s.* Ingenieur *m.*; Techniker, Maschinenbauer *m.*; *(mil.)* Pioneer *m.*

engineering *s.* Ingenieurwesen *n.*; Maschinenbaukunst *f.*; *electrical ~,* Elektrotechnik *f.*

England *s.* England *n.*

English *a.* englisch; ~ *s.* Englisch *n.*; **~man,** Engländer *m.*; **~woman** Engländerin *f.*

engraft *v.t.* pfropfen; einprägen.

engrain *v.t.* tief färben; einprägen.

engrave *v.t.* stechen, gravieren.

engraver *s.* Graveur *m.*; Bildstecher *m.*

engraving *s.* Kupferstich *m.*; Holzschnitt *m.*

engross *v.t.* ganz in Anspruch nehmen.

engulf *v.t.* versenken, verschlingen.

enhance *v.t.* verbessern; erhöhen, steigern.

enhancement *s.* Verbesserung; Erhöhung; Steigerung *f.*

enigma *s.* Rätsel *n.*

enigmatic(al) *a.*, **~ly** *adv.* rätselhaft.

enjoin *v.t.* einschärfen, anbefehlen.

enjoy *v.t.* genießen; *to ~ oneself,* sich gut unterhalten.

enjoyable *a.* angenehm; erfreulich.

enjoyment *s.* Vergnügen *n.*

enlarge *v.t.* erweitern, vergrößern; ~ *v.i.* sich verbreiten.

enlargement *s.* Erweiterung *f.*; (*phot.*) Vergrößerung *f.*

enlighten *v.t.* aufklären, erleuchten.

enlightened *a.* aufgeklärt.

enlightenment *s.* Aufklärung *f.*

enlist *v.t.* anwerben; ~ *v.i.* Dienste nehmen.

enlistment *s.* *(mil.)* Anwerbung *f.*

enliven *v.t.* beleben, ermuntern.

enmesh *v.t.* umgarnen, verstricken.

enmity *s.* Feindschaft *f.*

ennoble *v.t.* adeln; veredeln.

enormity *s.* Ungeheuerlichkeit *f.*

enormous *a.*, **~ly** *adv.* ungeheuer; riesig; gewaltig.

enormousness *s.* ungeheure Größe *f.*; Riesenhaftigkeit *f.*

enough *a. & adv.* genug; genügend.

enounce *v.t.* verkünden; aussprechen.

enrage *v.t.* in Wut versetzen; wütend machen.

enrapture *v.t.* entzücken.

enrich *v.t.* bereichern; anreichern.

enrichment *s.* Anreicherung *f.*; Bereicherung *f.*

enroll *v.t.* einschreiben; anwerben.

enrollment *s.* Einschreibung *f.*; Immatrikulation *f.*

enshrine *v.t.* einschließen; (als Heiligtum) aufbewahren.

enslave *v.t.* zum Sklaven machen.

ensnare *v.t.* verstricken, fangen.

ensue *v.i.* folgen; sich ergeben.

ensure *v.t.* (sich) sichern.

entail *v.t.* mit sich bringen.

entangle *v.t.* verwickeln; *to become ~d,* sich verfangen.

entanglement *s.* Verwirrung, Verwicklung *f.*, Verstrickung *f.*

enter *v.t. & i.* eintreten; hineingehen; einführen; einschreiben, eintragen.
enteric *a.* enterisch, Darm...
enteritis *s.* Darmkatarrh *m.*
enterprise *s.* Unternehmung *f.*
enterprising *a.* unternehmend.
entertain *v.t.* unterhalten; bewirten; hegen (Hoffnung).
entertainer *s.* Entertainer(in) *m.(f.)*
entertaining *a.* unterhaltsam.
entertainment *s.* Unterhaltung *f.*
entertainment tax *s.* Vergnügungssteuer *f.*
enthrall *v.t.* bezaubern, fesseln.
enthrone *v.t.* inthronisieren.
enthusiasm *s.* Begeisterung *f.*, Enthusiasmus *m.*
enthusiast *s.* Schwärmer *m.*
enthusiastic *a.* schwärmerisch, begeistert.
entice *v.t.* reizen, anlocken.
enticement *s.* Anlockung *f.*; Reiz *m.*
enticing *a.* verlockend.
entire *a.*, **~ly** *adv.* ganz, ungeteilt, vollständig.
entirety *s.* Ganzheit, Gesamtheit *f.*
entitle *v.t.* betiteln; berechtigen.
entity *s.* Einheit *f.*
entomb *v.t.* begraben.
entombment *s.* Begräbnis *n.*
entomologist *s.* Entomologe *m.*; Entomologin *f.*
entomology *s.* Insektenkunde *f.*
entourage *s.* Begleitung, Gefolge *f.*
entrails *s.pl.* Eingeweide *n.pl.*
entrance *s.* Eingang *m.*; Antritt *m.*; **~-examination**, Aufnahmeprüfung *f.*; **~-fee**, Aufnahmegebühr *f.*; **~-hall** *s.* Diele *f.*; Vorsaal *m.*; *no* ~, Eintritt verboten.
entrance *v.t.* entzücken.
entrant *s.* Beitretender (zu einem Verein) *m.*; Bewerber *m.*; Teilnehmer eines Wettbewerbs *m.*
entrap *v.t.* verleiten.
entreat *v.t.* anflehen, beschwören.
entreaty *s.* Bitte *f.*; Gesuch *n.*
entree *s.* Hauptgericht *n.*
entrench *v.t.* sich festsetzen (Idee); sich verwurzeln.
entrepreneur *s.* Unternehmer(in) *m.(f.)*
entrust *v.t.* anvertrauen.
entry *s.* Eingang *m.*; Eintragung *f.*; Meldung *f.* (*Sport*); gebuchter Posten *m.*; **~-permit**, Einreiseerlaubnis *f.*; *no* ~, Eintritt verboten, Einfahrt verboten.
entwine *v.t.* sich schlingen, sich winden.
enumerate *v.t.* aufzählen.
enumeration *s.* Aufzählung *f.*
enunciate *v.t.* aussagen, berichten; formulieren.
envelop *v.t.* einhüllen, einwickeln; (*mil.*) umfassen.
envelope *s.* Hülle *f.*; (Brief)umschlag *m.*
envenom *v.t.* vergiften; erbittern.
enviable *a.* beneidenswert.
envious *a.*, **~ly** *adv.* neidisch.
environment *s.* Umgebung *f.*
environmentalist *s.* Umweltschützer(in) *m.(f.)*
environs *s.pl.* Umgebung *f.*
envisage *v.t.* ins Auge fassen; sich etw. vorstellen.
envoy *s.* Gesandte *m./f.*; Bote *m.*, Botin *f.*
envy *s.* Neid *m.*; ~ *v.t.* beneiden.
enzyme *s.* Enzym *n.*

ephemeral *a.* kurzlebig, flüchtig, ephemer.
epic *a.* episch; ~ *s.* Epos *n.*
epicenter *s.* Epizentrum *n.*
epicure *s.* Epikuräer, Genußmensch *m.*
epicurean *a.* üppig lebend, epikuräisch.
epidemic *a.* epidemisch; ~ *s.* Seuche *f.*
epigram *s.* Sinngedicht *n.*, Epigramm *n.*
epilepsy *s.* Fallsucht *f.* Epilepsie *f.*
epileptic *a.* fallsüchtig., epileptisch.
epilogue *s.* Nachwort *n.*, Epilog *m.*
Epiphany *s.* Dreikönigsfest *n.*
episcopal *a.* bischöflich.
episcopate *s.* Episkopat *n.*
episode *s.* Episode *f.*; Folge *f.*
epistle *s.* Brief *m.*; Epistel *f.*
epitaph *s.* Grabschrift *f.*
epithet *s.* Beiwort *n.*; Beiname *m.*
epitome *s.* Inbegriff *m.*
epitomize *v.t.* verkörpern.
epoch *s.* Epoche *f.*
equable *a.* ausgeglichen.
equal *a.*, **~ly** *adv.* gleich; gewachsen; ~ *v.i.* gleichen, gleichkommen.
equality *s.* Gleichheit *f.*
equalize *v.t.* gleichmachen.
equal opportunity *s.* Chancengleichheit *f.*
equals sign *s.* (*math.*) Gleichheitszeichen *n.*
equanimity *s.* Gleichmut *m.*
equate *v.t.* gleichsetzen.
equation *s.* Gleichung *f.*
equator *s.* Äquator *m.*
equatorial *a.* äquatorial.
equestrian *a* reitend; Reiter...
equidistant *a.* gleich weit entfernt.
equilateral *a.* (*geom.*) gleichseitig, gleichschenkelig (Dreieck).
equilibrium *s.* Gleichgewicht *n.*
equinox *s.* Tagundnachtgleiche *f.*
equip *v.t.* ausrüsten.
equipment *s.* Ausrüstung *f.*
equipoise *s.* Gleichgewicht *n.*
equitable *a.*, **~bly** *adv.* gerecht; billig.
equity *s.* Billigkeit, Unparteilichkeit *f.*
equivalent *a.*, **~ly** *adv.* gleichbedeutend; ~ *s.* Gegenwert *m.*, Äquivalent *n.*
equivocal *a.*, **~ly** *adv.* zweideutig.
equivocate *v.i.* zweideutig reden; Ausflüchte gebrauchen.
equivocation *s.* Ausflucht *f.*
equivoque *s.* Zweideutigkeit *f.*
era *s.* Zeitrechnung *f.*; Ära, Zeit *f.*
eradicate *v.t.* ausrotten.
erase *v.t.* ausstreichen; ausradieren.
eraser *s.* Radiergummi *m.*; Tafelwischer *m.*
erasure *s.* Ausradierung *f.*
erect *v.t.* aufrichten; errichten; ~ *a.* aufrecht; erigiert.
erection *s.* Aufrichtung *f.*; Erhebung *f.*; Aufbau *m.*; Erektion *f.*
eremite *s.* Einsiedler *m.*
ermine *s.* Hermelin *n. & m.*
erode *v.t.* erodieren; auswaschen; zerfressen.
erosion *s.* Erosion *f.*, Zerfressung *f.*.
erotic *a.* erotisch.
erotically *adv.* erotisch.
err *v.i.* sich verirren; abweichen; irren.

errand *s.* Botengang *m.*
errand-boy *s.* Laufbursche *m.*
errant *a.* herumirrend (Ritter); umherziehend.
erratic *a.* irrend; erratisch.
erratum *s.* Druckfehler *m.*; Errata *pl.*
erroneous *a.*, **~ly** *adv.* irrig, irrtümlich.
error *s.* Irrtum, Fehler *m.*
erudite *a.*, **~ly** *adv.* gelehrt.
erudition *s.* Gelehrsamkeit *f.*
erupt *v.i.* ausbrechen.
eruption *s.* Ausbruch *m.*
escalate *v.i.* eskalieren.
escalation *s.* Eskalation *f.*
escalator *s.* Rolltreppe *f.*
escapade *s.* Eskapade *f.*, Seitensprung *m.*
escape *v.t. & i.* entrinnen, entlaufen; entweichen; vermeiden; ~ *s.* Entkommen *n.*; Ausflucht *f.*; ~ *of gas*, Ausströmen von Gas *n.*; *to have a narrow* ~, mit knapper Not davonkommen.
escapism *s.* Realitätsflucht *f.*
eschew *v.t.* meiden, scheuen.
escort *v.t.* geleiten, decken; ~ *s.* Bedeckung *f.*, Geleit *a.*, Begleit . . .; ~ *plane*, Begleitflugzeug *n.*
esophagus *s.* Speiseröhre *f.*
esoteric *a.* esoterisch, geheim.
especial *a.*, besonder; **~ly** *adv.* besonders.
espionage *s.* Spionage *f.*
espouse *v.t.* sich einer Sache annehmen.
essay *s.* Essay *m.*; Aufsatz *m.*
essence *s.* Wesen *n.*; Essenz *f.*
essential *a.*, **~ly** *adv.* wesentlich; ~ *s.* Hauptsache *f.*; wesentlicher Umstand *m.*
establish *v.t.* errichten, einsetzen; ansiedeln; bestätigen; festsetzen.
Established Church *s.* Staatskirche *f.*
establishment *s.* Einrichtung *f.*; Niederlassung *f.*; Anlage (von Fabriken, etc.) *f.*; (*mil.*) Mannschaftsbestand *m.* Establissement *n.*, Firma *f.*
estate *s.* Stand *m.*; Vermögen *n.*; Grundstück *n.*; Landgut *n.*; Nachlaß *m.*
esteem *v.t.* achten, schätzen; erachten; ~ *s.* Wertschätzung *f.*
estimable *a.* schätzbar, achtbar.
estimate *v.t.* schätzen; veranschlagen, berechnen; ~ *s.* Schätzung *f.*; Voranschlag *m.*; *rough* ~, ungefährer Überschlag *m.*; *budget estimates*, Haushaltsvoranschlag *m.*
estimation *s.* Schätzung *f.*; Achtung *f.*
Estonia *s.* Estland *n.*
Estonian *s.* Estländer(in) *m.*(*f.*); ~ *a.* estländisch.
estrange *v.t.* entfremden; entwenden.
estrangement *s.* Entfremdung *f.*
estuary *s.* Mündung *f.*; Seebucht *f.*
etch *v.t.* ätzen, radieren.
etching *s.* Radierung *f.*
eternal *a.*, **~ly** *adv.* ewig.
eternity *s.* Ewigkeit *f.*
ether *s.* Äther *m.*
ethereal *a.* ätherisch.
ethic *s.* Ethik *f.*
ethical *a.*, **~ly** *adv.* sittlich, ethisch.
ethics *s.pl.* Sittenlehre *f.*, Ethik *f.*
Ethiopia *s.* Äthiopien *n.*
Ethiopian *s.* Äthiopier(in) *m.*(*f.*); *a.* äthiopisch.
ethnic *a.* Volk. . . , ethnisch.
ethnography *s.* Völkerkunde *f.*; Ethnographie *f.*

ethyl *s.* Äthyl *n.*
etiquette *s.* (feine) Sitte, Etikette *f.*
etymology *s.* Etymologie *f.*
eucalyptus *s.* Eukalyptus *m.*
eugenics *s.pl.* Eugenik *f.*
eulogize *v.t.* loben.
eulogy *s.* Lobrede *f.*
eunuch *s.* Eunuch *m.*
euphemism *s.* Euphemismus *m.*
euphemistic *a.* euphemistisch.
euphonic *a.* wohlklingend.
euphony *s.* Wohlklang *m.*
euphoria *s.* Euphorie *f.*
euphoristic *a.* euphoristisch.
Europa *s.* Europa *n.*
European *s.* Europäen(in) *m.*(*f.*); ~*a.* europäisch.
European Community *s.* Europäische Gemeinschaft.
euthanasia *s.* Euthanasie *f.*
evacuate *v.t.* (*mil.*) räumen, evakuieren.
evacuation *s.* Räumung *f.*; Evakuierung *f.*
evade *v.t. & i.* ausweichen; umgehen; ~*taxes*, Steuern hinterziehen.
evaluate *v.t.* zahlenmäßig berechnen.
evaluation *s.* Evaluierung *f.*
evanescent *a.* verschwindend.
evangelical *a.* evangelisch.
evangelize *v.t.* evangelisieren.
evaporate *v.i.* verdunsten, verdampfen; ~ *v.t.* verdampfen; *evaporated milk*, Trockenmilch *f.*
evasion *s.* Umgehung *f.* (eines Gesetzes); (Steuer) Hinterziehung *f.*
evasive *s.* ausweichend.
eve *s.* Abend *m.*; Vorabend *m.*
even *a.*, **~ly** *adv.* eben, glatt; gerade; unparteiisch; quitt; ~ *adv.* sogar; *not* ~, nicht einmal; ~ *now*, jetzt; ~ *though*, selbst wenn.; ~ *v.t.* gleichmachen, ebnen.
even-handed *a.* unparteiisch.
evening *s.* Abend *m.*; **~-dress**, Abendkleidung *f.*
even-numbered *a.* gerade (Zahl).
evensong *s.* Abendgottesdienst *m.*
event *s.* Begebenheit *f.*; Vorfall *m.*; *at all* ~*s*, auf alle Fälle.
even-tempered *a.* ausgeglichen.
eventful *a.* ereignisreich.
eventual *a.* etwaig; zufällig; **~ly** *adv.* schließlich.
eventuality *s.* Eventualität *f.*, Möglichkeit *f.*, Fall *m.*
ever *adv.* je, jemals; immer; noch so.
evergreen *a.* immergrünend; ~ *s.* Immergrün *n.*
everlasting *a.*, **~ly** *adv.* immerwährend.
evermore *adv.* auf ewig.
every *a.* jeder, jede, jedes; ~ *one*, jeder(mann), alle *pl.*; **~thing**, alles; **~where**, überall.
evict *v.t.* zur Räumung zwingen.
eviction *s.* Räumungszwang *m.*
evidence *s.* Zeugnis *n.*; Beweis *m.*; *to admit in* ~, als Beweis zulassen; *to give* ~, aussagen; *to produce* ~, Beweis antreten.
evident *a.*, **~ly** *adv.* augenscheinlich, klar, offensichtlich.
evil *a.*, **~ly** *adv.* übel, böse; ~ *s.* Übel, Verbrechen *n.*; Unglück *n.*
evil: **~-doer** Übeltäter(in) *m.*(*f.*); **~-minded** *a.* bösartig.
evince *v.t.* an den Tag legen; zeugen von.

evocation *s.* Hervorrufung *f.*

evocative *a.* evozierend; aufrüttelnd.

evoke *v.t.* hervorrufen; beschwören, evozieren.

evolution *s.* Entwicklung *f.*; Evolution *f.*

evolutionary *a.* evolutionär.

evolve *v.t.* entwickeln; ~ *v.i.* sich entwickeln.

ewe *s.* Mutterschaf *n.*

exacerbate *v.t.* erbittern, verschlimmern.

exact *a.*, **~ly** *adv.* genau, gewissenhaft; ~ *v.t.* fordern, erpressen.

exacting *a.* streng, genau.

exaction *s.* Eintreibung *f.*

exactitude, exactness *s.* Genauigkeit *f.*

exaggerate *v.t.* übertreiben.

exaggeration *s.* Übertreibung *f.*

exalt *v.t.* (lob)preisen.

exaltation *s.* Erhöhung, Erhebung *f.*; Überschwang *m.*

exalted *a.* hoch, erhaben; überschwenglich.

examination *s.* Prüfung *f.*, Examen *n.*; Untersuchung *f.*; (*law*) Verhör *n.*, Vernehmung *f.*; *to be under* ~, erwogen werden; **~-board**, Prüfungskommission *f.*; *final* ~, Schlußexamen *n.*; **~-papers** *pl.* Prüfungsaufgaben *f.pl.*; Klausurarbeit *f.*

examine *v.t.* prüfen; verhören.

examinee *s.* Examenskandidat(in) *m.*(*f.*)

examiner *s.* Untersucher, Examinator *m.*

example *s.* Beispiel, Muster *n.*; *for* ~, zum Beispiel.

exasperate *v.t.* verärgern, zur Verzweiflung bringen.

exasperating *a.* ärgerlich.

exasperation *s.* Ärger *m.*; Verzweiflung *f.*

excavate *v.t.* aushöhlen; ausgraben.

excavation *s.* Ausgrabung *f.*

excavator *s.* Bagger *m.*

exceed *v.t.* überschreiten, übertreffen.

exceeding *a.*, **~ly** *adv.* außerordentlich, überaus; *not* ~, nicht mehr als.

excel *v.t.* übertreffen; ~ *v.i.* hervorstechen, sich auszeichnen.

excellence *s.* Vortrefflichkeit, *f.*; hervorragende Qualität.

excellency *s.* Exzellenz *f.*

excellent *a.*, **~ly** *adv.* vortrefflich.

except *v.t.* ausnehmen; Einwendungen machen; ~ *pr.* ausgenommen, außer.

exception *s.* Ausnahme *f.*; Einwendung *f.*; *to admit of no* ~, keine Ausnahme zulassen; *to take* ~ *to*, sich stossen an.

exceptional *a.*, **~ly** *adv.* außergewöhnlich, ausnahmsweise.

excerpt *v.t.* exzerpieren; ~ *s.* Auszug *m.*

excess *s.* Übermaß *n.*; Ausschweifung *f.*; ~ **fare** *s.* Zuschlag *m.*; ~ **baggage** *s.* Mehrgepäck *n.*

excessive *a.*, **~ly** *adv.* übermäßig.

exchange *v.t.* wechseln, tauschen; ~ *s.* Tausch, Wechsel *m.*; Börse *f.*; **~-rate** *s.* Wechselkurs *m.*; *foreign* ~, Devisen *f.pl.*; *foreign* ~ *control*, Devisenzwangswirtschaft *f.*

exchequer *s.* Schatzkammer *f.*; Staatskasse *f.*; Schatzamt *n.*; *Chancellor of the* ~, (englischer) Schatzkanzler *m.*

excise *s.* Akzise *f.* (Verbrauch-) Steuer *f.*; ~ *v.t.* besteuern; herausschneiden.

excision *s.* (*med.*) Ausschneidung *f.*

excitable *a.* reizbar; erregbar.

excite *v.t.* erregen, anfeuern, reizen.

excited *a.* aufgeregt.

excitement *s.* Begeisterung *f.*; Aufregung *f.*

exciting *a.* aufregend; spannend.

exclaim *v.t.* ausrufen.

exclamation *s.* Ausruf *m.*; **~-mark**, **~-point** Ausrufungszeichen *n.*

exclamatory *a.*, ausrufend, Ausrufungs. . .

exclude *v.t.* ausschließen.

exclusion *s.* Ausschluß *m.*

exclusive *a.* ausschließlich.

excommunicate *v.t.* exkommunizieren.

excommunication *s.* Exkommunikation *f.*

excrement *s.* Auswurf, Kot *m.*, Exkremente *pl.*

excretion *s.* Absonderung *f.*

excruciating *a.* qualvoll.

exculpate *v.t.* entschuldigen.

excursion *s.* Ausflug *m.*

excursionist *s.* Tourist(in), Ausflügler(in) *m.*(*f.*)

excursive *a.* abschweifend.

excusable *a.* verzeihlich, entschuldbar.

excuse *v.t.* entschuldigen, verzeihen; *excused from appearing*, vom Erscheinen befreit; ~ *s.* Entschuldigung *f.*

execrable *a.*, **~ly** *adv.* abscheulich.

execrate *v.t.* verwünschen, verabscheuen.

execration *s.* Verwünschung *f.*

execute *v.t.* ausführen, vollziehen; vortragen, spielen (Musik, Theater); hinrichten; *to* ~ *a deed*, eine Urkunde ausfertigen.

execution *s.* Ausführung, Vollziehung *f.*; Vortrag *m.*, Vortragsweise *f.*; Pfändung *f.*; Hinrichtung *f.*; Verheerung *f.*

executioner *s.* Scharfrichter *m.*

executive *a.* vollziehend; ~ *committee*, Vorstand *m.*; ~ *regulation*, Ausführungsbestimmung *f.*; ~ *s.* vollziehende Gewalt *f.*; leitende Angestellte *m.*/*f.*

executor *s.* Testamentsvollstrecker *m.*

exemplary *a.*, **~ily** *adv.* vorbildlich.

exemplify *v.t.* durch Beispiele erläutern.

exempt *a.* frei, ausgenommen; ~ *v.t.* ausnehmen, verschonen.

exemption *s.* Befreiung *f.*

exercise *s.* Übung, Ausübung *f.*; Bewegung *f.*; ~ *v.t.* ausüben; ~ *v.i.* sich üben; exerzieren.

exercise-book *s.* Schreibheft *n.*, Schulheft *n.*

exert *v.t.* ausüben; geltend machen; sich anstrengen.

exertion *s.* Anstrengung, Bemühung *f.*

exhalation *s.* Ausatmen *n.*; Verströmen *n.*

exhale *v.t.* ausatmen, verströmen.

exhaust *v.t.* erschöpfen; auspumpen; ~ *s.* Auspuff *m.*

exhausted *a.* ermüdet, erschöpft.

exhausting *a.* ermüdend, anstrengend.

exhaustion *s.* Erschöpfung *f.*

exhaustive *a.* umfassend, erschöpfend.

exhaust-pipe *s.* Auspuffrohr *n.*

exhibit *v.t.* darstellen; aufweisen; ausstellen; ~ *s.* ausgestellter Gegenstand *m.*

exhibition *s.* Darstellung *f.*; Ausstellung *f.*

exhibitionist *s.* Exhibitionist(in) *m.*(*f.*)

exhibitor *s.* Aussteller(in) *m.*(*f.*)

exhilarate *v.t.* aufheitern.

exhilarating *a.* erheiternd.

exhort *v.t.* ermahnen.

exhortation s. Ermahnung f.
exhumation s. Wiederausgrabung f.
exhume v.t. wieder ausgraben.
exigence(cy) s. Erfordernis n.; Not f.
exigent a. auspruchsvoll, dringend.
exile s. Verbannung f.; Verbannte m./f.; ~ v.t. verbannen.
exist v.i. existieren.
existence s. Dasein n.
existent a. vorhanden.
existential a. existentiell.
existentialism s. Existentialismus m.
existing a. bestehend.
exit s. Ausgang m.; Abtreten n.; ~**permit**, Ausreiseerlaubnis f.; ~**visa** s. Ausreisevisum n.
exodus s. Auszug m.
ex officio a. & adv. von Amts wegen, amtlich.
exonerate v.t. entlasten; entbinden (Pflicht).
exorbitant a., ~**ly** adv. maßlos; überhöht.
exorcise v.t. (böse Geister) bannen.
exorcism s. Geisterbeschwörung f.
exorcist s. Exorzist.
exotic a. ausländisch, exotisch.
expand v.t. erweitern; ~ v.i. sich ausdehnen.
expanse s. weiter Raum m.; weite Fläche f.
expansible s. ausdehnbar.
expansion s. Ausdehnung, Vergrößerung f.
expansive a. ausgedehnt; mitteilsam, überschwänglich.
expatriate v.t. ausbürgern; ~a. ausgebürgert; ~s. Ausgebürgerte m./f.
expatriation s. Verbannung f.; Auswanderung f.; Ausbürgerung f.
expect v.t. erwarten; denken, vermuten.
expectance(cy) s. Erwartung; Anwartschaft f.; life expectancy, Lebenserwartung f.
expectant a. erwartend; ~ mother, werdende Mutter f.; ~ s. Anwärter m.
expectation s. Erwartung f.
expediency s. Zweckmäßigkeit f.
expedient a., ~**ly** adv. zweckmäßig; ~ s. Mittel n., Ausweg m.
expedite v.t. beschleunigen; abfertigen.
expedition s. Abfertigung f.; Feldzug m.; Forschungsreise f.
expeditionary a. zu einem Feldzuge gehörig.
expeditious a., ~**ly** adv. hurtig, förderlich.
expel v.t. vertreiben; verstoßen.
expend v.t. ausgeben; aufwenden.
expenditure s. Kosten pl.; Ausgabe f.; Aufwand m.; (mil.) Verbrauch (von Munition) m.
expense s. Ausgabe f.; Preis m.; Kosten pl.; to bear the ~s, die Kosten tragen.
expensive a., teuer, kostspielig.
experience s. Erfahrung f.; Erlebnis n.; ~ v.t. erfahren; erleben.
experienced a. erfahren.
experiment s. Versuch m.; ~ v.i. Versuche anstellen, experimentieren.
experimental a. experimentell, erfahrungsmäßig.
experimentation s. Experimentieren n.
expert a., ~**ly** adv. erfahren, kundig; ~ s. Sachverständige, Fachmann m.; ~'s opinion, ~ evidence, Gutachten n.
expertise s. Fachkenntnisse pl.; Können n.
expertly adv. meisterhaft; fachmännisch.

expiate v.t. sühnen.
expiation s. Sühnung f.
expiration s. Ablauf m.; Verfallzeit f.
expire v.i. ablaufen; fällig werden.
explain v.t. erklären, erläutern.
explanation s. Erklärung f.
explanatory a. erklärend.
expletive s. Fluch m.; Kraftausdruck m.
explicable a. erklärbar.
explicit a., ~**ly** adv. ausdrücklich.
explode v.t. sprengen; ~ v.i. platzen, ausbrechen.
exploit s. Heldentat f.; ~ v.t. ausbeuten; ausnutzen.
exploitation s. Ausbeutung f.; Ausnutzung f.
exploration s. Erforschung f.
exploratory a. Forschungs . . .; ~**talks** Sondierungsgespräche pl.
explore v.t. erforschen, untersuchen.
explorer s. Entdeckungsreisende m./f.; Forschungsreisende m./f.
explosion s. Explosion f., Ausbruch m.
explosive a. explosiv; ~ s. Sprengstoff m.
exponent s. Exponent(in) m.(f.); Vertreter(in) m.(f.)
export s. Ausfuhr f.; ~ control office, Ausfuhrstelle f.; ~**-trade**, Ausfuhrhandel m.; ~ v.t. ausführen.
exporter s. Exporteur m.
expose v.t. bloßstellen; entlarven; belichten.
exposed a. ungeschützt.
exposition s. Darstellung f.; Ausstellung f.
exposure s. Bloßstellung f.; (phot.) Belichtung f.
expound v.t. auslegen.
express v.t. ausdrücken; äußern; ~ a., ~**ly** adv. deutlich, ausdrücklich; ~ letter, Eilbrief m.; ~ train s. Schnellzug m.; to send ~, durch Eilboten schicken.
expression s. Ausdruck m.; Redensart f.
expressionism s. Expressionismus m.
expressive a., ~**ly** adv. ausdrucksvoll.
expropriate v.t. enteignen.
expropriation s. Enteignung f.
expulsion s. Vertreibung f.
expunge v.t. ausstreichen, tilgen.
expurgate v.t. reinigen, ausmerzen.
expurgation s. Reinigung f.
exquisite a., ~**ly** adv. auserlesen.
ex-service man s. ehemaliger Soldat m.
extant a. noch vorhanden.
extemporaneous, extemporary a., ~**ily** adv. unvorbereitet, aus dem Stegreif.
extempore adv. aus dem Stegreif.
extemporize v.t. improvisieren, aus dem Stegreif darbieten.
extend v.t. ausdehnen; erweisen; ~ v.i. sich erstrecken; extending table, Ausziehtisch m.
extension s. Ausdehnung f.; (tel.) Nebenanschluß m.; ~**cable**. Verlängerungsschnur f.
extensive a., ~**ly** adv. ausgedehnt.
extent s. Ausdehnung, Weite f.; Umfang m.; Grad m.
extenuate v.t. verdünnen; schwächen; beschönigen; ~ing circumstances s.pl. mildernde Umstände m.pl.
exterior a., ~**ly** adv. äußerlich; ~ s. Äußere n.
exterminate v.t. ausrotten.
extermination s. Ausrottung f.
exterminator s. Kammerjäger m.

external *a.*, **~ly** *adv.* äußerlich; ~ *s.* Äußere *n.*; *for* ~ *use only*, äußerlich! (von Medizinen).

extinct *a.* erloschen; ausgestorben.

extinction *s.* Aussterben *n.*

extinguish *v.t.* auslöschen; vertilgen.

extinguisher *s.* Feuerlöscher *m.*

extirpate *v.t.* ausrotten, vertilgen.

extol *v.t.* erheben, preisen.

extort *v.t.* entwinden; erpressen.

extortion *s.* Erpressung, Plackerei *f.*

extortionate *a.* erpressend.

extra *a.* Extra. . ., Sonder. . ., Neben. . .; *coffee will be* ~, Kaffee wird besonders berechnet; **~s** *s.pl.* Nebenkosten *pl.*; *no* **~s**, keine Kosten außerdem; **film-~** *s.* Filmstatist *m.*

extract *v.t.* ausziehen; ableiten; ~ *s.* Auszug *m.*; Extrakt *m.*

extraction *s.* Extraktion *f.*; Gewinnung *f.*; Herkunft *f.*

extradite *v.t.* ausliefern.

extradition *s.* Auslieferung (von Verbrechern) *f.*

extra-marital *a.* außerehelich.

extraneous *a.* von außen; belanglos; nicht zur Sache gehörig.

extraordinary *a.*, **~ily** *adv.* außerordentlich.

ex(tra)territorial *a.* exterritorial.

ex(tra)territoriality *s.* Exterritorialität *f.*

extravagance *s.* Verschwendung *f.*; Übertriebenheit *f.*; Extravaganz *f.*

extravagant *a.*, **~ly** *adv.* verschwenderisch; übermäßig hoch; extravagant.

extreme *a.*, **~ly** *adv.* äußerst, höchst; radikal; ~ *s.* Äußerste *n.*; höchster Grad *m.*

extremist *s.* Extremist(in) *m.(f.)*

extremity *s.* Äußerste *n.*; Unglück *n.*; **~ies** *pl.* Gliedmassen *pl.*

extricate *v.t.* herauswickeln.

extrinsic *a.*, **~ally** *adv.* äußerlich, von außen.

extrovert *a.* extrovertiert.

exuberance *s.* Überfülle *f.*; Überschwang *m.*

exuberant *a.*, **~ly** *adv.* üppig; überschwenglich.

exude *v.t.* ausschwitzen.

exult *v.i.* frohlocken.

exultant *a.* frohlockend.

exultation *s.* Frohlocken *n.*

eye *s.* Auge *n.*; (Nadel-) Öhr *n.*; Knospe *f.*; *eyes front!* (*mil*) Augen gerade aus!: *eyes right!* (*mil.*) Augen rechts!; ~ *v.t.* ansehen.

eyeball *s.* Augapfel *m.*

eyebrow *s.* Augenbraue *f.*; **~-pencil**, Augenbrauenstift *m.*

eye-glass *s.* Zwicker *m.*, Brille *f.*

eyelash *s.* Augenwimper *f.*

eyelid *s.* Augenlid *n.*

eye shadow *s.* Lidschatten *m.*

eyesight *s.* Sehkraft *f.*

eyesore *s.* häßlicher Anblick *m.*; Dorn im Auge *m.*; Schandfleck *m.*

eyewash *s.* Augenwasser *n.*; (*fig.*) Quatsch *m.*

eyewitness *s.* Augenzeuge *m.*, Augenzeugin *f.*

F

F, f der Buchstabe F oder f *n.*; (*mus.*) F, f; **F-sharp** Fis, fis.

fable *s.* Fabel *f.*; Märchen *n.*; ~ *v.i.* fabeln; ~ *v.t.* erdichten.

fabric *s.* Bau *m.*; Gewebe *n.*; Stoff *m.*

fabricate *v.t.* erbauen; verfertigen; fälschen; erdichten.

fabrication *s.* Erdichtung, Fälschung *f.*

fabulous *a.*, **~ly** *adv.* fabelhaft.

facade *s.* Fassade *f.*

face *s.* Gesicht *n.*; Vorderseite *f.*; Uhrblatt *n.*; Fläche, Oberfläche *f.*; *in the* ~ *of*, angesichts; ~ *v.t.* ansehen; gegenüber liegen od. stehen; Trotz bieten; einfassen; (*arch.*) verkleiden; (*mech.*) glätten.

faceless *a.* anonym.

facelift *s.* Facelifting *n.*

facet *s.* geschliffene Ecke *f.*, Facette *f.*

facetious *a.*, **~ly** *adv.* drollig, scherzhaft, witzig.

facial *a.* Gesichts . . .; Gesichtsmassage *f.*

facile *a.* leicht; gefällig, banal.

facilitate *v.t.* erleichtern.

facility *s.* Leichtigkeit *f.*; Erleichterung *f.*; **facilities** *s.pl.* Anlagen, Einrichtungen *f.pl.*

facing *adv.* gegenüber; (Fenster) hinaus liegend; ~ *s.* Vorderseite *f.*; Aufschlag *m.*; Einfassung *f.* (Kleid).

facsimile *s.* genaue Nachbildung *f.*

fact *s.* Tatsache *f.*

faction *s.* Splittergruppe *f.*

factitious *a.* künstlich, gekünstelt.

factor *s.* Faktor *m.*

factory *s.* Fabrik *f.*; Faktorei *f.*; **~-guard**, Werkschutz *m.*; **~-hand**, Fabrikarbeiter *m.*

factual *a.* sachlich.

faculty *s.* Fähigkeit *f.*; Fakultät *f.*

fad *s.* Modeerscheinung *f.*; Marotte *f.*

fade *v.i.* verwelken; verschießen; vergehen; (*radio*) schwinden.; ~ **in** einblenden; ~ **out** ausblenden.

fag-end *s.* letztes (schlechtes) Ende *n.*

fagot, faggot *s.* Reisigbündel *n.*; ~ *v.t.* zusammenbinden.

Fahrenheit *a.* Fahrenheit.

fail *v.i.* fehlen, mangeln; versiegen; fehlschlagen; durchfallen; Bankrott machen; ~ *v.t.* verlassen, unterlassen; ~ *s.* Mangel *m.*

failed *a.* nicht bestanden; gescheitert.

failing *s.* Mangel, Fehler *m.*; ~ *pr.* in Ermangelung von.

failure *s.* Versäumnis *n.* Mangel *m.*; Mißerfolg, Fehlschlag *m.*; Bankrott *m.*; ~ *to do a thing*, Unterlassung etwas zu tun.

faint *v.i.* vergehen; in Ohnmacht fallen; ~ *a.*, **~ly** *adv.* schwach.

faintness *s.* Undeutlichkeit; Mattheit *f.*

fair *a.*, **~ly** *adv.* hübsch; rein; hell: günstig; ehrlich, aufrichtig; blond; billig; ~ **play** *s.* ehrliche Spiel *n.*; anständige Handeln *n.*; ~ *adv.* mäßig, gefällig, höflich; ~ *s.* (Handels) Messe *f.*; Jahrmarkt *m.*

fairly *adv.* ziemlich, leidlich; gehörig.

fairness *s.* Gerechtigkeit *f.*; Ehrlichkeit *f.*; Billigkeit *f.*

fairy *s.* Fee *f.*; Zauberin *f.*

fairy tale *s.* Märchen *n.*

faith s. Glaube m.; Treue f.; breach of ~, Treubruch m.; in good ~, in gutem Glauben, gutgläubig.
faithful a., ~ly adv. gläubig, treu; ehrlich; yours ~ly, hochachtungsvoll.
faith healing s. Gesundbeten n.
faithless a. ungläubig; treulos.
fake v.t. Betrug, Schwindel m.; ~ v.t. betrügen.
falcon s. Falke m.
falconer s. Falkner m.
fall v.i.st. fallen; sich ereignen; geraten; to ~ into, münden in (Fluß); to ~ off, abfallen; vergehen; to ~ out with, sich verkrachen mit; to ~ short of, zurückbleiben hinter; ~ s. Fall m.; Abnahme f.; Senkung f.; Herbst m.; Wasserfall m.
fallacious a., ~ly adv. irrig.
fallacy s. Täuschung f.; Betrug m.; Trugschluß m.
fallible a., ~bly adv. fehlbar.
fall-out s. Fallout m., radioaktiver Niederschlag m.
fallow a. falb; brach; ~ deer, Damwild n.; ~ s. Brache f.; ~ v.t. brachen.
false a., ~ly adv. falsch, unecht; ~ alarm, blinder Alarm m.; ~ key, Nachschlüssel m.
falsehood s. Unwahrheit f.; Falschheit f.
falseness s. Falschheit f.; Treulosigkeit f.
falsetto s. Fistelstimme f.
falsification s. Verfälschung f.
falsify v.t. verfälschen; verdrehen.
falsity s. Falschheit f.
falter v.i. straucheln; stammeln.
fame s. Ruhm, Ruf m.
familiar a., ~ly adv. vertraulich; vertraut; ~ s. Vertraute m. & f.
familiarity s. Vertrautheit f., Vertraulichkeit f.
familiarize v.t. vertraut machen.
family s. Familie f.; Gattung f.
family allowance s. Kindergeld n.
family doctor s. Hausarzt m.
family planning s. Familienplanung f.
family tree s. Stammbaum m.
famine s. Hungersnot f.
famished a. (fam.) verhungert.
famous a., ~ly adv. berühmt.
fan s. Fächer m.; Ventilator m.; Fan m.; ~ v.t. fächeln; anfachen.
fanatic(al) a., ~ally adv. eifervoll; ~ s. Fanatiker(in) m.(f.)
fanaticism s. Fanatismus m.
fan belt s. Keilriemen m.
fancier 's. Liebhaber(in), Züchter(in) (von Vögeln, Pflanzen, etc.) m.(f.)
fanciful a., ~ly adv. phantastisch.
fancy s. Einbildung, Phantasie f.; Vorliebe f.; (fig.) Grille f.; ~ v.i. sich einbilden; ~ v.t. Gefallen finden an; lieb haben; a. phantastisch; kunstvoll; elegant.
fancy-dress s. Maskenanzug m.; ~ ball, Maskenball, Kostümball m.
fancy-goods s.pl. Modeartikel m.pl.
fancy-price s. Liebhaberpreis m.
fanfare s. Fanfare f.
fang s. Fangzahn, Hauer m.; Klaue f.
fantasia s. (mus.) Fantasie f.
fantastic(al) a., ~ally adv. fantastisch.
fantasy s. Phantasie f.
far adv. weit, fern; ~ a. fern, entfernt; by ~, bei weitem.
far away a. entlegen; fern.

farce s. Posse f.; Farce f.
farcical a., possenhaft. (fig.) absurd.
fare s. Fahrt, Reise f.; Fuhre f.; Kost f.; Fahrgast m.; Fahrpreis m., Fahrgeld n.; at half-fares, zum halben Fahrpreis.
Far East s. the ~ der Ferne Osten.
Far Eastern a. fernöstlich.
farewell adv. lebe wohl; ~ s. Lebewohl n., Abschied m.
far fetched a. weit hergeholt.
far-flung a. weit ausgedehnt; weit entfernt.
farm s. Bauernhof m.; Landgut n.; ~-yard, Hof m; ~-manager, landwirtschaftlicher Betriebsleiter m.; ~ v.t. (ver)pachten.
farmer s. Landwirt(in) m.(f.); Bauer m., Bäuerin f.
farm-land s. Landarbeiter(in) m.(f.)
farmhouse s. Bauernhaus n.
farming s. Landwirtschaft f.
farmstead s. Gehöft n.
far-off a. weit entfernt.
far-reaching a. weitreichend.
far-seeing a. weitblickend.
far-sighted a. weitsichtig; weitblickend.
fart s. (vulg.) Furz m.; ~ v.i. furzen.
farther a. & adv. weiter, ferner.
farthest a. & adv. am weitesten.
Far West s. the ~ der Westen der USA.
fascinate v.t. bezaubern; faszinieren.
fascinated a. fasziniert.
fascinating a. faszinierend; bezaubernd.
fascination s. Zauber, Reiz m.
Fascism s. Faschismus m.
Fascist s. Faschist m.
fashion s. Form, Gestalt f.; Mode f.: ~ v.t. gestalten.
fashionable a., ~bly adv. elegant, modisch; modern.
fashion show s. Modeschau f.
fast v.i. fasten: ~ s. Fasten n.; Fasttag m.; ~ a. & adv. fest; stark, sehr; geschwind; flott, leichtlebig; the clock is ~, die Uhr geht vor.
fasten v.t. befestigen; verbinden.
fastener s. Verschluß m., Zwecke f.
fast-food restaurant s. Schnellimbiß m.
fastidious a., ~ly adv. wählerisch; pingelig; heikel.
fastness s. Festigkeit, Stärke f.; Festung f.
fast-train s. Schnellzug m.
fat a. fett, dick; ~ s. Fett m.
fatal a., ~ly adv. verhängnisvoll; tödlich.
fatalism s. Fatalismus m.
fatalist s. Fatalist(in) m.(f.)
fatalistic a. fatalistisch.
fatality s. Verhängnis n.; (tödlicher) Unglücksfall m.
fate s. Schicksal n., Verhängnis n.
fateful a. verhängnisvoll; entscheidend.
father s. Vater m.; Stammvater m.
Father Christmas s. Weihnachtsmann m.
fatherhood s. Vaterschaft f.
father-in-law s. Schwiegervater m.
fatherland s. Vaterland n.
fatherless a. vaterlos.
fatherly a. väterlich.
fathom s. Faden m.; Klafter f.; ~ v.t. umklaftern; ergründen.
fathomless a. unergründlich.
fatigue s. Müdigkeit, Mühseligkeit f.; ~ v.t.

ermüden.

fatness *s.* Fettigkeit *f.*; Fett *n.*

fatten *v.t.* mästen; ~ *v.i.* fett werden.

fattening *a.* dick machend.

fatty *a.* fettig, ölig; Fett . . .; ~ **acid** *s.* Fettsäure *f.*

fatuity *s.* Albernheit *f.*

fatuous *a.* albern.

faucet *s.* Wasserhahn *m.*

fault *s.* Fehler, Mangel *m.*; *to find* ~ *with*, etwas auszusetzen finden an . . ., tadeln.

fault finder *s.* Nörgler(in) *m.*(*f.*)

faultless *a.* fehlerfrei.

faulty *a.*, ~**ily** *adv.* fehlerhaft.

fauna *s.* Fauna *f.*

favor *s.* Gunst, Gewogenheit *f.*; Gefallen; *in* ~ *of*, zu Gunsten; *to do a person a* ~, einem einen Gefallen erweisen; ~**s** *pl.* Gunstbezeigungen *f.pl.*; ~ *v.t.* begünstigen, beehren.

favorable *a.*, ~**bly** *adv.* günstig.

favorite *s.* Günstling *m.*; ~ *a.* Lieblings. . .

favoritism *s.* Günstlingswirtschaft *f.*

fawn *s.* Rehkitz *n.*; Rehfarbe *f.*; ~ *a.* hellbraun; ~ *v.i.* kriechend schmeicheln.

fax *s.* (Tele)Fax *n.*; ~ *v.t.* faxen.

fax machine *s.* Faxgerät *n.*

fear *s.* Furcht *f.* Scheu *f.*; ~ *v.t. & i.* fürchten; sich fürchten.

fearful *a.*, ~**ly** *adv.* furchtsam.

fearless *a.*, ~**ly** *adv.* furchtlos.

fearsome *a.* furchterregend.

feasibility *s.* Ausführbarkeit *f.* Machbarkeit *f.*

feasible *a.*, ~**bly** *adv.* machbar; möglich.

feast *s.* Fest *n.*; Schmauserei *f.*; ~ *v.i.* schmausen; ~ *v.t.* bewirten.

feat *s.* Meisterleistung *f.*; Meisterwerk *n.*

feather *s.* Feder *f.*; ~ *v.t.* mit Federn schmücken/polstern.

feather: ~ **bed** *s.* mit Federn gefüllte Matratze; ~ **duster** *s.* Federwisch *m.*; ~**weight** *s.* Federgewicht *n.*

feathery *a.* gefiedert; locker.

feature *s.* Gesichtszug *m.*; Merkmal *n.*; ~ *v.t.* (*film*) darstellen.

featureless *a.* eintönig.

febrile *a.* fieberhaft.

February *s.* Februar *m.*

feces *s.pl.* Fäkalien *pl.*

fecundate *v.t.* befruchten.

fecundity *s.* Fruchtbarkeit *f.*

federal *a.* bundesmäßig; Bundes. . .

federalism *s.* Föderalismus *m.*

federate *a.* verbündet.

federation *s.* Bund *m.*

fee *s.* Lohn *m.*, Honorar *n.*; Gebühr *f.*; Lehen *n.*; *to charge a* ~ *for*, ein Honorar berechnen, eine Gebühr erheben; ~ *v.t.* bezahlen, besolden.

feeble *a.*, ~**bly** *adv.* schwach; ~ **minded** *a.* geistesschwach.

feebleness *s.* Schwäche *f.*

feed *v.t.ir.* füttern; widen; ~ *v.i.* essen; (*mech.*) Material zuführen, vorschieben; sich nähren; ~ *s.* Futter *n.*; Nahrung *f.*; (*mech.*) Vorschub *m.*

feedback *s.* Feedback *n.*; Rückkoppelung *f.*

feeder *s.* Zufluß *m.*

feeding-bottle *s.* Saugflasche *f.*

feeding-stuffs *pl.* Futtermittel *n.pl.*

feel *v.t. & i.ir.* (sich) fühlen, befühlen, empfinden; ~ *s.* Gefühl *n.*

feeler *s.* Fühler *m.*, Fühlhorn *n.*

feeling *p. & a.*, ~**ly** *adv.* fühlend, gefühlvoll; ~ *s.* Gefühl *n.*

feet *s.pl.* (von *foot*) Füsse *m.pl.*

feign *v.t. & i.* erdichten; heucheln, vorgeben.

feint *s.* Verstellung, Finte *f.*; (*mil.*) Scheinangriff *m.*

felicitate *v.t.* beglückwünschen.

felicitous *a.* glücklich.

felicity *s.* Glückseligkeit *f.*; Glück *n.*

feline *a.* katzenartig; ~*s.* Katze *f.*

fell *a.* (*poet.*) grausam; ~ *s.* Fell *n.*; Haut *f.*; ~ *v.t.* fällen, hinstrecken.

felloe *s.* Felge *f.*

fellow *s.* Genosse *m.*; Mitglied *n.*; Bursche *m.*; (in Zusammensetzungen) Mit. . .

fellow-being *s.* Mitmensch *m.*

fellow-citizen *s.* Mitbürger *m.*

fellow-countryman *s.* Landsmann *m.*

fellow-creature *s.* Mitmensch *m.*

fellow-feeling *s.* Mitgefühl *n.*; Zusammengehörigkeitsgefühl *n.*

fellowship *s.* Gemeinschaft, Genossenschaft *f.*; Stipendium *n.*

fellow-traveller *s.* Mitreisende *m.*/*f.*

felon *s.* Verbrecher *m.*

felonious *a.* verbrecherisch; treulos.

felony *s.* schweres Verbrechen *n.*.

felspar *s.* Feldspat *m.*

felt *s.* Filz *m.*; ~ *v.t.* filzen.

female *a.* weiblich; ~ *s.* weibliche Person *f.*; Weibchen *n.* (von Tieren).

feminine *a.* weiblich; feminin ~ *s.* (*gram.*) Femininum *n.*

feminism *s.* Feminismus *m.*

feminist *s.* Feministin *f.*; Feminist *m.*; *a.* feministisch.

femur *s.* Oberschenkelknochen *m.*

fen *s.* Sumpf *m.*, Moor *n.*

fence *s.* Zaun *m.*; Schutzwehr *f.*; ~ *v.t.* einhegen; verteidigen; ~ *v.i.* fechten; abwehren.

fencer *s.* Fechter(in) *m.*(*f.*)

fencing *s.* Einhegung *f.*; Fechtkunst *f.*

fend *v.t.* abwehren; parieren.

fender *s.* Kaminschutz *m.*; Kotflügel *m.*

fennel *s.* Fenchel *m.*

ferment *v.i.* gären; ~ *s.* Gärungsmittel *n.*

fermentation *s.* Gärung *f.*

fern *s.* Farnkraut *n.*

ferocious *a.*, ~**ly** *adv.* wild, grimmig.

ferocity *s.* Wildheit, Grausamkeit *f.*

ferret *s.* Frettchen *n.*; ~ *v.t.* durchsuchen; herumstöbern.

ferrous *a.* Eisen. . .

ferry *s.* Fähre *f.*; ~ *v.t.* übersetzen.

ferryman *s.* Fährmann *m.*

fertile *a.*, ~**ly** *adv.* fruchtbar.

fertility *s.* Fruchtbarkeit *f.*

fertilization *s.* Befruchtung *f.*

fertilize *v.t.* befruchten.

fertilizer *s.* Dünger *m.*

fervency *s.* Inbrunst *f.*; Eifer *m.*

fervent *a.*, ~**ly** *adv.* heiß, inbrünstig.

fervid *a.* heiß, glühend; eifrig.

fervor *s.* Leidenschaft *f.*; Inbrunst *f.*

festal, festive *a.* festlich.
fester *v.i.* eitern.
festival *s.* Fest *n.*; Festival *n.*
festive *a.* festlich.
festivity *s.* Festlichkeit *f.*
festoon *s.* Girlande *f.*; ~ *v.t.* schmücken.
fetal *a.* fötal; fetal.
fetch *v.t.* holen, beibringen.
fetching *a.* einnehmend, gewinnend.
fetid *a.* stinkend.
fetish *s.* Fetisch *m.*
fetishism *s.* Fetischismus *m.*
fetishist *s.* Fetischist(in) *m.*(*f.*)
fetter *v.t.* fesseln; ~ *s.* Fessel *f.*
fetus *s.* Fötus *m.*, Fetus *m.*
feud *s.* Fehde *f.*; Lehen *n.*
feudal *a.* feudal, Feudal. . .; Lehns. . .
feudalism *s.* Lehnswesen *n.*
fever *s.* Fieber *n.*
feverish *a.* fieberhaft.
few *a.* wenig *pl.* wenige; *a* ~, einige.
fiancé *s.* Verlobte, Bräutigam *m.*
fiancée *s.* Verlobte. Braut *f.*
fib *s.* kleine Lüge, Schwindelei *f.*; ~ *v.i.* flunkern.
fibber *s.* Flunkerer *m.*; Schwindler(in) *m.*(*f.*)
fiber *s.* Faser *f.*
fiberboard *s.* Faserbrett *n.*
fibrous *a.* faserig.
fickle *a.* veränderlich, unbeständig.
fiction *s.* Erdichtung *f.*; Romandichtung *f.*, Unterhaltungsliteratur.
fictional *a.* fiktional, erfunden.
fictitious *a.*, ~**ly** *adv.* erdichtet; ~ *transaction*, Scheingeschäft *n.*
fiddle *s.* Geige, Fiedel *f.*; ~ *v.i.* geigen.
fiddler *s.* Geiger(in) *m.*(*f.*)
fiddlestick *s.* Fiedelbogen *m.*; ~**s!** *i.* Unsinn! Larifari!
fiddlestring *s.* Violinsaite *f.*
fiddling *a.* belanglos.
fiddly *a.* knifflig; umständlich.
fidelity *s.* Treue *f.*; Klangtreue *f.*; Bildtreue *f.*
fidget *v.i.* sich ruhelos bewegen, zappeln; ~ *s.* nervöse Unruhe *f.*
fidgety *a.* unruhig, nervös.
fiduciary *a.* Vertrauens . . .; ~ *issue*, ungedeckte Notenausgabe *f.*; ~ *s.* Treuhänder *m.*
fie *i.* pfui!
fief *s.* Lehen *n.*
field *s.* Feld *n.*; Schlachtfeld *n.*; Arbeitsgebiet *n.*; ~**-glass**, Feldstecher *m.*; ~**-marshal** *s.* Feldmarshall *m.*; ~**-kitchen** *s.* Feldküche *f.*; ~**-officer**, Stabsoffizier *m.*; ~**-post** *s.* Fieldpost *f.*
fiend *s.* Teufel *m.*; Unhold *m.*
fiendish *a.* teuflisch, ummenschlich.
fierce *a.*, ~**ly** *adv.* wild, grimmig.
fiery *a.* feurig; jähzornig.
fife *s.* Querpfeife *f.*
fifteen *a.* fünfzehn.
fifth column *s.* fünfte Kolonne *f.*
fiftieth *a.* fünfzigst. . .
fifty *a.* fünfzig.
fig *s.* Feige *f.*
fight *v.t. & i.st.* kämpfen, streiten; ~ *s.* Gefecht *n.*; Kampf *m.*
fighter *s.* Jagdflugzeug *n.*; Kämpfer(in) *m.*(*f.*)

fighting *a.* Kampf . . .; ~*s.* Kämpfe *pl. m.*
figment *s.* Erdichtung *f.*; ~ *of the imagination*, reine Einbildung *f.*
figurative *a.*, ~**ly** *adv.* bildlich.
figure *s.* Gestalt *f.*; Ziffer *f.*; Zahl, Summe *f.*; ~**-head** Gallionsbild *n.*; (*fig.*) Strohpuppe *f.*; ~ *of speech*, Redewendung *f.*; ~ *v.i.* bilden, formen; vorstellen; ~ *v.i.* eine Rolle spielen, auftreten.
figured *a.* gemustert.
figure-skating *s.* Eiskunstlauf *m.*
figurine *s.* kleine Figur *f.*
Fiji Islands *pl.* Fidschi Inseln *pl.*
filament *s.* Faser *f.*; Faden (*m.*) der Glühlampe.
filch *a.* mausen.
file *s.* Liste *f.*; Reihe *f.*, (*mil.*) Rotte *f.*; Briefordner *m.*; Feile *f.*; Akt *m.*, Aktenbündel *n.*; *single* ~, Gänsemarsch *m.*; ~ *v.t.* aufreihen; einordnen; feilen; *to* ~ *a petition*, ein Gesuch einreichen.
file card *s.* Karteikarte *f.*
filial *a.*, ~**ly** *adv.* kindlich.
filibuster *s.* Verschleppungstaktik *f.*; Filibuster *n.*; ~*v.t.* Dauerreden halten.
filigree *s.* Filigranarbeit *f.*
filing-cabinet *s.* Aktenschrank *m.*
filings *s.pl.* Feilspäne *m.pl.*
fill *v.t.* füllen; einschenken; stopfen; *to* ~ *out, to* ~ *up*, ausfüllen (Formular); ~ *s.* Fülle, Genüge *f.*
filler *s.* Füllmaterial *n.*
fillet *s.* Lendenbraten *m.*, Filet *n.*
filling *s.* Füllung *f.*; Plombe *f.*
fillip *s.* Anreiz *m.*
filly *s.* Stutenfohlen *n.*
film *s.* Häutchen *n.* (*phot.*) Film, *m.*; ~ *v.t. & i.* (ver) filmen.
filter *v.t.* Filter *m & n.*; ~ *v.t.* filtern.
filth *s.* Schmutz, Kot *m.*
filthy *a.*, ~**ily** *adv.* kotig; unflätig.
filtrate *v.t. & i.* filtrieren.
fin *s.* Flosse *f.*
final *a.*, ~**ly** *adv.* endlich; endgültig; ~ *s.* (*Sport*) Schlußrunde *f.*; Endspiel *n.*
finale *s.* Finale *n.*
finalist *s.* Finalist(in) *m.*(*f.*)
finalize *v.t.* vollenden, abschließen.
finance *s.* Finanzwesen *n.*; ~ *v.t.* finanzieren; ~ *s.pl.* Finanzen *pl.*
financial *a.* finanziell; ~ *year*, Hautshaltsjahr *n.*
financier *s.* Finanzmann *m.*
finch *s.* Fink *m.*
find *v.t. & i.st.* finden, antreffen; bemerken; *to* ~ *out*, herausfinden, ausfindig machen; *the jury found him guilty*, die Geschworenen sprachen ihn schuldig; ~ *s.* Fund *m.*
finder *s.* Finder(in) *m.*(*f.*)
finding *s.* Befund *m.*, Ergebnis *n.*
fine *a.*, ~**ly** *adv.* fein, schön; zart; kostbar; schlau; ~ *s.* Geldbusse *f.*; ~ *v.t.* klären; eine Geldstrafe auflegen.
fine arts *pl.* schöne Künste *f.pl.*
finery *s.* Staat, Putz *m.*
finesse *s.* Feinheit *f.*
finger *s.* Finger *m.*; ~ *v.t.* betasten.
finger-bowl *s.* Fingerschale *f.*
finger-end *s.* Fingerspitze *f.*
fingering *s.* (*mus.*) Fingersatz *m.*
finger-mark *s.* Fingerabdruck *m.*

finger-nail *s.* Fingernagel *m.*
finger-print *s.* Fingerabdruck *m.*
fingertip *s.* Fingerspitze *f.*; *to have a thing at one's ~s,* etwas am Schnürchen haben.
finicking, finicky *a.* zimperlich, geziert; heikel.
finish *v.t.* endigen, vollenden; ~ *s.* letze Hand; Schluß *m.*; Appretur *f.*
finished goods *pl.* Fertigwaren *f.pl.*
finite *a.*, ~**ly** *adv.* begrenzt; endlich.
Finland *s.* Finnland *n.*
Finn *s.* Finne *m.*; Finnin *f.*
Finnish *a.* finnisch.
fiord *s.* Fjord *m.*
fir *s.* Tanne, Kiefer *f.*
fir-cone *s.* Tannenzapfen *m.*
fire *s.* Feuer *n.*; Feuersbrunst *f.*; (*fig.*) Leidenschaft *f.*; *to set on ~,* anzünden; ~ *v.t.* anzünden; anfeuern; abfeuern; (*fam.*) entlassen, herauswerfen: ~ *v.i.* Feuer fangen; schießen.
fire-alarm *s.* Feuermelder *m.*
fire-arms *s.pl.* Feuerwaffen *f.pl.*
fire-brand *s.* Feuerbrand *m.*; Aufwiegler *m.*
fire-brick *s.* feuerfester Ziegel *m.*
fire-department *s.* Feuerwehr *f.*
fire-eater *s.* Feuerschlucker *m.*
fire-engine *s.* Löschfahrzeng *n.*
fire-escape *s.* Rettungsleiter *f.*
fire-extinguisher *s.* Feuerlöscher *m.*
fire-fighting *s.* Feuerbekämpfung *f.*
firefly *s.* Leuchtkäfer *m.*
fire-guard *s.* Feuergitter (Kamin) *n.*
fire-insurance *s.* Feuerversicherung *f.*
fireman *s.* Feuerwehrmann *m.*
fire-place *s.* Kamin, Herd *m.*
fire-power *s.* (*mil.*) Feuerkraft *f.*
fire-proof *a.* feuerfest.
fireside *s.* Herd, Kamin *m.*
fire-station *s.* Feuerwache *f.*
fire-wood *s.* Brennholz *n.*
fire-works *s.pl.* Feuerwerk *n.*
firing *s.* Brennen *n.* (Ton); Abfeuern *s.*
firing-range *s.* (*mil.*) Schussweite *f.*; Schiesstand *m.*
firm *a.*, ~**ly** *adv.* fest, derb; entschlossen; ~ *s.* Firma *f.*
firmament *s.* Himmelsgewölbe *n.*
firmness *s.* Festigkeit *f.*
first *a. & adv.* ~**ly** *adv.* der, die, das erste; erstens; *at ~,* anfänglich, zuerst, zunächst; ~ *of all,* vor allen Dingen; ~ *come,* ~ *served,* wer zuerst kommt, mahlt zuerst.
first aid *s.* Erste Hilfe *f.*
first-rate *a.* erstklassig, vorzüglich.
fiscal *a.* fiskalisch; ~ *year,* Haushaltsjahr *n.*
fish *s.* Fisch *m.*; ~*v.t.* fischen.
fish-bone *s.* Fischgräte *f.*
fisher *s.* Fischer *m.*
fisherman *s.* Fischer *m.*
fishery *s.* Fischfang *m.*, Fischerei *f.*
fishing-boat *s.* Fischerboot *n.*
fishing-hook *s.* Fischangel *f.*
fishing-line *s.* Angelschnur *f.*
fishing-rod *s.* Angelrute *f.*
fishing-tackle *s.* Angelgerät *n.*
fishmonger *s.* Fischhändler *m.*
fishy *a.* fischartig; verdächtig.
fission *s.* Spaltung (Zelle, Atomkern) *f.*

fissure *s.* Spalte *f.*; Riß *m.*; ~ *v.t.* spalten.
fist *s.* Faust *f.*
fistful *s.* Handvoll *f.*
fistula *s.* Fistel *f.*
fit *s.* Anwandlung *f.*; Anfall *m.*; ~ *a.*, ~**ly** *adv.* passend; bequem; tauglich; in guter Form; ~ *v.t.* anpassen, versehen; zurechtmachen; ~ *up,* montieren; ~ *v.i.* sich schicken.
fitful *a.* launisch.
fitness *s.* Tauglichkeit; Schicklichkeit *f.*
fitted *a.* geeignet, passend.
fitter *s.* Monteur *m.*
fitting *a.*, ~**ly** *adv.* schicklich, passend; ~ *s.pl.* Zubehörteile *f.pl.*; Einrichtung *f.*; ~ *s.* Anprobe *f.* (beim Schneider).
five *a.* fünf.
fix *v.t.* befestigen, anbringen; festsetzen; bestimmen; in Ordnung bringen; (*phot.*) fixieren; ~ *v.i.* festwerden; ~ *s.* Verlegenheit, Klemme *f.*
fixation *s.* Fixierung *f.*; Festsetzung, Befestigung *f.*
fixed *p. & a.*, ~**ly** *adv.* festgesetzt, unverwandt; (*mil.*) ortsfest.
fixing solution *s.* (*phot.*) Fixierbad *n.*
fixture *s.* eingebautes Teil *n.*
fizz *v.i.* sprudeln; ~ *s.* Sprudeln *n.*
fizzle *v.i.* aischen, sprühen.
fizzy *a.* sprudelnd.
flabbergast *v.t.* völlig verblüffen.
flabby *a.* schlaff, welk.
flaccid *a.* schlapp, schlaff.
flag *s.* Fahne, Flagge *f.*; ~ *v.i.* erschlaffen.
flagellate *v.t.* geisseln.
flagon *s.* (Deckel-)Kanne *f.*; Flasche *f.*
flag-pole *s.* Flaggenmast *m.*
flagrant *a.*, ~**ly** *adv.* offenkundig; berüchtigt; abscheulich.
flag-ship *s.* Flaggschiff *n.*
flag-staff *s.* Flaggenstange *f.*
flail *s.* Dreschflegel *m.*
flair *s.* Gespür *n.*
flake *s.* Flocke *f.*; ~ *v.i.* sich flocken; abblättern.
flaky *a.* blättrig, bröckelig.
flamboyance *s.* Extravaganz *f.*; Grellheit *f.*
flamboyant *a.* extravagant; grell.
flame *s.* Flamme *f.*; ~ *v.i.* flammen.
flamethrower *s.* (*mil.*) Flammenwerfer *m.*
flaming *a.* feuerrot; flammend; leidenschaftlich.
flan *s.* Torte *f.*, Törtchen *n.*
flange *s.* Flansch *m.*
flank *s.* Seite, Weiche *f.*; Flanke *f.*; ~ *v.t.* in die Flanke fallen, flankieren.
flannel *s.* Flanell *m.*; Flanell . . .; Waschlappen *m.*; ~**s** *pl.* wollenes Unterzeug *n.*; Flanellhosen *pl.*
flap *s.* Lappen *m.*; Klaps *m.*; Rockschoß *m.*; ~ *v.t.* klapsen.
flapper *s.* Klappe *f.*
flare *v.i.* flackern; ausbrechen; ~ *s.* Lohe *f.*, Geflacker *n.*
flare-path *s.* (*avi.*) Leuchtpfad *m.*
flash *s.* schnelle Flamme *f.*; Blitz *m.*; ~ *v.i.* aufblitzen, auflodern.
flashback *s.* Rückblende *f.*
flashlight *s.* Taschenlampe *f.*; Blitzlicht *n.*
flashy *a.* schimmernd; oberflächlich anziehend.
flask *s.* Flasche *f.*; Reiseflasche, Feldflasche *f.*; Pulverhorn *n.*

flat *a.*, **~ly** *adv.* platt, flach, schal; matt; rundheraus; (*com.*) flau; (*mus.*) um halben Ton erniedrigt; ~ *rate*, (*com.*) Einheitssatz *m.*; ~ *tire*, Reifenpanne *f.*; ~ *s.* Plattheit; Fläche *f.*; Untiefe *f.*; Stockwerk *n.*; Etagenwohnung *f.*; (*mus.*) das B *n.*
flat-chested *a.* flachbrüstig; flachbusig.
flat-foot *s.* Plattfuß; ~ *a.* **flatfooted** plattfüßig.
flat-iron *s.* Bügeleisen *n.*
flatly *a.* rundweg, direkt.
flatness *s.* Flachheit *f.*
flatten *v.t.* flach machen; ~ *v.i.* schal werden.
flatter *v.t.* schmeicheln.
flatterer *s.* Schmeichler(in) *m.(f.)*
flattery *s.* Schmeichelei *f.*
flat tyre *s.* Reifenplatte *f.*; Platte *m.*
flatulence *s.* Blähung *f.*; Nichtigkeit *f.*
flatulent *a.* blähend; schwülstig.
flaunt *v.i. & t.* protzen, zur Schau stellen.
flautist *s.* Flötist(in) *m.(f.)*
flavor *s.* Geschmack *m.*; Aroma *n.*; Blume (des Weines) *f.*
flaw *s.* Fehler *m.*; Defekt *m.*
flawless *a.* fehlerfrei; einwandfrei.
flax *s.* Flachs *m.*
flaxen *a.* flachsen.
flay *a.* (die Haut) abziehen, schinden.
flea *s.* Floh *m.*; ~ **bite** *s.* Flohbiß *m.*; (*fig.*) Kleinigkeit *f.*
fleck *s.* Fleck *m.*; Tupfen *m.*; ~ *v.t.* sprenkeln.
fledge *v.t.* befiedern.
fledged *a.* flügge, befiedert.
fledgling *s.* Jungvogel *m.*
flee *v.i.ir.* fliehen.
fleece *s.* Vlies *n.*; ~ *v.t.* scheren; (*fig.*) prellen.
fleecy *a.* flauschig; wollig.
fleet *a.* Flotte *f.*
fleeting *a.* flüchtig; vergänglich.
Flemish *a.* flämisch.
flesh *s.* Fleisch *n.*
flesh-eating a. fleischfressend.
flesh wound *s.* Fleischwunde *f.*
fleshy *a.* fleischig.
flex *v.t.* beugen; (Muskel) anspannen.
flexibility *s.* Biegsamkeit *f.* Flexibilität *f.*
flexible *a.*, **~bly** *adv.* biegsam; flexibel.
flexion *s.* Biegung *f.*
flextime *s.* Gleitzeit *f.*
flick *v.t.* schnippen, schnellen.
flicker *v.i.* flackern; flimmern (Film).
flier *s.*, Flieger *m.*; Renner *m.*
flight *s.* Flucht *f.*; Flug *m.*; Schwarm *m.*; (*avi.*) Staffel *f.*; ~ (*of stairs*) *s.* Treppe *f.*
flight attendant *s.* Flugbegleiter(in) *m.(f.)*
flight-recorder *s.* Flugschreiber *m.*
flighty *a.* flatterhaft.
flimsy *a.* locker, dünn; schwach.
flinch *v.i.* zurückschaudern.
fling *v.t.st.* werfen, schleudern; ~ *s.* Wurf, Schlag *m.*; Austoben *n.*
flint *s.* Feuerstein, Kiesel *m.*
flip *v.t. & i.* schnellen; schnipsen; ~ *s.* Schnipsen *n.*
flippancy *s.* Leichtfertigkeit.
flippant *a.* leichtfertig, frivol.
flipper *s.* Flosse *f.*
flirt *v.t.* schnellen; ~ *v.i.* liebeln, kokettieren.
flirtation *s.* Liebelei *f.*, Flirt *m.*

flirtations *a.* kokett.
flit *v.i.* flattern; huschen; ausrücken.
float *s.* Floß *m.*; Schwimmer *m.*; (*avi.*) Schwimmgestell, *n.*; ~ *v.i.* obenauf schwimmen; dahintreiben; ~ *v.t.* flößen; überfluten; flott machen; ins Leben rufen.
floating *a.* schwimmend; treibend; schwebend; ~ **debts** *pl.* schwebende Schulden *f.pl.*; ~ **dock** *s.* Schwimmdock *n.*
flock *s.* Herde *f.*; Haufen *m.*; (Woll-) Flocke *f.*; ~ *v.i.* in Haufen ziehen, strömen, sich scharen.
flocky *a.* flockig.
floe *s.* Treibeis *n.*; Eisscholle *f.*
flog *v.t.* peitschen.
flogging s. Prügelstrafe *f.*
flood *s.* Flut *f.*; Hochwasser *n.*; ~ *v.t.* überschwemmen.
floodlight *s.* Scheinwerferlicht *n.*; ~ *v.t.* mit Scheinwerfer beleuchten.
floor *s.* Fußboden, Boden *m.*; Tenne *f.*; Stockwerk *n.*; ~ *v.t.* dielen; zu Boden schlagen.
floor lamp *s.* Stehlampe *f.*
floor leader *s.* Fraktionsführer(in) *m.(f.)*
floorshow *s.* Varietévorstellung *f.*
flop *v.i.* plumpsen; ~ *s.* Versager *m.*
floppy *a.* biegsam, weich; ~ **disk** *s.* (*comp.*) Diskette *f.*
flora *pl.* Flora *f.*
floral *a.* Blüten . . ., Blumen . . ..
floral tribute *s.* Blumenspende *f.*
florid *a.*, **~ly** *adv.* verschnörkelt; blumig.
florin *s.* Gulden *m.*
florist *s.* Blumenhändler(in) *m.(f.)*
flotilla *s.* Flotille *f.*
flotsam *s.* Treibgut *n.*
flounce *v.i.* auffahren, sich heftig bewegen.
flounder *s.* Flunder *m.* or *f.*; ~ *v.i.* zappeln; sich abmühen; Fehler machen.
flour *s.* feines Mehl *n.*
flourish *v.i.* blühen; prahlen; ~ *v.t.* schwingen; verzieren; ~ *s.* Schnörkel *m.*; Verzierung *f.*; Gepränge *m.*; Trompetenstoß *m.*
flout *v.i. & t.* mißachten.
flow *v.i.* fließen; fluten; ~ *s.* Flut *f.*; Redefluß *m.*
flow chart *s.* Flußdiagramm *n.*
flower *s.* Blume, Blüte *f.*; Beste *n.*; ~ *v.i.* blühen.
flower bed *s.* Blumenbeet *n.*
flowered *a.* geblümt.
flower-pot *s.* Blumentopf *m.*
flowershop *s.* Blumenladen *m.*
flowery *a.* blumig.
flowing *a.* fließend.
flu *s.* Grippe *f.*
fluctuate *v.i.* schwanken.
fluctuation *s.* Schwankung *f.*
flue *s.* Ofenrohr *m.* Luftkanal *m.*
fluency *s.* Fluß (der Rede) *m.*; Gewandtheit *f.*
fluent *a.*, **~ly** *adv.* fließend, flüssig; geläufig.
fluff *s.* Staubflocke, Fluse *f.*; Flaum *m.*; Fussel *f.*
fluffy *a.* weich, flauschig.
fluid *a.* flüssig; ~ *s.* Flüssigkeit *f.*
fluke *s.* (*fam.*) glücklicher Zufall *m.*
fluky *a.* glücklich, zufällig.
flunkey *s.* Lakai *m.*
fluorescence *s.* Fluoreszenz *f.*
fluorescent *a.* fluoreszierend.

fluoride *a.* Fluorid *n.*

flurry *s.* Windstoß *m.*; Unruhe f.; ~ *v.t.* beunruhigen.

flush *s.* fliegende Röte f.; Aufwallung f.; kurzer Regenguß *m.*; ~ *v.t.* ausspülen; erröten machen; ~ *v.i.* erröten.

fluster *v.t.* aufregen; verwirren.

flute *s.* Flöte f.; ~ *v.t.* riefeln.

flutist *s.* Flötist(in) *m.*(f.)

flutter *v.i.* flattern; unruhig sein; ~ *v.t.* scheuchen, beunruhigen; ~ *s.* Geflatter *n.*; Unruhe f.

flux *s.* Fluß *m.*; Abfluß *m.*

fly *v.i. & t.st.* fliegen; fliehen; jagen; ~ *s.* Fliege f.; offene Droschke f.

fly-fishing *s.* Angeln mit künstlichen Fliegen als Lockspeise *n.*

flying *a.* fliegend; ~ **boat** *s.* Flugboot *n.*; ~ **bomb** *s.* Flugbombe f.; ~**saucer** *s.* fliegende Untertasse f. ~**squad** *s.* Überfallkommando *n.*; ~ **suit** *s.* Flugan- zug *m.*

fly-leaf *s.* Vorsetzblatt *n.*; loses Blatt *n.*

fly-paper *s.* Fliegenpapier *n.*

fly-swatter *s.* Fliegenklatsche f.

flyweight *s.* Fliegengewicht *n.*

fly-wheel *s.* Schwungrad *n.*

foal *s.* Fohlen *n.*; ~ *v.i.* fohlen.

foam *s.* Schaum *m.*; ~ *v.i.* schäumen.

fob *v.t.* foppen, anführen.

focal *a.* im Brennpunkt.

focus *s.* Brennpunkt *m.*; ~ *v.t.* (*phot.*) einstellen.

fodder *s.* Viehfutter *n.*; ~ *v.t.* füttern.

foe *s.* Feind *m.*

fog *s.* Nebel(dichter) *n.*; ~**-signal** *s.* Nebelsignal *n.*

foggy *a.*, ~**ily** *adv.* nebelig, dunkel.

fog-horn *s.* Nebelhorn *n.*

fogy *s.* alter Opa *m.*, alte Oma f.

foible *s.* Schwäche f.; Eigenhert f.

foil *v.t.* vereiteln; ~ *s.* Foile f.; Laubwerk *n.*; Rapier *n.*; Metallblättchen *n.*; Einfassung f.

foist *v.t* unterschieben, zuschieben.

fold *s.* Falte f.; Falz *m.*; Schafhürde f.; ~ *v.t.* falten; pferchen; ~ *v.i.* sich schließen.

folder *s.* Falzbein *n.*; Broschüre f.; Aktendeckel *m.*, Mappe f.

folding *a.* zusammenklappbar; ~ **doors** *pl.*, Falttür f.

folding-knife *s.* Taschenmesser *n.*

folding-screen *s.* spanische Wand f.

foliage *s.* Laubwerk *n.*

folio *s.* Folio *n.*; Foliant *m.*

folk *s.* Volk *n.*; Leute *pl.*

folklore *s.* Volkskunde f.; Folklore f. Überlieferung f.

follow *v.t. & i.* (be-, nach-, ver-)folgen; *to* ~ *suit*, bedienen, Farbe bekennen (in der Karte); je- mandes Beispiel folgen.

follower *s.* Nachfolger *m.*; Anhänger *m.*

following *a.* folgend.

folly *s.* Torheit f.; Ausschweifung f.

foment *v.t.* schüren.

fond *a.*, ~**ly** *adv.* vernarrt; zärtlich; *to be* ~ *of*, gern haben, gern tun.

fondle *v.t.* liebkosen, verzärteln.

fondness *s.* Zärtlichkeit f.; Vorliebe f.

font *s.* Taufstein *m.*; Schriftguß *m.*; Schrifttype f.

food *s.* Speise f., Essen *n.*; Futter *n.*; *to go without* ~,

ohne Nahrung sein.

food-hoarder *s.* Hamsterer *m.*

food poisoning *s.* Lebensmittelvergiftung f.

food-processor *s.* Küchenmaschine f.

fool *s.* Narr *m.*; ~ *v.t.* zum besten haben.

foolery *s.* Narrheit f.

fool hardy *a.* tollkühn.

foolish *a.*, ~**ly** *adv.* töricht, närrisch.

foolproof *a.* kinderleicht; betriebssicher.

foolscap *s.* Kanzleipapier *n.*

foot *s.* Fuß *m.*; Tritt *m.*; *on* ~, zu Fuß; ~ *v.t. & i.* treten, fussen; zu Fuß gehen; ~ *the bill*, zahlen.

foot-and-mouth disease *s.* Maul-und Klauenseu- che f.

football *s.* Fußball (spiel) *n.*, Rugby *n.*

football-pool *s.* Fußballtoto *m.*

footbridge *s.* Steg *m.*; Brücke für Fußgänger f.

footfall *s.* Geräusch eines Schrittes *n.*

Foot-guards *s.pl.* Gardeinfanterie f.

foothold *s.* fester Stützpunkt *m.*

footing *s.* Halt; Stützpunkt *m.*; *war-*~, Kriegsstand *m.*

foot-lights *s.pl.* Rampenlichter *n.pl.*

foot-locker *s.* verschließbare Truhe f.

footman *s.* Lakai, Bediente *m.*

footnote *s.* Fußnote f.

footpace *s.* langsamer Schritt *m.*

footpath *s.* Fußweg *m.*

footprint *s.* Fußstapfe f.

footsore *a.* mit wunden Füssen.

footstep *s.* Schritt *m.*; Fußtritt *m.*

footstool *s.* Fußschemel *m.*

footsupport *s.* Schuheinlage f.

footwear *s.* Schuhwerk, -zeug *n.*

footwork *s.* Beinarbeit f.

fop *s.* Geck *m.*

foppery *s.* Narrheit f.; Ziererei f.

foppish *a.* geziert, geckenhaft.

for *pr & c.* für, mit, nach, wegen, um. . . willen; aus, an, auf, zu, zufolge; denn, deswegen; ~ *all that*, trotzdem; ~ *and on behalf of*, per procura (p.p.).

forage *s.* Futter *n.*; ~ *v.t.* fouragieren; stöbern.

foray *s.* Raubzug *m.*; ~ *v.t.* plündern.

forbear *v.i.st.* unterlassen, Geduld haben; ~ *v.t.* sich enthalten; ~ *s.* Ahne *m.*, Vorfahre *m.*

forbearance *s.* Vermeidung, Unterlassung; Nach- sicht f.

forbid *v.t.st.* verbieten, verhindern; *God* ~! Gott vehüte!

force *s.* Kraft, Gewalt, Gültigkeit f.; Mannschaft f.; ~**s** *pl.* Truppen f.pl.; *to be in* ~, in Kraft sein; *to come into* ~, in Kraft treten; ~ *v.t.* zwingen; Gewalt brauchen, notzüchtigen; erstürmen; ~*d labor s.* Zwangsarbeit f.; ~*d loan s.* Zwangsanleihe f.; ~*d march s.* Eilmarsch *m.*; ~*d rate of exchange s.* Zwangskur *m.*; ~*d sale*, Zwangsverkauf *m.*

forceful *a.* wirkungsvoll.

forcible *a.*, ~**bly** *adv.* kräftig, gewaltsam.

ford *s.* Furt f.; ~ *v.t.* durchwaten.

fore *a.* vorder; vorherig; ~ *adv.* vorn.

forebode *v.t.* vorbedeuten, ahnen.

forecast *v.t. & i.st.* voraussehen; ~ *s.* Voraussage f.

forecastle *s.* (*nav.*) Back f., Vorderdeck *n.*

foreclose *v.i.* ausschießen; vorwegnehmen.

foreclosure *s.* Verfallserklärung f.

foredoom *s.* Vorherbestimmung f; ~ *v.t.* zum

Untergang bestimmen.

forefather s. Vorfahr m.

forefinger s. Zeigefinger m.

forefront s. vorderste Reihe f.

forego v.i.st. vorhergehen.

foregone a. von vornherein bestimmt; ~ conclusion, ausgemachete Sache f.

foreground s. Vordergrund m.

forehand s. Vorhand (-schlag m.) f.

forehead s. Stirn f.

foreign a. ausländisch; fremd; ~ bill, Auslandswechsel m.; ~ Office s. Auswärtiges Amt n.

foreigner s. Ausländer(in) m.(f.)

foreknowledge s. Vorherwissen n.

foreland s. Vorgebirge n.

forelock s. Stirnhaar n.; Schopf m.

foreman s. Vorarbeiter m.; Sprecher m. (der Geschworenen).

foremast s. Fockmast m.

foremost a. vorderste, vornehmste.

forensic a. gerichtlich.

foreplay s. Vorspiel n.

forerunner s. Vorbote m.

foresee v.t.st. vorhersehen.

foreshadow v.t. vorausahnen lassen.

foreshorten v.t. verkürzen.

foresight s. Voraussicht f., Weitblick m.

foreskin s. Vorhaut f.

forest s. Forst, Wald m.; ~-**fire** s. Waldbrand m.

forestall v.t. vorwegnehmen, zuvorkommen.

forester s. Förster(in) m.(f.)

forestry s. Forstwirtschaft f.

foretaste s. Vorgeschmack m.; ~ v.t. einen Vorgeschmack haben.

foretell v.t.st. vorhersagen.

forethought s. Vorbedacht m.

forewarn v.t. vorwarnen.

forewoman s. Vorarbeiterin f.

foreword s. Vorwort n.

forfeit s. Geldbuße f.; Pfand (im Pfänderspiel) n.; ~ v.t. verwirken, verscherzen; ~ a. verwirkt, verfallen.

forfeiture s. Verlust m.; Einbuße f.

forge s. Schmiede f.; ~ v.t. schmieden; ersinnen; fälschen; ~ ahead, vorwärtsdrängen.

forger s. Fälscher(in) m.(f.)

forgery s. Fälschung f.

forget v.t.st. vergessen.

forgetful a. vergeßlich.

forgetfulness s. Vergeßlichkeit f.

forget-me-not s. Vergißmeinnicht n.

forgettable a. leich zu vergessen.

forgive v.t.st. vergeben, verzeihen.

forgiveness s. Verzeihung f.

forgo v.t. verzichten auf, aufgeben.

fork s. Gabel, Zinke f.

forked a. gabelförmig.

foundation s. Gründung f.; Fundament n.; Stiftung f.; Anstalt f.; ~-**stone**, Grundstein f.

founder s. Stifter(in) m.(f.); Gründer(in) m.(f.); ~ v.i. scheitern; sinken.

foundling s. Findelkind n.

foundry s. Gießerei f.

fount = **fountain.**

fountain s. Quelle f.; Springbrunnen m.; ~-**head** s. Urquell m.; ~-**pen** s. Füllfeder f.

four a. vier; ~ s. (sport) Vierer m.

four-engine(d) a.(avi.) viermotorig.

fourfold a. vierfach.

four-handed a. vierhändig.

four-in-hand s. Vierspänner m.

fourposter s. Himmelbett n.

fourteen a. vierzehn.

fowl s. Vogel m.; Huhn n.; Geflügel n.; ~ v.i. Vögel fangen.

fox s. Fuchs m.

fox-glove s. (bot.) Fingerhut m.

fox-hunt s. Fuchsjagd f.

fraction s. (ar.) Bruch; Bruchteil m.

fractional a. gebrochen, Bruch...; geringfügig.

fracture s. (Knocken-) Bruch m.; ~ v.t. brechen.

fragile a. zerbrechlich, schwach.

fragility s. Zerbrechlichkeit f.; Gebrechlichkeit f.

fragment s. Bruchstück n.

fragmentary a. fragmentarisch.

fragmented a. bruchstückhaft.

fragrance s. Wohlgeruch m., Duft m.

fragrant a., ~**ly** adv. wohlriechend.

frail a. gebrechlich; schwach.

frailty s. Gebrechlichkeit f.; Fehltritt m.; Schwachheit f.

frame s. Rahmen m.; Gerüst, Gestell n.; Gestalt, Form f.; Einfassung f.; ~ v.t. einfassen; bilden; erfinden.

framework s. Fachwerk n.; (fig.) Bau m., Rahmen m.; within the ~ of, im Rahmen von.

franchise s. Wahlrecht n.; Gerechtsame f.

France s. Frankreich n.

frank a., ~**ly** adv. frei; aufrichtig.

frankfurt(er) s. Frankfurter Würstchen n.

frankincense s. Weihrauch m.

frankness s. Offenheit f.

frantic a., ~**ally** adv. wahnsinnig; verzweifelt.

fraternal a., ~**ly** adv. brüderlich.

fraternity s. Brüderschaft f.; Brüderlichkeit f.

fraternization s. Verbrüderung f.

fraternize v.i. sich verbrüdern.

fratricidal a. brudermörderisch.

fratricide s. Brudermord m.; Brudermörder m.

fraud s. Betrug m.; Enttäuschung f.

fraudulent a., ~**ly** adv, betrügerisch.

fraught p. befrachtet; voll.

fray s. Schlägerei f.; ~ v.t. ausfransen; durchscheuern.

freak s. Mißbildung f.; Freak m.

freckle s. Sommersprosse f.

freckled, freckly a. sommersprossig.

free a., ~**ly** adv. frei; offenherzig; ohne Kosten; gutwillig; ~ on board (f.o.b), frei Schiff; ~ on rail, frei Eisenbahn; of my ~ will, freiwillig; ~ v.t. befreien; freigeben.

freebooter s. Freibeuter m.

freedom s. Freiheit f.; Bürgerrecht m.; ~ of association and assembly, Koalitions- und Versammlungsfreiheit.

freedom fighter s. Freiheitskämpfer m.

free enterprise s. freies Unternehmertum n.

freehand-drawing s. Freihandzeichnen n.

freehold s. Besitzrecht n.

freelance s. Freischaffende m./f.; ~ journalist, freier Journalist m.

free market s. freier Markt m.

freemason s. Freimaurer m.
freemasonry s. Freimaurerei f.
freeport s. Freihafen m.
free-range a. freilaufend (Huhn).
freesia s. Freesie f.
free speech s. Redefreiheit f.
freestone s. Sandstein m.
freethinker s. Freigeist m.
free-trade s. Freihandel m.
freeway s. Autobahn f.
freewheel s. Freilauf m.
freeze v.i.st. frieren, gefrieren; to ~ to death, erfrieren; ~ v.t. gefrieren machen; to ~ promotions, wages, Beförderungen aussetzen, Löhne nicht erhöhen.
freezing-point s. Gefrierpunkt m.
freight s. Fracht f.; ~-car s. Güterwagen m.; ~-train s. Güterzug; ~-yard s. Güterbahnhof.
French a. französisch; ~ s. Franzose m.; Französin f.; Franzosen n.pl.
French Canadian s. Frankokanadien(in) m.(f.); a. frankokanadisch.
French dressing s. Vinaigrette f.
French fries pl. Pommes frites pl.
French horn s. Waldhorn n.
Frenchman m. Franzose m.
French window s. Flügelfenster n., Verandatür f.
Frenchwoman f. Französin f.
frenetic a. rasend.
frenzied a. wahnsinnig.
frenzy s. Raserei f.
frequency s. Häufigkeit f.; (elek., Radio) Frequenz f.; high ~, Hochfrequenz f.
frequent a., ~ly adv. häufig, zahlreich.; ~ v.t. oft besuchen.
fresco s. Fresko n.
fresh a., ~ly adv. frisch; kühl; neu.
freshen v.t. erfrischen; auffrischen; ~ v.i. frisch, kühl werden.
freshman s. Erstsemester n.
freshness s. Frische f.
freshwater s. Süßwasser n.
fret s. ~ v.t. abreiben; zerfressen; erzürnen; ~ v.i. sich grämen, ärgern.
fretful a., ~ly adv. ärgerlich; verdrießlich; quengelig.
fret-saw s. Laubsäge, Stichsäge f.
fretwork s. Gitterwerk, feines Schnitzwerk n., Laubsägearbeit f.
Freudian a. Freudsche; ~ slip s. Freudsche Fehlleistung f.
friable a. zerreibbar.
friar s. Mönch, Frater m.
friction s. Reibung f.
Friday s. Freitag m.; Good ~, Karfreitag m.
fridge s. Kühlschrank m.
friend s. Freud(in) m.(f.)
friendliness s. Freundlichkeit f.
friendly a. freundschaftlich; freundlich.
friendship s. Freundschaft f.
frieze s. Fries m.
frigate s. Fregatte f.
fright s. Entsetzen n.; Schreckbild n.; Schrecken n.
frighten v.t. erschrecken.
frightened a. verängstigt.
frightening a. furchterregend.

frightful a., ~ly adv. schrecklich.
frigid a., ~ly adv. kalt, frostig.
frigidity s. Kälte f.; Kaltsinn m.
frill s. Krause f.
fringe s. Franse f.; Rand m.; ~ v.t. befransen; säumen.
frippery s. Trödelkram m.
frisk s. Sprung m.; ~ v.i. hüpfen.
frisky a. lustig, munter.
fritter v.t. vergeuden.
friviolity s. Leichtfertigkeit f.
frivolous a., ~ly adv. frivol.
frizz(le) s. Haarlocke f.; ~ v.t. kräuseln.
fro adv., to and ~, hin und her.
frock s. Rock m. Frauenkleid.
frog s. Frosch m.; ~-spawn s. Froschlaich m.
frolic a. frölich; ~ s. Scherz m.; ~ v.i. spassen; herumtollen.
frolicsome a., ~ly adv. lustig.
from pr. von, aus, nach, wegen; vor.
front s. Stirn f.; Vorderseite f., Front f.; Vorder...; ~-door s. Vordertür f.; ~-room s. Vorderzimmer n.; ~-view s. Vorderansicht f.; ~ v.t. gegenüberstehen.
frontage s. Vorderseite f.
frontal a. Stirn..., Front...; ~-attack s. (mil.) Stirnangriff m.
frontier s. Grenze f.; ~-readjustments pl. Grenzberichtigungen f.pl.
frontispiece s. Vorderseite (eines Gebäudes) f.; Titelbild n.
frost s. Frost m.; Reif m.
frostbite s. Frostbeulen f.pl.
frost-bitten a. vom Froste beschädigt.
frosted a. bereift, überfroren; ~ glass s. Mattglas n.
frosting s. Zuckerguß m.; Glasur f.
frosty a. frostig; bereift.
froth s. Schaum m.; ~ v.t. & i. schäumen.
frothy a. schaumig.
frown s. gerunzelte Stirn f.; ~ v.i. die Stirn runzeln; finster blicken.
frozen p. gefroren; ~ meat s. Gefrierfleisch n.
fructify v.t. befruchten.
frugal a., ~ly adv. sparsam; mäßig.
frugality s. Sparsamkeit, Mäßigkeit f.
fruit s. Frucht f.; Obst n.; Ertrag m.
fruiterer s. Obsthändler(in) m.(f.)
fruitful a., ~ly adv. fruchtbar.
fruition s. Genuß m.; Verwirklichung f.
fruitless a., ~ly adv. fruchtlos.
fruit-salad s. Fruchtsalat m.
fruity a. fruchtartig; fruchtig; geschwollen (Ausdrucksweise); schmalzig.
frump s.(pej.) Vogelscheuche f.
frustrate v.t. vereiteln, vernichten; frustrieren.
frustration s. Vereitlung f.; Frustration f.
fry s. Fischbrut f.; small ~, kleines Volk n.; ~ v.t. rösten, braten; backen (Fisch); fried egg s. Spiegelei n.
frying-pan s. Bratpfanne f., Pfanne f.
fuschia s. (bot.) Fuchsie f.
fuck (vulg.) v.t. & i. ficken; ~you! leck mich am Arsch.
fuddle v.t. & i. (fam.) (sich) berauschen verwirren.
fudge s. Karamelbonbon n.; Unsinn m.; ~ v.t. pfuschen.

fuel s. Brennmaterial n.; Feuerung f.

fuel oil s. Heizöl n.

fuel consumption s. Kraftstoffverbrauch m.

fugitive a. flüchtig; leicht verschwindend (Farbe); ~ s. Flüchtling m.

fugue s. (mus.) Fuge f.

fulfil v.t. erfüllen, vollziehen.

fulfilment s. Erfüllung, Vollziehung f.

full a. voll; gänzlich; ~ adv. völlig, genau, recht, gerade; in ~, vollständig, voll ausgeschrieben; ~ face s. Vorderansicht (des Gesichts) f.; ~ powers f.pl. Vollmacht f.; ~ stop s. Punkt (Interpunktion) m.; ~ s. Fülle f.

full-blooded a. vollblütig.

full-blown a. ganz aufgeblüht; ausgewachsen.

full-bodied a. vollmundig.

full-dress s. Abendkleidung f.

full fledged a. flügge; (fig.) richtig.

full-length a. in Lebensgröße; abendfüllend.

full-moon s. Vollmond m.

fulminate v.i. donnern; schelten.

fullness s. Fülle f.

fulsome a., ~ly adv. übertrieben.

fumble v.i.&i. tappen, betasten; stümpern.

fume s. Rauch m.; Dunst m.; Zorn m.; ~ v.i. rauchen, verdampfen; zornig sein; ~ v.t. räuchern.

fumigate v.t. räuchern.

fun s. Scherz, Spaß m.; to make ~ of, zum besten haben.

function s. Amt n.; Dienst m.; Tätigkeit f.; Funktion f.; gesellige Veranstaltung f.; ~ v.i. funktionieren; tätig sein.

functional a. funktionell, funktional.

fund s. Kapital n.; Fonds m.pl.; Vorrat m.; public ~s pl. Staatsschulden f.pl.; ~ v.t. finanzieren.

fundamental s., ~ly adv. grundlegend.

funeral s. Begräbnis n. ~ march s. Trauermarsch m.

funereal a. Trauer. . . , düster.

fungus s. Pilz m., (med.) Fungus m.

funicular a. Drahtseil. . .

funk s. grosse Angst f.; ~ v.t. & i. sich drücken.

funnel s. Trichter m.; Schornstein m.

funny a. spaßhaft, komisch.

funny bone s. Musikantenknochen m.

fur s. Pelz m.; Belag (auf der Zunge) m.; Kesselstein m.; ~ v.t. mit Pelz füttern.

furbish v.t. polieren; putzen.

furious a., ~ly adv. wütend, rasend.

furl v.t. aufrollen; (die Segel) aufziehen.

furlong s. ein Achtel engl. Meile, 201 m.

furlough s. Urlaub m.

furnace s. Ofen, Schmelzofen m.

furnish v.t. versehen, ausstatten, (aus-) möblieren.

furnishing s. Ausrüstung f.; ~s pl. Ausrüstungsgegenstände, Einrichtungsgegenstände m.pl.

furniture s. Möbel n.pl.; Hausgerät m.

furor s. Furore f.

furred a. belegt (Zunge).

furrier s. Kürschner m.

furrow s. Furche f.; Runzel f.; ~ v.t. furchen.

furry a. pelzig.; haarig.

further a. & adv. ferner, weiter; überdies; ~ to, in weiterer Bezugnahme auf (in Briefen); ~ v.t. befördern.

furtherance s. Förderung f.

furthermore adv. ferner, ausserdem.

furthermost a. äußerst. . . ; entlegenst. . .

furthest a. & adv. weitest; am weitesten.

furtive a., ~ly adv. verstohlen.

fury s. Tollheit, Wut, f.

fuse v.t. & i. (ver)schmelzen; to ~ mines, Minen schärfen; ~ s. Zünder m.; (elek.) Sicherung f.

fuselage s. Rumpf (m.) des Flugzeuges.

fusible a. schmelzbar.

fusion s. Schmelzen n.; (fig.) Verschmelzung f.

fuss s. Lärm m., Getue m.

fussy a. unruhig, übertrieben geschäftig.

futile a. nichtig, wertlos.

futility s. Nichtigkeit f.

future a. künftig; ~ s. Zunkunft f.; Futur n.; ~s pl. Termingeschäfte n.pl.

futuristic a. futuristisch.

fuzz s. leichter Flaum m.

fuzzy a. flaumig; bluschelig; unscharf.

G

G, g der Buchstabe G oder g n.; (mus.) G, g; **G sharp** Gis n.; **G flat** Ges n.

gab s. Mundwerk m.; (fam.) Geschwätzigkeit f.

gabble v.i. schnattern; plaudern; ~ s. Geschnatter, Geschwätz n.

gable s. Giebel m.

gabled a. gegiebelt.

gad v.i. herumstreichen.

gad-fly s. Bremse f.

gadget s. technische Vorrichtung f.; Apparat m.; Krimskrams m.

gadgetry s. (hochtechnisierte) Austrütung f.

Gaelic s. Gälisch; a gälisch.

gaff s. blow the ~ plaudern.

gaffe s. Fauxpas m.; Fehler m.

gag s. Knebel m.; (fam.) (auf dem Theater) Gag m.; witziger Einfall m.; ~ v.i. knebeln.

gaga a. verkalkt; vertrottelt.

gage s. Unterpfand n.; ~ v.t. verpfänden.

gaiety s. Fröhlichkeit f.

gaily adv. fröhlich.

gain s. Gewinn, Vorteil m.; ~ v.t. gewinnen, erlangen.

gainful a., ~ly adv. einträglich.

gainings s.pl. Gewinn m.

gainsay v.t.st. widersprechen; leugnen.

gait s. Gangart, Gehart f.

gaiter s. Gamasche f.

gala s. Fest n., Gala f.

galaxy s. Milchstraße f.; Galaxie f. (fig.) glänzende Versammlung f.

gale s. frischer Wind m.; Sturm m.; ~-**warning** s. Sturmwarnung f.

gall s. Galle f.; Gallapfel m.; Bitterkeit f.; ~ v.t. wund rieben; ärgern.

gallant a., ~ly adv. tapfer, stattlich; ~ a., adv. höflich; galant, artig (gegen Fräuen).

gallantry s. Tapferkeit f.; Galanterie f.

gallery s. Galerie f.; Stollen (Bergwerk) m.

galley s. Galeere f.; Kombüse f.

galley(-proof) *s.* Fahnenabzug *m.* (*typ.*)
Gallicism *s.* Gallizismus *m.*
gallon *s.* Gallone (3, 79 Liter) *f.*
gallop *v.i.* galoppieren; ~ *s.* Galopp *m.*
gallows *s.* Galgen *m.*
gallstone *s.* Gallenstein *m.*
galore *s. adv.* in Hülle und Fülle.
galosh *s.* Überschuh, Gummischuh *m.*
galvanize *v.t.* galvanisieren.
gamble *v.i.* (hoch) spielen; ~ *s.* Glücksspiel *n.*
gambler *s.* Spieler(in) *m.*(*f.*)
gambling *s.* Spiel(en) *n.*; Glücksspiel *n.*
gambol *s.* Luftsprung *m.*; lustiger Streich *m.*; ~ *v.i.* springen, hüpfen.
game *s.* Spiel *n.*; Scherz *m.*; Wild *n.* ~*of chance s.* Glücksspiel *n.*; ~**-law** *s.* Jagdgesetz *n.*; ~ *a.* mutig; ~ *v.i.* spielen.
gamekeeper *s.* Wildhüter *m.*
gamepark *s.* Wildpark.
gamester *s.* Spieler *m.*
gammon *s.* (geräucherter) Schinken *m.*
gamut *s.* Tonleiter *f.*; Skala *f.*
gander *s.* Gänserich *m.*
gang *s.* Bande *f.*; Trupp *m.*
gangrene *s.* (kalter) Brand *m.*
gangster *s.* Gangster *m.*
gangway *s.* Gangway *f.*; Durchgang *m.*; (*nav.*) Laufplanke *f.*
gantry *s.* Portal *n.*; Schilderbrücke *f.*
gap *s.* Lücke *f.*; Bresche *f.*; Riß *m.*
gape *v.i.* gaffen; gähnen; klaffen.
garage *s.* Garage *f.*
garb *s.* Gewand *n.*, Kleidung *f.*
garbage *s.* Dreck *m.*; Unrat *m.*
garbage can *s.* Mülleimer *m.*
garble *v.t.* auslesen; entstellen.
garden *s.* Garten *m.*; ~ *v.i.* Gartenbau treiben.
gardener *s.* Gärtner(in) *m.*(*f.*)
gardening *s.* Gärtnerei *f.*
garden shed *s.* Geräteschuppen *m.*
gargle *v.t.* gurgeln.; *s.* Gurgelmittel *n.*
gargoyle; *s.* Wasserspeier *m.*, Scheusal *n.*
garish *a.*, ~**ly** *adv.* grell; prunkend.
garland *s.* Girlande *f.*
garlic *s.* Knoblauch *m.*
garment *s.* Kleidungsstück *n.*; Kleidung *f.*
garnish *v.t.* schmücken; versorgen; garnieren; ~ *s.* Verzierung *f.*
garret *s.* Dachstube *f.*
garrison *s.* Garnison *f.* ~ *v.t.* in Garnison legen; ~**town** *s.* Garnison(s)stadt.
garrulity *s.* Schwatzhaftigkeit *f.*
garrulous *a.* schwatzhaft.
garter *s.* Strumpfband *n.*; Sockenhalter *m.*
gas *s.* Gas *n.*, Benzin *n.*
gas-burner *s.* Gasbrenner *m.*
gaseous *a.* gasförmig.
gash *s.* Schnittwunde *f.*; klaffende Wunde *f.* ~ *v.t.* tief verwunden; aufritzen.
gasket *s.* (*mech.*) (Flach-)Dichtung *f.*
gas-lighting *s.* Gasbeleuchtung *f.*
gas-meter *s.* Gasmesser *m.*
gasoline *s.* Benzin *n.*; ~**-station** *s.* Tankstelle *f.*
gasometer *s.* Gasometer *m.*
gasp *v.i.* keuchen; schnappen.
gas-pipe *s.* Gasrohr *n.*

gastric *a.* gastrisch, Magen. . .
gastronomic *a.* gastronomisch.
gastronomy *s.* Gastronomie *f.*; Kochkunst *f.*
gasworks *s.pl.* Gaswerk *n.*
gate *s.* Tor *n.*; Pforte *f.*
gate-crasher *s.* ungeladener Gast *m.*
gateway *s.* Tor *n.*; Torbogen *m.*
gather *v.t.* sammeln; pflücken, ernten; ~ *v.i.* sich versammeln.
gathering *s.* Versammlung *f.*
gauche *a.* linkisch.
gaudy *a.*, ~**ily** *adv.* geputzt, bunt.
gauge *v.t.* eichen; ausmessen; abschätzen; ~ *s.* Eichmass *n.*; Spurweite (der Eisenbahn) *f.*; (*mech.*) Lehre *f.*; *narrow--railway s.* Schmalspurbahn, Kleinbahn *f.*
gaunt *a.*, ~**ly** *adv.* dürr, hager.
gauntlet *s.* Fehdehandschuh *m.*; *to run the* ~, Spießruten laufen; *to take up the* ~, die Herausforderung annehmen.
gauze *s.* Gaze *f.*
gawk *v.t. & i.* glotzen.
gawky *a.* ungeschickt, albern.
gay *a.*, ~**ly** *adv.* munter, lustig; bunt.
gaze *v.i.* anstaunen, anstarren; ~ *s.* starrer Blick *m.*
gazelle *s.* Gazelle *f.*
gazette *s.* Zeitung *f.*, Amtsblatt *n.*; ~ *v.t.* amtlich veröffentlichen.
gazetteer *s.* geographisches Lexikon *n.*
gear *s.* Treibwerk *n.*; (*mech.*) Zahnrad *n.*; (*mech.*) Übersetzung *f.*, Gang *m.*; *to put in another* ~, einen anderen Gang einschalten; *high* ~, grosse Übersetzung (am Fahrrad) *f.*; *low* ~, klein Übersetzung *f.*
gearbox *s.* (*mech.*) Getriebe(-kasten) *m.*
gearing *s.* Getriebe *n.*; Übersetzung *f.*
gear-shift *s.* Gangschaltung *f.*
gear-stick *s.* Schalthebel *m.*
Geiger counter *s.* Geigerzähler *m.*
gel *s.* Gel *n.*
gelatine *s.* Gallerte *f.*; Gelatine *f.*
gelatinous *a.* gallertartig.
geld *v.t.* verschneiden; kastrieren.
gelding *s.* Wallach *m.*
gem *s.* Edelstein *m.*; Juwel *n.*
Gemini *s.* (*astr.*) Zwillinge *pl.*
gender *s.* Geschlecht *n.*
gene *s.* Gen *n.*
genealogical *a.* genealogisch, Stamm. . .
genealogy *s.* Genealogie *f.*
general *a.* allgemein; ~ *s.* General *m.*;
generality *s.* Allgemeinheit *f.*
generalization *s.* Verallgemeinerung *f.*
generalize *v.t.* verallgemeinern.
general knowledge *s.* Allgemeinwissen *n.*
generally *adv.* im allgemeinen.
general manager *s.* Direktor(in) *m.*(*f.*)
general meeting *s.* Generalversammlung *f.*
general practice *s.* Allgemeinmedizin *f.*
general practitioner *s.* Arzt/Ärztin (*m./f.*) für Allgemeinmedizin.
general staff *s.* Generalstad *n.*
general strike *s.* Generalstreik *m.*
generate *v.t.* erzeugen.
generation *s.* Generation *f.*; Erzeugung *f.*; Geschlecht *n.*; Zeitalter *n.*
generator *s.* Generator *m.*; Lichtmaschine *f.*

generic *a.* Gattungs. . .
generosity *s.* Großzügigkeit *f.*; Freigebigkeit *f.*
generous *a.*, **~ly** *adv.* großmütig; friegebig.
genesis *s.* Entstehung *f.*; Schöpfung *f.*; Genesis *f.*
genetic *a.* genetisch.
genetics *s.* Genetik *f.*
genial *a.*, **~ly** *adv.* heiter; freundlich.
geniality *s.* Freundlichkeit *f.*
genitals *s.pl.* Geschlechtsteile *m.pl.*, Geschlechtsorgane *n.pl.*
genitive *s.* Genitiv *m.*; *a.* genitivisch.
genius *s.* Schutzgeist *m.*; Genie *n.*
genocide *s.* Völkermord *m.*
genre *s.* Genre *n.*, Gattung *f.*
genteel *a.*, **~ly** *adv.* fein, vornehm.
gentian *s.* Enzian *m.*
gentility *s.* Vornehmheit *f.*
gentle *a.* sanft; vornehm; artig, fein; gütig; fromm (von Pferden).
gentleman *s.* Herr, Mann von Stande, feiner Mann *m.*; Gentleman *m.*; *gentlemen's agreement*, freundschaftliches Übereinkommen *n.*
gentlemanlike *a.* wohlgesittet, anständig.
gentleness *s.* Artigkeit, Sanftmut *f.*
gentlewoman *s.* Dame (aus gutem Hause) *f.*
gently *adv.* zärtlich; sanft; vorsichtig.
gentry *s.* niederer Adel *m.*
genuflection *s.* Kniebeugung *f.*
genuine *a.*, **~ly** *adv.* echt, rein; authentisch.
genus *s.* Gattung *f.*
geographer *s.* Geograph *m.*
geographical *a.*, **~ly** *adv.* geographisch.
geography *s.* Erdkunde *f.*
geological *a.* geologisch.
geologist *a.* Geologe, Erdkundige *m.*
geology *s.* Erdkunde *f.*
geometric *a.* geometrisch.
geometrician *s.* Geometer *m.*
geometry *s.* Geometrie *f.*; *plane ~*, ebene Geometrie *f.*
geranium *s.* Geranium *n.*
gerbil *s.* Wüstenmaus *f.*
geriatrics *s.* Geriatric *f.*; Altersheilkunde *f.*
germ *s.* Keim *m.*
German *a.* deutsch; *s.* Deutsche *m./f.*
germane *a.* verwandt; zugehörig.
Germanic *d.* germanisch.
Germanism *s.* Germanismus *m.*
Germany *s.* Deutschland *n.*
germfree *a.* keimfrei.
germicide *s.* bazillentötendes Mittel *n.*
germinal *a.* Keim. . .
germinate *v.i.* keimen, sprossen.
germination *s.* Keimung *f.*, Keimen *n.*
germ warfare *s.* Bakterienkrieg *m.*
gerund *s.* Gerundium *m.*
gestation *s.* Trächtigkeit *f.*; Schwangerschaft *f.*
gesticulate *v.i.* Gebärden machen, gestikulieren.
gesticulation *s.* Gesten *f.pl.*
gesture *s.* Gebärde, Stellung *f.*
get *v.t.st.* erhalten, bekommen; veranstalten; besorgen; erzeugen; *~ v.i.* werden; wohin geraten; sich wohin begeben; *to ~ into*, geraten; *to ~ off*, wegschaffen, entkommen; aussteigen; *to ~ on*, anziehen; vorwärts kommen; Erfolg haben; *to ~*

out, herausbringen; heraus(be)kommen; aussteigen; *to ~ over*, überwinden; *to ~ through*, durchkommen; fertig bringen; *to ~ together*, zusammenbringen; zusammenkommen; *to ~ up*, aufsteigen; sich erheben; aufstehen.
get-at-able *a.* erreichbar, zugänglich.
get-up *s.* Aufmachung *f.*
geyser *s.* Geysin *m.*
Ghana *s.* Ghana *n.*
Ghanaian *a.* ghanaisch; *s.* Ghanaer(in) *m.(f.)*
ghastly *a.* gräßlich; geisterhaft.
gherkin *s.* (kleine) Essiggurke *f.*
ghetto *s.* Ghetto *n.*
ghost *s.* Geist *m.*; Gespenst *n.*
ghostly *a.* gespenstisch.
ghost: **~story** *s.* Gespenstergeschichte *f.*; **~town** *s.* Geisterstadt *f.*; **~~writer** *s* Ghostwriter *m.*
ghoulish *a.* teuflisch, schauerlich.
giant *s.* Riese *m.*
giant panda *s.* Riesenpanda *m.*
gibber *v.i.* plappern.
gibberish *s.* Kauderwelsch *n.*
gibe *v.t. & i.* spotten, verhöhnen; *~ s.* Hohn *m.*
giblets *s.pl.* Gänseklein *n.*
giddiness *s.* Schwindel *m.*
giddy *a.*, **~ily** *adv.* schwind[e]lig; leichtsinnig.
gift *s.* Gabe *f.*; Geschenk *n.*; **~shop** *s.* Geschenkboutique *f.*
gifted *a.* begabt.
gift-wrap *v.t.* als Geschenk einpacken.
gig *s.* Kabriolett *n.*; leichtes Boot *n.*
gigantic *a.* riesenhaft; gigantisch.
giggle *v.i.* kichern.
gild *v.t.ir.* vergolden.
gilding, gilt *s.* Vergoldung *f.*
gill *s.* Kieme *f.*
gillyflower *s.* Goldlack *m.*; Levkoje *f.*
gitt *s.* Goldauflage *f.*; *a.* vergoldet.
gilt-edged *a.* (*com.*) mündelsicher.
gimcrack *s.* Tand *m.*
gimmick *s.* Gag *m.*
gin *s.* Wacholderbranntwein *m.*, Gin *m.*
ginger *s.* Ingwer *m.*; **~-beer**, Ingwerbier *n.*
gingerbread *s.* Ingwerkuchen *m.*
gingerly *a.* sachte, zimperlich.
gipsy *s.* Zigeuner(in) *m(f.)*
giraffe *s.* Giraffe *f.*
gird *v.t. & i.r. & ir.* gürten; sticheln, schmähen.
girder *s.* Bindebalken *m.*; Träger *m.*
girdle *s.* Gürtel *m.*; Hüfthalter *m.*; *~ v.t.* umgürten.
girl *s.* Mädchen *n.*
girlhood *s.* Mädchenjahre *n.pl.*; Mädchentum *n.*
girlish *a.*, **~ly** *adv.* mädchenhaft.
girth *s.* Gurt *m.*; Umfang *m.*
gist *s.* Wesentliche *n.*; Kern *m.*
give *v.t.st.* geben; schenken; *to ~ away*, verschenken; *to ~ birth to*, gebären; *to ~ in, to ~ way*, nachgeben; *to ~ up*, abgeben; *to ~ oneself up*, sich freiwillig stellen; *~ v.i.* nachgeben; sich werfen (vom Holze).
given *p.* bestimmt, festgesetzt.
give-and-take *s.* gegenseitiges Entgegenkommen *n.*
gizzard *s.* (Vogel-, Fisch-) Magen *m.*
glacé *a.* glasiert.
glacial *a.* eisig; Gletscher. . . , Eis. . .

glacier *s.* Gletscher *m.*
glad *a.*, **~ly** *adv.* heiter, froh; angenehm.
gladden *v.t.* erfreuen, erheitern.
glade *s.* Lichtung *f.*
gladiator *s.* Gladiator *m.*
gladiolus *s.* Gladiole *f.*
glamor *s.* Zauber *m.*, Ausstrahlung *f.*
glamorize *v.t.* verherrlichen; glorifizieren.
glamorous *a.* glanzvoll; mondän.
glance *s.* Schimmer, Blitz *m.*, Blick *m.*; ~ *v.t.* flüchtig anschauen; abgleiten; ~ *v.i.* schimmern; strahlen.
gland *s.* Drüse *f.*
glandular *a.* Glasbläser *m.*
glare *s.* Glanz, Schimmer *m.*; durchdringender Blick *m.*; ~ *v.i.* blendenden Glanz werfen; starr ansehen.
glaring *a.* grell; offenkundig.
glass *s.* Glas *n.*; Spiegel *m.*; Fernglas *n.*; ~ *a.* gläsern; ~ *v.t.* überglasen, verglasen.
glass-blower *s.* Glasbläser *m.*
glasses *pl.* Brille *f.*
glass-works *s.pl.* Glashütte *f.*
glassy *a.* gläsern, glasartig.
glaucoma *s.* Glaukoma *n.* grüner Star *m.*
glaze *v.t.* verglasen; glätten; mit Glasscheiben versehen; *s.* Glasur *f.*; Lasur *f.*
glazed paper *s.* Glanzpapier *n.*
glazier *s.* Glaser *m.*
gleam *s.* Strahl, Glanz *m.*; ~ *v.i.* strahlen, glänzen.
gleaming *a.* glänzend.
glean *v.t.* nachlesen, sammeln.
glee *s.* Fröhlichkeit *f.*; Schadenfreude *f.*
gleeful *a.* freudig; vergnügt.
glib *a.*, **~ly** *adv.* glatt; zungenfertig.
glide *v.i.* gleiten, schleichen; (*avi.*) einen Gleitflug (oder Segelflug) machen; ~ *s.* Gleitflug *m.*
glider *s.* Segelflugzeug *m.*
gliding *s.* Segelfliegen *n.*
glimmer *v.i.* schimmern; ~ *s.* Schimmer *m.*; Glimmen *n.*
glimpse *s.* (kurzer) Blick *m.*; flüchtigsehen.
glint *s.* Lichtschein *m.*; Funkeln *n.*; ~ *v.i.* gläzen; blinken.
glisten, *v.i.* glitzern, glänzen.
glitter *v.i.* glänzen, glitzern.
gloaming *s.* Zwielicht *n.*
gloat *v.i.* to ~ over, sich weiden an; sich hämisch freuen.
global *a.* global, weltweit.
globe *s.* Kugel *f.*; Globus *m.*; ~ trotter, Weltenbummler(in) *m.(f.)*, Globetrotter(in) *m.(f.)*
globular *a.* kugelförmig.
globule *s.* Kügelchen *n.*
gloom, gloominess *s.* Dunkelheit *f.*; Trübsinn *m.*
gloomy *a.*, **~ily** *adv.* düster; traurig.
glorification *s.* Verherrlichung *f.*
glorify *v.t.* verherrlichen;
glorious *a.*, **~ly** *adv.* glorreich; ruhmreich.
glory *s.* Ruhm *m.*; Herrlichkeit *f.*; Stolz *m.*; ~ *v.i.* sich rühmen.
gloss *s.* Glanz *m.*; Politur *f.*; Glosse *f.*; ~ *v.t.* polieren; Glossen machen; *to* ~ *over*, beschönigen, bemänteln.
glossary *s.* Glossar, *n.*
glossy *a.* glänzend, glatt.

glottal stop *s.* Knacklaut *m.*; Glottisschlag *m.*
glove *s.* Handschuh *m.*; ~**compartment** *s.* Handschuhfach *n.*
glow *v.i.* glühen; ~ *s.* Glut *f.*
glower *v.i.* finster dreinblicken.
glowing *a.* glühend, begeistert.
glow-worm *s.* Glühwürmchen *n.*
glucose *s.* Glucose *f.*
glue *s.* Leim *m.*; ~ *v.t.* leimen.
glum *a.* finster, mürrisch.
glut *v.t.* überladen; ~ *s.* Überfluß *m.*
glutinous *a.* klebrig.
glutton *s.* Fresser *m.*; Vielfraß *m.*
gluttonous *a.*, **~ly** *adv.* gefräßig.
gluttony *s.* Gefräßigkeit *f.*
glycerin *s.* Glyzerin *n.*
gnarled *a.* knorrig, ästig.
gnash *v.t.* knirschen.
gnat *s.* Mücke *f.*
gnaw *v.t.* nagen, zerfressen.
gnome *s.* Gnom, Erdgeist *m.*
go *v.i.st.* gehen; fahren; gelten; *the sirens* ~, die Sirenen gehen an; *it goes without saying,* es versteht sich von selbst; *to* ~ *back on one's word,* sein Versprechen nicht erfüllen od. zurücknehmen; *to* ~ *down,* fallen (Preise); *to* ~ *fishing,* zum Fischen gehen; *to* ~ *in for,* sich auf etwas legen; *to* ~ *off,* explodieren; *to* ~ *on,* weitermachen, fortfahren; *to* ~ *sour,* sauer werden; *to* ~ *through,* durchsehen; durchmachen; *to* ~ *up,* steigen (Preise); *to* ~ *to law,* eine Klage anstrengen; ~ *s.* Gang, Lauf *m.*; Bewegung *f.*, Schwung, Schneid *m.*
goad *s.* Treibestachel *m.*; ~*v.t.* stacheln; quälen.
go-ahead *a.* rührig, strebsam.
goal *s.* Mal *n.*; Grenzpfahl *m.*; Zeil *n.*; (Fußball) Tor *n.*
goalie, goal-keeper *s.* Torwart, Tormann *m.*
goat *s.* Ziege *f.*; *he-goat,* Ziegenbock *m.*
gobble *v.t.* gierig verschlingen.
go-between *s.* Vermittler *m.*
goblet *s.* Becher *m.*
goblin *s.* Kobold *m.*
god *s.* Gott *m.*
godchild *s.* Patenkind *n.*
goddess *s.* Göttin *f.*
godfather *s.* Pate *m.*
god-forsaken *a.* gottverlassen.
godless *a.* gottlos.
godlike *a.* göttlich.
godly *a.* gottselig, fromm.
godmother *s.* Patin *f.*
godparent *s.* Pate *m.*; Patin *f.*
godsend *s.* Gottesgabe *f.*
go-getter *s.* Draufgänger(in) *m.(f).*
goggle *v.i.* glotzen; die Augen verdrehen; ~**s** *s.pl.* Schutzbrille *f.*
goiter *s.* Kropf *m.*
gold *s.* Gold *n.*
golden *a.* golden. ~ **eagle** *s.* Steinadler *m.*; ~ **hamster** *s.* Goldhamster *m.*; ~ **rule** *s.* goldene Regel *f.*
goldfinch *s.* Stieglitz *m.*
goldfish *s.* Goldfisch *m.*
gold-leaf *s.* Goldblatt, Blattgold *n.*
gold-plated *a.* vergoldet.
goldsmith *s.* Goldschmied(in) *m.(f.)*
golf *s.* Golf *n.*; ~**-course, ~-links,** Golfplatz *m.*;

~-club *s.* Golfschläger; Golf Klub *m.*

golfer *s.* Golfspieler(in) *m.*(*f.*); Golfer(in) *m.*(*f.*)

gondola *s.* Gondel *f.*

gondolier *s.* Gondolier *m.*

gone *p. & a.* weg, fort; vergangen.

gong *s.* Gong *m. & n.*

gonorrhea *s.* (*med.*) Tripper *m.*

good *a.* gut, wohl; recht; **~-Friday**, Karfreitag *m.*; *be ~ enough*, seien Sie so freundlich; *to make ~*, vergüten, (Versprechen) erfüllen; sich durchsetzen, sich bewähren; *~ s.* Gut *n.*; *this is no ~*, das ist nichts wert; *~s pl.* Güter *pl.*; Habe *f.*; Waren *pl.*

good-bye *adv. & s.* lebe wohl!; Lebewohl *n*; auf Wiedersehen!

good-humored *a.* gutmütig; gutgelaunt.

goodies *s. pl.* Naschereien Süßigkeiten.

good-looking *a.* hübsch, schön.

goodly *a.* schön; beträchtlich.

good-natured *a.* gutmütig.

goodness *s.* Güte, *f.*; *for ~, sake*, um Himmels willen!; *~ gracious*, gütiger Himmel!; *thank ~*, Gott sei Dank!

good-tempered *a.* gutmütig; verträglich.

goodwill *s.* guter Ruf einer Firma *m.*

goof *s.* (*fam.*) Schnitzer *m.*; *~ v.i.* Mist machen.

goose *s.* Gans *f.*

gooseberry *s.* Stachelbeere *f.*

goose-flesh *s.* Gänsehaut *f.*

goose-pimples *s.pl.* *to have ~* Gänsehaut haben.

goose-step *s.* Paradeschritt *m.*

Gordian *a.* gordisch, verwickelt.

gore *s.* geronnenes Blut *n.*; Zwickel *m.*

gorge *s.* Kehle, Gurgel *f.*; Felsenschlucht *f.*; *~ v.t.* verschlucken; vollstopfen.

gorgeous *a.*, **~ly** *adv.* glänzend, prächtig.

gorilla *s.* Gorilla *m.*

gormandize *v.i.* schlemmen.

gorse *s.* Stechginster *m.*

gory *a.* blutig, mörderisch.

gosh (*fam.*) Gott!

gosling *s.* Gänseküken *n.*; Gössel *n.*

gospel *s.* Evangelium *n.*

gossamer *s*, Altweibersommer *m.*; Sommerfäden *m.pl.*

gossip *s.*; Klatschbase *f.*; Klatsch *m.*; *~ v.i.* klatschen.

Gothic *a.* gotisch; *Gothic letters pl.* (*typ.*) Fraktur *f.*

gouge *v.t.* aushöhlen.

goulash *s.* Gulasch *n.*

gourd *s.* Kürbis *m.*

gourmand *s.* Gourmand, Schlemmer *m.*

gourmet *s.* Gourmet *m.*, Feinschmecker *m.*

gout *s.* Gicht *f.*

gouty *a.* gichtisch.

govern *v.t.* regieren, lenken, beherrschen; *~ v.i.* herrschen.

governess *s.* Erzieherin *f.*

governing body *s.* Vorstand (Krankenhaus, Schule) *m.*

government *s.* Regierungsform, Regierung *f.*; **~-property**, Behördeneigentum *n.*

governor *s.* Gouverneur *m.*; (*fam.*) Chef, Vater *m.*; Prinzipal *m.*

gown *s.* Frauenkleid *n.*; Abendtoilette *f.*; Talar *m.* (*law & univ.*)

grab *v.t.* plötzlich greifen, packen; *~ s.* (*fig.*) Räuberei *f.*

grace *s.* Gnade *f.*; Anmut *f.*; Tischgebet *n.*; *Your ~*, (Titel) Euer Gnaden; *~ v.t.* begünstigen; schmücken.

graceful *a.*, **~ly** *adv.* anmutig, gnädig, graziös, reizend.

gracious *a.*, **~ly** *adv.* gnädig.

gradation *s.* Steigerung *f.*; Abstufung *f.*; Ablaut *m.*

grade *s.* Grad, Rang *m.*; Klasse *f.*; Note *f.* *~ v.t.* abstufen, einateilen.

gradient *s.* Steigung *f.*

gradual *a.*, **~ly** *adv.* allmählich.

graduate *v.t.* in Grade teilen; abstufen; *~ v.i.* einen Grad erlangen; *~ s.* Person (*f.*) mit akademischem Grad.

graduation *s.* Abtufung *f.*; Graduierung *f.*; Absolvieren *n.*

graffiti *s.pl.* Graffiti *pl.*

graft *s.* Pfropfreis *n.*; Transplantation *f.* *~ v.t.* pfropfen; transplantieren.

grain *s.* Korn, Samenkorn *n.*; Gran *m. & n.*; Holzfaser *f.*

gram *s.* Gramm *n.*

grammar *s.* Grammatik *f.*

grammarian *s.* Grammatiker *m.*

grammatical *a.*, **~ly** *adv.* grammatisch.

gramophone *s.* Grammophon *n.*

granary *s.* Kornboden *m.*; Kornkammer *f.* Getreidesilo *m.*

grand *a.* groß, erhaben; großartig.

grand-child *s.* Enkel(in) *m.*(*f.*)

granddaughter *s.* Enkelin *f.*

grandduke *s.* Großherzog *m.*

grandee *s.* Grande (in Spanien) *m.*; hoho Herr *m.*

grandeur *s.* Grösse *f.*; Pracht *f.*

grandfather *s.* Großvater *m.*

grandiloquent *a.* großprecherisch; hochtrabend.

grandiose *a.* hochtrabend; großartig.

grandly *adv.* großartig; aufwendig.

grandmother *s.* Großmutter *f.*

grandparent *s.* Großvater *m.*; Großmutter *f.*; **~s** *pl.* Großeltern.

grand piano *s.* (Konzert)Flügel *m.*

grandstand *s.* Tribüne *f.*

granite *s.* Granit *m.*

granny *s.* (*fam.*) Großmütterchen *n.*

grant *v.t.* zugestehen; bewilligen, verleihen; *~ s.* Beihilfe *f.*; stipendium *n.*

granular *a.* gekörnt, körnig, granuliert.

granulate *v.t.* (*v.i.* sich) körnen.

granulated sugar *s.* Kristallzucker *m.*

granule *s.* Körnchen *n.*

grape *s.* Weinbeere *f.*; *bunch of ~s*, Weintraube *f.*

grapefruit *s.* Grapefruit *f.*

graph *s.* Schaubild *n.*; Diagramm *n.*; graphische Darstellung *f.*

graphic *a.* graphisch, genau; anschaulich; *~ representation*, graphische Darstellung *f.*, Kurvenbild *n.*

graphically *adv.* plastisch, anschaulich; graphisch.

graphite *s.* Graphit *m.*

grapple *v.t.* packen, ergreifen; *~ v.i.* ringen (mit).

grasp *s.* Griff *m.*; Bereich *m.*; Fassungskraft *f.*; *~ v.t.* greifen, fassen; *~ v.i.* haschen; streben.

grasping *a.* gierig, habsüchtig.

grass *s.* Gras *n.*

grasshopper *s.* Grashüpfer *m.*

grassland *s.* Grasland *n.*; Weideland *n.*
grassroots *s.pl.* Wurzel *f.*; (*pol.*) Basis *f.*
grassplot *s.* Rasenplatz *m.*
grasssnake *s.* Ringelnatter *f.*
grass-widow *s.* Strohwitwe *f.*
grass-widower *s.* strohwitwer *m.*
grassy *a.* grasbedecht.
grate *s.* Feuerrost *m.*; ~ *v.t.* vergittern; raspeln; kränken; ~ *v.i.* knirschen.
grateful *a.*, ~**ly** *adv.* dankbar; angenehm.
grater *s.* Reibe *f.*, Raspel *f.*
gratification *s.* Befriedigung *f.*
gratify *v.t.* befriedigen; willfahren.
gratifying *a.* erfreulich.
grating *s.* Gitter *n.*
gratis *a.* unentgeltlich.
gratitude *s.* Dankbarkeit *f.*
gratuitous *a.*, ~**ly** *adv.* unentgeltlich; unberechtigt.
gratuity *s.* Trinkgeld *n.*
grave *a.* feierlich, ernst; tief (vom Tone); ~ *s.* Grab *n.*
grave-digger *s.* Totengräber *m.*
gravel *s.* Kies *m.*
gravestone *s.* Grabstein *m.*
graveyard *s.* Friedhof *m.*
gravitate *v.i.* gravitieren, zuneigen.
gravity *s.* Ernst *m.*; Schwere *f.*; Wichtigkeit *f.*; Schwerkraft *f.*; Gravitation *f.*
gravy *s.* Sauce *f.*, Bratensaft *m.* Saft des Fleisches *m.*; ~ **boat** *s.* Sauciere *f.*
gray *a.* grau; ~ *s.* Grau *n.*
grayish *a.* etwas grau, gräulich.
gray matter *s.* (*fig.*) graue Zellen *pl.*
graze *v.i.* weiden, grasen; ~ *v.t.* abweiden; streifen; *s.* Schürfwunde *f.*
grease *s.* Fett *n.*, Schmiere *f.*; ~ *v.t.* schmieren; bestechen.
greaseproof paper *s.* Butterbrotpapier *n.*; Pergamentpapier *n.*
greasy *a.*, ~**ily** *adv.* fett, schmierig.
great *a.* groß; ~~**grandfather,** etc. *s.* Urgroßvater, etc.
Great Britain *s.* Großbritannien.
greatly *adv.* sehr; stark.
greatness *s.* Größe, Macht *f.*
Grecian *a.* griechisch.
Greece *s.* Griechenland *n.*
greed, greediness *s.* Gier(igkeit) *f.*
greedy *a.*, ~**ily** *adv.* gierig.
Greek *a.* griechisch; *s.* Grieche *m.*; Griechin *f.*
green *a.*, ~**ly** *adv.* grün; frisch; unreif; unerfahren; ~ *s.* Rasenplatz *m.*; ~**s** *s.pl.* Gemüse *n.*
greenbelt *s.* Grüngürtel *m.*
greenery *s.* Grün *n.*
greengage *s.* Reineclaude (Pflaume) *f.*
greengrocer *s.* Gemüsehändler *m.*
greenhorn *s.* grüner Junge *m.*
greenhouse *s.* Gewächshaus *n.*
greenish *a.* grünlich.
Greenland *s.* Grönland *n.*
Green Party *s.* (*pol.*) die Grünen.
greet *v.t.* grüßen.
greeting *s.* Begrüßung *f.*, Gruß *n.*; ~ **card** *s.* Grußkarte *f.*
gregarious *a.*, ~**ly** *adv.* gesellig.
gremlin *s.* Kobald *m.*

grenade *s.* Granate *f.*
grenadier *s.* Grenadier *m.*
greyhound *s.*, Windhund *m.*
grid, *s.* Bratrost *m.*; (Gitter)Netz *n.*; Raster *n.*
grief *s.* Gram, Kummer *m.*
grievance *s.* Beschwerde *f.*
grieve *v.t.* kränken; ~ *v.i.* sich grämen.
grievous *a.*, ~**ly** *adv.* schmerzlich; schwer.
grill *v.t.* rösten; ~ *s.* Bratrost *m.*
grille *s.* Gitter *n.*
grim *a.*, ~**ly** *adv.* grimmig.
grimace *s.* Fratze, Grimasse *f.*
grimalkin *s.* (alte) Katze *f.*
grime *s.* Schmutz *m.*; ~ *v.t.* beschmutzen.
grimy *a.* schmutzig, rußig.
grin *s.* Grinsen *n.*; ~ *v.i.* grinsen.
grind *v.t.st.* mahlen; (Orgel) drehen; (*teeth*) knirschen; schleifen; quälen.
grinder *s.* Schleifmaschine *f.*; Mühle *f.*
grindstone *s.* Schleifstein *m.*
grip *s.* Griff; ~ *v.t.* fest greifen.
gripe *v.t.* (*fam.*) meckern, schimpfen ~ *s.* Meckern *n.* ~**s** *pl.* Bauchgrimmen *n.*
gripping *a.* packend.
grisly *a.* scheußlich.
grist *s.* Mahlgut *n.*
gristle *s.* Knorpel *m.*
grit *s.* Grieß *m.*; (*fig.*) Festigkeit *f.*
gritty *a.* sandig.
grizzled, grizzly *a.* grau; ~ **bear** *s.* Grizzlybär *m.*
groan *v.i.* seufzen, stöhnen; ~ *s.* Seufzer *m.*; Murren *n.*
grocer *s.* Lebensmittelhändler(in) *m.*(*f.*)
groceries *s.pl.* Lebensmittel *pl.*
grocery store *s.* Lebensmittelgeschäft *n.*
grog *s.* Grog *m.*
groin *s.* Leiste *f.*; Rippe *f.*; ~*ed arch,* Kreuzbogen *m.*
groom *s.* Aufwärter *m.*; Stallknecht *m.*; ~ *v.t.* ein Pferd warten.
groove *s.* Rille *f.* Nut *f.*; (*fig.*) Gleis *n.*; ~ *v.t.* auskehlen, falzen.
grope *v.i. & t.* tappen, tasten.
gross *a.*, ~**ly** *adv.* dick; dumm; grob, ordinär, zotig; Brutto . . .; ~ **national product** Bruttosozialprodukt ~ **weight** *s.* Bruttogewicht *n.*; ~ *s.* Ganze *n.*; Masse *f.*; Gros *n.*
grotesque *a.*, ~**ly** *adv.* grotesk.
grotto *s.* Grotte *f.*
grouch *s.* Miesepeter *m.*; Spielverderber(in) *m.*(*f.*); ~ *v.i.* nörgeln, meckern.
grouchy *a.* nörglerisch.
ground *s.* Grund, Boden *m.*; (Beweis-) Grund *m.*; (*elek.*) Erde *f.*; ~**s** *pl.* Bodensatz *m.*; ~ *v.t.* gründen; (*elek.*) erden; ~ **breaking** *a.* bahnbrechend.
ground control *s.* Flugsicherung *f.*
ground-floor *s.* Erdgeschoß *n.*
ground-forces *pl.* (*mil.*) Bodentruppen *pl.f.*
ground glass *s.* (*phot.*) Mattscheibe *f.*
grounding *s.* Anfangsgründe *m.pl.*; Grundwissen *n.*
groundless *a.*, ~**ly** *adv.* grundlos.
groundnut *s.* Erdnuß *f.*
ground-plan *s.* Grundriß *m.*
ground water *s.* Grundwasser *n.*
groundwork *s.* Grundlage *f.*
group *s.* Gruppe *f.*; (*avi.*) Gruppe *f.*; ~~**captain** *s.*

Gruppenkommandeur *m.*; ~ *v.t.* gruppieren.
grouping *s.* Gruppierung *f.*
grouse *s.* schottisches Moorhuhn *n.*; ~ *v.i.* meckern.
grout *s.* Mörtel *m.*
grove *s.* Hain *m.*, Gehölz *n.*
grovel *v.i.* kriechen.
grow *v.i.st.* wachsen; werden; ~ *v.t.* bauen, kultivieren.
grower *s.* Pflauzer(in) *m.(f.)*; Produzent(in) *m.(f.)*
growl *v.i.* brummen, knurren; ~ *s.* Brummen *n.*
grown-up *a.* erwachsen; ~ *s.* Erwachsene *m./f.*
growth *s.* Wachstum *n.*, Wuchs *m.*; Erzeugnis *n.*; Gewächs *n.*; ~ **industry** *s.* Wachstunsindustrie *f.*
grub *s.* Larve, Made *f.*; Wurm *m.*; Futter *n.*; (*sl.*) Essen *n.*; ~ *v.t.* wühlen; futtern.
grudge *v.t.* mißgönnen, ungern tun; ~ *s.* Groll, Neid *m.*
grudging *a.* ~ly *adv.* widerwillig.
gruel *s.* Haferschleim *m.*, Grütze *f.*
grueling *a.* erschöpfend, aufreibend.
gruesome *a.* grausig.
gruff *a.*, ~ly *adv.* mürrisch.
grumble *v.i.* murren, brummen.
grumbler *s.* Querulant(in) *m.(f.)*
grumpy *a.* mürrisch, böse.
grunt *v.i.* grunzen; *s.* Grunzen *n.*
guarantee *s.* Bürge *m.*, Bürgin *f.*; Bürgschaft, Pfandsumme *f.*; ~ *v.t.* verbürgen, garantieren.
guaranty *s.* Bürgschaft *f.*
guard *s.* Wache *f.*; Schutz *m.*; Stichblatt (Degen) *n.*; Garde *f.*; Schaffner *m.*; ~ *of honor s.* Ehrenwache *f.*; *on one's* ~, auf der Hut; *to be on* ~, Wache stehen; ~s *pl.* Leibwache *f.*; ~ *v.t.* bewachen, beschützen; ~ *v.i.* auf der Hut sein.
guarded *adv.* zurückhaltend; vorsichtig.
guardian *s.* Aufseher *m.*; Vormund *m.*; Beschützer *m.*; ~-**angel** Schutzengel *m.*; *to place under the care of a* ~, unter Vormundschaft stellen.
guardianship *s.* Vormundschaft *f.*
guard-rail *s.* Geländer *n.*
guardsman *s.* Gardist *m.*
guerilla *s.* Freischärler, Partisan *m.*; Guerillakämpfer(in) *m.(f.)*
guess *v.i. & t.* mutmassen, (er)raten; ~ *s.* Vermutung *f.*
guest *s.* Gast *m.*
guest; ~house *s.* Pension *f.*; ~**room** *s.* Gästezimmer *n.*
guffaw *s.* brüllendes Gelächter *n.*
guidance *s.* Führung, Leitung *f.*
guide *v.t.* leiten, führen; ~ *s.* Führer(in) *m.(f.)*
guidebook *s.* Reiseführer *m.*
guided missile *s.* (*mil.*) Lenkflugkörper *m.*
guide-dog *s.* Blindenhund *m.*
guided tour *s.* Fuhrung *f.*
guidelines *s.pl.* Richtlinien *f.pl.*
guild *s.* Gilde, Innung *f.*
guilder *s.* holländischer Gulden *m.*

guile *s.* Betrug *m.*; Arglist *f.*
guileless *a.* arglos, ehrlich.
guillotine *s.* Guillotine *f.*, Fallbeil *n.*
guilt *s.* Schuld *f.*
guiltless *a.* unschuldig.
guilty *a.*, ~ily *adv.* schuldig.
guinea pig *s.* Meerschweinchen *n.*
guise *s.* Gewand *n.*; Maske *f.*
guitar *s.* Gitarre *f.*
guitarist *s.* Gitarrist(in) *m.(f.)*.
gulch *s.* Schlucht *f.*
gulf *s.* Meerbusen *m.*; Abgrund *m.*
gull *s.* Möwe *f.*
gullet *s.* Gurgel *f.*; Schlund *m.*
gullible *a.* leichtgläubig.
gully *s.* Abfluß, *m.*, Gully *m.*
gulp *s.* Schluck, Zug *m.*; ~ *v.t.* schlucken.
gum *s.* Gummi *n.*; Zahnfleisch *n.*; ~ *v.t.* gummieren.
gumption *s.* (*fam.*) Grips *m.*; Verstand *m.*
gun *s.* Geschütz *n.*; Kanone *f.*; Flinte *f.*, Gewehr *n.*; Revolver *m.*; ~-**license** *s.* Waffenschein *m.*; ~-**running** *s.* Waffenschmuggel *m.*
gun-battle *s.* Schießerei *f.*
gun-boat *s.* Kanonenboot *n.*
gun carriage *s.* Lafette *f.*
gun-cotton *s.* Schießbaumwolle *f.*
gunpowder *s.* Schießpulver *n.*
gun-shot *s.* Schuß *m.*; Schußweite *f.*
gunsmith *s.* Büchsenmacher *m.*
gunwale *s.* (*nav.*) Schaudeck *n.*
gurgle *v.i.* gurgeln; rieseln.
gush *v.i.* strömen; ~ *s.* Guß *m.*; Schwall *m.*; Überschwenglichkeit *f.*
gushing *a.* reißend.
gusset *s.* Zwickel *m.*; Keil *m.*
gust *s.* Windstoß *m.*; Bö *f.*
gusto *s.* Eifer *m.*, Vernügen *n.*
gusty *a.* böig.
gut *s.* Darm *m.*; ~s *pl.* Eingeweide *n.*; ~ *v.t.* ausweiden; ausbrennen (ein Haus); **gutted** *p.* ausgebrannt.
gutter *s.* Rinne, Gosse *f.*
gutter press *s.* Sensationspresse *f.*
gutteral *a.* Kehl . . .; guttural; ~ *s.* Kehllaut *m.*
guy *s.* Halteseil *n.*; (*fam.*) Typ *m.*
guzzle ~ *v.t.* verschlingen.
gym *s.* (*fam.*) Turnhalle *f.*, Turnen *n.*
gymnasium *s.* Turnhalle *f.*
gymnastic(al) *a.*, ~ly *adv.* gymnastisch.
gymnastics *s.pl.* Turnen *n.*; Gymnastik *f.*
gym-shoe *s.* Turnschuh *m.*
gynecological *a.* gynäkologisch.
gynecologist *s.* Gynäkologe *m.*, Gynäkologin *f.*
gynecology *s.* Gynäkologie *f.*; Frauenheilkunde *f.*
gypsum *s.* Gips *m.*
gyrate *v.i.* wirbeln, kreiseln.
gyration *s.* Drehung *f.*
gyroscope *s.* Kreiselkompaß *m.*; Gyroskop *n.*

H

H, h der Buchstabe H oder h *n.*
habeas corpus *s.* Anordnung (*f.*) eines Haftprüfungstermins.
haberdashery *s.* Herrenmoden *pl.f.*
habit *s.* Gewohnheit *f.*; Zustand *m.*; Habit *m.*; *by ~,* aus Gewohnheit.
habitable *a.* bewohnbar.
habitat *s.* Habitat *n.*; Lebensraum *m.*
habitation *s.* Wohnung *f.*
habitual *a.,* **~ly** *adv.* gewohnt, gewohnheitsmäßig.
habituate *v.t.* gewöhnen.
habitué *s.* Stammgast *m.*
hack *v.t.* hacken; *~ s.* Hieb *m.*
hacker *s.* (*comp.*) Hacker *m.*
hackney-coach *s.* Mietskutsche *f.*
hackneyed *a.* abgedroschen.
hack-saw *s.* Metallsäge *f.*
hack-writer *s.* Lohnschreiber *m.*
haddock *s.* Schellfisch *m.*
haft *s.* Stiel *m.*; Heft *n.*; Griff *m.*
hag *s.* Hexe *f.*
haggard *a.,* **~ly** *adv.* wild; hager.
haggle *v.i.* handeln, feilschen.
hail *s.* Hagel *m.*; *~ v.i.* hageln; *~ s.* Ruf *m.*; *within ~,* in Rufweite; *~! i.* Glück! Heil!; *~ v.t.* grüßen; anrufen; stammen; *to ~ a taxi,* ein Auto herbeirufen.
hailstone *s.* Hagelkorn *n.*
hair *s.* Haar *n.*; *to do one's ~,* sich die Haare machen; *~-style, ~-do,* Frisur *f.*; *long-~ed a.* langhaarig; *short-~ed a.* kurzhaarig.
hairbrush *s.* Haarbürste *f.*
hair-cut *s.* Haarschnitt *m.*
hair-dresser *s.* Friseur *m.*, Friseuse *f.*
hair-drier *s.* Haartrockner *m.*
hairpin *s.* Haarnadel *f.*; *~-turn* Haarnadelkurve *f.*
hair-raising *a.* haarsträubend.
hair-splitting *s.* Wortklauberei *f.*
hair-style *s.* Frisur *f.*
hair-tonic *s.* Haarwuchsmittel *n.*
hairy *a.* haarig, behaart; (*fig.*) schwierig.
halberd *s.* Hellebarde *f.*
halcyon *a.* still, friedlich.
hale *a.* heil, frisch, gesund.
half *a.* halb; *~ past five,* halb sechs; *~ s.* Hälfte *f.*
half-back *s.* (Fußball) Läufer *m.*
half-blood *s.* Halbblut *n.*
half-breed *s.* Mischling *m.*
half-cast *s.* Halbblut *n.*
half-hearted *a,* halbherzlg.
half-pay *s.* Ruhegehalt *n.*, Pension *f.*
halfway *adv.* auf halbem Wege.
half-witted *a.* einfältig.
half-yearly *a.* halbjährlich.
halibut *s.* Heilbutte *m.*
halitosis *s.* Halitose *f.*; schlechter Mundgeruch *m.*
hall *s.* Saal *m.*; Halle *f.*; (Guts-) Herrenhaus *n.*; Hausflur *f.*
hallmark *s.* Feingehaltsstempel *m.*; Kennzeichen *n.*
hallo! *i.* hallo!
hallow *v.t.* weihen, heiligen.
Halloween *s.* Abend (*m.*) vor Allerheiligen.
hall-porter *s.* Hotelportier *m.*

hallstand *s.* Kleiderständer *m.*
hallucinate *v.i.* halluzinieren.
hallucination *s.* Halluzination *f.*
hallucinogenic *a.* halluzinogen.
hallway *s.* Flur *m.*; Korridor *m.*
halo *s.* Hof (um Sonne oder Mond), *m.*; Heiligenschein *m.*
halt *i.* halt!; *s.* Halt *m.*; *~ v.i.* anhalten; hinken; zögern.
halter *s.* Halfter *f.* & *m.*
halting *a.* schleppend; zögernd.
halve *v.t.* halbieren.
ham *s.* Schenkel *m.*; Schinken *m.*
hamburger *s.* Hamburger *m.*, Hacksteak *n.*
hamlet *s.* Weiler *m.*, Dörfchen *n.*
hammer *s.* Hammer *m.*; Hahn (am Gewehr) *m.*; *~ v.t.* hämmern, schmieden.
hammock *s.* Hängematte *f.*
hamper *v.t.* belästigen, behindern; *s.* (Deckel) Korb *m.*
hamster *s.* Hamster *m.*
hamstring *s.* Kniesehne *f.*
hand *s.* Hand *f.*; Handschrift *f.*; Uhrzeiger *m.*; Richtung, Seite *f.*; Arbeiter *m.*; Karten (*f.pl.*) eines Spielers; *at ~,* zur Hand, nah; *at the ~s of,* von Seiten; *by ~,* mit der Hand; *signed in his own ~,* eigenhändig unterschrieben; *on ~,* vorrätig, auf Lager; *to give* (*lend*) *a ~,* helfen, zugreifen; *to have on one's ~s,* auf den Hals haben; *on the one ~, on the other ~,* einerseits, andererseits; *out of ~,* unlenkbar; *off ~,* aus dem Stegreif; *the upper ~,* die Oberhand; *~ v.t.* einhändigen; reichen; *to ~ down* (*order, decision*), (Entscheidung) erlassen; *to ~ over,* übergeben, überstellen.
hand-bag *s.* Handtasche *f.*
hand-baggage *s.* Handgepäck *n.*
handbill *s.* (Werbe-) Zettel *m.*
handbook *s.* Handbuch *n.*
hand-brake *s.* Handbremse *f.*
hand-carved *a.* handgeschnitzt.
handcuff *s.* Handfessel *f.*
handful *s.* Handvoll *f.*
hand-grenade *s.* Handgranate *f.*
handicap *s.* Vorgabe *f.*; Belastung *f.*; (*fig.*) Behinderung *f.*; Vorgaberennen; *to ~, v.t.* belasten; hemmen.
handicapped *a.* behindert; *~ s.* Behinderte *m./f.*
handicraft *s.* (Kunst) Handwerk *n.*
handiwork *s.* Handarbeit *f.*
handkerchief *s.* Taschentuch *n.*
handle *s.* Griff *m.*; Henkel *m.*; *v.t.* anfassen; handhaben; umgehen mit.
handlebar *s.* Lenkstange *f.*
handmade *a.* handgearbeitet.
handmade paper *s.* Büttenpapier *n.*
hand-out *s.* Almosen *n.*; Handzettel *m.*; Handout *n.*
hand-painted *a.* handbemalt.
hand-picked *a.* handverlesen.
handrail *s.* Geländer *n.*
handset *s.* (Telefon) Hörer *m.*
handshake *s.* Händedruck *m.*
handsome *a.,* **~ly** *adv.* gutaussehend; schön.

ausehnlich.

handstand *s.* Handstand *m.*

hand-tailored *a.* handgeschneidert.

hand-to-hand fighting *s.* Handgemenge *n.*

handwriting *s.* Handschrift *f.*

handwritten *a.* handgeschrieben.

handy *a.*, **~ily** *adv.*; geschickt; handlich; griffbereit.

handyman *s.* Handwerker *m.*

hang *to get the* ~ *of it*, hinter etwas kommen, ~ *v.t.* hängen, behängen; *to* ~ *oneself*, sich aufhängen; ~ *v.i.* hängen, schweben.

hangar *s.* Flugzeughalle *f.*

hanger *s.* Kleiderbügel *m.*; Aufhänger *m.*

hang glider *s.* Drachenflieger(in) *m.(f.)*

hang gliding *s.* Drachenfliegen *n.*

hanging *a.* Hänge...

hangman *s.* Henker *m.*

hangover *s.* Kater *m.*, Katzenjammer *m.*

hank *s.* Strang *m.*

hanker *v.i.* sich sehnen, trachten.

hankering *s.* Verlangen *n.*

hanky *s.* Taschentuch *n.*; **~-panky** *s.* (*fam.*) Mauschelei *f.*

haphazard willkürlich; unbedacht.

hapless *a.* unglücklich.

happen *v.i.* sich ereignen; *I ~ed to be there*, ich war zufällig da.

happiness *s.* Glück *n.* Heiterkeit *f.*

happy *a.*, **~ily** *adv.* glücklich; heiter; froh.

happy ending *s.* Happyend *n.*

happy-go-lucky *a.* sorglos.

harass *v.t.* belästigen; schikanieren.

harrasment *s.* Belästigung *f.*

harbinger *s.* Vorbote *m.*

harbor *s.* Hafen *m.*; Zufluchtsort *m.*; **~-dues** *pl.* Hafengebühren *f.pl.*; ~ *v.t.* beherbergen; hegen; ~ *v.i.* vor Anker gehen.

hard *a. & adv.* hart; mühsam; **~up**, in Not, ohne Geld; ~ **cash** *s.* klingende Münze *f.*; ~ **coal** *s.* Steinkohle *f.*; ~ **drinks** *pl.* alkoholische Getränke *n. pl.*; ~ **rubber** *s.* Hartgummi *m.*

harden *v.t.* härten; ~ *v.i.* hart werden, sich verhärten; (Preise) anziehen.

hardened *a.* verhärtet; abgehärtet.

hardening *s.* Härten *n.*; Verhärtung *f.*

hard headed *a.* praktisch; starrköpfig.

hard hearted *a.* hartherzig.

hard-liner *s.* Befürworter(in) *m.(f.)* einer harten Linie.

hardly *adv.* kaum.

hardness *s.* Härte *f.*

hardship *s.* Beschwerde *f.*; Ungemach *n.*; Not *f.*

hardware *s.* Metallwaren *f.pl.*; Eisenwaren.

hard-working *a.* fleißig.

hardy *a.*, **~ily** *adv.* hart, fest, stark; tapfer; kühn; abgehärtet.

hardy: ~ **annual** *s.* winterharte einjährige Pflanze *f.*; ~ **perennial** *s.* winterharte mehrjährige Pflanze *f.*

hare *s.* Hase *m.*

hare-bell *s.* Glockenblume *f.*

hare-brained *a.* unüberlegt.

hare-lip *s.* Hasenscharte *f.*

harem *s.* Harem *m.*

haricot *s.* weisse Bohne *f.*

hark *v.i.* horchen; ~! *i.* horch!

harlequin *s.* Harlekin *m.*

harm *s.* Unrecht, Leid *n.*; Schaden *m.*; *to do* ~, schaden; ~ *v.t.* verletzen, beeinträchtigen.

harmful *a.*, **~ly** *adv.* schädlich.

harmless *a.* unschädlich, arglos, harmlos; unverletzt; *to render* ~, (Granate) blind machen.

harmonic *a.* wohlklingend.

harmonica *s.* Harmonika *f.*

harmonics *s.pl.* Harmonielehre *f.*

harmonious *a.* harmonisch.

harmonize *v.t.* in Einklang bringen; ~ *v.i.* übereinstimmen, harmonieren.

harmonium *s.* Harmonium *n.*

harmony *s.* Einklang *m.*

harness *s.* Pferdegeschirr *n.*; Harnisch *m.*; ~ *v.t.* anschirren.

harp *s.* Harfe *f.*; ~ *v.i.* dauernd reden; herumreiten auf.

harpist *s.* Harfenspieler(in) *m.(f.)*

harpoon *s.* Harpune *f.*; ~ *v.t.* harpunieren.

harpsichord *s.* Cembalo *n.*

Harpy *s.* Harpyie *f.*

harrow *s.* Egge *f.*; ~ *v.t.* eggen; quälen, heimsuchen.

harrowing *a.* entsetzlich; grauenhaft.

harry *v.t.* angreifen; bedrängen.

harsh *a.*, **~ly** *adv.* herb, rauh; barsch.

hart *s.* Hirsch *m.*

hartshorn *s.* Hirschhorn *n.*

harum-scarum *a.* Hals über Kopf, hastig.

harvest *s.* Ernte *f.*; ~ *v.t.* ernten.

harvester *s.* Erntemaschine *f.*; Erntearbeiter(in) *m.(f.)*

harvest-home *s.* Erntefest *n.*

hash *v.t.* zerhacken; ~ *s.* gehacktes Fleisch *n.*, Haschee *n.*

hashish *s* Haschisch *n.*

hasp *s.* Haspe *f.*

hassle *s.* Krach *m.*; Mühe *f.*

haste *s.* Eile, Hast *f.*; Eifer *m.*

hasten *v.n.* eilen; ~ *v.t.* beschleunigen.

hasty *a.*, **~ily** *adv.* eilig; hastig; hitzig.

hat *s.* Hut *m.*; **~-box** *s.* Hutschachtel *f.*; *to raise one's* ~ *to a person*, vor einem den Hut abnehmen.

hatch *v.t.* ausbrüten; ausschlüpfen; ~ *v.i.* im Werke sein; ~ *s.* Brut *f.*; Luke *f.* **~-back** *s.* (Auto *n.*) mit Heckklappe *f.*

hatchet *s.* Beil *n.*; Axt *f.*

hate *s.* Haß *m.*; ~ *v.t.* hassen.

hateful *a.*, **~ly** *adv.* verhaßt, gehässig.

hatred *s.* Haß *m.*

hatter *s.* Hutmacher *m.*

haughty *a.*, **~ily** *adv.* stolz, hochmütig.

haul *v.t.* ziehen, schleppen; ~ *s.* Ziehen; Schleppen *n.*; Fang.

haulage *s.* Transport *m.*; **~-contractor** *s.* Transportunternehmer *m.*

haunch *s.* Lendenstück *n.*; Keule *f.* ~ *of venison s.* Keule *f.*

haunt *v.t.* oft besuchen; beschweren, plagen; umgehen, spuken in.

haunted *p. & a.* nicht geheuer; *a* ~ *house*, ein Haus, in welchem es spukt.

have *v.t.ir.* haben; halten; bekommen; lassen; ~ *to*, müssen.

haven *s.* Hafen *m.*; geschütete Anlegestelle *f.*

haversack s. Brotbeutel m.
havoc s. Verwüstung, Zerstörung f.
haw s. Hagebutte f.
Hawaii s. Hawaii n.
Hawaiian a. hawaiisch; s. Hawaiianer(in) m.(f.)
hawk s. Habicht m.; Falke m.;. ~ v.i. mit Falken jagen; hausieren.
hawker s. Hausierer m.
hawser s. (nav.) Kabeltau n., Trosse f.
hawthorn s. (red) Rotdorn m., (white) Weißdorn m.
hay s. Heu n.
hay-cock s. Heuschober m.
hay-fever s. Heuschnupfen m.
hay-loft s. Heuboden m.
hay-stack s. Heuschober m.
hazard s. Gefahr f.; ~ v.t. aufs Spiel setzen.
hazardous a., **~ly** adv. gefährlich.
haze s. Dunst m.; leichter Nebel m.
hazel s. Haselnußstrauch m. ~ a. hasel.
hazel-nut s. Haselnuß f.
hazy a. nebelig; dunstig; unbestimmt.
he pn. er; ~ s. Männchen n.
head s. Haupt n.; Kopf m.; Spitze (einer Kolonne etc.) f.; Gipfel m.; Schiffschnabel m.; Kapitel n.; Punkt m.; Titel (Buch, Abschnitt) m.; Stück n.; Vorsteher m.; Ober . . . ; to bring to a ~, zur Entscheidung bringen; he could not make ~ or tail of it, er konnte daraus nicht klug werden; ~ v.t. & i. anführen, befehligen; mit einer Überschrift versehen; (nav.) einen Kurs nehmen.
headache s. Kopfweh n.
headboard s. Kopfende n.
head-dress s. Kopfputz m.
header s. Kopfsprung m., Kopfball m.
headgear s. Kopfbedeckung f.
headhunter s. Kopfjäger m.
heading s. Überschrift f.
headland s. Landspitze f.
headless a. kopflos, unbesonnen.
headlights pl. Scheinwerferlicht (Auto) n.
headlong a. & adv. kopfüber.
headmaster s. Schulleiter m.
headmistress s. Schulleiterin f.
headphone s. Kopfhörer m.
headquarters pl. Hauptgeschäftsstelle, Zentrale f.; Hauptquartier n.; vorgesetzte Stelle f.
headstrong a. halsstarrig.
head-waiter s. Oberkellner m.
headway s. Fortschritt m.
headwind s. Gegenwind m.
heady a. berauschend.
heal v.t. & i. heilen, zuheilen.
healing s. Heilung f.
health s. Gesundheit f.
health-food shop s. Reformhaus n.
health-insurance s. Krankenversicherung f.
health resort s. Kurort m.
health service s. Gesundheitsdienst m.
health visitor s. Krankenschwester f., Krankenpfleger m. im Sozialdienst.
healthy a., **~ily** adv. gesund.
heap s. Haufen m.; ~ v.t. häufen.
hear v.t. & i.ir. hören, anhören; erfahren; verhören; to ~ a case, (law) einen Fall verhandeln.

hearing s. Hören n.; Gehör n.; Verhör n., Verhandlung f. (law); Anhörung f.; Hearing n.; Hörweite f.; hard of ~, schwerhörig; ~ aid s. Hörgerät n.; to fix a ~, (law) einen Termin anberaumen.
hearsay s. Hörensagen n.; by ~, vom Hörensagen.
hearse s. Leichenwagen m.
heart s. Herz n.; Gemüt n.; at ~, im Grunde; by ~, auswendig; to take ~, Mut fassen; Herz (in der Karte).
heartache s. Qual f.
heart attack s. Herzanfall m.
heartbeat s. Herzschlag m.
heartbreaking a. herzzerreißend.
heartburn s. Sodbrennen n.
heart condition s. Herzleiden n.
hearten v.t. ermutigen.
heartening a. ermutigend.
heart-failure s. Herzversagen n.
heartfelt a. innig empfunden, herzlich.
hearth s. Kamin; m. **~rug** s. Kaminvorleger m.
heartless a., **~ly** adv. grausam; herzlos.
heartrending a. herzzerreißend.
heart-searching s. Gewissenserforschung f.
heart-shaped a. herzförmig.
heart-transplant s. Herztransplantation f.
heart-trouble s. Probleme (n.pl.) mit dem Herzen.
heart-warming a. herzerfreuend.
hearty a., **~ily** adv. herzlich, aufrichtig.
heat s. Hitze f.; Lauf m., Brunst(zeit) f.; (phys.) Wärme; **blood-~** s. Blutwärme; **body-~** s. Körperwärme f.; **~proof** a., wärmesicher; ~v.t. heizen; erhitzen.
heated a., **~ly** adv. hitzig.
heater s. Ofen m.; Boiler m.
heath s. Heide f.
heathen s. Heide m., Heidin f.; ~a. heidnisch.
heather s. Heidekraut n., Heide f.
heating s. Heizung f.; **~-unit** s. Heizkörper m.
heat-resistant a. hitzebeständig.
heat-stroke s. Hitzschlag m.
heatwave s. Hitzewelle f.
heave v.t. st. heben; erheben; (nav.) lichten; ~ v.i. schwellen; ~ s. Heben n.; Wogen n.
heaven s. Himmel m.
heavenly a. & adv. himmlisch.
heaviness s. Schwere f.; Gewicht n.
heavy a., **~ily** adv. schwer; träge; ~ artillery, schwerste Artillerie f.; ~ smoker, starker Raucher m.; ~ type, (typ.) Fettdruck m.; ~ traffic, starker Verkehr m.
heavy-duty a. strapazierfähig.
heavyweight s. Schwergewicht (Boxen) n.
Hebrew a. hebräisch; ~ s. Hebräer(in) m.(f.)
heckle v.t. (einen Redner) durch Zwischenrufe unterbrechen.
hectic a. hektisch.
hedge s. Hecke f.; Zaun m.; ~ v.t. einhegen; to ~ v.i. Ausflüchte machen.
hedgehog s. Igel m.; **~-position** s. (mil.) Igelstellung f.
hedgerow s. Hecke f.
heed s. Aufmerksamkeit f.; ~ v.t. beachten.
heedful a., **~ly** adv. vorsichtig.
heedless a., **~ly** adv. unachtsam.
heel s. Ferse f.; Absatz m.; ~ v.t. mit einem Absatz versehen; ~v.i. sich auf die Seite legen (nav.).

hefty *a.* handfest, unentwegt, stramm.
hegemony *s.* Vorherrschaft *f.*
height *s.* Höhe *f.*; Gipfel *m.*
heighten *v.t.* erhöhen, verbessern.
heinous *a.*, ~**ly** *adv.* abscheulich; schändlich.
heir *s.* Erbe *m.*; ~-**apparent** *s.* rechtmäßiger Erbe; ~-**at-law** *s.* gesetzlicher Erbe *m.*; ~-**presumptive** *s.* mutmaßlicher Erbe *m.*
heiress *s.* Erbin *f.*
heirloom *s.* Erbstück *n.*; Erbe *n.*
heist *s.* Raubüberfall *m.*; ~ *v.t.* rauben.
helical *a.* schraubenfömig, Spiral...
helicopter *s.* Hubschrauber *m.*, Helikopter *m.*
heliport *s.* Heliport *m.*
helix *s.* Spirale *f.*
hell *s.* Hölle *f.*
hellfire *s.* Höllenfeuer *n.*
hellish *a.*, ~**ly** *adv.* höllisch.
helm *s.* Steuerruder *n.*
helmet *s.* Helm *m.*
helmsman *s.* Steuermann *m.*
help *s.* Hilfe *f.*; ~*v.t. & i.* helfen; (bei Tische) bedienen; ~ *yourself!* langen Sie zu!; *Can I help you?* Kann ich Ihnen behilflich sein?; *I cannot ~ it,* ich kann es nicht ändern.
helper *s.* Helfer(in) *m.(f.)*
helpful *a.* behilflich, nützlich.
helping *s.* Portion (Essen), *f.*; *second ~*, zweite Portion *f.*
helpless *a.*, ~**ly** *adv.* hilflos.
helpmate *s.* Gehilfe *m.*; Gehilfin *f.*
helter-skelter *adv.* Hals über Kopf.; holterdiepolter.
hem *s.* Saum *m.*; Räuspern *n.*; ~ *v.t.* säumen; ~*vi.i* sich räuspern.
hemisphere *s.* Halbkugel *f.*; Hemisphäre *f.*
hemline *s.* Saum *m.*
hemlock *s.* Schierling *m.*
hemoglobin *s.* Hämoglobin.
hemophilia *s.* Hämophilie *f.*, Bluterkrankheit *f.*
hemorrhage *s.* Blutsturz *m.*
hemorrhoids *s.pl.* Hämorrhoiden *f.pl.*
hemostatic *a.* blutstillend.
hemp *s.* Hanf *m.*; Haschisch *n.*
hem-stitch *s.* Hohlsaum *m.*; ~ *v.t.* mit Hohlsam nähen.
hen *s.* Henne *f.*; Huhn *n.*
hence *adv.* von hier; von nun an; daher.
henceforth *adv.* von nun an: von da an.
henchman *s.* (*pol.*) Anhänger *m.*; Handlanger *m.*
henpecked *p.* unter dem Pantoffel stehend.
her *pn.* sie, ihr.; (*poss.*) ihr.
herald *s,.* Herold *m.*; ~ *v.t.* verkünden.
heraldry *s.* Wappenkunde *f.*; Heraldik *f.*
herb *s.* Kraut *n.*; Gras *n.*
herbaceous *a.* krautartig.
herbal *a.* Kräuter...
herbalist *s.* Kräuterkenner *m.*
herbarium *s.* Herbarium *n.*
herbivore *s.* Pflanzenfresser *m.*
herbivorous *a.* pflanzenfressend.
herd *s.* Herde *f.*
herdsman *s.* Hirte *m.*
here *adv.* hier; her.
hereafter *adv.* künftig.
hereat *adv.* hierbei.

hereby *adv.* hierdurch; hiermit.
hereditary *a.*, ~**ily** *adv.* erblich.
heredity *s.* Vererbung *f.*; Erblichkeit *f.*
herein *adv.* hierin; hier hinein.
hereinafter *adv.* im Folgenden.
hereof *adv.* hiervon.
hereon *adv.* hieran, hierauf, hierüber.
heresy *s.* Ketzerei *f.*
heretic *s.* Ketzer *m.*
heretical *a.*, ~**ly** *adv.* ketzerisch.
heretofore *adv.* ehemals.
herewith *adv.* hiermit.
heritage *s.* Erbgut *n.*, Erbschaft *f.*
hermaphrodite *s.* Zwitter *m.*
hermetic *a.*, ~**ally** *adv.* luftdicht.
hermit *s.* Einsiedler *m.*
hermitage *s.* Einsiedelei *f.*
hernia *s.* (*med.*) Bruch *m.*
hero *s.* Held *m.*
heroic *a.*, ~**ally** *adv.* heldenhaft, heroisch.
heroine *s.* Heldin *f.*
heroism *s.* Heldenmut *m.*
heron *s.* Reiher *m.*
herpes *s.* Herpes *m.*
herring *s.* Hering *m.*
hers *pn.* der, die, das ihrige.
herself *pn.* sie selbst, ihr selbst, sich.
hesitant *a.* zögernd; unsicher.
hesitate *v.i.* zögern.
hesitation *s.* Unschlüßigkeit *f.*; Unsicherheit *f.*
heterodox *a.* irrgläubig.
heterogeneous *a.* verschiedenartig.
heterosexual *a.* heterosexuell; ~ *s.* Heterosexuelle *m./f.*
hew *v.t.* hauen, hacken, fällen.
hex *v.t.* verhexen.
hexagon *s.* Sechseck *n.*
hexameter *s.* Hexameter *m.*
heyday *s.* Höhepunkt *m.*, Blüte *f.*
hibernate *v.i.* Winterschlaf halten.
hibernation *s.* Winterschlaf *m.*
hiatus *s.* Bruch *m.*; Unterbrechung *f.*
hiccup *s.* Schluckauf *m.*; ~*v.i.* den Schluckauf haben.
hide *s.* Hauf *f.*; Fell *n.*; ~ *v.t.st.* verstecken; ~ *v.i.st.* sich verstecken; ~ *and seek.* Versteckenspiel *n.*
hidebound *a.* engstirnig, engherzig.
hideous *a.*, ~**ly** *adv.* scheußlich.
hide-out *s.* Versteck *n.*
hiding *s.* Versteck *n.*; (*fam.*) Tracht Prügel *f.*
hiding-place *s.* Schulpfwinkel *m.*
hierarchic, hierarchical *a.*; ~**ly** *adv.* hierarchisch.
hierarchy *s.* Hierarchie *f.*
hieroglyphic *a.* hieroglyphisch; ~**s** *s.pl.* Hieroglyphen *f.pl.*
high *a.*, ~**ly** *adv.* hoch, erhaben; (Wild) angegangen; ~**life** *s.* vornehme Welt *f.*; *highly strung a.* nervös, reizbar; ~ *s.* Hoch (Wetterkunde) *n.*
high altar *s.* Hochaltar *m.*
high brow *s.* Intellektuelle *m./f.* ~ *a.* intellektuell; hochgestochen.
High Church *s.* Hochkirche *f.*
higher education *s.* Hochschulbildung *f.*
high explosive *s.* Sprengstoff *m.*
high-flown *a.* schwülstig.

high-flyer s. Hochbegabte m./f.; (fam.) Überflieger(in) m.(f.)
high-grade a. hochwertig.
high-handed a. selbstherrlich.
high-heeled a. hochhackig (Schuhe).
highland s. Hochland n.
highness s. Höhe f.; Hohheit f. (Titel).
high-powered a. Hochleistungs...; dynamisch.
high pressure s. Hochdruck m.
high priest s. Hohepriester m.
high-ranking a. hochrangig.
high-rise s. Hochhaus n.
highroad, highway s. Landstraße f.
high school s. Oberschule f.
high seas pl. hohe See f.
high season s. Hochsaison f.
high tech a. High-Tech-...
high tension, high voltage s. (elek.) Hochspannung f.; ~ **cable** s. Hochspannungsleitung f.
high water s. Hochwasser n.
highwayman s. Straßenräuber m.
highway robbery s. Straßenraub m.
hijack v.t. entführen.
hijacker s. Entführer(in) m.(f.)
hike v.i. wandern; to hitchhike per Anhalter fahren.
hiker s. Wanderer m., Wanderin f.
hilarious a. heiter, aufgeheitert.
hilarity s. Fröchlichkeit f.
hill s. Hügel m., Berg m.
hillbilly s. Hinterwäldler(in) m.(f.)
hillock s. kleiner Hügel m.
hillside s. Hang m.
hilltop s. Gipfel m.
hilly a. hügelig.
hilt s. Heft n.; Degengefäß n.
him pn. ihn, ihm; den, dem.
himself pn. er selbst, ihn selbst, ihm selbst; sich.
hind a. hinter; ~s. Hirschkuh f.
hinder v.t. hindern, stören.
hindmost a. hinterst.
hind-quarters s.pl. Hinterbeine (des Pferdes), n.pl.
hindrance s. Hindernis n.
hindsight s. **with**~ im nachhinein.
hinge s. Türangel f.; Scharnier n.; ~ v.i. (fig.) ~on, sich um etwas drehen.
hint s. Wink, Fingerzeig m.; Anspielung f.; ~ v.t. zu verstehen geben.
hinterland s. Hinterland n., Umland n.
hip s. Hüfte f.; Hagebutte f.
hip-bath s. Sitzbad n.
hip-bone s. Hüftknochen m.
hip flask s. Flachmann m.
hip-joint s. Hüftgelenk n.
hippie s. Hippie m.
hippodrome s. Rennbahn f.
hippopotamus s. Nilpferd n.
hire s. Miete f.; Lohn m.; on ~, zu vermieten; ~ v.t. mieten, vermieten; anwerben.
hirsute a. haarig, rauh.
his pn. sein; der, die, das seinige.
hiss v.i. zischen; ~ v.t. auszischen.; ~ s. Zischen n.
historian s. Geschichtsforscher(in) m.(f.)
historic a. historisch.
historical a., ~**ly** adv. geschichtlich.
historiographer s. Geschichtschreiber(in) m.(f.)
history s. Geschichte f.

histrionic a. dramatisch.
hit v.t.ir. schlagen, stossen; treffen; ~ v.i. anstossen; zusammenstossen; ~ s. Schlag, Stoss m.; Treffer, Zufall m.; (theat.) Schlager m.; (mil.) direct ~, Volltreffer m.
hitch v.t. & i. festmachen; (sich) ruckweise bewegen; ~ s. Ruck m.; (nav.) Knoten m.; Schwierigkeit f.
hitch-hike v.i. per Anhalter fahren.
hitch-hiker s. Anhalter(in) m.(f.)
hither adv. hierher; ~ a. diesseitig.
hitherto adv. bisher.
hit man s. (sl.) Killer m.
hive s. Bienenstock, Schwarm m.; ~ v.i. beisammen wohnen.
hoard s. Vorrat, Schatz m.; ~ v.t. & i. aufhäufen, sammeln; hamstern.
hoarder s. Hamsterer m., Hamsterin f.
hoarding s. Bretterzaun m.
hoar-frost s. Reif m.
hoarse a., ~**ly** adv. heiser.
hoary a. eisgrau; bereift.
hoax s. Schwindel m.; Streich m.; blinder Alarm m. ~ v.t. foppen.
hobble v.i. humpeln.
hobby s. Steckenpferd n.
hobgoblin s. Kobold m.
hobnail s. Nagel m.; hobnailed boots pl. genagelte Schuhe m.pl.
hob-nob v.i. vertaulich zusammen trinken (anstossen).
hobo s. Landstreicher m.
hock s. Rheinwein m. ~v.t. versetzen.
hockey s. Hockey n.
hockey-stick s. Hockeyschläger m.
hocus-pocus s. Taschenspielerei f.
hodge-podge s. Mischmasch m.
hoe s. Hacke f.; ~ v.t. hacken.
hog s. Schwein n.
hoggish a., ~**ly** adv. schweinisch.
hoi polloi s. breite Masse f.
hoist v.t. in die Höhe heben; hissen; ~ s. (Personen) Aufzug m.
hoity-toity a. hochnäsig; leichtsinnig.
hold v.t.st. halten; behalten; enthalten; meinen, schätzen; besitzen; ~ v.i. sich halten; beharren; to ~ forth, darstellen; hinreißen; vortragen; to ~ good, sich bestätigen; gültig sein; to ~ off, abhalten, ausweichen; ~ on!, ~ the line!, bleiben Sie am Telephon!; to ~ on to, (mil.) (eine Stellung) halten; to ~ out, ausstrecken; aushalten; anbieten; to ~ up, in die Höhe halten; aufrecht erhalten, unterstützen; ~! halt!; ~ s. Halten, Fassen n.; Griff m.; Gewalt f.; Schiffsraum m.; Lager n.; to get ~ of, habhaft werden; ~~all s. Reisekoffer m.
holder s. Inhaber m.; Halter m.
holding s. Pachtgut n.; Besitz m.; ~ **company** s. Dachgesellschaft f.; (mil.) ~~**line** s. Auffanglinie f.
hold-up s. Raubüberfall m.
hole s. Loch n.; (fig.) Klemme f.
holiday s. Feiertag m.; ~ of obligation, gebotener Feiertag m.; public ~, gesetzlicher Feiertag m.; on ~, in den Ferien; ~**s** pl. Ferien pl.; ~s with pay, bezahlter Urlaub m.
holiness s. Heiligkeit f.
Holland s. Holland n.

hollow *a.* hohl; falsch; ~ *s.* Höhle *f.*; ~ *v.t.* aushöhlen.

holly *s.* Stechpalme *f.*

hollyhock *s.* Stockrose *f.*

holm *s.* Holm, Werder *m.*; Uferland *n.*

holocaust *s.* Holocaust *m.*; Massenvernichtung *f.*

holograph *s.* eigenhändig geschriebenes Dokument *n.*

holster *s.* Halfter *f.* & *m.*

holy *a.* heilig; ~ *Saturday*, Karsamstag *m.*

holy-water *s.* Weihwasser *n.*

holy-week *s.* Karwoche *f.*

homage *s.* Huldigung *f.*; *to do* ~, huldigen.

home *s.* Heimat *f.*; Wohnung *f.*; ~ *a.* heimisch; **~-address** *s.* Heimatadresse *f.*; *~-for the elderly s.* Altersheim *n.*; **~-rule** *s.* Selbstverwaltung *f.*; **~-trade** *s.* Binnenhandel *m.*; *~adv.* heim; nach Hause; tüchtig, derb; *at* ~, zu Hause.

homeless *a.* obdachlos, heimatlos; *~s.* Obdachlose *m./f.*

homely *a.* & *adv.* einfach, schmucklos.

home-made *a.* zu Hause hergestellt.

homeopathic *a.* homöopathisch *f.*

homeopathy *s.* Homöopathie *f.*

homesick *a.* *be* ~ Heimweh haben.

homesickness *s.* Heimweh *n.*

homestead *s.* Heimstätte *f.*; Gehöft *n.*

hometown *s.* Heimatstadt *f.*

homeward(s) *adv.* heimwärts; ~ *bound*, auf der Rückreise.

homework *s.* Hausarbeiten, Hausaufgaben (des Schülers) *f.pl.*

homey *a.* gemütlich.

homicidal *a.* gemeingefährlich.

homicide *s.* Totschlag *m.*

homily *s.* Predigt *f.*

homing pigeon *s.* Brieftaube *f.*

homogeneous *a.* gleichartig.

homogenize *v.t.* homogenisieren.

homonym *s.* Homonym *n.*

homosexual *a.* homosexuell; *s.* Homosexuelle *m./f.*

homosexuality *s.* Homosexualität *f.*

hone *s.* Wetzstein *m.*; *~v.t.* wetzen.

honest *a.*, **~ly** *adv.* anständig; redlich.

honesty *s.* Ehrlichkeit, Ehrbarkeit *f.*

honey *s.* Honig *m.*; Süßigkeit *f.*

honey-comb *s.* Honigwabe *f.*

honeyed *a.* honigsüß.

honeymoon *s.* Flitterwochen *f.pl.*

honeysuckle *s.* Geißblatt *n.*

honk *s.* Hupen *n.*; *~v.i.* hupen.

honorary *a.* Ehren. . .

honor *s.* Ehre, Würde *f.*; ~ *v.t.* ehren, beehren; honorieren (Wechsel).

honorable *a.*, **~bly** *adv.* ehrenvoll, ehrbar, achtbar.

hood *s.* Haube *f.*; Kapuze *f.*

hoodlum *s.* Rowdy *m.*

hoodwink *v.t.* täuschen.

hoof *s.* Huf *m.*; Klaue *f.*

hook *s.* (Angel-)Haken *m.*; Gartenmesser *n.*; *by* ~ *or by crook*, so oder so; ~ *v.t.* anhaken.

hooked *p.* & *a.* gebogen, gekrümmt; (*fam.*) süchtig.

hooker *s.* (*fam.*) Nutte *f.*

hooligan *s.* Rowdy *m.*

hoop *s.* Reifen *m.*; Reifrock *m.*; ~ *v.t.* (ein Faß) binden; ~ *v.i.* laut rufen.

hooper *s.* Böttcher *m.*

hoot *v.i.* tuten, hupen, heulen.

hop *v.i.* hüpfen; ~ *v.t.* hopsen; ~ *s.* Hüpfen *n.*; Sprung *m.*; Hopsen *m.*; Hopfen *m.*; *~s pl.* (*com.*) Hopfen.

hope *s.* Hoffnung *f.*; ~ *v.i.* hoffen.

hopeful *a.*, **~ly** *adv.* hoffnungsvoll.

hopeless *a.* hoffnungslos.

horde *s.* Horde *f.*

horizon *s.* Horizont *m.*; (*avi.*) *artificial* ~, künstlicher Horizont *m.*

horizontal *a.*, **~ly** *adv.* waagerecht.

horizontal bar *s.* Reck (Turnen) *n.*

hormone *s.* Hormon *m.*

horn *s.* Horn *n.*; **~-signal** *s.* Hupsignal *n.*

horned *a.* gehörnt.

hornet *s.* Hornisse *f.*

horn-rimmed *a.* ~ *spectacles pl.* Hornbrille *f.*

horny *a.* hornig; (*vulg.*) geil.

horoscope *s.* Horoskop *n.*

horrendous *a.* schrecklich; horrend.

horrible *a.*, **~bly** *adv.* abscheulich.

horrid *a.* schrecklich.

horrific *a.* schreckenerregend.

horrify *v.t.* entsetzen.

horror *s.* Entsetzen *n.*; Greuel *m.*

horror-stricken, horror-struck *s.* von Entsetzen gepackt.

horse *s.* Pferd *n.*; *on ~-back*, zu Pferde; **~-riding** *s.* Reiten *n.*

horse-breaker *s.* Bereiter *m.*

horse-chestnut *s.* Roßkastanie *f.*

horse-dealer *s.* Pferdehändler *m.*

horsedrawn *a.* (*mil.*) Pferde. . . , bespannt; ~ *artillery*, bespannte Artillerie *f.*; ~ *vehicle*, Pferdefuhrwerk *n.*

horsehair *s.* Roßhaar *n.*

horseman *s.* Reiter *m.*

horsemanship *s.* Reitkunst *f.*

horse-play *s.* Balgerei *f.*

horse-power *s.* Pferdekraft *f.*

horse-race *s.* Pferderennen *n.*

horseradish *s.* Meerrettich *m.*

horseshoe *s.* Hufeisen *n.*

horse-trailer *s.* Pferdeanhänger *m.*

horsewoman *s.* Reiterin *f.*

horticultural *a.* zum Gartenbau gehörig.

horticulture *s.* Gartenbau *m.*

hose *s.* Strumpf *m.*; Spritzenschlauch *m.*

hosier *s.* Strumpfwarenhändler *m.*

hosiery *s.* Strumpfwaren *f.pl.*

hospice *s.* Hospiz *n.*; Sterbeklinik *f.*

hospitable *a.*, **~ly** *adv.* gastlich; gastfreundlich.

hospital *s.* Hospital, Krankenhaus *n.*; **~-ship** *s.* Lazarettschiff *n.*; **~-train** *s.* Lazarettzug *m.*

hospitality *s.* Gastlichkeit *f.*

hospitalize *v.t.* ins Krankenhaus einweisen.

host *s.* Gastgeber *m.*; Wirt *m.*; Heer *n.*, Schwarm *m.*

hostage *s.* Geisel *m.*

hostel *s.* Herberge *f.*

hostess *s.* Wirtin *f.*; Gastgeberin *f.*

hostile *a.*, **~ly** *adv.* feindlich.

hostility *s.* Feindseligkeit *f.*

hot *a.*, **~ly** *adv.* heiß; scharf (gewürzt).

hot air *s.* leeres Gerede.
hotbed *s.* Mistbeet *n.*, Frühbeet *n.*; (*fig.*) Brutstätte *f.*
hot-blooded *a.* heißblütig, hitzig.
hotchpotch *s.* Mischmasch *m.*
hotel *s.* Gasthof *m.*, Hotel *n.*
hot-house *s.* Treibhaus *n.*
hot line *s.* heißer Draht *m.*
hot plate *s.* Heizplatte *f.*
hot-water bottle *s.* Wärmflasche *f.*
hound *s.* Jagdhund, Hetzhund *m.*
hour *s.* Stunde *f.*
hour-glass *s.* Sanduhr *f.*
hour-hand *s.* Stundenzeiger *m.*
hourly *a. & adv.* stündlich.
house *s.* Haus *n.*; (*theat.*) Zuschauerraum *m.*; ~ *v.t.* beherbergen; ~ *v.i.* hausen.
house-agent *s.* Häusermakler *m.*
housebreaker *s.* Einbrecher *m.*
household *s.* Haushalt *m.*, Haushaltung *f.*; ~ *a.* häuslich, einfach.
householder *s.* Haushaltsvorstand *m.*
housekeeper *s.* Haushälterin *f.*
housekeeping *s.* Haushalten *n.*; ~ *a.* Haushalts. . .
house of correction *s.* Besserungsanstalt *f.*
house-search *s.* Haussuchung *f.*
house-warming party *s.* Einzugsparty *f.*
housewife *s.* Hausfrau *f.*
house work *s.* Hausarbeit *f.*
housing *s.* Wohnungen *pl.*; Obdach *n.*; Lagern *n.*; Satteldecke *f.*; **~-department,** **~-office** *s.* Wohnungsamt *n.*; **~-shortage** *s.* Wohnungsnot *f.*
hovel *s.* Schuppen *m.*; Hütte *f.*
hover *v.i.* schweben; schwanken; sich aufhalten.
hovercraft *s.* Luftkissenfahrzeug *n.*
how *adv.* wie.
however *adv.* wie dem auch sei, dennoch; aber, trotzdem; ~*c.* wie. . . auch.
howitzer *s.* Haubitze *f.*
howl *v.i.* heulen; ~ *s.* Geheul *n.*
howler *s.*(*sl.*) grober Fehler *m.*
hoyden *s.* Wildfang *m.*
hub *s.* Radnabe *f.*; Mittelpunkt *m.*
hubbub *s.* Tumult, Lärm *m.*
hubcap *s.* Radkappe *f.*
huckster *s.* Höker *m.*; ~ *v.i.* hökern.
huddle *s.* Verwirrung, Unordnung *f.*; ~ *v.t.* eilfertig verrichten, hudeln; ~ *v.i.* sich drängen; *to ~ oneself up*, sich zusammenkauern.
hue *s.* Farbe *f.*, Farbton *m.*; ~ *and cry*, Zetergeschrei *n.*; Hetze *f.*
huff *v.i.* keuchen, schnaufen.
hug *s.* Umarmung *f.*; ~ *v.t.* umarmen, liebkosen.
huge *a.* ungeheuer, riesig.
hulk *s.* Rumpf (des Schiffes) *m.*; Wrack *n.*
hull *s.* Schale, Hülse *f.*; Rumpf (des Schiffes) *m.*; Wanne (eines Panzers) *f.*; ~ *v.t.* schälen, enthülsen.
hullabaloo *s.* Spektakel, Klamauk *m.*
hullo *i.* hallo!
hum *s.* Gesumme, Gemurmel *n.*; ~! *i.* hm!; ~ *v.i.* summen, brummen.
human *a.*, **~ly** *adv.* menschlich; ~ *s.* Mensch *m.*
human being *s.* Mensch *m.*
humane *a.*, **~ly** *adv.* liebreich, menschenfreundlich.

humanism *s.* Humanismus *m.*
humanist *s.* Humanist(in) *m.*(*f.*)
humanitarian *a.* humanitär; ~ *s.* Menschenfreund *m.*
humanity *s.* Menschheit *f.*; Menschlichkeit *f.*; **~ties** *pl.* klassische Wissenschaft *f.*
humanize *v.t.* vermenschlichen, humanisieren.
humankind *s.* Menschengeschlecht *n.*
humble *a.*, **~bly** *adv.* bescheiden, unterwürfig; demütig; ~ *v.t.* demütigen.
humbug *s.* Schwindel *m.*; Humbug *m.*
humdrum *a.* langweilig; eintönig.
humid *a.* feucht, naß.
humidity *s.* Feuchtigkeit *f.*
humiliate *s.* erniedrigen; demütigen.
humiliation *s.* Demütigung *f.*
humility *s.* Unterwürfigkeit *f.*; Demut *f.*
humming-bird *s.* Kolbri *m.*
hummock *s.* Hügel *m.*
humor *s.* Humor *m.*; Komik *f.*; Komische *n.*; Laune *f.*
humorist *s.* Humorist(in) *m.*(*f.*)
humorless *a.* humorlos.
humorous *a.*, **~ly** *adv.* humoristisch; humorvoll.
hump, hump-back *s.* Höcker, Buckel *m.*
hump-backed *a.* buck[e]lig.
humus *s.* Humus *m.*
hunch *s.* Buckel *m.*; ~ *v.t.* krümmen.
hunch-back *s.* Buck[e]lige *m.*/*f.*
hundred *a.* hundert; ~ *s.* Hundert *n.*
hundred-weight *s.* (englischer) Zentner *m.* (112 Pfund; 50.8 kg.).
Hungarian *s.* Ungar(in) *m.*(*f.*)
Hungary *s.* Ungarn *n.*
hunger *s.* Hunger *m.*; ~ *v.i.* hungern; **~-strike** *s.* Hungerstreik *m.*
hungry *a.*, **~ily** *adv.* hungrig.
hunt *v.t. & i.* hetzen, jagen; nachspüren; ~ *s.* (Hetz-) Jagd *f.*
hunter *s.* Jäger(in) *m.*(*f.*); Jagdpferd *n.*
hunting *s.* (Hetz-) Jagd *f.*
hunting-license *s.* Jagdschein *m.*
huntsman *s.* Jäger *m.*
hurdle *s.* Hürde *f.* **~race** *s.* Hürdenlauf *m.*
hurdler *s.* Hürdenläufer(in) *m.*(*f.*)
hurl *v.t.* werfen, schleudern.
hurly-burly *s.* Wirrwarr *m.*; Tumult *m.*
hurrah *i.* hurra!
hurricane *s.* Orkan *m.*
hurried *a.* eilig, hastig; überstürzt.
hurry *s.* Eile, Unruhe *f.*; ~ *v.t.* beschleunigen, treiben; ~ *v.i.* eilen.
hurt *s.* ~ *v.t.ir.* verletzen; ~ *v.i.ir.* schmerzen, wehtun; ~*a.* verletzt; gekränkt.
hurtful *a.*, **~ly** *adv.* verletzend, kränkend.
husband *s.* Gatte, Ehemann *m.*; ~ *v.t.* haushalten.
husbandry *s.* Landwirtschaft *f.*; Haushaltung, Wirtschaftlichkeit *f.*
hush! *i.* still!; ~, stillen, beruhigen; *to ~ up*, vertuschen; ~ *v.i.* schweigen; *s.* Stille *f.*; Schweigen *n.*
hushed *a.* gedämpft.
hush-money *s.* Schweigegeld *n.*
husk *s.* Hülse *f.*; ~ *v.t.* aushülsen.
husky *a.* heiser, rauh; **~s.** Husky *m.*
hussar *s.* Husar *m.*
hussy *s* (*pej.*). Göre *f.*; Range *f.*

hustle *v.t.* stossen, drängen; eilen.
hut *s.* Hütte; Baracke *f.*
hyacinth *s.* Hyazinthe *f.*
hybrid *s.* Bastardtier *n.*, Bastardpflanze *f.*; ~ *a.* Zwitter...
hydrangea *s.* Hortensie *f.*
hydrant *s.* Wasserhahn *m.*; Hydrant *m.*
hydraulic *a.* hydraulisch.
hydrocarbon *s.* Kohlenwasserstoff *m.*
hydrocephalus *s.* Wasserkopf *m.*
hydrochloric acid *s.* Salzsäure *f.*
hydroelectric station *s.* Wasserkraftwerk *n.*
hydrogen *s.* Wasserstoff *m.*
hydrogenation *s.* Hydrierung *f.*
hydrogen bomb *s.* Wasserstoffbombe *f.*
hydrogen peroxide *s.* Wasserstoffsuperoxyd *n.*
hydro powerstation *s.* Wasserkraftwerk *n.*
hyena *s.* Hyäne *f.*
hygiene *s.* Hygiene *f.*
hygienic *a.* hygienisch.
hymen *s.* Jungfernhäutchen *n.*
hymn *s.* Loblied *n.*, Hymne *f.*; **church-~**, Kirchenlied *n.*; **~-book** *s.* Gesangsbuch *n.*
hype *s.* Reklameschwindel *m.*
hyperactive *a.* hyperaktiv.

hyperbola *s.* Hyperbel *f.*
hyperbole *s.* Übertreibung *f.*
hyperbolical *a.*, **~ly** *adv.* übertrieben.
hypercritical *a.* hyperkritisch.
hypersensitive *a.* übersensibel.
hyphen *s.* Bindestrich *m.*
hyphenated *a.* Bindestrich...
hypnosis *s.* Hypnose *f.*
hypnotic *a.* einschläfernd; hypnotisch.
hypnotism *s.* Hypnotismus *m.*
hypnotize *v.t.* hypnotisieren
hypochondria *s.* Hypochondrie *f.*
hypochondriac *s.* Hypochonder *m.*
hypocrisy *s.* Heuchelei *f.*
hypocrite *s.* Heuchler(in) *m.(f.)*
hypocritical *a.* heuchlerisch.
hypodermic *a.* subkutan.
hypothecary *a.* hypothekarisch.
hypothermia *s.* Unterkühlung *f.*
hypothesis *s.* Hypothese *f.*; Annahme *f.*
hypothetical *a.* hypothetisch.
hysterectomy *s.* Hysterektomie *f.*
hysteria *s.* Hysterie (bes. übertragen) *f.*
hysterical *a.* hysterisch.
hysterics *s.pl.* Hysterie *f.*; hysterischer Anfall *m.*

I

I, i der Buchstabe I oder i *n.*
I *pn.* ich; *it is* ~, ich bin's.
iamb *s.* Iambus *m.*
iambic *a.* iambisch.
Iberia *s.* Iberische Halbinsel *f.*
Iberian Peninsula *s.* Iberische Halbinsel *f.*
ibex *s.* Steinbock *m.*
ice *s.* Eis *n.*; Gefrorenes *n.*; ~ *v.t.* mit Eiskühlen; überzuckern.
ice age *s.* Eiszeit *f.*
iceberg *s.* Eisberg *m.*
ice-bound *a.* eingefroren.
icebox *s.* Kühlschrank *m.*
ice-breaker *s.* Eisbrecher *m.*
ice-cream *s.* Eis *n.*, Gefrorenes *n.*; **~-parlor** *s.* Eisdiele *f.*
ice-cube *s.* Eiswürfel *m.*
ice-floe *s.* Eisscholle *f.*
Iceland *s.* Island *n.*
Icelander *s.* Isländer(in) *m.(f.)*
Icelandic *a.* isländisch.
ice-pack *s.* Eispackung *f.*; Kühlakku *n.*
ice-rink *s.* Schlittschuhbahn *f.*
ice-skate *v.i.* eislaufen; Schlittschuh laufen.
ice-skating *s.* Schlittschuhlaufen *n.*
icicle *s.* Eiszapfen *m.*
icing *s.* Zuckerguß *m.*; Zuckerglasur *f.*
icon *s.* Ikone *f.*
iconoclast *s.* Bilderstürmer *m.*
icy *a.* eisig.
idea *s.* Begriff *m.*; Idee *f.*; Vorstellung *f.*; Gedanke *m.*
ideal *a.*, **~ly** *adv.* ideal; ~ *s.* Ideal *n.*
idealism *s.* Idealismus *m.*
idealist *s.* Idealist *m.*
idealistic *a.* idealistisch.
idealize *v.t.* idealisieren.

identic(al) *a.* identisch.
identifiable *a.* erkennbar; nachweisbar, bestimmbar.
identification, *s.* Identifizierung *f.*; **~card** *s.* Ausweis *m.*
identify *v.t.* identifizieren.
identity *s.* Identität *f.*; *to prove one's* ~, sich ausweisen.
ideological *a.* ideologisch, weltanschaulich.
ideology *s.* Ideologie, Weltanschauung *f.*
idiocy *s.* Blödsinn *m.*; Idiotie *f.*
idiom *s.* Mundart *f.*; Redewendung *f.*
idiomatic *a*; idiomatisch.
idiosyncrasy *s.* Eigentümlichkeit *f.*
idiosyncratic *a.* eigenwillig.
idiot *s.* Dummkopf *m.*; Idiot(in) *m.(f.)*
idiotic *a.* blödsinnig; einfältig.
idle *a.*, faul; unnütz; müßig, träge; stillgelegt; stillstehend; leerlaufend. **~away** *v.t.* vertändeln; **~hours** *pl.* Mußestunden *pl.*
idleness *s.* Müßiggang *m.*; Trägheit *f.*
isol *s.* Abgott *m.*; Götzenbild *n.*
idolatrous *a.*, **~ly** *adv.* abgöttisch.
idolatry *s.* Götzendienst *m.*; Vergötterung *f.*
idolize *v.t.* vergöttern.
idyll *s.* Idylle *f.*
idyllic *a.* idyllisch.
if *c.* wenn, falls; ob.
igloo *s.* Iglu *m.* od. *n.*
igneous *a.* feurig.
ignite *v.t.* anzünden, entzünden.
igniter *s.* Zünder *m.*
ignition *s.* Entzündung *f.*; Zündung *f.*; **~key** *s.* Zündschlüssel *m.*
ignoble *a.*, **~bly** *adv.* unedel, gemein.
ignominious *a.*, **~ly** *adv.* schimpflich, verwerflich.
ignominy *s.* Schmach, Schande *f.*

ignoramus s. Nichtswisser(in) m./f. Ignorant(in) m.(f.)

ignorance s. Unwissenheit f.

ignorant a., ~ly adv. unwissend.

ignore v.t. nicht wissen; unbeachtet lassen; ignorieren.

ilk s. of his~ seinesgleichen; Sorte f.

ill a. & adv. krank; unwohl; übel, böse; ~ at ease, unbehaglich; ~ s. Übel n.

ill-advised a. schlechtberaten; unbedacht.

ill-behaved a. ungezogen.

ill-bred a. schlecht erzogen, unmanierlich.

illegal a., ~ly adv. gesetzwidrig.

illegality s. Gesetzwidrigkeit f.

illegible a. unleserlich.

illegitimacy s. uneheliche Geburt f.

illegitimate a., ~ly adv. unrechtmäßig; unehelich; gesetzwidrig.

ill-fated a. unglücklich.

ill-feeling s. Verstimmung f.

ill-humored a. schlechtgelaunt.

illiberal a., ~ly adv. engherzig; karg.

illicit a. unerlaubt.

illiteracy s. Analphabetentum n.

illiterate a. des Lesens und Schreibens unkundig, analphabetisch; ~ s. Analphabet m.

ill-judged a. unüberlegt.

ill-luck s. Unglück n., Pech n.

ill-mannered a. ungehobelt.

ill-matched a. schlecht zusammenpassend.

ill-natured a. bösartig.

illness s. Krankheit f.

illogical a., ~ly adv. unlogisch.

ill-tempered a. schlechtgelaunt; übellaunig.

ill-timed a. ungelegen.

illtreat v.t. mißhandeln.

ill-treatment s. Mißhandlung f.

illuminate v.t. erleuchten; illuminieren.

illuminating a. aufschlußreich.

illumination s. Festbeleuchtung f.; Erleuchtung f.

ill-usage s. Mißhandlung f.

illusion s. Täuschung f.

illusive, illusory a. täuschend, trüglich.

illustrate v.t. erläutern; illustrieren.

illustration s. Erläuterung f.; Illustration, Abbildung f.

illustrative a., ~ly adv. erläuternd.

illustrator s. Illustrator(in) m.(f.)

illustrious a., ~ly adv. erlaucht.

ill-will s. Übelwollen n., Böswilligkeit f.

image s. Bild n., Bildnis n.; Image n.

imagery s. bildhafte Sprache f., Bilder pl., Metaphorik f.

imaginable a. denkbar.

imaginary a. eingebildet, imaginär.

imagination s. Phantasie f.

imaginative a. erfinderisch, phantasievoll.

imagine v.t. sich einbilden; ersinnen.

imbalance s. Unausgeglichenheit f.; Ungleichgewicht n.

imbecile a. schwachsinnig, idiotisch; ~s. Idiot m.

imbibe v.t. einsaugen, aufsaugen.

imbroglio s. Verwicklung f.

imbue v.t. durchdringen, tränken; erfüllen.

imitate v.t. nachahmen, nachbilden.

imitation s. Nachahmung f.

imitative a. nachahmend.

imitator s. Nachahmer(in) m.(f.)

immaculate a., ~ly adv. makellos; unbefleckt.

immanent a. innewohnend.

immaterial a., ~ly adv. unkörperlich; unwesentlich.

immature a., ~ly adv. unreif; unzeitig.

immaturity s. Unreife f.

immeasurable a., ~bly adv. unermeßlich.

immediate a. unmittelbar; unverzüglich; ~ly adv. sogleich.

immemorial a. undenklich.

immense a., ~ly adv. unermeßlich.

immensity s. Unermeßlichkeit f.; Ungeheuerlichkeit f.

immerse v.t. eintauchen, versenken.

immersion s. Eintauchen n.; ~heater s. Tauchsieder m.

immigrant s. Einwanderer m., Einwanderin f.

immigrate v.i. einwandern.

immigration s. Einwanderung f.

imminence s. Bevorstehen n.

imminent a. bevorstehend, drohend.

immobile a. unbeweglich.

immobility s. Unbeweglichkeit f.

immobilize v.t. unbeweglich machen; festlegen.

immoderate a., ~ly adv. unmäßig.

immodest a., ~ly adv. unbescheiden; unanständig.

immolate v.t. opfern.

immoral a. unsittlich; unmoralisch.

immorality s. Unsittlichkeit f.

immortal a., ~ly adv. unsterblich.

immortality s. Unsterblichkeit f.

immortalize v.t. unsterblich machen.

immovable a., ~bly adv. unbeweglich; ~s s.pl. unbewegliche Güter n.pl.

immune a. geschützt (gegen).

immunity s. Freiheit f.; Befreiung f.; Vorrecht n.; Immunität f.

immunization s. Schutzimpfung f.

immunize v.t. immunisieren.

immunology s. Immunologie f.

immure v.t. einmauern.

immutable a., ~bly adv. unveränderlich.

imp s. Kobold m.; kleiner Schelm m.

impact s. Stoß, Aufprall m.

impair v.t. vermindern, beeinträchtigen.

impale v.t. pfählen; aufspießen.

impart v.t. mitteilen; verleihen.

impartial a., ~ly adv. unparteiisch.

impartiality s. Unparteilichkeit f.

impassable a. unpassierbar.

impasse s. Sackgasse f.

impassible a. gefühllos; unverletzlich.

impassioned p. leidenschaftlich.

impassive a. unempfindlich; ausdruckslos.

impatience s. Ungeduld f.

impatient a., ~ly adv. ungeduldig.

impeach v.t. anfechten; anklagen.

impeachment s. Anklage f.

impeccable a. untadelig, einwandfrei.

impecunious a. geldlos.

impede v.t. verhindern; behindern.

impediment s. Hindernis n.; **marriage-~** s. Ehehindernis n.; **speech ~s.** Sprachfehler m.

impel v.t. antreiben.

impend *v.i.* (drohend) bevorstehen.
impenetrable *a.,* **~bly** *adv.* undurchdringlich; unerforschlich.
impenitent *a.,* **~ly** *adv.* unbußfertig.
imperative *a.,* **~ly** *adv.* gebieterisch; dringend nötig; *~s.* Imperativ *m.*
imperceptible *a.,* **~bly** *adv.* unmerklich.
imperfect *a.,* **~ly** *adv.* unvollkommen; *~ s.* (*gram.*) Imperfekt(um) *n.*
imperfection *s.* Unvollkommenheit *f.*
imperial *a.,* **~ly** *adv.* kaiserlich; Reichs. . .
imperialism *s.* Imperialismus *m.*
imperialist *s.* Imperialist(in) *m.*(*f.*)
imperil *v.t.* gefährden.
imperious *a.,* **~ly** *adv.* gebieterisch.
imperishable *a.* unverderblich, unvergänglich.
impermeable *a.* undurchlässig.
impermissible *a.* unzulässig.
impersonal *a.,* **~ly** *adv.* unpersönlich.
impersonate *v.t.* verkörpern; darstellen.
impersonation *s.* Verkörperung *f.,* Imitation *f.*
impersonator *s.* Imitator(in) *m.*(*f.*)
impertinence *s.* Anmassung *f.*; Unverschämtheit *f.*
impertinent *a.* frech.
imperturbable *a.* unerschütterlich.
impervious *a.* undurchlässig.
impetuosity *s.* Impulsivität *f.*
impetuous *a.,* **~ly** *adv.* ungestüm, impulsiv.
impetus *s.* Antrieb *m.*; Drang *m.*; Motivation *f.*
impiety *s.* Gottlosigkeit *f.*
impinge *v.i.* auftreffen; stoßen.
impious *a.,* **~ly** *adv.* gottlos.
impish *a.* schelmisch; lausbübisch.
implacable *a.,* **~bly** *adv.* unversöhnlich.
implant *v.t.* einpflanzen; einprägen.
implausible *a.* unglaubwürdig.
implement *s.* Zubehör *n.*; Gerät *n.*; *~ v.t.* durchführen, erfüllen.
implementation *s.* Ausführung *f.,* Durchführung *f.*
implicate *v.t.* belasten; verwickeln.
implication *s.* Implikation *f.,* Verwicklung *f.*; Folgerung *f.,* Voraussetzung *f.*
implicit, *a.,* **~ly** *adv.* implizit; unbedingt; stillschweigend einbegriffen.
implode *v.i.* implodieren.
implore *v.t.* anflehen; erflehen.
imploring *a.* flehend.
imploringly *adv.* flehentlich.
imply *v.t.* implizieren, in sich schließen; besagen; stillschweigend eischließen.
impolite *q.* unhöflich.
impoliteness *s.* Unhöflichkeit *f.*
impolitic *a.,* **~ly** *adv.* unklug.
imponderable *a.* unwägbar; *~s. pl.* unwägbare Dinge *n.pl.*
import *s.* Import *m.* Einfuhr *f.*; Wichtigkeit *f.*; *~ v.t.* importieren; einführen; bedeuten.
importance *s.* Wichtigkeit *f.*
important *a.,* **~ly** *adv.* wichtig; bedeutend.
importer *s.* Einführer (von Waren) *m.*
importunate *a.,* **~ly** *adv.* zudringlich.
importune *v.t.* beschweren, belästigen.
importunity *s.* Zudringlichkeit *f.*
impose *v.t.* auferlegen (Arbeit), verhängen (Strafe); *to ~ upon,* aufdrängen.

imposing *a.* imponierend.
imposition *s.* Auferlegung *f.*; Auflage *f.*; Belastung *f.*
impossibility *s.* Unmöglichkeit *f.*
impossible *a.,* **~bly** *adv.* unmöglich.
impost *s.* Steuer, Abgabe *f.*
impostor *s.* Betrüger *m.*
imposture *s.* Betrug *m.*
impotence *s.* Unvermögen *n.*; Impotenz *f.*
impotent *a.,* **~ly** *adv.* unvermögend, schwach; impotent.
impound *v.t.* beschlagnahmen; sperren.
impoverish *v.t.* arm machen.
impoverishment *s.* Verarmung *f.*
impracticable *a.* undurchführbar.
imprecate *v.t.* verfluchen, verwünschen.
imprecation *s.* Verwünschung *f.*
impregnable *a.,* **~bly** *adv.* uneinnehmbar.
impregnate *v.t.* schwängern; sättigen; imprägnieren.
impress *v.t.* beeindrucken, eindrucken, einprägen.
impression *s.* Eindruck *m.*; Abdruck, Abzug *m.*; Auflage *f.*
impressionable *a.* beeinflußbar; eindrucksfähig.
impressive *a.,* **~ly** *adv.* beeindruckend; imponierend.
imprint *v.t.* prägen; einprägen; *~ s.* Stempel *m.*
imprison *v.t.* gefangen setzen; in Haft nehmen.
imprisonment *s.* Haft *f.*; *false ~,* ungesetzliche Gefangensetzung *f.*; *sentence of ~,* Gefängnisstrafe, Freiheitsstrafe *f.*; *one year's ~,* ein Jahr Gefängnis; *~ on remand,* Untersuchungshaft *f.*
improbability *s.* Unwahrscheinlichkeit *f.*
improbable *a.,* **~bly** *adv.* unwahrscheinlich.
impromptu *s.* Stück (*n.*) aus dem Stegrief; *~ a.* aus dem Stegreif.
improper *a.,* **~ly** *adv.* uneigentlich; unpassend; unanständig; *~ assault,* (*law*) Sittlichkeitsvergehen *n.*; *~ use,* Mißbrauch *m.*
impropriety *s.* Unrichtigkeit *f.*; Unschicklichkeit *f.*
improvable *a.,* **~bly** *adv.* verbesserungsfähig.
improve *v.t.* verbessern; *~ v.i.* besser werden; Fortschritte machen.
improvement *s.* Verbesserung *f.*
improvident *a.,* **~ly** *adv.* unbedachtsam; sorglos.
improvise *v.t.* improvisieren.
imprudence *s.* Unklugheit *f.*
imprudent *a.,* **~ly** *adv.* unklug.
impudence *s.* Unverschämtheit *f.*
impudent *a.,* **~ly** *adv.* unverschämt.
impugn *v.t.* anfechten; bestrieten.
impulse, impulsion *s.* Antrieb *m.*; Stoß *m.*; Impuls *m.*
impulsive *a.* erregbar; antreibend.
impulsiveness *s.* Impulsivität *f.*
impunity *s.* Straflosigkeit *f.*; *with ~,* ungestraft.
impure *a.,* **~ly** *adv.* unrein, unkeusch.
impurity *s.* Unreinheit *f.*; Unkeuschheit *f.*
imputable *a.* zurechenbar.
imputation *s.* Anschuldigung *f.*; Zurechnung, Beimessung *f.*
impute *v.t.* Schuld geben; beimessen; unterstellen.
in *pr.* in, an, zu, bei, mit, auf; unter, während; *~ itself,* an und für sich; *~ adv.* hinein, herein, drinnen.

inability *s.* Unfähigkeit *f.*; ~ **to pay,** Zahlungsunfähigkeit *f.*

inaccessibility *s.* Unzugänglichkeit *f.*

inaccessible *a.*, **~bly** *adv.* unzugänglich.

inaccuracy *s.* Ungenauigkeit *f.*

inaccurate *a.* ungenau.

inaction *s.* Untätigkeit *f.*

inactive *a.*, **~ly** *adv.* untätig.

inactivity *s.* Untätigkeit *f.*; Trägheit *f.*

inadequacy *s.* Unzulänglichkeit *f.*

inadequate *a.* unzulänglich.

inadmissible *a.* unzulässig.

inadvertence *s.* Unachtsamkeit *f.*

inadvertent *a.* unachtsam, **~ly** *adv.* aus Versehen; versehentlich.

inadvisable *a.* nicht ratsam, unratsam.

inalienable *a.* unveräußerlich.

inalterable *a.* unveränderlich.

inane *a.* leer, fad, geistlos.

inanimate *a.* unbeseelt; leblos; flau.

inapplicable *a.* unanwendbar.

inappreciable *a.* unbemerkbar.

inapproachable *a.* unzugänglich.

inappropriate *a.* unpassend.

inapt *a.* unpassend; ungeschickt.

inaptutude *s.* Untauglichkeit *f.*

inarticulate *a.*, **~ly** *adv.* undeutlich; unverständlich; unfähig, sich klar auszudrücken.

inasmuch *adv.* isofern, weil.

inattention *s.* Unaufmerksamkeit *f.*; Nichtbeachten (einer Vorschrift) *n.*

inattentive *a.*, **~ly** *adv.* unaufmerksam.

inaudible *a.* unhörbar.

inaugural *a.* einweihend; ~ **address** *s.* Antrittsrede *f.*

inaugurate *v.t.* einweihen.

inauspicious *a.*, **~ly** *adv.* ungünstig.; unheilvoll.

inborn *a.* angeboren.

inbred *a.* angeboren, durch Unzucht erzeugt.

inbreeding *s.* Unzucht *f.*

incalculable *a.* unberechenbar.

incandescent *a.* weißglühend; leuchtend, strahlend. ~ **light** (Gas-) Glühlicht *n.*

incantation *s.* Bezauberung *f.*

incapability *s.* Unfähigkeit *f.*

incapable *a.* unfähig, untauglich.

incapacitate *v.t.* unfähig machen.

incapacity *s.* Unfähigkeit *f.*

incarcerate *v.t.* einkerkern.

incarnate *a.* fleischgeworden; personifiziert.

incarnation *s.* Menschwerdung *f.*; Verkörperung *f.*

incautious *a.*, **~ly** *adv.* unvorsichtig.

incendiary *s.* Brandstifter *m.*; Aufwiegler *m.*; *~a.* brandstifterisch; ~ **bomb** *s.* Brandbombe *f.*

incense *s.* Weihrauch *m.*; ~ *v.t.* entzünden; erzürnen.

incentive *s.* Anreiz *m.*

inception *s.* Anfang *m.*

inceptive *a.* Anfangs. . .

incertitude *s.* Ungewißheit *f.*

incessant *a.*, **~ly** *adv.* unaufhörlich.

incest *s.* Blutschande *f.*

incestuous *a.*, **~ly** *adv.* blutschänderisch.

inch *s.* Zoll *m.* (2.54 cm.)

incidence *s.* Vorkommen *n.*; (*phys.*) Einfall *m.*

incident *s.* Ereignis *n.*; Nebenumstand *m.*

incidental *a.* zufällig; ~ **to,** gehörig zu, verbunden mit; **~s** *pl.* Nebenausgaben *f. pl.*; **~ly** *adv.* übrigens, nebenbei bemerkt.

incidental music *s.* Begleitmusik *f.*

incinerate *v.t.* verbrennen.

incinerator *s.* Verbrennungsofen *m.*

incipient *a.* anfangend; anfänglich.

incision *s.* Einschnitt *m.*

incisive *a.* einschneidend.

incisor *s.* Schneidezahn *m.*

incite *v.t.* anreizen, antreiben.

incitement *s.* Aufstachelung *f.*; Anstiftung *f.*

incivility *s.* Unhöflichkeit *f.*

inclemency *s.* Unbarmherzigkeit *f.*

inclement *a.* umbarmherzig, rauh.

inclination *s.* Neigung *f.*

incline *v.t.* neigen; ~ *v.i.* sich neigen, geneigt sein; **~d plane** *s.* schiefe Ebene *f.*; ~ *s.* Neigung *f.*

include *v.t.* einschließen.

including *pr.* einschließflich.

inclusion *s.* Einschließung *f.*; Einbeziehung *f.*

inclusive *a.*, **~ly** *adv.* einschließlich; alles einbegriffen; *both dates* ~, beide Tage einbegriffen; ~ *terms pl.* Pensionspreis mit Licht und Bedienung *m.*

incognito *a.* inkognito.

incoherence *s.* Mangel an Zusammenhang *m.*

incoherent *a.*, **~ly** *adv.* unzusammenhängend.

incombustible *a.* unverbrennlich.

income *s.* Einkommen *n.*; *earned* ~, Einkommen durch Arbeit; *unearned* ~, Einkommen aus Vermögen.

income-tax *s.* Einkommensteuer *f.*

incoming *a.* einlaufend, eingehend; neu eintretend; **~s** *s.pl.* Eingänge *m. pl.*

incommensurable *a.* inkommensurabel.

incomparable *a.*, **~bly** *adv.* unvergleichlich.

incompatibility *s.* Unverträglichkeit *f.*

incompatible *a.*, **~bly** *adv.* unvereinbar.

incompetence, incompetency *s.* Unbefugtheit *f.*; Unzulänglichkeit *f.*

incompetent *a.*, **~ly** *adv.* unzuständig; unfähig; unbefugt; unzulänglich.

incomplete *a.* unvollständig.

incomprehensible *a.*, **~bly** *adv.* unbegreiflich.

incomprehensibility *s.* Unbegreiflichkeit *f.*

inconceivable *a.*, **~bly** *adv.* unbegreiflich.

inconclusive *a.* nicht überzeugend; nicht schlüssig.

incongruity *s.* Ungereimtheit *f.*

incongruous *a.*, **~ly** *adv.* nicht passend, unvereinbar.

inconsequential *a.* belanglos.

inconsiderable *a.*, **~bly** *adv.* unbedeutend, unwichtig.

inconsiderate *a.*, **~ly** *adv.* unbedachtsam, rücksichtslos.

inconsistency *s.* Inkonsequenz *f.*; Inkonsistenz *f.*; Widersprüchlichkeit *f.*

inconsistent *a.*, **~ly** *adv.* unvereinbar, ungereimt, widersprüchlich.

inconsolable *a.*, **~bly** *adv.* untröstlich.

inconspicuous *a.* unauffällig.

inconstant *a.* unbeständig.

incontestable *a.*, **~bly** *adv.* unbestreitbar.

incontinence *s.* Zügellosigkeit *f.*

401

incontinent *s.* unmäßig; zügellos; inkontinent.

incontrovertible *a.* unbestreitbar; unwiderlegbar.

inconvenience *s.* Unbequemlichkeit, Lästigkeit *f.*; ~ *v.t.* belästigen.

inconvenient *a.*, **~ly** *adv.* unbequem, ungelegen; unpassend.

incorporate *v.t.* einverleiben; (*law*) zu einer Gesellschaft machen; ~ *a.* einverleibt; **~d** *company* *s.* (eingetragene) Aktiengesellschaft *f.*

incorporation *s.* Einverleibung *f.*

incorrect *a.*, **~ly** *adv.* fehlerhaft; ungenau.

incorrigible *a.*, **~bly** *adv.* unverbesserlich.

incorruptible *a.*, **~bly** *adv.* unbestechlich; unverderblich.

increase *v.i.* wachsen, zunehmen; ~ *v.t.* vergrößern; ~ *s.* Zunahme *f.*

increasing *a.* zunehmend; steigend.

incredible *a.*, **~bly** *adv.* unglaublich.

incredulity *s.* Unglaube *m.*

incredulous *a.*, **~ly** *adv.* ungläubig.

increment *s.* Zuwachs *m.*, Zunahme *f.*; ~ **value** *s.* Wertzuwachs *m.*

incriminate *v.t.* belasten; beschuldigen; **~ing** *a.* belastend.

incubate *v.t.* brütten.

incubation *s.* Inkubation *f.*

incubator *s.* Brutkasten *m.*

incubus *s.* (*med.*) Alpdrücken *n.*; (*fig.*) Schreckgespenst *n.*

inculcate *v.t.* einschärfen, einprägen.

inculpate *v.t.* beschuldigen, tadeln.

incumbent *a.* obliegend; gegenwärtig.

incunabula *s.pl.* Wiegendrucke *m. pl.*

incur *v.t.* auf sich laden, sich zuziehen; *to* ~ *debts,* Schulden machen; *to* ~ *a fine,* in eine Geldstrafe verfallen; *to* ~ *an obligation,* eine Verpflichtung eingehen.

incurable *a.*, **~bly** unheilbar.

incursion *s.* Einfall, Streifzug *m.*

indebted *p. & a.* verschuldet; verpflichtet.

indebtedness *s.* Verschuldung *s.*

indecency *s.* Unanständigkeit *f.*

indecent *a.*, **~ly** *adv.* unanständig.

indecipherable *a.* nicht zu entziffern.

indecision *s.* Unentschlossenheit *f.*

indecisive *a.* unschlüssig; nicht entscheidend.

indecisiveness *s.* Unentschlossenheit *f.*

indecorous *a.* unanständig.

indeed *adv.* in der Tat, allerdings.

indefatigable *a.*, **~bly** *adv.* unermüdlich.

indefensible *a.* unhaltbar.

indefinable *a.* unbestimmbar.

indefinite *a.*, **~ly** *adv,.* unbestimmt, unbeschränkt.

indelible *a.*, **~bly** *adv.* unauslöschlich.

indelicacy *s.* Mangel (*m.*) an Zartgefühl.

indelicate *a.* geschmacklos; ungehörig.

indemnification *s.* Entschädigung *f.*

indemnify *v.t.* schadlos halten.

indemnity *s.* Absicherung *f.*; Schadenersatz *m.*

indent *v.t.* auszacken; einkerben; (Zeile) einrücken.

indentation *s.* Kerbe *f.*; Einschnitt *m.*

indenture *s.* Vertrag *m.*; Lehrbrief *m.*; ~ *v.t.* verdingen.

independence *s.* Unabhängigkeit *f.*

independent *a.*, **~ly** *adv.* unabhängig.

indescribable *a.* unbeschreiblich.

indestructible *a.* unzerstörbar.

indeterminate *a.*, **~ly** *adv.* unbestimmt.

index *s.* Anzeiger *m.*; Zeigefinger *m.*; Register *n.*; Index *m.*; ~ *v.t.* registrieren.

India *s.* Indien *n.*

Indian *a.* indisch; **American** ~ indianisch; **American** ~ *s.* Indianer(in) *m.*(*f.*)

Indian corn *s.* Mais *m.*

Indian Ocean *s.* Indischer Ozean *m.*

Indian summer *s.* Nachsommer *m.*; Altweibersommer *m.*

india-rubber *s.* Gummi *m.* or *n.*, Kautschuk *m.*

indicate *v.t.* anzeigen; erkeunen lassen.

indication *s.* Anzeichen *n.*

indicative *a.*, **~ly** *adv.* anzeigend; ~ *s.* (*gram.*) Indikativ *m.*

indicator *s.* Anzeiger *m.*

indict *v.t.* schriftlich anklagen, belangen.

indictable *a.* (*law*) klagbar.

indictment *s.* Anklagebeschluß *m.*

indifference *s.* Gleichgültigkeit *f.*

indifferent *a.*, **~ly** *adv.* gleichgültig; unparteiisch; leidlich; mäßig.

indigence *s.* Armut, Dürftigkeit *f.*

indigenous *a.* eingeboren.

indigent *a.*, **~ly** *adv.* dürftig; arm.

indigestible *a.* unverdaulich.

indigestion *s.* Verdauungsbeschwerde *f.* Magenverstimmung *f.*

indignant *a.*, **~ly** *adv.* entrüstet; indigniert.

indignation *s.* Entrüstung *f.*

indignity *s.* Unwürdigkeit.

indirect *a.* mittelbar, indirekt.

indirect object *s.* indirektes Objekt *n.*

indirect speech *s.* indirekte Rede *f.*

indiscernible *a.* nicht zu unterscheiden.

indiscipline *s.* Zuchtlosigkeit *f.*

indiscreet *a.*, **~ly** *adv.* unbedachtsam; unbescheiden; indiskret.

indiscretion *s.* Unbedachtsamkeit *f.*; Unbescheidenheit, Indiskretion *f.*

indiscriminate *a.*, **~ly** *adv.* nicht unterschieden, unbedingt; ohne Unterschied.

indispensable *a.*, **~ly** *adv.* unentbehrlich, unerlässlich.

indisposed *a.* unpässlich, abgeneigt.

indisposition *s.* Unpässlichkeit *f.*

indisputable *a.*, **~bly** *adv.* unbestreitbar.

indissoluble *a.*, **~bly** *adv.* unauflöslich.

indistinct *a.*, **~ly** *adv.* undeutlich; ohne Unterschied.

indistinguishable *a.* ununterschiedbar.

indite *v.t.* abfassen, schreiben.

individual *a.*, **~ly** *adv.* einzeln, persönlich; ~ *s.* Individuum *n.*, Person *f.*

individuality *s.* Individualität *f.*

indivisible *a.*, **~bly** *adv.* unteilbar.

indocile *a.* ungelehrig.

indoctrinate *v.t.* indoktrinieren.

indolence *s.* Trägheit *f.*

indolent *a.*, **~ly** *adv.* träge.

indomitable *a.* unbezähmbar.

Indonesia *s.* Indonesien *n.*

Indonesian *a.* indonesisch; ~ *s.* Indonesier(in) *m.*(*f.*)

indoor *a.* im Hause ~**pool** *s.* Hallenbad *n.*

indoors *adv.* im Hause, drinnen.

indubitable *a.*, ~**bly** *adv.* unzweifelhaft.

induce *v.t.* bewegen, veranlassen; *(elek.)* induzieren.

inducement *s.* Beweggrund, Anlaß *m.*

induction *s.* Einführung *f.*; Induktion *f.*

inductive *a.*, ~**ly** *adv.* bewegend; folgerungsmäßig; Induktions . . .

indulge *v.t.* nachsichtig sein, nachgeben; ~*v.i.* frönen.

indulgence *s.* Nachsicht *f.*; Ablaß *m.*; *plenary* ~, vollkommener Ablaß *m.*

indulgent *a.*, ~**ly** *adv.* nachsichtig.

industrial *a.* industriell, Gewerbe . . .; ~ *court*, Arbeitsgericht *n.*; ~ *dispute*, Arbeitsstreit *m.*; ~ *exhibition*, Gewerbeausstellung *f.*

industrious *a.*, ~**ly** *adv.* fleißig.

industry *s.* Fleiß *m.*; Industrie *f.*

inebriate *v.t.* betrunken machen, *(fig.)* berauschen.

inebriated *a.* betrunken; *(fig.)* berauscht.

inebriety *s.* Trunkenheit *f.*

inedible *a.* ungenießbar.

ineffable *a.*, ~**bly** *adv.* unaussprechlich.

ineffaceable *a.* unauslöschlich.

ineffective, ineffectual *a.*, ~**ly** *adv.* unwirksam.

inefficiency *s.* Unfähigkeit *f.*

inefficient *a.* unwirksam, untüchtig.

ineligible *a.* nicht wählbar.

inept *a.* unbeholfen; albern.

ineptitude *s.* Unbeholfenheit *f.*, Albernheit *f.*

inequality *s.* Ungleichheit *f.*

inequitable *a.* unbillig.

inert *a.*, ~**ly** *adv.* träge; reglos.

inertia *s.* *(phys.)* Trägheit *f.*

inescapable *a.* unausweichlich.

inessential *a.* unwesentlich.

inestimable *a.*, ~**bly** *adv.* unschätzbar.

inevitability *s.* Unvermeidlichkeit *f.*

inevitable *a.*, ~**bly** *adv.* unvermeidlich.

inexact *a.* ungenau.

inexcusable *a.*, ~**bly** *adv.* nicht zu entschuldigen.

inexhaustible *a.* unerschöpflich.

inexorable *a.*, ~**bly** *adv.* unerbittlich.

inexpediency *s.* Unzweckmäßigkeit *f.*

inexpedient *a.* unzweckmäßig, unpassend.

inexpensive *a.* nicht kostspielig; billig, preiswert.

inexperience *s.* Unerfahrenheit *f.*

inexperienced *a.* unerfahren.

inexpert *a.* unerfahren, ungeübt.

inexplicable *a.*, ~**bly** *adv.* unerklärlich.

inexpressible *a.*, unaussprechlich.

inextinguishable *a.* unauslöschlich.

inextricable *a.* unentwirrbar.

infallibility *s.* Unfehlbarkeit *f.*

infallible *a.*, ~**bly** *adv.* unfehlbar.

infamous *a.*, ~**ly** *adv.* verrufen, ehrlos.

infamy *s.* Ehrlosigkeit, Schande *f.*; Infamie *f.*

infancy *s.* frühe Kindheit *f.*

infant *s.* (kleines) Kind *n.*; Unmündige *m.*; ~ *mortality*, Säuglingssterblichkeit *f.*

infanta *s.* Infantin *f.*

infanticide *s.* Kindesmord *m.*

infantile *a.* kindlich; kindisch; ~ *paralysis*, spinale Kinderlähmung *f.*

infantry *s.* Infanterie *f.*, Fußvolk *n.*

infatuate *v.t.* betören.

infatuated *a.* betört, bezaubert.

infatuation *s.* Verblendung, Betörung *f.*

infeasible *a.* unausführbar.

infect *v.t.* anstecken; infizieren.

infection *s.* Ansteckung *f.*; Infektion *f.*

infectious *a.*, ~**ly** *adv.* ansteckend; infektiös.

infer *v.t.* schließen; folgern, herleiten.

inference *s.* Folgerung *f.*

inferior *a.* untergeordnet; niedriger; minderwertig; ~ *s.* Untergebene *m.*

inferiority *s.* Minderwertigkeit *f.*; Unterlegenheit *f.*

infernal *a.* höllisch.

inferno *s.* Inferno *n.*

infertile *a.* unfruchtbar.

infertility *s.* Unfruchtbarkeit *f.*

infest *v.t.* befallen; heimsuchen.

infidel *a.* ungläubig; ~ *s.* Ungläubige *m./f.*

infidelity *s.* Untreue *f.*; Unglaube *m.*

infighting *s.* interne Machtkämpfe *m. pl.*

infiltrate *v.i.* einsickern; infiltrieren.

infiltrator *s.* Eindringling *m.*

infinite *a.*, ~**ly** *adv.* unendlich.

infinitive *s.* *(gram.)* Infinitiv *m.*

infinitude, infinity *s.* Unendlichkeit *f.*

infirm *a.* kraftlos, schwach; gebrechlich.

infirmary *s.* Krankenstube *f.*

infirmity *s.* Schwäche *f.*

inflame *v.t.* anzünden; sich entzünden.

inflammable *a.* entzündlich.

inflammation *s.* Entzündung *f.*

inflammatory *a.* entzündend; aufreizend.

inflatable *a.* aufblasbar.

inflate *v.t.* aufblasen, aufblähen.

inflated *a.* aufgeblasen; geschwollen.

inflation *s.* Aufblähung *f.*; Aufgeblasenheit *f.*; Inflation *f.*

inflationary *a.* inflationär.

inflect *v.t.* beugen; flektieren.

inflection *s.* Beugung *f.*

inflexible *a.*, ~**ly** *adv.* unbeugsam.

inflict *v.t.* auferlegen, verhängen.

influence *s.* Einfluß *m.*; ~ *v.t.* Einfluß üben auf, einwirken, beeinflussen.

influential *a.* einflußreich.

influenza *s.* Influenza, Grippe *f.*

influx *s.* Einfließen *n.*; Zufluß *m.*

inform *v.t.* benachrichtigen; ~ *v.i.* *(against)* angeben, denunzieren.

informal *a.*, ~**ly** *adv.* formlos.

informant *s.* Informant(in) *m.(f.)*

information *s.* Unterweisung *f.*; Nachricht *f.*; Auskunft *f.*; *for (your) information*, zur Kenntnisnahme.

informative *a.* informativ.

informed *a.* informiert.

informer *s.* Informant(in) *m.(f.)*

infrared *a.* infrarot.

infrastructure *s.* Infrastruktur *f.*

infrequent *a.* selten, ungewöhnlich.

infringe *v.t.* übertreten, verletzen.

infringement *s.* Übertretung *f.*; Verstoß *m.*

infuriate *v.t.* wütend machen.

infuse *v.t.* aufgießen, einflößen.

infusion *s.* Aufguß (Tee) *m.*

ingenious *a.*, **~ly** *adv.* einfallsreich.
ingenuity *s.* Einfallsreichtum *m.*
ingenuous *a.* unbefangen; offen; bieder.
inglorious *a.*, **~ly** *adv.* unrühmlich.
ingot *s.* Metallbarren *m.*
ingrained *a.* eingefleischt.
ingratiate *v.t.* beliebt machen.
ingratiating *a.* schmeichlerisch.
ingratitude *s.* Undankbarkeit *f.*
ingredient *s.* Bestandteil *m.*; Zutat *f.*
inhabit *v.t.* bewohnen.
inhabitable *a.* bewohnbar.
inhabitant *s.* Einwohner *m.*
inhale *v.t.* einatmen; inhalieren.
inharmonious *a.* unharmonisch.
inhere *v.i.* anhaften, innewohnen.
inherent *a.* anhaftend; eigen.
inherit *v.t.* erben; bekommen.
inheritance *s.* Erbschaft *f.*; Erbgut *n.*; *law of ~,* Erbrecht *n.*
inhibit *v.t.* hindern; verbieten.
inhibited *a.* gehemmt.
inhospitable *a.*, **~bly** *adv.* ungastlich.
inhuman(e) *a.*, **~ly** *adv.* unmenschlich.
inhumanity *s.* Unmenschlichkeit *f.*
inimical *a.* schädlich.
inimitable *a.*, **~bly** *adv.* unnachahmlich.
iniquitous *a.* unbillig, frevelhaft.
iniquity *s.* Bosheit, Ungerechtigkeit *f.*
initial *a.*, **~ly** *adv.* anfänglich; ~ *s.* Anfangsbuchstabe *m.*; ~ *v.t.* paraphieren; abzeichnen.
initiate *v.t.* einführen, einweihen; einleiten (Maßnahmen).
initiation *s.* Initiation; Einleitung; Eröffnung *f.*
initiative *a.* einleitend; ~ *s.* Initiative *f.*
inject *v.t.* einspritzen.
injection *s.* Einspritzung *f.*
injudicious *a.*, **~ly** *adv.* unverständig; unklug.
injunction *s.* Vorschrift; Verfügung *f.*
injure *v.t.* verletzen, beeinträchtigen; schädigen; *the ~d person,* (*law*) der Geschädigte *m.*
injured *a.* verletzt.
injurious *a.*, **~ly** *adv.* nachteilig.
injury *s.* Nachteil *m.*; Verletzung *f.*
injustice *s.* Ungerechtigkeit *f.*
ink *s.* Tinte *f.*; Druckerschwärze *f.*
ink-lines *pl.* Linienblatt *n.*
inkling *s.* Ahnung *f.*; Wink *m.*
inkstand *s.* Tintenfaß *n.*, Schreibzeug *n.*
inky *a.* tintenbeschmiert; tintig.
inlaid *a.* eingelegt.
inland *a.* inländisch; ~ *s.* Binnenland *n.*; ~ *harbor,* ~ *port,* Binnenhafen *m.*
in-law *s.* angeheiratete Verwandte *m./f.*
inlay *v.t.ir.* einlegen.
inlet *s.* Zugang *m.*; Bucht *f.*; Einlage *f.*
inmate *s.* Insasse *m.*; Hausgenosse *m.*
inmost *a.* innerst.
inn *s.* Gasthof *m.*; Wirtshaus *n.*
innards *s. pl.* Eingeweide *pl.*; Innereien *pl.*
innate *a.*, **~ly** *adv.* angeboren.
inner *a.*, **~ly** *adv.* innerlich; geheim.
inner city *s.* Innenstadt *f.*
innermost *a.* innerst.
innkeeper *s.* Gastwirt(in) *m.*(*f.*)
innocence *s.* Unschuld *f.*

innocent *a.*, **~ly** *adv.* unschuldig.
innocuous *a.*, **~ly** *adv.* unschädlich.
innovate *v.i.* Neuerungen machen.
innovation *s.* Neuerung *f.*
innovator *s.* Neuerer *m.*
innuendo *s.* Wink, Fingerzeig *m.*; Andeutung *f.*
innumerable *a.*, **~bly** *adv.* unzählig; zahllos.
inoculate *v.t.* einimpfen; impfen.
inoculation *s.* Impfung *f.*
inoffensive *a.*, **~ly** *adv.* unanstößig, arglos.
inoperative *a.* unwirksam.
inopportune *a.* ungelegen.
inordinate *a.*, **~ly** *adv.* ausschweifend.
inorganic *a.*, **~ally** *adv.* anorganisch.
in-patient *s.* stationärer Patient(in) *m.*(*f.*)
input *s.* (Daten) Eingabe *f.*, Input *m.*; Investition.
inquest *s.* Leichenschau *f.*
inquietude *s.* Unruhe *f.*
inquire *v.i.* sich erkundigen; untersuchen; fragen.
inquiring *a.* fragend; forschend.
inquiry *s.* Untersuchung *f.*; Nachfrage, Erkundigung *f.*
inquisition *s.* Untersuchung *f.*; Ketzergericht *n.*; Inquisition *f.*
inquisitive *a.*, **~ly** *adv.* neugierig.
inquisitiveness *s.* Neugierde *f.*; Wißbegierde *f.*
inroad *s.* Einfall *m.*; Eingriff *m.*
insane *a.*, geisteskrank, wahnsinnig.
insanitary *a.* gesundheitsschädlich, unhygienisch.
insanity *s.* Wahnsinn *m.*
insatiable *a.*, **~bly** *adv.* unersättlich.
inscribe *v.t.* einschreiben; widmen.
inscription *s.* Inschrift *f.*; Aufschrift *f.*; Einschreibung *f.*
inscrutable *a.*, **~bly** *adv.* unerforschlich.
insect *s.* Insekt *n.*; **~bite** *s.* Insektenstich *m.*; **~-repellent** *s.* Insektenpulver *n.*
insecticide *s.* Insektizid *n.*
insecure *a.*, **~ly** *adv.* unsicher.
insecurity *s.* Unsicherheit *f.*
insensate *a.* unvernünftig.
insensibility *s.* Gefühllosigkeit *f.*; Unempfindlichkeit *f.*
insensible *a.*, **~bly** *adv.* unempfindlich; unmerklich.
insensitive *a.* unsensibel, gefühllos.
insensitiveness, insensitivity *s.* Gefühllosigkeit *f.*; Unempfindlichkeit *f.*
inseparable *a.*, **~bly** *adv.* unzertrennlich.
insert *v.t.* einfügen, einschalten.
insertion *s.* Einfügung, Einschaltung *f.*
inset *s.* Einsatz *m.*; Einsatzbild *n.*, Einsatzkarte *f.*, Nebenbild *n.*
inshore *adv.* nahe der Küste.
inside *s.* Innenseite *f.* *adv.* innen; *a.* inner . . . ; Innen . . . ; intern.
insider *s.* Insider(in) *m.*(*f.*)
insidious *a.*, **~ly** *adv.* hinterlistig.
insight *s.* Einsicht *f.*
insignia *s. pl.* Insignien *pl.*; Abzeichen *n. pl.*
insignificance *s.* Geringfügigkeit *f.*
insignificant *a.*, **~ly** *adv.* unbedeutend.
insincere *a.*, **~ly** *adv.* nicht aufrichtig.
insincerity *s.* Unaufrichtigkeit *f.*
insinuate *v.t.* zu verstehen geben; sich einschmeicheln.

insinuation *s.* Einschmeichelung *f.*; Unterstellung *f.*; Wink *m.*

insipid *a.*, **~ly** *adv.* geschmacklos, fade.

insist *v.i.* auf etwas bestehen.

insistence *s.* Beharen, Bestehen *n.*

insole *s.* Schuheinlage *f.*

insolence *s.* Frechheit *f.*

insolent *a.* unverschämt, frech.

insoluble *a.* unlöslich; unlösbar.

insolvency *s.* Zahlungsunfähigkeit *f.*

insolvent *a.* zahlungsunfähig.

insomnia *s.* Schlaflosigkeit *f.*

inspect *v.t.* besichtigen; inspizieren; kontrollieren.

inspection *s.* Besichtigung *f.*; Inspektion *f.*

inspector *s.* Kontrolleur(in) *m.*(*f.*), Inspektor(in) *m.*(*f.*)

inspiration *s.* Eingebung *f.*; Inspiration *f.*

inspire *v.t.* einhauchen, einflößen; begeistern; einatmen.

inspiring *a.* inspirierend.

instability *s.* Unbeständigkeit *f.*

install *v.t.* einsetzen; installieren.

installation *s.* Bestallung *f.*; Anlage *f.*

installment *s.* Teilzahlung *f.*; Rate *f.*; *by* ~s, in Raten.

instance *s.* dringende Bitte *f.*; Gelegenheit *f.*; Fall *m.*; Instanz *f.*; *for* ~, zum Beispiel.

instant *a.*, **~ly** *adv.* dringend; augenblicklich, sogleich; ~s. Augenblick *m.*

instantaneous *a.*, **~ly** *adv.* augenblicklich.

instantly *adv.* sofort.

instead *pr.* anstatt; ~*adv.* stattdessen.

instep *s.* Spann, Rist *m.*

instigate *v.t.* aufhetzen, anstiften.

instigation *s.* Anstiftung *f.*; Initierung *f.*

instigator *s.* Anstifter(in) *m.*(*f.*)

instill *v.t.* einflößen.

instinct *s.* Instinkt *m.*; ~ *a.* belebt.

instinctive *a.*, **~ly** *adv.* unwillkürlich.

institute *s.* Anstalt *f.*; Institut *n.*

institution *s.* Einsetzung *f.*; Verordnung *f.*; Anstalt *f.*; Einrichtung *f.*; Institution *f.*

institutional *a.* institutionell.

instruct *v.t.* unterrichten; unterweisen; beauftragen.

instruction *s.* Unterweisung *f.*; Unterricht *m.*; Vorschrift *f.*; Auftrag *m.*

instructions *pl.* Gebrauchsanweisung *f.*

instructive *a.* lehrreich.

instructor *s.* Lehrer(in) *m.*(*f.*)

instrument *s.* Werkzeug *n.*; Instrument *n.*

instrumental *a.*, **~ly** *adv.* als behilflich.

instrumentalist *s.* Instrumentalist(in) *m.*(*f.*)

insubordinate *a.* ungehorsam; aufsässig.

insubordination *s.* Ungehorsam *m.*

insubstantial *a.* dürftig; gering.

insufferable *a.*, **~bly** *adv.* unerträglich.

insufficiency *s.* Unzulänglichkeit *f.*

insufficient *a* . **~ly** *adv.* unzulänglich.

insular *a.* Insel . . .

insularity *s.* insulare Lage *f.*; Beschränktheit *f.*

insulate *v.t.* absondern, isolieren; (*elek.*) ~*ing tape*, Isolierband *n.*

insulation *s.* Isolierung *f.*

insulator *s.* Isolator *m.*

insult *v.t.* beschimpfen, beleidigen; ~ *s.* Beleidigung, Beschimpfung *f.*

insulting *a.* beleidigend.

insuperable *a.* unüberwindlich.

insupportable *a.* unerträglich.

insurable *a.* versicherungsfähig.

insurance *s.* Versicherung *f.*; **~-broker** *s.* Versicherungsmakler *m.*; **~-claim** *s.* Versicherungsanspruch *m.*; **~-policy** *s.* Versicherungspolice *f.*

insure *v.t.* versichern; sichern.

insurgents *s. pl.* Aufrührer *m. pl.*

insurmountable *a.* unüberwindlich.

insurrection *s.* Aufstand *m.*

intact *a.* unberührt; unversehrt.

intake *s.* Aufnahme *f.*; Zustrom *m.*; Einlaßöffnung *f.*

intangible *a.* nicht greifbar.

integer *a.* ganze Zahl *f.*

integral *a.* ganz, vollständig.

integrate *v.t.* integrieren; eingliedern.

integration *s.* integration *f.*

integrity *s.* Vollständigkeit *f.*; Rechtschaffenheit *f.*; Integrität *f.*

intellect *s.* Verstand *m.*; Intellekt *m.*

intellectual *a.* Verstandes . . . ; geistig; verständig; intellecktuell; ~ *s.* Intellektuelle *m.*/*f.*

intelligence *s.* Verstand *m.*, Verständnis *n.*; Einsicht *f.*; Nachricht *f.*

intelligence-service *s.* Nachrichtendienst *m.*

intelligent *a.*, **~ly** *adv.* verständig, einsichtig; intelligent.

intelligible *a.*, **~bly** *adv.* verständlich.

intemperance *s.* Unmäßigkeit *f.*

intemperate *a.* **~ly** *adv.* unmäßig.

intend *v.t.* beabsichtigen.

intendant *s.* Aufseher, Verwalter *m.*

intended *a.* beabsichtigt.

intending *a.* angehend; künftig.

intense *a.*, **~ly** *adv.* heftig; intensiv.

intensify *v.t.* steigern, verstärken.

intensity *s.* Heftigkeit *f.*; Intensität *f.*

intensive *a.*, **~ly** *adv.* angestrengt.

intensive care *s.* Intensivpflege *f.*

intent *a.*, begierig; aufmerksam. ~*s.* Vorhaben *n.*

intention *s.* Absicht *f.*; Intention *f.*

intentional *a.* absichtlich.

interact *v.i.* sich gegenseitig beeinflussen.

interaction *s.* Wechselwirkung *f.*

interactive *a.* interaktiv.

intercede *v.i.* dazwischen treten, vermitteln.

intercept *v.t.* abfangen; auffangen; unterbrechen.

intercession *s.* Fürsprache *f.*

interchange *v.t. & i.* tauschen; abwechseln; ~ *s.* Tausch, Verkehr *m.*; Abwechselung *f.*, Tauschhandel *m.*

interchangeable *a.* austauschbar.

intercom *s.* Sprechanlage *f.*

interconnect *v.t.* zusammenschalten; miteinander verbinden.

intercontinental *a.* interkontinental.

intercourse *s.* Verkehr, Umgang *m.*

interdependence *s.* gegenseitige Abhängigkeit *f.*

interdependent *a.* voneinander abhängig.

interdict *v.t.* untersagen.

interdiction *s.* Untersagung *f.*

interest *s.* Anteil *m.*; Nutzen *m.*; Zins *m.*; Zinsen *pl.*;

Interesse *n.*, Belang *m.*; *rate of* ~, Zinssatz *m.*; *to bear* ~, Zinsen tragen; ~ *v.t.* angehen, beteiligen, interessieren.
interested *p. & a.* interessiert (*an*); eigennützig.
interesting *a.* interessant.
interface *s.* Grenzfläche *f.*; (*comp.*) Schnittstelle *f.*
interfere *v.i.* sich einmengen; stören.
interference *s.* Dazwischenkunft *f.*; Einmischung *f.*; (*phys.*) Interferenz *f.*
interim *s.* Zwischenzeit *f.*; ~ *a. adv.* vorläufig, Zwischen...
interior *a.*, ~ly *adv.* innerlich; ~s. Innere *n.*; ~ **decoration** *s.* Innendekoration *f.*
interject *v.t.* einwerfen.
interjection *s.* (*gram.*) Interjektion *f.*
interlock *v.i.* ineinandergreifen.
interlope *v.i.* sich eindrängen.
interloper *s.* Eindringling *m.*
interlude *s.* Zwischenspiel *n.*
intermarriage *s.* Mischehe *f.*
intermarry *v.i.* Mischehen eingehen.
intermeddle *v.i.* sich einmischen.
intermediary *a.* vermittelnd; ~ *s.* Vermittler *m.*
intermediate *a.*, ~ly *adv.* dazwischenliegend, Zwischen..., Mittel...
interment *s.* Beerdigung *f.*
intermezzo *s.* (*mus.*) Intermezzo; (*fig.*) Zwischenspiel, Intermezzo *n.*
interminable *a.* unbegrenzt.
intermingle *v.t.* untermischen; ~ *v.i.* sich vermischen.
intermission *s.* Aussetzen *n.*, Pause *f.*
intermittent *a.* in Abständen auftretend.
intern *v.t.* internieren.
internal *a.*, ~ly *adv.* innerlich; ~ *combustion engine s.* Explosionsmotor, Verbrennungsmotor *m.*
internal medicine *s.* innere Medizin *f.*
internal Revenue Service *s.* Finanzamt *n.*
international *a.* international, zwischenstaatlich; Welt..., Völker..., ~ *call*, (*tel.*) Auslandsgespräch *n.*; ~ *law*, Völkerrecht *n.*; ~ *Monetary Fund s.* internationale Währungsfonds *m.*; ~ *relations pl.* auswärtige Beziehungen *f.pl.*
internee *s.* Internierte *m.*
internment *s.* Internierung *f.*
interplay *s.* Wechselspiel *n.*
interpolation *s.* Einschiebung *f.*
interpose *v.i.* dazwischen treten.
interpret *v.t.* auslegen; interpretieren.
interpretation *s.* Auslegung *f.*; Interpretation *f.*
interpreter *s.* Dolmetscher(in) *m.*(*f.*)
interelated *a.* zusammenhängend.
interrogate *v.t. & i.* befragen.
interrogation *s.* Frage *f.*; Befragen *n.*; Verhör *n.*; ~~**mark** *s.* Fragezeichen *n.*
interrogative *a.* fragend; ~ *s.* Fragewort *n.*
interrogatory *a.* fragend; ~ *s.* Verhör *n.*
interrupt *v.t.* unterbrechen.
interruption *s.* Unterbrechung *f.*
intersect *v.t. & i.* (sich) durchschneiden, sich kreuzen.
intersection *s.* Schnittpunkt *m.*; Straßenkreuzung *f.*
intersperse *v.t.* einstreuen.
interstate *a.* zwischenstaatlich.
interstice *s.* Zwischenraum *m.*; Lücke *f.*

intertwine *v.t. & i.* verflechten.
interval *s.* Zwischenraum *m.*; Pause *f.*; Abstand *m.*; Intervall *n.*
intervene *v.i.* sich einmischen; eintreten.
intervention *s.* Dazwischenkunft, Vermittlung *f.*; Einmischung, Intervention *f.*
interview *s.* Interview *n.*; Unterredung *f.*; ~ *v.t.* bei einem Besuch ausfragen, interviewen; *interviewing hours pl.* Sprechstunden (von Stellen und Behörden).
interviewee *s.* Interviewte *m.*/*f.*
interviewer *s.* Interviewer(in) *m.*(*f.*)
interweave *v.t.st.* verweben.
interzonal *a.* Zwischenzonen...
intestate *adv.* ohne Testament.
intestinal *a.* intestinal; Darm...
intestine *a.* inner; ~s *s.pl.* Eingeweide *n.*, Darm *m.*
intimacy *s.* Vertraulichkeit *f.*, Vertrautheit *f.*
intimate *s.*, ~ly *adv.* innig; vertraut; ~ *v.t.* andeuten, anzeigen.
intimation *s.* Andeutung *f.*; Wink *m.*
intimidate *v.t.* einschüchtern.
intimidation *s.* Einschüchterung *f.*
into *pr.* in; hinein.
intolerable *a.*, ~bly *adv.* unerträglich.
intolerance *s.* Unduldsamkeit *f.*
intolerant *a.* unduldsam, intolerant.
intonation *s.* Tonfall *m.*
intoxicate *v.t.* berauschen; *intoxicating liquors*, berauschende Getränke *n.pl.*
intoxication *s.* Rausch *m.*
intractable *a.* unlenksam, unbändig.
intransigence *s.* Kompromißlosigkeit *f.*
intransigent *a.* unnachgiebig.
intransitive *a.* intransitiv.
intravenous *a.* intravenös.
intrepid *a.*, ~ly *adv.* unerschrocken.
intricacy *s.* Verwicklung, Verlegenheit *f.*
intricate *a.*, ~ly *adv.* verworren, schwierig.
intrigue *s.* Verwicklung *f.*; Intrige *f.*; ~ *v.i.* Ränke schmieden; intrigieren; faszinieren.
intriguing *a.* ~ly *adv.* faszinierend.
intrinsic *a.*, ~ally *adv.* inner, wesentlich.
introduce *v.t.* einführen; vorstellen.
introduction *s.* Einführung, Einleitung *f.*; Vorstellung *f.*
introductory *a.* einleitend.
introspection *s.* Selbstbeobachtung *f.*
introspective *a.* nach innen gerichtet.
introversion *s.* Introversion *f.*
introvert *s.* introvierter Mensch *m.*
introverted *a.* introvertiert.
intrude *v.i.* sich eindrängen; ~ *v.t.* aufdrängen.
intruder *s.* Eindringling *m.*
intrusion *s.* Eindringen *n.*
intrusive *a.* aufdringlich.
intuition *s.* Intuition *f.*
intuitive *a.*, ~ly *adv.* intuitiv.
inundate *v.t.* überschwemmen.
inundation *s.* Überschwemmung *f.*
inure *v.t.* gewöhnen, abhärten.
invade *v.t.* einfallen; angreifen.
invader *s.* Angreifer(in) *m.*(*f.*)
invalid *a.* kränklich; dienstunfähig; ungültig; ~ *s.* Invalide *m.*; ~ **chair** *s.* Rollstuhl *m.*
invalidate *a.* ungültig machen.

invalidity *s.* Ungültigkeit *f.*
invaluable *a.* unschätzbar.
invariable *a.*, **~bly** *adv.* unveränderlich.
invasion *s.* Einfall, Angriff *m.*
invective *s.* Schmähung *f.*, Beschimpfung *f.*
inveigh *v.i.* schimpfen; schmähen.
inveigle *v.t.* verleiten, verführen.
invent *v.t.* erfinden.
invention *s.* Erfindung *f.*
inventive *a.* erfinderisch.
inventor *s.* Erfinder *m.*
inventory *s.* Verzeichnis; Inventar *n.*
inverse *a.*, **~ly** *adv.* umgekehrt.
inversion *s.* Umkehrung *f.*
invert *v.t.* umkehren; **~ed** *commas pl.* Anführungszeichen *n.*
invertebrate *s.* wirbellose Tiers *n.*; *a.* wirbellos.
invest *v.t.* bekleiden; erteilen; (eine Summe) anlegen; einschließen.; investieren.
investigate *v.t.* erforschen.
investigation before trial *s.* (*law*) Voruntersuchung *f.*
investigative *a.* detektivisch.
investiture *s.* Belehnung, Einsetzung *f.*
investment *s.* (Geld-) Anlage *f.*; Investition *f.*
investor *s.* Geldgeber(in) *m.*(*f.*)
inveterate *a.* eingefleischt; unverbesserlich; unübergehäßig; boshaft.
invidious *a.*, **~ly** *adv.* windbar.
invigorate *v.t.* stärken; beleben.
invincible *a.*, **~bly** *adv.* unüberwindlich.
inviolable *a.*, **~bly** *adv.* unverletzlich.
inviolate *a.* unverletzt.
invisibility *s.* Unsichtbarkeit *f.*
invisible *a.*, **~bly** *adv.* unsichtbar.
invisible mending *s.* Kunststopferei *f.*
invitation *s.* Einladung *f.*
invite *v.t.* einladen; auffordern.
inviting *a.* einladend.
invocation *s.* Anrufung *f.*
invoice *s.* Warenrechnung, Faktura *f.*; **~***v.t.* in Rechnung stellen.
invoke *v.t.* anrufen; sich berufen auf.
involuntary *a.*, **~ily** *adv.* unfeiwillig; unwillkürlich.
involve *v.t.* in sich schließen; verwickeln.
invulnerable *a.* unverwundbar.
inward *a. & adv.* **~ly** *adv.* innerlich; einwärts; **~** *s.* Innere *n.*
inwards *adv.* einwärts.
iodine *s.* Jod *n.*
ionize *v.t.* (*elek.*) ionisieren.
I.O.U. = I owe you *s.* Schuldschein *m.*
Iran *s.* Iran *m.*
Iranian *a.* iranisch; *s.* Iraner(in) *m.*(*f.*)
Iraq *s.* Irak *m.*
Iraqi *a.* irakisch; *s.* Iraker(in) *m.*(*f.*)
irascible *a.* jähzornig; reizbar.
irate *a.* erzürnt, zornig.
ire *s.* Zorn *m.*
Ireland *s.* Irland *n.*
iris *s.* Regenbogenhaut *f.*; Schwertlilie *f.*
Irish *a.* irisch; **~man** *s.* Ire *m.*; **~ Republic** *s.* Irische Republik *f.*; **~ sea** *s.* Irische See *f.*; **~woman** *s.* Irin *f.*
irk *v.t.* ärgern.

irksome *a.* ärgerlich; lästig.
iron *s.* Eisen *n.*; Bügeleisen *n.*; **~** *a.* eisern; fest; **~** *v.t.* bügeln.
ironclad *a.* gepanzert (von Schiffen).
ironic(al) *a.*, **~ally** *adv.* ironisch.
ironing-board *s.* Bügelbrett *n.*
ironmonger *s.* Eisenwarenhändler *m.*
iron ore *s.* Eisenerz *n.*
iron-works *s.pl.* Eisenhütte *f.*
irony *s.* Ironie *f.*
irradiate *v.t.* bestrahlen, bescheinen.
irrational *a.*, **~ly** *adv.* unvernünftig.
irreclaimable *a.* unwiederbringlich, unverbesserlich.
irreconcilable *a.*, **~bly** *adv.* unversöhnlich; unvereinbar.
irrecoverable *a.*, **~ly** *adv.* unwiederbringlich; unersetzlich; **~ debts** *pl.* uneinbringliche Forderungen *f.pl.*
irredeemable *a.* unablöslich, nicht tilgbar, nicht rückzahlbar; unverbesserlich.
irreducible *a.* nicht zu verringern; nicht zu verwandeln.
irrefutable *a.*, **~bly** *adv.* unwiderleglich.
irregular *a.*, **~ly** *adv.* unregelmäßig.
irregularity *s.* Unregelmäßigkeit *f.*
irrelevant *a.*, **~ly** *adv.* unerheblich.
irreligion *s.* Unglaube *m.*
irreligious *a.*, **~ly** *adv.* ungläubig.
irremediable *a.*, **~bly** *adv.* unheilbar, unersetzlich.
irremovable *a.* unabsetzbar.
irreparable *a.*, **~bly** *adv.* nicht wiedergutzumachend; irreparabel.
irreplaceable *a.*, **~ly** *adv.* unersetzlich.
irreprehensible *a.*, **~bly** *adv.* untadelhaft.
irrepressible *a.* ununterdrückbar; unbezähmbar.
irreproachable *a.*, **~bly** *adv.* untadelig.
irresistable *a.*, **~bly** *adv.* unwiderstehlich.
irresolute *a.*, **~ly** *adv.* unschlüssig.
irrespective *a.*, **~ly** *adv.* ohne Rücksicht auf; **~** *of,* ungeachtet.
irresponsibility *s.* Unverantwortlichkeit *f.*
irresponsible *a.* unverantwortlich.
irretrievable *a.*, **~bly** *adv.* unersetzlich, unwiederbringlich.
irreverent *a.*, **~ly** *adv.* respektlos; unehrerbietig.
irrevocable *a.*, **~bly** *adv.* unwiderruflich.
irrigate *v.t.* bewässern.
irrigation *s.* Bewässerung *f.*
irritability *s.* Reizbarkeit *f.*; Gereiztheit *f.*
irritable *a.* reizbar.
irritant *s.* Reizmittel *n.*
irritate *v.t.* reizen; erbittern.
irritation *s.* Erbitterung *f.*; Arger *m.*
irruption *s.* Einbruch *m.*
Islam *s.* Islam *m.*
Islamic *a.* islamisch.
island *s.* Insel *f.*; Schutzinsel *f.*
islander *s.* Inselbewohner *m.*
isle *s.* Insel *f.*
isolate *v.t.* absondern.; isolieren.
isolation *s.* Isolierung *f.*
isosceles *a.* gleichschenklig (Dreieck).
isotope *s.* Isotop *n.*
Israel *s.* Israel *n.*
Israeli *a.* israelisch; **~** *s.* Israeli *m.*(*f.*)

issuance *s.* Ausgabe *f.*

issue *s.* Ausgang *m.*; Erfolg *m.*; Notenausgabe, Emission *f.*; Nachkommen *pl.*; streitige Frage *f.*; ~ *of a paper*, Zeitungsausgabe *f.*; ~ *v.i.* herrühren, entspringen; endigen; ~ *v.t.* ergehen lassen; ausgeben, ausstellen (Wechsel).

isthmus *s.* Landenge *f.*

it *pn.* es, das; *with ~*, damit.

Italian *a.* italienisch; *s.* Italiener(in) *m.*(*f.*)

italic *s.* Kursivschrift *f.*; ~ *a.* kursiv.

Italy *s.* Italien *n.*

itch *s.* Jucken *n.*; Gelüst *n.*; ~ *v.i.* jucken; verlangen.

itchy *a.* juckend; kratzig.

item *adv.* desgleichen; ferner; ~ *s.* Posten *m.*; Stück *n.*; Punkt *m.*

itemize *v.t.* detaillieren.

itinerant *a.* wandernd.

itinerary *a.* reisend, wandernd; ~ *s.* Reiseroute *f.*; Reisebuch *n.*

its *pn.* sein, dessen.

itself *p.* es selbst, selbst, sich.

ivory *s.* Elfenbein *n.*; ~ *a.* elfenbeinern.

ivy *s.* Epheu *m.*

Ivy League *s.* Eliteuniversitäten in USA.

J

J, j der Buchstabe J oder j *n.*

jab *v.t.* stossen, stechen; ~s. Schlag *m.*, Stich *m.*

jabber *v.i.* schwatzen;; plappern.

jack *s.* Kerl, Matrose *m.*; Bube *m.* (Karte); (*nav.*) Gösch *f.*; Sägebock *m.*; (Hand-)Winde *f.*; Bratenwender *m.*; Stiefelknecht *m.*; Flaschenzug *m.*; (*mech.*) Hebebock, Wagenheber *m.*

jackal *s.* Schakal *m.*

jackass *s.* Eselhengst *m.*; (*fig.*) Esel *m.*

jack-boots *s.pl.* hohe Stiefel *m.pl.*

jackdaw *s.* Dohle *f.*

jacket *s.* Jacke *f.*; Schutzumschlag (eines Buches) *m.*

Jack-of-all-trades *s.* Hans Dampf in allen Gassen.

jade *s.* Jade *m.*, Jadegrün *n.*; Schindmähre *f.*; Weibsbild *n.*; ~d *a.* erschöpft; abgestumpft.

jag *v.t.* kerben; ~ *s.* Kerbe *f.*; Felszacken *m.*; Zahn *m.*

jagged *a.* zackig.

jail *s.* Gefängnis *n.*; ~ *v.t.* einkerkern.

jailbird *s.* (*fam.*) Knastbruder *m.*

jailbreak *s.* Gefängnisausbruch *m.*

jailer *s.* Gefangenwärter *m.*

jalopy *s.* alte Kiste *f.* (*Auto*).

jam *s.* Marmelade *f.*; ~ *v.t.* zusammenpressen; (*radio*) stören.

jamboree *s.* großes Treffen *n.*; ausgelassene Feier *f.*

jam-packed *a.* vollgestopft.

janitor *s.* Türhüter, Pförtner *m.*

January *s.* Januar *m.*

Japan *s.* Japan *n.*

Japanese *a.* japanisch; *s.* Japaner(in) *m.*(*f.*)

jape *s.* Scherz *m.*; Spaß *m.*

jar *v.i.* quietschen; knarren; mißtönen; ~ *s.* Quietschen *n.*; Krug *m.*

jargon *s.* Jargon *m.*

jasmine *s.* Jasmin *m.*

jasper *s.* Jaspis *m.*

jaundice *s.* Gelbsucht *f.*

jaundiced *a.* gelbsüchtig.

jaunt *v.i.* herumstreifen; ~ *s.* Ausflug *m.*

jaunty *a.*, ~ily *adv.* leicht, munter.

javelin *s.* Wurfspeer *m.*

jaw *s.* Kinnbacken, Kiefer *m.*; (*mech.*) Backen; ~s *s.pl.* Rachen *m.*; ~ *v.t.* schimpfen.

jawbone *s.* Kieferknochen *m.*

jay *s.* Häher *m.*

jazz *s.* Jazzmusik *f.*; ~-band *s.* Jazzband *f.*

jealous *a.*, ~ly *adv.* eifersüchtig.

jealousy *s.* Eifersucht *f.*; Argwohn *m.*

jeans *s.pl.* Jeans *pl.*

jeer *v.t.* & *i.* spotten; ~ *s.* Spott *m.*

jejune *a.* nüchtern; fade, trocken.

jell *v.i.* gelieren.

jelly *s.* Gallerte *f.*; Gelee *n.*

jelly-fish *s.* Qualle, Meduse *f.*

jeopardize *v.t.* gefährden; aufs Spiel setzen.

jeopardy *s.* Gefahr *f.*

jerk *s.* Ruck *m.*; Stoß *m.*; (*fam.*) Knülch *m.* ~ *v.t.* ruckeln; stossen.

jerky *a.* abgehackt; holprig.

jerry-built *a.* unsolide gebaut.

jersey *s.* Pullover *m.*; Jersey *n.*

jest *s.* Scherz *m.*; ~ *v.i.* scherzen.

jester *s.* Spaßvogel *m.*; Hofnarr *m.*

Jesuit *s.* Jesuit *m.*

Jesuitical *a.*, ~ly *adv.* jesuitisch.

jet *s.* Jet *n.*; Wasser(Gas-)-strahl *m.*; ~-fighter *s.* (*avi.*) Düsenjäger *m.*

jet-black *a.* pechschwarz.

jet lag *s.* Zeitverschiebung *f.*; Jet-travel-Syndrom *n.*

jet plane *s.* Düsenflugzeug *n.*

jetsam *s.* Strandgut *n.*

jettison *v.t.* über Bord werfen; ~able tank, (*avi.*) abwerfbare Tank *m.*

jetty *s.* Hafendamm *m.*, Mole *f.*

Jew *s.* Jude *m.*; Jüdin *f.*

jewel *s.* Juwel *n.*

jeweller *s.* Juwelier *m.*

jewelery *s.* Juwelen *pl.*

Jewish *a.* jüdisch.

Jewry *s.* Judenschaft *f.*; Judenviertel *n.*

jib *s.* Fock *f.*; Ausleger *m.*; ~ *v.i.* bocken; schenen.

jiff(y) *s.* *in a ~*, augenblicklich.

jig *s.* Gigue (Tanz) *f.*; (*mech.*) (Bohr) Schablone, (Bohr) Lehre *f.*

jiggle *v.t.* wackeln; schütteln.

jilt *v.i.* & *t.* (den Liebhaber) sitzen lassen.

jingle *v.t.* & *i.* klingeln, klimpern; ~ *s.* Geklingel *n.*

jingo *s.* Hurrapatriot, Chauvinist *m.*

jingoism *s.* Chauvinismus *m.*

jinx *s.* Fluch *m.*; ~ *v.t.* verhexen.

jitter *s.* (*fam.*) Angst *f.*; Baumel *m.*

job *s.* (geringe) Arbeit *f.*; Arbeitsstück *n.*; *odd ~s pl.* Gelegenheitsarbeiten *pl.*; ~ *v.i.* Lohnarbeit tun; jobben.

jobber *s.* Stückarbeiter, Handlanger, Jobber *m.*

job-hunting *s.* Arbeitssuche *f.*

jobless *a.* arbeitslos.

jockey s. Jockei, Reitknecht m.; Betrüger m.; ~ v.t. rangeln.
jocose a., ~**ly** adv. scherzhaft.
jocular a., ~**ly** adv. spaßhaft, lustig.
jocund a., ~**ly** adv. lustig, munter.
jog v.t. stossen; schütteln; ~ v.i. traben; joggen; ~ s. Schupp m.; Rütteln n.
jogger s. Jogger(in) m.(f.)
jogging s. Jogging n.; Joggen n.
joggle v.t. rütteln; ~ v.i. sich schütteln.
jogtrot s. Trott m.; ~ v.i. traben.
join v.t. zusammenfügen, verbinden, zugesellen; ~ v.i. sich berühren; sich verbinden; sich beteiligen; sich anschließen.
joiner s. Tischler(in) m.(f.)
joinery s. Tischlerei f.
joint a. vereinigt; ~ s. Verbindung f.; Gelenk n.; Fuge f.; Knoten m.; Bratenstück n.; ~ v.t. zusammenfügen; verbinden.
joint heir s. Miterbe m.
jointly adv. gemeinsam.
joint owner s. Mitinhaber m.
joint-stock company s. Aktiengesellschaft f.
joist s. Querbalken m.
joke s. Spaß, Scherz, Witz m.; ~ v.i. spassen.
jolly a., ~**ily** adv. fröhlich, lustig; (sl.) famos; ~ adv. sehr.
jolt v.t. & i. rütteln; ~ s. Stoß m.
Jordan s. Jordanien n.
Jordanian a. jordanisch; ~ s. Jordanier(in) m.(f.)
jostle v.t. stossen, anrennen.
jot s. Iota, Pünktchen n.; ~v.t. ~ down kurz niederschreiben.
jotter s. Notizbuch n.
jotting s. Notiz m.
journal s. Tagebuch n.; Zeitschrift f.; Zeitung f.
journalism s. Zeitungswesen n.; Journalismus m.
journalist s. Journalist(in) m.(f.)
journey s. Reise f.; Weg m.; ~ v.i. reisen.
journeyman s. Geselle m.
Jove s. by ~! bei Gott!
jovial a., ~**ly** adv. frohsinnig.
joviality s. Frohsinnigkeit f.
jowl s. Backe f.; Unterkiefer m.; cheek by ~, dicht zusammen.
joy s. Freude, Fröhlichkeit f.; ~ v.i. sich freuen.
joyful a. froh; freudig.
joyless a., ~**ly** adv. freudlos.
joyous a., ~**ly** adv. fröhlich, erfreulich.
joystick s. Knüppel m.; (comp.) Joystick m.
jubilant a. frohlockend.
jubilation s. Jubel m.
jubilee s. Jubeljahr n.; Jubiläum n.
Judaism s. Judentum n.
judge s. Richter(in) m.(f.); Kenner(in) m.(f.); associate ~, Beisitzer(in) (bei Gericht) m.(f.); ~ v.i. & t. richten; (be)urteilen; entscheiden.
judgment s. Urteil n.; Urteilskraft f.; to pronounce (pass) ~ on, ein Urteil fällen.
judicature s. Gerichtswesen.

judicial a., ~**ly** adv. gerichtlich.
judiciary s. Gerichtswesen n.; Richterstand m.
judicious a., ~**ly** adv. scharfsinnig, klug.
judo s. Judo n.
jug s. Krug m.
juggernaut s. (fig.) Moloch m.; schwerer Lastzug m.
juggle s. Gaukelei f.; ~ v.i. gaukeln.
juggler s. Gaukler(in) m. (f.).; Jongleur(in) m.(f.)
jugular a. Hals. . .; ~ s. Halsader f.
juice s. Saft m.
juicy a. saftig.
juke-box s. Musikbox f.
July s. Juli m.
jumble v.t. vermengen, verwirren; ~ s. Mischmasch m.; ~ **sale** s. Ramschverkauf m.
jump v.i. springen, hüpfen; stossen (vom Wagen); ~ v.t. überspringen; ~ s. Sprung m.; high ~, Hochsprung m.; long ~, Weitsprung m.
jumper s. Trägerrock m.; Trägerkleid n.; ~ **cable** s. Starthilfekabel n.
jumpy a. nervös.
junction s. Vereinigung f.; Knotenpunkt (m.) mehrerer Eisenbahnen.
juncture s. Verbindung f.; Gelenk n.; Fuge f.; (kritischer) Zeitpunkt m.
June s. Juni m.
jungle s. Dschungel m. or f.
junior a. jünger; Unter. . .
juniper s. Wacholder m.
junk s. Trödel m.; Gerümpel m.; Dschunke f.
junta s. Junta f.
Jupiter s. Jupiter m.
juridical a., ~**ly** adv. gerichtlich.
jurisdiction s. Gerichtsbarkeit f.; Rechtssprechung, Zuständigkeit f.; contentious ~, streitige Gerichtsbarkeit f.; lack of ~, Unzuständigkeit (des Gerichts).
jurisdictional a. Gerichtsbarkeits. . ., Zuständigkeits . . .
jurisprudence s. allgemeine Rechtswissenschaft f.
jurist s. Rechtsgelehrte m.; Jurist m.
juror s. Geschworene m./f.
jury s. Geschworene m.pl.; ~-**box**, Geschworenenbank f.; ~-**member** s. Geschworene m./f.
just a. gerecht, rechtschaffen; richtig, gehörig; vollständig; ~ adv. eben, bloß, gerade, fast.
justice s. Gerechtigkeit f.; Recht m.; to administer (dispense) ~, Recht sprechen.
justifiable a., ~**bly** adv. zu rechtfertigen.
justification s. Rechtfertigung f.
justify v.t. rechtfertigen.
justly adv. mit Recht; genau.
justness s. Rechtmäßigkeit f.
jut v.i. hervorragen, überhangen.
jute s. Jute f.
juvenile a. jung, jugendlich; ~ s. Jugendliche m./f.; **court** s. Jugendgericht n.; ~ **delinquency** s. Jugendkriminalität f.
juxtapose v.t. nebeneinanderstellen.
juxtaposition s. Nebeneinanderstellung f.

K

K, k der Buchstabe K oder k n.
kaleidoscope s. Kaleidoskop n.
kali s. Salzkraut n., Kali n.

Kampuchea s. Kamputschea n.
kangaroo s. Känguruh n.
kayak s. Kajak m.

keel *s.* Kiel *m.*; Kielraum *m.*; ~ *v.i.* umkippen; kentern.

keen *a.*, **~ly** *adv.* scharf, spitzig; eifrig; heftig; scharfsinnig; ~ *edge*, scharfe Schneide *f.*; ~ *on a thing*, hinter etwas her, auf etwas erpicht.

keenness *s.* Schärfe *f.*; Eifer *m.*

keep *v.t.ir.* halten; behalten; erhalten; aufbewahren; führen (Laden); hüten; unterhalten; beobachten; feiern; fortfahren; ~ *v.i.* sich halten, dauerhaft sein; sich aufhalten, bleiben; *he ~s repeating*, er wiederholt dauernd; *to ~ well*, sich weiter gut befinden; *to ~ away*, abhalten, sich fern halten; *to ~ house*, den Haushalt führen; *to ~ in touch*, in Verbindung bleiben; *to ~ off*, abhalten; davonbleiben; *to ~ on*, dabei bleiben, fortfahren; aufbehalten (*hat*); anbehalten (*dress*); *to ~ up*, aufrecht erhalten; unterhalten, sich erhalten; Schritt halten.

keeper *s.* Aufseher *m.*; (Tier) Wärter(in) *m.*(*f.*)

keeping *s.* Gewahrsam *m.*

keepsake *s.* Andenken *n.*

keg *s.* Fäßchen *n.*

ken *s.* Gesichtskreis *m.*

kennel *s.* Hundhütte *f.*; Hundezwinger *m.*

Kenya *s.* Kenia *n.*

Kenyan *a.* kenianisch; ~ *s.* Kenianer(in) *m.*(*f.*)

kerbstone *s.* Bordstein *m.*; Randstein *m.*

kerchief *s.* Kopf-, Halstuch *n.*

kernel *s.* Kern *m.*

kerosene *s.* Kerosin (Brennöl) *n.*

ketchup *s.* Pikante Sauce *f.*; Ketchup *m.* or *n.*

kettle *s.* Kessel *m.*

kettle-drum *s.* Kesselpauke *f.*

key *s.* Schlüssel *m.*; Tonart *f.*; Taste *f.*; (*mech.*) Keil *m.*; **~-position**, Schlüsselstellung *f.*; ~ **way**, *s.* (*mech.*) Nute *f.*

keyboard *s.* Tastatur *f.*; Klaviatur *f.*; Keyboard *n.*

keyhole *s.* Schlüsselloch *n.*

keynote *s.* Grundton *m.*

key signature *s.* (*mus.*) Vorzeichen *n.*

keystone *s.* Schlußstein *m.*

keyword *s.* Schlüsselwort *n.*

kibbutz *s.* Kibbuz *m.*

kick *v.t. & i.* mit dem Fusse stoßen, treten, ausschlagen; strampeln; ~ *s.* Tritt, Stoß *m.*

kid *s.* Zicklein *n.*; Kind *n.*

kid-gloves *s.pl.* Glacéhandschuhe *m.pl.*

kidnap *v.t.* Kinder entführen, Menschen rauben.

kidnapper *s.* Entführer(in) *m.*(*f.*); Kidnapper(in) *m.*(*f.*)

kidney *s.* Niere *f.*

kidney bean *s.* Weiße Bohne *f.*

kidney machine *s.* künstliche Niere *f.*

kill *v.t.* töten, schlachten; *to ~ weeds*, Unkraut vernichten.

killer *s.* Mörder(in) *m.*(*f.*)

killer whale *s.* Schwertwal *m.*

killing *a.* tödlich; vernichtend.

killjoy *s.* Spielverderber *m.*

kiln *s.* Brenn-, Darrofen *m.*

kilo *s.* Kilo *n.*

kilt *s.* Kilt *m.*, Schottenrock *m.*

kin *s.* Verwandtschaft *f.*; ~ *a.* verwandt.

kind *s.* Art *f.*; Gattung *f.*; *payment in ~*, Naturalleistung, *f.*; ~ *a.*, **~ly** *adv.* gütig, liebreich; nett.

kindergarten *s.* Vorschule.

kindle *v.t.* anzünden; ~ *v.i.* sich entzünden.

kindling *s.* Anmachholz *n.*

kindly *a.* gütig, freundlicherweise.

kindness *s.* Güte, Freundlichkeit *f.*

kindred *s.* Verwandtschaft, Schwägerschaft *f.*; ~ *a.* verwandt.

kinetic *a.* kinetisch.

king *s.* König *m.*

kingdom *s.* Königreich *n.*; Reich *n.*

kingfisher *s.* Eisvogel *m.*

kink *s.* Knick *m.* (im Draht); Schleife *f.* (im Tau); (*fig.*) Schrulle *f.*; Sparren *m.*

kinsfolk *s.* Sippe *f.*, Verwandten *pl.*

kinship *s.* Verwandtschaft *f.*

kinsman *s.* Verwandte *m.*

kinswoman *s.* Verwandte *f.*

kipper *s.* geräucherter Bückling *m.*

kiss *v.t.* küssen; ~ *s.* Kuß *m.*

kit *s.* Ausrüstung *f.*; **~-bag** *s.* Tornister *m.*

kitchen *s.* Küche *f.*; **~-appliances** *pl.* Küchenartikel *m.pl.*; **~-garden** Gemüsegarten *m.*; **~-maid** Küchenmädchen *n.*

kitchenette *s.* kleine Küche *f.*

kite *s.* Gabelweih *m.*; Papierdrache *m.*; (*fig.*) Versuchsballon.

kith *s.* ~ *and kin*, Freunde und Verwandte.

kitten *s.* Kätzchen *n.*

kitty *s.* Kätzchen *n.*

knack *s.* Kunstgriff *m.*; Geschick *n.*

knacker *s.* Abdecker *m.*

knapsack *s.* Tornister *m.*; Rucksack *m.*

knave *s.* Schurke *m.*; Bube (in der Karte) *m.*

knavish *a.*, **~ly** *adv.* schurkisch.

knead *v.t.* kneten.

knee *s.* Knie *n.* **~-cap** *s.* Kniescheibe *f.*; ~ **joint** *s.* Kniegelenk *n.*

kneel *v.i.ir.* knien.

knell *s.* Totenglocke *f.*

knicker-bockers *s.pl.* Kniehosen *f.pl.*

knickers *s.pl.* Schlüpfer *m.*

knick-knacks *s.pl.* Schnickschnack *m.*

knife *s.* Messer *n.*; **~-edge** *s.* Schneide *f.*

knife-rest *s.* Messerbänkchen *n.*

knight *s.* Ritter *m.*; Springer (im Schach) *m.*

knight-errant *s.* fahrender Ritter *m.*

knighthood *s.* Ritterwürde *f.*

knightly *a. or adv.* ritterlich.

knit *v.t.r. & ir.* stricken; knüpfen; runzeln.

knitting *s.* Strickzeug *n.*

knitting-needle *s.* Stricknadel *f.*

knitwear *s.* Strickwaren *f.pl.*

knob *s.* Knopf, Knorren *m.*; Quaste *f.*

knock *v.t. & i.* klopfen, pochen; schlagen, stossen; *to ~ about*, sich umhertreiben; *to ~ down*, zuschlagen (bei Versteigerungen); **~-down price**, äußerster Preis, Taxe (bei Versteigerungen) **~-kneed** *a.* x-beinig; **~-knees** *pl.* X-Beine *n.pl.*; *to ~ off*, mit der Arbeit aufhören; ~ *s.* Schlag *m.*; Anklopfen *n.*

knocker *s.* Türklopfer *m.*

knoll *s.* kleiner Hügel *m.*

knot *s.* Knoten *m.*; Schleife *f.*; Baumast, Baumknorren *m.*; Schwierigkeit *f.*; Seemeile *f.*; ~ *v.t.* verknüpfen; verwirren.

knotty *a.*, **~ily** *adv.* knotig; verwickelt.

knout *s.* Knute *f.*; ~ *v.t.* knuten.

know *v.t. & i.st.* wissen, kennen; erkennen;

können; *to let me ~*, mich benachrichtigen; *to get to ~*, erfahren.

know-how *s.* Kenntnisse *f.pl.*

knowing *p. & a.* bewußt, kundig, bewandert; schlau; *~ s.* Wissen *n.*; Kenntnis *f.*

knowingly *adv.* wissentlich.

knowledge *s.* Wissen *n.*; Wissenschaft *f.*; Erkenntnis *f.*; Bekanntschaft *f.*; *to the best of my ~ and belief*, nach bestem Wissen und Gewissen; *it is common ~*, es ist allgemein bekannt.

knuckle *s.* Knöchel *m.*; *~ of veal*, *s.* Kalbshaxe *f.*

knuckle-duster *s.* Schlagring *m.*

koala *s.* Koala *m.*

kook *s.* (*fam.*) Spinner *m.*

koran *s.* Koran *m.*

Korea *s.* Korea *m.*

Korean *a.* koreanisch; *~s.* Koreaner(in) *m.*(*f.*)

kosher *a.* koscher.

Kremlin *s.* Kreml *m.*

L

L, l der Buchstabe L oder l *n.*

lab *s.* Labor *n.*

label *s.* Zettel *m.*; Aufschrift *f.*; *~ v.t.* mit Zettel versehen, mit Aufschrift versehen.

labial *s.* Lippenlaut *m.*

labor *s.* Arbeit *f.*; Mühe *f.*; Geburtswehe *f.*; *~ v.i.* arbeiten; sich abmühen.

laboratory *s.* Laboratorium *n.*

laborer *s.* Arbeiter *m.*; Hilfsarbeiter *m.*; landwirtschaftlicher Arbeiter, Tagelöhner *m.*

labor-exchange *s.* Arbeitsamt *n.*

laborious *a.*, *~ly adv.* arbeitsam, mühsam; umständlich.

labor-union *s.* Gewerkschaft *f.*

laburnum *s.* (*bot.*) Goldregen *m.*

labyrinth *s.* Labyrinth *n.*

lace *s.* Schnur *f.*; Spitze, Tresse *f.*; *~ v.t.* zuschnüren; besetzen.

lace-bobbins *s.pl.* Spitzenklöppel *m.pl.*

lace-boots *s.pl.* Schnürstiefel *m.pl.*

lacerate *v.t.* zerreissen.

laceration *s.* Rißwunde *f.*; Schnittwunde *f.*

lachrymal *a.* Tränen. . .

lachrymose *a.* weinerlich.

lack *v.i.* bedürfen, nicht haben; fehlen; *~ s.* Mangel *m.*

lackadaisical *a.* lustlos; nachlässig.

lackey *s.* Lakai *m.*

lackluster *a.* matt; glanzlos.

laconic *a.* lakonisch.

lacquer *s.* Lack *m.*; *~v.t.* lackieren.

lacuna *s.* Lücke *f.*

lad *s.* Knabe, Junge *m.*

ladder *s.* Leiter *f.*; Laufmasche (*f.*) im Strumpf.

laden *a.* beladen.

la-di-da *a.* affektiert.

ladle *s.* Schöpflöffel *m.*; *~ v.t.* ausschöpfen, auslöffeln.

lady *s.* Dame *f.*; Gemahlin *f.*, Herrin *f.*; *~-bug*, Marienkäfer *m.*; *~-killer* Herzenbrecher *m.*

ladylike *a.* damenhaft; wohlerzogen.

lag *v.i.* zögern; zurückbleiben.

lager *s.* Lagerbier *n.*

laggard *a.* träge, langsam; *~ s.* Zauderer *m.*

lagoon *s.* Lagune *f.*

laid-back *a.* gelassen.

lair *s.* Unterschlupf *m.*; Schlupfwinkel *m.*

laird *s.* Gutsherr (in Schottland) *m.*

laity *s.* Laienstand *m.*

lake *s.* See *m.*

Lake Constance *s.* Bodensee *m.*

lama *s.* Lama *n.*

lamb *s.* Lamm *n.*; *~ v.i.* lammen.

lambaste *v.t.* (*fam.*) fertigmachen; verprügeln.

lamblike *a.* lammartig; fromm, sanft.

lame *a.*, lahm; *~ v.t.* lähmen.

lameness *s.* Lähmung *f.*

lament *v.i.* klagen, jammern; *~ s.* Wehklage *f.*

lamentable *a.*, *~bly adv.* kläglich.

lamentation *s.* Wehklage *f.*

lamina *s.pl.* Plättchen *n.*, Lamelle *f.*

laminated *a.* lamelliert.

lamp *s.* Lampe *f.*

lampoon *s.* Schmähschrift *f.*

lamp-post *s.* Laternenpfahl *m.*

lamprey *s.* Neunauge *n.*

lampshade *s.* Lampenschirm *m.*

lance *s.* Lanze *f.*; *~ corporal* *s.* Gefreite *m.*; *~ v.t.* aufstechen.

lancet *s.* Lanzette *f.*; Spitzbogen *m.*

land *s.* Land *n.*; Landschaft, Länderei *f.*; Boden *m.*; Grundstück *n.*; *~ v.t. & i.* landen.

landed *a.* Land. . ., Grund. . .

land-forces *s.pl.* Landmacht *f.*

landing *s.* Landung *f.*; Treppenabsatz *m.*; *~-stage* *s.* Landungsbrücke *f.*; *forced ~*, (*avi.*) Notlandung *f.*

landlady *s.* Hauswirtin; Gastwirtin *f.*

landlord *s.* Gutsbesitzer *m.*; Gastwirt *m.*; Hauswirt *m.*

land-lubber *s.* Landratte *f.*

landmark *s.* Grenzstein *m.*; Markstein *m.*

landowner *s.* Grundbesitzer *m.*

land-register *s.* Grundbuch *n.*

land-registry *s.* Grundbuchamt *n.*

landscape *s.* Landschaft *f.*

land-service *s.* Landhilfe *f.*

land-slide *s.* Erdrutsch *m.*; politischer Umschwung *m.*

landslip *s.* Erdrutsch *m.*

land-tax *s.* Grundsteuer *f.*

lane *s.* Heckengang *m.*; Gasse *f.*

language *s.* Sprache *f.*; Ausdrucksweise *f.*

languid *a.*, *~ly adv.* matt, langsam.

languish *v.i.* schmachten; (*fig.*) danieder liegen.

languor *s.* Mattigkeit *f.*; Trägheit *f.*; Lauheit *f.*; Schwüle *f.*

languorous *a.* einschläfernd, schwül.

lank, lanky *a.*, *~ly adv.* schlank; dünn; hager.

lantern *s.* Laterne *f.*

lap *s.* Schoß *m.*; Runde *f.*; *~ v.t.* wickeln, einwickeln; lecken.

lap-dog *s.* Schoßhund *m.*

lapel *s.* Revers *n.*; Aufschlag (*m.*) an einem Rock.

lapse *s.* Gleiten *n.*; Fehltritt *m.*; Versehen *n.*; Verlauf *m.*; ~ *of time,* Zeitablauf *m.*; ~ *v.i.* fallen; verfließen; verfallen.

laptop *s.* Laptop *n.*

larceny *s.* Diebstahl *m.*

larch *s.* Lärche *f.*

lard *s.* Schmalz, Schweinefett *n.*; ~ *v.t.* spicken.

larder *s.* Speisekammer *f.*

large *a.,* **~ly** *adv.* groß; weit, breit; stark; reichlich; *at* ~, in Freiheit.

lark *s.* Lerche *f.*; Schabernack *m.*

larva *s.* Larve, Puppe *f.*

laryngitis *s.* Kehlkopfentzündung *f.*

larynx *s.* Kehlkopf *m.*

lascivious *a.,* **~ly** *adv.* wollüstig, geil.

laser *s.* Laser *m.*

laser beam *s.* Laserstrahl *m.*

laser printer *s.* Laserdrucker *m.*

lash *s.* (Peitschen) Hieb *m.*; Schnur *f.*; Geißel *f.*; Rute *f.*; Augenwimper *f.*; ~ *v.t.* peitschen; schlagen; ~ *v.i.* ausschlagen; ausschweifen.

lass *s.* Mädchen *n.*

lassitude *s.* Mattigkeit *f.*

last *a.* letzte, äußerste; vorig; *at* ~, endlich; **~ly** *adv.* zuletzt; schließlich; ~ *s.* Leisten *m.*; ~ *v.i.* währen, dauern; sich halten.

last-ditch *a.* allerletzt; ~ **attempt** *s.* letzter verzweifelter Versuch *m.*

lasting *p. & a.* **~ly** *adv.* dauernd.

lastly *adv.* zuletzt, zum Schluß.

latch *s.* Schnappriegel *m.*; ~ *v.t.* zuklinken; Schnappschloß *n.*; einschnappen.

latch-key *s.* Wohnungsschlüssel *m.*

late *a. & adv.* spät, letzt; (von Zügen) verspätet; ehemalig; neulich; verstorben; *of* ~, neulich.

latecomer *s.* Zuspätkommende *m./f.*

lately *adv.* neulich, kürzlich.

lateness *s.* Verspätung *f.*

latent *a.* verborgen, latent; ~ **heat** *s.* gebundene Wärme *f.*

later *a. & adv.* später.

lateral *a.,* **~ly** *adv.* seitlich; Quer...

latest *a.* spätest; letzt.

lath *s.* Latte *f.*; ~ *v.t.* belatten.

lathe *s.* Drehbank *f.*

lather *s.* Seifenschaum *m.*; ~ *v.i.* schäumen; ~ *v.t.* einseifen; prügeln.

Latin *a.* lateinisch; ~ *s.* Latein *n.*

Latin America *s.* Lateinamerika *f.*

Latin American *a.* lateinamerikanisch; *s.* Lateinamerikaner(in) *m.(f.)*

latitude *s.* Breite *f.*; Spielraum *m.*

latter *a.* [der] letztere (von zweien), spätere; *the* ~, dieser, diese (*f. & pl.*)

lattice *s.* Gitter *n.*; ~ *v.t.* vergittern.

Latvia *s.* Lettland *n.*

Latvian *a.* lettisch; ~ *s.* Lette *m.*; Lettin *f.*

laudable *a.,* **~bly** *adv.* lobenswert.

laudatory *a.* lobend.

laugh *v.i.* lachen; ~ *s.* Gelächter *n.*

laughable *a.* lächerlich.

laughing gas *s.* Lachgas *n.*

laughing-stock *s.* Gegenstand des Gelächters *m.*

laughter *s.* Gelächter *n.*

launch *v.t.* schleudern; loslassen; vom Stapel lassen; in Gang setzen; ~ *v.i.* sich aufmachen; ~ *s.* Stapellauf *m.*; Barkasse *f.*

launching ~ **pad** *s.* Abschußrampe *f.*; ~ **site** *s.* Abschußbasis *f.*

launder *v.t.* (Wäsche) waschen.

laundromat *s.* Waschsalon *m.*

laundry *s.* Wäsche *f.*; Wäscherei *f.*

laundry-bill *s.* Waschzettel *m.*

Laureate *s.* *poet* ~, Preisträger(in) *m.(f.)*

laurel *s.* Lorbeer, Lorbeerbaum *m.*

lava *s.* Lava *f.*

lavatory *s.* Toilette *f.*

lavender *s.* Lavendel *m.*

lavish *a.,* **~ly** *adv.* verschwenderisch; ~ *v.t.* verschwenden.

law *s.* Gesetz *n.*; Recht *n.*; Prozeß *m.*; Rechtswissenschaft *f.*

law-abiding *a.* gesetzestreu.

law-court *s.* Gerichtshof *m.*

law firm *s.* Anwaltsfirma *f.*

lawful *a.,* **~ly** *adv.* gesetzmäßig; erlaubt.

lawless *a.,* **~ly** *adv.* gesetzlos.

lawn *s.* Rasenplatz *m.*; Batist *m.*

lawn-mower *s.* Rasenmäher *m.*

lawn-tennis *s.* Rasentennis *n.*

lawsuit *s.* Rechtsstreit, Prozeß *m.*

lawyer *s.* Rechtsgelehrte *m./f.* (Rechts)Anwalt *m.* (Rechts)Anwältin *f.*

lax *a.,* **~ly** *adv.* schlaff, locker.

laxative *s.* Abführmittel *n.*

laxity *s.* Schlaffheit *f.*

lay *v.t.* legen, stellen; lindern, dämpfen; *to* ~ *by,* zurücklegen (Geld); *to* ~ *in,* sich eindecken; *to* ~ *out,* anlegen (Garten); *to* ~ *the table,* den Tisch decken; *to* ~ *up,* abtakeln; *to be laid up,* krank im Bett liegen; *a.* weltlich, Laien...; **~-brother,** Laienbruder *m.*

layer *s.* Lage, Schicht *f.*; Ableger *m.*

layette *s.* Babywäsche *f.*

layman *s.* Laie *m.*

layoff *s.* Entlassung *f.*

layout *s.* Anlage (Garten, etc.) *f.*; Layout *n.*

laze *v.i.* faulenzen.

laziness *s.* Faulheit *f.*

lazy *a.,* **~ily** *adv.* faul, träge.

lazybones *s.* Faulenzer(in) *m.(f.)*

lea *s.* Wiese, Fläche *f.*; Garnmaß *n.*

lead *s.* Blei *n.*; Lot, Senkblei *n.*

lead *v.t.ir.* führen, leiten; verleiten; ~ *v.i.* vorangehen; **leading** *a.* führend, erste, vornehmste, Haupt...; ~ *s.* Führung, Leitung *f.*; Vorsprung *m.*; *leading article, leader,* Leitartikel *m.*

leaden *a.* bleiern.

leader *s.* Führer *m.*; Leitartikel *m.*

leadership *s.* Führung *f.*; Leitung *f.*; Führungseigenschaften *pl.*

leadfree *a* bleifrei.

leading *a.* führend; leitend.

leading question *s.* Suggestivfrage *f.*

leading strings *s.pl.* Gängelband *n.*

leading case *s.* (*law*) Präzedenzfall *m.*

lead pencil *s.* Bleistift *m.*

lead-poisoning *s.* Bleivergiftung *f.*

lead story *s.* Titelgeschichte *f.*

leaf *s.* Blatt *n.*; Türflügel *m.*; **gold-~,** Blattgold *n.*; ~ *v.i.* Blätter bekommen.

leafless *s.* blätterlos.

leaflet s. Blättchen n., Zettel m.
leafy a. belaubt.
league s. Bündnis n.; Liga f.; Meile f. (4.8 km.); ~ v.i. sich verbünden.
leak s. Leck m.; Durchsickern (von Geheimnissen) n.; ~ v.i. leck sein; (*fig.*) *to* ~ *out*, durchsickern.
leakage s. Lecksein n.; Verlust m.
leaky a. leck.
lean v.i.r. & ir. (sich) lehnen; ~ v.t. anlehnen; ~ a., ~ly adv. mager.
leaning s. Neigung, Richtung f.
leanness s. Hagerkeit f.; Magerkeit f.
leap v.i.st. springen, hüpfen; ~ s. Sprung m.
leap-frog s. Bockspringen n.
leapyear s. Schaltjahr n.
learn v.i. & t. lernen; erfahren.
learned a., ~ly adv. gelehrt; erfahren.
learner s. Lerner(in) m.(f.)
learning s. Gelehrsamkeit f.; Lernen n.
lease s. Pacht f.; Miete f.; ~ v.t. verpachten.
lease-hold s. Pachtung f.; Pacht...
leash s. (Koppel)leine f.; Koppel f.; ~ v.t. koppeln.
least a. kleinste, wenigste; ~ adv. am wenigsten; *at* ~, wenigstens.
leather s. Leder n.
leathery a. ledern.
leave s. Erlaubnis f.; Urlaub, Abschied m.; *to beg* ~, so frei sein; ~ v.t.ir. lassen; verlassen; hinterlassen; ~ v.i.ir. abstehen von etwas, aufhören; abreisen, weggehen; *leaving certificate*, Abgangszeugnis n.; *leaving examination*, Schlußexamen, Abitur n.
leaven s. Sauerteig m.; ~ v.t. säuern.
Lebanese a. libanesisch; ~ s. Libanese m.; Libanesin f.
Lebanon s. Libanon m.
lecherous a. lüstern; geil.
lechery s. Wollust f.
lectern s. Lesepult n.
lecture s. Vorlesung f.; Strafpredigt f., Vortrag m.; ~ v.t. abkanzeln; ~ v.i. Vorlesungen, Vorträge halten; ~-room, Vorlesungsraum m.
lecturer s. Vortragende m./f.; Dozent(in) m.(f.)
ledge s. Vorsprung m.; Sims m.
ledger s. (com.) Hauptbuch n.
lee s. (nav.) Leeseite f.
leech s. Blutegel m.
leek s. Lauch m.
leer s. Seitenblick m.; ~ v.i. schielen.
lees s.pl. Bodensatz m.
leeway s. Abtrift f.
left p. von *to leave*, übrig; *to be* ~ *till called-for*, zur Aufbewahrung; post-lagernd; ~ a. link: *lefthand side*, linke Seite; ~ s. Linke (in der Politik) f.; adv. links.
left-handed a. linkshändig.
left-overs s.pl. Reste pl.; Überbleibsal pl. **left-wing** a. (pl.) links, dem linken Flügel angehörend.
leg s. Bein n.; Keule f.; Stiefelschaft m.; ~ *of mutton, veal, etc.*, Hammelkeule, Kalbskeule f.; *three-legged, four-legged, etc.*, dreibeinig, vierbeinig.
legacy s. Vermächtnis n.; Erbe n.
legal a., ~ly adv. gesetzlich; ~ *remedy*, Rechtsmittel n., Rechtschilfe f.; ~ *status*, Rechtsstellung f.; ~ *tender*, gesetzliches Zahlungsmittel n.
legality s. Gesetzlichkeit f.; Rechtmäßigkeit f.; Legalität f.

legalize v.t. rechtskräftig machen; legalisieren.
legate s. (päpstlicher) Legat m.
legation s. Gesandtschaft f.
legend s. Legende f.; Sage f.; Zeichenerklärung f.
legendary a. sagenhaft; legendär.
legerdemain s. Taschenspielerei f.
leggings s.pl. Leggings pl., Gamaschen f.pl.
leggy a. hochbeinig.
legibility s. Lesbarkeit f.
legible a., ~bly adv. leserlich.
legion s. Legion f.; Menge f.
legislation s. Gesetzgebung f.
legislative a. gesetzgebend; ~ *body*, gesetzgebende Körperschaft f.
legislator s. Gesetzgeber m.
legislature s. Gesetzgebung f.
legitimacy s. Legitimität f.; Ehelichkeit f.
legitimate a., ~ly adv. zulässig, richtig; ehelich.
legitimization s. Gültigmachung f.; Ausweis m.; Ehelichkeitserklärung f.
legitimize v.t. legitimieren.
leg-room s. Beinfreiheit f.
leisure s. Musse f.; Freizeit f.
leisurely a. & adv. mit Musse, gemächlich.
lemon s. Zitrone f.
lemonade s. Limonade f.
lend v.t.ir. leihen, borgen.
lender s. Verleiher(in) m.(f.)
lending library s. Leihbibliothek f.
length s. Länge f.; Strecke f.; *at* ~, zuletzt, endlich; *a* ~ *of carpet*, ein Stück Teppich; *a trouser* ~, eine Hosenlänge (von Stoff).
lengthen v.t. & i. verlängern.
lengthways adv. längs.
lengthwise adv. der Länge nach.
lengthy a. weitschweifig.
leniency s. Milde, Nachsicht f.
lenient a. nachsichtig, mild.
lens s. (Glas) Linse f.
Lent s. Fastenzeit f.
lentil s. Linse f.
leopard s. Leopard m.
leotard s. Trikot m.
leper s. Aussätzige m./f.; Leprakranke m./f.
leprosy s. Aussatz m.; Lepra f.
leprous a. leprös.
lesbian s. Lesbierin f.; lesbisch a.
lesion s. (med.) Verletzung f.
less a. & adv. kleiner, weniger, geringer.
lessee s. Pächter(in) m.(f.)
lessen v.t. & i. vermindern; abnehmen.
lesser a. kleiner, weniger.
lesson s. Lektion, Stunde f.; Lehre f.
lessor s. Verpächter m.
lest c. damit nicht; daß.
let v.t.ir. lassen; gestatten; vermieten, verpachten; *rooms to* ~, Zimmer zu vermieten; ~ *alone*, geschweige denn; ~ **down,** v.t. im Stiche lassen.
lethal a. tödlich, Toten...
lethargic a. lethargisch, träge.
lethargy s. Trägheit f.; Lethargie f.
letter s. Buchstabe f.; (print.) Type f.; Brief m.; *by* ~, brieflich; ~**s** s.pl. Literatur f.
letter-box s. Briefkasten m.
letter-head s. Briefkopf m.
letter-weight s. Briefbeschwerer m.

lettuce *s.* Kopfsalat *m.*

leucocyte *s.* Leukozyt *m.*; weißes Blutkörperchen *n.*

leukemia *s.* Leukämie *f.*

levee *s.* Morgenempfang beim König *m.*; Schutzdamm (*m.*) an Flüssen.

level *a.* gleich, eben, flach; waagerecht; ~ *s.* Fläche *f.*; Niveau *n.*; Höhenlage *f.*; Wasserwaage *f.*; Pegel *m.*; *on top* ~, an höchster Stelle; ~ *v.t.* gleichmachen; dem Boden gleichmachen; ebnen; nivellieren; richten.

level-crossing *s.* schienengleicher Bahnübergang *m.*

lever *s.* Hebel *m.*

leverage *s.* Hebelkraft *f.*

levity *s.* Leichtigkeit *f.*; Leichtsinn *m.*

levy *v.t.* heben; erheben; ausheben; ~ *s.* Hebung; Aushebung *f.*; Erhebung (von Steuern).

lewd *a.*, ~**ly** *adv.* liederlich, unzüchtig; geil.

lexicon *s.* Wörterbuch *n.*

liability *s.* Verantwortlichkeit *f.*; Hang *m.*; Verbindlichkeit *f.*; Haftpflicht *f.*; *limited* ~ *s.* beschränkte Haftung *f.*; **liabilities** *pl.* Passiva *s.pl.*; ~ *of kin*, Sippenhaftung *f.*

liable *a.* ausgesetzt; haftbar; *to be* ~, haften; ~ *to duty*, zollpflichtig; *to render oneself* ~ *to prosecution*, sich strafbar machen.

liaison *s.* (*mil.*) Verbindung *f.*; Liaison *f.*; ~**-officer** *s.* Verbindungsoffizier *m.*

liar *s.* Lügner(in) *m.*(*f.*)

libel *s.* Klageschrift *f.*; Verleumdung *f.*; ~ *v.t.* beschimpfen; verleumden.

libelous *s.* ehrenrührig.

liberal *a.*, ~**ly** *adv.* freisinnig; freigebig; liberal (*polit.*).

liberality *s.* Großzügigkeit *f.*; Liberalität *f.*

liberate *v.t.* befreien.

liberation *s.* Befreiung *f.*

liberator *s.* Befreier(in) *m.*(*f.*)

libertine *a.* ausschweifend; ~ *s.* Wüstling *m.*

liberty *s.* Freiheit *f.*

libidinous *a.* unzüchtig.

Libra *s.* (*astro.*) Waage *f.*

librarian *s.* Bibliothekar(in) *m.*(*f.*)

library *s.* Bibliothek *f.*, Bücherei *f.*

libretto *s.* Libretto *n.*

Libya *s.* Libyen *n.*

Libyan *a.* libysch; *s.* Libyer(in) *m.*(*f.*)

license *s.* Freiheit, Erlaubnis *f.*; Lizenz *f.*; Zügellosigkeit *f.*; Konzession *f.*; Schankgerechtigkeit *f.*; *under* ~ *from the Government*, mit Regierungskonzession; *to take out a* ~, sich eine Konzession verschaffen; ~**d** *p.* mit Konzession.

license *v.t.* genehmigen.

licensee *s.* Lizenz-, Konzessionsinhaber, Lizenzträger *m.*

licentious *a.*, ~**ly** *adv.* ausschweifend.

lichen *s.* Flechte *f.*; Leberkraut *n.*

lick *v.t.* lecken; prügeln.

licking *s.* Tracht Prügel *f.*

lid *s.* Deckel *m.*; Augenlid *n.*

lie *s.* Lüge *f.*; Lage *f.*; ~ *v.i.* lügen; ~ *v.i.st.* liegen; ruhen.

liege *s.* Lehnsherr *m.*; Lehnsmann *m.*

lien *s.* Pfandrecht *n.*

lieu *s.* *in* ~ *of*, statt, anstatt.

lieutenant *s.* Leutnant *m.*; ~**-colonel** *s.* Oberstleutnant *m.*

life *s.* Leben *n.*; Lebensbeschreibung *f.*; Lebhaftigkeit *f.*; Lebensdauer (eines Abkommens, einer Maschine, etc.); *for* ~, auf Lebenszeit; ~**-interest** (*law*) lebenslänglicher Nießbrauch *m.*

life-annuity *s.* Lebensrente *f.*

life-belt *s.* Rettungsgürtel *m.*

life-boat *s.* Rettungsboot *n.*

life-guard *s.* Leibwache *f.*

life-insurance *s.* Lebensversicherung *f.*

life-jacket *s.* Schwimmweste *f.*

lifeless *a.*, ~**ly** *adv.* leblos.

lifelong *a.* lebenslang.

life-sentence *s.* lebenslange Freiheitsstrafe *f.*

life-size *a.* lebensgroß.

life-time *s.* Lebenszeit *f.*

lift *v.t.* heben, aufheben; entwenden; ~ *v.i.* sich heben, sich heben lassen; ~ *s.* Heben *n.*; Hebewerkzeug *n.*; Aufzug, Fahrstuhl *m.*.

ligament *s.* Band *n.*; Flechse *f.*

ligature *s.* Band *n.*; Bindung *f.*

light *s.* Licht *n.*; Beleuchtung *f.*; *will you give me a* ~?, kann ich Feuer haben?; ~ *v.t.r. & ir.* leuchten, anzünden; beleuchten; *to* ~ *on, v.i.* sich niederlassen auf; geraten auf; ~ *a. & adv.*, ~**ly** *adv.* leicht; unbedeutend; licht, hell; leichtsinnig; ~**-blue**, ~**-brown**, hellblau, hellbraun, etc.

light-bulb *s.* Glühbirne *f.*

lighted *a.* brennend; beleuchtet.

lighten *v.t.* erleuchten; erleichtern; lichten; löschen; ~ *v.i.* blitzen.

lighter *s.* Anzünder *m.*

light-hearted *a.* wohlgemut, fröhlich.

light-house *s.* Leuchtturm *m.*

lighting *s.* Beleuchtung *f.*

light metal *s.* Leichtmetall *n.*

lightmeter *s.* Lichtmesser *m.*

lightness *s.* Leichtigkeit *f.*; Heiterkeit *f.*

lightning *s.* Blitz *m.*; ~**-war** *s.* Blitzkrieg *m.*

lightning-conductor, lightning-rod *s.* Blitzableiter *m.*

lights *pl.* Lunge (der Tiere als Speise) *f.*

lightweight *s.* Leichtgewicht (Boxen) *n.*

ligneous *a.* hölzern; holzig.

lignite *s.* Braunkohle *f.*

likable *a.* liebenswert.

like *a. & adv.* gleich, ähnlich; fast; *it's just* ~ *him*, das sieht ihm ähnlich; ~ *s.* Gleiche, Ebenbild *n.*; ~ *v.t. & i.* mögen, gefallen, belieben; gern haben.

likelihood *s.* Wahrscheinlichkeit *f.*

likely *a. & adv.* wahrscheinlich.

liken *v.t.* vergleichen.

likeness *s.* Gleichheit *f.*; Ebenbild *n.*

likewise *adv.* gleichfalls.

liking *s.* Gefallen *m.*, Belieben *n.*

lilac *s.* Flieder *m.*; *a.* lila.

lilt *s.* flotter Rhythmus *m.*

lily *s.* Lilie *f.*; ~ *of the valley*, Maiglöckchen *n.*

limb *s.* Glied *n.*; Ast *m.*

limber *a.* geschmeidig; ~**up** auflockern.

limbo *s.* Vorhölle *f.*; Gefängnis *n.*; Vergessenheit *f.*

lime *s.* Leim *m.*; Kalk *m.*; Linde *f.*; Limone *f.*; ~**-juice** Limonensaft *m.*

lime-light *s.* *in the* ~, im Rampenlicht stehen.

limestone *s.* Kalkstein *m.*

limerick *s.* Limerick *m.*

limit *s.* Grenze *f.*; Schranke *f.*; (*com.*) Limite *f.*; *off ~s,* Zutritt gesperrt; *that is the ~,* das ist die Höhe; *~ v.t.* beschränken; *~ed company,* Gesellschaft mit beschränkter Haftung; *~ in scope,* von beschränktem Umfang.

limitation *s.* Einschränkung *f.*; (*law*) Verjährung *f.*; *period of ~,* Verjährungsfrist *f.*; *statute of ~s,* Verjährungsgesetz *n.*

limitless *a.* grenzenlos.

limp *a.* schlapp; matt; *~ v.i.* hinken.

limpid *a.* klar, durchsichtig.

linchpin *s.* Kernstück *n.*

line *s.* Linie, Zeile *f.*; Eisenbahnlinie *f.*; Telephonleitung, elektrische Leitung *f.*; Leine *f.*; Reihe *f.*; Vers *m.*; Geschäftszweig *m.*; Äquator *m.*; Stamm *m.*; Art und Weise *f.*; *in the direct ~,* in gerader Linie (verwandt); *in the ascending ~,* in aufsteigender Linie; *in the descending ~,* in absteigender Linie; *~ of communications,* (*mil.*) Zufuhrstraße, Verbindungslinie *f.*; *~ v.t.* liniieren; einfassen, füttern; *to ~ up,* sich in einer Reihe aufstellen, sich zusammenschließen; *~-up* *s.* Formierung *f.*; Zusammenschluß *m.*

lineage *s.* Abstammung *f.*; Geschlecht *n.*

lineal *a.*, *~ly adv.* in gerader Linie; linienweise.

lineament *s.* Gesichtszug *m.*

linear *a.* Linien..., linear.

linen *s.* Leinwand *f.*; Wäsche *f.*; *~ a.* leinen.

liner *s.* Linienschiff *n.*

linesman *s.* Linienrichter *m.*

lineswoman *s.* Linienrichterin *f.*

linger *v.i.* säumen, zögern.

lingo *s.* Kauderwelsch *n.*; Fachjargon *m.*

lingual *a.* Zungen...

linguist *s.* Linguist(in) *m.(f.)*

linguistic *a.* sprachwissenschaftlich.

linguistics *s.* Linguistik *f.*, Sprachwissenschaft *f.*

liniment *s.* Salbe *f.*

lining *s.* (Unter-)Futter *n.*; Verschalung *f.*

link *s.* (Ketten)glied *n.*; Band *n.*; Kette *f.*; *~ v.t.* verketten; *to ~ up with;* *~ v.i.* Verbindung herstellen mit.

linkage *s.* Verbindung *f.*

linnet *s.* Hänfling *m.*

linseed *s.* Leinsamen *m.*

linseed-oil *s.* Leinöl *n.*

lint *s.* Mull *m.*

lintel *s.* Türsturz *m.*

lion *s.* Löwe *m.*

lioness *s.* Löwin *f.*

lion tamer *s.* Löwenbändiger(in) *m.(f.)*

lip *s.* Lippe *f.*; Rand *m.*

lipstick *s.* Lippenstift *m.*

liquefy *v.t. & i.* verflüssigen.

liqueur *s.* Liqueur *m.*; Likör *m.*

liquid *a.* flüssig; klar, hell; wohltonend. *~ s.* Flüssigkeit *f.*

liquidate *v.t.* (*com.*) liquidieren, bezahlen; abwickeln.

liquidation *s.* (*com.*) Liquidation *f.*

liquidity *s.* Liquidität *f.*

liquidize *v.t.* auflösen; pürieren.

liquor *s.* alkoholisches Getränk *m.*; Flüssigkeit *f.*; *in ~,* betrunken.

liquorice *s.* Süßholz *n.*; Lakritze *f.*

liquor store *s.* Spirituosengeschäft *n.*

lisp *v.i.* lispeln; *~ s.* Lispeln *n.*

lissom(e) *a.* geschmeidig, gelenkig.

list *s.* Liste *f.*; Musterrolle *f.*; Saum *m.*; Salleiste *f.*; Schranke *f.*; Neigung *f.*; (*nav.*) Schlagseite *f.*; *~ v.t.* einschreiben; aufführen; *~ v.i.* gelüsten.

listen *v.i.* zuhören; lauschen.

listener *s.* Hörer(in) *m.(f.)*; Zuhörer(in) *m.(f.)*

listless *a.*, *~ly adv.* lustlos; verdrossen.

litany *s.* Litanei *f.*

literacy *s.* Kenntnis (*f.*) des Lesens und Schreibens.

literal *a.*, *~ly adv.* buchstäblich; wörtlich.

literary *a.* literarisch; *~ award s.* Literaturpreis *m.*; *~ critic s.* Literaturkritiker(in) *m.(f.)*; *~ historian s.* Literarhistoriker(in) *m.(f.)*

literate *a.* des Lesens und Schreibens kundig.

literature *s.* Literatur *f.*

lithe *a.* biegsam, geschmeidig.

lithograph *s.* Lithographie *f.*; Steindruck *m.*; *~ v.t.* lithographieren.

lithographer *s.* Lithograph(in) *m.(f.)*

lithography *s.* Lithographie *f.* (Technik); Steindruck *m.*

Lithuania *s.* Litauen *n.*

Lithuanian *a.* litauisch.

litigant *s.* streitende Partei *f.*

litigate *v.t. & i.* streiten; prozessieren.

litigation *s.* Prozeß *m.*

litigious *a.*, *~ly adv.* streitsüchtig.

litmus *s.* Lackmus *n.*

litter *s.* Sänfte *f.*; Wurf *m.*; Abfälle *m.pl.*; Streu *f.*; *~ v.t.* (Junge) werfen; umherstreuen.

little *a. & adv.* klein, wenig; gering; *~ by ~,* nach und nach.

littoral *a.* Ufer...; *~ s.* Küstenland *n.*

liturgy *s.* Liturgie *f.*

live *v.i.* leben; verleben; am Leben bleiben; wohnen; dauern; *~ a.* lebendig; (*elek.*) geladen; (Patrone) scharf; *~-stock,* Viehbestand *m.*; *~ coal s.* glühende Kohle *f.*

livelihood *s.* Unterhalt *m.*

liveliness *s.* Lebhaftigkeit *f.*

livelong *a.*, *the ~ day,* der liebe lange Tag.

lively *a.* lebhaft, munter.

liver *s.* Leber *f.*

liverish *a.* mürrisch.

livery *s.* Livree *f.*

live-stock *s.* Vieh(bestand) *m.*

livid *a.* bleifarbig, fahl.

living *s.* Leben *n.*; Unterhalt *m.*; Pfarrstelle, Pfründe *f.*; *to earn a ~,* sich sein Leben verdienen; *~ room s.* Wohnzimmer *n.*

lizard *s.* Eidechse *f.*

llama *s.* Lama *n.*; Lamawolle *f.*

load *s.* Ladung, Last *f.*; (*elek.*) Belastung *f.*; *~ v.t.* laden, aufladen; *~-line,* Ladelinie *f.*; *~ing ramp,* Laderampe *f.*

loaded *a.* geladen.

loaf *s.* Laib *m.*; Brot *n.*; (Zucker) Hut *m.*; *~ v.i.* umherlungern.

loam *s.* Lehmboden *m.*

loan *s.* Anleihe *f.*; *~ v.t.* leihen.

loath *a.* unwillig, abgeneigt.

loathe *v.t.* verabscheuen, hassen.

loathing *s.* Ekel *m.*

loathsome *a.*, *~ly adv.* ekelhaft.

lob *v.t.* (Tennis) lobben.

lobby *s.* Vorsaal *m.*; Wandelgang *m.*; Lobby *f.*; ~ *v.t.* Abgeordnete bearbeiten.

lobe *s.* Ohrläppchen *n.*

lobster *s.* Hummer *m.*

local *a.* örtlich, Orts...; ~ *authorities*, *pl.* Kommunalbehörden *f.pl.*; ~ *government*, Kommunalverwaltung *f.*; ~ *traffic*, Nahverkehr *m.*

locality *s.* Örtlichkeit *f.*

localize *v.t.* lokalisieren.

locate *v.t.* plazieren; einen Ort bestimmen.

location *s.* Lage *f.*; Ort *m.*; Standort *m.*; Feststellung (*f.*) eines Ortes.

loch *s.* See *m.*; Bucht *f.*

lock *s.* Schloß *n.*; Locke *f.*; Schleuse *f.*; Verschluß *m.*; Hemmung *f.*; *under* ~ *and key*, hinter Schloß und Riegel; ~ *v.t.* verschließen; hemmen (ein Rad); ~ *v.i.* ineinander greifen.

locker *s.* Schließfach *f.*; Schrank *m.*

locket *s.* Medaillon *n.*

lockjaw *s.* Mundsperre *f.*; Wundstarrkrampf *m.*

lock-out *s.* Aussperrung *f.*

locksmith *s.* Schlosser *m.*

lock-up *s.* Gefängniszelle *f.*

locomotion *s.* Fortbewegungs...

locomotive (engine) *s.* Lokomotive *f.*

locust *s.* Heuschrecke *f.*

locution *s.* Redensart *f.*; Ausdruck *m.*

lode *s.* Wasserlauf *m.*; Erzgang *m.*; ~**-star**, Leitstern, Polarstern *m.*

lodge *v.i.* wohnen; ~ *v.t.* beherbergen; ~ *s.* Häuschen *n.*; Loge *f.*

lodger *s.* Mieter(in) *m.(f.)*

lodging *s.* Zimmer *n.*; Unterkunft *f.*

lodgings *s.pl.* möblierte Zimmer *n.pl.*

loft *s.* Boden, Dachboden *m.*

lofty *a.*, ~**ily** *adv.* hoch, erhaben; stolz.

log *s.* Klotz *m.*; (*nav.*) Log *n.*

loganberry *s.* Loganbeere *f.*

logarithm *s.* Logarithmus *m.* (*math.*)

log-book *s.* Schiffstagebuch *n.*

log-cabin *s.* Blockhaus *n.*

loggerhead *s.*, *to be at* ~*s*, sich in den Haaren liegen.

logging *s.* Holzeinschlag *m.*

logic *s.* Logik *f.*

logical *a.*, ~**ly** *adv.* logisch.

logician *s.* Logiker *m.*

logistics *s.pl.* Logistik *f.*

loin *s.* Lendenbraten *m.*; ~*s* *s.pl.* Lenden *f.pl.*

loincloth *s.* Lendenschurz *m.*

loiter *v.i.* zaudern, trödeln, herumlungern.

loll *v.i.* sich lümmeln.

lollipop *s.* Lutscher *m.*

lone *a.*, ~**ly** *adv.* einsam; allein.

loneliness *s.* Einsamkeit *f.*

lonely, lonesome *a.* einsam.

loner *s.* Einzelgänger(in) *m.(f.)*

long *a. & adv.* lang; lange; ~**-term** langfristig; *I won't be* ~, ich werde nicht lange brauchen; *so* ~*!*, auf Wiedersehen!; ~ *v.t.* sich sehnen.

long-distance *a.* Fern...; Langstrecken...

longevity *s.* Langlebigkeit *f.*

longhand *s.* Langschrift *f.*

longing *s.* Sehnsucht *f.*

longitude *s.* geographische Länge *f.*

longitudinal *a.*, ~**ly** *adv.* der Länge nach; Längen...

long jump *s.* Weitsprung *m.*

long-lived *a.* langlebig; von langer Lebensdauer (Material).

long-range *a.* Langstrecken...; mit großer Reichweite; langfristig.

long-shoreman *s.* Werftarbeiter *m.*

long-sighted *a.* weitsichtig.

long-suffering *a.* langmütig.

long-term *a.* langfristig.

long wave *s.* Langwelle *f.* (*radio*).

long-winded *a.* langatmig.

look *v.t. & i.* sehen, hinsehen; aussehen; *to* ~ *after*, betreuen; *to* ~ *for*, suchen; *to* ~ *over*, sich anschauen; *to* ~ *through*, durchsehen, durchlesen.

look-alike *s.* Doppelgänger(in) *m.(f.)*

looker-on *s.* Zuschauer *m.*

looking-glass *s.* Spiegel *m.*

look-out *s.* Ausguck *m.*; Wache *f.*

loom *s.* Webstuhl *m.*; ~ *v.i.* sichtbar werden; ~*up*, aufragen; ~*large*, sich auftürmen.

loony *a.* (*fam.*) bekloppt; verrückt.

loop *s.* Schlinge *f.*; Schnürloch *n.*

loophole *s.* Ausflucht *f*; (*fig.*) Schlupfloch *n.*, Hintertürchen *n.*

loose *a.*, ~**ly** *adv.* lose, los; locker; liederlich; frei; ~*-leaf notebook* *s.* Loseblätterbuch *n.*

loosen *v.t.* lösen, locker machen.

loot *s.* Beute *f.*; ~ *v.t.* plündern.

lop *v.t.* ausästen; abhacken.

lope *v.i.* springen; beschwingt gehen.

lop-sided *a.* scheif, einseitig.

loquacious *a.* schwatzhaft.

loquacity *s.* Schwatzhaftigkeit *f.*

lord *s.* Lord *m.*; Herr *m.*; Gott *m.*

lordly *a.* vornehm, stolz.

lordship *s.* Herrschaft, Lordschaft *f.*; *Your Lordship* (Titel), Euer Gnaden.

lore *s.* Kunde *f.*; Lehre *f.*

lorry *s.* Lori, Lore *f.*; Lastwagen *m.*

lose *v.t.ir.* verlieren; *to* ~ *one's way*, sich verlaufen.

loser *s.* Verlierer(in) *m.(f.)*

loss *s.* Verlust *m.*; *at* ~, ratlos.

lost-property office *s.* Fundbüro *n.*

lot *s.* Los *n.*; Schicksal *n.*; Anteil *m.*; Menge *f.*; Posten *m.*; Partie *f.*; Stück Land *n.*; ~ *v.t.* verlosen.

lotion *s.* Hautwasser *n.*; Lotion *f.*

lottery *s.* Lotterie *f.*; ~**-ticket** *s.* Lotterielos *n.*

loud *a.*, ~**ly** *adv.* laut; grell (Farben).

loudness *s.* Lautstärke *f.*

loudspeaker *s.* (*radio*) Lautsprecher *m.*; ~**-van,** Lautsprecherwagen *m.*

lounge *v.i.* faulenzen; ~ *s.* (Hotel) Halle; Wartesaal *m.*; Foyer *n.*

louse *s.* Laus *f.*

lousy *a.* verlaust; widerlich; mies; (*sl.*) beschissen.

lout *s.* Lümmel *m.*

loutish *a.*, ~**ly** *adv.* plump, tölpisch.

lovable *a.* liebenswert.

love *v.t. & i.* lieben; gern haben; ~*s.* Liebe *f.*; Liebchen *n.*; *in* ~, verliebt; *to fall in* ~ *with*, sich verlieben in; *make*~ sich lieben; *send one's* ~ *to s.b.* jn. grüßen lassen; *there is no love lost between them*, sie haben nichts füreinander übrig.

love-affair *s.* Liebesaffäre *f.*

lovely *a.* liebenswürdig; lieblich; herrlich.

lovemaking s. (körperliche) Liebe f.
love-match s. Liebesheirat f.
lover s. Liebhaber m.; Geliebte f. Geliebte(r) m.; *they are ~s* sie lieben sich.
lovesick a. liebeskrank; an Liebeskummer leidend.
loving a., **~ly** adv. liebevoll; mit viel Liebe.
low a. & adv. niedrig; leise; niedergeschlagen; **~ brow** a. schlicht; anspruchslos; **~ calorie** a. kalorienarm; *in a ~ voice*, leise; **~ s.** Tief (Wetterkunde) **~ v.i.** brüllen.
lower a. niedriger; tiefer; **~deck** s. Zwischendeck n.; **~ v.t.** niederlassen; verringern; *to ~ a boat*, ein Boot aussetzen; *to ~ one's voice*, leiser reden; **~ v.i.** abnehmen.
lower case s. Kleinbuchstabe m.; klein.
lower deck s. Unterdeck.
Lower Saxony s. Niedersachsen n.
low-fat a. fettarm.
low-grade a. geringwertig.
low-key a. gedämpft; zurückhaltend.
lowland s. Tiefland n., Flachland.
lowly a. & adv. niedrig, bescheiden.
low-pressure s. Tiefdruck m.
low season s. Nebensaison f.
low-spirited a. niedergeschlagen, mutlos.
loyal a., **~ly** adv. treu, pflichttreu.
loyalty s. Treue f.
lozenge s. Raute f.; Pastille f.
lubber s. Tölpel, Grobian m.
lubricant s. Schmierstoff m.
lubricate v.t. einölen, schmieren.
lucid a. leuchtend; klar, licht, durchsichtig.
luck s. Glück n.; Zufall m.; Schicksal, Geschick n. *good ~*, Glück n.; *ill ~*, *bad ~*, Unglück n.
luckless a. glücklos.
lucky a., **~ily** adv. glücklich; glücklicherweise.
lucrative a. einträglich.
lucre s. Gewinn m., Geld n.; *filthy ~*, gemein Profitgier f.
lucubration s. nächtliches Studium n.; **~s** pl. gelehrte Abhandlungen f.pl.
ludicrous a., **~ly** adv. lächerlich, albern.
lug v.t. schleppen.
luggage s. Gepäck n.; **hand-~,** Handgepäck n.; *heavy ~*, großes Gepäck n.; **~-office,** Gepäckabfertigung f.; **left-~ office,** Gepäckaufbewahrungsstelle f.; **~-van,** Gepäckwagen m.
lugubrious a. schwermütig, traurig, trübsinnig.
lukewarm a., **~ly** adv. lau.
lull v.t. einlullen; **~ v.i.** sich legen (vom Winde).
lullaby s. Wiegenlied n.
lumbago s. Hexenschuß m.
lumber s. Gerümpel n.; Plunder m.; Bauholz n.
lumber-jack s. Holzfäller m.
lumber-mill s. Sägewerk n.
luminary s. Lichtkörper m.; (fig.) Leuchte f.

luminosity s. Helligkeit f.
luminous a. leuchtend; Leucht...; **~ watch** s. Leuchtuhr f.
lump s. Klumpen m.; Masse f.; *in the ~*, in Bausch und Bogen; **~-sugar,** Stückzucker m.; **~ sum,** Pauschalsumme f.; **~ v.t.** im ganzen nehmen; *to ~ together*, in einen Topf werfen.
lumpy a. klumpig.
lunacy s. Irrsinn, Wahnsinn m.
lunar a. Mond...
lunar eclipse s. Mondfinsternis f.
lunatic a. irrsinnig; **~ s.** Irre m./f.; **~ asylum** s. Irrenhaus n.
lunch, luncheon s. Mittagessen n., Lunch m. **~-basket** s. Imbißkorb m.; **~ v.i.** leichtes Mittagessen einnehmen.
lunch-hour s. Mittagspause f.
lunch-time s. Mittagszeit f.
lung s. Lunge f.
lunge s. Ausfall (beim Fechten) m.; Sprung (m.) vorwärts.
lupin s. Lupine f.
lurch s. *leave in the ~*, im Stich lassen; **~ v.i.** taumeln.
lure s. Köder m.; Lockung f.; Reiz m.; **~v.t.** Ködern; verlocken.
lurid a. fahl, grell; gespenstisch, düster.
lurk v.i. lauern.
luscious a. köstlich; lecker; üppig; knackig.
lush a. üppig.
lust s. Begierde f.; Trieb m.; Wollust f.; **~ v.i.** gelüsten.
luster s. Glanz m.; Kronleuchter m.
lustful a. lüstern, wollustig.
lustrous a. glänzend.
lusty a., **~ily** adv. munter; kräftig.
lute s. Laute f.; Kitt m.; **~ v.t.** verkitten.
Lutheran a. lutherisch; **~ s.** Lutheraner m.
Luxembourg, Luxemburg s. Luxemburg n.
luxuriance s. Üppigkeit f.
luxuriant a./adv. üppig, reichlich.
luxuriate v.i. schwelgen.
luxurious a., **~ly** adv. üppig; luxuriös.
luxury s. Üppigkeit f.; Luxus m.
lye s. Lauge f.
lying a. verlogen, lügnerisch.
lying-in s. Wochenbett n.
Lyme disease s. Borreliose f.
lymph s. Lymphe f.; Quellwasser n.
lynch v.t. lynchen.
lynch-law s. Pöbeljustiz, Lynchjustiz f.
lynx s. Luchs m.
lyre s. Laute f.; Lyra f.
lyric a. lyrisch; **~ poetry** s. lyrisches Gedicht n.
lyricism s. Lyrismus m.
lyricist s. Lyriker(in) m.(f.)

M

M, m der Buchstabe M oder m n.
macabre a. makaber.
macadam s. Schotter m.
macaroni s. Makkaroni f.pl.
macaroon s. Makrone f.
mace s. Amtsstab m.; Muskatblüte f. (Gewürz);

chemische Keule f.
macerate v.t. (cul.) einlegen (Fleisch).
machete s. Machete f.; Buschmesser n.
machiavellian a. machiavellistisch.
machination s. Machenschaft f.
machine s. Maschine f.; **~ v.t.** maschinell bearbeiten od. herstellen; **~-gun** s. Maschinengewehr

n.; **~-tool** *s.* Werkzeugmaschine *f.*
machinery *s.* Maschinerie *f.*
machinist *s.* Maschinist *m.*
machismo *s.* Machismo *m.*
macho *s.* Macho *m.*
mackerel *s.* Makrele *f.*
mackintosh *s.* Regenmantel *m.*
macroscopic *a.* makroskopisch.
mad *a.*, **~ly** *adv.* wahnsinnig, toll.
madam *s.* gnädige Frau *f.*
madcap *s.* Tollkopf *m.*; **~a.** unbesonnen, wild.
madden *v.t.* verrückt machen.
made-to-measure *a.* Maß...
made-up *a.* erfunden.
madhouse *s.* Tollhaus *n.*; Irrenanstalt *f.*
madman *s.* Wahnsinniger *m.*
madness *s.* Wahnsinn *m.*; Tollheit *f.*
madwoman *s.* Verrückte *f.*
maelstrom *s.* Strudel *m.*; Sog *m.*
Mafia *s.* Mafia *f.*
magazine *s.* Zeitschrift *f.*; Magazin *n.*; Lagerhaus *n.*; Pulvermagazin *n.*; **~-rifle** *s.* Mehrladegewehr *n.*
maggot *s.* Made *f.*; (*fig.*) Grille *f.*
magic *s.* Zauberkunst *f.*; ~ *a.* zauberhaft, magisch, Zauber...
magic carpet *s.* fliegender Teppich *m.*
magician *a.* Zauberer *m.*; Zauberin *f.*
magic wand *s.* Zauberstab *m.*
magistrate *s.* Friedensrichter(in) *m.*(*f.*); obrigkeitliche Person *f.*
magnanimity *s.* Großmut *f.*
magnanimous *a.*, **~ly** *adv.* großmütig.
magnate *s.* Magnat(in) *m.*(*f.*)
magnesia *s.* Magnesia *f.*
magnesium *s.* Magnesium *n.*
magnet *s.* Magnet *m.*
magnetic *a.* magnetisch.
magnetic field *s.* Magnetfeld *n.*
magnetic pole *s.* Magnetpol *m.*
magnetism *s.* Magnetismus *m.*
magnetize *v.t.* magnetisieren.
magneto *s.* Zündapparat *m.*
magnification *s.* Vergrößerung *f.* (Mikroskop, etc.).
magnificence *s.* Großartigkeit *f.*, Pracht *f.*
magnificent *a.*, **~ly** *adv.* prachtvoll, großartig, herrlich.
magnify *v.t.* vergrößern, verherrlichen.
magnifying glass *s.* Lupe *f.*; Vergrößerungsglas *n.*
magnitude *s.* Größe *f.*
magpie *s.* Elster *f.*
mahogany *s.* Mahagoni(holz) *n.*
maid *s.* Jungfer *f.*; Mädchen *n.*; Dienstmädchen *n.*; *old* ~, alte Jungfer.
maiden *s.* Jungfer *f.*; Magd *f.*; ~ *name s.* Mädchenname *m.*; ~ *speech s.* Jungfernrede *f.*
maidenhead, maidenhood *s.* Jungfernschaft *f.*
maid servant *s.* Hausangestellte *f.*
mail *s.* Briefpost *f.*; ~ *v.t.* mit der Post schicken.
mail-bag *s.* Briefbeutel *m.*
mailcarrier *s.* Briefträger(in) *m.*(*f.*)
mail box *s.* Briefkasten *m.*
mailing list *s.* Adressenliste *f.*
mailorder *a.* Versand...
mail-train *s.* Postzug *m.*

maim *v.t.* verstümmeln.
main *a.* hauptsächlich; Haupt...; groß; ~ *s.* Hauptteil *m.*; Hauptrohr *n.*; Hauptleitung *f.*; Weltmeer *n.*; Festland *n.*; *in the* ~, hauptsächlich, im allgemeinen; *the* ~ *chance*, der eigene Vorteil.
main: ~ **beam** *s.* Aufblendlicht *n.*; ~ **clause** *s.* Hauptsatz *m.*; **~land** *s.* Festland *n.*
mainly *adv.* hauptsächlich.
main: ~ **road** *s.* Hauptstraße *f.*; **~spring** *s.* Hauptfeder, Triebfeder *f.*; **~stay** *s.* Hauptstütze *f.*; **~stream** *s.* Hauptstrom *m.*; Hauptrichtung *f.*; ~ **street** *s.* Hauptstraße *f.*
maintain *v.t.* erhalten, unterhalten; ernähren; behaupten; verfechten.
maintenance *s.* Unterhalt *m.*; Instandhaltung, Unterhaltung, Wartung *f.*; **~-free** *a.* wartungsfrei.
maize *s.* Mais *m.*
majestic *a.*, **~ally** *adv.* majestätisch.
majesty *s.* Majestät *f.*
major *a.* größer; mündig; (*mus.*) Dur; ~ *s.* Major *m.*; Obersatz *m.*
majority *s.* Mehrheit *f.*; Mündigkeit *f.*
majority: ~ **rule** *s.* Mehrheitsentscheidung *f.*; ~ **verdict** *s.* Mehrheitsentscheid *m.*
make *v.t.ir.* machen; (veran)lassen; *to ~ good,* Erfolg haben, sich bewähren; *to ~ out,* ausschreiben, ausstellen (Scheck, Rechnung); *to ~ up,* verarbeiten; ~ *v.i.* sich wenden, wohin gehen; sich stellen; *to ~ for,* lossteuern auf; *to ~ out,* ausmachen; *to ~ up for,* entschädigen; ~ *s.* Machwerk *n.*; Gestalt *f.*; Sorte, Art *f.*
make-believe *s.* Phantasie...
maker *s.* Verfertiger *m.*; Schöpfer *m.*
makeshift *s.* Notbehelf *m.*
make-up *s.* Schminke *f.*; Make-up *n.*
making *s.* Herstellung *f.*; *in the* ~, im Entstehen.
maladjusted *a.* verhaltensgestört.
maladministration *s.* Mißwirtschaft *f.*
maladroit *a.* ungeschickt; taktlos.
malady *s.* Krankheit *f.*; Leiden *n.*; Übel *n.*
malaise *s.* Unbehagen *n.*
malaria *s.* Sumpffieber *n.*; Malaria *f.*
Malay *a.* malanisch; ~ *s.* Malaie *m.*, Malaiin *f.*
Malaya *s.* Malaya *n.*
Malaysia *s.* Malaysia *n.*
Malaysian *a.* malaysisch; ~ *s.* Malaysier *m.*; Malaysierin *f.*
malcontent *a.*, **~ly** *adv.* unzufrieden.
male *a.* männlich; ~ *s.* Mann *m.*; Männchen *n.*
malediction *s.* Fluch *m.*
malefactor *s.* Übeltäter *m.*
male nurse *s.* Krankenwärter *m.*
malevolence *s.* Bosheit *f.*
malevolent *a.*, **~ly** *adv.* böswillig.
malformation *s.* Mißbildung *f.*
malformed *a.* mißgebildet.
malice *s.* Bosheit *f.*, Groll *m.*; *with* ~ *aforethought,* (*law*) mit bösem Vorbedacht.
malicious *a.*, **~ly** *adv.* boshaft, tückisch.
malign *a.* schädlich; böse; bösartig; ~ *v.t.* verleumden.
malignancy *s.* Bösartigkeit *f.*
malignant *a.*, **~ly** *adv.* bösartig.
malignity *s.* Bosheit, Schadenfreude *f.*
malinger *v.i.* simulieren.
mall *s.* Einkaufszentrum *n.*

malleable *a.* formbar.
mallet *s.* Holzhammer *m.*
mallow *s.* Malve *f.*
malnutrition *s.* Unterernährung *f.*
malodorous *a.* übelriechend.
malpractice *s.* Amtsvergehen *n.*; (ärztlicher) Kunstfehler *m.*
malt *s.* Malz *n.*; ~ *v.i.* malzen.
maltreat *v.t.* mißhandeln.
maltreatment *s.* Mißhandlung *f.*
mam(m)a *s.* Mama *f.*
mammal *s.* Säugetier *n.*
mammoth *s.* Mammut *n.*; ~*a.* riesig.
man *s.* Mensch *m.*; Mann *m.*; ~ *v.t.* bemannen.
manacle *s.* Handschelle *f.*; ~ *v.t.* fesseln.
manage *v.t.* handhaben; verwalten; einrichten; leiten; fertig bringen; zureiten; ~ *v.i.* die Aufsicht führen; sich behelfen.
manageable *a.* handlich; lenksam.
management *s.* Verwaltung *f.*, Leitung *f.*, Direktion *f.*; Behandlung *f.*
manager *s.* Verwalter(in) *m.*(*f.*); Leiter(in) *m.*(*f.*); Direktor(in) *m.*(*f.*); *a good* ~, ein guter Haushalter; *general* ~, Generaldirektor *m.*; *works* ~, Betriebsleiter *m.*
managerial *a.* leitend; geschäftlich.
managing *a.* geschäftsführend, leitend.
mandarin *s.* Hochchinesisch *n.*; Parteibonze *m.*; Bürokrat(in) *m.*(*f.*)
mandate *s.* Mandat *n.*, Auftrag *m.*
mandatory *a.* befehlend; Mandats. . .
mandolin *s.* Mandoline *f.*
mandrake *s.* Alraun(e) *m.*(*f.*)
mandrel *s.* (*mech.*) Spindel, Docke *f.*
mane *s.* Mähne *f.*
maneuver *s.* Manöver *n.*; Kunstgriff *m.*; ~*v.t.* manövieren.
manful *a.*, ~**ly** *adv.* mannhaft, tapfer.
manganese *s.* Mangan *n.*
mange *s.* Räude *f.*
manger *s.* Krippe *f.*, Trog *m.*; *dog in the* ~, Neidhammel *m.*
mangle *v.t.* verstümmeln; zerstückeln.
mangold *s.* Mangold *m.*, Runkelrübe *f.*
mangrove *s.* Mangrovenbaum *m.*
mangy *a.* räudig; schäbig.
manhandle *v.t.* rauh anfassen.
manhole *s.* Einstiegsloch *n.*
manhood *s.* Mannheit *f.*; Tapferkeit *f.*; Mannesalter *n.*
manhour *s.* Arbeitsstunde *f.*
man-hunt *s.* Großfahndung *f.*
mania *s.* Wahnsinn *m.*; Sucht *f.*
maniac *a.* wahnsinnig; ~ *s.* Wahnsinnige *m.*/*f.*
manicure *s.* Maniküre *f.*; *v.t.* maniküren.
manifest *a.*, ~**ly** *adv.* offenbar; ~ *s.* Ladungsverzeichnis *n.*; ~ *v.t.* offenbaren; manifest werden.
manifestation *s.* Offenbarung *f.*; Anzeichen *n.*
manifesto *s.* Manifest *n.*
manifold *a.*, ~**ly** *adv.* veilfältig.
manikin *s.* Männlein *n.*; Gliederpuppe *f.*
manipulate *v.t.* manipulieren; handhaben.
manipulation *s.* Manipulation *f.*
manipulative *a.* manipulierend.
mankind *s.* Menschengeschlecht *f.*; Menschheit *f.*
manlike *a.* männlich.

manly *a.* männlich; mannhaft.
man-made *a.* künstlich; von Menschen geschaffen.
manned *a.* bemannt.
mannequin *s.* Mannequin *n.*; Schaufensterpuppe *f.*
manner *s.* Art *f.*; ~**s** *pl.* Sitten *f.pl.*; *in a* ~, gewissermaßen; *in a* ~ *of speaking*, sozusagen.
mannered *a.* manieriert; **ill/well** ~ schlechte/gute Manieren haben.
mannerism *s.* Manieriertheit *f.*
mannerly *a.* & *adv.* artig.
manometer *s.* Druckmesser *m.*
manor *s.* Rittergut *n.*; Herrenhaus *n.*
manor-house *s.* Herrenhaus *n.*
manpower *s.* Arbeitspotential *n.*; Arbeitskräfte *f.pl.*; ~**-allocation,** Arbeitseinsatz *m.*
man-servant *s.* Diener *m.*
mansion *s.* Villa *f.*
manslaughter *s.* Totschlag *m.*
mantel *s.* Kaminverkleidung *f.*
mantelpiece *s.* Kaminsims *m.*
mantle *s.* Umhang *m.*; Hülle *f.*
man-trap *s.* Fußangel *f.*
manual *a.* manuell; Hand. . .; ~ *s.* Handbuch *n.*
manufacture *s.* Fabrikation *f.*; Fabrikat *n.*; ~ *v.t.* fabrizieren; verarbeiten; ~*ed articles pl.* Fertigwaren *f.pl.*
manufacturer *s.* Fabrikant *m.*; Hersteller *m.*
manure *v.t.* düngen; ~ *s.* Dünger *m.*
manuscript *s.* Handschrift *f.*; Manuskript *n.*
many *a.* viele, viel; mancher, manche, manches; *as* ~ *as*, soviele als *or* wie.
map *s.* Landkarte *f.*, Stadtplan *m.*; ~ *v.t.* in Kartenform darstellen; (*mil.*) ~**-exercise** *s.* Planspiel *n.*; (*mil.*) ~**-maneuver** *s.* Kriegsspiel *n.*; ~**-scale** *s.* Kartenmaßstab *m.*
maple *s.* Ahorn *m.*
mar *v.t.* verderben; beschädigen.
marathon race *s.* Marathonlauf *m.*
maraud *v.i.* plündern.
marauder *s.* Plünderer *m.*
marble *s.* Marmor *m.*; Murmel *f.*; ~ *a.* marmorn.
March *s.* März *m.*
march *s.* Marsch; Zug *m.*; Mark *f.*, Grenzland *n.*; ~ *v.i.* marschieren; ~ *v.t.* marschieren lassen; ~ **past** *s.* Vorbeimarsch *m.*
marcher *s.* Demonstrant(in) *m.*(*f.*)
marchioness *s.* Markgräfin *f.*
mare *s.* Stute *f.*; ~*'s nest*, (*fig.*) Windei *n.*; Zeitungsente *f.*
margarine *s.* Margarine *f.*
margin *s.* Rand *m.*; Spielraum *m.*; Überschuß *m.*
marginal *a.* am Rande; Rand. . .; geringfügig; marginal; ~ **note** *s.* Randbemerkung *f.*
marginalize *v.t.* marginalisieren.
marigold *s.* Dotterblume *f.*
marinade *s.* Marinade *f.*
marinate *v.t.* marinieren.
marine *a.* See. . .; ~ *s.* Marine *f.*; Seesoldat *m.*
mariner *s.* Seemann *m.*
marionette *s.* Marionette *f.*
marital *a.* ehelich; ~ **status** *s.* Familienstand *m.*
maritime *a.* zur See gehörig; ~ **law** *s.* Seerecht *n.*
marjoram *s.* Majoran *m.*

mark s. Marke f.; Kennzeichen n.; Spur f.; Schutzmarke f.; (Zeugnis) Note m.; Ziel n.; *not quite up to the ~,* nicht ganz auf der Höhe; ~ v.t. & i. ziechnen; aufmerken; markieren; *to ~ off,* abstreichen; *to ~ out,* abstecken; *to ~ out for,* ausersehen für; *to ~ time,* auf der Stelle treten (*mil. & fig.*).
marked a., **~ly** adv. deutlich; ausgeprägt.
marker s. Markierung f.
market s. Markt m.; Absatz m.; ~ **forces** pl. Kräfte des Marktes; **~-gardener** s. Handelsgärtner m.; **~ing association** s. Absatzgenossenschaft f.; *to come into the ~,* auf den Markt kommen; *to place on the ~,* auf den Markt bringen.; **~place** s. Marktplatz m.; ~ **research** s. Konjunkturforschung f.; ~ v.t. auf den Markt bringen.
marketable a. verkäuflich, gangbar.
marking s. Musterung f.; Zeichnung (eines Fells) f.; (*mil.*) Hoheitsabzeichen n.; Zensieren n.; Benoten n.; **~-ink** s. (unauslöschliche) Zeichentinte f.; **~-iron** s. Brenneisen f.
marksman s. Schütze m.
marksmanship s. Schießfertigkeit, Zeilsichherheit f.
mark-up s. Preiserhöhung f.; Handelsspanne f.
marmalade s. Apfelsinenmarmelade f.
marmot s. Murmeltier n.
maroon a. kastanienbraun; **~v.t.** aussetzen; (fig.) im Stich lassen.
marquee s. Zeltdach n., Markise f.
marquess, marquis s. Marquis m.
marquetry s. eingelegte Arbeit f.
marriage s. Ehe, Heirat f.; **~-certificate** s. Trauschein m.; **~-counseling** s. Eheberatung f.; **~-settlement** s. Ehevertrag m.
marriageable a. heiratsfähig.
married a. verheiratet; ~ **couple** s. Ehepaar n.
marrow s. Mark n.; **~-bone** s. Markknochen m.
marry v.t. heiraten; verheiraten; trauen; ~ v.i. heiraten.
marsh s. Marsch f.; Stumpf m.
marshal s. Marschall m.; ~ v.t. ordnen; anführen.
marshalling yard s. Verschiebebahnhof m.
marshland s. Sumpfland n.
marshy a. sumpfig.
marsupial s. Beuteltier n.
marten s. Marder m.
martial a. kriegerisch, militärisch; ~ **law** s. Standrecht n.
martyr s. Märtyrer(in) m.(f.); ~ v.t. martern.
martyrdom s. Märtyrertum n.
marvel s. Wunder n.; ~ v.i. staunen.
marvelous a., **~ly** adv. wunderbar.
Marxism s. Marxismus m.
Marxist s. Marxist(in) m.(f.)
marzipan s. Marzipan n.
mascara s. Mascara n.; Wimperntusche f.
mascot s. Glücksbringer m., Maskottchen n.
masculine a. männlich; ~ s. (gram.) Maskulinum n.
masculinity s. Männlichkeit f.
mash s. Gemisch n.; Brei m.; ~ v.t. mengen, maischen, zerdrücken.
mashed potatoes pl. Kartoffelbrei m.
mask s. Maske f.; ~ v.t. & i. maskieren; sich verstellen.
masochism s. Masochismus m.

masochist s. Masochist(in) m.(f.)
masochistic a. masochistisch.
mason s. Maurer m.; Freimaurer m.
masonic a. freimaurerisch.
masonry s. Maurerei f.; Mauerwerk n.; Freimaurertum n.
masquerade s. Maskenball m.; Verkleidung f.; ~ v.i. maskiert gehen.
mass s. Masse, Menge f.; Messe f.; **high** ~ s. Hochamt n.; **low** ~ s. stille Messe; ~ v.t. & i. (sich) anhäufen, sich sammeln.
massacre s. Metzelei f.; Massaker n.; ~ v.t. niedermetzeln.
massage v.t. massieren; **~s.** Massage f.
mass communication s. Massenkommunikation f.
masseur s. Masseur m.
masseuse s. Masseurin f.
massive a. dicht, fest, massiv.
mass media s.pl. Massenmedien pl.
mass meeting s. Massenversammlung f.
mass production s. Massenproduktion f.
mast s. Mast(baum) m.; Mast f.
master s. Meister m.; Herr m.; Magister, Lehrer m.; ~ v.t. meistern.
master-builder s. Baumeister m.
masterful a. herrisch; meisterhaft.
master-key s. Hauptschlüssel m.
masterly a. & adv. meisterhaft.
mastermind s. führender Kopf m.
master-piece s. Meisterstück n.
master-switch s. Hauptschalter m.
mastery s. Herrschaft f.; Geschicklichkeit f.; (Sprache) Beherrschung f.
masticate v.t. & i. kauen.
mastiff s. Bulldogge f.
masturbate v.i. & t. masturbieren.
masturbation s. Masturbation f.
mat s. Matte f.; ~ v.t. mit Matten bedecken; mattieren.
match s. Lunte f.; Streichholz n.; Gleiche n.; Wette f.; Heirat f.; (Spiel)Partie f.; Wettspiel n.; ~ v.t. zusammenpassen, zusammenbringen; vergleichen; aufwiegen; ~ v.i. passen.
matchbox s. Streichholzschachtel f.
matchmaker s. Ehestifter(in) m.(f.)
matchpoint s. Matchball m.
matchless a., **~ly** adv. unvergleichlich.
mate s. Gefährte, Gehilfe m.; Geselle m.; Maat m.; Steuermann m.; Gatte m., Gattin f.; ~ adv. (schach) matt; ~ v.t. & i. (sich) paaren.
material a., **~ly** adv. körperlich; wesentlich; materiell; ~ s. Material n., Stoff m.; Kleiderstoff m.; raw ~, Rohstoff m.
materialism s. Materialismus m.
materialist Materialist(in) m.(f.)
materialistic a. materialistisch.
materialize v.t. verwirklichen; ~ v.i. sich verwirklichen, zu Stande kommen.
maternal a., **~ly** adv. mütterlich.
maternity s. Mutterschaft f.; ~ *hospital,* Entbindungsanstalt f.
maternity leave s. Mutterschaftsurlaub m.
mathematical a., **~ly** adv. mathematisch.
mathematician s. Mathematiker m.
mathematics s.pl. Mathematik f.

matinée *s.* Matinee *f.*, Nachmittagsvorstellung *f.*
matins *s.pl.* Frühmette *f.*
matricide *s.* Muttermord *m.*
matriculate *v.t.* einschreiben, immatrikulieren.
matrimonial *a.*, ~**ly** *adv.* ehelich.
matrimony *s.* Ehe *f.*
matrix *s.* Matrize *f.*
matron *s.* Matrone; Vorsteherin *f.*
matt *a.* matt.
matted *a.* verfilzt.
matter *s.* Stoff *m.*; Sache *m.*; Gegenstand *m.*; Eiter *m.*; (*typ.*) Satz *m.*; ~ *of course, s.* Selbstverständlichkeit; *as a* ~ *of fact,* tatsächlich; *matter-of-fact,* ~ *a.* sachlich, nüchtern; ~ *of opinion,* Ansichtssache *f.*; *what is the* ~?, was ist los? *no* ~ *how,* gleichgültig, wie . . .; ~ *v.i.* daran liegen, etwas ausmachen; *it does not* ~, es macht nichts.
mattock *s.* Hacke *f.*
mattress *s.* Matratze *f.*
mature *a.*, ~**ly** *adv.* reif; fällig; reiflich; ~ *v.t.* reifen; ~**d** *a.* abgelagert.
maturity *s.* Reife *f.*; Verfallzeit *f.*
maudlin *a.* (betrunken) weinerlich.
maul *v.t.* stampfen; schlagen; verletzen.
maunder *v.i.* faseln.
Maundy Thursday *s.* Gründonnerstag *m.*
mausoleum *s.* Mausoleum *n.*
mauve *a.* mauve, malvenfarbig.
maverick *s.* Einzelgänger(in) *m.*(*f.*)
maw *s.* Magen (der Tiere) *m.*; Kropf *m.*
mawkish *a.* widerlich; (*fig.*) empfindsam.
maxim *s.* Grundsatz *m.*
maximum *s.* Höchstmaß *n.*; Höchst. . .; Maximum *n.*; ~ *price,* Höchstpreis *m.*
may *v.i.ir.* dürfen, mögen, können; ~ *s.* Weißdorn *m.*
May *s.* Mai *m.*
maybe *adv.* vielleicht.
May-day *s.* der erste Mai *m.*
mayhem *s.* Chaos *n.*
mayonnaise *s.* Mayonnaise *f.*
mayor *s.* Bürgermeister(in) *m.*(*f.*)
mayoralty *s.* Bürgermeisteramt *n.*
Maypole *s.* Maibaum *m.*
maze *s.* Labyrinth *n.*; Wirrwarr *m.*
me *pn.* mich, mir.
mead *s.* Met *m.*
meadow *s.* Wiese *f.*
meager *a.*, ~**ly** *adv.* mager; dürftig.
meal *s.* Schrotmehl *n.*; Mahlzeit *f.*
meal-time *s.* Essenszeit *f.*
mealy-mouthed *a.* unaufrichtig.
mean *a.*, ~**ly** *adv.* niedrig, gemein; verächtlich; mittler, Durchschnitts. . ., mittelmäßig; *in the* ~ *time,* inzwischen; ~ *s.* Mittel(weg) *n.*; Mitte *f.*; ~ *v.t. & i.ir.* meinen, bedeuten; beabsichtigen.
meander *s.* Windung *f.*; ~ *v.i.* sich schlängeln.
meaning *s.* Sinn *m.*; Bedeutung *f.*
meaningful *a.* sinnvoll; bedeutungsvoll.
meaningless *a.* sinnlos.
meanness *s.* Gemeinheit *f.*; Filzigkeit *f.*
means *s.pl.* Mittel *n.*; Vermögen *n.*; ~ *of production,* Produktionsmittel *n.pl.*
meantime *s. in the* ~ in der Zwischenzeit.
meanwhile *adv.* inzwischen.
measles *s.pl.* Masern *f.pl.*; *German* ~, Röteln *pl.*

measly *a.* (*fam. pej.*) popelig; mickrig.
measurable *a.*, ~**ly** *adv.* meßbar.
measure *s.* Maß *n.*; Maßstab *m.*; (*mus.*) Takt *m.*; (*ar.*) Teilor, Faktor *m.*; Maßregel *f.*; *to* ~, nach Maß; **made-to-**~ *a.* maßgearbeitet; *to take* ~*s,* Maßnahmen ergreifen; ~ *v.t. & i.* messen, abmessen; enthalten; fassen.
measured *a.* rhythmisch, gleichmäßig; gemessen.
measurement *s.* Messung *f.*; Maß *n.*; *to take a person's* ~, einem Maß nehmen.
meat *s.* Fleisch *n.*; Speise *f.*; ~ *safe,* Fliegenschrank *m.*
meatball *s.* Fleischklößchen *n.*
meat-pie *s.* Fleischpastete *f.*
meaty *a.* fleischig; (*fig.*) gehaltvoll.
mechanic *s.* Mechaniker *m.*
mechanical *a.*, ~**ly** *adv.* mechanisch.
mechanics *s.* Mechanik *f.*; Mechanismus *m.*
mechanism *s.* Getriebe *n.*
mechanize *v.t.* mechanisieren.
medal *s.* Orden *m.*; Medaille *f.*
medalist *s.* Medaillengewinner(in) *m.*(*f.*)
medallion *s.* Medaillon *n.*
meddle *v.i.* sich mischen; sich abgeben.
meddlesome *a.* sich einmischend.
media *s.pl.* Medien *pl.*
mediate *v.i.* vermitteln.
mediation *s.* Vermittlung *f.*
mediator *s.* Vermittler, Fürsprecher *m.*
medical *a.*, ~**ly** *adv.* medizinisch; ~ *care,* ärztliche Betreuung *f.*; ~ *certificate,* ärztliches Attest *n.*; ~ *examination,* ärztliche Untersuchung *f.*; ~ *opinion,* ärztliches Gutachten *n.*; ~ *practitioner s.* praktischer Arzt *m.*; (*mil.*) ~ *service,* Sanitätsdienst *m.*
medicate *v.t.* mit Arznei versetzen; medizinisch behandeln.
medication *s.* Medikation *f.*; Medizin *f.*
medicinal *a.*, ~**ly** *adv.* medizinisch, Heil. . .
medicine *s.* Arznei *f.*; Medizin *f.*
medieval *a.* mittelalterlich; *the* ~ *period* Mittelalter *n.*
mediocre *a.* mittelmäßig.
mediocrity *s.* Mittelmäßigkeit *f.*
meditate *v.t. & i.* nachsinnen, überlegen; meditieren.
meditation *s.* Betrachtung *f.*; Meditation *f.*
Mediterranean *a.* Mittelmeer *n.*; ~ *a.* Mittelmeer. . ., mittelländisch.
medium *s.* Mittel *n.*; Bindemittel (Malerei) *n.*; Mittelding *n.*; Medium *n.*; ~ *a.* Mittel. . ., mittlere; ~ *artillery,* (*mil.*) schwere Artillerie *f.*; ~**-sized** *a.* mittelgroß; ~ *wave s.* (*radio*) Mittelwelle *f.*
medley *s.* Gemenge *n.*, Mischmasch *m.*
meek *a.*, ~**ly** *adv.* sanftmütig; demütig.
meet *v.t. & i.ir.* treffen; begegnen; entgegenkommen; versammeln; (Schuld) bezahlen; erleiden.
meeting *s.* Zusammentreffen *n.*; Versammlung, Sitzung *f.*; *to call a* ~ *for 10 o'clock,* eine Sitzung auf 10 Uhr einberufen.
meeting place *s.* Treffpunkt *m.*
megacycle *s.* (*radio*) Megahertz *n.*
megalomania *s.* Größenwahn *m.*
megaphone *s.* Megaphon *n.*
melancholic *a.* schwermütig.
melancholy *s.* Schwermut *f.*; ~ *a.* schwermütig.

mellow *a.* mürbe; mild; ~ *v.t.* zur Reife bringen; mürbe machen; ~ *v.i.* mürbe werden; sich mildern.
melodious *s.,* **~ly** *adv.* wohlklingend.
meoldrama *s.* Melodrama *n.*
melodramatic *a.* melodramatisch.
melody *s.* Singweise, Melodie *f.*
melon *s.* Melone *f.*
melt *v.t.* schmelzen; ~ *v.i.* schmelzen, zerfließen; *melting point, s.* Schmelzpunkt *m.; melting pot, s.* Schmelztiegel *m.*
member *s.* Glied *n.;* Mitglied *n.*
membership *s.* Mitgliedschaft *f.;* **~-card** *s.* Mitgliedskarte *f.;* **~-subscription** *s.* Mitgliedsbeitrag *m.*
membrane *s.* Häutchen *n.,* Membran *f.*
memento *s.* Andenken *n.*
memoir *s.* Denkschrift *f.;* **~s** *pl.* Memoiren *pl.*
memorable *a.* **~bly** *adv.* denkwürdig.
memorandum *s.* Notiz *f.;* Anmerkung *f.;* Denkschrift *f.*
memorial *s.* Denkmal *n.;* Denkschrift, Bittschrift *f.;* ~ *a.* Gedächnis. . .; **~-celebration** *s.* Gedenkfeier *f.;* **~-day** *s.* Gedenktag für die Gefallenen.
memorize *v.t.* auswendig lernen.
memory *s.* Gedächtnis *n.;* Andenken *n.*
menace *v.t.* drohen; bedrohen; ~ *s.* Drohung *f.*
menacing *a.* drohend.
mend *v.t.* (aus)bessern; ~ *v.i.* sich bessern.
mendacious *a.* lügenhaft.
mendacity *s.* Lügenhaftigkeit *f.*
mendicancy *s.* Bettelei *f.*
mendicant *a.* bettelnd; ~ *s.* Bettler, Bettelmönch *m.*
menfolk *s.* Männer *pl.*
menial *a.* Gesinde. . .; niedrig; gemein; ~ *s.* Diener *m.*
meningitis *s.* Hirnhautenzündung *f.*
menopause *s.* Wechseljahre *n. pl.;* Klimakterium *n.*
menstrual *a.* menstrual; Menstruations. . .
menstruation *s.* Menstruation *f.*
menswear *s.* Herrenbekleidung *f.*
mental *a.,* **~ly** *adv.* geistig, innerlich; ~ **case, patient** *s.* Geisteskranker *m.;* **~ly defective** *a.* schwachsinnig; ~ **deficiency** *s.* Schwachsinn *m.;* ~ **hospital** *s.* psychiatrische Klinik *f.;* ~ **illness** *s.* Geisteskrankheit *f.*
mentality *s.* Mentalität *f.*
menthol *s.* Menthol *n.*
mention *s.* Erwähnung *f.;* ~ *v.t.* erwähnen; *don't ~ it!,* bitte!; *not to ~,* geschweige denn.
mentor *s.* Mentor(in) *m.(f.)*
menu *s.* Speisenfolge *f.;* Speisekarte *f.;* Menü *n.*
men working! Baustelle!
meow *v.i.* miauen; **~s.** Miauen *n.*
mercantile *a.* kaufmännisch, Handels. . .
mercenary *a.* gedungen; ~ *s.* Söldner *m.*
mercer *s.* Schnittwaren-, Seidenhändler *m.*
merchandise *s.* Ware *f.*
merchant *s.* Kaufmann *m.;* **~-ship** *s.* Handelsschiff *n.;* ~ **navy** *s.* Handelsmarine *f.*
merciful *a.,* **~ly** *adv.* gnädig; barmherzig.
merciless *a.,* **~ly** *adv.* gnadenlos; unbarmherzig.
mercurial *a.* Quecksilber. . .; lebhaft.
mercury *s.* Quecksilber *n.*

mercy *s.* Barmherzigkeit, Gnade *f.*
mere *a.* bloß; lauter; **~ly** *adv.* nur.
meretricious *a.,* **~ly** *adv.* protzig; prunkhaft; falsch.
merge *v.t.* zusammenlegen; eintauchen; verschmelzen; ~ *v.i.* aufgehen (in).
merger *s.* Zusammenlegung, Fusion *f.*
meridian *s.* Meridian *m.;* Höhepunkt *m.*
meringue *s.* Meringe *f.;* Baiser *n.*
merit *s.* Verdienst *n.;* Wert *m.;* ~ *v.t.* verdienen.
meritocracy *s.* Meritokratie *f.*
meritorious *a.,* **~ly** *adv.* verdienstlich.
mermaid *s.* Seejungfer *f.*
merriment *s.* Fröhlichkeit, Belustigung *f.*
merry *a.,* **~ily** *adv.* lustig, fröhlich, munter; **~-go-round** *s.* Karussell *n.*
mesh *s.* Masche *f.;* Netz *n.;* ~ *v.t.* bestricken, fangen; *(mech.)* in Eingriff bringen; ~ *v.i. (mech.)* ineinandergreifen.
mesmerize *v.t.* hypnotisieren; faszinieren.
mess *s.* Offizierstisch *m.;* Unordnung *f.;* Sauerei *f.;* ~ *v.i.* zusammen speisen; ~ *v.t.* verpfuschen; durcheinanderbringen.
message *s.* Botschaft *f.;* Nachricht *f.; to give a ~,* etwas ausrichten; *to leave a ~,* etwas ausrichten lassen; **~-center** *s. (mil.)* Nachrichtenstelle, Meldesammelstelle *f.*
messenger *s.* Bote *m.;* Botin *f.;* ~ **boy** *s.* Botenjunge *m.*
Messiah *s.* Messias *m.*
mess-up *s.* Durcheinander *m.*
messy *a.* unordentlich; schmutzig.
metabolism *s.* Stoffwechsel *m.;* Metabolismus.
metal *s.* Metall *n.*
metal detector *s.* Metallsuchgerät *n.*
metallic *a.* metallisch.
metallurgy *s.* Metallurgie *f.;* Hüttenkunde *f.*
metamorphose *v.t.* umgestalten.
metamorphosis *s.* Verwandlung *f.*
metaphor *s.* Metapher *f.*
metaphorical *a.* bildlich, übertragen; metaphorisch.
metaphysical *a.* metaphysisch.
metaphysics *s.pl.* Metaphysik *f.*
mete ~ **out** *v.t.* zumessen.
meteor *s.* Meteor *n.*
meteorological *a.* meteorologisch, wetterkundlich; ~ **service** *s.* Wetterdienst *m.*
meteorology *s.* Wetterkunde *f.;* Meteorologie *f.*
meter *s.* Meßgerät *n.; (elek.)* Zähler *m.;* Versmaß *n.,* Metrum *n.*
meter maid *s.* (*fam.*) Politesse *f.*
meter reader *s.* Gas- oder Stromabaser *m.*
method *s.* Verfahren *n.;* Ordnung *f.;* Lehrweise *f.,* Methode *f.*
methodical *a.* methodisch.
Methodist *s.* Methodist *m.*
methodology *s.* Methodik *f.*
methyl *s.* Methyl *n.*
meticulous *a.,* **~ly** *adv.* peinlich genau.
metric *s.* metrisch, Meter. . .; ~ **system** *s.* metrisches System *n.*
metrical *a.,* **~ly** *adv.* metrisch, Vers. . .
metronome *s.* Metronom *n.*
metropolis *s.* Hauptstadt *f.;* Metropole *f.*
metropolitan *a.* hauptstädtisch.; ~ **New York**

Großraum New York.

mettle s. Naturanlage f.; Temperament n.; Eifer m., Mut m.; *be on one's ~,* vor Eifer brennen.

mettlesome a. mutig, feurig.

mew v.i. miauen; kreischen.

Mexican a. mexikanisch; ~ s. Mexikaner(in) m.(f.)

Mexico s. Mexiko n.

miaow v.i. miauen; ~s. Miauen n.

mica s. Glimmer m.

micro a. mikro..., Mikro...

microbe s. Mikrobe f.

microbiology s. Mikrobiologie f.

microchip s. Mikrochip m.

microdot s. Mikrat n.

microfiche s. Mikrofiche m.

micrometer s. Mikrometer n.

microorganism s. Mikroorganismus m.

microphone s. Mikrophon n.

microprocessor s. Mikroprozessor m.

microscope s. Mikroskop n.

microscopic a. mikroskopisch.

microwave s. Mikrowelle f.; Mikrowellenherd m.

mid a. mitten, mittel; **in ~-air,** mitten in der Luft; **~-June,** Mitte Juni.

midday s. Mittag m.

middle s. Mitte f.; ~ a. Mittel...

Middle Ages s.pl. Mittelalter n.

middle class s. Mittelschicht f.

Middle East s. Mittlerer Osten m.

middleman s. Zwischenhändler m.

middle-of-the-road a. gemäßigt.

middle weight s. Mittelgewicht n.

middling a. mittelmäßig.

midfield s. Mittelfeld n.

midge s. Mücke f.

midget s. Zwerg m.; Liliputaner(in) m.(f.)

midnight s. Mitternacht f.; ~ a. mitternächtlich; ~ **sun** s. Mitternachtssonne f.

midship s. Mitte (f.) des Schiffs.

midshipman s. Seekadett m.

midst s. Mitte f.

midsummer s. Sommersonnenwende f.; Hochsommer m.

midway adv. auf halbem Wege.

midwife s. Hebamme f.

midwifery s. Geburtshilfe f.

midwinter s. Wintersonnenwende f.; Mitte (f.) des Winters.

miff v.t. (fam.) verärgern.

might s. Macht, Gewalt f.

mighty a., ~**ily** adv. mächtig, überaus.

migraine s. Migräne f.

migrant s. Wanderer m., Wandertier n.; ~ a. Wander...

migrate v.i. wandern, fortziehen.

migration s. Wanderung f.

migratory a. wandernd, Zug...

mike s. (fam.) Mikro n.

mild a., ~**ly** adv. sanft, mild.

mildew s. Mehltau m.

mile s. Meile f.; 1609 m.

mileage s. Meilenzahl f.

milestone s. Meilenstein m.

militarism s. Militarismus m.

militant a. streitend, kriegführend.

militarize v.t. militarisieren.

military a. militärisch; ~ **bridge** s. Kriegsbrücke f.; ~ **code** s. Militärstrafgesetzbuch n.; ~ **law** s. Kriegsrecht n.; ~ **government** s. Militärregierung f.; ~ **post** s. Standort m.; ~ **target,** ~ **objective** s. kriegswichtiges Ziel n.; ~ s. Soldatenstand m.

militate v.i. ~against, sprechen gegen.

militia s. Milizia f.; Land-, Bürgerwehr f.

milk s. Milch f.; ~ v.t. melken.

milkbar s. Milchbar f.

milk-maid s. Milchmädchen n.

milk-sop s. Schwächling m.

milktooth s. Milchzahn m.

Milky-Way s. Milchstraße f.

mill s. Mühle f.; Fabrik f.; ~ v.t. mahlen; (Münzen) rändeln; walken.

millennium s. Millenium n.

miller s. Müller m.

millet s. Hirse f.

milliner s. Putzmacherin f.

millinery s. Putzwaren f.pl.

milling machine s. Fräsmaschine f.

million s. Million f.

millionaire s. Millionär m.

mime s. Pantomime f.; Pantomime m.; Pantomimin f.; ~v.i. pantomimisch darstellen.

mimeograph s. Mimeograph m.; ~ v.t. vervielfältigen.

mimic a. mimisch, Schein...; ~ s. Mime; ~ v.t. nachäffen.

mimicry s. Mimikrie f.; Nachahmen n.

minatory a. drohend.

mince v.t. kleinhacken; *to ~ matters,* sich ein Blatt vor den Mund nehmen; ~ v.i. sich zieren; ~**d meat** s. Hackfleisch n.

mincemeat s. Pastetenfüllung f. (Fett, Rosinen, Zitrone, etc.) *to make ~ of* (fig.) aus jm. Hackfleisch machen.

mincer s. Fleischwolf m.

mincingly adv. geziert, affektiert.

mincing-machine s. Hackmaschine f.

mind s. Gemüt n.; Geist, Verstand, Sinn m.; Neigung f.; *to make up one's ~,* sich entschließen; *to bear in ~,* sich merken; *to change one's ~,* sich anders besinnen; ~ v.t. merken; achten; sich bekümmern um; ~v.i. willens sein; *never ~!,* es macht nichts!

minded a. gesinnt, geneigt.

mindful a., ~**ly** adv. achtsam; eingedenk.

mine pn. mein, meinige; ~ s. Bergwerk n.; Grube f.; Mine f.; ~ v.t. graben; Minen legen.

minefield s. (mil.) Minenfeld n.

miner s. Bergmann m.

mineral s. Mineral n.; ~ a. mineralisch; ~ **water** Mineralwasser n.

mineralogy s. Mineralogie f.

minesweeper s. Minensucher m.

mingle v.t. & i. mischen; sich mischen.

miniature s. Miniatur f.; Miniatur...

minim s. (mus.) halbe Note f.

minimal a., ~**ly** adv. minimal.

minimize v.t. möglichst klein machen.

minimum s. Mindestmaß, Minimum n.

mining s. Bergbau m.; ~**-academy** s. Bergakademie f.; ~**-bureau** s. Bergamt n.; ~**-industry** s. Montanindustrie f.

minion s. Günstling m.

miniskirt *s.* Minirock *m.*
minister *s.* Diener *m.*; Minister, Gesandte *m.*; Geistliche *m.*; ~ *v.i.* dienen.
ministerial *a.*, ~**ly** *adv.* ministeriell; geistlich.
ministration *s.* Dienst *m.*; Amt *n.*
ministry *s.* Dienst *m.*; Ministerium *n.*
mink *s.* Nerz *m.*
minor *a.* kleiner, geringer; jünger; unmündig; (*mus.*) Moll.
minority *s.* Minderheit *f.*; Unmündigkeit *f.*
minster *s.* Münster *m.* or *n.*
minstrel *s.* Spielmann *m.*
mint *s.* Münze *f.*; Fundgrube *f.*; Minze (Pflanze) *f.*; ~ *v.t.* münzen, prägen.
mintage *s.* Prägen *n.*; Münzgebühr *f.*
mint-sauce *s.* Minzsoße *f.*
minuet *s.* Menuett *f.*
minus *pr.* minus.
minuscule *a.* winzig.
minute *a.* klein; umständlich; ~ *s.* Minute *f.*; Notiz *f.*; ~**s** *pl.* Protokoll *n.*; *to keep the* ~*s*, das Protokoll führen; ~ **hand** *s.* Minutenzeiger *m.*
minutely *adv.* genauestens, sorgfältig.
minutiae *s.pl.* Einzelheiten *f.pl.*
minx *s.* (kleines) Biest *n.*
miracle *s.* Wunder *n.*
miraculous *a.*, ~**ly** *adv.* wunderbar.
mirage *s.* Luftspiegelung *f.*, Fata Morgana *f.*
mire *s.* Schlamm *m.*
mirror *s.* Spiegel *m.*; ~ *v.t.* spiegeln; ~ **image** *s.* Spiegelbild *n.*
mirth *s.* Fröhlichkeit, Freude, Lust *f.*
misadventure *s.* Mißgeschick *n.*
misalliance *s.* Mißheirat *f.*
misanthrope *s.* Misanthrop *m.* Menschenfeind *m.*
misapplication *s.* falsche Anwendung *f.*
misapply *v.t.* falsch anwenden.
misapprehend *v.t.* mißverstehen.
misapprehension *s.* Mißverständnis *n.*
misappropriate *v.t.* unterschlagen, veruntreuen.
misbehave *v.i.* sich schlecht aufführen.
misbehavior *s.* schlechtes Benehmen *n.*
miscalculate *v.t.* falsch berechnen; falsch einschätzen.
miscalculation *s.* Rechenfehler *m.*; Fehleinschätzung *f.*
miscarriage *s.* Fehlgeburt *f.*; ~ *of justice*, Fehlurteil *n.*
miscarry *v.i.* eine Fehlgeburt haben; mißlingen.
miscellaneous *a.* gemischt.
miscellany *s.* Gemisch *n.*; vermischte Schriften *f.pl.*
mischance *s.* unglücklicher Zufall *m.*, Mißgeschick *n.*
mischief *s.* Unsinn *m.*; Unfug *m.*
mischief-maker *s.* Unheilstifter *m.*
mischievous *a.*, ~**ly** *adv.* schelmisch; boshaft; mutwillig.
misconceive *v.t.* falschauffassen.
misconception *s.* Mißverständnis *n.*
misconduct *s.* Fehltritt *m.*; schlechte Verwaltung *f.*
misconstruction *s.* Mißdeutung *f.*
misconstrue *v.t.* mißdeuten.
miscount *v.t.* sich verzählen.
miscreant *s.* Bösewicht *m.*
misdeed *s.* Missetat *f.*; Verbrechen *n.*

misdemeanor *s.* Vergehen *n.*
misdirect *v.t.* falsch leiten; falsch adressieren.
miser *s.* Geizhals *m.*
miserable *a.*, ~**bly** *adv.* elend.
miserly *a.* karg, geizig.
misery *s.* Elend *n.*, Not *f.*
misfire *v.i.* versagen (Gewehr); fehlzünden (motor).
misfit *s.* Außenseiter(in) *m.*(*f.*)
misfortune *s.* Unglück *n.*; Mißgeschick *n.*
misgiving *s.* Befürchtung *f.*; Bedenken *pl.*
misgovern *v.t.* schlecht regieren.
misguide *v.t.* verleiten.
mishandle *v.t.* schlecht handhaben; (*fam.*) verkorxen.
mishap *s.* Mißgeschick *n.*; Unfall *m.*
mishear *v.t. & i.* (sich) verhören.
mish-mash *s.* Mischmasch *m.*
misinform *v.t.* falsch berichten.
misinterpret *v.t.* mißdeuten.
misinterpretation *s.* falsche Auslegung *f.*, Mißdeutung.
misjudge *v.i. & t.* falsch urteilen, verkennen.
mislay *v.t.st.* verlegen.
mislead *v.t.st.* verleiten; irreführen.
misleading *a.* irreführend.
mismanage *v.t.* übel verwalten.
mismanagement *s.* Mißwirtschaft *f.*; schlechte Verwaltung *f.*
misnomer *s.* falsche Bezeichnung *f.*
misogynist *s.* Frauenhasser *m.*
misogyny *s.* Misogynie *f.*
misplace *v.t.* verlegen.
misplaced *a.* deplaziert; verlegt.
misprint *v.t.* verdrucken; ~ *s.* Druckfehler *m.*
mispronounce *v.t.* falsch aussprechen.
misquotation *s.* falsches Zitat *n.*
misquote *v.t.* falsch zitieren.
misread *v.t.* falschlesen; falsch deuten.
misrepresent *v.t.* falsch darstellen.
misrepresentation *s.* falsche Darstellung *f.*; Verdrehung *f.*
misrule *s.* schlechte Regierung *f.*
miss *v.t.* missen, vermissen; verfehlen, verpassen; versäumen; übersehen; auslassen; ~ *s.* Fehlstoß, -wurf, -schuß *m.*; ~ *s.* Fräulein *n.*; Frau *f.*
misshapen *a.* mißgestaltet.
missile *s.* Wurfgeschoß *n.*; Flugkörper *m.*
missing *a.* verloren, abwesend; (*mil.*) vermißt.
mission *s.* Sendung *f.*; Gesandtschaft *f.*; Mission *f.*; (*mil.*) Auftrag *m.*
missionary *s.* Missionar *m.*; Missionarin *f.*
misspell *v.t.r. & st.* falsch buchstabieren, unrichtig schreiben.
misspend *v.t.* verschwenden.
misstate *v.t.* falsch angeben, falsch darstellen.
misstatement *s.* falsche Angabe *f.*; falsche Darstellung *f.*
mist *s.* Dunst *m.*; Nebel *m.*
mistake *v.t.st.* mißverstehen; ~ *v.i.* sich irren; ~ *s.* Irrtum *m.*; Versehen *n.*; Fehler *m.*
mistaken *a.* irrig.
mistakenly *adv.* irrtümlicherweise.
Mister (Mr.) *s.* Herr (Titel) *m.*
mistimed *a.* unzeitig.
mistletoe *s.* Mistel *f.*

mistranslate *v.t.* falsch übersetzen.
mistranslation *s.* falsche Übersetzung *f.*; Übersetzungsfehler *m.*
mistreat *v.t.* mißhandeln.
mistreatment *s.* Mißhandlung *f.*
mistress *s.* Gebieterin *f.*; Lehrerin *f.*; Herrin; Meisterin *f.*; Geliebte *f.*; ~, (*Mrs.*) Frau (als Titel) *f.*
mistrust *s.* Mißtrauen *n.*; ~ *v.t.* mißtrauen.
mistrustful *a.*, ~ly *adv.* mißtrauisch.
misty *a.*, ~ily *adv.* neb(e)lig, trübe.
misunderstand *v.t.st.* mißverstehen.
misunderstanding *s.* Mißverständnis *n.*
misunderstood *a.* unverstanden; verkaunt.
misuse *v.t.* mißbrauchen; ~ *s.* Mißbrauch *m.*
mite *s.* Milbe *f.*; Scherflein *n.*; kleines Kind *n.*
mitigate *v.t.* lindern, mildern.
mitigation *s.* Linderung *f.*; Milderung *f.*
mitre *s.* Bischofsmütze *f.*
mitten *s.* Fausthandschuh *m.*
mix *v.t.* mischen, vermischen; (Salat) anmachen; ~ *v.i.* sich vermischen, verkehren; *to ~ up*, durcheinanderbringen, verswehseln; *~ed double*, *s.* (*tennis*) gemischtes Doppelspiel *n.*
mixer *s.* Mixer *m.*; Mischmaschine *f.*
mixture *s.* Mischung *f.*
mix-up *s.* Durcheinander *n.*; Mißverständnis *n.*; Verwechslung *f.*
mnemonic *s.* Gedächtnisstütze *f.*
moan *v.i.* stöhnen; ~ *v.t.* beklagen; ~ *s.* Stöhnen *n.*
moat *s.* Burggraben *m.*
mob *s.* Pöbel *m.*; ~ *v.t.* lärmend angreifen, belästigen.
mobile *a.* fahrbar, beweglich.
mobile home *s.* großer Wohnwagen *m.*
mobility *s.* Beweglichkeit *f.*
mobilization *s.* Mobilisierung *f.*
mobilize *v.t.* mobilisieren; mobil machen (Truppen).
moccasin *s.* Mokassin *n.*
mock *s.* Spott *m.*; ~ *a.* Pseudo... nachgemacht; ~-turtle *s.* falsche Schildkrötensuppe *f.*; ~ *v.i. & t.* verspotten, täuschen.
mockery *s.* Spötterei *f.*; Schein *m.*
mocking *a.* spöttisch; ~ *s.* Spott *m.*
modal *a.* modal; ~ **auxiliary** *s.* Modalverb *n.*
mode *s.* Art und Weise, Sitte *f.*
model *s.* Muster, Vorbild *n.*; Modell *n.*; Model *n.*; ~ *v.t.* modellieren, entwerfen; modeln.
modeling *s.* Formung *f.*; Modellieren *n.*
modem *s.* Modem *n.*
moderate *a.*, ~ly *adv.* mäßig; gemäßigt; mittelmäßig; ~ *v.t.* mäßigen.
moderation *s.* Mäßigung, Mäßigkeit *f.*
modern *a.* neu, modern.
modernism *s.* Modernismus *m.*
modernist *s.* Modernist(in) *m.(f.)*
modernity *s.* Modernität *f.*
modernize *v.t.* modernisieren.
modest *a.*, ~ly *adv.* bescheiden, sittsam.
modesty *s.* Sittsamkeit; Bescheidenheit *f.*
modicum *s.* geringe Menge *f.*
modifiable *a.* modifizierbar.
modification *s.* Abänderung *f.*; Einschränkung *f.*
modify *v.t.* abändern, einschränken, mildern.
modular *a.* Modul...
modulate *v.t.* modulieren; anpassen.

module *s.* Modul *n.*; Bauelement *n.*; Kapsel *f.*
mohair *s.* Mohair *n.*
moiety *s.* Hälfte *f.*
moist *a.* feucht.
moisten *v.t.* befeuchten.
moisture *s.* Feuchtigkeit *f.*
moisturizer *s.* Feuchtigkeits...
molar *s.* Backenzahn *m.*
molasses *s.* Melasse *f.*; Sirup *m.*
mold *s.* Form *f.*; Gießform *f.*; Schablone *f.*; Schimmel *m.*; Mutterboden *m.*; ~ *v.t.* formen; gießen; ~ *v.i.* schimmeln.
molder *v.i.* vermodern; zerbröckeln.
molding *s.* Fries *m.*, Simswerk *n.*
moldy *a.* schimm(e)lig, moderig.
molt *v.i.* (sich) mausern; häuten; haaren; ~ *s.* Mauser *f.*
mole *s.* Maulwurf *m.*; Steindamm *m.*; Muttermal *n.*
molecular *a.* molekular.
molecule *s.* Molekül *n.*
molehill *s.* Maulwurfshügel *m.*
molest *v.t.* belästigen, beschweren.
molestation *s.* Belästigung *f.*
moll *s.* Gangsterbraut *f.*
mollify *v.t.* erweichen; besänftigen.
mollusk *s.* Molluske *f.*, Weichtier *n.*
mollycoddle *s.* Weichling *m.*; ~ *v.t.* verzärteln.
molten *a.* geschmolzen, gegossen.
mom, mommy *s.* Mama, Mutti *f.*
moment *s.* Augenblick *m.*; Moment *m.*
momentary *a.*, ~ily *adv.* einen Augenblick dauernd.
momentous *a.* wichtig, von Bedeutung.
momentum *s.* Triebkraft *f.*; Moment *n.*
monarch *s.* Monarch(in) *m.(f.)*
monarchical *a.* monarchisch.
monarchist *s.* Monarchist(in) *m.(f.)*
monarchy *s.* Monarchie *f.*
monastery *s.* (Mönchs-) Kloster *n.*
monastic *a.*, ~ally *adv.* klösterlich.
Monday *s.* Montag *m.*
monetarism *s.* Monetarismus *m.*
monetarist *s.* Monetarist(in) *m.(f.)*
monetary *a.* Geld...; ~ **standard** *s.* Münzfuß *m.*; ~ **unit**, Geld-, Münzeinheit *f.*
money *s.* Geld *n.*; *ready ~*, *~ in hand*, bares Geld.
money-changer *s.* Geldwechsler *m.*
money-order *s.* Postanweisung *f.*
Mongol *s.* Mongole *m.*, Mongolin *f.*
Mongolia *s.* Mongolei *f.*
Mongolian *a.* mongolisch; ~ *s.* Mongole *m.*; Mongolin *f.*
mongrel *s.* Mischling, Bastard *m.*
monitor *s.* Ermahner *m.*; Klassenordner *n.*; Monitor *m.*; Panzerschiff *n.*; ~ *v.t.* abhören, mithören.
monk *s.* Mönch *m.*
monkey *s.* Affe *m.*
monkey business *s.* Schabernack *m.*; krumme Tour *f.*; Unfug *m.*
monkish *a.* mönchisch.
monochrome *a.* einfarbig.
monocle *s.* Monokel *n.*
monogamy *s.* Einehe, Monogamie *f.*
monogram *s.* Namenszug *m.*
monograph *s.* Monographie *f.*
monologue *s.* Selbstgespräch *n.*; Monolog *m.*

monomania s. fixe Idee f., Monomanie f.

monoplane s. Eindecker m.

monopolize v.t. Alleinhandel treiben; monopolisieren; (fig.) an sich reißen.

monopoly s. Alleinhandel m., Monopol n.

monosyllabic a. einsilbig.

monosyllable s. einsilbiges Wort n.

monotonous a. eintönig.

monotony s. Eintönigkeit f.

monsoon s. Monsun m.

monster s. Ungeheuer n.; Riesen. . .

monstrance s. Monstranz f.

monstrosity s. Ungeheuerlichkeit f.

monstrous a., **-ly** adv. ungeheuer; scheußlich.

montage s. Montage f.

month s. Monat m.

monthly a. & adv. monatlich; ~ s. Monatsschrift f.

monument s. Denkmal n.

monumental a., **-ly** adv. Denkmal. . . monumental; gewaltig.

moo v.i. muhen; ~s. Muhen n.

mood s. Stimmung, Laune f.; (gram.) Modus m.; (mus.) Tonart f.

moody a., **-ily** adv. mürrisch, launisch.

moon s. Mond m.; Monat m.; once in a blue ~, alle Jubeljahre.

moon-calf s. Mondkalb n.

moonlight s. Mondschein m.; ~v.i. schwarzarbeiten.

moonshine s. Unsinn m.

moon-struck a. mondsüchtig.

moor s. Mohr m.; Moor n.; ~ v.t. (nav.) vertäuen.

mooring s. Ankerplatz m.

moor-hen s. Wasserhuhn n.

moorish a. maurisch; moorig.

moose s. Elch m.

moot a. umstritten; strittig.

mop s. Mop m.; Wisch m.; Scheuertuch n.; (fig.) Wuschelkopf m.

mope v.i. Trübsal blasen.

moraine s. Moräne f.

moral a., **-ly** adv. sittlich; gut, moralisch; ~ s. Nutzanwendung f.; **-s** pl. Sitten f.pl. Moral f.

morale s. Moral, Stimmung f.

morality s. Sittenlehre, Sittlichkeit f.

moralize v.i. Sittlichkeit predigen; moralisieren.

morass s. Morast m.

moratorium s. Moratorium n., Schuldenstundung f., Zahlungsaufschub m.

morbid a. krankhaft; makaber.

mordant a., **-ly** adv. beißend, sarkastisch.

more a. & adv. mehr; ferner, noch; once ~, noch einmal.

moreover adv. überdies.

moribund a. sterbend; (fig.) zum Aussterben verurteilt.

Mormon s. Mormone m.; Mormonin f.

morning s. Morgen m.; **~-after pill** s. Pille (für den Morgen) danach; **~-coat** s. Cut m.; ~ star s. Morgenstern m.

Moroccan a. marokkanisch; s. Marokkaner(in) m.(f.)

Morocco s. Marokko n.

moron s. Schwachkopf m.

morose a., **-ly** adv. mürrisch.

morphine s. Morphium n.

morphological a. morphologisch.

morphology s. Morphologie f.

Morse s. Morsezeichen n.; Morseschrift f.

Morse code s. Morsealphabet.

morsel s. Bissen m.

mortal a., **-ly** adv. sterblich, tödlich; ~ sin, Todsünde f.; ~ s. Sterbliche m./f., Mensch m.

mortality s. Sterblichkeit f.; **~-rate** Sterblichkeitsziffer f.

mortar s. Mörsar m.; Mörtel m.; (mil.) Granatwerfer m.

mortgage s. Hypothek f.; to foreclose a ~, eine Hypothek für verfallen erklären; debt on ~, Hypothekenschuld f.; **~-bond, ~-deed** s. Pfandbrief m.; ~ credit bank, Bodenkreditbank f.; ~ v.t. mit einer Hypothek belasten, verpfänden.

mortician s. Leichenbestatter(in) m.(f.)

mortification s. Kränkung f., Ärger m.

mortify v.t. beschämen.

mortuary a. Begräbnis. . .; ~s. Leichenhalle f.

mosaic s. Mosaik n.

moselle s. Mosel f.; Moselwein m.

mosque s. Moschee f.

mosquito s. Moskito m.; Stechmücke f.

mosquito net s. Moskitonetz n.

moss s. Moos n.

mossy a. moosig; bemoost.

most a. meist, die meisten; ~ adv. meistenteils; höchst; ~ s. Meiste n.; at ~, höchstens.

mostly adv. meistenteils, meist, meistens.

motel s. Motel n.

motet s. Motette f.

moth s. Motte f.; Nachtfalter m.; **~-eaten** a. von Motten zerfressen; **~-powder** s. Mottenpulver n.; **~-proof** a. mottensicher.

mother s. Mutter f.; ~ of pearl, Perlmutter f.; ~ v.t. bemuttern.

mother country s. Mutterland n.

motherhood s. Mutterschaft f.

mother-in-law s. Schwiegermutter f.

motherland s. Mutterland n.

motherly a. mütterlich.

mother tongue s. Muttersprache f.

motif s. Motiv n.

motion s. Bewegung f.; Gang m.; Trieb m.; Antrag m.

motionless a. unbeweglich.

motion-picture s. Film m.

motivate v.t. motivieren, begründen.

motivation s. Motivation f.

motive a. bewegend; ~ s. Motiv n.

motley a. scheckig, bunt.

motor a. bewegend; ~ s. Motor m., Kraftmaschine f.; **~-ambulance** s. Krankenkraftwagen m.; **~-bicycle, ~-bike** s. Motorrad n.; **~-bus** s. Autobus m.; **~-car** s. Auto(mobil) n., Kraftwagen m.; **~-coach** s. Reiseomnibus m.; **~-highway** s. Autobahn f.; (nav.) Motorbarkasse f.; **~-pool** s. Kraftfahrpark m.; ~ **transport service** s. (mil.) Kraftfahrwesen n.; **~-vehicle** s. Motorfahrzeug n.; ~ v.i. mit dem Auto fahren.

motorist s. Motorfahrer m.

motorize v.t. motorisieren.

mottled a. gesprenkelt.

motto s. Wahl-, Sinnspruch m.

mound s. Erdhügel m.

mount *s.* Berg, Hügel *m.*; Reitpferd *n.*; (*mil.*) Lafette *f.*; ~ *v.i.* (hinauf)steigen; ~ *v.t.* erheben; besteigen; beschlagen (mit Silber, etc.); montieren; (Bilder) aufziehen; (Edelsteine) fassen; *to* ~ *guard,* auf Wache ziehen.
mountain *s.* Berg *m.*; ~**-ash,** Eberesche *f.*
mountaineer *s.* Bergsteiger(in) *m.*(*f.*)
mountaineering *s.* Bergsteigen *n.*; ~ **expedition** *s.* Bergpartie *f.*
mountainous *a.* gebirgig.
mountain: ~ **range** *s.* Gebirgszug *m.*; ~**side** *s.* Bergabhang *m.*; ~ **top** *s.* Berggipfel *m.*
mounted *a.* beritten.
mourn *v.i.* trauern; ~*v.t.* betrauern.
mourner *s.* Leidtragende *m.*/*f.*; Trauernde *m.*/*f.*
mournful *a.*, ~**ly** *adv.* traurig; klagend.
mourning *s.* Trauer *f.*
mouse *s.* Maus *f.*
mouse-hole *s.* Mauseloch *n.*
mouse-trap *s.* Mausefalle *f.*
moustache *s.* Schnurrbart *m.*
mousy *a.* mausgrau; schüchtern.
mouth *s.* Mund *m.*; Mündung *f.*; ~ *v.t.* in den Mund nehmen; ~*-to-~ resuscitation s.* Mund-zu-Mund-Beatmung.
mouthful *s.* Mundvoll *m.*
mouth-organ *s.* Mundharmonika *f.*
mouth-piece *s.* Mundstück *n.*; Wortführer *m.*; Sprachrohr *n.*
mouthwash *s.* Mundwasser *n.*
mouth-watering *a.* lecker.
movable *a.*, ~**bly** *adv.* beweglich; ~ *property,* bewegliche Habe *f.*; ~**s** *pl.* bewegliche Güter *n.pl.*
move *v.t.* bewegen, fortbewegen; anregen; beantragen; überreden, erregen; ~ *v.i.* sich bewegen, sich fortbewegen, vorrücken; umziehen; *to* ~ *into a house,* ein Haus beziehen; *to* ~ *up* (*mil.*) heranführen; nachrücken; ~ *s.* Bewegung *f.*; Zug (beim Spiele) *m.*; Maßregel *f.*
movement *s.* Bewegung *f.*; Gangwerk (Uhr) *n.*; (*mus.*) Satz *m.*; Tempo *n.*
mover *s.* Anreger *m.*
movie *s.* Film *m.*; ~**s.** Kino *n.*; *go to the* ~*s,* ins Kino gehen.
movie-goer *s.* Kinogänger(in) *m.*(*f.*)
moving *a.* beweglich; ergreifend, bewegend.
mow *v.t.* mähen.
mower *s.* Mäher, Schnitter *m.*
Mozambique *s.* Mozambik *n.*
much *a. & adv.* viel; sehr.
mucilage *s.* Pflanzenschleim *m.*; Klebstoff *m.*
muck *s.* Mist, Dünger *m.*; Dreck *m.*
mucous *a.* schleimig.
mucus *s.* Schleim *m.*
mud *s.* Schlamm, Lehm *m.*; ~ **bath** *s.* Schlammbad *n.*; ~**-guard** *s.* Kotflügel *m.*
muddle *v.t.* verwirren; verpfuschen; ~ *v.i.* wursteln; ~ *s.* Verwirrung *f.*; Durcheinander *n.*
muddled *a.* benebelt, verwörren.
muddle-headed *a.* wirr.
muddy *a.*, ~**ily** *adv.* schlammig; trübe.
mudpack *s.* Schlammpackung *f.*
mud pie *s.* Kuchen (aus Sand) *m.*
muesli *s.* Müsli *n.*
muff *s.* Muff *m.*; ~*v.t.* verpatzen; verderben.
muffin *s.* Muffin *n.*

muffle *v.t.* umwickeln; dämpfen (Trommel).
muffler *s.* Auspufftopf *m.*; dicke Schal *m.*
mufti *s.* Zivil *n.*; Kleidung *f.*
mug *s.* Krug, Becher *m.*; große Tasse *f.*; Fratze *f.*
mugger *s.* Straßenräuber(in) *m.*(*f.*)
mugging *s.* Straßenraub *m.*
muggy *a.* schwül; drückend.
mulatto *s.* Mulatte *m.*
mulberry *s.* Maulbeere *f.*
mulch *s.* Mulch *m.*; ~*v.t.* mulchen.
mule *s.* Maultier *m.*
muleteer *s.* Maultiertreiber *m.*
mulish *a.* störrig.
mull *v.t.* grübeln; nachdenken.
mulled wine *s.* Glühwein *m.*
mullion *s.* Fensterpfosten *m.*
multicolored *a.* vielfarbig.
multifarious *a.*, ~**ly** *adv.* mannigfaltig.
multiform *a.* vielförmig.
multilateral *a.* vielseitig; multilateral.
multimillionaire *s.* Multimillionär(in) *m.*(*f.*)
multinational *a.* multinational; ~*s.* multinationaler Konzern *m.*
multiple *a.* vielfach; ~ *s.* Vielfaches *n.*
multiplicand *s.* Vervielfältigungszahl *f.*
multiplication *s.* Vervielfältigung, Multiplikation *f.*
multiplication-table *s.* Einmaleins *n.*
multiplicity *s.* Menge, Mannigfaltigkeit *f.*
multiply *v.t.* multiplizieren, vervielfältigen.
multi-purpose *a.* Mehrzweck...
multiracial *a.* gemischtrassig.
multitude *s.* Vielheit *f.*, Menge *f.*
mum *a.* still; ~! *i.* still! st!
mumble *v.i. & t.* nuscheln.
mummer *s.* Schauspieler *m.*
mummy *s.* Mumie *f.*
mumps *s.pl.* (*med.*) Ziegenpeter *m.*; Mumps *m.*
munch *v.t. & i.* mampfen.
mundane *a.* weltlich.
municipal *a.* Stadt..., Gemeinde...; ~ *board,* Magistrat *m.*
municipality *s.* Gemeinde *f.*
munition *s.* Kriegsvorrat *m.*; Kriegsmaterial *n.*
mural *a.* Mauer...; Wandbild *n.*; Deckengemälde *n.*
murder *s.* Mord *m.*; ~ *with robbery,* Raubmord *m.*; ~ *v.t.* ermorden.
murderer *s.* Mörder(in) *m.*(*f.*)
murderous *a.*, ~**ly** *adv.* mörderisch.
murky *a.* dunkel, trübe.
murmur *s.* Gemurmel *n.*; ~ *v.i.* murmeln; murren.
muscle *s.* Muskel *m.*
muscular *a.* muskulär; muskulös.
muse *s.* Muse *f.*; ~ *v.i.* nachdenken.
museum *s.* Museum *n.*
mush *s.* Mus *n.*; Brei *m.*
mushroom *s.* Pilz *m.*
mushroom cloud *s.* Atompilz *m.*; Pilzwolke *f.*
mushy *a.* breiig.
music *s.* Musik *f.*; Noten *f.pl.*
musical *a.*, ~**ly** *adv.* musikalisch.
musical comedy *s.* Operette *f.*
music box *s.* Spieldose *f.*
music-hall *s.* Varieté *f.*
musician *s.* Musiker(in) *m.*(*f.*)

music-lesson s. Musikstunde f.
music-stand s. Notenpult n.
musk s. Moschus m.
musket s. Flinte, Muskete f.
musketeer s. Musketier m.
musk-rat s. Bisamratte f.
musky a. moschus.
Muslim a. muslimisch; ~ s. Muslim m.; Muslime f.
muslin s. Musselin m.
muss v.t. verstrubbeln; ~ s. Durcheinander n.
mussel s. Muschel f.
must v.i.ir. müssen; ~ s. Most m.
mustang s. Mustang m.
mustard s. Senf m.
muster v.t. mustern; einstellen; aufbringen; ~ s. Musterung, Musterrolle f.; Trupp m.
mustiness s. Muffigkeit f.
musty a., **~ily** adv. dumpfig, muffig.
mutable a. veränderlich.
mutant a. mutiert; ~ s. Mutant m.
mutate v.t. mutieren.
mutation s. Veränderung f.; Mutation f.
mute a., **~ly** adv. stumm.
muted a. gedämpft.
mutilate v.t. verstümmeln.
mutilation s. Verstümmelung f.
mutineer s. Meuterer m.

mutinous a., **~ly** adv. aufrüherisch.
mutiny s. Meuterei f.; ~ v.i. sich empören.
mutter v.i. & t. murren; murmeln; ~ s. Gemurmel n.
muttering s. Gemurmel n.
mutton s. Hammelfleisch n.; **~-chop** Hammelkotelett.
mutual a. gegenseitig.
muzzle s. Maulkorb m.; Mündung (eines Gewehrs) f.; ~ v.t. den Maulkorb anlegen.
muzzy a. verschwommen.
my pn. mein, meine.
myopia s. Myopie f.; Kurzsichtigkeit f.
myopic a. kurzsichtig.
myriad s. Myriade f.
myrrh s. Myrrhe f.
myrtle s. Myrtle f.
myself pn. (ich) selbst; mich, mir.
mysterious a., **~ly** adv. geheimnisvoll.
mystery s. Geheimnis n.; **~-novel** s. Kriminalroman m. ~ **tour** s., ~ **trip** s. Fahrt ins Blaue.
mystic(al) a., **~ly** adv. mystisch; dunkel; ~ s. Mystiker(in) m.(f.)
mystification s. Fopperei f.
mystify v.t. foppen; irreführen.
myth s. Mythos m.; Mythe f.; Erdichtung f.
mythological a. mythologisch.
mythology s. Mythologie f.

N

N, n der Buchstabe N oder n n.
nab v.t. (fam.) schnappen, erwischen.
nadir s. Nadir, Tiefpunkt m.
nag s. kleines Reitpferd n.; (sl.) Gaul m.; ~ v.t. & i. nörgeln.
nagging a. nörglerisch; quälend.
nail s. Nagel m.; ~ v.t. nageln.
nail-brush s. Nagelbürste f.
nail-file s. Nagelfeile f.
nail-polish s. Nagellack m.
nail-scissors s.pl. Nagelschere f.
naïve a. unbefangen, naiv.
naïveté s. Unbefangenheit f.; Naivität f.
naked a., **~ly** adv. nackt, bloß; wehrlos; offen; ~ light, ungeschütztes Licht n.; ~ eye, bloßes Auge n.
nakedness s. Nacktheit, Blöße f.
name s. Name m.; (guter) Ruf m.; Christian ~, first ~, Vorname m.; family ~, Familienname m.; proper ~, Eigenname s. of the ~ N., N. by ~, namens N.; in ~ only, nur dem Namen nach; to send in one's ~, sich anmelden; ~ v.t. nennen, ernennen.
name-calling s. Beschimpfungen pl.
nameday s. Namenstag m.
nameless a. namenlos.
namely adv. nämlich.
nameplate s. Namensschild n.
namesake s. Namensvetter m.
nanny s. Kindermädchen n.
nap s. Schläfchen n.; Nickerchen n.
nape s. Genick n., Nacken m.
napkin s. Serviette f.
napkin-ring s. Serviettenring m.
narcissism s. Narzißmus m.
narcissist s. Narzißt(in) m.(f.)

narcissistic a. narzißtisch.
narcissus s. Narzisse f.
narcosis s. Narkose f.
narcotic a. betäubend, narkotisch; ~ s. Betäubungsmittel n.
narcotize v.t. narkotisieren.
narrate v.t. erzählen.
narration s. Erzählung f.
narrative a., **~ly** adv. erzählend; ~ s. Erzählung f.
narrator s. Erzähler(in) m.(f.)
narrow a. eng[e]; schmal; **~ly** adv. mit knapper Not; ~ gauge, Schmalspur. . .; ~ s. Meerenge f.; ~ v.t. & i. (sich) verengen.
narrow-minded a. beschränkt; engstirnig.
nasal a. Nasen. . ., nasal; ~ s. (ling.) Nasenlaut m.
nascent a. entstehend, werdend.
nasturtium s. Kapuzinerkresse f.
nasty a., **~ily** adv. schmutzig; bösartig; ungünstig, unfreundlich.
natal a. Geburts. . .
nation s. Volk n., Nation f.
national a., **~ly** adv. national, Volks. . .; ~ s. Staatsangehöriger m.; Staatsangehörige f.; ~ **debt** s. Staatsschuld f.
nationalism s. Nationalismus m.
nationalist a. nationalistisch; s. Nationalist(in) m.(f.)
nationalistic a. nationalistisch.
nationality s. Staatsangehörigkeit f., Nationalität f.
nationalization s. Nationalisierung f.
nationalize v.t. verstaatlichen.
nationally adv. landesweit.

native *a.*, **~ly** *adv.* natürlich; angeboren; einheimisch; ~ **country** *s.* Heimat *f.*; ~ **language** *s.* Muttersprache *f.*; ~ *s.* Eingeborener *m.*
nativity *s.* Geburt *f.*
nativity play *s.* Krippenspiel *n.*
natty *a.* (*fam.*) schick; flott.
natural *a.*, **~ly** *adv.* natürlich; ~ *s.* Naturtalent *n.*
naturalism *s.* Naturalismus *m.*
naturalist *s.* Naturforscher(in) *m.*(*f.*)
naturalization *s.* Naturalisierung *f.*, Einbürgerung *f.*
naturalize *v.t.* einbürgern.
naturally *adv.* von Natur aus; naturgetren; natürlich.
naturalness *s.* Natürlichkeit *f.*
natural resources *s.pl.* natürliche Resourcen *pl.*
natural science *s.* Naturwissenschaft *f.*
nature *s.* Natur *f.*; Beschaffenheit *f.*; *law of* ~, *natural law*, *s.* Naturrecht, Naturgesetz *n.*
natured *a.* geartet.
nature lover *s.* Naturfreund(in) *m.*(*f.*)
nature reserve *s.* Naturschutzgebiet *n.*
naught *s.* Nichts *n.*; Null *f.*; *to come to* ~ zunichte werden; *to set at* ~, mißachten, in den Wind schlagen.
naughty *a.*, **~ily** *adv.* unartig.
nausea *s.* Übelkeit *f.*
nauseate *v.t.* sich ekeln vor; anekeln; jm. Übelkeit erregen.
nauseous *a.*, **~ly** *adv.* ekelhaft.
nautical *a.* nautisch, See. . .; ~ **mile** *s.* Seemeile *f.*
naval *a.* Schiffs. . ., See. . .; ~ **base** *s.* Kriegshafen *m.*
nave *s.* Schiff (einer Kirche) *n.*; Nabe *f.*
navel *s.* Nabel *m.*
navigable *a.* schiffbar; lenkbar.
navigate *v.i.* schiffen; ~ *v.t.* befahren.
navigation *s.* Seemannskunst *f.*; Schiffahrt *f.*; ~ **light**, Positionslicht, Kennlicht *n.*
navigator *s.* Seefahrer *m.*
navvy *s.* Bauarbeiter *m.*; Strassenarbeiter *m.*
navy *s.* (Kriegs-) Flotte *f.*; Marine *f.*; **~-yard** *s.* Marinewerft *f.*
nay *s.* Gegenstimme *f.*; Neinstimme *f.*
Nazi *s.* Nazi *m.*; Nationalsonzialist(in) *m.*(*f.*)
near *pr.* neben, in der Nähe von; ~ *a.* nahe; verwandt; ~ *adv.* beinahe; ~ *v.t. & i.* sich nähern.
nearby *a.* nahegelegen.
Near East *s.* Naher Osten *m.*
nearly *adv.* nahe, beinahe; genau, karg.
nearness *s.* Nähe *f.*
near-sighted *a.* kurzsichtig.
neat *a.*, **~ly** *adv.* nett, sauber.
neatness *s.* Sauberkeit *f.*; Ordentlichkeit *f.*
nebulous *a.* neblig, wolkig.
necessaries *s.pl.* Bedürfnisse *n.pl.*
necessary *a.*, **~ily** *adv.* notwendig.
necessitate *v.t.* erfordern; zwingen.
necessity *s.* Notwendigkeit *f.*; Bedürfnis *n.*
neck *s.* Hals *m.*; Busen *m.*
necklace *s.* Halsband *n.*
neckline *s.* (Hals) Ausschnitt *m.*
necktie *s.* Binde, Kravatte *f.*
necromancy *s.* schwarze Kunst *f.*
necrosis *s.* (*med.*) Nekrose *f.*
nectar *s.* Nektar, Göttertrank *m.*
nectarine *s.* Nektarine *f.*

nee *a.* geborene.
need *s.* Not *f.*, Mangel *m.*; *in case of* ~, im Notfall; ~ *v.t.* nötig haben; bedürfen; brauchen; ~ *v.i.* nötig sein.
needful *a.* notwendig.
needle *s.* Nähnadel *f.*; Nadel *f.*
needless *a.*, **~ly** *adv.* unnötig; ~ *to say*, selbstverständlich.
needle-woman *s.* Näherin *f.*
needlework *s.* Näharbeit *f.*
needy *a.*, **~ily** *adv.* dürftig, arm.
negate *v.t.* verneinen; aufheben.
negation *s.* Verneinung *f.*
negative *a.*, **~ly** *adv.* verneinend; ~ *s.* Verneinung *f.*; (*phot.*) Negativ *n.*; *to answer in the* ~, verneinend antworten.
neglect *v.t.* vernachlässigen; ~ *s.* Vernachlässigung *f.*; *gross* ~, (*law*) grobe Fahrlässigkeit *f.*; ~ *of duty*, Pflichtversäumnis *f.*
neglectful *a.* nachlässig; unachtsam.
negligence *s.* Nachlässigkeit *f.* Unachtsamkeit *f.* *contributory* ~, mitwirkendes Verschulden.
negligent *a.*, **~ly** *adv.* nachlässig.
negligible *a.* unerheblich.
negotiable *a.* verkäuflich; begebbar; *not* ~, nur zur Verrechnung (auf Schecks).
negotiate *v.i.* handeln; unterhandeln; ~ *v.t.* verhandeln über; (Wechsel) begeben; (Hindernis) überwinden.
negotiation *s.* Handel *m.*; Unterhandlung *f.*; *to enter into* ~*s*, Verhandlungen aufnehmen.
negotiator *s.* Unterhändler(in) *m.*(*f.*)
Negro *s.* Neger *m.*/*f.*
neigh *v.i.* wiehern; ~ *s.* Wiehern *n.*
neighbor *s.* Nachbar(in) *m.*(*f.*); Nächste *m.*; ~ *v.t. & i.* angrenzen.
neighborhood *s.* Nachbarschaft *f.*
neighboring *a.* benachbart; angrenzend.
neighborly *a.* nachbarlich, gefällig.
neither *pn.* keiner (von beiden); ~ *c.* weder; auch nicht.
neo- (*in Zus.*) neo . . ., Neo . . ., neu.
neoclassical *a.* klassizistisch.
neolithic *a.* neolithisch; jung steinzeitlich.
neologism *s.* Neubildung *f.*; Neologismus *m.*
neon *s.* Neon (Edelgas) *n.*; **~-lamp** *s.* Neonlampe; **~-tube** *s.* Neonröhre *f.*
neophyte *s.* Neubekehrte *m. & f.*
nephew *s.* Neffe *m.*
nephritis *s.* Nierenentzündung *f.*
nepotism *s.* Vetternwirtschaft *f.*
nerve *s.* Nerv *m.*; Sehne *f.*; (*fig.*) Kraft *f.*; *to get on s.b.'s* ~*s*, jm. auf die Nerven gehen; *to lose one's* ~, die Nerven verlieren; *v.t.* bestärken.
nerveless *a.* kraftlos; kaltblütig.
nerve-racking *a.* nervenaufreibend.
nervous *a.*, **~ly** *adv.* nervig; nervös.
nervous breakdown *s.* Nervenzusammenbruch *m.*
nervy *a.* unverschämt; unruhig.
nest *s.* Nest *n.*; **~-egg** *s.* Sparpfenning, Notpfennig *m.*; ~ *v.i.* nisten.
nestle *v.t.* sich schmiegen.
nestling *s.* Nestling *m.*
net *s.* Netz *n.*; ~ *v.t.* häkeln; einfangen; ~ *a.* netto. ~ **profit** *s.* Reingewinn *m.*

nettle *s.* Nessel *f.*; **~-rash,** Nesselfieber *n.*; ~ *v.t.* reizen.
network *s.* Netzwerk, Netz *n.*
neuralgia *s.* Nervenschmerz *m.*; Neuralgie *f.*
neuritis *s.* Nervenentzündung *f.*
neurological *a.* neurologisch.
neurologist *s.* Neurologe *m.*; Neurologin *f.*
neurosis *s.* Neurose *f.*
neurotic *a.* neurotisch.
neuter *a.* geschlechtslos; (*gram.*) sächlich; ~ *s.* Neutrum *n.*
neutral *a.*, **~ly** *adv.* neutral.
neutrality *s.* Neutralität *f.*
neutralize *v.t.* neutralisieren.
neutron *s.* Neutron *n.*
neutron bomb *s.* Neutronenbombe *f.*
never *adv.* nie, niemals.
nevertheless *adv.* nichtsdestoweniger.
new *a.* neu.
new-born *a.* neugeboren; **~s.** Neugeborenes *n.*
newcomer *s.* Neuankömmling, Fremde *m./f.*
newfangled *a.* neumodisch.
newly *adv.* kürzlich; neu.
newly-weds *s.pl.* Jungverheiratete *pl.*
new moon *s.* Neumond *m.*
newness *s.* Neuheit *f.*; Unerfahrenheit *f.*
news *s.* Neuigkeit *f.*; Nachricht; **~-medium** *s.* Mittel der Nachrichtenverbreitung *n.*
news-agent *s.* Zeitungsverkäufer *m.*
newsflash *s.* Kurzmeldung *f.*
news headline *s.* Schlagzeile *f.*
newspaper *s.* Zeitung *f.*; **~-clipping, ~-cutting,** Zeitungsausschnitt *m.*
newsprint *s.* Zeitungspapier *n.*
newsreel *s.* Filmwochenschau *f.*
news-vendor *s.* Zeitungsverkäufer *m.*
newsworthy *a.* berichtenswert.
newt *s.* Salamander *m.*
New Testament *s.* Neues Testament *n.*
New Year's Day *s.* Neujahrstag *m.*
New Year's Eve *s.* Silvester(abend) *m.*
New Zealand *s.* Neuseeland *n.*
New Zealander *s.* Neuseeländer(in) *m.*(*f.*)
next *a.* nächst, folgend; ~ *adv.* gleich darauf, hernach; ~ *door,* nebenan; ~ *of kin,* die nächsten Verwandten *pl.*
nib *s.* Spitze (besonders einer Schreibfeder) *f.*; Stahlfeder *f.*
nibble *v.i. & t.* benagen; anbeißen (von Fischen); knabbern.
Nicaragua *s.* Nicaragua *n.*
Nicaraguan *a.* nicaraguanisch; ~ *s.* Nicaraguaner(in) *m.*(*f.*)
nice *a.*, **~ly** *adv.* fein, nett; wählerisch; genau.
niceness *s.* Feinheit.
nicety *s.* Feinheit *f.*; Genauigkeit *f.*
niche *s.* Nische *f.*
nick *s.* Kerbe *f.*; rechter Augenblick *m.*; *Old Nick,* der Teufel; ~ *v.t.* kerben.
nickel *s.* Nickel *m.*
nickname *s.* Spitzname *m.*
nicotine *s.* Nikotin *n.*
niece *s.* Nichte *f.*
Nigeria *s.* Nigeria *n.*
Nigerian *a.* nigerisch; ~ *s.* Nigerianer(in) *m.*(*f.*)
niggard *s.* Filz, Knicker *m.*

niggardly *a.* karg, geizig.
niggle *v.i.* nörgeln; herumtüfteln.
niggling *a.* belanglos; nichtssagend.
nigh *a.* nahe; ~ *adv.* nahe, beinahe.
night *s.* Nacht *f.*; *by ~,* nachts; *last ~,* gestern Abend; **~-cap,** Schlafmütze *f.*; (*fig.*) Schlummertrunk *m.*; *first ~,* Erstaufführung *f.*; *opening ~ s.* Premiere *f.*
nightblindness *s.* Nachtblindheit *f.*
nightclub *s.* Nachtklub *m.*, Kabarett *n.*
nightdress *s.* Nachtkleid *n.*
nightfighter *s.* (*avi.*) Nachtjäger *m.*
nightfall *s.* Einbruch (*m.*) der Nacht.
nightgown *s.* Nachthemd *n.*
nightie *s.* Nachthemd *n.*
nightingale *s.* Nachtigall *f.*
nightly *a.* nächtlich; ~ *adv.* nachts; alle Nächte.
nightmare *s.* Alpdrücken *n.*; Alptraum *m.*
night school *s.* Abendschule *f.*
nightshade *s.* Nachtschatten *m.*
night shift *s.* Nachtschicht *f.*
night-time *s.* Nacht *f.*
nil *s.* nichts.
Nile *s.* Nil *m.*
nimble *a.*, **~bly** *adv.* hurtig, flink.
nimbus *s.* Strahlenkranz; Nimbus *m.*
nincompoop *s.* Einfaltspinsel *m.*; Trottel *m.*
nine *a.* neun; ~ *s.* Neun *f.*
ninefold *a.* neunfach.
nine-pins *s.pl.* Kegelspiel *n.*
nineteen *a.* neunzehn.
ninety *a.* neunzig.
ninny *s.* (*fam.*) Dummkopf *m.*, Trottel *m.*
ninth *a.* neunt...
nip *v.t.* kneifen; zwicken, schneiden (von der Kälte); *to ~ in the bud,* im Keim ersticken; ~ *s.* Kniff *m.*, Kneifen *n.*
nip *s.* Schlückchen *n.*
nippers *s.pl.* Kneifzange *f.*
nipple *s.* Brustwarze *f.*; Sauger *m.*
nippy *a.* frisch, kühl; spritzig.
nit *s.* Nisse *f.*
niter *s.* Salpeter *m.*
nitrate *s.* salpetersaures Salz *n.*; Nitrat *n.*
nitric acid *s.* Salpetersäure *f.*
nitrogen *s.* Stickstoff *m.*
nitroglycerine *s.* Nitroglyzerin *n.*
nitty-gritty *s.* der Kern einer Sache.
nit-wit *s.* (*fam.*) Trottel *m.*, Schwachkopf *m.*
no *adv.* nein, nicht; ~ *a.* kein.
nobility *s.* Adel *m.*
noble *a.*, **~bly** *adv.* adlig; edel; trefflich; ~ *s.* Adlige *m./f.*
nobleman *s.* Edelmann *m.*
noblewoman *s.* Adlige *f.*
nobody *s.* niemand, keiner.
no-claim(s) bonus *s.* Schadenfreiheitsrabatt *m.*
nocturnal *a.* nächtlich, Nacht...
nod *v.i. & t.* nicken, winken; schlummern; ~ *s.* Nicken *n.*; Wink *m.*
nodal *a.* Knoten...
node *s.* Knoten *m.*; Überbein *n.*
noise *s.* Lärm *m.*; Gerücht *n.*; ~ *v.t. & i.* lärmen.
noiseless *a.* geräuschlos.
noisome *a.*, **~ly** *adv.* schädlich; widrig.
noisy *a.*, **~ily** *adv.* geräuschvoll, laut.
nomad *s.* Nomade *m.*

nomadic *a.* nomadisch.
no man's land *s.* Niemandsland *n.*
nomenclature *s.* Terminologie *f.*
nominal *a.*, ~**ly** *adv.* dem Namen nach; Namen..., Nenn..., Titular...; sehr gering, unwesentlich; ~ *capital,* Stammkapital *n.*; ~ *value,* Nennwert *m.*
nominate *v.t.* ernennen; vorschlagen.
nomination *s.* Ernennung, Aufstellung eines Wahlkandidaten *f.*
nominative *s.* (*gram.*) Nominativ *m.*
nominee *s.* Vorgeschlagene *m./f.*
non-acceptance *s.* Nichtannahme *f.*
non-aggression *s.* Nichtangriff *m.*; Gewaltverzicht *m.*
non-alcoholic *a.* alkoholfrei.
non-aligned *a.* blockfrei.
non-attendance *s.* Nichterscheinen *n.*
non-belligerent *s.* Nichtkriegführender *m.*; ~ *a.* nichtkriegführend.
nonce *s., for the* ~, für dies eine Mal.
nonchalance *s.* Lässigkeit *f.*; Nonchalance *f.*
non-combatant *a.* nichtkämpfend; ~ *s.* Nichtkämpfende *m./f.*
non-commissioned *a.*, ~ *officer,* Unteroffizier *m.*
non-committal *a.* unverbindlich.
non-compliance *s.* Nichterfüllung *s.*
nonconformist *s.* Nonkonformist(in) *m.(f.)*
non-denominational *a.* konfessionslos.
nondescript *a.* unklassifizierbar, unauffällig.
none *a.* keiner, keine, keines; ~**theless,** *adv.* nichtsdestoweniger.
nonentity *s.* Nichtsein *n.*; (*fig.*) Nichts *n.*
nonessential *a.* unwesentlich.
nonevent *s.* Reinfall *m.*
nonexistence *s.* Nichtvorhandensein *n.*
nonfiction *s.* Sachbuch *n.*
non-fulfilment *s.* Nichterfüllung *s.*
non-intervention *s.* Nichteinmischung *s.*
non-member *s.* Nichtmitglied *m.*
non-observance *s.* Nichtbeachtung *f.*
no-nonsense *a.* nüchtern, sachlich.
non-party *a.* parteilich nicht gebunden.
non-payment *s.* Nichtzahlung *f.*
non-plus *v.t.* verblüffen.
non-profitmaking organization *s.* gemeinnütziges Unternehmen *n.*
non-resident *a.* nichtansässig; ~ *s.* Nichtansässige *m./f.*
non-returnable *a.* Einweg...
nonsense *s.* Unsinn *m.*
nonsensical *a.*, ~**ly** *adv.* unsinnig, albern.
non-smoker *s.* Nichtraucher(in) *m.(f.)*
non-stop *a.* durchgehend (Zug).
nonunion *a.* nichtorganisiert.
non-violence *s.* Gewaltlosigkeit *f.*
noodle *s.* Nudel *f.*
nook *s.* Winkel *m.*; Ecke *f.*
noon *s.* Mittag *m.*
noose *s.* Schlinge *f.*; ~ *v.t.* verstricken.
nor *c.* noch; auch nicht; weder.
norm *s.* Regel *f.*; Muster *n.*
normal *a.* normal; *s.* Normalstand *m.*
normality *s.* Normalität *f.*
normalize *v.t.* normalisieren; ~*v.i.* sich normalisieren.
normally *adv.* normalerweise.

north *s.* Norden *m.*; *a. & adv.* nördlich.
North Africa *s.* Nordafrika *n.*
North America *s.* Nordamerika *n.*
north-east *s.* Nordost(en) *m.*; ~ *a.* nordöstlich.
northeastern *a.* nordöstlich.
northerly, northern *a.* nördlich.
northern lights *s.pl.* Nordlicht *n.*
northernmost *a.* nördlichst...
northward *a.u.adv.* nördlich; nordwärts.
northwest *s.* Nordwest(en) *m.*; ~ *a.* nordwestlich.
northwestern *a.* nordwestlich.
Norway *s.* Norwegen *n.*
Norwegian *a.* norwegisch; ~ *s.* Norweger(in) *m.(f.)*
nose *s.* Nase *f.*; ~ *v.t.* auswittern.
nosebleed *s.* Nasenbluten *n.*
nose-dive *s.* (*avi.*) Sturzflug *m.*
nosegay *s.* Blumensträußchen *n.*
nose-landing, nose-over *s.* (*avi.*) Kopfstand *m.*
nosh *s.* Bissen *m.*; Happln *m.*
nostalgia *s.* Heimweh *n.*
nostalgic *a.* nostalgisch, wehmütig.
nostril *s.* Nasenloch *n.*, Nüster *f.*
nostrum *s.* Allheilmittel *n.*
not *adv.* nicht.
notable *a.*, ~**bly** *adv.* bemerkenswert; beträchtlich; merklich.
notary *s.* Notar *m.*
notation *s.* Notation *f.*; Notierung *f.*
notch *s.* Kerbe *f.*; ~ *v.t.* einkerben.
note *s.* Zeichen, Merkmal *n.*; Note *f.*; Schein *m.*; Anmerkung *f.*; Zettel *m.*; Briefchen *n.*; Rechnung *f.*; Wichtigkeit *f.*; ~ *of hand,* Schuldschein *m.*; ~ *v.t.* aufzeichnen; bermerken; *be it* ~*d,* wohlgemerkt.
notebook *s.* Notizbuch *n.*; Spiralheft *n.*
noted *a.*, ~**ly** *adv.* berühmt, bekannt.
notepad *s.* Notizblock *m.*
note-paper *s.* Briefpapier *n.*
noteworthy *a.* beachtenswert.
nothing *pn.* nichts; *for* ~, umsonst; ~ *s.* Nichts *n.*
nothingness *s.* Nichts *n.*; Nichtigkeit *f.*
notice *s.* Bemerkung *f.*; Kenntnis *f.*; Bekanntmachung *f.*; Nachricht *f.*; Kündigung *f.*; *to give* ~, kündigen; *until further* ~, bis auf weiteres; *at* (*subject to*) *a month's* ~, auf monatliche Kündigung; *period of* ~, Kündigungsfrist *f.*; ~ *v.t.* bemerken, Acht geben auf.
noticeable *a.* merklich; wahrnehmbar.
notice-board *s.* schwarzes Brett *n.*
notifiable *a.* meldepflichtig.
notification *s.* Benachrichtigung *f.*
notify *v.t.* (an)melden; benachrichtigen, formell anzeigen.
notion *s.* Begriff *m.*; Meinung *f.*
notoriety *s.* traurige Berühmtheit *f.*, schlechter Ruf *m.*
notorious *a.*, ~**ly** *adv.* allbekannt; offenkundig; berüchtigt.
notwithstanding *c. & pr.* ungeachtet; dennoch.
nought *s.* Null *f.*
noun *s.* Hauptwort *n.*, Substantiv *n.*
nourish *v.t. & i.* (er)nähren, unterhalten.
nourishing *a.* nahrhaft.
nourishment *s.* Nahrung *f.*
nouveau riche *s.* Neureiche *m./f.*
novel *s.* Roman *m.*; ~ *a.* neu, ungewöhnlich.

novelist s. Romanautor(in) m.(f.)
novella s. Novelle f.
novelty s. Neuheit f.
November s. November m.
novice s. Neuling m.; Novize m.; Novizin f.
now adv. jetzt, nun; **~adays,** heutzutage; ~ and then, zuweilen.
nowhere adv. nirgends.
noxious a., **~ly** adv. schädlich.
nozzle s. Tülle f.; Düse f.; Öffnung einer Röhre f.
nuance s. Nuance f.
nuclear a. (phys.) Kern. . .; Atom. . .
nuclear: ~ deterrent s. atomare Abschreckung f.; **~ disarmament** s. atomare Abrüstung f.; **~ energy** s. Atomenergie f.
nuclear family s. Kernfamilie f.; Kleinfamilie f.
nuclear: ~ fission s. Kernspaltung f.; **~-free** a. atomwaffenfrei; **~ physics** s. Atomphysik f.; **~ power** s. Atomkraft f.; **~ power station** s. Kernkraftwerk n.; **~ waste** s. Atommüll m.
nucleus s. Kern m.
nude a. nackt, bloß.
nudge v.t. leise anstoßen; **~s.** Stups m.
nudist s. Nudist(in) m.(f.); Anhänger(in) der Freikörperkultur (FKK).
nudity s. Nacktheit f.
nugget s. Klumpen m.; Goldklumpen m.
nuisance s. Ärgernis n., Plage f.; Unfug m.; Verdruß m.
nukes s.pl. Atomwaffen pl.
null a. nichtig, ungültig; ~ and void, null und nichtig.
nullify v.t. ungültig machen.
nullity s. Nichtigkeit f.; (law) ~ action, Nichtigkeitsklage f.; **~-appeal,** Nichtigkeitsbeschwerde f.
numb a. starr; taub.
number s. Zahl f.; Nummer f.; Lieferung f.; ~ v.t. zählen, rechnen.
numberless a. unzählbar.

number-plate s. Nummernschild n.
numbness s. Gefühllosigkeit f.
numeral a. Zahl. . .; ~ s. Zahlwort n.; Zahlzeichen n.; Ziffer (des Uhrblatts) f.
numerator s. Zähler m.
numerical a., **~ly** adv. numerisch.
numerous a. zahlreich.
numismatics s.pl. Münzkunde f.
nun s. Nonne f.
nuncio s. Nuntius m.
nunnery s. Nonnenkloster n.
nuptial a. hochzeitlich, ehelich.
nurse s. Amme f.; Krankenschwester f., Krankenpfleger(in) m.(f.); Kindermädchen n.; ~ v.i. säugen; pflegen, warten; hegen.
nursemaid s. Kindermädchen n.
nursery s. Kinderstube f.; Pflanzschule f.; Baumschule f.
nursery rhymes s.pl. Kinderlieder n.pl.
nursery school s. Kindergarten m.; ~ **teacher** s. Kindergärtner(in) m./f.
nursing s. (Kranken-)Pflege f.; ~ **home** s. Pflegeheim n.; Genesungsheim n.
nursling s. Pflegekind n.
nurture v.t. nähren, aufziehen.
nut s. Nuß f.; Schraubenmutter f.
nutcracker s. Nußknacker m.
nutmeg s. Muskatnuß f.
nutrient s. Nährstoff m.
nutriment s. Nahrung f.; Futter n.
nutrition s. Ernährung f.; Fütterung f.
nutritious a. nährend, nahrhaft.
nuts a. verrückt.
nutshell s. Nußschale f.
nutty a. nussig; (sl.) verrückt.
nuzzle v.i. kuscheln.
nylon s. Nylon n.
nymph s. Nymphe f.
nymphomaniac a. nymphoman, mannstoll; ~ s. Nymphomanin f.

O

O, o der Buchstabe O oder o n.
o i. o, ach.
oaf s. Tölpel m.
oak s. Eiche f.
oaken a. eichen.
oar s. Ruder n.; Riemen m.
oarsman s. Ruderer m.
oasis s. Oase f.
oath s. Eid, Schwur m.; Fluch m.; upon ~, eidlich, unter Eid; in lieu of an ~, eidesstattlich, an Eides Statt; to take an ~, einen Eid leisten.
oatmeal s. Hafermehl (n.), -grütze f.
oats s.pl. Hafer m.
obduracy s. Verstocktheit f.
obdurate a., **~ly** adv. verstockt.
obedience s. Gehorsam m.
obedient a., **~ly** adv. gehorsam.
obeisance s. Verbeugung f.
obelisk s. Obelisk m.
obese a. fettleibig, feist.
obesity s. Fettleibigkeit f.
obey v.t. gehorchen.

obituary s. Todesanzeige f.; Nachruf m.; ~ a. Todes. . ., Toten. . .
object s. Gegenstand m.; Zweck m.; Objekt n.; that is no ~, das ist nebensächlich, das spielt keine Rolle; ~ v.t. entgegensetzen; einwenden.
objection s. Einwand m.; no ~, nichts dagegen; to make an ~ to, einen Einwand erheben gegen.
objectionable a. verwerflich, anstößig.
objective a., **~ly** adv. sachlich; objektiv; ~ s. Ziel n.; (opt.) Objektiv n.
objectivity s. Objektivität f.
object lesson s. Paradebeispiel n.; Veranschaulichung f.
objector s. Gegner(in) m.(f.)
obligate v.t. verpflichten.
obligation s. Verpflichtung f.; Schuldverschreibung f.
obligatory a. verpflichtend, verbindlich.
oblige v.t. verpflichten, verbinden.
obliging a., **~ly** adv. verbindlich.
oblique a., **~ly** adv. schief, schräg; mittelbar.
obliterate a. auslöschen, ausstreichen.

oblivion s. Vergessenheit f.; (law) Straferlaß m.; Act of ~, Amnestie f.
oblivious a. vergeßlich, vergessend.
oblong a., ~ly adv. länglich; rechteckig.
obloquy s. Schmähung f.; Tadel m.
obnoxious a., ~ly adv. widerlich.
oboe s. Oboe f.
obscene a., ~ly adv. unzüchtig; obszön.
obscenity s. Unzüchtigkeit f.; Obszönität f.
obscure a., ~ly adv. dunkel; niedrig, verborgen; ~ v.t. verdunkeln.
obscurity s. Dunkelheit f.; Niedrigkeit f.
obsequies s.pl. Leichenbegängnis n.
obsequious a., ~ly adv. unterwürfig; kriecherisch.
obsequiousness s. Unterwürfigkeit f.
observance s. Beachtung f., Innehaltung f.; Vorschrift f., Regel f.
observant a. aufmerksam; achtsam.
observation s. Beobachtung f.
observatory s. Sternwarte f.; Observatorium n.
observe v.t. beobachten; bemerken.
observer s. Beobachter(in) m.(f.)
obsessed a. (with) besessen (von).
obsession s. Besessenheit f.; Obsession f.
obsessive a. zwanghaft, obsessiv.
obsolescence s. Veralten n.
obsolescent a. veraltend.
obsolete a. veraltet.
obstacle s. Hindernis n.
obstacle-race s. Hindernislauf m.
obstetric a. Geburts(hilfe) . . .
obstetrician s. Geburtshelfer(in) m.(f.)
obstetrics s. Geburtshilfe f.
obstinacy s. Hartnäckigkeit f.
obstinate a., ~ly adv. hartnäckig.
obstreperous a., ~ly adv. lärmend; widerspenstig.
obstruct v.t. verstopfen; hemmen; behindern.
obstruction s. Verstopfung f.; Hindernis n.; Hemmung f.
obtain v.t. erlangen; erreichen.
obtainable a. erlangbar, erhältlich.
obtrude v.t. aufdrängen.
obtrusive a. aufdringlich.
obtuse a., ~ly adv. stumpf; dumm; ~-angled a. (geom.) stumpfwinklig.
obviate v.t. vorbeugen.
obvious a. augenfällig, deutlich; einleuchtend; ~ly adv. selbstverständlich.
occasion s. Gelegenheit f.; Veranlassung f.; on this ~, dabei; ~ v.t. verursachen, veranlassen.
occasional a., ~ly adv. gelegentlich.
Occident s. Abendland n.
occidental a. westlich; abendländisch.
occult a., ~ly adv. verborgen, geheim, okkult.
occupant s. Inhaber(in) m.(f.) Insasse m.; Insassin f.
occupation s. Besitzergreifung f.; Besetzung f.; Besatzung f.; Beschäftigung f.
occupational a. beruflich; Berufs. . .
occupational therapy s. Beschäftigungstherapie f.
occupier s. Besitzer(in) m.(f.); Inhaber(in) m.(f.)
occupy v.t. in Besitz nehmen; beschäftigen; innehaben, bewohnen; bekleiden (Amt); besetzen.
occur v.i. sich ereignen; einfallen.
occurrence s. Ereignis n.; Vorfall m.
ocean s. Weltmeer n.; Ozean m.

ocean-going a. hochseetüchtig; Übersee. . .
ocher s. Ocker m.
o'clock Uhr: two ~, zwei Uhr.
octagon a. Achteck n.
octane s. Oktan n.; ~-rating s. Oktanzahl f.; Klopfwert m. (mot.).
octave s. Oktave f.
octavo s. Oktavformat n.
October s. Oktober m.
octogenarian s. Achtzigjährige m./f. ~ a. achtzigjährig.
octopus s. Krake m.
ocular a., ~ly adv. Augen. . .; augenscheinlich.
oculist s. Augenarzt m., Augenärztin f.
odd a., ~ly adv. ungerade; überzählig; übrig; einzeln; wunderlich; ungefähr, etwas über; a hundred ~, einige hundert.
oddity, oddness s. Seltsamkeit f.; Eigentümlichkeit f.
odds s. Ungleichheit f.; Wahrscheinlichkeit f.; Vorgabe f.; Streit m.
ode s. Ode f.
odious a., ~ly adv. verhaßt, widerlich.
odium s. Tadel m., Vorwurf m.
odor s. Geruch, Wohlgeruch m.
odorless a. geruchlos.
odorous a. duftig.
of pr. von, aus, vor, um, in Betreff.
off adv. & pr. von, ab, weg, davon; entfernt; (nav.) auf der Höhe von; ~! i. weg! fort!
offal s. Abfall m.; Aas m.
off-duty hours pl. Außerdienststunden f.pl.
offend v.t. beleidigen; ärgern; verletzen; the ~ed party, der Beleidigte m.
offender s. Beleidiger m.; Zuwiderhandelnder m.; Missetäter m.; first ~, nicht vorbestrafter Verbrecher m.
offense s. Beleidigung f.; Verdruß m.; Ärgernis n.; Vergehen n.; Anstoß m.; to give ~ to, Anstoß erregen; einen beleidigen; to take ~ at a thing, etwas übelnehmen.
offensive a., ~ly adv. anstößig; beleidigend; Angriffs. . .; ~ s. Offensive f.
offer v.t. anbieten, darbringen, opfern; ~ v.i. sich erbieten; ~ s. Anerbieten n.; Antrag m.; Offerte f.
offering s. Angebot n.; Opfer n.
offhand a. leichthin, beiläufig.
office s. Amt n.; Dienst m.; Gottesdienst m.; Büro n.; head ~, main ~, Hauptbüro n., Hauptgeschäftstelle f.; to resign ~, vom Amt zurücktreten; discharge from ~, Amtsenthebung f.; oath of ~, Dienstseid m.; term of ~, Amtszeit f.; ~-appliances pl. Büroartikel m.pl.; ~-holder, Amtsinhaber m.; ~-hours pl. Amtsstunden, Geschäftsstunden f.pl.; ~ worker, Büroangestellte m./f.
officer s. Beamte m.; Offizier m.; ~ candidate, Offiziersanwärter m.; ~'s mess, Kasino n.
official a., ~ly adv. amtlich, offiziell; ~ authority, Amtsgewalt f.; ~ journey s. Dienstreise f.; ~ s. Beamte m.; Beamtin f.; senior ~, höhere Beamte m.
officialdom s. Beamtentum n.; Bürokratie f.
officiate v.i. amtieren.
officious a., ~ly adv. übereifrig.
off-key a. verstimmt.
off-load v.t. abladen.
off-peak a. außerhalb der Spitzenzeit; abfallend.

off-putting *a.* abstossend, abschreckend.

offset *s.* Gegenrechnung *f.*; (*arch.*) Absatz *m.*; ~ *v.t.* ausgleichen.

offshoot *s.* Sproß, Ausläufer *m.*

offspring *s.* Nachkommenschaft *f.*

off-stage *adv.* in den Kulissen.

off-the-record *a. u. adv.* inoffiziell.

off-white *a.* naturweiß.

often *adv.* oft, öfters.

ogle *v.t.* (lieb)äugeln.

ogre *s.* Menschenfresser *m.*

oh! *i.* oh! ach!

ohm *s.* (*elek.*) Ohm *n.*; **~meter** *s.* Widerstandsmesser *m.*

oil *s.* Öl *n.*; ~ *v.t.* einölen.

oilcake *s.* Ölkuchen *m.*

oilcloth *s.* Wachstuch *n.*

oilcolor *s.* Ölfarbe *f.*

oil *s.* Öl *n.*; ~ *v.t.* einölen.

oilcake *s.* Ölkuchen *m.*

oilcloth *s.* Wachstuch *n.*

oilcolor *s.* Ölfarbe *f.*

oil-gauge *s.* (*mot., avi.*) Ölstandzeiger *m.*

oil-level *s.* (*mot., avi.*) Ölstand *m.*

oil painting *s.* Ölgemälde *n.*

oil pressure *s.* Öldruck *m.*

oil-refinery *s.* Ölraffinerie *f.*

oil-slick *s.* Ölteppich *m.*

oil-tanker *s.* Öltankschiff *n.*

oil-well *s.* Ölquelle *f.*

oily *a.* ölig, fett; schmierig.

ointment *s.* Salbe *f.*

OK, okay okay, in Ordnung.

old *a.* alt.

old age *s.* Alter *n.*, Greisenalter *n.*; ~ **insurance** *s.* Altersversicherung *f.*; ~ **pension** *s.* Alterspension *f.*

old-fashioned *a.* altmodisch.

oldish *a.* älter.

old maid *s.* alte Jungfer *f.*

old wives' tale *s.* Ammenmärchen *n.*

oleander *s.* Oleander *m.*

oleograph *s.* Öldruck *m.*

olfactory *a.* Geruchs . . .

oligarchy *s.* Oligarchie *f.*

olive *s.* Olive *f.*; Ölbaum *m.*; **~-branch** *s.* Ölzweig *m.*; (*fig.*) Friedensangebot *n.*

olive-oil *s.* Olivenöl *n.*

Olympic Games *s.pl.* Olympische Spiele *pl.*

Olympics *s.pl.* Olympiade *f.*

omelet *s.* Omelett *n.*

omen *s.* Vorbedeutung *f.*, Vorzeichen *n.*

ominous *a.*, **~ly** *adv.* ominös, unheilvoll.

omission *s.* Unterlassung *f.*; Auslassung *f.*

omit *v.t.* auslassen; unterlassen.

omnibus *s.* Omnibus *m.*

omnipotence *s.* Allmacht *f.*

omnipotent *a.*, **~ly** *adv.* allmächtig.

omnipresent *a.*, allgegenwärtig.

omniscient *a.* allwissend.

on *pr. & adv.* an, auf; in, zu, mit, bei, unter, von; zufolge; weiter, fort; *and so* ~, und so weiter.

once *adv.* einmal; einst, dereinst; ~ *more*, ~ *again*, noch einmal.

oncoming *a.* entgegenkommend.

one *a. & pn.* einer, eine, ein(s); man, jemand; *any*

~, irgend jemand, jeder; ~ *another*, einander, sich; *every* ~, jeder; *oneself*, sich selbst; ~ *by* ~, einer nach dem andern.

one-armed *a.* einarmig; **one-eyed** *a.* einäugig.

onerous *a.* lästig, beschwerlich.

one-sided *a.* einseitig.

one-time *a.* ehemalig; einmalig.

one-way street *s.* Einbahnstraße *f.*; **one-way traffic** *s.* Einbahnverkehr *m.*

ongoing *a.* andauernd, laufend.

onion *s.* Zwiebel *f.*

onlooker *s.* Zuschauer(in) *m.*(*f.*)

only *a.* einzig; ~ *adv.* allein, nur; erst.

on-off *a.* ein-aus . . .

onset *s.* Einsetzen *n.*; Einbruch *m.*; Anfall *m.*

onslaught *s.* Angriff *m.*

onus *s.* Last *f.*

onward *a. & adv.* vorwärts.

ooze *s.* Schlick *m.*; ~ *v.i.* sickern; (*fig.*) ausstromen.

opal *s.* Opal *m.*

opalescent *a.* schillernd; opalisierend.

opaque *a.* dunkel, undurchsichtig.

open *a.* **~ly** *adv.* offen; öffentlich; freimütig; aufrichtig; zugänglich; *in the* ~ *air*, im Freien; ~ *drive*, (*mot.*) freie Fahrt *f.*; ~ *v.t.* öffnen, eröffnen erschließen; ~ *v.i.* sich öffnen; *to* ~ *out*, aufgehen.

open-air *a.* Openair . . . ; ~ **swimming pool** *s.* Freibad *n.*

open-ended *a.* ohne Zeitbegrenzung.

opener *s.* Öffner *m.*

open-handed *a.* freigebig.

open-hearted *a.* aufrichtig; herzlich.

open-heart surgery *n.* Offenherzchirurgie *f.*

opening *s.* Öffnung *f.*; Eröffnung *f.*; (*com.*) Absatzweg *m.*; Gelegenheit, Aussicht *f.*; ~ **ceremony** *s.* feierliche Eröffnung. **~-hours** *pl.* Öffnungszeiten *f.pl.*

open market *s.* freier Markt *m.*

open-minded *a.* aufgeschlossen.

openness *s.* Offenheit *f.*; Empfänglichkeit *f.*

open season *s.* Jagdsaison *f.*

opera *s.* Oper *f.*

opera-glasses *s. pl.* Operngucker *m.*

opera-house *s.* Opernhaus *n.*

opera-singer *s.* Opernsänger(in) *m.*(*f.*)

operate *v.t.* wirken, operieren; (*mil.*) operieren, vorgehen; (*mech.*) handhaben, bedienen (Maschine); ~ *v.i.* (*mech.*) arbeiten, in Betrieb sein (Fabrik); *in operating condition*, in arbeitsfähigem Zustand; *to be* ~*d on*, sich operieren lassen.

operatic *a.* opernmässig.

operation *s.* Wirkung *f.*; Operation *s.*; (*chem.*) Verfahren *n.*; (*mech.*) Arbeitsgang *m.*; Betrieb (einer Fabrik) *m.*; (*mil.*) Unternehmen *n.*, Operation *f.*; *in* ~, in Kraft sein, in Betrieb; *out of* ~, außer Betrieb.

operational *a.* (*mil.*) operatív.

operative *a.* wirksam, tätig; ~ *s.* Arbeiter(in) *m.*(*f.*)

operator *s.* Operateur *m.*; Telefonist(in) *m.*(*f.*)

operetta *s.* Operette *f.*

ophthalmic *a.* Augen . . . ; augenärztlich.

ophthalmologist *s.* Augenarzt *m.*; -ärztin *f.*

ophthalmology *s.* Ophthalmologie *f.*; Augenheilkunde *f.*

opiate *s.* Opiat *n.*; ~ *a.* einschläfernd.

opine *v.i.* meinen.

opinion s. Meinung; Ansicht f.; (law) Urteilsbegründung f.

opinionated, a. starrsinnig; eigensinnig.

opinion poll s. Meinungsumfrage f.

opium s. Opium m.

opponent a. widerstreitend; ~ s. Gegner(in) m.(f.)

opportune a., ~**ly** adv. günstig, gelegen.

opportunist s. Opportunist(in) m.(f.)

opportunity s. (gute) Gelegenheit, Möglichkeit f., günstiger Augenblick m.; to miss an ~, die Gelegenheit verpassen; to take an ~, eine Gelegenheit ergreifen.

oppose v.t. entgegenstellen, sich widersetzen; ~ v.i. Widerstand leisten; einwenden.

opposed a. gegensetzlich, entgegengesetzt.

opposite a., ~**ly** adv. entgegengesetzt; widerstreitend; ~ number, der entsprechende Beamte (eines anderen Staates); ~ pr. gegenüber; ~ adv. gegenüber; ~ s. Gegentiel n.

opposition s. Opposition f.; Gegensatz m.; Opposition(spartei) f.; Widerstand m.

oppress v.t. unterdrücken, bedrücken.

oppression s. Unterdrückung f.

oppressive a., ~**ly** adv. bedrückend; repressiv; drückend.

oppressor s. Unterdrücker m.

opprobrious a., ~**ly** adv. schimpflich.

opprobrium s. Schimpf m.; Schande f.

opt v.i. sich entscheiden.

optic(al) a. optisch, Seh. . .

optician s. Optiker(in) m.(f.)

optics s.pl. Optik f.

optimism s. Optimismus m.

optimist s. Optimist(in) m.(f.)

optimistic a. optimistisch.

optimize v.t. optimieren.

optimum s. Optimum n.; a. optimal.

option s. Wahl f.; first ~, Vorkaufsrecht n., Vorhand f.

optional a. freigestellt, wahlfrei.

opulence s. Reichtum m.

opulent a. wohlhabend.

opus s. Opus n.; Werk n.

or c. oder; entweder; ~ else, sonst.

oracle s. Orakel n.

oracular a. orakelhaft.

oral a., ~**ly** adv. mündlich; Mund . . .

orange s. Orange f.; Apfelsine f.

orangeade s. Orangenlimonade f.

orangutan s. Orang-Utan m.

oration s. Rede f.

orator s. Redner(in) m.(f.)

oratorical a. rednerisch.

oratorio s. Oratorium n.

oratory s. Redekunst f.

orb s. Kugel f.; Augapfel m.

orbit s. Bereich m.; Kreis-, Umlaufbahn f.

orchard s. Obstgarten m.

orchestra s. Orchester n.

orchestral a. Orchester . . . ; ~ **music** s. Orchestermusik f.

orchestrate v.t. orchestrieren.

orchestration s. Orchestrierung f.

orchid s. Orchidee f.

ordain v.t. verordnen; einsetzen; to ~ priest, xum Priester weihen.

ordeal s. Gottesurteil n.; Heimsuchung f., Tortur f.

order s. Ordnung f.; Verordnung f.; Befehl m.; Bestellung f.; Auftrag m.; Anweisung f.; Gattung f.; Rang m.; Orden m.; Reihenfolge f.; in ~ to, um zu; by ~ of, auf Befehl von; out of ~, defekt, kaputt; to ~, auf Bestellung, nach Mass; to call to ~, zur Ordnung rufen; to establish ~, Ordnung schaffen; to take ~s, Aufträge, Bestellungen entgegennehmen; sich zum Priester weihen lassen; ~**-blank** s. Bestellungsformular n.; ~**-form** s. Bestellschein m.; ~ **of battle** s. (mil.) Schlachtaufstellung f.; ~**s** pl. geistlicher Stand m.; ~ v.t. orden, anordnen, befehlen; bestellen; to ~ again, nachbestellen.

orderly a. & adv. ordentlich, regelmäßig; gesittet; diensttuend; ~ **room** s. (mil.) Schreibstube f.

ordinal s. Ordnungszahl f.; Ordinalzahl f.

ordinance s. Verordnung, Regel f.

ordinary a., ~**ily** adv. gewöhnlich, üblich, mittelmäßig; gemein; ~ share, Stammaktie f.

ordination s. (Priester-) Weihe f.

ordure s. Kot, Schmutz m.

ore s. Erz, Metall n; high-grade ~, hochwertiges Erz; low-grade ~, geringwertiges Erz.

oregano s. Oregano n.

organ s. Werkzeug n.; Organ n.; Orgel f.; ~**-stop** s. Orgelregister n.

organ-grinder s. Orgeldreher m.

organic a., ~**ally** adv. organisch; biologisch; biodynamisch.

organism s. Organismus m.

organist s. Organist(in) m.(f.)

organization s. Organisation f.; Ordnung f.; Anordnung f.

organizational a., ~**ly** adv. organisatorisch.

organize v.t. einrichten, organisieren.

organized a. organisiert; geregelt.

organizer s. Organisator(in) m.(f.)

orgasm s. Orgasmus m.

orgy s. Orgie f.

oriel s. Erkerfenster n.

orient a. östlich; ~ s. Osten m., to ~ oneself, v.t. sich orientieren; **the O~** s. Orient m.; Morgenland n.

oriental a. östlich; orientalisch; ~ s. Asiate m.; Asiatin. f.

orientation s. Orientierung f.; general ~, Einführungsbesprechung f.

orifice s. Öffnung f.; Loch n.

origin s. Ursprung m.; Herkunft f.

original a., ~**ly** adv. ursprünglich, eigenartig; ~ sin s. Erbsünde f.; ~ s. Urbild n.; Urschrift f.; Original n.

originality s. Originalität f. Ursprünglichkeit f.

originate v.t. ins Leben rufen; schaffen; ~ v.i. entstehen, entspringen.

originator s. Urheber(in), Schöpfer(in) m.(f.)

ornament s. Verzierung f.; Putz m.; Zier, Schmuck m.; Schmuckstück n.

ornamental a., ~**ly** adv. zierend, Zier . . .

ornamentation s. Ausschmückung f.; Verzierung f.

ornate a. geziert, zierlich; schmuckreich.

ornithology s. Vogelkunde f.

orphan s. Waise m. & f.

orphanage s. Waisenhaus n.

orthodox a. rechtgläubig; üblich, landläufig.

orthodoxy s. Orthodoxie f.

orthographic(al) *a.* orthographisch.

orthography *s.* Rechtschreibung *f.*

orthopedic *a.* orthopädisch.

oscillate *v.i.* schwingen: schwanken.

oscillatiion *s.* Schwingung *f.*

osier *s.* Weide *f.*

osmosis *s.* Osmose *f.*

ossify *v.i.* ossifizieren, verknöchern.

ostensible *a.* scheinbar, vorgeblich.

ostentation *s.* Gepränge *n.*; Prahlerei *f.*

ostentatious *a.*, **~ly** *adv.* prahlerisch.

osteopath *s.* Osteopath *m.*, Knochenheilkundige *m./f.*

ostracism *s.* Ächtung *f.*

ostracize *v.t.* verbannen.

ostrich *s.* Strauß (Vogel) *m.*

other *a.* ander.

otherwise *adv.* anders, sonst.

otter *s.* Fischotter *f.*

ottoman *s.* Ruhebett *n.*

ought *v.i.ir.* sollen, müssen.

ounce *s.* Unze *f.* (28,35 g.)

our *pn.* unser, unsere.

ours *pn.* unser, der unsrige.

ourself *pn.* (wir) selbst, wir.

ourselves *pn.pl.* (wir) selbst, uns.

oust *v.t.* ausstoßen, verdrängen.

out *adv.* aus; draußen, außerhalb; heraus, hinaus; erloschen; ~ *of*, aus, aus . . . hinaus; *have it ~ with s.b.*, (*fig.*) die Sache mit jm. ausfechten; *be ~ of sth.*, etw. nicht mehr haben.

outbid *v.t.st.* überbieten.

outboard motor *s.* Außenbordmotor *m.*

outbreak *s.* Ausbruch *m.*

outbuilding *s.* Nebengebäude *n.*

outburst *s.* Ausbruch *m.*

outcast *p. & a.* verworfen; verbannt; ~ *s.* Verstoßene *m./f.*; Ausgestoßene *m./f.*

outcome *s.* Ergebnis *n.*

outcry *s.* Aufschrei *m.* (der Empörung/Entrüstung)

outdated *a.* veraltet.

outdistance *v.t.* hinter sich lassen.

outdo *v.t.st.* übertreffen.

outdoor *a.* im Freien; Außen . . . ; *out of doors*, im Freien.

outer *a.* äußer.

outermost *a.* äußerst.

outer space *s.* Weltraum *m.*

outfit *s.* Austrüstung *f.*; Ausstattung *f.*; Kleider *n.pl.*

outfitter *s.* Ausstatter(in) *m.(f.)*

outflow *s.* Ausfluß *m.*; Abfluß *m.*

outgoing *~s s.pl.* Ausgaben *f.pl.*; ~ *a.* abgehend; *the ~ president*, der ausscheidende Präsident *m.*; kontaktfreudig.

outgrow *v.t.st.* entwachsen.

outhouse *s.* Nebengebäude *n.*

outing *s.* Ausflug *m.*

outlandish *a.* seltsam, fremdartig.

outlast *v.t.* überdauern.

outlaw *s.* Geächtete *m.*; ~ *v.t.* ächten.; verbieten.

outlay *s.* Auslage *f.*; Ausgabe *f.*

outlet *s.* Ausgang *m.*; Ventil *n.*; Absatzmarkt *m.*, Verkaufsstelle *f.*

outline *s.* Umriß, Abriß *m.*; ~ *v.t.* kurz darstellen, umreißen.

outlive *v.t.* überleben.

outlook *s.* Ausblick *m.*, Aussicht *f.*

outlying *a.* fernliegend; abgelegen.

outmaneuver *v.t.* überlisten.

outmoded *a.* altmodisch.

outnumber *v.t.* an Zahl übertreffen.

outpatient *s.* ambulanter Patient(in) *m.(f.)*

outpost *s.* Vorposten *m.*

outpouring *s.* Erguß *m.*

output *s.* Ertrag *m.*; Produktion *f.*

outrage *v.t.* schmählich behandeln; vergewaltigen; ~ *s.* Greueltat *f.*; Gewalttat *f.*; Unverschämtheit *f.*

outrageous *a.*, **~ly** *adv.* abscheulich, greulich; unverschämt; übertrieben.

outright *adv.* gänzlich, völlig.

outrun *v.t.st.* im Laufen übertreffen.

outset *s.* Anfang *m.*

outshine *v.t.st.* überstrahlen.

outside *s.* Außenseite *f.*; ~ *adv. & pr.* außen; außerhalb; draußen; äußerst; hinaus.

outsider *s.* Außenseiter(in) *m.(f.)*

outsized *a.* übergroß.

outskirts *s.pl.* Stadtrand *m.*

outspoken *a.* freimütig, offen.

outstanding *a.* unbezahlt; hervorragend.

outstretched *p. & a.* ausgestreckt.

outstrip *v.t.* überholen.

outvote *v.t.* überstimmen.

outward *a.* der, die, das äußere, äußerlich; ~ *adv.* aussen, auswärts.

outwardly *adv.* äußerlich.

outward(s) *adv.* nach außen; **~bound** *a.* auf der Hinreise.

outweigh *v.t.* überwiegen.

outwit *v.t* überlisten.

outwork *s.* Heimarbeit *f.*

oval *a.* eirund; ~ *s.* Oval *n.*

ovary *s.* Eierstock *m.*

ovation *s.* Ovation *f.*

oven *s.* Backofen, Ofen *m.*

oven: **~-glove** *s.* Topfhandschuh *n.*; **~-proof** *a.* feuerfest; **~ware** *s.* feuerfestes Geschirr *n.*

over *pr. & adv.* über, darüber, hinüber, überhin; vorüber, vorbei, allzu; *all ~*, über und über; ganz vorbei; ~ *again*, noch einmal; *continued ~*, Fortsetzung umseitig; ~ *there*, da drüben.

over-abundant *a.* überreichlich.

overact *v.t. & i.* übertreiben.

overall *s.* Arbeitskittel *m.* ~ *size*, Einheitsgröße *f.* **~s** *pl.* Arbeitsanzug *m.*; **~a.** allgemein; *adv.* im grossen und ganzen.

overawe *v.t.* in Furcht halten.

overbalance *v.t.* umkippen; das Gleichgewicht verlieren.

overbear *v.t.st.* überwältigen.

overbearing *a.* anmaßend, stolz.

overbid *v.t.st.* überbieten.

overboard *adv.* über Bord.

overburden *v.t.* überladen.

overcast *v.t.st.* überziehen; ~ *a.* bewölkt.

overcharge *v.t.* überladen; überfordern.

overcloud *v.t.* überwölken.

overcoat *s.* Überzieher *m.*, Mantel *m.*

overcome *v.t.st.* überwältigen; überwinden.

overconfidence *s.* Vermessenheit *f.*

overcrowded *a.* überfüllt.

overdo *v.t.st.* zu viel tun, übertreiben.

overdose *v.t.* überdosieren.
overdraft *s.* überzogenes Konto *n.*
overdraw *v.t.* das Bankkonto überziehen.
overdress *v.t.* sich zu elegant anziehen.
overdue *a.* fällig; überfällig.
overeager *a.* übereifrig.
overeat *v.i.* zu viel essen.
overestimate *v.t.* überschätzen.
overexert *v.t.* sich überanstrengen.
overexpose *v.t.* überbelichten.
overexposure *s.* (*phot.*) Überbelichtung *f.*
overflow *v.i.* & *v.t.st.* überfließen; ~ *s.* Überlauf *m.*, Ausflußröhre *f.*; **~-meeting**, Parallelversammlung *f.*
overgrow *v.t.st.* überwachsen.
overgrown *p.* & *a.* überwachsen; überwuchert.
overgrowth *s.* Überwucherung *f.*
overhang *v.t.st.* überhängen.
overhaul *v.t.* gründlich prüfen; (*nav.*) überholen.
overhead *adv.* & *a.* oben, Ober . . . ; ~ *cable*, ~ *line*, ~ *wire*, (*elek.*) Freileitung, Oberleitung *f.*; ~ *clearance*, lichte Höhe *f.*; ~ *expenses pl.* laufende Ausgaben *f.pl.*; ~ *railway*, Hochbahn *f.*
overhear *v.t.ir.* zufällig hören; behorchen.
overheat *v.t.* überhitzen.
over-indulge *v.t.* zu sehr frönen; ~*v.i.* es übertreiben.
overjoy *v.t.* entzücken.
overkill *s.* Overkill *n.*
overland *a.* Überland . . .
overlap *v.t.* übereinander griefen, teilweise zusammenfallen.
overlay *v.t.ir.* belegen, überlagern.
overleaf *adv.* umseitig.
overload *v.t.* überladen.
overlook *v.t.* überblicken; durchsehen, prüfen; Nachsicht haben; übersehen.
overmuch *a.* zu viel.
overnight *adv.* über Nacht; ~ *accommodation*, Übernachtungsunterkunft *f.*
overpay *v.t.* zu reichlich bezahlen.
overpopulated *a.* überbevölkert.
overpower *v.t.* überwältigen.
overpriced *a.* zu teuer.
overprotective *a.* überfürsorglich.
overproduction *s.* Überproduktion *f.*
overrate *v.t.* überschätzen.
overreach *v.t.* überragen; übervorteilen; *to ~ oneself*, sich übernehmen.
over-reaction *s.* Überreaktion *f.*
override *v.t.* umstoßen; *of overriding importance*, von vorrangiger Wichtigkeit.
overripe *a.* überreif.
overrule *v.t.* als ungültig verwerfen; (Entscheidung) aufheben.
overrun *v.t.st.* überlaufen, überrennen.

oversea *a.* & *adv.*, **overseas** *adv.* überseeisch.
oversee *v.t.st.* beaufsichtigen.
overseer *s.* Aufseher *m.*
oversensitive *a.* überempfindlich.
overshadow *v.t.* überschatten.
overshoe *s.* Überschuh *m.*
overshoot *v.t.ir.* über das Ziel hinausschießen.
oversight *s.* Versehen *n.*
oversimplify *v.t.* zu stark vereinfachen.
oversleep *v.t.* *ir.* sich verschlafen.
overspend *v.i.* zuvielausgeben.
overspread *v.t.st.* überdecken.
overstaff *v.t.* überbesetzen.
overstate *v.t.* übertreiben.
overstatement *s.* Übertreibung *f.*
overstay *v.t.* (Zeit) überschreiten; *to ~ a date*, über einen Termin hinaus ausbleiben; *~ing of leave*, Urlaubsüberschreitung *f.*
overstep *v.t.* überschreiten.
overstrain *v.t.* (*v.i.* sich) überanstrengen.
overstretch *v.t.* überdehnen.
overt *a.*, **~ly** *adv.* offenbar, öffentlich.
overtake *v.t.st.* überholen, ereilen.
overtax *v.t.* zu hoch besteuern; überbürden.
overthrow *v.t.st.* umwerfen; umstürzen, vernichten; ~ *s.* Umsturz *m.*
overtime *s.* Überstunden *f.pl.*; *to work ~*, Überstunden machen.
overture *s.* Vorschlag, Antrag *m.*; Ouvertüre *f.*
overturn *v.t.* umwerfen; zerstören; ~ *v.i.* umkippen, umfallen; ~ *s.* Umsturz *m.*
overvalue *v.t.* zu hoch schätzen.
overview *s.* Überblick *m.*
overweening *a.*, **~ly** *adv.* anmaßend.
overweight *s.* Übergewicht *n.*
overwhelm *v.t.* überwältigen.
overwork *v.t.* & *i.* (sich) überarbeiten; ~ *s.* übermäßige Arbeit *f.*
oviduct *s.* Eileiter *m.*
oviparous *a.* eierlegend.
owe *v.t.* schuldig sein, verdanken.
owing *p.* schuldig; ~ *to pr.* dank . . . , infolge; *how much is ~ to you?*, wieviel ist an Sie zu zahlen?
owl *s.* Eule *f.*
own *a.* eigen; *on one's ~*, selbständig, für sich; *to come into one's ~*, zu seinem Rechte kommen.
owner *s.* Eigentümer *m.*; *at ~'s risk*, auf eigene Gefahr.
ownership *s.* Eigentum(srecht) *n.*
ox *s.* Ochs[e] *m.*; Rindvieh *n.*
oxidation *s.* Oxydation *f.*
oxide *s.* Oxyd *n.*
oxidize *v.t.* & *i.* oxydieren.
oxygen *s.* Sauerstoff *m.*; **~-apparatus** *s.* Sauerstoffapparat *m.*
oyster *s.* Auster *f.*; ~ *bed* *s.* Austernbank *f.*
ozone *s.* Ozone *n.*; ~ *layer* *s.* Ozonschicht *f.*

P

P, p der Buchstabe P oder p *n.*
pace *s.* Schritt, Gang *m.*; Tempo *n.*; ~ *v.i.* schreiten; paßgehen; ~ *v.t.* abschreiten; *to keep ~ with*, Schritt halten mit.
pacemaker *s.* Schrittmacher(in) *m.*(*f.*); Herzschrittmacher *m.*

pachyderm *s.* Dickhäuter *m.*
pacific *a.* friedlich, friedsam.
Pacific Ocean *s.* Pazifischer Ozean *m.*
pacifism *s.* Pazifismus *m.*
pacification *s.* Befriedung *f.*

pacifist *s.* Pazifist(in) *m.(f.)*
pacify *v.t.* Frieden stiften; beruhigen.
pack *s.* Packen, Ballen *m.*; Päckchen *n.*; Rudel *n.*, Meute *f.*; (Karten)Spiel *n.*; Tornister *m.*; **~-horse** *s.* Packpferd *n.*; ~ *radio set*, Tornisterempfänger *m.*; ~ *receiver,* Tornisterempfänger *m.* *(radio);* **~-saddle** *s.* Packsattel *m.*; ~ *v.t.* packen; parteüsch zusammensetzen; ~ *v.i.* einpacken; sich packen.
package *s.* Verpackung *f.*, Packet *n.*; *v.t.* verpacken.
package tour *s.* Pauschalreise *f.*
packaging *s.* Verpackung *f.*
packed *a.* gepackt; bepackt.
packet-boat *s.* Postschiff *n.*
packing *s.* Verpackungsmaterial *n.*; Verpacken *n.*
pack-thread *s.* Bindfaden *m.*
pact *s.* Vertrag *m.*
pad *s.* Block *(m.)* Papier; Polster *n.*, Kissen *n.*; Bausch, Wulst *m.*; Unterlage *f.*; ~ *v.t.* polstern, wattieren.
padded *a.* gepolstert.
padding *s.* Polsterung *f*
paddle *s.* Paddel *n.*; Rührholz *n.*; Schaufel *f.*; ~ *v.i.* paddeln; plätschern, waten.
paddle-steamer *s.* Raddampfer *m.*
paddle-wheel *s.* Schaufelrad *n.*
paddling pool *s.* Plauschbechen *n.*
paddock *s.* Gehege *n.*; Koppel *f.*
padlock *s.* Vorhängeschloß *n.*
pagan *s.* Heide *m.*; ~ *a.* heidnisch.
paganism *s.* Heidentum *n.*
page *s.* Page *m.*; Diener *m.*; (Buch)seite *f.*; ~ *v.t.* mit Seitenzahlen bezeichnen; ausrufen lassen; anpiepsen (Beeper, Telefon).
pageant *s.* Prunkaufzug, Festzug *m.* **beauty ~** Schönheitswettbewerb *m.*
pageantry *s.* Prunk *m.*; Gepränge *n.*
pager *s.* Piepser *m.*
paginate *v.t.* paginieren.
pagoda *s.* Pagode *f.*
pail *s.* Eimer *m.*
pain *s.* Schmerz *m.*; **~s** *pl.* Mühe *f.*; Leiden *n.pl.*; ~ *v.t.* Schmerzen bereiten.
painful *a.*, **~ly** *adv.* schmerzhaft; mühsam.
painkiller *s.* schmerzstillendes Mittel *n.*
painless *a.* schmerzlos.
painstaking *a.* äußerst sorgsam.
paint *v.t.* malen; anstreichen; ~ *v.i.* sich schminken; ~ *s.* Farbe *f.*; Schmink *f.*
paint-box *s.* Malkasten *m.*
paintbrush *s.* Pinsel *m.*
painter *s.* Maler(in) *m.(f.)*
painting *s.* Malerei *f.*; Gemälde *n.*
pair *s.* Paar *n.*; ~ *v.t.* (*v.i.* sich) paaren.
pajamas *s.pl.* Pyjama *m.*, Schlafanzug *m.*
Pakistan *s.* Pakistan *n.*
Pakistani *a.* pakistanisch; ~ *s.* Pakistani *m./f.*; Pakistaner(in) *m.(f.)*
pal *s.* *(sl.)* Kamerad, *m.* Kumpel *m.*
palace *s.* Palast *m.*
palatable *a.* schmackhaft.
palatal *a.* Gaumen . . .
palate *s.* Gaumen *m.*
palatial *s.* palastartig.
palaver *s.* Gespräch, Geschwätz *n.*; Umstrand *m.*
pale *a.*, **~ly** *adv.* blaß, bleich; **~-ale** *s.* helles Bier *n.*; ~ *s.* Pfahl *m.*; ~ *v.t.* pfählen; ~ *v.i.* bleich werden

(v.i.)
paleness *s.* Blässe *f.*
Palestine *s.* Palästina *n.*
Palestinian *s.* palästinensisch; ~ *s.* Palästinenser(in) *m.(f.)*
palette *s.* Palette *f.*
palfrey *s.* Zelter *m.*
palisade *s.* Pfahlwerk *n.*
pall *s.* Sargtuch *n.*; ~ *v.t.* *(fig.)* langweilen; ~ *v.i.* schal werden.
pall-bearer *s.* Sargträger(in) *m.(f.)*
pallet *s.* Strohsack *m.*; Palette *f.*
palliasse *s.* Strohsack *m.*
palliate *v.t.* bemänteln; lindern.
palliative *a.* beschönigend, lindernd; ~ *s.* Linderungsmittel *n.*
pallid *a.*, **~ly** *adv.* blaß, bleich.
pallor *s.* Blässe *f.*
palm *s.* Palme *f.*; Handfläche *f.*; ~ *v.t.* betrügen; ~ *off,* aufschwindeln.
palmistry *s.* Handlesekunst *f.*
Palm Sunday *s.* Palmsonntag *m.*
palm-tree *s.* Palme *f.*
palmy *a.* palmenreich; *(fig.)* siegreich; glücklich.
palpable *a.*, **~bly** *adv.* greifbar, fühlbar; deutlich.
palpitate *v.i.* pochen (vom Herzen).
palpitation *s.* Herzklopfen *n.*
palsied *a.* gelähmt.
palsy *s.* Lähmung *f.*
paltry *a.* armselig, erbärmlich.
pamper *v.t.* verwöhnen; verhätscheln.
pamphlet *s.* Flugschrift *f.*
pamphleteer *s.* Verfasser von Flugschriften *m.*
pan *s.* Kochtopf *m.*; Pfanne *f.*; *v.t. & i.* (die Kamera) schwenken.
panacea *s.* Allheilmittel *n.*
Panama *s.* Panama *n.*
Panamanian *a.* panamaisch; *s.* Panamer(in) *m.(f.)*
pancake *s.* Pfannkuchen *m.*
pancreas *s.*Bauchspeicheldrüse *f.*; Pankreas *m.*
panda *s.* Panda *m.*
pandemonium *s.* Tumult *m.*; Heidenlärm *m.*
pander *s.* Kuppler *m.*; ~ *v.i.* kuppeln; Vorschub leisten.
pane *s.* Glaßscheibe *f.*
panegyrist *s.* Lobredner *m.*
panel *s.* (Tür-) Füllung *f.*; Fach, Feld *n.*; Geschworenenliste *f.*; Kommission *f.*
paneling *s.* Täfelung *f.*
panelist *s.* Mitglied (Kommission, Gremium).
pang *s.* Stich, Schreck *m.*
panic *s.* Panik *f.*
panicky *a.* beunruhigend; unruhig.
panic-stricken *a.* von Panik erfaßt.
panoply *s.* völlige Rüstung *f.*
panorama *s.* Panorama *n.*
pansy *f.* *(bot.)* Stiefmütterchen *n.*
pant *v.i.* schnappen (nach Luft); keuchen; lechzen; pochen.
panther *s.* Panther *m.*
panties *s.pl.* Schlüpfer *m.*
pantomime *s.* Pantomime *f.*
pantry *s.* Speisekammer *f.*
pants *s.pl.* (Herren-) Unterhosen *f.pl.*; Hosen *f.pl.*
pap *s.* Kinderbrei *m.*
papa *s.* Papa *m.*

papacy s. Papsttum n.
papal a. päpstlich.
paper s. Papier n.; Zettel m.; Abhandlung f.; Zeitung f.; ~s pl. Schriften f.pl.; Akten, Legitimationspapiere pl.; to read a ~, einen Vortrag halten; to commit to ~, zu Papier bringen; ~**back** s. Taschenbach n.; ~**bag** s. Tüte f.; ~**clamp** s. (grosse) Papierklammer f.; ~**clip** s. (kleine) Papierklammer f.; ~**credit** s. Wechselkredit m.; ~**napkin** s. Papierserviette f.; ~**work** s. Büroarbeit f.; ~**bound** a. broschiert; ~ a. papieren; ~ v.t. tapezieren.
paper-chase s. Schnitzeljagd f.
paper-hanger s. Tapezier m.
paper-mill s. Papiermühle f.
paper money s. Papiergeld n.
paper napkin s. Papierserviette f.
paper-weight s. Briefbeschwerer m.
paperwork s. Schreibarbeit f.
papier-maché s. Papiermaché n.
papist s. Papist(in) m.(f.)
par s. Gleichheit f.; Pari n.; at ~, pari.
parable s. Parabel f.; Gleichnis n.
parabola s. (geom.) Parabel f.
parabolic a. gleichnisweise; parabolisch.
parachute s. Fallschirm m.; ~**flare** s. Fallschirmleuchtbombe f.
parachutist s. Fallschirmspringer(in) m.(f.)
parade s. Gepränge n.; Parade f.; ~ v.t. aufziehen; ~ v.t. prunken mit.
parade ground s. Exerzierplate m.
paradigm s. Beispiel n., Paradigma n.
paradise s. Paradies n.
paradox s. Paradox n.
paradoxical a., ~**ly** adv. paradox.
paraffin s. Paraffin n.; Petroleum n.
paragon s. Muster, Urbild n.
paragraph s. Abschnitt m.
parakeet s. Sittich m.
parallel a. parallel, gleichlaufend; entsprechend; ~ **bars** pl. Barren (Turnen) m.; (elek.) ~ **connection** s. Nebeneinanderschaltung f.; ~ s. Parallelinie f.; Ähnlichkeit, Vergleich m. ~ v.t. gleichmachen; gleichkommen, vergleichen.
paralysis s. Lähmung f.
paralytic a. gelähmt; ~ s. Gelähmte m./f.
paralyze v.t. lähmen.
parameter s. Parameter m.
paramilitary a. paramilitärisch.
paramount a. oberst, höchst.
paranoia s. Paranoia f.
parapet s. Brustwehr f.; Geländer n.
paraphernalia s. Drum und Dran n.
paraphrase s. Umschreibung f.; ~ v.t. umschreiben.
paraplegia s. Paraplegie f.; Querschnittslähmung f.
parasite s. Schmarotzer m.
parasitic s. parasitisch, parasitär.
parasol s. Sonnenschirm m.
paratroops s.pl. Fallschirmtruppen f.pl.
paratyphoid s. Paratyphus m.
parboil v.t. halbgar kochen, ankochen.
parcel s. Stück n.; Teil m.; Partie, Anzahl f., Posten (Ware) m.; Paket n., Päckchen n.; ~ of land, Parzelle f.; ~ post Paketpost f.; ~s company s. Paketfahrtgesellschaft f.; ~s office (rail.), Gepäckabfertigung f.; ~ v.t. teilen, zerstückeln.

parch v.t. dörren; austrocknen; ~ v.i. verdorren.
parchment s. Pergament n.
pardon s. Verzeihung, Begnadigung f.; beg your ~? was beliebt?; wie, bitte?; ~ v.t. verzeihen, begnadigen.
pardonable a., ~**bly** adv. verzeihlich.
pare v.t. schneiden; schälen.
parent s. Elternteil m.; Vater m.; Mutter f.; ~ **company** s. Muttergesellschaft; ~s pl. Eltern pl.
parentage s. Abstammung f.
parental a. elterlich.
parenthesis s. Klammer f., Parenthese f.
parenthetical a. eingeschaltet, beiläufig.
parenthood s. Elternschaft f.
paring s. Schale f.; Abfall m.
parish s. Kirchspiel n.; Pfarrbezirk m., Gemeinde f. ~**register** s. Kirchenbuch n.
parishioner s. Gemeindemitglied n.
parity s. Gleichheit f.; Umrechnungskurs m.
park s. Park m.; ~ v.t. (Autos) parken; No parking! Parken verboten! (fam.) deponieren.
parking; ~ attendant s. Parkplatzwächter m.; ~**meter** s. Parkuhr f.; ~**space** s. Parkplatz m.; ~**ticket** s. Strafzettel m.
parlance s. Redeweise f.
parliament s. Parlament n.
parliamentary a. Parlaments. . . , parlamentarisch; ~ division, Wahlbezirk m.
parlor s. Wohnzimmer n.; Salon m.
parochial a. Pfarr. . . , Gemeinde. . . ; (fig.) Kirchturms. . .
parody s. Parodie f.; ~ v.t. parodieren.
parole s. Ehrenwort n.; Losung f; bedingte Strafaussetzung f.
paroxysm s. heftiger Anfall m.; Krampf m.
parquet s. Parkett n.
parricide s. Vatermord m.; Vatermörder m.
parrot s. Papagei m.; ~ v.t. nachplappern.
parry v.t. & i. abwehren, parieren.
parsimonious a., ~**ly** adv. sparsam.
parsimony s. Sparsamkeit f.
parsley s. Petersilie f.
parsnip s. Pastinake f.
parson s. Pfarrer m.; (fam.) Pfaffe m.
parsonage s. Pfarrei f.; Pfarrhaus f.
part s. Teil, Anteil m.; Rolle f.; Schuldigkeit f.; Gegend f.; ~s pl. Anlagen pl., Talent n.; Gegenden f.pl.; in ~, teilweise; to take in good ~, gut aufnehmen; on my ~, meinerseits; ~**payment**, Teilzahlung, Abschlagszahlung f.; ~ v.t. teilen; trennen; ~ v.i. sich trennen; abreisen.
partake v.i.st. teilnehmen, teilhaben.
partial a., ~**ly** adv. teilweise; parteiisch.
partiality s. Vorliebe, Parteilichkeit f.
participant s. Teilnehmer(in) m.(f.)
participate v.i. teilnehmen, teilhaben.
participle s. (gram.) Partizip.
particle s. Teilchen n.; Partikel f.
particolored a. buntfarbig.
particular a., ~**ly** adv. besonder; einzeln; sondebar; seltsam; wählerisch, genau, einzeln; ~ s.. Einzelheit f.; besonderer Umstand m.; further ~ s, Näheres m.
particularity s. Besonderheit f.; Umständlichkeit f.
parting s. Scheiden f.; Scheitel m.; ~ a. Scheide. . .
partisan s. Parteigänger m.; Guerillakreiger, Partisan m.

partition s. Teilung f.; Scheidewand f.; ~ v.t. teilen, abteilen.
partitive a., ~ly adv. teilend, partitiv.
partly adv. teils, zum Teil.
partner s. Teilnehmer m.; Gefährte m.; Teilhaber m.; Tanzpartner(in) m.(f.); Speilgegner m.; silent ~, stiller Teilhaber m.
partnership s. Genossenschaft f.; Handelsgesellschaft f.; Teilhaberschaft f.; general ~, offene Handelsgesellschaft f.; to enter into ~ with, sich assoziieren mit.
partridge s. Rebhuhn n.
part-time a. Teilzeit...; Halbtags...
party s. Partei f.; Gesellschaft, Partie f.; Teilnehmer m.; to be a ~ to, beteiligt sein an; ~line s. Parteilinie f.; ~official s. Parteifunktionär m.; ~politics s.
parvenu s. Emporkömmling m.
paschal a. Oster...
pass v.i. gehen, vorübergehen; vergehen; fahren; felten; geschehen; to ~ away, sterben; to ~ in the opposite direction, (mot.) kreuzen; ~ v.t. verbringen; übertragen; überschicken; gehen lassen; bestätigen; (Gesetz) annehmen; verleben; passieren; überschreiten; (mot.) überholen; to ~ an examination, eine Prüfung bestehen; to ~ on, weiterleiten; to be ~ed as fit, für tauglich befunden werden; ~ s. Paß, Weg, Durchgang m.; Passierschein, Ausweis m.; Stoß (im Fechten) m.; Zustand m.; Lage f.
passable a., ~bly adv. gangbar; mittelmäßig.
passage s. Durchgang m.; Durchfahrt f.; Hausflur f.; Gang m.; Überfahrt f.; (Buch) Stelle f.; Verabschiedung f. (eines Gesetzes).
passage-way s. Gang m.
pass-book s. Kontobuch n.
passenger s. Reisende m./f.; Passagier m.; ~ train, Personenzug m.; ~ traffic, Personenverkehr m.
passer-by s. Passant(in) m.(f.)
passing a. vorübergehend, flüchtig; ~, ~ly adv. sehr, äusserst; in ~, im Vorübergehen.
passion s. Leidenschaft f.; Zorn m.; to fly into a ~, zornig werden; Passion of Christ, Leiden Christi n., Passion f.
passionate a.,~ly adv. leidenschaftlich.
passion-flower s. Passionsblume f.
passion-fruit s. Passionsfrucht f.
passive a., ~ly adv. leidend; untätig; passiv; ~ s. (gram.) Passivum n.
passiveness s., **passivity** s. Passivität f.
Passover s. Passah(fest) n.
passport s. Paß m.
password s. Losung f.; Kennwort n.
past a. & pr. vergangen, vorbei, über... hinaus; ~ master, Altmeister m.; Experte m.; ~ s. Vergangenheit f.
pasta a. Teigwaren pl.
paste s. Teig m.; Kleister m.; Paste f.; ~v.t. kleistern, pappen.
pasteboard s. Pappdeckel m., Karton m.
pastel s. Pastell n.
pastern s. Fessel am Pferdefuß f.
pasteurize v.t. pasteurisieren.
pastil(le) s. Räucherkerzchen n.
pastime s. Zeitvertreib m.
pastor s. Pfarrer m., Pastor m.
pastoral s. Hirten...; pastoral; ~letter s. Hirtenbrief m.; ~ s. Schäfergedicht n.

pastry s. Backwerk n., Kuchen m.
pastrycook s. Konditor m.
pasture s. Weide f.; ~ v.t. & i. weiden.
pat s. Schlag, Patsch m.; Scheibchen n.; ~ a. bequem, passend; ~ v.t. patschen, streicheln; klopfen.
patch s. Fleck m.; Stück n.; Flicken m.; Schönheitspflästerschen n.; ~ v.t. flicken, ausbessern
patchwork s. Patchwork n.
patchy a. ungleich, zusammengestoppelt.
patent a. offen; patentiert; letters ~, Freibrief m.; ~ s. Vorrecht, Patent n.; to take out a ~ for a thing, sich etwas patentieren lassen; ~ pending, angemeldetes Patent; renewal of a ~, Patentverlängerung f.; ~ agent, ~ lawyer s. Patentanwalt m.; ~grant, Patenterteilung; f. ~holder s. Patentinhaber m.; ~holding company, Patentinhabergesellschaft f.; ~ Office, Patentamt n.; ~ v.t. patentieren.
patent-leather s. Lackleder n.
paternal a. väterlich.
paternity s. Vaterschaft f.
path s. Pfad, Fußsteig m.; Weg m.
pathetic a., ~ally adv. rührend, traurig.
pathological a., ~ly adv. pathologisch.
pathology s. Krankheitslehre f., Pathologie f.
pathos s. Feierlichkeit f.; Rührung f.
pathway s. Fußweg m.
patience s. Geduld f.
patient a., ~ly adv. geduldig; ~ s. Kranke m./f., Patient(in) m.(f.)
patio s. Veranda f.; Terrasse f.; Patio m.
patriarch s. Patriarch m.
patriarchal a. patriarchalisch.
patrician s. Patrizier m.; ~ a. patrizisch.
patrimony s. Erbgut, Erbteil n.
patriot s. Patriot(in) m.(f.)
patriotic s. patriotisch.
patriotism s. Vaterlandsliebe f.; Patriotismus m.
patrol s. Patrouille f., Spähtrupp m.; ~activity, Spähtrupptätigkeit f.; ~ v.i. patrouillieren.
patron s. Gönner(in) m.(f.); Schirmherr(in) m.(f.)
patronage s. Gönnerschaft f.; Schutz m.
patronize v.t. beschützen, begünstigen; als Kunde besuchen; gönnerhaft behandeln.
patter v.i. prasseln; trippeln.; Prasseln n.; Trippeln n.
pattern s. Muster n.; Schnitt m., Schnittmuster n.
patty s. Pastetchen n.
paucity s. Mangel m.
paunch s. Wanst m.
pauper s. Arme m./f.
pause s. Ruhepunkt, Absatz m.; Pause f.; ~ v.i. pausieren; sich besinnen.
pave v.t. pflastern; bahnen.
pavement s. Pflaster n.; Bürgersteig m.
pavilion s. Zelt n.; Pavillon m.
paving-stone s. Pflasterstein m.
paw s. Pfote, Tatze f.; ~ v.t. scharren; streicheln; tölpisch angreifen.
pawn s. Pfand n.; Bauer (im Schach) m.; Pranke f. ~ v.t. verpfänden.
pawnbroker s. Pfandleiher m.
pawnshop s. Pfandhaus n.; Leihhaus n.
pawn-ticket s. Pfandschein m.
pay v.t.ir. zahlen; abstatten; to ~ for, bezahlen; to ~

down, bar bezahlen; *to ~ in*, einzahlen; *to ~ off*, abzahlen (Schuld); *to ~ in advance*, im voraus bezahlen; *to ~ after receipt*, nach Erhalt der Rechnung bezahlen; *to ~ attention*, achtgeben; *to ~ a call, visit*, einen Besuch abstatten; *to ~ the piper*, die Zeche bezahlen; *~ v.i.* sich lohnen, rentieeren; *~ s.* Bezahlung *f.*; Lohn *m.*; **~-day** *s.* Zahltag *m.*; **~-envelope** *s.* Lohntüte *f.*

payable *a.* zahlbar, fällig.

payee *s.* Zahlungsempfänger(in) *m.(f.)*

payer *s.* Zahler *m.*; Bezogene *m.*

paying guest *s.* zahlender Gast *m.*; *to take paying guests*, zahlende Gäste aufnehmen.

payload *s.* Nutzlast *f.*

paymaster *s.* Zahlmeister *m.*

payment *s.* Bezahlung *f.*; *against ~*, gegen Bezahlung; *~ order*, Zahlungsbefehl *m.*; *action for ~*, Schuldklage *f.*; *~ on account*, Abschlagszahlung *f.*; *to stop, suspend ~*, Zahlungen einstellen.

pay phone *s.* Münzfernsprecher *m.*

pay-rise *s.* Gehaltserhöhung *f.*

payroll *s.* Lohnliste *f.*

pay slip *s.* Gehaltsstreifen *m.*

pea *s.* Erbse *f.*; *sweet ~*, Edelwicke *f.*

peace *s.* Freide *m.*; Ruhe *f.*; *to keep the ~*, Ruhe halten; **~-maker** *s.* Freidensstifter *m.*; **~-treaty** *s.* Friedensvertrag *m.*

peaceable *a.*, **~bly** *adv.* friedfertig; friedlich.

peaceful *a.*, **~ly** *adv.* friedlich, ruhig.

peaceloving *a.* friedliebend.

peacemaker *s.* Friedensstifter(in) *m.(f.)*

peach *s.* Pfirsich *m.*

peacock *s.* Pfau *m.*

peahen *s.* Pfauhenne *f.*

pea-jacket *s.* (*nav.*) Tuchjacke *f.*

peak *s.* Gipfel *m.*; Spitze *f.*; Höhepunkt *m.*; Höchststand *m.*; *~v.i.* den Höhepunkt erreichen.

peak-hour *s.* Stoßzeit *f.*

peaky *a.* kränklich.

peal *s.* Schall *m.*; Geläut *n.*; Gekrach *n.*; *~ v.i.* schallen, krachen.

peanut *s.* Erdnuß *f.*

pear *s.* Birne *f.*

pearl *s.* Perle *f.*; Perlschrift *f.*; *real ~*, echte Perle; **~-barley**, Perlgraupen *pl.*

pearl-oyster *s.* Perlmuschel *f.*

pear-tree *s.* Birnbaum *m.*

peasant *s.* Bauer *m.*

peasantry *s.* Landvolk *n.*

peat *s.* Torf *m.*

pebble *s.* Kiesel *m.*

pebbly *a.* steinig.

peccadillo *s.* kleine Sünde *f.*; Fehler *m.*

peck *s.* Viertelscheffel *m.*; Menge *f.*; *~ v.t.* picken, hacken.

pecking order *s.* Hackordnung *f.*

peckish *a.* (*fam.*) hungrig.

pectin *s.* Pektin *n.*

pectoral *a.* Brust. . .

peculiar *a.* eigen, eigentümlich; **~ly** *adv.* besonders.

peculiarity *s.* Eigentümlichkeit *f.*

pecuniary *a.* Geld. . .

pedagogic(al) *a.* pädagogisch.

pedagogue *s.* Erzieher(in) *m.(f.)*; (*pej.*) Pedant *m.*

pedagogy *s.* Pädagogik *f.*

pedal *s.* Trittbrett *n.*, Pedal *n.*

pedant *s.* Pedant(in) *m.(f.)*

pedantic *a.* pedantisch.

pedantry *s.* Pedanterie *f.*

peddle *v.i.* hausieren.; Straßenhandel betrieben.

peddler *s.* Hausierer *m.*; *drug ~*, Drogenhändler(in) *m.(f.)*

pedestal *s.* Sockel *m.*

pedestrian *s.* Fußgänger(in) *m.(f.)*

pedestrian crossing *s.* Fußgängerüberweg *m.*

pedicure *s.* Pediküre *f.*

pedigree *s.* Stammbaum *m.*; **~-dog**, Rassehund, Zuchthund *m.*

peek *v.i.* (verstohlen) gucken; einen kurzen Blick werfen; *~s.* flüchtiger Blick *m.*

peel *s.* Schale, Rinde *f.*; *~ v.t.* (*v.i.* sich) schälen.

peeler *s.* (Kartoffel) Schäler *m.*

peelings *s.pl.* Schalen *pl.*

peep *v.i.* gucken, neugierig blicken; *~out*, zum Vorschein kommen, (*fam.*) hervorgucken; piepen; *~s.* Blick *m.*; Piepsen *n.*; (*sl*) Pieps *m.*

peep-hole *s.* Guckloch *n.*

peer *s.* Gefährte *m.*; Ebenbürtige *m.*; Peer, Hochadlige *m.*

peerage *s.* Peerswürde *f.*; Peers *m.pl.*; Handbuch des englischen Adels *n.*

peeress *s.* Gemahlin eines Peers *f.*

peer group *s.* Peer-group *f.*; Gleichaltrigengruppe *f.*

peerless *a.*, **~ly** *adv.* unvergleichlich.

peevish *a.*, **~ly** *adv.* verdrießlich; quengelig.

peewit *s.* Kiebitz *m.*

peg *s.* Pflock; Wirbel *m.*; Holzstift *m.*; *~ v.t.* stabilisieren, stützen.

pejorative *a.* pejorativ; abwertend.

pelican *s.* Pelikan *m.*

pellet *s.* Kügelchen *n.*

pell-mell *adv.* durcheinander.

pellucid *a.* durchsichtig.

pelt *s.* Fell *n.*; Haut *f.*; *~ v.t.* werfen, bewerfen; *~ v.i.* dicht fallen, stark regnen; *~ing rain*, Platzregen *m.*

pelvis *s.* Becken *n.*

pen *s.* Schreibfeder *f.*; Füllhalter *m.*; Kugelschreiber *m.*; Pferch *m.* *~ v.t.* niederschreiben; einpferchen.

penal *a.* Straf. . ., strafbar; *~ clause* (*law*) Strafklausel *f.*; *~ administration*, Strafvollzug *m.*; *~ code* *s.* Strafgesetzbuch *n.*; *~ law* *s.* Strafgesetz *n.*; *~ reform*, Strafrechtsreform *f.*; *~ servitude* *s.* Zuchthausstrafe *f.*; *~ servitude for life*, lebenslängliches Zuchthaus *n.*

penalize *v.t.* bestrafen; benachteiligen.

penalty *s.* Strafe, Buße *f.*; **~kick** *s.* Elfmeter *m.*

penance *s.* Buße *f.*

pencil *s.* Stift *m.*; Bleistift *m.*; *drawing ~*, Zeichenstift *m.*; *colored ~* Farbstift *m.*

pencil sharpener *s.* Bleistiftspitzer *m.*

pendant *s.* Anhänger (*m.*) an Kette.

pendent *a.* überhängend.

pending *a.* schwebend, unentschieden; *~ case*, (*law*) anhängige Sache *f.*

pendulum *s.* Pendel *n.*

penetrable *a.* durchdringlich.

penetrate *v.t. & i.* durchdringen; ergründen; (*mil.*) eindringen.

penetrating *a.* durchdringend; scharfsinnig.

penetration *s.* Durchdringung *f.* Eindringen *n.*;

Scharfsinn *m.*; (*mil.*) Einbruch *m.*
penguin *s.* Pinguin *m.*
pen-holder *s.* Federhalter *m.*
penicillin *s.* Penizillin *n.*
peninsula *s.* Halbinsel *f.*
penis *s.* Penis *m.*
penitence *s.* Buße, Reue *f.*
penitent *a.*, **~ly** *adv.* bußfertig; ~ *s.* Büßer(in) *m.(f.)*
penitentiary *s.* Strafvollzugsanstalt *f.*
pen-knife *s.* Federmesser *m.*
penmanship *s.* Schreibekunst *f.*
penname *s.* Schriftstellername *m.*
pennant, pennon *s.* Wimpel *m.*
penniless *a.* ohne Geld; mittellos.
penny *s.* Penny *m.*
penny-pinching *s.* Pfennigfuchserei *f.*
pen-pal *s.* Brieffreund(in) *m.(f.)*
pension *s.* Kostgeld *n.*; Ruhegehalt *n.*; ~, Pension *f.*; ~ *v.t.* pensionieren.
pensionable *a.* pensionsberechtigt, pensionsfähig.
pensioner *s.* Rentner(in) *m.(f.)*; Pensionär(in) *m.(f.)*
pensive *a.*, **~ly** *adv.* gedankenvoll, nachdenklich; tiefsinnig.
pent *a.* ~ *up*, aufgestaut, verhalten.
pentagon *s.* Fünfeck *n.*
pentathlon *s.* Fünfkampf *m.*
Pentecost *s.* Pfingsten *pl.*
penthouse *s.* Penthouse, -haus *n.*
penurious *a.*, **~ly** *adv.* karg; dürftig.
penury *s.* Dürftigkeit *f.*; Mangel *m.*
peony *s.* Päonie *f.*, Pfingstrose *f.*
people *s.* Volk *n.*; Leute *pl.*, (*fam.*) man; ~ *say*, man sagt; ~ *v.t.* bevölkern.
peopled *a.* bevölkert.
People's Republic of China *s.* Volksrepublik China *f.*
pep *s.* Schwung; *v.t.* aufpeppen.
pepper *s.* Pfeffer *m.*; (*red, green, yellow*) rote, grüne, gelbe Paprika *m.* ~ *v.t.* pfeffern.
peppercorn *s.* Pfefferkorn *n.*
pepper mill *s.* Pfeffermihle *f.*
peppermint *s.* Pfefferminze *f.*
peppery *n.* pfeffrig; scharf.
per *pr.* durch; *as* ~, laut; ~ *annum*, pro Jahr; ~ *cent*, Prozent *n.*; ~ *diem allowance*, Tagegeld *n.*; ~ *pound*, pro Pfund; ~ *rail*, per Bahn.
perceive *v.t.* wahrnehmen; merken.
percentage *s.* Prozentsatz *m.*; ~ **sign** *s.* Prozentzeichen *n.*
perceptible *a.*, **~bly** *adv.* wahrnehmbar.
perception *s.* Empfindung *f.*; Wahrnehmung *f.*; Anschauung, Vorstellung *f.*
perceptive *a.* einfühlsam; scharfsinnig.
perch *s.* Aufsitzstange, (*fam. fig.*) hoher Sitz; Hühnerstange *f.*; Barsch *m.*; Rute *f.* (5,029 m.); ~ *v.i.* aufsitzen (von Völgeln); ~ *v.t.* setzen.
percolate *v.t.* durchseihen, durchsickern; durchlaufen.
percolator *s.* Kaffeemaschine *f.*
percussion *s.* Schlagzeug *n.*
peregrination *s.* Reise, Wanderschaft *f.*
peremptory *a.*, **~ily** *adv.* bestimmt; endgültig; herrisch; dogmatisch.
perennial *a.* (Pflanzen) ausdauernd; dauernd.

perfect *a.*, **~ly** *adv.* vollkommen, vollendet; ~ *s.* (*gram.*) Perfekt(um) *n.*; ~ *v.t.* vervollkommnen.
perfection *s.* Vollkommenheit *f.*
perfectionism *s.* Perfektionismus *m.*
perfectionist *s.* Perfektionist(in) *m.(f.)*
perfidious *a.* treulos.
perfidy *s.* Treulosigkeit *f.*
perforate *v.t.* durchbohren.
perforation *s.* Perforation *f.*; Loch *n.*
perforator *s.* Locher, Lochapparat *m.*
perforce *adv.* notgedrungen.
perform *v.t.* vollziehen, erfüllen, verrichten, vollenden; durchführen, ausführen; ~ *v.i.* wirken; spielen (eine Rolle), aufführen; vortragen.
performance *s.* Leistung, Vollziehung *f.*; Aufführung *f.*
performer *s.* Ausführende *m./f.*
perfume *s.* Wohlgeruch *m.*; Parfüm, *n.*; ~ *v.t.* parfümieren.
perfumery *s.* Parfümerie(n) *f.pl.*
perfunctory *a.* oberfiächlich, sorglos.
perhaps *adv.* vielleicht.
peril *s.* Gefahr *f.*; *at your* ~, auf eigene Gefahr.
perilous *a.*, **~ly** *adv.* gefährlich.
perimeter *s.* Umkreis *m.*; Begrenzung *f.*
period *s.* Zeitraum *m.*; Periode *f.*; Punkt *m.*; (Unterrichts) Stunde *f.*; (*sp.*) Spielabschnitt *m.* ~ *furniture* *s.* Stilmöbel *pl.*
periodic(al) *a.*, **~ly** *adv.* periodisch; ~ *s.* Zeitschrift *f.*
periodicity *s.* regelmässige Wiederkehr *f.*
periodic table *s.* Periodensystem *n.*
peripheral *a.* peripher; marginal.
periphery *s.* Peripherie *f.*
periscope *s.* Sehrohr, Periskop *n.*
perish *v.i.* umkommen.
perishable *a.* leicht verderblich.
peritonitis *s.* Bauchfellentzündung *f.*
perjure *v.t.* ~*o.s.* meineidig werden.
perjury *s.* Meineid *m.*
perk *v.i.* munter werden; durchlaufen (Kaffee); *to* ~ *up*, sich emporstrecken; ~ *v.t.* aufrichten.
perky *a.* lebhaft; munter; keck.
perm *s.* Dauerwelle *f.*
permanence *s.* Fortdauer *f.*
permanent *a.*, **~ly** *adv.* (fort)dauernd, beständig; planmäßig (Beamte); ~ **waves** *pl.* Dauerwellen *f.pl.*
permeable *a.* durchdringlich; durchlässig.
permeate *v.t.* durchdringen.
permissible *a.* zulässig.
permission *s.* Erlaubnis *f.*; *to ask* ~, um Erlaubnis bitten; *by* ~ *of*, mit Erlaubnis von; *by special* ~, mit besonderer Genehmigung.
permissive *a.* tolerant; großzügig; permissiv.
permit *v.t.* gestatten; ~ *s.* Erlaubnisschein *m.*
permutation *s.* Umstellung *f.*; Anordnung *f.*
pernicious *a.*, **~ly** *adv.* verderblich.; bösartig; übel.
peroration *s.* Redeschluß *m.*
perpendicular *a.*, **~ly** *adv.* senkrecht; ~ *s.* senkrechte Linie *f.*, Lot *n.*
perpetrate *v.t.* verüben.
perpetrator *s.* (*law*) Täter(in) *m.(f.)*
perpetual *a.*, **~ly** *adv.* immerwährend.
perpetuate *v.t.* verewigen; fortsetzen.
perpetuity *s.* Ewigkeit *f.*; Fortdauer *f.*; *in* ~, auf

ewig, für immer.
perplex *v.t.* verwirren; bestürzt machen.
perplexed *a.* verwirrt; ratlos.
perplexity *s.* Bestürzung *f.*; Verwirrung *f.*
perquisite *s.* Vergünstigung *f.*
persecute *v.t.* verfolgen.
persecution *s.* Verfolgung *f.*
persecutor *s.* Verfolger(in) *m.*(*f.*)
perseverance *s.* Beharrlichkeit *f.*
persevere *v.i.* beharren, ausdauern.
Persian *a.* persisch; ~ **carpet** *s.* Perserteppich *m.*; ~ **cat** *s.* Perserkatze *f.*
persist *v.i.* beharren, bestehen.
persistence *s.* Beharrlichkeit *f.*
persistent *a.* beharrlich.
person *s.* Person *m.*; Mensch *m.*; *in* ~, persönlich.
personable *a.* sympathisch.
personage *s.* Persönlichkeit *f.*
personal *a.*, ~**ly** *adv.* persönlich; ~ *estate*, bewegliche Habe *f.*; ~ **files** *pl.* Handakten *pl.*
personality *s.* Persönlichkeit *f.*
personalize *v.t.* eine persönliche Note geben; mit Namen/Initialen versehen.
personal: ~ **organizer** *s.* Terminplaner *m.*; ~ **property** *s.* bewegliches Vermögen *n.*
personification *s.* Verkörperung *f.*
personify *v.t.* verkörpern.
personnel *s.* Personal *n.*; ~~**carrier** *s.* Mannschaftstransportwagen *m.*; ~~**file**, Personalakten *pl.*; ~~**section**, Personalabteilung *f.*
perspective *s.* Perspektive, Aussicht, Fernsicht (zeichnung) *f.*; ~ *a.*, ~**ly** *adv.* perspektivisch.
perspicacious *a.* scharfsichtig.
perspicacity *s.* Scharfblick *m.*
perspicuity *s.* Deutlichkeit *f.*
perspicuous *a.*, ~**ly** *adv.* durchsichtig; verständlich.
perspiration *s.* Schweiß *m.*
perspire *v.i.* ausdünsten, schwitzen.
persuadable *a.* leicht zu überreden.
persuade *v.t.* überreden, überzeugen.
persuasion *s.* Überredung *f.*; Überzeugung *f.*
persuasive *a.*, ~**ly** *adv.* überredend; überzeugend.
persuasiveness *s.* Überzeugungskraft *f.*
pert *a.*, ~**ly** *adv.* keck; vorlaut.
pertain *v.i.* gehören, betreffen.
pertinacious *a.*, ~**ly** *adv.* hartnäckig; beharrlich.
pertinacity *s.* Beharrlichkeit *f.*
pertinence *s.* Angemessenheit *f.*
pertinent *a.*, ~**ly** *adv.* angemessen, passend; treffend; relevant.
perturb *v.t.* verwirren, stören; beunruhigen.
perturbation *s.* Beunruhigung *f.*
Peru *s.* Peru *n.*
perusal *s.* Durchlesen *n.*; Durchsicht *f.*
peruse *v.t.* durchlesen; prüfen.
Peruvian *a.* peruavisch; *s.* Peruaner(in) *m.*(*f.*)
pervade *v.t.* durchdringen.
pervasive *a.* durchdringend.
perverse *a.*, ~**ly** *adv.* verkehrt; verstockt; verdorben; pervers.
perversion *s.* Verdrehung *f.*; Abkehr *f.*; Pervertierung *f.*; Perversion *f*
perversity *s.* Verkehrtheit *f.* Eingensinn *m.*; Verdorbenheit *f.*
pervert *v.t.* verdrehen; verführen.

perverted *a.* pervertiert; verdorben.
pesky *a.* (*fam.*) verdammt.
pessimism *s.* Pessimismus *m.*
pessimist *s.* Pessimist *m.*
pessimistic *a.*, ~**ally** *adv.* pessimistisch.
pest *s.* Plage *f.*, Plagegeist *m.*; Pflanzenschädling *m.*
pester *v.t.* belästigen, plagen.
pesticide *s.* Pestizid *s.*
pestiferous *a.* ansteckend; verpestet.
pestilence *s.* Seuche *f.*; Pest *f.*
pestilent *a.* verderblich; lästig.
pestilential *a.*, ~**ly** *adv.* pestartig.
pestle *s.* Mörserkeule *f.*, Stößel *m.*
pet *s.* Haustier *n.*; Liebling *m.*; ~ *a.* Lieblings. . . ; ~ *v.t.* hätscheln.
petal *s.* Blütenblatt *n.*
petard *s.* Sprengbüchse *f.*
peter out *v.i.* allmählich aufhören.; versanden.
pet-food *s.* Tierfutter *n.*
petit bourgeois *s.* Kleinbürger *m.*
petite *a.* zierlich.
petition *s* Gesuch *n.*; Bittschrift *f.*; ~ *v.t.* bitten, anhalten.
petitioner *s.* Bittsteller *m.*
petrel *s.* Sturmvogel *m.*
petrifaction *s.* Versteinerung *f.*
petrify *v.i.* versteinern.
petrol *s.* Benzin; ~ *station*, (*mot.*) Tankstelle *f.*
petroleum *s.* Endöl *n.* Petroleum *n.*; ~ **jelly** *s.* Vaseline *f.*
petticoat *s.* Unterrock *m.*
petty *a.* klein; gering; kleinlich.
petulance *s.* Mutwille *m.*; Verdrießlichkeit *f.*
petulant *a.*, ~**ly** *adv.* mutwillig, ärgerlich; (verdriesslich).
pew *s.* Kirchenstuhl *m.*
pewter *s.* Zinn *m.*
phallic *a.* phallisch.
phantasm *s.* Traumbild, Trugbild *n.*
phantom *s.* Phantom *n.*; Gespenst *n.*
Pharaoh *m.* Pharao *m.*
Pharisee *s.* Pharisäer *m.*
pharmaceutical *a.* pharmazeutisch.
pharmaceutics *s.pl.* Arzneikunde *f.*
pharmacist *s.* Pharmazent(in); Apotheker(in) *m.*(*f.*)
pharmacy *s.* Pharmazie *f.*
pharyngitis *s.* Rachenkatarrh *m.*
pharynx *s.* Rachen *m.*
phase *s.* Phase *f.*
pheasant *s.* Fasan *m.*
phenomenal *a.* phänomenal; Erscheinungs. . . ; außerordentlich groß, etc.
phenomenon *s.* Phänomen *n.*
phial *s.* Fläschchen *n.*
philanderer *s.* Schürzenjäger *m.*
philanthropic *a.* menschenfreundlich.
philanthropist *s.* Menschenfreund(in) *m.*(*f.*)
philanthropy *s.* Menschenliebe *f.*
philatelist *s.* Briefmarkensammler (in) *m.*(*f.*)
philately *s.* Philatelic *f.*; Briefmarkenkunde *f.*
philharmonic *a.* philharmonisch; *s.* Philharmonie *f.*
Philippines *s.pl.* Philippinen *pl.*
philistine *s.* Philister *m.*, Spießer *m.*
philological *a.* philologisch.

philologist s. Philologe m., Philologin f.
philology s. Philologie f.
philosopher s. Philosoph(in) m.(f.); ~'s stone, Stein der Weisen m.
philosophic(al) a., ~ly adv. philosophisch.
philosophize v.i. philosophieren.
philosophy s. Philosophie f.
phlebitis s. Venenentzündung f.
phlegm s. Schleim m.; Phlegma n.
phelgmatic a. phlegmatisch.
phobia s. Phobie f.
phoenix s. Phönix m.
phone s. Telefon n.; ~v.t. telefonieren.
phone: ~ **book** s. Telefonbuch n.; ~ **booth** s. Telefonzelle f.; ~ **call** s. Anruf m.; ~ **card** s. Telefonkarte f.; ~ **number** s. Telefonnummer f.; ~ **tapping** s. Abhören (n.) des Telefons.
phonetic a., ~ally adv. phonetisch.
phonetics s.pl. Phonetik f.
phon(e)y a. falsch; erfunden; ~s. Schwindler(in) m.(f.)
phonograph s. Grammophon n.
phosphate s. Phosphat n.
phosphorescent a, phosphoreszierend.
phosphorus s. Phosphor m.
photo s. Fotografie f., Foto n.
photocopier s. Fotokopierer m.; Fotokopiergerät n.
photocopy s. Fotokopie f.; ~v.t. fotokopieren.
photograph s. Fotografie f., Lichtbild n.; ~ v.t. fotographieren.
photographer s. Fotograph(in) m.(f.)
photographic s. fotographisch.
photography s. Fotografie f.
photosensitive a. lichtempfindlich.
photosynthesis s. Photosynthese f.
phrase s. Redensart f.; Satz m.; ~ v.t. ausdrücken, nennen.
phraseology s. Redeweise f.
physical a., ~ly adv. physikalisch, physisch; körperlich, Körper...; ~ **education** s. Sportunterricht m. ~ **pecularities** pl. besondere Merkmale n.pl. ~ly **disabled** a. körperbehindert.
physician s. Arzt m., Ärztin f.
physicist s. Physiker(in) m.(f.)
physics s. Physik f.
physiognomy s. Gesichtsausdruck m.
physiological a. physiologisch.
physiology s. Physiologie f.
physiotherapy a. Physiotherapie f.
physique s. Körperbeschaffenheit f., Körperbau m.
pianist s. Klavierspieler(in) m.(f.), Pianist(in) m.(f.)
piano s. Klavier n.; grand ~, Flügel m.;
piano: ~ **player** s. Klavierspieler(in) m.(f.); ~-**stool** s. Klavierschemel m.; ~-**tuner** s. Klavierstimmer(in) m.(f.)
piccolo s. Pikkoloflöte f.
pick v.t. & i. picken; hacken; stochern, stechen; pflücken; auflesen; wählen; zupfen; to ~ out, auswählen; to ~ up, aufheben, auflesen; (Passagiere) aufnehmen; (ab)holen; to ~ on a person, an einem herumkritisieren; to ~ a quarrel, mit einem anbinden; to ~ a person's pockets, Taschendiebstahl verüben; ~ s. Auswahl f.; Spitzhammer m.
pickaback adv. huckepack.

pickaxe s. Spitzhacke. f.
picket s. Streikposten m.
pickle s. Salzgurke f.; Gewurzgurke f.; Pökel m. Marinade f.; (fam.) mißliche Lage f.; ~ v.t. einpökeln.
picklock s. Dietrich m.
pick-me-up s. Stärkungsmittel n.
pickpocket s. Taschendieb m.
picnic s. Picknick n., Landpartie f.
pictorial a. illustriert; bildlich; ~ representation, bildliche Darstellung f.
picture s. Bild n.; Porträt n.; Foto n.; ~ v.t. malen; schildern.
picture: ~-**book** s. Bilderbuch n.; ~-**frame** s. Bildervahmen m.; ~-**gallery** s. Gemäldegalerie f.; ~-**hook** s. Bilderhaken m.
picturesque a. malerisch.
piddle v.i. pinkeln, Pipimachen; ~ **away** zeitvertrödeln.
pidgin s. Pidgin n.
pie s. Pastete f.; Elster f.
piebald a. scheckig.
piece s. Stück n.; Scherbe f.; a ~, pro Stück; pro Person; ~-**goods** pl. Stückgüter n.pl.; by the ~, stückweise; to take to ~s, auseinandernehmen; ~ v.t. stücken; flicken.
piecemeal a. & adv. stückweise.
piecework s. Akkordarbeit f.; to do ~, im Akkord arbeiten; ~-**(work) rates** pl. Akkordlöhne pl.
pier s. Pier m.; Pfeiler m.; Steindamm m.; Abfahrtsplatz m., Landungsbrücke f.
pierce v.t. durchstechen; durchbohren; ~ v.i. eindringen; rühren.
piercing a. durchdringend; schneidend.
piety s. Frömmigkeit f.
pig s. Ferkel, Schwein n.; Metallbarren m.
pigeon s. Taube f.; ~-**hole**, Fach n.
piggy: ~**back** adv. huckepack; ~ **bank** s. Sparschwein n.
pig-headed a. dickköpfig.
pig-iron s. Roheisen n.
piglet s. Ferkel n.
pigment s. Farbstoff m.
pigmy s. see pygmy.
pigskin s. Schweinsleder n.
pigsty s. Schweinestall m.
pig-tail s. Haarzopf m.; ~s pl. Ratenschwänzchen pl.
pike s. Pike f.; Hecht m.
pilaster s. Wandpfeiler m.
pilchard s. Sardine f.
pile s. Pfahl m.; Haufen, Stoß (Papier) m.; ~s pl. Hämorrhoiden f.pl.; ~ v.t. aufhäufen.
pile-dwelling s. Pfahlbau m.
pile-up s. Massenkarambolage f.
pilfer v.t. & i. stehlen, mausen.
pilgrim s. Pilger(in) m.(f.)
pilgrimage s. Pilgerfahrt f.
pill s. Pille f.
pillage s. Plünderung f.; ~ v.t. plündern.
pillar s. Pfeiler m.; Säule f.
pillar-box s. (Säulen) Briefkasten m.
pillar-drill s. (mech.) Säulenbohrmaschine f.
pillion s. Beifahrersitz m.
pillory s. Pranger f.; ~ v.t. an den Pranger stellen, anprangern.
pillow s. Kopfkissen n.

pillow-case *s.* Kissenüberzug *m.*

pilot *s.* Lotse *m.*, Lotsin *f.*; (*avi.*) Pilot(in) *m.*(*f.*); **~-plant**, Versuchsfabrik *f.*; **~-jet**, Stichflamme *f.*; ~ *v.t.* steuern, lotsen.

pimp *s.* Kuppler(in) *m.*(*f.*); Zuhälter(in) *m.*(*f.*); ~ *v.i.* kuppeln.

pimpernel *s.* Pimpernelle *f.*

pimple *s.* Pickel *m.*; Pustel *m.*

pimply *a.* pickelig.

pin *s.* Stecknadel *f.*; Stift, Pflock *m.*; Bolzen *m.*; (Instrumenten-)Wirbel *m.*; (Spiel-)Kegel *m.*; ~ *v.t.* anstecken; annageln; *to ~ down*, festnageln (*fig.*); *to ~ up*, anstecken.

pinafore *s.* Schürze *f.*

pin-ball *s.* Flippern; ~ **machine** *s.* Flipper *m.*

pincers *s.pl.* Kneifzange *f.*; Scheren *pl.* (Krebs).

pinch *v.t.* kneifen, zwicken; drücken (Schuh); bedrücken, quälen; (*fam.*) klauen, stibitzen; ~ *v.i.* knausern; darben; ~ *s.* Zwick *m.*; Prise (Tabak) *f.*; Druck *m.*; Not, Verlegenheit *f.*

pinchbeck *s.* Tombak *m.*; ~ *a.* falsch, unecht.

pincushion *s.* Nadelkissen *n.*

pine *s.* Kiefer *f.*; ~ *v.i.* schmachten; sich verzehren.

pineapple *s.* Ananas *f.*

pinecone *s.* Kiefernzapfen *m.*

pineneedle *s.* Kiefernnadel *f.*

ping-pong *s.* Tischtennis *n.*

pinhead *s.* Stecknadelkopf *m.*

pinion *s.* Ritzel *n.*; Zahnrad *n.*; ~ *v.t.* fesseln (an).

pink *a.* blaßrot, rosa.

pinkie *s.* kleiner Finger *m.*

pin-money *s.* Extrageld *n.*; Taschengeld *n.*

pinnacle *s.* Gipfel *m.*; Höhepunkt *m.*

pinpoint *v.t.* genau bestimmen.

pin-prick *s.* Nadelstich *m.*

pin-stripe *s.* Nadelstreifen *m.* (Anzug).

pint *s.* Pinte *f.*

pin-up *s.* Pin-up-Foto *n.*

pioneer *s.* Pionier *m.*; Bahnbrecher *m.*

pious *a.*, **~ly** *adv.* fromm; (*pej.*) heuchlerisch.

pip *s.* Pips *m.*; Auge (in der Karte) *n.*; Obstkern *m.*; ~*v.t.* besiegen.

pipe *s.* Röhre, *f.*; Pfeife *f.*; ~ *v.i.* pfeifen, kreischen.

pipe-cleaner *s.* Pfeifenreiniger *m.*

pipe-dream *s.* Wunschtraum *m.*

pipe-line *s.* Röhrenleitung *f.*; Pipeline *f.*

piper *s.* Pfeifer(in) *m.*(*f.*)

pipette *s.* Pipette *f.*

piping *s.* Zierstreifen *m.* (an Kleidern), Litzenbesatz *m.*; Rohrleitungssystem *n.*; ~ **hot** *a.* siedend heiß.

piquancy *s.* Schärfe *f.*; (*fig.*) Pikanterie *f.*

piquant *a.*, **~ly** *adv.* beißend; pikant.

pique *s.* Groll *m.*; ~ *v.t.* aufreizen; sich brüsten.

piracy *s.* Seeräuberei *f.*

pirate *s.* Seeräuber *m.*; illegaler Nachdrucker *m.*; ~ *v.t.* rauben; illegal nachdrucken.

piratical *a.*, **~ly** *adv.*, räuberisch.

pirouette *s.* Pirouette *f.*; ~ *v.i.* pirouettieren.

Pisces *s.pl.* (*astro.*) Fische *pl.*

pish! *i.* pfui!

piss *s.* (*vulg.*) Pisse *f. m.*; ~ *v.i.* pissen.

pissed off *a.* (*sl.*) stocksauer.

pistachio *s.* Pistazie *f.*

pistil *s.* (*bot.*) Sternpel *m.*

pistol *s.* Pistole *f.*

piston *s.* Kolben *m.*; **~-rod** *s.* Kolbenstange *f.*

pit *s.* Grube *f.*; Graben *m.*; (*theat.*) Parkett *n.*; ~ *v.t.* eingraben; gegeneinander hetzen.

pitch *s.* Pech *n.*; Wurf *m.*; Grad *m.*; Tonhöhe *f.*; Stimmlage *f.*; Tonlage *f.*; Steigung *f.*; ~ *v.t.* befestigen; werfen; aufstellen; orden; (*mus.*) abstimmen; ~ *v.i.* herabstürzen; aufschlagen (Ball); sich.

pitch-dark *a.* pechschwarz, stockfinster.

pitched roof *s.* Schräge Dach *n.*

pitcher *s.* Krug *m.*; Werfer *m.* (Baseball).

pitchfork *s.* Heugabel *f.*; Stimmgabel *f.*

piteous *a.*, **~ly** *adv.* kläglich, erbämlich.

pitfall *s.* Fallgrube, Falle *f.*

pith *s.* Mark *n.*; Kern *m.*; Kraft *f.*; Vorzüglichste *n.*

pithy *a.*, **~ily** *adv.* markig, kräftig.

pitiable *a.* erbärmlich.

pitiful *a.*, **~ly** *adv.* erbärmlich, mitleiderregend; bemitleidenswert.

pitiless *a.*, **~ly** *adv.* unbarmherzig; mitleidlos.

pittance *s.* Hungerlohn *m.*

pity *s.* Mitleid *n.*; *it is a ~*, es ist schade; ~ *v.t.* bemitleiden, bedauern.

pitying *a.* **~ly** *adv.* mitleidig.

pivot *s.* Zapfen *m.*; Drehpunkt *m.*; Angelpunkt *m.*; springender Punkt *m.*; *to ~ on*, *v.i.* sich drehen um.

pivotal *a.* zentral...

pixie *s.* Kobold *m.*

placard *s.* (öffentlicher) Anschlag *m.*, Plakat *n.*; ~ *v.t.* bekanntmachen.

placate *v.t.* besänftigen.

place *s.* Platz *n.*, Stelle *f.*; Ort *m.*; Amt, *n.*; *to take ~*, stattfinden; ~*s of interest, pl.* Sehenswürdigkeiten *pl*; ~ *v.t.* stellen; setzen; unterbringen (Kapital).

place-mat *s.* Set *n./m.* (Tisch).

place-name *s.* Ortsname *m.*

place-setting *s.* Gedeck *n.*

placenta *s.* Plazenta *f.*, Mutterkuchen *m.*

placid *a.*, **~ly** *adv.* gelassen, sanft.

plagiarism *s.* Plagiat *n.*

plagiarist *s.* Plagiator(in) *m.*(*f.*)

plagiarize *v.t.* plagiieren.

plagiary *s.* Plagiat *n.*

plague *s.* Seuche *f.* Plage *f.*; **~-spot** *s.* Pestbeule *f.*; Schandfleck *m.*

plaice *s.* (*zool.*) Scholle *f.*

plaid *s.* Plaid *n./m.*; ~*a.* kariert.

plain *a.* eben, flach; einfach, schlicht; aufrichtig; deutlich; häßlich; **~ly** *adv.* deutlich; ~ *s.* Fläche, Ebene *f.*

plain chocolate *s.* zartbittere Schokolade *f.*

plain clothes *pl.* Zivil(anzug) *n.*

plainness *s.* Klarheit *f.*; Offenheit *f.*;

plain-spoken *a.* ehrlich, aufrichtig.

plaint *s.* Klage *f.*; Beschwerde *f.*

plaintiff *s.* Kläger(in) *m.*(*f.*)

plaintive *a.*, **~ly** *adv.* klagend, kläglich.

plait *s.* Falte *f.*; Flechte *f.*, Zopf *m.*; ~ *v.t.* falten; verflechten.

plaited *a.* geflochten.

plan *s.* Plan, Grundriß *m.*; ~ *v.t.* entwerfen, modeln.

plane *s.* Fläche *f.*; Hobel *m.*; Platane *f.*; ~ *v.t.* ebnen, hobeln; abwärts gleiten.

planer *s.* Hobelmaschine *f.*

planet *s.* Planet *m.*

planetarium *s.* Planetarium *n.*

planetary *a.* planetarisch.

plank *s.* Planke, Bohle *f.*; ~ *v.t.* bohlen, dielen.

plankton *s.* (*biol.*) Plankton *n.*
planner *s.* Planer(in) *m.*(*f.*)
planning *s.* Planen *n.*; Planung *f.*
plant *s.* Pflanze *f.*; Werk *n.*, Fabrik *f.*; Bertriebsanlage *f.*; ~ *v.t. & i.* pflanzen, stiften.
plantation *s.* Pflanzung, Pflanzschule *f.*; Plantage *f.*
planter *s.* Pflanzer(in) *m.*(*f.*)
plaque *s.* Platte *f.*; Plakette *f.*
plash *v,.i.* plätschern.
plasma *s.* Plasma *n.*
plaster *s.* Pflaster *n.*; Mörtel *m.*, Verputz *m.*; ~ *of Paris*, Gips *m.*; ~ *v.t.* bepflastern; verputzen.
plasterboard *s.* Gipsplatte *f.*
plaster cast *s.* Gipsabdruck *m.*; Gipsverband *m,.*
plastered *a.* (*fam.*) voll, blau, betrunken.
plasterer *s.* Gipser *m.*
plastic *a.* plastisch, bildsam.; *s.* Plastik *n.*; Kunststoff *m.*
plastic surgery *s.* plastische Chirurgie *f.*
plate *s.* Metallplatte *f.*; Kupferstich, Stahlstich *m.*; (*phot.*) Platte *f.*; Teller *m.*; Silbergeschirr *n.*; ~ *v.t.* plattieren; (*with gold*) vergolden; panzern.
plateau *s.* Hochebene *f.*; Plateau *n.*
plate-rack *s.* Geschirrständer *m.*
platform *s.* (*rail.*) Bahnsteig *m.*; Rednerbühne *f.*; politische Programm *n.*; ~ **ticket** *s.* Bahnsteigkarte *f.*
platinum *s.* Platin *n.*
platitude *s.* Gemeinplatz *m.*; Platitüde *f.*
platonic *a.* platonisch.
platoon *s.* (*mil.*) Zug *m.*
platter *s.* Schüssel *f.*
plaudit *s.* lauter Beifall *m.*
plausibility *s.* Glaubwürdigkeit *f.*
plausible *a.*, **~bly** *adv.* einleuchtend; glaubwürdig.
play *s.* Spiel *n.*; Schauspiel *n.*, Stück *n.*; Spielraum *m.*; ~ *v.t.* spielen; *to ~ off against*, ausspielen gegen; ~ *v.i.* spielen; scherzen
playable *a.* bespielbar; bühnenreif.
play-bill *s.* Theaterzettel *m.*
player *s.* Spieler(in) *m.*(*f.*); Schauspieler(in) *m.*(*f.*)
playful *a.* spielend; scherzend.
play-ground *s.* Spielplatz *m.*
play group *s.* Spielgruppe *f.*
playhouse *s.* Schauspielhaus *n.*
playing field *s.* Sportplatz *m.*
playmate *s.* Spielkamerad(in) *m.*(*f.*)
play-off *s.* Entscheidungsspiel *n.*
play-pen *s.* Laufställchen *n.*
plaything *s.* Spielzeug *n.*
playwright *s.* Dramatiker(in) *m.*(*f.*)
plea *s.* Gesuch *n.*; Appell *m.*; Verteidigungsrede *f.*
plead *v.i.* vor Gericht reden; ~ *guilty*, sich schuldig bekennen; ~ *v.t.* als Beweis anführen, vorschützen; erörtern; verteidigen.
pleasant *a.*, **~ly** *adv.* angenehm; munter, lustig.
pleasantry *s.* Scherz *m.*
please *v.t. & i.* gefallen; belieben; befriedigen, besänftigen; ~! bitte!; ~ *yourself!*, wie Sie wünschen!
pleased *a.* zufrieden; erfrent.
pleasing *a.*, **~ly** *adv.* gefällig, angenehm.
pleasurable *a.*, **~bly** *adv.* angenehm.
pleasure *s.* Vergnügen *n.*; Belieben *n.*; ~ **cruise** *s.* Vergnügungsfahrt *f.*

pleat *s.* Falte *f.*; ~ *v.t.* fälteln, falten.
pleated *a.* gefältelt; Falten. . .
plebian *a.* pöbelhaft; ~ *s.* gemeiner Mensch *m.*; Pöbel *m.*
plebiscite *s.* Volksentscheid *m.*
plectrum *s.* Plektrum *n.*
pledge *s.* Pfand *n.*; Bürgschaft *f.*; ~ *v.t.* verpfänden, verpflichten; geloben.
plenary *a.*, **~ily** *adv.* vollständig, Voll. . ., Plenar. . .
plenary session *s.* Plenarsitzung *f.*
plenipotentiary *a.* bevollmächtigt; ~ *s.* Bevollmächtige *m.*
plenitude *s.* Fülle *f.*
plentiful *a.*, **~ly** *adv.* reichlich, ergiebig.
plenty *s.* Fülle *f.*; Überfluß *m.*; ~ *of*, vollauf, reichlich, mehr als genug.
pleonasm *s.* Pleonasmus *m.*
plethora *s.* Überfülle *f.*
pleurisy *s.* Brustfell-, Rippenfellentzündung *f.*
pliable *a.*, **~bly** *adv.* biegsam.
pliant *a.*, **~ly** *adv.* biegsam, geschmeidig.
pliers *s.pl.* Drahtzange *f.*
plight *s.* Notlage *f.*
plinth *s.* Sockel *m.*
plod *v.i.* trotten; sich anstrengen; ochsen
plop *v.i.* plumpsen; platschen; ~*s.* Plumps *m.*; Platsch *m.*
plot *s.* Stück (Land) *n.*; Fleck *m.*; Plan *m.*; Anschlag, Putsch *m.*; Verwicklung, Handlung *f.*; ~ *v.i.* sich verschwören, ~ *v.t.* aussinnen, anzetteln; *to ~ the course*, den Kurs abstecken.
plotter *s.* Verschwörer(in) *m.*(*f.*)
plow *s.* Pflug *m.*; ~ *v.t.* pflügen.
ploy *s.* Trick *m.*
pluck *s.* Zug, Ruck *m.*; (*fig.*) Mut *m.*, Schneid *m.*; ~ *v.t.* pflücken, rupfen; *to ~ up courage*, Mut fassen.
plucky *a.* mutig, schneidig.
plug *s.* Pflock, Stöpsel, Zapfen, Dübel *m.*; (*elek.*) Stecker *m.*; ~ *v.t.* zustopfen.
plum *s.* Pflaume, *f.*; Leckbissen *m.*
plumage *s.* Gefieder *n.*
plumb *s.* Bleilot *n.*; ~ *adv.* senkrecht; ~ *v.t.* sondieren; Klempnerarbeit machen.
plumber *s.* Klempner(in), Installateur(in) *m.*(*f.*)
plumbline *s.* Senkblei *n.*
plume *s.* (Schmuck-)Feder *f.*; ~ *v.t.* mit Federn schmücken; rupfen; ~ *v.i.* sich brüsten.
plummet *s.* Bleilot *n.*; ~*v.i.* stürzen.
plump *a.*, **~ly** *adv.* fleischig, dick; derb, gerade heraus; ~*v.i. & t.* schwellen; plumpsen; mästen.
plum-tree *s.* Pflaumenbaum *m.*
plunder *s.* Beute *f.*; Raub *m.*; Plünderung *f.*; ~ *v.t.* plündern.
plunge *v.t. & i.* undertauchen; hinabstürzen; (Pferd) ausschlagen, ~ *s.* Untertauchen *n.*; Sturz *m.*; (*fig.*) Wagnis *n.*
pluperfect *s.* (*gram.*) Plusquamperfekt(um) *n.*
plural *a.* (*gram.*) Mehrzahl *f.*
plurality *s.* Vielzahl *f.*; Pluralität *f.*
plus *a.* (*ar.*) plus; ~*adv.* zusammen mit.
plush *s.* Plüsch *m.*
plutonium *s.* Plutonium *n.*
ply *s.* Falte *f.*; ~*wood*, Sperrholz *n.*; *four~*, (Wolle) vierfach; ~*v.t.* handhaben, treiben; ~*v.i.* gebrauchen; nachgehen (Arbeit).
pneumatic *a.* Luft. . ., pneumatisch.
pneumatic: ~drill *s.* Preßuftbohrer *m.*; **~hammer**

s. Preßlufthammer *m*.
pneumonia *s*. Lungenentzündung *f*.
poach *v.t*. im Wasserbad kochen; wildern; ~ *v.i*. wildern; **~ed eggs** *s.pl*. verlorene Eier *n.pl*.
poacher *s*. Wilddieb *m*., Wilderer *m*.
pock *s*. Pocke, Blatter *f*.
pocket *s*. Tasche *f*.; Loch *n*. (Billiards); ~ *v.t*. einstecken.
pocket-book *s*. Handtasche *f*.
pocket-money *s*. Taschengeld *n*.
pocket-size *a*. im Taschenformat.
pock: ~-mark *s*. Pockennarbe *f*.; *a*. pockennarbig.
pod *s*. Hülse, Schale, Schote *f*.
podgy *a*. dicklich; mollig.
podium *s*. Podium *n*.
poem *s*. Gedicht *n*.
poet *s*. Dichter(in) *m./f*.
poetic(al) *a*., **~ly** *adv*. dichterisch.
poetics *s.pl*. Poetik *f*.
poetry *s*. Dichtkunst *f*.; Gedichte *n.pl*.
poignancy *s*. Schärfe *f*.; Schmerzlichkeit *f*.
poignant *a*., **~ly** *adv*. beißend, scharf; durchdringend.
point *s*. Punkt *m*.; Spitze *f*.; Auge (in der Karte) *n*.; Zweck *m*.; Kompaßstrich *m*.; **~s** *pl*. (*rail*.) Weiche *f*.; **~-blank** *adv*. & *a*. direkt, gerade heraus; *the case in* ~, der betreffende Fall; *on the* ~, im Begriff; *there is no* ~ *in doing that*, es hat keinen Zweck, das zu tun; *that is beside the* ~, das hat damit nichts zu tun; ~ *of view*, *s*. Gesichtspunkt *m*.; ~ *v.t*. hinweisen; *to* ~ *out*, hinweisen auf, anführen.
pointed *a*., **~ly** *adv*. zugespitzt; spitz; punktiert; beißend.
pointer *s*. Zeiger *m*.; Zeigestock *m*.; Vorstehhund *m*.
pointless *a*., sinnlos; belanglos; stumpf.
poise *s*. Gewicht, Gleichgewicht *n*.; Haltung *f*.; ~ *v.t*. wägen; im Gleichgewicht erhalten.
poised *a*. selbstsicher.
poison *s*. Gift *n*.; ~ *v.t*. vergiften.
poisoning *s*. Vergiftung *f*.
poisonous *a*., **~ly** *adv*. giftig.
poke *s*. Stoß *m*.; Puff *m*.; ~ *v.t*. tappen; schüren; stossen.
poker *s*. Schüreisen *n*.; Poker *n*.
poker-faced *a*. mit unbeweglichem Gesicht.
polar *a*. polar, Pol. . .
polar bear *s*. Eisbär *m*.
polarity *s*. Polarität *f*.
polarization *s*. Polarisierung *f*.
polarize *v.t*. polarisieren, spalten.
Pole *s*. Pole *m*.; Polin *f*.
pole *s*. Pol *m*.; Strange *f*.; Mast *m*.; Pfahl *m*.
pole-axe *s*. Streitaxt *f*.
polecat *s*. Iltis *m*.
polemic(al) *a*. Streit. . . ; *m*.; **~s** *pl*. Polemik *f*.
polemicist *s*. Polemiker(in) *m.(f.)*
pole-star *s*. Polarstern *m*.
pole: ~-vault *s*. Stabhochsprung; **~-vaulter** *s*. Stabhochspringer(in) *m.(f.)*; **~-vaulting** *s*. Stabhochspringen *n*.
police *s*. Polizei *f*.; **~-headquarters** *pl*. Polizeipräsidium *n*.; **~-informer** *s*. Polizeispitzel *m*.
policeman *s*. Polizist, Schutzmann *m*.
police-station *s*. Polizeiwache *f*.
policewoman *s*. Polizistin *f*.

policy *s*. Politik *f*.; Diplomatie *f*.; Versicherungspolice *f*.; **~-making** *a*. politisch maßgebend; **~-holder** *s*. Policeinhaber *m*.; *to take out a* ~ *on the life of his wife*, das Leben seiner Frau versichern.
polio *s*. Polio *f*.; Kinderlähmung *f*.
Polish *a*. polnisch.
polish *v.t*. glätten; zieren; ~ *s*. Glätte, Politur *f*.; Glanz *m*.; Schliff *m*.
polite *a*., **~ly** *adv*. höflich.
politeness *s*. Höflichkeit *f*.
politic *s*. weltklug, politisch.
political *a*., **~ly** *adv*. politisch, staatskundig, Staats. . . ; **~science** *s*. Politologie *f*.
politician *s*. Politiker(in) *m.(f.)*
politicize *v.t*. politisieren.
politics *s.pl*. Politik, Staatskunst *f*.
polka *s*. Polka *f*.; **~-dot** *s*. Tupfen *m*.
poll *s*. Abstimmung *f*.; ~ *v.t*. Stimmen erhalten; ~ *v.i*. stimmen.
pollen *s*. Blütenstaub *m*.
pollinate *v.t*. bestäuben.
pollination *s*. Bestäubung *f*.
polling-station *s*. Wahllokal *n*.
poll-tax *s*. Kopfsteuer *f*.
pollster *s*. Meinungsforscher(in) *m.(f.)*
pollutant *s*. (Umwelt) Schadstoff *m*.
pollute *v.t*. verschmutzen, verunreinigen.
pollution *s*. (Umwelt) Verschmutzung *f*.
polo *s*. Polo *n*.; **~-neck** *s*. Rollkragen *m*.
polygamist *s*. Polygamist(in) *m.(f.)*.
polygamy *s*. Mehrehe *f*.; Polygamie *f*.
polyglot *a*. vielsprachig.
polygon *s*. Vieleck *n*.
polygonal *a*. vieleckig.
polyp(e) *s*. Polyp *m*.
polypus *s*. (*med*.) Polyp *m*.
polysyllabic *a*. vielsilbig.
polytechnic *a*. polytechnisch; ~ *s*. Technische Hochschule *f*.
polytheism *s*. Vielgötterei *f*.
polyvalent *a*. mehrwertig.
pomade, pomatum *s*. Pomade *f*.
pomegranate *s*. Granatapfel *m*.; Granatbaum *m*.
pommel *s*. (Degen-, Sattel-)Knopf *m*.
pomp *s*. Pracht *f*.; Gepränge *n*.
pomposity *s*. Prahlerei *f*.; Schwulst *m*.
pompous *a*., **~ly** *adv*. hochtrabend.
pond *s*. Teich *m*.
ponder *v.t*. nachdenken; abwägen.
ponderable *a*. wägbar.
ponderous *a*., **~ly** *adv*. schwer; schwerfällig.
poniard *s*. Dolch *m*.; ~ *v.t*. erdolchen.
pontiff *s*. Hohepriester *m*.; Papst *m*.
pontifical *a*., **~ly** *adv*. päpstlich.
pontoon *s*. Brückenkahn *m*., Ponton *m*.
pony *s*. Pony *n*.
pony-tail *s*. Pferdeschwanz *m*.
poodle *s*. Pudel *m*.
pooh! poh! pah!
pooh-pooh *v.t*. (*fig*.) verächtlich ablehnen, nichts wissen wollen von.
pool *s*. Pfuhl, Teich *m*.; (Spiel-)Einsatz *m*.; (*com*.) Kartell *n*.; gemeinsame Fonds *m*.; ~ *v.t*. zusammenlegen, zusammenwerfen.
poop *s*. Heck *n*. (Schiff).
poor *a*., **~ly** *adv*. arm, dürftig; gering.

poorly *a. & adv.* ärmlich; unpässlich.
poorness *s.* Armut *f.*; Dürftigkeit *f.*
poor-relief *s.* Armenfürsorge *f.*
pop *s.* Puff, Knall *m.*; ~ *v.i.* knallen, paffen; huschen; ~ *v.t.* schnell bewegen, schnellen.
pop: ~**art** *s.* Popart *f.*, ~**concert** *s.* Popkonzert *n.*; ~**corn** *s.* Popcorn *n.*
pope *s.* Papst *m.*
popery *s.* Papisterei *f.*
pop-gun *s.* Spielzeuggewehr *n.*
poplar *s.* Pappel *f.*
poplin *s.* Poplin *m.*
poppy *s.* Mohn *m.*
populace *s.* Pöbel *m.*
popular *a.* volkstümlich, beliebt, volksmäßig; Volks...
popularize *v.t.* populär bekannt machen, popularisieren.
popularity *s.* Volkstümlichkeit *f.*
popularly *adv.* allgemein; volkstümlich.
popular music *s.* Unterhaltungsmusik *f.*
populate *v.t.* bevölkern.
population *s.* Bevölkerung *f.*; ~ **explosion** *s.* Bevölkerungsexplosion *f.*
populous *a.*, dichtbevölkert.
porcelain *s.* Porzellan *n.*
porch *s.* Vorhalle *f.*; Vordach *n.*; Vorbau *m.*; Veranda *f.*
porcupine *s.* Stachelschwein *n.*
pore *s.* Pore *f.*; ~ *v.i.* ~**over** studieren; nachdenken über.
pork *s.* Schweinefleisch *n.*
pork: ~ **chop** *s.* Schweinekotelett *n.*; ~ **sausage** *s.* Schweinswürstchen *n.*
pornographic *a.* pornographisch, Porno...
pornography *s.* Pornographie *f.*
porous *a.* porös.
porridge *s.* Haferbrei *m.*
port *s.* Hafen *m.*, Hafenstadt *f.*; (*nav.*) Pfortluke *f.*; Backbord *n.*; Portwein *m.*; ~ *of arrival,* Ankunftshafen *m.*; ~ *of call,* Anlegehafen *m.*; ~ *of destination,* Bestimmungshafen *m.*; ~ *of registry,* Heimathafen *m.*; ~**charges,** ~**dues** *pl.* Hafengebühren *f.pl.*
portable *a.* tragbar.
portal *s.* Portal *n.*
portcullis *s.* Fallgitter *n.*
portend *v.t.* vorbedeuten, deuten auf.
portent *s.* (üble) Vorbedeutung *f.*
portentous *a.* verhängnisvoll, fürchterlich.
porter *s.* Träger, Dienstmann *m.*; Portier *m.*; Schlafwagenschaffner *m.*
portfolio *s.* Mappe *f.*; Portefeuille *n.*; (*fig.*) Geschäftsbereich *m.*
porthole *s.* (*nav.*) Seitenfenster *n.*; Bullauge *n.*
portico *s.* Säulengang *m.*
portion *s.* Teil, Anteil *m.*; Portion *f.* Heiratsgut *n.*; *compulsory* ~, (*law*) Pflichtteil *n.*; ~ *v.t.* austeilen.
portly *a.* stattlich; wohlbeleibt.
portmanteau *s.* Reisekoffer *m.*
portrait *s.* Bildnis, Porträt *n.*
portraitist *s.* Porträtmaler(in) *m.*(*f.*)
portray *v.t.* abmalen; schildern.
Portugal *s.* Portugal *n.*
Portuguese *a.* portugiesisch; ~ *s.* Portugiese *m.*, Portugiesin *f.*

pose *s.* Pose, Stellung *f.*; ~ *v.t.* (eine Frage, Behauptung) aufstellen.
posh *a.* vornehm; nobel (*pej.*).
position *s.* Stellung, Lage *f.*; Stand *m.*; Standpunkt *m.*; ~**warfare** *s.* (*mil.*) Stellungskrieg *m.*; *to hold a* ~, ein Amt bekleiden.
positive *a.*, ~**ly** *adv.* ausdrücklich; sicher; bestimmt; positiv; konstruktiv.
posse *s.* (Polizei-) Aufgebot *n.*
possess *v.t.* besitzen; besetzen.
possessed *a.* besessen; ~*s.* Besessene *m.*/*f.*
possession *s.* Besitz *m.*; Besitzung *f.*; *to be in* ~ *of,* im Besitz von etwas sein.
possessive *a.* Besitz...; besitzergreifend (*gram.*) besitzanzeigend.
possessor *s.* Besitzer(in) *m.*(*f.*)
possibility *s.* Möglichkeit *f.*
possible *a.* möglich.
possibly *adv.* möglicherweise, vielleicht.
post *s.* Pfosten, Pfahl *m.*; Posten *m.*; Stelle *f.* Anstellung *f.*; Post *f.*; *by* ~, mit der Post; *Ministry of* ~, Postministerium *n.*; ~ *v.t.* anschlagen; hinstellen; auf die Post geben, (Brief) einstecken; ~ *v.i.* mit der Post reisen, eilen.
postage *s.* Porto *n.*, Postgebühr *f.*; ~ *due,* Strafporto *n.*, Nachgebühr *f.*; ~ *paid,* franko, portofrei.
postage-stamp *s.* Briefmarke *f.*
postal *a.* Post...; ~**order** (P.O.), Postanweisung *f.*; ~ **check,** ~**money order** *s.* Postscheck *m.*; ~ **expenses** *pl.* Portospesen *pl.*
postcard *s.* Postkarte *f.*; *color* ~, farbige Postkarte; *picture* ~, Ansichtspostkarte.
post-date *v.t.* nachdatieren.
poste restante *adv.* postlagernd; ~ *s.* Briefaufbewahrungsstelle *f.*
poster *s.* Plakat *n.*
posterior *a.* später; ~*s.* Hintere *m.*
posterity *s.* Nachwelt *f.*
post-haste *adv.* in grosser Eile.
posthumous *a.* nachgeboren, hinterlasen.
post-mark *s.* Poststempel *m.*
post-master *s.* Postmeister *m.*
post-mortem *s.* nach dem Tod; ~ **examination** *s.* Obduktion *f.*, Leichenschau *f.*
post-office *s.* Postamt *n.*; ~**box** (P.O. box) *s.* Postfach *n.*; ~ *savings bank,* Postsparkasse *f.*
postpone *v.t.* verschieben; aufschieben.
postponement *s.* Aufschub *m.*; Verschiebung *f.*
postscript *s.* Nachschrift *f.*
postulate *s.* Postulat *n.*, Forderung *f.*; ~ *v.t.* fordern; als richtig annehmen.
posture *s.* Stellung, Lage *f.*; (körperliche) Haltung *f.*
post-war Nachkriegs...
posy *s.* Blumenstrauß *m.*
pot *s.* Topf, Krug *m.*; Kanne *f.*; (*sl.*) Marijuana *n.*; Pot *n.* ~ *boiler,* Brotarbeit *f.*
potable *a.* trinkbar.
potash *s.* Pottasche *f.*; Kali *n.*
potassium *s.* Kalium *n.*
potato *s.* Kartoffel *f.*; **boiled** ~**es** *pl.* Salzkartoffeln *pl.*; **fried** ~**es** *pl.* Bratkartoffeln; **mashed** ~**es,** Kartoffelbrei *m.*; ~**blight,** Kartoffelkrankheit *f.*; ~*es in jackets, pl.* Pellkartoffeln *pl.*
pot-belly *s.* Schwerbauch *m.*
potency *s.* Kraft *f.*; Wirksamkeit *f.*; Potenz *f.*

potent *a.*, **~ly** *adv.* mächtig, stark, wirsam; potent.
potentate *s.* Machthaber *m.*
potential *a.*, **~ly** *adv.* möglich, potentiell; **military ~** *s.* Kriegspotential *n.*
potentialities *pl.* Möglichkeiten *f.pl.*
pother *s.* Lärm *m.*; ~ *v.i.* lärmen, poltern; ~ *v.t.* aufregen.
potion *s.* (Arznei-)Trank *m.*
potluck *s.* ~ **dinner** *s.* Essen, bei dem jeder etwas mitbringt.
pot-pourri *s.* (*mus.*) Potpourri *n.*; Allerei *n.*
potted *a.* eingemacht.
potter *s.* Töpfer(in) *m.*(*f.*)
potter's wheel *s.* Töpferscheibe *f.*
pottery *s.* Töpferei *f.*; Töpferwaren *f.pl.*
potty *s.* Töpfchen *n.*; **~-trained** *a.* sauber.
pouch *s.* Tasche *f.*; Beutel *m.*; ~ *v.t.* einstecken.
poultice *s.* Wickel *m.*; (warmer) Umschlag *m.*
poultry *s.* Federvieh, Geflügel *n.*
pounce *s.* Sprung *m.*; Satz *m.*; *v.i.* herfallen über.
pound *s.* Pfund *n.*; ~ *v.t.* zerstossen; (Vieh) einsperren; (*mil.*) belegen mit, bombardieren.
pounding *s.* Schlagen *n.*; Klopfen *n.*; Stampfen *n.*
pour *v.t.* gießen; ~ *v.i.* strömen.
pouring *a.* strömend.
pout *s.* üble Laune *f.*; Schmollmund *m.*; ~ *v.i.* schmollen.
poverty *s.* Armut *f.*; Mangel *m.*
poverty: ~line Armutsgrenze *f.*; **~-stricken** *a.* notleidend.
powder *s.* Pulver *n.*; Puder, Staub *m.*; ~ *v.t.* pudern; bestreuen.
power *s.* Macht, Gewalt *f.*; Kraft *f.*; Vollmacht *f.*; (*math.*) Potenz *f.*; (*elek.*) Starkstrom *m.*; ~ **cut** *s.* Stromsperre *f.*; ~ **failure** *s.* Stromausfall *m.* **~station** *s.* Kraftwerk *n.*
powerful *a.*, **~ly** *adv.* mächtig, kräftig.
powerless *a.* kraftlos, ohnmächtig.
powerloom *s.* mechanischer Webstuhl *m.*
pox *s.* Pocken *pl.*; (*fam.*) Syphilis *f.*
practicable *a.*, **~bly** *adv.* ausführbar; praktikabel.
practical *a.*, **~ly** *adv.* aussübend, praktisch; tatsächlich; ~ **joke**, Streich *m.*
practicality *s.* Durchführbarkeit *f.*
practice *s.* Ausübung *f.*; Übung *f.*; Praxis *f.* ~ *v.t.* üben; anwenden; ~ *v.i.* sich üben; treiben.
practiced *a.* erfahren; geübt.
practising *a.* praktizierend.
practitioner *s.* Praktiker(in) *m.*(*f.*)
pragmatic *a.*, **~ally**, adv. pragmatisch.
prairie *s.* Prärie *f.*
praise *s.* Lob *n.*; ~ *v.t.* loben.
praiseworthy *s.*, **~ily** *adv.* lobenswert.
prance *v.i.* stolzieren; täuzeln; herumspringen.
prank *s.* Possen, Streich *m.*;
prate *v.i.* schwatzen.
prattle *v.t.* schwatzen; plappern; ~ *s.* Geschwätz *n.* Geplapper *n.*
prawn *s.* Garnele *f.*
pray *v.i.* & *t.* beten; bitten.
prayer *s.* Gebet *n.*; Bitte *f.*; *the Lord's* ~, das Vaterunser.
prayerbook *s.* Gebetbuch *n.*
preach *v.t.* & *i.* predigen.
preacher *s.* Prediger(in) *m.*(*f.*)
preamble *s.* Einleitung, Vorrede *f.*

prearrange *v.t.* vorher anordnen; verabreden.
precarious *a.*, **~ly** *adv.* unsicher; instabil; gefährlich; abhängig; aufkündbar.
precaution *s.* Vorsicht, Vorischtsmaßregel *f.*; *to take ~s,* Vorischtsmaßnahmen treffen.
precautionary *a.*, vorbeugend, Vorsichts. . .
precede *v.t.* vorhergehen.
precedence *s.* Vortritt, Vorrang *m.*
precedent *s.* Präzedenzfall *m.*
precept *s.* Vorschrift, Regel *f.*
preceptor *s.* Lehrer *m.*; Tutor *m.*
precinct *s.* Viertel *n.*, Bezirk, Umfang *m.*
precious *a.*, **~ly** *adv.* kostbar; wertvoll.
precipice *s.* Abgrund *m.*
precipitate *v.t.* hinabstürzen; (*chem.*) fällen; überstürzen; heraufbeschwören; ~ *v.i.* herabstürzen; sich übereilen; vorschnell sein; ~ *a.*, **~ly** *adv.* übereilt; voreilig; **~tion** *s.*
precipitous *a.* sehr steil; schroff.
précis *s.* kurze Inhaltsangabe *f.*, Zusammenfassung *f.*
precise *a.*, **~ly** *adv.* genau; steif.
precision *s.* Bestimmtheit *f.*; (*mech.*) ~ **worker** *s.* Präzisionsarbeiter *m.*; ~ **tool** *s.* Präzisionswerkzeug *n.*
preclude *v.t.* ausschließen.
precocious *a.* frühreif; altklug.
precocity *s.* Frühreife *f.*
preconceive *v.t.* sich vorher denken.
preconceived *a.* vorgefaßt.
preconception *s.* Vorurteil *n.*; vorgefaßte Meinung *f.*
precondition *s.* Vorbedingung *f.*
pre-cooked *a.* vorgekocht.
precursor *s.* Vorläufer, Vorbote *m.*
pre-date *v.t.* zurückdatieren.
predatory *a.* räuberisch.
predecessor *s.* Vorgänger(in) *m.*(*f.*)
predestination *s.* Vorherbestimmung *f.*; Gnadenwahl *f.*
predestine *v.t.* vorherbestimmen.
predestined *a.* vorherbestimmt, prädestiniert.
predicament *s.* (mißliche Lage *f.*, Dilemma *n.*
predicate *s.* (*gram.*) Prädikat *n.*
predicative *a.* prädikativ.
predict *v.t.* vorhersagen.
predictable *a.* vorhersagbar; berechenbar.
prediction *s.* Vorhersage *f.*
predilection *s.* Vorliebe *f.*
predispose *v.t.* geneigt machen.
predisposition *s.* Neigung *f.*
predominance *s.* Übergewicht *n.*
predominant *a.*, **~ly** *adv.* vorherrschend.
predominate *v.i.* vorherrschen.
pre-eminence *s.* Vorrang *m.*
pre-eminent *a.*, **~ly** *adv.* hervorragend; herausragend.
pre-emption *s.* Vorkauf *m.*; Vorkaufsrecht *n.*
preen *v.t.* putzen; **~o.s.** sich putzen.
pre-exist *v.i.* vorher da sein.
prefab *s.* Fertighaus *n.*
prefabricated *a.* vorgefertigt.
preface *s.* Vorrede *f.*; ~ *v.t.* einleiten.
prefect *s.* Präfekt.
prefer *v.t.* vorziehen; **~red stock,** *s.* Vorzugsaktie *f.*
preferable *a.* vorzuziehen(d), vorzüglicher.

preferably *adv.* am besten; am liebsten; vorzugsweise.

preference *s.* Vorzug *m.*; Vorliebe *f.*

preferential *a.*, **~ly** *adv.* bevorzugt, Vorzugs...; **~ treatment**, Vorzugsbehandlung *f.*

prefigure *v.t.* sich ausmalen.

prefix *s.* Vorsilbe *f.*

pregnancy *s.* Schwangerschaft *f.* **~ test** *s.* Schwangerschaftstest *m.*

pregnant *a.*, **~ly** *adv.* schwanger; trächtig.

preheat *v.t.* vorheizen.

prehistoric *a.* prähistorisch, vorgeschichtlich.

prehistory *s.* Vorgeschichte *f.*

prejudge *v.t.* vorverurteilen; vorschnellbeurteilen.

prejudice *s.* Vorurteil *n.*; Nachteil *m.*; *without ~ to*, unbeschadet; **~** *v.t.* einnehmen (für/gegen); benachteiligen.

prejudicial *a.*, **~ly** *adv.* schädlich.

prelacy *s.* Prälatenwürde *f.*

prelate *s.* Prälat *m.*

preliminary *a.* vorläufig, Vor...; *(law)* **~** *examination*, Vorverhör *n.*; **~** *s.* Vorbereitung *f.*; **~ies** *pl.* Vorverhandlungen *f.pl.*

prelude *s.* Vorspiel *n.*, Auftakt *m.*

premarital *a.* vorehelich.

premature *a.*, **~ly** *adv.* vorschnell; frühreif.

premeditate *v.t.* vorher überlegen; **~d** *p.* vorbedacht, vorsätzlich.

premeditation *s.* Vorbedacht *m.*

premier *s.* Premierminister *m.*

premiere *s.* Premiere *f.*; Erstaufführung *f.*; Uraufführung *f.*

premilitary *a.* vormilitärisch.

premise *s.* Prämisse *f.*

premises *s.pl.* Vordersätze *m.pl.*; Haus (*n.*) mit Zubehör; Grundstücke *n.pl.*

premium *s.* Preis *m.*; Versicherungsprämie *f.*; *at a ~*, über pari; sehr gesucht.

premonition *s.* Warnung, Vorahnung *f.*

prenatal *a.* vorgeburtlich, pränatal; **~ care** *s.* Mutterschaftsfürsorge.

preoccupation *s.* Sorge *f.*; Hauptanliegen *n.*

preoccupy *v.t.* ganz in Anspruch nehmen; ausschließlich beschäftigen.

pre-packed *a.* abgepackt.

preparation *s.* Vorbereitung, Zubereitung *f.*; Präparat *n.*

preparatory *a.* vorbereitend; vorläufig.

prepare *v.t.* vorbereiten; zubereiten; **~** *v.i.* sich vorbereiten.

preparedness *s.* Bereitschaft *f.*

prepay *v.t.* vorausbezahlen; frankieren.

prepayment *s.* Vorausbezahlung.

preponderance *s.* Übergewicht *n.*

preponderant *a.* überwiegend.

preponderate *v.i.* überwiegen.

preposition *s.* (*gram.*) Präposition *f.*; Verhältniswort *n.*

prepossessed *a.* eingenommen sein.

prepossessing *a.* einnehmend, anziehend.

prepossession *s.* Voreingenommenheit *f.*

preposterous *a.* unsinnig.

prerequisite *s.* Bedingung, Voraussetzung *f.*

prerogative *s.* Vorrecht *n.*

presage *s.* Vorbedeutung *f.*; **~** *v.t.* vorhersagen; anzeigen.

presbyterian *a.* presbyterianisch; **~** *s.* Presbyterianer *m.*

pre-school *a.* Vorschul...

prescribe *v.t.* vorschreiben; **~** *v.i.* verschreiben.

prescription *s.* Vorschrift *f.*; Rezept *n.*; Verjährung *f.*

presence *s.* Gegenwart *f.*; **~** *of mind*, Geistesgegenwart *f.*

present *a.* Gegenwärtig; bereit; *at ~*, gegenwärtig; **~** *s.* (Zeit) Gegenwart *f.*; (*gram.*) Präsens *n.*; Geschenk *n.*

present *v.t.* vorlegen, unterbreiten; (Gesuch) einreichen; beschenken; vorschlagen, präsentieren; *to ~ a play*, ein Stück zeigen.

presentable *a.* präsentierbar.

presentation *s.* Darstellung *f.*; Vorzeigung *f.*

present-day *a.* heutig, zeitgemäß.

presenter *s.* Moderator(in) *m.*(*f.*)

presentiment *s.* Vorgefühl *n.*, Ahnung *f.*

presently *adv.* gleich; bald; nachher.

preservation *s.* Erhaltung, Bewahrung *f.*

preservative *a.* bewahrend; **~** *s.* Schutzmittel *n.*; Konservierungsmittel *n.*

preserve *v.t.* bewahren; einlegen, einmachen; **~** *s.* Eingemachtes *n.*

preside *v.i.* den Vorsitz führen.

presidency *s.* Vorsitz *m.*; Präsidentschaft *f.*

president *s.* Präsident(in) *m.*(*f.*) Vorsitzende *m.*/*f.*; (*Univ.*) Rektor(in) *m.*(*f.*)

presidential *a.* Präsidenten...; **~ campaign** *s.* Präsidentschaftswahlkampf *m.*

press *s.* Presse *f.*; Druck, Drang *m.*; Gedränge *n.*; *in the ~*, in der Presse; **~** *conference*, Pressekonferenz *f.*; **~** *v.t.* pressen; keltern; drängen; **~** *v.i.* drücken; dringen, drängen.

press-gallery *s.* Pressetribüne *f.*

pressing *a.*, **~ly** *adv.* dringend.

press release *s.* Presseerklärung *f.*

pressure *s.* Druck *m.*; *under ~*, unter Druck (arbeiten); *to put ~ on s.b.*, auf jn. Druck ausüben.

pressure-cooker *s.* Schnellkochtopf *m.*

pressure-group *s.* Pressure-group *f.*

prestige *s.* Ansehen *n.*, Geltung *f.*

prestigious *a.* angesehen.

presumable *a.* mutmaßlich.

presume *v.t.* & *i.* mutmaßen; sich anmaßen; sich verlassen; **~d** *dead*, verschollen, mutmaßlich tot.

presumption *s.* Mutmaßung *f.*; Dünkel *m.*; Vermessenheit *f.*

presumptive *a.*, **~ly** *adv.* mutmaßlich.

presumptuous *a.*, **~ly** *adv.* anmaßend.

presuppose *v.t.* voraussetzen.

pretend *v.t.* vorgeben; erheucheln; **~** *v.i.* sich verstellen; beanspruchen.

pretended *a.* vorgetäuscht, gespielt.

pretender *s.* (Thron-) Prätendent, Beansprucher *m.*

pretense *s.* Vorwand *m.*; Schein *m.*; *under false ~s*, unter Vorspiegelung falscher Tatsachen *f.*

pretension *s.* Anmaßung *f.*

pretentious *a.*, **~ly** *adv.* anspruchsvoll.

preterite *s.* (*gram.*) Präteritum *n.*

pretext *s.* Vorwand *m.*

pretty *a.* & *adv.* niedlich, nett; ziemlich.

pretzel *s.* Brezel *f.*

prevail *v.i.* (vor-) herrschen.

prevailing *a.* vorherrschend, aktuell.
prevalence *s.* Verbreitung *f.*; Vorhersehen *n.*
prevalent *a.*, **~ly** *adv.* vorhersehend.
prevaricate *v.i.* Ausflüchte machen.
prevarication *s.* Verdrehung, Ausflucht *f.*
prevent *v.t.* zuvorkommen; vorbeugen; verhindern.
prevention *s.* Verhütung *f.*; Vorbeugung *f.*
preventive *a.*, **~ly** *adv.* vorbeugend; ~ *s.* Verhütungsmittel *n.*
preview *s.* Vorschau *f.*; Voraufführung *f.*; Vorbesichtigung *f.*
previous *a.*, **~ly** *adv.* vorig, früher.
pre-war *a.* Vorkriegs...
prey *s.* Beute *f.*; *bird/beast of* ~ Raubvogel *m.*; Raubtier *n.*; ~ *v.i.* rauben, plündern.
price *s.* Preis *m.*; Wert *m.*; **~-control**, Preisüberwachung *f.*; *low* ~*d*, in niedriger Preislage.
price-cut *s.* Preissenkung *f.*
priceless *a.* unschätzbar.
price: ~ **list** *s.* Preisliste *f.*; **~-range** *s.* Preisspanne *f.*; **~-rise** *s.* Preisanstieg *m.*; ~ **tag** *s.* Preisschild *n.*
prick *v.t.* stechen, anstechen; spornen; spitzen; *to* ~ *one's ears*, die Ohren spitzen; ~ *v.i.* stechen, prikkeln; ~ *s.* Spitze *f.*; Stich *m.*; *(vulg.)* Penis *m.*, Schwanz *m.*
prickle *s.* Stachel *m.*; Dorn *m.*
prickly *a.* dornig; stachelig.
pride *s.* Stolz *m.*; Hochmut *m.*; ~*v.t.* stolz sein auf.
priest *s.* Priester *m.*
priestess *s.* Priesterin *f.*
priesthood *s.* Priesteramt *n.*; Geistlichkeit *f.*
priestly *a.* priesterlich.
prig *s.* Tugendbold *m.*
priggish *a.* (übertrieben) tugendhaft.
prim *a.* geziert, förmlich; gesetzt.
prima facie, auf den ersten Blick.
primacy *s.* Primat *m.*; Vorrang *m.*
primary *a.* ursprünglich, Anfangs..., Haupt...; **~ily** *adv.* vornehmlich.
primary: ~ **color** *s.* Grundfarbe *f.*; ~ **election** *s.* Vorwahl *f.*; ~ **school** *s.* Grundschule *f.*
primate *s.* Primas *m.*; *(zool.)* Primat *m.*
prime *a.*, **~ly** *adv.* Haupt...; vortrefflich; **~-cost** *s.* Gestehungskosten *pl.*; ~ *Minister*, Ministerpräsident *m.*; ~ **number** *s.* Primzahl *f.* ~ *s.* Blüte, Vollendung *f.*; Beste *n.*; ~ *v.t.* grundieren, unterrichten.
primer *s.* Fibel *f.*, Elementarbuch *n.*; Grundierlack *m.*
primeval *a.* urzeitlich; uralt.
primitive *a.*, **~ly** *adv.* unsprünglich; einfach, primitiv.
primogeniture *s.* Erstgeburt *f.*
primrose *s.* Primel *f.*; Schlüsselblume *f.*
prince *s.* Fürst, Prinz *m.*
Prince Charming *s.* Märchenprinz *m.*
prince consort *s.* Prinzgemahl *m.*
princely *a. & adv.* prinzlich, fürstlich.
princess *s.* Prinzessin, Fürstin *f.*
principal *a.*, **~ly** *adv.* vorzüglich, Haupt..., hauptsächlich; ~ *s.* Haupt *n.*; *(law)* Haupttäter *m.*; Direktor *m.*; Hauptsache *f.*; Kapital *n.*
principality *s.* Fürstentum *n.*
principally *adv.* in erster Linie.
principle *s.* Prinzip *n.*; Grundursache *f.*; Grundsatz

m.; *to lay down a* ~, einen Grundsatz aufstellen.
print *v.t.* drucken, abdrucken; in grossen Buchstaben schreiben; (*phot.*) absiehen; einprägen; ~ *s.* Druck *m.*; Abdruck *m.*; (*phot.*) Abzug *m.*, Kopie *f.*; Spur *f.*; (Stahl)Stick *m.*; *out of* ~, vergriffen; **~s** *pl.* gedruckte Kattunstoffe *m.pl.*
printable *a.* druckreif.
printed matter, printed paper *s.* Drucksache *f.*
printer *s.* *(comp.)* Drucker *m.*; Drucker(in) *m.*(*f.*)
printing *s.* Drucken *n.*; **~-house** *s.* Buchdruckerei *f.*; ~ *ink*, Druckerschwärze *f.*
print-out *s.* Ausdruck *m.*
prior *a.* früher; ~ *to*, vor; ~ *s.* Prior *m.*
prioress *s.* Priorin *f.*
priority *s.* Priorität *f.*; Vorrang *m.*
prism *s.* Prisma *f.*
prison *s.* Gefängnis *n.*
prison camp *s.* Gefangenenlager *n.*
prisoner *s.* Gefangene *m.*; ~ **of war** *s.* Kriegsgefangene *m.*
prison-guard *s.* Gefängniswärter(in) *m.*(*f.*)
prissy *a.* (*fam.*) zimperlich; überordentlich.
pristine *a.* ehemalig, alt.
privacy *s.* Verborgenheit *f.*
private *a.*, **~ly** *adv.* privat; geheim; nicht öffentlich; nicht amtlich; persönlich, Privat..., eigen; (*tel.*) ~ *call*, Privatgespräch; ~ *enterprise*, freie Wirtschaft *f.*; ~ *s.* gemeine Soldat *m.*; *in* ~, unter vier Augen.
private parts *s.pl.* Geschlechtsteile *pl.*
private practice *s.* Privatpraxis *f.*
privation *s.* Beraubung *f.*; Mangel *m.*
privatization *s.* Privatisierung *f.*
privatize *v.t.* privatisieren.
privet *s.*(*bot*) Liguster *m.*
privilege *s.* Vorrecht *n.*; Privileg *n.* ~ *v.t.* bevorrechten; privilegieren.
privileged *a.* privilegiert.
privy *a.* geheim, besonder; mitwissend; ~ *council*, Staatsrat *m.*; *Lord Privy Seal*, Geheimsiegelbewahrer; ~ *s.* Abort *m.*
prize *s.* Preis *m.*; Belohnung *f.*; ~ *v.t.* würdigen, schätzen; (mit Gewalt) öffnen.
prize-fighter *s.* Boxer *m.*
prize-winner *s.* Preisträger(in) *m.*(*f.*)
probability *s.* Wahrscheinlichkeit *f.*
probable *a.*, **~bly** *adv.* wahrscheinlich.
probate *s.* Testamentsbestätigung *f.*
probation *s.* Probezeit *f.*; Bewährungsfrist *f.*; *on* ~, auf Probe, widerruflich.
probationary *a.* Probe...; ~ **period** *s.* Probezeit *f.*
probationer *s.* Prüfling *m.*; Anwärter(in) *m.*(*f.*)
probe *s.* Sonde *f.*; ~ *v.t.* sondieren.
probing *a.* forschend; durchdringend.
probity *s.* Redlichkeit *f.*
problem *s.* Aufgabe *f.*, Problem *n.*
problematic *a.*, **~ally** *adv.* zweifelhaft; problematisch.
procedure *s.* Verfahren *n.*; *legal* ~, Prozeßverfahren *n.*
proceed *v.i.* fortfahren; verfahren; vorgehen; weitergehen; *to* ~ *from*, hervorgehen, herrühren; *to* ~ *to*, sich begeben nach, fortfahren nach.
proceeding *s.* Vorgehensweise *f.*; Verfahren; **(legal) ~s** *pl.* Prozeß, gerichtliches Verfahren *n.*; *to take* ~ *against*, gerichtlich vorgehen gegen.
proceeds *s.pl.* Ertrag, Gewinn *m.*

process *s.* Vorgang *m.*; Verfahren *n.*; Prozeß *m.*; ~ *v.t.* behandeln, bearbeiten (*chem.*)

procession *s.* Prozession *f.*; Umzug *m.*

processor *s.* (*comp.*) Prozessor *m.*

proclaim *v.t.* öffentlich bekanntmachen.

proclamation *s.* Verkündung *f.*; Bekanntmachung *f.*

proclivity *s.* Neigung *f.*, Hang *m.*

procrastinate *v.t. & i.* zandern; zögern.

procreate *v.t.* zeugen, erzeugen.

procure *v.t.* besorgen; verschaffen, liefern; ~ *v.i.* verkuppeln.

procurement *s.* Beschaffung *f.*

procurer *s.* Kuppler *m.*

procuress *s.* Kupplerin *f.*

prod *s.* Stupser *m.*; ~ *v.t.* stupsen; stoßen.

prodigal *a.*, ~**ly** *adv.* verschwenderisch; ~ *s.* Verschwender(in) *m.*(*f.*); ~ **son** *s.* verlorener Sohn *m.*

prodigality *s.* Verschwendung *f.*

prodigious *a.*, ~**ly** *adv.* ungeheur; außerordentlich.

prodigy *s.* Wunderding, *n.*; Talent *n.*; **child** ~ *s.* Wunderkind *n.*

produce *v.t.* vorführen; hervorbringen; vorstellen; vorzeigen; produzieren; *to* ~ *a play,* ein Stück einstudieren; *to* ~ *a witness,* einen Zeugen beibringen; ~ *s.* Erzeugnis *n.*; Ertrag *m.*; Produkte *n.pl.*; ~**exchange** *s.* Produktenbörse *f.*

producer *s.* Erzeuger(in) *m.*(*f.*); Produzent(in) *m.*(*f.*) ~ **gas** *s.* Generatorgas, Holzgas *n.*

product *s.* Erzeugnis, Produkt *n.*

production *s.* Vorführung *f.*; Erzeugnis *n.*; Vorlegung *f.*; Produktion *f.*; Erzeugung *f.*

production line *s.* Fertigungsstraße *f.*; Fließband *n.*

productive *a.* fruchtbar; schöpferisch; productiv.

productivity *s.* Produktivität *f.*

profanation *s.* Entweihung *f.*

profane *a.*, ~**ly** *adv.* ungeweiht; gottlos; weltlich; ~ *v.t.* entweihen.

profanity *s.* Gottlosigkeit, Ruchlosigkeit *f.*; Fluchen *n.*

profess *v.t.* bekennen; ausüben.

professed *a.* erklärt; angeblich.

professedly *adv.* erklärtermaßen, eingestandenermaßen.

profession *s.* Bekenntnis *n.*; Beruf *m.*

professional *a.* berufsmäßig, Berufs...; Fach...; ~ *s. by* ~, von Beruf *m.*; (*sp.*) Berufssportler(in) *m.*(*f.*)

professionalism *s.* Professionalismus *m.*

professor *s.* Professor(in) *m.*(*f.*)

professorship *s.* Professur *f.*, Lehrstuhl *m.*

proffer *v.t.* darbieten; anbieten; ~ *s.* Anerbieten *n.*

proficiency *s.* können *n.*; Tüchtigkeit *f.*

proficient *a.* tüchtig, bewandert.

profile *s.* Seitenansicht *f.*; Profil *n.*; Porträt *n.*; *keep a low* ~ sich zurückhalten.

profit *s.* Gewinn *m.*; Vorteil *m.*; *at a* ~, mit Gewinn; ~ *and loss,* Gewinn und Verlust; ~ **sharing** *s.* Gewinnbeteiligung *f.*; ~ *v.t. & i.* Vorteil bringen; Nutzen ziehen; nutzen; Fortschritte machen.

profitability *s.* Rentabilität *f.*

profitable *a.*, ~**bly** *adv.* einträglich.

profiteer *v.i.* sich bereichern; ~ *s.* Profitmacher(in) *m.*(*f.*)

profiteering *s.* Wucher *m.*

profit: ~~**-making** *a.* gewinnorientiert; ~ **margin** *s.* Gewinnspanne *f.*, ~ **sharing** *s.* Gewinnbeteiligung *f.*

profligacy *s.* Liederlichtkeit *f.*

profligate *a.*, ~**ly** *adv.* ruchlos; liederlich; verschwenderisch.

profound *a.*, ~**ly** *adv.* tief, dunkel; (*fig.*) gründlich.

profundity *s.* Tiefe *f.*; Ausmaß *n.*

profuse *a.*, ~**ly** *adv.* verschwenderisch.

profusion *s.* Überfluß *m.*

progenitor *s.* Vorvater, Ahn *m.*

progeny *s.* Nachkommenschaft *f.*

prognosis *s.* Prognose *f.*, Vorhersage *f.*

prognosticate *v.t.* vorhersagen.

program(me) *s.* Programm *n.*

programmer *s.* Progammierer(in) *m.*(*f.*)

progress *s.* Fortschritt, Gang *m.*; *to be in* ~, im Gange sein; ~ *v.i.* fortschreiten.

progression *s.* Fortschritt *m.*; Zunahme *f.*; Progression *f.*

progressive *a.* fortschreitend; ~**ly** *adv.* nach und nach.

progress report *s.* Tätigkeitsbericht *m.*; Lagebericht *m.*

prohibit *v.t.* verbieten, verhindern.

prohibition *s.* Verbot *n.*; Prohibition *f.*

prohibitive, prohibitory *a.* verbietend; ~ *duty,* Sperrzoll *m.*; ~ *price,* unerschwinglicher Preis *m.*

project *v.t.* entwerfen; ~ *v.i.* vorspringen; ~ *s.* Entwurf, Plan *m.*; Unternehmen *n.*; Aktion *f.*

projectile *a.* Wurf...; ~ *s.* Geschoß *n.*

projection *s.* Wurf *m.*; Entwurf, Riß *m.*; (*arch.*) Vorsprung *m.*; Projektion *f.*; ~~**-room** *s.* Vorführraum *m.* (für Lichtbilder).

projectionist *s.* Filmvorführer(in) *m.*(*f.*)

projector *s.* Projektionsapparat *m.*; Projektor *m.*

proletarian *a.* proletarisch; Arbeiter... *s.* Proletarier(in) *m.*(*f.*)

proletariat *s.* Proletariat *n.*

proliferate *v.i.* sich stark vermehren; proliferieren.

proliferation *s.* starke Vermehrung *f.*; Proliferation *f.*

prolific *a.*, ~**ally** *adv.* fruchtbar; produktiv.

prolix *a.*, ~**ly** *adv.* weitläufig, langwierig.

prolixity *s.* Weitschweifigkeit *f.*

prolog *s.* Prolog *m.*; Eröffnungsrede *f.*

prolong *v.t.* verlängern; (*com.*) prolongieren.

prolongation *s.* Verlängerung *f.*

prolonged *a* lang; lang anhaltend.

promenade *s.* Spazierweg *m.*; Promenade *f.* ~ *v.i.* spazieren(gehen).

prominence *s.* Bekanntheit *f.*; (Fels) Vorsprung *m.*

prominent *a.* hervorragend; vorspringend.

promiscuity *s.* Promiskuität *f.*

promiscuous *a.*, ~**ly** *adv.* promiskuitiv.

promise *s.* Versprechen *n.*; ~ *v.t.* versprechen.

promising *a.* vielversprechend.

promontory *s.* Vorgebirge *n.*

promote *v.t.* befördern; fördern; werben für.

promoter *s.* Förderer *m.*; Förderin *f.*; Veranstalter(in) *m.*(*f.*)

promotion *s.* Beförderung *f.*; Förderung *f.*; (Schule) Versetzung *f.*

prompt *a.*, ~**ly** *adv.* bereit; schnell; ~ *v.t.* vorsagen; anreizen; soufflieren.

prompt-book *s.* Souffleurbuch *n.*
prompter *s.* Souffleur *m.*, Souffleuse *f.*
promptitude, promptness *s.* Pünklichkeit *f.*
promulgate *v.t.* verkünden; verbreiten.
prone *a.*, **~ly** *adv.* geneigt, hingestreckt.
prong *s.* Gabel *f.*; Zinke *f.*
pronominal *s.* fürwörtlich; pronominal.
pronoun *s.* Fürwort *n.*
pronounce *v.t.* aussprechen; feierlich erklären.
pronounced *a.* erklärt; ausgeprägt.
pronouncement *s.* Verlautbarung, Äusserung *f.*; (Urteils-) Verkündigung *f.*
pronunciation *s.* Aussprache *f*
proof *s.* Beweis *m.*; Probe *f.*; Korrekturbogen *m.*; *in ~ of,* zum Beweis von; *burden of ~,* Beweislast *f.*; *to furnish ~,* Beweis liefern; ~ *a.* undurchlässig; bewährt.
proof-read *v.t.* Korrektur lesen.
proof-sheet *s.* Korrekturbogen *m.*
prop *s.* Stütze *f.*, Pfahl *m.*; Grubenklotz *m.*; Requisit *n.*; ~ *v.t.* stützen; *to ~ up,* aufstützen.
propaganda *s.* Propaganda *f.*
propagate *v.t.* fortpflanzen; ausbreiten; ~ *v.i.* sich fortpflanzen; sich vermehren.
propagation *s.* Vermehrung *f.*; Verbreitung *f.*
propel *v.t.* vorwärtstreiben.
propeller *s,* (Schiffs-, Luft-)Schraube *f.*; Propeller *m.*; **~-blade** *s.* Luftschraubenblatt *n.*; ~ **hub** *s.* Propellernabe *f.*; ~ **shaft** *s.* Kardanwelle *f.*
propensity *s.* Neigung *f.*; Hang *m.*
proper *a.*, **~ly** *adv.* eigen, eigentümlich; schicklich; eigentlich; tauglich.
property *s.* Eigentum *n.*; Eigenschaft *f.*; *(chem.)* Eigenschaft *f.*; Vermögen *n.*; *law of ~,* Sachenrecht *n.*
prophecy *s.* Prophezeiung *f.*; Vorhersage *f.*
prophesy *v.t.* prophezeien; vorhersagen.
prophet *s.* Prophet *m.*
prophetess *s.* Prophetin *f.*
prophetic *a.*, **~ally** *adv.* prophetisch.
prophylactic *a.* vorbeugend; ~ *s.* Vorbeugungsmittel *n.*
propitiate *v.t.* versöhnen.
propitious *a.*, **~ly** *adv.* gnädig, günstig.
proponent *s.* Befürworter(in) *m.(f.)*
proportion *s.* Verhältnis *n.*; Ebenmaß *n.*; Anteil *m.*; ~ *v.t.* ins Verhältnis bringen, anpassen; *inversely ~ed,* umgekehrt proportionell.
proportional *a.* verhältnismäßig, im Verhältnis stehend; ~ *representation,* Verhältniswahl *f.*
proportionate *a.*, **~ly** *adv.* entsprechend, im Verhältnis.
proportioned *a.* proportioniert.
proposal *s.* Vorschlag *m.*; Antrag *m.*
propose *v.t.* vorschlagen; sich vornehmen; ~ *v.i.* vorhaben; anhalten um.
proposition *s.* Vorschlag *m.*; Antrag *m.*; *(math.)* Satz *m.*; *(logic)* Aussage *f.*
propound *v.t.* darlegen; vortragen.
proprietary *a.* eigentümlich; gesetzlich geschützt; ~ *article,* Markenartikel *m.*; ~ *right,* Schutzrecht *n.*; ~ *s.* Eigentümer *m.pl.*
proprietor *s.* Eigentümer(in) *m.(f.)*; Inhaber(in) *m.(f.)*
propriety *s.* Anstand *m.*; Richtigkeit *f.*
proscription *s.* Ächtung *f.*; Verbot *n.*

propulsion *s.* Antrieb *m.*
prorogation *s.* Vertagung *f.*
prorogue *v.t.* vertagen.
prosaic *a.* prosaisch.
proscribe *v.t.* ächten.
prose *s.* Prosa *f.*
prosecute *v.t.* verfolgen; verklagen.
prosecution *s.* Verfolgung, Anklage *f.*; *(law)* Anklagebehörde; ~ *witness,* Belastungszeuge *m.*
prosecutor *s.* Kläger(in) *m.(f.)*; *public ~,* Staatsanwalt *m.*, Staatsanwaltin *f.*
proselyte *s.* Neubekehrte *m.*
prosody *s.* Prosodie *f.*
prospect *s.* Ansicht, Aussicht *f.*; ~ *v.i.* sich umschauen; schürfen.
prospective *a.* voraussichtlich; zukünftig; bevorstehend.
prospectus *s.* Prospekt *m.*
prosper *v.i.* gedeihen, geligen; ~ *v.t.* begünstigen; segnen.
prosperity *s.* Wohlstand *m.*, Glück *n.*
prosperous *a.*, **~ly** *adv.* glücklich, günstig.
prostitute *v.t.* prostituieren ~ *s.* Dirne *f.*; Prostituierte *f.*; *male* ~ Strichjunge *m.*
prostitution *s.* Prostitution *f.*
prostrate *a.* hingestreckt, ausgestreckt; ~ *v.t.* niederwerfen.
prostration *a.* Niedergeschlagenheit *f.*; Fußfall *m.*
prosy *a.* langweilig, weitschweifig.
protect *v.t.* schützen, bewahren.
protection *s.* Schutz *m.*; Zollschutz *m.*
protective *a.* beschützend; ~ *duty,* Schutzzoll *m.*
protector *s.* Beschützer(in) *m.* (*f.*)
protectorate *s.* Protektorat *n.*
protégé *s.* Protégé *m.*; Schützling *m.*
protein *s.* Eiweiß *n.*
protest *v.i. & t.* beteuern; sich verwahren, protestieren; zurückweisen; ~ *s.* Protest *m.*; Gegenerklärung *f.*
Protestant *a.* protestantisch; ~ *s.* Protestant(in) *m.* (*f.*)
Protestantism *s.* Protestantismus *m.*
protestation *s.* Beteurung *f.*; Protest *m.*
protester *s.* Protestierende *m.(f.)*; Demonstrant(in) *m.(f.)*
protocol *s.* Protokoll *n.*
protoplasm *s.* Protoplasma *n.*
prototype *s.* Urbild, Muster *n.*; Prototyp *m.*
protract *v.t.* in die Länge ziehen.
protraction *s.* Verzögerung *f.*
protractor *s.* Winkelmesser *m.*
protrude *v.i.* vordringen, hervorragen.
protruberance *s.* Auswuchs *m.*; Beule *f.*
protruberant *a.* (her)vorstehend.
proud *a.*, **~ly** *adv.* stolz.
prove *v.t.* beweisen; ~ *v.i.* sich bewähren, erweisen.
proven *p.* bewiesen.
proverb *s.* Sprichwort *n.*
proverbial *a.*, **~ly** *adv.* sprichwörtlich.
provide *v.t.* versehen; verschaffen, versorgen; festsetzen, bedingen, verordnen; ~ *v.i.* sich vorsehen; sorgen für; *to ~ against,* unmöglich machen; *to be ~d for,* versorgt sein.
provided *c.*, ~ *that,* vorausgesetzt daß.
providence *s.* Vorsehung *f.*
provident *a.*, **~ly** *adv.* vorsichtig; vorausblickend.

providential *a.*, **~ly** *adv.* schicksalhaft; glücklich.
provider *s.* Ernährer(in) *m.*(*f.*); Versorger(in) *m.*(*f.*)
province *s.* Gebiet *n.*; Provinz *f.*
provincial *a.* **~ly** *adv.* provinziell; Provinz. . . ; Provinzler(in) *m.*(*f.*)
provision *s.* Vorsorge, Vorkehrung *f.*; Vorrat *m.*; Bestimmung *f.*; **~s** *pl.* Lebensmittel *n.pl.*, Proviant *m.*; ~ *v.t.* mit Lebensmitteln versorgen.
provisional *s.*, **~ly** *adv.* vorläufig; provisorisch.
proviso *s.* Vorbehalt *m.*
provocation *s.* Herausforderung *f.*
provocative *a.* aufreizend.
provoke *v.t.* herausfordern; provozieren.
provoking *a.*, **~ly** *adv.* empörend.
prow *s.* Bug *m.*, Vorderteil (eines Schiffes) *n.*
prowess *s.*, Tapferkeit *f.*
prowl *v.i.* umherstreichen.
proximity *s.* Nähe, Nachbarschaft *f.*
proxy *s.* Vollmacht *f.*; Stellvertreter(in) *m.*(*f.*); Bevollmächtigte *m.*/*f.*; *by* ~, in Vertretung, per procura.
prude *s.* prüder Mensch *m.*
prudence *s.* Klugheit *f.*, Vernunft *f.*
prudent *a.*, **~ly** *adv.* klug, vorsichtig.
prudential *a.* klug, Klugheits. . .
prudery *s.* Prüderie *f.*
prudish *a.* prüde.
prune *s.* Backpflaume *f.*; ~ *v.t.* (Bäume) beschneiden; putzen.
pruning shears *s.pl.* Gartenschere *f.*
prurience *s.* Lüsternheit *f.*; Geilheit *f.*
prurient *a.* lüstern.
Prussian blue *a.* preussischblau.
prussic acid *s.* Blausäure *f.*
pry *v.i.* spähen, ausforschen.
prying *a.* neugierig, naseweis.
psalm *s.* Psalm *m.*
pseudo *a.* Pseudo. . . , unecht.
pseudonym *s.* Deckname *m.*; Pseudonym *n.*
pshaw! *i.* pah!
psoriasis *s.* Schuppenflechte *f.*
psyche *s.* Psyche *f.*
psychiatric *a.* psychiatrisch.
psychiatrist *s.* Psychiater(in) *m.*(*f.*)
psychiatry *s.* Psychiatrie *f.*
psychic *a.* psychisch; übersinnlich.
psycho *a.* verrückt; ~ *s.* Verrückte *m.*(*f.*)
psychoanalysis *s.* Psychoanalyse *f.*
psychoanalyst *s.* Psychoanalytiker(in) *m.*(*f.*)
psychoanalyze *v.t.* psychoanalysieren.
psychological *a.* psychologisch.
psychologist *s.*, Psychologe *m.*; Psychologin *f.*
psychology *s.* Psychologie *f.*
psychopath *s.* Psychopath(in) *m.*(*f.*)
psychopathic *a.* psychopathisch.
psychosis *s.* Psychose *f.*
psychosomatic *a.* psychosomatisch.
psychotherapist *s.* Psychotherapeut(in) *m.*(*f.*)
psychotherapy *s.* Psychotherapie *f.*
pub *s.* Kneipe *f.*
puberty *s.* Entwicklungsalter *n.*, Pubertät *f.*
pubescent *a.* pubertär.
pubic *a.* Scham. . .
public *a.*, **~ly** *adv.* öffentlich, allgemein; Staats. . . ; ~ *relations pl.* Presse und Propaganda, Werbung *f.*;

~utility, gemeinnütziges Unternehmen *n.*; ~ *s.* Publikum *n.*, Leute *pl.*
publication *s.* Bekanntmachung *f.*; Herausgabe *f.*; Veröffentlichung, Schrift *f.*; ~ *price*, Ladenpreis (eines Buches) *m.*
public-figure *s.* Persönlichkeit des öffentlichen Lebens.
public-house *s.* Wirtshaus *n.*
publicity *s.* Öffentlichkeit *f.*; Reklame *f.*; ~ **agent** *s.* Werbefachmann *m.*
publicize *v.t.* publizieren.
public library *s.* öffentliche Bücherei *f.*
publish *v.t.* herausgeben, verlegen.
publisher *s.* Verleger(in) *m.*(*f.*); Herausgeber(in) *m.*(*f.*)
publishing *s.* Verlagswesen *n.*; ~ **house** *s.* Verlag *m.*
pucker *v.t.* runzeln, falten ~ *v.i.* sich falten; ~ *s.* Falte *f.*
pudding *s.* Pudding *m.*
puddle *s.* Pfütze *f.*; ~ *v.t.* puddeln.
puerile *a.* kindisch.
Puerto Rican *a.* puertoricanisch; ~ *s.* Puertoricaner(in) *m.*(*f.*)
Puerto Rico *s.* Puerto Rico *n.*
puff *s.* Windstoss *m.*; Bausch *m.*; Reklame *f.*; ~ *v.i.* blasen, schnauben; aufschwellen; ~ *v.t.* aufblasen; stolz machen; anpreisen.
puff pastry *s.* Blätterteig *m.*
puffy *a.* bauschig; schwülstig.
pug *s.* Mops *m.*
pugilist *s.* Boxer *m.*
pugnacious *a.* kampfsüchtig.
pugnacity *s.* Kampflust *f.*
puke *v.i.* (*vulg.*) kotzen; ~ *s.* Kotze *f.*
pule *v.i.* piepen; winseln.
pull *v.t.* ziehen; reißen; rudern; ~ *through*, durchkommen; ~ *up*, anhalten; ~ *s.* Zug, Ruck, Stoß *m.*
pullet *s.* Hühnchen *n.*
pulley *s.* Rolle *f.*, Flaschenzug *f.*
pullover *s.* Pullover *m.*
pulmonary *a.* Lungen. . .
pulp *s.* Brei *m.*; Zellstoff *m.*; Fleisch (vom Obst), Mark *n.*
pulpit *s.* Kanzel *f.*
pulsate *v.i.* pulsieren.
pulsation *s.* Pulsschlag *n.*
pulse *s.* Puls *m.*; Hülsenfrucht *f.*
pulverize *v.t.* pulverisieren; zu Staub machen.
pumice *s.* Bimsstein *m.*
pump *s.* Pumpe *f.* ~ *v.t. & i.* pumpen; (*fig.*) ausforschen.
pumpkin *s.* Kürbis *m.*
pun *s.* Wortspiel *n.*; ~ *v.i.* witzeln.
punch *s.* Stoß *m.*; Punze *f.*; Locheisen *n.*; Punsch *m.*; Hanswurst *m.*; ~ *and Judy show*, Kasperletheater; ~ *v.t.* lochen, puffen, schlagen.
punching bag *s.* Sandsack *m.*
punch line *s.* Pointe *f.*
punchy *a.* doof; kräftig.
punctilio *s.* übertriebene Genauigkeit *f.*
punctilious *a.* ängstlich genau, spitzfindig.
punctual *a.*, **~ly** *adv.* pünktlich.
punctuality *s.* Pünktlichkeit *f.*
punctuate *v.t.* interpunktieren.
punctuation *s.* Interpunktion *f.*; Zeichensetzung *f.*;

~ mark *s.* Satzzeichen *n.*
puncture *s.* Stich *m.*; Punktur *f.*; Loch *n.*, Reifenpanne *f.*; Punktion *f.*; *~ v.t.* stechen.
pundit *s.* Experte *m.*; Expertin *f.*; Pandit, gelehrter
Hindu *m.*
pungency *s.* Schärfe *f.*
pungent *a.*, **~ly** *adv.* stechend; scharf.
punish *v.t.* strafen, bestrafen.
punishable *a.* strafbar.
punishing *a.* vernichtend; mörderisch; zerm-
ürbend.
punishment *s.* Strafe, Bestraufung *f.*
punitive *a.* Straf...
punster *s.* Wortspieler *m.*
punt *s.* flacher Kahn *m.*, Schauke *f.*; *~ v.i.* staken.
puny *a.* winzig; schwach.
pup *s.* junger Hund *m.*; *in ~,* trächtig (von
Hunden).
pupa *s.* (*zool.*) Puppe *f.*
pupate *v.i.* sich verpuppen.
pupil *s.* Pupille *f.*; Mündel *n.*; Zögling *m.*
puppet *s.* Puppe *f.*, Marionette *f.*
puppet-show *s.* Puppenspiel *n.*
puppy *s.* junger Hund *m.*; Laffe *m.*
purchase *s.* Kauf *m.*; **~-tax**, Verkaufssteuer *f.*; *~ v.t.*
kaufen; erwerben; *purchasing power*, Kaufkraft *f.*
purchaser *s.* Käufer(in) *m.(f.)*
pure *a.*, **~ly** *adv.* rein, echt; lauter.
purgation *s.* Reinigung *f.*
purgative *a.* reinigend; *~ s.* Abführmittel *n.*
purgatory *s.* Fegefeuer *n.*
purge *v.t.* reinigen; läutern; abführen; *~ s.* politische Säuberung *f.*
purification *s.* Reinigung.
purifier *s.* Reiniger *m.*
purify *v.t.* reinigen, klären.
purist *s.* Purist(in) *m.(f.)*
Puritan *s.* Puritaner(in) *m.(f.)*
puritanical *a.* puritanisch.
purity *s.* Reinheit, Keuschheit.
purl *s.* Geriesel *n.*; Gekräusel *n.*; linke Masche *f.* *~
v.i.* rieseln.
purlieu *s.* Umgebung *f.*
purloin *v.t.* entwenden.
purple *s.* Purpur *m.*; *~ a.* purpurn.
purport *s.* Inhalt *m.*; *~ v.t.* zum Inhalt haben;
scheinbar besagen; *~ed,* angeblich.
purpose *s.* Absicht *f.*; Zweck *m.*; Inhalt *m.*; Tendenz
f.; *on ~,* absichtlich; *to the ~,* zweckdienlich; *to no
~,* vergebens; *novel with a ~,* Tendenzroman *m.*; *~
v.t.* sich vornehmen.
purposeful *a.* entschlossen; zielstrebig.
purposeless *a.* zwecklos.
purposely *adv.* absichtlich.
purr *v.i.* schnurren (von Katsen).
purse *s.* Geldtäschchen *n.*; Börse *f.*; *~ v.t.* rümpfen,
runzeln.
purser *s.* Zahlmeister(in) *m.(f.)*
pursuance *s.* Verfolgung *f.*, Verfolg *m.*; *in ~ of,* in

Ausübung...
pursuant to *pr.* zufolge, gemäß.
pursue *v.t.* verfolgen; fortsetzen; fortfahren;
(Beruf) betrieben.
pursuit *s.* Verfolgung *f.*; Trachten *n.*; **~s** *pl.* Geschäfte *n.pl.*
purulent *a.* eitrig.
purvey *v.t.* versorgen, liefern.
purveyor *s.* Lieferant(in) *m.(f.)*
purview *s.* Verfügung *f.*; Bereich *m.*
pus *s.* Eiter *m.*
push *v.t. & i.* stoßen, schieben; beschleunigen; *~ s.*
Stoß, Schub *m.*
pusher *s.* Dealer; Pusher; Streber(in) *m.(f.)*
pushing *a.* aufdringlich, streberhaft.
pusillanimity *s.* Kleinmut *m.*
pusillanimous *a.*, **~ly** *adv.* kleinmütig.
puss, pussy *s.* Mieze (Katze) *f.*
pustule *s.* Bläschen *n.*
put *v.t.ir.* setzen, stellen, legen; stecken; *to ~ at,*
schätzen auf; *to ~ by,* beiseitelegen; *to ~ down,*
aufschreiben; *to ~ forward,* vorbringen; *to ~ in,* in
den Hafen einlaufen; *to ~ into operation, effect,* ausführen; *to ~ on,* anlegen; aufsetzen; anziehen;
umbinden; (*fig.*) annehmen, erheucheln; *to ~ on
flesh,* Fleisch ansetzen; *to ~ on weight,* zunehmen;
to ~ off, weglegen, hinhalten, aufschieben; *to ~ out,*
auslöschen; ärgern; ausfahren (Flotte); ausstrecken; *to ~ to,* hinzufügen; anspannen; *to ~
together,* zusammenstellen; *to ~ up,* aufstellen,
errichten, aufschlagen (Bett), einsetzen (Pflanze),
heraufsetzen (Preis); verpacken; unterbringen;
absteigen, einkehren; *to ~ up for sale,* meistbietend
verkaufen; *to ~ up with,* sich abfinden mit; **~-up**
job, abgekartete Sache *f.*; *to ~ through to,* (*tel.*) Verbindung herstellen mit.
putative *a.* vermeintlich; mutmaßlich.
putrefaction *s.* Zersetzung *f.*; Fäulnis *f.*
putrefy *v.i.* sichzersetzen; faul werden.
putrescent *a.* faulend.
putrid *a.* faul, verfault.
putty *s.* Glaserkitt *m.*
put-up job *s.* abgekartetes Spiel *n.*
puzzle *v.t.* verwirren, in Verlegenheit bringen *~ s.*
Verwirrung *f.*; Rätsel *n.*; Puzzle *n.*
puzzled *n.* ratlos.
puzzlement *s.* Verwirrung *f.*
puzzling *s.* rätselhaft.
pygmy *s.* Zwerg(in) *m.(f.)*; Pygmäe *m.* Pygmäin *f.*
pyjamas *pl.* Schlafanzug *m.*; Pyjama *m.*
pylon *s.* Mast *m.*
pyramid *s.* Pyramide *f.*
pyre *s.* Scheiterhaufen *m.*
Pyrenees *s.pl.* Pyrenäen *pl.*
pyromania *s.* Pyromanie *f.*
pyromaniac *a.* Pyromane *m.*; Pyromanin *f.*
pyrotechnics *s.pl.* Feuerwerkskunst *f.*
Pyrrhic victory *s.* Pyrrhussieg *m.*
python *s.* Python *f.*
pyx *s.* Pyxis *f.*; Hostienbehälter *m.*

Q

Q, q der Buchstabe Q oder q *n.*
quack *v.i.* quacken; marktschreierisch anpreisen; *~
s.* Quacksalber *m.*; Marktschreier *m.*

quackery *s.* Quacksalberei *f.*
quad *s.* Vierling *m.*; viereckiger Innenhof *m.*
quadrangle *s.* Viereck *n.*; Hof *m.*

quadraphonic *a.* quadrophon(isch).

quadratic *a.* quadratisch.

quadrilateral *a.* vierseitig.

quadrille *s.* Quadrille *f.*; Kontretanz *m.*

quadripartite *a.* Viermächte. . .

quadruped *a.* vierfüßig; ~ *s.* Vierfüßer *m.*

quadruple *a.,* **~ply** *adv.* vierfach; ~ *s.* Vierfache *n.*; ~ *v.t.* vervierfachen.

quadruplets *pl.* Vierlinge *pl.*

quaff *v.i. & t.* zechen.

quagmire *s.* Sumpf, Moorboden *m.*; Morast *m.*

quail *s.* Wachtel *f.*; ~ *v.i.* verzagen.

quaint *a.,* **~ly** *adv.* seltsam; niedlich.

quake *v.i.* zittern, beben.

Quaker *s.* Quäker(in) *m.(f.)*

qualification *s.* Eigenschaft *f.*; Befähigung *f.*; Beschränkung *f.*

qualified *a.* geeignet; qualifiziert; berechtigt; bestimmt; bedingt; eingeschränkt.

qualify *v.t.* befähigen; einschränken; bestimmen; ~ *v.i.* seine Befähigung nachweisen; *to ~ for,* Befähigung erwerben für; *~ing date,* Stichtag *m.*; *~ing match s.* Qualifikationsspiel *n. ~ing period,* Probezeit *f.*

qualitative *a.* qualitativ.

quality *s.* Eigenschaft, Beschaffenheit *f.*; Qualität *f.*; (hoher) Stand, Rang *m.*; ~ *papers,* Qualitätspapiere *pl.*

qualm *s.* Bedenken *pl.*; Zweifel *pl.*

quandary *s.* Dilemma *n.*; Ungewißheit *f.*; Verlegenheit *f.*

quantify *v.t.* quantifizieren.

quantitative *a.* der Menge nach.

quantity *s.* Menge, Anzahl *f.*; *(math.)* Grösse *f.*; Quantität *f.*

quantum *s.* Menge, Grösse *f.*; Betrag *m.*; Quant *n.*

quantum leap *s.* Quantensprung *m.*

quarantine *s.* Liegezeit, Quarantäne *f.*

quarrel *s.* Zank *m.*; Streit *m.*; ~ *v.i.* sich zanken, streiten.

quarrelsome *a.,* **~ly** *adv.* zänkisch.

quarry *s.* Steinbruch *m.*; verfolgtes Wild *n.*; Beute *f.* ~ *v.t.* Steine brechen.

quart *s.* Viertelmaß *n.*

quarter *s.* Viertel *n.*; Stadviertel *n.*; Vierteljahr *n.*; Wohnung *f.*; Quartier *n.*; **~s** *pl.* *(mil.)* Unterkunft *f.*; ~ *v.t.* vierteilen; beherbergen; einquartieren.

quarter-deck *s.* Achterdeck, Halbdeck *n.*

quarterly *a. & adv.* vierteljährlich; ~ *s.* Vierteljahrsschrift *f.*

quarter-master *s.* Quartiermeister *m.*

quarter-note *s.* Viertelnote *f.*

quartet(te) *s.* Quartett *n.*

quarto *s.* Quartformat *n.*; Quartband *m.*

quartz *s.* Quarz *m.*

quasar *s.* Quasar *m.*

quash *v.t.* unterdrücken; vernichten; (Urteil) aufheben.

quasi *a. & adv.* gewissermaßen, Halb. . . , scheinbar.

quaver *v.i.* zittern; trillern; ~ *s.* *(mus.)* Tremolo *n.*; Achtelnote *f.*

quay *s.* Kai *m.*

queasy *a.* übel, unwohl; überempfindlich.

queen *s.* Königin *f.*

queen bee *s.* Bienenkönigin *f.*

queer *a.,* **~ly** *adv.* wunderlich, seltsam; verdächtig;

unwohl, schwindlig.

quell *v.t.* dämpfen; unterdrücken; zügeln.

quench *v.t.* löschen; (den Durst) stillen.

querulous *a.,* **~ly** *adv.* reizbar; gereizt.

query *s.* Frage *f.*; ~ *v.t.* fragen, bezweifeln.

quest *s.* Suchen *n.*; Untersuchung *f.*; *in ~ of,* auf der Suche.

question *s.* Frage *f.*; Streitfrage *f.*; Untersuchung *f.*; Zweifel *m.*; *in ~,* fraglich, vorliegend; *~!,* zur Sache!; ~ *v.i.& t.* fragen, befragen; verhören, vernehmen; bezwiefeln.

questionable *a.* zweifelhaft, fraglich; fragwürdig.

questioning *a.* fragend; **~s.** Fragen *n.*; Befragung *f.*; Vernehmung *f.*

question-mark *s.* Fragezeichen *n.*

questionnaire *s.* Fragebogen *m.*

queue *s.* Zopf *m.*; Schlange (von Menschen); *to ~ up,* *v.i.* Schlange stehen.

quibble *s.* Wortspiel *n.*; Zweideutigkeit *f.*; Ausflucht *f.*; ~ *v.i.* (spitzfindig) witzeln; ausweichen.

quick *a. & adv.,* **~ly** *adv.* schnell; lebendig; lebhaft; hurtig; scharfsinnig; **~-acting** *a.* schnellwirkend; ~ **march!,** vorwärts marsch!; ~ **step,** Geschwindschritt *m.*

quicken *v.t.* beleben, beschleunigen; ~ *v.i.* lebendig werden.

quicklime *s.* ungelöschter Kalk *m.*

quickness *s.* Schnelligkeit *f.*; Schärfe *f.*

quicksand *s.* Treibsand *m.*

quicksilver *s.* Quecksilber *n.*

quick-tempered *a.* hitzig.

quick-witted *a.* geistesgegenwärtig.

quid *s.* Priemchen *n.*; Pfund *(n.)* Sterling.

quid-pro-quo *s.* Gegenleistung *f.*

quiescence *s.* Ruhe *f.*

quiescent *a.* ruhend.

quiet *a.,* **~ly** *adv.* ruhig, gelassen; still, leise; **~s.** Ruhe *f.*; ~ *v.t.* beruhigen.

quieten *v.t.* beruhigen.

quill *s.* Federkiel *m.*; Feder *f.*

quilt *s.* Steppdecke *f.*; ~ *v.t.* steppen.

quince *s.* Quitte *f.*

quinine *s.* Chinin *n.*

quinsy *s.* Bräune (Halskrankheit) *f.*

quint *s.* Quinte *f.*

quintessence *s.* Quintessenz *f.*

quintet(te) *s.* Quintett *n.*

quintuple *a.* fünffach.

quintuplets *s.pl.* Fünflinge *pl.*

quip *s.* Stichelei *f.*; Witzelei *f.*; **~v.i.** sticheln, witzeln.

quirk *s.* Stichelei *f.*; Kniff *m.*; Schnörkel *m.*

quit *a.* quitt, los, frei; ~ *v.t.* verlassen; lossprechen; fahren lassen; *notice to ~,* Kündigung *f.*

quite *adv.* völlig, gänzlich.

quits *adv.* quitt, abgemacht.

quiver *s.* Köcher *m.*; ~ *v.i.* zittern.

quixotic *a.* donquichottisch.

quiz *v.t.* ausfragen; ~ *s.* Examen *n.* Quiz *n.*

quoin *s.* Ecke (eines Hauses) *f.*; Keil *(m.)* des Setzers

quoit *s.* Wurfring *m.* (Spiel).

quondam *adv.* ehemalig.

quorum *s.* beschlußfähige Anzahl *f.*

quota *s.* Anteil *m.*, Quote *f.*; Zuteilung *f.*; Kontingent *n.*

quotation s. Anführung f.; Zitat n.; Preisangabe f.;
Notierung f.; ~ **marks** pl. Anführungszeichen n.
quote v.t. (Stellen) anführen; zitieren; (einen Preis)

notieren, berechnen.
quotient s. Quotient, Teilzähler m.

R

R, r der Buchstabe R oder r n.
rabbet s. Fuge f.; Falz m.; Nuthobel m.; ~v.t. ein-
fugen; abhobeln.
rabbi s. Rabbiner m.
rabbit s. Kaninchen n.
rabbit punch s. Genickschlag m.
rabbit-hutch s. Kaninchenstall m.
rabble s. Pöbel, Mob m.
rabid a. wütend, rasend.
rabies s. Tollwut f.
race s. Rasse f., Geschlecht n.; Wettlauf m.; Rennen
n.; ~s pl. Pferderennen n.; ~ v.i. wettrennen.
race-course s. Rennbahn f.
race-meeting s. Rennen n.
race-track s. Rennstrecke f.
racial a., ~ly adv. rassisch, völkisch; Rassen. . .
racism s. Rassismus m.
racist s. Rassist(in) m.(f.); ~a. rassistisch.
rack s. Foltenbank f.; Raufe f.; luggage ~, Gepäck-
netz n.; Gestell n.; ~ and ruin, gänzlich zu Grunde;
~ v.t. strecken, foltern; to ~ one's brains, sich den
Kopf zerbrechen.
racket s. Schläger m. (Sport); Lärm m.; Erpressung,
Schiebung f.
racketeer s. Scheiber m.; Wucherer m.
racking a. quälend.
racoon s. Waschbär m.
racy a. rassig; flott.
radar s. (mil.) Funkmeßgerät n.
radial a., ~ly adv. strahlenförmig; Radial. . .
radiance s. Glanz m.; Strahlen n.
radiant a. strahlend.
radiate v.t. & i. ausstrahlen, strahlen.
radiation s. Ausstrahlung f.
radiator s. Heizkörper m.; (mot.) Kühler m.
radical a., ~ly adv. Grund. . . ; eingewurzelt; radikal; ~ s. Wurzel f., Grundstoff m.; Radikale m.
radio s. Radio n., Funk m.; ~**active** a. radioaktiv;
~**activity** s. Radioaktivität f., ~**-carbon dating** s.
Radiokarbondatierung f.; ~**graphy** s. Radio-
graphie f.; ~**logy** s. Radiologie f. ~ **operator** s.
Funker, Bordfunker m.; ~**-set** s. Radioapparat m.;
~**-station** s. Rundfunksender m.
radiotherapy Radiotherapie f., Strahlentherapie f.
radish s. Radieschen n.; Rettich m.
radium s. Radium n.
radius s. Halbmesser m.; Strahl m.; Umkreis m.
radon s. Radon n.
raffia s. Raffiabast m,.
raffle s. Lotterie f.; Tombola f.; ~ v.i. verlosen.
raft s. Floß n.
rafter s. Dachsparren m.
rag s. Lumpfen m.; Ulk m.; ~v.t. necken.
ragamuffin s. Lumpenkerl m.
rage s. Wut, Raserei f.; Entzückung f.; ~ v.i. rasen.
ragged a. zerlumpt; rauh.

ragout s. Ragout n.
raid s. Überfall m.; Beutezug m.
raider s. Plünderer m.; Plünderin f.; Räuber(in)
m.(f.)
rail s. Riegel m.; Querholz n.; Geländer n.; Schiene
f.; (nav.) Reling f.; by ~, mit der Eisenbahn; ~ v.t.
mit einem Gitter versehen; ~ v.i. schimpfen.
railing s. Geländer n.; Zaun m.
raillery s. Spöttelei f.
railway, railroad s. Eisenbahn f.; ~**-network** s.
Eisenbahnnetz n.; ~**-shop** s. Eisenbahnwerkstatt f.
railway-guide s. Kursbuch n.
raiment s. Kleidung f.
rain s. Regen m.; ~ v.i. imp. regen; ~**-coat** s. Regenmantel m.; ~**fall** s. Niederschlagsmenge f.;
~**-soaked** a. vom Regen durchnäßt; ~**storm** s.
Regenguß m.; ~**wear** s. Regenkleidung f.
rainbow s. Regenbogen m.
rainforest s. Regenwald m.
rain-guage s. Regenmesser m.
rainproof a. wasserdicht.
rainy a. regnerisch, Regen. . . ; for a ~ day, für eine
Notzeit.
raise v.t. aufheben, erheben; errichten; erhöhen;
erregen, veranlassen; aufziehen; werben; auftreiben (Geld); ~s. Lohnerhöhung f.
raisin s. Rosine f.
rake s. Rechen m.; Wüstling m.; ~ v.t. harken; zu-
sammenschüren, scharren; durchstöbern;
rakish a., ~ly adv. flott, keß.
rally v.t. wieder sammeln; aufmuntern ~ v.i. sich
weider sammeln; sich erholen; ~ s. Sammlung f.;
Tagung, Treffen, Versammlung f.; (Autosport)
Sternfahrt f.
ram s. Widder m.; Schafbock m.; ~ v.t. einrammen.
ramble v.i. umherschweifen; abschweifen; ~ s.
Ausflug m.
rambler s. Wanderer m.; Wanderin f.
rambling a. zusammenhanglos; (von Gebäuden)
unregelmäßig.; verwinkelt- ~ **rose** s. Kletterrose f.
ramification s. Verzweigung f.; Auswirkungen pl.
ramify v.t. & i. (sich) verzweigen.
ramp v.i. sich drohend aufrichten (vom Tier);
toben; ~ s. Rampe; Schwindelei f.
rampage v.i. randalieren, wüten; go on the ~, Randale (f.) machen.
rampant a. dreist; überhandnehmend; wuchernd;
ansteigend.
rampart s. Wall m.; Wehrgang m.
ramshackle a. wack[e]lig, baufällig.
ranch s. Farm f.
rancid a. ranzig.
rancidity s. Ranzigkeit f.
rancor s. Groll m.; Erbitterung f.
rancorous a., ~ly adv. voller Groll, erbittert.
random a. zufällig, Zufalls. . . ; willkürlich at ~, aufs

Geradewohl, ins Blaue.

randy *a.* (*fam.*) scharf, geil.

range *s.* Reihe *f.*; Ordnung *f.*; Küchenherd *m.*; Umfang *m.*; Bereich *m.*; Spielraum *m.*; Schußweite *f.*; ~ *of prices*, Prieslage *f.*; ~ *v.i.* sich reihen; herumstreifen; sich erstrecken; ~ *v.t.* ordnen; schweifen über.

rangefinder *s.* (*phot.*) Entfernungsmesser *m.*

ranger *s.* Aufseher(in) *m.*(*f.*); Förster(in) *m.*(*f.*)

rank *s.* Reihe *f.*; Linie *f.*; Glied *n.*; Rang *m.*; *to serve in the* ~*s*, (*mil.*) als gemeiner Soldat dienen; ~ *v.t. & i.* reihen, sich reihen; zugehören; *it* ~*s third*, es steht an dritter Stelle; ~ *a.*, ~**ly** *adv.* üppig, übermäßig; ranzig; arg; Erz. . . , rein.

rankle *v.i.* sich entzünden; schmerzen; (*fig.*) nagen.

ransack *v.t.* plündern; durchstöbern.

ransom *s.* Lösegeld *n.*; ~ *v.t.* loskaufen.

rant *s.* schwülstige Gerede *n.* ~ *v.i.* schwülstig reden; eifern; wüten.

ranter *s.* Großsprecher *m.*

rap *v.t. & i.* schlagen, klopfen;- ~ *s.* Schlag *m.*; Klopfen *n.*; Nasenstüber *m.*

rapacious *a.*, ~**ly** *adv.* habgierig.

rapacity *s.* Habgier *f.*

rape *s.* Notzucht *f.*; Vergewaltigung *f.* ~ *v.i.* vergewaltigen, notzüchtigen.

rape *s.* Raps *m.*; ~ *oil* *s.* Rapsöl *n.*

rapid *a.*, ~**ly** *adv.* schnell, reißend; ~**s** *s.pl.* Stromschnellen *f.pl.*

rapidity *s.* Schnelligkeit *f.*

rapier *s.* Rapier *n.*

rapine *s.* Raub *m.*

rapist *s.* Vergewaltiger *m.*

rapport *s.* (harmonisches) Verhältnis *n.*

rapt *a.* hingerissen, entzückt.

rapture *s.* Entzückung *f.*; Verzückung *f.*

rapturous *a.* hinreißend; leidenschaftlich.

rare *a.*, ~**ly** *adv.* selten; kostbar; dünn; nicht durchgebraten, englisch gebraten.

rarefied *a.* dünn; exklusiv.

rarefy *v.t.* verdünnen.

rareness, rarity *s.* Seltenheit *f.*; Dünnheit *f.*

raring *a.* (*fam.*) **to be** ~ kaum abwarten können.

rascal *s.* Schurke *m.*; Schlingel *m.*

rascality *s.* Schurkerei *f.*

rash *a.*, ~**ly** *adv.* übereilt, unbesonnen; ~ *s.* Hautausschlag *m.*

rasher *s.* Scheibe (Speck) *f.*

rasp *v.t.* raspeln; wehtun; ~ *s.* Raspel *f.*

raspberry *s.* Himbeere *f.*

rasping *a.* krächzend; rasselnd.

rat *s.* Ratte *f.*; Spitzel *m.*

rate *s.* Preis *m.*; Taxe *f.*; Anteil *m.*, Satz *m.*, Rate (statistisch) *f.*; geringes Maß *n.*; Verhältnis *n.*; Grad, Rang *m.*; Klasse *f.*; *at any* ~, auf jeden Fall; ~ *v.t.* schätzen, einschätzen; tadeln; ~ *v.t.* rangieren, einen bestimmten Wert haben; *to* ~ *highly*, einen hohen Wert haben.

rather *adv.* vielmehr, lieber; ziemlich; *I had* ~, ich wollte lieber.

ratification *s.* Bestätigung *f.*; Ratifizierung *f.*

ratify *v.t.* bestätigen, ratifizieren.

rating *s.* Einschätzung *f.*; Einschaltquote *f.*; Dienstgrad *m.*

ratio *s.* Verhältnis *n.*

ration *s.* Ration *f.*, Zuteilung; ~**-book** *s.* Lebensmittelkarten *pl.*; ~ *v.t.* rationieren; ~*ing*, Rationierung *f.*

rational *a.*, ~**ly** *adv.* vernünftig; rational.

rationale *s.* rationale Erklärung *f.*; logische Grundlage *f.*

rationalization *s.* Rationalisierung *f.*

rationalize *v.t.* rationalisieren.

rattle *s.* Geklapper *n.*; Knarre *f.*; Geschnatter *n.*; Röcheln *n.*; ~ *v.t. & i.* rasseln; knarren; plappern.

rattle-snake *s.* Klapperschlange *f.*

rattling *a.* rasselnd; klappernd.

ratty *a.* (*fam.*) reizbar; (*fig.*) schäbig; verkommen, abgenutzt.

raucous *a.* heiser, rauh.

ravage *v.t.* verwüsten, verheeren; ~ *s.* Verwüstung *f.*

rave *v.i.* rasen, wüten; schwärmen.

ravel *v.t.* verwickeln; ~ *out*, ausfasern; ~ *v.i.* ~ **out,** sich auffasern, sich entwirren.

raven *s.* Rabe *m.*

ravenous *a.*, ~**ly** *adv.* gefräßig; gierig.

ravine *s.* Schlucht *f.*

raving *a.*, ~**ly** *adv.* rasend; faselnd; (*fam.*) phantastisch.

ravish *v.t.* hinreißen, entzücken.

ravishing *a.* hinreißend.

ravishment *s.* Entzückung *f.*

raw *a.*, ~**ly** *adv.* roh; unreif; rauh; neu, unerfahren; wund; unverdünnt (von Spirituosen).

raw material *s.* Rohmaterial *n.*

ray *s.* Strahl *m.*; Rochen *m.*; ~ *v.t.* strahlen.

rayon *s.* Kunstseide *f.*

raze *v.t.* schleifen, zerstören; radieren.

razor *s.* Rasiermesser *n.*; Rasierapparat *m.*; Rasierer *m.*

razor-blade *s.* Rasierklinge *f.*

razor-edge *s.* Rasierschneide *f.*; *be on the* ~, auf des Messers Schneide stehen.

razor-strop *s.* Streichriemen *m.*

razzia *s.* Razzia *f.*

re *pr.* betreffend.

reach *v.t.* reichen, langen; erreichen; ~ *v.i.* sich erstrecken; streben; ~ *s.* Reichweite *f.*; Strecke *f.*; Flußabschnitt, Strombaschnitt *m.*; Raum, Bereich *m.*; Hörweite, Schußweite *f.*; Fassungskraft *f.*

reachable *a.* erreichbar.

react *v.i.* rückwirken, gegenwirken; (*chem.*) reagieren.

reaction *s.* Rückwirkung *f.*; Reaktion *f.*; (*elek.*) Rückkopplung *s.*

reactionary *a.* reaktionär; ~ *s.* Reaktionär(in) *m.*(*f.*)

reactor *s.* (nuclear) Kernreaktor *m.*

read *v.t. & i.ir.* lesen, vorlesen; (fürs Examen) studieren; sich lesen, lauten, klingen; anzeigen (von Meßapparaten).

readable *a.* lesbar.

readdress *v.t.* umadressieren.

reader *s.* Leser(in) *m.*(*f.*); Vorleser(in) *m.*(*f.*); Lektor(in) *m.*(*f.*)

readership *s.* Leserschaft *f.*; Leserkreis *m.*

readiness *s.* Bereitwilligkeit *f.*

reading *s.* Lektüre *f.*; Belesenheit *f.*; Lesart *f.*; Stand *m.*, Ablesung *f.* (eines Meßapparates).

reading-glasses *s.pl.* Lesebrille *f.*

reading-knowledge *s.* Leseverstehen *n.*
reaching-list *s.* Literaturliste *f.*
reading-room *s.* Lesezimmer *n.*
readjust *v.i.* sich umstellen; ~*v.t.* einstellen.
readmission *s.* Wierderzulassung *f.*
readmit *v.t.* wieder zulassen.
ready *a.*, ~**ily** *adv.* bereit; fertig.
ready-made *a.* gebrauchsfertig; konfektions...
  ready-to-serve *a.* servierfertig; **ready-to-wear**
  a. Konfektions...
reaffirm *v.t.* bekräftigen.
reagent *s.* Reagens *n.*
real *a.*, ~**ly** *adv.* echt (auch Perle, Diamant, etc.); in
  der Tat, wesentlich, wirklich.
real estate *s.* Grundbesitz; ~ **register** *s.* Grundbuch, *n.*
realization *s.* Verwirklichung *f.*; Verwertung *f.*
realism *s.* Realismus *m.*
reality *s.* Wirklichkeit, Wesenheit *f.*
realize *v.t.* verwirklichen; erzielen; sich vorstellen;
  zu Geld machen.
real life *s.* wirkliches Leben *n.*
really *adv.* wirklich, in der Tat.
realm *s.* Königreich, Reich *n.*
realty *s.* Grundbesitz *m.*
ream *s.* Ries (Papier) *n.*; ~ *v.t.* (*mech.*) ausweiten,
  ausbohren.
reamer *s.* (*mech.*) Ausbohrwerkzeug *n.*, Aufräumer
  m.
reanimate *v.t.* wieder beleben.
reap *v.t. & i.* Korn schneiden; einernten.
reaper *s.* Schnitter *m.*; Mähmaschine *f.*
reappear *v.i.* wieder erscheinen, auftauchen.
reappearance *s.* Wiedererscheinen *n.*; Wiederauftauchen *n.*
reappraisal *s.* Neubewertung *f.*
reappraise *v.t.* bewerten.
rear *s.* hinterer Teil *m.*; Rückseite *f.* Hintergrund *m.*;
  Hinter... (*mil.*) rückwärtig; ~ **area** *s.* rückwärtiges
  Heeresgebiet *n.*; ~ **cover** *s.* Rückendeckung *f.*; ~
  light *s.* (*mot. und cycling*) Schlußlicht, Katzenauge
  n.; ~ **wheel** *s.* Hinterrad *n.*; ~ *v.t.* heben; erziehen,
  aufziehen; ~ *v.i.* sich aufbäumen.
rear-guard *s.* Nachhut *f.*
rearm *v.i.* aufrüsten.
rearmament *s.* Aufrüstung *f.*
rearrange *v.t.* umräumen; verlegen (Termin).
rearrangement *s.* Umräumen *n.*; Verlegen *n.*
reason *s.* Vernunft *f.*; Ursache *f.*; Grund *m.*; *it stands
  to* ~, es ist klar; ~ *v.i.* schließen; nachdenken; streiten; ~ *v.t.* durchdenken; erörtern.
reasonable *a.*, ~**ly** *adv.* vernünftig; billig; ziemlich;
  ~ *prices*, mäßige Preise *pl.*
reasoned *a.* durchdacht.
reasoning *s.* Urteilskraft, Beweisführung *f.*; *line of*
  ~, Gedankengang *m.*
reassemble *v.t.* (*v.i.* sich) wieder versammeln,
  zusammenbauen.
reassurance *s.* Bestätigung *f.*; Beruhigung *f.*
reassure *v.t.* beruhigen.; bestätigen.
reassuring *a.* beruhigend.
rebate *s.* Rabatt *m.*, Abzug *m.*
rebel *v.i.* sich empören; ~ *s.* Rebell, Empörer *m.*
rebellion *s.* Empörung *f.*
rebellious *a.*, ~**ly** *adv.* aufrührerisch; rebellisch.
rebirth *s.* Wiedergeburt *f.*

reborn *a.* wiedergeboren.
rebound *v.i.* zurückprallen; abprallen.
rebuff *s.* Rückstoß *m.*; Abweisung *f.*; ~ *v.t.* zurück-
  stoßen; abweisen.
rebuild *v.t.st.* wieder aufbauen; umbauen.
rebuke *v.t.* tadeln; auszanken; ~ *s.* Tadel, Verweis
  m.
rebut *v.t.* widerlegen, zurückweisen.
rebuttal *s.* Widerlegung *f.*, Gegenbeweis *m.*
recalcitrant *a.* widerstrebend, störrig.
recall *s.* Zurückberufung *f.*; Widerruf *m.*; ~ *v.t.*
  zurückrufen; sich erinnern; kündigen.
recant *v.t. & i.* widerrufen.
recantation *s.* Widerruf *m.*
recapitulate *v.t.* kurz wiederholen.
racapitulation *s.* Zusammenfassung *f.*
recapture *s.* Wieder(gefangen)nahme *f.*; Zurück-
  eroberung *f.* ~ *v.t.* wieder(gefangen)nehmen; Zu-
  rückerobern.
recast *v.t.* umschmelzen; umarbeiten; umformen.
recede *v.i.* zurückweichen; schwinden.
receding *a.* fliehend (Kinn, Stirn); zurückgehend.
receipt *s.* Empfang *m.*; Entgegennahme *f.*; Einnahme *f.*; Quittung *f.*; Aufnahme *f.*; Rezept *n.* ~
  v.t. quittieren.
receive *v.t.* empfangen, annehmen.
receiver *s.* Empfänger *m.* (auch Radio); (*tel.*) Hörer
  m.; Einnehmer *m.*; ~ *of stolen goods*, Hehler *m.*;
  official ~, Konkursverwalter *m.*
recent *a.* neu; frisch; ~**ly** *adv.* neulich.
receptacle *s.* Behälter *m.*
reception *s.* Aufnahme *f.*; Empfang *m.*
receptionist *s.* Empfangsdame *f.*; Empfangschef
  m.; Sprechstundenhilfe *f.*
receptive *a.* empfänglich.
recess *s.* Zurückgehen *n.*; Falte *f.*; Nische *f.*; Einbuchtung *f.*; Versteck *m.*; Ferien *pl.*; zeitweilige
  Vertagung (einer Sitzung) *f.*
recession *s.* Zurückweichen *n.*; Rezession *f.*
recharge *v.t.* aufladen; nachladen.
rechargeable *a.* wiederaufladbar.
recipe *s.* Rezept *n.*
recipient *s.* Empfänger(in) *m.*(*f.*)
reciprocal *a.*, ~**ly** *adv.* wechselseitig.
reciprocate *v.t. & i.* abwechseln; erwidern.
reciprocity *s.* Gegenseitigkeit *f.*
recital, recitation *s.* Vortrag *m.*; Musikvortrag *m.*;
  Hersagen *n.*; Erzählung *f.*
recitation *s.* Rezitation *f.*
recite *v.t.* vortragen; hersagen.
reckless *a.* unbekümmert, tollkühn; rücksichtslos.
recklessness *s.* Rücksichtslosigkeit *f.*
reckon *v.t. & i.* rechnen, schätzen, achten; meinen;
  to ~ *up*, zusammenrechnen; *to* ~ *over again*,
  nachrechnen.
reckoning Rechnen *n.*; Rechnung *f.*; Berechnung
  f.
reclaim *v.t.* zurückfordern; bekehren; (Land) urbar
  machen.
reclamation *s.* Zurückforderung *f.*; Urbarmachung
  f.
recline *v.t.* (*v.i.* sich) (zurück) lehnen.
recluse *s.* Einsiedler(in) *m.*(*f.*)
reclusive *a.* zurückgezogen.
recognition *s.* Wiedererkennen *n.*; Anerkennung
  f.

recognizable *a.* (wieder) erkennbar.

recognizance *s.* schriftliche Verpflichtung *f.* (vor Gericht).

recognize *v.t.* wiedererkennen; anerkennen.

recoil *v.i.* zurückprallen; zurückschrecken; ~ *s.* Rückstoß *m.*

recollect *v.i.* sich besinnen, sich erinnern.

recollection *s.* Erinnerung *f.*; Gedächtnis *n.*

recommend *v.t.* empfehlen.

recommendation *s.* Empfehlung *f.*

recompense *v.t.* vergelten; entschädigen; belohnen; ~ *s.* Vergeltung *f.*; Belohnung *f.*; Anerkennung *f.*

reconcilable *a.* versöhnbar; vereinbar.

reconcile *v.t.* versöhnen; vereinigen.

reconciliation *s.* Versöhnung *f.*

recondite *a.* verborgen; unverständlich.

recondition *v.t.* neu instandsetzen, überholen.

reconnaissance *s.* (*mil.*) Aufklärung *f.*; close ~, Nahaufklärung *f.*; long-range ~, Fernaufklärung *f.*

reconnoiter *v.t.* auskundschaften.

reconquer *v.t.* wiedererobern.

reconsider *v.t.* von neuem erwägen.

reconstruct *v.t.* wieder aufbauen; rekonstruieren.

record *v.t.* eintragen; ~ *s.* Verzeichnis *n.*; Urkunde *f.*; Protokoll *n.*; Bericht *m.*; Ruf *m.*; Höchstleistung *f.*; (Schall-) Platte *f.*; good ~, gutes Vorleben *n.*; bad ~, schlechtes Vorleben *n.*; no criminal ~, nicht vorbestraft; the worst on ~, der nachweisbar schlechteste; to place on ~, zu Protokoll geben; electric ~-player, elektrischer Plattenspieler *m.*; ~s *pl.* Akten *pl.*; Archiv *n.*; Chronik *f.*

recorded *a.* aufgezeichnet; überliefert.

recorder *s.* Kassettenrecorder *m.*; Tonbandgerät *n.*; Blockflöte *f.*

record-holder *s.* Rekordhalter(in) *m.*(*f.*); Rekordinhaber(in) *m.*(*f.*)

recording *s.* Aufnahme *f.*; ~ **session** *s.* Aufnahme *f.*; ~ **studio** *s.* Tonstudio *n.*

recount *v.t.* erzählen.

re-count *v.t.* nachzählen.

recoup *v.t.* entschädigen; wieder einbringen.

recourse *s.* Zuflucht *f.*; (*law*) Regreß, Rekurs *m.*; to have ~ to, sich an einen halten; zu ~, Regreß nehmen; person liable to ~, Regreßpflichtige *m.*

recover *v.t.* wiederbekommen; wieder gut machen; eintreiben; ~ *v.i.* sich erholen.

recoverable *a.* wiedererlangbar; debts ~ by law, klagbare Schulden.

recovery *s.* Erholung *f.*; Wiederherstellung *f.*; Genesung *f.*

recreant *a.* feigherzig; treulos; ruchlos; ~ *s.* Bösewicht *m.*; Abtrünnige *m.*

recreate *v.t.* (*v.i.* sich) erquicken.

recreation *s.* Erholung *f.*; Freizeitbeschäftigung *f.*

recreational *a.* Unterhaltungs. . ., Erholungs. . .

recreative *a.* erquickend, ergötzlich; Unterhaltungs. . .

recrimination *s.* Gegenbeschuldigung *f.*

recruit *v.t. & i.* ersetzen; rekrutieren; ~ *s.* Rekrut *m.*; Neuling *m.*

recruitment *s.* Anwerbung *f.*

rectangle *s.* Rechteck *n.*

rectangular *a.* rechtwinklig, rechteckig.

rectification *s.* Berichtigung *f.*

rectify *v.t.* berichtigen, verbessern.

rectilinear *a.* geradlinig.

rectitude *s.* Biederkeit, Redlichkeit *f.*

rector *s.* Rektor(in) *m.*(*f.*); Pfarrer *m.*

rectory *s.* Pfarre *f.*; Pfarrhaus *n.*

rectum *s.* Mastdarm *m.*; Rektum *n.*

recumbent *a.* liegend.

recuperate *v.t.* wiederherstellen; ~ *v.i.* sich erholen.

recuperation *s.* Erholung *f.*

recur *v.i.* sich wiederholen; wiederkehren.

recurrence *s.* Wiederkehr *f.*; Wiederholung *f.*

recurrent *a.* wiederkehrend.

recycle *v.t.* wiederverwerten; recyclen.

recycling *s.* Recyling *n.* Wiederaufbereitung *f.*

red *a.* rot; ~ **beet** *s.* rote Rübe *f.*; ~ **currant** *s.* (rote) Johannisbeere *f.*; ~ **herring** *s.* Bückling; (*fig.*) Ablenkungsversuch *m.*; ~ tape, Bürokratie *f.*; bürokratisch; ~ *s.* Rot *n.*; ~ *Ridinghood*, Rotkäppchen *n.*

redaction *s.* Abfassung, Neubearbeitung *f.*

redbreast *s.* Rotkehlchen *n.*

Red Cross *s.* Rotes Kreuz *n.*

redden *v.t.* röten; ~ *v.i.* erröten.

reddish *a.* rötlich.

redecorate *v.t.* neu dekorieren.

redeem *v.t.* loskaufen, auslösen, erlösen; büssen; entschädigen; einlösen; amortisieren, tilgen.

redeemable *a.* ablöslich, austilgbar.

Redeemer *s.* Erlöser *m.*; Heiland *m.*

redemption *s.* Loskaufung *f.*; Erlösung *f.*; Tilgung *f.*; Einlösung *f.*; Ablösung *f.*

redisgnate *v.t.* neu bezeichnen, neu benennen.

red-handed *a.* auf frischer Tat.

red-headed *a.* rothaarig.

red-hot *a.* rotglühend.

redirect *v.t.* (Brief) umadressieren; weiterleiten; nachsenden.

rediscover *v.t.* wiederentdecken.

redistribute *v.t.* umverteilen.

red-lead *s.* Mennig *m.*

red-letter ~ day, *s.* Wichtiger Kalendertag *m.*

red-light district *s.* Bordellviertel *n.*

redness *s.* Röte *f.*

redo *v.t.* wiederholen; erneuern; überarbeiten.

redolent *a.* stark riechend; duftend.

redouble *v.t.* (*v.i.*sich) verdoppeln.

redoubtable *a.* furchtbar; gewaltig.

redress *v.t.* bessern; abhelfen; wiedergutmachen; ~ *s.* Abhilfe *f.*; Entschädigung *f.*; Ersatz *m.*; right of ~, Ersatzanspruch *m.*

reduce *v.t.* reduzieren; herunterbringen; verkleinern; herabsetzen; bezwingen; (*mil.*) to ~ to the ranks, zum gemeinen Soldaten degradieren; at ~d rates, zu ermäßigten Preisen.

reducible *a.* verkleinerbar; reduzierbar.

reduction *s.* Herabsetzung *f.*; Bezwingung *f.*; Verminderung *f.*; Rabatt *m.*; (*phot.*) Verkleinerung *f.*; ~ of staff, Personalabbau *m.*

redundancy *s.* Redundanz *f.*; Überfluß *m.*

redundant *a.*, **~ly** *adv.* überflüssig.

reduplicate *v.t.* verdoppeln.

red-wine *s.* Rotwein *m.*

re-echo *v.t. & i.* widerhallen.

reed *s.* Schilfrohr *n.*; Ried *n.*; Flöte *f.*

reef *s.* Riff *n.*; Reff *n.*; ~ *v.t.* reffen.

reek *s.* Gestank *m.*; ~ *v.i.* stinken.

reel *s.* Haspel *f.*; (Garn-) Rolle *f.*; Spule *f.*; ~ *v.t.* haspeln; (*Film*) kurbeln; ~ *v.i.* taumeln.

re-elect *v.t.* wiederwählen.

re-election *s.* Wiederwahl *f.*

re-eligible *a.* wieder wählbar.

re-embark *v.t. & i.* (sich) wieder einschiffen; *to* ~ *upon*, erneut beginnen.

re-enact *v.t.* wieder in Kraft setzen; nachspielen (Szene).

re-engage *v.t.* wieder beginnen; wieder anstellen; ~ *v.i.* wieder Dienste nehmen.

re-enter *v.t.* wieder eintreten.

re-entry permit *s.* Wiedereinreiseerlaubnis *f.*

re-establish *v.t.* wiederherstellen.

re-examine *v.t.* nachprüfen.

re-export *v.t.* wieder ausführen.

ref *s.* Ringrichter *m.*

refashion *v.t.* umgestalten.

refectory *s.* Speisezimmer (im Kloster) *n.*; Mensa *f.*

refer *v.t.* verweisen; beziehen; ~ *v.i.* sich beziehen, sich berufen.

referee *s.* Schiedsrichter *m.*

reference *s.* Verweisung, Bezugnahme, Beziehung *f.*; Auskunftsgeber *m.*; ~ **-number** *s.* Aktenzeichen *n.*, Aktennummer *f.*, Geschäftsnummer *f.*, Verweisungszeichen *n.*; ~**s** *pl.* Referenzen, Empfehlungen *f.pl.*; Zeichenerklärung *f.*; ~**-date** *s.* Stichtag *m.*; ~**-book** *s.* Nachschlagewerk *n.*; ~**-library** *s.* Handbücherei, Nachschlagebibliothek *f.*

referendum (on) *s.* Volksentscheid (über) *m.*; Referendum *n.*

refill *v.t.* neu füllen; ~ *s.* Ersatzteil (für den Bleistifthalter); ~**-battery** *s.* Ersatzbatterie *f.*

refine *v.t.* raffinieren, reinigen; verfeinern; ~ *v.i.* sich verfeinern; klügeln.

refined *a.* raffiniert; kultiviert.

refinement *s.* Verfeinerung *f.*

refinery *s.* Raffinerie *f.*

refit *v.t.* wiederherstellen; ausbessern.

reflect *v.t.* zurückwerfen; widerspiegeln; ~ *v.i.* ~*on s.b.*, zurückfallen; ~(*up*)*on sth.*, betrachten, nachdenken.

reflection *s.* Zurückstrahlung *f.*; Widerschein *m.*; Betrachtung, Überlegung *f.*; Tadel *m.*

reflective *a.* nachdenkend.

reflector *s.* Reflektor *m.*

reflex *s.* Widerschein *m.*; Reflex *m.*; ~ **camera** *s.* Spiegelreflexkamera *f.*

reflexive *a.* zurückwirkend; (*gram.*) reflexiv.

reflex reaction *s.* Reflexreaktion *f.*

refloat *v.t.* wieder flott machen.

reflux *s.* Rückfluß *m.*

reform *v.t.* umändern; verbessern; reformieren; ~ *v.i.* sich bessern; ~ *s.* Verbesserung, Reform *f.*

reformation *s.* Umänderung *f.*; Besserung *f.*; Reformation *f.*

reformer *s.* Reformpolitiker(in) *m.*(*f.*)

refract *v.t.* (Strahlen) brechen.

refraction *s.* Strahlenbrechung *f.*

refractory *a.*, ~**ily** *adv.* widerspenstig.

refrain *v.t.* zügeln; ~ *v.i.* sich enthalten; ~ *s.* Kehrreim *m.*

refresh *v.t.* erfrischen; auffrischen.

refresher *s.* Erfrischung *f.*; ~ **course** *s.* Auffrischungskurs *m.*

refreshment *s.* Erfrischung *f.*; ~**-room,** Erfrischungsraum *m.*

refrigerate *v.t.* kühlen; kühl lagern.

refrigerator *s.* Kühlschrank *m.*

refuel *v.t. & i.* nachtanken; wieder mit Brennstoff füllen.

refuge *s.* Zuflucht *f.*

refugee *s.* Flüchtling *m.*; ~ **camp** *s.* Flüchtlingslager *n.*

refulgence *s.* Glanz *m.*

refulgent *a.* glänzend.

refund *v.t.* zurückzahlen; ~ *s.* Rückerstattung *f.*

refurbish *v.t.* renovieren; aufarbeiten.

refusal *s.* Verweigerung *f.*

refuse *v.t.* verweigern, abschlagen; verwerfen; ~ *s.* Abfall *m.*, Ausschuß *m.*; Auswurf *m.*; ~ **collection** *s.* Müllabfuhr *f.*

refutation *s.* Widerlegung *f.*

refute *v.t.* widerlegen.

regain *v.t.* wiedergewinnen.

regal *a.*, ~**ly** *adv.* königlich.

regale *v.t.* fürstlich bewirten; erfreuen.

regalia *s.pl.* Insignien *pl.*

regard *v.t.* ansehen; achten; beobachten; Rücksicht nehmen; sich beziehen; betrachten als; ~ *s.* Blick *m.*; Achtung *f.*; Ansicht *f.*; Rücksicht, Beziehung *f.*; ~**s** *pl.* Empfehlungen, Grüße *pl.*

regarding *prep.* hinsichtlich, betreffend.

regardless *adv.* ohne Rücksicht auf.

regency *s.* Regentschaft *f.*

regenerate *v.t.* wiedergebären; neu beleben; ~ *a.* wiedergeboren.

regeneration *s.* Wiedergeburt *f.*

regent *a.* regierend; ~ *s.* Regent *m.*

regicide *s.* Königsmord, Königsmörder *m.*

regime *s.* Regierungssystem *n.*; Regime *n.*

regimen *s.* Lebensweise *f.*; Diät *f.*

regiment *s.* Regierung *f.*; Regiment *n.*

regimentation *s.* Reglementierung *f.*

region *s.* Gegend *f.*; Gebiet *n.*; Bezirk *m.*

regional *a.*, ~**ly** *adv.* regional; Regional. . .

register *s.* Verzeichnis *n.*; Register *n.*; (Orgel-) Register *n.*; ~ *v.t.* eintragen; (einen Brief) einschreiben; (Gepäck) aufgeben.

registered *a.* eingeschrieben (Brief); gesetzlich geschützt.

registrar *s.* Registrator *m.*; Standesbeamte *m.*; ~'**s office** *s.* Standesamt *n.*

registration *s.* Registrierung *f.*; Anmeldung *f.*; Eintragung *f.*; ~ **slip** *s.* Gepäckaufgabeschein *m.*; ~ **number** *s.* polizeiliches Kennzeichen *n.*

registry *s.* Registratur *f.*; ~ **office** *s.* Standesamt *n.*

regret *s.* Bedauern *n.*; Kummer *m.*; ~ *v.t.* bedauern; bereuen.

regretful *a.* mit, voll Bedauern.

regrettable *a.* bedauerlich.

regroup *v.t. & i.* (sich) neugruppieren; umgruppieren; ~**ing** *s.* Umgruppierung *f.*

regular *a.*, ~**ly** *adv.* regelmäßig, ordentlich; ~ *s.* Stammkunde *m.*; Stammkundin *f.*; Stammgast *m.*, ~**s** *pl.* Linientruppen *f.pl.*

regular gas *s.* Normalbenzin *n.*

regularity *s.* Regelmäßigkeit *f.*

regularize *v.t.* regeln; gesetzlich regeln/festlegen.

regulate *v.t.* ordnen, regeln.

regulation s. Einrichtung, Vorschrift f.; ~ a. vorschriftsmäßig; **~s** pl. Satzungen, Ausführungsbestimmungen pl.
regulator s. Regler m.
rehabilitate v.t. rehabilitieren.
rehabilitation s. Wiedereinsetzung in den vorigen Stand f.; Rehabilitation f.
rehash v.t. aufwärmen; s. Aufguß m.
rehear v.t. (law) erneut verhandeln.
rehearsal s. Probe f.; Theaterprobe f.
rehearse v.t. proben.
rehouse v.t. umquartieren; neu unterbringen.
reign v.i. herrschen, regieren; ~ s. Regierung f.; Herrschaft f.
reimburse v.t. zurückerstatten; entschädigen.
reimbursement s. Entschädigung, Wiedererstattung f.
reimport v.t. wiedereinführen.
reimportation s. Wiedereinfuhr f.
rein s. Zügel m.; ~ v.t. zügeln.
reincarnation s. Reinkarnation f.
reindeer s. Rentier n.
reinforce v.t. verstärken.
reinforcement s. Verstärkung f.
reinstate v.t. wieder einsetzen.
reinsurance s. Rückversicherung f.
reinsure v.t. rückversichern.
reinterpret v.t. neu interpretieren.
reinvest v.t. (Geld) wieder anlegen.
reissue s. Neuauflage f.; ~v.t. neu herausbringen.
reiterate v.t. wiederholen.
reject v.t. verwerfen; ausschlagen; ablehnen.
rejection s. Verwerfung f.; Ablehnung f.
rejoice v.i. sich freuen; ~ v.t. erfreuen.
rejoicing s. Jubel m.; **~s** pl. Freudebezeugungen f.pl.
rejoin v.t. wieder vereinigen; sich wieder vereinigen mit; ~ v.i. erwidern.
rejoinder s. Erwiderung.
rejuvenate v.t. verjüngen.
relapse v.i. zurückfallen, einen Rückfall bekommen; ~ s. Rückfall m.
relate v.t. erzählen, berichten; ~ v.i. sich beziehen.
related a. verwandt.
relation s. Bericht m.; Beziehung f.; Verwandtschaft f.; Verwandte m. & f.
relationship s. Verwandtschaft f.
relative a., **~ly** adv. sich beziehend, bezüglich; verhältnismäßig; relativ; ~ s. Verwandte m. & f.
relative clause s. Relativsatz m.
relative pronoun s. Relativpronomen n.
relativity s. Relativität f.
relax v.t. lockern, entspannen; ~ v.i. erschlaffen; sich entspannen.
relaxation s. Erschlaffung f.; Erholung f.; Nachlassen n.; Erleichterung f.
relaxed a. entspannt, gelöst.
relaxing a. entspannend, erholsam.
relay s. Schicht f.; Staffel f.; Pferdewechsel m.; (elek.) Relais n.; Ablösungs. . .; ~ race, Stafettenlauf m.; ~ v.t. übertragen nach (radio).
release v.t. befreien; loslassen, entlassen; (Bomben) abwerfen; ~ s. Freilassung, Befreiung f.; Entbindung, Entlastung f.; Freigabe f. (für Veröffentlichung); (Bomben-) Abwurf m.; (phot.) Auslösung f.; **press** ~ s. (Presse) Verlautbarung.

relegate v.t. verweisen; absteigen.
relegation s. Verweisung f.; (sp.) Abstieg m.
relent v.i. weich werden; nachgeben.
relentless a. unerbittlich, unbarmherzig.
relevance s. Relevanz f.; Bedeutung f.
relevant a. erheblich; zur Sache gehörig.
reliability s. Zuverlässigkeit f.
reliable a. verlässlich, zuverlässig, vertrauenswürdig.
reliance s. Zuversicht f.; Vertrauen n.
reliant a. to be ~ on, angewiesen sein auf.
relic s. Überrest m.; Reliquie f.
relief s. Erleichterung f.; Unterstützung f.; Ablösung f.; Relief n.; low ~, Flachrelief n.; **~-fund** s. Hilfsfond m.; **~-train** s. Vorzug, Entlastungszug m.
relieve v.t. erleichtern; unterstützen; ablösen; entsetzen; beruhigen; (hervor) heben.
religion s. Religion f.
religious a., **~ly** adv. religiös, Religions. . .; Ordens. . .; (fig.) gewissenhaft.
relinquish v.t. verlassen; aufgeben.
relinquishment s. Verzicht m.
relish s. Geschmack m.; Beigeschmack m.; Würze f.; Genuß m.; ~ v.t. Geschmack finden an; schmackhaft machen; ~ v.i. schmecken, gefallen.
relocate v.t. umsiedeln, verlegen.
reluctance s. Widerstreben n.
reluctant a., **~ly** adv. widerstrebend.
rely v.i. sich verlassen, vertrauen.
remain v.i. bleiben; übrigbleiben, verharren; it ~s to be seen, es muß sich zeigen.
remainder s. Rest m.; Rückstand m.
remaining a. restlich, übrig.
remains s.pl. (sterbliche) Reste; Überbleibsel pl.; Relikte pl.
remake s. Remake n.; Neuverfilmung f.
remand v.t. (in Untersuchungshaft) behalten.
remark v.t. bemerken; wahrnehmen; ~ s. Anmerkung f.
remarkable a., **~bly** adv. bemerkenswert; hervorragend.
remarriage s. Wiederverheiratung f.
remarry v.i. & t. wieder heiraten.
remedial a. heilend.
remedy s. Heilmittel, Hilfsmittel n.; Ersatz m.; ~ v.t. beilen, abhelfen.
remember v.t. sich erinnern; empfehlen, grüssen; gedenken; (fam.) behalten; to ~ a person in one's will, einen im Testament bedenken.
remembrance s. Erinnerung f.; Andenken n.; Gedenken n.
remind v.t. erinnern, mahnen.
reminder s. Mahnung f.
reminiscence s. Erinnerung f.
reminiscent (of) a. erinnernd (an).
remiss a., **~ly** adv. schlaff; lässig.
remission s. Nachlassen n.; Milderung f., Erlassung, Vergebung f.
remit v.t. remittieren, übersenden; vermindern, nachlassen; erlassen.
remittance s. Überweisung f.
remnant s. Überrest, Rest m.
remodel v.t. umbilden; umfassionieren (Hut, Mantel).
remold v.t. umgestalten.
remonstrance s. Einwendung f.; Protest m.

remonstrate *v.i.* Einwendungen machen.

remorse *s.* Gewissensbiß *m.*

remorseful *a.* reuig, reuevoll.

remorseless *a.,* ~**ly** *adv.* hartherzig; erbarmungslos.

remote *a.,* ~**ly** *adv.* entlegen, entfernt.

remote control *s.* (*mech.*) Fernsteuerung *f.*; Fernbedienung *f.* ~**led** *a.* ferngesteuert.

remount *v.t.* wieder besteigen; ~ *s.* frisches Reitpferd *n.*

removable *a.* abnehmbar; entfernbar.

removal *s.* Wegschaffung, Absetzung *f.*; Entlassung *f.*

remove *v.t.* wegräumen; versetzen; absetzen; entfernen; ~ *v.i.* sich entfernen; ~ *s.* Abstand *m.*; Grad *m.*, Stufe *f.*

remunerate *v.t.* belohnen, vergüten.

remuneration *s.* Belohnung, Vergütung *f.*

remunerative *a.* gewinnbringend.

Renaissance *s.* Renaissance *f.*

rename *v.t.* umbenennen, umtaufen.

Renascence *s.* Wiedergeburt *f.*; Renaissance *f.*

rend *v.t.* & *i.st.* zerreißen.

render *v.t.* zurückgeben; überliefern; darstellen; übersetzen; leisten; machen; *to* ~ *account*, Rechenschaft ablegen; *to* ~ *judgment*, Urteil fällen; *to* ~ *service*, Dienst leisten; *per account* ~*ed*, laut erhaltener Rechnung.

rendering *s.* Wiedergabe *f.*; Übertragung *f.*

rendezvous *s.* Stelldichein *n.*; Verabredung *f.*; Rendezvous *n.*

rendition *s.* Wiedergabe *f.*; Übertragung *f.*

renegade *s.* Abtrünnige *m./f.*

renew *v.t.* erneuern; wiederholen.

renewable *a.* verlängerbar.

renewal *s.* Erneuerung *f.*; Verlängerung *f.*

renounce *v.t.* entsagen, abschwören, verzichten auf; verleugnen.

renovate *v.t.* renovieren; restaurieren.

renovation *s.* Renovierung *f.*; Restaurierung *f.*

renown *s.* Ruf, Ruhm *m.*

renowned *a.* berühmt.

rent *s.* Miete *f.*; Pacht *f.*; ~ *v.t.* (ver)mieten, (ver)pachten.

rental *s.* Miete *f.*; Mietsumme, Pachtsumme *f.*; **car** ~ *s.* Antoverleih *m.*

rent-controlled *a.* mietpreisgebunden.

renunciation *s.* Entsagung *f.*; Verzicht *m.*

reopen *v.t.* wieder eröffnen; ~ *v.i.* wieder eröffnet werden.

reorder *v.t.* nachbestellen; neu bestellen; umordnen.

reorganization *s.* Umorganisation *f.*; Umbildung *f.* Neugliederung *f.*

reorganize *v.t.* neugestalten; umorganisieren.

reorient *v.t.* sich umorientieren, neu ausrichten.

reorientation *s.* Neuorientierung *f.*

rep *s.* (*fam.*) Vertreter(in) *m.*(*f.*)

repair *v.t.* ersetzen; ausbessern; ~ *s.* Ausbesserung *f.*; Reparatur *f.*; *to keep in good* ~, in gutem Zustand halten; *out of* ~, baufällig; ~**-shop** *s.* Reparaturwerkstatt *f.*

repairable *a.,* ~**bly** *adv.* ausbesserungsfähig; ersetzbar.

reparation *s.* Ausbesserung *f.*; Ersatz *m.*; Entschädigung *f.*

repartee *s.* schnelle, treffende Antwort *f.*; Schlagfertigkeit *f.*

repast *s.* Mahlzeit *f.*

repatriate *v.t.* in die Heimat zurückbringen; repatriieren.

repatriation *s.* Rückführung, Repatriierung *f.*

repay *v.t.st.* zurückzahlen; vergelten.

repayable *a.* rückzahlbar.

repayment *s.* Rückzahlung *f.*

repeal *v.t.* widerrufen; aufheben; ~ *s.* Aufhebung *f.*; Widerruf *m.*

repeat *v.t.* wiederholen; hersagen; ~*s.* Wiederholung *f.*; ~ *order*, Nachbestellung *f.*; ~ *performance*, Wiederholung einer Aufführung *f.*

repeatedly *adv.* wiederholt.

repel *v.t.* zurückstossen; abstossen; zurückschlagen.

repellent *a.* abstossend.

repent *v.t.* & *i.* bereuen, Buße tun.

repentance *s.* Reue, Buße *f.*

repentant *a.* reuig, bußfertig.

repeople *v.t.* wieder bevölkern.

repercussion *s.* Widerhall *m.*

repertoire *s.* Repertoire *n.*

repertory *s.* Sachregister *n.*; Fundgrube *f.*; Repertoire *n.*; ~ *theater*, Theater mit wechselndem Spielplan; Repertoiretheater *n.*

repetition *s.* Wiederholung *f.*; Hersagen *n.*

repetitious *a.* sich stetig wiederholend.

repetitive *a.* eintönig.

rephrase *v.t.* umformulieren.

repine *v.i.* sich grämen; murren, klagen.

replace *v.t.* ersetzen; zurückstellen.

replacement *s.* Ersatz *m.*

replant *v.t.* umpflanzen.

replenish *v.t.* (wieder)anfüllen.

replete *a.* angefüllt, voll.

repletion *s.* Überfülle *f.*

replica *s.* Nachbildung *f.*; Abbild *n.*

reply *v.i.* erwidern; ~ *s.* Antwort *f.*; ~**-card,** Postkarte (*f.*) mit Antwort; ~**-coupon** *s.* Antwortschein *m.*

repolish *v.t.* wieder polieren.

report *v.t.* berichten, erzählen; melden, anzeigen; ~ *v.i.* sich melden; *to* ~ *out*, sich abmelden; *to* ~ *to the police*, sich bei der Polizei melden; ~ *s.* Gerücht *n.*; Ruf *m.*; Nachricht *f.*; Knall *m.*; Bericht *m.*; Schulzeugnis *n.*

reported speech *s.* indreckte Rede *f.*

reporter *s.* Berichterstatter(in) *m.*(*f.*); Reporter(in) *m.*(*f.*)

repose *v.i.* ruhen, beruhen; ~ *s.* Ruhe *f.*

repository *s.* Behältnis *n.*; Warenlager *n.*

repossess *v.t.* wieder in Besitz nehmen.

reprehend *v.t.* tadeln; rügen.

reprehensible *a.,* ~**bly** *adv.* tadelnswert.

reprehension *s.* Tadel *m.*; Rüge *f.*

reprehensive *a.* tadelnd.

represent *v.t.* darstellen, vorstellen; vertreten; zu Gemüt führen.

representation *s.* Vorstellung *f.*; Darstellung *f.*; Stellvertretung *f.*

representative *a.,* ~**ly** *adv.* vorstellend; stellvertretend; ~ *s.* Vertreter(in) *m.*(*f.*)

repress *v.t.* unterdrücken; Einhalt tun.

repressed *a.* unterdrückt; verdrängt.

repression *s.* Unterdrückung; Verdrängung *f.*

repressive *a.* repressiv; unterdrückend.

reprieve *v.t.* Frist geben; ~ *s.* Frist *f.*; Begnadigung *f.*

reprimand *s.* Verweis, Tadel *m.*; ~ *v.t.* tadeln.

reprint *v.t.* wieder drucken; ~ *s.* Nachdruck *m.*

reprisal *s.* Wiedervergeltung *f.*; *in ~ for*, als Vergeltungsmaßnahme für.

reproach *v.t.* vorwerfen; ~ *s.* Vorwurf *m.*; Schmach *f.*

reproachful *a.*, **~ly** *adv.* vorwurfsvoll.

reprobate *a.* verworfen, ruchlos; ~ *s.* Halunke *m.*; ~ *v.t.* verwerfen.

reprocess *v.t.* wiederaufbereiten.

reproduce *v.t.* wieder hervorbringen; nachbilden; ~*v.i.* sich fortpflanzen.

reproduction *s.* Nachbildung, Wiederholung *f.*; Fortpflanzung *f.*

reproductive *a.* wiedererzeugend; Fortpflanzungs..

reproof *s.* Vorwurf, Verweis *m.*

reprove *v.t.* tadeln, verweisen; schelten.

reptile *a.* kriechend; ~ *s.* Reptil *n.*

republic *s.* Republik *f.*

republican *a.* republikanisch; ~ *s.* Republikaner(in) *m.*(*f.*)

republish *v.t.* neu veröffentlichen.

repudiate *v.t.* zurückweisen, verstoßen; Schulden nicht anerkennen.

repugnance *s.* Widerwille *m.*; Abschen *f.*

repugnant *a.* widerspenstig; zuwider; **~ly** *adv.* mit Widerwillen.

repulse *v.t.* zurückschlagen; abschlagen; ~ *s.* Zurücktreibung *f.*

repulsion *s.* Zurückstoßung *f.*; Abweisung *f.*; Abscheu *f.*; (*phys.*) Abstoßung *f.*

repulsive *a.* abstoßend, widerwärtig.

repurchase *v.t.* wiederkaufen; ~ *s.* Rückkauf *m.*

reputable *a.*, **~bly** *adv.* angesehen.

reputation *s.* Ruf *m.*

repute *v.t.* halten für, achten; ~ *s.* Ruf *m.*

reputed *a.* angeblich, bekannt; *to be ~d*, den Ruf haben.

request *s.* Bitte *f.*; Gesuch *n.*; Nachfrage *f.*; *in ~*, gesucht, begehrt; ~ *v.t.* bitten, ersuchen.

require *v.t.* verlangen, fordern; brauchen.

requirement *s.* Forderung *f.*; Bedarf *m.*

requisite *a.*, **~ly** *adv.* erforderlich; ~ *s.* Erfordernis *n.*; Bedarfsartikel *m.*

requisition *s.* Forderung *f.*; Beschlag *m.*; Anforderung *f.*; ~ *v.t.* anfordern, requirieren.

requital *s.* Vergeltung *f.*

requite *v.t.* vergelten.

rerun *v.t.* wiederholen; ~*s.* Wiederholung *f.*

resale *s.* Wiederverkauf *m.*

reschedule *v.t.* zeitlich neu festlegen.

rescind *v.t.* aufheben; abschaffen.

rescission *s.* Umstossung, Aufhebung (einer Verordnung) *f.*

rescue *v.t.* befreien, retten; ~ *s.* Befreiung, Rettung *f.*; *to come to the ~ of*, einem zu Hilfe kommen.

rescuer *s.* Retter(in) *m.*(*f.*)

research *s.* Untersuchung *f.*, Forschung *f.*; ~ *v.i.* Forschung treiben.

research assistant *s.* wissenschaftliche Assistent(in) *m.*(*f.*)

researcher *s.* Forscher(in) *m.*(*f.*)

research fellowship *s.* Forschungsstipendium *n.*

resemblance *s.* Ähnlichkeit *f.*; Ebenbild *n.*

resemble *v.t.* ähneln; gleichen.

resent *v.t.* übelnehmen.

resentful *a.* übelnehmerisch; ärgerlich; rachgierig.

resentment *s.* Zorn *m.*; Verdruß *m.*; Groll *m.*; Unmut *m.*

reservation *s.* Aufbewahrung *f.*; Vorbehalt *m.*; Zurückhaltung *f.*; Vorbestellung *f.* Reservierung *f.*; **~-list** *s.* Warteliste *f.*

reserve *v.t.* vorbehalten, aufbewahren; reservieren; ~ *s.* Rückhalt *m.*, Reserve *f.*; Vorrat *m.*; Vorsicht *f.*; Zurückhaltung *f.*

reserved *a.*, **~ly** *adv.* zurückhaltend; vorsichtig; belegt.

reservist *s.* Reservist *m.*

reservoir *s.* Behälter *m.*

reset *v.t.* neu einfassen; (Edelstein); nachstellen (Zähler, Uhr).

resettle *v.t.* umsiedeln.

resettlement *s.* Umsiedlung *f.*

reshape *v.t.* neugestalten, neuformen.

reshuffle *s.* Umbildung (der Regierung) *f.*

reside *v.i.* wohnen, sich aufhalten.

residence *s.* Aufenthalt, Wohnsitz *m.*; Wohnung *f.*; Residenz *f.*; *place of ~*, Aufenthaltsort *m.*; ~ **permit** *s.* Aufenthaltsgenehmigung *f.*

resident *a.* wohnhaft, ansässig; ~ *s.* Bewohner(in) *m.*(*f.*); Einwohner(in) *m.*(*f.*)

residential *a.* Wohn.. .; ~ **club** *s.* Wohnklub *m.*; ~ **district** *s.* Wohnviertel *n.*, Wohnbezirk *m.*

residual *a.* zurückbleibend.

residue *a.* Rest, Rückstand *m.*

residuum *s.* Rückstand *m.*

resign *v.t.* entsagen, abtreten; aufgeben, sich ergeben in; ~ *v.i.* seine Stelle aufgeben.

resignation *s.* Abtretung, Entsagung, Verzichtleistung *f.*; (Amt) Niederlegung *f.*, Rücktritt *m.*; Ergebung *f.*

resigned *a.*, **~ly** *adv.* ergeben; resigniert.

resilience *s.* Schnellkraft, Spannkraft *f.*; Elastizität *f.*

resilient *a.* spannkräftig, elastisch.

resin *s.* Harz *n.*

resinous *a.* harzig.

resist *v.t. & i.* widerstehen.

resistance *s.* Widerstand *m.* (auch *elek.*).

resistant, resisting *a.* beständig; . . fest; *oil-~*, ölfest; *shock-~*, stoßfest.

resit *v.t.* wiederholen (Prüfung); ~*s.* Wiederholungsprüfung *f.*

resolute *a.*, **~ly** *adv.* entschlossen.

resolution *s.* Auflösung *f.*; Entschlossenheit *f.*; Vorsatz *m.*; Beschluß *m.*, Entschließung *f.*

resolve *v.t.* auflösen; aufklären; beschließen; ~ *v.i.* sich entschließen; schmelzen; ~ *s.* Entschluß *m.*

resonance *s.* Widerhall *m.*; Nachhall *m.*; Resonanz *f.*

resonant *a.* widerhallend; volltönend.

resonate *v.i.* mitklingen, mitschwingen.

resort *v.i.* sich wenden an; seine Zuflucht nehmen; ~ *s.* Zuflucht *f.*; *health ~*, Kurort *m.*; *ski ~*, Skiort *m.*

resound *v.i.* widerhallen.

resounding *a.* hallend; überwältigend.

resource *s.* Hilfsmittel *n.*; Zuflucht *f.*; ~s *pl.* Geld-
mittel *n.pl.*; (Erz-) Vorräte *pl.*; Fähigkeiten *f.pl.*
resourceful *a.* findig.
respect *v.t.* berücksichtigen; sich beziehen; (hoch)-
achten; ~ *s.* Rücksicht, Hinsicht, Beziehung *f.*;
Hochachtung *f.*; ~s *pl.* Empfehlung *f.*
respectability *s.* Achtbarkeit *f.*
respectable *a.*, ~**bly** *adv.* achtbar; ansehnlich;
anständig; leidlich.
respectful *a.*, ~**ly** *adv.* ehrerbietig, höflich.
respecting *pr.* hinsichtlich; bezüglich.
respective *a.* jeweilig, verschieden; ~**ly** *adv.*
beziehungsweise.
respiration *s.* Atmen *n.*; Atmung *f.*
respirator *s.* Atmenschutzgerät *n.*
respiratory *a.* Atmungs…
respire *v.t. & i.* atmen, einatmen.
respite *s.* Frist *f.*; Aufschub, Stillstand *m.*
resplendent *a.*, ~**ly** *adv.* glänzend; prächtig.
respond *v.i.* entsprechen; antworten.
respondent *s.* Beklagte *m./f.*
response *s.* Antwort *f.*
responsibility *s.* Verantwortlichkeit *f.*, Verantwortung *f.*
responsible *a.*, ~**bly** *adv.* verantwortlich.
responsive *a.* aufgeschlossen; antwortend;
empfänglich.
rest *s.* Ruhe, Rast *f.*; Ruhepunkt *m.*; Pause *f.*; Rest
m.; die übrigen *pl.* ~ *v.i.* ruhen, rasten; ~*assured,*
sich verlassen; *let a matter* ~, eine Sache auf sich
beruhen lassen; ~*against,* sich stützen gegen; ~ *v.t.*
ausruhen lassen; lehnen.
restart *v.t.* wieder anlassen; wieder aufnehmen.
restate *v.t.* neu formulieren.
restaurant *s.* Restaurant *n.*
restaurant-car *s.* Speisewagen *m.*
rested *a.* ausgeruht.
restful *a.* ruhig; beruhigend.
resting-place *s.* Ruheplatz *m.*
restitution *s.* Wiedererstattung *f.*; Wiederherstellung *f.*; ~**-law** *s.* Wiedergutmachungsgesetz *n.*
restive *a.* störrisch, widerspenstig.
restless *a.*, ~**ly** *adv.* ruhelos.
restoration *s.* Wiederherstellung *f.*; Restaurierung
f.; Restauration *f.*; Zurückerstattung *f.*
restorative *a.* stärkend; ~ *s.* kräftigendes Heilmittel
n.
restore *v.t.* wiedergeben; wiederherstellen;
restaurieren.
restorer *s.* Restaurator(in) *m.(f.)*
restrain *v.t.* zurückhalten, einschränken.
restrained *a.* zurückhaltend; beherrscht.
restraint *s.* Einschränkung *f.*; Zurückhaltung *f.*;
Zwang *m.*; *under* ~, in Gewahrsam.
restrict *v.t.* einschränken; ~**ed** *a.* beschränkt,
begrenzt.
restriction *s.* Einschränkung *f.*
restrictive *a.*, ~**ly** *adv.* einschränkend.
rest-room *s.* Toilette *f.*
restructure *v.t.* umstrukturieren.
restyle *v.t.* neu stylen.
result *v.i.* hervorgehen, folgen, sich ergeben; ~ *s.*
Ergebnis *n.*; Folge *f.*
resume *v.t.* zurücknehmen; wieder aufnehmen;
wieder anfangen; zusammenfassen.
résumé *s.* Zusammenfassung *f.*; Lebenslauf *m.*

resumption *s.* Zurückgewinnung *f.*; Wiederaufnahme *f.*
resurface *v.i.* wieder auftauchen; ~ *v.t.* (Straße)
neu belegen.
resurrection *s.* Auferstehung *f.*
resuscitate *v.t.* wiedererwecken; wiederbeleben.
retail *v.t.* im Einzelhandel verkaufen; ~ *s.* Einzel-
verkauf *m.*; ~**-trade** *s.* Einzelhandel *m.*; ~**-price** *s.*
Ladenpreis *m.*
retailer *s.* Einzelhändler(in) *m.(f.)*
retain *v.t.* behalten, beibehalten.
retainer *s.* Honorarverschuß *m.*; Verpflichtung (*f.*)
eines Anwalts.
retake *v.t.st.* wiedernehmen.
retaliate *v.i.* vergelten; zurückschlagen.
retaliation *s.* Wiedervergeltung *f.*; Gegenschlag *m.*
retaliatory *a.* Vergeltungs…
retard *v.t.* aufhalten; verzögern; retardieren.
retardation *s.* Verzögerung *f.*
retch *v.i.* würgen.
retention *s.* Zurückhalten *n.*; Beibehaltung *f.*; Ver-
haltung *f.*
retentive *a.* gut (Gedächtnis); bewahrend;
(zurück)haltend.
reticence *s.* Zurückhaltung *f.*
reticent *a.* zurückhaltend.
retina *s.* Netzhaut (des Auges) *f.*
retinue *s.* Gefolge *n.*
retire *v.i.* zich zurückziehen; zu Bett gehen; in den
Ruhestand treten; ~ *v.t.* in den Ruhestand
versetzen.
retired *p. & a.*, ~**ly** *adv.* zurückgezogen, eingezogen; pensioniert, im Ruhestand; ~ *list,* Liste der
Pensionierten.
retirement *s.* Zurückgezogenheit *f.*; Ausscheiden
n.; Pensionierung *f.*
retirement age *s.* Rentenalter *n.*; Altersgrenze *f.*
retiring *a.* zurückhaltend.
retort *v.t. & i.* erwidern; zurückgeben; ~ *s.* Erwiderung *f.*; Retorte *f.*
retouch *v.t.* überarbeiten; (*phot.*) retuschieren.
retrace *v.t.* wieder zeichnen; zurückgeben;
zurückverfolgen.
retract *v.t. & i.* zurückziehen; einziehen.
retractable *a.* einziehbar.
retraction *s.* Widerruf *m.*; Einziehen *n.*; Zurücknahme *f.*
retrain *v.t.* umschulen.
retraining *s.* Umschulung *f.*
retread *v.t.* runderneuern; ~*s.* runderneuerter
Reifen *m.*
retreat *s.* Rückzug *m.*; Zufluchtsort *m.*; Eingezo-
genheit *f.*
retrench *v.t.* einschränken; ~ *v.i.* seine Ausgaben
einschränken.
retrenchment *s.* Einschränkung *f.*; Ersparung *f.*
retrial *s.* (*law*) nochmalige Verhandlung *f.*; Wiederaufnahmeverfahren *n.*
retribution *s.* Vergeltung *f.*
retrieval *s.* Rettung *f.*; Wiedergutmachung *f.*
retrieve *v.t.* wiederbekommen; wieder ersetzen;
(*hunting*) apportieren.
retriever *s.* Retriever *m.*; Apportierhund *m.*
retroactive *a.* rückwirkend; *with* ~ *effect,* mit rück-
wirkender Kraft.
retrograde *a.* rückschrittlich; ~ *step s.* Rückschritt

m.

retrogression *s.* Rückgang *m.*
retrogressive *a.* rückschrittlich.
retrospect *s.* Rückblick *m.*
retrospective *a.*, **~ly** *adv.* rückwirkend; zurückblickend.
retry *v.t.* (*law*) von neuem verhandeln.
return *v.i.* umkehren, wiederkommen; antworten; ~ *v.t.* erstatten; erwidern; zurückschicken, wiederbringen; melden, berichten; wählen; ~ *s.* Rückkehr *f.*; Rückgabe *f.*; Gewinn *m.*; Rückzahlung *f.*; Erwiderung *f.*; Gegendienst *m.*; Bericht, Wahlbericht *m.*; **~s** *pl.* statistische Angaben *f.pl.*; Einnahme *f.*; *many happy returns of the day,* Geburtstagsglückwunsch *m.*; *in ~,* dafür, dagegen; *by ~ of post,* postwendend; **returnable** *a.* Rückgabe. . .
return: ~ **address** *s.* Absenderadresse, Rückanschrift *f.*; ~ **flight** *s.* Rückflug *m.*; ~ **journey** *s.* Rückreise *f.*; ~ **postage** *s.* Rückporto *m.*
return-ticket *s.* Rückfahrkarte *f.*
reunification *s.* Wiedervereinigung *f.*
reunion *s.* Wiedersehensfeier *f.*; Klassentreffen *n.*
reunite *v.t.* (*v.i.* sich) wieder vereinigen.
reuse *v.t.* wiederverwenden.
rev *s.* (*fam.*) Umdrehung *f.*; ~ **counter** *s.* Drehzahlmesser *m.*
revaluation *s.* Aufwertung *f.*
revamp *v.t.* aufmöbeln, aufpolieren.
reveal *v.t.* offenbaren; enthüllen.
revealing *a.* aufschlußreich.
reveille *s.* (*mil.*) Morgensignal *n.*
revel *v.i.* feiern; (*fig.*) schwärmen, schwelgen; ~ *s.* Gelage *n.*
revelation *s.* Offenbarung *f.*; Enthüllung *f.*
reveller *s.* Feiernde *m./f.*
revelry *s.* Feiern *n.*, lärmende Festlichkeit.
revenge *s.* Rache *f.*; ~ *v.t.* rächen.
revengeful *a.*, **~ly** *adv.* rachgierig.
revenue *s.* Einkommen *n.*; Ertrag *m.*; Staatseinnahmen *f.pl.*; ~ *and expenditure,* Einnahmen und Ausgaben *pl.*
reverberate *v.i.* widerhallen.
reverberation *s.* Widerhall *m.*
revere *v.t.* ehren, verehren.
reverence *s.* Ehrerbietung *f.*; Verneigung *f.*; Ehrwürden (Titel).
reverend *a.* ehrwürdig (Titel der Geistlichen).
reverent *a.*, **~ly** *adv.* ehrerbietig.
reverential *a.*, **~ly** *adv.* ehrerbietig.
reverie *s.* Träumerei *f.*
reversal *s.* Umstoßung (eines Urteils) *f.*; Umkehrung *f.*; Umsteuerung *f.*
reverse *v.t.* umkehren; umstoßen; umsteuern; ~ *s.* Wendung *f.*, Umschlag *m.*, Wechsel *m.*; Gegenteil *n.*; Rückseite *f.*; Schlappe *f.*; ~ *a.* Rückwärts. . .; **~-gear** *s.* (*mech.*) Rückwärtsgang *m.*
reversible *a.* reversibel; umkehrbar.
reversion *s.* Umkehrung *f.*; Heimfall *m.*
revert *v.t.* umkehren; zurückwerfen; ~ *v.i.* zurückkehren; heimfallen.
revertible *a.* heimfallend.
review *v.t.* wieder durchsehen; mustern; rezensieren; revidieren; ~ *s.* Übersicht, Durchsicht, Rezension *f.*; kritische Zeitschrift, Rundschau *f.*, (*law*) Revision *f.*

reviewer *s.* Rezensent *m.*
revile *v.t.* schmähen, schimpfen.
revise *v.t.* durchsehen.
revision *s.* Durchsicht, Revision *f.*
revisit *v.t.* wieder besuchen.
revitalize *v.t.* neu beleben.
revival *s.* Wiederbelebung *f.*; Revival *n.*
revive *v.t.* wieder aufleben; ~ *v.t.* wieder beleben.
revocable *a.* widerruflich.
revocation *s.* Zurückrufung *f.*; Widerruf *m.*
revoke *v.t.* widerrufen.
revolt *v.i.* sich empören; ~ *s.* Abfall *m.*; Empörung *f.*; Aufstand *m.*
revolting *a.* abstoßend; abscheulich.
revolution *s.* Revolution *f.*; Umwälzung *f.*; Umlauf *m.*; Umdrehung *f.*
revolutionary *a.* revolutionär.
revolutionize *v.t.* revolutionieren; (gänzlich) umgestalten.
revolve *v.t.* umwälzen; erwägen; ~ *v.i.* sich drehen, umlaufen.
revolver *s.* Revolver *m.*
revolving *a.* drehbar; Dreh. . .
revue *s.* Revue *f.*; Kabarett *n.*
revulsion *s.* Umschwung, Umschlag *m.*
reward *v.t.* vergelten, belohnen; ~ *s.* Belohnung *f.*
rewarding *a.* lohnend.
rewind *v.t.* zurückspulen; wieder aufziehen.
rewire *v.t.* neue Leitungen legen.
reword *v.t.* umformulieren.
rewrite *v.t.* umarbeiten; umschreiben.
rhapsody *s.* Rhapsodie *f.*; Schwärmerei *f.*
rhesus factor *s.* Rhesusfaktor *m.*
rhetoric *s.* Redekunst *f.*; Rhetorik *f.*; (*pej.*) Phrasen *pl.*
rhetorical *a.*, **~ly** *adv.* rednerisch; rhetorisch; (*pej.*) phrasenhaft.
rhetorician *s.* Rhetoriker(in) *m.*(*f.*)
rheumatic *a.* rheumatisch; *s.* Rheumatiker(in) *m.*(*f.*)
rheumatism *s.* Rheumatismus *m.*
rhino(ceros) *s.* Nashorn *n.*; Rhinozeros *n.*
rhombus *s.* (*geom.*) Raute *f.*; Rhombus *m.*
rhomboidal *a.* rautenförmig.
rhubarb *s.* Rhabarber *m.*
rhyme *s.* Reim *m.*; Vers *m.*; ~ *v.t.* & *i.* reimen.
rhythm *s.* Rhythmus *m.*
rhythmic(al) *a.*, **~ly** *adv.* rhythmisch.
rib *s.* Rippe *f.*; (*nav.*) Inholz *n.*; Kiel *m.*; Schaft *m.*; ~ *v.t.* rippen; (*sl.*) hänseln.
ribald *a.* frech, zotig.
ribaldry *s.* zotige Sprache *f.*
ribbon *s.* Band, Ordensband *n.*; Farbband *n.*; Streifen *m.*
rice *s.* Reis *m.*; ~ **paddy** *s.* Reisfeld *n.*
rich *a.*, **~ly** *adv.* reich; kostbar; nahrhaft, fett; (Kuchen) schwer.
riches *s.* Reichtum *m.*
richness *s.* Reichtum *m.*; Fülle *f.*
rick *s.* (Heu) Schober *m.*
rickets *s.pl.* Rachitis *f.*
rickety *a.* rachitisch; wack[e]lig.
rickshaw *s.* Rickscha *f.*
ricochet *v.i.* (*mil.*) abprallen; ~ *s.* Abpraller *m.*
rid *v.t.st.* befreien; wegschaffen; ~ *a.* entledigt; *to get ~ of,* loswerden.

466

riddance *s.* Befreiung, Entledigung *f.*
ridden *a.* geplagt; *bed* ~, bettlägerig.
riddle *s.* Rätsel *n.*; grobe Sieb *n.*; ~ *v.t.* sieben; durchlöchern.
ride *v.i. & st.* reiten; fahren; *to* ~ *at anchor*, vor Anker liegen; ~ *s.* Ritt *m.*; Fahrt *f.* Reitweg *m.*
rider *s.* Reiter(in) *m.(f.)*; Zusatzklausel *f.*
ridge *s.* Grat *m.*; Kamm *m.*; Rücken *m.*; Erhöhung *f.*, First *m.*; Furche *f.*; Bergkette *f.*; ~ *v.t.* furchen.
ridicule *s.* Spott *m.*; Lächerlichkeit *f.*; ~ *v.t.* lächerlich machen.
ridiculous *a.*, **~ly** *adv.* lächerlich.
riding *s.* Reiten *n.*; ~ *a.* Reit...; ~ **breeches** *pl.* Reithosen *pl.*; **~-habit** *s.* Reitkleid *n.*
rife *a.*, **~ly** *adv.* herrschend, allgemein.
riffraff *s.* Gesindel *n.*
rifle *v.t.* rauben, plündern; riefeln; *~s.* Gewehr *n.*
rifleman *s.* (*mil.*) Schütze *m.*; **rifle-regiment** *s.* Schützenregiment *n.*
rifle-range *s.* Schießstand *m.*
rift *s.* Unstimmigkeit *f.*; Riß *m.*; Spalte *f.*; ~ *v.i.* sich spalten.
rig *s.* Streich *m.*; Takelung *f.*; Putz *m.*; ~ *v.t.* auftakeln, ausrüsten; verfälschen; manipulieren.
rigging *s.* Takelwerk *n.*; Takelung *f.*
right *a. & adv.*, **~ly** *adv.* gerade; recht; richtig; sehr; echt, rechtmäßig; *to be* ~, recht haben; *all ~!*, alles in Ordnung!; schon gut; *~hand side*, rechte Seite; ~ *s.* Recht *n.*; rechte Seite *f.*; *by* ~, von Rechts wegen; *all ~s reserved*, alle Rechte vorbehalten; ~ *v.t.* Recht verschaffen; berichtigen.
right angle *s.* rechter Winkel *m.*
right-angled *a.* rechtwinkelig.
righteous *a.* gerecht, rechtschaffen.
righteousness *s.* Rechtschaffenheit *f.*
rightful *a.*, **~ly** *adv.* rechtmäßig, gerecht.
right-handed *a.* rechtshändig.
rightist *a.* rechtsgerichtet.
right-minded *a.* gerecht denkend.
right-wing *a.* (*pol.*) dem rechten Flügel angehörend, rechtsstehend.
rigid *a.*, **~ly** *adv.* steif; starr; streng.
rigidity *s.* Steifheit *f.*, Unbiegsamkeit *f.*
rigmarole *s.* Salbaderei *f.*
rigor *s.* Strenge *f.*
rigor mortis *s.* Leichenstarre *f.*
rigorous *a.*, **~ly** *adv.* streng; genau.
rile *v.t.* (*fam.*) ärgern.
rill *s.* Bach *m.*
rim *s.* Rand *m.*; Reifen *m.*, Radkranz *m.*; Einfassung *f.*
rimless *a.* randlos.
rime *s.* Reif *m.*; Frost *m.*
rind *s.* Rinde, Schale *f.*
ring *s.* Ring *m.*; Clique *f.*; Schall *m.*; Geläute *n.*; ~ *v.t.* klingeln; ~ *v.i.* läuten; erschallen; *to* ~ *up*, anklingeln, anrufen.
ringing *a.* schallend; klangvoll; *~s.* Läuten.
ringleader *s.* Rädelsführer(in) *m.(f.)*
ringlet *s.* Ringelchen *n.*; Ringellocke *f.*
rink *s.* Eisbahn *f.*; Rollschuhbahn *f.*
rinse *v.t.* spülen, ausschwenken; *~s.* Spülen *n.*
riot *s.* Schwelgerei *f.*; Tumult *m.*; Aufruhr *m.*; ~ *v.i.* schwärmen, schwelgen; Aufruhr stiften.
rioter *s.* Aufrührer(in) *m.(f.)*
riotous *a.*, **~ly** *adv.* schwelgerisch; ausgelassen;

aufrührerisch.
rip *v.t.* auftrennen, aufreißen; enthüllen; ~ *s.* Riß *m.*
ripe *a.*, **~ly** *adv.* reif, zeitig.
ripen *v.t. & i.* reifen.
rip-off *s.* (*fam.*) Nepp *m.*
riposte *s.* Replik *f.*; Entgegnung *f.*
ripple *v.i.* sich kräuseln; ~ *v.t.* riffeln.
rip-roaring *a.* (*fam.*) toll.
rise *v.i.* sich erheben, aufstehen; aufsteigen; aufgehen; heranwachsen; entstehen; steigen; ~ *s.* Anhöhe *f.*; Steigung *f.*; Ursprung *m.*; Steigen (im Preis) *n.*
riser: early ~ *s.* Frühaufsteher(in) *m.(f.)*; **late** ~ *s.* Spätaufsteher(in) *m.(f.)*
rising *s.* Aufstand *m.*; Aufstehen *n.*; Aufbruch *m.*; Anschwellung *f.*; *~a.* aufgehend; steigend.
risk *s.* Gefahr *f.*; Wagnis *n.*; ~ *v.t.* wagen.
risky *a.* gewagt. gefährlich.
risqué *a.* gewagt (Witz).
rite *s.* feierlicher Brauch *m.*, Ritus *m.*
ritual *a.*, **~ly** *adv.* feierlich; rituell.
rival *s.* Rivale *m.*; Rivalin *f.*; Nebenbuhler(in) *m.(f.)*; Konkurrent(in) *m.(f.)*; ~ *a.* rivalisierend; nebenbuhlerisch; ~ *v.t. & i.* wetteifern.
rivalry *s.* Rivalität *f.*; Konkurrenz *f.*
rive *v.t.st.* (*v.i.* sich) spalten.
river *s.* Fluß *m.*; Strom *m.*; ~ *crossing*, Flußübergang *m.*
rivet *s.* Niet *n.*; Klammer *f.* ~ *v.t.* nieten, vernieten; befestigen.
riveting *a.* fesselnd.
rivulet *s.* Bach *m.*
roach *s.* Rotauge *n.* (Fisch); Kakerlak *f.*
road *s.* Straße, Landstraße *f.*; *~s pl.* Reede *f.*; **~-bed** *s.* Straßenunterbau *m.*; **~-block** *s.* (*mil.*) Straßensperre *f.*; **~-hog** *s.* rücksichtsloser Fahrer *m.*; **~-sign** *s.* Verkehrsschild *n.*
roam *v.i.* umherstreifen; ~ *v.t.* durchwandern.
roan *a.* scheckig, gefleckt ~ *s.* Schecke *f.*
roar *v.i.* brüllen; lärmen; brausen; ~ *s.* Gebrüll *n.*; Brausen *n.*
roaring *a.* dröhnend, tosend.
roast *v.t.* braten, rösten; ~ *a.* gebraten; ~ *s.* Braten *m.*; ~ **mutton** *s.* Hammelbraten; ~ **chicken** *s.* Hühnerbraten.
roastbeef *s.* Rinderbraten *m.*
rob *v.t.* rauben, berauben, bestehlen.
robber *s.* Räuber(in) *m.(f.)*
robbery *s.* Räuberei *f.*; Raub *m.*
robe *s.* langer Rock *m.*; (*law & univ.*) Talar *m.*; Staatskleid *n.*; ~ *v.t. & i.* das Staatskleid anlegen, kleiden.
robin *s.* Rotkehlchen *n.*
robot *s.* Roboter *m.*
robust *a.* stark, rüstig; derb.
rock *s.* Felsen *m.*; ~ *v.t. & i.* rütteln; einwiegen; schaukeln.
rockery *s.* Steingarten *m.*
rocket *s.* Rakete *f.*; (*mil.*) **~-launcher, ~-projector,** Raketenwurfmaschine *f.*
rockfall *s.* Steinschlag *m.*
rock-garden *s.* Steingarten *m.*
rocking-chair *s.* Schaukelstuhl *m.*
rocking-horse *s.* Schaukelpferd *n.*
rocky *a.* felsig; felsenhart.

rococo *s.* Rokoko *n.*
rod *s.* Rute *f.*; Stange *f.*; Meßrute *f.*
rodent *s.* Nagetier *n.*
roe *s.* Reh *n.*; Hirschkuh *f.*; Fischrogen *m.*
roebuck *s.* Rehbock *m.*
roger verstanden! (Funkverkehr).
rogue *s.* Schelm *m.*; Schurke *m.*
roguery *s.* Spitzbüberei, Schelmerei *f.*
roguish *a.*, **~ly** *adv.* spitzbübisch.
roister *v.i.* lärmen, poltern.
role *s.* Rolle *f.*; ~ **playing** *s.* Rollenspiel *n.*; ~ **reversal** *s.* Rollentausch *m.*
roll *v.t.* rollen, wälzen; walzen, strecken; ~ *v.i.* sich wälzen, sich drehen; schlingern; ~ *s.* Rollen *n.*; Rolle, Walze *f.*; Brötchen *n.*, Semmel *f.*; Wirbel (auf der Trommel) *m.*; Urkunde, Liste *f.*; ~ *and butter*, Butterbrötchen.
roll-call *s.* Namensaufruf *m.*, (*mil.*) Appell *m.*
roller *s.* Rolle *f.*; Walze *f.*; Wickelband *n.*; ~ *skate*, Rollschuh *m.*
roller-bearing *s.* (*mech.*) Rollenlager *n.*
roller-blind *s.* Rollo *n.*
roller-coaster *s.* Achterbahn *f.*
roller-skate *v.i.* Rollschuh laufen.
roller-skating *s.* Rollschuhlaufen *n.*
rollfilm *s.* (*phot.*) Rollfilm *m.*
rollick *v.i.* ausgelassen sein.
rolling-mill *s.* Walzwerk *n.*
rolling-pin *s.* Nudelholz *n.*, Teigrolle *f.*
Roman *a.* römisch; ~ *numerals* pl. römische Zahlen; ~ *type*, Antiquaschrift *f.*; ~ **Catholic** *a.* römisch-katholisch; *s.* Katholik(in) *m.*(*f.*)
romance *s.* Romanze *f.*; Erdichtung *f.*; ~ *v.i.* erdichten; aufschneiden.
Romance *a.* romanisch; ~ **languages and literature** Romanistik *f.*
Romanesque *a.* (*arch.*) romanisch.
Romania *s.* Rumänien.
Romanian *a.* rumänisch; ~*s.* Rumäne *m.*; Rumänin *f.*
romantic *a.*, **~ly** *adv.* romantisch.
Romanticism *s.* Romantik *f.*
romanticize *v.t.* romantisieren.
Romany *s.* Romani (Sprache); ~*ies* pl. die Roma, (*fam.*) die Zigeuner.
romp *s.* Tollen, (*sp. fam.*) leichter Sieg. ~ *v.i.* ausgelassen sein, sich balgen.
rood *s.* Rute *f.*
roof *s.* Dach *n.*; Decke *f.*; ~-**garden** *s.* Dachgarten *m.*; ~ *v.t.* bedachen.
roofing *s.* Bedachung *f.*; ~-**felt** *s.* Dachpappe *f.*
roof-rack *s.* Dachgepäckträger *m.*
roof-top *s.* Dach *n.*
rook *s.* Saatkrähe *f.*; Turm (im Schach) *m.*; Gauner *m.*
rookery *s.* Krähenhorst *m.*
room *s.* Raum *m.*; Platz *m.*; Zimmer *n.*
room-mate *s.* Zimmergenosse *m.*; Zimmergenossin *f.*; Mitbewohner(in) *m.*(*f.*)
roomy *a.* geräumig.
roost *s.* Hühnerstange *f.*
root *s.* Wurzel *f.*; Ursprung *m.*; ~ *v.i.* (ein)wurzeln; ~ **out** *v.t.* ausrotten; ausjäten, (Rüben) ausziehen.
rooted *a.* & *p.* eingewurzelt, fest.
rootless *a.* wurzellos; nichtverwurzelt.
rope *s.* Seil *n.*; Tau *n.*; Strick *m.*; ~ *v.t.* anseilen.

rope-dancer, rope-walker *s.* Seiltänzer(in) *m.*(*f.*)
rope-ladder *s.* Strickleiter *f.*
rope-maker *s.* Seiler *m.*
rope-walk *s.* Seilbahn *f.*
rosary *s.* Rosenkranz *m.*
rose *s.* Rose *f.*; Rosette *f.*
roseate *a.* rosig, rosenfarben.
rosebud *s.* Rosenknospe *f.*
rosebush *s.* Rosenstrauch *m.*
rosemary *s.* Rosmarin *m.*
rosette *s.* Rosette (Verzierung) *f.*
rosin *s.* Harz *n.*; Kolophonium *m.*
roster *s.* Dienstplan *m.*, Namensliste *f.*
rostrum *s.pl.* Podium *n.*; Rednerpult *n.*
rosy *a.* rosig.
rot *v.i.* faulen, modern; ~ *s.* Fäulnis *f.*; Schund *m.*; Unsinn *m.*
rota *s.* Dienstturnus *m.*
rotary *a.* rotierend; Rotations. . .; *s.* Kreisverkehr *m.*
rotate *v.i.* & *t.* (sich) drehen, rotieren.
rotation *s.* Kreislauf *m.*; Umdrehung *f.*; Wechsel *m.*; ~ *of crops*, Fruchtwechsel *m.*; *in* ~, abwechselnd.
rote *s.* *by* ~, auswendig.
rotten *a.* verfault; verdorben; verfallen; scheußlich, übel; ~ *egg*, faules Ei *m.*
rotund *a.* rund, kreisförmig.
rotundity *s.* Rundheit *f.*
rouble *s.* Rubel *m.*
rouge *s.* Rouge *n.*
rough *a.*, **~ly** *adv.* rauh, holprig, roh; ungebildet, grob; heftig; ~ *draft*, erster Entwurf *m.*, Faustskizze *f.*, ~ *notes* pl. flüchtige Notizen *f.pl.*; ~ *calculation*, grobe Berechnung *f.*; ~ *s.* Rohheit *f.*, ~ *v.t.* roh bearbeiten; *to* ~ *it*, primitiv leben.
roughage *s.* grobe Nahrung *f.*, Ballaststoffe pl.
rough-cast *s.* roher Entwurf *m.*; Rohputz *m.*; ~ *v.t.* entwerfen.
rough copy *s.* Entwurf *m.*; Konzept *n.*
roughen *v.t.* rauh machen; aufrauhen.
rough neck *s.* Grobian *m.*
roughness *s.* Rauheit *f.*; Unebenheit *f.*
rough-shod *a.* rücksichtslos.
round *a.* rund; unverhohlen, offen; volltönend; *a* ~ *sum*, eine runde Summe *f.*; ~ *adv.* & *pr.* um, herum, rings; geradeheraus; ~ *s.* Runde *f.*; Salve *f.*; (Patrone) Schuß *m.*; ~ **up** *s.* Razzia *f.*; ~ *v.t.* rundmachen; umfahren; ~ *v.i.* sich runden; *to* ~ *up*, *v.t.* zusammentreiben.
roundabout *a.* umgebend, Um. . .; ~ *adv.* rundherum; ~ *s.* Karussell *n.*
roundelay *s.* Rundgesang *m.*
roundly *adv.* rund; geradeheraus.
roundness *s.* Rundung *f.*; Offenheit *f.*
round trip *s.* Hin- und Rückfahrt *f.*
rouse *v.t.* aufwecken; aufregen, auftreiben; ~ *v.i.* aufwachen.
rout *s.* Aufruhr *m.*; Rotte *f.*; wilde Flucht *f.*; ~ *v.t.* in die Flucht schlagen; aufreiben.
route *s.* Weg *m.*; Marschroute *f.*
routine *s.* Routine *f.*; Schlendrian *m.*; ~ *work*, laufende Arbeiten pl.; Rontinearbeit *f.*
rove *v.i.* herumschwärmen, wandern; ~ *v.t.* durchwandern.
row *s.* Reihe *f.*; ~ *v.t.* & *i.* rudern; ~ *s.* Lärm *m.*;

Auflauf, Streit *m.*
rowan *s.* Eberesche *f.*
row-boat *s.* Ruderboot *n.*
rowdy *s.* roher Kerl *m.;* Rowdy *m.;* ~ *a.* roh, lärmend.
rowel *s.* Spornrädchen *n.*
rowing-match *s.* Wettrudern *n.*
royal *a.,* ~**ly** *adv.* königlich; prächtig.
royalist *m. s.* Royalist(in) *m.(f.)*
royalty *s.* Königtum *n.;* Mitglied (*n.*) der Königsfamilie; Ertragsanteil *m.* (im Urheberrecht), Tantieme *f.*
rub *v.t.* reiben, scheuern, abwischen; ~ *v.i.* sich durchschlagen; ~ *s.* Reibung *f.;* Hindernis *n.;* to ~ *one's hands together,* sich die Hände reiben.
rubber *s.* Wischtuch *n.;* Robber (im Whistspiel) *m.;* Kautschuk *m.,* Gummi *m.;* (*sl.*) Pariser *m.* (Kondom); ~**s** *pl.* Gummischuhe *m.pl.;* ~ **band** *s.* Gummiband *n.;* ~**-dinghy** *s.* Schlauchboot *n.;* ~ **stamp** *s.* Stempel; ~**-stamp** *v.t.* abstempeln; (*fig.*) genehmigen.
rubbish *s.* Unsinn *m.;* Schutt *m.;* Kehricht *m. & n.*
rubbishy *a.* blödsinnig.
rubble *s.* Steinschutt *m.;* Trümmer *pl.*
rubella *s.* Röteln *pl.*
rubicund *a.* rot, rötlich.
rubric *s.* Rubrik *f.*
ruby *s.* Rubin *m.*
rudder *s.* (Steuer)Ruder *n.;* Steuer *n.*
ruddy *a.* rötlich.
rude *a.,* ~**ly** *adv.* unhöflich; rüde; grob.
rudeness *s.* Grobheit *f.,* ungehöriges Benehmen *n.*
rudimentary *a.* rudimentär, Anfangs. . .
rudiments *s.pl.* Grundzüge *pl.;* Grundlagen *pl.*
rue *s.* Raute (Pflanze) *f.;* ~ *v.t.* bereuen; beklagen.
rueful *a.,* ~**ly** *adv.* reuig, kläglich.
ruff *s.* Halskrause *f.*
ruffian *s.* roher Kerl *m.;* Raufbold *m.*
ruffianly *a.* wüst, brutal, bübisch.
ruffle *v.t.* kräuseln; zerknüllen; fälteln; aus der Fassung bringen; ~ *v.i.* rauh werden; flattern; ~ *s.* Krause, Rüsche *f.;* Gekräusel *n.;* Unruhe *f.*
rug *s.* Bettvorleger, Kaminvorleger *f.;* kleiner Teppich *m.*
rugby *s.* Rugby *n.*
rugged *a.,* ~**ly** *adv.* rauh, holp[e]rig; zerklüftet.
rugger *s.* = **rugby.**
ruin *s.* Einsturz *m.;* Ruine *f.;* Ruin *m.;* Untergang *m.;* Verderben *n.;* ~ *v.t.* zerstören; zu Grunde richten.
ruinous *a.,* ~**ly** *adv.* ruinös.
rule *s.* Regel *f.;* (gerichtliche) Verfügung *f.;* Ordnung *f.;* Lineal *n.;* Maßstab *m.;* Herrschaft *f.;* ~ *of thumb,* Erfahrungsregel *f.;* ~ *of the road,* Straßenverkehrsordnung, Fahrordnung *f.;* ~ *v.t.* lin(i)ieren; regeln; verordnen; beherrschen; ~ *v.i.* herrschen; *to* ~ *out,* ausschließen.
ruled *a.* liniert.
ruler *s.* Herrscher(in) *m.(f.);* Lineal *n.*
ruling *s.* Gerichtsentscheidung *f.; a.* herrschend; regierend.
rum *s.* Rum *m.*
rumble *v.i.* rumpeln, rasseln.
ruminant *s.* Wiederkäuer *m.*
ruminate *v.t. & i.* wiederkäuen; (*fig.*) grübeln.
rummage *v.t.* durchstöbern; wühlen; ~ *sale,*

Ramschverkauf *m.*
rummy *s.* Rommé *n.*
rumor *s.* Gerücht *n.;* ~ *v.t.* (ein Gerücht) verbreiten, aussprengen.
rump *s.* Hinterteil *n.;* Rest *m.*
rumple *s.* Runzel *f.;* Falte *f.;* ~ *v.t.* runzeln, zerknittern.
rumpsteak *s.* Rumpsteak *n.*
rumpus *s.* (*sl.*) Krach *m.,* Trubel *m.*
run *v.i. & st.* laufen; eilen; verstreichen; strömen; lauten; sich erstrecken; leiten; hetzen; *to* ~ *down,* niederrennen; abhetzen; heruntermachen; *to* ~ *into,* hineinfahren in, anfahren; *to* ~ *into debt,* Schulden machen; *to* ~ *off,* davonlaufen; *to* ~ *on,* fortschreiten, fortsetzen; *to* ~ *out,* auslaufen; zu Ende gehen; sich erschöpfen; *to* ~ *over,* überfahren; *to* ~ *short,* ausgehen; *to* ~ *to,* sich belaufen auf; *to* ~ *up,* in die Höhe laufen; anwachsen lassen; hinauftreiben, steigern; errichten, aufbauen; ~ *s.* Laufen *n.;* Lauf, Gang *m.;* Andrang, Ansturm; Weidegrund *m.;* starke Nachfrage *f.;* Aufführungsperiode (*f.*) eines Stücks; Laufmasche, *f.* (*in stocking*); *the common* ~, Durchschnittstyp *m.;* ~ *on a bank,* Ansturm (*m.*) auf eine Bank; *in the long* ~, auf die Dauer.
runaway *s.* Flüchtling *m.;* Ausreißer(in) *m.(f.)*
rune *s.* Rune *f.*
rung *s.* (Leiter)Sprosse *f.*
runic *a.* runisch, Runen. . .
runner *s.* Läufer(in) *m.* (*f.*); Bote *m.;* Botin *f.;* Kufe *f.;* ~**-beans** *pl.* grüne Bohnen *f.pl.;* ~**-up,** Zweite *m./f.*
running *a.,* laufend; fließend; hintereinander; ~**-board** *s.* (*mot.*) Trittbrett *n.;* ~ **costs** *pl.* Betriebskosten *pl.;* ~ **repairs** *s.* laufende Reparaturen *f.;* ~ **shoes** *pl.* Joggingschuhe *pl.;* ~ **mate** Vizepräsidentschaftskandidat(in) *m.(f.);* ~ **water,** laufendes Wasser *m.*
runny *a.* flüssig; laufend (Nase); tränend (Auge).
runway *s.* (*avi.*) Startbahn *f.;* Landebahn *f.*
rupee *s.* Rupie *f.*
rupture *s.* Bruch *m.;* Uneinigkeit *f.;* ~ *v.i.* brechen, bersten.
rural *a.,* ~**ly** *adv.* ländlich.
ruse *s.* List *f.,* Trick *m.*
rush *s.* Binse *f.;* Ansturm *m.;* Hetzerei, Hetze *f.;* Andrang *m.,* Gedränge *n.;* Sturz *m.;* ~ **hour** *s.* Stoßzeit *f.;* ~ **hours** *pl.* Hauptgeschäftszeiten *f.pl.;* ~ *v.i.* stürzen, schießen, rennen; rauschen; ~ *v.t.* (durch)hetzen, durchpeitschen.
rusk *s.* Zwieback *m.*
russet *a.* braunrot; ~ *s.* Reinette (Apfel) *f.*
Russia *s.* Rußland *f.*
Russian *a.* russisch, ~*s.* Russe *m.;* Russin *f.*
rust *s.* Rost *m.;* ~ *v.i.* rosten.
rustic *a.,* ~**ally** *adv.* ländlich, bäurisch; ~ *s.* Bauer *m.*
rusticity *s.* Ländlichkeit *f.*
rustle *v.i.* rauschen; säuseln; raschlen.
rustler *s.* Viehdieb *m.*
rusty *a.,* ~**ily** *adv.* rostig; eingerostet.
rut *s.* Spur *f.;* Geleise *n.;* Brunst *f.,* Brunft *f.;* ~ *v.t.* furchen; *v.i.* brunsten.
ruthless *a.,* ~**ly** *adv.* unbarmherzig.
rutted *a.* ausgefahren.
rutting-season *s.* Brunftzeit *f.*
rye *s.* Roggen *m.;* ~**-grass,** Lolch *m.*

S

S, s der Buchstabe S oder s *n*.
Sabbath *s*. Sabbat *m*.; Ruhetag *m*.
sabbatical *a*. ~ **term/year** Forschungssemester *n*./ Forschungsjahr *n*.
saber *s*. Säbel *m*.; ~ *v.t*. niedersäbeln; ~ **rattling** *s*. Säbelrasseln *n*.
sable *s*. Zobel *m*.; Zobelpelz *m*.
sabotage *s*. Sabotage *f*.; ~ *v.t*. sabotieren.
saccharin *s*. Saccharin *n*.
sacerdotal *a*. priesterlich.
sack *s*. Sack *m*.; Beutel *m*., Tüte *f*., (*fam*.) Plünderung *f*.; Laufpaß *m*.; ~ *v.t*. einsacken; plündern; entlassen.
sackcloth *s*. Sackleinwand *f*.
sack race *s*. Sackhüpfen *n*.
sacrament *s*. Sakrament *n*.; heiliges Abendmahl *n*.; *to take the* ~, zum Abendmahl gehen.
sacred *a*., **~ly** *adv*. heilig; ehrwürdig; ~ **cow** *s*. heilige Kuh *f*.
sacrifice *v.t*. & *i*. opfern; ~ *s*. Opfer *n*.; Opferung *f*.; Preisgabe *f*.
sacrificial *a*. Opfer...
sacrilege *s*. Kirchenraub, Frevel *m*.
sacrilegious *a*., **~ly** *adv*. frevelhaft; ruchlos.
sacristan *s*. Kirchner, Küster *m*.
sacristy *s*. Sakristei *f*.
sacrosanct *a*. sakrosankt.
sad *a*., **~ly** *adv*. dunkel; traurig; trübe, ernst; schlimm, arg.
sadden *v.t*. betrüben.
saddle *s*. Sattel *m*.; Rückenstück (*n*.); **~-horse,** Reitpferd *n*.; ~ *v.t*. satteln; belasten.
saddler *s*. Sattler *m*.
sadism *s*. Sadismus *m*.
sadist *s*. Sadist(in) *m*.(*f*.)
sadistic *a*., **~ally** *adv*. sadistisch.
sadness *s*. Traurigkeit, Schwermut *f*.; Ernst *m*.
safari *s*. Safari *f*.
safe *a*., **~ly** *adv*. sicher; unversehrt; ~ *s*. Geldschrank *m*.; Safe *m*.
safe-conduct *s*. sicheres Geleit *n*.; Schutzbrief *m*.
safeguard *s*. Schutzwache *f*.; Schutz *m*.; ~ *v.t*. schützen, sichern.
safety *s*. Sicherheit *f*.; ~ **belt** *s*. Sicherheitsgurt *m*.; **~-curtain** *s*. eiserner Vorhang *m*.; **~-glass** *s*. Plexiglas *n*.; **~-match** *s*. Sicherheitszündholz *n*.; **~-pin** *s*. Sicherheitsnadel *f*.; **~-razor** *s*. Rasierapparat *m*.; **~-valve** *s*. Sicherheitsventil *n*.
saffron *s*. Safran *m*.; ~ *a*. safrangelb.
sag *v.i*. sich senken, sacken; durchhängen.
saga *s*. Heldenepos *n*.; Saga *f*.
sagacious *a*., **~ly** *adv*. scharfsinnig.
sagacity *s*. Scharfsinn *m*.
sage *a*., **~ly** *adv*. weise, klug; ~ *s*. Weise *m*.; (Gewürz) Salbei *f*.
sagittarius *s*. (*astr*.) Schütze *m*.
sago *s*. Sago *m*.
sail *s*. Segel *n*.; Schiff *n*.; Windmühlenflügel *m*.; ~ *v.i*. segeln; abfahren (vom Schiff); ~ *v.t*. durchsegeln; **~ing-boat** *s*. Segelboot *n*.
sailor *s*. Matrose *m*.; *to be a good* ~, seefest sein.
saint *a*., **~ly** *adv*. heilig; ~ *s*. Heilige *m*./*f*.
saintly *a*. fromm, heilig.

sake *s*. *for God's* ~, um Gotteswillen; *for the* ~ *of*, um... ..willen; *for my* ~, um meinetwillen.
salacious *a*., **~ly** *adv*. lüstern; schlüpfrig; geil.
salad *s*. Salat *m*.; **~-dressing** Salatsoße *f*.
salamander *s*. Salamander *m*.
salami *s*. Salami(wurst) *f*.
salaried *a*. besoldet.
salary *s*. Gehalt *n*.; **~-scale** *s*. Gehaltsskala *f*.
sale *s*. Verkauf, Absatz *m*.; Ausverkauf *m*.; **~s assistant** *s*. Verkäufer(in) *m*.(*f*.); **~s clerk** *s*. Verkäufer(in) *m*. (*f*.); **~swoman** *s*. Verkäuferin *f*.; **~sman** *s*. Verkäufer *m*.; **~smanship** *s*. Verkaufstüchtigkeit, Verkaufsgewandtheit *f*.; *for* ~, verkäuflich.
salient *a*. springend; hervorragend.
saline *a*. salzartig; ~ *s*. Salzquelle *f*.
saliva *s*. Speichel *m*.
salivate *v.i*. speicheln.
sallow *a*. blaß; gelblich; ~ *s*. Salweide *f*.
sally *s*. Ausfall *m*.; Ausflug *m*.; witziger Einfall *m*.; ~ *v.i*. sich aufmachen; hervorbrechen.
salmon *s*. Lachs, Salm *m*.
salon *s*. Salon *m*.
saloon *s*. Saal, Salon *m*.; Kneipe *f*.; erste Klasse *f*. (Schiff); **~-car** *s*. (*mot*.) Limousine *f*., (*rail*.) Luxuswagen *m*.
salt *s*. Salz *n*.; (*fig*.) Seebär *m*.; Würze *f*.; Witz *m*.; ~ *a*., **~ly** *adv*. salzig; ~ *v.t*. (ein)salzen.
salt-cellar *s*. Salzfaß *n*.
salter *s*. Salzhändler *m*.
salt-shaker *s*. Salzfaß *n*.
salt-works *s.pl*. Saline *f*.
salty *a*. etwas salzig.
salubrious *a*. heilsam, gesund.
salubrity *s*. Heilsamkeit *f*.
salutary *a*. heilsam.
salutation *s*. Gruß *m*.; Anrede (Brief) *f*.
salute *v.t*. grüßen; ~ *s*. Gruß *m*.
salvage *s*. Bergung *f*.; Bergelohn *m*.; ~ *v.t*. bergen.
salvation *s*. Rettung, Seligkeit *f*.; **~-army,** 'Heilsarmee,' *f*.
salve *s*. Salbe *f*. ~ *v.t*. salben; lindern; bergen.
salver *s*. Präsentierteller *m*.
salvo *s*. Vorbehalt *m*.; Salve *f*.
same *pn*. derselbe, dieselbe, dasselbe; einerlei; *all the* ~, trotzdem.
sameness *s*. Gleichheit *f*.
sample *s*. Probe *f*., Muster *n*.; *according to* ~, nach Muster; ~ *v.t*. eine Probe nehmen.
sampler *s*. Stick(muster)tuch *n*.
sanatorium *s*. Heilanstalt *f*.
sanctification *s*. Heiligung, Einsegnung *f*.
sanctify *v.t*. heiligen.
sanctimonious *a*., **~ly** *adv*. scheinheilig.
sanction *s*. Bestätigung *f*., Genehmigung *f*.; Sanktion *f*.; Zwangsmaßnahme *f*.; Gesetzeskraft *f*.; ~ *v.t*. bestätigen; genehmigen.
sanctity *s*. Heiligkeit, Reinheit *f*.
sanctuary *s*. Heiligtum *n*.; Freistätte *f*.
sand *s*. Sand *m*.; **~s** *pl*. Sandwüste; Strand *m*.; Sandbank *f*.
sandal *s*. Sandale *f*.

sandalwood *s.* Sandelholz *n.*
sandbag *s.* Sandsack *m.*
sandbox *s.* Sandkasten *m.*
sand-castle *s.* Sandburg *f.*
sandpaper *s.* Sandpapier *n.*
sandstone *s.* Sandstein *m.*
sandwich *s.* belegtes Brot *n.*; Sandwich *n.*; ~ *v.t.* einklemmen; ~ **man** *s.* Plakatträger *m.*
sandy *a.* sandig; gelblichrot.
sane *a.* gesund (an Geist), vernünftig.
sangfroid *s.* Kaltblütigkeit *f.*
sanguinary *a.* blutig; blutdürstig.
sanguine *a.*, **~ly** *adv.* hoffnungsvoll.
sanitary *a.* gesundheitlich, Gesundheits. . .; ~ **napkin** *s.* Monatsbinde *f.*
sanitation *s.* Hygiene *f.*
sanity *s.* Gesundheit *f.*; gesunder Verstand *m.*
Santa Claus *s.* der Weihnachtsmann *m.*
sap *s.* Saft (der Bäume) *m.*; Splint *m.*; ~ *v.t. & i.* untergraben, sappen.
sapience *s.* Weisheit *f.*
sapient *a.* weise.
sapless *a.* saftlos.
sapling *s.* junger Baum *m.*
sapper *s.* Sappeur *m.*
sapphire *s.* Saphir *m.*
sappy *a.* saftig; weich; munter.
sarcasm *s.* beißender Spott *m.*; Sarkasmus *m.*
sarcastic *a.* beißend, sarkastisch.
sarcophagus *s.* Steinsarg *m.*
sardine *s.* Sardine *f.*
sardonic *a.* sardonisch, bitter, grimmig.
sartorial *a.* Schneider. . .
sash *s.* Schärpe *f.*; Fensterrahmen *m.*; (**~-window**) Schiebefenster *n.*
satanic *a.*, **~ally** *adv.* teuflisch.
satchel *s.* Schulmappe *f.*; Tasche *f.*
sate *v.t.* sättigen.
sateen *s.* Satin *m.*
satellite *s.* Satellit *m.*
satellite dish *s.* Parabolantenne *f.*
satiate *v.t.* sättigen.
satiety *s.* Sättigung *f.*; Überdruß *m.*
satin *s.* Atlas *m.*; Satin *m.*
satire *s.* Satire *f.*
satirical *a.*, **~ly** *adv.* satirisch.
satirist *s.* Satiriker(in) *m.(f.)*
satirize *v.t.* bespötteln.
satisfaction *s.* Genugtuung *f.*; Befriedigung, Freude *f.*
satisfactory *a.*, **~ily** *adv.* befriedigend.
satisfied *p. & a.* zufrieden.
satisfy *v.t. & i.* genugtun, genügen; befriedigen; überzeugen.
satisfying *a.* befriedigend.
saturate *v.t.* (*chem.*) sättigen; durchnässen.
saturated *a.* gesättigt; durchnäßt.
Saturday *s.* Sonnabend, Samstag *m.*
Saturn *s.* Saturn *m.*
saturnine *a.* mürrisch, finster.
sauce *s.* Sauce, Soße, Tunke *f.*; Würze *f.*; **~-boat** *s.* Sauciere *f.*
saucepan *s.* Kochtopf *m.*, Tiegel *m.*
saucer *s.* Untertasse *f.*
saucy *a.*, **~ily** *adv.* unverschämt; keck.
Saudi Arabia *s.* Saudi Arabien *n.*

Saudi Arabian *a.* saudiarabisch; **~s.** Saudi(araber) *m.*, Saudiaraberin *f.*
sauna *s.* Sauna *f.*
saunter *v.i.* schlendern; ~ *s.* Bummel *m.*
saurian *a.* Saurier. . .
sausage *s.* Wurst *f.*
savage *a.*, **~ly** *adv.* wild, grausam; ~ *s.* Wilde *m. f.*
savagery *s.* Brutalität *f.*
savanna(h) *s.* Grasfläche *f.*; Savanne *f.*
save *v.t.* retten, bergen; schonen; sparen, ersparen; aufheben; ~ *pr.* außer, ausgenommen.
saveloy *s.* Zervelatwurst *f.*
saving *a.*, **~ly** *adv.* sparsam; ~ *s.* Rettung *f.*; Vorbehalt *m.*; Ersparnis *f.*; ~ *pr.* außer; ~ *clause*, (*law*) Vorbehaltsklausel *f.*; **~s-bank** *s.* Sparkasse *f.*; **~s-certificate** *s.* Spargutschein *m.*
Savior *s.* Heiland *m.*; Retter(in) *m.(f.)*
savor *s.* Geschmack *m.*; Geruch, Duft *m.*; ~ *v.i. & t.* schmecken, riechen; nach etwas aussehen.
savory *a.* schmackhaft; wohlriechend; scharfgewürzt; ~ *s.* Häppchen *n.*
savoy *s.* Wirsing(kohl) *m.*
savvy *a.* (*fam.*) klug; mit viel Grips.
saw *s.* Säge *f.*; Spruch *m.*; ~ *v.t.* sägen.
sawdust *s.* Sägespäne *m.pl.*
saw-horse *s.* Sägebock *m.*
saw-mill *s.* Schneidemühle *f.*
Saxony *s.* Sachsen *n.*
saxophone *s.* Saxophon *n.*
saxophonist *s.* Saxophonist(in) *m.(f.)*
say *v.t. & i.st.* sagen; hersagen; erzählen.
saying *s.* Rede *f.*; Redensart *f.*; *it goes without ~*, es versteht sich von selbst.
scab *s.* Schorf *m.*; Krätze *f.*
scabbard *s.* Säbelscheide *f.*
scabby *a.* krätzig; schäbig.
scabies *s.* Krätze *f.*
scabrous *a.* heikel, schlüpfrig.
scaffold *s.* Gerüst, Schafott *n.*; ~ *v.t.* ein Gerüst aufschlagen; stützen.
scaffolding *s.* Gerüst *n.*; Bühne *f.*
scald *s.* Verbrühung *f.*; Brandwunde *f.*; Skalde *m.*; ~ *v.t.* brühen, verbrennen; (Milch) abkochen.
scalding-hot *a.* brühheiß.
scale *s.* Waagschale *f.*; Schuppe *f.*; Kesselstein *m.*; Maßtab *m.*; Tonleiter *f.*; Stufenleiter *f.*; Gradeinteilung *f.*; *pair of ~s*, Waage *f.*; *on a large ~*, im Großen, auf großem Fuße; ~ *v.t.* erklettern, stürmen; abschiefern, schuppen; ~ *v.i.* abblättern.
scaled *a.* schuppig.
scaling-ladder *s.* Sturmleiter *f.*; Feuerleiter *f.*
scallop *s.* Zacke *f.*, Langette *f.*; Muschel *f.*; ~ *v.t.* ausbogen.
scalp *s.* Kopfhaut *f.*; ~ *v.t.* skalpieren.
scalpel *s.* Skalpell *n.*
scaly *a.* schuppig, geschuppt.
scamp *s.* Taugenichts *m.*; Lausbub *m.*; ~ *v.t.* verpfuschen.
scamper *v.i.* rennen.
scan *v.t.* skandieren (Verse); genau ansehen, erwägen.
scandal *s.* Ärgernis *n.* Skandal *m.*; Schande *f.*
scandalize *v.t.* ärgern, Anstoß geben.
scandalous *a.*, **~ly** *adv.* schändlich.
Scandinavia *s.* Skandinavien *n.*
Scandinavian *a.* skandinavisch; ~ *s.* Skandinavier(in) *m.(f.)*

scanner s. Geigerzähler m.; (comp.) Scanner m.

scant a. knapp; sparsam.

scanty a. sparsam, karg, knapp; gering.

scapegoat s. Sündenbock m.

scar s. Narbe f.; ~ v.t. eine Narbe hinterlassen; ~ v.i. vernarben.

scarab s. Käfer m.; Skarabäus m.

scarce a. spärlich, knapp.

scarcely adv. kaum.

scarcity s. Seltenheit, Spärlichkeit f.; Knappheit f.

scare v.t. scheuchen, schrecken; ~ s. leerer Schreck m.; Panik f.

scarecrow s. Vogelscheuche f.

scared a. verängstigt; Angst haben.

scaremonger s. Panikmacher(in) m.(f.)

scarf s. Halstuch n.; Kopftuch n.; Schultertuch n.

scarlet s. Scharlach m.; ~ a. scharlachrot; ~-**fever** s. Scharlachfieber n.

scathing a. beißend; scharf.

scatter v.t. zerstreuen, verbreiten; verstreuen; ~ v.i. sich zerstreuen.

scatterbrained a. konfus; schusselig.

scavenge v.t. ~ on leben von; ~ in herumwühlen.

scavenger s. Aasfresser m.

scenario s. Szenario n.

scene s. Bühne f.; Schauplatz m.; Szene f.; Begebenheit f.; Kulisse f.; Auftritt m.; ~ of action, Schauplatz m.

scenery s. Landschaft, Gegend, Szenerie f.; Gemälde n.; Bühnengerät n.

scenic(al) a. bühnenmäßig; landschaftlich, Landschafts. . .

scent s. Geruch m.; Witterung f.; Fährte f.; ~ v.t. riechen, wittern; durchduften.

scented a. duftend.

scepter s. Zepter n.

sceptic a. skeptisch; s. Skeptiker(in) m. (f.).

scepticism s. Skeptik f.; Skeptizismus m.

schedule s. Verzeichnis n., Liste f.; Fahrplan m.; ~ v.t. aufzeichnen; on ~ adv. planmäßig, fahrplanmäßig.

scheduled a. planmäßig.

schematic a. schematisch.

scheme s. Plan, Entwurf m.; Figur f., Schema n.; ~ v.i. & t. Pläne machen, entwerfen; Ränke schmieden.

schemer s. Ränkeschmied m.

scheming a. intrigant.

schism s. Kirchenspaltung f.

schismatic a., ~**ally** adv. schismatisch.

schizophrenia s. Schizophrenie f.

schizophrenic a. schizophren.

scholar s. Gelehrte m./f.

scholarly a. wissenschaftlich; gelehrt.

scholarship s. Gelehrsamkeit f.; Stipendium n.

scholastic a., ~**ally** adv. schulmäßig; Schul. . .; scholastisch; ~ degree, Schulabgangszeugnis n.

school s. Schule f.; Schulhaus n.; ~-**age**, schulpflichtiges Alter n.; ~-**attendance**, Schulbesuch m.; ~-**leaving age**, Schulentlassungsalter n.; ~ v.t. schulen, unterrichten.

school-board s. Schulbehörde f.

schoolboy s. Schuljunge m.

schoolgirl s. Schulmädchen n.

schoolmaster s. Schullehrer m.

schoolmate s. Schulkamerad(in) m.(f.)

schoolmistress s. Lehrerin f.

schoolteacher s. Lehrer(in) m.(f.)

schoolyard s. Schulhof m.

school year s. Schuljahr n.

schooner s. Schoner (Fahrzeug) m.

sciatica s. Ischias f.

science s. Wissenschaft f.; Naturwissenschaft f.; Kenntnis f.

scientific a., ~**ally** adv. wissenschaftlich.

scientist s (Natur)Wissenschaftler(in) m.(f.)

scintillate v.i. funkeln.

scintillating a. sprühend; geistsprühend.

scion s. Sproß m., Sprößling m.

scissors s.pl. Schere f.

sclerosis s. Sklerose f.

scoff v.t. verspotten; verschlingen; ~ s. Hohn m.

scold v.t. & i. schelten, zanken.

scolding s. Schimpfen n., Schelte f.

sconce s. kleine Laterne f.; Wandleuchter m.

scone s. kleiner Mürbekuchen m.

scoop s. Schaufel; Spatel m.; Schöpflöffel m.; ~ v.t. schaufeln, schöpfen, aushöhlen.

scoot v.i. (fam). rasen; die Kurve kratzen

scooter s. Tretroller m.; Motorroller m.

scope s. Spielraum m., Umfang m.; Gesichtskreis m.; Zweck m.

scorch v.t. sengen, brennen; ~ v.i. ausdorren; scorched earth, (mil.) verbrannte Erde (Verwüstung des eigenen Landes durch eine zurückgehende Armee); ~ s. Brandfleck m.

scorching a. glühend heiß; sengend.

score s. Kerbholz n., Kerbe f.; Zeche f.; Schuld f.; Spielstand m.; (mus.) Partitur f.; ~ v.t. einkerben; anschreiben; Punkte machen; (mus.) instrumentieren; gewinnen; ~-**board** s. Anzeigetafel f.

scorn s. Spott m.; Geringschätzung f.; Verachtung f.; ~ v.t. & i. verspotten; verachten.

scornful a., ~**ly** adv. höhnisch; verächtlich.

Scorpio s. (astro.) Skorpion m.

scorpion s. Skorpion m.

Scot s. Schotte m.; Schottin f.

Scotch s. Scotch Whisky.

scotch fir s. Föhre, Kiefer f.

scotch tape s. Klebestreifen m.

scot-free a. unversehrt, ungeschoren.

Scotland s. Schottland n.

Scots a. schottisch; s. Schottisch n.

Scottish a. schottisch.

scoundrel s. Schurke m.

scour v.t. & i. scheuern, reinigen; durchstreifen.

scourer s. Topfreiniger m.

scourge s. Geißel f.; Strafe f.; ~ v.t. geißeln, züchtigen.

scout s. Späher, Kundschafter m.; **boy** ~ s. Pfadfinder m.; **girl** ~ s. Pfadfinderin f.; ~ v.i. ausspähen; ~ v.t. zurückweisen, verspotten.

scowl s. finsteres Gesicht n.; ~ v.i. finster aussehen.

scraggy a., ~**ily** adv. mager; dürr.

scram v.i. abhauen, Leine ziehen.

scramble v.i. sich reißen; klettern; ~ s. Raffen n.; Gedränge n.; Krabbelei f.

scrambled eggs s.pl. Rühreier n.pl.

scrap s. Stückchen n.; Fetzen m.; Balgerei f., Rauferei f.; ~**s** pl. Überbleibsel n.pl.; ~-**iron** Schrott m.; ~ v.t. verschrotten; zum alten Eisen werfen.

scrape *v.t. & i.* schaben, kratzen, zusammenscharren; ~ *s.* Schürfwunde *f.*

scraper *s.* Kratzeisen, Schabeisen *n.*; Kratzbürste *f.*; Kratzer *m.*; Schaber *m.*

scrappy *a.*, **-ily** *adv.* zusammengestückelt.

scrap value *s.* Schrottwert *m.*

scratch *v.t.* kratzen; ritzen, kritzeln; ~ *s.* Riß, Ritz *m.*; Schramme *f.*

scratchy *a.* kratzend; zerkratzt.

scrawl *v.t.* kritzeln; ~ *s.* Gekritzel *n.*

scrawny *a.* mager; dürr.

scream *v.i.* kreischen, schreien; ~ *s.* Schrei *m.*

scree *s.* Schutt *m.*; Geröll *n.*

screech *v.i.* schreien, kreischen.

screen *s.* Schirm *m.*; (Kino) Leinwand *f.*; (*mil.*) Schützenschleier *m.*; Sandsieb *n.*; ~ *v.t.* schützen; sieben; (Licht) abblenden; (*fig.*) überprüfen.

screw *s.* Schraube *f.*; ~ *v.t.* schrauben; quetschen, drücken.

screw-driver *s.* Schraubenzieher *m.*

screwed up *a.* neurotisch.

screwy *a.* (*fam.*) verrückt.

scribble *v.i. & t.* kritzeln; ~ *s.* Gekritzel *n.*

scribbler *s.* Schmierer, Sudler *m.*

scribe *s.* Schreiber(in) *m.*(*f.*); Schriftgelehrte *m./f.*

scrimmage *s.* Handgemenge *n.*

scrimp *v.i.* knausern.

script *s.* (*typ.*) Schrift *f.*; Schriftart *f.*; Schreibschrift *f.*; (*Film, Radio*) Drehbuch, Manuskript *n.*

scriptural *a.* schriftmäßig, biblisch.

Scripture *s.* Heilige Schrift *f.*

script writer *s.* Drehbuchautor(in) *m.*(*f.*)

scrivener *s.* Schreiber *m.*

scrofula *s.* Skrofeln *f.pl.*

scrofulous *a.* skrofulös.

scroll *s.* Rolle *f.*; Schnörkel *m.*

scrounge *v.t.* stehlen, klauen, schnorren.

scrounger *s.* Schnorrer(in) *m.*(*f.*)

scrub *v.t.* scheuern; ~ *v.i.* sich placken; ~ *s.* Gestrüpp *n.*; Buschwerk *n.*; Gebüsch *n.*

scrubby *a.* stoppelig; stachelig.

scruffy *a.* schmuddelig.

scrumptious *a.* lecker.

scrunch *v.t.* zerknüllen; ~ *v.i.* knirschen.

scruple *s.* Bedenken *f.*, Skrupel *m.*

scrupulous *a.*, **-ly** *adv.* bedenklich, gewissenhaft, skrupulös.

scrutinize *v.t. & i.* forschen; prüfen.

scrutiny *s.* genaue Untersuchung *f.*; Wahlprüfung *f.*

scuba *s.* Tauchgerät *n.*; ~ **diving** *s.* (Sport) Tauchen *n.*

scud *v.i.* fortlaufen; rennen; (*nav.*) lenzen.

scuff *v.t.* verkratzen; schlurfen.

scuffle *s.* Balgerei *f.*; Handgemenge *n.*; ~ *v.i.* sich balgen.

scull *s.* Heckriemen, *m.*; Skullboat *n.*; ~ *v.i.* skullen, wriggen.

scullion *s.* Küchenjunge *m.*

sculptor *s.* Bildhauer(in) *m.*(*f.*)

sculpture *s.* Bildhauerkunst *f.*; Skulptur *f.*; ~ *v.t.* schnitzen; formen.

scum *s.* Schaum *m.*; Abschaum, Auswurf *m.*; ~ *v.t.* abschäumen.

scurf *s.* Schuppe *f.*

scurrility *s.* grober Spaß *m.*

scurrilous *a.*, **-ly** *adv.* possenhaft; gemein, grob, zotig.

scurry *v.i.* dahineilen; ~ *s.* Hasten *n.*

scurvy *s.* Skorbut *m.*

scuttle *s.* Kohlenkasten *m.*; Luke *f.*; hastige Flucht *f.*; ~ *v.t.* (ein Schiff) durchlöchern, versenken; ~ *v.i.* flüchten.

scythe *s.* Sense *f.*

sea *s.* See *f.*; Meer *n.*; *at ~*, (*fig.*) ratlos.

seabed *s.* Meeresboden *m.*

seaboard *s.* Seeküste *f.*

sea-chart *s.* Seekarte *f.*

sea-coast *s.* Meeresküste *f.*

seafaring *a.* seefahrend.

sea-fight *s.* Seeschlacht *f.*

seafood *s.* Meeresfrüchte *pl.*

sea-going *a.* seetüchtig.

sea-green *a.* Meergrün *n.*

sea-gull *s.* Möwe *f.*

sea-horse *s.* Seepferdchen *n.*

seal *s.* Siegel, Petschaft *n.*; Bestätigung *f.*; Robbe *f.*, Seehund *m.*; *under my hand and ~*, unter Brief und Siegel; ~ *v.t. & i.* besiegeln, siegeln.

sealant *s.* Dichtungsmaterial *n.*

sea-level *s.* Meeresspiegel *m.*

sealing-wax *s.* Siegellack *n.*

sea-lion *s.* Seelöwe *m.*

sealskin *s.* Seehundsfell *n.*

seam *s.* Saum *m.*; Nacht *f.*; Fuge *f.*; Flöz *n.*

seaman *s.* Seemann *m.*

seamanship *s.* Seemannskunst *f.*

seamless *a.* nahtlos.

seamstress *s.* Näherin *f.*

seamy *a.* mit Nähten; ~ *side*, Schattenseite *f.*

sea-plane *s.* Wasserflugzeug *n.*

seaport *s.* Seehafen *m.*

sear *v.t.* brennen, sengen; brandmarken; verhärten.

search *v.t. & i.* suchen, untersuchen, prüfen; ~ *s.* Suchen, Durchsuchen, Nachforschen *n.*; Prüfung *f.*; ~-**warrant** *s.* Haussuchungsbefehl *m.*

searching *a.* prüfend; forschend.

search-light *s.* Scheinwerfer *m.*

searing *a.* brennend, stechend (Schmerz); sengend (Hitze).

sea-salt *s.* Meersalz *n.*

sea shell *s.* Muschel(schale) *f.*

seasick *a.* seekrank.

sea-sickness *s.* Seekrankheit *f.*

sea-side *s.* Strand *m.*; Küste *f.*; Seebad *n.*; *to the ~*, an die See.

season *s.* Jahreszeit *f.*; rechte Zeite *f.*; Saison *f.*; *to be in ~*, *out of ~*, saisongemäß, nichtsaisongemäß sein; ~ *v.t. & i.* reifen; trocknen; gewöhnen, abhärten; würzen; mildern.

seasonable *a.* zeitgemäß.

seasoned *a.* reif, abgelagert; gewürzt.

seasoning *s.* Würze *f.*

season-ticket *s.* (*rail.*) Dauerkarte *f.*

seat *s.* Sitz (auch Hosensitz) *m.*; Stuhl *m.*; Lage *f.*; Schauplatz *m.*; Landsitz *m.*; Platz (Bahn, Omnibus) *m.*; **corner-~**, Eckplatz *m.*; ~ *v.t.* setzen; *to be ~ed*, sitzen; *take a ~*, nehmen Sie Platz!

seat-belt *s.* Sicherheitsgurt *m.*

seated *a.* sitzend.

sea-urchin *s.* Seeigel *m.*

sea-water s. Meerwasser n.
seaward a. & adv. seewärts.
seaweed s. Tang m., Alge f.
seaworthy a. seetüchtig.
secede v.i. sich trennen.
secession s. Spaltung f.; Trennung f.
secessionist s. Abtrünnige m.; Sonderbündler m.
seclude v.t. ausschließen, absondern.
seclusion s. Absonderung f.; Zurückgezogenheit f.
second a. der, die, das zweite; nächste; geringer; ~ *cousin*, Vetter(Base) zweiten Grades; ~ *sight*, zweites Gesicht n.; *on ~ thought*, bei nochmaliger Überlegung; ~ s. Sekundant m.; Sekunde f.; ~ v.t. beistehen, (Antrag) unterstützen.
secondary a., ~**ily** adv. nächstfolgend; untergeordnet; Neben...; ~ *circuit*, (elek.) Nebenstromkreis m.; ~ *education* s. höhere Bildung f. ~ *school*, höhere Schule f.
second-best a. zweitbest; *come off ~*, adv. den kürzeren ziehen.
second-class a. zweitklassig, zweitrangig.
second-hand a. aus zweiter Hand; gebraucht; antiquarisch.
second home s. Zweitwohnung f.; Ferienhaus n.
secondly adv. zweitens.
second name s. Nachname f.; Zuname m.
second nature s. zweite Natur f.
second-rate a. zweitrangig.
second thoughts s.pl. *have ~*, es sich anders überlegen.
secrecy s. Heimlichkeit f.; Verschwiegenheit f.
secret a., ~**ly** adv. geheim, verborgen; verschwiegen; ~ *agent* s. Geheimagent(in) m.(f.); ~ *police*, Geheimpolizei f.; ~ *service*, Geheimdienst m.; ~ s. Geheimnis n.; *official ~*, Amtsgeheimnis n.
secretarial a. Sekretärs...; sekretariats...; Sekretärinnen...
secretariat s. Sekretariat n.
secretary s. Schriftführer(in) m.(f.); Sekretär m.; Sekretärin f.; ~ *of state* s. Außenminister(in) m. (f.); ~ *general* s. Generalsekretär(in) m.(f.)
secret ballot s. geheime Abstimmung f.
secrete v.t. absondern.
secretion s. Absonderung f.
secretive a. verschwiegen; geheimtuerisch.
sect s. Sekte f.
sectarian a. zu einer Sekte gehörig; ~ s. Sektierer m.
section s. Zerschneiden n.; Abteilung f.; Abschnitt m.; (rail.) Strecke f.; Durchschnitt m.
sectional a. Gruppen...; partikular...
sector s. Kreisausschnitt m.; (mil.) Geländeabschnitt m.
secular a., ~**ly** adv. weltlich, säkular.
secularize v.t. verweltlichen; säkularisieren.
secure a., ~**ly** adv. sicher; sorglos; ~ v.t. sichern, versichern; befestigen; sich verschaffen.
security s. Sicherheit, Sorglosigkeit f.; Schutz m.; Bürgschaft f.; **securities** pl. Wertpapiere n.pl.
sedan s. Sänfte f.; (mot.) Limousine f.
sedate a., ~**ly** adv. ruhig, gesetzt.
sedative a. stillend, beruhigend; ~ s. Sedativum n.; Beruhigungsmittel f.
sedentary a. sitzend, seßhaft.
sedge s. Schilfgras n., Binse f.
sediment s. Bodensatz m.; Ablagerung f.

sedition s. Aufstand m.; Empörung f.
seditious a., ~**ly** adv. aufrührerisch.
seduce v.t. verführen, verleiten.
seducer s. Verführer m.
seduction s. Verführung f.
seductive s. verführerisch.
sedulous a., ~**ly** adv. emsig, fleißig.
see v.t. & i.st. sehen; besuchen; *to ~ through*, durchschauen; *to ~ a thing through*, etwas bis ans Ende durchhalten; *to ~ to it*, dafür sorgen; *I'll be seeing you*, auf Wiedersehen!
seed s. Same m.; Saat f.; ~ v.i. in Samen schießen; ausfallen.
seedbed s. (Saat)Beet n.
seedless n. kernlos.
seedling s. Sämling m.
seedy a. samenreich; schäbig; elend.
seek v.t. & i.st. suchen, trachten; aufsuchen.
seem v.i. scheinen, erscheinen.
seeming a., ~**ly** adv. scheinbar; dem Anscheine nach.
seemly a. anständig, schicklich.
seep v.i. sickern.
seer s. Seher, Prophet m.
see-saw s. Wippe f.
seethe v.t. & i. sieden, kochen.
see-through a. durchsichtig.
segment s. Abschnitt m.
segregate v.t. & i. absondern; segregieren.
segregation s. Trennung f.; Rassentrennung f.
seismic a. seismisch.
seismometer s. Erdbebenmesser m.
seize v.t. ergreifen; wegnehmen; beschlagnahmen; *to be ~d with*, im Besitz sein von.
seizure s. Ergreifung f.; Verhaftung f.; Beschlagnahme f.; Krankheitsanfall m.
seldom adv. selten.
select v.t. auswählen, auslesen; ~ a. auserlesen.
selection s. Auswahl f.; Zuchtwahl f.
selective a. selektiv; wählerisch.
selectivity s. (radio) Trennschärfe f.
selenium s. Selen n.
self n. & pref. Selbst, Ich n.; selbst.
self-absorbed a. in sich selbst versunken.
self-assured a. selbstsicher.
self-centered a. ichbezogen.
self-command s. Selbstbeherrschung f.
self-conceit s. Eigendünkel m.
self-confidence s. Selbstvertrauen m.
self-conscious a., ~**ly** adv. befangen, gehemmt.
self-contained a. verschlossen; in sich vollständig.
self-control s. Selbstbeherrschung f.
self-defense s. Notwehr f.
self-denial s. Selbstverleugnung f.
self-determination s. Selbstbestimmung f.
self-educated a. ~ *person* s. Autodidakt(in) m.(f.)
self-effacing a. zurückhaltend.
self-employed a. selbständig.
self-esteem s. Selbstachtung f.
self-evident a. offenkundig.
self-explanatory a. selbsterklärend; *it is~*, es erklärt sich selbst.
self-governing a. autonom.
self-government s. Autonomie f.; Selbstverwaltung f.
self-help s. Selbsthilfe f.

self-indulgence *s.* Maßlosigkeit *f.*
self-indulgent *a.* maßlos.
self-interest *s.* Eigennutz *m.*
selfish *a.*, **~ly** *adv.* selbstsüchtig.
selfishness *s.* Selbstsucht *f.*
selfless *a.* selbstlos.
selflessness *s.* Selbstlosigkeit *f.*
self-made *a.* selbstgemacht; durch eigene Kraft emporgekommen.
self-opinionated *a.* eingebildet; rechthaberisch.
self-pity *s.* Selbstmitleid *n.*
self-portrait *s.* Selbstporträt *n.*
self-possession *s.* Selbstbeherrschung *f.*
self-preservation *s.* Selbsterhaltung *f.*
self-propelled *a.* (*mil.*) Selbstfahr. . .
self-raising flour *s.* Backpulvermehl *n.*
self-reliant *a.* selbstbewußt; selbstsicher.
self-respect *s.* Selebstachtung *f.*
self-respecting *a.* mit Selbstachtung.
self-restraint *s.* Selbstbeherrschung *f.*
self-righteous *a.* selbstgerecht.
self-sacrifice *s.* Selbstanfopferung *f.*
selfsame *a.* der-, die- dasselbe.
self-service *s. f.* Selbstbedienung *f.*
self-styled *a.* (*ironic*) von eigenen Gnaden.
self-sufficiency *s.* Autarkie *f.*; Unabhängigkeit *f.*
self-sufficient *a.* unabhängig; autark.
self-supporting *a.* sich selbst tragend; finanziell unabhängig.
self-taught *a.* autodidaktisch; selbsterlernt.
self-will *s.* Eigenwille, Eigensinn *m.*
self-willed *a.* eigenwillig.
sell *v.t.st.* verkaufen; (*fig.*) hereinlegen; ~ *v.i.* Absatz finden, gehen; *to be sold out*, ausverkauft sein.
seller *s.* Verkäufer *m.*
selling *s.* Verkauf *m.*; Verkaufen *n.*
semantic *a.* semantisch.
semantics *s.* Semantik *f.*
semaphore *s.* optische Signale *pl.*
semblance *s.* Ähnlichkeit *f.*; Anschein *m.*
semen *s.* Samen(flüßigkeit) *m.* (*f.*); Sperma *n.*
semester *s.* Semester *n.*
semibreve *s.* ganze Note *f.*
semicircle *s.* Halbkreis *m.*
semicircular *a.* halbkreisförmig.
semicolon *s.* Strichpunkt *m.*
semiconductor *s.* Halbleiter *m.*
semi-detached *a.* halbfreistehend; ~ *house*, *s.* Doppelhaushälfte *f.*
semi-final *s.* Halbfinale *m.*
semi-finished *a.* halbfertig.
seminal *a.* grundlegend.
seminar *s.* Seminar *n.*
semiquaver *s.* Sechzehntelnote *f.*
semi-skilled *a.* angelernt.
Semite *s.* Semite *m.*, Semitin *f.*
semitone *s.* Halbton *m.*
semolina *s.* Grieß *m.*
senate *s.* Senat, Rat *m.*
senator *s.* Senator(in) *m.*(*f.*)
senatorial *a.*, **~ly** *adv.* ratsherrlich.
send *v.t. & i.st.* schicken, senden; *to ~for*, holen lassen.
sender *s.* Absender(in) *m.*(*f.*)
senile *a.* greisenhaft; altersschwach, senil.
senility *s.* Altersschwäche *f.*; Senilität *f.*

senior *s.* Ältere, Älteste *m.*; ~ *a.* dienstälteste, rangälteste, Ober. . .
senior citizen *s.* Senior(in) *m.*(*f.*)
seniority *s.* höheres Alter *n.*; Dienstalter *n.*; Altersfolge *f.*
sensation *s.* Aufsehen *n.*; Eindruck *m.*; Empfindung *f.*; Sensation *f.*
sensational *a.* Aufsehen erregend; sensationell, Sensations. . .
sense *s.* Sinn, Verstand *m.*; Bedeutung *f.*; Gefühl *n.*; *common* ~, gesunder Menschenverstand *m.*
senseless *a.*, **~ly** *adv.* sinnlos; unvernünftig; gefühllos, bewußtlos.
sensibility *s.* Empfindlichkeit *f.*; Empfindsamkeit *f.*
sensible *a.*, **~bly** *adv.* empfindlich, fühlbar, merkbar; reizbar; empfindsam; vernünftig, klug.
sensitive *a.*, **~ly** *adv.* empfindsam, reizbar; ~ **plant** *s.* empfindliche Pflanze *f.*
sensitivity *s.* Empfindlichkeit *f.*; Sensibilität *f.*
sensitize *v.t.* sensibilisieren.
sensory *a.* Sinnes. . .
sensual *a.*, **~ly** *adv.* sinnlich.
sensualist *s.* sinnlicher Mensch *m.*
sensuality *s.* Sinnlichkeit *f.*
sensuous *a.* sinnlich, die Sinne betreffend.
sentence *s.* Richterspruch, Urteil *n.*; Satz *m.*; ~ *of death*, Todesurteil *n.*; *to pass* ~, das Urteil fällen; *to serve one's* ~, seine Strafe absitzen; ~ *v.t.* verurteilen.
sententious *a.* ~ly *adv.* moralisierend.
sentient *a.* empfindend.
sentiment *s.* Empfindung *f.*; Gefühl *n.*; Gesinnung *f.*; Meinung *f.*
sentimental *a.*, **~ly** *adv.* empfindsam, sentimental; ~ *value*, persönlicher Wert *m.*
sentimentality *s.* Rührseligkeit *f.*
sentinel, sentry *s.* Schildwache *f.*; **~-box**, Schilderhaus *n.*; Wachhäuschen *n.*; *line of sentries*, Postenkette *f.*
separable *a.* trennbar.
separate *v.t.* trennen; ~ *v.i.* sich trennen; ~ *a.* getrennt, einzeln; **~ly** *adv.* besonders.
separation *s.* Trennung *f.*; (*chem.*) Scheidung *f.*; Ehetrennung *f.*; ~ *allowance*, Scheidungsalimente *n.pl.*, Trennungszulage *f.*; (*mil.*) Familienunterstützung *f.*
separatist *s.* Separatist(in) *m.*(*f.*); ~ *a.* separatistisch.
September *a.* September *m.*
septennial *a.* siebenjährig; siebenjährlich.
septic *a.* septisch, Fäulnis. . .
septuagenarian *s.* Siebzigjährige *m. & f.*
sepulchral *a.* Grab. . ., Begräbnis. . .
sepulchre *s.* Grabmal *n.*; Gruft *f.*
sepulture *s.* Beerdigung *f.*; Begräbnis *n.*
sequel *s.* Folge *f.*
sequence *s.* (Reihen)folge, Ordnung *f.*
sequester, *v.t.* einziehen; absondern.
sequestration *s.* Absonderung *f.*; Beschlagnahme *f.*; Zwangsverwaltung *f.*
sequoia *s.* Mammutbaum *m.*
seraglio *s.* Serail *n.*
seraph *s.* Seraph *m.*
seraphic *a.* seraphisch.
Serb *a.* serbisch; *s.* Serbe *m.*, Serbin *f.*
Serbia *s.* Serbien *n.*

sere *a.* dürr, trocken.

serenade *s.* Ständchen *n.*

serene *a.*, **~ly** *adv.* heiter; ruhig.

serenity *s.* Heiterkeit, Gemütsruhe *f.*

serf *s.* Leibeigene *m.*

serfdom *s.* Leibeigenschaft *f.*

sergeant *s.* Sergeant *m.*; (Polizei- Wacht-meister *m.*; **~-major** *s.* Feldwebel *m.*

serial *a.* periodisch, Lieferungs . . .; ~ *number*, laufende Nummer *f.*; ~ *s.* Lieferungswertk *n.*, Zeitschrift *f.*

series *s.* Reihe, Folge *f.*; (*elek.*) ~ *connection*, Reihenschaltung *f.*

serious *a.* ernsthaft; wichtig; **~ly** *adv.* im Ernst; *to take an thing seriously*, etwas ernst nehmen.

seriousness *s.* Ernsthaftigkeit *f.*

sermon *s.* Predigt *f.*

serpent *s.* Schlange *f.*

serpentine *a.* schlangenförmig, geschlängelt.

serrated *a.* (*bot.*) gesägt, zackig; gezackt.

serum *s.* Blutwasser *n.*; Heilserum *n.*

servant *s.* Diener. Bediente *m.*; Magd *f.*; (Dienst)mädchen *n.*

serve *v.t. & i.* dienen; aufwarten, servieren; auftragen; dienlich sein; genügen; zustellen; (*tennis*) angeben, aufschlagen; *~s him right!*, geschieht ihm recht!

service *s.* Dienst *m.*; Bedienung *f.*; Dienstpflicht *f.*; Zustellung *f.*; Gefälligkeit *f.*; Nutzen *m.*; Gottesdienst *m.*; Tafelservice *n.*; (*tennis*) Aufschlag *m.*, Angabe *f.*; Verkehrsdienst *m.*; *steamship* ~, Dampferverkehr; *500 hours of* ~, 500 Stunden Arbeitsleistung (einer Maschine); *car* ~, Wagenpfege *f.*; ~ *station*, Tankstelle *f.*; ~ *flat*, Wohnung mit Bedienung *f.*; ~ *man*, Wehrmachtsangehöriger *m.*; **~s** *pl.* öffentliche Dienste, Betriebe (auch privater Gesellschaften), öffentliche Behörden; *the* (*fighting*) ~s, *pl.* die Wehrmacht *f.*; *all* ~s, Gas, Elektrisch, etc.; ~ *v.t.* bedienen (von öffentlichen Diensten, etc.).

serviceable *a.* **~ly** *adv.* nützlich, brauchbar, verwendungsfähig.

service industry *s.* Dienstleistungsbetrieb *m.*

servile *a.*, **~ly** *adv.* unterwürfig.

servility *s.* Unterwürfigkeit *f.*

serving *s.* Portion *f.*

servitude *s.* Knechtschaft, Sklaverei *f.*

session *s.* Sitzung *f.*

set *v.t.* setzen, stellen; ordnen; (Uhr) stellen; (Edelsteine) fassen; pflanzen; *to* ~ (*to music*), komponieren; ~ *v.i.* untergehen (Sonne); gerinnen; *to* ~ *about*, an etwas gehen, anfangen; *to* ~ *aside* (Urteil) aufheben; *to* ~ *down*, niedersetzen; aufschreiben; *to* ~ *forth*, dartun; ausdrücken; *to* ~ *in*, einsetzen; pflanzen; anfangen, eintreten; *to* ~ *off*, hervorheben; abreisen; *to* ~ *off against*, anrechnen gegen; *to* ~ *on*, anhetzen; angreifen; *to* ~ *out*, bestimmen, festsetzen, hervorheben; beginnen; aufbrechen; *to* ~ *the table*, den Tisch decken; *to* ~ *to*, anfangen, sich legen (auf); *to* ~ *up*, aufrichten; festsetzen; sich niederlassen; *to* ~ *up for*, sich ausgeben für; ~ *s.* Satz *m.*; Reihe *f.*; Gespann, Paar *n.*; Spiel *n.*; Besteck *n.*; Gattung; Bande *f.*; Garnitur *f.*; Service *n.*; ~ *p. & a.* festgesetzt, bestimmt; geordnet; starr; versessen auf.

setback *s.* Rückschlag *m.*

settee *s.* Sofa *n.*

setting *s.* Einfassung *f.*; Ordnen *n.*; Untergang (der Sonne) *f.*; Musikbegleitung *f.*

settle *v.t.* erledigen; festsetzen; einrichten, bestimmen; regeln; schlichten; bezahlen; (eine Summe) aussetzen; *to* ~ *an annuity on a person*, einem eine Leibrente aussetzen; ~ *v.i.* sich setzen, sich senken; sich ansiedeln; *to* ~ *down*, sich niederlassen (als Arzt, etc.), sich verheiraten; ~ *s.* Bank, Truhe *f.*; *settling day*, Abrechnungstag (Börse) *m.*

settled *a.* beständig; geregelt.

settlement *s.* Entscheidung *f.*; Anordnung, Versorgung *f.*; Leibrente *f.*, Vermächtnis *n.*, Familienrente *f.*; Niederlassung, Ansiedelung *f.*; Vergleich *m.*; Rechnungsabschluß *m.*; Schlichtung *f.*; Regelung *f.*; *in* ~, als Bezahlung.

settler *s.* Settler(in) *m.*(*f.*)

set-up *s.* Organisation *f.*; Aufban *m.*

seven sieben.

sevenfold *a. & adv.* siebenfach.

seventeen siebzehn.

seventh *a.* sieb(en)t. . .

seventy siebzig.

sever *v.t.* (*v.i.*) sich trennen, abschneiden.

several *a.* verschieden; getrennt, einzeln; mehrere.

severance *s.* Abbruch *m.*; Unterbrechung *f.*; ~ *pay* *s.* Abfindung *f.*

severe *a.*, **~ly** *adv.* streng; heftig.

severity *s.* Strenge, Härte *f.*; Ernst *m.*

sew *v.t. & i.* nähen, heften; *sewing kit*, Nähzeug *n.*; *sewing silk*, Nähseide *f.*

sewage *s.* Abwasser *n.*

sewer *s.* Abwasserkanal *m.*

sewerage *s.* Kanalwesen *n.*; abfließendes Wasser *n.*; Kanalbau *m.*

sewing-machine *s.* Nähmaschine *f.*

sewing-needle *s.* Nähnadel *f.*

sex *s.* Geschlecht *n.*

sexagenarian *s.* Sechzigjährige *m. & f.*

sex education *s.* Sexualerziehung *f.*

sexism *s.* Sexismus *m.*

sexist *a.* sexistisch; ~ *s.* Sexist(in) *m.*(*f.*)

sex life *s.* Geschlechtsleben *n.*

sex symbol *s.* Sexidol *n.*

sextant *s.* Sextant *m.*

sexton *s.* Küster *m.*; Totengräber *m.*

sexual *a.* geschlechtlich.

sexual harassment *s.* sexuelle Belästigung *f.*

sexual intercourse *s.* Geschlechtsverkehr *m.*

sexuality *s.* Sexualität *f.*

sexy *a.* (*fam.*) sexy; erotisch.

shabby *a.*, **~ily** *adv.* schäbig.

shack *s.* Hütte *f.*; Baracke *f.*

shackle *v.t.* fesseln; ~ *s.* Kettenglied *n.*; **~s** *s.pl.* Fesseln *f.pl.*

shade *s.* Schatten *m.*; Schattierung *f.*; (*fig.*) Schirm *m.*; Glasglocke *f.*; Abtönung *f.*; ~ *v.t.* beschatten; schattieren; schützen.

shading *s.* Schattierung *f.*; Lichtschutz *m.*

shadow *s.* Schatten *m.*; ~ *v.t.* beschatten; schattieren; schützen; heimlich folgen.

shadowy *a.* schattig, dunkel.

shady *a.* schattig; (*fam.*) anrüchig.

shaft *s.* Schaft *m.*; Pfeil; Deichsel *f.*; Schacht *m.*; (*mech.*) Welle, Spindel *f.*

shaggy *a.* zottig; buschig.

shake *v.t.st.* (ab)schütteln, rütteln; erschüttern; *to ~ hands*, sich die Hände geben; *to ~ off*, abschütteln; *~ v.i.* beben, wanken; *(mus.)* trillern; *~ s.* Erschütterung *f.*; Stoß *m.*; Triller *m.*; Schütteln *n.*; (Hände) Druck *m.*

shakedown *s.* Notlager *n.*

shaky *a.* wacklig, gebrechlich.

shallop *s.* Schaluppe *f.*

shallot *s.* Schalotte *f.*

shallow *a.*, **~ly** *adv.* seicht, matt; schwach, albern; *~ s.* Untiefe *f.*

sham *a.* unecht, nachgemacht; Schein . . .; *~ s.* Täuschung *f.*, Schein *m.*; *~ v.t. & i.* vortäuschen, betrügen.

shamble *v.i.* schlurfen.

shambles *s.pl.* Schlachthaus *n.*; Chaos *n.*

shame *s.* Scham *f.*; Schande *f.*; *for ~!*, pfui; *~ v.t.* beschämen; schänden.

shamefaced *a.*, **~ly** *adv.* betreten.

shameful *a.*, **~ly** *adv.* schändlich; beschämend.

shameless *a.*, **~ly** *adv.* unverschämt.

shampoo *v.t.* schamponieren; *~ s.* Shampoo *n.*

shamrock *s.* weiser Klee *m.*

shandy *s.* Bier (*n.*) mit Limonade, Radler *m.*

shank *s.* Schenkel *m.*; Stengel *m.*; *(mech.)* Stiel, Schaft *m.*

shanty *s.* Hütte, Bude *f.*; **~town** *s.* Elendsviertel *n.*

shape *s.* Form, Gestalt *f.*; Modell *n.*; Wuchs *m.*; *in good ~*, in guter Verfassung; *~ v.t.* bilden, gestalten; *~ v.i.* sich gestalten.

shaped *a.* geformt.

shapeless *a.* unförmig; formlos.

shapely *a.* wohlgebildet.

share *s.* Teil, Anteil *m.*; Aktie *f.*, Anteilschein *m.*; *ordinary ~*, Stammaktie *f.*; *preferred ~*, Vorzugsaktie *f.*; Pflugschar *f.*; *in equal ~s*, zu gleichen Teilen; *~ v.t.* verteilen; *~ v.i.* teilhaben, teilnehmen.

shareholder *s.* Aktionär(in) *m(.f.)*

shark *s.* Haifisch *m.*; Gauner *m.*

sharp *a.*, **~ly** *adv.* scharf; spitzig; streng; heftig; hitzig; beißend; spitzfindig; pfiffig; genau; *(mus.)* um einen halben Ton erhöt; *to look ~*, aufpassen; *at 10 o' clock ~*, pünktlich um 10 Uhr; *~ s. (mus.)* Kreuz *n.*

sharpen *v.t.* schärfen wertzen, (zu)spitzen.

sharpener *s.* Spitzer *m.*; Schleifstein *m.*

sharpness *s.* Schärfe *f.*

sharpshooter *s.* Scharfschütze *m.*

sharp-witted *a.* scharfsinnig.

shatter *v.t.* zerschmettern, zerstreuen; zerrütten; *~ v.i.* zerfallen.

shatterproof glass *s.* Sicherheitsglas *n.*

shave *v.t.r. & st.* schaben; scheren; rasieren; placken; leicht streifen; *~ v.i.* sich rasieren.

shaven *a.* rasiert.

shaver *s.* Rasierapparat *m.*; Rasierer *m.*

shaving *s.* Rasieren *n.*; Schnitzel *n.*; **~s** *pl.* Hobelspäne *m.pl.*; *~ cream s.* Rasierkreme *f.*; *~ soap, ~ stick*, Rasierseife *f.*; *~ things pl.* Rasiersachen *f.pl.*

shaving-brush *s.* Rasierpinsel *m.*

shawl *s.* Umschlagetuch *n.*, Schal *m.*

she *pn.* sie; *~ s.* Weibchen *n.*

sheaf *s.* Garbe *f.*

shear *v.t.st.* scheren; rupfen; *~ s.* Schur *f.*; **~s** *pl.* grosse Schere *f.*

sheath *s.* (Schwert) Scheide *f.*

sheathe *v.t.* in die Scheide stecken; überziehen.

sheathing *s.* Umhüllung *f.*; Verkleidung *f.*

shed *s.* Schuppen *m.*; Schirmdach *n.*; *~ v.t.* vergießen, ausschütten; abwerfen; verbreiten.

sheen *s.* Schimmer, Glanz *m.*

sheep *s.* Schaf *n.*; Dummkopf *m.*

sheepish *a.*, **~ly** *adv.* verlegen.

sheepskin *s.* Schaffell *n.*

sheer *a.* lauter, rein; senkrecht; *~ adv.* völlig; *~ v.i.* (*nav.*) gieren, abweichen.

sheet *s.* Bettuch *n.*; Laken *n.*; Platte *f.*; Bogen (Papier) *m.*

sheet-iron *s.* Eisenblech *n.*

sheet-lightning *s.* Wetterleuchten *n.*

sheet-metal *s.* Blech *n.*

sheik(h) *s.* Scheich *m.*

shelf *s.* Fach *n.*, Brett *n.*; Regal *n.*; Sims *m.* (& *n.*); **~life** *s.* Haltbarkeit *f.*

shell *s.* Schale, Hülse, Muschel *f.*; Gehäse *n.*; Granate *f.*; *~ v.t.* (*v.i. sich*) schälen, abschuppen; beschießen.

shellac *s.* Schellack *m.*

shell-fish *s.* Schalentier *n.*

shell-proof *a.* bombensicher.

shelter *s.* Obdach *n.*; Schutz *m.*; Schutzraum (Luftschutz) *m.*; *~ v.t.* decken; schützen, bergen, beherbergen; *~ v.i.* Schutz suchen.

sheltered *a.* geschützt; bemütet.

shelve *v.t.* auf ein Regal stellen; abschieben; auf die lange Bank schieben; *~ v.i.* sich neigen.

shelving *s.* Regale *pl.*

shepherd *s.* Schäfer, Hirt *m.*

shepherdess *s.* Schäferin, Hirtin *f.*

sherbet *s.* Sorbett *n.*

sheriff *s.* Sheriff *m.*

sherry *s.* Sherry(wein) *m.*

Shetland Islands *pl.* Shetlandinseln *pl.*

shield *s.* Schild *m.*; *~ v.t.* bedecken; beschirmen.

shift *v.t.* wechseln; auszeihen; umkleiden; versetzen, wegschieben, wegschaffen; *~ v.i.* schalten; drehen (Wind); *~ s.* Wechsel *m.*; Ausflucht *f.*; List *f.*; Schicht *f.*, Tagewerk *m.*; *to make ~*, sich behelfen.

shifting *a.*, **~ly** *adv.* listig, schlau; beweglich.

shiftless *a.* hilflos, ungewandt.

shifty *a.* verschlagen.

shilling *s.* Schilling *m.*

shilly-shally *v.i.* schwanken; zaudern.

shimmer *v.i.* schimmern; *s.* Schimmer *m.*

shin *s.* Schienbein *n.*

shindy *s.* Radau, Krach *m.* Rauferei *f.*

shine *v.i.* scheinen, leuchten, funkeln; *~ s.* Schein, Glanz *m.*

shingle *s.* Schindel *f.*; Kieselsteine *pl.* **~s** *s.pl.* Gürtelrose *f.*

shining, shiny, *a.* hell, glänzend.

ship *s.* Schiff *n.*; *~ v.t.* schiffen; einschiffen; verschiffen; versenden.

shipboard *s.* Schiffsbord *n.*

ship-broker *s.* Schiffsmakler *m.*

ship-builder *s.* Schiffbauer *m.*

shipmate *s.* Schiffsmaat *m.*

shipment *s.* Verschiffung *f.*; Warensendung *f.*; Versand *m.*

shipowner *s.* Reeder(in) *m.(f.)*

shipper *s.* Spediteur(in) *m.(f.)*

shipping s. Einschiffung f.; Schiffsbestand m.; Schiffahrt f.; ~ agent s. Schiffsspediteur m.; ~-**space** s. Schiffsraum m.
shipper s. Versender, Verlader m.
shipshape a. in bester Ordnung.
shipwreck s. Schiffbruch m.; ~ v.t. & i. scheitern, stranden.
shipwright s. Schiffbauer m.
ship-yard s. Werft f.
shirk v.t. & i. vermeiden; sich drücken.
shirker s. Drückeberger m.
shirt s. Hemd n.; ~ blouse s. Hemdbluse f.
shirtsleeve s. Hemdsärmel m.
shit s. (vulg.) Scheiße f.; ~ v.i.st. scheißen; ~**ty** a. beschissen.
shiver v.i. frösteln, zittern; ~ s. Schauer m.
shivery a. verfroren; zitternd.
shoal s. Schwarm m.; Menge f.; Untiefe f.; ~ a. seicht; ~ v.i. wimmeln; seicht werden.
shock s. Stoß m.; Angriff m.; Anstoß m., Ärgernis n.; Schock m., Haarschopf m.; elektrischer Schlag m.; ~ troops, (mil.) Stoßtruppen pl.; ~ v.t. anstossen; erschüttern; Anstoß geben, verletzen, ensetzen.
shock absorber s. Stoßdämpfer m.
shocking a., ~**ly** adv. schockierend.
shockproof a. stoßfest.
shock therapy s. Schocktherapie f.
shoddy a. schäbig; minderwertig.
shoe s. Schuh m.; Hufeisen n.; ~ v.t.st. beschuhen; beschlagen (ein Pferd).
shoe-black s. Schuhputzer m.
shoe-horn s. Schuhlöffel m.
shoe-lace s. Schuhlitze f.
shoe-maker s. Schuhmacher m.
shoe-polish s. Schuhwichse f.
shoeshine s. Schuhglanz m.
shoe-strings pl. Schuhbänder n.pl.
shoetree s. Schuhleisten m.
shoo v.t. (ver)scheuchen.
shoot v.t.st. schießen; abfeuern; drehen (Film); to ~ down, (avi.) abschießen; to ~ dead, to ~ to death, totschießen; to ~ a film, einen Film aufnehmen; ~ v.t. hervorschießen; sprießen; daherschießen; ~ s. Schößling m.; Gleitbahn f.
shooting s. Jagd f.; Schuß m.; ~-**box**, Jagdhütte f.; ~-**gallery**, Schießtand m.
shooting-star s. Sternschnuppe f.
shop s. Laden m.; Werkstatt f.; to talk ~ fachsimpeln; ~ v.i. einkaufen (gehen).
shop-front s. Schaufenster m.
shop-keeper s. Ladeninhaber m.
shop-lifter s. Ladendieb m.; ~-**lifting** s. Ladendiebstahl m.
shopper s. Käufer(in) m.(f.)
shopping s. Einkaufen n.; ~ center Einkaufszentrum n.
shop-steward s. Vertrauensmann m.; Vertrauensfrau f.
shore s. Gestade n.; Strand m.; stützbalken m.; v.t. ~ up abstützen.
short a. kurz; eng; beschränkt; in ~, kurzum; to cut ~, unterbrechen; in ~ supply, beschränkt verfügbar; to be ~ of, an etwas Mangel haben. ~**ly** adv. in Kürze; bald.
shortage s. Mangel m., Knappheit f.
shortbread s. Mürbegebäck n.

short-circuit s. Kurzschluß m.
shortcoming s. Mangel m., Unzulänglichkeit f.
short cut s. Abkürzungsweg m.
shorten v.t. abkürzen, verkürzen; ~ v.i. kürzer werden.
shorthand s. Stenographie f.
short-lived a. kurzlebig.
shortness s. Kürze f.; Knappheit f.
short pastry s. Mürbeteig m.
short-sighted a. kurzsichtig.
short sleeved a. kurzärmelig.
short story s. Kurzgeschichte f.
short tempered a. aufbrausend.
short-term a. kurzfristig.
short-wave s. (radio) Kurzwelle f.
shot s. Schuß m.; Schußweite f.; Schrot m. or n.; Kugel f.; Aufnahme f. (Film; Foto).
shotgun s. Jagdflinte, Schrotflinte f.
shot-proof a. kugelfest.
shoulder s. Schulter f.; Seitenstreifen m. (Straße); to turn a cold ~ on a person, einem die kalte Schulter zeigen; ~ v.t. auf die Schulter nehmen, schultern; drängen, stossen.
shoulder-bag s. Umhängetasche f.
shoulder-blade s. Schulterblatt n.
shoulder-strap s. Träger m.
shout v.i. laut rufen; jauchzen; schreien; ~ s. Geschrei n.; Zuruf m.
shouting s. Schreien m.; Geschrei n.
shove v.t. schieben, stossen; ~ s. Schub, Stoß m.
shovel s. Schaufel f.; Schippe f.; ~ v.t. schaufeln.
show v.t. zeigen; beweisen; to ~ round, herumführen; ~ v.i. sich zeigen, erscheinen; to ~ off, prahlen; ~ s. Schau f.; Schauspiel n.; Gepränge n.; Anschein m.; Ausstellung f.; by ~ of hands, durch Heben der Hände (bei Wahlen) f.; **flower-**~ s. Blumenausstellung f.; ~-**case** s. Schaukasten m.; ~-**man** s. Schaubudenbesitzer, Aussteller m.; Schowman m.; ~-**room** s. Ausstellungsraum m.
showdown s. endgültige Kraftprobe f.
shower s. Regenschauer m.; Fülle f.; Dusche f.; ~ v.i. schauern, regnen; ~ v.t. überschütten ~ v.i. (sich) duschen.
shower-bath s. Brausebad n.; Dusche f.
showery a. regnerisch, Regen. . .
showground s. Ausstellungsgelände n.
showing s. Vorführung f.; Sendung f.
show-piece s. Schaustück n.; Paradestück n.
show trial s. Schauprozeß m.
showy a. prunkend, Aufsehen erregend.
shrapnel s. Schrapnell n.
shred v.t. zerfetzen; schroten; ~ s. Abschnitzel n.; Fetzen m.
shrew s. zänkisches Weib n.; Spitzmaus f.
shrewd a., ~**ly** adv. schlau, verschlagen.
shrewdness s. Schlauheit f.
shriek v.i. kreischen; ~ s. Schrei m.
shrift s. short ~, kurze Frist f.
shrill a. gellend; schrill.
shrimp s. Garnele f., Krabbe f.
shrine s. Schrein m.
shrink v.i.st. einschrumpfen; einlaufen (Stoffe); ~ v.t. zusammenziehen.
shrinkage s. Einschrumpfen n.
shrive v.t.st. Beichte hören; ~ v.refl. beichten.

shrivel *v.t.* runzeln, zusammenziehen; ~ *v.i.* einschrumpfen, sich runzeln.

shroud *s.* Hülle *f.*; Leichentuch *n.*; ~ *v.t.* einhüllen.

Shrove-Tuesday *s.* Fastnachtsdienstag *m.*

shrub *s.* Staude *f.*, Strauch *m.*

shrubbery *s.* Gebüsch *n.*

shrug *v.t.* die Achseln zuckern; *to* ~ *one's shoulders,* mit den Achseln zucken; ~ *s.* Achselzucken *n.*

shudder *s.* Schauder *m.*; ~ *v.i.* schaudern.

shuffle *v.t.* mischen (Karten), mengen; *to* ~ *off,* abstreifen; ~ *v.i.* schlürfend gehen, ~ *s.* Schlurfen *n.*

shun *v.t.* meiden, scheuen.

shunt *s.* Nebengleis *n.*; Nebenanschluß *f.*; ~ *v.t.* (einen Zug) auf ein Seitengeleise schieben, rangieren.

shut *v.t.* zumachen, schließen; *to* ~ *down,* (Fabrik) stillegen; *to* ~ *up,* einsperren; ~ *v.i.* sich schließen, zugehen; ~ *up,* halts Maul!

shutdown *s.* Stillegung *f.*

shutter *s.* Fensterladen *m.*; (*phot.*) Verschluß *m.*

shuttle *s.* (Weber-)schiffchen *n.*; ~-**train** *s.* Pendelzug *m.*; ~-**service** *s.* Pendelverkehr *m.*

shuttlecock *s.* Federball *m.*

shy *a.* -**ly** *adv.* scheu, schüchtern; ~ *v.i.* scheuen (von Pferden).

shyness *s.* Scheuheit *f.*; Schüchternheit *f.*

siamese *a.* Siamesisch.

Siberia *s.* Sibirien *n.*

sibilant *a.* zischend; ~ *s.* Zischlaut *m.*

sibling *s.* Bruder *m.*; Schwester *f.*; Geschwister *pl.*

sibyl *s.* Sibylle, Prophetin *f.*

sibylline *a.* sibyllinisch.

Sicily *s.* Sizilien *n.*

sick *a.* krank; übel; (*fig.*) ~ *of,* überdrüssig; (*mil.*) ~-**bay**, ~-**ward** *s.* Revier *n.*; ~-**call** *s.* (*mil.*) Krankenappell *m.*; *to call in* ~, sich krank melden; ~-**leave** *s.* Krankenerlaub *m.*

sicken *v.t.* krank machen; ~ *v.i.* krank werden; Ekel empfinden.

sickening *a.* ekelerregend; widerlich; umerträglich.

sickle *s.* Sichel *f.*

sickly *a.* kränklich, schwächlich, siech.

sickness *a.* Krankheit, Übelkeit *f.*

sick-pay *s.* Krankengeld *n.*

side *s.* Seite *f.*; Rand *m.*; Partei *f.*; (*geom.*) Schenkel (des Dreiecks); ~ *of bacon,* Speckseite *f.*; *to take* ~s, Partei nehmen; *to* ~ *with, v.i.* jemandes Partei ergreifen.

side-arms *s.pl.* Seitengewehr *n.*

sideboard *s.* Anrichte *f.*

side-car *s.* Beiwagen (*m.*) (des Motorrades).

side-glance *s.* Seitenblick *m.*

side-light *s.* Streiflicht *m.*

sideline *s.* Nebenverdienst *m.*, Nebenbranche *f.*

sidelong *a. & adv.* seitwärts.

side-saddle *s.* Damensattel *m.*

sideshow *s.* Nebenattraktion *f.*

sidestep *v.i.* (*fig.*) ausweichen.

sidetrack *v.t.* ablenken; *to* ~ *the issue,* von der wirklichen Frage ablenken.

sidestroke *s.* Seitenschwimmen *n.*

side-table *s.* Beistelltisch *m.*

side-walk *s.* Bürgersteig *m.*

sideways *adv.* seitwärts.

siding *s.* Parteinahme *f.*; (*rail.*) Nebengleis *n.*

sidle *v.i.* schleichen.

siege *s.* Belagerung *f.*

sieve *s.* Sieb *n.*

sift *v.t.* sieben; sichten, prüfen.

sigh *v.i.* seufzen; ~ *v.t.* ausseufzen, beseufzen; ~ *s.* Seufzer *m.*

sight *s.* Gesicht *n.*; Sehkraft *f.*; Anblick *m.*; sehenswürdigkeit *f.*; Visier *n.*; *at first* ~, auf den ersten Blick; *by* ~, vom Sehen; *in* ~, in Sicht; *to lose* ~ *of,* aus dem Gesicht verlieren; ~s *pl.* Sehenswürdigkeiten *pl.*; ~ *v.t.* sichten, zielen.

sight-seeing *s.* Besichtigung (*f.*) von Sehenswürdigkeiten.

sign *s.* Zeichen *n.*; Kennzeichen *n.*; Aushängeschild *n.*; ~ *v.t. & i.* unterschreiben, unterzeichnen; winken; *to* ~, sich anwerben lassen; *authorized to* ~, zeichnungsberechtigt; ~ed 'gezeichnet' (gez.)

signal *s.* Zeichen *n.*; Signal *n.*; ~ *box* *s.* (*rail.*) Stellwerk *n.*; ~ *center* *s.* (*mil.*) Nachrichtenzentrale *f.*; ~ *communications pl.* (*mil.*) Nachrichtenwesen *n.*; ~-**man** *s.* (*rail.*) Signalwärter *m.*; ~ *troops pl.* (*mil.*) Nachrichtentruppen *pl.*; ~ *v.t.* signalisieren.

signatory *s.* Unterzeichner *m.*; ~ *a.* unterzeichnend; ~ *powers pl.* Signatarmächte *f.pl.*

signature *s.* Unterschrift *f.*; Zeichen, Kennzeichen *n.*

signboard *s.* Aushängeschild *n.*

signet *s.* Siegel *n.*; ~ *ring, s.* Siegelring *m.*

significance *s.* Bedeutung *f.*; Sinn *m.*

significant *a.*, -**ly** *adv.* bezeichnend; bedeutsam; bedeutend.

signification *s.* Bedeutung *f.*

signify *v.t. & i.* anzeigen; bedeuten.

sign-language *s.* Zeichensprache *f.*

sign-post *s.* Wegweiser *m.*

silence *s.* Ruhe *f.*, Stillschweigen *n.*; Verschwiegenheit *f.*; *to keep* ~, schweigen; ~!, *i.* still!; ~ *v.t.* zum Schweigen bringen.

silencer *s.* Schalldämpfer *m.*

silent *a.*, -**ly** *adv.* schweigend; stumm; verschwiegen; *to be* ~, schweigen; ~ **movie** *s.* Stummfilm *m.*; ~ **partner** *s.* stiller Teilhaber *m.*

silent majority *s.* schweigende Mehrheit *f.*, stiller Teilhaber *m.*

Silesia *s.* Schlesien *n.*

silhouette *s.* Silhouette *f.*

silica *s.* Kieselerde *f.*

silicon *s.* Silizium *n.*

silicone *s.* Silikon *n.*

silk *s.* Seide *f.*; Seidenzeug *n.*; ~s *pl.* Seidenstoffe *m.pl.*; ~ *a.* seiden.

silken *a.* seiden; seidenartig, weich.

silk-growing *s.* Seidenzucht *f.*

silkworm *s.* Seidenraupe *f.*

silky *a.* seiden; seidenartig.

sill *s.* Schwelle, Brüstung *f.*; Fensterbrett *n.*

silliness *s.* Dummheit *f.*; Blödheit *f.*

silly *a.*, -**ily** *adv.* einfältig, albern; ~ *season,* Sauregurkenzeit *f.*

silo *s.* Kornkeller *m.*; Kornlagerhaus *n.*, Silo *m./n.*

silt *v.i.* verschlammen; ~ *s.* Schlamm *m.*; Schlick *m.*

silver *s.* Silber *n.*; Silbergeld *n.*; ~ *lining,* Silberstreifen; ~-**plated** *a.* versilbert; ~ *a.* silbern; ~ *v.t.* versilbern.

silversmith *s.* Silberarbeiter *m.*

silvery *a.* silbern; silberhell.

similar *a.*, **~ly** *adv.* gleichartig, ähnlich.
similarity *s.* Ähnlichkeit *f.*
simile *s.* Vergleich *m.*
similitude *s.* Ähnlichkeit *f.*
simmer *v.i.* köcheln; brodeln.
simper *v.i.* einfältig lächeln; ~ *s.* geziertes Lächeln *n.*
simple *a.*, **simply** *adv.* einfach, einzeln; einfältig.
simple-minded *a.* arglos.
simpleton *s.* Tropf *m.*, Dummkopf *m.*
simplicity *s.* Einfachheit, Einfalt *f.*
simplification *s.* Vereinfachung *f.*
simplify *v.t.* vereinfachen.
simplistic *a.* simpel.
simulate *v.t.* & *i.* nachahmen; heucheln; vorschützen.
simulated *a.* Vorgetäuscht; simuliert.
simulation *s.* Simulation *f.* Verstellung *f.*
simultaneous *a.*, **~ly** *adv.* gleichzeitig.
simultaneous translation *s.* Simultandolmetschen *n.*
sin *s.* Sünde *f.*; ~ *v.i.* sündigen.
since *pr.* & *adv.* seit, seitdem; *long* ~, schon lange; ~ *c.* da; seit.
sincere *a.*, **~ly** *adv.* aufrichtig; *yours ~ly*, Ihr ergebener.
sincerity *s.* Aufrichtigkeit, Offenheit *f.*
sine *s.* (*math.*) Sinus *m.*
sinecure *s.* Sinekur *f.*; Pfründe *f.*
sinew *s.* Sehne *f.*; Nerv *m.*
sinewy *a.* sehnig; stark.
sinful *a.*, **~ly** *adv.* sündig, sündhaft.
sing *v.t.* & *i.st.* singen, besingen.
singe *v.t.* sengen, versengen.
singer *s.* Sänger(in) *m.*(*f.*)
single *a.* einzeln; einfach: ledig; **~-breasted** *a.* einreihig (Anzug); ~ *combat s.* Zweikampf *m.*; **~-handed** *a.* ohne Hilfe; ~ *journey f.*; Hinreise *f.*; ~ *room s.* einbettiges Zimmer *n.*; ~ *track a.* (*rail.*) eingleisig; ~ *s.* (*tennis*) Einzelspiel *n.*; ~ *out v.t.* absondern; aussuchen.
singleness *s.* Einzelheit *f.*; Einfachheit *f.*, Aufrichtigkeit *f.*
sing-song *s.* Singsang *m.*
singular *a.*, **~ly** *adv.* einzigartig; ungewöhnlich; ~ *s.* (*gram.*) Einzahl *f.*
singularity *s.* Einzigartigkeit *f.*, Sonderbarkeit *f.*
sinister *a.*, **~ly** *adv.* unheilvoll; schlimm, boshaft; (*her.*) link.
sink *v.i.st.* (ver)sinken; fallen; abnehmen; umkommen; ~ *v.t.* (ver)senken; unterdrücken, niederschlagen; in den Grund bohren; (Schuld) tilgen; ~ *s.* Spüle *f.*; Spülbecken *n.*
sinking *a.* sinkend; untergehend.
sinner *s.* Sünder(in) *m.*(*f.*)
sinuous *a.* geschlängelt, gewunden.
sinus *s.* (*anat.*) Nebenhöhle *f.*; Sinus *m.*
sinusitis *s.* Nebenhöhlenentzündung *f.*
sip *v.t.* nippen; schlürfen; ~ *s.* Schlückchen *n.*
siphon *s.* (Saug-) Heber *m.*; Siphonflasche *f.*
sir *s.* Herr (als Anrede) *m.*; Sir (Titel eines Ritters) *m.*
sire *s.* Vater *m.*; Sire *m.*; *v.t.* zeugen.
siren *s.* Sirene *f.*
sirloin *s.* Lendenbraten *m.*
sissy *s.* Weichling *m.*

sister *s.* Schwester *f.*; Nonne *f.*; Oberschwester (Krankenpflegerin) *f.*; **~-in-law** *s.* Schwägerin *f.*
sisterhood *s.* Schwesternschaft *f.*
sisterly *a.* schwesterlich.
sit *v.i.st.* sitzen; brüten; ~ *v.t. to ~ oneself*, sich setzen; *to ~ down*, sich setzen; *to ~ for an examination*, sich einer Prüfung unterziehen.
sitcom *s.*, **situation comedy** *s.* Situationskomödie *f.*
site *s.* Lage *f.*, Platz *m.*; Standort *m.*; ~ *v.t.* placieren, stationieren.
sitter *s.* Portraitmodell *n.*
sitting *s.* Sitzen *n.*; Sitzung *f.*
sitting-room *s.* Wohnzimmer *n.*
situate *v.t.* legen.
situated *a.* liegend, gelegen.
situation *s.* Lage *f.*; Zustand *m.*; Stellung, Stelle *f.*; ~ *estimate*, Lagebeurteilung *f.*, **~map**, Lagekarte *f.*, **~report**, Lagemeldung *f.*
six, sechs; *at ~es and sevens*, in Verwirrung.
six-footer *s.* Zwei-Meter-Mann *m.*; Zwei-Meter-Frau *f.*
sixteen, sechzehn.
sixteenth *a.* sechzehnt...
sixteenth-note *s.* Sechzehntelnote *f.*
sixth *a.* sechst...
sixtieth *a.* sechzigst...
sixty, sechzig.
size *s.* Größe *f.*; Maß *n.*; Format *n.*; ~ *v.t.* nach Größenordnen; *to ~ up*, (*fam.*) einschätzen; (*paint*) grundieren.
sizeable *a.*, **~ly** *adv.* ansehnlich.
sized *a.* von gewisser Größe; geleimt.
sizzle *v.i.* zischen; brutzeln; *s.* Zischen *n.*; Brutzeln *n.*
skate *s.* Schlittschuh *m.*; Roche[n] (Fisch) *m.*; ~ *v.i.* Schlittschuh laufen.
skateboard *s.* Skateboard *n.*
skater *s.* Schlittschuhläufer(in) *m.*(*f.*)
skating-rink *s.* Rollschuhbahn; Eisbahn *f.*
skedaddle *v.i.* davonlaufen.
skeleton *s.* Gerippe *n.*; Skelett *n.*; ~ *key*, Nachschlüssel *m.*; ~ *staff*, Minimalbesetzung *f.*
skeptic *s.* skeptisch.
sketch *s.* Entwurf *m.*; Skizze *f.*; ~ *v.t.* entwerfen, skizzieren.
sketchy *a.* flüchtig.
skew *a.* schräg; schief.
skewer *s.* (Brat)spieß *m.*; ~ *v.t.* aufspießen.
ski *s.* Ski *m.* (*pl.* Skier), Schi, *m.*; ~ *v.i.* skilaufen, schilaufen.
skid *s.* Hemmschuh *m.*; Kufe *f.*; ~ *v.t.* hemmen; ~ *v.i.* ausrutschen.
skier *s.* Skiläfer(in) *m.*(*f.*)
skiing *s.* Skilaufen *n.*; Skisport *m.*
ski-jump *s.* Sprungschanze *f.*
ski-jumping *s.* Skispringen *n.*
skiff *s.* Einer *m.* (Rudern).
ski-lift *s.* Skilift *m.*
skill *s.* Geschicklichkeit *f.*; Fertigkeit *f.*
skilled *a.* geschickt; ausgebildet; ~ *worker*, gelernte Arbeiter(in) *m.*(*f.*)
skillful *a.*, **~ly** *adv.* geschickt, erfahren.
skim *v.t.* abschäumen, (Milch) entrahmen; ~ *v.i.* flüchtig hingleiten; streifen; **~-milk** *s.* Magermilch *f.*

skimp *v.t.* knapp halten.
skimpy *a.* sparsam, karg.
skin *s.* Haut *f.*, Balg *m.*; Schale, Hülse *f.*; ~ *v.t.* häuten, abdecken; ~ *v.i.* zuheilen.
skin diving *s.* Schnorcheln *n.*
skin-graft *s.* Hauttransplantation *f.*
skinny *a.* mager.
skin-tight *a.* hauteng.
skip *v.i.* springen, hüpfen; ~ *v.t.* überhüpfen; übergehen; ~ *s.* Sprung *m.*
ski pole *s.* Skistock *m.*
skipper *s.* Schiffer *m.*; Hüpfer *m.*
ski resort *s.* Skiort *m.*
skirmish *s.* Scharmützel *n.*; ~ *v.i.* plänkeln.
skirt *s.* Frauenrock, Rock *m.*; Saum *m.*; Rockschoß *m.*; Einfassung *f.*; ~ *v.t.* einfassen, besetzen; am Rande entlang gehen.
skit *s.* Stichelei, Satire, Spottschrift *f.*
skittish *a.*, ~**ly** *adv.* scheu, unstet; leichtfertig, flüchtig.
skittle *s.* Kegel *m.*; ~*alley* *s.* Kegelbahn *f.*
skulk *v.i.* lauern, herumlungern, heimlich umherschleichen.
skull *s.* Schädel *m.*; Totenkopf *m.*
skunk *s.* Stinktier *n.*; Schuft *m.*
sky *s.* (Wolken) himmel *m.*, Himmel *m.*
sky-diver *s.* Fallschirmspringer(in) *m.*(*f.*)
skylark *s.* Feldlerche *f.*; ~ *v.i.* Possen treiben.
skylight *s.* Oberlicht *n.*; Dachfenster *n.*
skyline *s.* Kontur (einer Stadt) *f.*; Silhouette *f.*
skyscraper *s.* Wolkenkratzer *m.*
slab *s.* Platte, Steinplatte *f.*; Tafel *f.*
slack *a.*, ~**ly** *adv.* schlaff, locker; nachlässig.
slacken *v.t.* schlaff werden, abspannen; nachlassen; verringern; (Kalk) löschen; ~ *v.i.* erschlaffen.
slacker *s.* Drückeberger *m.*
slacks *pl.* weite Hosen *f.pl.*
slag *s.* Schlacke *f.*
slake *v.t.* (Kalk) löschen; stillen; dämpfen.
slalom *s.* Slalom *m.*
slam *v.t.* zuschmeißen; ~ *s.* Klatsch, Schlag *m.*
slander *s.* Verleumdung *f.*; ~ *v.t.* verleumden, verunglimpfen.
slanderous *a.*, ~**ly** *adv.* verleumderisch.
slang *s.* lässige Umgangssprache *f.*; Slang *m.*
slant *a.*, ~**ly** *adv.* schief, schräg; abschüssig, ~ *v.t.* seitwärts wenden; ~ *v.i.* abfallen (von der horizontalen Linie); ~ *s.* Tendenz.
slantwise *a.* schief, schräg.
slap *v.t. & i.* schlagen, klapsen; *to ~ someone's face,* einem ins Gesicht schlagen; ~ *s.* Klaps *m.*
slapdash *a.* heftig; nachlässig.
slash *v.t.* hauen; (auf)schlitzen; ~ *s.* Hieb *m.*; Schlitz *m.*; Schmarre *f.*
slat *s.* Leiste *f.*; Latte *f.*; Lamelle *f.*
slate *s.* Schiefer *m.*; Schiefertafel *f.*; ~ *v.t.* mit Schiefer decken; abkanzeln; *slated for,* festgesetzt, eingesetzt für. . .
slattern *s.* Schlampe *f.*
slaughter *s.* Metzelei *f.*, Blutbad *n.*; ~ *v.t.* schlachten, morden.
slaughter-house *s.* Schlachthaus *n.*
slav *s.* Slawe *m.*; Slawin *f.*
slave *s.* Sklave *m.*; Sklavin *f.*; ~ *v.i.* sich placken.

slave-driver *s.* Leuteschinder *m.*; Sklaventreiber(in) *m.*(*f.*)
slave labor *s.* Sklavenarbeit *f.*
slaver *v.i.* geifern.
slavery *s.* Sklaverei *f.*
slavish *a.*, ~**ly** *adv.* sklavisch.
slavonic *a.* slawisch.
slay *v.t.st.* erschlagen, töten.
sled *s.*, **sledge** *s.* Schlitten *m.*; Schleife *f.*
sledgehammer *s.* Vorschlaghammer *m.*
sleek *a.*, ~**ly** *adv.* glatt; weich; ~ *v.t.* glätten.
sleep *v.i.st.* schlafen; ~ *s.* Schlaf *m.*; *to go to ~,* einschlafen; *to put to ~,* einschläfern.
sleeper *s.* Schläfer(in) *m.*(*f.*); (*rail.*) Schwelle *f.*
sleeper *s.* Schlafwagen *m.*; Schlafwagenplatz *m.*
sleeping-bag *s.* Schlafsack *m.*
sleeping-car *s.* (Eisenbahn) Schlafwagen *m.*
sleeping pill *s.* Schlaftablette *f.*
sleeping sickness *s.* Schlafkrankheit *f.*
sleepless *a.*, ~**ly** *adv.* schlaflos.
sleep-walker *s.* Schlafwandler(in) *m.*(*f.*)
sleepy *a.*, ~**ily** *adv.* schläfrig, verschlafen.
sleet *s.* Schneeregen *m.*; ~ *v.i.* regnen und schneien.
sleeve *s.* Ärmel *m.*; *to laugh in one's ~,* sich ins Fäustchen lachen; *to have a plan up one's ~,* einen Plan in petto haben; *to roll up one's ~ s,* die Ärmel hochkrempeln.
sleeveless *a.* ärmellos.
sleigh *s.* Schlitten *m.*
sleigh-ride *s.* Schlittenfahrt *f.*
sleight *s.* List *f.*; Kunststück *n.*; ~ *of hand,* Taschenspielerstückchen *n.*
slender *a.*, ~**ly** *adv.* schlank; dünn; spärlich, karg; schwach.
sleuth *s.* Spürhund *m.*; Detektiv *m.*
slice *s.* Schnitte, Scheibe *f.*; Slice *m.* (Tennis); ~ *v.i.* (in Scheiben) zerschneiden; schneiden (Ball).
sliced *a.* aufgeschnitten; kleingeschnitten.
slick *a.* glatt, flott.
slide *v.i.st.* gleiten, ausgleiten; schlüpfen; rutschen; ~ *v.t.* hineinschieben; ~ *s.* Gleitbahn *f.*; (*mech.*) Schlitten (Drehbank, etc.); Dia(positiv) *n.*; Rutschbahn *f.*; ~ *rule* *s.* Rechenschieber *m.*; ~ *valve* *s.* Schiebeventil *n.*
sliding-door *s.* Schiebetür *f.*; ~~**scale** *s.* gleitende Skala *f.*; ~ *seat,* Rollsitz *m.*
slight *a.*, ~**ly** *adv.* klein, gering; unwichtig, schwach, dünn; ~ *s.* Geringschätzung *f.*; Verachtung *f.*; ~ *v.t.* geringschätzig behandeln.; brüskieren; herabsetzen.
slim *a.* schlank, schmächtig.
slime *s.* Schleim *m.*; Schlamm *m.*
slimming *s.* Abnehmen *n.*; Kürzung *f.*
slimy *a.* schleimig; schlammig.
sling *s.* Schlag, Wurf *m.*; Schleuder *f.*; Schlinge, Binde *f.*; ~ *v.t.st.* schleudern; über die Schulter hängen.
slink *v.i.st.* schleichen.
slinky *a.* aufreizend.
slip *v.i.* gleiten, ausgleiten; (ent-) schlüpfen; entfallen; ~ *v.t.* schlüpfen lassen, abreißen; loslassen; anziehen; ~ *s.* Ausgleiten *n.*; Entwischen *n.*; Versehen *n.*; Stückchen *n.*; Streifchen *n.*; Zettel *m.*; Unterrock *m.* (Kissen-)überzug *m.*; (*nav.*) Helling *f.*; ~ *of the pen,* Schreibfehler *m.*; ~ *of the tongue,* Versprecher *m.*; *to give the ~,* entwischen.

slipper *s.* Pantoffel *m.*
slippery *a.* schlüpfrig, glatt.
slip-shod *a.* nachlässig; schlampig.
slipway *s.* Laufweg *m.*; Helling *f.*
slit *v.t.* aufschneiden, durchschneiden; aufschlitzen; spalten; ~ *s.* Riß *m.*; Spalte *f.*
slither *v.i.* rutschen; schlittern.
sliver *s.* Holzsplitter *m.*
slob *s.* (*sl.*) Schwein *n.*
slobber *v.i.* sabbern.
sloe *s.* Schlehe *f.*
slog *v.t.* dreschen; draufschlagen.
slogan *s.* Wahlparole *f.*; Schlagwort *n.*
sloop *s.* Schaluppe *f.*
slop *v.t.* verschütten; schwappen.
slope *s.* Abhang *m.*; Gefälle *n.*; Piste *f.*; ~ *v.i.* abfallen; ~ *v.t.* abschrägen.
sloping *a.*, ~**ly** *adv.* schief, abschüssig.
sloppy *a.* schlampig; nachlässig.
slosh *v.i.* platschen; schwappen.
slot *s.* Spalte *f.*, Schlitz *m.*; ~ *machine* (Waren-, Spiel) Automat *m.*
sloth *s.* Trägheit *f.*; Faultier *n.*
slothful *a.*, ~**ly** *adv.* träge, faul.
slouch *v.i.* den Kopf hängen; krumm dastehen; ~ *s.* schlaffe Haltung *f.*; latschiger Gang *m.*
slough *s.* Morast, Sumpf *m.*; Haut *f.*; Schorf *m.*; ~ *v.i.* sich häuten.
Slovak *a.* slowakisch; *s.* Slowake *m.*; Slowakin *f.*
Slovakia *s.* Slowakei *f.*
slovenly *a.* & *adv.* liederlich, schlampig.
slow *a.*, ~**ly** *adv.* langsam, träge; schwerfällig, begriffsstützig; *to be* ~, (Uhr) nachgehen; ~*down s.* Verlangsamung *f.*; ~*train s.* Bummelzug *m.*; ~-*motion picture s.* Zeitlupenaufnahme *f.*; ~*down v.t.* verlangsamen.
slowness *s.* Langsamkeit *f.*
slow-witted *a.* schwerfällig.
slow-worm *s.* Blindschleiche *f.*
sludge *s.* Matsch *m.*; Schlamm *m.*
slug *s.* Nacktschnecke *f.*; Gewehrkugel *f.*; Schlag *m.*
sluggard *s.* Faulenzer *m.*; ~ *a.* träge.
sluggish *a.*, ~**ly** *adv.* langsam, träge.
sluice *s.* Schleuse *f.*; ~ *v.t.* ablassen.
slum *s.* Elendsviertel *n.*
slumber *s.* Schlummer *m.*; ~ *v.i.* schlummern.
slump *v.i.* fallen, stürzen; ~ *s.* Kurssturz *m.*; Baisse *f.*
slur *v.t.* besudeln; verleumden; (*mus.*) verschleifen; rasch darüberhingehen; ~ *s.* Beleidigung *f.*; undeutliche Aussprache *f.*
slush *s.* Schneematsch *m.*; sentimentaler Kitsch *m.*
slut *s.* Schlampe *f.*
sluttish *a.*, ~**ly** *adv.* schlampig, schmutzig.
sly *a.*, ~**ly** *adv.* schlau; *on the* ~, verstohlenerweise; ~ *digs pl.* Seitenhiebe *m.pl.*
smack *s.* Klaps *m.*; Schmatz *m.*; ~*v.i.* schmecken; schmatzen, schnalzen; ~ *v.t.* klatschen; prügeln.
small *a.* klein, gering; dünn; ~ *hours*, frühe Morgenstunden *f.pl.*; ~ *s.* dünner Teil *m*; ~ *of the back*, Kreuz *n.*
small-arms *s.pl.* Handfeuerwaffen *f.pl.*
small change *s.* Kleingeld *n.*
small-pox *s.* Pocken *f.pl.*
small print *s.* Kleingedruckte *n.*
small-scale *a.* in kleinen Maßstab.

small screen *s.* Biedschirm (TV).
small-talk *s.* Geplauder *n.*
smart *a.*, ~**ly** *adv.* klug, gescheit; scharf; lebhaft; schneidig, fesch; pfiffig; elegant; *s.* Schmerz *m.*; ~ *v.i.* schmerzen; ~ **aleck** *s.* Besserwisser *m.*; ~ **ass** (*vulg.*) *s.* Klugscheißer *m.*
smarten *v.t.* herrichten; in Ordnung bringen.
smartness *s.* Schlauheit *f.*; Schick *m.*
smash *s.* Schmiß, Fall *m.*; Bankerott *m.*; ~ *v.t.* zerschmettern.
smattering *s.* oberflächliche Kenntnis *f.*
smear *v.t.* beschmieren; ~ *s.* Fleck *m.* ~ **test** *s.* Abstrich *m.*
smell *v.t.* & *i.r.* & *st.* riechen; wittern; ~ *s.* Geruch *m.*
smelling salts *pl.* Riechsalz *n.*
smelly *a.* stinkend.
smelt *v.t.* (Erz) schmelzen.
smile *v.i.* lächeln; schmunzeln; ~ *s.* Lächeln *n.*
smirk *v.i.* grinsen; ~ *s.* Grinsen *n.*
smite *v.t.st.* schlagen, treffen; zerstören; heimsuchen.
smith *s.* Schmied *m.*
smithereens *s.pl.* Stückchen *n.pl.*, Splitter *m.*
smithy *s.* Schmiede *f.*
smitten *a.*, ~ *with a person*, stark verliebt, bezaubert.
smock *s.* Kittel *m.*
smog *s.* Smog *m.*
smoke *s.* Rauch *m.*; (*mil.*) Nebel; ~-**screen** *s.* Nebelwand *f.*; ~ **stack** *s.* Schornstein *m.*; ~ *v.i.* rauchen; *no smoking*, Rauchen verboten!; ~ *v.t.* rauchen; räuchern.
smoked *a.* geräuchert.
smokeless *a.* rauchlos; rauchfrei.
smoker *s.* Raucher(in) *m.*(*f.*)
smoking *s.* Rauchen *n.*
smoky *a.* rauchend, rauchig.
smolder *v.i.* schwelen.
smooth *a.*, ~**ly** *adv.* glatt, eben; sanft, lieblich; ~ *v.t.* ebnen; polieren; mildern.
smoothness *s.* Glätte *f.*; Weichheit *f.*; Reibungslosigkeit *f.*; Geschicklichkeit *f.*
smother *v.t.* ersticken.
smudge *s.* Schmutz, Schmier *m.*; ~ *v.t.* beschmutzen, verschmieren.
smug *a.*, ~**ly** *adv.* selbstgefällig.
smuggle *v.t.* & *i.* schmuggeln.
smuggler *s.* Schmuggler(in) *m.*(*f.*)
smuggling *s.* Schmuggelei *f.*; Schmuggel *m.*
smut *s.* Rußfleck *m.*; Schlüpfrigkeit *f.*; Getreidebrand *m.*
smutty *a.*, ~**ily** *adv.* russig, schmutzig; brandig (von Gewächsen); unflätig.
snack *s.* Bissen, Imbiß *m.*; ~ **bar** *s.* Imbißraum *m.*; Schnellimbiß *m.*
snaffle *s.* Trense *f.*; ~*bit*, Trensengebiß *n.*
snag *s.* Haken *m.*
snail *s.* Schnecke *f.*
snake *s.* Schlange *f.*; ~ *skin* *s.* Schlangenleder *n.*
snaky *a.* schlangenartig; gewunden.
snap *v.t.* & *i.* schnappen, abschnappen; beißen; bissig antworten; ~ *one's fingers*, mit den Fingern schnalzen; ~ *s.* Schnapp *m.*; Biß *m.*; Fang *m.*; Knall *m.*; Schnappschloß *n.*; ~ *a.* plötzlich, überraschend.

snapdragon *s.* (*bot.*) Löwenmaul *n.*

snappish *a.*, **~ly** *adv.* bissig, schnippisch.

snappy *a.*, **~ily** *adv.* schick; elegant.

snap-shot *s.* Momentaufnahme *f.*, Schnappschuß *m.*

snare *s.* Schlinge *f.*; ~ *v.t.* verstricken.

snarl *v.i.* knurren; verheddern; *s.* Knurren *n.*; Knoten *m.*

snatch *v.t.* schnappen, ergreifen, an sich reißen; ~ *v.i.* haschen; ~ *s.* schneller Griff *m.*; Ruck, Hui *m.*

sneak *v.i.* kriechen; schleichen; ~ *s.* Petze *f.* Kriecher m.

sneaky *a.* hinterhältig, Kriecher *m.*

sneer *v.i.* hohnlächeln; sticheln; grinsen; ~ *s.* Spott *m.*; Stichel *f.*

sneeze *v.i.* niesen.

snide *a.* abfällig.

sniff *v.i.* schnüffeln; schnuppern; schniefen; ~ *s.* Nasevoll *f.* Schnuppern *n.*

snigger *v.i.* kichern.

snip *v.t.* schneiden; schnippeln; ~ *s.* Schnitt *m.*; Schnipsel *n.*

snipe *s.* Schnepfe *f.*; ~ *v.i.* aus gedeckter Stellung schießen.

sniper *s.* Heckenschütze *m.*

snippet *s.* Schnipsel *n.*; Bruchstück *n.*; Gesprächsfetzen *m.*

snitch *v.i.* ~ *on s.o.*, jn. verpetzen.

snivel *v.i.* winseln; schniefen; weinerlich sein.

snob *s.* Geck *m.*; Snob *m.*

snobbery *s.* Snobismus *m.*

snobbish *a.* snobistisch.

snoop *v.i.* schnüffeln.

snooper *s.* Schnüffler(in) *m.*(*f.*)

snooty *a.*, **~ily** *adv.* hochnäsig.

snooze *v.i.* dösen; ~ *s.* Nickerchen *n.*

snore *v.i.* schnarchen; ~ *s.* Schnarchen *n.*

snorer *s.* Schnarcher(in) *m.*(*f.*)

snorkel *s.* Schnorchel *m.*; ~ *v.i.* schnorcheln.

snort *v.i.* schnaufen; schnauben.

snot *s.* (*fam.*) Rotz *m.*

snotty *a.* rotznäsig.

snout *s.* Schnauze *f.*; Rüssel *m.*

snow *s.* Schnee *m.*; ~ *v.i.* schneien; *~ed in, under, p.* verschneit, eingeschneit.

snowball *s.* Schneeball *m.*

snowbound *a.* eingeschneit.

snowdrift *s.* Schneewehe *f.*

snowdrop *s.* Schneeglöckchen *n.*

snowplow *s.* Schneepflug *m.*

snowshoe *s.* Schneeschuh *m.*

snow-white *a.* schneeweiß.

snowy *a.* schneeig; schneeweiß; schneereich.

snub *v.t.* zurechtweisen; brüskieren; ~ *s.* scharfe Rüge *f.*; Abfuhr *f.*

snub-nosed *a.* stupsnasig.

snuff *s.* Schnupftabak *m.*; ~ *v.t.* schnupfen; (Kerze) ausdrücken.

snuff-box *s.* Schnupftabaksdose *f.*

snuffle *v.i.* schnüffeln.

snug *a.*, **~ly** *adv.* geborgen; anheimelnd, gemütlich, nett.

snuggle *v.i.* sich anschmiegen.

so *adv.* & *c.* so; also, folglich; daher; *so and so,* so und so.

soak *v.t.* einsaugen; durchnässen; einweichen; ~

v.i. weich werden, durchziehen; saufen.

soaking *a.* tropfnaß.

soap *s.* Seife *f.*; *laundry ~,* Waschseife *f.*; *soft ~,* Schmierseife; (*fig.*) Schmus *m.*; ~ *v.t.* einseifen.

soap-bubble *s.* Seifenblase *f.*

soap-flakes *pl.* Seifenflocken *f.pl.*

soap-suds *s.pl.* Seifenschaum *m.*

soapy *a.* seifig; salbungsvoll.

soar *v.i.* sich aufschwingen, schweben; in die Höhe gehen.

soaring *a.* schwebend; sprunghaft ansteigend.

sob *v.i.* schluchzen; ~ *s.* Schluchzen *n.*

sober *a.*, **~ly** *adv.* nüchtern; besonnen; gesetzt; ~ *v.t.* ernüchtern; mäßigen.

sobering *a.* ernüchternd.

sobriety *s.* Nüchternheit, Mäßigkeit *f.*

so-called *a.* sogenannt.

soccer *s.* Fußball *m.*

sociable *a.*, **~bly** *adv.* gesellig.

social *a.* gesellschaftlich; gesellig; sozial; *~science,* Gesellschaftswissenschaft *f.*; *~worker,* Sozialarbeiter(in) *m.*(*f.*)

social class *s.* Gesellschaftsschicht *f.*

social climber *s.* Emporkömmling *m.*

Social Democrat *s.* Sozialdemokrat(in) *m.*(*f.*)

socialism *s.* Sozialismus *m.*

socialist *s.* Sozialist(in) *m.*(*f.*)

socialize *v.t.* sozialisieren, vergesellschaften.

social life *s.* gesellschaftliches Leben *n.*

society *s.* Gesellschaft *f.*; Verein *m.*

sociologist *s.* Soziologe *m.*; Soziologin *f.*

sociology *s.* Sozologie *f.*

sock *s.* Socke *f.*

socket *s.* Hülse *f.*; (Augen-, Zahn-)Höhle *f.*; (*elek.*) Steckdose *f.*; Fassung *f.*

sod *s.* Rasenstück *n.*; Sode *f.*

soda *s.* Soda *f.*; *~-water* Sodawasser *n.*

sodden *a.* durchnäßt; aufgeweicht.

sodium *s.* (*chem.*) Natrium *n.*; ~ *chloride s.* Kochsalz *n.*

sodomy *s.* Sodomie *f.*

sofa *s.* Sofa *n.*

soft *a.*, **~ly** *adv.* weich, mürbe; sanft, zärtlich; leise; nachgiebig. **~!**, *i.* gemach! gelassen! sachte!; ~ *drinks pl.* nichtalkoholische Getränke *n.pl.*; **~-boiled** *a.* weichgekocht (Ei).

soften *v.t.* & *i.* erweichen; mildern, besänftigen; weich werden.

softener *s.* Enthärter *m.*; Weichspülmittel *n.*

soft-hearted *a.* weichherzig.

soft-spoken *a.* sanftredend.

software *s.* (*comp.*) Software *f.*

soggy *a.* durchweicht, sumpfig.

soil *s.* Boden *m.*; Erdreich *n.*; Flecken *m.*; Schmutz *m.*; ~ *v.t.* besudeln, beschmutzen.

soiled *a.* schmutzig.

sojourn *s.* Aufenthalt *m.*; ~ *v.i.* sich aufhalten.

solace *s.* Trost *m.*; ~ *v.t.* erquicken, lindern, trösten.

solar *a.* Sonnen . . .; ~ **cell** *s.* Sonnenzelle *f.*; Solarzelle *f.*; ~ **eclipse** *s.* Sonnenfinsternis *f.*; ~ **energy** *s.* Sonnenenergie *f.*

solarium *s.* Solarium *n.*

solar plexus *s.* Solarplexus *m.*

solar system *s.* Sonnensystem *n.*

solder *v.t.* löten; ~ *s.* Lot *n.*

soldering iron *s.* Lötkolben *m.*

soldier s. Soldat m.

soldierly a. soldatisch.

sole a., **~ly** adv. allein, einzig; bloß; ledig; ~ *agent* s. (*com.*) Alleinvertreter m.; ~ s. Sohle f.; Grundfläche f.; Seezunge f.; ~ v.t. besohlen.

solemn a., **~ly** adv. feierlich, festlich.

solemnity s. Feierlichkeit f.; Ernst m.

solemnize v.t. feiern.

solicit v.t. (anhaltend) bitten; ansprechen.

solicitation s. Ansuchen, Anliegen n.

solicitor s. Anwalt, Notar m.

solicitous a., **~ly** adv. besorgt, ängstlich; fürsorglich.

solicitude s. Besorgnis f.; Sorgfalt f.

solid a., **~ly** adv. fest, gediegen; massiv, gründlich; ernst; echt; solide; ~ s. fester Körper m.

solidarity s. Solidarität f.

solidify v.t. verfestigen.

solidity s. Festigkeit, Dichtheit f.; Gründlichkeit, Echtheit f.

solid-state s. Festkörper m.

soliloquize v.i. ein Selbstgespräch führen.

soliloquy s. Selbstgespräch n.

solitaire s. Solitär(spiel) n.; (jewel) Solitär m.

solitary a., **~ily** adv. einsam; eingezogen; ~*confinement*, Einzelhaft f.; ~ s. Einsiedler(in) m.(f.)

solitude s. Einsamkeit f.; Einöde f.

solo s. Solo n.

soloist s. (*mus.*) Solist(in) m.(f.)

solstice s. Sonnenwende f.

soluble a. auflösbar; lösbar.

solution s. Auflösung f.; Lösung f.

solve v.t. lösen; erklären; (be)heben.

solvency s. Zahlungsfähigkeit f.

solvent a. zahlungsfähig; ~ s. Lösungsmittel n.

somber a. dunkel, düster.

some a. ein paar, manch; ein bißchen, einige, etliche, irgendein; etwas, ein wenig; ungefähr; ~*body*, jemand, einer; ~*how*, irgendwie; ~*thing*, etwas; ~*time*, einst, vormals; ~*times*, zuweilen; ~*what*, etwas; ~*where*, irgendwo.

somersault s. Purzelbaum m.; Salto m.

somnambulism s. Schlafwandeln n.

somnambulist s. Schlafwandler(in) m.(f.)

somnolent a. schläfrig.

son s. Sohn m.; ~*-in-law*, Schwiegersohn m.

sonata s. Sonate f.

song s. Gesang m.; Lied n.; *for a* ~, spottbillig.

sonic a. Schall. . .; ~**boom** s. Überschallknall m.

sonnet s. Sonett n.

sonorous a., **~ly** adv. resonant.

soon adv. bald; früh; gern; *as* ~ *as*, sobald (als).

sooner adv. eher, früher; lieber

soonest adv. ehestens.

soot s. Ruß m.; ~*ed up*, a. verrußt.

soothe v.t. besänftigen, lindern.

soothsayer s. Wahrsager m.

sooty a. rußig.

sop s. eingetunkter Bissen m.; (*fig.*) Köder m.; ~ v.t. eintunken.

sophism s. Trugschluß m.

sophist s. Sophist m.

sophistical a., **~ly** adv. sophistisch.

sophisticated a. kultiviert; anspruchsvoll; subtil; hochentwickelt.

sophistry s. Spitzfindigkeit f.

sophomore s. Student(in) im zweiten Studienjahr.

soporific a. einschläfernd.

soprano s. Sopran m.; Sopranistin f.

sorcerer s. Zauberer m.; Hexer m.

sorceress s. Hexe f.; Zauberin f.

sorcery s. Zauberei f.

sordid a., **~ly** adv. schmutzig; gemein.

sore a. wund; schmerzhaft, empfindlich; ~ s. ~*spot*, wunder Punkt m.; wunde Stelle f.

sorely adv. schmerzlich, in hohem Grade; dringend.

sorrel a. rötlich; ~ s. Rotfuchs m.; Sauerampfer m.

sorrow s. Kummer m., Sorge f.

sorrowful a., **~ly** adv. traurig.

sorry a., traurig, betrübt; erbärmlich, armselig; *I am* ~, es tut mir leid.

sort s. Gattung, Sorte, Art f.; *out of* ~s, verstimmt; nicht in Form; ~ v.t. sortieren.

sort code s. Bankleitzahl f.

sortie s. Ausfall m.

so so a. (*fam.*) so la la.

sot s. Trunkenbold m.

sought-after a. begehrt; gesucht.

soul s. Seele f. ~**destroying** a. nervtötend, geisttötend.

soulful a. gefühlvoll.

soul mate s. Seelenverwandte m./f.

soul-searching s. Gewissenspüfung f.

sound a. & adv., **~ly** adv. gesund, fest, stark, tüchtig; ~ s. Schall, Laut, Klang m.; Sonde f.; Schwimmblase (eines Fisches) f.; ~**film** s. Tonfilm m.; ~**insulation** Schalldämpfung f.; ~ v.i. klingen, tönen, lauten; ~ v.t. ertönen lassen; sondieren, ausforschen; loten; *to* ~ *the lungs*, die Lungen abhorchen.

sound barrier s. Schallmauer f.

sounding-board s. Resonanzboden m.

soundless a. klanglos.

soundness s. Gesundheit f.; Vernünftigkeit f.; Gründlichkeit f.

sound-proof a. schalldicht.

soundtrack s. (*film*) Tonspur f.; Filmmusik f.

soundwave s. Schallwelle f.

soup s. Suppe, Fleischbrühe f.

sour a., **~ly** adv. sauer, herb, bitter; mürrisch; ~ v.t. sauer machen; (*fig.*) verbittern; ~ v.i. sauer werden.

source s. Quelle f.; Ursprung m.; ~ *of supply*, Bezugsquelle f.

sourpuss s. Miesepeter m.

souse v.t. eintauchen.

south s. Süden m.; ~ a. & adv. südlich, gegen Süden.

South Africa s. Südafrika n.

South African a. südafrikanisch; s. Südafrikaner(in) m.(f.)

South America s. Südamerika n.

South American a. südamerikanisch; Südamerikaner(in) m.(f.)

southbound a. in Richtung Sünden.

southeast s. südosten m.; ~a. südöstlich.

south-eastern a. südöstlich.

southerly a. südlich.

southerner s. Bewohner(in) des Südens; Südstaatler(in) m.(f.)

southern a. südlich.

southernmost *a.* südlichst.
South Pole *s.* Südpol *m.*
South Seas *s.* Südsee *f.*
southward *adv.* südwärts.
southwest *s.* Südwesten *m.;* ~*a.* südwestlich.
southwester *s.* Südwestwind *m.*
souvenir *s.* Andenken *n.*
sovereign *a.* souverän; ~ *s.* Souverän *m.*, Landesherr *m.*
sovereignty *s.* Oberherrschaft *f.;* Souveränität *f.*
sow *s.* Sau *f.;* Trog *m.;* ~ *v.t.r. & st.* säen.
sowing machine *s.* Sämaschine *f.*
soy bean *s.* Soyabohne *f.*
spa *s.* Bad *n.*, Badeort *m.*
space *s.* Raum *m.;* Zeitraum *m.;* Weltraum *m.;* Weilchen *n.;* Strecke, Frist *f.;* ~ *v.t.* (Druck) sperren; **single-~d** einzeilig (Schreibmaschine); **double-~d,** zweizeilig.
space: **~age** *s.* Weltraumzeitalter *n.;* **~bar** *s.* Leertaste *f.;* **~craft** *s.* Raumfahrzeug *n.;* **~flight** *s.* Raumflug *m.;* **~-saving** *a.* raumsparend; **~ship** *s.* Raumschiff *n.;* **~shuttle** *s.* Raumfähre *f.;* **~station** *s.* Weltraumstation *f.;* **~suit** *s.* Weltraumanzug *m.*
spacious *a.*, **~ly** *adv.* geräumig.
spade *s.* Spaten *m.;* ~*s,* Grün, Pik (in der Karte) *n.;* **~work** *s.* Vorarbeit *f.*
Spain *s.* Spanien *n.*
span *s.* Spanne *f.;* Gespann *m.;* Spannweite *f.;* ~ *v.t.* spannen, (aus)messen.
spangle *s.* Flitter *m.*, Paillette *f.;* ~ *v.t.* übersäen.
Spaniard *s.* Spanier(in) *m.(f.)*
spaniel *s.* Wachtelhund *m.*
Spanish *a.* spanisch; *s.* Spanier(in) *m.(f.)*
spank *v.t.* durchwichsen; klapsen; ~ *v.i.* tüchtig ausschreiten.
spanking *s.* Tracht Prügel *f.*
spanner *s.* Schraubenschlüssel *m.;* *adjustable* ~ Engländer *m.*
spar *s.* Sparren *m.;* Scheinhieb *m.;* (*min.*) Spat *m.;* ~ *v.i.* boxen.
spare *v.t. & i.* sparen, scheuen; entbehren; (ver)schonen, Nachsicht haben; erübrigen; ~ *a.* sparsam, spärlich; mager; überzählig; ~ *s.* Ersatzteil *m.;* **~-part** *s.* Ersatzteil *m.;* **~-room** *s.* Fremdenzimmer *n.;* **~-wheel** *s.* Ersatzrad *n.*
sparing *a.*, **~ly** *adv.* sparsam, spärlich.
spark *s.* Funke *m.;* ~ *v.i.* Funken sprühen.
sparkle *s.* Funkeln *n.;* Glitzern *n.;* ~ *v.i.* funkeln; perlen (vom Wein); sprühen; *sparkling wine,* Schaumwein *m.*
spark plug *s.* Zündkerze *f.*
sparrow *s.* Sperling *m.;* **~-hawk,** Sperber *m.*
sparse *a.*, **~ly** *adv.* spärlich; dünn.
Spartan *a.* spartanisch; ~ *s.* Spartaner(in) *m.(f.)*
spasm *s.* Krampf *m.*
spasmodic *a.* krampfartig.
spastic *s.* Spastiker(in) *m.(f.);* ~*a.* spastisch.
spate *s.* Hochwasser *n.;* (*fig.*) Flut *f.*
spatial *a.* räumlich.
spatter *v.t.* bespritzen; besudeln.
spatula *s.* Spachtel *f.*
spavin *s.* (Pferdekrankheit) Spat *m.*
spawn *s.* Laich *m.;* Rogen *m.;* Brut *f.;* ~ *v.i.* laichen; ~ *v.t.* ausbrüten.
spay *v.t.* sterilisieren (weibliche Tiere).
speak *v.t. & i.st.* sprechen, reden.

speaker *s.* Sprecher(in), Redner(in) *m.(f.);* Präsident(in) *m.(f.)* des Unterhauses; (*elels.*) Lautsprecher *m.*
speaking *s.* sprechen *n.*
speaking-tube *s.* Sprachrohr *n.*
spear *s.* Speer, Spieß *m.*, Lanze *f.*
spearhead *s.* (*mil.*) Spitze *f.*
spearmint *s.* grüne Minze *f.*
special *a.*, besonder, eigen; vorzüglich; ~*correspondent,* Sonderberichterstatter *m.;* ~ *diet,* Diät *f.;* ~ *train* *s.* Extrazug, Sonderzug *m.;* **~ly** *adv.* besonders.
specialist *s.* Fachmann *m.* Fachfrau *f.;* Spezialist(in) *m.(f.)*
special offer *s.* Sonderangebot *n.*
specialty *s.* Besonderheit, Eigenheit *f.;* Sonderfach *n.*
specialize *v.i.* (*in*) als Spezialfach betreiben; spezialisieren.
specie *s.* Metallgeld *n.*
species *s.* Art, Gattung *f.;* Gestalt *f.*
specific *a.*, **~ally** *adv.* eigen, eigenartig; bestimmt; spezifisch; ~ *gravity,* spezifisches Gewicht *n.*
specification *s.* namentliche Angabe *f.;* (Patent-)Beschreibung *f.*
specify *v.t.* einzeln angeben.
specimen *s.* Probe *f.*, Muster *n.;* Exemplar *n.;* **~-copy,** Frei-, Probeexemplar *n.*
specious *a.*, **~ly** *adv.* trügerisch.
speck *s.* Fleck *m.;* Fleckchen *n.;* ~ *v.t.* flecken, sprenkeln.
speckle *s.* Fleckchen, Tüpfelchen *n.;* ~ *v.t.* flecken, sprenkeln.
spectacle *s.* Schauspiel *n.;* Anblick *m.;* ~*s pl.* Brille *f.;* **~-frame,** Brillengestell *n.*
spectacular *a.* spektakulär.
spectator *s.* Zuschauer(in) *m.(f.)*
specter *s.* Gespenst *n.*
spectral *a.* gespenstig; Spektral...
spectrum *s.* Spektrum *n.*
speculate *v.i.* nachsinnen, grübeln; spekulieren.
speculation *s.* Betrachtung *f.;* Nachsinnen *n.;* Vermutung *f.;* Spekulation *f.*
speculative *a.*, **~ly** *adv.* forschend; unternehmend, spekulativ.
speculator *s.* Spekulant(in) *m.(f.)*
speculum *s.* (*med.*) Spiegel *m.*
speech *s.* Rede *f.;* Sprache *f.;* *freedom of* ~, Redefreiheit *f.;* *to deliver a* ~, eine Rede halten.
speechday *s.* Schlußfeier (Schule) *f.*
speech defect *s.* Sprachfehler *m.*
speechless *a.* sprachlos.
speed *v.i.* sich beeilen, eilen; glücken; ~ *v.t.* beschleunigen, befördern; *to* ~ *up,* beschleunigen; ~ *s.* Eile *f.;* gute Erfolg *m.;* Geschwindigkeit *f.;* **~-limit** *s.* Höchstgeschwindigkeit *f.;* **~-boat** *s.* Schnellboot *n.*
speeding *s.* zu schnelles Fahren; Geschwindigkeitsüberschreitung *f.*
speedometer *s.* Geschwindigkeitsanzeiger *m.*
speed trap *s.* Geschwindigkeitskontrolle *f.*
speedy *a.*, **~ily** *adv.* eilig, schnell.
spell *v.i. & t.r. & st.* buchstabieren; (richtig) schreiben; bedeuten; *to* ~ *out,* entziffern, enträtseln; *to* ~ *out a number,* eine Zahl ausschreiben; ~ *s.* Zauber *m.;* kurze Zeit *f.;* Weile *f.*

spellbound *a.* (fest)gebannt.; verzaubert.

spelling *s.* Buchstabieren *n.*; Rechtschreibung *f.*; **~bee** *s.* Rechtschreibwettbewerb *m.* **~book** Fibel *f.* **~ mistake** *s.* Rechtschreibfehler *m.*

spelt *s.* Spelz, Dinkel *m.*

spend *v.t.* & *i.st.* verwenden; ausgeben; verschwenden; Aufwand machen; erschöpfen; (Zeit) zubringen.

spendthrift *s.* Verschwender(in) *m.*(*f.*)

spent *a.* erschöpft, kraftlos.

sperm *s.* Samen *m.*

sperm whale *s.* Pottwal *m.*; Sperma *n.*

spew *v.t.* ausspeien.

sphere *s.* Kugel *f.*; Erd-, Himmelskugel *f.*; Bereich, Wirkungskreis *m.*

spherical *a.*, **~ly** *adv.* kugelförmig.

spice *s.* Gewürz *n.*; Anflug, Beigeschmack *m.*; **~** *v.t.* würzen.

spick-and-span *adv.* blitzblank; funkelnagelneu.

spicy *a.* würzig, pikant, scharf.

spider *s.* Spinne f.; **~web** *s.* Spinnennetz *n.*

spidery *a.* spinnenförmig.

spigot *s.* Zapfen, Hahn *m.*

spike *s.* Spitze *f.*; langer Nagel; Kornähre *f.*; **~** *v.t.* festnageln; (ein Geschütz) vernageln.

spiky *a.* spitz; stachielig.

spill *v.t.r.* & *st.* verschütten, vergießen.

spillage *s.* Verschütten *n.*; Verschüttetes *n.*

spin *v.t.st.* spinnen; wirbeln; **~** *v.i.* kreiseln, sich drehen.

spinach *s.* Spinat *m.*

spinal *a.* Rückgrat. . .; **~ column** *s.* Wirbelsäule *f.* **~cord**, Rückenmark *n.*

spindle *s.* Spindel *f.*; Stengel *m.*

spindly *a.* spindeldürr.

spin-drier *s.* Wäscheschleuder *f.*

spin-dry *v.t.* schleudern.

spine *s.* Rückgrat *n.*; Dorn *m.* Stachel *m.*; Buchrücken *m.*

spine-chilling *a.* gruselig.

spineless *a.* rückgratlos (*fig.*).

spinnaker *s.* Spinnaker *m.* (Segel).

spinning: **~mill** Spinnerei *f.*; **~top** *s.* Kreisel *m.*; **~wheel** *s.* Spinnrad *n.*

spin-off *s.* Abfallprodukt *n.*; (positiver) Nebeneffekt *m.*

spinster *s.* ledige Frau *f.*

spiny *a.* stachelig; dornig.

spiral *a.*, **~ly** *adv.* spiralförmig; gewunden, schneckenförmig; **~** *s.* Schneckenlinie *f.*, Spirale *f.*; **~ staircase** *s.* Wendeltreppe *f.*

spire *s.* (Kirch)turm *m.*, Turmspitze *f.*; Turm *m.*

spirit *s.* Geist *m.*; Seele *f.*; Gespenst *n.*; Lebhaftigkeit, Energie *f.*; Gemütsart *f.*; **~s** *pl.* Lebensgeister *m.pl.*, gute Laune *f.*; geistige Getränke *n.pl.*; *in high* **~s,** munter; *in low* **~s,** verstimmt; **~** *v.t.* *to* **~** *away,* hinwegzaubern.

spirited *a.*, **~ly** *adv.* geistreich; lebhaft, mutig, feurig.

spiritism *s.* Spiritismus *m.*

spiritless *a.*, **~ly** *adv.* mutlos.

spirit-level *s.* Wasserwaage *f.*

spirit of wine *s.* Weingeist *m.*

spiritual *a.*, **~ly** *adv.* geistig; geistlich.

spiritualism *s.* Spiritualismus *m.*

spit *v.t.* & *i.st.* spucken; fauchen; aufspießen; **~** *s.*

Bratspieß *m.*; schmale Landzunge *f.*

spite *s.* Groll *m.*; Verdruß *m.*; *in ~ of,* trotz; **~** *v.t.* ärgern.

spiteful *a.*, **~ly** *adv.* boshaft, feindselig.

spitfire *s.* Brausekopf, Hitzkopf *m.*

spitting image *s.* *the ~ of sb.,* wie aus dem Gesicht geschnitten.

spittle *s.* Speichel *m.*

spiv *s.* Schwarzhändler(in) *m.*(*f.*); Schieber *m.*

splash *v.t.* bespritzen; **~** *s.* Spritzfleck *m.*; *to make a ~,* Aufsehen erregen.

splash-board *s.* Spritzbrett *n.*

splat *v.i.* klatschen.

splay *v.t.* spreizen (Finger).

spleen *s.* Milz *f.*; üble Laune *f.*

splendid *a.*, **~ly** *adv.* glänzend, prachtvoll.

splendor *s.* Glanz *m.*; Pracht *f.*

splice *v.t.* spleißen, einfügen.

splint *s.* Schiene *f.*; *v.t.* schienen.

splinter *s.* Splitter *m.*; **~ -proof** *a.* splittersicher; **~** *v.t.* splittern.

split *v.t.st.* spalten; **~** *v.i.* bersten; zerspringen; **~** *s.* Spalt, Riß *m.*; **~ second** *s.* Sekundenbruchteil *m.*

splutter *v.i.* herauspoltern; sprudeln, prusten.

spoil *v.t.* rauben, plündern; verderben, verwüsten; (Kinder) verziehen; **~** *v.i.* verderben; **~** *s.* Beute *f.*

spoil-sport *s.* Spielverderber(in) *m.*(*f.*)

spoilt *a.* verzogen.

spoke *s.* Speiche *f.*; Sprosse *f.*

spokesman *s.* Sprecher *m.*

spokesperson *s.* Sprecher(in) *m.*(*f.*)

spokeswoman *s.* Sprecherin *f.*

sponge *s.* Schwamm *m.*; **~** *v.t.* wegwischen; **~** *v.i.* in sich saugen; schmarotzen; *to throw in the ~,* die Flinte ins Korn werfen

sponge-cake *s.* Biskuitkuchen *m.*

sponger *s.* Schmarotzer *m.*

spongy *a.* schwammig.

sponsor *s.* Sponsor(in) *m.*(*f.*); Geldgeber(in) *m.*(*f.*); Bürge *m.* Bürgin *f.*; **~***v.t.* fördern, organisieren; **~***ing member,* förderndes Mitglied *n.*

sponsored *a.* gesponsert; finanziell gefördert.

sponsorship *s.* Sponsorschaft; Unterstützung *f.*

spontaneity *s.* Freiwilligkeit *f.*

spontaneous *a.*, **~ly** *adv.* spontan

spoof *s.* Veralberung *f.*; Parodie *f.*

spook *s.* Geist *m.*; Gespenst *n.*

spooky *a.* gespenstisch.

spool *s.* Spule *f.*; **~** *v.t.* spulen.

spoon *s.* Löffel *m.*;

spoon-feel *v.t.* füttern; (*fig.*) alles vorkauen.

sporadic *a.* sporadisch.

spore *s.* (*bot.*) Spore *f.*

sport *s.* Sport *m.*; Spiel *n.*; Scherz, Zeitvertreib *m.*; (*fig.*) Spielball *m.*; **~** *v.t.* & *i.* spielen; scherzen; belustigen; zur Schau tragen.

sporting *a.* sportlich; sport. . .

sportsman *s.* Sportsmann *m.*, Sportler *m.*

sportsmanship *s.* Auständigkeit *f.*; Fairness *f.*

sportswear *s.* Sportskleidung *f.*

sportswoman *s.* Sportlerin *f.*

sporty *a.* sportlich; sportbegeistert.

spot *s.* Platz *m.*; Stelle *f.*; Stück Land *n.*; Fleck *m.*; Spot *m.* (TV); **~** *v.t.* flecken, sprenkeln; genau erkennen; im voraus vestimmen.

spotless *a.* fleckenlos; unbefleckt.

spotlight s. Scheinwerferlicht n.

spotted a. gepunktet; getüpfelt; ~ *fever*, Fleckfieber n.

spotty a. fleckig, befleckt.

spouse s. Gatte m., Gattin f.

spout s. Rinne f.; Tülle f.; Wasserstrahl m.; Wasserhose f.; ~ v.t. & i. (aus) spritzen; deklamieren.

sprain v.t. verstauchen; ~ s. Verstauchung f.

sprat s. Sprotte f.

sprawl v.i. sich spreizen, räkeln; (bot.) wuchern.

spray s. Gischt m.; Spray n./m.; Strauß m. (Blumen); ~ v.t. zerstäuben; (Metall) spritzen; sprühen.

spray gun s. Spritzpistole f.

spread v.t.ir. (v.i. sich) ausbreiten; (be)decken; ~ s. Ausdehnung f.; Verbreitung f.; ~**sheet** s. Arbeitsblatt n.

spree s. Jux m.; Zecherei f.; Einkaufsorgie f.

sprig s. Sproß, Sprößling m.

sprightly a. lebhaft, munter.

spring v.i.st. springen; entspringen, aufsprießen; entstehen; ~ v.t. sprengen; aufstöbern; ~ s. Sprung m.; Leck n.; Quelle f.; Springbrunnen m.; Frühling m.; Springfeder f.

spring board s. Sprungbrett n.

spring-mattress s. Sprungfedermatratze f.

spring-steel s. (mech.) Federstahl m.

spring-tide s. Springflut f.

springy a. elastisch, federnd.

sprinkle v.t. & i. (be)sprengen; ausstreuen.

sprinkler s. Sprinkler m.

sprinkling s. dünne Schicht f.

sprint s. Sprint m.; ~v.i. rennen; sprinten.

sprinter s. Sprinter(in) m.(f.)

sprite s. Schrat m.; Gespenst n.

sprout v.i. sprießen; ~ s. Sprößling m.; *Brussels* ~s, pl. Rosenkohl m.

spruce a., ~**ly** adv. nett; geputzt; ~ s. Fichte f.; ~ v.t. (v.i. sich) herausputzen.

sprung a. gefedert; **well-**~, gut gefedert.

spry a. munter, lebhaft.

spud s. Kartoffel f.

spume s. Schaum m.; ~ v.i. schäumen.

spunk s. Mumm m.

spur s. Sporn, Stachel m.; Antrieb m.; Ausläufer einer Bergkette m.; ~ v.t. (auch *fig.*) anspornen; ~ v.i. eilen.

spurious a., ~**ly** adv. unecht; unaufrichtig; zweifelhaft.

spurn v.t. verschmähen; ~ v.i. ausschlagen; verschmähen.

spurt v.i. spritzen; ~ s. plötzliche Anstrengung f., Ruck m.

sputter v.i. sprudeln; ~ v.t. sprudelnd ausstoßen; ~ s. Gesprudel n.

spy s. Späher, Spion m.; ~ v.i. & t. (aus)spähen.

squabble v.i. zanken, Hähdel suchen; ~ s. Streit, Wortwechsel m.

squad s. Schar f. Gruppe f.; Trupp m.

squadron s. Schwadron f.; (nav.) Geschwader n.; (avi.) Staffel f.; (avi.) ~-*leader*, s. Staffelkapitän m.

squalid a. schmutzig.

squall s. laute Schrei m.; Windstoß m.; Bö f.; ~ v.i. laut schreien.

squalor s. Schmutz m.

squander v.t. verschwenden; vergeuden.

square a. viereckig, rechtwinklig; passend; quitt; redlich; ~ *deal*, ehrliche Behandlung; ~ s. Viereck, Quadrat n.; viereckiger Platz m.; Feld (Schach) n.; Winkelmaß n.; 10 *inches* ~, 10 Zoll im Quadrat; ~ v.t. viereckig machen; regeln, anpassen, ausgleichen; (math.) ins Quadrat erheben; ~ v.i. passen; übereinstimmen; ~ *measures* pl. Flächenmasse n.pl.; ~ **brackets** pl. eckige Klammern pl.

square-built a. vierschrötig.

squash v.t. zerquetschen; ~ s. Brei m., Gedränge n.; Fruchtsaft m.; Kürb m.

squat v.i. kauern, sich ansiedeln; ~ a. kauernd; stämmig.

squatter s. Besetzen(in) m.(f.)

squawk v.i. krähen; kreischen; keifen.

squeak v.i. quieken, schreien; ~ s. Quieken n.; Schrei m.

squeal v.i. schreien, winseln, kreischren.

squeamish a., ~**ly** adv. wählerisch; empfindlich.

squeeze v.t. drücken, pressen, quetschen; ~ v.i. sich (durch)drängen; ~ s. Druck m.; Quetschung f.; Gipsabguß m.

squelch v.i. glucksen.

squib s. Frosch (Feuerwerk) m.; Spottgedicht n.

squid s. Kalmar m.

squint v.i. schielen; ~ a. schielend.

squint[ing] s. Schielen n.

squire s. (obs.) Schildknappe m.; Landedelmann m.; (Land)junker m.

squirm v.i. sich winden.

squirrel s. Eichhörnchen n.

squirt v.t. spritzen; ~ s. Spritzer m.; Wasserstrahl m.

Sri Lanka s. Sri Lanka n.

Sri Lankan a. srilankisch; ~ s. Srilanker(in) m.(f.)

stab s. Stich m.; Stoß m.; Wunde f.; ~ v.t. & i. erstechen, stechen.

stabbing s. Messerstecherei f.; a. stechend.

stability s. Beständigkeit f., Stabilität f.

stabilization s. Stabilisierung f.; ~ *fund*, Währungsausgleichfonds m.

stabilize v.t. stabilisieren.

stable a. fest, dauerhaft; beständig; stabil (Währung); ~ s. Stall m.

stack s. Schober, Stapel m.; (Gewehr-) Pyramide f.; ~ v.t. aufschichten.

stadium s. Stadion n.

staff s. Stab, Stock m.; (General)stab m.; Personal n.; die fünf Notenlinien pl.; ~, v.t. mit Personal versehen.

stag s. Hirsch m.; (Börse) Konzertzeichner m.

stage s. Gerüst n.; Bühne f.; Schauplatz m.; Etappe f., Stadium n.; Stufe f.; Poststation f.; *to go on the* ~, zur Bühne gehen; ~ v.t. inszenieren, veranstalten.

stage-box s. Proszeniumsloge f.

stage-coach s. Postkutsche f.

stage direction s. Bühnenanweisung f.

stage-fright s. Lampenfieber n.

stage-manager s. Bühnenleiter m.

stage-manager s. Inspizient(in) m.(f.)

stagger v.i. wanken, taumeln; schwanken; ~ v.t. verblüffen; staffeln; ~*ed holidays*, pl. gestaffelte Ferien pl.; ~ s. (avi.) Staffelung (der Flügel) f.

staggering a. erschütternd; beunruhigend.

stagnant a. stillstehend, stockend.

stagnate v.i. stillstehen, stocken.

stagnation s. Stillstand m.; Stockung f.; Stagnation

f.

staid *a.* gesetzt, ernsthaft.

stain *s.* Flecken *m.*; Beize *f.*; Makel *m.*; ~ *v.t.* beflecken; färben; *~ed glass,* buntes Glas *n.,* Glasmalerei *f.*

stainless *a.* unbefleckt; rostfrei; *~steel s.* Edelstahl *m.*

stair *s.* Stufe *f.*; *~s pl.* Treppe *f.*; *~-carpet s.* Treppenläufer *m.*

staircase *s.* Treppe *f.*; Treppenhaus *n.*

stairway *s.* Treppenaufgang *m.*

stake *s.* Pfahl *m.*; Einsatz (im Spiel) *m.*; *at ~,* auf dem Spiele; *~ v.t.* aufs Spiel setzen.

stalactite *s.* Stalaktit *m.*

stalagmite *s.* Stalagmit *m.*

stale *a.* alt, altbacken; schal, geistlos;

stalemate *s.* Patt *n.*; ~ *v.t.* patt setzen; (*fig.*) lahmlegen.

stalk *s.* Stengel, Federkiel *m.*; gravitätischer Schritt *m.*; ~ *v.t. & i.* einherschreiten; stolzieren, beschleichen; verfolgen.

stall *s.* Stall *m.*; Stand *m.,* Box *f.* (im Stall); Sperrsitz *m.*; Chorstuhl *m.*; ~ *v.t.* zum Stehen bringen; ~ *v.i.* abwürgen (Motor).

stallion *s.* Hengst *m.*

stalwart *a.* stark, mutig; ~ *s.* treue Anhänger(in) *m.(f.)*

stamen *s.* Staubfäden *m.pl.*

stamina *s.* Ausdauer *f.*

stammer *v.i.* stammeln, stottern.

stammerer *s.* Stammler *m.*

stamp *v.t.* stampfen; stempeln, prägen; mit einer Marke versehen, (Brief) frankieren; *to ~ out,* austreten, unterdrücken; ~ *s.* Stampfe *f.*; Stempel *m.*; Gepräge *n.*; Abdruck *m.*; Briefmarke *f.,* Marke *f.*; ~ *collector,* Briefmarkensammler *m.*; ~ *pad,* Stempelkissen *n.*

stampede *s.* wilde Flucht *f.*; *~v.i.* (in wilder Flucht) davonstürmen; ~ *v.t.* in wilde Flucht jagen.

stanch *v.i. & t.* stillen, abbinden.

stand *v.i.ir.* stehen; aufstehen, stellen; sich verhalten; gelten; kosten, zu stehen kommen; *~v.t.ir.* stellen; aushalten, vertragen; standhalten; *to ~ by,* dabeistehen; *to ~ for,* eintreten für; *to ~ up,* aufrecht stehen; *to ~ up to,* aushalten; ~ *s.* Ständer *m.*; (*phot.*) Stativ *n.*; Stand *m.*; Gestell, Gerüst *n.*; *~-camera* (*phot.*) Stativkamera *f.*

standard *s.* Standarte *f.*; Ständer *m.*; Pfosten *m.*; Eichmaß *m.*; Maßstab *m.,* Regel, Richtschnur *f.,* Norm *f.*; Münzfuß *m.*; *gold ~,* Goldstandard *m.*; *~ of life,* Lebenshaltung *f.*; *~-lamp s.* Stehlampe *f.*; ~ *operating procedure* (SOP) (*mil.*) vorschriftsmäßiges Verfahren *n.*; ~ *a.* musterhaft, normal, klassisch.

standardize *v.t.* normieren.

standing *p. & a.* stehend, bleibend, beständig; ~ *s.* Stand, Platz *m.*; Rang *m.*; Dauer *f.*; Stellung *f.*; *of long (old) ~,* von lange her.

standing-order *s.* Dauerauftrag *m.*

standing-room *s.* Stehplatz *m.*

standpoint *s.* Standpunkt *m.*

stand-still *s.* Stillstand *m.*

stand-up *a.* regelrecht (vom Faustkampf); ~ *collar,* Stehkragen *m.*

stanza *s.* Stanze *f.*; Strophe *f.*

staple *s.* Heftklammer *f.*; ~, *v.t.* klammern, mit einer Heftklammer versehen; *staple goods pl.,*

Grundnahrungsmittel *n.*

stapler *s.* Hefter *m.,* Heftmaschine *f.*

star *s.* Stern *m.*; grosser Schauspieler, Star *m.*; ~ *v.t. & i.* besternen; eine Hauptrolle spielen; *~s and stripes,* Sternenbanner *n.*

starboard *s.* Steuerbord *n.*

starch *s.* Stärke (zur Wäsche) *f.*; ~ *v.t.* stärken.

stardom *s.* Starruhm *m.*

stare *s.* starrer Blick *m.*; Staunen *n.*; ~ *v.i.* anstarren.

starfish *s.* Seestern *m.*

staring *a.* starrend.

stark *a.,* *~ly* *adv.* kraß; öde; völlig; nackt (Wahrheit).

starlight *s.* Sternenlicht; ~ *night,* Sternennacht *f.*

starling *s.* Star (Vogel) *m.*

starlit *a.* sternklar.

starred *a.* gestirnt.

starry *a.* sternig; sternhell.

start *v.i.* (*rail.*) abgehen; (*Sport*) starten; anfangen; ~ *v.t.* aufjagen; stutzig machen; aufwerfen (Fragen); beginnen; (*mech.*) in Gang bringen, anlassen; (*Sport*) ablaufen lassen; ~ *s.* Abfahrt *f.*; Beginn *m.*; Vorsprung *m.*

starter *s.* Anreger *m.*; (*Sport*) Starter *m.*; (*mech.*) Anlasser *m.*; (Rennen) Teilnehmer(in) *m.(f.)*

startle *v.t.* erschrecken, überraschen.

startling *a.* erstaunlich; überraschend.

starvation *s.* Verhungern *n.*; ~ *wages pl.* Hungerlohn *m.*

starve *v.i.* Not leiden, verhungern; ~ *v.t.* verhungern lassen, aushungern.

state *s.* Zustand *m.*; Stand, Rang *m.*; Staat *m.*; Aufwand *m.*; *~-aided* *a.* staatlich unterstützt; *~-owned* *a.* im Staatsbesitz; *lying in ~,* Aufbahrung *f.*; ~ *v.t.* stellen, festsetzen; dartun, vortragen, erklären, sagen.

stately *a.* stattlich, prächtig; stolz.

statement *s.* Angabe, Aussage *f.*; Überschlag, Bericht *m.,* Angabe *f.*; ~ *of account s.* (Rechnungs) auszug *m.*

state-of-the-art *a.* auf dem neuesten Stand der Technik stehend.

statesman *s.* Staatsmann *m.*

statesmanlike *a.* staatsmännisch.

statesmanship *s.* Regierungskunst *f.*

stateswomen *s.* Staatsfrau *f.*

static *a.* statisch, gleichbleibend; ~ *s.* atmosphärische Störung *f.*

station *s.* Stand *m.*; Stelle *f.*; Amt *n.*; Rang *m.*; Standort *m.*; Bahnhof *m.*; *~s of the cross,* Kreuzwegstationen *pl.*; ~ *v.t.* hinstellen; (*mil.*) stationieren.

stationary *a.* feststehend

stationer *s.* Schreibwarenhändler(in) *m.(f.)*

stationery *s.* Schreibwaren *f.pl.*

station-master *s.* Bahnhofsvorsteher(in) *m.(f.)*

station wagon *s.* Kombiwagen *m.*

statistic(al) *a.* statistisch.

statistician *s.* Statistiker(in) *m.(f.)*

statistics *s.pl.* Statistik *f.*

statue *s.* Statue *f.*

statuette *s.* Statuette *f.*

stature *s.* Leibesgröße *f.*; Wuchs *m.*; Statur *f.*

status *s.* Lage *f.*; Status *m.*

statute *s.* Satzung *f.*; Gesetz *n.*; Parlamentsakte *f.*

statutory *a.* gesetzmäßig; ~ *corporation,* Körperschaft des öffentlichen Rechts; ~ *declaration,*

eidesstattliche Erklärung *f.*
staunch *a.* zuverlässig, treu; standhaft, fest.
stave *v.t. to ~ in,* den Boden ausschlagen; *to ~ off,* abwehren.
stay *v.i.st.* stillstehen, bleiben, warten; sohnen; ~ *v.t.* aufhalten, durchhalten; ~ *s.* Aufenthalt *m.*
stay-at-home *s.* häuslicher Mensch *m.*
staying power *s.* Durchhaltevermögen *n.*
stead *s.* Stelle *f.*; Platz *m.*; *in his ~,* an seiner Stelle; *in~ of,* statt.
steadfast *a.,* **~ly** *adv.* fest, standhaft.
steady *a.,* **~ily** *adv.* fest, standhaft; beständig; ~ *v.t.* beruhigen; ~*v.i.* sich beruhigen; stabilisieren.
steak *s.* Steak *n.*
steal *v.t.st.* stehlen; ~ *v.i.* schleichen.
stealth *s.* Heimlichkeit *f.*; *by ~,* verstohlen.
stealthy *a.* verstohlen, heimlich.
steam *s.* Dampf *m.*; ~ *v.t.* dämpfen; ~ *v.i.* dampfen.
steam-boat *s.* Dampfschiff *n.*
steam-engine *s.* Dampfmaschine *f.*; Dampflokomotive *f.*
steamer *s.* Dampfer *m.*; Dämpfer *m.*
steam-iron *s.* Dampfbügeleisen *n.*
steam-navigation *s.* Dampfschiffahrt *f.*
steam-pressure gauge *s.* Dampfdruckmesser *m.*
steam-roller *s.* Dampfwalze *f.*
steamship *s.* Dampfschiff *n.*
steam-tug *s.* Schleppdampfer *m.*
steamy *a.* dunstig; feucht.
steel *s.* Stahl *m.*; ~ *v.t.* stählen; ~ *cabinet,* Stahlschrank *m.*; ~-**engraving** *s.* Stahlstich *m.*; ~ *frame s.* Eisenkonstruktion *f.*; ~ *helmet s.* Stahlhelm *m.*; ~ *wool s.* Stahlwolle *f.*
steely *a.* stählern; stahlhart.
steelyard *s.* Schnellwaage *f.*
steep *a.,* **~ly** *adv.* jäh, steil; (*fam.*) übertrieben; ~ *v.t.* eintunken, einweichen; *to ~o.s. in,* versenken.
steepen *v.i.* steiler werden.
steeple *s.* Kirchturm *m.*
steeple-chase *s.* Hindernisrennen *n.*
steer *v.t. & i.* steuern; ~**ing column** *s.* (*mot.*) Lenksäule *f.*; ~**ing lock** *s.* Lenkradschloß *n.*; ~**ing wheel** *s.* Steuerrad *n.*
steerage *s.* Lenkung *f.*; Zwischendeck *n.*; ~-**passenger,** Zwischendeckpassagier *m.*
steersman *s.* Steuermann *m.*
stellar *a.* gestirnt, Sternen. . .
stem *s.* Stiel, Stengel *m.*; Stamm *m.*; ~ *v.t.* stemmen, ankämpfen; sich widersetzen.
stench *s.* Gestank *m.*
stencil *s.* Schablone *f.*, Matrize *f.*
stenographer *s.* Stenograph(in) *m.*(*f.*)
stenography *s.* Stenographie *f.*
stentorian *a.* überlaut.
step *v.i.* schreiten, treten; ~ *up v.t.* antreiben; *to ~ in,* sich ins Mittel legen; ~ *s.* Schritt, Tritt, Gang *m.*; Fußstapfe *f.*; Stufe *f.*; Trittbrett *n.*; ~ *by ~,* Schritt für Schritt; *to fall into ~ with,* in gleichen Schritt fallen mit; *to keep ~ with,* Schritt halten mit; *to take ~s,* Schritte tun, Maßnahmen ergreifen; ~**s** *pl.,* *ladder s.* Trittleiter *f.*; ~ *a.* Stief. . . (Bruder, etc.).
steppe *s.* Steppe *f.*
stepping-stone *s.* Steinstufe *f.*; (*fig.*) Sprungbrett *n.*
stereo *s.* Stereoanlage *f.*; Stereo *n.*
stereophonic *a.* stereophon.

stereoscope *s.* Stereoskop *n.*
stereoscopic *a.* stereoskopisch.
stereotype *s.* Stereotyp *n.*; ~ *a.* Stereotyp. . . (*typ.*); (*fig.*) abgedroschen, stereotyp; ~ *v.t.* stereotypieren; unveränderlich festlegen.
sterile *a.* unfruchtbar; steril.
sterilize *v.t.* keimfrei machen; sterilisieren.
sterility *s.* Unfruchtbarkeit *f.*
sterilization *s.* Sterilisation *f.*; Sterilisierung *f.*
sterilize *v.t.* sterilisieren.
sterling *s.* Sterling *m.*; *a pound ~,* ein Pfund Sterling; ~ *a.* echt, zuverlässig.
stern *a.,* **~ly** *adv.* ernst, starr; streng, grausam; ~ *s.* (*nav.*) Heck *n.*
stertorous *a.* röchelnd, schnarchend.
stethoscope *s.* Stethoskop *n.*
stew *s.* Eintopf *m.* geschmortes Fleisch *n.*; ~ *v.t.* schmoren, dämpfen; ~*ed fruit,* Kompott *n.*
steward *s.* Verwalter(in) *m.*(*f.*); Steward *m.*
stewardess *s.* Stewardess *f.*
stick *s.* Stock, Stecken *m.*; Stange *f.*; ~ *of wood,* Holzscheit *n.*; ~ *v.t.* stecken, ankleben; *to ~ together,* zusammenleimen, zusammenkleben ~ *v.i.* stocken; sich anhängen; *to ~ at nothing,* vor nichts zurückscheuen; *to ~ to,* beharren bei.
sticker *s.* Aufkleber *m.*
stick-in-the-mud *s.* (*fam.*) Trantüte *f.*; Rückschrittler(in) *m.*(*f.*)
stickleback *s.* Stichling *m.*
stickler *s.* Verfechter *m.*; Eiferer *m.*
stick-up *s.* Überfall *m.*
sticky *a.* klebrig.
stiff *a.,* **~ly** *adv.* steif; staff; schwierig; hartnäckig.
stiffen *v.t.* versteifen; stärken; ~ *v.i.* steif werden, erstarren.
stiffness *s.* Steifheit *f.*
stifle *a.* ersticken.
stifling *a.* erstickend; stickig; drückend.
stigma *s.* Brandmal *n.*; Schande *f.*
stigmatize *v.t.* brandmarken.
stile *s.* Zauntritt *m.*
still *a.* still, ruhig; ~ *adv.* stets, noch, immer noch; ~ *c.* doch, indessen; ~ *v.t.* stillen, beruhigen.
stillbirth *s.* Totgeburt *f.*
stillborn *a.* totgeboren.
still-life *s.* (*fig.*) Stilleben *n.*
stillness *s.* Bewegungslosigkeit *f.*
stilt *s.* Stelze *f.*
stilted *a.* hochtrabend, gespreizt.
stimulant *a.* anregend; ~ *s.* Reizmittel *n.*
stimulate *v.t.* anspornen, anreizen.
stimulation *s.* Stimulierung *f.*; Anregung *f.*
stimulative *a.* anreizend, antreibend.
stimulus *s.* Antrieb, Sporn *m.*; Reizmittel *n.*
sting *v.t.st.* stechen; schmerzen; anstacheln; (*fig.*) kränken; ~ *s.* Stachel *m.*; Stich *m.*; Biß *m.*; Spitze *f.*
stinging-nettle *s.* Brennessel *f.*
stingy *a.,* **~ily** *adv.* karg, geizig.
stink *v.i.st.* stinken; ~ *s.* Gestank *m.*
stink-bomb *s.* Stinkbombe *f.*
sting *s.* Beschränkung *f.*; Maß *n.*; ~ *v.t.* knapp halten; einschränken.
stipend *s.* Besoldung *f.*; Stipendium *n.*
stipulate *v.t.* vereinbaren, bedingen; *as ~d,* wie vereinbart.
stipulation *s.* Auflage *f.*; Übereinkunft *f.*;

Bedingung *f.*
stir *v.t.* regen, bewegen; aufrühren, schüren; umrühren; ~ *v.i.* sich regen; aufstehen; ~ *s.* Regung *f.;* Lärm, Aufruhr *m.;* Getümmel *n.*
stirring *a.* aufregend, bewegt; mitreißend.
stirrup *s.* Steigbügel *m.*
stitch *v.t. & i.* stechen; heften; säumen; ~ *s.* Stich *m.;* Masche *f.*
stoat *s.* Hermelin *n.*
stock *s.* Stock, Stamm, Klotz *m.;* (Gewehr-)Schaft *m.;* Grundstock *m.;* Vorrat *m.;* Lager *n.;* Aktie; Aktien *pl.,* (Stamm-)Kapital *n.;* Herkunft *f.;* Inventar *n.; in* ~, auf Lager; ~ *taking,* Bestandsaufnahme *f.;* ~-*in-trade,* *s.* Betriebsvorrat *m.* (auch *fig.*); ~ *v.t.* versehen mit; auf Lager haben.
stockade *s.* Palisade *f.*
stock breeder *s.* Viehzüchter(in) *m.(f.)*
stockbroker *s.* Börsenmakler(in) *m.(f.)*
stock-exchange *s.* (Fonds-) Börse *f.*
stock-holder *s.* Aktionär *m.*
stocking *s.* Strumpf *m.*
stock-market *s.* Börsengeschäft *n.*
stockpile *s.* Vorrat *m.;* ~ *v.t.* einen Vorrat sammeln.
stock-still *a.* unbeweglich.
stocky *a.* stämmig.
stodgy *a.* füllend, unverdaulich.
stoic *s.* Stoiker(in) *m.(f.)*
stoical *a.,* ~**ly** *adv.* stoisch, standhaft.
stoicism *s.* Gleichmut *m.*
stoke *v.t.* schüren, heizen.
stoker *s.* Heizer(in) *m.(f.)*
stole *s.* Stola *f.*
stolid *a.,* ~**ly** *adv.* dumm, dickhäutig.
stomach *s.* Magen *m.;* Bauch *m.;* ~*for,* Lust (*f.*) zu; ~-**ache,** Bauchweh *n.;* ~ *v.t.* sich gefallen lassen; vertragen.
stone *s.* Stein, (Obst-)Kern *m.;* Gewicht (*n.*) von 14 Pfund; ~ *a.* steinern; ~ *v.t.* steinigen; auskernen; *a* ~*'s throw,* eine kurze Entfernung.
Stone Age *s.* Steinzeit *f.*
stone-blind *a.* stockblind.
stone-dead *a.* mausetot.
stone-deaf *a.* stocktaub.
stone-fruit *s.* Steinobst *n.*
stone-mason *s.* Steinmetz *m.*
stoneware *s.* steingut *n.*
stony *a.* steinig; steinern; steinhart.
stool *s.* Schemel *m.;* Stuhl *m.*
stoop *v.i.* sich bücken; ~ *s.* Bücken *n.;* Herablassung *f.*
stop *v.t.* (ver)stopfen; hemmen, hindern; versperren; (Zahn) füllen; (Zahlungen) einstellen; *to* ~ *payment on a check,* einen Scheck sperren; ~ *v.i.* stillstehen; anhalten; stehenbleiben; aufhören; *to* ~ *at a hotel,* in einem Hotel absteigen; ~ *s.* Stillstand *m.;* Klappe *f.;* Pause *f.;* Unterbrechung, Hemmung *f.;* Verbot *n.;* Eden *n.;* Haltestelle *f.;* ~!, *i.* halt!
stop-cock *s.* Absperrhahn *m.*
stop-gap *s.* Notbehelf *m.*
stop-light *s.* rote Ampel *f.*
stopover *s.* Fahrtunterbrechung *f.;* Aufenthalt (im Bahnhof) *m.*
stoppage *s.* Verstopfung *f.;* Stillstand *m.;* Zahlungseinstellung *f.*
stopper *s.* Stöpsel *m.;* ~ *v.t.* zustöpseln.
stop-watch *s.* Stoppuhr *f.*

storage *s.* Lagern, *n.;* Lagerung *f.;* ~ *charge,* Lagergebühr *f.;* ~ *battery* *s.* Akkumulator *m.*
store *s.* Vorrat, Proviant *m.;* Fülle *f.;* Laden *m.;* ~-**room** *s.* Vorratskammer *f.; to put in* ~, einlagern; ~*s,* Warenhaus *n.;* Vorräte *m.pl.; military* ~*s,* Kriegsvorräte *pl.;* Magazin *n.;* ~ *v.t.* speichern, (Möbel) einlagern; (Schiff) verproviantieren.
store-house *s.* Lagerhaus *n.;* Schatzkammer *f.*
store-keeper *s.* Magazinaufseher *m.;* Lagerist(in) *m.(f.)*
stork *s.* Storch *m.*
storm *s.* Sturm (auch *mil.*) *m.;* Gewitter *n.;* Aufruhr *m.;* ~ *v.t. & i.* (be)stürmen; wüten.
stormy *a.* stürmisch; ungestüm.
story *s.* Geschichte *f.;* Erzählung *f.;* Lüge *f.;* Stock(werk) *n.,* Geschoß *n.,* Etage *f.* ~-**teller** *s.* Erzähler *m.;* Flunkerer *m.*
stout *a.,* ~**ly** *adv.* stark; standhaft, wacker, tapfer; wohlbeleibt; ~ *s.* dunkles Bier *n.*
stove *s.* Ofen *m.;* Herd *m.*
stovepipe *s.* Ofenrohr *n.*
stow *v.t.* stauen; schichten, packen.
stowage *s.* Stauen *n.;* Stauraum *m.;* Packerlohn *m.*
stowaway *s.* blinder Passagier *m.*
straddle *v.i.* mit gespreizten Beinen stehen; sich rittlings setzen.
straggle *v.i.* verstreut stehen; hinterherzockeln; wuchern (von Pflanzen).
straggler *s.* Nachzügler *m.*
straight *a. & adv.,* ~**ly** *adv.* gerade; unmittelbar, direkt; ~ *on,* ~ *ahead,* geradeaus; *to put* ~, in Ordnung bringen; ~ *away* *adv.* sofort, gleich.
straighten *v.t.* gerade, straff machen; *to* ~ *out,* in Ordnung bringen; *to* ~ *up,* aufrichten.
straight face *s.* unbewegtes Gesicht *n.*
straighforward *a.* freimütig.
strain *v.t.* spannen, strecken; quetschen, durchseihen; anstrengen; verstauchen; übertreiben; ~ *v.i.* sich anstrengen; ~ *s.* Anstrengung *f.;* Spannung *f.;* Inanspruchnahme *f.;* Verstauchung *f.;* Neigung *f.;* Tonart *f.,* Klänge *pl.;* Stamm *m.,* Klasse, Familie *f.;* Art *f.*
strained *p. & a.* gespannt; gezwungen.
strainer *s.* Filtriertrichter *m.;* (Tee)Seiher *m.;* Sieb *n.*
strait *a.,* ~**ly** *adv.* eng, knapp, genau, streng; schwierig; ~-**jacket** *s.* Zwangsjacke *f.;* ~ *laced* *a.* prüde; ~ *s.* Enge, Meerenge *f.;* ~**s** *pl.* Verlegenheit, Klemme *f.*
straiten *v.t.* verengen; in Verlegenheit setzen.
straitness *s.* Enge *f.;* Strenge *f.;* Einschränkung *f.;* Verlegenheit *f.*
strand *s.* Strand *m.;* Strähne *f.;* (*fig.*) Ader *f.;* ~ *v.i.* stranden.
strange *a.,* ~**ly** *adv.* fremd; seltsam.
stranger *s.* Fremde *m./f.;* Ausländer(in) *m.(f.)*
strangle *v.t.* erdrosseln; erwürgen.
stranglehold *s.* Würgegriff *m.*
strangulate *v.t.* abschnüren.
strangulation *s.* Erdrosselung *f.*
strap *s.* Riemen, Gurt *m.;* Strippe *f.;* (*mil.*) Achselschnur *f.;* ~-**hanger** *m.* (*fam.*) Stehplatzinhaber(in) *m./f.* ; ~ *v.t.* mit Riemen fest machen.
strapping *a.* stämmig *f.;* stramm.
stratagem *s.* Kriegslist *f.;* Schachzug *m.*
strategic *a.* strategisch.

strategist s. Stratege m.; Strategin f.
strategy s. Kriegskunst f.; List f.
stratify v.t. schichten.
stratosphere s. stratosphäre f.
stratum s. Lage, Schicht f.
straw s. Stroh n.; Strohhalm m.
strawberry s. Erdbeere f.
straw-cutter s. Häckselschneidemaschine f.
stray v.i. irregehen; umherstreifen; ~ a. verirrt, verlaufen.
streak s. Strich, Streifen m.; Strähne f.
streaker s. Blitzer(in) m.(f.)
streaky a. streifig; durchwachsen (Speck).
stream s. Bach m.; Wasserlauf m.; Strom m. ~ v.i. strömen, fließen.
streamer s. Wimpel f.; (flatterndes) Band n.; Papierschlange f.
streamlined a. Stromlinien...
street s. Straße, Gasse f.
streetcar s. Straßenbahnwagen m.
street-lamp s. Straßenlaterne f.
street lighting s. Straßenbeleuchtung f.
street vendor s. Straßenverkäufer m.
strength s. Stärke, Kraft f.; on the ~ of, auf Grund von; ~ report, (mil.) Stärkenachweisung f.
strength v.t. stärken; befestigen; bekräftigen; ~ v.i. erstarken.
strenuous a., ~ly adv. tapfer, wacker; tätig, eifrig; anstrengend.
stress s. Nachdruck m.; Gewicht n.; Hauptton m.; Anspannung f., Druck m.; ~ v.t. betonen.
stretch v.t. (v.i. sich) strecken, (aus)dehnen, anstrengen; übertreiben; ~ s. Ausdehnung, Strecke f.; Überanspannung f.; Anstrengung f.; at a ~, in einem Zuge, ununterbrochen.
stretcher s. Tragbahre f.; Spanner m.; ~-bearer s. Krankenträger m.
strew v.t.st. streuen, bedecken.
stricken a. betroffen (von); heimgesucht.
strict a., ~ly adv. eng; straff; genau; streng; ~ly speaking, streng genommen.
strictness s. Strenge f.
stricture s. Tadel m.; Kritik f.
stride s. (weiter) Schritt m.; ~ v.i.st. schreiten.
strident a. kreischend; schrill.
strife s. Streit m.; Wettstreit m.
strike v.t. & i. schlagen, stossen; treffen; rühren, bewegen; auffallen; (Flagge) streichen; (Zelt, Lager) abbrechen; (Handel) abschließen; die Arbeit einstellen, streiken; to ~ a balance, den Saldo ziehen; to ~ a match, Zündholz anzünden; to ~ a mine, auf eine Mine laufen; to ~ off, out, ausstreichen; to ~ a person off the list, einen von der Liste streichen; to ~ a chord, eine Saite anschlagen; to ~ up, (Lied) anstimmen; ~ s. Arbeitseinstellung f., Streik m.; on ~, streikend; ~ ballot s. Urabstimmung f. ~-breaker s. Streikbrecher m.
striker s. Streikende m./f.
striking a., ~ly adv. auffallend, ergreifend; treffend; ~ distance, Reichweite f.; ~ power, Schlagkraft f.
string s. Bindfaden m.; Schnur f.; Sehne f.; Saite f.; Reihe f.; ~ v.t. besaiten; aufreihen.
string-band s. Streichorchester n.
stringency s. Strenge f.; Knappheit f.
stringent a. streng; zusammenziehend; bindend.

stringy a. faserig.
strip v.t. abstreifen; berauben; ~ v.i. sich auskleiden; ~ s. Streifen m.
stripe s. Streifen m.; (mil.) Tresse f.
striped a. gestreift.
strip lighting s. Neonbeleuchtung f.
stripling s. Bürschchen n.
strip-tease s. Striptease m.
stripy a. gestreift.
strive v.i.st. streben; kämpfen um; sich bemühen.
stroke s. Streich, Schlag, Stoß m.; Schlag (der Uhr) m.; Schlaganfall m.; Strich m.; Zug, Federstrich m.; Kolbenhub m.; ~ v.t. streichen; streicheln.
stroll v.i. herumstreifen, herumschlendern; ~ s. Spaziergang m.
stroller s. Bummler(in) m.(f.); Buggy m.
strong a., ~ly adv. stark, kräftig; tüchtig, streng, nachdrücklich; 40 men ~, 40 Mann hoch; ~ drinks, pl. alkoholische Getränke n.pl.
strong-box s. Geldschrank m.
stronghold s. Feste f.; Bollwerk n.
strong language s. derbe Ausdrucksweise f.
strong-minded a. willensstark.
strong-room s. Stahlkammer f.
structural a., ~ly adv. strukturell, baulich.
structure s. Bau m.; Bauart, Einrichtung f.
struggle v.i. kämpfen; sich anstrengen; ringen; sich sträuben; ~ s. Sträuben n.; Kampf m.; Zuckung f.; ~ for life, Kampf (m.) ums Dasein.
strum v.t. klimpern.
strut v.i. stolzieren; ~ s. Stützbalken m., Strebe f.
strychnine s. Strychnin n.
stub s. Stumpf, Klotz m.; (Am.) Kontrollabschnitt m.
stubble s. Stoppel m.
stubborn a., ~ly adv. steif, unbiegsam, hart; standhaft; hartnäckig.
stubbornness s. Sturheit f.; Hartnäckigkeit f.
stucco s. Stuck m.
stud s. Knaufnagel m.; Knopf, Hemdenknopf m.; Ständer m.; Gestüt n.; Zuchthengst m.; ~ v.t. beschlagen; (fig.) besetzen.
stud-book s. Zuchtbuch n.
student s. Student m.; Gelehrte m.
studied a., ~ly adv. gelehrt; studiert; gekünstelt.
studio s. Atelier n.; (radio) Senderaum m.; (film) Aufnahmeatelier n.
studious a., ~ly adv. beflissen, fleißig; bedacht; geflissentlich.
study s. Studium n.; Studierstube f.; Studie f.; ~ v.i. studieren; nachsinnen, sich befleißigen; ~ v.t. einstudieren; genau untersuchen.
stuff s. Stoff m.; Zeug n.; Gerät n.; Unsinn m.; Plunder m.; ~ v.t. (aus)stopfen; füllen.
stuffing s. Füllung f.; Füllsel n.
stuffy a. stickig; spießig.
stultify v.t. lähmen.
stumble v.i. stolpern; stocken.
stumbling-block s. Stolperstein m.; Hindernis n.
stump s. Stumpf m.; (Zigarren)stummel m.; ~ v.t. stampfen; tappen.
stumpy a. gedrungen.
stun v.t. betäuben, verdutzen.
stunning a. erstaunlich; (fam.) toll.
stunt v.t. am Wachstum hindern; ~ s. (sl.) Kraftanstrengung f.; (Zeitung) Werbetrick m.; Sensation

f.; Kunststück *n.*
stupefaction *s.* Betäubung *f.*
stupefy *v.t.* betäuben, verblüffen.
stupendous *a.*, **~ly** *adv.* erstaunlich.
stupid *a.*, **~ly** *adv.* dumm, albern; langweilig.
stupidity *s.* Dummheit *f.*; Torheit *f.*
stupor *s.* Erstarrung *f.*; Staunen *n.*
sturdy *a.*, **~ily** *adv.* derb, stark; stabil; stämmig.
sturgeon *s.* Stör *m.*
stutter *v.i.* stottern; **~s.** Stottern *n.*
sty *s.* Schweinestall *m.*
sty(e) *s.* Gerstenkorn (am Auge) *n.*
style *s.* Stil *m.*; Schreibart *f.*; Machart, Aufmachung *f.*; Titel *m.*; **~** *v.t.* entwerfen
stylish *a.* elegant, modisch.
stylist *s.* Designer(in) *m.*(*f.*)
stylistic *a.* stilistisch.
styptic *a.* blutstillend.
suasion *s.* Überredung *f.*; *moral* **~**, gutes Zureden *n.*
suave *a.* mild, sanft; verbindlich.
suavity *s.* Lieblichkeit, Anmut *f.*
sub-committee *s.* Unterausschuß *m.*
subconscious *a.*, **~ly** *adv.* unterbewußt.
subcontract *s.* Unterkontrakt *m.*
subcontractor *s.* Subunternehmer(in) *m.* (*f.*).
sub culture *s.* Subkultur *f.*
subcutaneous *a.* unter der Haut.
subdivide *v.t.* unterteilen.
subdivision *s.* Unterabteilung *f.*; Unterteilung *f.*
subdue *v.t.* unterwerfen; dämpfen.
subdued *a.* gedämpft; ruhig.
subgroup *s.* Untergruppe *f.*
subheading *s.* Untertitel *m.*
subhuman *a.* unmenschlich.
subject *a.* unterworfen, ausgesetzt; zu Grunde liegend; **~** *to*, vorbehaltlich; **~** *to reservations*, unter Vorbehalt; **~** *s.* Untertan *m.*; Person *f.*; Gegenstand *m.*, Betreff *m.*; Subjekt *n.*; **~** *index s.* Sachregister *n.*; **~** *matter*, Gegenstand *m.*, Thema *n.*
subject *v.t.* unterwerfen; aussetzen.
subjection *s.* Unterwerfung *f.*
subjective *a.* subjektiv.
subjoin *v.t.* beifügen.
subjugate *v.t.* unterjochen.
subjunctive *s.* (*gram.*) Konjunktiv *m.*
sublet *v.t.* unterverpachten, weitervermieten.
sublimate *s.* (*chem.*) Sublimat *n.*
sublime *a.*, **~ly** *adv.* erhaben, hehr, hoch; großartig.
subliminal *a.* unterschwellig.
sublimity *s.* Erhabenheit *f.*
submachine gun *s.* Maschinenpistole *f.*
submarine *a.* unterseeisch; **~** *s.* Unterseeboot *n.*
submerge *v.t.* & *i.* untertauchen; überschwemmen.
submersion *s.* Untertauchen *n.*; Überschwemmung *f.*
submission *s.* Unterwürfigkeit, Demut, Ergebung *f.*; Eingabe *f.*
submissive *a.*, **~ly** *adv.* unterwürfig.
submit *v.t.* unterwerfen; unterbreiten; **~** *v.i.* sich fügen; *s.* unterwerfen.
subnormal *a.* unterdurchschnittlich.
subordinate *a.*, **~ly** *adv.* untergeordnet; **~** *clause*, (*gram.*) Nebensatz *m.*; **~** *s.* Untergeordnete, Untergebene *m.*/*f.*; **~** *v.t.* unterordnen.

suborn *v.t.* (zu falschem Zeugnis) verleiten.
subornation *s.* Anstiftung *f.*
subpoena *s.* Vorladung *f.*; *v.t.* vorladen.
subscribe *v.t.* unterschreiben; zeichnen; **~** *v.i.* abonnieren; einwilligen.
subscriber *s.* Abonnent(in) *m.*(*f.*)
subscription *s.* Unterzeichnung *f.*; Abonnement *n.*; (Geld) Beitrag *m.*; *annual* **~**, Jahresabonnement *n.*; *monthly* **~**, Monatsabonnement *n.*; **~** *list*, Subskriptionsliste, Zeichnungsliste *f.*; *to cancel one's* **~**, den Abonnement aufgeben.
subsection *s.* Unterabteilung *f.*
subsequent *a.*, nachfolgend, nachträglich; **~** *delivery*, Nachlieferung *f.*; **~** *payment*, Nachzahlung *f.*; **~ly** *adv.* nachher.
subservience *s.* Unterwürfigkeit *f.*
subservient *a.* dienlich; unterwürfig.
subside *v.i.* sinken, abnehmen; aufhören; zurückgehen.
subsidence *s.* Senkung *f.*; Sinken *n.*
subsidiary *a.* Hilfs. . ., helfend; **~** *company*, Tochtergesellschaft *f.*; **~** *subject*, Nebenfach *n.*; **~** *s.* Gehilfe *m.*/*f.*
subsidize *v.t.* mit Geld unterstützen, subventionieren.
subsidy *s.* Subvention *f.*
subsist *v.i.* bestehen, auskommen; **~** *v.t.* erhalten, ernähren.
subsistence *s.* Dasein, Bestehen, Auskommen *n.*; Lebensunterhalt *m.*; **~** *allowance* *s.* Verpflegungsgeld *n.*; **~** *level s.* Existenzminimum *n.*; *minimum of* **~**, Existenzminimum *n.*
subsoil *s.* Untergrund *m.*
subsonic *a.* Unterschall. . .
substance *s.* Wesen *n.*; Stoff *m.*, Substanz *f.*; Hauptinhalt *m.*; Vermögen *n.*
substandard *a.* unzulänglich.
substantial *a.*, **~ly** *adv.* wesentlich, wirklich, körperlich; nahrhaft; stark, zahlungsfähig, vermögend.
substantiality *s.* Wesenheit *f.*
substantiate *v.t.* dartun, nachweisen; erhärten.
substantive *s.* Hauptwort *n.*
substitute *v.t.* ersetzen; auswechseln; **~** *s.* Stellvertreter *m.*; Ersatzmittel *n.*; **~** *material*, Werkstoff *m.*
substitution *s.* Stellvertretung, Unterschiebung *f.*
substratum *s.* Unterlage, Grundlage *f.*
substructure *s.* Unterbau *f.*
subtenant *s.* Untermieter(in) *m.*(*f.*)
subterfuge *s.* Ausflucht *f.*
subterranean *a.* unterirdisch.
subtitle *s.* Untertitel *m.*
subtle *a.*, **~tly** *adv.* fein, schlau.
subtlety *s.* Schlauheit *f.*, Scharfsinn *m.*
subtotal *s.* Zwischensumme *f.*
subtract *v.t.* abziehen, subtrahieren.
subtraction *s.* Abziehen *n.*, Subtraktion *f.*
subtrahend *s.* (*ar.*) Subtrahend *m.*
subtropical *a.* subtropisch.
suburb *s.* Vorstadt *f.*
suburban *a.* vorstädtisch; **~** *traffic*, Vorortsverkehr *m.*; **~** *train*, Vorortszug *m.*
suburbia *s.* Vorort *m.*
subversion *s.* Umsturz *m.*
subversive *a.* umstürzend; **~** *activities pl.* Wühlarbeit *f.*

subvert *v.t.* umstürzen, zerstören.
subway *s.* Unterführung *f.*; U-Bahn *f.*, Untergrundbahn *f.*
succeed *v.t. & i.* nachfolgen; *to ~ to an estate*, ein Vermögen erben; *to ~ to a person*, einen beerben; *to ~ in doing*, gelingen.
success *s.* Erfolg *m.*, Glück *n.*
successful *a.*, **~ly** *adv.* erfolgreich.
succession *s.* Reihenfolge, Folge, Nachfolge *f.*; Erbfolge *f.*; *in ~*, hintereinander, nacheinander; *right of ~*, Erbfolge *f.*; *~ to the throne*, Thronfolge *f.*
successive *a.* einander folgend; **~ly** *adv.* der Reihe nach.
successor *s.* Nachfolger(in) *m.(f.)*
succinct *a.*, **~ly** *adv.* gedrängt, bündig; prägnant.
succinctness *s.* Knappheit *f.*; Prägnanz *f.*
succulent *a.* saftig.
succumb *v.i.* unterliegen.
such *pn.* solcher, solche, solches; von der Art, so groß; *~ a.* so ein; *~like*, dergleichen; *~ as*, die, welche...; *no ~ thing*, nichts dergleichen.
suck *v.t. & i.* (ein)saugen; pumpen; *~ s.* Saugen *n.*
sucker *s.* Saugkolben *m.*, Saugrohr *n.*; Wurzelsproß *m.*; (*fam.*) Gimpel *m.*
sucking-pump *s.* Saugpumpe *f.*
suckle *v.t.* säugen, stillen.
suckling-pig *s.* Spanferkel *n.*
suction *s.* Saugen *n.*; Saug...
Sudan *s.* Sudan *m.*
sudden *a.*, **~ly** *adv.* plötzlich; übereilt, hitzig; *all of a ~*, plötzlich.
suddenness *s.* Plötzlichkeit *f.*
suds *s.pl.* Seifenwasser *n.*
sue *v.i.* ansuchen; *v.t.* bitten, verklagen; *to ~ for damages*, auf Schadenersatz klagen.
suede *s.* Wildleder *n.*
suet *s.* Talg *m.*; Hammelfett *n.*
suffer *v.t. & i.* leiden, ausstehen; Strafe, Schaden leiden; gestatten.
sufferable *a.*, **~bly** *adv.* erträglich; zulässig.
sufferance *s.* Duldung *f.*
suffering *s.* Leiden *n.*
suffice *v.i.* genügen; *~ v.t.* Genüge leisten, befriedigen.
sufficiency *s.* Genüge *f.*; Zulänglichkeit *f.*
sufficient *a.*, **~ly** *adv.* hinlänglich.
suffix *s.* anhängen; *~ s.* Anhängesilbe *f.*
suffocate *v.t.* ersticken.
suffocation *s.* Erstickung *f.*
suffrage *s.* Wahlstimme *f.*; Beifall *m.*; Stimmrecht *n.*; *universal ~*, allgemeine Wahlrecht *n.*
suffragette *s.* Suffragette *f.*, Stimmrechtlerin *f.*
suffuse *v.t.* übergießen; durchfluten.
sugar *s.* Zucker *m.*; *~ tongs pl.* Zuckerzange *f.*; *~ v.t.* zuckern.
sugar-basin *s.* Zuckerschale *f.*
sugar-cane *s.* Zuckerrohr *n.*
sugar-loaf *s.* Zuckerhut *m.*
sugar-plum *s.* Bonbon *n.*
sugary *a.* zuckerig.
suggest *v.t.* eingeben, beibringen, vorschlagen; einflössen.
suggestion *s.* Rat *m.*, Vorschlag *m.*
suggestive *a.* andeutend; anregend; vielsagend; schlüpfrig.
suicidal *a.* selbstmörderisch.

suicide *s.* Selbstmord *m.*; Selbstmörder *m.*; *to commit ~*, Selbstmord begehen.
suit *s.* Folge *f.*; Farbe (Karte) *f.*; Gesuch *n.*; Prozeß *m.*; Anzug *m.*; Bitte *f.*; *~ v.t.* ordnen; passen; gefallen; geziemen; gut stehen; *~ v.i.* übereinstimmen.
suitability *s.* Eignung *f.*; Angemessenheit *f.*
suitable *a.*, **~bly** *adv.* gemäß, angemessen, schicklich, passend.
suitcase *s.* Koffer *m.*
suite *s.* Gefolge *n.*; Hotelsuite *f.*; Zimmereinrichtung *f.*
suitor *s.* Bittsteller *m.*; Bewerber, Freier *m.*
sulfate *s.* Sulfat *n.*
sulfide *s.* Sulphid *n.*
sulfur *s.* Schwefel *m.*
sulfuric *a.* Schwefel...; *~ acid* *s.* Schwefelsäure *f.*
sulfurous *a.*, **~ly** *adv.* schwef[e]lig.
sulfury *a.* schwefelgelb.
sulk *v.i.* schmollen.
sulky *a.*, **~ily** *adv.* schmollend, launisch.
sullen *a.*, **~ly** *adv.* düster, verdrießlich, mürrisch.
sully *v.t.* besudeln.
sultan *s.* Sultan *m.*
sultana *s.* (kernlose) Rosine *f.*, Sultanine *f.*
sultry *a.* schwül.
sum *s.* Summe *f.*; Rechenaufgabe *f.*; *~ total*, Gesamtsumme *f.*; *~ v.t.* zusammenzählen, rechnen; *to ~ up*, zusammenfassen, (*law*) Beweisaufnahme zusammenfassen.
summarize *v.t.* (kurz) zusammenfassen.
summary *a.*, **~ily** *adv.* summarisch, kurz; *~ s.* Auszug, kurze Inhaltsangabe *f.*; *~ jurisdiction*, *~ proceedings*, (*law*) Schnellverfahren, beschleunigtes Verfahren *n.*
summer *s.* Sommer *m.*; Tragbalken *m.*; *~ time*, Sommerzeit *f.*
summer-house *s.* Gartenhaus *n.*
summer school *s.* Sommerkurs *m.*
summer term *s.* Sommerhalbjahr *n.*
summery *a.* sommerlich.
summing-up *s.* Zusammenfassung *f.*
summit *s.* Gipfel *m.*, Spitze *f.*
summon *v.t.* vorladen, aufrufen; (Kraft) zusammennehmen.
summons *s.* Vorladung *f.*; Aufforderung *f.*
sumptuous *a.*, **~ly** *adv.* prachtig; luxuriös.
sun *s.* Sonne *f.*
sunbathe *v.i.* sonnenbaden.
sunbeam *s.* Sonnenstrahl *m.*
sunburn *s.* Sonnenbrand *m.*
sunburnt *a.* gebräunt, verbrannt.
Sunday *s.* Sonntag *m.*
sunder *v.t.* trennen, absondern.
sundial *s.* Sonnenuhr *f.*
sundown *s.* Sonnenuntergang *m.*
sundry *a.* mehrere, verschiedene.
sunflower *s.* Sonnenblume *f.*
sun-glasses, *pl.* Sonnenbrille *f.*
sunken *a.* versunken; (*fig*) eingefallen.
sun-lamp *s.* Ultraviolettlampe *f.*
sunlight *s.* Sonnenlicht *n.*
sunlit *a.* sonnenbeschienen.
sunny *a.* sonnig.
sunray *s.* Sonnenstrahl *m.*

sunrise *s.* Sonnenaufgang *m.*
sunroof *s.* Schiebedach *n.*; Dachterrasse *f.*
sunset *s.* Sonnenuntergang *m.*
sunshade *s.* Sonnenschirm *m.*
sunshine *s.* Sonnenschein *m.*
sun-spot *s.* Sonnenflecken *m.*
sunstroke *s.* Sonnenstich *m.*
suntan *s.* (Sonnen)bräune *f.*; ~**lotion** s. Sonnenschutzmittel *n.*
sunup *s.* Sonnenaufgang *m.*
super *a.* (*fam.*) super.
superarabundant *a.*, ~**ly** *adv.* überreichlich.
superb *a.*, ~**ly** *adv.* prächtig, herrlich.
supercilious *a.*, ~**ly** *adv.* anmassend.
superficial *a.*, ~**ly** *adv.* oberflächlich; seight.
superfluity *s.* Überfluß *m.*
superfluous *a.*, ~**ly** *adv.* überflüssig.
superhuman *a.* übermenschlich.
superintend *v.t.* die Aufsicht führen; überwachen.
superintendence *s.* Aufsicht *f.*
superintendent *s.* Inspektor, Aufseher *m.*
superior *a.* höher; größer; vorzüglich; überlegen; ~ *s.* Obere, Vorgesetzte *m.*; ~ *authority*, vorgesetzte Behörde *f.*
superiority *s.* Überlegenheit *f.*; Vorrang *m.*; Vorrecht *n.*
superlative *a.*, ~**ly** *adv.* unübertrefflich; im höchsten Grade; ~ *s.* Superlativ *m.*
superman *s.* Übermensch *m.*
supernatural *a.*, ~**ly** *adv.* übernatürlich.
supernumerary *a.* überzählig; ~ *s.* Überzählige *m.*; Figurant *m.*
superpower *s.* Supermacht *f.*
superscribe *v.t.* überschreiben.
superscription *s.* Überschrift *f.*
supersede *v.t.* verdrängen; ablösen.
supersession *s.* Ersatz *m.*, Verdrängung *f.*
supersonic *a.* Überschall. . .
superstition *s.* Aberglaube *m.*
superstitious *a.*, ~**ly** *adv.* abergläubisch.
superstore *s.* Großmarkt *m.*
superstructure *s.* Aufbau *m.*; Überbau *m.*
supervene *v.i.* hinzukommen.
supervention *s.* Hinzukommen.
supervise *v.t.* beaufsichtigen.
supervision *s.* Aufsicht *f.*
supervisor *s.* Aufseher *m.*
supervisory *a.* Aufsichts. . .
supper *s.* Abendessen *n.*; *the Last S~*, das letzte Abendmahl *n.*
supplant *v.t.* verdrängen, ausstechen.
supple *a.*, ~**ly** *adv.* geschmeidig, biegsam; nachgiebig.
supplement *s.* Ergänzung *f.*; Zusatz, Anhang *m.*; Beilage (Zeitung) *f.*; ~*v.t.* ergänzen.
supplemental, supplementary *a.* ergänzend; ~ *order*, Nachbestellung *f.*
suppliant *a.* demütig, flehend.
supplicate *v.t.* anflehen.
supplication *s.* demütige Bitte *f.*
supplier *s.* Versorger *m.*
supply *v.t.* ersetzen, ergänzen; liefern, versorgen; ~ *s.* Beschaffung *f.*; Zuschuß *m.*; Vorrat *m.*; (*mil.*) Nachschub *m.*; ~**depot** *s.* Nachschublager *n.*; ~ *and demand*, Angebot (*n.*) und Nachfrage (*f.*); ~**ies** *pl.* Bedarf *m.*, Vorrat *m.*

support *v.t.* unterstützen; erhalten, ernähren; tragen; bekräftigen; ~ *s.* Stütze *f.*; Unterstützung *f.*; Unterhalt *m.*; *in ~ of*, zum Beweis von.
supporter *s.* Unterstützer(in) *m.*(*f.*); Gönner(in) *m.* (*f.*); Anhänger(in) *m.*(*f.*)
supportive *a.* hilfreich.
suppose *v.t.* voraussetzen, vermuten.
supposedly *adv.* angeblich.
supposition *s.* Annahme *f.*; Vermutung *f.*
suppress *v.t.* unterdrücken; verhindern.
suppression *s.* Unterdrückung *f.*; Verheimlichung *f.*; Abschaffung *f.*
suppurate *v.i.* eitern.
supremacy *s.* Obergewalt *f.*; Übergewicht, Überlegenheit *f.*
supreme *a.*, ~**ly** *adv.* höchst, oberst.
surcharge *s.* Zuschlag.
sure *a.* & *adv.*, ~**ly** *adv.* sicher, gewiß, zuverlässig; *to be ~*, sicher wissen; *to make ~*, sich vergewissern; *for ~*, sicher.
surety *s.* Sicherheit *f.*; Bürge *m.*, Bürgschaft *f.*
surf *s.* Brandung *f.*
surface *s.* Oberfläche *f.*; Flächeninhalt *m.*; ~ *mail s.* gewöhnliche Post (nicht Luftpost) *f.*
surfeit *s.* Übermaß *n.*; Überangebot *n.*; ~*v.t.* überfüllen; ~*v.i.* sich übersättigen.
surfer *s.* Surfer(in) *m.*(*f.*)
surfing *s.* Surfen *n.*
surge *s.* Woge, Brandung *f.*; ~ *v.i.* wogen; steigen.
surgeon *s.* Chirurg(in) *m.*(*f.*)
surgery *s.* Chirurgie *f.*
surgical *a.* chirurgisch, wundärztlich.
surly *a.*, ~**ily** *adv.* grob, mürrisch.
surmise *v.t.* mutmassen; ~ *s.* Vermutung *f.*
surmount *v.t.* überragen; überwinden.
surname *s.* Zuname *m.*; Nachname *m.*; ~ *v.t.* einen Zunamen geben.
surpass *v.t.* übertreffen.
surplice *s.* Chorhemd *n.*
surplus *s.* Überschuß *m.*; Überrest *m.*; ~ *a.* überzählig, überschüssig.
surprise *s.* Überraschung *f.*; *v.t.* überraschen; erstaunen.
surprising *a.*, ~**ly** *adv.* erstaunlich.
surrender *v.t.* übergeben, überliefern; abreten; ~ *v.i.* sich ergeben; ~ *s.* Übergabe, Auslieferung *f.*
surreptious *a.*, ~**ly** *adv.* erschlichen, verstohlen; heimlich; ~ *passage*, gefälschte Stelle *f.*
surrogate *s.* Ersatz *m.*
surrogate mother *s.* Leihmutter *f.*
surround *v.t.* umgeben, einschließen.
surroundings *s.pl.* Umgebung *f.*
surtax *s.* Steuerzuschlag *m.*
surveillance *s.* Überwachung *f.*
survey *v.t.* überblicken, besichtigen; ausmessen; ~ *s.* Überblick *m.*; Besichtigung, Vermessung *f.*; Riß, Plan *m.*
surveying *s.* Landvermessung *f.*
surveyor *s.* Inspektor(in) *m.*(*f.*); Landvermessen(in) *m.*(*f.*)
survival *s.* Überleben *n.*
survive *v.t.* überleben; ~ *v.i.* übrig bleiben, noch leben, fortleben.
survivor *s.* Überlebende *m.*/*f.*
susceptibility *s.* Empfänglichkeit *f.* Anfälligkeit *f.*
susceptible *a.* empfänglich; empfindlich.

suspect *v.i.* Verdacht hegen, argwöhnen, besorgen; ~ *v.t.* in Verdacht haben; bezweifeln; ~ *s.* Verdächtige *m./f.; to be* ~, belastet sein.

suspected *a.* verdächtig.

suspend *v.t.* aufhängen; unterbrechen; suspendieren, zeitweise ausschließen; einstellen; aufschieben; absetzen.

suspenders *pl.* Hosenträger *pl.*

suspense *s.* Ungewißheit *f.;* Spannung *f.*

suspension *s.* Aufhängen *n.;* Aufschub *m.;* Einstellung *f.;* Stillstand *m.;* Suspension *f.;* ~ *of payments,* Zahlungseinstellung *f.*

suspension-bridge *s.* Hängebrücke *f.*

suspicion *s.* Verdacht, Argwohn *m.; above* ~, über allen Verdacht erhaben.

suspicious *a.,* ~**ly** *adv.* argwöhnisch; verdächtig.

sustain *v.t.* standhalten; widerstehen; stützen; aufrechthalten; (Verlust) erleiden; behaupten.

sustained *a.* anhaltend; ausdauernd.

sustenance *s.* Nahrung *f.;* Nährwert *m.*

suture *s.* Naht *f.*

suzerain *s.* Oberlehnsherr *m.*

svelte *a.* schlank.

swab *s.* (*med.*) Tupfer *m.*

Swabia *s.* Schwaben *n.*

swaddle *v.t.* windeln, wickeln.

swagger *v.i.* stolzieren; prahlen; großtun.

swallow *v.t.* (ver)schlucken; verschlingen; ~ *s.* Schwalbe *f.*

swamp *s.* Sumpf *m.;* ~ *v.t.* (in Morast) versenken; überschwemmen.

swampy *a.* sumpfig.

swan *s.* Schwan *m.*

swank *s.* (*fam.*) Großtuerei *f.;* ~ *v.i.* großtun, renommieren.

swanky *a.* protzig.

swansong *s.* Schwanengesang *m.*

swap *v.t.* tauschen; austauschen; *s.* Tausch *m.*

swarm *s.* Schwarm *m.;* Gewimmel *n.;* ~ *v.i.* wimmeln.

swarthy *a.,* ~**ily** *adv.* schwärzlich, dunkel.

swash *v.i.* plantschen.

swash-buckler *s.* Schwadroneur *m.;* Abenteurer *m.*

swastika *s.* Hakenkreuz *n.*

swat *v.t.* totschlagen (Fliege).

swatch *s.* Stoffmuster *n.*

swathe *v.t.* einhüllen.

sway *v.t.* schwenken; lenken, ~ *v.i.* schwanken; Einfluß haben, herrschen; ~ *s.* Schwung *m.;* Ausschlag (der Waage) *m.*

swear *v.i.st.* schwören; fluchen; ~ *v.t.* vereidigen; beschwören; *to* ~ *by, to* ~ *false,* falsch schwören; *to* ~ *in,* vereidigen.

swear-word *s.* Fluchwort *n.*

sweat *s.* Schweiß *m.;* ~ *v.i.* schwitzen; ~ *v.t.* schwitzen; (*fig.*) ausbeuten, für Hungerlohn beschäftigen.

sweater *s.* Sweater *m.,* Pullover *m.*

sweat-shop *s.* ausbeuterischer Betrieb *m.*

sweaty *a.* schweißig.

Swede *s.* Schwede *m.;* Schwedin *f.*

Sweden *s.* Schweden *n.*

Swedish *a.* schwedisch.

sweep *v.t.* fegen, kehren; ~ *s.* Zug, Schwung *m.;*

Schleppe *f.;* Schornsteinfeger *m.;* flacher Landstrich *m.*

sweeper *s.* Straßenfeger *m.*

sweeping *a.* reißend; weitgreifend; umfassend.

sweepstake *s.* Lotterie.

sweet *a.,* ~**ly** *adv.* süß; lieblich; freundlich; ~ *pea,* Edelwicke *f.;* ~ *william,* Bartnelke *f.;* ~ *tooth,* Leckermaul *n.;* ~ *s.* Süßigkeit, Lieblichkeit *f.;* Schätzchen *n.;* ~**s** *pl.* Zuckerwerk *n.*

sweeten *v.t.* versüßen; milde stimmen.

sweetener *s.* Süßstoff *m.*

sweetheart *s.* Liebchen *n.*

sweetness *s.* Süßigkeit, Lieblichkeit *f.*

sweet potato *s.* Batate *f.*

sweetroll *s.* Schnecke (Gebäck) *f.*

sweet-tempered *a.* sanftmütig.

swell *v.i.st.* schwellen; zunehmen; sich blähen; ~ *v.t.* aufblasen; vergrössern; ~ *s.* Anschwellen *n.;* Erhebung *f.;* Dünung *f.;* ~ *a.* vorzüglich; aufgedonnert.

swelling *s.* Schwellung *f.*

swelter *v.i.* lechzen; vor Hitze vergehen.

swerve *v.i.* abweichen; abschweifen.

swift *a.* ~**ly** *adv.* schnell, flüchtig; bereit; ~ *s.* Mauersegler *m.*

swiftness *s.* Schnelligkeit *f.*

swig *v.t.* schlucken; kippen.

swill *v.i. & t.* ausspülen; hinunterspülen.

swim *v.i.st.* schwimmen; schwindlig sein; verschwimmen; ~ *v.t.* durchschwimmen; schwemmen.

swimmer *s.* Schwimmer(in) *m.(f.)*

swimming-pool *s.* Schwimmbad *n.*

swim-suit *s.* Badeanzug *m.*

swindle *v.t.* beschwindeln; erschwindeln; ~ *s.* Schwindel *m.*

swindler *s.* Schwindler(in) *m.(f.)*

swine *s.* Schwein *n.* (*meist fig.*)

swing *v.t.* schwingen, schaukeln; ~ *v.i.* sich schwingen; schwanken; sich umdrehen; baumeln; (*nav.*) schwaien; ~ *s.* Schwung *m.;* Schaukel *f.;* Spielraum *m.;* Gang *m.; in full* ~, in vollem Gang; ~-*bridge,* Drehbrücke *f.;* ~*ing chair s.* Schaukelstuhl *m.* ~(*ing*) *door,* Pendeltür *f.;* ~*in lamp,* Hängelampe *f.*

swinish *a.,* ~**ly** *adv.* schweinisch.

swipe *v.t.* (*fam.*) eindreschen; (auf) knallen.

swirl *v.i.* wirbeln; ~ *s.* Strudel *m.*

swish *v.t.* schlagen; sausen lassen.

Swiss *a.* Schweizerisch; ~ Schweizer(in) *m.(f.)*

switch *s.* Gerte *f.;* (*rail.*) Weiche *f.;* (*elek.*) Schalter *m.;* (*elek.*) ~-**gear** *s.* Schaltgerät *n.;* ~ *v.t.* hauen; (*elek.*) (um)schalten; *to* ~ *on, off,* andrehen, abdrehen.

switchback, ~-**railway** *s.* Berg-und-Talbahn *f.*

switch-board *s.* Schalttafel *f.,* Schaltbrett *n.*

Switzerland *s.* Schweiz *f.*

swivel *s.* Drehzapfen *m.;* Drehgelenk *n.* ~-**bridge** *s.* Drehbrücke *f.;* ~-**chair** *s.* Drehstuhl *m.;* ~ *v.i. & t.* (sich) auf einem Zapfen drehen.

swollen *a.* geschwollen.

swoon *v.i.* in Ohnmacht fallen; ~ *s.* Ohnmacht *f.*

swoop *s.* Stoß *m.;* plötzliche Razzia *f.;* Sturzflug *m.* ~ *v.i. & t.* herabstoßen, herfallen über.

swop *s.* Tausch *m.;* ~ *v.t.* tauschen.

sword *s.* Schwert *n.;* Degen *m.*

swordfish s. Schwertfisch m.
swordsman s. Fechter m.
sworn a. beeidigt, vereidigt; ~ to, beschworen.
sybarite s. Genießer m.
sycamore s. Sykomore f.
sycophant s. Schmeichler m., Kriecher m.
syllabic(al) a. silbig, Silben...
syllabication s. Silbentrennung f.
syllable s. Silbe f.
syllabus s. Lehrplan m.; Literaturliste f.
syllogism s. (Vernunft-) Schluß m.
sylph s. Luftgeist m.
symbiosis s. Symbiose f.
symbol s. Sinnbild, Symbol n.; graphische, Zeichen n.
symbolical a., ~ly adv. sinnbildlich.
symbolize v.t. sinnbildlich darstellen, versinnbildlichen.
symmetrical a., ~ly adv. ebenmäßig; symmetrisch.
symmetry s. Ebenmaß n.; Symmetrie f.
sympathetic a. mitfühlend; (seelen)verwandt.
sympathize v.i. mitempfinden; übereinstimmen; sympathisieren.
sympathy s. Mitgefühl n.; Sympathie f.
symphönic a. sinfonisch; symphonisch.
symphony s. Symphonie, Sinfonie f.; ~ **orchestra** s. Sinfonieorchester n.
symptom s. Anzeichen n.
symptomatic a. bezeichnend.
synagogue s. Synagoge f.

synchronize v.t. gleichgehend machen; synchronisieren.
synchronous a. gleichzeitig.
syncopate v.t. (mus.) synkopieren.
syndicate s. Syndikat n., Konzern m.; Konsortium n.
syndrome s. Syndrom n.
synod s. Kirchenversammlung f.; Synode f.
synonym s. sinnverwandtes Wort n.; Synonym n.
synonymous a., ~ly adv. sinnverwandt.
synonymy s. Sinnverwandtschaft f.
synopsis s. kurzer Abriß m.
syntactic a. syntaktisch.
syntax s. Syntax f.
synthesis s. Synthese f.
synthesize v.t. synthetisieren.
synthesizer s. synthesizer m.
synthetic a., ~ally adv. synthetisch, künstlich(hergestellt); ~ material, Werkstoff m.; ~ petrol, künstliches Benzin n.; ~ rubber, künstlicher Gummi m.
syphilis s. Syphilis f.
Syria s. Syrien n.
Syrian a. Syrisch; Syrer(in) m.(f.)
syringe s. Spritze f.; ~ v.t. spritzen.
syrup, sirup s. Syrup m.
system s. System, Lehrgebäude n.
systematic(al) a., ~ally adv. systematisch, planmäßig.
systematize v.t. systematisieren.
systemic a. systemisch.
systems analyst s. Systemanalytiker(in) m.(f.)

T

T,t der Buchstabe T oder t n.
tab s. Lasche f.; Aufhänger m.; Schildchen, Etikett n.
tabby s. Tigerkatze f.
tabernacle s. Tabernakel m.
table s. Tafel f.; Tisch m.; Tabelle f.; ~ of contents, s. Inhaltsverzeichnis. f.; ~ v.t. auf den Tisch legen.
tableau vivant s. lebendes Bild n.
table-cloth s. Tischtuch n.
table manners s. pl. Tischmanieren pl.
table-mat s. set n.
tablespoon s. Eßlöffel m.; ~ful, s. Eßlöffelvoll m.
tablet s. Täfelchen n.; Tablette f.; Schreibtafel f.
table tennis s. Tischtennis n.
table-ware s. Geschirr n., Besteck n.
tabloid s. Boulevardzeitung f.
taboo s. Tabu n.; ~ a. verboten; tabuisiert.
tabular a. tabellarisch.
tabulate v.t. in Tabellen bringen; tabellarisch ordnen.
tachograph s. Fahrtenschreiber m.
tachometer s. (mot.) Umdrehungsmesser m.
tacit a., ~ly adv. stillschweigend.
taciturn a. schweigsam.
taciturnity s. Schweigsamkeit f.
tack s. Stift m.; Häkchen n.; Zwecke f.; (nav.) Kurs m.; ~ v.t. anheften, befestigen.
tackle, Takelwerk n.; Gerät n.; Flaschenzug m.; ~ v.t. takeln; in Angriff nehmen.
tacky a. klebrig; schäbig.
tact s. Feingefühl n.; Takt m.

tactful a., ~ly adv. taktvoll.
tactical a., ~ly adv. taktisch.
tactician s. Taktiker(in) m.(f.)
tactics s.pl. Kriegskunst, Taktik f.
tactless a., ~ly adv. taktlos.
tadpole s. Kaulquappe f.
taffeta s. Taft m.
tag s. Zettel m.; Anhängsel n.; Etikett n.; Schlaufe f.; Fangen n. ~ v.t. anheften; anhängen.
tail s. Schwanz m.; Ende n.; Rockschoß m.; ~ suit, tails, Frack m.
tail-light s. Rücklicht n.
tailor s. Schneider m.; ~-made, vom Schneider angefertigt; ~ v.t. & i. schneidern.
tail-wind s. Rückenwind m.
taint v.t. beflecken; verderben; anstecken; verführen; ~ s. Flecken m.; Ansteckung f.; Verderbnis f.
take v.t.st. (mit-, an-, ein-, fest-, weg-) nehmen, empfangen; ergreifen; dafürhalten, meinen; bringen; sich gefallen lassen, einstecken; (Feuer) fangen; ~ v.i. gefallen, anschlagen, ansprechen; it ~s (me) three hours, ich brauche drei Stunden; to ~ after, einem nachgeraten; to ~ down, aufschreiben, zu Protokoll nehmen; to ~ in, betrügen; to ~ in a paper, eine Zeitung bestellen; to ~ off, ausziehen, (Hut) abnehmen; abfliegen; to ~ to, Gefallen finden an; to ~ to heart, sich zu Herzen nehmen; to ~ for granted, als erwiesen annehmen; to ~ ill, amiss, übelnehmen; to ~ into account, in Betracht ziehen; to ~ part in, teilnehmen an; to ~ place,

stattfinden; *to ~ prisoner*, gefangennehmen; *to ~ a seat*, Platz nehmen; *to ~ one's time*, sich Zeit nehmen; *to ~ an examination*, *test*, eine Prüfung machen.

take-off *s.* Abflug *m.*, Abheben *n.*; Start *m.*

taker *s.* Abnehmer(in) *m.*(*f.*)

taking *s.* Nehmen *n.*; Einnahme *f.*; ~ *a.* einnehmend, packend.

talc, talcum *s.* Talk *m.*; **talcum powder** *s.* Körperpuder *m.*

tale *s.* Erzählung *f.*; Märchen *n.*

tale-bearer *s.* Zuträger *m.*

talent *s.* Talent *n.*, Begabung *f.*

talented *a.* talentvoll, begabt.

talk *v.i.* reden, sprechen; schwatzen; ~ *s.* Gespräch *n.*; Gerücht *n.*

talkative *a.*, **~ly** *adv.* gesprächig.

tall *a.* lang, groß; (*fig.*) geflunkert.

tallboy *s.* Kommode (*f.*) mit Aufsatz.

tallow *s.* Talg *m.*; ~ *v.t.* einschmieren.

tally *v.t.* einkerben; (*nav.*) anholen; ~ *v.i.* passen, entsprechen, stimmen; ~ *s.* Zählstand *m.*; *keep a ~ of*, Buch führen.

tally-ho *i.* hallo!; ~ *s.* Weidruf *m.*

talon *s.* Kralle, Klaue *f.*

tambour *s.* Handtrommel *f.*; Stickrahmen; ~ *v.t.* sticken.

tambourine *s.* Tamburin *n.*

tame *a.*, **~ly** *adv.* zahm; folgsam; ~ *v.t.* zähmen; bändigen.

tamper (with) *v.i.* such einmischen; an etwas herumpfuschen.

tampon *s.* Tampon *m.*

tan *s.* Lohe *f.*; Bräune *f.*; ~ *v.t.* lohen, gerben; bräunen; braun werden.

tandem *s.* Tandem *n.*

tang *s.* scharfer Geruch od. Geschmack *m.*

tangent *s.* Tangente *f.*

tangerine *s.* Mandarine *f.*

tangible *a.* greifbar, fühlbar.

tangle *v.t.* verwirren, verwickeln; ~ *s.* Knoten *m.*, Verwicklung *f.*

tangled *a.* verheddert; verworren.

tangy *a.* scharf; würzig.

tank *s.* Wasserbehälter *m.*; Tank *m.*; Panzer *m.*; ~ *car* *s.* (*rail.*) Kesselwagen, Tankwagen *m.*; ~ *driver* *s.* (*mil.*) Panzerfahrer *m.*; ~ *v.i.* tanken.

tankard *s.* Trinkgefäß *n.*; Krug *m.*

tanker *s.* Tanker *m.*

tanned *a.* braungebrannt.

tanner *s.* Lohgerber(in) *m.*(*f.*)

tannery *s.* Gerberei *f.*

tannin *s.* Gerbstoff *m.*

tantalize *v.t.* reizen; zappeln lassen.

tantalizing *a.* verlockend.

tantamount *a.* gleichwertig; gleichbedeutend.

tantrum *s.* Wutanfall *m.*, Trotzanfall *m.*

tap *s.* gelinder Schlag *m.*; Zapfen *m.*; Hahn *m.* (*mech.*) Gewindebohrer *m.*; ~ *wrench* *s.* Halter für Gewindebohrer; *on ~*, angezapft, erhältlich; ~ *v.t.* klopfen an, abklopfen; anzapfen; (Telegramme) abfangen, Telephon abhören.

tap-dance *s.* Steptanz *m.*

tap-dancer *s.* Steptänzer(in) *m.*(*f.*)

tape *s.* Kassette (Audio) *f.*; Video *n.*; (*Sport*) Zielband *n.*; (*tel.*) Papierstreifen *m.*

tape deck *s.* Kassettentrecorder *m.*; Tapedeck *n.*

tape-measure *s.* Bandmaß *n.*

taper *s.* Wachskerze *f.*; Wachsstock *m.*; ~ *v.t.* verjüngen, zuspitzen; *~off*, *~v.i.* spitz zulaufen, sich verjüngen.

tape recorder *s.* Kassettenrecorder *m.*

tapestry *s.* gewirkte Tapete *f.*, Gobelin *m.*

tapeworm *s.* Bandwurm *m.*

tapioca *s.* Tapioka *f.*

tap-room *s.* Schankstube *f.*

tap-water *s.* Leitungswasser *n.*

tar *s.* Teer *m.*; (*fam.*) Matrose *m.*; ~ *v.t.* teeren.

tarantula *s.* Tarantel *f.*

tardy *a.*, **~ily** *adv.* langsam; träge; spät.

tare *s.* Wicke *f.*; (*com.*) Tara *f.*

target *s.* (Schieß-)Scheibe; (*mil.*, *avi.*) Ziel *n.*; ~ *date*, Termin *m.*; ~ *practice*, Schießübung *f.*

tariff *s.* Zolltarif *m.*; **~-wall** *s.* Zollschranke *f.*

tarnish *v.t.* trübe machen; beschmutzen; ~ *v.i.* den Glanz verlieren.

tarnished *a.* stumpf; befleckt.

tarpaulin *s.* Plane *f.*; Persenning *f.*

tarragon *s.* Estragon *n.*

tarry *a.* teerig.

tart *s.* Obsttörtchen *n.*; ~ *a.*, **~ly** *adv.* herb, sauer.

tartan *s.* Plaid *n.*

tartar *s.* Weinstein *m.*; Zahnstein *m.*; *Tartar*, Tatar *m.*

tartaric *a.* Weinstein. . .; ~ *acid* *s.* Weinsäure *f.*

tartlet *s.* Törtchen *n.*

task *s.* Aufgabe *f.*; *take to ~*, zur Rede stellen; ins Gebet nehmen.

task force *s.* Sonderkommando *n.*

tassel *s.* Troddel, Quaste *f.*

taste *v.t. & i.* kosten, schmecken; versuchen; (*fig.*) empfinden; ~ *s.* Probe *f.*; Geschmack *m.*; Neigung *f.*

tasteful *a.* schmackhaft, geschmackvoll.

tasteless *a.* geschmacklos.

tasty *a.* lecker.

tat: tit for ~ wie du mir, so ich dir.

tatter *s.* Lumpen *m.*; ~ *v.t.* zerlumpen, zerfetzen.

tattle *v.i.* schwatzen; tratschen; klatschen; ~ *s.* Geschwätz *n.*; Tratsch *m.*

tattoo *s.* Tätowierung *f.*; ~ *v.t.* tätowieren.

tatty *a.* schäbig, zerfleddert; mies.

taunt *v.t.* verspotten; verhöhnen; ~ *s.* Hohn, Spott *m.*

taunting *s.* Spott *m.*; *~a.* verhöhnend.

Taurus *s.* (*astro.*) Stier *m.*

taut *a.* straff, steif.

tauten *v.t. & i.* straff machen, sich straffen.

tautology *s.* Tautologie *f.*

tavern *s.* Wirtshaus *n.*; Schenke *f.*

tawdry *a.* geschmacklos, verkommen, verlottert.

tawny *a.* lohfarbig, gelbbraun.

tax *s.* Steuer, Abgabe *f.*; ~ *v.t.* besteuern; belasten; ~ *allowance* *s.* Steuerfreibetrag *m.* ~ *free*, steuerfrei; ~ **payer** *s.* Steuerzahler *m.*; ~ **collector** *s.* Steuereinnehmer *m.*; ~ **remission**, Steuererlaß *m.*

taxable *a.* steuerbar, steuerpflichtig.

taxation *s.* Abschätzung *f.*; Besteuerung *f.*; *exempt from ~*, steuerfrei.

taxi, taxicab *s.* Taxi *n.*; ~ *stand*, *s.* Taxistand *m.*; ~ *v.i.* (*avi.*) rollen.

taximeter *s.* Taxameter *m.*

tax office s. Finanzamt n., Steueramt.

taxpayer s. Steuerzahler(in) m.(f.)

tax return s. Steuererklärung f.

tea s. Tee m.; ~ **kettle** s. Teekessel m.; ~ leaves pl. Teeblätter pl. ~pot s. Teekanne f.; ~ set s. Teeservice n.

teach v.t. & i.ir. lehren, unterrichten.

teachable a., ~**bly** adv. gelehrig.

teacher s. Lehrer m.; Lehrerin f.

teak-wood s. Teakholz n.

team s. Gespann n.; Mannschaft f.; ~ work, Zusammenspiel n.

team; ~ effort s. Gemeinschaftsarbeit f.; ~-**mate** s. Mannschaftskamerad(in) m. (f.); ~ **spirit** s. Teamgeist m.

teamster s. Lastwagenfahrer(in) m.(f.)

tea-party s. Teegesellschaft f.

tear s. Traäe f.; ~ v.t.st. reißen, zerreißen; ~ v.i. wüten; rasen; ~ s. Riß m.

teardrop s. Träne f.

tearful a. weinend; tränenreich; weinerlich.

tearing s. reißend; tobend; heftig.

tease v.t. necken, hänseln.

teasel s. Kardendistel f.; Karde f.

teaser s. (fam.) harte Nuß f.; brain ~, s. Denksportaufgabe f.

teasing a. neckend.

teat s. Zitze f.; Brustwarze f.

tea-things s.pl. Teegeschirr n.

tea-tree s. Teestrauch m.

technical a., ~**ly** adv. kunstmäßig, technisch; Fach. . .

technical consultant s. Fachberater m.

technicality s. technisches Detail n.

technician s. Techniker(in) m.(f.)

technique s. Technik f.

technological a. technologisch.

technologist s. Technologe f.; Technologin f.

technology s. Technologie f.

teddy-bear s. Teddybär m.

tedious a., ~**ly** adv. langweilig, lästig.

tedium s. Langweiligkeit f. Langeweile f.

teem v.i. wimmeln (von); strotzen; gießen.

teenager s. Teenager m.; Jugendliche m./f.

teens s.pl. Lebensjahre (n.pl.), die auf teen endigen (von 13-19); Teenagerjahre n.pl.

teeter v.i. wanken; schaukeln.

teeth s.pl. Zähne m.pl.

teethe v.i. zahnen.

teetotaller s. Abstinenzler m.

telecommunication s. Fernmeldeverkehr m.

telegram s. Telegramm n.

telegraph s. Telegraf m.; ~ v.t. telegraphieren.

telegraphic a. telegraphisch.

telegraphy s. Telegraphie f.

telepathy s. Telepathie f.

telephone s. Telefon n., Fernsprecher m.; ~ v.t. & i. telephonieren; ~ **booth** s. Telephonzelle f.; ~-**exchange** s. Fernsprechamt n.

telephone operator s. Telefonist(in) m.(f.)

teleprinter s. Fernschreiber m.

telescope s. Fernrohr n.; ~ v.t. & i. (sich) ineinanderschieben.

telescopic a. teleskopisch; ausziehbar.

teletext s. Bildschirmtext m.; Teletext m.

televise v.t. im Fernsehen übertragen.

television s. Fernsehen n.; ~ **set** s. Fernsehapparat m.

telex s. Telex n.

tell v.t. & i.ir. sagen; erzählen, melden, anzeigen; Wirkung tun; zählen; to ~ off, anschnauzen, abfahren lassen.

teller s. (Bank) Kassierer(in) m.(f.)

telling a. durchschlagend, wirkungsvoll.

tell-tale s. Klatschmaul n. ~ a. klatschaft; verräterisch.

temerity s. Tollkühnheit f.

temper v.t. mäßigen; mildern; (Stahl) tempern; ~ s. Gemütsstimmung f.; Mäßigung f.; Laune f.; Härte f.; to keep one's ~, die Ruhe behalten; to lose one's ~, heftig werden, die Fassung verlieren.

temperament s. Temperament n.

temperamental a., ~**ly** adv. launenhaft; reizbar; temperamentvoll.

temperance s. Mäßigkeit f.; Enthaltsamkeit f.

temperate a., ~**ly** adv. mäßig, gemäßigt; ruhig, gelassen.

temperature s. Temperatur f.; to have a ~, (leicht) Fieber haben; to take the ~, Temperatur messen, nehmen.

tempered a. good~, gutgelaunt; bad ~, schlechtgelaunt.

tempest s. Sturm m.; Ungewitter n.

tempestuous a., ~**ly** adv. stürmisch.

template s. Schablone f.

temple s. Tempel m.; Schläfe f.

temporal a., ~**ly** adv. zeitlich; weltlich; Schläfen. . .

temporary a., ~**ily** adv. vorübergehend; zeitweilig, vorläufig; ~ **duty**, (mil.) zeitweiliger Dienst m.

temporize v.i. die passende Zeit abwarten; hinhalten; Zeit zu gewinnen suchen.

tempt v.t. versuchen, verleiten.

temptation s. Versuchung f.

tempter s. Versucher m.

tempting a. verlockend.

temptress s. Versucherin f.

ten a. zehn; ~ s. Zehn f.

tenable a. haltbar.

tenacious a. festhaltend, zähe.

tenacity s. Zähigkeit f., Beharrlichkeit f.

tenancy s. Pacht-, Mietverhältnis n.

tenant s. Pächter, Mieter m.

Ten Commandments s.pl. die Zehn Gebote pl.

tend v.t. warten, pflegen; bedienen (Maschine); ~ v.i. abzielen, (zu-) neigen, tendieren.

tendency s. Richtung, Neigung f.; Tendenz f.

tendentious a. tendenziös.

tender a., ~**ly** adv. weich, zart; zärtlich, empfindlich; ~ s. Angebot n.; Wärter m.; (rail.) Tender m.; Zahlungsmittel n.; ~ v.t. anbieten; to ~ one's resignation, seine Entlassung beantragen.

tenderize v.t. (cul.) zart machen; weich klopfen.

tenderness s. Zartheit f.; Zärtlichkeit f.; Sorgfalt f., Empfindlichkeit f.

tendon s. Sehne, Flechse f.

tendril s. Ranke f., Trieb m.

tenement s. Mietshaus n.

tenet s. Satz, Grundsatz m.; Lehre f.

tenfold a. zehnfach.

tennis s. Tennisspiel n.; ~ **court**, Tennisplatz m.

tenon s. Fuge f.; Zapfen m.

tenor s. Tenor m.

tense *s.* *(gram.)* Zeitform *f.*, Tempus *n.*; ~ *a.* angespannt; straff.

tensile *a.* dehnbar; ~ *strength*, Zugfestigkeit *f.*

tension *s.* Spannung *f.*

tent *s.* Zelt *n.*

tentacle *s.* Fühler *m.*

tentative *a.* ~**ly** *adv.* vorläufig; versuchsweise.

tenter-hook *s.* Spannhaken *m.*; *to be on* ~*s*, wie auf Kohlen sitzen, in Ängsten sein.

tenuity *s.* Dünne *f.*; Zartheit *f.*; Armseligkeit *f.*

tenth *a.* zehnt. . .

tenuous *a.* dünn, fein; unsicher, unbestimmt.

tenure *s.* Besitzrecht *n.*; Amtszeit *f.*; Dauerstellung *f.*

tepid *a.*, lau, lauwarm.

term *s.* Grenze *f.*; Ausdruck *m.*; Begriff *m.*; Termin *m.*, Frist *f.*; Trimester *n.*; ~**s** *pl.* Preis *m.*; Bedingungen *pl.*; *prison* ~, Strafzeit *f.*; *inclusive* ~*s*, *pl.* Preis, in dem alles einbegriffen ist; *in* ~*s of numbers*, in Zahlen ausgedrückt; *to come to* ~*s with*, sich einigen über etw. mit jm.; *to be on good* ~*s with*, mit einem gut stehen; ~ *v.t.* nennen, benennen.

terminal *a.* letzt. . ., End. . .; ~ *s.* Endstück *n.*; *(elek.)* Pol, *m.*

terminate *v.t.* begrenzen; endigen; ~ *v.i.* enden.

termination *s.* Ende *n.*; Endung *f.*

terminology *s.* Terminologie *f.*

terminus *s.* Endstation *f.*

termite *s.* Termite *f.*

terrace *s.* Terrasse *f.*

terrain *s.* Gelände *n.*

terrestrial *a.*, ~**ly** *adv.* irdisch.

terrible *a.*, ~**bly** *adv.* fürchterlich.

terrier *s.* Terrier *m.*

terrific *a.* phantastisch, wahnsinnig, toll.

terrify *v.t.* erschrecken.

terrifying *a.* entsetzlich, erschreckend.

territorial *a.* Landes. . .; ~ *waters*, Hoheitsgewässer *pl.*; *limit of* ~ *waters*, Hoheitsgrenze *f.*

territory *s.* Gebiet *n.*; Landschaft *f.*

terror *s.* Schrecken *m.*; (Todes)Angst *f.* (*fam.*)

terrorism *s.* Terrorismus *m.* Teufel.

terrorist *s.* Terrorist(in) *m.*(*f.*)

terrorize *v.t.* terrorisieren; in Schrecken versetzen.

terry(cloth) *s.* Frottee *n.*

terse *a.*, ~**ly** *adv.* glatt; bündig; knapp.

tertiary *a.* tertiär.

test *s.* Klassenarbeit *f.*; Test *m.*; Prüfung, Probe *f.*; (*fig.*) Prüfstein *m.*; ~ *case*, Schulfall, Probefall *m.*; ~ *flight*, Probeflug *m.*; ~ *tube*, Reagenzglas *n.*; *to put to the* ~, auf die Probe stellen; ~ *v.t.* prüfen; testen; (*chem.*) untersuchen; *to* ~ *the heart*, das Herz abklopfen; *to* ~ *the sight*, das Sehvermögen prüfen.

testament *s.* Testament *n.*, letzter Wille *m.*

testamentary *a.* testamentarisch.

testator *s.* Erblasser(in) *m.*(*f.*)

testicle *s.* Hode *f.*

testify (to) *v.i.* etwas bezeugen.

testimonial *s.* schriftliches Zeugnis *n.*; Empfehlung *f.*, Ehrbeweis *m.*

testimony *s.* Zeugnis *n.*; *to bear* ~, Zeugnis ablegen.

test paper *s.* Indikatorpapier *n.*; Prüfungsbogen *m.*

test-tube *s.* Reagenzglas; ~ *baby* *s.* Retortenbaby *n.*

testy *a.*, ~**ily** *adv.* mürrisch, reizbar.

tetanus *s.* Starrkrampf *m.*

tetchy *a.* empfindlich.

tether *s.* Spannseil *n.*; (*fig.*) Fähigkeit *f.*, Kraft *f.*; *to be at the end of one's* ~, am Ende seiner Kraft sein; ~ *v.t.* anbinden.

Teutonic *a.* germanisch; teutonisch.

text *s.* Text *m.*; Bibelstelle *f.*

text-book *s.* Leitfaden *m.*; Lehrbuch *n.*

textile *a.* gewebt; Textil. . .; ~**s** *pl.* Textilien *f.pl.*

textual *a.* textgemäß, wörtlich.

texture *s.* Beschaffenheit *f.*; Struktur *f.*; Konsistenz *f.*

Thai *a.* thailändisch; ~ *s.* Thai *m.*/*f.*

Thailand *s.* Thailand *n.*

Thames *s.* Themse *f.*

than *c.* als.

thank *v.t.* danken; ~**s** *pl.* Dank *m.*

thankful *a.*, ~**ly** *adv.* dankbar.

thankless *a.* undankbar.

Thanksgiving *s.* Erntedankfest *n.*

thank-you *s.* Dankeschön *n.*

that *pn.* jener, jene, jenes; welcher, welche, welches; der, die, das; ~ *c.* daß, damit, weil.

thatch *s.* Dachstroh *n.*; Strohdach *n.*; ~ *v.t.* mit Stroh decken.

thaw *v.t. & i.* tauen, auftauen, ~ *s.* Tauwetter *n.*

the *art.* der, die, das, den; so, desto; ~ *less*, umsoweniger.

theater *s.* Theater *s.*; Schauplatz *m.*; ~ *of operations*, (*mil.*) Operationsgebiet; ~ *of war*, Kriegsschauplatz *m.*

theater-goer *s.* Theaterbesucher(in) *m.*(*f.*)

theatrical *a.*, ~**ly** *adv.* bühnenhaft, theatralisch.

thee *pn.* dir, dich.

theft *s.* Diebstahl *m.*

their *pn.* ihr, ihre.

theirs *pn.* ihr, ihre; der, die, das ihrige.

them *pn.pl.* sie, ihnen.

theme *s.* Gegenstand *m.*; Thema *n.*

theme music *s.* Titelmusik *f.*

themselves *pn.pl.* sie selbst, sich (selbst).

then *adv.* dann, alsdann, damals; *now and* ~, dann und wann; ~ *c.* dann, daher, folglich.

thence *adv.* von da, von dort, daher.

thenceforth *adv.* seitdem; von da ab.

theocracy *s.* Gottes-, Priesterherrschaft *f.*

theocratic *a.* theokratisch.

theologian *s.* Theologe *m.*

theological *a.*, ~**ly** *adv.* theologisch.

theology *s.* Theologie *f.*

theorem *s.* Lehrsatz, Grundsatz *m.*

theoretical *a.*, ~**ly** *adv.* theoretisch.

theorist *s.* Theoretiker(in) *m.*(*f.*)

theorize *v.i.* Theorien aufstellen.

theory *s.* Theorie *f.*; Lehre *f.*

theosophy *s.* Theosophie *f.*

therapeutics *s.pl.* Therapie, Heilkunde *f.*

therapist *s.* Therapeut(in) *m.*(*f.*)

therapy *s.* Heilverfahren *n.*

there *adv.* da, dort, dahin; hin; ~ *is*, ~ *are*, es gibt, es sind; ~ *about*, daherum; ~*after*, danach; ~*by*, damit, dadurch; ~*fore*; daher, folglich; also; ~*from*, davon, daraus; ~*in*, darin; ~*of*, davon; ~*on*, darauf, daran; ~*to*, dazu; ~*under*, darunter; ~*upon*, darauf, hierauf; deswegen; ~*with*, damit; ~*you are*, da hast du es!

thermal *a.* Wärme. . ., Thermal. . .

thermodynamics *s.* Thermodynamik *f.*

thermometer s. Thermometer n. or m.

thermos-flask s. Thermosflasche f.

these pn.pl. diese.

thesis s. These f.; Dissertation f.; Doktorarbeit f.

they pn.pl. sie, diejenigen; man; es.

thick a. & adv., ~**ly** adv. dick, dicht; trübe, häufig; unklar; vertraut; ~ s. dicke Ende n.; Gewühl n.

thicken v.t. verdicken, verdichten; vermehren; ~ v.i. dick, trübe werden; sich verstärken.

thicket s. Dickicht n.

thickheaded a. strohdumm.

thickness s. Dicke, Dichtheit f.; Lage, Schicht f.

thick-set a. untersetzt, gedrungen.

thief s. Dieb m.; Räuber (am Licht) m.

thieve v.i. stehlen.

thievery s. Dieberei f.

thievish a., ~**ly** adv. diebisch.

thigh s. Schenkel m.; Lende f.

thimble s. Fingerhut m.

thin a., ~**ly** adv. dünn; mager, schwach; spärlich; ~ paper, Dünndruckpapier n.; ~ v.t. verdünnen; lichten.

thine pn. dein; der/die/das deinige.

thing s. Ding n., Sache f.; ~s pl. Sachen f.pl.

think v.t. & i.r. denken, nachdenken; meinen, to ~ over, überlegen.

thinker s. Denker(in) m.(f.)

thinking s. Denken n., Meinung f.

think-tank s. (fam.) Denkfabrik f.

thinner s. Verdünnungsmittel n.

thirdly adv. drittens.

third party s. (law) dritte Person f.; ~ **insurance** s. Haftpflichtversicherung f.

thirst s. Durst m.; Begierde f.; ~ v.i. dursten.

thirsty a., ~**ily** adv. durstig.

thirteen a. dreizehn.

thirteenth s. dreizehnt.

thirtieth a. dreißigst.

thirty a. dreißig.

this pn. dieser, diese, dies(es); ~ way!, hierher!

thistle s. Distel f.

thither adv. dorthin, dahin.

thong s. Riemen m.; Peitschenschnur f.

thorax s. Brustkasten m.

thorn s. Dorn m.

thorny a. dornig; heikel.

thorough a. gänzlich; gründlich; ~**ly** adv. durch und durch.

thoroughbred s. Vollblut n.; ~a. vollblütig (Pferd).

thoroughfare s. Durchgang m.; Verkehrsstraße f.

thorough-going a. gründlich.

thoroughness s. Gründlichkeit f.

those pn.pl. diejenigen, jene.

thou pn. du.

though c. obgleich, obschon, obwohl, doch; wenn auch; as ~, als wenn.

thought s. Gedanke m.; Meinung f.; Idee f.; Denken n.

thoughtful a., ~**ly** adv. gedankenvoll; nachdenklich; achtsam, rücksichtsvoll.

thoughtless a., ~**ly** adv. gedankenlos; nachlässig.

thought-provoking a. anregend.

thousand a. tausend; ~ s. Tausend n.

thousandfold a. & adv. tausendfach.

thrash v.t. dreschen; prügeln; ~ out, eingehend erörtern.

thrashing s. (fig.) Prügel m.

thread s. Faden, Zwirn m.; Schraubengang m., Gewinde n.; (Reifen) Profil n.; ~ v.t. einfädeln.

threadbare a. abgenutzt; abgedroschen; verschlissen.

threat s. Drohung f.

threaten v.t. drohen; ~ing letter, Drohbrief m.

three a. drei.

three-dimensional a. dreidimensional.

threefold a. dreifach.

threescore a. sechzig, Schock n.

thresh v.t. dreschen.

threshold s. (Tür)Schwelle f.

thrice adv. dreimal.

thrift s. Sparsamkeit f.

thriftshop s. Secondhandladen m.

thrifty a. sparsam, wirtschaftlich.

thrill v.t. faszinieren; begeistern; ~ v.i. beben; schauern; ~ a. Schauer m. Erregung f.

thriller s. Sensationsdrama n.; Schmöker m.

thrilling a. spannend; packend.

thrive v.i.st. wachsen; gedeihen.

thriving a., ~**ly** adv. blühend.

throat s. Schlund m.; Kehle f., Hals m.; to clear one's ~, sich räuspern.

throaty a. kehlig.

throb v.i. pochen, klopfen; ~ s. Klopfen, Schlagen n.

throes s.pl. Qualen f.pl.

thrombosis s. Thrombose f.

throne s. Thron m.

throng s. Gedränge n., Schar f.; ~ v.i. sich drängen.

throttle s. Drossel... ~ v.t. erdrosseln; (mech.) abdrosseln.

throttle-valve s. Drosselventil n.

through pr. & adv. durch, mittels; ~ carriage, Kurswagen m. (rail.); ~ **train** s. durchgehender Zug m.; ~ **traffic** s. Durchgangsverkehr m.; wet ~, durchnäßt.

throughout pr. & adv. ganz durch; durchaus, überall.

throughway s. Schnellstraße f.

throw v.t. & i.st. (hin-, um-) werfen; to ~ off, von sich werfen, entsagen; to ~ open, weit öffnen; to ~ out, verwerfen; to ~ over, aufgeben; to ~ up, in die Höhe werfen; aufgeben; ~ s. Schlag m.; Wurf m.

thrush s. Drossel f.

thrust v.t. & i.ir. stossen; schleudern; drücken, pressen; drängen; to ~ upon, aufdrängen; ~ s. Stoß, Stich, Angriff m.

thud s. dröhnender, dumpfer Schlag m.

thug s. Schläger m.

thumb s. Daumen m.; ~ v.t. durchblättern; per Anhalter fahren; under a person's ~, unter jemandes Gewalt.

thumbscrew s. Daumenschraube f.

thumbtack s. Reißnagel m.

thump s. Schlag, Stoß m.; ~ v.t. schlagen, stossen, puffen.

thumping a. (fam.) sehr groß, kolossal.

thunder s. Donner m.; ~ v.t. & i. donnern.

thunder-bolt s. Donnerkeil, Blitz m.

thunder-clap s. Donnerschlag m.

thunder-cloud s. Gewitterwolke f.

thunderous a. donnernd.

thunderstorm s. Gewitter n.

thunder-struck *a.* wie vom Donner entsetzt.
Thursday *s.* Donnerstag *m.*
thus *adv.* so, also, in solcher Weise.
thwart *v.a.* durchkreuzen; vereiteln.
thy *pn.* dein, deine.
thyme *s.* Thymian *m.*
thyroid gland *s.* Schilddrüse *f.*
thyself *pn.* du selbst, selbst; dich, dir.
tiara *s.* Tiara *f.*
Tibet *s.* Tibet *n.*
Tibetan *a.* tibetisch; *s.* Tibeter(in) *m.*(*f.*)
tibia *s.* Schienbein *n.*
tic *s.* nervöses Zucken *n.*; Tick *m.*
tick *s.* Zecke *f.*; Ticken *n.*; *on* ~, auf Pump; ~ *v.i.* ticken; ~ *off,* abhaken, markieren.
ticket *s.* Zettel *m.*; Billett *n.*, Fahrkarte *f.*; Los *n.*; Pfandschein *m.*; Wahlliste *f. n.*; *to take a* ~, ein Billett lösen; ~ *v.t.* einen Zettel anheften.
ticket-office *s.* Fahrkartenausgabe *f.*
tickle *v.t.* kitzeln.
ticklish *a.* kitzlig; heikel; verfänglich.
tidal *a.* Gezeiten. . ., Flut. . .; ~**wave** *s.* Flutwelle *f.*
tidbit *s.* Leckerbissen *m.*
tide *s.* Gezeiten *f.pl.*, Ebbe und Flut *f.*; Flut (*fig.*) *f.*; *the* ~ *turns,* das Blatt wendet sich; *the turning of the* ~, Umschwung *m.*; ~ *over, v.t.* hinwegkommen über, überbrücken.
tidiness *s.* Ordentlichkeit *f.*
tidings *s.pl.* (*lit.*) Kunde.
tidy *a.*, ~**ily** *adv.* ordentlich, niedlich, nett; ~ *v.t.* sauber machen, ordnen.
tie *v.t.* (an)binden, knüpfen; verpflichten; (*mus.*) (ver)binden; ~ *up,* zubinden; ~ *down* (*mil.*) (Kräfte) binden; ~ *s.* Knoten *m.*; Krawatte, Halsbinde *f.*; Schleife *f.*; (*mus.*) Bindung *f.*; (*Sport*) Gleichstand *m.*
tiepin *s.* Schlipsnadel, Krawattennadel *f.*
tier *s.* Reihe, Linie *f.*; Rang *m.*
tiff *s.* Zank *m.*
tiger *s.* Tiger *m.*
tight *a.*, ~**ly** *adv.* fest, dicht; knapp, eng, straff; genau; betrunken; ~ *corner,* Klemme *f.*; ~ *fitting,* eng anliegend; ~ *rope,* Drahtseil *n.*; ~ *ropewalker, s.* Seiltänzer(in) *m.*(*f.*)
tighten *v.t.* festziehen, schnüren; enger machen.
tights *s.pl.* Trikothose *pl.*; Trikot *n.*
tigress *s.* Tigerin *f.*
tile *s.* Ziegel *m.*; Kachel *f.*; Fliese *f.* ~ *v.t.* mit Ziegeln decken; kacheln.
till *pr. & c.* bis; ~ *v.t.* pflügen, ackern; ~ *s.* Ladenkasse *f.*
tillage *s.* Ackern *n.*; Ackerbau *m.*
tiller *s.* Pinne *f.* Ruder *n.*
tilt *s.* Turnier *n.*; Neigung; ~ *v.t.* stoßen, überschlagen; überdecken; ~ *v.i.* turnieren; kippen, umschlagen, schwanken.
timber *s.* Bauholz *n.*; Holz *n.*; Balken *m.*; ~ **line** *s.* Baumgrenze *f.*
timber-yard *s.* Holzlager *n.*
timbre *s.* Klangfarbe *f.*; Timbre *n.*
time *s.* Zeit *f.*; Zeitmaß *n.*; Mal, *n.*; Tempo *n.*, Takt *m.*; *at a* ~, zugleich; *at the same* ~, zugleich, gleichzeitig; *in* ~, rechtzeitig; über der Zeit; *in no* ~, im Handumdrehen; *behind* ~, verspätet; *what is the* ~?, wieviel Uhr ist es?; *to tell the* ~, sagen, wieviel Uhr es ist; *I am having a good* ~, es geht mir gut; ich

amüsiere mich; *I am having a bad* ~, es geht mir schlecht; *high* ~, hohe, höchste Zeit; *to beat* ~, den Takt schlagen; *full-*~ *job,* volle Stelle *f.* *half-*~ *job,* halbe Stelle; *f.* ~ *v.t.* abmessen; Zeit festsetzen für.
time-bomb *s.* Zeitbombe *f.*
time-consuming *a.* zeitraubend.
time-fuse *s.* Zeitzünder *m.*
time-keeper *s.* Uhr *f.*; Kontrolleur *m.*
time-limit *s.* Frist *f.*
timely *a. & adv.* (recht)zeitig.
time-signal *s.* Zeitzeichen *n.*
time-table *s.* Fahrplan *m.*; Stundenplan *m.*
time-worn *a.* abgenutzt.
timid *a.* schüchtern.
timidity *s.* Schüchternheit *f.*
timpani *s. pl.* Kesselpauke *f.*
tin *s.* Zinn *n.*; Weißblech *n.*; (Blech-) Büchse (zum Einmachen) *f.*; ~ *v.t.* verzinnen; in Büchsen einmachen.
tinder *s.* Zunder *m.*
tinfoil *s.* Stanniol *n.*; Alufolie *f.*
tinge *v.t.* färben; tönen; ~ *s.* Anstrich *m.*; Färbung *f.*
tingle *v.i.* kribbeln; prickeln.
tin-hat *s.* (*fam.*) Stahlhelm *m.*
tinker *s.* Kesselflicker *m.*; ~ *v.t.* flicken; pfuschen.
tinkle *v.i.* klingen.
tin-opener *s.* Büchsenöffner *m.*
tinplate *s.* Weißblech *n.*
tinsel *s.* Lametta *n.*
tint *s.* Farbe *f.*; (Farb-) Ton *m.*, Tönung *f.*; ~ *v.t.* färben; abtönen.
tiny *a.* winzig.
tip *s.* Spitze *f.*; leichte Berührung *f.*; Wink *m.*; Trinkgeld *n.*; ~ *v.t.* bespitzen; antupfen; kippen; Trinkgeld geben.
tipple *s.* alkoholisches Getränk *n.*; ~ *v.i.* zechen.
tipsy *a.* berauscht, benebelt.
tiptoe *s.* Zehenspitze *f.*; ~ *v.i.* auf den Zehenspitzen gehen.
tiptop *a.* ausgezeichnet.
tirade *s.* Wortschwall *m.*; Scheltrede *f.*
tire *s.* Reifen *m.*; ~**gauge** *s.* Reifendruckprüfer *m.*; ~ **pressure** *s.* Reifendruck *m.*; ~ *v.t. & i.* ermüden; müde werden.
tired *a.* müde; überdrüssig.
tiredness *s.* Müdigkeit *f.*
tireless *a.* unermüdlich.
tiresome *a.*, ~**ly** *adv.* ermüdend, langweilig.
tiring *a.* ermüdend; anstrengend.
tissue *s.* Gewebe *n.*; Papiertuch *n.*; Papiertaschentuch *n.*
tissue-paper *s.* Seidenpapier *n.*
tit *s.* (*fam.*) Brust *f.*; Brustwarze *f.*; Meise *f.*; ~ *for tat,* wie du mir, so ich dir.
titanic *a.* titanisch.
tithe *s.* Zehnte *m.*; ~ *v.t.* zehnten.
title *s.* Titel *m.*; Name *m.*; Anspruch *m.*, Recht *n.*; ~ *v.t.* benennen.
titled *a.* adelig.
title-deed *s.* Eigentumsurkunde *f.*
title-page *s.* Titelblatt *n.*
titmouse *s.* Meise *f.*
titter *v.i.* kichern; ~ *s.* Kichern *n.*
tittle *s.* Tüttelchen *n.*
tittle-tattle *s.* Geschwätz *n.*

titular *a.* Titular...

to *pr.* zu, nach, an, auf, mit, gegen, für, um, in Ansehung, bis, vor; ~ *adv.* zu; ~ *and fro*, hin und her.

toad *s.* Kröte *f.*

toad-stool *s.* Pilz *m.*; Giftpilz *m.*

toady *s.* Schmeichler(in) *m.(f.)*; Kriecher(in) *m.(f.)*; ~*v.i.* (vor jm.) kriechen.

toast *v.t.* rösten; toasten; trinken auf; ~ *s.* geröstete Brotschnitte *f.*; Trinkspruch *m.*

toaster *s.* Toaster *m.*

tobacco *s.* Tabak *m.*; ~-**pouch** Tabaksbeutel *m.*

tobacconist *s.* Tabakhändler *m.*

toboggan *s.* Rodelschlitten *m.*

today *adv.* heute.

toddle *v.i.* watscheln; herumschlendern.

toddler *s.* kleinkind *n.*

to-do *s.* Aufheben *n.*, Lärm *m.*

toe *s.* Zehe *f.*; Vorderhuf *m.*

together *adv.* zusammen; ~ *with*, samt.

togetherness *s.* Zusammengehörigkeit *f.*

toil *s.* schwere Arbeit, Mühseligkeit *f.*; ~ *v.i.* sich abarbeiten.

toilet *s.* Toilette *f.*; Putztisch *m.*; ~-**bag** *s.* Kulturbeutel *m.* ~ *paper* Toilettenpapier *n.*; ~ *requisites pl.* Toilettenartikel *pl.*; ~ *set,* Toilettengarnitur *f.*

toilsome *a.* mühselig, mühsam.

token *s.* Zeichen *n.*; Gutschein *m.*; Marke *f.*

tolerable *a.*, ~**bly** *adv.* leidlich; annehmbar.

tolerance *s.* Duldung *f.*; Toleranz *f.* (*mech.*) zulässige Abweichung *f.*

tolerant *a.* duldsam; tolerant.

tolerate *v.t.* ertragen, dulden.

toleration *s.* Duldung, Nachsicht *f.*

toll *s.* Zoll *m.*; Läuten *n.*; ~ *v.t.* läuten.

toll-bar *s.* Schlagbaum *m.*

toll-bridge *s.* gebührenpflichtige Brücke *f.*

toll-call *s.* gebührenpflichtiges Gespräch *n.*

tomato *s.* Tomate *f.*

tomb *s.* Grab, Grabmal *n.*; ~ *stone s.* Grabstein *m.*

tomboy *s.* Wildfang (Mädchen) *m.*

tom-cat *s.* Kater *m.*

tome *s.* Band *m.*, dickes Buch *n.*

tomfoolery *s.* Narretei *f.*

tommy-gun *s.* Maschinenpistole *f.*

tomorrow *adv.* morgen.

tomtit *s.* Meise *f.*

ton *s.* Tonne (Gewicht: 1016 kg.; Schiffsmaß: 40 Kubikfuß) *f.*

tone *s.* Ton, Klang, Laut *m.*; ~ *v.t.* abtönen.

tongs *pl.* Zange *f.*

tongue *s.* Zunge *f.*; ~ **in cheek**, scherzhaft, ~ **twister** *s.* Zungenbrecher *m.*

tonic *a.* tonisch; stärkend; ~ *s.* Stärkungsmittel *n.*; Tonikum *n.*

tonight *adv.* heute abend, heute nacht.

tonnage *s.* Tonnengehalt *m.*, Raumgehalt (Schiff) *m.*

tonsil *s.* Halsdrüse *f.*, Mandel *f.*

tonsillitis *s.* Mandelentzündung *f.*

tonsure *s.* Tonsur *f.*

too *adv.* zu, allzu; gleichfalls, auch.

tool *s.* Werkzeug, Gerät *n.*

toot *v.t. & i.* blasen, tuten.

tooth *s.* Zahn *m.*

tooth-ache *s.* Zahnweh *n.*

toothbrush *s.* Zahnbürste *f.*

tooth-filling *s.* Zahnfüllung *f.*

toothless *a.* zahnlos.

toothpaste *s.* Zahnpaste *f.*

tooth-pick *s.* Zahnstocher *m.*

top *s.* Gipfel, Wipfel *m.*; Spitze *f.*; Kreisel *m.*; Haupt *n.*; Obere *n.*; höchster Rang *m.*; ~ *a.* oberst, Haupt...; *from* ~ *to toe*, vom Scheitel bis zur Sohle; ~ *coat s.* (*Am.*) Überzieher *m.*; ~ *floor*, oberster Stockwerk *n.*; ~ *righthand corner*, obere rechte Ecke; ~ *secret a.* ganz geheim, *s.* (*mil.*) geheime Kommandosache; ~ *speed*, Höchstgeschwindigkeit *f.*; ~ *v.i.* sich erheben, hervorstechen; ~ *v.t.* übertreffen.

topaz *s.* Topas *m.*

top-gallant *s.* Bramsegel *n.*

top-hat *s.* Zylinderhut *m.*

top-heavy *a.* oberlastig.

topic *s.* Gegenstand *m.*, Thema *n.*

topical *a.*, ~**ly** *adv.* aktuell; örtlich, lokal.

topicality *s.* Aktualität *f.*

topless *a.* ohne Oberteil.

topmast *s.* Topmast *m.*

topmost *a.* oberst, höchst.

top-notch *a.* hervorragend; phantastisch.

topography *s.* Ortsbeschreibung *f.*

topping *s.* Glasur *f.*; Guß *m.*

topple *v.i.* vorwärts fallen, hinstürzen; ~*v.t.* fällen, umstürzen.

topsail *s.* Marssegel *n.*

topsy-turvy *adv.* das unterste zu oberst.

torch *s.* Fackel *f.*; ~-**light procession,** Fackelzug *m.*

torment *v.t.* peinigen, martern; quälen; ~ *s.* Qual, Marter *f.*

tormentor *s.* Peiniger *m.*

tornado *s.* Wirbelsturm *m.*

torpedo *s.* Torpedo *m.*; ~ *boat s.* Torpedoboot *n.*; ~(*boat*) *destroyer s.* Torpedo(boot)zerstörer *m.*; ~ *tube s.* Lanzierrohr *n.*

torpid *a.* starr; träge.

torpor *s.* Erstarrung *f.*; Trägheit *f.*

torrent *s.* Gießbach *m.*; (*fig.*) Strom *m.*

torrential *a.* strömend; reißend.

torrid *a.* (*also fig.*) brennend heiß, sengend.

torsion *s.* Drehung, Windung *f.*

tortoise *s.* Schildkröte *f.*

tortoise-shell *s.* Schildpatt *n.*

tortuous *a.* gewunden; verschlungen; kompliziert.

torture *s.* Folter *f.*; Marter *f.*; ~ *v.t.* foltern, martern.

torture-chamber *s.* Folterkammer *f.*

Tory *s.* Tory, englischer Konservative *m.*

toss *v.t.* schleudern; losen; hochwerfen. ~ *s.* Wurf *m.*; Aufwerfen *n.* (einer Münze), Losen *n.*

toss-up *s.* Hochwerfen einer Münze.

tot *s.* kleines Kind *n.*; Schlückchen, Gläschen *n.*

tot ~ *up, v.t.* (*fam.*) zusammenziehen; ~*v.i.* sich summieren.

total *a.*, ~**ly** *adv.* ganz, gänzlich; ~ *s.* Gesamtsumme *f.*, Gesamtbetrag *m.*; ~ *v.i.* sich belaufen auf; ~ *eclipse, s.* totale Finsternis *f.* ~ *loss,* Totalausfall *m.*; ~ *war,* totaler Krieg *m.*

totalitarian *a.* totalitär.

totality *s.* Ganze *n.*, Vollständigkeit *f.*

tote *v.t.* schleppen.

totem-pole *s.* Totempfahl *m.*

totter *v.i.* wanken, wackeln.

touch *v.t.* (be)fühlen; betreffen; anstossen, rühren, berühren; *to ~ up*, auffrischen, restaurieren; *~ v.i.* sich berühren; sich beziehen auf; *~ wood!* unberufen!; *~ s.* Berührung *f.*; Gefühl *n.*; Anflug, Anstrich *m.*; (*mus.*) Anschlag *m.*; *to get in ~ with*, sich in Verbindung setzen mit.
touch-and-go, unsicher, gewagt.
touched *a.* gerührt.
touching *a.* rührend, treffend; *~ pr.* betreffend, in betreff.
touch-line *s.* Seitenlinie *f.*
touch-stone *s.* Prüfstein *m.*
touch-type *v.i.* blindschreiben.
touchy *a.* empfindlich, reizbar.
tough *a.*, **~ly** *adv.* zäh; hart; fest; schwer.
toughen *v.t.* zäh machen; abhärten. *~ v.i.* zäh werden.
toughness *s.* Festigkeit *f.*; Zähigkeit *f.*
tour *s.* (Rund-)Reise *f.*; Ausflug *m.*; *~ v.t. & i.* (be)reisen.
tourism *s.* Tourismus *m.*
tourist *s.* Tourist(in) *m.* (*f.*); *~ agent*, Reiseagent *m.*; *~traffic*, Fremdenverkehr *m.*
tournament *s.* Turnier *m.*
tour operator *s.* Reiseveranstalter(in) *m.*(*f.*)
tousled *a.* zerzaust.
tout *v.i.* Kunden locken; *~ s.* Schlepper(in) *m.*(*f.*); Kundenwerber(in) *m.*(*f.*)
tow *s.* Werg *n.*; Schlepptau *n.*; *~ v.t.* schleppen; *~ away v.i.* abschleppen.
toward, towards *pr.* gegen, zu, bis an, entgegen; auf. . .zu.
towel *s.* Handtuch *n.*; *~ horse*, Handtuchständer *m.*; *face-~*, Gesichtshandtuch *n.*; *roller ~*, Rollhandtuch *n.*; *to ~ oneself*, *v.t.* sich mit dem Handtuch abreiben.
tower *s.* Turm *m.*; Zwinger *m.*; Festung *f.*; *~ v.i.* hoch ragen, sich erheben.
towering *s.* hoch aufragend.
towing-boat *s.* Schleppboot *n.*
town *s.* Ort *m.*; (Klein)Stadt *f.*
town-hall *s.* Rathaus *n.*
town-planning *s.* Städtebau *m.*
township *s.* Stadt-, Ortsgemeinde *f.*
townsman *s.* Städter, Bürger *m.*
tow-path *s.* Leinpfad *m.*
towrope *s.* Abschleppseil *n.*
toxic *a.* giftig; toxisch.
toy *s.* Spielzeug *n.*; *~ v.i.* spielen (Essen; Gedanken).
trace *s.* Spur, Fußtapfe *f.*; Strang *m.*, Zugseil *n.*; *~ v.t.* nachspüren; zeichnen, entwerfen; abstecken; durchpausen.
traceable *a.* auffindbar.
trace element *s.* Spurenelement *n.*
tracer-bullet *s.* Leuchtspurgeschoß *n.*
trachea *s.* Luftröhre *f.*
tracing *s.* Durchpausen *n.*; Pauszeichnung *n.*; Aufriß *m.*; **~-paper** *s.* Pauspapier *n.*
track *s.* Spur *f.*; Fährte *f.*; Geleise *f.*; Pfad *f.*; (Panzer)Kette *f.*; Bahn *f.* (Rennen); *~ed vehicles*, pl. Raupenfahrzeuge *pl.*; *to be on the wrong ~*, auf der falschen Fährte sein; *~ v.t.* der Spur folgen; *to ~ down*, aufspüren.
track events *s.pl.* Laufdisziplinen (Sport).
trackless *a.* spurlos, pfadlos.
track record *s.* Bahnrekord *m.*

track shoe *s.* Rennschuh *m.*
tract *s.* Gebiet *n.*; Trakt *m.*; Traktat *m.*, Flugschrift *f.*
traction *s.* Ziehen *n.*; Zug *m.*; *~ engine*, Zugmaschine *f.*
tractor *s.* Traktor *m.*
trade *s.* Handel *m.*; Gewerbe, Geschäft *n.*; *~ v.i.* Handel treiben; austauschen; *foreign ~*, Außenhandel *m.*; *~ name*, Firmenname *m.*; *~ price*, Engrospreis *m.*; *~ school*, Gewerbeschule *f.*
trade-mark *s.* Warenzeichen *n.*
trader *s.* Händler(in) *m.*(*f.*)
tradesman *s.* Einzelhändler(in) *m.*(*f.*); *~'s entrance* Lieferanteneingang *m.*
trade(s)-union *s.* Gewerkschaft *f.*
trade-unionist *s.* Gewerkschaftler(in) *m.*(*f.*)
trade-wind *s.* Passatwind *m.*
trading *s.* Handel *m.*
trading estate *s.* Gewerbegebiet *n.*
tradition *s.* Tradition *f.*; Überlieferung *f.*; Brauch *m.*
traditional *a.* **~ly** *adv.* traditionell; überleifert; herkömmlich.
traffic *s.* Handel *m.*; Verkehr *m.*; *goods ~*, Güterverkehr *m.*; *passenger ~*, Personenverkehr *m.*; *~circle*, Kreisverkehr *m.* *~ code*, Verkehrsregeln *pl.*; *~ jam*, Verkehrsstockung *f.*; *~ light*, Verkehrsampel *f.*; *~ regulation*, Verkehrsregelung *f.*; *~ sign*, Verkehrszeichen *n.*; *~ v.i.* Handel treiben.
tragedy *s.* Trauerspiel *n.*, Tragödie *f.*
tragic *a.*, **~ally** *adv.* tragisch.
tragicomedy *s.* Tragikomödie *f.*
trail *s.* Spur, Fährte *f.*; Pfad *m.*; *~ v.t.* nachspüren; nachschleppen; *~ v.i.* sich in die Länge ziehen.
trailer *s.* (*mot.*) Anhängewagen *m.*
train *s.* Schweif *m.*; Schleppe *f.*; Reihe *f.*; Gefolge *n.*; (*rail.*) Zug *m.*; *~ v.t.* ziehen, schleppen; abrichten; ausbilden, trainieren; (Geschütz) richten; *~ v.i.* sich trainieren.
train-driver *s.* Lokomotivführer(in) *m.*(*f.*)
trained *a.* ausgebildet; geschult; trainiert.
trainee *s.* Auszubildende *m.*/*f.*; Lehrling *m.*
trainer *s.* Trainer(in) *m.*(*f.*); Behandler(in) *m.*(*f.*)
train fare *s.* Fahrpreis *m.*
training *s.* Ausbildung *s.*; Training *n.*; *to be in ~*, trainieren; in Formsein; *to be under ~*, ausgebildet werden; **~-center** *s.* Ausbildungsstelle *f.*; **~-college** *s.* Lehrerseminar *n.*; **~-ship** *s.* Schulschiff *n.*
train-oil *s.* Fischtran *m.*
train service *s.* Zugverbindung *f.*
train station *s.* Bahnhof *m.*
trait *s.* Zug, *m.*; Eigenschaft *f.*
traitor *s.* Verräter(in) *m.*(*f.*)
traitorous *a.*, **~ly** *adv.* verräterisch.
trajectory *s.* Flugbahn *f.*
tram *s.* Strassenbahn *f.*
tramp *s.* Landstreicher(in) *m.*(*f.*); *~ v.i. & t.* umherstreifen; trampeln.
trample *v.i. & t.* trampeln; *to ~ upon*, mit Füßen treten (*fig.*).
trampoline *s.* Trampolin *n.*
tramway *s.* Straßenbahn *f.*
trance *s.* Trancezustand *m.*
tranquil *a.* ruhig, gelassen.
tranquility *s.* Ruhe *f.*
tranquilize *v.t.* beruhigen; (*med.*) betäuben.

transact *v.t.* abmachen; verrichten (Geschäft).

transaction *s.* Geschäft *n.*; Verhandlung *f.*

transalpine *a.* jenseits der Alpen.

transatlantic *a.* transatlantisch.

transcend *v.t.* übersteigen; übertreffen; transzendieren.

transcendental *a.* transzendental.

transcontinental *a.* transkontinental.

transcribe *v.t.* abschreiben; übertragen.

transcript *s.* Abschrift *f.*; Umschrift *f.*; (*law*) Protokoll *n.*

transept *s.* (Kirche) Kreuzflügel *m.*; Querschiff *n.*

transfer *v.t.* übertragen; versetzen, verlegen; (Geld) überweisen; ~ *s.* Übertragung *f.*; Überweisung *f.*; Verlegung, Versetzung *f.*; *disciplinary* ~, Strafversetzung *f.*; **~-paper** *s.* Umdruckpapier *n.*

transferable *a.* übertragbar.

transference *s.* Übertragung *f.*

transfiguration *s.* Verklärung *f.*

transfigure *v.i.* verwandeln; verklären.

transfix *v.t.* durchbohren.

transform *v.t.* umgestalten, verwandeln.

transformation *s.* Verwandlung *f.*

transformer *s.* (*elek.*) Transformator *m.*; **~-station**, Transformatorenhaus *n.*

transfusion *s.* Transfusion *f.*; Übertragung *f.*

transgress *v.t.* überschreiten, verletzen.

transgression *s.* Überschreitung *f.*; Vergehen *n.*

transgressor *s.* Übertreter(in) *m.(f.)*

transient *a.*, **~ly** *adv.* vergänglich; vorübergehend.

transit *s.* Durchgang *m.*; (*mil.*) Durchmarsch *m.*; *in* ~, unterwegs, auf dem Transport; ~ *duty*, Durchgangszoll *m.*; ~ *trade*, Durchgangshandel *m.*; ~ *traffic*, Durchgangsverkehr *m.*

transition *s.* Übergang *m.*

transitional *a.* Übergangs...

transitive *a.*, **~ly** *adv.* (*gram.*) transitiv.

transitory *a.*, **~ily** *adv.* vorübergehend, vergänglich; flüchtig.

translate *v.t.* übersetzen; versetzen.

translation *s.* Übersetzung *f.*

translator *s.* Übersetzer(in) *m.(f.)*

translucent *a.* durchscheinend.

transmigration *s.* ~ *of souls*, Seelenwanderung *f.*

transmissible *a.* übertragbar; vererblich.

transmission *s.* Übertragung *f.*; Übersendung *f.*; (*phys.*) Fortpflanzung; (*mech.*) Transmission.

transmit *v.t.* übersenden, übertragen; (*phys.*) leiten; vererben.

transmitter *s.* (*tel.*, *radio*) Sender *m.*

transmutation *s.* Verwandlung *f.*, Umwandlung *f.*

transmute *v.t.* umwandeln.

transparency *s.* Durchsichtigkeit *f.*

transparent *a.*, **~ly** *adv.* durchsichtig.

transpire *v.t.* ausdünsten; ~ *v.i.* schwitzen; verlauten passieren

transplant *v.t.* verpflanzen; (*med.*) transplantieren; ~*s.* Transplantat *n.*

transplantation *s.* Verpflanzung *f.*; (*med.*) Transplantation *f.*

transport *v.t.* befördern, transportieren; hinreissen, entzücken; ~ *s.* Versendung, Beförderung *f.*, Transportschiff *n.*; Transport *m.*; Entzückung *f.*; *charges pl.* Speditionskosten *pl*; ~ *plane*, Transportflugzeug *n.*; *Minister of* ~, Verkehrsminister *m.*

transportation *s.* Fortschaffung *f.*; Deportierung *f.*;

Transport *m.*, Transportmittel *n.*

transpose *v.t.* umstellen.

transposition *s.* Umstellung *f.*

tranship *v.t.* umladen.

transhipment *s.* Umladung *f.*, Umschlag *m.*; **~-harbor**, Umschlagshafen *m.*

transubstantiation *s.* Wesensverwandlung *f.*; (*eccl.*) Transsubstantiation *f.*

transverse *a.*, **~ly** *adv.* schräg, quer.

transvestite *s.* Transvestit *m.*

trap *s.* Falle *f.*; Klappe *f.*; ~ *v.t.* ertappen; **~ped** *p.* eingeklemmt.

trap-door *s.* Falltür *f.*

trapeze *s.* Trapez *n.*; ~ *artist* *s.* Trapezkünstler(in) *m.(f.)*

trapper *s.* Fallensteller *m.*

trappings *s.pl.* Schmuck *m.*

trash *s.* Plunder, Abfall *m.*; (*fig.*) Blech *n.*, Unsinn *m.*; Schund *m.* Kitsch *m.*

trashcan *s.* Mülltonne *f.*

trashy *a.* Schund. ..; minderwertig.

trauma *s.* Trauma *n.*; Shock *m.*

travel *v.i.* reisen; sich bewegen; ~ *v.t.* bereisen; ~ *s.* Reise *f.*; *away on* ~, verreist; ~ *agency*, Reiseagentur *f.*; ~ *goods pl.* Reiseartikel *pl.*; ~ *order* (*mil.*) Fahrtbefehl *m.*, Fahrtausweis *m.*

traveler *s.* Reisende, Geschäftsreisende *m.*; **~s'** *check*, Reisescheck *m.*

traveling bag, Reisetasche *f.*

travelog *s.* Reisebericht *m.*

travel-sickness *s.* Reisekrankheit *f.*

traverse *s.* Querholz *n.*; (*mech.*) Querstück *n.*, Querträger *m.*, Traverse *f.*; (*fig.*) Querstrich *m.*; Quergang *m.*; ~ *v.t.* durchkreuzen; durchwandern; durchforschen; (durch)queren; ~*a. & adv.* quer.

travesty *s.* Travestie *f.*; ~ *v.t.* travestieren.

trawl *v.t.* mit einem Schleppnetz fischen.

trawler *s.* Fischtrawler *m.*

tray *s.* Tablett *n.*; Ablagekorb *m.*; *ash-~* Aschenbecher *m.*

treacherous *a.*, **~ly** *adv.* verräterisch, heimtückisch.

treachery *s.* Heimtücke *f.*, Verrat *m.*

treacle *s.* Sirup *m.*

tread *v.i. & i.st.* (be)treten; ~ *s.* Schritt, Tritt *m.*; Lauffläche, (Reifen)Profil *n.*

treadle *s.* Trittbrett *n.*

treadmill *s.* Tretmühle *f.*

treason *s.* Verrat *m.*; *high* ~, *capital* ~, Hochverrat *m.*

treasonable *a.*, **~bly** *adv.* verräterisch.

treasure *s.* Schatz *m.*; ~ *v.t.* aufhäufen; wertschätzen.

treasurer *s.* Schatzmeister(in) *m.(f.)*; Leiter(in) der Finanzabteilung.

treasury *s.* Schatzkammer *f.*; Schatzamt *n.*; ~ *bill* *s.* Schatzwechsel *m.*; ~ *bond,* ~ *certificate,* Schatzanweisung *f.*

treat *v.t. & i.* handeln, behandeln; unterhandeln; freihalten; ~ *s.* Vergnügen *n.*; Leckerbissen *m.*; Schmaus *m.*; Genuss *m.*

treatise *s.* Abhandlung *f.*

treatment *s.* Behandlung *f.*

treaty *s.* Vertrag *m.*

treble *a.* dreifach; ~ *s.* Sopranstimme *f.*; Diskant *m.*; ~ *v.t.* verdreifachen; ~ *clef* *s.* Violinschlüssel *m.*

tree *s.* Baum *m.*

tree: ~-**lined** *a.* von Bäumen gesäumt; ~- **top** *s.* Baumwipfel *m.*; ~-**trunk** *s.* Baumstamm *m.*

trefoil *s.* Klee *m.*

trellis *s.* Gitter *n.*; Spalier *n.*

tremble *v.i.* zittern; ~ *s.* Zittern *n.*

trembling *a.* zitternd; ~ *s.* Zittern *n.*

tremendous *a.*, ~**ly** *adv.* schrecklich, furchtbar; ungeheuer groß.

tremor *s.* Zittern, Beben *n.*

tremulous *a.* zitternd; flackernd.

trench *s.* (Schützen-) Graben *m.*; ~-**coat**, Wettermantel *m.*

trenchant *a.* schneidend, scharf; deutlich.

trend *v.i.* verlaufen; sich entwickeln; ~ *s.* Richtung *f.*; Trend *m.*; Tendenz *f.*

trendy *a.* modisch.

trepidation *s.* Beklommenheit *f.*

trespass *v.i.* übertreten, sich vergehen; unbefugt betreten; ~ *s.* Übertretung *f.*; Eingriff *m.*; unbefugtes Betreten *n.*

tress *s.* Haarlocke *f.*

trestle *s.* Bockgestell *n.*

trial *s.* Prozeß *m.*, Gerichtsverhandlung *f.*; Versuch *m.*, Probe *f.*, Prüfung *f.*; ~ *by jury*, Schwurgerichtsverhandlung *f.*; ~ *in absentia*, Verhandlung in Abwesenheit des Angeklagten; *to be on ~, to stand ~ for*, unter Anklage stehen; *to bring to ~*, vor Gericht stellen; ~ *run*, Probefahrt (Auto) *f.*

triangle *s.* Dreieck *n.*; Triangel *f.*

triangular *a.*, ~**ly** *adv.* dreieckig.

tribal *a.* Stammes...

tribe *s.* Stamm *m.*; Sippe *f.*

tribesman *s.* Stammesangehörige *m.*

tribeswoman *s.* Stammesangehörige *f.*

tribulation *s.* Trübsal *f.*

tribunal *s.* Tribunal *n.*, Gerichtshof *m.*

tributary *s.* Nebenfluß *m.*

tribute *s.* Tribut *m.*

trice *s.* Augenblick *m.*, Nu *m.* or *n.*

trick *s.* Trick *m.*; Kniff *m.*; Streich, Betrug *m.*; Eigentümlichkeit *f.*; Kartenstich *m.*; *to play a person a ~*, einem einen Streich spielen; ~ *v.t.* betrügen, anführen.

trickery *s.* Betrügerei, List *f.*

trickle *v.i.* tröpfeln; ~ *s.* Getröpfel *n.*

trickster *s.* Betrüger(in) *m.(f.)*

tricky *a.* verzwickt; heikel.

tricolor *s.* Trikolore *f.*

tricycle *s.* Dreirad *n.*

trident *s.* Dreizack *m.*

tried *a.* erprobt.

triennial *a.*, ~**ly** *adv.* dreijährlich.

trifle *s.* Kleinigkeit, Lappalie *f.*; Biskuit (*n.*) mit Kompott; ~ *v.i.* tändeln, spielen, scherzen.

trifling *a.*, ~**ly** *adv.* geringfügig; unbedeutend.

trigger *s.* Drücker *m.* (am Gewehr).

trigonometry *s.* Trigonometrie *f.*

trike *s.* Dreirad *n.*

trilateral *a.* dreiseitig.

trill *s.* Triller *m.*; ~ *v.t.* trillern.

trillion *s.* (*US*) Billion *f.*; (*Brit.*) Trillion *f.*

trilogy *s.* Trilogie *f.*

trim *a.*, ~**ly** *adv.* in Ordnung; geputzt; niedlich; ~ *s.* Putz, Besatz *m.*; Ausrüstung *f.*; ~ *v.t.* putzen; schneiden; stutzen; einfassen; (*nav.*) trimmen.

trimming *s.* Besatz *m.*; Verzierung *f.*; Beilagen *pl.*

Trinity *s.* Dreieinigkeit *f.*

trinket *s.* billiges Schmuckstück *n.*

trio *s.* Trio *n.*; Terzett *n.*

trip *v.i.* trippeln; stolpern; straucheln, fehlen; ~ *v.t. to ~ up*, ein Bein stellen, erwischen; ~ *s.* Fehltritt *m.*; Ausflug *m.*; Reise *f.*

tripartite *a.* dreiteilig, Dreimächte...; ~ *commission*, Dreierkommission *f.*; ~ *pact*, Dreierpakt *m.*

tripe *s.* Kaldaunen (Nahrung) *pl.*; Eingeweide *pl.*, Quatsch *m.*

triple *a.* dreifach; ~ *v.t.* verdreifachen.

triplet *s.* Drilling *m.*

triplicate *a.* dreifach; in dreifacher Ausführung; ~ *s.* Triplikat *n.*; *in ~*, in dreifacher Ausführung.

tripod *s.* Dreifuß *m.*; dreifüßiger Ständer *m.*

tripping *a.* leicht(füßig); munter; strauchelnd.

triptych *s.* Triptychon *n.*

tripwire *s.* Stolperdraht *m.*

trisyllable *s.* dreisilbiges Wort *n.*

trite *a.*, ~**ly** *adv.* abgedroschen; banal.

triumph *s.* Triumph, Sieg *m.*; ~ *v.i.* triumphieren; siegen.

triumphant *a.*, ~**ly** *adv.* triumphierend.

trivia *s.pl.* Bagatellen *pl.*, Belanglosigkeiten *f.pl.*

trivial *a.*, ~**ly** *adv.* alltäglich, platt; trivial.

triviality *s.* Plattheit *f.*, Trivialität *f.*

trivialize *v.t.* trivialisieren.

trolley *s.* Straßenbahn *f.*; Förderkarren *m.*; Handwagen *m.*; ~-**bus**, elektrischer Omnibus *m.*

trollop *s.* Schlampe, Dirne *f.*

trombone *s.* Posaune *f.*

troop *s.* Haufen *m.*, Schar *f.*; Trupp *m.*; ~**s** *pl.* Truppen *f.pl.*; ~ *carrier* *s.* Truppentransporter *m.*; ~ *ship* *s.* Truppentransportschiff *n.*; ~ *training ground*, Truppenübungsplatz *m.*; ~ *v.i.* sich scharen, in Scharen ziehen.

trope *s.* bildlicher Ausdruck, Tropus *m.*

trophy *s.* Siegeszeichen *n*; Trophäe *f.*

tropic *s.* Wendekreis *m.*; ~*s*, Tropen *f.pl.*

tropical *a.*, ~**ly** *adv.* tropisch; bildlich.

trot *v.i.* traben; ~ *s.* Trab, Trott *m.*

troth *s.* Treuegelöbnis *n.*

trotter *s.* Traber *m.*; Fuß (*m.*) eines Tieres.

trouble *v.t.* trüben, stören; beunruhigen; bemühen; quälen; ~ *v.i.* sich kümmern, sich Sorgen machen um; ~ *s.* Unruhe, Sorge *f.*; Kummer, Verdruß *m.*; Ärger *m.*

troubled *a.* besorgt; unruhig; bewegt.

trouble: ~-**free** *a.* problemlos; ~-**maker** *s.* Unruhestifter(in) *m.(f.)*; ~-**shooter** *s.* Vermittler(in) *m.(f.)*

troublesome *a.*, ~**ly** *adv.* beschwerlich.

trouble-spot *s.* Unruheherd *m.*; Schwachstelle *f.*

trough *s.* Trog *m.*; Wellental *n.*; Tief *n.*

trounce *v.t.* haushoch besiegen.

troupe *s.* (Theater) Truppe *f.*

trousers *pl.* Hosen *pl.*

trousseau *s.* Aussteuer *f.*

trout *s.* Forelle *f.*

trowel *s.* Kelle *f.*

troy-weight *s.* Gold- und Silbergewicht *n.*

truant *a.* müßig, träge; ~ *s.* Schulschwänzer(in) *m.(f.)*; Faulenzer(in) *m.(f.)*

truce *s.* Waffenstillstand *m.*

truck *s.* (*rail.*) Güterwagen *m.*; Lastwagen *m.*

truculent *a.* aufsässig; trotzig.

trudge *v.i.* stapfen; trotten.

true *a.* wahr; echt; treu, aufrichtig, redlich; richtig.

truffle *s.* Trüffel *f.*

truism *s.* Gemeinplatz *m.*

truly *adv.* wirklich, wahrhaftig; aufrichtig; *yours ~,* Ihr ergebener.

trump *s.* Trumpf *m.;* ~ *v.t.* trumpfen; *to ~ up,* erdichten.

trumpet *s.* Trompete *f.;* ~ *v.t.* ausposaunen.

trumpeter *s.* Trompeter(in) *m.(f.)*

truncate *v.t.* stutzen; kürzen.

truncheon *s.* Schlagstock *m.*

trundle *v.t. & i.* rollen, (sich) wälzen; ~ *s.* Rolle, Walze *f.*

trunk *s.* Stamm *m.;* Stumpf *m.;* Rumpf *m.;* Rüssel *m.;* Schrankkoffer *m.;* Kofferraum *m.*

truss *v.t.* fesseln; aufbinden; ~ *s.* Band, Bruchband *n.*

trust *s.* Vertrauen *n.;* Kredit *m.;* Obhut, Treuhand *f.;* anvertrautes Gut *n.;* Trust *m.; in ~,* zu treuen Händen; *on ~,* auf Treu und Glauben; *to take on ~,* auf Treu und Glauben hinnehmen; *breach of ~,* Vertrauensbruch *m.; position of ~,* Vertrauensstellung *f.;* **~-company,** Treuhandgesellschaft *f.;* ~ *v.i. & t.* (ver)trauen, sich verlassen; anvertrauen.

trustee *s.* Treuhänder(in) *m.(f.);* Kurator(in) *m.(f.)*

trustful *a.* vertrauensvoll.

trustworthy *a.* vertrauenswürdig.

trusty *a.* treu, zuverlässig.

truth *s.* Wahrheit *f.;* Wirklichkeit *f.;* Wahrhaftigkeit, Redlichkeit, Treue *f.*

truthful *a.* wahrhaftig.

try *v.t.* versuchen, sich bemühen; untersuchen, probieren, prüfen, verhören; *(law)* Prozeß verhandeln; *to ~ on,* anprobieren.

trying *a.* schwierig; mißlich.

try-out *s.* Erprobung *f.*

tub *s.* Faß *n.;* Zuber *m.;* Kübel *m.;* Badewanne *f.*

tuba *s.* Tuba *f.*

tubby *a.* rundlich; pummelig.

tube *s.* Rohr *n.,* Röhre *f.;* Schlauch (Fahrrad) *m.;* *(fam.)* die Röhre *f.* (TV).

tuber *s.* Knolle *f.*

tubercle *s.* Knötchen *n.;* Tuberkel *f.*

tuberculosis *s.* Tuberkulose *f.*

tubing *s.* Röhrenmaterial *n.;* Rohre *n. pl.*

tubular *a.* röhrenförmig.

tuck *s.* Falte *f.;* Biese *f.;* Umschlag (am Kleid) *m.;* ~ *v.t.* stecken einschlagen, einwickeln.

Tuesday *s.* Dienstag *m.*

tufa, tuff *s.* Tuffstein *m.*

tuft *s.* Büschel *m.* or *n.;* Quaste *f.;* ~ *v.t.* bequasten.

tug *v.t. & i.* ziehen, zerren; ~ *s.* Ziehen, Zerren *n.;* Schlepper *m.; seagoing ~,* Hochseeschlepper *m.; ~ of war,* Tauziehen *n.*

tuition *s.* Schulgeld *n.;* Unterricht *m.;* Erziehung *f.*

tulip *s.* Tulpe *f.*

tulle *s.* Tüll *m.*

tumble *v.i.* umfallen, stürzen; sich wälzen; ~ *v.t.* werfen, umwenden; zerknittern; ~ *s.* Fall, Sturz *m.*

tumble-down *a.* baufällig.

tumble-dry *v.t.* im Automaten trocknen.

tumbler *s.* Trinkglas *n.*

tumid *a.* geschwollen.

tummy *s.* *(fam.)* Bauch *m.;* Bäuchlein *n.*

tumor *s.* Geschwulst *f.;* Tumor *m.*

tumult *s.* Getümmel *n.;* Aufruhr *m.*

tumultuous *a.,* **~ly** *adv.* lärmend, aufrührerisch.

tun *s.* Tonne *f.;* Faß *n.*

tuna *s.* Thunfisch *m.*

tune *s.* Ton *m.;* Melodie *f.;* Tonstück *n.;* Stimmung *f.; out of ~,* verstimmt; ~ *v.t.* stimmen; *(radio)* einstellen; *tuning dial s.* *(radio)* Einstellscheibe *f.*

tuneful *a.* wohlklingend; melodisch.

tuneless *a.* unmelodisch.

tuner *s.* (Klavier-), Stimmer(in) *m.(f.)*

tungsten *s.* Wolfram *n.*

tunic *s.* Tunika *f.;* Waffenrock *m.*

tuning-fork *s.* Stimmgabel *f.*

tunnel *s.* Tunnel *m.*

turban *s.* Turban *m.*

turbid *a.,* **~ly** *adv.* trübe, dick.

turbine *s.* Kreiselrad *n.,* Turbine *f.*

turbot *s.* Steinbutt *m.*

turbulence *s.* Ungestüm *n.;* Aufruhr *m.;* Verwirrung *f.*

turbulent *a.,* **~ly** *adv.* aufrührerisch; stürmisch.

tureen *s.* Suppenschüssel *f.;* Terrine *f.*

turf *s.* Rasen *m.;* Rennbahn *f.;* Pferderennen *n.*

turgid *a.* geschwollen, gedunsen; schwülstig.

Turk *s.* Türke *m.;* Türkin *f.*

Turkey *s.* Türkei *f.*

turkey *s.* Truthahn *m.,* Truthenne *f.;* Puter *m.,* Putl *f.*

Turkish *a.* türkisch.

Turkish bath *s.* türkisches Bad, Schwitzbad *n.*

turmeric *s.* Kurkuma *f.*

turmoil *s.* Unruhe *f.;* Aufruhr *m.*

turn *v.t.* drehen, (um)wenden; drechseln; umlegen; ~ *v.i.* sich (um)drehen; sich verwandeln; werden; umschlagen, verderben; *to ~ down,* zurückweisen, ablehnen; (Gas) kleindrehen; *to ~ in,* abgeben; *to ~ off,* ablenken; abdrehen, ausdrehen; *to ~ on,* andrehen; *to ~ out,* ausfallen, sich erweisen; hinaustreiben; antreten; (Waren) herstellen; *to ~ over,* übertragen, (um)wenden, durchblättern; übergeben, überstellen; umsetzen (Waren); *please ~ over* (PTO), bitte wenden!; *to ~ round,* sich herumdrehen; *to ~ up,* aufschlagen; auftauchen, erscheinen; ~ *s.* Umdrehung, Schwenkung *f.;* Änderung *f.;* Wechsel *m.;* Streich *m.;* Neigung *f.;* Gestalt, Beschaffenheit *f.; a good ~,* eine Gefälligkeit *f.; it is your ~,* Sie sind an der Reihe; *by ~s,* wechselweise, abwechselnd.

turncoat *s.* Überläufer *m.*

turn-down, ~ collar *s.* (Klapp-) Umlegekragen *m.*

turner *s.* Drechsler *m.;* Eisendreher *m.*

turning *s.* Drechseln, Drehen *n.;* Wendung *f.;* Krümmung *f.;* Querstraße *f.*

turning-point *s.* Wendepunkt *m.*

turnip *s.* (Weiße) Rübe *f.*

turn-out *s.* Gesamtertrag *m.;* Antreten *(n.)* zur Arbeit.

turnover *s.* Umsatz *m.;* ~ *tax,* Umsatzsteuer *f.*

turnpike *s.* gebührenpflichtige Straße *f.*

turnstile *s.* Drehkreuz *n.*

turntable *s.* *(rail.)* Drehscheibe *f.;* Plattenteller *m.*

turn-up *s.* Hosenaufschlag *m.*

turpentine *s.* Terpentin *m.*

turquoise, *s.* Türkis *m.;* ~*a.* türkis.

turret *s.* Türmchen *n.*; Panzerturm *m.*
turtle *s.* Seeschildkröte *f.*; ~-**neck** *s.* Rollkragen
tusk *s.* Fangzahn *m.*
tussle *s.* Gerangel *n*, Rauferei *f.*
tussock *s.* Grasbüschel *n.*
tutelage *s.* Vormundschaft *f.*; Unmündigkeit *f.*
tutelary *a.* vormundschaftlich.
tutor *s.* Hauslehrer *m.*; Lehrer *m.*; ~ *v.t.* unterrichten.
tutorial Lehr. . ., Lehrer. .
tuxedo *s.* Smoking *m.*
twaddle *s.* Quatsch *m.*; Unsinn *m.*
twang *v.i.* schwirren; näseln; ~ *s.* näselnde Aussprache *f.*
tweak *v.t.* zwichen, kneifen.
tweed *s.* Tweed *m.* Halbtuch *n.*
tweezers *s.pl.* **pair of** ~ Pinzette *f.*
Twelfth Night *s.* Dreikönigsfest *n.*
twelve *a.* zwölf.
twentieth *a.* zwanzigst. . .
twenty *a.* zwanzig.
twerp *s.* (*fam.*) Blödmann *m.*
twice *adv.* zweimal, doppelt.
twiddle *v.t.* herumdrehen an; (*fam.*) herumfummeln.
twig *s.* Zweig *m.*; Rute *f.*
twilight *s.* Zwielicht *n.*; Dämmerung *f.*
twin *s.* Zwilling *m.*; *a.* Doppel. . .; ~ **bed** *s.* Doppelbett *n.*; ~ **engine(d),** *a.* (*avi.*) zweimotorig.
twine *v.t.* drehen, zwirnen; ~ *v.i.* sich winden ~ *s.* Bindfaden *m.*; Zwirn *m.*; Windung *f.*
twinge *s.* Stechen *n.*; stechender Schmerz *m.*
twinkle *v.i.* blinken, blinzeln; ~ *s.* Funkeln *n.*; Glitzern *n.*; Blinzeln.
twinkling *s.* in the ~ of an eye, im Handumdrehen.
twirl *v.t. & i.* quirlen; wirbeln; ~ *s.* Wirbel *m.*; Schnörkel *m.*
twist *v.t.* (*v.i.* sich) drehen, verdrehen, flechten, spinnen; verzerren; ~ *s.* Geflecht *n.*; Biegung *f.*;

Windung *f.*
twisted *a.* verbogen; verdreht.
twitch *v.t.* zupfen, zwicken; zucken; ~ *s.* Zupfen, *n.*; Zucken *n.*
twitter *v.i.* zwitschern; kichern, zittern; ~ *s.* Gezwitscher *n.*
two *a.* zwei; ~-**bit** *a.* klein; unbedeutend; ~-**speed** (*mech.*) *a.* mit zwei Gängen; ~-**piece suit,** zweiteiliger Anzug *m.*; in ~, entzwei.
two-handed *a.* zweihändig.
twofold *a* zweifach.
twosome *s.* Paar *n.*; Zweier *m.*
two-time *a.* zweimalig; ~-*v.t.* (*fam.*) untreu sein.
two-way *a.* zweibahnig; mit Gegenverkehr.
tympanum *s.* Trommelfell *n.*; Giebelfeld *n.*
type *s.* Typ, Typus *m.*; Schrift *f.*; Drucktype *f.*; ~ *v.t.* auf der Schreibmaschine schreiben, tippen.
type-cast *v.t.* auf ein Rollenfach festlegen.
typescript *s.* Maschinenschrift *f.*; ~ *a.* maschinengeschrieben.
typesetter *s.* (Schrift-) Setzer(in) *m.*(*f.*)
type-write *v.t. & i.* mit der Schreibmaschine schreiben, tippen.
typewriter *s.* Schreibmaschine *f.*; ~ **ribbon,** Schreibmaschinenfarbband *n.*
typhoid *s.* Typhus *m.*
typhoon *s.* Teifun *m.*
typhus *s.* Fleckfieber *n.*
typical *a.* ~**ly** *adv.* typisch.
typify *v.t.* darstellen; typisch sein für; kennzeichnen.
typist *s.* Schreibkraft *f.*
typographic(al) *a.,* ~**ly** *adv.* typographisch.
typography *s.* Typographie *f.*
tyrannical *a.,* ~**ly** *adv.* tyrannisch.
tyrannize *v.t.* tyrannisieren.
tyranny *s.* Tyrannei *f.*
tyrant *s.* Tyrann *m.*
Tyrol *s.* Tirol *n.*

U

U,u der Buchstabe U oder u *n.*
ubiquitous *a.* allgegenwärtig.
ubiquity *s.* Allgegenwart *f.*
U-boat *s.* U-boot *n.*
udder *s.* Euter *n.*
Uganda *s.* Uganda *n.*
Ugandan *a.* Ugandisch; ~ *s.* Ugander(in) *m.*(*f.*)
ugh *i.* bah pfui!
ugliness *s.* Häßlichkeit *f.*
ugly *a.* häßlich, ekelhaft.
Ukraine *s.* Ukraine *s.*
Ukrainian *a.* ukrainisch; ~ *s.* Ukrainer(in) *m.*(*f.*)
ulcer *s.* Geschwür.
ulcerate *v.i.* schwären; Geschwür hervorrufen.
ulterior *a.* hintergründig; geheim.
ultimate *a.,* ~**ly** *adv.* letzt, zuletzt, endlich.
ultimatum *s.* Ultimatum *n.*
ultra *a.* ultra. . .; hyper. . .
ultra shortwave *s.* (*radio*) Ultrakurzwelle *f.*
ultrasonic *a.* Ultraschall. . .
ultrasound *s.* Ultraschall *m.*
ultraviolet *a.* ultraviolett.
umbel *s.* Dolde *f.*

umber *s.* Umbra (Farbe) *f.*
umbilical cord *s.* Nabelschnur *f.*
umbrage *s* Anstoß, Ärger *m.*
umbrella *s.* Regenschirm, Schirm *m.*; ~ **stand,** Regenschirmständer *m.*
umlaut *s.* Umlaut *m.*
umpire *s.* Schiedsrichter(in) *m.*(*f.*)
umpteen *a.* x-mal; zig.
umpteenth *a.* for the ~ time, zum x-sten Mal.
unabashed *a.* ungeniert; schamlos.
unabated *a.* unvermindert.
unable *a.* unfähig, unvermögend.
unabridged *a.* ungekürzt.
unaccented *a.* unbetont.
unacceptable *a.,* ~**bly** *adv.* unannehmbar.
unaccommodating *a.* unnachgiebig.
unaccompanied *a.* unbegleitet.
unaccountable *a.,* ~**bly** *adv.* unerklärlich.
unaccounted *a.* ~-*for* unauffindbar; vermißt.
unaccustomed *a.* ungewohnt; ungewöhnlich.
unacquainted *a.* unbekannt.
unadorned *a.* schmucklos.
unadulterated *a.* unverfälscht, echt.

unadventurous *a.* bieder; ereignislos; ohne Unternehmungsgeist.
unadvisable *a.* nicht ratsam, unklug.
unadvised *a.*, **~ly** *adv.* unberaten; unbesonnen.
unaffected *a.*, **~ly** *adv.* ungerührt; unbeeinflußt; ungekünstelt.
unafraid *a.* furchtlos.
unaided *a.* ohne Hilfe, allein, (Auge) bloß.
unalloyed *a.* unvermischt.
unalterable *a.*, **~bly** *adv.* unveränderlich.
unaltered *a.* unverändert.
unambiguous *a.*, **~ly** *adv.* unzweideutig.
un-American *a.* unamerikanisch; antiamerikanisch.
unanimity *s.* Einmütigkeit *f.*
unanimous *a.*, **~ly** *adv.* einmütig.
unanswerable *a.*, **~bly** *adv.* unwiderleglich.
unaswered *a.* unbeantwortet.
unappetizing *a.* unappetitlich.
unappreciated *a.* unbeachtet.
unapproachable *a.* unerreicht; unzugänglich.
unapt *a.* **~ly** *adv.* untauglich, unpassend.
unarmed *a.* unbewaffnet, wehrlos.
unashamed *a.* schamlos, unverhohlen.
unasked *a.* ungefordert, ungebeten.
unassailable *a.* uneinnehmbar.
unassisted *a.* ohne Hilfe.
unassuming *a.* anspruchslos.
unattached *a.* unverbunden.
unattainable *a.* unerreichbar.
unattained *a.* unerreicht.
unattempted *a.* unversucht.
unattended *a.* unbeaufsichtigt; unbegleitet.
unattractive *a.* unattraktiv; reizlos.
unauthentic *a.* unverbürgt.
unauthorized *a.* unberechtigt.
unavailing *a.* vergeblich, nutzlos.
unavailable *a.* nicht erhältlich.
unavenged *a.* ungerächt.
unavoidable *a.*, **~bly** *adv.* unvermeidlich.
unaware (of) *a.* ohne Kenntnis von, unbewußt; **~s** *adv.* unversehens.
unbalanced *a.* nicht im Gleichgewicht.
unbearable *a.* unerträglich.
unbeaten *a.* unbesiegt, unübertroffen.
unbecoming *a.*, **~ly** *adv.* nicht kleidsam; ungeziemend.
unbeknown(st) *a.* ohne Wissen, unbekannt.
unbelief *s.* Unglaube *m.*
unbelievable *a.* unglaublich, unglaubhaft.
unbeliever *s.* Ungläubiger *m./f.*
unbelieving *a.* ungläubig.
unbend *v.t.i.r.;* geradebiegen, entspannen, nachlassen; **~** *v.i.* gemütlich werden.
unbending *a.* unbiegsam; starr.
unbiased *a.*, **~ly** *adv.* vorurteilsfrei.
unbid(den) *a.* ungebeten, freiwillig.
unbind *v.t.st.* losbinden.
unbleached *a.* ungebleicht.
unblemished *a.* unbefleckt, tadellos.
unblushing *a.* schamlos.
unbolt *v.t.* aufriegeln, öffnen.
unborn *a.* ungeboren.
unbosom *v.t.* (Herz) ausschütten.
unbound *a.* ungebunden.
unbounded *a.* unbegrenzt.

unbridle *v.t.* abzäumen; **~d** *a.* zügellos.
unbroken *a.* ungebrochen.
unbuckle *v.t.* aufschnallen.
unburden *v.t.* entlasten.
unbusinesslike *a.* nicht geschäftsmäßig; unpraktisch.
unbutton *v.t.* aufknöpfen.
uncalled, uncalled-for *a.* ungerufen; unnötig; unaufgefordert; nicht eingefordert.
uncanny *a.* unheimlich.
uncared-for *a.* vernachlässigt.
unceasing *a.* fortwährend, unaufhörlich.
unceremonious *a.* ungezwungen, einfach.
uncertain *a.*, **~ly** *adv.* ungewiß; unzuverlässig.
uncertainty *s.* Ungewißheit *f.*
unchain *v.t.* entfesseln.
unchallenged *a.* unbestritten.
unchanged *a.* unverändert.
unchanging *a.* unveränderlich, bleibend.
uncharitable *a.*, **~bly** *adv.* lieblos.
unchecked *a.* ungehindert; unkontrolliert.
unchristain *a.*, **~ly** *adv.* unchristlich.
uncivil *a.* unhöflich.
uncivilized *a.* ungesittet.
unclaimed *a.* unverlangt, nicht beansprucht; unbestellbar.
unclassified *a.* nicht klassifiziert; nicht geheim.
uncle *s.* Onkel, Oheim *m.*
unclean *a.*, **~ly** *adv.* unrein.
unclothed *a.* unbekleidet.
unclouded *a.* unbewölkt; heiter.
uncoil *v.t.* abwickeln.
uncolored *a.* ungefärbt.
uncombed *a.* ungekämmt.
uncomfortable *a.*, **~bly** *adv.* unbehaglich.
uncommon *a.*, **~ly** *adv.* ungewöhnlich.
uncommunicative *a.* unkommunikativ; verschlossen.
uncomplaining *a.* nicht klagend.
uncompromising *a.* unnachgiebig.
unconcern *s.* Gleichgültigkeit *f.*
unconcerned *a.*, **~ly** *adv.* gleichgültig; sorglos.
unconditional *a.* bedingungslos.
unconfined *a.*, **~ly** *adv.* unbegrenzt.
unconfirmed *a.* unbestätigt.
uncongenial *a.* unsympathisch; nicht zusagend.
unconnected *a.* unverbunden.
unconquerable *a.*, **~bly** *adv.* unüberwindlich.
unconquered *a.* unbesiegt.
unconscious *a.* unbewußt; bewußtlos.
unconsciousness *s.* Bewußtlosigkeit *f.*
unconsecrated *a.* ungeweiht.
unconstitutional *a.* verfassungswidrig.
unconstrained *a.*, **~ly** *adv.* ungezwungen.
uncontaminated *a.* unverschmutzt; nicht verseucht.
uncontested, uncontradicted *a.* unbestritten, unwidersprochen.
uncontrollable *a.*, **~bly** *adv.* unkontrollierbar.
uncontrolled *a.*, **~ly** *adv.* unkontrolliert.
uncontroversial *a.* nicht kontrovers.
unconventional *a.* unkonventionell.
unconvinced *a.* unüberzeugt.
unconvincing *a.* nicht überzeugend.
uncooked *a.* roh.
uncork *v.t.* entkorken.

uncorrected *a.* unberichtigt.
uncorrupted *a.* unverdorben.
uncourteous *a.*, **~ly** *adv.* unhöflich.
uncouth *a.*, **~ly** *adv.* ungeschlacht, grob.
uncover *v.t.* aufdecken; entblössen.
uncritical *a.* unkritisch.
uncrowned *a.* ungekrönt.
unction *s.* Salbung *f.*; Salbe *f.*; *extreme* ~, letzte Ölung *f.*
unctuous *a.* ölig, fettig; salbungsvoll.
uncultivated *a.* nicht kultiviert; ungebildet.
uncurbed *a.* ungezähmt, ausgelassen.
undamaged *a.* unbeschädigt.
undated *a.* nicht datiert.
undaunted *a.*, **~ly** *adv.* unerschrocken.
undeceive *v.t.* einem die Augen öffnen.
undecided *a.* unentschieden.
undecipherable *a.* nicht zu entziffern.
undefeated *a.* unbesiegt.
undefended *a.* nicht verteidigt.
undefined *a.* unbestimmt.
undemanding *a.* anspruchslos.
undemonstrative *a.* zurückhaltend, ruhig.
undeniable *a.*, **~bly** *adv.* unleugbar.
under *pr. & adv.* unter; weniger, geringer; unten; **~age**, unmündig.
underbid *v.t.st.* unterbieten.
undercarriage *s.* (*avi.*) Fahrgestell *n.*
underclothing *s.* Unterzeug *n.*
undercover *a.* getarnt; verdeckt.
undercurrent *s.* Unterströmung *f.*
undercut *v.t.* unterbieten.
underdeveloped *a.* unterentwickelt.
underdevelopment *s.* Unterentwicklung *f.*
underdog *s.* Unterlegene *m./f.*
underdone *a.* nicht gar.
underestimate *v.t.* unterschätzen; ~ *s.* Unterschätzung *f.*
underexposure *s* (*phot.*) Unterbelichtung *f.*
underfed *a.* unterernährt.
underfoot *adv.* unter den Füssen.
undergo *v.t.st.* sich unterziehen; ausstehen; erfahren.
undergraduate *s.* Student(in) *m.(f.)* vor dem Vordiplom (B.A.).
underground *a.* unterirdisch; (*rail.*) Untergrundbahn *f.*; ~ (*Movement*), politische Widerstandsbewegung *f.*
undergrowth *s.* Unterholz *n.*
underhand *a. & adv.* heimlich; hinterlistig; tückisch; (*Tennis*) Tief.. .
underlie *v.i.* liegen unter; zugrunde liegen.
underline *v.t.* unterstreichen.
underling *s.* (*pej.*) Untergebene *m./f.*
undermine *v.t.* untergraben.
undermost *a.* unterst.
underneath *adv.* unten, darunter; ~ *pr.* unter.
undernourished *a.* unterernährt.
underpaid *a.* schlecht bezahlt.
underpass *s.* Unterführung *f.*
underpin *v.t.* unterbauen; stützen.
underplay *v.t.* herunterspielen.
underprivileged *a.* unterprivilegiert.
underproduction *s.* Unterproduktion *f.*
underprop *v.t.* unterstützen.
underrate *v.t.* unterschätzen.

underscore *v.t.* unterstreichen.
under secretary *s.* Unterstaatssekretär *m.*
undersell *v.t.ir.* unterbieten.
undershot *a.* unterschlächtig.
underside *s.* Unterseite *f.*
undersigned *a.* unterschrieben; *I, the* ~, der/die Unterzeichnete.
undersized *a.* unter normaler Größe.
understaffed *a.* unterbesetzt.
understand *v.t. & i.st.* verstehen; vernehmen, hören, erfahren.
understandable *a.* verständlich.
understanding *a.* verständnisvoll; ~ *s.* Verstand *m.*, Einsicht *f.*; Einverständnis *n.*; *to come to an* ~ *with*, sich verständigen mit; *on the* ~ *that*, unter der Voraussetzung, daß.
understate *v.t.* herunterspielen; zu gering angeben.
understatement *s.* Untertreibung *f.* zu maßvolle Darstellung *f.*
understudy *s.* zweite Besetzung *f.*
undertake *v.t.st.* unternehmen, übernehmen; sich verpflichten, garantieren.
undertaker *s.* Leichenbestatter *m.*
undertaking *s.* Unternehmen *n.*; Betrieb *m.*; Übernahme *f.*
undertone *s.* halbleise Rede *f.*; Unterton *m.*
undertow *s.* Unterströmung *f.*
undervalue *v.t.* unterschätzen.
underwear *s.* Unterwäsche *f.*
underweight *a.* untergewichtig.
underwood *s.* Unterholz *n.*
underwrite *v.t.st.* (*com.*) unterzeichnen; versichern; unterstützen.
underwriter *s.* Versicherer, Assekurant *m.*
undeserved *a.*, **~ly** *adv.* unverdient.
undeserving *a.* unwürdig, unwert.
undesigned *a.*, **~ly** *adv.* unbeabsichtigt.
undesirable *a.* unerwünscht.
undetected *a.* unentdeckt.
undetermined *a.* unentschieden.
undeterred *a.* nicht entmutigt, unbeeindruckt.
undeveloped *a.* unentwickelt.
undigested *a.* unverdaut.
undignified *a.* würdelos.
undiminished *a.* unvermindert.
undiplomatic *a.* undiplomatisch.
undiscerned *a.*, **~ly** *adv.* unbemerkt, unentdeckt.
undiscernible *a.*, **~bly** *adv.* ununterscheidbar, unbemerklich.
undiscerning *a.* einsichtslos.
undisciplined *a.* ungeschult; zuchtlos.
undiscovered *a.* unentdeckt.
undiscriminating *a.* wahllos.
undisguised *a.* unverstellt, offen.
undismayed *a.* unverzagt.
undisputed *a.* unbestritten.
undistinguished *a.* mittelmäßig.
undisturbed *a.*, **~ly** *adv.* ungestört.
undivided *a.*, **~ly** *adv.* ungeteilt, ganz.
undo *v.t.st.* aufmachen; auflösen; zerstören; ungeschehen machen.
undoing *s.* Aufmachen *n.*; Verderben *n.*
undone *a.* unerledigt; (*fig.*) ruiniert, hin.
undoubted *a.*, **~ly** *adv.* unzweifelhaft.
undreamt-of *a.* ungeahnt.

undress *v.t.* (*v.i.* sich) auskleiden.
undressed *a.* unbekleidet; ausgezogen.
undrinkable *a.* untrinkbar.
undue *a.* ungebührlich; übermäßig.
undulate *v.t. & i.* wogen, wellen.
unduly *adv.* ungebührlich.
undutiful *a.*, ~**ly** *adv.* pflichtvergessen.
undying *a.* unsterblich.
unearned *a.* unverdient.
unearth *v.t.* ausgraben; aufstöbern.
unearthly *a.* unirdisch, überirdisch.
uneasy *a.*, ~**ily** *adv.* unruhig, ängstlich.
uneatable *a.* ungenießbar.
uneconomic *a.*, ~**ally** *adv.* unwirtschaftlich.
unedifying *a.* unerbaulich.
uneducated *a.* unerzogen, ungebildet.
unembarrassed *a.* nicht verlegen.
unemotional *a.* temperamentlos.
unemployable *a.* verwendungsunfähig.
unemployed *a.* arbeitslos.
unemployment *s.* Arbeitslosigkeit *f.*; ~ *insurance,* Arbeitslosenversicherung *f.*
unencumbered *a.* unbelastet; ohne Hypotheken.
unending *a.* endlos.
unendurable *a.* unerträglich.
unenterprising *a.* nicht unternehmend.
unenviable *a.* nicht beneidenswert.
unequal *a.*, ~**ly** *adv.* ungleich; unangemessen; nicht gewachsen.
unequalled *a.* unvergleichlich, unerreicht.
unequivocal *a.* unzweideutig.
unerring *a.*, ~**ly** *adv.* untrüglich.
unessential *a.* unwesentlich.
unethical *a.* unmoralisch.
uneven *a.*, ~**ly** *adv.* uneben, ungleich; ungerade.
uneventful *a.* ereignislos.
unexampled *a.* Beispiellos, unerhört.
unexceptional *a.*, ~**ly** *adv.* alltäglich; durchschnittlich.
unexpected *a.*, ~**ly** *adv.* unerwartet.
unexpired *a.* nicht abgelaufen, noch in Kraft.
unexplained *a.* unerklärt.
unexplored *a.* unerforscht.
unexpurgated *a.* nicht gereinigt, ungekürzt.
unfaded *a.* unverwelkt; unverschossen.
unfading *a.* unverwelklich; echt.
unfailing *a.* unfehlbar, gewiss; zuverlässig; unerschöpflich.
unfair *a.*, ~**ly** *adv.* unfair; unsportlich; unbillig, unredlich; ~ *competition,* unlauterer Wettbewerb *m.*
unfaithful *a.*, ~**ly** *adv.* untreu.
unfaltering *a.* nicht schwankend, sicher; fest.
unfamiliar *a.* ungewöhnt.
unfashionable *a.*, ~**bly** *adv.* unmodern.
unfasten *v.t.* losmachen, losbinden.
unfathomable *a.*, ~**bly** *adv.* unergründlich, unermeßlich.
unfavorable *a.*, ~**bly** *adv.* ungünstig.
unfeeling *a.* gefühllos.
unfeigned *a.*, ~**ly** *adv.* aufrichtig.
unfermented *a.* ungegoren; ungesäuert.
unfetter *v.t.* entfesseln.
unfilial *a.* lieb-, respektlos (Kind).
unfinished *a.* unvollendet.
unfit *a.*, ~**ly** *adv.* ungeeignet; untauglich; ~ *v.t.*

untüchtig machen.
unfix *v.t.* losmachen; lösen.
unflagging *a.* unermüdlich.
unflattering *a.* wenig schmeichelhaft.
unflinching *a.* unerschrocken.
unfold *v.t.* entfalten; darlegen.
unforeseeable unvorhersehbar.
unforeseen *a.* unvorhergesehen.
unforgettable *a.* unvergeßlich.
unforgivable *a.* unverzeihlich.
unforgiving *a.* unversöhnlich; nachtragend.
unforgotten *a.* unvergessen.
unfortified *a.* unbefestigt; schwach.
unfortunate *a.*, ~**ly** *adv.* unglücklich; leidig.
unfortunately *adv.* leider.
unfounded *a.* unbegründet; grundlos.
unfreeze *v.t.* auftauen.
unfrequented *a.* unbesucht.
unfriendly *a.* unfreundlich.
unfruitful *a.*, ~**ly** *adv.* unfruchtbar.
unfulfilled *a.* unerfüllt.
unfurl *v.t.* aufspannen, entfalten (Segel).
unfurnished *a.* nicht ausgestattet (mit); unmöbliert; entblößt.
ungainly *a.* plump, ungeschickt.
ungentle *a.*, ~**tly** *adv.* unsanft, grob.
ungentlemanly *a.* ungebildet; unfein.
unglazed *a.* unglasiert; unverglast.
ungodly *a.* gottlos.
ungovernable *a.* unvergleichlich, unlenksam.
ungracious *a.*, ~**ly** *adv.* ungnädig; ungünstig; mißfällig.
ungrammatical *a.* ungrammatisch.
ungrateful *a.*, ~**ly** *adv.* undankbar.
ungrounded *a.* nicht stichhaltig.
ungrudging *a.*, ~**ly** *adv.* gern, ohne Murren.
unguarded *a.*, ~**ly** *adv.* unbewacht.
unguent *s.* Salbe *f.*
unguided *a.* ohne Führung; ungeleitet.
unhallowed *a.* verrucht; ungeweiht.
unhampered *a.* ungehindert.
unhandy *a.* unhandlich; ungeschickt.
unhappiness *s.* Unglück *n.*
unhappy *a.*, ~**ily** *adv.* unglücklich.
unharmed *a.* unversehrt.
unharness *v.t.* abschirren.
unhealthiness *s.* Ungesundheit *f.*
unhealthy *a.*, ~**ily** *adv.* ungesund.
unheard *a.* ungehört; ~ *of,* unerhört.
unheeded *a.* unbeachtet.
unheedful, unheeding *a.* unachtsam.
unhesitating *a.* ohne Zögern.
unhindered *a.* ungehindert.
unhinge *v.t.* aus den Angeln heben; (*fig.*) zerrütten; (*fig.*) aus dem Gleichgewicht bringen.
unhistoric *a.*, ~**ally** *adv.* unhistorisch.
unholy *a.* unheilig, gottlos; verrucht.
unhook *v.t.* loshaken.
unhoped (for) *a.* unverhofft.
unhorse *v.t.* aus dem Sattel heben.
unhuman *a.*, ~**ly** *adv.* nicht menschlich, überirdisch.
unhurt *a.* unverletzt.
unhygienic *a.* unhygienisch.
unicorn *s.* Einhorn *n.*
unidentified *a.* nicht identifiziert.

unification *s.* Vereinigung *f.*, Vereinheitlichung *f.*
uniform *a.*, **~ly** *adv.* einförmig, gleichförmig; ~ *s.* Uniform *f.*
uniformity *s.* Gleichförmigkeit *f.*
unify *v.t.* vereinigen, vereinheitlichen.
unilateral *a.* einseitig.
unimaginable *a.* undenkbar.
unimaginative *a.* phantasielos, einfallslos.
unimpaired *a.* unvermindert; unverletzt.
unimpeded *a.* ungehemmt.
unimportant *a.* unwichtig.
unimpressed *a.* unbeeindruckt.
unimpressive *a.* eindruckslos.
unimproved *a.* unverbessert; unbenutzt (Land).
uninfluenced *a.* unbeeinflußt.
uninformed *a* ununterrichtet, uninformiert.
uninhabitable *a.* unbewohnbar.
uninhabited *a.* unbewohnt.
uninhibited *a.* ungehemmt.
uninitiated *a.* uneingeweiht.
uninjured *a.* unverletzt.
uninspired *a.* einfallslos.
uninspiring *a.* langweilig.
uninstructed *a.* ununterrichtet.
uninsured *a.* nicht versichert.
unintelligible *a.*, **~bly** *adv.* unverständlich.
unintended, unintentional *a.* unbeabsichtigt.
uninterested *a.* uninteressiert.
uninteresting *a.* uninteressant.
uninterrupted *a.*, **~ly** *adv.* ununterbrochen.
uninvited *a.* ungeladen.
uninviting *a* nicht anziehend; wenig einladend.
union *s.* Vereinigung *f.*, Bund *m.*; Verein *m.*; Verband *m.*; Gewerkschaft *f.*; **~-Jack**, britische Nationalflagge *f.*
unique *a.* enzigartig.
unison *s.* Einklang *m.*; Einmütigkeit *f.*
unit *s.* Einheit *f.*
unite *v.t.* (*v.i.* sich) vereinigen.
united *a.* vereint.
United Kingdom *s.* Vereinigtes Königreich (Großbritannien).
United Nations *s.pl.* Vereinte Nationen *f.pl.*
United States (of America) Vereinigte Staaten (von Amerika).
unity *s.* Einheit, Eintracht *f.*
universal *a.*, **~ly** *adv.* allgemein; allumfassend; Welt. . .; universal.
universe *s.* Weltall, Universum *n.*
university *s.* Universität *f.*
univocal *a.* eindeutig.
unjust *a.*, **~ly** *adv.* ungerecht.
unjustifiable *a.*, **~bly** *adv.* nicht zu rechtfertigen; unverantwortlich.
unjustified *a.* nicht gerechtfertigt.
unkempt *a.* ungekämmt.
unkind *a.*, **~ly** *adv.* unfreundlich, lieblos.
unkindness *s.* Unfreundlichkeit *f.*
unknowing *a.*, **~ly** *adv.* unwissend.
unknown *a.* unbekannt.
unlace *v.t.* aufschnüren.
unlamented *a.* unbeklagt.
unlatch *v.t.* aufklinken.
unlawful *a.*, **~ly** *adv.* ungesetzlich.
unleaded *a.* bleifrei.
unlearn *v.t.* verlernen.

unlearned *a.* **~ly** *adv.* ungelehrt.
unleavened *a.* ungesäuert.
unless *c.* wenn nicht, außer wenn.
unlettered *a.* ungelehrt.
unlicensed *a.* ohne Konzession.
unlike *a.*, **~ly** *adv.* ungleich, anders als.
unlikelihood *s.* Unwahrscheinlichkeit *f.*
unlikley *a.* & *adv.* unwahrscheinlich.
unlimited *a.*, **~ly** *adv.* unbegrenzt; unbestimmt.
unlined *a.* ungefüttert; ohne Linien.
unliquidated *a.* unbezahlt.
unlisted *a.* **~ number** *s.* Geheimnummer *f.*
unlit *a.* unbeleuchtet.
unload *v.t.* abladen.
unlock *v.t.* aufschließen.
unlooked-for *a.* unerwartet, unvermutet.
unloving *a.* lieblos.
unlucky *a.* unglücklich.
unmanageable *a.* unlenksam, unbändig.
unmanly *a.* unmännlich.
unmannerly *a.* ungesittet, unartig.
unmanufactured *a.* unverarbeitet.
unmarked *a.* nicht gekennzeichnet.
unmarketable *a.* unverkäuflich.
unmarried *a.* unverheiratet, ledig.
unmask *v.t.* (*v.i.* sich) entlarven.
unmatched *a.* unvergleichlich.
unmeasured *a.* ungemessen.
unmentionable *a.* unaussprechlich.
unmentioned *a.* nicht erwähnt.
unmerciful *a.*, **~ly** *adv.* unbarmherzig.
unmerited *a.* unverdient.
unmethodical *a.* unmethodisch.
unmindful *a.* uneingedenk, unachtsam.
unmingled *a.* unvermischt.
unmistakable *a.* unverkennbar.
unmitigated *a.* ungemildert, völlig.
unmolested *a.* unbelästigt.
unmotherly *a.* unmütterlich.
unmounted *a.* (Bild) nicht aufgezogen; (Stein) nicht gefaßt.
unmoved *a.* unbewegt; unverändert.
unmusical *a.* unmusikalisch.
unnamed *a.* ungenannt, namenlos.
unnatural *a.*, **~ly** *adv.* unnatürlich.
unnecessary *a.* unnötig.
unnerve *v.t.* entnerven, entkräften.
unnerving *a.* entnervend.
unnoticed *a.* unbemerkt.
unnumbered *a.* ungezählt.
unobjectionable *a.* einwandfrei; unanfechtbar.
unobservant *a.* unachtsam.
unobserved *a.*, **~ly** *adv.* unbeobachtet.
unobstructed *a.* nicht verstopft; ungehindert.
unobtainable *a.* nicht erhältlich; unerreichbar.
unobtrusive *a.* unaufdringlich, bescheiden.
unoccupied *a.* unbesetzt; unbenutzt; unbebaut; unbeschäftigt.
unoffending *a.* unschädlich, harmlos.
unofficial *a.* nicht amtlich.
unopened *a.* ungeöffnet.
unopposed *a.* ohne Widerstand.
unorganized *a.* unorganisiert.
unorthodox *a.* unorthodox; unüblich.
unpack *v.t.* auspacken; aufmachen.
unpaid *a.* unbezahlt.

unpalatable *a.* ungenießbar.
unparalleled *a.* unvergleichlich.
unpardonable *a.*, **~bly** *adv.* unverzeihlich.
unparliamentary *a.* unparlamentarisch.
unpatriotic *a.* unpatriotisch.
unpaved *a.* ungepflastert.
unperceived *a.*, **~ly** *adv.* unbemerkt.
unperturbed *a.* nicht beunruhigt, gelassen.
unpick *v.t.* auftrennen.
unpin *v.t.* losheften, abnehmen.
unplanned *a.* ungeplant.
unpleasant *a.*, **~ly** *adv.* unangenehm.
unpleasantness *s.* Unannehmlichkeit *f.*; Unfreundlichkeit *f.*
unplowed *a.* ungepflügt.
unpoetical *a.*, **~ly** *adv.* unpoetisch.
unpolished *a.* unpoliert; (*fig.*) ungeschliffen.
unpolitical *a.* unpolitisch.
unpolluted *a.* sauber; nicht verschmutzt.
unpopular *a.* unbeliebt.
unpopularity *s.* Unbeliebtheit *f.*
unpractical *a.* unpraktisch.
unpractised *a.* ungeübt, unerfahren.
unprecedented *a.* beispiellos, unerhört.
unpredictable *a.* unberechenbar.
unprejudiced *a.* vorurteilsfrei; unvoreingenommen.
unpremeditated *a.* nicht vorsätzlich.
unprepared *a.* unvorbereitet.
unprepossessing *a.* nicht einnehmend.
unpretentious *a.* anspruchslos.
unpriced *a.* ohne Preisangabe.
unprincipled *a.* gewissenlos.
unprintable *a.* nicht druckreif.
unprinted *a.* ungedruckt.
unprivileged *a.* nicht bevorrechtigt.
unproductive *a.* unfruchtbar, unergiebig.
unprofessional *a.* unfachmännisch, stümperhaft; standeswidrig.
unprofitable *a.*, **~bly** *adv.* unrentabel, unnütz.
unpromising *a.* nicht vielversprechend.
unpronounceable *a.* unaussprechbar.
unpropitious *a.* ungünstig.
unproportioned *a.* unverhältnismäßig.
unprotected *a.* unbeschützt.
unproved *a.* ungeprüft; unbewiesen.
unprovided *a.* unversorgt; unvorhergesehen.
unprovoked *a.* unprovoziert, grundlos.
unpublished *a.* unveröffentlicht.
unpunctual *a.* unpünktlich.
unpunctuality *s.* Unpünktlichkeit *f.*
unpunished *a.* ungestraft.
unpurified *a.* ungereinigt.
unqualified *a.* nicht fähig, ungeeignet; unberechtigt; uneingeschränkt.
unquestionable *a.*, **~bly** *adv.* zweifellos.
unquestioned *a.* unbefragt; unbestritten.
unquestioning *a.* bedingungslos, blind.
unquiet *a.*, **~ly** *adv.* unruhig, ungestüm.
unravel *v.t.* ausfasern; entwirren.
unread *a.* ungelesen; unbelesen.
unreadable *a.* nicht lesenswert.
unready *a.*, **~ily** *adv.* nicht bereit.
unreal *a.* nicht wirklich.
unrealistic *a.* unrealistisch.

unrealizable *a.* nicht realisierbar, nicht verkäuflich.
unreasonable *a.*, **~bly** *adv.* unvernünftig; unbillig, ohne Grund.
unreasoning *a.* blind, vernunftlos.
unreclaimed *a.* nicht zurückgefordert; unangebaut; nicht gebessert.
unrecognizable *a.*, **~ly** *adv.* nicht wiederzuerkennen.
unreconciled *a.* unversöhnt.
unrecorded *a.* nicht aufgezeichnet.
unredeemed *a.* nicht losgekauft; unerlöst; ungemildert.
unreel *v.t.* abspulen; abwickeln.
unrefined *a.* ungeläutert.
unreflecting *a.* gedankenlos, unüberlegt.
unregarded *a.* unberücksichtigt.
unrelated *a.* unzusammenhängend; nicht verwandt.
unrelenting *a.* unbeugsam, unerbittlich.
unreliable *a.* unzuverlässig.
unrelieved *a.* ungemildert, ununterbrochen.
unremitting *a.* unablässig, unaufhörlich.
unremunerative *a.* uneinträglich.
unrepeatable *a.* einzigartig; einmalig.
unrepresentative *a.* nicht repräsentativ.
unrepentant *a.* reuelos.
unrequited *a.* unerwidert.
unreserved *a.*, **~ly** *adv.* rückhaltlos; nicht numeriert.
unresisting *a.* widerstandslos; wehrlos.
unresolved *a.* unentschlossen.
unresponsive *a.* teilnahmslos.
unrest *s.* Unruhe *f.*
unrestored *a.* nicht wiederhergestellt.
unrestrained *a.* unbeschränkt; zügellos.
unrestricted *a.*, **~ly** *adv.* uneingeschränkt, unbeschränkt.
unreturned *a.* nicht zurückgegeben; nicht gewählt.
unrevoked *a.* unwiderrufen.
unrewarded *a.* unbelohnt.
unrewarding *a.* unbefriedigend; undankbar.
unrig *v.t.* abtakeln.
unripe *a.* unreif.
unrivalled *a.* unvergleichlich; beispiellos.
unroll *v.t.* aufrollen.
unromantic *a.* unromantisch.
unruffled *a.* ruhig; glatt (vom Meer).
unruliness *s.* Ungebärdigkeit *f.*
unruly *a.* unlenksam, unbändig.
unsaddle *v.t.* absatteln.
unsafe *a.*, **~ly** *adv.* unsicher, gefährlich.
unsaid *a.* ungesagt.
unsalaried *a.* unbesoldet.
unsaleable *a.* unverkäuflich.
unsalted *a.* ungesalzen.
unsanctioned *a.* unbestätigt.
unsanitary *a.* unhygienisch.
unsatisfactory *a.*, **~ily** *adv.* unzulänglich, unbefriedigend.
unsatisfied *a.* unbefriedigt; unzufrieden.
unsatisfying *a.* unbefriedigend.
unsavory *a.*, **~ily** *adv.* (*fig.*) geschmacklos; unangenehm (Geruch...)
unscathed *a.* unversehrt.

unscented *a.* nicht parfümiert.
unscheduled *a.* außerplanmäßig.
unschooled *a.* ungeschult.
unscientific *a.* unwissenschaftlich.
unscramble *v.t.* entwirren.
unscrew *v.t.* losschrauben.
unscrupulous *a.* gewissenlos; skrupellos.
unseal *v.t.* entsiegeln
unseasonable *a.* unzeitig; unschicklich, unpassend; **~bly** *adv.* zur Unzeit.
unseasoned *a.* ungewürzt.
unseat *v.t.* abwerfen, absetzen.
unsecured *a.* (*com.*) ungedeckt, nicht sichergestellt; ungesichert; unbefestigt.
unseeded *a.* (*sp.*) ungesetzt.
unseemly *a.* unziemlich.
unseen *a.* ungesehen, unsichtbar.
unselfish *a.* selbstlos, uneigennützig.
unsettle *v.t.* durcheinanderbringen; verwirren.
unsettled *a.* ungeordnet; unbeständig, unsicher, veränderlich; unbezahlt.
unshackle *v.t.* entfesseln.
unshaken *a.* unerschüttert; fest.
unshaven *a.* nicht rasiert.
unsheltered *a.* unbedeckt; ungeschützt.
unshorn *a.* ungeschoren.
unshrinkable *a.*, **~ly** *adv.* nicht einlaufend (Stoff).
unshrinking *a.* unverzagt; nicht einlaufend.
unsightly *a.* unschön.
unsigned *a.* unsigniert, nicht unterzeichnet.
unskilful *a.*, **~ly** *adv.* ungeschickt, unkundig.
unskilled *a.* unerfahren; ungelernt; **~ worker**, ungelernter Arbeiter *m.*
unslaked *a.* ungelöscht.
unsociable *a.*, **~bly** *adv.* ungesellig.
unsocial *a.* unsozial.
unsoiled *a.* unbeschmutzt.
unsold *a.* unverkauft.
unsolicited *a.* unverlangt, ungefordert.
unsolved *a.* ungelöst.
unsophisticated *a.* unverfälscht; unverdorben, natürlich.
unsound *a.* ungesund; nicht stichhaltig; verdorben; nicht echt, nicht aufrichtig; *of ~ mind*, geisteskrank.
unsounded *a.* unergründet.
unsparing *a.* reichlich; schonungslos.
unspeakable *a.*, **~bly** *adv.* unsäglich.
unspecified *a.* nicht spezifiziert.
unspent *a.* unerschöpft, unverbraucht.
unspoiled *a.* unverdorben.
unspoken *a.* unausgesprochen.
unsportsmanlike *a.* nicht sportsmäßig.
unspotted *a.* unbefleckt.
unstable *a.* nicht fest, unbeständig.
unstained *a.* unbefleckt; ungefärbt.
unstamped *a.* ungestempelt, ohne Marke.
unsteady *a.*, **~ily** *adv.* unbeständig, veränderlich, wankelmütig.
unstinted *a.* ungeschmälert, freigebig.
unstrained *a.* ungezwungen.
unstressed *a.* unbelastet; (*ling.*) unbetont.
unstring *v.t.st.* abspannnen, lösen.
unstudied *a.* unstudiert; ungekünstelt.
unstuffed *a.* ungefüllt.
unsubstantial *a.* unkörperlich; wesenlos.

unsuccessful *a.*, **~ly** *adv.* erfolglos.
unsuitable *a.*, **~bly** *adv.* nicht passend.
unsuited *a.* nicht passend, ungeeignet.
unsung *a.* unbesungen.
unsure *a.* unsicher.
unsurpassed *a.* unübertroffen.
unsurprisingly *adv.* ohne Überraschung.
unsuspected *a.*, **~ly** *adv.* unverdächtig.
unsuspecting *a.* arglos, unbefangen.
unsuspicious *a.* nicht argwöhnisch.
unswayed *a.* unbeeinflußt.
unsymmetrical *a.* asymmetrisch.
untained *a.*, **~ly** *adv.* unverdorben.
untamed *a.* ungezähmt.
untarnished *a.* ungetrübt.
untasted *a.* ungekostet, unversucht.
untaxed *a.* unbesteuert.
unteachable *a.* ungelehrig.
untempered *a.* ungemildert.
untenable *a.* unhaltbar.
untested *a.* ungeprüft.
unthankful *a.*, **~ly** *adv.* undankbar.
unthinkable *a.* undenkbar.
unthinking *a.* gedankenlos, sorglos.
unthought *a.* **~ of** unvermutet.
unthread *v.t.* ausfädeln.
untidy *a.* unordentlich, unreinlich.
untie *v.t.* aufbinden, lösen.
until *c.* bis; **~** *pr.* bis (an), bis zu.
untimely *a.* & *adv.* unzeitig, vorschnell.
untinged *a.* nicht gefärbt.
untiring *a.* unermüdet.
unto *pr.* zu, an, bis, bis an.
untold *a.* ungezählt; ungesagt.
untouchable *a.* unberührbar.
untouched *a.* unberührt, ungerührt.
untowards *a.*, **~ly** *adv.* widrig, ungünstig.
untraceable *a.* unaufspürbar.
untrained *a.* ungelernt; trainiert.
untranslatable *a.* unübersetzbar.
untravelled *a.* ungereist; unbereist.
untried *a.* unversucht; unverhört; unerprobt; unerfahren.
untrimmed *a.* ungeschmückt.
untroubled *a.* ungestört, ungetrübt.
untrue *a.* unwahr, falsch.
untruly *adv.* fälschlich.
untrustworthy *a.* unzuverlässig.
untruth *s.* Unwahrheit *f.*
untuned *a.* verstimmt; (*fig.*) verwirrt.
untwine *v.t.* aufwickeln, auftrennen.
untwist *v.t.* aufrebbeln, aufdrehen.
unused *a.* ungebraucht; ungewohnt.
unusual *a.*, **~ly** *adv.* ungewöhnlich.
unutterable *a.*, **~bly** *adv.* unausprechlich.
unvaccinated *a.* ungeimpft.
unvalued *a.* ungeschätzt.
unvaried *a.* unverändert.
unvarnished *a.* ungeschminkt.
unvarying *a.* unveränderlich.
unveil *v.t.* entschleiern.
unventilated *a.* ungelüftet; (*fig.*) ununtersucht, unerörtert.
unversed *a.* unbewandert.
unvisited *a.* unbesucht.
unvoiced *a.* unausgesprochen; stimmlos.

unwanted *a.* unerwünscht.
unwarranted *a.* ungerechtfertigt; unverbürgt.
unwary *a.* unbehutsam; unvorsichtig.
unwashed *a.* ungewaschen.
unwavering *a.* fest (Blick); unerschütterlich.
unwearied *a.* unermüdet.
unwedded *s.* unverheiratet.
unweighed *a.* ungewogen; unerworgen.
unwelcome *a.* unwillkommen.
unwell *a.* unwohl, unpässlich.
unwholesome *a.* ungesund.
unwieldy *a.*, **~ily** *adv.* schwerfällig, unhandlich.
unwilling *a.* **~ly** *adv.* widerwillig.
unwillingness *s.* Unwille *m.*
unwind *v.t.st.* loswinden, abwickeln; entspannen.
unwise *a.*, **~ly** *adv.* töricht, unklug.
unwished *a.* **~ for**, unerwünscht.
unwitting *a.*, **~ly** *adv.* unwissentlich.
unwomanly *a.* unweiblich, unfraulich.
unwonted *a.* ungewohnt; ungewöhnlich.
unworkable *a.* unpraktisch.
unworldy *a.* weltfremd.
unworn *a.* ungetragen.
unworthy *a.*, **~ily** *adv.* unwürdig.
unwrap *v.t.* auswickeln.
unwritten *a.* ungeschrieben.
unwrought *a.* unbearbeitet; roh.
unyielding *a.* unnachgiebig, unbeugsam.
up *adv. & pr.* auf, aufwärts hinauf; empor, oben; *the second ~*, der zweite von unten; *it is ~ to him*, es ist seine Sache; **~ to date** *a.* modern, auf der Höhe; *be ~ against*, (*fam.*) gegenüberstehen.
upbringing *s.* Erziehung *f.*
upgrade *v.t.* befördern, verbessern; aufbessern.
upheaval *s.* Erhebung *f.*, Aufruhr *m.*
upheave *v.t.st.* emporheben.
uphill *a.* bergauf führend, ansteigend; **~** *adv.* bergauf; aufwarts.
uphold *v.t.st.* aufrecht(er)halten; unterstützen.
upholsterer *s.* Tapezierer *m.*
upkeep *s.* Instandhaltung *f.*
uplift *v.t.* aufrichten; **~s.** Auftrieb geben.
upon *pr.* auf, an, bei, nach.
upper *a.* ober, höher; Ober. . .; **~ case** *s.* Großbuchstabe *m.*; **~ circle** *s.* (*theat.*) erste Rang *m.*; **~class** *s.* Oberschicht *f.* **~ leather** *s.* Oberleder *n.*; *down on one's ~s*, in zerlumpten Schuhen, heruntergekommen.
uppermost *a.* höchst, oberst.
uppity *a.* hochnäsig.
upright *a.*, **~ly** *adv.* aufrecht, gerade; aufrichtig; **~** *s.* Ständer *m.*; **~ size**, Hochformat *n.*
uprising *s.* Aufstand *m.*
uproar *s.* Aufruhr *m.*; heftige Getöse *n.*
uproarious *a.* aufrührerisch, lärmend.
uproot *v.t.* ausreißen, entwurzeln.
upset *v.t.* umstürzen; außer Fassung bringen; *~ stomach*, verdorbener Magen *m.*
upsetting *a.* erschütternd; ärgerlich.
upshot *s.* Ausgang *m.*; Ergebnis *n.*
upside *s.* Oberseite *f.*; *~ down*, das Oberste zu unterst, drunter und drüber.
upstage *v.t.* jm. die Schau stehlen.
upstairs *adv.* oben (im Hause), nach oben.
upstart *s.* Emporkömmling *m.*
upstate *a.* nördlicher Teil eines Staates.

upstream *a. & adv.* flußaufwärts.
upsurge *s.* Aufschwellen *n.*; Aufwallung *f.*
uptight *a.* nervös, reizbar; verklemmt.
upturn *s.* Aufschwung *m.*
upward(s) *adv.* aufwärts, oben; *~ of*, mehr als.
Urals *s.pl.* Ural *m.*
uranium *s.* Uran *n.*
urban *a.* Stadt. . ., städtisch.
urbane *a.* weltmännisch; gewandt.
urbanity *s.* Höflichkeit *f.*
urchin *s.* (kleiner) Schelm *m.*
urethra *s.* Harnröhre *f.*
urge *v.t.* treiben, drängen; eifrig betreiben; darauf bestehen.
urgency *s.* Dringlichkeit *f.*
urgent *a.*, **~ly** *adv.* dringend, heftig.
uric *a.* Harn. . .; **~ acid**, Harnsäure *f.*
urinate *v.i.* urinieren.
urine *s.* Urin, Harn *m.*
urn *s.* Urne *f.*; Teekessel *m.*
Uruguay *s.* Uruguay *n.*
Uruguayan *a.* uruguayisch; **~** *s.* Uruguayer(in) *m.*(*f.*)
us *pn.* uns.
US, USA *s.* United States of America.
usable *a.* brauchbar; gebräuchlich.
usage *s.* Gebrauch *m.*; Sitte *f.*
use *s.* Gebrauch, Brauch *m.*; Verwendung *f.*; *in ~*, üblich, gebräuchlich; (*of*) *no ~*, unnütz, zwecklos; *to make ~ of*, Gebrauch machen von; **~** *v.t.* gebrauchen; sich bedienen; anwenden; gewöhnen; behandeln; ausüben; *to ~ up*, aufbrauchen; **~** *v.i.* pflegen, gewohnt sein.
used *a.* gewöhnt; benutzt; gebraucht; *more widely ~*, gebräuchlicher; **~up**, verbraucht.
useful *a.*, **~ly** *adv.* nützlich, dienlich.
usefulness *s.* Nützlichkeit *f.*
useless *a.*, **~ly** *adv.* unnütz, unbrauchbar.
user *s.* Benutzer(in) *m.*(*f.*)
usher *s.* Gerichtsdiener *m.*; Platzanweiser(in) *m.*(*f.*); **~** *v.t.* **~ in**, einführen, anmelden.
usual *a.*, **~ly** *adv.* gebräuchlich, üblich.
usufruct *s.* Nutznießung *f.*
usurer *s.* Wucherer *m.*
usurious *a.* wucherisch.
usurp *v.t.* unrechtmäßig an sich reißen, usurpieren.
usurpation *s.* widerrechtliche Besitzergreifung, Aneignung *f.*
usurper *s.* unrechtmäßiger Machthaber, Inhaber *m.*
usury *s.* Wucher *m.*
utensil *s.* Gerät, Guschirr *n.*
uterine *a.* Gebärmutter. . .
uterus *s.* Gebärmutter *f.*
utilitarian *s.* Utilitarier *m.*; **~a.** Nützlichkeits. . .; utilitaristisch.
utility *s.* Nützlichkeit *f.*; Nutzen *m.*; **~** *a.* Gebrauchs . . . (ohne Verschönerung, z.B. *~ shirt*, *~ furniture*, etc.); *public utilities*, gemeinnützige Anstalten *pl.*
utilization *s.* Nutzung *f.*
utilize *v.t.* nutzen.
utmost *a.* äußerst, höchst.
Utopia *s.* Utopia *n.*
Utopian *a.* utopisch, schwärmerhaft.
utter *a.* äußerst; gänzlich; **~v.t.** sprechen, äußern.

utterance s. Äußerung f.
utterly adv. äußerst, gänzlich, durchaus.

U-turn s. Wende (um 180°) f.
uvula s. Zäpfchen (im Halse) n.

V

V, v der Buchstabe V oder v n.
vacancy s. Leere f.; freie Stelle f.; ~**cies** pl. Zimmer frei.
vacant a. leer, erledigt; gedankenarm.
vacate v.t. räumen; (Amt) niederlegen.
vacation s. Räumung f.; Ferien f.pl.
vaccinate v.t. impfen.
vaccination s. Impfung f.
vaccine s. Impfstoff m.
vacillate v.i. wanken; schwanken.
vacuum s. luftleerer Raum m.; ~cleaner, Staubsauger s.; ~ bottle s. Thermosflasche f.
vagabond a. umherstreifend; ~s. Landstricher m.
vagary s. Grille, Laune f.
vagina s. (Mutter-) Scheide f., Vagina f.
vagrancy s. Landstreicherei f.
vagrant s. Landstreicher(in) m.(f.); ~ a. wandernd, unstet.
vague a. unbestimmt, vage.
vain a., ~**ly** adv. leer, nichtig, eitel, vergeblich; in ~, vergebens.
vale s. Tal n.
valediction s. Abschied m.
valedictory a. Abschieds . . .
valentine s. Grußkarte (f.) am Valentinstage (14. Februar); (Valentins-) Schatz m.
valet s. Kammerdiener, Lakai m.; ~ service s. Reinigungsservice.
valetudinarian a. kränklich, siech; ~ s. Kranke m.
valiant a., ~**ly** adv. tapfer, brav.
valid a., ~**ly** adv. rechtskräftig; gültig.
validate v.t. bestätigen; beweisen; für gültig erklären.
validity s. Gültigkeit f.; Wert m.
valley s. Tal n.
valor s. Tapferkeit f.
valorous a., ~**ly** adv. tapfer.
valuable a. schätzbar; kostbar; ~s pl. Wertsachen f.pl.
valuation s. Schätzung f.
value s. Wert, Preis m.; ~ v.t. schätzen, Achtung erweisen; trassieren.
value added tax s. Mehrwertsteuer f.
valued a. geschätzt; wertvoll.
value-judgment s. Werturteil n.
valueless a. wertlos.
valuer s. Schätzer(in) m.(f.)
valve s. Ventil n.; Klappe f.
vamp s. Vamp m.
vampire s. Vampir m.
van s. Vorhut f.; Möbelwagen m.; Lieferwagen m.
vandalism s. Vandalismus m.
vandalize v.t. zerstören; beschädigen.
vane s. Wetterfahne f.
vanguard s. Vorhut f.
vanilla s. Vanille f.
vanish v.i. verschwinden, zergehen.
vanity s. Eitelkeit, Nichtigkeit f.; ~ bag s. Kosmetiktäschchen n.
vanquish v.t. besiegen.

vantage-point s. Aussichtspunkt m.; from my ~ aus meiner Sicht.
vapid a. schal; geistlos.
vapor s. Dunst, Dampf m.; Schwaden f.pl.
vaporize v.i. verdampfen.
vaporous a. dunstig; nebelhaft, nichtig.
variable a. ~**bly** adv. veränderlich.
variance s. Uneinigkeit, Mißhelligkeit f.; to be at ~, uneinig sein; nicht übereinstimmen.
variant s. Variante f.; ~ a. abweichend.
variation s. Veränderung f.; Verschiedenheit, Abweichung f.
varicose veins pl. Krampfadern pl.
varied a. mannigfaltig.
variegated a. bunt.
variety s. mannigfaltigkeit, Abwechslung, Veränderung f.; Spielart f.; ~ entertainment, Varieteaufführung f.
various a. verschieden; mannigfach.
varnish s. Firnis m.; Anstrich m.; ~ v.t. firnissen, lackieren; (fig.) bemänteln.
vary v.t. (v.i.sich) verändern; verschieden sein, abweichen.
varying a. wechselnd; wechselhaft.
vascular a. (med.) Gefäß . . .
vase s. Vase f.
vasectomy s. Vasektomie f.
vaseline s. Vaselin n.
vassal s. Lehnsmann, Untertan m.
vassalage s. Lehnsverhältnis f.
vast a., ~**ly** adv. sehr groß, weit.
vastness s. Weite f.; ungeheure Größe f.
vat s. Faß n.; Bottich m.
Vatican s. Vatikan m.
vault s. Gewölbe n.; Gruft f.; Sprung m.; Tresorraum m.; ~v.i. ~s. schwingen; ~ v.t. wölben; ~ing horse, Pferd (Turnen) n.
vaulted a. gewölbt.
vaunt v.t. preisen, loben; ~v.i. prahlen; sich rühmen.
veal s. Kalbfleisch n.
veer v.i. sich drehen; (nav.) (ab)fieren.
vegetable s. (meist pl.) Gemüse n.; ~ a. Pflanzen . . ., pflanzenartig; ~fat, Pflanzenfett n.; ~ kingdom, Pflanzenreich n.; ~ oil, Pflanzenöl n.; to be just a ~, nur noch dahinvegetieren.
vegetarian s. Vegetarier(in) m.(f.); ~ a. vegetarisch.
vegetate v.t. nur noch dahinvegetieren.
vegetation s. Vegetation f.
vehemence s. Heftigkeit f.; Eifer m.
vehement a.; ~**ly** adv. heftig, ungestüm.
vehicle s. Fuhrwerk n.; Träger m.
vehicular a. Fahr . . .
veil s. Schleier m; ~ v.t. verschleiern.
veiled a. verschleiert; (fig.) versteckt.
vein s. Blutader f.; Vene f.; Ader (im Holze, etc.) f.; Laune, Stimmung f.; Metallader f.
Velcro s. Klettverschluß m.
vellum s. Pergament n.

velocity s. Geschwindigkeit f.; Schnelligkeit f.
velvet s. Samt m.; ~ a. samten.
velveteen s. Plüsch m.
velvety a. samtig.
venal a. käuflich; korrupt.
venality s. Feilheit f.; Bestechlichkeit f.
vend v.t. verkaufen.
vender, vendor s. Verkäufer(in) m.(f.)
vendible a. verkäuflich.
vending-machine s. (Verkaufs-)Automat m.
veneer v.t. fournieren, auslegen; ~ s. Fournier n.
venerable a., **~bly** adv. ehrwürdig.
venerate v.t. verehren.
veneration s. Verehrung f.; Ehrfurcht f.
veneral disease s. (VD) Geschlechtskrankheit f.
venetian blind s. Jalousie f.
Venezuela s. Venezuela n.
Venezuelan a. venezolanisch; ~ s. Venezolaner(in) m.(f.)
vengeance s. Rache f.
vengeful a. rachsüchtig.
venial a. verzeihlich; lässlich (Sünde).
venison s. Wildbret n.
venom s. Gift n.
venomous a., **~ly** adv. giftig; boshaft.
venous a. venös, Venen . . .
vent s. ; Abzug m.; Öffnung f.; Schlitz m.; to give ~, Luft machen; ~ v.t. lüften.
ventilate v.t. lüften; erörtern.
ventilation s. Lüftung f.; Belüftung f.
ventilator s. Ventilator m.
ventricle s. Herzkammer f.
ventriloquist s. Bauchredner(in) m.(f.)
venture s. Wagnis n.; Unternehmung f.; Einsatz m.; at a ~, auf gut Glück; ~ v.i. & t. wagen; joint ~, s. Gemeinschaftsunternehmen n.
venturesome a., **~ly** adv. verwegen.
venue s. Gerichtsstand, zuständiger Gerrichtshof m.; Treffpunkt m.
veracious a. wahrhaft, aufrichtig.
veracity s. Wahrhaftigkeit f.
veranda(h) s. Veranda f.
verb s. Verb n., Zeitwort n.
verbal a. **~ly** adv. sprachlich, mündlich.
verbatim adv. wörtlich; im Wortlaut.
verbiage s. Wortschwall m.
verbose a. wortreich, weitschweifig.
verdant a. grün, grünend.
verdict s. Entscheidung f.; Urteil n.
verdigris s. Grünspan m.
verge s. Rand m; Grenze f.; on the ~ of, am Rande, dicht vor; ~ v.i. sich neigen, grenzen, streifen.
verger s. Küster m.
verifiable a. nachprüfbar; verifizierbar.
verification s. Bestätigung f.; Nachprüfung f.; Beweis m.
verify v.t. überprüfen; bestätigen.
veritable a. wahr; echt; richtig.
vermicelli s.pl. Fadennudeln f.pl.
vermilion s. Zinnober m.; ~ v.t. rot färben.
vermin s. Ungeziefer n.
vermouth s. Wermut m.
vernacular s. Landessprache f.; ~ a. einheimisch, Landes . . .
versatile a. vielseitig; veränderlich.
versatility s. Vielseitigkeit f.

verse s. Vers m.
versed a. bewandert, erfahren.
versification s. Versbau m.
versify v.t. & i. reimen.
version s. Übersetzung f.; Lesart f.; Darstellung f.
versus pr. gegen.
vertebra s. Rückenwirbel m.
vertebral a. Wirbel . . .
vertebrate s. Wirbeltier m.
vertex s. Scheitelpunkt m.; Spitze f.
vertical a., **~ly** adv. senkrecht, lotrecht.
vertigo s. Schwindel m.; Schwindelgefühl n.
verve s. Schwung m.; Energie f.
very a. wahr, wirklich, echt; völlig; gerade, gar; ~adv. sehr; the ~ same, genau der, die, das selbe; the ~ best, der, die, das allerbeste.
vesicle s. Bläschen n.
vespers s.pl. Abendgottesdienst m.
vessel s. Gefäß n.; Fahrzeug n., Schiff n.
vest s. Unterjacke f.; Weste f.; ~ v.t. bekleiden; verleihen.
vestal v. Vestalin f.
vested p. & a., altbegründet, gesetzlich festgestellt, verbrieft; to be ~ in, jemandem zustehen; ~ interests, pl. Privatinteressen pl..
vestibule s. Vorhalle f.
vestige s. Spur f.
vestment s. Gewand n.; Ornat n.
vestry s. Sakristei; Gemeindeversammlung f.; **~-men** pl. Kirchenälteste m.pl.
vet s. (fam.) Tierarzt m., Tierärztin f.
vetch s. Wicke f.
veteran s. alter Soldat m.; ~ a. erfahren.
veterinarian s. Tierarzt m., Tierärztin f.
veterinary a. tierärztlich, veterinär.
veto s. Veto n.; Einspruch m.; ~ v.t. Einspruch erheben.
vex v.t. plagen, ärgern; ~ v.i. sich grämen.
vexation s. Plage f.; Verärgerung f.
vexatious a., **~ly** adv. unausstehlich; ärgerlich; schikanös.
via pr. über.
viability s. Lebensfähigkeit f.; Realisierbarkeit f.
viable a. lebensfähig, realisierbar.
viaduct s. Bahnbrücke f.
vial s. Phiole f.; Fläschchen n.
vibrant a. vibrierend; lebenssprühend.
vibrate v.i. zittern, beben, vibrieren.
vibration s. Schwingung f., Vibration f.
vibrato s. Vibrato n.
vicar s. Pfarrer m.
vicarage s. Pfarrstelle f.; Pfarrhaus n.
vicarious a. stellvertretend.
vice s. Laster n.; Fehler, Mangel m.; Schraubstock m.; ~pr. an Stelle von; ~ (in Zus.) Vize..., Unter...
vice-admiral s. Vizeadmiral m.
vice-chairman s. stellvertretende Vorsitzende m.
viceroy s. Vizekönig m.
vice-versa adv. umgekehrt.
vicinity s. Nachbarschaft, Nähe f.
vicious a., **~ly** adv. lasterhaft; bösartig (Tier); ~ circle, Teufelskreis m.
vicissitude s. Wechsel(fall), Umschlag m.
victim s. Opfer n.
victimization s. Schikanierung f.
victimize v.t. schikanieren; (auf-)opfern; betrügen.

victor *s.* Sieger(in) *m.(f.)*
Victorian *a.* viktorianisch.
victorious *a.*, ~**ly** *adv.* siegreich.
victory *s.* Sieg *m.*
victuals *s.pl.* Lebensmittel *n.pl.*
vie *v.i.* wetteifern.
Vienna *s.* Wien *n.*
Viennese *a.* Wiener; ~ *s.* Wiener(in) *m.(f.)*
Vietnam *s.* Vietnam *n.*
Vietnamese *a.* vietnamesisch; ~ *s.* Vietnamese *m.*, Vietnamesin *f.*
view *s.* Aussicht *f.*; Ansicht *f.*; Anblick *m.*; *in ~ of*, in Hinblick auf; *with a ~ to*, mit der Absicht zu . . .; ~ *v.t.* besichtigen, betrachten; prüfen.
viewer *s.* Zuschauer(in) *m.(f.)* Betrachter(in) *m.(f.)*
viewfinder *s.* (*phot.*) Sucher *m.*
viewpoint *s.* Standpunkt *m.*; Sichtweise *f.*
vigil *s.* Nachtwache *f.*; Vorabend (*m.*) eines Festtages.
vigilance *s.* Wachsamkeit *f.*
vigilant *a.*, ~**ly** *adv.* wachsam.
vigilantes *pl.* Bürgerwehr *f.*
vigor *s.* Stärke, Kraft *f.*; Energie *f.*
vigorous *a.*, ~**ly** *adv.* kräftig, rüstig.
Viking *s.* Wikinger(in) *m.(f.)*
vile *a.*, gemein, abstoßend; (*fig.*) scheußlich.
vilify *v.t.* erniedrigen, beschimpfen.
villa *s.* Landhaus *n.*; Villa *f.*
village *s.* Dorf *n.*
villager *s.* Dorfbewohner *m.*
villain *s.* Schurke *m.*; Bösewicht *m.*
villainous *a.*, ~**ly** *adv.* niederträchtig; abschenlich.
villainy *s.* Schändlichkeit, Niederträchtigkeit *f.*
vindicate *v.t.* verteidigen; rehabilitieren.
vindication *s.* Verteidigung *f.*; Rehabilitation *f.*
vindictive *a.* nachtragend; rachsüchtig.
vine *s.* Weinstock *m.*; Rebe, Ranke *f.*
vinegar *s.* (Wein-)Essig *m.*
vine-grower *s.* Winzer(in) *m.(f.)*, Weinbauer(in) *m.(f.)*
vine-growing *s.* Weinbau *m.*
vineyard *s.* Weinberg *m.*
vintage *s.* Weinlese *f.*; (Wein)Jahrgang *m.*; ~ *a.* erlesen; herrlich.
vintner *s.* Weinhändler(in) *m.(f.)*; Winzer(in) *m(f.)*
viola *s.* Bratsche *f.*
violate *v.t.* verletzen; schänden.
violation *s.* Verletzung *f.*; Schändung *f.*
vilence *s.* Heftigkeit, Gewalt.
violent *a.*, ~**ly** *adv.* heftig; gewalttätig.
violet *s.* Veilchen *n.*
violin *s.* Violine, Geige *f.*; ~ **case** *s.* Geigenkasten *m.*
violinist *s.* Geiger(in) *m.(f.)*; Violinist(in) *m.(f.)*
violoncello *s.* Cello *n.*, kleine Baßgeige *f.*
viper *s.* Viper, Natter *f.*
viral *a.* Virus . . .
virago *s.* Xantippe *f.*
virgin *s.* Jungfrau *f.*
virginal *a.* jungfräulich.
virginity *s.* Jungfräulichkeit *f.*
Virgo *s.* (*astr.*) Jungfrau *f.*
virile *a.* männlich, viril.
virility *s.* Männlichkeit *f.*

virtual *a.*, ~**ly** *adv.* eigentlich, so gut wie.
virtue *s.* Tugend *f.*; *in ~ of*, zufolge; *by ~ of*, kraft.
virtuoso *s.* Virtuose *m.*; Virtuosin *f.*
virtuous *a.*, ~**ly** *adv.* tugendhaft, sittsam.
virulence *s.* Bösartigkeit *f.*
virulent *a.*, ~**ly** *adv.* giftig; bösartig.
virus *s.* (*med.*) Virus; (*fig.*) Gift *n.*
visa *s.* Sichtvermerk *m.*, Visum *n.*; ~ *v.t.* mit Sichtvermerk versehen.
vis-à-vis *pr.* gegenüber.
viscosity *s.* Zähflüßigkeit *f.*
viscount *s.* Vicomte *m.*
viscountess *s.* Vicomtesse *f.*
viscous *a.* zähflüßig; klebrig.
visibility *s.* Sichtbarkeit *f.*; Sichtverhältnisse *n. pl.*
visible *a.*, sichtbar.
visibly *adv.* sichtlich.
vision *s.* Sehkraft *f.*; Erscheinung *f.*; Vision *f.*
visionary *s.* Visionär(in) *m.(f.)*; ~ *a.* eingebildet; seherhaft.
visit *s..* Besuch *m.*; Besichtigung *f.*; ~ *v.t. & i.* besuchen; besichtigen; heimsuchen.
visitation *s.* Besuch *m.*; Besichtigung *f.*; Inspektion *f.*
visiting card *s.* Visitenkarte *f.*
visitor *s.* Besucher(in) *m.(f.)*; Sommergast *m.*; ~**s' book,** Fremdenbuch *n.*, ~**'s bureau,** Fremdenamt, *n.*
visor *s.* Visier *n.*; Mützenschirm *m.*
vista *s.* Aussicht *f.*
visual *a.* Seh . . ., Gesichts . . .
visualize *v.t.* sich im Geiste vorstellen; ins Auge fassen.
vital *a.*, ~**ly** *adv.* Lebens . . .; unentbehrlich, wesentlich; vital; ~**s** *s.pl* edle Teile *m.pl.*
vitality *s.* Lebenskraft *f.*; Vitalität *f.*
vitamin *s.* Vitamin *n.*; ~ **pill** *s.* Vitamintablette *f.*
vitiate *v.t.* beeinträchtigen; hinfällig machen (Vertrag).
viticulture *s.* Weinbau *m.*
vitreous *a.* gläsern, glasartig.
vitriolic *a.* ätzend; giftig.
vituperate *v.t.* tadeln, schmähen.
vituperation *s.* Schmähung *f.*
vituperative *a.* schmähend.
vivacious *a.* munter, lebhaft.
vivacity *s.* Lebhaftigkeit *f.*
viva voce *adv.* mündlich.
vivid *a.*, ~**ly** *adv.* lebhaft, strahlend; kräftig.
vividness *s.* Lebhaftigkeit *f.*
vivify *v.t.* beleben.
viviparous *a.* lebendige Junge gebärend.
vivisection *s.* Vivisektion *f.*
vixen *s.* Füchsin *f.*; zänkisches Weib *n.*
viz *adv.* nämlich.; d.h.
vizier *s.* Wesir *m.*
V-neck *s.* V-Ausschnitt *m.*
vocabulary *s.* Wörterverzeichnis *n.*; Wortschatz *m.*
vocal *a.* Stimm . . ., stimmhaft; Vokal. . .; ~ *chord*, Stimmband *n.*
vocalist *s.* Sänger(in) *m.(f.)*
vocation *s.* Neigung *f.*; Berufung *f.*; Begabung *f.*
vocational *a.* Berufs. . .; ~ **guidance** *s.* Berufsberatung *f.*
vociferate *v.i. & a.* heftig schreien.
vociferous *s.* schreiend, brüllend.

vogue s. Mode f.
voice s. Stimme f.; at the top of one's ~, aus voller Kehle; ~ v.t. äußern; stimmhaft aussprechen; ~ **box** s. Kehlkopf m.
voiced a. stimmhaft.
voiceless a. stimmlos.
void a. leer; ungültig, nichtig; öd; ~ s. Leere f. Öde f.; ~ v.t. (aus)leeren; räumen, aufheben; ungültig machen.
volatile a. unbeständig; flüchtig.
volatilize v.t. verflüchtigen.
volcanic a. vulkanisch.
volcano s. Vulkan m.
volition s. Wille m.
volley s. Salve f.; ~**ball** s. Volleyball m.
volt s. Volt n.
voltage s. (elek.) Spannung f.
volte-face s. Kehrtwendung f.
voltmeter s. (elek.) Voltmesser m.
voluble a., ~**bly** adv. redselig; gesprächig.
volume s. (Buch) Band m., Masse f.; Umfang f.; Rauminhalt m.; (Radio) Lautstärke f.; ~ control, Lautstärkeneinstellung f.
voluminous a., ~**ly** adv. umfangreich.
voluntary a. freiwillig; absichtlich.
volunteer s. Freiwillige m/f.; v.t. freiwillig dienen; ~v.i. sich freiwillig melden.
voluptuary s. Wollüstling m.
voluptuous a., ~**ly** adv. wollüstig; üppig.

volute s. Windung f., Schnecke f.
vomit v.i. sich erbrechen; s. übergeben; ~v.t. ausspeien, auswerfen; ~ s. Auswurf m.; Erbrochene n.
voracious a., ~**ly** adv. gefräßig, gierig.
voracity s. Gefräßigkeit, Raubsucht f.
vortex s. Wirbel m.; Strudel m.
vote s. Wahlstimme f.; Beschluß, m.; ~ v.t. & i. wählen, stimmen, abstimmen.
voter s. Wähler(in) m.(f.)
voting s. Abstimmung f.; ~ **system** s. Wahlsystem n.
votive a. gelobt, Weih . . .
vouch v.t. bezeugen; verbürgen; ~ v.i. Gewährleisten.
voucher s. Beleg, Schein, Gutschein m.
vow s. Gelübde, feierliches Versprechen n.; ~ v.t. & i. geloben.
vowel s. Selbstlaut, Vokal m.
voyage s. Reise f. Seereise f.; ~ v.t. & i. bereisen; zur See reisen; ~ out, Ausfahrt, Hinfahrt f.
V-shaped a. V-förmig.
vulcanize v.t. vulkanisieren.
vulgar a., ~**ly** adv. gemein; vulgär; pöbelhaft; landesüblich.
vulgarity s. Gemeinheit f.
vulgarize v.t. herabwürdigen.
vulnerable a. verwundbar.
vulpine a. fuchsartig.
vulture s. Geier m.

W

W, w der Buchstabe W oder w n.
wad s. (Watte-) Bausch m.; Pfropfen m.; Knäuel n.; ~ v.t. wattieren.
wadding s. Wattierung f.; Futter n.; Füllmaterial n.
waddle v.i. watscheln, wackeln.
wade v.t. & i. (durch)waten.
wafer s. Oblate f.; Hostie f.; Eiswaffel f.; ~ v.t. mit Oblate siegeln.
waffle s. Waffel f.; Geschwafel n.; Faselei f.; ~ v.i. faseln; schwafeln.
waft v.i. wehen; ziehen; ~ s. Hauch f.
wag v.t. schütteln; wedeln; ~ v.i. wackeln; ~ s. Spaßvogel m.
wage s. Lohn m.; ~**-earner** s. Lohn-empfänger m.; ~**-tariff** s. Lohntarif m.; ~v.t. to ~ war, Krieg führen.
wager s. Wette f.; ~ v.t. & i. wetten.
wages s.pl.(Arbeits)Lohn m.
waggish a., ~**ly** adv. schalkhaft.
waggle v.i. wackeln, wanken.
wag(g)on s. Wagon, Güterwagen m.
wagtail s. Bachstelze f.
wail v.t. beklagen; ~ v.i. wehklagen; ~ s. Klage f. Geheul n.
wain s. (poet.) Wagen m.; Charles's ~, der grosse Bär.
wainscot s. Täfelung f.; Wandleiste f; ~ täfeln.
waist s. Taille f.; schmalste Stelle f.; Damenbluse f.
waistband s. Gürtelbund m.; Hosen/Rockbund m.
waistcoat s. Weste f.
waist-deep a. bis zur Taille reichend.
waistline s. Taille f.
wait v.i. warten; aufwarten; to keep a person ~ing,

einen warten lassen; lie in ~, lauern; ~ on, bedienen; ~ s. Lauer f.; Hinterhalt m.
waiter s. Aufwärter, Kellner m.
waiting-room s. Wartesaal m.
waiting-woman s. Kammermädchen n.
waitress s. Kellnerin f.
waive v.t. aufgeben, verzichten (auf).
wake ~ up, v.i. & t., st. wachen; aufwachen; aufwecken; ~ s. Wachen n.; Kielwasser n.
wakeful a., ~**ly** adv. wachsam; schlaflos.
waken v.t. aufwecken; ~ v.i. aufwachen.
walk v.t. & i. (im Schritte) gehen; spazierengehen; im Schritt gehen lassen; ~ s. Gang, Schritt m.; Spaziergang m.
walkabout s. Bad in der Menge.
walker s. Fußgänger(in), Spaziergänger(in) m.(f.); Geher(in) m.(f.)
walkie-talkie s. Walkie-Talkie n.
walking s. Spazierengehen n.; Wandern n.
walking shoe s. Wanderschuh m.
walking-stick s. Spazierstock m.
walking-tour s. Fußtour f.
Walkman s. Walkman m.
walk-on part s. Statistenrolle f.
walk-out s. Arbeitsniederlegung f.
walk-over s. leichter Sieg m.; Spaziergang m.
walkway s. Fußweg m.
wall s. Wand, Mauer f.; ~ v.t. ummauern; befestigen.; ~**-to** ~ carpeting Teppichboden m.
wall bars s. pl. Sprossenwand f.
wallet s. Tasche f.; Brieftasche f.; Geldtasche f.
wallflower s. (bot.) Goldlack m.; (fig.) Mauerblümchen n.

wallop *v.t.* prügeln; schlagen; ~ *s.* Schlag *m.*
wallow *v.i.* sich wälzen; schlingern; schwelgen.
wallpainting *s.* Wandgemälde *n.*
wallpaper *s.* Tapete *f.*
wallsocket *s.* Wandsteckdose *f.*
wall-unit *s.* Hängeschrank *m.*
walnut *s.* Walnuß *f.*
walrus *s.* Walroß *n.*
waltz *s.* Walzer *m.*; ~ *v.i.* walzen.
wan *a.* blaß, bleich.
wand *s.* Stab *m.*; Gerte *f.*
wander *v.i.* wandern; schlendern; abschweifen, irre reden.
wane *v.i.* abnehmen, welken; ~ *s.* Abnahme *f.*, Verfall *m.*
wangle *v.t.* organisieren; ~ *s.* Kniff *m.*
want *v.t.* nötig haben, brauchen, Mangel haben (an); wollen; wünschen; ~ *v.i.* mangeln, fehlen; ~ *s.* Bedürfnis *n.*; Mangel *m.*; Not *f.*
wanting *s.* Mangel *m.*; Bedürfnis *n.*; ~ *a.* mangelnd, fehlend.
wanton *a.*, **~ly** *adv.* üppig, ausgelassen, mutwillig; zwecklos; liederlich, geil; ~ *s.* liederliche Person *f.*; ~ *v.i.* schäkern, schwärmen.
wantonness *s.* Mutwille *m.*; Geilheit *f.*; Üppigkeit *f.*; Zwecklosigkeit *f.*
war *s.* Krieg *m.*; ~ *v.i.* Krieg führen.
warble *v.t. & i.* wirbeln; trillern.
warbler *s.* Grasmücke *f.*
war-blinded *a. & s.* Kriegsblinde *m.*
war correspondent *s.* Kriegsberichterstatter(in) *m.(f.)*
war crime *s.* Kriegsverbrechen *n.*
war criminal *s.* Kriegsverbrecher(in) *m.(f.)*
war-cry *s.* Kriegsruf, Schlachtruf *m.*
ward *s.* Gewahrsam *m.*; Vormundschaft *f.*; Stadtbezirk *m.*; Mündel *f.*; (Hospital-)Saal *m.*; ~ *v.t.* bewachen; abwehren.
warden *s.* Aufseher(in) *m.(f.)*; Rektor(in) *m.(f.)*; Heimleiter(in) *m.(f.)*
warder *s.* Wächter, Hüter, Wärter *m.*
wardrobe *s.* Kleiderschrank *m.*; Garderobe *f.*
ware *s.* Ware *f.*, Geschirr *n.*
warehouse *s.* Warenlager, Magazin *n.*; ~ *clerk s.* Lagerist *m.*; ~ *v.t.* einlagern.
warfare *s.* Krieg *m.*; Kriegsführung *f.*
war-game *s.* Kriegsspiel *n.*
warhead *s.* Sprengkopf *m.*
warlike *a.* kriegerisch, Kriegs . . .
warm *a.*, **~ly** *adv.* warm; eifrig; feurig, hitzig; ~ *v.t. (v.i.* sich) erwärmen.
warm-blooded *a.* warmblütig.
war memorial *s.* Kriegsdenkmal *n.*
warm-hearted *a.* warmherzig.
warmonger *s.* Kriegshetzer(in) *m.(f.)*
warmth *s.* Wärme *f.*; Eifer *m.*
warn *v.t.* warnen, ermahnen; ankündigen, wissen lassen.
warning *s.* Warnung *f.*; Ankündigung *f.*; Bescheid *m.*; *at a minute's* ~, fristlos.
war-office *s.* Kriegsministerium *n.*
warp *v.i.* sich verbiegen; ~ verziehen; abweichen; ~ *v.t.* krümmen; ~ *s.* Weberkette *f.*; Krümmung *f.*
war-paint *s.* Kriegsbemalung *f.*
warrant *s.* Durchsuchungsbefehl *m.*; Haftbefehl *m.*; ~ *v.t.* rechtfertigen.

warranty *s.* Garantie *f.*
warren *s.* Kaninchengehege *n.*
warring *a.* kriegführend.
warrior *s.* Krieger *m.*
war-risk *s.* Kriegsrisiko *n.*
warship *s.* Kriegsschiff *n.*
wart *s.* Warze *f.*
wart-hog *s.* Warzenschwein *n.*
wartime *s.* Kriegszeit *f.*
wary *a.* vorsichtig; schlau.
wash *v.t. &* (sich) waschen; bespülen; ~ *s.* Wäsche *f.*; Wellenschlag *m.*; Schwemmland *n.*; Anstrich *m.*; Spülwasser *n.*; **~-basin** *s.* Waschbecken *n.*; **~-day** *s.* Waschtag *m.*; **~-tub** *s.* Waschfaß *n.*; ~ *up s.* Aufwaschen *n.*; **~ing powder** *s.* Waschpulver *n.*
washable *a.* waschbar.
wash-bill *s.* Waschzettel *m.*
washed-out *a.* verwaschen; (*fig.*) abgehetzt.
washer *s.* Waschen *n.*; Waschmaschine *f.*; Dichtungsring *m.*
washing *s.* Waschen *n.*; Wäsche *f.*
washing-machine *s.* Waschmaschine *f.*
wash-out *s.* Pleite *f.*; Reinfall *m.*
wasp *s.* Wespe *f.*
waspish *a.*, **~ly** *adv.* reizbar, zänkisch.
wastage *s.* Schwund *m.*
waste *v.t.* verwüsten, zerstören; verschwenden; ~ *v.i.* abnehmen; schwinden; ~ *a.* verwüstet, öde; unnütz; ~ *s.* Verwüstung *f.*; Abnahme *f.*; Auszehrung *f.*; Einöde *f.*; Vergeudung *f.*; Verschwendung *f.*; Abfall *m.*; ~ *of time,* Zeitvergeudung *f.*; ~ *land s.* Ödland *n.*; ~ *product s.* Abfallprodukt *n.*; ~ (*water*) *s.* Abwasser *n.*
waste-book *s.* Kladde *f.*
waste disposal *s.* Abfallbeseitigung *f.*; Entsorgung *f.*
wasteful *a.*, **~ly** *adv.* verschwenderisch.
waste-paper *s.* Papierbfall *m.* ~ *basket,* Papierkorb *m.*
waste-pipe *s.* Abflußrohr *n.*
wastrel *s.* Verschwender *m.*
watch *s.* Wache, Wachsamkeit *f.*; Posten *m.*; Armband- Taschenuhr *f.*; ~ *v.t.* bewachen; beobachten; aufpassen; ~ *v.i.* wachen.
watchband, watchbracelet *s.* Uhrenarmband *n.*
watchdog *s.* Wachhund *m.*
watchful *a.*, **~ly** *adv.* wachsam.
watch-maker *s.* Uhrmacher(in) *m.(f.)*
watchman *s.* Nachtwächter *m.*
watchstrap *s.* Uhrenarmband *n.*
watchtower *s.* Wachturm *m.*
watchword *s.* Losung *f.*
water *s.* Wasser *n.*; *to make,* ~ *sein Wasser abschlagen; ~s pl.* (Heil) Brunnen *m.*; ~ *v.t.* wässern, begießen, tränken; verwässern; **~ing-can** *s.* Gießkanne *f.*
watercart *s.* Sprengwagen *m.*
water-closet *s.* Wasserklosett *n.*; Toilette *f.*
water-color *s.* Aquarell *n.*
water-colorist *s.* Aquarellist *m.*
watercourse *s.* Wasserlauf *m.*
water-cress *s.* Brunnenkresse *f.*
water-diviner *s.* Rutengänger(in) *m.(f.)*
waterfall *s.* Wasserfall *m.*
water-fowl *s.* Wassergeflügel *n.*

waterfront s. Ufer n.
water-glass s. Wasserglas n.
water-level s. Wasserstand m.
water-lily s. Seerose f.
waterlogged a. wasserdurchtränkt.
water-main s. Hauptwasserleitung f.
waterman s. Bootsführer m.
watermark s. Wasserzeichen n.
water-melon s. Wassermelone f.
water-mill s. Wassermühle f.
water-pipe s. Wasserrohr n.; Wasserpfeife f.
water-power s. Wasserkraft f.
waterproof a. wasserdicht.
water-rate s. Wassergeld n.
water-repellent a. wasserabstoßend.
water-resistant a. wasserundurchlässig.
water-shed s. Wasserscheide f.
water-spout s. Dachtraufe f.
water-supply s. Wasserversorgung f.
water-table s. Grundwasserspiegel m.
water tap s. Wasserhahn m.
water-tight a. wasserdicht.
water-tower s. Wasserturm m.
waterways pl. Wasserstraßen pl.
water-works s. Wasserwerk n.
watery a. wässerig, wasserreich.
watt s. (elek.) Watt n.
wattage s. elektrische Leistung f.
wave s. Welle, Woge f.; ~ v.i. wogen; winken; ~ v.t. schwingen.
wave-band s. (radio) Wellenband n.
wavelength s. (radio) Wellenlänge f.
waver v.i. schwanken; wanken.
wavy a. wogend; wellig.
wax s. Wachs n.; Siegellack n.; Ohrenschmalz n.; Schusterpech n.; ~ v.t. wachsen; wichsen, bohnern. ~ v.i. wachsen, zunehmen; werden.
waxen a. wächsern, Wachs . . .
waxwork s. Wachsfigur f.
waxy a. wachsartig.
way s. Weg m.; Richtung f.; Bahn f.; Art und Weise f.; Verfahren n.; Mittel n.; the ~ out, Ausgang m., Ausweg m.; right of ~, Wegerecht n.; by the ~, beiläufig, übrigens; by ~ of excuse, als Entschuldigung; this ~, so, auf diese Weise; this ~ or that, so oder so; to make ~ for, ausweichen; to lead the ~, vorgehen, vorangehen; to lose one's ~, sich verlaufen; to find one's ~, sich zurechtfinden; on his ~, under ~, unterwegs.
way-bill s. Beförderungsschein m.
wayfarer s. Wanderer m., Wanderin f. Reisende m./f.
waylay v.t.ir. auflauern, überfallen.
wayside s. Wegrand m.; by the ~, am Wege.
wayward a., ~ly adv. eigensinnig.
we pn. wir.
weak a. schwach, schwächlich.
weak current s. (elek.) Schwachstrom m.
weaken v.t. schwächen, entkräften.
weak-kneed a. schwach; feige.
weakling s. Schwächling m.
weakly a. & adv. schwächlich.
weakness s. Schwäche, Schwachheit f.
weak-willed a. willensschwach.
weal s. striemen m.
wealth s. Wohlstand m., Reichtum n.

wealthy a., ~ily adv. wohlhabend, reich.
wean v.t. entwöhnen; abgewöhnen.
weapon s. Waffe f.
weaponry s. Waffen pl.
wear v.t.st. tragen; anhaben; ~ v.i. st. sich tragen; to ~ off, sich abnutzen, sich verlieren; to ~ out, abtragen, abnutzen; ~ s. Tragen n.; Abnutzung f.; Tracht f.; Anzug m.; ~ and tear, Abnutzung f.; hard ~, starke Beanspruchung f.; to have longer ~, länger halten; resistance to ~, Strapazierfähigkeit f.; ~ing apparel s. Kleidungsstücke pl.
wearisome a., ~ly adv. ermüdend.
weary a., ~ily adv. müde, matt; überdrüssig; ~ v.t. ermüden; ~ v.i. müde werden.
weasel s. Wiesel n.
weather s. Wetter n.; Witterung f.; ~ bureau s. Wetterwarte f.; ~ outlook, Wetteraussichten pl.; ~ permitting, bei gutem Wetter; ~ v.t. der Luft aussetzen, lüften; verwittern; verblassen.
weather-beaten a. verwittert; wettergeerbt.
weather-chart s. Wetterkarte f.
weather-forecast s. Wetterbericht m., Wettervorhersage f.
weather-map s. Wetterkarte f.
weatherproof a. wetterfest; ~ v.t. wetterfest machen.
weather satellite s. Wettersatellit m.
weather-vane s. Wetterfahne f.
weave v.t. & i.st. weben, flechten, torkeln.
weaver s. Weber(in) m.(f.)
web s. Netz n.; Gewebe n.; Schwimmhaut f.
web-footed a. mit Schwimmfüssen.
wed v.t. & i. heiraten; ehelichen; trauen.
wedded a. eingetraut, verheiratet.
wedding s. Hochzeit f.; ~-ring, Trauring m.
wedge s. Keil m.; ~ v.t. (ver)keilen; durchzwängen.
wedlock s. Ehe f.; Ehestand m.
Wednesday s. Mittwoch m.
wee a. winzig, klein.; ~v.i. (fam.) Pipimachen.
weed s. Unkraut n.; ~s pl. Unkraut n.; ~ v.t. jäten.
weeding s. Unkrautjäten n.
weedy a. voll Unkraut.
week s. Woche f.; a ~ from tomorrow, morgen über acht Tage; a ~ ago yesterday, gestern vor acht Tagen.
weekday s. Wochentag m.
weekend s. Wochenende n.
weekly a. & adv. wöchentlich; ~ s. Wochenblatt n.
weeny a. (fam.) klitzeklein, winzig.
weep v.i. & t.ir. weinen; beweinen.
weeping-willow s. Trauerweide f.
weevil s. Rüsselkäfer m.
weigh v.t. wiegen, wägen, erwägen; schätzen; to ~ out, ausweigen; ~ v.i. wiegen, (nieder)drücken.
weighing-machine s. Hebelwaage f.
weight s. Gewicht n.; Wucht f.; Schwergewicht n.; Nachdruck m.; ~ v.t. beschweren; to carry ~ with, viel gelten bei; to gain ~, zunehmen; to lose ~, abnehmen.
weight-bridge s. Brückenwaage f.
weightless a. schwerelos.
weightlessness s. Schwerelosigkeit f.
weight-lifting s. Gewichtheben n.
weighty a., ~ily adv. gewichtig; schwer.
weir s. Wehr n.
weird a. unheimlich, seltsam.

welcome *a. & i.* willkommen; ~ *s.* Willkomm *m.*; *to bid* ~, willkommen heißen; ~ *v.t.* bewillkommen; *you are* ~, bitte!

welcoming *a.* einladend.

weld *v.t.* zusammen(schweißen).

welder *s.* Schweißer(in) *m.(f.)*

welfare *s.* Wohlfahrt *f.*; ~ *officer*, *s.* Fürsorgebeamter *m.*; ~ *state*, *s.* Wohlfahrtsstaat *m.* ~ *work*, *s.* Fürsorge, Sozialarbeit *f.*

well *s.* Quelle *f.*; Brunnen *m.*; ~**s** *pl.* Heilquelle *f.*; ~ *v.i.* quellen; ~ *a. & adv.* wohl, gut; gesund; leicht; gern; *as* ~ *as*, so wohl als auch.

well-advised *a.* klug (Plan).

well-appointed *a.* gut ausgestattet.

well-authenticated *a.* wohlverbürgt.

well-balanced *a.* dusgeglichen, ausgewogen.

well-behaved *a.* Wohlerzogen.

well-being *s.* Wohlsein *n.*

well-bred *a.* anständig; gut erzogen.

well-chosen *a.* wohlgesetzt (Worte); gewählt.

well-deserved *a.* wohlverdient.

well-done *a.* 'durch' (Braten).

well-groomed *a.* gepflegt, gut aussehend.

well-nigh *adv.* beinahe.

well-off, **well-to-do** *a.* wohlhabend.

well-read *a.* belesen.

well-wisher *s.* Gönner(in), Freund(in) *m.(f.)*

Welsh *a.* walfisich; *s.* Waliser(in) *m.(f.)* ~**-rabbit** *s.* Käse auf geröstetem Brot *m.*; ~ *v.i.* nicht bezahlen (Restaurant).

welter *v.i.* swich wälzen; ~ *s.* Wirrwarr *m.*

wend *v.i. & t.* gehen, (sich) wenden.

wer(e)wolf *s.* Werwolf *m.*

west *s.* Westen, Abend *m.*; ~ *a. & adv.* westlich; ~**bound** *a.* in Richtung Westen.

westerly, **western** *a.* westlich.

westerner *s.* Abendländer(in) *m.(f.)*

westernize *v.t.* verwestlichen.

westernmost *a.* westlichst . . .

Westphalia *s.* Westfalen *n.*

westward *a.*, ~**ly** adv. westwärts; westlich.

wet *a.* naß, feucht, regnerisch; ~ *paint!*, frisch gestrichen! ~ *s.* Nässe *f.*; ~ *v.t.* nässen, anfeuchten.

wether *s.* Hammel *m.*

wet-nurse *s.* Amme *f.*

whack *v.t.* tüchtig schlagen, prügeln; hauen.

whale *s.* Walfisch *m.*

whalebone *s.* Fischbein *n.*

whaler *s.* Walfischfänger *m.*

whale-oil *s.* Tran *m.*

wharf *s.* Kai *m.*; Landeplatz *m.*

what *pn.* was; welcher, welches; was für ein; ~ . . . ~, teils . . . teils.

what(so)ever *pn.* was auch (immer).

wheat *s.* Weizen *m.*

wheedle *v.t.* schmeicheln; beschwatzen.

wheel *s.* Rad, Spinnrad *n.*; Töpferscheibe *f.*; (*mil.*) Schwenkung *f.*; ~ *v.t.* (*v.i.*) sich) drehen, rollen; (*mil.*) schwenken, einschwenken; fahren; *right* ~!, (*mil.*) rechts schwenkt!; *left* ~!, (*mil.*) links schwenkt!

wheelbarrow *s.* Schubkarren *m.*

wheelchair *s.* Fahrstuhl, Rollstuhl *m.*

wheeze *v.i.* keuchen, schnaufen, röcheln.

wheezy *a.* keuchend; pfeifend.

whelp *s.* Junge *n.*; junger Hund *m.*; ~ *v.i.* Jungen

werfen.

when *adv. & c.* wenn, wann, da, als; wo.

whence *adv.* woher, von wo.

where *adv.* wo, wohin; ~*abouts*, wo ungefähr etwa; worüber, *s.pl.* ~*abouts*, Aufenthalt *m.*; ~*as*, da, doch, während; ~*at*, wobei, woran, worauf; ~*by*, wodurch, womit; ~*fore*, weshalb, wofür; ~*in*, worin; ~*into*, worin; ~*of*, wovon, woraus; ~*on*, woran, worauf; ~*so*, ~*soever*, wo auch immer; ~*to*, wozu, worauf; ~*upon*, worauf; ~*with*, womit; ~*withal*, womit auch.

wherever *adv.* wo immer, überall wo.

wherewithal *s.* Mittel *n.*

whet *v.t.* wetzen; schärfen.

whether *c.* ob.

whetstone *s.* Wetzstein, Schleifstein *m.*

whey *s.* Molke *f.*

which *pn.* welcher, welche, welches; wer, was; der, die, das.

whichever *pn.* welcher auch immer, was auch.

whiff *s.* Hauch, Luftzug *m.*

while *s.* Weile, Zeit, *f.*; ~ *v.t.* verbringen, ~**away**, vertreiben.

while, **whilst** *c.* indem, während, solange (als).

whim *s.* Grille *f.*; Einfall *m.*

whimper *v.i.* winseln; wimmern; ~*s.* Wimmern *n.*

whimsical *a.*, ~**ly** *adv.* grillenhaft, launenhaft.

whine *v.i.* weinen, wimmern; ~ *s.* Gewimmer *n.*

whip *s.* Peitsche, Geissel *f.*; (Parlament) Einpeitscher *m.*; Aufforderung (*f.*) an Parteimitglieder im Parlament; ~ *v.t.* peitschen, geißeln; übernähen; ~ *v.i.* springen, flitzen; ~*ped cream*, *s.* Schlagsahne *f.*, Schlagrahm *m.*

whip-hand *s.* Oberhand *f.*

whipping *s.* Prügel *f.*; ~**-top**, Kreisel *m.*

whirl *s.* Wirbel, Strudel *m.*; ~ *v.t.* wirbeln; ~ *v.i.* herumwirbeln.

whirl-pool *s.* Strudel, Wirbel *m.*

whirr *v.i.* surren; *s.* Surren *n.*

whirlwind *s.* Wirbelwind *m.*

whisk *s.* Wedel *m.*; Schneebesen *m.*; ~ *v.t.* schlagen (Sahne); wischen; ~ *v.i.* schwirren, huschen.

whisker *s.* Backenbart *m.*; Schnurrhaar *n.*; Bartborste *f.*

whisky *s.* Whisky *m.*

whisper *v.t. & i.* wispern, flüstern; zuraunen; ~ *s.* Geflüster *n.*

whist *s.* Whist(spiel) *n.*

whist-drive *s.* Whistturnier *n.*

whistle *v.i. & t.* pfeifen; ~ *s.* Pfeifen *n.*; Pfiff *m.*; Pfeife *f.*

whit *s.* Punkt *m.*; Kleinigkeit *f.*; *not a* ~, nicht im geringsten.

white *a.* weiß; bleich; rein; ~ *horse*, Schimmel *m.*

whitebait *s.* junger Hering *m.*, Sprotte *f.*

white-collar worker *s.* Büroangestellte *m./f.*

white-heat *s.* Weißglut *f.*

white-hot *a.* weißglühend.

whiten *v.t.* weißen; weiß machen.

whiteness *s.* Blässe *f.*; Reinheit *f.*

white-wash *s.* Tünche *f.*; ~ *v.t.* weißen, tünchen; weiß waschen.

whither *adv.* wohin; ~*soever*, wohin auch.

white wine *s.* Weißwein *m.*

whiting *s.* Weißling (Fisch) *m.*; Kreide *f.*

whitish *a.* weißlich, etwas blaß.

Whitsunday s. Pfingsten n.

whittle v.t. schneiden; schnitzeln.

whiz v.i. zischen, sausen, schwirren; ~ s. Zischen, Sausen n.

whiz-kid s. Senkrechtstarter(in) m.(f.)

who pn. wer; welcher; der, die, das.

whodunit s. (fam.) Krimi m.

whoever pn. wer auch (immer); jeder; der, die, das.

whole a. ganz; heil, gesund; ~ number, ganze Zahl f.; ~ s. Ganze n.; on the ~, im Ganzen.

wholefood s. Vollwertkost f.

wholehearted a., ~ly adv. mit ganzem Herzen.

whole note s. ganze Note f.

wholesale a. Groß. . ., im großen, Großhandels. . .; ~ s. Großhandel m.; ~ a. im großen.

wholesome a., ~ly adv. gesund, heilsam.

whole wheat a. Vollkorn . . .

wholly adv. gänzlich, völlig.

whom pron. wen; wem; den, die, dem.

whoop s. Schrei m.; Jauchzer m.; ~ v.i. jauchzen; schreien.

whooping-cough s. Keuchhusten m.

whore s. Hure f.

whorl s. Quirl m.; Windung f.

whortleberry s. Heidelbeere f.

whose pn. dessen; deren; wessen.

whosever pn. wer auch (immer).

why adv. warum; weshalb.

wick s. Docht m.

wicked a., ~ly adv. böse; schlecht; niederträchtig.

wickedness s. Bosheit f., Niedertracht f.

wicker s. Weidenzweig m.; ~ a. aus Zweigen geflochten, Korb. . .; Weiden. . . ~ furniture, s. Korbmöbel pl.

wickerwork s. Korbflechtwaren pl.

wicket s. Pförtchen n.; Schalter m.; ~s pl. Tor n. (beim Kricket).

wide a., ~ly adv. weit; breit; fern; sehr; far and ~, weit und breit.

wide-angle lens s. Weitwinkelobjektiv n.

wide-awake s. ganz wach; pfiffig.

wide-eyed a. mit grossen Augen.

widen v.t. (v.i. sich) erweitern; verbreiten.

wide-open a. weit aufstehend, aufgerissen.

wide-ranging a. weitreichend; weitgehend.

widespread a. weit verbreitet.

widow s. Witwe f.; ~ v.t. zur Witwe machen.

widowed a. verwitwet.

widower s. Witwer m.

widowhood s. Witwenstand m.

width s. Weite, Breite f.

wield v.t. handhaben; schwingen.

wife s. Frau f.; Weib n.; Ehefrau f.

wig s. Perücke f.

wiggle v.t. hin- und herbewegen, wacheln.

wight s. Wicht, Kerl m.

wigwam s. Wigwam m., Indianerzelt n.

wild a., ~ly adv. wild.

wildcat s. Wildkatze f.

wildcat a. ~strike s. Wilder Streik m.

wilderness s. Wildnis f.

wildfire s. Lauffeuer m.

wildfowl s. Wildgeflügel n.

wildness s. Wildheit f.

Wild West s. der Wilde Westen m.

wile s. List, Tücke f.; Streich m.

wilful as., eigensinnig; vorsätzlich; willkürlich.

will s. Wille m.; Testament n.; ~ v.i. letztwillig verfügen.

willed a. gesonnen, geneigt.

willies s.pl. (fam.) Nervösitat f., Nervenschwäche f., get the ~, Zustände kommen.

willing a., ~ly adv. willig; willens; gern.

willingness s. Bereitwilligkeit f, Bereitschaft f.

will-o'-the-wisp Irrlicht n.

willow s. Weide f.; (mech.) Wolf m.

will-power s. Willenskraft f.

willy-nilly adv. wohl oder übel.

wilt v.i. welken.

wily a. schlau, verschmitzt.

wimp s. (fam. pej.) Schlappschwanz m.

win v.t. & i.st. gewinnen; einnehmen; (be)siegen; erobern; to ~ over, gewinnen für.

wince v.i. zucken; zurückfahren.

winch s. Kurbel f.; Winde f., Kran m.

wind s. Wind m.; Atem m.; ~ v.t.st. winden, wickeln; drehen, wenden; to ~ up, aufziehen (Uhr); liquidieren (Geschäfte).

windbag s. (fig.) Schaumschläger m; Schwätzer m.

wind-break s. Windschutz m.

windbreaker s. Windjacke f.

windfall s. Fallobst n.; (fig.) Glücksfall m.

winding s. Windung, Krümmung f.; (elek.) Wicklung f.; ~ a. gewunden; ~-stairs s.pl. Wendeltreppe f.

wind instrument s. Blasinstrument n.

windlass s. Winde f.

windmill s. Windmühle f.; Windrädchen n.

window s. Fenster n.; ~ cleaner s. Fensterputzer m.; ~ dresser s. Schaufensterdekorateur(in) m.(f.).; ~ dressing, Schaufensterdekoration f., Aufmachung f., ~shopping s. Schaufensterbummel m.

windpipe s. Luftröhre f.

windshield s. (mot.) Windschutz, Windscheibe f.; ~-wiper s. Scheibenwischer m.

windsurfing s. Windsurfen n.

windswept a. windgepeitscht.

windtunnel s. Windkanal m.

windward a. luvwärts; s. Luvseite f.

windy a. windig; nichtig.

wine s. Wein m.

wine-cellar s. Weinkeller m.

wine-list s. Weinkarte f.

wine-press s. Kelter f.

winery s. Weinkellerei f.

wine-tasting s. Weinprobe f.

wing s. Flügel m.; Schwinge f.; Kulisse f.; (avi.) Tragfläche f.; (avi.) Geschwader n.; ~commander s. Geschwaderkommandeur m.; on the ~, im Fluge; ~ v.t. beflügeln; ~ v.i. fliegen.

winged a. geflügelt, schnell.

winger s. Außenstürmer(in) m.(f.)

wingspan, wingspread s. Flugelspannweite f.

wink s. Blinzeln n.; ~ v.i. (zu)blinzeln; (fig.) ~ at sth. ein Auge zudrücken bei etw.

winker s. Blinker m.

winner s. Gewinner(in) m.(f.); Sieger(in) m.(f.)

winning p. & a. gewinnend, einnehmend; siegreich; ~ s. Gewinn m.

winter s. Winter m.

winterize v.t. winterfest machen.

wintry *a.* winterlich.

wipe *v.t.* wischen, abwischen; abtrocknen; *to ~ out,* (*mil.*) vernichten; *~ s.* Wischen *n.*

wiper *s.* Wischer *m.*

wire *s.* Draht *m.*; Drahtnachricht *f.*; *~ v.t.* drahten; *~* **brush** *s.* Drahtbürste *f.*; *~-***netting** *s.* Drahtgeflecht *n.*; *~-***rope** *s.* Drahtseil *n.*

wiredraw *v.i.* Draht ziehen; (*fig.*) in die Länge ziehen.

wireless *a.* drahtlos; *~ v.i.* funken; *~ s.* Rundfunk *m.*, Radio *n.*, Funker *m.*

wire-puller *s.* Marionettenspieler *m.*; (*fig.*) Drahtzieher *m.*

wire-pulling *s.* heimliche Umtriebe *pl.*, Intrigen *pl.*

wiring *s.* (elektrische) Leitungen *f.pl.*

wiry *a.* aus Draht; (*fig.*) zäh, sehnig.

wisdom *s.* Weisheit, Klugheit *f.*; *~***tooth** *s.* Weisheitszahn *m.*

wise *a.* *~ly adv.* weise; verständig, erfahren.

wisecrack *v.i.* witzeln; *s.* Witzelei *f.*

wiseguy *s.* (*vulg.*) Klugscheißer(in) *m.*(*f.*)

wish *v.t. & i.* wünschen; *~ s.* Wunsch *m.*

wishful *a.*, *~ly adv.* wünschend, sehnlich; *~ thinking,* Wunschdenken *n.*

wishy-washy *a.* wässerig; (*fig.*) lasch, schlapp.

wisp *s.* Bündel *n.*; Büschel *n.*

wistful *a.*, *~ly adv.* sehnsüchtig; melancholisch.

wit *s.* Witz *m.*; Geist *m.*; witziger Kopf *m.*; Witzbold *m. to ~,* nämlich, das heißt; *to be at one's ~'s end,* nicht mehr ein und aus wissen.

witch *s.* Hexe, Zauberin *f.*

witchcraft *s.* Hexerei *f.*

witchhunt *s.* Hexenjagd *f.*

withdraw *v.t.st.* zurücknehmen, zurückziehen; abberufen; (Geld) abheben; *~ v.i.* sich zurückziehen.

withdrawal *s.* Zurückziehung, Zurücknahme *f.*; Abhebung *f.*

withdrawn *a.* verschlossen, zurückgezogen.

wither *v.t. & i.* ausdörren, verwelken, vertrocknen, vergehen.

withered *a.* verwelkt.

withering *a.* vernichtend; sengend.

withhold *v.t.st.* zurückhalten; vorenthalten; verhindern.

within *pr.* in, innerhalb, binnen; *~ adv.* drinnen, im Innern.

without *pr.* außerhalb, vor; ohne; *~ adv.* außerhalb; draußen.

withstand *v.t.st.* widerstehen; standhalten.

witless *a.* geistlos; geistesgestört.

witness *s.* Zeugnis *n.*; Zeuge *m.*; *~ box,* Zeugenbank *f.*; *to bear ~,* Zeugnis ablegen; *to take the ~ stand,* in den Zeugenstand treten; *~ for the prosecution,* Belastungszeuge *m.*; *~ for the defense,* Entlastungszeuge *m.*; *~ summons,* Zeugenvorladung *f.*; *~ v.t.* bezeugen; zugegen sein, erleben.

witticism *s.* Witz *m.*, Witzelei *f.*

wittingly *adv.* wissentlich, vorsätzlich.

witty *a.*, *~ily adv.* witzig; geistreich.

wizard *s.* Zauberer *m.*

wizened *a.* runzelig.

wobble *v.i.* wackeln; zittern.

woe *s.* Weh *n.*; Leid *n.*; *~! i.* weh!

woebegone *a.* jammervoll.

woeful *a.*, *~ly adv.* traurig; erbärmlich.

wolf *s.* Wolf *m.*

wolfish *a.* wölfisch, gefrässig.

wolfram *s.* Wolfram(erz) *n.*

woman *s.* Frau *f.*, Weib *n.*

womanhood *s.* Weiblichkeit *f.*, Fraulichkeit *f.*

womanish *a.*, *~ly adv.* weibisch.

womanizer *s.* Schürzenjäger *m.*

womankind *s.* weibliches Geschlecht *n.*

womanliness *s.* Weiblichkeit *f.*, Fraulichkeit *f.*

womanly *a.* fraulich, weiblich.

womb *s.* Gebärmutter *f.*

Women's Liberation *s.* Frauenbewegung *f.*

women's rights *s.pl.* Frauenrechte *pl.*

wonder *s.* Wunder *n.*; Verwunderung *f.*; *~ v.i.* sich wundern; sich fragen, gern wissen mögen.

wonderful *a.*, *~ly adv.* wunderbar.

wondering *a.* staunend, fragend.

wonderland *s.* Paradies *n.*; Wunderland *n.*

wonderment *s.* Verwunderung *f.*

wondrous *a.*, *~ly adv.* wunderbar, außerordentlich.

won't = **will not.**

wont *s.* Gewohnheit *f.*; *use and ~,* fester Gebrauch *m.*; *~ a.* gewohnt.

wonted *a.* gewohnt; gewöhnlich.

woo *v.t. & i.* freien, werben; zustreben.

wood *s.* Wald *m.*; Holz *n.*

wood-bine *s.* Geißblatt *n.*

wood-carver *s.* Holzschnitzer *m.*

wood-carving *s.* Holzschnitzerei *f.*

wood-cut *s.* Holtzschnitt *m.*

wooded *a.* holzreich; waldig, bewaldet.

wooden *a.* hölzern; (*fig.*) steif.

wood-engraver *s.* Holzschneider *m.*

wood-land *s.* Waldung *f.*

wood-lark *s.* Heiderlerche *f.*

wood-louse *s.* Assel *f.*

woodman *s.* Holzhacker *m.*; Förster *m.*

woodpecker *s.* Specht *m.*

woodpulp *s.* Holzzellstoff *m.*

wood-ruff *s.* Waldmeister (Pflanze) *m.*

woodshaving *s.* Holzspan *m.*

wood-shed *s.* Holzschuppen *m.*

wood-wind *s.* Holzblasinstrument *n.*

woodwool *s.* Holzwolle *f.*

woodwork *s.* Holzarbeit *f.*; Holzwerk *n.*; Täfelung *f.*

woodworker *s.* Holzarbeiter *m.*

woodworm *s.* Holzwurm *m.*

woody *a.* waldig, holzig.

wooer *s.* Freier, Bewerber *m.*

woofer *s.* Baßlautsprecher *m.*

wool *s.* Wolle *f.*

woollen *a.* wollen; *~s s.pl.* Wollwaren *f.pl.*

woolly *a.* wollig; verworren, unklar.

word *s.* Wort *n.*; Nachricht *f.*; *~ for ~,* Wort für Wort; *in other ~s,* mit anderen Worten; *~ v.t.* in Worte fassen.

wording *s.* Formulierung *f.*; Stil *m.*

word order *s.* Wortstellung *f.*

word processing *s.* Textverarbeitung *f.*

word processor *s.* Textverarbeitungssystem *n.*

wordy *a.* wortreich; weitschweifig.

work *s.* Arbeit *f.*; Werk *n.*; Getriebe *n.*; Handarbeit

f.; *hours of* ~, Arbeitsstunden *pl.*; ~**-basket**, Arbeits-
korb *m.*, ~**-box**, Arbeitskästchen *n.* (Handarbeit);
~**-order** *s.* Werkstattauftrag *m.*; ~**-permit** *s.*
Arbeitserlaubnis *f.*; ~**s** *pl.* Fabrik *f.*, Werk *n.*; Getriebe, Werk *n.* (Uhr, Klavier); Schriften *f.pl.*; ~ *v.i.*
arbeiten; wirken; gären; funktionieren; ~ *v.t.* bearbeiten; behandeln; arbeiten lassen; in Betrieb
haben; bedienen (Handwerkszeug), arbeiten mit;
to ~ *out*, berechnen; *to* ~ *out at*, kommen auf; *to* ~
up, aufarbeiten, verarbeiten.
workable *a.* bearbeitungsfähig; betriebsfähig.
workaday *a.* Alltags. . .; alltäglich.
workaholic *a.* (*fam.*) arbeitswütig; ~*s.* arbeits-
wütiger Mensch *m.*; Arbeitstier.
workday *s.* Arbeitstag *m.*
worker *s.* Arbeiter(in) *m.*(*f.*); *heavy* ~, Schwer-
arbeiter *m.*
workforce *s.* Beligschaft *f.*
working *a.* Arbeits. . .; ~ *capacity*, Leistungsfähigkeit *f.*; ~ *capital*, Betriebskapital *n.*; ~ **class** *s.* Arbei-
terklasse *f.*; ~**-day** *s.* Arbeitstag *m.*, ~ *expenses* *pl.*
Betriebsunkosten *pl.*; ~ *hours* *pl.* Arbeitsstunden
pl.; ~ **knowledge** *s.* ausreichende Kenntnisse *f.pl.*;
~ *majority*, arbeitsfähige Mehrheit *f.*; ~ *partner*,
aktiver Teilhaber *m.*
work-load *s.* Arbeitslast *f.*
workman *s.* Arbeiter *m.*
workmanship *s.* Werk *n.*; Arbeit *f.*; Geschicklichkeit *f.*; Stil *m.*
workshop *s.* Werkstatt *f.*; Workshop *m.*
work-to-rule *s.* Dienst nach Vorschrift *f.*
world *s.* Welt *f.*; Erde *f.*
World Bank *s.* Weltbank *f.*
worldly *a.* weltlich, irdisch; Welt . . .
world power *s.* Weltmacht *f.*
world war *s.* Weltkrieg *m.*
world-wide *a.* weltweit.
worm *s.* Wurm *m.*; Gewinde *n.*; ~ *v.t. & i.* wühlen,
bohren; sich einschleichen.
worm-eaten *a.* wurmstichig.
worm's-eye-view *s.* Froschperspektive *f.*
wormwood *s.* Wermut *m.*
worn-out *a.* abgenutzt; erschöpft.
worried *a.* besorgt; ängstlich.
worry *v.t.* sich Sorgen machen; ängstigen, plagen;
~ *s.* Quälerei *f.*, Sorge *f.*
worrying *a.* sorgenvoll.
worse *a. & adv.* schlechter, schlimmer, ärger; *the* ~,
desto schlimmer.
worsen *v.i.* schlechter werden; verschlechtern;
verschlimmern.
worship *s.* Verehrung *f.*; Ehrerbietung *f.*; Gottesdienst *m.*; ~ *v.t. & i.* verehren; anbeten.
worshipper *s.* Anbeter(in) *m.*(*f.*); Andächtige *m.*
worst *a. & adv.* schlechtest, schlimmst; ~ *s.*
Schlimmste, Ärgste *n.*; *to get the* ~ *of it*, den kürzeren ziehen; *if the* ~ *comes to the* ~, wenn alle
Stricke reißen.
worsted *s.* Wollgarn, Kammgarn *n.*
wort *s.* Kraut *n.*; (Bier) Würze.
worth *s.* Wert *m.*; Würdigkeit *f.*; ~ *a.* wert; ~ *while*,
der Mühe wert.
worthless *a.* unwürdig; wertlos.
worthy *a.*, ~**ily** *adv.* würdig.

would-be *a.* vorgeblich, Schein. . .; Möchtegern. . .
wound *s.* Wunde *f.*; ~ *v.t.* verwunden.
wraith *s.* Gespenst *n.*
wrangle *v.i.* zanken, streiten; ~ *s.* Zank, Streit *m.*
wrap *v.t.* wickeln, einwickeln.
wrapper *s.* Umschlagetuch *n.*; Hülle *f.*; Kreuzband
n.; Deckblatt *n.*
wrapping *s.* Verpackung *f.*
wrapping-paper *s.* Packpapier *n.*
wrath *s.* Zorn, *m.*
wrathful *a.*, ~**ly** *adv.* zornig.
wreak *v.t.* rächen; (ver)üben.
wreath *s.* Gewinde *n.*; Flechte *f.*; Locke *f.*; Kranz
m.; ~**e** *v.t.* flechten, winden, bekränzen; ~ *v.i.* sich
ringeln.
wreck *s.* Schiffbruch *m.*; Wrack *n.*; Verwüstung *f.*;
Strandgut *n.*; ~ *v.t. & i.* zertrümmern; zum Scheitern bringen; scheitern.
wreckage *s.* Trümmer *pl.*
wren *s.* Zaunkönig *m.*
wrench *v.t.* heftig ziehen, entwinden; verrenken;
~ *s.* Ruck *m.*; Verrenkung *f.*; Schraubenschlüssel
m.
wrest *v.t.* drehen, zerren; (ent)reissen; verdrehen.
wrestle *v.i.* ringen, kämpfen.
wrestler *s.* Ringer(in) *m.*(*f.*).
wrestling *s.* Ringkampf *m.*
wretch *s.* Elende *m.*; Schuft *m.*
wretched *a.*, ~**ly** *adv.* unglücklich, elend.
wretchedness *s.* Elend *n.*; Erbärmlichkeit *f.*
wriggle *v.i.* sich biegen, sich winden.
wring *v.t.st.* wringen; auswringen; drücken; ~ *s.*
Händeringen *n.*
wrinkle *s.* Runzel *f.*; Falte *f.*; Kniff *m.*; ~ *v.t.* (*v.i.*
sich) runzeln; rümpfen; zerknittern.
wrinkled *a.* runz(e)lig.
wrinkly *a.* runz(e)lig.
wrist *s.* Handgelenk *n.*
wrist-band *s.* Manschette *f.*; Armband *n.*
wristwatch *s.* Armbanduhr *f.*
writ *s.* Verfügung *f.*; Gerichtsbefehl *m.*
write *v.t. & i.st.* schreiben; *to* ~ *off*, abschreiben
(Schuld); *to* ~ *out*, ausschreiben.
writer *s.* Schriftsteller(in) *m.*(*f.*); Verfasser(in)
m.(*f.*); Schreiber(in) *m.*(*f.*)
writhe *v.t.* drehen, winden, verdrehen; ~ *v.i.* sich
krümmen, sich winden.
writing *s.* Schreiben *n.*; Schrift, Urkunde *f.*; Aufsatz
m.; Schriftstellerei *f.*; ~**-book**, Schreibheft *n.*;
~**-case**, Schreibmappe *f.*; ~**-desk**, Schreibtisch *m.*;
~**-pad**, ~**-tablet**, Schreibblock *m.*; ~**-paper**,
Schreibpapier *n.*; *in* ~, schriftlich.
wrong *a. & adv.*, ~**ly** *adv.* unrecht; verkehrt; falsch;
to be ~, unrecht haben; ~ *s.* Unrecht *n.*; Irrtum *m.*;
to put a person in the ~, einen ins Unrecht setzen; ~
v.t. unrecht tun, Schaden zufügen; kränken.
wrongdoer *s.* Missetäter(in) *m.*(*f.*)
wrongdoing *s.* Missetat *f.*
wrongful *a.*, ~**ly** *adv.* ungerecht.
wrong-headed *a.* starrköpfig.
wroth *a.* zornig.
wrought *p. & a.* gearbeitet; gewirkt; ~ *iron*, *s.*
Schmiedeeisen *n.*; ~*a.* schmeideeisern.
wry *a.*, ~**ly** *adv.* ironisch; sarkastisch.
wry-neck *s.* Wendehals *m.*

X

X, x der Buchstabe X oder x *n.*
xerox *s.* Xerographie *f.*
Xmas *s.* (*fam.*) (*Christmas*) Weihnachten.

X-ray *s.* Röntgenstrahl *m.; x-ray tube,* Röntgenröhre *f.*
xylophone *s.* Xylophon *n.*

Y

Y, y der Buchstabe Y oder y *n.*
yacht *s.* Jacht *f.; ~ v.i.* mit einer Jacht fahren.
yachting *s.* Segeln *n.*
yachtsman *s.* Segler *m.*
yank *v.t.* reißen an; *~out v.t.* herausreißen.
Yankee *s.* Nordamerikaner *m.*
yard *s.* Hof *m.;* Yard *n.* (0,914 m.); Werft *f.*
yardstick *s.* Maßstab *m.*
yarn *s.* Garn *n.;* (*fig.*) Erzählung *f.*
yarrow *s.* Schafgarbe (Pflanze) *f.*
yawn *v.i.* gähnen; *~ s.* Gähnen *n.*
ye *pr.* ihr, euch.
yea *adv.* ja, ja doch.
year *s.* Jahr *n.; ~ by ~,* Jahr um Jahr.
yearbook *s.* Jahrbuch *n.*
yearlong *a.* einjährig.
yearly *a. & adv.* jährlich.
yearn *v.i.* sich sehnen, verlangen.
yearning *s.* Sehnsucht *f.*
year-round *a.* ganzjährig.
yeast *s.* Hefe *f.*
yell *v.i.* gellen, schreien, kreischen; *~ s.* Angstgeschrei, Gellen *n.*
yellow *a.* gelb; *~ fever,* gelbes Fieber *n.; ~ pages s.pl.* Branchenverzeichnis *n.; ~v.i.* vergilben.; *~ s.* Gelb *n.*
yellowish *a.* gelblich.
yelp *v.i.* kläffen, bellen.
yeoman *s.* Freisasse, Pächter *m.*
yes *adv.* ja, jawohl.

yesterday *adv.* gestern.
yet *c.* doch, dennoch, aber; *~ adv.* noch, sogar; schon; *as ~,* bisher, *not ~,* noch nicht.
yew-tree *s.* Eibe *f.*
Yiddish *a.* jiddisch; *~s.* Jiddisch *n.*
yield *v.t.* hergeben; hervorbringen, gestatten; aufgeben, übergeben; abwerfen, einbringen; *~ v.i.* sich ergeben; nachgeben; weichen; *~ s.* Ertrag *m.*
yodel *v.i.* jodeln; *~ s.* Jodler *m.*
yoga *s.* Joga *n.*
yog(h)urt *s.* Joghurt *m./n.*
yoke *s.* Joch *n.; ~ v.t.* zusammenkoppeln.
yokel *s.* dummer Bauer *m.*
yolk *s.* Eidotter *n.;* Eigelb *n.*
yon, yonder *a.* jener, jene, jenes; *~ adv.* an jenem Ort, da drüben.
yore *adv.; of ~,* ehedem, vormals.
you *pn.* Sie, du, ihr, euch; man, einen.
young *a.* jung; *~ s.* Junge *n.*
youngish *a.* jugendlich.
youngster *s.* Junge *m.*
your *pn.* euer, Ihr, dein.
yours *pn.* euer, eurig, eurige, Ihr, dein, *etc.*
yourself, yourselves *pn.* euch, euch selbst; ihr selbst, Sie (selbst) etc.
youth *s.* Jugend *f.;* Jugendlicher *m. ~ hostel* *s.* Jugendherberge *f.*
youthful *a., ~ly adv.* jugendlich.
Yule *s.* Weihnachten *pl.*
yummy *a.* (*fam.*) lecker.

Z

Z, z der Buchstabe Z oder Z *n.*
Zaire *s.* Zaire *n.*
Zambia *s.* Sambia *n.*
zany *a.* verrückt; blöd.
zeal *s.* Eifer *m.*
zealot *s.* Eiferer, Zelot *m.*
zealous *a., ~ly adv.* eifrig, warm, innig.
zebra *s.* Zebra *n.*
zenith *s.* Scheitelpunkt, Zenit *m.*
Zephir *s.* Zephyr, Westwind *m.*
zero *s.* Null *f.;* Nullpunkt *m.; ~ hour,* (*mil.*) Nullzeit *f.,* x Uhr.
zest *s.* erhöhter Geschmack, Genuß *m.;* Eifer *m.*
zigzag *s.* Zickzack *n.; ~ a.* zickzackförmig.
zilch *s.* rein gar nichts.
Zimbabwe *s.* Simbabwe *n.*
zinc *s.* Zink *n.*

Zionism *s.* Zionismus *m.*
Zionist *s.* Zionist(in) *m.(f.)*
Zip code *s.* Postleitzahl *f.*
zipper *s.* Reißverschluß *m.*
zither *s.* Zither *f.*
zodiac *s.* Tierkreis *m.*
zonal *a.* Zonen . . .
zone *s.* Gürtel *m.;* Erdstrich *m.;* Gebiet *n.,* Zone *f.; ~ of occupation,* Besatzungszone *f.; ~ of operations,* Operationsgebiet *n.*
Zoo (*=Zoological Gardens*) *s.* Zoo *m.*
zoo-keeper *s.* Zoowärter(in) *m.(f.)*
zoological *a.* zoologisch.
zoologist *s.* Zoologe *m.;* Zoologin *f.*
zoology *s.* Zoologie *f.,* Tierkunde *f.*
zoom *v.i.* heranholen; vorbeisausen.
zoom-lens *s.* Gummilinse *f.,* Zoom *m.*

Geographical Names

Abyssinia, Abessinien; **Abyssinian**, Abessinier, abessinisch.

Adriatic, das Adriatische Meer.

Ægæan, the ~ Sea, das Ägäische Meer.

Africa, Afrika; **African**, Afrikaner, afrikanisch.

Aix-la-Chapelle, Aachen.

Albania, Albanien; **Albanian**, Albanese, albanisch.

Alexandria, Alexandrien.

Algiers, Algier.

Alps, die Alpen; **Alpine**, Alpen...

Alsace, Elsaß; **Alsatian**, Elsässer, elsässisch.

Amazon, der Amazonenstrom.

America, Amerika; **American**, Amerikaner, amerikanisch.

Andalusia, Andalusien; **Andalusian**, Andalusier, andalusisch.

Andes, die Anden.

Anglo-Saxon, Angelsachse; angelsächsisch.

Antilles, die Antillen.

Antioch, Antiochien.

Antwerp, Antwerpen.

Apennines, die Apenninen.

Arabia, Arabien; **Arab**, Araber; Arabian, arabisch.

Aragon, Aragonien; **Aragonese**, aragonier, aragonisch.

Arctic Circle, Nördlicher Polarkreis.

Arctic Ocean, Nördliches Eismeer.

Ardennes, die Ardennen.

Argentina, Argentinien; **Argentine**, argentinisch.

Armenia, Armenien; **Armenian**, Armenier, armenisch.

Asia, Asien; **Asiatic**, Asiate, asiatisch.

Asia Minor, Kleinasien.

Asturias, Asturien; **Asturian**, Asturier, asturisch.

Athens, Athen; **Athenian**, Athener, athenisch.

Atlantic, das Atlantische Meer.

Australia, Australien; **Australian**, Australier, australisch.

Austria, Österreich; **Austrian**, Österreicher, österreichisch.

Avon, Avon.

Azores, die Azoren.

Bale, Basel.

Balearic,~Islands,die Balearen.

Baltic, baltisch.

Baltic, die Ostsee.

Barbadoes, die Barbaden Inseln.

Barbary, die Berberei.

Bavaria, Bayern; **Bavarian**, Bayer, bayrisch.

Belarus, Weißrußland.

Belgium, Belgien; **Belgian**, Belgier, belgisch.

Bengal, Bengalen; **Bengali**, Bengale, bengalisch.

Bessarabia, Bessarabien.

Biscay, Biskaya; **Biscayan**, Biskayer, biskayisch.

Black Forest, der Schwarzwald.

Black Sea, das Schwarze Meer.

Bœotia, Böotien.

Bohemia, Böhmen; **Bohemian**, Böhme, böhmisch.

Bosnia, Bosnien; **Bosnian**, Bosnier, bosnisch.

Bothnia, the Gulf of ~, der Bottnische Meerbusen.

Brazil, Brasilien; **Brazilian,** Brasil(an)er, brasil(ani)sch.

Britain, Great ~, Grossbritannien; **British,** britisch; **Briton,** Brite.

Britanny, die Bretagne; **Breton,** Bretone, bretonisch.

Bruges, Brügge.

Brunswick, Braunschweig.

Brussels, Brüssel.

Bulgaria, Bulgarien; **Bulgarian,** Bulgare, bulgarisch.

Burgundy, Burgund; **Burgundian,** Burgunder, burgundisch.

Burma, Birma; **Burmese,** Birmane, birmanisch.

Byzantium, Byzanz; **Byzantine,** Byzantiner, byzantinisch.

Cadiz, Cadix, Kadiz.

Calabria, Kalabrien; **Calabrian,** Calabrese, Kalabrier, kalabrisch.

California, Kalifornien; **Californian,** Kalifornier, kalifornisch.

Cambodia, Kambodscha.

Cameroon, Kamerun.

Canaries, Canary Islands, die Kanarischen Inseln.

Candian, Kandiot, kretisch.

Caribbee, the ~ **Islands,** die Karibischen Inseln.

Carinthia, Kärnten.

Carniola, Krain.

Carpathians, die Karpathen.

Cashmere, Kaschmir.

Caspian, the ~ **Sea,** das Kaspische Meer.

Castile, Kastilien.

Catalonia, Katalonien; **Catalonian,** Katalonier, katalonisch.

Caucasus, der Kaukasus.

Celt, Kelte.

Central America, Mittelamerika.

China, China; **Chinese,** Chinese, chinesisch.

Circassia, Zirkassien; **Circassian,** Zirkassier, zirkassisch.

Cleves, Kleve.

Cologne, Köln.

Constance, Lake ~, der Bodensee.

Copenhagen, Kopenhagen.

Cordileras, die Kordilleren.

Corsican, Korse, korsisch.

Courland, Kurland.

Cossack, Kosak.

Cracow, Krakau.

Crete, Kreta, Kandia; **Cretan,** Kreter, kretisch.

Crimea, die Krim.

Croatia, Kroatien; **Croatian,** Kroate, kroatisch.

Cyprus, Cypern.

Czech, Tscheche.

Czech Republic, Tschechien.

Czechoslovakia *s.* die Tschechoslovakei *f.*

Dalmatia, Dalmatien; **Dalmatian,** Dalmatiner, dalmatisch.

Dane, Däne; **Danish,** dänisch.

Danube, die Donau.

Dauphiny, die Dauphiné.

Dead Sea, das Tote Meer.

Denmark, Dänemark.

Dunkirk, Dünkirchen.

Dutch, holländisch; **the** ~, die Holländer; ~**man,** Holländer.

East Indies, Ostindien.

Egypt, Ägypten; **Egyptian,** Ägypter, ägyptisch.

England, England; **English,** englisch; **the** ~, die Engländer; **the** ~ **Channel,** der Ärmelkanal; **Englishman,** Engländer.

Estonia, Estland; **Estonian,**

Estländer, estnisch.
Ethiopia, Äthiopien.
Europe, Europa; **European**, Europäer, europäisch.

Far East, der Ferne Osten.
Flanders, Flandern.
Fleming, Flamländer; **Flemish**, flämisch.
Florence, Florenz; **Florentine**, Florentiner, florentinisch.
France, Frankreich.
Franconia, Franken.
French, französisch; **the ~**, die Franzosen; **~man**, Franzose.
Frisian, Friese, friesisch.

Gael, Gäle; **Gaelic**, gälisch.
Galicia, Galizien; **Galician**, Galizier, galizisch.
Galilee, Galiläa.
Gascony, die Gascogne; **Gascon**, Gascogner, gascognisch.
Gaul, Gallien; Gallier.
Geneva, Genf; **Genevan**, Genevese, Genfer, genferisch.
Genoa, Genua; **Genoese**, Genuese, genuesisch.
Germany, Deutschland; **German**, Deutsche, deutsch.
Ghent, Gent.
Greece, Griechenland; **Greek**, Grieche, griechisch.
Greenland, Grönland.

The Hague, der Haag.
Hainault, Hennegau.
Hanover, Hannover; **Hanoverian**, Hannoveraner, hannöversch.
Hebrew, Hebräer, hebräisch.
the Hebrides, die Hebriden.
Heligoland, Helgoland.
Helvetia, Helvetien, die Schweiz.
Hesse, Hessen; **Hessian**, Hesse, Hessisch.
Hindoo, Hindu.

Hungary, Ungarn; **Hungarian**, Ungar, ungarisch.

Iceland, Island; **Icelander**, Isländer; **Icelandic**, isländisch.
Illyria, Illyrien.
India, Indien; **the Indies**, Indien; **Indian**, Inder, indisch.
Ingria, Ingermanland.
Ionia, Ionien; **Ionian**, Ionier, ionisch.
Iraq, Irak.
Ireland, Irland; **Irish**, irisch; **the ~**, die Iren, Irländer; **Irishman**, Irländer.
Istria, Istrien.
Italy, Italien; **Italian**, Italiener, italienisch.

Japanese, Japaner, japanisch.
Jordan, Jordanien.
Judea, Judäa.

Lapland, Lappland; **Lapp**, **Laplander**, Lappe; **Lappisch**, lappländisch.
Latvia, Lettland.
Lebanon, Libanon.
Leeward Isles, die kleinen Antillen.
Leghorn, Livorno.
Leipsic, Leipzig.
Lett, lettisch; **the ~**, der Lette.
Levant, die Levante.
Liege, Lüttich.
Lisbon, Lissabon.
Lisle, Lille.
Lithuania, Litauen; **Lithuanien**, Litauer, litauisch.
Livonia, Livland; **Livonian**, Livländer, livländisch.
Lombardy, Lombardei; **Lombard**, Lombarde, lombardisch.
Lorraine, Lothringen.
Louvain, Löwen.

Low Countries, die Niederlande.
Lucerne, Luzern; **the Lake of** ~, der Vierwaldstädter See.
Lusatia, die Lausitz; **Lusatian**, Lausitzer, lausitzisch.
Lyons, Lyon.

Macedonia, Mazedonien; **Macedonian**, Mazedonier, mazedonisch.
Madeira, Madeira.
Malay, Malaie; malaiisch.
Maltese, Malteser, maltesisch.
Manxman, Bewohner der Insel Man.
Marches, die Marken.
Marseilles, Marseille.
Mayence, Mainz.
Mediterranean, das Mittelländische Meer.
Middle East, der Mittlere Osten.
Milan, Mailand.
Moldavia, die Moldau.
Molucas, die Molukken.
Mongolia, die Mongolei; **Mongol**, Mongole, mongolisch.
Moor, Maure, Mohr; **Moorish**, maurisch.
Moravia, Mähren; **Moravian**, Mähre, mährisch; **the Moravian Brethren**, die Herrnhuter.
Morocco, Marokko; **Moroccan**, Marokkaner, marokkanisch.
Moscovy, Moskovien.
Moscow, Moskau.
Moselle, die Mosel.
Mozambique, Mozambik.
Munich, München.

Naples, Neapel; **Neapolitan**, Neapolitaner, Neapeler, neapolitanisch.
Netherlands, die Niederlande.
Neu(f)chatel, Neuenburg.

Newfoundland, Neufundland.
Nice, Nizza.
Nile, der Nil.
Normandy, die Normandie; **Norman**, Normanne, normannisch.
North Africa, Nordafrika.
North America, Nordamerika.
Norway, Norwegen; **Norwegian**, Norweger, norwegisch.
Nova Scotia, Neuschottland.
Nubia, Nubien; **Nubian**, Nubier, nubisch.
Nuremberg, Nürnberg.

Orange, Oranien.
the Orcades *or* **Orkenys**, die Orkaden Inseln.
Ostend, Ostende.
Ottoman, **the** ~ **Empire**, das Osmanische Reich.
Oxonian, Oxforder.

Pacific, der Stille Ozean.
Palatinate, die Pfalz; **Palatine**, Pfälzer, pfälzisch.
Palestine, Palästina.
Patagonia, Patagonien; **Patagonian**, Patagonier, patagonisch.
Pennsylvania, Pennsylvanien.
Persia, Persien; **Persian**, Perser, persisch.
Peruvian, Peruaner, peruanisch.
Piedmont, Piemont; **Piedmontese**, Piemontese, piemontesisch.
Poland, Polen; **Pole**, Pole; **Polish**, polnisch.
Pomerania, Pommern; **Pomeranian**, Pommer, pommerisch.
Portuguese, Portugiese, portugiesisch.
Prague, Prag.
Prussia, Preußen; **Prussian**, Preusse, preussisch.

Pyrenees, die Pyrenäen.

Ratisbon, Regensburg.
Rhenish, rheinisch.
Rhine, der Rhein.
Rhineland, Rheinland.
Rhodes, Rhodos.
Rocky Mountains, das Felsengebirge.
Rome, Rom; **Roman**, Römer, römisch.
R(o)umania, Rumänien; **R(o)umanian**, Rumäne, rumänisch.
Russia, Rußland; **Russian**, Russe, russisch.

Saracen, Sarazene, sarazenisch.
Sardinia, Sardinien; **Sardinian**, Sardinier, sardinisch.
Savoy, Savoyen; **Savoyard**, Savoyarde.
Saxony, Sachsen; **Saxon**, Sachse, sächsisch.
Scandinavia, Skandinavien; **Scandinavian**, Skandinavier, skandinavisch.
Scania, Schonen.
the Scheldt, die Schelde.
Scotland, Schottland; **Scottish**, schottisch; **the Scotch**, **Scots**, die **Schotten; Scotsman**, **Scot**, Schotte.
Serbia, Serbien; **Serbian**, Serbe, serbisch.
Silberia, Sibirien; **Siberian**, Sibirier, sibirisch.
Sicily, Sizilien; **Sicilian**, Sizili[an]er, sizili[an]isch.
Silesia, Schlesien; **Silesian**, Schlesier, schlesisch.
Slavonia, Slavonien; **Slavonian**, Slavonier, slavonisch.
Sound, der Sund.
South Africa, Südafrika.
South America, Südamerika.
Spain, Spanien; **Spaniard**, Spanier; **Spanish**, spanisch.

Spires, Speyer.
Styria, Steiermark; **Styrian**, Steiermärker, stei[e]risch.
Swabia, Schwaben; **Swabian**, Schwabe, schwäbisch.
Sweden, Schweden; **Swede**, Schwede; **Swedish**, schwedisch.
Switzerland, die Schweiz; **Swiss**, Schweizer, schweizerisch.
Syracuse, Syrakus.
Syria, Syrien; **Syrian**, Syr[i]er, syrisch.

Tagus, der Tajo.
Tangier, Tanger.
Tartary, die Tatarei; **Tartar**, Tatare, tatarisch.
Teuton, Germane, Teutone; **Teutonic**, germanisch.
Thames, die Themse.
Thermopyl–, die Thermopylen.
Thessaly, Thessalien; **Thessalian**, Thessalier, thessalisch.
Thrace, Thrazien; **Thracian**, Thrazier, thrazisch.
Thuringia, Thüringen; **Thuringian**, Thüringer, thüringisch.
Translyvania, Siebenbürgen.
Trent, Trient.
Treves, Trier.
Troy, Troja; **Trojan**, Trojaner, trojanisch.
Turkey, die Türkei; **Turk**, Türke; **Turkish**, türkisch.
Tuscany, Toskana; **Tuscan**, Toskaner, toskanisch.
Tyre, Tyrus.
Tyrol, Tirol; **Tyrolese**, Tiroler, tirolisch.

Umbria, Umbrien.
United States, die Vereinigten Staaten.

Valais, Wallis.
Valtelline, Veltlin.
Vaud, Waadt, Waadtland.
Venice, Venedig; **Venetian**, Venediger, Venezianer, venezianisch.
Vesuvius, der Vesuv.
Vienna, Wien; **Viennese**, Wiener, wienerisch.
Vistula, die Weichsel.
Vosges, die Vogesen.

Wallachia, die Wallachei; **Wallachian**, Wallache, wallachisch.
Walloon, Wallone, wallonisch.
Warsaw, Warschau.

Welsh, walisisch; **the** ~, die Waliser.
West Indies, Westindien; **West Indian**, Westindier, westindisch.
Westphalia, Westfalen; **Westphalian**, Westfale, westfälisch.
Wurtemberg, Württemberg.

Yugoslavia, Jugoslavien.

Zealand, Seeland.
Zimbabwe, Simbabwe.
Zuider Zee, die *or* der Zuidersee.

Table of English Strong and Irregular Weak Verbs

Present	Past Tense	Past Participle	Present	Past Tense	Past Participle
abide	abode*	abode*	**forsake**	forsook	forsaken
arise	arose	arisen	**forswear**	forswore	forsworn
awake	awoke*	awoken*	**freeze**	froze	frozen
be	was/were	been	**get**	got	got, gotten
bear	bore	borne, born	**gild**	gilt*	gilt*
beat	beat	beaten	**give**	gave	given
become	became	become	**go**	went	gone
befall	befell	befallen	**grind**	ground	ground
beget	begot	begotten	**grow**	grew	grown
begin	began	begun	**hang**	hung*	hung*
bend	bent	bent	**have**	had	had
bereave	bereft*	bereft*	**hear**	heard	heard
beseech	besought*	besought*	**heave**	hove*	hove*
bid	bade, bid	bidden, bid	**hew**	hewed	hewn*
bind	bound	bound	**hide**	hid	hidden, hid
bite	bit	bitten	**hit**	hit	hit
bleed	bled	bled	**hold**	held	held
blow	blew	blown	**hurt**	hurt	hurt
break	broke	broken	**keep**	kept	kept
breed	bred	bred	**kneel**	knelt*	knelt*
bring	brought	brought	**knit**	knit*	knit*
build	built	built	**know**	knew	known
burn	burnt*	burnt*	**lay**	laid	laid
burst	burst	burst	**lead**	led	led
buy	bought	bought	**lean**	leant*	leant*
can	could	—	**leap**	leapt*	leapt*
cast	cast	cast	**learn**	learnt*	learnt*
chide	chid*	chid(den)*	**leave**	left	left
choose	chose	chosen	**lend**	lent	lent
cleave	cleft, clove	cleft, cloven	**let**	let	let
			lie (liegen)	lay	lain
cling	clung	clung	**light**	lit*	lit*
clothe	clad*	clad*	**lose**	lost	lost
come	came	come	**make**	made	made
cost	cost	cost	**may**	(subj.)	—
creep	crept	crept		might	
cut	cut	cut	**mean**	meant	meant
deal	dealt	dealt	**meet**	met	met
dig	dug	dug	**melt**	melted	molten*
do	did	done	**mow**	mowed	mown*
draw	drew	drawn	**pay**	paid	paid
dream	dreamt*	dreamt*	**pen** (ein-	pent*	pent*
drink	drank	drunk	schließen)		
drive	drove	driven	**plead**	pled*	pled*
dwell	dwelt*	dwelt*	**prove**	proved	proven
eat	ate	eaten	**put**	put	put
fall	fell	fallen	**quit**	quit(ted)	quit(ted)
feed	fed	fed	**read**	read	read
feel	felt	felt	**rid**	rid, ridded	rid, ridded
fight	fought	fought	**ride**	rode	ridden
find	found	found	**ring**	rang	rung
flee	fled	fled	**rise**	rose	risen
fling	flung	flung	**rive**	rived	riven
fly	flew	flown	**run**	ran	run
forbear	forbore	forborne	**saw**	sawed	sawn*
forbid	forbade	forbidden	**say**	said	said
forego	forewent	foregone	**see**	saw	seen
foretell	foretold	foretold	**seek**	sought	sought
forget	forgot	forgotten	**sell**	sold	sold
forgive	forgave	forgiven	**send**	sent	sent

Verbs marked * are more commonly conjugated in the regular weak form.

Present	Past Tense	Past Participle	Present	Past Tense	Past Participle
set	set	set	**stave**	stove*	stove*
sew	sewed	sewn*	**steal**	stole	stolen
shake	shook	shaken	**stick**	stuck	stuck
shall	(*subj.*)	—	**sting**	stung	stung
	should		**stink**	stank,	stunk
shear	sheared	shorn*		stunk	
shed	shed	shed	**strew**	strewed	strewn*
shine	shone	shone	**stride**	strode	stridden
shoe	shod	shod	**strike**	struck	struck
shoot	shot	shot			(stricken)
show	showed	shown*	**string**	strung	strung
shred	shred,	shred,	**strive**	strove	striven
	shredded	shredded	**strow**	strowed	strown
shrink	shrunk,	shrunk	**swear**	swore	sworn
	shrank		**sweep**	swept	swept
shut	shut	shut	**swell**	swelled	swollen*
sing	sang	sung	**swim**	swam	swum
sink	sank, sunk	sunk	**swing**	swung	swung
sit	sat	sat	**take**	took	taken
slay	slew	slain	**teach**	taught	taught
sleep	slept	slept	**tear**	tore	torn
slide	slid	slid	**tell**	told	told
sling	slung	slung	**think**	thought	thought
slink	slunk	slunk	**thrive**	throve*	thriven*
slit	slit	slit	**throw**	threw	thrown
smell	smelt*	smelt*	**thrust**	thrust	thrust
smite	smote	smitten	**tread**	trod	trod,
sow	sowed	sown*			trodden
speak	spoke	spoken	**wake**	woke,	waked,
speed	sped*	sped*		waked	woke[n]
spell	spelt*	spelt*	**wear**	wore	worn
spend	spent	spent	**weave**	wove	woven
spill	spilt*	spilt*	**weep**	wept	wept
spin	spun	spun	**wet**	wet, wetted	wet, wetted
spit	spit, spat	spit, spat	**will**	would	—
split	split	split	**win**	won	won
spoil	spoilt*	spoilt*	**wind**	wound	wound
spread	spread	spread	**work**	wrought*	wrought*
spring	sprung,	sprung	**wring**	wrung	wrung
	sprang		**write**	wrote	written
stand	stood	stood			

Verbs marked * are more commonly conjugated in the regular weak form.

English Abbreviations

A, *answer,* Antwort, Antw.; *ampere,* Ampere, A.

A.B., *able-bodied,* dienstfähiger Matrose *m.; Bachelor of Arts,* Bakkalaureus der Philosophie.

abbr., *abbreviation,* Abkürzung, Abk.

AC, *alternating current,* Wechselstrom.

A.C., *ante Christum,* vor Christi Geburt.

a/c, *account,* Rechnung.

A.D., *anno Domini,* im Jahre des Herrn, nach Christus, n. Chr.

adj., *adjective,* Adjektiv, Adj.

Adm., *Admiral,* Admiral *m.*

adv., *adverb,* Adverb, Adv.

advt., *advertisement,* Inserat.

AFL-CIO, *American Federation of Labor & Congress of Industrial Organizations,* Gewerkschaftsverband.

AM, *amplitude modulation,* Kurz- Mittel- u. Longwelle.

a.m., *ante meridiem,* vormittags.

anon., *anonymous,* anonym.

a/o, *account of,* auf Rechnung von.

AP, *Associated Press,* amerikanische Nachrichten Agentur.

approx., *approximately.*

Apr., *April,* April, Apr.

apt., *apartment,* Wohnung, Wng.

arr., *arrival,* Ankunft, Ank.

ASCII, *American Standard Code for Information Interchange,* standardisierter Code zur Darstellung alphanumerischer zeichen.

asst., *assistant,* Assistent(in), Asst.

attn., *attention (of),* zu Händen (von), z. Hdn.

Aug., *August,* August, Aug.

av., *average,* Durchschnitt.

Ave., *Avenue,* Allee.

b., *born,* geboren, geb.

B.A., *Bachelor of Arts,* Bakkalaureus der Philosophie.

B&B, *bed and breakfast,* Übernachtung mit Frühstück.

B.C., *before Christ,* vor Christus.

B.D., *Bachelor of Divinity,* Bakkalaureus der Theologie.

B/E, *bill of exchange,* Wechsel.

bk, *book,* Buch; *bank,* Bank.

B.L., *Bachelor of Law,* Bakkalaureus der Rechte.

B/L, *bill of lading,* Frachtbrief.

bl., *barrel,* Faß; *bale,* Ballen.

Blvd., *Boulevard,* Boulevard.

B.M., *Bachelor of Medicine,* Bakkalaureus der Medizin.

B.Mus., *Bachelor of Music,* Bakkalaureus der Musik.

BO, *branch office,* Filiale.

Bros., *brothers,* Gebrüder *pl.,* Gebr.

B.Sc., *Bachelor of Science,* Bakkalaureus der Naturwissenschaften.

B/W, *black and white,* schwarzweiß, s/w.

C., *centigrade,* Grad Celsius.

c., *cent,* Cent; *century,* Jahrhundert, jh.

ca., *circa,* etwa.

Can., *Canada,* Kanada.

Capt., *Captain,* Kapitän; Hauptmann.

CB, *Citizens Band,* CB-Funk.

C.C., *City Council,* Stadtrat.

CD, *compact disk,* CD; *corps diplomatique,* diplomatisches Korps, CD.

C.E., *Civil Engineer,* Ingenieur.

cert., *certificate,* Bescheinigung.

CET, *Central European Time,* mitteleuropäische Zeit, MEZ.

cf., *confer,* Vergleiche, vgl.

ch., *Chapter,* Kapitel, Kap.

CIA, *Central Intelligence Agency,* (US-Geheimdienst).

C in C, *Commander in Chief,* Oberbefehlshaber.

cl., *centiliter,* Zentiliter; *class,* Klasse, Kl.

cm., *centimeter,* Zentimeter.

Co., *Company,* Gesellschaft; *County,* Verwaltungsbezirk.

c/o, *care of,* bei per Adresse, p.A.

C.O.D., *cash on delivery,* per Nachnahme.

Col., *Colonel,* Oberst.

col., *column,* Spalte, Sp.

cont(d)., *continued,* Fortsetzung, Forts.

CP, *Canadian Press,* (Nachrichtenagentur); *Communist Party,* Kommunistische Partei, KP.

cp., *compare,* vergleiche, vgl.

CPA, *certified public accountant,* antlich zugelassener Wirtschaftsprüfer.

cu., *cubic,* Kubik.

CV, *curriculum vitae,* Lebenslauf.

C.W.O., *cash with order,*

cwt., *hundredweight,* Zentner *m.*

d. *died,* gestorben, gest.; *depth,* Tiefe, T.

DA, *deposit account,* Depositenkonto.

DC, *direct current,* Glichstrom; *District of Columbia* (District der amerikanischen Haupstadt Washington).

D.C.L., *Doctor of Civil Law,* Doktor des bürgerlichen Rechts.

D.D., *Doctor of Divinity,* Doktor der Theologie.

D.D.S. *Doctor of Dental Surgery,* Doktor der Zahnmedizin, Dr. med. dent.

DDT, *dichlorodiphenyltrichloroethane,* Dichlordiphenyl-trichloräthan, DDT.

Dec., *December,* Dezember, Dez.

dec., *decd, deceased,* gestorben, gest.

deg., *degree,* Grad *m.*

dep., *departure,* Abfahrt, Abf.

dept., *department,* Abteilung, *f.* Abt.

Dip., *dip., diploma,* Diplom, dipl.

Dir., *dir., director,* Direktor, Dir.

disc., *discount,* Abzug *m.,* Rabatt *m.*

div., *divorced,* geschieden, gesch.; *division,* Abteilung,, Abt.

DJ, *disk jockey,* Disk Jockey.

D.Litt., *Doctor of Literature,* Doktor der Literatur.

D.Mus., *Doctor of Music,* Doktor der Musik.

do., *ditto,* dito, desgleichen, dgl.

dol., *dollar,* Dollar.

doz., *dozen,* Dutzend *n.*

D.Phil., *Doctor of Philosophy,* Doktor der Philosophie.

Dpt., *department,* Abteilung *f.,* Abt.

Dr., *Doctor,* Doktor *m,* Dr.; *drive,* Fahrweg

D.Sc., *Doctor of Science,* Doktor der Naturwissenschaften, Dr. rer. nat.

D.V.M., *Doctor of Veterinary Medicine,* Doktor der Tiermedizine.

E., *east,* Osten, *m.,* O.

E. & O.E. *errors and omissions excepted,* Irrtümer und Auslassungen vorbehalten.

ECOSOC, *Economic and Social Council,* Wirtschafts- und Sozialrat der UN.

ECU, *European Currency Unit,* Europäische Währungseinheit.

Ed., *ed., edited,* herausgegeben, h(rs)g.; *edition,* Auflage, Aufl., *editor,* Herausgeber(in), H(rs)g.

EDP, *electronic data processing,* elektronische Datenverarbeitung, EDV.

E.E., e.e., *errors excepted,* Irrtümer vorbehalten.

e.g., *exempli gratia,* zum Beispiel.

enc(l)., *enclosure(s),* Anlage, Anl.

ESA, *European Space Agency,* Europäische Weltraumbehörde.

esp., *especially,* besonders, bes., bsd.

Esq., *Esquire,* Herrn.

est., *established,* gegründet, gegr.; *estimated,* geschätzt, gesch.

EDTA, *estimated time of arrival,* voraussichtliche Ankunftszeit.

etc., *et cetera,* usw.

ETD, *estimated time of departure,* voraussichtliche Abflug-oder Abfahrtszeit.

EURATOM, *European Atomic Energy Community,* Europäische Atomgemeinschaft, Euratom.

excl., *exclusive, excluding,* ausschließlich, ausschl.

ext., *extension,* Apparat (teleph.), App.; *external, exterior,* äußerlich, Außen ...

F., *Fahrenheit,* Fahrenheit.

F.A., *Football Association,* Fußballverband.

FAO, *Food and Agriculture Organization,* Organisation für Ernährung und Landwirtschaft der UN.

FBI, *Federal Bureau of Investigation,* US-Bundeskriminalamt.

Feb., *February,* Februar, Feb.

fed., *federal,* Bundes. . .

fig., *figure,* Abbildungen, Abb.

fl., *floor,* stock.

FM, *frequency modulation,* Ultrakurzwellen, UKW.

f.o.b., *free on board,* frei (Schiff).

fo., fol., *folio,* Folio.

foll., *following,* folgend, folg.

fr., *franc,* Franc, Franken.

FRG, *Federal Republic of Germany,* Bundesrepublik Deutschland, BRD.

Fri., *Friday,* Freitag, Fr.

ft., *foot, feet,* Fuß.

fth., fthm., *fathom,* Klafter.

fur., *furlong,* Achtelmeile *f.*

g, *gram,* Gramm, g.

gal., *gallon,* Gallone (3,785 l).

GATT, *General Agreement on Tariffs and Trade,* Allgemeines Zoll-und Handelsabkommen.

G.B., *Great Britain,* Großbritannien.

GDP, *gross domestic product,* Bruttoinlandsprodukt, BIP.

Gen., *general,* General.

gen., *generally,* allgemein.

gm, *gram,* Gramm.

GMT, *Greenwich Mean Time,* Westeuropäische Zeit, WEZ.

GNP, *gross national product,* Bruttosozialprodukt, BNP.

Gov., *government,* Regierung; *governor,* Gouverneur.

G.P., *General Practitioner,* praktischer Arzt *m.*

G.P.O., *General Post Office,* Hauptpostamt *n.*

gr. wt., *gross weight,* Bruttogewicht.

gtd., guar., *guaranteed,* garantiert.

h., hr., *hour,* Stunde *f.,* hrs., *hours,* Stunden; *height,* Höhe.

H.B.M., *His (or Her) Britannic Majesty,* Seine (Ihre) Majestät

der König (die Königin) von Großritannien.
hdbk, *handbook,* Handbuch.
HE, *high explosive,* hochexplosiv.
hf., *half,* halb.
H.M., *His/Her Majesty,* Seine/Ihre Majestät.
H.M.S., *His/Her Majesty's Ship,* Seiner/Ihrer Majestät Schiff.
HO, *head office,* Hauptgeschäftsstelle, Zentrale.
Hon., *Honorable,* Ehrenwert; *Honorary,* Ehren...
h.p., *horse-power,* Pferdestärke *f.*
HQ, *Headquarters,* Hauptquartier.
H.S., *High School,* höhere Schule.
ht., *height,* Höhe, H.

IATA, *International Air Transport Association,* Internationaler Luftverkehrsverband.
ib(id), *ibidem* (*in the same place*), ebenda, ebd.
IBRD, *International Bank for Reconstruction and Development,* Internationale Bank für Wiederaufbau und Entwicklung.
IC, *integrated circuit,* integrierter Schaltkreis.
ICU, *intensive care unit,* Intensivstation.
ID, *identification,* Ausweis.

i.e., *id est,* das heißt, d.h.
ill., *illustration,* Abbildung, Abd.
in., *inches,* Zoll.
Inc., *incorporated,* eingetragen.
incl., *inclusive, including,* einschließlich, einschl.
inst., *instant, of the present month,* dieses Monats, d.M.
I.O.U., *I owe you,* ich schulde Ihnen; Schuldschein *m.*
IQ, *intelligence quotient,* Intelligenzquotient, IQ.
ISBN, *international standard book number,* ISBN-Nummer.
ital., *italics,* Kursivdruck *m.*
IUD, *intrauterine device,* Intrauterinpessar.
IYHF, *International Youth Hostel Federation,* Internationaler Jugendherbergsverband.

J, *Joule,* Joule, J.
J., *Judge,* Richter.
Jan., *January,* Januar, Jan.
JCD, *Juris Civilis Doctor* (*Doctor of Civil Law*), Doktor des Zivilrechts.
J.P., *Justice of the Peace,* Friedensrichter *m.*
Jr., *Junior,* der Jüngere, jr., jun.
JUD, *Juris Utriusque Doctor* (*Doctor of Canon and Civil Law*), Doktor beider Rechte.
Jul., *July,* Juli.
Jun., *June,* Juni.

K.C., *Knight Commander,* Komtur, Großmeister *m.;* King's Counsel, Justizrat *m.*
k., *kilogram,* Kilogramm k, kg.
km., *kilometer,* Kilometer, Km.
Kn, *knot,* Knoten, kn.
KO, *knockout,* Knockout, K.o.
kph, *kilometer(s) per hour,* Stundenkilometer, km/h.
kV, *kv, kilovolt,* Kilovolt, kV.
kW, *kw, Kilowatt,* Kilowatt, kW.

L, *large,* groß; *Lake,* See.
L., £, *libra, pound sterling,* Pfund (sterling) *n.*
l., *left,* links, l.; *line,* Zeile, z; *liter,* Liter, l.
LA, *Los Angeles.*
lat., *Latitude,* Breite *f.*
lb., *libra, pound,* Pfund *n.*
l.c., *loco citato,* am angeführten Orte. **L/C,** *letter of credit,* Kreditbrief *m.*
LCD, *liquid crystal display,* Flüssigkristallanzeige.

Lieut., Lt., *Lieutenant,* Leutnant *m.*
lit., *literally,* wörtlich.
Litt.D., *Litterarum Doctor* (*Doctor of Letters*), Doktor der Literatur.
ll. *lines,* Zeilen, Z.
LL.D., *Legum Doctor,* Doktor der Rechte.
loc. cit., *loco citato* (*at the place already cited*), an angeführten Ort, a.a.O.
long., *longitude,* Länge *f.*
LP, *long playing,* Langspielplatte, LP.
l.p., *low pressure,* Tiefdruck.
Ltd., *limited* (*liability company*), (Gesellschaft) mit beschränkter Haftung, m.b.H.
LW, *long wave,* Langwelle, LW.

M, *medium,* mittelgroß.
m., *male, masculine,* männlich; *meter,* Meter *m.; mile, Meile f.; minute,* Minute *f.* min.; *married,* verheiratet, verh.; *million,* Million, Mio., Mill.
M.A., *Master of Arts,* Magister der Philosophie.
Maj., *major,* Major.
Maj.-Gen., *major-general,* Generalmajor.
Mar., *March,* März.
masc., *masculine,* maskulin.
MBA, *Master of Business Administration,* Magister der Betriebswirtschaftslehre.
M.C., *master of ceremonies,* Zeremonienmeister, Conférencier.
M.D., *Medicinae Doctor,* Doktor der Medizin, Dr. med.
med., *medical,* medizinisch; *medium,* mittelgroß; *medieval,* mittelalterlich.
MEP, *Member of the European Parliament,* Mitglied des Europaparlaments.
Messrs., *Messieurs,* Herren.

mfd., *manufactured,* angefertigt.
mg, *milligram,* Milligramm, mg.
mo., *month,* Monat.
M.O., *Money Order,* Postanweisung *f.*
Mon., *Monday,* Montag.
mos., *months,* Monate.
MP, *Member of Parliament,* Parlamentsmitglied; *military police,* Militärpolizei.
mph, *miles per hour,* Stundenmeilen.
Mr., *Mister,* Herr.
Mrs., *Mistress,* Frau *f.*
Ms., Frau, Fräulein.
MS., *manuscript,* Handschrift *f.,* Ms.
M.Sc., *Master of Science,* Magister der Naturwissenschaften.
MSS., *manuscripts,* Handschriften.
Mt., *Mount,* Berg *m.*
mth, *month,* Monat.
Mus.D., *Doctor of Music,* Doktor der Musik.
MW, *medium wave,* Mittelwelle, MW.

N., *north,* Norden, N; *Nitrogen,* Stickstoff *m.; n., name,* Name; *noun,* substantiv, subst.; *neuter,* sächlich.
N.B., *nota bene* (note well), notabene, NB.
n.d., *no date,* ohne Datum.
N.E., *northeast,* Nordost, NO.
neg., *negative,* negativ, neg.
net., *netto,* netto.
NNE, *north-north-east,* Nord-Nordost.
NNW, *north-north-west,* Nord-Nordwest.
no., *numero,* Nummer *f.*
nos., *numbers,* Nummern.
Nov., *November,* November, Nov.
n.s., *not specified,* nicht angegeben.

539

NT, *New Testament,* Neues Testament, NT.

nt. wt., *net weight,* Nettogewicht.

NW, *north-west,* Nordwest.

N.Y., *New York.*

N.Z., *New Zealand,* Neuseeland.

O., *Oxygen,* Sauerstoff.

Ob., *obiit* (=*died*), gestorben, gest.

Oct., *October,* Oktober, Okt.

OECD, *Organization for Economic Cooperation and Development,* Organisation für wirtschaftliche Zusammenarbeit und Entwicklung.

O.H.M.S., *On His/Her Majesty's Service,* im Dienste Sr/Ihr. Majestät; Dienstsache.

o.n.o., *or nearest offer,* Verhandlungsbasis, VB.

OPEC, *Organization of Petroleum Exporting Countries,* Organisation der Erdöl exportierenden Länder.

O.T., *Old Testament,* Altes Testament, AT.

oz., *ounce,* Unze.

p., *page,* Seite.

p.a., *per annum* (*per year*), pro Jahr.

par., *paragraph,* Absatz, Abs., Abschnitt, Abschn.

PC, *Personal computer,* Personalcomputer, PC; *police constable,* Schutzmann.

p.c., *postcard,* Postkarte *f.*; % *per cent,* Prozent, %.

PD, *Police Department,* Polizeibehörde.

pd, *paid,* bezahlt, bez.

p.d., *per diem* (*by the day*), pro Tag.

PEN (*International Association of*) *Poets, Playwrights, Editors,* *Essayists, and Novelists,* PEN-Club, (internationaler Schriftstellerverband).

per pro, *per procurationem,* (by proxy); per Prokura, pp.

Ph.D., *philosophiae doctor* (*Doctor of Philosophy*), Doktor der Philosophie, Dr. phil.

PIN *personal identification number,* (Nummer auf Scheckkarten).

Pk., *Park,* Park.

Pl., *Place,* Platz, Pl.

pl., *plural,* Plural, Pl., pl.

p.m., *post meridiem,* nachmittags.

P.O., *Post Office,* Postamt *n.*; *postal order,* Postanweisung.

P.O.B., *post office box,* Postfach, Pf.

P.O.D., *pay on delivery,* per Nachnahme; *Post Office Department,* Postministerium.

P.O.O., *Post Office Order,* Postanweisung *f.*

pop., *population,* Einwohner, Einw.

POW, *prisoner of war,* Kriegsgefangene.

pp., *pages,* Seiten *pl.*

PR, *public relations,* Öffentlichkeitsarbeit.

Pres., *president,* Präsident.

Prof., *Professor,*Professor.

P.S., *Postscript,* Nachschrift *f.*

pt., *pint,* Pinte *f.*; *part,* Teil, T.; *payment,* Zahlung.

PTA, *Parent Teacher Association,* Eltern-Lehrer-Vereinigung.

P.T.O., *Please turn over,* bitte wenden.

Pvt., *private,* Gemeiner Soldat.

qr., *quarter,* Viertel.

quot., *quotation,* Kurs-Preisnotierung.

qt., *quart,* Quart.

qto., *quarto,* Quartformat *n.*

r., *right,* rechts, r.
RAM, *random access memory,* Direktzugriffsspeicher.
RC, *Roman Catholic,* römisch-Katholisch, r.-k.
rcpt., *receipt,* Quittung *f.*
Rd, *Road,* Straße, Str.
recd., *received,* erhalten, erh.
ref., *reference,* (mit) Bezug (auf).
regd., *registered,* eingetragen.
Regt., *Regiment,* Regiment *n.*
res., *research,* Forschungs...; *residence,* Wohnsitz.
ret., *retd., retired,* im Ruhestand, i.R., außer Dienst, a.D.
Rev., *reverend,* Ehrwürden, Hochwürden, Ehrw.
rm., *room,* Zimmer, Zi.
ROM, *read only memory,* Nur-Lese-Speicher.
r.p.m., *revolutions per minute,* Umdrehungen pro Minute, U/min.
RR, *railroad,* Eisenbahn.
RSVP, *répondez s'il vous plaît* (*please reply*), um Antwort wird gebeten, u.A.w.g.
rt., *right,* rechts, r.
Rt. Hon., *Right Honorable,* Hochwohlgeboren.

s, *second,* Sekunde, Sek.
S., *south,* Süden, S.; *Saint,* Sankt; *Society,* Verein.
$, *dollar,* Dollar.
S.A., *South Africa,* Südafrika.
SASE, *self-addressed stamped envelope,* frankierter Rückumschlag.
sc., scil., *scilicet* (*namely*), nämlich.
Sc.D. = D.Sc.
SE, *south-east,* Südost, so.
Sec., *Secretary,* Sekretär(in), Sekr.; Minister, Min.
sec., *second,* sekunde, sek.
Sen., *senior,* Senior, der Ältere, d.Ä., sen.

Sept., *September,* September, Sept.
Sgt., *Sergeant,* Sergeant *m.*
soc., *society,* Gesellschaft, Verein.
Sq., *Square,* Platz *m.*
sq., *square,* Quadrat. . .
Sr. *sister* eccl. (Ordens)Schwester; *senior,* Senior, der Ältere, d.Ä., sen.
S.S., *Saints,* Heilige *pl.*
S.S., *steamship,* Dampfer *m.*
SSE, *south-southeast,* Südsüdost, SSO.
SSW, *south-south-west,* Südsüdwest, SSW.
St., *Saint,* Heilige *m.*; *Street,* Straße *f.*
STA, *scheduled time of arrival,* planmäßige Ankunftszeit.
Sta., *Station,* Bahnhof, Bhf.
STD, *Scheduled time of departure,* planmäßge Abfahrtszeit.
stg., *sterling,* Sterling.
stn, *station,* Bahnhof, Bhf.
Sun., *Sunday,* Sonntag, So.
suppl., *supplement,* Nachtrag.
Surg., *surgery,* Chirurgie *f.*; *surgeon,* Chirurg *m.*
SW, *southwest,* Südwest, SW; *short wave,* Kurzwelle, KW.

t, *ton,* Tonne, t.
TB, *tuberculosis,* Tuberkulose, Tb(c).
tbsp., *tablespoon,* Eßlöffel, Eßl.
tel., *telephone,* Telefon, Tel.
Thur., *Thursday,* Donnerstag, Do.
TM, *trademark,* Warenzeichen, Wz.
T.O., *Turn over,* umschlagen.
tsp., *teaspoon,* Teelöffel, Teel.
TU, *trade union,* Gewerkschaft.
Tues., *Tuesday,* Dienstag, Di.

UEFA, *Union of European Football Associations,* UEFA.
UFO, *unidentified flying object,*

Ufo.

UHF, *ultrahigh frequency,* Ultrahochfrequenzbereich, UHF.

U.K., *United Kingdom,* Vereinigtes Königreich *n.,* Großbritannien.

UN, *United Nations,* Vereinte Nationen, UN.

UNESCO, *United Nations Educational, Scientific, and Cultural Organization,* (Organisation der Vereinten Nationen für Erziehung, Wissenschaft, und Kultur).

UNICEF, *United Nations Children's Fund,* (Kinderhilfswerk der Vereinten Nationen).

UPI, *United Press International,* (amerikanische Nachrichtenagentur).

U.S., *United States,* Vereinigte Staaten, *n.pl.*

U.S.A., *United States of America,* Vereinigte Staaten von Nordamerika; *United States Army,* Heer (*n.*) der Vereinigten Staaten.

USW, *ultrashort wave,* Ultrakurzwelle.

V, *volt,* Volt, V.

VAT, *value-added tax,* Mehrwertsteuer, Mwst.

VCR, *video cassette recorder,* Videorecorder.

VD, *venereal disease,* Geschlechtskrankheit.

VHF, *very high frequency,* Ultrakurzwelle, VHF, UKW.

v., *vide,* siehe; *verse,* Vers *m*; *versus,* gegen.

Ven., *Venerable,* Ehrwürden.

VIP, *very important person,* (prominente Persönlichkeit), VIP.

viz., *videlicet* (namely), nämlich.

vol., *volume,* Band *m.*; vols., *volumes,* Bände *m.pl.*

vs., *versus,* contra, gegen.

VSOP, *very superior old pale,* (Qualitätsbezeichnung für 20–25 Jahre alten Weinbrand u.ä.).

v.v., *verses,* Verse; *vice versa,* umgekehrt, v.v.

W., *west,* Western, W.

W.C., *water closet,* Abort *m.*

Wed., *Wednesday,* Mittwoch, Mi.

WHO, *World Health Organization,* Weltgesundheitsorganisation, WGO.

wk., *week,* Woche, Wo.; *work,* Arbeit.

wkly., *weekly,* wöchentlich.

wks., *weeks,* Wochen, Wo.

WNW, *west-north-west,* West-Nordwest, WNW.

w/o, *without,* ohne, o.

WP, *word processor,* Textverarbeitungssystem; *word processing,* Textverarbeitung; *weather permitting,* wenn es das Wetter erlaubt.

w.p.m., *words per minute,* Wörter pro Minute.

WSW, *west-south-west,* West-Südwest, WSW.

wt., *weight,* Gewicht, Gew.

XL, *extra large,* extragroß.

Xmas, *Christmas,* Weihnachten *n.*

Xroads, *crossroads,* Straßenkreuzung.

XS, *extra small,* extraklein.

yd., *yard,* Yard *n.*

Y.M.C.A., *Young Men's Christian Association,* Christlicher Verein junger Männer, CVJM.

yr, *year,* Jahr.

Y.W.C.A., *Young Women's Christian Association,* Christlicher Verein junger Frauen, CFJF.

Days of the Week

Sunday	der Sonntag
Monday	der Montag
Tuesday	der Dienstag
Wednesday	der Mittwoch
Thursday	der Donnerstag
Friday	der Freitag
Saturday	der Sonnabend *or* der Samstag

Months

January	der Januar	July	der Juli
February	der Februar	August	der August'
March	der März	September	der Septem'ber
April	der April'	October	der Okto'ber
May	der Mai	November	der Novem'ber
June	der Juni	December	der Dezem'ber

Signs

Vorsicht	Caution	Raucher	For smokers
Achtung	Watch out	Nichtraucher	For non-smokers
Ausgang	Exit		
Eingang	Entrance	Rauchen verboten	No smoking
Halt	Stop	Kein Zutritt	No admittance
Geschlossen	Closed	Damen (*or*) Frauen	Women
Geöffnet	Open		
Langsam	Slow	Herren (*or*) Männer	Men
Verboten	Prohibited		
Gesperrt	Road closed	Abort	Toilet
Einbahnstraße	One way street		

Weights and Measures

The Germans use the *Metric System* of weights and measures, which is a decimal system in which multiples are shown by the prefixes: Dezi- (one tenth); Zeni- (one hundredth); Milli- (one thousandth); Deka- (ten); Hekto- (hundred); Kilo- (thousand).

1 **Zentimeter** = .3937 inches
1 **Meter** = 39.37 inches
1 **Kilometer** = .621 mile
1 **Zentigramm** = .1543 grain
1 **Gram** = 15.432 grain
1 **Pfund (1/2 Kilogramm)** = 1.1023 pounds
1 **Kilogramm** = 2.2046 pounds
1 **Tonne** = 2,204 pounds
1 **Zentiliter** = 2,204 pounds
1 **Zentiliter** = .338 ounces
1 **Liter** = 1.0567 quart (liquid);
.908 quart (dry)
1 **Kiloliter** = 264.18 gallons

Useful Words and Phrases

Hello (*or*) How do you do?	Guten Tag. Grüß Gott.
Good morning.	Guten Morgen. Grüß Gott.
Good afternoon.	Guten Tag. Grüß Gott.
Good evening.	Guten Abend.
How are you?	Wie geht es Ihnen?
Fine, thanks, and you?	Gut, danke, und Ihnen?
I'm fine, too, thanks.	Auch gut, danke.
Please.	Bitte.
Thank you.	Danke schön.
You're welcome.	Bitte schön.
Pardon me.	Entschul'digen Sie, bitte. Verzei'hung.
I am sorry, I made a mistake.	Es tut mir leid, ich habe mich geirrt.
Do you mind?	Macht es Ihnen etwas aus?
Good luck.	Alles Gute.
Good night.	Gute Nacht.
Good-bye.	Auf Wiedersehen.
Can you please help me?	Können Sie mir bitte helfen?
Do you understand me?	Verste'hen Sie mich?
I don't understand you.	Ich verste'he Sie nicht.
Please speak slowly.	Sprechen Sie bitte langsam.
Please say it again.	Sagen Sie es bitte noch einmal.
I don't speak German very well.	Ich spreche nicht sehr gut Deutsch.
Do you speak English?	Sprechen Sie Englisch?
What do you call that in German?	Wie heißt das auf deutsch?
How do you say . . . in German?	Wie sagt man . . . auf deutsch?
What's your name, please?	Wie heißen Sie bitte?
My name is . . .	Ich heiße . . .
May I introduce . . .	Darf ich Ihnen . . . vorstellen?
What time is it?	Wieviel Uhr ist es?
How much does that cost?	Wie viel kostet das?
I would like . . .	Ich möchte gern . . .; Ich hätte gern . . .
May I see something better?	Könnten Sie mir etwas Besseres zeigen?
May I see something cheaper?	Könnten Sie mir etwas Billigeres zeigen?
It is not exactly what I want.	Es ist nicht ganz das, was ich suche.
I'd like to buy . . .	Ich möchte gern . . . kaufen.
I'd like to eat.	Ich möchte gern essen.
Where is there a good restaurant?	Wo ist hier ein gutes Restaurant?
I'm hungry (thirsty).	Ich habe Hunger (Durst).
Please give me . . .	Bitte geben Sie mir . . .
Please bring me . . .	Bitte bringen Sie mir . . .
May I see the menu?	Ich hätte gern die Speisekarte.
The check, please.	Bitte zahlen.
Is service included in the bill?	Ist das mit Bedie'nung?
Where is there a good hotel?	Wo ist hier ein gutes Hotel'?
Please help me with my luggage.	Helfen Sie mir bitte mit meinem Gepäck'.
Where can I get a taxi?	Wo bekom'me (finde) ich eine Taxe?
What is the fare to . . . ?	Was kostet die Fahrt nach (bis) . . .?
Please take me to this address.	Bitte bringen (fahren) Sie mich zu dieser Adres'se.
Please let me off at . . .	Bitte halten Sie . . .
I am lost.	Ich habe mich verlau'fen (verfah'ren).
I have a reservation.	Ich habe . . . reserviert'.
Where is the men's (ladies') room?	Wo ist die Toilet'te, bitte?
How do I get to the station?	Wie komme ich zum Bahnhof?
Where can I check my baggage?	Wo ist die Gepäckauf'bewahrung?
Is this a non-stop flight?	Ist dies ein direkt'er Flug?
I'm sick.	Ich bin krank.
I need a doctor.	Ich brauche einen Arzt.
Where is the nearest drugstore?	Wo ist die nächste Drogerie'?
Where is the next pharmacy?	Wo ist die nächte Apotheke?

Useful Words and Phrases

Is there any mail for me?	Ist Post für mich da?
Where can I mail this letter?	Wo kann ich diesen Brief einstecken?
I want to send a fax.	Ich möchte gern ein Fax schicken.
Where is the nearest bank?	Wo ist die nächste Bank?
Where can I change money?	Wo kann ich hier Geld wechseln?
Do you accept travelers checks?	Nehmen Sie Reiseschecks?
May I have the bill, please?	Könnte ich bitte die Rechnung haben?
Right away.	Sofort'.
Help!	Hilfe!
Please call the police.	Rufen sie bitte die Polizei'.
Who is it?	Wer ist dort?
Come in.	Herein'.
Just a minute!	Einen Augenblick, bitte!
Hello (*on telephone*).	Hier . . . (*say your name*).
Look out!	Vorsicht! Achtung!
Hurry.	Schnell.
As soon as possible.	So bald wie möglich.
To the right.	Rechts.
To the left.	Links.
Straight ahead.	Gera'de aus.

Food Terms

apple	Apfel		**lobster**	Hummer
asparagus	Spargel		**meat**	Fleisch
bacon	Speck		**milk**	Milch
banana	Bana'ne		**mushroom**	Pilz
beans	Bohnen		**noodle**	Nudel
beer	Bier		**nuts**	Nüsse
bread	Brot		**orange**	Apfelsi'ne
butter	Butter		**pastry**	Gebäck'
cake	Kuchen		**peach**	Pfirsich
carrot	Mohrrübe		**pear**	Birne
cauliflower	Blumenkohl		**pepper**	Pfeffer
celery	Sellerie		**pie**	Obstkuchen
cheese	Käse		**pineapple**	Ananas
chicken	Huhn		**pork**	Schweinefleisch
chocolate	Schokola'de		**potato**	Kartof'fel
coffee	Kaffee		**rice**	Reis
cookie	Keks		**salad**	Salat'
cream	Sahne		**salmon**	Lachs
cucumber	Gurke		**salt**	Salz
dessert	Nachtisch		**sandwich**	beleg'tes Brot
duck	Ente		**shrimp**	Garne'le
egg	Ei		**soup**	Suppe
fish	Fisch		**spinach**	Spinat'
fowl	Geflü'gel		**steak**	Beefsteak
fruit	Frucht, Obst		**strawberry**	Erdbeere
goose	Gans		**sugar**	Zucker
grape	Weintraube		**tea**	Tee
grapefruit	Pampelmu'se		**tomato**	Toma'te
ham	Schinken		**trout**	Forel'le
ice cream	Sahneneis		**turkey**	Truthahn
juice	Saft		**veal**	Kalbfleisch
lamb	Lammfleisch		**vegetable**	Gemüse
lemonade	Limona'de		**water**	Wasser
lettuce	Kopf		**wine**	Wein

Decimals

Instead of a decimal point, a comma is used:
English: 3.82 "three point eight two"
German: 3,82 "drei Komma acht zwei"

Fractions

the half; half a pound	die Hälfte; ein halbes Pfund
one and a half	anderthalb, eineinhalb
the third; two-thirds	das Drittel; zweidrittel
the fourth; three-fourths	das Viertel; dreiviertel
the fifth; four-fifths	das Fünftel; vierfünftel

Numerals

Cardinal		Ordinal	
1	eins	1st	erst
2	zwei	2nd	zweit-
3	drei	3rd	dritt-
4	vier	4th	viert-
5	fünf	5th	fünft-
6	sechs	6th	sechst-
7	sieben	7th	sieb(en)t-
8	acht	8th	acht-
9	neun	9th	neunt-
10	zehn	10th	zehnt-
11	elf	11th	elft-
12	zwölf	12th	zwölft-
13	dreizehn	13th	dreizehnt-
14	vierzehn	14th	vierzehnt-
15	fünfzehn	15th	fünfzehnt-
16	sechzehn	16th	sechzehnt-
17	siebzehn	17th	siebzehnt-
18	achtzehn	18th	achtzehnt-
19	neunzehn	19th	neunzehnt-
20	zwanzig	20th	zwanzigst
21	einundzwanzig	21st	einundzwanzigst-
30	dreißig	30th	dreißigst-
32	zweiunddreißig	32nd	zweiunddreißigst-
40	vierzig	40th	vierzigst-
43	dreiundvierzig	43rd	dreiundvierzigst-
50	fünfzig	50th	fünfzigst-
54	vierundfünfzig	54th	vierundfünfzigst-
60	sechzig	60th	sechzigst-
65	fünfundsechzig	65th	fünfundsechzigst-
70	siebzig	70th	siebzigst-
76	sechsundsiebzig	76th	sechsundsiebzigst-
80	achtzig	80th	achtzigst-
87	siebenundachtzig	87th	siebenundachtzigst-
90	neunzig	90th	neunzigst-
98	achtundneunzig	98th	achtundneunzigst-
100	hundert	100th	hundertst-
101	hunderteins	101th	hundertst-
202	zweihundertzwei	202nd	zweihundertzweit-
1,000	tausend	1,000th	tausendst-
1,000,000	eine Million'	1,000,000	millionst'-